DECISION GUIDES
Graduate School

GRADUATE PROGRAMS IN Engineering and Computer Science 2004

THOMSON

PETERSON'S

Australia • Canada • Mexico • Singapore • Spain • United Kingdom • United States

THOMSON

PETERSON'S

About The Thomson Corporation and Peterson's

With revenues of US$7.2 billion, The Thomson Corporation (www.thomson.com) is a leading global provider of integrated information solutions for business, education, and professional customers. Its Learning businesses and brands (www.thomsonlearning.com) serve the needs of individuals, learning institutions, and corporations with products and services for both traditional and distributed learning.

Peterson's, part of The Thomson Corporation, is one of the nation's most respected providers of lifelong learning online resources, software, reference guides, and books. The Education Supersite[SM] at www.petersons.com—the Internet's most heavily traveled education resource—has searchable databases and interactive tools for contacting U.S.-accredited institutions and programs. In addition, Peterson's serves more than 105 million education consumers annually.

For more information, contact Peterson's, 2000 Lenox Drive, Lawrenceville, NJ 08648; 800-338-3282; or find us on the World Wide Web at www.petersons.com/about.

ISSN 1528-6223
ISBN 0-7689-1179-6

Printed in Canada

10 9 8 7 6 5 4 3 2 1   05 04 03

Table of Contents

Table of Contents

The *Decision Guides* are a collaborative effort between Peterson's and Educational Testing Service (ETS) and the Graduate Record Examinations (GRE) Board. This collaboration builds upon Peterson's survey research and publication capabilities and the GRE Program's long-term relationship with the graduate education community, including administration of the Graduate Record Examinations. This collaboration enables a greater range of potential graduate students to access comprehensive information as they make decisions about pursuing graduate education. At the same time, it enables institutions to achieve greater promotion and awareness of their graduate offerings.

The graduate and professional programs in this *Decision Guide* are offered by colleges, universities, and professional schools and specialized institutions in the United States and U.S. territories. They are accredited by U.S. accrediting bodies recognized by the Department of Education or the Council on Higher Education Accreditation. Most are regionally accredited.

This volume is divided into the subject fields in which graduate degrees are offered. There are two overarching supersections, Computer Science and Engineering. The Computer Science supersection has a single main section and ten narrower subject areas (Artificial Intelligence/Robotics; Bioinformatics; Computer Science; Financial Engineering; Health Informatics; Human-Computer Interaction; Information Science; Medical Informatics; Software Engineering; and Systems Science). The Engineering supersection has nineteen sections. Each section covers an identifiable category of degree specialization. The nineteen sections in the Engineering

supersection are: Engineering and Applied Sciences; Aerospace/Aeronautical Engineering; Agricultural Engineering; Architectural Engineering; Bioengineering, Biomedical Engineering, and Biotechnology; Chemical Engineering; Civil and Environmental Engineering; Electrical and Computer Engineering; Energy and Power Engineering; Engineering Design; Engineering Physics; Geological, Mineral/Mining, and Petroleum Engineering; Industrial Engineering; Management of Engineering and Technology; Materials Sciences and Engineering; Mechanical Engineering and Mechanics; Ocean Engineering; Paper and Textile Engineering; and Telecommunications. These major sections are subdivided into narrower subject areas.

How Information Is Organized

Graduate program information in this *Decision Guide* is presented in profile form. The format of the profiles is consistent throughout the book, making it easy to compare one institution with another and one program with another. Any item that does not apply to or was not provided by a graduate unit is omitted from its listing. The following outline describes the profile information.

    Identifying Information. In the conventional university-college-department organizational structure, the parent institution's name is followed by the name of the administrative unit or units under which the degree program is offered and then the specific unit that offers the degree program. (For example, University of Notre Dame, College of Arts and Letters, Division of Humanities, Department of Art, Art History, and Design, Concentration in Design.) The last unit listed is the one to which all information in the profile pertains. The institution's city, state, and postal code follow.

Awards. Each postbaccalaureate degree awarded is listed; fields of study offered by the unit may also be listed. Frequently, fields of study are divided into subspecializations, and those appear following the degrees awarded. Students enrolled in the graduate program would be able to specialize in any of the fields mentioned.

Part-Time and Evening/Weekend Programs. When information regarding the availability of part-time or evening/weekend study appears in the profile, it means that students are able to earn a degree exclusively through such study.

Postbaccalaureate Distance Learning Degrees. A postbaccalaureate distance learning degree program signifies that course requirements can be fulfilled with minimal or no on-campus study.

Faculty. Figures on the number of faculty members actively involved with graduate students through teaching or research are separated into full- and part-time as well as men and women whenever the information has been supplied.

Students. Figures for the number of students enrolled in graduate and professional programs pertain to the semester of highest enrollment from the 2001–02 academic year. These figures are divided into full- and part-time and men and women whenever the data have been supplied. Information on the number of students who are members of a minority group or are international students appears here. The average age of the students is followed by the number of applicants, the percentage accepted, and the number enrolled for fall 2001. This section also includes the number of degrees awarded in calendar year 2001. Many doctoral programs offer a terminal master's degree if students leave the program after completing only part of the requirements for a doctoral degree; that is indicated here. All degrees are classified into one of four types: master's, doctoral, first-professional, and other advanced degrees. A unit may award one or several degrees at a given level; however, the data are only collected by type and may therefore represent several different degree programs.

Degree Requirements. The information in this section is also broken down by type of degree, and all information for a degree level pertains to all degrees of that type unless otherwise specified. Degree requirements are collected in a simplified form to provide some very basic information on the nature of the program and on foreign language, thesis or dissertation, comprehensive exam, and registration requirements. Some units may also provide a short list of additional requirements, such as fieldwork or internships. Information on the median amount of time required to earn the degree for full-time and part-time students is presented here. For complete information on graduation requirements, contact the graduate school or program directly.

Entrance Requirements. Entrance requirements are divided into the levels of master's, doctoral, first-professional, and other advanced degrees. Within each level, information may be provided in two basic categories, entrance exams and other requirements. The entrance exams use the standard acronyms used by the testing agencies, unless they are not well known. Other entrance requirements are quite varied, but they often contain an undergraduate or graduate grade point average (GPA). Unless otherwise stated, the GPA is calculated on a 4.0 scale and is listed as a minimum required for admission.

Application. The standard application **deadline,** any nonrefundable application **fee,** and whether electronic applications are accepted may be listed here. Note that the deadline should be used for reference only; these dates are subject to change, and students interested in applying should contact the graduate unit directly about application procedures and deadlines.

Expenses. Cost of study may be quite complex at a graduate institution. There are often sliding scales for part-time study, a different cost for first-year students, and other variables that make it impossible to completely cover the cost of study for each graduate program. To provide the most usable information, figures are given for full-time study for a full year where available and for part-time study in terms of a per-unit rate (per credit, per semester hour, etc.) **if** these costs are reported to be the **same** as the parent institution. If specific program costs have been reported as different from the parent institution, the reader is advised to contact the institution for expense information. Because expenses are always subject to change, this is good advice at any time.

Financial Support. This section contains data on the number of awards administered by the institution and given to graduate students during the 2001–02 academic year. The first figure given represents the total number of students enrolled in that unit who received financial aid. If the unit has provided information on graduate appointments, these are broken down into three major categories: *fellowships* give money to graduate students to cover the cost of study and living expenses and are not based on a work obligation or research commitment, *research assistantships* provide stipends to graduate students for assistance in a formal research project with a faculty member, and *teaching assistantships* provide stipends to graduate students for teaching or for assisting faculty members in teaching undergraduate classes.

In addition to graduate appointments, the availability of several other financial aid sources is covered in this section. *Career-related internships* or *fieldwork* offer money to students who are participating in a formal off-campus research project or practicum. *Federal Work-Study* is made available to students who demonstrate need and meet the federal guidelines; this form of aid normally includes 10 or more hours of work per week in an office of the institution or off campus in a nonprofit agency. *Tuition waivers* are routinely part of a graduate appointment, but units sometimes waive part or all of a student's tuition even if a graduate appointment is not available. *Institutionally sponsored loans* are low-interest loans available to graduate students to cover both educational and living expenses. The availability of grants, scholarships, traineeships, unspecified assistantships, and financial aid to part-time students is also indicated here.

Some programs list the financial aid application deadline and the forms that need to be completed for students to be eligible for financial aid. There are two forms: FAFSA, the Free Application for Federal Student Aid, which is required for federal aid; and the CSS Financial Aid PROFILE.

Faculty Research. Each unit has the opportunity to list several keyword phrases describing the current research involving faculty members and graduate students. Space limitations prevent the unit from listing complete information on all research programs. The total expenditure for funded research from the previous academic year may also be included.

Unit Head and Application Contact. The head of the graduate program for each unit is listed with the academic title and telephone and fax numbers and e-mail addresses, if available. In addition to the unit head, many graduate programs list separate contacts for application and admission information. Unit Web sites are provided, if available. If no unit head or application contact is given, you should contact the overall institution for information.

For Further Information

Many programs offer more in-depth, narrative style information that can be located at www.petersons.com/gradchannel. There is a notation to this effect at the end of those program profiles.

How This Information Was Gathered

The information published in this book was collected through *Peterson's Annual Survey of Graduate and Professional Institutions.* Each spring and summer, this survey is sent to more than 1,800 institutions offering postbaccalaureate degree programs, including accredited institutions in the United States and U.S. territories. (See article entitled "Accreditation and Accrediting Agencies.") Deans and other administrators provide information on specific programs as well as overall institutional information. Peterson's editorial staff then goes over each returned survey carefully and verifies or revises responses after further research and discussion with administrators at the institutions.

While every effort is made to ensure the accuracy and completeness of the data, information is sometimes unavailable or changes occur after publication deadlines. The omission of any particular item from a directory or profile signifies either that the item is not applicable to the institution or program or that information was not available.

The Admissions
Process

Generalizations about graduate admissions practices are not always helpful because each institution has its own set of guidelines and procedures. Nevertheless, some broad statements can be made about the admissions process that may help you plan your strategy.

General Requirements

Graduate schools and departments have requirements that applicants for admission must meet. Typically, these requirements include undergraduate transcripts (which provide information about undergraduate grade point average and course work applied toward a major), admission test scores, and letters of recommendation. Most graduate programs also ask for an essay or personal statement that describes your personal reasons for seeking graduate study. In some fields, such as art and music, portfolios or auditions may be required in addition to other evidence of talent. Some institutions require that the applicant have an undergraduate degree in the same subject as the intended graduate major.

Most institutions evaluate each applicant on the basis of the applicant's total record, and the weight accorded any given factor varies widely from institution to institution and from program to program.

Admission Tests

The major testing program used in graduate admissions is the Graduate Record Examinations (GRE) testing program, sponsored by the GRE Board and administered by Educational Testing Service, Princeton, New Jersey.

The Graduate Record Examinations testing program consists of a General Test and eight Subject Tests. The General Test measures verbal reasoning, quantitative reasoning, and analytical writing skills. It is offered as a computer-adaptive test (CAT) in the United States, Canada, and many other countries. In the CAT, the computer determines which question to present next by adjusting to your previous responses. Paper-based General Test administrations are offered in some parts of the world.

The computer-adaptive General Test consists of a 30-minute verbal section, a 45-minute quantitative section, and a 75-minute analytical writing section. In addition, an unidentified verbal or quantitative section that doesn't count toward a score may be included and an identified research section that is not scored may also be included.

The paper-based General Test consists of two 30-minute verbal sections, two 30-minute quantitative sections, and a 75-minute analytical writing section. In addition, an unidentified verbal or quantitative section that doesn't count toward a score may be included.

The Subject Tests measure achievement and assume undergraduate majors or extensive background in the following eight disciplines:

- Biochemistry, Cell and Molecular Biology
- Biology
- Chemistry
- Computer Science
- Literature in English
- Mathematics
- Physics
- Psychology

The Subject Tests are available at regularly scheduled paper-based administrations at test centers around the world. Testing time is approximately 2 hours and 50 minutes. You can obtain more information about the GRE tests by visiting the GRE Web site at www.gre.org or consulting the *GRE Information and Registration Bulletin*. The *Bulletin* can be obtained at many undergraduate colleges. You can also download it from the GRE Web site or obtain it by contacting Graduate Record Examinations, Educational Testing Service, Princeton, NJ 08541-6000, telephone 1-609-771-7670.

If you expect to apply for admission to a program that requires any of the GRE tests, you should select a test date well in advance of the application deadline. Scores on the computer-adaptive General Test are reported within ten to fifteen days; however, if you choose to handwrite your essay responses on the analytical writing section, score reporting will take approximately six weeks. Scores on the paper-based General Test and the Subject Tests are reported within six weeks.

Another testing program, the Miller Analogies Test (MAT), is administered at more than 600 licensed testing centers in the United States, Canada, and other countries. Testing time is 50 minutes. The test consists entirely of analogies. You can obtain the *Candidate Information Booklet*, which contains a list of test centers and instructions for taking the test, by calling The Psychological Corporation, Controlled Test Center, at 1-800-622-3231.

Check the specific requirements of the programs to which you are applying.

Factors Involved in Selecting a Graduate School or Program

Selecting a graduate school and a specific program of study is a complex matter. Quality of the faculty; program and course offerings; the nature, size, and location of the institution; admission requirements; cost; and the availability of financial assistance are among the many factors that affect one's choice of institution. Other considerations are job placement and achievements of the program's graduates and the institution's resources, such as libraries, laboratories, and computer facilities. If you are to make the best possible choice, you need to learn as much as you can about the schools and programs you are considering before you apply.

The following steps may help you narrow your choices.

- Talk to alumni of the programs or institutions you are considering to get their impressions of how well they were prepared for work in their fields of study.
- Remember that graduate school requirements change, so be sure to get the most up-to-date information possible.
- Talk to department faculty and the graduate adviser at your undergraduate institution. They often have information about programs of study at other institutions.
- Visit the Web sites of the graduate schools in which you are interested to request a graduate catalog. Contact the department chair in your chosen field of study for additional information about the department and the field.
- Visit as many campuses as possible. Call ahead for an appointment with the graduate adviser in your field of interest and be sure to check out the facilities and talk to students.

Tips for Minority Students: Indicators of a university's values in terms of diversity are found both in its recruitment programs and its resources directed to student success. Important questions: Does the institution vigorously recruit minorities for its graduate programs? Is there funding available to help with the costs associated with visiting the school? Are minorities represented in the institution's brochures or Web site or on their faculty rolls? What campus-based resources or services (including assistance in locating housing or career counseling and placement) are available? Is funding available to members of underrepresented groups?

At the program level, it is particularly important for minority students to investigate the "climate" of a program under consideration. How many minority students are enrolled and how many have graduated? What opportunities are there to work with diverse faculty and mentors whose research interests match yours? How are conflicts resolved or concerns addressed? How interested are faculty in building strong and supportive relations with students? "Climate" concerns should be addressed by posing questions to various individuals, including faculty members, current students, and alumni.

Information is also available through various organizations, such as the Hispanic Association of Colleges and Universities (HACU), and publications, such as *Black Issues in Higher Education* and *Hispanic Outlook* magazine. There are also books devoted to this topic, such as *The Multicultural Student's Guide to Colleges* by Robert Mitchell.

When and How to Apply

You should begin the application process at least one year before you expect to begin your graduate study. Find out the application deadline for each institution (many are provided in the profile section of this volume). Go to the institution Web site and find out if you can apply online. If not, request a paper application form. Fill out this form thoroughly and neatly. Assume that the school needs all the information it is requesting and that the admissions officer will be sensitive to the neatness and overall quality of what you submit. Do not supply more information than the school requires.

The institution may ask at least one question that will require a three- or four-paragraph answer. Compose your response on the assumption that the admissions officer is interested in both what you think and how you express yourself. Keep your statement brief and to the point, but, at the same time, include all pertinent information about your past experiences and your educational goals. Individual statements vary greatly in style and content, which helps admissions officers to differentiate among applicants. Many graduate departments give considerable weight to the statement in making their admissions decisions, so be sure to take the time to prepare a thoughtful and concise statement.

If recommendations are a part of the admissions requirements, choose carefully the individuals you ask to write them. It is generally best to ask current or former professors to write the recommendations, provided they are able to attest to your intellectual ability and motivation for doing the work required of a graduate student. It is advisable to provide stamped, preaddressed envelopes to people being asked to submit recommendations on your behalf.

Completed applications, including references and transcripts and admission test scores, should be received at the institution by the specified date.

Be advised that institutions do not usually make admissions decisions until all materials have been received. Enclose a self-addressed postcard with your application, requesting confirmation of receipt. Allow at least 10 days for the return of the postcard before making further inquiries.

If you plan to apply for financial support, it is imperative that you file your application early.

How Admission Decisions Are Made

The program you apply to is directly involved in the admissions process. Although the final decision is usually made by the graduate dean (or an associate) or by the faculty admissions committee, recommendations from faculty members in your intended field are important. At some institutions, an interview is incorporated into the decision process.

A Special Note for International Students

In addition to the steps already described, there are some special considerations for international students who intend to apply for graduate study in the United States. All graduate schools require an indication of competence in English. The purpose of the Test of English as a Foreign Language (TOEFL) is to evaluate the English proficiency of people who are nonnative speakers of English and want to study at colleges and universities where English is the language of instruction. The TOEFL is administered by Educational Testing

Service (ETS) under the general direction of a policy board established by the College Board and the Graduate Record Examinations Board.

The TOEFL is administered as a computer-based test throughout most of the world and is available year-round by appointment only. It is not necessary to have previous computer experience to take the test. The test consists of four sections—listening, reading, structure, and writing. Total testing time is approximately 4 hours.

The TOEFL is offered in the paper-based format in areas of the world where computer-based testing is not available. The paper-based TOEFL consists of three sections—listening comprehension, structure and written expression, and reading comprehension. Testing time is approximately 3 hours. The Test of Written English (TWE) is also given. TWE is a 30-minute essay that measures the examinee's ability to compose in English. Examinees receive a TWE score separate from their TOEFL score. The

Information Bulletin contains information on local fees and registration procedures.

Additional information and registration materials are available from TOEFL Services, Educational Testing Service, P.O. Box 6151, Princeton, New Jersey 08541-6151. Telephone: 1-609-771-7100. E-mail: toefl@ets.org. World Wide Web: http://www.toefl.org.

International students should apply especially early because of the number of steps required to complete the admissions process. Furthermore, many United States graduate schools have a limited number of spaces for international students, and many more students apply than the schools can accommodate.

International students may find financial assistance from institutions very limited. The U.S. government requires international applicants to submit a certification of support, which is a statement attesting to the applicant's financial resources. In addition, international students *must* have health insurance coverage.

Financial
Support

The range of financial support at the graduate level is very broad. The following descriptions will give you a general idea of what you might expect and what will be expected of you as a financial support recipient.

Fellowships, Scholarships, and Grants

These are usually outright awards of a few hundred to many thousands of dollars with no service to the institution required in return. Fellowships and scholarships are usually awarded on the basis of merit and are highly competitive. Grants are made on the basis of financial need or special talent in a field of study. Many grants not only cover tuition, fees, and supplies but also include stipends for living expenses with allowances for dependents. However, the terms of each grant should be examined because some do not permit recipients to supplement their income with outside work. Fellowships, scholarships, and grants may vary in the number of years for which they are awarded.

In addition to the availability of these funds at the university or program level, many excellent fellowship programs are available at the national level and may be applied for before and during enrollment in a graduate program. A listing of many of these programs can be found at the Council of Graduate Schools' Web site: http://www.cgsnet.org/ResourcesForStudents/fellowships.htm.

Assistantships and Internships

As described here, many graduate students receive financial support through assistantships, particularly involving teaching or research duties. It is important to recognize that such appointments should not be simply employment relationships but rather should constitute an integral and important part of a student's graduate education. As such, the appointments should be accompanied by strong faculty mentoring and increasingly responsible apprenticeship experiences (these are often lacking for teaching assistantships). The specific nature of these appointments in a given program should be factor considered in selecting that graduate program.

Teaching Assistantships

These usually provide a salary and full or partial tuition remission, and they may also provide health benefits. Unlike fellowships, scholarships, and grants, which require no service to the institution, teaching assistantships require recipients to provide the institution with a specific amount of undergraduate teaching, ideally related to the student's field of study. Some teaching assistants are limited to grading papers, compiling bibliographies, or monitoring laboratories. At some graduate schools, teaching assistants must carry lighter course loads than regular full-time students.

Research Assistantships

These are very similar to teaching assistantships in the manner in which financial assistance is provided. The difference is that recipients are given basic research assignments in their disciplines rather than teaching responsibilities. The work required is normally related to the student's field of study; in most instances, the assistantship supports the student's thesis or dissertation research.

Administrative Internships

These are similar to assistantships in application of financial assistance funds, but the student is given an assignment on a part-time basis, usually as a special assistant to one of the university's administrative officers. The assignment may not necessarily be directly related to the recipient's discipline.

Residence Hall and Counseling Assistantships

These are frequently assigned to graduate students in psychology, counseling, and social work. Duties can vary from being available in a dean's office for a specific number of hours for consultation with undergraduates to living in campus residences and being responsible for both counseling and administrative tasks or advising student activity groups. Residence hall assistantships sometimes include room and board in addition to tuition and stipends.

Health Insurance

The availability and affordability of health insurance is an important issue and one that should be considered in an applicant's choice of institution and program. While often included with assistantships and fellowships, this is not always the case and, even if provided, the benefits may be very limited. It is important to note that the U.S. government requires international students to have health insurance.

The GI Bill

This provides financial assistance for students who are veterans of the United States armed forces. If you are a veteran, contact your local Veterans Administration office to determine your eligibility and to get full details about benefits.

Federal Work-Study Program (FWS)

Employment is another way some students finance their graduate studies. The federally funded Federal Work-Study Program provides eligible students with employment opportunities, usually in public and private nonprofit organizations. Federal funds pay up to 75 percent of the wages, with the remainder paid by the employing agency. FWS is available to graduate students who demonstrate financial need. Not all schools have these funds, and some only award them to undergraduates. Each school sets its application deadline and work-study earnings limits. Wages vary and are related to the type of work done.

Loans

Many graduate students borrow to finance their graduate programs when other sources of assistance (which do not have to be repaid) prove insufficient. You should always read and understand the terms of any loan program before submitting your application.

Federal Loans

Federal Stafford Loans. The Federal Stafford Loan Program offers government-sponsored, low-interest loans to students through a private lender such as a bank, credit union, or savings and loan association.

There are two components of the Federal Stafford Loan program. Under the *subsidized* component of the program, the federal government pays the interest accruing on the loan while you are enrolled in graduate school on at least a half-time basis. Under the *unsubsidized* component of the program, you pay the interest on the loan from the day proceeds are issued. Eligibility for the federal subsidy is based on demonstrated financial need as determined by the financial aid office from the information you provide on the Free Application for Federal Student Aid (FAFSA). (See "Applying for Need-Based Financial Aid" for more information on the FAFSA.) A cosigner is not required, since the loan is not based on creditworthiness.

Although *unsubsidized* Federal Stafford Loans may not be as desirable as *subsidized* Federal Stafford Loans from the consumer's perspective, they are a useful source of support for those who may not qualify for the subsidized loans or who need additional financial assistance.

Graduate students may borrow up to $18,500 per year through the Stafford Loan

Program, up to a cumulative maximum of $138,500, including undergraduate borrowing. This may include up to $8500 in Subsidized Stafford Loans annually, depending on eligibility, up to a cumulative maximum of $65,500, including undergraduate borrowing. The amount of the loan borrowed through the *unsubsidized* Stafford Program equals the total amount of the loan (as much $18,500) minus your eligibility for a Subsidized Stafford Loan (as much as $8500). You may borrow up to the cost of the school in which you are enrolled or will attend, minus estimated financial assistance from other federal, state, and private sources, up to a maximum of $18,500.

The interest rate for the Federal Stafford Loans varies annually and is set every July. The rate during in-school, grace, and deferment periods is based on the 91-Day U.S. Treasury Bill rate plus 1.7 percent, capped at 8.25 percent. The rate during repayment is based on the 91-Day U.S. Treasury Bill rate plus 2.3 percent, capped at 8.25 percent. The 2002–03 rate is 4.06 percent.

Two fees may be deducted from the loan proceeds upon disbursement: a guarantee fee of up to 1 percent, which is deposited in an insurance pool to ensure repayment to the lender if the borrower defaults, and a federally mandated 3 percent origination fee, which is used to offset the administrative cost of the Federal Stafford Loan Program.

Under the *subsidized* Federal Stafford Loan Program, repayment begins six months after your last enrollment on at least a half-time basis. Under the *unsubsidized* program, repayment of interest begins within thirty days from disbursement of the loan proceeds, and repayment of the principal begins six months after your last enrollment on at least a half-time basis. Some borrowers may choose to defer interest payments while they are in school. The accrued interest is added to the loan balance when the borrower begins repayment. There are several repayment options.

Federal Direct Loans. Some schools participate in the Department of Education's Direct Lending Program instead of offering Federal Stafford Loans. The two programs are essentially the same except that with the Direct Loans, schools themselves generate the loans with funds provided from the federal government. Terms and interest rates are virtually the same except that there are a few more repayment options with Federal Direct Loans.

Federal Perkins Loans. The Federal Perkins Loan is available to students demonstrating financial need and is administered directly by the school. Not all schools have these funds, and some may award them to undergraduates only. Eligibility is determined from the information you provide on the FAFSA. The school will notify you of your eligibility.

Eligible graduate students may borrow up to $6000 per year, up to a maximum of $40,000, including undergraduate borrowing (even if your previous Perkins Loans have been repaid). The interest rate for Federal Perkins Loans is 5 percent, and no interest accrues while you remain in school at least half-time. There are no guarantee, loan, or disbursement fees. Repayment begins nine months after your last enrollment on at least a half-time basis and may extend over a maximum of ten years with no prepayment penalty.

Deferring Your Federal Loan Repayments. If you borrowed under the Federal Stafford Loan Program or the Federal Perkins Loan Program for previous undergraduate or graduate study, your repayments may be deferred when you return to graduate school, depending on when you borrowed and under which program.

There are other deferment options available if you are temporarily unable to repay your loan. Information about these deferments is provided at your entrance and exit interviews. If you believe you are eligible for a deferment of your loan repayments, you must contact your lender to complete a deferment form. The deferment must be filed prior to the time your repayment is due, and it must be refiled when it expires if you remain eligible for deferment at that time.

Supplemental (Private) Loans

Many lending institutions offer supplemental loan programs and other financing plans, such as the ones described below, to students seeking additional assistance in meeting their educational expenses. Some loan programs target all types of graduate students; others are designed specifically for business, law, or medical students. In addition, you can use private loans not specifically designed for education to help finance your graduate degree.

If you are considering borrowing through a supplemental or private loan program, you should carefully consider the terms and be sure to "read the fine print." Check with the program sponsor for the most current terms that will be applicable to the amounts you intend to borrow for graduate study. Most supplemental loan programs for graduate study offer unsubsidized, credit-based loans. In general, a credit-ready borrower is one who has a satisfactory credit history or no credit history at all. A creditworthy borrower generally must pass a credit test to be eligible to borrow or act as a cosigner for the loan funds.

Many supplemental loan programs have a minimum annual loan limit and a maximum annual loan limit. Some offer amounts equal to the cost of attendance minus any other aid you will receive for graduate study. If you are planning to borrow for several years of graduate study, consider whether there is a cumulative or aggregate limit on the amount you may borrow. Often this cumulative or aggregate limit will include any amounts you borrowed and have not repaid for undergraduate or previous graduate study.

The combination of the annual interest rate, loan fees, and the repayment terms you choose will determine how much you will repay over time. Compare these features in combination before you decide which loan program to use. Some loans offer interest rates that are adjusted monthly, some quarterly, some annually. Some offer interest rates that are lower during the in-school, grace, and deferment periods, and then increase when you begin repayment. Most programs include a loan "origination" fee, which is usually deducted from the principal amount you receive when the loan is disbursed, and must be repaid along with the interest and other principal when you graduate, withdraw from school, or drop below half-time study. Sometimes the loan fees are reduced if you borrow with a qualified cosigner. Some programs allow you to defer interest and/or principal payments while you are enrolled in graduate school.

Many programs allow you to capitalize your interest payments; the interest due on your loan is added to the outstanding balance of your loan, so you don't have to repay immediately, but this increases the amount you owe. Other programs allow you to pay the interest as you go, which will reduce the amount you later have to repay.

Some examples of supplemental programs follow.

CitiAssist Loans. Offered by Citibank, these no-fee loans help graduate students fill the gap between the financial aid they receive and the money they need for school. Visit www.studentloan.com for more loan information from Citibank.

EXCEL Loan. This program, sponsored by Nellie Mae, is designed for students who are not ready to borrow on their own and wish to borrow with a creditworthy cosigner. Visit www.nelliemae.com for more information.

Key Alternative Loan. This loan can bridge the gap between education costs and traditional funding. Visit www.keybank.com for more information.

Graduate Access Loan. Sponsored by the Access Group, this is for graduate students enrolled at least half-time. The Web site is www.accessgroup.com.

Signature Student Loan. A loan program for students who are enrolled at least half-time, this is sponsored by Sallie Mae. Visit www.salliemae.com for more information.

Remember that these are generalized statements about financial assistance at the graduate level. Because each institution allots its aid differently, you should communicate directly with the school and the specific department of interest to you. It is not unusual, for example, to find that an endowment vested within a specific department supports one or more fellowships. You may fit its requirements and specifications precisely.

Applying for Need-Based Financial Aid

Schools that award federal and institutional financial assistance based on need will require you to complete the FAFSA and, in some cases, an institutional financial aid application.

If you are applying for federal student assistance, you **must** complete the FAFSA. A service of the U.S. Department of Education, it is free to all applicants. You must send the FAFSA to the address listed in the FAFSA instructions or you can apply online at http://www.fafsa.ed.gov.

After your FAFSA information has been processed, you will receive a Student Aid Report (SAR). If you are an entering student, you may want to make copies of the SAR and send them to the school(s) to which you are applying. If you are a continuing student, you should make a copy of the SAR and forward the original document to the school you are attending.

Follow the instructions on the SAR if your situation changes and you need to correct information reported on your original application.

If you would like more information on federal student financial aid, visit the FAFSA Web site or request *The Student Guide 2003–2004* from the following address: Federal Student Aid Information Center, P.O. Box 84, Washington, DC 20044.

The U.S. Department of Education also has a toll-free number for questions concerning federal student aid programs. The number is 1-800-4-FED AID (1-800-433-3243). If you are hearing impaired, call toll-free, 1-800-730-8913.

Accreditation
and Accrediting Agencies

Colleges and universities in the United States, and their individual academic and professional programs, are accredited by nongovernmental agencies concerned with monitoring the quality of education in this country. Agencies with both regional and national jurisdictions grant accreditation to institutions as a whole, while specialized bodies acting on a nationwide basis—often national professional associations—grant accreditation to departments and programs in specific fields.

Institutional and specialized accrediting agencies share the same basic concerns: the purpose an academic unit—whether university or program—has set for itself and how well it fulfills that purpose, the adequacy of its financial and other resources, the quality of its academic offerings, and the level of services it provides. Agencies that grant institutional accreditation take a broader view, of course, and examine university-wide or college-wide services that a specialized agency may not concern itself with.

Both types of agencies follow the same general procedures when considering an application for accreditation. The academic unit prepares a self-evaluation, which focuses on the concerns mentioned above and includes an assessment of both its strengths and weaknesses; a team of representatives of the accrediting body reviews this evaluation, visits the campus, and makes its own report; and finally, the accrediting body makes a decision on the application. Often, even when accreditation is granted, the agency makes a recommendation regarding how the institution or program can improve. All institutions and programs are reviewed every few years to determine whether they continue to meet

established standards; if they do not, they may lose their accreditation.

Accrediting agencies themselves are reviewed and evaluated periodically by the U.S. Department of Education and the Council for Higher Education Accreditation (CHEA). Agencies recognized adhere to certain standards and practices, and their authority in matters of accreditation is widely accepted in the educational community.

This does not mean, however, that accreditation is a simple matter, either for schools wishing to become accredited or for students deciding where to apply. Indeed, in certain fields the very meaning and methods of accreditation are the subject of a good deal of debate. **Those who are applying to graduate school should be aware of the safeguards provided by regional accreditation, especially in terms of degree acceptance and institutional longevity. Indeed, many institutions that offer graduate study will accept only those applicants whose undergraduate degree is from a regionally accredited institution.** (NOTE: Most institutions profiled in the *Decision Guides* are regionally accredited.) Beyond this, applicants should understand the role that specialized accreditation plays in their field, as this varies considerably from one discipline to another. In certain professional fields, it is necessary to have graduated from a program that is accredited in order to be eligible for a license to practice, and, in some fields, the federal government also makes this a hiring requirement.

Institutions and programs that present themselves for accreditation are sometimes granted the status of candidate for accreditation, or what is known as "preaccreditation." This may happen, for example, when an academic unit is too new to have met all the requirements for accreditation. Such status signifies initial recognition and indicates that the school or program in question is working to fulfill all requirements; it does not, however, guarantee that accreditation will be granted.

Readers are advised to contact agencies directly for answers to their questions about accreditation. The names and addresses of all agencies recognized by the U.S. Department of Education and the Council for Higher Education Accreditation are listed below.

Institutional Accrediting Agencies—Regional

MIDDLE STATES ASSOCIATION OF COLLEGES AND SCHOOLS

Accredits institutions in Delaware, District of Columbia, Maryland, New Jersey, New York, Pennsylvania, Puerto Rico, and the Virgin Islands.

Jean Avnet Morse, Executive Director
Commission on Higher Education
3624 Market Street
Philadelphia, Pennsylvania 19104-2680
Telephone: 215-662-5606
Fax: 215-662-5501
E-mail: jamorse@msache.org
World Wide Web: http://www.msache.org

NEW ENGLAND ASSOCIATION OF SCHOOLS AND COLLEGES

Accredits institutions in Connecticut, Maine, Massachusetts, New Hampshire, Rhode Island, and Vermont.

Charles M. Cook, Director
Commission on Institutions of Higher
    Education
209 Burlington Road
Bedford, Massachusetts 01730-1433
Telephone: 781-271-0022
Fax: 781-271-0950
E-mail: CIHE@neasc.org
World Wide Web: http://www.neasc.org

NORTH CENTRAL ASSOCIATION OF COLLEGES AND SCHOOLS

Accredits institutions in Arizona, Arkansas, Colorado, Illinois, Indiana, Iowa, Kansas, Michigan, Minnesota, Missouri, Nebraska, New Mexico, North Dakota, Ohio, Oklahoma, South Dakota, West Virginia, Wisconsin, and Wyoming.

Steven D. Crow, Executive Director
The Higher Learning Commission
30 North LaSalle, Suite 2400
Chicago, Illinois 60602-2504
Telephone: 312-263-0456
Fax: 312-263-7462
E-mail: scrow@hlcommission.org
World Wide Web: http://www.
    ncahigherlearningcommission.org

NORTHWEST ASSOCIATION OF SCHOOLS AND COLLEGES

Accredits institutions in Alaska, Idaho, Montana, Nevada, Oregon, Utah, and Washington.

Sandra E. Elman, Executive Director
Commission on Colleges and Universities
8060 165th Avenue, NE, Suite 100
Redmond, Washington 98052
Telephone: 425-558-4224
Fax: 425-376-0596
E-mail: pjarnold@nwccu.org
World Wide Web: http://www.nwccu.org

SOUTHERN ASSOCIATION OF COLLEGES AND SCHOOLS

Accredits institutions in Alabama, Florida, Georgia, Kentucky, Louisiana, Mississippi, North Carolina, South Carolina, Tennessee, Texas, and Virginia.

James T. Rogers, Executive Director
Commission on Colleges
1866 Southern Lane
Decatur, Georgia 30033
Telephone: 404-679-4500
Fax: 404-679-4528
E-mail: jrogers@sacscoc.org
World Wide Web: http://www.sacscoc.org

WESTERN ASSOCIATION OF SCHOOLS AND COLLEGES

Accredits institutions in California, Guam, and Hawaii.

Ralph A. Wolff, Executive Director
The Senior College Commission
985 Atlantic Avenue, Suite 100
Alameda, California 94501
Telephone: 510-748-9001
Fax: 510-748-9797
E-mail: rwolff@wascsenior.org
World Wide Web: http://www.wascweb.org

Institutional Accrediting Agencies—Other

ACCREDITING COUNCIL FOR INDEPENDENT COLLEGES AND SCHOOLS

Dr. Steven A. Eggland, Executive Director
750 First Street, NE, Suite 980
Washington, D.C. 20002-4241
Telephone: 202-336-6780
Fax: 202-842-2593
E-mail: steve@acics.org
World Wide Web: http://www.acics.org

DISTANCE EDUCATION AND TRAINING COUNCIL

Michael P. Lambert, Executive Secretary
1601 Eighteenth Street, NW
Washington, D.C. 20009
Telephone: 202-234-5100
Fax: 202-332-1386
E-mail: detc@detc.org
World Wide Web: http://www.detc.org

Specialized Accrediting Agencies

ENGINEERING

George D. Peterson, Executive Director
Accreditation Board for Engineering and
    Technology, Inc.
111 Market Place, Suite 1050
Baltimore, Maryland 21202
Telephone: 410-347-7700
Fax: 410-625-2238
E-mail: gpeterson@abet.org
World Wide Web: http://www.abet.org

TECHNOLOGY

Elise Scanlon, Executive Director
Accrediting Commission of Career Schools
    and Colleges of Technology
2101 Wilson Boulevard, Suite 302
Arlington, Virginia 22201
Telephone:703-247-4212
Fax: 703-247-4533
E-mail: info@accsct.org
World Wide Web: http://www.accsct.org

Graduate Programs in
Computer Science

17

Computer Science and Information Technology

ARTIFICIAL INTELLIGENCE/ ROBOTICS

■ CARNEGIE MELLON UNIVERSITY

Carnegie Institute of Technology, Department of Civil and Environmental Engineering, Pittsburgh, PA 15213-3891

AWARDS Civil engineering (MS, PhD); civil engineering and industrial management (MS); civil engineering and robotics (PhD); civil engineering/bioengineering (PhD); civil engineering/engineering and public policy (MS, PhD). Part-time programs available. Terminal master's awarded for partial completion of doctoral program.

Degree requirements: For master's, thesis (for some programs); for doctorate, thesis/dissertation, qualifying exam.
Entrance requirements: For master's and doctorate, GRE General Test, TOEFL.
Faculty research: Computer-aided engineering and management, structured and computational machines, civil systems. *Web site:* http://www.ce.cmu.edu/

Find an in-depth description at www.petersons.com/gradchannel.

■ CARNEGIE MELLON UNIVERSITY

School of Computer Science and Carnegie Institute of Technology and Graduate School of Industrial Administration, Robotics Institute, Pittsburgh, PA 15213-3891

AWARDS MS, PhD.

Degree requirements: For doctorate, thesis/dissertation.
Entrance requirements: For doctorate, GRE General Test, GRE Subject Test, TOEFL.
Faculty research: Perception, cognition, manipulation, robot systems, manufacturing. *Web site:* http://www.ri.cmu.edu/
Find an in-depth description at www.petersons.com/gradchannel.

■ THE CATHOLIC UNIVERSITY OF AMERICA

School of Engineering, Department of Mechanical Engineering, Washington, DC 20064

AWARDS Design (D Engr, PhD); design and robotics (MME, D Engr, PhD); fluid mechanics and thermal science (MME, D Engr, PhD);

mechanical design (MME); ocean and structural acoustics (MME, MS Engr, PhD). Part-time and evening/weekend programs available.
Faculty: 6 full-time (1 woman).
Students: 7 full-time (0 women), 16 part-time (3 women); includes 4 minority (2 African Americans, 2 Asian Americans or Pacific Islanders), 8 international. Average age 34. 14 applicants, 36% accepted, 2 enrolled. In 2001, 3 master's, 3 doctorates awarded.
Degree requirements: For master's, thesis optional; for doctorate, thesis/dissertation, oral exams, comprehensive exam.
Entrance requirements: For master's, minimum GPA of 3.0; for doctorate, minimum GPA of 3.5. *Application deadline:* For fall admission, 8/1 (priority date); for spring admission, 12/1. Applications are processed on a rolling basis. *Application fee:* $55. Electronic applications accepted.
Expenses: Tuition: Full-time $20,050; part-time $770 per credit. Required fees: $430 per term. Tuition and fees vary according to program.
Financial support: Research assistantships, teaching assistantships, career-related internships or fieldwork, Federal Work-Study, institutionally sponsored loans, and tuition waivers (full and partial) available. Support available to part-time students. Financial award application deadline: 2/1.
Faculty research: Automated engineering. Dr. Ji Steven Brown, Chair, 202-319-5170.

■ CORNELL UNIVERSITY

Graduate School, Graduate Fields of Engineering, Field of Computer Science, Ithaca, NY 14853-0001

AWARDS Algorithms (M Eng, PhD); applied logic and automated reasoning (M Eng, PhD); artificial intelligence (M Eng, PhD); computer graphics (M Eng, PhD); computer science (M Eng, PhD); computer vision (M Eng, PhD); concurrency and distributed computing (M Eng, PhD); information organization and retrieval (M Eng, PhD); operating systems (M Eng, PhD); parallel computing (M Eng, PhD); programming environments (M Eng, PhD); programming languages and methodology (M Eng, PhD); robotics (M Eng, PhD); scientific computing (M Eng, PhD); theory of computation (M Eng, PhD).
Faculty: 39 full-time.
Students: 171 full-time (24 women); includes 23 minority (1 African American, 20 Asian Americans or Pacific Islanders, 2 Hispanic Americans), 88 international. 881 applicants, 19% accepted. In 2001, 92 master's, 17 doctorates awarded. Terminal master's awarded for partial completion of doctoral program.

Degree requirements: For doctorate, thesis/dissertation.
Entrance requirements: For master's, GRE General Test, TOEFL, 2 letters of recommendation; for doctorate, GRE General Test, GRE Subject Test (or mathematics), TOEFL, 2 letters of recommendation. *Application deadline:* For fall admission, 1/1 (priority date). *Application fee:* $65. Electronic applications accepted.
Expenses: Tuition: Full-time $25,970. Required fees: $50.
Financial support: In 2001–02, 87 students received support, including 20 fellowships with full tuition reimbursements available, 47 research assistantships with full tuition reimbursements available, 20 teaching assistantships with full tuition reimbursements available; institutionally sponsored loans, scholarships/grants, tuition waivers (full and partial), and unspecified assistantships also available. Financial award applicants required to submit FAFSA.
Faculty research: Artificial intelligence, operating systems and databases, programming languages and security, scientific computing, theory of computing.
Application contact: Graduate Field Assistant, 607-255-8593, *E-mail:* phd@cs.cornell.edu—meng@cs.cornell.edu. *Web site:* http://www.gradschool.cornell.edu/grad/fields_1/comp-sci.html

Find an in-depth description at www.petersons.com/gradchannel.

■ OHIO UNIVERSITY

Graduate Studies, Russ College of Engineering and Technology, Integrated Engineering Program, Athens, OH 45701-2979

AWARDS Geotechnical and environmental engineering (PhD); intelligent systems (PhD); materials processing (PhD).

Faculty: 39 full-time (1 woman).
Students: 16 full-time (1 woman), 8 part-time (1 woman), 21 international. 34 applicants, 88% accepted. In 2001, 3 degrees awarded.
Degree requirements: For doctorate, thesis/dissertation, comprehensive exam.
Entrance requirements: For doctorate, GRE General Test, MS in engineering or related field. *Application deadline:* For fall admission, 3/15. Applications are processed on a rolling basis. *Application fee:* $30.
Expenses: Tuition, state resident: full-time $6,585. Tuition, nonresident: full-time $12,254.
Financial support: In 2001–02, 3 fellowships with full tuition reimbursements (averaging $10,500 per year), 3 research assistantships with full tuition reimbursements (averaging $10,500 per year) were

awarded. Federal Work-Study, institutionally sponsored loans, and tuition waivers (full) also available. Financial award application deadline: 3/15.

Faculty research: Material processing, expert systems, environmental geotechnical manufacturing. *Total annual research expenditures:* $1.5 million.

Dr. Jerrel Mitchell, Associate Dean for Research and Graduate Studies, 740-593-1482, *E-mail:* mitchell@ bobcat.ent.ohiou.edu.

Find an in-depth description at www.petersons.com/gradchannel.

■ SAN JOSE STATE UNIVERSITY

Graduate Studies, College of Engineering, Department of Computer, Information and Systems Engineering, Program in Computer Engineering, San Jose, CA 95192-0001

AWARDS Computer engineering (MS); computer software (MS); computerized robots and computer applications (MS); microprocessors and microcomputers (MS).

Faculty: 5 full-time (0 women), 12 part-time/adjunct (1 woman).
Students: 62 full-time (36 women), 124 part-time (45 women); includes 119 minority (4 African Americans, 115 Asian Americans or Pacific Islanders), 33 international. Average age 28. 236 applicants, 39% accepted. In 2001, 53 degrees awarded.
Degree requirements: For master's, thesis, comprehensive exam.
Entrance requirements: For master's, GRE General Test, BS in computer science or 24 credits in related area. *Application deadline:* For fall admission, 6/29; for spring admission, 11/30. Applications are processed on a rolling basis. *Application fee:* $59. Electronic applications accepted.
Expenses: Tuition, nonresident: part-time $246 per unit. Required fees: $678 per semester. Tuition and fees vary according to course load.
Financial support: Teaching assistantships, career-related internships or fieldwork, Federal Work-Study, and institutionally sponsored loans available. Support available to part-time students. Financial award application deadline: 5/1; financial award applicants required to submit FAFSA.
Faculty research: Robotics, database management systems, computer networks.
Application contact: Dr. Haluk Ozemek, Coordinator, 408-924-4100.

■ SOUTHERN NEW HAMPSHIRE UNIVERSITY

School of Business, Graduate Programs, Program in Business Administration, Manchester, NH 03106-1045

AWARDS Accounting (Certificate); artificial intelligence (Certificate); business administration (MBA); computer informations systems (Certificate); database management (Certificate); finance (Certificate); health administration (Certificate); human resource management (Certificate); international business (Certificate); marketing (Certificate); operations management (Certificate); school business administration (Certificate); taxation (Certificate); telecommunications and networking (Certificate); training and development (Certificate). Part-time and evening/weekend programs available.

Faculty: 29 full-time (3 women), 104 part-time/adjunct (28 women).
Students: 122 full-time (45 women), 1,003 part-time (438 women), 95 international. Average age 32. In 2001, 411 degrees awarded.
Degree requirements: For master's, thesis or alternative.
Entrance requirements: For master's, minimum GPA of 2.7 during previous 2 years, 2.5 overall. *Application deadline:* Applications are processed on a rolling basis. *Application fee:* $0.
Expenses: Tuition: Full-time $11,340; part-time $1,260 per course. One-time fee: $540 full-time. Full-time tuition and fees vary according to course load, degree level and program.
Financial support: In 2001–02, 4 research assistantships were awarded; career-related internships or fieldwork, Federal Work-Study, and institutionally sponsored loans also available. Support available to part-time students.
Application contact: Patricia Gerard, Assistant Dean, Academic Services, School of Business, 603-644-3102, *Fax:* 603-644-3144, *E-mail:* p.gerard@snhu.edu.

Find an in-depth description at www.petersons.com/gradchannel.

■ UNIVERSITY OF CALIFORNIA, SAN DIEGO

Graduate Studies and Research, Department of Electrical and Computer Engineering, La Jolla, CA 92093

AWARDS Applied ocean science (MS, PhD); applied physics (MS, PhD); communication theory and systems (MS, PhD); computer engineering (MS, PhD); electrical engineering (M Eng); electronic circuits and systems (MS, PhD); intelligent systems, robotics and control (MS, PhD); photonics (MS, PhD); signal and image processing (MS, PhD).

Faculty: 35.

Students: 334 (44 women). 1,149 applicants, 20% accepted, 114 enrolled. In 2001, 51 master's, 12 doctorates awarded.
Entrance requirements: For master's and doctorate, GRE General Test. *Application deadline:* For fall admission, 1/12. *Application fee:* $40. Electronic applications accepted.
Expenses: Tuition, nonresident: full-time $10,434. Required fees: $4,883.
Charles Tu, Chair.
Application contact: Graduate Coordinator, 858-534-6606.

■ UNIVERSITY OF GEORGIA

Graduate School, College of Arts and Sciences, Program in Artificial Intelligence, Athens, GA 30602

AWARDS MS.

Faculty: 1 full-time (0 women).
Students: 21 full-time (5 women), 5 part-time (2 women), 21 international. 32 applicants, 38% accepted. In 2001, 5 degrees awarded.
Degree requirements: For master's, thesis.
Entrance requirements: For master's, GRE General Test. *Application deadline:* For fall admission, 7/1 (priority date); for spring admission, 11/15. *Application fee:* $30. Electronic applications accepted.
Expenses: Tuition, state resident: full-time $2,376; part-time $132 per credit hour. Tuition, nonresident: full-time $9,504; part-time $528 per credit hour. Required fees: $236 per semester.
Financial support: Unspecified assistantships available.
Dr. Donald Nute, Director, 706-542-0358, *Fax:* 706-542-8864, *E-mail:* dnute@ ai.uga.edu.
Application contact: Dr. Walter Don Potter, Graduate Coordinator, 706-542-0361, *Fax:* 706-542-8864, *E-mail:* potter@ cs.uga.edu. *Web site:* http://ai.uga.edu/

■ UNIVERSITY OF SOUTHERN CALIFORNIA

Graduate School, School of Engineering, Department of Computer Science, Program in Robotics and Automation, Los Angeles, CA 90089

AWARDS MS.

Entrance requirements: For master's, GRE General Test.
Expenses: Tuition: Full-time $25,060; part-time $844 per unit. Required fees: $473.
Faculty research: Neural computation, molecular computation.

■ THE UNIVERSITY OF TENNESSEE

Graduate School, College of Engineering, Department of Mechanical and Aerospace Engineering and Engineering Science, Program in Engineering Science, Knoxville, TN 37996

AWARDS Applied artificial intelligence (MS); biomedical engineering (MS, PhD); composite materials (MS, PhD); computational mechanics (MS, PhD); engineering science (MS, PhD); fluid mechanics (MS, PhD); industrial engineering (PhD); optical engineering (MS, PhD); product development and manufacturing (MS); solid mechanics (MS, PhD). Part-time programs available.

Students: 25 full-time (5 women), 16 part-time (2 women); includes 6 minority (2 African Americans, 2 Asian Americans or Pacific Islanders, 1 Hispanic American, 1 Native American), 9 international. 20 applicants, 70% accepted. In 2001, 6 master's, 6 doctorates awarded.
Degree requirements: For master's, thesis or alternative; for doctorate, thesis/dissertation.
Entrance requirements: For master's and doctorate, TOEFL, minimum GPA of 2.7. *Application deadline:* For fall admission, 2/1 (priority date). Applications are processed on a rolling basis. *Application fee:* $35. Electronic applications accepted.
Expenses: Tuition, state resident: full-time $4,280; part-time $233 per hour. Tuition, nonresident: full-time $12,066; part-time $666 per hour. Tuition and fees vary according to program.
Financial support: Career-related internships or fieldwork, Federal Work-Study, and institutionally sponsored loans available. Financial award application deadline: 2/1; financial award applicants required to submit FAFSA.
Application contact: Dr. Majid Keyhani, Graduate Representative, 865-974-4795, *E-mail:* keyhani@utk.edu.

BIOINFORMATICS

■ BOSTON UNIVERSITY

Graduate School of Arts and Sciences and College of Engineering, Program in Bioinformatics, Boston, MA 02215

AWARDS MS, PhD.

Students: 46 full-time (10 women), 16 part-time (5 women); includes 7 minority (4 African Americans, 3 Asian Americans or Pacific Islanders), 16 international. Average age 29.
Expenses: Tuition: Full-time $25,872; part-time $340 per credit. Required fees: $40 per semester. Part-time tuition and fees vary according to class time, course level and program.

Application contact: Graduate Program Administrator, 617-358-0752, *Fax:* 617-353-5929, *E-mail:* bioinfo@bu.edu.
Find an in-depth description at www.petersons.com/gradchannel.

■ GEORGE MASON UNIVERSITY

College of Arts and Sciences, Department of Biology, Master's Program in Biology, Fairfax, VA 22030-4444

AWARDS Bioinformatics (MS); ecology, systematics and evolution (MS); environmental science and public policy (MS); interpretive biology (MS); molecular, microbial, and cellular biology (MS); organismal biology (MS). Part-time programs available.

Faculty: 18 full-time (8 women), 40 part-time/adjunct (25 women).
Students: 7 full-time (3 women), 52 part-time (32 women); includes 4 minority (1 African American, 1 Asian American or Pacific Islander, 2 Hispanic Americans), 6 international. Average age 31. 44 applicants, 61% accepted, 17 enrolled. In 2001, 16 degrees awarded.
Degree requirements: For master's, thesis or alternative.
Entrance requirements: For master's, GRE General Test, GRE Subject Test, bachelor's degree in biology or equivalent. *Application deadline:* For fall admission, 5/1; for spring admission, 11/1. *Application fee:* $30. Electronic applications accepted.
Expenses: Tuition, state resident: full-time $3,168; part-time $132 per credit hour. Tuition, nonresident: full-time $11,280; part-time $470 per credit hour. Required fees: $1,416; $59 per credit hour.
Financial support: Available to part-time students. Application deadline: 3/1; *Web site:* http://www.gmu.edu/departments/biology/sublevelgradpro3.html

■ INDIANA UNIVERSITY BLOOMINGTON

School of Informatics, Bloomington, IN 47405

AWARDS Bioinformatics (MS); chemical informatics (MS); human computer interaction (MS); new media (MS), including media arts and science.

Students: 13 full-time (4 women), 2 part-time (1 woman); includes 2 minority (both Asian Americans or Pacific Islanders), 5 international. Average age 30.
Application fee: $45 ($55 for international students).
Expenses: Tuition, state resident: full-time $4,720; part-time $197 per credit. Tuition, nonresident: full-time $13,748; part-time $573 per credit. Required fees: $642.
Financial support: In 2001–02, fellowships (averaging $5,000 per year)
J. Michael Dunn, Dean. *Web site:* http://www.informatics.indiana.edu/

■ IOWA STATE UNIVERSITY OF SCIENCE AND TECHNOLOGY

Graduate College, Interdisciplinary Programs, Bioinformatics and Computational Biology Program, Ames, IA 50011-3260

AWARDS PhD.

Students: 40 full-time (12 women); includes 2 minority (both African Americans), 28 international. 257 applicants, 9% accepted, 9 enrolled.
Degree requirements: For doctorate, thesis/dissertation.
Entrance requirements: For doctorate, GRE General Test, TOEFL or IELTS. *Application deadline:* For fall admission, 2/1 (priority date). Electronic applications accepted.
Expenses: Tuition, state resident: full-time $1,851. Tuition, nonresident: full-time $5,449. Tuition and fees vary according to program.
Financial support: In 2001–02, 28 research assistantships with full tuition reimbursements (averaging $16,600 per year), 1 teaching assistantship with full tuition reimbursement (averaging $12,028 per year) were awarded. Fellowships with full tuition reimbursements, scholarships/grants, traineeships, health care benefits, and unspecified assistantships also available.
Faculty research: Functional and structural genomics, genome evolution, macromolecular structure and function, mathematical biology and computational modeling, metabolic and developmental networks.
Dr. Daniel Voytas, Chair, 515-294-5122, *Fax:* 515-294-6790, *E-mail:* bcb@iastate.edu.
Application contact: Kathy Wiederin, Program Assistant, 888-569-8509, *Fax:* 515-294-6790, *E-mail:* bcb@iastate.edu. *Web site:* http://www.bcb.iastate.edu/
Find an in-depth description at www.petersons.com/gradchannel.

■ MARQUETTE UNIVERSITY

Graduate School, Program in Bioinformatics, Milwaukee, WI 53201-1881

AWARDS MS.

Students: 3 full-time (2 women), 3 part-time; includes 3 minority (all Asian Americans or Pacific Islanders), 2 international. Average age 32.
Application fee: $40.
Expenses: Tuition: Full-time $10,170; part-time $445 per credit hour. Tuition and fees vary according to course load.
Dr. Anne Clough, Head, 414-288-5238, *E-mail:* clough@mscs.mu.edu. *Web site:* http://www.brc.mcw.edu/ap

■ NORTH CAROLINA STATE UNIVERSITY

Graduate School, Program in Genomic Sciences, Program in Bioinformatics, Raleigh, NC 27695

AWARDS MB, PhD.

Faculty: 87 full-time (22 women), 2 part-time/adjunct (0 women).
Students: 31 full-time (13 women), 8 part-time (3 women); includes 10 minority (3 African Americans, 7 Asian Americans or Pacific Islanders), 15 international. Average age 30. 72 applicants, 21% accepted. In 2001, 4 degrees awarded.
Entrance requirements: For master's and doctorate, GRE, TOEFL, minimum B average. *Application deadline:* For fall admission, 6/25; for spring admission, 11/25. *Application fee:* $55.
Expenses: Tuition, state resident: full-time $1,748. Tuition, nonresident: full-time $6,904.
Financial support: In 2001–02, 12 fellowships (averaging $6,805 per year), 11 research assistantships (averaging $5,980 per year), 1 teaching assistantship (averaging $5,545 per year) were awarded. Financial award application deadline: 1/15.
Faculty research: Statistical genetics, molecular evolution, pedigree analysis, quantitative genetics, protein structure. Dr. Barbara Sherry, Director of Graduate Programs, 919-515-4480, *Fax:* 919-515-3044, *E-mail:* barbara_sherry@ncsu.edu.

Find an in-depth description at www.petersons.com/gradchannel.

■ RENSSELAER POLYTECHNIC INSTITUTE

Graduate School, School of Science, Department of Bioinformatics, Troy, NY 12180-3590

AWARDS MS.

Application deadline: For fall admission, 1/15. Applications are processed on a rolling basis. *Application fee:* $45. Electronic applications accepted.
Expenses: Tuition: Full-time $26,400; part-time $1,320 per credit hour. Required fees: $1,437.
Application contact: Elena M. Quiroz, Assistant Dean, 518-276-6142, *E-mail:* bioinformatics@rpi.edu.

■ UNIVERSITY OF CALIFORNIA, RIVERSIDE

Graduate Division, Interdepartmental Program in Genetics, Riverside, CA 92521-0102

AWARDS Genomics and bioinformatics (PhD); molecular genetics, evolutionary and population genetics (PhD).

Students: 7 full-time (5 women); includes 2 minority (both Asian Americans or Pacific Islanders), 1 international. In 2001, 1 degree awarded.

Degree requirements: For doctorate, thesis/dissertation, qualifying exams, teaching experience.
Entrance requirements: For doctorate, GRE General Test, TOEFL, minimum GPA of 3.2. *Application deadline:* For fall admission, 5/1; for spring admission, 12/1. Applications are processed on a rolling basis. *Application fee:* $40.
Expenses: Tuition, state resident: full-time $5,001. Tuition, nonresident: full-time $15,897.
Financial support: Fellowships, research assistantships, teaching assistantships, career-related internships or fieldwork, Federal Work-Study, institutionally sponsored loans, and tuition waivers (full and partial) available. Financial award application deadline: 2/1; financial award applicants required to submit FAFSA.
Faculty research: Molecular genetics, microbial genetics, plant genetics, population genetics, evolutionary genetics. Dr. Bradley Hyman, Chair.
Application contact: 909-787-5688, *Fax:* 909-787-5517, *E-mail:* genetics@ucrac1.ucr.edu. *Web site:* http://molecular-evolutionary.genetics.ucr.edu/

Find an in-depth description at www.petersons.com/gradchannel.

■ UNIVERSITY OF CALIFORNIA, SAN DIEGO

Graduate Studies and Research, Interdisciplinary Doctoral Program in Bioinformatics, La Jolla, CA 92093

AWARDS PhD. Offered through the Departments of Bioengineering, Biology, Biomedical Sciences, Chemistry and Biochemistry, Computer Sciences and Engineering, Mathematics, and Physics.

Faculty: 49.
Students: 9 (3 women). 96 applicants, 15% accepted, 9 enrolled.
Entrance requirements: For doctorate, GRE General Test. *Application deadline:* For fall admission, 1/16. *Application fee:* $40. Electronic applications accepted.
Expenses: Tuition, nonresident: full-time $10,434. Required fees: $4,883. Dr. Shankar Subramaniam, Chair, 858-822-4948.
Application contact: Annie Perez, Graduate Coordinator, 858-822-4948, *E-mail:* aperez@ucsd.edu.

Find an in-depth description at www.petersons.com/gradchannel.

■ UNIVERSITY OF CALIFORNIA, SANTA CRUZ

Division of Graduate Studies, School of Engineering, Program in Bioinformatics, Santa Cruz, CA 95064

AWARDS MS, PhD.

Degree requirements: For master's and doctorate, thesis/dissertation.

Entrance requirements: For master's and doctorate, GRE General Test.
Expenses: Tuition: Full-time $19,857.

■ UNIVERSITY OF MEDICINE AND DENTISTRY OF NEW JERSEY

School of Health Related Professions, Department of Health Informatics, Program in Biomedical Informatics, Newark, NJ 07107-3001

AWARDS MS, PhD.

Application deadline: For fall admission, 6/1; for spring admission, 10/1.
Expenses: Tuition, state resident: part-time $292 per credit. Tuition, nonresident: part-time $440 per credit. Full-time tuition and fees vary according to degree level, program and student level.
Application contact: Dr. Laura B. Nelson, Associate Dean of Academic and Student Services, 973-972-5454, *Fax:* 973-972-7028, *E-mail:* shrp.adm@umdnj.edu.

■ UNIVERSITY OF MICHIGAN

Horace H. Rackham School of Graduate Studies, Program in Bioinformatics, Ann Arbor, MI 48109

AWARDS MS, PhD. Part-time programs available.

Faculty: 27 full-time (7 women), 2 part-time/adjunct (1 woman).
Students: 7 full-time (0 women), 1 (woman) part-time; includes 1 minority (Hispanic American), 5 international. 140 applicants, 10% accepted, 6 enrolled.
Degree requirements: For master's, summer internship, thesis optional; for doctorate, thesis/dissertation, 3 rotations, comprehensive exam, registration.
Entrance requirements: For master's and doctorate, GRE or MCAT, TOEFL. *Application deadline:* For fall admission, 1/5. *Application fee:* $50. Electronic applications accepted.
Faculty research: Mathematical modeling, molecular modeling, statistical methods for computational biology.
Application contact: Alicia Marie Mastronardi, Administrative Assistant I, 734-615-8895, *Fax:* 734-615-6553, *E-mail:* allegria@umich.edu. *Web site:* http://www.bioinformatics.med.umich.edu/

■ UNIVERSITY OF PITTSBURGH

School of Medicine, Biomedical Informatics Training Program, Pittsburgh, PA 15260

AWARDS MS, PhD, Certificate. Part-time programs available. Terminal master's awarded for partial completion of doctoral program.

Degree requirements: For master's, written research report or thesis, thesis optional; for doctorate, thesis/dissertation, comprehensive exam, registration; for Certificate, written research report or thesis.

University of Pittsburgh (continued)
Expenses: Tuition, state resident: full-time $9,410; part-time $385 per credit. Tuition, nonresident: full-time $19,376; part-time $797 per credit. Required fees: $480; $90 per term. Tuition and fees vary according to program.
Faculty research: Artificial intelligence; probability theory; data mining; machine learning; evaluation methods; dental, radiology, and pathology imaging. *Web site:* http://www.cbmi.upmc.edu

■ THE UNIVERSITY OF TEXAS AT EL PASO

Graduate School, College of Science, Department of Biological Sciences, Program in Bioinformatics, El Paso, TX 79968-0001

AWARDS MS.

Expenses: Tuition, state resident: full-time $2,450. Tuition, nonresident: full-time $6,000.
Application contact: Dr. Eppie D. Rael, Student Information Contact, 915-747-5844, *Fax:* 915-747-5808, *E-mail:* erael@miners.utep.edu.

■ UNIVERSITY OF WASHINGTON

School of Medicine and Graduate School, Graduate Programs in Medicine, Department of Medical Education and Health Informatics, Division of Biomedical and Health Informatics, Seattle, WA 98195

AWARDS MS.

Entrance requirements: For master's, GRE General Test, TOEFL, minimum GPA of 3.0; previous undergraduate course work in biology, computer programming, and mathematics. *Application deadline:* For fall admission, 2/1. *Application fee:* $50. Electronic applications accepted.
Expenses: Tuition, state resident: full-time $5,539. Tuition, nonresident: full-time $14,376. Required fees: $390. Tuition and fees vary according to course load and program.
Dr. Ira Kalet, Director.
Application contact: Jennifer Hoffman, Program Manager, *Fax:* 206-543-3461, *E-mail:* informat@u.washington.edu.

■ VANDERBILT UNIVERSITY

Graduate School, Department of Biomedical Informatics, Nashville, TN 37240-1001

AWARDS MS, PhD.

Faculty: 13 full-time (3 women).
Students: 3 full-time (1 woman), 1 part-time, 2 international.
Degree requirements: For doctorate, thesis/dissertation, final and qualifying exams.
Application deadline: For fall admission, 1/15. *Application fee:* $40.

Expenses: Tuition: Full-time $28,350.
Randolph A. Miller, Chair, 615-936-1556, *Fax:* 615-936-1427, *E-mail:* randolph.a.miller@vanderbilt.edu.
Application contact: Dominik Aronsky, Director of Graduate Studies, 615-936-1425, *Fax:* 615-936-1427, *E-mail:* dominik.aronsky@mcmail.vanderbilt.edu.

■ YALE UNIVERSITY

Graduate School of Arts and Sciences, Department of Molecular, Cellular, and Developmental Biology, Program in Developmental Biology, New Haven, CT 06520

AWARDS PhD.

Degree requirements: For doctorate, thesis/dissertation.
Entrance requirements: For doctorate, GRE General Test, GRE Subject Test.
Find an in-depth description at www.petersons.com/gradchannel.

■ YALE UNIVERSITY

School of Medicine and Graduate School of Arts and Sciences, Combined Program in Biological and Biomedical Sciences (BBS), Bioinformatics and Computational Biology Track, New Haven, CT 06520

AWARDS PhD, MD/PhD.

Dr. Perry Miller, Director of Graduate Studies, *E-mail:* dgs.bioinfo@yale.edu. *Web site:* http://info.med.yale.edu/bbs

COMPUTER SCIENCE

■ ADELPHI UNIVERSITY

Graduate School of Arts and Sciences, Department of Mathematics and Computer Science, Garden City, NY 11530

AWARDS MS, DA. Part-time and evening/weekend programs available.

Students: Average age 53.
Degree requirements: For doctorate, thesis/dissertation.
Application deadline: Applications are processed on a rolling basis. *Application fee:* $50.
Expenses: Tuition: Full-time $12,960; part-time $540 per credit. One-time fee: $400 part-time. Tuition and fees vary according to course load, degree level and program.
Financial support: Fellowships, teaching assistantships, tuition waivers (full) available. Financial award application deadline: 2/15; financial award applicants required to submit FAFSA.
Dr. William Quirin, Chairperson, 516-877-4480.

■ AIR FORCE INSTITUTE OF TECHNOLOGY

School of Engineering and Management, Department of Electrical and Computer Engineering, Dayton, OH 45433-7765

AWARDS Computer engineering (MS, PhD); computer systems/science (MS); electrical engineering (MS, PhD); electro-optics (MS, PhD). Part-time programs available.

Degree requirements: For master's and doctorate, thesis/dissertation.
Entrance requirements: For master's and doctorate, GRE General Test, minimum GPA of 3.0, U.S. citizenship.
Faculty research: Remote sensing, information survivability, microelectronics, computer networks, artificial intelligence. *Web site:* http://en.afit.edu/bng/

■ ALABAMA AGRICULTURAL AND MECHANICAL UNIVERSITY

School of Graduate Studies, School of Arts and Sciences, Department of Mathematics and Computer Science, Huntsville, AL 35811

AWARDS MS. Evening/weekend programs available.

Faculty: 4 full-time (0 women), 2 part-time/adjunct (0 women).
Students: 16 full-time (6 women), 29 part-time (17 women); includes 10 minority (8 African Americans, 2 Asian Americans or Pacific Islanders), 31 international. Average age 30. In 2001, 15 degrees awarded.
Degree requirements: For master's, thesis optional.
Entrance requirements: For master's, GRE General Test, TOEFL. *Application deadline:* For fall admission, 5/1. *Application fee:* $15 ($20 for international students).
Expenses: Tuition, state resident: full-time $1,380. Tuition, nonresident: full-time $2,500.
Financial support: In 2001–02, 5 research assistantships with tuition reimbursements (averaging $4,900 per year) were awarded; career-related internships or fieldwork also available. Financial award application deadline: 4/1.
Faculty research: Computer-assisted instruction, database management, software engineering, operating systems, neural networks.
Dr. Surendar Pulusami, Chair, 256-851-4119.

■ ALCORN STATE UNIVERSITY

School of Graduate Studies, School of Arts and Sciences, Department of Mathematical Sciences, Alcorn State, MS 39096-7500

AWARDS Computer and information sciences (MS).

Application deadline: For fall admission, 7/15 (priority date); for spring admission,

11/25. Applications are processed on a rolling basis. *Application fee:* $0 ($10 for international students).

Expenses: Tuition, state resident: full-time $6,418; part-time $924 per credit. Tuition, nonresident: full-time $12,497; part-time $1,656 per credit.

Dr. Keith Alford, Chairperson, 601-877-6420.

■ AMERICAN COLLEGE OF COMPUTER & INFORMATION SCIENCES

Department of Computer Science, Birmingham, AL 35205

AWARDS MSCS. Part-time and evening/weekend programs available. Postbaccalaureate distance learning degree programs offered (no on-campus study).

Faculty: 1 (woman) full-time.

Students: Average age 35. 244 applicants, 28% accepted. In 2001, 10 degrees awarded.

Entrance requirements: For master's, bachelor's degree in related field. *Application deadline:* Applications are processed on a rolling basis. *Application fee:* $20. Electronic applications accepted.

Expenses: Tuition: Full-time $5,580.

Cheryl Mills, Program Director, 800-767-2427, *Fax:* 205-326-3822, *E-mail:* faculty@accis.edu.

Application contact: Natalie Nixon, Director of Admissions, 800-767-2427, *Fax:* 205-328-2229, *E-mail:* admiss@accis.edu. *Web site:* http://www.accis.edu/

■ AMERICAN UNIVERSITY

College of Arts and Sciences, Department of Computer Science and Information Systems, Program in Computer Science, Washington, DC 20016-8001

AWARDS MS. Part-time and evening/weekend programs available.

Students: 16 full-time (9 women), 23 part-time (4 women); includes 7 minority (2 African Americans, 4 Asian Americans or Pacific Islanders, 1 Hispanic American), 23 international. Average age 29. In 2001, 20 degrees awarded.

Degree requirements: For master's, thesis or alternative, comprehensive exam.

Entrance requirements: For master's, minimum GPA of 3.0. *Application deadline:* For fall admission, 2/1 (priority date); for spring admission, 10/1. Applications are processed on a rolling basis. *Application fee:* $50.

Expenses: Tuition: Full-time $14,274; part-time $793 per credit. Required fees: $290. Tuition and fees vary according to program.

Financial support: Fellowships with full tuition reimbursements, career-related internships or fieldwork, Federal Work-Study, institutionally sponsored loans, tuition waivers (full and partial), and

unspecified assistantships available. Financial award application deadline: 2/1.

Faculty research: Artificial intelligence, database systems, software engineering, expert systems. *Web site:* http://www.csis.american.edu/

■ AMERICAN UNIVERSITY

College of Arts and Sciences, Department of Mathematics and Statistics, Program in Statistical Computing, Washington, DC 20016-8001

AWARDS MS. Part-time and evening/weekend programs available.

Degree requirements: For master's, one foreign language, thesis optional.

Entrance requirements: For master's, BA in mathematics. *Application deadline:* For fall admission, 2/1; for spring admission, 10/1. *Application fee:* $50.

Expenses: Tuition: Full-time $14,274; part-time $793 per credit. Required fees: $290. Tuition and fees vary according to program.

Financial support: Fellowships, teaching assistantships, career-related internships or fieldwork, Federal Work-Study, and institutionally sponsored loans available. Support available to part-time students. Financial award application deadline: 2/1.

Faculty research: Data analysis; random processes; environmental, meteorological, and biological applications.

■ APPALACHIAN STATE UNIVERSITY

Cratis D. Williams Graduate School, College of Arts and Sciences, Department of Computer Science, Boone, NC 28608

AWARDS MS.

Faculty: 9 full-time (3 women).

Students: 14 full-time (2 women), 4 part-time (1 woman); includes 1 African American, 1 Hispanic American, 4 international. 17 applicants, 65% accepted, 7 enrolled. In 2001, 1 degree awarded.

Degree requirements: For master's, one foreign language, comprehensive exam.

Entrance requirements: For master's, GRE General Test. *Application deadline:* For fall admission, 7/1 (priority date); for spring admission, 11/1. *Application fee:* $35.

Expenses: Tuition, state resident: full-time $1,286. Tuition, nonresident: full-time $9,354. Required fees: $1,116.

Financial support: In 2001–02, fellowships (averaging $2,000 per year), 5 research assistantships (averaging $8,000 per year), 1 teaching assistantship (averaging $8,000 per year) were awarded. Scholarships/grants and unspecified assistantships also available. Financial award application deadline: 7/1; financial award applicants required to submit FAFSA. *Total annual research expenditures:* $36,000.

Dr. Ed Pekarek, Chairperson, 828-262-2612.

Application contact: Dr. James Wilkes, Adviser, 828-262-3050, *Fax:* 828-265-8617, *E-mail:* wilkesjt@appstate.edu.

■ ARIZONA STATE UNIVERSITY

Graduate College, College of Engineering and Applied Sciences, Department of Computer Science and Engineering, Tempe, AZ 85287

AWARDS Computer science (MCS, MS, PhD).

Degree requirements: For master's, thesis or alternative; for doctorate, thesis/dissertation.

Entrance requirements: For master's and doctorate, GRE General Test (recommended).

Faculty research: Software engineering, graphics, computer-aided geometric design microprocessor applications, digital system design.

Find an in-depth description at www.petersons.com/gradchannel.

■ ARKANSAS STATE UNIVERSITY

Graduate School, College of Arts and Sciences, Department of Computer Science and Mathematics, Jonesboro, State University, AR 72467

AWARDS Computer science (MS); mathematics (MS, MSE). Part-time programs available.

Faculty: 12 full-time (2 women).

Students: 20 full-time (5 women), 5 part-time (1 woman); includes 4 minority (3 Asian Americans or Pacific Islanders, 1 Hispanic American), 11 international. Average age 28. In 2001, 11 degrees awarded.

Degree requirements: For master's, thesis or alternative, comprehensive exam.

Entrance requirements: For master's, GRE General Test or MAT, appropriate bachelor's degree. *Application deadline:* For fall admission, 7/1 (priority date); for spring admission, 11/15 (priority date). Applications are processed on a rolling basis. *Application fee:* $15 ($25 for international students). Electronic applications accepted.

Expenses: Tuition, state resident: full-time $3,384; part-time $141 per hour. Tuition, nonresident: full-time $8,520; part-time $355 per hour. Required fees: $742; $28 per hour. $25 per semester. One-time fee: $15 full-time. Tuition and fees vary according to degree level.

Financial support: Teaching assistantships, Federal Work-Study and scholarships/grants available. Support available to part-time students. Financial award application deadline: 7/1; financial award applicants required to submit FAFSA.

Dr. Jeff Jenness, Chair, 870-972-3090, *Fax:* 870-972-3950, *E-mail:* jeffj@astate.edu. *Web site:* http://www.csm.astate.edu/

■ AUBURN UNIVERSITY

Graduate School, College of Engineering, Department of Computer Science and Software Engineering, Auburn University, AL 36849

AWARDS MS, MSWE, PhD. Part-time programs available.

Faculty: 12 full-time (0 women).
Students: 59 full-time (16 women), 45 part-time (18 women); includes 8 minority (6 African Americans, 2 Asian Americans or Pacific Islanders), 60 international. 138 applicants, 44% accepted. In 2001, 33 master's, 4 doctorates awarded.
Degree requirements: For master's, thesis (for some programs); for doctorate, thesis/dissertation.
Entrance requirements: For master's and doctorate, GRE General Test, GRE Subject Test. *Application deadline:* For fall admission, 7/7; for spring admission, 11/24. Applications are processed on a rolling basis. *Application fee:* $25 ($50 for international students). Electronic applications accepted.
Financial support: Research assistantships, teaching assistantships, Federal Work-Study available. Support available to part-time students. Financial award application deadline: 3/15.
Faculty research: Parallelizable, scalable software translations; graphical representations of algorithms, structures, and processes; graph drawing. *Total annual research expenditures:* $400,000.
Dr. James Cross, Chair, 334-844-4330.
Application contact: Dr. John F. Pritchett, Dean of the Graduate School, 334-844-4700, *E-mail:* hatchlb@ mail.auburn.edu. *Web site:* http:// www.eng.auburn.edu/department/cse/

■ AZUSA PACIFIC UNIVERSITY

College of Liberal Arts and Sciences, Department of Computer Science, Azusa, CA 91702-7000

AWARDS Applied computer science and technology (MS), including client/server technology, computer information systems, end-user support, inter-emphasis, technical programming, telecommunications; client/ server technology (Certificate); computer information systems (Certificate); computer science (Certificate); end-user training and support (Certificate); software engineering (MSE); technical programming (Certificate); telecommunications (Certificate). Part-time and evening/weekend programs available.

Students: 34 full-time (8 women), 98 part-time (30 women); includes 44 minority (6 African Americans, 28 Asian Americans or Pacific Islanders, 10 Hispanic Americans), 57 international. 126 applicants, 94% accepted. In 2001, 51 degrees awarded.
Degree requirements: For master's, thesis or alternative, project.
Entrance requirements: For master's, minimum GPA of 3.0; proficiency in 1 programming language, college-level algebra, and applied calculus. *Application deadline:* For fall admission, 9/1 (priority date). Applications are processed on a rolling basis. *Application fee:* $45 ($65 for international students).
Expenses: Contact institution.
Financial support: Teaching assistantships, career-related internships or fieldwork available. Support available to part-time students.
Faculty research: Applied artificial intelligence, programming languages, engineering, database systems.
Dr. Samuel Sambasivam, Acting Chairman, 626-815-5310, *Fax:* 626-815-5323, *E-mail:* ssambasivam@apu.edu. *Web site:* http:// www.apu.edu/~cs/

Find an in-depth description at www.petersons.com/gradchannel.

■ BALL STATE UNIVERSITY

Graduate School, College of Sciences and Humanities, Department of Computer Science, Muncie, IN 47306-1099

AWARDS MA, MS.

Faculty: 9.
Students: 33 full-time (9 women), 32 part-time (7 women). Average age 30. 78 applicants, 81% accepted. In 2001, 50 degrees awarded.
Entrance requirements: For master's, GRE General Test. *Application fee:* $25 ($35 for international students).
Expenses: Tuition, state resident: full-time $4,068; part-time $2,542. Tuition, nonresident: full-time $10,944; part-time $6,462. Required fees: $1,000; $500 per term.
Financial support: In 2001–02, 12 teaching assistantships with full tuition reimbursements (averaging $7,272 per year) were awarded. Financial award application deadline: 3/1.
Faculty research: Numerical methods, programmer productivity, graphics.
Dr. Norman Gibbs, Chairperson, 765-285-8641, *Fax:* 765-285-2614, *E-mail:* ngibbs@ bsu.edu.
Application contact: Dr. J. Michael McGrew, Graduate Program Director, 765-285-8641, *Fax:* 765-285-2614, *E-mail:* mmcgrew@bsu.edu. *Web site:* http:// www.cs.bsu.edu/

■ BAYLOR UNIVERSITY

Graduate School, School of Engineering and Computer Science, Waco, TX 76798

AWARDS Computer science (MS). Part-time programs available.

Students: 14 full-time (1 woman), 5 part-time (1 woman), 13 international. In 2001, 3 degrees awarded.
Degree requirements: For master's, thesis optional.
Entrance requirements: For master's, GRE General Test, minimum GPA of 3.0. *Application deadline:* For fall admission, 8/1; for spring admission, 12/1. Applications are processed on a rolling basis. *Application fee:* $25.
Expenses: Tuition: Part-time $379 per semester hour. Required fees: $42 per semester hour. $101 per semester. Tuition and fees vary according to program.
Financial support: Teaching assistantships available. Financial award application deadline: 3/15.
Faculty research: Database systems, advanced architecture, operations research.
Dr. Greg Speegle, Director of Graduate Studies, 254-710-3876, *Fax:* 254-710-3839, *E-mail:* greg_speegle@baylor.edu.
Application contact: Suzanne Keener, Administrative Assistant, 254-710-3588, *Fax:* 254-710-3870, *E-mail:* graduate_ school@baylor.edu. *Web site:* http:// cs.baylor.edu/

■ BOISE STATE UNIVERSITY

Graduate College, College of Arts and Sciences, Program in Computer Science, Boise, ID 83725-0399

AWARDS MS. Part-time programs available.

Degree requirements: For master's, thesis, comprehensive exam.
Entrance requirements: For master's, GRE General Test, minimum GPA of 3.0. Electronic applications accepted.

■ BOSTON UNIVERSITY

Graduate School of Arts and Sciences, Department of Computer Science, Boston, MA 02215

AWARDS MA, PhD.

Students: 66 full-time (18 women), 7 part-time (2 women); includes 4 minority (3 Asian Americans or Pacific Islanders, 1 Native American), 47 international. Average age 28. 517 applicants, 19% accepted, 30 enrolled. In 2001, 139 master's, 2 doctorates awarded.
Degree requirements: For master's, one foreign language, registration; for doctorate, one foreign language, thesis/ dissertation, oral and written qualifying exams.
Entrance requirements: For master's and doctorate, GRE General Test, TOEFL, 3 letters of recommendation. *Application deadline:* For fall admission, 1/1; for spring admission, 10/1. *Application fee:* $60.
Expenses: Tuition: Full-time $25,872; part-time $340 per credit. Required fees: $40 per semester. Part-time tuition and fees vary according to class time, course level and program.
Financial support: In 2001–02, 40 students received support, including 6 fellowships, 13 research assistantships (averaging $13,500 per year), 18 teaching assistantships with full tuition reimbursements available (averaging $13,500 per year); Federal Work-Study and

scholarships/grants also available. Support available to part-time students. Financial award application deadline: 1/15; financial award applicants required to submit FAFSA.
Azer Bestavros, Chairman, 617-353-9726, *Fax:* 617-353-6457, *E-mail:* best@bu.edu.
Application contact: Jennifer Streubel, Program Coordinator, 617-353-8919, *Fax:* 617-353-6457, *E-mail:* jenn4@bu.edu. *Web site:* http://cs-www.bu.edu/

■ BOSTON UNIVERSITY

Metropolitan College, Program in Computer Science, Boston, MA 02215

AWARDS Computer information systems (MS); computer science (MS); telecommunications (MS). Part-time and evening/weekend programs available.

Faculty: 8 full-time (1 woman).
Students: 34 full-time (12 women), 341 part-time (87 women); includes 73 minority (5 African Americans, 65 Asian Americans or Pacific Islanders, 3 Hispanic Americans), 50 international. Average age 34. 113 applicants, 99% accepted, 112 enrolled. In 2001, 64 degrees awarded.
Application deadline: For fall admission, 6/1 (priority date); for winter admission, 10/1 (priority date); for spring admission, 3/1 (priority date). Applications are processed on a rolling basis. *Application fee:* $60.
Expenses: Tuition: Full-time $25,872; part-time $340 per credit. Required fees: $40 per semester. Part-time tuition and fees vary according to class time, course level and program.
Financial support: In 2001–02, 21 students received support, including 21 research assistantships with partial tuition reimbursements available; career-related internships or fieldwork, Federal Work-Study, and tuition waivers (full and partial) also available. Support available to part-time students.
Faculty research: Software engineering, information systems architecture, process control, operating systems, parallel processing.
Dr. Tanya Zlateva, Chairman, 617-353-2566, *Fax:* 617-353-2367, *E-mail:* csinfo@bu.edu.
Application contact: Sarah-Grace H. Thomas, Administrative Secretary, 617-353-2566, *Fax:* 617-353-2367, *E-mail:* csinfo@bu.edu. *Web site:* http://bumetb.bu.edu/compsci.html

■ BOWIE STATE UNIVERSITY

Graduate Programs, Program in Computer Science, Bowie, MD 20715-9465

AWARDS MS. Part-time and evening/weekend programs available.

Degree requirements: For master's, research paper, thesis optional.
Faculty research: Holographics, launch vehicle ground truth ephemera.

■ BOWLING GREEN STATE UNIVERSITY

Graduate College, College of Arts and Sciences, Department of Computer Science, Bowling Green, OH 43403

AWARDS MS. Part-time programs available.

Faculty: 10.
Students: 33 full-time (8 women), 8 part-time (3 women); includes 4 minority (1 African American, 3 Asian Americans or Pacific Islanders), 24 international. Average age 28. 84 applicants, 42% accepted, 16 enrolled. In 2001, 20 degrees awarded.
Degree requirements: For master's, thesis or alternative.
Entrance requirements: For master's, GRE General Test, TOEFL. *Application fee:* $30. Electronic applications accepted.
Expenses: Tuition, state resident: full-time $7,376; part-time $342 per credit hour. Tuition, nonresident: full-time $13,628; part-time $640 per credit hour.
Financial support: In 2001–02, 4 research assistantships with full tuition reimbursements (averaging $7,300 per year), 20 teaching assistantships with full tuition reimbursements (averaging $6,095 per year) were awarded. Career-related internships or fieldwork, tuition waivers (full and partial), and unspecified assistantships also available. Financial award applicants required to submit FAFSA.
Faculty research: Artificial intelligence, real time and concurrent programming languages, behavioral aspects of computing, network protocols.
Dr. Julie Barnes, Chair, 419-372-8142.
Application contact: Dr. Lee Miller, Graduate Coordinator, 419-372-8706.

■ BRADLEY UNIVERSITY

Graduate School, College of Liberal Arts and Sciences, Department of Computer Science, Peoria, IL 61625-0002

AWARDS Computer information systems (MS); computer science (MS). Part-time and evening/weekend programs available.

Students: 51 full-time, 48 part-time. 202 applicants, 60% accepted. In 2001, 35 degrees awarded.
Degree requirements: For master's, thesis or alternative, comprehensive exam.
Entrance requirements: For master's, TOEFL. *Application deadline:* For fall admission, 7/1 (priority date); for spring admission, 11/1. Applications are processed on a rolling basis. *Application fee:* $40 ($50 for international students).
Expenses: Tuition: Part-time $7,615 per semester. Tuition and fees vary according to course load.
Financial support: In 2001–02, 11 research assistantships with partial tuition reimbursements (averaging $1,219 per

year) were awarded; teaching assistantships, scholarships/grants and tuition waivers (partial) also available. Financial award application deadline: 3/1.
Dr. James Miller, Chairperson, 309-677-2459.
Application contact: Dr. Jiang-Bo Liu, Graduate Adviser, 309-677-2386.

■ BRANDEIS UNIVERSITY

Graduate School of Arts and Sciences, Michtom School of Computer Science, Waltham, MA 02454-9110

AWARDS MA, PhD. Part-time programs available.

Faculty: 10 full-time (1 woman).
Students: 53 full-time (9 women); includes 5 minority (all Asian Americans or Pacific Islanders), 25 international. 120 applicants, 38% accepted. In 2001, 5 master's, 4 doctorates awarded.
Degree requirements: For doctorate, thesis/dissertation, thesis proposal.
Entrance requirements: For master's and doctorate, resumé, 3 letters of recommendation. *Application deadline:* For fall admission, 2/15. *Application fee:* $60. Electronic applications accepted.
Expenses: Tuition: Full-time $27,392. Required fees: $35.
Financial support: In 2001–02, 40 students received support, including research assistantships with tuition reimbursements available (averaging $18,000 per year), teaching assistantships with tuition reimbursements available (averaging $18,000 per year); institutionally sponsored loans and tuition waivers (full and partial) also available. Financial award application deadline: 4/15; financial award applicants required to submit CSS PROFILE or FAFSA.
Faculty research: Artificial intelligence, programming languages, parallel computing, computer linguistics, data compression.
Dr. James Pustejovsky, Director of Graduate Studies, 781-736-2709, *Fax:* 781-736-2741.
Application contact: Myrna Fox, Department Administrator, 781-736-2701, *E-mail:* maf@cs.brandeis.edu. *Web site:* http://www.cs.brandeis.edu/

■ BRIDGEWATER STATE COLLEGE

School of Graduate and Continuing Education, School of Arts and Sciences, Department of Mathematics and Computer Science, Bridgewater, MA 02325-0001

AWARDS Computer science (MS); mathematics (MAT). Part-time and evening/weekend programs available.

Entrance requirements: For master's, GRE General Test. *Application deadline:* For fall admission, 3/1 (priority date); for

Bridgewater State College (continued)
spring admission, 10/1 (priority date).
Application fee: $50.
Expenses: Tuition, state resident: part-time $135 per credit. Tuition, nonresident: part-time $294 per credit. Tuition and fees vary according to class time.

■ BRIGHAM YOUNG UNIVERSITY

Graduate Studies, College of Physical and Mathematical Sciences, Department of Computer Science, Provo, UT 84602-1001

AWARDS MS, PhD.

Faculty: 25 full-time (0 women), 3 part-time/adjunct (1 woman).
Students: 33 full-time (6 women), 60 part-time (8 women); includes 1 minority (Hispanic American), 23 international. Average age 26. 44 applicants, 70% accepted. In 2001, 26 master's, 2 doctorates awarded. Terminal master's awarded for partial completion of doctoral program.
Degree requirements: For master's, thesis; for doctorate, thesis/dissertation, residency, comprehensive exam.
Entrance requirements: For master's, GRE General Test, TOEFL, minimum GPA of 3.0 in last 60 hours; for doctorate, GRE General Test, GRE Subject Test, TOEFL, minimum GPA of 3.0 in last 60 hrs. Undergraduate degree in computer science. *Application deadline:* For fall admission, 2/15; for winter admission, 5/15; for spring admission, 9/15. *Application fee:* $50. Electronic applications accepted.
Expenses: Tuition: Full-time $3,860; part-time $214 per hour.
Financial support: In 2001–02, 73 students received support, including 8 fellowships with full tuition reimbursements available (averaging $15,000 per year), 57 research assistantships with full tuition reimbursements available (averaging $13,000 per year), 8 teaching assistantships with full tuition reimbursements available (averaging $13,500 per year); scholarships/grants and tuition waivers (full and partial) also available. Financial award application deadline: 2/20.
Faculty research: Graphics, image processing, neural networks and machine learning, computer systems. *Total annual research expenditures:* $2.6 million.
Dr. Tony R. Martinez, Chair, 801-422-6464, *Fax:* 801-378-7775, *E-mail:* martinez@cs.byu.edu.
Application contact: Dr. David W. Embley, Graduate Coordinator, 801-422-6470, *Fax:* 801-378-7775, *E-mail:* gradinfo@cs.byu.edu. *Web site:* http://www.cs.byu.edu/homepage.html

■ BROOKLYN COLLEGE OF THE CITY UNIVERSITY OF NEW YORK

Division of Graduate Studies, Department of Computer and Information Science, Brooklyn, NY 11210-2889

AWARDS Computer and information science (MA, PhD); computer science and health science (MS); economics and computer and information science (MPS); information systems (MS). Part-time and evening/weekend programs available.

Students: 43 full-time (17 women), 408 part-time (145 women); includes 226 minority (70 African Americans, 146 Asian Americans or Pacific Islanders, 10 Hispanic Americans), 137 international. 356 applicants, 67% accepted. In 2001, 49 degrees awarded.
Degree requirements: For master's, thesis or alternative, comprehensive exam or thesis, comprehensive exam.
Entrance requirements: For master's, TOEFL, GRE, previous course work in computer science. *Application deadline:* For fall admission, 3/1; for spring admission, 11/1. *Application fee:* $40.
Expenses: Tuition, state resident: full-time $4,350; part-time $185 per credit. Tuition, nonresident: full-time $7,600; part-time $320 per credit.
Financial support: In 2001–02, 5 research assistantships with full tuition reimbursements (averaging $15,000 per year), 13 teaching assistantships with full tuition reimbursements (averaging $15,000 per year) were awarded. Fellowships, career-related internships or fieldwork, Federal Work-Study, institutionally sponsored loans, scholarships/grants, and tuition waivers (partial) also available. Support available to part-time students. Financial award application deadline: 5/1; financial award applicants required to submit FAFSA.
Faculty research: Networks and distributed systems, programming languages, modeling and computer applications, algorithms, artificial intelligence, theoretical computer science.
Dr. Aaron H. Tenenbaum, Chairperson, 718-951-5657.
Application contact: Gerald Weiss, Graduate Counselor, 718-951-5217, *Fax:* 718-951-4842, *E-mail:* weiss@sci.brooklyn.cuny.edu.

■ BROWN UNIVERSITY

Graduate School, Department of Computer Science, Providence, RI 02912

AWARDS Sc M, PhD.

Degree requirements: For master's, thesis or alternative; for doctorate, one foreign language, thesis/dissertation, comprehensive exam.

Entrance requirements: For master's and doctorate, GRE General Test, GRE Subject Test.

■ CALIFORNIA INSTITUTE OF TECHNOLOGY

Division of Engineering and Applied Science, Option in Computer Science, Pasadena, CA 91125-0001

AWARDS MS, PhD.

Faculty: 10 full-time (0 women).
Students: 27 full-time (4 women); includes 2 minority (both Asian Americans or Pacific Islanders), 14 international. 314 applicants, 5% accepted, 8 enrolled. In 2001, 5 master's, 2 doctorates awarded.
Degree requirements: For master's and doctorate, thesis/dissertation.
Application deadline: For fall admission, 1/15. *Application fee:* $0. Electronic applications accepted.
Financial support: In 2001–02, 11 fellowships, 14 research assistantships were awarded. Teaching assistantships
Faculty research: VLSI systems, concurrent computation, high-level programming languages, signal and image processing, graphics.
Dr. Leonard Schulman, Head, 626-395-6839.

■ CALIFORNIA POLYTECHNIC STATE UNIVERSITY, SAN LUIS OBISPO

College of Engineering, Department of Computer Science, San Luis Obispo, CA 93407

AWARDS MSCS. Part-time programs available.

Faculty: 19 full-time (2 women), 22 part-time/adjunct (3 women).
Students: 14 full-time (5 women), 32 part-time (10 women). 45 applicants, 58% accepted, 15 enrolled. In 2001, 8 degrees awarded.
Degree requirements: For master's, thesis.
Entrance requirements: For master's, GRE General Test, TWE, minimum GPA of 3.0 in last 90 quarter units. *Application deadline:* For fall admission, 5/31 (priority date); for spring admission, 2/28. Applications are processed on a rolling basis. *Application fee:* $55. Electronic applications accepted.
Expenses: Tuition, nonresident: part-time $164 per unit. One-time fee: $2,153 part-time.
Financial support: In 2001–02, 20 teaching assistantships were awarded; career-related internships or fieldwork, Federal Work-Study, and institutionally sponsored loans also available. Financial award application deadline: 3/2; financial award applicants required to submit FAFSA.
Faculty research: Computer systems, software, graphics, hardware design, expert

systems, software engineering and computer networks.

Dr. James Beug, Chair, 805-756-2824, *Fax:* 805-756-2956, *E-mail:* jlbeug@calpoly.edu. *Web site:* http://www.csc.calpoly.edu/

■ CALIFORNIA STATE POLYTECHNIC UNIVERSITY, POMONA

Academic Affairs, College of Science, Program in Computer Science, Pomona, CA 91768-2557

AWARDS MS. Part-time and evening/weekend programs available.

Students: 22 full-time (3 women), 14 part-time (3 women); includes 8 minority (all Asian Americans or Pacific Islanders), 22 international. Average age 29. 82 applicants, 22% accepted. In 2001, 2 degrees awarded.
Degree requirements: For master's, thesis.
Entrance requirements: For master's, GRE General Test. *Application deadline:* For fall admission, 5/1 (priority date); for winter admission, 10/15 (priority date); for spring admission, 1/20 (priority date). Applications are processed on a rolling basis. *Application fee:* $55. Electronic applications accepted.
Expenses: Tuition, nonresident: part-time $164 per unit. Required fees: $1,850.
Financial support: Career-related internships or fieldwork, Federal Work-Study, and institutionally sponsored loans available. Support available to part-time students. Financial award application deadline: 3/2; financial award applicants required to submit FAFSA.
Dr. Norton Riley, Graduate Coordinator, 909-869-3444, *E-mail:* hnriley@ csupomona.edu. *Web site:* http:// www.csupomona.edu/~cs/

■ CALIFORNIA STATE UNIVERSITY, CHICO

Graduate School, College of Engineering, Computer Science, and Technology, Department of Computer Science, Chico, CA 95929-0722

AWARDS MS.

Students: 110 full-time, 49 part-time; includes 80 minority (2 African Americans, 76 Asian Americans or Pacific Islanders, 2 Hispanic Americans). 170 applicants, 62% accepted, 37 enrolled. In 2001, 31 degrees awarded.
Degree requirements: For master's, thesis or alternative, oral exam.
Application deadline: For fall admission, 4/1; for spring admission, 10/1. Applications are processed on a rolling basis. *Application fee:* $55. Electronic applications accepted.
Expenses: Tuition, state resident: full-time $2,148. Tuition, nonresident: full-time $6,576.

Financial support: Fellowships, research assistantships, teaching assistantships, career-related internships or fieldwork available.
Anne Keuneke, Chair, 530-898-6442.
Application contact: Susan Ledgerwood, Graduate Coordinator, 530-898-4010.

■ CALIFORNIA STATE UNIVERSITY, FRESNO

Division of Graduate Studies, College of Engineering and Computer Science, Department of Computer Science, Fresno, CA 93740-8027

AWARDS MS. Part-time and evening/weekend programs available.

Faculty: 7 full-time (2 women).
Students: 36 full-time (8 women), 54 part-time (8 women); includes 14 minority (1 African American, 11 Asian Americans or Pacific Islanders, 2 Hispanic Americans), 68 international. Average age 31. 137 applicants, 75% accepted, 38 enrolled. In 2001, 11 degrees awarded.
Degree requirements: For master's, thesis or alternative. *Median time to degree:* Master's–2.5 years full-time, 3.5 years part-time.
Entrance requirements: For master's, GRE General Test, TOEFL, minimum GPA of 2.75. *Application deadline:* For fall admission, 8/1 (priority date); for spring admission, 12/1. Applications are processed on a rolling basis. *Application fee:* $55. Electronic applications accepted.
Expenses: Tuition, nonresident: part-time $246 per unit. Required fees: $605 per semester. Tuition and fees vary according to course load.
Financial support: In 2001–02, 12 teaching assistantships were awarded; fellowships, research assistantships, career-related internships or fieldwork, Federal Work-Study, scholarships/grants, and unspecified assistantships also available. Support available to part-time students. Financial award application deadline: 3/1; financial award applicants required to submit FAFSA.
Faculty research: Software design, parallel processing, computer engineering, autoline research.
Dr. Brent Auernheimer, Chair, 559-278-4373, *Fax:* 559-278-4197.
Application contact: Lan Jin, Coordinator, 559-278-4373, *Fax:* 559-278-4197, *E-mail:* lan_jin@csufresno.edu.

■ CALIFORNIA STATE UNIVERSITY, FULLERTON

Graduate Studies, College of Engineering and Computer Science, Department of Computer Science, Fullerton, CA 92834-9480

AWARDS Applications administrative information systems (MS); applications mathematical methods (MS); computer science (MS); information processing systems (MS). Part-time programs available.

Faculty: 17 full-time (5 women), 45 part-time/adjunct.
Students: 164 full-time (47 women), 152 part-time (38 women); includes 134 minority (2 African Americans, 122 Asian Americans or Pacific Islanders, 10 Hispanic Americans), 128 international. Average age 31. 354 applicants, 63% accepted, 101 enrolled. In 2001, 28 degrees awarded.
Degree requirements: For master's, project or thesis.
Entrance requirements: For master's, GRE General Test, minimum undergraduate GPA of 2.5. *Application fee:* $55.
Expenses: Tuition, nonresident: part-time $246 per unit. Required fees: $964.
Financial support: Career-related internships or fieldwork, Federal Work-Study, institutionally sponsored loans, and scholarships/grants available. Support available to part-time students. Financial award application deadline: 3/1.
Faculty research: Software engineering, development of computer networks.
Dr. Ning Chen, Chair, 714-278-3700.
Application contact: Dr. Susamma Barua, Adviser, 714-278-3700.

■ CALIFORNIA STATE UNIVERSITY, HAYWARD

Academic Programs and Graduate Studies, School of Science, Department of Mathematics and Computer Science, Computer Science Program, Hayward, CA 94542-3000

AWARDS MS.

Students: 301 applicants, 31% accepted. In 2001, 117 degrees awarded.
Degree requirements: For master's, comprehensive exam or thesis.
Entrance requirements: For master's, GRE, minimum GPA of 3.0 in field, 2.75 overall. *Application deadline:* For fall admission, 6/15; for winter admission, 10/27; for spring admission, 1/5. Applications are processed on a rolling basis. *Application fee:* $55. Electronic applications accepted.
Expenses: Tuition, nonresident: part-time $164 per unit. Required fees: $405 per semester.
Financial support: Career-related internships or fieldwork, Federal Work-Study, and institutionally sponsored loans available. Support available to part-time students. Financial award application deadline: 3/1.
Donald L. Wolitzer, Coordinator, 510-885-3467.
Application contact: Jennifer Cason, Graduate Program Coordinator/ Operations Analyst, 510-885-3286, *Fax:* 510-885-4777, *E-mail:* jcason@ csuhayward.edu.

■ CALIFORNIA STATE UNIVERSITY, LONG BEACH

Graduate Studies, College of Engineering, Department of Computer Engineering and Computer Science, Long Beach, CA 90840

AWARDS Computer engineering (MS); computer science (MS). Part-time programs available.

Faculty: 17 full-time (3 women), 8 part-time/adjunct (0 women).
Students: 71 full-time (27 women), 140 part-time (47 women); includes 89 minority (2 African Americans, 80 Asian Americans or Pacific Islanders, 7 Hispanic Americans), 76 international. Average age 33. 261 applicants, 11% accepted. In 2001, 62 degrees awarded.
Degree requirements: For master's, thesis or alternative.
Entrance requirements: For master's, TOEFL. *Application deadline:* For fall admission, 8/1; for spring admission, 12/1. *Application fee:* $55. Electronic applications accepted.
Financial support: Teaching assistantships, Federal Work-Study, institutionally sponsored loans, scholarships/grants, and unspecified assistantships available. Financial award application deadline: 3/2.
Faculty research: Artificial intelligence, software engineering, computer simulation and modeling, user-interface design, networking.
Dr. Sandra Cynar, Chair, 562-985-4285, *Fax:* 562-985-7561, *E-mail:* cynar@csulb.edu.
Application contact: Dr. Dar Liu, Graduate Adviser, 562-985-1594, *Fax:* 562-985-7561, *E-mail:* liu@csulb.edu.

■ CALIFORNIA STATE UNIVERSITY, NORTHRIDGE

Graduate Studies, College of Engineering and Computer Science, Department of Civil and Manufacturing Engineering, Northridge, CA 91330

AWARDS Applied mechanics (MSE); civil engineering (MS); engineering and computer science (MS); engineering management (MS); industrial engineering (MS); materials engineering (MS); mechanical engineering (MS), including aerospace engineering, applied engineering, machine design, mechanical engineering, structural engineering, thermofluids; mechanics (MS). Part-time and evening/weekend programs available.

Faculty: 14 full-time, 2 part-time/adjunct.
Students: 25 full-time (4 women), 72 part-time (9 women). Average age 31. 64 applicants, 77% accepted, 22 enrolled. In 2001, 34 degrees awarded.
Degree requirements: For master's, thesis.
Entrance requirements: For master's, GRE General Test, TOEFL, minimum

GPA of 2.5. *Application deadline:* For fall admission, 11/30. *Application fee:* $55.
Expenses: Tuition, nonresident: part-time $631 per semester. Required fees: $246 per unit.
Financial support: Teaching assistantships available. Financial award application deadline: 3/1.
Faculty research: Composite study.
Dr. Stephen Gadomski, Chair, 818-677-2166.
Application contact: Dr. Ileana Costa, Graduate Coordinator, 818-677-3299.

■ CALIFORNIA STATE UNIVERSITY, NORTHRIDGE

Graduate Studies, College of Engineering and Computer Science, Department of Computer Science, Northridge, CA 91330

AWARDS MS. Part-time and evening/weekend programs available.

Faculty: 18 full-time, 24 part-time/adjunct.
Students: 50 full-time (24 women), 46 part-time (10 women); includes 14 minority (2 African Americans, 10 Asian Americans or Pacific Islanders, 2 Hispanic Americans), 51 international. Average age 31. 179 applicants, 59% accepted, 23 enrolled. In 2001, 16 degrees awarded.
Degree requirements: For master's, thesis.
Entrance requirements: For master's, GRE General Test, TOEFL, minimum GPA of 2.5. *Application deadline:* For fall admission, 11/30. *Application fee:* $55.
Expenses: Tuition, nonresident: part-time $631 per semester. Required fees: $246 per unit.
Financial support: Application deadline: 3/1.
Faculty research: Radar data processing.
Steven G. Stepanek, Chair, 818-677-3398.

■ CALIFORNIA STATE UNIVERSITY, SACRAMENTO

Graduate Studies, College of Engineering and Computer Science, Department of Computer Science, Sacramento, CA 95819-6048

AWARDS Computer systems (MS); software engineering (MS). Part-time and evening/weekend programs available.

Students: 76 full-time (15 women), 67 part-time (18 women); includes 34 minority (1 African American, 29 Asian Americans or Pacific Islanders, 3 Hispanic Americans, 1 Native American), 68 international.
Degree requirements: For master's, thesis or alternative, writing proficiency exam.
Entrance requirements: For master's, TOEFL. *Application deadline:* For fall admission, 4/15; for spring admission, 11/1. *Application fee:* $55.

Expenses: Tuition, state resident: full-time $1,965; part-time $668 per semester. Tuition, nonresident: part-time $246 per unit.
Financial support: Research assistantships, teaching assistantships, career-related internships or fieldwork and Federal Work-Study available. Support available to part-time students. Financial award application deadline: 3/1.
Dr. Don Warner, Chair, 916-278-5843.
Application contact: Dr. Cui Zhang, Coordinator, 916-278-5769.

■ CALIFORNIA STATE UNIVERSITY, SAN BERNARDINO

Graduate Studies, College of Natural Sciences, Department of Computer Science, San Bernardino, CA 92407-2397

AWARDS MS.

Students: Average age 30. 107 applicants, 61% accepted. In 2001, 7 degrees awarded. *Application deadline:* For fall admission, 8/31 (priority date). *Application fee:* $55.
Expenses: Tuition, nonresident: full-time $4,428. Required fees: $1,733.
Dr. Arturo I. Concepcion, Chair, 909-880-5326, *Fax:* 909-80-7004, *E-mail:* concep@csusb.edu.

■ CALIFORNIA STATE UNIVERSITY, SAN MARCOS

College of Arts and Sciences, Program in Computer Science, San Marcos, CA 92096-0001

AWARDS MS. Part-time programs available.

Faculty: 7 full-time (3 women).
Students: 17 full-time (10 women), 17 part-time (5 women); includes 9 minority (all Asian Americans or Pacific Islanders), 13 international. Average age 32. 36 applicants, 25% accepted. In 2001, 4 degrees awarded.
Degree requirements: For master's, thesis (for some programs).
Entrance requirements: For master's, GRE General Test, GRE Subject Test (recommended), TOEFL. *Application deadline:* For fall admission, 5/30; for spring admission, 11/30. *Application fee:* $55.
Expenses: Tuition, state resident: part-time $567 per semester. Tuition, nonresident: part-time $813 per semester.
Financial support: In 2001–02, 7 research assistantships (averaging $7,000 per year), 2 teaching assistantships (averaging $4,400 per year) were awarded.
Faculty research: Networks, multimedia, parallel algorithms, software engineering, artificial intelligence.
Rochelle L. Boehning, Chair, 760-750-4118, *Fax:* 760-750-3439, *E-mail:* chelle@csusm.edu.

Application contact: JoAnn Espinosa, Administrative Coordinator, 760-750-4118, *Fax:* 760-750-3439, *E-mail:* jespinoz@csusm.edu.

■ CAPITOL COLLEGE

Graduate Programs, Laurel, MD 20708-9759

AWARDS Computer science (MS); electrical engineering (MS); electronic commerce management (MS); information and telecommunications systems management (MS); information architecture (MS); network security (MS). Part-time and evening/weekend programs available. Postbaccalaureate distance learning degree programs offered (no on-campus study).

Faculty: 3 full-time (0 women), 34 part-time/adjunct (4 women).
Students: 6 full-time (3 women), 625 part-time (175 women). Average age 35. 400 applicants, 75% accepted, 275 enrolled. In 2001, 52 degrees awarded. *Median time to degree:* Master's–2 years part-time.
Entrance requirements: For master's, GRE General Test and TOEFL (for international students), minimum GPA of 2.5. *Application deadline:* For fall admission, 7/1 (priority date); for winter admission, 12/1 (priority date); for spring admission, 3/1 (priority date). Applications are processed on a rolling basis. *Application fee:* $100 for international students. Electronic applications accepted.
Expenses: Tuition: Part-time $354 per credit.
Financial support: In 2001–02, 2 students received support. Available to part-time students. Applicants required to submit FAFSA.
Pat Smit, Dean of Academics, 301-369-2800 Ext. 3044, *Fax:* 301-953-3876, *E-mail:* gradschool@capitol-college.edu.
Application contact: Ken Crockett, Director of Graduate Admissions, 301-369-2800 Ext. 3026, *Fax:* 301-953-3876, *E-mail:* gradschool@capitol-college.edu. *Web site:* http://www.capitol-college.edu/

■ CARNEGIE MELLON UNIVERSITY

School of Computer Science, Department of Computer Science, Pittsburgh, PA 15213-3891

AWARDS Algorithms, combinatorics, and optimization (PhD); computer science (PhD); pure and applied logic (PhD).

Degree requirements: For doctorate, thesis/dissertation.
Entrance requirements: For doctorate, GRE General Test, GRE Subject Test, TOEFL, BS in computer science or equivalent.
Faculty research: Software systems, theory of computations, artificial intelligence, computer systems, programming

languages. *Web site:* http://www.cs.cmu.edu/

Find an in-depth description at www.petersons.com/gradchannel.

■ CARNEGIE MELLON UNIVERSITY

School of Computer Science, Language Technologies Institute, Pittsburgh, PA 15213-3891

AWARDS MLT, PhD. Terminal master's awarded for partial completion of doctoral program.

Degree requirements: For doctorate, thesis/dissertation.
Entrance requirements: For master's and doctorate, GRE General Test, GRE Subject Test, TOEFL.
Faculty research: Machine translation, natural language processing, speech and information retrieval, literacy. *Web site:* http://www.lti.cs.cmu.edu/

■ CASE WESTERN RESERVE UNIVERSITY

School of Graduate Studies, The Case School of Engineering, Department of Electrical Engineering and Computer Science, Cleveland, OH 44106

AWARDS Computer engineering (MS, PhD); computing and information science (MS, PhD); electrical engineering (MS, PhD); systems and control engineering (MS, PhD). Part-time and evening/weekend programs available. Postbaccalaureate distance learning degree programs offered (minimal on-campus study).

Faculty: 29 full-time (2 women), 15 part-time/adjunct (1 woman).
Students: 61 full-time (17 women), 72 part-time (6 women); includes 8 minority (3 African Americans, 5 Asian Americans or Pacific Islanders), 85 international. Average age 25. 843 applicants, 16% accepted, 27 enrolled. In 2001, 33 master's, 16 doctorates awarded. Terminal master's awarded for partial completion of doctoral program.
Degree requirements: For master's, thesis; for doctorate, thesis/dissertation, qualifying exam, teaching experience.
Entrance requirements: For master's and doctorate, GRE General Test, TOEFL. *Application deadline:* For fall admission, 2/1; for spring admission, 11/1. Applications are processed on a rolling basis. *Application fee:* $25.
Financial support: In 2001–02, 34 fellowships with full and partial tuition reimbursements (averaging $15,240 per year), 22 research assistantships with full and partial tuition reimbursements (averaging $14,220 per year) were awarded. Career-related internships or fieldwork, Federal Work-Study, and institutionally sponsored loans also available. Support available to part-time students. Financial

award application deadline: 3/1; financial award applicants required to submit FAFSA.
Faculty research: Computational biology and biorobotics; HEHS and solid state, VSLI system design and testing; databases, software engineering, computer systems; systems optimization, planning and decision making; digital signal processing, control and filtering theory. *Total annual research expenditures:* $3.2 million.
Dr. B. Ross Barmish, Chairman, 216-368-2833, *Fax:* 216-368-6888, *E-mail:* brb8@po.cwru.edu.
Application contact: Elizabethanne M. Fuller, Department Assistant, 216-368-4080, *Fax:* 216-368-2668, *E-mail:* emf4@po.cwru.edu. *Web site:* http://eecs.cwru.edu/

■ THE CATHOLIC UNIVERSITY OF AMERICA

School of Engineering, Department of Electrical Engineering and Computer Science, Washington, DC 20064

AWARDS MEE, MS Engr, MSCS, D Engr, PhD. Part-time and evening/weekend programs available.

Faculty: 8 full-time (0 women), 3 part-time/adjunct (0 women).
Students: 6 full-time (1 woman), 31 part-time (4 women); includes 4 minority (1 African American, 1 Asian American or Pacific Islander, 2 Hispanic Americans), 17 international. Average age 33. 64 applicants, 69% accepted, 10 enrolled. In 2001, 6 master's, 2 doctorates awarded.
Degree requirements: For master's, thesis optional; for doctorate, thesis/dissertation, oral exams, comprehensive exam.
Entrance requirements: For master's, TOEFL, minimum GPA of 3.0; for doctorate, TOEFL, minimum GPA of 3.4. *Application deadline:* For fall admission, 8/1 (priority date); for spring admission, 12/1. Applications are processed on a rolling basis. *Application fee:* $55. Electronic applications accepted.
Expenses: Tuition: Full-time $20,050; part-time $770 per credit. Required fees: $430 per term. Tuition and fees vary according to program.
Financial support: Research assistantships, career-related internships or fieldwork, Federal Work-Study, institutionally sponsored loans, tuition waivers (full and partial), and unspecified assistantships available. Support available to part-time students. Financial award application deadline: 2/1.
Faculty research: Signal and image processing, computer communications, robotics, intelligent controls, bioelectromagnetics, properties of materials.
Dr. Nader Namazi, Chair, 202-319-5193.

■ CENTRAL CONNECTICUT STATE UNIVERSITY

School of Graduate Studies, School of Arts and Sciences, Department of Computer Science, New Britain, CT 06050-4010

AWARDS MS.

Faculty: 10 full-time (5 women), 6 part-time/adjunct (0 women).
Students: 43 full-time (17 women), 77 part-time (26 women); includes 45 minority (5 African Americans, 35 Asian Americans or Pacific Islanders, 4 Hispanic Americans, 1 Native American), 15 international. Average age 34. 73 applicants, 71% accepted. *Application deadline:* For fall admission, 8/10 (priority date); for spring admission, 12/10. Applications are processed on a rolling basis. *Application fee:* $40.
Expenses: Tuition, state resident: full-time $2,772; part-time $245 per credit. Tuition, nonresident: full-time $7,726; part-time $245 per credit. Required fees: $2,102. Tuition and fees vary according to course level and degree level.
Financial support: Application deadline: 3/15.
Dr. Joan Calvert, Director, 860-832-2715, *E-mail:* calvertj@ccsu.edu.

■ CENTRAL MICHIGAN UNIVERSITY

College of Graduate Studies, College of Science and Technology, Department of Computer Science, Mount Pleasant, MI 48859

AWARDS MS.

Degree requirements: For master's, thesis or alternative.
Entrance requirements: For master's, TOEFL, minimum GPA of 2.5 in last 2 undergraduate years.
Faculty research: Compiler construction, artificial intelligence, database theory, software engineering, operating systems. *Web site:* http://www.cps.cmich.edu/

■ CHICAGO STATE UNIVERSITY

Graduate Studies, College of Arts and Sciences, Department of Mathematics and Computer Science, Chicago, IL 60628

AWARDS MS.

Faculty: 5 full-time (1 woman).
Students: 29 (15 women); includes 22 minority (17 African Americans, 2 Asian Americans or Pacific Islanders, 2 Hispanic Americans, 1 Native American) 2 international.
Degree requirements: For master's, oral exam, thesis optional.
Entrance requirements: For master's, minimum GPA of 2.75. *Application deadline:* For fall admission, 7/1; for spring admission, 11/10. *Application fee:* $25.

Financial support: Research assistantships available.
Dr. Howard Silver, Chairperson, 773-995-2102, *Fax:* 773-995-3767, *E-mail:* h-silver@csu.edu.
Application contact: Anika Miller, Graduate Studies Office, 773-995-2404, *E-mail:* g-studies1@csu.edu.

■ CHRISTOPHER NEWPORT UNIVERSITY

Graduate Studies, Department of Physics, Computer Science, and Engineering, Newport News, VA 23606-2998

AWARDS Applied physics and computer science (MS). Part-time and evening/weekend programs available.

Faculty: 15 full-time (2 women).
Students: 5 full-time (1 woman), 42 part-time (14 women); includes 13 minority (6 African Americans, 6 Asian Americans or Pacific Islanders, 1 Hispanic American). Average age 37. 6 applicants, 100% accepted. In 2001, 5 degrees awarded.
Degree requirements: For master's, thesis or alternative, comprehensive exam.
Entrance requirements: For master's, GRE, minimum GPA of 3.0. *Application deadline:* For fall admission, 7/1 (priority date); for spring admission, 11/15. Applications are processed on a rolling basis. *Application fee:* $40. Electronic applications accepted.
Expenses: Tuition, state resident: full-time $1,782; part-time $99 per credit. Tuition, nonresident: full-time $6,138; part-time $341 per credit. Required fees: $49 per credit hour. $20 per term.
Financial support: In 2001–02, 5 fellowships with full tuition reimbursements (averaging $3,300 per year), 1 research assistantship with full and partial tuition reimbursement (averaging $2,000 per year) were awarded. Career-related internships or fieldwork and Federal Work-Study also available. Support available to part-time students. Financial award application deadline: 3/1; financial award applicants required to submit FAFSA.
Faculty research: Advanced programming methodologies, experimental nuclear physics, computer architecture, semiconductor nanophysics, laser and optical fiber sensors.
Dr. David Hibler, Coordinator, 757-594-7360, *Fax:* 757-594-7919, *E-mail:* dhibler@pcs.cnu.edu.
Application contact: Susan R. Chittenden, Graduate Admissions, 757-594-7359, *Fax:* 757-594-7333, *E-mail:* gradstdy@cnu.edu. *Web site:* http://www.cnu.edu/

■ CITY COLLEGE OF THE CITY UNIVERSITY OF NEW YORK

Graduate School, School of Engineering, Department of Computer Sciences, New York, NY 10031-9198

AWARDS MS, PhD.

Students: 234. In 2001, 94 degrees awarded.
Degree requirements: For master's, thesis optional; for doctorate, one foreign language, thesis/dissertation, comprehensive exam.
Entrance requirements: For master's, TOEFL; for doctorate, GRE General Test, TOEFL. *Application deadline:* Applications are processed on a rolling basis. *Application fee:* $40.
Expenses: Tuition, state resident: part-time $185 per credit. Tuition, nonresident: part-time $320 per credit. Required fees: $43 per term.
Financial support: Fellowships, teaching assistantships, Federal Work-Study and tuition waivers (partial) available. Support available to part-time students. Financial award application deadline: 6/1.
Faculty research: Complexities of algebraic research, human issues in computer science, scientific computing, supercompilers, parallel algorithms.
Douglas Troeger, Chairman, 212-650-6152.
Application contact: Graduate Admissions Office, 212-650-6977.

■ CITY UNIVERSITY

Graduate Division, School of Business and Management, Bellevue, WA 98005

AWARDS C++ programming (Certificate); computer systems—C++ programming (MS); computer systems—individual (MS); computer systems—web programming language (MS); computer systems-web development (MS); e-commerce (MBA, Certificate); financial management (MBA, Certificate); general management (MBA, MPA, Certificate); general management-Europe (MBA); human resource management (MBA, MPA); human resources management (Certificate); individualized study (MBA, MPA); information systems (MBA, MPA, Certificate); managerial leadership (MBA, MPA, Certificate); marketing (MBA, Certificate); organizational management-general management (MS); organizational management-human resource management (MS); organizational management-individualized study (MS); organizational management-project management (MS); personal financial planning (MBA, Certificate); project management (MBA, MPA, MS, Certificate); public administration (Certificate); web development (Certificate); web programming language (Certificate). Part-time and evening/weekend programs available. Postbaccalaureate distance learning degree programs offered (no on-campus study).

Faculty: 15 full-time (8 women), 513 part-time/adjunct (148 women).
Students: 289 full-time, 2,769 part-time; includes 819 minority (140 African Americans, 615 Asian Americans or Pacific Islanders, 49 Hispanic Americans, 15 Native Americans), 19 international. Average age 37. 786 applicants, 100% accepted, 215 enrolled. In 2001, 849 degrees awarded.
Degree requirements: For master's, thesis (for some programs).
Application deadline: Applications are processed on a rolling basis. *Application fee:* $75 ($175 for international students). Electronic applications accepted.
Expenses: Tuition: Part-time $324 per credit.
Financial support: In 2001–02, 90 students received support. Federal Work-Study available. Support available to part-time students. Financial award applicants required to submit FAFSA.
Carl Adams, Dean, 425-637-1010 Ext. 5392, *Fax:* 425-709-5363, *E-mail:* ksmith@ cityu.edu.
Application contact: 800-426-5596, *Fax:* 425-709-5363, *E-mail:* info@cityu.edu. *Web site:* http://www.cityu.edu/

■ CLAREMONT GRADUATE UNIVERSITY

Graduate Programs, Independent Programs, Department of Mathematics, Claremont, CA 91711-6160

AWARDS Computer science (PhD); engineering mathematics (PhD); financial engineering (MS); operations research and statistics (MA, MS); physical applied mathematics (MA, MS); pure mathematics (MA, MS, PhD); scientific computing (MA, MS); systems and control theory (MA, MS). Part-time programs available.

Faculty: 3 full-time (0 women), 1 part-time/adjunct (0 women).
Students: 28 full-time (8 women), 11 part-time; includes 11 minority (1 African American, 8 Asian Americans or Pacific Islanders, 2 Hispanic Americans), 8 international. Average age 38. In 2001, 4 master's, 2 doctorates awarded. Terminal master's awarded for partial completion of doctoral program.
Degree requirements: For doctorate, 2 foreign languages, thesis/dissertation.
Entrance requirements: For master's and doctorate, GRE General Test. *Application deadline:* For fall admission, 2/15 (priority date). Applications are processed on a rolling basis. *Application fee:* $50. Electronic applications accepted.
Expenses: Tuition: Full-time $22,984; part-time $1,000 per unit. Required fees: $160; $80 per semester.
Financial support: Fellowships, research assistantships, career-related internships or fieldwork, Federal Work-Study, institutionally sponsored loans, and tuition waivers

(full and partial) available. Support available to part-time students. Financial award application deadline: 2/15; financial award applicants required to submit FAFSA.
John Angus, Chair, 909-621-8080, *Fax:* 909-607-9261, *E-mail:* john.angus@ cgu.edu.
Application contact: Mary Solberg, Administrative Assistant, 909-621-8080, *Fax:* 909-607-9261, *E-mail:* math@cgu.edu. *Web site:* http://www.cgu.edu/math/ index.html

■ CLARK ATLANTA UNIVERSITY

School of Arts and Sciences, Department of Computer and Information Science, Atlanta, GA 30314

AWARDS MS.

Degree requirements: For master's, one foreign language, thesis.
Entrance requirements: For master's, GRE General Test, minimum GPA of 2.5.

■ CLARK ATLANTA UNIVERSITY

School of Arts and Sciences, Department of Mathematical Sciences, Atlanta, GA 30314

AWARDS Applied mathematics (MS); computer science (MS). Part-time programs available.

Degree requirements: For master's, one foreign language, thesis.
Entrance requirements: For master's, GRE General Test, minimum GPA of 2.5.
Faculty research: Numerical methods for operator equations, Ada language development.

■ CLARKSON UNIVERSITY

Graduate School, Interdisciplinary Studies, Program in Interdisciplinary Computer Science, Potsdam, NY 13699

AWARDS MS.

Faculty: 6 full-time (2 women).
Students: 11 full-time (4 women); includes 1 minority (Asian American or Pacific Islander), 4 international. Average age 24. 65 applicants, 40% accepted. In 2001, 3 master's awarded. *Median time to degree:* Master's–2 years full-time.
Entrance requirements: For master's, GRE, TOEFL. *Application deadline:* For fall admission, 5/15; for spring admission, 10/15. Applications are processed on a rolling basis. *Application fee:* $25 ($35 for international students).
Expenses: Tuition: Part-time $714 per credit. Required fees: $108 per semester.
Financial support: In 2001–02, 7 students received support, including 2 research assistantships (averaging $17,000 per year), 5 teaching assistantships (averaging $17,000 per year); tuition waivers (partial) also available.

Dr. Susan E. Conroy, Chair, 315-268-6510, *Fax:* 315-268-7994, *E-mail:* conroy@ clarkson.edu.
Application contact: Donna Brockway, Assistant to Dean/Foreign Student Advisor, 315-268-6447, *Fax:* 315-268-7994, *E-mail:* brockway@clarkson.edu.

■ CLARKSON UNIVERSITY

Graduate School, School of Science, Department of Mathematics and Computer Science, Potsdam, NY 13699

AWARDS Computer science (MS); mathematics (MS, PhD).

Faculty: 10 full-time (1 woman).
Students: 7 full-time (5 women), 4 international. Average age 31. 17 applicants, 59% accepted. In 2001, 2 master's, 1 doctorate awarded. Terminal master's awarded for partial completion of doctoral program.
Degree requirements: For doctorate, thesis/dissertation, departmental qualifying exam. *Median time to degree:* Master's–2.3 years full-time; doctorate–6 years full-time.
Entrance requirements: For master's, GRE, TOEFL. *Application deadline:* For fall admission, 5/15 (priority date); for spring admission, 10/15 (priority date). Applications are processed on a rolling basis. *Application fee:* $25 ($35 for international students).
Expenses: Tuition: Part-time $714 per credit. Required fees: $108 per semester.
Financial support: In 2001–02, 5 students received support, including 1 research assistantship (averaging $17,000 per year), 4 teaching assistantships (averaging $17,000 per year); fellowships, scholarships/grants also available.
Faculty research: Fiber optics, hydrodynamics, inverse scattering, nonlinear optics, nonlinear waves. *Total annual research expenditures:* $127,435.
Dr. David L. Powers, Division Head, 315-268-2369, *Fax:* 315-268-2371, *E-mail:* dpowers@clarkson.edu.
Application contact: Donna Brockway, Assistant to Dean/Foreign Student Advisor, 315-268-6447, *Fax:* 315-268-7994, *E-mail:* brockway@clarkson.edu.

Find an in-depth description at www.petersons.com/gradchannel.

■ CLEMSON UNIVERSITY

Graduate School, College of Engineering and Science, Department of Computer Science, Clemson, SC 29634

AWARDS MS, PhD.

Students: 109 full-time (23 women), 14 part-time (3 women); includes 1 minority (African American), 71 international. 359 applicants, 50% accepted, 53 enrolled. In 2001, 62 degrees awarded. Terminal master's awarded for partial completion of doctoral program.

Clemson University (continued)

Degree requirements: For master's, thesis optional; for doctorate, thesis/dissertation.

Entrance requirements: For master's and doctorate, GRE General Test, TOEFL. *Application deadline:* For fall admission, 5/1; for spring admission, 10/1. Applications are processed on a rolling basis. *Application fee:* $40.

Expenses: Tuition, state resident: full-time $5,310. Tuition, nonresident: full-time $11,284.

Financial support: Fellowships, research assistantships, teaching assistantships, institutionally sponsored loans available. Financial award application deadline: 3/1; financial award applicants required to submit FAFSA.

Faculty research: Parallel computation, performance modeling, operating systems, software engineering, design and analysis of algorithms. *Total annual research expenditures:* $537,017.

Dr. Stephen T. Hedetniemi, Chair, 864-656-5858, *Fax:* 864-656-0145, *E-mail:* hedet@cs.clemson.edu.

Application contact: Dr. James Westall, Graduate Coordinator, 864-656-3444, *Fax:* 864-656-0145, *E-mail:* westall@clemson.edu. *Web site:* http://www.cs.clemson.edu/homepage.html

Find an in-depth description at www.petersons.com/gradchannel.

■ **COLLEGE OF CHARLESTON**

Graduate School, Department of Computer Science, Charleston, SC 29424-0001

AWARDS Computer and information sciences (MS).

Expenses: Tuition, state resident: part-time $200 per hour. Tuition, nonresident: part-time $455 per hour. Required fees: $2 per hour. $15 per term. One-time fee: $45 part-time.

■ **THE COLLEGE OF SAINT ROSE**

Graduate Studies, School of Mathematics and Sciences, Program in Computer Information Systems, Albany, NY 12203-1419

AWARDS MS. Part-time and evening/weekend programs available.

Faculty: 7 full-time (3 women).

Students: 1 (woman) full-time, 41 part-time (18 women); includes 10 minority (5 African Americans, 5 Asian Americans or Pacific Islanders), 2 international. 12 applicants, 92% accepted, 11 enrolled. In 2001, 9 degrees awarded.

Application deadline: For fall admission, 7/15 (priority date); for spring admission, 12/1. Applications are processed on a rolling basis. *Application fee:* $30.

Expenses: Tuition: Full-time $8,712. Required fees: $190.

Financial support: Research assistantships, career-related internships or fieldwork and tuition waivers (partial) available. Support available to part-time students. Financial award application deadline: 3/1; financial award applicants required to submit FAFSA.

Dr. Neal Mazur, Department Chair, 518-454-5174, *Fax:* 518-458-5446, *E-mail:* mazurn@mail.strose.edu.

Application contact: 518-454-5136, *Fax:* 518-458-5479, *E-mail:* ace@mail.strose.edu.

■ **COLLEGE OF STATEN ISLAND OF THE CITY UNIVERSITY OF NEW YORK**

Graduate Programs, Program in Computer Science, Staten Island, NY 10314-6600

AWARDS MS, PhD. Part-time and evening/weekend programs available.

Students: 20 full-time (6 women), 41 part-time (13 women); includes 20 minority (19 Asian Americans or Pacific Islanders, 1 Hispanic American). Average age 29. In 2001, 31 degrees awarded.

Degree requirements: For master's, thesis optional; for doctorate, thesis/dissertation.

Entrance requirements: For master's, previous undergraduate course work in computer science. *Application deadline:* For fall admission, 6/1 (priority date); for spring admission, 12/1. Applications are processed on a rolling basis. *Application fee:* $40.

Expenses: Tuition, state resident: full-time $4,350; part-time $185 per credit. Tuition, nonresident: full-time $7,600; part-time $320 per credit. Required fees: $53 per semester.

Financial support: Fellowships, research assistantships, teaching assistantships available.

Dr. Emile Chi, Chair, 718-982-2845, *E-mail:* chi@postbox.csi.cuny.edu.

Application contact: Mary Beth Reilly, Director of Admissions, 718-982-2010, *Fax:* 718-982-2500, *E-mail:* reilly@postbox.csi.cuny.edu. *Web site:* http://www.csi.cuny.edu/

■ **THE COLLEGE OF WILLIAM AND MARY**

Faculty of Arts and Sciences, Department of Computer Science, Williamsburg, VA 23187-8795

AWARDS Computational operations research (MS); computer science (MS, PhD), including computational science (PhD). Part-time programs available.

Faculty: 15 full-time (4 women), 4 part-time/adjunct (0 women).

Students: 53 full-time (20 women), 20 part-time (3 women); includes 3 minority (1 African American, 1 Asian American or Pacific Islander, 1 Hispanic American), 25 international. Average age 28. 243 applicants, 23% accepted. In 2001, 14 master's, 3 doctorates awarded. Terminal master's awarded for partial completion of doctoral program.

Degree requirements: For master's, research project, thesis optional; for doctorate, thesis/dissertation, oral exam.

Entrance requirements: For master's, GRE General Test, minimum GPA of 2.5; for doctorate, GRE General Test, minimum GPA of 3.0. *Application deadline:* For fall admission, 3/1 (priority date); for spring admission, 11/1. Applications are processed on a rolling basis. *Application fee:* $30.

Expenses: Tuition, state resident: full-time $3,262; part-time $175 per credit hour. Tuition, nonresident: full-time $14,768; part-time $550 per credit hour. Required fees: $2,478.

Financial support: In 2001–02, 39 students received support, including 3 fellowships with tuition reimbursements available (averaging $17,000 per year), 8 research assistantships with tuition reimbursements available (averaging $14,000 per year), 28 teaching assistantships with tuition reimbursements available (averaging $14,000 per year). Financial award application deadline: 3/1; financial award applicants required to submit FAFSA.

Faculty research: Distributed and parallel systems, simulation, stochastic modeling, computer architecture, scientific computing, metaheuristics, reliability, optimization, statistics. *Total annual research expenditures:* $821,769.

Dr. Richard H. Prosl, Chair, 757-221-3455, *Fax:* 757-221-1717, *E-mail:* chair@cs.wm.edu.

Application contact: Vanessa Godwin, Administrative Director, 757-221-3455, *Fax:* 757-221-1717, *E-mail:* gradinfo@cs.wm.edu. *Web site:* http://www.cs.wm.edu/

■ **COLORADO SCHOOL OF MINES**

Graduate School, Department of Mathematical and Computer Sciences, Golden, CO 80401-1887

AWARDS MS, PhD. Part-time programs available.

Faculty: 18 full-time (2 women), 11 part-time/adjunct (5 women).

Students: 22 full-time (12 women), 11 part-time (4 women); includes 4 minority (all Asian Americans or Pacific Islanders), 16 international. 56 applicants, 63% accepted, 12 enrolled. In 2001, 8 master's awarded.

Degree requirements: For master's, thesis/dissertation; for doctorate, thesis/dissertation, comprehensive exam. *Median time to degree:* Master's–2 years full-time.

Entrance requirements: For master's and doctorate, GRE General Test. *Application* *deadline:* For fall admission, 12/1 (priority date); for spring admission, 5/1 (priority date). Applications are processed on a rolling basis. *Application fee:* $40. Electronic applications accepted.

Expenses: Tuition, state resident: full-time $4,940; part-time $246 per credit. Tuition, nonresident: full-time $16,070; part-time $803 per credit. Required fees: $341 per semester.

Financial support: In 2001–02, 1 fellowship (averaging $3,000 per year), 7 research assistantships (averaging $3,714 per year), 7 teaching assistantships (averaging $3,000 per year) were awarded. Unspecified assistantships also available. Support available to part-time students. Financial award applicants required to submit FAFSA.

Faculty research: Applied statistics, numerical computation, artificial intelligence, linear optimization. *Total annual research expenditures:* $410,734.

Dr. Graeme Fairweather, Head, 303-273-3860, *E-mail:* gfairwea@mines.edu.

Application contact: Paul Martin, Associate Professor, 303-273-3895, *Fax:* 303-273-3875, *E-mail:* pamartin@mines.edu. *Web site:* http://www.mines.edu/academic/macs/

■ COLORADO STATE UNIVERSITY

Graduate School, College of Natural Sciences, Department of Computer Science, Fort Collins, CO 80523-0015

AWARDS MS, PhD. Part-time programs available. Postbaccalaureate distance learning degree programs offered (no on-campus study).

Faculty: 18 full-time (3 women).

Students: 55 full-time (10 women), 71 part-time (22 women); includes 10 minority (1 African American, 6 Asian Americans or Pacific Islanders, 3 Hispanic Americans), 73 international. Average age 31. 200 applicants, 69% accepted, 39 enrolled. In 2001, 35 degrees awarded. Terminal master's awarded for partial completion of doctoral program.

Degree requirements: For master's, thesis or alternative; for doctorate, thesis/dissertation, qualifying, preliminary, and final exams.

Entrance requirements: For master's, GRE General Test, TOEFL, computer science background, minimum GPA of 3.2; for doctorate, GRE General Test, TOEFL, BSC in computer science, minimum GPA of 3.2. *Application deadline:* For fall admission, 2/1 (priority date); for spring admission, 9/1 (priority date). Applications are processed on a rolling basis. *Application fee:* $30. Electronic applications accepted.

Expenses: Tuition, state resident: full-time $2,880; part-time $160 per credit. Tuition, nonresident: full-time $11,412; part-time $634 per credit. Required fees: $750; $34 per credit.

Financial support: In 2001–02, 5 fellowships with tuition reimbursements (averaging $2,700 per year), 17 research assistantships with tuition reimbursements (averaging $15,000 per year), 38 teaching assistantships with tuition reimbursements (averaging $15,000 per year) were awarded. Career-related internships or fieldwork and Federal Work-Study also available. Financial award application deadline: 2/10.

Faculty research: Architecture, artificial intelligence, parallel and distributed computing, software engineering, computer vision/graphics. *Total annual research expenditures:* $1.2 million.

Dr. Dale H. Grit, Chairman, 970-491-5862, *Fax:* 970-491-2466, *E-mail:* grit@cs.colostate.edu.

Application contact: Graduate Coordinator, 970-491-5792, *Fax:* 970-491-2466, *E-mail:* gradinfo@cs.colostate.edu. *Web site:* http://www.cs.colostate.edu/

Find an in-depth description at www.petersons.com/gradchannel.

■ COLORADO TECHNICAL UNIVERSITY

Graduate Studies, Program in Computer Science, Colorado Springs, CO 80907-3896

AWARDS Computer science (DCS); computer systems security (MSCS); software engineering (MSCS); software project management (MSCS). Part-time and evening/weekend programs available.

Faculty: 6 full-time (2 women), 10 part-time/adjunct (3 women).

Students: 77 full-time (15 women), 10 part-time (2 women); includes 10 minority (4 African Americans, 6 Asian Americans or Pacific Islanders), 2 international. Average age 38. 31 applicants, 94% accepted, 27 enrolled. In 2001, 33 master's, 1 doctorate awarded.

Degree requirements: For master's, thesis or alternative; for doctorate, thesis/dissertation. *Median time to degree:* Master's–2 years full-time, 3 years part-time; doctorate–3.5 years full-time.

Entrance requirements: For doctorate, minimum graduate GPA of 3.0, 5 years of related work experience. *Application deadline:* For fall admission, 10/2; for winter admission, 1/3; for spring admission, 4/3. Applications are processed on a rolling basis. *Application fee:* $100.

Expenses: Tuition: Full-time $6,960; part-time $290 per credit. Required fees: $40 per quarter. One-time fee: $100. Tuition and fees vary according to course load and degree level.

Financial support: Career-related internships or fieldwork and Federal Work-Study available. Financial award applicants required to submit FAFSA.

Faculty research: Software engineering, systems engineering.

Dr. Jack Klag, Dean, 719-590-6850, *Fax:* 719-590-6817.

Application contact: Judy Galante, Graduate Admissions, 719-590-6720, *Fax:* 719-598-3740, *E-mail:* jgalante@coloradotech.edu. *Web site:* http://www.coloradotech.edu/

■ COLORADO TECHNICAL UNIVERSITY DENVER CAMPUS

Program in Computer Science, Greenwood Village, CO 80111

AWARDS Computer systems security (MSCS); software engineering (MSCS); software project management (MSCS). Part-time and evening/weekend programs available.

Faculty: 4 full-time (2 women), 4 part-time/adjunct (2 women).

Students: 24 full-time (4 women), 2 part-time (1 woman); includes 9 minority (3 African Americans, 6 Asian Americans or Pacific Islanders). Average age 34. 6 applicants, 83% accepted, 5 enrolled. In 2001, 10 master's awarded.

Degree requirements: For master's, thesis or alternative. *Median time to degree:* Master's–2 years full-time, 3 years part-time.

Entrance requirements: For master's, minimum undergraduate GPA of 3.0, resume. *Application deadline:* For fall admission, 10/2; for winter admission, 1/3; for spring admission, 4/3. Applications are processed on a rolling basis. *Application fee:* $100.

Expenses: Tuition: Full-time $6,960; part-time $290 per credit. Required fees: $40 per quarter. One-time fee: $100. Tuition and fees vary according to course load and degree level.

Financial support: Federal Work-Study and scholarships/grants available. Support available to part-time students. Financial award applicants required to submit FAFSA.

Dr. Jack Klag, Dean of Computer Science, 719-590-6850, *Fax:* 719-598-3740, *E-mail:* jklag@coloradotech.edu.

Application contact: Suzanne Hyman, Director of Admissions, 303-694-6600, *Fax:* 303-694-6673, *E-mail:* shyman@coloradotech.edu. *Web site:* http://www.coloradotech.edu/

■ COLUMBIA UNIVERSITY

Fu Foundation School of Engineering and Applied Science, Department of Computer Science, New York, NY 10027

AWARDS MS, PhD, CSE. PhD offered through the Graduate School of Arts and Sciences. Part-time programs available. Postbaccalaureate distance learning degree programs offered (no on-campus study).

Faculty: 29 full-time (4 women), 3 part-time/adjunct (0 women).

Columbia University (continued)
Students: 123 full-time (29 women), 86 part-time (20 women); includes 20 minority (1 African American, 17 Asian Americans or Pacific Islanders, 2 Hispanic Americans), 124 international. Average age 23. 555 applicants, 36% accepted, 64 enrolled. In 2001, 74 master's, 8 doctorates awarded. Terminal master's awarded for partial completion of doctoral program. **Degree requirements:** For master's, thesis optional; for doctorate, thesis/dissertation, candidacy exam, qualifying exam. *Median time to degree:* Master's–1.5 years full-time; doctorate–7 years full-time. **Entrance requirements:** For master's, doctorate, and CSE, GRE General Test, GRE Subject Test, TOEFL. *Application deadline:* For fall admission, 1/5 (priority date); for spring admission, 10/1 (priority date). *Application fee:* $55. Electronic applications accepted.
Expenses: Tuition: Full-time $27,528. Required fees: $1,638.
Financial support: In 2001–02, 2 fellowships (averaging $20,000 per year), 86 research assistantships (averaging $15,876 per year), 11 teaching assistantships (averaging $15,876 per year) were awarded. Federal Work-Study and outside fellowships also available. Financial award application deadline: 1/5; financial award applicants required to submit FAFSA.
Faculty research: Algorithms and complexity, robotics, software systems, parallel processing, artificial intelligence. *Total annual research expenditures:* $8 million.
Dr. Kathleen R. McKeown, Chairman, 212-939-7000, *Fax:* 212-666-0140, *E-mail:* kathy@cs.columbia.edu.
Application contact: Genevive Goubourn, Graduate Program Officer, 212-939-7000, *Fax:* 212-666-0140, *E-mail:* gradinfo@columbia.edu. *Web site:* http://www.cs.columbia.edu/

Find an in-depth description at www.petersons.com/gradchannel.

■ **COLUMBUS STATE UNIVERSITY**

Graduate Studies, College of Science, Department of Computer Science, Columbus, GA 31907-5645

AWARDS Applied computer science (MS); information technology management (MS). Part-time and evening/weekend programs available.

Faculty: 2 full-time (0 women).
Students: 15 full-time (1 woman), 77 part-time (23 women); includes 11 minority (5 African Americans, 4 Asian Americans or Pacific Islanders, 2 Hispanic Americans), 10 international. Average age 37. 67 applicants, 46% accepted. In 2001, 13 degrees awarded.
Entrance requirements: For master's, GRE General Test, minimum GPA of

2.75. *Application deadline:* For fall admission, 7/6 (priority date); for spring admission, 12/14. *Application fee:* $25.
Expenses: Tuition, state resident: full-time $1,166. Tuition, nonresident: full-time $7,386.
Financial support: In 2001–02, 3 research assistantships with partial tuition reimbursements (averaging $3,000 per year) were awarded; career-related internships or fieldwork, Federal Work-Study, institutionally sponsored loans, scholarships/grants, tuition waivers (partial), and unspecified assistantships also available. Support available to part-time students. Financial award application deadline: 5/1; financial award applicants required to submit FAFSA.
Dr. Wayne Summers, Chair, 706-568-2410, *Fax:* 706-565-3529, *E-mail:* zanev_vladimir@colstate.edu.
Application contact: Katie Thornton, Graduate Admissions Specialist, 706-568-2279, *Fax:* 706-568-2462, *E-mail:* thornton_katie@colstate.edu. *Web site:* http://www.cs.colstate.edu/

■ **CORNELL UNIVERSITY**

Graduate School, Graduate Fields of Engineering, Field of Computer Science, Ithaca, NY 14853-0001

AWARDS Algorithms (M Eng, PhD); applied logic and automated reasoning (M Eng, PhD); artificial intelligence (M Eng, PhD); computer graphics (M Eng, PhD); computer science (M Eng, PhD); computer vision (M Eng, PhD); concurrency and distributed computing (M Eng, PhD); information organization and retrieval (M Eng, PhD); operating systems (M Eng, PhD); parallel computing (M Eng, PhD); programming environments (M Eng, PhD); programming languages and methodology (M Eng, PhD); robotics (M Eng, PhD); scientific computing (M Eng, PhD); theory of computation (M Eng, PhD).

Faculty: 39 full-time.
Students: 171 full-time (24 women); includes 23 minority (1 African American, 20 Asian Americans or Pacific Islanders, 2 Hispanic Americans), 88 international. 881 applicants, 19% accepted. In 2001, 92 master's, 17 doctorates awarded. Terminal master's awarded for partial completion of doctoral program.
Degree requirements: For doctorate, thesis/dissertation.
Entrance requirements: For master's, GRE General Test, TOEFL, 2 letters of recommendation; for doctorate, GRE General Test, GRE Subject Test (or mathematics), TOEFL, 2 letters of recommendation. *Application deadline:* For fall admission, 1/1 (priority date). *Application fee:* $65. Electronic applications accepted.
Expenses: Tuition: Full-time $25,970. Required fees: $50.
Financial support: In 2001–02, 87 students received support, including 20 fellowships with full tuition reimbursements available, 47 research assistantships

with full tuition reimbursements available, 20 teaching assistantships with full tuition reimbursements available; institutionally sponsored loans, scholarships/grants, tuition waivers (full and partial), and unspecified assistantships also available. Financial award applicants required to submit FAFSA.
Faculty research: Artificial intelligence, operating systems and databases, programming languages and security, scientific computing, theory of computing.
Application contact: Graduate Field Assistant, 607-255-8593, *E-mail:* phd@cs.cornell.edu—meng@cs.cornell.edu. *Web site:* http://www.gradschool.cornell.edu/grad/fields_1/comp-sci.html

Find an in-depth description at www.petersons.com/gradchannel.

■ **CREIGHTON UNIVERSITY**

Graduate School, College of Arts and Sciences, Program in Computer Sciences, Omaha, NE 68178-0001

AWARDS MCS.

Students: 4 full-time (1 woman), 6 part-time (3 women); includes 4 minority (1 African American, 3 Asian Americans or Pacific Islanders), 2 international. In 2001, 7 degrees awarded.
Entrance requirements: For master's, GRE General Test, TOEFL. *Application deadline:* For fall admission, 3/1. Applications are processed on a rolling basis. *Application fee:* $40.
Dr. Mark Wierman, Director, *E-mail:* wierman@creighton.edu.
Application contact: Dr. Barbara J. Braden, Dean, Graduate School, 402-280-2870, *Fax:* 402-280-5762, *E-mail:* bbraden@creighton.edu.

■ **DAKOTA STATE UNIVERSITY**

College of Business and Information Systems, Madison, SD 57042-1799

AWARDS MSIS. Part-time and evening/weekend programs available. Postbaccalaureate distance learning degree programs offered (minimal on-campus study).

Faculty: 12 full-time (0 women).
Students: 30 full-time (11 women), 49 part-time (20 women); includes 2 minority (1 African American, 1 Asian American or Pacific Islander), 16 international. Average age 34. 46 applicants, 83% accepted, 27 enrolled. In 2001, 22 degrees awarded.
Degree requirements: For master's, core ICCP examination, integrative project. *Median time to degree:* Master's–1.67 years full-time, 2 years part-time.
Entrance requirements: For master's, GRE General Test or GMAT, minimum GPA of 2.7. *Application deadline:* For fall admission, 8/1; for winter admission, 10/1. Applications are processed on a rolling basis. *Application fee:* $35 ($85 for international students). Electronic applications accepted.

Expenses: Tuition, state resident: part-time $95 per credit hour. Tuition, nonresident: part-time $182 per credit hour. Tuition and fees vary according to course load, campus/location and reciprocity agreements.
Financial support: In 2001–02, 30 students received support, including 13 research assistantships with partial tuition reimbursements available (averaging $4,035 per year), 5 teaching assistantships with partial tuition reimbursements available (averaging $5,800 per year); Federal Work-Study, scholarships/grants, and unspecified assistantships also available. Support available to part-time students. Financial award applicants required to submit FAFSA.
Faculty research: Effectiveness of technology in economics education, e-commerce, human computer interface, data mining and data warehousing.
Dr. Richard Christoph, Dean, 605-256-5176, *Fax:* 605-256-5316.
Application contact: Laurie B. Dennis, Director, Graduate Programs, 605-256-5263, *Fax:* 605-256-5316, *E-mail:* laurie.dennis@dsu.edu. *Web site:* http://www.departments.dsu.edu/bis/

Find an in-depth description at www.petersons.com/gradchannel.

■ DARTMOUTH COLLEGE

School of Arts and Sciences, Department of Computer Science, Hanover, NH 03755

AWARDS MS, PhD.

Faculty: 14 full-time (2 women).
Students: 56 full-time (11 women); includes 2 minority (both Asian Americans or Pacific Islanders), 36 international. 414 applicants, 10% accepted, 17 enrolled. In 2001, 4 master's, 2 doctorates awarded. Terminal master's awarded for partial completion of doctoral program.
Degree requirements: For master's and doctorate, thesis/dissertation.
Entrance requirements: For master's and doctorate, GRE General Test, GRE Subject Test. *Application deadline:* For fall admission, 2/1 (priority date). *Application fee:* $30.
Expenses: Tuition: Full-time $26,425.
Financial support: In 2001–02, 56 students received support, including fellowships with full tuition reimbursements available (averaging $16,440 per year), research assistantships with full tuition reimbursements available (averaging $16,440 per year); career-related internships or fieldwork, institutionally sponsored loans, scholarships/grants, and tuition waivers (full and partial) also available. Support available to part-time students. Financial award application deadline: 2/1.
Dr. David Nicol, Chair, 603-646-3385.
Application contact: Delia Mauceli, Administrative Assistant, 603-646-0129,

E-mail: delia.mauceli@dartmouth.edu. *Web site:* http://www.cs.dartmouth.edu/

Find an in-depth description at www.petersons.com/gradchannel.

■ DEPAUL UNIVERSITY

School of Computer Science, Telecommunications, and Information Systems, Program in Computer Science, Chicago, IL 60604-2287

AWARDS MS, PhD. Part-time and evening/weekend programs available. Postbaccalaureate distance learning degree programs offered.

Faculty: 24 full-time (3 women), 11 part-time/adjunct (3 women).
Students: 372 full-time (136 women), 310 part-time (72 women); includes 178 minority (41 African Americans, 121 Asian Americans or Pacific Islanders, 16 Hispanic Americans), 186 international. Average age 32. 978 applicants, 72% accepted, 413 enrolled. In 2001, 103 degrees awarded.
Degree requirements: For master's, capstone course; for doctorate, thesis/dissertation, comprehensive exam.
Entrance requirements: For doctorate, GRE, master's degree in computer science. *Application deadline:* For fall admission, 8/1 (priority date); for winter admission, 11/5 (priority date); for spring admission, 3/1 (priority date). Applications are processed on a rolling basis. *Application fee:* $25. Electronic applications accepted.
Expenses: Tuition: Part-time $362 per credit hour. Tuition and fees vary according to program.
Financial support: Fellowships, research assistantships, teaching assistantships, Federal Work-Study, tuition waivers (full and partial), and unspecified assistantships available. Support available to part-time students. Financial award application deadline: 4/1; financial award applicants required to submit FAFSA.
Faculty research: Quantum computation, human-computer interaction, image processing, programming languages, combinatorial algorithms.
Dr. Martin Kalin, Associate Dean, 312-362-8864, *E-mail:* mkalin@cs.depaul.edu.
Application contact: Anne B. Morley, Assistant Dean, 312-362-8714, *Fax:* 312-362-6116. *Web site:* http://www.cs.depaul.edu/

■ DREXEL UNIVERSITY

Graduate School, College of Arts and Sciences, Department of Mathematics and Computer Science, Program in Computer Science, Philadelphia, PA 19104-2875

AWARDS MS, PhD.

Faculty: 39 full-time (9 women), 3 part-time/adjunct (1 woman).
Students: 19 full-time (4 women), 50 part-time (13 women); includes 8 minority (1

African American, 7 Asian Americans or Pacific Islanders), 32 international. Average age 27. 144 applicants, 49% accepted, 19 enrolled. In 2001, 37 degrees awarded.
Entrance requirements: For master's, GRE, TOEFL, TSE (financial award applicants for teaching assistantships). *Application deadline:* For fall admission, 8/21. Applications are processed on a rolling basis. *Application fee:* $50. Electronic applications accepted.
Expenses: Tuition: Full-time $20,088; part-time $558 per credit. Required fees: $78 per term. One-time fee: $200. Tuition and fees vary according to course load, degree level and program.
Financial support: Research assistantships, teaching assistantships, unspecified assistantships available. Financial award application deadline: 2/1.
Application contact: Director of Graduate Admissions, 215-895-6700, *Fax:* 215-895-5939, *E-mail:* enroll@drexel.edu.

Find an in-depth description at www.petersons.com/gradchannel.

■ DUKE UNIVERSITY

Graduate School, Department of Computer Science, Durham, NC 27708-0586

AWARDS MS, PhD.

Faculty: 24 full-time, 9 part-time/adjunct.
Students: 79 full-time (19 women); includes 5 minority (1 African American, 3 Asian Americans or Pacific Islanders, 1 Hispanic American), 51 international. 290 applicants, 16% accepted, 18 enrolled. In 2001, 12 master's, 8 doctorates awarded.
Degree requirements: For doctorate, thesis/dissertation.
Entrance requirements: For master's, GRE General Test; for doctorate, GRE General Test, GRE Subject Test (recommended). *Application deadline:* For fall admission, 12/31. *Application fee:* $75.
Expenses: Tuition: Full-time $24,600.
Financial support: Fellowships, research assistantships, teaching assistantships, Federal Work-Study available. Financial award application deadline: 12/31.
Robert Wagner, Director of Graduate Studies, 919-660-6538, *Fax:* 919-660-6519, *E-mail:* dgs@cs.duke.edu. *Web site:* http://www.cs.duke.edu/

Find an in-depth description at www.petersons.com/gradchannel.

■ EAST CAROLINA UNIVERSITY

Graduate School, School of Computer Science and Communication, Greenville, NC 27858-4353

AWARDS MS.

Faculty: 6 full-time (0 women).
Students: 8 full-time (2 women), 12 part-time (2 women); includes 1 minority (Asian American or Pacific Islander), 9 international. Average age 28. 23

East Carolina University (continued)
applicants, 30% accepted. In 2001, 3 degrees awarded.
Entrance requirements: For master's, GRE General Test, TOEFL. *Application fee:* $45.
Expenses: Tuition, state resident: full-time $2,636. Tuition, nonresident: full-time $11,365.
Dr. Michael Poteat, Interim Dean, 252-328-6461, *Fax:* 252-328-6071, *E-mail:* poteatg@mail.ecu.edu.
Application contact: Dr. Ronnie Smith, Director of Graduate Studies, 252-328-1905, *Fax:* 252-328-6414, *E-mail:* smithr@mail.ecu.edu. *Web site:* http://www.ecu.edu/

■ EASTERN MICHIGAN UNIVERSITY

Graduate School, College of Arts and Sciences, Department of Computer Science, Ypsilanti, MI 48197

AWARDS MS.

Faculty: 16 full-time.
Students: 37 full-time, 33 part-time; includes 1 minority (Hispanic American), 49 international. In 2001, 18 degrees awarded.
Degree requirements: For master's, thesis or alternative.
Entrance requirements: For master's, TOEFL. *Application deadline:* For fall admission, 5/15. *Application fee:* $30.
Expenses: Tuition, state resident: part-time $285 per credit hour. Tuition, nonresident: part-time $510 per credit hour.
Financial support: Application deadline: 3/15.
Dr. Hartmut Hoft, Head, 734-487-1063.

■ EASTERN WASHINGTON UNIVERSITY

Graduate School Studies, College of Science, Mathematics and Technology, Department of Computer Science, Cheney, WA 99004-2431

AWARDS M Ed, MS. Part-time programs available.

Faculty: 15 full-time (2 women).
Students: 8 full-time (2 women), 8 part-time; includes 1 minority (Native American), 2 international. 22 applicants, 27% accepted, 3 enrolled. In 2001, 8 degrees awarded.
Degree requirements: For master's, thesis or alternative, comprehensive exam.
Entrance requirements: For master's, minimum GPA of 3.0. *Application deadline:* For fall admission, 4/1 (priority date); for spring admission, 1/15. Applications are processed on a rolling basis. *Application fee:* $35.
Expenses: Tuition, state resident: full-time $1,586; part-time $159 per credit hour. Tuition, nonresident: full-time $4,677;

part-time $468 per credit hour. Required fees: $222; $159 per credit. $74 per quarter.
Financial support: In 2001–02, 7 teaching assistantships with partial tuition reimbursements (averaging $12,000 per year) were awarded; career-related internships or fieldwork, Federal Work-Study, institutionally sponsored loans, scholarships/grants, health care benefits, tuition waivers (partial), and unspecified assistantships also available. Support available to part-time students. Financial award application deadline: 2/1.
Dr. Ray Hamel, Chair, 509-359-6260, *Fax:* 509-358-2061.
Application contact: Dr. Timothy Rolfe, Adviser, 509-359-4276, *Fax:* 509-359-2215.

■ EAST STROUDSBURG UNIVERSITY OF PENNSYLVANIA

Graduate School, School of Arts and Sciences, Department of Computer Science, East Stroudsburg, PA 18301-2999

AWARDS MS. Part-time and evening/weekend programs available.

Faculty: 5 full-time (0 women).
Students: 15 full-time (6 women), 3 part-time; includes 2 minority (both Asian Americans or Pacific Islanders), 11 international. Average age 29. In 2001, 2 degrees awarded.
Degree requirements: For master's, thesis or alternative, comprehensive exam.
Entrance requirements: For master's, bachelor's degree in computer science or related field. *Application deadline:* For fall admission, 7/31 (priority date); for spring admission, 11/30. Applications are processed on a rolling basis. *Application fee:* $25.
Expenses: Tuition, state resident: full-time $4,600; part-time $256 per credit. Tuition, nonresident: full-time $7,554; part-time $420 per credit. Required fees: $806; $45 per credit.
Financial support: In 2001–02, 15 research assistantships with full tuition reimbursements (averaging $5,000 per year) were awarded; career-related internships or fieldwork, Federal Work-Study, and institutionally sponsored loans also available. Financial award application deadline: 3/1; financial award applicants required to submit FAFSA.
Dr. Richard Prince, Graduate Coordinator, 570-422-0666, *Fax:* 570-422-3490, *E-mail:* rprince@po-box.esu.edu. *Web site:* http://www.esu.edu/cpsc/

■ EAST TENNESSEE STATE UNIVERSITY

School of Graduate Studies, College of Applied Science and Technology, Department of Computer and Information Sciences, Johnson City, TN 37614

AWARDS Computer science (MS); information systems science (MS); software engineering (MS). Part-time and evening/weekend programs available.

Faculty: 11 full-time (0 women).
Students: 25 full-time (6 women), 17 part-time (6 women); includes 1 minority (African American), 17 international. Average age 30. In 2001, 12 degrees awarded.
Degree requirements: For master's, thesis, comprehensive exam.
Entrance requirements: For master's, GRE General Test, TOEFL, minimum GPA of 2.5. *Application deadline:* For fall admission, 7/15 (priority date); for spring admission, 11/15. Applications are processed on a rolling basis. *Application fee:* $25 ($35 for international students).
Expenses: Tuition, state resident: part-time $181 per hour. Tuition, nonresident: part-time $270 per hour. Required fees: $220 per term.
Financial support: Research assistantships with full tuition reimbursements, teaching assistantships with full tuition reimbursements, scholarships/grants available. Support available to part-time students. Financial award application deadline: 7/1; financial award applicants required to submit FAFSA.
Faculty research: Operating systems, database design, artificial intelligence, simulation, parallel algorithms.
Dr. Terry Countermine, Chair, 423-439-5332, *Fax:* 423-439-7119, *E-mail:* counter@etsu.edu. *Web site:* http://www.etsu.edu/

■ EDINBORO UNIVERSITY OF PENNSYLVANIA

Graduate Studies, School of Science, Management and Technology, Department of Mathematics and Computer Science, Edinboro, PA 16444

AWARDS Certificate. Part-time and evening/weekend programs available.

Faculty: 1 full-time (0 women).
Students: 1 full-time (0 women), 18 part-time (8 women), 1 international. Average age 35.
Application deadline: Applications are processed on a rolling basis. *Application fee:* $25. Electronic applications accepted.
Expenses: Tuition, state resident: full-time $4,600; part-time $256 per credit. Tuition, nonresident: full-time $7,554; part-time $420 per credit. Required fees: $68 per credit.

Financial support: Career-related internships or fieldwork, Federal Work-Study, institutionally sponsored loans, scholarships/grants, and unspecified assistantships available. Support available to part-time students. Financial award application deadline: 5/1; financial award applicants required to submit FAFSA. Patricia Hillman, Head, 814-732-2760, *E-mail:* hillman@edinboro.edu.
Application contact: Dr. Mary Margaret Bevevino, Dean of Graduate Studies, 814-732-2856, *Fax:* 814-732-2611, *E-mail:* mbevevino@edinboro.edu.

■ ELMHURST COLLEGE

Graduate Programs, Program in Computer Network Systems, Elmhurst, IL 60126-3296

AWARDS MS. Part-time and evening/weekend programs available.

Faculty: 2 full-time (1 woman).
Students: 45 applicants, 71% accepted, 28 enrolled. In 2001, 26 degrees awarded.
Degree requirements: For master's, thesis optional.
Application deadline: For fall admission, 4/1 (priority date). Applications are processed on a rolling basis. *Application fee:* $25.
Expenses: Tuition: Part-time $555 per hour.
Financial support: Federal Work-Study and scholarships/grants available. Support available to part-time students. Financial award application deadline: 6/1; financial award applicants required to submit FAFSA.
Application contact: Elizabeth D. Kuebler, Director of Graduate Admission, 630-617-3069, *Fax:* 630-617-5501, *E-mail:* gradadm@elmhurst.edu.

■ EMORY UNIVERSITY

Graduate School of Arts and Sciences, Department of Mathematics and Computer Science, Atlanta, GA 30322-1100

AWARDS Mathematics (PhD); mathematics/computer science (MS).

Faculty: 25 full-time (5 women), 4 part-time/adjunct (0 women).
Students: 35 full-time (11 women); includes 4 minority (3 African Americans, 1 Hispanic American), 13 international. 140 applicants, 19% accepted, 10 enrolled. In 2001, 6 master's, 7 doctorates awarded. Terminal master's awarded for partial completion of doctoral program.
Degree requirements: For master's, thesis, registration; for doctorate, one foreign language, thesis/dissertation, comprehensive exam, registration.
Entrance requirements: For master's and doctorate, GRE General Test, TOEFL.
Application deadline: For fall admission, 1/20. *Application fee:* $50. Electronic applications accepted.

Expenses: Tuition: Full-time $24,770. Required fees: $100. Tuition and fees vary according to program and student level.
Financial support: Fellowships, teaching assistantships, scholarships/grants available. Financial award application deadline: 1/20. *Total annual research expenditures:* $1.1 million.
Dr. Dwight Duffus, Chairman, 404-727-7580, *Fax:* 404-727-5611.
Application contact: Ron Gould, Director of Graduate Studies, 404-727-7580, *Fax:* 404-727-5611, *E-mail:* dgs@mathcs.emory.edu. *Web site:* http://www.mathcs.emory.edu/

■ EMPORIA STATE UNIVERSITY

School of Graduate Studies, College of Liberal Arts and Sciences, Department of Mathematics, Computer Science and Economics, Emporia, KS 66801-5087

AWARDS Mathematics (MS).

Faculty: 13 full-time (2 women).
Students: 1 full-time (0 women), 4 part-time (3 women). 2 applicants, 0% accepted. In 2001, 1 degree awarded.
Degree requirements: For master's, comprehensive exam or thesis.
Entrance requirements: For master's, TOEFL. *Application deadline:* For fall admission, 8/15 (priority date). Applications are processed on a rolling basis.
Application fee: $30 ($75 for international students). Electronic applications accepted.
Expenses: Tuition, state resident: full-time $2,632; part-time $119 per credit hour. Tuition, nonresident: full-time $6,734; part-time $290 per credit hour.
Financial support: In 2001–02, 1 teaching assistantship with full tuition reimbursement (averaging $5,273 per year) was awarded; fellowships, research assistantships, career-related internships or fieldwork, Federal Work-Study, institutionally sponsored loans, health care benefits, and unspecified assistantships also available. Financial award application deadline: 3/15; financial award applicants required to submit FAFSA.
Dr. Larry Scott, Chair, 620-341-5281, *Fax:* 620-341-6055, *E-mail:* scottlar@emporia.edu.
Application contact: Dr. Joe Yanik, Graduate Coordinator, 620-341-5639, *E-mail:* yanikjoe@emporia.edu. *Web site:* http://www.emporia.edu/math-cs/home.htm

■ FAIRLEIGH DICKINSON UNIVERSITY, METROPOLITAN CAMPUS

University College: Arts, Sciences, and Professional Studies, School of Computer Science and Information Systems, Program in Computer Science, Teaneck, NJ 07666-1914

AWARDS MS.

Students: 180 full-time (43 women), 86 part-time (29 women); includes 23 minority (4 African Americans, 17 Asian Americans or Pacific Islanders, 1 Hispanic American, 1 Native American), 203 international. Average age 28. 431 applicants, 72% accepted, 60 enrolled. In 2001, 70 degrees awarded.
Application deadline: Applications are processed on a rolling basis. *Application fee:* $40.
Expenses: Tuition: Full-time $11,484; part-time $638 per credit. Required fees: $420; $97.
Dr. Gilbert Steiner, Interim Director, School of Computer Science and Information Systems, 201-692-2261, *Fax:* 201-692-2773, *E-mail:* steiner@fdu.edu.

Find an in-depth description at www.petersons.com/gradchannel.

■ FITCHBURG STATE COLLEGE

Division of Graduate and Continuing Education, Program in Computer Science, Fitchburg, MA 01420-2697

AWARDS MS. Part-time and evening/weekend programs available.

Students: 22 full-time (11 women), 16 part-time (8 women); includes 2 minority (1 African American, 1 Asian American or Pacific Islander), 32 international. In 2001, 12 degrees awarded.
Entrance requirements: For master's, GRE General Test or MAT, appropriate bachelor's degree, interview. *Application deadline:* Applications are processed on a rolling basis. *Application fee:* $10.
Expenses: Tuition, state resident: part-time $150 per credit. Required fees: $7 per credit. $65 per term. Tuition and fees vary according to course load.
Financial support: In 2001–02, research assistantships with partial tuition reimbursements (averaging $5,500 per year), teaching assistantships with partial tuition reimbursements (averaging $5,500 per year) were awarded. Federal Work-Study and unspecified assistantships also available. Support available to part-time students. Financial award application deadline: 3/1; financial award applicants required to submit FAFSA.
Dr. Nadimpalli Mahadev, Chair, 978-665-3270, *Fax:* 978-665-3658, *E-mail:* gce@fsc.edu.
Application contact: Director of Admissions, 978-665-3144, *Fax:* 978-665-4540, *E-mail:* admissions@fsc.edu. *Web site:* http://www.fsc.edu/

■ FLORIDA ATLANTIC UNIVERSITY

College of Engineering, Department of Computer Science and Engineering, Program in Computer Science, Boca Raton, FL 33431-0991

AWARDS MS, PhD. Part-time and evening/weekend programs available.

Florida Atlantic University (continued)

Faculty: 11 full-time (1 woman).

Students: 72 full-time (29 women), 42 part-time (11 women); includes 32 minority (3 African Americans, 20 Asian Americans or Pacific Islanders, 9 Hispanic Americans), 66 international. Average age 30. 190 applicants, 67% accepted, 39 enrolled. In 2001, 22 master's, 1 doctorate awarded.

Degree requirements: For master's, thesis optional; for doctorate, thesis/dissertation, qualifying exam.

Entrance requirements: For master's, GRE General Test, TOEFL, minimum GPA of 3.0 in last 60 hours of undergraduate course work; for doctorate, TOEFL, minimum GPA of 3.5, master's degree. *Application deadline:* For fall admission, 4/10 (priority date); for spring admission, 10/1. Applications are processed on a rolling basis. *Application fee:* $20.

Expenses: Tuition, state resident: full-time $3,098; part-time $172 per credit. Tuition, nonresident: full-time $10,427; part-time $579 per credit.

Financial support: In 2001–02, 20 research assistantships with partial tuition reimbursements (averaging $10,098 per year), 10 teaching assistantships with full tuition reimbursements (averaging $11,936 per year) were awarded. Fellowships, career-related internships or fieldwork, Federal Work-Study, and unspecified assistantships also available. Support available to part-time students. Financial award application deadline: 4/1; financial award applicants required to submit FAFSA.

Faculty research: Software engineering, artificial intelligence, performance evaluation, queuing theory.

Application contact: Donna Rubinoff, Graduate Admissions Coordinator, 561-297-3855, *Fax:* 561-297-2800, *E-mail:* donna@cse.fau.edu. *Web site:* http://www.cse.fau.edu/

■ FLORIDA GULF COAST UNIVERSITY

College of Business, Program in Computer and Information Systems, Fort Myers, FL 33965-6565

AWARDS MS.

Faculty: 31 full-time (9 women), 14 part-time/adjunct (3 women).

Students: 5 full-time (2 women), 12 part-time (3 women); includes 8 minority (1 African American, 2 Asian Americans or Pacific Islanders, 3 Hispanic Americans, 2 Native Americans). 8 applicants, 25% accepted, 0 enrolled. In 2001, 6 degrees awarded.

Entrance requirements: For master's, GMAT, minimum GPA 3.0. *Application deadline:* Applications are processed on a rolling basis. *Application fee:* $20. Electronic applications accepted.

Expenses: Tuition, state resident: part-time $164 per credit hour. Tuition,

nonresident: part-time $571 per credit hour. Required fees: $36 per semester. Dr. Walter Rodriguez, Chair, 239-590-7360, *Fax:* 239-590-7330, *E-mail:* wrodrigz@fgcu.edu.

Application contact: Carol Burnette, Assistant Dean, 239-590-7350, *Fax:* 239-590-7330, *E-mail:* burnette@fgcu.edu.

■ FLORIDA INSTITUTE OF TECHNOLOGY

Graduate Programs, College of Engineering, Computer Science Department, Melbourne, FL 32901-6975

AWARDS Computer information systems (MS); computer science (MS, PhD); software engineering (MS). Part-time and evening/weekend programs available.

Faculty: 11 full-time (1 woman), 5 part-time/adjunct (1 woman).

Students: 59 full-time (14 women), 121 part-time (32 women); includes 21 minority (4 African Americans, 8 Asian Americans or Pacific Islanders, 9 Hispanic Americans), 106 international. Average age 30. 381 applicants, 58% accepted. In 2001, 35 degrees awarded. Terminal master's awarded for partial completion of doctoral program.

Degree requirements: For master's, thesis optional; for doctorate, thesis/dissertation, comprehensive exam.

Entrance requirements: For master's, minimum GPA of 3.0; for doctorate, GRE General Test, GRE Subject Test (computer science), minimum GPA of 3.5, resumé. *Application deadline:* Applications are processed on a rolling basis. *Application fee:* $50. Electronic applications accepted.

Expenses: Tuition: Part-time $650 per credit.

Financial support: In 2001–02, 50 students received support, including 30 research assistantships with full and partial tuition reimbursements available (averaging $10,708 per year), 20 teaching assistantships with full and partial tuition reimbursements available (averaging $8,672 per year); career-related internships or fieldwork and tuition remissions also available. Financial award application deadline: 3/1; financial award applicants required to submit FAFSA.

Faculty research: Artificial intelligence, software engineering, management and processes, programming languages, database systems. *Total annual research expenditures:* $1.5 million.

Dr. William D. Shoaff, Chair, 321-674-8066, *Fax:* 321-674-7046, *E-mail:* wds@cs.fit.edu.

Application contact: Carolyn P. Farrior, Director of Graduate Admissions, 321-674-7118, *Fax:* 321-723-9468, *E-mail:* cfarrior@fit.edu. *Web site:* http://www.cs.fit.edu/

Find an in-depth description at www.petersons.com/gradchannel.

■ FLORIDA INSTITUTE OF TECHNOLOGY

Graduate Programs, School of Extended Graduate Studies, Melbourne, FL 32901-6975

AWARDS Acquisition and contract management (MS, MSM, PMBA); aerospace engineering (MS); business administration (PMBA); computer information systems (MS); computer science (MS); ebusiness (MSM); electrical engineering (MS); engineering management (MS); health management (MS); human resource management (MSM, PMBA); human resources management (MS); information systems (MSM, PMBA); logistics management (MS, MSM); management (MS); material acquisition management (MS); mechanical engineering (MS); operations research (MS); project management (MS), including information systems, operations research; public administration (MPA); software engineering (MS); space systems (MS); space systems management (MS); systems management (MS), including information systems, operations research; transportation management (MSM). Part-time and evening/weekend programs available. Postbaccalaureate distance learning degree programs offered (no on-campus study).

Faculty: 10 full-time (2 women), 131 part-time/adjunct (15 women).

Students: 57 full-time (29 women), 1,198 part-time (455 women); includes 277 minority (183 African Americans, 38 Asian Americans or Pacific Islanders, 51 Hispanic Americans, 5 Native Americans), 16 international. Average age 37. 299 applicants, 42% accepted. In 2001, 434 degrees awarded.

Entrance requirements: For master's, minimum GPA of 3.0. *Application deadline:* Applications are processed on a rolling basis. *Application fee:* $50. Electronic applications accepted.

Expenses: Tuition: Part-time $650 per credit.

Financial support: Institutionally sponsored loans available. Financial award application deadline: 3/1; financial award applicants required to submit FAFSA. Dr. Ronald L. Marshall, Dean, School of Extended Graduate Studies, 321-674-8880.

Application contact: Carolyn P. Farrior, Director of Graduate Admissions, 321-674-7118, *Fax:* 321-723-9468, *E-mail:* cfarrior@fit.edu. *Web site:* http://www.segs.fit.edu/

■ FLORIDA INTERNATIONAL UNIVERSITY

College of Arts and Sciences, School of Computer Science, Miami, FL 33199

AWARDS MS, PhD. Part-time and evening/weekend programs available.

Faculty: 25 full-time (3 women).

Students: 32 full-time (12 women), 8 part-time (3 women); includes 6 minority (all

Hispanic Americans), 29 international. Average age 30. 278 applicants, 46% accepted, 30 enrolled. In 2001, 27 master's, 4 doctorates awarded.

Degree requirements: For master's, thesis optional; for doctorate, thesis/dissertation.

Entrance requirements: For master's and doctorate, GRE General Test, TOEFL. *Application deadline:* For fall admission, 4/1 (priority date); for spring admission, 10/1. Applications are processed on a rolling basis. *Application fee:* $20.

Expenses: Tuition, state resident: full-time $2,916; part-time $162 per credit hour. Tuition, nonresident: full-time $10,245; part-time $569 per credit hour. Required fees: $168 per term.

Financial support: Application deadline: 4/1.

Faculty research: Computer graphics, database management systems, simulation. Dr. Jainendra Navlakha, Director, 305-348-2744, *Fax:* 305-348-3549, *E-mail:* navlakha@cs.fiu.edu.

Find an in-depth description at www.petersons.com/gradchannel.

■ FLORIDA STATE UNIVERSITY

Graduate Studies, College of Arts and Sciences, Department of Computer Science, Tallahassee, FL 32306

AWARDS Computer and network system administration (MA, MS); computer science (MA, MS, PhD); software engineering (MA, MS). Part-time programs available.

Faculty: 28 full-time (2 women), 2 part-time/adjunct (1 woman).

Students: 124 full-time, 25 part-time; includes 13 minority (10 African Americans, 3 Asian Americans or Pacific Islanders), 102 international. Average age 26. 725 applicants, 43% accepted. In 2001, 26 master's, 1 doctorate awarded.

Degree requirements: For master's, thesis or alternative; for doctorate, thesis/dissertation.

Entrance requirements: For master's, GRE General Test, minimum undergraduate GPA of 3.0; for doctorate, GRE General Test, minimum GPA of 3.0. *Application deadline:* For fall admission, 3/3 (priority date); for spring admission, 9/3 (priority date). Applications are processed on a rolling basis. *Application fee:* $20. Electronic applications accepted.

Expenses: Tuition, state resident: part-time $163 per credit hour. Tuition, nonresident: part-time $570 per credit hour. Tuition and fees vary according to program.

Financial support: In 2001–02, 4 fellowships with full tuition reimbursements (averaging $12,000 per year), 20 research assistantships with full tuition reimbursements (averaging $13,500 per year), 81 teaching assistantships with full tuition reimbursements (averaging $13,000 per year) were awarded. Career-related internships or fieldwork, Federal Work-Study,

institutionally sponsored loans, and unspecified assistantships also available. Financial award application deadline: 3/3; financial award applicants required to submit FAFSA.

Faculty research: Expert systems, compiler design, artificial intelligence, neural networks, database theory and design, real time systems, logic, networking. *Total annual research expenditures:* $1.3 million.
Theodore P. Baker, Chairman, 850-644-4029, *Fax:* 850-644-0058, *E-mail:* baker@cs.fsu.edu.

Application contact: David Gaitros, Graduate Admissions, 850-644-4055, *Fax:* 850-644-0058, *E-mail:* gaitrosd@cs.fsu.edu. *Web site:* http://www.cs.fsu.edu/

■ FORDHAM UNIVERSITY

Graduate School of Arts and Sciences, Department of Computer Science and Information Systems, New York, NY 10458

AWARDS Computer science (MS). Part-time and evening/weekend programs available.

Faculty: 11 full-time (1 woman).

Students: 4 full-time (1 woman), 22 part-time (11 women); includes 5 minority (3 Asian Americans or Pacific Islanders, 2 Hispanic Americans), 10 international. Average age 31. 63 applicants, 49% accepted. In 2001, 9 degrees awarded.

Degree requirements: For master's, comprehensive exam.

Entrance requirements: For master's, GRE General Test. *Application deadline:* For fall admission, 1/15 (priority date); for spring admission, 12/1. *Application fee:* $65. Electronic applications accepted.

Expenses: Tuition: Part-time $720 per credit. Required fees: $135 per semester.

Financial support: In 2001–02, 5 students received support, including research assistantships with tuition reimbursements available (averaging $12,000 per year), 1 teaching assistantship with tuition reimbursement available (averaging $12,000 per year); career-related internships or fieldwork, institutionally sponsored loans, tuition waivers (full and partial), and unspecified assistantships also available. Financial award application deadline: 1/16.
Dr. D. Frank Hsu, Chair, 718-817-4480, *Fax:* 718-817-4488, *E-mail:* hsu@fordham.edu.

Application contact: Dr. Craig W. Pilant, Assistant Dean, 718-817-4420, *Fax:* 718-817-3566, *E-mail:* pilant@fordham.edu. *Web site:* http://www.fordham.edu/gsas/

■ FRANKLIN UNIVERSITY

Computer Science Program, Columbus, OH 43215-5399

AWARDS MS. Part-time and evening/weekend programs available.

Degree requirements: For master's, thesis or alternative, registration.

Entrance requirements: For master's, minimum undergraduate GPA of 2.75. Electronic applications accepted.

Expenses: Tuition: Part-time $315 per credit hour. Tuition and fees vary according to program. *Web site:* http://www.franklin.edu

■ FROSTBURG STATE UNIVERSITY

Graduate School, College of Liberal Arts and Sciences, Department of Computer Science, Program in Applied Computer Science, Frostburg, MD 21532-1099

AWARDS MS.

Faculty: 4 full-time (1 woman), 2 part-time/adjunct (0 women).

Students: 15 full-time (5 women), 9 part-time; includes 2 minority (1 African American, 1 Asian American or Pacific Islander), 8 international. Average age 29. 21 applicants, 43% accepted.
Application deadline: Applications are processed on a rolling basis. *Application fee:* $30. Electronic applications accepted.

Expenses: Tuition, area resident: Part-time $187 per credit hour. Tuition, state resident: full-time $3,366; part-time $187 per credit hour. Tuition, nonresident: full-time $3,906; part-time $217 per credit hour. Required fees: $812; $34 per credit hour. One-time fee: $9 full-time.

Financial support: In 2001–02, 5 research assistantships with full tuition reimbursements (averaging $5,000 per year) were awarded. Financial award application deadline: 3/1.
Dr. Mohsen Chitsaz, Program Coordinator, 301-687-4787, *E-mail:* mchitsaz@frostburg.edu.

Application contact: Patricia C. Spiker, Director of Graduate Services, 301-687-7053, *Fax:* 301-687-4597, *E-mail:* pspiker@frostburg.edu.

■ GEORGE MASON UNIVERSITY

School of Information Technology and Engineering, Department of Computer Science, Fairfax, VA 22030-4444

AWARDS MS, PhD. Part-time and evening/weekend programs available.

Faculty: 27 full-time (6 women), 22 part-time/adjunct (4 women).

Students: 76 full-time (35 women), 281 part-time (68 women); includes 63 minority (7 African Americans, 55 Asian Americans or Pacific Islanders, 1 Hispanic American), 175 international. Average age 31. 364 applicants, 60% accepted, 116 enrolled. In 2001, 92 master's, 3 doctorates awarded.

Degree requirements: For master's, thesis optional; for doctorate, thesis/dissertation, comprehensive oral and written exams.

Entrance requirements: For master's, GRE General Test, TOEFL, minimum

George Mason University (continued)
GPA of 3.0 in last 60 hours. *Application deadline:* For fall admission, 5/1; for spring admission, 11/1. *Application fee:* $30. Electronic applications accepted.
Expenses: Tuition, state resident: full-time $3,168; part-time $132 per credit hour. Tuition, nonresident: full-time $11,280; part-time $470 per credit hour. Required fees: $1,416; $59 per credit hour.
Financial support: Fellowships, research assistantships, teaching assistantships, career-related internships or fieldwork and Federal Work-Study available. Support available to part-time students. Financial award application deadline: 3/1; financial award applicants required to submit FAFSA.
Faculty research: Artificial intelligence, image processing/graphics, parallel/distributed systems, software engineering systems. *Total annual research expenditures:* $1.8 million.
Dr. Henry J. Hamburger, Chairman, 703-993-1530, *Fax:* 703-993-1710, *E-mail:* csinfo@cs.gmu.edu. *Web site:* http://ite.gmu.edu/

■ THE GEORGE WASHINGTON UNIVERSITY

School of Engineering and Applied Science, Department of Computer Science, Washington, DC 20052

AWARDS MS, D Sc, App Sc, Engr. Part-time and evening/weekend programs available.

Faculty: 14 full-time (3 women), 9 part-time/adjunct (1 woman).
Students: 99 full-time (31 women), 203 part-time (52 women); includes 55 minority (14 African Americans, 38 Asian Americans or Pacific Islanders, 3 Hispanic Americans), 154 international. Average age 32. 259 applicants, 79% accepted. In 2001, 76 master's, 10 doctorates, 2 other advanced degrees awarded.
Degree requirements: For master's, thesis optional; for doctorate and other advanced degree, dissertation defense, qualifying exam.
Entrance requirements: For master's, TOEFL or George Washington University English as a Foreign Language Test, appropriate bachelor's degree, minimum GPA of 3.0; for doctorate, TOEFL or George Washington University English as a Foreign Language Test, appropriate bachelor's or master's degree, minimum GPA of 3.3, GRE required if highest earned degree is BS; for other advanced degree, TOEFL or George Washington University English as a Foreign Language Test, 2 years experience, appropriate master's degree, minimum GPA of 3.4. *Application deadline:* For fall admission, 3/1 (priority date); for spring admission, 10/1. Applications are processed on a rolling basis. *Application fee:* $55.
Expenses: Tuition: Part-time $810 per credit. Required fees: $1 per credit.

Financial support: In 2001–02, 27 fellowships with tuition reimbursements (averaging $7,000 per year), 23 teaching assistantships with tuition reimbursements (averaging $4,200 per year) were awarded. Research assistantships, career-related internships or fieldwork and institutionally sponsored loans also available. Financial award application deadline: 3/1; financial award applicants required to submit FAFSA.
Faculty research: Computer graphics, multimedia, VLSI, parallel processing.
Dr. Bhagirath Narahari, Chair, 202-994-7181, *Fax:* 202-994-0227, *E-mail:* cs@seas.gwu.edu.
Application contact: Howard M. Davis, Manager, Office of Admissions and Student Records, 202-994-6158, *Fax:* 202-994-0909, *E-mail:* data:adms@seas.gwu.edu. *Web site:* http://www.gwu.edu/~gradinfo/

Find an in-depth description at www.petersons.com/gradchannel.

■ GEORGIA INSTITUTE OF TECHNOLOGY

Graduate Studies and Research, College of Computing, Atlanta, GA 30332-0001

AWARDS Algorithms, combinatorics, and optimization (PhD); computer science (MS, MSCS, PhD); human computer interaction (MSHCI). Part-time programs available. Terminal master's awarded for partial completion of doctoral program.

Degree requirements: For master's, thesis optional; for doctorate, thesis/dissertation, comprehensive exam.
Entrance requirements: For master's, GRE General Test, GRE Subject Test, TOEFL, minimum GPA of 3.0; for doctorate, GRE General Test, GRE Subject Test, TOEFL, minimum GPA of 3.3.
Faculty research: Computer systems, graphics, intelligent systems and artificial intelligence, networks and telecommunications, software engineering. *Web site:* http://www.cc.gatech.edu/

Find an in-depth description at www.petersons.com/gradchannel.

■ GEORGIA SOUTHWESTERN STATE UNIVERSITY

Graduate Studies, School of Computer and Information Science, Americus, GA 31709-4693

AWARDS Computer information systems (MS); computer science (MS). Part-time programs available.

Faculty: 5 full-time (0 women).
Students: 18 full-time (3 women), 16 part-time (10 women); includes 8 minority (6 African Americans, 2 Asian Americans or Pacific Islanders), 17 international. Average

age 29. 20 applicants, 25% accepted. In 2001, 9 degrees awarded.
Degree requirements: For master's, thesis (for some programs).
Entrance requirements: For master's, GRE General Test, minimum GPA of 3.0. *Application deadline:* For fall admission, 8/1; for spring admission, 12/15. Applications are processed on a rolling basis. *Application fee:* $20.
Expenses: Tuition, area resident: Part-time $97 per semester hour. Tuition, state resident: full-time $1,160. Tuition, nonresident: full-time $4,640; part-time $387 per semester hour. Required fees: $277; $217 per year.
Financial support: In 2001–02, 10 students received support, including 10 teaching assistantships with full tuition reimbursements available; fellowships, scholarships/grants also available. Financial award application deadline: 9/1.
Faculty research: Database, Internet technologies, computational complexity, encryption.
Dr. Boris V. Peltsverger, Interim Dean, 912-931-2818 Ext. 2113, *Fax:* 912-931-2270, *E-mail:* plz@canes.gsw.edu.
Application contact: Lois Oliver, Graduate Admissions Specialist, 912-931-2002, *Fax:* 912-931-2021, *E-mail:* loliver@canes.gsw.edu. *Web site:* http://www.gsu.edu/~cais/

■ GEORGIA STATE UNIVERSITY

College of Arts and Sciences, Department of Computer Science, Atlanta, GA 30303-3083

AWARDS MS, PhD. Part-time and evening/weekend programs available.

Faculty: 14 full-time (2 women).
Students: 79 full-time (31 women), 16 part-time (5 women); includes 70 minority (1 African American, 69 Asian Americans or Pacific Islanders). Average age 24. 357 applicants, 22% accepted, 33 enrolled. In 2001, 25 degrees awarded.
Degree requirements: For master's, thesis or alternative, comprehensive exam, registration; for doctorate, thesis/dissertation, qualifying exam. *Median time to degree:* Master's–1.67 years full-time, 2.25 years part-time.
Entrance requirements: For master's, GRE General Test, TOEFL, letters of recommendation (3); for doctorate, transcripts, letters of recommendation (3). *Application deadline:* For fall admission, 8/1; for spring admission, 12/1. Applications are processed on a rolling basis. *Application fee:* $25. Electronic applications accepted.
Financial support: In 2001–02, 60 students received support, including 20 research assistantships with full tuition reimbursements available (averaging $7,000 per year), 40 teaching assistantships with full tuition reimbursements available (averaging $7,000 per year); institutionally sponsored loans, tuition waivers (full), and unspecified assistantships also available.

Financial award application deadline: 2/15; financial award applicants required to submit FAFSA.

Faculty research: Computer architecture, computer networks, databases, software engineering, artificial intelligence. *Total annual research expenditures:* $1.2 million. Dr. Martin D. Fraser, Chair, 404-651-2253, *Fax:* 404-651-2246, *E-mail:* mfraser@cs.gsu.edu.

Application contact: Dr. Raj Sunderraman, Chair, 404-651-2253, *Fax:* 404-651-2246, *E-mail:* rsunderraman@cs.gsu.edu. *Web site:* http://www.cs.gsu.edu/

Find an in-depth description at www.petersons.com/gradchannel.

■ GOVERNORS STATE UNIVERSITY

College of Arts and Sciences, Division of Science, Program in Computer Science, University Park, IL 60466-0975

AWARDS MS. Part-time and evening/weekend programs available.

Faculty: 8 full-time (1 woman), 8 part-time/adjunct (1 woman).
Students: 83 (26 women). Average age 32. In 2001, 20 degrees awarded.
Degree requirements: For master's, thesis or alternative.
Entrance requirements: For master's, minimum GPA of 2.75. *Application deadline:* For fall admission, 7/15 (priority date); for spring admission, 11/10. Applications are processed on a rolling basis. *Application fee:* $0.
Expenses: Tuition, state resident: part-time $111 per hour. Tuition, nonresident: part-time $333 per hour.
Financial support: Research assistantships, career-related internships or fieldwork, Federal Work-Study, institutionally sponsored loans, and scholarships/grants available. Support available to part-time students. Financial award application deadline: 5/1.
Dr. Edwin Cehelnik, Chairperson, Division of Science, 708-534-4520.

■ GRADUATE SCHOOL AND UNIVERSITY CENTER OF THE CITY UNIVERSITY OF NEW YORK

Graduate Studies, Program in Computer Science, New York, NY 10016-4039

AWARDS PhD.

Faculty: 56 full-time (12 women).
Students: 80 full-time (20 women), 1 (woman) part-time; includes 16 minority (5 African Americans, 8 Asian Americans or Pacific Islanders, 3 Hispanic Americans), 40 international. Average age 36. 136 applicants, 41% accepted, 22 enrolled. In 2001, 4 degrees awarded.
Degree requirements: For doctorate, one foreign language, thesis/dissertation.

Entrance requirements: For doctorate, GRE General Test. *Application deadline:* For fall admission, 4/15. *Application fee:* $40.
Expenses: Tuition, state resident: part-time $245 per credit. Tuition, nonresident: part-time $425 per credit. Required fees: $72 per semester.
Financial support: In 2001–02, 36 students received support, including 26 fellowships, 3 teaching assistantships; research assistantships Financial award application deadline: 2/1; financial award applicants required to submit FAFSA.
Dr. Ted Brown, Executive Officer, 212-817-8191, *Fax:* 212-817-1510, *E-mail:* tbrown@gc.cuny.edu.

■ HAMPTON UNIVERSITY

Graduate College, Department of Computer Science, Hampton, VA 23668

AWARDS MS. Part-time and evening/weekend programs available.

Degree requirements: For master's, thesis or alternative.
Entrance requirements: For master's, GRE General Test.
Faculty research: Software testing, neural networks, parallel processing, computer graphics, natural language processing.

■ HARVARD UNIVERSITY

Graduate School of Arts and Sciences, Division of Engineering and Applied Sciences, Center for Research in Computing Technology, Cambridge, MA 02138

AWARDS PhD.

Degree requirements: For doctorate, thesis/dissertation.
Entrance requirements: For doctorate, GRE General Test, GRE Subject Test, TOEFL.
Expenses: Tuition: Full-time $23,370. Required fees: $816. Full-time tuition and fees vary according to program and student level.

■ HOFSTRA UNIVERSITY

College of Liberal Arts and Sciences, Division of Natural Sciences, Mathematics, Engineering, and Computer Science, Department of Computer Science, Hempstead, NY 11549

AWARDS MA, MS. Part-time and evening/weekend programs available.

Faculty: 3 full-time (1 woman), 1 part-time/adjunct (0 women).
Students: 1 (woman) full-time, 36 part-time (9 women); includes 2 minority (both Asian Americans or Pacific Islanders). Average age 34. In 2001, 12 degrees awarded.
Degree requirements: For master's, thesis, projects (MA).

Entrance requirements: For master's, GRE General Test, minimum GPA of 3.0. *Application deadline:* Applications are processed on a rolling basis. *Application fee:* $40 ($75 for international students).
Expenses: Tuition: Full-time $12,408. Tuition and fees vary according to course load and program.
Financial support: Institutionally sponsored loans and scholarships/grants available. Support available to part-time students. Financial award applicants required to submit FAFSA.
Faculty research: Data filming, robotics, graphics, algorithm optimization, natural language programming. *Total annual research expenditures:* $90,000.
Dr. David M. Burghardt, Director, 516-463-5550, *E-mail:* eggdmb@hofstra.edu.
Application contact: Mary Beth Carey, Vice President of Enrollment Services, *Fax:* 516-560-7660, *E-mail:* hofstra@hofstra.edu.

■ HOLLINS UNIVERSITY

Graduate Programs, Program in Liberal Studies, Roanoke, VA 24020-1603

AWARDS Computer studies (MALS); humanities (MALS); interdisciplinary studies (MALS); liberal studies (CAS); social science (MALS). Part-time and evening/weekend programs available.

Faculty: 21 full-time (9 women), 9 part-time/adjunct (4 women).
Students: 43 full-time (35 women), 132 part-time (105 women); includes 16 minority (12 African Americans, 2 Hispanic Americans, 2 Native Americans). Average age 37. 61 applicants, 100% accepted, 54 enrolled. In 2001, 51 master's, 2 other advanced degrees awarded.
Degree requirements: For master's, thesis.
Entrance requirements: For master's, letters of recommendation, interview. *Application deadline:* For fall admission, 8/1 (priority date); for spring admission, 1/10 (priority date). Applications are processed on a rolling basis. *Application fee:* $35. Electronic applications accepted.
Expenses: Tuition: Part-time $765 per course.
Financial support: In 2001–02, 57 students received support. Available to part-time students. Application deadline: 7/15;
Faculty research: Elderly blacks, film, feminist economics, U.S. voting patterns, Wagner, diversity.
Dr. Leslie V. Willett, Dean of Graduate Studies, 540-362-7431, *Fax:* 540-362-6288, *E-mail:* lwillett@hollins.edu.
Application contact: Cathy S. Koon, Coordinator of Graduate Studies, 540-362-6575, *Fax:* 540-362-6288, *E-mail:* hugrad@hollins.edu. *Web site:* http://www.hollins.edu/

■ HOOD COLLEGE

Graduate School, Programs in Computer and Information Sciences, Frederick, MD 21701-8575

AWARDS Computer science (MS); information technology (MS). Part-time and evening/weekend programs available.

Faculty: 8 full-time (2 women), 2 part-time/adjunct (0 women).
Students: 11 full-time (5 women), 105 part-time (31 women); includes 20 minority (9 African Americans, 9 Asian Americans or Pacific Islanders, 2 Hispanic Americans), 8 international. Average age 33. 36 applicants, 67% accepted, 23 enrolled. In 2001, 37 degrees awarded.
Degree requirements: For master's, thesis or alternative, registration.
Entrance requirements: For master's, TOEFL, minimum GPA of 2.5. *Application deadline:* Applications are processed on a rolling basis. *Application fee:* $30.
Expenses: Tuition: Full-time $5,670; part-time $315 per credit. Required fees: $20 per term.
Financial support: Institutionally sponsored loans available. Financial award applicants required to submit FAFSA.
Faculty research: Systems engineering, natural language, processing, database design, artificial intelligence and parallel distributed computing.
Dr. Betty Mayfield, Chairperson, 301-696-3763, *Fax:* 301-696-3597, *E-mail:* mayfield@hood.edu.
Application contact: 301-696-3600, *Fax:* 301-696-3597, *E-mail:* hoodgrad@hood.edu.

■ HOWARD UNIVERSITY

College of Engineering, Architecture, and Computer Sciences, School of Engineering and Computer Science, Department of Systems and Computer Science, Washington, DC 20059-0002

AWARDS MCS. Offered through the Graduate School of Arts and Sciences. Part-time programs available.

Students: In 2001, 7 degrees awarded.
Degree requirements: For master's, thesis.
Entrance requirements: For master's, GRE General Test, TOEFL, minimum GPA of 3.0. *Application deadline:* For fall admission, 4/1 (priority date); for spring admission, 11/1. Applications are processed on a rolling basis. *Application fee:* $45.
Financial support: In 2001–02, 5 research assistantships with full tuition reimbursements, 5 teaching assistantships with full tuition reimbursements were awarded. Fellowships, career-related internships or fieldwork, institutionally sponsored loans, and scholarships/grants also available. Financial award application deadline: 4/1; financial award applicants required to submit FAFSA.

Faculty research: Software engineering, software fault-tolerance, software reliability, artificial intelligence.
Dr. Ronald J. Leach, Chair, 202-806-6595, *Fax:* 202-806-4531, *E-mail:* rjl@scs.howard.edu. *Web site:* http://www.howard.edu/

■ ILLINOIS INSTITUTE OF TECHNOLOGY

Graduate College, Armour College of Engineering and Sciences, Department of Computer Science, Chicago, IL 60616-3793

AWARDS Computer science (MS, PhD); teaching (MST); telecommunications and software engineering (MTSE). Part-time and evening/weekend programs available. Postbaccalaureate distance learning degree programs offered (no on-campus study).

Faculty: 18 full-time (3 women), 14 part-time/adjunct (1 woman).
Students: 378 full-time (78 women), 425 part-time (105 women); includes 86 minority (9 African Americans, 67 Asian Americans or Pacific Islanders, 9 Hispanic Americans, 1 Native American), 595 international. Average age 28. 1,741 applicants, 9% accepted. In 2001, 249 master's, 9 doctorates awarded. Terminal master's awarded for partial completion of doctoral program.
Degree requirements: For master's, thesis (for some programs), comprehensive exam; for doctorate, thesis/dissertation, comprehensive exam.
Entrance requirements: For master's and doctorate, GRE General Test, TOEFL, minimum undergraduate GPA of 3.0. *Application deadline:* For fall admission, 7/1; for spring admission, 11/1. Applications are processed on a rolling basis. *Application fee:* $30. Electronic applications accepted.
Expenses: Tuition: Part-time $590 per credit hour.
Financial support: In 2001–02, 1 fellowship, 9 research assistantships, 46 teaching assistantships were awarded. Federal Work-Study, institutionally sponsored loans, scholarships/grants, and unspecified assistantships also available. Support available to part-time students. Financial award application deadline: 3/1; financial award applicants required to submit FAFSA.
Faculty research: Artificial intelligence, computer architecture, medical imaging, concurrent programming, distributed systems. *Total annual research expenditures:* $214,441.
Dr. Edward Reingold, Chairman, 312-567-3309, *Fax:* 312-567-5067, *E-mail:* reingold@iit.edu.
Application contact: Dr. Ali Cinar, Dean of Graduate College, 312-567-3637, *Fax:* 312-567-7517, *E-mail:* gradstu@iit.edu. *Web site:* http://www.csam.iit.edu/

■ ILLINOIS STATE UNIVERSITY

Graduate School, College of Applied Science and Technology, Department of Applied Computer Science, Normal, IL 61790-2200

AWARDS MS.

Faculty: 14 full-time (3 women).
Students: 46 full-time (15 women), 48 part-time (17 women); includes 6 minority (1 African American, 5 Asian Americans or Pacific Islanders), 52 international. 147 applicants, 21% accepted. In 2001, 25 degrees awarded.
Degree requirements: For master's, thesis (for some programs).
Entrance requirements: For master's, GRE General Test, minimum GPA of 3.0 in last 60 hours; proficiency in COBOL, FORTRAN, Pascal, or P12. *Application deadline:* Applications are processed on a rolling basis. *Application fee:* $30.
Expenses: Tuition, state resident: full-time $2,691; part-time $112 per credit hour. Tuition, nonresident: full-time $5,880; part-time $245 per credit hour. Required fees: $1,146; $48 per credit hour.
Financial support: In 2001–02, 21 research assistantships (averaging $7,963 per year), 23 teaching assistantships (averaging $7,049 per year) were awarded. Fellowships, tuition waivers (full) and unspecified assistantships also available. Financial award application deadline: 4/1. *Total annual research expenditures:* $80,000.
Dr. Robert Zant, Chairperson, 309-438-8338. *Web site:* http://www.acs.ilstu.edu/

■ INDIANA UNIVERSITY BLOOMINGTON

Graduate School, College of Arts and Sciences, Department of Computer Science, Bloomington, IN 47405

AWARDS Computer science (MS, PhD); computer science/cognitive science (PhD); computer science/logic (PhD). PhD offered through the University Graduate School.

Faculty: 19 full-time (1 woman).
Students: 112 full-time (32 women), 36 part-time (7 women); includes 5 minority (2 African Americans, 3 Asian Americans or Pacific Islanders), 103 international. Average age 28. In 2001, 33 master's, 3 doctorates awarded. Terminal master's awarded for partial completion of doctoral program.
Degree requirements: For master's, thesis optional; for doctorate, thesis/dissertation, oral and written exams.
Entrance requirements: For master's and doctorate, GRE General Test, TOEFL. *Application deadline:* For fall admission, 1/15 (priority date); for spring admission, 9/1 (priority date). Applications are processed on a rolling basis. *Application fee:* $45 ($55 for international students). Electronic applications accepted.
Expenses: Tuition, state resident: full-time $4,720; part-time $197 per credit. Tuition,

nonresident: full-time $13,748; part-time $573 per credit. Required fees: $642.

Financial support: In 2001–02, 8 fellowships with full tuition reimbursements (averaging $15,000 per year), 22 research assistantships with full tuition reimbursements (averaging $11,400 per year), 54 teaching assistantships with full tuition reimbursements (averaging $11,400 per year) were awarded. Federal Work-Study and traineeships also available. Financial award application deadline: 2/1.

Faculty research: Hardware/VLSI, parallel programming, graphics/visualization, programming language, cognitive science/artificial intelligence.

Dr. Daniel Friedman, Chairman, 812-855-6488, *Fax:* 812-855-4829.

Application contact: Pam Larson, Admissions Secretary, 812-855-6487, *Fax:* 812-855-4829, *E-mail:* admissions@cs.indiana.edu. *Web site:* http://www.cs.indiana.edu/

Find an in-depth description at www.petersons.com/gradchannel.

■ INDIANA UNIVERSITY–PURDUE UNIVERSITY FORT WAYNE

School of Engineering, Technology, and Computer Science, Department of Computer Science, Fort Wayne, IN 46805-1499

AWARDS Applied computer science (MS). Part-time programs available.

Faculty: 4 full-time (0 women).
Students: 2 full-time (1 woman), 27 part-time (8 women); includes 4 minority (3 Asian Americans or Pacific Islanders, 1 Hispanic American), 3 international. Average age 36. 22 applicants, 68% accepted, 12 enrolled. In 2001, 6 degrees awarded.
Entrance requirements: For master's, GRE, minimum GPA of 3.0. *Application deadline:* For fall admission, 8/1 (priority date); for spring admission, 11/1. Applications are processed on a rolling basis. *Application fee:* $30.
Expenses: Tuition, state resident: full-time $2,845; part-time $158 per credit hour. Tuition, nonresident: full-time $6,323; part-time $351 per credit hour. Required fees: $9 per credit hour. Tuition and fees vary according to course load.
Financial support: In 2001–02, teaching assistantships with partial tuition reimbursements (averaging $7,350 per year); career-related internships or fieldwork, Federal Work-Study, scholarships/grants, and unspecified assistantships also available. Support available to part-time students. Financial award application deadline: 3/1; financial award applicants required to submit FAFSA.
Dr. David Erbach, Chair, 260-481-6803, *Fax:* 260-481-6880, *E-mail:* erbachd@ipfw.edu. *Web site:* http://www.engr.ipfw.edu/cs/

■ INDIANA UNIVERSITY–PURDUE UNIVERSITY INDIANAPOLIS

School of Science, Department of Computer and Information Science, Indianapolis, IN 46202-5132

AWARDS Computer science (MS). Part-time and evening/weekend programs available.

Students: 4 full-time (all women), 45 part-time (9 women); includes 4 minority (1 African American, 3 Asian Americans or Pacific Islanders), 27 international. Average age 30. In 2001, 12 degrees awarded.
Degree requirements: For master's, thesis optional.
Entrance requirements: For master's, GRE, BS or equivalent in computer science. *Application deadline:* For fall admission, 1/15 (priority date); for spring admission, 9/15. Applications are processed on a rolling basis. *Application fee:* $45 ($55 for international students). Electronic applications accepted.
Expenses: Tuition, state resident: full-time $4,480; part-time $187 per credit. Tuition, nonresident: full-time $12,926; part-time $539 per credit. Required fees: $177.
Financial support: In 2001–02, 8 students received support, including 1 fellowship, 5 research assistantships with tuition reimbursements available; teaching assistantships with tuition reimbursements available, career-related internships or fieldwork, institutionally sponsored loans, and tuition waivers (full and partial) also available. Support available to part-time students. Financial award application deadline: 1/15; financial award applicants required to submit FAFSA.
Faculty research: Artificial intelligence, graphics and visualization, computational geometry, database systems, distributed computing.
Mathew J. Palakal, Chair, 317-274-9727, *Fax:* 317-274-9742, *E-mail:* grad_advisor@cs.iupui.edu.
Application contact: 317-274-9727, *Fax:* 317-274-9742, *E-mail:* admissions@cs.iupui.edu. *Web site:* http://www.cs.iupui.edu/

■ INDIANA UNIVERSITY SOUTH BEND

College of Liberal Arts and Sciences, Program in Applied Mathematics and Computer Science, South Bend, IN 46634-7111

AWARDS MS.

Faculty: 19 full-time (4 women).
Expenses: Tuition, state resident: full-time $3,664; part-time $153. Tuition, nonresident: full-time $8,929; part-time $372. Required fees: $390. Tuition and fees vary according to program.
Dr. James Wolfer, Graduate Director, 574-237-6521, *Fax:* 574-237-4335, *E-mail:* amcs@iusb.edu.

■ INTER AMERICAN UNIVERSITY OF PUERTO RICO, METROPOLITAN CAMPUS

Division of Science and Technology, Program in Open Information Systems, San Juan, PR 00919-1293

AWARDS MS.

Degree requirements: For master's, 2 foreign languages.

■ IONA COLLEGE

School of Arts and Science, Program in Computer Science, New Rochelle, NY 10801-1890

AWARDS MS. Part-time and evening/weekend programs available.

Faculty: 7 full-time (2 women).
Students: Average age 29. In 2001, 8 degrees awarded.
Degree requirements: For master's, thesis or alternative.
Entrance requirements: For master's, minimum GPA of 3.0. *Application deadline:* Applications are processed on a rolling basis. *Application fee:* $25.
Expenses: Contact institution.
Financial support: Tuition waivers (partial) and unspecified assistantships available. Support available to part-time students.
Faculty research: Telecommunications, computer graphics, expert systems, database design, compiler design.
Dr. Robert Schiaffino, Chair, 914-633-2338, *E-mail:* rschiaffino@iona.edu.
Application contact: Alyce Ware, Associate Director of Graduate Recruitment, 914-633-2420, *Fax:* 914-633-2023, *E-mail:* aware@iona.edu. *Web site:* http://www.iona.edu/

■ IOWA STATE UNIVERSITY OF SCIENCE AND TECHNOLOGY

Graduate College, College of Liberal Arts and Sciences, Department of Computer Science, Ames, IA 50011

AWARDS MS, PhD.

Faculty: 19 full-time, 2 part-time/adjunct.
Students: 55 full-time (15 women), 30 part-time (9 women), 68 international. 568 applicants, 20% accepted, 24 enrolled. In 2001, 46 master's, 2 doctorates awarded.
Degree requirements: For master's and doctorate, thesis/dissertation. *Median time to degree:* Master's–2.2 years full-time; doctorate–6.4 years full-time.
Entrance requirements: For master's and doctorate, GRE General Test, TOEFL or IELTS. *Application deadline:* For fall admission, 2/1 (priority date); for spring admission, 9/15 (priority date). *Application fee:* $20 ($50 for international students). Electronic applications accepted.

Iowa State University of Science and Technology (continued)

Expenses: Tuition, state resident: full-time $1,851. Tuition, nonresident: full-time $5,449. Tuition and fees vary according to program.
Financial support: In 2001–02, 40 research assistantships with partial tuition reimbursements (averaging $13,575 per year), 31 teaching assistantships with partial tuition reimbursements (averaging $12,206 per year) were awarded. Fellowships, scholarships/grants, health care benefits, and unspecified assistantships also available.
Dr. David Fernandez-Baca, Chair, 515-294-4377, *Fax:* 515-294-0258, *E-mail:* grad_adm@cs.iastate.edu.
Application contact: Melanie Eckhart, Information Contact, 515-294-8361, *E-mail:* grad_adm@cs.iastate.edu. *Web site:* http://www.cs.iastate.edu/

Find an in-depth description at www.petersons.com/gradchannel.

■ **JACKSON STATE UNIVERSITY**

Graduate School, School of Science and Technology, Department of Computer Science, Jackson, MS 39217
AWARDS MS. Part-time and evening/weekend programs available.

Degree requirements: For master's, thesis, comprehensive exam.
Entrance requirements: For master's, GRE General Test, TOEFL.

■ **JACKSONVILLE STATE UNIVERSITY**

College of Graduate Studies and Continuing Education, College of Arts and Sciences, Program in Computer Systems and Software Design, Jacksonville, AL 36265-1602
AWARDS MS.

Degree requirements: For master's, thesis optional.

■ **JAMES MADISON UNIVERSITY**

College of Graduate and Professional Programs, College of Integrated Science and Technology, Department of Computer Science, Harrisonburg, VA 22807
AWARDS MS. Postbaccalaureate distance learning degree programs offered (no on-campus study).

Faculty: 9 full-time (0 women), 2 part-time/adjunct (0 women).
Students: 21 full-time (5 women), 102 part-time (18 women); includes 7 minority (2 African Americans, 2 Asian Americans or Pacific Islanders, 2 Hispanic Americans, 1 Native American), 14 international. Average age 29. In 2001, 44 degrees awarded.

Degree requirements: For master's, thesis or alternative.
Entrance requirements: For master's, GRE General Test. *Application deadline:* For fall admission, 7/1 (priority date). Applications are processed on a rolling basis. *Application fee:* $55.
Expenses: Tuition, state resident: part-time $143 per credit hour. Tuition, nonresident: part-time $465 per credit hour.
Financial support: Teaching assistantships, Federal Work-Study and unspecified assistantships available. Financial award application deadline: 3/1; financial award applicants required to submit FAFSA.
Dr. Malcolm G. Lane, Head, 540-568-2770.

■ **JOHNS HOPKINS UNIVERSITY**

G. W. C. Whiting School of Engineering, Department of Computer Science, Baltimore, MD 21218-2699
AWARDS MSE, PhD.

Faculty: 16 full-time (0 women), 4 part-time/adjunct (0 women).
Students: 105 full-time (22 women), 3 part-time; includes 9 minority (7 Asian Americans or Pacific Islanders, 2 Hispanic Americans), 62 international. Average age 26. 432 applicants, 13% accepted, 55 enrolled. In 2001, 35 master's, 5 doctorates awarded. Terminal master's awarded for partial completion of doctoral program.
Degree requirements: For master's, thesis optional; for doctorate, thesis/dissertation, oral exam.
Entrance requirements: For master's, GRE General Test,, TOEFL; for doctorate, GRE General Test TOEFL. *Application deadline:* For fall admission, 1/15; for spring admission, 12/1. *Application fee:* $0. Electronic applications accepted.
Expenses: Tuition: Full-time $27,390.
Financial support: In 2001–02, 101 students received support, including 3 fellowships with full and partial tuition reimbursements available (averaging $16,000 per year), 40 research assistantships with full tuition reimbursements available (averaging $16,000 per year), 16 teaching assistantships with full tuition reimbursements available (averaging $16,000 per year); Federal Work-Study, institutionally sponsored loans, scholarships/grants, tuition waivers (full), and unspecified assistantships also available. Financial award application deadline: 1/15.
Faculty research: Algorithms, distributed computing, natural language processing, human-computer interaction, computer medical systems. *Total annual research expenditures:* $4.6 million.
Dr. S. Rao Kosaraju, Chair, 410-516-8133, *Fax:* 410-516-6134, *E-mail:* kosaraju@cs.jhu.edu.
Application contact: Linda Rorke, Admissions Coordinator, 410-516-8775, *Fax:* 410-516-6134, *E-mail:* linda@cs.jhu.edu. *Web site:* http://www.cs.jhu.edu/

Find an in-depth description at www.petersons.com/gradchannel.

■ **KANSAS STATE UNIVERSITY**

Graduate School, College of Engineering, Department of Computing and Information Sciences, Manhattan, KS 66506

AWARDS Computer science (MS, PhD); software engineering (MSE). Part-time programs available. Postbaccalaureate distance learning degree programs offered (minimal on-campus study).

Faculty: 16 full-time (2 women).
Students: 144 full-time (34 women), 50 part-time (13 women); includes 5 minority (all Asian Americans or Pacific Islanders), 160 international. 446 applicants, 39% accepted, 73 enrolled. In 2001, 39 master's, 2 doctorates awarded. Terminal master's awarded for partial completion of doctoral program.
Degree requirements: For master's, thesis or alternative; for doctorate, thesis/dissertation, preliminary exams.
Entrance requirements: For master's, GRE, TOEFL, bachelor's degree in computer science, minimum GPA of 3.0; for doctorate, GRE General Test, GRE Subject Test, TOEFL, master's degree in computer science or bachelor's degree plus advanced strong computer knowledge. *Application deadline:* For fall admission, 3/1 (priority date); for spring admission, 9/1. Applications are processed on a rolling basis. *Application fee:* $0 ($25 for international students). Electronic applications accepted.
Expenses: Tuition, state resident: part-time $113 per credit hour. Tuition, nonresident: part-time $358 per credit hour.
Financial support: In 2001–02, 51 research assistantships with partial tuition reimbursements (averaging $10,000 per year), 42 teaching assistantships with full tuition reimbursements (averaging $10,000 per year) were awarded. Career-related internships or fieldwork, institutionally sponsored loans, and scholarships/grants also available. Support available to part-time students. Financial award application deadline: 3/15; financial award applicants required to submit FAFSA.
Faculty research: Parallel distributed computing systems, programming languages, database systems, software engineering, real-time systems. *Total annual research expenditures:* $1 million.
Dr. Virgil E. Wallentine, Head, 785-532-6350, *Fax:* 785-532-7353, *E-mail:* virg@cis.ksu.edu.
Application contact: Dr. David Gustafson, Graduate Program Director, 785-532-6350, *Fax:* 785-532-7353, *E-mail:*

dag@cis.ksu.edu. *Web site:* http://www.cis.ksu.edu/home.shtml/
Find an in-depth description at www.petersons.com/gradchannel.

■ KNOWLEDGE SYSTEMS INSTITUTE

Program in Computer and Information Sciences, Skokie, IL 60076

AWARDS MS. Part-time and evening/weekend programs available. Postbaccalaureate distance learning degree programs offered (minimal on-campus study).

Faculty: 5 full-time (0 women), 14 part-time/adjunct (4 women).
Students: 69 full-time (21 women), 27 part-time (7 women); includes 15 minority (4 African Americans, 10 Asian Americans or Pacific Islanders, 1 Hispanic American), 62 international. Average age 28. 59 applicants, 93% accepted. In 2001, 14 degrees awarded.
Application deadline: Applications are processed on a rolling basis. *Application fee:* $40. Electronic applications accepted.
Expenses: Tuition: Full-time $5,670; part-time $315 per credit. Required fees: $30; $5 per course. $50 per term. One-time fee: $5.
Financial support: In 2001–02, 15 students received support. Federal Work-Study available. Financial award applicants required to submit FAFSA.
Faculty research: Data mining, web development, database programming and administration.
Judy Pan, Executive Director, 847-679-3135, *Fax:* 847-679-3166, *E-mail:* office@ksi.edu.
Application contact: Margaret M. Price, Office Manager, 847-679-3135, *Fax:* 847-679-3166, *E-mail:* mprice@ksi.edu. *Web site:* http://www.ksi.edu/

■ KUTZTOWN UNIVERSITY OF PENNSYLVANIA

College of Graduate Studies and Extended Learning, College of Liberal Arts and Sciences, Program in Computer and Information Science, Kutztown, PA 19530-0730

AWARDS MS. Part-time and evening/weekend programs available.

Faculty: 16 part-time/adjunct (3 women).
Students: 15 full-time (11 women), 8 part-time (1 woman), 12 international. Average age 33. In 2001, 11 degrees awarded.
Degree requirements: For master's, comprehensive exam or thesis.
Entrance requirements: For master's, GRE General Test, TOEFL, TSE.
Application deadline: Applications are processed on a rolling basis. *Application fee:* $35.
Expenses: Tuition, state resident: full-time $4,600; part-time $256 per credit. Tuition,

nonresident: full-time $7,554; part-time $420 per credit. Required fees: $835.
Financial support: Career-related internships or fieldwork, Federal Work-Study, and unspecified assistantships available. Financial award application deadline: 3/15; financial award applicants required to submit FAFSA.
Faculty research: Artificial intelligence, expert systems, neural networks.
William Bateman, Chairperson, 610-683-4410, *E-mail:* bateman@kutztown.edu. *Web site:* http://www.kutztown.edu/acad/

■ LAMAR UNIVERSITY

College of Graduate Studies, College of Engineering, Department of Computer Science, Beaumont, TX 77710

AWARDS MS. Part-time programs available.

Faculty: 6 full-time (1 woman).
Students: 124 full-time (18 women), 21 part-time (5 women); includes 1 minority (Asian American or Pacific Islander), 142 international. Average age 26. 279 applicants, 54% accepted. In 2001, 32 degrees awarded.
Degree requirements: For master's, comprehensive exams and project or thesis.
Entrance requirements: For master's, GRE General Test, TOEFL, minimum GPA of 3.3 in last 60 hours of undergraduate course work or 3.0 overall.
Application deadline: For fall admission, 5/15 (priority date); for spring admission, 10/1 (priority date). Applications are processed on a rolling basis. *Application fee:* $25 ($50 for international students).
Expenses: Tuition, state resident: full-time $1,114. Tuition, nonresident: full-time $3,670.
Financial support: In 2001–02, 2 research assistantships with tuition reimbursements (averaging $6,000 per year), 50 teaching assistantships with tuition reimbursements (averaging $6,000 per year) were awarded. Institutionally sponsored loans, scholarships/grants, and tuition waivers (partial) also available. Financial award application deadline: 4/1.
Faculty research: Artificial intelligence, object oriented databases, symbolic computation, computer networks, graphics. *Total annual research expenditures:* $10,000.
Dr. Lawrence J. Osborne, Chair, 409-880-8775, *Fax:* 409-880-2364, *E-mail:* osborne@hal.lamar.edu.
Application contact: Sandy Drane, Coordinator of Graduate Admissions, 409-880-8356, *Fax:* 409-880-8414, *E-mail:* gradmissions@hal.lamar.edu. *Web site:* http://www.lamar.edu/

■ LA SALLE UNIVERSITY

School of Arts and Sciences, Program in Computer Information Science, Philadelphia, PA 19141-1199

AWARDS Computer information science (MS); information technology leadership (MS). Part-time and evening/weekend programs available.

Faculty: 8 full-time (3 women), 2 part-time/adjunct (0 women).
Students: 1 full-time (0 women), 87 part-time (31 women); includes 12 minority (5 African Americans, 7 Asian Americans or Pacific Islanders), 3 international. Average age 35. 44 applicants, 27% accepted, 11 enrolled. In 2001, 24 degrees awarded.
Entrance requirements: For master's, GRE or MAT, 18 undergraduate credits in computer science, professional experience. *Application deadline:* Applications are processed on a rolling basis. *Application fee:* $30.
Expenses: Contact institution.
Financial support: Institutionally sponsored loans and scholarships/grants available. Support available to part-time students. Financial award application deadline: 7/15; financial award applicants required to submit FAFSA.
Faculty research: Human-computer interaction, networks, technology trends, databases, groupware.
Dr. Linda Elliot, Director, 215-951-1133, *Fax:* 215-951-1805, *E-mail:* macis@lasalle.edu. *Web site:* http://www.lasalle.edu/academ/grad/

■ LAWRENCE TECHNOLOGICAL UNIVERSITY

College of Arts and Sciences, Southfield, MI 48075-1058

AWARDS Computer science (MS); science education (MSE); technical communication (MS). Part-time and evening/weekend programs available.

Faculty: 26 full-time (7 women), 14 part-time/adjunct (4 women).
Students: 15 full-time (2 women), 133 part-time (55 women); includes 38 minority (4 African Americans, 28 Asian Americans or Pacific Islanders, 1 Hispanic American, 5 Native Americans), 33 international. Average age 34. 100 applicants, 97 enrolled. In 2001, 41 degrees awarded.
Entrance requirements: For master's, GRE. *Application deadline:* For fall admission, 8/1 (priority date); for winter admission, 12/1 (priority date); for spring admission, 5/1. Applications are processed on a rolling basis. *Application fee:* $50. Electronic applications accepted.
Expenses: Tuition: Part-time $460 per credit hour.
Financial support: Application deadline: 3/1.

Lawrence Technological University
(continued)
Dr. James Rodgers, Dean, 248-204-3500, *Fax:* 248-204-3518, *E-mail:* scidean@ltu.edu.
Application contact: Jane Rohrback, Interim Director of Admissions, 248-204-3160, *Fax:* 248-204-3188, *E-mail:* admission@ltu.edu. *Web site:* http://www.ltu.edu/

■ LEHIGH UNIVERSITY

P.C. Rossin College of Engineering and Applied Science, Department of Computer Science, Program in Computer Science, Bethlehem, PA 18015-3094

AWARDS MS, PhD. Part-time programs available.

Faculty: 14 full-time (1 woman).
Students: 38 full-time (7 women), 17 part-time (6 women); includes 9 minority (1 African American, 8 Asian Americans or Pacific Islanders), 16 international. Average age 24. 231 applicants, 13% accepted. In 2001, 4 master's, 1 doctorate awarded.
Degree requirements: For master's, oral presentation of thesis; for doctorate, thesis/dissertation, qualifying, general, and oral exams. *Median time to degree:* Master's–2 years full-time; doctorate–1 year full-time.
Entrance requirements: For master's, GRE General Test, TOEFL, minimum GPA of 3.0; for doctorate, GRE General Test, TOEFL, MS, minimum GPA of 3.25. *Application deadline:* For fall admission, 4/15; for spring admission, 11/1. Applications are processed on a rolling basis. *Application fee:* $50. Electronic applications accepted.
Expenses: Tuition: Part-time $468 per credit hour. Required fees: $200; $100 per semester. Tuition and fees vary according to program.
Financial support: In 2001–02, 3 fellowships with full tuition reimbursements (averaging $15,000 per year), 2 research assistantships with full tuition reimbursements (averaging $11,700 per year), 10 teaching assistantships with full tuition reimbursements (averaging $12,330 per year) were awarded. Financial award application deadline: 1/15.
Application contact: Anne Nierer, Graduate Coordinator, 610-758-4072, *Fax:* 610-758-6279, *E-mail:* aln3@lehigh.edu. *Web site:* http://www.eecs.lehigh.edu/
Find an in-depth description at www.petersons.com/gradchannel.

■ LEHMAN COLLEGE OF THE CITY UNIVERSITY OF NEW YORK

Division of Natural and Social Sciences, Department of Mathematics and Computer Science, Program in Computer Science, Bronx, NY 10468-1589

AWARDS MS.

Students: 38 full-time (16 women), 25 part-time (9 women); includes 9 minority (3 African Americans, 4 Asian Americans or Pacific Islanders, 2 Hispanic Americans), 1 international. Average age 36. In 2001, 24 degrees awarded.
Degree requirements: For master's, one foreign language, thesis or alternative. *Median time to degree:* Master's–1 year full-time.
Application deadline: For fall admission, 4/1; for spring admission, 11/1. Applications are processed on a rolling basis. *Application fee:* $40.
Expenses: Tuition, state resident: part-time $185 per credit. Tuition, nonresident: part-time $320 per credit. Required fees: $40 per term.
Financial support: Federal Work-Study and tuition waivers (full and partial) available. Support available to part-time students. Financial award application deadline: 5/15; financial award applicants required to submit FAFSA.
Charles Berger, Adviser, 718-960-8117, *Fax:* 718-960-8969.

■ LONG ISLAND UNIVERSITY, BROOKLYN CAMPUS

School of Business, Public Administration and Information Sciences, Department of Computer Science, Brooklyn, NY 11201-8423

AWARDS MS.

Entrance requirements: For master's, GMAT or GRE. Electronic applications accepted.

■ LONG ISLAND UNIVERSITY, C.W. POST CAMPUS

College of Information and Computer Science, Department of Computer Science/Management Engineering, Brookville, NY 11548-1300

AWARDS Computer science education (MS); information systems (MS); management engineering (MS). Part-time and evening/weekend programs available.

Faculty: 11 full-time (3 women), 7 part-time/adjunct (0 women).
Students: 41 full-time (16 women), 100 part-time (38 women). 96 applicants, 90% accepted, 42 enrolled. In 2001, 31 degrees awarded.
Degree requirements: For master's, thesis or alternative, comprehensive exam.
Entrance requirements: For master's, bachelor's degree in science, mathematics, or engineering; minimum GPA of 2.5.
Application deadline: Applications are processed on a rolling basis. *Application fee:* $30. Electronic applications accepted.
Expenses: Tuition: Full-time $10,296; part-time $572 per credit. Required fees: $380; $190 per semester.
Financial support: Career-related internships or fieldwork, Federal Work-Study, institutionally sponsored loans, unspecified assistantships, and management engineering prize available. Support available to part-time students. Financial award application deadline: 5/15; financial award applicants required to submit CSS PROFILE or FAFSA.
Faculty research: Inductive music learning, re-engineering business process, technology and ethics.
Dr. Susan Fife-Dorchak, Chair, 516-299-2293, *E-mail:* susan.dorchak@liu.edu.
Application contact: Christopher Malinowski, Director of Graduate Programs, 516-299-2663, *E-mail:* cmalinow@liu.edu. *Web site:* http://www.liu.edu/postlas/

■ LOUISIANA STATE UNIVERSITY AND AGRICULTURAL AND MECHANICAL COLLEGE

Graduate School, College of Basic Sciences, Department of Computer Science, Baton Rouge, LA 70803

AWARDS Computer science (MSSS, PhD); systems science (MSSS). Part-time programs available.

Faculty: 12 full-time (3 women).
Students: 74 full-time (15 women), 19 part-time (8 women); includes 9 minority (7 African Americans, 1 Asian American or Pacific Islander, 1 Hispanic American), 68 international. Average age 29. 200 applicants, 37% accepted, 27 enrolled. In 2001, 23 master's, 5 doctorates awarded. Terminal master's awarded for partial completion of doctoral program.
Degree requirements: For master's and doctorate, thesis/dissertation.
Entrance requirements: For master's and doctorate, GRE General Test, minimum GPA of 3.0. *Application deadline:* For fall admission, 2/1; for spring admission, 10/1. Applications are processed on a rolling basis. *Application fee:* $25.
Expenses: Tuition, state resident: full-time $2,551. Tuition, nonresident: full-time $5,551. Required fees: $854. Part-time tuition and fees vary according to course load.
Financial support: In 2001–02, 6 fellowships (averaging $14,750 per year), 24 research assistantships with partial tuition reimbursements (averaging $11,520 per year), 27 teaching assistantships with partial tuition reimbursements (averaging $12,098 per year) were awarded. Unspecified assistantships also available. Financial award application deadline: 2/1; financial award applicants required to submit FAFSA.
Faculty research: Robotics, artificial intelligence, algorithms, database software engineering, high-performance computing. *Total annual research expenditures:* $732,006.
Dr. Sitharama S. Iyengar, Chair, 225-578-1495, *Fax:* 225-578-1465, *E-mail:* iyengar@csc.lsu.edu.
Application contact: Dr. Peter Chen, Graduate Coordinator, 225-578-1495, *Fax:*

225-578-1465, *E-mail:* chen@csc.lsu.edu. *Web site:* http://bit.csc.lsu.edu/

■ LOUISIANA TECH UNIVERSITY

Graduate School, College of Engineering and Science, Department of Computer Science, Ruston, LA 71272

AWARDS MS. Part-time programs available.

Degree requirements: For master's, thesis or alternative.

Entrance requirements: For master's, GRE General Test, TOEFL, minimum GPA of 3.0 in last 60 hours.

Faculty research: Computer systems organization, artificial intelligence, expert systems, graphics, program language.

■ LOYOLA MARYMOUNT UNIVERSITY

Graduate Division, College of Science and Engineering, Department of Electrical Engineering and Computer Science, Program in Computer Science, Los Angeles, CA 90045-2659

AWARDS MS. Part-time and evening/weekend programs available.

Faculty: 4 full-time (1 woman), 3 part-time/adjunct (0 women).

Students: 12 full-time (2 women), 11 part-time (3 women); includes 10 minority (5 African Americans, 5 Asian Americans or Pacific Islanders), 7 international. 41 applicants, 61% accepted, 12 enrolled. In 2001, 7 degrees awarded.

Degree requirements: For master's, research seminar.

Entrance requirements: For master's, TOEFL. *Application deadline:* Applications are processed on a rolling basis. *Application fee:* $45. Electronic applications accepted.

Expenses: Tuition: Part-time $612 per credit hour. Required fees: $86 per term. Tuition and fees vary according to program.

Financial support: In 2001–02, 1 student received support. Scholarships/grants available. Support available to part-time students. Financial award application deadline: 7/1; financial award applicants required to submit FAFSA. *Web site:* http://www.lmu.edu/acad/gd/graddiv.htm

■ LOYOLA UNIVERSITY CHICAGO

Graduate School, Department of Computer Sciences, Chicago, IL 60611-2196

AWARDS Computer science (MS). Part-time and evening/weekend programs available.

Faculty: 25 full-time (2 women), 10 part-time/adjunct (0 women).

Students: 91 full-time (43 women), 55 part-time (28 women); includes 9 minority (2 African Americans, 7 Asian Americans or Pacific Islanders), 110 international.

Average age 27. 236 applicants, 86% accepted. In 2001, 85 degrees awarded.

Degree requirements: For master's, comprehensive exam.

Entrance requirements: For master's, GRE General Test, TOEFL, minimum B average. *Application deadline:* For fall admission, 7/1; for spring admission, 11/15. Applications are processed on a rolling basis. *Application fee:* $40. Electronic applications accepted.

Expenses: Tuition: Part-time $529 per credit hour.

Financial support: In 2001–02, 20 students received support, including 5 research assistantships with full tuition reimbursements available (averaging $8,000 per year), 9 teaching assistantships with full tuition reimbursements available (averaging $11,000 per year); career-related internships or fieldwork, Federal Work-Study, and institutionally sponsored loans also available. Financial award application deadline: 2/1; financial award applicants required to submit FAFSA.

Faculty research: Algorithms, logic, parallel/distributed computing, programming languages, theory of computation. *Total annual research expenditures:* $1.3 million.

Dr. Joseph H. Mayne, Chair, 773-508-3558, *Fax:* 773-508-2123, *E-mail:* jhm@math.luc.edu.

Application contact: Cecilia Murphy, Graduate Secretary, 773-508-3322, *Fax:* 773-508-2123, *E-mail:* gradinfo-cs@cs.luc.edu.

Find an in-depth description at www.petersons.com/gradchannel.

■ MAHARISHI UNIVERSITY OF MANAGEMENT

Graduate Studies, Program in Computer Science, Fairfield, IA 52557

AWARDS MS.

Degree requirements: For master's, thesis or alternative.

Entrance requirements: For master's, GRE General Test, TOEFL, minimum GPA of 3.0.

Faculty research: Parallel processing, computer systems in architecture.

■ MARIST COLLEGE

Graduate Programs, School of Computer Science and Mathematics, Poughkeepsie, NY 12601-1387

AWARDS Computer science (MS), including information systems, software development. Part-time and evening/weekend programs available.

Faculty: 11 full-time (3 women), 5 part-time/adjunct (1 woman).

Students: 50 full-time (15 women), 93 part-time (28 women); includes 63 minority (4 African Americans, 57 Asian Americans or Pacific Islanders, 2 Hispanic

Americans), 2 international. Average age 33. In 2001, 34 degrees awarded.

Degree requirements: For master's, thesis optional.

Application deadline: For fall admission, 8/1 (priority date); for spring admission, 12/15. Applications are processed on a rolling basis. *Application fee:* $30.

Expenses: Tuition: Full-time $4,320; part-time $480 per credit. Required fees: $30 per semester.

Financial support: Federal Work-Study and tuition waivers (partial) available. Support available to part-time students. Financial award application deadline: 8/15; financial award applicants required to submit FAFSA.

Dr. Roger Norton, Dean, 845-575-3000, *E-mail:* roger.norton@marist.edu.

Application contact: Dr. John DeJoy, Acting Dean of Graduate and Continuing Education, 845-575-3530, *Fax:* 845-575-3640, *E-mail:* john.dejoy@marist.edu.

■ MARLBORO COLLEGE

The Graduate Center of Marlboro College, Program in Internet Engineering, Brattleboro, VT 05301

AWARDS MS. Evening/weekend programs available. Postbaccalaureate distance learning degree programs offered (minimal on-campus study).

Faculty: 4 part-time/adjunct (0 women).

Students: 26 full-time (12 women). In 2001, 13 degrees awarded.

Degree requirements: For master's, capstone project.

Application deadline: For fall admission, 3/1 (priority date). Applications are processed on a rolling basis. *Application fee:* $0. Electronic applications accepted.

Expenses: Tuition: Part-time $3,000 per term. Tuition and fees vary according to program.

Financial support: Applicants required to submit FAFSA.

Application contact: Margaret J. Donahue, Admissions Officer, 802-258-9209, *Fax:* 802-258-9201, *E-mail:* mdonahue@gradcenter.marlboro.edu. *Web site:* http://www.gradcenter.marlboro.edu/

■ MARQUETTE UNIVERSITY

Graduate School, College of Arts and Sciences, Department of Mathematics, Statistics, and Computer Science, Milwaukee, WI 53201-1881

AWARDS Algebra (PhD); bio-mathematical modeling (PhD); computers (MS); mathematics (MS); mathematics education (MS); statistics (MS). Part-time programs available.

Faculty: 24 full-time (3 women).

Students: 26 full-time (10 women), 10 part-time (2 women); includes 1 minority (Asian American or Pacific Islander), 27 international. Average age 31. 76 applicants, 76% accepted. In 2001, 22 master's, 2 doctorates awarded. Terminal

Marquette University (continued)
master's awarded for partial completion of doctoral program.

Degree requirements: For master's, thesis or alternative, comprehensive exam; for doctorate, 2 foreign languages, thesis/dissertation, comprehensive exam.

Entrance requirements: For master's, TOEFL; for doctorate, TOEFL, sample of scholarly writing. *Application fee:* $40.

Expenses: Tuition: Full-time $10,170; part-time $445 per credit hour. Tuition and fees vary according to course load.

Financial support: In 2001–02, 2 research assistantships, 20 teaching assistantships were awarded. Federal Work-Study, institutionally sponsored loans, scholarships/grants, and tuition waivers (full and partial) also available. Support available to part-time students. Financial award application deadline: 2/15.

Faculty research: Models of physiological systems, mathematical immunology, computational group theory, mathematical logic. *Total annual research expenditures:* $442,234.

Dr. John Simms, Chairman, 414-288-7573, *Fax:* 414-288-1578.

Application contact: Dr. Naveen Bansal, Director of Graduate Studies, 414-288-5290.

■ MARQUETTE UNIVERSITY

Graduate School, Program in Computing, Milwaukee, WI 53201-1881

AWARDS MS.

Students: 52 full-time (22 women), 65 part-time (19 women); includes 8 minority (1 African American, 6 Asian Americans or Pacific Islanders, 1 Hispanic American), 76 international. Average age 31. In 2001, 28 degrees awarded.

Application deadline: Applications are processed on a rolling basis. *Application fee:* $40. Electronic applications accepted.

Expenses: Tuition: Full-time $10,170; part-time $445 per credit hour. Tuition and fees vary according to course load.

Dr. George Corliss, Head, *E-mail:* george.corliss@marquette.edu. *Web site:* http://www.comp.mu.edu

■ MARYMOUNT UNIVERSITY

School of Arts and Sciences, Program in Math and Computer Science, Arlington, VA 22207-4299

AWARDS MS, Certificate.

Students: 6 full-time (3 women), 32 part-time (7 women); includes 13 minority (4 African Americans, 7 Asian Americans or Pacific Islanders, 2 Hispanic Americans), 4 international. Average age 33. 22 applicants, 100% accepted, 11 enrolled. In 2001, 4 degrees awarded.

Degree requirements: For master's, thesis or alternative.

Entrance requirements: For master's, GRE, interview. *Application deadline:* Applications are processed on a rolling

basis. *Application fee:* $35. Electronic applications accepted.

Expenses: Tuition: Part-time $512 per credit. Required fees: $5 per credit.

Financial support: Research assistantships with full tuition reimbursements, career-related internships or fieldwork and scholarships/grants available. Support available to part-time students. Financial award applicants required to submit FAFSA.

Dr. Elsa Schaefer, Chair, 703-284-1566, *Fax:* 703-284-3859, *E-mail:* elsa.schaefer@marymount.edu. *Web site:* http://www.marymount.edu/

■ MASSACHUSETTS INSTITUTE OF TECHNOLOGY

School of Engineering, Department of Electrical Engineering and Computer Science, Cambridge, MA 02139-4307

AWARDS Computer science (EE); electrical engineering (EE); electrical engineering and computer science (M Eng, SM, PhD, Sc D).

Faculty: 111 full-time (11 women), 2 part-time/adjunct (0 women).

Students: 853 full-time (170 women), 3 part-time (1 woman); includes 220 minority (22 African Americans, 180 Asian Americans or Pacific Islanders, 15 Hispanic Americans, 3 Native Americans), 238 international. Average age 22. 2,491 applicants, 21% accepted, 306 enrolled. In 2001, 314 master's, 73 doctorates awarded. Terminal master's awarded for partial completion of doctoral program.

Degree requirements: For master's, thesis/dissertation; for doctorate, thesis/dissertation, comprehensive exam.

Entrance requirements: For master's and doctorate, TOEFL. *Application deadline:* For fall admission, 1/1. *Application fee:* $60. Electronic applications accepted.

Expenses: Tuition: Full-time $26,960. Full-time tuition and fees vary according to program.

Financial support: In 2001–02, 781 students received support, including 163 fellowships, 594 research assistantships, 123 teaching assistantships; career-related internships or fieldwork, Federal Work-Study, institutionally sponsored loans, scholarships/grants, health care benefits, and unspecified assistantships also available. Financial award applicants required to submit FAFSA.

Faculty research: Modem control and system theory, radio astronomy, knowledge-based application systems, artificial intelligence, electrohydrodynamics. *Total annual research expenditures:* $50.5 million.

Dr. John V. Guttag, Head, 617-253-4001, *Fax:* 617-258-7354, *E-mail:* guttag@eecs.mit.edu.

Application contact: Peggy Carney, Administrator, 617-253-4603, *Fax:* 617-258-7354, *E-mail:* grad-ap@eecs.mit.edu. *Web site:* http://www.eecs.mit.edu/

■ MCNEESE STATE UNIVERSITY

Graduate School, College of Science, Department of Mathematics, Computer Science, and Statistics, Lake Charles, LA 70609

AWARDS Computer science (MS); mathematics (MS); statistics (MS). Evening/weekend programs available.

Faculty: 10 full-time (3 women).

Students: 27 full-time (8 women), 17 part-time (7 women); includes 3 minority (1 African American, 2 Hispanic Americans), 21 international. In 2001, 9 degrees awarded.

Degree requirements: For master's, thesis or alternative, written exam, comprehensive exam.

Entrance requirements: For master's, GRE General Test. *Application deadline:* For fall admission, 7/15 (priority date). Applications are processed on a rolling basis. *Application fee:* $20 ($30 for international students).

Expenses: Tuition, state resident: part-time $1,208 per semester. Tuition, nonresident: part-time $4,378 per semester.

Financial support: Teaching assistantships available. Financial award application deadline: 5/1.

Sid Bradley, Head, 337-475-5788, *Fax:* 337-475-5799, *E-mail:* sbradley@mail.mcneese.edu.

■ MICHIGAN STATE UNIVERSITY

Graduate School, College of Engineering, Department of Computer Science and Engineering, East Lansing, MI 48824

AWARDS Computer science (MS, PhD).

Faculty: 25.

Students: 71 full-time (10 women), 69 part-time (10 women); includes 14 minority (8 African Americans, 6 Asian Americans or Pacific Islanders), 95 international. Average age 27. 388 applicants, 13% accepted. In 2001, 24 master's, 11 doctorates awarded.

Degree requirements: For master's, written exam or substantial design project; for doctorate, thesis/dissertation, qualifying exams, comprehensive exam.

Entrance requirements: For master's, GRE General Test, GRE Subject Test, TOEFL; for doctorate, GRE General Test, GRE Subject Test, TOEFL, sample of published work. *Application deadline:* For fall admission, 1/15. Applications are processed on a rolling basis. *Application fee:* $30 ($40 for international students). Electronic applications accepted.

Expenses: Tuition, state resident: part-time $244 per credit hour. Tuition, nonresident: part-time $494 per credit hour. Required fees: $268 per semester. Tuition and fees vary according to course load, degree level and program.

Financial support: In 2001–02, 15 fellowships (averaging $3,949 per year), 4

research assistantships (averaging $13,940 per year), 62 teaching assistantships with tuition reimbursements (averaging $13,170 per year) were awarded. Financial award applicants required to submit FAFSA.
Faculty research: Analysis of embedded systems, sequential decision making, reconfigurable adaptable micro-robots. *Total annual research expenditures:* $1.9 million.
Dr. Wayne Dyksen, Chair, 517-353-3148, *Fax:* 517-432-1061, *E-mail:* cseinfo@ cse.msu.edu.
Application contact: Graduate Director, 517-353-3293, *E-mail:* gradir@ cps.msu.edu. *Web site:* http:// www.cse.msu.edu/

Find an in-depth description at www.petersons.com/gradchannel.

■ MICHIGAN TECHNOLOGICAL UNIVERSITY

Graduate School, College of Sciences and Arts, Department of Computer Science, Houghton, MI 49931-1295
AWARDS Computer science (MS). Part-time programs available.

Entrance requirements: For master's, GRE General Test, TOEFL. Electronic applications accepted.
Faculty research: Software engineering, parallel algorithms, graphics and computational biology, geometric modeling/graphics, instruction level parallelism. *Web site:* http://www.cs.mtu.edu/ grad-prog.html
Find an in-depth description at www.petersons.com/gradchannel.

■ MIDDLE TENNESSEE STATE UNIVERSITY

College of Graduate Studies, College of Basic and Applied Sciences, Department of Computer Science, Murfreesboro, TN 37132
AWARDS MS. Part-time programs available.

Faculty: 10 full-time (4 women).
Students: 6 full-time (2 women), 38 part-time (8 women); includes 26 minority (2 African Americans, 22 Asian Americans or Pacific Islanders, 2 Hispanic Americans). Average age 31. 21 applicants, 90% accepted. In 2001, 11 degrees awarded.
Degree requirements: For master's, one foreign language, thesis, comprehensive exam.
Entrance requirements: For master's, GRE or MAT. *Application deadline:* For fall admission, 8/1 (priority date). Applications are processed on a rolling basis. *Application fee:* $25. Electronic applications accepted.
Expenses: Tuition, state resident: full-time $1,716; part-time $191 per hour. Tuition, nonresident: full-time $4,952; part-time $461 per hour. Required fees: $14 per hour. $58 per semester.

Financial support: In 2001–02, 7 teaching assistantships were awarded; institutionally sponsored loans and scholarships/grants also available. Support available to part-time students. Financial award application deadline: 5/1; financial award applicants required to submit FAFSA. *Total annual research expenditures:* $1,969.
Dr. Richard Detmer, Chair, 615-898-2397, *Fax:* 615-898-5567, *E-mail:* rdetmer@ mtsu.edu.

■ MIDWESTERN STATE UNIVERSITY

Graduate Studies, College of Science and Mathematics, Computer Science Program, Wichita Falls, TX 76308
AWARDS MS. Part-time and evening/weekend programs available.

Faculty: 5 full-time (1 woman).
Students: 12 full-time (1 woman), 25 part-time (6 women); includes 5 minority (4 Asian Americans or Pacific Islanders, 1 Hispanic American), 24 international. Average age 30. 14 applicants, 93% accepted. In 2001, 14 degrees awarded.
Degree requirements: For master's, thesis or alternative.
Entrance requirements: For master's, GRE General Test, TOEFL. *Application deadline:* For fall admission, 8/7; for spring admission, 12/15. *Application fee:* $0 ($50 for international students).
Expenses: Tuition, state resident: full-time $936. Tuition, nonresident: full-time $4,734. Required fees: $1,280. One-time fee: $190. Tuition and fees vary according to course load.
Financial support: In 2001–02, 2 research assistantships were awarded; teaching assistantships with partial tuition reimbursements, Federal Work-Study, institutionally sponsored loans, tuition waivers (partial), and unspecified assistantships also available. Support available to part-time students.
Dr. Ranette Halverson, Program Chair, 940-397-4189.
Application contact: Dr. Stewart Carpenter, Graduate Coordinator, Computer Science, 940-397-4279. *Web site:* http://www.mwsu.edu/

■ MILLS COLLEGE

Graduate Studies, New Horizons Program in Mathematics and Computer Science, Oakland, CA 94613-1000
AWARDS Computer science (Certificate). Part-time programs available.

Faculty: 6 full-time (4 women), 4 part-time/adjunct (1 woman).
Students: 4 full-time (3 women), 1 (woman) part-time. Average age 32. 15 applicants, 80% accepted, 7 enrolled.
Entrance requirements: For degree, TOEFL. *Application deadline:* For fall admission, 2/1 (priority date); for spring

admission, 11/1. Applications are processed on a rolling basis. *Application fee:* $50. Electronic applications accepted.
Expenses: Tuition: Full-time $12,700; part-time $3,250 per credit. Required fees: $480. One-time fee: $480 part-time.
Financial support: In 2001–02, 5 fellowships (averaging $625 per year), 7 teaching assistantships (averaging $3,000 per year) were awarded. Career-related internships or fieldwork, institutionally sponsored loans, scholarships/grants, and residence awards also available. Support available to part-time students. Financial award application deadline: 2/1; financial award applicants required to submit FAFSA.
Faculty research: Dynamical systems, human interface, parallel computation, compiling techniques, fault tolerance, operating systems.
Ellen Spertus, Director, 510-430-2011, *Fax:* 510-430-3314.
Application contact: Ron B. Clement, Associate Director of Graduate Studies, 510-430-2355, *Fax:* 510-430-2159, *E-mail:* rclement@mills.edu. *Web site:* http:// www.mills.edu/

■ MILLS COLLEGE

Graduate Studies, Program in Interdisciplinary Computer Science, Oakland, CA 94613-1000
AWARDS MA. Part-time programs available.

Faculty: 6 full-time (4 women), 4 part-time/adjunct (1 woman).
Students: 11 full-time (9 women). Average age 35. 16 applicants, 69% accepted, 7 enrolled. In 2001, 1 degree awarded.
Degree requirements: For master's, thesis.
Entrance requirements: For master's, TOEFL. *Application deadline:* For fall admission, 2/1 (priority date); for spring admission, 11/1. Applications are processed on a rolling basis. *Application fee:* $50. Electronic applications accepted.
Expenses: Tuition: Full-time $12,700; part-time $3,250 per credit. Required fees: $480. One-time fee: $480 part-time.
Financial support: In 2001–02, 9 fellowships with partial tuition reimbursements (averaging $4,000 per year), 7 teaching assistantships with partial tuition reimbursements (averaging $3,000 per year) were awarded. Career-related internships or fieldwork, institutionally sponsored loans, scholarships/grants, and residence awards also available. Support available to part-time students. Financial award application deadline: 2/1; financial award applicants required to submit CSS PROFILE or FAFSA.
Faculty research: Dynamical systems, linear programming, theory of computer viruses, interface design, intelligent tutoring systems.
Ellen Spertus, Director, 510-430-2011, *Fax:* 510-430-3314.
Application contact: Ron B. Clement, Associate Director of Graduate Studies,

Mills College (continued)
510-430-2355, *Fax:* 510-430-2159, *E-mail:* rclement@mills.edu. *Web site:* http://www.mills.edu/

Find an in-depth description at www.petersons.com/gradchannel.

■ MINNESOTA STATE UNIVERSITY, MANKATO

College of Graduate Studies, College of Science, Engineering and Technology, Department of Computer Science, Mankato, MN 56001

AWARDS MS.

Faculty: 15 full-time (2 women).
Students: 15 full-time (5 women), 7 part-time (2 women). Average age 31. In 2001, 4 degrees awarded.
Degree requirements: For master's, thesis or alternative, comprehensive exam.
Entrance requirements: For master's, GRE General Test, minimum GPA of 3.0 during previous 2 years. *Application deadline:* For fall admission, 7/9 (priority date); for spring admission, 11/27. Applications are processed on a rolling basis. *Application fee:* $20.
Expenses: Tuition, state resident: full-time $3,253; part-time $157 per credit. Tuition, nonresident: full-time $4,893; part-time $248 per credit. Required fees: $24 per credit. Tuition and fees vary according to reciprocity agreements.
Financial support: Research assistantships with full tuition reimbursements, teaching assistantships with full tuition reimbursements available. Financial award application deadline: 3/15; financial award applicants required to submit FAFSA.
Dr. C. Veltsos, Head, 507-389-6765.
Application contact: Joni Roberts, Admissions Coordinator, 507-389-5244, *Fax:* 507-389-5974, *E-mail:* grad@mankato.msus.edu.

■ MINNESOTA STATE UNIVERSITY, MANKATO

College of Graduate Studies, College of Science, Engineering and Technology, Department of Mathematics and Statistics, Program in Computers, Mankato, MN 56001

AWARDS Mathematics: computer science (MS).

Students: Average age 32.
Degree requirements: For master's, one foreign language, thesis or alternative, comprehensive exam.
Entrance requirements: For master's, GRE General Test, GRE Subject Test, minimum GPA of 3.0 during previous 2 years. *Application deadline:* For fall admission, 7/9 (priority date); for spring admission, 11/27. Applications are processed on a rolling basis. *Application fee:* $20.
Expenses: Tuition, state resident: full-time $3,253; part-time $157 per credit. Tuition,

nonresident: full-time $4,893; part-time $248 per credit. Required fees: $24 per credit. Tuition and fees vary according to reciprocity agreements.
Financial support: Fellowships with full tuition reimbursements, research assistantships with full tuition reimbursements, teaching assistantships with full tuition reimbursements, Federal Work-Study and institutionally sponsored loans available. Support available to part-time students. Financial award application deadline: 3/15; financial award applicants required to submit FAFSA.
Dr. Lee Cornell, Chairperson, 507-389-2968.
Application contact: Joni Roberts, Admissions Coordinator, 507-389-5244, *Fax:* 507-389-5974, *E-mail:* grad@mankato.msus.edu.

■ MISSISSIPPI COLLEGE

Graduate School, College of Arts and Sciences, Department of Mathematics and Computer Science, Clinton, MS 39058

AWARDS Computer science (MS); mathematics (MS).

Degree requirements: For master's, comprehensive exam.
Entrance requirements: For master's, minimum GPA of 2.5.

■ MISSISSIPPI STATE UNIVERSITY

College of Engineering, Department of Computer Science, Mississippi State, MS 39762

AWARDS MS, PhD. Part-time programs available. Postbaccalaureate distance learning degree programs offered (minimal on-campus study).

Faculty: 18 full-time (6 women), 8 part-time/adjunct (0 women).
Students: 100 full-time (30 women), 45 part-time (9 women); includes 9 minority (5 African Americans, 3 Asian Americans or Pacific Islanders, 1 Native American), 109 international. Average age 27. 400 applicants, 52% accepted. In 2001, 20 master's, 1 doctorate awarded.
Degree requirements: For master's and doctorate, thesis/dissertation, comprehensive oral or written exam.
Entrance requirements: For master's, GRE General Test, TOEFL, minimum GPA of 2.75; for doctorate, GRE, TOEFL. *Application deadline:* For fall admission, 7/1; for spring admission, 11/1. Applications are processed on a rolling basis. *Application fee:* $25 for international students. Electronic applications accepted.
Expenses: Tuition, state resident: full-time $3,586; part-time $150 per credit hour. Tuition, nonresident: full-time $8,128; part-time $339 per credit hour. Tuition and fees vary according to course load and campus/location.

Financial support: In 2001–02, 3 fellowships with full tuition reimbursements (averaging $9,000 per year), 24 research assistantships with full tuition reimbursements (averaging $9,900 per year), 14 teaching assistantships with full tuition reimbursements (averaging $9,000 per year) were awarded. Federal Work-Study, institutionally sponsored loans, and unspecified assistantships also available. Financial award applicants required to submit FAFSA.
Faculty research: Artificial intelligence, software engineering, visualization, high performance computing. *Total annual research expenditures:* $1 million.
Dr. Julia E. Hodges, Head, 662-325-2756, *Fax:* 662-325-8997, *E-mail:* hodges@cs.msstate.edu.
Application contact: Jerry B. Inmon, Director of Admissions, 662-325-2224, *Fax:* 662-325-7360, *E-mail:* admit@admissions.msstate.edu. *Web site:* http://www.cs.msstate.edu/

Find an in-depth description at www.petersons.com/gradchannel.

■ MONMOUTH UNIVERSITY

Graduate School, Department of Computer Science, West Long Branch, NJ 07764-1898

AWARDS MS. Part-time and evening/weekend programs available.

Faculty: 6 full-time (1 woman), 7 part-time/adjunct (0 women).
Students: 81 full-time (42 women), 63 part-time (16 women). Average age 29. 274 applicants, 48% accepted, 50 enrolled. In 2001, 23 degrees awarded.
Degree requirements: For master's, thesis optional.
Entrance requirements: For master's, minimum GPA of 3.0 in major, 2.75 overall. *Application deadline:* For fall admission, 8/15 (priority date); for spring admission, 12/15 (priority date). Applications are processed on a rolling basis. *Application fee:* $35. Electronic applications accepted.
Expenses: Tuition: Full-time $9,900; part-time $549 per credit. Required fees: $568.
Financial support: In 2001–02, 95 students received support, including 76 fellowships (averaging $2,503 per year), 34 research assistantships (averaging $5,002 per year); scholarships/grants and unspecified assistantships also available. Support available to part-time students. Financial award application deadline: 3/1; financial award applicants required to submit FAFSA.
Faculty research: Databases, natural language processing, protocols, performance analysis, communications networks (systems), telecommunications.
Dr. Al Fredericks, Director, 732-571-3441, *Fax:* 732-263-5202.
Application contact: Kevin Roane, Director, Office of Graduate Admissions, 732-571-3452, *Fax:* 732-263-5123, *E-mail:*

gradadm@monmouth.edu. *Web site:* http://www.monmouth.edu/~cs/cs.html

Find an in-depth description at www.petersons.com/gradchannel.

■ MONTANA STATE UNIVERSITY–BOZEMAN

College of Graduate Studies, College of Engineering, Department of Computer Science, Bozeman, MT 59717

AWARDS Computer science (MS); computer sciences (PhD); engineering (PhD). Part-time programs available.

Students: 20 full-time (7 women), 19 part-time (10 women); includes 1 minority (Asian American or Pacific Islander), 8 international. Average age 32. 30 applicants, 90% accepted, 13 enrolled. In 2001, 9 degrees awarded.
Degree requirements: For master's, thesis (for some programs); for doctorate, thesis/dissertation.
Entrance requirements: For master's, GRE General Test, TOEFL, minimum GPA of 3.0; for doctorate, GRE General Test, TOEFL, minimum GPA of 3.2. *Application deadline:* For fall admission, 7/8; for spring admission, 11/24. Applications are processed on a rolling basis. *Application fee:* $50. Electronic applications accepted.
Expenses: Tuition, state resident: full-time $3,894; part-time $198 per credit. Tuition, nonresident: full-time $10,661; part-time $480 per credit. International tuition: $10,811 full-time. Tuition and fees vary according to course load and program.
Financial support: In 2001–02, 35 students received support, including 7 research assistantships with full tuition reimbursements available (averaging $10,500 per year), 13 teaching assistantships with full tuition reimbursements available (averaging $7,500 per year); institutionally sponsored loans, scholarships/grants, and unspecified assistantships also available. Financial award application deadline: 3/1; financial award applicants required to submit FAFSA.
Faculty research: Computational biology, graphics, CS education, graph theory, artificial intelligence. *Total annual research expenditures:* $155,986.
Dr. J. Denbigh Starkey, Head, 406-994-4780, *Fax:* 406-994-4376, *E-mail:* gradappl@cs.montana.edu. *Web site:* http://www.cs.montana.edu/

■ MONTCLAIR STATE UNIVERSITY

The School of Graduate, Professional and Continuing Education, College of Science and Mathematics, Department of Computer Science, Upper Montclair, NJ 07043-1624

AWARDS Applied mathematics (MS); applied statistics (MS); informatics (MS); object oriented computing (Certificate). Part-time and evening/weekend programs available.

Degree requirements: For master's, comprehensive exam.
Entrance requirements: For master's, minimum GPA of 2.67, 15 undergraduate math credits, bachelors degree in computer science, math, science or engineering. Electronic applications accepted.

■ MONTCLAIR STATE UNIVERSITY

The School of Graduate, Professional and Continuing Education, College of Science and Mathematics, Department of Mathematics, Upper Montclair, NJ 07043-1624

AWARDS Mathematics (MS), including computer science, mathematics education, pure and applied mathematics, statistics. Part-time and evening/weekend programs available.

Degree requirements: For master's, comprehensive exam.
Entrance requirements: For master's, minimum GPA of 2.67.

■ MONTCLAIR STATE UNIVERSITY

The School of Graduate, Professional and Continuing Education, College of Science and Mathematics, Department of Mathematics, Programs in Mathematics, Concentration in Computer Science, Upper Montclair, NJ 07043-1624

AWARDS MS.

Degree requirements: For master's, comprehensive exam.
Entrance requirements: For master's, minimum GPA of 2.67. Electronic applications accepted.

■ NATIONAL TECHNOLOGICAL UNIVERSITY

Programs in Engineering, Fort Collins, CO 80526-1842

AWARDS Chemical engineering (MS); computer engineering (MS); computer science (MS); electrical engineering (MS); engineering management (MS); environmental systems management (MS); management of technology (MS); manufacturing systems engineering (MS); materials science and engineering (MS); mechanical engineering (MS); microelectronics and semiconductor engineering (MS); software engineering (MS); special majors (MS); systems engineering (MS). Part-time programs available. Postbaccalaureate distance learning degree programs offered (no on-campus study).

Students: In 2001, 114 degrees awarded.
Degree requirements: For master's, comprehensive exam.

Entrance requirements: For master's, BS in engineering or related field; 2.9 minimum GPA. *Application deadline:* Applications are processed on a rolling basis. *Application fee:* $50. Electronic applications accepted.
Expenses: Tuition: Part-time $660 per credit hour. Part-time tuition and fees vary according to course load, campus/location and program.
Dr. Andre Vacroux, President, 970-495-6400, *Fax:* 970-484-0668, *E-mail:* andre@ntu.edu.
Application contact: Rhonda Bonham, Admissions Officer, 970-495-6400, *Fax:* 970-498-0601, *E-mail:* rhonda@ntu.edu. *Web site:* http://www.ntu.edu/

■ NAVAL POSTGRADUATE SCHOOL

Graduate Programs, Department of Computer Science, Monterey, CA 93943

AWARDS MS, PhD. Program only open to commissioned officers of the United States and friendly nations and selected United States federal civilian employees. Part-time programs available. Postbaccalaureate distance learning degree programs offered (minimal on-campus study).

Degree requirements: For master's, thesis; for doctorate, one foreign language, thesis/dissertation.

■ NEW JERSEY INSTITUTE OF TECHNOLOGY

Office of Graduate Studies, College of Computing Science, Program in Computer Science, Newark, NJ 07102

AWARDS MS, PhD. Part-time and evening/weekend programs available.

Faculty: 42 full-time (5 women).
Students: 331 full-time (121 women), 355 part-time (84 women); includes 161 minority (12 African Americans, 132 Asian Americans or Pacific Islanders, 16 Hispanic Americans, 1 Native American), 356 international. Average age 29. 1,513 applicants, 41% accepted, 198 enrolled. In 2001, 320 master's, 5 doctorates awarded.
Degree requirements: For doctorate, thesis/dissertation.
Entrance requirements: For master's, GRE General Test; for doctorate, GRE General Test, minimum graduate GPA of 3.5. *Application deadline:* For fall admission, 6/5 (priority date); for spring admission, 10/15. Applications are processed on a rolling basis. *Application fee:* $50. Electronic applications accepted.
Expenses: Tuition, state resident: full-time $7,812; part-time $434 per credit. Tuition, nonresident: full-time $10,746; part-time $597 per credit. Required fees: $47 per credit. $76 per semester.
Financial support: Fellowships with full and partial tuition reimbursements, research assistantships with full and partial

New Jersey Institute of Technology
(continued)
tuition reimbursements, teaching assistant-ships with full and partial tuition reimbursements, career-related internships or fieldwork, Federal Work-Study, institutionally sponsored loans, and unspecified assistantships available. Financial award application deadline: 3/15. Dr. James McHugh, Chairperson.
Application contact: Kathryn Kelly, Director of Admissions, 973-596-3300, *Fax:* 973-596-3461, *E-mail:* admissions@njit.edu.

■ **NEW MEXICO HIGHLANDS UNIVERSITY**

Graduate Studies, College of Arts and Sciences, Program in Media Arts and Computer Science, Las Vegas, NM 87701

AWARDS Cognitive science (MA, MS); computer graphics (MA, MS); design studies (MA); digital audio and video production (MA); multimedia systems (MS); networking technology (MA, MS).

Faculty: 13 full-time (2 women).
Students: 10 full-time (4 women), 8 part-time (6 women); includes 5 minority (all Hispanic Americans), 6 international. Aver-age age 34. In 2001, 2 degrees awarded.
Expenses: Tuition, state resident: full-time $2,238. Tuition, nonresident: full-time $9,366.
Financial support: Research assistantships with full and partial tuition reimburse-ments available.
Dr. Tomas Salazar, Dean, 505-454-3080, *Fax:* 505-454-3389, *E-mail:* salazar_t@nmhu.edu.
Application contact: Dr. Linda LaGrange, Associate Dean of Graduate Studies, 505-454-3266, *Fax:* 505-454-3558, *E-mail:* lagrange_l@nmhu.edu.

■ **NEW MEXICO INSTITUTE OF MINING AND TECHNOLOGY**

Graduate Studies, Department of Computer Science, Socorro, NM 87801
AWARDS MS, PhD. Part-time programs avail-able.
Faculty: 3 full-time (0 women), 3 part-time/adjunct (0 women).
Students: 36 full-time (4 women), 4 part-time (3 women); includes 2 minority (1 Asian American or Pacific Islander, 1 Hispanic American), 28 international. Average age 25. 104 applicants, 36% accepted, 14 enrolled. In 2001, 13 degrees awarded.
Degree requirements: For master's, thesis optional; for doctorate, thesis/dissertation.
Entrance requirements: For master's, GRE General Test, TOEFL; for doctor-ate, GRE General Test, GRE Subject Test, TOEFL. *Application deadline:* For fall admission, 3/1 (priority date); for spring

admission, 6/1 (priority date). Applications are processed on a rolling basis. *Application fee:* $16 ($30 for international students). Electronic applications accepted.
Expenses: Tuition, state resident: part-time $1,084 per semester. Tuition, nonresident: part-time $4,367 per semester. Required fees: $429 per semester.
Financial support: In 2001–02, 10 research assistantships (averaging $13,505 per year), 20 teaching assistantships with full and partial tuition reimbursements (averaging $12,714 per year) were awarded. Fellowships, Federal Work-Study and institutionally sponsored loans also available. Financial award application deadline: 3/1; financial award applicants required to submit CSS PROFILE or FAFSA.
Dr. Andrew Sung, Chairman, 505-835-5949, *Fax:* 505-835-5587, *E-mail:* sung@nmt.edu.
Application contact: Dr. David B. Johnson, Dean of Graduate Studies, 505-835-5513, *Fax:* 505-835-5476, *E-mail:* graduate@nmt.edu. *Web site:* http://www.cs.nmt.edu/

■ **NEW MEXICO STATE UNIVERSITY**

Graduate School, College of Arts and Sciences, Department of Computer Science, Las Cruces, NM 88003-8001
AWARDS MS, PhD. Part-time programs avail-able.
Faculty: 7 full-time (0 women), 8 part-time/adjunct (0 women).
Students: 57 full-time (13 women), 17 part-time (4 women); includes 9 minority (2 Asian Americans or Pacific Islanders, 7 Hispanic Americans), 50 international. Average age 29. 140 applicants, 82% accepted, 13 enrolled. In 2001, 18 master's, 3 doctorates awarded.
Degree requirements: For master's, thesis or alternative; for doctorate, one foreign language, thesis/dissertation.
Entrance requirements: For master's and doctorate, GRE General Test. *Application deadline:* For fall admission, 7/1 (priority date); for spring admission, 11/1. Applica-tions are processed on a rolling basis. *Application fee:* $15 ($35 for international students). Electronic applications accepted.
Expenses: Tuition, state resident: full-time $3,234; part-time $135 per credit. Tuition, nonresident: full-time $9,420; part-time $428 per credit. Required fees: $858.
Financial support: In 2001–02, 5 research assistantships, 20 teaching assistantships were awarded. Career-related internships or fieldwork and Federal Work-Study also available. Support available to part-time students. Financial award application deadline: 3/1.
Faculty research: Programming languages, artificial intelligence, databases, operating systems, computer networks.

Dr. Roger Hartley, Head, 505-646-3723, *Fax:* 505-646-1002, *E-mail:* arthur@nmsu.edu.
Application contact: Dr. Joseph J. Pfeiffer, Chair, Graduate Committee, 505-646-1605, *Fax:* 505-646-1002, *E-mail:* pfeiffer@nmsu.edu. *Web site:* http://www.cs.nmsu.edu/

■ **NEW YORK INSTITUTE OF TECHNOLOGY**

Graduate Division, School of Engineering and Technology, Program in Computer Science, Old Westbury, NY 11568-8000

AWARDS MS. Part-time and evening/weekend programs available.

Students: 219 full-time (57 women), 151 part-time (41 women); includes 60 minor-ity (9 African Americans, 50 Asian Americans or Pacific Islanders, 1 Hispanic American), 227 international. Average age 32. 312 applicants, 63% accepted, 77 enrolled. In 2001, 97 degrees awarded.
Degree requirements: For master's, project.
Entrance requirements: For master's, GRE General Test, TOEFL, minimum QPA of 2.85, BS in computer science or related field. *Application deadline:* For fall admission, 7/1 (priority date); for spring admission, 12/1 (priority date). Applica-tions are processed on a rolling basis. *Application fee:* $50. Electronic applications accepted.
Expenses: Tuition: Part-time $545 per credit. Tuition and fees vary according to course load, degree level, program and student level.
Financial support: In 2001–02, 37 research assistantships with partial tuition reimbursements were awarded; fellowships, institutionally sponsored loans, tuition waivers (partial), and unspecified assistant-ships also available. Support available to part-time students. Financial award applicants required to submit FAFSA.
Faculty research: Image processing, multimedia CD-ROM, prototype modules of the DTV application environment.
Dr. Ayat Jafari, Chair, 516-686-7523, *E-mail:* ajafari@nyit.edu.
Application contact: Jacquelyn Nealon, Dean of Admissions and Financial Aid, 516-686-7925, *Fax:* 516-686-7613, *E-mail:* jnealon@nyit.edu.

■ **NEW YORK UNIVERSITY**

Graduate School of Arts and Science, Courant Institute of Mathematical Sciences, Department of Computer Science, New York, NY 10012-1019

AWARDS Computer science (MS, PhD); information systems (MS); scientific comput-ing (MS). Part-time and evening/weekend programs available.
Faculty: 30 full-time (1 woman).

Students: 151 full-time (39 women), 292 part-time (89 women); includes 50 minority (1 African American, 44 Asian Americans or Pacific Islanders, 5 Hispanic Americans), 257 international. Average age 27. 805 applicants, 38% accepted, 125 enrolled. In 2001, 111 master's, 9 doctorates awarded.

Degree requirements: For doctorate, thesis/dissertation, oral and written exams.

Entrance requirements: For master's and doctorate, GRE General Test, GRE Subject Test, TOEFL. *Application deadline:* For fall admission, 1/4; for spring admission, 11/1. *Application fee:* $60.

Expenses: Tuition: Full-time $19,536; part-time $814 per credit. Required fees: $1,330; $38 per credit. Tuition and fees vary according to course load and program.

Financial support: Fellowships with tuition reimbursements, research assistantships with tuition reimbursements, teaching assistantships with tuition reimbursements, Federal Work-Study and institutionally sponsored loans available. Financial award application deadline: 1/4; financial award applicants required to submit FAFSA.

Faculty research: Distributed parallel and secure computing, computer graphics and vision, algorithmic and theory of computation, natural language processing, computational biology.
Margaret Wright, Director, 212-998-3011, *Fax:* 212-995-4124.

Application contact: Denis Zorin, Director of Graduate Studies, 212-998-3011, *Fax:* 212-995-4124, *E-mail:* admissions@cs.nyu.edu. *Web site:* http://cs.nyu.edu/

Find an in-depth description at www.petersons.com/gradchannel.

■ **NORTH CAROLINA AGRICULTURAL AND TECHNICAL STATE UNIVERSITY**

Graduate School, College of Engineering, Department of Computer Science, Greensboro, NC 27411

AWARDS MSCS. Part-time programs available.

Faculty: 9 full-time (1 woman), 1 part-time/adjunct (0 women).

Students: 49 full-time (27 women), 30 part-time (15 women); includes 22 minority (all Asian Americans or Pacific Islanders). Average age 25. 51 applicants, 47% accepted. In 2001, 23 degrees awarded.

Degree requirements: For master's, thesis (for some programs), comprehensive exam.

Application deadline: For fall admission, 7/1 (priority date); for spring admission, 1/9. Applications are processed on a rolling basis. *Application fee:* $35.

Financial support: In 2001–02, 24 students received support, including 16 research assistantships, 4 teaching assistantships; fellowships, career-related

internships or fieldwork also available. Financial award application deadline: 3/30.

Faculty research: Object-oriented analysis, artificial intelligence, distributed computing, societal implications of computing, testing. *Total annual research expenditures:* $49,140.
Dr. Ken Williams, Chairperson, 336-334-7245, *Fax:* 336-334-7244, *E-mail:* williams@ncat.edu.

Application contact: Dr. Huiming Yu, Graduate Coordinator, 336-334-7245, *Fax:* 336-334-7244, *E-mail:* cshmyu@ncat.edu. *Web site:* http://www.cs.ncat.edu/graddirector/

■ **NORTH CAROLINA STATE UNIVERSITY**

Graduate School, College of Engineering, Department of Computer Science, Raleigh, NC 27695

AWARDS MC Sc, MS, PhD. Part-time programs available.

Faculty: 37 full-time (4 women), 12 part-time/adjunct (0 women).

Students: 210 full-time (49 women), 105 part-time (28 women); includes 63 minority (11 African Americans, 47 Asian Americans or Pacific Islanders, 5 Hispanic Americans), 171 international. Average age 28. 446 applicants, 43% accepted. In 2001, 80 master's, 5 doctorates awarded.

Degree requirements: For master's, thesis (for some programs); for doctorate, thesis/dissertation.

Entrance requirements: For master's, GRE General Test, GRE Subject Test, TOEFL, minimum GPA of 3.0; for doctorate, GRE General Test, GRE Subject Test, TOEFL, minimum GPA of 3.5. *Application deadline:* For fall admission, 4/1 (priority date); for spring admission, 10/1. *Application fee:* $45.

Expenses: Tuition, state resident: full-time $1,748. Tuition, nonresident: full-time $6,904.

Financial support: In 2001–02, 4 fellowships (averaging $6,005 per year), 45 research assistantships (averaging $5,873 per year), 38 teaching assistantships (averaging $6,223 per year) were awarded. Career-related internships or fieldwork and institutionally sponsored loans also available. Financial award application deadline: 2/1.

Faculty research: Networking and performance analysis, theory and algorithms of computation, data mining, graphics and human computer interaction, software engineering and information security. *Total annual research expenditures:* $6 million.
Dr. Alan L. Tharp, Head, 919-515-7435, *Fax:* 919-515-7896, *E-mail:* tharp@adm.csc.ncsu.edu.

Application contact: Dr. Edward Davis, Interim Director of Graduate Programs, 919-515-7045, *Fax:* 919-515-7896, *E-mail:* davis@csc.ncsu.edu. *Web site:* http://www.csc.ncsu.edu/

■ **NORTH CAROLINA STATE UNIVERSITY**

Graduate School, College of Engineering, Department of Electrical and Computer Engineering, Program in Computer Networking, Raleigh, NC 27695

AWARDS MS.

Faculty: 31 full-time (5 women).

Students: 116 full-time (23 women), 50 part-time (13 women); includes 29 minority (7 African Americans, 21 Asian Americans or Pacific Islanders, 1 Hispanic American), 110 international. Average age 27. 206 applicants, 54% accepted. In 2001, 45 degrees awarded.

Entrance requirements: For master's, GRE General Test, GRE Subject Test. *Application fee:* $45.

Expenses: Tuition, state resident: full-time $1,748. Tuition, nonresident: full-time $6,904.

Financial support: In 2001–02, 2 fellowships (averaging $4,688 per year), 17 research assistantships (averaging $5,569 per year), 12 teaching assistantships (averaging $5,879 per year) were awarded.
Dr. Edward W. Davis, Interim Director of Graduate Programs, 919-515-7045, *Fax:* 919-515-7896, *E-mail:* davis@csc.ncsu.edu.

■ **NORTH CAROLINA STATE UNIVERSITY**

Graduate School, College of Management, Program in Management, Raleigh, NC 27695

AWARDS Biotechnology (MS); computer science (MS); engineering (MS); forest resources management (MS); general business (MS); management information systems (MS); operations research (MS); statistics (MS); telecommunications systems engineering (MS); textile management (MS); total quality management (MS). Part-time programs available.

Faculty: 14 full-time (6 women), 3 part-time/adjunct (0 women).

Students: 60 full-time (18 women), 138 part-time (47 women); includes 27 minority (12 African Americans, 13 Asian Americans or Pacific Islanders, 2 Hispanic Americans), 17 international. Average age 32. 225 applicants, 44% accepted. In 2001, 67 degrees awarded.

Entrance requirements: For master's, GMAT or GRE, TOEFL, minimum undergraduate GPA of 3.0. *Application deadline:* For fall admission, 6/25; for spring admission, 11/25. Applications are processed on a rolling basis. *Application fee:* $45.

Expenses: Tuition, state resident: full-time $1,748. Tuition, nonresident: full-time $6,904.

Financial support: In 2001–02, fellowships (averaging $3,551 per year), 32 teaching assistantships (averaging $3,027

North Carolina State University
(continued)

per year) were awarded. Research assistantships Financial award application deadline: 3/1.
Faculty research: Manufacturing strategy, information systems, technology commercialization, managing research and development, historical stock returns. *Total annual research expenditures:* $69,089.
Dr. Stephen G. Allen, Head, 919-515-5584, *Fax:* 919-515-5073, *E-mail:* steve_allen@ncsu.edu. *Web site:* http://www.mgt.ncsu.edu/facdep/bizmgmt/bizman.html

■ **NORTH CENTRAL COLLEGE**

Graduate Programs, Department of Computer Science, Naperville, IL 60566-7063

AWARDS MS. Part-time and evening/weekend programs available.

Faculty: 5 full-time, 10 part-time/adjunct.
Students: 5 full-time (1 woman). Average age 28. 22 applicants, 73% accepted. In 2001, 13 degrees awarded.
Degree requirements: For master's, project.
Entrance requirements: For master's, interview. *Application deadline:* For fall admission, 8/15; for winter admission, 12/1; for spring admission, 2/1. Applications are processed on a rolling basis. *Application fee:* $25.
Expenses: Tuition: Full-time $8,145; part-time $552 per credit hour.
Financial support: Scholarships/grants available. Support available to part-time students.
Faculty research: Experimental broadband network.
Dr. Judy Walters, Coordinator, 630-637-5177, *Fax:* 630-637-5844, *E-mail:* jcw@noctrl.edu.
Application contact: Frank Johnson, Director of Graduate Programs, 630-637-5840, *Fax:* 630-637-5844, *E-mail:* frjohnson@noctrl.edu.

■ **NORTH DAKOTA STATE UNIVERSITY**

The Graduate School, College of Science and Mathematics, Department of Computer Science, Fargo, ND 58105

AWARDS Computer science (MS, PhD); operations research (MS). Part-time programs available.

Faculty: 11 full-time (0 women), 5 part-time/adjunct (2 women).
Students: 95 full-time (25 women), 29 part-time (7 women); includes 90 minority (5 African Americans, 85 Asian Americans or Pacific Islanders). Average age 24. 113 applicants, 33% accepted. In 2001, 29 master's, 2 doctorates awarded.
Degree requirements: For master's, thesis optional; for doctorate, thesis/dissertation, qualifying exam.

Entrance requirements: For master's, TOEFL, minimum GPA of 3.0, BS in computer science or related field; for doctorate, TOEFL, minimum GPA of 3.25, MS in computer science or related field. *Application deadline:* For fall admission, 8/15 (priority date); for spring admission, 12/15 (priority date). *Application fee:* $35.
Expenses: Tuition, state resident: part-time $124 per credit. Tuition, nonresident: part-time $325 per credit. Required fees: $22 per credit. Tuition and fees vary according to reciprocity agreements.
Financial support: In 2001–02, 31 research assistantships with full tuition reimbursements (averaging $10,000 per year), 13 teaching assistantships with full tuition reimbursements (averaging $8,000 per year) were awarded. Career-related internships or fieldwork, Federal Work-Study, and institutionally sponsored loans also available. Financial award application deadline: 4/15.
Faculty research: Networking, software engineering, artificial intelligence, database, programming languages.
Dr. Kendall E. Nygard, Chair, 701-231-8562, *Fax:* 701-231-8255, *E-mail:* kendall_nygard@ndsu.nodak.edu.
Application contact: Mimi E. Monson, Secretary, 701-231-9460, *Fax:* 701-231-8255, *E-mail:* mimi_monson@ndsu.nodak.edu. *Web site:* http://www.cs.ndsu.nodak.edu

■ **NORTH DAKOTA STATE UNIVERSITY**

The Graduate School, College of Science and Mathematics, Department of Statistics, Fargo, ND 58105

AWARDS Applied statistics (MS); computer science and statistics (MS); statistics (PhD).

Faculty: 5 full-time (1 woman).
Students: 24 full-time (10 women), 1 (woman) part-time; includes 1 minority (African American), 11 international. Average age 24. 12 applicants, 100% accepted, 8 enrolled. In 2001, 2 master's, 1 doctorate awarded.
Degree requirements: For master's and doctorate, thesis/dissertation, comprehensive exam.
Entrance requirements: For master's and doctorate, TOEFL. *Application deadline:* Applications are processed on a rolling basis. *Application fee:* $35.
Expenses: Tuition, state resident: part-time $124 per credit. Tuition, nonresident: part-time $325 per credit. Required fees: $22 per credit. Tuition and fees vary according to reciprocity agreements.
Financial support: In 2001–02, 1 fellowship with full tuition reimbursement, 4 research assistantships with full tuition reimbursements, 7 teaching assistantships with full tuition reimbursements were awarded. Career-related internships or fieldwork, Federal Work-Study, institutionally sponsored loans, and tuition waivers

(full) also available. Financial award application deadline: 4/15.
Faculty research: Nonparametric statistics, survival analysis, multivariate analysis, distribution theory, inference modeling, biostatistics.
Dr. Rhonda Magel, Chair, 701-231-7177, *Fax:* 701-231-8734, *E-mail:* ndsu.stats@ndsu.nodak.edu.
Application contact: Susan Foster, Graduate Studies and Research, 701-231-7033, *Fax:* 702-231-6524, *E-mail:* susan.foster@ndsu.nodak.edu. *Web site:* http://www.ndsu.nodak.edu/statistics/

■ **NORTHEASTERN ILLINOIS UNIVERSITY**

Graduate College, College of Arts and Sciences, Department of Computer Science, Program in Computer Science, Chicago, IL 60625-4699

AWARDS MS. Part-time and evening/weekend programs available.

Faculty: 14 full-time (3 women), 9 part-time/adjunct (1 woman).
Students: 44 full-time (14 women), 70 part-time (18 women). Average age 33. 80 applicants, 38% accepted. In 2001, 30 degrees awarded.
Degree requirements: For master's, research project, or thesis.
Entrance requirements: For master's, minimum GPA of 2.75, proficiency in 2 higher-level computer languages, 1 course in discrete mathematics. *Application deadline:* For fall admission, 4/1 (priority date); for spring admission, 8/15. Applications are processed on a rolling basis. *Application fee:* $25.
Expenses: Tuition, area resident: Full-time $2,882; part-time $107 per semester hour. Tuition, nonresident: part-time $320 per semester hour. International tuition: $8,646 full-time. Required fees: $20 per semester hour.
Financial support: In 2001–02, 22 students received support, including 10 research assistantships with full tuition reimbursements available (averaging $6,600 per year); career-related internships or fieldwork, Federal Work-Study, institutionally sponsored loans, and tuition waivers (full and partial) also available. Support available to part-time students. Financial award applicants required to submit FAFSA.
Faculty research: Telecommunications, database inference problems, decision making under uncertainty, belief networks, analysis of algorithms.
Dr. Rich Neopolitan, Chairperson, 773-442-4734, *Fax:* 773-442-4900, *E-mail:* re-neapolitan@neiu.edu.
Application contact: Dr. Mohan K. Sood, Dean of the Graduate College, 773-442-6010, *Fax:* 773-442-6020, *E-mail:* m-sood@neiu.edu.

■ NORTHEASTERN UNIVERSITY

College of Computer Science, Boston, MA 02115-5096

AWARDS MS, PhD. Part-time and evening/weekend programs available.

Faculty: 18 full-time (5 women), 3 part-time/adjunct (0 women).
Students: 110 full-time (44 women), 44 part-time (10 women); includes 4 minority (1 African American, 2 Asian Americans or Pacific Islanders, 1 Native American), 107 international. Average age 29. 313 applicants, 59% accepted. In 2001, 50 master's, 2 doctorates awarded. Terminal master's awarded for partial completion of doctoral program.
Degree requirements: For master's, thesis optional; for doctorate, thesis/dissertation, comprehensive exam.
Entrance requirements: For master's and doctorate, GRE General Test, TOEFL. *Application deadline:* For fall admission, 8/15; for winter admission, 11/1; for spring admission, 2/1. Applications are processed on a rolling basis. *Application fee:* $50.
Expenses: Contact institution.
Financial support: In 2001–02, 23 research assistantships with full tuition reimbursements (averaging $13,125 per year), 10 teaching assistantships with full tuition reimbursements (averaging $13,125 per year) were awarded. Fellowships, career-related internships or fieldwork, Federal Work-Study, and institutionally sponsored loans also available. Financial award application deadline: 2/15.
Faculty research: Database theory, parallel computing, programming languages and software development, artificial intelligence, network and cryptography. *Total annual research expenditures:* $1.2 million.
Dr. Larry A. Finkelstein, Dean, 617-373-2462, *Fax:* 617-373-5121.
Application contact: Dr. Agnes Chan, Associate Dean and Director of Graduate Program, 617-373-2462, *Fax:* 617-373-5121. *Web site:* http://www.ccs.neu.edu/

Find an in-depth description at www.petersons.com/gradchannel.

■ NORTHERN ILLINOIS UNIVERSITY

Graduate School, College of Liberal Arts and Sciences, Department of Computer Science, De Kalb, IL 60115-2854

AWARDS MS. Part-time and evening/weekend programs available.

Faculty: 9 full-time (1 woman).
Students: 124 full-time (31 women), 48 part-time (15 women); includes 19 minority (2 African Americans, 17 Asian Americans or Pacific Islanders), 121 international. Average age 26. 289 applicants, 36% accepted, 39 enrolled. In 2001, 66 degrees awarded.

Degree requirements: For master's, comprehensive exam.
Entrance requirements: For master's, GRE General Test, TOEFL, minimum GPA of 2.75. *Application deadline:* For fall admission, 6/1; for spring admission, 11/1. Applications are processed on a rolling basis. *Application fee:* $30.
Expenses: Tuition, state resident: full-time $5,124; part-time $148 per credit hour. Tuition, nonresident: full-time $8,666; part-time $295 per credit hour. Required fees: $51 per term.
Financial support: In 2001–02, 2 research assistantships with full tuition reimbursements, 1 teaching assistantship with full tuition reimbursement were awarded. Fellowships with full tuition reimbursements, career-related internships or fieldwork, Federal Work-Study, tuition waivers (full), and unspecified assistantships also available. Support available to part-time students.
Faculty research: Databases, theorem proving.
Dr. Rodney Angotti, Chair, 815-753-0378, *Fax:* 815-753-0342.

■ NORTHERN KENTUCKY UNIVERSITY

School of Graduate Programs, Program in Computer Science, Highland Heights, KY 41099

AWARDS MSCS.

Faculty: 5 full-time (0 women).
Students: Average age 34.
Application fee: $25.
Expenses: Tuition, state resident: full-time $2,958; part-time $149 per credit hour. Tuition, nonresident: full-time $7,872; part-time $422 per credit hour.
Dr. Thomas K. Kearns, Interim Chairperson, 859-572-5328.
Application contact: Peg Griffin, Graduate Coordinator, 859-572-6364, *E-mail:* griffinp@nku.edu.

■ NORTHWESTERN POLYTECHNIC UNIVERSITY

School of Engineering, Fremont, CA 94539-7482

AWARDS Computer science (MS); computer systems engineering (MS); electrical engineering (MS). Part-time and evening/weekend programs available.

Faculty: 7 full-time (0 women), 53 part-time/adjunct (4 women).
Students: 239 full-time (119 women), 210 part-time (108 women). Average age 30. 132 applicants, 55% accepted. In 2001, 148 degrees awarded.
Degree requirements: For master's, thesis optional.
Entrance requirements: For master's, TOEFL, minimum GPA of 2.0. *Application deadline:* For fall admission, 8/12 (priority date); for spring admission, 2/11 (priority

date). Applications are processed on a rolling basis. *Application fee:* $50 ($75 for international students).
Expenses: Tuition: Full-time $8,100; part-time $450 per unit. Required fees: $45; $15 per term.
Financial support: In 2001–02, 160 teaching assistantships with full and partial tuition reimbursements (averaging $1,000 per year) were awarded; career-related internships or fieldwork and unspecified assistantships also available.
Faculty research: Computer networking; database design; internet technology; software engineering; digital signal processing.
Dr. Pochang Hsu, Dean, 510-657-5911, *Fax:* 510-657-8975, *E-mail:* npuadm@npu.edu.
Application contact: Jack Xie, Director of Admissions, 510-657-5913, *Fax:* 510-657-8975, *E-mail:* jack@npu.edu. *Web site:* http://www.npu.edu/engineeringindex.htm

■ NORTHWESTERN UNIVERSITY

McCormick School of Engineering and Applied Science, Department of Computer Science, Evanston, IL 60208

AWARDS MS, PhD. Admissions and degrees offered through The Graduate School.

Faculty: 12 full-time (1 woman), 3 part-time/adjunct (0 women).
Students: 33 full-time (8 women), 3 part-time; includes 7 minority (1 African American, 6 Asian Americans or Pacific Islanders), 5 international. Average age 25. 280 applicants, 7% accepted. In 2001, 6 master's, 4 doctorates awarded.
Degree requirements: For master's and doctorate, thesis/dissertation. *Median time to degree:* Master's–3 years full-time; doctorate–6 years full-time. *Application deadline:* For fall admission, 1/15. *Application fee:* $50 ($55 for international students).
Expenses: Tuition: Full-time $26,526.
Financial support: In 2001–02, 5 fellowships with full tuition reimbursements (averaging $12,843 per year), 13 research assistantships with partial tuition reimbursements (averaging $12,843 per year), 9 teaching assistantships with full tuition reimbursements (averaging $12,843 per year) were awarded. Federal Work-Study, institutionally sponsored loans, and scholarships/grants also available. Financial award application deadline: 1/15; financial award applicants required to submit FAFSA.
Faculty research: Autonomous mobile robots, education and technology, intelligent information, qualitative reasoning, systems research.
Lawrence Birnbaum, Chair, 847-491-3500, *E-mail:* l-birnbaum@infolab.northwestern.edu.
Application contact: Student Services Coordinator, 847-491-3500, *E-mail:*

Northwestern University (continued)
cs-info@cs.northwestern.edu. *Web site:*
http://www.cs.northwestern.edu/

**Find an in-depth description at
www.petersons.com/gradchannel.**

■ NORTHWEST MISSOURI STATE UNIVERSITY

Graduate School, Melvin and Valorie Booth College of Business and Professional Studies, Department of Computer Science and Information Systems, Maryville, MO 64468-6001

AWARDS School computer studies (MS). Part-time programs available.

Faculty: 8 full-time (3 women).
Students: 1 full-time (0 women), 2 part-time (1 woman), 2 international. 3 applicants, 100% accepted, 1 enrolled. In 2001, 2 degrees awarded.
Degree requirements: For master's, comprehensive exam.
Entrance requirements: For master's, GRE General Test, TOEFL, minimum GPA of 3.0. *Application deadline:* Applications are processed on a rolling basis. *Application fee:* $0 ($50 for international students).
Expenses: Tuition, state resident: full-time $2,777; part-time $154 per hour. Tuition, nonresident: full-time $4,626; part-time $257 per hour. Tuition and fees vary according to course level and course load.
Financial support: In 2001–02, 1 student received support, including 1 research assistantship (averaging $5,250 per year), 1 teaching assistantship (averaging $5,250 per year) Financial award application deadline: 3/1.
Dr. Phillip Heeler, Chairperson, 660-562-1200.
Application contact: Dr. Frances Shipley, Dean of Graduate School, 660-562-1145, *Fax:* 660-562-0000, *E-mail:* gradsch@mail.nwmissouri.edu.

■ NOVA SOUTHEASTERN UNIVERSITY

School of Computer and Information Sciences, Fort Lauderdale, FL 33314-7721

AWARDS Computer information systems (MS, PhD); computer science (MS, PhD); computing technology in education (MS, Ed D, PhD); information science (PhD); information systems (PhD); management information systems (MS). Part-time and evening/weekend programs available.
Postbaccalaureate distance learning degree programs offered (no on-campus study).

Faculty: 18 full-time (4 women), 12 part-time/adjunct (3 women).
Students: 832 full-time (297 women); includes 195 minority (97 African Americans, 39 Asian Americans or Pacific Islanders, 56 Hispanic Americans, 3 Native Americans), 63 international. Average age

41. 286 applicants, 80% accepted, 169 enrolled. In 2001, 114 master's, 27 doctorates awarded. Terminal master's awarded for partial completion of doctoral program.
Degree requirements: For master's, thesis optional; for doctorate, thesis/dissertation.
Entrance requirements: For master's, minimum undergraduate GPA of 2.5, minimum major GPA of 3.0; for doctorate, master's degree, minimum graduate GPA of 3.25. *Application deadline:* Applications are processed on a rolling basis. *Application fee:* $50.
Expenses: Contact institution.
Financial support: In 2001–02, 2 teaching assistantships with full tuition reimbursements (averaging $25,000 per year) were awarded; Federal Work-Study, scholarships/grants, and unspecified assistantships also available. Support available to part-time students. Financial award application deadline: 5/1.
Faculty research: Artificial intelligence, database management, human-computer interaction, distance education, computer education.
Dr. Edward Lieblein, Dean.
Application contact: Sherese Young, Marketing Coordinator, 954-262-2005, *Fax:* 954-262-3915, *E-mail:* scisinfo@nova.edu. *Web site:* http://www.scis.nova.edu/

**Find an in-depth description at
www.petersons.com/gradchannel.**

■ OAKLAND UNIVERSITY

Graduate Study and Lifelong Learning, School of Engineering and Computer Science, Program in Computer Science and Engineering, Rochester, MI 48309-4401

AWARDS Computer science (MS); embedded systems (MS); software engineering (MS). Part-time and evening/weekend programs available.

Faculty: 15 full-time (2 women).
Students: 83 full-time (33 women), 98 part-time (35 women); includes 26 minority (2 African Americans, 24 Asian Americans or Pacific Islanders), 77 international. Average age 33. 135 applicants, 81% accepted. In 2001, 56 degrees awarded.
Entrance requirements: For master's, minimum GPA of 3.0 for unconditional admission. *Application deadline:* For fall admission, 8/1 (priority date); for winter admission, 12/1 (priority date); for spring admission, 4/1 (priority date). Applications are processed on a rolling basis. *Application fee:* $30. Electronic applications accepted.
Expenses: Tuition, state resident: full-time $5,904; part-time $246 per credit hour. Tuition, nonresident: full-time $12,192; part-time $508 per credit hour. Required fees: $472; $236 per term.
Financial support: Federal Work-Study, institutionally sponsored loans, and tuition waivers (full) available. Financial award

application deadline: 3/1; financial award applicants required to submit FAFSA.
Dr. Ishwar K. Sethi, Chair, 248-370-2820.

■ OGI SCHOOL OF SCIENCE & ENGINEERING AT OREGON HEALTH & SCIENCE UNIVERSITY

Graduate Studies, Department of Computer Science and Engineering, Beaverton, OR 97006-8921

AWARDS Computational finance (MS, Certificate); computer science and engineering (MS, PhD). Part-time and evening/weekend programs available.

Faculty: 20 full-time (2 women), 28 part-time/adjunct (3 women).
Students: 47 full-time, 124 part-time. Average age 31. 279 applicants, 51% accepted. In 2001, 35 master's, 3 doctorates awarded. Terminal master's awarded for partial completion of doctoral program.
Degree requirements: For master's, thesis optional; for doctorate, oral defense of dissertation.
Entrance requirements: For master's and doctorate, GRE General Test, TOEFL. *Application deadline:* For fall admission, 3/1 (priority date). Applications are processed on a rolling basis. *Application fee:* $50. Electronic applications accepted.
Expenses: Tuition: Full-time $4,905; part-time $545 per credit hour. Required fees: $466.
Financial support: In 2001–02, 41 students received support, including 39 research assistantships with full and partial tuition reimbursements available, 3 teaching assistantships; fellowships, scholarships/grants also available. Financial award application deadline: 3/1.
Faculty research: Computer systems architecture, intelligent and interactive systems, programming models and systems, theory of computation. *Total annual research expenditures:* $6.8 million.
Dr. James Hook, Head, 503-748-1169, *E-mail:* hook@cse.ogi.edu.
Application contact: Shirley Kapsch, Enrollment Manager, 503-748-1255, *Fax:* 503-748-1285, *E-mail:* kapsch@cse.ogi.edu. *Web site:* http://www.cse.ogi.edu/

**Find an in-depth description at
www.petersons.com/gradchannel.**

■ OGI SCHOOL OF SCIENCE & ENGINEERING AT OREGON HEALTH & SCIENCE UNIVERSITY

Graduate Studies, Department of Electrical and Computer Engineering, Beaverton, OR 97006-8921

AWARDS Computer engineering (MS, PhD); electrical engineering (MS, PhD). Part-time programs available.

Faculty: 23 full-time (2 women), 31 part-time/adjunct (0 women).
Students: 54 full-time (19 women), 75 part-time (23 women). Average age 29. 184

applicants, 97% accepted. In 2001, 25 master's, 2 doctorates awarded. Terminal master's awarded for partial completion of doctoral program.
Degree requirements: For master's, thesis optional; for doctorate, oral defense of dissertation.
Entrance requirements: For master's, TOEFL; for doctorate, GRE General Test, GRE Subject Test, TOEFL. *Application deadline:* For fall admission, 3/1 (priority date). Applications are processed on a rolling basis. *Application fee:* $50. Electronic applications accepted.
Expenses: Tuition: Full-time $4,905; part-time $545 per credit hour. Required fees: $466.
Financial support: In 2001–02, 20 students received support, including 19 research assistantships with full and partial tuition reimbursements available; fellowships, Federal Work-Study also available. Financial award application deadline: 3/1.
Faculty research: Semiconductor materials, microwave circuits, atmospheric optics, surface physics, electron and ion optics. *Total annual research expenditures:* $3.5 million.
John Carruthers, Head, 503-748-1616, *Fax:* 503-748-1406.
Application contact: Barbara Olsen, Enrollment Manager, 503-748-1418, *Fax:* 503-748-1406, *E-mail:* bolsen@ece.ogi.edu. *Web site:* http://www.eeap.ogi.edu/
Find an in-depth description at www.petersons.com/gradchannel.

■ THE OHIO STATE UNIVERSITY

Graduate School, College of Engineering, Department of Computer and Information Science, Columbus, OH 43210

AWARDS MS, PhD.

Degree requirements: For master's, thesis optional; for doctorate, thesis/dissertation.
Entrance requirements: For master's and doctorate, GRE General Test, TSE.

■ OHIO UNIVERSITY

Graduate Studies, Russ College of Engineering and Technology, School of Electrical Engineering and Computer Science, Athens, OH 45701-2979

AWARDS Computer science (MS); electrical engineering (MS, PhD).

Faculty: 31 full-time (2 women), 10 part-time/adjunct (3 women).
Students: 95 full-time (19 women), 28 part-time (9 women); includes 5 minority (1 African American, 4 Asian Americans or Pacific Islanders), 98 international. 549 applicants, 51% accepted, 43 enrolled. In 2001, 16 master's, 4 doctorates awarded.
Degree requirements: For master's, thesis; for doctorate, thesis/dissertation, qualifying exams, comprehensive exam.

Median time to degree: Master's–3 years full-time; doctorate–5 years full-time.
Entrance requirements: For master's, GRE, BSEE, minimum GPA of 3.0; for doctorate, GRE, MSEE, minimum GPA of 3.0. *Application fee:* $30.
Expenses: Tuition, state resident: full-time $6,585. Tuition, nonresident: full-time $12,254.
Financial support: In 2001–02, 11 fellowships with full tuition reimbursements (averaging $14,000 per year), 5 research assistantships with full tuition reimbursements (averaging $12,000 per year), 5 teaching assistantships with full tuition reimbursements (averaging $10,500 per year) were awarded. Federal Work-Study and institutionally sponsored loans also available.
Faculty research: Avionics, networking/communications, intelligent distribution, real-time computing, control systems, optical properties of semiconductors. *Total annual research expenditures:* $9 million.
Application contact: Dr. David M. Chelberg, Graduate Chair, 740-593-1922, *Fax:* 740-593-0007, *E-mail:* chelberg@ohio.edu. *Web site:* http://webeers.ent.ohiou.edu
Find an in-depth description at www.petersons.com/gradchannel.

■ OKLAHOMA CITY UNIVERSITY

Petree College of Arts and Sciences, Division of Mathematics and Science, Oklahoma City, OK 73106-1402

AWARDS Computer science (MS). Part-time and evening/weekend programs available.

Degree requirements: For master's, thesis optional.
Entrance requirements: For master's, minimum GPA of 3.0.
Expenses: Contact institution.
Faculty research: Parallel processing, pedagogical techniques, databases, numerical analysis, gesture recognition. *Web site:* http://www.okcu.edu/

■ OKLAHOMA STATE UNIVERSITY

Graduate College, College of Arts and Sciences, Department of Computer Science, Stillwater, OK 74078

AWARDS Computer education (Ed D); computer science (MS, PhD).

Faculty: 15 full-time (1 woman).
Students: 85 full-time (26 women), 88 part-time (29 women); includes 20 minority (6 African Americans, 12 Asian Americans or Pacific Islanders, 1 Hispanic American, 1 Native American), 134 international. Average age 31. 330 applicants, 46% accepted. In 2001, 15 master's awarded.
Degree requirements: For master's and doctorate, thesis/dissertation.

Entrance requirements: For master's, GRE General Test, TOEFL; for doctorate, GRE General Test, GMAT, TOEFL. *Application deadline:* For fall admission, 7/1 (priority date). *Application fee:* $25.
Expenses: Tuition, state resident: part-time $92 per credit hour. Tuition, nonresident: part-time $297 per credit hour. Required fees: $21 per credit hour. $14 per semester. One-time fee: $20. Tuition and fees vary according to course load.
Financial support: In 2001–02, 37 students received support, including 11 research assistantships (averaging $12,366 per year), 31 teaching assistantships (averaging $9,338 per year); career-related internships or fieldwork, Federal Work-Study, and tuition waivers (partial) also available. Support available to part-time students. Financial award application deadline: 3/1.
Dr. George Hedrick, III, Head, 405-744-5668, *Fax:* 405-774-9097, *E-mail:* geh@okstate.edu. *Web site:* http://www.cs.okstate.edu/
Find an in-depth description at www.petersons.com/gradchannel.

■ OLD DOMINION UNIVERSITY

College of Engineering and Technology, Program in Modeling and Simulation, Norfolk, VA 23529

AWARDS ME, MS, PhD. Part-time and evening/weekend programs available. Postbaccalaureate distance learning degree programs offered.

Faculty: 11 full-time (1 woman), 6 part-time/adjunct (0 women).
Students: 6 full-time (2 women), 17 part-time (4 women); includes 4 minority (2 African Americans, 2 Asian Americans or Pacific Islanders), 2 international. Average age 38. In 2001, 9 degrees awarded. Terminal master's awarded for partial completion of doctoral program.
Degree requirements: For master's, thesis (for some programs); for doctorate, thesis/dissertation.
Application deadline: For fall admission, 6/15 (priority date); for spring admission, 10/15 (priority date). Applications are processed on a rolling basis. *Application fee:* $30.
Expenses: Tuition, state resident: part-time $202 per credit. Tuition, nonresident: part-time $534 per credit. Required fees: $76 per semester.
Financial support: In 2001–02, 4 students received support, including 2 research assistantships with partial tuition reimbursements available (averaging $18,000 per year); career-related internships or fieldwork, scholarships/grants, and unspecified assistantships also available. Financial award application deadline: 4/15.
Faculty research: HLA, virtual systems, human-computer interface, discrete-event systems. *Total annual research expenditures:* $3.5 million.

Old Dominion University (continued)
Dr. Ralph Rogers, Graduate Program Director, 757-683-4938, *Fax:* 757-683-5640, *E-mail:* globaleng@odu.edu. *Web site:* http://www.odu.edu/webroot/orgs/engr/wlengineer.nsf/pages/ms_home

■ OLD DOMINION UNIVERSITY

College of Sciences, Program in Computer Science, Norfolk, VA 23529
AWARDS MS, PhD. Part-time programs available.

Faculty: 22 full-time (2 women).
Students: 96 full-time (24 women), 87 part-time (14 women); includes 9 minority (5 African Americans, 3 Asian Americans or Pacific Islanders, 1 Hispanic American), 149 international. Average age 27. 264 applicants, 61% accepted. In 2001, 25 master's, 6 doctorates awarded. Terminal master's awarded for partial completion of doctoral program.
Degree requirements: For master's, comprehensive diagnostic exam, thesis optional; for doctorate, thesis/dissertation, comprehensive exam.
Entrance requirements: For master's, GRE General Test, TOEFL, minimum GPA of 3.0 in major, 2.5 overall; for doctorate, GRE General Test, TOEFL. *Application deadline:* For fall admission, 7/1. Applications are processed on a rolling basis. *Application fee:* $30.
Expenses: Tuition, state resident: part-time $202 per credit. Tuition, nonresident: part-time $534 per credit. Required fees: $76 per semester.
Financial support: In 2001–02, 98 students received support, including 1 fellowship (averaging $2,021 per year), 27 research assistantships with tuition reimbursements available (averaging $8,736 per year), 28 teaching assistantships with tuition reimbursements available (averaging $7,926 per year); career-related internships or fieldwork, scholarships/grants, and tuition waivers (partial) also available. Support available to part-time students. Financial award application deadline: 2/15; financial award applicants required to submit FAFSA.
Faculty research: Software engineering, artificial intelligence, foundations, high-performance computing, networking. *Total annual research expenditures:* $1.4 million.
Dr. Christian Wild, Graduate Program Director, 757-683-4679, *Fax:* 757-683-4900, *E-mail:* csgpd@odu.edu. *Web site:* http://www.cs.odu.edu/

■ PACE UNIVERSITY

School of Computer Science and Information Systems, New York, NY 10038
AWARDS Computer communications and networks (Certificate); computer science (MS); computing studies (DPS); information systems (MS); object-oriented programming (Certificate); telecommunications (MS, Certificate). Part-time and evening/weekend programs available.

Faculty: 23 full-time, 9 part-time/adjunct.
Students: 210 full-time (70 women), 446 part-time (165 women); includes 129 minority (49 African Americans, 61 Asian Americans or Pacific Islanders, 19 Hispanic Americans), 197 international. Average age 28. 474 applicants, 72% accepted. In 2001, 112 master's, 6 other advanced degrees awarded.
Entrance requirements: For master's, GRE General Test. *Application deadline:* For fall admission, 7/31 (priority date); for spring admission, 11/30. Applications are processed on a rolling basis. *Application fee:* $65. Electronic applications accepted.
Expenses: Contact institution.
Financial support: Research assistantships, career-related internships or fieldwork available. Support available to part-time students. Financial award applicants required to submit FAFSA.
Dr. Susan Merritt, Dean, 914-422-4375.
Application contact: Joanna Broda, Director of Admissions, 212-346-1652, *Fax:* 212-346-1585, *E-mail:* gradnyc@pace.edu. *Web site:* http://www.pace.edu/
Find an in-depth description at www.petersons.com/gradchannel.

■ PACE UNIVERSITY, WHITE PLAINS CAMPUS

School of Computer Science and Information Systems, White Plains, NY 10603
AWARDS Computer communications and networks (Certificate); computer science (MS); computing studies (DPS); information systems (MS); object-oriented programming (Certificate); telecommunications (MS, Certificate). Part-time and evening/weekend programs available.

Faculty: 14 full-time, 6 part-time/adjunct.
Students: 73 full-time (30 women), 307 part-time (117 women); includes 122 minority (37 African Americans, 60 Asian Americans or Pacific Islanders, 25 Hispanic Americans), 50 international. Average age 31. 262 applicants, 65% accepted, 117 enrolled. In 2001, 65 master's, 9 other advanced degrees awarded.
Entrance requirements: For master's, GRE General Test. *Application deadline:* For fall admission, 8/1 (priority date); for spring admission, 12/1 (priority date). Applications are processed on a rolling basis. *Application fee:* $65. Electronic applications accepted.
Expenses: Contact institution.
Financial support: Research assistantships, career-related internships or fieldwork available. Support available to part-time students. Financial award applicants required to submit FAFSA.
Dr. Susan Merritt, Dean, 914-422-4375.
Application contact: Joanna Broda, Director of Admissions, 914-422-4283,

Fax: 914-422-4287, *E-mail:* gradwp@pace.edu. *Web site:* http://www.pace.edu/

■ PACIFIC STATES UNIVERSITY

College of Computer Science, Los Angeles, CA 90006

AWARDS MSCS. Part-time and evening/weekend programs available.

Faculty: 1 full-time (0 women), 2 part-time/adjunct (0 women).
Students: 15 full-time (7 women); all minorities (all Asian Americans or Pacific Islanders). In 2001, 8 degrees awarded.
Entrance requirements: For master's, TOEFL, bachelor's degree in physics, engineering, computer science, or applied mathematics; minimum undergraduate GPA of 2.5 during last 90 hours. *Application deadline:* For fall admission, 8/15 (priority date); for winter admission, 10/15 (priority date); for spring admission, 1/15 (priority date). Applications are processed on a rolling basis. *Application fee:* $100. Electronic applications accepted.
Expenses: Tuition: Full-time $9,600. Required fees: $1,050.
Financial support: Applicants required to submit FAFSA.
Muyung Yoo, Dean, 888-200-0383, *Fax:* 323-731-7276, *E-mail:* admission@psuca.edu.
Application contact: Mai A. Diep, Registrar, 888-200-0383, *Fax:* 323-731-7276, *E-mail:* admission@psuca.edu. *Web site:* http://www.psuca.edu/science.htm

■ THE PENNSYLVANIA STATE UNIVERSITY HARRISBURG CAMPUS OF THE CAPITAL COLLEGE

Graduate Center, School of Science, Engineering and Technology, Department of Computer Science, Middletown, PA 17057-4898

AWARDS MS.

Students: 16 full-time (10 women), 31 part-time (10 women). In 2001, 3 degrees awarded.
Degree requirements: For master's, thesis.
Entrance requirements: For master's, TOEFL. *Application deadline:* For fall admission, 7/26. *Application fee:* $45.
Expenses: Tuition, state resident: full-time $7,882; part-time $333 per credit. Tuition, nonresident: full-time $14,384; part-time $600 per credit.
Dr. Thang Bui, Chair, 717-948-6088.

■ THE PENNSYLVANIA STATE UNIVERSITY UNIVERSITY PARK CAMPUS

Graduate School, College of Engineering, Department of Computer Science and Engineering, State College, University Park, PA 16802-1503

AWARDS M Eng, MS, PhD.

Students: 110 full-time (27 women), 50 part-time (16 women). In 2001, 47 master's, 10 doctorates awarded.
Degree requirements: For doctorate, thesis/dissertation.
Entrance requirements: For master's and doctorate, GRE General Test. *Application fee:* $45.
Expenses: Tuition, state resident: full-time $7,882; part-time $333 per credit. Tuition, nonresident: full-time $16,142; part-time $673 per credit. Required fees: $124 per semester.
Raj Acharya, Head, 814-865-9505.
Find an in-depth description at www.petersons.com/gradchannel.

■ POLYTECHNIC UNIVERSITY, BROOKLYN CAMPUS

Department of Computer and Information Science, Major in Computer Science, Brooklyn, NY 11201-2990

AWARDS MS, PhD. Part-time and evening/weekend programs available.

Degree requirements: For doctorate, thesis/dissertation.
Entrance requirements: For master's, BA or BS in computer science, mathematics, science, or engineering; working knowledge of a high-level program; for doctorate, GRE General Test, GRE Subject Test, qualifying exam, BA or BS in science, engineering, or management; MS or 1 year of graduate course work. Electronic applications accepted.
Find an in-depth description at www.petersons.com/gradchannel.

■ POLYTECHNIC UNIVERSITY, LONG ISLAND GRADUATE CENTER

Graduate Programs, Department of Computer and Information Science, Major in Computer Science, Melville, NY 11747

AWARDS MS, PhD.

Degree requirements: For master's, thesis (for some programs).
Electronic applications accepted.

■ POLYTECHNIC UNIVERSITY, WESTCHESTER GRADUATE CENTER

Graduate Programs, Department of Computer and Information Science, Major in Computer Science, Hawthorne, NY 10532-1507

AWARDS MS, PhD.

Degree requirements: For master's, thesis (for some programs); for doctorate, thesis/dissertation.
Electronic applications accepted.

■ PORTLAND STATE UNIVERSITY

Graduate Studies, College of Engineering and Computer Science, Department of Computer Science, Portland, OR 97207-0751

AWARDS MS. Part-time programs available.

Faculty: 17 full-time (4 women), 9 part-time/adjunct (1 woman).
Students: 37 full-time (17 women), 41 part-time (12 women); includes 7 minority (all Asian Americans or Pacific Islanders), 53 international. Average age 30. 130 applicants, 63% accepted. In 2001, 23 degrees awarded.
Degree requirements: For master's, thesis optional.
Entrance requirements: For master's, GRE General Test, TOEFL, minimum GPA of 3.0 in upper-division course work or 2.75 overall. *Application deadline:* For fall admission, 3/15 (priority date). Applications are processed on a rolling basis. *Application fee:* $50.
Financial support: In 2001–02, 5 research assistantships (averaging $9,878 per year), 5 teaching assistantships with full tuition reimbursements (averaging $8,285 per year) were awarded. Career-related internships or fieldwork and Federal Work-Study also available. Support available to part-time students. Financial award application deadline: 3/1; financial award applicants required to submit FAFSA.
Faculty research: Formal methods, database systems, parallel programming environments, computer security, software tools. *Total annual research expenditures:* $172,484.
Cynthia Brown, Head, 503-725-4036, *Fax:* 503-725-3211, *E-mail:* brown@cs.pdx.edu.
Application contact: Beth Phelps, Office Coordinator, 503-725-4036, *Fax:* 503-725-3211, *E-mail:* phelps@cs.pdx.edu. *Web site:* http://www.cs.pdx.edu/
Find an in-depth description at www.petersons.com/gradchannel.

■ PRINCETON UNIVERSITY

Graduate School, School of Engineering and Applied Science, Department of Computer Science, Princeton, NJ 08544-1019

AWARDS M Eng, MSE, PhD.

Degree requirements: For doctorate, thesis/dissertation.
Entrance requirements: For master's and doctorate, GRE General Test, GRE Subject Test.
Faculty research: Algorithms, complexity, systems, VLSI.
Find an in-depth description at www.petersons.com/gradchannel.

■ PURDUE UNIVERSITY

Graduate School, School of Science, Department of Computer Sciences, West Lafayette, IN 47907

AWARDS MS, PhD. Part-time programs available.

Faculty: 30 full-time (2 women), 7 part-time/adjunct (1 woman).
Students: 108 full-time (16 women), 37 part-time (8 women). Average age 26. 607 applicants, 21% accepted. In 2001, 56 master's, 11 doctorates awarded. Terminal master's awarded for partial completion of doctoral program.
Degree requirements: For master's, thesis optional; for doctorate, thesis/dissertation.
Entrance requirements: For master's and doctorate, GRE General Test, TOEFL, TWE, minimum GPA of 3.5. *Application deadline:* For fall admission, 12/15. *Application fee:* $30. Electronic applications accepted.
Expenses: Tuition, state resident: full-time $4,164; part-time $149 per credit hour. Tuition, nonresident: full-time $13,872; part-time $458 per credit hour. Tuition and fees vary according to campus/location and program.
Financial support: In 2001–02, 140 students received support, including 2 fellowships with full and partial tuition reimbursements available (averaging $20,000 per year), 79 research assistantships with partial tuition reimbursements available (averaging $12,140 per year), 59 teaching assistantships with partial tuition reimbursements available (averaging $11,250 per year) Financial award application deadline: 12/15.
Faculty research: Computer systems, geometric modeling, information security, scientific computing, software systems, theory and algorithms. *Total annual research expenditures:* $3.9 million.
Prof. Ahmed H. Sameh, Head, 765-494-6003.
Application contact: Dr. William J. Gorman, Assistant to the Head, 765-494-6004, *Fax:* 765-494-0739, *E-mail:*

Purdue University (continued)
gradinfo-p@cs.purdue.edu. *Web site:* http://
www.cs.purdue.edu/

**Find an in-depth description at
www.petersons.com/gradchannel.**

■ PURDUE UNIVERSITY

**Graduate School, School of Science,
Department of Statistics, West
Lafayette, IN 47907**

AWARDS Applied statistics (MS); statistics
(PhD); statistics and computer science (MS);
statistics/computational finance (MS);
theoretical statistics (MS).

Faculty: 24 full-time (5 women).
Students: 62 full-time (24 women), 2 part-
time (both women), 44 international. Average age 29. 175 applicants. In 2001, 20
master's, 2 doctorates awarded.
Degree requirements: For doctorate,
thesis/dissertation.
Entrance requirements: For master's and
doctorate, GRE General Test, TOEFL.
Application deadline: For fall admission,
1/15. *Application fee:* $30. Electronic
applications accepted.
Expenses: Tuition, state resident: full-time
$4,164; part-time $149 per credit hour.
Tuition, nonresident: full-time $13,872;
part-time $458 per credit hour. Tuition
and fees vary according to campus/location
and program.
Financial support: In 2001–02, 5 fellowships with full tuition reimbursements
(averaging $20,000 per year), 8 research
assistantships with full tuition reimbursements (averaging $13,500 per year), 38
teaching assistantships with full tuition
reimbursements (averaging $13,500 per
year) were awarded. Career-related internships or fieldwork also available. Support
available to part-time students. Financial
award applicants required to submit
FAFSA.
Faculty research: Bayesian analysis,
computational finance, design of experiments, probability theory.
Dr. M. E. Bock, Head, 765-494-3141, *Fax:*
765-494-0558, *E-mail:* mbock@
stat.purdue.edu.
Application contact: Carmen Kennedy,
Graduate Secretary, 765-494-5794, *Fax:*
765-494-0558, *E-mail:* graduate@
stat.purdue.edu. *Web site:* http://
www.stat.purdue.edu/

**Find an in-depth description at
www.petersons.com/gradchannel.**

■ QUEENS COLLEGE OF THE CITY UNIVERSITY OF NEW YORK

**Division of Graduate Studies,
Mathematics and Natural Sciences
Division, Department of Computer
Science, Flushing, NY 11367-1597**

AWARDS MA. Part-time and evening/weekend
programs available.

Students: 33 full-time (16 women), 164
part-time (70 women). 251 applicants,
65% accepted. In 2001, 44 degrees
awarded.
Degree requirements: For master's,
thesis optional.
Entrance requirements: For master's,
GRE, TOEFL, minimum GPA of 3.0.
Application deadline: For fall admission, 4/1;
for spring admission, 11/1. Applications
are processed on a rolling basis. *Application
fee:* $40.
Expenses: Tuition, state resident: full-time
$2,175; part-time $185 per credit. Tuition,
nonresident: full-time $3,800; part-time
$320 per credit. Required fees: $114; $57
per semester. Tuition and fees vary according to course load.
Financial support: Career-related internships or fieldwork, Federal Work-Study,
institutionally sponsored loans, tuition
waivers (partial), unspecified assistantships,
and adjunct lectureships available. Support
available to part-time students. Financial
award application deadline: 4/1; financial
award applicants required to submit
FAFSA.
Faculty research: Fifth-generation
computing, hardware/software development, analysis of algorithms and theoretical computer science.
Dr. Ishin Phillips, Chairperson, 718-997-
3500, *E-mail:* yun@cs.qc.edu.
Application contact: Dr. K. Yukawa,
Graduate Adviser, 718-997-3500, *E-mail:*
keitaro_yukawa@qc.edu.

■ REGIS UNIVERSITY

**School for Professional Studies,
Program in Computer Information
Technology, Denver, CO 80221-1099**

AWARDS Database technologies (MSCIT,
Certificate), including database administrator
(Certificate), Oracle application development
(Certificate), Oracle e-commerce enterprise
and Web/Internet Protocol programming
(Certificate); e-commerce engineering (MSCIT,
Certificate), including advanced e-commerce
(Certificate), management of technology
(Certificate), Oracle e-commerce enterprise
and Web/Internet Protocol programming
(Certificate), portal management (Certificate);
management of technology (MSCIT); network-
ing technologies (MSCIT); networking
technology (Certificate), including
e-commerce, network engineering, telecom-
munications; object-oriented technologies
(MSCIT); object-oriented technology
(Certificate), including C++ programming,
Java programming, Visual Basic program-
ming. Offered at Boulder Campus, Northwest
Denver Campus, Southeast Denver Campus,
Fort Collins Campus, Colorado Springs
Campus, and Broomfield Campus. Part-time
and evening/weekend programs available.
Postbaccalaureate distance learning degree
programs offered (no on-campus study).

Students: 343. Average age 36. In 2001,
40 degrees awarded.

Degree requirements: For master's and
Certificate, final research project.
Entrance requirements: For master's and
Certificate, GMAT, TOEFL, or university-
based test (international applicants), 2
years of related experience, resumé.
Application deadline: Applications are
processed on a rolling basis. *Application fee:*
$75.
Expenses: Contact institution.
Financial support: Federal Work-Study
available. Support available to part-time
students. Financial award applicants
required to submit FAFSA.
Don Archer, Chair, 303-458-4302, *Fax:*
303-964-5538.
Application contact: 800-677-9270 Ext.
4080, *Fax:* 303-964-5538, *E-mail:*
masters@regis.edu. *Web site:* http://
www.regis.edu/spsgraduate/

■ RENSSELAER AT HARTFORD

**Department of Computer and
Information Science, Hartford, CT
06120-2991**

AWARDS Computer science (MS). Part-time
and evening/weekend programs available.

Faculty: 7 full-time (2 women), 11 part-
time/adjunct (1 woman).
Students: 12 full-time (5 women), 364
part-time (79 women); includes 58 minority (3 African Americans, 46 Asian
Americans or Pacific Islanders, 7 Hispanic
Americans, 2 Native Americans), 47
international. Average age 31. 99
applicants, 69% accepted, 52 enrolled. In
2001, 65 degrees awarded.
Degree requirements: For master's,
seminar, thesis optional.
Entrance requirements: For master's,
TOEFL. *Application deadline:* For fall
admission, 8/6 (priority date). Applications
are processed on a rolling basis. *Application
fee:* $45. Electronic applications accepted.
Expenses: Tuition: Full-time $11,700;
part-time $650 per credit.
Financial support: Research assistantships,
tuition waivers (full and partial) and
unspecified assistantships available. Sup-
port available to part-time students.
Financial award applicants required to
submit FAFSA.
James McKim, Chair, 860-548-2455,
E-mail: jcm@rh.edu.
Application contact: Rebecca Danchak,
Director of Admissions, 860-548-2420,
Fax: 860-548-7823, *E-mail:* rdanchak@
rh.edu.

■ RENSSELAER AT HARTFORD

**Department of Engineering, Hartford,
CT 06120-2991**

AWARDS ME, MS. Part-time and evening/
weekend programs available.

Faculty: 11 full-time (2 women), 34 part-
time/adjunct (1 woman).
Students: 2 full-time (0 women), 225 part-
time (30 women). Average age 31. In 2001,
66 degrees awarded.

Degree requirements: For master's, seminar.

Entrance requirements: For master's, TOEFL. *Application deadline:* For fall admission, 8/6 (priority date). Applications are processed on a rolling basis. *Application fee:* $45.

Expenses: Tuition: Full-time $11,700; part-time $650 per credit.

Financial support: Research assistantships, career-related internships or fieldwork, tuition waivers (full and partial), and unspecified assistantships available. Support available to part-time students. Financial award applicants required to submit FAFSA.

James McKim, Chair, 860-548-2455, *E-mail:* jcm@rh.edu.

Application contact: Rebecca Danchak, Director of Admissions, 860-548-2420, *Fax:* 860-548-7823, *E-mail:* rdanchak@rh.edu.

■ RENSSELAER POLYTECHNIC INSTITUTE

Graduate School, School of Science, Department of Computer Science, Troy, NY 12180-3590

AWARDS MS, PhD. Part-time programs available. Postbaccalaureate distance learning degree programs offered (no on-campus study).

Faculty: 22 full-time (3 women), 1 part-time/adjunct (0 women).

Students: 147 full-time (39 women), 47 part-time (14 women); includes 13 minority (9 African Americans, 4 Asian Americans or Pacific Islanders), 101 international. 652 applicants, 16% accepted, 56 enrolled. In 2001, 41 master's, 2 doctorates awarded.

Degree requirements: For master's, thesis (for some programs); for doctorate, thesis/dissertation. *Median time to degree:* Doctorate–7.5 years full-time.

Entrance requirements: For master's and doctorate, GRE General Test, TOEFL. *Application deadline:* For fall admission, 1/15 (priority date); for spring admission, 10/1 (priority date). Applications are processed on a rolling basis. *Application fee:* $45. Electronic applications accepted.

Expenses: Tuition: Full-time $26,400; part-time $1,320 per credit hour. Required fees: $1,437.

Financial support: In 2001–02, 50 students received support, including 23 research assistantships with full tuition reimbursements available, 30 teaching assistantships with full tuition reimbursements available (averaging $12,615 per year); fellowships with full tuition reimbursements available, career-related internships or fieldwork and institutionally sponsored loans also available. Financial award application deadline: 1/15.

Faculty research: Computer vision, parallel computing, computational science, database systems, robotics.

Dr. David Spooner, Acting Chair, 518-276-8326, *Fax:* 518-276-4033, *E-mail:* spoonerd@rpi.edu.

Application contact: Terry Hayden, Coordinator of Graduate Admissions, 518-276-8419, *Fax:* 518-276-4033, *E-mail:* grad-adm@cs.rpi.edu. *Web site:* http://www.cs.rpi.edu/

Find an in-depth description at www.petersons.com/gradchannel.

■ RICE UNIVERSITY

Graduate Programs, George R. Brown School of Engineering, Department of Computer Science, Houston, TX 77251-1892

AWARDS Computer science (MCS, MS, PhD); computer science in bioinformatics (MCS).

Faculty: 15 full-time (2 women), 9 part-time/adjunct (0 women).

Students: 61 full-time (6 women), 6 part-time; includes 8 minority (7 Asian Americans or Pacific Islanders, 1 Hispanic American), 41 international. 506 applicants, 10% accepted, 24 enrolled. In 2001, 12 master's, 5 doctorates awarded. Terminal master's awarded for partial completion of doctoral program.

Degree requirements: For master's, thesis (for some programs), registration; for doctorate, thesis/dissertation, qualifying exam, teaching assistant, PhD proposal defense. *Median time to degree:* Doctorate–6.4 years full-time.

Entrance requirements: For master's and doctorate, GRE General Test, GRE Subject Test, TOEFL, minimum GPA of 3.0. *Application deadline:* For fall admission, 2/1 (priority date); for spring admission, 10/15. Applications are processed on a rolling basis. *Application fee:* $25. Electronic applications accepted.

Expenses: Tuition: Full-time $17,300. Required fees: $250.

Financial support: In 2001–02, 17 fellowships with tuition reimbursements (averaging $22,667 per year), 30 research assistantships with tuition reimbursements (averaging $22,667 per year), 1 teaching assistantship with tuition reimbursement (averaging $23,667 per year) were awarded. Financial award application deadline: 2/1; financial award applicants required to submit FAFSA.

Faculty research: Operating systems, distributed systems, programming languages, algorithms, automatic program testing. *Total annual research expenditures:* $10.5 million.

Moshe Y. Vardi, Chairman, 713-527-4834.

Application contact: Melissa Cisneros, Staff Assistant, 713-348-4834, *Fax:* 713-348-5930, *E-mail:* mcisnero@rice.edu. *Web site:* http://www.cs.rice.edu/

Find an in-depth description at www.petersons.com/gradchannel.

■ RIVIER COLLEGE

School of Graduate Studies, Department of Computer Science and Mathematics, Nashua, NH 03060-5086

AWARDS Computer science (MS); information science (MS); mathematics (MAT). Part-time and evening/weekend programs available.

Faculty: 3 full-time (1 woman), 11 part-time/adjunct (2 women).

Students: 37 full-time (25 women), 61 part-time (28 women); includes 8 minority (all Asian Americans or Pacific Islanders), 32 international. Average age 36. 53 applicants, 62% accepted. In 2001, 61 degrees awarded.

Entrance requirements: For master's, GRE Subject Test. *Application deadline:* Applications are processed on a rolling basis. *Application fee:* $25. Electronic applications accepted.

Expenses: Tuition: Part-time $360 per credit. Required fees: $25 per year. Part-time tuition and fees vary according to course level and course load.

Financial support: Available to part-time students. Application deadline: 2/1.

Dr. A. Darien Lauten, Director, 603-888-1311, *E-mail:* dlauten@rivier.edu.

Application contact: Diane Monahan, Director of Graduate Admissions, 603-897-8129, *Fax:* 603-897-8810, *E-mail:* gradadm@rivier.edu.

■ ROCHESTER INSTITUTE OF TECHNOLOGY

Graduate Enrollment Services, Golisano College of Computing and Information Sciences, Department of Computer Science, Program in Computer Science, Rochester, NY 14623-5698

AWARDS MS.

Students: 116 full-time (18 women), 72 part-time (16 women); includes 13 minority (1 African American, 10 Asian Americans or Pacific Islanders, 2 Hispanic Americans), 123 international. 312 applicants, 82% accepted, 85 enrolled. In 2001, 33 degrees awarded.

Degree requirements: For master's, thesis.

Entrance requirements: For master's, GRE General Test, TOEFL, minimum GPA of 3.0. *Application deadline:* For fall admission, 3/1 (priority date). Applications are processed on a rolling basis. *Application fee:* $50.

Expenses: Tuition: Full-time $20,928; part-time $587 per hour. Required fees: $162. Tuition and fees vary according to program.

Financial support: Research assistantships, teaching assistantships, scholarships/grants available.

Roger Goborski, Graduate Coordinator, 585-475-7801, *E-mail:* rsg@cs.rit.edu.

ROOSEVELT UNIVERSITY

Graduate Division, College of Arts and Sciences, School of Computer Science and Telecommunications, Program in Computer Science, Chicago, IL 60605-1394

AWARDS MSC. Part-time and evening/weekend programs available.

Faculty: 6 full-time (0 women), 4 part-time/adjunct (0 women).
Application deadline: For fall admission, 6/1 (priority date). Applications are processed on a rolling basis. *Application fee:* $25 ($35 for international students).
Expenses: Tuition: Full-time $9,090; part-time $505 per credit hour. Required fees: $100 per term.
Financial support: Application deadline: 2/15.
Faculty research: Artificial intelligence, software engineering, distributed databases, parallel processing. *Total annual research expenditures:* $40,000.
Application contact: Joanne Canyon-Heller, Coordinator of Graduate Admissions, 312-281-3250, *Fax:* 312-341-3523, *E-mail:* applyru@roosevelt.edu.

RUTGERS, THE STATE UNIVERSITY OF NEW JERSEY, NEW BRUNSWICK

Graduate School, Program in Computer Science, New Brunswick, NJ 08901-1281

AWARDS MS, PhD. Part-time programs available. Terminal master's awarded for partial completion of doctoral program.

Degree requirements: For master's, thesis or alternative; for doctorate, thesis/dissertation.
Entrance requirements: For master's and doctorate, GRE General Test, GRE Subject Test.
Faculty research: Theoretical computer science, distributed/networked/wireless systems, artificial intelligence, compiling.
Web site: http://athos.rutgers.edu/
Find an in-depth description at www.petersons.com/gradchannel.

SACRED HEART UNIVERSITY

Graduate Studies, College of Arts and Sciences, Department of Computer Science and Information Technology, Fairfield, CT 06432-1000

AWARDS Computer science (MS, CPS); e-commerce (CPS); information technology (MS, CPS); multimedia (CPS). Part-time and evening/weekend programs available. Postbaccalaureate distance learning degree programs offered (minimal on-campus study).

Students: 14 full-time, 178 part-time; includes 60 minority (15 African Americans, 38 Asian Americans or Pacific Islanders, 5 Hispanic Americans, 2 Native Americans), 17 international. Average age 31. 79 applicants, 29% accepted. In 2001, 7 degrees awarded.

Degree requirements: For master's, thesis optional.
Application deadline: Applications are processed on a rolling basis. *Application fee:* $45 ($100 for international students).
Expenses: Tuition: Full-time $16,128; part-time $435 per credit. Required fees: $285 per term.
Financial support: In 2001–02, 10 students received support. Career-related internships or fieldwork and unspecified assistantships available. Support available to part-time students. Financial award applicants required to submit FAFSA.
Faculty research: Contemporary market software.
Domenick Pinto, Academic Director and Chairperson, 203-371-7789, *Fax:* 203-371-0506, *E-mail:* pintod@sacredheart.edu.
Application contact: William Farrell, Director of Graduate Admissions, MSCIS and MBA Programs, 203-365-7619, *Fax:* 203-365-4732, *E-mail:* farrellw@sacredheart.edu. *Web site:* http://www.sacredheart.edu/graduate/computer/

ST. CLOUD STATE UNIVERSITY

School of Graduate Studies, College of Science and Engineering, Department of Computer Science, St. Cloud, MN 56301-4498

AWARDS MS.

Faculty: 9 full-time (2 women), 1 part-time/adjunct (0 women).
Students: 17 full-time (12 women), 11 part-time (8 women); includes 23 minority (2 African Americans, 20 Asian Americans or Pacific Islanders, 1 Native American). 54 applicants, 30% accepted. In 2001, 3 degrees awarded.
Degree requirements: For master's, thesis or alternative.
Entrance requirements: For master's, GRE General Test, minimum GPA of 2.75. *Application deadline:* For fall admission, 3/1; for spring admission, 10/1. *Application fee:* $35.
Expenses: Tuition, state resident: part-time $156 per credit. Tuition, nonresident: part-time $244 per credit. Required fees: $20 per credit.
Financial support: Unspecified assistantships available. Financial award application deadline: 3/1.
Dr. Larry Grover, Chairperson, 320-255-4966.
Application contact: Lindalou Krueger, Graduate Studies Office, 320-255-2113, *Fax:* 320-654-5371, *E-mail:* lekrueger@stcloudstate.edu.

ST. JOHN'S UNIVERSITY

St. John's College of Liberal Arts and Sciences, Department of Mathematics and Computer Science, Jamaica, NY 11439

AWARDS Algebra (MA); analysis (MA); applied mathematics (MA); computer science (MA); geometry-topology (MA); logic and foundations (MA); probability and statistics (MA). Part-time and evening/weekend programs available.

Faculty: 19 full-time (1 woman), 14 part-time/adjunct (5 women).
Students: 3 full-time (2 women), 4 part-time (2 women); includes 2 minority (both African Americans), 2 international. Average age 26. 10 applicants, 60% accepted, 3 enrolled. In 2001, 3 degrees awarded.
Degree requirements: For master's, thesis optional.
Entrance requirements: For master's, minimum GPA of 3.0. *Application deadline:* Applications are processed on a rolling basis. *Application fee:* $40.
Expenses: Tuition: Full-time $14,520; part-time $605 per credit. Required fees: $150; $75 per term. Tuition and fees vary according to class time, course load, degree level, campus/location, program and student level.
Financial support: Research assistantships with full tuition reimbursements, scholarships/grants available. Support available to part-time students. Financial award application deadline: 3/1; financial award applicants required to submit FAFSA.
Faculty research: Development of a computerized metabolic map.
Dr. Charles Traina, Chair, 718-990-6166, *E-mail:* trainac@stjohns.edu.
Application contact: Matthew Whelan, Director, Office of Admission, 718-990-2000, *Fax:* 718-990-2096, *E-mail:* admissions@stjohns.edu. *Web site:* http://www.stjohns.edu/

SAINT JOSEPH'S UNIVERSITY

College of Arts and Sciences, Program in Computer Science, Philadelphia, PA 19131-1395

AWARDS MS. Part-time and evening/weekend programs available.

Entrance requirements: For master's, GRE General Test, TOEFL.
Expenses: Contact institution.

ST. MARY'S UNIVERSITY OF SAN ANTONIO

Graduate School, Department of Computer Science, Program in Computer Information Systems, San Antonio, TX 78228-8507

AWARDS MS.

Faculty: 3 full-time (2 women).
Students: 14 full-time (6 women), 81 part-time (30 women); includes 38 minority (3

African Americans, 5 Asian Americans or Pacific Islanders, 29 Hispanic Americans, 1 Native American), 14 international. Average age 30. In 2001, 32 degrees awarded. **Degree requirements:** For master's, thesis optional. **Entrance requirements:** For master's, GMAT or GRE General Test. *Application deadline:* Applications are processed on a rolling basis. *Application fee:* $15. Electronic applications accepted. **Expenses:** Tuition: Full-time $8,190; part-time $455 per credit hour. Required fees: $375. **Financial support:** Research assistantships, career-related internships or fieldwork and institutionally sponsored loans available. Financial award application deadline: 2/15; financial award applicants required to submit FAFSA. **Faculty research:** Artificial intelligence, database/knowledge base, software engineering, expert systems. Dr. Douglas L. Hall, Graduate Program Director, 210-436-3317.

■ ST. MARY'S UNIVERSITY OF SAN ANTONIO

Graduate School, Department of Computer Science, Program in Computer Science, San Antonio, TX 78228-8507

AWARDS MS.

Faculty: 3 full-time (2 women). **Students:** 8 full-time (0 women), 13 part-time (2 women); includes 12 minority (1 African American, 2 Asian Americans or Pacific Islanders, 9 Hispanic Americans), 4 international. In 2001, 2 degrees awarded. **Entrance requirements:** For master's, GRE. *Application deadline:* Applications are processed on a rolling basis. Electronic applications accepted. **Expenses:** Tuition: Full-time $8,190; part-time $455 per credit hour. Required fees: $375. **Financial support:** Application deadline: 2/15. Dr. Douglas L. Hall, Graduate Program Director, 210-436-3317.

■ SAINT XAVIER UNIVERSITY

Graduate Studies, School of Arts and Sciences, Department of Mathematics and Computer Science, Chicago, IL 60655-3105

AWARDS Applied computer science in Internet information systems (MS).

Faculty: 1 (woman) full-time. **Students:** 10 full-time (3 women), 6 part-time (4 women). Average age 32. **Degree requirements:** For master's, thesis optional. *Application deadline:* For fall admission, 8/15. *Application fee:* $35. **Expenses:** Tuition: Full-time $4,500; part-time $500 per credit. Required fees: $40 per term.

Dr. Florence Appel, Associate Professor and Associate Chair/Computer Science, 773-298-3398, *Fax:* 773-779-9061, *E-mail:* appel@sxu.edu. **Application contact:** Beth Gierach, Managing Director of Admission, 773-298-3053, *Fax:* 773-298-3076, *E-mail:* gierach@sxu.edu. **Find an in-depth description at www.petersons.com/gradchannel.**

■ SAM HOUSTON STATE UNIVERSITY

College of Arts and Sciences, Department of Mathematical and Information Sciences, Huntsville, TX 77341

AWARDS Computing science (M Ed, MS); mathematics (M Ed, MA, MS); statistics (MS). Part-time programs available.

Students: 25 full-time (9 women), 21 part-time (12 women); includes 2 minority (1 African American, 1 Asian American or Pacific Islander), 23 international. Average age 31. In 2001, 11 degrees awarded. **Entrance requirements:** For master's, GRE General Test, TOEFL. *Application deadline:* For fall admission, 8/1; for spring admission, 12/1. Applications are processed on a rolling basis. *Application fee:* $20. **Expenses:** Tuition, area resident: Part-time $69 per credit. Tuition, state resident: full-time $1,380; part-time $69 per credit. Tuition, nonresident: full-time $5,600; part-time $280 per credit. Required fees: $748. Tuition and fees vary according to course load. **Financial support:** Teaching assistantships, institutionally sponsored loans available. Support available to part-time students. Financial award application deadline: 5/31; financial award applicants required to submit FAFSA. **Faculty research:** Applied mathematics, applied mathematical statistics, computer science. Dr. Jaimie Hebert, Chair, 936-294-1563, *Fax:* 936-294-1882, *E-mail:* mth_gem@ shsu.edu. *Web site:* http://www.shsu.edu/~mcss_www/

■ SAN DIEGO STATE UNIVERSITY

Graduate and Research Affairs, College of Sciences, Department of Mathematical Sciences, Program in Computer Science, San Diego, CA 92182

AWARDS MS.

Degree requirements: For master's, comprehensive exam or thesis. **Entrance requirements:** For master's, GRE General Test, TOEFL.

■ SAN FRANCISCO STATE UNIVERSITY

Graduate Division, College of Science and Engineering, Department of Computer Science, San Francisco, CA 94132-1722

AWARDS MS. Part-time programs available.

Degree requirements: For master's, thesis or alternative. **Entrance requirements:** For master's, GRE, minimum GPA of 2.5 in last 60 units. **Faculty research:** Parallel computing, real time systems, database systems, neural networks, computer graphics.

■ SAN JOSE STATE UNIVERSITY

Graduate Studies, College of Engineering, Department of Computer, Information and Systems Engineering, Program in Computer Engineering, San Jose, CA 95192-0001

AWARDS Computer engineering (MS); computer software (MS); computerized robots and computer applications (MS); microprocessors and microcomputers (MS).

Faculty: 5 full-time (0 women), 12 part-time/adjunct (1 woman). **Students:** 62 full-time (36 women), 124 part-time (45 women); includes 119 minority (4 African Americans, 115 Asian Americans or Pacific Islanders), 33 international. Average age 28. 236 applicants, 39% accepted. In 2001, 53 degrees awarded. **Degree requirements:** For master's, thesis, comprehensive exam. **Entrance requirements:** For master's, GRE General Test, BS in computer science or 24 credits in related area. *Application deadline:* For fall admission, 6/29; for spring admission, 11/30. Applications are processed on a rolling basis. *Application fee:* $59. Electronic applications accepted. **Expenses:** Tuition, nonresident: part-time $246 per unit. Required fees: $678 per semester. Tuition and fees vary according to course load. **Financial support:** Teaching assistantships, career-related internships or fieldwork, Federal Work-Study, and institutionally sponsored loans available. Support available to part-time students. Financial award application deadline: 5/1; financial award applicants required to submit FAFSA. **Faculty research:** Robotics, database management systems, computer networks. **Application contact:** Dr. Haluk Ozemek, Coordinator, 408-924-4100.

■ SAN JOSE STATE UNIVERSITY

Graduate Studies, College of Science, Department of Mathematics and Computer Science, San Jose, CA 95192-0001

AWARDS Computer science (MS); mathematics (MA, MS). Part-time and evening/weekend programs available.

Faculty: 51 full-time (5 women), 3 part-time/adjunct (0 women).
Students: 48 full-time (24 women), 103 part-time (42 women); includes 89 minority (2 African Americans, 85 Asian Americans or Pacific Islanders, 2 Hispanic Americans), 30 international. Average age 31. 363 applicants, 16% accepted. In 2001, 33 degrees awarded.
Degree requirements: For master's, thesis (for some programs), comprehensive exam.
Entrance requirements: For master's, GRE Subject Test. *Application deadline:* For fall admission, 6/29; for spring admission, 11/30. Applications are processed on a rolling basis. *Application fee:* $59. Electronic applications accepted.
Expenses: Tuition, nonresident: part-time $246 per unit. Required fees: $678 per semester. Tuition and fees vary according to course load.
Financial support: In 2001–02, 20 teaching assistantships were awarded; career-related internships or fieldwork and Federal Work-Study also available. Support available to part-time students. Financial award applicants required to submit FAFSA.
Faculty research: Artificial intelligence, algorithms, numerical analysis, software database, number theory.
David Hayes, Chair, 408-924-5100, *Fax:* 408-924-5080.
Application contact: Dr. John Mitchem, Graduate Adviser, 408-924-5135.

■ SANTA CLARA UNIVERSITY

School of Engineering, Department of Computer Science and Engineering, Santa Clara, CA 95053

AWARDS Computer science and engineering (MSCSE, PhD); high performance computing (Certificate); software engineering (MS, Certificate). Part-time and evening/weekend programs available.

Students: 90 full-time (52 women), 144 part-time (62 women); includes 54 minority (3 African Americans, 51 Asian Americans or Pacific Islanders), 148 international. Average age 28. 233 applicants, 44% accepted. In 2001, 103 degrees awarded.
Degree requirements: For master's, thesis or alternative; for doctorate and Certificate, thesis/dissertation.
Entrance requirements: For master's, GRE General Test, TOEFL, minimum GPA of 2.75; for doctorate, GRE General Test, GRE Subject Test, TOEFL, master's degree or equivalent; for Certificate,

master's degree, published paper. *Application deadline:* For fall admission, 6/1; for spring admission, 1/1. Applications are processed on a rolling basis. *Application fee:* $45 ($55 for international students). Electronic applications accepted.
Expenses: Tuition: Part-time $320 per unit. Tuition and fees vary according to class time, degree level, program and student level.
Financial support: Fellowships, research assistantships, teaching assistantships, Federal Work-Study available. Support available to part-time students. Financial award application deadline: 3/1; financial award applicants required to submit FAFSA. *Total annual research expenditures:* $13,156.
Dr. Daniel W. Lewis, Chair, 408-554-5281.
Application contact: Tina Samms, Assistant Director of Graduate Admissions, 408-554-4313, *Fax:* 408-554-5474, *E-mail:* engr-grad@scu.edu.

■ SHIPPENSBURG UNIVERSITY OF PENNSYLVANIA

School of Graduate Studies and Research, College of Arts and Sciences, Department of Mathematics, Shippensburg, PA 17257-2299

AWARDS Computer science (MS); information systems (MS). Part-time and evening/weekend programs available.

Faculty: 10 full-time (2 women).
Students: 26 full-time (5 women), 43 part-time (16 women); includes 2 minority (1 Hispanic American, 1 Native American), 32 international. Average age 30. 94 applicants, 60% accepted, 10 enrolled. In 2001, 15 degrees awarded.
Degree requirements: For master's, Project. *Median time to degree:* Master's– 1.92 years full-time, 2.58 years part-time.
Entrance requirements: For master's, TOEFL, GRE General Test, minimum GPA of 2.75. *Application deadline:* Applications are processed on a rolling basis. *Application fee:* $30. Electronic applications accepted.
Expenses: Tuition, state resident: full-time $4,600; part-time $256 per credit hour. Tuition, nonresident: full-time $7,554; part-time $420 per credit hour. Required fees: $290; $145 per semester.
Financial support: In 2001–02, 22 research assistantships with full tuition reimbursements were awarded; career-related internships or fieldwork and unspecified assistantships also available. Support available to part-time students. Financial award application deadline: 3/1; financial award applicants required to submit FAFSA.
Dr. Fred Nordai, Chairperson, 717-477-1431, *Fax:* 717-477-4009, *E-mail:* flnord@ship.edu.
Application contact: Renee Payne, Associate Dean of Graduate Admissions, 717-477-1231, *Fax:* 717-477-4016, *E-mail:*

rmpayn@ship.edu. *Web site:* http://www.ship.edu/academic/artcps.html

■ SOUTH DAKOTA SCHOOL OF MINES AND TECHNOLOGY

Graduate Division, Department of Computer Science, Rapid City, SD 57701-3995

AWARDS MS. Part-time programs available.

Entrance requirements: For master's, TOEFL, TWE. Electronic applications accepted.
Faculty research: Database systems, remote sensing, numerical modeling, artificial intelligence, neural networks.

■ SOUTH DAKOTA STATE UNIVERSITY

Graduate School, College of Engineering, Department of Computer Science, Brookings, SD 57007

AWARDS Engineering (MS), including computer science.

Degree requirements: For master's, thesis, oral exam.
Entrance requirements: For master's, TOEFL.

■ SOUTHEASTERN UNIVERSITY

College of Graduate Studies, Department of Computer Science and Information Studies, Washington, DC 20024-2788

AWARDS MBA, MS. Part-time and evening/weekend programs available.

Faculty: 4 full-time (1 woman), 31 part-time/adjunct (1 woman).
Students: 97 full-time (54 women), 57 part-time (30 women); includes 8 minority (all Asian Americans or Pacific Islanders), 143 international. Average age 34. In 2001, 153 degrees awarded.
Entrance requirements: For master's, GRE General Test, TOEFL. *Application deadline:* Applications are processed on a rolling basis. *Application fee:* $45.
Expenses: Tuition: Full-time $7,695; part-time $285 per credit hour. One-time fee: $45.
Financial support: In 2001–02, 7 students received support. Federal Work-Study available. Support available to part-time students. Financial award application deadline: 8/21; financial award applicants required to submit CSS PROFILE or FAFSA.
Dr. Abe Eftekari, Head, 202-488-8162 Ext. 254, *Fax:* 202-488-8093.
Application contact: Information Contact, 202-265-5343, *Fax:* 202-488-8093.

■ SOUTHERN ILLINOIS UNIVERSITY CARBONDALE

Graduate School, College of Science, Department of Computer Science, Carbondale, IL 62901-6806

AWARDS MS.

Faculty: 12 full-time (0 women).
Students: 40 full-time (7 women), 15 part-time (4 women); includes 5 minority (2 African Americans, 2 Asian Americans or Pacific Islanders, 1 Native American), 42 international. 104 applicants, 28% accepted. In 2001, 16 degrees awarded.
Degree requirements: For master's, thesis.
Entrance requirements: For master's, TOEFL, previous undergraduate course work in computer science, minimum GPA of 2.7. *Application deadline:* Applications are processed on a rolling basis. *Application fee:* $20.
Expenses: Tuition, state resident: full-time $3,794; part-time $154 per hour. Tuition, nonresident: full-time $6,566; part-time $308 per hour. Required fees: $277 per hour.
Financial support: In 2001–02, 32 students received support, including 3 research assistantships with full tuition reimbursements available, 22 teaching assistantships with full tuition reimbursements available; fellowships with full tuition reimbursements available, Federal Work-Study, institutionally sponsored loans, and tuition waivers (full) also available. Support available to part-time students. Financial award application deadline: 3/1.
Faculty research: Analysis of algorithms, VLSI testing, database systems, artificial intelligence, computer architecture.
Dr. William Wright, Chairperson, 618-453-6042.
Application contact: Georgia L. Marine, Graduate Program Secretary, 618-536-2327, *Fax:* 618-453-6044, *E-mail:* csinfo@cs.siu.edu. *Web site:* http://www.cs.siu.edu/
Find an in-depth description at www.petersons.com/gradchannel.

■ SOUTHERN ILLINOIS UNIVERSITY EDWARDSVILLE

Graduate Studies and Research, School of Engineering, Department of Computer Information Systems, Edwardsville, IL 62026-0001

AWARDS MS. Part-time programs available.

Students: 34 full-time (7 women), 48 part-time (15 women); includes 2 minority (1 Asian American or Pacific Islander, 1 Native American), 67 international. Average age 33. 94 applicants, 46% accepted, 25 enrolled. In 2001, 30 degrees awarded.
Degree requirements: For master's, thesis or research paper, final exam.
Median time to degree: Master's–2.5 years full-time, 4.5 years part-time.

Entrance requirements: For master's, GMAT or GRE, TOEFL. *Application deadline:* For fall admission, 7/20; for spring admission, 12/7. *Application fee:* $25.
Expenses: Tuition, state resident: full-time $2,712; part-time $113 per credit hour. Tuition, nonresident: full-time $5,424; part-time $226 per credit hour. Required fees: $250; $125 per term. $125 per term. Tuition and fees vary according to course load, campus/location and reciprocity agreements.
Financial support: In 2001–02, 1 research assistantship with full tuition reimbursement, 12 teaching assistantships with full tuition reimbursements were awarded. Fellowships with full tuition reimbursements, career-related internships or fieldwork, Federal Work-Study, institutionally sponsored loans, scholarships/grants, traineeships, and unspecified assistantships also available. Support available to part-time students. Financial award application deadline: 3/1; financial award applicants required to submit FAFSA.
Dr. Marilyn Livingston, Chairperson, 618-650-2386, *E-mail:* mliving@siue.edu.
Application contact: Dr. Greg Stephen, Program Director, 618-650-3459, *E-mail:* gstephe@siue.edu.

■ SOUTHERN METHODIST UNIVERSITY

School of Engineering, Department of Computer Science and Engineering, Dallas, TX 75275

AWARDS Computer engineering (MS Cp E, PhD); computer science (MS, PhD); engineering management (MSEM, DE); operations research (MS, PhD); software engineering (MS). Part-time and evening/weekend programs available. Postbaccalaureate distance learning degree programs offered (no on-campus study).

Faculty: 9 full-time (3 women).
Students: 53 full-time (15 women), 163 part-time (37 women); includes 73 minority (16 African Americans, 43 Asian Americans or Pacific Islanders, 14 Hispanic Americans), 49 international. Average age 32. 307 applicants, 78% accepted. In 2001, 59 master's, 4 doctorates awarded. Terminal master's awarded for partial completion of doctoral program.
Degree requirements: For master's, thesis optional; for doctorate, thesis/dissertation, oral and written qualifying exams, oral final exam (PhD).
Entrance requirements: For master's, GRE General Test, TOEFL, minimum GPA of 3.0 in last 2 years; bachelor's degree in engineering, mathematics, or sciences; for doctorate, preliminary counseling exam (PhD), minimum GPA of 3.0, bachelor's degree in related field, MA (DE). *Application deadline:* For fall admission, 7/1 (priority date); for spring admission, 11/15. Applications are processed on a rolling basis. *Application fee:* $50.

Expenses: Tuition: Part-time $285 per credit hour.
Financial support: In 2001–02, 14 research assistantships with full tuition reimbursements (averaging $15,000 per year), 11 teaching assistantships with full tuition reimbursements (averaging $9,000 per year) were awarded. Financial award applicants required to submit FAFSA.
Faculty research: Trusted and high performance network computing, software engineering and management, knowledge engineering and management, computer arithmetic. *Total annual research expenditures:* $126,192.
Hesham El-Rewini, Head, 214-768-3278.
Application contact: Jim Dees, Director, Student Administration, 214-768-1456, *Fax:* 214-768-3845, *E-mail:* jdees@engr.smu.edu. *Web site:* http://www.seas.sm.edu/cse/

Find an in-depth description at www.petersons.com/gradchannel.

■ SOUTHERN OREGON UNIVERSITY

Graduate Office, School of Sciences, Ashland, OR 97520

AWARDS Environmental education (MA, MS); mathematics/computer science (MA, MS); science (MA, MS). Part-time programs available.

Faculty: 46 full-time (9 women), 5 part-time/adjunct (3 women).
Students: 20 full-time (9 women), 13 part-time (5 women); includes 1 minority (Hispanic American), 8 international. Average age 35. 23 applicants, 48% accepted, 6 enrolled. In 2001, 17 degrees awarded.
Degree requirements: For master's, thesis (for some programs), comprehensive exam (MA), comprehensive exam (for some programs).
Entrance requirements: For master's, GRE General Test, minimum GPA of 3.0. *Application deadline:* For fall admission, 4/15 (priority date); for winter admission, 10/15 (priority date); for spring admission, 1/15 (priority date). *Application fee:* $50.
Expenses: Tuition, state resident: full-time $5,184; part-time $192 per credit. Tuition, nonresident: full-time $9,828; part-time $364 per credit. Required fees: $927. One-time fee: $75 full-time. Full-time tuition and fees vary according to course load, program and reciprocity agreements.
Financial support: In 2001–02, 5 teaching assistantships with tuition reimbursements (averaging $3,519 per year) were awarded; institutionally sponsored loans and unspecified assistantships also available.
Faculty research: Ferroelectric, ecology environmental science, biotechnology, material science. *Total annual research expenditures:* $318,923.
Dr. Joseph Graf, Dean, 541-552-6474.
Application contact: Susan Koralek, Administrative Assistant, 541-552-6474.

■ SOUTHERN POLYTECHNIC STATE UNIVERSITY

School of Computing and Software Engineering, Program in Computer Science and Software Engineering, Marietta, GA 30060-2896

AWARDS Computer science (MS); software engineering (MSSE). Part-time and evening/weekend programs available.

Students: 97 full-time (50 women), 151 part-time (55 women); includes 55 minority (25 African Americans, 26 Asian Americans or Pacific Islanders, 4 Hispanic Americans), 126 international. Average age 32. In 2001, 82 degrees awarded.
Degree requirements: For master's, thesis.
Entrance requirements: For master's, GRE, 2 years full-time software development experience (MSSE), recommendations (3). *Application deadline:* For fall admission, 7/1 (priority date); for spring admission, 11/1. Applications are processed on a rolling basis. *Application fee:* $20. Electronic applications accepted.
Expenses: Tuition, state resident: full-time $1,746; part-time $97 per credit. Tuition, nonresident: full-time $6,966; part-time $387 per credit. Required fees: $221 per term.
Financial support: Career-related internships or fieldwork, Federal Work-Study, scholarships/grants, and unspecified assistantships available. Support available to part-time students. Financial award application deadline: 5/1; financial award applicants required to submit FAFSA.
Dr. Venu Dasigi, Head, 770-528-7406, *Fax:* 770-528-5511, *E-mail:* vdasigi@spsu.edu.
Application contact: Virginia A. Head, Director of Admissions, 770-528-7281, *Fax:* 770-528-7292, *E-mail:* vhead@spsu.edu. *Web site:* http://www.cs.spsu.edu/csdept/

■ SOUTHERN UNIVERSITY AND AGRICULTURAL AND MECHANICAL COLLEGE

Graduate School, College of Sciences, Department of Computer Science, Baton Rouge, LA 70813

AWARDS Information systems (MS); micro/minicomputer architecture (MS); operating systems (MS). Part-time programs available. Postbaccalaureate distance learning degree programs offered (minimal on-campus study).

Faculty: 6 full-time (0 women).
Students: 46 full-time (22 women), 13 part-time (8 women); includes 20 minority (18 African Americans, 2 Asian Americans or Pacific Islanders), 39 international. Average age 31. 41 applicants, 66% accepted. In 2001, 12 degrees awarded.
Degree requirements: For master's, thesis.

Entrance requirements: For master's, GRE General Test, TOEFL, minimum GPA of 3.0, bachelor's degree in computer science or related field. *Application deadline:* For fall admission, 6/1 (priority date); for spring admission, 11/1. Applications are processed on a rolling basis. *Application fee:* $25.
Expenses: Tuition, state resident: full-time $1,323. Tuition, nonresident: full-time $2,583. International tuition: $2,613 full-time. Tuition and fees vary according to program.
Financial support: In 2001–02, 10 research assistantships with tuition reimbursements (averaging $7,000 per year), 3 teaching assistantships with tuition reimbursements (averaging $7,000 per year) were awarded. Career-related internships or fieldwork, scholarships/grants, and unspecified assistantships also available. Financial award application deadline: 4/15.
Faculty research: Network theory, computational complexity, high speed computing, neural networking, data warehousing/mining. *Total annual research expenditures:* $500,000.
Dr. Erold W. Hinds, Chair, 225-771-2060, *Fax:* 225-771-4223, *E-mail:* ewhinds@aol.com.
Application contact: Dr. John A. Dyer, Professor, 225-771-2060, *Fax:* 225-771-4223, *E-mail:* dyera@mail.cmps.subr.edu.

■ SOUTHWEST MISSOURI STATE UNIVERSITY

Graduate College, College of Business Administration, Department of Computer Science, Springfield, MO 65804-0094

AWARDS MS. Part-time and evening/weekend programs available. Postbaccalaureate distance learning degree programs offered.

Degree requirements: For master's, thesis or alternative, comprehensive exam.
Entrance requirements: For master's, GMAT, minimum GPA of 2.75. *Application deadline:* For fall admission, 7/5 (priority date); for spring admission, 12/20 (priority date). Applications are processed on a rolling basis. Electronic applications accepted.
Expenses: Tuition, state resident: full-time $2,286; part-time $127 per credit. Tuition, nonresident: full-time $4,572; part-time $254 per credit. Required fees: $151 per semester. Tuition and fees vary according to course level and program.
Financial support: Research assistantships, teaching assistantships, career-related internships or fieldwork, Federal Work-Study, institutionally sponsored loans, scholarships/grants, tuition waivers (partial), and unspecified assistantships available. Support available to part-time students. Financial award application deadline: 3/31.
Dr. Jerry Chin, Head.

■ SOUTHWEST TEXAS STATE UNIVERSITY

Graduate School, College of Science, Department of Computer Science, San Marcos, TX 78666

AWARDS Computer science (MA, MS); software engineering (MS). Part-time programs available.

Faculty: 11 full-time (2 women).
Students: 124 full-time (64 women), 65 part-time (28 women); includes 24 minority (19 Asian Americans or Pacific Islanders, 5 Hispanic Americans), 127 international. Average age 31. 142 applicants, 62% accepted, 57 enrolled. In 2001, 39 degrees awarded.
Degree requirements: For master's, thesis (for some programs), comprehensive exam.
Entrance requirements: For master's, GRE General Test, TOEFL, minimum GPA of 2.75 in last 60 hours. *Application deadline:* For fall admission, 6/15 (priority date); for spring admission, 10/15 (priority date). Applications are processed on a rolling basis. *Application fee:* $40 ($90 for international students).
Expenses: Tuition, state resident: full-time $1,512; part-time $84 per credit hour. Tuition, nonresident: full-time $5,310; part-time $295 per credit hour. Required fees: $864; $29 per credit hour. $195 per term. Full-time tuition and fees vary according to course load.
Financial support: In 2001–02, 2 research assistantships (averaging $8,535 per year), 14 teaching assistantships (averaging $8,856 per year) were awarded. Career-related internships or fieldwork, Federal Work-Study, and institutionally sponsored loans also available. Support available to part-time students. Financial award application deadline: 4/1; financial award applicants required to submit FAFSA.
Faculty research: Software engineering, artificial intelligence, multimedia, distributed/parallel computing, database systems, operating systems.
Dr. Moonis Ali, Chair, 512-245-3409, *Fax:* 512-245-8750, *E-mail:* ma04@swt.edu.
Application contact: Dr. Khosrow Kaikhah, Graduate Adviser, 512-245-3666, *Fax:* 512-245-8750, *E-mail:* kk02@swt.edu. *Web site:* http://www.gradcollege.swt.edu/
Find an in-depth description at www.petersons.com/gradchannel.

■ STANFORD UNIVERSITY

School of Engineering, Department of Computer Science, Stanford, CA 94305-9991

AWARDS MS, PhD.

Faculty: 37 full-time (4 women).
Students: 401 full-time (83 women), 80 part-time (11 women); includes 110 minority (4 African Americans, 98 Asian Americans or Pacific Islanders, 8 Hispanic Americans), 209 international. Average age

25. 928 applicants, 21% accepted. In 2001, 162 master's, 20 doctorates awarded. Terminal master's awarded for partial completion of doctoral program.
Degree requirements: For doctorate, thesis/dissertation.
Entrance requirements: For master's, GRE General Test, TOEFL; for doctorate, GRE General Test, GRE Computer Science Subject Test, TOEFL. *Application deadline:* For fall admission, 12/15. *Application fee:* $65 ($80 for international students). Electronic applications accepted. Hector Garcia-Molina, Chair, 650-723-0685, *Fax:* 650-725-7411, *E-mail:* hector@cs.stanford.edu.
Application contact: Graduate Administrator, 650-723-1519. *Web site:* http://www.cs.stanford.edu/

■ STANFORD UNIVERSITY

School of Engineering, Program in Scientific Computing and Computational Mathematics, Stanford, CA 94305-9991
AWARDS MS, PhD.
Students: 40 full-time (7 women), 10 part-time (1 woman); includes 9 minority (7 Asian Americans or Pacific Islanders, 2 Hispanic Americans), 25 international. Average age 28. 38 applicants, 66% accepted. In 2001, 6 master's, 3 doctorates awarded. Terminal master's awarded for partial completion of doctoral program.
Degree requirements: For doctorate, thesis/dissertation, qualifying exam.
Entrance requirements: For master's, GRE General Test, TOEFL; for doctorate, GRE General Test, GRE Subject Test, TOEFL. *Application deadline:* For fall admission, 2/15. *Application fee:* $65 ($80 for international students). Electronic applications accepted.
Dr. Gene H. Golub, Director, 650-723-3124, *Fax:* 650-723-2411, *E-mail:* golub@sccm.stanford.edu.
Application contact: Admissions Coordinator, 650-723-0572. *Web site:* http://www-sccm.stanford.edu/

■ STATE UNIVERSITY OF NEW YORK AT ALBANY

College of Arts and Sciences, Department of Computer Science, Albany, NY 12222-0001
AWARDS MS, PhD.
Students: 48 full-time (20 women), 16 part-time (4 women); includes 2 minority (both Asian Americans or Pacific Islanders), 48 international. Average age 29. 125 applicants, 53% accepted. In 2001, 29 degrees awarded.
Degree requirements: For master's, project or thesis; for doctorate, thesis/dissertation, area exams, comprehensive exam.
Entrance requirements: For master's and doctorate, GRE General Test, TOEFL.

Application deadline: For fall admission, 8/1; for spring admission, 11/1. *Application fee:* $50.
Expenses: Tuition, state resident: full-time $2,550; part-time $213 per credit. Tuition, nonresident: full-time $4,208; part-time $351 per credit. Required fees: $470; $470 per year.
Financial support: Fellowships, research assistantships, teaching assistantships, career-related internships or fieldwork and Federal Work-Study available. Financial award application deadline: 3/1.
Faculty research: Algorithm design and analysis, artificial intelligence, computational logic, databases, numerical analysis.
Neil Murray, Chair, 518-442-4270.

■ STATE UNIVERSITY OF NEW YORK AT BINGHAMTON

Graduate School, School of Arts and Sciences, Department of Mathematical Sciences, Binghamton, NY 13902-6000
AWARDS Computer science (MA, PhD); probability and statistics (MA, PhD). Part-time programs available.
Faculty: 24 full-time (4 women), 11 part-time/adjunct (6 women).
Students: 36 full-time (10 women), 9 part-time (4 women); includes 4 minority (2 Asian Americans or Pacific Islanders, 2 Hispanic Americans), 13 international. Average age 30. 44 applicants, 57% accepted, 11 enrolled. In 2001, 3 master's, 8 doctorates awarded. Terminal master's awarded for partial completion of doctoral program.
Degree requirements: For master's, thesis or alternative; for doctorate, 2 foreign languages, thesis/dissertation.
Entrance requirements: For master's and doctorate, GRE General Test, GRE Subject Test, TOEFL. *Application deadline:* For fall admission, 4/15 (priority date); for spring admission, 11/1. Applications are processed on a rolling basis. Electronic applications accepted.
Expenses: Tuition, state resident: full-time $5,100; part-time $213 per credit. Tuition, nonresident: full-time $8,416; part-time $351 per credit. Required fees: $811.
Financial support: In 2001–02, 37 students received support, including 9 fellowships with full tuition reimbursements available (averaging $2,943 per year), 2 research assistantships with full tuition reimbursements available (averaging $7,800 per year), 32 teaching assistantships with full tuition reimbursements available (averaging $9,821 per year); career-related internships or fieldwork, Federal Work-Study, institutionally sponsored loans, tuition waivers (full and partial), and unspecified assistantships also available. Support available to part-time students. Financial award application deadline: 2/15.
Dr. Erik Pederson, Chairperson, 607-777-2147.

■ STATE UNIVERSITY OF NEW YORK AT BINGHAMTON

Graduate School, Thomas J. Watson School of Engineering and Applied Science, Department of Computer Science, Binghamton, NY 13902-6000
AWARDS M Eng, MS, PhD. Part-time programs available.
Faculty: 16 full-time (2 women), 15 part-time/adjunct (6 women).
Students: 104 full-time (27 women), 75 part-time (20 women); includes 17 minority (3 African Americans, 12 Asian Americans or Pacific Islanders, 1 Hispanic American, 1 Native American), 114 international. Average age 28. 475 applicants, 35% accepted, 40 enrolled. In 2001, 51 master's, 3 doctorates awarded.
Degree requirements: For master's, thesis or alternative; for doctorate, thesis/dissertation.
Entrance requirements: For master's and doctorate, GRE General Test, GRE Subject Test, TOEFL. *Application deadline:* For fall admission, 4/15 (priority date); for spring admission, 11/1. Applications are processed on a rolling basis. Electronic applications accepted.
Expenses: Tuition, state resident: full-time $5,100; part-time $213 per credit. Tuition, nonresident: full-time $8,416; part-time $351 per credit. Required fees: $811.
Financial support: In 2001–02, 66 students received support, including 4 fellowships with full tuition reimbursements available (averaging $6,747 per year), 21 research assistantships with full tuition reimbursements available (averaging $5,104 per year), 42 teaching assistantships with full tuition reimbursements available (averaging $7,637 per year); career-related internships or fieldwork, Federal Work-Study, scholarships/grants, and unspecified assistantships also available. Financial award application deadline: 2/15.
Dr. Kanad Ghose, Chair, 607-777-4608.

■ STATE UNIVERSITY OF NEW YORK AT NEW PALTZ

Graduate School, School of Physical Sciences and Engineering, Department of Computer Science, New Paltz, NY 12561
AWARDS MS.
Students: 29 full-time (11 women), 30 part-time (13 women); includes 19 minority (all Asian Americans or Pacific Islanders), 29 international. In 2001, 18 degrees awarded.
Degree requirements: For master's, thesis (for some programs), comprehensive exam.
Entrance requirements: For master's, GRE General Test, minimum GPA of 3.0, proficiency in program assembly. *Application deadline:* For fall admission, 3/15 (priority date). Applications are processed on a rolling basis. *Application fee:* $50.

State University of New York at New Paltz (continued)

Expenses: Tuition, state resident: full-time $5,100; part-time $213 per credit. Tuition, nonresident: full-time $8,416; part-time $351 per credit. Required fees: $624; $21 per credit. $60 per semester.
Financial support: Teaching assistantships, tuition waivers (full) available.
Dr. Paul Zuckerman, Chair, 845-257-3516, *Fax:* 845-257-3996.
Application contact: Keqin Li, Graduate Adviser, 914-257-3535.

■ STATE UNIVERSITY OF NEW YORK AT NEW PALTZ

Graduate School, School of Physical Sciences and Engineering, Department of Mathematics, New Paltz, NY 12561

AWARDS Computer science (MS); mathematics (MA, MAT, MS Ed).

Students: In 2001, 20 degrees awarded.
Entrance requirements: For master's, GRE General Test, minimum GPA of 3.0. *Application deadline:* For fall admission, 3/15 (priority date). Applications are processed on a rolling basis. *Application fee:* $50.
Expenses: Tuition, state resident: full-time $5,100; part-time $213 per credit. Tuition, nonresident: full-time $8,416; part-time $351 per credit. Required fees: $624; $21 per credit. $60 per semester.
Financial support: Teaching assistantships, Federal Work-Study, institutionally sponsored loans, and tuition waivers (full) available.
Faculty research: Universal algebra, lattice theory, mathematical logic, operator theory, combinatorics.
Dr. Sunday Chikwendu, Chair, 845-257-3564.
Application contact: H. P. Sankappanavar, Graduate Adviser, 845-257-3535.

■ STATE UNIVERSITY OF NEW YORK INSTITUTE OF TECHNOLOGY AT UTICA/ROME

School of Information Systems and Engineering Technology, Program in Computer and Information Science, Utica, NY 13504-3050

AWARDS MS. Part-time and evening/weekend programs available.
Faculty: 11 full-time (2 women).
Students: 28 full-time (4 women), 42 part-time (9 women); includes 3 minority (1 African American, 2 Asian Americans or Pacific Islanders), 22 international. Average age 30. 48 applicants, 92% accepted. In 2001, 17 degrees awarded.
Degree requirements: For master's, thesis or project.
Entrance requirements: For master's, GRE General Test, TOEFL, minimum GPA of 3.0, letter of recommendation (1).

Application deadline: For fall admission, 6/15 (priority date). Applications are processed on a rolling basis. *Application fee:* $50.
Expenses: Tuition, state resident: full-time $5,100; part-time $213 per credit hour. Tuition, nonresident: full-time $8,416; part-time $351 per credit hour. Required fees: $525; $21 per credit hour. Tuition and fees vary according to course load.
Financial support: In 2001–02, 15 students received support. Federal Work-Study, scholarships/grants, and unspecified assistantships available. Financial award applicants required to submit FAFSA.
Faculty research: Artificial intelligence, combinatorics, distributed database systems, data security, systems theory/methodology.
Dr. Jorge Novillo, Chair, 315-792-7352, *Fax:* 315-792-7399, *E-mail:* jorge@sunyit.edu.
Application contact: Marybeth Lyons, Director of Admissions, 315-792-7500, *Fax:* 315-792-7837, *E-mail:* smbl@sunyit.edu.

Find an in-depth description at www.petersons.com/gradchannel.

■ STATE UNIVERSITY OF WEST GEORGIA

Graduate School, College of Arts and Sciences, Department of Computer Science, Carrollton, GA 30118

AWARDS Applied computer science (MS). Part-time and evening/weekend programs available.

Faculty: 7 full-time (1 woman).
Degree requirements: For master's, thesis optional.
Entrance requirements: For master's, GRE. *Application deadline:* For fall admission, 8/1 (priority date); for spring admission, 12/18. *Application fee:* $20. Electronic applications accepted.
Expenses: Tuition, state resident: full-time $232; part-time $97 per credit hour. Tuition, nonresident: full-time $928; part-time $387 per credit hour. Required fees: $536; $14 per credit. $100 per semester.
Faculty research: Artificial intelligence, software engineering, web technologies, database. *Total annual research expenditures:* $47,000.
Dr. Adel M. Abunawass, Chair, 770-836-6795, *E-mail:* adel@westga.edu.
Application contact: Dr. Jack O. Jenkins, Dean, Graduate School, 770-836-6419, *Fax:* 770-836-2301, *E-mail:* jjenkins@westga.edu.

■ STEPHEN F. AUSTIN STATE UNIVERSITY

Graduate School, College of Business, Department of Computer Science, Nacogdoches, TX 75962

AWARDS MS. Part-time programs available.

Faculty: 6 full-time (1 woman).
Students: 11 full-time (3 women), 3 part-time, 6 international. 8 applicants, 75% accepted. In 2001, 4 degrees awarded.
Degree requirements: For master's, thesis optional.
Entrance requirements: For master's, GRE General Test, TOEFL. *Application deadline:* For fall admission, 8/1 (priority date); for spring admission, 12/1. Applications are processed on a rolling basis. *Application fee:* $0 ($50 for international students).
Expenses: Tuition, state resident: full-time $1,008; part-time $42 per credit. Tuition, nonresident: full-time $6,072; part-time $253 per credit. Required fees: $1,248; $52 per credit. Tuition and fees vary according to course load.
Financial support: In 2001–02, 7 teaching assistantships (averaging $7,500 per year) were awarded; research assistantships, Federal Work-Study also available. Support available to part-time students. Financial award application deadline: 3/1.
Dr. Craig A. Wood, Chair, 409-468-2508.

■ STEVENS INSTITUTE OF TECHNOLOGY

Graduate School, School of Applied Sciences and Liberal Arts, Department of Computer Science, Hoboken, NJ 07030

AWARDS Advanced programming: theory, design and verification (Certificate); artificial intelligence and robotics (MS, PhD); computer and information systems (MS, PhD); computer architecture and digital system design (MS, PhD); database systems (Certificate); elements of computer science (Certificate); information systems (MS, Certificate); network and graph theory (Certificate); software design (MS, PhD); software engineering (Certificate); theoretical computer science (MS, PhD, Certificate); wireless communications (Certificate). MS and Certificate offered in cooperation with the Program in Information Systems. Part-time and evening/weekend programs available.

Faculty: 12 full-time (5 women).
Students: 50 full-time (19 women), 196 part-time (51 women); includes 57 minority (6 African Americans, 44 Asian Americans or Pacific Islanders, 7 Hispanic Americans), 91 international. 327 applicants, 57% accepted. In 2001, 72 master's, 2 doctorates awarded. Terminal master's awarded for partial completion of doctoral program.
Degree requirements: For master's, thesis optional; for doctorate, variable foreign language requirement, thesis/dissertation, comprehensive exam.
Entrance requirements: For master's and doctorate, GRE, TOEFL, minimum GPA of 3.0. *Application deadline:* Applications are processed on a rolling basis. *Application fee:* $50. Electronic applications accepted.

Expenses: Tuition: Full-time $13,950; part-time $775 per credit. Required fees: $180. One-time fee: $180 part-time. Full-time tuition and fees vary according to degree level and program.
Financial support: Fellowships, Federal Work-Study available. Financial award application deadline: 4/15.
Faculty research: Semantics, reliability theory, programming language, cyber security.
Stephen L. Bloom, Director, 201-216-5439, *Fax:* 201-216-8246, *E-mail:* bloom@cs.stevens-tech.edu. *Web site:* http://www.cs.stevens-tech.edu/
Find an in-depth description at www.petersons.com/gradchannel.

■ STEVENS INSTITUTE OF TECHNOLOGY

Graduate School, Wesley J. Howe School of Technology Management, Program in Information Systems, Computer Science Track, Hoboken, NJ 07030

AWARDS MS.

Expenses: Tuition: Full-time $13,950; part-time $775 per credit. Required fees: $180. One-time fee: $180 part-time. Full-time tuition and fees vary according to degree level and program.

■ STONY BROOK UNIVERSITY, STATE UNIVERSITY OF NEW YORK

Graduate School, College of Engineering and Applied Sciences, Department of Computer Science, Stony Brook, NY 11794

AWARDS Computer science (MS, PhD); software engineering (Certificate).

Faculty: 29 full-time (3 women), 3 part-time/adjunct (0 women).
Students: 184 full-time (46 women), 60 part-time (9 women); includes 19 minority (3 African Americans, 16 Asian Americans or Pacific Islanders), 196 international. 634 applicants, 40% accepted. In 2001, 57 master's, 7 doctorates, 1 other advanced degree awarded.
Degree requirements: For master's, thesis or alternative; for doctorate, thesis/dissertation, comprehensive exam.
Entrance requirements: For master's and doctorate, GRE General Test, TOEFL. *Application deadline:* For fall admission, 1/15. *Application fee:* $50.
Expenses: Tuition, state resident: full-time $5,100; part-time $213 per credit. Tuition, nonresident: full-time $8,416; part-time $351 per credit. Required fees: $496.
Financial support: In 2001–02, 3 fellowships, 73 research assistantships, 98 teaching assistantships were awarded.

Faculty research: Artificial intelligence, computer architecture, database management systems, VLSI, operating systems. *Total annual research expenditures:* $2.2 million.
Dr. Arie Kaufman, Chairman, 631-632-8470.
Application contact: Dr. Michael Kiefer, Director, 631-632-8443, *Fax:* 631-632-8334, *E-mail:* mkiefer@notes.cc.sunysb.edu. *Web site:* http://www.cs.sunysb.edu/
Find an in-depth description at www.petersons.com/gradchannel.

■ SUFFOLK UNIVERSITY

College of Arts and Sciences, Department of Mathematics and Computer Science, Boston, MA 02108-2770

AWARDS Computer science (MS). Part-time and evening/weekend programs available.

Students: 26 full-time (7 women), 14 part-time (6 women); includes 3 minority (all Asian Americans or Pacific Islanders), 30 international. Average age 27. 43 applicants, 70% accepted, 7 enrolled. In 2001, 5 degrees awarded.
Degree requirements: For master's, thesis optional.
Application deadline: For fall admission, 6/15 (priority date); for spring admission, 11/15 (priority date). Applications are processed on a rolling basis. *Application fee:* $35.
Expenses: Contact institution.
Financial support: In 2001–02, 24 students received support, including 2 fellowships with full and partial tuition reimbursements available (averaging $5,310 per year); career-related internships or fieldwork, Federal Work-Study, and institutionally sponsored loans also available. Financial award application deadline: 3/15; financial award applicants required to submit FAFSA.
Dan Stefanescu, Graduate Program Director, 617-573-8251, *Fax:* 617-573-8591, *E-mail:* dstefane@suffolk.edu.
Application contact: Judith Reynolds, Director of Graduate Admissions, 617-573-8302, *Fax:* 617-523-0116, *E-mail:* grad.admission@suffolk.edu. *Web site:* http://www.cs.suffolk.edu/gradcs/html

■ SYRACUSE UNIVERSITY

Graduate School, L. C. Smith College of Engineering and Computer Science, Department of Electrical Engineering and Computer Science, Program in Computer and Information Science, Syracuse, NY 13244-0003

AWARDS Computer and information science (PhD); computer science (MS).

Students: 239 full-time (14 women), 14 part-time (4 women), 228 international. Average age 28. In 2001, 176 master's, 77 doctorates awarded.

Degree requirements: For master's and doctorate, thesis/dissertation.
Entrance requirements: For master's and doctorate, GRE General Test, GRE Subject Test. *Application deadline:* Applications are processed on a rolling basis. *Application fee:* $50.
Expenses: Tuition: Full-time $15,528; part-time $647 per credit. Required fees: $420; $38 per term. Tuition and fees vary according to program.
Financial support: Fellowships, research assistantships, teaching assistantships, Federal Work-Study and tuition waivers (partial) available. Financial award application deadline: 1/10.
Dr. Kishan Mehrotra, Program Director, 315-443-2811, *Fax:* 315-443-2583, *E-mail:* kishan@ecs.syr.edu.
Application contact: Barbara Hazard, Information Contact, 315-443-2655, *Fax:* 315-443-2583, *E-mail:* bahazard@syr.edu. *Web site:* http://www.ecs.syr.edu/
Find an in-depth description at www.petersons.com/gradchannel.

■ TARLETON STATE UNIVERSITY

College of Graduate Studies, College of Business Administration, Stephenville, TX 76402

AWARDS Business administration (MBA); computer and information systems (MS). Part-time and evening/weekend programs available. Postbaccalaureate distance learning degree programs offered (minimal on-campus study).

Degree requirements: For master's, comprehensive exam.
Entrance requirements: For master's, GMAT or GRE General Test. *Web site:* http://www.tarleton.edu

■ TEMPLE UNIVERSITY

Graduate School, College of Science and Technology, Department of Computer and Information Sciences, Philadelphia, PA 19122-6096

AWARDS MS, PhD. Part-time programs available. Terminal master's awarded for partial completion of doctoral program.

Degree requirements: For doctorate, thesis/dissertation.
Entrance requirements: For master's and doctorate, GRE General Test, TOEFL, minimum GPA of 2.8. Electronic applications accepted.
Expenses: Tuition, state resident: full-time $8,487; part-time $369 per credit hour. Tuition, nonresident: full-time $12,282; part-time $534 per credit hour. Required fees: $350. Tuition and fees vary according to course load, program and reciprocity agreements.
Faculty research: Artificial intelligence, information systems, software engineering, network-distributed systems. *Web site:* http://www.cis.temple.edu/

■ TEXAS A&M UNIVERSITY

College of Engineering, Department of Computer Science, College Station, TX 77843

AWARDS Computer engineering (MCE, MS, PhD); computer science (MCS, MS, PhD). Part-time programs available.

Faculty: 39.
Students: 263 (59 women). Average age 28.
Degree requirements: For master's, thesis (MS); for doctorate, thesis/dissertation.
Entrance requirements: For master's and doctorate, GRE General Test, TOEFL. *Application deadline:* For fall admission, 5/1 (priority date). *Application fee:* $50 ($75 for international students).
Expenses: Tuition, state resident: full-time $11,872. Tuition, nonresident: full-time $17,892.
Financial support: Fellowships with full tuition reimbursements, research assistantships, teaching assistantships available. Financial award application deadline: 3/1.
Faculty research: Software development, numerical applications and controls, data structures.
Dr. Jennifer Welch, Interim Head, 979-845-5534, *Fax:* 979-847-8578, *E-mail:* csdept@cs.tamu.edu.
Application contact: Dr. S. Bart Childs, Graduate Advisor, 979-845-8981, *E-mail:* grad-advisor@cs.tamu.edu. *Web site:* http://www.cs.tamu.edu/

Find an in-depth description at www.petersons.com/gradchannel.

■ TEXAS A&M UNIVERSITY– COMMERCE

Graduate School, College of Arts and Sciences, Department of Computer Science and Information Systems, Commerce, TX 75429-3011

AWARDS Computer science (MS). Part-time programs available.

Faculty: 9 full-time (1 woman).
Students: 180 full-time (21 women), 57 part-time (12 women); includes 10 minority (8 Asian Americans or Pacific Islanders, 1 Hispanic American, 1 Native American), 215 international. Average age 36. 56 applicants, 96% accepted. In 2001, 54 degrees awarded.
Degree requirements: For master's, thesis (for some programs), comprehensive exam.
Entrance requirements: For master's, GMAT or GRE General Test. *Application deadline:* For fall admission, 6/1 (priority date); for spring admission, 11/1 (priority date). Applications are processed on a rolling basis. *Application fee:* $0 ($25 for international students). Electronic applications accepted.
Expenses: Tuition, state resident: full-time $2,221. International tuition: $7,285 full-time.

Financial support: In 2001–02, research assistantships (averaging $7,875 per year), teaching assistantships (averaging $7,875 per year) were awarded. Federal Work-Study and institutionally sponsored loans also available. Financial award application deadline: 5/1; financial award applicants required to submit FAFSA.
Faculty research: Programming.
Dr. Sam Saffer, Head, 903-886-5409, *Fax:* 903-886-5404.
Application contact: Tammi Higginbotham, Graduate Admissions Adviser, 843-886-5167, *Fax:* 843-886-5165, *E-mail:* tammi_higginbotham@tamu-commerce.edu. *Web site:* http://www.bobcat.tamu-commerce.edu/homepage

■ TEXAS A&M UNIVERSITY– CORPUS CHRISTI

Graduate Programs, College of Science and Technology, Program in Computing and Mathematical Sciences, Corpus Christi, TX 78412-5503

AWARDS Computer science (MS); mathematics (MS). Part-time and evening/weekend programs available.

Degree requirements: For master's, thesis.
Entrance requirements: For master's, GRE General Test. Electronic applications accepted.

■ TEXAS A&M UNIVERSITY– KINGSVILLE

College of Graduate Studies, College of Engineering, Department of Electrical Engineering and Computer Science, Program in Computer Science, Kingsville, TX 78363

AWARDS MS.

Students: 14 full-time (1 woman), 3 part-time, (all international). Average age 24. In 2001, 3 degrees awarded.
Degree requirements: For master's, thesis or alternative, comprehensive exam.
Entrance requirements: For master's, GRE General Test, TOEFL, minimum GPA of 3.0. *Application deadline:* For fall admission, 6/1; for spring admission, 11/15. Applications are processed on a rolling basis. *Application fee:* $15 ($25 for international students).
Expenses: Tuition, state resident: part-time $42 per hour. Tuition, nonresident: part-time $253 per hour. Required fees: $56 per hour. One-time fee: $46 part-time. Tuition and fees vary according to program.
Financial support: Research assistantships available. Financial award application deadline: 5/15.
Faculty research: Operating systems, programming languages, database systems, computer architecture, artificial intelligence.

Dr. Rajab Challoo, Coordinator, 361-593-2001.
Application contact: H. D. Gorakhpurwalla, Graduate Coordinator, 361-593-2004.

■ TEXAS TECH UNIVERSITY

Graduate School, College of Engineering, Department of Computer Science, Lubbock, TX 79409

AWARDS Computer science (MS, PhD); software engineering (MS). Part-time programs available.

Faculty: 11 full-time (2 women).
Students: 59 full-time (13 women), 18 part-time (5 women); includes 4 minority (1 Asian American or Pacific Islander, 3 Hispanic Americans), 59 international. Average age 28. 224 applicants, 38% accepted, 17 enrolled. In 2001, 15 master's, 1 doctorate awarded.
Degree requirements: For master's and doctorate, thesis/dissertation.
Entrance requirements: For master's and doctorate, GRE General Test, minimum GPA of 3.0. *Application deadline:* Applications are processed on a rolling basis. *Application fee:* $25 ($50 for international students). Electronic applications accepted.
Expenses: Tuition, state resident: full-time $1,926; part-time $107 per credit hour. Tuition, nonresident: full-time $5,724; part-time $318 per credit hour. Required fees: $779; $737 per year. Tuition and fees vary according to course level, course load and program.
Financial support: In 2001–02, 22 students received support, including 8 research assistantships with partial tuition reimbursements available (averaging $12,015 per year), 12 teaching assistantships with partial tuition reimbursements available (averaging $10,100 per year); fellowships, Federal Work-Study and institutionally sponsored loans also available. Support available to part-time students. Financial award application deadline: 5/1; financial award applicants required to submit FAFSA.
Faculty research: Generic controller software development, neural networks/speech recognition, neural-type network for solving 2-point boundary value. *Total annual research expenditures:* $766,366.
Dr. Daniel Earl Cooke, Chair, 806-742-3527, *Fax:* 806-742-3519.
Application contact: Graduate Adviser, 806-742-3527, *Fax:* 806-742-3519. *Web site:* http://www.cs.ttu.edu/

■ TOWSON UNIVERSITY

Graduate School, Program in Computer Science, Towson, MD 21252-0001

AWARDS MS. Part-time and evening/weekend programs available.

Faculty: 4 full-time (0 women).
Students: 211. In 2001, 78 degrees awarded.

Degree requirements: For master's, exam, thesis optional.
Application deadline: Applications are processed on a rolling basis. *Application fee:* $40. Electronic applications accepted.
Expenses: Tuition, state resident: part-time $211 per credit. Tuition, nonresident: part-time $435 per credit. Required fees: $52 per credit.
Financial support: Federal Work-Study and unspecified assistantships available. Support available to part-time students. Financial award application deadline: 4/1; financial award applicants required to submit FAFSA.
Faculty research: Deductive databases, neural nets, software engineering, data communications and networks.
Dr. Ramesh Karne, Director, 410-704-3955, *Fax:* 410-704-3868, *E-mail:* rkarne@towson.edu.
Application contact: 410-704-2501, *Fax:* 410-704-4675, *E-mail:* grads@towson.edu.

■ TUFTS UNIVERSITY

Division of Graduate and Continuing Studies and Research, Graduate and Professional Studies, Computer Science Program, Medford, MA 02155
AWARDS Certificate. Part-time and evening/weekend programs available.

Students: Average age 29. 1 applicant, 100% accepted. In 2001, 2 degrees awarded.
Application deadline: For fall admission, 8/15 (priority date); for spring admission, 12/12 (priority date). Applications are processed on a rolling basis. *Application fee:* $50. Electronic applications accepted.
Expenses: Tuition: Full-time $26,853. Full-time tuition and fees vary according to program.
Financial support: Available to part-time students. Application deadline: 5/1.
Alida Poirier, Assistant Director, 617-627-3395, *Fax:* 617-627-3016, *E-mail:* pcs@ase.tufts.edu.
Application contact: Information Contact, 617-627-3395, *Fax:* 617-627-3016, *E-mail:* pcs@ase.tufts.edu. *Web site:* http://ase.tufts.edu/gradstudy

■ TUFTS UNIVERSITY

Division of Graduate and Continuing Studies and Research, Graduate and Professional Studies, Post-baccalaureate Minor Program in Computer Science, Medford, MA 02155
AWARDS Certificate. Part-time and evening/weekend programs available.

Students: Average age 28. 8 applicants, 100% accepted. In 2001, 2 degrees awarded.
Application deadline: For fall admission, 8/15 (priority date); for spring admission, 12/12 (priority date). Applications are processed on a rolling basis. *Application fee:* $50. Electronic applications accepted.

Expenses: Tuition: Full-time $26,853. Full-time tuition and fees vary according to program.
Financial support: Application deadline: 5/1.
Alida Poirier, Assistant Director, 617-627-3395, *Fax:* 617-627-3016, *E-mail:* pcs@ase.tufts.edu.
Application contact: Information Contact, 617-627-3395, *Fax:* 617-627-3016, *E-mail:* pcs@ase.tufts.edu. *Web site:* http://ase.tufts.edu/gradstudy

■ TUFTS UNIVERSITY

Division of Graduate and Continuing Studies and Research, Graduate School of Arts and Sciences, School of Engineering, Department of Electrical Engineering and Computer Science, Medford, MA 02155
AWARDS Computer science (MS, PhD); electrical engineering (MS, PhD). Part-time programs available.

Faculty: 17 full-time, 5 part-time/adjunct.
Students: 123 (37 women); includes 16 minority (1 African American, 10 Asian Americans or Pacific Islanders, 4 Hispanic Americans, 1 Native American) 43 international. 154 applicants, 49% accepted. In 2001, 30 master's, 2 doctorates awarded. Terminal master's awarded for partial completion of doctoral program.
Degree requirements: For master's, thesis or alternative; for doctorate, thesis/dissertation.
Entrance requirements: For master's and doctorate, GRE General Test, TOEFL.
Application deadline: For fall admission, 3/1; for spring admission, 10/15. Applications are processed on a rolling basis. *Application fee:* $50. Electronic applications accepted.
Expenses: Tuition: Full-time $26,853. Full-time tuition and fees vary according to program.
Financial support: Research assistantships with full and partial tuition reimbursements, teaching assistantships with full and partial tuition reimbursements, Federal Work-Study, scholarships/grants, and tuition waivers (partial) available. Financial award application deadline: 2/15; financial award applicants required to submit FAFSA.
Jim Schmolze, Chair, 617-627-3217, *Fax:* 617-627-3220.
Application contact: Anselm Blumer, Information Contact, 617-623-3217, *Fax:* 617-627-3220, *E-mail:* webmaster@eecs.tufts.edu. *Web site:* http://www.cs.tufts.edu/

■ TULANE UNIVERSITY

School of Engineering, Department of Computer Science, New Orleans, LA 70118-5669
AWARDS MS, MSCS, PhD, Sc D. MS and PhD offered through the Graduate School. Part-time programs available. Terminal

master's awarded for partial completion of doctoral program.
Degree requirements: For master's, thesis or alternative; for doctorate, thesis/dissertation.
Entrance requirements: For master's and doctorate, GRE General Test, TOEFL, minimum B average in undergraduate course work.
Expenses: Tuition: Full-time $24,675. Required fees: $2,210.
Faculty research: Software engineering, robotics, artificial intelligence, fuzzy sets, programming languages, neural nets.

■ UNION COLLEGE

Center for Graduate Education and Special Programs, Division of Engineering and Computer Science, Department of Computer Science, Schenectady, NY 12308-2311
AWARDS MS.

Students: 4 full-time (0 women), 11 part-time (1 woman), 2 international. Average age 35. 2 applicants, 100% accepted, 2 enrolled. In 2001, 7 degrees awarded.
Degree requirements: For master's, project, or thesis.
Entrance requirements: For master's, minimum GPA of 3.0. *Application deadline:* Applications are processed on a rolling basis. *Application fee:* $50.
Expenses: Contact institution.
Financial support: Health care benefits available.
Faculty research: Microprocessor applications.
Dr. David Hemmendinger, Chair, 518-388-6319.
Application contact: Rhonda Sheehan, Coordinator of Recruiting and Admissions, 518-388-6238, *Fax:* 518-388-6754, *E-mail:* sheehanr@union.edu. *Web site:* http://www.engineering.union.edu

■ UNIVERSITY AT BUFFALO, THE STATE UNIVERSITY OF NEW YORK

Graduate School, School of Engineering and Applied Sciences, Department of Computer Science and Engineering, Buffalo, NY 14260
AWARDS Computer science (MS, PhD). Part-time programs available.

Faculty: 31 full-time (6 women), 3 part-time/adjunct (1 woman).
Students: 173 full-time (46 women), 48 part-time (7 women); includes 5 minority (all Asian Americans or Pacific Islanders), 173 international. Average age 27. 584 applicants, 42% accepted. In 2001, 79 master's, 9 doctorates awarded. Terminal master's awarded for partial completion of doctoral program.
Degree requirements: For master's, thesis or alternative, registration; for

University at Buffalo, The State University of New York (continued)
doctorate, thesis/dissertation, comprehensive qualifying exam.
Entrance requirements: For master's and doctorate, GRE General Test, GRE Subject Test (computer science), TOEFL. *Application deadline:* For fall admission, 12/15. *Application fee:* $35. Electronic applications accepted.
Expenses: Tuition, state resident: full-time $6,118. Tuition, nonresident: full-time $9,434.
Financial support: In 2001–02, 99 students received support, including 3 fellowships with tuition reimbursements available (averaging $4,000 per year), 26 research assistantships with tuition reimbursements available (averaging $11,000 per year), 69 teaching assistantships with tuition reimbursements available (averaging $11,000 per year); career-related internships or fieldwork, Federal Work-Study, institutionally sponsored loans, and unspecified assistantships also available. Financial award application deadline: 12/15; financial award applicants required to submit FAFSA.
Faculty research: Artificial intelligence, computer vision, parallel architecture, operating systems, theory, VLSI, databases. *Total annual research expenditures:* $2.4 million.
Dr. Bharadwaj Jayaraman, Chairman, 716-645-3180 Ext. 141, *Fax:* 716-645-3464, *E-mail:* cse-chair@cse.buffalo.edu.
Application contact: Dr. Xin He, Director of Graduate Studies, 716-645-3180 Ext. 128, *Fax:* 716-645-3464, *E-mail:* cse-dgs@cse.buffalo.edu. *Web site:* http://www.cse.buffalo.edu/
Find an in-depth description at www.petersons.com/gradchannel.

■ **THE UNIVERSITY OF AKRON**

Graduate School, Buchtel College of Arts and Sciences, Department of Computer Science, Akron, OH 44325-0001
AWARDS MS.
Students: 36 full-time (13 women), 26 part-time (9 women); includes 4 minority (all Asian Americans or Pacific Islanders), 47 international. Average age 28. 55 applicants, 82% accepted, 21 enrolled. In 2001, 14 degrees awarded.
Degree requirements: For master's, seminar and comprehensive exam or thesis.
Entrance requirements: For master's, minimum GPA of 2.75. *Application deadline:* For fall admission, 3/1. Applications are processed on a rolling basis. *Application fee:* $25 ($50 for international students).
Expenses: Tuition, state resident: full-time $6,562; part-time $219 per credit. Tuition, nonresident: full-time $9,027; part-time $383 per credit. Required fees: $272; $11 per credit. Tuition and fees vary according to course load.

Financial support: Application deadline: 3/1.
Dr. Wolfgang Pelz, Chair, 330-972-7400, *E-mail:* wolfgangpelz@uakron.edu. *Web site:* http://www.cs.uakron.edu/

■ **THE UNIVERSITY OF AKRON**

Graduate School, Buchtel College of Arts and Sciences, Department of Theoretical and Applied Mathematics, Akron, OH 44325-0001
AWARDS Applied mathematics (MS); computer science (MS); mathematics (MS). Part-time and evening/weekend programs available.
Faculty: 27 full-time (6 women), 3 part-time/adjunct (0 women).
Students: 6 full-time (2 women), 4 part-time (2 women), 1 international. Average age 32. 21 applicants, 81% accepted, 5 enrolled. In 2001, 3 degrees awarded.
Degree requirements: For master's, seminar and comprehensive exam or thesis.
Entrance requirements: For master's, minimum GPA of 2.75. *Application deadline:* For fall admission, 3/1. Applications are processed on a rolling basis. *Application fee:* $40 ($50 for international students).
Expenses: Tuition, state resident: full-time $6,562; part-time $219 per credit. Tuition, nonresident: full-time $9,027; part-time $383 per credit. Required fees: $272; $11 per credit. Tuition and fees vary according to course load.
Financial support: In 2001–02, 1 research assistantship with full tuition reimbursement, 28 teaching assistantships with full tuition reimbursements were awarded. Tuition waivers (full) also available. Financial award application deadline: 3/1.
Faculty research: Numerical analysis.
Dr. Jianping Zhu, Chair, 330-972-7400, *E-mail:* jzhu@uakron.edu. *Web site:* http://www.math.uakron.cou/

■ **THE UNIVERSITY OF ALABAMA**

Graduate School, College of Engineering, Department of Computer Science, Tuscaloosa, AL 35487
AWARDS MSCS, PhD.
Faculty: 17 full-time (4 women).
Students: 44 full-time (13 women), 3 part-time (2 women); includes 1 minority (African American), 37 international. Average age 27. 218 applicants, 24% accepted, 19 enrolled. In 2001, 15 master's, 1 doctorate awarded.
Degree requirements: For master's, thesis or alternative; for doctorate, thesis/dissertation.
Entrance requirements: For master's, GRE General Test, minimum GPA of 3.0 in last 60 hours; for doctorate, GRE General Test, minimum GPA of 3.0. *Application deadline:* For fall admission, 7/6. Applications are processed on a rolling basis. *Application fee:* $25.
Expenses: Tuition, state resident: full-time $3,292; part-time $183 per credit hour.

Tuition, nonresident: full-time $8,912; part-time $495 per credit hour. Tuition and fees vary according to course load, campus/location and program.
Financial support: In 2001–02, 23 students received support, including 1 fellowship with full tuition reimbursement available, 8 research assistantships with full tuition reimbursements available (averaging $8,500 per year), 14 teaching assistantships with full tuition reimbursements available (averaging $8,500 per year); Federal Work-Study also available.
Faculty research: Software engineering, artificial intelligence, database management, algorithms, human-computer interaction. *Total annual research expenditures:* $4.9 million.
Dr. David Cordes, Head, 205-348-1671, *Fax:* 205-348-0219, *E-mail:* cs@cs.us.edu.
Application contact: Dr. Hui-Chuan Chen, Professor, 205-348-6363, *Fax:* 205-348-0219. *Web site:* http://cs.ua.edu/

■ **THE UNIVERSITY OF ALABAMA AT BIRMINGHAM**

Graduate School, School of Natural Sciences and Mathematics, Department of Computer and Information Sciences, Birmingham, AL 35294
AWARDS MS, PhD.
Students: 51 full-time (12 women), 29 part-time (10 women); includes 10 minority (all Asian Americans or Pacific Islanders), 61 international. 345 applicants, 51% accepted. In 2001, 30 master's, 2 doctorates awarded.
Degree requirements: For master's, thesis optional; for doctorate, thesis/dissertation.
Entrance requirements: For master's and doctorate, GRE General Test. *Application deadline:* Applications are processed on a rolling basis. *Application fee:* $35 ($60 for international students).
Expenses: Tuition, state resident: full-time $3,058. Tuition, nonresident: full-time $5,746. Tuition and fees vary according to course load, degree level and program.
Financial support: In 2001–02, 7 fellowships with full tuition reimbursements (averaging $13,200 per year), 2 research assistantships with full tuition reimbursements (averaging $13,200 per year), 9 teaching assistantships with full tuition reimbursements (averaging $13,200 per year) were awarded. Career-related internships or fieldwork, Federal Work-Study, institutionally sponsored loans, tuition waivers (full and partial), and unspecified assistantships also available. Support available to part-time students. Financial award application deadline: 3/10.
Faculty research: Theory and software systems, intelligent systems, systems architecture.

Dr. Warren T. Jones, Chairman, 205-934-2213, *Fax:* 205-934-5473, *E-mail:* wjones@uab.edu. *Web site:* http://www.cis.uab.edu/
Find an in-depth description at www.petersons.com/gradchannel.

■ THE UNIVERSITY OF ALABAMA IN HUNTSVILLE

School of Graduate Studies, College of Science, Department of Computer Science, Huntsville, AL 35899

AWARDS Computer science (MS, PhD); software engineering (Certificate). Part-time and evening/weekend programs available.

Faculty: 13 full-time (3 women), 2 part-time/adjunct (1 woman).
Students: 66 full-time (18 women), 65 part-time (14 women); includes 17 minority (6 African Americans, 10 Asian Americans or Pacific Islanders, 1 Hispanic American), 71 international. Average age 30. 134 applicants, 82% accepted, 54 enrolled. In 2001, 48 master's, 2 doctorates awarded.
Degree requirements: For master's, thesis or alternative, oral and written exams, comprehensive exam, registration; for doctorate, thesis/dissertation, oral and written exams, comprehensive exam, registration.
Entrance requirements: For master's and doctorate, GRE General Test, GRE Subject Test, minimum GPA of 3.0. *Application deadline:* For fall admission, 7/24 (priority date); for spring admission, 11/15 (priority date). Applications are processed on a rolling basis. *Application fee:* $35.
Expenses: Tuition, area resident: Part-time $175 per hour. Tuition, state resident: full-time $4,408. Tuition, nonresident: full-time $9,054; part-time $361 per hour.
Financial support: In 2001–02, 32 students received support, including 17 research assistantships with full and partial tuition reimbursements available (averaging $9,573 per year), 13 teaching assistantships with full and partial tuition reimbursements available (averaging $6,879 per year); fellowships with full and partial tuition reimbursements available, career-related internships or fieldwork, Federal Work-Study, institutionally sponsored loans, scholarships/grants, health care benefits, tuition waivers (full and partial), and unspecified assistantships also available. Support available to part-time students. Financial award application deadline: 4/1; financial award applicants required to submit FAFSA.
Faculty research: Numerical analysis, programming languages, software systems, artificial intelligence, visualization systems. *Total annual research expenditures:* $620,635.
Dr. Phillip Richards, Chair, 256-824-6088, *Fax:* 256-824-5093, *E-mail:* nrichardso@cs.uah.edu. *Web site:* http://www.merlin.cs.uah.edu/

■ UNIVERSITY OF ALASKA FAIRBANKS

Graduate School, College of Science, Engineering and Mathematics, Department of Mathematical Sciences, Fairbanks, AK 99775-7480

AWARDS Computer science (MS); mathematics (MAT, MS, PhD); statistics (MS). Part-time programs available.

Faculty: 16 full-time (2 women), 4 part-time/adjunct (0 women).
Students: 21 full-time (6 women), 5 part-time (3 women); includes 2 minority (1 African American, 1 Asian American or Pacific Islander), 14 international. Average age 30. 34 applicants, 65% accepted, 15 enrolled. In 2001, 7 degrees awarded. Terminal master's awarded for partial completion of doctoral program.
Degree requirements: For master's, project; for doctorate, one foreign language, thesis/dissertation, comprehensive exam.
Entrance requirements: For master's and doctorate, GRE General Test, GRE Subject Test, TOEFL. *Application deadline:* For fall admission, 4/1 (priority date); for spring admission, 11/1. *Application fee:* $35.
Expenses: Tuition, state resident: full-time $4,272; part-time $178 per credit. Tuition, nonresident: full-time $8,328; part-time $347 per credit. Required fees: $960; $60 per term. Part-time tuition and fees vary according to course load.
Financial support: In 2001–02, fellowships with tuition reimbursements (averaging $10,000 per year), research assistantships with tuition reimbursements (averaging $12,000 per year), teaching assistantships with tuition reimbursements (averaging $12,000 per year) were awarded. Career-related internships or fieldwork, Federal Work-Study, and scholarships/grants also available. Financial award application deadline: 4/1.
Faculty research: Numerical analysis, graph theory, statistics, theoretical computer science, algebra topology.
Dr. Dana L. Thomas, Head, 907-474-7332, *E-mail:* ffdlt@uaf.edu.

■ THE UNIVERSITY OF ARIZONA

Graduate College, College of Science, Department of Computer Science, Tucson, AZ 85721

AWARDS MS, PhD. Part-time programs available.

Faculty: 15 full-time (1 woman).
Students: 116 full-time (20 women), 3 part-time (1 woman); includes 2 minority (1 Asian American or Pacific Islander, 1 Hispanic American), 97 international. Average age 25. 508 applicants, 33% accepted, 61 enrolled. In 2001, 32 master's awarded. Terminal master's awarded for partial completion of doctoral program.
Degree requirements: For master's, thesis optional; for doctorate, thesis/dissertation. *Median time to degree:* Master's–2 years full-time; doctorate–6 years full-time.
Entrance requirements: For master's, GRE General Test, TOEFL, minimum GPA of 3.2; for doctorate, GRE General Test, GRE Subject Test, TOEFL, minimum undergraduate GPA of 3.5. *Application deadline:* For fall admission, 12/1; for spring admission, 6/1. Applications are processed on a rolling basis. *Application fee:* $45.
Expenses: Tuition, state resident: full-time $2,490; part-time $436 per unit. Tuition, nonresident: full-time $10,300; part-time $436 per unit. Full-time tuition and fees vary according to degree level and program.
Financial support: In 2001–02, 2 fellowships with full tuition reimbursements (averaging $10,000 per year), 27 research assistantships with full tuition reimbursements (averaging $12,719 per year), 19 teaching assistantships with full tuition reimbursements (averaging $12,719 per year) were awarded. Career-related internships or fieldwork, institutionally sponsored loans, scholarships/grants, and tuition waivers (full and partial) also available. Financial award application deadline: 12/1.
Faculty research: Operating systems, theory of computation, programming languages, databases, algorithms, networks, web searching, parallel and distributed systems. *Total annual research expenditures:* $2.5 million.
Dr. Peter J. Downey, Head, 520-621-2207, *Fax:* 520-621-4246.
Application contact: Sonia A. Economou, Graduate Coordinator, 520-621-4049, *Fax:* 520-621-4246, *E-mail:* gradadmissions@cs.arizona.edu. *Web site:* http://www.cs.arizona.edu/

■ UNIVERSITY OF ARKANSAS

Graduate School, J. William Fulbright College of Arts and Sciences, Department of Computer Science, Fayetteville, AR 72701-1201

AWARDS MS, PhD.

Students: 22 full-time (7 women), 8 part-time (3 women); includes 2 Asian Americans or Pacific Islanders, 18 international. 39 applicants, 54% accepted. In 2001, 12 degrees awarded.
Degree requirements: For doctorate, thesis/dissertation.
Application fee: $40 ($50 for international students).
Expenses: Tuition, state resident: full-time $3,553; part-time $197 per credit. Tuition, nonresident: full-time $8,411; part-time $467 per credit. Required fees: $42 per credit. Tuition and fees vary according to course load and program.
Financial support: In 2001–02, 11 fellowships, 32 research assistantships, 3 teaching assistantships were awarded. Career-related internships or fieldwork and Federal

University of Arkansas (continued)
Work-Study also available. Support available to part-time students. Financial award application deadline: 4/1; financial award applicants required to submit FAFSA. Aicha Elshabini, Chair, 479-575-6427.

■ UNIVERSITY OF ARKANSAS AT LITTLE ROCK

Graduate School, College of Information Science and Systems Engineering, Department of Computer Science, Little Rock, AR 72204-1099

AWARDS MS. Part-time and evening/weekend programs available.

Degree requirements: For master's, thesis optional.
Entrance requirements: For master's, GRE General Test, minimum GPA of 3.0; bachelor's degree in computer science, mathematics, or appropriate alternative.
Expenses: Tuition, state resident: full-time $3,006; part-time $107 per credit. Tuition, nonresident: full-time $6,012; part-time $357 per credit. Required fees: $22 per credit. Tuition and fees vary according to program.

■ UNIVERSITY OF BRIDGEPORT

School of Engineering, Department of Computer Science and Engineering, Bridgeport, CT 06601

AWARDS Computer engineering (MS); computer science (MS).

Faculty: 6 full-time (0 women), 5 part-time/adjunct (0 women).
Students: 127 full-time (30 women), 319 part-time (119 women); includes 2 African Americans, 27 Asian Americans or Pacific Islanders, 1 Native American, 404 international. Average age 30. 626 applicants, 69% accepted, 71 enrolled. In 2001, 109 degrees awarded.
Degree requirements: For master's, thesis optional.
Entrance requirements: For master's, TOEFL. *Application deadline:* For fall admission, 8/1 (priority date); for spring admission, 12/1 (priority date). Applications are processed on a rolling basis. *Application fee:* $25 ($35 for international students). Electronic applications accepted.
Expenses: Tuition: Part-time $385 per credit hour. Required fees: $50 per term. Tuition and fees vary according to degree level and program.
Financial support: In 2001–02, 58 students received support; research assistantships, teaching assistantships, career-related internships or fieldwork, Federal Work-Study, institutionally sponsored loans, and tuition waivers (partial) available. Support available to part-time students. Financial award application deadline: 6/1; financial award applicants required to submit FAFSA.

Dr. Stephen F. Grodzinsky, Chairman, 203-576-4145, *Fax:* 203-576-4766, *E-mail:* grodzinsky@bridgeport.edu.
Find an in-depth description at www.petersons.com/gradchannel.

■ UNIVERSITY OF CALIFORNIA, BERKELEY

Graduate Division, College of Engineering, Department of Electrical Engineering and Computer Sciences, Computer Science Division, Berkeley, CA 94720-1500

AWARDS MS, PhD.

Degree requirements: For master's, comprehensive exam or thesis; for doctorate, thesis/dissertation, qualifying exam.
Entrance requirements: For master's and doctorate, GRE General Test, GRE Subject Test, TOEFL, minimum GPA of 3.0.
Expenses: Tuition, nonresident: full-time $10,704. Required fees: $4,349.

■ UNIVERSITY OF CALIFORNIA, DAVIS

Graduate Studies, College of Engineering, Graduate Group in Computer Science, Davis, CA 95616

AWARDS MS, PhD.

Faculty: 42 full-time (1 woman).
Students: 121 full-time (29 women); includes 26 minority (23 Asian Americans or Pacific Islanders, 2 Hispanic Americans, 1 Native American), 47 international. Average age 27. 371 applicants, 35% accepted, 44 enrolled. In 2001, 33 master's, 8 doctorates awarded.
Degree requirements: For master's, thesis optional; for doctorate, thesis/dissertation.
Entrance requirements: For master's and doctorate, GRE General Test, GRE Subject Test, minimum GPA of 3.0. *Application deadline:* For fall admission, 1/15 (priority date). Applications are processed on a rolling basis. *Application fee:* $60. Electronic applications accepted.
Expenses: Tuition, state resident: full-time $4,831. Tuition, nonresident: full-time $15,725.
Financial support: In 2001–02, 96 students received support, including 23 fellowships with full and partial tuition reimbursements available (averaging $5,832 per year), 52 research assistantships with full and partial tuition reimbursements available (averaging $10,349 per year), 39 teaching assistantships with partial tuition reimbursements available (averaging $14,033 per year); career-related internships or fieldwork, Federal Work-Study, institutionally sponsored loans, scholarships/grants, traineeships, tuition waivers (full and partial), and readerships also available. Financial award

application deadline: 1/15; financial award applicants required to submit FAFSA.
Faculty research: Intrusion detection, malicious code detection, next generation light wave computer networks, biological algorithms, parallel processing.
Chip Martel, Graduate Chair, 530-754-2651, *Fax:* 530-752-4767, *E-mail:* martel@cs.ucdavis.edu.
Application contact: Kim Reinking, Graduate Staff Assistant, 530-752-7224, *Fax:* 530-752-4767, *E-mail:* reinking@cs.ucdavis.edu. *Web site:* http://www.cs.ucdavis.edu/

■ UNIVERSITY OF CALIFORNIA, IRVINE

Office of Research and Graduate Studies, Department of Information and Computer Science, Irvine, CA 92697

AWARDS MS, PhD.

Faculty: 39.
Students: 217 full-time (44 women), 14 part-time (4 women); includes 51 minority (49 Asian Americans or Pacific Islanders, 2 Hispanic Americans), 105 international. Average age 31. 755 applicants, 17% accepted, 60 enrolled. In 2001, 39 master's, 4 doctorates awarded. Terminal master's awarded for partial completion of doctoral program.
Degree requirements: For master's and doctorate, thesis/dissertation.
Entrance requirements: For master's and doctorate, GRE General Test, GRE Subject Test. *Application deadline:* For fall and spring admission, 1/15 (priority date); for winter admission, 10/15 (priority date). Applications are processed on a rolling basis. *Application fee:* $60. Electronic applications accepted.
Expenses: Tuition, nonresident: full-time $10,704. Required fees: $8,396. Tuition and fees vary according to course load, program and student level.
Financial support: Fellowships, research assistantships, teaching assistantships, institutionally sponsored loans and tuition waivers (full and partial) available. Financial award application deadline: 3/2; financial award applicants required to submit FAFSA.
Faculty research: Artificial intelligence, computer system design, software, biomedical computing, theory.
Debra J. Richardson, Chair, 949-824-7405, *Fax:* 949-824-3976, *E-mail:* djr@uci.edu.
Application contact: Kris Domiccio, Contact, 949-824-2277. *Web site:* http://www.ics.uci.edu/

Find an in-depth description at www.petersons.com/gradchannel.

■ UNIVERSITY OF CALIFORNIA, LOS ANGELES

Graduate Division, School of Engineering and Applied Science, Department of Computer Science, Los Angeles, CA 90095

AWARDS MS, PhD, MBA/MS.

Faculty: 26 full-time, 23 part-time/ adjunct.
Students: 273 full-time (43 women); includes 72 minority (2 African Americans, 63 Asian Americans or Pacific Islanders, 7 Hispanic Americans), 133 international. 649 applicants, 33% accepted, 78 enrolled. In 2001, 40 master's, 18 doctorates awarded.
Degree requirements: For master's, comprehensive exam or thesis; for doctorate, thesis/dissertation, qualifying exams.
Entrance requirements: For master's, GRE General Test, GRE Subject Test, minimum GPA of 3.0; for doctorate, GRE General Test, GRE Subject Test, minimum GPA of 3.25. *Application deadline:* For fall admission, 1/15; for winter admission, 8/15. *Application fee:* $60. Electronic applications accepted.
Expenses: Tuition, nonresident: full-time $10,244. Required fees: $3,609. Full-time tuition and fees vary according to program.
Financial support: In 2001–02, 15 fellowships, 170 research assistantships, 132 teaching assistantships were awarded. Federal Work-Study, institutionally sponsored loans, and tuition waivers (full and partial) also available. Financial award application deadline: 1/15; financial award applicants required to submit FAFSA.
Dr. Milos Ercegovac, Chair, 310-825-5414.
Application contact: Verra Morgan, Student Affairs Officer, 310-825-6830, *Fax:* 310-UCLA-CSD, *E-mail:* verra@ cs.ucla.edu. *Web site:* http:// www.cs.ucla.edu/

■ UNIVERSITY OF CALIFORNIA, RIVERSIDE

Graduate Division, Graduate Program in Computer Science, Riverside, CA 92521-0102

AWARDS Computer science (MS, PhD). Part-time programs available.

Faculty: 21 full-time (0 women), 1 part-time/adjunct (0 women).
Students: 83 full-time (28 women), 5 part-time (1 woman); includes 7 Asian Americans or Pacific Islanders, 63 international. Average age 29. 407 applicants, 18% accepted, 27 enrolled. In 2001, 17 master's, 1 doctorate awarded.
Degree requirements: For master's, project; for doctorate, thesis/dissertation, qualifying exams. *Median time to degree:* Master's–2 years full-time; doctorate–4 years full-time.

Entrance requirements: For master's and doctorate, GRE General Test, TOEFL, minimum GPA of 3.2. *Application deadline:* For fall admission, 5/1; for spring admission, 12/1. Applications are processed on a rolling basis. *Application fee:* $40.
Expenses: Tuition, state resident: full-time $5,001. Tuition, nonresident: full-time $15,897.
Financial support: In 2001–02, teaching assistantships (averaging $14,000 per year); fellowships, research assistantships, career-related internships or fieldwork, Federal Work-Study, institutionally sponsored loans, and tuition waivers (full and partial) also available. Financial award application deadline: 2/1; financial award applicants required to submit FAFSA.
Faculty research: Compiler construction, operating systems, theory of computation, computer architecture, computer networks, design automation.
Dr. Mart Molle, Chair, 909-787-7354, *Fax:* 909-787-4643.
Application contact: Terri Phonharath, Graduate Student Affairs, 909-787-5639, *Fax:* 909-787-4643, *E-mail:* gradadmissions@cs.ucr.edu. *Web site:* http:// www.cs.ucr.edu/graduate/

■ UNIVERSITY OF CALIFORNIA, SAN DIEGO

Graduate Studies and Research, Department of Computer Science and Engineering, La Jolla, CA 92093

AWARDS Computer engineering (MS, PhD); computer science (MS, PhD).

Faculty: 18.
Students: 207 (44 women). 1,086 applicants, 16% accepted, 72 enrolled. In 2001, 44 master's, 12 doctorates awarded.
Degree requirements: For doctorate, thesis/dissertation.
Entrance requirements: For master's and doctorate, GRE General Test. *Application deadline:* For fall admission, 1/8. *Application fee:* $40. Electronic applications accepted.
Expenses: Tuition, nonresident: full-time $10,434. Required fees: $4,883.
Faculty research: Analysis of algorithms, combinatorial algorithms, discrete optimization.
Mohan Paturi, Chair, 858-534-1126, *Fax:* 858-534-7029, *E-mail:* paturi@cs.ucsd.edu.
Application contact: Graduate Coordinator, 858-534-6005.

Find an in-depth description at www.petersons.com/gradchannel.

■ UNIVERSITY OF CALIFORNIA, SAN DIEGO

Graduate Studies and Research, Interdisciplinary Program in Cognitive Science, La Jolla, CA 92093

AWARDS Cognitive science/anthropology (PhD); cognitive science/communication (PhD); cognitive science/computer science and engineering (PhD); cognitive science/

linguistics (PhD); cognitive science/ neuroscience (PhD); cognitive science/ philosophy (PhD); cognitive science/ psychology (PhD); cognitive science/sociology (PhD). Admissions through affiliated departments.

Faculty: 57 full-time (12 women).
Students: 8 full-time (4 women). Average age 26. 2 applicants. In 2001, 2 degrees awarded.
Degree requirements: For doctorate, thesis/dissertation.
Entrance requirements: For doctorate, GRE General Test. *Application deadline:* Applications are processed on a rolling basis. *Application fee:* $0.
Expenses: Tuition, nonresident: full-time $10,434. Required fees: $4,883.
Faculty research: Cognition, neurobiology of cognition, artificial intelligence, neural networks, psycholinguistics.
Gary Cottrell, Director, 858-534-7141, *Fax:* 858-534-1128, *E-mail:* gcottrell@ ucsd.edu.
Application contact: Graduate Coordinator, 858-534-7141, *Fax:* 858-534-1128, *E-mail:* gradinfo@cogsci.ucsd.edu. *Web site:* http://cogsci.ucsd.edu/CURRENT/Cog-interdisciplinary.html

■ UNIVERSITY OF CALIFORNIA, SANTA BARBARA

Graduate Division, College of Engineering, Department of Computer Science, Santa Barbara, CA 93106

AWARDS MS, PhD.

Degree requirements: For master's, thesis or alternative; for doctorate, thesis/ dissertation.
Entrance requirements: For master's, GRE, TOEFL, minimum GPA of 3.0; for doctorate, GRE, TOEFL, minimum GPA of 3.5. Electronic applications accepted. *Web site:* http://www.cs.ucsb.edu/

■ UNIVERSITY OF CALIFORNIA, SANTA CRUZ

Division of Graduate Studies, School of Engineering, Department of Computer Science, Santa Cruz, CA 95064

AWARDS MS, PhD.

Faculty: 15 full-time.
Students: 105 full-time (31 women); includes 9 minority (1 African American, 5 Asian Americans or Pacific Islanders, 3 Hispanic Americans), 41 international. 437 applicants, 31% accepted. In 2001, 11 master's, 2 doctorates awarded.
Degree requirements: For master's, thesis; for doctorate, one foreign language, thesis/dissertation, qualifying exam. *Median time to degree:* Master's–9 years full-time; doctorate–4 years full-time.
Entrance requirements: For master's and doctorate, GRE General Test, GRE

University of California, Santa Cruz (continued)

Subject Test. *Application deadline:* For fall admission, 2/1. *Application fee:* $40.
Expenses: Tuition: Full-time $19,857.
Financial support: Fellowships, research assistantships, teaching assistantships, Federal Work-Study and institutionally sponsored loans available. Financial award application deadline: 2/1.
Faculty research: Algorithm analysis, artificial intelligence, computer graphics, information and communication theory, problem-solving techniques.
Dr. Phokion Kolaitis, Chairperson, 831-459-4768.
Application contact: Carol Mullane, Graduate Admissions, 831-459-2576, *E-mail:* jodi@cse.ucsc.edu. *Web site:* http://www.ucsc.edu/

Find an in-depth description at www.petersons.com/gradchannel.

■ **UNIVERSITY OF CENTRAL FLORIDA**

College of Engineering and Computer Sciences, Program in Computer Science, Orlando, FL 32816

AWARDS MS, PhD. Part-time and evening/weekend programs available.

Faculty: 26 full-time (3 women), 8 part-time/adjunct (2 women).
Students: 110 full-time (23 women), 66 part-time (13 women); includes 35 minority (4 African Americans, 25 Asian Americans or Pacific Islanders, 6 Hispanic Americans), 93 international. Average age 27. 329 applicants, 62% accepted, 63 enrolled. In 2001, 44 master's, 5 doctorates awarded.
Degree requirements: For master's, thesis or alternative; for doctorate, thesis/dissertation, candidacy exam, departmental qualifying exam.
Entrance requirements: For master's, GRE General Test, GRE Subject Test, TOEFL, minimum GPA of 3.0 in last 60 hours; for doctorate, GRE Subject Test, TOEFL, minimum GPA of 3.0 in last 60 hours. *Application deadline:* For fall admission, 7/15 (priority date); for spring admission, 12/1 (priority date). *Application fee:* $20. Electronic applications accepted.
Expenses: Tuition, state resident: part-time $162 per hour. Tuition, nonresident: part-time $569 per hour.
Financial support: In 2001–02, 17 fellowships with partial tuition reimbursements (averaging $3,338 per year), 192 research assistantships with partial tuition reimbursements (averaging $3,490 per year), 94 teaching assistantships with partial tuition reimbursements (averaging $5,143 per year) were awarded. Career-related internships or fieldwork, Federal Work-Study, institutionally sponsored loans, tuition waivers (partial), and unspecified assistantships also available. Financial award application deadline: 3/1;

financial award applicants required to submit FAFSA.
Faculty research: Parallel processing, databases, algorithms, virtual reality.
Dr. Erol Gelenbe, Chair, 407-823-2311, *Fax:* 407-823-5419, *E-mail:* erol@cs.ucf.edu.
Application contact: Dr. Ronald Dutton, Coordinator, 407-823-2341, *Fax:* 407-823-5419, *E-mail:* dutton@cs.ucf.edu. *Web site:* http://www.ucf.edu/

■ **UNIVERSITY OF CENTRAL OKLAHOMA**

College of Graduate Studies and Research, College of Mathematics and Science, Department of Mathematics and Statistics, Edmond, OK 73034-5209

AWARDS Applied mathematical sciences (MS), including computer science, mathematics, mathematics/computer science teaching, statistics. Part-time programs available.

Degree requirements: For master's, thesis.
Faculty research: Curvature, FAA, math education. *Web site:* http://www.ucok.edu/graduate.applied.htm

■ **UNIVERSITY OF CHICAGO**

Division of the Physical Sciences, Department of Computer Science, Chicago, IL 60637-1513

AWARDS SM, PhD.

Faculty: 15 full-time (1 woman), 2 part-time/adjunct (0 women).
Students: 41 full-time (13 women); includes 2 minority (1 Asian American or Pacific Islander, 1 Hispanic American), 32 international. Average age 25. 181 applicants, 10% accepted. In 2001, 5 master's, 2 doctorates awarded. Terminal master's awarded for partial completion of doctoral program.
Degree requirements: For master's, thesis; for doctorate, one foreign language, thesis/dissertation.
Entrance requirements: For doctorate, GRE General Test, GRE Subject Test (strongly recommended). *Application deadline:* For fall admission, 1/5. Applications are processed on a rolling basis. *Application fee:* $55.
Expenses: Tuition: Full-time $16,548.
Financial support: In 2001–02, research assistantships with tuition reimbursements (averaging $13,950 per year), teaching assistantships with tuition reimbursements (averaging $14,400 per year) were awarded. Fellowships Financial award application deadline: 1/5.
Faculty research: Theory of computing, artificial intelligence, programming languages, computational geometry, scientific computing.
Prof. Stuart A. Kurtz, Chairman, 773-702-8070, *Fax:* 773-702-8487, *E-mail:* chair@cs.uchicago.edu.

Application contact: Margaret P. Jaffey, Student Support Representative, 773-702-6011, *Fax:* 773-702-8487, *E-mail:* admissions@cs.uchicago.edu. *Web site:* http://www.cs.uchicago.edu/

■ **UNIVERSITY OF CHICAGO**

Division of the Physical Sciences, Professional Master's Program in Computer Science, Chicago, IL 60637-1513

AWARDS SM. Program offered by the Department of Computer Science. Part-time and evening/weekend programs available.

Faculty: 5 full-time (0 women), 4 part-time/adjunct (1 woman).
Students: 49 full-time (17 women), 87 part-time (26 women); includes 45 minority (7 African Americans, 34 Asian Americans or Pacific Islanders, 4 Hispanic Americans), 12 international. Average age 30. 188 applicants. In 2001, 63 degrees awarded.
Entrance requirements: For master's, GRE. *Application deadline:* For fall admission, 6/1 (priority date); for winter admission, 10/1 (priority date); for spring admission, 12/1 (priority date). Applications are processed on a rolling basis. *Application fee:* $70. Electronic applications accepted.
Expenses: Tuition: Full-time $16,548.
Financial support: Institutionally sponsored loans available. Financial award applicants required to submit FAFSA.
Dr. Leo J. Irakliotis, Associate Chairman of the Computer Science Department and Program Director, 773-702-8070, *Fax:* 773-702-6209, *E-mail:* questions@masters.cs.uchicago.edu.
Application contact: Margaret P. Jaffey, Student Support Representative, 773-702-6011, *Fax:* 773-702-8487, *E-mail:* questions@masters.cs.uchicago.edu. *Web site:* http://www.masters.cs.uchicago.edu/

■ **UNIVERSITY OF CINCINNATI**

Division of Research and Advanced Studies, College of Engineering, Department of Electrical and Computer Engineering and Computer Science, Program in Computer Science, Cincinnati, OH 45221

AWARDS MS.

Degree requirements: For master's, thesis, registration.
Entrance requirements: For master's, GRE General Test, TOEFL. *Application deadline:* For fall admission, 2/1 (priority date). *Application fee:* $40.
Expenses: Tuition, state resident: part-time $2,698 per quarter. Tuition, nonresident: part-time $4,977 per quarter.
Financial support: Fellowships, tuition waivers (full) and unspecified assistantships available. Financial award application deadline: 2/1.

Application contact: Dieter Schmidt, Graduate Program Director, 513-556-1816, *Fax:* 513-556-7326, *E-mail:* dieter.schmidt@uc.edu. *Web site:* http://www.ececs.uc.edu/

Find an in-depth description at www.petersons.com/gradchannel.

■ UNIVERSITY OF CINCINNATI

Division of Research and Advanced Studies, College of Engineering, Department of Electrical and Computer Engineering and Computer Science, Program in Computer Science and Engineering, Cincinnati, OH 45221

AWARDS PhD.

Degree requirements: For doctorate, thesis/dissertation, registration.
Entrance requirements: For doctorate, GRE General Test, TOEFL. *Application deadline:* For fall admission, 2/1 (priority date). *Application fee:* $40.
Expenses: Tuition, state resident: part-time $2,698 per quarter. Tuition, nonresident: part-time $4,977 per quarter.
Financial support: Fellowships, tuition waivers (full) and unspecified assistantships available. Financial award application deadline: 2/1.
Application contact: Dieter Schmidt, Graduate Program Director, 513-556-1816, *Fax:* 513-556-7326, *E-mail:* dieter.schmidt@uc.edu. *Web site:* http://www.ececs.uc.edu/

Find an in-depth description at www.petersons.com/gradchannel.

■ UNIVERSITY OF COLORADO AT BOULDER

Graduate School, College of Engineering and Applied Science, Department of Computer Science, Boulder, CO 80309

AWARDS ME, MS, PhD.

Faculty: 27 full-time (3 women).
Students: 117 full-time (27 women), 24 part-time (9 women); includes 19 minority (1 African American, 13 Asian Americans or Pacific Islanders, 5 Hispanic Americans), 50 international. Average age 31. 211 applicants, 43% accepted. In 2001, 46 master's, 6 doctorates awarded.
Degree requirements: For master's, thesis or alternative, comprehensive exam; for doctorate, one foreign language, thesis/dissertation.
Entrance requirements: For master's, minimum undergraduate GPA of 3.0. *Application deadline:* For fall admission, 3/1 (priority date). Applications are processed on a rolling basis. *Application fee:* $50 ($60 for international students).
Expenses: Tuition, state resident: full-time $3,474. Tuition, nonresident: full-time $16,624.

Financial support: In 2001–02, 13 fellowships (averaging $5,320 per year), 16 research assistantships (averaging $18,744 per year), 12 teaching assistantships (averaging $17,543 per year) were awarded. Tuition waivers (full) also available. Financial award application deadline: 3/1.
Faculty research: Artificial intelligence, databases, hardware systems, hypermedia, machine learning. *Total annual research expenditures:* $6.2 million.
Clayton Lewis, Chair, 303-492-6657, *Fax:* 303-492-2844.
Application contact: Vicki Kunz, Graduate Adviser, 303-492-6361, *Fax:* 303-492-2844, *E-mail:* vicki@cs.colorado.edu. *Web site:* http://www.cs.colorado.edu/

■ UNIVERSITY OF COLORADO AT COLORADO SPRINGS

Graduate School, College of Engineering and Applied Science, Department of Computer Science, Colorado Springs, CO 80933-7150

AWARDS MS, PhD. Part-time programs available.

Faculty: 9 full-time (1 woman), 2 part-time/adjunct (1 woman).
Students: 57 full-time (18 women), 28 part-time (7 women); includes 4 minority (1 African American, 2 Asian Americans or Pacific Islanders, 1 Hispanic American), 11 international. Average age 33. In 2001, 18 master's awarded.
Degree requirements: For master's, oral final exam, thesis optional.
Entrance requirements: For master's, GRE General Test, TOEFL, minimum GPA of 3.0, 2 semesters of calculus, 1 other math course, previous course work in computer science. *Application deadline:* For fall admission, 7/1 (priority date); for spring admission, 12/1. Applications are processed on a rolling basis. *Application fee:* $60 ($75 for international students).
Expenses: Tuition, state resident: full-time $2,900; part-time $174 per credit. Tuition, nonresident: full-time $9,961; part-time $591 per credit. Required fees: $14 per credit. $141 per semester. Tuition and fees vary according to course load, program and student level.
Financial support: Teaching assistantships available.
Faculty research: Analytical intelligence, software engineering, networks, database systems, graphics. *Total annual research expenditures:* $170,000.
Dr. Robert W. Sebesta, Chairman, 719-262-3325, *Fax:* 719-262-3369, *E-mail:* rws@sneffels.uccs.edu.
Application contact: Marijke Augusteijn, Academic Adviser, 719-262-3325, *Fax:* 719-262-3369, *E-mail:* mfa@antero.uccs.edu. *Web site:* http://csweb.uccs.edu/

■ UNIVERSITY OF COLORADO AT DENVER

Graduate School, College of Engineering and Applied Science, Department of Computer Science, Denver, CO 80217-3364

AWARDS MS. Part-time and evening/weekend programs available.

Faculty: 10 full-time (2 women).
Students: 24 full-time (18 women), 96 part-time (76 women); includes 19 minority (1 African American, 15 Asian Americans or Pacific Islanders, 3 Hispanic Americans), 32 international. Average age 28. 102 applicants, 76% accepted, 42 enrolled. In 2001, 40 degrees awarded.
Degree requirements: For master's, thesis or alternative.
Entrance requirements: For master's, GRE. *Application deadline:* For fall admission, 2/1; for spring admission, 10/1. Applications are processed on a rolling basis. *Application fee:* $50 ($60 for international students). Electronic applications accepted.
Expenses: Tuition, state resident: full-time $3,284; part-time $198 per credit hour. Tuition, nonresident: full-time $13,380; part-time $802 per credit hour. Required fees: $444; $222 per semester.
Financial support: Research assistantships, teaching assistantships, career-related internships or fieldwork and Federal Work-Study available. Financial award application deadline: 3/1; financial award applicants required to submit FAFSA. *Total annual research expenditures:* $77,440.
Krzysztof Cios, Chair, 303-556-6314, *Fax:* 303-556-8369, *E-mail:* krys.clos@cudenver.edu.
Application contact: Laura Cuellar, Program Assistant, 303-556-4083, *Fax:* 303-556-8369, *E-mail:* lcuellar@carbon.cudenver.edu. *Web site:* http://carbon.cudenver.edu/public/compsci/

■ UNIVERSITY OF CONNECTICUT

Graduate School, School of Engineering, Field of Computer Science and Engineering, Storrs, CT 06269

AWARDS Artificial intelligence (MS, PhD); computer architecture (MS, PhD); computer science (MS, PhD); operating systems (MS, PhD); robotics (MS, PhD); software engineering (MS, PhD). Terminal master's awarded for partial completion of doctoral program.

Degree requirements: For master's, thesis or alternative; for doctorate, thesis/dissertation.
Entrance requirements: For master's and doctorate, GRE General Test.

■ UNIVERSITY OF DAYTON

Graduate School, College of Arts and Sciences, Department of Computer Science, Dayton, OH 45469-1300

AWARDS MCS. Part-time and evening/weekend programs available.

Faculty: 9 full-time (2 women), 8 part-time/adjunct (4 women).

Students: 5 full-time (1 woman), 32 part-time (7 women); includes 3 minority (all Asian Americans or Pacific Islanders), 20 international. Average age 23. 47 applicants, 77% accepted, 7 enrolled. In 2001, 8 degrees awarded.

Degree requirements: For master's, thesis or alternative, project or additional coursework. *Median time to degree:* Master's–2 years full-time, 3.5 years part-time.

Entrance requirements: For master's, GRE General Test, 4 undergraduate courses in computer science, minimum undergraduate GPA of 3.0. *Application deadline:* For fall admission, 8/1. Applications are processed on a rolling basis. *Application fee:* $30. Electronic applications accepted.

Expenses: Tuition: Full-time $5,436; part-time $453 per credit hour. Required fees: $50; $25 per term.

Financial support: In 2001–02, 5 students received support, including 4 teaching assistantships with tuition reimbursements available (averaging $9,000 per year)

Faculty research: Software engineering, networking, databases. *Total annual research expenditures:* $50,000.

Dr. James P. Buckley, Graduate Director, 937-229-3808, *Fax:* 937-229-4000, *E-mail:* james.buckley@notes.udayton.edu.

Application contact: Dr. Raghava Gowda, Graduate Director, 937-229-3808, *Fax:* 937-229-4000, *E-mail:* raghava.gowda@notes.udayton.edu. *Web site:* http://www.udayton.edu/~cps/graduate.html

■ UNIVERSITY OF DELAWARE

College of Arts and Science, Department of Computer and Information Sciences, Newark, DE 19716

AWARDS MS, PhD. Part-time programs available.

Faculty: 23 full-time (3 women), 3 part-time/adjunct (0 women).

Students: 97 full-time (26 women), 13 part-time (3 women); includes 10 minority (4 African Americans, 5 Asian Americans or Pacific Islanders, 1 Hispanic American), 66 international. Average age 30. 232 applicants, 42% accepted, 55 enrolled. In 2001, 24 master's, 6 doctorates awarded. Terminal master's awarded for partial completion of doctoral program.

Degree requirements: For master's, thesis optional; for doctorate, thesis/dissertation.

Entrance requirements: For master's and doctorate, GRE General Test, TOEFL.

Application deadline: For fall admission, 7/1; for spring admission, 12/1. Applications are processed on a rolling basis. *Application fee:* $50. Electronic applications accepted.

Expenses: Tuition, state resident: full-time $4,770; part-time $265 per credit. Tuition, nonresident: full-time $13,860; part-time $770 per credit. Required fees: $414.

Financial support: In 2001–02, 66 students received support, including 3 fellowships with full tuition reimbursements available (averaging $13,000 per year), 44 research assistantships with full tuition reimbursements available (averaging $13,000 per year), 19 teaching assistantships with full tuition reimbursements available (averaging $13,000 per year); tuition waivers (full) and unspecified assistantships also available. Financial award application deadline: 2/1.

Faculty research: Theory, computer algebra, graphics and computer vision, bioinformatics, high performance computing. *Total annual research expenditures:* $1.5 million.

Prof. M. Sandra Carberry, Chair, 302-831-2711, *Fax:* 302-831-8458, *E-mail:* gradprgm@cis.udel.edu.

Application contact: Dr. Paul D. Amer, Graduate Coordinator, 302-831-1944, *Fax:* 302-831-8458, *E-mail:* gradprgm@cis.udel.edu. *Web site:* http://www.cis.udel.edu/

Find an in-depth description at www.petersons.com/gradchannel.

■ UNIVERSITY OF DENVER

Graduate Studies, Faculty of Natural Sciences, Mathematics and Engineering, Department of Engineering, Denver, CO 80208

AWARDS Computer science and engineering (MS); electrical engineering (MS); management and general engineering (MSMGEN); materials science (PhD); mechanical engineering (MS). Part-time and evening/weekend programs available.

Faculty: 13 full-time (2 women), 3 part-time/adjunct (0 women).

Students: 17 (6 women) 11 international. 50 applicants, 62% accepted. In 2001, 11 degrees awarded. Terminal master's awarded for partial completion of doctoral program.

Degree requirements: For master's, thesis (for some programs); for doctorate, thesis/dissertation.

Entrance requirements: For master's and doctorate, GRE General Test, TOEFL, TSE. *Application deadline:* Applications are processed on a rolling basis. *Application fee:* $45.

Expenses: Tuition: Full-time $21,456.

Financial support: In 2001–02, 11 students received support, including 6 research assistantships with full and partial tuition reimbursements available (averaging $9,999 per year), 7 teaching assistantships with full and partial tuition reimbursements available (averaging

$10,782 per year); fellowships with full and partial tuition reimbursements available, career-related internships or fieldwork, Federal Work-Study, institutionally sponsored loans, and scholarships/grants also available. Financial award application deadline: 3/1; financial award applicants required to submit FAFSA.

Faculty research: Microelectrics, digital signal processing, robotics, speech recognition, microwaves, aerosols, x-ray analysis, acoustic emissions. *Total annual research expenditures:* $1 million.

Dr. James C. Wilson, Chair, 303-871-2102.

Application contact: Susie Montoya, Assistant to Chair, 303-871-2102. *Web site:* http://littlebird.engr.du.edu/

■ UNIVERSITY OF DENVER

Graduate Studies, Faculty of Natural Sciences, Mathematics and Engineering, Department of Mathematics and Computer Science, Denver, CO 80208

AWARDS Applied mathematics (MA, MS); computer science (MS); mathematics and computer science (PhD). Part-time programs available.

Faculty: 18 full-time (7 women), 1 (woman) part-time/adjunct.

Students: 61 (20 women); includes 6 minority (1 African American, 2 Asian Americans or Pacific Islanders, 1 Hispanic American, 2 Native Americans) 39 international. 121 applicants, 88% accepted. In 2001, 42 degrees awarded. Terminal master's awarded for partial completion of doctoral program.

Degree requirements: For master's, computer language, foreign language, or laboratory experience; for doctorate, one foreign language, thesis/dissertation, oral and written exams.

Entrance requirements: For master's and doctorate, GRE General Test, TOEFL. *Application deadline:* Applications are processed on a rolling basis. *Application fee:* $45.

Expenses: Tuition: Full-time $21,456.

Financial support: In 2001–02, 21 students received support, including 5 fellowships with full and partial tuition reimbursements available, 2 research assistantships with full and partial tuition reimbursements available (averaging $9,081 per year), 14 teaching assistantships with full and partial tuition reimbursements available (averaging $9,972 per year); career-related internships or fieldwork, Federal Work-Study, institutionally sponsored loans, and scholarships/grants also available. Support available to part-time students. Financial award application deadline: 3/1; financial award applicants required to submit FAFSA.

Faculty research: Real-time software, convex bodies, multidimensional data, parallel computer clusters. *Total annual research expenditures:* $163,312.

Dr. Scott Leuteneqqer, Chairperson, 303-871-2821.
Application contact: Roy James Rosa, Graduate Secretary, 303-871-3017. *Web site:* http://www.cs.du.edu/

■ UNIVERSITY OF DENVER

University College, Denver, CO 80208

AWARDS Applied communication (MSS); computer information systems (MCIS); environmental policy and management (MEPM); healthcare systems (MHS); liberal studies (MLS); library and information services (MLIS); public health (MPH); technology management (MoTM); telecommunications (MTEL). Part-time and evening/weekend programs available. Postbaccalaureate distance learning degree programs offered (no on-campus study).

Faculty: 167 part-time/adjunct (52 women).
Students: 1,244 (618 women); includes 177 minority (65 African Americans, 53 Asian Americans or Pacific Islanders, 54 Hispanic Americans, 5 Native Americans) 76 international. 54 applicants, 85% accepted. In 2001, 274 degrees awarded.
Entrance requirements: For master's, minimum undergraduate GPA of 3.0. *Application deadline:* For fall admission, 7/15 (priority date); for winter admission, 10/14 (priority date); for spring admission, 2/10 (priority date). Applications are processed on a rolling basis. *Application fee:* $25.
Expenses: Contact institution.
Financial support: In 2001–02, 174 students received support. *Total annual research expenditures:* $59,206.
Mike Bloom, Dean, 303-871-3141.
Application contact: Cindy Kraft, Admission Coordinator, 303-871-3969, *Fax:* 303-871-3303. *Web site:* http://www.du.edu/ucol/

■ UNIVERSITY OF DETROIT MERCY

College of Engineering and Science, Department of Mathematics and Computer Science, Program in Computer Science, Detroit, MI 48219-0900

AWARDS MSCS. Evening/weekend programs available.

Faculty: 5 full-time (1 woman).
Students: 24 full-time (6 women), 42 part-time (9 women); includes 4 minority (all Asian Americans or Pacific Islanders), 54 international. Average age 29. In 2001, 23 degrees awarded.
Entrance requirements: For master's, minimum GPA of 3.0. *Application deadline:* For fall admission, 8/1 (priority date). Applications are processed on a rolling basis. *Application fee:* $30 ($50 for international students).
Expenses: Tuition: Full-time $10,620; part-time $590 per credit hour. Required

fees: $400. Tuition and fees vary according to program.
Financial support: Fellowships, career-related internships or fieldwork available. Dr. Kevin Daimi, Director, 313-993-1022, *Fax:* 313-993-1166, *E-mail:* daimikj@udmercy.edu.

■ UNIVERSITY OF FLORIDA

Graduate School, College of Engineering, Department of Computer and Information Science and Engineering, Gainesville, FL 32611

AWARDS Computer and information science and engineering (ME); computer organization (MS, PhD, Engr); information systems (MS, PhD, Engr); manufacturing systems engineering (Certificate); software systems (MS, PhD, Engr).

Degree requirements: For master's, thesis (for some programs); for doctorate, thesis/dissertation.
Entrance requirements: For master's and doctorate, GRE General Test, minimum GPA of 3.0; for other advanced degree, GRE General Test. Electronic applications accepted.
Expenses: Tuition, state resident: part-time $164 per hour. Tuition, nonresident: part-time $571 per hour. Tuition and fees vary according to course level and program.
Faculty research: Artificial intelligence, networks security, distributed computing, parallel processing system, vision and visualization, database systems. *Web site:* http://www.cise.ufl.edu/academic/grad/

Find an in-depth description at www.petersons.com/gradchannel.

■ UNIVERSITY OF GEORGIA

Graduate School, College of Arts and Sciences, Department of Computer Science, Athens, GA 30602

AWARDS Applied mathematical science (MAMS); computer science (MS, PhD).

Faculty: 20 full-time (1 woman).
Students: 61 full-time (14 women), 15 part-time (6 women); includes 1 minority (African American), 60 international. 192 applicants, 23% accepted. In 2001, 26 master's awarded.
Degree requirements: For doctorate, thesis/dissertation.
Entrance requirements: For master's and doctorate, GRE General Test. *Application deadline:* For fall admission, 7/1 (priority date); for spring admission, 11/15. *Application fee:* $30. Electronic applications accepted.
Expenses: Tuition, state resident: full-time $2,376; part-time $132 per credit hour. Tuition, nonresident: full-time $9,504; part-time $528 per credit hour. Required fees: $236 per semester.
Financial support: Fellowships, research assistantships, teaching assistantships, unspecified assistantships available.

Dr. E. Rodney Canfield, Head, 706-542-3455, *Fax:* 706-542-2966, *E-mail:* erc@cs.uga.edu.
Application contact: Dr. John A. Miller, Graduate Coordinator, 706-542-3440, *Fax:* 706-542-2966, *E-mail:* jam@cs.uga.edu. *Web site:* http://www.cs.uga.edu/

■ UNIVERSITY OF HAWAII AT MANOA

Graduate Division, College of Arts and Sciences, College of Natural Sciences, Department of Information and Computer Sciences, Honolulu, HI 96822

AWARDS Communication and information science (PhD); computer science (PhD); information and computer sciences (MS); library and information science (MLI Sc, MLIS, PhD, Certificate, JD/MLI Sc, MLI Sc/MA, MLI Sc/MS), including advanced library and information science (Certificate), communication and information science (PhD), library and information science (MLI Sc). Part-time programs available.

Faculty: 17 full-time (2 women), 1 part-time/adjunct (0 women).
Students: 46 full-time (19 women), 14 part-time (2 women); includes 14 Asian Americans or Pacific Islanders. Average age 33. 73 applicants, 68% accepted. In 2001, 22 degrees awarded.
Application deadline: For fall admission, 10/15; for spring admission, 8/10. *Application fee:* $25 ($50 for international students).
Expenses: Tuition, state resident: full-time $2,160; part-time $1,980 per year. Tuition, nonresident: full-time $5,190; part-time $4,829 per year.
Financial support: In 2001–02, 23 students received support, including 8 research assistantships (averaging $15,375 per year), 10 teaching assistantships (averaging $13,173 per year); tuition waivers (full and partial) also available.
Faculty research: Software engineering, telecommunications, artificial intelligence, multimedia.
Dr. Stephen Y. Itoga, Chair, 808-956-7420, *E-mail:* itoga@hawaii.edu.
Application contact: Dr. Jan Stelovsky, Graduate Field Chairperson, 808-956-7175, *Fax:* 808-956-3548, *E-mail:* janst@hawaii.edu.

■ UNIVERSITY OF HOUSTON

College of Natural Sciences and Mathematics, Department of Computer Science, Houston, TX 77204

AWARDS MS, PhD. Part-time programs available. Postbaccalaureate distance learning degree programs offered.

Faculty: 15 full-time (1 woman), 10 part-time/adjunct (0 women).
Students: 191 full-time (52 women), 131 part-time (46 women); includes 39 minority (1 African American, 38 Asian

University of Houston (continued)

Americans or Pacific Islanders), 242 international. Average age 30. 460 applicants, 64% accepted. In 2001, 87 master's, 6 doctorates awarded. Terminal master's awarded for partial completion of doctoral program.

Degree requirements: For master's, thesis (for some programs); for doctorate, thesis/dissertation.

Entrance requirements: For master's and doctorate, GRE General Test, TOEFL. *Application deadline:* For fall admission, 10/1 (priority date); for spring admission, 5/1 (priority date). *Application fee:* $0 ($75 for international students).

Expenses: Tuition, state resident: full-time $1,512. Tuition, nonresident: full-time $5,310. Required fees: $1,308. Tuition and fees vary according to program.

Financial support: In 2001–02, 123 students received support, including 44 research assistantships with full tuition reimbursements available (averaging $9,990 per year), 63 teaching assistantships with full tuition reimbursements available (averaging $9,297 per year); Federal Work-Study and institutionally sponsored loans also available. Support available to part-time students. Financial award application deadline: 3/1; financial award applicants required to submit FAFSA.

Faculty research: Parallel and distributed systems, software engineering, numerical analysis, databases, graphics and virtual reality. *Total annual research expenditures:* $396,567.

Dr. Shou-Hsuan Huang, Interim Chair, 713-743-3381.

Application contact: Amanda Vaughan, Graduate Academic Adviser, 713-743-3364, *Fax:* 713-743-3335, *E-mail:* vaughan@cs.uh.edu. *Web site:* http://www.cs.uh.edu/

Find an in-depth description at www.petersons.com/gradchannel.

■ UNIVERSITY OF HOUSTON

College of Technology, Houston, TX 77204

AWARDS Construction management (MT); manufacturing systems (MT); microcomputer systems (MT); occupational technology (MSOT). Part-time and evening/weekend programs available.

Faculty: 11 full-time (5 women), 13 part-time/adjunct (4 women).

Students: 36 full-time (17 women), 60 part-time (21 women); includes 28 minority (16 African Americans, 4 Asian Americans or Pacific Islanders, 8 Hispanic Americans), 17 international. Average age 35. 33 applicants, 82% accepted. In 2001, 25 degrees awarded.

Entrance requirements: For master's, GMAT, GRE, or MAT (MSOT); GRE (MT), minimum GPA of 3.0 in last 60

hours. *Application deadline:* For fall admission, 7/1; for spring admission, 11/1. *Application fee:* $35 ($110 for international students).

Expenses: Tuition, state resident: full-time $1,512. Tuition, nonresident: full-time $5,310. Required fees: $1,308. Tuition and fees vary according to program.

Financial support: Fellowships, research assistantships, teaching assistantships, career-related internships or fieldwork, Federal Work-Study, and institutionally sponsored loans available. Support available to part-time students.

Faculty research: Educational delivery systems, technical curriculum development, computer-integrated manufacturing, neural networks. *Total annual research expenditures:* $354,283.

Uma G. Gupta, Dean, 713-743-4032, *Fax:* 713-743-4032.

Application contact: Holly Rosenthal, Graduate Academic Adviser, 713-743-4098, *Fax:* 713-743-4032, *E-mail:* hrosenthal@uh.edu. *Web site:* http://www.tech.uh.edu/

■ UNIVERSITY OF HOUSTON–CLEAR LAKE

School of Natural and Applied Sciences, Program in Computer Science, Houston, TX 77058-1098

AWARDS MS. Part-time and evening/weekend programs available.

Students: 204; includes 50 minority (46 Asian Americans or Pacific Islanders, 4 Hispanic Americans), 118 international. Average age 30. In 2001, 72 degrees awarded.

Entrance requirements: For master's, GRE General Test. *Application deadline:* For fall admission, 8/1; for spring admission, 12/1. Applications are processed on a rolling basis. *Application fee:* $30 ($70 for international students).

Expenses: Tuition, state resident: full-time $2,016; part-time $84 per credit hour. Tuition, nonresident: full-time $6,072; part-time $253 per credit hour. Tuition and fees vary according to course load.

Financial support: Research assistantships, teaching assistantships, career-related internships or fieldwork, Federal Work-Study, institutionally sponsored loans, and scholarships/grants available. Support available to part-time students. Financial award application deadline: 5/1.

Dr. Sadegh Davari, Chair, 281-283-3850, *Fax:* 281-283-3707, *E-mail:* davari@cl.uh.edu.

Application contact: Dr. Robert Ferebee, Associate Dean, 281-283-3700, *Fax:* 281-283-3707, *E-mail:* ferebee@cl.uh.edu.

■ UNIVERSITY OF IDAHO

College of Graduate Studies, College of Engineering, Department of Computer Science, Moscow, ID 83844-2282

AWARDS MS, PhD.

Faculty: 14 full-time (2 women).

Students: 22 full-time (8 women), 45 part-time (8 women); includes 4 minority (2 Asian Americans or Pacific Islanders, 2 Hispanic Americans), 29 international. 84 applicants, 52% accepted. In 2001, 8 master's, 1 doctorate awarded.

Degree requirements: For master's and doctorate, thesis/dissertation.

Entrance requirements: For master's, GRE General Test, TOEFL, minimum GPA of 3.0; for doctorate, minimum undergraduate GPA of 2.8, 3.0 graduate. *Application deadline:* For fall admission, 8/1; for spring admission, 12/15. *Application fee:* $35 ($45 for international students).

Expenses: Tuition, state resident: full-time $1,613. Tuition, nonresident: full-time $3,000.

Financial support: In 2001–02, 6 research assistantships (averaging $4,791 per year), 8 teaching assistantships (averaging $9,785 per year) were awarded. Career-related internships or fieldwork also available. Financial award application deadline: 2/15.

Faculty research: Artificial intelligence, theory of computation, software engineering.

Dr. John W. Dickinson, Interim Chair, 208-885-7227. *Web site:* http://www.cs.uidaho.edu/

Find an in-depth description at www.petersons.com/gradchannel.

■ UNIVERSITY OF ILLINOIS AT CHICAGO

Graduate College, College of Engineering, Department of Electrical Engineering and Computer Science, Program in Computer Science, Chicago, IL 60607-7128

AWARDS MS, PhD. Evening/weekend programs available.

Students: 134 full-time (28 women), 107 part-time (22 women); includes 19 minority (7 African Americans, 12 Asian Americans or Pacific Islanders, 178 international. Average age 26. 791 applicants, 13% accepted, 51 enrolled.

Degree requirements: For master's, thesis or alternative; for doctorate, thesis/dissertation, departmental qualifying exam.

Entrance requirements: For master's, TOEFL, BS in related field, minimum GPA of 3.75 on a 5.0 scale; for doctorate, GRE General Test, TOEFL, minimum GPA of 3.75 on a 5.0 scale, MS in related field. *Application deadline:* For fall admission, 6/7; for spring admission, 11/1. *Application fee:* $40 ($50 for international students).

Expenses: Tuition, state resident: full-time $3,060. Tuition, nonresident: full-time $6,688.

Financial support: In 2001–02, 127 students received support; fellowships, research assistantships, teaching assistantships, tuition waivers (full) available. Ugo Buy, Head, 313-996-8679.

Find an in-depth description at www.petersons.com/gradchannel.

■ UNIVERSITY OF ILLINOIS AT CHICAGO

Graduate College, College of Liberal Arts and Sciences, Department of Mathematics, Statistics, and Computer Science, Chicago, IL 60607-7128

AWARDS Applied mathematics (MS, DA, PhD); computer science (MS, DA, PhD); probability and statistics (MS, DA, PhD); pure mathematics (MS, DA, PhD); teaching of mathematics (MST).

Faculty: 69 full-time (4 women).
Students: 131 full-time (45 women), 26 part-time (8 women); includes 15 minority (1 African American, 6 Asian Americans or Pacific Islanders, 8 Hispanic Americans), 100 international. Average age 30. 222 applicants, 34% accepted, 24 enrolled. In 2001, 79 master's, 5 doctorates awarded.
Degree requirements: For master's, comprehensive exam; for doctorate, one foreign language, thesis/dissertation.
Entrance requirements: For master's and doctorate, GRE General Test, TOEFL, minimum GPA of 3.75 on a 5.0 scale. *Application deadline:* For fall admission, 6/1; for spring admission, 11/1. Applications are processed on a rolling basis. *Application fee:* $40 ($50 for international students). Electronic applications accepted.
Expenses: Tuition, state resident: full-time $3,060. Tuition, nonresident: full-time $6,688.
Financial support: In 2001–02, 107 students received support; fellowships with full tuition reimbursements available, research assistantships with full tuition reimbursements available, teaching assistantships with full tuition reimbursements available, Federal Work-Study and tuition waivers (full) available. Financial award application deadline: 3/1; financial award applicants required to submit FAFSA.
Jeremy Teitelbaum, Head, 312-996-3041, *E-mail:* jeremy@uic.edu.
Application contact: David Marker, Director of Graduate Studies, 312-996-3041.

Find an in-depth description at www.petersons.com/gradchannel.

■ UNIVERSITY OF ILLINOIS AT SPRINGFIELD

Graduate Programs, College of Liberal Arts and Sciences, Program in Computer Science, Springfield, IL 62703-5404

AWARDS MA.

Faculty: 5 full-time (1 woman), 11 part-time/adjunct (4 women).
Students: 56 full-time (14 women), 77 part-time (15 women); includes 12 minority (3 African Americans, 4 Asian Americans or Pacific Islanders, 5 Hispanic Americans), 69 international. Average age 29. 203 applicants, 71% accepted, 45 enrolled. In 2001, 12 degrees awarded.
Entrance requirements: For master's, GRE General Test, TOEFL, minimum undergraduate GPA of 2.7. *Application deadline:* Applications are processed on a rolling basis.
Expenses: Tuition, state resident: full-time $2,680. Tuition, nonresident: full-time $8,064. Required fees: $626. One-time fee: $626.
Financial support: In 2001–02, 73 students received support, including 19 research assistantships (averaging $6,300 per year); scholarships/grants also available. Financial award applicants required to submit FAFSA.
Faculty research: Software engineering, especially testing: reliability computer ethics, graph theoretic aspects of system communication, especially VSLI circuit layout. Ted Mims, Convener, 217-206-7326.

■ UNIVERSITY OF ILLINOIS AT URBANA–CHAMPAIGN

Graduate College, College of Engineering, Department of Computer Science, Champaign, IL 61820

AWARDS MCS, MS, MST, PhD.

Faculty: 38 full-time.
Students: 434 full-time (76 women); includes 41 minority (1 African American, 37 Asian Americans or Pacific Islanders, 1 Hispanic American, 2 Native Americans), 276 international. 987 applicants, 15% accepted. In 2001, 142 master's, 23 doctorates awarded.
Degree requirements: For master's and doctorate, thesis/dissertation.
Entrance requirements: For master's and doctorate, GRE General Test, minimum GPA of 3.0. *Application deadline:* For fall admission, 12/20. Applications are processed on a rolling basis. *Application fee:* $40 ($50 for international students). Electronic applications accepted.
Expenses: Tuition, state resident: part-time $3,227 per degree program. Tuition, nonresident: part-time $7,169 per degree program. Tuition and fees vary according to program.
Financial support: In 2001–02, 28 fellowships, 248 research assistantships, 96 teaching assistantships were awarded. Tuition

waivers (full and partial) also available. Financial award application deadline: 1/15. Marc Snir, Head, 217-333-3373, *Fax:* 217-333-3501, *E-mail:* snir@uiuc.edu.
Application contact: Barbara Cicone, Officer, 217-333-3425, *Fax:* 217-333-3501, *E-mail:* cicone@cs.uiuc.edu. *Web site:* http://www.cs.uiuc.edu/

Find an in-depth description at www.petersons.com/gradchannel.

■ THE UNIVERSITY OF IOWA

Graduate College, College of Liberal Arts and Sciences, Department of Computer Science, Iowa City, IA 52242-1316

AWARDS MCS, MS, PhD.

Faculty: 17 full-time, 1 part-time/adjunct.
Students: 47 full-time (14 women), 31 part-time (12 women); includes 7 minority (3 African Americans, 3 Asian Americans or Pacific Islanders, 1 Hispanic American), 54 international. 202 applicants, 10% accepted, 15 enrolled. In 2001, 29 master's, 4 doctorates awarded.
Degree requirements: For doctorate, thesis/dissertation, comprehensive exam.
Entrance requirements: For master's, GRE General Test, GRE Subject Test, TOEFL; for doctorate, GRE General Test, GRE Subject Test, TOEFL, minimum GPA of 3.0. *Application deadline:* For fall admission, 3/1; for spring admission, 10/1. *Application fee:* $30 ($50 for international students). Electronic applications accepted.
Expenses: Tuition, state resident: full-time $3,702; part-time $206 per semester hour. Tuition, nonresident: full-time $11,924; part-time $206 per semester hour. Required fees: $101 per semester. Tuition and fees vary according to course load and program.
Financial support: In 2001–02, 16 research assistantships, 41 teaching assistantships were awarded. Fellowships Financial award applicants required to submit FAFSA.
Steven C. Bruell, Chair, 319-335-0713.

■ UNIVERSITY OF KANSAS

Graduate School, School of Engineering, Department of Electrical Engineering and Computer Science, Program in Computer Science, Lawrence, KS 66045

AWARDS MS, PhD.

Students: 97 full-time (14 women), 16 part-time (5 women); includes 5 minority (3 Asian Americans or Pacific Islanders, 1 Hispanic American, 1 Native American), 70 international. Average age 26. 325 applicants, 19% accepted, 29 enrolled. In 2001, 15 master's, 1 doctorate awarded. Terminal master's awarded for partial completion of doctoral program.
Degree requirements: For master's, exam, thesis optional; for doctorate, one

University of Kansas (continued)
foreign language, thesis/dissertation, qualifying exams, comprehensive exam.
Entrance requirements: For master's, GRE, TOEFL, minimum GPA of 3.0; for doctorate, GRE, TOEFL, minimum GPA of 3.5. *Application deadline:* For fall admission, 2/1 (priority date); for spring admission, 10/15. Applications are processed on a rolling basis. *Application fee:* $40.
Expenses: Tuition, state resident: full-time $2,722; part-time $113 per credit. Tuition, nonresident: full-time $8,586; part-time $358 per credit. Required fees: $551; $46 per credit. Tuition and fees vary according to campus/location, program and reciprocity agreements.
Financial support: Fellowships, research assistantships with partial tuition reimbursements, teaching assistantships with full and partial tuition reimbursements, career-related internships or fieldwork available.
Application contact: John M. Gauch, Graduate Director, 785-864-4487, *Fax:* 785-864-3226, *E-mail:* grad_admissions@ eecs.ku.edu.

■ UNIVERSITY OF KENTUCKY

Graduate School, Graduate School Programs from the College of Engineering, Program in Computer Science, Lexington, KY 40506-0032

AWARDS MS, PhD.

Faculty: 21 full-time (2 women).
Students: 131 full-time (35 women), 25 part-time (6 women); includes 4 minority (all Asian Americans or Pacific Islanders), 120 international. 446 applicants, 51% accepted. In 2001, 43 degrees awarded.
Degree requirements: For master's, thesis optional; for doctorate, one foreign language, thesis/dissertation, comprehensive exam.
Entrance requirements: For master's, GRE General Test, minimum undergraduate GPA of 2.5; for doctorate, GRE General Test, minimum graduate GPA of 3.0. *Application deadline:* For fall admission, 7/19. Applications are processed on a rolling basis. *Application fee:* $30 ($35 for international students).
Expenses: Tuition, state resident: full-time $4,075; part-time $213 per credit hour. Tuition, nonresident: full-time $11,295; part-time $614 per credit hour.
Financial support: In 2001–02, 3 fellowships, 48 research assistantships, 34 teaching assistantships were awarded. Federal Work-Study and institutionally sponsored loans also available. Support available to part-time students.
Faculty research: Artificial intelligence and databases, communication networks and operating systems, graphics and vision, numerical analysis, theory. *Total annual research expenditures:* $174,500.
Dr. Jun Zhang, Director of Graduate Studies, 859-257-3892, *Fax:* 859-257-1971, *E-mail:* jzhang@cs.engr.uky.edu.

Application contact: Dr. Jeannine Blackwell, Associate Dean, 859-257-4905, *Fax:* 859-323-1928.

Find an in-depth description at www.petersons.com/gradchannel.

■ UNIVERSITY OF LOUISIANA AT LAFAYETTE

Graduate School, College of Engineering, Center for Advanced Computer Studies, Lafayette, LA 70504

AWARDS Computer engineering (MS, PhD); computer science (MS, PhD). Part-time programs available.

Faculty: 24 full-time (1 woman).
Students: 137 full-time (23 women), 34 part-time (8 women); includes 2 minority (1 Asian American or Pacific Islander, 1 Hispanic American), 153 international. 502 applicants, 57% accepted, 54 enrolled. In 2001, 73 master's, 6 doctorates awarded. Terminal master's awarded for partial completion of doctoral program.
Degree requirements: For master's, thesis or alternative; for doctorate, thesis/dissertation, final oral exam.
Entrance requirements: For master's, GRE General Test, TOEFL, minimum GPA of 2.75; for doctorate, GRE General Test, TOEFL, minimum GPA of 3.0. *Application deadline:* For fall admission, 5/15. *Application fee:* $20 ($30 for international students).
Expenses: Tuition, state resident: full-time $2,317; part-time $79 per credit. Tuition, nonresident: full-time $8,882; part-time $369 per credit. International tuition: $9,018 full-time.
Financial support: In 2001–02, 5 fellowships with full tuition reimbursements (averaging $13,900 per year), 34 research assistantships with full tuition reimbursements (averaging $6,868 per year), 23 teaching assistantships with full tuition reimbursements (averaging $6,868 per year) were awarded. Federal Work-Study and tuition waivers (full) also available. Financial award application deadline: 3/1.
Dr. Magdy A. Bayoumi, Chair, 337-482-6147.
Application contact: Dr. William Edwards, Graduate Coordinator, 337-482-6338.

Find an in-depth description at www.petersons.com/gradchannel.

■ UNIVERSITY OF LOUISIANA AT LAFAYETTE

Graduate School, College of Sciences, Department of Computer Science, Lafayette, LA 70504

AWARDS MS.

Students: 137 full-time (23 women), 34 part-time (8 women); includes 2 minority (1 Asian American or Pacific Islander, 1 Hispanic American), 153 international. 502

applicants, 57% accepted, 54 enrolled. In 2001, 65 degrees awarded.
Degree requirements: For master's, thesis or alternative.
Entrance requirements: For master's, GRE General Test, minimum GPA of 2.75. *Application deadline:* For fall admission, 5/15. *Application fee:* $20 ($30 for international students).
Expenses: Tuition, state resident: full-time $2,317; part-time $79 per credit. Tuition, nonresident: full-time $8,882; part-time $369 per credit. International tuition: $9,018 full-time.
Dr. Magdy A. Bayoumi, Chair, 337-482-6147. *Web site:* http://www.utc.edu/ ~bschool/

■ UNIVERSITY OF LOUISVILLE

Graduate School, Speed Scientific School, Department of Computer Engineering and Computer Science, Program in Computer Engineering and Computer Science, Louisville, KY 40292-0001

AWARDS M Eng, MS.

Students: 15 full-time (2 women), 37 part-time (9 women); includes 13 minority (2 African Americans, 10 Asian Americans or Pacific Islanders, 1 Hispanic American), 1 international. Average age 28. In 2001, 10 degrees awarded.
Degree requirements: For master's, thesis.
Entrance requirements: For master's, GRE General Test. *Application deadline:* Applications are processed on a rolling basis. *Application fee:* $25.
Expenses: Tuition, state resident: full-time $4,134. Tuition, nonresident: full-time $11,486.
Dr. Khaled A. Kamel, Chair, Department of Computer Engineering and Computer Science, 502-852-6304.

■ UNIVERSITY OF LOUISVILLE

Graduate School, Speed Scientific School, Department of Computer Engineering and Computer Science, Program in Computer Science, Louisville, KY 40292-0001

AWARDS MS.

Students: 26 full-time (11 women), 59 part-time (8 women); includes 5 minority (2 African Americans, 3 Asian Americans or Pacific Islanders), 69 international. In 2001, 41 degrees awarded.
Expenses: Tuition, state resident: full-time $4,134. Tuition, nonresident: full-time $11,486.
Dr. Khaled A. Kamel, Chair, Department of Computer Engineering and Computer Science, 502-852-6304.

■ UNIVERSITY OF LOUISVILLE

Graduate School, Speed Scientific School, Department of Computer Engineering and Computer Science, Program in Computer Science and Engineering, Louisville, KY 40292-0001

AWARDS PhD.

Students: 32 full-time (5 women), 4 part-time; includes 2 minority (both Asian Americans or Pacific Islanders), 27 international. Average age 29. In 2001, 2 degrees awarded.
Degree requirements: For doctorate, thesis/dissertation.
Entrance requirements: For doctorate, GRE General Test. *Application deadline:* Applications are processed on a rolling basis. *Application fee:* $25.
Expenses: Tuition, state resident: full-time $4,134. Tuition, nonresident: full-time $11,486.
Dr. Peter Aronhime, Director.

■ UNIVERSITY OF MAINE

Graduate School, College of Liberal Arts and Sciences, Department of Computer Science, Orono, ME 04469

AWARDS MS, PhD. Part-time programs available.

Faculty: 5 full-time (0 women), 1 part-time/adjunct (0 women).
Students: 14 full-time (8 women), 3 part-time (1 woman); includes 2 minority (1 Asian American or Pacific Islander, 1 Hispanic American), 11 international. 34 applicants, 32% accepted, 8 enrolled. In 2001, 1 master's, 1 doctorate awarded.
Degree requirements: For master's, thesis optional; for doctorate, thesis/dissertation.
Entrance requirements: For master's and doctorate, GRE General Test, GRE Subject Test, TOEFL. *Application deadline:* For fall admission, 2/1 (priority date). Applications are processed on a rolling basis. *Application fee:* $50. Electronic applications accepted.
Expenses: Tuition, state resident: full-time $3,780; part-time $210 per credit hour. Tuition, nonresident: full-time $10,782; part-time $599 per credit hour. Required fees: $9.5 per credit hour. $32 per semester. Tuition and fees vary according to reciprocity agreements.
Financial support: In 2001–02, 2 research assistantships with tuition reimbursements (averaging $15,775 per year), 9 teaching assistantships with tuition reimbursements (averaging $14,275 per year) were awarded. Career-related internships or fieldwork, Federal Work-Study, institutionally sponsored loans, and tuition waivers (full) also available. Financial award application deadline: 3/1.
Faculty research: Theory, software engineering, graphics, applications, artificial intelligence.

Dr. George Markowsky, Chair, 207-581-3941, *Fax:* 207-581-4977.
Application contact: Scott G. Delcourt, Director of the Graduate School, 207-581-3218, *Fax:* 207-581-3232, *E-mail:* graduate@maine.edu. *Web site:* http://www.umaine.edu/graduate/

■ UNIVERSITY OF MARYLAND, BALTIMORE COUNTY

Graduate School, College of Engineering, Department of Computer Science and Electrical Engineering, Program in Computer Science, Baltimore, MD 21250-5398

AWARDS MS, PhD.

Degree requirements: For doctorate, thesis/dissertation.
Entrance requirements: For master's and doctorate, GRE General Test, GRE Subject Test, minimum GPA of 3.2.
Faculty research: Artificial intelligence, quantum computation, computer and communication security, electronic commerce cryptology, computer graphics and animation.

■ UNIVERSITY OF MARYLAND, COLLEGE PARK

Graduate Studies and Research, College of Computer, Mathematical and Physical Sciences, Department of Computer Science, College Park, MD 20742

AWARDS MS, PhD. Part-time and evening/weekend programs available.

Faculty: 52 full-time (7 women), 8 part-time/adjunct (0 women).
Students: 152 full-time (30 women), 80 part-time (13 women); includes 15 minority (3 African Americans, 8 Asian Americans or Pacific Islanders, 3 Hispanic Americans, 1 Native American), 153 international. 751 applicants, 13% accepted, 38 enrolled. In 2001, 27 master's, 20 doctorates awarded. Terminal master's awarded for partial completion of doctoral program.
Degree requirements: For master's, thesis or alternative; for doctorate, thesis/dissertation.
Entrance requirements: For master's and doctorate, GRE General Test, GRE Subject Test, minimum GPA of 3.0. *Application deadline:* For fall admission, 1/15; for spring admission, 10/15. Applications are processed on a rolling basis. *Application fee:* $50 ($70 for international students). Electronic applications accepted.
Expenses: Tuition, state resident: part-time $289 per credit hour. Tuition, nonresident: part-time $448 per credit hour. One-time fee: $436 part-time. Full-time tuition and fees vary according to course load, campus/location and program.
Financial support: In 2001–02, 12 fellowships with full tuition reimbursements

(averaging $10,132 per year), 41 research assistantships with tuition reimbursements (averaging $14,821 per year), 81 teaching assistantships with tuition reimbursements (averaging $14,330 per year) were awarded. Career-related internships or fieldwork, Federal Work-Study, and scholarships/grants also available. Support available to part-time students. Financial award applicants required to submit FAFSA.
Faculty research: Artificial intelligence, computer applications, information processing.
Dr. Larry Davis, Chairperson, 301-405-2662, *Fax:* 301-405-6707.
Application contact: Trudy Lindsey, Director, Graduate Admissions and Records, 301-405-6991, *Fax:* 301-314-9305, *E-mail:* grschool@deans.umd.edu.

■ UNIVERSITY OF MARYLAND EASTERN SHORE

Graduate Programs, Department of Mathematics and Computer Sciences, Princess Anne, MD 21853-1299

AWARDS Applied computer science (MS).

Degree requirements: For master's, thesis or alternative, research project.
Entrance requirements: For master's, GRE General Test, TOEFL, minimum GPA of 3.0. Electronic applications accepted.
Faculty research: Parallel processing.

■ UNIVERSITY OF MASSACHUSETTS AMHERST

Graduate School, College of Natural Sciences and Mathematics, Department of Computer Science, Amherst, MA 01003

AWARDS MS, PhD. Part-time programs available.

Faculty: 32 full-time (1 woman).
Students: 55 full-time (16 women), 148 part-time (34 women); includes 12 minority (1 African American, 9 Asian Americans or Pacific Islanders, 2 Hispanic Americans), 108 international. Average age 27. 1,230 applicants, 11% accepted. In 2001, 19 master's, 9 doctorates awarded. Terminal master's awarded for partial completion of doctoral program.
Degree requirements: For doctorate, thesis/dissertation.
Entrance requirements: For master's and doctorate, GRE General Test, TOEFL, TWE. *Application deadline:* For fall admission, 1/15 (priority date); for spring admission, 10/1. Applications are processed on a rolling basis. *Application fee:* $40 ($50 for international students).
Expenses: Tuition, state resident: full-time $1,980; part-time $110 per credit. Tuition, nonresident: full-time $7,456; part-time $414 per credit. Required fees: $4,112. One-time fee: $115 full-time.

University of Massachusetts Amherst (continued)

Financial support: In 2001–02, 17 fellowships with full tuition reimbursements (averaging $7,226 per year), 123 research assistantships with full tuition reimbursements (averaging $14,041 per year), 39 teaching assistantships with full tuition reimbursements (averaging $7,214 per year) were awarded. Career-related internships or fieldwork, Federal Work-Study, scholarships/grants, traineeships, and unspecified assistantships also available. Support available to part-time students. Financial-award application deadline: 1/15.
Faculty research: Artificial intelligence, systems, theory, robotics.
Dr. Bruce Croft, Director, 413-545-2742, *Fax:* 413-545-1294, *E-mail:* csinfo@cs.umass.edu.
Application contact: Chair, Admissions Committee, 413-545-3640, *E-mail:* gradinfo@dpc.umassp.edu.
Find an in-depth description at www.petersons.com/gradchannel.

■ UNIVERSITY OF MASSACHUSETTS BOSTON

Office of Graduate Studies and Research, College of Arts and Sciences, Faculty of Sciences, Program in Computer Science, Boston, MA 02125-3393

AWARDS MS, PhD. Part-time and evening/weekend programs available.

Degree requirements: For master's, capstone final project, thesis optional; for doctorate, thesis/dissertation, oral exams, comprehensive exam.
Entrance requirements: For master's and doctorate, GRE General Test, minimum GPA of 2.75.
Faculty research: Queuing theory, database design theory, computer networks, theory of database query languages, real-time systems.

■ UNIVERSITY OF MASSACHUSETTS DARTMOUTH

Graduate School, College of Engineering, Program in Computer Science, North Dartmouth, MA 02747-2300

AWARDS MS, Certificate. Part-time programs available.

Faculty: 11 full-time (1 woman), 2 part-time/adjunct (1 woman).
Students: 57 full-time (14 women), 26 part-time (8 women); includes 2 minority (1 Asian American or Pacific Islander, 1 Hispanic American), 65 international. Average age 29. 95 applicants, 79% accepted, 25 enrolled. In 2001, 31 degrees awarded.
Degree requirements: For master's, thesis or alternative.

Entrance requirements: For master's, GRE General Test, TOEFL. *Application deadline:* For fall admission, 4/20 (priority date); for spring admission, 11/15 (priority date). Applications are processed on a rolling basis. *Application fee:* $25 ($45 for international students).
Expenses: Tuition, state resident: full-time $2,071; part-time $86 per credit. Tuition, nonresident: full-time $8,099; part-time $337 per credit. Part-time tuition and fees vary according to course load and reciprocity agreements.
Financial support: In 2001–02, 6 research assistantships (averaging $2,500 per year), 9 teaching assistantships (averaging $4,278 per year) were awarded. Federal Work-Study and unspecified assistantships also available. Support available to part-time students. Financial award application deadline: 3/1; financial award applicants required to submit FAFSA.
Faculty research: Visualization methods, mathematical models and metrics of ocean data, non-linear simulations of olfactory system. *Total annual research expenditures:* $234,000.
Dr. Jan Bergandy, Director, 508-999-8293, *Fax:* 508-999-9144, *E-mail:* jbergandy@umassd.edu.
Application contact: Maria E. Lomba, Graduate Admissions Officer, 508-999-8604, *Fax:* 508-999-8183, *E-mail:* graduate@umassd.edu.

■ UNIVERSITY OF MASSACHUSETTS LOWELL

Graduate School, College of Arts and Sciences, Department of Computer Science, Lowell, MA 01854-2881

AWARDS MS, PhD, Sc D. Part-time programs available.

Degree requirements: For master's, thesis optional; for doctorate, thesis/dissertation.
Entrance requirements: For master's and doctorate, GRE General Test.
Faculty research: Networks, multimedia systems, human-computer interaction, graphics and visualization databases.

■ THE UNIVERSITY OF MEMPHIS

Graduate School, College of Arts and Sciences, Department of Mathematical Sciences, Memphis, TN 38152-3420

AWARDS Applied mathematics (MS); applied statistics (PhD); bioinformatics (MS); computer science (PhD); computer sciences (MS); mathematics (MS, PhD); statistics (MS, PhD). Part-time programs available.

Faculty: 28 full-time (4 women), 7 part-time/adjunct (1 woman).
Students: Average age 30. 139 applicants, 37% accepted. In 2001, 31 master's, 8 doctorates awarded. Terminal master's awarded for partial completion of doctoral program.

Degree requirements: For master's, comprehensive exam; for doctorate, one foreign language, thesis/dissertation, oral exams.
Entrance requirements: For master's, GRE General Test, MAT, TOEFL, minimum GPA of 2.5; for doctorate, GRE General Test, TOEFL, minimum GPA of 2.5. *Application deadline:* For fall admission, 8/1; for spring admission, 12/1. Applications are processed on a rolling basis. *Application fee:* $25 ($50 for international students). Electronic applications accepted.
Expenses: Tuition, state resident: full-time $2,026. Tuition, nonresident: full-time $4,528.
Financial support: In 2001–02, 58 students received support, including fellowships with full tuition reimbursements available (averaging $17,500 per year), 9 research assistantships with full tuition reimbursements available (averaging $9,000 per year), 30 teaching assistantships with full tuition reimbursements available (averaging $9,000 per year); career-related internships or fieldwork and scholarships/grants also available. Financial award application deadline: 2/2.
Faculty research: Combinatorics, ergodic theory, graph theory, Ramsey theory, applied statistics. *Total annual research expenditures:* $3.3 million.
Dr. James E. Jamison, Chairman, 901-678-2482, *Fax:* 901-678-2480, *E-mail:* jjamison@memphis.edu.
Application contact: Dr. Anna Kaminska, Coordinator of Graduate Studies, 901-678-2482, *Fax:* 901-678-2480, *E-mail:* dfwilson@memphis.edu. *Web site:* http://www.msci@memphis.edu

■ UNIVERSITY OF MIAMI

Graduate School, College of Arts and Sciences, Department of Computer Science, Coral Gables, FL 33124

AWARDS MS.

Application fee: $50.
Expenses: Tuition: Part-time $960 per credit hour. Required fees: $85 per semester. Tuition and fees vary according to program.
Financial support: Applicants required to submit FAFSA.
Dr. Victor Milenkovic, Chair, 305-284-4194.

■ UNIVERSITY OF MICHIGAN

Horace H. Rackham School of Graduate Studies, College of Engineering, Department of Electrical Engineering and Computer Science, Division of Computer Science and Engineering, Ann Arbor, MI 48109

AWARDS MS, MSE, PhD.

Faculty: 40 full-time (4 women), 2 part-time/adjunct (0 women).
Students: 221 full-time (33 women), 11 part-time (2 women); includes 28 minority

(3 African Americans, 23 Asian Americans or Pacific Islanders, 1 Hispanic American, 1 Native American), 95 international. Average age 25. 1,230 applicants, 24% accepted. In 2001, 60 master's, 13 doctorates awarded. Terminal master's awarded for partial completion of doctoral program. **Degree requirements:** For doctorate, thesis/dissertation, oral defense of dissertation, preliminary exams. **Entrance requirements:** For master's and doctorate, GRE General Test, TOEFL. *Application deadline:* For fall admission, 5/1. Applications are processed on a rolling basis. *Application fee:* $55. Electronic applications accepted. **Financial support:** In 2001–02, 171 students received support, including 30 fellowships with full tuition reimbursements available (averaging $20,220 per year), 100 research assistantships with full tuition reimbursements available (averaging $20,220 per year), 41 teaching assistantships with full tuition reimbursements available (averaging $18,880 per year); health care benefits also available. Financial award application deadline: 1/15. **Faculty research:** Intelligent systems, hardware systems, software systems, theory of computation, VLSI. *Total annual research expenditures:* $10.4 million. Dr. John E. Laird, Chair, 734-764-2390, *Fax:* 734-763-1503, *E-mail:* admit@ eecs.umich.edu. **Application contact:** Dawn Freysinger, Student Services Associate, 734-764-2390, *Fax:* 734-764-1503, *E-mail:* admit@ eecs.umich.edu. *Web site:* http:// www.eecs.umich.edu/

■ UNIVERSITY OF MICHIGAN–DEARBORN

College of Engineering and Computer Science, Department of Computer and Information Science, Dearborn, MI 48128-1491

AWARDS Computer and information science (MS); software engineering (MS). Part-time and evening/weekend programs available.

Faculty: 13 full-time (1 woman), 6 part-time/adjunct (3 women). **Students:** 11 full-time (4 women), 115 part-time (35 women); includes 35 minority (2 African Americans, 32 Asian Americans or Pacific Islanders, 1 Hispanic American). Average age 29. 117 applicants, 60% accepted, 33 enrolled. In 2001, 42 degrees awarded. **Degree requirements:** For master's, thesis optional. *Median time to degree:* Master's–5 years full-time. **Entrance requirements:** For master's, TOEFL, bachelor's degree in mathematics, computer science, or engineering; minimum GPA of 3.0. *Application deadline:* For fall admission, 6/15; for winter admission, 9/15; for spring admission, 2/15. Applications are processed on a rolling basis. *Application fee:* $55.

Expenses: Tuition, state resident: part-time $300 per credit hour. Tuition, nonresident: part-time $756 per credit hour. Required fees: $90 per semester. Tuition and fees vary according to course level, course load and program. **Financial support:** In 2001–02, 1 research assistantship with full tuition reimbursement, 1 teaching assistantship were awarded. Financial award application deadline: 4/1; financial award applicants required to submit FAFSA. **Faculty research:** Information systems, geometric modeling, networks, databases. Dr. K. Akingbehin, Acting Chair, 313-436-9145, *Fax:* 313-593-4256, *E-mail:* kiumi@ umich.edu. **Application contact:** Kate Markotan, Graduate Secretary, 313-436-9145, *Fax:* 313-593-4256, *E-mail:* tabatha@ umd.umich.edu. *Web site:* http:// www.engin.umd.umich.edu/

■ UNIVERSITY OF MINNESOTA, DULUTH

Graduate School, College of Science and Engineering, Department of Computer Science, Duluth, MN 55812-2496

AWARDS MS. Part-time programs available.

Faculty: 9 full-time (2 women). **Students:** 29 full-time (8 women), 28 international. Average age 27. 94 applicants, 57% accepted, 14 enrolled. In 2001, 11 degrees awarded. **Degree requirements:** For master's, thesis (for some programs). **Entrance requirements:** For master's, GRE General Test, TOEFL, minimum GPA of 3.0. *Application deadline:* For fall admission, 7/15. Applications are processed on a rolling basis. *Application fee:* $50 ($55 for international students). **Expenses:** Tuition, state resident: full-time $2,932; part-time $489 per credit. Tuition, nonresident: full-time $5,758; part-time $960 per credit. Tuition and fees vary according to course load. **Financial support:** In 2001–02, 27 students received support, including 1 fellowship with partial tuition reimbursement available, 7 research assistantships with full and partial tuition reimbursements available (averaging $10,826 per year), 19 teaching assistantships with full and partial tuition reimbursements available (averaging $10,826 per year); Federal Work-Study, institutionally sponsored loans, and tuition waivers (partial) also available. Financial award application deadline: 3/15. **Faculty research:** Information retrieval, artificial intelligence, machine learning, parallel/distributed computing, graphics. Dr. Carolyn J. Crouch, Director of Graduate Studies, 218-726-7607, *Fax:* 218-726-8240, *E-mail:* cs@d.umn.edu. *Web site:* http://www.d.umn.edu/cs/grad/

■ UNIVERSITY OF MINNESOTA, TWIN CITIES CAMPUS

Graduate School, Institute of Technology, Department of Computer Science and Engineering, Minneapolis, MN 55455-0213

AWARDS Computer and information sciences (MCIS, MS, PhD). Part-time programs available. Terminal master's awarded for partial completion of doctoral program.

Degree requirements: For doctorate, thesis/dissertation. **Entrance requirements:** For master's and doctorate, GRE General Test. **Expenses:** Tuition, state resident: full-time $2,932; part-time $489 per credit. Tuition, nonresident: full-time $5,758; part-time $960 per credit. Part-time tuition and fees vary according to course load, program and reciprocity agreements. **Faculty research:** Software systems, numerical analysis, theory, artificial intelligence. *Web site:* http://www.cs.umn.edu/

■ UNIVERSITY OF MINNESOTA, TWIN CITIES CAMPUS

Graduate School, Scientific Computation Program, Minneapolis, MN 55455-0213

AWARDS MS, PhD. Part-time programs available.

Faculty: 44 full-time (2 women), 1 part-time/adjunct (0 women). **Students:** 9 full-time (1 woman), 3 part-time (1 woman); includes 1 minority (Asian American or Pacific Islander), 6 international. 15 applicants, 60% accepted, 2 enrolled. In 2001, 1 master's, 2 doctorates awarded. **Degree requirements:** For master's and doctorate, thesis/dissertation. **Entrance requirements:** For doctorate, GRE. *Application deadline:* For fall admission, 1/2 (priority date). Applications are processed on a rolling basis. *Application fee:* $50 ($55 for international students). Electronic applications accepted. **Expenses:** Tuition, state resident: full-time $2,932; part-time $489 per credit. Tuition, nonresident: full-time $5,758; part-time $960 per credit. Part-time tuition and fees vary according to course load, program and reciprocity agreements. **Financial support:** In 2001–02, 2 fellowships with full tuition reimbursements were awarded; research assistantships, teaching assistantships, career-related internships or fieldwork and Federal Work-Study also available. **Faculty research:** Parallel computations, quantum mechanical dynamics, computational materials science, computational fluid dynamics, computational neuroscience. David Ferguson, Director of Graduate Studies, 612-626-2601, *E-mail:* ferguson@ umn.edu.

University of Minnesota, Twin Cities Campus (continued)

Application contact: Kathleen Clinton, Graduate Program Administrator, 612-625-8424, *Fax:* 612-625-9442. *Web site:* http://www.scicomp.umn.edu/

■ UNIVERSITY OF MISSOURI– COLUMBIA

Graduate School, College of Engineering, Department of Computer Engineering and Computer Science, Columbia, MO 65211

AWARDS MS, PhD. Part-time programs available.

Faculty: 16 full-time (3 women).
Students: 53 full-time (21 women), 45 part-time (11 women); includes 6 minority (1 African American, 4 Asian Americans or Pacific Islanders, 1 Hispanic American), 74 international. 32 applicants, 47% accepted. In 2001, 22 master's, 3 doctorates awarded.
Degree requirements: For doctorate, thesis/dissertation.
Entrance requirements: For master's, GRE General Test, minimum GPA of 3.0; for doctorate, GRE General Test, TOEFL. *Application deadline:* For fall admission, 4/15 (priority date); for winter admission, 9/15 (priority date). Applications are processed on a rolling basis. *Application fee:* $25 ($50 for international students).
Expenses: Tuition, state resident: part-time $179 per credit hour. Tuition, nonresident: part-time $539 per credit hour. Required fees: $122 per semester. Tuition and fees vary according to program.
Financial support: Research assistantships, teaching assistantships, institutionally sponsored loans available.
Dr. Hongchi Shi, Director of Graduate Studies, 573-882-3088, *E-mail:* shih@cecs.missouri.edu. *Web site:* http://www.engineering.missouri.edu/computer.htm

■ UNIVERSITY OF MISSOURI– KANSAS CITY

School of Interdisciplinary Computing and Engineering, Kansas City, MO 64110-2499

AWARDS Computer networking (MS, PhD); software engineering (MS); telecommunications networking (MS, PhD). PhD offered through the School of Graduate Studies. Part-time programs available.

Faculty: 26 full-time (3 women), 18 part-time/adjunct (1 woman).
Students: 105 full-time (37 women), 103 part-time (27 women); includes 12 minority (3 African Americans, 8 Asian Americans or Pacific Islanders, 1 Hispanic American), 171 international. Average age 29. In 2001, 37 degrees awarded.

Degree requirements: For doctorate, thesis/dissertation.
Entrance requirements: For master's, GRE General Test, minimum GPA of 3.0; for doctorate, GRE General Test, minimum GPA of 3.5. *Application deadline:* For fall admission, 3/1 (priority date); for spring admission, 10/1. Applications are processed on a rolling basis. *Application fee:* $25.
Expenses: Tuition, state resident: part-time $233 per credit hour. Tuition, nonresident: part-time $623 per credit hour. Tuition and fees vary according to course load.
Financial support: In 2001–02, 15 research assistantships, 15 teaching assistantships were awarded. Career-related internships or fieldwork, Federal Work-Study, institutionally sponsored loans, and tuition waivers (partial) also available. Support available to part-time students. Financial award application deadline: 3/1.
Faculty research: Multimedia networking, distributed systems/databases, data/network security.
Dr. William Osbourne, Dean, 816-235-1193, *Fax:* 816-235-5159. *Web site:* http://www.cstp.umkc.edu/

Find an in-depth description at www.petersons.com/gradchannel.

■ UNIVERSITY OF MISSOURI– ROLLA

Graduate School, College of Arts and Sciences, Department of Computer Science, Rolla, MO 65409-0910

AWARDS MS, PhD. Part-time programs available. Terminal master's awarded for partial completion of doctoral program.

Degree requirements: For doctorate, thesis/dissertation, departmental qualifying exam.
Entrance requirements: For master's, GRE General Test; for doctorate, GRE Subject Test. Electronic applications accepted.
Faculty research: Intelligent systems, artificial intelligence software engineering, distributed systems, database systems, computer systems.

■ UNIVERSITY OF MISSOURI–ST. LOUIS

Graduate School, College of Arts and Sciences, Department of Mathematical Sciences, St. Louis, MO 63121-4499

AWARDS Applied mathematics (MA, PhD); computer science (MS); telecommunications science (Certificate). Part-time and evening/weekend programs available.

Faculty: 18.
Students: 36 full-time (22 women), 59 part-time (17 women); includes 10 minority (all Asian Americans or Pacific Islanders), 46 international. In 2001, 4 degrees awarded.

Degree requirements: For master's, thesis optional; for doctorate, thesis/dissertation.
Entrance requirements: For master's, GRE if no BS in computer science; for doctorate, GRE General Test. *Application deadline:* For fall admission, 5/1 (priority date); for spring admission, 12/1. Applications are processed on a rolling basis. *Application fee:* $25 ($40 for international students). Electronic applications accepted.
Expenses: Tuition, state resident: part-time $231 per credit hour. Tuition, nonresident: part-time $621 per credit hour.
Financial support: In 2001–02, 1 fellowship with full tuition reimbursement (averaging $12,000 per year), 2 research assistantships with full tuition reimbursements (averaging $12,884 per year), 13 teaching assistantships with full and partial tuition reimbursements (averaging $11,787 per year) were awarded.
Faculty research: Applied mathematics, statistics, algebra, analysis, computer science. *Total annual research expenditures:* $402,989.
Dr. Haiyun Cai, Director of Graduate Studies, 314-516-5741, *Fax:* 314-516-5400, *E-mail:* caih@msx.umsl.edu.
Application contact: Graduate Admissions, 314-516-5458, *Fax:* 314-516-5310, *E-mail:* gradadm@umsl.edu.

■ THE UNIVERSITY OF MONTANA–MISSOULA

Graduate School, College of Arts and Sciences, Department of Computer Science, Missoula, MT 59812-0002

AWARDS MS. Part-time programs available.

Faculty: 7 full-time (0 women).
Students: 12 full-time (4 women), 11 part-time (3 women); includes 3 minority (1 African American, 2 Asian Americans or Pacific Islanders), 11 international. Average age 33. 17 applicants, 76% accepted, 3 enrolled. In 2001, 1 degree awarded.
Degree requirements: For master's, thesis (for some programs), project or thesis.
Entrance requirements: For master's, GRE General Test, TOEFL. *Application deadline:* For fall admission, 3/15 (priority date). Applications are processed on a rolling basis. *Application fee:* $45.
Expenses: Tuition, state resident: full-time $2,482; part-time $1,700 per year. Tuition, nonresident: full-time $7,372; part-time $5,000 per year. Required fees: $1,900. Tuition and fees vary according to degree level.
Financial support: In 2001–02, 5 research assistantships (averaging $9,400 per year), 8 teaching assistantships with full tuition reimbursements (averaging $8,665 per year) were awarded. Federal Work-Study and unspecified assistantships also available. Financial award application deadline: 3/1; financial award applicants required to submit FAFSA.

Faculty research: Parallel and distributed systems, neural networks, genetic algorithms, machine learning, data visualization, artificial intelligence. *Total annual research expenditures:* $923,085. Dr. Jerry Esmay, Chair, 406-243-2883. **Application contact:** Kathy Lockridge, Graduate Secretary, 406-243-2883, *E-mail:* gradadvisor@cs.umt.edu. *Web site:* http://www.cs.umt.edu/

■ UNIVERSITY OF NEBRASKA AT OMAHA

Graduate Studies and Research, College of Information Science and Technology, Department of Computer Science, Omaha, NE 68182

AWARDS MA, MS. Part-time and evening/weekend programs available.

Faculty: 10 full-time (0 women).
Students: 66 full-time (17 women), 73 part-time (24 women); includes 7 minority (1 African American, 4 Asian Americans or Pacific Islanders, 1 Hispanic American, 1 Native American), 89 international. Average age 34. 115 applicants, 67% accepted, 43 enrolled. In 2001, 18 degrees awarded.
Degree requirements: For master's, thesis (for some programs), comprehensive exam.
Entrance requirements: For master's, GRE General Test, minimum GPA of 3.0, previous course work in computer science. *Application deadline:* For fall admission, 7/1 (priority date); for spring admission, 12/1 (priority date). Applications are processed on a rolling basis. *Application fee:* $35. Electronic applications accepted.
Expenses: Tuition, state resident: part-time $116 per credit hour. Tuition, nonresident: part-time $291 per credit hour. Required fees: $13 per credit hour. $4 per semester. One-time fee: $52 part-time.
Financial support: In 2001–02, 58 students received support; research assistantships, teaching assistantships, Federal Work-Study, institutionally sponsored loans, scholarships/grants, tuition waivers (full), and unspecified assistantships available. Support available to part-time students. Financial award application deadline: 3/1; financial award applicants required to submit FAFSA. Dr. Stanley Wileman, Chairperson, 402-554-2423.

■ UNIVERSITY OF NEBRASKA– LINCOLN

Graduate College, College of Arts and Sciences and College of Engineering and Technology, Department of Computer Science and Engineering, Lincoln, NE 68588

AWARDS Computer engineering (PhD); computer science (MS, PhD).

Faculty: 18.

Students: 138 (34 women); includes 1 minority (Asian American or Pacific Islander) 120 international. Average age 31. 339 applicants, 36% accepted, 58 enrolled. In 2001, 21 master's, 3 doctorates awarded.
Degree requirements: For master's, thesis optional; for doctorate, thesis/dissertation, comprehensive exam.
Entrance requirements: For master's and doctorate, GRE General Test, TOEFL. *Application deadline:* For fall admission, 3/1; for spring admission, 10/1. *Application fee:* $35. Electronic applications accepted.
Expenses: Tuition, state resident: full-time $2,412; part-time $134 per credit. Tuition, nonresident: full-time $6,223; part-time $346 per credit. Tuition and fees vary according to course load.
Financial support: In 2001–02, 1 fellowship, 53 research assistantships, 33 teaching assistantships were awarded. Federal Work-Study, health care benefits, and unspecified assistantships also available. Support available to part-time students. Financial award application deadline: 1/15.
Faculty research: Software engineering, geo- and bio-informatics, scientific computation, secure communication. Dr. Richard Sincovec, Chair, 402-472-2401, *Fax:* 402-472-7767.
Application contact: Dr. Hong Jiang, Graduate Committee Chair. *Web site:* http://www.cse.unl.edu

Find an in-depth description at www.petersons.com/gradchannel.

■ UNIVERSITY OF NEVADA, LAS VEGAS

Graduate College, Howard R. Hughes College of Engineering, Department of Computer Science, Las Vegas, NV 89154-9900

AWARDS MS, PhD. Part-time programs available.

Faculty: 13 full-time (0 women).
Students: 20 full-time (9 women), 19 part-time (6 women); includes 3 minority (2 Asian Americans or Pacific Islanders, 1 Hispanic American), 20 international. 41 applicants, 44% accepted, 11 enrolled. In 2001, 9 master's awarded.
Degree requirements: For master's, project, thesis optional; for doctorate, thesis/dissertation, comprehensive exam. *Median time to degree:* Doctorate–5 years full-time.
Entrance requirements: For master's, GRE General Test, minimum GPA of 3.0; for doctorate, GRE General Test, GRE Subject Test, minimum GPA of 3.3. *Application deadline:* For fall admission, 6/15; for spring admission, 11/15. Applications are processed on a rolling basis. *Application fee:* $40 ($55 for international students).
Expenses: Tuition, state resident: full-time $1,926; part-time $107 per credit. Tuition, nonresident: full-time $9,376; part-time

$220 per credit. Tuition and fees vary according to course load.
Financial support: In 2001–02, 3 research assistantships (averaging $7,417 per year), 14 teaching assistantships with partial tuition reimbursements (averaging $10,000 per year) were awarded. Financial award application deadline: 3/1. Dr. Hal Berghal, Chair, 702-895-3681.
Application contact: Graduate College Admissions Evaluator, 702-895-3320, *Fax:* 702-895-4180, *E-mail:* gradcollege@ccmail.nevada.edu. *Web site:* http://www.cs.unlv.edu/

■ UNIVERSITY OF NEVADA, RENO

Graduate School, College of Engineering, Department of Computer Science, Reno, NV 89557

AWARDS MS.

Faculty: 8.
Students: 45 full-time (16 women), 12 part-time (3 women); includes 8 minority (all Asian Americans or Pacific Islanders), 28 international. Average age 30. In 2001, 11 degrees awarded.
Degree requirements: For master's, thesis optional.
Entrance requirements: For master's, GRE, TOEFL, minimum GPA of 2.75. *Application deadline:* For fall admission, 3/1 (priority date). Applications are processed on a rolling basis. *Application fee:* $40.
Expenses: Tuition, state resident: full-time $2,067; part-time $108 per credit. Tuition, nonresident: full-time $9,282; part-time $109 per credit. Required fees: $57 per semester. Tuition and fees vary according to course load.
Financial support: In 2001–02, 5 research assistantships, 12 teaching assistantships were awarded. Financial award application deadline: 3/1. Dr. Sushil Louis, Graduate Program Director, 775-784-4313, *Fax:* 775-784-1877.
Application contact: Director of Graduate Studies, 775-784-4315.

■ UNIVERSITY OF NEW HAMPSHIRE

Graduate School, College of Engineering and Physical Sciences, Department of Computer Science, Durham, NH 03824

AWARDS MS, PhD. Part-time and evening/weekend programs available.

Faculty: 13 full-time.
Students: 37 full-time (10 women), 28 part-time (2 women); includes 1 minority (Asian American or Pacific Islander), 44 international. Average age 33. 47 applicants, 74% accepted, 8 enrolled. In 2001, 14 degrees awarded.
Degree requirements: For master's, thesis or alternative; for doctorate, thesis/dissertation.

University of New Hampshire (continued)

Entrance requirements: For master's and doctorate, GRE General Test. *Application deadline:* For fall admission, 4/1 (priority date); for winter admission, 12/1 (priority date). Applications are processed on a rolling basis. *Application fee:* $50. Electronic applications accepted.

Expenses: Tuition, state resident: full-time $6,300; part-time $350 per credit. Tuition, nonresident: full-time $15,720; part-time $643 per credit. Required fees: $560; $280 per term. One-time fee: $15 part-time. Tuition and fees vary according to course load.

Financial support: In 2001–02, 24 research assistantships, 15 teaching assistantships were awarded. Fellowships, career-related internships or fieldwork, Federal Work-Study, scholarships/grants, and tuition waivers (full and partial) also available. Support available to part-time students.

Faculty research: Programming languages, compiler design, parallel algorithms, computer graphics, artificial intelligence.
Dr. Ted Sparr, Chairperson, 603-862-3778, *E-mail:* tms@cc.unh.edu.
Application contact: James Weiner, Graduate Coordinator, 603-862-2691, *E-mail:* jlw@cs.unh.edu. *Web site:* http://www.cs.unh.edu/

■ UNIVERSITY OF NEW HAVEN

Graduate School, School of Engineering and Applied Science, Program in Computer and Information Science, West Haven, CT 06516-1916

AWARDS Applications software (MS); management information systems (MS); systems software (MS). Part-time and evening/weekend programs available.

Students: 54 full-time (23 women), 147 part-time (41 women); includes 13 minority (1 African American, 11 Asian Americans or Pacific Islanders, 1 Hispanic American), 81 international. In 2001, 53 degrees awarded.
Degree requirements: For master's, thesis or alternative.
Application deadline: Applications are processed on a rolling basis. *Application fee:* $50.
Expenses: Tuition: Full-time $12,015; part-time $445 per credit hour. Required fees: $30. One-time fee: $100 full-time.
Financial support: Federal Work-Study available. Support available to part-time students. Financial award application deadline: 5/1; financial award applicants required to submit FAFSA.
Dr. Tahany Fergany, Coordinator, 203-932-7067.

■ UNIVERSITY OF NEW MEXICO

Graduate School, School of Engineering, Department of Computer Science, Albuquerque, NM 87131-2039

AWARDS MS, PhD. Part-time programs available.

Faculty: 19 full-time (2 women), 4 part-time/adjunct (1 woman).
Students: 113 full-time (21 women), 32 part-time (11 women); includes 9 minority (7 Asian Americans or Pacific Islanders, 2 Hispanic Americans), 85 international. Average age 31. 259 applicants, 78% accepted, 51 enrolled. In 2001, 17 master's, 3 doctorates awarded.
Degree requirements: For doctorate, thesis/dissertation.
Entrance requirements: For master's and doctorate, GRE General Test, minimum GPA of 3.0. *Application deadline:* For fall admission, 6/30; for spring admission, 11/15. *Application fee:* $40.
Expenses: Tuition, state resident: full-time $2,771; part-time $115 per credit hour. Tuition, nonresident: full-time $11,207; part-time $467 per credit hour. Required fees: $570; $24 per credit hour. Part-time tuition and fees vary according to course load and program.
Financial support: In 2001–02, 49 students received support. Health care benefits available. Financial award application deadline: 3/1; financial award applicants required to submit FAFSA.
Faculty research: Artificial life, genetic algorithms, database systems, complexity theory, interactive computer graphics. *Total annual research expenditures:* $1.5 million.
Dr. Deepak Kapur, Chair, 505-277-3112, *Fax:* 505-277-6927, *E-mail:* kapur@unm.edu.
Application contact: Lynne Jacobsen, Program Advisement Coordinator, 505-277-3135, *Fax:* 505-277-6927, *E-mail:* ljake@cs.unm.edu. *Web site:* http://www.cs.unm.edu/

■ UNIVERSITY OF NEW ORLEANS

Graduate School, College of Sciences, Department of Computer Science, New Orleans, LA 70148

AWARDS MS.

Faculty: 5 full-time (0 women).
Students: 48 full-time (14 women), 32 part-time (7 women); includes 15 minority (5 African Americans, 9 Asian Americans or Pacific Islanders, 1 Hispanic American), 44 international. Average age 29. 143 applicants, 57% accepted, 19 enrolled. In 2001, 15 degrees awarded.
Entrance requirements: For master's, GRE General Test. *Application deadline:* For fall admission, 7/1 (priority date); for spring admission, 11/15 (priority date). Applications are processed on a rolling basis. *Application fee:* $20. Electronic applications accepted.

Expenses: Tuition, state resident: full-time $2,748; part-time $435 per credit. Tuition, nonresident: full-time $9,792; part-time $1,773 per credit.
Financial support: Applicants required to submit FAFSA.
Dr. Mahdi Abdelguerfi, Chairman, 504-280-7076, *Fax:* 504-280-7228, *E-mail:* mabdelgu@uno.edu.
Application contact: Dr. Eduardo Kortright, Graduate Coordinator, 504-280-6626, *Fax:* 504-280-7228, *E-mail:* mkortrig@uno.edu.

■ THE UNIVERSITY OF NORTH CAROLINA AT CHAPEL HILL

Graduate School, College of Arts and Sciences, Department of Computer Science, Chapel Hill, NC 27599

AWARDS MS, PhD.

Degree requirements: For master's, comprehensive exam; for doctorate, thesis/dissertation, comprehensive exam.
Entrance requirements: For master's and doctorate, GRE General Test, minimum GPA of 3.0.
Expenses: Tuition, state resident: full-time $2,864. Tuition, nonresident: full-time $12,030.
Find an in-depth description at www.petersons.com/gradchannel.

■ THE UNIVERSITY OF NORTH CAROLINA AT CHARLOTTE

Graduate School, College of Information Technology, Department of Computer Science, Charlotte, NC 28223-0001

AWARDS MS.

Faculty: 17 full-time (2 women), 12 part-time/adjunct (2 women).
Students: 87 full-time (26 women), 58 part-time (18 women); includes 12 minority (5 African Americans, 6 Asian Americans or Pacific Islanders, 1 Hispanic American), 110 international. Average age 26. 296 applicants, 66% accepted, 52 enrolled. In 2001, 59 degrees awarded.
Degree requirements: For master's, thesis optional.
Entrance requirements: For master's, GRE General Test, minimum GPA of 3.0 during previous 2 years, 2.8 overall. *Application deadline:* For fall admission, 7/15; for spring admission, 11/15. Applications are processed on a rolling basis. *Application fee:* $35. Electronic applications accepted.
Expenses: Tuition, state resident: full-time $1,483; part-time $371 per year. Tuition, nonresident: full-time $9,850; part-time $2,463 per year. Required fees: $1,043; $277 per year. Tuition and fees vary according to course load.
Financial support: In 2001–02, 6 research assistantships, 16 teaching assistantships were awarded. Fellowships, career-related

internships or fieldwork, Federal Work-Study, institutionally sponsored loans, scholarships/grants, and unspecified assistantships also available. Support available to part-time students. Financial award application deadline: 4/1; financial award applicants required to submit FAFSA.
Faculty research: Adaptive computations; artificial intelligence; data mining; parallel distributed processing; information integration, security, and privacy.
Dr. Richard A. Lejk, Interim Chair, 704-687-4881, *Fax:* 704-687-3516, *E-mail:* lejk@uncc.edu.
Application contact: Kathy Barringer, Director of Graduate Admissions, 704-687-3366, *Fax:* 704-687-3279, *E-mail:* gradadm@email.uncc.edu. *Web site:* http://www.uncc.edu/gradmiss/

■ THE UNIVERSITY OF NORTH CAROLINA AT GREENSBORO

Graduate School, College of Arts and Sciences, Department of Mathematics, Greensboro, NC 27412-5001

AWARDS Computer science (MA); mathematical science (M Ed, MA). Part-time programs available.

Faculty: 17 full-time (6 women), 1 part-time/adjunct (0 women).
Students: 12 full-time (5 women), 25 part-time (9 women); includes 7 minority (1 African American, 5 Asian Americans or Pacific Islanders, 1 Hispanic American), 11 international. 44 applicants, 45% accepted, 10 enrolled. In 2001, 6 degrees awarded.
Degree requirements: For master's, thesis (for some programs), comprehensive exam.
Entrance requirements: For master's, GRE General Test, TOEFL. *Application deadline:* For fall admission, 6/15; for spring admission, 11/1. Applications are processed on a rolling basis. *Application fee:* $35.
Expenses: Tuition, state resident: part-time $344 per course. Tuition, nonresident: part-time $2,457 per course.
Financial support: In 2001–02, 9 research assistantships with full tuition reimbursements (averaging $6,333 per year), 1 teaching assistantship with full tuition reimbursement (averaging $7,500 per year) were awarded. Career-related internships or fieldwork, Federal Work-Study, scholarships/grants, traineeships, and unspecified assistantships also available. Support available to part-time students.
Faculty research: General and geometric topology, statistics, computer networks, symbolic logic, mathematics education.
Dr. Paul Duvall, Head, 336-334-5836, *Fax:* 336-334-5949, *E-mail:* duvallp@uncg.edu.
Application contact: Dr. James Lynch, Director of Graduate Recruitment and Information Services, 336-334-4881, *Fax:* 336-334-4424. *Web site:* http://www.uncg.edu/mat/

■ UNIVERSITY OF NORTH DAKOTA

Graduate School, John D. Odegard School of Aerospace Sciences, Department of Computer Science, Grand Forks, ND 58202

AWARDS MS. Part-time programs available.

Faculty: 10 full-time (0 women).
Students: 29 applicants, 83% accepted, 6 enrolled. In 2001, 8 degrees awarded.
Degree requirements: For master's, thesis or alternative, comprehensive exam.
Entrance requirements: For master's, GRE General Test, TOEFL, minimum GPA of 3.0. *Application deadline:* For fall admission, 3/1 (priority date); for spring admission, 10/15 (priority date). Applications are processed on a rolling basis. *Application fee:* $30.
Expenses: Tuition, state resident: full-time $3,298. Tuition, nonresident: full-time $7,998.
Financial support: In 2001–02, 19 students received support, including 6 research assistantships with full tuition reimbursements available (averaging $8,775 per year), 11 teaching assistantships with full tuition reimbursements available (averaging $8,775 per year); fellowships, Federal Work-Study, institutionally sponsored loans, scholarships/grants, tuition waivers (full and partial), and unspecified assistantships also available. Support available to part-time students. Financial award application deadline: 3/15; financial award applicants required to submit FAFSA.
Faculty research: Operating systems, simulation, parallel computation, hypermedia, graph theory.
Dr. Ronald A. Marsh, Director, 701-777-4013, *Fax:* 701-777-3330, *E-mail:* rmarsh@cs.und.edu. *Web site:* http://www.cs.und.edu/

■ UNIVERSITY OF NORTHERN IOWA

Graduate College, College of Natural Sciences, Department of Computer Science, Cedar Falls, IA 50614

AWARDS MA, MS.

Students: 15 full-time (2 women), 7 part-time (3 women); includes 3 minority (1 African American, 2 Asian Americans or Pacific Islanders), 11 international. 19 applicants, 74% accepted. In 2001, 10 degrees awarded.
Degree requirements: For master's, thesis or alternative.
Application deadline: For fall admission, 8/1 (priority date). Applications are processed on a rolling basis. *Application fee:* $20 ($50 for international students).
Expenses: Tuition, state resident: full-time $3,704; part-time $206 per credit hour. Tuition, nonresident: full-time $9,122; part-time $501 per credit hour. Required

fees: $324; $108 per semester. Part-time tuition and fees vary according to course load.
Financial support: Application deadline: 3/1.
Dr. Bart L. Bergquist, Acting Head, 319-273-2618, *Fax:* 319-273-7123. *Web site:* http://www.cs.uni.edu/

■ UNIVERSITY OF NORTH FLORIDA

College of Computer Sciences and Engineering, Jacksonville, FL 32224-2645

AWARDS Computer and information sciences (MS). Part-time programs available.

Faculty: 18 full-time (2 women).
Students: 11 full-time (7 women), 33 part-time (12 women); includes 11 minority (1 African American, 9 Asian Americans or Pacific Islanders, 1 Hispanic American), 4 international. Average age 33. 66 applicants, 27% accepted, 11 enrolled. In 2001, 9 degrees awarded.
Degree requirements: For master's, thesis optional.
Entrance requirements: For master's, GRE General Test, minimum GPA of 3.0 in last 60 hours. *Application deadline:* For fall admission, 7/6 (priority date); for winter admission, 11/2 (priority date); for spring admission, 3/10 (priority date). Applications are processed on a rolling basis. *Application fee:* $20. Electronic applications accepted.
Expenses: Tuition, state resident: full-time $2,411; part-time $134 per credit hour. Tuition, nonresident: full-time $9,391; part-time $522 per credit hour. Required fees: $670; $37 per credit hour.
Financial support: In 2001–02, 14 students received support, including 3 teaching assistantships (averaging $4,992 per year); Federal Work-Study and tuition waivers (partial) also available. Support available to part-time students. Financial award application deadline: 4/1; financial award applicants required to submit FAFSA.
Faculty research: Parallel and distributed computing; networks; generic programming; algorithms; multimedia and temporal databases. *Total annual research expenditures:* $105,672.
Dr. Neal Coulter, Dean, 904-620-1350, *E-mail:* ncoulter@unf.edu.
Application contact: Dr. Charles Winton, Director of Graduate Studies, 904-620-2985, *E-mail:* cwinton@unf.edu. *Web site:* http://www.unf.edu/coce/cis/

■ UNIVERSITY OF NORTH TEXAS

Robert B. Toulouse School of Graduate Studies, College of Arts and Sciences, Department of Computer Sciences, Denton, TX 76203

AWARDS MA, MS, PhD.

University of North Texas (continued)

Faculty: 15 full-time (2 women), 3 part-time/adjunct (1 woman).

Students: 154 full-time (49 women), 119 part-time (46 women); includes 25 minority (7 African Americans, 11 Asian Americans or Pacific Islanders, 7 Hispanic Americans), 165 international. In 2001, 59 master's, 2 doctorates awarded. Terminal master's awarded for partial completion of doctoral program.

Degree requirements: For master's, thesis (for some programs), comprehensive exam; for doctorate, thesis/dissertation, comprehensive exam.

Entrance requirements: For master's, GRE General Test, minimum undergraduate GPA of 3.0; for doctorate, GRE General Test, minimum GPA of 3.5. *Application deadline:* For fall admission, 7/17. *Application fee:* $25 ($50 for international students).

Expenses: Tuition, state resident: part-time $1,861 per hour. Tuition, nonresident: part-time $319 per hour. Required fees: $88; $21 per hour.

Financial support: Fellowships, research assistantships, teaching assistantships, career-related internships or fieldwork, Federal Work-Study, and institutionally sponsored loans available. Financial award application deadline: 4/1.

Faculty research: Parallel algorithms, artificial intelligence, operating systems, software engineering, databases.

Dr. Roy T. Jacob, Chair, 940-565-2767, *Fax:* 940-565-2799, *E-mail:* jacob@cs.unt.edu.

Application contact: Dr. Steve R. Tate, Graduate Adviser, 940-565-2767, *Fax:* 940-565-2799, *E-mail:* srt@cs.unt.edu.

Find an in-depth description at www.petersons.com/gradchannel.

■ **UNIVERSITY OF NOTRE DAME**

Graduate School, College of Engineering, Department of Computer Science and Engineering, Notre Dame, IN 46556

AWARDS MS, PhD. Part-time programs available.

Faculty: 14 full-time (1 woman), 2 part-time/adjunct (0 women).

Students: 51 full-time (15 women), 2 part-time; includes 8 minority (3 African Americans, 3 Asian Americans or Pacific Islanders, 1 Hispanic American, 1 Native American), 26 international. 133 applicants, 21% accepted, 13 enrolled. In 2001, 6 master's, 1 doctorate awarded. Terminal master's awarded for partial completion of doctoral program.

Degree requirements: For master's, comprehensive exam; for doctorate, thesis/dissertation. *Median time to degree:* Doctorate–4 years full-time.

Entrance requirements: For master's and doctorate, GRE General Test, TOEFL. *Application deadline:* For fall admission, 2/1 (priority date); for spring admission, 10/1.

Applications are processed on a rolling basis. *Application fee:* $50. Electronic applications accepted.

Expenses: Tuition: Full-time $24,220; part-time $1,346 per credit hour. Required fees: $155.

Financial support: In 2001–02, 51 students received support, including 9 fellowships with full tuition reimbursements available (averaging $16,000 per year), 13 research assistantships with full tuition reimbursements available (averaging $13,700 per year), 18 teaching assistantships with full tuition reimbursements available (averaging $13,700 per year); tuition waivers (full) also available. Financial award application deadline: 2/1.

Faculty research: Parallel architectures, VLSI design, VLSI CAD, parallel and distributed computing, operating systems. *Total annual research expenditures:* $1.1 million.

Dr. Kevin W. Bowyer, Chair, 574-631-8320, *Fax:* 574-631-9260, *E-mail:* cse@cse.nd.edu.

Application contact: Dr. Terrence J. Akai, Director of Graduate Admissions, 574-631-7706, *Fax:* 574-631-4183, *E-mail:* gradad@nd.edu. *Web site:* http://www.cse.nd.edu/

Find an in-depth description at www.petersons.com/gradchannel.

■ **UNIVERSITY OF OKLAHOMA**

Graduate College, College of Engineering, School of Computer Science, Norman, OK 73019-0390

AWARDS MS, PhD. Part-time programs available.

Faculty: 12 full-time (2 women).

Students: 128 full-time (27 women), 27 part-time (9 women); includes 6 minority (1 African American, 3 Asian Americans or Pacific Islanders, 2 Native Americans), 132 international. 137 applicants, 80% accepted, 57 enrolled. In 2001, 45 master's, 2 doctorates awarded. Terminal master's awarded for partial completion of doctoral program.

Degree requirements: For master's, oral exams, qualifying exam, thesis optional; for doctorate, thesis/dissertation, general exam, qualifying exam.

Entrance requirements: For master's and doctorate, GRE General Test, TOEFL. *Application deadline:* For fall admission, 4/1 (priority date); for spring admission, 9/1. Applications are processed on a rolling basis. *Application fee:* $25 ($50 for international students).

Expenses: Tuition, state resident: full-time $2,208; part-time $92 per credit hour. Tuition, nonresident: part-time $297 per credit hour. Tuition and fees vary according to course level, course load and program.

Financial support: In 2001–02, 45 research assistantships with partial tuition reimbursements (averaging $9,928 per year), 20 teaching assistantships with

partial tuition reimbursements (averaging $9,646 per year) were awarded. Career-related internships or fieldwork, Federal Work-Study, scholarships/grants, traineeships, tuition waivers (full and partial), and unspecified assistantships also available. Support available to part-time students. Financial award application deadline: 4/15; financial award applicants required to submit FAFSA.

Faculty research: Database systems, telecommunications and networking, parallel and distributive computing, intelligent systems, software engineering, embedded systems. *Total annual research expenditures:* $923,638.

John Antonio, Director, 405-325-4042, *Fax:* 405-325-4044, *E-mail:* antoio@ou.edu.

Application contact: Dr. S. K. Dhall, Associate Professor, 405-325-2972, *Fax:* 405-325-4044, *E-mail:* sdhall@ou.edu.

■ **UNIVERSITY OF OREGON**

Graduate School, College of Arts and Sciences, Department of Computer and Information Science, Eugene, OR 97403

AWARDS MA, MS, MSE, PhD. Part-time programs available.

Faculty: 18 full-time (3 women), 4 part-time/adjunct (2 women).

Students: 51 full-time (14 women), 11 part-time (4 women); includes 1 minority (Hispanic American), 27 international. 141 applicants, 26% accepted. In 2001, 13 master's, 7 doctorates awarded. Terminal master's awarded for partial completion of doctoral program.

Degree requirements: For doctorate, thesis/dissertation.

Entrance requirements: For master's and doctorate, GRE General Test, TOEFL, minimum GPA of 3.0. *Application deadline:* For fall admission, 2/1. *Application fee:* $50.

Expenses: Tuition, state resident: full-time $4,968; part-time $501 per credit hour. Tuition, nonresident: full-time $8,400; part-time $691 per credit hour.

Financial support: In 2001–02, 47 teaching assistantships were awarded; fellowships, research assistantships, Federal Work-Study and institutionally sponsored loans also available. Financial award application deadline: 2/1.

Faculty research: Artificial intelligence, graphics, natural-language processing, expert systems, operating systems.

Sarah A. Douglas, Head, 541-346-4408.

Application contact: Star Holmberg, Graduate Secretary, 541-346-1377, *Fax:* 541-346-5373, *E-mail:* star@cs.uoregon.edu. *Web site:* http://www.cs.uoregon.edu/

Find an in-depth description at www.petersons.com/gradchannel.

■ UNIVERSITY OF PENNSYLVANIA

School of Engineering and Applied Science, Department of Computer and Information Science, Philadelphia, PA 19104

AWARDS MCIT, MSE, PhD. Part-time programs available.

Faculty: 28 full-time (4 women), 37 part-time/adjunct (8 women).
Students: 239 full-time (51 women), 46 part-time (11 women); includes 12 minority (3 African Americans, 8 Asian Americans or Pacific Islanders, 1 Hispanic American), 169 international. 792 applicants, 29% accepted, 82 enrolled. In 2001, 64 master's, 17 doctorates awarded. Terminal master's awarded for partial completion of doctoral program.
Degree requirements: For master's, thesis optional; for doctorate, thesis/dissertation. *Median time to degree:* Master's–1.5 years full-time, 2.5 years part-time; doctorate–5 years full-time.
Entrance requirements: For master's and doctorate, GRE General Test, TOEFL. *Application deadline:* For fall admission, 12/15. Applications are processed on a rolling basis. *Application fee:* $65. Electronic applications accepted.
Financial support: In 2001–02, 18 fellowships with full tuition reimbursements, 112 research assistantships with full tuition reimbursements were awarded. Teaching assistantships, institutionally sponsored loans also available. Financial award application deadline: 1/2.
Faculty research: AI, computer systems graphics, information management, robotics, software systems theory. *Total annual research expenditures:* $35 million.
Dr. Benjamin C. Pierce, Graduate Group Chair, 215-898-2012, *Fax:* 215-898-0587, *E-mail:* bcpierce@cis.upenn.edu.
Application contact: Mike Felker, Graduate Coordinator, 215-898-9672, *Fax:* 215-898-0587, *E-mail:* mfelker@cis.upenn.edu. *Web site:* http://www.cis.upenn.edu

Find an in-depth description at www.petersons.com/gradchannel.

■ UNIVERSITY OF PHOENIX–PHOENIX CAMPUS

College of Information Systems and Technology, Phoenix, AZ 85040-1958

AWARDS MSCIS. Evening/weekend programs available. Postbaccalaureate distance learning degree programs offered (no on-campus study).

Students: 95 full-time, 76 part-time. Average age 33. In 2001, 111 degrees awarded.
Degree requirements: For master's, thesis or alternative.
Entrance requirements: For master's, TOEFL, 3 years of work experience, comprehensive cognitive assessment, minimum GPA of 2.5. *Application deadline:*

Applications are processed on a rolling basis. *Application fee:* $85.
Expenses: Tuition: Full-time $7,680; part-time $320 per credit. Full-time tuition and fees vary according to campus/location and program.
Financial support: Applicants required to submit FAFSA.
Dr. Adam Honea, Dean, 480-557-1659, *E-mail:* adam.honea@phoenix.edu.
Application contact: 480-966-7400. *Web site:* http://www.phoenix.edu/

■ UNIVERSITY OF PITTSBURGH

Faculty of Arts and Sciences, Department of Computer Science, Pittsburgh, PA 15260

AWARDS MS, PhD. Part-time programs available.

Faculty: 17 full-time (3 women).
Students: 53 full-time (10 women), 19 part-time (6 women); includes 3 minority (all Asian Americans or Pacific Islanders), 38 international. Average age 24. 246 applicants, 20% accepted, 21 enrolled. In 2001, 17 master's, 7 doctorates awarded. Terminal master's awarded for partial completion of doctoral program.
Degree requirements: For master's, thesis or alternative; for doctorate, thesis/dissertation, preliminary exams, comprehensive exam. *Median time to degree:* Master's–2 years full-time, 4 years part-time; doctorate–5 years full-time.
Entrance requirements: For master's and doctorate, GRE General Test, TOEFL. *Application deadline:* For fall admission, 3/1; for spring admission, 10/1. Applications are processed on a rolling basis. Electronic applications accepted.
Expenses: Tuition, state resident: full-time $9,410; part-time $385 per credit. Tuition, nonresident: full-time $19,376; part-time $797 per credit. Required fees: $480; $90 per term. Tuition and fees vary according to program.
Financial support: In 2001–02, 48 students received support, including 16 research assistantships with tuition reimbursements available (averaging $11,980 per year), 35 teaching assistantships with tuition reimbursements available (averaging $11,980 per year); fellowships with tuition reimbursements available, career-related internships or fieldwork, Federal Work-Study, scholarships/grants, health care benefits, and tuition waivers (partial) also available. Financial award application deadline: 2/1.
Faculty research: Algorithms and theory, artificial intelligence, parallel and distributed systems, software systems and interfaces. *Total annual research expenditures:* $1.8 million.
Dr. Rami Melhem, Chairman, 412-624-8493, *Fax:* 412-624-8854, *E-mail:* melhem@cs.pitt.edu.
Application contact: Loretta Shabatura, Graduate Secretary, 412-624-8495, *Fax:*

412-624-8854, *E-mail:* loretta@cs.pitt.edu. *Web site:* http://www.cs.pitt.edu/

■ UNIVERSITY OF RHODE ISLAND

Graduate School, College of Arts and Sciences, Department of Computer Science and Statistics, Kingston, RI 02881

AWARDS MS, PhD.

Students: In 2001, 4 degrees awarded.
Degree requirements: For master's, thesis optional; for doctorate, one foreign language, thesis/dissertation.
Entrance requirements: For master's, GRE Subject Test. *Application deadline:* For fall admission, 4/15 (priority date). Applications are processed on a rolling basis. *Application fee:* $35.
Expenses: Tuition, state resident: full-time $3,756; part-time $209 per credit. Tuition, nonresident: full-time $10,774; part-time $599 per credit. Required fees: $1,586; $76 per credit. $76 per credit. One-time fee: $60 full-time.
Financial support: Unspecified assistantships available.
Dr. James Kowalski, Chair, 401-874-2701.

■ UNIVERSITY OF ROCHESTER

The College, Arts and Sciences, Department of Computer Science, Rochester, NY 14627-0250

AWARDS MS, PhD.

Faculty: 11.
Students: 44 full-time (10 women), 3 part-time (2 women); includes 2 minority (1 Asian American or Pacific Islander, 1 Hispanic American), 30 international. 431 applicants, 6% accepted, 10 enrolled. In 2001, 9 master's, 3 doctorates awarded. Terminal master's awarded for partial completion of doctoral program.
Degree requirements: For doctorate, thesis/dissertation, qualifying exam.
Entrance requirements: For master's, GRE General Test; for doctorate, GRE General Test, TOEFL. *Application deadline:* For fall admission, 2/1 (priority date). *Application fee:* $25.
Expenses: Tuition: Part-time $755 per credit hour.
Financial support: Fellowships, research assistantships, teaching assistantships, tuition waivers (full and partial) available. Financial award application deadline: 2/1.
Mitsunori Ogihara, Chair, 585-275-5478.
Application contact: Peggy Meeker, Graduate Program Secretary, 585-275-7737.

Find an in-depth description at www.petersons.com/gradchannel.

■ UNIVERSITY OF SAN FRANCISCO

College of Arts and Sciences, Department of Computer Science, San Francisco, CA 94117-1080

AWARDS MS. Part-time programs available.

Faculty: 7 full-time (0 women), 2 part-time/adjunct (0 women).
Students: 22 full-time (4 women), 3 part-time (1 woman); includes 1 minority (Asian American or Pacific Islander), 23 international. Average age 25. 70 applicants, 81% accepted, 9 enrolled. In 2001, 5 degrees awarded.
Degree requirements: For master's, thesis optional.
Entrance requirements: For master's, GRE General Test, GRE Subject Test, TOEFL, BS in computer science or related field. *Application deadline:* For fall admission, 7/1 (priority date); for spring admission, 12/1. Applications are processed on a rolling basis. *Application fee:* $55 ($65 for international students).
Expenses: Tuition: Full-time $14,400; part-time $800 per unit. Tuition and fees vary according to degree level, campus/location and program.
Financial support: In 2001–02, 10 students received support; fellowships, teaching assistantships, career-related internships or fieldwork and Federal Work-Study available. Financial award application deadline: 3/2; financial award applicants required to submit FAFSA.
Faculty research: Software engineering, computer graphics, computer networks.
Dr. Peter Pacheco, Chairman, 415-422-6630.
Application contact: Dr. Benjamin Wells, Graduate Adviser, 415-422-6530, *E-mail:* wells@usfca.edu.

■ UNIVERSITY OF SOUTH ALABAMA

Graduate School, Division of Computer and Information Sciences, Mobile, AL 36688-0002

AWARDS Computer science (MS); information science (MS). Part-time and evening/weekend programs available.

Faculty: 10 full-time (1 woman).
Students: 102 full-time (17 women), 27 part-time (4 women); includes 7 minority (3 African Americans, 3 Asian Americans or Pacific Islanders, 1 Native American), 88 international. 153 applicants, 60% accepted. In 2001, 25 degrees awarded.
Degree requirements: For master's, project, thesis optional.
Entrance requirements: For master's, GRE General Test, minimum GPA of 2.5. *Application deadline:* For fall admission, 9/1 (priority date). Applications are processed on a rolling basis. *Application fee:* $25.
Expenses: Tuition, state resident: full-time $3,048. Tuition, nonresident: full-time $6,096. Required fees: $320.

Financial support: In 2001–02, 4 research assistantships were awarded; career-related internships or fieldwork and institutionally sponsored loans also available. Support available to part-time students. Financial award application deadline: 4/1.
Faculty research: Numerical analysis, artificial intelligence, simulation, medical applications, software engineering.
Dr. David Feinstein, Dean, 334-460-6390.

■ UNIVERSITY OF SOUTH CAROLINA

The Graduate School, College of Engineering and Information Technology, Department of Computer Science and Engineering, Columbia, SC 29208

AWARDS Computer science and engineering (ME, MS, PhD); software engineering (MS). Part-time and evening/weekend programs available. Postbaccalaureate distance learning degree programs offered (minimal on-campus study).

Faculty: 20 full-time (3 women).
Students: 136 full-time (26 women), 41 part-time (10 women); includes 149 minority (5 African Americans, 143 Asian Americans or Pacific Islanders, 1 Hispanic American). Average age 27. 399 applicants, 48% accepted. In 2001, 126 master's, 2 doctorates awarded.
Degree requirements: For master's, thesis (for some programs), registration; for doctorate, thesis/dissertation, comprehensive exam, registration.
Entrance requirements: For master's and doctorate, GRE General Test, TOEFL. *Application deadline:* For fall admission, 3/1 (priority date); for spring admission, 10/1. *Application fee:* $35. Electronic applications accepted.
Expenses: Tuition, state resident: full-time $4,434. Tuition, nonresident: full-time $9,854. Tuition and fees vary according to program.
Financial support: In 2001–02, 5 fellowships (averaging $9,600 per year), 29 research assistantships with partial tuition reimbursements (averaging $15,000 per year), 24 teaching assistantships with partial tuition reimbursements (averaging $13,000 per year) were awarded. Career-related internships or fieldwork also available.
Faculty research: Computer security and computer vision, artificial intelligence, multiagent systems, conceptual modeling. *Total annual research expenditures:* $1.3 million.
Dr. Duncan A. Buell, Professor and Chair, 803-777-2880, *Fax:* 803-777-3767, *E-mail:* buell@cse.sc.edu.
Application contact: Jewel Rogers, Administrative Assistant, 803-777-7849, *Fax:* 803-777-3767, *E-mail:* jewel@engr.sc.edu. *Web site:* http://www.cse.sc.edu/

■ THE UNIVERSITY OF SOUTH DAKOTA

Graduate School, College of Arts and Sciences, Department of Computer Science, Vermillion, SD 57069-2390

AWARDS MA.

Faculty: 5 full-time (0 women), 1 part-time/adjunct (0 women).
Students: 25 full-time (9 women), 13 part-time (8 women); includes 22 minority (20 Asian Americans or Pacific Islanders, 2 Native Americans). 25 applicants, 32% accepted. In 2001, 12 degrees awarded.
Degree requirements: For master's, thesis.
Entrance requirements: For master's, GRE General Test. *Application deadline:* Applications are processed on a rolling basis. *Application fee:* $35.
Expenses: Tuition, state resident: full-time $1,700; part-time $95 per credit hour. Tuition, nonresident: full-time $5,027; part-time $279 per credit hour. Required fees: $1,062; $59 per credit hour.
Financial support: Teaching assistantships available. Support available to part-time students. Financial award applicants required to submit FAFSA.
John Lushbough, Chair, 605-677-5388.
Application contact: Dr. Rich McBride, Graduate Adviser, 605-677-5388. *Web site:* http://www.usd.edu/csci/

■ UNIVERSITY OF SOUTHERN CALIFORNIA

Graduate School, School of Engineering, Department of Computer Science, Program in Computer Science, Los Angeles, CA 90089

AWARDS MS, PhD.

Degree requirements: For doctorate, thesis/dissertation.
Entrance requirements: For master's and doctorate, GRE General Test.
Expenses: Tuition: Full-time $25,060; part-time $844 per unit. Required fees: $473.
Faculty research: Multi-media and virtual reality, databases.

Find an in-depth description at www.petersons.com/gradchannel.

■ UNIVERSITY OF SOUTHERN MAINE

School of Applied Science, Engineering, and Technology, Department of Computer Science, Portland, ME 04104-9300

AWARDS MS. Part-time programs available.

Degree requirements: For master's, thesis.
Entrance requirements: For master's, GRE Subject Test, minimum GPA of 3.0.
Expenses: Tuition, state resident: part-time $200 per credit. Tuition, nonresident: part-time $560 per credit.

Faculty research: Computer networks, database systems, software engineering, theory of computability, human factors. *Web site:* http://www.cs.usm.maine.edu/

■ UNIVERSITY OF SOUTHERN MISSISSIPPI

Graduate School, College of Science and Technology, School of Mathematical Sciences, Department of Computer Science, Hattiesburg, MS 39406-5106

AWARDS MS.

Faculty: 15 full-time (2 women), 5 part-time/adjunct (0 women).
Students: 20 full-time (6 women), 1 part-time; includes 10 minority (all Asian Americans or Pacific Islanders). Average age 30. 47 applicants, 45% accepted. In 2001, 18 degrees awarded.
Degree requirements: For master's, thesis or alternative, comprehensive exam.
Entrance requirements: For master's, GRE General Test, TOEFL, minimum GPA of 2.75. *Application deadline:* For fall admission, 8/6 (priority date). Applications are processed on a rolling basis. *Application fee:* $0 ($25 for international students).
Expenses: Tuition, state resident: full-time $3,416; part-time $190 per credit hour. Tuition, nonresident: full-time $7,932; part-time $441 per credit hour.
Financial support: Research assistantships with full tuition reimbursements, teaching assistantships with full tuition reimbursements, Federal Work-Study and institutionally sponsored loans available. Financial award application deadline: 3/15.
Faculty research: Satellite telecommunications, advanced life-support systems, artificial intelligence.
Dr. Adel Ali, Chair, 601-266-4949.

■ UNIVERSITY OF SOUTHERN MISSISSIPPI

Graduate School, College of Science and Technology, School of Mathematical Sciences, Program in Scientific Computing, Hattiesburg, MS 39406

AWARDS PhD. Part-time programs available.

Faculty: 2 part-time/adjunct (0 women).
Students: Average age 35. 24 applicants, 54% accepted. In 2001, 1 doctorate awarded.
Degree requirements: For doctorate, 2 foreign languages, thesis/dissertation, comprehensive exam.
Entrance requirements: For doctorate, GRE General Test, TOEFL, minimum GPA of 3.5. *Application deadline:* For fall admission, 8/6 (priority date). Applications are processed on a rolling basis. *Application fee:* $0 ($25 for international students).
Expenses: Tuition, state resident: full-time $3,416; part-time $190 per credit hour. Tuition, nonresident: full-time $7,932; part-time $441 per credit hour.

Financial support: Teaching assistantships, Federal Work-Study and institutionally sponsored loans available. Financial award application deadline: 3/15.

■ UNIVERSITY OF SOUTH FLORIDA

College of Graduate Studies, College of Engineering, Department of Computer Science and Engineering, Tampa, FL 33620-9951

AWARDS Computer engineering (M Cp E, MS Cp E); computer science (MCS, MSCS); computer science and engineering (PhD). Part-time programs available.

Faculty: 19 full-time (2 women).
Students: 109 full-time (32 women), 33 part-time (6 women); includes 20 minority (2 African Americans, 14 Asian Americans or Pacific Islanders, 4 Hispanic Americans), 85 international. Average age 30. 648 applicants, 26% accepted, 53 enrolled. In 2001, 4 master's, 4 doctorates awarded. Terminal master's awarded for partial completion of doctoral program.
Degree requirements: For doctorate, thesis/dissertation, 2 tools of research as specified by dissertation committee.
Entrance requirements: For master's, GRE General Test, minimum GPA of 3.0 during previous 2 years; for doctorate, GRE General Test. *Application deadline:* For fall admission, 6/1; for spring admission, 10/15. *Application fee:* $20. Electronic applications accepted.
Expenses: Tuition, state resident: part-time $166 per credit hour. Tuition, nonresident: part-time $573 per credit hour. Required fees: $17 per term.
Financial support: Fellowships with full tuition reimbursements, research assistantships with full tuition reimbursements, teaching assistantships with full tuition reimbursements, career-related internships or fieldwork, Federal Work-Study, institutionally sponsored loans, and tuition waivers (partial) available. Support available to part-time students. Financial award applicants required to submit FAFSA.
Faculty research: Computer vision, databases, VLSI design and test, networks, artificial intelligence. *Total annual research expenditures:* $1.2 million.
Dr. Abe Kandel, Chairperson, 813-974-3652, *Fax:* 813-974-5456, *E-mail:* kandel@csee.usf.edu.
Application contact: Dr. Dmitry B. Goldgof, Graduate Director, 813-974-3033, *Fax:* 813-974-5456, *E-mail:* msphd@csee.usf.edu. *Web site:* http://www.csee.usf.edu/

Find an in-depth description at www.petersons.com/gradchannel.

■ THE UNIVERSITY OF TENNESSEE

Graduate School, College of Arts and Sciences, Department of Computer Science, Knoxville, TN 37996

AWARDS MS, PhD. Part-time programs available.

Faculty: 16 full-time (0 women).
Students: 58 full-time (14 women), 55 part-time (16 women); includes 9 minority (3 African Americans, 5 Asian Americans or Pacific Islanders, 1 Hispanic American), 44 international. 149 applicants, 36% accepted. In 2001, 29 master's, 2 doctorates awarded.
Degree requirements: For master's, thesis or alternative; for doctorate, thesis/dissertation.
Entrance requirements: For master's and doctorate, GRE General Test, TOEFL, minimum GPA of 2.7. *Application deadline:* For fall admission, 2/1 (priority date). Applications are processed on a rolling basis. *Application fee:* $35. Electronic applications accepted.
Expenses: Tuition, state resident: full-time $4,280; part-time $233 per hour. Tuition, nonresident: full-time $12,066; part-time $666 per hour. Tuition and fees vary according to program.
Financial support: In 2001–02, 1 fellowship, 19 research assistantships, 34 teaching assistantships were awarded. Federal Work-Study, institutionally sponsored loans, and unspecified assistantships also available. Financial award application deadline: 2/1; financial award applicants required to submit FAFSA.
Dr. Robert Ward, Head, 865-974-5067, *Fax:* 865-974-4404, *E-mail:* ward@cs.utk.edu.
Application contact: Dr. David Straight, Graduate Representative, *E-mail:* straight@cs.utk.edu.

Find an in-depth description at www.petersons.com/gradchannel.

■ THE UNIVERSITY OF TENNESSEE AT CHATTANOOGA

Graduate Division, College of Engineering and Computer Sciences, Department of Computer Science, Chattanooga, TN 37403-2598

AWARDS MS. Part-time and evening/weekend programs available.

Faculty: 5 full-time (1 woman), 1 part-time/adjunct (0 women).
Students: 9 full-time (2 women), 25 part-time (6 women); includes 1 minority (African American), 13 international. Average age 33. 46 applicants, 41% accepted, 8 enrolled. In 2001, 7 degrees awarded.
Degree requirements: For master's, thesis.
Entrance requirements: For master's, GRE General Test. *Application deadline:* For fall admission, 8/1 (priority date); for

The University of Tennessee at Chattanooga (continued)

spring admission, 12/1 (priority date). Applications are processed on a rolling basis. *Application fee:* $25.

Expenses: Tuition, state resident: full-time $3,752; part-time $228 per hour. Tuition, nonresident: full-time $10,282; part-time $565 per hour.

Financial support: Fellowships, research assistantships, Federal Work-Study and institutionally sponsored loans available. Support available to part-time students. Financial award application deadline: 4/1; financial award applicants required to submit FAFSA.

Dr. Stephanie Smullen, Acting Head, 423-425-4395, *Fax:* 423-425-5229, *E-mail:* stephanie-smullen@utc.edu.

Application contact: Dr. Deborah E. Arfken, Dean of Graduate Studies, 865-425-1740, *Fax:* 865-425-5223, *E-mail:* deborah-arfken@utc.edu. *Web site:* http://www.utc.edu/

■ THE UNIVERSITY OF TEXAS AT ARLINGTON

Graduate School, College of Engineering, Department of Computer Science and Engineering, Arlington, TX 76019

AWARDS M Engr, M Sw En, MCS, MS, PhD. Part-time and evening/weekend programs available. Postbaccalaureate distance learning degree programs offered.

Faculty: 16 full-time (2 women), 3 part-time/adjunct (0 women).

Students: 320 full-time (73 women), 141 part-time (28 women); includes 44 minority (1 African American, 39 Asian Americans or Pacific Islanders, 4 Hispanic Americans), 371 international. 845 applicants, 62% accepted, 124 enrolled. In 2001, 111 master's, 5 doctorates awarded.

Degree requirements: For master's, thesis optional; for doctorate, thesis/dissertation, comprehensive exam.

Entrance requirements: For master's, GRE General Test, TOEFL, minimum GPA of 3.2; for doctorate, GRE General Test, TOEFL, minimum GPA of 3.5. *Application deadline:* For fall admission, 6/16. Applications are processed on a rolling basis. *Application fee:* $25 ($50 for international students).

Expenses: Tuition, area resident: Full-time $2,268. Tuition, nonresident: full-time $6,264. Required fees: $839. Tuition and fees vary according to course load.

Financial support: In 2001–02, 23 fellowships (averaging $1,000 per year), 80 teaching assistantships (averaging $12,000 per year) were awarded. Research assistantships, career-related internships or fieldwork, scholarships/grants, and tuition waivers (partial) also available. Financial award application deadline: 6/1; financial award applicants required to submit FAFSA.

Dr. Behrooz A. Shirazi, Chairman, 817-272-3065, *Fax:* 817-272-3784, *E-mail:* shirazi@uta.edu.

Application contact: Dr. Ramesh Yerraballi, Graduate Adviser, 817-272-5128, *Fax:* 817-272-3784, *E-mail:* ramesh@uta.edu. *Web site:* http://www.cse.uta.edu/

Find an in-depth description at www.petersons.com/gradchannel.

■ THE UNIVERSITY OF TEXAS AT AUSTIN

Graduate School, College of Natural Sciences, Department of Computer Sciences, Austin, TX 78712-1111

AWARDS MA, MSCS, PhD.

Faculty: 37 full-time (5 women), 31 part-time/adjunct (10 women).

Students: 238 full-time (27 women), 24 part-time (2 women); includes 16 minority (14 Asian Americans or Pacific Islanders, 2 Hispanic Americans), 177 international. Average age 26. 595 applicants, 25% accepted, 63 enrolled. In 2001, 63 master's, 10 doctorates awarded.

Degree requirements: For master's, thesis optional; for doctorate, thesis/dissertation, oral proposal, final defense.

Entrance requirements: For master's and doctorate, GRE General Test, GRE Subject Test, TOEFL. *Application deadline:* For fall admission, 1/2; for spring admission, 9/1. Applications are processed on a rolling basis. *Application fee:* $50 ($75 for international students). Electronic applications accepted.

Expenses: Tuition, state resident: full-time $3,159. Tuition, nonresident: full-time $6,957. Tuition and fees vary according to program.

Financial support: In 2001–02, 14 fellowships with full tuition reimbursements (averaging $18,000 per year), 85 research assistantships with partial tuition reimbursements (averaging $18,968 per year), 109 teaching assistantships with partial tuition reimbursements (averaging $13,500 per year) were awarded. Institutionally sponsored loans also available. Financial award application deadline: 1/2.

Faculty research: Artificial intelligence, distributed computing, networks, algorithms, experimental systems. *Total annual research expenditures:* $7 million.

Dr. J. Strother Moore, Chairman, 512-471-9500.

Application contact: Katherine Utz, Admissions Secretary, 512-471-9503, *Fax:* 512-471-7866, *E-mail:* csadmis@cs.utexas.edu. *Web site:* http://www.cs.utexas.edu/

Find an in-depth description at www.petersons.com/gradchannel.

■ THE UNIVERSITY OF TEXAS AT DALLAS

Erik Jonsson School of Engineering and Computer Science, Program in Computer Science, Richardson, TX 75083-0688

AWARDS MS, PhD. Part-time and evening/weekend programs available.

Faculty: 33 full-time (4 women), 3 part-time/adjunct (2 women).

Students: 591 full-time (176 women), 255 part-time (86 women); includes 101 minority (3 African Americans, 96 Asian Americans or Pacific Islanders, 1 Hispanic American, 1 Native American), 677 international. Average age 27. 1,664 applicants, 47% accepted. In 2001, 245 master's, 7 doctorates awarded.

Degree requirements: For master's, thesis optional; for doctorate, thesis/dissertation.

Entrance requirements: For master's, GRE General Test, TOEFL, minimum GPA of 3.0 in undergraduate course work, 3.3 in quantitative course work; for doctorate, GRE General Test, TOEFL, minimum GPA of 3.5. *Application deadline:* For fall admission, 7/15; for spring admission, 11/15. Applications are processed on a rolling basis. *Application fee:* $25 ($75 for international students). Electronic applications accepted.

Expenses: Tuition, state resident: full-time $1,440; part-time $84 per credit. Tuition, nonresident: full-time $5,310; part-time $295 per credit. Required fees: $1,835; $87 per credit. $138 per term.

Financial support: In 2001–02, 61 research assistantships with full tuition reimbursements (averaging $5,198 per year), 70 teaching assistantships with full tuition reimbursements (averaging $5,162 per year) were awarded. Fellowships, career-related internships or fieldwork, Federal Work-Study, institutionally sponsored loans, and scholarships/grants also available. Support available to part-time students. Financial award application deadline: 4/30; financial award applicants required to submit FAFSA.

Faculty research: Telecommunication networks, parallel processing, nanotechnology, artificial intelligence, software engineering.

Dr. Dung T. Huynh, Head, 972-883-2169, *Fax:* 972-883-2349, *E-mail:* huynh@utdallas.edu.

Application contact: Information Contact, 972-883-2185, *Fax:* 972-883-2349, *E-mail:* cs-grad-info@utdallas.edu. *Web site:* http://www.utdallas.edu/dept/cs/

Find an in-depth description at www.petersons.com/gradchannel.

■ THE UNIVERSITY OF TEXAS AT EL PASO

Graduate School, College of Engineering, Department of Computer Science, El Paso, TX 79968-0001

AWARDS MIT, MS. Part-time and evening/weekend programs available.

Students: 124 (33 women); includes 42 minority (2 African Americans, 3 Asian Americans or Pacific Islanders, 37 Hispanic Americans) 25 international. Average age 34. 15 applicants, 93% accepted. In 2001, 13 degrees awarded. **Degree requirements:** For master's, thesis optional.
Entrance requirements: For master's, GRE General Test, TOEFL, minimum GPA of 3.0. *Application deadline:* For fall admission, 7/1 (priority date); for spring admission, 11/1 (priority date). Applications are processed on a rolling basis. *Application fee:* $15 ($65 for international students). Electronic applications accepted.
Expenses: Tuition, state resident: full-time $2,450. Tuition, nonresident: full-time $6,000.
Financial support: In 2001–02, research assistantships with partial tuition reimbursements (averaging $21,125 per year), teaching assistantships with partial tuition reimbursements (averaging $16,900 per year) were awarded. Fellowships with partial tuition reimbursements, Federal Work-Study, institutionally sponsored loans, scholarships/grants, and tuition waivers (partial) also available. Financial award application deadline: 3/15; financial award applicants required to submit FAFSA.
Dr. Daniel G. Novick, Chairperson, 915-747-5480, *Fax:* 915-747-5030, *E-mail:* novick@cs.utep.edu.
Application contact: Dr. Charles H. Ambler, Dean of the Graduate School, 915-747-5491 Ext. 7886, *Fax:* 915-747-5788, *E-mail:* cambler@miners.utep.edu.

■ THE UNIVERSITY OF TEXAS AT SAN ANTONIO

College of Sciences, Department of Computer Science, San Antonio, TX 78249-0617

AWARDS MS, PhD.

Faculty: 9 full-time (1 woman).
Students: 50 full-time (13 women), 23 part-time (4 women); includes 9 minority (1 African American, 4 Asian Americans or Pacific Islanders, 2 Hispanic Americans, 2 Native Americans), 46 international. Average age 29. 96 applicants, 52% accepted, 28 enrolled. In 2001, 14 master's, 1 doctorate awarded.
Degree requirements: For master's, thesis optional; for doctorate, thesis/dissertation, comprehensive exam, registration.
Entrance requirements: For master's, GRE General Test, minimum GPA of 3.0

in last 60 hours; for doctorate, GRE General Test, TOEFL, minimum GPA of 3.3 in last 60 hours. *Application deadline:* For fall admission, 7/1. Applications are processed on a rolling basis. *Application fee:* $25.
Expenses: Tuition, state resident: full-time $2,268; part-time $126 per credit hour. Tuition, nonresident: full-time $6,066; part-time $337 per credit hour. Required fees: $781. Tuition and fees vary according to course load. *Total annual research expenditures:* $590,200.
Dr. Kleanthis Psarris, Chair, 210-458-4436.

■ THE UNIVERSITY OF TEXAS AT TYLER

Graduate Studies, College of Engineering and Computer Science, Department of Computer Science, Tyler, TX 75799-0001

AWARDS Computer information systems (MAT); computer science (MS); interdisciplinary studies (MAIS, MSIS).

Faculty: 5 full-time (0 women).
Students: 13 full-time (1 woman), 16 part-time (6 women); includes 8 minority (3 African Americans, 4 Asian Americans or Pacific Islanders, 1 Hispanic American), 6 international. Average age 31. 29 applicants, 100% accepted, 4 enrolled. In 2001, 4 degrees awarded.
Degree requirements: For master's, comprehensive exam, project or thesis.
Entrance requirements: For master's, GRE General Test, previous course work in data structures and computer organization, 6 hours of calculus and statistics. *Application deadline:* For fall admission, 6/15 (priority date); for spring admission, 10/15 (priority date). Applications are processed on a rolling basis. *Application fee:* $0. Electronic applications accepted.
Expenses: Tuition, state resident: part-time $44 per credit hour. Tuition, nonresident: part-time $262 per credit hour. Required fees: $58 per credit hour. $76 per semester.
Financial support: In 2001–02, 5 research assistantships with tuition reimbursements (averaging $2,333 per year), 1 teaching assistantship (averaging $2,333 per year) were awarded. Financial award application deadline: 7/1; financial award applicants required to submit FAFSA.
Faculty research: Database design, software engineering, distributed objects, client-server architecture, visual programming.
Dr. Ron King, Chair, 903-566-7097, *Fax:* 903-566-7189, *E-mail:* rking@mail.uttyl.edu.
Application contact: Carol A. Hodge, Office of Graduate Studies, 903-566-5642, *Fax:* 903-566-7068, *E-mail:* chodge@mail.uttly.edu.

■ THE UNIVERSITY OF TEXAS–PAN AMERICAN

College of Science and Engineering, Department of Computer Science, Edinburg, TX 78539-2999

AWARDS MS. Part-time and evening/weekend programs available. Postbaccalaureate distance learning degree programs offered (minimal on-campus study).

Degree requirements: For master's, final written exam, project.
Entrance requirements: For master's, GRE General Test, TOEFL, minimum GPA of 3.0 in last 60 hours.
Expenses: Tuition, state resident: part-time $212 per semester hour. Tuition, nonresident: part-time $367 per semester hour.
Faculty research: Artificial intelligence, distributed systems internet computing, theoretical computer sciences, information visualization. *Web site:* http://www.cs.panam.edu/

■ UNIVERSITY OF TOLEDO

Graduate School, College of Engineering, Department of Electrical Engineering and Computer Science, Toledo, OH 43606-3398

AWARDS Computer science (MS); electrical engineering (MS); engineering sciences (PhD). Part-time and evening/weekend programs available.

Faculty: 22 full-time (2 women).
Students: 53 full-time (5 women), 149 part-time (23 women); includes 2 minority (both African Americans), 183 international. Average age 25. 945 applicants, 22% accepted. In 2001, 71 master's, 1 doctorate awarded.
Degree requirements: For master's, thesis or alternative; for doctorate, thesis/dissertation.
Entrance requirements: For master's, GRE General Test, TOEFL, minimum GPA of 2.7; for doctorate, GRE General Test, TOEFL. *Application deadline:* For fall admission, 5/31 (priority date). Applications are processed on a rolling basis. *Application fee:* $30. Electronic applications accepted.
Expenses: Tuition, state resident: full-time $7,278; part-time $303 per hour. Tuition, nonresident: full-time $15,731; part-time $699 per hour. Required fees: $43 per hour.
Financial support: In 2001–02, 182 students received support, including 19 research assistantships with full tuition reimbursements available, 28 teaching assistantships with full tuition reimbursements available; fellowships with full tuition reimbursements available, Federal Work-Study, scholarships/grants, and tuition waivers (full) also available. Support available to part-time students. Financial award application deadline: 4/1.

University of Toledo (continued)

Faculty research: Power electronics, digital television, satellite communications, computer networks, fault-tolerant computing, weather and intelligent transportation. *Total annual research expenditures:* $8,495. Dr. Demetrios Kazakos, Interim Chairman, 419-530-8140.

Application contact: Ezzatollah Salari, Director of Graduate Program, 419-530-8148, *Fax:* 419-530-8146, *E-mail:* esalari@uoft2.utoledo.edu. *Web site:* http://www.eecs.utoledo.edu/

Find an in-depth description at www.petersons.com/gradchannel.

■ **UNIVERSITY OF TULSA**

Graduate School, College of Business Administration and College of Engineering and Natural Sciences, Department of Engineering and Technology Management, Tulsa, OK 74104-3189

AWARDS Chemical engineering (METM); computer science (METM); electrical engineering (METM); geological science (METM); mathematics (METM); mechanical engineering (METM); petroleum engineering (METM). Part-time and evening/weekend programs available.

Students: 2 full-time (1 woman), 1 part-time, 2 international. Average age 26. 3 applicants, 100% accepted, 1 enrolled. In 2001, 2 degrees awarded.

Entrance requirements: For master's, GRE General Test, TOEFL. *Application deadline:* Applications are processed on a rolling basis. *Application fee:* $30. Electronic applications accepted.

Expenses: Tuition: Full-time $9,540; part-time $530 per credit hour. Required fees: $80. One-time fee: $230 full-time.

Financial support: Fellowships, research assistantships, teaching assistantships, Federal Work-Study, scholarships/grants, tuition waivers (partial), and unspecified assistantships available. Support available to part-time students. Financial award application deadline: 2/1; financial award applicants required to submit FAFSA.

Application contact: Information Contact, *E-mail:* graduate-business@utulsa.edu. *Web site:* http://www.cba.utulsa.edu/academic.asp#graduate_studies/

■ **UNIVERSITY OF TULSA**

Graduate School, College of Engineering and Natural Sciences, Department of Mathematical and Computer Sciences, Program in Computer Science, Tulsa, OK 74104-3189

AWARDS MS, PhD. Part-time programs available.

Students: 48 full-time (7 women), 27 part-time (14 women); includes 4 minority (1 African American, 2 Asian Americans or Pacific Islanders, 1 Native American), 48 international. Average age 28. 116 applicants, 93% accepted, 37 enrolled. In 2001, 11 master's, 2 doctorates awarded.

Degree requirements: For master's, thesis optional; for doctorate, thesis/dissertation, comprehensive exam.

Entrance requirements: For master's and doctorate, GRE General Test, TOEFL. *Application deadline:* Applications are processed on a rolling basis. *Application fee:* $30. Electronic applications accepted.

Expenses: Tuition: Full-time $9,540; part-time $530 per credit hour. Required fees: $80. One-time fee: $230 full-time.

Financial support: In 2001–02, 4 fellowships with full and partial tuition reimbursements (averaging $2,500 per year), 16 research assistantships with full and partial tuition reimbursements (averaging $8,200 per year), 6 teaching assistantships with full and partial tuition reimbursements (averaging $7,200 per year) were awarded. Federal Work-Study, scholarships/grants, tuition waivers (partial), and unspecified assistantships also available. Support available to part-time students. Financial award application deadline: 2/1; financial award applicants required to submit FAFSA.

Faculty research: Genetic algorithms, medical imaging, parallel and scientific computation, database security, fuzzy control.

Application contact: Dr. Roger L. Wainwright, Adviser, 918-631-3143, *Fax:* 918-631-3077, *E-mail:* grad@utulsa.edu. *Web site:* http://www.mcs.utulsa.edu/

■ **UNIVERSITY OF UTAH**

Graduate School, College of Engineering, School of Computing, Salt Lake City, UT 84112-1107

AWARDS M Phil, MS, PhD.

Faculty: 23 full-time (3 women).

Students: 58 full-time (11 women), 30 part-time (2 women); includes 20 minority (19 Asian Americans or Pacific Islanders, 1 Hispanic American), 14 international. Average age 28. 97 applicants, 29% accepted. In 2001, 7 master's, 2 doctorates awarded.

Degree requirements: For master's, thesis (MS); for doctorate, thesis/dissertation.

Entrance requirements: For master's and doctorate, GRE General Test, GRE Subject Test, TOEFL, minimum GPA of 3.0. *Application deadline:* For fall admission, 7/1. *Application fee:* $40 ($60 for international students).

Expenses: Tuition, state resident: part-time $320 per semester hour. Tuition, nonresident: part-time $1,135 per semester hour. Required fees: $143 per semester hour. Tuition and fees vary according to course load, degree level and program.

Financial support: Fellowships, research assistantships, teaching assistantships available. Financial award applicants required to submit FAFSA.

Faculty research: Computer-aided graphic design, VLSI, information retrieval, portable artificial intelligence systems, functional programming. Dr. Thomas C. Henderson, Director, 801-581-8224, *Fax:* 801-581-5843, *E-mail:* tch@cs.utah.edu.

Application contact: Al Davis, Director of Graduate Studies, 801-581-8224, *Fax:* 801-581-5843, *E-mail:* ald@cs.utah.edu. *Web site:* http://www.coe.utah.edu/

Find an in-depth description at www.petersons.com/gradchannel.

■ **UNIVERSITY OF VERMONT**

Graduate College, College of Engineering and Mathematics, Department of Computer Science and Electrical Engineering, Program in Computer Science, Burlington, VT 05405

AWARDS MS.

Degree requirements: For master's, thesis or alternative.

Entrance requirements: For master's, GRE General Test, TOEFL.

Expenses: Tuition, state resident: part-time $335 per credit. Tuition, nonresident: part-time $838 per credit.

■ **UNIVERSITY OF VIRGINIA**

School of Engineering and Applied Science, Department of Computer Science, Charlottesville, VA 22903

AWARDS MCS, MS, PhD.

Faculty: 27 full-time (3 women), 1 part-time/adjunct (0 women).

Students: 90 full-time (14 women), 5 part-time (1 woman); includes 4 minority (1 African American, 2 Asian Americans or Pacific Islanders, 1 Hispanic American), 52 international. Average age 25. 435 applicants, 21% accepted, 39 enrolled. In 2001, 17 master's, 6 doctorates awarded.

Degree requirements: For master's, thesis (for some programs); for doctorate, thesis/dissertation, comprehensive exam.

Entrance requirements: For master's and doctorate, GRE General Test. *Application deadline:* For fall admission, 8/1; for spring admission, 12/1. Applications are processed on a rolling basis. *Application fee:* $40. Electronic applications accepted.

Expenses: Tuition, state resident: full-time $3,988. Tuition, nonresident: full-time $17,078. Required fees: $1,190.

Financial support: Fellowships available. Financial award application deadline: 2/1; financial award applicants required to submit FAFSA.

Faculty research: Systems programming, operating systems, analysis of programs and computation theory, programming languages, software engineering.

John A. Stankovic, Chairman, 434-982-2275, *Fax:* 434-982-2214.
Application contact: Kathryn Thornton, Assistant Dean, 434-924-3897, *Fax:* 434-982-2214, *E-mail:* inquiry@cs.virginia.edu. *Web site:* http://www.cs.virginia.edu/
Find an in-depth description at www.petersons.com/gradchannel.

■ UNIVERSITY OF WASHINGTON

Graduate School, College of Engineering, Department of Computer Science and Engineering, Seattle, WA 98195

AWARDS Computer science (MS, PhD). Part-time programs available.

Faculty: 39 full-time (4 women).
Students: 160 full-time (25 women); includes 9 minority (1 African American, 8 Asian Americans or Pacific Islanders), 67 international. Average age 28. 543 applicants, 16% accepted, 28 enrolled. In 2001, 30 master's, 10 doctorates awarded. Terminal master's awarded for partial completion of doctoral program.
Degree requirements: For master's, thesis or alternative; for doctorate, thesis/dissertation, depth exam, comprehensive exam. *Median time to degree:* Master's–2.12 years full-time; doctorate–6 years full-time.
Entrance requirements: For master's and doctorate, GRE General Test, TOEFL, minimum GPA of 3.0. *Application deadline:* For fall admission, 1/1. *Application fee:* $50. Electronic applications accepted.
Expenses: Tuition, state resident: full-time $5,539. Tuition, nonresident: full-time $14,376. Required fees: $390. Tuition and fees vary according to course load and program.
Financial support: In 2001–02, 121 students received support, including 20 fellowships with full tuition reimbursements available (averaging $17,217 per year), 76 research assistantships with partial tuition reimbursements available (averaging $16,565 per year), 45 teaching assistantships with partial tuition reimbursements available (averaging $16,585 per year) Financial award application deadline: 1/1; financial award applicants required to submit FAFSA.
Faculty research: Theory, systems, artificial intelligence, graphics, databases. *Total annual research expenditures:* $5.9 million.
Dr. David Notkin, Chair, 206-543-1695.
Application contact: Lindsay Michimoto, Graduate Admissions, Information Contact, 206-543-1695, *E-mail:* grad_admissions@cs.washington.edu. *Web site:* http://www.cs.washington.edu/
Find an in-depth description at www.petersons.com/gradchannel.

■ UNIVERSITY OF WEST FLORIDA

College of Arts and Sciences: Sciences, Department of Computer Science, Pensacola, FL 32514-5750

AWARDS Computer science (MS); systems and control engineering (MS). Part-time and evening/weekend programs available.

Faculty: 7 full-time (2 women), 1 part-time/adjunct (0 women).
Students: 19 full-time (5 women), 42 part-time (14 women); includes 14 minority (3 African Americans, 6 Asian Americans or Pacific Islanders, 4 Hispanic Americans, 1 Native American), 6 international. Average age 34. 61 applicants, 31% accepted, 9 enrolled. In 2001, 38 degrees awarded.
Degree requirements: For master's, thesis optional.
Entrance requirements: For master's, GRE General Test. *Application deadline:* For fall admission, 6/30; for spring admission, 11/1. Applications are processed on a rolling basis. *Application fee:* $20.
Expenses: Tuition, state resident: full-time $3,995; part-time $166 per credit hour. Tuition, nonresident: full-time $13,766; part-time $574 per credit hour. Tuition and fees vary according to campus/location.
Financial support: Fellowships, research assistantships available.
Dr. Mohsen Guizani, Chairperson, 850-474-2542.

■ UNIVERSITY OF WISCONSIN–MADISON

Graduate School, College of Letters and Science, Department of Computer Sciences, Madison, WI 53706-1380

AWARDS MS, PhD. Part-time programs available. Terminal master's awarded for partial completion of doctoral program.

Degree requirements: For doctorate, thesis/dissertation.
Entrance requirements: For master's and doctorate, GRE General Test, GRE Subject Test. Electronic applications accepted.
Expenses: Tuition, state resident: full-time $7,361; part-time $399 per credit. Tuition, nonresident: full-time $20,499; part-time $1,282 per credit. Required fees: $34 per credit. Full-time tuition and fees vary according to course load, program, reciprocity agreements and student level. *Web site:* http://www.cs.wisc.edu/

■ UNIVERSITY OF WISCONSIN–MILWAUKEE

Graduate School, College of Engineering and Applied Science, Department of Electrical Engineering and Computer Science, Milwaukee, WI 53201-0413

AWARDS Computer science (MS, PhD). Part-time programs available.

Faculty: 23 full-time (1 woman).
Students: 20 full-time (7 women), 52 part-time (19 women); includes 9 minority (1 African American, 8 Asian Americans or Pacific Islanders), 38 international. 101 applicants, 47% accepted. In 2001, 10 degrees awarded.
Degree requirements: For master's, thesis or alternative; for doctorate, thesis/dissertation, internship.
Entrance requirements: For master's, minimum GPA of 2.75; for doctorate, minimum GPA of 3.5. *Application deadline:* For fall admission, 1/1 (priority date); for spring admission, 9/1. Applications are processed on a rolling basis. *Application fee:* $45 ($75 for international students).
Expenses: Tuition, state resident: full-time $6,180; part-time $535 per credit. Tuition, nonresident: full-time $19,482; part-time $1,366 per credit. Tuition and fees vary according to course load, program and reciprocity agreements.
Financial support: In 2001–02, 1 fellowship, 4 research assistantships, 13 teaching assistantships were awarded. Career-related internships or fieldwork and unspecified assistantships also available. Support available to part-time students. Financial award application deadline: 4/15.
K. Vairavan, Co-Chair, 414-229-5357, *Fax:* 414-229-6958, *E-mail:* kv@uwm.edu. *Web site:* http://www.uwm.edu/CEAS/

■ UNIVERSITY OF WISCONSIN–PARKSIDE

School of Business and Technology, Program in Computer and Information Systems, Kenosha, WI 53141-2000
AWARDS MSCIS.

Faculty: 7 full-time (1 woman).
Students: 12 applicants, 75% accepted, 7 enrolled.
Entrance requirements: For master's, GRE General Test or GMAT, 3 letters of recommendation, minimum GPA of 3.0. *Application deadline:* For fall admission, 8/1 (priority date). Applications are processed on a rolling basis. *Application fee:* $45.
Expenses: Tuition, area resident: Full-time $4,542; part-time $264 per credit. Tuition, nonresident: full-time $14,366; part-time $810 per credit. Required fees: $236; $27 per credit. Tuition and fees vary according to program.
Faculty research: Distributed systems, data bases, natural language processing, event-driven systems.

University of Wisconsin–Parkside (continued)

Dr. Timothy V. Fossum, Chair, Computer Science Department, 262-595-2314, *Fax:* 262-595-2114, *E-mail:* timothy.fossum@cs.uwp.edu.

■ UNIVERSITY OF WYOMING

Graduate School, College of Engineering, Department of Computer Science, Laramie, WY 82071

AWARDS MS, Pro MS, PhD. Part-time programs available.

Faculty: 7 full-time (0 women).
Students: 26 full-time (3 women), 8 part-time (4 women), 20 international. 58 applicants, 45% accepted. In 2001, 23 degrees awarded. Terminal master's awarded for partial completion of doctoral program.
Degree requirements: For master's and doctorate, thesis/dissertation.
Entrance requirements: For master's and doctorate, GRE General Test, minimum GPA of 3.0. *Application deadline:* For fall admission, 3/1 (priority date); for spring admission, 10/1 (priority date). Applications are processed on a rolling basis. *Application fee:* $40. Electronic applications accepted.
Expenses: Tuition, state resident: full-time $2,895; part-time $161 per credit hour. Tuition, nonresident: full-time $8,367; part-time $465 per credit hour. Required fees: $491; $10 per credit hour. $2 per credit hour. Tuition and fees vary according to course load and program.
Financial support: Research assistantships, teaching assistantships, career-related internships or fieldwork, Federal Work-Study, and tuition waivers (partial) available. Financial award application deadline: 3/1.
Faculty research: Fault-tolerant computing, distributed systems, knowledge representation, automated reasoning, parallel database access, formal methods. *Total annual research expenditures:* $169,701. Dr. Jeffrey Van Baalen, Chairman, 307-766-5190, *Fax:* 307-766-4036.
Application contact: Graduate Coordinator, 307-766-5190, *Fax:* 307-766-4036, *E-mail:* cosc@uwyo.edu. *Web site:* http://www.cs.uwyo.edu/

■ UTAH STATE UNIVERSITY

School of Graduate Studies, College of Science, Department of Computer Science, Logan, UT 84322

AWARDS MCS, MS, PhD. Part-time and evening/weekend programs available. Postbaccalaureate distance learning degree programs offered.

Faculty: 12 full-time (1 woman), 2 part-time/adjunct (0 women).
Students: 56 full-time (14 women), 72 part-time (20 women); includes 3 minority (2 Asian Americans or Pacific Islanders, 1 Hispanic American), 99 international.

Average age 24. 267 applicants, 50% accepted. In 2001, 26 degrees awarded.
Degree requirements: For master's, thesis (for some programs), research project; for doctorate, thesis/dissertation.
Entrance requirements: For master's, GRE General Test, GRE Subject Test, TOEFL, minimum GPA of 3.0; for doctorate, GRE General Test, TOEFL, minimum GPA of 3.25. *Application deadline:* For fall admission, 6/15 (priority date); for spring admission, 10/15. Applications are processed on a rolling basis. *Application fee:* $40.
Expenses: Tuition, state resident: full-time $1,693. Tuition, nonresident: full-time $4,233. Required fees: $501. Tuition and fees vary according to program.
Financial support: In 2001–02, 1 fellowship with partial tuition reimbursement, 12 research assistantships with partial tuition reimbursements, 8 teaching assistantships with partial tuition reimbursements were awarded. Career-related internships or fieldwork, Federal Work-Study, institutionally sponsored loans, and tuition waivers (partial) also available. Support available to part-time students. Financial award application deadline: 2/16.
Faculty research: Artificial intelligence, software engineering, parallelism. *Total annual research expenditures:* $1.5 million. Donald H. Cooley, Head, 435-797-2451, *Fax:* 435-797-3265, *E-mail:* usucs@cc.usu.edu.
Application contact: Greg Jones, Graduate Adviser, 435-797-3267, *Fax:* 435-797-3265, *E-mail:* jones@greg.cs.usu.edu. *Web site:* http://www.cs.usu.edu/

■ VANDERBILT UNIVERSITY

School of Engineering, Department of Electrical Engineering and Computer Science, Program in Computer Science, Nashville, TN 37240-1001

AWARDS M Eng, MS, PhD. MS and PhD offered through the Graduate School. Part-time programs available.

Faculty: 12 full-time (2 women), 1 (woman) part-time/adjunct.
Students: 44 full-time (17 women), 1 part-time; includes 4 minority (3 African Americans, 1 Asian American or Pacific Islander), 27 international. Average age 24. 132 applicants, 20% accepted, 26 enrolled. In 2001, 23 master's, 4 doctorates awarded. Terminal master's awarded for partial completion of doctoral program.
Degree requirements: For master's, thesis (for some programs); for doctorate, thesis/dissertation, comprehensive exam. *Median time to degree:* Master's–2 years full-time; doctorate–5 years full-time.
Entrance requirements: For master's and doctorate, GRE General Test, TOEFL, 3 letters of recommendation. *Application deadline:* For fall admission, 1/15; for spring admission, 11/1. *Application fee:* $40. Electronic applications accepted.
Expenses: Tuition: Full-time $28,350.

Financial support: In 2001–02, 40 students received support, including 4 fellowships with full tuition reimbursements available (averaging $5,000 per year), 17 research assistantships with full tuition reimbursements available (averaging $22,189 per year), 23 teaching assistantships with full tuition reimbursements available (averaging $12,274 per year); institutionally sponsored loans, scholarships/grants, health care benefits, and tuition waivers (full and partial) also available. Financial award application deadline: 1/15.
Faculty research: Artificial intelligence, performance evaluation, databases, software engineering, computational science. *Total annual research expenditures:* $8.5 million.
Application contact: Dr. Gaulam Biswas, Director of Graduate Studies, 615-343-7549, *Fax:* 615-322-0677, *E-mail:* csgradapp@vuse.vanderbilt.edu. *Web site:* http://www.eecs.vuse.vanderbilt.edu/

■ VILLANOVA UNIVERSITY

Graduate School of Liberal Arts and Sciences, Department of Computing Sciences, Villanova, PA 19085-1699

AWARDS MS. Part-time and evening/weekend programs available.

Students: 70 full-time (30 women), 136 part-time (49 women); includes 8 minority (5 African Americans, 3 Asian Americans or Pacific Islanders), 134 international. Average age 29. 145 applicants, 46% accepted. In 2001, 67 degrees awarded.
Degree requirements: For master's, independent study project, thesis optional.
Entrance requirements: For master's, minimum GPA of 3.0. *Application deadline:* For fall admission, 8/1 (priority date); for spring admission, 12/1. *Application fee:* $40.
Expenses: Contact institution.
Financial support: Research assistantships, Federal Work-Study and scholarships/grants available. Financial award application deadline: 4/1; financial award applicants required to submit FAFSA. Dr. Robert Beck, Chair, 610-519-7310. *Web site:* http://www.csc.villanova.edu/academics/grads.html

■ VIRGINIA COMMONWEALTH UNIVERSITY

School of Graduate Studies, School of Engineering, Program in Computer Science, Richmond, VA 23284-9005

AWARDS MS.

Students: 10 full-time, 20 part-time; includes 19 minority (2 African Americans, 17 Asian Americans or Pacific Islanders). 62 applicants, 50% accepted. In 2001, 10 degrees awarded.
Degree requirements: For master's, thesis optional.
Entrance requirements: For master's, GRE General Test. *Application deadline:*

For fall admission, 7/1; for spring admission, 11/15. *Application fee:* $30.
Expenses: Tuition, state resident: full-time $4,276; part-time $238 per credit. Tuition, nonresident: full-time $12,672; part-time $704 per credit. Required fees: $1,167; $43 per credit.
Application contact: Dr. James A. Ames, Program Head. *Web site:* http://www.mas.vcu.edu/

VIRGINIA POLYTECHNIC INSTITUTE AND STATE UNIVERSITY

Graduate School, College of Arts and Sciences, Department of Computer Science, Department of Computer Science, Blacksburg, VA 24061

AWARDS MS, PhD. Part-time and evening/weekend programs available.

Students: 205 full-time (55 women), 70 part-time (15 women); includes 19 minority (4 African Americans, 13 Asian Americans or Pacific Islanders, 2 Hispanic Americans), 186 international. 902 applicants, 30% accepted, 87 enrolled. In 2001, 92 master's, 2 doctorates awarded.
Degree requirements: For master's, thesis optional; for doctorate, thesis/dissertation.
Entrance requirements: For master's and doctorate, GRE General Test, TOEFL. *Application deadline:* For fall admission, 2/1; for spring admission, 10/15. Applications are processed on a rolling basis. *Application fee:* $45. Electronic applications accepted.
Expenses: Tuition, state resident: part-time $241 per hour. Tuition, nonresident: part-time $406 per hour. Tuition and fees vary according to program.
Financial support: In 2001–02, 104 students received support. Application deadline: 2/1.
Application contact: Office of Admissions, *E-mail:* gradprog@cs.vt.edu. *Web site:* http://www.cs.vt.edu

Find an in-depth description at www.petersons.com/gradchannel.

WAKE FOREST UNIVERSITY

Graduate School, Department of Computer Science, Winston-Salem, NC 27109

AWARDS MS. Part-time programs available.

Degree requirements: For master's, one foreign language, thesis optional.
Entrance requirements: For master's, GRE General Test, GRE Subject Test.

WASHINGTON STATE UNIVERSITY

Graduate School, College of Engineering and Architecture, School of Electrical Engineering and Computer Science, Program in Computer Science, Pullman, WA 99164

AWARDS MS, PhD.

Faculty: 10 full-time (1 woman), 3 part-time/adjunct (0 women).
Students: 32 full-time (10 women), 9 part-time (2 women), 32 international. In 2001, 10 master's, 2 doctorates awarded.
Degree requirements: For master's, oral exam, thesis optional; for doctorate, thesis/dissertation, oral exam, qualifying exam.
Entrance requirements: For master's and doctorate, GRE General Test, GRE Subject Test, TOEFL, minimum GPA of 3.0. *Application deadline:* For fall admission, 3/1 (priority date). Applications are processed on a rolling basis. *Application fee:* $35.
Expenses: Tuition, state resident: full-time $6,088; part-time $304 per semester. Tuition, nonresident: full-time $14,918; part-time $746 per semester. Tuition and fees vary according to program.
Financial support: In 2001–02, 6 research assistantships with full and partial tuition reimbursements, 19 teaching assistantships with full and partial tuition reimbursements were awarded. Career-related internships or fieldwork, Federal Work-Study, institutionally sponsored loans, tuition waivers (partial), and teaching associateships also available. Financial award application deadline: 4/1; financial award applicants required to submit FAFSA.
Faculty research: Networks, software engineering, database systems, computer graphics, algorithmics. *Total annual research expenditures:* $3.3 million.
Dr. Thomas R. Fischer, Director, 509-335-8148, *Fax:* 509-335-3818.
Application contact: Dr. Krishna Sivalingam, Graduate Coordinator, 509-335-6601, *Fax:* 509-335-3818, *E-mail:* krishna@eecs.wsu.edu.

WASHINGTON STATE UNIVERSITY SPOKANE

Graduate Programs, Program in Computer Science, Spokane, WA 99201-3899

AWARDS MS.

WASHINGTON UNIVERSITY IN ST. LOUIS

Henry Edwin Sever Graduate School of Engineering and Applied Science, Department of Computer Science, St. Louis, MO 63130-4899

AWARDS MS, D Sc. Part-time programs available.

Faculty: 17 full-time (2 women), 7 part-time/adjunct (0 women).
Students: 86 full-time (15 women), 51 part-time (6 women); includes 10 minority (1 African American, 8 Asian Americans or Pacific Islanders, 1 Hispanic American), 57 international. 299 applicants, 25% accepted, 57 enrolled. In 2001, 20 master's, 5 doctorates awarded. Terminal master's awarded for partial completion of doctoral program.
Degree requirements: For master's, thesis optional; for doctorate, thesis/dissertation.
Entrance requirements: For master's, GRE General Test, TOEFL, TWE, minimum undergraduate GPA of 2.75; for doctorate, GRE General Test, TOEFL, TWE. *Application deadline:* For fall admission, 5/1; for spring admission, 9/15. *Application fee:* $20. Electronic applications accepted.
Expenses: Tuition: Full-time $26,900.
Financial support: In 2001–02, fellowships (averaging $18,250 per year), research assistantships with tuition reimbursements (averaging $19,680 per year), teaching assistantships with tuition reimbursements (averaging $19,680 per year) were awarded. Career-related internships or fieldwork, Federal Work-Study, scholarships/grants, and unspecified assistantships also available. Financial award application deadline: 1/15.
Faculty research: Artificial intelligence, computational science, computer and systems architecture, media and machines, networking and communication, software systems. *Total annual research expenditures:* $4.3 million.
Dr. Gruia-Catalin Roman, Chair, 314-935-6132, *Fax:* 314-935-7302, *E-mail:* roman@cs.wustl.edu.
Application contact: Jean Grothe, Graduate Admissions Coordinator, 314-935-6160, *Fax:* 314-935-7302, *E-mail:* admissions@cs.wustl.edu. *Web site:* http://www.cs.wustl.edu/

Find an in-depth description at www.petersons.com/gradchannel.

WAYNE STATE UNIVERSITY

Graduate School, College of Science, Department of Computer Science, Detroit, MI 48202

AWARDS Computer science (MA, MS, PhD); electronics and computer control systems (MS); scientific computing (Certificate).

Faculty: 9 full-time.

Wayne State University (continued)

Students: 187. 673 applicants, 20% accepted, 65 enrolled. In 2001, 57 master's, 8 doctorates, 2 other advanced degrees awarded.
Degree requirements: For master's, thesis (for some programs); for doctorate, thesis/dissertation.
Entrance requirements: For master's and doctorate, GRE General Test, TOEFL. *Application deadline:* For fall admission, 7/1. *Application fee:* $20 ($30 for international students).
Expenses: Tuition, state resident: full-time $3,764. Tuition and fees vary according to degree level and program.
Financial support: In 2001–02, 1 fellowship, 17 research assistantships, 31 teaching assistantships were awarded. Career-related internships or fieldwork and Federal Work-Study also available.
Faculty research: Neural computation, artificial intelligence, software engineering, distributed systems, databases. *Total annual research expenditures:* $391,330.
William Hase, Chairperson, 313-577-2477, *Fax:* 313-577-6868.
Application contact: Farshad Fotouhi, Graduate Director, 313-577-3107, *Fax:* 313-588-6868, *E-mail:* fotouhi@cs.wayne.edu.

■ WEBSTER UNIVERSITY

School of Business and Technology, Department of Mathematics and Computer Science, St. Louis, MO 63119-3194

AWARDS Computer distributed systems (Certificate); computer science (MS).

Students: 57 full-time (18 women), 211 part-time (51 women); includes 53 minority (16 African Americans, 23 Asian Americans or Pacific Islanders, 13 Hispanic Americans, 1 Native American), 43 international. Average age 36. In 2001, 52 master's, 2 other advanced degrees awarded.
Entrance requirements: For master's, 36 hours of graduate course work. *Application deadline:* Applications are processed on a rolling basis. *Application fee:* $25 ($50 for international students).
Expenses: Tuition: Full-time $7,164; part-time $398 per credit hour.
Financial support: Federal Work-Study available. Support available to part-time students. Financial award application deadline: 4/1; financial award applicants required to submit FAFSA.
Faculty research: Databases, computer information systems networks, operating systems, computer architecture.
Al Cawns, Chair, 314-961-2660 Ext. 7569, *Fax:* 314-963-6050.
Application contact: Denise Harrell, Associate Director of Graduate and Evening Student Admissions, 314-968-6983, *Fax:* 314-968-7116, *E-mail:* gadmit@webster.edu. *Web site:* http://www.webster.edu/depts/business/mathcs/

■ WEST CHESTER UNIVERSITY OF PENNSYLVANIA

Graduate Studies, College of Arts and Sciences, Department of Computer Science, West Chester, PA 19383

AWARDS MS, Certificate. Part-time and evening/weekend programs available.

Faculty: 8.
Students: 19 full-time (9 women), 11 part-time (5 women); includes 5 minority (all Asian Americans or Pacific Islanders), 19 international. Average age 30. 62 applicants, 61% accepted. In 2001, 10 degrees awarded.
Degree requirements: For master's, comprehensive exam.
Entrance requirements: For master's, GRE General Test, interview; for Certificate, GRE General Test. *Application deadline:* For fall admission, 4/15 (priority date); for spring admission, 10/15. Applications are processed on a rolling basis. *Application fee:* $25.
Expenses: Tuition, state resident: full-time $4,600; part-time $256 per credit. Tuition, nonresident: full-time $7,554; part-time $420 per credit. Required fees: $44 per credit.
Financial support: In 2001–02, 2 research assistantships with full tuition reimbursements (averaging $5,000 per year) were awarded. Support available to part-time students. Financial award application deadline: 2/15; financial award applicants required to submit FAFSA.
Faculty research: Automata theory, compilers, non well-founded sets.
Dr. John Weaver, Chair, 610-436-2204.
Application contact: Dr. Elaine Milito, Graduate Coordinator, 610-436-2690, *E-mail:* emilito@wcupa.edu.

■ WESTERN CAROLINA UNIVERSITY

Graduate School, College of Arts and Sciences, Department of Mathematics and Computer Science, Cullowhee, NC 28723

AWARDS Comprehensive education-mathematics (MA Ed). Part-time and evening/weekend programs available.

Faculty: 14 full-time (4 women).
Students: 4 full-time (1 woman), 10 part-time (6 women), 1 international. 9 applicants, 78% accepted, 7 enrolled. In 2001, 4 degrees awarded.
Degree requirements: For master's, thesis optional.
Entrance requirements: For master's, GRE General Test, GRE Subject Test (applied mathematics applicants). *Application deadline:* For fall admission, 5/1 (priority date); for spring admission, 10/1 (priority date). Applications are processed on a rolling basis. *Application fee:* $35.
Expenses: Tuition, state resident: full-time $1,072. Tuition, nonresident: full-time $8,704. Required fees: $1,171.

Financial support: In 2001–02, 3 students received support, including 2 research assistantships with full and partial tuition reimbursements available (averaging $6,507 per year), 1 teaching assistantship with full and partial tuition reimbursement available (averaging $6,507 per year); fellowships, Federal Work-Study, institutionally sponsored loans, and scholarships/grants also available. Financial award application deadline: 3/15; financial award applicants required to submit FAFSA.
Dr. Charles Wallis, Head, 828-227-7245, *Fax:* 828-227-7240, *E-mail:* cwallis@email.wcu.edu.
Application contact: Josie Bewsey, Assistant to the Dean, 828-227-7398, *Fax:* 828-227-7480, *E-mail:* jbewsey@email.wcu.edu. *Web site:* http://www.cs.wcu.edu/

■ WESTERN CONNECTICUT STATE UNIVERSITY

Division of Graduate Studies, School of Arts and Sciences, Department of Mathematics and Computer Science, Danbury, CT 06810-6885

AWARDS Mathematics and computer science (MA); theoretical mathematics (MA). Part-time and evening/weekend programs available.

Faculty: 1 full-time (0 women).
Students: Average age 34. In 2001, 1 degree awarded.
Degree requirements: For master's, thesis or research project.
Entrance requirements: For master's, minimum GPA of 2.5. *Application deadline:* For fall admission, 8/1 (priority date). Applications are processed on a rolling basis. *Application fee:* $40.
Expenses: Tuition, state resident: full-time $2,772; part-time $215 per credit hour. Tuition, nonresident: full-time $7,726. Required fees: $30 per term.
Financial support: Fellowships, career-related internships or fieldwork available. Support available to part-time students. Financial award application deadline: 5/1; financial award applicants required to submit FAFSA.
Dr. C. Edward Sandifer, Professor, 203-837-9351.
Application contact: Chris Shankle, Associate Director of Graduate Admissions, 203-837-8244, *Fax:* 203-837-8338, *E-mail:* shanklec@wcsu.edu. *Web site:* http://www.wcsu.edu/mathcs

■ WESTERN ILLINOIS UNIVERSITY

School of Graduate Studies, College of Business and Technology, Department of Computer Science, Macomb, IL 61455-1390

AWARDS MS. Part-time programs available.

Faculty: 11 full-time (2 women).
Students: 45 full-time (13 women), 17 part-time (3 women); includes 1 minority

(Asian American or Pacific Islander), 43 international. Average age 28. 92 applicants, 15% accepted. In 2001, 40 degrees awarded.
Degree requirements: For master's, thesis or alternative.
Entrance requirements: For master's, proficiency in Java. *Application deadline:* Applications are processed on a rolling basis. *Application fee:* $0 ($25 for international students). Electronic applications accepted.
Expenses: Tuition, state resident: part-time $108 per credit hour. Tuition, nonresident: part-time $216 per credit hour. Required fees: $33 per credit hour.
Financial support: In 2001–02, 27 students received support, including 19 research assistantships with full tuition reimbursements available (averaging $5,720 per year), 8 teaching assistantships with full tuition reimbursements available (averaging $7,140 per year) Financial award applicants required to submit FAFSA.
Faculty research: Space-based life support, public Internet services, artificial intelligence, artificial languages, algorithmic fluency.
Dr. Kathleen Neumann, Chairperson, 309-298-1452.
Application contact: Dr. Barbara Baily, Director of Graduate Studies, 309-298-1806, *Fax:* 309-298-2345, *E-mail:* grad-office@wiu.edu. *Web site:* http://www.wiu.edu/

■ WESTERN KENTUCKY UNIVERSITY

Graduate Studies, Ogden College of Science, and Engineering, Department of Computer Science, Bowling Green, KY 42101-3576

AWARDS MS.

Faculty: 9 full-time (4 women).
Students: In 2001, 8 degrees awarded.
Degree requirements: For master's, comprehensive exam.
Entrance requirements: For master's, GRE General Test, minimum GPA of 2.75. *Application deadline:* For fall admission, 7/1 (priority date); for spring admission, 11/1. Applications are processed on a rolling basis. *Application fee:* $30.
Expenses: Tuition, area resident: Part-time $167 per credit. Tuition, state resident: full-time $2,490. Tuition, nonresident: full-time $6,660; part-time $399 per credit. Required fees: $554. Part-time tuition and fees vary according to campus/location and reciprocity agreements.
Financial support: Research assistantships with partial tuition reimbursements, teaching assistantships with partial tuition reimbursements, Federal Work-Study, institutionally sponsored loans, tuition waivers (partial), unspecified assistantships, and service awards available. Support available to part-time students. Financial award

application deadline: 4/1; financial award applicants required to submit FAFSA.
Faculty research: Visual studio, assessment. *Total annual research expenditures:* $232.
Dr. Arthur Shindhelm, Head, 270-745-4642, *Fax:* 270-745-6449, *E-mail:* art.shindhelm@wku.edu.

■ WESTERN MICHIGAN UNIVERSITY

Graduate College, College of Arts and Sciences, Department of Mathematics, Kalamazoo, MI 49008-5202

AWARDS Applied mathematics (MS); computational mathematics (MS); graph theory and computer science (PhD); mathematics (MA, PhD), including mathematics (MA), mathematics education.

Faculty: 28 full-time (9 women).
Students: 22 full-time (11 women), 20 part-time (12 women); includes 2 minority (1 Hispanic American, 1 Native American), 9 international. 29 applicants, 62% accepted, 14 enrolled. In 2001, 19 master's, 1 doctorate awarded.
Degree requirements: For doctorate, one foreign language, thesis/dissertation, 3 comprehensive exams.
Entrance requirements: For doctorate, GRE General Test. *Application deadline:* For fall admission, 2/15 (priority date). Applications are processed on a rolling basis. *Application fee:* $25.
Expenses: Tuition, state resident: part-time $186 per credit hour. Tuition, nonresident: part-time $442 per credit hour. Required fees: $602. One-time fee: $132 part-time. Tuition and fees vary according to course load.
Financial support: Fellowships, research assistantships, teaching assistantships, Federal Work-Study available. Financial award application deadline: 2/15; financial award applicants required to submit FAFSA.
Dr. Jay A. Wood, Chairperson, 616-387-4513.
Application contact: Admissions and Orientation, 616-387-2000, *Fax:* 616-387-2355.

■ WESTERN MICHIGAN UNIVERSITY

Graduate College, College of Engineering and Applied Sciences, Department of Computer Science, Kalamazoo, MI 49008-5202

AWARDS MS, PhD.

Faculty: 14 full-time (2 women).
Students: 137 full-time (28 women), 11 part-time (3 women); includes 2 minority (both Asian Americans or Pacific Islanders), 130 international. 601 applicants, 50% accepted, 47 enrolled. In 2001, 62 degrees awarded.

Degree requirements: For master's, oral exams, thesis optional; for doctorate, 2 foreign languages, thesis/dissertation.
Entrance requirements: For master's and doctorate, GRE General Test. *Application deadline:* For fall admission, 2/15 (priority date). Applications are processed on a rolling basis. *Application fee:* $25.
Expenses: Tuition, state resident: part-time $186 per credit hour. Tuition, nonresident: part-time $442 per credit hour. Required fees: $602. One-time fee: $132 part-time. Tuition and fees vary according to course load.
Financial support: Fellowships, research assistantships, teaching assistantships, career-related internships or fieldwork and institutionally sponsored loans available. Financial award application deadline: 2/15; financial award applicants required to submit FAFSA.
Dr. J. Donald Nelson, Interim Chairperson, 616-387-5646.
Application contact: Admissions and Orientation, 616-387-2000, *Fax:* 616-387-2355.

■ WESTERN WASHINGTON UNIVERSITY

Graduate School, College of Arts and Sciences, Department of Computer Science, Bellingham, WA 98225-5996

AWARDS MS. Part-time programs available.

Degree requirements: For master's, project, thesis optional.
Entrance requirements: For master's, GRE General Test, TOEFL, minimum GPA of 3.0 in last 60 semester hours or last 90 quarter hours.

■ WEST VIRGINIA UNIVERSITY

College of Engineering and Mineral Resources, Lane Department of Computer Science and Electrical Engineering, Program in Computer Science, Morgantown, WV 26506

AWARDS MS, PhD.

Students: 71 full-time (15 women), 21 part-time (7 women); includes 3 minority (all Asian Americans or Pacific Islanders), 67 international. Average age 26. 155 applicants, 46% accepted. In 2001, 28 master's, 3 doctorates awarded.
Degree requirements: For master's, thesis; for doctorate, one foreign language, thesis/dissertation, comprehensive exam.
Entrance requirements: For master's, GRE General Test, TOEFL, minimum GPA of 3.0; for doctorate, GRE General Test, GRE Subject Test, TOEFL. *Application deadline:* For fall admission, 3/15 (priority date). Applications are processed on a rolling basis. *Application fee:* $45.
Expenses: Tuition, state resident: full-time $2,791. Tuition, nonresident: full-time $8,659. Required fees: $1,002. Tuition and fees vary according to program.

West Virginia University (continued)

Financial support: In 2001–02, 23 research assistantships, 28 teaching assistantships were awarded. Federal Work-Study, institutionally sponsored loans, tuition waivers (full and partial), and graduate administrative assistantships also available. Financial award application deadline: 2/1; financial award applicants required to submit FAFSA.

Faculty research: Artificial intelligence, knowledge-based simulation, data communications, mathematical computations, software engineering.

Application contact: Dr. John Atkins, Professor, 304-293-0405 Ext. 2570, *Fax:* 304-293-8602, *E-mail:* john.atkins@mail.wvu.edu. *Web site:* http://www.cs.wvu.edu/

■ WICHITA STATE UNIVERSITY

Graduate School, Fairmount College of Liberal Arts and Sciences, Department of Computer Science, Wichita, KS 67260

AWARDS MS.

Faculty: 8 full-time (1 woman).
Students: 94 full-time (17 women), 61 part-time (18 women); includes 15 minority (all Asian Americans or Pacific Islanders), 113 international. Average age 29. 387 applicants, 56% accepted, 43 enrolled. In 2001, 21 degrees awarded.
Degree requirements: For master's, project, thesis optional.
Entrance requirements: For master's, GRE, TOEFL, minimum GPA of 2.75. *Application deadline:* For spring admission, 1/1. Applications are processed on a rolling basis. *Application fee:* $25 ($40 for international students). Electronic applications accepted.
Expenses: Tuition, state resident: full-time $1,888; part-time $105 per credit. Tuition, nonresident: full-time $6,129; part-time $341 per credit. Required fees: $345; $19 per credit. $17 per semester. Tuition and fees vary according to course load and program.
Financial support: In 2001–02, 7 teaching assistantships with full tuition reimbursements (averaging $4,400 per year) were awarded; research assistantships, unspecified assistantships also available. Financial award application deadline: 4/1.
Faculty research: Software engineering, database systems.
Dr. Prakash Ramanan, Chair, 316-978-3920, *Fax:* 316-978-3984, *E-mail:* prakash.ramanan@wichita.edu. *Web site:* http://www.wichita.edu/

■ WORCESTER POLYTECHNIC INSTITUTE

Graduate Studies, Department of Computer Science, Worcester, MA 01609-2280

AWARDS MS, PhD, Advanced Certificate, Certificate. Part-time and evening/weekend programs available.

Faculty: 20 full-time (5 women), 8 part-time/adjunct (2 women).
Students: 126 full-time (40 women), 59 part-time (13 women); includes 16 minority (1 African American, 14 Asian Americans or Pacific Islanders, 1 Hispanic American), 127 international. 426 applicants, 67% accepted, 61 enrolled. In 2001, 55 master's, 1 doctorate awarded. Terminal master's awarded for partial completion of doctoral program.
Degree requirements: For master's, thesis optional; for doctorate, thesis/dissertation.
Entrance requirements: For master's and doctorate, GRE General Test, TOEFL. *Application deadline:* For fall admission, 2/1 (priority date); for spring admission, 10/15 (priority date). Applications are processed on a rolling basis. *Application fee:* $60. Electronic applications accepted.
Expenses: Tuition: Part-time $796 per credit. Required fees: $20; $752 per credit. One-time fee: $30 full-time.
Financial support: In 2001–02, 51 students received support, including 4 fellowships with full tuition reimbursements available (averaging $11,306 per year), 8 research assistantships with full and partial tuition reimbursements available (averaging $17,256 per year), 25 teaching assistantships with full and partial tuition reimbursements available (averaging $12,942 per year); career-related internships or fieldwork, institutionally sponsored loans, and scholarships/grants also available. Financial award application deadline: 2/15; financial award applicants required to submit FAFSA.
Faculty research: Artificial intelligence, computer networks and distributed systems, database systems, analysis of algorithms, computer graphics and visualization. *Total annual research expenditures:* $429,458.
Dr. Micha Hofri, Head, 508-831-5670, *Fax:* 508-831-5776, *E-mail:* hofri@cs.wpi.edu.
Application contact: Dr. Elke Rundensteiner, Graduate Coordinator, 508-831-5815, *Fax:* 508-831-5776, *E-mail:* rundenst@cs.wpi.edu. *Web site:* http://www.wpi.edu/Academics/Depts/CS/
Find an in-depth description at www.petersons.com/gradchannel.

■ WRIGHT STATE UNIVERSITY

School of Graduate Studies, College of Engineering and Computer Science, Department of Computer Science and Engineering, Computer Science Program, Dayton, OH 45435

AWARDS MS.

Students: 62 full-time (21 women), 18 part-time (6 women); includes 4 minority (all Asian Americans or Pacific Islanders), 59 international. 244 applicants, 66% accepted. In 2001, 35 degrees awarded.
Degree requirements: For master's, thesis optional.
Entrance requirements: For master's, GRE General Test, TOEFL, minimum GPA of 3.0 in major, 2.7 overall. *Application fee:* $25.
Expenses: Tuition, state resident: full-time $7,161; part-time $225 per quarter hour. Tuition, nonresident: full-time $12,324; part-time $385 per quarter hour. Tuition and fees vary according to course load, degree level and program.
Financial support: Fellowships, research assistantships, teaching assistantships, unspecified assistantships available. Support available to part-time students. Financial award application deadline: 3/31; financial award applicants required to submit FAFSA.
Application contact: Dr. Jay E. Dejongh, Graduate Program Director, 937-775-5136, *Fax:* 937-775-5133, *E-mail:* jay.dejongh@wright.edu.
Find an in-depth description at www.petersons.com/gradchannel.

■ WRIGHT STATE UNIVERSITY

School of Graduate Studies, College of Engineering and Computer Science, Department of Computer Science and Engineering, Program in Computer Science and Engineering, Dayton, OH 45435

AWARDS PhD.

Students: 21 full-time (3 women), 5 part-time, 16 international. 34 applicants, 68% accepted.
Degree requirements: For doctorate, thesis/dissertation, candidacy and general exams.
Entrance requirements: For doctorate, GRE General Test, TOEFL, minimum GPA of 3.3. *Application fee:* $25.
Expenses: Tuition, state resident: full-time $7,161; part-time $225 per quarter hour. Tuition, nonresident: full-time $12,324; part-time $385 per quarter hour. Tuition and fees vary according to course load, degree level and program.
Financial support: Application deadline: 3/31.
Dr. Nikolas G. Bourbakis, Director, 937-775-5138, *Fax:* 937-775-5133, *E-mail:* nikolas.bourbakis@wright.edu.

▪ YALE UNIVERSITY

Graduate School of Arts and Sciences, Department of Computer Science, New Haven, CT 06520

AWARDS PhD.

Degree requirements: For doctorate, thesis/dissertation.

Entrance requirements: For doctorate, GRE General Test, GRE Subject Test.

Find an in-depth description at www.petersons.com/gradchannel.

FINANCIAL ENGINEERING

▪ CLAREMONT GRADUATE UNIVERSITY

Graduate Programs, Independent Programs, Department of Mathematics, Claremont, CA 91711-6160

AWARDS Computer science (PhD); engineering mathematics (PhD); financial engineering (MS); operations research and statistics (MA, MS); physical applied mathematics (MA, MS); pure mathematics (MA, MS, PhD); scientific computing (MA, MS); systems and control theory (MA, MS). Part-time programs available.

Faculty: 3 full-time (0 women), 1 part-time/adjunct (0 women).

Students: 28 full-time (8 women), 11 part-time; includes 11 minority (1 African American, 8 Asian Americans or Pacific Islanders, 2 Hispanic Americans), 8 international. Average age 38. In 2001, 4 master's, 2 doctorates awarded. Terminal master's awarded for partial completion of doctoral program.

Degree requirements: For doctorate, 2 foreign languages, thesis/dissertation.

Entrance requirements: For master's and doctorate, GRE General Test. *Application deadline:* For fall admission, 2/15 (priority date). Applications are processed on a rolling basis. *Application fee:* $50. Electronic applications accepted.

Expenses: Tuition: Full-time $22,984; part-time $1,000 per unit. Required fees: $160; $80 per semester.

Financial support: Fellowships, research assistantships, career-related internships or fieldwork, Federal Work-Study, institutionally sponsored loans, and tuition waivers (full and partial) available. Support available to part-time students. Financial award application deadline: 2/15; financial award applicants required to submit FAFSA. John Angus, Chair, 909-621-8080, *Fax:* 909-607-9261, *E-mail:* john.angus@cgu.edu.

Application contact: Mary Solberg, Administrative Assistant, 909-621-8080,

Fax: 909-607-9261, *E-mail:* math@cgu.edu. *Web site:* http://www.cgu.edu/math/index.html

▪ CLAREMONT GRADUATE UNIVERSITY

Graduate Programs, Independent Programs, Program in Financial Engineering, Claremont, CA 91711-6160

AWARDS MSFE, MSFE/EMBA, MSFE/MBA, MSFE/PhD.

Students: 6 full-time (1 woman), 3 part-time; includes 2 minority (1 Asian American or Pacific Islander, 1 Hispanic American), 4 international. Average age 29. In 2001, 14 degrees awarded.

Entrance requirements: For master's, GRE General Test or GMAT. *Application deadline:* For fall admission, 2/15 (priority date). *Application fee:* $50.

Expenses: Tuition: Full-time $22,984; part-time $1,000 per unit. Required fees: $160; $80 per semester.

Financial support: Application deadline: 2/15.
Richard Smith, Director, 909-607-3310, *Fax:* 909-621-9104, *E-mail:* fineng@cgu.edu.

Application contact: Kate Rogel, Secretary, 909-607-3310, *Fax:* 909-621-9104, *E-mail:* fineng@cgu.edu. *Web site:* http://www.cgu.edu/mafe/

▪ CLAREMONT GRADUATE UNIVERSITY

Graduate Programs, Peter F. Drucker Graduate School of Management, Claremont, CA 91711-6160

AWARDS Executive management (EMBA, MA, MSAM, PhD, Certificate), including advanced management (MSAM), executive management (EMBA, MA, PhD, Certificate); financial engineering (MS); management (MBA), including business administration, finance, international business, marketing, strategic management. Part-time programs available.

Faculty: 13 full-time (2 women), 9 part-time/adjunct (1 woman).

Students: 139 full-time (48 women), 198 part-time (76 women); includes 75 minority (9 African Americans, 46 Asian Americans or Pacific Islanders, 19 Hispanic Americans, 1 Native American), 80 international. Average age 38. In 2001, 126 master's, 4 doctorates awarded.

Entrance requirements: For doctorate, GMAT or GRE General Test. *Application deadline:* For fall admission, 2/15 (priority date). Applications are processed on a rolling basis. *Application fee:* $50. Electronic applications accepted.

Expenses: Tuition: Full-time $22,984; part-time $1,000 per unit. Required fees: $160; $80 per semester.

Financial support: Fellowships, research assistantships, teaching assistantships,

career-related internships or fieldwork, Federal Work-Study, and institutionally sponsored loans available. Support available to part-time students. Financial award application deadline: 2/15; financial award applicants required to submit FAFSA.

Faculty research: Strategy and leadership, brand management, cost management and control, organizational transformation, general management.
Cornelis de Kluyver, Dean, 909-607-3778, *Fax:* 909-621-8543, *E-mail:* drucker@cgu.edu.

Application contact: Go Yoshida, Assistant Director/Market Research, 909-607-7810, *Fax:* 909-621-8543, *E-mail:* drucker@cgu.edu. *Web site:* http://www.drucker.cgu.edu

▪ COLUMBIA UNIVERSITY

Fu Foundation School of Engineering and Applied Science, Department of Industrial Engineering and Operations Research, New York, NY 10027

AWARDS Financial engineering (MS); industrial engineering (MS, Eng Sc D, PhD, Engr); operations research (MS, Eng Sc D, PhD). Part-time and evening/weekend programs available. Postbaccalaureate distance learning degree programs offered (no on-campus study).

Faculty: 16 full-time (0 women), 10 part-time/adjunct (0 women).

Students: 91 full-time (31 women), 69 part-time (21 women); includes 9 minority (8 Asian Americans or Pacific Islanders, 1 Native American), 125 international. Average age 26. 482 applicants, 46% accepted, 72 enrolled. In 2001, 76 master's, 4 doctorates awarded. Terminal master's awarded for partial completion of doctoral program.

Degree requirements: For doctorate, thesis/dissertation, oral and written qualifying exams.

Entrance requirements: For master's, doctorate, and Engr, GRE General Test, TOEFL. *Application deadline:* For fall admission, 1/5; for spring admission, 10/1. *Application fee:* $55. Electronic applications accepted.

Expenses: Tuition: Full-time $27,528. Required fees: $1,638.

Financial support: In 2001–02, 2 fellowships (averaging $5,000 per year), 12 research assistantships with full tuition reimbursements (averaging $19,200 per year), 12 teaching assistantships with full tuition reimbursements (averaging $19,200 per year) were awarded. Federal Work-Study also available. Financial award application deadline: 1/5; financial award applicants required to submit FAFSA.

Faculty research: Discrete event stochastic systems, optimization, production planning and scheduling, inventory control, yield management, simulation, mathematical programming, combinatorial

Columbia University (continued)
optimization, queuing, financial engineering. *Total annual research expenditures:* $682,685.
Dr. Donald Goldfarb, Chairman, 212-854-8011, *Fax:* 212-854-8103, *E-mail:* gold@ieor.columbia.edu.
Application contact: Nathaniel C. Farrell, Program Coordinator, 212-854-4351, *Fax:* 212-854-8103, *E-mail:* nat@ieor.columbia.edu. *Web site:* http://www.ieor.columbia.edu/
Find an in-depth description at www.petersons.com/gradchannel.

■ KENT STATE UNIVERSITY

Graduate School of Management, Program in Financial Engineering, Kent, OH 44242-0001

AWARDS MSFE.

Faculty: 10 full-time (2 women).
Degree requirements: For master's, capstone project.
Entrance requirements: For master's, GMAT or GRE. *Application deadline:* For fall admission, 4/1 (priority date). Applications are processed on a rolling basis. *Application fee:* $30. Electronic applications accepted.
Financial support: In 2001–02, 3 research assistantships (averaging $12,000 per year) were awarded; Federal Work-Study also available. Financial award application deadline: 4/1.
Faculty research: Stochastic models, financial derivatives.
Dr. Mark E. Holder, Assistant Professor, 330-672-2282, *Fax:* 330-672-9806, *E-mail:* mholder@kent.edu.
Application contact: *E-mail:* msfe@kent.edu.

■ POLYTECHNIC UNIVERSITY, BROOKLYN CAMPUS

Department of Management, Major in Financial Engineering, Brooklyn, NY 11201-2990

AWARDS MS.

Degree requirements: For master's, thesis or alternative.
Entrance requirements: For master's, GMAT, minimum B average in undergraduate course work. Electronic applications accepted.

■ POLYTECHNIC UNIVERSITY, LONG ISLAND GRADUATE CENTER

Graduate Programs, Department of Management, Major in Financial Engineering, Melville, NY 11747

AWARDS MS.

Electronic applications accepted.

■ POLYTECHNIC UNIVERSITY, WESTCHESTER GRADUATE CENTER

Graduate Programs, Division of Management, Major in Financial Engineering, Hawthorne, NY 10532-1507

AWARDS MS.

Electronic applications accepted.

■ PRINCETON UNIVERSITY

Graduate School, School of Engineering and Applied Science, Department of Operations Research and Financial Engineering, Princeton, NJ 08544-1019

AWARDS Financial engineering (M Eng); operations research and financial engineering (MSE, PhD). *Web site:* http://www.orfe.princeton.edu/

■ UNIVERSITY OF CALIFORNIA, BERKELEY

Graduate Division, Haas School of Business, Concurrent Program in Business Administration and Financial Engineering, Berkeley, CA 94720-1500

AWARDS MBA/MFE.

Electronic applications accepted.
Expenses: Tuition, nonresident: full-time $10,704. Required fees: $4,349.
Faculty research: Financial economics, modern portfolio theory, valuation of exotic options, mortgage markets. *Web site:* http://www.haas.berkeley.edu/MFE

■ UNIVERSITY OF CALIFORNIA, BERKELEY

Graduate Division, Haas School of Business, Program in Financial Engineering, Berkeley, CA 94720-1500

AWARDS MFE.

Faculty: 13 full-time (1 woman), 3 part-time/adjunct (0 women).
Students: 48 full-time (4 women); includes 5 minority (3 Asian Americans or Pacific Islanders, 2 Hispanic Americans), 35 international. Average age 29. 240 applicants, 25% accepted, 48 enrolled. In 2001, 45 degrees awarded.
Degree requirements: For master's, applied finance project. *Median time to degree:* Master's–1 year full-time.
Entrance requirements: For master's, GMAT or GRE. *Application deadline:* For spring admission, 10/2. Applications are processed on a rolling basis. *Application fee:* $125. Electronic applications accepted.
Expenses: Contact institution.
Financial support: In 2001–02, 8 students received support. Career-related internships or fieldwork available. Support available to part-time students. Financial award

application deadline: 3/1; financial award applicants required to submit FAFSA.
Faculty research: Financial economics, modern portfolio theory, valuation of exotic options, mortgage markets.
John O'Brien, Executive Director, Master's of Engineering Program, 510-642-4417, *Fax:* 510-643-4345, *E-mail:* mfe@haas.berkeley.edu.
Application contact: Yong No, Information Contact, 510-642-4417, *Fax:* 510-643-4345, *E-mail:* mfe@haas.berkeley.edu. *Web site:* http://www.haas.berkeley.edu/MFE

■ UNIVERSITY OF MICHIGAN

Horace H. Rackham School of Graduate Studies, College of Engineering, Program in Financial Engineering, Ann Arbor, MI 48109

AWARDS MS. Part-time programs available.

Faculty: 6 full-time (1 woman).
Students: 42 full-time (12 women), 5 part-time; includes 7 minority (3 African Americans, 3 Asian Americans or Pacific Islanders, 1 Native American), 32 international. Average age 29. 162 applicants, 63% accepted, 38 enrolled. In 2001, 12 degrees awarded.
Degree requirements: For master's, registration. *Median time to degree:* Master's–1.5 years full-time.
Entrance requirements: For master's, GRE or GMAT, TOEFL. *Application deadline:* For fall admission, 5/1; for winter admission, 10/1. Applications are processed on a rolling basis. *Application fee:* $55. Electronic applications accepted.
Financial support: In 2001–02, 2 fellowships with full tuition reimbursements (averaging $25,704 per year), 2 teaching assistantships with full tuition reimbursements (averaging $12,852 per year) were awarded. Career-related internships or fieldwork also available. Financial award applicants required to submit FAFSA.
Prof. Romesh Saigal, Director, 734-763-7544, *Fax:* 734-647-0079, *E-mail:* rsaigal@umich.edu.
Application contact: Henia Kamil, Program Manager, 734-763-1134, *Fax:* 734-647-0079, *E-mail:* autoeng@umich.edu. *Web site:* http://interpro.engin.umich.edu/fep/
Find an in-depth description at www.petersons.com/gradchannel.

■ UNIVERSITY OF TULSA

Graduate School, College of Business Administration, Program in Finance, Tulsa, OK 74104-3189

AWARDS Corporate finance (MS); international finance (MS); investment and portfolio management (MS); risk management/financial engineering (MS). Part-time and evening/weekend programs available.

Faculty: 5 full-time (0 women).

Students: 4 full-time (1 woman), 12 part-time (4 women); includes 1 minority (Native American), 5 international. 21 applicants, 100% accepted, 14 enrolled. **Entrance requirements:** For master's, GMAT, TOEFL. *Application deadline:* Applications are processed on a rolling basis. *Application fee:* $30.
Expenses: Tuition: Full-time $9,540; part-time $530 per credit hour. Required fees: $80. One-time fee: $230 full-time.
Financial support: In 2001–02, 5 teaching assistantships with full and partial tuition reimbursements (averaging $5,250 per year) were awarded; career-related internships or fieldwork, Federal Work-Study, institutionally sponsored loans, scholarships/grants, and unspecified assistantships also available. Support available to part-time students. Financial award application deadline: 2/1; financial award applicants required to submit FAFSA. *Web site:* http://www.cba.utulsa.edu/msfinance/

HEALTH INFORMATICS

■ THE COLLEGE OF ST. SCHOLASTICA

Graduate Studies, Department of Health Information Management, Duluth, MN 55811-4199

AWARDS MA. Part-time programs available. Postbaccalaureate distance learning degree programs offered (minimal on-campus study).

Faculty: 5 full-time (2 women), 9 part-time/adjunct (7 women).
Students: 1 (woman) full-time, 20 part-time (18 women); includes 2 minority (both African Americans). Average age 43. 17 applicants, 53% accepted, 7 enrolled. In 2001, 17 degrees awarded.
Degree requirements: For master's, thesis.
Entrance requirements: For master's, interview, minimum GPA of 3.0. *Application deadline:* Applications are processed on a rolling basis. *Application fee:* $50. Electronic applications accepted.
Expenses: Tuition: Part-time $565 per credit. Tuition and fees vary according to course load and program.
Financial support: In 2001–02, 2 students received support. Scholarships/grants available. Support available to part-time students. Financial award applicants required to submit FAFSA.
Shirley Eichenwald, Director, 218-723-6011, *Fax:* 218-733-2239, *E-mail:* seichenw@css.edu. *Web site:* http://www.css.edu/depts/grad/him/him_grad.html

■ DUKE UNIVERSITY

School of Nursing, Durham, NC 27708-0586

AWARDS Adult acute care (Certificate); adult cardiovascular (Certificate); adult oncology/HIV (Certificate); adult primary care (Certificate); clinical nurse specialist (MSN), including adult oncology/HIV, gerontology, neonatal, pediatric, pediatric acute care; clinical research management (MSN, Certificate); family (Certificate); gerontology (Certificate); health and nursing ministries (MSN, Certificate); health systems leadership and outcomes (MSN, Certificate); leadership in community based long term care (MSN, Certificate); neonatal (Certificate); nurse anesthetist (MSN, Certificate); nurse practitioner (MSN), including adult acute care, adult cardiovascular, adult oncology/HIV, adult primary care, family, gerontology, neonatal, pediatric, pediatric acute care; nursing informatics (Certificate); pediatric (Certificate); pediatric acute care (Certificate). Part-time programs available. Postbaccalaureate distance learning degree programs offered (minimal on-campus study).

Faculty: 29 full-time, 5 part-time/adjunct.
Students: 99 full-time (92 women), 85 part-time (80 women); includes 28 minority (17 African Americans, 6 Asian Americans or Pacific Islanders, 4 Hispanic Americans, 1 Native American). Average age 37. 106 applicants, 74% accepted, 54 enrolled. In 2001, 89 master's, 17 other advanced degrees awarded.
Degree requirements: For master's, thesis optional.
Entrance requirements: For master's, GRE General Test or MAT, 1 year of nursing experience, BSN, minimum GPA of 3.0, previous course work in statistics; for Certificate, MSN. *Application deadline:* For fall admission, 3/1 (priority date); for spring admission, 10/1 (priority date). Applications are processed on a rolling basis. *Application fee:* $50.
Expenses: Contact institution.
Financial support: Career-related internships or fieldwork, institutionally sponsored loans, scholarships/grants, and traineeships available. Support available to part-time students. Financial award application deadline: 6/30; financial award applicants required to submit FAFSA.
Faculty research: Gerontology, care of premature infants, sudden infant death syndrome, symptom distress in cancer, Latino health. *Total annual research expenditures:* $730,720.
Dr. Mary T. Champagne, Dean, 919-684-3786, *Fax:* 919-681-8899, *E-mail:* champ001@mc.duke.edu.
Application contact: Jennifer Avery, Admissions Officer, 919-684-4248, *Fax:* 919-681-8899, *E-mail:* avery014@mc.duke.edu. *Web site:* http://son3.mc.duke.edu/

■ LA SALLE UNIVERSITY

Program in Nursing, Philadelphia, PA 19141-1199

AWARDS Adult health and illness, clinical nurse specialist (MSN); clinical research (Certificate); nursing administration (MSN); nursing education (Certificate); nursing informatics (Certificate); primary care of adults-nurse practitioner (MSN); public health nursing (MSN); school nurse (Certificate); wound, ostomy, and continence nursing (MSN, Certificate). Part-time programs available. Postbaccalaureate distance learning degree programs offered (minimal on-campus study).

Faculty: 13 full-time (12 women), 8 part-time/adjunct (5 women).
Students: 11 full-time (6 women), 179 part-time (165 women); includes 12 minority (8 African Americans, 2 Asian Americans or Pacific Islanders, 2 Hispanic Americans). Average age 37. 93 applicants, 85% accepted, 75 enrolled. In 2001, 30 degrees awarded.
Entrance requirements: For master's, GRE or MAT, 1 year of professional work experience, BSN, Pennsylvania RN license. *Application deadline:* Applications are processed on a rolling basis. *Application fee:* $30.
Expenses: Contact institution.
Financial support: In 2001–02, 49 students received support; teaching assistantships, institutionally sponsored loans, scholarships/grants, and traineeships available. Support available to part-time students. Financial award application deadline: 7/1.
Faculty research: Medication errors, wound care, metacognition, education of RN students.
Dr. Zane R. Wolf, Dean, 215-951-1430, *Fax:* 215-951-1896, *E-mail:* wolf@lasalle.edu.
Application contact: Dr. Janice Beitz, Graduate Director, 215-951-1430, *Fax:* 215-951-1896, *E-mail:* beitz@lasalle.edu.

■ LOMA LINDA UNIVERSITY

School of Allied Health Professions, Department of Health Information Systems, Loma Linda, CA 92350

AWARDS MHIS.

Faculty: 10 full-time (8 women), 8 part-time/adjunct (6 women).
Students: 20 full-time (18 women), 80 part-time (76 women).
Application fee: $50.
Expenses: Tuition: Part-time $420 per unit.
Marilyn H. Davidian, Chair.

■ MEDICAL UNIVERSITY OF SOUTH CAROLINA

College of Health Professions, Department of Health Administration and Policy, Program in Health Information Administration, Charleston, SC 29425-0002

AWARDS MHS, MHA/MHS. Part-time and evening/weekend programs available. Postbaccalaureate distance learning degree programs offered.

Medical University of South Carolina (continued)

Faculty: 2 full-time (both women).
Students: 4 full-time (1 woman), 10 part-time (4 women); includes 1 minority (African American), 1 international. Average age 35. In 2001, 4 degrees awarded.
Degree requirements: For master's, 20 hours of community service.
Entrance requirements: For master's, GRE General Test, TOEFL, minimum GPA of 3.0. *Application deadline:* For fall admission, 7/31 (priority date); for winter admission, 12/1 (priority date); for spring admission, 4/15 (priority date). Applications are processed on a rolling basis. *Application fee:* $55.
Expenses: Tuition, state resident: part-time $210 per term. Tuition, nonresident: part-time $279 per term. Required fees: $70 per term. Tuition and fees vary according to degree level and program.
Financial support: Fellowships, research assistantships, Federal Work-Study and scholarships/grants available. Support available to part-time students. Financial award application deadline: 3/15; financial award applicants required to submit FAFSA.
Faculty research: Computer-based patient records, Internet use in health care, health information networks, continuous quality improvement, organizational behavior.
Dr. Karen A. Wager, Director, 843-792-4492, *Fax:* 843-792-3327, *E-mail:* wagerka@musc.edu.
Application contact: Holly Rorabaugh, Student Services Coordinator, 843-792-8510, *Fax:* 843-792-3327, *E-mail:* rorabaugh@musc.edu. *Web site:* http://www.musc.edu/hap/mhsmain.html

■ NEW YORK MEDICAL COLLEGE

School of Public Health, Program in Health Informatics, Valhalla, NY 10595-1691

AWARDS MPH.

Degree requirements: For master's, thesis.
Entrance requirements: For master's, TOEFL, Undergraduate GPA of 3.0 or better.

■ NEW YORK UNIVERSITY

The Steinhardt School of Education, Division of Nursing, Programs in Advanced Practice Nursing, New York, NY 10012-1019

AWARDS Advance practice nursing: adult primary care nurse practitioner (MA); advanced practice nursing: adult acute care nurse practitioner (MA, Advanced Certificate); advanced practice nursing: adult primary care nurse practitioner (Advanced Certificate); advanced practice nursing: adult primary care/geriatrics (Advanced Certificate); advanced practice nursing: children with special needs (Advanced Certificate); advanced practice nursing: geriatrics (MA, Advanced Certificate); advanced practice nursing: holistic nursing (MA, Advanced Certificate); advanced practice nursing: home health nursing (Advanced Certificate); advanced practice nursing: mental health (MA, Advanced Certificate); advanced practice nursing: pediatrics (Advanced Certificate); advanced practice nursing: pediatrics/children with special needs (MA); midwifery (MA, Advanced Certificate); nursing administration (MA, Advanced Certificate); nursing informatics (MA, Advanced Certificate); palliative care (MA, Advanced Certificate); teaching of nursing (MA). Part-time and evening/weekend programs available.

Faculty: 29 full-time (26 women).
Students: 42 full-time (39 women), 365 part-time (348 women); includes 107 minority (45 African Americans, 41 Asian Americans or Pacific Islanders, 21 Hispanic Americans). 152 applicants, 83% accepted, 93 enrolled. In 2001, 90 master's, 14 other advanced degrees awarded.
Degree requirements: For master's, thesis (for some programs).
Entrance requirements: For master's, TOEFL, B.S. in nursing; for Advanced Certificate, TOEFL, master's degree. *Application deadline:* For fall admission, 2/1 (priority date); for spring admission, 12/1. Applications are processed on a rolling basis. *Application fee:* $40 ($60 for international students).
Expenses: Tuition: Full-time $19,536; part-time $814 per credit. Required fees: $1,330; $38 per credit. Tuition and fees vary according to course load and program.
Financial support: Career-related internships or fieldwork, Federal Work-Study, institutionally sponsored loans, scholarships/grants, and tuition waivers (partial) available. Support available to part-time students. Financial award application deadline: 3/1; financial award applicants required to submit FAFSA.
Faculty research: Elderly black diabetics, families and illness, public health nursing, parent-child nursing, health policy costs.
Judi Haber, Director, 212-998-5300.
Application contact: 212-998-5030, *Fax:* 212-995-4328, *E-mail:* grad.admissions@nyu.edu.

■ TOURO COLLEGE

Barry Z. Levine School of Health Sciences, Dix Hills, NY 11746

AWARDS Biomedical sciences (MS); health information management (Certificate); occupational therapy (MS); physical therapy (MS).

Entrance requirements: For degree, minimum GPA of 2.5.
Expenses: Contact institution.

■ THE UNIVERSITY OF ALABAMA AT BIRMINGHAM

Graduate School, School of Health Related Professions, Department of Health Services Administration, Program in Health Informatics, Birmingham, AL 35294

AWARDS MS.

Students: 25 full-time (9 women), 26 part-time (14 women); includes 14 minority (11 African Americans, 2 Asian Americans or Pacific Islanders, 1 Native American), 10 international. 120 applicants, 43% accepted.
Degree requirements: For master's, thesis or alternative.
Entrance requirements: For master's, GRE General Test, MAT, minimum GPA of 3.0, previous course work in computing fundamentals and programming. *Application fee:* $35 ($60 for international students). Electronic applications accepted.
Expenses: Tuition, state resident: full-time $3,058. Tuition, nonresident: full-time $5,746. Tuition and fees vary according to course load, degree level and program.
Financial support: Career-related internships or fieldwork and Federal Work-Study available.
Faculty research: Healthcare/medical informatics, natural language processing, application of expert systems, graphical user interface design.
Dr. Helmuth F. Orthner, Director, 205-934-3509, *Fax:* 205-975-6608, *E-mail:* horthner@uab.edu.

■ UNIVERSITY OF CENTRAL FLORIDA

College of Health and Public Affairs, Program in Health Services, Orlando, FL 32816

AWARDS Health care information systems (Certificate); health services administration (MS); managed care (Certificate); medical group management (Certificate); risk quality management (Certificate). Part-time and evening/weekend programs available.

Faculty: 19 full-time (6 women), 18 part-time/adjunct (12 women).
Students: 35 full-time (23 women), 80 part-time (56 women); includes 42 minority (29 African Americans, 5 Asian Americans or Pacific Islanders, 8 Hispanic Americans), 1 international. Average age 31. 58 applicants, 84% accepted, 27 enrolled. In 2001, 38 degrees awarded.
Degree requirements: For master's, thesis or alternative, research report, comprehensive exam.
Entrance requirements: For master's, GRE General Test, TOEFL. *Application deadline:* For fall admission, 7/15; for spring admission, 10/1. *Application fee:* $20. Electronic applications accepted.
Expenses: Tuition, state resident: part-time $162 per hour. Tuition, nonresident: part-time $569 per hour.

Financial support: In 2001–02, 5 fellowships with partial tuition reimbursements (averaging $6,150 per year), 13 research assistantships with partial tuition reimbursements (averaging $2,408 per year), 21 teaching assistantships with partial tuition reimbursements (averaging $2,274 per year) were awarded. Career-related internships or fieldwork, Federal Work-Study, institutionally sponsored loans, and unspecified assistantships also available. Financial award application deadline: 3/1; financial award applicants required to submit FAFSA.
Dr. Aaron Liberman, Head, 407-823-3264, *E-mail:* aliberma@pegasus.cc.ucf.edu. *Web site:* http://www.ucf.edu/

■ **UNIVERSITY OF LA VERNE**

School of Public Affairs and Health Administration, Department of Health Services Management and Gerontology, Program in Health Administration, La Verne, CA 91750-4443

AWARDS Health administration (MHA); healthcare information management (MHA); managed care (MHA). Part-time programs available.

Faculty: 3 full-time (2 women), 2 part-time/adjunct (1 woman).
Students: 4 full-time (2 women), 23 part-time (15 women); includes 16 minority (6 African Americans, 4 Asian Americans or Pacific Islanders, 4 Hispanic Americans, 2 Native Americans), 2 international. Average age 37. In 2001, 1 degree awarded. *Application deadline:* Applications are processed on a rolling basis. *Application fee:* $40.
Expenses: Tuition: Full-time $4,410; part-time $245 per unit. Required fees: $60. Tuition and fees vary according to course load, degree level, campus/location and program.
Financial support: In 2001–02, 11 students received support. Application deadline: 3/2.
Application contact: Jo Nell Baker, Director, Graduate Admissions and Academic Services, 909-593-3511 Ext. 4504, *Fax:* 909-392-2761, *E-mail:* bakerj@ulv.edu. *Web site:* http://www.ulv.edu/mha/

■ **UNIVERSITY OF MEDICINE AND DENTISTRY OF NEW JERSEY**

School of Nursing, Program in Nursing Informatics—Newark, Newark, NJ 07107-3001

AWARDS MSN.

Application deadline: For fall admission, 4/15; for spring admission, 10/15. Applications are processed on a rolling basis. *Application fee:* $30.
Expenses: Tuition: state resident: part-time $292 per credit. Tuition, nonresident: part-time $440 per credit. Full-time

tuition and fees vary according to degree level, program and student level.
Financial support: Application deadline: 5/1.
Application contact: Joan Shields, Manager, Enrollment and Student Services, 973-972-5447, *Fax:* 973-972-7453, *E-mail:* shieldjo@umdnj.edu.

■ **UNIVERSITY OF MEDICINE AND DENTISTRY OF NEW JERSEY**

School of Nursing, Program in Nursing Informatics—Stratford, Newark, NJ 07107-3001

AWARDS MSN.

Application deadline: For fall admission, 4/15; for spring admission, 10/15. Applications are processed on a rolling basis. *Application fee:* $30.
Expenses: Tuition, state resident: part-time $292 per credit. Tuition, nonresident: part-time $440 per credit. Full-time tuition and fees vary according to degree level, program and student level.
Financial support: Application deadline: 5/1.
Dr. Joseph Kristoff, Track Coordinator, 856-566-7158, *Fax:* 856-566-6203.
Application contact: Davida E. Wedington, Admissions Information, 856-566-6200, *Fax:* 856-566-6203, *E-mail:* wedingda@umdnj.edu.

■ **UNIVERSITY OF MINNESOTA, TWIN CITIES CAMPUS**

Graduate School, Program in Health Informatics, Minneapolis, MN 55455-0213

AWARDS MS, PhD. Part-time programs available.

Faculty: 18 full-time (5 women), 7 part-time/adjunct (1 woman).
Students: 32 full-time (16 women); includes 12 minority (all Asian Americans or Pacific Islanders), 13 international. Average age 32. 82 applicants, 43% accepted, 14 enrolled. In 2001, 6 degrees awarded.
Degree requirements: For master's, thesis or alternative; for doctorate, thesis/dissertation. *Median time to degree:* Master's–6 years full-time.
Entrance requirements: For master's and doctorate, GRE General Test, previous course work in life sciences, programming, differential equations. *Application deadline:* For fall admission, 6/30. Applications are processed on a rolling basis. *Application fee:* $50 ($55 for international students). Electronic applications accepted.
Expenses: Tuition, state resident: full-time $2,932; part-time $489 per credit. Tuition, nonresident: full-time $5,758; part-time $960 per credit. Part-time tuition and fees vary according to course load, program and reciprocity agreements.

Financial support: In 2001–02, 24 students received support, including 7 fellowships with full tuition reimbursements available (averaging $35,220 per year), 16 research assistantships with full and partial tuition reimbursements available (averaging $13,250 per year), 1 teaching assistantship with full and partial tuition reimbursement available (averaging $13,250 per year); Federal Work-Study, scholarships/grants, traineeships, and tuition waivers (full and partial) also available. Financial award application deadline: 1/15.
Faculty research: Medical decision making, physiological control systems, population studies, clinical information systems, telemedicine. *Total annual research expenditures:* $1.4 million.
Dr. Stuart Speedie, Director, 612-625-8440, *Fax:* 612-625-7166, *E-mail:* speed002@umn.edu.
Application contact: Doreen Gruebele, Principal Secretary, 612-625-8440, *Fax:* 612-625-7166, *E-mail:* doreen@umn.edu. *Web site:* http://www.hinf.umn.edu/

■ **UNIVERSITY OF MISSOURI–COLUMBIA**

Graduate School, Department of Health Management and Informatics, Columbia, MO 65211

AWARDS Health administration (MHA); health informatics (MHA); health services management (MHA). Part-time programs available.

Faculty: 12 full-time (4 women).
Students: 49 full-time (24 women), 4 part-time (2 women); includes 3 minority (2 Hispanic Americans, 1 Native American), 13 international. In 2001, 23 degrees awarded.
Entrance requirements: For master's, GRE General Test or GMAT, minimum GPA of 3.0. *Application fee:* $25 ($50 for international students).
Expenses: Tuition, state resident: part-time $179 per credit hour. Tuition, nonresident: part-time $539 per credit hour. Required fees: $122 per semester. Tuition and fees vary according to program.
Financial support: Research assistantships, teaching assistantships, institutionally sponsored loans available.
Dr. Joseph W. Hales, Director of Graduate Studies, 573-884-3915, *E-mail:* halesj@missouri.edu. *Web site:* http://www.hmi.missouri.edu/

■ **UNIVERSITY OF PUERTO RICO, MEDICAL SCIENCES CAMPUS**

College of Health Related Professions, Program in Health Information Management, San Juan, PR 00936-5067

AWARDS MS. Part-time programs available.

Faculty: 4 full-time (all women), 1 (woman) part-time/adjunct.

University of Puerto Rico, Medical Sciences Campus (continued)

Students: 13 full-time (all women), 9 part-time (7 women). Average age 27. 18 applicants, 56% accepted. In 2001, 8 degrees awarded.
Degree requirements: For master's, one foreign language, thesis or alternative, internship.
Entrance requirements: For master's, PAEG, interview. *Application deadline:* For fall admission, 2/15 (priority date). Applications are processed on a rolling basis. *Application fee:* $25.
Financial support: In 2001–02, 13 students received support, including 10 research assistantships with full tuition reimbursements available (averaging $7,000 per year), 1 teaching assistantship with full tuition reimbursement available (averaging $7,000 per year); career-related internships or fieldwork, Federal Work-Study, institutionally sponsored loans, scholarships/grants, and tuition waivers (partial) also available. Financial award application deadline: 4/30.
Faculty research: Quality of medical records, health information data.
Ana Orabona, Director, 787-758-2525 Ext. 4507.
Application contact: Genoveva Ruiz, Student Affairs Office Director, 787-758-2525 Ext. 4000.

■ UNIVERSITY OF VIRGINIA

College and Graduate School of Arts and Sciences, Department of Health Evaluation Sciences, Charlottesville, VA 22903

AWARDS Clinical investigation (MS); epidemiology (MS); health care informatics (MS); health care resource management (MS); health services research and outcomes evaluation (MS). Part-time programs available.

Faculty: 25 full-time (8 women), 3 part-time/adjunct (2 women).
Students: 15 full-time (8 women), 6 part-time (3 women); includes 2 minority (1 African American, 1 Asian American or Pacific Islander), 3 international. Average age 33. 54 applicants, 59% accepted, 16 enrolled. In 2001, 21 degrees awarded.
Degree requirements: For master's, thesis (for some programs).
Entrance requirements: For master's, GRE or MCAT. *Application deadline:* For fall admission, 3/1 (priority date). *Application fee:* $40. Electronic applications accepted.
Expenses: Tuition, state resident: full-time $3,988. Tuition, nonresident: full-time $17,078. Required fees: $1,190.
Financial support: Career-related internships or fieldwork available. Financial award applicants required to submit FAFSA.
William A. Knaus, Director, 434-924-8430, *Fax:* 434-924-8437.

Application contact: Robyn Kells, Coordinator, 434-924-8646, *Fax:* 434-924-8437, *E-mail:* ms-hes@virginia.edu. *Web site:* http://www.med.virginia.edu/docs/hes/ms-program/

■ UNIVERSITY OF WASHINGTON

School of Medicine and Graduate School, Graduate Programs in Medicine, Department of Medical Education and Health Informatics, Division of Biomedical and Health Informatics, Seattle, WA 98195

AWARDS MS.

Entrance requirements: For master's, GRE General Test, TOEFL, minimum GPA of 3.0; previous undergraduate course work in biology, computer programming, and mathematics. *Application deadline:* For fall admission, 2/1. *Application fee:* $50. Electronic applications accepted.
Expenses: Tuition, state resident: full-time $5,539. Tuition, nonresident: full-time $14,376. Required fees: $390. Tuition and fees vary according to course load and program.
Dr. Ira Kalet, Director.
Application contact: Jennifer Hoffman, Program Manager, *Fax:* 206-543-3461, *E-mail:* informat@u.washington.edu.

HUMAN-COMPUTER INTERACTION

■ CARNEGIE MELLON UNIVERSITY

School of Computer Science, Department of Human-Computer Interaction, Pittsburgh, PA 15213-3891

AWARDS MHCI, PhD.

Entrance requirements: For master's, GRE General Test, GRE Subject Test. *Web site:* http://www.cs.cmu.edu/

Find an in-depth description at www.petersons.com/gradchannel.

■ DEPAUL UNIVERSITY

School of Computer Science, Telecommunications, and Information Systems, Program in Human-Computer Interaction, Chicago, IL 60604-2287

AWARDS MS. Part-time and evening/weekend programs available. Postbaccalaureate distance learning degree programs offered.

Faculty: 8 full-time (3 women), 9 part-time/adjunct (2 women).
Students: 76 full-time (46 women), 46 part-time (32 women); includes 31 minority (7 African Americans, 13 Asian Americans or Pacific Islanders, 11 Hispanic Americans), 13 international.

Average age 32. 92 applicants, 86% accepted, 53 enrolled. In 2001, 34 degrees awarded.
Degree requirements: For master's, capstone course.
Application deadline: For fall admission, 8/1 (priority date); for winter admission, 11/15 (priority date); for spring admission, 3/1 (priority date). Applications are processed on a rolling basis. *Application fee:* $25. Electronic applications accepted.
Expenses: Tuition: Part-time $362 per credit hour. Tuition and fees vary according to program.
Financial support: In 2001–02, 6 students received support; fellowships, research assistantships, teaching assistantships, Federal Work-Study, tuition waivers (full and partial), and unspecified assistantships available. Support available to part-time students. Financial award application deadline: 4/1; financial award applicants required to submit FAFSA.
Faculty research: Computer graphics, human and computer interaction, cognitive science, animation computational geometry, physical based modeling.
Dr. Martin Kalin, Associate Dean, 312-362-8864, *E-mail:* mkalin@cs.depaul.edu.
Application contact: Genaro Balcazar, Director of Admissions, 312-362-8714, *Fax:* 312-362-6116, *E-mail:* ctiadmissions@cs.depaul.edu. *Web site:* http://www.cs.depaul.edu/

■ GEORGIA INSTITUTE OF TECHNOLOGY

Graduate Studies and Research, Ivan Allen College of Policy and International Affairs, Multidisciplinary Program in Human Computer Interaction, Atlanta, GA 30332-0001

AWARDS MSHCI.

Entrance requirements: For master's, TOEFL.

■ INDIANA UNIVERSITY BLOOMINGTON

School of Informatics, Bloomington, IN 47405

AWARDS Bioinformatics (MS); chemical informatics (MS); human computer interaction (MS); new media (MS), including media arts and science.

Students: 13 full-time (4 women), 2 part-time (1 woman); includes 2 minority (both Asian Americans or Pacific Islanders), 5 international. Average age 30.
Application fee: $45 ($55 for international students).
Expenses: Tuition, state resident: full-time $4,720; part-time $197 per credit. Tuition, nonresident: full-time $13,748; part-time $573 per credit. Required fees: $642.
Financial support: In 2001–02, fellowships (averaging $5,000 per year)
J. Michael Dunn, Dean. *Web site:* http://www.informatics.indiana.edu/

■ NAVAL POSTGRADUATE SCHOOL

Graduate Programs, Program in Modeling Virtual Environments and Simulations, Monterey, CA 93943

AWARDS MS, PhD. Program only open to commissioned officers of the United States and friendly nations and selected United States federal civilian employees. Part-time programs available.

Degree requirements: For master's, thesis; for doctorate, one foreign language, thesis/dissertation.

■ TUFTS UNIVERSITY

Division of Graduate and Continuing Studies and Research, Graduate and Professional Studies, Human-Computer Interaction Program, Medford, MA 02155

AWARDS Certificate. Part-time and evening/weekend programs available.

Students: Average age 32. 6 applicants, 100% accepted. In 2001, 2 degrees awarded.
Application deadline: For fall admission, 8/15 (priority date); for spring admission, 12/12 (priority date). Applications are processed on a rolling basis. *Application fee:* $50. Electronic applications accepted.
Expenses: Tuition: Full-time $26,853. Full-time tuition and fees vary according to program.
Financial support: Available to part-time students. Application deadline: 5/1.
Alida Poirier, Assistant Director, 617-627-3395, *Fax:* 617-627-3016, *E-mail:* pcs@ase.tufts.edu.
Application contact: Information Contact, 617-627-3395, *Fax:* 617-627-3016, *E-mail:* pcs@ase.tufts.edu. *Web site:* http://ase.tufts.edu/gradstudy

■ UNIVERSITY OF BALTIMORE

Graduate School, College of Liberal Arts, School of Information Arts and Technologies, Program in Interaction Design and Information Architecture, Baltimore, MD 21201-5779

AWARDS MS, DCD.

Degree requirements: For master's, project or thesis.
Entrance requirements: For master's, General GRE or Miller Analogy Test, undergraduate GPA of 3.0. Electronic applications accepted.
Expenses: Tuition, state resident: full-time $5,508; part-time $306 per credit. Tuition, nonresident: full-time $8,352; part-time $464 per credit. Required fees: $37 per credit. $60 per semester. Tuition and fees vary according to course load and degree level.

Find an in-depth description at www.petersons.com/gradchannel.

■ UNIVERSITY OF MICHIGAN

Horace H. Rackham School of Graduate Studies, School of Information, Ann Arbor, MI 48109

AWARDS Archives and records management (MS); human-computer interaction (MS); information (PhD); information economics, management and policy (MS); library and information services (MS). Part-time programs available.

Entrance requirements: For master's and doctorate, GRE General Test. *Web site:* http://www.si.umich.edu/

Find an in-depth description at www.petersons.com/gradchannel.

INFORMATION SCIENCE

■ ALCORN STATE UNIVERSITY

School of Graduate Studies, School of Arts and Sciences, Department of Mathematical Sciences, Alcorn State, MS 39096-7500

AWARDS Computer and information sciences (MS).

Application deadline: For fall admission, 7/15 (priority date); for spring admission, 11/25. Applications are processed on a rolling basis. *Application fee:* $0 ($10 for international students).
Expenses: Tuition, state resident: full-time $6,418; part-time $924 per credit. Tuition, nonresident: full-time $12,497; part-time $1,656 per credit.
Dr. Keith Alford, Chairperson, 601-877-6420.

■ AMERICAN INTERCONTINENTAL UNIVERSITY

Program in Information Technology, Atlanta, GA 30328

AWARDS MIT. Part-time and evening/weekend programs available.

Faculty: 40 full-time (10 women), 6 part-time/adjunct (2 women).
Students: 34 full-time (13 women), 190 part-time (91 women); includes 124 minority (106 African Americans, 13 Asian Americans or Pacific Islanders, 5 Hispanic Americans). 189 applicants, 46% accepted, 86 enrolled.
Degree requirements: For master's, technical proficiency demonstration.
Median time to degree: Master's–1.5 years part-time.
Entrance requirements: For master's, Computer Programmer Aptitude Battery Exam, interview. *Application deadline:* For fall admission, 11/27 (priority date); for winter admission, 1/28 (priority date); for spring admission, 4/8 (priority date). Applications are processed on a rolling

basis. *Application fee:* $50. Electronic applications accepted.
Expenses: Tuition: Part-time $3,485 per term. Required fees: $300 per term. Tuition and fees vary according to program.
Financial support: Institutionally sponsored loans available. Support available to part-time students. Financial award application deadline: 4/30; financial award applicants required to submit FAFSA.
Faculty research: Operating systems, security issues, networks and routing, computer hardware.
Ed Malin, Dean, 404-965-6500 Ext. 6536, *Fax:* 404-965-6502, *E-mail:* emalin@aiuniv.edu.
Application contact: Karen Thurgood, Director of Admissions, 404-965-6500 Ext. 8072, *Fax:* 404-965-6502, *E-mail:* kthurgood@aiuniv.edu. *Web site:* http://www.aiuniv.edu/

Find an in-depth description at www.petersons.com/gradchannel.

■ AMERICAN INTERCONTINENTAL UNIVERSITY ONLINE

Program in Information Technology, Hoffman Estates, IL 60192

AWARDS MIT.

Application deadline: Applications are processed on a rolling basis. *Application fee:* $50.
Expenses: Tuition: Full-time $18,000. Required fees: $2,300. One-time fee: $175 full-time. Full-time tuition and fees vary according to program.
Dr. Robin Throne, Chief Academic Officer, 847-585-2002, *Fax:* 847-585-2042, *E-mail:* rthrone@aiu-online.com.
Application contact: Stephen Fireng, Vice President of Admissions, 877-701-3800, *Fax:* 847-585-2695, *E-mail:* sfireng@careered.com.

■ AMERICAN UNIVERSITY

College of Arts and Sciences, Department of Computer Science and Information Systems, Program in Information Systems, Washington, DC 20016-8001

AWARDS MS, Certificate. Part-time and evening/weekend programs available.

Students: 31 full-time (12 women), 89 part-time (34 women); includes 34 minority (24 African Americans, 6 Asian Americans or Pacific Islanders, 4 Hispanic Americans), 46 international. Average age 32. In 2001, 73 degrees awarded.
Degree requirements: For master's, thesis or alternative, comprehensive exam.
Entrance requirements: For master's, minimum GPA of 3.0. *Application deadline:* For fall admission, 2/1 (priority date); for spring admission, 10/1. Applications are processed on a rolling basis. *Application fee:* $50.

American University (continued)

Expenses: Tuition: Full-time $14,274; part-time $793 per credit. Required fees: $290. Tuition and fees vary according to program.
Financial support: Fellowships with full tuition reimbursements, teaching assistantships, career-related internships or fieldwork, Federal Work-Study, institutionally sponsored loans, and unspecified assistantships available. Financial award application deadline: 2/1.
Faculty research: Artificial intelligence, database systems, software engineering, expert systems. *Web site:* http://www.csis.american.edu/

■ **ARIZONA STATE UNIVERSITY EAST**

College of Technology and Applied Sciences, Department of Information and Management Technology, Mesa, AZ 85212

AWARDS MS. Part-time and evening/weekend programs available.

Faculty: 11 full-time (2 women).
Students: 26 full-time (15 women), 81 part-time (43 women); includes 15 minority (2 African Americans, 5 Asian Americans or Pacific Islanders, 8 Hispanic Americans), 32 international. Average age 33. 46 applicants, 52% accepted, 20 enrolled. In 2001, 24 degrees awarded.
Degree requirements: For master's, thesis or applied project and oral defense. *Median time to degree:* Master's–2 years full-time, 3 years part-time.
Entrance requirements: For master's, GRE, TOELF. *Application deadline:* Applications are processed on a rolling basis. *Application fee:* $45. Electronic applications accepted.
Expenses: Tuition, state resident: full-time $2,412; part-time $126 per credit hour. Tuition, nonresident: full-time $10,278; part-time $428 per credit hour. Required fees: $26. Tuition and fees vary according to course load.
Financial support: In 2001–02, 26 students received support, including 6 research assistantships with partial tuition reimbursements available (averaging $5,542 per year); teaching assistantships, career-related internships or fieldwork, Federal Work-Study, scholarships/grants, tuition waivers (full and partial), and unspecified assistantships also available. Support available to part-time students. Financial award application deadline: 3/1; financial award applicants required to submit FAFSA.
Faculty research: Digital imaging; digital publishing, Internet development/e-commerce, information databases, multimedia, animation, 3-D modeling, perishability studies of technology; hazardous materials and waste management; environmental regulations, remediation processes, operations management, quality

assurance, industrial training. *Total annual research expenditures:* $357,999.
Dr. Thomas Schildgen, Chair, 480-727-1005, *Fax:* 480-727-1684, *E-mail:* ts@asu.edu.

■ **ARKANSAS TECH UNIVERSITY**

Graduate Studies, School of System Science, Department of Computer and Information Science, Russellville, AR 72801-2222

AWARDS Information technology (MS).

Faculty: 7 full-time (2 women).
Students: 89 (32 women); includes 6 minority (4 Asian Americans or Pacific Islanders, 2 Hispanic Americans) 51 international. 27 applicants, 96% accepted, 17 enrolled. In 2001, 9 degrees awarded.
Degree requirements: For master's, comprehensive exam (for some programs). *Application deadline:* For fall admission, 3/1 (priority date); for spring admission, 10/1 (priority date). Applications are processed on a rolling basis. *Application fee:* $0 ($30 for international students). Electronic applications accepted.
Expenses: Tuition: Part-time $125 per hour.
Financial support: In 2001–02, 5 students received support, including teaching assistantships (averaging $4,000 per year); unspecified assistantships also available. Financial award application deadline: 4/15; financial award applicants required to submit FAFSA.
Application contact: Dr. Larry Morell, Head, 479-968-0355, *E-mail:* larry.morell@mail.atu.edu. *Web site:* http://www.atu.edu

■ **BALL STATE UNIVERSITY**

Graduate School, College of Communication, Information, and Media, Center for Information and Communication Sciences, Muncie, IN 47306-1099

AWARDS MS.

Faculty: 8.
Students: 96 full-time (24 women), 55 part-time (16 women); includes 9 minority (4 African Americans, 2 Asian Americans or Pacific Islanders, 2 Hispanic Americans, 1 Native American), 16 international. Average age 28. 127 applicants, 86% accepted. In 2001, 99 degrees awarded. *Application fee:* $25 ($35 for international students).
Expenses: Tuition, state resident: full-time $4,068; part-time $2,542. Tuition, nonresident: full-time $10,944; part-time $6,462. Required fees: $1,000; $500 per term.
Financial support: In 2001–02, 20 teaching assistantships with full tuition reimbursements (averaging $5,893 per year) were awarded. Financial award application deadline: 3/1.
Dr. Rayford Steele, Director, 765-285-1889, *Fax:* 765-285-1516, *E-mail:* rsteele@bsu.edu. *Web site:* http://www.cics.bsu.edu/

■ **BARRY UNIVERSITY**

School of Adult and Continuing Education, Program in Information Technology, Miami Shores, FL 33161-6695

AWARDS MS. Part-time and evening/weekend programs available.

Entrance requirements: For master's, GRE or MAT, bachelor's degree in information technology, related area or professional experience. *Application deadline:* Applications are processed on a rolling basis. *Application fee:* $30.
Expenses: Tuition: Full-time $12,480. Tuition and fees vary according to degree level and program.
Financial support: Applicants required to submit FAFSA.
Dr. Larry Beebe, Academic Coordinator, 305-899-3300, *Fax:* 305-899-3346, *E-mail:* lbeebe@mail.barry.edu.
Application contact: Mary Hernandez, Director, 305-899-3300, *Fax:* 305-899-3346, *E-mail:* mhernandez@mail.barry.edu.

■ **BELLEVUE UNIVERSITY**

Graduate School, Program in Computer Information Systems, Bellevue, NE 68005-3098

AWARDS MS.

Application fee: $50.
Expenses: Tuition, state resident: part-time $265 per credit. One-time fee: $50 part-time.
Financial support: Federal Work-Study and scholarships/grants available.
Application contact: Elizabeth A. Wall, Director of Marketing and Enrollment, 402-293-3702, *Fax:* 402-293-3730, *E-mail:* eaw@scholars.bellevue.edu.

Find an in-depth description at www.petersons.com/gradchannel.

■ **BENTLEY COLLEGE**

The Elkin B. McCallum Graduate School of Business, Program in Information Technology, Waltham, MA 02452-4705

AWARDS MSIT.

Entrance requirements: For master's, GMAT or GRE General Test, TOEFL. *Application deadline:* For fall admission, 6/1 (priority date); for spring admission, 11/1. Applications are processed on a rolling basis. *Application fee:* $50. Electronic applications accepted.
Expenses: Tuition: Full-time $18,640; part-time $777 per credit. Required fees: $100.
Financial support: Career-related internships or fieldwork, Federal Work-Study, and unspecified assistantships available. Support available to part-time students. Financial award application deadline: 4/15; financial award applicants required to submit CSS PROFILE or FAFSA.

Application contact: Debbie K. Love, Senior Associate Director of Graduate Admissions, 781-891-2108, *Fax:* 781-891-2464.

■ BRADLEY UNIVERSITY

Graduate School, College of Liberal Arts and Sciences, Department of Computer Science, Peoria, IL 61625-0002

AWARDS Computer information systems (MS); computer science (MS). Part-time and evening/weekend programs available.

Students: 51 full-time, 48 part-time. 202 applicants, 60% accepted. In 2001, 35 degrees awarded.
Degree requirements: For master's, thesis or alternative, comprehensive exam.
Entrance requirements: For master's, TOEFL. *Application deadline:* For fall admission, 7/1 (priority date); for spring admission, 11/1. Applications are processed on a rolling basis. *Application fee:* $40 ($50 for international students).
Expenses: Tuition: Part-time $7,615 per semester. Tuition and fees vary according to course load.
Financial support: In 2001–02, 11 research assistantships with partial tuition reimbursements (averaging $1,219 per year) were awarded; teaching assistantships, scholarships/grants and tuition waivers (partial) also available. Financial award application deadline: 3/1.
Dr. James Miller, Chairperson, 309-677-2459.
Application contact: Dr. Jiang-Bo Liu, Graduate Adviser, 309-677-2386.

■ BROOKLYN COLLEGE OF THE CITY UNIVERSITY OF NEW YORK

Division of Graduate Studies, Department of Computer and Information Science, Brooklyn, NY 11210-2889

AWARDS Computer and information science (MA, PhD); computer science and health science (MS); economics and computer and information science (MPS); information systems (MS). Part-time and evening/weekend programs available.

Students: 43 full-time (17 women), 408 part-time (145 women); includes 226 minority (70 African Americans, 146 Asian Americans or Pacific Islanders, 10 Hispanic Americans), 137 international. 356 applicants, 67% accepted. In 2001, 49 degrees awarded.
Degree requirements: For master's, thesis or alternative, comprehensive exam or thesis, comprehensive exam.
Entrance requirements: For master's, TOEFL, GRE, previous course work in computer science. *Application deadline:* For fall admission, 3/1; for spring admission, 11/1. *Application fee:* $40.
Expenses: Tuition, state resident: full-time $4,350; part-time $185 per credit. Tuition,

nonresident: full-time $7,600; part-time $320 per credit.
Financial support: In 2001–02, 5 research assistantships with full tuition reimbursements (averaging $15,000 per year), 13 teaching assistantships with full tuition reimbursements (averaging $15,000 per year) were awarded. Fellowships, career-related internships or fieldwork, Federal Work-Study, institutionally sponsored loans, scholarships/grants, and tuition waivers (partial) also available. Support available to part-time students. Financial award application deadline: 5/1; financial award applicants required to submit FAFSA.
Faculty research: Networks and distributed systems, programming languages, modeling and computer applications, algorithms, artificial intelligence, theoretical computer science.
Dr. Aaron H. Tenenbaum, Chairperson, 718-951-5657.
Application contact: Gerald Weiss, Graduate Counselor, 718-951-5217, *Fax:* 718-951-4842, *E-mail:* weiss@sci.brooklyn.cuny.edu.

■ BRYANT COLLEGE

Graduate School, College of Business Administration, Program in Information Systems, Smithfield, RI 02917-1284

AWARDS MSIS. Part-time and evening/weekend programs available.

Faculty: 7 full-time (1 woman).
Students: 5 full-time (1 woman), 24 part-time (7 women), 2 international. Average age 32. 37 applicants, 65% accepted, 24 enrolled.
Application deadline: For fall admission, 7/15 (priority date); for spring admission, 11/15. Applications are processed on a rolling basis. *Application fee:* $60 ($80 for international students). Electronic applications accepted.
Expenses: Tuition: Part-time $433 per credit. Tuition and fees vary according to program.
Financial support: Research assistantships with full tuition reimbursements, unspecified assistantships available. Support available to part-time students.
Dr. Wallace Wood, Chair, 401-232-6247, *Fax:* 401-232-6319, *E-mail:* woodshed@bryant.edu.
Application contact: Kristopher T. Sullivan, Director of Graduate Programs, 401-232-6230, *Fax:* 401-232-6494, *E-mail:* gradprog@bryant.edu.

■ CALIFORNIA STATE UNIVERSITY, FULLERTON

Graduate Studies, College of Engineering and Computer Science, Department of Computer Science, Fullerton, CA 92834-9480

AWARDS Applications administrative information systems (MS); applications mathematical

methods (MS); computer science (MS); information processing systems (MS). Part-time programs available.

Faculty: 17 full-time (5 women), 45 part-time/adjunct.
Students: 164 full-time (47 women), 152 part-time (38 women); includes 134 minority (2 African Americans, 122 Asian Americans or Pacific Islanders, 10 Hispanic Americans), 128 international. Average age 31. 354 applicants, 63% accepted, 101 enrolled. In 2001, 28 degrees awarded.
Degree requirements: For master's, project or thesis.
Entrance requirements: For master's, GRE General Test, minimum undergraduate GPA of 2.5. *Application fee:* $55.
Expenses: Tuition, nonresident: part-time $246 per unit. Required fees: $964.
Financial support: Career-related internships or fieldwork, Federal Work-Study, institutionally sponsored loans, and scholarships/grants available. Support available to part-time students. Financial award application deadline: 3/1.
Faculty research: Software engineering, development of computer networks.
Dr. Ning Chen, Chair, 714-278-3700.
Application contact: Dr. Susamma Barua, Adviser, 714-278-3700.

■ CAPELLA UNIVERSITY

Graduate School, School of Technology, Minneapolis, MN 55402

AWARDS Information technology (MS). Part-time and evening/weekend programs available. Postbaccalaureate distance learning degree programs offered (no on-campus study).

Faculty: 10 full-time, 50 part-time/adjunct.
Students: Average age 35. 373 applicants, 64% accepted, 194 enrolled. In 2001, 1 degree awarded. Terminal master's awarded for partial completion of doctoral program.
Degree requirements: For master's, project, thesis optional. *Median time to degree:* Master's–1.5 years full-time, 3 years part-time.
Entrance requirements: For master's, TOEFL, minimum GPA of 2.7. *Application deadline:* Applications are processed on a rolling basis. Electronic applications accepted.
Expenses: Tuition: Part-time $1,210 per course. Tuition and fees vary according to degree level and program.
Financial support: Institutionally sponsored loans and scholarships/grants available. Support available to part-time students. Financial award applicants required to submit FAFSA.
Dr. Kurt Linberg, Dean, 888-CAPELLA, *E-mail:* klinberg@capella.edu.
Application contact: Liz Krummen, Associate Dean of Enrollment Services, 888-CAPELLA, *E-mail:* info@capella.edu.

■ CAPITOL COLLEGE

Graduate Programs, Laurel, MD 20708-9759

AWARDS Computer science (MS); electrical engineering (MS); electronic commerce management (MS); information and telecommunications systems management (MS); information architecture (MS); network security (MS). Part-time and evening/weekend programs available. Postbaccalaureate distance learning degree programs offered (no on-campus study).

Faculty: 3 full-time (0 women), 34 part-time/adjunct (4 women).
Students: 6 full-time (3 women), 625 part-time (175 women). Average age 35. 400 applicants, 75% accepted, 275 enrolled. In 2001, 52 degrees awarded. *Median time to degree:* Master's–2 years part-time.
Entrance requirements: For master's, GRE General Test and TOEFL (for international students), minimum GPA of 2.5. *Application deadline:* For fall admission, 7/1 (priority date); for winter admission, 12/1 (priority date); for spring admission, 3/1 (priority date). Applications are processed on a rolling basis. *Application fee:* $100 for international students. Electronic applications accepted.
Expenses: Tuition: Part-time $354 per credit.
Financial support: In 2001–02, 2 students received support. Available to part-time students. Applicants required to submit FAFSA.
Pat Smit, Dean of Academics, 301-369-2800 Ext. 3044, *Fax:* 301-953-3876, *E-mail:* gradschool@capitol-college.edu.
Application contact: Ken Crockett, Director of Graduate Admissions, 301-369-2800 Ext. 3026, *Fax:* 301-953-3876, *E-mail:* gradschool@capitol-college.edu. *Web site:* http://www.capitol-college.edu/

■ CARNEGIE MELLON UNIVERSITY

Carnegie Institute of Technology, Information Networking Institute, Pittsburgh, PA 15213-3891

AWARDS MS.

Degree requirements: For master's, thesis.
Entrance requirements: For master's, GRE General Test, previous course work in computer science, computer engineering, or electrical engineering.
Expenses: Contact institution.
Faculty research: Wireless, including protocols, architecture, innovative platforms, compression research, human factors, high speed networks, and prototype for industrial clients. *Web site:* http://www.ini.cmu.edu/
Find an in-depth description at www.petersons.com/gradchannel.

■ CARNEGIE MELLON UNIVERSITY

School of Computer Science, Language Technologies Institute, Pittsburgh, PA 15213-3891

AWARDS MLT, PhD. Terminal master's awarded for partial completion of doctoral program.

Degree requirements: For doctorate, thesis/dissertation.
Entrance requirements: For master's and doctorate, GRE General Test, GRE Subject Test, TOEFL.
Faculty research: Machine translation, natural language processing, speech and information retrieval, literacy. *Web site:* http://www.lti.cs.cmu.edu/

■ CARNEGIE MELLON UNIVERSITY

School of Computer Science, Program in Knowledge Discovery and Data Mining, Pittsburgh, PA 15213-3891

AWARDS MS. *Web site:* http://www.cs.cmu.edu/

■ CASE WESTERN RESERVE UNIVERSITY

School of Graduate Studies, The Case School of Engineering, Department of Electrical Engineering and Computer Science, Cleveland, OH 44106

AWARDS Computer engineering (MS, PhD); computing and information science (MS, PhD); electrical engineering (MS, PhD); systems and control engineering (MS, PhD). Part-time and evening/weekend programs available. Postbaccalaureate distance learning degree programs offered (minimal on-campus study).

Faculty: 29 full-time (2 women), 15 part-time/adjunct (1 woman).
Students: 61 full-time (17 women), 72 part-time (6 women); includes 8 minority (3 African Americans, 5 Asian Americans or Pacific Islanders), 85 international. Average age 25. 843 applicants, 16% accepted, 27 enrolled. In 2001, 33 master's, 16 doctorates awarded. Terminal master's awarded for partial completion of doctoral program.
Degree requirements: For master's, thesis; for doctorate, thesis/dissertation, qualifying exam, teaching experience.
Entrance requirements: For master's and doctorate, GRE General Test, TOEFL. *Application deadline:* For fall admission, 2/1; for spring admission, 11/1. Applications are processed on a rolling basis. *Application fee:* $25.
Financial support: In 2001–02, 34 fellowships with full and partial tuition reimbursements (averaging $15,240 per year), 22 research assistantships with full and partial tuition reimbursements (averaging $14,220 per year) were awarded.

Career-related internships or fieldwork, Federal Work-Study, and institutionally sponsored loans also available. Support available to part-time students. Financial award application deadline: 3/1; financial award applicants required to submit FAFSA.
Faculty research: Computational biology and biorobotics; HEHS and solid state, VSLI system design and testing; databases, software engineering, computer systems; systems optimization, planning and decision making; digital signal processing, control and filtering theory. *Total annual research expenditures:* $3.2 million.
Dr. B. Ross Barmish, Chairman, 216-368-2833, *Fax:* 216-368-6888, *E-mail:* brb8@po.cwru.edu.
Application contact: Elizabethanne M. Fuller, Department Assistant, 216-368-4080, *Fax:* 216-368-2668, *E-mail:* emf4@po.cwru.edu. *Web site:* http://eecs.cwru.edu/

■ CENTRAL WASHINGTON UNIVERSITY

Graduate Studies and Research, College of Education and Professional Studies, Department of Information Technology and Administrative Management, Ellensburg, WA 98926-7463

AWARDS Business and distributive education (M Ed). Part-time programs available.

Faculty: 12 full-time (6 women).
Students: 1 (woman) full-time, 3 part-time (2 women). 2 applicants, 100% accepted, 2 enrolled. In 2001, 6 degrees awarded.
Degree requirements: For master's, thesis or alternative.
Entrance requirements: For master's, minimum GPA of 3.0. *Application deadline:* For fall admission, 4/1 (priority date); for winter admission, 10/1; for spring admission, 1/1. Applications are processed on a rolling basis. *Application fee:* $35.
Expenses: Tuition, state resident: full-time $4,848; part-time $162 per credit. Tuition, nonresident: full-time $14,772; part-time $492 per credit. Required fees: $324.
Financial support: In 2001–02, 1 teaching assistantship with partial tuition reimbursement (averaging $7,120 per year) was awarded; research assistantships with partial tuition reimbursements, Federal Work-Study also available. Financial award application deadline: 3/1; financial award applicants required to submit FAFSA.
Dr. V. Wayne Klemin, Chair, 509-963-2611.
Application contact: Barbara Sisko, Office Assistant, Graduate Studies and Research, 509-963-3103, *Fax:* 509-963-1799, *E-mail:* masters@cwu.edu. *Web site:* http://www.cwu.edu/

■ CLAREMONT GRADUATE UNIVERSITY

Graduate Programs, School of Information Science, Claremont, CA 91711-6160

AWARDS Electronic commerce (MSEC); information systems (MIS); management of information systems (MSMIS, PhD). Part-time programs available.

Faculty: 6 full-time (0 women), 5 part-time/adjunct (1 woman).
Students: 65 full-time (16 women), 59 part-time (21 women); includes 38 minority (11 African Americans, 22 Asian Americans or Pacific Islanders, 5 Hispanic Americans), 42 international. Average age 35. 99 applicants, 60% accepted. In 2001, 40 master's, 4 doctorates awarded.
Degree requirements: For doctorate, thesis/dissertation, portfolio, comprehensive exam.
Entrance requirements: For master's and doctorate, GMAT, GRE General Test. *Application deadline:* For fall admission, 2/15 (priority date). Applications are processed on a rolling basis. *Application fee:* $50. Electronic applications accepted.
Expenses: Tuition: Full-time $22,984; part-time $1,000 per unit. Required fees: $160; $80 per semester.
Financial support: Fellowships, research assistantships, teaching assistantships, Federal Work-Study and institutionally sponsored loans available. Support available to part-time students. Financial award application deadline: 2/15; financial award applicants required to submit FAFSA.
Faculty research: GPSS, man-machine interaction, organizational aspects of computing, implementation of information systems, information systems practice.
Lorne Olfman, Dean, 909-621-8209, *Fax:* 909-621-8564, *E-mail:* lorne.olfman@ cgu.edu.
Application contact: Nancy Back, Program Coordinator, 909-621-8209, *Fax:* 909-621-8564, *E-mail:* infosci@cgu.edu. *Web site:* http://www.cgu.edu/is/
Find an in-depth description at www.petersons.com/gradchannel.

■ CLARK ATLANTA UNIVERSITY

School of Arts and Sciences, Department of Computer and Information Science, Atlanta, GA 30314

AWARDS MS.

Degree requirements: For master's, one foreign language, thesis.
Entrance requirements: For master's, GRE General Test, minimum GPA of 2.5.

■ CLARKSON UNIVERSITY

Graduate School, Interdisciplinary Studies, Program in Information Technology, Potsdam, NY 13699

AWARDS MS.

Students: 17 full-time (3 women), 4 part-time; includes 1 minority (Asian American or Pacific Islander), 12 international. Average age 26. 34 applicants, 71% accepted.
Entrance requirements: For master's, TOEFL. *Application deadline:* For fall admission, 5/15 (priority date); for spring admission, 10/15 (priority date). Applications are processed on a rolling basis. *Application fee:* $25 ($35 for international students).
Expenses: Tuition: Part-time $714 per credit. Required fees: $108 per semester.
Financial support: In 2001–02, 1 student received support, including 1 research assistantship (averaging $17,000 per year)
Dr. William D. Horn, Chair, 315-268-6420, *Fax:* 315-268-7994, *E-mail:* horn@ clarkson.edu.
Application contact: Donna Brockway, Assistant to Dean/Foreign Student Advisor, 315-268-6447, *Fax:* 315-268-7994, *E-mail:* brockway@clarkson.edu.
Find an in-depth description at www.petersons.com/gradchannel.

■ CLARK UNIVERSITY

Graduate School, College of Professional and Continuing Education, Program in Information Technology, Worcester, MA 01610-1477

AWARDS MIT.

Students: Average age 29. 2 applicants, 100% accepted, 2 enrolled.
Application fee: $50.
Expenses: Tuition: Full-time $24,400; part-time $763 per credit. Required fees: $10.
Financial support: In 2001–02, fellowships with partial tuition reimbursements (averaging $4,700 per year), research assistantships with partial tuition reimbursements (averaging $4,700 per year), teaching assistantships with partial tuition reimbursements (averaging $4,700 per year) were awarded. Tuition waivers (partial) also available.
Max E. Hess, Director of Graduate Studies, 508-793-7217, *Fax:* 508-793-7232.
Application contact: Julia Parent, Director of Marketing, Communications, and Admissions, 508-793-7217, *Fax:* 508-793-7232, *E-mail:* jparent@clarku.edu. *Web site:* http://www.copace.clarku.edu/

■ COLEMAN COLLEGE

Graduate Program in Information Technology, La Mesa, CA 91942-1532

AWARDS MSIT. Evening/weekend programs available.

Faculty: 7 full-time (1 woman), 3 part-time/adjunct (1 woman).
Students: 27 full-time (5 women). Average age 35. 32 applicants, 91% accepted, 29 enrolled.
Entrance requirements: For master's, minimum GPA of 3.0. *Application deadline:*

Applications are processed on a rolling basis. *Application fee:* $100.
Expenses: Tuition: Part-time $200 per credit.
Financial support: Applicants required to submit FAFSA.
Dr. Marianne Liszkay, Director of Graduate Studies, 619-465-3990 Ext. 168, *Fax:* 619-463-0162, *E-mail:* mliszkay@ coleman.edu.
Application contact: Debbie Coleman, Registrar, 619-465-3990 Ext. 102, *Fax:* 619-463-0162, *E-mail:* debcoleman@ coleman.edu.

■ THE COLLEGE OF SAINT ROSE

Graduate Studies, School of Mathematics and Sciences, Program in Computer Information Systems, Albany, NY 12203-1419

AWARDS MS. Part-time and evening/weekend programs available.

Faculty: 7 full-time (3 women).
Students: 1 (woman) full-time, 41 part-time (18 women); includes 10 minority (5 African Americans, 5 Asian Americans or Pacific Islanders), 2 international. 12 applicants, 92% accepted, 11 enrolled. In 2001, 9 degrees awarded.
Application deadline: For fall admission, 7/15 (priority date); for spring admission, 12/1. Applications are processed on a rolling basis. *Application fee:* $30.
Expenses: Tuition: Full-time $8,712. Required fees: $190.
Financial support: Research assistantships, career-related internships or fieldwork and tuition waivers (partial) available. Support available to part-time students. Financial award application deadline: 3/1; financial award applicants required to submit FAFSA.
Dr. Neal Mazur, Department Chair, 518-454-5174, *Fax:* 518-458-5446, *E-mail:* mazurn@mail.strose.edu.
Application contact: 518-454-5136, *Fax:* 518-458-5479, *E-mail:* ace@ mail.strose.edu.

■ COLORADO TECHNICAL UNIVERSITY

Graduate Studies, Program in Management, Colorado Springs, CO 80907-3896

AWARDS Business administration (MBA); business management (MSM); business technology (MSM); database management (MSM); human resources management (MSM); information technology (MSM); logistics management (MSM); management (DM); organizational leadership (MSM); project management (MSM). Part-time and evening/weekend programs available.

Faculty: 9 full-time (2 women), 6 part-time/adjunct (0 women).
Students: 224 full-time (79 women), 37 part-time (9 women); includes 43 minority (19 African Americans, 9 Asian Americans

Colorado Technical University (continued)
or Pacific Islanders, 15 Hispanic Americans), 7 international. Average age 38. 94 applicants, 96% accepted, 82 enrolled. In 2001, 112 master's, 2 doctorates awarded.

Degree requirements: For master's, thesis or alternative; for doctorate, thesis/dissertation. *Median time to degree:* Master's–2 years full-time, 3 years part-time; doctorate–3.5 years full-time.

Entrance requirements: For doctorate, minimum graduate GPA of 3.0, 5 years of related work experience. *Application deadline:* For fall admission, 10/2; for winter admission, 1/3; for spring admission, 4/3. Applications are processed on a rolling basis. *Application fee:* $100.

Expenses: Tuition: Full-time $6,960; part-time $290 per credit. Required fees: $40 per quarter. One-time fee: $100. Tuition and fees vary according to course load and degree level.

Financial support: Career-related internships or fieldwork and Federal Work-Study available. Financial award applicants required to submit FAFSA.

Faculty research: Sexual harassment, performance evaluation, critical thinking. Dr. Eric Goodman, Dean, 719-590-6772, *Fax:* 719-598-3740, *E-mail:* egoodman@coloradotech.edu.

Application contact: Judy Galante, Graduate Admissions, 719-590-6720, *Fax:* 719-598-3740, *E-mail:* jgalante@coloradotech.edu. *Web site:* http://www.coloradotech.edu/

■ DAKOTA STATE UNIVERSITY

College of Business and Information Systems, Madison, SD 57042-1799

AWARDS MSIS. Part-time and evening/weekend programs available. Postbaccalaureate distance learning degree programs offered (minimal on-campus study).

Faculty: 12 full-time (0 women).
Students: 30 full-time (11 women), 49 part-time (20 women); includes 2 minority (1 African American, 1 Asian American or Pacific Islander), 16 international. Average age 34. 46 applicants, 83% accepted, 27 enrolled. In 2001, 22 degrees awarded.
Degree requirements: For master's, core ICCP examination, integrative project. *Median time to degree:* Master's–1.67 years full-time, 2 years part-time.
Entrance requirements: For master's, GRE General Test or GMAT, minimum GPA of 2.7. *Application deadline:* For fall admission, 8/1; for winter admission, 10/1. Applications are processed on a rolling basis. *Application fee:* $35 ($85 for international students). Electronic applications accepted.
Expenses: Tuition, state resident: part-time $95 per credit hour. Tuition, nonresident: part-time $182 per credit hour. Tuition and fees vary according to course load, campus/location and reciprocity agreements.

Financial support: In 2001–02, 30 students received support, including 13 research assistantships with partial tuition reimbursements available (averaging $4,035 per year), 5 teaching assistantships with partial tuition reimbursements available (averaging $5,800 per year); Federal Work-Study, scholarships/grants, and unspecified assistantships also available. Support available to part-time students. Financial award applicants required to submit FAFSA.
Faculty research: Effectiveness of technology in economics education, e-commerce, human computer interface, data mining and data warehousing. Dr. Richard Christoph, Dean, 605-256-5176, *Fax:* 605-256-5316.
Application contact: Laurie B. Dennis, Director, Graduate Programs, 605-256-5263, *Fax:* 605-256-5316, *E-mail:* laurie.dennis@dsu.edu. *Web site:* http://www.departments.dsu.edu/bis/

Find an in-depth description at www.petersons.com/gradchannel.

■ DEPAUL UNIVERSITY

School of Computer Science, Telecommunications, and Information Systems, Program in Information Systems, Chicago, IL 60604-2287

AWARDS MS. Part-time and evening/weekend programs available.

Faculty: 6 full-time (1 woman), 11 part-time/adjunct (2 women).
Students: 291 full-time (115 women), 211 part-time (87 women); includes 164 minority (45 African Americans, 101 Asian Americans or Pacific Islanders, 18 Hispanic Americans), 128 international. Average age 30. 523 applicants, 71% accepted, 223 enrolled. In 2001, 105 degrees awarded.
Degree requirements: For master's, thesis optional.
Application deadline: For fall admission, 8/1 (priority date); for winter admission, 11/15 (priority date); for spring admission, 5/1 (priority date). Applications are processed on a rolling basis. *Application fee:* $25.
Expenses: Tuition: Part-time $362 per credit hour. Tuition and fees vary according to program.
Financial support: Fellowships, research assistantships, teaching assistantships, Federal Work-Study, tuition waivers (partial), and unspecified assistantships available. Support available to part-time students. Financial award application deadline: 4/1; financial award applicants required to submit FAFSA. Dr. Martin Kalin, Associate Dean, 312-362-8864, *E-mail:* mkalin@cs.depaul.edu.
Application contact: Genaro Balcazar, Director of Admissions, 312-362-8714, *Fax:* 312-362-6116, *E-mail:* ctiadmissions@cs.depaul.edu. *Web site:* http://www.cs.depaul.edu/

■ DESALES UNIVERSITY

Graduate Division, Program in Information Systems, Center Valley, PA 18034-9568

AWARDS MSIS. Part-time and evening/weekend programs available.

Faculty: 2 full-time (0 women), 9 part-time/adjunct (1 woman).
Students: 104. 35 applicants, 100% accepted. In 2001, 5 degrees awarded.
Degree requirements: For master's, thesis optional.
Application deadline: For fall admission, 8/30 (priority date). Applications are processed on a rolling basis. *Application fee:* $35.
Expenses: Contact institution.
Financial support: Unspecified assistantships available. Financial award applicants required to submit FAFSA.
Faculty research: Digital communication, numerical analysis, database design. Dr. Julius G. Bede, Director, 610-282-1100 Ext. 1280, *Fax:* 610-282-2254, *E-mail:* julius.bede@desales.edu.
Application contact: Debra Hockenberry, Associate Director, 610-282-1100 Ext. 1451, *E-mail:* debra.hockenberry@desales.edu. *Web site:* http://www.desales.edu

■ DREXEL UNIVERSITY

Graduate School, College of Information Science and Technology, Program in Information Science and Technology, Philadelphia, PA 19104-2875

AWARDS PhD. Part-time and evening/weekend programs available.

Faculty: 27 full-time (13 women), 11 part-time/adjunct (2 women).
Students: Average age 40. 19 applicants, 47% accepted, 5 enrolled.
Degree requirements: For doctorate, thesis/dissertation.
Application deadline: For fall admission, 8/21. Applications are processed on a rolling basis. *Application fee:* $50. Electronic applications accepted.
Expenses: Tuition: Full-time $20,088; part-time $558 per credit. Required fees: $78 per term. One-time fee: $200. Tuition and fees vary according to course load, degree level and program.
Financial support: Research assistantships, teaching assistantships, career-related internships or fieldwork, Federal Work-Study, institutionally sponsored loans, tuition waivers (partial), and unspecified assistantships available. Support available to part-time students. Financial award application deadline: 2/1.
Application contact: Director of Graduate Admissions, 215-895-6700, *Fax:* 215-895-5939, *E-mail:* enroll@drexel.edu.

■ EAST CAROLINA UNIVERSITY

Graduate School, School of Education, Department of Business, Vocational, and Technical Education, Greenville, NC 27858-4353

AWARDS Information technologies (MS); vocation education (MA Ed).

Faculty: 5 full-time (2 women).
Students: 4 full-time (all women), 4 part-time (3 women); includes 3 minority (2 African Americans, 1 Hispanic American). Average age 34. 4 applicants, 100% accepted. In 2001, 2 degrees awarded.
Degree requirements: For master's, comprehensive exam.
Entrance requirements: For master's, GRE or MAT, TOEFL. *Application deadline:* For fall admission, 6/1 (priority date). Applications are processed on a rolling basis. *Application fee:* $45.
Expenses: Tuition, state resident: full-time $2,636. Tuition, nonresident: full-time $11,365.
Financial support: Federal Work-Study available. Support available to part-time students. Financial award application deadline: 6/1.
Dr. Lilla Holsey, Director of Graduate Studies, 252-328-6983, *Fax:* 252-328-6835, *E-mail:* holseyl@mail.ecu.edu.
Application contact: Dr. Paul D. Tschetter, Senior Associate Dean of the Graduate School, 252-328-6012, *Fax:* 252-328-6071, *E-mail:* gradschool@mail.ecu.edu.

■ EAST TENNESSEE STATE UNIVERSITY

School of Graduate Studies, College of Applied Science and Technology, Department of Computer and Information Sciences, Johnson City, TN 37614

AWARDS Computer science (MS); information systems science (MS); software engineering (MS). Part-time and evening/weekend programs available.

Faculty: 11 full-time (0 women).
Students: 25 full-time (6 women), 17 part-time (6 women); includes 1 minority (African American), 17 international. Average age 30. In 2001, 12 degrees awarded.
Degree requirements: For master's, thesis, comprehensive exam.
Entrance requirements: For master's, GRE General Test, TOEFL, minimum GPA of 2.5. *Application deadline:* For fall admission, 7/15 (priority date); for spring admission, 11/15. Applications are processed on a rolling basis. *Application fee:* $25 ($35 for international students).
Expenses: Tuition, state resident: part-time $181 per hour. Tuition, nonresident: part-time $270 per hour. Required fees: $220 per term.
Financial support: Research assistantships with full tuition reimbursements, teaching

assistantships with full tuition reimbursements, scholarships/grants available. Support available to part-time students. Financial award application deadline: 7/1; financial award applicants required to submit FAFSA.
Faculty research: Operating systems, database design, artificial intelligence, simulation, parallel algorithms.
Dr. Terry Countermine, Chair, 423-439-5332, *Fax:* 423-439-7119, *E-mail:* counter@etsu.edu. *Web site:* http://www.etsu.edu/

■ EDINBORO UNIVERSITY OF PENNSYLVANIA

Graduate Studies, School of Science, Management and Technology, Program in Information Technology, Edinboro, PA 16444

AWARDS Certificate. Part-time and evening/weekend programs available.

Students: 1 full-time (0 women), 18 part-time (8 women), 1 international. Average age 35.
Application deadline: Applications are processed on a rolling basis. *Application fee:* $25. Electronic applications accepted.
Expenses: Tuition, state resident: full-time $4,600; part-time $256 per credit. Tuition, nonresident: full-time $7,554; part-time $420 per credit. Required fees: $68 per credit.
Financial support: Career-related internships or fieldwork, Federal Work-Study, institutionally sponsored loans, scholarships/grants, and unspecified assistantships available. Support available to part-time students. Financial award application deadline: 5/1; financial award applicants required to submit FAFSA.
Application contact: Dr. Mary Margaret Bevevino, Dean of Graduate Studies, 814-732-2856, *Fax:* 814-732-2611, *E-mail:* mbevevino@edinboro.edu.

■ FLORIDA GULF COAST UNIVERSITY

College of Business, Program in Computer and Information Systems, Fort Myers, FL 33965-6565

AWARDS MS.

Faculty: 31 full-time (9 women), 14 part-time/adjunct (3 women).
Students: 5 full-time (2 women), 12 part-time (3 women); includes 8 minority (1 African American, 2 Asian Americans or Pacific Islanders, 3 Hispanic Americans, 2 Native Americans). 8 applicants, 25% accepted, 0 enrolled. In 2001, 6 degrees awarded.
Entrance requirements: For master's, GMAT, minimum GPA 3.0. *Application deadline:* Applications are processed on a rolling basis. *Application fee:* $20. Electronic applications accepted.
Expenses: Tuition, state resident: part-time $164 per credit hour. Tuition,

nonresident: part-time $571 per credit hour. Required fees: $36 per semester.
Dr. Walter Rodriguez, Chair, 239-590-7360, *Fax:* 239-590-7330, *E-mail:* wrodrigz@fgcu.edu.
Application contact: Carol Burnette, Assistant Dean, 239-590-7350, *Fax:* 239-590-7330, *E-mail:* burnette@fgcu.edu.

■ FLORIDA INSTITUTE OF TECHNOLOGY

Graduate Programs, College of Engineering, Computer Science Department, Melbourne, FL 32901-6975

AWARDS Computer information systems (MS); computer science (MS, PhD); software engineering (MS). Part-time and evening/weekend programs available.

Faculty: 11 full-time (1 woman), 5 part-time/adjunct (1 woman).
Students: 59 full-time (14 women), 121 part-time (32 women); includes 21 minority (4 African Americans, 8 Asian Americans or Pacific Islanders, 9 Hispanic Americans), 106 international. Average age 30. 381 applicants, 58% accepted. In 2001, 35 degrees awarded. Terminal master's awarded for partial completion of doctoral program.
Degree requirements: For master's, thesis optional; for doctorate, thesis/dissertation, comprehensive exam.
Entrance requirements: For master's, minimum GPA of 3.0; for doctorate, GRE General Test, GRE Subject Test (computer science), minimum GPA of 3.5, resumé. *Application deadline:* Applications are processed on a rolling basis. *Application fee:* $50. Electronic applications accepted.
Expenses: Tuition: Part-time $650 per credit.
Financial support: In 2001–02, 50 students received support, including 30 research assistantships with full and partial tuition reimbursements available (averaging $10,708 per year), 20 teaching assistantships with full and partial tuition reimbursements available (averaging $8,672 per year); career-related internships or fieldwork and tuition remissions also available. Financial award application deadline: 3/1; financial award applicants required to submit FAFSA.
Faculty research: Artificial intelligence, software engineering, management and processes, programming languages, database systems. *Total annual research expenditures:* $1.5 million.
Dr. William D. Shoaff, Chair, 321-674-8066, *Fax:* 321-674-7046, *E-mail:* wds@cs.fit.edu.
Application contact: Carolyn P. Farrior, Director of Graduate Admissions, 321-674-7118, *Fax:* 321-723-9468, *E-mail:* cfarrior@fit.edu. *Web site:* http://www.cs.fit.edu/

Find an in-depth description at www.petersons.com/gradchannel.

■ GEORGE MASON UNIVERSITY

School of Information Technology and Engineering, Department of Information and Software Engineering, Fairfax, VA 22030-4444

AWARDS Information systems (MS); software systems engineering (MS). Part-time and evening/weekend programs available.

Faculty: 14 full-time (0 women), 11 part-time/adjunct (1 woman).
Students: 135 full-time (69 women), 457 part-time (176 women); includes 154 minority (26 African Americans, 115 Asian Americans or Pacific Islanders, 12 Hispanic Americans, 1 Native American), 209 international. Average age 33. 287 applicants, 70% accepted. In 2001, 148 degrees awarded.
Degree requirements: For master's, thesis optional.
Entrance requirements: For master's, GMAT or GRE General Test, TOEFL, minimum GPA of 3.0 in last 60 hours. *Application deadline:* For fall admission, 5/1; for spring admission, 11/1. *Application fee:* $30. Electronic applications accepted.
Expenses: Tuition, state resident: full-time $3,168; part-time $132 per credit hour. Tuition, nonresident: full-time $11,280; part-time $470 per credit hour. Required fees: $1,416; $59 per credit hour.
Financial support: Fellowships, research assistantships, teaching assistantships available. Support available to part-time students. Financial award application deadline: 3/1; financial award applicants required to submit FAFSA.
Faculty research: Security, database management, real time systems, software quality. *Total annual research expenditures:* $380,638.
Dr. Sushil Jajodia, Chairperson, 703-993-1640, *Fax:* 703-993-1638, *E-mail:* ise@gmu.edu. *Web site:* http://ise.gmu.edu/

■ GEORGIA SOUTHWESTERN STATE UNIVERSITY

Graduate Studies, School of Computer and Information Science, Americus, GA 31709-4693

AWARDS Computer information systems (MS); computer science (MS). Part-time programs available.

Faculty: 5 full-time (0 women).
Students: 18 full-time (3 women), 16 part-time (10 women); includes 8 minority (6 African Americans, 2 Asian Americans or Pacific Islanders), 17 international. Average age 29. 20 applicants, 25% accepted. In 2001, 9 degrees awarded.
Degree requirements: For master's, thesis (for some programs).
Entrance requirements: For master's, GRE General Test, minimum GPA of 3.0. *Application deadline:* For fall admission, 8/1; for spring admission, 12/15. Applications are processed on a rolling basis. *Application fee:* $20.

Expenses: Tuition, area resident: Part-time $97 per semester hour. Tuition, state resident: full-time $1,160. Tuition, nonresident: full-time $4,640; part-time $387 per semester hour. Required fees: $277; $217 per year.
Financial support: In 2001–02, 10 students received support, including 10 teaching assistantships with full tuition reimbursements available; fellowships, scholarships/grants also available. Financial award application deadline: 9/1.
Faculty research: Database, Internet technologies, computational complexity, encryption.
Dr. Boris V. Peltsverger, Interim Dean, 912-931-2818 Ext. 2113, *Fax:* 912-931-2270, *E-mail:* plz@canes.gsw.edu.
Application contact: Lois Oliver, Graduate Admissions Specialist, 912-931-2002, *Fax:* 912-931-2021, *E-mail:* loliver@canes.gsw.edu. *Web site:* http://www.gsu.edu/~cais/

■ GRAND VALLEY STATE UNIVERSITY

Science and Mathematics Division, Department of Computer Science and Information Systems, Allendale, MI 49401-9403

AWARDS Information systems (MS); software engineering (MS). Part-time and evening/weekend programs available.

Faculty: 7 full-time (0 women), 1 part-time/adjunct (0 women).
Students: 17 full-time (4 women), 72 part-time (14 women); includes 11 minority (3 African Americans, 7 Asian Americans or Pacific Islanders, 1 Hispanic American), 19 international. Average age 33. 25 applicants, 80% accepted. In 2001, 25 degrees awarded.
Degree requirements: For master's, thesis or alternative.
Entrance requirements: For master's, GMAT or GRE General Test. *Application deadline:* For fall admission, 2/1. Applications are processed on a rolling basis. *Application fee:* $20.
Expenses: Tuition, state resident: part-time $202 per credit hour. Tuition, nonresident: part-time $437 per credit hour.
Financial support: Research assistantships available.
Faculty research: Object technology, distributed computing, information systems management.
Paul Leidig, Professor, 616-895-2048, *Fax:* 616-895-2106, *E-mail:* leidigp@gvsu.edu. *Web site:* http://www.csis.gvsu.edu/

■ HARVARD UNIVERSITY

Extension School, Cambridge, MA 02138-3722

AWARDS Applied sciences (CAS); English for graduate and professional studies (DGP); environmental management (CEM); information technology (ALM); liberal arts (ALM);

museum studies (CMS); premedical studies (Diploma); public health (CPH); publication and communication (CPC); special studies in administration and management (CSS); technologies of education (CTE). Part-time and evening/weekend programs available.

Faculty: 450 part-time/adjunct.
Students: Average age 33. In 2001, 79 master's, 303 Diplomas awarded.
Degree requirements: For master's, thesis.
Entrance requirements: For master's and other advanced degree, TOEFL, TWE. *Application deadline:* Applications are processed on a rolling basis. *Application fee:* $75.
Expenses: Contact institution.
Financial support: In 2001–02, 213 students received support. Scholarships/grants available. Support available to part-time students. Financial award application deadline: 8/11; financial award applicants required to submit FAFSA.
Michael Shinagel, Dean.
Application contact: Program Director, 617-495-4024, *Fax:* 617-495-9176. *Web site:* http://www.extension.harvard.edu/

■ HOOD COLLEGE

Graduate School, Program in Management Information Technology, Frederick, MD 21701-8575

AWARDS MS. Part-time and evening/weekend programs available.

Faculty: 7 full-time (3 women), 1 part-time/adjunct (0 women).
Students: 3 full-time (1 woman), 10 part-time (4 women); includes 1 minority (Native American). Average age 33. 6 applicants, 83% accepted. In 2001, 1 degree awarded.
Degree requirements: For master's, thesis.
Entrance requirements: For master's, TOEFL, minimum GPA of 2.5. *Application deadline:* Applications are processed on a rolling basis. *Application fee:* $30. Electronic applications accepted.
Expenses: Tuition: Full-time $5,670; part-time $315 per credit. Required fees: $20 per term.
Financial support: Career-related internships or fieldwork and institutionally sponsored loans available. Support available to part-time students.
Faculty research: Systems engineering, parallel distributed computing, strategy, business ethics, entrepreneurship.
Dr. Regina S. Lightfoot, Director, 301-696-3724, *E-mail:* rlightfoot@hood.edu.
Application contact: Margot Rhoades, Graduate School Office, 301-696-3600, *Fax:* 301-696-3597, *E-mail:* hoodgrad@hood.edu.

■ HOOD COLLEGE

Graduate School, Programs in Computer and Information Sciences, Frederick, MD 21701-8575

AWARDS Computer science (MS); information technology (MS). Part-time and evening/weekend programs available.

Faculty: 8 full-time (2 women), 2 part-time/adjunct (0 women).
Students: 11 full-time (5 women), 105 part-time (31 women); includes 20 minority (9 African Americans, 9 Asian Americans or Pacific Islanders, 2 Hispanic Americans), 8 international. Average age 33. 36 applicants, 67% accepted, 23 enrolled. In 2001, 37 degrees awarded.
Degree requirements: For master's, thesis or alternative, registration.
Entrance requirements: For master's, TOEFL, minimum GPA of 2.5. *Application deadline:* Applications are processed on a rolling basis. *Application fee:* $30.
Expenses: Tuition: Full-time $5,670; part-time $315 per credit. Required fees: $20 per term.
Financial support: Institutionally sponsored loans available. Financial award applicants required to submit FAFSA.
Faculty research: Systems engineering, natural language, processing, database design, artificial intelligence and parallel distributed computing.
Dr. Betty Mayfield, Chairperson, 301-696-3763, *Fax:* 301-696-3597, *E-mail:* mayfield@hood.edu.
Application contact: 301-696-3600, *Fax:* 301-696-3597, *E-mail:* hoodgrad@hood.edu.

■ INDIANA UNIVERSITY BLOOMINGTON

School of Informatics, Bloomington, IN 47405

AWARDS Bioinformatics (MS); chemical informatics (MS); human computer interaction (MS); new media (MS), including media arts and science.

Students: 13 full-time (4 women), 2 part-time (1 woman); includes 2 minority (both Asian Americans or Pacific Islanders), 5 international. Average age 30.
Application fee: $45 ($55 for international students).
Expenses: Tuition, state resident: full-time $4,720; part-time $197 per credit. Tuition, nonresident: full-time $13,748; part-time $573 per credit. Required fees: $642.
Financial support: In 2001–02, fellowships (averaging $5,000 per year)
J. Michael Dunn, Dean. *Web site:* http://www.informatics.indiana.edu/

■ INDIANA UNIVERSITY BLOOMINGTON

School of Library and Information Science, Bloomington, IN 47405

AWARDS MIS, MLS, PhD, Spec. JD/MLS, MIS/MA, MLS/MA, MPA/MIS, MPA/MLS. PhD offered through the University Graduate School. Part-time programs available.

Faculty: 13 full-time (5 women), 1 part-time/adjunct (0 women).
Students: 168 full-time (105 women), 104 part-time (75 women); includes 30 minority (12 African Americans, 10 Asian Americans or Pacific Islanders, 7 Hispanic Americans, 1 Native American), 20 international. Average age 31. In 2001, 115 master's, 7 doctorates awarded.
Degree requirements: For doctorate, thesis/dissertation.
Entrance requirements: For master's, GRE General Test, TOEFL, minimum GPA of 3.0; for doctorate, GRE General Test, minimum GPA of 3.5. *Application deadline:* For fall admission, 5/15 (priority date); for spring admission, 11/1 (priority date). Applications are processed on a rolling basis. *Application fee:* $45 ($55 for international students).
Expenses: Tuition, state resident: full-time $4,720; part-time $197 per credit. Tuition, nonresident: full-time $13,748; part-time $573 per credit. Required fees: $642.
Financial support: In 2001–02, fellowships with partial tuition reimbursements (averaging $9,811 per year); career-related internships or fieldwork and tuition waivers (partial) also available.
Faculty research: Scholarly communication, interface design, public library policy, computer-mediated communication, information retrieval. *Total annual research expenditures:* $179,634.
Dr. Blaise Cronin, Dean, 812-855-2018, *Fax:* 812-855-6166.
Application contact: Rhonda Spencer, Information Contact, 812-855-2018, *Fax:* 812-855-6166. *Web site:* http://www.slis.indiana.edu/

Find an in-depth description at www.petersons.com/gradchannel.

■ IOWA STATE UNIVERSITY OF SCIENCE AND TECHNOLOGY

Graduate College, Interdisciplinary Programs, Program in Information Assurance, Ames, IA 50011

AWARDS MS.

Students: 11 full-time (2 women), 2 part-time (1 woman), 7 international. 9 applicants, 56% accepted, 4 enrolled.
Application fee: $20 ($50 for international students).
Expenses: Tuition, state resident: full-time $1,851. Tuition, nonresident: full-time $5,449. Tuition and fees vary according to program.
Financial support: In 2001–02, 10 research assistantships with partial tuition

reimbursements (averaging $11,997 per year), 1 teaching assistantship with partial tuition reimbursement (averaging $12,208 per year) were awarded. Health care benefits and unspecified assistantships also available.
Dr. Doug Jacobson, Chair of Supervising Committee, 515-294-8307, *E-mail:* infas@iac.iastate.edu. *Web site:* http://www.iac.iastate.edu/infas.html

■ ISIM UNIVERSITY

Programs in Information Management, Program in Information Technology, Denver, CO 80246

AWARDS MS. Part-time and evening/weekend programs available. Postbaccalaureate distance learning degree programs offered (no on-campus study).

Application deadline: Applications are processed on a rolling basis. *Application fee:* $75. Electronic applications accepted.
Expenses: Tuition: Part-time $1,245 per course.
Application contact: Robin Thompson, Admissions Mentor, 303-333-4224 Ext. 177, *Fax:* 303-336-1144, *E-mail:* rthompson@isim.edu.

■ KANSAS STATE UNIVERSITY

Graduate School, College of Engineering, Department of Computing and Information Sciences, Manhattan, KS 66506

AWARDS Computer science (MS, PhD); software engineering (MSE). Part-time programs available. Postbaccalaureate distance learning degree programs offered (minimal on-campus study).

Faculty: 16 full-time (2 women).
Students: 144 full-time (34 women), 50 part-time (13 women); includes 5 minority (all Asian Americans or Pacific Islanders), 160 international. 446 applicants, 39% accepted, 73 enrolled. In 2001, 39 master's, 2 doctorates awarded. Terminal master's awarded for partial completion of doctoral program.
Degree requirements: For master's, thesis or alternative; for doctorate, thesis/dissertation, preliminary exams.
Entrance requirements: For master's, GRE, TOEFL, bachelor's degree in computer science, minimum GPA of 3.0; for doctorate, GRE General Test, GRE Subject Test, TOEFL, master's degree in computer science or bachelor's degree plus advanced strong computer knowledge.
Application deadline: For fall admission, 3/1 (priority date); for spring admission, 9/1. Applications are processed on a rolling basis. *Application fee:* $0 ($25 for international students). Electronic applications accepted.
Expenses: Tuition, state resident: part-time $113 per credit hour. Tuition, nonresident: part-time $358 per credit hour.

Kansas State University (continued)
Financial support: In 2001–02, 51 research assistantships with partial tuition reimbursements (averaging $10,000 per year), 42 teaching assistantships with full tuition reimbursements (averaging $10,000 per year) were awarded. Career-related internships or fieldwork, institutionally sponsored loans, and scholarships/grants also available. Support available to part-time students. Financial award application deadline: 3/15; financial award applicants required to submit FAFSA.
Faculty research: Parallel distributed computing systems, programming languages, database systems, software engineering, real-time systems. *Total annual research expenditures:* $1 million.
Dr. Virgil E. Wallentine, Head, 785-532-6350, *Fax:* 785-532-7353, *E-mail:* virg@cis.ksu.edu.
Application contact: Dr. David Gustafson, Graduate Program Director, 785-532-6350, *Fax:* 785-532-7353, *E-mail:* dag@cis.ksu.edu. *Web site:* http://www.cis.ksu.edu/home.shtml/

Find an in-depth description at www.petersons.com/gradchannel.

■ KENNESAW STATE UNIVERSITY

College of Science and Mathematics, Program in Information Systems, Kennesaw, GA 30144-5591

AWARDS MSIS.

Faculty: 5 full-time (1 woman), 3 part-time/adjunct (1 woman).
Students: 52 full-time (15 women), 75 part-time (21 women); includes 23 minority (12 African Americans, 9 Asian Americans or Pacific Islanders, 2 Hispanic Americans), 39 international. Average age 34. 90 applicants, 79% accepted, 36 enrolled. In 2001, 13 degrees awarded.
Entrance requirements: For master's, GMAT or GRE General Test, minimum GPA of 2.75. *Application deadline:* For fall admission, 7/7; for spring admission, 10/20. *Application fee:* $20.
Expenses: Tuition, state resident: part-time $97 per credit hour. Tuition, nonresident: part-time $387 per credit hour. Required fees: $178 per semester.
Financial support: In 2001–02, 2 research assistantships with full tuition reimbursements (averaging $15,000 per year) were awarded
Merle King, Director, 770-423-6354, *Fax:* 770-423-6731, *E-mail:* mking@kennesaw.edu.
Application contact: Sinem Hamitoglu, Assistant Director of Graduate Admissions, 770-420-4377, *Fax:* 770-420-4435, *E-mail:* ksugrad@kennesaw.edu. *Web site:* http://www.kennesaw.edu/

■ KNOWLEDGE SYSTEMS INSTITUTE

Program in Computer and Information Sciences, Skokie, IL 60076

AWARDS MS. Part-time and evening/weekend programs available. Postbaccalaureate distance learning degree programs offered (minimal on-campus study).

Faculty: 5 full-time (0 women), 14 part-time/adjunct (4 women).
Students: 69 full-time (21 women), 27 part-time (7 women); includes 15 minority (4 African Americans, 10 Asian Americans or Pacific Islanders, 1 Hispanic American), 62 international. Average age 28. 59 applicants, 93% accepted. In 2001, 14 degrees awarded.
Application deadline: Applications are processed on a rolling basis. *Application fee:* $40. Electronic applications accepted.
Expenses: Tuition: Full-time $5,670; part-time $315 per credit. Required fees: $30; $5 per course. $50 per term. One-time fee: $5.
Financial support: In 2001–02, 15 students received support. Federal Work-Study available. Financial award applicants required to submit FAFSA.
Faculty research: Data mining, web development, database programming and administration.
Judy Pan, Executive Director, 847-679-3135, *Fax:* 847-679-3166, *E-mail:* office@ksi.edu.
Application contact: Margaret M. Price, Office Manager, 847-679-3135, *Fax:* 847-679-3166, *E-mail:* mprice@ksi.edu. *Web site:* http://www.ksi.edu/

■ KUTZTOWN UNIVERSITY OF PENNSYLVANIA

College of Graduate Studies and Extended Learning, College of Liberal Arts and Sciences, Program in Computer and Information Science, Kutztown, PA 19530-0730

AWARDS MS. Part-time and evening/weekend programs available.

Faculty: 16 part-time/adjunct (3 women).
Students: 15 full-time (11 women), 8 part-time (1 woman), 12 international. Average age 33. In 2001, 11 degrees awarded.
Degree requirements: For master's, comprehensive exam or thesis.
Entrance requirements: For master's, GRE General Test, TOEFL, TSE.
Application deadline: Applications are processed on a rolling basis. *Application fee:* $35.
Expenses: Tuition, state resident: full-time $4,600; part-time $256 per credit. Tuition, nonresident: full-time $7,554; part-time $420 per credit. Required fees: $835.
Financial support: Career-related internships or fieldwork, Federal Work-Study, and unspecified assistantships available. Financial award application deadline: 3/15;

financial award applicants required to submit FAFSA.
Faculty research: Artificial intelligence, expert systems, neural networks.
William Bateman, Chairperson, 610-683-4410, *E-mail:* bateman@kutztown.edu. *Web site:* http://www.kutztown.edu/acad/

■ LAMAR UNIVERSITY

College of Graduate Studies, College of Business, Beaumont, TX 77710

AWARDS Accounting (MBA); information systems (MBA); management (MBA). Part-time and evening/weekend programs available.

Faculty: 21 full-time (3 women).
Students: 31 full-time (16 women), 33 part-time (13 women); includes 11 minority (4 African Americans, 5 Asian Americans or Pacific Islanders, 2 Hispanic Americans), 10 international. Average age 29. 49 applicants, 45% accepted, 19 enrolled. In 2001, 23 degrees awarded.
Degree requirements: For master's, thesis optional.
Entrance requirements: For master's, GMAT, TOEFL, minimum GPA of 2.5 required. *Application deadline:* For fall admission, 3/15 (priority date); for spring admission, 10/1 (priority date). Applications are processed on a rolling basis. *Application fee:* $25 ($50 for international students).
Expenses: Tuition, state resident: full-time $1,114. Tuition, nonresident: full-time $3,670.
Financial support: In 2001–02, 12 students received support, including 3 research assistantships with partial tuition reimbursements available; fellowships with tuition reimbursements available, career-related internships or fieldwork, Federal Work-Study, institutionally sponsored loans, scholarships/grants, and tuition waivers (partial) also available. Support available to part-time students. Financial award application deadline: 4/1; financial award applicants required to submit FAFSA.
Faculty research: Marketing, finance, quantitative methods, MIS. *Total annual research expenditures:* $200,000.
Dr. Robert A. Swerdlow, Associate Dean, 409-880-8604, *Fax:* 409-880-8088, *E-mail:* swerdlowra@hal.lamar.edu. *Web site:* http://www.cob.lamar.edu/

■ LEHIGH UNIVERSITY

College of Business and Economics, Bethlehem, PA 18015-3094

AWARDS Accounting and information analysis (MS); business (MBA, PhD), including business (PhD), business administration (MBA); economics (MS, PhD); new ventures (Certificate); project management (Certificate);

supply chain management (Certificate). Part-time and evening/weekend programs available. Postbaccalaureate distance learning degree programs offered (minimal on-campus study).

Faculty: 53 full-time (7 women), 7 part-time/adjunct (1 woman).
Students: 70 full-time (22 women), 283 part-time (95 women); includes 43 minority (6 African Americans, 33 Asian Americans or Pacific Islanders, 3 Hispanic Americans, 1 Native American), 36 international. Average age 30. 262 applicants, 76% accepted, 136 enrolled. In 2001, 108 master's, 2 doctorates awarded. Terminal master's awarded for partial completion of doctoral program.
Degree requirements: For master's, thesis optional; for doctorate, thesis/dissertation, proposal defense, comprehensive exam.
Entrance requirements: For master's, GMAT, GRE, TOEFL; for doctorate, GMAT or GRE, TOEFL. *Application deadline:* For fall admission, 7/15; for spring admission, 12/1. Applications are processed on a rolling basis. *Application fee:* $50. Electronic applications accepted.
Expenses: Contact institution.
Financial support: In 2001–02, 57 students received support, including 2 fellowships with full tuition reimbursements available (averaging $12,000 per year), 1 research assistantship with full and partial tuition reimbursement available (averaging $1,000 per year), 24 teaching assistantships with full tuition reimbursements available (averaging $11,350 per year); career-related internships or fieldwork, scholarships/grants, and tuition waivers (full and partial) also available. Support available to part-time students. Financial award application deadline: 1/15.
Faculty research: Public finance, energy, investments, activity-based costing, management information systems.
Kathleen A. Trexler, Associate Dean and Director, 610-758-4450, *Fax:* 610-758-5283, *E-mail:* kat3@lehigh.edu.
Application contact: Mary- Theresa Taglang, Director of Recruitment and Admissions, 610-758-5285, *Fax:* 610-758-5283, *E-mail:* mtt4@lehigh.edu. *Web site:* http://www.lehigh.edu/~incbe/incbe.html

Find an in-depth description at www.petersons.com/gradchannel.

■ LEHIGH UNIVERSITY

College of Business and Economics, Department of Accounting, Program in Accounting and Information Analysis, Bethlehem, PA 18015-3094

AWARDS MS. Part-time programs available.

Faculty: 6 full-time (1 woman).
Students: 12 full-time (6 women); includes 1 minority (Asian American or Pacific Islander), 3 international. Average age 25. 22 applicants, 73% accepted, 12 enrolled.

Entrance requirements: For master's, GMAT, TOEFL. *Application deadline:* For fall admission, 5/1. Applications are processed on a rolling basis. *Application fee:* $50. Electronic applications accepted.
Expenses: Tuition: Part-time $468 per credit hour. Required fees: $200; $100 per semester. Tuition and fees vary according to program.
Financial support: In 2001–02, 4 students received support, including 4 research assistantships with partial tuition reimbursements available (averaging $1,000 per year); scholarships/grants also available. Financial award application deadline: 2/1.
Faculty research: Behavioral accounting, internal control, information systems, supply chain management, financial accounting, auditing.
Dr. Jack W. Paul, Director M.S. in Accounting and Information Analysis Program, 610-758-4452, *Fax:* 610-758-6429, *E-mail:* jwp1@lehigh.edu.
Application contact: Mary- Theresa Taglang, Director of Recruitment and Admissions, 610-758-5285, *Fax:* 610-758-5283, *E-mail:* mtt4@lehigh.edu.

Find an in-depth description at www.petersons.com/gradchannel.

■ LONG ISLAND UNIVERSITY, C.W. POST CAMPUS

College of Information and Computer Science, Department of Computer Science/Management Engineering, Brookville, NY 11548-1300

AWARDS Computer science education (MS); information systems (MS); management engineering (MS). Part-time and evening/weekend programs available.

Faculty: 11 full-time (3 women), 7 part-time/adjunct (0 women).
Students: 41 full-time (16 women), 100 part-time (38 women). 96 applicants, 90% accepted, 42 enrolled. In 2001, 31 degrees awarded.
Degree requirements: For master's, thesis or alternative, comprehensive exam.
Entrance requirements: For master's, bachelor's degree in science, mathematics, or engineering; minimum GPA of 2.5. *Application deadline:* Applications are processed on a rolling basis. *Application fee:* $30. Electronic applications accepted.
Expenses: Tuition: Full-time $10,296; part-time $572 per credit. Required fees: $380; $190 per semester.
Financial support: Career-related internships or fieldwork, Federal Work-Study, institutionally sponsored loans, unspecified assistantships, and management engineering prize available. Support available to part-time students. Financial award application deadline: 5/15; financial award applicants required to submit CSS PROFILE or FAFSA.

Faculty research: Inductive music learning, re-engineering business process, technology and ethics.
Dr. Susan Fife-Dorchak, Chair, 516-299-2293, *E-mail:* susan.dorchak@liu.edu.
Application contact: Christopher Malinowski, Director of Graduate Programs, 516-299-2663, *E-mail:* cmalinow@liu.edu. *Web site:* http://www.liu.edu/postlas/

■ MARIST COLLEGE

Graduate Programs, School of Computer Science and Mathematics, Poughkeepsie, NY 12601-1387

AWARDS Computer science (MS), including information systems, software development. Part-time and evening/weekend programs available.

Faculty: 11 full-time (3 women), 5 part-time/adjunct (1 woman).
Students: 50 full-time (15 women), 93 part-time (28 women); includes 63 minority (4 African Americans, 57 Asian Americans or Pacific Islanders, 2 Hispanic Americans), 2 international. Average age 33. In 2001, 34 degrees awarded.
Degree requirements: For master's, thesis optional.
Application deadline: For fall admission, 8/1 (priority date); for spring admission, 12/15. Applications are processed on a rolling basis. *Application fee:* $30.
Expenses: Tuition: Full-time $4,320; part-time $480 per credit. Required fees: $30 per semester.
Financial support: Federal Work-Study and tuition waivers (partial) available. Support available to part-time students. Financial award application deadline: 8/15; financial award applicants required to submit FAFSA.
Dr. Roger Norton, Dean, 845-575-3000, *E-mail:* roger.norton@marist.edu.
Application contact: Dr. John DeJoy, Acting Dean of Graduate and Continuing Education, 845-575-3530, *Fax:* 845-575-3640, *E-mail:* john.dejoy@marist.edu.

■ MARSHALL UNIVERSITY

Graduate College, College of Information, Technology and Engineering, Division of Information Systems and Technology Management, Program in Information Systems, Huntington, WV 25755

AWARDS MS. Part-time and evening/weekend programs available.

Students: 32 full-time (13 women), 46 part-time (16 women); includes 6 minority (2 African Americans, 3 Asian Americans or Pacific Islanders, 1 Hispanic American), 113 international. Average age 32. In 2001, 17 degrees awarded.
Degree requirements: For master's, final project, oral exam.
Entrance requirements: For master's, GRE General Test or MAT, minimum undergraduate GPA of 2.5.

Marshall University (continued)

Expenses: Tuition, state resident: part-time $147 per credit. Tuition, nonresident: part-time $468 per credit. Tuition and fees vary according to campus/location and reciprocity agreements.
Financial support: Tuition waivers (full) available. Support available to part-time students. Financial award application deadline: 8/1; financial award applicants required to submit FAFSA.
Dr. Tom Hankins, Director, 304-746-2044, *E-mail:* thankins@marshall.edu.
Application contact: Ken O'Neal, Assistant Vice President, Adult Student Services, 304-746-2500 Ext. 1907, *Fax:* 304-746-1902, *E-mail:* oneal@marshall.edu.

■ MONTCLAIR STATE UNIVERSITY

The School of Graduate, Professional and Continuing Education, College of Science and Mathematics, Department of Computer Science, Upper Montclair, NJ 07043-1624

AWARDS Applied mathematics (MS); applied statistics (MS); informatics (MS); object oriented computing (Certificate). Part-time and evening/weekend programs available.

Degree requirements: For master's, comprehensive exam.
Entrance requirements: For master's, minimum GPA of 2.67, 15 undergraduate math credits, bachelors degree in computer science, math, science or engineering. Electronic applications accepted.

■ NAVAL POSTGRADUATE SCHOOL

Graduate Programs, Program in Information Systems, Monterey, CA 93943

AWARDS MS. Program open only to commissioned officers of the United States and friendly nations and selected United States federal civilian employees. Part-time programs available.

Degree requirements: For master's, thesis.

■ NAVAL POSTGRADUATE SCHOOL

Graduate Programs, Program in Information Systems and Operations, Monterey, CA 93943

AWARDS MS.

Degree requirements: For master's, thesis.

■ NEW JERSEY INSTITUTE OF TECHNOLOGY

Office of Graduate Studies, College of Computing Science, Program in Information Systems, Newark, NJ 07102

AWARDS MS, PhD. Part-time and evening/weekend programs available.

Faculty: 20 full-time (5 women).
Students: 135 full-time (45 women), 174 part-time (48 women); includes 77 minority (13 African Americans, 54 Asian Americans or Pacific Islanders, 10 Hispanic Americans), 157 international. Average age 30. 429 applicants, 38% accepted, 80 enrolled. In 2001, 72 degrees awarded. Terminal master's awarded for partial completion of doctoral program.
Degree requirements: For master's and doctorate, thesis/dissertation.
Entrance requirements: For master's, GRE General Test; for doctorate, GRE General Test, minimum graduate GPA of 3.5. *Application deadline:* For fall admission, 6/5 (priority date); for spring admission, 10/15. Applications are processed on a rolling basis. *Application fee:* $50. Electronic applications accepted.
Expenses: Tuition, state resident: full-time $7,812; part-time $434 per credit. Tuition, nonresident: full-time $10,746; part-time $597 per credit. Required fees: $47 per credit. $76 per semester.
Financial support: Fellowships with full and partial tuition reimbursements, research assistantships with full and partial tuition reimbursements, teaching assistantships with full and partial tuition reimbursements, career-related internships or fieldwork, Federal Work-Study, institutionally sponsored loans, and unspecified assistantships available. Financial award application deadline: 3/15.
Dr. Murray Turoff, Chairperson, 973-596-3399, *E-mail:* murray.turoff@njit.edu.
Application contact: Kathryn Kelly, Director of Admissions, 973-596-3300, *Fax:* 973-596-3461, *E-mail:* admissions@njit.edu. *Web site:* http://www.njit.edu/

■ NORTHEASTERN UNIVERSITY

College of Engineering, Information Systems Program, Boston, MA 02115-5096

AWARDS MS. Part-time programs available.

Faculty: 13 part-time/adjunct (1 woman).
Students: 169 full-time (114 women), 79 part-time (35 women); includes 11 minority (3 African Americans, 8 Asian Americans or Pacific Islanders), 145 international. Average age 26. 137 applicants, 65% accepted, 42 enrolled. In 2001, 122 degrees awarded.
Degree requirements: For master's, thesis optional. *Median time to degree:* Master's–3 years full-time, 5 years part-time.

Entrance requirements: For master's, GRE General Test. *Application deadline:* For fall admission, 2/15 (priority date). Applications are processed on a rolling basis. *Application fee:* $50. Electronic applications accepted.
Expenses: Tuition: Part-time $535 per credit hour. Required fees: $56. Tuition and fees vary according to program.
Financial support: In 2001–02, 24 students received support, including 5 research assistantships with full tuition reimbursements available (averaging $13,560 per year), 4 teaching assistantships with full tuition reimbursements available (averaging $13,560 per year); fellowships, career-related internships or fieldwork, Federal Work-Study, scholarships/grants, tuition waivers (full), and unspecified assistantships also available. Support available to part-time students. Financial award application deadline: 2/15; financial award applicants required to submit FAFSA.
Faculty research: Simulation analysis.
Dr. Ronald Perry, Head, 617-373-4835.
Application contact: Stephen L. Gibson, Associate Director, 617-373-2711, *Fax:* 617-373-2501, *E-mail:* grad-eng@coe.neu.edu. *Web site:* http://www.coe.neu.edu/

■ NORTHERN KENTUCKY UNIVERSITY

School of Graduate Programs, Program in Information Systems, Highland Heights, KY 41099

AWARDS MSIS.

Faculty: 8 full-time (1 woman).
Students: 13 full-time (5 women), 12 part-time (5 women); includes 2 minority (both Asian Americans or Pacific Islanders), 4 international. Average age 33.
Application fee: $25.
Expenses: Tuition, state resident: full-time $2,958; part-time $149 per credit hour. Tuition, nonresident: full-time $7,872; part-time $422 per credit hour.
Dr. Margaret Meyers, Interim Chairperson, 859-572-6527.
Application contact: Peg Griffin, Graduate Coordinator, 859-572-6364, *E-mail:* griffinp@nku.edu.

■ NORTHWESTERN UNIVERSITY

McCormick School of Engineering and Applied Science, Department of Electrical and Computer Engineering, Program in Information Technology, Evanston, IL 60208

AWARDS MIT.

Faculty: 15 part-time/adjunct (0 women).
Students: Average age 32. 62 applicants, 56% accepted, 32 enrolled. In 2001, 27 degrees awarded.
Entrance requirements: For master's, GRE General Test, 2 years of professional experience. *Application deadline:* For fall

admission, 6/15. Applications are processed on a rolling basis. *Application fee:* $30.
Expenses: Tuition: Full-time $26,526.
Financial support: Employers reimbursement available.
Abraham Haddad, Chair, 847-491-3641, *Fax:* 847-491-4455.
Application contact: Carol Henes, Information Contact, 847-467-6557, *E-mail:* carolh@ece.northwestern.edu. *Web site:* http://www.ece.northwestern.edu/itp/

■ NOVA SOUTHEASTERN UNIVERSITY

School of Computer and Information Sciences, Fort Lauderdale, FL 33314-7721

AWARDS Computer information systems (MS, PhD); computer science (MS, PhD); computing technology in education (MS, Ed D, PhD); information science (PhD); information systems (PhD); management information systems (MS). Part-time and evening/weekend programs available.
Postbaccalaureate distance learning degree programs offered (no on-campus study).

Faculty: 18 full-time (4 women), 12 part-time/adjunct (3 women).
Students: 832 full-time (297 women); includes 195 minority (97 African Americans, 39 Asian Americans or Pacific Islanders, 56 Hispanic Americans, 3 Native Americans), 63 international. Average age 41. 286 applicants, 80% accepted, 169 enrolled. In 2001, 114 master's, 27 doctorates awarded. Terminal master's awarded for partial completion of doctoral program.
Degree requirements: For master's, thesis optional; for doctorate, thesis/dissertation.
Entrance requirements: For master's, minimum undergraduate GPA of 2.5, minimum major GPA of 3.0; for doctorate, master's degree, minimum graduate GPA of 3.25. *Application deadline:* Applications are processed on a rolling basis. *Application fee:* $50.
Expenses: Contact institution.
Financial support: In 2001–02, 2 teaching assistantships with full tuition reimbursements (averaging $25,000 per year) were awarded; Federal Work-Study, scholarships/grants, and unspecified assistantships also available. Support available to part-time students. Financial award application deadline: 5/1.
Faculty research: Artificial intelligence, database management, human-computer interaction, distance education, computer education.
Dr. Edward Lieblein, Dean.
Application contact: Sherese Young, Marketing Coordinator, 954-262-2005, *Fax:* 954-262-3915, *E-mail:* scisinfo@ nova.edu. *Web site:* http:// www.scis.nova.edu/

Find an in-depth description at www.petersons.com/gradchannel.

■ OAKLAND UNIVERSITY

Graduate Study and Lifelong Learning, School of Business Administration, Rochester, MI 48309-4401

AWARDS Accounting (M Acc); business administration (MBA, Certificate); information technology management (MS). Part-time and evening/weekend programs available.

Faculty: 55 full-time (10 women), 13 part-time/adjunct (2 women).
Students: 52 full-time (23 women), 484 part-time (164 women); includes 38 minority (11 African Americans, 18 Asian Americans or Pacific Islanders, 7 Hispanic Americans, 2 Native Americans), 39 international. Average age 31. 250 applicants, 76% accepted. In 2001, 152 master's, 7 other advanced degrees awarded.
Entrance requirements: For master's, GMAT, minimum GPA of 3.0 for unconditional admission. *Application deadline:* For fall admission, 8/15 (priority date); for winter admission, 12/1 (priority date); for spring admission, 4/15 (priority date). Applications are processed on a rolling basis. *Application fee:* $30. Electronic applications accepted.
Expenses: Tuition, state resident: full-time $5,904; part-time $246 per credit hour. Tuition, nonresident: full-time $12,192; part-time $508 per credit hour. Required fees: $472; $236 per term.
Financial support: Career-related internships or fieldwork, Federal Work-Study, institutionally sponsored loans, and tuition waivers (full) available. Financial award application deadline: 3/1; financial award applicants required to submit FAFSA.
Faculty research: Health care, economics, auto industry forecasting, computers in management. *Total annual research expenditures:* $17,073.
Dr. John Gardner, Dean, 248-370-3286.
Application contact: Darla Null, Coordinator, 248-370-3281. *Web site:* http://www.sba.oakland.edu

■ THE OHIO STATE UNIVERSITY

Graduate School, College of Engineering, Department of Computer and Information Science, Columbus, OH 43210

AWARDS MS, PhD.

Degree requirements: For master's, thesis optional; for doctorate, thesis/dissertation.
Entrance requirements: For master's and doctorate, GRE General Test, TSE.

■ PACE UNIVERSITY

School of Computer Science and Information Systems, New York, NY 10038

AWARDS Computer communications and networks (Certificate); computer science (MS); computing studies (DPS); information

systems (MS); object-oriented programming (Certificate); telecommunications (MS, Certificate). Part-time and evening/weekend programs available.

Faculty: 23 full-time, 9 part-time/adjunct.
Students: 210 full-time (70 women), 446 part-time (165 women); includes 129 minority (49 African Americans, 61 Asian Americans or Pacific Islanders, 19 Hispanic Americans), 197 international. Average age 28. 474 applicants, 72% accepted. In 2001, 112 master's, 6 other advanced degrees awarded.
Entrance requirements: For master's, GRE General Test. *Application deadline:* For fall admission, 7/31 (priority date); for spring admission, 11/30. Applications are processed on a rolling basis. *Application fee:* $65. Electronic applications accepted.
Expenses: Contact institution.
Financial support: Research assistantships, career-related internships or fieldwork available. Support available to part-time students. Financial award applicants required to submit FAFSA.
Dr. Susan Merritt, Dean, 914-422-4375.
Application contact: Joanna Broda, Director of Admissions, 212-346-1652, *Fax:* 212-346-1585, *E-mail:* gradnyc@ pace.edu. *Web site:* http://www.pace.edu/

Find an in-depth description at www.petersons.com/gradchannel.

■ PACE UNIVERSITY, WHITE PLAINS CAMPUS

School of Computer Science and Information Systems, White Plains, NY 10603

AWARDS Computer communications and networks (Certificate); computer science (MS); computing studies (DPS); information systems (MS); object-oriented programming (Certificate); telecommunications (MS, Certificate). Part-time and evening/weekend programs available.

Faculty: 14 full-time, 6 part-time/adjunct.
Students: 73 full-time (30 women), 307 part-time (117 women); includes 122 minority (37 African Americans, 60 Asian Americans or Pacific Islanders, 25 Hispanic Americans), 50 international. Average age 31. 262 applicants, 65% accepted, 117 enrolled. In 2001, 65 master's, 9 other advanced degrees awarded.
Entrance requirements: For master's, GRE General Test. *Application deadline:* For fall admission, 8/1 (priority date); for spring admission, 12/1 (priority date). Applications are processed on a rolling basis. *Application fee:* $65. Electronic applications accepted.
Expenses: Contact institution.
Financial support: Research assistantships, career-related internships or fieldwork available. Support available to part-time students. Financial award applicants required to submit FAFSA.
Dr. Susan Merritt, Dean, 914-422-4375.

Pace University, White Plains Campus (continued)

Application contact: Joanna Broda, Director of Admissions, 914-422-4283, *Fax:* 914-422-4287, *E-mail:* gradwp@pace.edu. *Web site:* http://www.pace.edu/

■ THE PENNSYLVANIA STATE UNIVERSITY GREAT VALLEY CAMPUS

Graduate Studies and Continuing Education, School of Graduate Professional Studies, Department of Engineering and Information Science, Program in Information Science, Malvern, PA 19355-1488

AWARDS MS.

Students: 55 full-time (23 women), 384 part-time (123 women). Average age 34. In 2001, 126 degrees awarded.
Application fee: $45.
Expenses: Tuition, state resident: part-time $415 per credit. Tuition, nonresident: part-time $680 per credit. Tuition and fees vary according to program.
Application contact: 610-648-3242, *Fax:* 610-889-1334.

■ THE PENNSYLVANIA STATE UNIVERSITY UNIVERSITY PARK CAMPUS

Graduate School, School of Information Sciences and Technology, Department of Information Sciences and Technology, State College, University Park, PA 16802-1503

AWARDS PhD.

Application fee: $45.
Expenses: Tuition, state resident: full-time $7,882; part-time $333 per credit. Tuition, nonresident: full-time $16,142; part-time $673 per credit. Required fees: $124 per semester.
Dr. David Hall, Associate Dean for Research and Graduate Programs, 814-865-3528.

■ POLYTECHNIC UNIVERSITY, BROOKLYN CAMPUS

Department of Computer and Information Science, Major in Information Systems Engineering, Brooklyn, NY 11201-2990

AWARDS MS. Part-time and evening/weekend programs available.

Entrance requirements: For master's, BA or BS in computer science, mathematics, science, or engineering; working knowledge of a high-level program. Electronic applications accepted.

Find an in-depth description at www.petersons.com/gradchannel.

■ POLYTECHNIC UNIVERSITY, LONG ISLAND GRADUATE CENTER

Graduate Programs, Department of Computer and Information Science, Major in Information Systems Engineering, Melville, NY 11747

AWARDS MS.

Degree requirements: For master's, thesis (for some programs). Electronic applications accepted.

■ POLYTECHNIC UNIVERSITY, WESTCHESTER GRADUATE CENTER

Graduate Programs, Department of Computer and Information Science, Major in Information Systems Engineering, Hawthorne, NY 10532-1507

AWARDS MS.

Degree requirements: For master's, thesis (for some programs). Electronic applications accepted.

■ PRINCETON UNIVERSITY

Graduate School, School of Engineering and Applied Science, Department of Electrical Engineering, Princeton, NJ 08544-1019

AWARDS Computer engineering (PhD); electrical engineering (M Eng); electronic materials and devices (PhD); information sciences and systems (PhD); optoelectronics (PhD). Part-time programs available.

Degree requirements: For doctorate, thesis/dissertation.
Entrance requirements: For master's and doctorate, GRE General Test, TOEFL. Electronic applications accepted.
Faculty research: Nanostructures, computer architecture, multimedia. *Web site:* http://www.princeton.edu/

■ REGIS UNIVERSITY

School for Professional Studies, Program in Computer Information Technology, Denver, CO 80221-1099

AWARDS Database technologies (MSCIT, Certificate), including database administrator (Certificate), Oracle application development (Certificate), Oracle e-commerce enterprise and Web/Internet Protocol programming (Certificate); e-commerce engineering (MSCIT, Certificate), including advanced e-commerce (Certificate), management of technology (Certificate), Oracle e-commerce enterprise and Web/Internet Protocol programming (Certificate), portal management (Certificate); management of technology (MSCIT); networking technologies (MSCIT); networking technology (Certificate), including

e-commerce, network engineering, telecommunications; object-oriented technologies (MSCIT); object-oriented technology (Certificate), including C++ programming, Java programming, Visual Basic programming. Offered at Boulder Campus, Northwest Denver Campus, Southeast Denver Campus, Fort Collins Campus, Colorado Springs Campus, and Broomfield Campus. Part-time and evening/weekend programs available. Postbaccalaureate distance learning degree programs offered (no on-campus study).

Students: 343. Average age 36. In 2001, 40 degrees awarded.
Degree requirements: For master's and Certificate, final research project.
Entrance requirements: For master's and Certificate, GMAT, TOEFL, or university-based test (international applicants), 2 years of related experience, resumé.
Application deadline: Applications are processed on a rolling basis. *Application fee:* $75.
Expenses: Contact institution.
Financial support: Federal Work-Study available. Support available to part-time students. Financial award applicants required to submit FAFSA.
Don Archer, Chair, 303-458-4302, *Fax:* 303-964-5538.
Application contact: 800-677-9270 Ext. 4080, *Fax:* 303-964-5538, *E-mail:* masters@regis.edu. *Web site:* http://www.regis.edu/spsgraduate/

■ RENSSELAER POLYTECHNIC INSTITUTE

Graduate School, School of Science, Interdisciplinary Program in Information Technology, Troy, NY 12180-3590

AWARDS MS. Part-time and evening/weekend programs available. Postbaccalaureate distance learning degree programs offered (no on-campus study).

Students: 33 full-time (14 women), 12 part-time (4 women); includes 7 minority (3 African Americans, 1 Asian American or Pacific Islander, 3 Hispanic Americans), 30 international. 120 applicants, 27% accepted, 27 enrolled. In 2001, 16 degrees awarded. *Median time to degree:* Master's– 1.5 years full-time, 2.5 years part-time.
Entrance requirements: For master's, TOEFL. *Application deadline:* For fall admission, 1/15 (priority date). Applications are processed on a rolling basis. *Application fee:* $45. Electronic applications accepted.
Expenses: Tuition: Full-time $26,400; part-time $1,320 per credit hour. Required fees: $1,437.
Financial support: In 2001–02, 8 students received support, including 3 teaching assistantships with full tuition reimbursements available (averaging $12,500 per year); career-related internships or fieldwork also available.

Faculty research: Database systems, software design, human-computer interaction, networking, bioinformatics.
Dr. David Spooner, Acting Chair, 518-276-8326, *Fax:* 518-276-4033, *E-mail:* spoonerd@rpi.edu.
Application contact: Gail Gere, Director of Program Development, 518-276-2660, *Fax:* 518-276-6687, *E-mail:* gereg@rpi.edu. *Web site:* http://www.it.rpi.edu/

Find an in-depth description at www.petersons.com/gradchannel.

■ RIVIER COLLEGE

School of Graduate Studies, Department of Computer Science and Mathematics, Nashua, NH 03060-5086

AWARDS Computer science (MS); information science (MS); mathematics (MAT). Part-time and evening/weekend programs available.

Faculty: 3 full-time (1 woman), 11 part-time/adjunct (2 women).
Students: 37 full-time (25 women), 61 part-time (28 women); includes 8 minority (all Asian Americans or Pacific Islanders), 32 international. Average age 36. 53 applicants, 62% accepted. In 2001, 61 degrees awarded.
Entrance requirements: For master's, GRE Subject Test. *Application deadline:* Applications are processed on a rolling basis. *Application fee:* $25. Electronic applications accepted.
Expenses: Tuition: Part-time $360 per credit. Required fees: $25 per year. Part-time tuition and fees vary according to course level and course load.
Financial support: Available to part-time students. Application deadline: 2/1.
Dr. A. Darien Lauten, Director, 603-888-1311, *E-mail:* dlauten@rivier.edu.
Application contact: Diane Monahan, Director of Graduate Admissions, 603-897-8129, *Fax:* 603-897-8810, *E-mail:* gradadm@rivier.edu.

■ ROBERT MORRIS UNIVERSITY

Graduate Studies, School of Communications and Information Systems, Program in Communications and Information Systems, Moon Township, PA 15108-1189

AWARDS Communications and information systems (MS); information systems management (MS); Internet information systems (MS). Only part-time programs offered. Part-time and evening/weekend programs available.

Faculty: 24 full-time (3 women), 34 part-time/adjunct (8 women).
Students: In 2001, 100 degrees awarded.
Entrance requirements: For master's, letters of recommendation. *Application deadline:* For fall admission, 8/1 (priority date); for spring admission, 11/30 (priority date). Applications are processed on a rolling basis. *Application fee:* $35. Electronic applications accepted.

Expenses: Contact institution.
Financial support: Institutionally sponsored loans and unspecified assistantships available. Support available to part-time students. Financial award application deadline: 5/1; financial award applicants required to submit FAFSA.
Dr. Frederick G. Kohun, Associate Dean, 412-262-8395, *Fax:* 412-299-2481, *E-mail:* kohun@rmu.edu.
Application contact: Kellie Laurenzi, Director of Enrollment Services, 800-762-0097, *Fax:* 412-299-2425, *E-mail:* laurenzi@rmu.edu. *Web site:* http://www.rmu.edu/

■ ROBERT MORRIS UNIVERSITY

Graduate Studies, School of Communications and Information Systems, Program in Information Systems and Communications, Moon Township, PA 15108-1189

AWARDS D Sc. Part-time and evening/weekend programs available.

Faculty: 5 full-time (0 women).
Entrance requirements: For doctorate, GRE or equivalent. *Application deadline:* For fall admission, 8/1 (priority date). *Application fee:* $35.
Expenses: Contact institution.
Financial support: Application deadline: 5/1.
Dr. Frederick G. Kohun, Associate Dean, 412-262-8395, *Fax:* 412-299-2481, *E-mail:* kohun@rmu.edu.
Application contact: Kellie Laurenzi, Director of Enrollment Services, 800-762-0097, *Fax:* 412-299-2425, *E-mail:* laurenzi@rmu.edu. *Web site:* http://www.rmu.edu/

■ ROCHESTER INSTITUTE OF TECHNOLOGY

Graduate Enrollment Services, Golisano College of Computing and Information Sciences, Department of Information Technology, Program in Information Technology, Rochester, NY 14623-5698

AWARDS MS.

Students: 188 full-time (65 women), 280 part-time (91 women); includes 45 minority (6 African Americans, 29 Asian Americans or Pacific Islanders, 7 Hispanic Americans, 3 Native Americans), 205 international. 267 applicants, 67% accepted, 119 enrolled. In 2001, 56 degrees awarded.
Entrance requirements: For master's, minimum GPA of 3.0. *Application deadline:* For fall admission, 3/1 (priority date). Applications are processed on a rolling basis. *Application fee:* $50.
Expenses: Tuition: Full-time $20,928; part-time $587 per hour. Required fees: $162. Tuition and fees vary according to program.

Diane Bills, Graduate Coordinator, 585-475-6971, *E-mail:* dpb@it.rit.edu.

■ SACRED HEART UNIVERSITY

Graduate Studies, College of Arts and Sciences, Department of Computer Science and Information Technology, Fairfield, CT 06432-1000

AWARDS Computer science (MS, CPS); e-commerce (CPS); information technology (MS, CPS); multimedia (CPS). Part-time and evening/weekend programs available. Postbaccalaureate distance learning degree programs offered (minimal on-campus study).

Students: 14 full-time, 178 part-time; includes 60 minority (15 African Americans, 38 Asian Americans or Pacific Islanders, 5 Hispanic Americans, 2 Native Americans), 17 international. Average age 31. 79 applicants, 29% accepted. In 2001, 7 degrees awarded.
Degree requirements: For master's, thesis optional.
Application deadline: Applications are processed on a rolling basis. *Application fee:* $45 ($100 for international students).
Expenses: Tuition: Full-time $16,128; part-time $435 per credit. Required fees: $285 per term.
Financial support: In 2001–02, 10 students received support. Career-related internships or fieldwork and unspecified assistantships available. Support available to part-time students. Financial award applicants required to submit FAFSA.
Faculty research: Contemporary market software.
Domenick Pinto, Academic Director and Chairperson, 203-371-7789, *Fax:* 203-371-0506, *E-mail:* pintod@sacredheart.edu.
Application contact: William Farrell, Director of Graduate Admissions, MSCIS and MBA Programs, 203-365-7619, *Fax:* 203-365-4732, *E-mail:* farrellw@sacredheart.edu. *Web site:* http://www.sacredheart.edu/graduate/computer/

■ ST. MARY'S UNIVERSITY OF SAN ANTONIO

Graduate School, Department of Computer Science, Program in Computer Information Systems, San Antonio, TX 78228-8507

AWARDS MS.

Faculty: 3 full-time (2 women).
Students: 14 full-time (6 women), 81 part-time (30 women); includes 38 minority (3 African Americans, 5 Asian Americans or Pacific Islanders, 29 Hispanic Americans, 1 Native American), 14 international. Average age 30. In 2001, 32 degrees awarded.
Degree requirements: For master's, thesis optional.
Entrance requirements: For master's, GMAT or GRE General Test. *Application deadline:* Applications are processed on a rolling basis. *Application fee:* $15. Electronic applications accepted.

St. Mary's University of San Antonio
(continued)

Expenses: Tuition: Full-time $8,190; part-time $455 per credit hour. Required fees: $375.

Financial support: Research assistantships, career-related internships or fieldwork and institutionally sponsored loans available. Financial award application deadline: 2/15; financial award applicants required to submit FAFSA.

Faculty research: Artificial intelligence, database/knowledge base, software engineering, expert systems.
Dr. Douglas L. Hall, Graduate Program Director, 210-436-3317.

■ SAINT XAVIER UNIVERSITY

Graduate Studies, School of Arts and Sciences, Department of Mathematics and Computer Science, Chicago, IL 60655-3105

AWARDS Applied computer science in Internet information systems (MS).

Faculty: 1 (woman) full-time.
Students: 10 full-time (3 women), 6 part-time (4 women). Average age 32.
Degree requirements: For master's, thesis optional.
Application deadline: For fall admission, 8/15. *Application fee:* $35.
Expenses: Tuition: Full-time $4,500; part-time $500 per credit. Required fees: $40 per term.
Dr. Florence Appel, Associate Professor and Associate Chair/Computer Science, 773-298-3398, *Fax:* 773-779-9061, *E-mail:* appel@sxu.edu.
Application contact: Beth Gierach, Managing Director of Admission, 773-298-3053, *Fax:* 773-298-3076, *E-mail:* gierach@sxu.edu.

Find an in-depth description at www.petersons.com/gradchannel.

■ SAN JOSE STATE UNIVERSITY

Graduate Studies, College of Engineering, Department of Computer, Information and Systems Engineering, Program in Information and Systems Engineering, San Jose, CA 95192-0001

AWARDS MS. Part-time programs available.

Faculty: 5 full-time (0 women), 9 part-time/adjunct (1 woman).
Students: 21 full-time (7 women), 20 part-time (5 women); includes 15 minority (1 African American, 11 Asian Americans or Pacific Islanders, 3 Hispanic Americans), 19 international. Average age 28. 17 applicants, 53% accepted. In 2001, 9 degrees awarded.
Degree requirements: For master's, comprehensive exam.
Entrance requirements: For master's, minimum GPA of 3.0. *Application deadline:* For fall admission, 6/29; for spring admission, 11/30. Applications are processed on

a rolling basis. *Application fee:* $59. Electronic applications accepted.
Expenses: Tuition, nonresident: part-time $246 per unit. Required fees: $678 per semester. Tuition and fees vary according to course load.
Financial support: Federal Work-Study available. Financial award applicants required to submit FAFSA.
Application contact: Dr. Louis Freund, Graduate Coordinator, 408-924-3890.

■ SHIPPENSBURG UNIVERSITY OF PENNSYLVANIA

School of Graduate Studies and Research, College of Arts and Sciences, Department of Mathematics, Shippensburg, PA 17257-2299

AWARDS Computer science (MS); information systems (MS). Part-time and evening/weekend programs available.

Faculty: 10 full-time (2 women).
Students: 26 full-time (5 women), 43 part-time (16 women); includes 2 minority (1 Hispanic American, 1 Native American), 32 international. Average age 30. 94 applicants, 60% accepted, 10 enrolled. In 2001, 15 degrees awarded.
Degree requirements: For master's, Project. *Median time to degree:* Master's–1.92 years full-time, 2.58 years part-time.
Entrance requirements: For master's, TOEFL, GRE General Test, minimum GPA of 2.75. *Application deadline:* Applications are processed on a rolling basis. *Application fee:* $30. Electronic applications accepted.
Expenses: Tuition, state resident: full-time $4,600; part-time $256 per credit hour. Tuition, nonresident: full-time $7,554; part-time $420 per credit hour. Required fees: $290; $145 per semester.
Financial support: In 2001–02, 22 research assistantships with full tuition reimbursements were awarded; career-related internships or fieldwork and unspecified assistantships also available. Support available to part-time students. Financial award application deadline: 3/1; financial award applicants required to submit FAFSA.
Dr. Fred Nordai, Chairperson, 717-477-1431, *Fax:* 717-477-4009, *E-mail:* flnord@ship.edu.
Application contact: Renee Payne, Associate Dean of Graduate Admissions, 717-477-1231, *Fax:* 717-477-4016, *E-mail:* rmpayn@ship.edu. *Web site:* http://www.ship.edu/academic/artcps.html

■ SOUTHERN METHODIST UNIVERSITY

School of Engineering, Department of Engineering Management, Information and Systems, Dallas, TX 75275

AWARDS Applied science (MS); engineering management (MSEM, DE); operations research (MS, PhD); systems engineering

(MS). Part-time and evening/weekend programs available. Postbaccalaureate distance learning degree programs offered.

Faculty: 6 full-time (1 woman).
Students: 10 full-time (1 woman), 100 part-time (22 women); includes 29 minority (6 African Americans, 11 Asian Americans or Pacific Islanders, 10 Hispanic Americans, 2 Native Americans), 10 international. 55 applicants, 78% accepted. In 2001, 25 master's, 5 doctorates awarded. Terminal master's awarded for partial completion of doctoral program.
Degree requirements: For master's, thesis optional; for doctorate, thesis/dissertation, oral and written qualifying exams.
Entrance requirements: For master's, GRE General, TOEFL, minimum GPA of 3.0 in last 2 years; bachelor's degree in engineering, mathematics, or sciences; for doctorate, bachelor's degree in related field. *Application deadline:* For fall admission, 7/1; for spring admission, 11/15. Applications are processed on a rolling basis. *Application fee:* $50.
Expenses: Tuition: Part-time $285 per credit hour.
Faculty research: Telecommunications, decision systems, information engineering, operations research, software.
Richard S. Barr, Chair, 214-768-2605, *E-mail:* emis@engr.smu.edu.
Application contact: Marc Valerin, Associate Director of Graduate Admissions, 214-768-3484, *E-mail:* valerin@seas.smu.edu.

Find an in-depth description at www.petersons.com/gradchannel.

■ SOUTHERN POLYTECHNIC STATE UNIVERSITY

School of Computing and Software Engineering, Program in Information Technology, Marietta, GA 30060-2896

AWARDS MSIT. Part-time and evening/weekend programs available.

Students: 39 full-time (19 women), 27 part-time (12 women); includes 23 minority (15 African Americans, 8 Asian Americans or Pacific Islanders), 29 international. Average age 31.
Entrance requirements: For master's, GRE General Test or GMAT, letters of recommendation (3). *Application deadline:* For fall admission, 7/1 (priority date); for spring admission, 11/1. Applications are processed on a rolling basis. *Application fee:* $20. Electronic applications accepted.
Expenses: Tuition, state resident: full-time $1,746; part-time $97 per credit. Tuition, nonresident: full-time $6,966; part-time $387 per credit. Required fees: $221 per term.
Financial support: Career-related internships or fieldwork, Federal Work-Study, scholarships/grants, and unspecified assistantships available. Support available to part-time students. Financial award

application deadline: 5/1; financial award applicants required to submit FAFSA. Dr. Rebecca A. Rutherford, Head, 770-528-7540, *Fax:* 770-528-5511, *E-mail:* brutherf@spsu.edu.
Application contact: Virginia A. Head, Director of Admissions, 770-528-7281, *Fax:* 770-528-7292, *E-mail:* vhead@ spsu.edu. *Web site:* http://www.cs.spsu.edu/ csdept/

■ STATE UNIVERSITY OF NEW YORK AT ALBANY

School of Information Science and Policy, Albany, NY 12222-0001

AWARDS Information science (MS, PhD); information science and policy (CAS); library science (MLS). Part-time and evening/ weekend programs available.

Students: 127 full-time (96 women), 102 part-time (81 women); includes 8 minority (4 African Americans, 3 Hispanic Americans, 1 Native American), 29 international. Average age 35. 172 applicants, 76% accepted. In 2001, 81 master's, 5 doctorates awarded.
Degree requirements: For doctorate, thesis/dissertation.
Entrance requirements: For doctorate, GRE General Test. *Application deadline:* For fall admission, 7/1; for spring admission, 11/1. *Application fee:* $50.
Expenses: Tuition, state resident: full-time $2,550; part-time $213 per credit. Tuition, nonresident: full-time $4,208; part-time $351 per credit. Required fees: $470; $470 per year.
Financial support: Fellowships, Federal Work-Study available. Financial award application deadline: 4/1.
Philip Eppard, Dean, 518-442-5115.
Application contact: Florance Bolton, Assistant to the Dean of Graduate Studies, 518-442-5200.

■ STATE UNIVERSITY OF NEW YORK INSTITUTE OF TECHNOLOGY AT UTICA/ROME

School of Arts and Sciences, Program in Information Design and Technology, Utica, NY 13504-3050

AWARDS MS. Part-time and evening/weekend programs available.

Faculty: 5 full-time (0 women), 1 (woman) part-time/adjunct.
Students: 3 full-time (2 women), 14 part-time (8 women). Average age 35. 16 applicants, 88% accepted.
Degree requirements: For master's, thesis or project.
Entrance requirements: For master's, GRE General Test, TOEFL, minimum GPA of 3.0, letters of recommendation (2), portfolio (recommended). *Application deadline:* For fall admission, 6/15 (priority date). Applications are processed on a rolling basis. *Application fee:* $50.

Expenses: Tuition, state resident: full-time $5,100; part-time $213 per credit hour. Tuition, nonresident: full-time $8,416; part-time $351 per credit hour. Required fees: $525; $21 per credit hour. Tuition and fees vary according to course load.
Financial support: In 2001–02, 1 student received support. Federal Work-Study, scholarships/grants, and unspecified assistantships available. Financial award applicants required to submit FAFSA.
Faculty research: Technical communication, digital media and computer-mediated communication.
Application contact: Marybeth Lyons, Director of Admissions, 315-792-7500, *Fax:* 315-792-7837, *E-mail:* smbl@ sunyit.edu.

■ STATE UNIVERSITY OF NEW YORK INSTITUTE OF TECHNOLOGY AT UTICA/ROME

School of Information Systems and Engineering Technology, Program in Computer and Information Science, Utica, NY 13504-3050

AWARDS MS. Part-time and evening/weekend programs available.

Faculty: 11 full-time (2 women).
Students: 28 full-time (4 women), 42 part-time (9 women); includes 3 minority (1 African American, 2 Asian Americans or Pacific Islanders), 22 international. Average age 30. 48 applicants, 92% accepted. In 2001, 17 degrees awarded.
Degree requirements: For master's, thesis or project.
Entrance requirements: For master's, GRE General Test, TOEFL, minimum GPA of 3.0, letter of recommendation (1). *Application deadline:* For fall admission, 6/15 (priority date). Applications are processed on a rolling basis. *Application fee:* $50.
Expenses: Tuition, state resident: full-time $5,100; part-time $213 per credit hour. Tuition, nonresident: full-time $8,416; part-time $351 per credit hour. Required fees: $525; $21 per credit hour. Tuition and fees vary according to course load.
Financial support: In 2001–02, 15 students received support. Federal Work-Study, scholarships/grants, and unspecified assistantships available. Financial award applicants required to submit FAFSA.
Faculty research: Artificial intelligence, combinatorics, distributed database systems, data security, systems theory/ methodology.
Dr. Jorge Novillo, Chair, 315-792-7352, *Fax:* 315-792-7399, *E-mail:* jorge@ sunyit.edu.
Application contact: Marybeth Lyons, Director of Admissions, 315-792-7500, *Fax:* 315-792-7837, *E-mail:* smbl@ sunyit.edu.

Find an in-depth description at www.petersons.com/gradchannel.

■ STEVENS INSTITUTE OF TECHNOLOGY

Graduate School, Wesley J. Howe School of Technology Management, Program in Information Systems, Hoboken, NJ 07030

AWARDS Computer science (MS); e-commerce (MS, Certificate); information management (MS, Certificate); project management (MS, Certificate); telecommunications management (MS, Certificate). Offered in cooperation with the Department of Computer Science.

Degree requirements: For master's, thesis optional.
Entrance requirements: For master's, GMAT, GRE, TOEFL. Electronic applications accepted.
Expenses: Tuition: Full-time $13,950; part-time $775 per credit. Required fees: $180. One-time fee: $180 part-time. Full-time tuition and fees vary according to degree level and program.

■ SYRACUSE UNIVERSITY

Graduate School, L. C. Smith College of Engineering and Computer Science, Department of Electrical Engineering and Computer Science, Program in Computer and Information Science, Syracuse, NY 13244-0003

AWARDS Computer and information science (PhD); computer science (MS).

Students: 239 full-time (14 women), 14 part-time (4 women), 228 international. Average age 28. In 2001, 176 master's, 77 doctorates awarded.
Degree requirements: For master's and doctorate, thesis/dissertation.
Entrance requirements: For master's and doctorate, GRE General Test, GRE Subject Test. *Application deadline:* Applications are processed on a rolling basis. *Application fee:* $50.
Expenses: Tuition: Full-time $15,528; part-time $647 per credit. Required fees: $420; $38 per term. Tuition and fees vary according to program.
Financial support: Fellowships, research assistantships, teaching assistantships, Federal Work-Study and tuition waivers (partial) available. Financial award application deadline: 1/10.
Dr. Kishan Mehrotra, Program Director, 315-443-2811, *Fax:* 315-443-2583, *E-mail:* kishan@ecs.syr.edu.
Application contact: Barbara Hazard, Information Contact, 315-443-2655, *Fax:* 315-443-2583, *E-mail:* bahazard@syr.edu. *Web site:* http://www.ecs.syr.edu/

Find an in-depth description at www.petersons.com/gradchannel.

■ SYRACUSE UNIVERSITY

Graduate School, L. C. Smith College of Engineering and Computer Science, Department of Electrical Engineering and Computer Science, Program in Systems and Information Science, Syracuse, NY 13244-0003

AWARDS MS.

Students: 2 full-time (1 woman), 6 part-time, 1 international. Average age 33. In 2001, 8 degrees awarded.
Entrance requirements: For master's, GRE General Test, GRE Subject Test. *Application deadline:* Applications are processed on a rolling basis. *Application fee:* $50.
Expenses: Tuition: Full-time $15,528; part-time $647 per credit. Required fees: $420; $38 per term. Tuition and fees vary according to program.
Financial support: Fellowships, research assistantships, teaching assistantships, Federal Work-Study and tuition waivers (partial) available. Financial award application deadline: 1/10.
Dr. Kishan Mehrotra, Program Director, 315-443-2811, *Fax:* 315-443-2583, *E-mail:* kishan@ecs.syr.edu.
Application contact: Barbara Hazard, Information Contact, 315-443-2655, *Fax:* 315-443-2583, *E-mail:* bahazard@syr.edu. *Web site:* http://www.ecs.syr.edu/
Find an in-depth description at www.petersons.com/gradchannel.

■ TARLETON STATE UNIVERSITY

College of Graduate Studies, College of Business Administration, Stephenville, TX 76402

AWARDS Business administration (MBA); computer and information systems (MS). Part-time and evening/weekend programs available. Postbaccalaureate distance learning degree programs offered (minimal on-campus study).

Degree requirements: For master's, comprehensive exam.
Entrance requirements: For master's, GMAT or GRE General Test. *Web site:* http://www.tarleton.edu

■ TEMPLE UNIVERSITY

Graduate School, College of Science and Technology, Department of Computer and Information Sciences, Philadelphia, PA 19122-6096

AWARDS MS, PhD. Part-time programs available. Terminal master's awarded for partial completion of doctoral program.

Degree requirements: For doctorate, thesis/dissertation.
Entrance requirements: For master's and doctorate, GRE General Test, TOEFL, minimum GPA of 2.8. Electronic applications accepted.
Expenses: Tuition, state resident: full-time $8,487; part-time $369 per credit hour.

Tuition, nonresident: full-time $12,282; part-time $534 per credit hour. Required fees: $350. Tuition and fees vary according to course load, program and reciprocity agreements.
Faculty research: Artificial intelligence, information systems, software engineering, network-distributed systems. *Web site:* http://www.cis.temple.edu/

■ TOWSON UNIVERSITY

Graduate School, Program in Information Security and Assurance, Towson, MD 21252-0001

AWARDS Certificate. Part-time and evening/weekend programs available.

Application fee: $40.
Expenses: Tuition, state resident: part-time $211 per credit. Tuition, nonresident: part-time $435 per credit. Required fees: $52 per credit.
Financial support: Application deadline: 4/1.
Dr. Ali Behforooz, Director, 410-704-3035, *Fax:* 410-704-3868, *E-mail:* abehforooz@towson.edu.
Application contact: 410-704-2501, *Fax:* 410-704-4675, *E-mail:* grads@towson.edu.

■ TOWSON UNIVERSITY

Graduate School, Program in Internet Application Development, Towson, MD 21252-0001

AWARDS Certificate. Part-time and evening/weekend programs available.

Application fee: $40. Electronic applications accepted.
Expenses: Tuition, state resident: part-time $211 per credit. Tuition, nonresident: part-time $435 per credit. Required fees: $52 per credit.
Financial support: Application deadline: 4/1.
Dr. Ali Behforooz, Director, 410-704-3035, *Fax:* 410-704-3868, *E-mail:* abehforooz@towson.edu.
Application contact: 410-704-2501, *Fax:* 410-704-4675, *E-mail:* grads@towson.edu.

■ TOWSON UNIVERSITY

Graduate School, Program in Networking Technologies, Towson, MD 21252-0001

AWARDS Certificate. Part-time and evening/weekend programs available.

Application fee: $40.
Expenses: Tuition, state resident: part-time $211 per credit. Tuition, nonresident: part-time $435 per credit. Required fees: $52 per credit.
Financial support: Application deadline: 4/1.
Dr. Ali Behforooz, Director, 410-704-3035, *Fax:* 410-704-3868, *E-mail:* abehforooz@towson.edu.
Application contact: 410-704-2501, *Fax:* 410-704-4675.

■ THE UNIVERSITY OF ALABAMA AT BIRMINGHAM

Graduate School, School of Natural Sciences and Mathematics, Department of Computer and Information Sciences, Birmingham, AL 35294

AWARDS MS, PhD.

Students: 51 full-time (12 women), 29 part-time (10 women); includes 10 minority (all Asian Americans or Pacific Islanders), 61 international. 345 applicants, 51% accepted. In 2001, 30 master's, 2 doctorates awarded.
Degree requirements: For master's, thesis optional; for doctorate, thesis/dissertation.
Entrance requirements: For master's and doctorate, GRE General Test. *Application deadline:* Applications are processed on a rolling basis. *Application fee:* $35 ($60 for international students).
Expenses: Tuition, state resident: full-time $3,058. Tuition, nonresident: full-time $5,746. Tuition and fees vary according to course load, degree level and program.
Financial support: In 2001–02, 7 fellowships with full tuition reimbursements (averaging $13,200 per year), 2 research assistantships with full tuition reimbursements (averaging $13,200 per year), 9 teaching assistantships with full tuition reimbursements (averaging $13,200 per year) were awarded. Career-related internships or fieldwork, Federal Work-Study, institutionally sponsored loans, tuition waivers (full and partial), and unspecified assistantships also available. Support available to part-time students. Financial award application deadline: 3/10.
Faculty research: Theory and software systems, intelligent systems, systems architecture.
Dr. Warren T. Jones, Chairman, 205-934-2213, *Fax:* 205-934-5473, *E-mail:* wjones@uab.edu. *Web site:* http://www.cis.uab.edu/
Find an in-depth description at www.petersons.com/gradchannel.

■ UNIVERSITY OF BALTIMORE

Graduate School, College of Liberal Arts, School of Information Arts and Technologies, Program in Interaction Design and Information Architecture, Baltimore, MD 21201-5779

AWARDS MS, DCD.

Degree requirements: For master's, project or thesis.
Entrance requirements: For master's, General GRE or Miller Analogy Test, undergraduate GPA of 3.0. Electronic applications accepted.
Expenses: Tuition, state resident: full-time $5,508; part-time $306 per credit. Tuition, nonresident: full-time $8,352; part-time $464 per credit. Required fees: $37 per

credit. $60 per semester. Tuition and fees vary according to course load and degree level.

Find an in-depth description at www.petersons.com/gradchannel.

■ UNIVERSITY OF CALIFORNIA, IRVINE

Office of Research and Graduate Studies, Department of Information and Computer Science, Irvine, CA 92697

AWARDS MS, PhD.

Faculty: 39.
Students: 217 full-time (44 women), 14 part-time (4 women); includes 51 minority (49 Asian Americans or Pacific Islanders, 2 Hispanic Americans), 105 international. Average age 31. 755 applicants, 17% accepted, 60 enrolled. In 2001, 39 master's, 4 doctorates awarded. Terminal master's awarded for partial completion of doctoral program.
Degree requirements: For master's and doctorate, thesis/dissertation.
Entrance requirements: For master's and doctorate, GRE General Test, GRE Subject Test. *Application deadline:* For fall and spring admission, 1/15 (priority date); for winter admission, 10/15 (priority date). Applications are processed on a rolling basis. *Application fee:* $60. Electronic applications accepted.
Expenses: Tuition, nonresident: full-time $10,704. Required fees: $8,396. Tuition and fees vary according to course load, program and student level.
Financial support: Fellowships, research assistantships, teaching assistantships, institutionally sponsored loans and tuition waivers (full and partial) available. Financial award application deadline: 3/2; financial award applicants required to submit FAFSA.
Faculty research: Artificial intelligence, computer system design, software, biomedical computing, theory.
Debra J. Richardson, Chair, 949-824-7405, *Fax:* 949-824-3976, *E-mail:* djr@uci.edu.
Application contact: Kris Domiccio, Contact, 949-824-2277. *Web site:* http://www.ics.uci.edu/

Find an in-depth description at www.petersons.com/gradchannel.

■ UNIVERSITY OF COLORADO AT COLORADO SPRINGS

Graduate School, College of Engineering and Applied Science, Department of Mechanical and Aerospace Engineering, Colorado Springs, CO 80933-7150

AWARDS Engineering management (ME); information operations (ME); manufacturing (ME); mechanical engineering (MS); software

engineering (ME); space operations (ME). Part-time and evening/weekend programs available.

Faculty: 7 full-time (0 women), 5 part-time/adjunct (3 women).
Students: 16 full-time (3 women), 14 part-time (1 woman); includes 1 minority (Asian American or Pacific Islander), 1 international. Average age 35. In 2001, 26 degrees awarded.
Degree requirements: For master's, thesis optional.
Entrance requirements: For master's, GRE General Test, TOEFL, bachelor's degree in engineering or related degree, minimum GPA of 3.0. *Application deadline:* For fall admission, 7/15; for spring admission, 12/10. Applications are processed on a rolling basis. *Application fee:* $60 ($75 for international students).
Expenses: Tuition, state resident: full-time $2,900; part-time $174 per credit. Tuition, nonresident: full-time $9,961; part-time $591 per credit. Required fees: $14 per credit. $141 per semester. Tuition and fees vary according to course load, program and student level.
Faculty research: Neural networks, artificial intelligence, robust control, space operations, space propulsion.
Dr. Peter Gorder, Chair, 719-262-3168, *Fax:* 719-262-3589, *E-mail:* pgorder@eas.uccs.edu.
Application contact: Siew Nylund, Academic Adviser, 719-262-3243, *Fax:* 719-262-3042, *E-mail:* snylund@uccs.edu. *Web site:* http://mepo-b.uccs.edu/newsletter.html

■ UNIVERSITY OF DELAWARE

College of Arts and Science, Department of Computer and Information Sciences, Newark, DE 19716

AWARDS MS, PhD. Part-time programs available.

Faculty: 23 full-time (3 women), 3 part-time/adjunct (0 women).
Students: 97 full-time (26 women), 13 part-time (3 women); includes 10 minority (4 African Americans, 5 Asian Americans or Pacific Islanders, 1 Hispanic American), 66 international. Average age 30. 232 applicants, 42% accepted, 55 enrolled. In 2001, 24 master's, 6 doctorates awarded. Terminal master's awarded for partial completion of doctoral program.
Degree requirements: For master's, thesis optional; for doctorate, thesis/dissertation.
Entrance requirements: For master's and doctorate, GRE General Test, TOEFL. *Application deadline:* For fall admission, 7/1; for spring admission, 12/1. Applications are processed on a rolling basis. *Application fee:* $50. Electronic applications accepted.
Expenses: Tuition, state resident: full-time $4,770; part-time $265 per credit. Tuition, nonresident: full-time $13,860; part-time $770 per credit. Required fees: $414.

Financial support: In 2001–02, 66 students received support, including 3 fellowships with full tuition reimbursements available (averaging $13,000 per year), 44 research assistantships with full tuition reimbursements available (averaging $13,000 per year), 19 teaching assistantships with full tuition reimbursements available (averaging $13,000 per year); tuition waivers (full) and unspecified assistantships also available. Financial award application deadline: 2/1.
Faculty research: Theory, computer algebra, graphics and computer vision, bioinformatics, high performance computing. *Total annual research expenditures:* $1.5 million.
Prof. M. Sandra Carberry, Chair, 302-831-2711, *Fax:* 302-831-8458, *E-mail:* gradprgm@cis.udel.edu.
Application contact: Dr. Paul D. Amer, Graduate Coordinator, 302-831-1944, *Fax:* 302-831-8458, *E-mail:* gradprgm@cis.udel.edu. *Web site:* http://www.cis.udel.edu/

Find an in-depth description at www.petersons.com/gradchannel.

■ UNIVERSITY OF FLORIDA

Graduate School, College of Engineering, Department of Computer and Information Science and Engineering, Gainesville, FL 32611

AWARDS Computer and information science and engineering (ME); computer organization (MS, PhD, Engr); information systems (MS, PhD, Engr); manufacturing systems engineering (Certificate); software systems (MS, PhD, Engr).

Degree requirements: For master's, thesis (for some programs); for doctorate, thesis/dissertation.
Entrance requirements: For master's and doctorate, GRE General Test, minimum GPA of 3.0; for other advanced degree, GRE General Test. Electronic applications accepted.
Expenses: Tuition, state resident: part-time $164 per hour. Tuition, nonresident: part-time $571 per hour. Tuition and fees vary according to course level and program.
Faculty research: Artificial intelligence, networks security, distributed computing, parallel processing system, vision and visualization, database systems. *Web site:* http://www.cise.ufl.edu/academic/grad/

Find an in-depth description at www.petersons.com/gradchannel.

■ UNIVERSITY OF GREAT FALLS

Graduate Studies Division, Programs in Information Systems, Great Falls, MT 59405

AWARDS MIS. Part-time and evening/weekend programs available.
Postbaccalaureate distance learning degree programs offered (minimal on-campus study).

University of Great Falls (continued)

Faculty: 2 full-time (0 women), 2 part-time/adjunct (1 woman).
Students: 6 full-time (2 women), 4 part-time. Average age 30. 13 applicants, 100% accepted. In 2001, 5 degrees awarded. *Median time to degree:* Master's–1 year full-time, 2 years part-time.
Entrance requirements: For master's, GRE General Test or MAT. *Application deadline:* For fall admission, 8/15 (priority date); for winter admission, 11/15 (priority date); for spring admission, 12/15 (priority date). Applications are processed on a rolling basis. *Application fee:* $35.
Expenses: Tuition: Part-time $440 per credit. One-time fee: $35 full-time.
Financial support: Application deadline: 3/1.
Dr. Lyndon Marshall, Director, 406-791-5340, *E-mail:* lmarshall@ugf.edu.

■ **UNIVERSITY OF HAWAII AT MANOA**

Graduate Division, College of Arts and Sciences, College of Natural Sciences, Department of Information and Computer Sciences, Program in Communication and Information Science, Honolulu, HI 96822

AWARDS PhD. Part-time programs available.
Faculty: 57 full-time (13 women), 3 part-time/adjunct (1 woman).
Students: 26 full-time (12 women), 12 part-time (8 women); includes 1 African American, 9 Asian Americans or Pacific Islanders. Average age 41. 61 applicants, 64% accepted, 26 enrolled. In 2001, 2 degrees awarded.
Degree requirements: For doctorate, thesis/dissertation.
Entrance requirements: For doctorate, GMAT or GRE, TOEFL, master's degree in closely related field, knowledge of computer programming. *Application deadline:* For fall admission, 1/15. *Application fee:* $25 ($50 for international students).
Expenses: Tuition, state resident: full-time $2,160; part-time $1,980 per year. Tuition, nonresident: full-time $5,190; part-time $4,829 per year.
Financial support: In 2001–02, 5 research assistantships (averaging $15,710 per year), 8 teaching assistantships (averaging $14,037 per year) were awarded. Tuition waivers (full and partial) also available. Financial award application deadline: 2/1.
Faculty research: Data communications, organizational communications, communication policies, information systems, computer software systems, human-computer interaction.
Dr. Rebecca Knuth, Chair, 808-956-7321, *Fax:* 808-956-5835, *E-mail:* knuth@hawaii.edu.
Application contact: William Remus, Head, 808-956-7608, *Fax:* 808-956-9889, *E-mail:* remus@hawaii.edu.

■ **UNIVERSITY OF HOUSTON**

C. T. Bauer College of Business, Decision and Information Sciences Program, Houston, TX 77204

AWARDS MBA, PhD. Part-time and evening/weekend programs available.

Students: 61 full-time (26 women), 86 part-time (30 women); includes 32 minority (3 African Americans, 26 Asian Americans or Pacific Islanders, 3 Hispanic Americans), 55 international. Average age 30. In 2001, 59 degrees awarded.
Application deadline: For fall admission, 5/1; for spring admission, 10/1. Applications are processed on a rolling basis. *Application fee:* $75 ($150 for international students).
Expenses: Tuition, state resident: full-time $1,512. Tuition, nonresident: full-time $5,310. Required fees: $1,308. Tuition and fees vary according to program.
Financial support: Career-related internships or fieldwork and Federal Work-Study available. Support available to part-time students. Financial award application deadline: 3/1; financial award applicants required to submit FAFSA.
Dr. Dennis Adams, Chair, 713-743-4747, *E-mail:* adams@uh.edu.
Application contact: 713-743-4900, *Fax:* 713-743-4942, *E-mail:* oss@uh.edu.

■ **UNIVERSITY OF HOUSTON– CLEAR LAKE**

School of Natural and Applied Sciences, Program in Computer Information Systems, Houston, TX 77058-1098

AWARDS MA. Part-time and evening/weekend programs available.

Students: 115; includes 28 minority (1 African American, 25 Asian Americans or Pacific Islanders, 2 Hispanic Americans), 75 international. Average age 32. In 2001, 38 degrees awarded.
Entrance requirements: For master's, GRE General Test. *Application deadline:* For fall admission, 8/1; for spring admission, 12/1. Applications are processed on a rolling basis. *Application fee:* $30 ($70 for international students).
Expenses: Tuition, state resident: full-time $2,016; part-time $84 per credit hour. Tuition, nonresident: full-time $6,072; part-time $253 per credit hour. Tuition and fees vary according to course load.
Financial support: Research assistantships, teaching assistantships, career-related internships or fieldwork, Federal Work-Study, institutionally sponsored loans, and scholarships/grants available. Support available to part-time students. Financial award application deadline: 5/1.
Dr. Kwok-Bun Yue, Chair, 281-283-3850, *Fax:* 281-283-3707, *E-mail:* yue@cl.uh.edu.
Application contact: Dr. Robert Ferebee, Associate Dean, 281-283-3700, *Fax:* 281-283-3707, *E-mail:* ferebee@cl.uh.edu.

■ **UNIVERSITY OF MARYLAND, BALTIMORE COUNTY**

Graduate School, Department of Information Systems, Baltimore, MD 21250-5398

AWARDS MS, PhD. Part-time and evening/weekend programs available. Terminal master's awarded for partial completion of doctoral program.

Entrance requirements: For master's, minimum GPA of 3.0; for doctorate, GRE General Test, minimum GPA of 3.0. Electronic applications accepted.
Faculty research: Human-computer interaction, medical informatics, security, networking.
Find an in-depth description at www.petersons.com/gradchannel.

■ **UNIVERSITY OF MARYLAND UNIVERSITY COLLEGE**

Graduate School of Management and Technology, Program in Information Technology, Adelphi, MD 20783

AWARDS Exec MS, MS. Part-time and evening/weekend programs available. Postbaccalaureate distance learning degree programs offered (no on-campus study).

Students: 66 full-time (16 women), 357 part-time (111 women); includes 189 minority (117 African Americans, 54 Asian Americans or Pacific Islanders, 16 Hispanic Americans, 2 Native Americans), 41 international. 200 applicants, 98% accepted.
Degree requirements: For master's, thesis or alternative.
Application deadline: Applications are processed on a rolling basis. *Application fee:* $50. Electronic applications accepted.
Expenses: Tuition, state resident: full-time $5,418; part-time $301 per credit hour. Tuition, nonresident: full-time $8,892; part-time $494 per credit hour.
Financial support: Federal Work-Study and scholarships/grants available. Support available to part-time students. Financial award application deadline: 6/1; financial award applicants required to submit FAFSA.
Dr. Donald Goff, Chair, 301-985-7200, *Fax:* 301-985-4611, *E-mail:* dgoff@umuc.edu.
Application contact: Coordinator, Graduate Admissions, 301-985-7155, *Fax:* 301-985-7175, *E-mail:* gradinfo@nova.umuc.edu. *Web site:* http://www.umuc.edu/grad/msit.html

■ UNIVERSITY OF MICHIGAN–DEARBORN

College of Engineering and Computer Science, Department of Computer and Information Science, Dearborn, MI 48128-1491

AWARDS Computer and information science (MS); software engineering (MS). Part-time and evening/weekend programs available.

Faculty: 13 full-time (1 woman), 6 part-time/adjunct (3 women).
Students: 11 full-time (4 women), 115 part-time (35 women); includes 35 minority (2 African Americans, 32 Asian Americans or Pacific Islanders, 1 Hispanic American). Average age 29. 117 applicants, 60% accepted, 33 enrolled. In 2001, 42 degrees awarded.
Degree requirements: For master's, thesis optional. *Median time to degree:* Master's–5 years full-time.
Entrance requirements: For master's, TOEFL, bachelor's degree in mathematics, computer science, or engineering; minimum GPA of 3.0. *Application deadline:* For fall admission, 6/15; for winter admission, 9/15; for spring admission, 2/15. Applications are processed on a rolling basis. *Application fee:* $55.
Expenses: Tuition, state resident: part-time $300 per credit hour. Tuition, nonresident: part-time $756 per credit hour. Required fees: $90 per semester. Tuition and fees vary according to course level, course load and program.
Financial support: In 2001–02, 1 research assistantship with full tuition reimbursement, 1 teaching assistantship were awarded. Financial award application deadline: 4/1; financial award applicants required to submit FAFSA.
Faculty research: Information systems, geometric modeling, networks, databases.
Dr. K. Akingbehin, Acting Chair, 313-436-9145, *Fax:* 313-593-4256, *E-mail:* kiumi@umich.edu.
Application contact: Kate Markotan, Graduate Secretary, 313-436-9145, *Fax:* 313-593-4256, *E-mail:* tabatha@umd.umich.edu. *Web site:* http://www.engin.umd.umich.edu/

■ UNIVERSITY OF MICHIGAN–DEARBORN

College of Engineering and Computer Science, Department of Industrial and Systems Engineering, Dearborn, MI 48128-1491

AWARDS Engineering management (MS); industrial and systems engineering (MSE); information systems and technology (MS). Part-time and evening/weekend programs available.

Faculty: 12 full-time (0 women), 8 part-time/adjunct (2 women).
Students: 7 full-time (2 women), 239 part-time (61 women); includes 45 minority (7 African Americans, 26 Asian Americans or

Pacific Islanders, 12 Hispanic Americans). Average age 31. 107 applicants, 91% accepted. In 2001, 78 degrees awarded.
Degree requirements: For master's, thesis optional.
Entrance requirements: For master's, bachelor's degree in applied mathematics, computer science, engineering, or physical science; minimum GPA of 3.0. *Application deadline:* For fall admission, 8/1 (priority date); for winter admission, 12/1 (priority date); for spring admission, 4/1. Applications are processed on a rolling basis. *Application fee:* $55.
Expenses: Tuition, state resident: part-time $300 per credit hour. Tuition, nonresident: part-time $756 per credit hour. Required fees: $90 per semester. Tuition and fees vary according to course level, course load and program.
Financial support: Fellowships, research assistantships, teaching assistantships, Federal Work-Study available. Financial award application deadline: 4/1; financial award applicants required to submit FAFSA.
Faculty research: Health care systems, databases, human factors, machine diagnostics, precision machining.
Dr. S. K. Kachhal, Chair, 313-593-5361, *Fax:* 313-593-3692.
Application contact: Shelly A. Harris, Graduate Secretary, 313-593-5361, *Fax:* 313-593-3692, *E-mail:* saharris@engin.umd.umich.edu. *Web site:* http://www.engin.umd.umich.edu/

■ UNIVERSITY OF MINNESOTA, TWIN CITIES CAMPUS

Graduate School, Institute of Technology, Department of Computer Science and Engineering, Minneapolis, MN 55455-0213

AWARDS Computer and information sciences (MCIS, MS, PhD). Part-time programs available. Terminal master's awarded for partial completion of doctoral program.

Degree requirements: For doctorate, thesis/dissertation.
Entrance requirements: For master's and doctorate, GRE General Test.
Expenses: Tuition, state resident: full-time $2,932; part-time $489 per credit. Tuition, nonresident: full-time $5,758; part-time $960 per credit. Part-time tuition and fees vary according to course load, program and reciprocity agreements.
Faculty research: Software systems, numerical analysis, theory, artificial intelligence. *Web site:* http://www.cs.umn.edu/

■ UNIVERSITY OF NEW HAVEN

Graduate School, School of Engineering and Applied Science, Program in Computer and Information Science, West Haven, CT 06516-1916

AWARDS Applications software (MS); management information systems (MS);

systems software (MS). Part-time and evening/weekend programs available.

Students: 54 full-time (23 women), 147 part-time (41 women); includes 13 minority (1 African American, 11 Asian Americans or Pacific Islanders, 1 Hispanic American), 81 international. In 2001, 53 degrees awarded.
Degree requirements: For master's, thesis or alternative.
Application deadline: Applications are processed on a rolling basis. *Application fee:* $50.
Expenses: Tuition: Full-time $12,015; part-time $445 per credit hour. Required fees: $30. One-time fee: $100 full-time.
Financial support: Federal Work-Study available. Support available to part-time students. Financial award application deadline: 5/1; financial award applicants required to submit FAFSA.
Dr. Tahany Fergany, Coordinator, 203-932-7067.

■ THE UNIVERSITY OF NORTH CAROLINA AT CHARLOTTE

Graduate School, College of Information Technology, Program in Information Technology, Charlotte, NC 28223-0001

AWARDS MS, PhD.

Faculty: 3 part-time/adjunct (0 women).
Students: 35 full-time (14 women), 32 part-time (14 women); includes 10 minority (4 African Americans, 6 Asian Americans or Pacific Islanders), 25 international. Average age 32. 86 applicants, 66% accepted, 37 enrolled. In 2001, 2 doctorates awarded.
Degree requirements: For doctorate, thesis/dissertation.
Application deadline: For fall admission, 7/15; for spring admission, 11/15. Applications are processed on a rolling basis. *Application fee:* $35. Electronic applications accepted.
Expenses: Tuition, state resident: full-time $1,483; part-time $371 per year. Tuition, nonresident: full-time $9,850; part-time $2,463 per year. Required fees: $1,043; $277 per year. Tuition and fees vary according to course load.
Financial support: In 2001–02, 2 research assistantships, 9 teaching assistantships were awarded. Fellowships, career-related internships or fieldwork, Federal Work-Study, institutionally sponsored loans, scholarships/grants, and unspecified assistantships also available. Support available to part-time students. Financial award application deadline: 4/1; financial award applicants required to submit FAFSA.
Faculty research: Enterprise integration and information environments, information security and privacy, intelligent systems/knowledge technology, multimedia computing and communications.
Dr. Bill Chu, Chair, 704-687-3119.

The University of North Carolina at Charlotte (continued)

Application contact: Kathy Barringer, Director of Graduate Admissions, 704-687-3366, *Fax:* 704-687-3279, *E-mail:* gradadm@email.uncc.edu. *Web site:* http://www.uncc.edu/gradmiss/

■ **UNIVERSITY OF NORTH FLORIDA**

College of Computer Sciences and Engineering, Jacksonville, FL 32224-2645

AWARDS Computer and information sciences (MS). Part-time programs available.

Faculty: 18 full-time (2 women).

Students: 11 full-time (7 women), 33 part-time (12 women); includes 11 minority (1 African American, 9 Asian Americans or Pacific Islanders, 1 Hispanic American), 4 international. Average age 33. 66 applicants, 27% accepted, 11 enrolled. In 2001, 9 degrees awarded.

Degree requirements: For master's, thesis optional.

Entrance requirements: For master's, GRE General Test, minimum GPA of 3.0 in last 60 hours. *Application deadline:* For fall admission, 7/6 (priority date); for winter admission, 11/2 (priority date); for spring admission, 3/10 (priority date). Applications are processed on a rolling basis. *Application fee:* $20. Electronic applications accepted.

Expenses: Tuition, state resident: full-time $2,411; part-time $134 per credit hour. Tuition, nonresident: full-time $9,391; part-time $522 per credit hour. Required fees: $670; $37 per credit hour.

Financial support: In 2001–02, 14 students received support, including 3 teaching assistantships (averaging $4,992 per year); Federal Work-Study and tuition waivers (partial) also available. Support available to part-time students. Financial award application deadline: 4/1; financial award applicants required to submit FAFSA.

Faculty research: Parallel and distributed computing; networks; generic programming; algorithms; multimedia and temporal databases. *Total annual research expenditures:* $105,672.

Dr. Neal Coulter, Dean, 904-620-1350, *E-mail:* ncoulter@unf.edu.

Application contact: Dr. Charles Winton, Director of Graduate Studies, 904-620-2985, *E-mail:* cwinton@unf.edu. *Web site:* http://www.unf.edu/coce/cis/

■ **UNIVERSITY OF NORTH TEXAS**

Robert B. Toulouse School of Graduate Studies, Interdisciplinary Studies, Denton, TX 76203

AWARDS Information science (PhD); interdisciplinary studies (MA, MS). Part-time programs available.

Students: 16. In 2001, 13 degrees awarded.

Degree requirements: For master's, thesis optional; for doctorate, one foreign language, thesis/dissertation.

Entrance requirements: For master's, GRE General Test, minimum GPA of 2.8. *Application deadline:* For fall admission, 7/17. *Application fee:* $25 ($50 for international students).

Expenses: Tuition, state resident: part-time $1,861 per hour. Tuition, nonresident: part-time $319 per hour. Required fees: $88; $21 per hour.

Financial support: Career-related internships or fieldwork, Federal Work-Study, and institutionally sponsored loans available. Financial award application deadline: 4/1.

Donna Hughes, Head, 940-565-2383, *Fax:* 940-565-2141, *E-mail:* hughesd@unt.edu.

Application contact: Dr. Sandra L. Terrell, Associate Dean, 940-565-2383, *Fax:* 940-565-2141, *E-mail:* terrell@unt.edu.

■ **UNIVERSITY OF OREGON**

Graduate School, College of Arts and Sciences, Department of Computer and Information Science, Eugene, OR 97403

AWARDS MA, MS, MSE, PhD. Part-time programs available.

Faculty: 18 full-time (3 women), 4 part-time/adjunct (2 women).

Students: 51 full-time (14 women), 11 part-time (4 women); includes 1 minority (Hispanic American), 27 international. 141 applicants, 26% accepted. In 2001, 13 master's, 7 doctorates awarded. Terminal master's awarded for partial completion of doctoral program.

Degree requirements: For doctorate, thesis/dissertation.

Entrance requirements: For master's and doctorate, GRE General Test, TOEFL, minimum GPA of 3.0. *Application deadline:* For fall admission, 2/1. *Application fee:* $50.

Expenses: Tuition, state resident: full-time $4,968; part-time $501 per credit hour. Tuition, nonresident: full-time $8,400; part-time $691 per credit hour.

Financial support: In 2001–02, 47 teaching assistantships were awarded; fellowships, research assistantships, Federal Work-Study and institutionally sponsored loans also available. Financial award application deadline: 2/1.

Faculty research: Artificial intelligence, graphics, natural-language processing, expert systems, operating systems.

Sarah A. Douglas, Head, 541-346-4408.

Application contact: Star Holmberg, Graduate Secretary, 541-346-1377, *Fax:* 541-346-5373, *E-mail:* star@cs.uoregon.edu. *Web site:* http://www.cs.uoregon.edu/

Find an in-depth description at www.petersons.com/gradchannel.

■ **UNIVERSITY OF PENNSYLVANIA**

School of Engineering and Applied Science, Department of Computer and Information Science, Philadelphia, PA 19104

AWARDS MCIT, MSE, PhD. Part-time programs available.

Faculty: 28 full-time (4 women), 37 part-time/adjunct (8 women).

Students: 239 full-time (51 women), 46 part-time (11 women); includes 12 minority (3 African Americans, 8 Asian Americans or Pacific Islanders, 1 Hispanic American), 169 international. 792 applicants, 29% accepted, 82 enrolled. In 2001, 64 master's, 17 doctorates awarded. Terminal master's awarded for partial completion of doctoral program.

Degree requirements: For master's, thesis optional; for doctorate, thesis/dissertation. *Median time to degree:* Master's–1.5 years full-time, 2.5 years part-time; doctorate–5 years full-time.

Entrance requirements: For master's and doctorate, GRE General Test, TOEFL. *Application deadline:* For fall admission, 12/15. Applications are processed on a rolling basis. *Application fee:* $65. Electronic applications accepted.

Financial support: In 2001–02, 18 fellowships with full tuition reimbursements, 112 research assistantships with full tuition reimbursements were awarded. Teaching assistantships, institutionally sponsored loans also available. Financial award application deadline: 1/2.

Faculty research: AI, computer systems graphics, information management, robotics, software systems theory. *Total annual research expenditures:* $35 million.

Dr. Benjamin C. Pierce, Graduate Group Chair, 215-898-2012, *Fax:* 215-898-0587, *E-mail:* bcpierce@cis.upenn.edu.

Application contact: Mike Felker, Graduate Coordinator, 215-898-9672, *Fax:* 215-898-0587, *E-mail:* mfelker@cis.upenn.edu. *Web site:* http://www.cis.upenn.edu

Find an in-depth description at www.petersons.com/gradchannel.

■ **UNIVERSITY OF PHOENIX–PHOENIX CAMPUS**

College of Information Systems and Technology, Phoenix, AZ 85040-1958

AWARDS MSCIS. Evening/weekend programs available. Postbaccalaureate distance learning degree programs offered (no on-campus study).

Students: 95 full-time, 76 part-time. Average age 33. In 2001, 111 degrees awarded.

Degree requirements: For master's, thesis or alternative.

Entrance requirements: For master's, TOEFL, 3 years of work experience, comprehensive cognitive assessment, minimum GPA of 2.5. *Application deadline:*

Applications are processed on a rolling basis. *Application fee:* $85.
Expenses: Tuition: Full-time $7,680; part-time $320 per credit. Full-time tuition and fees vary according to campus/location and program.
Financial support: Applicants required to submit FAFSA.
Dr. Adam Honea, Dean, 480-557-1659, *E-mail:* adam.honea@phoenix.edu.
Application contact: 480-966-7400. *Web site:* http://www.phoenix.edu/

■ UNIVERSITY OF PITTSBURGH

Faculty of Arts and Sciences, Intelligent Systems Program, Pittsburgh, PA 15260

AWARDS MS, PhD.

Students: 26 full-time (6 women); includes 11 minority (all Asian Americans or Pacific Islanders), 11 international. 60 applicants, 13% accepted, 8 enrolled. In 2001, 1 degree awarded. Terminal master's awarded for partial completion of doctoral program.
Degree requirements: For doctorate, thesis/dissertation.
Entrance requirements: For master's and doctorate, GRE General Test, TOEFL. *Application deadline:* For fall admission, 2/1 (priority date). Applications are processed on a rolling basis. *Application fee:* $40. Electronic applications accepted.
Expenses: Tuition, state resident: full-time $9,410; part-time $385 per credit. Tuition, nonresident: full-time $19,376; part-time $797 per credit. Required fees: $480; $90 per term. Tuition and fees vary according to program.
Financial support: In 2001–02, 7 fellowships with full tuition reimbursements (averaging $15,000 per year) were awarded; Federal Work-Study, institutionally sponsored loans, scholarships/grants, traineeships, and unspecified assistantships also available. Financial award application deadline: 2/1.
Faculty research: Medical artificial intelligence, expert systems, clinical decision support, plan generation and recognition, special cognition.
Bruce G. Buchanan, Director, 412-624-8737, *Fax:* 412-624-8561, *E-mail:* buchanan@cs.pitt.edu.
Application contact: Keena Walker, Administrator, 412-624-5755, *Fax:* 412-624-8561, *E-mail:* ispmail@pitt.edu. *Web site:* http://www.isp.pitt.edu/

■ UNIVERSITY OF PITTSBURGH

School of Information Sciences, Department of Information Science and Telecommunications, Program in Information Science, Pittsburgh, PA 15260

AWARDS MSIS, PhD, Certificate, MSIS/MPA, MSIS/MPIA. Part-time and evening/weekend programs available.

Degree requirements: For master's, thesis optional; for doctorate, thesis/dissertation, comprehensive exam, registration.
Entrance requirements: For master's, GRE General Test, previous course work in statistics and a structural programming language; for doctorate, GRE General Test, master's degree; minimum QPA of 3.3; previous course work in statistics and a structural programming language.
Expenses: Tuition, state resident: full-time $9,410; part-time $385 per credit. Tuition, nonresident: full-time $19,376; part-time $797 per credit. Required fees: $480; $90 per term. Tuition and fees vary according to program.
Faculty research: Visualization, systems analysis and design, telecommunications and networking, cognitive science, geoinformatics. *Web site:* http://www.sis.pitt.edu/~dist/

Find an in-depth description at www.petersons.com/gradchannel.

■ UNIVERSITY OF SOUTH ALABAMA

Graduate School, Division of Computer and Information Sciences, Mobile, AL 36688-0002

AWARDS Computer science (MS); information science (MS). Part-time and evening/weekend programs available.

Faculty: 10 full-time (1 woman).
Students: 102 full-time (17 women), 27 part-time (4 women); includes 7 minority (3 African Americans, 3 Asian Americans or Pacific Islanders, 1 Native American), 88 international. 153 applicants, 60% accepted. In 2001, 25 degrees awarded.
Degree requirements: For master's, project, thesis optional.
Entrance requirements: For master's, GRE General Test, minimum GPA of 2.5. *Application deadline:* For fall admission, 9/1 (priority date). Applications are processed on a rolling basis. *Application fee:* $25.
Expenses: Tuition, state resident: full-time $3,048. Tuition, nonresident: full-time $6,096. Required fees: $320.
Financial support: In 2001–02, 4 research assistantships were awarded; career-related internships or fieldwork and institutionally sponsored loans also available. Support available to part-time students. Financial award application deadline: 4/1.
Faculty research: Numerical analysis, artificial intelligence, simulation, medical applications, software engineering.
Dr. David Feinstein, Dean, 334-460-6390.

■ THE UNIVERSITY OF TENNESSEE

Graduate School, College of Communications, Knoxville, TN 37996

AWARDS Advertising (MS, PhD); broadcasting (MS, PhD); communications (MS, PhD); information sciences (PhD); journalism (MS, PhD); public relations (MS, PhD); speech communication (MS, PhD). Part-time and evening/weekend programs available. Postbaccalaureate distance learning degree programs offered (no on-campus study).

Faculty: 25 full-time (8 women).
Students: 62 full-time (41 women), 38 part-time (23 women); includes 11 minority (10 African Americans, 1 Hispanic American), 15 international. 153 applicants, 39% accepted. In 2001, 29 master's, 7 doctorates awarded.
Degree requirements: For master's, thesis or alternative; for doctorate, thesis/dissertation.
Entrance requirements: For master's and doctorate, GRE General Test, TOEFL, minimum GPA of 2.7. *Application deadline:* For fall admission, 2/1 (priority date). Applications are processed on a rolling basis. *Application fee:* $35. Electronic applications accepted.
Expenses: Tuition, state resident: full-time $4,280; part-time $233 per hour. Tuition, nonresident: full-time $12,066; part-time $666 per hour. Tuition and fees vary according to program.
Financial support: In 2001–02, 1 fellowship, 1 research assistantship, 19 teaching assistantships were awarded. Career-related internships or fieldwork, Federal Work-Study, institutionally sponsored loans, and unspecified assistantships also available. Financial award application deadline: 2/1; financial award applicants required to submit FAFSA.
Dr. Dwight Teeter, Dean, 865-974-3031, *Fax:* 865-974-3896.
Application contact: Dr. Edward Caudill, Head, 865-974-6651, *Fax:* 865-974-3896, *E-mail:* ccaudill@utk.edu.

■ THE UNIVERSITY OF TEXAS AT SAN ANTONIO

College of Business, Department of Information Systems, San Antonio, TX 78249-0617

AWARDS MSIT.

Faculty: 2 full-time (0 women), 1 part-time/adjunct (0 women).
Students: 16 full-time (4 women), 29 part-time (9 women); includes 11 minority (2 African Americans, 1 Asian American or Pacific Islander, 8 Hispanic Americans), 7 international. Average age 33. 28 applicants, 43% accepted, 7 enrolled. In 2001, 4 degrees awarded.
Degree requirements: For master's, thesis optional.
Entrance requirements: For master's, GMAT, minimum GPA of 3.0.
Expenses: Tuition, state resident: full-time $2,268; part-time $126 per credit hour. Tuition, nonresident: full-time $6,066; part-time $337 per credit hour. Required fees: $781. Tuition and fees vary according to course load.
Dr. Glenn Dietrich, 210-458-5354.

■ THE UNIVERSITY OF TEXAS AT TYLER

Graduate Studies, College of Engineering and Computer Science, Department of Computer Science, Tyler, TX 75799-0001

AWARDS Computer information systems (MAT); computer science (MS); interdisciplinary studies (MAIS, MSIS).

Faculty: 5 full-time (0 women).
Students: 13 full-time (1 woman), 16 part-time (6 women); includes 8 minority (3 African Americans, 4 Asian Americans or Pacific Islanders, 1 Hispanic American), 6 international. Average age 31. 29 applicants, 100% accepted, 4 enrolled. In 2001, 4 degrees awarded.
Degree requirements: For master's, comprehensive exam, project or thesis.
Entrance requirements: For master's, GRE General Test, previous course work in data structures and computer organization, 6 hours of calculus and statistics. *Application deadline:* For fall admission, 6/15 (priority date); for spring admission, 10/15 (priority date). Applications are processed on a rolling basis. *Application fee:* $0. Electronic applications accepted.
Expenses: Tuition, state resident: part-time $44 per credit hour. Tuition, nonresident: part-time $262 per credit hour. Required fees: $58 per credit hour. $76 per semester.
Financial support: In 2001–02, 5 research assistantships with tuition reimbursements (averaging $2,333 per year), 1 teaching assistantship (averaging $2,333 per year) were awarded. Financial award application deadline: 7/1; financial award applicants required to submit FAFSA.
Faculty research: Database design, software engineering, distributed objects, client-server architecture, visual programming.
Dr. Ron King, Chair, 903-566-7097, *Fax:* 903-566-7189, *E-mail:* rking@ mail.uttyl.edu.
Application contact: Carol A. Hodge, Office of Graduate Studies, 903-566-5642, *Fax:* 903-566-7068, *E-mail:* chodge@ mail.uttly.edu.

■ UNIVERSITY OF WASHINGTON

Graduate School, The Information School, Seattle, WA 98195

AWARDS Information management (MSIM); information science (PhD); library and information science (MLIS). Part-time and evening/weekend programs available. Postbaccalaureate distance learning degree programs offered.

Faculty: 10 full-time (5 women), 10 part-time/adjunct (6 women).
Students: 173 full-time (130 women), 130 part-time (96 women); includes 41 minority (6 African Americans, 26 Asian Americans or Pacific Islanders, 8 Hispanic Americans, 1 Native American), 8

international. Average age 33. 308 applicants, 63% accepted, 142 enrolled. In 2001, 86 degrees awarded.
Degree requirements: For master's, thesis optional; for doctorate, thesis/ dissertation.
Entrance requirements: For master's, GRE General Test, TOEFL, GMAT, minimum GPA of 3.0; for doctorate, GRE General Test, TOEFL, minimum GPA of 3.0. *Application deadline:* For fall admission, 1/15. *Application fee:* $50.
Expenses: Tuition, state resident: full-time $5,539. Tuition, nonresident: full-time $14,376. Required fees: $390. Tuition and fees vary according to course load and program.
Financial support: In 2001–02, 71 students received support, including 28 fellowships with tuition reimbursements available (averaging $11,340 per year), 8 research assistantships with tuition reimbursements available (averaging $11,340 per year), 4 teaching assistantships with tuition reimbursements available (averaging $11,340 per year); career-related internships or fieldwork, Federal Work-Study, institutionally sponsored loans, scholarships/grants, health care benefits, tuition waivers (full and partial), and unspecified assistantships also available. Financial award application deadline: 2/28; financial award applicants required to submit FAFSA.
Faculty research: Metadata, impact of networked information, augmented reality, human factors in information and communication technology, delivery of information resources in a networked environment. *Total annual research expenditures:* $664,080.
Michael B. Eisenberg, Dean, 206-685-9937, *Fax:* 206-616-3152, *E-mail:* mbe@ u.washington.edu.
Application contact: Student Services, 206-543-1794, *Fax:* 206-616-3152, *E-mail:* studentservices@ischool.washington.edu. *Web site:* http:// www.ischool.washington.edu/

■ UNIVERSITY OF WISCONSIN–PARKSIDE

School of Business and Technology, Program in Computer and Information Systems, Kenosha, WI 53141-2000

AWARDS MSCIS.

Faculty: 7 full-time (1 woman).
Students: 12 applicants, 75% accepted, 7 enrolled.
Entrance requirements: For master's, GRE General Test or GMAT, 3 letters of recommendation, minimum GPA of 3.0. *Application deadline:* For fall admission, 8/1 (priority date). Applications are processed on a rolling basis. *Application fee:* $45.
Expenses: Tuition, area resident: Full-time $4,542; part-time $264 per credit. Tuition, nonresident: full-time $14,366; part-time $810 per credit. Required fees: $236; $27

per credit. Tuition and fees vary according to program.
Faculty research: Distributed systems, data bases, natural language processing, event-driven systems.
Dr. Timothy V. Fossum, Chair, Computer Science Department, 262-595-2314, *Fax:* 262-595-2114, *E-mail:* timothy.fossum@ cs.uwp.edu.

■ VILLA JULIE COLLEGE

School of Graduate and Professional Studies, Stevenson, MD 21153

AWARDS Advanced Information Technologies (MS); Business and Technology Management (MS); E-Commerce (MS). Part-time and evening/weekend programs available.

Faculty: 6 full-time (1 woman), 6 part-time/adjunct (1 woman).
Students: Average age 35. In 2001, 18 degrees awarded.
Degree requirements: For master's, thesis.
Entrance requirements: For master's, GRE General Test. *Application deadline:* For fall admission, 8/1; for spring admission, 12/31. Applications are processed on a rolling basis. *Application fee:* $25.
Expenses: Tuition: Part-time $385 per credit. Required fees: $100 per semester. One-time fee: $25 part-time. Part-time tuition and fees vary according to degree level.
Dr. Jean Blosser, Dean, 410-653-6400, *Fax:* 410-653-6405, *E-mail:* masters@ vjc.edu.
Application contact: Judith B. Snyder, Admissions and Enrollment Services, 410-653-6400, *Fax:* 410-653-6405, *E-mail:* jsnyder@atec.vjc.edu. *Web site:* http:// www.atec.vjc.edu/

■ VIRGINIA POLYTECHNIC INSTITUTE AND STATE UNIVERSITY

Graduate School, College of Arts and Sciences, Department of Computer Science, Program in Information Systems, Blacksburg, VA 24061

AWARDS MIS. Part-time and evening/ weekend programs available.

Students: 6 full-time (5 women), 14 part-time (7 women); includes 4 minority (3 Asian Americans or Pacific Islanders, 1 Hispanic American), 7 international. 44 applicants, 34% accepted, 8 enrolled. In 2001, 10 degrees awarded.
Degree requirements: For master's, thesis optional.
Entrance requirements: For master's, GRE General Test, TOEFL. *Application deadline:* For fall admission, 2/1 (priority date). Applications are processed on a rolling basis. *Application fee:* $45. Electronic applications accepted.
Expenses: Tuition, state resident: part-time $241 per hour. Tuition, nonresident:

part-time $406 per hour. Tuition and fees vary according to program.
Financial support: Federal Work-Study available. Financial award application deadline: 4/1.
Dr. Athman Bouguettaya, Director, 703-538-8403, *Fax:* 703-538-8348, *E-mail:* athman@vt.edu. *Web site:* http://www.nvc.cs.vt.edu

Find an in-depth description at www.petersons.com/gradchannel.

MEDICAL INFORMATICS

■ COLUMBIA UNIVERSITY

College of Physicians and Surgeons and Graduate School of Arts and Sciences, Graduate School of Arts and Sciences at the College of Physicians and Surgeons, Department of Medical Informatics, New York, NY 10032

AWARDS M Phil, MA, PhD, MD/PhD.

Degree requirements: For doctorate, thesis/dissertation.
Entrance requirements: For master's and doctorate, GRE General Test, TOEFL, knowledge of computational techniques. Electronic applications accepted.
Expenses: Tuition: Full-time $27,528. Required fees: $1,638.

Find an in-depth description at www.petersons.com/gradchannel.

■ EMORY UNIVERSITY

The Rollins School of Public Health, Program in Public Health Informatics, Atlanta, GA 30322-1100

AWARDS MSPH.

Degree requirements: For master's, thesis, practicum.
Entrance requirements: For master's, GRE General Test, TOEFL. *Application deadline:* For fall admission, 2/1 (priority date). Applications are processed on a rolling basis. *Application fee:* $50.
Expenses: Contact institution.
Financial support: Research assistantships, career-related internships or fieldwork and scholarships/grants available. Financial award application deadline: 2/1; financial award applicants required to submit FAFSA.
Dr. Vicki Stover Hertzberg, Chair, 404-727-3968, *Fax:* 404-727-1370.
Application contact: Mary Glenn Costley, Assistant Director of Academic Programs, 404-727-3968, *E-mail:* mcostle@sph.emory.edu. *Web site:* http://www.sph.emory.edu/bios/phi/html

Find an in-depth description at www.petersons.com/gradchannel.

■ HARVARD UNIVERSITY

Medical School and Graduate School of Arts and Sciences, Division of Health Sciences and Technology, Cambridge, MA 02138

AWARDS Medical engineering/medical physics (PhD, Sc D), including applied physics (PhD), engineering sciences (PhD), medical engineering/medical physics (Sc D), physics (PhD); medical informatics (SM); medical sciences (MD); speech and hearing sciences (PhD, Sc D).

Degree requirements: For doctorate, thesis/dissertation.
Entrance requirements: For doctorate, bachelor's degree in engineering or science.
Expenses: Contact institution. *Web site:* http://hst.mit.edu; http://hst.harvard.edu

■ KIRKSVILLE COLLEGE OF OSTEOPATHIC MEDICINE

Arizona School of Health Sciences, Mesa, AZ 85206

AWARDS Audiology (Au D); medical informatics (MS); occupational therapy (MS); physical therapy (MS, DPT); physician assistant (MS); sports health care (MS). Postbaccalaureate distance learning degree programs offered (no on-campus study).

Faculty: 34 full-time (19 women), 50 part-time/adjunct (25 women).
Students: 313 full-time (213 women), 189 part-time (141 women); includes 60 minority (12 African Americans, 27 Asian Americans or Pacific Islanders, 15 Hispanic Americans, 6 Native Americans), 2 international. Average age 32. 735 applicants, 43% accepted. In 2001, 91 master's, 191 doctorates awarded.
Degree requirements: For master's and doctorate, thesis/dissertation (for some programs). *Median time to degree:* Master's–2.5 years full-time; doctorate–2.5 years full-time.
Entrance requirements: For master's, GRE General Test, minimum GPA of 2.50; for doctorate, GRE General Test (DPT), Evaluation of Practicing EPAC (Au D.) Audiologists Capabilities (Au D), current state licensure (Au D); master's degree in audiology (Au D); minimum GPA of 2.70 (DPT). *Application deadline:* For fall admission, 2/1 (priority date). Applications are processed on a rolling basis. *Application fee:* $50.
Expenses: Contact institution.
Financial support: In 2001–02, 314 students received support. Federal Work-Study available. Financial award application deadline: 6/1; financial award applicants required to submit FAFSA.
Faculty research: Older adult, medically underserved, Native American, technology and learning mobility.
Dr. Craig Phelps, Provost, 480-219-6000, *Fax:* 480-219-6110, *E-mail:* cphelps@ashs.edu.

Application contact: Lori A. Haxton, Assistant Dean for Student Affairs/Director of Admissions, 660-626-2237, *Fax:* 660-626-2969, *E-mail:* admissions@kcom.edu. *Web site:* http://www.ashs.edu/

■ MASSACHUSETTS INSTITUTE OF TECHNOLOGY

Whitaker College of Health Sciences and Technology, Division of Health Sciences and Technology, Program in Medical Informatics, Cambridge, MA 02139-4307

AWARDS SM.

Faculty: 9 full-time (1 woman).
Students: 15 full-time (4 women); includes 1 minority (Asian American or Pacific Islander), 7 international. Average age 33. 7 applicants, 43% accepted. In 2001, 7 degrees awarded.
Degree requirements: For master's, thesis. *Median time to degree:* Master's–1.22 years full-time.
Entrance requirements: For master's, MD or current enrollment in an MD program. *Application deadline:* For fall admission, 1/15; for spring admission, 10/1. *Application fee:* $55.
Expenses: Tuition: Full-time $26,960. Full-time tuition and fees vary according to program.
Financial support: In 2001–02, 15 students received support, including 12 fellowships with full and partial tuition reimbursements available (averaging $17,653 per year), 5 research assistantships with full and partial tuition reimbursements available (averaging $39,916 per year); career-related internships or fieldwork, institutionally sponsored loans, and traineeships also available. Financial award application deadline: 1/15.
Faculty research: Bioinformatics, clinical decision-making.
Dr. Robert A. Greenes, Program Director, 617-732-6281, *E-mail:* greenes@harvard.edu.

■ MEDICAL COLLEGE OF WISCONSIN

Graduate School of Biomedical Sciences, Program in Medical Informatics, Milwaukee, WI 53226-0509

AWARDS MS. Part-time and evening/weekend programs available.

Faculty: 15 part-time/adjunct (4 women).
Students: 31 (17 women). Average age 30. 34 applicants, 79% accepted. In 2001, 3 degrees awarded.
Degree requirements: For master's, thesis or alternative.
Entrance requirements: For master's, GMAT or GRE, TOEFL. *Application deadline:* For fall admission, 2/15 (priority date). Applications are processed on a rolling basis. *Application fee:* $30.
Expenses: Tuition: Full-time $9,693; part-time $540 per credit.

Medical College of Wisconsin (continued)
Financial support: Career-related internships or fieldwork available. Support available to part-time students. Financial award application deadline: 2/15; financial award applicants required to submit FAFSA.
Faculty research: Computer science. Director, 414-456-8218, *E-mail:* gradschool@mcw.edu.
Application contact: John Traxler, Head, 414-277-2218.

■ MILWAUKEE SCHOOL OF ENGINEERING

School of Business, Milwaukee, WI 53202-3109

AWARDS Engineering management (MS); medical informatics (MS). Part-time and evening/weekend programs available.

Faculty: 4 full-time (1 woman), 27 part-time/adjunct (2 women).
Students: 9 full-time (4 women), 230 part-time (48 women); includes 9 minority (5 African Americans, 4 Asian Americans or Pacific Islanders), 4 international. Average age 25. 80 applicants, 60% accepted, 31 enrolled.
Degree requirements: For master's, thesis or alternative, thesis defense or capstone project, comprehensive exam, registration.
Entrance requirements: For master's, GMAT or GRE General Test or MCAT, BS in engineering, science, business or related fields; letters of recommendation. *Application deadline:* Applications are processed on a rolling basis. *Application fee:* $35. Electronic applications accepted.
Expenses: Tuition: Part-time $440 per credit. Tuition and fees vary according to course load.
Financial support: In 2001–02, 10 students received support. Career-related internships or fieldwork available. Support available to part-time students. Financial award applicants required to submit FAFSA.
Joseph Papp, Chairman, 414-277-7352, *Fax:* 414-277-7479, *E-mail:* papp@msoe.edu.
Application contact: Paul Borens, Admissions Director, 800-332-6763, *Fax:* 414-277-7475, *E-mail:* borens@msoe.edu. *Web site:* http://www.msoe.edu/

■ OREGON HEALTH & SCIENCE UNIVERSITY

School of Medicine, Graduate Programs in Medicine, Division of Medical Informatics and Outcomes Research, Portland, OR 97239-3098

AWARDS Medical informatics (MS, Certificate). Part-time programs available.

Degree requirements: For master's, thesis.
Entrance requirements: For master's, GRE General Test, MCAT.

Faculty research: Information retrieval, telemedicine, consumer health informatics, information needs assessment. *Web site:* http://www.ohsu.edu/bicc.informatics/ms/
Find an in-depth description at www.petersons.com/gradchannel.

■ STANFORD UNIVERSITY

School of Medicine, Graduate Programs in Medicine, Biomedical Informatics Program, Stanford, CA 94305-9991

AWARDS MS, PhD.

Students: 20 full-time (6 women), 8 part-time; includes 11 minority (1 African American, 9 Asian Americans or Pacific Islanders, 1 Hispanic American), 6 international. Average age 29. 83 applicants, 4% accepted. In 2001, 2 master's, 1 doctorate awarded. Terminal master's awarded for partial completion of doctoral program.
Degree requirements: For master's and doctorate, thesis/dissertation.
Entrance requirements: For doctorate, GRE or MCAT, TOEFL. *Application deadline:* For fall admission, 1/1. *Application fee:* $65 ($80 for international students). Electronic applications accepted.
Russ B. Altman, Director, 650-725-3394, *E-mail:* russ.altman@stanford.edu.
Application contact: Darlene Vian, Administrator, 650-725-3388, *Fax:* 650-725-7944, *E-mail:* vian@smi.stanford.edu. *Web site:* http://www.smi.stanford.edu/
Find an in-depth description at www.petersons.com/gradchannel.

■ UNIVERSITY OF CALIFORNIA, DAVIS

Graduate Studies, Graduate Group in Medical Informatics, Davis, CA 95616

AWARDS MS.

Faculty: 29 full-time (2 women), 3 part-time/adjunct (all women).
Students: 15 full-time (2 women), 1 (woman) part-time; includes 1 minority (African American), 5 international. Average age 38. 55 applicants, 51% accepted, 12 enrolled. In 2001, 13 degrees awarded. *Application fee:* $60.
Expenses: Tuition, state resident: full-time $4,831. Tuition, nonresident: full-time $15,725.
Financial support: In 2001–02, 5 students received support, including 3 fellowships with full and partial tuition reimbursements available (averaging $1,588 per year), 1 teaching assistantship with partial tuition reimbursement available (averaging $14,145 per year); research assistantships with full and partial tuition reimbursements available, Federal Work-Study, institutionally sponsored loans, scholarships/grants, and tuition waivers (full and partial) also available. Financial

award application deadline: 1/15; financial award applicants required to submit FAFSA.
Richard Walters, Graduate Chair, 530-752-3241, *E-mail:* walters@cs.ucdavis.edu.
Application contact: Margarita Brice, Administrative Assistant, 530-752-2981, *Fax:* 530-752-4767, *E-mail:* mrbrice@ucdavis.edu. *Web site:* http://informatics.ucdmc.ucdavis.edu/Academics/

■ UNIVERSITY OF CALIFORNIA, SAN FRANCISCO

School of Pharmacy and Graduate Division, Graduate Program in Biological and Medical Informatics, San Francisco, CA 94143

AWARDS MS, PhD.

Faculty: 43 full-time (11 women), 9 part-time/adjunct (2 women).
Students: 21 full-time (6 women); includes 11 minority (10 Asian Americans or Pacific Islanders, 1 Hispanic American), 2 international. Average age 30. 63 applicants, 11% accepted, 4 enrolled. In 2001, 1 degree awarded. Terminal master's awarded for partial completion of doctoral program.
Degree requirements: For master's, thesis or alternative, research project; for doctorate, thesis/dissertation, cumulative qualifying exams, proposal defense. *Median time to degree:* Doctorate–3 years full-time.
Entrance requirements: For master's and doctorate, GRE General Test, TOEFL, minimum GPA of 3.0. *Application deadline:* For fall admission, 1/15. *Application fee:* $60.
Financial support: In 2001–02, 15 students received support, including 9 fellowships with full tuition reimbursements available (averaging $23,000 per year), 7 research assistantships with full tuition reimbursements available (averaging $23,000 per year); career-related internships or fieldwork, institutionally sponsored loans, scholarships/grants, traineeships, and tuition waivers (full) also available.
Faculty research: Bioinformatics, biomedical computing, decision science and engineering, imaging informatics, knowledge management/telehealth/health services research.
Thomas E. Ferrin, Director, 415-476-2299, *Fax:* 415-502-1755, *E-mail:* bmi@cgl.ucsf.edu.
Application contact: Barbara J. Paschke, Administrator, 415-514-0249, *Fax:* 415-514-0502, *E-mail:* bmi@cgl.ucsf.edu. *Web site:* http://www.pharmacy.ucsf.edu/

UNIVERSITY OF MEDICINE AND DENTISTRY OF NEW JERSEY

School of Health Related Professions, Department of Health Informatics, Program in Biomedical Informatics, Newark, NJ 07107-3001

AWARDS MS, PhD.

Application deadline: For fall admission, 6/1; for spring admission, 10/1.
Expenses: Tuition, state resident: part-time $292 per credit. Tuition, nonresident: part-time $440 per credit. Full-time tuition and fees vary according to degree level, program and student level.
Application contact: Dr. Laura B. Nelson, Associate Dean of Academic and Student Services, 973-972-5454, *Fax:* 973-972-7028, *E-mail:* shrp.adm@umdnj.edu.

UNIVERSITY OF UTAH

School of Medicine and Graduate School, Graduate Programs in Medicine, Department of Medical Informatics, Salt Lake City, UT 84112-1107

AWARDS MS, PhD. Part-time programs available.

Degree requirements: For master's and doctorate, thesis/dissertation.
Entrance requirements: For master's, GRE General Test, TOEFL, minimum GPA of 3.3; for doctorate, GRE, TOEFL, minimum GPA of 3.3. Electronic applications accepted.
Expenses: Tuition, state resident: part-time $320 per semester hour. Tuition, nonresident: part-time $1,135 per semester hour. Required fees: $143 per semester hour. Tuition and fees vary according to course load, degree level and program.
Faculty research: Health information systems, expert systems, genetic epidemiology, medical imaging. *Web site:* http://www.med.utah.edu/medinfo/

UNIVERSITY OF WASHINGTON

School of Medicine and Graduate School, Graduate Programs in Medicine, Department of Medical Education and Health Informatics, Division of Biomedical and Health Informatics, Seattle, WA 98195

AWARDS MS.

Entrance requirements: For master's, GRE General Test, TOEFL, minimum GPA of 3.0; previous undergraduate course work in biology, computer programming, and mathematics. *Application deadline:* For fall admission, 2/1. *Application fee:* $50. Electronic applications accepted.
Expenses: Tuition, state resident: full-time $5,539. Tuition, nonresident: full-time $14,376. Required fees: $390. Tuition and fees vary according to course load and program.
Dr. Ira Kalet, Director.

Application contact: Jennifer Hoffman, Program Manager, *Fax:* 206-543-3461, *E-mail:* informat@u.washington.edu.

SOFTWARE ENGINEERING

ANDREWS UNIVERSITY

School of Graduate Studies, College of Technology, Department of Engineering, Computer Science, and Engineering Technology, Berrien Springs, MI 49104

AWARDS Software engineering (MS).

Faculty: 6 full-time.
Students: 19 full-time (5 women), 20 part-time (8 women); includes 5 minority (2 African Americans, 2 Asian Americans or Pacific Islanders, 1 Hispanic American), 32 international. Average age 30. In 2001, 2 degrees awarded.
Entrance requirements: For master's, GMAT, TOEFL, minimum GPA of 2.6. *Application deadline:* Applications are processed on a rolling basis. *Application fee:* $40.
Expenses: Tuition: Full-time $12,600; part-time $525 per semester. Required fees: $268. Tuition and fees vary according to degree level.
Dr. Ronald L. Johnson, Chairman, 616-471-3420.
Application contact: Carolyn Hurst, Supervisor of Graduate Admission, 800-253-2874, *Fax:* 616-471-3228, *E-mail:* enroll@andrews.edu.

AUBURN UNIVERSITY

Graduate School, College of Engineering, Department of Computer Science and Software Engineering, Auburn University, AL 36849

AWARDS MS, MSWE, PhD. Part-time programs available.

Faculty: 12 full-time (0 women).
Students: 59 full-time (16 women), 45 part-time (18 women); includes 8 minority (6 African Americans, 2 Asian Americans or Pacific Islanders), 60 international. 138 applicants, 44% accepted. In 2001, 33 master's, 4 doctorates awarded.
Degree requirements: For master's, thesis (for some programs); for doctorate, thesis/dissertation.
Entrance requirements: For master's and doctorate, GRE General Test, GRE Subject Test. *Application deadline:* For fall admission, 7/7; for spring admission, 11/24. Applications are processed on a rolling basis. *Application fee:* $25 ($50 for international students). Electronic applications accepted.

Financial support: Research assistantships, teaching assistantships, Federal Work-Study available. Support available to part-time students. Financial award application deadline: 3/15.
Faculty research: Parallelizable, scalable software translations; graphical representations of algorithms, structures, and processes; graph drawing. *Total annual research expenditures:* $400,000.
Dr. James Cross, Chair, 334-844-4330.
Application contact: Dr. John F. Pritchett, Dean of the Graduate School, 334-844-4700, *E-mail:* hatchlb@mail.auburn.edu. *Web site:* http://www.eng.auburn.edu/department/cse/

AZUSA PACIFIC UNIVERSITY

College of Liberal Arts and Sciences, Department of Computer Science, Azusa, CA 91702-7000

AWARDS Applied computer science and technology (MS), including client/server technology, computer information systems, end-user support, inter-emphasis, technical programming, telecommunications; client/server technology (Certificate); computer information systems (Certificate); computer science (Certificate); end-user training and support (Certificate); software engineering (MSE); technical programming (Certificate); telecommunications (Certificate). Part-time and evening/weekend programs available.

Students: 34 full-time (8 women), 98 part-time (30 women); includes 44 minority (6 African Americans, 28 Asian Americans or Pacific Islanders, 10 Hispanic Americans), 57 international. 126 applicants, 94% accepted. In 2001, 51 degrees awarded.
Degree requirements: For master's, thesis or alternative, project.
Entrance requirements: For master's, minimum GPA of 3.0; proficiency in 1 programming language, college-level algebra, and applied calculus. *Application deadline:* For fall admission, 9/1 (priority date). Applications are processed on a rolling basis. *Application fee:* $45 ($65 for international students).
Expenses: Contact institution.
Financial support: Teaching assistantships, career-related internships or fieldwork available. Support available to part-time students.
Faculty research: Applied artificial intelligence, programming languages, engineering, database systems.
Dr. Samuel Sambasivam, Acting Chairman, 626-815-5310, *Fax:* 626-815-5323, *E-mail:* ssambasivam@apu.edu. *Web site:* http://www.apu.edu/~cs/

Find an in-depth description at www.petersons.com/gradchannel.

■ CALIFORNIA STATE UNIVERSITY, SACRAMENTO

Graduate Studies, College of Engineering and Computer Science, Department of Computer Science, Sacramento, CA 95819-6048

AWARDS Computer systems (MS); software engineering (MS). Part-time and evening/weekend programs available.

Students: 76 full-time (15 women), 67 part-time (18 women); includes 34 minority (1 African American, 29 Asian Americans or Pacific Islanders, 3 Hispanic Americans, 1 Native American), 68 international.
Degree requirements: For master's, thesis or alternative, writing proficiency exam.
Entrance requirements: For master's, TOEFL. *Application deadline:* For fall admission, 4/15; for spring admission, 11/1. *Application fee:* $55.
Expenses: Tuition, state resident: full-time $1,965; part-time $668 per semester. Tuition, nonresident: part-time $246 per unit.
Financial support: Research assistantships, teaching assistantships, career-related internships or fieldwork and Federal Work-Study available. Support available to part-time students. Financial award application deadline: 3/1.
Dr. Don Warner, Chair, 916-278-5843.
Application contact: Dr. Cui Zhang, Coordinator, 916-278-5769.

■ CARNEGIE MELLON UNIVERSITY

Graduate School of Industrial Administration, Pittsburgh, PA 15213-3891

AWARDS Accounting (PhD); algorithms, combinatorics, and optimization (MS, PhD); business management and software engineering (MBMSE); civil engineering and industrial management (MS); computational finance (MSCF); economics (MS, PhD); electronic commerce (MS); environmental engineering and management (MEEM); finance (PhD); financial economics (PhD); industrial administration (MBA), including administration and public management; information systems (PhD); management of manufacturing and automation (MOM, PhD), including industrial administration (PhD), manufacturing (MOM); marketing (PhD); mathematical finance (PhD); operations research (PhD); organizational behavior and theory (PhD); political economy (PhD); production and operations management (PhD); public policy and management (MS, MSED); software engineering and business management (MS). Part-time programs available. Terminal master's awarded for partial completion of doctoral program.

Degree requirements: For doctorate, thesis/dissertation.

Entrance requirements: For master's, GMAT, TOEFL.
Expenses: Contact institution. *Web site:* http://www.gsia.cmu.edu/

■ CARNEGIE MELLON UNIVERSITY

School of Computer Science, Software Engineering Program, Pittsburgh, PA 15213-3891

AWARDS MSE, PhD.

Entrance requirements: For master's, GRE General Test, GRE Subject Test (computer science), 2 years of experience in large-scale software development project. *Web site:* http://www.cs.cmu.edu/
Find an in-depth description at www.petersons.com/gradchannel.

■ CARROLL COLLEGE

Program in Software Engineering, Waukesha, WI 53186-5593

AWARDS MSE. Part-time and evening/weekend programs available.

Degree requirements: For master's, professional experience.
Electronic applications accepted.

■ CENTRAL MICHIGAN UNIVERSITY

College of Extended Learning, Program in Administration, Mount Pleasant, MI 48859

AWARDS General administration (MSA); health services administration (MSA, Certificate); hospitality and tourism (MSA, Certificate); human resources administration (MSA, Certificate); information resource management (MSA, Certificate); international administration (MSA, Certificate); leadership (MSA, Certificate); public administration (MSA, Certificate); software engineering administration (MSA, Certificate). Part-time and evening/weekend programs available. Postbaccalaureate distance learning degree programs offered (no on-campus study).

Faculty: 1,800 part-time/adjunct (0 women).
Students: Average age 38.
Entrance requirements: For master's, minimum GPA of 2.7 in major. *Application fee:* $50.
Financial support: Available to part-time students. Applicants required to submit FAFSA.
Dr. Terry Rawls, Director, 989-774-6525.
Application contact: 800-950-1144 Ext. 1205, *Fax:* 989-774-2461, *E-mail:* celinfo@mail.cel.cmich.edu. *Web site:* http://www.cel.cmich.edu/

■ CENTRAL MICHIGAN UNIVERSITY

College of Graduate Studies, Interdisciplinary Programs, Program in Administration, Mount Pleasant, MI 48859

AWARDS General administration (MSA); health service administration (MSA); hospitality and tourism administration (MSA); human resource administration (MSA); information resource administration (MSA); international administration (MSA); leadership (MSA); organizational communications (MSA); public administration (MSA); recreation and park administration (MSA); software engineering (MSA); sports administration (MSA).

Degree requirements: For master's, thesis or alternative.
Entrance requirements: For master's, minimum undergraduate GPA of 2.5.

■ COLORADO TECHNICAL UNIVERSITY

Graduate Studies, Program in Computer Science, Colorado Springs, CO 80907-3896

AWARDS Computer science (DCS); computer systems security (MSCS); software engineering (MSCS); software project management (MSCS). Part-time and evening/weekend programs available.

Faculty: 6 full-time (2 women), 10 part-time/adjunct (3 women).
Students: 77 full-time (15 women), 10 part-time (2 women); includes 10 minority (4 African Americans, 6 Asian Americans or Pacific Islanders), 2 international. Average age 38. 31 applicants, 94% accepted, 27 enrolled. In 2001, 33 master's, 1 doctorate awarded.
Degree requirements: For master's, thesis or alternative; for doctorate, thesis/dissertation. *Median time to degree:* Master's–2 years full-time, 3 years part-time; doctorate–3.5 years full-time.
Entrance requirements: For doctorate, minimum graduate GPA of 3.0, 5 years of related work experience. *Application deadline:* For fall admission, 10/2; for winter admission, 1/3; for spring admission, 4/3. Applications are processed on a rolling basis. *Application fee:* $100.
Expenses: Tuition: Full-time $6,960; part-time $290 per credit. Required fees: $40 per quarter. One-time fee: $100. Tuition and fees vary according to course load and degree level.
Financial support: Career-related internships or fieldwork and Federal Work-Study available. Financial award applicants required to submit FAFSA.
Faculty research: Software engineering, systems engineering.
Dr. Jack Klag, Dean, 719-590-6850, *Fax:* 719-590-6817.
Application contact: Judy Galante, Graduate Admissions, 719-590-6720, *Fax:*

719-598-3740, *E-mail:* jgalante@ coloradotech.edu. *Web site:* http:// www.coloradotech.edu/

■ COLORADO TECHNICAL UNIVERSITY DENVER CAMPUS

Program in Computer Science, Greenwood Village, CO 80111

AWARDS Computer systems security (MSCS); software engineering (MSCS); software project management (MSCS). Part-time and evening/weekend programs available.

Faculty: 4 full-time (2 women), 4 part-time/adjunct (2 women).
Students: 24 full-time (4 women), 2 part-time (1 woman); includes 9 minority (3 African Americans, 6 Asian Americans or Pacific Islanders). Average age 34. 6 applicants, 83% accepted, 5 enrolled. In 2001, 10 master's awarded.
Degree requirements: For master's, thesis or alternative. *Median time to degree:* Master's–2 years full-time, 3 years part-time.
Entrance requirements: For master's, minimum undergraduate GPA of 3.0, resume. *Application deadline:* For fall admission, 10/2; for winter admission, 1/3; for spring admission, 4/3. Applications are processed on a rolling basis. *Application fee:* $100.
Expenses: Tuition: Full-time $6,960; part-time $290 per credit. Required fees: $40 per quarter. One-time fee: $100. Tuition and fees vary according to course load and degree level.
Financial support: Federal Work-Study and scholarships/grants available. Support available to part-time students. Financial award applicants required to submit FAFSA.
Dr. Jack Klag, Dean of Computer Science, 719-590-6850, *Fax:* 719-598-3740, *E-mail:* jklag@coloradotech.edu.
Application contact: Suzanne Hyman, Director of Admissions, 303-694-6600, *Fax:* 303-694-6673, *E-mail:* shyman@ coloradotech.edu. *Web site:* http:// www.coloradotech.edu/

■ DEPAUL UNIVERSITY

School of Computer Science, Telecommunications, and Information Systems, Program in Software Engineering, Chicago, IL 60604-2287

AWARDS MS. Part-time and evening/weekend programs available.

Faculty: 6 full-time (0 women), 16 part-time/adjunct (1 woman).
Students: 77 full-time (18 women), 84 part-time (17 women); includes 41 minority (13 African Americans, 22 Asian Americans or Pacific Islanders, 6 Hispanic Americans), 29 international. Average age 32. 159 applicants, 71% accepted, 64 enrolled. In 2001, 29 degrees awarded.
Degree requirements: For master's, thesis optional.

Application deadline: For fall admission, 8/1 (priority date); for winter admission, 11/15 (priority date); for spring admission, 5/1 (priority date). Applications are processed on a rolling basis. *Application fee:* $25.
Expenses: Tuition: Part-time $362 per credit hour. Tuition and fees vary according to program.
Financial support: Fellowships, research assistantships, teaching assistantships, Federal Work-Study, tuition waivers (full), and unspecified assistantships available. Financial award application deadline: 4/1; financial award applicants required to submit FAFSA.
Faculty research: Formal methods, object-oriented technology, measurement of human-computer interaction, architecture.
Dr. Martin Kalin, Associate Dean, 312-362-8864, *E-mail:* mkalin@cs.depaul.edu.
Application contact: Genaro Balcazar, Assistant Dean, 312-362-8714, *Fax:* 312-362-6116, *E-mail:* ctiadmissions@ cs.depaul.edu.

■ DREXEL UNIVERSITY

Graduate School, College of Arts and Sciences, Department of Mathematics and Computer Science, Program in Software Engineering, Philadelphia, PA 19104-2875

AWARDS MSSE.

Faculty: 39 full-time (9 women), 3 part-time/adjunct (1 woman).
Students: 8 full-time (3 women), 28 part-time (3 women); includes 5 minority (4 Asian Americans or Pacific Islanders, 1 Hispanic American), 6 international. Average age 28. 29 applicants, 66% accepted, 9 enrolled. In 2001, 6 degrees awarded.
Entrance requirements: For master's, GRE, TOEFL, TSE (financial award applicants for teaching assistantships). *Application deadline:* For fall admission, 8/21. Applications are processed on a rolling basis. *Application fee:* $50. Electronic applications accepted.
Expenses: Tuition: Full-time $20,088; part-time $558 per credit. Required fees: $78 per term. One-time fee: $200. Tuition and fees vary according to course load, degree level and program.
Financial support: Application deadline: 2/1.
Application contact: Director of Graduate Admissions, 215-895-6700, *Fax:* 215-895-5939, *E-mail:* enroll@drexel.edu.

Find an in-depth description at www.petersons.com/gradchannel.

■ EAST TENNESSEE STATE UNIVERSITY

School of Graduate Studies, College of Applied Science and Technology, Department of Computer and Information Sciences, Johnson City, TN 37614

AWARDS Computer science (MS); information systems science (MS); software engineering (MS). Part-time and evening/weekend programs available.

Faculty: 11 full-time (0 women).
Students: 25 full-time (6 women), 17 part-time (6 women); includes 1 minority (African American), 17 international. Average age 30. In 2001, 12 degrees awarded.
Degree requirements: For master's, thesis, comprehensive exam.
Entrance requirements: For master's, GRE General Test, TOEFL, minimum GPA of 2.5. *Application deadline:* For fall admission, 7/15 (priority date); for spring admission, 11/15. Applications are processed on a rolling basis. *Application fee:* $25 ($35 for international students).
Expenses: Tuition, state resident: part-time $181 per hour. Tuition, nonresident: part-time $270 per hour. Required fees: $220 per term.
Financial support: Research assistantships with full tuition reimbursements, teaching assistantships with full tuition reimbursements, scholarships/grants available. Support available to part-time students. Financial award application deadline: 7/1; financial award applicants required to submit FAFSA.
Faculty research: Operating systems, database design, artificial intelligence, simulation, parallel algorithms.
Dr. Terry Countermine, Chair, 423-439-5332, *Fax:* 423-439-7119, *E-mail:* counter@etsu.edu. *Web site:* http:// www.etsu.edu/

■ EMBRY-RIDDLE AERONAUTICAL UNIVERSITY

Daytona Beach Campus Graduate Program, Department of Computing and Mathematics, Daytona Beach, FL 32114-3900

AWARDS Software engineering (MSE). Part-time and evening/weekend programs available.

Faculty: 4 full-time (0 women), 2 part-time/adjunct (0 women).
Students: 14 full-time (3 women), 20 part-time (5 women); includes 4 minority (3 African Americans, 1 Asian American or Pacific Islander), 20 international. Average age 27. 36 applicants, 28% accepted, 7 enrolled. In 2001, 21 degrees awarded.
Degree requirements: For master's, thesis or alternative.
Entrance requirements: For master's, TOEFL, minimum GPA of 3.0 in senior year, 2.5 overall; previous course work in

Embry-Riddle Aeronautical University (continued)
computer science. *Application deadline:* For fall admission, 8/1 (priority date); for spring admission, 12/1 (priority date). Applications are processed on a rolling basis. *Application fee:* $30 ($50 for international students).
Expenses: Tuition: Full-time $13,140; part-time $730 per credit. Required fees: $250; $250 per year. $125 per semester. Tuition and fees vary according to program.
Financial support: In 2001–02, 20 students received support, including 10 research assistantships with partial tuition reimbursements available (averaging $8,100 per year), 7 teaching assistantships with partial tuition reimbursements available (averaging $8,100 per year); fellowships with partial tuition reimbursements available, career-related internships or fieldwork, Federal Work-Study, and unspecified assistantships also available. Financial award application deadline: 4/15; financial award applicants required to submit FAFSA.
Faculty research: Guidant corporation, software competency study, metrics based flight operations, risk assessment system, software process improvement training and tools. *Total annual research expenditures:* $284,919.
Dr. David Gluch, Program Coordinator, 386-226-6455, *Fax:* 386-226-6678, *E-mail:* gluchd@erau.edu.
Application contact: Christine Castetter, Graduate Admissions, 800-388-3728, *Fax:* 386-226-7111, *E-mail:* gradmit@erau.edu.
Find an in-depth description at www.petersons.com/gradchannel.

■ FAIRFIELD UNIVERSITY

School of Engineering, Fairfield, CT 06824

AWARDS Management of technology (MS); software engineering (MS). Part-time and evening/weekend programs available.

Faculty: 2 full-time (0 women), 16 part-time/adjunct (2 women).
Students: 9 full-time (2 women), 215 part-time (43 women); includes 35 minority (8 African Americans, 21 Asian Americans or Pacific Islanders, 6 Hispanic Americans), 39 international. 53 applicants, 100% accepted, 42 enrolled. In 2001, 47 degrees awarded.
Degree requirements: For master's, thesis, final exam.
Entrance requirements: For master's, interview, minimum GPA of 2.8. *Application deadline:* For fall admission, 6/30 (priority date). Applications are processed on a rolling basis. *Application fee:* $55.
Expenses: Contact institution.
Financial support: Tuition waivers (partial) available. Financial award applicants required to submit FAFSA.

Faculty research: Vehicle dynamics, image processing, digital signal processing, modeling, multimedia.
Dr. Evangelos Hadjimichael, Dean, 203-254-4000 Ext. 4147, *Fax:* 203-254-4013, *E-mail:* hadjm@fair1.fairfield.edu.
Application contact: Dr. Richard G. Weber, Associate Dean, 203-254-4000 Ext. 4147, *Fax:* 203-254-4013, *E-mail:* rweber@fair1.fairfield.edu. *Web site:* http://www.fairfield.edu/
Find an in-depth description at www.petersons.com/gradchannel.

■ FLORIDA INSTITUTE OF TECHNOLOGY

Graduate Programs, College of Engineering, Computer Science Department, Melbourne, FL 32901-6975

AWARDS Computer information systems (MS); computer science (MS, PhD); software engineering (MS). Part-time and evening/weekend programs available.

Faculty: 11 full-time (1 woman), 5 part-time/adjunct (1 woman).
Students: 59 full-time (14 women), 121 part-time (32 women); includes 21 minority (4 African Americans, 8 Asian Americans or Pacific Islanders, 9 Hispanic Americans), 106 international. Average age 30. 381 applicants, 58% accepted. In 2001, 35 degrees awarded. Terminal master's awarded for partial completion of doctoral program.
Degree requirements: For master's, thesis optional; for doctorate, thesis/dissertation, comprehensive exam.
Entrance requirements: For master's, minimum GPA of 3.0; for doctorate, GRE General Test, GRE Subject Test (computer science), minimum GPA of 3.5, resumé. *Application deadline:* Applications are processed on a rolling basis. *Application fee:* $50. Electronic applications accepted.
Expenses: Tuition: Part-time $650 per credit.
Financial support: In 2001–02, 50 students received support, including 30 research assistantships with full and partial tuition reimbursements available (averaging $10,708 per year), 20 teaching assistantships with full and partial tuition reimbursements available (averaging $8,672 per year); career-related internships or fieldwork and tuition remissions also available. Financial award application deadline: 3/1; financial award applicants required to submit FAFSA.
Faculty research: Artificial intelligence, software engineering, management and processes, programming languages, database systems. *Total annual research expenditures:* $1.5 million.
Dr. William D. Shoaff, Chair, 321-674-8066, *Fax:* 321-674-7046, *E-mail:* wds@cs.fit.edu.

Application contact: Carolyn P. Farrior, Director of Graduate Admissions, 321-674-7118, *Fax:* 321-723-9468, *E-mail:* cfarrior@fit.edu. *Web site:* http://www.cs.fit.edu/
Find an in-depth description at www.petersons.com/gradchannel.

■ FLORIDA INSTITUTE OF TECHNOLOGY

Graduate Programs, School of Extended Graduate Studies, Melbourne, FL 32901-6975

AWARDS Acquisition and contract management (MS, MSM, PMBA); aerospace engineering (MS); business administration (PMBA); computer information systems (MS); computer science (MS); ebusiness (MSM); electrical engineering (MS); engineering management (MS); health management (MS); human resource management (MSM, PMBA); human resources management (MS); information systems (MSM, PMBA); logistics management (MS, MSM); management (MS); material acquisition management (MS); mechanical engineering (MS); operations research (MS); project management (MS), including information systems, operations research; public administration (MPA); software engineering (MS); space systems (MS); space systems management (MS); systems management (MS), including information systems, operations research; transportation management (MSM). Part-time and evening/weekend programs available. Postbaccalaureate distance learning degree programs offered (no on-campus study).

Faculty: 10 full-time (2 women), 131 part-time/adjunct (15 women).
Students: 57 full-time (29 women), 1,198 part-time (455 women); includes 277 minority (183 African Americans, 38 Asian Americans or Pacific Islanders, 51 Hispanic Americans, 5 Native Americans), 16 international. Average age 37. 299 applicants, 42% accepted. In 2001, 434 degrees awarded.
Entrance requirements: For master's, minimum GPA of 3.0. *Application deadline:* Applications are processed on a rolling basis. *Application fee:* $50. Electronic applications accepted.
Expenses: Tuition: Part-time $650 per credit.
Financial support: Institutionally sponsored loans available. Financial award application deadline: 3/1; financial award applicants required to submit FAFSA.
Dr. Ronald L. Marshall, Dean, School of Extended Graduate Studies, 321-674-8880.
Application contact: Carolyn P. Farrior, Director of Graduate Admissions, 321-674-7118, *Fax:* 321-723-9468, *E-mail:* cfarrior@fit.edu. *Web site:* http://www.segs.fit.edu/

■ FLORIDA STATE UNIVERSITY

Graduate Studies, College of Arts and Sciences, Department of Computer Science, Tallahassee, FL 32306

AWARDS Computer and network system administration (MA, MS); computer science (MA, MS, PhD); software engineering (MA, MS). Part-time programs available.

Faculty: 28 full-time (2 women), 2 part-time/adjunct (1 woman).
Students: 124 full-time, 25 part-time; includes 13 minority (10 African Americans, 3 Asian Americans or Pacific Islanders), 102 international. Average age 26. 725 applicants, 43% accepted. In 2001, 26 master's, 1 doctorate awarded.
Degree requirements: For master's, thesis or alternative; for doctorate, thesis/dissertation.
Entrance requirements: For master's, GRE General Test, minimum undergraduate GPA of 3.0; for doctorate, GRE General Test, minimum GPA of 3.0. *Application deadline:* For fall admission, 3/3 (priority date); for spring admission, 9/3 (priority date). Applications are processed on a rolling basis. *Application fee:* $20. Electronic applications accepted.
Expenses: Tuition, state resident: part-time $163 per credit hour. Tuition, nonresident: part-time $570 per credit hour. Tuition and fees vary according to program.
Financial support: In 2001–02, 4 fellowships with full tuition reimbursements (averaging $12,000 per year), 20 research assistantships with full tuition reimbursements (averaging $13,500 per year), 81 teaching assistantships with full tuition reimbursements (averaging $13,000 per year) were awarded. Career-related internships or fieldwork, Federal Work-Study, institutionally sponsored loans, and unspecified assistantships also available. Financial award application deadline: 3/3; financial award applicants required to submit FAFSA.
Faculty research: Expert systems, compiler design, artificial intelligence, neural networks, database theory and design, real time systems, logic, networking. *Total annual research expenditures:* $1.3 million.
Theodore P. Baker, Chairman, 850-644-4029, *Fax:* 850-644-0058, *E-mail:* baker@cs.fsu.edu.
Application contact: David Gaitros, Graduate Admissions, 850-644-4055, *Fax:* 850-644-0058, *E-mail:* gaitrosd@cs.fsu.edu. *Web site:* http://www.cs.fsu.edu/

■ GANNON UNIVERSITY

School of Graduate Studies, College of Sciences, Engineering, and Health Sciences, School of Engineering and Computer Science, Program in Engineering, Erie, PA 16541-0001

AWARDS Electrical engineering (MS); embedded software engineering (MS); mechanical engineering (MS). Part-time and evening/weekend programs available.

Degree requirements: For master's, thesis or alternative, comprehensive exam.
Entrance requirements: For master's, GRE Subject Test, bachelor's degree in engineering, minimum QPA of 2.5. *Web site:* http://www.gannon.edu/

■ GEORGE MASON UNIVERSITY

School of Information Technology and Engineering, Department of Information and Software Engineering, Fairfax, VA 22030-4444

AWARDS Information systems (MS); software systems engineering (MS). Part-time and evening/weekend programs available.

Faculty: 14 full-time (0 women), 11 part-time/adjunct (1 woman).
Students: 135 full-time (69 women), 457 part-time (176 women); includes 154 minority (26 African Americans, 115 Asian Americans or Pacific Islanders, 12 Hispanic Americans, 1 Native American), 209 international. Average age 33. 287 applicants, 70% accepted. In 2001, 148 degrees awarded.
Degree requirements: For master's, thesis optional.
Entrance requirements: For master's, GMAT or GRE General Test, TOEFL, minimum GPA of 3.0 in last 60 hours. *Application deadline:* For fall admission, 5/1; for spring admission, 11/1. *Application fee:* $30. Electronic applications accepted.
Expenses: Tuition, state resident: full-time $3,168; part-time $132 per credit hour. Tuition, nonresident: full-time $11,280; part-time $470 per credit hour. Required fees: $1,416; $59 per credit hour.
Financial support: Fellowships, research assistantships, teaching assistantships available. Support available to part-time students. Financial award application deadline: 3/1; financial award applicants required to submit FAFSA.
Faculty research: Security, database management, real time systems, software quality. *Total annual research expenditures:* $380,638.
Dr. Sushil Jajodia, Chairperson, 703-993-1640, *Fax:* 703-993-1638, *E-mail:* ise@gmu.edu. *Web site:* http://ise.gmu.edu/

■ GRAND VALLEY STATE UNIVERSITY

Science and Mathematics Division, Department of Computer Science and Information Systems, Allendale, MI 49401-9403

AWARDS Information systems (MS); software engineering (MS). Part-time and evening/weekend programs available.

Faculty: 7 full-time (0 women), 1 part-time/adjunct (0 women).
Students: 17 full-time (4 women), 72 part-time (14 women); includes 11 minority (3 African Americans, 7 Asian Americans or Pacific Islanders, 1 Hispanic American), 19 international. Average age 33. 25 applicants, 80% accepted. In 2001, 25 degrees awarded.
Degree requirements: For master's, thesis or alternative.
Entrance requirements: For master's, GMAT or GRE General Test. *Application deadline:* For fall admission, 2/1. Applications are processed on a rolling basis. *Application fee:* $20.
Expenses: Tuition, state resident: part-time $202 per credit hour. Tuition, nonresident: part-time $437 per credit hour.
Financial support: Research assistantships available.
Faculty research: Object technology, distributed computing, information systems management.
Paul Leidig, Professor, 616-895-2048, *Fax:* 616-895-2106, *E-mail:* leidigp@gvsu.edu. *Web site:* http://www.csis.gvsu.edu/

■ ILLINOIS INSTITUTE OF TECHNOLOGY

Graduate College, Armour College of Engineering and Sciences, Department of Computer Science, Chicago, IL 60616-3793

AWARDS Computer science (MS, PhD); teaching (MST); telecommunications and software engineering (MTSE). Part-time and evening/weekend programs available. Postbaccalaureate distance learning degree programs offered (no on-campus study).

Faculty: 18 full-time (3 women), 14 part-time/adjunct (1 woman).
Students: 378 full-time (78 women), 425 part-time (105 women); includes 86 minority (9 African Americans, 67 Asian Americans or Pacific Islanders, 9 Hispanic Americans, 1 Native American), 595 international. Average age 28. 1,741 applicants, 57% accepted. In 2001, 249 master's, 9 doctorates awarded. Terminal master's awarded for partial completion of doctoral program.
Degree requirements: For master's, thesis (for some programs), comprehensive exam; for doctorate, thesis/dissertation, comprehensive exam.
Entrance requirements: For master's and doctorate, GRE General Test, TOEFL, minimum undergraduate GPA of 3.0. *Application deadline:* For fall admission, 7/1; for spring admission, 11/1. Applications are processed on a rolling basis. *Application fee:* $30. Electronic applications accepted.
Expenses: Tuition: Part-time $590 per credit hour.
Financial support: In 2001–02, 1 fellowship, 9 research assistantships, 46 teaching assistantships were awarded. Federal Work-Study, institutionally sponsored loans, scholarships/grants, and unspecified assistantships also available. Support available to part-time students. Financial award application deadline: 3/1; financial award applicants required to submit FAFSA.

Illinois Institute of Technology (continued)
Faculty research: Artificial intelligence, computer architecture, medical imaging, concurrent programming, distributed systems. *Total annual research expenditures:* $214,441.
Dr. Edward Reingold, Chairman, 312-567-3309, *Fax:* 312-567-5067, *E-mail:* reingold@iit.edu.
Application contact: Dr. Ali Cinar, Dean of Graduate College, 312-567-3637, *Fax:* 312-567-7517, *E-mail:* gradstu@iit.edu. *Web site:* http://www.csam.iit.edu/

■ INTERNATIONAL TECHNOLOGICAL UNIVERSITY

Program in Software Engineering, Santa Clara, CA 95050

AWARDS MSSE.

Faculty: 1 full-time (0 women), 15 part-time/adjunct (3 women).
Students: 45 full-time (20 women), 19 part-time (2 women). In 2001, 19 degrees awarded.
Degree requirements: For master's, thesis or alternative.
Entrance requirements: For master's, TOEFL, 3 semesters of calculus, minimum GPA of 2.5. *Application deadline:* For fall admission, 8/31 (priority date); for winter admission, 12/31 (priority date); for spring admission, 3/30 (priority date). *Application fee:* $30 ($80 for international students).
Expenses: Tuition: Full-time $6,800; part-time $425 per unit.
Faculty research: Software testing, web management, client service and the Internet.
Dr. Russell Quong, Chairman of Computer Engineering, 408-556-9010, *Fax:* 408-556-9012.
Application contact: Dr. Chun-Mou Peng, Director of Research and Development Center, 408-556-9010, *Fax:* 408-556-9212, *E-mail:* chunmou@itu.edu.

■ JACKSONVILLE STATE UNIVERSITY

College of Graduate Studies and Continuing Education, College of Arts and Sciences, Program in Computer Systems and Software Design, Jacksonville, AL 36265-1602

AWARDS MS.

Degree requirements: For master's, thesis optional.

■ KANSAS STATE UNIVERSITY

Graduate School, College of Engineering, Department of Computing and Information Sciences, Program in Software Engineering, Manhattan, KS 66506

AWARDS MSE. Part-time programs available. Postbaccalaureate distance learning degree programs offered (no on-campus study).

Students: Average age 28. In 2001, 33 degrees awarded.
Degree requirements: For master's, thesis or alternative.
Application deadline: For fall admission, 2/1 (priority date); for spring admission, 10/1. Applications are processed on a rolling basis. *Application fee:* $0 ($25 for international students). Electronic applications accepted.
Expenses: Tuition, state resident: part-time $113 per credit hour. Tuition, nonresident: part-time $358 per credit hour.
Financial support: In 2001–02, 3 research assistantships, 11 teaching assistantships were awarded. Institutionally sponsored loans and scholarships/grants also available. Support available to part-time students. Financial award application deadline: 3/1; financial award applicants required to submit FAFSA.
Faculty research: Distributed systems, database systems. *Total annual research expenditures:* $750,000.
Application contact: Dr. David Gustafson, Graduate Program Director, 785-532-6350, *Fax:* 785-532-7353, *E-mail:* dag@cis.ksu.edu. *Web site:* http://www.cis.ksu.edu/

Find an in-depth description at www.petersons.com/gradchannel.

■ MERCER UNIVERSITY

Graduate Studies, Macon Campus, School of Engineering, Macon, GA 31207-0003

AWARDS Biomedical engineering (MSE); electrical engineering (MSE); engineering management (MSE); mechanical engineering (MSE); software engineering (MSE); software systems (MS); technical communications management (MS); technical management (MS). Part-time and evening/weekend programs available.

Faculty: 10 full-time (1 woman), 5 part-time/adjunct (1 woman).
Students: 3 full-time (2 women), 104 part-time (31 women); includes 19 minority (13 African Americans, 6 Asian Americans or Pacific Islanders), 5 international. Average age 36. 31 applicants, 97% accepted, 27 enrolled. In 2001, 32 degrees awarded.
Degree requirements: For master's, thesis or alternative, registration.
Entrance requirements: For master's, GRE, minimum undergraduate GPA of 3.0. *Application deadline:* For fall admission, 7/1; for spring admission, 11/15. Applications are processed on a rolling basis. *Application fee:* $35 ($50 for international students).
Expenses: Contact institution.
Financial support: Federal Work-Study available.
Dr. M. Dayne Aldridge, Dean, 478-301-2459, *Fax:* 478-301-5593, *E-mail:* aldridge_md@mercer.edu.

Application contact: Kathy Olivier, Graduate Administrative Coordinator, 478-301-2196, *E-mail:* olivier_kk@mercer.edu. *Web site:* http://www.mercer.edu/engineer.htm

■ MONMOUTH UNIVERSITY

Graduate School, Department of Software and Electrical Engineering, West Long Branch, NJ 07764-1898

AWARDS Software development (Certificate); software engineering (MS, Certificate). Part-time and evening/weekend programs available.

Faculty: 6 full-time (2 women), 3 part-time/adjunct (0 women).
Students: 24 full-time (12 women), 90 part-time (31 women); includes 30 minority (10 African Americans, 15 Asian Americans or Pacific Islanders, 5 Hispanic Americans), 23 international. Average age 31. 140 applicants, 59% accepted, 40 enrolled. In 2001, 9 degrees awarded.
Degree requirements: For master's, thesis optional.
Entrance requirements: For master's, bachelor's degree in computer science, engineering, mathematics, or physics; minimum GPA of 3.0; 1 year of software development experience. *Application deadline:* For fall admission, 8/15 (priority date); for spring admission, 12/15 (priority date). Applications are processed on a rolling basis. *Application fee:* $35. Electronic applications accepted.
Expenses: Contact institution.
Financial support: In 2001–02, 24 students received support, including 23 fellowships (averaging $1,956 per year), 10 research assistantships (averaging $4,418 per year); career-related internships or fieldwork, scholarships/grants, tuition waivers (partial), and unspecified assistantships also available. Support available to part-time students. Financial award application deadline: 3/1; financial award applicants required to submit FAFSA.
Faculty research: Formal protocol modeling with abstract data types and finite state machines, network computing, object orientation, distributed object base, artificial intelligence, real time systems.
James McDonald, Chairperson, 732-571-7501, *Fax:* 732-263-5253, *E-mail:* jamesmc@monmouth.edu.
Application contact: Kevin Roane, Director, Office of Graduate Admissions, 732-571-3452, *Fax:* 732-263-5123, *E-mail:* gradadm@monmouth.edu. *Web site:* http://www.monmouth.edu/~segrad/

Find an in-depth description at www.petersons.com/gradchannel.

■ NATIONAL TECHNOLOGICAL UNIVERSITY

Programs in Engineering, Fort Collins, CO 80526-1842

AWARDS Chemical engineering (MS); computer engineering (MS); computer science (MS); electrical engineering (MS); engineering management (MS); environmental systems management (MS); management of technology (MS); manufacturing systems engineering (MS); materials science and engineering (MS); mechanical engineering (MS); microelectronics and semiconductor engineering (MS); software engineering (MS); special majors (MS); systems engineering (MS). Part-time programs available. Postbaccalaureate distance learning degree programs offered (no on-campus study).

Students: In 2001, 114 degrees awarded.
Degree requirements: For master's, comprehensive exam.
Entrance requirements: For master's, BS in engineering or related field; 2.9 minimum GPA. *Application deadline:* Applications are processed on a rolling basis. *Application fee:* $50. Electronic applications accepted.
Expenses: Tuition: Part-time $660 per credit hour. Part-time tuition and fees vary according to course load, campus/location and program.
Dr. Andre Vacroux, President, 970-495-6400, *Fax:* 970-484-0668, *E-mail:* andre@ntu.edu.
Application contact: Rhonda Bonham, Admissions Officer, 970-495-6400, *Fax:* 970-498-0601, *E-mail:* rhonda@ntu.edu. *Web site:* http://www.ntu.edu/

■ NATIONAL UNIVERSITY

Academic Affairs, School of Business and Technology, Department of Technology, La Jolla, CA 92037-1011

AWARDS Biotechnology (MBA); electronic commerce (MBA, MS); environmental management (MBA); software engineering (MS); space commerce (MBA); technology management (MBA, MS); telecommunications systems management (MS). Part-time and evening/weekend programs available. Postbaccalaureate distance learning degree programs offered (minimal on-campus study).

Faculty: 9 full-time (0 women), 148 part-time/adjunct (20 women).
Students: 349 full-time (108 women), 130 part-time (44 women); includes 145 minority (45 African Americans, 76 Asian Americans or Pacific Islanders, 21 Hispanic Americans, 3 Native Americans), 138 international. 82 applicants, 100% accepted. In 2001, 250 degrees awarded.
Entrance requirements: For master's, interview, minimum GPA of 2.5. *Application deadline:* Applications are processed on a rolling basis. *Application fee:* $60 ($100 for international students).
Expenses: Tuition: Part-time $221 per quarter hour.

Financial support: Institutionally sponsored loans, scholarships/grants, and tuition waivers (full and partial) available. Support available to part-time students. Financial award application deadline: 5/1; financial award applicants required to submit FAFSA.
Dr. Leonid Preiser, Chair, 858-642-8425, *Fax:* 858-642-8716, *E-mail:* lpreiser@nu.edu.
Application contact: Nancy Rohland, Director of Enrollment Management, 858-642-8180, *Fax:* 858-642-8710, *E-mail:* advisor@nu.edu. *Web site:* http://www.nu.edu/

■ OAKLAND UNIVERSITY

Graduate Study and Lifelong Learning, School of Engineering and Computer Science, Program in Computer Science and Engineering, Rochester, MI 48309-4401

AWARDS Computer science (MS); embedded systems (MS); software engineering (MS). Part-time and evening/weekend programs available.

Faculty: 15 full-time (2 women).
Students: 83 full-time (33 women), 98 part-time (35 women); includes 26 minority (2 African Americans, 24 Asian Americans or Pacific Islanders), 77 international. Average age 33. 135 applicants, 81% accepted. In 2001, 56 degrees awarded.
Entrance requirements: For master's, minimum GPA of 3.0 for unconditional admission. *Application deadline:* For fall admission, 8/1 (priority date); for winter admission, 12/1 (priority date); for spring admission, 4/1 (priority date). Applications are processed on a rolling basis. *Application fee:* $30. Electronic applications accepted.
Expenses: Tuition, state resident: full-time $5,904; part-time $246 per credit hour. Tuition, nonresident: full-time $12,192; part-time $508 per credit hour. Required fees: $472; $236 per term.
Financial support: Federal Work-Study, institutionally sponsored loans, and tuition waivers (full) available. Financial award application deadline: 3/1; financial award applicants required to submit FAFSA.
Dr. Ishwar K. Sethi, Chair, 248-370-2820.

■ THE PENNSYLVANIA STATE UNIVERSITY GREAT VALLEY CAMPUS

Graduate Studies and Continuing Education, School of Graduate Professional Studies, Department of Engineering and Information Science, Program in Software Engineering, Malvern, PA 19355-1488

AWARDS MSE.
Students: 12 full-time (5 women), 164 part-time (45 women).
Application fee: $45.

Expenses: Tuition, state resident: part-time $415 per credit. Tuition, nonresident: part-time $680 per credit. Tuition and fees vary according to program.
Application contact: 610-648-3242, *Fax:* 610-889-1334.

■ ROCHESTER INSTITUTE OF TECHNOLOGY

Graduate Enrollment Services, Golisano College of Computing and Information Sciences, Department of Information Technology, Program in Software Development and Management, Rochester, NY 14623-5698

AWARDS MS.

Students: 4 full-time (2 women), 70 part-time (18 women); includes 12 minority (4 African Americans, 7 Asian Americans or Pacific Islanders, 1 Hispanic American), 6 international. 40 applicants, 75% accepted, 14 enrolled. In 2001, 36 degrees awarded.
Degree requirements: For master's, thesis.
Entrance requirements: For master's, GRE General Test, TOEFL, minimum GPA of 3.0. *Application deadline:* For fall admission, 3/1 (priority date). Applications are processed on a rolling basis. *Application fee:* $50.
Expenses: Tuition: Full-time $20,928; part-time $587 per hour. Required fees: $162. Tuition and fees vary according to program.
Financial support: Scholarships/grants and unspecified assistantships available.
Dr. Rayno Niemi, Graduate Coordinator, 716-475-2202, *E-mail:* rdn@it.rit.edu.

■ ST. MARY'S UNIVERSITY OF SAN ANTONIO

Graduate School, Department of Engineering, Program in Software Engineering, San Antonio, TX 78228-8507

AWARDS MS.
Faculty: 6 full-time, 3 part-time/adjunct.
Students: 1 (woman) full-time, 15 part-time (2 women); includes 6 minority (1 Asian American or Pacific Islander, 5 Hispanic Americans), 4 international. In 2001, 2 degrees awarded.
Entrance requirements: For master's, GRE or GMAT. *Application deadline:* Applications are processed on a rolling basis. *Application fee:* $15. Electronic applications accepted.
Expenses: Tuition: Full-time $8,190; part-time $455 per credit hour. Required fees: $375.
Financial support: Application deadline: 2/15.
Dr. Abe Yazdani, Graduate Program Director, 210-436-3305, *Fax:* 210-431-6895.

■ SAN JOSE STATE UNIVERSITY

Graduate Studies, College of Engineering, Department of Computer, Information and Systems Engineering, Program in Computer Engineering, San Jose, CA 95192-0001

AWARDS Computer engineering (MS); computer software (MS); computerized robots and computer applications (MS); microprocessors and microcomputers (MS).

Faculty: 5 full-time (0 women), 12 part-time/adjunct (1 woman).
Students: 62 full-time (36 women), 124 part-time (45 women); includes 119 minority (4 African Americans, 115 Asian Americans or Pacific Islanders), 33 international. Average age 28. 236 applicants, 39% accepted. In 2001, 53 degrees awarded.
Degree requirements: For master's, thesis, comprehensive exam.
Entrance requirements: For master's, GRE General Test, BS in computer science or 24 credits in related area. *Application deadline:* For fall admission, 6/29; for spring admission, 11/30. Applications are processed on a rolling basis. *Application fee:* $59. Electronic applications accepted.
Expenses: Tuition, nonresident: part-time $246 per unit. Required fees: $678 per semester. Tuition and fees vary according to course load.
Financial support: Teaching assistantships, career-related internships or fieldwork, Federal Work-Study, and institutionally sponsored loans available. Support available to part-time students. Financial award application deadline: 5/1; financial award applicants required to submit FAFSA.
Faculty research: Robotics, database management systems, computer networks.
Application contact: Dr. Haluk Ozemek, Coordinator, 408-924-4100.

■ SANTA CLARA UNIVERSITY

School of Engineering, Department of Computer Science and Engineering, Santa Clara, CA 95053

AWARDS Computer science and engineering (MSCSE, PhD); high performance computing (Certificate); software engineering (MS, Certificate). Part-time and evening/weekend programs available.

Students: 90 full-time (52 women), 144 part-time (62 women); includes 54 minority (3 African Americans, 51 Asian Americans or Pacific Islanders), 148 international. Average age 28. 233 applicants, 44% accepted. In 2001, 103 degrees awarded.
Degree requirements: For master's, thesis or alternative; for doctorate and Certificate, thesis/dissertation.
Entrance requirements: For master's, GRE General Test, TOEFL, minimum GPA of 2.75; for doctorate, GRE General Test, GRE Subject Test, TOEFL, master's

degree or equivalent; for Certificate, master's degree, published paper. *Application deadline:* For fall admission, 6/1; for spring admission, 1/1. Applications are processed on a rolling basis. *Application fee:* $45 ($55 for international students). Electronic applications accepted.
Expenses: Tuition: Part-time $320 per unit. Tuition and fees vary according to class time, degree level, program and student level.
Financial support: Fellowships, research assistantships, teaching assistantships, Federal Work-Study available. Support available to part-time students. Financial award application deadline: 3/1; financial award applicants required to submit FAFSA. *Total annual research expenditures:* $13,156.
Dr. Daniel W. Lewis, Chair, 408-554-5281.
Application contact: Tina Samms, Assistant Director of Graduate Admissions, 408-554-4313, *Fax:* 408-554-5474, *E-mail:* engr-grad@scu.edu.

■ SEATTLE UNIVERSITY

School of Science and Engineering, Program in Software Engineering, Seattle, WA 98122

AWARDS MSE. Part-time and evening/weekend programs available.

Faculty: 10 full-time (3 women), 5 part-time/adjunct (0 women).
Students: 8 full-time (3 women), 42 part-time (11 women); includes 9 minority (7 Asian Americans or Pacific Islanders, 1 Hispanic American, 1 Native American), 18 international. Average age 32. 29 applicants, 62% accepted, 10 enrolled. In 2001, 25 degrees awarded.
Degree requirements: For master's, thesis or alternative.
Entrance requirements: For master's, GRE General Test, 2 years of related work experience. *Application deadline:* For fall admission, 7/1. *Application fee:* $55.
Expenses: Tuition: Full-time $7,740; part-time $430 per credit hour. Tuition and fees vary according to course load, degree level and program.
Financial support: Career-related internships or fieldwork and Federal Work-Study available. Support available to part-time students. Financial award applicants required to submit FAFSA.
Dr. Everald Mills, Director, 206-296-5511, *Fax:* 206-296-2071.
Application contact: Janet Shandley, Associate Dean of Graduate Admissions, 206-296-5900, *Fax:* 206-298-5656, *E-mail:* grad_admissions@seattleu.edu. *Web site:* http://www.seattleu.edu/

■ SOUTHERN ADVENTIST UNIVERSITY

School of Computing, Collegedale, TN 37315-0370

AWARDS MSE. Part-time programs available.

Faculty: 1 full-time (0 women), 4 part-time/adjunct (0 women).
Students: 4 full-time (0 women), 5 part-time. Average age 26. 5 applicants, 60% accepted, 3 enrolled. In 2001, 1 degree awarded.
Degree requirements: For master's, professional software development portfolio. *Median time to degree:* Master's–2 years full-time.
Entrance requirements: For master's, GRE General Test, minimum GPA of 3.0. *Application deadline:* For fall admission, 3/1 (priority date); for winter admission, 10/1 (priority date). Applications are processed on a rolling basis. *Application fee:* $25. Electronic applications accepted.
Expenses: Tuition: Full-time $5,580; part-time $310 per credit hour.
Financial support: In 2001–02, 5 students received support. Career-related internships or fieldwork and tuition waivers (partial) available. Financial award application deadline: 3/1; financial award applicants required to submit FAFSA.
Faculty research: Component-based technologies, web-based development, large scale systems architecture, database integration.
Dr. Jared Bruckner, Dean, 423-238-2935, *Fax:* 423-238-2234, *E-mail:* bruckner@southern.edu.
Application contact: Darlene J. Williams, Application Coordinator, 423-238-2936, *Fax:* 423-238-2234, *E-mail:* mse@southern.edu. *Web site:* http://www.cs.southern.edu/

■ SOUTHERN METHODIST UNIVERSITY

School of Engineering, Department of Computer Science and Engineering, Dallas, TX 75275

AWARDS Computer engineering (MS Cp E, PhD); computer science (MS, PhD); engineering management (MSEM, DE); operations research (MS, PhD); software engineering (MS). Part-time and evening/weekend programs available. Postbaccalaureate distance learning degree programs offered (no on-campus study).

Faculty: 9 full-time (3 women).
Students: 53 full-time (15 women), 163 part-time (37 women); includes 73 minority (16 African Americans, 43 Asian Americans or Pacific Islanders, 14 Hispanic Americans), 49 international. Average age 32. 307 applicants, 78% accepted. In 2001, 59 master's, 4 doctorates awarded. Terminal master's awarded for partial completion of doctoral program.
Degree requirements: For master's, thesis optional; for doctorate, thesis/dissertation, oral and written qualifying exams, oral final exam (PhD).
Entrance requirements: For master's, GRE General Test, TOEFL, minimum GPA of 3.0 in last 2 years; bachelor's degree in engineering, mathematics, or

sciences; for doctorate, preliminary counseling exam (PhD), minimum GPA of 3.0, bachelor's degree in related field, MA (DE). *Application deadline:* For fall admission, 7/1 (priority date); for spring admission, 11/15. Applications are processed on a rolling basis. *Application fee:* $50.
Expenses: Tuition: Part-time $285 per credit hour.
Financial support: In 2001–02, 14 research assistantships with full tuition reimbursements (averaging $15,000 per year), 11 teaching assistantships with full tuition reimbursements (averaging $9,000 per year) were awarded. Financial award applicants required to submit FAFSA.
Faculty research: Trusted and high performance network computing, software engineering and management, knowledge engineering and management, computer arithmetic. *Total annual research expenditures:* $126,192.
Hesham El-Rewini, Head, 214-768-3278.
Application contact: Jim Dees, Director, Student Administration, 214-768-1456, *Fax:* 214-768-3845, *E-mail:* jdees@ engr.smu.edu. *Web site:* http:// www.seas.sm.edu/cse/

Find an in-depth description at www.petersons.com/gradchannel.

■ SOUTHERN POLYTECHNIC STATE UNIVERSITY

School of Computing and Software Engineering, Program in Computer Science and Software Engineering, Marietta, GA 30060-2896

AWARDS Computer science (MS); software engineering (MSSE). Part-time and evening/ weekend programs available.

Students: 97 full-time (50 women), 151 part-time (55 women); includes 55 minority (25 African Americans, 26 Asian Americans or Pacific Islanders, 4 Hispanic Americans), 126 international. Average age 32. In 2001, 82 degrees awarded.
Degree requirements: For master's, thesis.
Entrance requirements: For master's, GRE, 2 years full-time software development experience (MSSE), recommendations (3). *Application deadline:* For fall admission, 7/1 (priority date); for spring admission, 11/1. Applications are processed on a rolling basis. *Application fee:* $20. Electronic applications accepted.
Expenses: Tuition, state resident: full-time $1,746; part-time $97 per credit. Tuition, nonresident: full-time $6,966; part-time $387 per credit. Required fees: $221 per term.
Financial support: Career-related internships or fieldwork, Federal Work-Study, scholarships/grants, and unspecified assistantships available. Support available to part-time students. Financial award application deadline: 5/1; financial award applicants required to submit FAFSA.

Dr. Venu Dasigi, Head, 770-528-7406, *Fax:* 770-528-5511, *E-mail:* vdasigi@ spsu.edu.
Application contact: Virginia A. Head, Director of Admissions, 770-528-7281, *Fax:* 770-528-7292, *E-mail:* vhead@ spsu.edu. *Web site:* http://www.cs.spsu.edu/ csdept/

■ SOUTHWEST TEXAS STATE UNIVERSITY

Graduate School, College of Science, Department of Computer Science, Program in Software Engineering, San Marcos, TX 78666

AWARDS MS.

Students: 6 full-time (3 women), 8 part-time (2 women); includes 2 minority (both Hispanic Americans), 4 international. Average age 33. 14 applicants, 71% accepted, 5 enrolled. In 2001, 5 degrees awarded.
Degree requirements: For master's, thesis (for some programs), comprehensive exam.
Entrance requirements: For master's, GRE General Test, TOEFL, minimum GPA of 2.75 in last 60 hours. *Application deadline:* For fall admission, 6/15 (priority date); for spring admission, 10/15 (priority date). Applications are processed on a rolling basis. *Application fee:* $40 ($90 for international students).
Expenses: Tuition, state resident: full-time $1,512; part-time $84 per credit hour. Tuition, nonresident: full-time $5,310; part-time $295 per credit hour. Required fees: $864; $29 per credit hour. $195 per term. Full-time tuition and fees vary according to course load.
Dr. Khosrow Kaikhah, Graduate Adviser, 512-245-3666, *Fax:* 512-245-8750, *E-mail:* kk02@swt.edu.

■ STEVENS INSTITUTE OF TECHNOLOGY

Graduate School, School of Applied Sciences and Liberal Arts, Department of Computer Science, Program in Software Engineering, Hoboken, NJ 07030

AWARDS Certificate.

Expenses: Tuition: Full-time $13,950; part-time $775 per credit. Required fees: $180. One-time fee: $180 part-time. Full-time tuition and fees vary according to degree level and program.

■ STONY BROOK UNIVERSITY, STATE UNIVERSITY OF NEW YORK

Graduate School, College of Engineering and Applied Sciences, Department of Computer Science, Stony Brook, NY 11794

AWARDS Computer science (MS, PhD); software engineering (Certificate).

Faculty: 29 full-time (3 women), 3 part-time/adjunct (0 women).
Students: 184 full-time (46 women), 60 part-time (9 women); includes 19 minority (3 African Americans, 16 Asian Americans or Pacific Islanders), 196 international. 634 applicants, 40% accepted. In 2001, 57 master's, 7 doctorates, 1 other advanced degree awarded.
Degree requirements: For master's, thesis or alternative; for doctorate, thesis/ dissertation, comprehensive exam.
Entrance requirements: For master's and doctorate, GRE General Test, TOEFL. *Application deadline:* For fall admission, 1/15. *Application fee:* $50.
Expenses: Tuition, state resident: full-time $5,100; part-time $213 per credit. Tuition, nonresident: full-time $8,416; part-time $351 per credit. Required fees: $496.
Financial support: In 2001–02, 3 fellowships, 73 research assistantships, 98 teaching assistantships were awarded.
Faculty research: Artificial intelligence, computer architecture, database management systems, VLSI, operating systems. *Total annual research expenditures:* $2.2 million.
Dr. Arie Kaufman, Chairman, 631-632-8470.
Application contact: Dr. Michael Kiefer, Director, 631-632-8443, *Fax:* 631-632-8334, *E-mail:* mkiefer@notes.cc.sunysb.edu. *Web site:* http://www.cs.sunysb.edu/

Find an in-depth description at www.petersons.com/gradchannel.

■ TEXAS TECH UNIVERSITY

Graduate School, College of Engineering, Department of Computer Science, Lubbock, TX 79409

AWARDS Computer science (MS, PhD); software engineering (MS). Part-time programs available.

Faculty: 11 full-time (2 women).
Students: 59 full-time (13 women), 18 part-time (5 women); includes 4 minority (1 Asian American or Pacific Islander, 3 Hispanic Americans), 59 international. Average age 28. 224 applicants, 38% accepted, 17 enrolled. In 2001, 15 master's, 1 doctorate awarded.
Degree requirements: For master's and doctorate, thesis/dissertation.
Entrance requirements: For master's and doctorate, GRE General Test, minimum GPA of 3.0. *Application deadline:* Applications are processed on a rolling basis. *Application fee:* $25 ($50 for international students). Electronic applications accepted.
Expenses: Tuition, state resident: full-time $1,926; part-time $107 per credit hour. Tuition, nonresident: full-time $5,724; part-time $318 per credit hour. Required fees: $779; $737 per year. Tuition and fees vary according to course level, course load and program.
Financial support: In 2001–02, 22 students received support, including 8 research assistantships with partial tuition

Texas Tech University (continued)
reimbursements available (averaging $12,015 per year), 12 teaching assistantships with partial tuition reimbursements available (averaging $10,100 per year); fellowships, Federal Work-Study and institutionally sponsored loans also available. Support available to part-time students. Financial award application deadline: 5/1; financial award applicants required to submit FAFSA.
Faculty research: Generic controller software development, neural networks/speech recognition, neural-type network for solving 2-point boundary value. *Total annual research expenditures:* $766,366.
Dr. Daniel Earl Cooke, Chair, 806-742-3527, *Fax:* 806-742-3519.
Application contact: Graduate Adviser, 806-742-3527, *Fax:* 806-742-3519. *Web site:* http://www.cs.ttu.edu/

■ TOWSON UNIVERSITY

Graduate School, Program in Applied Information Technology, Towson, MD 21252-0001

AWARDS Applied information technology (MS); information security and assurance (Certificate); information systems management (Certificate); internet application development (Certificate); networking technologies (Certificate); software engineering (Certificate).

Students: 157.
Application deadline: Applications are processed on a rolling basis. *Application fee:* $40. Electronic applications accepted.
Expenses: Tuition, state resident: part-time $211 per credit. Tuition, nonresident: part-time $435 per credit. Required fees: $52 per credit.
Financial support: Application deadline: 4/1.
Dr. Ali Behforooz, Director, 410-704-3035, *Fax:* 410-704-3868, *E-mail:* abehforooz@towson.edu.
Application contact: 410-704-2501, *Fax:* 410-704-4675, *E-mail:* grads@towson.edu.

■ TOWSON UNIVERSITY

Graduate School, Program in Software Engineering, Towson, MD 21252-0001

AWARDS Certificate. Part-time and evening/weekend programs available.

Application fee: $40. Electronic applications accepted.
Expenses: Tuition, state resident: part-time $211 per credit. Tuition, nonresident: part-time $435 per credit. Required fees: $52 per credit.
Financial support: Fellowships, career-related internships or fieldwork, Federal Work-Study, and unspecified assistantships available. Support available to part-time students. Financial award application deadline: 4/1; financial award applicants required to submit FAFSA.

Dr. Ali Behforooz, Director, 410-704-3035, *Fax:* 410-704-3868, *E-mail:* abehforooz@towson.edu.
Application contact: 410-704-2501, *Fax:* 410-704-4675, *E-mail:* grads@towson.edu.

■ THE UNIVERSITY OF ALABAMA IN HUNTSVILLE

School of Graduate Studies, College of Science, Department of Computer Science, Huntsville, AL 35899

AWARDS Computer science (MS, PhD); software engineering (Certificate). Part-time and evening/weekend programs available.

Faculty: 13 full-time (3 women), 2 part-time/adjunct (1 woman).
Students: 66 full-time (18 women), 65 part-time (14 women); includes 17 minority (6 African Americans, 10 Asian Americans or Pacific Islanders, 1 Hispanic American), 71 international. Average age 30. 134 applicants, 82% accepted, 54 enrolled. In 2001, 48 master's, 2 doctorates awarded.
Degree requirements: For master's, thesis or alternative, oral and written exams, comprehensive exam, registration; for doctorate, thesis/dissertation, oral and written exams, comprehensive exam, registration.
Entrance requirements: For master's and doctorate, GRE General Test, GRE Subject Test, minimum GPA of 3.0.
Application deadline: For fall admission, 7/24 (priority date); for spring admission, 11/15 (priority date). Applications are processed on a rolling basis. *Application fee:* $35.
Expenses: Tuition, area resident: Part-time $175 per hour. Tuition, state resident: full-time $4,408. Tuition, nonresident: full-time $9,054; part-time $361 per hour.
Financial support: In 2001–02, 32 students received support, including 17 research assistantships with full and partial tuition reimbursements available (averaging $9,573 per year), 13 teaching assistantships with full and partial tuition reimbursements available (averaging $6,879 per year); fellowships with full and partial tuition reimbursements available, career-related internships or fieldwork, Federal Work-Study, institutionally sponsored loans, scholarships/grants, health care benefits, tuition waivers (full and partial), and unspecified assistantships also available. Support available to part-time students. Financial award application deadline: 4/1; financial award applicants required to submit FAFSA.
Faculty research: Numerical analysis, programming languages, software systems, artificial intelligence, visualization systems. *Total annual research expenditures:* $620,635.
Dr. Phillip Richards, Chair, 256-824-6088, *Fax:* 256-824-5093, *E-mail:* nrichardso@cs.uah.edu. *Web site:* http://www.merlin.cs.uah.edu/

■ UNIVERSITY OF COLORADO AT COLORADO SPRINGS

Graduate School, College of Engineering and Applied Science, Department of Mechanical and Aerospace Engineering, Colorado Springs, CO 80933-7150

AWARDS Engineering management (ME); information operations (ME); manufacturing (ME); mechanical engineering (MS); software engineering (ME); space operations (ME). Part-time and evening/weekend programs available.

Faculty: 7 full-time (0 women), 5 part-time/adjunct (3 women).
Students: 16 full-time (3 women), 14 part-time (1 woman); includes 1 minority (Asian American or Pacific Islander), 1 international. Average age 35. In 2001, 26 degrees awarded.
Degree requirements: For master's, thesis optional.
Entrance requirements: For master's, GRE General Test, TOEFL, bachelor's degree in engineering or related degree, minimum GPA of 3.0. *Application deadline:* For fall admission, 7/15; for spring admission, 12/10. Applications are processed on a rolling basis. *Application fee:* $60 ($75 for international students).
Expenses: Tuition, state resident: full-time $2,900; part-time $174 per credit. Tuition, nonresident: full-time $9,961; part-time $591 per credit. Required fees: $14 per credit. $141 per semester. Tuition and fees vary according to course load, program and student level.
Faculty research: Neural networks, artificial intelligence, robust control, space operations, space propulsion.
Dr. Peter Gorder, Chair, 719-262-3168, *Fax:* 719-262-3589, *E-mail:* pgorder@eas.uccs.edu.
Application contact: Siew Nylund, Academic Adviser, 719-262-3243, *Fax:* 719-262-3042, *E-mail:* snylund@uccs.edu. *Web site:* http://mepo-b.uccs.edu/newsletter.html

■ UNIVERSITY OF CONNECTICUT

Graduate School, School of Engineering, Field of Computer Science and Engineering, Storrs, CT 06269

AWARDS Artificial intelligence (MS, PhD); computer architecture (MS, PhD); computer science (MS, PhD); operating systems (MS, PhD); robotics (MS, PhD); software engineering (MS, PhD). Terminal master's awarded for partial completion of doctoral program.

Degree requirements: For master's, thesis or alternative; for doctorate, thesis/dissertation.
Entrance requirements: For master's and doctorate, GRE General Test.

■ UNIVERSITY OF HOUSTON–CLEAR LAKE

School of Natural and Applied Sciences, Program in Software Engineering, Houston, TX 77058-1098

AWARDS MS. Part-time and evening/weekend programs available.

Students: 43; includes 17 minority (4 African Americans, 9 Asian Americans or Pacific Islanders, 4 Hispanic Americans), 10 international. Average age 33. In 2001, 7 degrees awarded.
Entrance requirements: For master's, GRE General Test. *Application deadline:* For fall admission, 8/1; for spring admission, 12/1. Applications are processed on a rolling basis. *Application fee:* $30 ($70 for international students).
Expenses: Tuition, state resident: full-time $2,016; part-time $84 per credit hour. Tuition, nonresident: full-time $6,072; part-time $253 per credit hour. Tuition and fees vary according to course load.
Financial support: Research assistantships, teaching assistantships, career-related internships or fieldwork, Federal Work-Study, institutionally sponsored loans, and scholarships/grants available. Support available to part-time students. Financial award application deadline: 5/1.
Dr. Sharon White, Chair, 281-283-3850, *Fax:* 281-283-3707, *E-mail:* white5@cl.uh.edu.
Application contact: Dr. Robert Ferebee, Associate Dean, 281-283-3700, *Fax:* 281-283-3707, *E-mail:* ferebee@cl.uh.edu.

■ UNIVERSITY OF MARYLAND, COLLEGE PARK

Graduate Studies and Research, College of Computer, Mathematical and Physical Sciences, Software Engineering Program, College Park, MD 20742

AWARDS MS, MSWE. Part-time programs available.

Students: In 2001, 26 degrees awarded.
Entrance requirements: For master's, one year experience in software design, course in discrete MAM, imperative programming language. *Application deadline:* For fall admission, 7/1; for spring admission, 11/30. Applications are processed on a rolling basis. *Application fee:* $50 ($70 for international students).
Expenses: Tuition, state resident: part-time $289 per credit hour. Tuition, nonresident: part-time $448 per credit hour. One-time fee: $436 part-time. Full-time tuition and fees vary according to course load, campus/location and program.
Financial support: Federal Work-Study and scholarships/grants available. Support available to part-time students. Financial award applicants required to submit FAFSA.
Dr. Hafan Sayani, Director, 301-985-4616.

Application contact: Scott Wibbert, Admissions Representative, University College, 301-985-7155.

■ UNIVERSITY OF MARYLAND UNIVERSITY COLLEGE

Graduate School of Management and Technology, Program in Software Engineering, Adelphi, MD 20783

AWARDS M Sw E. Part-time and evening/weekend programs available. Postbaccalaureate distance learning degree programs offered (no on-campus study).

Students: 9 full-time (6 women), 242 part-time (80 women); includes 99 minority (58 African Americans, 34 Asian Americans or Pacific Islanders, 6 Hispanic Americans, 1 Native American), 13 international. 73 applicants, 99% accepted. In 2001, 27 degrees awarded.
Degree requirements: For master's, thesis or alternative.
Entrance requirements: For master's, programming language, software development experience, previous course work in discrete mathematics. *Application deadline:* Applications are processed on a rolling basis. *Application fee:* $50. Electronic applications accepted.
Expenses: Tuition, state resident: full-time $5,418; part-time $301 per credit hour. Tuition, nonresident: full-time $8,892; part-time $494 per credit hour.
Financial support: Federal Work-Study and scholarships/grants available. Support available to part-time students. Financial award application deadline: 6/1; financial award applicants required to submit FAFSA.
Dr. Donald Goff, Chair, 301-985-7200, *Fax:* 301-985-4611, *E-mail:* dgoff@umuc.edu.
Application contact: Coordinator, Graduate Admissions, 301-985-7155, *Fax:* 301-985-7175, *E-mail:* gradinfo@nova.umuc.edu. *Web site:* http://www.umuc.edu/prog/gsmt/mswe.html

■ UNIVERSITY OF MICHIGAN–DEARBORN

College of Engineering and Computer Science, Department of Computer and Information Science, Dearborn, MI 48128-1491

AWARDS Computer and information science (MS); software engineering (MS). Part-time and evening/weekend programs available.

Faculty: 13 full-time (1 woman), 6 part-time/adjunct (3 women).
Students: 11 full-time (4 women), 115 part-time (35 women); includes 35 minority (2 African Americans, 32 Asian Americans or Pacific Islanders, 1 Hispanic American). Average age 29. 117 applicants, 60% accepted, 33 enrolled. In 2001, 42 degrees awarded.

Degree requirements: For master's, thesis optional. *Median time to degree:* Master's–5 years full-time.
Entrance requirements: For master's, TOEFL, bachelor's degree in mathematics, computer science, or engineering; minimum GPA of 3.0. *Application deadline:* For fall admission, 6/15; for winter admission, 9/15; for spring admission, 2/15. Applications are processed on a rolling basis. *Application fee:* $55.
Expenses: Tuition, state resident: part-time $300 per credit hour. Tuition, nonresident: part-time $756 per credit hour. Required fees: $90 per semester. Tuition and fees vary according to course level, course load and program.
Financial support: In 2001–02, 1 research assistantship with full tuition reimbursement, 1 teaching assistantship were awarded. Financial award application deadline: 4/1; financial award applicants required to submit FAFSA.
Faculty research: Information systems, geometric modeling, networks, databases.
Dr. K. Akingbehin, Acting Chair, 313-436-9145, *Fax:* 313-593-4256, *E-mail:* kiumi@umich.edu.
Application contact: Kate Markotan, Graduate Secretary, 313-436-9145, *Fax:* 313-593-4256, *E-mail:* tabatha@umd.umich.edu. *Web site:* http://www.engin.umd.umich.edu/

■ UNIVERSITY OF MINNESOTA, TWIN CITIES CAMPUS

Graduate School, Institute of Technology, Center for the Development of Technological Leadership, Program in Software Engineering, Minneapolis, MN 55455-0213

AWARDS MS. Part-time and evening/weekend programs available.

Faculty: 13 part-time/adjunct (1 woman).
Students: 72 (20 women); includes 15 minority (1 African American, 10 Asian Americans or Pacific Islanders, 4 Hispanic Americans). Average age 26. 82 applicants, 48% accepted. In 2001, 18 degrees awarded.
Degree requirements: For master's, thesis, capstone project.
Entrance requirements: For master's, 1 year of work experience in software field, preferably in Twin-Cities area; minimum undergraduate GPA of 3.0. *Application deadline:* For fall admission, 6/15. Applications are processed on a rolling basis. *Application fee:* $50 ($55 for international students). Electronic applications accepted.
Expenses: Tuition, state resident: full-time $2,932; part-time $489 per credit. Tuition, nonresident: full-time $5,758; part-time $960 per credit. Part-time tuition and fees vary according to course load, program and reciprocity agreements.

University of Minnesota, Twin Cities Campus (continued)
Financial support: Institutionally sponsored loans available. Support available to part-time students. Financial award applicants required to submit FAFSA.
Faculty research: Database systems, human-computer interaction, software development, high performance neural systems, data mining.
Application contact: Shelli Burns, Admissions, 612-624-4380, *Fax:* 612-624-7510, *E-mail:* shelli@cdtl.umn.edu. *Web site:* http://www.cdtl.umn.edu/

■ UNIVERSITY OF MISSOURI–KANSAS CITY

School of Interdisciplinary Computing and Engineering, Kansas City, MO 64110-2499

AWARDS Computer networking (MS, PhD); software engineering (MS); telecommunications networking (MS, PhD). PhD offered through the School of Graduate Studies. Part-time programs available.

Faculty: 26 full-time (3 women), 18 part-time/adjunct (1 woman).
Students: 105 full-time (37 women), 103 part-time (27 women); includes 12 minority (3 African Americans, 8 Asian Americans or Pacific Islanders, 1 Hispanic American), 171 international. Average age 29. In 2001, 37 degrees awarded.
Degree requirements: For doctorate, thesis/dissertation.
Entrance requirements: For master's, GRE General Test, minimum GPA of 3.0; for doctorate, GRE General Test, minimum GPA of 3.5. *Application deadline:* For fall admission, 3/1 (priority date); for spring admission, 10/1. Applications are processed on a rolling basis. *Application fee:* $25.
Expenses: Tuition, state resident: part-time $233 per credit hour. Tuition, nonresident: part-time $623 per credit hour. Tuition and fees vary according to course load.
Financial support: In 2001–02, 15 research assistantships, 15 teaching assistantships were awarded. Career-related internships or fieldwork, Federal Work-Study, institutionally sponsored loans, and tuition waivers (partial) also available. Support available to part-time students. Financial award application deadline: 3/1.
Faculty research: Multimedia networking, distributed systems/databases, data/network security.
Dr. William Osbourne, Dean, 816-235-1193, *Fax:* 816-235-5159. *Web site:* http://www.cstp.umkc.edu/
Find an in-depth description at www.petersons.com/gradchannel.

■ UNIVERSITY OF NEW HAVEN

Graduate School, School of Engineering and Applied Science, Program in Computer and Information Science, West Haven, CT 06516-1916

AWARDS Applications software (MS); management information systems (MS); systems software (MS). Part-time and evening/weekend programs available.

Students: 54 full-time (23 women), 147 part-time (41 women); includes 13 minority (1 African American, 11 Asian Americans or Pacific Islanders, 1 Hispanic American), 81 international. In 2001, 53 degrees awarded.
Degree requirements: For master's, thesis or alternative.
Application deadline: Applications are processed on a rolling basis. *Application fee:* $50.
Expenses: Tuition: Full-time $12,015; part-time $445 per credit hour. Required fees: $30. One-time fee: $100 full-time.
Financial support: Federal Work-Study available. Support available to part-time students. Financial award application deadline: 5/1; financial award applicants required to submit FAFSA.
Dr. Tahany Fergany, Coordinator, 203-932-7067.

■ UNIVERSITY OF ST. THOMAS

Graduate Studies, Graduate School of Applied Science and Engineering, Program in Software Engineering, St. Paul, MN 55105-1096

AWARDS MS, MSDD, MSS, Certificate. Part-time and evening/weekend programs available.

Faculty: 9 full-time (2 women), 46 part-time/adjunct (6 women).
Students: 134 full-time (49 women), 765 part-time (238 women); includes 171 minority (52 African Americans, 114 Asian Americans or Pacific Islanders, 4 Hispanic Americans, 1 Native American), 326 international. Average age 32. 271 applicants, 98% accepted, 162 enrolled. In 2001, 219 master's, 24 other advanced degrees awarded.
Degree requirements: For master's, thesis optional.
Entrance requirements: For master's and Certificate, TOEFL. *Application deadline:* For fall admission, 8/1 (priority date); for spring admission, 1/1 (priority date). Applications are processed on a rolling basis. *Application fee:* $30.
Expenses: Tuition: Part-time $401 per credit. Tuition and fees vary according to degree level and program.
Financial support: In 2001–02, 230 students received support; fellowships, research assistantships, institutionally sponsored loans and scholarships/grants available. Support available to part-time students. Financial award application deadline: 4/1; financial award applicants required to submit FAFSA.

Faculty research: Distributed databases, fault tolerant computing, expert systems, object-oriented software.
Dr. Bernice Folz, Director, 651-962-5501, *E-mail:* gradsoftware@stthomas.edu.
Application contact: Douglas J. Stubeda, Assistant Director, 651-962-5503, *Fax:* 651-962-5543, *E-mail:* djstubeda@stthomas.edu. *Web site:* http://www.gps.stthomas.edu/
Find an in-depth description at www.petersons.com/gradchannel.

■ THE UNIVERSITY OF SCRANTON

Graduate School, Program in Software Engineering, Scranton, PA 18510

AWARDS MS. Part-time and evening/weekend programs available.

Faculty: 8 full-time (0 women).
Students: 12 full-time (3 women), 13 part-time (6 women); includes 2 minority (both Asian Americans or Pacific Islanders), 11 international. Average age 31. 19 applicants, 100% accepted. In 2001, 4 degrees awarded.
Degree requirements: For master's, thesis, capstone experience.
Entrance requirements: For master's, GMAT or GRE, TOEFL, minimum GPA of 3.0. *Application deadline:* For fall admission, 3/1 (priority date). *Application fee:* $50.
Expenses: Tuition: Part-time $539 per credit. Required fees: $25 per term.
Financial support: In 2001–02, 7 students received support, including 7 teaching assistantships (averaging $8,200 per year); career-related internships or fieldwork, Federal Work-Study, and teaching fellowships also available. Support available to part-time students. Financial award application deadline: 3/1.
Faculty research: Database, parallel and distributed systems, computer network, real time systems.
Dr. Yaodong Bi, Director, 570-941-6108, *Fax:* 570-941-4250, *E-mail:* biy1@scranton.edu. *Web site:* http://www.cs.uofs.edu/

■ UNIVERSITY OF SOUTH CAROLINA

The Graduate School, College of Engineering and Information Technology, Department of Computer Science and Engineering, Columbia, SC 29208

AWARDS Computer science and engineering (ME, MS, PhD); software engineering (MS). Part-time and evening/weekend programs available. Postbaccalaureate distance learning degree programs offered (minimal on-campus study).

Faculty: 20 full-time (3 women).

Students: 136 full-time (26 women), 41 part-time (10 women); includes 149 minority (5 African Americans, 143 Asian Americans or Pacific Islanders, 1 Hispanic American). Average age 27. 399 applicants, 48% accepted. In 2001, 126 master's, 2 doctorates awarded.
Degree requirements: For master's, thesis (for some programs), registration; for doctorate, thesis/dissertation, comprehensive exam, registration.
Entrance requirements: For master's and doctorate, GRE General Test, TOEFL. *Application deadline:* For fall admission, 3/1 (priority date); for spring admission, 10/1. *Application fee:* $35. Electronic applications accepted.
Expenses: Tuition, state resident: full-time $4,434. Tuition, nonresident: full-time $9,854. Tuition and fees vary according to program.
Financial support: In 2001–02, 5 fellowships (averaging $9,600 per year), 29 research assistantships with partial tuition reimbursements (averaging $15,000 per year), 24 teaching assistantships with partial tuition reimbursements (averaging $13,000 per year) were awarded. Career-related internships or fieldwork also available.
Faculty research: Computer security and computer vision, artificial intelligence, multiagent systems, conceptual modeling. *Total annual research expenditures:* $1.3 million.
Dr. Duncan A. Buell, Professor and Chair, 803-777-2880, *Fax:* 803-777-3767, *E-mail:* buell@cse.sc.edu.
Application contact: Jewel Rogers, Administrative Assistant, 803-777-7849, *Fax:* 803-777-3767, *E-mail:* jewel@engr.sc.edu. *Web site:* http://www.cse.sc.edu/

■ UNIVERSITY OF SOUTHERN CALIFORNIA

Graduate School, School of Engineering, Department of Computer Science, Program in Software Engineering, Los Angeles, CA 90089
AWARDS MS.

Entrance requirements: For master's, GRE General Test.
Expenses: Tuition: Full-time $25,060; part-time $844 per unit. Required fees: $473.

■ THE UNIVERSITY OF TEXAS AT ARLINGTON

Graduate School, College of Engineering, Department of Computer Science and Engineering, Arlington, TX 76019
AWARDS M Engr, M Sw En, MCS, MS, PhD. Part-time and evening/weekend programs available. Postbaccalaureate distance learning degree programs offered.

Faculty: 16 full-time (2 women), 3 part-time/adjunct (0 women).
Students: 320 full-time (73 women), 141 part-time (28 women); includes 44 minority (1 African American, 39 Asian Americans or Pacific Islanders, 4 Hispanic Americans), 371 international. 845 applicants, 62% accepted, 124 enrolled. In 2001, 111 master's, 5 doctorates awarded.
Degree requirements: For master's, thesis optional; for doctorate, thesis/dissertation, comprehensive exam.
Entrance requirements: For master's, GRE General Test, TOEFL, minimum GPA of 3.2; for doctorate, GRE General Test, TOEFL, minimum GPA of 3.5. *Application deadline:* For fall admission, 6/16. Applications are processed on a rolling basis. *Application fee:* $25 ($50 for international students).
Expenses: Tuition, area resident: Full-time $2,268. Tuition, nonresident: full-time $6,264. Required fees: $839. Tuition and fees vary according to course load.
Financial support: In 2001–02, 23 fellowships (averaging $1,000 per year), 80 teaching assistantships (averaging $12,000 per year) were awarded. Research assistantships, career-related internships or fieldwork, scholarships/grants, and tuition waivers (partial) also available. Financial award application deadline: 6/1; financial award applicants required to submit FAFSA.
Dr. Behrooz A. Shirazi, Chairman, 817-272-3065, *Fax:* 817-272-3784, *E-mail:* shirazi@uta.edu.
Application contact: Dr. Ramesh Yerraballi, Graduate Adviser, 817-272-5128, *Fax:* 817-272-3784, *E-mail:* ramesh@uta.edu. *Web site:* http://www.cse.uta.edu/
Find an in-depth description at www.petersons.com/gradchannel.

■ WAYNE STATE UNIVERSITY

Graduate School, College of Science, Department of Computer Science, Detroit, MI 48202
AWARDS Computer science (MA, MS, PhD); electronics and computer control systems (MS); scientific computing (Certificate).

Faculty: 9 full-time.
Students: 187. 673 applicants, 20% accepted, 65 enrolled. In 2001, 57 master's, 8 doctorates, 2 other advanced degrees awarded.
Degree requirements: For master's, thesis (for some programs); for doctorate, thesis/dissertation.
Entrance requirements: For master's and doctorate, GRE General Test, TOEFL. *Application deadline:* For fall admission, 7/1. *Application fee:* $20 ($30 for international students).
Expenses: Tuition, state resident: full-time $3,764. Tuition and fees vary according to degree level and program.

Financial support: In 2001–02, 1 fellowship, 17 research assistantships, 31 teaching assistantships were awarded. Career-related internships or fieldwork and Federal Work-Study also available.
Faculty research: Neural computation, artificial intelligence, software engineering, distributed systems, databases. *Total annual research expenditures:* $391,330.
William Hase, Chairperson, 313-577-2477, *Fax:* 313-577-6868.
Application contact: Farshad Fotouhi, Graduate Director, 313-577-3107, *Fax:* 313-588-6868, *E-mail:* fotouhi@cs.wayne.edu.

■ WEST VIRGINIA UNIVERSITY

College of Engineering and Mineral Resources, Lane Department of Computer Science and Electrical Engineering, Program in Software Engineering, Morgantown, WV 26506
AWARDS MS, MSSE.

Students: 2 full-time (1 woman), 31 part-time (8 women), 1 international. Average age 32. In 2001, 10 degrees awarded.
Application fee: $45.
Expenses: Tuition, state resident: full-time $2,791. Tuition, nonresident: full-time $8,659. Required fees: $1,002. Tuition and fees vary according to program.
Financial support: In 2001–02, 1 teaching assistantship was awarded. Financial award application deadline: 2/1.
Application contact: Dr. Wils L. Cooley, Graduate Coordinator, 304-293-0405 Ext. 2527, *Fax:* 304-293-8602, *E-mail:* wils.cooley@mail.wvu.edu. *Web site:* http://www.csee.wvu.edu/students/grad/msse.html

■ WIDENER UNIVERSITY

School of Engineering, Program in Computer and Software Engineering, Chester, PA 19013-5792
AWARDS ME, ME/MBA. Part-time and evening/weekend programs available.

Degree requirements: For master's, thesis optional.
Entrance requirements: For master's, GMAT (ME/MBA).
Expenses: Tuition: Part-time $500 per credit. Required fees: $25 per semester.
Faculty research: Computer and software engineering, computer network fault-tolerant computing, and optical computing.

SYSTEMS SCIENCE

■ COLORADO TECHNICAL UNIVERSITY

Graduate Studies, Program in Computer Science, Colorado Springs, CO 80907-3896

AWARDS Computer science (DCS); computer systems security (MSCS); software engineering (MSCS); software project management (MSCS). Part-time and evening/weekend programs available.

Faculty: 6 full-time (2 women), 10 part-time/adjunct (3 women).
Students: 77 full-time (15 women), 10 part-time (2 women); includes 10 minority (4 African Americans, 6 Asian Americans or Pacific Islanders), 2 international. Average age 38. 31 applicants, 94% accepted, 27 enrolled. In 2001, 33 master's, 1 doctorate awarded.
Degree requirements: For master's, thesis or alternative; for doctorate, thesis/dissertation. *Median time to degree:* Master's–2 years full-time, 3 years part-time; doctorate–3.5 years full-time.
Entrance requirements: For doctorate, minimum graduate GPA of 3.0, 5 years of related work experience. *Application deadline:* For fall admission, 10/2; for winter admission, 1/3; for spring admission, 4/3. Applications are processed on a rolling basis. *Application fee:* $100.
Expenses: Tuition: Full-time $6,960; part-time $290 per credit. Required fees: $40 per quarter. One-time fee: $100. Tuition and fees vary according to course load and degree level.
Financial support: Career-related internships or fieldwork and Federal Work-Study available. Financial award applicants required to submit FAFSA.
Faculty research: Software engineering, systems engineering.
Dr. Jack Klag, Dean, 719-590-6850, *Fax:* 719-590-6817.
Application contact: Judy Galante, Graduate Admissions, 719-590-6720, *Fax:* 719-598-3740, *E-mail:* jgalante@coloradotech.edu. *Web site:* http://www.coloradotech.edu/

■ COLORADO TECHNICAL UNIVERSITY DENVER CAMPUS

Program in Computer Science, Greenwood Village, CO 80111

AWARDS Computer systems security (MSCS); software engineering (MSCS); software project management (MSCS). Part-time and evening/weekend programs available.

Faculty: 4 full-time (2 women), 4 part-time/adjunct (2 women).
Students: 24 full-time (4 women), 2 part-time (1 woman); includes 9 minority (3 African Americans, 6 Asian Americans or Pacific Islanders). Average age 34. 6

applicants, 83% accepted, 5 enrolled. In 2001, 10 master's awarded.
Degree requirements: For master's, thesis or alternative. *Median time to degree:* Master's–2 years full-time, 3 years part-time.
Entrance requirements: For master's, minimum undergraduate GPA of 3.0, resume. *Application deadline:* For fall admission, 10/2; for winter admission, 1/3; for spring admission, 4/3. Applications are processed on a rolling basis. *Application fee:* $100.
Expenses: Tuition: Full-time $6,960; part-time $290 per credit. Required fees: $40 per quarter. One-time fee: $100. Tuition and fees vary according to course load and degree level.
Financial support: Federal Work-Study and scholarships/grants available. Support available to part-time students. Financial award applicants required to submit FAFSA.
Dr. Jack Klag, Dean of Computer Science, 719-590-6850, *Fax:* 719-598-3740, *E-mail:* jklag@coloradotech.edu.
Application contact: Suzanne Hyman, Director of Admissions, 303-694-6600, *Fax:* 303-694-6673, *E-mail:* shyman@coloradotech.edu. *Web site:* http://www.coloradotech.edu/

■ FAIRLEIGH DICKINSON UNIVERSITY, METROPOLITAN CAMPUS

University College: Arts, Sciences, and Professional Studies, Program in Systems Science, Teaneck, NJ 07666-1914

AWARDS MS.

Students: 2 full-time (0 women), 2 part-time, 2 international. Average age 45. 12 applicants, 67% accepted, 7 enrolled. In 2001, 4 degrees awarded.
Entrance requirements: For master's, GRE General Test. *Application deadline:* Applications are processed on a rolling basis. *Application fee:* $40.
Expenses: Tuition: Full-time $11,484; part-time $638 per credit. Required fees: $420; $97.
Dr. John Snyder, Dean, University College: Arts, Sciences, and Professional Studies, 201-692-2132, *Fax:* 201-692-2729, *E-mail:* rednys@fdu.edu.

■ FLORIDA INSTITUTE OF TECHNOLOGY

Graduate Programs, School of Extended Graduate Studies, Melbourne, FL 32901-6975

AWARDS Acquisition and contract management (MS, MSM, PMBA); aerospace engineering (MS); business administration (PMBA); computer information systems (MS); computer science (MS); ebusiness (MSM); electrical engineering (MS); engineering

management (MS); health management (MS); human resource management (MSM, PMBA); human resources management (MS); information systems (MSM, PMBA); logistics management (MS, MSM); management (MS); material acquisition management (MS); mechanical engineering (MS); operations research (MS); project management (MS), including information systems, operations research; public administration (MPA); software engineering (MS); space systems (MS); space systems management (MS); systems management (MS), including information systems, operations research; transportation management (MSM). Part-time and evening/weekend programs available. Postbaccalaureate distance learning degree programs offered (no on-campus study).

Faculty: 10 full-time (2 women), 131 part-time/adjunct (15 women).
Students: 57 full-time (29 women), 1,198 part-time (455 women); includes 277 minority (183 African Americans, 38 Asian Americans or Pacific Islanders, 51 Hispanic Americans, 5 Native Americans), 16 international. Average age 37. 299 applicants, 42% accepted. In 2001, 434 degrees awarded.
Entrance requirements: For master's, minimum GPA of 3.0. *Application deadline:* Applications are processed on a rolling basis. *Application fee:* $50. Electronic applications accepted.
Expenses: Tuition: Part-time $650 per credit.
Financial support: Institutionally sponsored loans available. Financial award application deadline: 3/1; financial award applicants required to submit FAFSA.
Dr. Ronald L. Marshall, Dean, School of Extended Graduate Studies, 321-674-8880.
Application contact: Carolyn P. Farrior, Director of Graduate Admissions, 321-674-7118, *Fax:* 321-723-9468, *E-mail:* cfarrior@fit.edu. *Web site:* http://www.segs.fit.edu/

■ HOOD COLLEGE

Graduate School, Program in Management Information Technology, Frederick, MD 21701-8575

AWARDS MS. Part-time and evening/weekend programs available.

Faculty: 7 full-time (3 women), 1 part-time/adjunct (0 women).
Students: 3 full-time (1 woman), 10 part-time (4 women); includes 1 minority (Native American). Average age 33. 6 applicants, 83% accepted. In 2001, 1 degree awarded.
Degree requirements: For master's, thesis.
Entrance requirements: For master's, TOEFL, minimum GPA of 2.5. *Application deadline:* Applications are processed on a rolling basis. *Application fee:* $30. Electronic applications accepted.

Expenses: Tuition: Full-time $5,670; part-time $315 per credit. Required fees: $20 per term.
Financial support: Career-related internships or fieldwork and institutionally sponsored loans available. Support available to part-time students.
Faculty research: Systems engineering, parallel distributed computing, strategy, business ethics, entrepreneurship.
Dr. Regina S. Lightfoot, Director, 301-696-3724, *E-mail:* rlightfoot@hood.edu.
Application contact: Margot Rhoades, Graduate School Office, 301-696-3600, *Fax:* 301-696-3597, *E-mail:* hoodgrad@hood.edu.

■ LOUISIANA STATE UNIVERSITY AND AGRICULTURAL AND MECHANICAL COLLEGE

Graduate School, College of Basic Sciences, Department of Computer Science, Baton Rouge, LA 70803

AWARDS Computer science (MSSS, PhD); systems science (MSSS). Part-time programs available.

Faculty: 12 full-time (3 women).
Students: 74 full-time (15 women), 19 part-time (8 women); includes 9 minority (7 African Americans, 1 Asian American or Pacific Islander, 1 Hispanic American), 68 international. Average age 29. 200 applicants, 37% accepted, 27 enrolled. In 2001, 23 master's, 5 doctorates awarded. Terminal master's awarded for partial completion of doctoral program.
Degree requirements: For master's and doctorate, thesis/dissertation.
Entrance requirements: For master's and doctorate, GRE General Test, minimum GPA of 3.0. *Application deadline:* For fall admission, 2/1; for spring admission, 10/1. Applications are processed on a rolling basis. *Application fee:* $25.
Expenses: Tuition, state resident: full-time $2,551. Tuition, nonresident: full-time $5,551. Required fees: $854. Part-time tuition and fees vary according to course load.
Financial support: In 2001–02, 6 fellowships (averaging $14,750 per year), 24 research assistantships with partial tuition reimbursements (averaging $11,520 per year), 27 teaching assistantships with partial tuition reimbursements (averaging $12,098 per year) were awarded. Unspecified assistantships also available. Financial award application deadline: 2/1; financial award applicants required to submit FAFSA.
Faculty research: Robotics, artificial intelligence, algorithms, database software engineering, high-performance computing. *Total annual research expenditures:* $732,006.
Dr. Sitharama S. Iyengar, Chair, 225-578-1495, *Fax:* 225-578-1465, *E-mail:* iyengar@csc.lsu.edu.
Application contact: Dr. Peter Chen, Graduate Coordinator, 225-578-1495, *Fax:*

225-578-1465, *E-mail:* chen@csc.lsu.edu.
Web site: http://bit.csc.lsu.edu/

■ LOUISIANA STATE UNIVERSITY IN SHREVEPORT

College of Sciences, Shreveport, LA 71115-2399

AWARDS Systems technology (MST). Part-time and evening/weekend programs available.

Degree requirements: For master's, comprehensive exam.
Entrance requirements: For master's, GRE General Test.
Expenses: Tuition, area resident: Full-time $1,890; part-time $105 per credit. Tuition, nonresident: full-time $6,000; part-time $175 per credit. Required fees: $220; $55 per credit.
Faculty research: Graphics, software quality, programming languages, tutoring systems. *Web site:* http://www.lsus.edu/

■ MIAMI UNIVERSITY

Graduate School, School of Engineering and Applied Science, Department of Systems Analysis, Oxford, OH 45056

AWARDS MS.

Faculty: 7 full-time (0 women), 3 part-time/adjunct (1 woman).
Students: 25 full-time (9 women); includes 8 minority (all Asian Americans or Pacific Islanders), 10 international. 57 applicants, 65% accepted, 10 enrolled. In 2001, 19 degrees awarded.
Degree requirements: For master's, thesis, final exam.
Entrance requirements: For master's, GRE, minimum undergraduate GPA of 3.0 during previous 2 years or 2.75 overall. *Application deadline:* For fall admission, 3/1 (priority date). Applications are processed on a rolling basis. *Application fee:* $35.
Expenses: Tuition, state resident: full-time $7,155; part-time $295 per semester hour. Tuition, nonresident: full-time $14,829; part-time $615 per semester hour. Tuition and fees vary according to degree level and campus/location.
Financial support: In 2001–02, 15 fellowships (averaging $9,552 per year) were awarded; research assistantships, teaching assistantships, Federal Work-Study and tuition waivers (full) also available. Financial award application deadline: 3/1.
Dr. Doug Troy, Chair, 513-529-5950.
Application contact: Dr. Mufit Ozden, Director of Graduate Studies, *E-mail:* sangrad@muohio.edu. *Web site:* http://www.sas.muohio.edu/san/

■ NORTHERN KENTUCKY UNIVERSITY

School of Graduate Programs, Program in Information Systems, Highland Heights, KY 41099

AWARDS MSIS.

Faculty: 8 full-time (1 woman).
Students: 13 full-time (5 women), 12 part-time (5 women); includes 2 minority (both Asian Americans or Pacific Islanders), 4 international. Average age 33.
Application fee: $25.
Expenses: Tuition, state resident: full-time $2,958; part-time $149 per credit hour. Tuition, nonresident: full-time $7,872; part-time $422 per credit hour.
Dr. Margaret Meyers, Interim Chairperson, 859-572-6527.
Application contact: Peg Griffin, Graduate Coordinator, 859-572-6364, *E-mail:* griffinp@nku.edu.

■ OAKLAND UNIVERSITY

Graduate Study and Lifelong Learning, School of Engineering and Computer Science, Program in Computer Science and Engineering, Rochester, MI 48309-4401

AWARDS Computer science (MS); embedded systems (MS); software engineering (MS). Part-time and evening/weekend programs available.

Faculty: 15 full-time (2 women).
Students: 83 full-time (33 women), 98 part-time (35 women); includes 26 minority (2 African Americans, 24 Asian Americans or Pacific Islanders), 77 international. Average age 33. 135 applicants, 81% accepted. In 2001, 56 degrees awarded.
Entrance requirements: For master's, minimum GPA of 3.0 for unconditional admission. *Application deadline:* For fall admission, 8/1 (priority date); for winter admission, 12/1 (priority date); for spring admission, 4/1 (priority date). Applications are processed on a rolling basis. *Application fee:* $30. Electronic applications accepted.
Expenses: Tuition, state resident: full-time $5,904; part-time $246 per credit hour. Tuition, nonresident: full-time $12,192; part-time $508 per credit hour. Required fees: $472; $236 per term.
Financial support: Federal Work-Study, institutionally sponsored loans, and tuition waivers (full) available. Financial award application deadline: 3/1; financial award applicants required to submit FAFSA.
Dr. Ishwar K. Sethi, Chair, 248-370-2820.

■ OLD DOMINION UNIVERSITY

College of Engineering and Technology, Program in Operations Research and System Analysis, Norfolk, VA 23529

AWARDS ME.

Old Dominion University (continued)
Students: 3 full-time (2 women), 7 part-time (2 women), 3 international. Average age 35. In 2001, 4 degrees awarded.
Expenses: Tuition, state resident: part-time $202 per credit. Tuition, nonresident: part-time $534 per credit. Required fees: $76 per semester.
Dr. Charles Keating, Graduate Program Director, 757-683-5753, *Fax:* 757-683-5640, *E-mail:* enmagpd@odu.edu. *Web site:* http://www.odu.edu/engr/enma/

■ PORTLAND STATE UNIVERSITY

Graduate Studies, College of Engineering and Computer Science, Systems Science Program, Portland, OR 97207-0751

AWARDS Systems science/anthropology (PhD); systems science/business administration (PhD); systems science/civil engineering (PhD); systems science/economics (PhD); systems science/engineering management (PhD); systems science/general (PhD); systems science/mathematical sciences (PhD); systems science/mechanical engineering (PhD); systems science/psychology (PhD); systems science/sociology (PhD).

Faculty: 4 full-time (0 women).
Students: 47 full-time (19 women), 32 part-time (10 women); includes 9 minority (4 Asian Americans or Pacific Islanders, 3 Hispanic Americans, 2 Native Americans), 15 international. Average age 36. 52 applicants, 38% accepted. In 2001, 8 degrees awarded.
Degree requirements: For doctorate, variable foreign language requirement, thesis/dissertation.
Entrance requirements: For doctorate, GMAT, GRE General Test, TOEFL, minimum undergraduate GPA of 3.0. *Application deadline:* For fall admission, 2/1; for spring admission, 11/1. *Application fee:* $50.
Financial support: In 2001–02, 1 research assistantship with full tuition reimbursement (averaging $6,839 per year) was awarded; teaching assistantships with full tuition reimbursements, career-related internships or fieldwork, Federal Work-Study, and institutionally sponsored loans also available. Support available to part-time students. Financial award application deadline: 3/1; financial award applicants required to submit FAFSA.
Faculty research: Systems theory and methodology, artificial intelligence neural networks, information theory, nonlinear dynamics/chaos, modeling and simulation. *Total annual research expenditures:* $106,413.
Dr. Nancy Perrin, Director, 503-725-4960, *E-mail:* perrinn@pdx.edu.
Application contact: Dawn Kuenle, Coordinator, 503-725-4960, *E-mail:* dawn@sysc.pdx.edu. *Web site:* http://www.sysc.pdx.edu/

■ RENSSELAER AT HARTFORD

Department of Engineering, Program in Computer and Systems Engineering, Hartford, CT 06120-2991

AWARDS ME.

Students: 18 applicants, 44% accepted, 6 enrolled.
Expenses: Tuition: Full-time $11,700; part-time $650 per credit.
James McKim, Chair, 860-548-2455, *E-mail:* jcm@rh.edu.
Application contact: Rebecca Danchak, Director of Admissions, 860-548-2420, *Fax:* 860-548-7823, *E-mail:* rdanchak@rh.edu.

■ SOUTHERN METHODIST UNIVERSITY

School of Engineering, Department of Engineering Management, Information and Systems, Dallas, TX 75275

AWARDS Applied science (MS); engineering management (MSEM, DE); operations research (MS, PhD); systems engineering (MS). Part-time and evening/weekend programs available. Postbaccalaureate distance learning degree programs offered.

Faculty: 6 full-time (1 woman).
Students: 10 full-time (1 woman), 100 part-time (22 women); includes 29 minority (6 African Americans, 11 Asian Americans or Pacific Islanders, 10 Hispanic Americans, 2 Native Americans), 10 international. 55 applicants, 78% accepted. In 2001, 25 master's, 5 doctorates awarded. Terminal master's awarded for partial completion of doctoral program.
Degree requirements: For master's, thesis optional; for doctorate, thesis/dissertation, oral and written qualifying exams.
Entrance requirements: For master's, GRE General, TOEFL, minimum GPA of 3.0 in last 2 years; bachelor's degree in engineering, mathematics, or sciences; for doctorate, bachelor's degree in related field. *Application deadline:* For fall admission, 7/1; for spring admission, 11/15. Applications are processed on a rolling basis. *Application fee:* $50.
Expenses: Tuition: Part-time $285 per credit hour.
Faculty research: Telecommunications, decision systems, information engineering, operations research, software.
Richard S. Barr, Chair, 214-768-2605, *E-mail:* emis@engr.smu.edu.
Application contact: Marc Valerin, Associate Director of Graduate Admissions, 214-768-3484, *E-mail:* valerin@seas.smu.edu.

Find an in-depth description at www.petersons.com/gradchannel.

■ STATE UNIVERSITY OF NEW YORK AT BINGHAMTON

Graduate School, Thomas J. Watson School of Engineering and Applied Science, Department of Systems Science and Industrial Engineering, Binghamton, NY 13902-6000

AWARDS M Eng, MS, MSAT, PhD. Part-time and evening/weekend programs available.

Faculty: 10 full-time (3 women), 4 part-time/adjunct (0 women).
Students: 80 full-time (8 women), 41 part-time (7 women); includes 5 minority (1 African American, 4 Asian Americans or Pacific Islanders), 80 international. Average age 29. 200 applicants, 54% accepted, 21 enrolled. In 2001, 24 master's, 2 doctorates awarded. Terminal master's awarded for partial completion of doctoral program.
Degree requirements: For master's, thesis or alternative; for doctorate, thesis/dissertation.
Entrance requirements: For master's and doctorate, GRE General Test, GRE Subject Test, TOEFL. *Application deadline:* For fall admission, 4/15 (priority date); for spring admission, 11/1. Applications are processed on a rolling basis. Electronic applications accepted.
Expenses: Tuition, state resident: full-time $5,100; part-time $213 per credit. Tuition, nonresident: full-time $8,416; part-time $351 per credit. Required fees: $811.
Financial support: In 2001–02, 58 students received support, including 1 fellowship with full tuition reimbursement available (averaging $7,500 per year), 42 research assistantships with full tuition reimbursements available (averaging $5,621 per year), 15 teaching assistantships with full tuition reimbursements available (averaging $6,457 per year); career-related internships or fieldwork, Federal Work-Study, institutionally sponsored loans, tuition waivers (full and partial), and unspecified assistantships also available. Support available to part-time students. Financial award application deadline: 2/15.
Faculty research: Problem restructuring, protein modeling.
Dr. Robert Emerson, Chair, 607-777-6509.

■ SYRACUSE UNIVERSITY

Graduate School, L. C. Smith College of Engineering and Computer Science, Department of Electrical Engineering and Computer Science, Program in Systems and Information Science, Syracuse, NY 13244-0003

AWARDS MS.

Students: 2 full-time (1 woman), 6 part-time, 1 international. Average age 33. In 2001, 8 degrees awarded.
Entrance requirements: For master's, GRE General Test, GRE Subject Test. *Application deadline:* Applications are processed on a rolling basis. *Application fee:* $50.

Expenses: Tuition: Full-time $15,528; part-time $647 per credit. Required fees: $420; $38 per term. Tuition and fees vary according to program.
Financial support: Fellowships, research assistantships, teaching assistantships, Federal Work-Study and tuition waivers (partial) available. Financial award application deadline: 1/10.
Dr. Kishan Mehrotra, Program Director, 315-443-2811, *Fax:* 315-443-2583, *E-mail:* kishan@ecs.syr.edu.
Application contact: Barbara Hazard, Information Contact, 315-443-2655, *Fax:* 315-443-2583, *E-mail:* bahazard@syr.edu.
Web site: http://www.ecs.syr.edu/

Find an in-depth description at www.petersons.com/gradchannel.

■ UNIVERSITY OF MICHIGAN–DEARBORN

College of Engineering and Computer Science, Department of Industrial and Systems Engineering, Dearborn, MI 48128-1491

AWARDS Engineering management (MS); industrial and systems engineering (MSE); information systems and technology (MS). Part-time and evening/weekend programs available.

Faculty: 12 full-time (0 women), 8 part-time/adjunct (2 women).
Students: 7 full-time (2 women), 239 part-time (61 women); includes 45 minority (7 African Americans, 26 Asian Americans or Pacific Islanders, 12 Hispanic Americans). Average age 31. 107 applicants, 91% accepted. In 2001, 78 degrees awarded.
Degree requirements: For master's, thesis optional.
Entrance requirements: For master's, bachelor's degree in applied mathematics,

computer science, engineering, or physical science; minimum GPA of 3.0. *Application deadline:* For fall admission, 8/1 (priority date); for winter admission, 12/1 (priority date); for spring admission, 4/1. Applications are processed on a rolling basis. *Application fee:* $55.
Expenses: Tuition, state resident: part-time $300 per credit hour. Tuition, nonresident: part-time $756 per credit hour. Required fees: $90 per semester. Tuition and fees vary according to course level, course load and program.
Financial support: Fellowships, research assistantships, teaching assistantships, Federal Work-Study available. Financial award application deadline: 4/1; financial award applicants required to submit FAFSA.
Faculty research: Health care systems, databases, human factors, machine diagnostics, precision machining.
Dr. S. K. Kachhal, Chair, 313-593-5361, *Fax:* 313-593-3692.
Application contact: Shelly A. Harris, Graduate Secretary, 313-593-5361, *Fax:* 313-593-3692, *E-mail:* saharris@engin.umd.umich.edu. *Web site:* http://www.engin.umd.umich.edu/

■ WASHINGTON UNIVERSITY IN ST. LOUIS

Henry Edwin Sever Graduate School of Engineering and Applied Science, Department of Systems Science and Mathematics, St. Louis, MO 63130-4899

AWARDS Control engineering (MCE); systems science and mathematics (MS, D Sc); systems science and mathematics and economics (D Sc). Part-time programs available.

Faculty: 7 full-time (0 women), 8 part-time/adjunct (0 women).
Students: 26 full-time (4 women), 8 part-time, 21 international. Average age 23. 49 applicants, 18% accepted, 6 enrolled. In 2001, 4 master's, 4 doctorates awarded. Terminal master's awarded for partial completion of doctoral program.
Degree requirements: For master's, thesis optional; for doctorate, thesis/dissertation, departmental qualifying exam.
Entrance requirements: For master's, TOEFL; for doctorate, GRE, TOEFL. *Application deadline:* For fall admission, 2/15; for spring admission, 10/14 (priority date). *Application fee:* $20. Electronic applications accepted.
Expenses: Tuition: Full-time $26,900.
Financial support: In 2001–02, 21 research assistantships with full tuition reimbursements (averaging $15,000 per year), 2 teaching assistantships with full tuition reimbursements (averaging $21,500 per year) were awarded. Career-related internships or fieldwork, Federal Work-Study, and institutionally sponsored loans also available. Financial award application deadline: 2/15.
Faculty research: Linear and nonlinear control systems, robotics and automation, scheduling and transportation systems, biocybernetics, computational mathematics. *Total annual research expenditures:* $2 million.
Dr. I. Norman Katz, Chairman, 314-935-6001, *Fax:* 314-935-6121, *E-mail:* katz@zach.wustl.edu.
Application contact: Sandra Devereaux, Administrative Secretary, 314-935-6001, *Fax:* 314-935-6121, *E-mail:* sandra@zach.wustl.edu. *Web site:* http://www.ssm.wustl.edu/

Find an in-depth description at www.petersons.com/gradchannel.

Graduate Programs in Engineering

Engineering and Applied Sciences

ENGINEERING AND APPLIED SCIENCES—GENERAL

■ AIR FORCE INSTITUTE OF TECHNOLOGY

School of Engineering and Management, Dayton, OH 45433-7765

AWARDS MS, PhD. Part-time programs available.

Degree requirements: For master's and doctorate, thesis/dissertation.
Entrance requirements: For master's, GRE General Test, minimum GPA of 3.0; for doctorate, GRE General Test. *Web site:* http://en.afit.edu/

■ ALABAMA AGRICULTURAL AND MECHANICAL UNIVERSITY

School of Graduate Studies, School of Engineering and Technology, Huntsville, AL 35811

AWARDS M Ed, MS. Part-time and evening/weekend programs available.

Faculty: 4 full-time (1 woman).
Students: In 2001, 8 degrees awarded.
Degree requirements: For master's, thesis optional.
Entrance requirements: For master's, GRE General Test. *Application deadline:* For fall admission, 5/1. *Application fee:* $15 ($20 for international students).
Expenses: Tuition, state resident: full-time $1,380. Tuition, nonresident: full-time $2,500.
Financial support: Research assistantships with tuition reimbursements, career-related internships or fieldwork available. Financial award application deadline: 4/1.
Faculty research: Ionized gases, hypersonic flow phenomenology, robotics systems development.
Dr. Arthur Bond, Dean, 256-851-5560.

■ ANDREWS UNIVERSITY

School of Graduate Studies, College of Technology, Berrien Springs, MI 49104

AWARDS MS.

Faculty: 6 full-time.
Students: 19 full-time (5 women), 20 part-time (8 women); includes 5 minority (2 African Americans, 2 Asian Americans or Pacific Islanders, 1 Hispanic American), 32 international. Average age 30. In 2001, 2 degrees awarded.
Entrance requirements: For master's, GMAT, TOEFL, minimum GPA of 2.6.

Application deadline: Applications are processed on a rolling basis. *Application fee:* $40.
Expenses: Tuition: Full-time $12,600; part-time $525 per semester. Required fees: $268. Tuition and fees vary according to degree level.
Dr. M. Wesley Schultz, Head, 616-471-3413.
Application contact: Carolyn Hurst, Supervisor of Graduate Admission, 800-253-2874, *Fax:* 616-471-3228, *E-mail:* enroll@andrews.edu.

■ ARIZONA STATE UNIVERSITY

Graduate College, College of Engineering and Applied Sciences, Tempe, AZ 85287

AWARDS M Eng, MCS, MS, MSE, PhD, MSE/MIMOT. Part-time programs available.

Degree requirements: For doctorate, thesis/dissertation.
Faculty research: Aerodynamics, computer design, environmental fluid dynamics, solar energy, thermosciences. *Web site:* http://www.eas.asu.edu/
Find an in-depth description at www.petersons.com/gradchannel.

■ ARIZONA STATE UNIVERSITY EAST

College of Technology and Applied Sciences, Mesa, AZ 85212

AWARDS MS. Part-time and evening/weekend programs available.

Faculty: 32 full-time (5 women), 2 part-time/adjunct (0 women).
Students: 107 full-time (43 women), 167 part-time (71 women); includes 35 minority (5 African Americans, 18 Asian Americans or Pacific Islanders, 12 Hispanic Americans), 129 international. Average age 32. 185 applicants, 62% accepted, 68 enrolled. In 2001, 58 degrees awarded.
Degree requirements: For master's, thesis or applied project and oral defense. *Median time to degree:* Master's–2 years full-time, 2.5 years part-time.
Entrance requirements: For master's, TOEFL, 3 letters of recommendation, minimum GPA of 3.0, resumé. *Application deadline:* Applications are processed on a rolling basis. *Application fee:* $45. Electronic applications accepted.
Expenses: Tuition, state resident: full-time $2,412; part-time $126 per credit hour. Tuition, nonresident: full-time $10,278; part-time $428 per credit hour. Required fees: $26. Tuition and fees vary according to course load.
Financial support: In 2001–02, 91 students received support, including 27

research assistantships with partial tuition reimbursements available (averaging $5,472 per year), 11 teaching assistantships with partial tuition reimbursements available (averaging $4,534 per year); career-related internships or fieldwork, Federal Work-Study, scholarships/grants, tuition waivers (full and partial), and unspecified assistantships also available. Support available to part-time students. Financial award application deadline: 3/1; financial award applicants required to submit FAFSA. *Total annual research expenditures:* $1.3 million.
Dr. Albert L. McHenry, Dean, 480-727-1093, *Fax:* 480-727-1089, *E-mail:* iacaxm@asuvm.inre.asu.edu. *Web site:* http://www.asu.edu/east/

■ AUBURN UNIVERSITY

Graduate School, College of Engineering, Auburn University, AL 36849

AWARDS M Ch E, M Mtl E, MAE, MCE, MEE, MIE, MME, MS, MSWE, PhD. Part-time programs available.

Faculty: 118 full-time (5 women).
Students: 244 full-time (57 women), 203 part-time (53 women); includes 29 minority (19 African Americans, 5 Asian Americans or Pacific Islanders, 4 Hispanic Americans, 1 Native American), 210 international. 699 applicants, 39% accepted. In 2001, 102 master's, 51 doctorates awarded.
Degree requirements: For master's, thesis (for some programs); for doctorate, thesis/dissertation.
Entrance requirements: For master's and doctorate, GRE General Test. *Application deadline:* For fall admission, 7/7; for spring admission, 11/24. Applications are processed on a rolling basis. *Application fee:* $25 ($50 for international students). Electronic applications accepted.
Financial support: Fellowships, research assistantships, teaching assistantships, Federal Work-Study available. Support available to part-time students. Financial award application deadline: 3/15.
Dr. Larry Benefield, Dean, 334-844-2308.
Application contact: Dr. John F. Pritchett, Dean of the Graduate School, 334-844-4700, *E-mail:* hatchlb@mail.auburn.edu. *Web site:* http://www.eng.auburn.edu/

■ BOSTON UNIVERSITY

College of Engineering, Boston, MA 02215

AWARDS MS, PhD, MBA/MS, MD/PhD. Part-time programs available. Postbaccalaureate distance learning degree programs offered (no on-campus study).

Faculty: 114 full-time (11 women), 30 part-time/adjunct (1 woman).
Students: 315 full-time (77 women), 53 part-time (14 women); includes 24 minority (5 African Americans, 13 Asian Americans or Pacific Islanders, 6 Hispanic Americans), 176 international. Average age 28. 1,205 applicants, 25% accepted, 120 enrolled. In 2001, 83 master's, 25 doctorates awarded.
Degree requirements: For doctorate, thesis/dissertation, comprehensive exam.
Entrance requirements: For master's and doctorate, GRE General Test, TOEFL. *Application deadline:* For fall admission, 4/1; for spring admission, 10/1. Applications are processed on a rolling basis. *Application fee:* $60. Electronic applications accepted.
Expenses: Tuition: Full-time $25,872; part-time $340 per credit. Required fees: $40 per semester. Part-time tuition and fees vary according to class time, course level and program.
Financial support: In 2001–02, 244 students received support, including 18 fellowships with full tuition reimbursements available (averaging $15,500 per year), 131 research assistantships with full tuition reimbursements available (averaging $13,500 per year), 48 teaching assistantships with full tuition reimbursements available (averaging $13,500 per year); career-related internships or fieldwork, Federal Work-Study, institutionally sponsored loans, scholarships/grants, and tuition waivers (full and partial) also available. Financial award application deadline: 1/15; financial award applicants required to submit FAFSA.
Faculty research: Acoustics, biotechnology, nano-technology, photonics, systems engineering. *Total annual research expenditures:* $36.2 million.
Dr. David Campbell, Dean, 617-353-2800, *Fax:* 617-353-6322.
Application contact: Cheryl Kelley, Director of Graduate Programs, 617-353-9760, *Fax:* 617-353-0259, *E-mail:* enggrad@bu.edu. *Web site:* http://www.bu.edu/eng/grad/
Find an in-depth description at www.petersons.com/gradchannel.

■ BRADLEY UNIVERSITY

Graduate School, College of Engineering and Technology, Peoria, IL 61625-0002

AWARDS MSCE, MSEE, MSIE, MSME, MSMFE. Part-time and evening/weekend programs available.

Faculty: 45.
Students: 44 full-time, 112 part-time. 534 applicants, 68% accepted. In 2001, 69 degrees awarded.
Degree requirements: For master's, comprehensive exam.
Entrance requirements: For master's, TOEFL, minimum GPA of 3.0. *Application deadline:* For fall admission, 7/1 (priority

date); for spring admission, 11/1. Applications are processed on a rolling basis. *Application fee:* $40 ($50 for international students).
Expenses: Tuition: Part-time $7,615 per semester. Tuition and fees vary according to course load.
Financial support: In 2001–02, 29 research assistantships with full and partial tuition reimbursements (averaging $1,405 per year) were awarded; teaching assistantships, institutionally sponsored loans, scholarships/grants, and tuition waivers (partial) also available. Support available to part-time students. Financial award application deadline: 3/1.
Dr. Richard Johnson, Dean, 309-677-2721.

■ BRIGHAM YOUNG UNIVERSITY

Graduate Studies, College of Engineering and Technology, Provo, UT 84602-1001

AWARDS MS, PhD, MBA/MS. Part-time programs available.

Faculty: 94 full-time (0 women).
Students: 314 full-time (28 women). Average age 26. 369 applicants, 51% accepted, 125 enrolled. In 2001, 113 master's, 11 doctorates awarded.
Degree requirements: For doctorate, thesis/dissertation.
Application deadline: For fall admission, 2/15. Applications are processed on a rolling basis. *Application fee:* $50. Electronic applications accepted.
Expenses: Tuition: Full-time $3,860; part-time $214 per hour.
Financial support: In 2001–02, 11 fellowships with full tuition reimbursements (averaging $13,000 per year), 73 research assistantships with partial tuition reimbursements (averaging $5,000 per year), 93 teaching assistantships with partial tuition reimbursements (averaging $6,300 per year) were awarded. Career-related internships or fieldwork, institutionally sponsored loans, and scholarships/grants also available. Support available to part-time students. Financial award application deadline: 3/15; financial award applicants required to submit FAFSA.
Faculty research: Combustion, catalysis, computer modeling, composites, microwave remote sensing, VSLI design tools. *Total annual research expenditures:* $7 million.
Dr. Douglas M. Chabries, Dean, 801-422-4327, *Fax:* 801-422-0218, *E-mail:* college@et.byu.edu. *Web site:* http://www.et.byu.edu/

■ BROWN UNIVERSITY

Graduate School, Division of Engineering, Providence, RI 02912

AWARDS Aerospace engineering (Sc M, PhD); biomedical engineering (Sc M); electrical sciences (Sc M, PhD); fluid mechanics, thermodynamics, and chemical processes

(Sc M, PhD); materials science (Sc M, PhD); mechanics of solids and structures (Sc M, PhD).

Degree requirements: For doctorate, thesis/dissertation, preliminary exam.
Find an in-depth description at www.petersons.com/gradchannel.

■ BUCKNELL UNIVERSITY

Graduate Studies, College of Engineering, Lewisburg, PA 17837

AWARDS MS, MS Ch E, MSCE, MSEE, MSME. Part-time programs available.

Faculty: 37 full-time (3 women).
Students: 19 full-time (4 women), 1 part-time, 10 international.
Degree requirements: For master's, thesis.
Entrance requirements: For master's, GRE General Test, GRE Subject Test, TOEFL, minimum GPA of 2.8. *Application deadline:* For fall admission, 6/1 (priority date); for spring admission, 12/1 (priority date). Applications are processed on a rolling basis. *Application fee:* $25.
Expenses: Tuition: Part-time $2,875 per course.
Financial support: Fellowships, research assistantships, teaching assistantships, unspecified assistantships available. Financial award application deadline: 3/1.
Dr. James Orbison, Interim Dean, 570-577-3711. *Web site:* http://www.bucknell.edu/

■ CALIFORNIA INSTITUTE OF TECHNOLOGY

Division of Engineering and Applied Science, Pasadena, CA 91125-0001

AWARDS Aeronautics (MS, PhD, Engr); applied and computational mathematics (MS, PhD); applied mechanics (MS, PhD); applied physics (MS, PhD); bioengineering (MS, PhD); civil engineering (MS, PhD); computation and neural systems (MS, PhD); computer science (MS, PhD); control and dynamical systems (MS, PhD); electrical engineering (MS, PhD); engineering science (PhD); environmental science and engineering (MS, PhD); materials science (MS, PhD); mechanical engineering (MS, PhD, Engr).

Faculty: 88 full-time (4 women).
Students: 458 full-time (93 women). 1,884 applicants, 14% accepted, 138 enrolled. In 2001, 87 master's, 81 doctorates awarded. Terminal master's awarded for partial completion of doctoral program.
Degree requirements: For doctorate, thesis/dissertation.
Entrance requirements: For master's and doctorate, GRE (strongly recommended), TOEFL, minimum GPA of 3.5. *Application deadline:* For fall admission, 1/15. *Application fee:* $50. Electronic applications accepted.
Financial support: Fellowships, research assistantships, teaching assistantships,

California Institute of Technology (continued)
Federal Work-Study and institutionally sponsored loans available. Support available to part-time students.
Dr. Richard M. Murray, Chair, 626-395-4101, *Fax:* 626-585-1729, *E-mail:* murray@caltech.edu. *Web site:* http://www.eas.caltech.edu

■ CALIFORNIA NATIONAL UNIVERSITY FOR ADVANCED STUDIES

College of Engineering, North Hills, CA 91343

AWARDS MS Eng. Part-time programs available. Postbaccalaureate distance learning degree programs offered (no on-campus study).

Degree requirements: For master's, thesis or alternative, project.
Entrance requirements: For master's, minimum GPA of 3.0. *Web site:* http://www.cnuas.edu/

■ CALIFORNIA POLYTECHNIC STATE UNIVERSITY, SAN LUIS OBISPO

College of Engineering, San Luis Obispo, CA 93407

AWARDS MS, MSAE, MSCS, MBA/MS, MCRP/MS. Part-time programs available.

Faculty: 98 full-time (8 women), 82 part-time/adjunct (14 women).
Students: 91 full-time (14 women), 72 part-time (15 women); includes 21 Asian Americans or Pacific Islanders, 19 international. 135 applicants, 59% accepted, 56 enrolled. In 2001, 42 degrees awarded.
Entrance requirements: For master's, GRE General Test. *Application deadline:* For fall admission, 5/31 (priority date). Applications are processed on a rolling basis. *Application fee:* $55. Electronic applications accepted.
Expenses: Tuition, nonresident: part-time $164 per unit. One-time fee: $2,153 part-time.
Financial support: Fellowships, research assistantships, teaching assistantships, career-related internships or fieldwork, Federal Work-Study, and institutionally sponsored loans available. Financial award application deadline: 3/2; financial award applicants required to submit FAFSA.
Faculty research: Artificial intelligence, fuel systems, solar power, advanced materials, traffic systems.
Dr. Peter Y. Lee, Dean, 805-756-2131, *Fax:* 805-756-6503, *E-mail:* plee@calpoly.edu.
Application contact: Dr. Daniel W. Walsh, Associate Dean, 805-756-2131, *Fax:* 805-756-6503, *E-mail:* dwalsh@calpoly.edu. *Web site:* http://synner.ceng.calpoly.edu/

■ CALIFORNIA STATE POLYTECHNIC UNIVERSITY, POMONA

Academic Affairs, College of Engineering, Pomona, CA 91768-2557

AWARDS Electrical engineering (MSEE); engineering (MSE). Part-time programs available.

Faculty: 106 full-time (15 women), 34 part-time/adjunct (1 woman).
Students: 48 full-time (10 women), 101 part-time (11 women); includes 66 minority (57 Asian Americans or Pacific Islanders, 9 Hispanic Americans), 34 international. Average age 28. 133 applicants, 68% accepted. In 2001, 49 degrees awarded.
Degree requirements: For master's, thesis or comprehensive exam.
Entrance requirements: For master's, TOEFL, GRE General Test or minimum GPA of 3.0 in upper-level course work. *Application deadline:* For fall admission, 5/1 (priority date); for winter admission, 10/15 (priority date); for spring admission, 1/2 (priority date). Applications are processed on a rolling basis. *Application fee:* $55. Electronic applications accepted.
Expenses: Tuition, nonresident: part-time $164 per unit. Required fees: $1,850.
Financial support: In 2001–02, 1 fellowship, 6 research assistantships, 5 teaching assistantships were awarded. Career-related internships or fieldwork, Federal Work-Study, institutionally sponsored loans, and unspecified assistantships also available. Support available to part-time students. Financial award application deadline: 3/2; financial award applicants required to submit FAFSA.
Faculty research: Aerospace; alternative vehicles; communications, computers, and controls; engineering management. *Total annual research expenditures:* $650,000.
Dr. Ed Hohmann, Dean, 909-869-2472, *Fax:* 909-869-4370, *E-mail:* echohmann@csupomona.edu.
Application contact: Dr. Rajan Chandra, Director, 909-869-2476, *Fax:* 909-869-4687, *E-mail:* rmchandra@csupomona.edu. *Web site:* http://www.csupomona.edu/~engineering/

■ CALIFORNIA STATE UNIVERSITY, CHICO

Graduate School, College of Engineering, Computer Science, and Technology, Chico, CA 95929-0722

AWARDS MS. Part-time programs available.

Faculty: 20.
Students: 122 full-time, 53 part-time; includes 89 minority (2 African Americans, 84 Asian Americans or Pacific Islanders, 3 Hispanic Americans). Average age 31. 215 applicants, 65% accepted, 48 enrolled. In 2001, 34 degrees awarded.

Degree requirements: For master's, thesis or alternative, oral exam.
Entrance requirements: For master's, letters of recommendation (2). *Application deadline:* For fall admission, 4/1; for spring admission, 10/1. Applications are processed on a rolling basis. *Application fee:* $55. Electronic applications accepted.
Expenses: Tuition, state resident: full-time $2,148. Tuition, nonresident: full-time $6,576.
Financial support: Fellowships, research assistantships, teaching assistantships, career-related internships or fieldwork and Federal Work-Study available. Support available to part-time students.
Dr. Kenneth Derucher, Dean, 530-898-5963.

■ CALIFORNIA STATE UNIVERSITY, FRESNO

Division of Graduate Studies, College of Engineering and Computer Science, Fresno, CA 93740-8027

AWARDS MS. Part-time and evening/weekend programs available.

Faculty: 26 full-time (2 women).
Students: 50 full-time (12 women), 76 part-time (10 women); includes 21 minority (2 African Americans, 15 Asian Americans or Pacific Islanders, 4 Hispanic Americans), 79 international. Average age 31. 194 applicants, 72% accepted, 52 enrolled. In 2001, 24 degrees awarded.
Degree requirements: For master's, thesis or alternative. *Median time to degree:* Master's–2.5 years full-time, 3.5 years part-time.
Entrance requirements: For master's, GRE General Test, TOEFL. *Application deadline:* For fall admission, 8/1 (priority date); for spring admission, 12/1. Applications are processed on a rolling basis. *Application fee:* $55. Electronic applications accepted.
Expenses: Tuition, nonresident: part-time $246 per unit. Required fees: $605 per semester. Tuition and fees vary according to course load.
Financial support: In 2001–02, 12 teaching assistantships were awarded; career-related internships or fieldwork, Federal Work-Study, scholarships/grants, and unspecified assistantships also available. Financial award application deadline: 3/1; financial award applicants required to submit FAFSA.
Faculty research: Exhaust emission, blended fuel testing, waste management.
Dr. Karl Longley, Dean, 559-278-2500, *Fax:* 559-278-7071, *E-mail:* karl_longley@csufresno.edu.
Application contact: Dr. Jesus Larralde-Muro, Graduate Program Coordinator, 559-278-2566, *E-mail:* jesus_larralde-muro@csufresno.edu.

■ CALIFORNIA STATE UNIVERSITY, FULLERTON

Graduate Studies, College of Engineering and Computer Science, Fullerton, CA 92834-9480

AWARDS MS. Part-time programs available.

Faculty: 45 full-time (7 women), 62 part-time/adjunct.
Students: 211 full-time (57 women), 238 part-time (54 women); includes 195 minority (6 African Americans, 170 Asian Americans or Pacific Islanders, 19 Hispanic Americans), 166 international. Average age 31. 508 applicants, 59% accepted, 140 enrolled. In 2001, 73 degrees awarded.
Degree requirements: For master's, project or thesis.
Entrance requirements: For master's, minimum undergraduate GPA of 2.5. *Application fee:* $55.
Expenses: Tuition, nonresident: part-time $246 per unit. Required fees: $964.
Financial support: Career-related internships or fieldwork, Federal Work-Study, institutionally sponsored loans, and scholarships/grants available. Support available to part-time students. Financial award application deadline: 3/1.
Dr. Raman Unnikrishnan, Dean, 714-278-3362.
Application contact: Dr. David Falconer, Associate Dean, 714-278-3362.

■ CALIFORNIA STATE UNIVERSITY, LONG BEACH

Graduate Studies, College of Engineering, Long Beach, CA 90840

AWARDS MS, MSAE, MSCE, MSE, MSEE, MSME, PhD, CE. Part-time and evening/weekend programs available.

Faculty: 83 full-time (7 women), 44 part-time/adjunct (3 women).
Students: 153 full-time (36 women), 394 part-time (78 women); includes 227 minority (18 African Americans, 172 Asian Americans or Pacific Islanders, 37 Hispanic Americans), 150 international. Average age 32. 523 applicants, 37% accepted. In 2001, 135 degrees awarded. Terminal master's awarded for partial completion of doctoral program.
Degree requirements: For doctorate, one foreign language, thesis/dissertation.
Entrance requirements: For master's, TOEFL. *Application deadline:* For fall admission, 8/1; for spring admission, 12/1. *Application fee:* $55. Electronic applications accepted.
Financial support: Research assistantships, teaching assistantships, career-related internships or fieldwork, Federal Work-Study, institutionally sponsored loans, scholarships/grants, and unspecified assistantships available. Financial award application deadline: 3/2.

Faculty research: Computational fluid dynamics, biomedical engineering, separation and purification, structural engineering, advanced database management. *Total annual research expenditures:* $5.8 million.
Dr. Michael Mahoney, Interim Dean, 562-985-5190, *Fax:* 562-985-7561, *E-mail:* mahoney@csulb.edu.
Application contact: Dr. Mihir K. Das, Associate Dean for Instruction, 562-985-5257, *Fax:* 562-985-7561, *E-mail:* mdas@engr.csulb.edu.

■ CALIFORNIA STATE UNIVERSITY, LOS ANGELES

Graduate Studies, College of Engineering, Computer Science, and Technology, Los Angeles, CA 90032-8530

AWARDS MA, MS. Part-time and evening/weekend programs available.

Faculty: 30 full-time, 28 part-time/adjunct.
Students: 53 full-time (13 women), 158 part-time (24 women); includes 101 minority (8 African Americans, 57 Asian Americans or Pacific Islanders, 35 Hispanic Americans, 1 Native American), 63 international. In 2001, 57 degrees awarded.
Entrance requirements: For master's, TOEFL. *Application deadline:* For fall admission, 6/30; for spring admission, 2/1. Applications are processed on a rolling basis. *Application fee:* $55.
Expenses: Tuition, nonresident: part-time $164 per unit.
Financial support: Federal Work-Study available. Support available to part-time students. Financial award application deadline: 3/1.
Dr. Kuei-wu Tsai, Dean, 323-343-4500.

■ CALIFORNIA STATE UNIVERSITY, NORTHRIDGE

Graduate Studies, College of Engineering and Computer Science, Northridge, CA 91330

AWARDS MS, MSE. Part-time and evening/weekend programs available.

Faculty: 59 full-time, 34 part-time/adjunct.
Students: 108 full-time (31 women), 207 part-time (30 women); includes 84 minority (3 African Americans, 58 Asian Americans or Pacific Islanders, 22 Hispanic Americans, 1 Native American), 100 international. Average age 33. 538 applicants, 42% accepted, 68 enrolled. In 2001, 72 degrees awarded.
Entrance requirements: For master's, GRE General Test, TOEFL, minimum GPA of 2.5. *Application deadline:* For fall admission, 11/30. *Application fee:* $55.
Expenses: Tuition, nonresident: part-time $631 per semester. Required fees: $246 per unit.

Financial support: Teaching assistantships, career-related internships or fieldwork and Federal Work-Study available. Support available to part-time students. Financial award application deadline: 3/1.
Dr. Laurence Caretto, Interim Dean, 818-677-4501.

■ CALIFORNIA STATE UNIVERSITY, SACRAMENTO

Graduate Studies, College of Engineering and Computer Science, Sacramento, CA 95819-6048

AWARDS MS. Part-time and evening/weekend programs available.

Students: 178 full-time (32 women), 183 part-time (33 women); includes 64 minority (3 African Americans, 51 Asian Americans or Pacific Islanders, 9 Hispanic Americans, 1 Native American), 184 international.
Degree requirements: For master's, writing proficiency exam.
Entrance requirements: For master's, TOEFL. *Application deadline:* For fall admission, 4/15; for spring admission, 11/1. *Application fee:* $55.
Expenses: Tuition, state resident: full-time $1,965; part-time $668 per semester. Tuition, nonresident: part-time $246 per unit.
Financial support: Research assistantships, teaching assistantships, career-related internships or fieldwork and Federal Work-Study available. Support available to part-time students. Financial award application deadline: 3/1.
Dr. Braja Das, Dean, 916-278-6366.

■ CARNEGIE MELLON UNIVERSITY

Carnegie Institute of Technology, Pittsburgh, PA 15213-3891

AWARDS M Ch E, ME, MS, PhD. Part-time and evening/weekend programs available.

Degree requirements: For doctorate, qualifying exam.
Entrance requirements: For master's and doctorate, GRE General Test, TOEFL. *Web site:* http://www.cit.cmu.edu/

■ CASE WESTERN RESERVE UNIVERSITY

School of Graduate Studies, The Case School of Engineering, Cleveland, OH 44106

AWARDS ME, MS, PhD, MD/PhD. Part-time and evening/weekend programs available. Postbaccalaureate distance learning degree programs offered.

Faculty: 109 full-time (6 women), 80 part-time/adjunct (10 women).
Students: 309 full-time (86 women), 296 part-time (58 women); includes 55 minority (7 African Americans, 42 Asian

Case Western Reserve University (continued)

Americans or Pacific Islanders, 6 Hispanic Americans), 295 international. Average age 24. 1,912 applicants, 26% accepted, 116 enrolled. In 2001, 131 master's, 51 doctorates awarded. Terminal master's awarded for partial completion of doctoral program. **Degree requirements:** For doctorate, thesis/dissertation, qualifying exam, teaching experience.
Entrance requirements: For master's, TOEFL; for doctorate, GRE, TOEFL. *Application deadline:* Applications are processed on a rolling basis. *Application fee:* $25.
Financial support: In 2001–02, 175 fellowships with full and partial tuition reimbursements (averaging $16,524 per year), 184 research assistantships with full and partial tuition reimbursements (averaging $16,413 per year), 5 teaching assistantships (averaging $18,600 per year) were awarded. Career-related internships or fieldwork, Federal Work-Study, and institutionally sponsored loans also available. Support available to part-time students. Financial award applicants required to submit FAFSA. *Total annual research expenditures:* $26.6 million.
Dr. Robert F. Savinell, Interim Dean, 216-368-4436, *Fax:* 216-368-6939, *E-mail:* rfs2@po.cwru.edu. *Web site:* http://www.case.cwru.edu/

Find an in-depth description at www.petersons.com/gradchannel.

■ THE CATHOLIC UNIVERSITY OF AMERICA

School of Engineering, Washington, DC 20064

AWARDS MBE, MCE, MEE, MME, MS Engr, MSCS, D Engr, PhD. Part-time and evening/weekend programs available.

Faculty: 26 full-time (2 women), 14 part-time/adjunct (2 women).
Students: 21 full-time (2 women), 86 part-time (16 women); includes 16 minority (9 African Americans, 5 Asian Americans or Pacific Islanders, 2 Hispanic Americans), 42 international. Average age 33. 123 applicants, 60% accepted, 17 enrolled. In 2001, 47 master's, 7 doctorates awarded.
Degree requirements: For master's, thesis optional; for doctorate, thesis/dissertation, oral exams, comprehensive exam.
Entrance requirements: For master's, minimum GPA of 3.0. *Application deadline:* For fall admission, 7/31; for spring admission, 12/10. Applications are processed on a rolling basis. *Application fee:* $55. Electronic applications accepted.
Expenses: Contact institution.
Financial support: Fellowships, research assistantships, teaching assistantships, career-related internships or fieldwork, Federal Work-Study, institutionally sponsored loans, tuition waivers (full and

partial), and unspecified assistantships available. Support available to part-time students. Financial award application deadline: 2/1.
Faculty research: Controls, signal processing, multiphase flow, robotics, composite structures.
Dr. Charles C. Nguyen, Dean, 202-319-5160, *Fax:* 202-319-4499.
Application contact: Peggy Wheeler, Administrative Assistant, 202-319-5160, *Fax:* 202-319-4499. *Web site:* http://www.ee.cua.edu/

Find an in-depth description at www.petersons.com/gradchannel.

■ CENTRAL CONNECTICUT STATE UNIVERSITY

School of Graduate Studies, School of Technology, Department of Engineering Technology, New Britain, CT 06050-4010

AWARDS MS. Part-time and evening/weekend programs available.

Entrance requirements: For master's, TOEFL, minimum GPA of 2.7. *Application deadline:* Applications are processed on a rolling basis. *Application fee:* $40.
Expenses: Tuition, state resident: full-time $2,772; part-time $245 per credit. Tuition, nonresident: full-time $7,726; part-time $245 per credit. Required fees: $2,102. Tuition and fees vary according to course level and degree level.
Financial support: Federal Work-Study available. Financial award application deadline: 3/15; financial award applicants required to submit FAFSA.
Dr. John Bean, Chair, 860-832-1825.

■ CENTRAL MISSOURI STATE UNIVERSITY

School of Graduate Studies, College of Applied Sciences and Technology, Warrensburg, MO 64093

AWARDS MS, MSE, Ed S. Part-time programs available.

Faculty: 43 full-time (12 women), 15 part-time/adjunct (5 women).
Students: 45 full-time (16 women), 144 part-time (54 women); includes 16 minority (7 African Americans, 6 Hispanic Americans, 3 Native Americans), 23 international. Average age 35. 71 applicants, 76% accepted. In 2001, 75 master's, 4 other advanced degrees awarded.
Application deadline: Applications are processed on a rolling basis. *Application fee:* $25 ($50 for international students).
Expenses: Tuition, area resident: Full-time $4,200; part-time $175 per credit hour. Tuition, nonresident: full-time $8,352; part-time $348 per credit hour.
Financial support: In 2001–02, 1 fellowship with tuition reimbursement (averaging $12,000 per year), 7 research assistantships

with full and partial tuition reimbursements (averaging $6,386 per year), 35 teaching assistantships with full and partial tuition reimbursements (averaging $6,552 per year) were awarded. Federal Work-Study, scholarships/grants, unspecified assistantships, and administrative and laboratory assistantships also available. Support available to part-time students. Financial award application deadline: 3/1; financial award applicants required to submit FAFSA.
Dr. Alice Greife, Interim Dean, 660-543-4450, *Fax:* 660-543-8031, *E-mail:* greiffe@cmsu1.cmsu.edu. *Web site:* http://www.cmsu.edu

■ CENTRAL WASHINGTON UNIVERSITY

Graduate Studies and Research, College of Education and Professional Studies, Department of Industrial and Engineering Technology, Ellensburg, WA 98926-7463

AWARDS Engineering technology (MS). Part-time programs available.

Faculty: 8 full-time (0 women).
Students: 3 full-time (1 woman), 27 part-time (2 women); includes 8 minority (3 African Americans, 3 Asian Americans or Pacific Islanders, 1 Hispanic American, 1 Native American), 1 international. 20 applicants, 85% accepted, 14 enrolled.
Degree requirements: For master's, thesis or alternative.
Entrance requirements: For master's, minimum GPA of 3.0. *Application deadline:* For fall admission, 4/1 (priority date); for winter admission, 10/1; for spring admission, 1/1. Applications are processed on a rolling basis. *Application fee:* $35.
Expenses: Tuition, state resident: full-time $4,848; part-time $162 per credit. Tuition, nonresident: full-time $14,772; part-time $492 per credit. Required fees: $324.
Financial support: In 2001–02, 1 research assistantship with partial tuition reimbursement (averaging $7,120 per year), 1 teaching assistantship with partial tuition reimbursement (averaging $7,120 per year) were awarded. Career-related internships or fieldwork and Federal Work-Study also available.
Dr. Walter Kaminski, Chair, 509-963-1756.
Application contact: Barbara Sisko, Office Assistant, Graduate Studies and Research, 509-963-3103, *Fax:* 509-963-1799, *E-mail:* masters@cwu.edu.

■ CHRISTIAN BROTHERS UNIVERSITY

Graduate Programs, School of Engineering, Memphis, TN 38104-5581

AWARDS MEM. Part-time and evening/weekend programs available.

Faculty: 3 full-time (0 women), 4 part-time/adjunct (3 women).

Students: 16 full-time (6 women), 34 part-time (6 women); includes 13 minority (11 African Americans, 2 Asian Americans or Pacific Islanders). Average age 32. In 2001, 7 degrees awarded.
Degree requirements: For master's, engineering management project.
Entrance requirements: For master's, GRE. *Application fee:* $25.
Expenses: Tuition: Full-time $4,050; part-time $450 per hour. One-time fee: $50.
Financial support: Institutionally sponsored loans available.
Dr. Sinipong Malasri, Dean, 901-321-3408, *Fax:* 901-321-3494.
Application contact: Dr. Neal Jackson, Director, 901-321-3283, *Fax:* 901-321-3494, *E-mail:* njackson@cbu.edu.

■ CITY COLLEGE OF THE CITY UNIVERSITY OF NEW YORK

Graduate School, School of Engineering, New York, NY 10031-9198
AWARDS ME, MS, PhD. Part-time programs available.

Students: 424; includes 201 minority (45 African Americans, 131 Asian Americans or Pacific Islanders, 25 Hispanic Americans). 521 applicants, 45% accepted. In 2001, 152 degrees awarded.
Degree requirements: For master's, thesis optional; for doctorate, one foreign language, thesis/dissertation, comprehensive exam.
Entrance requirements: For master's, TOEFL; for doctorate, GRE General Test, TOEFL. *Application deadline:* Applications are processed on a rolling basis. *Application fee:* $40.
Expenses: Tuition, state resident: part-time $185 per credit. Tuition, nonresident: part-time $320 per credit. Required fees: $43 per term.
Financial support: Fellowships, research assistantships, teaching assistantships, Federal Work-Study, institutionally sponsored loans, and tuition waivers (full and partial) available. Support available to part-time students.
Dr. Muntaz G. Kassir, Associate Dean for Graduate Studies, 212-650-8030.
Application contact: Graduate Admissions Office, 212-650-6977.
Find an in-depth description at www.petersons.com/gradchannel.

■ CLARKSON UNIVERSITY

Graduate School, School of Engineering, Potsdam, NY 13699
AWARDS ME, MS, PhD. Part-time programs available.

Faculty: 58 full-time (10 women), 5 part-time/adjunct (0 women).
Students: 136 full-time (39 women), 1 part-time; includes 2 minority (1 Asian American or Pacific Islander, 1 Hispanic American), 82 international. Average age

26. 679 applicants, 58% accepted. In 2001, 45 master's, 16 doctorates awarded.
Degree requirements: For master's, thesis; for doctorate, thesis/dissertation, departmental qualifying exam. *Median time to degree:* Master's–1.5 years full-time; doctorate–5 years full-time.
Entrance requirements: For master's, GRE, TOEFL. *Application deadline:* For fall admission, 5/15 (priority date); for spring admission, 10/15 (priority date). Applications are processed on a rolling basis. *Application fee:* $25 ($35 for international students).
Expenses: Tuition: Part-time $714 per credit. Required fees: $108 per semester.
Financial support: In 2001–02, 101 students received support, including 16 fellowships (averaging $20,000 per year), 56 research assistantships (averaging $17,000 per year), 29 teaching assistantships (averaging $17,000 per year). Scholarships/grants and tuition waivers (partial) also available.
Faculty research: Turbulent flow, structural dynamics, fluid dynamics, solid dynamics, electronic manufacturing. *Total annual research expenditures:* $5.2 million.
Dr. Norbert L. Ackermann, Dean, 315-268-6446, *Fax:* 315-268-3841, *E-mail:* nla@clarkson.edu.
Application contact: Donna Brockway, Assistant to Dean/Foreign Student Advisor, 315-268-6447, *Fax:* 315-268-7994, *E-mail:* brockway@clarkson.edu.
Find an in-depth description at www.petersons.com/gradchannel.

■ CLEMSON UNIVERSITY

Graduate School, College of Engineering and Science, Clemson, SC 29634
AWARDS M Engr, MS, PhD. Part-time programs available.

Faculty: 273 full-time (35 women), 13 part-time/adjunct (5 women).
Students: 839 full-time (223 women), 114 part-time (23 women); includes 32 minority (22 African Americans, 4 Asian Americans or Pacific Islanders, 6 Hispanic Americans), 520 international. 2,606 applicants, 47% accepted, 296 enrolled. In 2001, 298 master's, 46 doctorates awarded.
Degree requirements: For doctorate, thesis/dissertation.
Entrance requirements: For master's and doctorate, GRE General Test, TOEFL. *Application fee:* $40. Electronic applications accepted.
Expenses: Tuition, state resident: full-time $5,310. Tuition, nonresident: full-time $11,284.
Financial support: Fellowships, research assistantships, teaching assistantships, career-related internships or fieldwork, institutionally sponsored loans, and unspecified assistantships available. Support available to part-time students. Financial award applicants required to submit FAFSA.

Dr. Thomas M. Keinath, Dean, 864-656-3202, *Fax:* 864-656-0859, *E-mail:* keinath@clemson.edu.
Application contact: Dr. Christian Przirembel, Associate Dean, 864-656-3200, *Fax:* 864-656-0859, *E-mail:* rutgers@clemson.edu. *Web site:* http://www.eng.clemson.edu/
Find an in-depth description at www.petersons.com/gradchannel.

■ CLEVELAND STATE UNIVERSITY

College of Graduate Studies, Fenn College of Engineering, Cleveland, OH 44115
AWARDS MS, D Eng. Part-time and evening/weekend programs available.

Faculty: 46 full-time (3 women), 23 part-time/adjunct (3 women).
Students: 22 full-time (3 women), 217 part-time (41 women); includes 11 minority (3 African Americans, 4 Asian Americans or Pacific Islanders, 4 Hispanic Americans), 157 international. Average age 28. 422 applicants, 69% accepted. In 2001, 29 master's, 9 doctorates awarded.
Degree requirements: For master's, thesis or alternative; for doctorate, thesis/dissertation, candidacy and qualifying exams.
Entrance requirements: For master's, GRE General Test, TOEFL; for doctorate, GRE General Test, TOEFL, BS or MS in engineering. *Application deadline:* For fall admission, 7/15 (priority date). Applications are processed on a rolling basis. *Application fee:* $25. Electronic applications accepted.
Expenses: Tuition, state resident: full-time $6,838; part-time $263 per credit hour. Tuition, nonresident: full-time $13,526; part-time $520 per credit hour.
Financial support: In 2001–02, 34 students received support, including 1 fellowship with full tuition reimbursement available, 17 research assistantships with full tuition reimbursements available (averaging $14,000 per year), 16 teaching assistantships with full and partial tuition reimbursements available (averaging $12,000 per year); career-related internships or fieldwork, Federal Work-Study, institutionally sponsored loans, tuition waivers (full and partial), and unspecified assistantships also available. Support available to part-time students. Financial award application deadline: 3/30.
Faculty research: Structural mechanics, environmental, manufacturing systems, instrumentation and controls, biomedical engineering. *Total annual research expenditures:* $2.7 million.
Dr. John H, Hemann, Interim Dean, 216-687-2555.
Application contact: Dr. Joanne Belovich, Associate Dean, 216-687-2555, *E-mail:*

Cleveland State University (continued)
engineering@csvax.csuohio.edu. *Web site:*
http://csaxp.csuohio.edu/

**Find an in-depth description at
www.petersons.com/gradchannel.**

■ COLORADO SCHOOL OF MINES

Graduate School, Golden, CO 80401-1887

AWARDS ME, MS, PhD, Diplôme d'ingénieur, Diploma. Part-time programs available.

Faculty: 274 full-time (83 women), 34 part-time/adjunct (15 women).
Students: 505 full-time (161 women), 187 part-time (43 women); includes 39 minority (4 African Americans, 19 Asian Americans or Pacific Islanders, 13 Hispanic Americans, 3 Native Americans), 286 international. 777 applicants, 74% accepted, 180 enrolled. In 2001, 136 master's, 48 doctorates awarded. *Median time to degree:* Master's–2 years full-time; doctorate–4 years full-time.
Entrance requirements: For master's, doctorate, and other advanced degree, GRE General Test. *Application deadline:* For fall admission, 12/1 (priority date); for spring admission, 5/1 (priority date). Applications are processed on a rolling basis. *Application fee:* $40. Electronic applications accepted.
Expenses: Tuition, state resident: full-time $4,940; part-time $246 per credit. Tuition, nonresident: full-time $16,070; part-time $803 per credit. Required fees: $341 per semester.
Financial support: In 2001–02, 585 students received support, including 130 fellowships (averaging $4,651 per year), 359 research assistantships (averaging $4,987 per year), 311 teaching assistantships (averaging $5,262 per year); career-related internships or fieldwork, Federal Work-Study, institutionally sponsored loans, and unspecified assistantships also available. Support available to part-time students. Financial award applicants required to submit FAFSA.
Faculty research: Energy, environment, materials, minerals, engineering systems. *Total annual research expenditures:* $20.6 million.
Dr. Phillip R. Romig, Dean of Graduate Studies and Research, 303-273-3247, *Fax:* 303-273-3244, *E-mail:* grad-school@ mines.edu.
Application contact: Linda Powell, Graduate Admissions Officer, 303-273-3248, *Fax:* 303-273-3244, *E-mail:* lpowell@ mines.edu. *Web site:* http://www.mines.edu/

■ COLORADO STATE UNIVERSITY

Graduate School, College of Engineering, Fort Collins, CO 80523-0015

AWARDS M Eng, ME, MS, PhD. Part-time programs available.

Degree requirements: For doctorate, thesis/dissertation.
Entrance requirements: For master's, GRE General Test, TOEFL, minimum GPA of 3.0; for doctorate, GRE General Test, TOEFL. Electronic applications accepted.
Expenses: Tuition, state resident: full-time $2,880; part-time $160 per credit. Tuition, nonresident: full-time $11,412; part-time $634 per credit. Required fees: $750; $34 per credit.
Faculty research: Atmospheric science, optoelectronics, water resources, chemical and bioresource engineering, manufacturing, engine and energy conversion. *Web site:* http://www.engr.colostate.edu/

■ COLUMBIA UNIVERSITY

Fu Foundation School of Engineering and Applied Science, New York, NY 10027

AWARDS ME, MS, Eng Sc D, PhD, CSE, EE, EM, Engr, Met E, MBA/MS. Part-time programs available. Postbaccalaureate distance learning degree programs offered (no on-campus study).

Faculty: 129 full-time (7 women), 65 part-time/adjunct (4 women).
Students: 495 full-time (112 women), 327 part-time (70 women); includes 65 minority (6 African Americans, 54 Asian Americans or Pacific Islanders, 4 Hispanic Americans, 1 Native American), 543 international. Average age 24. 2,959 applicants, 31% accepted, 300 enrolled. In 2001, 276 master's, 64 doctorates awarded. Terminal master's awarded for partial completion of doctoral program.
Degree requirements: For doctorate, thesis/dissertation, qualifying exam.
Entrance requirements: For master's, doctorate, and other advanced degree, GRE General Test, TOEFL. *Application deadline:* For fall admission, 1/5 (priority date); for spring admission, 10/1 (priority date). Applications are processed on a rolling basis. *Application fee:* $55. Electronic applications accepted.
Expenses: Contact institution.
Financial support: In 2001–02, 42 fellowships (averaging $15,000 per year), 209 research assistantships (averaging $15,000 per year), 82 teaching assistantships (averaging $17,000 per year) were awarded. Career-related internships or fieldwork, Federal Work-Study, institutionally sponsored loans, scholarships/grants, unspecified assistantships, and outside fellowships also available. Support available to part-time students. Financial award

application deadline: 1/5; financial award applicants required to submit FAFSA.
Zvi Galil, Dean, 212-854-2993, *Fax:* 212-854-5900, *E-mail:* seasgradmit@ columbia.edu.
Application contact: Thomas P. Rock, Assistant Dean, 212-854-6438, *Fax:* 212-854-5900, *E-mail:* tpr4@columbia.edu. *Web site:* http://www.seas.columbia.edu/

**Find an in-depth description at
www.petersons.com/gradchannel.**

■ CORNELL UNIVERSITY

Graduate School, Graduate Fields of Engineering, Ithaca, NY 14853-0001

AWARDS M Eng, MPS, MS, PhD, M Eng/ MBA.

Faculty: 384 full-time.
Students: 1,037 full-time (196 women); includes 147 minority (9 African Americans, 116 Asian Americans or Pacific Islanders, 20 Hispanic Americans, 2 Native Americans), 556 international. 3,737 applicants, 34% accepted. In 2001, 427 master's, 91 doctorates awarded. Terminal master's awarded for partial completion of doctoral program.
Degree requirements: For doctorate, thesis/dissertation.
Entrance requirements: For master's and doctorate, TOEFL. *Application fee:* $65. Electronic applications accepted.
Expenses: Tuition: Full-time $25,970. Required fees: $50.
Financial support: In 2001–02, 640 students received support, including 168 fellowships with full tuition reimbursements available, 302 research assistantships with full tuition reimbursements available, 170 teaching assistantships with full tuition reimbursements available; career-related internships or fieldwork, institutionally sponsored loans, scholarships/grants, tuition waivers (full and partial), and unspecified assistantships also available. Financial award applicants required to submit FAFSA.
Dr. Harold G Craighead, Interim Dean.
Application contact: Graduate School Application Requests, Caldwell Hall, 607-255-5816. *Web site:* http:// www.gradschool.cornell.edu/

■ DARTMOUTH COLLEGE

Thayer School of Engineering, Hanover, NH 03755

AWARDS MEM, MS, PhD, MBA/MEM, MD/PhD.

Faculty: 33 full-time (4 women), 18 part-time/adjunct (1 woman).
Students: 136 full-time (27 women), 4 part-time; includes 20 minority (4 African Americans, 12 Asian Americans or Pacific Islanders, 4 Hispanic Americans), 57 international. Average age 24. 230 applicants, 43% accepted, 72 enrolled. In 2001, 46 master's, 6 doctorates awarded.
Degree requirements: For doctorate, thesis/dissertation, candidacy oral exam.

Median time to degree: Master's–2 years full-time; doctorate–4 years full-time.
Entrance requirements: For master's and doctorate, GRE General Test. *Application deadline:* For fall admission, 1/1 (priority date). *Application fee:* $40 ($50 for international students). Electronic applications accepted.
Expenses: Tuition: Full-time $26,425.
Financial support: In 2001–02, 4 fellowships with full tuition reimbursements (averaging $16,920 per year), 64 research assistantships with full tuition reimbursements (averaging $18,120 per year), 27 teaching assistantships with partial tuition reimbursements (averaging $5,800 per year) were awarded. Career-related internships or fieldwork, institutionally sponsored loans, scholarships/grants, and tuition waivers (full and partial) also available. Financial award application deadline: 1/15; financial award applicants required to submit CSS PROFILE.
Faculty research: Biomedical engineering, electrical and computer engineering, materials and mechanical engineering, environmental science and engineering, engineering physics. *Total annual research expenditures:* $11.3 million.
Dr. Lewis M. Duncan, Dean, 603-646-2238, *Fax:* 603-646-2580, *E-mail:* lewis.m.duncan@dartmouth.edu.
Application contact: Candace S. Potter, Graduate Admissions Administrator, 603-646-3844, *Fax:* 603-646-1620, *E-mail:* candace.potter@dartmouth.edu. *Web site:* http://engineering.dartmouth.edu/
Find an in-depth description at www.petersons.com/gradchannel.

■ DREXEL UNIVERSITY

Graduate School, College of Engineering, Philadelphia, PA 19104-2875

AWARDS MS, MSEE, PhD. Part-time and evening/weekend programs available.

Faculty: 100 full-time (9 women), 13 part-time/adjunct (1 woman).
Students: 93 full-time (21 women), 374 part-time (66 women); includes 43 minority (12 African Americans, 23 Asian Americans or Pacific Islanders, 7 Hispanic Americans, 1 Native American), 188 international. Average age 31. 909 applicants, 66% accepted, 76 enrolled. In 2001, 117 master's, 15 doctorates awarded.
Degree requirements: For doctorate, thesis/dissertation.
Entrance requirements: For master's and doctorate, TOEFL. *Application deadline:* For fall admission, 8/21. Applications are processed on a rolling basis. *Application fee:* $50. Electronic applications accepted.
Expenses: Tuition: Full-time $20,088; part-time $558 per credit. Required fees: $78 per term. One-time fee: $200. Tuition and fees vary according to course load, degree level and program.
Financial support: Research assistantships, teaching assistantships, career-related

internships or fieldwork, Federal Work-Study, institutionally sponsored loans, tuition waivers (full and partial), and unspecified assistantships available. Support available to part-time students. Financial award application deadline: 2/1. Dr. Selcuk Güçedil;eri, Dean, 215-895-2210.
Application contact: Director of Graduate Admissions, 215-895-6700, *Fax:* 215-895-5939, *E-mail:* enroll@drexel.edu.
Find an in-depth description at www.petersons.com/gradchannel.

■ DUKE UNIVERSITY

Graduate School, School of Engineering, Durham, NC 27708-0586
AWARDS MEM, MS, PhD, JD/MS, MBA/MS. Part-time programs available.

Students: In 2001, 45 master's, 35 doctorates awarded.
Degree requirements: For doctorate, thesis/dissertation.
Entrance requirements: For master's and doctorate, GRE General Test.
Expenses: Tuition: Full-time $24,600.
Financial support: Fellowships, research assistantships, teaching assistantships, Federal Work-Study available. Financial award application deadline: 12/31.
Dr. Kristina M. Johnson, Dean, 919-660-5389, *Fax:* 919-684-4860.

■ EAST CAROLINA UNIVERSITY

Graduate School, School of Industry and Technology, Greenville, NC 27858-4353

AWARDS MS. Part-time programs available.
Faculty: 9 full-time (1 woman), 1 part-time/adjunct (0 women).
Students: 23 full-time (7 women), 116 part-time (21 women); includes 9 minority (7 African Americans, 2 Hispanic Americans), 1 international. Average age 34. 47 applicants, 68% accepted. In 2001, 27 degrees awarded.
Degree requirements: For master's, comprehensive exam.
Application deadline: For fall admission, 6/1 (priority date). Applications are processed on a rolling basis. *Application fee:* $45.
Expenses: Tuition, state resident: full-time $2,636. Tuition, nonresident: full-time $11,365.
Financial support: Fellowships, research assistantships, teaching assistantships, Federal Work-Study available. Support available to part-time students. Financial award application deadline: 6/1.
Dr. Ruben M. Desmond, Dean, 252-328-6704, *Fax:* 252-328-4250, *E-mail:* desmondr@mail.ecu.edu.
Application contact: Dr. Paul D. Tschetter, Senior Associate Dean of the Graduate School, 252-328-6012, *Fax:* 252-328-6071, *E-mail:* gradschool@mail.ecu.edu. *Web site:* http://www.sit.ecu.edu/

■ EASTERN ILLINOIS UNIVERSITY

Graduate School, Lumpkin College of Business and Applied Sciences, School of Technology, Charleston, IL 61920-3099

AWARDS MS. Part-time and evening/weekend programs available.

■ EAST TENNESSEE STATE UNIVERSITY

School of Graduate Studies, College of Applied Science and Technology, Johnson City, TN 37614

AWARDS MS. Part-time and evening/weekend programs available. Postbaccalaureate distance learning degree programs offered (no on-campus study).

Faculty: 28 full-time (6 women).
Students: 74 full-time (25 women), 41 part-time (10 women); includes 6 minority (2 African Americans, 4 Asian Americans or Pacific Islanders), 21 international. Average age 32. In 2001, 48 degrees awarded.
Degree requirements: For master's, exam.
Entrance requirements: For master's, TOEFL. *Application deadline:* Applications are processed on a rolling basis. *Application fee:* $25 ($35 for international students).
Expenses: Tuition, state resident: part-time $181 per hour. Tuition, nonresident: part-time $270 per hour. Required fees: $220 per term.
Financial support: Research assistantships with full tuition reimbursements, teaching assistantships with full tuition reimbursements, career-related internships or fieldwork, Federal Work-Study, scholarships/grants, and unspecified assistantships available. Support available to part-time students. Financial award application deadline: 7/1; financial award applicants required to submit FAFSA.
Faculty research: Total quality management, software engineering. *Total annual research expenditures:* $54,867.
Dr. Carroll Hyder, Interim Dean, 423-439-7500, *Fax:* 423-439-7868, *E-mail:* hyder@etsu.edu. *Web site:* http://www.etsu.edu

■ FAIRFIELD UNIVERSITY

School of Engineering, Fairfield, CT 06824

AWARDS Management of technology (MS). Software engineering (MS). Part-time and evening/weekend programs available.

Faculty: 2 full-time (0 women), 16 part-time/adjunct (2 women).
Students: 9 full-time (2 women), 215 part-time (43 women); includes 35 minority (8 African Americans, 21 Asian Americans or Pacific Islanders, 6 Hispanic Americans),

Fairfield University (continued)
39 international. 53 applicants, 100% accepted, 42 enrolled. In 2001, 47 degrees awarded.
Degree requirements: For master's, thesis, final exam.
Entrance requirements: For master's, interview, minimum GPA of 2.8. *Application deadline:* For fall admission, 6/30 (priority date). Applications are processed on a rolling basis. *Application fee:* $55.
Expenses: Contact institution.
Financial support: Tuition waivers (partial) available. Financial award applicants required to submit FAFSA.
Faculty research: Vehicle dynamics, image processing, digital signal processing, modeling, multimedia.
Dr. Evangelos Hadjimichael, Dean, 203-254-4000 Ext. 4147, *Fax:* 203-254-4013, *E-mail:* hadjm@fair1.fairfield.edu.
Application contact: Dr. Richard G. Weber, Associate Dean, 203-254-4000 Ext. 4147, *Fax:* 203-254-4013, *E-mail:* rweber@fair1.fairfield.edu. *Web site:* http://www.fairfield.edu/

Find an in-depth description at www.petersons.com/gradchannel.

■ FAIRLEIGH DICKINSON UNIVERSITY, METROPOLITAN CAMPUS

University College: Arts, Sciences, and Professional Studies, School of Engineering and Engineering Technology, Teaneck, NJ 07666-1914

AWARDS Computer engineering (MS); electrical engineering (MSEE).

Students: 85 full-time (8 women), 16 part-time (3 women); includes 5 minority (1 African American, 3 Asian Americans or Pacific Islanders, 1 Hispanic American), 86 international. Average age 26. 300 applicants, 87% accepted, 50 enrolled. In 2001, 10 degrees awarded.
Application deadline: Applications are processed on a rolling basis. *Application fee:* $40.
Expenses: Tuition: Full-time $11,484; part-time $638 per credit. Required fees: $420; $97.
Dr. Alfredo Tan, Director, 201-692-2347, *Fax:* 201-692-2130, *E-mail:* tan@fdu.edu.

Find an in-depth description at www.petersons.com/gradchannel.

■ FLORIDA AGRICULTURAL AND MECHANICAL UNIVERSITY

Division of Graduate Studies, Research, and Continuing Education, FAMU-FSU College of Engineering, Tallahassee, FL 32307-3200

AWARDS MS, PhD. College administered jointly by Florida State University.

Entrance requirements: For master's, GRE General Test, minimum GPA of 3.0.

■ FLORIDA ATLANTIC UNIVERSITY

College of Engineering, Boca Raton, FL 33431-0991

AWARDS MS, PhD. Part-time and evening/weekend programs available. Postbaccalaureate distance learning degree programs offered (minimal on-campus study).

Faculty: 70 full-time (4 women), 5 part-time/adjunct (0 women).
Students: 189 full-time (58 women), 123 part-time (23 women); includes 63 minority (10 African Americans, 30 Asian Americans or Pacific Islanders, 23 Hispanic Americans), 180 international. Average age 30. 490 applicants, 69% accepted, 95 enrolled. In 2001, 106 master's, 12 doctorates awarded. Terminal master's awarded for partial completion of doctoral program.
Degree requirements: For master's, thesis optional; for doctorate, thesis/dissertation, qualifying exam.
Entrance requirements: For master's, GRE General Test, TOEFL, minimum GPA of 3.0; for doctorate, GRE General Test, TOEFL. *Application deadline:* Applications are processed on a rolling basis. *Application fee:* $20.
Expenses: Tuition, state resident: full-time $3,098; part-time $172 per credit. Tuition, nonresident: full-time $10,427; part-time $579 per credit.
Financial support: In 2001–02, research assistantships with partial tuition reimbursements (averaging $15,000 per year), teaching assistantships with partial tuition reimbursements (averaging $15,000 per year) were awarded. Fellowships, career-related internships or fieldwork, Federal Work-Study, and unspecified assistantships also available. Support available to part-time students. Financial award applicants required to submit FAFSA.
Faculty research: Automated underwater vehicles, communication systems, computer networks, materials, neural networks. *Total annual research expenditures:* $10,782.
Dr. Karl Stevens, Interim Dean, 561-297-3400, *Fax:* 561-297-2659, *E-mail:* stevens@fau.edu. *Web site:* http://www.eng.fau.edu/index.htm

■ FLORIDA INSTITUTE OF TECHNOLOGY

Graduate Programs, College of Engineering, Melbourne, FL 32901-6975

AWARDS MS, PhD. Part-time and evening/weekend programs available.

Faculty: 65 full-time (3 women), 23 part-time/adjunct (3 women).
Students: 145 full-time (32 women), 326 part-time (73 women); includes 49 minority (10 African Americans, 17 Asian Americans or Pacific Islanders, 22 Hispanic Americans), 231 international.

Average age 30. 1,146 applicants, 54% accepted. In 2001, 105 master's, 6 doctorates awarded. Terminal master's awarded for partial completion of doctoral program.
Degree requirements: For doctorate, thesis/dissertation, comprehensive exam.
Entrance requirements: For master's, minimum GPA of 3.0. *Application deadline:* Applications are processed on a rolling basis. *Application fee:* $50. Electronic applications accepted.
Expenses: Tuition: Part-time $650 per credit.
Financial support: In 2001–02, 125 students received support, including 2 fellowships with full and partial tuition reimbursements available (averaging $13,000 per year), 60 research assistantships with full and partial tuition reimbursements available (averaging $8,398 per year), 64 teaching assistantships with full and partial tuition reimbursements available (averaging $9,120 per year); career-related internships or fieldwork, institutionally sponsored loans, and tuition remissions also available. Financial award application deadline: 3/1; financial award applicants required to submit FAFSA.
Faculty research: Electrical and computer science and engineering; aerospace, chemical, civil, mechanical, and ocean engineering; environmental science and oceanography. *Total annual research expenditures:* $3.9 million.
Dr. J. Ronald Bailey, Dean, 321-674-7318, *Fax:* 321-674-7270, *E-mail:* jrbailey@fit.edu.
Application contact: Carolyn P. Farrior, Director of Graduate Admissions, 321-674-7118, *Fax:* 321-723-9468, *E-mail:* cfarrior@fit.edu. *Web site:* http://www.fit.edu/

■ FLORIDA INTERNATIONAL UNIVERSITY

College of Engineering, Miami, FL 33199

AWARDS MS, PhD. Part-time and evening/weekend programs available.

Faculty: 53 full-time (6 women).
Students: 226 full-time (38 women), 179 part-time (46 women); includes 142 minority (15 African Americans, 7 Asian Americans or Pacific Islanders, 120 Hispanic Americans), 222 international. Average age 32. 758 applicants, 46% accepted, 125 enrolled. In 2001, 76 master's, 5 doctorates awarded.
Degree requirements: For doctorate, thesis/dissertation.
Entrance requirements: For master's and doctorate, GRE General Test, TOEFL. *Application deadline:* For fall admission, 4/1 (priority date); for spring admission, 10/1. Applications are processed on a rolling basis. *Application fee:* $20.
Expenses: Tuition, state resident: full-time $2,916; part-time $162 per credit hour. Tuition, nonresident: full-time $10,245;

part-time $569 per credit hour. Required fees: $168 per term.

Financial support: Fellowships, research assistantships, teaching assistantships, career-related internships or fieldwork, Federal Work-Study, and institutionally sponsored loans available.

Dr. Vish Prasad, Acting Dean, 305-348-6050, *Fax:* 305-348-1401, *E-mail:* prasad@fiu.edu.

■ FLORIDA STATE UNIVERSITY

Graduate Studies, FAMU/FSU College of Engineering, Tallahassee, FL 32306

AWARDS MS, PhD. Part-time programs available. Postbaccalaureate distance learning degree programs offered (minimal on-campus study).

Degree requirements: For doctorate, thesis/dissertation, preliminary exam, qualifying exam.

Entrance requirements: For master's and doctorate, GRE General Test. Electronic applications accepted.

Expenses: Tuition, state resident: part-time $163 per credit hour. Tuition, nonresident: part-time $570 per credit hour. Tuition and fees vary according to program.

Faculty research: Fluid mechanics, aerodynamics, electromagnetics, digital signal processing, polymer processing. *Web site:* http://www.eng.fsu.edu/

■ GANNON UNIVERSITY

School of Graduate Studies, College of Sciences, Engineering, and Health Sciences, School of Engineering and Computer Science, Program in Engineering, Erie, PA 16541-0001

AWARDS Electrical engineering (MS); embedded software engineering (MS); mechanical engineering (MS). Part-time and evening/weekend programs available.

Degree requirements: For master's, thesis or alternative, comprehensive exam.

Entrance requirements: For master's, GRE Subject Test, bachelor's degree in engineering, minimum QPA of 2.5. *Web site:* http://www.gannon.edu/

■ GEORGE MASON UNIVERSITY

School of Information Technology and Engineering, Fairfax, VA 22030-4444

AWARDS MS, PhD. Part-time and evening/weekend programs available.

Faculty: 100 full-time (15 women), 68 part-time/adjunct (12 women).

Students: 345 full-time (130 women), 1,582 part-time (438 women); includes 464 minority (106 African Americans, 309 Asian Americans or Pacific Islanders, 45 Hispanic Americans, 4 Native Americans), 608 international. Average age 32. 1,531 applicants, 71% accepted, 658 enrolled. In 2001, 322 master's, 29 doctorates awarded.

Degree requirements: For master's, thesis optional; for doctorate, thesis/dissertation, comprehensive oral and written exams.

Entrance requirements: For master's, TOEFL, minimum GPA of 3.0 in last 60 hours; for doctorate, GRE General Test, TOEFL, minimum graduate GPA of 3.5. *Application deadline:* For fall admission, 5/1; for spring admission, 11/1. *Application fee:* $30. Electronic applications accepted.

Expenses: Tuition, state resident: full-time $3,168; part-time $132 per credit hour. Tuition, nonresident: full-time $11,280; part-time $470 per credit hour. Required fees: $1,416; $59 per credit hour.

Financial support: Fellowships, research assistantships, teaching assistantships, career-related internships or fieldwork, Federal Work-Study, institutionally sponsored loans, and unspecified assistantships available. Support available to part-time students. Financial award application deadline: 3/1; financial award applicants required to submit FAFSA.

Faculty research: Systems management, quality assurance, decision support systems, cognitive ergonomics. *Total annual research expenditures:* $8.9 million.

Lloyd Griffiths, Dean, 703-993-1500, *Fax:* 703-993-1734, *E-mail:* lgriffiths@gmu.edu.

Application contact: Dr. Stephen G. Nash, Information Contact, 703-993-1505, *Fax:* 703-993-1734, *E-mail:* itegrad@gmu.edu. *Web site:* http://ite.gmu.edu/

Find an in-depth description at www.petersons.com/gradchannel.

■ THE GEORGE WASHINGTON UNIVERSITY

School of Engineering and Applied Science, Washington, DC 20052

AWARDS MEM, MS, D Sc, App Sc, Engr, MEM/MS. Part-time and evening/weekend programs available.

Faculty: 76 full-time (10 women), 83 part-time/adjunct (5 women).

Students: 435 full-time (98 women), 1,138 part-time (316 women); includes 309 minority (131 African Americans, 122 Asian Americans or Pacific Islanders, 51 Hispanic Americans, 5 Native Americans), 515 international. Average age 34. 963 applicants, 90% accepted. In 2001, 381 master's, 13 doctorates, 2 other advanced degrees awarded.

Degree requirements: For master's, thesis optional; for doctorate, thesis/dissertation, qualifying exam.

Entrance requirements: For master's, TOEFL or George Washington University English as a Foreign Language Test, appropriate bachelor's degree; for doctorate, TOEFL or George Washington University English as a Foreign Language Test, appropriate bachelor's or master's degree, GRE required if highest earned degree is BS; for other advanced degree, TOEFL or George Washington University English as a Foreign Language Test, appropriate master's degree. *Application deadline:* For fall admission, 3/1; for spring admission, 10/1. Applications are processed on a rolling basis. *Application fee:* $55.

Expenses: Tuition: Part-time $810 per credit. Required fees: $1 per credit.

Financial support: In 2001–02, 77 fellowships with full and partial tuition reimbursements (averaging $6,200 per year), 133 research assistantships with full and partial tuition reimbursements, 71 teaching assistantships with full and partial tuition reimbursements (averaging $3,800 per year) were awarded. Career-related internships or fieldwork, Federal Work-Study, institutionally sponsored loans, and tuition waivers (full and partial) also available. Financial award application deadline: 3/1; financial award applicants required to submit FAFSA.

Faculty research: Fatigue fracture and structural reliability, computer-integrated manufacturing, materials engineering, artificial intelligence and expert systems, quality assurance. *Total annual research expenditures:* $6.3 million.

Dr. Timothy Tong, Dean, 202-994-6080, *Fax:* 202-994-4522, *E-mail:* tong@seas.gwu.edu.

Application contact: Howard M. Davis, Manager, Office of Admissions and Student Records, 202-994-6158, *Fax:* 202-994-0909, *E-mail:* data:adms@seas.gwu.edu. *Web site:* http://www.seas.gwu.edu/

Find an in-depth description at www.petersons.com/gradchannel.

■ GEORGIA INSTITUTE OF TECHNOLOGY

Graduate Studies and Research, College of Engineering, Atlanta, GA 30332-0001

AWARDS MS, MS Bio E, MS Ch E, MS Env E, MS Poly, MS Stat, MS Text, MSAE, MSCE, MSEE, MSESM, MSHP, MSHS, MSIE, MSME, MSMSE, MSNE, MSOR, MST Ch, MSTE, PhD, Certificate, MCP/MSCE, MD/PhD. Part-time programs available. Postbaccalaureate distance learning degree programs offered. Terminal master's awarded for partial completion of doctoral program.

Degree requirements: For doctorate, thesis/dissertation.

Entrance requirements: For master's and doctorate, TOEFL. Electronic applications accepted.

■ GEORGIA SOUTHERN UNIVERSITY

Jack N. Averitt College of Graduate Studies, Allen E. Paulson College of Science and Technology, School of Technology, Statesboro, GA 30460

AWARDS M Tech. Part-time and evening/weekend programs available.

Georgia Southern University (continued)
Faculty: 13 full-time (0 women), 1 part-time/adjunct (0 women).
Students: 13 full-time (7 women), 12 part-time (6 women); includes 4 minority (2 African Americans, 2 Asian Americans or Pacific Islanders). Average age 31. 10 applicants, 100% accepted, 9 enrolled. In 2001, 3 degrees awarded.
Degree requirements: For master's, thesis, terminal exam.
Entrance requirements: For master's, GRE General Test, minimum GPA of 2.5. *Application deadline:* For fall admission, 7/1 (priority date); for spring admission, 11/15 (priority date). Applications are processed on a rolling basis. *Application fee:* $0. Electronic applications accepted.
Expenses: Tuition, state resident: full-time $1,746; part-time $97 per credit hour. Tuition, nonresident: full-time $6,966; part-time $387 per credit hour. Required fees: $294 per semester.
Financial support: In 2001–02, 8 students received support, including 3 research assistantships with tuition reimbursements available (averaging $5,700 per year); career-related internships or fieldwork and unspecified assistantships also available. Financial award application deadline: 4/15; financial award applicants required to submit FAFSA.
Faculty research: Ergonomics, imaging science, printability, productivity, manufacturing technology. *Total annual research expenditures:* $62,330.
Dr. John Wallace, Director, 912-681-5761, *Fax:* 912-871-1455, *E-mail:* wallacej@gasou.edu.
Application contact: Dr. John R. Diebolt, Associate Graduate Dean, 912-681-5384, *Fax:* 912-681-0740, *E-mail:* gradschool@gasou.edu. *Web site:* http://www2.gasou.edu/cost/sot/School_of_Technology.html

■ GOLDEN GATE UNIVERSITY

School of Technology and Industry, San Francisco, CA 94105-2968

AWARDS Hospitality administration and tourism (MS); information systems (MS, Certificate); telecommunications management (MS, Certificate). Part-time and evening/weekend programs available.

Entrance requirements: For master's, GMAT (MBA), TOEFL, minimum GPA of 2.5.

■ GRADUATE SCHOOL AND UNIVERSITY CENTER OF THE CITY UNIVERSITY OF NEW YORK

Graduate Studies, Program in Engineering, New York, NY 10016-4039

AWARDS Chemical engineering (PhD); civil engineering (PhD); electrical engineering (PhD); mechanical engineering (PhD).

Faculty: 68 full-time (1 woman).

Students: 125 full-time (28 women), 6 part-time (1 woman); includes 13 minority (9 African Americans, 2 Asian Americans or Pacific Islanders, 2 Hispanic Americans), 95 international. Average age 32. 205 applicants, 63% accepted, 26 enrolled. In 2001, 22 degrees awarded.
Degree requirements: For doctorate, thesis/dissertation.
Entrance requirements: For doctorate, GRE General Test. *Application deadline:* For fall admission, 4/15. *Application fee:* $40.
Expenses: Tuition, state resident: part-time $245 per credit. Tuition, nonresident: part-time $425 per credit. Required fees: $72 per semester.
Financial support: In 2001–02, 67 students received support, including 64 fellowships; research assistantships, teaching assistantships, Federal Work-Study, institutionally sponsored loans, and tuition waivers (full and partial) also available. Financial award application deadline: 2/1; financial award applicants required to submit FAFSA.
Dr. Mumtaz Kassir, Acting Executive Officer, 212-650-8031, *Fax:* 212-650-8029, *E-mail:* kassir@ce-mail.engr.ccny.cuny.edu.
Find an in-depth description at www.petersons.com/gradchannel.

■ GRAND VALLEY STATE UNIVERSITY

Science and Mathematics Division, Seymour and Esther Padnos School of Engineering, Allendale, MI 49401-9403

AWARDS Manufacturing engineering (MSE); manufacturing operations (MSE); mechanical engineering (MSE). Part-time programs available.

Faculty: 10 full-time (1 woman), 3 part-time/adjunct (1 woman).
Students: 5 full-time (1 woman), 42 part-time (7 women); includes 4 minority (1 African American, 2 Asian Americans or Pacific Islanders, 1 Hispanic American), 2 international. Average age 31. 37 applicants, 57% accepted, 15 enrolled. In 2001, 2 degrees awarded.
Degree requirements: For master's, project. *Median time to degree:* Master's–3 years part-time.
Entrance requirements: For master's, engineering degree with minimum GPA of 3.0. *Application deadline:* Applications are processed on a rolling basis. *Application fee:* $20.
Expenses: Tuition, state resident: part-time $202 per credit hour. Tuition, nonresident: part-time $437 per credit hour.
Financial support: In 2001–02, 2 research assistantships with full tuition reimbursements (averaging $11,000 per year), 3 teaching assistantships with full tuition reimbursements (averaging $8,000 per

year) were awarded. Career-related internships or fieldwork, Federal Work-Study, institutionally sponsored loans, scholarships/grants, and unspecified assistantships also available.
Faculty research: Digital signal processing, computer aided design, computer aided manufacturing, manufacturing simulation, biomechanics. *Total annual research expenditures:* $300,000.
Dr. Paul Plotkowski, Director, 616-771-6750, *Fax:* 616-336-7215, *E-mail:* plotkowp@gvsu.edu.
Application contact: Dr. Hugh Jack, Graduate Coordinator, 616-771-6750, *Fax:* 616-336-7215, *E-mail:* jackh@gvsu.edu. *Web site:* http://www.engineer.gvsu.edu/

■ HARVARD UNIVERSITY

Graduate School of Arts and Sciences, Division of Engineering and Applied Sciences, Cambridge, MA 02138

AWARDS Applied mathematics (ME, SM, PhD); applied physics (ME, SM, PhD); computer science (ME, SM, PhD); computing technology (PhD); engineering science (ME); engineering sciences (SM, PhD); medical engineering/medical physics (PhD, Sc D), including applied physics (PhD), engineering sciences (PhD), medical engineering/medical physics (Sc D), physics (PhD). Terminal master's awarded for partial completion of doctoral program.

Degree requirements: For doctorate, thesis/dissertation.
Entrance requirements: For master's and doctorate, GRE General Test, GRE Subject Test, TOEFL.
Expenses: Tuition: Full-time $23,370. Required fees: $816. Full-time tuition and fees vary according to program and student level. *Web site:* http://www.deas.harvard.edu/

Find an in-depth description at www.petersons.com/gradchannel.

■ HOWARD UNIVERSITY

College of Engineering, Architecture, and Computer Sciences, School of Engineering and Computer Science, Washington, DC 20059-0002

AWARDS M Eng, MCS, MS, PhD. Part-time programs available.

Faculty: 44 full-time (4 women), 12 part-time/adjunct (1 woman).
Students: 50 full-time (19 women), 36 part-time (11 women); includes 42 minority (38 African Americans, 1 Asian American or Pacific Islander, 2 Hispanic Americans, 1 Native American), 44 international. 125 applicants, 50% accepted, 18 enrolled. In 2001, 16 master's, 4 doctorates awarded. Terminal master's awarded for partial completion of doctoral program.

Degree requirements: For doctorate, one foreign language, thesis/dissertation, preliminary exam.
Entrance requirements: For master's and doctorate, GRE General Test, TOEFL, minimum GPA of 3.0. *Application deadline:* For fall admission, 4/1; for spring admission, 11/1. Applications are processed on a rolling basis. *Application fee:* $45. Electronic applications accepted.
Financial support: In 2001–02, 20 research assistantships with full tuition reimbursements, 14 teaching assistantships with full and partial tuition reimbursements were awarded. Fellowships with full tuition reimbursements, career-related internships or fieldwork, institutionally sponsored loans, scholarships/grants, and unspecified assistantships also available. Financial award application deadline: 4/1; financial award applicants required to submit FAFSA.
Faculty research: Environmental engineering, solid-state electronics, dynamics and control of large flexible space structures, power systems, reaction kinetics. *Total annual research expenditures:* $9.3 million. *Web site:* http://www.howard.edu/

■ IDAHO STATE UNIVERSITY

Office of Graduate Studies, College of Engineering, Pocatello, ID 83209

AWARDS Engineering and applied science (PhD); engineering structures and mechanics (MS); environmental engineering (MS); measurement and control engineering (MS); nuclear science and engineering (MS); waste management and environmental science (MS). Part-time programs available.

Faculty: 13 full-time (0 women), 1 part-time/adjunct (0 women).
Students: 34 full-time (8 women), 18 part-time (1 woman); includes 7 minority (1 African American, 5 Asian Americans or Pacific Islanders, 1 Hispanic American), 15 international. Average age 34. In 2001, 12 master's, 1 doctorate awarded.
Degree requirements: For master's and doctorate, thesis/dissertation.
Entrance requirements: For master's and doctorate, GRE General Test, TOEFL. *Application deadline:* For fall admission, 7/1 (priority date); for spring admission, 12/1. Applications are processed on a rolling basis. *Application fee:* $35.
Expenses: Tuition, area resident: Full-time $3,432. Tuition, state resident: part-time $172 per credit. Tuition, nonresident: full-time $10,196; part-time $262 per credit. International tuition: $9,672 full-time. Part-time tuition and fees vary according to course load, program and reciprocity agreements.
Financial support: In 2001–02, 7 research assistantships with full and partial tuition reimbursements (averaging $10,740 per year), 16 teaching assistantships with full and partial tuition reimbursements (averaging $6,775 per year) were awarded. Federal

Work-Study and institutionally sponsored loans also available. Support available to part-time students. Financial award application deadline: 2/15.
Faculty research: Isotope separation, control technology, two-phase flow, photosynolysis, criticality calculations. *Total annual research expenditures:* $293,915. Dr. Jay Kunze, Dean, 208-282-2902, *Fax:* 208-282-4538. *Web site:* http://www.coe.isu.edu/engrg/

■ ILLINOIS INSTITUTE OF TECHNOLOGY

Graduate College, Armour College of Engineering and Sciences, Chicago, IL 60616-3793

AWARDS M Ch E, M Chem, M Eng, M Env E, M Geoenv E, M Trans E, MAC, MCEM, MECE, MGE, MHP, MMAE, MME, MMME, MPA, MPW, MS, MSE, MST, MTSE, PhD, JD/MPA, MBA/MPA. Part-time and evening/weekend programs available. Postbaccalaureate distance learning degree programs offered (no on-campus study).

Faculty: 153 full-time (18 women), 85 part-time/adjunct (10 women).
Students: 794 full-time (164 women), 1,010 part-time (227 women); includes 189 minority (37 African Americans, 117 Asian Americans or Pacific Islanders, 34 Hispanic Americans, 1 Native American), 1,227 international. Average age 28. 4,568 applicants, 53% accepted. In 2001, 488 master's, 38 doctorates awarded. Terminal master's awarded for partial completion of doctoral program.
Degree requirements: For master's, thesis (for some programs), comprehensive exam; for doctorate, thesis/dissertation, comprehensive exam.
Entrance requirements: For master's, GRE General Test; for doctorate, GRE General Test, TOEFL, minimum undergraduate GPA of 3.0. *Application deadline:* For fall admission, 7/1; for spring admission, 11/1. Applications are processed on a rolling basis. *Application fee:* $30. Electronic applications accepted.
Expenses: Tuition: Part-time $590 per credit hour.
Financial support: In 2001–02, 12 fellowships, 90 research assistantships, 129 teaching assistantships were awarded. Career-related internships or fieldwork, Federal Work-Study, institutionally sponsored loans, scholarships/grants, and unspecified assistantships also available. Support available to part-time students. Financial award application deadline: 3/1; financial award applicants required to submit FAFSA.
Faculty research: Polymers, wastewater control, soil-structure interaction, digital and computer systems, fluid dynamics. *Total annual research expenditures:* $13.1 million.
Dr. Allan Myerson, Dean, 312-567-3163, *Fax:* 312-567-7018, *E-mail:* myerson@iit.edu.

Application contact: Dr. Ali Cinar, Dean of Graduate College, 312-567-3637, *Fax:* 312-567-7517, *E-mail:* gradstu@iit.edu. *Web site:* http://www.armour.iit.edu/

■ INDIANA STATE UNIVERSITY

School of Graduate Studies, School of Technology, Terre Haute, IN 47809-1401

AWARDS MA, MS, PhD.

Degree requirements: For doctorate, thesis/dissertation.
Entrance requirements: For master's, TOEFL, bachelor's degree in industrial technology or related field, minimum undergraduate GPA of 2.5; for doctorate, GRE General Test. Electronic applications accepted.

■ INDIANA UNIVERSITY–PURDUE UNIVERSITY FORT WAYNE

School of Engineering, Technology, and Computer Science, Fort Wayne, IN 46805-1499

AWARDS MS. Part-time programs available.

Faculty: 4 full-time (0 women).
Students: 2 full-time (1 woman), 27 part-time (8 women); includes 4 minority (3 Asian Americans or Pacific Islanders, 1 Hispanic American), 3 international. Average age 36. 22 applicants, 68% accepted, 12 enrolled. In 2001, 6 degrees awarded.
Entrance requirements: For master's, GRE, minimum GPA of 3.0. *Application deadline:* For fall admission, 8/1 (priority date); for spring admission, 11/1. Applications are processed on a rolling basis. *Application fee:* $30.
Expenses: Tuition, state resident: full-time $2,845; part-time $158 per credit hour. Tuition, nonresident: full-time $6,323; part-time $351 per credit hour. Required fees: $9 per credit hour. Tuition and fees vary according to course load.
Financial support: In 2001–02, teaching assistantships (averaging $7,350 per year); career-related internships or fieldwork, Federal Work-Study, scholarships/grants, and unspecified assistantships also available. Support available to part-time students. Financial award application deadline: 3/1; financial award applicants required to submit FAFSA.
Faculty research: Antenna theory, two-phase heat transfer, experimental stress analysis, power electronics and motor drives. *Total annual research expenditures:* $23,127.
Dr. C. Wayne Unsell, Dean, Interim, 260-481-6839, *Fax:* 260-481-5734, *E-mail:* unsell@ipfw.edu.
Application contact: Dr. David Erbach, Chair of Computer Science, 260-481-6867, *Fax:* 260-481-5734, *E-mail:* erbach@ipfw.edu. *Web site:* http://www.engr.ipfw.edu/

■ INDIANA UNIVERSITY–PURDUE UNIVERSITY INDIANAPOLIS

School of Engineering and Technology, Interdisciplinary Program in Engineering, Indianapolis, IN 46202-2896

AWARDS MS, MSE. Part-time and evening/weekend programs available.

Students: 1 full-time (0 women), 1 international. Average age 22.
Degree requirements: For master's, thesis optional.
Entrance requirements: For master's, GRE, TOEFL, minimum B average. *Application deadline:* For fall admission, 7/1. *Application fee:* $45 ($55 for international students).
Expenses: Tuition, state resident: full-time $4,480; part-time $187 per credit. Tuition, nonresident: full-time $12,926; part-time $539 per credit. Required fees: $177.
Financial support: In 2001–02, 1 student received support; fellowships with tuition reimbursements available, research assistantships with tuition reimbursements available, Federal Work-Study and tuition waivers (partial) available. Support available to part-time students. Financial award application deadline: 3/1.
Faculty research: Computational fluid dynamics, heat and mass transfer, robotics and automation, signal processing, biomechanics.
Nasser Paydar, Associate Dean for Academic Programs, 317-274-9716, *Fax:* 317-274-4567.
Application contact: Valerie Lim, Graduate Program, 317-278-4960, *Fax:* 317-278-1671, *E-mail:* grad@engr.iupui.edu. *Web site:* http://www.engr.iupui.edu

■ IOWA STATE UNIVERSITY OF SCIENCE AND TECHNOLOGY

Graduate College, College of Engineering, Ames, IA 50011

AWARDS M Eng, MS, PhD. Part-time programs available.

Faculty: 218 full-time, 18 part-time/adjunct.
Students: 506 full-time (94 women), 234 part-time (35 women); includes 23 minority (11 African Americans, 7 Asian Americans or Pacific Islanders, 5 Hispanic Americans), 446 international. 1,870 applicants, 19% accepted, 163 enrolled. In 2001, 145 master's, 42 doctorates awarded.
Degree requirements: For doctorate, thesis/dissertation.
Application fee: $20 ($50 for international students). Electronic applications accepted.
Expenses: Tuition, state resident: full-time $1,851. Tuition, nonresident: full-time $5,449. Tuition and fees vary according to program.
Financial support: In 2001–02, 398 research assistantships with partial tuition reimbursements (averaging $14,220 per year), 126 teaching assistantships with

partial tuition reimbursements (averaging $11,758 per year) were awarded. Fellowships, Federal Work-Study, scholarships/grants, health care benefits, and unspecified assistantships also available. Support available to part-time students. Dr. James L. Melsa, Dean, 515-294-5933, *E-mail:* melsa@iastate.edu.
Application contact: Nancy Knight, Information Contact, 515-294-3241. *Web site:* http://www1.eng.iastate.edu/coe/grad.asp/

Find an in-depth description at www.petersons.com/gradchannel.

■ JOHNS HOPKINS UNIVERSITY

G. W. C. Whiting School of Engineering, Baltimore, MD 21218-2699

AWARDS M Mat SE, MA, MCE, MS, MSE, PhD, MD/PhD. Part-time and evening/weekend programs available.

Faculty: 123 full-time (11 women), 43 part-time/adjunct (2 women).
Students: 449 full-time (124 women), 23 part-time (3 women); includes 33 minority (5 African Americans, 19 Asian Americans or Pacific Islanders, 9 Hispanic Americans), 257 international. Average age 27. 1,743 applicants, 19% accepted, 168 enrolled. In 2001, 137 master's, 46 doctorates awarded. Terminal master's awarded for partial completion of doctoral program.
Degree requirements: For doctorate, thesis/dissertation, oral exam.
Entrance requirements: For master's and doctorate, GRE General Test, TOEFL. *Application fee:* $0. Electronic applications accepted.
Expenses: Tuition: Full-time $27,390.
Financial support: In 2001–02, 463 students received support, including 103 fellowships with full and partial tuition reimbursements available (averaging $17,041 per year), 200 research assistantships with full tuition reimbursements available (averaging $16,825 per year), 68 teaching assistantships with full and partial tuition reimbursements available (averaging $15,787 per year); Federal Work-Study, institutionally sponsored loans, scholarships/grants, tuition waivers (full), unspecified assistantships, and training grants also available. Support available to part-time students. Financial award applicants required to submit FAFSA.
Faculty research: Biomedical engineering, environmental systems and engineering, materials science and engineering, signal and image processing, structural dynamics and geomechanics. *Total annual research expenditures:* $19.4 million.
Dr. Ilene J. Busch-Vishniac, Dean, 410-516-8350 Ext. 3, *Fax:* 410-516-8627, *E-mail:* jeannie@jhu.edu. *Web site:* http://www.jhu.edu/~wsel/indexf.html

Find an in-depth description at www.petersons.com/gradchannel.

■ KANSAS STATE UNIVERSITY

Graduate School, College of Engineering, Manhattan, KS 66506

AWARDS MEM, MS, MSE, PhD. Part-time programs available. Postbaccalaureate distance learning degree programs offered (minimal on-campus study).

Faculty: 134.
Students: 332 full-time (82 women), 134 part-time (20 women); includes 9 minority (7 Asian Americans or Pacific Islanders, 2 Hispanic Americans), 310 international. 1,349 applicants, 31% accepted, 159 enrolled. In 2001, 93 master's, 18 doctorates awarded.
Entrance requirements: For master's and doctorate, GRE, TOEFL. *Application deadline:* Applications are processed on a rolling basis. *Application fee:* $0 ($25 for international students). Electronic applications accepted.
Expenses: Tuition, state resident: part-time $113 per credit hour. Tuition, nonresident: part-time $358 per credit hour.
Financial support: In 2001–02, 160 research assistantships (averaging $12,476 per year), 52 teaching assistantships (averaging $12,555 per year) were awarded. Fellowships, career-related internships or fieldwork, Federal Work-Study, institutionally sponsored loans, and scholarships/grants also available. Support available to part-time students. Financial award application deadline: 3/1; financial award applicants required to submit FAFSA. *Total annual research expenditures:* $14.5 million.
Terry S. King, Dean, 785-532-5590, *Fax:* 785-532-7810, *E-mail:* tsking@ksu.edu.
Application contact: Jan Rundquist, Secretary, 785-532-5846, *Fax:* 785-532-7810, *E-mail:* janr@ksu.edu. *Web site:* http://www.engg.ksu.edu/

Find an in-depth description at www.petersons.com/gradchannel.

■ KENT STATE UNIVERSITY

School of Technology, Kent, OH 44242-0001

AWARDS MA.

Degree requirements: For master's, thesis optional.
Entrance requirements: For master's, minimum GPA of 2.75.

■ KETTERING UNIVERSITY

Graduate School, Flint, MI 48504-4898

AWARDS MS Eng, MSMM, MSMO, MSOM. Part-time and evening/weekend programs available. Postbaccalaureate distance learning degree programs offered (no on-campus study).

Faculty: 35 full-time (5 women).
Students: 9 full-time (2 women), 684 part-time (187 women); includes 88 minority (63 African Americans, 13 Asian Americans

or Pacific Islanders, 11 Hispanic Americans, 1 Native American), 55 international. 437 applicants, 72% accepted. In 2001, 194 degrees awarded. **Degree requirements:** For master's, thesis (for some programs), registration. *Median time to degree:* Master's–3 years full-time, 6 years part-time. **Entrance requirements:** For master's, TOEFL, Letters of Recommendation from supervisors. *Application deadline:* For fall admission, 7/15. Applications are processed on a rolling basis. *Application fee:* $0. Electronic applications accepted. **Expenses:** Tuition: Full-time $8,370; part-time $465 per credit. **Financial support:** Fellowships with full tuition reimbursements, research assistantships with full tuition reimbursements, teaching assistantships with full tuition reimbursements, Federal Work-Study, scholarships/grants, and tuition waivers (partial) available. Support available to part-time students. Financial award application deadline: 7/15; financial award applicants required to submit CSS PROFILE or FAFSA. Dr. Tony Hain, Dean, Graduate Studies, 810-762-9616, *Fax:* 810-762-9935, *E-mail:* thain@kettering.edu. **Application contact:** Betty L. Bedore, Coordinator of Publicity, 810-762-7494, *Fax:* 810-762-9935, *E-mail:* bbedore@ kettering.edu. *Web site:* http:// www.kettering.edu

■ LAMAR UNIVERSITY

College of Graduate Studies, College of Engineering, Beaumont, TX 77710

AWARDS ME, MEM, MES, MS, DE. Part-time and evening/weekend programs available.

Faculty: 40 full-time (3 women), 2 part-time/adjunct (0 women).
Students: 281 full-time (29 women), 60 part-time (16 women); includes 9 minority (2 African Americans, 5 Asian Americans or Pacific Islanders, 2 Hispanic Americans), 313 international. Average age 26. 821 applicants, 45% accepted, 151 enrolled. In 2001, 123 master's, 5 doctorates awarded. Terminal master's awarded for partial completion of doctoral program. **Degree requirements:** For doctorate, thesis/dissertation. **Entrance requirements:** For master's and doctorate, GRE General Test, TOEFL. *Application deadline:* For fall admission, 5/15 (priority date); for spring admission, 10/1 (priority date). Applications are processed on a rolling basis. *Application fee:* $25 ($50 for international students). **Expenses:** Tuition, state resident: full-time $1,114. Tuition, nonresident: full-time $3,670. **Financial support:** In 2001–02, fellowships with partial tuition reimbursements (averaging $6,000 per year), research assistantships with partial tuition reimbursements (averaging $7,500 per year), teaching assistantships with partial

tuition reimbursements (averaging $7,500 per year) were awarded. Career-related internships or fieldwork, Federal Work-Study, institutionally sponsored loans, scholarships/grants, tuition waivers (full and partial), and laboratory assistantships, graders also available. Support available to part-time students. Financial award application deadline: 4/1. **Faculty research:** Energy alternatives; process analysis, design, and control; pollution prevention. *Total annual research expenditures:* $1.2 million. Dr. Jack Hopper, Chair, 409-880-8784, *Fax:* 409-880-2197, *E-mail:* che_dept@ hal.lamar.edu. **Application contact:** Sandy Drane, Coordinator of Graduate Admissions, 409-880-8356, *Fax:* 409-880-8414, *E-mail:* gradmissions@hal.lamar.edu.

■ LAWRENCE TECHNOLOGICAL UNIVERSITY

College of Engineering, Southfield, MI 48075-1058

AWARDS Automotive engineering (MAE); civil engineering (MCE); electrical and computer engineering (MS); manufacturing systems (MEMS, DE). Part-time and evening/weekend programs available.

Faculty: 27 full-time (2 women), 11 part-time/adjunct (1 woman).
Students: Average age 32. 133 applicants, 38 enrolled. In 2001, 43 degrees awarded. *Application deadline:* For fall admission, 8/1 (priority date); for winter admission, 12/1 (priority date); for spring admission, 5/1. Applications are processed on a rolling basis. *Application fee:* $50. Electronic applications accepted. **Expenses:** Tuition: Part-time $460 per credit hour. **Financial support:** Institutionally sponsored loans available. Support available to part-time students. Financial award application deadline: 3/1; financial award applicants required to submit FAFSA. **Faculty research:** Advanced composite materials in bridges, strengthening existing bridges with carbon and glass fiber sheets, development of drive shafts using composite materials. *Total annual research expenditures:* $150,000. Dr. Laird Johnston, Dean, 248-204-2500, *Fax:* 248-204-2509, *E-mail:* lejohnston@ ltu.edu. **Application contact:** Jane Rohrback, Interim Director of Admissions, 248-204-3160, *Fax:* 248-204-3188, *E-mail:* admission@ltu.edu.

■ LEHIGH UNIVERSITY

College of Business and Economics, Department of Finance and Law, Program in Business Administration and Engineering, Bethlehem, PA 18015-3094

AWARDS MBA/E. Part-time and evening/weekend programs available.

Postbaccalaureate distance learning degree programs offered (minimal on-campus study).
Students: 3 full-time, 17 part-time. 16 applicants.
Application deadline: For fall admission, 7/15; for spring admission, 12/1. Applications are processed on a rolling basis. *Application fee:* $50. Electronic applications accepted. **Expenses:** Tuition: Part-time $468 per credit hour. Required fees: $200; $100 per semester. Tuition and fees vary according to program. **Financial support:** Fellowships, research assistantships, teaching assistantships, tuition waivers (partial) available. Financial award application deadline: 2/1. **Application contact:** Mary- Theresa Taglang, Director of Recruitment and Admissions, 610-758-5285, *Fax:* 610-758-5283, *E-mail:* mtt4@lehigh.edu. *Web site:* http://www.lehigh.edu/~incbe/incbe.html

Find an in-depth description at www.petersons.com/gradchannel.

■ LEHIGH UNIVERSITY

P.C. Rossin College of Engineering and Applied Science, Bethlehem, PA 18015-3094

AWARDS M Eng, MS, PhD, MBA/M Eng. Part-time and evening/weekend programs available. Postbaccalaureate distance learning degree programs offered (no on-campus study).

Faculty: 121 full-time (4 women), 8 part-time/adjunct (0 women).
Students: 386 full-time (66 women), 123 part-time (21 women); includes 62 minority (13 African Americans, 36 Asian Americans or Pacific Islanders, 13 Hispanic Americans), 216 international. Average age 24. 1,986 applicants, 25% accepted, 134 enrolled. In 2001, 109 master's, 43 doctorates awarded. **Degree requirements:** For doctorate, thesis/dissertation. **Entrance requirements:** For master's and doctorate, TOEFL. *Application deadline:* For fall admission, 7/15; for spring admission, 12/1. Applications are processed on a rolling basis. *Application fee:* $50. Electronic applications accepted. **Expenses:** Contact institution. **Financial support:** In 2001–02, 36 fellowships with full and partial tuition reimbursements (averaging $12,600 per year), 148 research assistantships with full and partial tuition reimbursements (averaging $16,500 per year), 39 teaching assistantships with full and partial tuition reimbursements (averaging $12,330 per year) were awarded. Career-related internships or fieldwork, Federal Work-Study, institutionally sponsored loans, scholarships/grants, and tuition waivers (full and partial) also available. Support available to part-time students. Financial award application deadline: 1/15. *Total annual research expenditures:* $20.7 million.

Lehigh University (continued)
Dr. John P. Coulter, Associate Dean, 610-758-6310, *Fax:* 610-758-5623, *E-mail:* john.coulter@lehigh.edu.
Application contact: Lynn M. Walters, Administrative Coordinator, 610-758-6310, *Fax:* 610-758-5623, *E-mail:* lmw7@lehigh.edu. *Web site:* http://www.lehigh.edu
Find an in-depth description at www.petersons.com/gradchannel.

■ **LOUISIANA STATE UNIVERSITY AND AGRICULTURAL AND MECHANICAL COLLEGE**

Graduate School, College of Agriculture, Department of Biological and Agricultural Engineering, Baton Rouge, LA 70803

AWARDS Biological and agricultural engineering (MSBAE); engineering science (MS, PhD). Part-time programs available.

Faculty: 9 full-time (2 women).
Students: 9 full-time (5 women), 4 part-time (2 women); includes 1 minority (African American), 8 international. Average age 27. 13 applicants, 54% accepted, 5 enrolled. In 2001, 3 degrees awarded. Terminal master's awarded for partial completion of doctoral program.
Degree requirements: For master's and doctorate, thesis/dissertation.
Entrance requirements: For master's and doctorate, GRE General Test, minimum GPA of 3.0. *Application deadline:* For fall admission, 1/25 (priority date). Applications are processed on a rolling basis. *Application fee:* $25.
Expenses: Tuition, state resident: full-time $2,551. Tuition, nonresident: full-time $5,551. Required fees: $854. Part-time tuition and fees vary according to course load.
Financial support: In 2001–02, 9 research assistantships with partial tuition reimbursements (averaging $14,667 per year) were awarded; fellowships, teaching assistantships with partial tuition reimbursements, career-related internships or fieldwork also available. Financial award application deadline: 7/1; financial award applicants required to submit FAFSA.
Faculty research: Machine development, aquaculture, environmental engineering, microprocessor applications, ergonomics engineering, bioprocessing, hydrology, biosensors, food engineering. *Total annual research expenditures:* $11,895.
Dr. Richard Bengtson, Acting Head, 225-578-3153, *Fax:* 225-578-3492, *E-mail:* bengston@bae.lsu.edu.
Application contact: Dr. David C. Blouin, Associate Dean, 225-578-8303, *Fax:* 225-578-2526, *E-mail:* dblouin@lsu.edu. *Web site:* http://www.coa.lsu.edu/bioen/bioen.html

■ **LOUISIANA STATE UNIVERSITY AND AGRICULTURAL AND MECHANICAL COLLEGE**

Graduate School, College of Engineering, Department of Industrial and Manufacturing Systems Engineering, Baton Rouge, LA 70803

AWARDS Engineering science (PhD); industrial engineering (MSIE).

Faculty: 8 full-time (0 women).
Students: 14 full-time (1 woman), 4 part-time, 17 international. Average age 26. 101 applicants, 44% accepted, 7 enrolled. In 2001, 7 degrees awarded. Terminal master's awarded for partial completion of doctoral program.
Degree requirements: For master's and doctorate, thesis/dissertation.
Entrance requirements: For master's and doctorate, GRE General Test, minimum GPA of 3.0. *Application deadline:* For fall admission, 1/25 (priority date). Applications are processed on a rolling basis. *Application fee:* $25.
Expenses: Tuition, state resident: full-time $2,551. Tuition, nonresident: full-time $5,551. Required fees: $854. Part-time tuition and fees vary according to course load.
Financial support: In 2001–02, 1 student received support; fellowships, research assistantships with partial tuition reimbursements available, teaching assistantships with partial tuition reimbursements available, institutionally sponsored loans and unspecified assistantships available. Financial award application deadline: 5/1; financial award applicants required to submit FAFSA.
Faculty research: Ergonomics/human factors engineering, industrial hygiene, production systems, operations research, manufacturing engineering and maintenance. *Total annual research expenditures:* $76,608.
Dr. Thomas Ray, Interim Chair, 225-578-5369, *Fax:* 225-578-5109, *E-mail:* tray@lsu.edu.
Application contact: Dr. F. Aghazadeh, Graduate Adviser, 225-578-5112, *E-mail:* aghazadeh@lsu.edu. *Web site:* http://www.imse.lsu.edu

■ **LOUISIANA STATE UNIVERSITY AND AGRICULTURAL AND MECHANICAL COLLEGE**

Graduate School, College of Engineering, Interdepartmental Programs in Engineering, Baton Rouge, LA 70803

AWARDS Engineering science (MSES, PhD). Part-time and evening/weekend programs available.

Students: 45 full-time (11 women), 17 part-time (2 women); includes 7 minority (3 African Americans, 2 Asian Americans or Pacific Islanders, 2 Hispanic Americans), 45 international. Average age 29. 12 applicants, 75% accepted, 4 enrolled. In 2001, 19 master's, 4 doctorates awarded. Terminal master's awarded for partial completion of doctoral program.
Degree requirements: For master's, thesis optional; for doctorate, thesis/dissertation.
Entrance requirements: For master's and doctorate, GRE General Test, TOEFL, minimum GPA of 3.0. *Application deadline:* For fall admission, 1/25 (priority date). Applications are processed on a rolling basis. *Application fee:* $25.
Expenses: Tuition, state resident: full-time $2,551. Tuition, nonresident: full-time $5,551. Required fees: $854. Part-time tuition and fees vary according to course load.
Financial support: In 2001–02, 2 fellowships (averaging $14,333 per year), 21 research assistantships with partial tuition reimbursements (averaging $10,903 per year), 7 teaching assistantships with partial tuition reimbursements (averaging $14,163 per year) were awarded. Unspecified assistantships also available. Financial award application deadline: 3/1; financial award applicants required to submit FAFSA.
Faculty research: Environmental engineering, transportation engineering, enhanced oil recovery, microelectrical-mechanical systems, manufacturing. *Total annual research expenditures:* $140,467.
Dr. Julius Langlinais, Associate Dean, 225-578-5731, *Fax:* 225-578-1559, *E-mail:* eglang@lsu.edu. *Web site:* http://www.eng.lsu.edu/

■ **LOUISIANA TECH UNIVERSITY**

Graduate School, College of Engineering and Science, Ruston, LA 71272

AWARDS MS, D Eng, PhD. Part-time programs available. Terminal master's awarded for partial completion of doctoral program.

Degree requirements: For doctorate, thesis/dissertation.
Entrance requirements: For master's, GRE General Test, TOEFL, minimum GPA of 3.0 in last 60 hours; for doctorate, TOEFL.
Faculty research: Trenchless technology, micromanufacturing, radionuclide transport, microbial liquefaction, hazardous waste treatment. *Web site:* http://www.latech.edu/tech/general.html

■ **LOYOLA COLLEGE IN MARYLAND**

Graduate Programs, College of Arts and Sciences, Engineering Science Program, Baltimore, MD 21210-2699

AWARDS MES, MS. Part-time and evening/weekend programs available.

Students: 5 full-time (2 women), 124 part-time (21 women). 43 applicants, 77% accepted, 21 enrolled. In 2001, 46 degrees awarded. *Application deadline:* For fall admission, 9/1 (priority date); for spring admission, 12/1 (priority date). Applications are processed on a rolling basis. **Expenses:** Contact institution. **Financial support:** Research assistantships available. Financial award applicants required to submit FAFSA. Dr. Paul Coyne, Head, 410-617-2512. **Application contact:** Scott Greatorex, Director, Graduate Admissions, 410-617-5020 Ext. 2407, *Fax:* 410-617-2002, *E-mail:* sgreatorex@loyola.edu.

■ LOYOLA MARYMOUNT UNIVERSITY

Graduate Division, College of Science and Engineering, Los Angeles, CA 90045-2659

AWARDS MS, MSE. Part-time and evening/weekend programs available.

Faculty: 61 full-time (13 women), 44 part-time/adjunct (11 women). **Students:** 46 full-time (9 women), 46 part-time (9 women); includes 37 minority (8 African Americans, 20 Asian Americans or Pacific Islanders, 9 Hispanic Americans), 15 international. 97 applicants, 59% accepted, 31 enrolled. In 2001, 39 degrees awarded. **Entrance requirements:** For master's, TOEFL. *Application fee:* $45. Electronic applications accepted. **Expenses:** Tuition: Part-time $612 per credit hour. Required fees: $86 per term. Tuition and fees vary according to program. **Financial support:** In 2001–02, 23 students received support, including 4 research assistantships (averaging $2,717 per year); Federal Work-Study, scholarships/grants, and instructorships also available. Support available to part-time students. Financial award application deadline: 7/1; financial award applicants required to submit FAFSA. Dr. Gerald S. Jakubowski, Dean, 310-338-2834, *Fax:* 310-338-7399, *E-mail:* gjakubow@lmu.edu. **Application contact:** Dr. Bo A. Oppenheim, Director, 310-338-2825, *E-mail:* boppenhe@lmu.edu. *Web site:* http://www.lmu.edu/acad/gd/graddiv/htm

■ MANHATTAN COLLEGE

Graduate Division, School of Engineering, Riverdale, NY 10471

AWARDS Chemical engineering (MS); civil engineering (MS); computer engineering (MS); electrical engineering (MS); environmental engineering (ME, MS); mechanical engineering (MS). Part-time and evening/weekend programs available.

Entrance requirements: For master's, GRE, TOEFL, minimum GPA of 3.0. **Expenses:** Contact institution.

Find an in-depth description at www.petersons.com/gradchannel.

■ MARQUETTE UNIVERSITY

Graduate School, College of Engineering, Milwaukee, WI 53201-1881

AWARDS MS, PhD. Part-time and evening/weekend programs available.

Faculty: 45 full-time (4 women), 51 part-time/adjunct (6 women). **Students:** 124 full-time (33 women), 166 part-time (23 women); includes 21 minority (6 African Americans, 11 Asian Americans or Pacific Islanders, 3 Hispanic Americans, 1 Native American), 80 international. 276 applicants, 60% accepted. In 2001, 28 master's, 6 doctorates awarded. **Degree requirements:** For doctorate, thesis/dissertation. *Median time to degree:* Master's–2 years full-time, 3 years part-time. **Entrance requirements:** For master's, TOEFL; for doctorate, GRE General Test, TOEFL. *Application deadline:* Applications are processed on a rolling basis. *Application fee:* $40. Electronic applications accepted. **Expenses:** Tuition: Full-time $10,170; part-time $445 per credit hour. Tuition and fees vary according to course load. **Financial support:** In 2001–02, 55 students received support, including 21 fellowships with tuition reimbursements available, 24 research assistantships with tuition reimbursements available, 31 teaching assistantships with tuition reimbursements available; Federal Work-Study, institutionally sponsored loans, scholarships/grants, and tuition waivers (full and partial) also available. Support available to part-time students. Financial award application deadline: 2/15. **Faculty research:** Urban watershed management, microsensors for environmental pollutants, orthopedic rehabilitation engineering, telemedicine, ergonomics. *Total annual research expenditures:* $6 million. Dr. Douglas M. Green, Dean, 414-288-6591, *Fax:* 414-288-6025, *E-mail:* douglas.green@marquette.edu. **Application contact:** Craig Pierce, Director of Admissions, 414-288-7137, *Fax:* 414-288-1902, *E-mail:* mugs@vms.csd.mu.edu. *Web site:* http://www.eng.mu.edu/

Find an in-depth description at www.petersons.com/gradchannel.

■ MARSHALL UNIVERSITY

Graduate College, College of Information, Technology and Engineering, Huntington, WV 25755

AWARDS MS, MSE. Part-time and evening/weekend programs available.

Faculty: 15 full-time (1 woman), 13 part-time/adjunct (3 women). **Students:** 60 full-time (19 women), 163 part-time (37 women); includes 10 minority (4 African Americans, 3 Asian Americans or Pacific Islanders, 1 Hispanic American, 2 Native Americans), 15 international. Average age 36. In 2001, 51 degrees awarded. **Degree requirements:** For master's, final project, oral exam. **Expenses:** Contact institution. **Financial support:** Fellowships, tuition waivers (full) available. Support available to part-time students. Financial award application deadline: 8/1; financial award applicants required to submit FAFSA. Dr. James Hooper, Dean, 304-696-6204, *E-mail:* hooper@marshall.edu. **Application contact:** Ken O'Neal, Assistant Vice President, Adult Student Services, 304-746-2500 Ext. 1907, *Fax:* 304-746-1902, *E-mail:* oneal@marshall.edu.

■ MASSACHUSETTS INSTITUTE OF TECHNOLOGY

School of Engineering, Cambridge, MA 02139-4307

AWARDS M Eng, MST, SM, PhD, Sc D, CE, EAA, EE, EE, Mat E, Mech E, Met E, NE, Naval E, Ocean E, SM/MBA, SM/SM.

Faculty: 343 full-time (35 women), 5 part-time/adjunct (0 women). **Students:** 2,584 full-time (593 women), 14 part-time (3 women); includes 402 minority (54 African Americans, 291 Asian Americans or Pacific Islanders, 53 Hispanic Americans, 4 Native Americans), 1,023 international. Average age 23. 5,523 applicants, 30% accepted, 830 enrolled. In 2001, 872 master's, 243 doctorates awarded. Terminal master's awarded for partial completion of doctoral program. **Degree requirements:** For master's, thesis (for some programs); for doctorate, thesis/dissertation, comprehensive exam. *Application fee:* $60. Electronic applications accepted. **Expenses:** Tuition: Full-time $26,960. Full-time tuition and fees vary according to program. **Financial support:** In 2001–02, 2,378 students received support, including 588 fellowships, 1,624 research assistantships, 272 teaching assistantships; career-related internships or fieldwork, Federal Work-Study, institutionally sponsored loans, scholarships/grants, traineeships, health care benefits, and unspecified assistantships also available. Financial award applicants

Massachusetts Institute of Technology (continued)
required to submit FAFSA. *Total annual research expenditures:* $189.7 million.
Thomas L. Magnanti, Dean, 617-253-6604, *Fax:* 617-253-8549, *E-mail:* magnanti@mit.edu. *Web site:* http://web.mit.edu/engineering/

■ **MCNEESE STATE UNIVERSITY**

Graduate School, College of Engineering and Technology, Lake Charles, LA 70609

AWARDS Chemical engineering (M Eng); civil engineering (M Eng); electrical engineering (M Eng); mechanical engineering (M Eng). Part-time and evening/weekend programs available.

Faculty: 14 full-time (1 woman).
Students: 24 full-time (5 women), 5 part-time; includes 1 minority (Asian American or Pacific Islander), 23 international. In 2001, 5 degrees awarded.
Degree requirements: For master's, thesis or alternative.
Entrance requirements: For master's, GRE General Test, TOEFL, minimum undergraduate GPA of 3.0. *Application deadline:* For fall admission, 7/15 (priority date). Applications are processed on a rolling basis. *Application fee:* $20 ($30 for international students).
Expenses: Tuition, state resident: part-time $1,208 per semester. Tuition, nonresident: part-time $4,378 per semester.
Financial support: Federal Work-Study available. Support available to part-time students. Financial award application deadline: 5/1.
Dr. O. C. Karkalits, Dean, 337-475-5875, *Fax:* 337-475-5237, *E-mail:* ckarkal@mail.mcneese.edu.
Application contact: Dr. Jay O. Uppot, Director of Graduate Studies, 337-475-5874, *Fax:* 37-475-5286, *E-mail:* juppot@mail.mcneese.edu.

■ **MERCER UNIVERSITY**

Graduate Studies, Macon Campus, School of Engineering, Macon, GA 31207-0003

AWARDS Biomedical engineering (MSE); electrical engineering (MSE); engineering management (MSE); mechanical engineering (MSE). Software engineering (MSE). Software systems (MS); technical communications management (MS); technical management (MS). Part-time and evening/weekend programs available.

Faculty: 10 full-time (1 woman), 5 part-time/adjunct (1 woman).
Students: 3 full-time (2 women), 104 part-time (31 women); includes 19 minority (13 African Americans, 6 Asian Americans or Pacific Islanders), 5 international. Average age 36. 31 applicants, 97% accepted, 27 enrolled. In 2001, 32 degrees awarded.

Degree requirements: For master's, thesis or alternative, registration.
Entrance requirements: For master's, GRE, minimum undergraduate GPA of 3.0. *Application deadline:* For fall admission, 7/1; for spring admission, 11/15. Applications are processed on a rolling basis. *Application fee:* $35 ($50 for international students).
Expenses: Contact institution.
Financial support: Federal Work-Study available.
Dr. M. Dayne Aldridge, Dean, 478-301-2459, *Fax:* 478-301-5593, *E-mail:* aldridge_md@mercer.edu.
Application contact: Kathy Olivier, Graduate Administrative Coordinator, 478-301-2196, *E-mail:* olivier_kk@mercer.edu. *Web site:* http://www.mercer.edu/engineer.htm

■ **MIAMI UNIVERSITY**

Graduate School, School of Engineering and Applied Science, Oxford, OH 45056

AWARDS MS.

Faculty: 12 full-time (0 women), 4 part-time/adjunct (1 woman).
Students: 30 full-time (9 women); includes 8 minority (all Asian Americans or Pacific Islanders), 14 international. 74 applicants, 66% accepted, 13 enrolled. In 2001, 23 degrees awarded.
Degree requirements: For master's, thesis, final exam.
Entrance requirements: For master's, GRE, minimum undergraduate GPA of 3.0 during previous 2 years or 2.75 overall. *Application deadline:* For fall admission, 3/1 (priority date). Applications are processed on a rolling basis. *Application fee:* $35.
Expenses: Tuition, state resident: full-time $7,155; part-time $295 per semester hour. Tuition, nonresident: full-time $14,829; part-time $615 per semester hour. Tuition and fees vary according to degree level and campus/location.
Financial support: In 2001–02, 22 fellowships (averaging $10,057 per year) were awarded; research assistantships, teaching assistantships, Federal Work-Study and tuition waivers (full) also available. Financial award application deadline: 3/1.
Dr. Marek Dollár, Chair, 513-529-4036. *Web site:* http://www.sas.muohio.edu/

■ **MICHIGAN STATE UNIVERSITY**

Graduate School, College of Engineering, East Lansing, MI 48824

AWARDS MS, PhD. Part-time programs available. Postbaccalaureate distance learning degree programs offered (minimal on-campus study).

Faculty: 128.
Students: 376 full-time (67 women), 214 part-time (39 women); includes 82 minority (27 African Americans, 32 Asian Americans or Pacific Islanders, 23 Hispanic Americans), 365 international.

Average age 27. 2,244 applicants, 14% accepted. In 2001, 173 master's, 50 doctorates awarded. Terminal master's awarded for partial completion of doctoral program.
Degree requirements: For doctorate, thesis/dissertation.
Entrance requirements: For master's and doctorate, GRE. *Application deadline:* Applications are processed on a rolling basis. *Application fee:* $30 ($40 for international students). Electronic applications accepted.
Expenses: Tuition, state resident: part-time $244 per credit hour. Tuition, nonresident: part-time $494 per credit hour. Required fees: $268 per semester. Tuition and fees vary according to course load, degree level and program.
Financial support: In 2001–02, 174 fellowships with tuition reimbursements (averaging $3,471 per year), 235 research assistantships with tuition reimbursements (averaging $13,915 per year), 156 teaching assistantships with tuition reimbursements (averaging $13,076 per year) were awarded. Federal Work-Study also available. Support available to part-time students. Financial award applicants required to submit FAFSA.
Faculty research: Materials, environment, and energy; information and computation; biotechnology; transportation and automotive engineering; manufacturing and processing. *Total annual research expenditures:* $16.9 million.
Dr. Janie Fouke, Dean, 517-355-5113, *Fax:* 517-355-2288.
Application contact: Dr. Anthony Wojcik, Associate Dean for Graduate Studies and Research, 517-432-2464, *Fax:* 517-353-7782, *E-mail:* egrgrad@egr.msu.edu. *Web site:* http://www.egr.msu.edu/egr/

■ **MICHIGAN TECHNOLOGICAL UNIVERSITY**

Graduate School, College of Engineering, Houghton, MI 49931-1295

AWARDS ME, MS, PhD. Part-time programs available.

Degree requirements: For doctorate, thesis/dissertation.
Entrance requirements: For master's and doctorate, TOEFL. Electronic applications accepted. *Web site:* http://www.doe.mtu.edu/

Find an in-depth description at www.petersons.com/gradchannel.

■ **MILWAUKEE SCHOOL OF ENGINEERING**

Department of Electrical Engineering and Computer Science, Program in Engineering, Milwaukee, WI 53202-3109

AWARDS Perfusion (MS). Evening/weekend programs available.

Faculty: 2 full-time (0 women), 9 part-time/adjunct (1 woman).

Students: 8 full-time (4 women), 2 part-time (1 woman). Average age 25. 18 applicants, 39% accepted, 7 enrolled. In 2001, 10 degrees awarded.
Degree requirements: For master's, thesis or alternative, thesis defense, comprehensive exam, registration.
Entrance requirements: For master's, GRE General Test, BS in engineering, biology, chemistry or related field. *Application deadline:* Applications are processed on a rolling basis. *Application fee:* $35. Electronic applications accepted.
Expenses: Tuition: Part-time $440 per credit. Tuition and fees vary according to course load.
Financial support: In 2001–02, 4 students received support; research assistantships, career-related internships or fieldwork available. Support available to part-time students. Financial award applicants required to submit FAFSA.
Faculty research: Microprocessors, materials, thermodynamics, artificial intelligence, fluid power/hydraulics. *Total annual research expenditures:* $1.3 million.
Dr. Glenn Wrate, Chairman, 414-277-7330, *Fax:* 414-277-7465.
Application contact: Paul Borens, Admissions Director, 800-332-6763, *Fax:* 414-277-7475, *E-mail:* borens@msoe.edu. *Web site:* http://www.msoe.edu/

Find an in-depth description at www.petersons.com/gradchannel.

■ MISSISSIPPI STATE UNIVERSITY

College of Engineering, Mississippi State, MS 39762

AWARDS MS, PhD. Part-time programs available. Postbaccalaureate distance learning degree programs offered (no on-campus study).

Degree requirements: For doctorate, thesis/dissertation.
Entrance requirements: For master's, GRE General Test, TOEFL, minimum GPA of 2.75.
Expenses: Tuition, state resident: full-time $3,586; part-time $150 per credit hour. Tuition, nonresident: full-time $8,128; part-time $339 per credit hour. Tuition and fees vary according to course load and campus/location.
Faculty research: Fluid dynamics, combustion, composite materials, computer design, high-voltage phenomena. *Web site:* http://www.engr.msstate.edu/

■ MONTANA STATE UNIVERSITY–BOZEMAN

College of Graduate Studies, College of Engineering, Bozeman, MT 59717

AWARDS MS, PhD. Part-time programs available.

Students: 97 full-time (21 women), 58 part-time (21 women); includes 3 minority

(all Asian Americans or Pacific Islanders), 39 international. Average age 28. 165 applicants, 80% accepted, 59 enrolled. In 2001, 70 degrees awarded.
Degree requirements: For master's, thesis or alternative; for doctorate, thesis/dissertation.
Entrance requirements: For master's and doctorate, GRE General Test, TOEFL. *Application deadline:* For fall admission, 6/1; for spring admission, 11/1. Applications are processed on a rolling basis. *Application fee:* $50. Electronic applications accepted.
Expenses: Tuition, state resident: full-time $3,894; part-time $198 per credit. Tuition, nonresident: full-time $10,661; part-time $480 per credit. International tuition: $10,811 full-time. Tuition and fees vary according to course load and program.
Financial support: Fellowships with partial tuition reimbursements, research assistantships with partial tuition reimbursements, teaching assistantships with partial tuition reimbursements, career-related internships or fieldwork, Federal Work-Study, scholarships/grants, and tuition waivers (full and partial) available. Financial award application deadline: 3/1; financial award applicants required to submit FAFSA. *Total annual research expenditures:* $10 million.
Dr. Robert Marley, Interim Dean, 406-994-2272, *Fax:* 406-994-6665, *E-mail:* rmarley@montana.edu. *Web site:* http://www.coe.montana.edu/

■ MONTANA TECH OF THE UNIVERSITY OF MONTANA

Graduate School, Butte, MT 59701-8997

AWARDS MPEM, MS. Part-time and evening/weekend programs available.
Postbaccalaureate distance learning degree programs offered (no on-campus study).

Faculty: 46 full-time (6 women).
Students: 64 full-time (22 women), 16 part-time (9 women); includes 3 minority (1 Asian American or Pacific Islander, 2 Hispanic Americans). 76 applicants, 78% accepted, 29 enrolled. In 2001, 46 degrees awarded.
Degree requirements: For master's, thesis (for some programs), comprehensive exam (for some programs), registration.
Entrance requirements: For master's, GRE General Test, TOEFL. *Application deadline:* For fall admission, 4/1 (priority date); for spring admission, 10/1 (priority date). Applications are processed on a rolling basis. *Application fee:* $30.
Expenses: Tuition, state resident: full-time $3,717; part-time $196 per credit. Tuition, nonresident: full-time $11,770; part-time $324 per credit.
Financial support: In 2001–02, 61 students received support, including 13 research assistantships with full tuition reimbursements available (averaging $8,000 per year), 40 teaching assistantships

with partial tuition reimbursements available (averaging $5,440 per year); career-related internships or fieldwork, institutionally sponsored loans, and tuition waivers (full and partial) also available. Financial award application deadline: 4/1; financial award applicants required to submit FAFSA.
Faculty research: Mineral processing, environmental restoration, endophytic fungi, production and delivery, sonic technology. *Total annual research expenditures:* $5.3 million.
Dr. Joseph Figueira, Vice Chancellor, Research and Graduate Studies, 406-496-4102.
Application contact: Cindy Dunstan, Administrator, Graduate School, 406-496-4304, *Fax:* 406-496-4334, *E-mail:* cdunstan@mtech.edu. *Web site:* http://www.mtech.edu/

■ MORGAN STATE UNIVERSITY

School of Graduate Studies, School of Engineering, Baltimore, MD 21251

AWARDS MS, D Eng. Part-time and evening/weekend programs available.

Students: 82 (26 women); includes 43 minority (36 African Americans, 2 Asian Americans or Pacific Islanders, 5 Hispanic Americans) 17 international. In 2001, 7 degrees awarded.
Degree requirements: For master's and doctorate, thesis/dissertation, comprehensive exam or equivalent.
Entrance requirements: For master's, GRE, TOEFL, minimum undergraduate GPA of 2.5; for doctorate, GRE, TOEFL, minimum GPA of 3.0. *Application deadline:* For fall admission, 2/1; for spring admission, 10/1. Applications are processed on a rolling basis. *Application fee:* $0.
Expenses: Tuition, state resident: part-time $193 per credit. Tuition, nonresident: part-time $364 per credit. Required fees: $40 per credit.
Financial support: Fellowships, research assistantships, career-related internships or fieldwork and Federal Work-Study available. Financial award application deadline: 4/1.
Dr. Eugene DeLoatch, Dean, 443-885-3231.
Application contact: Dr. James E. Waller, Admissions and Programs Officer, 443-885-3185, *Fax:* 443-319-3837, *E-mail:* jwaller@moac.morgan.edu.

■ NATIONAL TECHNOLOGICAL UNIVERSITY

Programs in Engineering, Fort Collins, CO 80526-1842

AWARDS Chemical engineering (MS); computer engineering (MS); computer science (MS); electrical engineering (MS); engineering management (MS); environmental systems management (MS); management of technology (MS); manufacturing systems

National Technological University (continued)

engineering (MS); materials science and engineering (MS); mechanical engineering (MS); microelectronics and semiconductor engineering (MS). Software engineering (MS). Special majors (MS). Systems engineering (MS). Part-time programs available. Postbaccalaureate distance learning degree programs offered (no on-campus study).

Students: In 2001, 114 degrees awarded.
Degree requirements: For master's, comprehensive exam.
Entrance requirements: For master's, BS in engineering or related field; 2.9 minimum GPA. *Application deadline:* Applications are processed on a rolling basis. *Application fee:* $50. Electronic applications accepted.
Expenses: Tuition: Part-time $660 per credit hour. Part-time tuition and fees vary according to course load, campus/location and program.
Dr. Andre Vacroux, President, 970-495-6400, *Fax:* 970-484-0668, *E-mail:* andre@ntu.edu.
Application contact: Rhonda Bonham, Admissions Officer, 970-495-6400, *Fax:* 970-498-0601, *E-mail:* rhonda@ntu.edu. *Web site:* http://www.ntu.edu/

■ NATIONAL UNIVERSITY

Academic Affairs, School of Business and Technology, Department of Technology, La Jolla, CA 92037-1011

AWARDS Biotechnology (MBA); electronic commerce (MBA, MS); environmental management (MBA). Software engineering (MS). Space commerce (MBA); technology management (MBA, MS); telecommunications systems management (MS). Part-time and evening/weekend programs available. Postbaccalaureate distance learning degree programs offered (minimal on-campus study).

Faculty: 9 full-time (0 women), 148 part-time/adjunct (20 women).
Students: 349 full-time (108 women), 130 part-time (44 women); includes 145 minority (45 African Americans, 76 Asian Americans or Pacific Islanders, 21 Hispanic Americans, 3 Native Americans), 138 international. 82 applicants, 100% accepted. In 2001, 250 degrees awarded.
Entrance requirements: For master's, interview, minimum GPA of 2.5. *Application deadline:* Applications are processed on a rolling basis. *Application fee:* $60 ($100 for international students).
Expenses: Tuition: Part-time $221 per quarter hour.
Financial support: Institutionally sponsored loans, scholarships/grants, and tuition waivers (full and partial) available. Support available to part-time students. Financial award application deadline: 5/1; financial award applicants required to submit FAFSA.

Dr. Leonid Preiser, Chair, 858-642-8425, *Fax:* 858-642-8716, *E-mail:* lpreiser@nu.edu.
Application contact: Nancy Rohland, Director of Enrollment Management, 858-642-8180, *Fax:* 858-642-8710, *E-mail:* advisor@nu.edu. *Web site:* http://www.nu.edu/

■ NEW JERSEY INSTITUTE OF TECHNOLOGY

Office of Graduate Studies, Newark, NJ 07102

AWARDS M Arch, MA, MAT, MBA, MIP, MS, PhD, Engineer, M Arch/MIP, M Arch/MS. Part-time and evening/weekend programs available.

Faculty: 418 full-time (71 women), 272 part-time/adjunct (47 women).
Students: 1,253 full-time (382 women), 1,391 part-time (345 women); includes 584 minority (135 African Americans, 339 Asian Americans or Pacific Islanders, 108 Hispanic Americans, 2 Native Americans), 1,194 international. Average age 30. 5,061 applicants, 49% accepted, 847 enrolled. In 2001, 905 master's, 65 doctorates, 64 other advanced degrees awarded.
Degree requirements: For doctorate, residency.
Application deadline: For fall admission, 6/5 (priority date); for spring admission, 10/15. Applications are processed on a rolling basis. Electronic applications accepted.
Expenses: Tuition, state resident: full-time $7,812; part-time $434 per credit. Tuition, nonresident: full-time $10,746; part-time $597 per credit. Required fees: $47 per credit. $76 per semester.
Financial support: Fellowships with full and partial tuition reimbursements, research assistantships with full and partial tuition reimbursements, teaching assistantships with full and partial tuition reimbursements, career-related internships or fieldwork, Federal Work-Study, institutionally sponsored loans, and unspecified assistantships available. Financial award application deadline: 3/15.
Faculty research: Toxic and hazardous waste management, transportation, biomedical engineering, computer-integrated manufacturing, management of technology. *Total annual research expenditures:* $31 million.
Dr. Ron Kane, Dean of Graduate Studies, 973-596-3462, *Fax:* 973-596-6479, *E-mail:* ronald.kane@njit.edu.
Application contact: Kathryn Kelly, Director of Admissions, 973-596-3300, *Fax:* 973-596-3461, *E-mail:* admissions@njit.edu. *Web site:* http://www.njit.edu/

■ NEW MEXICO STATE UNIVERSITY

Graduate School, College of Engineering, Las Cruces, NM 88003-8001

AWARDS MS Ch E, MS Env E, MSCE, MSEE, MSIE, MSME, PhD. Part-time programs available.

Faculty: 59 full-time (3 women), 11 part-time/adjunct (2 women).
Students: 180 full-time (36 women), 109 part-time (19 women); includes 58 minority (2 African Americans, 6 Asian Americans or Pacific Islanders, 46 Hispanic Americans, 4 Native Americans), 137 international. Average age 30. 327 applicants, 75% accepted, 71 enrolled. In 2001, 97 master's, 12 doctorates awarded.
Degree requirements: For doctorate, thesis/dissertation.
Application deadline: For fall admission, 7/1 (priority date); for spring admission, 11/1. Applications are processed on a rolling basis. *Application fee:* $15 ($35 for international students). Electronic applications accepted.
Expenses: Tuition, state resident: full-time $3,234; part-time $135 per credit. Tuition, nonresident: full-time $9,420; part-time $428 per credit. Required fees: $858.
Financial support: In 2001–02, 54 research assistantships, 79 teaching assistantships were awarded. Fellowships, career-related internships or fieldwork and Federal Work-Study also available. Support available to part-time students. Financial award application deadline: 3/1.
Faculty research: Structures and nondestructive testing, environmental science and engineering, telecommunication theory and systems, manufacturing methods and systems, high performance computing and software engineering.
Dr. Kenneth White, Interim Dean, 505-646-2914, *Fax:* 505-646-3549, *E-mail:* krwhite@nmsu.edu. *Web site:* http://www.nmsu.edu/~coe/

■ NEW YORK INSTITUTE OF TECHNOLOGY

Graduate Division, School of Engineering and Technology, Old Westbury, NY 11568-8000

AWARDS MS, Advanced Certificate. Part-time and evening/weekend programs available. Postbaccalaureate distance learning degree programs offered.

Students: 268 full-time (66 women), 279 part-time (53 women); includes 96 minority (23 African Americans, 66 Asian Americans or Pacific Islanders, 7 Hispanic Americans), 268 international. Average age 33. 456 applicants, 65% accepted, 113 enrolled. In 2001, 150 degrees awarded.
Entrance requirements: For master's, minimum QPA of 2.85. *Application deadline:* For fall admission, 7/1 (priority date); for spring admission, 12/1 (priority date).

Applications are processed on a rolling basis. *Application fee:* $50. Electronic applications accepted.

Expenses: Tuition: Part-time $545 per credit. Tuition and fees vary according to course load, degree level, program and student level.

Financial support: In 2001–02, 42 research assistantships with partial tuition reimbursements were awarded; fellowships, career-related internships or fieldwork, institutionally sponsored loans, tuition waivers (full and partial), and unspecified assistantships also available. Support available to part-time students. Financial award applicants required to submit FAFSA.

Faculty research: Develop hybrid vehicle, system design of photovoltaic cells, prototype module of DTV application environment, adaptive target detection in nonhomogeneous environment.

Dr. Heskia Heskiaoff, Dean, 516-686-7931, *Fax:* 516-625-5801.

Application contact: Jacquelyn Nealon, Dean of Admissions and Financial Aid, 516-686-7925, *Fax:* 516-686-7613, *E-mail:* jnealon@nyit.edu. *Web site:* http://www.nyit.edu/

■ NORTH CAROLINA AGRICULTURAL AND TECHNICAL STATE UNIVERSITY

Graduate School, College of Engineering, Greensboro, NC 27411

AWARDS MSAE, MSCE, MSCS, MSE, MSEE, MSISE, MSME, PhD. Part-time programs available.

Faculty: 74 full-time (4 women), 15 part-time/adjunct (1 woman).
Students: 270 full-time (113 women), 7 part-time (2 women); includes 187 minority (167 African Americans, 20 Asian Americans or Pacific Islanders), 61 international. Average age 25. 790 applicants, 82% accepted, 339 enrolled. In 2001, 83 master's, 5 doctorates awarded. *Application deadline:* For fall admission, 7/1 (priority date); for spring admission, 1/9. Applications are processed on a rolling basis. *Application fee:* $35.
Financial support: Fellowships, research assistantships, teaching assistantships, career-related internships or fieldwork and unspecified assistantships available. Support available to part-time students.
Dr. Joseph Monroe, Dean, 336-334-7589, *Fax:* 336-334-7540, *E-mail:* monroe@ncat.edu.
Application contact: Dr. Kenneth Murray, Interim Dean of the Graduate School, 336-334-7920, *Fax:* 336-334-7282, *E-mail:* kmurray@ncat.edu. *Web site:* http://www.eng.ncat.edu/

Find an in-depth description at www.petersons.com/gradchannel.

■ NORTH CAROLINA STATE UNIVERSITY

Graduate School, College of Engineering, Raleigh, NC 27695

AWARDS M Ch E, M Eng, MBAE, MC Sc, MCE, MIE, MIMS, MME, MMSE, MNE, MOR, MS, MSIE, PhD, PD. Part-time programs available. Terminal master's awarded for partial completion of doctoral program.

Degree requirements: For doctorate, thesis/dissertation.
Expenses: Tuition, state resident: full-time $1,748. Tuition, nonresident: full-time $6,904. *Web site:* http://www.engr.ncsu.edu/

Find an in-depth description at www.petersons.com/gradchannel.

■ NORTH DAKOTA STATE UNIVERSITY

The Graduate School, College of Engineering and Architecture, Fargo, ND 58105

AWARDS MS, PhD. Part-time and evening/weekend programs available. Postbaccalaureate distance learning degree programs offered (minimal on-campus study). Terminal master's awarded for partial completion of doctoral program.

Degree requirements: For doctorate, thesis/dissertation.
Entrance requirements: For master's and doctorate, TOEFL.
Expenses: Tuition, state resident: part-time $124 per credit. Tuition, nonresident: part-time $325 per credit. Required fees: $22 per credit. Tuition and fees vary according to reciprocity agreements.
Faculty research: Theoretical mechanics, robotics, automation, CAD/CAM, environmental engineering.

■ NORTHEASTERN UNIVERSITY

College of Engineering, Boston, MA 02115-5096

AWARDS MS, PhD. Part-time programs available.

Faculty: 80 full-time (6 women), 29 part-time/adjunct (2 women).
Students: 498 full-time (199 women), 403 part-time (77 women); includes 86 minority (17 African Americans, 42 Asian Americans or Pacific Islanders, 26 Hispanic Americans, 1 Native American), 435 international. Average age 25. 1,265 applicants, 49% accepted, 216 enrolled. In 2001, 296 master's, 18 doctorates awarded.
Entrance requirements: For master's and doctorate, GRE General Test. *Application deadline:* For fall admission, 2/15 (priority date). Applications are processed on a rolling basis. *Application fee:* $50. Electronic applications accepted.
Expenses: Contact institution.
Financial support: In 2001–02, 258 students received support, including 5 fellowships with tuition reimbursements available, 120 research assistantships with full tuition reimbursements available (averaging $13,560 per year), 88 teaching assistantships with full tuition reimbursements available (averaging $13,560 per year); career-related internships or fieldwork, Federal Work-Study, scholarships/grants, tuition waivers (full), and unspecified assistantships also available. Support available to part-time students. Financial award application deadline: 2/15; financial award applicants required to submit FAFSA. *Total annual research expenditures:* $15.1 million.
Dr. Yaman Yener, Associate Dean of Engineering for Research and Graduate Studies, 617-373-2711, *Fax:* 617-373-2501.
Application contact: Stephen L. Gibson, Associate Director, 617-373-2711, *Fax:* 617-373-2501, *E-mail:* grad-eng@coe.neu.edu. *Web site:* http://www.coe.neu.edu/

Find an in-depth description at www.petersons.com/gradchannel.

■ NORTHERN ARIZONA UNIVERSITY

Graduate College, College of Engineering, Flagstaff, AZ 86011

AWARDS M Eng.

Faculty: 34 full-time (6 women).
Students: 9 full-time (3 women), 7 part-time (4 women); includes 2 minority (both Hispanic Americans), 1 international. 25 applicants, 64% accepted, 10 enrolled. In 2001, 1 degree awarded.
Entrance requirements: For master's, minimum GPA of 3.0 in final 60 hours of undergraduate course work. *Application fee:* $45.
Expenses: Tuition, state resident: full-time $2,488. Tuition, nonresident: full-time $10,354.
Dr. Mason Somerville, Dean, 928-523-5252.
Application contact: Ernesto Penado, Graduate Coordinator, 928-523-9453, *E-mail:* m.eng@nau.edu. *Web site:* http://www.triuniv.engr.arizona.edu/

■ NORTHERN ILLINOIS UNIVERSITY

Graduate School, College of Engineering and Engineering Technology, De Kalb, IL 60115-2854

AWARDS MS. Part-time and evening/weekend programs available.

Faculty: 34 full-time (1 woman), 3 part-time/adjunct (0 women).
Students: 108 full-time (21 women), 78 part-time (9 women); includes 14 minority (1 African American, 13 Asian Americans or Pacific Islanders), 111 international. Average age 26. In 2001, 43 degrees awarded.
Degree requirements: For master's, thesis optional.

Northern Illinois University (continued)
Entrance requirements: For master's, GRE General Test, TOEFL, minimum GPA of 2.75. *Application deadline:* For fall admission, 6/1; for spring admission, 11/1. Applications are processed on a rolling basis. *Application fee:* $30.
Expenses: Tuition, state resident: full-time $5,124; part-time $148 per credit hour. Tuition, nonresident: full-time $8,666; part-time $295 per credit hour. Required fees: $51 per term.
Financial support: Fellowships with full tuition reimbursements, research assistantships with full tuition reimbursements, teaching assistantships with full tuition reimbursements, career-related internships or fieldwork, Federal Work-Study, tuition waivers (full), and unspecified assistantships available. Support available to part-time students.
Dr. Romualdas Kasuba, Dean, 815-753-1281, *Fax:* 815-753-1310.

Find an in-depth description at www.petersons.com/gradchannel.

■ NORTHWESTERN POLYTECHNIC UNIVERSITY

School of Engineering, Fremont, CA 94539-7482
AWARDS Computer science (MS); computer systems engineering (MS); electrical engineering (MS). Part-time and evening/weekend programs available.
Faculty: 7 full-time (0 women), 53 part-time/adjunct (4 women).
Students: 239 full-time (119 women), 210 part-time (108 women). Average age 30. 132 applicants, 55% accepted. In 2001, 148 degrees awarded.
Degree requirements: For master's, thesis optional.
Entrance requirements: For master's, TOEFL, minimum GPA of 2.0. *Application deadline:* For fall admission, 8/12 (priority date); for spring admission, 2/11 (priority date). Applications are processed on a rolling basis. *Application fee:* $50 ($75 for international students).
Expenses: Tuition: Full-time $8,100; part-time $450 per unit. Required fees: $45; $15 per term.
Financial support: In 2001–02, 160 teaching assistantships with full and partial tuition reimbursements (averaging $1,000 per year) were awarded; career-related internships or fieldwork and unspecified assistantships also available.
Faculty research: Computer networking; database design; internet technology. Software engineering; digital signal processing.
Dr. Pochang Hsu, Dean, 510-657-5911, *Fax:* 510-657-8975, *E-mail:* npuadm@npu.edu.
Application contact: Jack Xie, Director of Admissions, 510-657-5913, *Fax:* 510-657-8975, *E-mail:* jack@npu.edu. *Web site:* http://www.npu.edu/engineeringindex.htm

■ NORTHWESTERN UNIVERSITY

McCormick School of Engineering and Applied Science, Evanston, IL 60208
AWARDS MEM, MIT, MME, MMM, MPM, MS, PhD, Certificate. MS and PhD admissions and degrees offered through The Graduate School. Part-time and evening/weekend programs available.
Faculty: 155 full-time.
Students: 777 full-time (183 women), 181 part-time (31 women); includes 154 minority (18 African Americans, 106 Asian Americans or Pacific Islanders, 29 Hispanic Americans, 1 Native American), 347 international. Average age 26. 2,762 applicants, 23% accepted. In 2001, 251 master's, 106 doctorates awarded.
Degree requirements: For doctorate, thesis/dissertation. *Median time to degree:* Master's–1.5 years full-time, 3 years part-time; doctorate–5 years full-time, 7 years part-time.
Entrance requirements: For master's and doctorate, GRE General Test, TOEFL. *Application deadline:* Applications are processed on a rolling basis. *Application fee:* $50 ($55 for international students). Electronic applications accepted.
Expenses: Tuition: Full-time $26,526.
Financial support: In 2001–02, 128 fellowships with full tuition reimbursements (averaging $19,800 per year), 358 research assistantships with partial tuition reimbursements (averaging $19,200 per year), 88 teaching assistantships with full tuition reimbursements (averaging $12,845 per year) were awarded. Career-related internships or fieldwork, Federal Work-Study, and institutionally sponsored loans also available. Financial award application deadline: 1/15; financial award applicants required to submit FAFSA. *Total annual research expenditures:* $45.2 million.
John Birge, Dean, 847-491-5520.
Application contact: Melissa W. Grady, Information Contact, 847-491-3553, *Fax:* 847-491-5341, *E-mail:* m-grady@northwestern.edu. *Web site:* http://www.tech.northwestern.edu/

Find an in-depth description at www.petersons.com/gradchannel.

■ OAKLAND UNIVERSITY

Graduate Study and Lifelong Learning, School of Engineering and Computer Science, Rochester, MI 48309-4401
AWARDS MS, PhD. Part-time and evening/weekend programs available.
Faculty: 39 full-time (6 women), 10 part-time/adjunct (0 women).
Students: 270 full-time (75 women), 378 part-time (96 women); includes 89 minority (17 African Americans, 65 Asian Americans or Pacific Islanders, 5 Hispanic Americans, 2 Native Americans), 167 international. Average age 30. 404 applicants, 81% accepted. In 2001, 173 master's, 8 doctorates awarded.

Degree requirements: For doctorate, thesis/dissertation.
Entrance requirements: For master's and doctorate, minimum GPA of 3.0 for unconditional admission. *Application deadline:* For fall admission, 8/1 (priority date); for winter admission, 12/1 (priority date); for spring admission, 4/1 (priority date). Applications are processed on a rolling basis. *Application fee:* $30. Electronic applications accepted.
Expenses: Tuition, state resident: full-time $5,904; part-time $246 per credit hour. Tuition, nonresident: full-time $12,192; part-time $508 per credit hour. Required fees: $472; $236 per term.
Financial support: Federal Work-Study, institutionally sponsored loans, and tuition waivers (full) available. Financial award application deadline: 3/1; financial award applicants required to submit FAFSA. *Total annual research expenditures:* $2.7 million.
Dr. Pieter Frick, Dean, 248-370-2233.
Application contact: Information Contact, 248-370-2233.

■ THE OHIO STATE UNIVERSITY

Graduate School, College of Engineering, Columbus, OH 43210
AWARDS M Arch, M Land Arch, MCRP, MS, PhD. Part-time and evening/weekend programs available.
Degree requirements: For doctorate, thesis/dissertation.

■ OHIO UNIVERSITY

Graduate Studies, Russ College of Engineering and Technology, Athens, OH 45701-2979
AWARDS MS, PhD. Part-time programs available.
Faculty: 106 full-time (5 women), 15 part-time/adjunct (4 women).
Students: 237 full-time (40 women), 78 part-time (17 women); includes 10 minority (4 African Americans, 6 Asian Americans or Pacific Islanders), 250 international. 933 applicants, 66% accepted. In 2001, 83 master's, 14 doctorates awarded. Terminal master's awarded for partial completion of doctoral program.
Degree requirements: For master's and doctorate, thesis/dissertation.
Entrance requirements: For doctorate, GRE. *Application fee:* $30. Electronic applications accepted.
Expenses: Tuition, state resident: full-time $6,585. Tuition, nonresident: full-time $12,254.
Financial support: In 2001–02, 16 fellowships with full tuition reimbursements (averaging $14,000 per year), 46 research assistantships with full tuition reimbursements (averaging $10,000 per year), 37 teaching assistantships with full tuition reimbursements (averaging $9,500 per year) were awarded. Career-related internships or fieldwork, Federal Work-Study, institutionally sponsored loans, tuition

waivers (full and partial), and unspecified assistantships also available.

Faculty research: Avionics engineering, coal research, transportation engineering, software systems integration, materials processing. *Total annual research expenditures:* $9.2 million.
Dr. Dennis Irwin, Interim Dean, 740-593-1482, *Fax:* 740-593-0659, *E-mail:* mitchell@ohio.edu.
Application contact: Roger Radcliff, Associate Dean, *Fax:* 740-593-0007, *E-mail:* radcliff@ohio.edu.

■ OKLAHOMA STATE UNIVERSITY

Graduate College, College of Engineering, Architecture and Technology, Stillwater, OK 74078

AWARDS M Arch, M Arch E, M Bio E, M En, M Gen E, MIE Mgmt, MS, PhD.

Faculty: 123 full-time (5 women), 14 part-time/adjunct (0 women).
Students: 368 full-time (52 women), 341 part-time (43 women); includes 42 minority (9 African Americans, 12 Asian Americans or Pacific Islanders, 10 Hispanic Americans, 11 Native Americans), 415 international. Average age 29. 1,158 applicants, 66% accepted. In 2001, 137 master's, 19 doctorates awarded.
Degree requirements: For doctorate, thesis/dissertation.
Entrance requirements: For master's and doctorate, TOEFL. *Application deadline:* For fall admission, 7/1 (priority date). *Application fee:* $25.
Expenses: Tuition, state resident: part-time $92 per credit hour. Tuition, nonresident: part-time $297 per credit hour. Required fees: $21 per credit hour. $14 per semester. One-time fee: $20. Tuition and fees vary according to course load.
Financial support: In 2001–02, 260 students received support, including 148 research assistantships (averaging $10,566 per year), 110 teaching assistantships (averaging $6,869 per year); fellowships, career-related internships or fieldwork, Federal Work-Study, and tuition waivers (partial) also available. Support available to part-time students. Financial award application deadline: 3/1.
Dr. Karl N. Reid, Dean, 405-744-5140.
Find an in-depth description at www.petersons.com/gradchannel.

■ OLD DOMINION UNIVERSITY

College of Engineering and Technology, Norfolk, VA 23529

AWARDS ME, MEM, MS, PhD. Part-time and evening/weekend programs available. Postbaccalaureate distance learning degree programs offered.

Faculty: 88 full-time (7 women), 28 part-time/adjunct (8 women).

Students: 217 full-time (40 women), 335 part-time (59 women); includes 73 minority (34 African Americans, 30 Asian Americans or Pacific Islanders, 8 Hispanic Americans, 1 Native American), 245 international. Average age 30. 468 applicants, 87% accepted. In 2001, 106 master's, 12 doctorates awarded.
Entrance requirements: For master's, TOEFL, GRE, minimum GPA of 3.0; for doctorate, TOEFL, GRE, minimum GPA of 3.5. *Application deadline:* Applications are processed on a rolling basis. *Application fee:* $30. Electronic applications accepted.
Expenses: Tuition, state resident: part-time $202 per credit. Tuition, nonresident: part-time $534 per credit. Required fees: $76 per semester.
Financial support: In 2001–02, 186 students received support, including 6 fellowships with full and partial tuition reimbursements available (averaging $9,000 per year), 140 research assistantships with full and partial tuition reimbursements available (averaging $12,100 per year), 20 teaching assistantships with full and partial tuition reimbursements available (averaging $9,000 per year); career-related internships or fieldwork, Federal Work-Study, institutionally sponsored loans, scholarships/grants, tuition waivers (partial), and unspecified assistantships also available. Support available to part-time students. Financial award applicants required to submit FAFSA.
Faculty research: Physical electronics, computational applied mechanics, structural dynamics, computational fluid dynamics, coastal engineering of water resources. *Total annual research expenditures:* $11.5 million.
Dr. William Swart, Dean, 757-683-3787, *Fax:* 757-683-4898, *E-mail:* wswart@odu.edu.
Application contact: Dr. Oktay Baysal, Associate Dean, 757-683-3789, *Fax:* 757-683-4898, *E-mail:* obaysal@odu.edu. *Web site:* http://www.odu.edu/engr/coet/
Find an in-depth description at www.petersons.com/gradchannel.

■ OREGON STATE UNIVERSITY

Graduate School, College of Engineering, Corvallis, OR 97331

AWARDS M Agr, M Eng, M Oc E, MA, MAIS, MS, PhD. Part-time programs available.

Faculty: 108 full-time (12 women), 2 part-time/adjunct (1 woman).
Students: 427 full-time (85 women), 69 part-time (5 women); includes 22 minority (1 African American, 16 Asian Americans or Pacific Islanders, 4 Hispanic Americans, 1 Native American), 332 international. Average age 28. In 2001, 116 master's, 16 doctorates awarded. Terminal master's awarded for partial completion of doctoral program.
Degree requirements: For doctorate, thesis/dissertation.

Entrance requirements: For master's and doctorate, TOEFL, minimum GPA of 3.0 in last 90 hours. *Application deadline:* Applications are processed on a rolling basis. *Application fee:* $50.
Expenses: Tuition, area resident: Full-time $15,933. Tuition, state resident: full-time $28,937.
Financial support: Fellowships, research assistantships, teaching assistantships, career-related internships or fieldwork, Federal Work-Study, institutionally sponsored loans, and instructorships available. Support available to part-time students. Financial award application deadline: 3/1.
Faculty research: Molecular beam epitaxy, wave-structure interaction, pavement materials, toxic wastes, mechanical design methodology.
Ronald L. Adams, Dean, 541-737-7722, *Fax:* 541-737-1805, *E-mail:* ronald.lynn.adams@orst.edu.
Application contact: Roy C. Rathja, Assistant Dean, 541-737-5236, *Fax:* 541-737-3124, *E-mail:* roy.rathja@orst.edu. *Web site:* http://www.engr.orst.edu/
Find an in-depth description at www.petersons.com/gradchannel.

■ THE PENNSYLVANIA STATE UNIVERSITY AT ERIE, THE BEHREND COLLEGE

Graduate Center, Program in Manufacturing Systems Engineering, Erie, PA 16563-0001

AWARDS M Eng.

Entrance requirements: For master's, GRE General Test. *Application deadline:* For fall admission, 7/26. *Application fee:* $50.
Expenses: Tuition, state resident: full-time $7,882; part-time $333 per credit. Tuition, nonresident: full-time $13,348; part-time $557 per credit.
Dr. Robert Simoneau, Director, 814-898-6153.

■ THE PENNSYLVANIA STATE UNIVERSITY HARRISBURG CAMPUS OF THE CAPITAL COLLEGE

Graduate Center, School of Science, Engineering and Technology, Program in Engineering Science, Middletown, PA 17057-4898

AWARDS M Eng. Evening/weekend programs available.

Students: 3 full-time (0 women), 30 part-time (10 women). Average age 33. In 2001, 5 degrees awarded.
Degree requirements: For master's, thesis.
Entrance requirements: For master's, GRE General Test, TOEFL, minimum

The Pennsylvania State University Harrisburg Campus of the Capital College (continued)
GPA of 2.5. *Application deadline:* For fall admission, 7/26. *Application fee:* $45.
Expenses: Tuition, state resident: full-time $7,882; part-time $333 per credit. Tuition, nonresident: full-time $14,384; part-time $600 per credit.
Dr. Seroj Mackertich, Chair, 717-948-6131.

■ THE PENNSYLVANIA STATE UNIVERSITY UNIVERSITY PARK CAMPUS

Graduate School, College of Engineering, State College, University Park, PA 16802-1503

AWARDS M Eng, MAE, MS, PhD.

Students: 902 full-time (172 women), 276 part-time (37 women).
Application fee: $45.
Expenses: Tuition, state resident: full-time $7,882; part-time $333 per credit. Tuition, nonresident: full-time $16,142; part-time $673 per credit. Required fees: $124 per semester.
Financial support: Fellowships, research assistantships, teaching assistantships available.
Dr. David N. Wormley, Dean, 814-865-7537.

Find an in-depth description at www.petersons.com/gradchannel.

■ PITTSBURG STATE UNIVERSITY

Graduate School, College of Technology, Department of Engineering Technology, Pittsburg, KS 66762

AWARDS MET.

Students: 10 full-time (3 women), 10 part-time (1 woman).
Degree requirements: For master's, thesis or alternative.
Application fee: $0 ($40 for international students).
Expenses: Tuition, state resident: full-time $2,676; part-time $114 per credit hour. Tuition, nonresident: full-time $6,778; part-time $285 per credit hour.
James Otter, Chairperson, 620-235-4349.

■ PITTSBURG STATE UNIVERSITY

Graduate School, College of Technology, Department of Technology Studies, Pittsburg, KS 66762

AWARDS Technology education (MS).

Students: 11 full-time (2 women), 7 part-time.
Degree requirements: For master's, thesis or alternative.

Application fee: $0 ($40 for international students).
Expenses: Tuition, state resident: full-time $2,676; part-time $114 per credit hour. Tuition, nonresident: full-time $6,778; part-time $285 per credit hour.
Financial support: Teaching assistantships, career-related internships or fieldwork and Federal Work-Study available.
Dr. John Iley, Chairperson, 620-235-4371.
Application contact: Marvene Darraugh, Administrative Officer, 620-235-4220, *Fax:* 620-235-4219, *E-mail:* mdarraug@pittstate.edu.

■ PORTLAND STATE UNIVERSITY

Graduate Studies, College of Engineering and Computer Science, Portland, OR 97207-0751

AWARDS M Eng, ME, MS, PhD, Certificate. Part-time and evening/weekend programs available.

Faculty: 53 full-time (6 women), 19 part-time/adjunct (3 women).
Students: 118 full-time (34 women), 161 part-time (35 women); includes 29 minority (3 African Americans, 19 Asian Americans or Pacific Islanders, 5 Hispanic Americans, 2 Native Americans), 142 international. Average age 31. 297 applicants, 67% accepted. In 2001, 101 master's, 2 doctorates awarded.
Degree requirements: For doctorate, one foreign language, thesis/dissertation, oral and written exams.
Entrance requirements: For master's, TOEFL, minimum GPA of 3.0 in upper-division course work or 2.75 overall; for doctorate, GRE General Test, GRE Subject Test, minimum GPA of 3.0 in upper-division course work. *Application deadline:* For fall admission, 3/1 (priority date). Applications are processed on a rolling basis. *Application fee:* $50.
Financial support: In 2001–02, 18 research assistantships with full tuition reimbursements (averaging $6,292 per year), 11 teaching assistantships with full tuition reimbursements (averaging $6,752 per year) were awarded. Career-related internships or fieldwork, Federal Work-Study, and institutionally sponsored loans also available. Support available to part-time students. Financial award application deadline: 3/1; financial award applicants required to submit FAFSA. *Total annual research expenditures:* $2.4 million.
Dr. Robert D. Dryden, Dean, 503-725-4631, *Fax:* 503-725-4298, *E-mail:* drydenr@eas.pdx.edu.
Application contact: Alisia Walton, Administrative Assistant, 503-725-4631, *Fax:* 503-725-4298, *E-mail:* waltona@eas.pdx.edu. *Web site:* http://www.eas.pdx.edu/

Find an in-depth description at www.petersons.com/gradchannel.

■ PRAIRIE VIEW A&M UNIVERSITY

Graduate School, College of Engineering, Prairie View, TX 77446-0188

AWARDS MS Engr. Part-time and evening/weekend programs available.

Faculty: 24 full-time (0 women), 1 part-time/adjunct (0 women).
Students: 13 full-time (3 women), 12 part-time (1 woman); includes 16 minority (10 African Americans, 6 Asian Americans or Pacific Islanders), 8 international. Average age 31. 16 applicants, 100% accepted, 8 enrolled. In 2001, 15 degrees awarded.
Degree requirements: For master's, thesis optional. *Median time to degree:* Master's–2 years full-time, 3 years part-time.
Entrance requirements: For master's, GRE General Test, bachelor's degree in engineering from an ABET accredited institution. *Application deadline:* For fall admission, 7/1 (priority date); for spring admission, 11/1 (priority date). Applications are processed on a rolling basis. *Application fee:* $50.
Expenses: Tuition, state resident: full-time $864; part-time $48 per credit hour. Tuition, nonresident: full-time $4,716; part-time $262 per credit hour. Required fees: $1,324; $59 per credit hour. $131 per term.
Financial support: In 2001–02, 12 students received support, including 11 research assistantships (averaging $14,000 per year), 1 teaching assistantship (averaging $12,000 per year); career-related internships or fieldwork, Federal Work-Study, institutionally sponsored loans, and scholarships/grants also available. Support available to part-time students. Financial award application deadline: 4/1; financial award applicants required to submit FAFSA.
Faculty research: Applied radiation research, lightweight structural materials and processing, thermal science, computational fluid dynamics, analog mixed signal. *Total annual research expenditures:* $3.7 million.
Dr. Milton R. Bryant, Dean, 936-857-2211, *Fax:* 936-857-2222.
Application contact: Dr. Shield B. Lin, Graduate Director, 936-857-4200, *Fax:* 936-857-4246, *E-mail:* shield_lin@pvamu.edu.

■ PRINCETON UNIVERSITY

Graduate School, School of Engineering and Applied Science, Princeton, NJ 08544-1019

AWARDS M Eng, MSE, PhD.

Degree requirements: For doctorate, thesis/dissertation.
Entrance requirements: For master's and doctorate, GRE General Test.

■ PURDUE UNIVERSITY

Graduate School, Schools of Engineering, West Lafayette, IN 47907

AWARDS MS, MS Bm E, MS Met E, MSAAE, MSABE, MSCE, MSE, MSIE, MSME, MSNE, PhD. Part-time and evening/weekend programs available. Postbaccalaureate distance learning degree programs offered (no on-campus study).

Students: 1,275 full-time (179 women), 658 part-time (119 women); includes 166 minority (41 African Americans, 77 Asian Americans or Pacific Islanders, 44 Hispanic Americans, 4 Native Americans), 1,010 international. Average age 28. 3,973 applicants, 36% accepted, 568 enrolled. In 2001, 399 master's, 142 doctorates awarded.

Degree requirements: For doctorate, thesis/dissertation.

Entrance requirements: For master's and doctorate, TOEFL. *Application fee:* $30. Electronic applications accepted.

Expenses: Tuition, state resident: full-time $4,164; part-time $149 per credit hour. Tuition, nonresident: full-time $13,872; part-time $458 per credit hour. Tuition and fees vary according to campus/location and program.

Financial support: Fellowships, research assistantships, teaching assistantships, career-related internships or fieldwork available. Support available to part-time students. Financial award applicants required to submit FAFSA.

Dr. Linda P. Katehi, Dean, 765-494-5345.

Find an in-depth description at www.petersons.com/gradchannel.

■ PURDUE UNIVERSITY CALUMET

Graduate School, School of Engineering, Mathematics, and Science, Department of Engineering, Hammond, IN 46323-2094

AWARDS MSE. Evening/weekend programs available.

Entrance requirements: For master's, TOEFL.

■ RENSSELAER AT HARTFORD

Department of Engineering, Hartford, CT 06120-2991

AWARDS ME, MS. Part-time and evening/ weekend programs available.

Faculty: 11 full-time (2 women), 34 part-time/adjunct (1 woman).

Students: 2 full-time (0 women), 225 part-time (30 women). Average age 31. In 2001, 66 degrees awarded.

Degree requirements: For master's, seminar.

Entrance requirements: For master's, TOEFL. *Application deadline:* For fall admission, 8/6 (priority date). Applications are processed on a rolling basis. *Application fee:* $45.

Expenses: Tuition: Full-time $11,700; part-time $650 per credit.

Financial support: Research assistantships, career-related internships or fieldwork, tuition waivers (full and partial), and unspecified assistantships available. Support available to part-time students. Financial award applicants required to submit FAFSA.

James McKim, Chair, 860-548-2455, *E-mail:* jcm@rh.edu.

Application contact: Rebecca Danchak, Director of Admissions, 860-548-2420, *Fax:* 860-548-7823, *E-mail:* rdanchak@rh.edu.

■ RENSSELAER POLYTECHNIC INSTITUTE

Graduate School, School of Engineering, Troy, NY 12180-3590

AWARDS M Eng, MS, D Eng, PhD, MBA/M Eng. Part-time and evening/weekend programs available. Postbaccalaureate distance learning degree programs offered (no on-campus study).

Faculty: 141 full-time (7 women), 30 part-time/adjunct (5 women).

Students: 664 full-time (121 women), 481 part-time (90 women); includes 116 minority (38 African Americans, 52 Asian Americans or Pacific Islanders, 26 Hispanic Americans), 515 international. 2,438 applicants, 37% accepted, 409 enrolled. In 2001, 324 master's, 62 doctorates awarded. Terminal master's awarded for partial completion of doctoral program.

Degree requirements: For master's, thesis (for some programs); for doctorate, thesis/dissertation.

Entrance requirements: For master's and doctorate, GRE, TOEFL. *Application deadline:* For fall admission, 1/15 (priority date). Applications are processed on a rolling basis. *Application fee:* $45. Electronic applications accepted.

Expenses: Tuition: Full-time $26,400; part-time $1,320 per credit hour. Required fees: $1,437.

Financial support: In 2001–02, fellowships with full tuition reimbursements (averaging $15,000 per year), research assistantships with full and partial tuition reimbursements (averaging $12,600 per year), teaching assistantships with full and partial tuition reimbursements (averaging $12,600 per year) were awarded. Career-related internships or fieldwork, institutionally sponsored loans, scholarships/grants, tuition waivers (full and partial), and unspecified assistantships also available. Financial award application deadline: 2/1; financial award applicants required to submit FAFSA.

Faculty research: Computer networking, materials, computational mechanics and modeling, microelectronic technology, data mining. *Total annual research expenditures:* $41.3 million.

Dr. William A. Baeslack, Dean, 518-276-6298, *Fax:* 518-276-8788, *E-mail:* baeslack@rpi.edu. *Web site:* http://www.eng.rpi.edu/

Find an in-depth description at www.petersons.com/gradchannel.

■ RICE UNIVERSITY

Graduate Programs, George R. Brown School of Engineering, Houston, TX 77251-1892

AWARDS M Ch E, M Stat, MA, MCAM, MCE, MCS, MEE, MEE, MES, MME, MMS, MS, PhD, MD/PhD. Part-time programs available.

Faculty: 98 full-time, 27 part-time/adjunct.

Students: 385 full-time (96 women), 25 part-time (8 women); includes 48 minority (10 African Americans, 22 Asian Americans or Pacific Islanders, 15 Hispanic Americans, 1 Native American), 206 international. 1,668 applicants, 16% accepted, 138 enrolled. In 2001, 65 master's, 51 doctorates awarded. Terminal master's awarded for partial completion of doctoral program.

Degree requirements: For master's, thesis (for some programs); for doctorate, thesis/dissertation.

Entrance requirements: For master's and doctorate, GRE General Test, GRE Subject Test, TOEFL, minimum GPA of 3.0. *Application deadline:* For fall admission, 2/1 (priority date); for spring admission, 11/1. Applications are processed on a rolling basis. *Application fee:* $25. Electronic applications accepted.

Expenses: Tuition: Full-time $17,300. Required fees: $250.

Financial support: In 2001–02, 182 fellowships with full tuition reimbursements (averaging $18,856 per year), 212 research assistantships with full tuition reimbursements (averaging $18,703 per year), 18 teaching assistantships with full tuition reimbursements (averaging $18,072 per year) were awarded. Federal Work-Study and tuition waivers (full) also available. Financial award applicants required to submit FAFSA.

Faculty research: Computational engineering, parallel computing, digital signal processing, tissue engineering, groundwater remediation. *Total annual research expenditures:* $23.3 million.

C. Sidney Burrus, Dean of Engineering, 713-348-4009, *Fax:* 713-348-5300, *E-mail:* grbsoe@rice.edu. *Web site:* http://www.engr.rice.edu/

■ ROBERT MORRIS UNIVERSITY

Graduate Studies, School of Engineering, Mathematics and Science, Moon Township, PA 15108-1189

AWARDS MS. Part-time and evening/weekend programs available.

Faculty: 3 full-time (0 women).

Entrance requirements: For master's, letters of recommendation. *Application*

Robert Morris University (continued)
deadline: For fall admission, 8/1 (priority date); for spring admission, 11/30 (priority date). Applications are processed on a rolling basis. *Application fee:* $35. Electronic applications accepted.
Expenses: Contact institution.
Financial support: Federal Work-Study, institutionally sponsored loans, and unspecified assistantships available. Financial award application deadline: 5/1; financial award applicants required to submit FAFSA.
Dr. Yildirim Omurtag, Dean, 412-604-2559, *Fax:* 412-262-8494, *E-mail:* omurtag@rmu.edu.
Application contact: Kellie Laurenzi, Director of Enrollment Services, 800-762-0097, *Fax:* 412-299-2425, *E-mail:* laurenzi@rmu.edu. *Web site:* http://www.rmu.edu/

■ ROCHESTER INSTITUTE OF TECHNOLOGY

Graduate Enrollment Services, College of Engineering, Rochester, NY 14623-5698

AWARDS ME, MS, MSEE, MSME, AC. Part-time and evening/weekend programs available.

Students: 58 full-time (12 women), 137 part-time (28 women); includes 21 minority (5 African Americans, 8 Asian Americans or Pacific Islanders, 8 Hispanic Americans), 62 international. 543 applicants, 53% accepted, 72 enrolled. In 2001, 79 master's, 6 other advanced degrees awarded.
Entrance requirements: For master's, TOEFL, minimum GPA of 3.0. *Application deadline:* For fall admission, 3/1 (priority date). Applications are processed on a rolling basis. *Application fee:* $50.
Expenses: Tuition: Full-time $20,928; part-time $587 per hour. Required fees: $162. Tuition and fees vary according to program.
Financial support: Fellowships, research assistantships, teaching assistantships, career-related internships or fieldwork, Federal Work-Study, institutionally sponsored loans, and tuition waivers (partial) available. Support available to part-time students.
Faculty research: Microprocessors, energy, communication systems.
Dr. Harvey Palmer, Dean, 585-475-2146.
Application contact: Dr. Richard Reeve, Associate Dean, 585-475-5382, *E-mail:* nrreie@rit.edu.

■ ROSE-HULMAN INSTITUTE OF TECHNOLOGY

Faculty of Engineering and Applied Sciences, Terre Haute, IN 47803-3920

AWARDS MS, MD/MS. Part-time and evening/weekend programs available.

Postbaccalaureate distance learning degree programs offered (minimal on-campus study).
Faculty: 62 full-time (7 women), 4 part-time/adjunct (1 woman).
Students: 57 full-time (11 women), 115 part-time (9 women); includes 8 minority (1 African American, 7 Asian Americans or Pacific Islanders), 40 international. Average age 28. 90 applicants, 81% accepted, 55 enrolled. In 2001, 25 degrees awarded.
Entrance requirements: For master's, GRE, TOEFL, minimum GPA of 3.0. *Application deadline:* For fall admission, 2/1 (priority date). Applications are processed on a rolling basis. *Application fee:* $0.
Expenses: Tuition: Full-time $21,792; part-time $615 per credit hour. Required fees: $405.
Financial support: In 2001–02, 68 students received support; fellowships with full and partial tuition reimbursements available, research assistantships with full and partial tuition reimbursements available, institutionally sponsored loans, scholarships/grants, and tuition waivers (full and partial) available. Financial award application deadline: 2/1.
Faculty research: Optical instrument design and prototypes, biomaterials, adsorption and adsorptin-based separations, image and speech processing, groundwater, solid and hazardous waste. *Total annual research expenditures:* $20 million.
Dr. Daniel J. Moore, Interim Associate Dean of the Faculty, 812-877-8110, *Fax:* 812-877-8061, *E-mail:* daniel.j.moore@rose-hulman.edu. *Web site:* http://www.rose-hulman.edu

Find an in-depth description at www.petersons.com/gradchannel.

■ ROWAN UNIVERSITY

Graduate School, College of Engineering, Glassboro, NJ 08028-1701

AWARDS MS. Part-time and evening/weekend programs available.

Students: 14 full-time (1 woman), 7 part-time (1 woman); includes 2 minority (both Asian Americans or Pacific Islanders). Average age 28. 8 applicants, 50% accepted, 4 enrolled. In 2001, 9 degrees awarded.
Application deadline: Applications are processed on a rolling basis. *Application fee:* $50. Electronic applications accepted.
Expenses: Tuition, state resident: full-time $7,080; part-time $295 per semester hour. Tuition, nonresident: full-time $11,328; part-time $472 per semester hour. Required fees: $855; $39 per semester hour. Tuition and fees vary according to degree level.
Financial support: Career-related internships or fieldwork, Federal Work-Study, and unspecified assistantships available. Support available to part-time students.
Dr. Dianne Dorland, Dean, 856-256-5300.

Application contact: Dr. T. R. Chandrupata, Program Adviser, 856-256-5342.

■ RUTGERS, THE STATE UNIVERSITY OF NEW JERSEY, NEW BRUNSWICK

Programs in Engineering, New Brunswick, NJ 08901-1281

AWARDS MS, PhD. Degrees offered through the Graduate School.

■ SAGINAW VALLEY STATE UNIVERSITY

College of Science, Engineering, and Technology, University Center, MI 48710

AWARDS MS. Part-time and evening/weekend programs available.

Faculty: 11 full-time (1 woman).
Students: 19 full-time (7 women), 23 part-time (5 women); includes 5 minority (3 African Americans, 1 Asian American or Pacific Islander, 1 Hispanic American), 5 international. Average age 33. 20 applicants, 75% accepted, 6 enrolled. In 2001, 10 degrees awarded. *Median time to degree:* Master's–2.32 years full-time, 2.5 years part-time.
Entrance requirements: For master's, TOEFL, minimum GPA of 3.0. *Application deadline:* Applications are processed on a rolling basis. *Application fee:* $25.
Expenses: Tuition, state resident: full-time $2,263; part-time $189 per credit. Tuition, nonresident: full-time $4,480; part-time $373 per credit. Required fees: $201; $17 per credit.
Financial support: In 2001–02, 1 fellowship with partial tuition reimbursement, 1 research assistantship with full tuition reimbursement (averaging $2,500 per year) were awarded. Federal Work-Study also available. Support available to part-time students. Financial award application deadline: 4/1; financial award applicants required to submit FAFSA.
Dr. Thomas Kullgren, Dean, 989-790-4144, *Fax:* 989-790-2717, *E-mail:* kullgren@svsu.edu.
Application contact: Barb Sageman, Director, Graduate Admissions, 989-249-1696, *Fax:* 989-790-0180, *E-mail:* gradadm@svsu.edu. *Web site:* http://www.svsu.edu/gradadm/mstp/index.html

■ ST. CLOUD STATE UNIVERSITY

School of Graduate Studies, College of Science and Engineering, St. Cloud, MN 56301-4498

AWARDS MA, MS.

Faculty: 70 full-time (21 women), 3 part-time/adjunct (1 woman).
Students: 32 full-time (15 women), 21 part-time (13 women); includes 27 minority (2 African Americans, 24 Asian

Americans or Pacific Islanders, 1 Native American). 90 applicants, 40% accepted. In 2001, 9 degrees awarded.
Degree requirements: For master's, thesis or alternative.
Entrance requirements: For master's, GRE General Test, minimum GPA of 2.75. *Application fee:* $35.
Expenses: Tuition, state resident: part-time $156 per credit. Tuition, nonresident: part-time $244 per credit. Required fees: $20 per credit.
Financial support: Federal Work-Study and unspecified assistantships available. Financial award application deadline: 3/1. Dr. A. I. Musah, Dean, 320-255-3909, *Fax:* 320-255-4262, *E-mail:* cose@ stcloudstate.edu.
Application contact: Lindalou Krueger, Graduate Studies Office, 320-255-2113, *Fax:* 320-654-5371, *E-mail:* lekrueger@ stcloudstate.edu.

■ ST. MARY'S UNIVERSITY OF SAN ANTONIO

Graduate School, Department of Engineering, San Antonio, TX 78228-8507

AWARDS Electrical engineering (MS); electrical/computer engineering (MS); engineering administration (MS); engineering computer applications (MS); engineering management (MS); engineering systems management (MS); industrial engineering (MS); operations research (MS). Software engineering (MS). Part-time and evening/weekend programs available.

Faculty: 6 full-time, 3 part-time/adjunct.
Students: 10 full-time (3 women), 48 part-time (9 women); includes 20 minority (1 African American, 3 Asian Americans or Pacific Islanders, 16 Hispanic Americans), 10 international. Average age 25. In 2001, 15 degrees awarded.
Degree requirements: For master's, thesis.
Entrance requirements: For master's, GRE General Test. *Application deadline:* For fall admission, 8/1. *Application fee:* $15.
Expenses: Tuition: Full-time $8,190; part-time $455 per credit hour. Required fees: $375.
Financial support: Teaching assistantships, Federal Work-Study available.
Faculty research: Image processing, control, communication, artificial intelligence, robotics.
Dr. Rafael Moras, Chairperson, 210-436-3305, *E-mail:* moras@stmarytx.edu.

■ SAN DIEGO STATE UNIVERSITY

Graduate and Research Affairs, College of Engineering, San Diego, CA 92182

AWARDS MS, PhD. Part-time and evening/weekend programs available. Terminal

master's awarded for partial completion of doctoral program.
Degree requirements: For doctorate, thesis/dissertation.
Entrance requirements: For master's, GRE General Test, TOEFL.

■ SAN FRANCISCO STATE UNIVERSITY

Graduate Division, College of Science and Engineering, School of Engineering, San Francisco, CA 94132-1722

AWARDS MS.

Entrance requirements: For master's, minimum GPA of 2.5 in last 60 units.
Faculty research: Signal processing, control systems, rehabilitation technology, computer engineering, power systems.

■ SAN JOSE STATE UNIVERSITY

Graduate Studies, College of Engineering, San Jose, CA 95192-0001

AWARDS MS. Part-time programs available.

Faculty: 60 full-time (5 women), 82 part-time/adjunct (7 women).
Students: 300 full-time (145 women), 776 part-time (227 women); includes 682 minority (14 African Americans, 639 Asian Americans or Pacific Islanders, 27 Hispanic Americans, 2 Native Americans), 165 international. Average age 29. 771 applicants, 56% accepted. In 2001, 237 degrees awarded.
Application deadline: For fall admission, 6/29; for spring admission, 11/30. Applications are processed on a rolling basis.
Application fee: $59. Electronic applications accepted.
Expenses: Tuition, nonresident: part-time $246 per unit. Required fees: $678 per semester. Tuition and fees vary according to course load.
Financial support: Teaching assistantships, career-related internships or fieldwork, Federal Work-Study, and institutionally sponsored loans available. Support available to part-time students. Financial award applicants required to submit FAFSA.
Dr. Don Kirk, Dean, 408-924-3800, *Fax:* 408-924-3818.

■ SANTA CLARA UNIVERSITY

School of Engineering, Santa Clara, CA 95053

AWARDS MS, MSAM, MSCE, MSCSE, MSE, MSE Mgt, MSEE, MSME, PhD, Certificate, Engineer. Part-time and evening/weekend programs available.

Faculty: 42 full-time (11 women), 54 part-time/adjunct (4 women).
Students: 146 full-time (67 women), 459 part-time (117 women); includes 206 minority (8 African Americans, 183 Asian Americans or Pacific Islanders, 15 Hispanic Americans), 253 international.

Average age 30. 441 applicants, 49% accepted. In 2001, 196 master's, 2 doctorates, 1 other advanced degree awarded.
Degree requirements: For master's, thesis or alternative; for doctorate and other advanced degree, thesis/dissertation.
Entrance requirements: For master's, GRE General Test, TOEFL, minimum GPA of 2.75; for doctorate, GRE General Test, TOEFL, master's degree or equivalent; for other advanced degree, master's degree, published paper. *Application deadline:* For fall admission, 6/1; for spring admission, 1/1. Applications are processed on a rolling basis. *Application fee:* $45 ($55 for international students). Electronic applications accepted.
Expenses: Contact institution.
Financial support: Fellowships, research assistantships, teaching assistantships, career-related internships or fieldwork, Federal Work-Study, institutionally sponsored loans, and scholarships/grants available. Support available to part-time students. Financial award application deadline: 3/1; financial award applicants required to submit FAFSA. *Total annual research expenditures:* $622,362.
Dr. Terry E. Shoup, Dean, 408-554-4600.
Application contact: Tina Samms, Assistant Director of Graduate Admissions, 408-554-4313, *Fax:* 408-554-5474, *E-mail:* engr-grad@scu.edu. *Web site:* http://www-eng.scu.edu/

Find an in-depth description at www.petersons.com/gradchannel.

■ SEATTLE UNIVERSITY

School of Science and Engineering, Seattle, WA 98122

AWARDS MSE. Part-time and evening/weekend programs available.

Faculty: 10 full-time (3 women), 5 part-time/adjunct (0 women).
Students: 8 full-time (3 women), 42 part-time (11 women); includes 9 minority (7 Asian Americans or Pacific Islanders, 1 Hispanic American, 1 Native American), 18 international. Average age 34. 29 applicants, 62% accepted, 10 enrolled. In 2001, 25 degrees awarded.
Degree requirements: For master's, thesis or alternative.
Entrance requirements: For master's, GRE General Test, 2 years of related work experience. *Application deadline:* For fall admission, 7/1. *Application fee:* $55.
Expenses: Contact institution.
Financial support: Career-related internships or fieldwork and Federal Work-Study available. Support available to part-time students. Financial award applicants required to submit FAFSA.
Dr. George Simmons, Dean, 206-296-5500, *Fax:* 206-296-2071.
Application contact: Janet Shandley, Associate Dean of Graduate Admissions, 206-296-5900, *Fax:* 206-298-5656, *E-mail:* grad_admissions@seattleu.edu. *Web site:* http://www.seattleu.edu/

■ SOUTH DAKOTA STATE UNIVERSITY

Graduate School, College of Engineering, Brookings, SD 57007

AWARDS MS, PhD. Part-time programs available.

Degree requirements: For master's, thesis, oral exam; for doctorate, thesis/dissertation, preliminary oral and written exams.
Entrance requirements: For master's and doctorate, TOEFL.
Faculty research: Process control and management, ground source heat pumps, water quality, heat transfer, power systems.

■ SOUTHERN ILLINOIS UNIVERSITY CARBONDALE

Graduate School, College of Engineering, Carbondale, IL 62901-6806

AWARDS MS, PhD.

Faculty: 55 full-time (3 women), 3 part-time/adjunct (0 women).
Students: 169 full-time (25 women), 109 part-time (25 women); includes 25 minority (11 African Americans, 10 Asian Americans or Pacific Islanders, 1 Hispanic American, 3 Native Americans), 174 international. 327 applicants, 32% accepted. In 2001, 60 master's, 3 doctorates awarded.
Degree requirements: For master's, comprehensive exam; for doctorate, thesis/dissertation.
Entrance requirements: For master's, TOEFL, minimum GPA of 2.7; for doctorate, GRE General Test, TOEFL, minimum GPA of 3.5. *Application deadline:* Applications are processed on a rolling basis. *Application fee:* $20.
Expenses: Tuition, state resident: full-time $3,794; part-time $154 per hour. Tuition, nonresident: full-time $6,566; part-time $308 per hour. Required fees: $277 per hour.
Financial support: In 2001–02, 112 students received support, including 1 fellowship, 58 research assistantships, 95 teaching assistantships; Federal Work-Study, institutionally sponsored loans, and tuition waivers (full) also available. Support available to part-time students.
Faculty research: Electrical systems, all facets of fossil energy, mechanics.
Dr. George Swisher, Dean, 618-536-2368.
Application contact: Dr. James Evers, Associate Dean of Research and Graduate Programs, 618-453-4321, *Fax:* 618-453-4235, *E-mail:* evers@sysa.c_engri.siu.edu.
Find an in-depth description at www.petersons.com/gradchannel.

■ SOUTHERN ILLINOIS UNIVERSITY EDWARDSVILLE

Graduate Studies and Research, School of Engineering, Edwardsville, IL 62026-0001

AWARDS MS. Part-time programs available.

Faculty: 40 full-time (3 women), 9 part-time/adjunct (1 woman).
Students: 145 full-time (24 women), 146 part-time (30 women); includes 10 minority (3 African Americans, 6 Asian Americans or Pacific Islanders, 1 Native American), 208 international. Average age 33. 336 applicants, 56% accepted, 80 enrolled. In 2001, 91 degrees awarded.
Degree requirements: For master's, thesis or research paper, final exam. *Median time to degree:* Master's–2.5 years full-time, 4 years part-time.
Entrance requirements: For master's, TOEFL. *Application deadline:* For fall admission, 7/20; for spring admission, 12/7. *Application fee:* $25.
Expenses: Tuition, state resident: full-time $2,712; part-time $113 per credit hour. Tuition, nonresident: full-time $5,424; part-time $226 per credit hour. Required fees: $250; $125 per term. $125 per term. Tuition and fees vary according to course load, campus/location and reciprocity agreements.
Financial support: In 2001–02, 11 research assistantships with full tuition reimbursements, 12 teaching assistantships with full tuition reimbursements were awarded. Fellowships with full tuition reimbursements, career-related internships or fieldwork, Federal Work-Study, institutionally sponsored loans, scholarships/grants, traineeships, and unspecified assistantships also available. Support available to part-time students. Financial award application deadline: 3/1; financial award applicants required to submit FAFSA.
Dr. Paul Seaburg, Dean, 618-650-2861, *E-mail:* pseabur@siue.edu.
Application contact: Dr. Jacob Van Roekel, Associate Dean, 618-650-2534, *E-mail:* jvanroe@siue.edu.

■ SOUTHERN METHODIST UNIVERSITY

School of Engineering, Dallas, TX 75275

AWARDS MS, MS Cp E, MSEE, MSEM, MSME, DE, PhD. Part-time programs available. Postbaccalaureate distance learning degree programs offered (no on-campus study).

Faculty: 48 full-time (5 women).
Students: 795 (164 women); includes 223 minority (49 African Americans, 125 Asian Americans or Pacific Islanders, 47 Hispanic Americans, 2 Native Americans) 197 international. Average age 32. 777 applicants, 42% accepted. In 2001, 217 master's, 18 doctorates awarded. Terminal master's awarded for partial completion of doctoral program.
Degree requirements: For master's, thesis optional; for doctorate, thesis/dissertation, oral and written qualifying exams.
Entrance requirements: For master's, GRE General Test, TOEFL, minimum GPA of 3.0 in last 2 years; bachelor's degree in engineering, mathematics, or sciences; for doctorate, bachelor's degree in related field. *Application deadline:* For fall admission, 7/1; for spring admission, 11/15. Applications are processed on a rolling basis. *Application fee:* $30.
Expenses: Contact institution.
Financial support: Fellowships, research assistantships, teaching assistantships, career-related internships or fieldwork, Federal Work-Study, institutionally sponsored loans, scholarships/grants, and tuition waivers (full and partial) available. Financial award applicants required to submit FAFSA.
Faculty research: Mobile and fault-tolerant computing, manufacturing systems, telecommunications, solid state devices and materials, fluid and thermal sciences. *Total annual research expenditures:* $3 million.
Dr. Stephen A. Szygenda, Dean, 214-768-3051, *Fax:* 214-768-3845, *E-mail:* szygenda@engr.smu.edu.
Application contact: Jim Dees, Director, Student Administration, 214-768-1456, *Fax:* 214-768-3845, *E-mail:* jdees@engr.smu.edu. *Web site:* http://www.seas.smu.edu/

■ SOUTHERN POLYTECHNIC STATE UNIVERSITY

School of Engineering Technology and Management, Marietta, GA 30060-2896

AWARDS MS. Part-time and evening/weekend programs available. Postbaccalaureate distance learning degree programs offered.

Faculty: 16 part-time/adjunct (2 women).
Students: 19 full-time (11 women), 129 part-time (36 women); includes 48 minority (36 African Americans, 7 Asian Americans or Pacific Islanders, 5 Hispanic Americans), 22 international. Average age 36. In 2001, 40 degrees awarded.
Application deadline: For fall admission, 7/15 (priority date); for spring admission, 12/1. Applications are processed on a rolling basis. *Application fee:* $20. Electronic applications accepted.
Expenses: Tuition, state resident: full-time $1,746; part-time $97 per credit. Tuition, nonresident: full-time $6,966; part-time $387 per credit. Required fees: $221 per term.
Financial support: Teaching assistantships, career-related internships or fieldwork, Federal Work-Study, scholarships/grants, and unspecified assistantships available. Support available to part-time students. Financial award

application deadline: 5/1; financial award applicants required to submit FAFSA. Dr. Richard M. Aynsley, Dean, 770-528-7234, *Fax:* 770-528-7134, *E-mail:* raynsley@spsu.edu.

Application contact: Virginia A. Head, Director of Admissions, 770-528-7281, *Fax:* 770-528-7292, *E-mail:* vhead@ spsu.edu. *Web site:* http://www.spsu.edu/ etm/

■ STANFORD UNIVERSITY

School of Engineering, Stanford, CA 94305-9991

AWARDS MS, PhD, Eng, MBA/MS.

Faculty: 219 full-time (19 women).
Students: 2,472 full-time (533 women), 574 part-time (107 women); includes 589 minority (65 African Americans, 439 Asian Americans or Pacific Islanders, 81 Hispanic Americans, 4 Native Americans), 1,401 international. Average age 26. 4,518 applicants, 39% accepted. In 2001, 1,009 master's, 196 doctorates awarded.
Degree requirements: For doctorate and Eng, thesis/dissertation.
Entrance requirements: For master's, doctorate, and Eng, GRE General Test, TOEFL. *Application fee:* $65 ($80 for international students). Electronic applications accepted.
Expenses: Contact institution.
James D. Plummer, Dean, 650-723-3938, *Fax:* 650-723-8545, *E-mail:* plummer@ ee.stanford.edu.
Application contact: 650-723-4291, *E-mail:* ck.gaa@stanford.edu. *Web site:* http://soe.stanford.edu/

■ STATE UNIVERSITY OF NEW YORK AT BINGHAMTON

Graduate School, Thomas J. Watson School of Engineering and Applied Science, Binghamton, NY 13902-6000

AWARDS M Eng, MS, MSAT, PhD. Part-time and evening/weekend programs available.

Faculty: 50 full-time (6 women), 24 part-time/adjunct (6 women).
Students: 277 full-time (47 women), 210 part-time (44 women); includes 46 minority (13 African Americans, 30 Asian Americans or Pacific Islanders, 2 Hispanic Americans, 1 Native American), 282 international. Average age 29. 1,055 applicants, 41% accepted, 105 enrolled. In 2001, 123 master's, 10 doctorates awarded. Terminal master's awarded for partial completion of doctoral program.
Degree requirements: For doctorate, thesis/dissertation.
Entrance requirements: For master's and doctorate, GRE General Test, GRE Subject Test, TOEFL. *Application deadline:* For fall admission, 4/15 (priority date); for spring admission, 11/1. Applications are processed on a rolling basis. Electronic applications accepted.
Expenses: Tuition, state resident: full-time $5,100; part-time $213 per credit. Tuition,

nonresident: full-time $8,416; part-time $351 per credit. Required fees: $811.
Financial support: In 2001–02, 198 students received support, including 7 fellowships with full tuition reimbursements available (averaging $6,476 per year), 112 research assistantships with full tuition reimbursements available (averaging $6,360 per year), 80 teaching assistantships with full tuition reimbursements available (averaging $7,583 per year); career-related internships or fieldwork, Federal Work-Study, institutionally sponsored loans, tuition waivers (full and partial), and unspecified assistantships also available. Support available to part-time students. Financial award application deadline: 2/15. Dr. Charles R. Westgate, Dean, 607-777-2871. *Web site:* http:// watson.binghamton.edu

Find an in-depth description at www.petersons.com/gradchannel.

■ STATE UNIVERSITY OF NEW YORK INSTITUTE OF TECHNOLOGY AT UTICA/ROME

School of Information Systems and Engineering Technology, Utica, NY 13504-3050

AWARDS Advanced technology (MS); computer and information science (MS); telecommunications (MS). Part-time and evening/weekend programs available.

Faculty: 20 full-time (3 women), 2 part-time/adjunct (0 women).
Students: 52 full-time (12 women), 74 part-time (15 women); includes 8 minority (4 African Americans, 4 Asian Americans or Pacific Islanders), 41 international. Average age 32. 96 applicants, 88% accepted. In 2001, 25 degrees awarded.
Entrance requirements: For master's, GRE General Test, TOEFL, minimum GPA of 3.0. *Application deadline:* For fall admission, 6/15 (priority date). Applications are processed on a rolling basis. *Application fee:* $50.
Expenses: Tuition, state resident: full-time $5,100; part-time $213 per credit hour. Tuition, nonresident: full-time $8,416; part-time $351 per credit hour. Required fees: $525; $21 per credit hour. Tuition and fees vary according to course load.
Financial support: In 2001–02, 39 students received support. Federal Work-Study, scholarships/grants, and unspecified assistantships available. Financial award applicants required to submit FAFSA. Dr. Orlando Baiocchi, Dean, 315-792-7234, *Fax:* 315-792-7800, *E-mail:* baiocco@sunyit.edu.
Application contact: Marybeth Lyons, Director of Admissions, 315-792-7500, *Fax:* 315-792-7837, *E-mail:* smbl@ sunyit.edu. *Web site:* http:// www.cs.sunyit.edu/ISET/

■ STEVENS INSTITUTE OF TECHNOLOGY

Graduate School, Charles V. Schaefer Jr. School of Engineering, Hoboken, NJ 07030

AWARDS M Eng, MS, PhD, Certificate, Engr. Part-time and evening/weekend programs available. Postbaccalaureate distance learning degree programs offered. Terminal master's awarded for partial completion of doctoral program.

Degree requirements: For doctorate, thesis/dissertation.
Entrance requirements: For master's and doctorate, TOEFL. Electronic applications accepted.
Expenses: Tuition: Full-time $13,950; part-time $775 per credit. Required fees: $180. One-time fee: $180 part-time. Full-time tuition and fees vary according to degree level and program.

Find an in-depth description at www.petersons.com/gradchannel.

■ STEVENS INSTITUTE OF TECHNOLOGY

Graduate School, Program in Interdisciplinary Sciences and Engineering, Hoboken, NJ 07030

AWARDS M Eng, MS, PhD.

Degree requirements: For doctorate, thesis/dissertation.
Entrance requirements: For master's and doctorate, TOEFL. Electronic applications accepted.
Expenses: Tuition: Full-time $13,950; part-time $775 per credit. Required fees: $180. One-time fee: $180 part-time. Full-time tuition and fees vary according to degree level and program.

■ STEVENS INSTITUTE OF TECHNOLOGY

Graduate School, School of Applied Sciences and Liberal Arts, Hoboken, NJ 07030

AWARDS M Eng, MS, PhD, Certificate. Part-time and evening/weekend programs available. Terminal master's awarded for partial completion of doctoral program.

Degree requirements: For doctorate, thesis/dissertation.
Entrance requirements: For master's and doctorate, TOEFL. Electronic applications accepted.
Expenses: Tuition: Full-time $13,950; part-time $775 per credit. Required fees: $180. One-time fee: $180 part-time. Full-time tuition and fees vary according to degree level and program.

■ STONY BROOK UNIVERSITY, STATE UNIVERSITY OF NEW YORK

Graduate School, College of Engineering and Applied Sciences, Stony Brook, NY 11794

AWARDS MBA, MS, PhD, Certificate. Part-time and evening/weekend programs available.

Faculty: 167 full-time (21 women), 22 part-time/adjunct (0 women).
Students: 580 full-time (195 women), 339 part-time (92 women); includes 94 minority (19 African Americans, 62 Asian Americans or Pacific Islanders, 13 Hispanic Americans), 614 international. 1,714 applicants, 46% accepted. In 2001, 221 master's, 44 doctorates, 1 other advanced degree awarded.
Degree requirements: For doctorate, thesis/dissertation, comprehensive exam.
Entrance requirements: For master's, TOEFL; for doctorate, GRE General Test, TOEFL. *Application deadline:* For fall admission, 1/15. *Application fee:* $50.
Expenses: Tuition, state resident: full-time $5,100; part-time $213 per credit. Tuition, nonresident: full-time $8,416; part-time $351 per credit. Required fees: $496.
Financial support: In 2001–02, 19 fellowships, 185 research assistantships, 260 teaching assistantships were awarded. Career-related internships or fieldwork also available. *Total annual research expenditures:* $17 million.
Dr. Yacov Shamash, Dean, 631-632-8380. *Web site:* http://www.ceas.sunysb.edu/

■ SYRACUSE UNIVERSITY

Graduate School, L. C. Smith College of Engineering and Computer Science, Syracuse, NY 13244-0003

AWARDS ME, MS, PhD, CE, EE, JD/MS. Part-time and evening/weekend programs available.

Faculty: 27 full-time (3 women), 15 part-time/adjunct (1 woman).
Students: 614 full-time (66 women), 222 part-time (27 women); includes 18 minority (5 African Americans, 13 Asian Americans or Pacific Islanders), 569 international. Average age 29. 979 applicants, 85% accepted, 297 enrolled. In 2001, 215 master's, 15 doctorates awarded.
Degree requirements: For doctorate, thesis/dissertation.
Entrance requirements: For master's and doctorate, GRE General Test, GRE Subject Test. *Application deadline:* Applications are processed on a rolling basis. *Application fee:* $50.
Expenses: Tuition: Full-time $15,528; part-time $647 per credit. Required fees: $420; $38 per term. Tuition and fees vary according to program.
Financial support: In 2001–02, 16 fellowships with full tuition reimbursements (averaging $13,680 per year), 101 research

assistantships with full tuition reimbursements (averaging $11,000 per year), 71 teaching assistantships with full tuition reimbursements (averaging $11,000 per year) were awarded. Federal Work-Study and tuition waivers (partial) also available. Financial award application deadline: 1/10.
Faculty research: Environmental systems, information assurance, biomechanics, solid mechanics and materials, software engineering.
Dr. Edward Bogucz, Dean, 315-443-4341, *Fax:* 315-443-4936, *E-mail:* bogucz@syr.edu.
Application contact: Dr. Eric F. Spina, Associate Dean, 315-443-3604, *Fax:* 315-443-4936, *E-mail:* efspina@syr.edu. *Web site:* http://www.ecs.syr.edu/

Find an in-depth description at www.petersons.com/gradchannel.

■ TEMPLE UNIVERSITY

Graduate School, College of Science and Technology, College of Engineering, Philadelphia, PA 19122-6096

AWARDS Civil and environmental engineering (MSE); electrical and computer engineering (MSE); engineering (PhD); environmental health sciences (MS), including environmental health; mechanical engineering (MSE). Part-time programs available.

Faculty: 28 full-time (2 women), 7 part-time/adjunct (1 woman).
Students: 48 full-time (16 women), 48 part-time (3 women); includes 6 minority (3 African Americans, 3 Asian Americans or Pacific Islanders), 43 international. 154 applicants, 49% accepted. In 2001, 32 master's, 1 doctorate awarded.
Degree requirements: For master's, thesis optional; for doctorate, thesis/dissertation, 2 published papers, comprehensive exam.
Entrance requirements: For master's, GRE General Test, TOEFL, minimum undergraduate GPA of 3.0; for doctorate, GRE General Test, TOEFL, minimum graduate GPA of 3.5, MS. *Application deadline:* For fall admission, 7/1 (priority date); for spring admission, 11/1 (priority date). Applications are processed on a rolling basis. *Application fee:* $40. Electronic applications accepted.
Expenses: Tuition, state resident: full-time $8,487; part-time $369 per credit hour. Tuition, nonresident: full-time $12,282; part-time $534 per credit hour. Required fees: $350. Tuition and fees vary according to course load, program and reciprocity agreements.
Financial support: In 2001–02, 30 students received support, including 2 fellowships with full tuition reimbursements available (averaging $15,000 per year), 3 research assistantships with full tuition reimbursements available (averaging $13,000 per year), 25 teaching assistantships with full tuition reimbursements available (averaging $11,400 per year);

career-related internships or fieldwork, Federal Work-Study, and institutionally sponsored loans also available. Financial award application deadline: 2/15.
Faculty research: Computer engineering, digital systems, bioengineering, transportation, materials.
Dr. Saroj Biswas, Director of Graduate Studies, 215-204-8403, *Fax:* 215-204-6936, *E-mail:* sbiswas@unix.temple.edu. *Web site:* http://www.eng.temple.edu/

Find an in-depth description at www.petersons.com/gradchannel.

■ TENNESSEE STATE UNIVERSITY

Graduate School, College of Engineering and Technology, Nashville, TN 37209-1561

AWARDS ME. Part-time and evening/weekend programs available.

Faculty: 20 full-time (0 women), 5 part-time/adjunct (0 women).
Students: 30 full-time (10 women), 28 part-time (5 women); includes 48 minority (21 African Americans, 24 Asian Americans or Pacific Islanders, 3 Hispanic Americans). Average age 27. 92 applicants, 88% accepted. In 2001, 14 degrees awarded.
Degree requirements: For master's, project.
Application deadline: Applications are processed on a rolling basis. *Application fee:* $15. Electronic applications accepted.
Expenses: Tuition, state resident: full-time $3,884; part-time $247 per hour. Tuition, nonresident: full-time $10,356; part-time $517 per hour.
Financial support: In 2001–02, 7 research assistantships (averaging $13,646 per year), 6 teaching assistantships (averaging $16,665 per year) were awarded. Fellowships Financial award application deadline: 4/30.
Faculty research: Intelligence/robotics, computational fluid dynamics, design methodologies, intelligent manufacturing, neural networks. *Total annual research expenditures:* $1.2 million.
Dr. Decatur B. Rogers, Dean, 615-963-5409, *Fax:* 615-963-5397.
Application contact: Dr. Mohan J. Malkani, Associate Dean, 615-963-5400, *Fax:* 615-963-5397, *E-mail:* malkani@harpo.tnstate.edu.

■ TENNESSEE TECHNOLOGICAL UNIVERSITY

Graduate School, College of Engineering, Cookeville, TN 38505

AWARDS MS, PhD. Part-time programs available.

Faculty: 76 full-time (2 women).
Students: 131 full-time (14 women), 43 part-time (9 women); includes 123 minority (4 African Americans, 119 Asian

Americans or Pacific Islanders). Average age 28. 965 applicants, 47% accepted. In 2001, 57 master's, 5 doctorates awarded.
Degree requirements: For master's, thesis; for doctorate, one foreign language, thesis/dissertation.
Entrance requirements: For master's, GRE General Test, TOEFL; for doctorate, GRE Subject Test, TOEFL, minimum GPA of 3.5. *Application deadline:* For fall admission, 3/1 (priority date); for spring admission, 8/1. *Application fee:* $25 ($30 for international students).
Expenses: Tuition, state resident: full-time $4,000; part-time $215 per hour. Tuition, nonresident: full-time $10,500; part-time $495 per hour. Required fees: $1,971 per semester.
Financial support: In 2001–02, 1 fellowship (averaging $10,000 per year), 91 research assistantships (averaging $9,293 per year), 29 teaching assistantships (averaging $7,223 per year) were awarded. Career-related internships or fieldwork also available. Support available to part-time students. Financial award application deadline: 4/1.
Dr. Glen Johnson, Dean, 931-372-3172, *Fax:* 931-372-6172.
Application contact: Dr. Francis O. Otuonye, Associate Vice President for Research and Graduate Studies, 931-372-3233, *Fax:* 931-372-3497, *E-mail:* fotuonye@tntech.edu.
Find an in-depth description at www.petersons.com/gradchannel.

■ TEXAS A&M UNIVERSITY

College of Engineering, College Station, TX 77843
AWARDS M Eng, MCE, MCS, MID, MS, D Eng, DE, PhD. Part-time programs available. Postbaccalaureate distance learning degree programs offered (minimal on-campus study).
Faculty: 437.
Students: 1,976 (328 women); includes 82 minority (18 African Americans, 30 Asian Americans or Pacific Islanders, 34 Hispanic Americans) 1,550 international. 4,692 applicants, 36% accepted, 515 enrolled. In 2001, 434 master's, 128 doctorates awarded. Terminal master's awarded for partial completion of doctoral program.
Entrance requirements: For master's and doctorate, GRE General Test, TOEFL. *Application fee:* $50 ($75 for international students). Electronic applications accepted.
Expenses: Tuition, state resident: full-time $11,872. Tuition, nonresident: full-time $17,892.
Financial support: Fellowships, research assistantships, teaching assistantships, career-related internships or fieldwork, institutionally sponsored loans, scholarships/grants, health care benefits, and unspecified assistantships available. Financial award applicants required to

submit FAFSA. *Total annual research expenditures:* $139.9 million.
C. Roland Haden, Dean, 979-845-7203, *Fax:* 979-845-8986, *E-mail:* r-haden@ tamu.edu.
Application contact: Karen Butler-Purry, Assistant Dean, 979-845-7200, *Fax:* 979-847-8654, *E-mail:* eapo@tamu.edu. *Web site:* http://aggieengineer.tamu.edu/

■ TEXAS A&M UNIVERSITY–KINGSVILLE

College of Graduate Studies, College of Engineering, Kingsville, TX 78363
AWARDS ME, MS. Part-time and evening/weekend programs available.
Faculty: 25 full-time (3 women).
Students: 142 full-time (18 women), 80 part-time (7 women); includes 25 minority (1 African American, 3 Asian Americans or Pacific Islanders, 21 Hispanic Americans), 188 international. Average age 26. In 2001, 69 degrees awarded.
Degree requirements: For master's, comprehensive exam.
Entrance requirements: For master's, GRE General Test, TOEFL. *Application deadline:* For fall admission, 6/1; for spring admission, 11/15. Applications are processed on a rolling basis. *Application fee:* $15 ($25 for international students).
Expenses: Tuition, state resident: part-time $42 per hour. Tuition, nonresident: part-time $253 per hour. Required fees: $56 per hour. One-time fee: $46 part-time. Tuition and fees vary according to program.
Financial support: Fellowships, research assistantships, teaching assistantships, career-related internships or fieldwork, Federal Work-Study, institutionally sponsored loans, tuition waivers (partial), and unspecified assistantships available. Support available to part-time students. Financial award application deadline: 5/15.
Dr. Phil V. Compton, Dean, 361-593-2001.
Find an in-depth description at www.petersons.com/gradchannel.

■ TEXAS TECH UNIVERSITY

Graduate School, College of Engineering, Lubbock, TX 79409
AWARDS M Engr, M Env E, MS, MS Ch E, MS Pet E, MSCE, MSEE, MSETM, MSIE, MSME, MSSEM, PhD. Part-time programs available.
Faculty: 91 full-time (8 women), 4 part-time/adjunct (0 women).
Students: 341 full-time (53 women), 88 part-time (17 women); includes 20 minority (2 African Americans, 3 Asian Americans or Pacific Islanders, 14 Hispanic Americans; 1 Native American), 284 international. Average age 28. 980 applicants, 33% accepted, 121 enrolled. In 2001, 107 master's, 15 doctorates awarded.

Degree requirements: For master's, thesis (for some programs); for doctorate, thesis/dissertation.
Entrance requirements: For master's and doctorate, GRE General Test, minimum GPA of 3.0. *Application deadline:* Applications are processed on a rolling basis. *Application fee:* $25 ($50 for international students). Electronic applications accepted.
Expenses: Contact institution.
Financial support: In 2001–02, 188 research assistantships with partial tuition reimbursements (averaging $10,087 per year), 36 teaching assistantships with partial tuition reimbursements (averaging $10,027 per year) were awarded. Fellowships, career-related internships or fieldwork, Federal Work-Study, and institutionally sponsored loans also available. Support available to part-time students. Financial award application deadline: 5/1; financial award applicants required to submit FAFSA.
Faculty research: Fluid mechanics/wind engineering, alternative fuels, pulsed power for space, environmental engineering, human factors/performance in the workplace. *Total annual research expenditures:* $10.7 million.
Dr. William M. Marcy, Dean, 806-742-3451, *Fax:* 806-742-3493.
Application contact: Graduate Adviser, 806-742-3451, *Fax:* 806-742-3493. *Web site:* http://www.coe.ttu.edu/

■ TUFTS UNIVERSITY

Division of Graduate and Continuing Studies and Research, Graduate School of Arts and Sciences, School of Engineering, Medford, MA 02155
AWARDS ME, MS, MSEM, PhD. Part-time programs available.
Faculty: 64 full-time, 24 part-time/adjunct.
Students: 371 (113 women); includes 36 minority (3 African Americans, 23 Asian Americans or Pacific Islanders, 9 Hispanic Americans, 1 Native American) 89 international. 347 applicants, 60% accepted. In 2001, 113 master's, 5 doctorates awarded. Terminal master's awarded for partial completion of doctoral program.
Degree requirements: For doctorate, thesis/dissertation.
Entrance requirements: For master's, TOEFL; for doctorate, GRE General Test, TOEFL. *Application deadline:* Applications are processed on a rolling basis. *Application fee:* $50. Electronic applications accepted.
Expenses: Tuition: Full-time $26,853. Full-time tuition and fees vary according to program.
Financial support: Research assistantships with full and partial tuition reimbursements, teaching assistantships with full and partial tuition reimbursements, Federal Work-Study, scholarships/grants, and tuition waivers (partial) available. Support available to part-time students. Financial

Tufts University (continued)
award application deadline: 2/15; financial award applicants required to submit FAFSA.
Dr. Ioannis Miaoulis, Dean, 617-627-3237, *Fax:* 617-627-3819. *Web site:* http://www.ase.tufts.edu/engineering/

Find an in-depth description at www.petersons.com/gradchannel.

■ **TULANE UNIVERSITY**

School of Engineering, New Orleans, LA 70118-5669

AWARDS MS, MSCS, MSE, PhD, Sc D. MS and PhD offered through the Graduate School. Part-time programs available.

Faculty: 55 full-time, 1 part-time/adjunct.
Students: 533 applicants, 22% accepted. In 2001, 38 master's, 13 doctorates awarded.
Degree requirements: For doctorate, thesis/dissertation.
Entrance requirements: For master's and doctorate, GRE General Test, TOEFL, minimum B average in undergraduate course work. *Application fee:* $35.
Expenses: Tuition: Full-time $24,675. Required fees: $2,210.
Financial support: Fellowships, research assistantships, teaching assistantships, career-related internships or fieldwork, Federal Work-Study, institutionally sponsored loans, and tuition waivers (full and partial) available. Financial award application deadline: 2/1.
Dr. Nicholas Altiero, Acting Dean, 504-865-5766, *Fax:* 504-862-8747.
Application contact: Dr. E. Michaelides, Associate Dean, 504-865-5764.

■ **TUSKEGEE UNIVERSITY**

Graduate Programs, College of Engineering, Architecture and Physical Sciences, Tuskegee, AL 36088

AWARDS MSEE, MSME, PhD.

Faculty: 19 full-time (0 women).
Students: 27 full-time (3 women), 20 part-time (3 women); includes 20 minority (19 African Americans, 1 Asian American or Pacific Islander), 25 international. Average age 24. 104 applicants, 59% accepted. In 2001, 17 degrees awarded.
Degree requirements: For master's, thesis or alternative.
Entrance requirements: For master's, GRE General Test, GRE Subject Test. *Application deadline:* For fall admission, 7/15. Applications are processed on a rolling basis. *Application fee:* $25 ($35 for international students).
Expenses: Tuition: Full-time $5,163; part-time $612 per credit hour.
Financial support: Fellowships, research assistantships, teaching assistantships, career-related internships or fieldwork, Federal Work-Study, and institutionally

sponsored loans available. Support available to part-time students. Financial award application deadline: 4/15.
Dr. Legand L. Burge, Acting Dean, 334-727-8356.

■ **UNION COLLEGE**

Center for Graduate Education and Special Programs, Division of Engineering and Computer Science, Schenectady, NY 12308-2311

AWARDS MS. Part-time and evening/weekend programs available.

Students: 11 full-time (3 women), 32 part-time (4 women); includes 1 minority (African American), 5 international. Average age 32. 8 applicants, 100% accepted, 6 enrolled. In 2001, 21 degrees awarded.
Entrance requirements: For master's, minimum GPA of 3.0. *Application deadline:* Applications are processed on a rolling basis. *Application fee:* $50.
Expenses: Contact institution.
Financial support: Research assistantships, health care benefits available. Support available to part-time students.
Application contact: Rhonda Sheehan, Coordinator of Recruiting and Admissions, 518-388-6238, *Fax:* 518-388-6754, *E-mail:* sheehanr@union.edu. *Web site:* http://www.engineering.union.edu

■ **UNIVERSITY AT BUFFALO, THE STATE UNIVERSITY OF NEW YORK**

Graduate School, School of Engineering and Applied Sciences, Buffalo, NY 14260

AWARDS M Eng, MS, PhD. Part-time and evening/weekend programs available. Postbaccalaureate distance learning degree programs offered (minimal on-campus study).

Faculty: 124 full-time (12 women), 30 part-time/adjunct (4 women).
Students: 637 full-time (110 women), 220 part-time (39 women); includes 42 minority (10 African Americans, 26 Asian Americans or Pacific Islanders, 4 Hispanic Americans, 2 Native Americans), 602 international. Average age 25. 2,307 applicants, 59% accepted, 357 enrolled. In 2001, 250 master's, 59 doctorates awarded. Terminal master's awarded for partial completion of doctoral program.
Degree requirements: For doctorate, thesis/dissertation.
Entrance requirements: For master's and doctorate, GRE General Test, TOEFL. *Application deadline:* Applications are processed on a rolling basis. *Application fee:* $35. Electronic applications accepted.
Expenses: Tuition, state resident: full-time $6,118. Tuition, nonresident: full-time $9,434.
Financial support: In 2001–02, 22 fellowships with full tuition reimbursements (averaging $16,000 per year), 210 research assistantships with full and partial tuition

reimbursements (averaging $14,000 per year), 180 teaching assistantships with full tuition reimbursements (averaging $10,700 per year) were awarded. Career-related internships or fieldwork, Federal Work-Study, institutionally sponsored loans, scholarships/grants, tuition waivers (full and partial), and unspecified assistantships also available. Support available to part-time students. Financial award applicants required to submit FAFSA.
Faculty research: Bioengineering, infrastructure and environmental engineering, electronic and photonic materials, simulation and visualization, information technology and computing. *Total annual research expenditures:* $24.9 million.
Dr. Mark H. Karwan, Dean, 716-645-2771, *Fax:* 716-645-2495.
Application contact: Dr. Andres Soom, Associate Dean, 716-645-2772, *Fax:* 716-645-2495, *E-mail:* soom@eng.buffalo.edu. *Web site:* http://www.eng.buffalo.edu/

■ **THE UNIVERSITY OF AKRON**

Graduate School, College of Engineering, Akron, OH 44325-0001

AWARDS MS, PhD, MD/PhD. Part-time and evening/weekend programs available.

Faculty: 54 full-time (6 women), 26 part-time/adjunct (0 women).
Students: 178 full-time (33 women), 102 part-time (16 women); includes 8 minority (2 African Americans, 2 Asian Americans or Pacific Islanders, 3 Hispanic Americans, 1 Native American), 167 international. Average age 29. 263 applicants, 74% accepted, 60 enrolled. In 2001, 71 master's, 21 doctorates awarded. Terminal master's awarded for partial completion of doctoral program.
Degree requirements: For master's, thesis or alternative; for doctorate, one foreign language, thesis/dissertation, candidacy exam, qualifying exam.
Entrance requirements: For master's, TOEFL; for doctorate, GRE, TOEFL. *Application deadline:* Applications are processed on a rolling basis. *Application fee:* $40 ($50 for international students).
Expenses: Tuition, state resident: full-time $6,562; part-time $219 per credit. Tuition, nonresident: full-time $9,027; part-time $383 per credit. Required fees: $272; $11 per credit. Tuition and fees vary according to course load.
Financial support: In 2001–02, 183 students received support, including 52 research assistantships with full tuition reimbursements available, 90 teaching assistantships with full tuition reimbursements available; fellowships with full tuition reimbursements available, career-related internships or fieldwork, Federal Work-Study, and tuition waivers (full) also available. Financial award application deadline: 3/1.

Faculty research: Computational mechanics, signal processing, reaction engineering, control engineering, thermodynamic heat transfer.
Dr. S. Graham Kelly, Interim Dean, 330-972-6978, *E-mail:* sgraham@uakron.edu.
Web site: http://ecgfhp01.ecgf.uakron.edu/

■ THE UNIVERSITY OF ALABAMA

Graduate School, College of Engineering, Tuscaloosa, AL 35487

AWARDS MS Ch E, MS Met E, MSAE, MSCE, MSCS, MSE, MSEE, MSESM, MSIE, MSME, PhD. Part-time and evening/weekend programs available. Postbaccalaureate distance learning degree programs offered.

Faculty: 96 full-time (9 women), 3 part-time/adjunct (0 women).
Students: 252 full-time (40 women), 100 part-time (11 women); includes 18 minority (9 African Americans, 4 Asian Americans or Pacific Islanders, 4 Hispanic Americans, 1 Native American), 232 international. Average age 28. 889 applicants, 25% accepted, 100 enrolled. In 2001, 83 master's, 19 doctorates awarded. Terminal master's awarded for partial completion of doctoral program.
Degree requirements: For doctorate, thesis/dissertation.
Application deadline: Applications are processed on a rolling basis. *Application fee:* $25. Electronic applications accepted.
Expenses: Tuition, state resident: full-time $3,292; part-time $183 per credit hour. Tuition, nonresident: full-time $8,912; part-time $495 per credit hour. Tuition and fees vary according to course load, campus/location and program.
Financial support: In 2001–02, 188 students received support, including 7 fellowships with full tuition reimbursements available, 117 research assistantships with full tuition reimbursements available (averaging $10,269 per year), 71 teaching assistantships with full tuition reimbursements available (averaging $10,319 per year); career-related internships or fieldwork, Federal Work-Study, and institutionally sponsored loans also available.
Faculty research: Energy, global environmental change, magnetic information technology, solidification modeling. *Total annual research expenditures:* $16.6 million.
Dr. Timothy J. Greene, Dean, 205-348-6405, *Fax:* 205-348-8573, *E-mail:* tgreene@coe.eng.ua.edu.
Application contact: Ronald Rogers, Assistant Vice President for Academic Affairs and Dean, Graduate School, 205-348-8280, *Fax:* 205-348-0400, *E-mail:* rrogers@aalan.ua.edu. *Web site:* http://coeweb.eng.ua.edu/
Find an in-depth description at www.petersons.com/gradchannel.

■ THE UNIVERSITY OF ALABAMA AT BIRMINGHAM

Graduate School, School of Engineering, Birmingham, AL 35294

AWARDS MS Mt E, MSBME, MSCE, MSEE, MSME, PhD. Evening/weekend programs available.

Students: 142 full-time (30 women), 110 part-time (19 women); includes 30 minority (19 African Americans, 9 Asian Americans or Pacific Islanders, 2 Hispanic Americans), 120 international. Average age 28. 667 applicants, 62% accepted. In 2001, 50 master's, 9 doctorates awarded.
Degree requirements: For doctorate, thesis/dissertation.
Entrance requirements: For master's, GRE General Test. *Application deadline:* Applications are processed on a rolling basis. *Application fee:* $35 ($60 for international students). Electronic applications accepted.
Expenses: Tuition, state resident: full-time $3,058. Tuition, nonresident: full-time $5,746. Tuition and fees vary according to course load, degree level and program.
Financial support: Fellowships with full tuition reimbursements, research assistantships with full tuition reimbursements, career-related internships or fieldwork, Federal Work-Study, institutionally sponsored loans, and tuition waivers (full and partial) available. Support available to part-time students.
Dr. Linda C. Lucas, Dean, 205-934-8420, *Fax:* 205-975-4919. *Web site:* http://www.eng.uab.edu/

■ THE UNIVERSITY OF ALABAMA IN HUNTSVILLE

School of Graduate Studies, College of Engineering, Huntsville, AL 35899

AWARDS MSE, MSOR, PhD. Part-time and evening/weekend programs available. Postbaccalaureate distance learning degree programs offered (no on-campus study).

Faculty: 57 full-time (6 women), 8 part-time/adjunct (0 women).
Students: 179 full-time (32 women), 268 part-time (60 women); includes 45 minority (22 African Americans, 18 Asian Americans or Pacific Islanders, 4 Hispanic Americans, 1 Native American), 117 international. Average age 34. 584 applicants, 49% accepted, 137 enrolled. In 2001, 83 master's, 19 doctorates awarded.
Degree requirements: For master's, thesis or alternative, oral and written exams, comprehensive exam, registration; for doctorate, thesis/dissertation, oral and written exams, comprehensive exam, registration.
Entrance requirements: For master's and doctorate, GRE General Test, minimum GPA of 3.0. *Application deadline:* For fall admission, 7/24 (priority date); for spring admission, 11/15 (priority date). Applications are processed on a rolling basis. *Application fee:* $35.
Expenses: Tuition, area resident: Part-time $175 per hour. Tuition, state resident: full-time $4,408. Tuition, nonresident: full-time $9,054; part-time $361 per hour.
Financial support: In 2001–02, 118 students received support, including 3 fellowships with full and partial tuition reimbursements available (averaging $13,000 per year), 66 research assistantships with full and partial tuition reimbursements available (averaging $9,304 per year), 47 teaching assistantships with full and partial tuition reimbursements available (averaging $7,834 per year); career-related internships or fieldwork, Federal Work-Study, institutionally sponsored loans, scholarships/grants, health care benefits, and tuition waivers (full and partial) also available. Support available to part-time students. Financial award application deadline: 4/1; financial award applicants required to submit FAFSA.
Faculty research: Propulsion, missile systems, automation, robotics, plasma. *Total annual research expenditures:* $3.2 million.
Dr. Jorge Aunon, Dean, 256-824-6474, *Fax:* 256-824-6843, *E-mail:* aunon@eb.uah.edu. *Web site:* http://www.eb.uah.edu/

■ UNIVERSITY OF ALASKA ANCHORAGE

School of Engineering, Anchorage, AK 99508-8060

AWARDS MCE, MS. Part-time and evening/weekend programs available.

Entrance requirements: For master's, GRE General Test.

■ THE UNIVERSITY OF ARIZONA

Graduate College, College of Engineering and Mines, Tucson, AZ 85721

AWARDS M Eng, MS, PhD. Part-time programs available.

Faculty: 243.
Students: 631 full-time (121 women), 167 part-time (37 women); includes 67 minority (5 African Americans, 31 Asian Americans or Pacific Islanders, 24 Hispanic Americans, 7 Native Americans), 475 international. Average age 29. 1,412 applicants, 49% accepted, 227 enrolled. In 2001, 123 master's, 44 doctorates awarded.
Degree requirements: For doctorate, thesis/dissertation.
Entrance requirements: For master's and doctorate, TOEFL. *Application fee:* $35.
Expenses: Tuition, state resident: full-time $2,490; part-time $436 per unit. Tuition, nonresident: full-time $10,300; part-time

The University of Arizona (continued)
$436 per unit. Full-time tuition and fees vary according to degree level and program.
Financial support: Fellowships, research assistantships, teaching assistantships, institutionally sponsored loans and scholarships/grants available.
Dr. Thomas W. Peterson, Dean, 520-621-6594, *Fax:* 520-621-2232, *E-mail:* peterson@erc.arizona.edu.

■ UNIVERSITY OF ARKANSAS

Graduate School, College of Engineering, Fayetteville, AR 72701-1201

AWARDS MS, MS Ch E, MS En E, MS Tc E, MSBAE, MSCE, MSCSE, MSE, MSEE, MSIE, MSME, MSOR, MSTE, PhD.

Students: 182 full-time (38 women), 144 part-time (32 women); includes 42 minority (23 African Americans, 11 Asian Americans or Pacific Islanders, 5 Hispanic Americans, 3 Native Americans), 149 international. 254 applicants, 85% accepted. In 2001, 120 master's, 7 doctorates awarded.
Degree requirements: For doctorate, one foreign language, thesis/dissertation. *Application fee:* $40 ($50 for international students).
Expenses: Tuition, state resident: full-time $3,553; part-time $197 per credit. Tuition, nonresident: full-time $8,411; part-time $467 per credit. Required fees: $42 per credit. Tuition and fees vary according to course load and program.
Financial support: In 2001–02, 97 research assistantships, 74 teaching assistantships were awarded. Fellowships, career-related internships or fieldwork and Federal Work-Study also available. Support available to part-time students. Financial award application deadline: 4/1; financial award applicants required to submit FAFSA.
Dr. Otto Loewer, Dean, 479-575-3054.

■ UNIVERSITY OF BRIDGEPORT

School of Engineering, Bridgeport, CT 06601

AWARDS MS. Part-time and evening/weekend programs available.
Faculty: 11 full-time (0 women), 15 part-time/adjunct (0 women).
Students: 263 full-time (43 women), 354 part-time (122 women); includes 40 minority (4 African Americans, 27 Asian Americans or Pacific Islanders, 1 Hispanic American, 8 Native Americans), 567 international. Average age 28. 1,209 applicants, 80% accepted, 159 enrolled. In 2001, 121 degrees awarded.
Degree requirements: For master's, thesis optional.
Entrance requirements: For master's, TOEFL. *Application deadline:* For fall admission, 8/1 (priority date); for spring

admission, 12/1 (priority date). Applications are processed on a rolling basis. *Application fee:* $25 ($35 for international students). Electronic applications accepted.
Expenses: Contact institution.
Financial support: In 2001–02, 76 students received support; fellowships, research assistantships, teaching assistantships, career-related internships or fieldwork, Federal Work-Study, institutionally sponsored loans, and tuition waivers (partial) available. Support available to part-time students. Financial award application deadline: 6/1; financial award applicants required to submit FAFSA.
Faculty research: Atmospheric chemistry, minicomputers, heat transfer.
Dr. Tarek M. Sobh, Director, 203-576-4111, *Fax:* 203-576-4766, *E-mail:* sobh@bridgeport.edu.
Find an in-depth description at www.petersons.com/gradchannel.

■ UNIVERSITY OF CALIFORNIA, BERKELEY

Graduate Division, College of Engineering, Berkeley, CA 94720-1500

AWARDS M Eng, MS, D Eng, PhD, M Arch/MS, MCP/MS, MPP/MS.

Degree requirements: For doctorate, thesis/dissertation, exam.
Entrance requirements: For master's and doctorate, GRE General Test, minimum GPA of 3.0.
Expenses: Tuition, nonresident: full-time $10,704. Required fees: $4,349.

■ UNIVERSITY OF CALIFORNIA, DAVIS

Graduate Studies, College of Engineering, Davis, CA 95616

AWARDS M Engr, MS, D Engr, PhD, Certificate, M Engr/MBA. Part-time programs available.

Faculty: 231 full-time, 9 part-time/adjunct.
Students: 756 full-time (194 women), 4 part-time; includes 141 minority (9 African Americans, 112 Asian Americans or Pacific Islanders, 18 Hispanic Americans, 2 Native Americans), 257 international. Average age 29. 1,960 applicants, 39% accepted, 223 enrolled. In 2001, 141 master's, 70 doctorates awarded. Terminal master's awarded for partial completion of doctoral program.
Degree requirements: For doctorate, thesis/dissertation.
Entrance requirements: For doctorate, GRE. *Application deadline:* Applications are processed on a rolling basis. *Application fee:* $60. Electronic applications accepted.
Expenses: Tuition, state resident: full-time $4,831. Tuition, nonresident: full-time $15,725.
Financial support: In 2001–02, 579 students received support, including 204 fellowships with full and partial tuition reimbursements available (averaging

$5,561 per year), 367 research assistantships with full and partial tuition reimbursements available (averaging $9,650 per year), 149 teaching assistantships with partial tuition reimbursements available (averaging $11,582 per year); career-related internships or fieldwork, Federal Work-Study, institutionally sponsored loans, scholarships/grants, and tuition waivers (full and partial) also available. Support available to part-time students. Financial award application deadline: 1/15; financial award applicants required to submit FAFSA.
Dr. Zuhair A. Munir, Interim Dean, 530-752-0554.
Application contact: Donna Davies, Information Contact, 530-752-0592, *Fax:* 530-752-8058, *E-mail:* dedavies@ucdavis.edu. *Web site:* http://www.engr.ucdavis.edu/

■ UNIVERSITY OF CALIFORNIA, IRVINE

Office of Research and Graduate Studies, School of Engineering, Irvine, CA 92697

AWARDS MS, PhD. Part-time programs available.

Faculty: 77.
Students: 346 full-time (69 women), 57 part-time (6 women); includes 97 minority (2 African Americans, 82 Asian Americans or Pacific Islanders, 13 Hispanic Americans), 161 international. Average age 29. 991 applicants, 35% accepted, 155 enrolled. In 2001, 69 master's, 20 doctorates awarded. Terminal master's awarded for partial completion of doctoral program.
Degree requirements: For doctorate, thesis/dissertation.
Entrance requirements: For master's, GRE General Test, minimum GPA of 3.0; for doctorate, GRE General Test, completion of MS degree. *Application deadline:* For fall and spring admission, 1/15 (priority date); for winter admission, 10/15 (priority date). Applications are processed on a rolling basis. *Application fee:* $60. Electronic applications accepted.
Expenses: Tuition, nonresident: full-time $10,704. Required fees: $8,396. Tuition and fees vary according to course load, program and student level.
Financial support: In 2001–02, 45 fellowships with tuition reimbursements (averaging $1,250 per year), 119 research assistantships with tuition reimbursements (averaging $1,120 per year), 38 teaching assistantships with tuition reimbursements (averaging $1,480 per year) were awarded. Institutionally sponsored loans and tuition waivers (full and partial) also available. Financial award application deadline: 3/2; financial award applicants required to submit FAFSA.
Faculty research: Chemical and biochemical engineering, civil and environmental engineering, electrical and computer engineering, mechanical and

aerospace engineering, materials science. *Total annual research expenditures:* $9.3 million.
Dr. Nicolaos G. Alexopoulos, Dean, 949-824-6002, *Fax:* 949-824-7966, *E-mail:* alfios@uci.edu.
Application contact: John Sommerhauser, Graduate Counselor, 949-824-6475, *Fax:* 949-824-3440, *E-mail:* jdsommer@uci.edu. *Web site:* http://www.eng.uci.edu/

Find an in-depth description at www.petersons.com/gradchannel.

■ UNIVERSITY OF CALIFORNIA, LOS ANGELES

Graduate Division, School of Engineering and Applied Science, Los Angeles, CA 90095

AWARDS MS, PhD, MBA/MS.

Faculty: 135 full-time, 105 part-time/adjunct.
Students: 1,165 full-time (210 women); includes 324 minority (10 African Americans, 285 Asian Americans or Pacific Islanders, 29 Hispanic Americans), 576 international. 2,873 applicants, 37% accepted, 362 enrolled. In 2001, 191 master's, 91 doctorates awarded.
Degree requirements: For master's, comprehensive exam or thesis; for doctorate, thesis/dissertation, qualifying exams.
Entrance requirements: For master's, GRE General Test, minimum GPA of 3.0; for doctorate, GRE General Test, minimum GPA of 3.25. *Application fee:* $60. Electronic applications accepted.
Expenses: Tuition, nonresident: full-time $10,244. Required fees: $3,609. Full-time tuition and fees vary according to program.
Financial support: In 2001–02, 215 fellowships, 662 research assistantships, 416 teaching assistantships were awarded. Career-related internships or fieldwork, Federal Work-Study, institutionally sponsored loans, and tuition waivers (full and partial) also available. Financial award applicants required to submit FAFSA.
Dr. Stephen E. Jacobsen, Associate Dean, Academic and Student Affairs, 310-825-1704.
Application contact: Diane Golomb, Student Affairs Officer, 310-825-1704, *Fax:* 310-825-2473, *E-mail:* diane@ea.ucla.edu. *Web site:* http://www.seas.ucla.edu/

Find an in-depth description at www.petersons.com/gradchannel.

■ UNIVERSITY OF CALIFORNIA, SANTA BARBARA

Graduate Division, College of Engineering, Santa Barbara, CA 93106

AWARDS MS, PhD. Terminal master's awarded for partial completion of doctoral program.

Degree requirements: For doctorate, thesis/dissertation.
Entrance requirements: For master's and doctorate, GRE, TOEFL. Electronic applications accepted. *Web site:* http://www.engineering.ucsb.edu/

■ UNIVERSITY OF CENTRAL FLORIDA

College of Engineering and Computer Sciences, Orlando, FL 32816

AWARDS MS, MS Cp E, MS Env E, MSAE, MSCE, MSEE, MSIE, MSME, MSMSE, PhD, Certificate. Part-time and evening/weekend programs available.

Faculty: 117 full-time (13 women), 40 part-time/adjunct (4 women).
Students: 450 full-time (92 women), 522 part-time (116 women); includes 215 minority (37 African Americans, 105 Asian Americans or Pacific Islanders, 69 Hispanic Americans, 4 Native Americans), 379 international. Average age 29. 1,432 applicants, 65% accepted, 317 enrolled. In 2001, 232 master's, 41 doctorates awarded.
Degree requirements: For doctorate, thesis/dissertation, candidacy exam, departmental qualifying exam.
Entrance requirements: For master's, GRE General Test, TOEFL, minimum GPA of 3.0 in last 60 hours; for doctorate, TOEFL, minimum GPA of 3.5 in last 60 hours, resumé. *Application deadline:* For fall admission, 7/15; for spring admission, 12/1. *Application fee:* $20. Electronic applications accepted.
Expenses: Tuition, state resident: part-time $162 per hour. Tuition, nonresident: part-time $569 per hour.
Financial support: In 2001–02, 156 fellowships with partial tuition reimbursements (averaging $4,015 per year), 1,041 research assistantships with partial tuition reimbursements (averaging $3,221 per year), 285 teaching assistantships with partial tuition reimbursements (averaging $3,673 per year) were awarded. Career-related internships or fieldwork, Federal Work-Study, institutionally sponsored loans, tuition waivers (partial), and unspecified assistantships also available. Financial award application deadline: 3/1; financial award applicants required to submit FAFSA.
Faculty research: Electro-optics, lasers, materials, simulation, microelectronics.
Dr. Martin Wanielista, Dean, 407-823-2156, *E-mail:* wanielis@ucf1vm.cc.ucf.edu.
Application contact: Dr. Issa Batarseh, Graduate Coordinator, 407-823-0185, *E-mail:* batarseh@pegasus.cc.ucf.edu. *Web site:* http://www.ucf.edu/

Find an in-depth description at www.petersons.com/gradchannel.

■ UNIVERSITY OF CINCINNATI

Division of Research and Advanced Studies, College of Engineering, Cincinnati, OH 45221

AWARDS MS, PhD, MBA/MS. Part-time and evening/weekend programs available.

Faculty: 110 full-time.
Students: 775 full-time (127 women), 251 part-time (46 women); includes 71 minority (23 African Americans, 38 Asian Americans or Pacific Islanders, 10 Hispanic Americans), 684 international. 2,085 applicants, 33% accepted. In 2001, 252 master's, 59 doctorates awarded. Terminal master's awarded for partial completion of doctoral program.
Degree requirements: For doctorate, thesis/dissertation.
Entrance requirements: For master's and doctorate, GRE General Test, TOEFL. *Application deadline:* For fall admission, 2/1 (priority date). *Application fee:* $40.
Expenses: Tuition, state resident: part-time $2,698 per quarter. Tuition, nonresident: part-time $4,977 per quarter.
Financial support: Fellowships, research assistantships, teaching assistantships, career-related internships or fieldwork, tuition waivers (full), and unspecified assistantships available. Support available to part-time students. Financial award application deadline: 2/1. *Total annual research expenditures:* $18.4 million.
Dr. Stephen T. Kowel, Dean, 513-556-2933, *Fax:* 513-556-3626. *Web site:* http://www.eng.uc.edu/

■ UNIVERSITY OF COLORADO AT BOULDER

Graduate School, College of Engineering and Applied Science, Boulder, CO 80309

AWARDS ME, MS, PhD, MBA/MS. Part-time programs available. Postbaccalaureate distance learning degree programs offered.

Faculty: 156 full-time (17 women).
Students: 786 full-time (188 women), 196 part-time (45 women); includes 95 minority (11 African Americans, 54 Asian Americans or Pacific Islanders, 28 Hispanic Americans, 2 Native Americans), 366 international. Average age 29. 1,184 applicants, 56% accepted. In 2001, 369 master's, 63 doctorates awarded.
Degree requirements: For doctorate, thesis/dissertation.
Application fee: $50 ($60 for international students). Electronic applications accepted.
Expenses: Contact institution.
Financial support: In 2001–02, 93 fellowships with full tuition reimbursements (averaging $4,765 per year), 190 research assistantships with full tuition reimbursements (averaging $16,271 per year), 89 teaching assistantships with full tuition reimbursements (averaging $15,839 per year) were awarded. Career-related internships or fieldwork, scholarships/grants,

University of Colorado at Boulder (continued)

traineeships, and tuition waivers (full) also available. *Total annual research expenditures:* $40.5 million.
Ross Corotis, Dean, 303-492-7006, *Fax:* 303-492-2199, *E-mail:* corotis@colorado.edu. *Web site:* http://www.colorado.edu/engineering/

Find an in-depth description at www.petersons.com/gradchannel.

■ UNIVERSITY OF COLORADO AT COLORADO SPRINGS

Graduate School, College of Engineering and Applied Science, Colorado Springs, CO 80933-7150

AWARDS ME, MS, PhD. Part-time and evening/weekend programs available.

Faculty: 30 full-time (1 woman), 10 part-time/adjunct (4 women).
Students: 129 full-time (34 women), 93 part-time (15 women); includes 21 minority (2 African Americans, 13 Asian Americans or Pacific Islanders, 6 Hispanic Americans), 21 international. Average age 33. In 2001, 56 master's, 1 doctorate awarded.
Degree requirements: For doctorate, thesis/dissertation, comprehensive exam.
Entrance requirements: For master's, GRE General Test, TOEFL, minimum GPA of 3.0; for doctorate, GRE General Test, TOEFL, minimum GPA of 3.3. *Application deadline:* Applications are processed on a rolling basis. *Application fee:* $60 ($75 for international students).
Expenses: Contact institution.
Financial support: Fellowships, research assistantships, teaching assistantships, career-related internships or fieldwork and Federal Work-Study available.
Faculty research: Ferroelectronics, electronics communication, computer-aided design, electromagnetics.
Dr. John Trapp, Dean, 719-262-3246, *Fax:* 719-262-3542, *E-mail:* jtrapp@uccs.edu. *Web site:* http://piglet.uccs.edu/

■ UNIVERSITY OF COLORADO AT DENVER

Graduate School, College of Engineering and Applied Science, Denver, CO 80217-3364

AWARDS ME, MS, PhD. Part-time and evening/weekend programs available.

Faculty: 39 full-time (7 women).
Students: 46 full-time (18 women), 260 part-time (119 women); includes 57 minority (8 African Americans, 32 Asian Americans or Pacific Islanders, 14 Hispanic Americans, 3 Native Americans), 52 international. Average age 33. 195 applicants, 72% accepted, 75 enrolled. In 2001, 84 master's, 2 doctorates awarded.
Degree requirements: For doctorate, one foreign language, thesis/dissertation.

Entrance requirements: For master's and doctorate, GRE. *Application deadline:* Applications are processed on a rolling basis. *Application fee:* $50 ($60 for international students). Electronic applications accepted.
Expenses: Contact institution.
Financial support: Research assistantships, teaching assistantships, career-related internships or fieldwork and Federal Work-Study available. Financial award application deadline: 3/1; financial award applicants required to submit FAFSA. *Total annual research expenditures:* $906,886.
Peter Jenkins, Chair, 303-556-2871, *Fax:* 303-556-2511, *E-mail:* pjenkins@cse.cudenver.edu.
Application contact: Judith Stalnaker, Associate Dean, 303-556-8405, *Fax:* 303-556-2368, *E-mail:* judy.stalnaker@cudenver.edu. *Web site:* http://www.cudenver.edu/public/engineer/

■ UNIVERSITY OF CONNECTICUT

Graduate School, School of Engineering, Storrs, CT 06269

AWARDS MS, PhD.

Degree requirements: For doctorate, thesis/dissertation.

■ UNIVERSITY OF DAYTON

Graduate School, School of Engineering, Dayton, OH 45469-1300

AWARDS MS Ch E, MS Mat E, MSAE, MSCE, MSE, MSEE, MSEM, MSEM, MSEO, MSME, MSMS, DE, PhD. Part-time and evening/weekend programs available.

Faculty: 54 full-time (1 woman), 53 part-time/adjunct (3 women).
Students: 215 full-time (42 women), 146 part-time (31 women); includes 43 minority (16 African Americans, 10 Asian Americans or Pacific Islanders, 17 Hispanic Americans), 91 international. Average age 24. In 2001, 86 master's, 25 doctorates awarded.
Degree requirements: For doctorate, thesis/dissertation, departmental qualifying exam.
Entrance requirements: For master's, TOEFL. *Application deadline:* For fall admission, 8/1 (priority date). Applications are processed on a rolling basis. *Application fee:* $30. Electronic applications accepted.
Expenses: Tuition: Full-time $5,436; part-time $453 per credit hour. Required fees: $50; $25 per term.
Financial support: In 2001–02, 3 fellowships with full tuition reimbursements (averaging $18,000 per year), 76 research assistantships with full tuition reimbursements (averaging $13,500 per year), 9 teaching assistantships with full tuition reimbursements (averaging $10,000 per year) were awarded. Career-related internships or fieldwork, institutionally sponsored loans, and tuition waivers (full and partial) also available.

Faculty research: Aerodynamics, energy systems, composite materials, rare-earth magnetics, artificial intelligence.
Dr. Blake Cherrington, Dean, 937-229-2736, *Fax:* 937-229-2756.
Application contact: Dr. Donald L. Moon, Associate Dean, 937-229-2241, *Fax:* 937-229-2471, *E-mail:* dmoon@notes.udayton.edu.

Find an in-depth description at www.petersons.com/gradchannel.

■ UNIVERSITY OF DELAWARE

College of Engineering, Newark, DE 19716

AWARDS M Ch E, MAS, MCE, MEE, MEM, MMSE, MS, MSME, PhD. Part-time and evening/weekend programs available. Postbaccalaureate distance learning degree programs offered (minimal on-campus study).

Faculty: 82 full-time (5 women).
Students: 379 full-time (93 women), 66 part-time (13 women); includes 25 minority (9 African Americans, 9 Asian Americans or Pacific Islanders, 7 Hispanic Americans), 247 international. Average age 27. 1,441 applicants, 24% accepted, 141 enrolled. In 2001, 47 master's, 38 doctorates awarded.
Degree requirements: For doctorate, thesis/dissertation.
Entrance requirements: For master's and doctorate, GRE General Test. *Application fee:* $50. Electronic applications accepted.
Expenses: Tuition, state resident: full-time $4,770; part-time $265 per credit. Tuition, nonresident: full-time $13,860; part-time $770 per credit. Required fees: $414.
Financial support: In 2001–02, 304 students received support, including 16 fellowships with full tuition reimbursements available (averaging $14,000 per year), 216 research assistantships with full tuition reimbursements available (averaging $16,040 per year), 42 teaching assistantships with full tuition reimbursements available (averaging $14,400 per year); career-related internships or fieldwork, Federal Work-Study, and institutionally sponsored loans also available. Support available to part-time students. Financial award applicants required to submit FAFSA. *Total annual research expenditures:* $17.8 million.
Dr. Eric W. Kaler, Dean, 302-831-8017, *Fax:* 302-831-8179, *E-mail:* kaler@udel.edu. *Web site:* http://www.udel.edu/engg/

Find an in-depth description at www.petersons.com/gradchannel.

■ UNIVERSITY OF DENVER

Graduate Studies, Faculty of Natural Sciences, Mathematics and Engineering, Department of Engineering, Denver, CO 80208

AWARDS Computer science and engineering (MS); electrical engineering (MS); management and general engineering (MSMGEN);

materials science (PhD); mechanical engineering (MS). Part-time and evening/weekend programs available.

Faculty: 13 full-time (2 women), 3 part-time/adjunct (0 women).
Students: 17 (6 women) 11 international. 50 applicants, 62% accepted. In 2001, 11 degrees awarded. Terminal master's awarded for partial completion of doctoral program.
Degree requirements: For master's, thesis (for some programs); for doctorate, thesis/dissertation.
Entrance requirements: For master's and doctorate, GRE General Test, TOEFL, TSE. *Application deadline:* Applications are processed on a rolling basis. *Application fee:* $45.
Expenses: Tuition: Full-time $21,456.
Financial support: In 2001–02, 11 students received support, including 6 research assistantships with full and partial tuition reimbursements available (averaging $9,999 per year), 7 teaching assistantships with full and partial tuition reimbursements available (averaging $10,782 per year); fellowships with full and partial tuition reimbursements available, career-related internships or fieldwork, Federal Work-Study, institutionally sponsored loans, and scholarships/grants also available. Financial award application deadline: 3/1; financial award applicants required to submit FAFSA.
Faculty research: Microelectrics, digital signal processing, robotics, speech recognition, microwaves, aerosols, x-ray analysis, acoustic emissions. *Total annual research expenditures:* $1 million.
Dr. James C. Wilson, Chair, 303-871-2102.
Application contact: Susie Montoya, Assistant to Chair, 303-871-2102. *Web site:* http://littlebird.engr.du.edu/

■ UNIVERSITY OF DETROIT MERCY

College of Engineering and Science, Detroit, MI 48219-0900

AWARDS M Eng Mgt, MATM, ME, MS, MSCS, DE. Part-time and evening/weekend programs available.

Faculty: 40 full-time (11 women).
Students: 74 full-time (16 women), 227 part-time (50 women); includes 50 minority (30 African Americans, 13 Asian Americans or Pacific Islanders, 5 Hispanic Americans, 2 Native Americans), 109 international. Average age 31. In 2001, 132 master's, 2 doctorates awarded.
Degree requirements: For doctorate, thesis/dissertation.
Application deadline: For fall admission, 8/1 (priority date). Applications are processed on a rolling basis. *Application fee:* $30 ($50 for international students).
Expenses: Contact institution.

Financial support: Fellowships, teaching assistantships, career-related internships or fieldwork and Federal Work-Study available.
Dr. Leo Hanifin, Dean, 313-993-1216, *Fax:* 313-993-1187, *E-mail:* hanifinl@udmercy.edu.

■ UNIVERSITY OF FLORIDA

Graduate School, College of Engineering, Gainesville, FL 32611

AWARDS MCE, ME, MS, PhD, Certificate, Engr, MD/PhD. Part-time programs available.

Degree requirements: For doctorate, thesis/dissertation.
Entrance requirements: For master's, GRE General Test, minimum GPA of 3.0; for doctorate and other advanced degree, GRE General Test. Electronic applications accepted.
Expenses: Tuition, state resident: part-time $164 per hour. Tuition, nonresident: part-time $571 per hour. Tuition and fees vary according to course level and program. *Web site:* http://www.eng.ufl.edu/
Find an in-depth description at www.petersons.com/gradchannel.

■ UNIVERSITY OF FLORIDA

Graduate School, Graduate Engineering and Research Center (GERC), Gainesville, FL 32611

AWARDS Aerospace engineering (ME, MS, PhD, Engr); electrical and computer engineering (ME, MS, PhD, Engr); engineering mechanics (ME, MS, PhD, Engr); industrial and systems engineering (ME, MS, PhD, Engr). Part-time programs available. Postbaccalaureate distance learning degree programs offered. Terminal master's awarded for partial completion of doctoral program.

Degree requirements: For master's, thesis optional; for doctorate and Engr, thesis/dissertation.
Entrance requirements: For master's, GRE General Test, TOEFL, minimum GPA of 3.0; for doctorate, GRE General Test, written and oral qualifying exams, TOEFL, minimum GPA of 3.0, master's degree in engineering; for Engr, GRE General Test, TOEFL, minimum GPA of 3.0, master's degree in engineering. Electronic applications accepted.
Expenses: Contact institution.
Faculty research: Aerodynamics, terradynamics, and propulsion; composite materials and stress analysis; optical processing of microwave signals and photonics; holography, radar, and communications. System and signal theory; digital signal processing. *Web site:* http://www.gerc.eng.ufl.edu/

■ UNIVERSITY OF HARTFORD

College of Engineering, West Hartford, CT 06117-1599

AWARDS M Eng, MBA/M Eng. Part-time and evening/weekend programs available.

Faculty: 8 full-time (1 woman), 6 part-time/adjunct (0 women).
Students: 35 full-time (0 women), 66 part-time (12 women); includes 5 minority (1 African American, 2 Asian Americans or Pacific Islanders, 2 Hispanic Americans), 43 international. Average age 30. 118 applicants, 73% accepted. In 2001, 9 degrees awarded.
Degree requirements: For master's, thesis.
Entrance requirements: For master's, GRE General Test, TOEFL, minimum GPA of 3.0. *Application deadline:* Applications are processed on a rolling basis. *Application fee:* $40 ($55 for international students). Electronic applications accepted.
Expenses: Contact institution.
Financial support: In 2001–02, 20 students received support, including research assistantships (averaging $5,000 per year); Federal Work-Study and unspecified assistantships also available. Support available to part-time students. Financial award application deadline: 6/1; financial award applicants required to submit FAFSA.
Faculty research: Real-time fault diagnostics of electrical power transformers using wavelet transforms and supersonic sensors.
Alan Hadad, Dean, 860-768-4112, *Fax:* 860-768-5073, *E-mail:* hadad@mail.hartford.edu.
Application contact: Laurie Granstrand, Manager of Student Services, 860-768-4858, *E-mail:* granstran@mail.hartford.edu. *Web site:* http://www.hartford.edu/

■ UNIVERSITY OF HAWAII AT MANOA

Graduate Division, College of Engineering, Honolulu, HI 96822

AWARDS MS, PhD. Part-time programs available.

Faculty: 59 full-time (4 women), 14 part-time/adjunct (0 women).
Students: 97 full-time (23 women), 44 part-time (9 women). 182 applicants, 85% accepted. In 2001, 40 master's, 6 doctorates awarded.
Degree requirements: For doctorate, thesis/dissertation, exams.
Application deadline: Applications are processed on a rolling basis. *Application fee:* $25 ($50 for international students).
Expenses: Tuition, state resident: full-time $2,160; part-time $1,980 per year. Tuition, nonresident: full-time $5,190; part-time $4,829 per year.
Financial support: In 2001–02, 51 research assistantships (averaging $15,177 per year), 12 teaching assistantships (averaging $13,249 per year) were awarded. Fellowships, career-related internships or fieldwork, Federal Work-Study, and tuition waivers (full and partial) also available. Financial award applicants required to submit FAFSA.

University of Hawaii at Manoa (continued)
Dr. Wai-Fah Chen, Dean, 808-956-7727, *Fax:* 808-956-2291.

■ UNIVERSITY OF HOUSTON

College of Technology, Houston, TX 77204

AWARDS Construction management (MT); manufacturing systems (MT); microcomputer systems (MT); occupational technology (MSOT). Part-time and evening/weekend programs available.

Faculty: 11 full-time (5 women), 13 part-time/adjunct (4 women).
Students: 36 full-time (17 women), 60 part-time (21 women); includes 28 minority (16 African Americans, 4 Asian Americans or Pacific Islanders, 8 Hispanic Americans), 17 international. Average age 35. 33 applicants, 82% accepted. In 2001, 25 degrees awarded.
Entrance requirements: For master's, GMAT, GRE, or MAT (MSOT); GRE (MT), minimum GPA of 3.0 in last 60 hours. *Application deadline:* For fall admission, 7/1; for spring admission, 11/1. *Application fee:* $35 ($110 for international students).
Expenses: Tuition, state resident: full-time $1,512. Tuition, nonresident: full-time $5,310. Required fees: $1,308. Tuition and fees vary according to program.
Financial support: Fellowships, research assistantships, teaching assistantships, career-related internships or fieldwork, Federal Work-Study, and institutionally sponsored loans available. Support available to part-time students.
Faculty research: Educational delivery systems, technical curriculum development, computer-integrated manufacturing, neural networks. *Total annual research expenditures:* $354,283.
Uma G. Gupta, Dean, 713-743-4032, *Fax:* 713-743-4032.
Application contact: Holly Rosenthal, Graduate Academic Adviser, 713-743-4098, *Fax:* 713-743-4032, *E-mail:* hrosenthal@uh.edu. *Web site:* http://www.tech.uh.edu/

■ UNIVERSITY OF HOUSTON

Cullen College of Engineering, Houston, TX 77204

AWARDS M Ch E, MCE, MEE, MIE, MME, MS, MS Ch E, MS Env E, MSCE, MSEE, MSIE, MSME, PhD, MBA/MIE. Part-time and evening/weekend programs available.

Faculty: 85 full-time (5 women), 9 part-time/adjunct (0 women).
Students: 392 full-time (87 women), 255 part-time (56 women); includes 107 minority (21 African Americans, 50 Asian Americans or Pacific Islanders, 36 Hispanic Americans), 355 international. Average age 29. 1,042 applicants, 46%

accepted. In 2001, 144 master's, 25 doctorates awarded. Terminal master's awarded for partial completion of doctoral program.
Degree requirements: For master's, thesis (for some programs); for doctorate, thesis/dissertation, departmental qualifying exam.
Entrance requirements: For master's and doctorate, GRE General Test, TOEFL. *Application deadline:* Applications are processed on a rolling basis. *Application fee:* $25 ($75 for international students).
Expenses: Tuition, state resident: full-time $1,512. Tuition, nonresident: full-time $5,310. Required fees: $1,308. Tuition and fees vary according to program.
Financial support: In 2001–02, 290 fellowships with partial tuition reimbursements (averaging $1,440 per year), 198 research assistantships with partial tuition reimbursements (averaging $13,200 per year), 82 teaching assistantships with partial tuition reimbursements (averaging $12,000 per year) were awarded. Career-related internships or fieldwork, Federal Work-Study, institutionally sponsored loans, scholarships/grants, and tuition waivers (partial) also available.
Faculty research: Superconducting materials, microantennas for space packs, direct numerical simulation of pairing vortices. *Total annual research expenditures:* $7.8 million.
Dr. Raymond W. Flumerfelt, Dean, 713-743-4207, *Fax:* 713-743-4214, *E-mail:* rwf@uh.edu.
Application contact: Dr. Earl Joseph Charlson, Associate Dean, Graduate Programs, 713-743-4200, *Fax:* 713-743-4205, *E-mail:* jcharlson@uh.edu. *Web site:* http://www.egr.uh.edu/

■ UNIVERSITY OF IDAHO

College of Graduate Studies, College of Engineering, Moscow, ID 83844-2282

AWARDS M Engr, MS, PhD.

Faculty: 69 full-time (5 women), 6 part-time/adjunct (1 woman).
Students: 106 full-time (28 women), 236 part-time (23 women); includes 26 minority (1 African American, 15 Asian Americans or Pacific Islanders, 7 Hispanic Americans, 3 Native Americans), 91 international. 390 applicants, 57% accepted. In 2001, 55 master's, 4 doctorates awarded.
Degree requirements: For doctorate, thesis/dissertation.
Entrance requirements: For doctorate, minimum undergraduate GPA of 2.8, graduate GPA of 3.0. *Application deadline:* For fall admission, 8/1; for spring admission, 12/15. *Application fee:* $35 ($45 for international students).
Expenses: Tuition, state resident: full-time $1,613. Tuition, nonresident: full-time $3,000.
Financial support: In 2001–02, 34 research assistantships (averaging $5,157

per year), 38 teaching assistantships (averaging $3,387 per year) were awarded. Fellowships, career-related internships or fieldwork and Federal Work-Study also available. Support available to part-time students. Financial award application deadline: 2/15.
Dr. David E. Thompson, Dean, 208-885-6479. *Web site:* http://www.uidaho.edu/engr/

■ UNIVERSITY OF ILLINOIS AT CHICAGO

Graduate College, College of Engineering, Chicago, IL 60607-7128

AWARDS MS, PhD, MD/PhD. Part-time and evening/weekend programs available.

Faculty: 85 full-time (1 woman).
Students: 547 full-time (128 women), 400 part-time (80 women); includes 111 minority (26 African Americans, 67 Asian Americans or Pacific Islanders, 18 Hispanic Americans), 615 international. Average age 27. 2,584 applicants, 23% accepted, 263 enrolled. In 2001, 244 master's, 31 doctorates awarded. Terminal master's awarded for partial completion of doctoral program.
Degree requirements: For doctorate, thesis/dissertation.
Entrance requirements: For master's, TOEFL; for doctorate, GRE, TOEFL. *Application deadline:* For fall admission, 6/1. Applications are processed on a rolling basis. *Application fee:* $40 ($50 for international students). Electronic applications accepted.
Expenses: Contact institution.
Financial support: In 2001–02, 469 students received support; fellowships with full tuition reimbursements available, research assistantships with full tuition reimbursements available, teaching assistantships with full tuition reimbursements available, career-related internships or fieldwork, Federal Work-Study, and tuition waivers (full) available. Financial award application deadline: 3/1; financial award applicants required to submit FAFSA.
Lawrence A. Kennedy, Dean, 312-996-2400.

Find an in-depth description at www.petersons.com/gradchannel.

■ UNIVERSITY OF ILLINOIS AT URBANA–CHAMPAIGN

Graduate College, College of Engineering, Champaign, IL 61820

AWARDS MCS, MS, MST, PhD, M Arch/MS, MBA/MS. Postbaccalaureate distance learning degree programs offered.

Faculty: 360 full-time, 21 part-time/adjunct.
Students: 2,069 full-time (323 women); includes 190 minority (11 African Americans, 141 Asian Americans or Pacific Islanders, 33 Hispanic Americans, 5 Native

Americans), 1,134 international. 5,093 applicants, 17% accepted. In 2001, 471 master's, 215 doctorates awarded. Terminal master's awarded for partial completion of doctoral program.

Degree requirements: For doctorate, thesis/dissertation.

Application deadline: Applications are processed on a rolling basis. *Application fee:* $40 ($50 for international students). Electronic applications accepted.

Expenses: Contact institution.

Financial support: In 2001–02, 126 fellowships, 1,215 research assistantships, 395 teaching assistantships were awarded. Federal Work-Study, institutionally sponsored loans, scholarships/grants, and tuition waivers (full and partial) also available.

Dr. David E. Daniel, Dean, 217-333-2150, *Fax:* 217-333-5847, *E-mail:* dedaniel@ uiuc.edu. *Web site:* http:// www.engr.uiuc.edu/

Find an in-depth description at www.petersons.com/gradchannel.

■ THE UNIVERSITY OF IOWA

Graduate College, College of Engineering, Iowa City, IA 52242-1316

AWARDS MS, PhD.

Faculty: 81 full-time (5 women), 13 part-time/adjunct (0 women).

Students: 192 full-time (48 women), 146 part-time (30 women); includes 13 minority (4 African Americans, 6 Asian Americans or Pacific Islanders, 3 Hispanic Americans), 216 international. Average age 28. 893 applicants, 38% accepted, 90 enrolled. In 2001, 65 master's, 23 doctorates awarded.

Degree requirements: For master's, exam, thesis optional; for doctorate, thesis/dissertation, comprehensive exam.

Entrance requirements: For master's and doctorate, GRE, TOEFL. *Application fee:* $30 ($50 for international students). Electronic applications accepted.

Expenses: Tuition, state resident: full-time $3,702; part-time $206 per semester hour. Tuition, nonresident: full-time $11,924; part-time $206 per semester hour. Required fees: $101 per semester. Tuition and fees vary according to course load and program.

Financial support: In 2001–02, 5 fellowships, 133 research assistantships, 80 teaching assistantships were awarded. Financial award applicants required to submit FAFSA. *Total annual research expenditures:* $21 million.

Dr. P. Barry Butler, Dean, 319-335-5766, *Fax:* 319-335-6086, *E-mail:* patrick-butler@uiowa.edu. *Web site:* http:// www.engineering.uiowa.edu/

Find an in-depth description at www.petersons.com/gradchannel.

■ UNIVERSITY OF KANSAS

Graduate School, School of Engineering, Lawrence, KS 66045

AWARDS MCE, MCM, ME, MS, DE, PhD. Part-time and evening/weekend programs available. Postbaccalaureate distance learning degree programs offered (no on-campus study).

Faculty: 99.

Students: 303 full-time (50 women), 332 part-time (59 women); includes 39 minority (6 African Americans, 21 Asian Americans or Pacific Islanders, 8 Hispanic Americans, 4 Native Americans), 300 international. Average age 29. 1,103 applicants, 31% accepted, 141 enrolled. In 2001, 132 master's, 16 doctorates awarded. Terminal master's awarded for partial completion of doctoral program.

Degree requirements: For doctorate, thesis/dissertation, comprehensive exam.

Entrance requirements: For master's, GRE, TOEFL, minimum GPA of 3.0; for doctorate, GRE, TOEFL, minimum GPA of 3.5. *Application deadline:* Applications are processed on a rolling basis. *Application fee:* $40.

Expenses: Contact institution.

Financial support: Fellowships, research assistantships with partial tuition reimbursements, teaching assistantships with full and partial tuition reimbursements, career-related internships or fieldwork and Federal Work-Study available.

Faculty research: Telecommunications, oil recovery, airplane design, structured materials, robotics.

Stuart R. Bell, Dean, 785-864-3881, *E-mail:* kuengr@ku.edu.

Application contact: Robb Sorem, Associate Dean, 785-864-2983, *Fax:* 785-864-5445, *E-mail:* sorem@ku.edu. *Web site:* http://www.engr.ku.edu/

Find an in-depth description at www.petersons.com/gradchannel.

■ UNIVERSITY OF KENTUCKY

Graduate School, Graduate School Programs from the College of Engineering, Lexington, KY 40506-0032

AWARDS M Eng, MCE, MME, MS, MS Ch E, MS Min, MSAE, MSCE, MSEE, MSEM, MSMAE, MSME, MSMSE, PhD. Part-time programs available.

Faculty: 179 full-time (18 women).

Students: 424 full-time (96 women), 101 part-time (13 women); includes 14 minority (2 African Americans, 11 Asian Americans or Pacific Islanders, 1 Hispanic American), 342 international. 1,118 applicants, 56% accepted. In 2001, 121 master's, 10 doctorates awarded.

Degree requirements: For master's, comprehensive exam; for doctorate, thesis/dissertation, comprehensive exam.

Entrance requirements: For master's, GRE General Test; for doctorate, GRE General Test, minimum graduate GPA of 3.0. *Application deadline:* For fall admission, 7/19. Applications are processed on a rolling basis. *Application fee:* $30 ($35 for international students).

Expenses: Tuition, state resident: full-time $4,075; part-time $213 per credit hour. Tuition, nonresident: full-time $11,295; part-time $614 per credit hour.

Financial support: In 2001–02, 24 fellowships, 202 research assistantships, 82 teaching assistantships were awarded. Career-related internships or fieldwork, Federal Work-Study, and institutionally sponsored loans also available. Support available to part-time students.

Dr. Thomas W. Lester, Dean, 859-257-1687.

Application contact: Dr. Jeannine Blackwell, Associate Dean, 859-257-4905, *Fax:* 859-323-1928.

■ UNIVERSITY OF LOUISIANA AT LAFAYETTE

Graduate School, College of Engineering, Lafayette, LA 70504

AWARDS MS, MSE, MSET, MSTC, PhD. Part-time and evening/weekend programs available.

Faculty: 56 full-time (5 women).

Students: 147 full-time (31 women), 48 part-time (7 women); includes 6 minority (5 African Americans, 1 Asian American or Pacific Islander), 148 international. 537 applicants, 56% accepted, 68 enrolled. In 2001, 53 master's, 5 doctorates awarded. Terminal master's awarded for partial completion of doctoral program.

Degree requirements: For master's, thesis or alternative; for doctorate, thesis/dissertation, final oral exam.

Entrance requirements: For master's, GRE General Test; for doctorate, GRE General Test, minimum GPA of 3.0. *Application deadline:* For fall admission, 5/15. *Application fee:* $20 ($30 for international students).

Expenses: Tuition, state resident: full-time $2,317; part-time $79 per credit. Tuition, nonresident: full-time $8,882; part-time $369 per credit. International tuition: $9,018 full-time.

Financial support: In 2001–02, 5 fellowships with full tuition reimbursements (averaging $13,900 per year), 51 research assistantships with full tuition reimbursements (averaging $6,412 per year), 23 teaching assistantships with full tuition reimbursements (averaging $6,868 per year) were awarded. Federal Work-Study and tuition waivers (full and partial) also available. Support available to part-time students.

Dr. Anthony B. Ponter, Dean, 337-482-6685.

■ UNIVERSITY OF LOUISVILLE

Graduate School, Speed Scientific School, Louisville, KY 40292-0001

AWARDS M Eng, MS, PhD, M Eng/MBA. Part-time programs available.

Faculty: 87 full-time (9 women), 18 part-time/adjunct (1 woman).

Students: 288 full-time (75 women), 360 part-time (63 women); includes 60 minority (20 African Americans, 30 Asian Americans or Pacific Islanders, 9 Hispanic Americans, 1 Native American), 267 international. Average age 29. In 2001, 205 master's, 4 doctorates awarded. Terminal master's awarded for partial completion of doctoral program.

Degree requirements: For master's and doctorate, thesis/dissertation.

Entrance requirements: For master's and doctorate, GRE General Test. *Application deadline:* Applications are processed on a rolling basis. *Application fee:* $25. Electronic applications accepted.

Expenses: Tuition, state resident: full-time $4,134. Tuition, nonresident: full-time $11,486.

Financial support: In 2001–02, 19 fellowships with full tuition reimbursements (averaging $18,000 per year), 51 research assistantships with full tuition reimbursements (averaging $14,700 per year), 34 teaching assistantships with full tuition reimbursements (averaging $15,150 per year) were awarded. Federal Work-Study and scholarships/grants also available. Dr. Thomas R. Hanley, Dean, 502-852-6281, *Fax:* 502-852-7033, *E-mail:* trhanl01@gwise.louisville.edu.

Application contact: Dr. Mickey R. Wilhelm, Associate Dean, 502-852-08002, *Fax:* 502-852-1577, *E-mail:* wilhelm@louisville.edu.

Find an in-depth description at www.petersons.com/gradchannel.

■ UNIVERSITY OF MAINE

Graduate School, College of Engineering, Orono, ME 04469

AWARDS MS, PhD. Part-time programs available.

Faculty: 55.

Students: 99 full-time (22 women), 31 part-time (4 women); includes 3 minority (2 Hispanic Americans, 1 Native American), 53 international. 142 applicants, 48% accepted, 29 enrolled. In 2001, 30 master's, 6 doctorates awarded. Terminal master's awarded for partial completion of doctoral program.

Degree requirements: For doctorate, thesis/dissertation.

Entrance requirements: For master's and doctorate, GRE General Test, TOEFL. *Application deadline:* For fall admission, 2/1 (priority date). Applications are processed on a rolling basis. *Application fee:* $50. Electronic applications accepted.

Expenses: Tuition, state resident: full-time $3,780; part-time $210 per credit hour.

Tuition, nonresident: full-time $10,782; part-time $599 per credit hour. Required fees: $9.5 per credit hour. $32 per semester. Tuition and fees vary according to reciprocity agreements.

Financial support: Fellowships, research assistantships with tuition reimbursements, teaching assistantships with tuition reimbursements, Federal Work-Study, institutionally sponsored loans, scholarships/grants, and tuition waivers (full and partial) available. Financial award application deadline: 3/1.
Dr. Larryl K. Matthews, Dean, 207-581-2216, *Fax:* 207-581-2220.

Application contact: Scott G. Delcourt, Director of the Graduate School, 207-581-3218, *Fax:* 207-581-3232, *E-mail:* graduate@maine.edu. *Web site:* http://www.umaine.edu/graduate/

■ UNIVERSITY OF MARYLAND, BALTIMORE COUNTY

Graduate School, College of Engineering, Baltimore, MD 21250-5398

AWARDS MS, PhD. Part-time and evening/weekend programs available. Terminal master's awarded for partial completion of doctoral program.

Degree requirements: For master's, thesis optional; for doctorate, thesis/dissertation.

Entrance requirements: For master's and doctorate, GRE General Test. Electronic applications accepted.

Faculty research: Biochemical/biomedical engineering, wireless and mobile computing, photonics, biomechanics, signal processing, manufacturing. *Web site:* http://www.umbc.edu/engineering

Find an in-depth description at www.petersons.com/gradchannel.

■ UNIVERSITY OF MARYLAND, COLLEGE PARK

Graduate Studies and Research, A. James Clark School of Engineering, College Park, MD 20742

AWARDS M Eng, ME, MS, PhD. Part-time and evening/weekend programs available. Postbaccalaureate distance learning degree programs offered.

Faculty: 310 full-time (39 women), 92 part-time/adjunct (8 women).

Students: 857 full-time (154 women), 569 part-time (119 women); includes 159 minority (65 African Americans, 71 Asian Americans or Pacific Islanders, 22 Hispanic Americans, 1 Native American), 830 international. 2,938 applicants, 23% accepted, 391 enrolled. In 2001, 314 master's, 93 doctorates awarded.

Degree requirements: For doctorate, thesis/dissertation.

Application deadline: Applications are processed on a rolling basis. *Application fee:*

$50 ($70 for international students). Electronic applications accepted.

Expenses: Tuition, state resident: part-time $289 per credit hour. Tuition, nonresident: part-time $448 per credit hour. One-time fee: $436 part-time. Full-time tuition and fees vary according to course load, campus/location and program.

Financial support: In 2001–02, 46 fellowships (averaging $11,832 per year), 509 research assistantships (averaging $14,390 per year), 178 teaching assistantships (averaging $13,313 per year) were awarded. Career-related internships or fieldwork, Federal Work-Study, institutionally sponsored loans, and scholarships/grants also available. Support available to part-time students. Financial award applicants required to submit FAFSA. *Total annual research expenditures:* $52.9 million.
Dr. Nariman Farvardin, Dean, 301-405-3868, *Fax:* 301-314-9281, *E-mail:* farvar@eng.umd.edu.

Application contact: Trudy Lindsey, Director, Graduate Admissions and Records, 301-405-6991, *Fax:* 301-314-9305, *E-mail:* grschool@deans.umd.edu.

■ UNIVERSITY OF MASSACHUSETTS AMHERST

Graduate School, College of Engineering, Amherst, MA 01003

AWARDS MS, PhD. Part-time and evening/weekend programs available.

Faculty: 86 full-time (8 women).

Students: 242 full-time (64 women), 206 part-time (32 women); includes 25 minority (2 African Americans, 14 Asian Americans or Pacific Islanders, 7 Hispanic Americans, 2 Native Americans), 266 international. Average age 28. 1,741 applicants, 20% accepted. In 2001, 105 master's, 29 doctorates awarded. Terminal master's awarded for partial completion of doctoral program.

Degree requirements: For doctorate, thesis/dissertation.

Entrance requirements: For master's and doctorate, GRE General Test. *Application deadline:* Applications are processed on a rolling basis. *Application fee:* $40 ($50 for international students).

Expenses: Tuition, state resident: full-time $1,980; part-time $110 per credit. Tuition, nonresident: full-time $7,456; part-time $414 per credit. Required fees: $4,112. One-time fee: $115 full-time.

Financial support: In 2001–02, 93 fellowships with full tuition reimbursements (averaging $8,272 per year), 328 research assistantships with full tuition reimbursements (averaging $11,839 per year), 81 teaching assistantships with full tuition reimbursements (averaging $5,551 per year) were awarded. Career-related internships or fieldwork, Federal Work-Study, scholarships/grants, traineeships, and unspecified assistantships also available. Support available to part-time students. Financial award application deadline: 2/1.

Dr. Joseph I. Goldstein, Dean, 413-545-0300, *Fax:* 413-545-0724, *E-mail:* jigo@ecs.umass.edu.

Find an in-depth description at www.petersons.com/gradchannel.

■ UNIVERSITY OF MASSACHUSETTS DARTMOUTH

Graduate School, College of Engineering, North Dartmouth, MA 02747-2300

AWARDS MS, PhD, Certificate. Part-time programs available.

Faculty: 63 full-time (6 women), 10 part-time/adjunct (2 women).
Students: 147 full-time (30 women), 73 part-time (19 women); includes 4 minority (1 African American, 1 Asian American or Pacific Islander, 2 Hispanic Americans), 172 international. Average age 28. 423 applicants, 74% accepted, 68 enrolled. In 2001, 54 master's, 3 doctorates awarded.
Degree requirements: For master's, thesis or alternative; for doctorate, thesis/dissertation, comprehensive exam.
Entrance requirements: For master's, TOEFL. *Application deadline:* For fall admission, 4/20; for spring admission, 11/15. Applications are processed on a rolling basis. *Application fee:* $25 ($45 for international students).
Expenses: Tuition, state resident: full-time $2,071; part-time $86 per credit. Tuition, nonresident: full-time $8,099; part-time $337 per credit. Part-time tuition and fees vary according to course load and reciprocity agreements.
Financial support: In 2001–02, 74 research assistantships with full tuition reimbursements (averaging $7,315 per year), 40 teaching assistantships with full tuition reimbursements (averaging $5,864 per year) were awarded. Federal Work-Study and unspecified assistantships also available. Support available to part-time students. Financial award application deadline: 3/1; financial award applicants required to submit FAFSA.
Faculty research: North Atlantic property fluxes, bio-active fabrics, nano composite fibers, remote sensing. *Total annual research expenditures:* $2.1 million.
Dr. Farhad Azadivar, Dean, 508-999-8539, *Fax:* 508-999-9137, *E-mail:* fazadivar@umassd.edu.
Application contact: Maria E. Lomba, Graduate Admissions Officer, 508-999-8604, *Fax:* 508-999-8183, *E-mail:* graduate@umassd.edu.

Find an in-depth description at www.petersons.com/gradchannel.

■ UNIVERSITY OF MASSACHUSETTS LOWELL

Graduate School, James B. Francis College of Engineering, Lowell, MA 01854-2881

AWARDS MS, MS Eng, D Eng, PhD, Sc D. Part-time and evening/weekend programs available. Terminal master's awarded for partial completion of doctoral program.
Degree requirements: For doctorate, thesis/dissertation.
Entrance requirements: For master's and doctorate, GRE General Test.

Find an in-depth description at www.petersons.com/gradchannel.

■ THE UNIVERSITY OF MEMPHIS

Graduate School, Herff College of Engineering, Memphis, TN 38152

AWARDS MS, PhD. Part-time programs available.
Degree requirements: For doctorate, thesis/dissertation.
Entrance requirements: For master's, GRE General Test. Electronic applications accepted.
Expenses: Tuition, state resident: full-time $2,026. Tuition, nonresident: full-time $4,528.
Faculty research: Soil structure, expert systems development, automatic computer troubleshooting, surface tension experiments.

■ UNIVERSITY OF MIAMI

Graduate School, College of Engineering, Coral Gables, FL 33124

AWARDS MS, MSAE, MSBE, MSCE, MSECE, MSEVH, MSIE, MSME, MSOES, DA, PhD, MBA/MSIE. Part-time and evening/weekend programs available.
Faculty: 43 full-time (2 women), 33 part-time/adjunct (2 women).
Students: 132 full-time (25 women), 11 part-time (3 women). Average age 28. 228 applicants, 82% accepted. In 2001, 51 master's, 15 doctorates awarded.
Degree requirements: For master's, thesis (for some programs); for doctorate, thesis/dissertation.
Entrance requirements: For master's and doctorate, GRE General Test, TOEFL. *Application deadline:* Applications are processed on a rolling basis. *Application fee:* $50.
Expenses: Tuition: Part-time $960 per credit hour. Required fees: $85 per semester. Tuition and fees vary according to program.
Financial support: In 2001–02, 53 students received support, including 7 fellowships with tuition reimbursements available (averaging $29,140 per year), 38 research assistantships with tuition reimbursements available (averaging $23,457 per year), 23 teaching assistantships with tuition reimbursements available

(averaging $34,374 per year); career-related internships or fieldwork, Federal Work-Study, institutionally sponsored loans, scholarships/grants, tuition waivers (partial), and unspecified assistantships also available. Support available to part-time students. Financial award application deadline: 2/1; financial award applicants required to submit FAFSA. *Total annual research expenditures:* $1.7 million.
Dr. M. Lewis Temares, Dean, 305-284-2404, *Fax:* 305-284-4792, *E-mail:* mtemares@miami.edu.
Application contact: Thomas D. Waite, Associate Dean, 305-284-2408, *Fax:* 305-284-2885, *E-mail:* twaite@miami.edu. *Web site:* http://www.eng.miami.edu/

Find an in-depth description at www.petersons.com/gradchannel.

■ UNIVERSITY OF MICHIGAN

Horace H. Rackham School of Graduate Studies, College of Engineering, Ann Arbor, MI 48109

AWARDS M Eng, MS, MSE, D Eng, PhD, Aerospace E, App ME, CE, Certificate, Ch E, EE, IOE, Mar Eng, Nav Arch, Nuc E, M Arch/M Eng, M Arch/MSE, MBA/M Eng, MBA/MS, MBA/MSE, MHSA/MS, MSE/MS. Part-time programs available. Postbaccalaureate distance learning degree programs offered.
Faculty: 309 full-time (30 women).
Students: 1,916 full-time (391 women), 359 part-time (68 women); includes 270 minority (66 African Americans, 157 Asian Americans or Pacific Islanders, 40 Hispanic Americans, 7 Native Americans), 1,109 international. Average age 26. 5,182 applicants, 34% accepted, 683 enrolled. In 2001, 581 master's, 184 doctorates awarded.
Degree requirements: For doctorate, thesis/dissertation.
Application deadline: Applications are processed on a rolling basis. Electronic applications accepted.
Expenses: Contact institution.
Financial support: In 2001–02, 244 fellowships with full tuition reimbursements (averaging $20,200 per year), 838 research assistantships with full tuition reimbursements (averaging $20,200 per year), 216 teaching assistantships with full tuition reimbursements (averaging $13,468 per year) were awarded. Career-related internships or fieldwork, Federal Work-Study, institutionally sponsored loans, scholarships/grants, traineeships, tuition waivers (full and partial), and unspecified assistantships also available. Support available to part-time students. Financial award applicants required to submit FAFSA. *Total annual research expenditures:* $135 million.
Stephen W. Director, Dean, 734-647-7010, *Fax:* 734-647-7009.

University of Michigan (continued)
Application contact: James Bean, Associate Dean, Graduate Education, 734-647-7009, *Fax:* 734-647-7045. *Web site:* http://www.engin.umich.edu/

Find an in-depth description at www.petersons.com/gradchannel.

■ UNIVERSITY OF MICHIGAN–DEARBORN

College of Engineering and Computer Science, Dearborn, MI 48128-1491

AWARDS MS, MSE, D Eng, MBA/MSE. Part-time and evening/weekend programs available.

Faculty: 53 full-time (3 women), 30 part-time/adjunct (6 women).
Students: 44 full-time (11 women), 741 part-time (151 women); includes 164 minority (22 African Americans, 111 Asian Americans or Pacific Islanders, 30 Hispanic Americans, 1 Native American). Average age 30. 440 applicants, 68% accepted, 102 enrolled. In 2001, 229 degrees awarded.
Degree requirements: For master's, thesis optional. *Median time to degree:* Master's–5 years full-time.
Application deadline: For fall admission, 6/15; for winter admission, 12/1; for spring admission, 2/15. Applications are processed on a rolling basis. *Application fee:* $55. Electronic applications accepted.
Expenses: Tuition, state resident: part-time $300 per credit hour. Tuition, nonresident: part-time $756 per credit hour. Required fees: $90 per semester. Tuition and fees vary according to course level, course load and program.
Financial support: Fellowships, research assistantships, teaching assistantships, Federal Work-Study available. Financial award application deadline: 4/1; financial award applicants required to submit FAFSA.
Faculty research: CAD/CAM, expert systems, acoustics, vehicle electronics, engines and fuels.
Dr. Subrata Sengupta, Dean, 313-593-5290, *Fax:* 313-593-9967, *E-mail:* razal@umich.edu.
Application contact: Dr. Kashev Varde, Associate Dean, 313-593-5117, *Fax:* 313-593-9967, *E-mail:* varde@umich.edu. *Web site:* http://www.engin.umd.umich.edu/

Find an in-depth description at www.petersons.com/gradchannel.

■ UNIVERSITY OF MINNESOTA, TWIN CITIES CAMPUS

Graduate School, Institute of Technology, Minneapolis, MN 55455-0213

AWARDS M Aero E, M Ch E, M Comp E, M Geo E, M Mat SE, MA, MCE, MCIS, MEE, MS, MS Ch E, MS Mat SE, MSEE, MSIE, MSME, MSMOT, PhD, MD/PhD. Part-time and evening/weekend programs available. Postbaccalaureate distance learning degree programs offered (minimal on-campus study).
Electronic applications accepted.
Expenses: Tuition, state resident: full-time $2,932; part-time $489 per credit. Tuition, nonresident: full-time $5,758; part-time $960 per credit. Part-time tuition and fees vary according to course load, program and reciprocity agreements. *Web site:* http://www.technology.umn.edu/

■ UNIVERSITY OF MISSISSIPPI

Graduate School, School of Engineering, Oxford, University, MS 38677

AWARDS Engineering science (MS, PhD).
Faculty: 45 full-time (4 women).
Students: 160 full-time (37 women), 17 part-time (3 women); includes 9 minority (7 African Americans, 2 Asian Americans or Pacific Islanders), 132 international. In 2001, 37 master's, 6 doctorates awarded.
Degree requirements: For master's, thesis (for some programs); for doctorate, thesis/dissertation.
Entrance requirements: For master's, GRE General Test, TOEFL, minimum GPA of 3.0; for doctorate, GRE General Test, TOEFL. *Application deadline:* For fall admission, 8/1. Applications are processed on a rolling basis. *Application fee:* $0 ($25 for international students).
Expenses: Tuition, state resident: full-time $3,626; part-time $202 per hour. Tuition, nonresident: full-time $8,172; part-time $454 per hour.
Financial support: Application deadline: 3/1.
Dr. Kai-Fong Lee, Dean, 662-915-7407, *Fax:* 662-915-1287, *E-mail:* engineer@olemiss.edu.

■ UNIVERSITY OF MISSOURI–COLUMBIA

Graduate School, College of Engineering, Columbia, MO 65211

AWARDS MS, PhD. Part-time programs available.
Faculty: 103 full-time (9 women), 1 (woman) part-time/adjunct.
Students: 228 full-time (53 women), 133 part-time (25 women); includes 28 minority (7 African Americans, 8 Asian Americans or Pacific Islanders, 13 Hispanic Americans), 248 international. 614 applicants, 53% accepted. In 2001, 78 master's, 13 doctorates awarded.
Degree requirements: For doctorate, thesis/dissertation.
Entrance requirements: For master's and doctorate, GRE General Test, TOEFL. *Application deadline:* Applications are processed on a rolling basis. *Application fee:* $25 ($50 for international students).
Expenses: Tuition, state resident: part-time $179 per credit hour. Tuition, nonresident: part-time $539 per credit

hour. Required fees: $122 per semester. Tuition and fees vary according to program.
Financial support: Fellowships, research assistantships, teaching assistantships, institutionally sponsored loans available.
Dr. James Thompson, Dean, 573-882-4375, *E-mail:* thompsonje@missouri.edu. *Web site:* http://www.engineering.missouri.edu

■ UNIVERSITY OF MISSOURI–ROLLA

Graduate School, School of Engineering, Rolla, MO 65409-0910

AWARDS M Eng, MS, DE, PhD. Part-time and evening/weekend programs available. Terminal master's awarded for partial completion of doctoral program.

Degree requirements: For doctorate, thesis/dissertation.
Electronic applications accepted. *Web site:* http://www.eng.umr.edu/

Find an in-depth description at www.petersons.com/gradchannel.

■ UNIVERSITY OF NEBRASKA–LINCOLN

Graduate College, College of Engineering and Technology, Lincoln, NE 68588

AWARDS M Eng, MS, PhD, MS/MCRP.

Faculty: 143.
Students: 315 (63 women); includes 14 minority (3 African Americans, 7 Asian Americans or Pacific Islanders, 4 Hispanic Americans) 196 international. Average age 30. 736 applicants, 29% accepted, 75 enrolled. In 2001, 83 master's, 10 doctorates awarded.
Degree requirements: For doctorate, thesis/dissertation, comprehensive exam.
Entrance requirements: For master's and doctorate, GRE General Test, TOEFL. *Application fee:* $35. Electronic applications accepted.
Expenses: Tuition, state resident: full-time $2,412; part-time $134 per credit. Tuition, nonresident: full-time $6,223; part-time $346 per credit. Tuition and fees vary according to course load.
Financial support: In 2001–02, 3 fellowships with full tuition reimbursements, 146 research assistantships with full tuition reimbursements, 30 teaching assistantships were awarded. Federal Work-Study also available. Support available to part-time students. Financial award application deadline: 2/15.
Dr. David H. Allen, Dean, 402-472-3181, *Fax:* 402-472-7792.

Find an in-depth description at www.petersons.com/gradchannel.

UNIVERSITY OF NEVADA, LAS VEGAS

Graduate College, Howard R. Hughes College of Engineering, Las Vegas, NV 89154-9900

AWARDS MS, MSE, PhD. Part-time programs available.

Faculty: 72 full-time (2 women).
Students: 80 full-time (23 women), 87 part-time (23 women); includes 20 minority (4 African Americans, 13 Asian Americans or Pacific Islanders, 3 Hispanic Americans), 73 international. 137 applicants, 50% accepted, 44 enrolled. In 2001, 34 master's, 3 doctorates awarded.
Degree requirements: For master's, comprehensive exam (for some programs); for doctorate, thesis/dissertation, comprehensive exam.
Entrance requirements: For master's, minimum GPA of 3.0; for doctorate, GRE General Test. *Application deadline:* For fall admission, 6/15; for spring admission, 11/15. *Application fee:* $40 ($55 for international students).
Expenses: Tuition, state resident: full-time $1,926; part-time $107 per credit. Tuition, nonresident: full-time $9,376; part-time $220 per credit. Tuition and fees vary according to course load.
Financial support: In 2001–02, 47 research assistantships with full and partial tuition reimbursements (averaging $8,354 per year), 48 teaching assistantships with partial tuition reimbursements (averaging $11,000 per year) were awarded. Fellowships, tuition waivers (full) also available. Financial award application deadline: 3/1.
Dr. Darrell Pepper, Interim Dean, 702-895-3699.
Application contact: Graduate College Admissions Evaluator, 702-895-3320, *Fax:* 702-895-4180, *E-mail:* gradcollege@ccmail.nevada.edu.

Find an in-depth description at www.petersons.com/gradchannel.

UNIVERSITY OF NEVADA, RENO

Graduate School, College of Engineering, Reno, NV 89557

AWARDS MS, PhD.

Faculty: 48.
Students: 158 full-time (37 women), 44 part-time (5 women); includes 18 minority (15 Asian Americans or Pacific Islanders, 3 Hispanic Americans), 117 international. Average age 29. In 2001, 45 master's, 5 doctorates awarded. Terminal master's awarded for partial completion of doctoral program.
Degree requirements: For master's, thesis optional; for doctorate, thesis/dissertation.
Entrance requirements: For master's, TOEFL, minimum GPA of 2.75; for doctorate, TOEFL, minimum GPA of 3.0. *Application deadline:* For fall admission, 3/1

(priority date). Applications are processed on a rolling basis. *Application fee:* $40.
Expenses: Tuition, state resident: full-time $2,067; part-time $108 per credit. Tuition, nonresident: full-time $9,282; part-time $109 per credit. Required fees: $57 per semester. Tuition and fees vary according to course load.
Financial support: In 2001–02, 50 research assistantships, 32 teaching assistantships were awarded. Fellowships, Federal Work-Study, institutionally sponsored loans, and tuition waivers (full) also available. Financial award application deadline: 3/1.
Dr. Theodore Batchman, Dean, 775-784-6925.

UNIVERSITY OF NEW HAVEN

Graduate School, School of Engineering and Applied Science, West Haven, CT 06516-1916

AWARDS MS, MSEE, MSIE, MSME, Certificate, MBA/MSIE. Part-time and evening/weekend programs available.

Students: 71 full-time (28 women), 218 part-time (48 women); includes 19 minority (4 African Americans, 13 Asian Americans or Pacific Islanders, 2 Hispanic Americans), 110 international. In 2001, 80 degrees awarded.
Degree requirements: For master's, thesis or alternative.
Application deadline: Applications are processed on a rolling basis. *Application fee:* $50.
Expenses: Tuition: Full-time $12,015; part-time $445 per credit hour. Required fees: $30. One-time fee: $100 full-time.
Financial support: Federal Work-Study available. Support available to part-time students. Financial award application deadline: 5/1; financial award applicants required to submit FAFSA.
Dr. Zulma Turo-Ramos, Dean, 203-932-7167.

Find an in-depth description at www.petersons.com/gradchannel.

UNIVERSITY OF NEW MEXICO

Graduate School, School of Engineering, Albuquerque, NM 87131-2039

AWARDS MEHWE, MEME, MS, PhD. Part-time and evening/weekend programs available.

Faculty: 105 full-time (10 women), 47 part-time/adjunct (4 women).
Students: 381 full-time (73 women), 182 part-time (40 women); includes 83 minority (5 African Americans, 22 Asian Americans or Pacific Islanders, 49 Hispanic Americans, 7 Native Americans), 269 international. Average age 32. 952 applicants, 46% accepted, 143 enrolled. In 2001, 97 master's, 21 doctorates awarded.
Degree requirements: For doctorate, thesis/dissertation.

Entrance requirements: For master's and doctorate, GRE General Test, minimum GPA of 3.0. *Application deadline:* Applications are processed on a rolling basis. *Application fee:* $40.
Expenses: Tuition, state resident: full-time $2,771; part-time $115 per credit hour. Tuition, nonresident: full-time $11,207; part-time $467 per credit hour. Required fees: $570; $24 per credit hour. Part-time tuition and fees vary according to course load and program.
Financial support: In 2001–02, 207 students received support. Application deadline: 3/1; *Total annual research expenditures:* $11.2 million.
Dr. Joseph L. Cecchi, Dean, 505-277-5431, *Fax:* 505-277-5433, *E-mail:* cecchi@unm.edu. *Web site:* http://www.unm.edu/~soe/index.html/

Find an in-depth description at www.petersons.com/gradchannel.

UNIVERSITY OF NEW ORLEANS

Graduate School, College of Engineering, New Orleans, LA 70148

AWARDS MS, PhD, Certificate. Part-time and evening/weekend programs available.

Faculty: 17 full-time (2 women), 4 part-time/adjunct (0 women).
Students: 116 full-time (30 women), 97 part-time (26 women). Average age 29. 510 applicants, 39% accepted, 45 enrolled. In 2001, 52 master's, 6 doctorates awarded.
Degree requirements: For master's, thesis optional; for doctorate, thesis/dissertation.
Entrance requirements: For master's, GRE General Test, minimum GPA of 3.0; for doctorate, GRE General Test. *Application deadline:* For fall admission, 7/1 (priority date). Applications are processed on a rolling basis. *Application fee:* $20. Electronic applications accepted.
Expenses: Tuition, state resident: full-time $2,748; part-time $435 per credit. Tuition, nonresident: full-time $9,792; part-time $1,773 per credit.
Financial support: Fellowships, research assistantships, teaching assistantships, institutionally sponsored loans available. Financial award applicants required to submit FAFSA.
Faculty research: Electrical, civil, environmental, mechanical, naval architecture, and marine engineering.
Dr. John N. Crisp, Dean, 504-280-6825, *Fax:* 504-280-7413, *E-mail:* jcrisp@uno.edu.
Application contact: Dr. Paul Chirlian, Associate Director, 504-280-5504, *Fax:* 504-280-7413, *E-mail:* pchirlia@uno.edu.

Find an in-depth description at www.petersons.com/gradchannel.

■ THE UNIVERSITY OF NORTH CAROLINA AT CHARLOTTE

Graduate School, The William States Lee College of Engineering, Charlotte, NC 28223-0001

AWARDS ME, MS, MSCE, MSE, MSEE, MSME, PhD. Part-time and evening/weekend programs available.

Faculty: 50 full-time (2 women), 12 part-time/adjunct (0 women).
Students: 119 full-time (24 women), 135 part-time (18 women); includes 27 minority (16 African Americans, 10 Asian Americans or Pacific Islanders, 1 Hispanic American), 110 international. Average age 28. 401 applicants, 74% accepted, 81 enrolled. In 2001, 40 master's, 9 doctorates awarded.
Entrance requirements: For master's, GRE General Test. *Application deadline:* For fall admission, 7/15; for spring admission, 11/15. Applications are processed on a rolling basis. *Application fee:* $35. Electronic applications accepted.
Expenses: Tuition, state resident: full-time $1,483; part-time $371 per year. Tuition, nonresident: full-time $9,850; part-time $2,463 per year. Required fees: $1,043; $277 per year. Tuition and fees vary according to course load.
Financial support: In 2001–02, 1 fellowship (averaging $4,000 per year), 57 research assistantships, 45 teaching assistantships were awarded. Career-related internships or fieldwork, Federal Work-Study, institutionally sponsored loans, scholarships/grants, and unspecified assistantships also available. Support available to part-time students. Financial award application deadline: 4/1; financial award applicants required to submit FAFSA.
Dr. Robert E. Johnson, Dean, 704-687-2301, *Fax:* 704-687-2352, *E-mail:* robejohn@email.uncc.edu.
Application contact: Kathy Barringer, Director of Graduate Admissions, 704-687-3366, *Fax:* 704-687-3279, *E-mail:* gradadm@email.uncc.edu. *Web site:* http://www.uncc.edu/gradmiss/
Find an in-depth description at www.petersons.com/gradchannel.

■ UNIVERSITY OF NORTH DAKOTA

Graduate School, School of Engineering and Mines, Grand Forks, ND 58202

AWARDS M Engr, MA, MS, PhD. Part-time programs available.

Faculty: 40 full-time (0 women).
Students: 20 full-time (2 women), 33 part-time (5 women). 71 applicants, 89% accepted, 15 enrolled. In 2001, 14 master's, 2 doctorates awarded.
Degree requirements: For doctorate, thesis/dissertation, comprehensive final exam, final exam.

Entrance requirements: For master's, GRE General Test, TOEFL, minimum GPA of 3.0 (MS), 2.5 (M Engr); for doctorate, GRE General Test, TOEFL, minimum GPA of 3.5. *Application deadline:* For fall admission, 3/1 (priority date); for spring admission, 10/15 (priority date). Applications are processed on a rolling basis. *Application fee:* $30.
Expenses: Tuition, state resident: full-time $3,298. Tuition, nonresident: full-time $7,998.
Financial support: In 2001–02, 34 students received support, including 28 research assistantships with full tuition reimbursements available (averaging $10,100 per year), 29 teaching assistantships with full tuition reimbursements available (averaging $10,100 per year); fellowships, career-related internships or fieldwork, Federal Work-Study, institutionally sponsored loans, scholarships/grants, tuition waivers (full and partial), and unspecified assistantships also available. Support available to part-time students. Financial award application deadline: 3/15; financial award applicants required to submit FAFSA. *Total annual research expenditures:* $57,629.
Dr. John L. Watson, Dean, 701-777-3411, *Fax:* 701-777-4838, *E-mail:* john_watson@mail.und.nodak.edu. *Web site:* http://www.und.edu/dept/sem/

■ UNIVERSITY OF NORTH TEXAS

Robert B. Toulouse School of Graduate Studies, College of Arts and Sciences, Department of Engineering Technology, Denton, TX 76203

AWARDS MS. Part-time programs available.

Faculty: 13 full-time (1 woman), 5 part-time/adjunct (0 women).
Students: 25 full-time (9 women), 16 part-time (3 women); includes 5 minority (2 African Americans, 2 Asian Americans or Pacific Islanders, 1 Hispanic American), 25 international. Average age 30. In 2001, 2 degrees awarded.
Entrance requirements: For master's, GRE General Test, BS in related field. *Application deadline:* For fall admission, 7/17. *Application fee:* $25 ($50 for international students).
Expenses: Tuition, state resident: part-time $1,861 per hour. Tuition, nonresident: part-time $319 per hour. Required fees: $88; $21 per hour.
Financial support: Fellowships, research assistantships, teaching assistantships, career-related internships or fieldwork, Federal Work-Study, and institutionally sponsored loans available. Financial award application deadline: 4/1.
Faculty research: Computer-aided design, robotics, computer-integrated manufacturing, automation, pattern recognition.
Dr. Albert BIlly Grubbs, Chair, 940-565-2022, *Fax:* 940-565-2666, *E-mail:* grubbs@unt.edu.

Application contact: Dr. Michael Kozak, Graduate Adviser, 940-565-2022, *Fax:* 940-565-2666, *E-mail:* kozak@cas.unt.edu.

■ UNIVERSITY OF NOTRE DAME

Graduate School, College of Engineering, Notre Dame, IN 46556

AWARDS ME, MEME, MS, PhD. Part-time programs available.

Faculty: 97 full-time (4 women), 7 part-time/adjunct (1 woman).
Students: 321 full-time (79 women), 11 part-time (3 women); includes 18 minority (6 African Americans, 7 Asian Americans or Pacific Islanders, 3 Hispanic Americans, 2 Native Americans), 204 international. Average age 25. 826 applicants, 27% accepted, 97 enrolled. In 2001, 62 master's, 18 doctorates awarded. Terminal master's awarded for partial completion of doctoral program.
Degree requirements: For master's, comprehensive exam; for doctorate, thesis/dissertation. *Median time to degree:* Doctorate–5.5 years full-time.
Entrance requirements: For master's and doctorate, GRE General Test, TOEFL. *Application deadline:* For fall admission, 2/1 (priority date). Applications are processed on a rolling basis. *Application fee:* $50. Electronic applications accepted.
Expenses: Tuition: Full-time $24,220; part-time $1,346 per credit hour. Required fees: $155.
Financial support: In 2001–02, 323 students received support, including 92 fellowships with full tuition reimbursements available (averaging $18,800 per year), 156 research assistantships with full tuition reimbursements available (averaging $19,500 per year), 49 teaching assistantships with full tuition reimbursements available (averaging $18,300 per year). Scholarships/grants, tuition waivers (full), and unspecified assistantships also available. Financial award application deadline: 2/1.
Faculty research: Aero/fluid dynamics, controls and communications, hazardous waste, nano electronics, catalysis and surface dynamics. *Total annual research expenditures:* $11.8 million.
Dr. Frank P. Incropera, Dean, 574-631-5534, *Fax:* 574-631-8007, *E-mail:* incropera.1@nd.edu.
Application contact: Dr. Terrence J. Akai, Director of Graduate Admissions, 574-631-7706, *Fax:* 574-631-4183, *E-mail:* gradad@nd.edu. *Web site:* http://www.edu/~engineer/eng_home.html

■ UNIVERSITY OF OKLAHOMA

Graduate College, College of Engineering, Norman, OK 73019-0390

AWARDS M Env Sc, MS, D Engr, PhD. Part-time and evening/weekend programs available.

Faculty: 91 full-time (9 women), 6 part-time/adjunct (1 woman).

Students: 456 full-time (86 women), 182 part-time (30 women); includes 37 minority (7 African Americans, 15 Asian Americans or Pacific Islanders, 8 Hispanic Americans, 7 Native Americans), 457 international. 534 applicants, 82% accepted, 158 enrolled. In 2001, 159 master's, 27 doctorates awarded.
Degree requirements: For doctorate, thesis/dissertation, qualifying exam.
Entrance requirements: For master's and doctorate, TOEFL. *Application fee:* $25 ($50 for international students).
Expenses: Tuition, state resident: full-time $2,208; part-time $92 per credit hour. Tuition, nonresident: part-time $297 per credit hour. Tuition and fees vary according to course level, course load and program.
Financial support: In 2001–02, 5 fellowships (averaging $5,000 per year), 216 research assistantships with partial tuition reimbursements (averaging $10,257 per year), 97 teaching assistantships with partial tuition reimbursements (averaging $9,815 per year) were awarded. Career-related internships or fieldwork, Federal Work-Study, institutionally sponsored loans, and tuition waivers (full and partial) also available. Support available to part-time students. Financial award applicants required to submit FAFSA. *Total annual research expenditures:* $8.8 million.
Dr. Arthur Porter, Dean, 405-325-2621.

■ UNIVERSITY OF PENNSYLVANIA

School of Engineering and Applied Science, Philadelphia, PA 19104

AWARDS MCIT, MS, MSE, PhD, AC, M Arch/MSE, MD/PhD, MSE/MBA, MSE/MCP, VMD/PhD. Part-time and evening/weekend programs available. Terminal master's awarded for partial completion of doctoral program.
Degree requirements: For doctorate, thesis/dissertation.
Entrance requirements: For master's, TOEFL. Electronic applications accepted. *Web site:* http://www.seas.upenn.edu/
Find an in-depth description at www.petersons.com/gradchannel.

■ UNIVERSITY OF PITTSBURGH

School of Engineering, Pittsburgh, PA 15260

AWARDS MS Ch E, MS Met E, MSBENG, MSCEE, MSEE, MSIE, MSME, MSMSE, MSMfSE, MSPE, PhD, Certificate, MD/PhD, MS Ch E/MSPE. Part-time and evening/weekend programs available.
Postbaccalaureate distance learning degree programs offered (no on-campus study).
Faculty: 89 full-time (7 women), 25 part-time/adjunct (0 women).
Students: 309 full-time (70 women), 203 part-time (31 women); includes 37 minority (12 African Americans, 20 Asian

Americans or Pacific Islanders, 5 Hispanic Americans), 198 international. 1,180 applicants, 40% accepted, 132 enrolled. In 2001, 100 master's, 43 doctorates awarded. Terminal master's awarded for partial completion of doctoral program.
Degree requirements: For doctorate, thesis/dissertation, final oral exams, comprehensive exam.
Entrance requirements: For master's and doctorate, TOEFL. *Application deadline:* For fall admission, 8/1 (priority date); for spring admission, 12/1 (priority date). Applications are processed on a rolling basis. *Application fee:* $40.
Expenses: Contact institution.
Financial support: In 2001–02, 226 students received support, including 11 fellowships with full tuition reimbursements available (averaging $20,074 per year), 162 research assistantships with full tuition reimbursements available (averaging $18,118 per year), 53 teaching assistantships with full tuition reimbursements available (averaging $18,244 per year). Scholarships/grants, traineeships, and tuition waivers (full and partial) also available. Financial award application deadline: 2/15.
Faculty research: Artificial organs, biotechnology, signal processing, construction management, fluid dynamics. *Total annual research expenditures:* $19.3 million.
Dr. Gerald D. Holder, Dean, 412-624-9811, Fax: 412-624-0412, *E-mail:* holder@engrng.pitt.edu.
Application contact: 412-624-9800, *Fax:* 412-624-9808, *E-mail:* admin@engrng.pitt.edu. *Web site:* http://www.engrng.pitt.edu/~engwww/

■ UNIVERSITY OF PORTLAND

Graduate School, Multnomah School of Engineering, Portland, OR 97203-5798

AWARDS ME. Part-time and evening/weekend programs available.

Faculty: 16 full-time (0 women).
Students: 2 full-time (0 women), 1 part-time. 27 applicants, 63% accepted. In 2001, 5 degrees awarded.
Entrance requirements: For master's, GRE General Test, TOEFL, minimum GPA of 3.0. *Application deadline:* For fall admission, 8/1 (priority date); for spring admission, 12/1. Applications are processed on a rolling basis. *Application fee:* $45.
Expenses: Contact institution.
Financial support: Teaching assistantships, career-related internships or fieldwork, Federal Work-Study, and institutionally sponsored loans available. Support available to part-time students. Financial award application deadline: 3/15.
Dr. Zia Yamayee, Dean, 503-943-7314.
Application contact: Dr. Khalid Khan, Graduate Program Director, 503-943-7276, *E-mail:* khan@up.edu.

■ UNIVERSITY OF PUERTO RICO, MAYAGÜEZ CAMPUS

Graduate Studies, College of Engineering, Mayagüez, PR 00681-9000

AWARDS M Ch E, M Co E, MCE, MEE, MME, MMSE, MS, PhD. Part-time programs available.

Degree requirements: For master's, comprehensive exam; for doctorate, one foreign language, thesis/dissertation.
Entrance requirements: For master's and doctorate, minimum GPA of 2.5, proficiency in English and Spanish.

■ UNIVERSITY OF RHODE ISLAND

Graduate School, College of Engineering, Kingston, RI 02881

AWARDS MS, PhD. Part-time programs available.

Application deadline: For fall admission, 4/15 (priority date). Applications are processed on a rolling basis. *Application fee:* $35.
Expenses: Tuition, state resident: full-time $3,756; part-time $209 per credit. Tuition, nonresident: full-time $10,774; part-time $599 per credit. Required fees: $1,586; $76 per credit. $76 per credit. One-time fee: $60 full-time.
Financial support: Research assistantships, teaching assistantships, tuition waivers (full) available.
Arun Shukla, Interim Dean, 401-874-2186.
Application contact: Dr. David Shao, Associate Dean, 401-874-2186.

■ UNIVERSITY OF ROCHESTER

The College, School of Engineering and Applied Sciences, Rochester, NY 14627-0250

AWARDS MS, PhD. Part-time programs available.

Faculty: 53.
Students: 212 full-time (41 women), 26 part-time (7 women); includes 17 minority (4 African Americans, 8 Asian Americans or Pacific Islanders, 5 Hispanic Americans), 120 international. 980 applicants, 13% accepted, 59 enrolled. In 2001, 44 master's, 23 doctorates awarded. Terminal master's awarded for partial completion of doctoral program.
Degree requirements: For master's, thesis optional; for doctorate, thesis/dissertation, preliminary and oral exams.
Entrance requirements: For master's and doctorate, GRE, TOEFL. *Application deadline:* For fall admission, 2/1 (priority date). *Application fee:* $25.
Expenses: Tuition: Part-time $755 per credit hour.
Financial support: Fellowships, research assistantships, teaching assistantships,

University of Rochester (continued)
tuition waivers (full and partial) available. Financial award application deadline: 2/1. Kevin Parker, Dean, 716-275-4151.

Find an in-depth description at www.petersons.com/gradchannel.

■ UNIVERSITY OF ST. THOMAS

Graduate Studies, Graduate School of Applied Science and Engineering, St. Paul, MN 55105-1096

AWARDS MMSE, MS, MSDD, MSS, Certificate. Part-time and evening/weekend programs available.

Faculty: 12 full-time (2 women), 78 part-time/adjunct (7 women).
Students: 136 full-time (49 women), 984 part-time (277 women); includes 194 minority (62 African Americans, 123 Asian Americans or Pacific Islanders, 7 Hispanic Americans, 2 Native Americans), 332 international. Average age 32. 331 applicants, 98% accepted. In 2001, 248 master's, 29 other advanced degrees awarded.
Application deadline: For fall admission, 8/1 (priority date); for spring admission, 1/1 (priority date). Applications are processed on a rolling basis. *Application fee:* $30. Electronic applications accepted.
Expenses: Contact institution.
Financial support: In 2001–02, 236 students received support; fellowships, research assistantships, institutionally sponsored loans and scholarships/grants available. Support available to part-time students. Financial award application deadline: 4/1; financial award applicants required to submit FAFSA.
Application contact: Dr. Angeline Barretta-Herman, Associate Vice President for Academic Affairs, 651-962-6033, *Fax:* 651-962-6702, *E-mail:* a9barrettahe@stthomas.edu.

■ UNIVERSITY OF SOUTH ALABAMA

Graduate School, College of Engineering, Mobile, AL 36688-0002

AWARDS MS Ch E, MSEE, MSME. Part-time programs available.

Faculty: 22 full-time (0 women).
Students: 102 full-time (13 women), 34 part-time (4 women); includes 4 minority (2 African Americans, 2 Asian Americans or Pacific Islanders), 120 international. 215 applicants, 66% accepted. In 2001, 18 degrees awarded.
Degree requirements: For master's, project or thesis.
Entrance requirements: For master's, GRE General Test, BS in engineering, minimum GPA of 3.0. *Application deadline:* For fall admission, 9/1 (priority date). Applications are processed on a rolling basis. *Application fee:* $25.

Expenses: Tuition, state resident: full-time $3,048. Tuition, nonresident: full-time $6,096. Required fees: $320.
Financial support: In 2001–02, 4 research assistantships were awarded; career-related internships or fieldwork and institutionally sponsored loans also available. Support available to part-time students. Financial award application deadline: 4/1.
Dr. B. Keith Harrison, Interim Associate Dean, 334-460-6140.
Application contact: Dr. Russell M. Hayes, Director of Graduate Studies, 334-460-6117.

■ UNIVERSITY OF SOUTH CAROLINA

The Graduate School, College of Engineering and Information Technology, Columbia, SC 29208

AWARDS ME, MS, PhD. Part-time and evening/weekend programs available. Postbaccalaureate distance learning degree programs offered (minimal on-campus study).

Faculty: 86 full-time (7 women).
Students: 324 full-time (76 women), 146 part-time (21 women); includes 334 minority (16 African Americans, 309 Asian Americans or Pacific Islanders, 9 Hispanic Americans). Average age 30. 827 applicants, 49% accepted. In 2001, 163 master's, 22 doctorates awarded.
Degree requirements: For master's, thesis (for some programs); for doctorate, thesis/dissertation.
Entrance requirements: For master's and doctorate, GRE General Test, TOEFL. *Application deadline:* For fall admission, 3/1 (priority date); for spring admission, 11/1. Applications are processed on a rolling basis. *Application fee:* $40. Electronic applications accepted.
Expenses: Tuition, state resident: full-time $4,434. Tuition, nonresident: full-time $9,854. Tuition and fees vary according to program.
Financial support: In 2001–02, 5 fellowships (averaging $9,600 per year), 177 research assistantships with partial tuition reimbursements (averaging $15,000 per year), 42 teaching assistantships with partial tuition reimbursements (averaging $14,400 per year) were awarded. Career-related internships or fieldwork, institutionally sponsored loans, and scholarships/grants also available.
Faculty research: Electrochemical engineering/fuel cell technology, fracture mechanics and nondestructive evaluation, virtual prototyping for electric power systems, wideband-gap electronics materials behavior/composites and smart materials. *Total annual research expenditures:* $18.5 million.
Dr. Ralph E. White, Dean, 803-777-3270, *Fax:* 803-777-9597, *E-mail:* white@engr.sc.edu.
Application contact: Mike Perkins, Student Services Manager, 803-777-4177, *Fax:* 803-777-0027, *E-mail:* perkins@

engr.sc.edu. *Web site:* http://www.engr.sc.edu/

■ UNIVERSITY OF SOUTHERN CALIFORNIA

Graduate School, School of Engineering, Los Angeles, CA 90089

AWARDS MCM, ME, MS, PhD, Certificate, Engr, MBA/MS. Part-time programs available.

Degree requirements: For doctorate, thesis/dissertation.
Entrance requirements: For master's, doctorate, and other advanced degree, GRE General Test.
Expenses: Contact institution.

Find an in-depth description at www.petersons.com/gradchannel.

■ UNIVERSITY OF SOUTHERN COLORADO

College of Education, Engineering and Professional Studies, Pueblo, CO 81001-4901

AWARDS MS. Part-time and evening/weekend programs available.

Faculty: 5 full-time (1 woman), 1 part-time/adjunct (0 women).
Students: 16 full-time (4 women), 18 part-time (3 women); includes 5 minority (1 African American, 3 Hispanic Americans, 1 Native American), 20 international. Average age 29. 30 applicants, 87% accepted. In 2001, 23 degrees awarded.
Degree requirements: For master's, thesis optional.
Entrance requirements: For master's, GRE General Test, TOEFL. *Application deadline:* For fall admission, 7/19 (priority date); for spring admission, 11/30 (priority date). *Application fee:* $35.
Expenses: Tuition, state resident: full-time $1,746; part-time $97 per credit. Tuition, nonresident: full-time $8,298; part-time $461 per credit. Required fees: $445; $97 per credit. $582 per semester. Tuition and fees vary according to course load.
Financial support: In 2001–02, 1 fellowship (averaging $17,000 per year), 1 research assistantship with partial tuition reimbursement (averaging $13,000 per year), 2 teaching assistantships with partial tuition reimbursements (averaging $8,300 per year) were awarded. Career-related internships or fieldwork, Federal Work-Study, institutionally sponsored loans, and scholarships/grants also available. Financial award application deadline: 3/1; financial award applicants required to submit FAFSA.
Faculty research: Computer-integrated manufacturing, reliability, economic development, design of experiments, scheduling. *Total annual research expenditures:* $60,000.
Dr. Hector R. Carrasco, Dean, 719-549-2696, *Fax:* 719-549-2519, *E-mail:* carrasco@uscolo.edu.

Application contact: Dr. Huseyin Sarper, Graduate Coordinator, 719-549-2889, *Fax:* 719-549-2519, *E-mail:* sarper@uscolo.edu. *Web site:* http://www.ceeps.edu

■ UNIVERSITY OF SOUTHERN INDIANA

Graduate Studies, School of Science and Engineering Technology, Evansville, IN 47712-3590

AWARDS MS. Part-time and evening/weekend programs available.

Faculty: 5 full-time (0 women).
Students: Average age 35. 9 applicants, 56% accepted, 3 enrolled.
Degree requirements: For master's, project.
Entrance requirements: For master's, minimum GPA of 2.5, BS in engineering or engineering technology. *Application deadline:* Applications are processed on a rolling basis. *Application fee:* $25.
Expenses: Tuition, state resident: full-time $1,361; part-time $151 per hour. Tuition, nonresident: full-time $2,732; part-time $304 per hour. Required fees: $60; $23 per semester. Tuition and fees vary according to course load.
Financial support: In 2001–02, 2 students received support. Federal Work-Study, institutionally sponsored loans, scholarships/grants, tuition waivers (full and partial), and unspecified assistantships available. Financial award application deadline: 3/1; financial award applicants required to submit FAFSA.
Dr. Jerome Cain, Dean, 812-464-1977, *E-mail:* jcain@usi.edu. *Web site:* http://www.usi.edu/

■ UNIVERSITY OF SOUTHERN MISSISSIPPI

Graduate School, College of Science and Technology, School of Engineering Technology, Hattiesburg, MS 39406

AWARDS MS. Part-time programs available.
Faculty: 25 full-time (0 women).
Students: 26 full-time (9 women), 15 part-time (5 women); includes 5 minority (3 African Americans, 1 Asian American or Pacific Islander, 1 Hispanic American). Average age 28. 43 applicants, 60% accepted. In 2001, 14 degrees awarded.
Degree requirements: For master's, thesis optional.
Entrance requirements: For master's, GMAT or GRE General Test, TOEFL, minimum GPA of 2.75. *Application deadline:* For fall admission, 8/6 (priority date). Applications are processed on a rolling basis. *Application fee:* $0 ($25 for international students).
Expenses: Tuition, state resident: full-time $3,416; part-time $190 per credit hour. Tuition, nonresident: full-time $7,932; part-time $441 per credit hour.

Financial support: Research assistantships, teaching assistantships, career-related internships or fieldwork and Federal Work-Study available. Financial award application deadline: 3/15.
Faculty research: Robotics; CAD/CAM. Simulation; computer integrated manufacturing processes; construction scheduling, estimating, and computer systems. *Total annual research expenditures:* $1.9 million.
Dr. Ruth Ann Cade, Director, 601-266-4896, *Fax:* 601-266-5829.
Application contact: Graduate Admissions, 601-266-5137. *Web site:* http://www.set.usm.edu/

■ UNIVERSITY OF SOUTH FLORIDA

College of Graduate Studies, College of Engineering, Tampa, FL 33620-9951

AWARDS M Ch E, M Cp E, MCE, MCS, ME, MIE, MME, MS, MS Ch E, MS Cp E, MSBE, MSCE, MSCS, MSE, MSEE, MSEM, MSES, MSIE, MSME, PhD. Part-time and evening/weekend programs available.

Faculty: 87 full-time (7 women), 1 part-time/adjunct (0 women).
Students: 432 full-time (108 women), 268 part-time (43 women); includes 93 minority (17 African Americans, 39 Asian Americans or Pacific Islanders, 35 Hispanic Americans, 2 Native Americans), 373 international. 1,620 applicants, 43% accepted, 210 enrolled. In 2001, 55 master's, 4 doctorates awarded. Terminal master's awarded for partial completion of doctoral program.
Degree requirements: For doctorate, thesis/dissertation, 2 tools of research as specified by dissertation committee.
Entrance requirements: For master's, GRE General Test, minimum GPA of 3.0 during previous 2 years; for doctorate, GRE General Test. *Application deadline:* For fall admission, 6/1; for spring admission, 10/15. Applications are processed on a rolling basis. *Application fee:* $20. Electronic applications accepted.
Expenses: Tuition, state resident: part-time $166 per credit hour. Tuition, nonresident: part-time $573 per credit hour. Required fees: $17 per term.
Financial support: Fellowships with full tuition reimbursements, research assistantships with full and partial tuition reimbursements, teaching assistantships with full tuition reimbursements, career-related internships or fieldwork, Federal Work-Study, institutionally sponsored loans, tuition waivers (partial), and unspecified assistantships available. Support available to part-time students. Financial award applicants required to submit FAFSA.
Louis A. Martin-Vega, Associate Dean, 813-974-3780, *Fax:* 813-974-5094, *E-mail:*

csmith@eng.usf.edu. *Web site:* http://www.eng.usf.edu/academic.html
Find an in-depth description at www.petersons.com/gradchannel.

■ THE UNIVERSITY OF TENNESSEE

Graduate School, College of Engineering, Knoxville, TN 37996

AWARDS MS, PhD, MS/MBA. Part-time and evening/weekend programs available. Postbaccalaureate distance learning degree programs offered.

Faculty: 134 full-time (5 women), 11 part-time/adjunct (1 woman).
Students: 297 full-time (66 women), 252 part-time (48 women); includes 31 minority (18 African Americans, 9 Asian Americans or Pacific Islanders, 3 Hispanic Americans, 1 Native American), 175 international. 771 applicants, 53% accepted. In 2001, 155 master's, 36 doctorates awarded.
Degree requirements: For master's, thesis or alternative; for doctorate, thesis/dissertation.
Entrance requirements: For master's and doctorate, TOEFL, minimum GPA of 2.7. *Application deadline:* For fall admission, 2/1 (priority date). Applications are processed on a rolling basis. *Application fee:* $35. Electronic applications accepted.
Expenses: Tuition, state resident: full-time $4,280; part-time $233 per hour. Tuition, nonresident: full-time $12,066; part-time $666 per hour. Tuition and fees vary according to program.
Financial support: In 2001–02, 11 fellowships, 130 research assistantships, 46 teaching assistantships were awarded. Career-related internships or fieldwork, Federal Work-Study, institutionally sponsored loans, and unspecified assistantships also available. Financial award application deadline: 2/1; financial award applicants required to submit FAFSA.
Dr. Fred Tompkins, Interim Dean, 865-974-5321.
Find an in-depth description at www.petersons.com/gradchannel.

■ THE UNIVERSITY OF TENNESSEE AT CHATTANOOGA

Graduate Division, College of Engineering and Computer Sciences, Chattanooga, TN 37403-2598

AWARDS MS. Part-time and evening/weekend programs available.

Faculty: 16 full-time (3 women), 1 part-time/adjunct (0 women).
Students: 18 full-time (5 women), 71 part-time (13 women); includes 8 minority (6 African Americans, 2 Asian Americans or Pacific Islanders), 28 international. Average age 33. 88 applicants, 48% accepted, 18 enrolled. In 2001, 10 degrees awarded.

The University of Tennessee at Chattanooga (continued)

Degree requirements: For master's, thesis.
Entrance requirements: For master's, GRE General Test. *Application deadline:* For fall admission, 8/1 (priority date); for spring admission, 12/1 (priority date). Applications are processed on a rolling basis. *Application fee:* $25.
Expenses: Tuition, state resident: full-time $3,752; part-time $228 per hour. Tuition, nonresident: full-time $10,282; part-time $565 per hour.
Financial support: Fellowships, research assistantships, Federal Work-Study and institutionally sponsored loans available. Support available to part-time students. Financial award application deadline: 4/1; financial award applicants required to submit FAFSA.
Dr. Phil M. Kazemersky, Acting Dean, 423-425-4121, *Fax:* 423-425-5229, *E-mail:* phil-kazemersky@utc.edu.
Application contact: Dr. Deborah E. Arfken, Dean of Graduate Studies, 865-425-1740, *Fax:* 865-425-5223, *E-mail:* deborah-arfken@utc.edu. *Web site:* http://www.utc.edu/

■ THE UNIVERSITY OF TENNESSEE SPACE INSTITUTE

Graduate Programs, Tullahoma, TN 37388-9700

AWARDS MS, PhD. Part-time programs available. Postbaccalaureate distance learning degree programs offered.

Faculty: 41 full-time (1 woman), 8 part-time/adjunct (0 women).
Students: 53 full-time (11 women), 129 part-time (18 women); includes 6 minority (2 African Americans, 3 Asian Americans or Pacific Islanders, 1 Hispanic American), 29 international. 72 applicants, 69% accepted, 35 enrolled. In 2001, 56 master's, 8 doctorates awarded. Terminal master's awarded for partial completion of doctoral program.
Degree requirements: For doctorate, one foreign language, thesis/dissertation. *Application deadline:* Applications are processed on a rolling basis. *Application fee:* $35. Electronic applications accepted.
Expenses: Tuition, state resident: full-time $4,730; part-time $208 per semester hour. Tuition, nonresident: full-time $15,028; part-time $627 per semester hour. Required fees: $10 per semester hour. One-time fee: $35.
Financial support: In 2001–02, 5 fellowships with full and partial tuition reimbursements, 53 research assistantships with full tuition reimbursements were awarded. Career-related internships or fieldwork, Federal Work-Study, and tuition waivers (full and partial) also available. Financial award applicants required to submit FAFSA.
Faculty research: Energy conversion, materials processing, computational fluid

dynamics, aerodynamics, laser applications. *Total annual research expenditures:* $6.3 million.
Dr. John Caruthers, Chief Operating Officer, 931-394-7213, *Fax:* 931-394-7211, *E-mail:* jcaruthe@utsi.edu.
Application contact: Dr. Alfonso Pujol, Assistant Vice President and Dean for Student Affairs, 931-393-7432, *Fax:* 931-393-7346, *E-mail:* apujol@utsi.edu.

Find an in-depth description at www.petersons.com/gradchannel.

■ THE UNIVERSITY OF TEXAS AT ARLINGTON

Graduate School, College of Engineering, Arlington, TX 76019

AWARDS M Engr, M Sw En, MCS, MS, PhD. Part-time programs available.

Faculty: 89 full-time (5 women), 12 part-time/adjunct (1 woman).
Students: 971 full-time (183 women), 426 part-time (76 women); includes 126 minority (12 African Americans, 95 Asian Americans or Pacific Islanders, 17 Hispanic Americans, 2 Native Americans), 1,077 international. Average age 27. 2,269 applicants, 80% accepted, 442 enrolled. In 2001, 251 master's, 20 doctorates awarded.
Degree requirements: For master's, thesis optional; for doctorate, thesis/dissertation.
Entrance requirements: For master's and doctorate, GRE General Test, TOEFL. *Application deadline:* For fall admission, 6/16. Applications are processed on a rolling basis. *Application fee:* $25 ($50 for international students).
Expenses: Tuition, area resident: Full-time $2,268. Tuition, nonresident: full-time $6,264. Required fees: $839. Tuition and fees vary according to course load.
Financial support: Fellowships, research assistantships, teaching assistantships, career-related internships or fieldwork, Federal Work-Study, institutionally sponsored loans, scholarships/grants, and tuition waivers (partial) available. Financial award application deadline: 6/1; financial award applicants required to submit FAFSA.
Dr. Bill D. Carroll, Dean, 817-272-5725, *Fax:* 817-272-5110, *E-mail:* carroll@uta.edu.
Application contact: Dr. Theresa A. Maldonado, Associate Dean for Research and Graduate Studies, 817-272-5725, *Fax:* 817-272-2548, *E-mail:* maldonado@uta.edu. http://www.engineering.uta.edu/

Find an in-depth description at www.petersons.com/gradchannel.

■ THE UNIVERSITY OF TEXAS AT AUSTIN

Graduate School, College of Engineering, Austin, TX 78712-1111

AWARDS MA, MS, MSE, PhD, MBA/MSE, MD/PhD, MP Aff/MSE. Part-time and evening/weekend programs available.

Faculty: 227 full-time (21 women), 72 part-time/adjunct (6 women).
Students: 1,475 full-time (277 women), 411 part-time (71 women); includes 170 minority (26 African Americans, 92 Asian Americans or Pacific Islanders, 48 Hispanic Americans, 4 Native Americans), 1,070 international. Average age 28. 4,000 applicants, 27% accepted, 371 enrolled. In 2001, 416 master's, 132 doctorates awarded.
Entrance requirements: For master's and doctorate, GRE General Test. *Application fee:* $50 ($75 for international students). Electronic applications accepted.
Expenses: Tuition, state resident: full-time $3,159. Tuition, nonresident: full-time $6,957. Tuition and fees vary according to program.
Financial support: In 2001–02, 293 fellowships with partial tuition reimbursements (averaging $3,160 per year), 756 research assistantships with full tuition reimbursements (averaging $14,000 per year), 305 teaching assistantships with partial tuition reimbursements (averaging $13,000 per year) were awarded. Career-related internships or fieldwork, Federal Work-Study, institutionally sponsored loans, scholarships/grants, tuition waivers (partial), and academic assistantships, tutorships also available. Support available to part-time students. Financial award applicants required to submit FAFSA. *Total annual research expenditures:* $91.4 million.
Dr. Ben G. Streetman, Dean, 512-471-1166, *Fax:* 512-475-7072, *E-mail:* bstreet@mail.utexas.edu. *Web site:* http://www.engr.utexas.edu/

Find an in-depth description at www.petersons.com/gradchannel.

■ THE UNIVERSITY OF TEXAS AT DALLAS

Erik Jonsson School of Engineering and Computer Science, Richardson, TX 75083-0688

AWARDS MS, MSEE, MSTE, PhD. Part-time and evening/weekend programs available.

Faculty: 59 full-time (5 women), 8 part-time/adjunct (3 women).
Students: 786 full-time (214 women), 381 part-time (104 women); includes 153 minority (9 African Americans, 134 Asian Americans or Pacific Islanders, 9 Hispanic Americans, 1 Native American), 889 international. Average age 27. 2,614 applicants, 40% accepted. In 2001, 313 master's, 14 doctorates awarded.
Degree requirements: For doctorate, thesis/dissertation.

Entrance requirements: For master's, GRE General Test, TOEFL; for doctorate, GRE General Test, TOEFL, minimum GPA of 3.5. *Application deadline:* For fall admission, 7/15; for spring admission, 11/15. Applications are processed on a rolling basis. *Application fee:* $25 ($75 for international students). Electronic applications accepted.
Expenses: Tuition, state resident: full-time $1,440; part-time $84 per credit. Tuition, nonresident: full-time $5,310; part-time $295 per credit. Required fees: $1,835; $87 per credit. $138 per term.
Financial support: In 2001–02, 4 fellowships with full tuition reimbursements (averaging $3,000 per year), 101 research assistantships with full tuition reimbursements (averaging $5,234 per year), 105 teaching assistantships with full tuition reimbursements (averaging $5,130 per year) were awarded. Career-related internships or fieldwork, Federal Work-Study, institutionally sponsored loans, and scholarships/grants also available. Support available to part-time students. Financial award application deadline: 4/30; financial award applicants required to submit FAFSA.
Faculty research: Telecommunications, optical devices, software engineering, materials and systems, artificial intelligence. *Total annual research expenditures:* $2.7 million.
Dr. William P. Osborne, Dean, 972-883-2974, *Fax:* 972-883-2813, *E-mail:* wosborne@utdallas.edu.
Application contact: Sheila R. Fleming, Student Development Specialist for Engineering and Computer Science, 972-883-4155, *Fax:* 972-883-2813, *E-mail:* fleming@utdallas.edu. *Web site:* http://www.utdallas.edu/dept/eecs/

■ THE UNIVERSITY OF TEXAS AT EL PASO

Graduate School, College of Engineering, El Paso, TX 79968-0001

AWARDS MEENE, MIT, MS, MSENE, PhD. Part-time and evening/weekend programs available.

Students: 382 (87 women); includes 115 minority (3 African Americans, 5 Asian Americans or Pacific Islanders, 107 Hispanic Americans) 102 international. Average age 28. In 2001, 78 degrees awarded.
Degree requirements: For doctorate, thesis/dissertation.
Entrance requirements: For master's, GRE General Test, TOEFL; for doctorate, GRE General Test, TOEFL, minimum graduate GPA of 3.5. *Application deadline:* For fall admission, 7/1 (priority date); for spring admission, 11/1 (priority date). Applications are processed on a rolling basis. *Application fee:* $15 ($65 for international students). Electronic applications accepted.
Expenses: Contact institution.

Financial support: In 2001–02, research assistantships with partial tuition reimbursements (averaging $21,125 per year), teaching assistantships with partial tuition reimbursements (averaging $16,900 per year) were awarded. Fellowships with partial tuition reimbursements, career-related internships or fieldwork, Federal Work-Study, institutionally sponsored loans, scholarships/grants, and tuition waivers (partial) also available. Financial award application deadline: 3/15; financial award applicants required to submit FAFSA.
Dr. Andrew H. Swift, Dean, 915-747-5460.
Application contact: Dr. Charles H. Ambler, Dean of the Graduate School, 915-747-5491 Ext. 7886, *Fax:* 915-747-5788, *E-mail:* cambler@miners.utep.edu. *Web site:* http://www.utep.edu/engineer/

■ THE UNIVERSITY OF TEXAS AT SAN ANTONIO

College of Engineering, San Antonio, TX 78249-0617

AWARDS MSCE, MSEE, MSME. Part-time and evening/weekend programs available.

Faculty: 21 full-time (1 woman), 4 part-time/adjunct (0 women).
Students: 53 full-time (11 women), 70 part-time (11 women); includes 29 minority (2 African Americans, 6 Asian Americans or Pacific Islanders, 21 Hispanic Americans), 49 international. Average age 29. 98 applicants, 91% accepted, 49 enrolled. In 2001, 22 degrees awarded.
Degree requirements: For master's, thesis optional.
Entrance requirements: For master's, GRE General Test, minimum GPA of 3.0 in last 60 hours of bachelors degree. *Application deadline:* For fall admission, 7/1; for spring admission, 12/1. Applications are processed on a rolling basis. *Application fee:* $25.
Expenses: Tuition, state resident: full-time $2,268; part-time $126 per credit hour. Tuition, nonresident: full-time $6,066; part-time $337 per credit hour. Required fees: $781. Tuition and fees vary according to course load.
Financial support: Research assistantships, teaching assistantships, career-related internships or fieldwork, institutionally sponsored loans, and scholarships/grants available. Financial award application deadline: 3/31. *Total annual research expenditures:* $361,969.
Dr. Zorica Pantic-Tanner, Dean, 210-458-5526.

■ THE UNIVERSITY OF TEXAS AT TYLER

Graduate Studies, College of Engineering and Computer Science, Department of Engineering, Tyler, TX 75799-0001

AWARDS M Engr. Part-time programs available.

Faculty: 10 full-time (1 woman).
Students: 1 full-time (0 women), 5 part-time (1 woman); includes 1 minority (Asian American or Pacific Islander), 1 international. Average age 36. 5 applicants, 100% accepted, 2 enrolled. In 2001, 2 degrees awarded.
Degree requirements: For master's, engineering project.
Entrance requirements: For master's, GRE, bachelor's degree in engineering. *Application deadline:* For fall admission, 10/30; for spring admission, 5/30. Applications are processed on a rolling basis. *Application fee:* $0 ($50 for international students).
Expenses: Tuition, state resident: part-time $44 per credit hour. Tuition, nonresident: part-time $262 per credit hour. Required fees: $58 per credit hour. $76 per semester.
Financial support: Application deadline: 7/1;
Faculty research: Mechatronics vibration analysis, fluid dynamics, electronics and instrumentation, manufacturing processes.
Application contact: Dr. R. Lindsay Wells, Program Coordinator, 903-565-5610, *Fax:* 903-566-7148, *E-mail:* lwells@mail.uttyl.edu. *Web site:* http://cecs.uttyler.edu/

■ UNIVERSITY OF TOLEDO

Graduate School, College of Engineering, Department of General Engineering, Toledo, OH 43606-3398

AWARDS MS.

Faculty: 1 full-time (0 women), 2 part-time/adjunct (0 women).
Students: 22 applicants, 100% accepted. In 2001, 6 degrees awarded.
Entrance requirements: For master's, GRE General Test, minimum GPA of 2.7, industrial experience. *Application fee:* $30.
Expenses: Tuition, state resident: full-time $7,278; part-time $303 per hour. Tuition, nonresident: full-time $15,731; part-time $699 per hour. Required fees: $43 per hour. *Total annual research expenditures:* $404,000.
Daniel Solarek, Chairman, 419-530-3159, *Fax:* 419-530-3068.
Application contact: Dr. Ella Fridman, Graduate Program Director, 419-530-3273, *Fax:* 419-530-3068.

■ UNIVERSITY OF TULSA

Graduate School, College of Engineering and Natural Sciences, Tulsa, OK 74104-3189

AWARDS ME, METM, MS, MSE, PhD, JD/MS. Part-time programs available.

Faculty: 72 full-time (6 women), 3 part-time/adjunct (0 women).

Students: 189 full-time (44 women), 93 part-time (16 women); includes 9 minority (1 African American, 5 Asian Americans or Pacific Islanders, 2 Hispanic Americans, 1 Native American), 212 international. Average age 28. 377 applicants, 79% accepted, 154 enrolled. In 2001, 43 master's, 13 doctorates awarded.

Degree requirements: For doctorate, thesis/dissertation.

Entrance requirements: For master's and doctorate, GRE General Test, TOEFL. *Application deadline:* Applications are processed on a rolling basis. *Application fee:* $30. Electronic applications accepted.

Expenses: Tuition: Full-time $9,540; part-time $530 per credit hour. Required fees: $80. One-time fee: $230 full-time.

Financial support: Fellowships with full and partial tuition reimbursements, research assistantships with full and partial tuition reimbursements, teaching assistantships with full and partial tuition reimbursements, career-related internships or fieldwork, Federal Work-Study, scholarships/grants, tuition waivers (partial), and unspecified assistantships available. Support available to part-time students. Financial award application deadline: 2/1; financial award applicants required to submit FAFSA. *Total annual research expenditures:* $15.8 million.

Dr. Steve J. Bellovich, Dean, 918-631-2288, *E-mail:* steven-bellovich@utulsa.edu.

Application contact: Information Contact, *E-mail:* grad@utulsa.edu. *Web site:* http://www.ens.utulsa.edu/

■ UNIVERSITY OF UTAH

Graduate School, College of Engineering, Salt Lake City, UT 84112-1107

AWARDS M Phil, ME, MS, PhD, EE. Part-time programs available.

Faculty: 90 full-time (12 women), 15 part-time/adjunct (2 women).

Students: 381 full-time (66 women), 192 part-time (33 women); includes 178 minority (4 African Americans, 159 Asian Americans or Pacific Islanders, 11 Hispanic Americans, 4 Native Americans), 99 international. Average age 29. 903 applicants, 45% accepted. In 2001, 68 master's, 29 doctorates awarded. Terminal master's awarded for partial completion of doctoral program.

Entrance requirements: For master's and doctorate, TOEFL, minimum GPA of 3.0. *Application fee:* $40 ($60 for international students).

Expenses: Tuition, state resident: part-time $320 per semester hour. Tuition, nonresident: part-time $1,135 per semester hour. Required fees: $143 per semester hour. Tuition and fees vary according to course load, degree level and program.

Financial support: Fellowships, research assistantships, teaching assistantships, career-related internships or fieldwork, Federal Work-Study, institutionally sponsored loans, and traineeships available. Support available to part-time students. Financial award applicants required to submit FAFSA.

Faculty research: Biomaterials, wastewater treatment, computer-aided graphics design, semiconductors, polymers.

Gerald B. Stringfellow, Dean, 801-581-6911, *Fax:* 801-581-8692, *E-mail:* stringfellow@coe.utah.edu.

Application contact: Carolee Stout, Advisor, 801-581-6911, *Fax:* 801-581-8692, *E-mail:* cstout@coe.utah.edu. *Web site:* http://www.coe.utah.edu/

■ UNIVERSITY OF VERMONT

Graduate College, College of Engineering and Mathematics, Burlington, VT 05405

AWARDS MAT, MS, MST, PhD. Part-time programs available.

Degree requirements: For doctorate, thesis/dissertation.

Entrance requirements: For master's and doctorate, TOEFL.

Expenses: Tuition, state resident: part-time $335 per credit. Tuition, nonresident: part-time $838 per credit.

Find an in-depth description at www.petersons.com/gradchannel.

■ UNIVERSITY OF VIRGINIA

School of Engineering and Applied Science, Charlottesville, VA 22903

AWARDS MAM, MCS, ME, MEP, MMSE, MS, PhD, ME/MBA. Part-time programs available. Postbaccalaureate distance learning degree programs offered (no on-campus study).

Faculty: 165 full-time (23 women), 17 part-time/adjunct (3 women).

Students: 560 full-time (129 women), 36 part-time (6 women); includes 41 minority (9 African Americans, 27 Asian Americans or Pacific Islanders, 5 Hispanic Americans), 274 international. Average age 27. 1,569 applicants, 24% accepted, 173 enrolled. In 2001, 127 master's, 39 doctorates awarded. Terminal master's awarded for partial completion of doctoral program.

Degree requirements: For doctorate, thesis/dissertation, comprehensive exam.

Entrance requirements: For master's and doctorate, GRE General Test. *Application deadline:* For fall admission, 8/1; for spring admission, 12/1. Applications are processed on a rolling basis. *Application fee:* $40. Electronic applications accepted.

Expenses: Contact institution.

Financial support: Fellowships with full tuition reimbursements, research assistantships with full tuition reimbursements, teaching assistantships with full tuition reimbursements, career-related internships or fieldwork available. Financial award application deadline: 2/1; financial award applicants required to submit FAFSA.

Richard W. Miksad, Dean, 434-924-3593. **Application contact:** Bill Thurneck, 424-924-3155. *Web site:* http://www.seas.virginia.edu/

■ UNIVERSITY OF WASHINGTON

Graduate School, College of Engineering, Seattle, WA 98195

AWARDS EMCIS, MAE, MME, MS, MS Ch E, MSAA, MSCE, MSE, MSEE, MSIE, MSME, PhD, MBA/MSE. Part-time and evening/weekend programs available. Postbaccalaureate distance learning degree programs offered (minimal on-campus study).

Faculty: 179 full-time (25 women), 11 part-time/adjunct (1 woman).

Students: 967 full-time (254 women), 343 part-time (90 women); includes 163 minority (16 African Americans, 115 Asian Americans or Pacific Islanders, 24 Hispanic Americans, 8 Native Americans), 478 international. Average age 29. 2,066 applicants, 36% accepted, 311 enrolled. In 2001, 327 master's, 81 doctorates awarded. Terminal master's awarded for partial completion of doctoral program.

Degree requirements: For master's, thesis (for some programs), comprehensive exam; for doctorate, thesis/dissertation, comprehensive exam. *Median time to degree:* Master's–4 years full-time; doctorate–4 years full-time.

Entrance requirements: For master's, GRE, TOEFL, letters of recommendation; for doctorate, GRE, TOEFL, departmental qualifying exam. *Application deadline:* For fall admission, 7/1; for winter admission, 11/1; for spring admission, 2/1. *Application fee:* $50. Electronic applications accepted.

Expenses: Tuition, state resident: full-time $5,539. Tuition, nonresident: full-time $14,376. Required fees: $390. Tuition and fees vary according to course load and program.

Financial support: In 2001–02, 105 fellowships with full tuition reimbursements (averaging $14,389 per year), 518 research assistantships with full tuition reimbursements (averaging $13,759 per year), 218 teaching assistantships with full tuition reimbursements (averaging $13,281 per year) were awarded. Career-related internships or fieldwork, Federal Work-Study, institutionally sponsored loans, scholarships/grants, traineeships, health care benefits, tuition waivers (full), unspecified assistantships, and stipend supplements also available. Support available to part-time students. Financial award application deadline: 2/28; financial award applicants required to submit FAFSA.

Faculty research: Advanced materials and manufacturing, biotechnology, computer systems and software, microelectronics, earthquake engineering. *Total annual research expenditures:* $61 million.
Dr. Denice D. Denton, Dean, 206-543-0340, *Fax:* 206-685-0666, *E-mail:* denton@engr.washington.edu.
Application contact: Frank Ashby, Director, Student and Community Relations, 206-543-1770, *Fax:* 206-616-8554, *E-mail:* engradv@engr.washington.edu. *Web site:* http://www.engr.washington.edu/

■ UNIVERSITY OF WISCONSIN–MADISON

Graduate School, College of Engineering, Madison, WI 53706-1380

AWARDS ME, MS, PhD, PDD. Part-time programs available. Postbaccalaureate distance learning degree programs offered (minimal on-campus study).

Faculty: 176 full-time (14 women), 16 part-time/adjunct (3 women).
Students: 1,024 full-time (188 women), 127 part-time (15 women); includes 74 minority (16 African Americans, 29 Asian Americans or Pacific Islanders, 17 Hispanic Americans, 12 Native Americans), 526 international. 2,145 applicants, 33% accepted. In 2001, 232 master's, 107 doctorates awarded.
Degree requirements: For doctorate, thesis/dissertation.
Application deadline: Applications are processed on a rolling basis. *Application fee:* $45. Electronic applications accepted.
Expenses: Tuition, state resident: full-time $7,361; part-time $399 per credit. Tuition, nonresident: full-time $20,499; part-time $1,282 per credit. Required fees: $34 per credit. Full-time tuition and fees vary according to course load, program, reciprocity agreements and student level.
Financial support: Fellowships with full and partial tuition reimbursements, research assistantships with full tuition reimbursements, teaching assistantships with full tuition reimbursements, career-related internships or fieldwork, Federal Work-Study, institutionally sponsored loans, scholarships/grants, and unspecified assistantships available. Support available to part-time students. *Total annual research expenditures:* $90.2 million.
Paul S. Peercy, Dean, 608-262-3482, *Fax:* 608-262-6400, *E-mail:* peercy@engr.wisc.edu.
Application contact: Graduate Admissions, 608-262-2433, *Fax:* 608-262-5134, *E-mail:* gradadmiss@mail.bascom.wisc.edu. *Web site:* http://www.engr.wisc.edu/
Find an in-depth description at www.petersons.com/gradchannel.

■ UNIVERSITY OF WISCONSIN–MADISON

Graduate School, Department of Engineering Professional Development, Madison, WI 53706-1380

AWARDS Engineering (PDD); professional practice (ME); technical Japanese (ME). Part-time programs available. Postbaccalaureate distance learning degree programs offered.

Entrance requirements: For master's, TOEFL, 4 years of engineering experience, minimum GPA of 3.0.
Expenses: Contact institution.

■ UNIVERSITY OF WISCONSIN–MILWAUKEE

Graduate School, College of Engineering and Applied Science, Milwaukee, WI 53201-0413

AWARDS MS, PhD, MUP/MS. Part-time programs available.

Faculty: 59 full-time (3 women).
Students: 83 full-time (15 women), 160 part-time (33 women); includes 27 minority (8 African Americans, 17 Asian Americans or Pacific Islanders, 1 Hispanic American, 1 Native American), 124 international. 320 applicants, 52% accepted. In 2001, 43 master's, 11 doctorates awarded.
Degree requirements: For master's, thesis or alternative; for doctorate, thesis/dissertation, internship.
Entrance requirements: For master's, minimum GPA of 2.75; for doctorate, minimum GPA of 3.5. *Application deadline:* For fall admission, 1/1 (priority date); for spring admission, 9/1. Applications are processed on a rolling basis. *Application fee:* $45 ($75 for international students).
Expenses: Tuition, state resident: full-time $6,180; part-time $535 per credit. Tuition, nonresident: full-time $19,482; part-time $1,366 per credit. Tuition and fees vary according to course load, program and reciprocity agreements.
Financial support: In 2001–02, 8 fellowships, 22 research assistantships, 54 teaching assistantships were awarded. Career-related internships or fieldwork, Federal Work-Study, and unspecified assistantships also available. Support available to part-time students. Financial award application deadline: 4/15.
Dr. William Gregory, Dean, 414-229-4126, *E-mail:* wgregory@uwm.edu. *Web site:* http://www.uwm.edu/CEAS/

■ UNIVERSITY OF WISCONSIN–PLATTEVILLE

School of Graduate Studies, Distance Learning Center, Online Program in Engineering, Platteville, WI 53818-3099

AWARDS ME. Postbaccalaureate distance learning degree programs offered (no on-campus study).

Degree requirements: For master's, thesis or alternative.
Electronic applications accepted.
Expenses: Tuition, state resident: full-time $4,564; part-time $224 per credit. Tuition, nonresident: full-time $14,388; part-time $769 per credit. Part-time tuition and fees vary according to course load.

■ UNIVERSITY OF WYOMING

Graduate School, College of Engineering, Laramie, WY 82071

AWARDS MS, Pro MS, PhD. Part-time programs available.

Faculty: 60 full-time (2 women), 5 part-time/adjunct (1 woman).
Students: 122 full-time (26 women), 44 part-time (9 women); includes 2 minority (both Hispanic Americans), 80 international. Average age 27. 180 applicants, 49% accepted. In 2001, 61 master's, 2 doctorates awarded.
Entrance requirements: For master's and doctorate, GRE General Test, TOEFL, minimum GPA of 3.0. *Application deadline:* Applications are processed on a rolling basis. *Application fee:* $40. Electronic applications accepted.
Expenses: Tuition, state resident: full-time $2,895; part-time $161 per credit hour. Tuition, nonresident: full-time $8,367; part-time $465 per credit hour. Required fees: $491; $10 per credit hour. $2 per credit hour. Tuition and fees vary according to course load and program.
Financial support: Fellowships, research assistantships, teaching assistantships, career-related internships or fieldwork, Federal Work-Study, and institutionally sponsored loans available. Support available to part-time students. *Total annual research expenditures:* $5.8 million.
Dr. Ovid A. Plumb, Dean, 307-766-4257, *Fax:* 307-766-4444, *E-mail:* gplumb@uwyo.edu. *Web site:* http://www.uwyo.edu/

■ UTAH STATE UNIVERSITY

School of Graduate Studies, College of Engineering, Logan, UT 84322

AWARDS ME, MS, PhD, CE, EE. Part-time and evening/weekend programs available.

Students: 174 full-time (25 women), 103 part-time (12 women); includes 7 minority (1 African American, 2 Asian Americans or Pacific Islanders, 2 Hispanic Americans, 2 Native Americans), 162 international. Average age 28. 662 applicants, 44% accepted. In 2001, 77 master's, 7 doctorates awarded. Terminal master's awarded for partial completion of doctoral program.
Degree requirements: For doctorate, thesis/dissertation.
Entrance requirements: For master's and doctorate, GRE General Test, TOEFL, minimum GPA of 3.0. *Application deadline:* For fall admission, 6/15; for spring admission, 10/15. Applications are processed on a rolling basis. *Application fee:* $40.

Utah State University (continued)
Expenses: Tuition, state resident: full-time $1,693. Tuition, nonresident: full-time $4,233. Required fees: $501. Tuition and fees vary according to program.
Financial support: Fellowships with partial tuition reimbursements, research assistantships with partial tuition reimbursements, teaching assistantships with partial tuition reimbursements, career-related internships or fieldwork, Federal Work-Study, institutionally sponsored loans, and tuition waivers (partial) available. Support available to part-time students.
A. Bruce Bishop, Dean, 435-797-2775.

Find an in-depth description at www.petersons.com/gradchannel.

■ **VANDERBILT UNIVERSITY**

School of Engineering, Nashville, TN 37240-1001

AWARDS M Eng, MS, PhD, MD/PhD. MS and PhD offered through the Graduate School. Part-time programs available.

Faculty: 135 full-time (10 women), 12 part-time/adjunct (2 women).
Students: 340 full-time (88 women), 25 part-time (4 women); includes 55 minority (20 African Americans, 31 Asian Americans or Pacific Islanders, 4 Hispanic Americans), 157 international. Average age 26. 642 applicants, 31% accepted, 114 enrolled. In 2001, 76 master's, 25 doctorates awarded. Terminal master's awarded for partial completion of doctoral program.
Degree requirements: For master's, thesis (for some programs), comprehensive exam (for some programs), registration (for some programs); for doctorate, thesis/dissertation, comprehensive exam (for some programs), registration (for some programs).
Entrance requirements: For master's and doctorate, GRE General Test. *Application deadline:* For fall admission, 1/15; for spring admission, 11/1. *Application fee:* $40. Electronic applications accepted.
Expenses: Tuition: Full-time $28,350.
Financial support: In 2001–02, 202 students received support, including 42 fellowships with full and partial tuition reimbursements available (averaging $10,299 per year), 161 research assistantships with full and partial tuition reimbursements available (averaging $17,268 per year), 114 teaching assistantships with full tuition reimbursements available (averaging $14,068 per year); career-related internships or fieldwork, Federal Work-Study, institutionally sponsored loans, scholarships/grants, traineeships, and tuition waivers (full and partial) also available. Support available to part-time students. Financial award application deadline: 1/15; financial award applicants required to submit CSS PROFILE or FAFSA.

Faculty research: Robotics, microelectronics, laser diagnostics, reliability in design, environmental remediation. *Total annual research expenditures:* $18 million.
Dr. Kenneth F. Galloway, Dean, 615-322-0720, *Fax:* 615-343-8006, *E-mail:* kenneth.f.galloway@vanderbilt.edu.
Application contact: Dr. Arthur K. Overholser, Associate Dean, 615-343-3773, *Fax:* 615-343-8006, *E-mail:* knowles.a.overholser@vanderbilt.edu. *Web site:* http://www.vuse.vanderbilt.edu/

Find an in-depth description at www.petersons.com/gradchannel.

■ **VILLANOVA UNIVERSITY**

College of Engineering, Villanova, PA 19085-1699

AWARDS M Ch E, MCE, MME, MSCE, MSEE, MSTE, MSWREE, Certificate. Part-time and evening/weekend programs available.

Faculty: 51 full-time (4 women), 17 part-time/adjunct (0 women).
Students: 80 full-time (19 women), 158 part-time (29 women); includes 24 minority (4 African Americans, 16 Asian Americans or Pacific Islanders, 4 Hispanic Americans), 51 international. Average age 26. 201 applicants, 60% accepted, 56 enrolled. In 2001, 65 degrees awarded.
Degree requirements: For master's, thesis optional. *Median time to degree:* Master's–2 years full-time, 4 years part-time.
Entrance requirements: For master's, GRE General Test (applicants with degrees from foreign universities), minimum GPA of 3.0. *Application deadline:* For fall admission, 8/1 (priority date); for spring admission, 12/1. Applications are processed on a rolling basis. *Application fee:* $40. Electronic applications accepted.
Expenses: Contact institution.
Financial support: In 2001–02, 58 students received support, including 10 research assistantships with full tuition reimbursements available (averaging $10,265 per year), 31 teaching assistantships with full tuition reimbursements available (averaging $10,265 per year); Federal Work-Study, scholarships/grants, and tuition waivers (full and partial) also available. Support available to part-time students.
Faculty research: Composite materials, economy and risk, heat transfer, signal detection.
Barry C. Johnson, Dean, 610-519-4940, *Fax:* 610-519-4941, *E-mail:* barry.johnson@villanova.edu. *Web site:* http://www.engineering.villanova.edu

Find an in-depth description at www.petersons.com/gradchannel.

■ **VIRGINIA COMMONWEALTH UNIVERSITY**

School of Graduate Studies, School of Engineering, Richmond, VA 23284-9005

AWARDS MS, PhD, MD/PhD.

Students: 17 full-time, 5 part-time; includes 7 minority (1 African American, 6 Asian Americans or Pacific Islanders). 45 applicants, 67% accepted. In 2001, 1 degree awarded.
Degree requirements: For doctorate, thesis/dissertation, comprehensive oral and written exams.
Entrance requirements: For master's and doctorate, GRE General Test. *Application deadline:* For fall admission, 2/15; for spring admission, 11/15. *Application fee:* $30.
Expenses: Tuition, state resident: full-time $4,276; part-time $238 per credit. Tuition, nonresident: full-time $12,672; part-time $704 per credit. Required fees: $1,167; $43 per credit.
Faculty research: Artificial hearts, orthopedic implants, medical imaging, medical instrumentation and sensors, cardiac monitoring.
Dr. Robert J. Mattauch, Dean, 804-828-0190, *Fax:* 804-828-9866, *E-mail:* rjmatta@vcu.edu.
Application contact: Dr. Gerald E. Miller, Associate Dean for Graduate Affairs, 804-828-7263, *Fax:* 804-828-4454, *E-mail:* gemiller@vcu.edu. *Web site:* http://www.vcu.edu/egrweb/

Find an in-depth description at www.petersons.com/gradchannel.

■ **VIRGINIA POLYTECHNIC INSTITUTE AND STATE UNIVERSITY**

Graduate School, College of Engineering, Blacksburg, VA 24061

AWARDS M Eng, MEA, MS, PhD. Part-time and evening/weekend programs available.

Faculty: 263 full-time (19 women).
Students: 1,179 full-time (203 women), 452 part-time (85 women); includes 140 minority (44 African Americans, 63 Asian Americans or Pacific Islanders, 32 Hispanic Americans, 1 Native American), 699 international. 3,196 applicants, 36% accepted. In 2001, 389 master's, 103 doctorates awarded. Terminal master's awarded for partial completion of doctoral program.
Entrance requirements: For master's and doctorate, TOEFL. *Application deadline:* For fall admission, 12/1 (priority date). Applications are processed on a rolling basis. *Application fee:* $45. Electronic applications accepted.
Expenses: Tuition, state resident: part-time $241 per hour. Tuition, nonresident: part-time $406 per hour. Tuition and fees vary according to program.

Financial support: In 2001–02, 106 fellowships, 639 research assistantships, 249 teaching assistantships were awarded. Career-related internships or fieldwork, Federal Work-Study, institutionally sponsored loans, tuition waivers (full and partial), and unspecified assistantships also available. Support available to part-time students. Financial award application deadline: 1/15.
Dr. Malcolm J. McPherson, Interim Dean, 540-231-6641. *Web site:* http://www.eng.vt.edu/

Find an in-depth description at www.petersons.com/gradchannel.

■ WASHINGTON STATE UNIVERSITY

Graduate School, College of Engineering and Architecture, Pullman, WA 99164
AWARDS MS, PhD.
Faculty: 107.
Students: 241 full-time (56 women), 31 part-time (10 women); includes 11 minority (1 African American, 7 Asian Americans or Pacific Islanders, 3 Hispanic Americans), 154 international. In 2001, 114 master's, 17 doctorates awarded. Terminal master's awarded for partial completion of doctoral program.
Degree requirements: For master's, oral exam; for doctorate, thesis/dissertation, oral exam.
Application deadline: For fall admission, 3/1 (priority date). Applications are processed on a rolling basis. *Application fee:* $35.
Expenses: Tuition, state resident: full-time $6,088; part-time $304 per semester. Tuition, nonresident: full-time $14,918; part-time $746 per semester. Tuition and fees vary according to program.
Financial support: In 2001–02, 80 research assistantships with full and partial tuition reimbursements, 90 teaching assistantships with full and partial tuition reimbursements were awarded. Fellowships, career-related internships or fieldwork, Federal Work-Study, institutionally sponsored loans, tuition waivers (partial), and teaching associateships also available. Financial award applicants required to submit FAFSA. *Total annual research expenditures:* $8.3 million.
Dr. Anjan Bose, Dean, 509-335-5593. *Web site:* http://www.cea.wsu.edu/

■ WASHINGTON UNIVERSITY IN ST. LOUIS

Henry Edwin Sever Graduate School of Engineering and Applied Science, St. Louis, MO 63130-4899
AWARDS MCE, MCE, MCM, MEM, MIM, MS, MSCE, MSE, MSEE, MSEE, MTM, D Sc, M Arch/MCM, MD/D Sc. Part-time and evening/weekend programs available.
Faculty: 81 full-time (6 women), 156 part-time/adjunct.

Students: 299 full-time (57 women), 278 part-time (61 women); includes 61 minority (14 African Americans, 44 Asian Americans or Pacific Islanders, 3 Hispanic Americans), 175 international. 1,193 applicants, 31% accepted, 191 enrolled. In 2001, 172 master's, 30 doctorates awarded. Terminal master's awarded for partial completion of doctoral program.
Degree requirements: For master's, thesis (for some programs), comprehensive exam (for some programs); for doctorate, thesis/dissertation, comprehensive exam.
Entrance requirements: For master's and doctorate, GRE, TOEFL. *Application deadline:* For fall admission, 2/1. *Application fee:* $20. Electronic applications accepted.
Expenses: Tuition: Full-time $26,900.
Financial support: In 2001–02, 147 students received support, including 12 fellowships with full tuition reimbursements available, 131 research assistantships with full tuition reimbursements available, 4 teaching assistantships; career-related internships or fieldwork, Federal Work-Study, institutionally sponsored loans, scholarships/grants, health care benefits, and unspecified assistantships also available. Financial award applicants required to submit FAFSA. *Total annual research expenditures:* $30.5 million.
Christopher I. Byrnes, Dean, 314-935-6166.
Application contact: Elaine Halley, Director, Graduate Recruiting, 314-935-4849, *E-mail:* elainehalley@seas.wustl.edu. *Web site:* http://www.seas.wustl.edu/

■ WAYNE STATE UNIVERSITY

Graduate School, College of Engineering, Detroit, MI 48202
AWARDS MS, PhD, Certificate. Part-time programs available.
Faculty: 85 full-time.
Students: 586 full-time (98 women), 969 part-time (166 women); includes 142 minority (46 African Americans, 89 Asian Americans or Pacific Islanders, 7 Hispanic Americans), 1,028 international. 3,185 applicants, 42% accepted, 490 enrolled. In 2001, 516 master's, 32 doctorates, 14 other advanced degrees awarded. Terminal master's awarded for partial completion of doctoral program.
Degree requirements: For master's, thesis optional; for doctorate, thesis/dissertation.
Application deadline: For fall admission, 7/1 (priority date); for spring admission, 3/15. Applications are processed on a rolling basis. *Application fee:* $20 ($30 for international students).
Expenses: Tuition, state resident: full-time $3,764. Tuition and fees vary according to degree level and program.
Financial support: In 2001–02, 7 fellowships, 83 research assistantships, 46 teaching assistantships were awarded. Career-related internships or fieldwork, Federal Work-Study, institutionally sponsored

loans, scholarships/grants, and tuition waivers (full and partial) also available. Support available to part-time students.
Faculty research: Smart sensors and integrated microelectronics, biomedical engineering, civil infrastructures, nanotechnology, manufacturing and automotive engineering.
Dr. Ralph Kummler, Interim Dean, 313-577-3780, *Fax:* 313-577-5300, *E-mail:* rkummler@che.eng.wayne.edu.
Application contact: Steven Salley, Associate Dean, 313-577-3861, *E-mail:* ssalley@wayne.edu.

Find an in-depth description at www.petersons.com/gradchannel.

■ WESTERN MICHIGAN UNIVERSITY

Graduate College, College of Engineering and Applied Sciences, Kalamazoo, MI 49008-5202
AWARDS MS, MSE, PhD. Part-time programs available.
Faculty: 85 full-time (9 women), 1 part-time/adjunct.
Students: 489 full-time (78 women), 123 part-time (20 women); includes 25 minority (8 African Americans, 13 Asian Americans or Pacific Islanders, 4 Hispanic Americans), 468 international. 1,511 applicants, 61% accepted, 223 enrolled. In 2001, 103 master's, 2 doctorates awarded.
Degree requirements: For doctorate, thesis/dissertation, oral exam.
Entrance requirements: For master's, minimum GPA of 3.0; for doctorate, GRE General Test, minimum GPA of 3.0.
Application deadline: For fall admission, 2/15 (priority date). Applications are processed on a rolling basis. *Application fee:* $25.
Expenses: Tuition, state resident: part-time $186 per credit hour. Tuition, nonresident: part-time $442 per credit hour. Required fees: $602. One-time fee: $132 part-time. Tuition and fees vary according to course load.
Financial support: In 2001–02, 4 fellowships (averaging $4,056 per year), 17 research assistantships (averaging $9,839 per year), 64 teaching assistantships (averaging $4,802 per year) were awarded. Career-related internships or fieldwork and Federal Work-Study also available. Financial award application deadline: 2/15; financial award applicants required to submit FAFSA.
Dr. Daniel M. Litynski, Dean, 616-387-4017.
Application contact: Admissions and Orientation, 616-387-2000, *Fax:* 616-387-2355.

Find an in-depth description at www.petersons.com/gradchannel.

■ WESTERN NEW ENGLAND COLLEGE

School of Engineering, Springfield, MA 01119-2654

AWARDS MSEE, MSEM, MSME. Part-time and evening/weekend programs available.

Faculty: 17 full-time (0 women), 2 part-time/adjunct (0 women).
Students: Average age 29. 11 applicants, 27% accepted. In 2001, 12 degrees awarded.
Degree requirements: For master's, thesis optional.
Entrance requirements: For master's, GRE, bachelor's degree in engineering or related field. *Application deadline:* Applications are processed on a rolling basis. *Application fee:* $30.
Expenses: Tuition: Part-time $429 per credit. Required fees: $9 per credit. $20 per semester.
Financial support: Teaching assistantships available. Support available to part-time students. Financial award application deadline: 4/1; financial award applicants required to submit FAFSA.
Faculty research: Fluid mechanics, control systems.
Dr. Carl E. Rathmann, Dean, 413-782-1273 Ext. 1285, *E-mail:* crathman@wnec.edu.
Application contact: Dr. Janet Castleman, Director of Continuing Education, 413-782-1750, *Fax:* 413-782-1779, *E-mail:* jcastlem@wnec.edu.

■ WEST TEXAS A&M UNIVERSITY

College of Agriculture, Nursing, and Natural Sciences, Department of Mathematics, Physical Sciences and Engineering Technology, Program in Engineering Technology, Canyon, TX 79016-0001

AWARDS MS. Part-time programs available.

Faculty: 2 full-time (0 women).
Students: 3 full-time (0 women), 8 part-time (1 woman); includes 1 minority (Hispanic American), 3 international. Average age 34. 6 applicants, 100% accepted, 6 enrolled. In 2001, 4 degrees awarded.
Degree requirements: For master's, thesis optional. *Median time to degree:* Master's–2 years full-time, 4 years part-time.
Entrance requirements: For master's, GRE General Test. *Application deadline:* Applications are processed on a rolling basis. *Application fee:* $25 ($75 for international students). Electronic applications accepted.
Expenses: Tuition, state resident: part-time $120 per hour. Tuition, nonresident: part-time $253 per hour.
Financial support: In 2001–02, research assistantships (averaging $6,500 per year), 1 teaching assistantship (averaging $6,500

per year) were awarded. Federal Work-Study, institutionally sponsored loans, and tuition waivers (partial) also available. Support available to part-time students. Financial award applicants required to submit FAFSA.
Faculty research: Composites, firearms technology, small arms research and development.
Application contact: Dr. Gerald Chen, Graduate Adviser, 806-651-2449, *Fax:* 806-651-2733, *E-mail:* gchen@mail.wtamu.edu.

■ WEST VIRGINIA UNIVERSITY

College of Engineering and Mineral Resources, Morgantown, WV 26506

AWARDS MS, MS Ch E, MS Min E, MSAE, MSCE, MSE, MSEE, MSEM, MSIE, MSME, MSPNGE, MSSE, PhD. Part-time programs available.

Faculty: 112 full-time (9 women), 13 part-time/adjunct (2 women).
Students: 480 full-time (88 women), 172 part-time (50 women); includes 17 minority (3 African Americans, 12 Asian Americans or Pacific Islanders, 2 Hispanic Americans), 367 international. Average age 27. 814 applicants, 66% accepted. In 2001, 213 master's, 21 doctorates awarded. Terminal master's awarded for partial completion of doctoral program.
Degree requirements: For master's, thesis optional; for doctorate, thesis/dissertation, comprehensive exam.
Entrance requirements: For master's and doctorate, TOEFL. *Application fee:* $45.
Expenses: Contact institution.
Financial support: In 2001–02, 242 research assistantships, 84 teaching assistantships were awarded. Fellowships, career-related internships or fieldwork, Federal Work-Study, institutionally sponsored loans, tuition waivers (full and partial), and graduate administrative assistantships also available. Financial award application deadline: 2/1; financial award applicants required to submit FAFSA.
Faculty research: Composite materials, software engineering, information systems, aerodynamics, vehicle propulsion and emission, manufacturing, longwall mining, transportation planning, biomedical engineering. *Total annual research expenditures:* $12.2 million.
Dr. Eugene Cilento, Dean, 304-293-2111 Ext. 2413, *Fax:* 304-293-4139, *E-mail:* eugene.cilento@mail.wvu.edu.
Application contact: Dr. Afzel Noore, Associate Dean, Academic Affairs, 304-293-4821 Ext. 2210, *Fax:* 304-293-2037, *E-mail:* afzel.noore@mail.wvu.edu. *Web site:* http://www.cemr.wvu.edu/
Find an in-depth description at www.petersons.com/gradchannel.

■ WEST VIRGINIA UNIVERSITY INSTITUTE OF TECHNOLOGY

College of Engineering, Montgomery, WV 25136

AWARDS MS. Part-time programs available.

Faculty: 10 full-time (1 woman).
Students: 20 full-time (5 women), 1 part-time, 20 international. Average age 24. 35 applicants, 77% accepted. In 2001, 2 degrees awarded.
Degree requirements: For master's, thesis or alternative, fieldwork.
Entrance requirements: For master's, GRE General Test, TOEFL, minimum GPA of 3.0. *Application deadline:* For fall admission, 3/15 (priority date). Applications are processed on a rolling basis. *Application fee:* $10.
Expenses: Tuition, state resident: full-time $3,248; part-time $180 per credit. Tuition, nonresident: full-time $7,852; part-time $436 per credit.
Financial support: In 2001–02, 21 teaching assistantships with full tuition reimbursements (averaging $4,000 per year) were awarded; career-related internships or fieldwork, Federal Work-Study, and institutionally sponsored loans also available. Financial award application deadline: 3/15.
Dr. M. Sathyamoorthy, Dean, 304-442-3161, *Fax:* 304-442-1006.
Application contact: Robert P. Scholl, Registrar, 304-442-3167, *Fax:* 304-442-3097, *E-mail:* rscholl@wvutech.edu.

■ WICHITA STATE UNIVERSITY

Graduate School, College of Engineering, Wichita, KS 67260

AWARDS MEM, MS, PhD. Part-time and evening/weekend programs available.

Faculty: 40 full-time (1 woman), 2 part-time/adjunct (0 women).
Students: 347 full-time (26 women), 330 part-time (43 women); includes 70 minority (5 African Americans, 57 Asian Americans or Pacific Islanders, 7 Hispanic Americans, 1 Native American), 461 international. Average age 27. 893 applicants, 59% accepted, 182 enrolled. In 2001, 98 master's, 15 doctorates awarded. Terminal master's awarded for partial completion of doctoral program.
Degree requirements: For doctorate, one foreign language, thesis/dissertation, comprehensive exam.
Entrance requirements: For master's and doctorate, GRE, TOEFL. *Application deadline:* For fall admission, 7/1 (priority date); for spring admission, 1/1. Applications are processed on a rolling basis. *Application fee:* $25 ($40 for international students). Electronic applications accepted.
Expenses: Tuition, state resident: full-time $1,888; part-time $105 per credit. Tuition, nonresident: full-time $6,129; part-time $341 per credit. Required fees: $345; $19

per credit. $17 per semester. Tuition and fees vary according to course load and program.

Financial support: In 2001–02, 110 research assistantships (averaging $4,832 per year), 34 teaching assistantships with full tuition reimbursements (averaging $4,298 per year) were awarded. Fellowships, career-related internships or fieldwork, Federal Work-Study, institutionally sponsored loans, scholarships/grants, traineeships, and unspecified assistantships also available. Support available to part-time students. Financial award application deadline: 4/1; financial award applicants required to submit FAFSA.

Faculty research: Composite dynamics, controls, propulsion, optics, electronics manufacturing. *Total annual research expenditures:* $6.5 million.

Dr. Dennis Siginer, Dean, 316-978-3400, *Fax:* 316-978-3853, *E-mail:* dennis.siginer@wichita.edu. *Web site:* http://www.wichita.edu/

■ WIDENER UNIVERSITY

School of Engineering, Chester, PA 19013-5792

AWARDS ME, ME/MBA. Part-time and evening/weekend programs available.

Degree requirements: For master's, thesis optional.

Expenses: Contact institution.

Find an in-depth description at www.petersons.com/gradchannel.

■ WRIGHT STATE UNIVERSITY

School of Graduate Studies, College of Engineering and Computer Science, Dayton, OH 45435

AWARDS MS, MSCE, MSE, PhD. Part-time and evening/weekend programs available.

Degree requirements: For master's, thesis optional; for doctorate, thesis/dissertation, candidacy and general exams.

Entrance requirements: For master's, TOEFL; for doctorate, GRE General Test, TOEFL, minimum GPA of 3.3.

Expenses: Tuition, state resident: full-time $7,161; part-time $225 per quarter hour. Tuition, nonresident: full-time $12,324; part-time $385 per quarter hour. Tuition and fees vary according to course load, degree level and program.

Faculty research: Robotics, heat transfer, fluid dynamics, microprocessors, mechanical vibrations. *Web site:* http://www.cs.wright.edu/

Find an in-depth description at www.petersons.com/gradchannel.

■ YALE UNIVERSITY

Graduate School of Arts and Sciences, Programs in Engineering and Applied Science, New Haven, CT 06520

AWARDS Applied physics (MS, PhD); chemical engineering (MS, PhD); electrical engineering (MS, PhD); mechanical engineering (M Phil, MS, PhD), including applied mechanics and mechanical engineering. Part-time programs available. Terminal master's awarded for partial completion of doctoral program.

Degree requirements: For doctorate, thesis/dissertation, exam.

Entrance requirements: For master's and doctorate, GRE General Test, TOEFL.

Find an in-depth description at www.petersons.com/gradchannel.

■ YOUNGSTOWN STATE UNIVERSITY

Graduate School, William Rayen College of Engineering, Youngstown, OH 44555-0001

AWARDS MSE. Part-time and evening/weekend programs available.

Degree requirements: For master's, thesis optional.

Entrance requirements: For master's, TOEFL, minimum GPA of 2.75 in field.

Faculty research: Structural mechanics, water quality, wetlands engineering, control systems, power systems, heat transfer, kinematics and dynamics.

APPLIED SCIENCE AND TECHNOLOGY

■ CAPELLA UNIVERSITY

Graduate School, School of Technology, Minneapolis, MN 55402

AWARDS Information technology (MS). Part-time and evening/weekend programs available. Postbaccalaureate distance learning degree programs offered (no on-campus study).

Faculty: 10 full-time, 50 part-time/adjunct.

Students: Average age 35. 373 applicants, 64% accepted, 194 enrolled. In 2001, 1 degree awarded. Terminal master's awarded for partial completion of doctoral program.

Degree requirements: For master's, project, thesis optional. *Median time to degree:* Master's–1.5 years full-time, 3 years part-time.

Entrance requirements: For master's, TOEFL, minimum GPA of 2.7. *Application deadline:* Applications are processed on a rolling basis. Electronic applications accepted.

Expenses: Tuition: Part-time $1,210 per course. Tuition and fees vary according to degree level and program.

Financial support: Institutionally sponsored loans and scholarships/grants available. Support available to part-time students. Financial award applicants required to submit FAFSA.

Dr. Kurt Linberg, Dean, 888-CAPELLA, *E-mail:* klinberg@capella.edu.

Application contact: Liz Krummen, Associate Dean of Enrollment Services, 888-CAPELLA, *E-mail:* info@capella.edu.

■ THE COLLEGE OF WILLIAM AND MARY

Faculty of Arts and Sciences, Department of Applied Science, Williamsburg, VA 23187-8795

AWARDS MS, PhD. Part-time programs available. Postbaccalaureate distance learning degree programs offered.

Faculty: 6 full-time (0 women), 2 part-time/adjunct (1 woman).

Students: 32 full-time (6 women), 7 part-time (2 women); includes 5 minority (2 African Americans, 2 Asian Americans or Pacific Islanders, 1 Hispanic American), 14 international. Average age 31. 56 applicants, 30% accepted. In 2001, 3 master's, 4 doctorates awarded. Terminal master's awarded for partial completion of doctoral program.

Degree requirements: For master's, thesis optional; for doctorate, thesis/dissertation.

Entrance requirements: For master's and doctorate, GRE General Test, GRE Subject Test, TOEFL, minimum GPA of 3.0. *Application deadline:* For fall admission, 2/1 (priority date); for spring admission, 10/1 (priority date). *Application fee:* $30.

Expenses: Tuition, state resident: full-time $3,262; part-time $175 per credit hour. Tuition, nonresident: full-time $14,768; part-time $550 per credit hour. Required fees: $2,478.

Financial support: In 2001–02, 25 students received support, including 23 research assistantships with full tuition reimbursements available (averaging $16,500 per year); career-related internships or fieldwork, Federal Work-Study, and scholarships/grants also available. Financial award application deadline: 4/1; financial award applicants required to submit FAFSA.

Faculty research: Interface/surface science, nondestructive evaluation, applied mathematics and modeling, polymer and composite materials, patent practice. *Total annual research expenditures:* $2.2 million.

Dr. Roy Champion, Chair, 757-221-3510.

Application contact: Marcy Rosa Bourges, Office Assistant, 757-221-2563, *Fax:* 757-221-2050, *E-mail:* marcy@as.wm.edu.

■ HARVARD UNIVERSITY

Extension School, Cambridge, MA 02138-3722

AWARDS Applied sciences (CAS); English for graduate and professional studies (DGP); environmental management (CEM); information technology (ALM); liberal arts (ALM); museum studies (CMS); premedical studies

Harvard University (continued)
(Diploma); public health (CPH); publication and communication (CPC). Special studies in administration and management (CSS); technologies of education (CTE). Part-time and evening/weekend programs available.
Faculty: 450 part-time/adjunct.
Students: Average age 33. In 2001, 79 master's, 303 Diplomas awarded.
Degree requirements: For master's, thesis.
Entrance requirements: For master's and other advanced degree, TOEFL, TWE. *Application deadline:* Applications are processed on a rolling basis. *Application fee:* $75.
Expenses: Contact institution.
Financial support: In 2001–02, 213 students received support. Scholarships/grants available. Support available to part-time students. Financial award application deadline: 8/11; financial award applicants required to submit FAFSA.
Michael Shinagel, Dean.
Application contact: Program Director, 617-495-4024, *Fax:* 617-495-9176. *Web site:* http://www.extension.harvard.edu/

■ JAMES MADISON UNIVERSITY

College of Graduate and Professional Programs, College of Integrated Science and Technology, Department of Integrated Science and Technology, Harrisonburg, VA 22807

AWARDS MS.
Faculty: 4 full-time (3 women).
Students: 5 full-time (0 women), 3 part-time (1 woman), 2 international. Average age 29.
Degree requirements: For master's, thesis or alternative.
Entrance requirements: For master's, GRE General Test. *Application deadline:* For fall admission, 7/1 (priority date). Applications are processed on a rolling basis. *Application fee:* $55.
Expenses: Tuition, state resident: part-time $143 per credit hour. Tuition, nonresident: part-time $465 per credit hour.
Financial support: In 2001–02, 2 teaching assistantships with full tuition reimbursements (averaging $7,170 per year) were awarded; Federal Work-Study and unspecified assistantships also available. Financial award application deadline: 3/1; financial award applicants required to submit FAFSA.
Dr. Ronald G. Kander, Head, 540-568-2740.

■ OKLAHOMA STATE UNIVERSITY

Graduate College, Program in Natural and Applied Science, Stillwater, OK 74078

AWARDS MS.

Students: 26 full-time (18 women), 66 part-time (39 women); includes 11 minority (4 African Americans, 1 Asian American or Pacific Islander, 3 Hispanic Americans, 3 Native Americans), 3 international. Average age 35. 42 applicants, 81% accepted. In 2001, 45 degrees awarded.
Entrance requirements: For master's, TOEFL. *Application fee:* $25.
Expenses: Tuition, state resident: part-time $92 per credit hour. Tuition, nonresident: part-time $297 per credit hour. Required fees: $21 per credit hour. $14 per semester. One-time fee: $20. Tuition and fees vary according to course load.
Financial support: In 2001–02, 6 research assistantships (averaging $8,215 per year), 6 teaching assistantships (averaging $9,135 per year) were awarded.
Dr. Al Carlozzi, Associate Dean, 405-744-6368, *Fax:* 405-744-0355, *E-mail:* grad_i@okstate.edu.

■ RENSSELAER POLYTECHNIC INSTITUTE

Graduate School, School of Science, Masters Program in Applied Science, Troy, NY 12180-3590

AWARDS MS.
Students: 1 full-time (0 women), 1 (woman) part-time, 1 international. 7 applicants, 57% accepted. In 2001, 1 degree awarded.
Entrance requirements: For master's, GRE General Test, TOEFL. *Application deadline:* For fall admission, 1/15 (priority date). Applications are processed on a rolling basis. *Application fee:* $45. Electronic applications accepted.
Expenses: Tuition: Full-time $26,400; part-time $1,320 per credit hour. Required fees: $1,437.
Financial support: Application deadline: 2/1.
Faculty research: Bioinformatics.
Dr. Samuel C. Wait, Associate Dean, 518-276-6305, *E-mail:* waitsc@rpi.edu.

■ SOUTHERN METHODIST UNIVERSITY

School of Engineering, Department of Engineering Management, Information and Systems, Dallas, TX 75275

AWARDS Applied science (MS); engineering management (MSEM, DE); operations research (MS, PhD). Systems engineering (MS). Part-time and evening/weekend programs available. Postbaccalaureate distance learning degree programs offered.
Faculty: 6 full-time (1 woman).
Students: 10 full-time (1 woman), 100 part-time (22 women); includes 29 minority (6 African Americans, 11 Asian Americans or Pacific Islanders, 10 Hispanic Americans, 2 Native Americans), 10 international. 55 applicants, 78%

accepted. In 2001, 25 master's, 5 doctorates awarded. Terminal master's awarded for partial completion of doctoral program.
Degree requirements: For master's, thesis optional; for doctorate, thesis/dissertation, oral and written qualifying exams.
Entrance requirements: For master's, GRE General, TOEFL, minimum GPA of 3.0 in last 2 years; bachelor's degree in engineering, mathematics, or sciences; for doctorate, bachelor's degree in related field. *Application deadline:* For fall admission, 7/1; for spring admission, 11/15. Applications are processed on a rolling basis. *Application fee:* $50.
Expenses: Tuition: Part-time $285 per credit hour.
Faculty research: Telecommunications, decision systems, information engineering, operations research, software.
Richard S. Barr, Chair, 214-768-2605, *E-mail:* emis@engr.smu.edu.
Application contact: Marc Valerin, Associate Director of Graduate Admissions, 214-768-3484, *E-mail:* valerin@seas.smu.edu.

Find an in-depth description at www.petersons.com/gradchannel.

■ SOUTHERN METHODIST UNIVERSITY

School of Engineering, Department of Environmental and Civil Engineering, Dallas, TX 75275

AWARDS Applied science (MS, PhD); civil engineering (MS); environmental engineering (MS); environmental systems management (MS). Part-time and evening/weekend programs available. Postbaccalaureate distance learning degree programs offered.

Students: 2 full-time (1 woman), 26 part-time (9 women); includes 12 minority (6 African Americans, 2 Asian Americans or Pacific Islanders, 4 Hispanic Americans). In 2001, 23 degrees awarded. Terminal master's awarded for partial completion of doctoral program.
Degree requirements: For master's, thesis optional; for doctorate, thesis/dissertation, oral and written qualifying exams.
Entrance requirements: For master's, GRE General Test, TOEFL, minimum GPA of 3.0 in last 2 years; bachelor's degree in engineering, mathematics, or sciences; for doctorate, bachelor's degree in related field. *Application deadline:* For fall admission, 7/1; for spring admission, 11/15. Applications are processed on a rolling basis. *Application fee:* $50.
Expenses: Tuition: Part-time $285 per credit hour.
Dr. Edward Forest, Head, 214-768-2280, *Fax:* 214-768-3845, *E-mail:* eforest@seas.smu.edu.

Application contact: Marc Valerin, Associate Director of Graduate Admissions, 214-768-3484, *E-mail:* valerin@ seas.smu.edu.

Find an in-depth description at www.petersons.com/gradchannel.

■ SOUTHWEST MISSOURI STATE UNIVERSITY

Graduate College, College of Natural and Applied Sciences, Program in Natural and Applied Sciences-Interdisciplinary, Springfield, MO 65804-0094

AWARDS MNAS. Part-time programs available.

Faculty: 1 full-time (0 women).
Students: 11 full-time (8 women), 10 part-time (7 women). In 2001, 10 degrees awarded.
Degree requirements: For master's, thesis or alternative, comprehensive exam.
Entrance requirements: For master's, GRE General Test, minimum undergraduate GPA of 3.0. *Application deadline:* For fall admission, 8/5 (priority date); for spring admission, 12/20 (priority date). Applications are processed on a rolling basis. *Application fee:* $25. Electronic applications accepted.
Expenses: Tuition, state resident: full-time $2,286; part-time $127 per credit. Tuition, nonresident: full-time $4,572; part-time $254 per credit. Required fees: $151 per semester. Tuition and fees vary according to course level and program.
Financial support: In 2001–02, research assistantships with full tuition reimbursements (averaging $6,150 per year), teaching assistantships with full tuition reimbursements (averaging $6,150 per year) were awarded. Federal Work-Study and scholarships/grants also available. Financial award application deadline: 3/31. Dr. William Cheek, Graduate Director, 417-836-5249, *Fax:* 417-836-6934.

■ UNIVERSITY OF ARKANSAS AT LITTLE ROCK

Graduate School, College of Information Science and Systems Engineering, Department of Applied Science, Little Rock, AR 72204-1099

AWARDS Instrumental sciences (MS, PhD). Part-time programs available.

Degree requirements: For master's, oral exams, thesis optional; for doctorate, thesis/dissertation, 2 semesters of residency, candidacy exams.
Entrance requirements: For master's, GRE General Test, TOEFL, interview, minimum GPA of 3.0; for doctorate, GRE General Test, TOEFL, interview, minimum graduate GPA of 3.5.
Expenses: Tuition, state resident: full-time $3,006; part-time $107 per credit. Tuition, nonresident: full-time $6,012; part-time $357 per credit. Required fees: $22 per credit. Tuition and fees vary according to program.
Faculty research: Particle and powder science and technology, optical sensors, process control and automation, signal and image processing, biomedical measurement systems.

■ UNIVERSITY OF CALIFORNIA, BERKELEY

Graduate Division, Group in Applied Science and Technology, Berkeley, CA 94720-1500

AWARDS PhD.

Degree requirements: For doctorate, thesis/dissertation, preliminary exam, qualifying exam.
Entrance requirements: For doctorate, GRE General Test, BA or BS in engineering, physics, mathematics, chemistry, or related field; minimum GPA of 3.0.
Expenses: Tuition, nonresident: full-time $10,704. Required fees: $4,349. *Web site:* http://www.coe.berkeley.edu/~ast-ids/

■ UNIVERSITY OF CALIFORNIA, DAVIS

Graduate Studies, College of Engineering, Program in Applied Science, Davis, CA 95616

AWARDS MS, PhD. Part-time programs available.

Faculty: 21 full-time (4 women), 3 part-time/adjunct (1 woman).
Students: 69 full-time (17 women); includes 10 minority (2 African Americans, 5 Asian Americans or Pacific Islanders, 3 Hispanic Americans), 21 international. Average age 30. 47 applicants, 74% accepted, 19 enrolled. In 2001, 7 master's, 5 doctorates awarded. Terminal master's awarded for partial completion of doctoral program.

Degree requirements: For master's and doctorate, thesis/dissertation.
Entrance requirements: For master's and doctorate, GRE General Test, minimum GPA of 3.3. *Application deadline:* For fall admission, 1/15 (priority date). Applications are processed on a rolling basis. *Application fee:* $60. Electronic applications accepted.
Expenses: Tuition, state resident: full-time $4,831. Tuition, nonresident: full-time $15,725.
Financial support: In 2001–02, 29 students received support, including 24 fellowships with full and partial tuition reimbursements available (averaging $5,908 per year), 11 research assistantships with full and partial tuition reimbursements available (averaging $9,699 per year), 4 teaching assistantships with partial tuition reimbursements available (averaging $13,683 per year); career-related internships or fieldwork, Federal Work-Study, and tuition waivers (full and partial) also available. Financial award application deadline: 1/15; financial award applicants required to submit FAFSA.
Faculty research: Plasma physics, scientific computing, fusion technology, laser physics and nonlinear optics. Richard R. Freeman, Graduate Chair, 925-422-9287, *Fax:* 510-422-8681, *E-mail:* mfreeman@llnl.gov.
Application contact: Dee Kindelt, Graduate Administrative Assistant, 510-754-8858, *Fax:* 510-752-2444, *E-mail:* mkindelt@ ucdavis.edu. *Web site:* http://das.ucdavis.edu

■ UNIVERSITY OF MISSISSIPPI

Graduate School, School of Applied Sciences, Oxford, University, MS 38677

AWARDS MA, MS, PhD.

Faculty: 17.
Students: 45 full-time (32 women), 13 part-time (8 women). In 2001, 23 master's, 7 doctorates awarded.
Entrance requirements: For master's, GRE General Test, TOEFL, minimum GPA of 3.0. *Application deadline:* For fall admission, 8/1. Applications are processed on a rolling basis. *Application fee:* $0 ($25 for international students).
Expenses: Tuition, state resident: full-time $3,626; part-time $202 per hour. Tuition, nonresident: full-time $8,172; part-time $454 per hour.
Financial support: Application deadline: 3/1. Dr. Thomas Crowe, Chairman, 662-915-7652, *Fax:* 662-915-5717, *E-mail:* tcrowe@ olemiss.edu.

Aerospace/Aeronautical Engineering

AEROSPACE/ AERONAUTICAL ENGINEERING

■ AIR FORCE INSTITUTE OF TECHNOLOGY

School of Engineering and Management, Department of Aeronautics and Astronautics, Dayton, OH 45433-7765

AWARDS Aeronautical engineering (MS, PhD); astronautical engineering (MS, PhD); materials science (MS, PhD). Space operations (MS). Systems engineering (MS). Part-time programs available.

Degree requirements: For master's and doctorate, thesis/dissertation.
Entrance requirements: For master's and doctorate, GRE General Test, minimum GPA of 3.0, U.S. citizenship.
Faculty research: Computational fluid dynamics, experimental aerodynamics, computational structural mechanics, experimental structural mechanics, aircraft and spacecraft stability and control. *Web site:* http://en.afit.edu/bny

■ ARIZONA STATE UNIVERSITY

Graduate College, College of Engineering and Applied Sciences, Department of Mechanical and Aerospace Engineering, Tempe, AZ 85287

AWARDS Aerospace engineering (MS, MSE, PhD); engineering science (MS, MSE, PhD); mechanical engineering (MS, MSE, PhD).

Degree requirements: For master's, thesis or alternative; for doctorate, thesis/dissertation.
Entrance requirements: For master's and doctorate, GRE General Test.
Faculty research: Aerodynamics, fluid mechanics, propulsion and space power, advanced structures and materials, robotics and automation.

■ ARIZONA STATE UNIVERSITY EAST

College of Technology and Applied Sciences, Department of Aeronautical Management Technology, Mesa, AZ 85212

AWARDS MS. Part-time and evening/weekend programs available.

Faculty: 6 full-time (1 woman).
Students: 4 full-time (1 woman), 15 part-time (2 women); includes 1 minority (Hispanic American), 6 international. Average age 35. 10 applicants, 70% accepted, 3 enrolled.
Degree requirements: For master's, thesis or applied project and oral defense.
Entrance requirements: For master's, GRE, TOEFL. *Application deadline:* Applications are processed on a rolling basis. *Application fee:* $45. Electronic applications accepted.
Expenses: Tuition, state resident: full-time $2,412; part-time $126 per credit hour. Tuition, nonresident: full-time $10,278; part-time $428 per credit hour. Required fees: $26. Tuition and fees vary according to course load.
Financial support: In 2001–02, 5 students received support, including 5 research assistantships with partial tuition reimbursements available (averaging $4,850 per year); career-related internships or fieldwork, Federal Work-Study, scholarships/grants, tuition waivers (full and partial), and unspecified assistantships also available. Support available to part-time students. Financial award application deadline: 3/1; financial award applicants required to submit FAFSA.
Faculty research: Aviation training and education, human factors, aviation psychology, hypobarics, hyperbarics. *Total annual research expenditures:* $42,715.
Dr. William K. McCurry, Chair, 480-727-1998, *Fax:* 480-727-1730, *E-mail:* mccurry@asu.edu.

■ ARIZONA STATE UNIVERSITY EAST

College of Technology and Applied Sciences, Department of Manufacturing and Aeronautical Engineering Technology, Mesa, AZ 85212

AWARDS MS. Part-time and evening/weekend programs available.

Faculty: 6 full-time (0 women), 1 part-time/adjunct (0 women).
Students: 8 full-time (0 women), 8 part-time (1 woman); includes 1 minority (Hispanic American), 6 international. Average age 29. 16 applicants, 56% accepted, 4 enrolled. In 2001, 5 degrees awarded.
Degree requirements: For master's, thesis or applied project and oral defense. *Median time to degree:* Master's–2.5 years part-time.
Entrance requirements: For master's, GRE Subject Test (science and mathematics), TOEFL. *Application deadline:* Applications are processed on a rolling basis. *Application fee:* $45. Electronic applications accepted.
Expenses: Tuition, state resident: full-time $2,412; part-time $126 per credit hour.

Tuition, nonresident: full-time $10,278; part-time $428 per credit hour. Required fees: $26. Tuition and fees vary according to course load.
Financial support: In 2001–02, 9 students received support, including 5 research assistantships with partial tuition reimbursements available (averaging $3,325 per year); teaching assistantships, career-related internships or fieldwork, Federal Work-Study, scholarships/grants, tuition waivers (full and partial), and unspecified assistantships also available. Support available to part-time students. Financial award application deadline: 3/1; financial award applicants required to submit FAFSA.
Faculty research: Manufacturing modeling and simulation. Semiconductor fabrication process; "smart" materials (composite materials, hydrogen generation, optimization of turbine engines, and machinability and manufacturing processes design). *Total annual research expenditures:* $55,051.
Dr. Scott Danielson, Chair, 480-727-1185, *Fax:* 480-727-1549, *E-mail:* scottda@asu.edu.

■ AUBURN UNIVERSITY

Graduate School, College of Engineering, Department of Aerospace Engineering, Auburn University, AL 36849

AWARDS MAE, MS, PhD. Part-time programs available.

Faculty: 10 full-time (0 women).
Students: 13 full-time (3 women), 12 part-time (4 women), 6 international. 23 applicants, 39% accepted. In 2001, 6 master's, 1 doctorate awarded.
Degree requirements: For master's, thesis (MS), exam; for doctorate, thesis/dissertation, exams.
Entrance requirements: For master's and doctorate, GRE General Test. *Application deadline:* For fall admission, 7/7; for spring admission, 11/24. Applications are processed on a rolling basis. *Application fee:* $25 ($50 for international students). Electronic applications accepted.
Financial support: Fellowships, research assistantships, teaching assistantships, Federal Work-Study available. Support available to part-time students. Financial award application deadline: 3/15.
Faculty research: Aerodynamics, flight dynamics and simulation, propulsion, structures and aeroelasticity, aerospace smart structures.
Dr. John E. Cochran, Head, 334-844-4874.
Application contact: Dr. John F. Pritchett, Dean of the Graduate School, 334-844-4700, *E-mail:* hatchlb@

mail.auburn.edu. *Web site:* http://www.eng.auburn.edu/department/ae/

Find an in-depth description at www.petersons.com/gradchannel.

■ BOSTON UNIVERSITY

College of Engineering, Department of Aerospace and Mechanical Engineering, Boston, MA 02215

AWARDS Aerospace engineering (MS, PhD); mechanical engineering (MS, PhD). Part-time programs available.

Faculty: 24 full-time (1 woman), 6 part-time/adjunct (0 women).
Students: 47 full-time (7 women), 6 part-time (1 woman), 31 international. Average age 27. 223 applicants, 17% accepted, 14 enrolled. In 2001, 9 master's, 4 doctorates awarded. Terminal master's awarded for partial completion of doctoral program.
Degree requirements: For master's, thesis optional; for doctorate, thesis/dissertation, comprehensive exam.
Entrance requirements: For master's and doctorate, GRE General Test, TOEFL. *Application deadline:* For fall admission, 4/1; for spring admission, 10/1. Applications are processed on a rolling basis. *Application fee:* $60. Electronic applications accepted.
Expenses: Tuition: Full-time $25,872; part-time $340 per credit. Required fees: $40 per semester. Part-time tuition and fees vary according to class time, course level and program.
Financial support: In 2001–02, 43 students received support, including 3 fellowships with full tuition reimbursements available (averaging $15,500 per year), 21 research assistantships with full tuition reimbursements available (averaging $13,500 per year), 12 teaching assistantships with full tuition reimbursements available (averaging $13,500 per year); career-related internships or fieldwork, Federal Work-Study, institutionally sponsored loans, and scholarships/grants also available. Financial award application deadline: 1/15; financial award applicants required to submit FAFSA.
Faculty research: Acoustics and vibrations, fluid mechanics, MEMS, nanotechnology, robotics. *Total annual research expenditures:* $2.1 million.
Dr. John Baillieul, Chairman, 617-353-9848, *Fax:* 617-353-5548.
Application contact: Cheryl Kelley, Director of Graduate Programs, 617-353-9760, *Fax:* 617-353-0259, *E-mail:* enggrad@bu.edu. *Web site:* http://www.bu.edu/eng/grad/

Find an in-depth description at www.petersons.com/gradchannel.

■ BROWN UNIVERSITY

Graduate School, Division of Engineering, Program in Aerospace Engineering, Providence, RI 02912
AWARDS Sc M, PhD.

Degree requirements: For doctorate, thesis/dissertation, preliminary exam.

■ CALIFORNIA INSTITUTE OF TECHNOLOGY

Division of Engineering and Applied Science, Option in Aeronautics, Pasadena, CA 91125-0001
AWARDS MS, PhD, Engr.
Faculty: 10 full-time (0 women).
Students: 53 full-time (9 women); includes 2 minority (both Asian Americans or Pacific Islanders), 34 international. 102 applicants, 24% accepted, 14 enrolled. In 2001, 12 master's, 18 doctorates awarded.
Degree requirements: For doctorate, thesis/dissertation.
Application deadline: For fall admission, 1/15. *Application fee:* $0.
Financial support: In 2001–02, 13 fellowships, 19 research assistantships, 11 teaching assistantships were awarded.
Faculty research: Computational fluid dynamics, technical fluid dynamics, structural mechanics, mechanics of fracture, aeronautical engineering and propulsion.
Dr. Hans G. Hornung, Executive Officer, 626-395-4551.
Application contact: Dr. Joseph E. Shepherd, Representative, 626-395-3283, *E-mail:* jeshep@galcit.caltech.edu.

■ CALIFORNIA POLYTECHNIC STATE UNIVERSITY, SAN LUIS OBISPO

College of Engineering, Department of Aerospace Engineering, San Luis Obispo, CA 93407
AWARDS MSAE. Part-time programs available.
Faculty: 6 full-time (0 women), 4 part-time/adjunct (1 woman).
Students: 2 full-time (0 women), 10 part-time. 2 applicants, 50% accepted, 1 enrolled. In 2001, 5 degrees awarded.
Degree requirements: For master's, thesis.
Entrance requirements: For master's, GRE General Test, minimum GPA of 2.5 during last 2 years. *Application deadline:* For fall admission, 5/31 (priority date); for spring admission, 12/31. Applications are processed on a rolling basis. *Application fee:* $55.
Expenses: Tuition, nonresident: part-time $164 per unit. One-time fee: $2,153 part-time.
Financial support: Research assistantships, teaching assistantships, career-related internships or fieldwork available. Financial award application deadline: 3/2; financial award applicants required to submit FAFSA.
Faculty research: Aerodynamics, fluid dynamics, computational fluid dynamics,

aircraft structures, propulsion, flight simulation and control.
Dr. Daniel J. Biezad, Chair, 805-756-5126, *Fax:* 805-756-2376, *E-mail:* dbiezad@calpoly.edu. *Web site:* http://www.calpoly.edu/~aero/

■ CALIFORNIA STATE UNIVERSITY, LONG BEACH

Graduate Studies, College of Engineering, Department of Aerospace Engineering, Long Beach, CA 90840
AWARDS MSAE. Part-time programs available.
Faculty: 7 full-time (1 woman), 6 part-time/adjunct (0 women).
Students: 1 full-time (0 women), 12 part-time; includes 5 minority (1 African American, 3 Asian Americans or Pacific Islanders, 1 Hispanic American), 2 international. Average age 35. 10 applicants, 70% accepted. In 2001, 1 degree awarded.
Degree requirements: For master's, thesis or alternative.
Entrance requirements: For master's, TOEFL. *Application deadline:* For fall admission, 8/1; for spring admission, 12/1. *Application fee:* $55. Electronic applications accepted.
Financial support: Career-related internships or fieldwork, Federal Work-Study, institutionally sponsored loans, scholarships/grants, and unspecified assistantships available. Financial award application deadline: 3/2.
Faculty research: Aerodynamic flows, ice accretion, stability and transition.

■ CALIFORNIA STATE UNIVERSITY, NORTHRIDGE

Graduate Studies, College of Engineering and Computer Science, Department of Civil and Manufacturing Engineering, Northridge, CA 91330
AWARDS Applied mechanics (MSE); civil engineering (MS); engineering and computer science (MS); engineering management (MS); industrial engineering (MS); materials engineering (MS); mechanical engineering (MS), including aerospace engineering, applied engineering, machine design, mechanical engineering, structural engineering, thermofluids; mechanics (MS). Part-time and evening/weekend programs available.
Faculty: 14 full-time, 2 part-time/adjunct.
Students: 25 full-time (4 women), 72 part-time (9 women). Average age 31. 64 applicants, 77% accepted, 22 enrolled. In 2001, 34 degrees awarded.
Degree requirements: For master's, thesis.
Entrance requirements: For master's, GRE General Test, TOEFL, minimum GPA of 2.5. *Application deadline:* For fall admission, 11/30. *Application fee:* $55.

California State University, Northridge (continued)

Expenses: Tuition, nonresident: part-time $631 per semester. Required fees: $246 per unit.
Financial support: Teaching assistantships available. Financial award application deadline: 3/1.
Faculty research: Composite study.
Dr. Stephen Gadomski, Chair, 818-677-2166.
Application contact: Dr. Ileana Costa, Graduate Coordinator, 818-677-3299.

■ CALIFORNIA STATE UNIVERSITY, NORTHRIDGE

Graduate Studies, College of Engineering and Computer Science, Department of Civil and Manufacturing Engineering, Department of Mechanical Engineering, Northridge, CA 91330

AWARDS Aerospace engineering (MS); applied engineering (MS); machine design (MS); mechanical engineering (MS). Structural engineering (MS); thermofluids (MS). Part-time and evening/weekend programs available.

Faculty: 8 full-time, 2 part-time/adjunct.
Students: 6 full-time (0 women), 42 part-time (6 women); includes 19 minority (14 Asian Americans or Pacific Islanders, 4 Hispanic Americans, 1 Native American), 3 international. Average age 34. 24 applicants, 79% accepted, 6 enrolled. In 2001, 4 degrees awarded.
Degree requirements: For master's, thesis or alternative.
Entrance requirements: For master's, GRE General Test, TOEFL, minimum GPA of 2.5. *Application deadline:* For fall admission, 11/30. *Application fee:* $55.
Expenses: Tuition, nonresident: part-time $631 per semester. Required fees: $246 per unit.
Financial support: Application deadline: 3/1.
Dr. Sidney H. Schwartz, Chair, 818-677-2187.
Application contact: Dr. Tom Mincer, Graduate Coordinator, 818-677-2007.

■ CASE WESTERN RESERVE UNIVERSITY

School of Graduate Studies, The Case School of Engineering, Department of Mechanical and Aerospace Engineering, Cleveland, OH 44106

AWARDS Aerospace engineering (MS, PhD); fluid and thermal engineering sciences (MS); fluid and thermal engineering sciences (PhD); mechanical engineering (MS, PhD). Part-time programs available. Postbaccalaureate distance learning degree programs offered (no on-campus study).

Faculty: 16 full-time (1 woman), 9 part-time/adjunct (1 woman).

Students: 34 full-time (4 women), 49 part-time (7 women); includes 7 minority (6 Asian Americans or Pacific Islanders, 1 Hispanic American), 31 international. Average age 24. 290 applicants, 21% accepted, 14 enrolled. In 2001, 19 master's, 9 doctorates awarded.
Degree requirements: For master's, thesis (for some programs); for doctorate, thesis/dissertation, qualifying exam, teaching experience.
Entrance requirements: For master's, TOEFL; for doctorate, GRE, TOEFL. *Application deadline:* For fall admission, 7/1 (priority date). Applications are processed on a rolling basis. *Application fee:* $25.
Expenses: Contact institution.
Financial support: In 2001–02, 27 fellowships with full and partial tuition reimbursements (averaging $16,200 per year), 23 research assistantships with full and partial tuition reimbursements (averaging $16,200 per year) were awarded. Institutionally sponsored loans and tuition waivers (full and partial) also available. Financial award application deadline: 3/1; financial award applicants required to submit FAFSA.
Faculty research: Microgravity studies of combustion and fluid interfaces; molecular dynamics of transport processes; mechanical analysis of materials and biomaterials; machinery diagnostics and control; biorobotics; DPIV and LDV measurements in two-phase flows. *Total annual research expenditures:* $4.7 million.
Dr. Joseph M. Prahl, Chairman, 216-368-2941, *Fax:* 216-368-6445, *E-mail:* jmp@po.cwru.edu.
Application contact: Angelika Szakacs, Secretary, 216-368-5403, *Fax:* 216-368-3007, *E-mail:* mechgac@po.cwru.edu. *Web site:* http://www.scl.cwru.edu/cse/emae/

■ CORNELL UNIVERSITY

Graduate School, Graduate Fields of Engineering, Field of Aerospace Engineering, Ithaca, NY 14853-0001

AWARDS M Eng, MS, PhD.

Faculty: 25 full-time.
Students: 18 full-time (4 women); includes 1 minority (Asian American or Pacific Islander), 11 international. 88 applicants, 17% accepted. In 2001, 4 master's, 1 doctorate awarded. Terminal master's awarded for partial completion of doctoral program.
Degree requirements: For master's, thesis (MS); for doctorate, one foreign language, thesis/dissertation.
Entrance requirements: For master's and doctorate, GRE General Test, TOEFL, 3 letters of recommendation. *Application deadline:* For fall admission, 1/15. *Application fee:* $65. Electronic applications accepted.
Expenses: Tuition: Full-time $25,970. Required fees: $50.

Financial support: In 2001–02, 13 students received support, including 5 fellowships with full tuition reimbursements available, 4 research assistantships with full tuition reimbursements available, 4 teaching assistantships with full tuition reimbursements available; institutionally sponsored loans, scholarships/grants, tuition waivers (full and partial), and unspecified assistantships also available. Financial award applicants required to submit FAFSA.
Faculty research: Aerodynamics, fluid mechanics, turbulence, combustion/propulsion, aeroacoustics.
Application contact: Graduate Field Assistant, 607-255-5250, *E-mail:* maegrad@cornell.edu. *Web site:* http://www.gradschool.cornell.edu/grad/fields_1/aero-engr.html

■ EMBRY-RIDDLE AERONAUTICAL UNIVERSITY

Daytona Beach Campus Graduate Program, Department of Aeronautical Science, Daytona Beach, FL 32114-3900

AWARDS MAS. Part-time and evening/weekend programs available.

Faculty: 8 full-time (2 women).
Students: 19 full-time (3 women), 55 part-time (15 women); includes 9 minority (6 African Americans, 1 Asian American or Pacific Islander, 2 Hispanic Americans), 29 international. Average age 29. 49 applicants, 59% accepted, 13 enrolled. In 2001, 19 degrees awarded.
Degree requirements: For master's, thesis optional.
Entrance requirements: For master's, TOEFL, minimum GPA of 2.5. *Application deadline:* For fall admission, 8/1 (priority date); for spring admission, 12/1 (priority date). Applications are processed on a rolling basis. *Application fee:* $30 ($50 for international students). Electronic applications accepted.
Expenses: Tuition: Full-time $13,140; part-time $730 per credit. Required fees: $250; $250 per year. $125 per semester. Tuition and fees vary according to program.
Financial support: In 2001–02, 28 students received support, including 4 research assistantships with partial tuition reimbursements available (averaging $8,100 per year), 3 teaching assistantships with partial tuition reimbursements available (averaging $8,100 per year); fellowships with partial tuition reimbursements available, career-related internships or fieldwork, Federal Work-Study, and unspecified assistantships also available. Support available to part-time students. Financial award application deadline: 4/15; financial award applicants required to submit FAFSA.

Faculty research: Agate program, situation awareness for general aviation, retention of women in collegiate aviation programs. *Total annual research expenditures:* $794,586.
Dr. Marvin Smith, Program Coordinator, 386-226-6448, *Fax:* 386-226-6012, *E-mail:* smithm@erau.edu.
Application contact: Christine Castetter, Graduate Admissions, 800-388-3728, *Fax:* 386-226-7111, *E-mail:* gradmit@erau.edu.
Find an in-depth description at www.petersons.com/gradchannel.

■ EMBRY-RIDDLE AERONAUTICAL UNIVERSITY

Daytona Beach Campus Graduate Program, Department of Aerospace Engineering, Daytona Beach, FL 32114-3900

AWARDS MSAE. Part-time and evening/weekend programs available.

Faculty: 8 full-time (0 women).
Students: 19 full-time (2 women), 11 part-time (1 woman); includes 1 minority (Asian American or Pacific Islander), 22 international. Average age 25. 48 applicants, 31% accepted, 5 enrolled. In 2001, 10 degrees awarded.
Degree requirements: For master's, thesis optional.
Entrance requirements: For master's, TOEFL, BS in aeronautical engineering or equivalent; minimum GPA of 3.0 in junior and senior years, 2.5 overall. *Application deadline:* For fall admission, 8/1 (priority date); for spring admission, 12/1 (priority date). Applications are processed on a rolling basis. *Application fee:* $30 ($50 for international students). Electronic applications accepted.
Expenses: Tuition: Full-time $13,140; part-time $730 per credit. Required fees: $250; $250 per year. $125 per semester. Tuition and fees vary according to program.
Financial support: In 2001–02, 13 students received support, including 12 teaching assistantships with partial tuition reimbursements available (averaging $8,100 per year); fellowships with partial tuition reimbursements available, research assistantships with partial tuition reimbursements available, career-related internships or fieldwork, Federal Work-Study, and unspecified assistantships also available. Support available to part-time students. Financial award application deadline: 4/15; financial award applicants required to submit FAFSA.
Faculty research: Composite propeller, fatigue on landing gears on small airplanes. *Total annual research expenditures:* $107,279.
Dr. Lakshmanan Narayanaswami, Program Coordinator, 386-226-6736, *Fax:* 386-226-6747, *E-mail:* swamil@erau.edu.

Application contact: Christine Castetter, Graduate Admissions, 800-388-3728, *Fax:* 386-226-7111, *E-mail:* gradmit@erau.edu.
Find an in-depth description at www.petersons.com/gradchannel.

■ EMBRY-RIDDLE AERONAUTICAL UNIVERSITY

Department of Physical Sciences, Program in Space Science, Daytona Beach, FL 32114-3900

AWARDS MS.

Expenses: Tuition: Full-time $13,140; part-time $730 per credit. Required fees: $250; $250 per year. $125 per semester. Tuition and fees vary according to program.

■ EMBRY-RIDDLE AERONAUTICAL UNIVERSITY, EXTENDED CAMPUS

Graduate Resident Centers, Department of Aeronautical Science, Daytona Beach, FL 32114-3900

AWARDS MAS. Part-time and evening/weekend programs available. Postbaccalaureate distance learning degree programs offered (minimal on-campus study).

Faculty: 55 full-time (5 women), 253 part-time/adjunct (16 women).
Students: 38 full-time (4 women), 1,636 part-time (221 women); includes 218 minority (92 African Americans, 39 Asian Americans or Pacific Islanders, 69 Hispanic Americans, 18 Native Americans), 33 international. Average age 36. 417 applicants, 92% accepted, 221 enrolled. In 2001, 687 degrees awarded.
Degree requirements: For master's, thesis optional.
Application deadline: Applications are processed on a rolling basis. *Application fee:* $30 ($50 for international students). Electronic applications accepted.
Expenses: Tuition: Full-time $5,880; part-time $245 per credit.
Financial support: In 2001–02, 38 students received support. Available to part-time students. Applicants required to submit FAFSA.
Dr. Stephen O'Brien, Chair, 386-226-8050, *E-mail:* obriens@erau.edu.
Application contact: Pam Thomas, Director of Admissions and Records, 386-226-6910, *Fax:* 386-226-6984, *E-mail:* ecinfo@erau.edu. *Web site:* http://www.embryriddle.edu/

■ FLORIDA INSTITUTE OF TECHNOLOGY

Graduate Programs, College of Engineering, Mechanical and Aerospace Engineering Department, Melbourne, FL 32901-6975

AWARDS Aerospace engineering (MS, PhD); mechanical engineering (MS, PhD). Part-time programs available.

Faculty: 12 full-time (0 women), 2 part-time/adjunct (0 women).
Students: 14 full-time (3 women), 22 part-time (1 woman); includes 2 minority (both Hispanic Americans), 16 international. Average age 29. 146 applicants, 50% accepted. In 2001, 4 master's, 2 doctorates awarded.
Degree requirements: For master's, thesis optional; for doctorate, thesis/dissertation, comprehensive exam.
Entrance requirements: For master's, GRE General Test, GRE Subject Test, minimum GPA of 3.0; for doctorate, GRE General Test, minimum GPA of 3.2, resumé. *Application deadline:* Applications are processed on a rolling basis. *Application fee:* $50. Electronic applications accepted.
Expenses: Tuition: Part-time $650 per credit.
Financial support: In 2001–02, 15 students received support, including 5 research assistantships with full and partial tuition reimbursements available (averaging $7,182 per year), 10 teaching assistantships with full and partial tuition reimbursements available (averaging $6,734 per year); career-related internships or fieldwork and tuition remissions also available. Financial award application deadline: 3/1; financial award applicants required to submit FAFSA.
Faculty research: Dynamic systems, robotics, and controls. Structures, solid mechanics, and materials; thermal-fluid sciences, optical tomography, composite/recycled materials. *Total annual research expenditures:* $338,000.
Dr. John J. Engblom, Department Head, 321-674-7132, *Fax:* 321-674-8813, *E-mail:* engblom@fit.edu.
Application contact: Carolyn P. Farrior, Director of Graduate Admissions, 321-674-7118, *Fax:* 321-723-9468, *E-mail:* cfarrior@fit.edu. *Web site:* http://www.fit.edu/
Find an in-depth description at www.petersons.com/gradchannel.

■ FLORIDA INSTITUTE OF TECHNOLOGY

Graduate Programs, School of Aeronautics, Melbourne, FL 32901-6975

AWARDS Airport development and management (MSA); applied aviation safety (MSA); aviation human factors (MS). Part-time and evening/weekend programs available.

Florida Institute of Technology (continued)

Faculty: 6 full-time (1 woman).
Students: 9 full-time (5 women), 8 part-time (4 women); includes 3 minority (1 African American, 2 Hispanic Americans), 8 international. Average age 26. 26 applicants, 65% accepted. In 2001, 4 degrees awarded.
Degree requirements: For master's, thesis.
Entrance requirements: For master's, GRE General Test or GRE Subject Test, minimum undergraduate GPA of 3.0. *Application deadline:* For fall admission, 8/1; for spring admission, 12/1. Applications are processed on a rolling basis. *Application fee:* $50. Electronic applications accepted.
Expenses: Tuition: Part-time $650 per credit.
Financial support: In 2001–02, 1 student received support, including 1 teaching assistantship with full and partial tuition reimbursement available (averaging $6,840 per year); research assistantships with full and partial tuition reimbursements available, career-related internships or fieldwork, institutionally sponsored loans, unspecified assistantships, and tuition remissions also available. Financial award application deadline: 3/1.
Faculty research: Aircraft cockpit design; medical human factors; operating room human factors; hypobaric chamber operations and effects; aviation professional education. *Total annual research expenditures:* $157,100.
Dr. Nathaniel Villaire, Chairman of Graduate Studies, 321-674-8120, *Fax:* 321-674-8059, *E-mail:* villaire@fit.edu.
Application contact: Carolyn P. Farrior, Director of Graduate Admissions, 321-674-7118, *Fax:* 321-723-9468, *E-mail:* cfarrior@fit.edu. *Web site:* http://www.fit.edu/soa/

Find an in-depth description at www.petersons.com/gradchannel.

■ **FLORIDA INSTITUTE OF TECHNOLOGY**

Graduate Programs, School of Extended Graduate Studies, Melbourne, FL 32901-6975

AWARDS Acquisition and contract management (MS, MSM, PMBA); aerospace engineering (MS); business administration (PMBA); computer information systems (MS); computer science (MS); ebusiness (MSM); electrical engineering (MS); engineering management (MS); health management (MS); human resource management (MSM, PMBA); human resources management (MS); information systems (MSM, PMBA); logistics management (MS, MSM); management (MS); material acquisition management (MS); mechanical engineering (MS); operations research (MS); project management (MS), including information systems, operations research; public administration (MPA). Software engineering (MS). Space systems

(MS). Space systems management (MS). Systems management (MS), including information systems, operations research; transportation management (MSM). Part-time and evening/weekend programs available. Postbaccalaureate distance learning degree programs offered (no on-campus study).

Faculty: 10 full-time (2 women), 131 part-time/adjunct (15 women).
Students: 57 full-time (29 women), 1,198 part-time (455 women); includes 277 minority (183 African Americans, 38 Asian Americans or Pacific Islanders, 51 Hispanic Americans, 5 Native Americans), 16 international. Average age 37. 299 applicants, 42% accepted. In 2001, 434 degrees awarded.
Entrance requirements: For master's, minimum GPA of 3.0. *Application deadline:* Applications are processed on a rolling basis. *Application fee:* $50. Electronic applications accepted.
Expenses: Tuition: Part-time $650 per credit.
Financial support: Institutionally sponsored loans available. Financial award application deadline: 3/1; financial award applicants required to submit FAFSA.
Dr. Ronald L. Marshall, Dean, School of Extended Graduate Studies, 321-674-8880.
Application contact: Carolyn P. Farrior, Director of Graduate Admissions, 321-674-7118, *Fax:* 321-723-9468, *E-mail:* cfarrior@fit.edu. *Web site:* http://www.segs.fit.edu/

■ **THE GEORGE WASHINGTON UNIVERSITY**

School of Engineering and Applied Science, Department of Mechanical and Aerospace Engineering, Washington, DC 20052

AWARDS MS, D Sc, App Sc, Engr. Part-time and evening/weekend programs available.

Faculty: 12 full-time (1 woman), 13 part-time/adjunct (0 women).
Students: 46 full-time (8 women), 97 part-time (19 women); includes 17 minority (4 African Americans, 4 Asian Americans or Pacific Islanders, 9 Hispanic Americans), 37 international. Average age 29. 89 applicants, 97% accepted. In 2001, 28 master's, 2 doctorates awarded.
Degree requirements: For master's, thesis optional; for doctorate, thesis/dissertation, final and qualifying exams.
Entrance requirements: For master's, TOEFL or George Washington University English as a Foreign Language Test, appropriate bachelor's degree, minimum GPA of 3.0; for doctorate, TOEFL or George Washington University English as a Foreign Language Test, appropriate bachelor's or master's degree, minimum GPA of 3.4, GRE required if highest earned degree is BS; for other advanced degree, TOEFL or George Washington University English as a Foreign Language Test, appropriate master's degree,

minimum GPA of 3.0. *Application deadline:* For fall admission, 3/1 (priority date); for spring admission, 10/1. Applications are processed on a rolling basis. *Application fee:* $55.
Expenses: Tuition: Part-time $810 per credit. Required fees: $1 per credit.
Financial support: In 2001–02, 7 fellowships with tuition reimbursements (averaging $3,900 per year), 8 teaching assistantships with tuition reimbursements (averaging $3,000 per year) were awarded. Research assistantships, career-related internships or fieldwork and institutionally sponsored loans also available. Financial award application deadline: 3/1; financial award applicants required to submit FAFSA.
Dr. Michael K. Myers, Chair, 202-994-6749, *Fax:* 202-994-0238, *E-mail:* mkmyers@seas.gwu.edu.
Application contact: Howard M. Davis, Manager, Office of Admissions and Student Records, 202-994-6158, *Fax:* 202-994-0909, *E-mail:* data:adms@seas.gwu.edu. *Web site:* http://www.gwu.edu/~gradinfo/

Find an in-depth description at www.petersons.com/gradchannel.

■ **GEORGIA INSTITUTE OF TECHNOLOGY**

Graduate Studies and Research, College of Engineering, School of Aerospace Engineering, Atlanta, GA 30332-0001

AWARDS Aerospace engineering (MS, MSAE, PhD); biomedical engineering (MS Bio E). Part-time programs available. Terminal master's awarded for partial completion of doctoral program.

Degree requirements: For master's, thesis optional; for doctorate, thesis/dissertation.
Entrance requirements: For master's, GRE, TOEFL, minimum GPA of 3.0; for doctorate, GRE, TOEFL, minimum GPA of 3.25.
Faculty research: Structural mechanics and dynamics, fluid mechanics, flight mechanics and controls, combustion and propulsion, system design and optimization.

Find an in-depth description at www.petersons.com/gradchannel.

■ **ILLINOIS INSTITUTE OF TECHNOLOGY**

Graduate College, Armour College of Engineering and Sciences, Department of Mechanical, Materials and Aerospace Engineering, Mechanical and Aerospace Engineering Division, Chicago, IL 60616-3793

AWARDS MMAE, MS, PhD. Part-time programs available.

Faculty: 17 full-time (2 women), 8 part-time/adjunct (0 women).
Students: 66 full-time (10 women), 58 part-time (2 women); includes 7 minority (all Asian Americans or Pacific Islanders), 92 international. Average age 28. 539 applicants, 39% accepted. In 2001, 36 master's, 2 doctorates awarded. Terminal master's awarded for partial completion of doctoral program.
Degree requirements: For master's, thesis (for some programs), comprehensive exam; for doctorate, thesis/dissertation, comprehensive exam.
Entrance requirements: For master's and doctorate, GRE General Test, TOEFL, minimum undergraduate GPA of 3.0. *Application deadline:* For fall admission, 7/1; for spring admission, 11/1. Applications are processed on a rolling basis. *Application fee:* $30. Electronic applications accepted.
Expenses: Tuition: Part-time $590 per credit hour.
Financial support: In 2001–02, 13 research assistantships, 10 teaching assistantships were awarded. Federal Work-Study, institutionally sponsored loans, scholarships/grants, and unspecified assistantships also available. Financial award application deadline: 3/1; financial award applicants required to submit FAFSA.
Faculty research: Solid and structural mechanics, fluid dynamics, thermal sciences, transportation engineering, design and manufacturing.
Dr. Candace Wark, Associate Chair, Mechanical Engineering, 312-567-3209, *Fax:* 312-567-7230, *E-mail:* wark@iit.edu.
Application contact: Dr. Ali Cinar, Dean of Graduate College, 312-567-3637, *Fax:* 312-567-7517, *E-mail:* gradstu@iit.edu. *Web site:* http://www.mmae.iit.edu/

■ IOWA STATE UNIVERSITY OF SCIENCE AND TECHNOLOGY

Graduate College, College of Engineering, Department of Aerospace Engineering and Engineering Mechanics, Ames, IA 50011

AWARDS Aerospace engineering (M Eng, MS, PhD); engineering mechanics (M Eng, MS, PhD).

Faculty: 34 full-time.
Students: 47 full-time (11 women), 7 part-time; includes 3 minority (2 African Americans, 1 Asian American or Pacific Islander), 40 international. 83 applicants, 34% accepted, 17 enrolled. In 2001, 7 master's, 2 doctorates awarded.
Degree requirements: For master's, thesis (for some programs); for doctorate, thesis/dissertation. *Median time to degree:* Master's–2.2 years full-time; doctorate–4.2 years full-time.
Entrance requirements: For master's and doctorate, GRE General Test, TOEFL or IELTS. *Application deadline:* For fall admission, 3/1 (priority date); for spring admission, 10/1 (priority date). *Application fee:*

$20 ($50 for international students). Electronic applications accepted.
Expenses: Tuition, state resident: full-time $1,851. Tuition, nonresident: full-time $5,449. Tuition and fees vary according to program.
Financial support: In 2001–02, 18 research assistantships with partial tuition reimbursements (averaging $11,139 per year), 28 teaching assistantships with partial tuition reimbursements (averaging $11,144 per year) were awarded. Fellowships, scholarships/grants, health care benefits, and unspecified assistantships also available.
Dr. Thomas J. Rudolphi, Chair, 515-294-5666, *E-mail:* aeem_info@iastate.edu.
Application contact: Dr. Ambar Mitra, Director of Graduate Education, 515-294-2694, *E-mail:* aeem_info@iastate.edu. *Web site:* http://www1.eng.iastate.edu/coe/grad.asp

■ MASSACHUSETTS INSTITUTE OF TECHNOLOGY

School of Engineering, Department of Aeronautics and Astronautics, Cambridge, MA 02139-4307

AWARDS M Eng, SM, PhD, Sc D, EAA.

Faculty: 33 full-time (4 women), 1 part-time/adjunct (0 women).
Students: 229 full-time (57 women), 1 part-time; includes 26 minority (4 African Americans, 15 Asian Americans or Pacific Islanders, 7 Hispanic Americans), 112 international. Average age 23. 308 applicants, 55% accepted, 76 enrolled. In 2001, 65 master's, 13 doctorates awarded.
Degree requirements: For master's, thesis/dissertation; for doctorate, thesis/dissertation, comprehensive exam.
Entrance requirements: For master's, GRE General Test, TOEFL; for doctorate, GRE General Test, TOEFL, MS. *Application deadline:* For fall admission, 1/15; for spring admission, 11/1. *Application fee:* $60. Electronic applications accepted.
Expenses: Tuition: Full-time $26,960. Full-time tuition and fees vary according to program.
Financial support: In 2001–02, 230 students received support, including 36 fellowships, 169 research assistantships, 14 teaching assistantships; Federal Work-Study, institutionally sponsored loans, scholarships/grants, health care benefits, and unspecified assistantships also available. Financial award applicants required to submit FAFSA.
Faculty research: Composite materials, structural dynamics, aerodynamic design and optimization, computational fluid dynamics, micromachines and devices. *Total annual research expenditures:* $24 million.
Dr. Edward F. Crawley, Head, 617-253-7510, *Fax:* 617-258-7566, *E-mail:* crawley@mit.edu.

Application contact: Marie Stuppard, Coordinator, Academic Programs, 617-253-2279, *Fax:* 617-258-7566, *E-mail:* mas@mit.edu. *Web site:* http://web.mit.edu/aeroastro/www/

■ MIDDLE TENNESSEE STATE UNIVERSITY

College of Graduate Studies, College of Basic and Applied Sciences, Department of Aerospace, Murfreesboro, TN 37132

AWARDS Aerospace education (M Ed); airport/airline management (MS); asset management (MS); aviation administration (MS). Part-time and evening/weekend programs available.

Students: 5 full-time, 22 part-time; includes 4 minority (2 African Americans, 2 Hispanic Americans). Average age 33. 4 applicants, 100% accepted. In 2001, 5 degrees awarded.
Degree requirements: For master's, one foreign language, comprehensive exam.
Entrance requirements: For master's, GRE General Test or MAT. *Application deadline:* For fall admission, 8/1 (priority date). *Application fee:* $25.
Expenses: Tuition, state resident: full-time $1,716; part-time $191 per hour. Tuition, nonresident: full-time $4,952; part-time $461 per hour. Required fees: $14 per hour. $58 per semester.
Financial support: In 2001–02, 2 teaching assistantships were awarded. Financial award application deadline: 5/1.
Paul Craig, Interim Chair, 615-898-2788, *E-mail:* rferrara@frank.mtsu.edu.

■ MISSISSIPPI STATE UNIVERSITY

College of Engineering, Department of Aerospace Engineering, Mississippi State, MS 39762

AWARDS Aerospace engineering (MS); engineering mechanics (MS). Part-time programs available.

Faculty: 15 full-time (0 women).
Students: 12 full-time (3 women), 5 part-time (1 woman), 5 international. Average age 26. 31 applicants, 94% accepted, 4 enrolled. In 2001, 1 degree awarded.
Degree requirements: For master's, thesis optional.
Entrance requirements: For master's, GRE General Test, TOEFL, minimum GPA of 2.75. *Application deadline:* For fall admission, 7/1; for spring admission, 11/1. Applications are processed on a rolling basis. *Application fee:* $25 for international students. Electronic applications accepted.
Expenses: Tuition, state resident: full-time $3,586; part-time $150 per credit hour. Tuition, nonresident: full-time $8,128; part-time $339 per credit hour. Tuition and fees vary according to course load and campus/location.

Mississippi State University (continued)
Financial support: In 2001–02, 11 research assistantships with partial tuition reimbursements (averaging $12,000 per year), 1 teaching assistantship with partial tuition reimbursement (averaging $12,000 per year) were awarded. Federal Work-Study, institutionally sponsored loans, and unspecified assistantships also available. Financial award applicants required to submit FAFSA.
Faculty research: Computational fluid dynamics, flight mechanics, aerodynamics, composite structures, prototype development. *Total annual research expenditures:* $5.1 million.
Dr. John C. McWhorter, Head, 662-325-3623, *Fax:* 662-325-7730, *E-mail:* mcwho@ae.msstate.edu.
Application contact: Jerry B. Inmon, Director of Admissions, 662-325-2224, *Fax:* 662-325-7360, *E-mail:* admit@admissions.msstate.edu. *Web site:* http://www.ae.msstate.edu/

■ **NAVAL POSTGRADUATE SCHOOL**

Graduate Programs, Department of Aeronautics and Astronautics, Monterey, CA 93943

AWARDS MS, D Eng, PhD, Eng. Program only open to commissioned officers of the United States and friendly nations and selected United States federal civilian employees. Part-time programs available.

Degree requirements: For master's and Eng, thesis; for doctorate, one foreign language, thesis/dissertation.

■ **NAVAL POSTGRADUATE SCHOOL**

Graduate Programs, Program in Space Systems, Monterey, CA 93943

AWARDS MS. Program only open to commissioned officers of the United States and friendly nations and selected United States federal civilian employees. Part-time programs available.

Degree requirements: For master's, thesis.

■ **NORTH CAROLINA STATE UNIVERSITY**

Graduate School, College of Engineering, Department of Mechanical and Aerospace Engineering, Program in Aerospace Engineering, Raleigh, NC 27695

AWARDS MS, PhD.

Faculty: 38 full-time (3 women), 45 part-time/adjunct (1 woman).
Students: 31 full-time (6 women), 2 part-time; includes 3 minority (1 African American, 2 Asian Americans or Pacific Islanders), 6 international. Average age 27.

30 applicants, 67% accepted. In 2001, 6 master's, 2 doctorates awarded.
Degree requirements: For master's, thesis, oral exam; for doctorate, thesis/dissertation, oral and preliminary exams.
Entrance requirements: For master's and doctorate, GRE General Test. *Application deadline:* For fall admission, 7/15; for spring admission, 12/15. Applications are processed on a rolling basis. *Application fee:* $45.
Expenses: Tuition, state resident: full-time $1,748. Tuition, nonresident: full-time $6,904.
Financial support: In 2001–02, 4 fellowships (averaging $8,878 per year), 16 research assistantships (averaging $5,852 per year), 5 teaching assistantships (averaging $5,849 per year) were awarded. Career-related internships or fieldwork and institutionally sponsored loans also available.
Faculty research: Vibration and control, fluid dynamics, thermal sciences, structure and materials, aerodynamics acoustics.
Dr. Richard D. Gould, Director of Graduate Programs, 919-515-5236, *Fax:* 919-515-7968, *E-mail:* gould@eos.ncsu.edu.

Find an in-depth description at www.petersons.com/gradchannel.

■ **THE OHIO STATE UNIVERSITY**

Graduate School, College of Engineering, Program in Aeronautical and Astronautical Engineering, Columbus, OH 43210

AWARDS MS, PhD.

Degree requirements: For master's, thesis optional; for doctorate, thesis/dissertation.
Entrance requirements: For master's and doctorate, GRE General Test.

■ **OLD DOMINION UNIVERSITY**

College of Engineering and Technology, Program in Aerospace Engineering, Norfolk, VA 23529

AWARDS Aerospace engineering (ME, MS, PhD); aerospace engineering mechanics (ME, MS, PhD), including experimental methods (ME). Part-time and evening/weekend programs available. Postbaccalaureate distance learning degree programs offered (no on-campus study).

Faculty: 10 full-time (0 women).
Students: 42 full-time (3 women), 12 part-time (1 woman); includes 3 minority (1 African American, 2 Asian Americans or Pacific Islanders), 38 international. Average age 29. 55 applicants, 80% accepted. In 2001, 8 master's, 6 doctorates awarded.
Degree requirements: For master's, thesis, comprehensive exam; for doctorate, thesis/dissertation, candidacy exam.
Entrance requirements: For master's, minimum GPA of 3.0; for doctorate, minimum GPA of 3.25. *Application deadline:*

For fall admission, 7/1; for spring admission, 10/1. Applications are processed on a rolling basis. *Application fee:* $30. Electronic applications accepted.
Expenses: Tuition, state resident: part-time $202 per credit. Tuition, nonresident: part-time $534 per credit. Required fees: $76 per semester.
Financial support: In 2001–02, 2 fellowships with tuition reimbursements (averaging $16,000 per year), 31 research assistantships with tuition reimbursements (averaging $15,000 per year) were awarded. Teaching assistantships, career-related internships or fieldwork, scholarships/grants, and tuition waivers (partial) also available. Support available to part-time students. Financial award application deadline: 2/15; financial award applicants required to submit FAFSA.
Faculty research: Computational fluid dynamics, experimental fluid dynamics, structural mechanics, dynamics and control, multidisciplinary problems. *Total annual research expenditures:* $1 million.
Dr. Brett Newman, Graduate Program Director, 757-683-5860, *Fax:* 757-683-3200, *E-mail:* aeroinfo@aero.odu.edu. *Web site:* http://www.odu.edu/aero/

■ **OLD DOMINION UNIVERSITY**

College of Engineering and Technology, Program in Engineering Mechanics (Aerospace Emphasis), Norfolk, VA 23529

AWARDS ME, MS, PhD.

Students: 2 full-time (0 women), 2 part-time, 1 international. Average age 32. In 2001, 1 master's, 2 doctorates awarded.
Expenses: Tuition, state resident: part-time $202 per credit. Tuition, nonresident: part-time $534 per credit. Required fees: $76 per semester.
Dr. Brett Newman, Graduate Program Director, 757-683-5860, *Fax:* 757-683-3200, *E-mail:* aeroinfo@aero.odu.edu. *Web site:* http://www.odu.edu/webroot/orgs/engr/aero.nsf

■ **THE PENNSYLVANIA STATE UNIVERSITY UNIVERSITY PARK CAMPUS**

Graduate School, College of Engineering, Department of Aerospace Engineering, State College, University Park, PA 16802-1503

AWARDS M Eng, MS, PhD.

Students: 57 full-time (7 women), 3 part-time. In 2001, 10 master's, 12 doctorates awarded.
Degree requirements: For master's and doctorate, thesis/dissertation.
Entrance requirements: For master's and doctorate, GRE General Test. *Application fee:* $45.
Expenses: Tuition, state resident: full-time $7,882; part-time $333 per credit. Tuition,

nonresident: full-time $16,142; part-time $673 per credit. Required fees: $124 per semester.
Dr. Dennis K. McLaughlin, Head, 814-865-6431.

Find an in-depth description at www.petersons.com/gradchannel.

■ POLYTECHNIC UNIVERSITY, BROOKLYN CAMPUS

Department of Mechanical, Aerospace and Manufacturing Engineering, Major in Aeronautics and Astronautics, Brooklyn, NY 11201-2990

AWARDS MS. Part-time programs available.

Entrance requirements: For master's, BS in aerospace or mechanical engineering. Electronic applications accepted.
Faculty research: UV filter, fuel efficient hydrodynamic containment for gas core fission, turbulent boundary layer research.

■ POLYTECHNIC UNIVERSITY, LONG ISLAND GRADUATE CENTER

Graduate Programs, Department of Mechanical, Aerospace and Manufacturing Engineering, Major in Aeronautics and Astronautics, Melville, NY 11747

AWARDS MS.

Electronic applications accepted.

■ PRINCETON UNIVERSITY

Graduate School, School of Engineering and Applied Science, Department of Mechanical and Aerospace Engineering, Princeton, NJ 08544-1019

AWARDS Applied physics (M Eng, MSE, PhD); computational methods (M Eng, MSE); dynamics and control systems (M Eng, MSE, PhD); energy and environmental policy (M Eng, MSE, PhD); energy conversion, propulsion, and combustion (M Eng, MSE, PhD); flight science and technology (M Eng, MSE, PhD); fluid mechanics (M Eng, MSE, PhD).

Faculty: 26 full-time (2 women).
Students: 70 full-time (12 women), 42 international. Average age 26. 256 applicants, 18% accepted. In 2001, 8 master's, 9 doctorates awarded.
Degree requirements: For master's, thesis/dissertation; for doctorate, thesis/dissertation, comprehensive exam (for some programs).
Entrance requirements: For master's and doctorate, GRE General Test. *Application deadline:* For fall admission, 1/3. Electronic applications accepted.
Financial support: Fellowships, research assistantships, teaching assistantships, Federal Work-Study and institutionally sponsored loans available. Financial award

application deadline: 1/3. *Total annual research expenditures:* $5.3 million.
Prof. Naomi Enrich Leonard, Director of Graduate Studies, 609-258-5129, *Fax:* 609-258-6109, *E-mail:* maegrad@princeton.edu.
Application contact: Jessica H. Buchanan, Graduate Administrator, 609-258-4683, *Fax:* 609-258-6109, *E-mail:* maegrad@princeton.edu. *Web site:* http://www.princeton.edu/~mae/maegrad/index.html

Find an in-depth description at www.petersons.com/gradchannel.

■ PURDUE UNIVERSITY

Graduate School, Schools of Engineering, School of Aeronautics and Astronautics, West Lafayette, IN 47907

AWARDS MS, MSAAE, MSE, PhD.

Faculty: 24 full-time (1 woman), 1 part-time/adjunct (0 women).
Students: 139 full-time (10 women), 12 part-time (2 women); includes 7 minority (1 African American, 2 Asian American or Pacific Islander, 4 Hispanic Americans, 1 Native American), 73 international. Average age 28. 200 applicants, 97% accepted, 45 enrolled. In 2001, 23 master's, 20 doctorates awarded.
Degree requirements: For doctorate, variable foreign language requirement, thesis/dissertation.
Entrance requirements: For master's and doctorate, GRE General Test, TOEFL. *Application fee:* $30. Electronic applications accepted.
Expenses: Tuition, state resident: full-time $4,164; part-time $149 per credit hour. Tuition, nonresident: full-time $13,872; part-time $458 per credit hour. Tuition and fees vary according to campus/location and program.
Financial support: In 2001–02, 12 fellowships, 57 research assistantships, 26 teaching assistantships were awarded. Career-related internships or fieldwork also available. Support available to part-time students. Financial award applicants required to submit FAFSA.
Faculty research: Structures and materials, propulsion, aerodynamics, dynamics and control.
Dr. Thomas N. Farris, Head, 765-494-5117, *Fax:* 765-494-0307, *E-mail:* farrist@ecn.purdue.edu.
Application contact: Linda Flack, Administrative Assistant, 765-494-5152, *Fax:* 765-494-0307, *E-mail:* flack@ecn.purdue.edu. *Web site:* http://aae.www.ecn.purdue.edu/

Find an in-depth description at www.petersons.com/gradchannel.

■ RENSSELAER POLYTECHNIC INSTITUTE

Graduate School, School of Engineering, Department of Mechanical, Aerospace, and Nuclear Engineering, Program in Aerospace Engineering, Troy, NY 12180-3590

AWARDS M Eng, MS, D Eng, PhD, MBA/M Eng. Part-time and evening/weekend programs available.

Faculty: 29 full-time (2 women), 2 part-time/adjunct (0 women).
Students: 9 full-time (0 women), 4 international. 39 applicants, 49% accepted. In 2001, 3 master's, 5 doctorates awarded.
Degree requirements: For master's, thesis (for some programs); for doctorate, thesis/dissertation.
Entrance requirements: For master's and doctorate, GRE, TOEFL. *Application deadline:* For fall admission, 1/15 (priority date). Applications are processed on a rolling basis. *Application fee:* $45. Electronic applications accepted.
Expenses: Tuition: Full-time $26,400; part-time $1,320 per credit hour. Required fees: $1,437.
Financial support: Fellowships, research assistantships, teaching assistantships, career-related internships or fieldwork, institutionally sponsored loans, and tuition waivers (partial) available. Financial award application deadline: 2/1.
Faculty research: Vehicular performance and flight mechanics, gas dynamics, aerodynamics, structural dynamics, advanced propulsion, fluids. *Total annual research expenditures:* $2.5 million.
Application contact: Dr. Kevin C. Craig, Director, 518-276-6620, *Fax:* 518-276-4860, *E-mail:* craigk@rpi.edu. *Web site:* http://www.rpi.edu/dept/meaem/

Find an in-depth description at www.petersons.com/gradchannel.

■ RUTGERS, THE STATE UNIVERSITY OF NEW JERSEY, NEW BRUNSWICK

Graduate School, Program in Mechanical and Aerospace Engineering, New Brunswick, NJ 08901-1281

AWARDS Computational fluid dynamics (MS, PhD); design and dynamics (MS, PhD); fluid mechanics (MS, PhD); heat transfer (MS, PhD). Solid mechanics (MS, PhD). Part-time and evening/weekend programs available.

Degree requirements: For master's, thesis (for some programs); for doctorate, thesis/dissertation.
Entrance requirements: For master's, GRE General Test, BS in mechanical/aerospace engineering or related field; for doctorate, GRE General Test, MS in mechanical/aerospace engineering or related field. *Web site:* http://cronos.rutgers.edu/~mechaero/

■ SAINT LOUIS UNIVERSITY

Graduate School, Parks College of Engineering and Aviation, Department of Aerospace and Mechanical Engineering, St. Louis, MO 63103-2097

AWARDS Aerospace engineering (MS, MS(R)).

Faculty: 11 full-time (2 women), 8 part-time/adjunct (0 women).
Students: 8 full-time (3 women), 9 part-time; includes 1 minority (Hispanic American), 12 international. Average age 26. 5 applicants, 100% accepted, 4 enrolled. In 2001, 4 degrees awarded.
Degree requirements: For master's, thesis (for some programs), comprehensive exam.
Entrance requirements: For master's, GRE General Test. *Application deadline:* For fall admission, 7/1; for spring admission, 11/1. Applications are processed on a rolling basis. *Application fee:* $40.
Expenses: Tuition: Part-time $630 per credit hour.
Financial support: In 2001–02, 11 students received support, including 5 research assistantships with tuition reimbursements available, 4 teaching assistantships with tuition reimbursements available Financial award application deadline: 4/1; financial award applicants required to submit FAFSA.
Faculty research: Hypersonic vehicle design, high temperature lubrication, design optimization, research on free shear layer flows mechanical design methodology. *Total annual research expenditures:* $191,132.
Dr. Krishnaswamy Ravindra, Chairperson, 314-977-8331, *Fax:* 314-977-8403, *E-mail:* ravindrak@slu.edu.
Application contact: Dr. Marcia Buresch, Associate Dean of the Graduate School, 314-977-2240, *Fax:* 314-977-3943, *E-mail:* bureschm@slu.edu.

■ SAN DIEGO STATE UNIVERSITY

Graduate and Research Affairs, College of Engineering, Department of Aerospace Engineering and Engineering Mechanics, San Diego, CA 92182

AWARDS Aerospace engineering (MS); engineering mechanics (MS); engineering sciences and applied mechanics (PhD); flight dynamics (MS); fluid dynamics (MS). Terminal master's awarded for partial completion of doctoral program.

Degree requirements: For doctorate, thesis/dissertation.
Entrance requirements: For master's, GRE General Test, TOEFL.
Faculty research: Organized structures in post-stall flow over wings/three dimensional separated flow, airfoil growth effect, probabilities, structural mechanics.

■ SAN JOSE STATE UNIVERSITY

Graduate Studies, College of Engineering, Department of Mechanical and Aerospace Engineering, Program in Aerospace Engineering, San Jose, CA 95192-0001

AWARDS MS.

Students: 1 full-time (0 women), 12 part-time (3 women); includes 6 minority (4 Asian Americans or Pacific Islanders, 2 Hispanic Americans). Average age 30. 11 applicants, 91% accepted. In 2001, 2 degrees awarded.
Application deadline: For fall admission, 6/29; for spring admission, 11/30. Applications are processed on a rolling basis.
Application fee: $59. Electronic applications accepted.
Expenses: Tuition, nonresident: part-time $246 per unit. Required fees: $678 per semester. Tuition and fees vary according to course load.
Financial support: Applicants required to submit FAFSA.
Application contact: Dick Desautel, Acting Chair, 408-924-3900, *Fax:* 408-924-4004.

■ STANFORD UNIVERSITY

School of Engineering, Department of Aeronautics and Astronautics, Stanford, CA 94305-9991

AWARDS MS, PhD, Eng.

Faculty: 15 full-time (1 woman).
Students: 157 full-time (21 women), 49 part-time (6 women); includes 28 minority (4 African Americans, 18 Asian Americans or Pacific Islanders, 6 Hispanic Americans), 90 international. Average age 27. 220 applicants, 76% accepted. In 2001, 55 master's, 23 doctorates awarded. Terminal master's awarded for partial completion of doctoral program.
Degree requirements: For doctorate and Eng, thesis/dissertation.
Entrance requirements: For master's and Eng, GRE General Test, GRE Subject Test, TOEFL; for doctorate, GRE General Test, GRE Engineering Subject Test, TOEFL. *Application deadline:* For fall admission, 1/15. Applications are processed on a rolling basis. *Application fee:* $65 ($80 for international students). Electronic applications accepted.
Financial support: Institutionally sponsored loans available.
George Springer, Chairman, 650-723-4135, *Fax:* 650-723-0062, *E-mail:* gspringer@stanford.edu.
Application contact: Graduate Admissions Coordinator, 650-723-2757. *Web site:* http://aa.stanford.edu

Find an in-depth description at www.petersons.com/gradchannel.

■ TEXAS A&M UNIVERSITY

College of Engineering, Department of Aerospace Engineering, College Station, TX 77843

AWARDS M Eng, MS, PhD.

Faculty: 29.
Students: 101 (10 women). Average age 27.
Degree requirements: For master's, thesis (MS); for doctorate, thesis/dissertation.
Entrance requirements: For master's and doctorate, GRE General Test, TOEFL. *Application deadline:* For fall admission, 1/15 (priority date); for spring admission, 9/15. Applications are processed on a rolling basis. *Application fee:* $50 ($75 for international students). Electronic applications accepted.
Expenses: Tuition, state resident: full-time $11,872. Tuition, nonresident: full-time $17,892.
Financial support: Fellowships, research assistantships, teaching assistantships available. Financial award application deadline: 3/1; financial award applicants required to submit FAFSA.
Faculty research: Materials and structures, aerodynamics and CFD, flight dynamics and control.
Dr. Terry Alfriend, Head, 979-845-7541.
Application contact: Dr. Dimitris Lagoudas, Graduate Adviser, 979-845-5520, *Fax:* 979-845-6051, *E-mail:* karer@aero.tamu.edu.

■ UNIVERSITY AT BUFFALO, THE STATE UNIVERSITY OF NEW YORK

Graduate School, School of Engineering and Applied Sciences, Department of Mechanical and Aerospace Engineering, Buffalo, NY 14260

AWARDS Aerospace engineering (M Eng, MS, PhD); mechanical engineering (M Eng, MS, PhD). Part-time programs available.

Faculty: 25 full-time (3 women), 3 part-time/adjunct (0 women).
Students: 150 full-time (7 women), 48 part-time (6 women); includes 7 minority (6 Asian Americans or Pacific Islanders, 1 Hispanic American), 136 international. Average age 24. 454 applicants, 48% accepted. In 2001, 48 master's, 17 doctorates awarded. Terminal master's awarded for partial completion of doctoral program.
Degree requirements: For master's, project, or thesis; for doctorate, thesis/dissertation.
Entrance requirements: For master's and doctorate, GRE General Test, GRE Subject Test, TOEFL. *Application deadline:* For fall admission, 2/1; for spring admission, 10/1. Applications are processed on a rolling basis. *Application fee:* $35.

Expenses: Tuition, state resident: full-time $6,118. Tuition, nonresident: full-time $9,434.

Financial support: In 2001–02, 70 students received support, including 3 fellowships with tuition reimbursements available, 41 research assistantships with tuition reimbursements available (averaging $12,500 per year), 29 teaching assistantships with tuition reimbursements available (averaging $10,740 per year); Federal Work-Study, institutionally sponsored loans, tuition waivers (full), and unspecified assistantships also available. Financial award application deadline: 2/1; financial award applicants required to submit FAFSA.

Faculty research: Fluid and thermal sciences, systems and design, mechanics and materials. *Total annual research expenditures:* $1.4 million.

Dr. Christina L. Bloebaum, Chair, 716-645-2593 Ext. 2231, *Fax:* 716-645-3875, *E-mail:* clb@eng.buffalo.edu.

Application contact: Dr. Dale B. Taulbee, Director of Graduate Studies, 716-645-2593 Ext. 2307, *Fax:* 716-645-3875, *E-mail:* trldale@eng.buffalo.edu. *Web site:* http://www.eng.buffalo.edu/dept/mae/

Find an in-depth description at www.petersons.com/gradchannel.

■ THE UNIVERSITY OF ALABAMA

Graduate School, College of Engineering, Department of Aerospace Engineering and Mechanics, Tuscaloosa, AL 35487

AWARDS MSAE, MSESM, PhD. Part-time programs available. Postbaccalaureate distance learning degree programs offered (no on-campus study).

Faculty: 12 full-time (1 woman).
Students: 21 full-time (2 women), 18 part-time (2 women); includes 3 minority (1 African American, 2 Asian Americans or Pacific Islanders), 22 international. Average age 28. 46 applicants, 46% accepted, 13 enrolled. In 2001, 13 master's, 3 doctorates awarded. Terminal master's awarded for partial completion of doctoral program.
Degree requirements: For master's, thesis or alternative; for doctorate, thesis/dissertation.
Entrance requirements: For master's and doctorate, GRE General Test. *Application deadline:* For fall admission, 7/6 (priority date). Applications are processed on a rolling basis. *Application fee:* $25.
Expenses: Tuition, state resident: full-time $3,292; part-time $183 per credit hour. Tuition, nonresident: full-time $8,912; part-time $495 per credit hour. Tuition and fees vary according to course load, campus/location and program.
Financial support: In 2001–02, 25 students received support, including 5 fellowships with full tuition reimbursements available, 12 research assistantships with full tuition reimbursements available, 8 teaching assistantships with full tuition

reimbursements available; Federal Work-Study and institutionally sponsored loans also available. Financial award application deadline: 7/6.
Faculty research: Flight simulation, advanced mechanical behavior in materials, fluid and solid computational mechanics, hypersonic aerodynamics, intelligent systems. *Total annual research expenditures:* $3.8 million.

Dr. Charles L. Karr, Associate Professor, Interim Head, 205-348-0066, *Fax:* 205-348-7240, *E-mail:* ckarr@coe.eng.ua.edu.
Application contact: Dr. Amnon Katz, Information Contact, 205-348-7300, *Fax:* 205-348-7240.

■ THE UNIVERSITY OF ALABAMA IN HUNTSVILLE

School of Graduate Studies, College of Engineering, Department of Mechanical and Aerospace Engineering, Huntsville, AL 35899

AWARDS Aerospace engineering (MSE); mechanical engineering (MSE, PhD). Part-time and evening/weekend programs available.

Faculty: 15 full-time (0 women), 4 part-time/adjunct (0 women).
Students: 40 full-time (6 women), 29 part-time (6 women); includes 4 minority (2 Asian Americans or Pacific Islanders, 2 Hispanic Americans), 26 international. Average age 31. 91 applicants, 60% accepted, 21 enrolled. In 2001, 8 master's, 4 doctorates awarded.
Degree requirements: For master's, thesis or alternative, oral and written exams, comprehensive exam, registration; for doctorate, thesis/dissertation, oral and written exams, comprehensive exam, registration.
Entrance requirements: For master's, GRE General Test, BSE, minimum GPA of 3.0; for doctorate, GRE General Test, minimum GPA of 3.0. *Application deadline:* For fall admission, 7/24 (priority date); for spring admission, 11/15 (priority date). Applications are processed on a rolling basis. *Application fee:* $35.
Expenses: Tuition, area resident: Part-time $175 per hour. Tuition, state resident: full-time $4,408. Tuition, nonresident: full-time $9,054; part-time $361 per hour.
Financial support: In 2001–02, 29 students received support, including 21 research assistantships with full and partial tuition reimbursements available (averaging $9,936 per year), 8 teaching assistantships with full and partial tuition reimbursements available (averaging $7,100 per year); fellowships with full and partial tuition reimbursements available, career-related internships or fieldwork, Federal Work-Study, institutionally sponsored loans, scholarships/grants, health care benefits, and tuition waivers (full and partial) also available. Support available to part-time students. Financial

award application deadline: 4/1; financial award applicants required to submit FAFSA.
Faculty research: Combustion, fluid dynamics, solar energy, propulsion, laser diagnostics. *Total annual research expenditures:* $1.6 million.
Dr. Francis C. Wessling, Chair, 256-824-6469, *Fax:* 256-824-6758, *E-mail:* wesslif@eb.uah.edu. *Web site:* http://www.eb-p5.eb.uah.edu/mae/

■ THE UNIVERSITY OF ARIZONA

Graduate College, College of Engineering and Mines, Department of Aerospace and Mechanical Engineering, Program in Aerospace Engineering, Tucson, AZ 85721

AWARDS MS, PhD. Part-time programs available.

Degree requirements: For master's, thesis or alternative; for doctorate, one foreign language, thesis/dissertation.
Entrance requirements: For master's and doctorate, GRE General Test, GRE Subject Test, TOEFL, minimum GPA of 3.0.
Expenses: Tuition, state resident: full-time $2,490; part-time $436 per unit. Tuition, nonresident: full-time $10,300; part-time $436 per unit. Full-time tuition and fees vary according to degree level and program.
Faculty research: Fluid mechanics, structures, computer-aided design, stability and control, combustion.

Find an in-depth description at www.petersons.com/gradchannel.

■ UNIVERSITY OF CALIFORNIA, DAVIS

Graduate Studies, College of Engineering, Program in Mechanical and Aeronautical Engineering, Davis, CA 95616

AWARDS Aeronautical engineering (M Engr, MS, D Engr, PhD, Certificate); mechanical engineering (M Engr, MS, D Engr, PhD, Certificate).

Faculty: 29 full-time (1 woman).
Students: 106 full-time (18 women); includes 25 minority (3 African Americans, 20 Asian Americans or Pacific Islanders, 2 Hispanic Americans), 28 international. Average age 28. 234 applicants, 69% accepted, 38 enrolled. In 2001, 25 master's, 8 doctorates awarded.
Degree requirements: For master's, thesis optional; for doctorate, thesis/dissertation.
Entrance requirements: For master's and doctorate, GRE General Test, minimum GPA of 3.0. *Application deadline:* For fall admission, 3/15. *Application fee:* $60. Electronic applications accepted.
Expenses: Tuition, state resident: full-time $4,831. Tuition, nonresident: full-time $15,725.

University of California, Davis (continued)
Financial support: In 2001–02, 80 students received support, including 13 fellowships with full and partial tuition reimbursements available (averaging $2,246 per year), 53 research assistantships with full and partial tuition reimbursements available (averaging $9,707 per year), 20 teaching assistantships with partial tuition reimbursements available (averaging $9,897 per year); career-related internships or fieldwork, Federal Work-Study, institutionally sponsored loans, scholarships/grants, and tuition waivers (full and partial) also available. Financial award application deadline: 1/15; financial award applicants required to submit FAFSA.
Rida T. Farouki, Chairperson, 530-752-1779, *Fax:* 530-752-4158, *E-mail:* farouki@ucdavis.edu.
Application contact: Susan Fann, Academic Assistant, 530-752-0581, *Fax:* 530-752-4158, *E-mail:* sfann@ucdavis.edu. *Web site:* http://mae.ucdavis.edu/

■ UNIVERSITY OF CALIFORNIA, IRVINE

Office of Research and Graduate Studies, School of Engineering, Department of Mechanical and Aerospace Engineering, Irvine, CA 92697

AWARDS MS, PhD. Part-time programs available.

Students: 62 full-time (10 women), 14 part-time (3 women); includes 20 minority (16 Asian Americans or Pacific Islanders, 4 Hispanic Americans), 16 international. 180 applicants, 33% accepted, 19 enrolled. In 2001, 18 master's, 4 doctorates awarded. Terminal master's awarded for partial completion of doctoral program.
Degree requirements: For doctorate, thesis/dissertation.
Entrance requirements: For master's, GRE General Test, minimum GPA of 3.0; for doctorate, GRE General Test. *Application deadline:* For fall and spring admission, 1/15 (priority date); for winter admission, 10/15 (priority date). Applications are processed on a rolling basis. *Application fee:* $60. Electronic applications accepted.
Expenses: Tuition, nonresident: full-time $10,704. Required fees: $8,396. Tuition and fees vary according to course load, program and student level.
Financial support: In 2001–02, 14 fellowships with tuition reimbursements (averaging $1,250 per year), 24 research assistantships with tuition reimbursements (averaging $1,120 per year), 12 teaching assistantships with tuition reimbursements (averaging $1,480 per year) were awarded. Institutionally sponsored loans and tuition waivers (full and partial) also available. Financial award application deadline: 3/2; financial award applicants required to submit FAFSA.

Faculty research: Thermal and fluid sciences, combustion and propulsion, control systems, robotics. *Total annual research expenditures:* $3.5 million.
Dr. Said Elghobashi, Chair, 949-824-6131, *Fax:* 949-824-8585, *E-mail:* selghoba@uci.edu.
Application contact: Dorothy Miles, Graduate Coordinator, 949-824-5469, *Fax:* 949-824-8585, *E-mail:* djmiles@uci.edu. *Web site:* http://www.eng.uci.edu/

Find an in-depth description at www.petersons.com/gradchannel.

■ UNIVERSITY OF CALIFORNIA, LOS ANGELES

Graduate Division, School of Engineering and Applied Science, Department of Mechanical and Aerospace Engineering, Program in Aerospace Engineering, Los Angeles, CA 90095

AWARDS MS, PhD.

Students: 31 full-time (2 women); includes 6 minority (1 African American, 5 Asian Americans or Pacific Islanders), 11 international. 56 applicants, 66% accepted, 10 enrolled. In 2001, 4 master's, 1 doctorate awarded.
Degree requirements: For master's, comprehensive exam or thesis; for doctorate, thesis/dissertation, qualifying exams.
Entrance requirements: For master's, GRE General Test, GRE Subject Test (international applicants), minimum GPA of 3.0; for doctorate, GRE General Test, GRE Subject Test (international applicants), minimum GPA of 3.25. *Application deadline:* For fall admission, 1/5; for spring admission, 12/31. *Application fee:* $60. Electronic applications accepted.
Expenses: Tuition, nonresident: full-time $10,244. Required fees: $3,609. Full-time tuition and fees vary according to program.
Financial support: In 2001–02, 37 research assistantships, 9 teaching assistantships were awarded. Fellowships, Federal Work-Study, institutionally sponsored loans, and tuition waivers (full and partial) also available. Financial award application deadline: 1/5; financial award applicants required to submit FAFSA.
Application contact: Dr. Angie Castillo, Student Affairs Officer, 310-825-7793, *Fax:* 310-206-4830, *E-mail:* angie@ea.ucla.edu.

■ UNIVERSITY OF CALIFORNIA, SAN DIEGO

Graduate Studies and Research, Department of Mechanical and Aerospace Engineering, Program in Aerospace Engineering, La Jolla, CA 92093

AWARDS MS, PhD. Part-time programs available.

Degree requirements: For master's, comprehensive exam or thesis; for doctorate, thesis/dissertation, qualifying exam.
Entrance requirements: For master's and doctorate, GRE General Test, TOEFL, minimum GPA of 3.0.
Expenses: Tuition, nonresident: full-time $10,434. Required fees: $4,883.
Faculty research: Aerospace structures, turbulence, gas dynamics and combustion. *Web site:* http://www-ames.ucsd.edu/

Find an in-depth description at www.petersons.com/gradchannel.

■ UNIVERSITY OF CENTRAL FLORIDA

College of Engineering and Computer Sciences, Department of Mechanical, Materials, and Aerospace Engineering, Program in Aerospace Engineering, Orlando, FL 32816

AWARDS MSAE.

Faculty: 19 full-time (1 woman), 5 part-time/adjunct (0 women).
Students: 2 full-time (1 woman), 13 part-time (2 women); includes 3 minority (2 African Americans, 1 Hispanic American), 3 international. Average age 28. 11 applicants, 73% accepted, 2 enrolled. In 2001, 3 degrees awarded.
Degree requirements: For master's, thesis or alternative.
Application deadline: For fall admission, 7/15 (priority date); for spring admission, 12/1 (priority date). *Application fee:* $20. Electronic applications accepted.
Expenses: Tuition, state resident: part-time $162 per hour. Tuition, nonresident: part-time $569 per hour.
Financial support: In 2001–02, 1 fellowship (averaging $17,550 per year), 13 research assistantships (averaging $1,915 per year), 5 teaching assistantships (averaging $3,216 per year) were awarded. Career-related internships or fieldwork, institutionally sponsored loans, scholarships/grants, tuition waivers (partial), and unspecified assistantships also available.
Application contact: Dr. A. J. Kassab, Coordinator, 407-823-2416, *Fax:* 407-823-0208, *E-mail:* kassab@mail.ucf.edu.

Find an in-depth description at www.petersons.com/gradchannel.

■ UNIVERSITY OF CINCINNATI

Division of Research and Advanced Studies, College of Engineering, Department of Aerospace Engineering, Cincinnati, OH 45221

AWARDS MS, PhD. Part-time programs available.

Faculty: 19 full-time (1 woman), 2 part-time/adjunct (0 women).
Students: 92 full-time (12 women), 21 part-time (6 women). 111 applicants, 26%

accepted. In 2001, 18 master's, 5 doctorates awarded. Terminal master's awarded for partial completion of doctoral program. **Degree requirements:** For master's, thesis or alternative, project or thesis; for doctorate, thesis/dissertation, registration. *Median time to degree:* Master's–1.8 years full-time, 2.5 years part-time; doctorate–6 years full-time. **Entrance requirements:** For master's and doctorate, GRE General Test, TOEFL. *Application deadline:* For fall admission, 2/1 (priority date). *Application fee:* $40. Electronic applications accepted. **Expenses:** Tuition, state resident: part-time $2,698 per quarter. Tuition, nonresident: part-time $4,977 per quarter. **Financial support:** In 2001–02, 1 fellowship with full tuition reimbursement (averaging $18,000 per year), 18 research assistantships with full tuition reimbursements (averaging $19,200 per year), 14 teaching assistantships with full tuition reimbursements (averaging $10,200 per year) were awarded. Tuition waivers (full) and unspecified assistantships also available. Financial award application deadline: 2/1. **Faculty research:** Computational fluid mechanics/propulsion, large space structures, dynamics and guidance of VTOL vehicles. *Total annual research expenditures:* $3.6 million. Dr. Awatef Hamed, Head, 513-556-3553, *Fax:* 513-556-5038, *E-mail:* a.hamed@ uc.edu. **Application contact:** Dr. Bruce K. Walker, Director of Graduate Studies, 513-556-3552, *Fax:* 513-556-5038, *E-mail:* bruce.walker@uc.edu. *Web site:* http:// www.ase.uc.edu/

■ UNIVERSITY OF COLORADO AT BOULDER

Graduate School, College of Engineering and Applied Science, Department of Aerospace Engineering Sciences, Boulder, CO 80309

AWARDS ME, MS, PhD. Postbaccalaureate distance learning degree programs offered.

Faculty: 24 full-time (3 women). **Students:** 112 full-time (24 women), 21 part-time (5 women); includes 10 minority (1 African American, 5 Asian Americans or Pacific Islanders, 3 Hispanic Americans, 1 Native American), 16 international. Average age 28. 96 applicants, 85% accepted. In 2001, 40 master's, 11 doctorates awarded. Terminal master's awarded for partial completion of doctoral program. **Degree requirements:** For master's, thesis or alternative, comprehensive exam; for doctorate, thesis/dissertation, comprehensive final exam. **Entrance requirements:** For master's, GRE General Test, minimum undergraduate GPA of 3.25; for doctorate, minimum undergraduate GPA of 3.25. *Application deadline:* For fall admission, 2/1 (priority

date). Applications are processed on a rolling basis. *Application fee:* $50 ($60 for international students). **Expenses:** Tuition, state resident: full-time $3,474. Tuition, nonresident: full-time $16,624. **Financial support:** In 2001–02, 21 fellowships (averaging $5,009 per year), 46 research assistantships with full tuition reimbursements (averaging $16,646 per year), 27 teaching assistantships with full tuition reimbursements (averaging $16,592 per year) were awarded. Career-related internships or fieldwork, Federal Work-Study, and scholarships/grants also available. Support available to part-time students. Financial award application deadline: 2/15. **Faculty research:** Aerodynamics, gas dynamics and fluid mechanics, atmospheric and oceanic sciences. *Total annual research expenditures:* $11.7 million. Charbel Farhat, Interim Chair, 303-492-3992, *Fax:* 303-492-7881, *E-mail:* charbel.farhat@colorado.edu. **Application contact:** Robin Basile, Graduate Coordinator, 303-492-6416, *Fax:* 303-792-7881, *E-mail:* basiller@ spot.colorado.edu. *Web site:* http:// aerospace.colorado.edu/

■ UNIVERSITY OF COLORADO AT COLORADO SPRINGS

Graduate School, College of Engineering and Applied Science, Department of Mechanical and Aerospace Engineering, Colorado Springs, CO 80933-7150

AWARDS Engineering management (ME); information operations (ME); manufacturing (ME); mechanical engineering (MS). Software engineering (ME). Space operations (ME). Part-time and evening/weekend programs available.

Faculty: 7 full-time (0 women), 5 part-time/adjunct (3 women). **Students:** 16 full-time (3 women), 14 part-time (1 woman); includes 1 minority (Asian American or Pacific Islander), 1 international. Average age 35. In 2001, 26 degrees awarded. **Degree requirements:** For master's, thesis optional. **Entrance requirements:** For master's, GRE General Test, TOEFL, bachelor's degree in engineering or related degree, minimum GPA of 3.0. *Application deadline:* For fall admission, 7/15; for spring admission, 12/10. Applications are processed on a rolling basis. *Application fee:* $60 ($75 for international students). **Expenses:** Tuition, state resident: full-time $2,900; part-time $174 per credit. Tuition, nonresident: full-time $9,961; part-time $591 per credit. Required fees: $14 per credit. $141 per semester. Tuition and fees vary according to course load, program and student level.

Faculty research: Neural networks, artificial intelligence, robust control, space operations, space propulsion. Dr. Peter Gorder, Chair, 719-262-3168, *Fax:* 719-262-3589, *E-mail:* pgorder@ eas.uccs.edu. **Application contact:** Siew Nylund, Academic Adviser, 719-262-3243, *Fax:* 719-262-3042, *E-mail:* snylund@uccs.edu. *Web site:* http://mepo-b.uccs.edu/ newsletter.html

■ UNIVERSITY OF CONNECTICUT

Graduate School, School of Engineering, Department of Mechanical Engineering, Storrs, CT 06269

AWARDS Aerospace engineering (MS, PhD); biomedical engineering (MS, PhD); mechanical engineering (MS, PhD); ocean engineering (MS, PhD). Terminal master's awarded for partial completion of doctoral program.

Degree requirements: For master's, thesis or alternative; for doctorate, thesis/ dissertation. **Entrance requirements:** For master's and doctorate, GRE General Test, GRE Subject Test. **Faculty research:** Design, applied mechanics, dynamics and control, energy and thermal sciences, manufacturing.

■ UNIVERSITY OF DAYTON

Graduate School, School of Engineering, Department of Mechanical and Aerospace Engineering, Dayton, OH 45469-1300

AWARDS Aerospace engineering (MSAE, DE, PhD); mechanical engineering (MSME, DE, PhD). Part-time programs available.

Faculty: 14 full-time (0 women), 10 part-time/adjunct (1 woman). **Students:** 38 full-time (4 women), 18 part-time (4 women); includes 9 minority (2 African Americans, 1 Asian American or Pacific Islander, 6 Hispanic Americans), 16 international. Average age 26. In 2001, 10 master's, 5 doctorates awarded. **Degree requirements:** For doctorate, variable foreign language requirement, thesis/dissertation, departmental qualifying exam. **Entrance requirements:** For master's, TOEFL. *Application deadline:* For fall admission, 8/1 (priority date). Applications are processed on a rolling basis. *Application fee:* $30. **Expenses:** Tuition: Full-time $5,436; part-time $453 per credit hour. Required fees: $50; $25 per term. **Financial support:** In 2001–02, 1 fellowship with full tuition reimbursement (averaging $18,000 per year), 20 research assistantships with full tuition reimbursements (averaging $13,500 per year), 1 teaching assistantship with full tuition reimbursement (averaging $9,000 per year) were awarded. Institutionally sponsored

University of Dayton (continued)
loans and tuition waivers (full and partial) also available.

Faculty research: Turbine blade convection, jet engine combustion, energy storage, heat pipes surface transfer, surface coating friction and wear. *Total annual research expenditures:* $400,000.
Dr. Kevin Hallinan, Chairperson, 937-229-2835, *Fax:* 937-229-2756, *E-mail:* khallinan@engr.udayton.edu.
Application contact: Dr. Donald L. Moon, Associate Dean, 937-229-2241, *Fax:* 937-229-2471, *E-mail:* dmoon@ notes.udayton.edu.

■ **UNIVERSITY OF FLORIDA**

Graduate School, College of Engineering, Department of Aerospace Engineering, Mechanics, and Engineering Science, Program in Aerospace Engineering, Gainesville, FL 32611

AWARDS ME, MS, PhD, Certificate, Engr.

Degree requirements: For master's and other advanced degree, thesis optional; for doctorate, thesis/dissertation.
Entrance requirements: For master's and doctorate, GRE General Test, TOEFL, minimum GPA of 3.0; for other advanced degree, GRE General Test. Electronic applications accepted.
Expenses: Tuition, state resident: part-time $164 per hour. Tuition, nonresident: part-time $571 per hour. Tuition and fees vary according to course level and program.

■ **UNIVERSITY OF FLORIDA**

Graduate School, Graduate Engineering and Research Center (GERC), Gainesville, FL 32611

AWARDS Aerospace engineering (ME, MS, PhD, Engr); electrical and computer engineering (ME, MS, PhD, Engr); engineering mechanics (ME, MS, PhD, Engr); industrial and systems engineering (ME, MS, PhD, Engr). Part-time programs available. Postbaccalaureate distance learning degree programs offered. Terminal master's awarded for partial completion of doctoral program.

Degree requirements: For master's, thesis optional; for doctorate and Engr, thesis/dissertation.
Entrance requirements: For master's, GRE General Test, TOEFL, minimum GPA of 3.0; for doctorate, GRE General Test, written and oral qualifying exams, TOEFL, minimum GPA of 3.0, master's degree in engineering; for Engr, GRE General Test, TOEFL, minimum GPA of 3.0, master's degree in engineering. Electronic applications accepted.
Expenses: Contact institution.
Faculty research: Aerodynamics, terradynamics, and propulsion; composite materials and stress analysis; optical processing of microwave signals and photonics; holography, radar, and communications. System and signal theory; digital signal processing. *Web site:* http://www.gerc.eng.ufl.edu/

■ **UNIVERSITY OF HOUSTON**

Cullen College of Engineering, Department of Mechanical Engineering, Houston, TX 77204

AWARDS Aerospace engineering (MS, PhD); biomedical engineering (MS); computer and systems engineering (MS, PhD); environmental engineering (MS, PhD); materials engineering (MS, PhD); mechanical engineering (MME, MSME); petroleum engineering (MS). Part-time and evening/weekend programs available.

Faculty: 16 full-time (0 women), 1 part-time/adjunct (0 women).
Students: 34 full-time (4 women), 26 part-time (2 women); includes 7 minority (3 Asian Americans or Pacific Islanders, 4 Hispanic Americans), 32 international. Average age 28. 114 applicants, 64% accepted. In 2001, 20 master's, 3 doctorates awarded. Terminal master's awarded for partial completion of doctoral program.
Degree requirements: For master's, thesis (for some programs); for doctorate, thesis/dissertation, departmental qualifying exam.
Entrance requirements: For master's and doctorate, GRE General Test, TOEFL. *Application deadline:* For fall admission, 7/3 (priority date); for spring admission, 12/4. Applications are processed on a rolling basis. *Application fee:* $25 ($75 for international students).
Expenses: Tuition, state resident: full-time $1,512. Tuition, nonresident: full-time $5,310. Required fees: $1,308. Tuition and fees vary according to program.
Financial support: In 2001–02, 20 research assistantships (averaging $14,400 per year), 13 teaching assistantships (averaging $14,400 per year) were awarded. Fellowships, career-related internships or fieldwork and Federal Work-Study also available. Financial award application deadline: 2/15.
Faculty research: Experimental and computational turbulence, composites, rheology, phase change/heat transfer, characterization of superconducting materials. *Total annual research expenditures:* $396,172.
Dr. Lewis T. Wheeler, Interim Chair, 713-743-4500, *Fax:* 713-743-4503.
Application contact: Susan Sanderson-Clobe, Graduate Admissions Analyst, 713-743-4505, *Fax:* 713-743-4503, *E-mail:* megrad@uh.edu. *Web site:* http://www.mc.uh.edu

Find an in-depth description at www.petersons.com/gradchannel.

■ **UNIVERSITY OF ILLINOIS AT URBANA–CHAMPAIGN**

Graduate College, College of Engineering, Department of Aeronautical and Astronautical Engineering, Champaign, IL 61820

AWARDS MS, PhD.

Faculty: 18 full-time.
Students: 69 full-time (11 women); includes 4 minority (2 Asian Americans or Pacific Islanders, 2 Hispanic Americans), 29 international. 132 applicants, 21% accepted. In 2001, 10 master's, 3 doctorates awarded.
Degree requirements: For master's and doctorate, thesis/dissertation.
Entrance requirements: For master's and doctorate, GRE General Test, TOEFL. *Application deadline:* For fall admission, 2/1; for spring admission, 11/1. Applications are processed on a rolling basis. *Application fee:* $40 ($50 for international students). Electronic applications accepted.
Expenses: Tuition, state resident: part-time $3,227 per degree program. Tuition, nonresident: part-time $7,169 per degree program. Tuition and fees vary according to program.
Financial support: In 2001–02, 4 fellowships, 40 research assistantships, 17 teaching assistantships were awarded. Financial award application deadline: 2/20.
Dr. Michael B. Bragg, Head, 217-333-2651, *Fax:* 217-244-0720, *E-mail:* mbragg@uiuc.edu.
Application contact: Sandee G. Moore, Administrative Secretary, 217-333-2651, *Fax:* 217-244-0720, *E-mail:* sgmoore@ uiuc.edu. *Web site:* http://www.aae.uiuc.edu/

Find an in-depth description at www.petersons.com/gradchannel.

■ **UNIVERSITY OF KANSAS**

Graduate School, School of Engineering, Department of Aerospace Engineering, Lawrence, KS 66045

AWARDS ME, MS, DE, PhD.

Faculty: 8.
Students: 16 full-time (2 women), 10 part-time; includes 2 minority (both Asian Americans or Pacific Islanders), 15 international. Average age 29. 36 applicants, 64% accepted, 5 enrolled. In 2001, 3 master's, 1 doctorate awarded.
Degree requirements: For master's, thesis or alternative, exam; for doctorate, variable foreign language requirement, thesis/dissertation, comprehensive exam.
Entrance requirements: For master's, GRE, Michigan English Language Battery, TOEFL, minimum GPA of 3.0; for doctorate, GRE, Michigan English Language Battery, TOEFL, minimum GPA of 3.5. *Application deadline:* Applications are processed on a rolling basis. *Application fee:* $40 ($45 for international students).

Expenses: Tuition, state resident: full-time $2,722; part-time $113 per credit. Tuition, nonresident: full-time $8,586; part-time $358 per credit. Required fees: $551; $46 per credit. Tuition and fees vary according to campus/location, program and reciprocity agreements.
Financial support: In 2001–02, 13 research assistantships with partial tuition reimbursements (averaging $9,265 per year), 2 teaching assistantships with full and partial tuition reimbursements (averaging $9,000 per year) were awarded. Fellowships, career-related internships or fieldwork also available.
Faculty research: Control systems, aerodynamics, propulsion.
Mark Ewing, Chair, 785-864-4267, *Fax:* 785-864-3597, *E-mail:* aerohawk@ku.edu.
Application contact: Jan Roskam, Graduate Advisor, 785-864-4267, *Fax:* 785-864-3597, *E-mail:* aerohawk@ku.edu. *Web site:* http://www.engr.ku.edu/ae/

■ UNIVERSITY OF MARYLAND, COLLEGE PARK

Graduate Studies and Research, A. James Clark School of Engineering, Department of Aerospace Engineering, College Park, MD 20742

AWARDS M Eng, ME, MS, PhD. Part-time and evening/weekend programs available. Postbaccalaureate distance learning degree programs offered.

Faculty: 37 full-time (1 woman), 12 part-time/adjunct (0 women).
Students: 88 full-time (12 women), 33 part-time (2 women); includes 12 minority (4 African Americans, 6 Asian Americans or Pacific Islanders, 2 Hispanic Americans), 54 international. 140 applicants, 35% accepted, 28 enrolled. In 2001, 22 master's, 5 doctorates awarded.
Degree requirements: For master's, thesis optional; for doctorate, variable foreign language requirement, thesis/dissertation.
Entrance requirements: For master's and doctorate, GRE General Test (recommended), minimum GPA of 3.2. *Application deadline:* For fall admission, 8/1; for spring admission, 1/1. Applications are processed on a rolling basis. *Application fee:* $50 ($70 for international students). Electronic applications accepted.
Expenses: Tuition, state resident: part-time $289 per credit hour. Tuition, nonresident: part-time $448 per credit hour. One-time fee: $436 part-time. Full-time tuition and fees vary according to course load, campus/location and program.
Financial support: In 2001–02, 7 fellowships with full tuition reimbursements (averaging $12,509 per year), 83 research assistantships with tuition reimbursements (averaging $19,833 per year), 13 teaching assistantships with tuition reimbursements (averaging $16,214 per year) were awarded. Federal Work-Study and scholarships/grants also available. Support

available to part-time students. Financial award applicants required to submit FAFSA.
Faculty research: Aerodynamics and propulsion, structural mechanics, flight dynamics, rotor craft, space robotics.
Dr. William Fourney, Chairman, 301-405-1129, *Fax:* 301-314-9001.
Application contact: Trudy Lindsey, Director, Graduate Admissions and Records, 301-405-6991, *Fax:* 301-314-9305, *E-mail:* grschool@deans.umd.edu.

■ UNIVERSITY OF MARYLAND, COLLEGE PARK

Graduate Studies and Research, A. James Clark School of Engineering, Professional Program in Engineering, College Park, MD 20742

AWARDS Aerospace engineering (M Eng); chemical engineering (M Eng); civil engineering (M Eng); electrical engineering (M Eng); fire protection engineering (M Eng); materials science and engineering (M Eng); mechanical engineering (M Eng); reliability engineering (M Eng). Systems engineering (M Eng). Part-time and evening/weekend programs available. Postbaccalaureate distance learning degree programs offered.

Faculty: 11 part-time/adjunct (0 women).
Students: 19 full-time (4 women), 144 part-time (31 women); includes 41 minority (17 African Americans, 18 Asian Americans or Pacific Islanders, 6 Hispanic Americans), 27 international. 71 applicants, 80% accepted, 50 enrolled. In 2001, 64 degrees awarded.
Application deadline: For fall admission, 8/15; for spring admission, 1/10. Applications are processed on a rolling basis.
Application fee: $50 ($70 for international students). Electronic applications accepted.
Expenses: Tuition, state resident: part-time $289 per credit hour. Tuition, nonresident: part-time $448 per credit hour. One-time fee: $436 part-time. Full-time tuition and fees vary according to course load, campus/location and program.
Financial support: In 2001–02, 1 research assistantship with tuition reimbursement (averaging $20,655 per year), 5 teaching assistantships with tuition reimbursements (averaging $11,114 per year) were awarded. Fellowships, Federal Work-Study and scholarships/grants also available. Support available to part-time students. Financial award applicants required to submit FAFSA.
Dr. George Syrmos, Acting Director, 301-405-5256, *Fax:* 301-314-9477.
Application contact: Trudy Lindsey, Director, Graduate Admissions and Records, 301-405-6991, *Fax:* 301-314-9305, *E-mail:* grschool@deans.umd.edu.

■ UNIVERSITY OF MICHIGAN

Horace H. Rackham School of Graduate Studies, College of Engineering, Department of Aerospace Engineering, Ann Arbor, MI 48109

AWARDS M Eng, MS, MSE, PhD, Aerospace E. Part-time programs available.

Faculty: 21 full-time (0 women).
Students: 97 full-time (5 women), 6 part-time; includes 4 minority (1 African American, 1 Asian American or Pacific Islander, 1 Hispanic American, 1 Native American), 53 international. Average age 26. 212 applicants, 83% accepted, 39 enrolled. In 2001, 37 master's, 10 doctorates awarded. Terminal master's awarded for partial completion of doctoral program.
Degree requirements: For doctorate, oral defense of dissertation, preliminary exams. *Median time to degree:* Master's–1.5 years full-time, 4 years part-time; doctorate–3.5 years full-time.
Entrance requirements: For master's, GRE General Test; for doctorate, GRE General Test, master's degree. *Application deadline:* For fall and spring admission, 1/15 (priority date); for winter admission, 10/15 (priority date). Applications are processed on a rolling basis. *Application fee:* $55. Electronic applications accepted.
Financial support: In 2001–02, 8 fellowships with full tuition reimbursements (averaging $19,200 per year), 36 research assistantships with full tuition reimbursements (averaging $20,200 per year), 6 teaching assistantships with full tuition reimbursements (averaging $12,853 per year) were awarded. Federal Work-Study, health care benefits, and tuition waivers (full and partial) also available. Financial award application deadline: 1/15.
Faculty research: Fluid dynamics, combustion, propulsion, composites, aeroelasticity. *Total annual research expenditures:* $5.7 million.
Dr. David C. Hyland, Chair, 734-764-3311, *Fax:* 734-763-0578, *E-mail:* dihiland@umich.edu.
Application contact: Margaret A. Fillion, Student Services Assistant, 734-764-3311, *Fax:* 734-763-0578, *E-mail:* mafn@engin.umich.edu. *Web site:* http://www.engin.umich.edu/dept/aero/

■ UNIVERSITY OF MICHIGAN

Horace H. Rackham School of Graduate Studies, College of Engineering, Department of Atmospheric, Oceanic, and Space Sciences, Ann Arbor, MI 48109

AWARDS Atmospheric and space sciences (MS, PhD); oceanography: physical (MS, PhD); remote sensing and geoinformation (M Eng). Space and planetary physics (PhD). Space systems (M Eng). Part-time programs available.

Faculty: 22 full-time (2 women), 9 part-time/adjunct (0 women).

University of Michigan (continued)

Students: 43 full-time (19 women), 4 part-time (2 women); includes 3 minority (all Asian Americans or Pacific Islanders), 19 international. Average age 25. 63 applicants, 48% accepted, 15 enrolled. In 2001, 11 master's, 5 doctorates awarded. Terminal master's awarded for partial completion of doctoral program.
Degree requirements: For master's, thesis (for some programs); for doctorate, thesis/dissertation, oral defense of dissertation, preliminary exams.
Entrance requirements: For master's and doctorate, GRE General Test, TOEFL. *Application deadline:* For fall admission, 1/15 (priority date). Applications are processed on a rolling basis. *Application fee:* $60. Electronic applications accepted.
Financial support: In 2001–02, 11 fellowships with tuition reimbursements (averaging $20,200 per year), 19 research assistantships with tuition reimbursements (averaging $20,200 per year), 2 teaching assistantships with tuition reimbursements (averaging $19,500 per year) were awarded. Career-related internships or fieldwork, Federal Work-Study, and institutionally sponsored loans also available. Support available to part-time students. Financial award application deadline: 3/15; financial award applicants required to submit FAFSA.
Faculty research: Far ultraviolet images/Comet Shoemaker Levy 9, remote sensing of Earth's atmosphere and oceans/MEDSAT timed space mission to investigate Earth's atmosphere with Fabry-Perot interferometer, study of formation of ozone and other oxidants, Doppler lidar. *Total annual research expenditures:* $16.7 million.
Lennard Fisk, Chair, 734-647-3660, *Fax:* 734-764-4585, *E-mail:* lafisk@umich.edu.
Application contact: Margaret Reid, Academic Services Assistant, 734-647-3660, *Fax:* 734-764-4585, *E-mail:* aoss.um@umich.edu. *Web site:* http://www.engin.umich.edu/dept/aoss/

■ UNIVERSITY OF MINNESOTA, TWIN CITIES CAMPUS

Graduate School, Institute of Technology, Department of Aerospace Engineering and Mechanics, Minneapolis, MN 55455-0213

AWARDS Aerospace engineering (M Aero E, MS, PhD); mechanics (MS, PhD). Part-time programs available.

Faculty: 17 full-time (2 women).
Students: 65 full-time (12 women), 1 part-time, 44 international. Average age 24. 141 applicants, 57% accepted, 23 enrolled. In 2001, 7 master's, 2 doctorates awarded.
Degree requirements: For doctorate, thesis/dissertation. *Median time to degree:* Master's–2 years full-time; doctorate–5 years full-time.

Application deadline: For fall admission, 6/15; for spring admission, 10/15. Applications are processed on a rolling basis.
Application fee: $50 ($55 for international students). Electronic applications accepted.
Expenses: Tuition, state resident: full-time $2,932; part-time $489 per credit. Tuition, nonresident: full-time $5,758; part-time $960 per credit. Part-time tuition and fees vary according to course load, program and reciprocity agreements.
Financial support: In 2001–02, 1 fellowship with full tuition reimbursement (averaging $13,500 per year), 43 research assistantships with full and partial tuition reimbursements (averaging $13,500 per year), 13 teaching assistantships with full and partial tuition reimbursements (averaging $13,500 per year) were awarded. Partial departmental scholarships also available. Financial award application deadline: 1/31.
Faculty research: Fluid mechanics, solid and continuum mechanics, computational mechanics, dynamical systems and controls. *Total annual research expenditures:* $4.5 million.
William L. Garrard, Head, 612-625-8000, *Fax:* 612-626-1558, *E-mail:* dept@aem.umn.edu.
Application contact: Ruth A. Robinson, Graduate Program Coordinator, 612-625-5000, *Fax:* 612-626-1558, *E-mail:* dept@aem.umn.edu. *Web site:* http://www.aem.umn.edu/

Find an in-depth description at www.petersons.com/gradchannel.

■ UNIVERSITY OF MISSOURI–COLUMBIA

Graduate School, College of Engineering, Department of Mechanical and Aerospace Engineering, Columbia, MO 65211

AWARDS MS, PhD.

Faculty: 18 full-time (1 woman).
Students: 44 full-time (3 women), 12 part-time (1 woman); includes 4 minority (2 African Americans, 2 Hispanic Americans), 36 international. 23 applicants, 52% accepted. In 2001, 18 master's, 3 doctorates awarded.
Degree requirements: For master's, thesis; for doctorate, one foreign language, thesis/dissertation.
Entrance requirements: For master's and doctorate, GRE General Test, TOEFL, minimum GPA of 3.0. *Application deadline:* Applications are processed on a rolling basis. *Application fee:* $25 ($50 for international students).
Expenses: Tuition, state resident: part-time $179 per credit hour. Tuition, nonresident: part-time $539 per credit hour. Required fees: $122 per semester. Tuition and fees vary according to program.

Financial support: Research assistantships, teaching assistantships, institutionally sponsored loans available.
Dr. Uee Wan Cho, Director of Graduate Studies, 573-882-3778, *E-mail:* chou@missouri.edu. *Web site:* http://www.engineering.missouri.edu/mechanical.htm

■ UNIVERSITY OF MISSOURI–ROLLA

Graduate School, School of Engineering, Department of Mechanical and Aerospace Engineering and Engineering Mechanics, Program in Aerospace Engineering, Rolla, MO 65409-0910

AWARDS MS, PhD. Part-time programs available.

Degree requirements: For master's, thesis (for some programs); for doctorate, thesis/dissertation.
Entrance requirements: For master's, GRE General Test, TOEFL, minimum GPA of 3.0; for doctorate, GRE General Test, TOEFL, minimum GPA of 3.5. Electronic applications accepted.
Faculty research: Aerodynamics, stability and control, fluid dynamics and propulsion, acoustics, radiative transfer. *Web site:* http://www.maem.umr.edu/~grad/

■ UNIVERSITY OF NOTRE DAME

Graduate School, College of Engineering, Department of Aerospace and Mechanical Engineering, Notre Dame, IN 46556

AWARDS Aerospace and mechanical engineering (PhD); aerospace engineering (MS); mechanical engineering (MEME, MS). Part-time programs available.

Faculty: 27 full-time (0 women).
Students: 75 full-time (10 women), 4 part-time (1 woman); includes 2 minority (both Asian Americans or Pacific Islanders), 54 international. 147 applicants, 50% accepted, 24 enrolled. In 2001, 26 master's, 5 doctorates awarded. Terminal master's awarded for partial completion of doctoral program.
Degree requirements: For master's, thesis or alternative, comprehensive exam; for doctorate, thesis/dissertation. *Median time to degree:* Doctorate–6.2 years full-time.
Entrance requirements: For master's and doctorate, GRE General Test, TOEFL. *Application deadline:* For fall admission, 2/1 (priority date); for spring admission, 10/15. Applications are processed on a rolling basis. *Application fee:* $50. Electronic applications accepted.
Expenses: Tuition: Full-time $24,220; part-time $1,346 per credit hour. Required fees: $155.
Financial support: In 2001–02, 73 students received support, including 8 fellowships with full tuition reimbursements

available (averaging $18,000 per year), 32 research assistantships with full tuition reimbursements available (averaging $13,100 per year), 22 teaching assistantships with full tuition reimbursements available (averaging $13,100 per year); tuition waivers (full) and unspecified assistantships also available. Financial award application deadline: 2/1. **Faculty research:** Aerodynamics/fluid dynamics, design and manufacturing, controls/robotics, solid mechanics/biomechanics. *Total annual research expenditures:* $3.4 million. Dr. Robert C. Nelson, Chair, 574-631-5430, *Fax:* 574-631-8341, *E-mail:* amedept.1@nd.edu. **Application contact:** Dr. Terrence J. Akai, Director of Graduate Admissions, 574-631-7706, *Fax:* 574-631-4183, *E-mail:* gradad@nd.edu. *Web site:* http://www.nd.edu/~ame/

Find an in-depth description at www.petersons.com/gradchannel.

■ UNIVERSITY OF OKLAHOMA

Graduate College, College of Engineering, School of Aerospace and Mechanical Engineering, Program in Aerospace Engineering, Norman, OK 73019-0390

AWARDS MS, PhD.

Students: 5 full-time (0 women), 1 part-time; includes 2 minority (1 Asian American or Pacific Islander, 1 Hispanic American), 3 international. 15 applicants, 87% accepted, 1 enrolled. In 2001, 3 master's, 1 doctorate awarded. **Degree requirements:** For master's, thesis or alternative, comprehensive exam; for doctorate, thesis/dissertation, qualifying exam, comprehensive exam. **Entrance requirements:** For master's, GRE General Test, TOEFL, BS in engineering or physical sciences; for doctorate, GRE General Test, TOEFL, MS in aerospace engineering or equivalent. *Application deadline:* For fall admission, 6/1 (priority date). Applications are processed on a rolling basis. *Application fee:* $25 ($50 for international students). **Expenses:** Tuition, state resident: full-time $2,208; part-time $92 per credit hour. Tuition, nonresident: part-time $297 per credit hour. Tuition and fees vary according to course level, course load and program. **Financial support:** In 2001–02, 2 students received support; fellowships, research assistantships with partial tuition reimbursements available, teaching assistantships with partial tuition reimbursements available, career-related internships or fieldwork, Federal Work-Study, scholarships/grants, tuition waivers (partial), and unspecified assistantships available. Financial award application

deadline: 3/1; financial award applicants required to submit FAFSA. **Find an in-depth description at www.petersons.com/gradchannel.**

■ UNIVERSITY OF SOUTHERN CALIFORNIA

Graduate School, School of Engineering, Department of Aerospace and Mechanical Engineering, Los Angeles, CA 90089

AWARDS MS, PhD, Engr. Part-time and evening/weekend programs available. Postbaccalaureate distance learning degree programs offered. Terminal master's awarded for partial completion of doctoral program.

Degree requirements: For master's, thesis optional; for doctorate, thesis/dissertation. **Entrance requirements:** For master's, doctorate, and Engr, GRE General Test, GRE Subject Test. **Expenses:** Tuition: Full-time $25,060; part-time $844 per unit. Required fees: $473. **Faculty research:** Aerodynamics of air/ground vehicles, gas dynamics; astronautics and space science; geophysical and microgravity flows, planetary physics; power MEMs and MEMS. **Find an in-depth description at www.petersons.com/gradchannel.**

■ THE UNIVERSITY OF TENNESSEE

Graduate School, College of Engineering, Department of Mechanical and Aerospace Engineering and Engineering Science, Program in Aerospace Engineering, Knoxville, TN 37996

AWARDS MS, PhD. Part-time programs available.

Students: 13 full-time (2 women), 9 part-time; includes 1 minority (African American), 8 international. 37 applicants, 70% accepted. In 2001, 5 master's, 2 doctorates awarded. **Degree requirements:** For master's, thesis or alternative; for doctorate, thesis/dissertation. **Entrance requirements:** For master's and doctorate, TOEFL, minimum GPA of 2.7. *Application deadline:* For fall admission, 2/1 (priority date). Applications are processed on a rolling basis. *Application fee:* $35. Electronic applications accepted. **Expenses:** Tuition, state resident: full-time $4,280; part-time $233 per hour. Tuition, nonresident: full-time $12,066; part-time $666 per hour. Tuition and fees vary according to program. **Financial support:** Application deadline: 2/1. **Application contact:** Dr. Majid Keyhani, Graduate Representative, 865-974-4795, *E-mail:* keyhani@utk.edu.

■ THE UNIVERSITY OF TENNESSEE SPACE INSTITUTE

Graduate Programs, Program in Aerospace Engineering, Tullahoma, TN 37388-9700

AWARDS MS, PhD. Part-time programs available.

Faculty: 8 full-time (0 women). **Students:** 11 full-time (2 women), 6 part-time; includes 1 minority (African American), 4 international. 7 applicants, 100% accepted. In 2001, 1 degree awarded. **Degree requirements:** For master's, thesis (for some programs); for doctorate, one foreign language, thesis/dissertation. **Entrance requirements:** For master's and doctorate, GRE General Test. *Application deadline:* Applications are processed on a rolling basis. *Application fee:* $35. Electronic applications accepted. **Expenses:** Tuition, state resident: full-time $4,730; part-time $208 per semester hour. Tuition, nonresident: full-time $15,028; part-time $627 per semester hour. Required fees: $10 per semester hour. One-time fee: $35. **Financial support:** Fellowships with full and partial tuition reimbursements, research assistantships with full tuition reimbursements, career-related internships or fieldwork, Federal Work-Study, and tuition waivers (full and partial) available. Financial award applicants required to submit FAFSA. Dr. Roy Schulz, Degree Program Chairman, 931-393-7425, *Fax:* 931-393-7530, *E-mail:* rschuhlz@utsi.edu. **Application contact:** Dr. Alfonso Pujol, Assistant Vice President and Dean for Student Affairs, 931-393-7432, *Fax:* 931-393-7346, *E-mail:* apujol@utsi.edu.

■ THE UNIVERSITY OF TEXAS AT ARLINGTON

Graduate School, College of Engineering, Department of Mechanical and Aerospace Engineering, Program in Aerospace Engineering, Arlington, TX 76019

AWARDS M Engr, MS, PhD. Part-time and evening/weekend programs available. Postbaccalaureate distance learning degree programs offered (no on-campus study).

Students: 16 full-time (1 woman), 21 part-time (4 women); includes 3 minority (2 Asian Americans or Pacific Islanders, 1 Hispanic American), 15 international. 25 applicants, 96% accepted, 11 enrolled. In 2001, 3 master's, 1 doctorate awarded. Terminal master's awarded for partial completion of doctoral program. **Degree requirements:** For master's, thesis optional; for doctorate, thesis/dissertation, comprehensive exam. **Entrance requirements:** For master's, GRE General Test, TOEFL, minimum GPA of 3.3; for doctorate, GRE General

The University of Texas at Arlington (continued)
Test, TOEFL, minimum GPA of 3.5. *Application deadline:* For fall admission, 6/16. Applications are processed on a rolling basis. *Application fee:* $25 ($50 for international students).
Expenses: Tuition, area resident: Full-time $2,268. Tuition, nonresident: full-time $6,264. Required fees: $839. Tuition and fees vary according to course load.
Financial support: In 2001–02, 5 fellowships (averaging $1,000 per year), 6 research assistantships (averaging $12,000 per year), 8 teaching assistantships (averaging $14,000 per year) were awarded. Financial award application deadline: 6/1; financial award applicants required to submit FAFSA.
Application contact: Dr. Tom S. Lund, Graduate Adviser, 817-272-7053, *Fax:* 817-272-5010, *E-mail:* lund@chandra.uta.edu. *Web site:* http://www.mae.uta.edu/
Find an in-depth description at www.petersons.com/gradchannel.

■ **THE UNIVERSITY OF TEXAS AT AUSTIN**

Graduate School, College of Engineering, Department of Aerospace Engineering and Engineering Mechanics, Program in Aerospace Engineering, Austin, TX 78712-1111

AWARDS MSE, PhD.

Students: 101 full-time (16 women), 13 part-time (1 woman); includes 4 minority (1 African American, 2 Hispanic Americans, 1 Native American), 51 international. 166 applicants, 33% accepted, 22 enrolled. In 2001, 17 master's, 9 doctorates awarded.
Entrance requirements: For master's and doctorate, GRE General Test. *Application deadline:* For fall admission, 1/15 (priority date); for spring admission, 10/1 (priority date). Applications are processed on a rolling basis. *Application fee:* $50 ($75 for international students). Electronic applications accepted.
Expenses: Tuition, state resident: full-time $3,159. Tuition, nonresident: full-time $6,957. Tuition and fees vary according to program.
Financial support: In 2001–02, 87 students received support, including 15 fellowships with tuition reimbursements available, 71 research assistantships with full tuition reimbursements available, 19 teaching assistantships with tuition reimbursements available Financial award application deadline: 1/15.
Prof. David G. Hull, Graduate Advisor, 512-471-4908, *E-mail:* dghull@mail.utexas.edu.
Application contact: Nita Pollard, Graduate Coordinator, 512-471-7595, *Fax:* 512-471-3788, *E-mail:* ase.grad@

mail.ae.utexas.edu. *Web site:* http://www.ae.utexas.edu/
Find an in-depth description at www.petersons.com/gradchannel.

■ **UNIVERSITY OF VIRGINIA**

School of Engineering and Applied Science, Department of Mechanical and Aerospace Engineering, Charlottesville, VA 22903
AWARDS ME, MS, PhD.

Faculty: 30 full-time (1 woman).
Students: 51 full-time (6 women), 3 part-time (1 woman), 24 international. Average age 26. 160 applicants, 14% accepted, 11 enrolled. In 2001, 19 master's, 4 doctorates awarded.
Degree requirements: For master's, thesis (MS); for doctorate, thesis/dissertation, comprehensive exam.
Entrance requirements: For master's, GRE General Test; for doctorate, GRE General Test, TOEFL. *Application deadline:* For fall admission, 8/1 (priority date); for spring admission, 12/1. Applications are processed on a rolling basis. *Application fee:* $40. Electronic applications accepted.
Expenses: Tuition, state resident: full-time $3,988. Tuition, nonresident: full-time $17,078. Required fees: $1,190.
Financial support: Fellowships, research assistantships, teaching assistantships available. Financial award application deadline: 2/1; financial award applicants required to submit FAFSA.
Joseph A.C. Humprey, Chair, 434-924-7422, *Fax:* 434-982-2037, *E-mail:* mae-adm@virginia.edu.
Application contact: Kathryn Thornton, Assistant Dean, 434-924-3897, *Fax:* 434-982-2214, *E-mail:* inquiry@cs.virginia.edu. *Web site:* http://www.mae.virginia.edu/
Find an in-depth description at www.petersons.com/gradchannel.

■ **UNIVERSITY OF WASHINGTON**

Graduate School, College of Engineering, Department of Aeronautics and Astronautics, Seattle, WA 98195
AWARDS MAE, MSAA, PhD. Part-time programs available. Postbaccalaureate distance learning degree programs offered (minimal on-campus study).

Faculty: 18 full-time.
Students: 54 full-time (5 women), 17 part-time (5 women); includes 2 minority (both Asian Americans or Pacific Islanders), 20 international. Average age 28. 83 applicants, 90% accepted, 17 enrolled. In 2001, 23 master's, 7 doctorates awarded.
Degree requirements: For master's, thesis optional; for doctorate, thesis/dissertation, registration. *Median time to degree:* Master's–1.75 years full-time, 2.5 years part-time; doctorate–4.92 years full-time, 9.75 years part-time.

Entrance requirements: For master's, GRE General Test, TOEFL, minimum GPA of 3.0; for doctorate, GRE General Test, TOEFL, minimum GPA of 3.35. *Application deadline:* For fall admission, 7/1; for winter admission, 11/1; for spring admission, 2/1. Applications are processed on a rolling basis. *Application fee:* $50. Electronic applications accepted.
Expenses: Tuition, state resident: full-time $5,539. Tuition, nonresident: full-time $14,376. Required fees: $390. Tuition and fees vary according to course load and program.
Financial support: In 2001–02, 7 fellowships (averaging $4,178 per year), 27 research assistantships with full tuition reimbursements (averaging $11,682 per year), 13 teaching assistantships with full tuition reimbursements (averaging $11,403 per year) were awarded. Federal Work-Study, health care benefits, tuition waivers (full), and unspecified assistantships also available. Financial award application deadline: 2/15.
Faculty research: Space systems, aircraft systems, energy systems, composites/structures, fluid dynamics. *Total annual research expenditures:* $4.2 million.
Dr. Adam P. Bruckner, Chair, 206-543-1950, *Fax:* 206-543-0217, *E-mail:* bruckner@aa.washington.edu.
Application contact: Wanda Frederick, Manager of Graduate Programs and External Relations, 206-616-1113, *Fax:* 206-543-0217, *E-mail:* wanda@aa.washington.edu. *Web site:* http://www.aa.washington.edu/

■ **UTAH STATE UNIVERSITY**

School of Graduate Studies, College of Engineering, Department of Mechanical and Aerospace Engineering, Logan, UT 84322
AWARDS Aerospace engineering (MS, PhD); mechanical engineering (ME, MS, PhD).

Faculty: 14 full-time (0 women), 3 part-time/adjunct (1 woman).
Students: 31 full-time (4 women), 18 part-time (5 women), 27 international. Average age 25. 186 applicants, 24% accepted. In 2001, 11 degrees awarded. Terminal master's awarded for partial completion of doctoral program.
Degree requirements: For master's, thesis (for some programs); for doctorate, thesis/dissertation.
Entrance requirements: For master's, GRE General Test, TOEFL, minimum GPA of 3.0; for doctorate, GRE General Test, GRE Subject Test, TOEFL, minimum GPA of 3.0. *Application deadline:* For fall admission, 3/15 (priority date); for spring admission, 10/15. Applications are processed on a rolling basis. *Application fee:* $40.
Expenses: Tuition, state resident: full-time $1,693. Tuition, nonresident: full-time $4,233. Required fees: $501. Tuition and fees vary according to program.

Financial support: In 2001–02, 25 students received support, including 1 fellowship with partial tuition reimbursement available (averaging $12,000 per year), 20 research assistantships with partial tuition reimbursements available (averaging $12,000 per year), 5 teaching assistantships with partial tuition reimbursements available (averaging $10,000 per year); Federal Work-Study and institutionally sponsored loans also available. Financial award application deadline: 3/15.
Faculty research: In-space instruments, cryogenic cooling, thermal science, space structures, composite materials.
Dr. J. Clair Batty, Head, 435-797-2868, *Fax:* 435-797-2417.
Application contact: Joan P. Smith, Graduate Student Adviser, 435-797-0330, *Fax:* 435-797-2417, *E-mail:* jpsmith@mae.usu.edu. *Web site:* http://www.mae.usu.edu/

■ VIRGINIA POLYTECHNIC INSTITUTE AND STATE UNIVERSITY

Graduate School, College of Engineering, Department of Aerospace and Ocean Engineering, Program in Aerospace Engineering, Blacksburg, VA 24061

AWARDS M Eng, MS, PhD.

Faculty: 18 full-time (0 women), 2 part-time/adjunct (0 women).
Students: 67 full-time (3 women), 12 part-time (2 women); includes 5 minority (1 African American, 2 Asian Americans or Pacific Islanders, 2 Hispanic Americans), 38 international. 116 applicants, 46% accepted. In 2001, 16 master's, 9 doctorates awarded.
Degree requirements: For master's, thesis (for some programs); for doctorate, thesis/dissertation.
Entrance requirements: For master's and doctorate, GRE, TOEFL. *Application deadline:* For fall admission, 12/1 (priority date). Applications are processed on a rolling basis. *Application fee:* $45. Electronic applications accepted.
Expenses: Tuition, state resident: part-time $241 per hour. Tuition, nonresident: part-time $406 per hour. Tuition and fees vary according to program.
Financial support: In 2001–02, 8 fellowships with full tuition reimbursements (averaging $1,800 per year), research assistantships with full tuition reimbursements (averaging $1,450 per year) were awarded. Institutionally sponsored loans and unspecified assistantships also available. Financial award application deadline: 4/1.
Faculty research: Aerodynamics, spacecraft attitude control formation flying, multidisciplinary design. *Total annual research expenditures:* $3.5 million.
Application contact: Dr. Frederick H. Lutze, Chairman, Graduate Committee,

540-231-6409, *Fax:* 540-231-9632, *E-mail:* lutze@aoe.vt.edu.

■ WEBSTER UNIVERSITY

School of Business and Technology, Department of Business, St. Louis, MO 63119-3194

AWARDS Business (MA, MBA); computer resources and information management (MA, MBA); computer science/distributed systems (MS); environmental management (MS); finance (MA, MBA); health care management (MA); health services management (MA, MBA); human resources development (MA, MBA); human resources management (MA); international business (MA, MBA); management (MA, MBA); marketing (MA, MBA); procurement and acquisitions management (MA, MBA); public administration (MA); real estate management (MA, MBA). Security management (MA, MBA). Space systems management (MA, MBA, MS); telecommunications management (MA, MBA).

Students: 1,415 full-time (661 women), 3,483 part-time (1,566 women); includes 1,604 minority (1,183 African Americans, 166 Asian Americans or Pacific Islanders, 220 Hispanic Americans, 35 Native Americans), 606 international. Average age 33. In 2001, 1439 degrees awarded. *Application deadline:* Applications are processed on a rolling basis. *Application fee:* $25 ($50 for international students).
Expenses: Tuition: Full-time $7,164; part-time $398 per credit hour.
Financial support: Federal Work-Study available. Support available to part-time students. Financial award application deadline: 4/1; financial award applicants required to submit FAFSA.
Steve Hinson, Chair, 314-968-7017, *Fax:* 314-968-7077.
Application contact: Denise Harrell, Associate Director of Graduate and Evening Student Admissions, 314-968-6983, *Fax:* 314-968-7116, *E-mail:* gadmit@webster.edu.

■ WEST VIRGINIA UNIVERSITY

College of Engineering and Mineral Resources, Department of Mechanical and Aerospace Engineering, Program in Aerospace Engineering, Morgantown, WV 26506

AWARDS Aerospace engineering (MSAE, PhD); engineering (MSE). Part-time programs available.

Students: 5 full-time (2 women), 2 international. Average age 28. 20 applicants, 85% accepted. In 2001, 4 master's, 1 doctorate awarded. Terminal master's awarded for partial completion of doctoral program.
Degree requirements: For master's, thesis/dissertation; for doctorate, thesis/dissertation, comprehensive exam.
Entrance requirements: For master's and doctorate, GRE General Test, TOEFL,

minimum GPA of 3.0. *Application deadline:* For fall admission, 4/1 (priority date); for spring admission, 10/1. Applications are processed on a rolling basis. *Application fee:* $45.
Expenses: Tuition, state resident: full-time $2,791. Tuition, nonresident: full-time $8,659. Required fees: $1,002. Tuition and fees vary according to program.
Financial support: In 2001–02, 1 research assistantship, 3 teaching assistantships were awarded. Fellowships, Federal Work-Study, institutionally sponsored loans, and tuition waivers (partial) also available. Financial award application deadline: 2/1; financial award applicants required to submit FAFSA.
Faculty research: Transonic aerodynamics, viscous/inviscid interactions, combustion, aerospace structures, space mechanics.
Application contact: Dr. Gary J. Morris, Graduate Director and Interim Chair, 304-293-4111 Ext. 2342, *Fax:* 304-293-8823, *E-mail:* gary.morris@mail.wvu.edu. *Web site:* http://www.cemr.wvu.edu/

■ WICHITA STATE UNIVERSITY

Graduate School, College of Engineering, Department of Aerospace Engineering, Wichita, KS 67260

AWARDS MS, PhD. Part-time programs available.

Faculty: 10 full-time (0 women).
Students: 24 full-time (2 women), 73 part-time (11 women); includes 10 minority (8 Asian Americans or Pacific Islanders, 2 Hispanic Americans), 35 international. Average age 30. 53 applicants, 75% accepted, 17 enrolled. In 2001, 13 master's, 6 doctorates awarded. Terminal master's awarded for partial completion of doctoral program.
Degree requirements: For master's, oral or written exam, thesis optional; for doctorate, one foreign language, thesis/dissertation, comprehensive exam.
Entrance requirements: For master's and doctorate, GRE, TOEFL. *Application deadline:* For fall admission, 7/1 (priority date); for spring admission, 1/1. Applications are processed on a rolling basis. *Application fee:* $25 ($40 for international students). Electronic applications accepted.
Expenses: Tuition, state resident: full-time $1,888; part-time $105 per credit. Tuition, nonresident: full-time $6,129; part-time $341 per credit. Required fees: $345; $19 per credit. $17 per semester. Tuition and fees vary according to course load and program.
Financial support: In 2001–02, 20 research assistantships (averaging $8,239 per year), 3 teaching assistantships with full tuition reimbursements (averaging $5,666 per year) were awarded. Fellowships, Federal Work-Study, institutionally sponsored loans, and unspecified assistantships also available. Financial award application deadline: 4/1.

Wichita State University (continued)
Faculty research: Composite materials and structures, electro-impulse de-icing, computational fluid dynamics, stall-spin aerodynamics and simulation, water droplet trajectories on and around aircraft surfaces.
Dr. Walter Horn, Chairperson, 316-978-3410, *Fax:* 316-978-3307, *E-mail:* walter.horn@wichita.edu. *Web site:* http://www.wichita.edu/

AVIATION

■ CENTRAL MISSOURI STATE UNIVERSITY

School of Graduate Studies, College of Applied Sciences and Technology, Department of Power and Transportation, Warrensburg, MO 64093

AWARDS Aviation safety (MS). Part-time programs available.

Faculty: 5 full-time (0 women), 6 part-time/adjunct (1 woman).
Students: 15 full-time (5 women), 29 part-time (4 women); includes 2 minority (both African Americans), 8 international. Average age 33. 19 applicants, 89% accepted. In 2001, 33 degrees awarded.
Degree requirements: For master's, comprehensive exam.
Entrance requirements: For master's, minimum GPA of 2.5. *Application deadline:* Applications are processed on a rolling basis. *Application fee:* $25 ($50 for international students).
Expenses: Tuition, area resident: Full-time $4,200; part-time $175 per credit hour. Tuition, nonresident: full-time $8,352; part-time $348 per credit hour.
Financial support: In 2001–02, 1 research assistantship with full and partial tuition reimbursement (averaging $8,000 per year), 3 teaching assistantships with full and partial tuition reimbursements (averaging $6,875 per year) were awarded. Federal Work-Study, scholarships/grants, unspecified assistantships, and administrative and laboratory assistantships also available. Support available to part-time students. Financial award application deadline: 3/1; financial award applicants required to submit FAFSA.
Faculty research: Survey of aircraft manufacturing to determine the extent of the use of depleted uranium in aircraft control counterweights, computer assisted fluid power instruction, effects of composition of aftermarket auto brake pads on performance, continuous process improvement program at CMSU-a case study.
Dr. Scott Wilson, Interim Chair, 660-543-4975, *Fax:* 660-543-4979, *E-mail:* swilson@cmsu1.cmsu.edu. *Web site:* http://www.cmsu.edu/

■ MIDDLE TENNESSEE STATE UNIVERSITY

College of Graduate Studies, College of Basic and Applied Sciences, Department of Aerospace, Murfreesboro, TN 37132

AWARDS Aerospace education (M Ed); airport/airline management (MS); asset management (MS); aviation administration (MS). Part-time and evening/weekend programs available.

Students: 5 full-time, 22 part-time; includes 4 minority (2 African Americans, 2 Hispanic Americans). Average age 33. 4 applicants, 100% accepted. In 2001, 5 degrees awarded.
Degree requirements: For master's, one foreign language, comprehensive exam.
Entrance requirements: For master's, GRE General Test or MAT. *Application deadline:* For fall admission, 8/1 (priority date). *Application fee:* $25.
Expenses: Tuition, state resident: full-time $1,716; part-time $191 per hour. Tuition, nonresident: full-time $4,952; part-time $461 per hour. Required fees: $14 per hour. $58 per semester.
Financial support: In 2001–02, 2 teaching assistantships were awarded. Financial award application deadline: 5/1.
Paul Craig, Interim Chair, 615-898-2788, *E-mail:* rferrara@frank.mtsu.edu.

■ UNIVERSITY OF NEW HAVEN

Graduate School, School of Public Safety and Professional Studies, Program in Aviation Science, West Haven, CT 06516-1916

AWARDS MS.

Students: 1 full-time (0 women), 4 part-time. In 2001, 1 degree awarded.
Degree requirements: For master's, thesis or alternative.
Application fee: $50.
Expenses: Tuition: Full-time $12,015; part-time $445 per credit hour. Required fees: $30. One-time fee: $100 full-time.
Financial support: Application deadline: 5/1.
George D. Lainas, Director, 203-932-7472.

■ UNIVERSITY OF NORTH DAKOTA

Graduate School, John D. Odegard School of Aerospace Sciences, Program in Aviation, Grand Forks, ND 58202

AWARDS MS.

Students: 2 full-time (0 women), 1 part-time. 3 applicants, 100% accepted, 3 enrolled.
Degree requirements: For master's, comprehensive exam.
Application deadline: For fall admission, 3/1 (priority date); for spring admission, 10/15

(priority date). Applications are processed on a rolling basis. *Application fee:* $30.
Expenses: Tuition, state resident: full-time $3,298. Tuition, nonresident: full-time $7,998.
Financial support: Application deadline: 3/15.
Dr. Paul D. Lindseth, Director, 701-777-2917, *Fax:* 701-777-3016, *E-mail:* lindseth@aero.und.edu. *Web site:* http://www.aero.und.edu/avitms/

■ THE UNIVERSITY OF TENNESSEE

Graduate School, Intercollegiate Programs, Program in Aviation Systems, Knoxville, TN 37996

AWARDS MS. Part-time programs available. Postbaccalaureate distance learning degree programs offered (no on-campus study).

Students: 11 full-time (1 woman), 47 part-time (3 women); includes 5 minority (2 African Americans, 3 Hispanic Americans), 3 international. 13 applicants, 31% accepted. In 2001, 21 degrees awarded.
Degree requirements: For master's, thesis optional.
Entrance requirements: For master's, TOEFL, minimum GPA of 2.7. *Application deadline:* For fall admission, 2/1 (priority date). Applications are processed on a rolling basis. *Application fee:* $35. Electronic applications accepted.
Expenses: Tuition, state resident: full-time $4,280; part-time $233 per hour. Tuition, nonresident: full-time $12,066; part-time $666 per hour. Tuition and fees vary according to program.
Financial support: Application deadline: 2/1.
Dr. Ralph Kimberlin, Head, 931-393-7411, *Fax:* 931-393-7409, *E-mail:* rkimberl@utsi.edu.

■ THE UNIVERSITY OF TENNESSEE SPACE INSTITUTE

Graduate Programs, Program in Aviation Systems, Tullahoma, TN 37388-9700

AWARDS MS.

Faculty: 4 full-time (0 women), 1 part-time/adjunct (0 women).
Students: 4 full-time (0 women), 50 part-time (6 women); includes 1 minority (Asian American or Pacific Islander), 1 international. 15 applicants, 93% accepted, 14 enrolled. In 2001, 22 degrees awarded.
Degree requirements: For master's, thesis (for some programs).
Application deadline: Applications are processed on a rolling basis. *Application fee:* $35.
Expenses: Tuition, state resident: full-time $4,730; part-time $208 per semester hour. Tuition, nonresident: full-time $15,028; part-time $627 per semester hour. Required fees: $10 per semester hour. One-time fee: $35.

Financial support: Fellowships, research assistantships, career-related internships or fieldwork, Federal Work-Study, and tuition waivers (full and partial) available. Financial award applicants required to submit FAFSA.

Faculty research: Helicopter terminal instrument procedures, alternate fuels for general aviation, aircraft certification. *Total annual research expenditures:* $150,000. Dr. Frank Collins, Co-Chairman, 931-393-7459, *Fax:* 931-393-7533, *E-mail:* fcollins@utsi.edu.

Application contact: Dr. Alfonso Pujol, Assistant Vice President and Dean for Student Affairs, 931-393-7432, *Fax:* 931-393-7346, *E-mail:* apujol@utsi.edu.

Agricultural Engineering

AGRICULTURAL ENGINEERING

■ COLORADO STATE UNIVERSITY

Graduate School, College of Engineering, Department of Civil Engineering, Program in Bioresource and Agricultural Engineering, Fort Collins, CO 80523-0015

AWARDS MS, PhD. Part-time programs available.

Faculty: 7 full-time (0 women).
Students: 5 full-time (4 women), 11 part-time (1 woman), 5 international. Average age 33. 14 applicants, 50% accepted, 2 enrolled. In 2001, 2 master's, 1 doctorate awarded. Terminal master's awarded for partial completion of doctoral program.
Degree requirements: For master's, thesis or alternative; for doctorate, thesis/dissertation.
Entrance requirements: For master's and doctorate, GRE General Test, TOEFL, minimum GPA of 3.0. *Application deadline:* For fall admission, 3/1 (priority date); for spring admission, 9/1 (priority date). Applications are processed on a rolling basis. *Application fee:* $30. Electronic applications accepted.
Expenses: Tuition, state resident: full-time $2,880; part-time $160 per credit. Tuition, nonresident: full-time $11,412; part-time $634 per credit. Required fees: $750; $34 per credit.
Financial support: In 2001–02, 7 students received support, including 1 fellowship, 6 research assistantships (averaging $15,600 per year), 2 teaching assistantships (averaging $11,700 per year); career-related internships or fieldwork, Federal Work-Study, and institutionally sponsored loans also available.
Faculty research: Irrigation, water quality, environmental engineering, groundwater, farm machinery. *Total annual research expenditures:* $660,000.
Application contact: Laurie Howard, Student Adviser, 970-491-5844, *Fax:* 970-491-7727, *E-mail:* lhoward@engr.colostate.edu.

■ CORNELL UNIVERSITY

Graduate School, Graduate Fields of Agriculture and Life Sciences and Graduate Fields of Engineering, Field of Agricultural and Biological Engineering, Ithaca, NY 14853-0001

AWARDS Biological engineering (M Eng, MPS, MS, PhD); energy (M Eng, MPS, MS, PhD); environmental engineering (M Eng, MPS, MS, PhD); environmental management (MPS); food processing engineering (M Eng, MPS, MS, PhD); international agriculture (M Eng, MPS, MS, PhD); local roads (M Eng, MPS, MS, PhD); machine systems (M Eng, MPS, MS, PhD). Soil and water engineering (M Eng, MPS, MS, PhD). Structures and environment (M Eng, MPS, MS, PhD).

Faculty: 28 full-time.
Students: 68 full-time (33 women); includes 12 minority (2 African Americans, 9 Asian Americans or Pacific Islanders, 1 Hispanic American), 27 international. 79 applicants, 56% accepted. In 2001, 15 master's, 1 doctorate awarded. Terminal master's awarded for partial completion of doctoral program.
Degree requirements: For master's, thesis (MS); for doctorate, thesis/dissertation.
Entrance requirements: For master's, 3 letters of recommendation (M Eng, MPS, MS); for doctorate, GRE General Test, TOEFL, 3 letters of recommendation. *Application deadline:* For fall admission, 1/15; for spring admission, 10/1. Applications are processed on a rolling basis. *Application fee:* $65. Electronic applications accepted.
Expenses: Tuition: Full-time $25,970. Required fees: $50.
Financial support: In 2001–02, 46 students received support, including 10 fellowships with full tuition reimbursements available, 26 research assistantships with full tuition reimbursements available, 10 teaching assistantships with full tuition reimbursements available; institutionally sponsored loans, scholarships/grants, tuition waivers (full and partial), and unspecified assistantships also available. Financial award applicants required to submit FAFSA.
Faculty research: Biological and food engineering, environmental, soil and water engineering, international agricultural engineering, structures and controlled environments, machine systems and energy.
Application contact: Graduate Field Assistant, 607-255-2173, *Fax:* 607-255-4080, *E-mail:* abengradfield@cornell.edu. *Web site:* http://www.gradschool.cornell.edu/grad/fields_1/ag-bioengr.html

■ IOWA STATE UNIVERSITY OF SCIENCE AND TECHNOLOGY

Graduate College, College of Engineering, Department of Agricultural and Biosystems Engineering, Ames, IA 50011

AWARDS M Eng, MS, PhD.

Faculty: 23 full-time, 3 part-time/adjunct.
Students: 26 full-time (5 women), 15 part-time (2 women); includes 3 minority (1 African American, 2 Hispanic Americans), 22 international. 24 applicants, 25% accepted, 4 enrolled. In 2001, 8 master's, 4 doctorates awarded.
Degree requirements: For master's, thesis (for some programs); for doctorate, thesis/dissertation. *Median time to degree:* Master's–1.8 years full-time; doctorate–5.2 years full-time.
Application deadline: For fall admission, 5/1 (priority date); for spring admission, 10/1. Applications are processed on a rolling basis. *Application fee:* $20 ($50 for international students). Electronic applications accepted.
Expenses: Tuition, state resident: full-time $1,851. Tuition, nonresident: full-time $5,449. Tuition and fees vary according to program.
Financial support: In 2001–02, 26 research assistantships with partial tuition reimbursements (averaging $14,893 per year), 1 teaching assistantship with partial tuition reimbursement (averaging $12,534 per year) were awarded. Fellowships, scholarships/grants, health care benefits, and unspecified assistantships also available.
Faculty research: Grain processing and quality, tillage systems, simulation and controls, water management, environmental quality.

Iowa State University of Science and Technology (continued)
Ramesh Kanwar, Head, 515-294-0462, *Fax:* 515-294-6633, *E-mail:* ageng@iastate.edu.
Application contact: Dr. James L. Baker, Director of Graduate Education, 515-294-4025, *E-mail:* ageng@iastate.edu. *Web site:* http://www.eng.iastate.edu/coe/grad.asp/

■ KANSAS STATE UNIVERSITY

Graduate School, College of Agriculture, Department of Grain Science and Industry, Manhattan, KS 66506

AWARDS MS, PhD. Part-time programs available.

Faculty: 18 full-time (4 women).
Students: 32 full-time (14 women), 11 part-time (4 women); includes 3 minority (1 Asian American or Pacific Islander, 1 Hispanic American, 1 Native American), 30 international. Average age 32. 13 applicants, 23% accepted, 3 enrolled. In 2001, 7 master's, 7 doctorates awarded. Terminal master's awarded for partial completion of doctoral program.
Degree requirements: For master's, thesis, oral exam; for doctorate, thesis/dissertation, preliminary exam.
Application deadline: For fall admission, 2/1 (priority date); for spring admission, 10/1. Applications are processed on a rolling basis. *Application fee:* $0 ($25 for international students).
Expenses: Tuition, state resident: part-time $113 per credit hour. Tuition, nonresident: part-time $358 per credit hour.
Financial support: In 2001–02, 28 research assistantships (averaging $9,500 per year), 3 teaching assistantships (averaging $7,000 per year) were awarded. Federal Work-Study, institutionally sponsored loans, and scholarships/grants also available. Support available to part-time students. Financial award application deadline: 3/1; financial award applicants required to submit FAFSA.
Faculty research: Particle management, grain and cereal product research, value added products using soy beans and wheat in plastics or adhesives, grain stored wheat. *Total annual research expenditures:* $500,000.
Brendan J. Donnelly, Head, 785-532-6161, *Fax:* 785-532-7010, *E-mail:* bjd@wheat.ksu.edu.
Application contact: Katherine Tilley, Graduate Program Director, 785-532-4811, *Fax:* 785-532-7010, *E-mail:* kat@wheat.ksu.edu. *Web site:* http://www.oznet.ksu.edu/dp-grsi/

■ KANSAS STATE UNIVERSITY

Graduate School, College of Engineering, Department of Biological and Agricultural Engineering, Manhattan, KS 66506

AWARDS MS, PhD.

Faculty: 25 full-time (1 woman).
Students: 20 full-time (7 women), 6 part-time (2 women), 17 international. 11 applicants, 82% accepted, 8 enrolled. In 2001, 1 master's, 3 doctorates awarded. Terminal master's awarded for partial completion of doctoral program.
Degree requirements: For master's and doctorate, thesis/dissertation.
Entrance requirements: For master's, GRE, TOEFL, bachelor's degree in agricultural engineering; for doctorate, GRE, TOEFL. *Application deadline:* For fall admission, 3/1; for spring admission, 10/1. Applications are processed on a rolling basis. *Application fee:* $0 ($25 for international students). Electronic applications accepted.
Expenses: Tuition, state resident: part-time $113 per credit hour. Tuition, nonresident: part-time $358 per credit hour.
Financial support: In 2001–02, 19 research assistantships (averaging $10,000 per year) were awarded; fellowships, teaching assistantships, Federal Work-Study, institutionally sponsored loans, and scholarships/grants also available. Support available to part-time students. Financial award application deadline: 3/1; financial award applicants required to submit FAFSA.
Faculty research: Water quality, animal production systems, agricultural machinery, irrigation systems, grain processing. *Total annual research expenditures:* $2.3 million.
Dr. James K. Koelliker, Head, 785-532-5580, *Fax:* 785-532-5825, *E-mail:* contact-1@bae.ksu.edu.
Application contact: Naiqian Zhang, Graduate Coordinator, 785-532-5580, *Fax:* 785-532-5825, *E-mail:* contact-1@bae.ksu.edu. *Web site:* http://www.bae.ksu.edu/

■ LOUISIANA STATE UNIVERSITY AND AGRICULTURAL AND MECHANICAL COLLEGE

Graduate School, College of Agriculture, Department of Biological and Agricultural Engineering, Baton Rouge, LA 70803

AWARDS Biological and agricultural engineering (MSBAE); engineering science (MS, PhD). Part-time programs available.

Faculty: 9 full-time (2 women).
Students: 9 full-time (5 women), 4 part-time (2 women); includes 1 minority (African American), 8 international. Average age 27. 13 applicants, 54% accepted, 5 enrolled. In 2001, 3 degrees awarded. Terminal master's awarded for partial completion of doctoral program.
Degree requirements: For master's and doctorate, thesis/dissertation.
Entrance requirements: For master's and doctorate, GRE General Test, minimum GPA of 3.0. *Application deadline:* For fall admission, 1/25 (priority date). Applications are processed on a rolling basis. *Application fee:* $25.
Expenses: Tuition, state resident: full-time $2,551. Tuition, nonresident: full-time $5,551. Required fees: $854. Part-time tuition and fees vary according to course load.
Financial support: In 2001–02, 9 research assistantships with partial tuition reimbursements (averaging $14,667 per year) were awarded; fellowships, teaching assistantships with partial tuition reimbursements, career-related internships or fieldwork also available. Financial award application deadline: 7/1; financial award applicants required to submit FAFSA.
Faculty research: Machine development, aquaculture, environmental engineering, microprocessor applications, ergonomics engineering, bioprocessing, hydrology, biosensors, food engineering. *Total annual research expenditures:* $11,895.
Dr. Richard Bengtson, Acting Head, 225-578-3153, *Fax:* 225-578-3492, *E-mail:* bengston@bae.lsu.edu.
Application contact: Dr. David C. Blouin, Associate Dean, 225-578-8303, *Fax:* 225-578-2526, *E-mail:* dblouin@lsu.edu. *Web site:* http://www.coa.lsu.edu/bioen/bioen.html

■ MICHIGAN STATE UNIVERSITY

Graduate School, College of Agriculture and Natural Resources and College of Engineering, Department of Agricultural Engineering, Program in Agricultural Technology and Systems Management, East Lansing, MI 48824

AWARDS MS, PhD.

Students: 1. Average age 31.
Entrance requirements: For master's, GRE General Test; for doctorate, GRE General Test, MS. *Application deadline:* Applications are processed on a rolling basis. *Application fee:* $30 ($40 for international students). Electronic applications accepted.
Expenses: Tuition, state resident: part-time $244 per credit hour. Tuition, nonresident: part-time $494 per credit hour. Required fees: $268 per semester. Tuition and fees vary according to course load, degree level and program.
Financial support: Applicants required to submit FAFSA.
Dr. Ajit K. Srivastava, Chairperson, Department of Agricultural Engineering, 517-355-4720, *Fax:* 517-432-2892, *E-mail:* srivasta@pilot.msu.edu.

■ MICHIGAN STATE UNIVERSITY

Graduate School, College of Agriculture and Natural Resources and College of Engineering, Department of Agricultural Engineering, Program in Biosystems Engineering, East Lansing, MI 48824

AWARDS MS, PhD.

Students: 22 full-time (6 women); includes 3 minority (2 Asian Americans or Pacific Islanders, 1 Hispanic American), 8 international. Average age 29.
Degree requirements: For doctorate, thesis/dissertation.
Entrance requirements: For master's, GRE General Test; for doctorate, GRE General test, MS. *Application deadline:* Applications are processed on a rolling basis. *Application fee:* $30 ($40 for international students). Electronic applications accepted.
Expenses: Tuition, state resident: part-time $244 per credit hour. Tuition, nonresident: part-time $494 per credit hour. Required fees: $268 per semester. Tuition and fees vary according to course load, degree level and program.
Financial support: Applicants required to submit FAFSA.

■ NORTH CAROLINA AGRICULTURAL AND TECHNICAL STATE UNIVERSITY

Graduate School, College of Engineering, Department of Architectural, Agricultural, Civil and Environmental Engineering, Greensboro, NC 27411

AWARDS MSAE, MSCE, MSE. Part-time programs available.

Faculty: 14 full-time (1 woman), 4 part-time/adjunct (0 women).
Students: 28 full-time (10 women), 10 part-time (4 women), 12 international. Average age 24. 22 applicants, 41% accepted. In 2001, 4 degrees awarded.
Degree requirements: For master's, thesis defense.
Entrance requirements: For master's, GRE General Test, GRE Subject Test (recommended), TOEFL (MSCE). *Application deadline:* For fall admission, 7/1; for spring admission, 1/9. Applications are processed on a rolling basis. *Application fee:* $35.
Financial support: In 2001–02, 1 fellowship (averaging $12,000 per year), 3 research assistantships (averaging $12,000 per year), 2 teaching assistantships (averaging $10,000 per year) were awarded. Career-related internships or fieldwork and unspecified assistantships also available.
Faculty research: Lightning, indoor air quality, material behavior HVAC controls, structural masonry systems. *Total annual research expenditures:* $800,000.

Dr. Peter Rojeski, Chairperson, 336-344-7575, *Fax:* 336-344-7126.
Application contact: Dr. W. Mark McGinley, Graduate Coordinator, 336-334-7575, *Fax:* 336-334-7126, *E-mail:* mcginley@garfield.ncat.edu.

■ NORTH CAROLINA STATE UNIVERSITY

Graduate School, College of Agriculture and Life Sciences and College of Engineering, Department of Biological and Agricultural Engineering, Raleigh, NC 27695

AWARDS MBAE, MS, PhD. Part-time programs available.

Faculty: 33 full-time (2 women), 13 part-time/adjunct (2 women).
Students: 32 full-time (13 women), 8 part-time (3 women); includes 6 minority (4 African Americans, 1 Asian American or Pacific Islander, 1 Hispanic American), 7 international. Average age 30. 21 applicants, 29% accepted. In 2001, 5 master's, 1 doctorate awarded.
Degree requirements: For master's, thesis or alternative; for doctorate, thesis/dissertation.
Entrance requirements: For master's and doctorate, GRE (international applicants only), TOEFL. *Application deadline:* For fall admission, 6/25. Applications are processed on a rolling basis. *Application fee:* $45.
Expenses: Tuition, state resident: full-time $1,748. Tuition, nonresident: full-time $6,904.
Financial support: In 2001–02, 3 fellowships (averaging $7,058 per year), 25 research assistantships (averaging $5,007 per year) were awarded. Teaching assistantships, career-related internships or fieldwork also available. Financial award application deadline: 2/28.
Faculty research: Bioinstrumentation, animal waste management, water quality engineering, machine systems, controlled environment agriculture. *Total annual research expenditures:* $7.3 million.
Dr. James H. Young, Director of Graduate Programs, 919-515-6710, *Fax:* 919-515-6719, *E-mail:* jim_young@ncsu.edu.
Application contact: Dr. Daniel H. Willits, Director of Graduate Programs, 919-515-6755, *Fax:* 919-515-7760, *E-mail:* bae_gradprog@ncsu.edu. *Web site:* http://www.bae.ncsu.edu/bae/

■ NORTH DAKOTA STATE UNIVERSITY

The Graduate School, College of Engineering and Architecture, Department of Agricultural and Biosystems Engineering, Fargo, ND 58105

AWARDS Agricultural and biosystems engineering (MS); engineering (PhD); natural resource management (MS). Part-time programs available.

Faculty: 7 full-time (0 women).
Students: 10 full-time (1 woman), 4 part-time; includes 10 minority (all Asian Americans or Pacific Islanders). Average age 25. 13 applicants, 15% accepted, 2 enrolled. In 2001, 3 degrees awarded.
Degree requirements: For master's and doctorate, thesis/dissertation. *Median time to degree:* Master's–2 years full-time.
Entrance requirements: For master's, TOEFL. *Application deadline:* For fall admission, 7/1. Applications are processed on a rolling basis. *Application fee:* $35.
Expenses: Tuition, state resident: part-time $124 per credit. Tuition, nonresident: part-time $325 per credit. Required fees: $22 per credit. Tuition and fees vary according to reciprocity agreements.
Financial support: In 2001–02, 7 students received support, including 7 research assistantships with full tuition reimbursements available (averaging $11,000 per year); career-related internships or fieldwork, Federal Work-Study, institutionally sponsored loans, and tuition waivers (full) also available. Financial award application deadline: 4/15.
Faculty research: Agricultural power and machine systems, irrigation, crop processing, food engineering, environmental resources.
E. C. Stegman, Chair, 701-231-7261, *Fax:* 701-231-1008, *E-mail:* earl.stegman@ndsu.nodak.edu. *Web site:* http://www.ageng.ndsu.nodak.edu/

■ THE OHIO STATE UNIVERSITY

Graduate School, College of Food, Agricultural, and Environmental Sciences, Department of Food, Agricultural, and Biological Engineering, Columbus, OH 43210

AWARDS MS, PhD.

Degree requirements: For master's, thesis optional; for doctorate, thesis/dissertation.
Entrance requirements: For master's, GRE General Test, (international students and non-engineering majors); for doctorate, GRE General Test (international students and non-engineering majors).

■ OKLAHOMA STATE UNIVERSITY

Graduate College, College of Agricultural Sciences and Natural Resources and College of Engineering, Architecture and Technology, School of Biosystems and Agricultural Engineering, Stillwater, OK 74078

AWARDS M Bio E, MS, PhD.

Faculty: 22 full-time (1 woman).
Students: 11 full-time (0 women), 19 part-time (5 women); includes 1 minority (Hispanic American), 18 international. Average age 27. 1 applicant, 100% accepted. In 2001, 1 degree awarded.

Oklahoma State University (continued)
Degree requirements: For master's and doctorate, thesis/dissertation.
Entrance requirements: For master's and doctorate, TOEFL. *Application deadline:* For fall admission, 6/1 (priority date). *Application fee:* $25.
Expenses: Tuition, state resident: part-time $92 per credit hour. Tuition, nonresident: part-time $297 per credit hour. Required fees: $21 per credit hour. $14 per semester. One-time fee: $20. Tuition and fees vary according to course load.
Financial support: In 2001–02, 28 students received support, including 27 research assistantships (averaging $12,589 per year), 2 teaching assistantships (averaging $19,150 per year); career-related internships or fieldwork, Federal Work-Study, and tuition waivers (partial) also available. Support available to part-time students. Financial award application deadline: 3/1.
Dr. Ron Elliot, Head, 405-744-5431, *Fax:* 405-744-6059.

■ THE PENNSYLVANIA STATE UNIVERSITY UNIVERSITY PARK CAMPUS

Graduate School, College of Engineering, Department of Agricultural and Biological Engineering, State College, University Park, PA 16802-1503

AWARDS Agricultural engineering (MS, PhD).

Students: 28 full-time (7 women), 12 part-time (3 women). In 2001, 6 master's, 4 doctorates awarded.
Degree requirements: For master's and doctorate, thesis/dissertation.
Entrance requirements: For master's and doctorate, GRE General Test. *Application fee:* $45.
Expenses: Tuition, state resident: full-time $7,882; part-time $333 per credit. Tuition, nonresident: full-time $16,142; part-time $673 per credit. Required fees: $124 per semester.
Dr. Roy E. Young, Head, 814-865-7792.

■ PURDUE UNIVERSITY

Graduate School, Schools of Engineering, Department of Agricultural and Biological Engineering, West Lafayette, IN 47907

AWARDS MS, MSABE, MSE, PhD. Part-time programs available.

Faculty: 23 full-time (1 woman), 8 part-time/adjunct (1 woman).
Students: 45 full-time (13 women), 7 part-time (1 woman); includes 4 minority (2 African Americans, 2 Hispanic Americans), 22 international. Average age 28. 44 applicants, 27% accepted. In 2001, 7 master's, 6 doctorates awarded. Terminal master's awarded for partial completion of doctoral program.

Degree requirements: For master's, thesis (for some programs); for doctorate, thesis/dissertation.
Entrance requirements: For master's and doctorate, GRE General Test, TOEFL. *Application deadline:* For fall admission, 6/15 (priority date); for spring admission, 10/1 (priority date). Applications are processed on a rolling basis. *Application fee:* $30. Electronic applications accepted.
Expenses: Tuition, state resident: full-time $4,164; part-time $149 per credit hour. Tuition, nonresident: full-time $13,872; part-time $458 per credit hour. Tuition and fees vary according to campus/location and program.
Financial support: In 2001–02, 7 fellowships (averaging $17,110 per year), 32 research assistantships (averaging $15,158 per year), 4 teaching assistantships (averaging $14,827 per year) were awarded. Career-related internships or fieldwork, scholarships/grants, unspecified assistantships, and instructorships also available. Support available to part-time students. Financial award applicants required to submit FAFSA.
Faculty research: Food and biological engineering, environmental engineering, machine systems, biotechnology, machine intelligence. *Total annual research expenditures:* $2.3 million.
Dr. Vincent F. Bralts, Head, 765-494-1162, *Fax:* 765-496-1115, *E-mail:* bralts@ecn.purdue.edu.
Application contact: Graduate Secretary, 765-494-1166, *Fax:* 765-496-1115, *E-mail:* abegrad@ecn.purdue.edu. *Web site:* http://www.purdue.edu/ABE

■ RUTGERS, THE STATE UNIVERSITY OF NEW JERSEY, NEW BRUNSWICK

Graduate School, Program in Bioresource Engineering, New Brunswick, NJ 08901-1281

AWARDS MS. Part-time programs available.

Degree requirements: For master's, thesis, seminar.
Entrance requirements: For master's, GRE General Test.
Faculty research: Greenhouse engineering, energy and environment, machine vision, flexible automation and robotics, systems analysis. *Web site:* http://www.rci.rutgers.edu/~biorengg/

■ SOUTH DAKOTA STATE UNIVERSITY

Graduate School, College of Engineering, Department of Agricultural Engineering, Brookings, SD 57007

AWARDS MS, PhD.

Degree requirements: For master's, thesis, oral exam; for doctorate, thesis/dissertation, preliminary oral and written exams.

Entrance requirements: For master's and doctorate, TOEFL.
Faculty research: Water resources, machine visions, food engineering, environmental engineering, machine design.

■ TEXAS A&M UNIVERSITY

College of Agriculture and Life Sciences and College of Engineering, Department of Biological and Agricultural Engineering, College Station, TX 77843

AWARDS M Agr, M Eng, MS, PhD. Part-time programs available.

Faculty: 35.
Students: 39 (12 women). Average age 27.
Degree requirements: For master's, thesis (MS), preliminary and final exams; for doctorate, thesis/dissertation, preliminary and final exams.
Entrance requirements: For master's and doctorate, GRE General Test, TOEFL. *Application deadline:* For fall admission, 2/1 (priority date); for spring admission, 10/1. Applications are processed on a rolling basis. *Application fee:* $50 ($75 for international students). Electronic applications accepted.
Expenses: Tuition, state resident: full-time $11,872. Tuition, nonresident: full-time $17,892.
Financial support: In 2001–02, fellowships (averaging $12,000 per year), research assistantships (averaging $14,250 per year), teaching assistantships (averaging $14,271 per year) were awarded. Career-related internships or fieldwork and tuition waivers (partial) also available. Financial award application deadline: 3/1; financial award applicants required to submit FAFSA. *Total annual research expenditures:* $1.2 million.
James R. Gilley, Head, 979-845-3931, *Fax:* 979-862-3442, *E-mail:* gilley@zeus.tamu.edu.
Application contact: Jeana Goodson, Academic Programs Assistant, 979-845-0609, *Fax:* 979-862-3442, *E-mail:* j-goodson@tamu.edu. *Web site:* http://agen.tamu.edu/

■ THE UNIVERSITY OF ARIZONA

Graduate College, College of Agriculture and Life Sciences, Department of Agricultural and Biosystems Engineering, Tucson, AZ 85721

AWARDS MS, PhD.

Faculty: 15.
Students: 15 full-time (8 women), 6 part-time (2 women); includes 2 minority (1 Asian American or Pacific Islander, 1 Hispanic American), 14 international. Average age 33. 9 applicants, 44% accepted, 2 enrolled. In 2001, 2 master's, 7 doctorates awarded. Terminal master's awarded for partial completion of doctoral program.

Degree requirements: For master's and doctorate, thesis/dissertation.

Entrance requirements: For master's and doctorate, TOEFL, minimum GPA of 3.0 in last 2 years of undergraduate study. *Application deadline:* For fall admission, 3/1. Applications are processed on a rolling basis. *Application fee:* $45.

Expenses: Tuition, state resident: full-time $2,490; part-time $436 per unit. Tuition, nonresident: full-time $10,300; part-time $436 per unit. Full-time tuition and fees vary according to degree level and program.

Financial support: Fellowships, research assistantships, teaching assistantships, Federal Work-Study, institutionally sponsored loans, scholarships/grants, and tuition waivers (full and partial) available. Financial award application deadline: 5/1.

Faculty research: Irrigation system design, energy-use management, equipment for alternative crops, food properties enhancement.
Donald Slack, Head, 520-621-3691, *Fax:* 520-6213963, *E-mail:* slackd@ u.arizona.edu.

Application contact: Lindy Fletcher, Graduate Secretary, 520-621-1753, *Fax:* 520-621-3963, *E-mail:* fletcher@ ag.arizona.edu.

■ UNIVERSITY OF ARKANSAS

Graduate School, College of Engineering, Department of Biological and Agricultural Engineering, Fayetteville, AR 72701-1201

AWARDS MSBAE, MSE, PhD.

Students: 1 (woman) full-time, 7 part-time (2 women), 4 international. 12 applicants, 33% accepted. In 2001, 1 master's, 2 doctorates awarded.

Degree requirements: For master's, thesis; for doctorate, one foreign language, thesis/dissertation.
Application fee: $40 ($50 for international students).

Expenses: Tuition, state resident: full-time $3,553; part-time $197 per credit. Tuition, nonresident: full-time $8,411; part-time $467 per credit. Required fees: $42 per credit. Tuition and fees vary according to course load and program.

Financial support: In 2001–02, 9 research assistantships were awarded; career-related internships or fieldwork and Federal Work-Study also available. Support available to part-time students. Financial award application deadline: 4/1; financial award applicants required to submit FAFSA.
Lalit R. Verma, Head, 479-575-2351.

■ UNIVERSITY OF CALIFORNIA, DAVIS

Graduate Studies, College of Engineering, Program in Biological and Agricultural Engineering, Davis, CA 95616

AWARDS M Engr, MS, D Engr, PhD, M Engr/ MBA. Part-time programs available.

Faculty: 28 full-time (3 women).
Students: 48 full-time (15 women); includes 6 minority (5 Asian Americans or Pacific Islanders, 1 Hispanic American), 24 international. Average age 30. 24 applicants, 79% accepted, 11 enrolled. In 2001, 4 master's, 6 doctorates awarded. Terminal master's awarded for partial completion of doctoral program.
Degree requirements: For master's and doctorate, thesis/dissertation.
Entrance requirements: For master's, minimum GPA of 3.0; for doctorate, GRE, minimum graduate GPA of 3.25. *Application deadline:* For fall admission, 4/1 (priority date). *Application fee:* $60. Electronic applications accepted.
Expenses: Tuition, state resident: full-time $4,831. Tuition, nonresident: full-time $15,725.
Financial support: In 2001–02, 43 students received support, including 21 fellowships with full and partial tuition reimbursements available (averaging $4,445 per year), 27 research assistantships with full and partial tuition reimbursements available (averaging $10,562 per year), 6 teaching assistantships with partial tuition reimbursements available (averaging $14,145 per year); Federal Work-Study, institutionally sponsored loans, scholarships/grants, and tuition waivers (full and partial) also available. Financial award application deadline: 1/15; financial award applicants required to submit FAFSA.
Faculty research: Forestry, irrigation and drainage, power and machinery, structures and environment, information and energy technologies.
Bruce R. Hartsough, Chair, 530-752-8331, *E-mail:* bioageng@ucdavis.edu.
Application contact: Leigh Ann Empie, Information Contact, 530-752-1451, *Fax:* 530-752-2780, *E-mail:* laempie@ ucdavis.edu. *Web site:* http:// www.engr.ucdavis.edu/~bae/

■ UNIVERSITY OF DAYTON

Graduate School, School of Engineering, Department of Civil Engineering, Dayton, OH 45469-1300

AWARDS Engineering mechanics (MSEM); environmental engineering (MSCE). Soil mechanics (MSCE). Structural engineering (MSCE); transport engineering (MSCE). Part-time programs available.

Faculty: 8 full-time (0 women), 2 part-time/adjunct (0 women).

Students: 8 full-time (6 women), 7 part-time (4 women), 6 international. In 2001, 2 degrees awarded.
Degree requirements: For master's, thesis or alternative.
Entrance requirements: For master's, TOEFL. *Application deadline:* For fall admission, 8/1. Applications are processed on a rolling basis. *Application fee:* $30.
Expenses: Tuition: Full-time $5,436; part-time $453 per credit hour. Required fees: $50; $25 per term.
Financial support: In 2001–02, 5 research assistantships with full tuition reimbursements (averaging $12,000 per year), 2 teaching assistantships with full tuition reimbursements (averaging $10,000 per year) were awarded. Institutionally sponsored loans also available.
Faculty research: Tire/soil interaction, tilt-up structures, viscoelastic response of restraint systems, composite materials.
Dr. Joseph E. Saliba, Chairperson, 937-229-3847, *E-mail:* jsaliba@ engr.udayton.edu.
Application contact: Dr. Donald L. Moon, Associate Dean, 937-229-2241, *Fax:* 937-229-2471, *E-mail:* dmoon@ notes.udayton.edu.

■ UNIVERSITY OF FLORIDA

Graduate School, College of Engineering and College of Agricultural and Life Sciences, Department of Agricultural and Biological Engineering, Gainesville, FL 32611

AWARDS Agricultural and biological engineering (ME, MS, PhD, Engr); agricultural operations management (MS, PhD). Part-time programs available. Terminal master's awarded for partial completion of doctoral program.

Degree requirements: For master's and Engr, thesis optional; for doctorate, thesis/dissertation.
Entrance requirements: For master's and doctorate, GRE General Test, minimum GPA of 3.0; for Engr, GRE General Test. Electronic applications accepted.
Expenses: Tuition, state resident: part-time $164 per hour. Tuition, nonresident: part-time $571 per hour. Tuition and fees vary according to course level and program.
Faculty research: Soil and water engineering, structures and environments, power and machinery, biological processing, food engineering, remote sensing hydrology, geographic information systems. *Web site:* http://www.agen.ufl.edu/

■ UNIVERSITY OF GEORGIA

Graduate School, College of Agricultural and Environmental Sciences, Department of Biological and Agricultural Engineering, Athens, GA 30602

AWARDS Agricultural engineering (MS); biological and agricultural engineering (PhD); biological engineering (MS).

Faculty: 30 full-time (1 woman).
Students: 15 full-time (5 women), 8 part-time (1 woman); includes 1 minority (Hispanic American), 9 international. 36 applicants, 36% accepted. In 2001, 3 master's, 1 doctorate awarded.
Degree requirements: For master's, thesis; for doctorate, one foreign language, thesis/dissertation.
Entrance requirements: For master's and doctorate, GRE General Test. *Application deadline:* For fall admission, 7/1 (priority date); for spring admission, 11/15. *Application fee:* $30. Electronic applications accepted.
Expenses: Tuition, state resident: full-time $2,376; part-time $132 per credit hour. Tuition, nonresident: full-time $9,504; part-time $528 per credit hour. Required fees: $236 per semester.
Financial support: Fellowships, research assistantships, teaching assistantships, unspecified assistantships available.
Dr. E. Dale Threadgill, Head, 706-542-1653, *Fax:* 706-542-8806, *E-mail:* tgill@engr.uga.edu.
Application contact: Dr. E. William Tollner, Contact, 706-542-3047, *Fax:* 706-542-6063, *E-mail:* btollner@engr.uga.edu. *Web site:* http://www.engr.uga.edu/index.html

Find an in-depth description at www.petersons.com/gradchannel.

■ UNIVERSITY OF IDAHO

College of Graduate Studies, College of Agriculture and College of Engineering, Department of Biological and Agricultural Engineering, Moscow, ID 83844-2282

AWARDS M Engr, MS, PhD.

Faculty: 4 full-time (0 women).
Students: 10 full-time (3 women), 6 part-time (1 woman), 7 international. 8 applicants, 50% accepted. In 2001, 3 master's, 1 doctorate awarded.
Degree requirements: For master's, thesis or alternative; for doctorate, one foreign language, thesis/dissertation.
Entrance requirements: For master's, minimum GPA of 2.8; for doctorate, minimum undergraduate GPA of 2.8, 3.0 graduate. *Application deadline:* For fall admission, 8/1; for spring admission, 12/15. *Application fee:* $35 ($45 for international students).
Expenses: Tuition, state resident: full-time $1,613. Tuition, nonresident: full-time $3,000.

Financial support: In 2001–02, 7 research assistantships (averaging $10,611 per year), 1 teaching assistantship (averaging $10,499 per year) were awarded. Career-related internships or fieldwork also available. Financial award application deadline: 2/15.
Faculty research: Irrigation, soil and water conservation, agricultural mechanization.
Dr. James De Shazer, Head, 208-885-6182. *Web site:* http://www.uidaho.edu/bae/bae.html

Find an in-depth description at www.petersons.com/gradchannel.

■ UNIVERSITY OF ILLINOIS AT URBANA–CHAMPAIGN

Graduate College, College of Agricultural, Consumer and Environmental Sciences, Department of Agricultural Engineering, Champaign, IL 61820

AWARDS MS, PhD.

Faculty: 16 full-time, 1 part-time/adjunct.
Students: 35 full-time (7 women); includes 4 minority (1 African American, 1 Asian American or Pacific Islander, 2 Hispanic Americans), 17 international. 26 applicants, 23% accepted.
Degree requirements: For master's and doctorate, thesis/dissertation.
Application deadline: Applications are processed on a rolling basis. *Application fee:* $40 ($50 for international students). Electronic applications accepted.
Expenses: Tuition, state resident: part-time $3,227 per degree program. Tuition, nonresident: part-time $7,169 per degree program. Tuition and fees vary according to program.
Financial support: In 2001–02, 10 fellowships, 20 research assistantships were awarded. Teaching assistantships, tuition waivers (full and partial) also available. Financial award application deadline: 2/15.
Loren E. Bode, Head, 217-333-3570, *Fax:* 217-244-0323, *E-mail:* l-bode@uiuc.edu.
Application contact: Dini Reid, Assistant to the Head, 217-244-9528, *Fax:* 217-244-0323, *E-mail:* dinireid@uiuc.edu. *Web site:* http://www.age.uiuc.edu/

■ UNIVERSITY OF KENTUCKY

Graduate School, Graduate School Programs from the College of Engineering, Program in Biosystems and Agricultural Engineering, Lexington, KY 40506-0032

AWARDS MSAE, PhD. Part-time programs available.

Faculty: 15 full-time (2 women).
Students: 15 full-time (8 women), 1 part-time; includes 2 minority (both African Americans), 2 international. 23 applicants, 30% accepted. In 2001, 3 master's, 1 doctorate awarded.

Degree requirements: For master's, thesis optional; for doctorate, thesis/dissertation, comprehensive exam.
Entrance requirements: For master's, GRE General Test, minimum undergraduate GPA of 2.5; for doctorate, GRE General Test, minimum graduate GPA of 3.0. *Application deadline:* For fall admission, 7/19. Applications are processed on a rolling basis. *Application fee:* $30 ($35 for international students).
Expenses: Tuition, state resident: full-time $4,075; part-time $213 per credit hour. Tuition, nonresident: full-time $11,295; part-time $614 per credit hour.
Financial support: In 2001–02, 5 fellowships, 7 research assistantships, 2 teaching assistantships were awarded. Federal Work-Study and institutionally sponsored loans also available. Support available to part-time students.
Faculty research: Machine systems, food engineering, fermentation, hydrology, water quality.
Dr. Richard Gates, Director of Graduate Studies, 859-257-3000 Ext. 220, *Fax:* 859-257-5671, *E-mail:* dgs@bae.uky.edu.
Application contact: Dr. Jeannine Blackwell, Associate Dean, 859-257-4905, *Fax:* 859-323-1928.

■ UNIVERSITY OF MARYLAND, COLLEGE PARK

Graduate Studies and Research, College of Agriculture and Natural Resources, Department of Biological Resources Engineering, College Park, MD 20742

AWARDS MS, PhD.

Faculty: 16 full-time (2 women), 3 part-time/adjunct (1 woman).
Students: 31 full-time (18 women), 19 part-time (8 women); includes 8 minority (5 African Americans, 3 Asian Americans or Pacific Islanders), 17 international. 39 applicants, 56% accepted, 11 enrolled. In 2001, 1 degree awarded.
Degree requirements: For master's, thesis optional; for doctorate, thesis/dissertation.
Entrance requirements: For master's, GRE General Test, minimum GPA of 3.0. *Application deadline:* For fall admission, 6/1 (priority date); for spring admission, 10/1. Applications are processed on a rolling basis. *Application fee:* $50 ($70 for international students). Electronic applications accepted.
Expenses: Tuition, state resident: part-time $289 per credit hour. Tuition, nonresident: part-time $448 per credit hour. One-time fee: $436 part-time. Full-time tuition and fees vary according to course load, campus/location and program.
Financial support: In 2001–02, 2 fellowships with full tuition reimbursements (averaging $9,771 per year), 17 research assistantships with tuition reimbursements (averaging $15,399 per year), 5 teaching assistantships with tuition reimbursements

(averaging $15,588 per year) were awarded. Career-related internships or fieldwork also available. Financial award applicants required to submit FAFSA.
Faculty research: Engineering aspects of production; harvesting, processing, and marketing of terrestrial and aquatic food and fiber.
Dr. Frederick Wheaton, Chairman, 301-405-1193, *Fax:* 301-314-9023.
Application contact: Trudy Lindsey, Director, Graduate Admissions and Records, 301-405-6991, *Fax:* 301-314-9305, *E-mail:* grschool@deans.umd.edu.

Find an in-depth description at www.petersons.com/gradchannel.

■ UNIVERSITY OF MINNESOTA, TWIN CITIES CAMPUS

Graduate School, College of Agricultural, Food, and Environmental Sciences, Department of Biosystems and Agricultural Engineering, Minneapolis, MN 55455-0213
AWARDS MBAE, MSBAE, PhD. Part-time programs available.
Faculty: 15 full-time (0 women), 2 part-time/adjunct (0 women).
Students: 12 full-time (1 woman), 3 part-time (1 woman), 9 international. 16 applicants, 69% accepted, 6 enrolled. In 2001, 7 master's, 4 doctorates awarded.
Degree requirements: For master's, thesis (for some programs), seminar; for doctorate, thesis/dissertation, seminar.
Entrance requirements: For master's and doctorate, TOEFL, BS in engineering or related field. *Application deadline:* For fall admission, 6/15; for spring admission, 10/15. Applications are processed on a rolling basis. *Application fee:* $50 ($55 for international students).
Expenses: Tuition, state resident: full-time $2,932; part-time $489 per credit. Tuition, nonresident: full-time $5,758; part-time $960 per credit. Part-time tuition and fees vary according to course load, program and reciprocity agreements.
Financial support: In 2001–02, 12 students received support, including 1 fellowship with full tuition reimbursement available (averaging $21,000 per year), 11 research assistantships with full tuition reimbursements available (averaging $16,671 per year). Scholarships/grants also available. Support available to part-time students. Financial award application deadline: 2/15.
Faculty research: Water quality, bioprocessing, food engineering, terramechanics, process and machine control. *Total annual research expenditures:* $3.1 million.
Dr. Kevin A. Janni, Head, 612-625-7733, *Fax:* 612-624-3005, *E-mail:* kjanni@umn.edu.
Application contact: Jonathan Chaplin, Director of Graduate Studies, 612-625-8146, *Fax:* 612-624-3005, *E-mail:*

jchaplin@umn.edu. *Web site:* http://www.bae.umn.edu/

■ UNIVERSITY OF MISSOURI–COLUMBIA

Graduate School, College of Engineering and College of Agriculture, Food and Natural Resources, Department of Biological Engineering, Columbia, MO 65211
AWARDS Agricultural engineering (MS); biological engineering (MS, PhD).
Faculty: 15 full-time (2 women).
Students: 7 full-time (3 women), 8 part-time (1 woman); includes 1 minority (Asian American or Pacific Islander), 12 international. 1 applicant, 0% accepted. In 2001, 4 master's, 1 doctorate awarded.
Degree requirements: For master's and doctorate, thesis/dissertation.
Entrance requirements: For master's and doctorate, GRE General Test, TOEFL, minimum GPA of 3.0. *Application deadline:* For fall admission, 4/1 (priority date). Applications are processed on a rolling basis. *Application fee:* $25 ($50 for international students).
Expenses: Tuition, state resident: part-time $179 per credit hour. Tuition, nonresident: part-time $539 per credit hour. Required fees: $122 per semester. Tuition and fees vary according to program.
Financial support: Research assistantships, teaching assistantships, institutionally sponsored loans available.
Dr. Fu-hung Hsieh, Director of Graduate Studies, 573-882-2444, *E-mail:* hsiehf@missouri.edu. *Web site:* http://www.engineering.missouri.edu/biological.htm

■ UNIVERSITY OF NEBRASKA–LINCOLN

Graduate College, College of Engineering and Technology, Department of Biological Systems Engineering, Program in Agricultural and Biological Systems Engineering, Lincoln, NE 68588
AWARDS MS.
Faculty: 30.
Students: 3 (1 woman). 9 applicants, 11% accepted, 0 enrolled. In 2001, 4 degrees awarded.
Degree requirements: For master's, thesis optional.
Entrance requirements: For master's, GRE General Test, curriculum vitae. *Application deadline:* For fall admission, 3/1 (priority date). *Application fee:* $35. Electronic applications accepted.
Expenses: Tuition, state resident: full-time $2,412; part-time $134 per credit. Tuition, nonresident: full-time $6,223; part-time $346 per credit. Tuition and fees vary according to course load.

Financial support: In 2001–02, 4 research assistantships were awarded; fellowships, health care benefits and unspecified assistantships also available. Financial award application deadline: 2/15.
Faculty research: Hydrological engineering, tractive performance, biomedical engineering, irrigation systems.
Dr. Derrel L. Martin, Graduate Committee Chair, 402-472-1586, *Fax:* 402-472-6338, *E-mail:* dlmartin@unlnotes.unl.edu. *Web site:* http://bse.unl.edu/

■ THE UNIVERSITY OF TENNESSEE

Graduate School, College of Agricultural Sciences and Natural Resources, Department of Agricultural and Biosystems Engineering, Program in Biosystems Engineering, Knoxville, TN 37996
AWARDS MS, PhD.
Students: 8 full-time (3 women), 5 part-time (1 woman); includes 1 minority (Native American), 3 international. 6 applicants, 67% accepted. In 2001, 4 master's, 1 doctorate awarded.
Degree requirements: For master's and doctorate, thesis/dissertation.
Entrance requirements: For master's, GRE General Test,, TOEFL, minimum GPA of 2.7; for doctorate, GRE General Test, TOEFL, minimum GPA of 2.7. *Application deadline:* For fall admission, 2/1 (priority date). Applications are processed on a rolling basis. *Application fee:* $35. Electronic applications accepted.
Expenses: Tuition, state resident: full-time $4,280; part-time $233 per hour. Tuition, nonresident: full-time $12,066; part-time $666 per hour. Tuition and fees vary according to program.
Financial support: Application deadline: 2/1.
Application contact: Dr. Ronald E. Yoder, Head, 865-974-7266, *Fax:* 865-974-4514, *E-mail:* ryoder@utk.edu.

■ THE UNIVERSITY OF TENNESSEE

Graduate School, College of Agricultural Sciences and Natural Resources, Department of Agricultural and Biosystems Engineering, Program in Biosystems Engineering Technology, Knoxville, TN 37996
AWARDS MS.
Students: 3 full-time (1 woman), 5 part-time (1 woman), 1 international. 3 applicants, 67% accepted. In 2001, 2 degrees awarded.
Degree requirements: For master's, thesis or alternative.
Entrance requirements: For master's, GRE General Test, TOEFL, minimum GPA of 2.7. *Application deadline:* For fall admission, 2/1 (priority date). Applications

The University of Tennessee (continued) are processed on a rolling basis. *Application fee:* $35. Electronic applications accepted.
Expenses: Tuition, state resident: full-time $4,280; part-time $233 per hour. Tuition, nonresident: full-time $12,066; part-time $666 per hour. Tuition and fees vary according to program.
Financial support: Application deadline: 2/1.
Application contact: Dr. Ronald E. Yoder, Head, 865-974-7266, *Fax:* 865-974-4514, *E-mail:* ryoder@utk.edu.

■ UNIVERSITY OF WISCONSIN–MADISON

Graduate School, College of Agricultural and Life Sciences, Department of Biological Systems Engineering, Madison, WI 53706

AWARDS MS, PhD. Part-time programs available.

Faculty: 16 full-time (0 women), 7 part-time/adjunct (0 women).
Students: 15 full-time (3 women), 1 part-time. Average age 30. 13 applicants, 85% accepted, 6 enrolled. In 2001, 2 degrees awarded. Terminal master's awarded for partial completion of doctoral program.
Degree requirements: For master's, thesis optional; for doctorate, thesis/dissertation. *Median time to degree:* Master's–2 years full-time.
Entrance requirements: For master's, GRE, TOEFL. *Application deadline:* Applications are processed on a rolling basis. *Application fee:* $45. Electronic applications accepted.
Expenses: Tuition, state resident: full-time $7,361; part-time $399 per credit. Tuition, nonresident: full-time $20,499; part-time $1,282 per credit. Required fees: $34 per credit. Full-time tuition and fees vary according to course load, program, reciprocity agreements and student level.
Financial support: In 2001–02, 1 fellowship with full tuition reimbursement (averaging $17,940 per year), 16 research assistantships with full tuition reimbursements (averaging $16,350 per year) were awarded. Federal Work-Study and institutionally sponsored loans also available. Support available to part-time students. Financial award application deadline: 11/1; financial award applicants required to submit FAFSA.
Faculty research: Waste systems, food engineering, power and machinery, structures and environment, construction

management. *Total annual research expenditures:* $20.9 million.
Ronald T. Schuler, Chair, 608-262-3310, *Fax:* 608-262-1228.
Application contact: Debby Sumwalt, Graduate Admissions Coordinator, 608-262-3310, *Fax:* 608-262-1228, *E-mail:* dsumwalt@facstaff.wisc.edu. *Web site:* http://bse.wisc.edu/

■ UTAH STATE UNIVERSITY

School of Graduate Studies, College of Engineering, Department of Biological and Irrigation Engineering, Logan, UT 84322

AWARDS Biological and agricultural engineering (MS, PhD); irrigation engineering (MS, PhD). Part-time programs available.

Faculty: 10 full-time (0 women).
Students: 27 full-time (5 women), 12 part-time (1 woman); includes 3 minority (1 African American, 2 Hispanic Americans), 30 international. Average age 28. 22 applicants, 59% accepted. In 2001, 10 master's, 3 doctorates awarded. Terminal master's awarded for partial completion of doctoral program.
Degree requirements: For master's, thesis (for some programs); for doctorate, thesis/dissertation.
Entrance requirements: For master's and doctorate, GRE General Test, TOEFL, minimum GPA of 3.0. *Application deadline:* For fall admission, 6/15 (priority date); for spring admission, 10/15. Applications are processed on a rolling basis. *Application fee:* $40.
Expenses: Tuition, state resident: full-time $1,693. Tuition, nonresident: full-time $4,233. Required fees: $501. Tuition and fees vary according to program.
Financial support: In 2001–02, 15 fellowships with partial tuition reimbursements, 15 research assistantships with partial tuition reimbursements, 2 teaching assistantships with partial tuition reimbursements were awarded. Tuition waivers (partial) also available. Support available to part-time students.
Faculty research: Surge flow, on-farm water management, crop-water yield modeling, drainage, groundwater modeling.
Wynn Walker, Head, 435-797-2788, *Fax:* 435-797-1248, *E-mail:* wynnwalk@cc.usu.edu.
Application contact: Lyman Willardson, Graduate Adviser, 435-797-2789, *Fax:* 435-797-1248, *E-mail:* fath8@cc.usu.edu. *Web site:* http://www.engineering.usu.edu/bie/

■ VIRGINIA POLYTECHNIC INSTITUTE AND STATE UNIVERSITY

Graduate School, College of Engineering, Department of Biological Systems Engineering, Blacksburg, VA 24061

AWARDS Bio-process engineering (M Eng, MS, PhD); food engineering (M Eng, MS, PhD); land and water engineering (M Eng, MS, PhD); nonpoint source pollution control (M Eng, MS, PhD); watershed engineering (M Eng, MS, PhD); wood engineering (M Eng, MS, PhD).

Faculty: 12 full-time (0 women), 8 part-time/adjunct (0 women).
Students: 24 full-time (13 women), 5 part-time; includes 1 minority (Asian American or Pacific Islander), 10 international. Average age 25. 19 applicants, 58% accepted. In 2001, 3 master's, 1 doctorate awarded.
Degree requirements: For master's and doctorate, thesis/dissertation. *Median time to degree:* Master's–2 years full-time; doctorate–3 years full-time.
Entrance requirements: For master's and doctorate, GRE General Test, TOEFL. *Application deadline:* For fall admission, 12/1 (priority date); for spring admission, 9/1 (priority date). Applications are processed on a rolling basis. *Application fee:* $45. Electronic applications accepted.
Expenses: Tuition, state resident: part-time $241 per hour. Tuition, nonresident: part-time $406 per hour. Tuition and fees vary according to program.
Financial support: In 2001–02, 4 fellowships with full tuition reimbursements (averaging $17,000 per year), 7 research assistantships with full tuition reimbursements (averaging $16,500 per year), 2 teaching assistantships with full tuition reimbursements (averaging $16,500 per year) were awarded. Career-related internships or fieldwork, institutionally sponsored loans, tuition waivers (full and partial), and unspecified assistantships also available. Support available to part-time students. Financial award application deadline: 4/1.
Faculty research: Soil and water engineering, alternative energy sources for agriculture and agricultural mechanization. *Total annual research expenditures:* $800,000.
Dr. John V. Perumpral, Head, 540-231-6615, *E-mail:* perump@vt.edu.
Application contact: Dr. S. Mostaghimi, Chairman, 540-231-7605, *E-mail:* smostagh@vt.edu. *Web site:* http://www.bse.vt.edu/

Architectural Engineering

ARCHITECTURAL ENGINEERING

■ ILLINOIS INSTITUTE OF TECHNOLOGY

Graduate College, Armour College of Engineering and Sciences, Department of Civil and Architectural Engineering, Chicago, IL 60616-3793

AWARDS M Geoenv E, M Trans E, MCEM, MGE, MPW, MS, MSE, PhD. Part-time and evening/weekend programs available.

Faculty: 9 full-time (0 women), 7 part-time/adjunct (0 women).
Students: 42 full-time (6 women), 57 part-time (7 women); includes 10 minority (2 African Americans, 7 Asian Americans or Pacific Islanders, 1 Hispanic American), 69 international. Average age 29. 180 applicants, 64% accepted. In 2001, 22 master's, 3 doctorates awarded. Terminal master's awarded for partial completion of doctoral program.
Degree requirements: For master's, thesis (for some programs), comprehensive exam; for doctorate, thesis/dissertation, comprehensive exam.
Entrance requirements: For master's and doctorate, GRE General Test, TOEFL, minimum undergraduate GPA of 3.0. *Application deadline:* For fall admission, 7/1; for spring admission, 11/1. Applications are processed on a rolling basis. *Application fee:* $30. Electronic applications accepted.
Expenses: Tuition: Part-time $590 per credit hour.
Financial support: In 2001–02, 10 teaching assistantships were awarded; Federal Work-Study, institutionally sponsored loans, scholarships/grants, and unspecified assistantships also available. Support available to part-time students. Financial award application deadline: 3/1; financial award applicants required to submit FAFSA.
Faculty research: Structural faligue, behavior of steel-reinforced concrete structures, soil-structure interaction, geosynthetics. *Total annual research expenditures:* $3,988.
Dr. J. Mohammadi, Chairman, 312-567-3540, *Fax:* 312-567-3519, *E-mail:* mohammadi@iit.edu.
Application contact: Dr. Ali Cinar, Dean of Graduate College, 312-567-3637, *Fax:* 312-567-7517, *E-mail:* gradstu@iit.edu. *Web site:* http://www.iit.edu/~ce/

■ KANSAS STATE UNIVERSITY

Graduate School, College of Engineering, Department of Architectural Engineering and Construction Science, Manhattan, KS 66506

AWARDS Architectural engineering (MS).
Faculty: 12 full-time (1 woman).
Students: 11 full-time (3 women), 1 part-time; includes 1 minority (Asian American or Pacific Islander). 9 applicants, 100% accepted, 4 enrolled. In 2001, 11 degrees awarded.
Degree requirements: For master's, thesis or alternative.
Entrance requirements: For master's, GRE, TOEFL, minimum GPA of 3.25. *Application deadline:* For fall admission, 2/1 (priority date); for spring admission, 10/1 (priority date). Applications are processed on a rolling basis. *Application fee:* $0 ($25 for international students). Electronic applications accepted.
Expenses: Tuition, state resident: part-time $113 per credit hour. Tuition, nonresident: part-time $358 per credit hour.
Financial support: In 2001–02, 2 research assistantships (averaging $8,000 per year) were awarded; fellowships, career-related internships or fieldwork, Federal Work-Study, institutionally sponsored loans, and scholarships/grants also available. Support available to part-time students. Financial award application deadline: 3/1; financial award applicants required to submit FAFSA.
Faculty research: Building electrical/lighting systems, building HVAC and plumbing systems, structural systems design and analysis, building systems integration, construction sciences, methods and management. *Total annual research expenditures:* $15,270.
David Fritchen, Head, 785-532-3566, *Fax:* 785-532-6944, *E-mail:* arecns@ksu.edu.
Application contact: Charles Burton, Graduate Program Director, 785-532-5964, *Fax:* 785-532-6944, *E-mail:* arecns@ksu.edu. *Web site:* http://www.engg.ksu.edu/AREDEPT/

■ NORTH CAROLINA AGRICULTURAL AND TECHNICAL STATE UNIVERSITY

Graduate School, College of Engineering, Department of Architectural, Agricultural, Civil and Environmental Engineering, Greensboro, NC 27411

AWARDS MSAE, MSCE, MSE. Part-time programs available.

Faculty: 14 full-time (1 woman), 4 part-time/adjunct (0 women).
Students: 28 full-time (10 women), 10 part-time (4 women), 12 international. Average age 24. 22 applicants, 41% accepted. In 2001, 4 degrees awarded.
Degree requirements: For master's, thesis defense.
Entrance requirements: For master's, GRE General Test, GRE Subject Test (recommended), TOEFL (MSCE). *Application deadline:* For fall admission, 7/1; for spring admission, 1/9. Applications are processed on a rolling basis. *Application fee:* $35.
Financial support: In 2001–02, 1 fellowship (averaging $12,000 per year), 3 research assistantships (averaging $12,000 per year), 2 teaching assistantships (averaging $10,000 per year) were awarded. Career-related internships or fieldwork and unspecified assistantships also available.
Faculty research: Lightning, indoor air quality, material behavior HVAC controls, structural masonry systems. *Total annual research expenditures:* $800,000.
Dr. Peter Rojeski, Chairperson, 336-344-7575, *Fax:* 336-344-7126.
Application contact: Dr. W. Mark McGinley, Graduate Coordinator, 336-334-7575, *Fax:* 336-334-7126, *E-mail:* mcginley@garfield.ncat.edu.

■ OKLAHOMA STATE UNIVERSITY

Graduate College, College of Engineering, Architecture and Technology, School of Architecture, Program in Architectural Engineering, Stillwater, OK 74078

AWARDS M Arch E.

Faculty: 16 full-time (1 woman).
Students: 1 full-time (0 women), 2 part-time; includes 1 minority (Native American), 1 international. Average age 27. 8 applicants, 0% accepted. In 2001, 1 degree awarded.
Degree requirements: For master's, thesis or alternative.
Entrance requirements: For master's, TOEFL. *Application deadline:* For fall admission, 7/1 (priority date). *Application fee:* $25.
Expenses: Tuition, state resident: part-time $92 per credit hour. Tuition, nonresident: part-time $297 per credit hour. Required fees: $21 per credit hour. $14 per semester. One-time fee: $20. Tuition and fees vary according to course load.
Financial support: Teaching assistantships, career-related internships or fieldwork, Federal Work-Study, and tuition

Oklahoma State University (continued)
waivers (partial) available. Support available to part-time students. Financial award application deadline: 3/1.
Dr. Randy Seitsinger, Head, School of Architecture, 405-744-6043.

■ THE PENNSYLVANIA STATE UNIVERSITY UNIVERSITY PARK CAMPUS

Graduate School, College of Engineering, Department of Architectural Engineering, State College, University Park, PA 16802-1503

AWARDS M Eng, MAE, MS, PhD.
Students: 21 full-time (5 women), 7 part-time. In 2001, 47 master's, 1 doctorate awarded.
Degree requirements: For master's and doctorate, thesis/dissertation.
Entrance requirements: For master's and doctorate, GRE General Test. *Application fee:* $45.
Expenses: Tuition, state resident: full-time $7,882; part-time $333 per credit. Tuition, nonresident: full-time $16,142; part-time $673 per credit. Required fees: $124 per semester.
Dr. Richard Behr, Head, 814-863-2078.
Application contact: Graduate Program Officer, 814-863-2078.
Find an in-depth description at www.petersons.com/gradchannel.

■ RENSSELAER POLYTECHNIC INSTITUTE

Graduate School, School of Architecture, Program in Lighting, Troy, NY 12180-3590

AWARDS MS. Part-time programs available.
Faculty: 15 full-time (3 women), 5 part-time/adjunct (1 woman).
Students: 22 full-time (10 women), 1 (woman) part-time; includes 2 minority (1 Asian American or Pacific Islander, 1 Hispanic American), 10 international. Average age 30. 31 applicants, 32% accepted, 8 enrolled. In 2001, 8 degrees awarded.
Degree requirements: For master's, thesis.
Entrance requirements: For master's, GRE General Test, TOEFL, portfolio. *Application deadline:* For fall admission, 4/1 (priority date). Applications are processed on a rolling basis. Electronic applications accepted.
Expenses: Tuition: Full-time $26,400; part-time $1,320 per credit hour. Required fees: $1,437.
Financial support: In 2001–02, 16 students received support; research assistantships with tuition reimbursements available, career-related internships or fieldwork and institutionally sponsored

loans available. Financial award application deadline: 4/1.
Faculty research: Energy-efficient lighting, lighting product development, lighting design demonstration, daylighting, transportation lighting. *Total annual research expenditures:* $2 million.
Dr. Mark Rea, Director, Lighting Research Center, 518-687-7100.
Application contact: Daniel Frering, Manager of Education, 518-687-7149, *Fax:* 518-687-7120, *E-mail:* frerid@rpi.edu. *Web site:* http://www.lrc.rpi.edu/

■ UNIVERSITY OF COLORADO AT BOULDER

Graduate School, College of Engineering and Applied Science, Department of Civil, Environmental, and Architectural Engineering, Boulder, CO 80309

AWARDS Building systems (MS, PhD); construction engineering and management (MS, PhD); environmental engineering (MS, PhD); geoenvironmental engineering (MS, PhD); geotechnical engineering (MS, PhD). Structural engineering (MS, PhD); water resource engineering (MS, PhD).
Faculty: 37 full-time (2 women).
Students: 167 full-time (49 women), 44 part-time (12 women); includes 14 minority (1 African American, 4 Asian Americans or Pacific Islanders, 9 Hispanic Americans), 88 international. Average age 30. 280 applicants, 59% accepted. In 2001, 59 master's, 13 doctorates awarded.
Degree requirements: For master's, thesis or alternative, comprehensive exam; for doctorate, thesis/dissertation.
Entrance requirements: For master's, GRE General Test, minimum undergraduate GPA of 3.0. *Application deadline:* For fall admission, 4/30; for spring admission, 10/31. *Application fee:* $50 ($60 for international students).
Expenses: Tuition, state resident: full-time $3,474. Tuition, nonresident: full-time $16,624.
Financial support: In 2001–02, 19 fellowships (averaging $5,252 per year), 45 research assistantships (averaging $15,638 per year), 14 teaching assistantships (averaging $13,821 per year) were awarded. Financial award application deadline: 2/15.
Faculty research: Building systems engineering, construction engineering and management, environmental engineering, geoenvironmental engineering, geotechnical engineering. *Total annual research expenditures:* $8.3 million.
Hon-Yim Ko, Chair, 303-492-6716, *Fax:* 303-492-7317, *E-mail:* ko@spot.colorado.edu.
Application contact: Jan Demay, Graduate Secretary, 303-492-7316, *Fax:* 303-492-7317, *E-mail:* demay@spot.colorado.edu. *Web site:* http://www.civil.colorado.edu/

■ UNIVERSITY OF DETROIT MERCY

School of Architecture, Detroit, MI 48219-0900

AWARDS M Arch.
Entrance requirements: For master's, BS in architecture, minimum GPA of 3.0, portfolio. *Application deadline:* Applications are processed on a rolling basis. *Application fee:* $30 ($50 for international students).
Expenses: Tuition: Full-time $10,620; part-time $590 per credit hour. Required fees: $400. Tuition and fees vary according to program.
Stephen Vogel, Dean, 313-993-1149, *Fax:* 313-993-1512, *E-mail:* architecture@udmercy.edu.

■ UNIVERSITY OF KANSAS

Graduate School, School of Engineering, Department of Civil, Environmental, and Architectural Engineering, Lawrence, KS 66045

AWARDS Architectural engineering (MS); civil engineering (MCE, MS, DE, PhD); construction management (MCM); environmental engineering (MS, PhD); environmental science (MS, PhD); water resources engineering (MS); water resources science (MS).
Faculty: 27.
Students: 38 full-time (11 women), 97 part-time (20 women); includes 12 minority (4 African Americans, 3 Asian Americans or Pacific Islanders, 4 Hispanic Americans, 1 Native American), 37 international. Average age 32. 105 applicants, 31% accepted, 19 enrolled. In 2001, 32 master's, 4 doctorates awarded.
Degree requirements: For master's, thesis or alternative, exam; for doctorate, thesis/dissertation, comprehensive exam.
Entrance requirements: For master's, GRE, Michigan English Language Assessment Battery, TOEFL, minimum GPA of 3.0; for doctorate, GRE, Michigan English Language Assessment Battery, TOEFL, minimum GPA of 3.5. *Application deadline:* Applications are processed on a rolling basis. *Application fee:* $40.
Expenses: Tuition, state resident: full-time $2,722; part-time $113 per credit. Tuition, nonresident: full-time $8,586; part-time $358 per credit. Required fees: $551; $46 per credit. Tuition and fees vary according to campus/location, program and reciprocity agreements.
Financial support: In 2001–02, 21 research assistantships with partial tuition reimbursements (averaging $10,367 per year), 6 teaching assistantships with full and partial tuition reimbursements (averaging $8,615 per year) were awarded. Fellowships, career-related internships or fieldwork also available.
Faculty research: Structures (fracture mechanics), transportation, environmental health.
Steve L. McCabe, Chair, 785-864-3766.

Application contact: David Parr, Graduate Director, *E-mail:* aparr@engr.ukans.edu. *Web site:* http://www.ceae.ku.edu/

■ UNIVERSITY OF LOUISIANA AT LAFAYETTE

Graduate School, College of the Arts, School of Architecture, Lafayette, LA 70504

AWARDS M Arch.

Faculty: 7 full-time (1 woman).
Entrance requirements: For master's, GRE General Test. *Application deadline:* For fall admission, 5/15. *Application fee:* $20 ($30 for international students).
Expenses: Tuition, state resident: full-time $2,317; part-time $79 per credit. Tuition, nonresident: full-time $8,882; part-time $369 per credit. International tuition: $9,018 full-time.
Robert W. McKinney, Director, 337-482-5319.
Application contact: Andrew Chandler, Graduate Coordinator, 337-482-5315.

■ THE UNIVERSITY OF MEMPHIS

Graduate School, Herff College of Engineering, Department of Engineering Technology, Memphis, TN 38152

AWARDS Architectural technology (MS); electronics engineering technology (MS); manufacturing engineering technology (MS). Part-time and evening/weekend programs available.

Faculty: 7 full-time (1 woman), 3 part-time/adjunct (1 woman).
Students: 76 full-time (15 women), 6 part-time (4 women), 77 international. Average age 28. 25 applicants, 68% accepted. In 2001, 26 degrees awarded.
Degree requirements: For master's, thesis optional.
Entrance requirements: For master's, GRE General Test, minimum undergraduate GPA of 2.5. *Application deadline:* For fall admission, 8/1; for spring admission, 12/1. Applications are processed on a rolling basis. *Application fee:* $25 ($50 for international students). Electronic applications accepted.
Expenses: Tuition, state resident: full-time $2,026. Tuition, nonresident: full-time $4,528.

Financial support: In 2001–02, 56 research assistantships with full tuition reimbursements (averaging $1,700 per year) were awarded; career-related internships or fieldwork also available. Financial award application deadline: 9/1.
Faculty research: Teacher education services-technology education; flexible manufacturing control systems; embedded, dedicated, and real-time computer systems; network, Internet, and web-based programming; analog and digital electronic communication systems. *Total annual research expenditures:* $68,205.
Ronald L. Day, Chairman, 901-678-2238, *Fax:* 901-678-5145, *E-mail:* rday@memphis.edu.
Application contact: Dr. Dean L. Smith, Coordinator of Graduate Studies, 901-678-3300, *Fax:* 901-678-5145, *E-mail:* dlsmith@memphis.edu. *Web site:* http://www.people.memphis.edu/~engtech/grad.htm

■ UNIVERSITY OF MIAMI

Graduate School, College of Engineering, Department of Civil, Architectural, and Environmental Engineering, Coral Gables, FL 33124

AWARDS Architectural engineering (MSAE); civil engineering (MSCE, DA, PhD). Part-time and evening/weekend programs available.

Faculty: 11 full-time (1 woman).
Students: 18 full-time (6 women), 2 part-time; includes 15 minority (5 African Americans, 8 Asian Americans or Pacific Islanders, 2 Hispanic Americans). Average age 29. 42 applicants, 45% accepted. In 2001, 3 master's, 2 doctorates awarded.
Degree requirements: For master's, thesis (for some programs); for doctorate, thesis/dissertation, oral and qualifying exams.
Entrance requirements: For master's and doctorate, GRE General Test, TOEFL, minimum GPA of 3.0. *Application deadline:* For fall admission, 2/1 (priority date); for spring admission, 10/1 (priority date). Applications are processed on a rolling basis. *Application fee:* $50. Electronic applications accepted.
Expenses: Tuition: Part-time $960 per credit hour. Required fees: $85 per semester. Tuition and fees vary according to program.

Financial support: Fellowships with tuition reimbursements, research assistantships with tuition reimbursements, teaching assistantships with tuition reimbursements, institutionally sponsored loans and tuition waivers (partial) available.
Faculty research: Wastewater treatment, water management, structural reliability, structural dynamics, wind engineering, water resources.
Dr. David A. Chin, Chairman, 305-284-3391, *Fax:* 305-284-3492, *E-mail:* dchin@miami.edu.
Application contact: Dr. Helena M. Solo-Gabriele, Adviser, 305-284-3391, *Fax:* 305-284-3492, *E-mail:* hmsolo@miami.edu. *Web site:* http://www.eng.miami.edu/~caegrad

■ THE UNIVERSITY OF TEXAS AT AUSTIN

Graduate School, College of Engineering, Program in Architectural Engineering, Austin, TX 78712-1111

AWARDS MSE. Part-time programs available.
Faculty: 8 full-time (0 women), 2 part-time/adjunct (1 woman).
Students: 5 full-time (2 women), 1 part-time; includes 1 minority (Hispanic American), 2 international. 15 applicants, 33% accepted. In 2001, 1 degree awarded.
Degree requirements: For master's, thesis.
Entrance requirements: For master's, GRE General Test. *Application deadline:* For fall admission, 1/15 (priority date); for spring admission, 9/1 (priority date). Applications are processed on a rolling basis. *Application fee:* $50 ($75 for international students). Electronic applications accepted.
Expenses: Tuition, state resident: full-time $3,159. Tuition, nonresident: full-time $6,957. Tuition and fees vary according to program.
Financial support: Fellowships, research assistantships, teaching assistantships, career-related internships or fieldwork available. Support available to part-time students. Financial award application deadline: 2/1.
Faculty research: Materials engineering, structural engineering, construction engineering, project management. *Total annual research expenditures:* $2 million.
Dr. Gerald E. Speitel, Chairman, Department of Civil Engineering, 512-471-4921, *Fax:* 512-471-0592, *E-mail:* speitel@mail.utexas.edu.
Application contact: James T. O'Connor, Graduate Adviser, 512-471-4645, *Fax:* 512-471-3191, *E-mail:* jtoconnor@mail.utexas.edu.

Bioengineering, Biomedical Engineering, and Biotechnology

BIOENGINEERING

■ ALFRED UNIVERSITY

Graduate School, New York State College of Ceramics, School of Ceramic Engineering and Materials Science, Alfred, NY 14802-1205

AWARDS Biomedical materials engineering science (MS); ceramic engineering (MS); ceramics (PhD); glass science (MS, PhD); materials science (MS).

Students: 51 full-time (14 women), 10 part-time (2 women). Average age 24. 108 applicants, 25% accepted. In 2001, 16 master's, 5 doctorates awarded.
Degree requirements: For master's and doctorate, thesis/dissertation.
Entrance requirements: For master's and doctorate, TOEFL. *Application deadline:* Applications are processed on a rolling basis. *Application fee:* $50. Electronic applications accepted.
Expenses: Contact institution.
Financial support: Fellowships, research assistantships, teaching assistantships, tuition waivers (full and partial) available. Financial award applicants required to submit FAFSA.
Faculty research: Fine-particle technology, x-ray diffraction, superconductivity, electronic materials.
Dr. Ronald S. Gordon, Dean, 607-871-2441, *E-mail:* gordon@alfred.edu.
Application contact: Cathleen R. Johnson, Coordinator of Graduate Admissions, 607-871-2141, *Fax:* 607-871-2198, *E-mail:* johnsonc@alfred.edu. *Web site:* http://www.alfred.edu/gradschool
Find an in-depth description at www.petersons.com/gradchannel.

■ ARIZONA STATE UNIVERSITY

Graduate College, College of Engineering and Applied Sciences, Department of Chemical, Bio and Materials Engineering, Program in Bioengineering, Tempe, AZ 85287

AWARDS MS, PhD.

Degree requirements: For doctorate, thesis/dissertation.
Entrance requirements: For master's and doctorate, GRE General Test.
Faculty research: Biotechnology, biocontrol, biomechanics, bioinstrumentation and materials, biosystems engineering/biotransport.
Find an in-depth description at www.petersons.com/gradchannel.

■ AUBURN UNIVERSITY

Graduate School, College of Agriculture, Department of Biosystems Engineering, Auburn University, AL 36849

AWARDS MS, PhD. Part-time programs available.

Faculty: 9 full-time (0 women).
Students: In 2001, 1 master's awarded.
Degree requirements: For master's and doctorate, thesis/dissertation.
Entrance requirements: For master's, GRE General Test; for doctorate, GRE General Test, GRE Subject Test, master's degree. *Application deadline:* For fall admission, 7/7; for spring admission, 11/24. Applications are processed on a rolling basis. *Application fee:* $25 ($50 for international students). Electronic applications accepted.
Financial support: Fellowships, research assistantships, teaching assistantships available. Financial award application deadline: 3/15.
Faculty research: Power and machinery, environmental engineering, forest engineering, waste management, food engineering.
Dr. Clifford A. Flood, Chair, 334-844-4180.
Application contact: Dr. John F. Pritchett, Dean of the Graduate School, 334-844-4700, *E-mail:* hatchlb@mail.auburn.edu. *Web site:* http://www.aeng.auburn.edu/department/an/index.html

■ BAYLOR COLLEGE OF MEDICINE

Medical School, Department of Bioengineering, Houston, TX 77030-3498

AWARDS MD/PhD.

Students: 2 full-time (0 women); includes 1 minority (Asian American or Pacific Islander). Average age 27. 121 applicants, 29% accepted.
Application deadline: For fall admission, 11/1 (priority date). Applications are processed on a rolling basis. *Application fee:* $35. Electronic applications accepted.
Expenses: Tuition, state resident: full-time $6,550. Tuition, nonresident: full-time $19,650. Required fees: $933. Full-time tuition and fees vary according to program and student level.
Financial support: Federal Work-Study, institutionally sponsored loans, and tuition waivers (full and partial) available. Financial award application deadline: 3/29.

Dr. James R. Lupski, Director, 713-798-5264, *Fax:* 713-798-6325, *E-mail:* mstp@bcm.tmc.edu.
Application contact: 713-798-4842, *Fax:* 713-798-5563, *E-mail:* melodym@bcm.tcm.edu. *Web site:* http://www.bcm.tmc.edu/mstp/

■ CALIFORNIA INSTITUTE OF TECHNOLOGY

Division of Engineering and Applied Science, Option in Bioengineering, Pasadena, CA 91125-0001

AWARDS MS, PhD.

Faculty: 1 full-time (0 women).
Students: 2 full-time (0 women); includes 1 minority (Asian American or Pacific Islander). 28 applicants, 29% accepted, 2 enrolled.
Degree requirements: For master's and doctorate, thesis/dissertation.
Application deadline: For fall admission, 1/15.
Faculty research: Biosynthesis and analysis, biometrics.
Dr. Morteza Gharib, Head, 626-395-4453.

■ CALIFORNIA POLYTECHNIC STATE UNIVERSITY, SAN LUIS OBISPO

College of Engineering, Program in Engineering, San Luis Obispo, CA 93407

AWARDS Biochemical engineering (MS); industrial engineering (MS); integrated technology management (MS); materials engineering (MS); water engineering (MS), including bioengineering, biomedical engineering, manufacturing engineering.

Faculty: 98 full-time (8 women), 82 part-time/adjunct (14 women).
Students: 20 full-time (4 women), 9 part-time (1 woman). 25 applicants, 68% accepted, 15 enrolled. In 2001, 22 degrees awarded.
Entrance requirements: For master's, GRE General Test, minimum GPA of 2.5 in last 90 quarter units. *Application fee:* $55.
Expenses: Tuition, nonresident: part-time $164 per unit. One-time fee: $2,153 part-time.
Financial support: Application deadline: 3/2.
Dr. Peter Y. Lee, Dean, 805-756-2131, *Fax:* 805-756-6503, *E-mail:* plee@calpoly.edu.
Application contact: Dr. Daniel W. Walsh, Associate Dean, 805-756-2131, *Fax:* 805-756-6503, *E-mail:* dwalsh@

calpoly.edu. *Web site:* http://www.synner.ceng.calpoly.edu/

■ CARNEGIE MELLON UNIVERSITY

Carnegie Institute of Technology, Biomedical and Health Engineering Program, Pittsburgh, PA 15213-3891

AWARDS Bioengineering (MS, PhD).

Degree requirements: For master's, thesis; for doctorate, thesis/dissertation, qualifying exam.

Entrance requirements: For master's and doctorate, GRE General Test, TOEFL. Electronic applications accepted.

Faculty research: Cellular and molecular systematics, signal and image processing, materials and mechanics. *Web site:* http://www.cmu.edu/cit/biomed/

■ CARNEGIE MELLON UNIVERSITY

Carnegie Institute of Technology, Department of Civil and Environmental Engineering, Pittsburgh, PA 15213-3891

AWARDS Civil engineering (MS, PhD); civil engineering and industrial management (MS); civil engineering and robotics (PhD); civil engineering/bioengineering (PhD); civil engineering/engineering and public policy (MS, PhD). Part-time programs available. Terminal master's awarded for partial completion of doctoral program.

Degree requirements: For master's, thesis (for some programs); for doctorate, thesis/dissertation, qualifying exam.

Entrance requirements: For master's and doctorate, GRE General Test, TOEFL.

Faculty research: Computer-aided engineering and management, structured and computational machines, civil systems. *Web site:* http://www.ce.cmu.edu/

Find an in-depth description at www.petersons.com/gradchannel.

■ CASE WESTERN RESERVE UNIVERSITY

School of Medicine and School of Graduate Studies, Graduate Programs in Medicine, Department of Physiology and Biophysics, Cleveland, OH 44106

AWARDS Biophysics and bioengineering (PhD); cell physiology (PhD); exerscise physiology (MS); physiology and biophysics (PhD); physiology and biotechnology (MS). Systems physiology (PhD).

Faculty: 64.

Students: 41 full-time (13 women), 1 part-time; includes 31 minority (23 African Americans, 7 Asian Americans or Pacific Islanders, 1 Hispanic American), 18 international. Average age 27. 63 applicants, 35% accepted, 12 enrolled. In 2001, 1 master's, 11 doctorates awarded.

Terminal master's awarded for partial completion of doctoral program.

Degree requirements: For master's and doctorate, thesis/dissertation.

Entrance requirements: For master's, minimum GPA of 3.28; for doctorate, GRE General Test, TOEFL, minimum GPA of 3.6. *Application deadline:* For fall admission, 3/15 (priority date). Applications are processed on a rolling basis. *Application fee:* $25.

Financial support: In 2001–02, 14 fellowships with tuition reimbursements (averaging $18,000 per year), 34 research assistantships (averaging $18,000 per year) were awarded. Scholarships/grants and tuition waivers (full) also available. Financial award application deadline: 3/31.

Faculty research: Cardiovascular physiology, calcium metabolism, epithelial cell biology. *Total annual research expenditures:* $9.1 million.

Dr. Antonio Scarpa, Chairman and Professor, 216-368-5298, *Fax:* 216-368-5586, *E-mail:* axs15@po.cwru.edu.

Application contact: A. Thompson, Coordinator, Graduate Training Programs, 216-368-2084, *Fax:* 216-368-5586, *E-mail:* axt36@po.cwru.edu. *Web site:* http://physiology.cwru.edu/

Find an in-depth description at www.petersons.com/gradchannel.

■ CLEMSON UNIVERSITY

Graduate School, College of Agriculture, Forestry and Life Sciences, Department of Agricultural and Biological Engineering, Program in Biosystems Engineering, Clemson, SC 29634

AWARDS M Engr, MS, PhD. Part-time programs available.

Degree requirements: For master's, thesis (for some programs); for doctorate, thesis/dissertation.

Entrance requirements: For master's, GRE General Test, TOEFL, minimum GPA of 3.0; for doctorate, GRE General Test, TOEFL, minimum GPA of 3.0.

Expenses: Tuition, state resident: full-time $5,310. Tuition, nonresident: full-time $11,284.

Dr. Robert Williamson, Graduate Coordinator, 864-656-4074.

■ CLEMSON UNIVERSITY

Graduate School, College of Engineering and Science, Department of Bioengineering, Clemson, SC 29634

AWARDS MS, PhD. Part-time programs available.

Students: 39 full-time (16 women), 3 part-time (2 women); includes 1 minority (Hispanic American), 15 international. Average age 23. 108 applicants, 58% accepted, 15 enrolled. In 2001, 10 degrees awarded.

Degree requirements: For master's, thesis optional; for doctorate, thesis/dissertation.

Entrance requirements: For master's and doctorate, GRE General Test, TOEFL. *Application deadline:* For fall admission, 6/1; for spring admission, 11/1. *Application fee:* $40.

Expenses: Tuition, state resident: full-time $5,310. Tuition, nonresident: full-time $11,284.

Financial support: Fellowships, research assistantships, teaching assistantships, career-related internships or fieldwork available. Financial award application deadline: 2/15; financial award applicants required to submit FAFSA.

Faculty research: Biomaterials, biomechanics.

Dr. R. Larry Dooley, Chair, 864-656-3051, *Fax:* 864-656-4466, *E-mail:* dooley@eng.clemson.edu.

Application contact: Dr. Robert Latour, Graduate Student Coordinator, 864-656-5552, *Fax:* 864-656-4466, *E-mail:* latourr@eng.clemson.edu. *Web site:* http://www.eng.clemson.edu/bio/

Find an in-depth description at www.petersons.com/gradchannel.

■ COLORADO STATE UNIVERSITY

Graduate School, College of Engineering, Department of Mechanical Engineering, Fort Collins, CO 80523-0015

AWARDS Bioengineering (MS, PhD); energy and environmental engineering (MS, PhD); energy conversion (MS, PhD); engineering management (MS); heat and mass transfer (MS, PhD); industrial and manufacturing systems engineering (MS, PhD); mechanical engineering (MS, PhD); mechanics and materials (MS, PhD). Part-time programs available.

Faculty: 17 full-time (2 women).

Students: 36 full-time (6 women), 63 part-time (11 women); includes 5 minority (2 Asian Americans or Pacific Islanders, 2 Hispanic Americans, 1 Native American), 22 international. Average age 32. 234 applicants, 83% accepted, 32 enrolled. In 2001, 10 master's, 3 doctorates awarded. Terminal master's awarded for partial completion of doctoral program.

Degree requirements: For doctorate, thesis/dissertation.

Entrance requirements: For master's and doctorate, GRE General Test, TOEFL, minimum GPA of 3.0. *Application deadline:* For fall admission, 2/1 (priority date). Applications are processed on a rolling basis. *Application fee:* $30. Electronic applications accepted.

Expenses: Tuition, state resident: full-time $2,880; part-time $160 per credit. Tuition, nonresident: full-time $11,412; part-time $634 per credit. Required fees: $750; $34 per credit.

Colorado State University (continued)

Financial support: In 2001–02, 2 fellowships, 15 research assistantships (averaging $15,792 per year), 14 teaching assistantships (averaging $11,844 per year) were awarded. Traineeships also available.
Faculty research: Space propulsion, controls and systems, engineering and materials. *Total annual research expenditures:* $2.1 million.
Dr. Allan T. Kirkpatrick, Head, 970-491-6559, *Fax:* 970-491-3827, *E-mail:* allan@engr.colostate.edu. *Web site:* http://www.engr.colostate.edu/depts/me/index.html

■ **CORNELL UNIVERSITY**

Graduate School, Graduate Fields of Agriculture and Life Sciences and Graduate Fields of Engineering, Field of Agricultural and Biological Engineering, Ithaca, NY 14853-0001

AWARDS Biological engineering (M Eng, MPS, MS, PhD); energy (M Eng, MPS, MS, PhD); environmental engineering (M Eng, MPS, MS, PhD); environmental management (MPS); food processing engineering (M Eng, MPS, MS, PhD); international agriculture (M Eng, MPS, MS, PhD); local roads (M Eng, MPS, MS, PhD); machine systems (M Eng, MPS, MS, PhD). Soil and water engineering (M Eng, MPS, MS, PhD). Structures and environment (M Eng, MPS, MS, PhD).

Faculty: 28 full-time.
Students: 68 full-time (33 women); includes 12 minority (2 African Americans, 9 Asian Americans or Pacific Islanders, 1 Hispanic American), 27 international. 79 applicants, 56% accepted. In 2001, 15 master's, 1 doctorate awarded. Terminal master's awarded for partial completion of doctoral program.
Degree requirements: For master's, thesis (MS); for doctorate, thesis/dissertation.
Entrance requirements: For master's, 3 letters of recommendation (M Eng, MPS, MS); for doctorate, GRE General Test, TOEFL, 3 letters of recommendation. *Application deadline:* For fall admission, 1/15; for spring admission, 10/1. Applications are processed on a rolling basis. *Application fee:* $65. Electronic applications accepted.
Expenses: Tuition: Full-time $25,970. Required fees: $50.
Financial support: In 2001–02, 46 students received support, including 10 fellowships with full tuition reimbursements available, 26 research assistantships with full tuition reimbursements available, 10 teaching assistantships with full tuition reimbursements available; institutionally sponsored loans, scholarships/grants, tuition waivers (full and partial), and unspecified assistantships also available. Financial award applicants required to submit FAFSA.
Faculty research: Biological and food engineering, environmental, soil and water

engineering, international agricultural engineering, structures and controlled environments, machine systems and energy.
Application contact: Graduate Field Assistant, 607-255-2173, *Fax:* 607-255-4080, *E-mail:* abengradfield@cornell.edu. *Web site:* http://www.gradschool.cornell.edu/grad/fields_1/ag-bioengr.html

■ **GEORGIA INSTITUTE OF TECHNOLOGY**

Graduate Studies and Research, College of Engineering, GA Tech/Emory Department of Biomedical Engineering, Atlanta, GA 30332-0001

AWARDS MS Bio E, PhD, Certificate, MD/PhD. Terminal master's awarded for partial completion of doctoral program.

Degree requirements: For master's and doctorate, thesis/dissertation.
Entrance requirements: For master's and doctorate, TOEFL.
Faculty research: Biomechanics and tissue engineering, bioinstrumentation and medical imaging. *Web site:* http://www.bioeng.gatech.edu/

Find an in-depth description at www.petersons.com/gradchannel.

■ **KANSAS STATE UNIVERSITY**

Graduate School, College of Engineering, Department of Biological and Agricultural Engineering, Manhattan, KS 66506

AWARDS MS, PhD.

Faculty: 25 full-time (1 woman).
Students: 20 full-time (7 women), 6 part-time (2 women), 17 international. 11 applicants, 82% accepted, 8 enrolled. In 2001, 1 master's, 3 doctorates awarded. Terminal master's awarded for partial completion of doctoral program.
Degree requirements: For master's and doctorate, thesis/dissertation.
Entrance requirements: For master's, GRE, TOEFL, bachelor's degree in agricultural engineering; for doctorate, GRE, TOEFL. *Application deadline:* For fall admission, 3/1; for spring admission, 10/1. Applications are processed on a rolling basis. *Application fee:* $0 ($25 for international students). Electronic applications accepted.
Expenses: Tuition, state resident: part-time $113 per credit hour. Tuition, nonresident: part-time $358 per credit hour.
Financial support: In 2001–02, 19 research assistantships (averaging $10,000 per year) were awarded; fellowships, teaching assistantships, Federal Work-Study, institutionally sponsored loans, and scholarships/grants also available. Support available to part-time students. Financial

award application deadline: 3/1; financial award applicants required to submit FAFSA.
Faculty research: Water quality, animal production systems, agricultural machinery, irrigation systems, grain processing. *Total annual research expenditures:* $2.3 million.
Dr. James K. Koelliker, Head, 785-532-5580, *Fax:* 785-532-5825, *E-mail:* contact-1@bae.ksu.edu.
Application contact: Naiqian Zhang, Graduate Coordinator, 785-532-5580, *Fax:* 785-532-5825, *E-mail:* contact-1@bae.ksu.edu. *Web site:* http://www.bae.ksu.edu/

■ **KANSAS STATE UNIVERSITY**

Graduate School, College of Engineering, Department of Electrical and Computer Engineering, Manhattan, KS 66506

AWARDS Bioengineering (MS, PhD); communications (MS, PhD); computer engineering (MS, PhD); control systems (MS, PhD); electric energy systems (MS, PhD); instrumentation (MS, PhD). Signal processing (MS, PhD). Postbaccalaureate distance learning degree programs offered (no on-campus study).

Faculty: 22 full-time (3 women).
Students: 34 full-time (8 women), 15 part-time (1 woman); includes 1 minority (Hispanic American), 23 international. 325 applicants, 8% accepted, 16 enrolled. In 2001, 15 master's, 4 doctorates awarded.
Degree requirements: For master's, thesis or alternative, final exam; for doctorate, thesis/dissertation, preliminary exams.
Entrance requirements: For master's, GRE General Test, TOEFL, bachelor's degree in electrical engineering or computer science; minimum GPA of 3.0; for doctorate, GRE General Test, TOEFL. *Application deadline:* For fall admission, 3/1; for spring admission, 9/1. Applications are processed on a rolling basis. *Application fee:* $0 ($25 for international students). Electronic applications accepted.
Expenses: Tuition, state resident: part-time $113 per credit hour. Tuition, nonresident: part-time $358 per credit hour.
Financial support: In 2001–02, 17 research assistantships with partial tuition reimbursements (averaging $9,900 per year), 7 teaching assistantships with full tuition reimbursements (averaging $9,900 per year) were awarded. Career-related internships or fieldwork, institutionally sponsored loans, and scholarships/grants also available. Support available to part-time students. Financial award application deadline: 3/1; financial award applicants required to submit FAFSA.
Faculty research: Communications systems and signal processing, real-time embedded systems, integrated circuits and

devices, bioengineering, power systems. *Total annual research expenditures:* $1.3 million.

Dr. David Soldan, Head, 785-532-5600, *Fax:* 785-532-1188, *E-mail:* grad@eece.ksu.edu.

Application contact: Anil Pahwa, Graduate Program Director, 785-532-5600, *Fax:* 785-532-1188, *E-mail:* pahw@ksu.edu. *Web site:* http://www.eece.ksu.edu/

■ LOUISIANA STATE UNIVERSITY AND AGRICULTURAL AND MECHANICAL COLLEGE

Graduate School, College of Agriculture, Department of Biological and Agricultural Engineering, Baton Rouge, LA 70803

AWARDS Biological and agricultural engineering (MSBAE); engineering science (MS, PhD). Part-time programs available.

Faculty: 9 full-time (2 women).
Students: 9 full-time (5 women), 4 part-time (2 women); includes 1 minority (African American), 8 international. Average age 27. 13 applicants, 54% accepted, 5 enrolled. In 2001, 3 degrees awarded. Terminal master's awarded for partial completion of doctoral program.
Degree requirements: For master's and doctorate, thesis/dissertation.
Entrance requirements: For master's and doctorate, GRE General Test, minimum GPA of 3.0. *Application deadline:* For fall admission, 1/25 (priority date). Applications are processed on a rolling basis. *Application fee:* $25.
Expenses: Tuition, state resident: full-time $2,551. Tuition, nonresident: full-time $5,551. Required fees: $854. Part-time tuition and fees vary according to course load.
Financial support: In 2001–02, 9 research assistantships with partial tuition reimbursements (averaging $14,667 per year) were awarded; fellowships, teaching assistantships with partial tuition reimbursements, career-related internships or fieldwork also available. Financial award application deadline: 7/1; financial award applicants required to submit FAFSA.
Faculty research: Machine development, aquaculture, environmental engineering, microprocessor applications, ergonomics engineering, bioprocessing, hydrology, biosensors, food engineering. *Total annual research expenditures:* $11,895.
Dr. Richard Bengtson, Acting Head, 225-578-3153, *Fax:* 225-578-3492, *E-mail:* bengston@bae.lsu.edu.
Application contact: Dr. David C. Blouin, Associate Dean, 225-578-8303, *Fax:* 225-578-2526, *E-mail:* dblouin@lsu.edu. *Web site:* http://www.coa.lsu.edu/bioen/bioen.html

■ MASSACHUSETTS INSTITUTE OF TECHNOLOGY

School of Engineering, Biological Engineering Division, Cambridge, MA 02139-4307

AWARDS Bioengineering (PhD); biomedical engineering (M Eng); toxicology (SM, PhD, Sc D).

Faculty: 9 full-time (2 women), 1 part-time/adjunct (0 women).
Students: 84 full-time (41 women); includes 14 minority (2 African Americans, 9 Asian Americans or Pacific Islanders, 3 Hispanic Americans), 32 international. Average age 24. 213 applicants, 17% accepted, 25 enrolled. In 2001, 2 master's, 8 doctorates awarded. Terminal master's awarded for partial completion of doctoral program.
Degree requirements: For master's, thesis; for doctorate, thesis/dissertation, oral and written qualifying exams.
Entrance requirements: For master's and doctorate, GRE General Test, TOEFL. *Application deadline:* For fall admission, 1/15. *Application fee:* $60. Electronic applications accepted.
Expenses: Tuition: Full-time $26,960. Full-time tuition and fees vary according to program.
Financial support: In 2001–02, 84 students received support, including 36 fellowships, 35 research assistantships, 7 teaching assistantships; Federal Work-Study, institutionally sponsored loans, scholarships/grants, health care benefits, and unspecified assistantships also available. Financial award application deadline: 1/15; financial award applicants required to submit FAFSA.
Faculty research: Biological imaging, biological microanalytics, biological transport process, biomaterials, cell and tissue engineering. *Total annual research expenditures:* $9 million.
Douglas A. Lauffenburger, Co-Director, 617-252-1629, *E-mail:* lauffen@mit.edu.
Application contact: Dalia Gabour, Academic Administrator, 617-253-5804, *Fax:* 617-258-8676, *E-mail:* be-www@mit.edu. *Web site:* http://web.mit.edu/beh/

Find an in-depth description at www.petersons.com/gradchannel.

■ MISSISSIPPI STATE UNIVERSITY

College of Engineering, Department of Agricultural and Biological Engineering, Mississippi State, MS 39762

AWARDS Biological engineering (MS); biomedical engineering (MS, PhD); engineering (PhD).

Faculty: 8 full-time (0 women), 1 part-time/adjunct (0 women).
Students: 10 full-time (4 women), 7 part-time (3 women); includes 2 minority (both

African Americans), 4 international. Average age 29. 7 applicants, 57% accepted. In 2001, 3 degrees awarded.
Degree requirements: For master's, thesis; for doctorate, thesis/dissertation, preliminary exam.
Entrance requirements: For master's, GRE General Test, TOEFL, minimum GPA of 2.75, minimum GPA of 3.0 for biomedical program; for doctorate, GRE General Test, TOEFL, minimum GPA of 3.0 for biomedical program. *Application deadline:* For fall admission, 7/1; for spring admission, 11/1. Applications are processed on a rolling basis. *Application fee:* $25 for international students.
Expenses: Tuition, state resident: full-time $3,586; part-time $150 per credit hour. Tuition, nonresident: full-time $8,128; part-time $339 per credit hour. Tuition and fees vary according to course load and campus/location.
Financial support: In 2001–02, 1 fellowship with tuition reimbursement (averaging $15,000 per year), 2 research assistantships with tuition reimbursements (averaging $12,500 per year), 1 teaching assistantship with tuition reimbursement (averaging $12,500 per year) were awarded. Federal Work-Study, institutionally sponsored loans, and unspecified assistantships also available. Financial award applicants required to submit FAFSA.
Faculty research: Bioenvironmental engineering, bioinstrumentation, biomechanics/biomaterials, precision agriculture, tissue engineering. *Total annual research expenditures:* $950,000.
Dr. Jerome A. Gilbert, Head, 662-325-3280, *Fax:* 662-325-3853, *E-mail:* jgilbert@abe.msstate.edu.
Application contact: Jerry B. Inmon, Director of Admissions, 662-325-2224, *Fax:* 662-325-7360, *E-mail:* admit@admissions.msstate.edu. *Web site:* http://www.abe.msstate.edu/

■ NORTH CAROLINA STATE UNIVERSITY

Graduate School, College of Agriculture and Life Sciences and College of Engineering, Department of Biological and Agricultural Engineering, Raleigh, NC 27695

AWARDS MBAE, MS, PhD. Part-time programs available.

Faculty: 33 full-time (2 women), 13 part-time/adjunct (2 women).
Students: 32 full-time (13 women), 8 part-time (3 women); includes 6 minority (4 African Americans, 1 Asian American or Pacific Islander, 1 Hispanic American), 7 international. Average age 30. 21 applicants, 29% accepted. In 2001, 5 master's, 1 doctorate awarded.
Degree requirements: For master's, thesis or alternative; for doctorate, thesis/dissertation.
Entrance requirements: For master's and doctorate, GRE (international applicants

North Carolina State University (continued)

only), TOEFL. *Application deadline:* For fall admission, 6/25. Applications are processed on a rolling basis. *Application fee:* $45.
Expenses: Tuition, state resident: full-time $1,748. Tuition, nonresident: full-time $6,904.
Financial support: In 2001–02, 3 fellowships (averaging $7,058 per year), 25 research assistantships (averaging $5,007 per year) were awarded. Teaching assistantships, career-related internships or fieldwork also available. Financial award application deadline: 2/28.
Faculty research: Bioinstrumentation, animal waste management, water quality engineering, machine systems, controlled environment agriculture. *Total annual research expenditures:* $7.3 million.
Dr. James H. Young, Director of Graduate Programs, 919-515-6710, *Fax:* 919-515-6719, *E-mail:* jim_young@ncsu.edu.
Application contact: Dr. Daniel H. Willits, Director of Graduate Programs, 919-515-6755, *Fax:* 919-515-7760, *E-mail:* bae_gradprog@ncsu.edu. *Web site:* http://www.bae.ncsu.edu/bae/

■ THE OHIO STATE UNIVERSITY

Graduate School, College of Food, Agricultural, and Environmental Sciences, Department of Food, Agricultural, and Biological Engineering, Columbus, OH 43210
AWARDS MS, PhD.

Degree requirements: For master's, thesis optional; for doctorate, thesis/dissertation.
Entrance requirements: For master's, GRE General Test, (international students and non-engineering majors); for doctorate, GRE General Test (international students and non-engineering majors).

■ OKLAHOMA STATE UNIVERSITY

Graduate College, College of Agricultural Sciences and Natural Resources and College of Engineering, Architecture and Technology, School of Biosystems and Agricultural Engineering, Stillwater, OK 74078
AWARDS M Bio E, MS, PhD.

Faculty: 22 full-time (1 woman).
Students: 11 full-time (0 women), 19 part-time (5 women); includes 1 minority (Hispanic American), 18 international. Average age 27. 1 applicant, 100% accepted. In 2001, 1 degree awarded.
Degree requirements: For master's and doctorate, thesis/dissertation.
Entrance requirements: For master's and doctorate, TOEFL. *Application deadline:* For fall admission, 6/1 (priority date). *Application fee:* $25.

Expenses: Tuition, state resident: part-time $92 per credit hour. Tuition, nonresident: part-time $297 per credit hour. Required fees: $21 per credit hour. $14 per semester. One-time fee: $20. Tuition and fees vary according to course load.
Financial support: In 2001–02, 28 students received support, including 27 research assistantships (averaging $12,589 per year), 2 teaching assistantships (averaging $19,150 per year); career-related internships or fieldwork, Federal Work-Study, and tuition waivers (partial) also available. Support available to part-time students. Financial award application deadline: 3/1.
Dr. Ron Elliot, Head, 405-744-5431, *Fax:* 405-744-6059.

■ OREGON STATE UNIVERSITY

Graduate School, College of Engineering, Department of Bioengineering, Corvallis, OR 97331
AWARDS M Agr, MAIS, MS, PhD.

Students: 22 full-time (11 women), 2 part-time, 10 international. Average age 31. In 2001, 3 master's, 3 doctorates awarded. Terminal master's awarded for partial completion of doctoral program.
Degree requirements: For master's, thesis or alternative; for doctorate, thesis/dissertation.
Entrance requirements: For master's and doctorate, TOEFL, minimum GPA of 3.0 in last 90 hours. *Application deadline:* For fall admission, 3/1. Applications are processed on a rolling basis. *Application fee:* $50.
Expenses: Contact institution.
Financial support: Fellowships, research assistantships, teaching assistantships, Federal Work-Study and institutionally sponsored loans available. Support available to part-time students. Financial award application deadline: 2/1.
Faculty research: Bioengineering, water resources engineering, food engineering, cell culture and fermentation, vadose zone transport, regional hydrology modeling, bioseparations, post-harvest processing, biomedical engineering, nonpoint pollution abatement, drug formulation and delivery, waste management, stochastic hydrology, biological modeling.
Dr. James A. Moore, Head, 541-737-6299, *Fax:* 541-737-2082, *E-mail:* mooreja@engr.orst.edu. *Web site:* http://www.bioe.orst.edu/

■ THE PENNSYLVANIA STATE UNIVERSITY MILTON S. HERSHEY MEDICAL CENTER

Graduate School Programs in the Biomedical Sciences, Intercollege Bioengineering Graduate Program, Hershey, PA 17033-2360
AWARDS MS, PhD, MD/PhD.

Students: 8 full-time (4 women), 5 international. Terminal master's awarded for partial completion of doctoral program.
Degree requirements: For master's, thesis/dissertation, registration; for doctorate, thesis/dissertation, comprehensive exam, registration.
Entrance requirements: For master's and doctorate, GRE, TOEFL. *Application deadline:* Applications are processed on a rolling basis. *Application fee:* $45. Electronic applications accepted.
Expenses: Tuition, state resident: full-time $20,500. Tuition, nonresident: full-time $28,500. Full-time tuition and fees vary according to degree level.
Financial support: In 2001–02, 1 fellowship with full tuition reimbursement, 1 research assistantship with full tuition reimbursement were awarded. Scholarships/grants and unspecified assistantships also available. Financial award applicants required to submit FAFSA.
Dr. Gerson Rosenberg, Head, *E-mail:* grad-hmc@psu.edu.
Application contact: Dr. William Weiss, Co-Director, Bioengineering Institute of Hershey, *E-mail:* grad-hmc@psu.edu. *Web site:* http://www.hmc.psu.edu/bioengineering_program/index.html

■ THE PENNSYLVANIA STATE UNIVERSITY UNIVERSITY PARK CAMPUS

Graduate School, Intercollege Graduate Programs, Department of Bioengineering, State College, University Park, PA 16802-1503
AWARDS MS, PhD.

Students: 26 full-time (9 women), 7 part-time (1 woman). In 2001, 7 master's, 1 doctorate awarded. Terminal master's awarded for partial completion of doctoral program.
Degree requirements: For master's and doctorate, thesis/dissertation.
Entrance requirements: For master's and doctorate, GRE General Test, TOEFL. *Application fee:* $45.
Expenses: Tuition, state resident: full-time $7,882; part-time $333 per credit. Tuition, nonresident: full-time $16,142; part-time $673 per credit. Required fees: $124 per semester.
Dr. Herbert H. Lipowsky, Head, 814-865-1407.
Find an in-depth description at www.petersons.com/gradchannel.

■ PURDUE UNIVERSITY

Graduate School, Schools of Engineering, School of Electrical and Computer Engineering, West Lafayette, IN 47907
AWARDS Biomedical engineering (MS Bm E, PhD); computer engineering (MS, PhD); electrical engineering (MS, PhD). Part-time

programs available. Postbaccalaureate distance learning degree programs offered (no on-campus study).

Faculty: 63 full-time (5 women), 10 part-time/adjunct (0 women).
Students: 355 full-time (46 women), 109 part-time (22 women); includes 27 minority (5 African Americans, 17 Asian Americans or Pacific Islanders, 5 Hispanic Americans), 353 international. Average age 27. 1,506 applicants, 27% accepted. In 2001, 123 master's, 38 doctorates awarded.
Degree requirements: For master's, thesis optional; for doctorate, thesis/dissertation.
Entrance requirements: For master's and doctorate, GRE General Test, TOEFL. *Application deadline:* For fall admission, 1/15 (priority date); for spring admission, 9/1. Applications are processed on a rolling basis. *Application fee:* $30. Electronic applications accepted.
Expenses: Tuition, state resident: full-time $4,164; part-time $149 per credit hour. Tuition, nonresident: full-time $13,872; part-time $458 per credit hour. Tuition and fees vary according to campus/location and program.
Financial support: In 2001–02, 305 students received support, including 28 fellowships with partial tuition reimbursements available (averaging $16,200 per year), 179 research assistantships with partial tuition reimbursements available (averaging $15,000 per year), 98 teaching assistantships with partial tuition reimbursements available (averaging $11,900 per year) Financial award application deadline: 1/5.
Faculty research: Biomedical communications and signal processing, solid-state materials and devices fields and optics, automatic controls, energy sources and systems, VLSI and circuit design. *Total annual research expenditures:* $13.9 million.
Dr. W. K. Fuchs, Head, 765-494-3539, *Fax:* 765-494-3544, *E-mail:* fuchs@purdue.edu.
Application contact: Dr. A. M. Weiner, Director of Admissions, 765-494-3392, *Fax:* 765-494-3393, *E-mail:* ecegrad@ecn.purdue.edu. *Web site:* http://www.ece.purdue.edu/ECE/
Find an in-depth description at www.petersons.com/gradchannel.

■ PURDUE UNIVERSITY

Graduate School, Schools of Engineering, School of Mechanical Engineering, West Lafayette, IN 47907

AWARDS Biomedical engineering (MS Bm E, PhD); mechanical engineering (MS, MSE, MSME, PhD).

Faculty: 53 full-time (3 women), 2 part-time/adjunct (0 women).
Students: 311 full-time (28 women), 33 part-time (7 women); includes 15 minority (5 African Americans, 6 Asian Americans or Pacific Islanders, 4 Hispanic

Americans), 210 international. Average age 23. 645 applicants, 33% accepted, 123 enrolled. In 2001, 88 master's, 18 doctorates awarded.
Degree requirements: For doctorate, thesis/dissertation.
Entrance requirements: For master's and doctorate, TOEFL. *Application fee:* $30. Electronic applications accepted.
Expenses: Tuition, state resident: full-time $4,164; part-time $149 per credit hour. Tuition, nonresident: full-time $13,872; part-time $458 per credit hour. Tuition and fees vary according to campus/location and program.
Financial support: In 2001–02, 209 students received support, including 23 fellowships with full tuition reimbursements available (averaging $18,450 per year), 140 research assistantships with full tuition reimbursements available (averaging $18,900 per year), 46 teaching assistantships with full tuition reimbursements available (averaging $15,300 per year); career-related internships or fieldwork also available. Support available to part-time students. Financial award applicants required to submit FAFSA.
Faculty research: Design, manufacturing, thermal/fluid sciences, mechanics, electromechanical systems.
Dr. E. Dan Hirleman, Head, 765-494-5688.
Application contact: Susan K. Fisher, Graduate Administrator, 765-494-5729, *Fax:* 765-496-7534.
Find an in-depth description at www.petersons.com/gradchannel.

■ RICE UNIVERSITY

Graduate Programs, George R. Brown School of Engineering, Department of Bioengineering, Houston, TX 77251-1892

AWARDS MS, PhD, MD/PhD.

Faculty: 17 full-time (3 women), 18 part-time/adjunct (0 women).
Students: 56 full-time (14 women); includes 21 minority (2 African Americans, 17 Asian Americans or Pacific Islanders, 2 Hispanic Americans). Average age 25. 215 applicants, 12% accepted. In 2001, 2 degrees awarded. Terminal master's awarded for partial completion of doctoral program.
Degree requirements: For master's, thesis, registration; for doctorate, thesis/dissertation, qualifying exam, internship.
Entrance requirements: For master's and doctorate, GRE General Test, TOEFL. *Application deadline:* For fall admission, 2/1. *Application fee:* $25. Electronic applications accepted.
Expenses: Tuition: Full-time $17,300. Required fees: $250.
Financial support: In 2001–02, 26 fellowships with full tuition reimbursements (averaging $18,500 per year), 17 research assistantships with full tuition reimbursements (averaging $18,500 per year), 1

teaching assistantship with full tuition reimbursement (averaging $9,250 per year) were awarded. Scholarships/grants, traineeships, and tuition waivers (full) also available.
Faculty research: Biomaterials, tissue engineering, laser-tissue interactions, biochemical engineering, gene therapy. *Total annual research expenditures:* $3.5 million.
Dr. Larry V. McIntire, Chair, 713-348-4903, *Fax:* 713-348-5877, *E-mail:* mcintire@rice.edu.
Application contact: Mauricio A. Benitez, Department Coordinator, 713-348-2871, *Fax:* 713-348-5877, *E-mail:* bioeng@ruf.rice.edu. *Web site:* http://www.ruf.rice.edu/~bioeng/

■ RICE UNIVERSITY

Graduate Programs, George R. Brown School of Engineering, Department of Electrical and Computer Engineering, Houston, TX 77251-1892

AWARDS Bioengineering (MS, PhD); circuits, controls, and communication systems (MS, PhD); computer science and engineering (MS, PhD); electrical engineering (MEE); lasers, microwaves, and solid-state electronics (MS, PhD). Part-time programs available.

Faculty: 20 full-time (2 women), 4 part-time/adjunct (0 women).
Students: 98 full-time (18 women), 8 part-time (2 women); includes 6 minority (1 African American, 3 Asian Americans or Pacific Islanders, 2 Hispanic Americans), 72 international. 337 applicants, 19% accepted, 34 enrolled. In 2001, 12 master's, 9 doctorates awarded.
Degree requirements: For master's, thesis (for some programs); for doctorate, thesis/dissertation.
Entrance requirements: For master's and doctorate, GRE General Test, GRE Subject Test, TOEFL, minimum GPA of 3.0. *Application deadline:* For fall admission, 2/1; for spring admission, 11/1. Applications are processed on a rolling basis. *Application fee:* $25.
Expenses: Tuition: Full-time $17,300. Required fees: $250.
Financial support: In 2001–02, 29 fellowships with tuition reimbursements, 60 research assistantships with tuition reimbursements, 2 teaching assistantships with tuition reimbursements were awarded. Federal Work-Study also available.
Faculty research: Physical electronics, systems, computer engineering, bioengineering. *Total annual research expenditures:* $4.5 million.
Don H. Johnson, Chairman, 713-348-4020.
Application contact: Bea Sparks, Information Contact, 713-348-4020, *E-mail:* elec@rice.edu. *Web site:* http://www.ece.rice.edu/

■ RUTGERS, THE STATE UNIVERSITY OF NEW JERSEY, NEW BRUNSWICK

Graduate School, Program in Bioresource Engineering, New Brunswick, NJ 08901-1281

AWARDS MS. Part-time programs available.

Degree requirements: For master's, thesis, seminar.
Entrance requirements: For master's, GRE General Test.
Faculty research: Greenhouse engineering, energy and environment, machine vision, flexible automation and robotics, systems analysis. *Web site:* http://www.rci.rutgers.edu/~biorengg/

■ SYRACUSE UNIVERSITY

Graduate School, L. C. Smith College of Engineering and Computer Science, Department of Bioengineering and Neuroscience, Syracuse, NY 13244-0003

AWARDS Bioengineering (ME, MS, PhD); neuroscience (MS).

Faculty: 9 full-time (3 women), 3 part-time/adjunct (0 women).
Students: 38 full-time (8 women), 1 (woman) part-time; includes 4 minority (all Asian Americans or Pacific Islanders), 7 international. In 2001, 9 degrees awarded.
Entrance requirements: For master's, GRE General Test, GRE Subject Test.
Application deadline: Applications are processed on a rolling basis. *Application fee:* $50.
Expenses: Tuition: Full-time $15,528; part-time $647 per credit. Required fees: $420; $38 per term. Tuition and fees vary according to program.
Financial support: In 2001–02, 3 fellowships with full tuition reimbursements (averaging $13,680 per year), 10 research assistantships with full tuition reimbursements (averaging $11,000 per year), 1 teaching assistantship with full tuition reimbursement (averaging $11,000 per year) were awarded. Financial award application deadline: 1/10.
Faculty research: Audition, taction, multisensory, computational neuroscience. *Total annual research expenditures:* $2.1 million.
Dr. Jeremy Gilbert, Chair, 315-443-5629, *Fax:* 315-443-1184, *E-mail:* gilbert@ecs.syr.edu.
Application contact: Dr. Laurel Carney, Information Contact, 315-443-9749, *Fax:* 315-443-1184, *E-mail:* lacarney@syr.edu. *Web site:* http://www.ecs.syr.edu/
Find an in-depth description at www.petersons.com/gradchannel.

■ TEXAS A&M UNIVERSITY

College of Agriculture and Life Sciences and College of Engineering, Department of Biological and Agricultural Engineering, College Station, TX 77843

AWARDS M Agr, M Eng, MS, PhD. Part-time programs available.

Faculty: 35.
Students: 39 (12 women). Average age 27.
Degree requirements: For master's, thesis (MS), preliminary and final exams; for doctorate, thesis/dissertation, preliminary and final exams.
Entrance requirements: For master's and doctorate, GRE General Test, TOEFL.
Application deadline: For fall admission, 2/1 (priority date); for spring admission, 10/1. Applications are processed on a rolling basis. *Application fee:* $50 ($75 for international students). Electronic applications accepted.
Expenses: Tuition, state resident: full-time $11,872. Tuition, nonresident: full-time $17,892.
Financial support: In 2001–02, fellowships (averaging $12,000 per year), research assistantships (averaging $14,250 per year), teaching assistantships (averaging $14,271 per year) were awarded. Career-related internships or fieldwork and tuition waivers (partial) also available. Financial award application deadline: 3/1; financial award applicants required to submit FAFSA. *Total annual research expenditures:* $1.2 million.
James R. Gilley, Head, 979-845-3931, *Fax:* 979-862-3442, *E-mail:* gilley@zeus.tamu.edu.
Application contact: Jeana Goodson, Academic Programs Assistant, 979-845-0609, *Fax:* 979-862-3442, *E-mail:* j-goodson@tamu.edu. *Web site:* http://agen.tamu.edu/

■ TUFTS UNIVERSITY

Division of Graduate and Continuing Studies and Research, Graduate and Professional Studies, Program in Bioengineering, Medford, MA 02155

AWARDS Certificate. Part-time and evening/weekend programs available.

Students: Average age 30. 3 applicants, 100% accepted. In 2001, 1 degree awarded.
Application deadline: For fall admission, 8/15 (priority date); for spring admission, 12/12 (priority date). Applications are processed on a rolling basis. *Application fee:* $50. Electronic applications accepted.
Expenses: Tuition: Full-time $26,853. Full-time tuition and fees vary according to program.
Financial support: Available to part-time students. Application deadline: 5/1.
Alida Poirier, Assistant Director, 617-627-3395, *Fax:* 617-627-3016, *E-mail:* pcs@ase.tufts.edu.

Application contact: Information Contact, 617-627-3395, *Fax:* 617-627-3016, *E-mail:* pcs@ase.tufts.edu. *Web site:* http://ase.tufts.edu/gradstudy

■ UNIVERSITY OF ARKANSAS

Graduate School, College of Engineering, Department of Biological and Agricultural Engineering, Fayetteville, AR 72701-1201

AWARDS MSBAE, MSE, PhD.

Students: 1 (woman) full-time, 7 part-time (2 women), 4 international. 12 applicants, 33% accepted. In 2001, 1 master's, 2 doctorates awarded.
Degree requirements: For master's, thesis; for doctorate, one foreign language, thesis/dissertation.
Application fee: $40 ($50 for international students).
Expenses: Tuition, state resident: full-time $3,553; part-time $197 per credit. Tuition, nonresident: full-time $8,411; part-time $467 per credit. Required fees: $42 per credit. Tuition and fees vary according to course load and program.
Financial support: In 2001–02, 9 research assistantships were awarded; career-related internships or fieldwork and Federal Work-Study also available. Support available to part-time students. Financial award application deadline: 4/1; financial award applicants required to submit FAFSA.
Lalit R. Verma, Head, 479-575-2351.

■ UNIVERSITY OF CALIFORNIA, BERKELEY

Graduate Division, Group in Bioengineering, Berkeley, CA 94720-1708

AWARDS PhD.

Degree requirements: For doctorate, thesis/dissertation, qualifying exam.
Entrance requirements: For doctorate, GRE General Test, minimum GPA of 3.0.
Expenses: Tuition, nonresident: full-time $10,704. Required fees: $4,349.
Faculty research: Imaging, biomechanics, biomems modeling, neuroscience, biomedical computing, vision. *Web site:* http://bioeng.berkeley.edu

■ UNIVERSITY OF CALIFORNIA, DAVIS

Graduate Studies, College of Engineering, Program in Biological and Agricultural Engineering, Davis, CA 95616

AWARDS M Engr, MS, D Engr, PhD, M Engr/MBA. Part-time programs available.

Faculty: 28 full-time (3 women).
Students: 48 full-time (15 women); includes 6 minority (5 Asian Americans or Pacific Islanders, 1 Hispanic American), 24 international. Average age 30. 24 applicants, 79% accepted, 11 enrolled. In

2001, 4 master's, 6 doctorates awarded. Terminal master's awarded for partial completion of doctoral program.

Degree requirements: For master's and doctorate, thesis/dissertation.

Entrance requirements: For master's, minimum GPA of 3.0; for doctorate, GRE, minimum graduate GPA of 3.25. *Application deadline:* For fall admission, 4/1 (priority date). *Application fee:* $60. Electronic applications accepted.

Expenses: Tuition, state resident: full-time $4,831. Tuition, nonresident: full-time $15,725.

Financial support: In 2001–02, 43 students received support, including 21 fellowships with full and partial tuition reimbursements available (averaging $4,445 per year), 27 research assistantships with full and partial tuition reimbursements available (averaging $10,562 per year), 6 teaching assistantships with partial tuition reimbursements available (averaging $14,145 per year); Federal Work-Study, institutionally sponsored loans, scholarships/grants, and tuition waivers (full and partial) also available. Financial award application deadline: 1/15; financial award applicants required to submit FAFSA.

Faculty research: Forestry, irrigation and drainage, power and machinery, structures and environment, information and energy technologies.

Bruce R. Hartsough, Chair, 530-752-8331, *E-mail:* bioageng@ucdavis.edu.

Application contact: Leigh Ann Empie, Information Contact, 530-752-1451, *Fax:* 530-752-2780, *E-mail:* laempie@ucdavis.edu. *Web site:* http://www.engr.ucdavis.edu/~bae/

■ UNIVERSITY OF CALIFORNIA, SAN DIEGO

Graduate Studies and Research, Department of Bioengineering, La Jolla, CA 92093

AWARDS M Eng, MS, PhD.

Students: 113 (39 women). 355 applicants, 40% accepted, 47 enrolled. In 2001, 18 master's, 6 doctorates awarded.

Entrance requirements: For master's and doctorate, GRE General Test, TOEFL, minimum GPA of 3.0. *Application deadline:* For fall admission, 1/16. *Application fee:* $40. Electronic applications accepted.

Expenses: Tuition, nonresident: full-time $10,434. Required fees: $4,883.

David Gough, Chair.

Application contact: Graduate Coordinator, 858-534-6884.

Find an in-depth description at www.petersons.com/gradchannel.

■ UNIVERSITY OF CALIFORNIA, SAN FRANCISCO

Graduate Division, Program in Bioengineering, San Francisco, CA 94143

AWARDS PhD.

Degree requirements: For doctorate, thesis/dissertation, qualifying exam.

Entrance requirements: For doctorate, GRE General Test, minimum GPA of 3.0.

Faculty research: Imaging, biomechanics, modeling, neuroscience, biomedical computing, vision. *Web site:* http://bioeng.berkeley.edu/

■ UNIVERSITY OF CONNECTICUT

Graduate School, School of Engineering, Field of Electrical and Systems Engineering, Storrs, CT 06269

AWARDS Biological engineering (MS); control and communication systems (MS, PhD); electromagnetics and physical electronics (MS, PhD). Terminal master's awarded for partial completion of doctoral program.

Degree requirements: For master's, thesis or alternative; for doctorate, thesis/dissertation.

Entrance requirements: For master's and doctorate, GRE General Test, TOEFL.

■ UNIVERSITY OF FLORIDA

Graduate School, College of Engineering and College of Agricultural and Life Sciences, Department of Agricultural and Biological Engineering, Gainesville, FL 32611

AWARDS Agricultural and biological engineering (ME, MS, PhD, Engr); agricultural operations management (MS, PhD). Part-time programs available. Terminal master's awarded for partial completion of doctoral program.

Degree requirements: For master's and Engr, thesis optional; for doctorate, thesis/dissertation.

Entrance requirements: For master's and doctorate, GRE General Test, minimum GPA of 3.0; for Engr, GRE General Test. Electronic applications accepted.

Expenses: Tuition, state resident: part-time $164 per hour. Tuition, nonresident: part-time $571 per hour. Tuition and fees vary according to course level and program.

Faculty research: Soil and water engineering, structures and environments, power and machinery, biological processing, food engineering, remote sensing hydrology, geographic information systems. *Web site:* http://www.agen.ufl.edu/

■ UNIVERSITY OF GEORGIA

Graduate School, College of Agricultural and Environmental Sciences, Department of Biological and Agricultural Engineering, Athens, GA 30602

AWARDS Agricultural engineering (MS); biological and agricultural engineering (PhD); biological engineering (MS).

Faculty: 30 full-time (1 woman).

Students: 15 full-time (5 women), 8 part-time (1 woman); includes 1 minority (Hispanic American), 9 international. 36 applicants, 36% accepted. In 2001, 3 master's, 1 doctorate awarded.

Degree requirements: For master's, thesis; for doctorate, one foreign language, thesis/dissertation.

Entrance requirements: For master's and doctorate, GRE General Test. *Application deadline:* For fall admission, 7/1 (priority date); for spring admission, 11/15. *Application fee:* $30. Electronic applications accepted.

Expenses: Tuition, state resident: full-time $2,376; part-time $132 per credit hour. Tuition, nonresident: full-time $9,504; part-time $528 per credit hour. Required fees: $236 per semester.

Financial support: Fellowships, research assistantships, teaching assistantships, unspecified assistantships available.

Dr. E. Dale Threadgill, Head, 706-542-1653, *Fax:* 706-542-8806, *E-mail:* tgill@engr.uga.edu.

Application contact: Dr. E. William Tollner, Contact, 706-542-3047, *Fax:* 706-542-6063, *E-mail:* btollner@engr.uga.edu. *Web site:* http://www.engr.uga.edu/index.html

Find an in-depth description at www.petersons.com/gradchannel.

■ UNIVERSITY OF HAWAII AT MANOA

Graduate Division, College of Tropical Agriculture and Human Resources, Department of Molecular Biosciences and Bioengineering, Honolulu, HI 96822

AWARDS Biosystems engineering (MS); molecular biosystems and bioengineering (MS, PhD). Part-time programs available.

Faculty: 39 full-time (4 women), 13 part-time/adjunct (2 women).

Students: 30 full-time (11 women), 6 part-time (2 women); includes 5 Asian Americans or Pacific Islanders, 1 Hispanic American. Average age 30. 37 applicants, 41% accepted, 5 enrolled.

Degree requirements: For master's, thesis.

Application deadline: For fall admission, 3/1; for spring admission, 9/1. *Application fee:* $25 ($50 for international students).

Expenses: Tuition, state resident: full-time $2,160; part-time $1,980 per year. Tuition,

University of Hawaii at Manoa (continued)

nonresident: full-time $5,190; part-time $4,829 per year.
Financial support: In 2001–02, 4 research assistantships (averaging $14,958 per year), 3 teaching assistantships (averaging $12,786 per year) were awarded. Fellowships, Federal Work-Study, institutionally sponsored loans, and tuition waivers (full) also available.
Faculty research: Mechanization, agricultural systems, waste management, water management, cell culture.
Dr. Charles M. Kinoshita, Chairperson, 808-956-8186, *Fax:* 808-956-9269, *E-mail:* kinoshi@wiliki.eng.hawaii.edu.
Application contact: Dr. Dulal Borthakur, Graduate Chair, 808-956-6600, *Fax:* 808-956-3542, *E-mail:* dulal@hawaii.edu.

■ **UNIVERSITY OF ILLINOIS AT CHICAGO**

Graduate College, College of Engineering, Bioengineering Department, Chicago, IL 60607-7128

AWARDS MS, PhD, MD/PhD.

Students: 85 full-time (25 women), 32 part-time (13 women); includes 26 minority (5 African Americans, 18 Asian Americans or Pacific Islanders, 3 Hispanic Americans), 53 international. Average age 27. 170 applicants, 45% accepted, 34 enrolled. In 2001, 13 master's, 5 doctorates awarded. Terminal master's awarded for partial completion of doctoral program.
Degree requirements: For master's and doctorate, thesis/dissertation.
Entrance requirements: For master's and doctorate, GRE Subject Test, TOEFL, minimum GPA of 4.0 on a 5.0 scale. *Application deadline:* For fall admission, 6/1; for spring admission, 11/1. Applications are processed on a rolling basis. *Application fee:* $40 ($50 for international students). Electronic applications accepted.
Expenses: Tuition, state resident: full-time $3,060. Tuition, nonresident: full-time $6,688.
Financial support: In 2001–02, 65 students received support; fellowships with full tuition reimbursements available, research assistantships with full tuition reimbursements available, teaching assistantships with full tuition reimbursements available, career-related internships or fieldwork, Federal Work-Study, and tuition waivers (full) available. Financial award application deadline: 3/1; financial award applicants required to submit FAFSA.
Faculty research: Imaging systems, bioinstrumentation, electrophysiology, biological control, laser scattering.
Dr. William O'Neill, Head, 312-413-2294.
Find an in-depth description at www.petersons.com/gradchannel.

■ **UNIVERSITY OF MAINE**

Graduate School, College of Engineering, Department of Chemical and Biological Engineering, Program in Biological Engineering, Orono, ME 04469

AWARDS MS. Part-time programs available.

Students: 1 (woman) full-time, 1 international. 2 applicants, 100% accepted, 1 enrolled. In 2001, 1 degree awarded. Terminal master's awarded for partial completion of doctoral program.
Degree requirements: For master's, thesis (for some programs).
Entrance requirements: For master's, GRE General Test, TOEFL. *Application deadline:* For fall admission, 2/1 (priority date). Applications are processed on a rolling basis. *Application fee:* $50. Electronic applications accepted.
Expenses: Tuition, state resident: full-time $3,780; part-time $210 per credit hour. Tuition, nonresident: full-time $10,782; part-time $599 per credit hour. Required fees: $9.5 per credit hour. $32 per semester. Tuition and fees vary according to reciprocity agreements.
Financial support: Federal Work-Study available. Financial award application deadline: 3/1.
Dr. Darrell Donahue, Coordinator, 207-581-2728, *Fax:* 207-581-2725.
Application contact: Scott G. Delcourt, Director of the Graduate School, 207-581-3218, *Fax:* 207-581-3232, *E-mail:* graduate@maine.edu. *Web site:* http://www.umaine.edu/graduate/

■ **UNIVERSITY OF MARYLAND, COLLEGE PARK**

Graduate Studies and Research, College of Agriculture and Natural Resources, Department of Biological Resources Engineering, College Park, MD 20742

AWARDS MS, PhD.

Faculty: 16 full-time (2 women), 3 part-time/adjunct (1 woman).
Students: 31 full-time (18 women), 19 part-time (8 women); includes 8 minority (5 African Americans, 3 Asian Americans or Pacific Islanders), 17 international. 39 applicants, 56% accepted, 11 enrolled. In 2001, 1 degree awarded.
Degree requirements: For master's, thesis optional; for doctorate, thesis/dissertation.
Entrance requirements: For master's, GRE General Test, minimum GPA of 3.0. *Application deadline:* For fall admission, 6/1 (priority date); for spring admission, 10/1. Applications are processed on a rolling basis. *Application fee:* $50 ($70 for international students). Electronic applications accepted.
Expenses: Tuition, state resident: part-time $289 per credit hour. Tuition, nonresident: part-time $448 per credit

hour. One-time fee: $436 part-time. Full-time tuition and fees vary according to course load, campus/location and program.
Financial support: In 2001–02, 2 fellowships with full tuition reimbursements (averaging $9,771 per year), 17 research assistantships with tuition reimbursements (averaging $15,399 per year), 5 teaching assistantships with tuition reimbursements (averaging $15,588 per year) were awarded. Career-related internships or fieldwork also available. Financial award applicants required to submit FAFSA.
Faculty research: Engineering aspects of production; harvesting, processing, and marketing of terrestrial and aquatic food and fiber.
Dr. Frederick Wheaton, Chairman, 301-405-1193, *Fax:* 301-314-9023.
Application contact: Trudy Lindsey, Director, Graduate Admissions and Records, 301-405-6991, *Fax:* 301-314-9305, *E-mail:* grschool@deans.umd.edu.
Find an in-depth description at www.petersons.com/gradchannel.

■ **UNIVERSITY OF MISSOURI–COLUMBIA**

Graduate School, College of Engineering and College of Agriculture, Food and Natural Resources, Department of Biological Engineering, Columbia, MO 65211

AWARDS Agricultural engineering (MS); biological engineering (MS, PhD).

Faculty: 15 full-time (2 women).
Students: 7 full-time (3 women), 8 part-time (1 woman); includes 1 minority (Asian American or Pacific Islander), 12 international. 1 applicant, 0% accepted. In 2001, 4 master's, 1 doctorate awarded.
Degree requirements: For master's and doctorate, thesis/dissertation.
Entrance requirements: For master's and doctorate, GRE General Test, TOEFL, minimum GPA of 3.0. *Application deadline:* For fall admission, 4/1 (priority date). Applications are processed on a rolling basis. *Application fee:* $25 ($50 for international students).
Expenses: Tuition, state resident: part-time $179 per credit hour. Tuition, nonresident: part-time $539 per credit hour. Required fees: $122 per semester. Tuition and fees vary according to program.
Financial support: Research assistantships, teaching assistantships, institutionally sponsored loans available.
Dr. Fu-hung Hsieh, Director of Graduate Studies, 573-882-2444, *E-mail:* hsiehf@missouri.edu. *Web site:* http://www.engineering.missouri.edu/biological.htm

■ UNIVERSITY OF NEBRASKA–LINCOLN

Graduate College, College of Engineering and Technology, Department of Biological Systems Engineering, Program in Agricultural and Biological Systems Engineering, Lincoln, NE 68588

AWARDS MS.

Faculty: 30.
Students: 3 (1 woman). 9 applicants, 11% accepted, 0 enrolled. In 2001, 4 degrees awarded.
Degree requirements: For master's, thesis optional.
Entrance requirements: For master's, GRE General Test, curriculum vitae. *Application deadline:* For fall admission, 3/1 (priority date). *Application fee:* $35. Electronic applications accepted.
Expenses: Tuition, state resident: full-time $2,412; part-time $134 per credit. Tuition, nonresident: full-time $6,223; part-time $346 per credit. Tuition and fees vary according to course load.
Financial support: In 2001–02, 4 research assistantships were awarded; fellowships, health care benefits and unspecified assistantships also available. Financial award application deadline: 2/15.
Faculty research: Hydrological engineering, tractive performance, biomedical engineering, irrigation systems.
Dr. Derrel L. Martin, Graduate Committee Chair, 402-472-1586, *Fax:* 402-472-6338, *E-mail:* dlmartin@unlnotes.unl.edu. *Web site:* http://bse.unl.edu/

■ UNIVERSITY OF NOTRE DAME

Graduate School, College of Engineering, Department of Civil Engineering and Geological Sciences, Notre Dame, IN 46556

AWARDS Bioengineering (MS); civil engineering (MS); civil engineering and geological sciences (PhD); environmental engineering (MS); geological sciences (MS).

Faculty: 15 full-time (1 woman).
Students: 42 full-time (16 women), 4 part-time (1 woman); includes 3 minority (1 African American, 1 Asian American or Pacific Islander, 1 Hispanic American), 13 international. 118 applicants, 19% accepted, 12 enrolled. In 2001, 5 master's, 3 doctorates awarded. Terminal master's awarded for partial completion of doctoral program.
Degree requirements: For master's, comprehensive exam; for doctorate, thesis/dissertation. *Median time to degree:* Doctorate–5.5 years full-time.
Entrance requirements: For master's and doctorate, GRE General Test, TOEFL. *Application deadline:* For fall admission, 2/1 (priority date); for spring admission, 10/15. Applications are processed on a rolling basis. *Application fee:* $50. Electronic applications accepted.

Expenses: Tuition: Full-time $24,220; part-time $1,346 per credit hour. Required fees: $155.
Financial support: In 2001–02, 46 students received support, including 7 fellowships with full tuition reimbursements available (averaging $18,000 per year), 16 research assistantships with full tuition reimbursements available (averaging $12,800 per year), 17 teaching assistantships with full tuition reimbursements available (averaging $12,800 per year); tuition waivers (full) also available. Financial award application deadline: 2/1.
Faculty research: Structural analysis, finite-element methods, environmental modeling, biological-waste treatment, petrology, environmental geology, geochemistry. *Total annual research expenditures:* $1.4 million.
Dr. Peter C. Burns, Director of Graduate Studies, 574-631-5380, *Fax:* 574-631-9236, *E-mail:* cegeos@nd.edu.
Application contact: Dr. Terrence J. Akai, Director of Graduate Admissions, 574-631-7706, *Fax:* 574-631-4183, *E-mail:* gradad@nd.edu. *Web site:* http://www.nd.edu/~gradsch/degreeprograms/Engineering/CE/CEMenu.html

■ UNIVERSITY OF PENNSYLVANIA

School of Engineering and Applied Science, Department of Bioengineering, Philadelphia, PA 19104

AWARDS MSE, PhD, MD/PhD, VMD/PhD. Terminal master's awarded for partial completion of doctoral program.

Degree requirements: For master's, thesis optional; for doctorate, thesis/dissertation.
Entrance requirements: For master's and doctorate, GRE General Test, TOEFL. Electronic applications accepted.
Faculty research: Biomaterials and biomechanics, biofluid mechanics and transport, bioelectric phenomena, computational neuroscience. *Web site:* http://www.seas.upenn.edu/be/index.html

■ UNIVERSITY OF PITTSBURGH

School of Engineering, Department of Bioengineering, Pittsburgh, PA 15260

AWARDS MSBENG, PhD, MD/PhD. Part-time and evening/weekend programs available.

Faculty: 7 full-time (0 women), 23 part-time/adjunct (1 woman).
Students: 70 full-time (21 women), 7 part-time (4 women); includes 15 minority (2 African Americans, 10 Asian Americans or Pacific Islanders, 3 Hispanic Americans). Average age 23. 110 applicants, 45% accepted, 29 enrolled. In 2001, 5 master's, 7 doctorates awarded. Terminal master's awarded for partial completion of doctoral program.

Degree requirements: For master's, thesis; for doctorate, thesis/dissertation, final oral exams, comprehensive exam. *Median time to degree:* Master's–2 years full-time; doctorate–5 years full-time.
Entrance requirements: For master's and doctorate, GRE General Test, TOEFL, minimum QPA of 3.0. *Application deadline:* For fall admission, 8/1 (priority date); for spring admission, 12/1. Applications are processed on a rolling basis. *Application fee:* $40.
Financial support: In 2001–02, 30 students received support, including 4 fellowships with full tuition reimbursements available (averaging $18,000 per year), 22 research assistantships with full tuition reimbursements available (averaging $18,000 per year), 4 teaching assistantships with full tuition reimbursements available (averaging $18,000 per year). Scholarships/grants and traineeships also available. Financial award application deadline: 2/15.
Faculty research: Artificial organs, biomechanics, biomaterials, signal processing, biotechnology. *Total annual research expenditures:* $2.7 million.
Harvey S. Borovetz, Director, 412-383-9713, *Fax:* 412-383-8788, *E-mail:* borovetzhs@msx.upmc.edu.
Application contact: Lynette R. Spataro, Academic Administrator, 412-624-6445, *Fax:* 412-383-8788, *E-mail:* spataro@engr.pitt.edu. *Web site:* http://www.engrng.pitt.edu/~wwwbiotc/
Find an in-depth description at www.petersons.com/gradchannel.

■ UNIVERSITY OF TOLEDO

Graduate School, College of Engineering, Department of Bioengineering, Toledo, OH 43606-3398

AWARDS MS, PhD.

Faculty: 10 full-time (1 woman).
Students: 26 full-time (9 women), 5 part-time, 21 international. Average age 26. 69 applicants, 68% accepted. In 2001, 6 master's, 4 doctorates awarded. Terminal master's awarded for partial completion of doctoral program.
Degree requirements: For master's, thesis optional; for doctorate, thesis/dissertation.
Entrance requirements: For master's, GRE General Test, TOEFL, minimum GPA of 3.3; for doctorate, GRE General Test, TOEFL. *Application deadline:* For fall admission, 5/31 (priority date). Applications are processed on a rolling basis. *Application fee:* $30. Electronic applications accepted.
Expenses: Tuition, state resident: full-time $7,278; part-time $303 per hour. Tuition, nonresident: full-time $15,731; part-time $699 per hour. Required fees: $43 per hour.
Financial support: In 2001–02, 10 research assistantships with full tuition reimbursements, 21 teaching assistantships

University of Toledo (continued)
with full tuition reimbursements were awarded. Fellowships, scholarships/grants, tuition waivers (full), and unspecified assistantships also available. Financial award application deadline: 4/1.
Faculty research: Artificial organs, biochemical engineering, bioelectrical systems, biomechanics, cellular engineering. *Total annual research expenditures:* $895,556.
Dr. Vijay Goel, Chairman, 419-530-8030, *Fax:* 419-530-8076, *E-mail:* vgoel@cng.utoledo.edu.
Application contact: Dr. Patricia Relue, Academic Program Director, 419-530-8098, *Fax:* 419-530-8076, *E-mail:* prelue@eng.utoledo.edu. *Web site:* http://bioe.eng.utoledo.edu/
Find an in-depth description at www.petersons.com/gradchannel.

■ **UNIVERSITY OF UTAH**
Graduate School, College of Engineering, Department of Bioengineering, Salt Lake City, UT 84112-1107

AWARDS ME, MS, PhD.

Faculty: 9 full-time (1 woman), 6 part-time/adjunct (2 women).
Students: 68 full-time (18 women), 16 part-time (6 women); includes 24 minority (23 Asian Americans or Pacific Islanders, 1 Hispanic American), 7 international. Average age 28. In 2001, 9 master's, 5 doctorates awarded. Terminal master's awarded for partial completion of doctoral program.
Degree requirements: For master's, thesis (MS); written project, oral presentation (ME); for doctorate, thesis/dissertation.
Entrance requirements: For master's and doctorate, GRE, TOEFL, minimum GPA of 3.0. *Application deadline:* For fall admission, 5/1. *Application fee:* $40 ($60 for international students).
Expenses: Tuition, state resident: part-time $320 per semester hour. Tuition, nonresident: part-time $1,135 per semester hour. Required fees: $143 per semester hour. Tuition and fees vary according to course load, degree level and program.
Financial support: Fellowships, research assistantships, traineeships available. Financial award application deadline: 5/1; financial award applicants required to submit FAFSA.
Faculty research: Bioinstrumentation, biomaterials, ultrasonic bioinstrumentation, medical imaging, neuroprosthesis.
Dr. Vladimir Hlady, Chair, 801-581-5042, *Fax:* 801-585-5361, *E-mail:* vladimir.hlady@m.cc.utah.edu.
Application contact: Richard Rabbitt, Graduate Advisor, 801-581-8528, *Fax:* 801-585-5361, *E-mail:* r.rabbitt@

m.cc.utah.edu. *Web site:* http://www.coe.utah.edu/
Find an in-depth description at www.petersons.com/gradchannel.

■ **UNIVERSITY OF WASHINGTON**
Graduate School, College of Engineering and School of Medicine, Department of Bioengineering, Seattle, WA 98195

AWARDS MME, MS, PhD.

Faculty: 30 full-time (3 women), 28 part-time/adjunct (3 women).
Students: 121 full-time (47 women), 43 part-time (11 women); includes 31 minority (3 African Americans, 20 Asian Americans or Pacific Islanders, 7 Hispanic Americans, 1 Native American), 30 international. 320 applicants, 18% accepted, 25 enrolled. In 2001, 6 master's, 15 doctorates awarded. Terminal master's awarded for partial completion of doctoral program.
Degree requirements: For master's, thesis; for doctorate, thesis/dissertation, qualifying exam, general exam. *Median time to degree:* Master's–2.7 years full-time, 4.5 years part-time; doctorate–5.5 years full-time.
Entrance requirements: For master's and doctorate, GRE General Test, TOEFL, minimum GPA of 3.0. *Application deadline:* For fall admission, 1/15. *Application fee:* $45. Electronic applications accepted.
Expenses: Tuition, state resident: full-time $5,539. Tuition, nonresident: full-time $14,376. Required fees: $390. Tuition and fees vary according to course load and program.
Financial support: In 2001–02, 20 fellowships with tuition reimbursements (averaging $19,883 per year), 92 research assistantships with tuition reimbursements (averaging $20,016 per year), 1 teaching assistantship with tuition reimbursement (averaging $20,016 per year) were awarded. Federal Work-Study, institutionally sponsored loans, traineeships, and tuition waivers (full) also available. Support available to part-time students. Financial award application deadline: 1/15.
Faculty research: Distributed diagnosis and home healthcare, engineered biomaterials, molecular bioengineering and nanotechnology, medical imaging and image-guided therapy, computational bioengineering.
Dr. Yongmin Kim, Chair, 206-685-2000, *Fax:* 206-685-3300.
Application contact: Jennifer Gouine, Graduate Academic Counselor, 206-685-2000, *Fax:* 206-685-3300, *E-mail:* jgouine@u.washington.edu. *Web site:* http://depts.washington.edu.bioe

■ **VIRGINIA POLYTECHNIC INSTITUTE AND STATE UNIVERSITY**
Graduate School, College of Engineering, Department of Biological Systems Engineering, Blacksburg, VA 24061

AWARDS Bio-process engineering (M Eng, MS, PhD); food engineering (M Eng, MS, PhD); land and water engineering (M Eng, MS, PhD); nonpoint source pollution control (M Eng, MS, PhD); watershed engineering (M Eng, MS, PhD); wood engineering (M Eng, MS, PhD).

Faculty: 12 full-time (0 women), 8 part-time/adjunct (0 women).
Students: 24 full-time (13 women), 5 part-time; includes 1 minority (Asian American or Pacific Islander), 10 international. Average age 25. 19 applicants, 58% accepted. In 2001, 3 master's, 1 doctorate awarded.
Degree requirements: For master's and doctorate, thesis/dissertation. *Median time to degree:* Master's–2 years full-time; doctorate–3 years full-time.
Entrance requirements: For master's and doctorate, GRE General Test, TOEFL. *Application deadline:* For fall admission, 12/1 (priority date); for spring admission, 9/1 (priority date). Applications are processed on a rolling basis. *Application fee:* $45. Electronic applications accepted.
Expenses: Tuition, state resident: part-time $241 per hour. Tuition, nonresident: part-time $406 per hour. Tuition and fees vary according to program.
Financial support: In 2001–02, 4 fellowships with full tuition reimbursements (averaging $17,000 per year), 7 research assistantships with full tuition reimbursements (averaging $16,500 per year), 2 teaching assistantships with full tuition reimbursements (averaging $16,500 per year) were awarded. Career-related internships or fieldwork, institutionally sponsored loans, tuition waivers (full and partial), and unspecified assistantships also available. Support available to part-time students. Financial award application deadline: 4/1.
Faculty research: Soil and water engineering, alternative energy sources for agriculture and agricultural mechanization. *Total annual research expenditures:* $800,000.
Dr. John V. Perumpral, Head, 540-231-6615, *E-mail:* perump@vt.edu.
Application contact: Dr. S. Mostaghimi, Chairman, 540-231-7605, *E-mail:* smostagh@vt.edu. *Web site:* http://www.bse.vt.edu/

BIOMEDICAL ENGINEERING

■ ARIZONA STATE UNIVERSITY

Graduate College, College of Engineering and Applied Sciences, Department of Chemical, Bio and Materials Engineering, Program in Bioengineering, Tempe, AZ 85287

AWARDS MS, PhD.

Degree requirements: For doctorate, thesis/dissertation.
Entrance requirements: For master's and doctorate, GRE General Test.
Faculty research: Biotechnology, biocontrol, biomechanics, bioinstrumentation and materials, biosystems engineering/biotransport.
Find an in-depth description at www.petersons.com/gradchannel.

■ BOSTON UNIVERSITY

College of Engineering, Department of Biomedical Engineering, Boston, MA 02215

AWARDS MS, PhD, MD/PhD. Part-time programs available.

Faculty: 30 full-time (5 women), 15 part-time/adjunct (1 woman).
Students: 89 full-time (31 women); includes 10 minority (6 Asian Americans or Pacific Islanders, 4 Hispanic Americans), 27 international. Average age 26. 183 applicants, 38% accepted, 29 enrolled. In 2001, 8 master's, 10 doctorates awarded. Terminal master's awarded for partial completion of doctoral program.
Degree requirements: For master's, thesis/dissertation; for doctorate, thesis/dissertation, comprehensive exam.
Entrance requirements: For master's and doctorate, GRE General Test, TOEFL. *Application deadline:* For fall admission, 4/1; for spring admission, 10/1. Applications are processed on a rolling basis. *Application fee:* $60. Electronic applications accepted.
Expenses: Tuition: Full-time $25,872; part-time $340 per credit. Required fees: $40 per semester. Part-time tuition and fees vary according to class time, course level and program.
Financial support: In 2001–02, 80 students received support, including 5 fellowships with full tuition reimbursements available (averaging $15,500 per year), 53 research assistantships with full tuition reimbursements available (averaging $13,500 per year), 9 teaching assistantships with full tuition reimbursements available (averaging $13,500 per year); career-related internships or fieldwork, Federal Work-Study, institutionally sponsored loans, and scholarships/grants also available. Financial award application deadline: 1/15; financial award applicants required to submit FAFSA.

Faculty research: Biomechanics, bio-MEMS, biomolecular engineering, hearing research, neuroscience. *Total annual research expenditures:* $17.3 million.
Dr. Kenneth R. Lutchen, Chairman, 617-353-2805, *Fax:* 617-353-6766.
Application contact: Cheryl Kelley, Director of Graduate Programs, 617-353-9760, *Fax:* 617-353-0259, *E-mail:* enggrad@bu.edu. *Web site:* http://www.bu.edu/eng/grad/
Find an in-depth description at www.petersons.com/gradchannel.

■ BROWN UNIVERSITY

Graduate School, Division of Biology and Medicine, Program in Artificial Organs/Biomaterials/Cellular Technology, Providence, RI 02912

AWARDS MA, Sc M, PhD.

Faculty: 4 full-time (2 women), 5 part-time/adjunct (2 women).
Students: 10 full-time (5 women); includes 3 minority (1 African American, 2 Asian Americans or Pacific Islanders), 2 international. Average age 24. 30 applicants, 10% accepted. In 2001, 3 degrees awarded. Terminal master's awarded for partial completion of doctoral program.
Degree requirements: For doctorate, thesis/dissertation, preliminary exam.
Entrance requirements: For master's and doctorate, GRE General Test, GRE Subject Test. *Application deadline:* For fall admission, 1/2 (priority date). Applications are processed on a rolling basis. *Application fee:* $60. Electronic applications accepted.
Financial support: In 2001–02, 3 fellowships, 1 research assistantship, 6 teaching assistantships were awarded. Financial award application deadline: 1/2.
Dr. Edith Mathiowitz, Director, 401-863-1358, *Fax:* 401-863-1753, *E-mail:* edith_mathiowitz@brown.edu.
Application contact: Susan Hirsch, Administrative Assistant, 401-863-3262, *Fax:* 401-863-1753, *E-mail:* susan_hirsch@brown.edu.

■ BROWN UNIVERSITY

Graduate School, Division of Engineering and Division of Biology and Medicine, Program in Biomedical Engineering, Providence, RI 02912

AWARDS Sc M.

Degree requirements: For master's, thesis.

■ CALIFORNIA POLYTECHNIC STATE UNIVERSITY, SAN LUIS OBISPO

College of Engineering, Program in Engineering, San Luis Obispo, CA 93407

AWARDS Biochemical engineering (MS); industrial engineering (MS); integrated

technology management (MS); materials engineering (MS); water engineering (MS), including bioengineering, biomedical engineering, manufacturing engineering.

Faculty: 98 full-time (8 women), 82 part-time/adjunct (14 women).
Students: 20 full-time (4 women), 9 part-time (1 woman). 25 applicants, 68% accepted, 15 enrolled. In 2001, 22 degrees awarded.
Entrance requirements: For master's, GRE General Test, minimum GPA of 2.5 in last 90 quarter units. *Application fee:* $55.
Expenses: Tuition, nonresident: part-time $164 per unit. One-time fee: $2,153 part-time.
Financial support: Application deadline: 3/2.
Dr. Peter Y. Lee, Dean, 805-756-2131, *Fax:* 805-756-6503, *E-mail:* plee@calpoly.edu.
Application contact: Dr. Daniel W. Walsh, Associate Dean, 805-756-2131, *Fax:* 805-756-6503, *E-mail:* dwalsh@calpoly.edu. *Web site:* http://www.synner.ceng.calpoly.edu/

■ CALIFORNIA STATE UNIVERSITY, NORTHRIDGE

Graduate Studies, College of Engineering and Computer Science, Department of Electrical and Computer Engineering, Northridge, CA 91330

AWARDS Biomedical engineering (MS); communications/radar engineering (MS); control engineering (MS); digital/computer engineering (MS); electronics engineering (MS); microwave/antenna engineering (MS). Part-time and evening/weekend programs available.

Faculty: 19 full-time, 6 part-time/adjunct.
Students: 31 full-time (3 women), 81 part-time (9 women); includes 30 minority (1 African American, 21 Asian Americans or Pacific Islanders, 8 Hispanic Americans), 32 international. Average age 33. 77 applicants, 73% accepted, 19 enrolled. In 2001, 22 degrees awarded.
Degree requirements: For master's, thesis or alternative.
Entrance requirements: For master's, GRE General Test, TOEFL, minimum GPA of 2.5. *Application deadline:* For fall admission, 11/30. *Application fee:* $55.
Expenses: Tuition, nonresident: part-time $631 per semester. Required fees: $246 per unit.
Financial support: Application deadline: 3/1.
Faculty research: Reflector antenna study, radome study.
Dr. Nagwa Bekir, Chair, 818-677-2190.
Application contact: Nagi El Naga, Graduate Coordinator, 818-677-2180.

■ CARNEGIE MELLON UNIVERSITY

Carnegie Institute of Technology, Biomedical and Health Engineering Program, Pittsburgh, PA 15213-3891

AWARDS Bioengineering (MS, PhD).

Degree requirements: For master's, thesis; for doctorate, thesis/dissertation, qualifying exam.

Entrance requirements: For master's and doctorate, GRE General Test, TOEFL. Electronic applications accepted.

Faculty research: Cellular and molecular systematics, signal and image processing, materials and mechanics. *Web site:* http://www.cmu.edu/cit/biomed/

■ CARNEGIE MELLON UNIVERSITY

Carnegie Institute of Technology, Department of Electrical and Computer Engineering, Concentration in Biomedical Engineering, Pittsburgh, PA 15213-3891

AWARDS MS, PhD. Part-time programs available.

Degree requirements: For master's, thesis; for doctorate, thesis/dissertation, qualifying exam, teaching experience.

Entrance requirements: For master's and doctorate, GRE General Test, TOEFL. *Web site:* http://www.ece.cmu.edu/

■ CASE WESTERN RESERVE UNIVERSITY

School of Graduate Studies, The Case School of Engineering, Department of Biomedical Engineering, Cleveland, OH 44106

AWARDS MS, PhD, MD/PhD.

Faculty: 19 full-time (0 women), 19 part-time/adjunct (4 women).

Students: 90 full-time (25 women), 46 part-time (13 women); includes 21 minority (2 African Americans, 16 Asian Americans or Pacific Islanders, 3 Hispanic Americans), 63 international. Average age 25. 177 applicants, 24% accepted, 26 enrolled. In 2001, 11 master's, 13 doctorates awarded. Terminal master's awarded for partial completion of doctoral program.

Degree requirements: For master's, thesis (for some programs); for doctorate, thesis/dissertation, qualifying exam, teaching experience.

Entrance requirements: For master's and doctorate, GRE, TOEFL. *Application deadline:* For fall admission, 2/1 (priority date); for spring admission, 10/1 (priority date). Applications are processed on a rolling basis. *Application fee:* $25.

Financial support: In 2001–02, 49 fellowships with full tuition reimbursements (averaging $17,028 per year), 71 research assistantships with full and partial tuition reimbursements (averaging $17,268 per

year) were awarded. Traineeships also available. Financial award application deadline: 2/15; financial award applicants required to submit FAFSA.

Faculty research: Biomaterials/tissue engineering; cardiac bioelectricity; neural engineering and neural prostheses; biomedical imaging, sensing, and guided intervention; transport and metabolic systems engineering. *Total annual research expenditures:* $6.4 million.

Dr. Patrick E. Crago, Chairman, 216-368-3977, *Fax:* 216-368-4969, *E-mail:* pec3@po.cwru.edu.

Application contact: Yolanda Cunningham, Admissions Coordinator, 216-368-4094, *Fax:* 216-368-4969, *E-mail:* ywc3@po.cwru.edu. *Web site:* http://bme.cwru.edu/

Find an in-depth description at www.petersons.com/gradchannel.

■ THE CATHOLIC UNIVERSITY OF AMERICA

School of Engineering, Department of Biomedical Engineering, Washington, DC 20064

AWARDS MBE, MS Engr, PhD. Part-time and evening/weekend programs available.

Faculty: 6 full-time (1 woman).

Students: 2 full-time (0 women), 9 part-time (4 women); includes 1 minority (African American), 5 international. Average age 33. 17 applicants, 59% accepted, 1 enrolled. In 2001, 7 master's, 1 doctorate awarded.

Degree requirements: For master's, thesis optional; for doctorate, thesis/dissertation, oral exams, comprehensive exam.

Entrance requirements: For master's, minimum GPA of 3.0; for doctorate, minimum GPA of 3.5. *Application deadline:* For fall admission, 8/1 (priority date); for spring admission, 12/1. Applications are processed on a rolling basis. *Application fee:* $55. Electronic applications accepted.

Expenses: Tuition: Full-time $20,050; part-time $770 per credit. Required fees: $430 per term. Tuition and fees vary according to program.

Financial support: Research assistantships, teaching assistantships, career-related internships or fieldwork, Federal Work-Study, institutionally sponsored loans, and tuition waivers (full and partial) available. Support available to part-time students. Financial award application deadline: 2/1.

Faculty research: Cell and tissue engineering, biomechanics, rehabilitation engineering, neural engineering, medical instrumentation.

Dr. Mark Mirotznik, Director, 202-319-5671, *Fax:* 202-319-4287.

■ CLEMSON UNIVERSITY

Graduate School, College of Engineering and Science, Department of Bioengineering, Clemson, SC 29634

AWARDS MS, PhD. Part-time programs available.

Students: 39 full-time (16 women), 3 part-time (2 women); includes 1 minority (Hispanic American), 15 international. Average age 23. 108 applicants, 58% accepted, 15 enrolled. In 2001, 10 degrees awarded.

Degree requirements: For master's, thesis optional; for doctorate, thesis/dissertation.

Entrance requirements: For master's and doctorate, GRE General Test, TOEFL. *Application deadline:* For fall admission, 6/1; for spring admission, 11/1. *Application fee:* $40.

Expenses: Tuition, state resident: full-time $5,310. Tuition, nonresident: full-time $11,284.

Financial support: Fellowships, research assistantships, teaching assistantships, career-related internships or fieldwork available. Financial award application deadline: 2/15; financial award applicants required to submit FAFSA.

Faculty research: Biomaterials, biomechanics.

Dr. R. Larry Dooley, Chair, 864-656-3051, *Fax:* 864-656-4466, *E-mail:* dooley@eng.clemson.edu.

Application contact: Dr. Robert Latour, Graduate Student Coordinator, 864-656-5552, *Fax:* 864-656-4466, *E-mail:* latourr@eng.clemson.edu. *Web site:* http://www.eng.clemson.edu/bio/

Find an in-depth description at www.petersons.com/gradchannel.

■ CLEVELAND STATE UNIVERSITY

College of Graduate Studies, Fenn College of Engineering, Doctoral Program in Applied Biomedical Engineering, Cleveland, OH 44115

AWARDS D Eng. Part-time and evening/weekend programs available.

Faculty: 9 full-time (1 woman), 15 part-time/adjunct (2 women).

Students: 20 full-time (7 women), 5 part-time (2 women); includes 1 minority (Asian American or Pacific Islander), 19 international. Average age 26. 25 applicants.

Degree requirements: For doctorate, thesis/dissertation.

Entrance requirements: For doctorate, GRE; TOEFL, minimum undergraduate GPA of 2.75; MS or MD GPA of 3.25; one prior degree in engineering. *Application deadline:* For fall admission, 5/15; for spring admission, 12/15. Applications are processed on a rolling basis. *Application fee:* $25.

Expenses: Tuition, state resident: full-time $6,838; part-time $263 per credit hour. Tuition, nonresident: full-time $13,526; part-time $520 per credit hour.
Financial support: In 2001–02, 11 research assistantships with full tuition reimbursements (averaging $16,500 per year) were awarded; career-related internships or fieldwork and tuition waivers (full) also available.
Faculty research: Biomechanics, drug delivery systems, medical imaging, tissue engineering, artificial heart valves.
Dr. Orhan Talu, Chairperson, 216-687-3539, *Fax:* 216-687-9220, *E-mail:* talu@csaxp.egr.csuohio.edu.
Application contact: Becky Caird, Administrative Coordinator, 216-687-9385, *Fax:* 216-687-9220, *E-mail:* che@csvax.egr.csuohio.edu. *Web site:* http://www.csaxp.csuohio.edu/fenn.ccfabm.html

■ **COLORADO STATE UNIVERSITY**

Graduate School, College of Engineering, Department of Mechanical Engineering, Fort Collins, CO 80523-0015

AWARDS Bioengineering (MS, PhD); energy and environmental engineering (MS, PhD); energy conversion (MS, PhD); engineering management (MS); heat and mass transfer (MS, PhD); industrial and manufacturing systems engineering (MS, PhD); mechanical engineering (MS, PhD); mechanics and materials (MS, PhD). Part-time programs available.

Faculty: 17 full-time (2 women).
Students: 36 full-time (6 women), 63 part-time (11 women); includes 5 minority (2 Asian Americans or Pacific Islanders, 2 Hispanic Americans, 1 Native American), 22 international. Average age 32. 234 applicants, 83% accepted, 32 enrolled. In 2001, 10 master's, 3 doctorates awarded. Terminal master's awarded for partial completion of doctoral program.
Degree requirements: For doctorate, thesis/dissertation.
Entrance requirements: For master's and doctorate, GRE General Test, TOEFL, minimum GPA of 3.0. *Application deadline:* For fall admission, 2/1 (priority date). Applications are processed on a rolling basis. *Application fee:* $30. Electronic applications accepted.
Expenses: Tuition, state resident: full-time $2,880; part-time $160 per credit. Tuition, nonresident: full-time $11,412; part-time $634 per credit. Required fees: $750; $34 per credit.
Financial support: In 2001–02, 2 fellowships, 15 research assistantships (averaging $15,792 per year), 14 teaching assistantships (averaging $11,844 per year) were awarded. Traineeships also available.
Faculty research: Space propulsion, controls and systems, engineering and

materials. *Total annual research expenditures:* $2.1 million.
Dr. Allan T. Kirkpatrick, Head, 970-491-6559, *Fax:* 970-491-3827, *E-mail:* allan@engr.colostate.edu. *Web site:* http://www.engr.colostate.edu/depts/me/index.html

■ **COLUMBIA UNIVERSITY**

Fu Foundation School of Engineering and Applied Science, Department of Biomedical Engineering, New York, NY 10027

AWARDS MS, Eng Sc D. Part-time programs available.

Faculty: 14 full-time (1 woman), 4 part-time/adjunct (0 women).
Students: 39 full-time (14 women), 18 part-time (2 women); includes 1 African American, 13 Asian Americans or Pacific Islanders. Average age 24. 184 applicants, 15% accepted. In 2001, 13 master's, 1 doctorate awarded.
Degree requirements: For doctorate, thesis/dissertation, qualifying exam.
Entrance requirements: For master's and doctorate, GRE General Test, TOEFL. *Application deadline:* For fall admission, 1/5; for spring admission, 10/1. *Application fee:* $55. Electronic applications accepted.
Expenses: Tuition: Full-time $27,528. Required fees: $1,638.
Financial support: In 2001–02, 6 fellowships with full tuition reimbursements (averaging $16,500 per year), 14 research assistantships with full tuition reimbursements (averaging $16,000 per year), 7 teaching assistantships with full tuition reimbursements (averaging $12,000 per year) were awarded. Federal Work-Study also available. Financial award application deadline: 1/5; financial award applicants required to submit FAFSA.
Faculty research: Artificial organs, orthopedic and musculoskeletal biomechanics, cellular and tissue engineering, artificial organs, cardiovascular biomechanics. *Total annual research expenditures:* $1.5 million.
Dr. Van C. Mow, Chair, 212-854-8458, *Fax:* 212-854-8725, *E-mail:* vcm1@columbia.edu.
Application contact: Jeffrey W. Holmes, Assistant Professor of Biomedical Engineering, 212-854-6530, *Fax:* 212-854-8725, *E-mail:* jh553@columbia.edu. *Web site:* http://www.seas.columbia.edu/~BME/
Find an in-depth description at www.petersons.com/gradchannel.

■ **CORNELL UNIVERSITY**

Graduate School, Graduate Fields of Engineering, Field of Biomedical Engineering, Ithaca, NY 14853-0001

AWARDS MS, PhD.

Faculty: 20 full-time.
Students: 9 full-time (4 women); includes 2 minority (both Asian Americans or

Pacific Islanders), 3 international. 84 applicants, 23% accepted. In 2001, 1 degree awarded.
Degree requirements: For master's and doctorate, thesis/dissertation.
Entrance requirements: For master's and doctorate, GRE General Test, GRE Subject Test (engineering), TOEFL, preapplication for international applicants, 3 letters of recommendation. *Application deadline:* For fall admission, 1/5. *Application fee:* $65. Electronic applications accepted.
Expenses: Tuition: Full-time $25,970. Required fees: $50.
Financial support: In 2001–02, 8 students received support, including 5 fellowships with full tuition reimbursements available, 3 research assistantships with full tuition reimbursements available; teaching assistantships, institutionally sponsored loans, scholarships/grants, tuition waivers (full and partial), and unspecified assistantships also available.
Faculty research: Biomaterials, biomedical instrumentation and diagnostics; biomedical mechanics; drug delivery, design, and metabolism.
Application contact: Graduate Field Assistant, 607-255-1003, *E-mail:* biomedeng@cornell.edu. *Web site:* http://www.gradschool.cornell.edu/grad/fields_1/biomed.html

■ **DARTMOUTH COLLEGE**

Thayer School of Engineering, Program in Biomedical Engineering, Hanover, NH 03755

AWARDS MS, PhD, MD/PhD.

Degree requirements: For master's, thesis; for doctorate, thesis/dissertation, candidacy oral exam.
Entrance requirements: For master's and doctorate, GRE General Test. *Application deadline:* For fall admission, 1/1 (priority date). *Application fee:* $40 ($50 for international students).
Expenses: Tuition: Full-time $26,425.
Financial support: Fellowships, research assistantships, teaching assistantships, career-related internships or fieldwork, Federal Work-Study, institutionally sponsored loans, and tuition waivers (full and partial) available. Financial award application deadline: 1/15.
Faculty research: Imaging and image processing, physiological modeling, cancer hyperthermia and radiation therapy, bioelectromagnetics, biomedical optics. *Total annual research expenditures:* $3.7 million.
Application contact: Candace S. Potter, Graduate Admissions Administrator, 603-646-3844, *Fax:* 603-646-1620, *E-mail:* candace.potter@dartmouth.edu. *Web site:* http://engineering.dartmouth.edu/

■ DREXEL UNIVERSITY

Graduate School, School of Biomedical Engineering, Science and Health Systems, Program in Biomedical Engineering, Philadelphia, PA 19104-2875

AWARDS MS, PhD.

Faculty: 11 full-time (2 women), 2 part-time/adjunct (0 women).
Students: 17 full-time (4 women), 27 part-time (1 woman); includes 5 minority (1 African American, 4 Asian Americans or Pacific Islanders), 18 international. Average age 29. 84 applicants, 69% accepted, 4 enrolled. In 2001, 2 master's, 1 doctorate awarded.
Degree requirements: For master's, thesis (for some programs); for doctorate, thesis/dissertation.
Application deadline: For fall admission, 8/21. Applications are processed on a rolling basis. *Application fee:* $50. Electronic applications accepted.
Expenses: Tuition: Full-time $20,088; part-time $558 per credit. Required fees: $78 per term. One-time fee: $200. Tuition and fees vary according to course load, degree level and program.
Financial support: Research assistantships, teaching assistantships, career-related internships or fieldwork, Federal Work-Study, institutionally sponsored loans, tuition waivers (full and partial), and unspecified assistantships available. Financial award application deadline: 2/1.
Application contact: Director of Graduate Admissions, 215-895-6700, *Fax:* 215-895-5939, *E-mail:* enroll@drexel.edu.

■ DUKE UNIVERSITY

Graduate School, School of Engineering, Department of Biomedical Engineering, Durham, NC 27708-0586

AWARDS MS, PhD.

Faculty: 32 full-time, 3 part-time/adjunct.
Students: 100 full-time (35 women); includes 12 minority (4 African Americans, 7 Asian Americans or Pacific Islanders, 1 Hispanic American), 25 international. 244 applicants, 20% accepted, 27 enrolled. In 2001, 8 master's, 13 doctorates awarded.
Degree requirements: For doctorate, thesis/dissertation.
Entrance requirements: For master's and doctorate, GRE General Test. *Application deadline:* For fall admission, 12/31; for spring admission, 11/1. *Application fee:* $75.
Expenses: Tuition: Full-time $24,600.
Financial support: Fellowships, research assistantships, teaching assistantships, Federal Work-Study available. Financial award application deadline: 12/31.
Dr. Monty Reichert, Director of Graduate Studies, 919-660-5132, *Fax:* 919-684-4488,

E-mail: kwb@acpub.duke.edu. *Web site:* http://www.bme_www.egr.duke.edu/
Find an in-depth description at www.petersons.com/gradchannel.

■ FLORIDA INTERNATIONAL UNIVERSITY

College of Engineering, Department of Mechanical Engineering, Program in Biomedical Engineering, Miami, FL 33199

AWARDS MS. Part-time and evening/weekend programs available.

Students: 20 full-time (4 women), 6 part-time (1 woman); includes 9 minority (1 African American, 1 Asian American or Pacific Islander, 7 Hispanic Americans), 15 international. 25 applicants, 76% accepted, 13 enrolled.
Degree requirements: For master's, thesis.
Entrance requirements: For master's, GRE General Test, TOEFL.
Expenses: Tuition, state resident: full-time $2,916; part-time $162 per credit hour. Tuition, nonresident: full-time $10,245; part-time $569 per credit hour. Required fees: $168 per term.

■ GEORGIA INSTITUTE OF TECHNOLOGY

Graduate Studies and Research, College of Engineering, GA Tech/Emory Department of Biomedical Engineering, Atlanta, GA 30332-0001

AWARDS MS Bio E, PhD, Certificate, MD/PhD. Terminal master's awarded for partial completion of doctoral program.

Degree requirements: For master's and doctorate, thesis/dissertation.
Entrance requirements: For master's and doctorate, TOEFL.
Faculty research: Biomechanics and tissue engineering, bioinstrumentation and medical imaging. *Web site:* http://www.bioeng.gatech.edu/
Find an in-depth description at www.petersons.com/gradchannel.

■ HARVARD UNIVERSITY

Graduate School of Arts and Sciences, Department of Physics, Cambridge, MA 02138

AWARDS Experimental physics (AM, PhD); medical engineering/medical physics (PhD, Sc D), including applied physics (PhD), engineering sciences (PhD), medical engineering/medical physics (Sc D), physics (PhD); theoretical physics (AM, PhD).

Degree requirements: For doctorate, thesis/dissertation, final exams, laboratory experience.
Entrance requirements: For master's, GRE General Test, TOEFL; for doctorate, GRE General Test, GRE Subject Test, TOEFL.

Expenses: Tuition: Full-time $23,370. Required fees: $816. Full-time tuition and fees vary according to program and student level.
Faculty research: Particle physics, condensed matter physics, atomic physics.

Find an in-depth description at www.petersons.com/gradchannel.

■ HARVARD UNIVERSITY

Graduate School of Arts and Sciences, Division of Engineering and Applied Sciences, Cambridge, MA 02138

AWARDS Applied mathematics (ME, SM, PhD); applied physics (ME, SM, PhD); computer science (ME, SM, PhD); computing technology (PhD); engineering science (ME); engineering sciences (SM, PhD); medical engineering/medical physics (PhD, Sc D), including applied physics (PhD), engineering sciences (PhD), medical engineering/medical physics (Sc D), physics (PhD). Terminal master's awarded for partial completion of doctoral program.

Degree requirements: For doctorate, thesis/dissertation.
Entrance requirements: For master's and doctorate, GRE General Test, GRE Subject Test, TOEFL.
Expenses: Tuition: Full-time $23,370. Required fees: $816. Full-time tuition and fees vary according to program and student level. *Web site:* http://www.deas.harvard.edu/

Find an in-depth description at www.petersons.com/gradchannel.

■ HARVARD UNIVERSITY

Medical School and Graduate School of Arts and Sciences, Division of Health Sciences and Technology and Department of Physics and Division of Engineering and Applied Sciences, Program in Medical Engineering/Medical Physics, Cambridge, MA 02138

AWARDS Applied physics (PhD); engineering sciences (PhD); medical engineering/medical physics (Sc D); physics (PhD).

Degree requirements: For doctorate, thesis/dissertation, oral and written qualifying exams.
Entrance requirements: For doctorate, bachelor's degree in engineering or science.
Expenses: Contact institution.

Find an in-depth description at www.petersons.com/gradchannel.

■ ILLINOIS INSTITUTE OF TECHNOLOGY

Graduate College, Armour College of Engineering and Sciences, Pritzker Institute of Medical Engineering, Chicago, IL 60616-3793

AWARDS Biomedical engineering (PhD). Part-time programs available.

Students: 11 full-time (7 women), 10 international. Average age 26. 26 applicants, 42% accepted.
Degree requirements: For doctorate, thesis/dissertation, comprehensive exam.
Entrance requirements: For doctorate, GRE General Test, TOEFL. *Application deadline:* For fall admission, 7/1; for spring admission, 11/1. Applications are processed on a rolling basis. *Application fee:* $30. Electronic applications accepted.
Expenses: Tuition: Part-time $590 per credit hour.
Financial support: Research assistantships, institutionally sponsored loans, scholarships/grants, and unspecified assistantships available. Financial award applicants required to submit FAFSA.
Faculty research: Cardiovascular electrophysiology, electronic implants, neural and muscular protheses, medical signal and image processing, medical imaging. *Total annual research expenditures:* $276,627.
Dr. Vincent Turitto, Director, 312-567-6927, *Fax:* 312-567-5707, *E-mail:* turitto@iit.edu.
Application contact: Dr. Ali Cinar, Dean of Graduate College, 312-567-3637, *Fax:* 312-567-7517, *E-mail:* gradstu@iit.edu. *Web site:* http://www.iit.edu/~bme

Find an in-depth description at www.petersons.com/gradchannel.

■ INDIANA UNIVERSITY–PURDUE UNIVERSITY INDIANAPOLIS

School of Engineering and Technology, Biomedical Engineering Program, Indianapolis, IN 46202-2896

AWARDS MS Bm E, PhD. Part-time and evening/weekend programs available.

Students: 4 full-time (2 women), 3 part-time (all women), 5 international. Average age 26.
Degree requirements: For master's, thesis optional.
Entrance requirements: For master's, GRE, TOEFL, minimum B average; for doctorate, GRE General Test, TOEFL. *Application deadline:* For fall admission, 5/1. *Application fee:* $45 ($55 for international students).
Expenses: Contact institution.
Financial support: Fellowships with tuition reimbursements, research assistantships with full and partial tuition reimbursements, teaching assistantships, Federal Work-Study and institutionally

sponsored loans available. Support available to part-time students. Financial award application deadline: 3/1.
Dr. Edward Berbari, Chair, 317-274-9721, *Fax:* 317-274-4493.
Application contact: Mary DeBruicker, Graduate Office, 765-494-3649, *Fax:* 765-494-6440, *E-mail:* bmeprogram@ecn.purdue.edu. *Web site:* http://www.ecn.purdue.edu/biomed/

■ JOHNS HOPKINS UNIVERSITY

G. W. C. Whiting School of Engineering and School of Medicine, Department of Biomedical Engineering, Baltimore, MD 21205

AWARDS MSE.

Faculty: 22 full-time (2 women), 6 part-time/adjunct (0 women).
Students: 32 full-time (9 women); includes 3 minority (all Asian Americans or Pacific Islanders), 12 international. Average age 24. 123 applicants, 24% accepted, 13 enrolled. In 2001, 12 degrees awarded.
Degree requirements: For master's, thesis.
Entrance requirements: For master's, GRE General Test, TOEFL. *Application deadline:* For fall admission, 1/10. *Application fee:* $0. Electronic applications accepted.
Expenses: Tuition: Full-time $27,390.
Financial support: In 2001–02, 27 students received support, including 27 fellowships with full tuition reimbursements available (averaging $13,104 per year); research assistantships, teaching assistantships, training grants also available. Financial award application deadline: 1/10.
Faculty research: Cardiovascular system, biomaterials and imaging, cell and tissue engineering, theoretical and computational biology, systems neuroscience. *Total annual research expenditures:* $731,289.
Dr. Murray B. Sachs, Director, 410-955-3131, *Fax:* 410-955-0549, *E-mail:* msachs@bme.jhu.edu.
Application contact: Dr. Eric D. Young, Director, PhD Program, 410-955-3277, *Fax:* 410-955-9826, *E-mail:* eyoung@bme.jhu.edu. *Web site:* http://www.bme.jhu.edu/

Find an in-depth description at www.petersons.com/gradchannel.

■ LOUISIANA TECH UNIVERSITY

Graduate School, College of Engineering and Science, Department of Biomedical Engineering, Ruston, LA 71272

AWARDS MS, PhD. Part-time programs available. Terminal master's awarded for partial completion of doctoral program.

Degree requirements: For master's and doctorate, thesis/dissertation.
Entrance requirements: For master's, GRE General Test, TOEFL, minimum

GPA of 3.0 in last 60 hours; for doctorate, TOEFL, minimum graduate GPA of 3.25 (MS) or GRE General Test.
Faculty research: Microbiosensors and microcirculatory transport, speech recognition, artificial intelligence, rehabilitation engineering, bioelectromagnetics.

■ MARQUETTE UNIVERSITY

Graduate School, College of Engineering, Department of Biomedical Engineering, Milwaukee, WI 53201-1881

AWARDS Bioinstrumentation/computers (MS, PhD); biomechanics/biomaterials (MS, PhD); functional imaging (PhD); healthcare technologies management (MS). Systems physiology (MS, PhD). Part-time and evening/weekend programs available.

Faculty: 16 full-time (2 women), 39 part-time/adjunct (6 women).
Students: 41 full-time (13 women), 25 part-time (6 women); includes 7 minority (6 Asian Americans or Pacific Islanders, 1 Hispanic American), 8 international. 61 applicants, 75% accepted. In 2001, 12 master's, 1 doctorate awarded. Terminal master's awarded for partial completion of doctoral program.
Degree requirements: For master's, thesis, comprehensive exam; for doctorate, dissertation defense, qualifying exam.
Entrance requirements: For master's and doctorate, GRE General Test, TOEFL. *Application deadline:* For fall admission, 2/15 (priority date); for spring admission, 11/15 (priority date). Applications are processed on a rolling basis. *Application fee:* $40. Electronic applications accepted.
Expenses: Tuition: Full-time $10,170; part-time $445 per credit hour. Tuition and fees vary according to course load.
Financial support: In 2001–02, 12 fellowships with full tuition reimbursements, 14 research assistantships with full tuition reimbursements, 6 teaching assistantships with full tuition reimbursements were awarded. Scholarships/grants also available. Financial award application deadline: 2/15.
Faculty research: Cell and organ physiology, signal processing, gait analysis, orthopedic rehabilitation engineering, telemedicine. *Total annual research expenditures:* $3.6 million.
Dr. John M. Winters, Chair, 414-288-3375, *Fax:* 414-288-7938, *E-mail:* jack.winters@marquette.edu.
Application contact: Brigid J. Lagerman, Assistant Chair, 414-288-7856, *Fax:* 414-288-7938, *E-mail:* brigid.lagerman@marquette.edu. *Web site:* http://www.eng.mu.edu/bien/

Find an in-depth description at www.petersons.com/gradchannel.

■ MASSACHUSETTS INSTITUTE OF TECHNOLOGY

School of Engineering, Biological Engineering Division, Cambridge, MA 02139-4307

AWARDS Bioengineering (PhD); biomedical engineering (M Eng); toxicology (SM, PhD, Sc D).

Faculty: 9 full-time (2 women), 1 part-time/adjunct (0 women).
Students: 84 full-time (41 women); includes 14 minority (2 African Americans, 9 Asian Americans or Pacific Islanders, 3 Hispanic Americans), 32 international. Average age 24. 213 applicants, 17% accepted, 25 enrolled. In 2001, 2 master's, 8 doctorates awarded. Terminal master's awarded for partial completion of doctoral program.
Degree requirements: For master's, thesis; for doctorate, thesis/dissertation, oral and written qualifying exams.
Entrance requirements: For master's and doctorate, GRE General Test, TOEFL. *Application deadline:* For fall admission, 1/15. *Application fee:* $60. Electronic applications accepted.
Expenses: Tuition: Full-time $26,960. Full-time tuition and fees vary according to program.
Financial support: In 2001–02, 84 students received support, including 36 fellowships, 35 research assistantships, 7 teaching assistantships; Federal Work-Study, institutionally sponsored loans, scholarships/grants, health care benefits, and unspecified assistantships also available. Financial award application deadline: 1/15; financial award applicants required to submit FAFSA.
Faculty research: Biological imaging, biological microanalytics, biological transport process, biomaterials, cell and tissue engineering. *Total annual research expenditures:* $9 million.
Douglas A. Lauffenburger, Co-Director, 617-252-1629, *E-mail:* lauffen@mit.edu.
Application contact: Dalia Gabour, Academic Administrator, 617-253-5804, *Fax:* 617-258-8676, *E-mail:* be-www@ mit.edu. *Web site:* http://web.mit.edu/beh/
Find an in-depth description at www.petersons.com/gradchannel.

■ MASSACHUSETTS INSTITUTE OF TECHNOLOGY

Whitaker College of Health Sciences and Technology, Division of Health Sciences and Technology, Medical Engineering/Medical Physics Program, Cambridge, MA 02139-4307

AWARDS Medical engineering (PhD); medical engineering and medical physics (Sc D); medical physics (PhD).

Students: 83 full-time (26 women); includes 17 minority (14 Asian Americans or Pacific Islanders, 3 Hispanic

Americans), 27 international. Average age 27. 132 applicants, 16% accepted. In 2001, 13 degrees awarded.
Degree requirements: For doctorate, thesis/dissertation, oral and written departmental qualifying exams. *Median time to degree:* Doctorate–3.31 years full-time.
Entrance requirements: For doctorate, bachelor's degree in engineering or science. *Application deadline:* For fall admission, 1/15. *Application fee:* $55.
Expenses: Contact institution.
Financial support: In 2001–02, 80 students received support, including 27 fellowships with full and partial tuition reimbursements available (averaging $48,046 per year), 48 research assistantships with full and partial tuition reimbursements available (averaging $22,056 per year), 5 teaching assistantships with full and partial tuition reimbursements available (averaging $16,789 per year); career-related internships or fieldwork and traineeships also available. Financial award application deadline: 1/15.
Faculty research: Imaging; informatics, genomics and proteomics; mathematical modeling; digital signal processing. Spectroscopy.
Dr. Martha L. Gray, Director, 617-253-2307, *E-mail:* mgray@mit.edu.
Application contact: Catherine A. Modica, Admissions Coordinator, 617-253-2307, *Fax:* 617-253-6692, *E-mail:* cmodica@mit.edu. *Web site:* http://hst.mit.edu
Find an in-depth description at www.petersons.com/gradchannel.

■ MAYO GRADUATE SCHOOL

Graduate Programs in Biomedical Sciences, Program in Biomedical Engineering, Rochester, MN 55905

AWARDS PhD.

Faculty: 60 full-time (3 women).
Students: 25 full-time (9 women); includes 4 minority (1 African American, 1 Asian American or Pacific Islander, 2 Hispanic Americans), 11 international. In 2001, 6 doctorates awarded.
Degree requirements: For doctorate, oral defense of dissertation, qualifying oral and written exam.
Entrance requirements: For doctorate, GRE, TOEFL, 2 years of chemistry; 1 year of biology, calculus, and physics. *Application deadline:* For fall admission, 12/31 (priority date). Applications are processed on a rolling basis. *Application fee:* $0. Electronic applications accepted.
Expenses: Tuition: Full-time $17,900.
Financial support: In 2001–02, 24 students received support, including 24 fellowships with full tuition reimbursements available (averaging $19,800 per year); tuition waivers (full) also available.
Dr. Gary C. Sieck, Education Coordinator, 507-255-7481, *E-mail:* sieck.gary@ mayo.edu.

Application contact: Melissa L. Berg, Admissions Coordinator, 507-538-1160, *Fax:* 507-284-0999, *E-mail:* phd.training@ mayo.edu.
Find an in-depth description at www.petersons.com/gradchannel.

■ MERCER UNIVERSITY

Graduate Studies, Macon Campus, School of Engineering, Macon, GA 31207-0003

AWARDS Biomedical engineering (MSE); electrical engineering (MSE); engineering management (MSE); mechanical engineering (MSE). Software engineering (MSE). Software systems (MS); technical communications management (MS); technical management (MS). Part-time and evening/weekend programs available.

Faculty: 10 full-time (1 woman), 5 part-time/adjunct (1 woman).
Students: 3 full-time (2 women), 104 part-time (31 women); includes 19 minority (13 African Americans, 6 Asian Americans or Pacific Islanders), 5 international. Average age 36. 31 applicants, 97% accepted, 27 enrolled. In 2001, 32 degrees awarded.
Degree requirements: For master's, thesis or alternative, registration.
Entrance requirements: For master's, GRE, minimum undergraduate GPA of 3.0. *Application deadline:* For fall admission, 7/1; for spring admission, 11/15. Applications are processed on a rolling basis. *Application fee:* $35 ($50 for international students).
Expenses: Contact institution.
Financial support: Federal Work-Study available.
Dr. M. Dayne Aldridge, Dean, 478-301-2459, *Fax:* 478-301-5593, *E-mail:* aldridge_md@mercer.edu.
Application contact: Kathy Olivier, Graduate Administrative Coordinator, 478-301-2196, *E-mail:* olivier_kk@mercer.edu. *Web site:* http://www.mercer.edu/ engineer.htm

■ MILWAUKEE SCHOOL OF ENGINEERING

Department of Electrical Engineering and Computer Science, Program in Engineering, Milwaukee, WI 53202-3109

AWARDS Perfusion (MS). Evening/weekend programs available.

Faculty: 2 full-time (0 women), 9 part-time/adjunct (1 woman).
Students: 8 full-time (4 women), 2 part-time (1 woman). Average age 25. 18 applicants, 39% accepted, 7 enrolled. In 2001, 10 degrees awarded.
Degree requirements: For master's, thesis or alternative, thesis defense, comprehensive exam, registration.
Entrance requirements: For master's, GRE General Test, BS in engineering,

biology, chemistry or related field. *Application deadline:* Applications are processed on a rolling basis. *Application fee:* $35. Electronic applications accepted.
Expenses: Tuition: Part-time $440 per credit. Tuition and fees vary according to course load.
Financial support: In 2001–02, 4 students received support; research assistantships, career-related internships or fieldwork available. Support available to part-time students. Financial award applicants required to submit FAFSA.
Faculty research: Microprocessors, materials, thermodynamics, artificial intelligence, fluid power/hydraulics. *Total annual research expenditures:* $1.3 million.
Dr. Glenn Wrate, Chairman, 414-277-7330, *Fax:* 414-277-7465.
Application contact: Paul Borens, Admissions Director, 800-332-6763, *Fax:* 414-277-7475, *E-mail:* borens@msoe.edu. *Web site:* http://www.msoe.edu/

Find an in-depth description at www.petersons.com/gradchannel.

■ MISSISSIPPI STATE UNIVERSITY

College of Engineering, Department of Agricultural and Biological Engineering, Mississippi State, MS 39762

AWARDS Biological engineering (MS); biomedical engineering (MS, PhD); engineering (PhD).
Faculty: 8 full-time (0 women), 1 part-time/adjunct (0 women).
Students: 10 full-time (4 women), 7 part-time (3 women); includes 2 minority (both African Americans), 4 international. Average age 29. 7 applicants, 57% accepted. In 2001, 3 degrees awarded.
Degree requirements: For master's, thesis; for doctorate, thesis/dissertation, preliminary exam.
Entrance requirements: For master's, GRE General Test, TOEFL, minimum GPA of 2.75, minimum GPA of 3.0 for biomedical program; for doctorate, GRE General Test, TOEFL, minimum GPA of 3.0 for biomedical program. *Application deadline:* For fall admission, 7/1; for spring admission, 11/1. Applications are processed on a rolling basis. *Application fee:* $25 for international students.
Expenses: Tuition, state resident: full-time $3,586; part-time $150 per credit hour. Tuition, nonresident: full-time $8,128; part-time $339 per credit hour. Tuition and fees vary according to course load and campus/location.
Financial support: In 2001–02, 1 fellowship with tuition reimbursement (averaging $15,000 per year), 2 research assistantships with tuition reimbursements (averaging $12,500 per year), 1 teaching assistantship with tuition reimbursement (averaging $12,500 per year) were awarded. Federal Work-Study, institutionally sponsored

loans, and unspecified assistantships also available. Financial award applicants required to submit FAFSA.
Faculty research: Bioenvironmental engineering, bioinstrumentation, biomechanics/biomaterials, precision agriculture, tissue engineering. *Total annual research expenditures:* $950,000.
Dr. Jerome A. Gilbert, Head, 662-325-3280, *Fax:* 662-325-3853, *E-mail:* jgilbert@abe.msstate.edu.
Application contact: Jerry B. Inmon, Director of Admissions, 662-325-2224, *Fax:* 662-325-7360, *E-mail:* admit@admissions.msstate.edu. *Web site:* http://www.abe.msstate.edu/

■ NEW JERSEY INSTITUTE OF TECHNOLOGY

Office of Graduate Studies, Department of Biomedical Engineering, Newark, NJ 07102

AWARDS MS. Part-time and evening/weekend programs available.

Faculty: 10 full-time (2 women).
Students: 18 full-time (9 women), 13 part-time (5 women); includes 11 minority (3 African Americans, 8 Asian Americans or Pacific Islanders), 7 international. 84 applicants, 49% accepted, 14 enrolled. In 2001, 8 degrees awarded. Terminal master's awarded for partial completion of doctoral program.
Degree requirements: For master's, thesis.
Entrance requirements: For master's, GRE General Test. *Application deadline:* For fall admission, 6/5 (priority date); for spring admission, 10/15. Applications are processed on a rolling basis. *Application fee:* $50. Electronic applications accepted.
Expenses: Tuition, state resident: full-time $7,812; part-time $434 per credit. Tuition, nonresident: full-time $10,746; part-time $597 per credit. Required fees: $47 per credit. $76 per semester.
Financial support: Fellowships with full and partial tuition reimbursements, research assistantships with full and partial tuition reimbursements, teaching assistantships with full and partial tuition reimbursements, career-related internships or fieldwork, Federal Work-Study, institutionally sponsored loans, and unspecified assistantships available. Financial award application deadline: 3/15.
Dr. David Kristol, Chairperson, 973-596-3584, *Fax:* 973-596-2222, *E-mail:* david.kristol@njit.edu.
Application contact: Kathryn Kelly, Director of Admissions, 973-596-3300, *Fax:* 973-596-3461, *E-mail:* admissions@njit.edu.

■ NORTHWESTERN UNIVERSITY

McCormick School of Engineering and Applied Science, Department of Biomedical Engineering, Evanston, IL 60208

AWARDS MS, PhD. Admissions and degrees offered through The Graduate School. Part-time programs available.

Faculty: 38 full-time (3 women), 3 part-time/adjunct (0 women).
Students: 74 full-time (23 women); includes 16 minority (3 African Americans, 11 Asian Americans or Pacific Islanders, 2 Hispanic Americans), 20 international. Average age 26. 116 applicants, 57% accepted. In 2001, 20 master's, 11 doctorates awarded. Terminal master's awarded for partial completion of doctoral program.
Degree requirements: For master's, thesis or alternative; for doctorate, thesis/dissertation. *Median time to degree:* Master's–2 years full-time; doctorate–5.5 years full-time.
Application deadline: For fall admission, 8/30. *Application fee:* $50 ($55 for international students).
Expenses: Tuition: Full-time $26,526.
Financial support: In 2001–02, 12 fellowships with full tuition reimbursements (averaging $19,200 per year), 36 research assistantships with partial tuition reimbursements (averaging $18,000 per year), 6 teaching assistantships with full tuition reimbursements (averaging $18,000 per year) were awarded. Career-related internships or fieldwork, Federal Work-Study, institutionally sponsored loans, scholarships/grants, and traineeships also available. Financial award application deadline: 1/15; financial award applicants required to submit FAFSA.
Faculty research: Biomechanics and transport, rehabilitation engineering, neuroscience, biomaterials, cellular engineering. *Total annual research expenditures:* $4.2 million.
Matthew R. Glucksberg, Chair, 847-491-7121, *Fax:* 847-491-4928, *E-mail:* m-glucksberg@northwestern.edu.
Application contact: Mary Anne Peruchini, Business Administrator, 847-491-5635, *Fax:* 847-491-4928, *E-mail:* mperuchini@northwestern.edu. *Web site:* http://www.northwestern.edu/bme/

Find an in-depth description at www.petersons.com/gradchannel.

■ THE OHIO STATE UNIVERSITY

Graduate School, College of Engineering, Program in Biomedical Engineering, Columbus, OH 43210

AWARDS MS, PhD. Evening/weekend programs available.

Degree requirements: For master's, thesis optional; for doctorate, thesis/dissertation.

The Ohio State University (continued)

Entrance requirements: For master's and doctorate, GRE General Test.

Find an in-depth description at www.petersons.com/gradchannel.

■ THE PENNSYLVANIA STATE UNIVERSITY UNIVERSITY PARK CAMPUS

Graduate School, Intercollege Graduate Programs, Department of Bioengineering, State College, University Park, PA 16802-1503

AWARDS MS, PhD.

Students: 26 full-time (9 women), 7 part-time (1 woman). In 2001, 7 master's, 1 doctorate awarded. Terminal master's awarded for partial completion of doctoral program.
Degree requirements: For master's and doctorate, thesis/dissertation.
Entrance requirements: For master's and doctorate, GRE General Test, TOEFL. *Application fee:* $45.
Expenses: Tuition, state resident: full-time $7,882; part-time $333 per credit. Tuition, nonresident: full-time $16,142; part-time $673 per credit. Required fees: $124 per semester.
Dr. Herbert H. Lipowsky, Head, 814-865-1407.

Find an in-depth description at www.petersons.com/gradchannel.

■ PURDUE UNIVERSITY

Graduate School, Schools of Engineering, Department of Biomedical Engineering, West Lafayette, IN 47907

AWARDS MS Bm E, PhD.

Students: 26 full-time (13 women); includes 1 minority (African American), 6 international. Average age 26. 168 applicants, 12% accepted.
Application deadline: For fall admission, 1/15 (priority date). *Application fee:* $30. Electronic applications accepted.
Expenses: Tuition, state resident: full-time $4,164; part-time $149 per credit hour. Tuition, nonresident: full-time $13,872; part-time $458 per credit hour. Tuition and fees vary according to campus/location and program.
Financial support: Fellowships, research assistantships, teaching assistantships available. Support available to part-time students. Financial award applicants required to submit FAFSA.
Faculty research: Biomaterials, biomechanics, medical image and signal processing, medical instrumentation, tissue engineering.
Dr. G. R. Wodicka, Founding Head, 765-494-2998, *Fax:* 765-494-1193, *E-mail:* wodicka@ecn.purdue.edu.
Application contact: Mary DeBruicker, Biomedical Engineering Graduate Office,

765-494-7054, *Fax:* 765-494-1193, *E-mail:* bmeprogram@ecn.purdue.edu. *Web site:* http://www.ecn.purdue.edu/biomed/

Find an in-depth description at www.petersons.com/gradchannel.

■ RENSSELAER POLYTECHNIC INSTITUTE

Graduate School, School of Engineering, Department of Biomedical Engineering, Troy, NY 12180-3590

AWARDS M Eng, MS, D Eng, PhD. Part-time programs available.

Faculty: 7 full-time (2 women).
Students: 34 full-time (13 women), 1 (woman) part-time; includes 2 minority (1 African American, 1 Asian American or Pacific Islander), 12 international. 100 applicants, 40% accepted. In 2001, 7 master's, 4 doctorates awarded.
Degree requirements: For master's, thesis (for some programs); for doctorate, thesis/dissertation.
Entrance requirements: For master's and doctorate, GRE, TOEFL. *Application deadline:* For fall admission, 2/1 (priority date). Applications are processed on a rolling basis. *Application fee:* $45. Electronic applications accepted.
Expenses: Tuition: Full-time $26,400; part-time $1,320 per credit hour. Required fees: $1,437.
Financial support: In 2001–02, 4 research assistantships with full and partial tuition reimbursements (averaging $5,850 per year), 12 teaching assistantships with full and partial tuition reimbursements (averaging $11,700 per year) were awarded. Fellowships, career-related internships or fieldwork and institutionally sponsored loans also available. Financial award application deadline: 2/1.
Faculty research: Internal and electrical impedance, computational mechanics, biomechanics and biomaterials, cellular and tissue bioengineering. *Total annual research expenditures:* $400,000.
Dr. Robert Spilker, Chair, 518-276-6548, *Fax:* 518-276-3035.
Application contact: Lorrie Citarella, Coordinator of Student Affairs, 518-276-6547, *Fax:* 518-276-3035, *E-mail:* citarl@rpi.edu. *Web site:* http://www.rpi.edu/dept/biomed/WWW/

Find an in-depth description at www.petersons.com/gradchannel.

■ RICE UNIVERSITY

Graduate Programs, George R. Brown School of Engineering, Department of Bioengineering, Houston, TX 77251-1892

AWARDS MS, PhD, MD/PhD.

Faculty: 17 full-time (3 women), 18 part-time/adjunct (0 women).
Students: 56 full-time (14 women); includes 21 minority (2 African Americans,

17 Asian Americans or Pacific Islanders, 2 Hispanic Americans). Average age 25. 215 applicants, 12% accepted. In 2001, 2 degrees awarded. Terminal master's awarded for partial completion of doctoral program.
Degree requirements: For master's, thesis, registration; for doctorate, thesis/dissertation, qualifying exam, internship.
Entrance requirements: For master's and doctorate, GRE General Test, TOEFL. *Application deadline:* For fall admission, 2/1. *Application fee:* $25. Electronic applications accepted.
Expenses: Tuition: Full-time $17,300. Required fees: $250.
Financial support: In 2001–02, 26 fellowships with full tuition reimbursements (averaging $18,500 per year), 17 research assistantships with full tuition reimbursements (averaging $18,500 per year), 1 teaching assistantship with full tuition reimbursement (averaging $9,250 per year) were awarded. Scholarships/grants, traineeships, and tuition waivers (full) also available.
Faculty research: Biomaterials, tissue engineering, laser-tissue interactions, biochemical engineering, gene therapy. *Total annual research expenditures:* $3.5 million.
Dr. Larry V. McIntire, Chair, 713-348-4903, *Fax:* 713-348-5877, *E-mail:* mcintire@rice.edu.
Application contact: Mauricio A. Benitez, Department Coordinator, 713-348-2871, *Fax:* 713-348-5877, *E-mail:* bioeng@ruf.rice.edu. *Web site:* http://www.ruf.rice.edu/~bioeng/

■ ROSE-HULMAN INSTITUTE OF TECHNOLOGY

Faculty of Engineering and Applied Sciences, Interdisciplinary Program in Biomedical Engineering, Terre Haute, IN 47803-3920

AWARDS MS, MD/MS. Part-time programs available.

Faculty: 7 full-time (2 women).
Students: 19 full-time (2 women), 5 part-time; includes 1 minority (Asian American or Pacific Islander), 6 international. Average age 24. 16 applicants, 88% accepted, 7 enrolled. In 2001, 2 degrees awarded.
Degree requirements: For master's, thesis.
Entrance requirements: For master's, GRE, TOEFL, minimum GPA of 3.0. *Application deadline:* For fall admission, 2/1 (priority date). Applications are processed on a rolling basis. *Application fee:* $0.
Expenses: Tuition: Full-time $21,792; part-time $615 per credit hour. Required fees: $405.
Financial support: In 2001–02, 22 students received support; fellowships with full and partial tuition reimbursements available, research assistantships with full and partial tuition reimbursements available, institutionally sponsored loans,

scholarships/grants, and tuition waivers (full and partial) available. Financial award application deadline: 2/1.

Faculty research: Retinal blood flow, biomaterials, design of artificial organs and prosthetic devices, biomedical optics, biomedical fluid mechanics. *Total annual research expenditures:* $206,000.

Dr. Lee Waite, Chair, 812-877-8404, *Fax:* 812-877-3198, *E-mail:* lee.waite@rose-hulman.edu.

Application contact: Dr. Daniel J. Moore, Interim Associate Dean of the Faculty, 812-877-8110, *Fax:* 812-877-8061, *E-mail:* daniel.j.moore@rose-hulman.edu.

■ RUTGERS, THE STATE UNIVERSITY OF NEW JERSEY, NEW BRUNSWICK

Graduate School, Program in Biomedical Engineering, New Brunswick, NJ 08901-1281

AWARDS MS, PhD. Part-time programs available. Terminal master's awarded for partial completion of doctoral program.

Degree requirements: For master's and doctorate, thesis/dissertation.

Entrance requirements: For master's and doctorate, GRE General Test, minimum GPA of 3.0.

Faculty research: Biomedical instrumentation, biomechanics and biomaterials, vision and imaging. *Web site:* http://biomedical.rutgers.edu/

■ STANFORD UNIVERSITY

School of Engineering, Department of Mechanical Engineering, Program in Biomechanical Engineering, Stanford, CA 94305-9991

AWARDS MS.

Entrance requirements: For master's, GRE General Test, TOEFL. *Application deadline:* For fall admission, 1/15. *Application fee:* $65 ($80 for international students). Electronic applications accepted.

Application contact: Admissions Office, 650-723-3148.

Find an in-depth description at www.petersons.com/gradchannel.

■ STONY BROOK UNIVERSITY, STATE UNIVERSITY OF NEW YORK

Graduate School, College of Engineering and Applied Sciences, Department of Biomedical Engineering, Stony Brook, NY 11794

AWARDS MS, PhD, Certificate.

Faculty: 27 full-time (4 women).

Students: 29 full-time (12 women), 4 part-time; includes 4 minority (3 Asian Americans or Pacific Islanders, 1 Hispanic American), 13 international. 67 applicants, 42% accepted. In 2001, 6 degrees awarded.

Degree requirements: For doctorate, thesis/dissertation, qualifying exams.

Entrance requirements: For master's and doctorate, GRE General Test, TOEFL. *Application deadline:* For fall admission, 1/15. *Application fee:* $50.

Expenses: Tuition, state resident: full-time $5,100; part-time $213 per credit. Tuition, nonresident: full-time $8,416; part-time $351 per credit. Required fees: $496.

Financial support: In 2001–02, 13 research assistantships, 13 teaching assistantships were awarded. *Total annual research expenditures:* $411,982.

Dr. Clint T. Rubin, Chair, 631-632-2302, *Fax:* 631-632-1539, *E-mail:* clint@bone.ortho.sunysb.edu.

Application contact: Anne Marie Dusatko, Administrative Secretary, 631-632-2302, *Fax:* 631-632-1539, *E-mail:* anne@bone.ortho.sunysb.edu. *Web site:* http://clio-yad.sunysb.edu/bmc/index.html

Find an in-depth description at www.petersons.com/gradchannel.

■ SYRACUSE UNIVERSITY

Graduate School, L. C. Smith College of Engineering and Computer Science, Department of Bioengineering and Neuroscience, Syracuse, NY 13244-0003

AWARDS Bioengineering (ME, MS, PhD); neuroscience (MS).

Faculty: 9 full-time (3 women), 3 part-time/adjunct (0 women).

Students: 38 full-time (8 women), 1 (woman) part-time; includes 4 minority (all Asian Americans or Pacific Islanders), 7 international. In 2001, 9 degrees awarded.

Entrance requirements: For master's, GRE General Test, GRE Subject Test. *Application deadline:* Applications are processed on a rolling basis. *Application fee:* $50.

Expenses: Tuition: Full-time $15,528; part-time $647 per credit. Required fees: $420; $38 per term. Tuition and fees vary according to program.

Financial support: In 2001–02, 3 fellowships with full tuition reimbursements (averaging $13,680 per year), 10 research assistantships with full tuition reimbursements (averaging $11,000 per year), 1 teaching assistantship with full tuition reimbursement (averaging $11,000 per year) were awarded. Financial award application deadline: 1/10.

Faculty research: Audition, taction, multisensory, computational neuroscience. *Total annual research expenditures:* $2.1 million.

Dr. Jeremy Gilbert, Chair, 315-443-5629, *Fax:* 315-443-1184, *E-mail:* gilbert@ecs.syr.edu.

Application contact: Dr. Laurel Carney, Information Contact, 315-443-9749, *Fax:*

315-443-1184, *E-mail:* lacarney@syr.edu. *Web site:* http://www.ecs.syr.edu/

Find an in-depth description at www.petersons.com/gradchannel.

■ TEXAS A&M UNIVERSITY

College of Engineering, Department of Biomedical Engineering, College Station, TX 77843

AWARDS M Eng, MS, D Eng, PhD. Part-time programs available.

Faculty: 6 full-time (0 women), 2 part-time/adjunct (0 women).

Students: 63 full-time (25 women), 6 part-time (2 women); includes 1 minority (Hispanic American), 50 international. Average age 27. 114 applicants, 47% accepted, 25 enrolled. In 2001, 4 master's, 6 doctorates awarded.

Degree requirements: For master's, thesis (for some programs), thesis (MS); for doctorate, thesis/dissertation, dissertation (PhD). *Median time to degree:* Master's–2.5 years full-time; doctorate–5 years full-time.

Entrance requirements: For master's and doctorate, GRE General Test, TOEFL. *Application deadline:* Applications are processed on a rolling basis. *Application fee:* $50 ($75 for international students). Electronic applications accepted.

Expenses: Tuition, state resident: full-time $11,872. Tuition, nonresident: full-time $17,892.

Financial support: In 2001–02, 25 students received support, including fellowships with partial tuition reimbursements available (averaging $12,600 per year), 16 research assistantships with partial tuition reimbursements available, 9 teaching assistantships; career-related internships or fieldwork, health care benefits, and unspecified assistantships also available. Financial award application deadline: 4/15; financial award applicants required to submit FAFSA.

Faculty research: Medical lasers, optical biosensors, medical instrumentation, cardiovascular mechanics, orthopedic mechanics, optical bioimaging. *Total annual research expenditures:* $1.4 million.

Dr. William A. Hyman, Interim Head, 979-845-5532, *Fax:* 979-845-4450, *E-mail:* w-hyman@tamu.edu.

Application contact: Dr. Gerard L. Coté, Graduate Advisor, 979-845-5532, *Fax:* 979-845-4450, *E-mail:* cote@tamu.edu.

■ THOMAS JEFFERSON UNIVERSITY

College of Graduate Studies, Program in Cell and Tissue Engineering, Philadelphia, PA 19107

AWARDS PhD.

Faculty: 5 full-time (2 women), 6 part-time/adjunct (2 women).

Students: 8 full-time (2 women); includes 3 minority (all Asian Americans or Pacific

Thomas Jefferson University (continued)
Islanders), 1 international. Average age 25. 9 applicants, 11% accepted, 1 enrolled.
Degree requirements: For doctorate, thesis/dissertation, comprehensive exam, registration.
Entrance requirements: For doctorate, GRE General Test, TOEFL, minimum GPA of 3.2. *Application deadline:* For fall admission, 3/1 (priority date). Applications are processed on a rolling basis. *Application fee:* $40. Electronic applications accepted.
Expenses: Tuition: Full-time $13,440. Tuition and fees vary according to degree level and program.
Financial support: In 2001–02, 8 fellowships with full tuition reimbursements were awarded; Federal Work-Study, institutionally sponsored loans, and traineeships also available. Support available to part-time students. Financial award application deadline: 5/1; financial award applicants required to submit FAFSA.
Faculty research: Skeletal development, biomaterials, bone implant interaction, tissue engineering, high resolution imaging. Dr. Irving Shapiro, Director, 215-955-7217, *Fax:* 215-955-9159.
Application contact: Jessie F. Pervall, Director of Admissions, 215-503-0155, *Fax:* 215-503-3433, *E-mail:* jessie.pervall@ mail.tju.edu.

Find an in-depth description at www.petersons.com/gradchannel.

■ TULANE UNIVERSITY

School of Engineering, Department of Biomedical Engineering, New Orleans, LA 70118-5669

AWARDS MS, MSE, PhD, Sc D. MS and PhD offered through the Graduate School. Terminal master's awarded for partial completion of doctoral program.
Degree requirements: For master's and doctorate, thesis/dissertation.
Entrance requirements: For master's and doctorate, GRE General Test, TOEFL, minimum B average in undergraduate course work.
Expenses: Tuition: Full-time $24,675. Required fees: $2,210.
Faculty research: Pulmonary and biofluid mechanics and biomechanics of bone, biomaterials science, finite element analysis, electric fields of the brain. *Web site:* http://www.omen.tulane.edu/

Find an in-depth description at www.petersons.com/gradchannel.

■ THE UNIVERSITY OF AKRON

Graduate School, College of Engineering, Department of Biomedical Engineering, Akron, OH 44325-0001

AWARDS MS. Part-time and evening/weekend programs available.
Faculty: 6 full-time (1 woman), 2 part-time/adjunct (0 women).

Students: 16 full-time (5 women), 5 part-time (2 women), 13 international. Average age 26. 39 applicants, 72% accepted, 7 enrolled. In 2001, 3 degrees awarded. Terminal master's awarded for partial completion of doctoral program.
Degree requirements: For master's, thesis.
Entrance requirements: For master's, GRE General Test, TOEFL, minimum GPA of 3.0. *Application deadline:* For fall admission, 3/1. Applications are processed on a rolling basis. *Application fee:* $40 ($50 for international students).
Expenses: Tuition, state resident: full-time $6,562; part-time $219 per credit. Tuition, nonresident: full-time $9,027; part-time $383 per credit. Required fees: $272; $11 per credit. Tuition and fees vary according to course load.
Financial support: In 2001–02, 5 research assistantships with full tuition reimbursements, 6 teaching assistantships with full tuition reimbursements were awarded. Fellowships with full tuition reimbursements, career-related internships or fieldwork, Federal Work-Study, scholarships/grants, and tuition waivers (full) also available. Financial award application deadline: 3/1.
Faculty research: Signal and image processing, gait analysis, biomechanics, biocontrols instrumentation, vascular dynamics. Dr. Daniel Sheffer, Interim Chair, 330-972-7691, *E-mail:* mverstraete@ uakron.edu. *Web site:* http:// www.biomed.uakron.edu/

■ THE UNIVERSITY OF ALABAMA AT BIRMINGHAM

Graduate School, School of Engineering, Department of Biomedical Engineering, Birmingham, AL 35294

AWARDS MSBME, PhD.
Students: 48 full-time (17 women), 7 part-time (1 woman); includes 8 minority (4 African Americans, 2 Asian Americans or Pacific Islanders, 2 Hispanic Americans), 16 international. 140 applicants, 22% accepted. In 2001, 15 master's, 7 doctorates awarded.
Degree requirements: For master's, thesis or alternative, oral exam; for doctorate, thesis/dissertation, comprehensive exam.
Entrance requirements: For master's and doctorate, GRE General Test, TOEFL. *Application deadline:* For fall admission, 4/15. Applications are processed on a rolling basis. *Application fee:* $35 ($60 for international students). Electronic applications accepted.
Expenses: Tuition, state resident: full-time $3,058. Tuition, nonresident: full-time $5,746. Tuition and fees vary according to course load, degree level and program.
Financial support: In 2001–02, 48 students received support; fellowships with full tuition reimbursements available,

research assistantships, career-related internships or fieldwork, Federal Work-Study, and institutionally sponsored loans available.
Dr. William M. Smith, Interim Chair, 205-934-8420, *E-mail:* macsmith@uab.edu. *Web site:* http://bmewww.eng.uab.edu/ BME/

■ UNIVERSITY OF CALIFORNIA, BERKELEY

Graduate Division, Group in Bioengineering, Berkeley, CA 94720-1708

AWARDS PhD.
Degree requirements: For doctorate, thesis/dissertation, qualifying exam.
Entrance requirements: For doctorate, GRE General Test, minimum GPA of 3.0.
Expenses: Tuition, nonresident: full-time $10,704. Required fees: $4,349.
Faculty research: Imaging, biomechanics, biomems modeling, neuroscience, biomedical computing, vision. *Web site:* http://bioeng.berkeley.edu

■ UNIVERSITY OF CALIFORNIA, DAVIS

Graduate Studies, College of Engineering, Graduate Group in Biomedical Engineering, Davis, CA 95616

AWARDS MS, PhD.
Faculty: 47 full-time (7 women), 2 part-time/adjunct (0 women).
Students: 59 full-time (23 women); includes 9 minority (8 Asian Americans or Pacific Islanders, 1 Hispanic American), 9 international. Average age 28. 109 applicants, 50% accepted, 9 enrolled. In 2001, 9 master's, 2 doctorates awarded.
Degree requirements: For master's and doctorate, thesis/dissertation.
Entrance requirements: For master's and doctorate, GRE General Test, minimum GPA of 3.25. *Application deadline:* For fall admission, 1/15 (priority date). Applications are processed on a rolling basis. *Application fee:* $60. Electronic applications accepted.
Expenses: Tuition, state resident: full-time $4,831. Tuition, nonresident: full-time $15,725.
Financial support: In 2001–02, 51 students received support, including 10 fellowships with full and partial tuition reimbursements available (averaging $5,810 per year), 37 research assistantships with full and partial tuition reimbursements available (averaging $7,666 per year), 13 teaching assistantships with partial tuition reimbursements available (averaging $9,245 per year); career-related internships or fieldwork, Federal Work-Study, institutionally sponsored loans, and tuition waivers (full and partial) also available. Financial award application deadline:

1/15; financial award applicants required to submit FAFSA.

Faculty research: Orthopedic biomechanics, cell/molecular biomechanics and transport, biosensors and instrumentation, human movement, biomedical image analysis, spectroscopy.

Jeffery Gibeling, Graduate Group Chair, 530-752-7037, *E-mail:* jcibeling@ ucdavis.edu.

Application contact: Frances Gamez, Administrative Assistant, 530-752-2611, *Fax:* 530-752-2123, *E-mail:* fmgamez@ ucdavis.edu. *Web site:* http:// www.bme.ucdavis.edu/

■ UNIVERSITY OF CALIFORNIA, IRVINE

Office of Research and Graduate Studies, School of Engineering, Department of Chemical and Biochemical Engineering and Materials Science, Program in Biomedical Engineering, Irvine, CA 92697

AWARDS MS, PhD. Part-time programs available.

Students: 19 full-time (5 women); includes 9 minority (1 African American, 7 Asian Americans or Pacific Islanders, 1 Hispanic American), 4 international. 64 applicants, 38% accepted, 8 enrolled. In 2001, 1 degree awarded. Terminal master's awarded for partial completion of doctoral program.

Degree requirements: For doctorate, thesis/dissertation.

Entrance requirements: For master's, GRE General Test, minimum GPA of 3.0; for doctorate, GRE General Test. *Application deadline:* For fall and spring admission, 1/15 (priority date); for winter admission, 10/15 (priority date). Applications are processed on a rolling basis. *Application fee:* $60. Electronic applications accepted.

Expenses: Tuition, nonresident: full-time $10,704. Required fees: $8,396. Tuition and fees vary according to course load, program and student level.

Financial support: In 2001–02, 4 fellowships (averaging $1,250 per year) were awarded; research assistantships, teaching assistantships, institutionally sponsored loans also available. Financial award application deadline: 3/2; financial award applicants required to submit FAFSA. Steve George, Director, 949-824-3941, *Fax:* 949-824-3440, *E-mail:* scgeorge@ uci.edu.

Application contact: Dee Pleasant, Admissions Assistant, 949-824-3494, *Fax:* 949-824-1727, *E-mail:* jpleasant@uci.edu. *Web site:* http://www.eng.uci.edu/

■ UNIVERSITY OF CALIFORNIA, LOS ANGELES

Graduate Division, School of Engineering and Applied Science, Interdepartmental Graduate Program in Biomedical Engineering, Los Angeles, CA 90095

AWARDS MS, PhD.

Faculty: 43 full-time, 56 part-time/ adjunct.

Students: 96 full-time (40 women); includes 35 minority (1 African American, 32 Asian Americans or Pacific Islanders, 2 Hispanic Americans), 36 international. 169 applicants, 66% accepted, 41 enrolled. In 2001, 2 master's, 2 doctorates awarded.

Degree requirements: For master's, comprehensive exam or thesis; for doctorate, thesis/dissertation, qualifying exams.

Entrance requirements: For master's, GRE General Test, minimum GPA of 3.0; for doctorate, GRE General Test, minimum GPA of 3.25. *Application deadline:* For fall admission, 1/15. *Application fee:* $60. Electronic applications accepted.

Expenses: Tuition, nonresident: full-time $10,244. Required fees: $3,609. Full-time tuition and fees vary according to program.

Financial support: In 2001–02, 17 fellowships, 32 research assistantships, 6 teaching assistantships were awarded.
Dr. Carlo D. Montemagno, Chair, 310-794-7270.

Application contact: Cheri Smith, Student Affairs Officer, 310-794-5945, *Fax:* 310-794-5956, *E-mail:* cheri@ ea.ucla.edu. *Web site:* http:// www.biomedengr.ucla.edu/

■ UNIVERSITY OF CALIFORNIA, SAN DIEGO

Graduate Studies and Research, Department of Bioengineering, La Jolla, CA 92093

AWARDS M Eng, MS, PhD.

Students: 113 (39 women). 355 applicants, 40% accepted, 47 enrolled. In 2001, 18 master's, 6 doctorates awarded.

Entrance requirements: For master's and doctorate, GRE General Test, TOEFL, minimum GPA of 3.0. *Application deadline:* For fall admission, 1/16. *Application fee:* $40. Electronic applications accepted.

Expenses: Tuition, nonresident: full-time $10,434. Required fees: $4,883.
David Gough, Chair.

Application contact: Graduate Coordinator, 858-534-6884.

Find an in-depth description at www.petersons.com/gradchannel.

■ UNIVERSITY OF CALIFORNIA, SAN FRANCISCO

Graduate Division, Program in Bioengineering, San Francisco, CA 94143

AWARDS PhD.

Degree requirements: For doctorate, thesis/dissertation, qualifying exam.
Entrance requirements: For doctorate, GRE General Test, minimum GPA of 3.0.
Faculty research: Imaging, biomechanics, modeling, neuroscience, biomedical computing, vision. *Web site:* http:// bioeng.berkeley.edu/

■ UNIVERSITY OF CONNECTICUT

Graduate School, School of Engineering, Department of Mechanical Engineering, Field of Biomedical Engineering, Storrs, CT 06269

AWARDS MS, PhD. Terminal master's awarded for partial completion of doctoral program.

Degree requirements: For master's, thesis or alternative; for doctorate, thesis/ dissertation.
Entrance requirements: For master's and doctorate, GRE General Test, TOEFL.

■ UNIVERSITY OF FLORIDA

Graduate School, College of Engineering, Biomedical Engineering Program, Gainesville, FL 32611

AWARDS ME, MS, PhD, Certificate, Engr.

Degree requirements: For master's, thesis optional; for doctorate, thesis/ dissertation.
Entrance requirements: For master's, GRE General Test, TOEFL, minimum GPA of 3.1; for doctorate, GRE General Test, TOEFL, minimum GPA of 3.3. Electronic applications accepted.
Expenses: Tuition, state resident: part-time $164 per hour. Tuition, nonresident: part-time $571 per hour. Tuition and fees vary according to course level and program. *Web site:* http://www.bme.ufl.edu/

■ UNIVERSITY OF FLORIDA

Graduate School, College of Engineering, Department of Nuclear and Radiological Engineering, Gainesville, FL 32611

AWARDS Biomedical engineering (ME, MS, PhD, Certificate, Engr); engineering physics (ME, MS, PhD, Engr); health physics (MS, PhD); medical physics (MS, PhD); nuclear engineering sciences (ME, PhD, Engr); nuclear sciences engineering (MS).

Degree requirements: For master's and doctorate, one foreign language, thesis/ dissertation; for other advanced degree, thesis optional.

University of Florida (continued)
Entrance requirements: For master's and doctorate, GRE General Test, TOEFL, minimum GPA of 3.0; for other advanced degree, GRE General Test. Electronic applications accepted.
Expenses: Tuition, state resident: part-time $164 per hour. Tuition, nonresident: part-time $571 per hour. Tuition and fees vary according to course level and program.
Faculty research: Robotics, Florida radon mitigation, nuclear space power, radioactive waste management, internal dosimetry. *Web site:* http://www.nucegn.ufl.edu/

■ UNIVERSITY OF HOUSTON

Cullen College of Engineering, Department of Mechanical Engineering, Houston, TX 77204

AWARDS Aerospace engineering (MS, PhD); biomedical engineering (MS); computer and systems engineering (MS, PhD); environmental engineering (MS, PhD); materials engineering (MS, PhD); mechanical engineering (MME, MSME); petroleum engineering (MS). Part-time and evening/weekend programs available.

Faculty: 16 full-time (0 women), 1 part-time/adjunct (0 women).
Students: 34 full-time (4 women), 26 part-time (2 women); includes 7 minority (3 Asian Americans or Pacific Islanders, 4 Hispanic Americans), 32 international. Average age 28. 114 applicants, 64% accepted. In 2001, 20 master's, 3 doctorates awarded. Terminal master's awarded for partial completion of doctoral program.
Degree requirements: For master's, thesis (for some programs); for doctorate, thesis/dissertation, departmental qualifying exam.
Entrance requirements: For master's and doctorate, GRE General Test, TOEFL. *Application deadline:* For fall admission, 7/3 (priority date); for spring admission, 12/4. Applications are processed on a rolling basis. *Application fee:* $25 ($75 for international students).
Expenses: Tuition, state resident: full-time $1,512. Tuition, nonresident: full-time $5,310. Required fees: $1,308. Tuition and fees vary according to program.
Financial support: In 2001–02, 20 research assistantships (averaging $14,400 per year), 13 teaching assistantships (averaging $14,400 per year) were awarded. Fellowships, career-related internships or fieldwork and Federal Work-Study also available. Financial award application deadline: 2/15.
Faculty research: Experimental and computational turbulence, composites, rheology, phase change/heat transfer, characterization of superconducting materials. *Total annual research expenditures:* $396,172.
Dr. Lewis T. Wheeler, Interim Chair, 713-743-4500, *Fax:* 713-743-4503.

Application contact: Susan Sanderson-Clobe, Graduate Admissions Analyst, 713-743-4505, *Fax:* 713-743-4503, *E-mail:* megrad@uh.edu. *Web site:* http://www.mc.uh.edu

Find an in-depth description at www.petersons.com/gradchannel.

■ UNIVERSITY OF ILLINOIS AT CHICAGO

Graduate College, College of Engineering, Bioengineering Department, Chicago, IL 60607-7128

AWARDS MS, PhD, MD/PhD.

Students: 85 full-time (25 women), 32 part-time (13 women); includes 26 minority (5 African Americans, 18 Asian Americans or Pacific Islanders, 3 Hispanic Americans), 53 international. Average age 27. 170 applicants, 45% accepted, 34 enrolled. In 2001, 13 master's, 5 doctorates awarded. Terminal master's awarded for partial completion of doctoral program.
Degree requirements: For master's and doctorate, thesis/dissertation.
Entrance requirements: For master's and doctorate, GRE Subject Test, TOEFL, minimum GPA of 4.0 on a 5.0 scale. *Application deadline:* For fall admission, 6/1; for spring admission, 11/1. Applications are processed on a rolling basis. *Application fee:* $40 ($50 for international students). Electronic applications accepted.
Expenses: Tuition, state resident: full-time $3,060. Tuition, nonresident: full-time $6,688.
Financial support: In 2001–02, 65 students received support; fellowships with full tuition reimbursements available, research assistantships with full tuition reimbursements available, teaching assistantships with full tuition reimbursements available, career-related internships or fieldwork, Federal Work-Study, and tuition waivers (full) available. Financial award application deadline: 3/1; financial award applicants required to submit FAFSA.
Faculty research: Imaging systems, bioinstrumentation, electrophysiology, biological control, laser scattering.
Dr. William O'Neill, Head, 312-413-2294.

Find an in-depth description at www.petersons.com/gradchannel.

■ THE UNIVERSITY OF IOWA

Graduate College, College of Engineering, Department of Biomedical Engineering, Iowa City, IA 52242-1316

AWARDS MS, PhD. Part-time programs available.

Faculty: 11 full-time (1 woman), 2 part-time/adjunct (0 women).
Students: 21 full-time (8 women), 14 part-time (3 women); includes 3 minority (2 African Americans, 1 Hispanic American),

19 international. Average age 27. 54 applicants, 59% accepted, 10 enrolled. In 2001, 9 master's, 5 doctorates awarded.
Degree requirements: For master's, written and oral exam, thesis optional; for doctorate, thesis/dissertation, written and oral exam, comprehensive exam.
Entrance requirements: For master's, GRE, TOEFL, minimum undergraduate GPA of 3.0; for doctorate, GRE, TOEFL. *Application deadline:* For fall admission, 4/15 (priority date); for winter admission, 10/1 (priority date); for spring admission, 3/1 (priority date). Applications are processed on a rolling basis. *Application fee:* $30 ($50 for international students). Electronic applications accepted.
Expenses: Tuition, state resident: full-time $3,702; part-time $206 per semester hour. Tuition, nonresident: full-time $11,924; part-time $206 per semester hour. Required fees: $101 per semester. Tuition and fees vary according to course load and program.
Financial support: In 2001–02, 1 fellowship with tuition reimbursement, 22 research assistantships with partial tuition reimbursements (averaging $14,700 per year), 7 teaching assistantships with tuition reimbursements (averaging $14,700 per year) were awarded. Scholarships/grants, health care benefits, and unspecified assistantships also available. Support available to part-time students. Financial award application deadline: 3/15.
Faculty research: Musculoskeletal biomechanics, cardiovascular biomechanics, biomaterials, tissue engineering, biomedical imaging and signal processing. *Total annual research expenditures:* $2 million.
Dr. Krishnan B. Chandran, Departmental Executive Officer, 319-335-5640, *Fax:* 319-335-5631, *E-mail:* krishnan-chandran@uiowa.edu.

Application contact: Lorena Lovetinsky, Secretary, 319-384-0671, *Fax:* 319-335-5631, *E-mail:* bme@engineering.uiowa.edu. *Web site:* http://www.bme.engineering.uiowa.edu

Find an in-depth description at www.petersons.com/gradchannel.

■ UNIVERSITY OF KENTUCKY

Graduate School, Program in Biomedical Engineering, Lexington, KY 40506-0032

AWARDS MSBE, PhD.

Faculty: 19 full-time (1 woman).
Students: 13 full-time (3 women), 3 part-time (1 woman); includes 2 minority (1 African American, 1 Asian American or Pacific Islander), 7 international. 57 applicants, 30% accepted. In 2001, 7 master's, 1 doctorate awarded.
Degree requirements: For master's, thesis optional; for doctorate, thesis/dissertation, comprehensive exam.
Entrance requirements: For master's, GRE General Test, minimum undergraduate GPA of 2.5; for doctorate, GRE

General Test, minimum graduate GPA of 3.0. *Application deadline:* For fall admission, 7/19. Applications are processed on a rolling basis. *Application fee:* $30 ($35 for international students).

Expenses: Tuition, state resident: full-time $4,075; part-time $213 per credit hour. Tuition, nonresident: full-time $11,295; part-time $614 per credit hour.

Financial support: In 2001–02, 4 fellowships, 11 research assistantships, 1 teaching assistantship were awarded.

Faculty research: Signal processing and dynamical systems, cardiopulmonary mechanics and systems, bioelectromagnetics, neuromotor control and electrical stimulation, biomaterials and musculoskeletal biomechanics. *Total annual research expenditures:* $875,194.

Dr. David Puleo, Director of Graduate Studies, 859-257-2405, *Fax:* 859-257-1856, *E-mail:* puleo@pop.uky.edu.

Application contact: Dr. Jeannine Blackwell, Associate Dean, 859-257-4905, *Fax:* 859-323-1928.

■ UNIVERSITY OF MASSACHUSETTS WORCESTER

Graduate School of Biomedical Sciences, Program in Biomedical Engineering and Medical Physics, Worcester, MA 01655-0115

AWARDS PhD.

Degree requirements: For doctorate, thesis/dissertation.

Entrance requirements: For doctorate, GRE General Test. *Application deadline:* For fall admission, 1/1 (priority date). Applications are processed on a rolling basis. *Application fee:* $25 ($50 for international students).

Expenses: Tuition, state resident: full-time $2,640. Tuition, nonresident: full-time $9,856. Required fees: $1,338.

Financial support: In 2001–02, research assistantships with full tuition reimbursements (averaging $19,000 per year); unspecified assistantships also available.

Faculty research: Tissue engineering, imaging.

Dr. Peter Grigg, Director, 508-856-2457.

Find an in-depth description at www.petersons.com/gradchannel.

■ UNIVERSITY OF MEDICINE AND DENTISTRY OF NEW JERSEY

Graduate School of Biomedical Sciences, Graduate Programs in Biomedical Sciences–Piscataway, Program in Biomedical Engineering, Piscataway, NJ 08854-5635

AWARDS MS, PhD.

Degree requirements: For master's and doctorate, thesis/dissertation, qualifying exam.

Entrance requirements: For master's and doctorate, GRE General Test, TOEFL.

Application deadline: For fall admission, 2/1; for spring admission, 10/1. *Application fee:* $40.

Expenses: Tuition, state resident: part-time $292 per credit. Tuition, nonresident: part-time $440 per credit. Full-time tuition and fees vary according to degree level, program and student level.

Financial support: Fellowships, research assistantships, teaching assistantships available. Financial award application deadline: 5/1.

Stanley M. Dunn, Director, 732-445-3706, *Fax:* 732-445-3753.

Find an in-depth description at www.petersons.com/gradchannel.

■ THE UNIVERSITY OF MEMPHIS

Graduate School, Herff College of Engineering, Program in Biomedical Engineering, Memphis, TN 38152

AWARDS MS, PhD.

Faculty: 19 full-time (3 women), 20 part-time/adjunct (4 women).

Students: 48 full-time (16 women), 15 part-time (5 women); includes 7 minority (3 African Americans, 4 Asian Americans or Pacific Islanders), 41 international. Average age 26. 155 applicants, 48% accepted. In 2001, 4 master's, 2 doctorates awarded.

Degree requirements: For master's, thesis or alternative, level A/oral exam; for doctorate, thesis/dissertation, level A and level B exams.

Entrance requirements: For master's, GRE General Test or MAT, minimum undergraduate GPA of 3.0; for doctorate, GRE General Test, minimum undergraduate GPA of 3.25 or master's degree in biomedical engineering. *Application deadline:* For fall admission, 8/1 (priority date); for spring admission, 12/1. Applications are processed on a rolling basis. *Application fee:* $25 ($50 for international students). Electronic applications accepted.

Expenses: Tuition, state resident: full-time $2,026. Tuition, nonresident: full-time $4,528.

Financial support: In 2001–02, fellowships with full tuition reimbursements (averaging $15,000 per year), research assistantships with full tuition reimbursements (averaging $9,500 per year) were awarded. Career-related internships or fieldwork and scholarships/grants also available. Financial award application deadline: 3/15.

Faculty research: Biomechanics, including orthopedic implants, prosthetic devices, and design; cell and tissue engineering with a focus on the cardiovascular system, artificial organs, biomaterials, and hemodynamics; electrophysiology, including measurement methods, modeling and computation, signal analysis, and biosensors and microfabrication; imaging including novel medical image-acquisition devices, computational image processing,

and quantitative analysis techniques. *Total annual research expenditures:* $859,000.

Dr. Eugene C. Eckstein, Chairman, 901-678-3733, *Fax:* 901-678-5281, *E-mail:* eckstein@memphis.edu.

Application contact: Dr. Steven M. Slack, Coordinator of Graduate Studies, 901-678-3733, *Fax:* 901-678-5281, *E-mail:* sslack@memphis.edu. *Web site:* http://memphis.mecca.org/bme

Find an in-depth description at www.petersons.com/gradchannel.

■ UNIVERSITY OF MIAMI

Graduate School, College of Engineering, Department of Biomedical Engineering, Coral Gables, FL 33124

AWARDS MSBE, PhD. Part-time programs available.

Faculty: 6 full-time (1 woman), 30 part-time/adjunct (1 woman).

Students: 32 full-time (3 women), 9 part-time (2 women); includes 26 minority (2 African Americans, 11 Asian Americans or Pacific Islanders, 12 Hispanic Americans, 1 Native American). Average age 26. 33 applicants, 79% accepted. In 2001, 12 master's, 5 doctorates awarded.

Degree requirements: For master's, oral exam or thesis; for doctorate, thesis/dissertation, oral and qualifying exams.

Entrance requirements: For master's and doctorate, GRE General Test, TOEFL, minimum GPA of 3.0. *Application deadline:* For fall admission, 5/1 (priority date); for spring admission, 10/1 (priority date). Applications are processed on a rolling basis. *Application fee:* $50.

Expenses: Tuition: Part-time $960 per credit hour. Required fees: $85 per semester. Tuition and fees vary according to program.

Financial support: In 2001–02, 40 students received support, including 2 fellowships with tuition reimbursements available (averaging $46,780 per year), 23 research assistantships with tuition reimbursements available (averaging $13,000 per year), 3 teaching assistantships with tuition reimbursements available (averaging $12,000 per year); career-related internships or fieldwork also available. Support available to part-time students.

Faculty research: Biomedical signal processing and instrumentation, cardiovascular engineering, optics and lasers, rehabilitation engineering, tissue mechanics. *Total annual research expenditures:* $386,622.

Dr. Ozcan Ozdamar, Chairman, 305-284-2136, *Fax:* 305-284-6494, *E-mail:* oozdamar@miami.edu.

Application contact: Yesy Capi, Staff Associate, 305-284-2445, *Fax:* 305-284-6494, *E-mail:* ycapi@miami.edu. *Web site:* http://www.eng.miami.edu/

■ UNIVERSITY OF MICHIGAN

Horace H. Rackham School of Graduate Studies, College of Engineering, Department of Biomedical Engineering and Center for Biomedical Engineering Research, Ann Arbor, MI 48109

AWARDS MS, MSE, PhD.

Faculty: 43 full-time (7 women), 63 part-time/adjunct (8 women).
Students: 167 full-time (60 women); includes 45 minority (12 African Americans, 27 Asian Americans or Pacific Islanders, 5 Hispanic Americans, 1 Native American), 49 international. Average age 26. 238 applicants, 60% accepted, 44 enrolled. In 2001, 31 master's, 7 doctorates awarded.
Degree requirements: For master's, thesis optional; for doctorate, oral defense of dissertation.
Entrance requirements: For master's, GRE General Test, TOEFL; for doctorate, GRE General Test, TOEFL, master's degree. *Application deadline:* For fall admission, 1/15 (priority date); for winter admission, 10/1 (priority date); for spring admission, 2/1 (priority date). Applications are processed on a rolling basis. *Application fee:* $55. Electronic applications accepted.
Financial support: In 2001–02, 17 fellowships with full tuition reimbursements (averaging $20,000 per year), 81 research assistantships with full tuition reimbursements (averaging $20,202 per year), 7 teaching assistantships with full tuition reimbursements (averaging $19,280 per year) were awarded. Federal Work-Study, scholarships/grants, and traineeships also available. Financial award application deadline: 1/15; financial award applicants required to submit FAFSA.
Faculty research: Biomedical imaging, biomechanics, biotechnology, bio-MEMS, biomaterials. *Total annual research expenditures:* $4.6 million.
Dr. Matthew O'Donnell, Chair, Biomedical Engineering, 734-764-9588, *Fax:* 734-936-1905, *E-mail:* biomede@umich.edu.
Application contact: Maria E. Steele, Student Services Assistant, 734-764-9588, *Fax:* 734-936-1905, *E-mail:* msteele@umich.edu. *Web site:* http://www.bme.umich.edu

Find an in-depth description at www.petersons.com/gradchannel.

■ UNIVERSITY OF MINNESOTA, TWIN CITIES CAMPUS

Graduate School, Institute of Technology and Medical School, Department of Biomedical Engineering, Minneapolis, MN 55455-0213

AWARDS MS, PhD, MD/PhD. Part-time programs available. Terminal master's awarded for partial completion of doctoral program.

Degree requirements: For master's, thesis optional; for doctorate, thesis/dissertation.
Entrance requirements: For master's and doctorate, GRE General Test.
Expenses: Tuition, state resident: full-time $2,932; part-time $489 per credit. Tuition, nonresident: full-time $5,758; part-time $960 per credit. Part-time tuition and fees vary according to course load, program and reciprocity agreements.
Faculty research: Biomedical microelectromechanical systems, tissue engineering, biomechanics and blood/fluid dynamics, biomaterials, soft tissue mechanics, biomedical imaging. *Web site:* http://www.bme.umn.edu

■ UNIVERSITY OF NEVADA, RENO

School of Medicine and Graduate School, Graduate Programs in Medicine, Program in Biomedical Engineering, Reno, NV 89557

AWARDS MS, PhD.

Faculty: 4.
Students: 6 full-time (1 woman), 2 part-time (both women); includes 1 minority (Hispanic American). Average age 32.
Degree requirements: For doctorate, thesis/dissertation.
Entrance requirements: For master's, GRE General Test, minimum GPA of 2.75; for doctorate, GRE General Test, minimum GPA of 3.0. *Application deadline:* For fall admission, 3/1; for spring admission, 11/1. Applications are processed on a rolling basis. *Application fee:* $40.
Expenses: Tuition, state resident: full-time $2,067; part-time $108 per credit. Tuition, nonresident: full-time $9,282; part-time $109 per credit. Required fees: $57 per semester. Tuition and fees vary according to course load.
Financial support: Application deadline: 3/1.
Dr. Nelson G. Publicover, Graduate Program Director, 775-784-4952, *E-mail:* bmeadmin@unr.edu.

■ THE UNIVERSITY OF NORTH CAROLINA AT CHAPEL HILL

School of Medicine and Graduate School, Graduate Programs in Medicine, Department of Biomedical Engineering, Chapel Hill, NC 27599

AWARDS MS, PhD.

Faculty: 19 full-time (3 women), 20 part-time/adjunct (2 women).
Students: 71 full-time (23 women); includes 12 minority (6 African Americans, 6 Asian Americans or Pacific Islanders), 26 international. In 2001, 6 master's, 5 doctorates awarded. Terminal master's awarded for partial completion of doctoral program.
Degree requirements: For master's, thesis, comprehensive exam; for doctorate, one foreign language, thesis/dissertation, qualifying exam.
Entrance requirements: For master's and doctorate, GRE General Test, minimum GPA of 3.0. *Application deadline:* For fall admission, 2/1. *Application fee:* $60. Electronic applications accepted.
Expenses: Tuition, state resident: full-time $2,864. Tuition, nonresident: full-time $12,030.
Financial support: In 2001–02, 10 fellowships, 43 research assistantships were awarded. Teaching assistantships, career-related internships or fieldwork and unspecified assistantships also available.
Faculty research: Medical imaging, medical informatics, biomaterials, microelectronics instrumentation, neuroscience engineering. *Total annual research expenditures:* $1.4 million.
Dr. Benjamin M. W. Tsui, Interim Chair, 919-966-1175, *Fax:* 919-966-2963, *E-mail:* chairman@bme.unc.edu.
Application contact: Dr. Stephen B. Knisley, Director of Graduate Studies, 919-966-1175, *Fax:* 919-966-2963, *E-mail:* knisley@bme.unc.research. *Web site:* http://www.bme.unc.edu/

Find an in-depth description at www.petersons.com/gradchannel.

■ UNIVERSITY OF PENNSYLVANIA

School of Engineering and Applied Science, Department of Bioengineering, Philadelphia, PA 19104

AWARDS MSE, PhD, MD/PhD, VMD/PhD. Terminal master's awarded for partial completion of doctoral program.

Degree requirements: For master's, thesis optional; for doctorate, thesis/dissertation.
Entrance requirements: For master's and doctorate, GRE General Test, TOEFL. Electronic applications accepted.
Faculty research: Biomaterials and biomechanics, biofluid mechanics and transport, bioelectric phenomena, computational neuroscience. *Web site:* http://www.seas.upenn.edu/be/index.html

■ UNIVERSITY OF PITTSBURGH

School of Engineering, Department of Bioengineering, Pittsburgh, PA 15260

AWARDS MSBENG, PhD, MD/PhD. Part-time and evening/weekend programs available.

Faculty: 7 full-time (0 women), 23 part-time/adjunct (1 woman).
Students: 70 full-time (21 women), 7 part-time (4 women); includes 15 minority (2 African Americans, 10 Asian Americans or Pacific Islanders, 3 Hispanic Americans). Average age 23. 110 applicants, 45% accepted, 29 enrolled. In 2001, 5 master's, 7 doctorates awarded. Terminal master's awarded for partial completion of doctoral program.

Degree requirements: For master's, thesis; for doctorate, thesis/dissertation, final oral exams, comprehensive exam. *Median time to degree:* Master's–2 years full-time; doctorate–5 years full-time. **Entrance requirements:** For master's and doctorate, GRE General Test, TOEFL, minimum QPA of 3.0. *Application deadline:* For fall admission, 8/1 (priority date); for spring admission, 12/1. Applications are processed on a rolling basis. *Application fee:* $40.
Financial support: In 2001–02, 30 students received support, including 4 fellowships with full tuition reimbursements available (averaging $18,000 per year), 22 research assistantships with full tuition reimbursements available (averaging $18,000 per year), 4 teaching assistantships with full tuition reimbursements available (averaging $18,000 per year). Scholarships/grants and traineeships also available. Financial award application deadline: 2/15.
Faculty research: Artificial organs, biomechanics, biomaterials, signal processing, biotechnology. *Total annual research expenditures:* $2.7 million.
Harvey S. Borovetz, Director, 412-383-9713, *Fax:* 412-383-8788, *E-mail:* borovetzhs@msx.upmc.edu.
Application contact: Lynette R. Spataro, Academic Administrator, 412-624-6445, *Fax:* 412-383-8788, *E-mail:* spataro@engr.pitt.edu. *Web site:* http://www.engrng.pitt.edu/~wwwbiotc/
Find an in-depth description at www.petersons.com/gradchannel.

■ UNIVERSITY OF ROCHESTER

The College, School of Engineering and Applied Sciences and Graduate Programs in Medicine and Dentistry, Department of Biomedical Engineering, Rochester, NY 14627-0250
AWARDS MS, PhD. Part-time programs available.
Faculty: 4.
Students: 23 full-time (8 women); includes 4 minority (3 Asian Americans or Pacific Islanders, 1 Hispanic American), 9 international. 81 applicants, 21% accepted, 8 enrolled. In 2001, 4 master's, 1 doctorate awarded. Terminal master's awarded for partial completion of doctoral program.
Degree requirements: For master's, comprehensive exam; for doctorate, thesis/dissertation, qualifying exam.
Entrance requirements: For doctorate, GRE General Test, TOEFL. *Application deadline:* For fall admission, 2/1. *Application fee:* $25.
Expenses: Tuition: Part-time $755 per credit hour.
Financial support: Fellowships, research assistantships, teaching assistantships, tuition waivers (full and partial) available. Financial award application deadline: 2/1.
Dr. Richard Waugh, Chair, 585-275-3768.

Application contact: Donna Porcelli, Graduate Program Secretary, 585-275-4042.

■ UNIVERSITY OF SOUTHERN CALIFORNIA

Graduate School, School of Engineering, Department of Biomedical Engineering, Los Angeles, CA 90089
AWARDS Biomedical engineering (MS, PhD); biomedical imaging and telemedicine (MS). Terminal master's awarded for partial completion of doctoral program.
Degree requirements: For master's, thesis (for some programs); for doctorate, thesis/dissertation.
Entrance requirements: For master's and doctorate, GRE General Test, GRE Subject Test.
Expenses: Tuition: Full-time $25,060; part-time $844 per unit. Required fees: $473.
Faculty research: Bio-signal processing, physiological system modeling; neural engineering; neural prosthesis.

■ UNIVERSITY OF SOUTH FLORIDA

College of Graduate Studies, College of Engineering, Program in Biomedical Engineering, Tampa, FL 33620-9951
AWARDS MSBE.
Students: 3 full-time (1 woman), 3 part-time (1 woman); includes 2 minority (1 African American, 1 Asian American or Pacific Islander), 1 international. *Application deadline:* For fall admission, 6/1; for spring admission, 10/15.
Expenses: Tuition, state resident: part-time $166 per credit hour. Tuition, nonresident: part-time $573 per credit hour. Required fees: $17 per term.
William Lee, Head, 813-974-2136, *E-mail:* lee@eng.usf.edu.

■ THE UNIVERSITY OF TENNESSEE

Graduate School, College of Engineering, Department of Mechanical and Aerospace Engineering and Engineering Science, Program in Engineering Science, Knoxville, TN 37996
AWARDS Applied artificial intelligence (MS); biomedical engineering (MS, PhD); composite materials (MS, PhD); computational mechanics (MS, PhD); engineering science (MS, PhD); fluid mechanics (MS, PhD); industrial engineering (PhD); optical engineering (MS, PhD); product development and manufacturing (MS). Solid mechanics (MS, PhD). Part-time programs available.
Students: 25 full-time (5 women), 16 part-time (2 women); includes 6 minority (2

African Americans, 2 Asian Americans or Pacific Islanders, 1 Hispanic American, 1 Native American), 9 international. 20 applicants, 70% accepted. In 2001, 6 master's, 6 doctorates awarded.
Degree requirements: For master's, thesis or alternative; for doctorate, thesis/dissertation.
Entrance requirements: For master's and doctorate, TOEFL, minimum GPA of 2.7. *Application deadline:* For fall admission, 2/1 (priority date). Applications are processed on a rolling basis. *Application fee:* $35. Electronic applications accepted.
Expenses: Tuition, state resident: full-time $4,280; part-time $233 per hour. Tuition, nonresident: full-time $12,066; part-time $666 per hour. Tuition and fees vary according to program.
Financial support: Career-related internships or fieldwork, Federal Work-Study, and institutionally sponsored loans available. Financial award application deadline: 2/1; financial award applicants required to submit FAFSA.
Application contact: Dr. Majid Keyhani, Graduate Representative, 865-974-4795, *E-mail:* keyhani@utk.edu.

■ THE UNIVERSITY OF TENNESSEE HEALTH SCIENCE CENTER

College of Graduate Health Sciences, School of Biomedical Engineering, Memphis, TN 38163-0002
AWARDS MS, PhD. Part-time programs available.
Faculty: 7 full-time (0 women).
Students: 37 full-time (14 women); includes 19 minority (3 African Americans, 16 Asian Americans or Pacific Islanders). Average age 25. 112 applicants, 12% accepted. In 2001, 10 degrees awarded. Terminal master's awarded for partial completion of doctoral program.
Degree requirements: For master's, thesis, comprehensive exam; for doctorate, thesis/dissertation, oral and written preliminary and comprehensive exams.
Entrance requirements: For master's and doctorate, GRE General Test, TOEFL, minimum B average; bachelor's degree in engineering, physics, chemistry, computer or mathematical science, biology, or a closely related field. *Application deadline:* For fall admission, 5/15. *Application fee:* $0. Electronic applications accepted.
Financial support: Research assistantships, teaching assistantships, career-related internships or fieldwork, Federal Work-Study, institutionally sponsored loans, and tuition waivers (full) available. Support available to part-time students. Financial award application deadline: 2/25.
Dr. Frank A. DiBianca, Chairman, 901-448-7099, *Fax:* 901-448-7387, *E-mail:* fdibianca@utmem.edu.

The University of Tennessee Health Science Center (continued)

Application contact: Ida Mosby, Director of Admissions, 901-448-5560, *Fax:* 901-448-7772, *E-mail:* lmosby@utmem.edu.

Find an in-depth description at www.petersons.com/gradchannel.

■ THE UNIVERSITY OF TEXAS AT ARLINGTON

Graduate School, College of Engineering, Biomedical Engineering Department, Arlington, TX 76019

AWARDS MS, PhD. Part-time programs available.

Faculty: 5 full-time (1 woman), 1 part-time/adjunct (0 women).
Students: 22 full-time (8 women), 15 part-time (5 women); includes 3 minority (1 African American, 2 Asian Americans or Pacific Islanders), 28 international. 36 applicants, 94% accepted, 15 enrolled. In 2001, 4 degrees awarded.
Degree requirements: For master's, thesis optional; for doctorate, thesis/dissertation, qualifying exam.
Entrance requirements: For master's, GRE General Test, TOEFL, minimum GPA of 3.0 based on last 60 hours of course work; for doctorate, GRE General Test, TOEFL, minimum GPA of 3.4 based on last 60 hours of course work. *Application deadline:* For fall admission, 6/16. Applications are processed on a rolling basis. *Application fee:* $25 ($50 for international students).
Expenses: Tuition, area resident: Full-time $2,268. Tuition, nonresident: full-time $6,264. Required fees: $839. Tuition and fees vary according to course load.
Financial support: In 2001–02, 3 fellowships (averaging $1,000 per year), 52 research assistantships (averaging $10,000 per year) were awarded. Teaching assistantships, career-related internships or fieldwork, Federal Work-Study, institutionally sponsored loans, scholarships/grants, and tuition waivers (partial) also available. Financial award application deadline: 6/1; financial award applicants required to submit FAFSA.
Faculty research: Instrumentation, mechanics, materials.
Dr. Khosrow Behbehani, Chair, 817-272-2249, *Fax:* 817-272-2251, *E-mail:* kb@uta.edu.
Application contact: Dr. Charles Chuong, Graduate Adviser, 817-272-2052, *Fax:* 817-272-2251, *E-mail:* chuong@uta.edu.

Find an in-depth description at www.petersons.com/gradchannel.

■ THE UNIVERSITY OF TEXAS AT AUSTIN

Graduate School, College of Engineering, Program in Biomedical Engineering, Austin, TX 78712-1111

AWARDS MSE, PhD. MD/PhD. Part-time programs available.

Degree requirements: For doctorate, thesis/dissertation.
Entrance requirements: For master's and doctorate, GRE General Test. Electronic applications accepted.
Expenses: Tuition, state resident: full-time $3,159. Tuition, nonresident: full-time $6,957. Tuition and fees vary according to program.
Faculty research: Biomechanics, bioengineering, tissue engineering, tissue optics, biothermal studies. *Web site:* http://www.ece.utexas.edu/bme

Find an in-depth description at www.petersons.com/gradchannel.

■ THE UNIVERSITY OF TEXAS SOUTHWESTERN MEDICAL CENTER AT DALLAS

Southwestern Graduate School of Biomedical Sciences, Biomedical Engineering Program, Dallas, TX 75390

AWARDS MS, PhD.

Faculty: 29 full-time (2 women), 6 part-time/adjunct (all women).
Students: 14 full-time (7 women); includes 2 minority (both Asian Americans or Pacific Islanders), 7 international. Average age 25. 83 applicants, 27% accepted. In 2001, 9 degrees awarded.
Degree requirements: For master's, comprehensive exam or thesis; for doctorate, thesis/dissertation, comprehensive exam.
Entrance requirements: For master's, GRE General Test, minimum GPA of 3.0; for doctorate, GRE General Test, TOEFL, minimum GPA of 3.4. *Application deadline:* For fall admission, 5/15 (priority date); for spring admission, 10/15. *Application fee:* $0.
Expenses: Tuition, state resident: full-time $990. Tuition, nonresident: full-time $6,062. Required fees: $843.
Financial support: In 2001–02, 1 fellowship with partial tuition reimbursement (averaging $900 per year), 24 research assistantships (averaging $774 per year) were awarded. Career-related internships or fieldwork, institutionally sponsored loans, scholarships/grants, and tuition waivers (partial) also available. Financial award application deadline: 3/15; financial award applicants required to submit FAFSA.
Faculty research: Noninvasive image analysis, biomaterials development, rehabilitation engineering, biomechanics, bioinstrumentation.

Dr. Peter P. Antich, Chair, 214-648-2503, *Fax:* 214-648-2991, *E-mail:* peter.antich@utsouthwestern.edu.
Application contact: Kaywana Emerson, Program Assistant, 214-648-2503, *Fax:* 214-648-2991, *E-mail:* kaywana.emerson@utsouthwestern.edu. *Web site:* http://www.swmed.edu/home_pages/bme/index.bme.html

Find an in-depth description at www.petersons.com/gradchannel.

■ UNIVERSITY OF UTAH

Graduate School, College of Engineering, Department of Bioengineering, Salt Lake City, UT 84112-1107

AWARDS ME, MS, PhD.

Faculty: 9 full-time (1 woman), 6 part-time/adjunct (2 women).
Students: 68 full-time (18 women), 16 part-time (6 women); includes 24 minority (23 Asian Americans or Pacific Islanders, 1 Hispanic American), 7 international. Average age 28. In 2001, 9 master's, 5 doctorates awarded. Terminal master's awarded for partial completion of doctoral program.
Degree requirements: For master's, thesis (MS); written project, oral presentation (ME); for doctorate, thesis/dissertation.
Entrance requirements: For master's and doctorate, GRE, TOEFL, minimum GPA of 3.0. *Application deadline:* For fall admission, 5/1. *Application fee:* $40 ($60 for international students).
Expenses: Tuition, state resident: part-time $320 per semester hour. Tuition, nonresident: part-time $1,135 per semester hour. Required fees: $143 per semester hour. Tuition and fees vary according to course load, degree level and program.
Financial support: Fellowships, research assistantships, traineeships available. Financial award application deadline: 5/1; financial award applicants required to submit FAFSA.
Faculty research: Bioinstrumentation, biomaterials, ultrasonic bioinstrumentation, medical imaging, neuroprosthesis.
Dr. Vladimir Hlady, Chair, 801-581-5042, *Fax:* 801-585-5361, *E-mail:* vladimir.hlady@m.cc.utah.edu.
Application contact: Richard Rabbitt, Graduate Advisor, 801-581-8528, *Fax:* 801-585-5361, *E-mail:* r.rabbitt@m.cc.utah.edu. *Web site:* http://www.coe.utah.edu/

Find an in-depth description at www.petersons.com/gradchannel.

■ UNIVERSITY OF VERMONT

Graduate College, College of Engineering and Mathematics, Department of Computer Science and Electrical Engineering, Program in Biomedical Engineering, Burlington, VT 05405

AWARDS MS.

Degree requirements: For master's, thesis.
Entrance requirements: For master's, TOEFL.
Expenses: Tuition, state resident: part-time $335 per credit. Tuition, nonresident: part-time $838 per credit.

■ UNIVERSITY OF VIRGINIA

School of Engineering and Applied Science, Department of Biomedical Engineering, Charlottesville, VA 22903

AWARDS ME, MS, PhD.

Faculty: 10 full-time (0 women).
Students: 51 full-time (19 women), 1 (woman) part-time; includes 11 minority (1 African American, 10 Asian Americans or Pacific Islanders), 13 international. Average age 25. 140 applicants, 21% accepted, 13 enrolled. In 2001, 8 master's, 5 doctorates awarded.
Degree requirements: For master's, project or thesis; for doctorate, thesis/dissertation, comprehensive exam.
Entrance requirements: For master's and doctorate, GRE General Test. *Application deadline:* For fall admission, 8/1; for spring admission, 12/1. *Application fee:* $40. Electronic applications accepted.
Expenses: Tuition, state resident: full-time $3,988. Tuition, nonresident: full-time $17,078. Required fees: $1,190.
Financial support: Fellowships, research assistantships, teaching assistantships available. Financial award application deadline: 2/1; financial award applicants required to submit FAFSA.
Faculty research: Cardiopulmonary and neural engineering, cellular engineering, image processing, orthopedics and rehabilitation engineering.
Dr. K. F. Ley, Chairman, 434-924-1722, *E-mail:* kf13f@virginia.edu. *Web site:* http://www.med.virginia.edu/bme/
Find an in-depth description at www.petersons.com/gradchannel.

■ UNIVERSITY OF WASHINGTON

Graduate School, College of Engineering and School of Medicine, Department of Bioengineering, Seattle, WA 98195

AWARDS MME, MS, PhD.

Faculty: 30 full-time (3 women), 28 part-time/adjunct (3 women).
Students: 121 full-time (47 women), 43 part-time (11 women); includes 31 minority (3 African Americans, 20 Asian Americans or Pacific Islanders, 7 Hispanic Americans, 1 Native American), 30 international. 320 applicants, 18% accepted, 25 enrolled. In 2001, 6 master's, 15 doctorates awarded. Terminal master's awarded for partial completion of doctoral program.
Degree requirements: For master's, thesis; for doctorate, thesis/dissertation, qualifying exam, general exam. *Median time to degree:* Master's–2.7 years full-time, 4.5 years part-time; doctorate–5.5 years full-time.
Entrance requirements: For master's and doctorate, GRE General Test, TOEFL, minimum GPA of 3.0. *Application deadline:* For fall admission, 1/15. *Application fee:* $45. Electronic applications accepted.
Expenses: Tuition, state resident: full-time $5,539. Tuition, nonresident: full-time $14,376. Required fees: $390. Tuition and fees vary according to course load and program.
Financial support: In 2001–02, 20 fellowships with tuition reimbursements (averaging $19,883 per year), 92 research assistantships with tuition reimbursements (averaging $20,016 per year), 1 teaching assistantship with tuition reimbursement (averaging $20,016 per year) were awarded. Federal Work-Study, institutionally sponsored loans, traineeships, and tuition waivers (full) also available. Support available to part-time students. Financial award application deadline: 1/15.
Faculty research: Distributed diagnosis and home healthcare, engineered biomaterials, molecular bioengineering and nanotechnology, medical imaging and image-guided therapy, computational bioegineering.
Dr. Yongmin Kim, Chair, 206-685-2000, *Fax:* 206-685-3300.
Application contact: Jennifer Gouine, Graduate Academic Counselor, 206-685-2000, *Fax:* 206-685-3300, *E-mail:* jgouine@u.washington.edu. *Web site:* http://depts.washington.edu.bioe

■ UNIVERSITY OF WISCONSIN–MADISON

Graduate School, College of Engineering, Department of Biomedical Engineering, Madison, WI 53706-1380

AWARDS MS, PhD. Part-time programs available.

Faculty: 3 full-time (0 women), 6 part-time/adjunct (2 women).
Students: 58 full-time (22 women), 3 part-time (all women); includes 14 minority (3 African Americans, 11 Native Americans). 174 applicants, 43% accepted, 17 enrolled. In 2001, 8 master's, 3 doctorates awarded. Terminal master's awarded for partial completion of doctoral program.
Degree requirements: For master's, thesis optional; for doctorate, thesis/dissertation, comprehensive exam, registration. *Median time to degree:* Master's–2 years full-time, 4 years part-time; doctorate–3.5 years full-time.
Entrance requirements: For master's, GRE, TOEFL, bachelors in engineering or a physical science (chemistry or physics; for doctorate, GRE, TOEFL, bachelor and master in biomedical engineering. *Application deadline:* For fall admission, 4/1; for spring admission, 10/1. *Application fee:* $45. Electronic applications accepted.
Expenses: Tuition, state resident: full-time $7,361; part-time $399 per credit. Tuition, nonresident: full-time $20,499; part-time $1,282 per credit. Required fees: $34 per credit. Full-time tuition and fees vary according to course load, program, reciprocity agreements and student level.
Financial support: In 2001–02, 3 fellowships with full tuition reimbursements (averaging $16,440 per year), 15 research assistantships with full tuition reimbursements (averaging $16,350 per year), 7 teaching assistantships with full tuition reimbursements (averaging $11,270 per year) were awarded. Financial award application deadline: 12/1.
Faculty research: Ergonomics; design, fabrication, and testing of novel micro fabrication techniques; magnetic resonance; tissue engineering; biomedical optics. *Total annual research expenditures:* $4.2 million.
Dr. Robert G. Radwin, Professor and Chair, 608-263-4660, *Fax:* 608-265-9239, *E-mail:* radwin@engr.wisc.edu.
Application contact: Cindy Schkirkie, Graduate Admissions Coordinator, 608-263-4660, *Fax:* 608-265-9239, *E-mail:* clschkir@facstaff.wisc.edu.

■ VANDERBILT UNIVERSITY

School of Engineering and Graduate School, Department of Biomedical Engineering, Nashville, TN 37240-1001

AWARDS M Eng, MS, PhD, MD/PhD.

Faculty: 12 full-time (2 women).
Students: 48 full-time (12 women); includes 7 minority (5 African Americans, 2 Asian Americans or Pacific Islanders), 2 international. Average age 25. 78 applicants, 40% accepted, 10 enrolled. In 2001, 9 master's, 4 doctorates awarded.
Degree requirements: For master's and doctorate, thesis/dissertation.
Entrance requirements: For master's, GRE General Test (except M Eng); for doctorate, GRE General Test. *Application deadline:* For fall admission, 1/15; for spring admission, 11/1. *Application fee:* $40. Electronic applications accepted.
Expenses: Tuition: Full-time $28,350.
Financial support: In 2001–02, 7 fellowships with full tuition reimbursements, 23 research assistantships with full tuition reimbursements, 11 teaching assistantships with full tuition reimbursements were awarded. Institutionally sponsored loans, scholarships/grants, traineeships, and

Vanderbilt University (continued)
tuition waivers (partial) also available. Support available to part-time students. Financial award application deadline: 1/15.
Faculty research: Quantitative physiology, bio-optics, medical informatics and computing, medical instrumentation, physiological transport phenomena, bioengineering education. *Total annual research expenditures:* $3.7 million.
Dr. Thomas R. Harris, Chair, 615-322-0842, *Fax:* 615-343-7919, *E-mail:* thomas.r.harris@vanderbilt.edu.
Application contact: Dr. Robert J. Roselli, Director of Graduate Studies, 615-322-2602, *Fax:* 615-343-7919, *E-mail:* robert.j.roselli@vanderbilt.edu. *Web site:* http://www.bme.vanderbilt.edu/

Find an in-depth description at www.petersons.com/gradchannel.

■ VIRGINIA COMMONWEALTH UNIVERSITY

School of Graduate Studies, School of Engineering, Department of Biomedical Engineering, Richmond, VA 23284-9005

AWARDS MS, PhD, MD/PhD.

Students: 23 full-time, 17 part-time; includes 23 minority (1 African American, 20 Asian Americans or Pacific Islanders, 2 Hispanic Americans). 125 applicants, 78% accepted. In 2001, 7 master's, 2 doctorates awarded.
Degree requirements: For master's, thesis; for doctorate, thesis/dissertation, comprehensive oral and written exams.
Entrance requirements: For master's and doctorate, GRE General Test. *Application deadline:* For fall admission, 2/15; for spring admission, 11/15. *Application fee:* $30.
Expenses: Tuition, state resident: full-time $4,276; part-time $238 per credit. Tuition, nonresident: full-time $12,672; part-time $704 per credit. Required fees: $1,167; $43 per credit.
Faculty research: Clinical instrumentation, mathematical modeling, neurosciences, radiation physics and rehabilitation.
Dr. Gerald E. Miller, Associate Dean for Graduate Education, 804-828-7263, *Fax:* 804-828-4454, *E-mail:* gemiller@vcu.edu.
Application contact: Dr. Jennifer S. Wayne, Graduate Program Director, 804-828-2595, *Fax:* 804-828-4454, *E-mail:* jswayne@vcu.edu. *Web site:* http://www.vcu.edu/egrweb/bme/bmehome.html

Find an in-depth description at www.petersons.com/gradchannel.

■ WAKE FOREST UNIVERSITY

School of Medicine and Graduate School, Graduate Programs in Medicine, Program in Medical Engineering, Winston-Salem, NC 27109

AWARDS PhD.

Faculty: 10 full-time (0 women).
Students: 6 full-time (0 women). Average age 26. 11 applicants, 0% accepted. In 2001, 1 degree awarded.
Degree requirements: For doctorate, thesis/dissertation.
Entrance requirements: For doctorate, GRE General Test, GRE Subject Test. *Application deadline:* For fall admission, 2/1 (priority date). Applications are processed on a rolling basis. *Application fee:* $25. Electronic applications accepted.
Financial support: In 2001–02, 6 students received support, including 4 fellowships, 2 research assistantships. Scholarships/grants and tuition waivers (full) also available. Financial award application deadline: 1/2. *Total annual research expenditures:* $216,219.
Dr. Pete Santago, Director, 336-716-2703.

■ WASHINGTON UNIVERSITY IN ST. LOUIS

Henry Edwin Sever Graduate School of Engineering and Applied Science, Department of Biomedical Engineering, St. Louis, MO 63130-4899

AWARDS MS, D Sc, MD/D Sc.

Faculty: 10 full-time (1 woman), 78 part-time/adjunct (2 women).
Students: 38 full-time (16 women), 1 part-time; includes 1 minority (African American), 11 international. Average age 23. 105 applicants, 26% accepted. In 2001, 4 master's, 2 doctorates awarded. Terminal master's awarded for partial completion of doctoral program.
Degree requirements: For master's, thesis optional; for doctorate, thesis/dissertation. *Median time to degree:* Master's–2 years full-time; doctorate–5 years full-time.
Entrance requirements: For master's, GRE, TOEFL, minimum GPA of 3.0; for doctorate, GRE General Test, TOEFL, minimum GPA of 3.5. *Application deadline:* For fall admission, 2/1 (priority date). *Application fee:* $20. Electronic applications accepted.
Expenses: Tuition: Full-time $26,900.
Financial support: In 2001–02, 27 fellowships with full tuition reimbursements (averaging $18,000 per year), research assistantships with full tuition reimbursements (averaging $18,000 per year), teaching assistantships with full tuition reimbursements (averaging $18,000 per year) were awarded. Federal Work-Study, institutionally sponsored loans, traineeships, and tuition waivers (partial) also available. Financial award application

deadline: 2/1; financial award applicants required to submit FAFSA.
Faculty research: Biomedical and biological imaging, cardiovascular engineering, cell and tissue engineering, computational molecular biology, computational neuroscience. *Total annual research expenditures:* $700,000.
Dr. Frank C. P. Yin, Chairman, 314-935-6164, *Fax:* 314-935-7448, *E-mail:* yin@biomed.wustl.edu.
Application contact: Shirley Eisenhauer, Department Secretary, 314-935-6164, *Fax:* 314-935-7448, *E-mail:* shirley@biomed.wustl.edu. *Web site:* http://www.seas.wustl.edu/academicprograms/biomed/

Find an in-depth description at www.petersons.com/gradchannel.

■ WAYNE STATE UNIVERSITY

Graduate School, College of Engineering, Department of Biomedical Engineering, Detroit, MI 48202

AWARDS MS, PhD.

Students: 75. In 2001, 13 degrees awarded.
Degree requirements: For master's, thesis optional; for doctorate, thesis/dissertation.
Application deadline: For fall admission, 7/1 (priority date). *Application fee:* $20 ($30 for international students). Electronic applications accepted.
Expenses: Tuition, state resident: full-time $3,764. Tuition and fees vary according to degree level and program.
Financial support: In 2001–02, 1 fellowship was awarded
Faculty research: Impact injury, neurophysiology of pain, smart sensors, biomaterials, orthopedic biomechanics.
Albert King, Director, 313-577-1344, *Fax:* 313-577-8333, *E-mail:* king@rrb.eng.wayne.edu.
Application contact: Michele Grimm, Graduate Director, 313-577-8395, *E-mail:* mgrimm@wayne.edu.

■ WORCESTER POLYTECHNIC INSTITUTE

Graduate Studies, Department of Biomedical Engineering, Worcester, MA 01609-2280

AWARDS Biomedical engineering (M Eng, MS, PhD, Certificate); clinical engineering (M Eng). Part-time and evening/weekend programs available.

Faculty: 6 full-time (0 women), 4 part-time/adjunct (0 women).
Students: 25 full-time (10 women); includes 2 minority (both Asian Americans or Pacific Islanders), 7 international. 78 applicants, 42% accepted, 9 enrolled. In 2001, 15 master's, 1 doctorate awarded. Terminal master's awarded for partial completion of doctoral program.

Degree requirements: For master's, thesis optional; for doctorate, thesis/dissertation.

Entrance requirements: For master's and doctorate, GRE General Test, TOEFL. *Application deadline:* For fall admission, 2/1 (priority date); for spring admission, 10/15 (priority date). Applications are processed on a rolling basis. *Application fee:* $60. Electronic applications accepted.

Expenses: Tuition: Part-time $796 per credit. Required fees: $20; $752 per credit. One-time fee: $30 full-time.

Financial support: In 2001–02, 14 students received support, including 9 fellowships with full and partial tuition reimbursements available (averaging $11,898 per year), 2 research assistantships with partial tuition reimbursements available (averaging $17,256 per year), 2 teaching assistantships with full and partial tuition reimbursements available (averaging $12,942 per year); career-related internships or fieldwork, institutionally sponsored loans, and scholarships/grants also available. Financial award application deadline: 2/15; financial award applicants required to submit FAFSA.

Faculty research: Biomedical sensors and instrumentation, biomechanics, nuclear magnetic resonance image and spectroscopy, medical imaging and in vitro optical imaging, cardiac electrophysiology. *Total annual research expenditures:* $306,352. Dr. Christopher H. Sotak, Head, 508-831-5447, *Fax:* 508-831-5541, *E-mail:* rapeura@wpi.edu.

Application contact: Dr. Ross Shonat, Graduate Coordinator, 508-831-6086, *Fax:* 508-831-5541, *E-mail:* shonat@wpi.edu. *Web site:* http://www.wpi.edu/Academics/Depts/BioMedEng/

Find an in-depth description at www.petersons.com/gradchannel.

BIOTECHNOLOGY

■ BROWN UNIVERSITY

Graduate School, Division of Biology and Medicine, Program in Artificial Organs/Biomaterials/Cellular Technology, Providence, RI 02912

AWARDS MA, Sc M, PhD.

Faculty: 4 full-time (2 women), 5 part-time/adjunct (2 women).

Students: 10 full-time (5 women); includes 3 minority (1 African American, 2 Asian Americans or Pacific Islanders), 2 international. Average age 24. 30 applicants, 10% accepted. In 2001, 3 degrees awarded. Terminal master's awarded for partial completion of doctoral program.

Degree requirements: For doctorate, thesis/dissertation, preliminary exam.

Entrance requirements: For master's and doctorate, GRE General Test, GRE Subject Test. *Application deadline:* For fall

admission, 1/2 (priority date). Applications are processed on a rolling basis. *Application fee:* $60. Electronic applications accepted.

Financial support: In 2001–02, 3 fellowships, 1 research assistantship, 6 teaching assistantships were awarded. Financial award application deadline: 1/2.

Dr. Edith Mathiowitz, Director, 401-863-1358, *Fax:* 401-863-1753, *E-mail:* edith_mathiowitz@brown.edu.

Application contact: Susan Hirsch, Administrative Assistant, 401-863-3262, *Fax:* 401-863-1753, *E-mail:* susan_hirsch@brown.edu.

■ DARTMOUTH COLLEGE

Thayer School of Engineering, Program in Biotechnology and Biochemical Engineering, Hanover, NH 03755

AWARDS MS, PhD.

Degree requirements: For master's, thesis; for doctorate, thesis/dissertation, candidacy oral exam.

Entrance requirements: For master's and doctorate, GRE General Test. *Application deadline:* For fall admission, 1/1 (priority date). *Application fee:* $40 ($50 for international students).

Expenses: Tuition: Full-time $26,425.

Financial support: Fellowships, research assistantships, teaching assistantships, career-related internships or fieldwork, Federal Work-Study, institutionally sponsored loans, and tuition waivers (full and partial) available. Financial award application deadline: 1/15.

Faculty research: Biomass processing, metabolic engineering, bioplastic synthesis, kinetics and reactor design, applied microbiology. *Total annual research expenditures:* $200,000.

Application contact: Candace S. Potter, Graduate Admissions Administrator, 603-646-3844, *Fax:* 603-646-1620, *E-mail:* candace.potter@dartmouth.edu. *Web site:* http://engineering.dartmouth.edu/

■ EAST CAROLINA UNIVERSITY

Graduate School, College of Arts and Sciences, Department of Biology, Greenville, NC 27858-4353

AWARDS Biology (MS); molecular biology/biotechnology (MS). Part-time programs available.

Faculty: 19 full-time (5 women).

Students: 40 full-time (19 women), 40 part-time (18 women); includes 7 minority (4 African Americans, 3 Asian Americans or Pacific Islanders), 2 international. Average age 28. 51 applicants, 63% accepted. In 2001, 23 degrees awarded.

Degree requirements: For master's, one foreign language, thesis, comprehensive exam.

Entrance requirements: For master's, GRE General Test, GRE Subject Test, TOEFL. *Application deadline:* For fall admission, 6/1 (priority date); for spring

admission, 10/15. Applications are processed on a rolling basis. *Application fee:* $45.

Expenses: Tuition, state resident: full-time $2,636. Tuition, nonresident: full-time $11,365.

Financial support: Fellowships with partial tuition reimbursements, research assistantships with partial tuition reimbursements, teaching assistantships with partial tuition reimbursements, career-related internships or fieldwork, Federal Work-Study, scholarships/grants, and unspecified assistantships available. Support available to part-time students. Financial award application deadline: 6/1.

Faculty research: Biochemistry, microbiology, cell biology.

Dr. Gerhard W. Kalmus, Director of Graduate Studies, 252-328-6722, *Fax:* 252-328-4178, *E-mail:* kalmusg@mail.ecu.edu.

Application contact: Dr. Paul D. Tschetter, Senior Associate Dean of the Graduate School, 252-328-6012, *Fax:* 252-328-6071, *E-mail:* gradschool@mail.ecu.edu.

Find an in-depth description at www.petersons.com/gradchannel.

■ FLORIDA INSTITUTE OF TECHNOLOGY

Graduate Programs, College of Science and Liberal Arts, Department of Biological Sciences, Melbourne, FL 32901-6975

AWARDS Biological sciences (PhD); biotechnology (MS); cell and molecular biology (PhD); ecology (MS); marine biology (MS). Part-time programs available.

Faculty: 15 full-time (1 woman), 3 part-time/adjunct (0 women).

Students: 11 full-time (6 women), 45 part-time (24 women); includes 3 minority (1 Asian American or Pacific Islander, 2 Hispanic Americans), 9 international. Average age 30. 137 applicants, 20% accepted. In 2001, 12 degrees awarded.

Degree requirements: For master's, thesis; for doctorate, departmental qualifying exams, oral defense of dissertation.

Entrance requirements: For master's, GRE General Test, minimum GPA of 3.0, resumé; for doctorate, GRE General Test, GRE Subject Test, minimum GPA of 3.2. *Application deadline:* Applications are processed on a rolling basis. *Application fee:* $50. Electronic applications accepted.

Expenses: Tuition: Part-time $650 per credit.

Financial support: In 2001–02, 28 students received support, including 6 research assistantships with full and partial tuition reimbursements available (averaging $11,924 per year), 22 teaching assistantships with full and partial tuition reimbursements available (averaging $7,030 per year); career-related internships or fieldwork and tuition remissions also available. Financial award application

Florida Institute of Technology (continued)
deadline: 3/1; financial award applicants required to submit FAFSA.

Faculty research: Reactions and components in initiation of protein synthesis in eukaryotic cells, fixation of radioactive carbon, changes in DNA molecule and differential expression of genetic information during aging, endangered or threatened avian and mammalian species, hydroacoustics and feeding preference of the West Indian manatee. *Total annual research expenditures:* $1.1 million.

Dr. Gary N. Wells, Head, 321-674-8034, *Fax:* 321-674-7238, *E-mail:* gwells@fit.edu.

Application contact: Carolyn P. Farrior, Director of Graduate Admissions, 321-674-7118, *Fax:* 321-723-9468, *E-mail:* cfarrior@fit.edu. *Web site:* http://www.fit.edu/

■ HOWARD UNIVERSITY

College of Medicine, Department of Biochemistry and Molecular Biology, Washington, DC 20059-0002

AWARDS Biochemistry and molecular biology (PhD); biotechnology (MS). Part-time programs available.

Degree requirements: For master's, externship; for doctorate, thesis/dissertation, comprehensive exam.

Entrance requirements: For master's and doctorate, GRE General Test, minimum GPA of 3.0.

Faculty research: Cellular and molecular biology of olfaction, gene regulation and expression, enzymology, NMR spectroscopy of molecular structure, hormone regulation/metabolism.

Find an in-depth description at www.petersons.com/gradchannel.

■ ILLINOIS INSTITUTE OF TECHNOLOGY

Graduate College, Armour College of Engineering and Sciences, Department of Biological, Chemical and Physical Sciences, Biology Division, Chicago, IL 60616-3793

AWARDS Biochemistry (MS); biology (PhD); biotechnology (MS); cell biology (MS); microbiology (MS). Part-time and evening/weekend programs available.

Faculty: 8 full-time (0 women), 2 part-time/adjunct (0 women).

Students: 21 full-time (7 women), 44 part-time (18 women); includes 6 minority (3 African Americans, 2 Asian Americans or Pacific Islanders, 1 Hispanic American), 33 international. Average age 32. 158 applicants, 35% accepted. In 2001, 11 master's, 6 doctorates awarded. Terminal master's awarded for partial completion of doctoral program.

Degree requirements: For master's, thesis (for some programs), comprehensive exam; for doctorate, thesis/dissertation, comprehensive exam.

Entrance requirements: For master's and doctorate, GRE General Test, TOEFL, minimum undergraduate GPA of 3.0. *Application deadline:* For fall admission, 7/1; for spring admission, 11/1. Applications are processed on a rolling basis. *Application fee:* $30. Electronic applications accepted.

Expenses: Tuition: Part-time $590 per credit hour.

Financial support: In 2001–02, 7 fellowships, 1 research assistantship, 5 teaching assistantships were awarded. Federal Work-Study, institutionally sponsored loans, scholarships/grants, and unspecified assistantships also available. Support available to part-time students. Financial award application deadline: 3/1; financial award applicants required to submit FAFSA.

Faculty research: Genetics, molecular biology.

Dr. Benjamin Stark, Associate Chair, 312-567-3980, *Fax:* 312-567-3494, *E-mail:* starkb@iit.edu.

Application contact: Dr. Ali Cinar, Dean of Graduate College, 312-567-3637, *Fax:* 312-567-7517, *E-mail:* gradstu@iit.edu. *Web site:* http://www.iit.edu/~bcps/database/search.cgi/:/frontend/grad/ms-phd/biol_degrees

■ ILLINOIS STATE UNIVERSITY

Graduate School, College of Arts and Sciences, Department of Biological Sciences, Program in Biotechnology, Normal, IL 61790-2200

AWARDS MS.

Students: 2 full-time (1 woman).

Degree requirements: For master's, thesis or alternative.

Entrance requirements: For master's, GRE General Test, minimum GPA of 2.6 in last 60 hours. *Application deadline:* Applications are processed on a rolling basis. *Application fee:* $30.

Expenses: Tuition, state resident: full-time $2,691; part-time $112 per credit hour. Tuition, nonresident: full-time $5,880; part-time $245 per credit hour. Required fees: $1,146; $48 per credit hour.

Financial support: Teaching assistantships available. Financial award application deadline: 4/1.

Application contact: Dr. R. K. Jayaswal, Director, 309-438-5128, *Fax:* 309-438-3722, *E-mail:* drjay@ilstu.edu. *Web site:* http://www.bio.ilstu.edu/biotech

■ KEAN UNIVERSITY

School of Natural, Applied and Health Sciences, Department of Biotechnology, Union, NJ 07083

AWARDS MS.

Faculty: 18 full-time (7 women), 13 part-time/adjunct.

Students: 10 full-time (5 women), 8 part-time (2 women); includes 8 minority (2 African Americans, 2 Asian Americans or Pacific Islanders, 4 Hispanic Americans), 1 international.

Degree requirements: For master's, thesis or alternative.

Application deadline: For fall admission, 6/15; for spring admission, 11/15. *Application fee:* $35.

Expenses: Tuition, state resident: full-time $7,372. Tuition, nonresident: full-time $9,004. Required fees: $1,006.

Financial support: In 2001–02, 1 research assistantship with full tuition reimbursement (averaging $3,000 per year) was awarded.

Dr. K. Reilly, Coordinator, 908-527-2472.

Application contact: Joanne Morris, Director of Graduate Admissions, 908-527-2665, *Fax:* 908-527-2286, *E-mail:* grad_adm@kean.edu.

Find an in-depth description at www.petersons.com/gradchannel.

■ KECK GRADUATE INSTITUTE OF APPLIED LIFE SCIENCES

Program in Biosciences, Claremont, CA 91711

AWARDS MBS.

Faculty: 12 full-time (3 women), 1 part-time/adjunct (0 women).

Students: 58 full-time (28 women). Average age 25. 130 applicants, 35% accepted.

Degree requirements: For master's, project.

Entrance requirements: For master's, GRE General Test or MCAT. *Application deadline:* For fall admission, 2/15 (priority date). Applications are processed on a rolling basis. *Application fee:* $60. Electronic applications accepted.

Expenses: Tuition: Full-time $28,800.

Financial support: In 2001–02, 58 students received support, including 49 fellowships with full and partial tuition reimbursements available (averaging $7,000 per year); career-related internships or fieldwork, institutionally sponsored loans, scholarships/grants, and tuition waivers (full and partial) also available.

Faculty research: Computational biology, drug discovery and development, molecular and cellular biology, biomedical engineering, biomaterials and tissue engineering.

Henry E. Riggs, President, 909-607-7855, *Fax:* 909-607-8086.

Application contact: John Friesman, Director of Admissions and Student Services, 909-607-8590, *Fax:* 909-607-8086, *E-mail:* admissions@kgi.edu. *Web site:* http://www.kgi.edu/

Find an in-depth description at www.petersons.com/gradchannel.

■ MANHATTAN COLLEGE

Graduate Division, School of Science, Program in Biotechnology, Riverdale, NY 10471

AWARDS MS.

Faculty research: Tissue culture, protein structure, molecular biochemistry.

■ NATIONAL UNIVERSITY

Academic Affairs, School of Business and Technology, Department of Technology, La Jolla, CA 92037-1011

AWARDS Biotechnology (MBA); electronic commerce (MBA, MS); environmental management (MBA). Software engineering (MS). Space commerce (MBA); technology management (MBA, MS); telecommunications systems management (MS). Part-time and evening/weekend programs available. Postbaccalaureate distance learning degree programs offered (minimal on-campus study).

Faculty: 9 full-time (0 women), 148 part-time/adjunct (20 women).

Students: 349 full-time (108 women), 130 part-time (44 women); includes 145 minority (45 African Americans, 76 Asian Americans or Pacific Islanders, 21 Hispanic Americans, 3 Native Americans), 138 international. 82 applicants, 100% accepted. In 2001, 250 degrees awarded.

Entrance requirements: For master's, interview, minimum GPA of 2.5. *Application deadline:* Applications are processed on a rolling basis. *Application fee:* $60 ($100 for international students).

Expenses: Tuition: Part-time $221 per quarter hour.

Financial support: Institutionally sponsored loans, scholarships/grants, and tuition waivers (full and partial) available. Support available to part-time students. Financial award application deadline: 5/1; financial award applicants required to submit FAFSA.

Dr. Leonid Preiser, Chair, 858-642-8425, *Fax:* 858-642-8716, *E-mail:* lpreiser@nu.edu.

Application contact: Nancy Rohland, Director of Enrollment Management, 858-642-8180, *Fax:* 858-642-8710, *E-mail:* advisor@nu.edu. *Web site:* http://www.nu.edu/

■ NORTH CAROLINA STATE UNIVERSITY

Graduate School, College of Management, Program in Management, Raleigh, NC 27695

AWARDS Biotechnology (MS); computer science (MS); engineering (MS); forest resources management (MS); general business (MS); management information systems (MS); operations research (MS). Statistics (MS); telecommunications systems engineering (MS); textile management (MS); total quality management (MS). Part-time programs available.

Faculty: 14 full-time (6 women), 3 part-time/adjunct (0 women).

Students: 60 full-time (18 women), 138 part-time (47 women); includes 27 minority (12 African Americans, 13 Asian Americans or Pacific Islanders, 2 Hispanic

Americans), 17 international. Average age 32. 225 applicants, 44% accepted. In 2001, 67 degrees awarded.

Entrance requirements: For master's, GMAT or GRE, TOEFL, minimum undergraduate GPA of 3.0. *Application deadline:* For fall admission, 6/25; for spring admission, 11/25. Applications are processed on a rolling basis. *Application fee:* $45.

Expenses: Tuition, state resident: full-time $1,748. Tuition, nonresident: full-time $6,904.

Financial support: In 2001–02, fellowships (averaging $3,551 per year), 32 teaching assistantships (averaging $3,027 per year) were awarded. Research assistantships Financial award application deadline: 3/1.

Faculty research: Manufacturing strategy, information systems, technology commercialization, managing research and development, historical stock returns. *Total annual research expenditures:* $69,089.

Dr. Stephen G. Allen, Head, 919-515-5584, *Fax:* 919-515-5073, *E-mail:* steve_allen@ncsu.edu. *Web site:* http://www.mgt.ncsu.edu/facdep/bizmgmt/bizman.html

■ NORTHWESTERN UNIVERSITY

The Graduate School and Judd A. and Marjorie Weinberg College of Arts and Sciences, Interdepartmental Biological Sciences Program (IBiS), Evanston, IL 60208

AWARDS Biochemistry, molecular biology, and cell biology (PhD), including biochemistry, cell and molecular biology, molecular biophysics, structural biology; biotechnology (PhD); cell and molecular biology (PhD); developmental biology and genetics (PhD); hormone action and signal transduction (PhD); neuroscience (PhD). Structural biology, biochemistry, and biophysics (PhD). Participants in the Interdepartmental Biological Sciences Program include the Departments of Biochemistry, Molecular Biology, and Cell Biology; Chemistry; Neurobiology and Physiology; Chemical Engineering; Civil Engineering; and Evanston Hospital.

Faculty: 63 full-time (13 women).

Students: 93 full-time (60 women); includes 6 minority (3 African Americans, 1 Hispanic American, 2 Native Americans), 11 international. 254 applicants, 21% accepted, 22 enrolled. In 2001, 15 degrees awarded.

Degree requirements: For doctorate, thesis/dissertation, 2 quarters of teaching experience. Seminar participation, comprehensive exam, registration.

Entrance requirements: For doctorate, GRE General Test, TOEFL, TSE. *Application deadline:* For fall admission, 12/31. Applications are processed on a rolling basis. *Application fee:* $50 ($55 for international students). Electronic applications accepted.

Expenses: Tuition: Full-time $26,526.

Financial support: In 2001–02, 79 students received support, including 15 fellowships with full tuition reimbursements available (averaging $21,000 per year), 51 research assistantships with full tuition reimbursements available (averaging $21,000 per year), 15 teaching assistantships with full tuition reimbursements available (averaging $21,000 per year); career-related internships or fieldwork, Federal Work-Study, institutionally sponsored loans, scholarships/grants, traineeships, health care benefits, and unspecified assistantships also available. Financial award application deadline: 12/31; financial award applicants required to submit FAFSA.

Faculty research: Developmental genetics, gene regulation, DNA-protein interactions, biological clocks, bioremediation, ion channels, neurobiology.

Dr. Robert A. Holmgren, Director, 847-491-5460, *Fax:* 847-467-1380, *E-mail:* ibis@northwestern.edu.

Application contact: Latonia Trimuel, Program Assistant, 800-545-1761, *Fax:* 847-467-1380, *E-mail:* ibis@northwestern.edu. *Web site:* http://www.biochem.northwestern.edu/ibis/

Find an in-depth description at www.petersons.com/gradchannel.

■ SALEM INTERNATIONAL UNIVERSITY

Program in Bioscience, Salem, WV 26426-0500

AWARDS Biotechnology/molecular biology (MS).

Faculty: 2 full-time (1 woman).

Students: 5 full-time (1 woman), 4 international. Average age 27. 10 applicants, 50% accepted.

Degree requirements: For master's, thesis.

Entrance requirements: For master's, GRE, TOEFL, minimum undergraduate GPA of 3.0. *Application deadline:* Applications are processed on a rolling basis. *Application fee:* $25. Electronic applications accepted.

Expenses: Contact institution.

Financial support: In 2001–02, 4 students received support, including 3 research assistantships with full tuition reimbursements available (averaging $7,200 per year); fellowships, teaching assistantships, career-related internships or fieldwork and tuition waivers (full) also available. Financial award application deadline: 4/15; financial award applicants required to submit FAFSA.

Faculty research: Genetic engineering of seed storage proteins, virus replication and infection, gene therapy, programmed cell death, cell protocols for creation of gene transfer.

Dr. Patrick Lai, Director of Graduate Bioscience Program, 304-782-5575, *Fax:* 304-782-5579, *E-mail:* bio@salemiu.edu.

Salem International University
(continued)

Application contact: William M. Martin, Director of Admissions, 304-782-5336, *Fax:* 304-782-5592, *E-mail:* admissions@salemiu.edu.

■ STEPHEN F. AUSTIN STATE UNIVERSITY

Graduate School, College of Sciences and Mathematics, Department of Chemistry, Program in Biotechnology, Nacogdoches, TX 75962

AWARDS MS.

Faculty: 2 full-time (both women), 37 part-time/adjunct (12 women).
Students: 23 full-time (11 women), 11 part-time (7 women); includes 7 minority (2 Asian Americans or Pacific Islanders, 2 Hispanic Americans, 3 Native Americans), 15 international. 21 applicants, 95% accepted. In 2001, 9 degrees awarded.
Degree requirements: For master's, thesis, comprehensive exam.
Entrance requirements: For master's, GRE General Test, TOEFL, minimum GPA of 2.8 in last 60 hours, 2.5 overall. *Application deadline:* For fall admission, 8/1 (priority date); for spring admission, 12/15. Applications are processed on a rolling basis. *Application fee:* $0 ($50 for international students).
Expenses: Tuition, state resident: full-time $1,008; part-time $42 per credit. Tuition, nonresident: full-time $6,072; part-time $253 per credit. Required fees: $1,248; $52 per credit. Tuition and fees vary according to course load.
Financial support: In 2001–02, 15 research assistantships (averaging $6,750 per year) were awarded; Federal Work-Study, health care benefits, and unspecified assistantships also available. Financial award application deadline: 3/1.
Dr. Beatrice Clack, Director, 936-468-3606.

■ TEXAS A&M UNIVERSITY

Interdisciplinary Faculty of Biotechnology, College Station, TX 77843

AWARDS MBIOT. Program begins in Summer term.

Faculty: 49 full-time.
Students: 11 full-time (6 women); includes 5 minority (1 African American, 4 Asian Americans or Pacific Islanders). Average age 25. 20 applicants, 55% accepted, 11 enrolled. In 2001, 5 degrees awarded.
Degree requirements: For master's, professional internship. *Median time to degree:* Master's–1.25 years full-time.
Entrance requirements: For master's, GRE, TOEFL, minimum undergraduate GPA of 3.0, 3.25 in science. *Application fee:* $50 ($75 for international students). Electronic applications accepted.

Expenses: Tuition, state resident: full-time $11,872. Tuition, nonresident: full-time $17,892.
Financial support: Fellowships, research assistantships, scholarships/grants available. Financial award applicants required to submit FAFSA.
Dr. Jorge Piedrahita, Head, 979-845-0732, *Fax:* 979-862-4790.
Application contact: Jeannine Kantz, Program Coordinator, 979-862-4935, *Fax:* 979-862-4790, *E-mail:* jkantz@tamu.edu.

■ TEXAS TECH UNIVERSITY

Graduate School, College of Arts and Sciences, Department of Chemistry and Biochemistry, Lubbock, TX 79409

AWARDS Biotechnology (MS); chemistry (MS, PhD). Part-time programs available.

Faculty: 23 full-time (1 woman).
Students: 61 full-time (15 women), 5 part-time (3 women); includes 4 minority (1 African American, 2 Asian Americans or Pacific Islanders, 1 Native American), 44 international. Average age 28. 39 applicants, 64% accepted, 15 enrolled. In 2001, 10 master's, 10 doctorates awarded.
Degree requirements: For master's and doctorate, thesis/dissertation.
Entrance requirements: For master's and doctorate, GRE General Test. *Application deadline:* Applications are processed on a rolling basis. *Application fee:* $25 ($50 for international students). Electronic applications accepted.
Expenses: Tuition, state resident: full-time $1,926; part-time $107 per credit hour. Tuition, nonresident: full-time $5,724; part-time $318 per credit hour. Required fees: $779; $737 per year. Tuition and fees vary according to course level, course load and program.
Financial support: In 2001–02, 38 research assistantships with partial tuition reimbursements (averaging $12,335 per year), 39 teaching assistantships with partial tuition reimbursements (averaging $13,402 per year) were awarded. Fellowships, career-related internships or fieldwork, Federal Work-Study, and institutionally sponsored loans also available. Support available to part-time students. Financial award application deadline: 5/1; financial award applicants required to submit FAFSA.
Faculty research: Biochemistry and molecular biology of phytosterols, biomedical optics and fluoroscence endoscopy, chemical reactions induced by ultrasound, ionic and molecular recognition with synthetic host molecules, ultratrace atmospheric analysis. *Total annual research expenditures:* $3.1 million.
Dr. Richard Bartsch, Chair, 806-742-3069, *Fax:* 806-742-1289.
Application contact: Graduate Adviser, 806-742-3069, *Fax:* 806-742-1289. *Web site:* http://www.ttu.edu/~chem/

■ TEXAS TECH UNIVERSITY HEALTH SCIENCES CENTER

Program in Biotechnology, Lubbock, TX 79430

AWARDS MS. Offered jointly with the General Academic Campus of TTU (science/argiculture track).

Find an in-depth description at www.petersons.com/gradchannel.

■ THOMAS JEFFERSON UNIVERSITY

College of Graduate Studies, Program in Cell and Tissue Engineering, Philadelphia, PA 19107

AWARDS PhD.

Faculty: 5 full-time (2 women), 6 part-time/adjunct (2 women).
Students: 8 full-time (2 women); includes 3 minority (all Asian Americans or Pacific Islanders), 1 international. Average age 25. 9 applicants, 11% accepted, 1 enrolled.
Degree requirements: For doctorate, thesis/dissertation, comprehensive exam, registration.
Entrance requirements: For doctorate, GRE General Test, TOEFL, minimum GPA of 3.2. *Application deadline:* For fall admission, 3/1 (priority date). Applications are processed on a rolling basis. *Application fee:* $40. Electronic applications accepted.
Expenses: Tuition: Full-time $13,440. Tuition and fees vary according to degree level and program.
Financial support: In 2001–02, 8 fellowships with full tuition reimbursements were awarded; Federal Work-Study, institutionally sponsored loans, and traineeships also available. Support available to part-time students. Financial award application deadline: 5/1; financial award applicants required to submit FAFSA.
Faculty research: Skeletal development, biomaterials, bone implant interaction, tissue engineering, high resolution imaging.
Dr. Irving Shapiro, Director, 215-955-7217, *Fax:* 215-955-9159.
Application contact: Jessie F. Pervall, Director of Admissions, 215-503-0155, *Fax:* 215-503-3433, *E-mail:* jessie.pervall@mail.tju.edu.

Find an in-depth description at www.petersons.com/gradchannel.

■ TUFTS UNIVERSITY

Division of Graduate and Continuing Studies and Research, Graduate and Professional Studies, Biotechnology Engineering Program, Medford, MA 02155

AWARDS Certificate. Part-time and evening/weekend programs available.

Students: Average age 26. 3 applicants, 100% accepted. In 2001, 3 degrees awarded.

Application deadline: For fall admission, 8/15 (priority date); for spring admission, 12/12 (priority date). Applications are processed on a rolling basis. *Application fee:* $50. Electronic applications accepted.
Expenses: Tuition: Full-time $26,853. Full-time tuition and fees vary according to program.
Financial support: Available to part-time students. Application deadline: 5/1. Alida Poirier, Assistant Director, 617-627-3395, *Fax:* 617-627-3016, *E-mail:* pcs@ase.tufts.edu.
Application contact: Information Contact, 617-627-3395, *Fax:* 617-627-3016, *E-mail:* pcs@ase.tufts.edu. *Web site:* http://ase.tufts.edu/gradstudy

■ TUFTS UNIVERSITY

Division of Graduate and Continuing Studies and Research, Graduate and Professional Studies, Biotechnology Program, Medford, MA 02155

AWARDS Certificate. Part-time and evening/weekend programs available.

Students: Average age 32. 7 applicants, 100% accepted. In 2001, 4 degrees awarded.
Application deadline: For fall admission, 8/15 (priority date); for spring admission, 12/12 (priority date). Applications are processed on a rolling basis. *Application fee:* $50. Electronic applications accepted.
Expenses: Tuition: Full-time $26,853. Full-time tuition and fees vary according to program.
Financial support: Available to part-time students. Application deadline: 5/1. Alida Poirier, Assistant Director, 617-627-3395, *Fax:* 617-627-3016, *E-mail:* pcs@ase.tufts.edu.
Application contact: Information Contact, 617-627-3395, *Fax:* 617-627-3016, *E-mail:* pcs@ase.tufts.edu. *Web site:* http://ase.tufts.edu/gradstudy

■ THE UNIVERSITY OF ALABAMA IN HUNTSVILLE

School of Graduate Studies, College of Engineering, Department of Chemical and Materials Engineering, Huntsville, AL 35899

AWARDS Biotechnology science and engineering (PhD); chemical engineering (MSE). Part-time and evening/weekend programs available.

Faculty: 4 full-time (0 women).
Students: 16 full-time (6 women), 1 part-time; includes 2 minority (1 African American, 1 Asian American or Pacific Islander), 11 international. Average age 25. 72 applicants, 21% accepted, 9 enrolled. In 2001, 6 degrees awarded.
Degree requirements: For master's, thesis or alternative, oral and written exams, comprehensive exam, registration; for doctorate, thesis/dissertation, comprehensive exam, registration.

Entrance requirements: For master's, GRE General Test, appropriate bachelor's degree, minimum GPA of 3.0. *Application deadline:* For fall admission, 7/24 (priority date); for spring admission, 11/15 (priority date). Applications are processed on a rolling basis. *Application fee:* $35.
Expenses: Tuition, area resident: Part-time $175 per hour. Tuition, state resident: full-time $4,408. Tuition, nonresident: full-time $9,054; part-time $361 per hour.
Financial support: In 2001–02, 11 students received support, including 1 fellowship with full and partial tuition reimbursement available (averaging $10,800 per year), 6 research assistantships with full and partial tuition reimbursements available (averaging $9,424 per year), 4 teaching assistantships with full and partial tuition reimbursements available (averaging $9,150 per year); career-related internships or fieldwork, Federal Work-Study, institutionally sponsored loans, scholarships/grants, health care benefits, and tuition waivers (full and partial) also available. Support available to part-time students. Financial award application deadline: 4/1; financial award applicants required to submit FAFSA.
Faculty research: Turbulence modeling, computational fluid dynamics, microgravity processing, multiphase transport, blood materials transport. *Total annual research expenditures:* $265,040.
Dr. Ramon Cerro, Chair, 256-824-6810, *Fax:* 256-824-6839, *E-mail:* rlc@eb.uah.edu. *Web site:* http://www.eb-p5.eb.uah.edu/che/

■ THE UNIVERSITY OF ALABAMA IN HUNTSVILLE

School of Graduate Studies, College of Engineering and College of Science, Interdisciplinary Program in Biotechnology Science and Engineering, Huntsville, AL 35899

AWARDS PhD.

Degree requirements: For doctorate, thesis/dissertation, oral and written exams, comprehensive exam, registration.
Expenses: Tuition, area resident: Part-time $175 per hour. Tuition, state resident: full-time $4,408. Tuition, nonresident: full-time $9,054; part-time $361 per hour.

■ UNIVERSITY OF CONNECTICUT

Graduate School, College of Liberal Arts and Sciences, Biological Sciences Group, Storrs, CT 06269

AWARDS Ecology and evolutionary biology (MS, PhD), including botany, ecology, entomology, systematics, zoology; molecular and cell biology (MS, PhD), including biochemistry, biophysics, biotechnology (MS), cell and developmental biology, genetics, microbiology, plant molecular and cell biology; physiology and neurobiology (MS, PhD), including neurobiology, physiology.

Degree requirements: For doctorate, thesis/dissertation.
Entrance requirements: For master's and doctorate, GRE General Test, GRE Subject Test, TOEFL.

■ UNIVERSITY OF CONNECTICUT

Graduate School, College of Liberal Arts and Sciences, Biological Sciences Group, Department of Molecular and Cell Biology, Field of Biotechnology, Storrs, CT 06269

AWARDS MS.

Entrance requirements: For master's, GRE General Test, GRE Subject Test, TOEFL.

■ UNIVERSITY OF DELAWARE

College of Arts and Science, Department of Biological Sciences, Newark, DE 19716

AWARDS Biotechnology (MS, PhD); cell and extracellular matrix biology (MS, PhD); cell and systems physiology (MS, PhD); ecology and evolution (MS, PhD); microbiology (MS, PhD); molecular biology and genetics (MS, PhD); plant biology (MS, PhD).

Faculty: 37 full-time (10 women).
Students: 33 full-time (22 women), 1 part-time; includes 6 minority (3 African Americans, 1 Asian American or Pacific Islander, 1 Hispanic American, 1 Native American), 9 international. Average age 26. 102 applicants, 32% accepted, 11 enrolled. In 2001, 2 master's, 1 doctorate awarded.
Degree requirements: For master's and doctorate, thesis/dissertation.
Entrance requirements: For master's and doctorate, GRE General Test. *Application deadline:* For fall admission, 4/15. Applications are processed on a rolling basis. *Application fee:* $50. Electronic applications accepted.
Expenses: Tuition, state resident: full-time $4,770; part-time $265 per credit. Tuition, nonresident: full-time $13,860; part-time $770 per credit. Required fees: $414.
Financial support: In 2001–02, 26 students received support, including 2 fellowships with full tuition reimbursements available (averaging $18,000 per year), 4 research assistantships with full tuition reimbursements available (averaging $18,000 per year), 11 teaching assistantships with full tuition reimbursements available (averaging $18,000 per year); tuition waivers (partial) also available. Financial award application deadline: 4/15.
Faculty research: Cell interactions, microorganisms, functional genomics, population ecology. *Total annual research expenditures:* $1.8 million.
Dr. Daniel D. Carson, Chair, 302-831-6977, *Fax:* 302-831-2281, *E-mail:* dcarson@udel.edu.
Application contact: Dr. Norman J. Karin, Graduate Coordinator, 302-831-1841, *Fax:* 302-831-2281, *E-mail:*

University of Delaware (continued)
ccoletta@udel.edu. *Web site:* http://
www.udel.edu/bio

**Find an in-depth description at
www.petersons.com/gradchannel.**

■ UNIVERSITY OF DELAWARE

**Delaware Biotechnology Institute,
Newark, DE 19716**

AWARDS PhD.

Expenses: Tuition, state resident: full-time
$4,770; part-time $265 per credit. Tuition,
nonresident: full-time $13,860; part-time
$770 per credit. Required fees: $414.

■ UNIVERSITY OF MARYLAND UNIVERSITY COLLEGE

**Graduate School of Management and
Technology, Program in
Biotechnology Studies, Adelphi, MD
20783**

AWARDS MS. Part-time and evening/weekend
programs available. Postbaccalaureate
distance learning degree programs offered
(no on-campus study).

Students: 26 applicants, 100% accepted.
Degree requirements: For master's,
thesis or alternative.
Application deadline: Applications are
processed on a rolling basis. *Application fee:*
$50. Electronic applications accepted.
Expenses: Tuition, state resident: full-time
$5,418; part-time $301 per credit hour.
Tuition, nonresident: full-time $8,892;
part-time $494 per credit hour.
Financial support: Federal Work-Study
and scholarships/grants available. Support
available to part-time students. Financial
award application deadline: 6/1; financial
award applicants required to submit
FAFSA.
Dr. Robert Ouellette, Acting Chair, 301-
985-7200, *Fax:* 301-985-4611, *E-mail:*
rouellette@umuc.edu.
Application contact: Coordinator, Graduate Admissions, 301-985-7155, *Fax:* 301-
985-7175, *E-mail:* gradinfo@
nova.umuc.edu. *Web site:* http://
www.umuc.edu/grad/msbt.html

■ UNIVERSITY OF MASSACHUSETTS BOSTON

**Office of Graduate Studies and
Research, College of Arts and
Sciences, Faculty of Sciences,
Program in Biotechnology and
Biomedical Science, Boston, MA
02125-3393**

AWARDS MS. Part-time and evening/weekend
programs available.

Degree requirements: For master's, oral
exams, thesis optional.
Entrance requirements: For master's,
GRE General Test, GRE Subject Test,
minimum GPA of 2.75, 3.0 in science and
math.

Faculty research: Evolutionary and
molecular immunology, molecular genetics,
tissue culture, computerized laboratory
technology.

■ UNIVERSITY OF MASSACHUSETTS LOWELL

**Graduate School, College of Arts and
Sciences, Department of Biological
Sciences, Lowell, MA 01854-2881**

AWARDS Biochemistry (PhD); biological sciences (MS); biotechnology (MS). Part-time
programs available.

Degree requirements: For master's and
doctorate, thesis/dissertation.
Entrance requirements: For master's and
doctorate, GRE General Test. Electronic
applications accepted.

■ UNIVERSITY OF MINNESOTA, TWIN CITIES CAMPUS

**Medical School and Graduate School,
Graduate Programs in Medicine and
Institute of Technology, Program in
Microbial Engineering, Minneapolis,
MN 55455-0213**

AWARDS MS. Part-time programs available.
Faculty: 32 full-time (3 women).
Students: 6 full-time (2 women), 1
(woman) part-time; includes 1 minority
(Asian American or Pacific Islander), 3
international. Average age 25. 5 applicants,
40% accepted. In 2001, 2 degrees awarded.
Degree requirements: For master's,
thesis.
Entrance requirements: For master's,
GRE General Test, TOEFL. *Application
deadline:* For fall admission, 1/31 (priority
date). *Application fee:* $50 ($55 for
international students).
Expenses: Tuition, state resident: full-time
$2,932; part-time $489 per credit. Tuition,
nonresident: full-time $5,758; part-time
$960 per credit. Part-time tuition and fees
vary according to course load, program
and reciprocity agreements.
Financial support: In 2001–02, 1 fellowship, 6 research assistantships were
awarded. Health care benefits and unspecified assistantships also available. Financial
award application deadline: 2/1.
Faculty research: Microbial genetics,
oncogenesis, gene transfer, fermentation,
bioreactors, genetics of antibiotic
biosynthesis. *Total annual research
expenditures:* $2.5 million.
Dr. Michael J. Sadowsky, Director of
Graduate Studies, 612-624-6774, *Fax:* 612-
625-1700, *E-mail:* sadowsky@
soils.umn.edu.
Application contact: Gayle Nance,
Principal Secretary, 612-625-0212, *Fax:*
612-625-1700, *E-mail:* bpti@
biosci.cbs.umn.edu. *Web site:* http://
bio.cbs.umn.edu/bpti/bpti.html

**Find an in-depth description at
www.petersons.com/gradchannel.**

■ UNIVERSITY OF MISSOURI–ST. LOUIS

**Graduate School, College of Arts and
Sciences, Department of Biology, St.
Louis, MO 63121-4499**

AWARDS Biology (MS, PhD), including animal
behavior (MS), biochemistry, biotechnology
(MS), conservation biology (MS), development (MS), ecology (MS), environmental
studies (PhD), evolution (MS), genetics (MS),
molecular biology and biotechnology (PhD),
molecular/cellular biology (MS), physiology
(MS), plant systematics, population biology
(MS), tropical biology (MS); biotechnology
(Certificate); tropical biology and conservation
(Certificate). Part-time programs available.

Faculty: 55.
Students: 27 full-time (15 women), 88
part-time (52 women); includes 17 minor-
ity (2 African Americans, 7 Asian
Americans or Pacific Islanders, 8 Hispanic
Americans), 31 international. In 2001, 11
master's, 6 doctorates awarded.
Degree requirements: For master's,
thesis or alternative; for doctorate, one
foreign language, thesis/dissertation, 1
semester of teaching experience.
Entrance requirements: For doctorate,
GRE General Test. *Application deadline:*
For fall admission, 7/1 (priority date); for
spring admission, 11/1 (priority date).
Applications are processed on a rolling
basis. *Application fee:* $25 ($40 for
international students). Electronic applications accepted.
Expenses: Tuition, state resident: part-
time $231 per credit hour. Tuition,
nonresident: part-time $621 per credit
hour.
Financial support: In 2001–02, 9 fellowships with full tuition reimbursements
(averaging $13,644 per year), 13 research
assistantships with full and partial tuition
reimbursements (averaging $12,644 per
year), 20 teaching assistantships with full
and partial tuition reimbursements (averaging $14,100 per year) were awarded.
Career-related internships or fieldwork and
Federal Work-Study also available. Support available to part-time students.
Financial award application deadline: 2/1.
Total annual research expenditures: $1.1 mil-
lion.
Director of Graduate Studies, 314-516-
6203, *Fax:* 314-516-6233, *E-mail:* icte@
umsl.edu.
Application contact: Clara Jackson,
Graduate Admissions Counselor, 314-516-
6946, *Fax:* 314-516-5310, *E-mail:*
gradadm@umsl.edu. *Web site:* http://
www.umsl.edu/divisions/artscience/biology/

■ UNIVERSITY OF NORTH TEXAS HEALTH SCIENCE CENTER AT FORT WORTH

Graduate School of Biomedical Sciences, Fort Worth, TX 76107-2699

AWARDS Anatomy and cell biology (MS, PhD); biochemistry and molecular biology (MS, PhD); biomedical sciences (MS, PhD); biotechnology (MS); forensic genetics (MS); integrative physiology (MS, PhD); medical science (MS); microbiology and immunology (MS, PhD); pharmacology (MS, PhD). Science education (MS).

Faculty: 68 full-time (11 women), 7 part-time/adjunct (0 women).
Students: 101 full-time (61 women), 35 part-time (19 women); includes 36 minority (13 African Americans, 7 Asian Americans or Pacific Islanders, 16 Hispanic Americans), 32 international. Average age 29. 90 applicants, 84% accepted, 42 enrolled. In 2001, 11 master's, 13 doctorates awarded. Terminal master's awarded for partial completion of doctoral program.
Degree requirements: For master's and doctorate, thesis/dissertation.
Entrance requirements: For master's and doctorate, GRE General Test, TOEFL. *Application deadline:* For fall admission, 5/1; for spring admission, 11/1. Applications are processed on a rolling basis. *Application fee:* $25 ($50 for international students).
Expenses: Tuition, state resident: full-time $6,550; part-time $858 per year. Tuition, nonresident: full-time $19,650; part-time $3,633 per year. Required fees: $1,300; $473 per year. Tuition and fees vary according to program.
Financial support: In 2001–02, 80 research assistantships (averaging $16,000 per year) were awarded; fellowships, teaching assistantships, career-related internships or fieldwork, Federal Work-Study, institutionally sponsored loans, scholarships/grants, and traineeships also available. Support available to part-time students. Financial award application deadline: 4/1; financial award applicants required to submit FAFSA.
Faculty research: Alzheimer's disease, aging, eye diseases, cancer, cardiovascular disease. *Total annual research expenditures:* $10.1 million.
Dr. Thomas Yorio, Dean, 817-735-2560, *Fax:* 817-735-0243, *E-mail:* yoriot@hsc.unt.edu.
Application contact: Carla Lee, Director of Graduate Admissions and Services, 817-735-2560, *Fax:* 817-735-0243, *E-mail:* gsbs@hsc.unt.edu. *Web site:* http://www.hsc.unt.edu/

Find an in-depth description at www.petersons.com/gradchannel.

■ UNIVERSITY OF PENNSYLVANIA

School of Engineering and Applied Science, Program in Biotechnology, Philadelphia, PA 19104

AWARDS MS. Part-time programs available.

Entrance requirements: For master's, GRE General Test, TOEFL, bachelor's degree in science or undergraduate course work in molecular biology. Electronic applications accepted. *Web site:* http://www.upenn.edu/BioTech/

Find an in-depth description at www.petersons.com/gradchannel.

■ THE UNIVERSITY OF TEXAS AT SAN ANTONIO

College of Sciences, Division of Life Sciences, Programs in Biology and Biotechnology, San Antonio, TX 78249-0617

AWARDS Biology (MS); biotechnology (MS). Part-time programs available.

Degree requirements: For master's, thesis optional.
Entrance requirements: For master's, GRE General Test, minimum GPA of 3.0.
Expenses: Tuition, state resident: full-time $2,268; part-time $126 per credit hour. Tuition, nonresident: full-time $6,066; part-time $337 per credit hour. Required fees: $781. Tuition and fees vary according to course load.
Faculty research: Plant ecology, bioremediation, neurophysiology, neurotoxicology, neuroendocrinology, neural circuit analysis.

■ UNIVERSITY OF THE SCIENCES IN PHILADELPHIA

College of Graduate Studies, Program in Cell Biology and Biotechnology, Philadelphia, PA 19104-4495

AWARDS MS. Part-time and evening/weekend programs available.

Faculty: 8 full-time (2 women).
Students: Average age 29. 8 applicants, 88% accepted, 3 enrolled.
Degree requirements: For master's, thesis (for some programs), registration.
Entrance requirements: For master's, GRE General Test, TOEFL. *Application deadline:* For fall admission, 5/1; for spring admission, 10/1. Applications are processed on a rolling basis. *Application fee:* $45.
Expenses: Tuition: Full-time $17,122; part-time $713 per credit. Required fees: $26 per credit.
Financial support: In 2001–02, 1 student received support; fellowships with full tuition reimbursements available, scholarships/grants and tuition waivers (full) available. Financial award application deadline: 5/1.
Faculty research: Invertebrate cell adhesion, plant-microbe interactions, natural

product mechanisms, cell signal transduction, gene regulation and organization. *Total annual research expenditures:* $30,000.
Dr. John R. Porter, Director, 215-596-8917, *Fax:* 215-596-8710, *E-mail:* j.porter@usip.edu.
Application contact: Dr. Rodney J. Wigent, Dean, 215-596-8937, *Fax:* 215-895-1185, *E-mail:* graduate@usip.edu. *Web site:* http://www.usip.edu/graduate/

■ UNIVERSITY OF VIRGINIA

College and Graduate School of Arts and Sciences, Interdisciplinary Program in Biotechnology, Charlottesville, VA 22903

AWARDS PhD. PhD awarded by related department.

Degree requirements: For doctorate, thesis/dissertation.
Application fee: $40.
Expenses: Tuition, state resident: full-time $3,988. Tuition, nonresident: full-time $17,078. Required fees: $1,190.
Dr. Gordon W. Laurie, Director, 434-924-2181, *Fax:* 434-924-0140, *E-mail:* medgpo32@virginia.edu.

Find an in-depth description at www.petersons.com/gradchannel.

■ UNIVERSITY OF WASHINGTON

Graduate School, College of Arts and Sciences, Department of Genome Sciences, Seattle, WA 98195

AWARDS Genome sciences (PhD).

Degree requirements: For doctorate, thesis/dissertation, general exam.
Entrance requirements: For doctorate, GRE General Test, TOEFL, minimum GPA of 3.0. Electronic applications accepted.
Expenses: Tuition, state resident: full-time $5,539. Tuition, nonresident: full-time $14,376. Required fees: $390. Tuition and fees vary according to course load and program.
Faculty research: Genetics of bacteria, yeast, plants, and mammals. *Web site:* http://depts.washington.edu/genetics/

Find an in-depth description at www.petersons.com/gradchannel.

■ WILLIAM PATERSON UNIVERSITY OF NEW JERSEY

College of Science and Health, Department of Biology, Program in Biotechnology, Wayne, NJ 07470-8420

AWARDS MS. Part-time and evening/weekend programs available.

Students: 6 full-time (3 women), 17 part-time (14 women); includes 12 minority (1 African American, 7 Asian Americans or Pacific Islanders, 4 Hispanic Americans). 20 applicants, 55% accepted. In 2001, 5 degrees awarded.

William Paterson University of New Jersey (continued)

Degree requirements: For master's, exit exam.

Entrance requirements: For master's, GRE General Test, GRE Subject Test (biology), minimum GPA of 2.75. *Application deadline:* Applications are processed on a rolling basis. *Application fee:* $35. Electronic applications accepted.

Expenses: Tuition, state resident: part-time $322 per credit. Tuition, nonresident: part-time $468 per credit.

Financial support: In 2001–02, 1 student received support; research assistantships with full tuition reimbursements available, career-related internships or fieldwork and unspecified assistantships available. Support available to part-time students. Financial award application deadline: 4/1; financial award applicants required to submit FAFSA.

Faculty research: DNA cloning, genetic engineering, plant tissue culture, molecular genetics, *Drosophila* gene expression.

Application contact: Danielle Liautaud, Graduate Admissions Counselor, 973-720-3579, *Fax:* 973-720-2035, *E-mail:* liautaudd@wpunj.edu. *Web site:* http://www.wpunj.edu/

■ **WORCESTER POLYTECHNIC INSTITUTE**

Graduate Studies, Department of Biology and Biotechnology, Worcester, MA 01609-2280

AWARDS Biology (MS); biomedical sciences (PhD); biotechnology (MS, PhD).

Faculty: 12 full-time (4 women), 1 (woman) part-time/adjunct.

Students: 30 full-time (14 women), 2 part-time (both women); includes 1 minority (Hispanic American), 8 international. 59 applicants, 41% accepted, 13 enrolled. In 2001, 11 degrees awarded.

Degree requirements: For master's, thesis; for doctorate, thesis/dissertation, qualifying exam.

Entrance requirements: For master's and doctorate, GRE General Test, TOEFL. *Application deadline:* For fall admission, 2/1 (priority date); for spring admission, 10/15 (priority date). Applications are processed on a rolling basis. *Application fee:* $60. Electronic applications accepted.

Expenses: Tuition: Part-time $796 per credit. Required fees: $20; $752 per credit. One-time fee: $30 full-time.

Financial support: In 2001–02, 20 students received support, including 3 fellowships with full tuition reimbursements available (averaging $16,952 per year), 3 research assistantships with full and partial tuition reimbursements available (averaging $17,256 per year), 11 teaching assistantships with full and partial tuition reimbursements available (averaging $12,942 per year); career-related internships or fieldwork, institutionally sponsored loans, scholarships/grants, and tuition waivers (full and partial) also available. Financial award application deadline: 2/15; financial award applicants required to submit FAFSA.

Faculty research: Molecular biology, plant physiology, immunology and neurobiology, biomedication, genetic engineering. *Total annual research expenditures:* $435,250.

Dr. Jill Rulfs, Interim Department Head, 508-831-5786, *Fax:* 508-831-5936, *E-mail:* jrulfs@wpi.edu.

Application contact: Dr. Daniel Gibson, Graduate Coordinator, 508-831-5543, *Fax:* 508-831-5936, *E-mail:* digibson@wip.edu. *Web site:* http://www.wpi.edu/Academics/Depts/Bio/

Find an in-depth description at www.petersons.com/gradchannel.

■ **WORCESTER STATE COLLEGE**

Graduate Studies, Program in Biotechnology, Worcester, MA 01602-2597

AWARDS MS. Part-time and evening/weekend programs available.

Faculty: 10 full-time (5 women), 6 part-time/adjunct (0 women).

Students: 3 full-time (2 women), 14 part-time (9 women); includes 1 minority (African American). In 2001, 3 degrees awarded.

Degree requirements: For master's, one foreign language, thesis, comprehensive exam.

Entrance requirements: For master's, GRE General Test or MAT, TOEFL, minimum undergraduate QPA of 3.0 in biology. *Application deadline:* Applications are processed on a rolling basis. *Application fee:* $10 ($40 for international students).

Expenses: Tuition: Part-time $120 per credit hour.

Financial support: Career-related internships or fieldwork, Federal Work-Study, institutionally sponsored loans, scholarships/grants, and unspecified assistantships available. Support available to part-time students. Financial award application deadline: 3/1; financial award applicants required to submit FAFSA.

Faculty research: Effects of insulin in invertebrates, ecology of freshwater turtles, symbiotic relations of plants and animals.

Dr. Peter Bradley, Coordinator, 508-929-8571, *Fax:* 508-929-8171, *E-mail:* pbradley@worcester.edu.

Application contact: Andrea Wetmore, Graduate Admissions Counselor, 508-929-8120, *Fax:* 508-929-8100, *E-mail:* awetmore@worcester.edu.

Chemical Engineering

BIOCHEMICAL ENGINEERING

■ **CALIFORNIA POLYTECHNIC STATE UNIVERSITY, SAN LUIS OBISPO**

College of Engineering, Program in Engineering, San Luis Obispo, CA 93407

AWARDS Biochemical engineering (MS); industrial engineering (MS); integrated technology management (MS); materials engineering (MS); water engineering (MS), including bioengineering, biomedical engineering, manufacturing engineering.

Faculty: 98 full-time (8 women), 82 part-time/adjunct (14 women).

Students: 20 full-time (4 women), 9 part-time (1 woman). 25 applicants, 68% accepted, 15 enrolled. In 2001, 22 degrees awarded.

Entrance requirements: For master's, GRE General Test, minimum GPA of 2.5 in last 90 quarter units. *Application fee:* $55.

Expenses: Tuition, nonresident: part-time $164 per unit. One-time fee: $2,153 part-time.

Financial support: Application deadline: 3/2.

Dr. Peter Y. Lee, Dean, 805-756-2131, *Fax:* 805-756-6503, *E-mail:* plee@calpoly.edu.

Application contact: Dr. Daniel W. Walsh, Associate Dean, 805-756-2131, *Fax:* 805-756-6503, *E-mail:* dwalsh@calpoly.edu. *Web site:* http://www.synner.ceng.calpoly.edu/

■ CORNELL UNIVERSITY

Graduate School, Graduate Fields of Engineering, Field of Chemical Engineering, Ithaca, NY 14853-0001

AWARDS Advanced materials processing (M Eng, MS, PhD); applied mathematics and computational methods (M Eng, MS, PhD); biochemical engineering (M Eng, MS, PhD); chemical reaction engineering (M Eng, MS, PhD); classical and statistical thermodynamics (M Eng, MS, PhD); fluid dynamics, rheology and biorheology (M Eng, MS, PhD); heat and mass transfer (M Eng, MS, PhD); kinetics and catalysis (M Eng, MS, PhD); polymers (M Eng, MS, PhD). Surface science (M Eng, MS, PhD).

Faculty: 18 full-time.
Students: 81 full-time (20 women); includes 12 minority (9 Asian Americans or Pacific Islanders, 3 Hispanic Americans), 44 international. 151 applicants, 50% accepted. In 2001, 17 master's, 6 doctorates awarded.
Degree requirements: For master's, thesis (MS); for doctorate, thesis/dissertation.
Entrance requirements: For master's and doctorate, GRE General Test, TOEFL, pre-application, 2 letters of recommendation. *Application deadline:* For fall admission, 1/15. *Application fee:* $65. Electronic applications accepted.
Expenses: Tuition: Full-time $25,970. Required fees: $50.
Financial support: In 2001–02, 64 students received support, including 19 fellowships with full tuition reimbursements available, 33 research assistantships with full tuition reimbursements available, 12 teaching assistantships with full tuition reimbursements available; institutionally sponsored loans, scholarships/grants, tuition waivers (full and partial), and unspecified assistantships also available. Financial award applicants required to submit FAFSA.
Faculty research: Biochemical and biomedical engineering, fluid dynamics, stability and rheology, surface science, kinetics and reactor design, electronics materials design and processing, polymer science and engineering.
Application contact: Graduate Field Assistant, 607-255-4550, *E-mail:* dgs@cheme.cornell.edu. *Web site:* http://www.gradschool.cornell.edu/grad/fields_1/chem-engr.html

■ DARTMOUTH COLLEGE

Thayer School of Engineering, Program in Biotechnology and Biochemical Engineering, Hanover, NH 03755

AWARDS MS, PhD.

Degree requirements: For master's, thesis; for doctorate, thesis/dissertation, candidacy oral exam.

Entrance requirements: For master's and doctorate, GRE General Test. *Application deadline:* For fall admission, 1/1 (priority date). *Application fee:* $40 ($50 for international students).
Expenses: Tuition: Full-time $26,425.
Financial support: Fellowships, research assistantships, teaching assistantships, career-related internships or fieldwork, Federal Work-Study, institutionally sponsored loans, and tuition waivers (full and partial) available. Financial award application deadline: 1/15.
Faculty research: Biomass processing, metabolic engineering, bioplastic synthesis, kinetics and reactor design, applied microbiology. *Total annual research expenditures:* $200,000.
Application contact: Candace S. Potter, Graduate Admissions Administrator, 603-646-3844, *Fax:* 603-646-1620, *E-mail:* candace.potter@dartmouth.edu. *Web site:* http://engineering.dartmouth.edu/

■ DREXEL UNIVERSITY

Graduate School, College of Engineering, Department of Chemical Engineering, Program in Biochemical Engineering, Philadelphia, PA 19104-2875

AWARDS MS. Part-time and evening/weekend programs available.

Faculty: 14 full-time (1 woman).
Students: Average age 35. 8 applicants, 25% accepted, 0 enrolled. In 2001, 3 degrees awarded.
Degree requirements: For master's, thesis.
Entrance requirements: For master's, TOEFL, minimum GPA of 3.0 in chemical engineering or biological sciences. *Application deadline:* For fall admission, 8/21. Applications are processed on a rolling basis. *Application fee:* $50. Electronic applications accepted.
Expenses: Tuition: Full-time $20,088; part-time $558 per credit. Required fees: $78 per term. One-time fee: $200. Tuition and fees vary according to course load, degree level and program.
Financial support: Research assistantships, teaching assistantships, career-related internships or fieldwork, Federal Work-Study, tuition waivers (full and partial), and unspecified assistantships available. Financial award application deadline: 2/1.
Faculty research: Monitoring and control of bioreactors, sensors for bioreactors, large-scale production of monoclonal antibodies.
Dr. Rajakkannu Mutharasan, Director, 215-895-2236.
Application contact: Director of Graduate Admissions, 215-895-6700, *Fax:* 215-895-5939, *E-mail:* enroll@drexel.edu.

■ RUTGERS, THE STATE UNIVERSITY OF NEW JERSEY, NEW BRUNSWICK

Graduate School, Program in Chemical and Biochemical Engineering, New Brunswick, NJ 08901-1281

AWARDS MS, PhD. Part-time and evening/weekend programs available. Terminal master's awarded for partial completion of doctoral program.

Degree requirements: For master's, thesis or alternative; for doctorate, thesis/dissertation.
Entrance requirements: For master's, GRE General Test, TOEFL; for doctorate, GRE General Test.
Faculty research: Biotechnology, environmental engineering, statistical thermodynamics, polymers, pharmaceutical engineering. *Web site:* http://sol.rutgers.edu/

■ UNIVERSITY OF CALIFORNIA, IRVINE

Office of Research and Graduate Studies, School of Engineering, Department of Chemical and Biochemical Engineering and Materials Science, Irvine, CA 92697

AWARDS Biomedical engineering (MS, PhD); chemical and biochemical engineering (MS, PhD). Part-time programs available.

Faculty: 12.
Students: 54 full-time (14 women), 1 part-time; includes 14 minority (1 African American, 12 Asian Americans or Pacific Islanders, 1 Hispanic American), 23 international. 133 applicants, 37% accepted, 24 enrolled. In 2001, 5 master's, 4 doctorates awarded. Terminal master's awarded for partial completion of doctoral program.
Degree requirements: For doctorate, thesis/dissertation.
Entrance requirements: For master's, GRE General Test, minimum GPA of 3.0; for doctorate, GRE General Test. *Application deadline:* For fall and spring admission, 1/15 (priority date); for winter admission, 10/15 (priority date). Applications are processed on a rolling basis. *Application fee:* $60. Electronic applications accepted.
Expenses: Tuition, nonresident: full-time $10,704. Required fees: $8,396. Tuition and fees vary according to course load, program and student level.
Financial support: In 2001–02, 10 fellowships with tuition reimbursements (averaging $1,250 per year), research assistantships with tuition reimbursements (averaging $1,120 per year), 7 teaching assistantships with tuition reimbursements (averaging $1,480 per year) were awarded. Institutionally sponsored loans also available. Financial award application deadline:

University of California, Irvine (continued)
3/2; financial award applicants required to submit FAFSA.
Faculty research: Bioreactors, recombinant cells, separation operations. *Total annual research expenditures:* $2.2 million.
Dr. Enrique J. Lavernia, Chair, 949-824-8277, *Fax:* 949-824-2541, *E-mail:* lavernia@uci.edu.
Application contact: Nancy Carter-Fields, Graduate Coordinator, 949-824-9250, *Fax:* 949-824-2541, *E-mail:* nvcarter@uci.edu. *Web site:* http://www.eng.uci.edu/cbe/
Find an in-depth description at www.petersons.com/gradchannel.

■ **THE UNIVERSITY OF IOWA**
Graduate College, College of Engineering, Department of Chemical and Biochemical Engineering, Iowa City, IA 52242-1316
AWARDS MS, PhD. Part-time programs available.
Faculty: 9 full-time (2 women), 4 part-time/adjunct (0 women).
Students: 21 full-time (7 women), 19 part-time (7 women); includes 3 minority (1 African American, 1 Asian American or Pacific Islander, 1 Hispanic American), 25 international. Average age 27. 93 applicants, 27% accepted, 9 enrolled. In 2001, 5 master's, 2 doctorates awarded.
Degree requirements: For master's, thesis (for some programs), comprehensive exam (for some programs), registration; for doctorate, thesis/dissertation, comprehensive exam, registration.
Entrance requirements: For master's and doctorate, GRE, TOEFL, minimum undergraduate GPA of 3.0. *Application deadline:* For fall admission, 2/1 (priority date); for spring admission, 10/1 (priority date). Applications are processed on a rolling basis. *Application fee:* $30 ($50 for international students). Electronic applications accepted.
Expenses: Tuition, state resident: full-time $3,702; part-time $206 per semester hour. Tuition, nonresident: full-time $11,924; part-time $206 per semester hour. Required fees: $101 per semester. Tuition and fees vary according to course load and program.
Financial support: In 2001–02, 34 students received support, including 6 fellowships (averaging $20,000 per year), 33 research assistantships with tuition reimbursements available (averaging $20,000 per year), 9 teaching assistantships (averaging $20,000 per year); health care benefits and unspecified assistantships also available. Financial award applicants required to submit FAFSA.
Faculty research: Photopolymerization, regional atmospheric modeling, biomaterials, medical engineering, cellular engineering. *Total annual research expenditures:* $3.1 million.

Dr. Alec Scranton, Departmental Executive Officer, 319-335-1414, *Fax:* 319-335-1415, *E-mail:* alec-scranton@uiowa.edu.
Application contact: Linda Wheatley, Secretary, 319-335-1400, *Fax:* 319-335-1415, *E-mail:* chemeng@engineering.uiowa.edu. *Web site:* http://www.cbe.engineering.uiowa.edu

■ **UNIVERSITY OF MARYLAND, BALTIMORE COUNTY**
Graduate School, College of Engineering, Department of Chemical and Biochemical Engineering, Baltimore, MD 21250-5398
AWARDS MS, PhD.
Entrance requirements: For master's, GRE General Test, minimum GPA of 3.0; for doctorate, GRE General Test, GRE Subject Test, TOEFL, minimum GPA of 3.0.
Faculty research: Bioengineering, mammalian cell culture, protein purification, adsorptive separation.
Find an in-depth description at www.petersons.com/gradchannel.

CHEMICAL ENGINEERING

■ **ARIZONA STATE UNIVERSITY**
Graduate College, College of Engineering and Applied Sciences, Department of Chemical, Bio and Materials Engineering, Program in Chemical Engineering, Tempe, AZ 85287
AWARDS MS, MSE, PhD.
Degree requirements: For doctorate, thesis/dissertation.
Entrance requirements: For master's and doctorate, GRE General Test.
Faculty research: Biomedical and clinical engineering, chemical process engineering, energy and materials conversion, environmental control.
Find an in-depth description at www.petersons.com/gradchannel.

■ **AUBURN UNIVERSITY**
Graduate School, College of Engineering, Department of Chemical Engineering, Auburn University, AL 36849
AWARDS M Ch E, MS, PhD. Part-time programs available.
Faculty: 14 full-time (0 women).
Students: 39 full-time (6 women), 6 part-time (1 woman); includes 6 minority (4 African Americans, 1 Asian American or Pacific Islander, 1 Hispanic American), 21 international. 113 applicants, 21%

accepted. In 2001, 15 master's, 5 doctorates awarded.
Degree requirements: For master's, thesis (for some programs); for doctorate, thesis/dissertation, comprehensive exam.
Entrance requirements: For master's and doctorate, GRE General Test. *Application deadline:* For fall admission, 7/7; for spring admission, 11/24. Applications are processed on a rolling basis. *Application fee:* $25 ($50 for international students). Electronic applications accepted.
Financial support: Fellowships, research assistantships, teaching assistantships, Federal Work-Study available. Support available to part-time students. Financial award application deadline: 3/15.
Faculty research: Coal liquefaction, asphalt research, pulp and paper engineering, surface science, biochemical engineering, microfibrous materials manufacturing. Dr. Robert P. Chambers, Head, 334-844-4827.
Application contact: Dr. John F. Pritchett, Dean of the Graduate School, 334-844-4700, *E-mail:* hatchlb@mail.auburn.edu. *Web site:* http://www.eng.auburn.edu/department/che/

■ **BRIGHAM YOUNG UNIVERSITY**
Graduate Studies, College of Engineering and Technology, Department of Chemical Engineering, Provo, UT 84602-1001
AWARDS Chemical (PhD); chemical engineering (MS).
Faculty: 13 full-time (0 women), 2 part-time/adjunct (0 women).
Students: 33 full-time (3 women); includes 1 minority (Hispanic American), 15 international. Average age 25. 40 applicants, 23% accepted, 7 enrolled. In 2001, 3 master's, 7 doctorates awarded.
Degree requirements: For master's and doctorate, thesis/dissertation. *Median time to degree:* Master's–1.5 years full-time; doctorate–4.5 years full-time.
Entrance requirements: For master's, minimum GPA of 3.0 in upper-division course work in major; for doctorate, minimum GPA of 3.3. *Application deadline:* For fall admission, 2/15. *Application fee:* $50. Electronic applications accepted.
Expenses: Tuition: Full-time $3,860; part-time $214 per hour.
Financial support: In 2001–02, 2 fellowships (averaging $18,000 per year), 30 research assistantships (averaging $18,290 per year), 3 teaching assistantships (averaging $4,052 per year) were awarded. Career-related internships or fieldwork, institutionally sponsored loans, and scholarships/grants also available. Financial award application deadline: 3/15.
Faculty research: Biomedical engineering, materials science, computer simulation, oil reservoir simulation, electrochemical engineering. *Total annual research expenditures:* $3.3 million.

Dr. W. Vincent Wilding, Chair, 801-422-2586, *Fax:* 801-422-7799, *E-mail:* cheme@byu.edu.
Application contact: Thomas H. Fletcher, Graduate Coordinator, 801-422-6236, *Fax:* 801-422-7799, *E-mail:* tom_fletcher@byu.edu. *Web site:* http://www.et.byu.edu/cheme/

■ BROWN UNIVERSITY

Graduate School, Division of Engineering, Program in Fluid Mechanics, Thermodynamics, and Chemical Processes, Providence, RI 02912

AWARDS Sc M, PhD.

Degree requirements: For doctorate, thesis/dissertation, preliminary exam.

■ BUCKNELL UNIVERSITY

Graduate Studies, College of Engineering, Department of Chemical Engineering, Lewisburg, PA 17837

AWARDS MS, MS Ch E. Part-time programs available.

Faculty: 10 full-time (1 woman).
Students: 3 full-time (1 woman), 2 international.
Degree requirements: For master's, thesis.
Entrance requirements: For master's, GRE General Test, GRE Subject Test, TOEFL, minimum GPA of 2.8. *Application deadline:* For fall admission, 6/1 (priority date); for spring admission, 12/1 (priority date). Applications are processed on a rolling basis. *Application fee:* $25.
Expenses: Tuition: Part-time $2,875 per course.
Financial support: In 2001–02, 3 students received support; research assistantships, teaching assistantships, unspecified assistantships available. Financial award application deadline: 3/1.
Faculty research: Computer-aided design, software engineering, applied mathematics and modeling, polymer science, digital process control.
Dr. Michael Hanyak, Chairman, 570-577-1114. *Web site:* http://www.bucknell.edu/

■ CALIFORNIA INSTITUTE OF TECHNOLOGY

Division of Chemistry and Chemical Engineering, Program in Chemical Engineering, Pasadena, CA 91125-0001

AWARDS MS, PhD.

Faculty: 10 full-time (2 women).
Students: 59 full-time (14 women). Average age 24. 183 applicants, 9% accepted, 16 enrolled. In 2001, 8 master's, 8 doctorates awarded. Terminal master's awarded for partial completion of doctoral program.
Degree requirements: For master's and doctorate, thesis/dissertation.

Application deadline: For fall admission, 1/15. *Application fee:* $0. Electronic applications accepted.
Financial support: In 2001–02, 59 students received support, including 37 fellowships, 35 research assistantships, 15 teaching assistantships; Federal Work-Study, institutionally sponsored loans, scholarships/grants, traineeships, health care benefits, and unspecified assistantships also available. Financial award application deadline: 1/15.
Faculty research: Chemical reaction engineering, transport phenomena, biochemical engineering, catalysis, ceramics and electronic materials.
Dr. Mark E. Davis, Executive Officer, 626-395-4251, *E-mail:* mdavis@cheme.caltech.edu.
Application contact: Kathy J. Bubash, Graduate Secretary, 626-395-4193, *Fax:* 626-568-8743, *E-mail:* kathy@cheme.caltech.edu. *Web site:* http://www.che.caltech.edu/

■ CARNEGIE MELLON UNIVERSITY

Carnegie Institute of Technology, Department of Chemical Engineering, Pittsburgh, PA 15213-3891

AWARDS Chemical engineering (M Ch E, MS, PhD); colloids, polymers and surfaces (MS). Part-time and evening/weekend programs available. Terminal master's awarded for partial completion of doctoral program.

Degree requirements: For doctorate, thesis/dissertation, qualifying exam.
Entrance requirements: For master's and doctorate, GRE General Test, GRE Subject Test, TOEFL.
Faculty research: Computer-aided design in process engineering, biomedical engineering, biotechnology, complex fluids. *Web site:* http://www.cheme.cmu.edu/

■ CASE WESTERN RESERVE UNIVERSITY

School of Graduate Studies, The Case School of Engineering, Department of Chemical Engineering, Cleveland, OH 44106

AWARDS MS, PhD. Part-time and evening/weekend programs available. Postbaccalaureate distance learning degree programs offered.

Faculty: 12 full-time (0 women), 10 part-time/adjunct (1 woman).
Students: 20 full-time (4 women), 16 part-time (4 women); includes 4 minority (all Asian Americans or Pacific Islanders), 15 international. Average age 25. 131 applicants, 17% accepted, 6 enrolled. In 2001, 7 master's, 2 doctorates awarded. Terminal master's awarded for partial completion of doctoral program.
Degree requirements: For master's, thesis (for some programs); for doctorate,

thesis/dissertation, qualifying exam, research proposal, teaching experience.
Entrance requirements: For master's, TOEFL; for doctorate, GRE, TOEFL. *Application deadline:* For fall admission, 2/15 (priority date); for spring admission, 11/1. Applications are processed on a rolling basis. *Application fee:* $25.
Financial support: In 2001–02, 8 fellowships with full and partial tuition reimbursements (averaging $18,600 per year), 17 research assistantships with full and partial tuition reimbursements (averaging $18,600 per year), 5 teaching assistantships (averaging $18,600 per year) were awarded. Federal Work-Study and institutionally sponsored loans also available. Financial award application deadline: 3/1; financial award applicants required to submit FAFSA.
Faculty research: Engineering aspects of materials and materials processing; electrochemical engineering and power generation; electrochemical sensors and advanced electroplating. Surfaces and collars; chemical process engineering, control and intensification. *Total annual research expenditures:* $2.1 million.
John C. Angus, Interim Co-Chair, 216-368-4182, *Fax:* 216-368-3016, *E-mail:* nxg3@po.cwru.edu.
Application contact: Kathleen Bates, Business Manager, 216-368-3840, *Fax:* 216-368-3016, *E-mail:* kmb4@po.cwru.edu. *Web site:* http://cheme.cwru.edu

■ CITY COLLEGE OF THE CITY UNIVERSITY OF NEW YORK

Graduate School, School of Engineering, Department of Chemical Engineering, New York, NY 10031-9198

AWARDS ME, MS, PhD. Part-time programs available.

Students: 11. In 2001, 7 degrees awarded.
Degree requirements: For master's, thesis optional; for doctorate, one foreign language, thesis/dissertation, comprehensive exam.
Entrance requirements: For master's, TOEFL; for doctorate, GRE General Test, TOEFL. *Application deadline:* Applications are processed on a rolling basis. *Application fee:* $40.
Expenses: Tuition, state resident: part-time $185 per credit. Tuition, nonresident: part-time $320 per credit. Required fees: $43 per term.
Financial support: Fellowships, research assistantships available.
Faculty research: Theoretical turbulences, bio-fluid dynamics, polymers, fluidization, transport phenomena.
Robert Graff, Chairman, 212-690-8136.
Application contact: Graduate Admissions Office, 212-650-6977.

■ CLARKSON UNIVERSITY

Graduate School, School of Engineering, Department of Chemical Engineering, Potsdam, NY 13699
AWARDS ME, MS, PhD. Part-time programs available.

Faculty: 11 full-time (2 women), 1 part-time/adjunct (0 women).
Students: 34 full-time (7 women), 1 part-time, 28 international. Average age 26. 109 applicants, 35% accepted. In 2001, 5 master's, 7 doctorates awarded.
Degree requirements: For master's, thesis; for doctorate, thesis/dissertation, departmental qualifying exam. *Median time to degree:* Master's–2 years full-time; doctorate–4 years full-time.
Entrance requirements: For master's, GRE, TOEFL. *Application deadline:* For fall admission, 5/15 (priority date); for spring admission, 10/15 (priority date). Applications are processed on a rolling basis. *Application fee:* $25 ($35 for international students).
Expenses: Tuition: Part-time $714 per credit. Required fees: $108 per semester.
Financial support: In 2001–02, 26 students received support, including 2 fellowships (averaging $20,000 per year), 18 research assistantships (averaging $17,000 per year), 6 teaching assistantships (averaging $17,000 per year). Scholarships/grants and tuition waivers (partial) also available.
Faculty research: Separation techniques, fluid mechanics, computational thermodynamics, corrosion, surface studies, electronic manufacturing. *Total annual research expenditures:* $1.5 million.
Dr. Ross Taylor, Chairman, 315-268-6652, *Fax:* 315-268-6654, *E-mail:* taylor@clarkson.edu.
Application contact: Donna Brockway, Assistant to Dean/Foreign Student Advisor, 315-268-6447, *Fax:* 315-268-7994, *E-mail:* brockway@clarkson.edu.

■ CLEMSON UNIVERSITY

Graduate School, College of Engineering and Science, Department of Chemical Engineering, Clemson, SC 29634
AWARDS MS, PhD.

Students: 32 full-time (10 women), 3 part-time (1 woman), 20 international. Average age 25. 127 applicants, 13% accepted, 6 enrolled. In 2001, 5 master's, 2 doctorates awarded.
Degree requirements: For master's and doctorate, thesis/dissertation.
Entrance requirements: For master's and doctorate, GRE General Test, TOEFL. *Application deadline:* For fall admission, 6/1. *Application fee:* $40.
Expenses: Tuition, state resident: full-time $5,310. Tuition, nonresident: full-time $11,284.
Financial support: Fellowships, research assistantships, teaching assistantships, career-related internships or fieldwork

available. Financial award applicants required to submit FAFSA.
Faculty research: Polymer processing, catalysis, process automation, thermodynamics, separation processes. *Total annual research expenditures:* $800,000.
Dr. Charles H. Gooding, Chair, 864-656-3055, *Fax:* 864-656-0784, *E-mail:* chgdng@clemson.edu.
Application contact: Dr. A. A. Ogale, Graduate Coordinator, 864-656-5483, *Fax:* 864-656-0784, *E-mail:* ogale@clemson.edu. *Web site:* http://www.ces.clemson.edu/chemeng/pages/gsadmis.htm

■ CLEVELAND STATE UNIVERSITY

College of Graduate Studies, Fenn College of Engineering, Department of Chemical Engineering, Cleveland, OH 44115
AWARDS MS, D Eng. Part-time programs available.

Degree requirements: For master's, project or thesis; for doctorate, thesis/dissertation, candidacy and qualifying exams.
Entrance requirements: For master's, GRE General Test, GRE Subject Test, TOEFL, minimum GPA of 2.75; for doctorate, GRE General Test, GRE Subject Test, TOEFL, minimum GPA of 3.25.
Expenses: Tuition, state resident: full-time $6,838; part-time $263 per credit hour. Tuition, nonresident: full-time $13,526; part-time $520 per credit hour.
Faculty research: Heterogeneous transport, absorption equilibrium and dynamics, transfer process in non-Newtonian fluids, tribology, optimization of mammalian cell culture, simulation and modeling. *Web site:* http://www.csuohio.edu/chemical-engineering

■ COLORADO SCHOOL OF MINES

Graduate School, Department of Chemical Engineering, Golden, CO 80401-1887
AWARDS MS, PhD. Part-time programs available.

Faculty: 24 full-time (3 women), 4 part-time/adjunct (0 women).
Students: 34 full-time (12 women), 11 part-time (2 women), 23 international. 75 applicants, 47% accepted, 11 enrolled. In 2001, 6 master's, 7 doctorates awarded.
Degree requirements: For master's, thesis (for some programs); for doctorate, thesis/dissertation, comprehensive exam. *Median time to degree:* Master's–2 years full-time; doctorate–4 years full-time.
Entrance requirements: For master's and doctorate, GRE General Test. *Application deadline:* For fall admission, 12/1 (priority date); for spring admission, 5/1 (priority

date). Applications are processed on a rolling basis. *Application fee:* $40. Electronic applications accepted.
Expenses: Tuition, state resident: full-time $4,940; part-time $246 per credit. Tuition, nonresident: full-time $16,070; part-time $803 per credit. Required fees: $341 per semester.
Financial support: In 2001–02, 18 fellowships (averaging $3,537 per year), 52 research assistantships (averaging $5,480 per year), 20 teaching assistantships (averaging $5,522 per year) were awarded. Unspecified assistantships also available. Support available to part-time students. Financial award applicants required to submit FAFSA.
Faculty research: Liquid fuels for the future, responsible management of hazardous substances, surface and interfacial engineering, advanced computational methods and process control, gas hydrates. *Total annual research expenditures:* $1 million.
Dr. James F. Ely, Head, 303-273-3885, *E-mail:* jely@mines.edu.
Application contact: Anthony M. Dean, Professor, 303-273-3643, *Fax:* 303-273-3730, *E-mail:* amdean@mines.edu. *Web site:* http://www.mines.edu/academic/chemeng/

■ COLORADO STATE UNIVERSITY

Graduate School, College of Engineering, Department of Chemical Engineering, Program in Chemical Engineering, Fort Collins, CO 80523-0015
AWARDS MS, PhD. Part-time programs available.

Faculty: 9 full-time (1 woman).
Students: 15 full-time (4 women), 18 part-time (5 women); includes 3 minority (1 African American, 1 Asian American or Pacific Islander, 1 Hispanic American), 13 international. Average age 28. 110 applicants, 16% accepted, 10 enrolled. In 2001, 4 degrees awarded. Terminal master's awarded for partial completion of doctoral program.
Degree requirements: For master's, thesis or alternative; for doctorate, thesis/dissertation.
Entrance requirements: For master's and doctorate, GRE General Test, TOEFL, minimum GPA of 3.0. *Application deadline:* For fall admission, 2/1 (priority date). Applications are processed on a rolling basis. *Application fee:* $30. Electronic applications accepted.
Expenses: Tuition, state resident: full-time $2,880; part-time $160 per credit. Tuition, nonresident: full-time $11,412; part-time $634 per credit. Required fees: $750; $34 per credit.
Financial support: In 2001–02, 2 fellowships (averaging $19,200 per year), 14 research assistantships (averaging $19,200 per year), 4 teaching assistantships (averaging $19,200 per year) were awarded.

Career-related internships or fieldwork, Federal Work-Study, and institutionally sponsored loans also available.
Faculty research: Heat and mass transfer, semiconductor materials, biochemical engineering, advanced materials, environmental engineering.
Dr. A. Ted Watson, Professor and Department Head, 970-491-5252, *Fax:* 970-491-7369, *E-mail:* atw@engr.colostate.edu.

■ COLUMBIA UNIVERSITY

Fu Foundation School of Engineering and Applied Science, Department of Chemical Engineering, New York, NY 10027

AWARDS MS, Eng Sc D, PhD, Engr. PhD offered through the Graduate School of Arts and Sciences. Part-time programs available.

Faculty: 11 full-time, 7 part-time/adjunct (1 woman).
Students: 18 full-time (5 women), 10 part-time (3 women); includes 3 minority (2 Asian Americans or Pacific Islanders, 1 Hispanic American), 13 international. 163 applicants, 15% accepted, 10 enrolled. In 2001, 7 master's, 4 doctorates awarded.
Degree requirements: For master's, thesis; for doctorate, thesis/dissertation, qualifying exam.
Entrance requirements: For master's, doctorate, and Engr, GRE General Test, TOEFL. *Application deadline:* For fall admission, 1/5; for spring admission, 10/1. *Application fee:* $55. Electronic applications accepted.
Expenses: Tuition: Full-time $27,528. Required fees: $1,638.
Financial support: In 2001–02, 1 fellowship with full tuition reimbursement (averaging $18,500 per year), 10 research assistantships with tuition reimbursements (averaging $18,500 per year), 7 teaching assistantships with tuition reimbursements (averaging $18,500 per year) were awarded. Federal Work-Study also available. Financial award application deadline: 1/5; financial award applicants required to submit FAFSA.
Faculty research: Electrochemistry, synthetic membrane applications, chemical process analysis, applied polymer physics. *Total annual research expenditures:* $2.6 million.
Dr. Jeffrey T. Koberstein, Head, 212-854-4453, *Fax:* 212-854-3054, *E-mail:* jk1191@columbia.edu.
Application contact: Teresa Colaizzo, Departmental Administrator, 212-854-4453, *Fax:* 212-854-3054, *E-mail:* tc16@columbia.edu. *Web site:* http://www.seas.columbia.edu/columbia/departments/chemical_engineering/

■ CORNELL UNIVERSITY

Graduate School, Graduate Fields of Engineering, Field of Chemical Engineering, Ithaca, NY 14853-0001

AWARDS Advanced materials processing (M Eng, MS, PhD); applied mathematics and computational methods (M Eng, MS, PhD); biochemical engineering (M Eng, MS, PhD); chemical reaction engineering (M Eng, MS, PhD); classical and statistical thermodynamics (M Eng, MS, PhD); fluid dynamics, rheology and biorheology (M Eng, MS, PhD); heat and mass transfer (M Eng, MS, PhD); kinetics and catalysis (M Eng, MS, PhD); polymers (M Eng, MS, PhD). Surface science (M Eng, MS, PhD).

Faculty: 18 full-time.
Students: 81 full-time (20 women); includes 12 minority (9 Asian Americans or Pacific Islanders, 3 Hispanic Americans), 44 international. 151 applicants, 50% accepted. In 2001, 17 master's, 6 doctorates awarded.
Degree requirements: For master's, thesis (MS); for doctorate, thesis/dissertation.
Entrance requirements: For master's and doctorate, GRE General Test, TOEFL, pre-application, 2 letters of recommendation. *Application deadline:* For fall admission, 1/15. *Application fee:* $65. Electronic applications accepted.
Expenses: Tuition: Full-time $25,970. Required fees: $50.
Financial support: In 2001–02, 64 students received support, including 19 fellowships with full tuition reimbursements available, 33 research assistantships with full tuition reimbursements available, 12 teaching assistantships with full tuition reimbursements available; institutionally sponsored loans, scholarships/grants, tuition waivers (full and partial), and unspecified assistantships also available. Financial award applicants required to submit FAFSA.
Faculty research: Biochemical and biomedical engineering, fluid dynamics, stability and rheology, surface science, kinetics and reactor design, electronics materials design and processing, polymer science and engineering.
Application contact: Graduate Field Assistant, 607-255-4550, *E-mail:* dgs@cheme.cornell.edu. *Web site:* http://www.gradschool.cornell.edu/grad/fields_1/chem-engr.html

■ DREXEL UNIVERSITY

Graduate School, College of Engineering, Department of Chemical Engineering, Program in Chemical Engineering, Philadelphia, PA 19104-2875

AWARDS MS, PhD.

Faculty: 14 full-time (1 woman).
Students: 12 full-time (3 women), 28 part-time (6 women); includes 3 minority (1

African American, 2 Asian Americans or Pacific Islanders), 23 international. Average age 26. In 2001, 4 master's, 2 doctorates awarded.
Degree requirements: For doctorate, thesis/dissertation.
Entrance requirements: For master's, TOEFL, minimum GPA of 3.0; for doctorate, TOEFL, minimum GPA of 3.5, MS in chemical engineering. *Application deadline:* For fall admission, 8/21. Applications are processed on a rolling basis. *Application fee:* $50. Electronic applications accepted.
Expenses: Tuition: Full-time $20,088; part-time $558 per credit. Required fees: $78 per term. One-time fee: $200. Tuition and fees vary according to course load, degree level and program.
Financial support: Research assistantships, teaching assistantships, unspecified assistantships available. Financial award application deadline: 2/1.
Application contact: Director of Graduate Admissions, 215-895-6700, *Fax:* 215-895-5939, *E-mail:* enroll@drexel.edu.

■ FLORIDA AGRICULTURAL AND MECHANICAL UNIVERSITY

Division of Graduate Studies, Research, and Continuing Education, FAMU-FSU College of Engineering, Department of Chemical Engineering, Tallahassee, FL 32310-6046

AWARDS MS, PhD.

Entrance requirements: For master's, GRE General Test, minimum GPA of 3.0.
Expenses: Contact institution.
Faculty research: Macromolecular transport, polymer processing, biochemical engineering, process control, environmental engineering.

■ FLORIDA INSTITUTE OF TECHNOLOGY

Graduate Programs, College of Engineering, Chemical Engineering Department, Melbourne, FL 32901-6975

AWARDS MS, PhD. Part-time programs available.

Faculty: 5 full-time (1 woman), 1 part-time/adjunct (0 women).
Students: 5 full-time (1 woman), 4 part-time (3 women); includes 1 minority (Hispanic American), 5 international. Average age 25. 54 applicants, 61% accepted. In 2001, 5 degrees awarded. Terminal master's awarded for partial completion of doctoral program.
Degree requirements: For master's and doctorate, thesis/dissertation.
Entrance requirements: For master's, TOEFL, minimum GPA of 3.0; for doctorate, GRE General Test, GRE Subject Test, minimum GPA of 3.5, resumé. *Application deadline:* Applications

Florida Institute of Technology (continued) are processed on a rolling basis. *Application fee:* $50. Electronic applications accepted.
Expenses: Tuition: Part-time $650 per credit.
Financial support: In 2001–02, 3 students received support, including 3 teaching assistantships with full and partial tuition reimbursements available (averaging $6,361 per year); research assistantships with full and partial tuition reimbursements available, career-related internships or fieldwork and tuition remissions also available. Financial award application deadline: 3/1; financial award applicants required to submit FAFSA.
Faculty research: Space technology, biotechnology, materials synthesis and processing, supercritical fluids, water treatment, process control. *Total annual research expenditures:* $22,000.
Dr. Paul A. Jennings, Chair, 321-674-8068, *Fax:* 321-674-7565, *E-mail:* jennings@fit.edu.
Application contact: Carolyn P. Farrior, Director of Graduate Admissions, 321-674-7118, *Fax:* 321-723-9468, *E-mail:* cfarrior@fit.edu. *Web site:* http://www.fit.edu/

■ FLORIDA STATE UNIVERSITY

Graduate Studies, FAMU/FSU College of Engineering, Department of Chemical Engineering, Tallahassee, FL 32310-6046

AWARDS MS, PhD. Part-time programs available.

Degree requirements: For master's, thesis; for doctorate, thesis/dissertation, preliminary exam, qualifying exam.
Entrance requirements: For master's, GRE General Test, BS in chemical engineering, minimum GPA of 3.3; for doctorate, GRE General Test.
Expenses: Contact institution.
Faculty research: Macromolecular transport, polymer processing, biochemical engineering, process control, environmental engineering, thermodynamics. *Web site:* http://www.eng.fsu.edu/home_pages/vinals/cheme.html/

■ GEORGIA INSTITUTE OF TECHNOLOGY

Graduate Studies and Research, College of Engineering, School of Chemical Engineering, Atlanta, GA 30332-0001

AWARDS Biomedical engineering (MS Bio E); chemical engineering (MS Ch E, PhD); polymers (MS Poly); pulp and paper engineering (Certificate).

Degree requirements: For master's and doctorate, thesis/dissertation.
Entrance requirements: For master's and doctorate, GRE, TOEFL, minimum GPA of 2.7. Electronic applications accepted.

Faculty research: Biochemical engineering; process modeling, synthesis, and control; polymer science and engineering; thermodynamics and separations. Surface and particle science.

■ GRADUATE SCHOOL AND UNIVERSITY CENTER OF THE CITY UNIVERSITY OF NEW YORK

Graduate Studies, Program in Engineering, New York, NY 10016-4039

AWARDS Chemical engineering (PhD); civil engineering (PhD); electrical engineering (PhD); mechanical engineering (PhD).

Faculty: 68 full-time (1 woman).
Students: 125 full-time (28 women), 6 part-time (1 woman); includes 13 minority (9 African Americans, 2 Asian Americans or Pacific Islanders, 2 Hispanic Americans), 95 international. Average age 32. 205 applicants, 63% accepted, 26 enrolled. In 2001, 22 degrees awarded.
Degree requirements: For doctorate, thesis/dissertation.
Entrance requirements: For doctorate, GRE General Test. *Application deadline:* For fall admission, 4/15. *Application fee:* $40.
Expenses: Tuition, state resident: part-time $245 per credit. Tuition, nonresident: part-time $425 per credit. Required fees: $72 per semester.
Financial support: In 2001–02, 67 students received support, including 64 fellowships; research assistantships, teaching assistantships, Federal Work-Study, institutionally sponsored loans, and tuition waivers (full and partial) also available. Financial award application deadline: 2/1; financial award applicants required to submit FAFSA.
Dr. Mumtaz Kassir, Acting Executive Officer, 212-650-8031, *Fax:* 212-650-8029, *E-mail:* kassir@ce-mail.engr.ccny.cuny.edu.

Find an in-depth description at www.petersons.com/gradchannel.

■ HOWARD UNIVERSITY

College of Engineering, Architecture, and Computer Sciences, School of Engineering and Computer Science, Department of Chemical Engineering, Washington, DC 20059-0002

AWARDS MS. Offered through the Graduate School of Arts and Sciences. Part-time programs available.

Students: Average age 25.
Degree requirements: For master's, thesis.
Entrance requirements: For master's, GRE General Test, TOEFL, minimum GPA of 3.0. *Application deadline:* For fall admission, 4/1; for spring admission, 11/1. Applications are processed on a rolling basis.

Financial support: In 2001–02, 1 teaching assistantship with full tuition reimbursement was awarded; research assistantships with full tuition reimbursements, tuition waivers (partial) also available.
Faculty research: Bioengineering, computational fluid mechanics, process control, reaction kinetics, reactor modeling.
Dr. Mobolaji E. Aluko, Chair, 202-806-6624, *Fax:* 202-806-4635, *E-mail:* maluko@scs.howard.edu. *Web site:* http://www.howard.edu/

■ ILLINOIS INSTITUTE OF TECHNOLOGY

Graduate College, Armour College of Engineering and Sciences, Department of Chemical and Environmental Engineering, Chemical Engineering Division, Chicago, IL 60616-3793

AWARDS M Ch E, MS, PhD. Part-time and evening/weekend programs available.

Faculty: 12 full-time (0 women), 5 part-time/adjunct (0 women).
Students: 75 full-time (15 women), 49 part-time (8 women); includes 9 minority (3 African Americans, 5 Asian Americans or Pacific Islanders, 1 Hispanic American), 99 international. Average age 28. 309 applicants, 61% accepted. In 2001, 23 master's, 5 doctorates awarded. Terminal master's awarded for partial completion of doctoral program.
Degree requirements: For master's, thesis (for some programs), comprehensive exam; for doctorate, thesis/dissertation, comprehensive exam.
Entrance requirements: For master's and doctorate, GRE General Test, TOEFL, minimum undergraduate GPA of 3.0. *Application deadline:* For fall admission, 7/1; for spring admission, 11/1. Applications are processed on a rolling basis. *Application fee:* $30. Electronic applications accepted.
Expenses: Tuition: Part-time $590 per credit hour.
Financial support: In 2001–02, 43 research assistantships, 13 teaching assistantships were awarded. Fellowships, Federal Work-Study, institutionally sponsored loans, and scholarships/grants also available. Support available to part-time students. Financial award application deadline: 3/1; financial award applicants required to submit FAFSA.
Faculty research: Multiphase flow, polymers, bioengineering, process control, energy conversion.
Dr. Ali Cinar, Dean of Graduate College, 312-567-3637, *Fax:* 312-567-7517, *E-mail:* gradstu@iit.edu. *Web site:* http://www.chee.iit.edu/grad/grad.htm

■ INSTITUTE OF PAPER SCIENCE AND TECHNOLOGY

Graduate Programs, Program in Chemical Engineering, Atlanta, GA 30318-5794

AWARDS MS, PhD. Part-time programs available. Terminal master's awarded for partial completion of doctoral program.

Degree requirements: For master's, industrial experience, research project; for doctorate, thesis/dissertation.

Entrance requirements: For master's and doctorate, GRE, minimum GPA of 3.0. *Web site:* http://www.ipst.edu/

■ IOWA STATE UNIVERSITY OF SCIENCE AND TECHNOLOGY

Graduate College, College of Engineering, Department of Chemical Engineering, Ames, IA 50011

AWARDS M Eng, MS, PhD.

Faculty: 16 full-time.
Students: 44 full-time (12 women), 3 part-time; includes 1 minority (Hispanic American), 22 international. 130 applicants, 18% accepted, 9 enrolled. In 2001, 3 master's, 9 doctorates awarded.
Degree requirements: For master's, thesis (for some programs); for doctorate, thesis/dissertation. *Median time to degree:* Master's–2.5 years full-time; doctorate–5 years full-time.
Entrance requirements: For master's and doctorate, GRE General Test (international applicants), TOEFL. *Application deadline:* For fall admission, 2/1 (priority date); for spring admission, 10/1. *Application fee:* $20 ($50 for international students). Electronic applications accepted.
Expenses: Tuition, state resident: full-time $1,851. Tuition, nonresident: full-time $5,449. Tuition and fees vary according to program.
Financial support: In 2001–02, 39 research assistantships with partial tuition reimbursements (averaging $15,907 per year) were awarded; teaching assistantships, scholarships/grants, health care benefits, and unspecified assistantships also available.
Dr. Charles E. Glatz, Chair, 515-294-7643, *Fax:* 515-294-2689, *E-mail:* chemengr@iastate.edu.
Application contact: Dr. Surya Mallapragada, Director of Graduate Education, 515-294-7407. *Web site:* http://www1.eng.iastate.edu/coe/grad.asp/

■ JOHNS HOPKINS UNIVERSITY

G. W. C. Whiting School of Engineering, Department of Chemical Engineering, Baltimore, MD 21218-2699

AWARDS MSE, PhD. Part-time programs available.

Faculty: 11 full-time (1 woman), 2 part-time/adjunct (0 women).
Students: 40 full-time (14 women), 1 part-time; includes 4 minority (3 Asian Americans or Pacific Islanders, 1 Hispanic American), 19 international. Average age 25. 79 applicants, 22% accepted, 14 enrolled. In 2001, 5 master's, 11 doctorates awarded.
Degree requirements: For master's, thesis; for doctorate, thesis/dissertation, oral exam.
Entrance requirements: For master's and doctorate, GRE General Test, TOEFL. *Application deadline:* For fall admission, 2/1. *Application fee:* $0. Electronic applications accepted.
Expenses: Tuition: Full-time $27,390.
Financial support: In 2001–02, 41 students received support, including 41 fellowships with full tuition reimbursements available (averaging $19,200 per year); research assistantships, teaching assistantships, Federal Work-Study, institutionally sponsored loans, unspecified assistantships, and training grants also available. Support available to part-time students. Financial award application deadline: 3/14.
Faculty research: Biotechnology, polymers and complex fluids, bioengineering, nucleation, thermodynamics and transport at surfaces. *Total annual research expenditures:* $2.4 million.
Dr. Michael Paulaitis, Chair, 410-516-7170, *Fax:* 410-516-5510, *E-mail:* michaelp@jhunix.hcf.jhu.edu.
Application contact: Lynn Johnson, Information Contact, 410-516-5455, *Fax:* 410-516-5510, *E-mail:* che@jhu.edu. *Web site:* http://www.jhu.edu/~chemel/

■ KANSAS STATE UNIVERSITY

Graduate School, College of Engineering, Department of Chemical Engineering, Manhattan, KS 66506

AWARDS MS, PhD. Postbaccalaureate distance learning degree programs offered.

Faculty: 10 full-time (0 women).
Students: 20 full-time (7 women), 6 part-time, 19 international. 83 applicants, 16% accepted, 8 enrolled. In 2001, 4 master's, 1 doctorate awarded.
Degree requirements: For master's, thesis or alternative; for doctorate, thesis/dissertation.
Entrance requirements: For master's and doctorate, GRE, TOEFL. *Application deadline:* For fall admission, 2/1 (priority date); for spring admission, 9/1 (priority date). Applications are processed on a rolling basis. *Application fee:* $0 ($25 for international students). Electronic applications accepted.
Expenses: Tuition, state resident: part-time $113 per credit hour. Tuition, nonresident: part-time $358 per credit hour.
Financial support: In 2001–02, fellowships with partial tuition reimbursements (averaging $15,000 per year), 20 research assistantships with partial tuition reimbursements (averaging $12,000 per year), teaching assistantships with partial tuition reimbursements (averaging $15,000 per year) were awarded. Institutionally sponsored loans and scholarships/grants also available. Support available to part-time students. Financial award application deadline: 3/1; financial award applicants required to submit FAFSA.
Faculty research: Transport phenomena, catalysis and reaction engineering, biochemical and environmental engineering, process systems engineering, materials science and engineering. *Total annual research expenditures:* $1.4 million.
Stevin Gehrke, Head, 785-532-5584, *Fax:* 785-532-7372, *E-mail:* chemail@ chem.ksu.edu.
Application contact: James H. Edgar, Graduate Program Director, 785-532-5584, *Fax:* 785-532-7372, *E-mail:* chemail@chem.ksu.edu. *Web site:* http://www.engg.ksu.edu/CHEDPT/home.html/

■ LAMAR UNIVERSITY

College of Graduate Studies, College of Engineering, Department of Chemical Engineering, Beaumont, TX 77710

AWARDS ME, MES, DE.

Faculty: 6 full-time (0 women), 1 part-time/adjunct (0 women).
Students: 32 full-time (2 women), 17 part-time (3 women); includes 2 minority (1 African American, 1 Asian American or Pacific Islander), 44 international. Average age 26. 120 applicants, 58% accepted. In 2001, 12 degrees awarded.
Degree requirements: For master's, thesis (for some programs); for doctorate, thesis/dissertation.
Entrance requirements: For master's and doctorate, GRE General Test, TOEFL. *Application deadline:* For fall admission, 5/15 (priority date); for spring admission, 10/1 (priority date). Applications are processed on a rolling basis. *Application fee:* $25 ($50 for international students).
Expenses: Tuition, state resident: full-time $1,114. Tuition, nonresident: full-time $3,670.
Financial support: In 2001–02, 24 students received support, including 10 fellowships with partial tuition reimbursements available, 23 research assistantships with partial tuition reimbursements available, 4 teaching assistantships with partial tuition reimbursements available; tuition waivers (full and partial) also available. Financial award application deadline: 4/1.
Faculty research: Industrial waste water treatment, air pollution, soil bioremediation, fluidization and fluidized bed, combustion, metal and sulfur emission control. *Total annual research expenditures:* $600,000.

Lamar University (continued)
Dr. Kuyen Li, Interim Chair, 409-880-8784, *Fax:* 409-880-2197, *E-mail:* che_dept@hal.lamar.edu.
Application contact: Sandy Drane, Coordinator of Graduate Admissions, 409-880-8356, *Fax:* 409-880-8414, *E-mail:* gradmissions@hal.lamar.edu. *Web site:* http://hal.lamar.edu/~che_dept/

■ LEHIGH UNIVERSITY

P.C. Rossin College of Engineering and Applied Science, Department of Chemical Engineering, Bethlehem, PA 18015-3094

AWARDS M Eng, MS, PhD. Part-time programs available. Postbaccalaureate distance learning degree programs offered (no on-campus study).

Faculty: 16 full-time (0 women).
Students: 73 full-time (11 women), 28 part-time (6 women); includes 7 minority (1 African American, 6 Asian Americans or Pacific Islanders), 59 international. Average age 25. 179 applicants, 21% accepted, 20 enrolled. In 2001, 17 master's, 9 doctorates awarded. Terminal master's awarded for partial completion of doctoral program.
Degree requirements: For doctorate, thesis/dissertation, qualifying and general exams.
Entrance requirements: For master's and doctorate, GRE General Test, TOEFL. *Application deadline:* For fall admission, 7/15; for spring admission, 12/1. Applications are processed on a rolling basis. *Application fee:* $50.
Expenses: Tuition: Part-time $468 per credit hour. Required fees: $200; $100 per semester. Tuition and fees vary according to program.
Financial support: In 2001–02, 45 students received support, including 5 fellowships with full tuition reimbursements available (averaging $18,000 per year), 32 research assistantships with full tuition reimbursements available (averaging $16,800 per year), 8 teaching assistantships with full tuition reimbursements available (averaging $16,800 per year); career-related internships or fieldwork, institutionally sponsored loans, and unspecified assistantships also available. Financial award application deadline: 1/15.
Faculty research: Emulsion polymers, process control, biochemical engineering, biotechnology, catalysis, surface science, reaction engineering. *Total annual research expenditures:* $2.8 million.
Dr. Gary W. Poehlein, Visiting Professor and Interim Chair, 610-758-4260, *Fax:* 610-758-5057, *E-mail:* gap3@lehigh.edu.
Application contact: Ralph Joseph Gabriel, PE, Administrative Associate for Graduate Studies, 610-758-5055, *Fax:* 610-758-5057, *E-mail:* inchegs@mail.lehigh.edu. *Web site:* http://www.lehigh.edu/~inchm/inchm.html

Find an in-depth description at www.petersons.com/gradchannel.

■ LOUISIANA STATE UNIVERSITY AND AGRICULTURAL AND MECHANICAL COLLEGE

Graduate School, College of Engineering, Gordon A. and Mary Cian Department of Chemical Engineering, Baton Rouge, LA 70803

AWARDS MS Ch E, PhD. Part-time and evening/weekend programs available.

Faculty: 14 full-time (1 woman), 1 part-time/adjunct (0 women).
Students: 34 full-time (2 women), 9 part-time (1 woman); includes 1 minority (Asian American or Pacific Islander), 36 international. Average age 28. 122 applicants, 18% accepted, 7 enrolled. In 2001, 8 master's, 2 doctorates awarded. Terminal master's awarded for partial completion of doctoral program.
Degree requirements: For master's, comprehensive exam or thesis; for doctorate, thesis/dissertation, general exam, qualifying exam.
Entrance requirements: For master's and doctorate, GRE General Test, minimum GPA of 3.0. *Application deadline:* For fall admission, 1/25 (priority date). Applications are processed on a rolling basis. *Application fee:* $25.
Expenses: Tuition, state resident: full-time $2,551. Tuition, nonresident: full-time $5,551. Required fees: $854. Part-time tuition and fees vary according to course load.
Financial support: In 2001–02, 1 fellowship (averaging $16,200 per year), 32 research assistantships with partial tuition reimbursements (averaging $20,306 per year) were awarded. Financial award application deadline: 4/15; financial award applicants required to submit FAFSA.
Faculty research: Reaction engineering, control, thermodynamic and transport phenomena, polymer processing and properties, biochemical engineering. *Total annual research expenditures:* $799,380.
Dr. F. Carl Knopf, Chair, 225-578-1426, *Fax:* 225-578-1476, *E-mail:* knopf@che.lsu.edu.
Application contact: Dr. Sharon Broussard, Coordinator, 225-578-3242, *Fax:* 225-578-1476, *E-mail:* broussard@che.lsu.edu. *Web site:* http://www.che.lsu.edu/

Find an in-depth description at www.petersons.com/gradchannel.

■ LOUISIANA TECH UNIVERSITY

Graduate School, College of Engineering and Science, Department of Chemical Engineering, Ruston, LA 71272

AWARDS MS, D Eng. Part-time programs available. Terminal master's awarded for partial completion of doctoral program.

Degree requirements: For master's and doctorate, thesis/dissertation.

Entrance requirements: For master's, GRE General Test, TOEFL, minimum GPA of 3.0 in last 60 hours; for doctorate, TOEFL, minimum graduate GPA of 3.25 (with MS) or GRE General Test.
Faculty research: Artificial intelligence, biotechnology, hazardous waste process safety.

■ MANHATTAN COLLEGE

Graduate Division, School of Engineering, Program in Chemical Engineering, Riverdale, NY 10471

AWARDS MS. Part-time and evening/weekend programs available.

Degree requirements: For master's, thesis or alternative.
Entrance requirements: For master's, GRE, TOEFL, minimum GPA of 3.0.
Faculty research: Advanced separation processes, environmental management, combustion.

■ MASSACHUSETTS INSTITUTE OF TECHNOLOGY

School of Engineering, Department of Chemical Engineering, Cambridge, MA 02139-4307

AWARDS SM, PhD, Sc D.

Faculty: 32 full-time (4 women), 1 part-time/adjunct (0 women).
Students: 206 full-time (57 women), 1 part-time; includes 21 minority (4 African Americans, 13 Asian Americans or Pacific Islanders, 3 Hispanic Americans, 1 Native American), 67 international. Average age 25. 378 applicants, 24% accepted, 45 enrolled. In 2001, 40 master's, 21 doctorates awarded. Terminal master's awarded for partial completion of doctoral program.
Degree requirements: For master's, thesis (for some programs); for doctorate, thesis/dissertation, comprehensive exam.
Entrance requirements: For master's and doctorate, GRE General Test, TOEFL. *Application deadline:* For fall admission, 1/2; for spring admission, 11/1. *Application fee:* $60. Electronic applications accepted.
Expenses: Tuition: Full-time $26,960. Full-time tuition and fees vary according to program.
Financial support: In 2001–02, 207 students received support, including 49 fellowships, 163 research assistantships, 25 teaching assistantships; career-related internships or fieldwork, Federal Work-Study, institutionally sponsored loans, scholarships/grants, health care benefits, and unspecified assistantships also available. Financial award applicants required to submit FAFSA.
Faculty research: Biochemical engineering, metabolic engineering, biomedical engineering, catalysis and chemical kinetics, combustion engineering. *Total annual research expenditures:* $19.2 million.

Dr. Robert C. Armstrong, Head, 617-253-4581, *Fax:* 617-258-8992, *E-mail:* rca@mit.edu.
Application contact: Suzanne Easterly, Academic Administrator, 617-253-4577, *Fax:* 617-253-9695, *E-mail:* chemegrad@mit.edu. *Web site:* http://web.mit.edu/cheme

■ MCNEESE STATE UNIVERSITY

Graduate School, College of Engineering and Technology, Lake Charles, LA 70609

AWARDS Chemical engineering (M Eng); civil engineering (M Eng); electrical engineering (M Eng); mechanical engineering (M Eng). Part-time and evening/weekend programs available.

Faculty: 14 full-time (1 woman).
Students: 24 full-time (5 women), 5 part-time; includes 1 minority (Asian American or Pacific Islander), 23 international. In 2001, 5 degrees awarded.
Degree requirements: For master's, thesis or alternative.
Entrance requirements: For master's, GRE General Test, TOEFL, minimum undergraduate GPA of 3.0. *Application deadline:* For fall admission, 7/15 (priority date). Applications are processed on a rolling basis. *Application fee:* $20 ($30 for international students).
Expenses: Tuition, state resident: part-time $1,208 per semester. Tuition, nonresident: part-time $4,378 per semester.
Financial support: Federal Work-Study available. Support available to part-time students. Financial award application deadline: 5/1.
Dr. O. C. Karkalits, Dean, 337-475-5875, *Fax:* 337-475-5237, *E-mail:* ckarkal@mail.mcneese.edu.
Application contact: Dr. Jay O. Uppot, Director of Graduate Studies, 337-475-5874, *Fax:* 37-475-5286, *E-mail:* juppot@mail.mcneese.edu.

■ MICHIGAN STATE UNIVERSITY

Graduate School, College of Engineering, Department of Chemical Engineering and Materials Science, East Lansing, MI 48824

AWARDS Chemical engineering (MS, PhD), including environmental toxicology (PhD); engineering mechanics (MS, PhD); materials science and engineering (MS, PhD); mechanics (PhD); metallurgy (MS, PhD). Part-time programs available.

Faculty: 22.
Students: 41 full-time (10 women), 5 part-time (1 woman); includes 9 minority (2 African Americans, 4 Asian Americans or Pacific Islanders, 3 Hispanic Americans), 21 international. Average age 26. 99 applicants, 14% accepted. In 2001, 8 master's, 6 doctorates awarded. Terminal master's awarded for partial completion of doctoral program.

Degree requirements: For doctorate, thesis/dissertation.
Entrance requirements: For master's, GRE, TOEFL, minimum GPA of 3.0; for doctorate, GRE, TOEFL. *Application deadline:* For fall admission, 1/15 (priority date); for spring admission, 11/1. Applications are processed on a rolling basis. *Application fee:* $30 ($40 for international students). Electronic applications accepted.
Expenses: Tuition, state resident: part-time $244 per credit hour. Tuition, nonresident: part-time $494 per credit hour. Required fees: $268 per semester. Tuition and fees vary according to course load, degree level and program.
Financial support: In 2001–02, 26 fellowships with tuition reimbursements (averaging $3,950 per year), 49 research assistantships with tuition reimbursements (averaging $14,052 per year), 19 teaching assistantships with tuition reimbursements (averaging $12,741 per year) were awarded. Financial award applicants required to submit FAFSA.
Faculty research: Agricultural bioprocessing, impact resistance of thermoplastic composite materials, durability of polymer composites. *Total annual research expenditures:* $989,316.
Dr. Martin Hawley, Interim Chair, 517-355-5135, *Fax:* 517-353-9842.
Application contact: Information Contact, 517-355-5135, *Fax:* 517-432-1105, *E-mail:* chems@egr.msu.edu. *Web site:* http://www.chems.msu.edu/

■ MICHIGAN TECHNOLOGICAL UNIVERSITY

Graduate School, College of Engineering, Department of Chemical Engineering, Houghton, MI 49931-1295

AWARDS MS, PhD. Part-time programs available.

Degree requirements: For master's and doctorate, thesis/dissertation.
Entrance requirements: For master's and doctorate, GRE General Test, TOEFL. Electronic applications accepted.
Faculty research: Polymer engineering, thermodynamics, chemical process safety, surface science/catalysis, environmental chemical engineering. *Web site:* http://www.chem.mtu.edu/chem-eng/

Find an in-depth description at www.petersons.com/gradchannel.

■ MISSISSIPPI STATE UNIVERSITY

College of Engineering, David C. Swalm School of Chemical Engineering, Mississippi State, MS 39762

AWARDS Chemical engineering (MS); engineering (PhD).

Faculty: 11 full-time (2 women).

Students: 19 full-time (6 women), 4 part-time; includes 2 minority (1 African American, 1 Hispanic American), 15 international. Average age 26. 79 applicants, 32% accepted, 2 enrolled. In 2001, 4 degrees awarded.
Degree requirements: For master's, thesis, comprehensive oral or written exam; for doctorate, thesis/dissertation, comprehensive exam. *Median time to degree:* Master's–3 years full-time.
Entrance requirements: For master's, GRE General Test, TOEFL, minimum GPA of 3.00; for doctorate, GRE, TOEFL. *Application deadline:* For fall admission, 4/1 (priority date); for spring admission, 8/1 (priority date). Applications are processed on a rolling basis. *Application fee:* $25 for international students.
Expenses: Tuition, state resident: full-time $3,586; part-time $150 per credit hour. Tuition, nonresident: full-time $8,128; part-time $339 per credit hour. Tuition and fees vary according to course load and campus/location.
Financial support: In 2001–02, 3 fellowships with full tuition reimbursements (averaging $16,000 per year), 19 research assistantships with full tuition reimbursements (averaging $13,200 per year) were awarded. Teaching assistantships with tuition reimbursements, Federal Work-Study, institutionally sponsored loans, and unspecified assistantships also available. Financial award applicants required to submit FAFSA.
Faculty research: Thermodynamics, composite materials, catalysis, surface science, environmental engineering. *Total annual research expenditures:* $1.4 million.
Dr. Kirk H. Schulz, Director, 662-325-2480, *Fax:* 662-325-2482.
Application contact: Jerry B. Inmon, Director of Admissions, 662-325-2224, *Fax:* 662-325-7360, *E-mail:* admit@admissions.msstate.edu. *Web site:* http://www.che.msstate.edu/

■ MONTANA STATE UNIVERSITY–BOZEMAN

College of Graduate Studies, College of Engineering, Department of Chemical Engineering, Bozeman, MT 59717

AWARDS Engineering (PhD). Part-time programs available. Postbaccalaureate distance learning degree programs offered (no on-campus study).

Students: 8 full-time (1 woman), 9 part-time (5 women); includes 1 minority (Asian American or Pacific Islander), 4 international. Average age 29. 18 applicants, 72% accepted, 6 enrolled.
Degree requirements: For doctorate, thesis/dissertation.
Entrance requirements: For doctorate, GRE General Test, TOEFL, minimum GPA of 3.0. *Application deadline:* For fall admission, 6/1; for spring admission, 11/15. Applications are processed on a

Montana State University–Bozeman (continued)

rolling basis. *Application fee:* $50. Electronic applications accepted.
Expenses: Tuition, state resident: full-time $3,894; part-time $198 per credit. Tuition, nonresident: full-time $10,661; part-time $480 per credit. International tuition: $10,811 full-time. Tuition and fees vary according to course load and program.
Financial support: In 2001–02, 11 students received support, including 10 research assistantships with partial tuition reimbursements available (averaging $12,000 per year), 1 teaching assistantship with partial tuition reimbursement available (averaging $12,000 per year). Scholarships/grants and unspecified assistantships also available. Financial award application deadline: 3/1. *Total annual research expenditures:* $370,571.
Dr. Ron W. Larsen, Head, 406-994-2221, *Fax:* 406-994-5308, *E-mail:* che_b@ coe.montana.edu. *Web site:* http://www.coe.montana.edu/che/

■ NATIONAL TECHNOLOGICAL UNIVERSITY

Programs in Engineering, Fort Collins, CO 80526-1842

AWARDS Chemical engineering (MS); computer engineering (MS); computer science (MS); electrical engineering (MS); engineering management (MS); environmental systems management (MS); management of technology (MS); manufacturing systems engineering (MS); materials science and engineering (MS); mechanical engineering (MS); microelectronics and semiconductor engineering (MS). Software engineering (MS). Special majors (MS). Systems engineering (MS). Part-time programs available. Postbaccalaureate distance learning degree programs offered (no on-campus study).

Students: In 2001, 114 degrees awarded.
Degree requirements: For master's, comprehensive exam.
Entrance requirements: For master's, BS in engineering or related field; 2.9 minimum GPA. *Application deadline:* Applications are processed on a rolling basis. *Application fee:* $50. Electronic applications accepted.
Expenses: Tuition: Part-time $660 per credit hour. Part-time tuition and fees vary according to course load, campus/location and program.
Dr. Andre Vacroux, President, 970-495-6400, *Fax:* 970-484-0668, *E-mail:* andre@ ntu.edu.
Application contact: Rhonda Bonham, Admissions Officer, 970-495-6400, *Fax:* 970-498-0601, *E-mail:* rhonda@ntu.edu. *Web site:* http://www.ntu.edu/

■ NEW JERSEY INSTITUTE OF TECHNOLOGY

Office of Graduate Studies, Department of Chemical Engineering, Chemistry, and Environmental Science, Program in Chemical Engineering, Newark, NJ 07102

AWARDS MS, PhD. Part-time and evening/weekend programs available.

Faculty: 24 full-time (0 women).
Students: 30 full-time (6 women), 15 part-time (7 women); includes 10 minority (1 African American, 6 Asian Americans or Pacific Islanders, 3 Hispanic Americans), 26 international. Average age 28. 142 applicants, 19% accepted, 9 enrolled. In 2001, 10 master's, 5 doctorates awarded. Terminal master's awarded for partial completion of doctoral program.
Degree requirements: For doctorate, thesis/dissertation, residency.
Entrance requirements: For master's, GRE General Test; for doctorate, GRE General Test, minimum graduate GPA of 3.5. *Application deadline:* For fall admission, 6/5 (priority date); for spring admission, 10/15. Applications are processed on a rolling basis. *Application fee:* $50.
Expenses: Tuition, state resident: full-time $7,812; part-time $434 per credit. Tuition, nonresident: full-time $10,746; part-time $597 per credit. Required fees: $47 per credit. $76 per semester.
Financial support: In 2001–02, 1 fellowship with full and partial tuition reimbursement, 15 research assistantships with full and partial tuition reimbursements, 2 teaching assistantships with full and partial tuition reimbursements were awarded. Career-related internships or fieldwork, Federal Work-Study, institutionally sponsored loans, and unspecified assistantships also available. Financial award application deadline: 3/15.
Application contact: Kathryn Kelly, Director of Admissions, 973-596-3300, *Fax:* 973-596-3461, *E-mail:* admissions@ njit.edu. *Web site:* http://www.njit.edu/

■ NEW MEXICO STATE UNIVERSITY

Graduate School, College of Engineering, Department of Chemical Engineering, Las Cruces, NM 88003-8001

AWARDS MS Ch E, PhD. Part-time programs available.

Faculty: 6 full-time (2 women), 1 part-time/adjunct (0 women).
Students: 15 full-time (3 women), 10 part-time (1 woman); includes 2 minority (1 Asian American or Pacific Islander, 1 Hispanic American), 12 international. Average age 32. 27 applicants, 15% accepted, 3 enrolled. In 2001, 2 master's, 2 doctorates awarded.
Degree requirements: For master's, thesis (for some programs); for doctorate, thesis/dissertation.
Entrance requirements: For master's and doctorate, GRE General Test. *Application deadline:* For fall admission, 3/1; for spring admission, 11/1. *Application fee:* $15 ($35 for international students). Electronic applications accepted.
Expenses: Tuition, state resident: full-time $3,234; part-time $135 per credit. Tuition, nonresident: full-time $9,420; part-time $428 per credit. Required fees: $858.
Financial support: In 2001–02, 3 research assistantships, 7 teaching assistantships were awarded. Fellowships with full tuition reimbursements, career-related internships or fieldwork, Federal Work-Study, and tuition waivers (partial) also available. Support available to part-time students. Financial award application deadline: 2/1.
Faculty research: Advanced materials, semiconductors, environmental engineering, biochemical engineering, biomedical engineering, food technology, computer-aided design, actinide separations and computer simulation of chemical and thermodynamic properties.
Dr. Charles L. Johnson, Head, 505-646-8637, *Fax:* 505-646-7706, *E-mail:* cjohnson@nmsu.edu.
Application contact: Dr. Sarah W. Harcum, Associate Professor, 505-646-4145, *Fax:* 505-646-7706, *E-mail:* harcum@nmsu.edu. *Web site:* http://chemeng.nmsu.edu/

■ NORTH CAROLINA AGRICULTURAL AND TECHNICAL STATE UNIVERSITY

Graduate School, College of Engineering, Department of Chemical Engineering, Greensboro, NC 27411

AWARDS MSE. Part-time programs available.

Faculty: 8 full-time (0 women).
Students: 19 full-time (8 women), 4 part-time (3 women); includes 13 minority (11 African Americans, 2 Asian Americans or Pacific Islanders), 8 international. Average age 23. 39 applicants, 41% accepted. In 2001, 1 degree awarded.
Degree requirements: For master's, thesis (for some programs).
Entrance requirements: For master's, GRE General Test, GRE Subject Test (recommended), TOEFL. *Application deadline:* For fall admission, 7/1 (priority date); for spring admission, 1/9. Applications are processed on a rolling basis. *Application fee:* $35.
Financial support: In 2001–02, 22 students received support, including 2 fellowships with full and partial tuition reimbursements available (averaging $14,000 per year), 10 research assistantships with full and partial tuition reimbursements available (averaging $14,000 per year), 10 teaching assistantships with full and partial tuition

reimbursements available (averaging $14,000 per year) Financial award application deadline: 4/30.

Faculty research: Thermodynamics, bioremediation, membrane reactors, environmental engineering, fuel cells. *Total annual research expenditures:* $299,823.
Dr. Franklin G. King, Chairperson, 336-334-7564 Ext. 40, *Fax:* 336-334-7904, *E-mail:* king@ncat.edu.

Application contact: Dr. Keith Schimmel, Graduate Coordinator, 336-334-7564 Ext. 41, *Fax:* 336-334-7904, *E-mail:* schimmel@ncat.edu.

■ NORTH CAROLINA STATE UNIVERSITY

Graduate School, College of Engineering, Department of Chemical Engineering, Raleigh, NC 27695

AWARDS M Ch E, MS, PhD. Part-time programs available.

Faculty: 25 full-time (2 women), 10 part-time/adjunct (0 women).
Students: 72 full-time (20 women), 7 part-time (4 women); includes 7 minority (4 African Americans, 3 Asian Americans or Pacific Islanders), 28 international. Average age 27. 178 applicants, 21% accepted. In 2001, 16 master's, 8 doctorates awarded. Terminal master's awarded for partial completion of doctoral program.
Degree requirements: For master's and doctorate, thesis/dissertation.
Entrance requirements: For master's and doctorate, GRE General Test, TOEFL. *Application deadline:* For fall admission, 6/25 (priority date); for spring admission, 11/25. Applications are processed on a rolling basis. *Application fee:* $45.
Expenses: Tuition, state resident: full-time $1,748. Tuition, nonresident: full-time $6,904.
Financial support: In 2001–02, 12 fellowships (averaging $7,578 per year), 70 research assistantships (averaging $6,765 per year), 11 teaching assistantships (averaging $6,904 per year) were awarded.
Faculty research: Molecular themodynamics and computer simulation; catalysis, kinetics, electrochemical reaction engineering, biochemical engineering. *Total annual research expenditures:* $10.7 million.
Dr. Peter K. Kilpatrick, Head, 919-515-7129, *Fax:* 919-515-3465, *E-mail:* peter_k@eos.ncsu.edu.
Application contact: Dr. Saad A. Khan, Director of Graduate Programs, 919-515-4519, *Fax:* 919-515-3465, *E-mail:* khan@eos.ncsu.edu. *Web site:* http://www.che.ncsu.edu

■ NORTHEASTERN UNIVERSITY

College of Engineering, Department of Chemical Engineering, Boston, MA 02115-5096

AWARDS MS, PhD. Part-time programs available.

Faculty: 8 full-time (2 women), 2 part-time/adjunct (0 women).
Students: 19 full-time (13 women), 8 part-time (2 women); includes 2 minority (both Hispanic Americans), 10 international. Average age 25. 60 applicants, 35% accepted, 6 enrolled. In 2001, 10 degrees awarded.
Degree requirements: For master's, thesis optional; for doctorate, thesis/dissertation, departmental qualifying exam. *Median time to degree:* Master's–2.5 years full-time, 5 years part-time.
Entrance requirements: For master's and doctorate, GRE General Test. *Application deadline:* For fall admission, 2/15 (priority date). Applications are processed on a rolling basis. *Application fee:* $50. Electronic applications accepted.
Expenses: Tuition: Part-time $535 per credit hour. Required fees: $56. Tuition and fees vary according to program.
Financial support: In 2001–02, 19 students received support, including 12 research assistantships with full tuition reimbursements available (averaging $13,560 per year), 7 teaching assistantships with full tuition reimbursements available (averaging $13,560 per year); fellowships with tuition reimbursements available, career-related internships or fieldwork, Federal Work-Study, scholarships/grants, tuition waivers (full), and unspecified assistantships also available. Support available to part-time students. Financial award application deadline: 2/15; financial award applicants required to submit FAFSA.
Faculty research: Aerogel, catalysts, advanced microgravity materials processing, biomaterials, catalyst development, biochemical reactions. *Total annual research expenditures:* $3.8 million.
Dr. Ronald Willey, Acting Chairman, 617-373-2996, *Fax:* 617-373-2501.
Application contact: Stephen L. Gibson, Associate Director, 617-373-2711, *Fax:* 617-373-2501, *E-mail:* grad-eng@coe.neu.edu. *Web site:* http://www.coe.neu.edu/

■ NORTHWESTERN UNIVERSITY

McCormick School of Engineering and Applied Science, Department of Chemical Engineering, Evanston, IL 60208

AWARDS MS, PhD. Admissions and degrees offered through The Graduate School. Part-time programs available.

Faculty: 19 full-time (5 women), 2 part-time/adjunct (0 women).
Students: 67 full-time (21 women), 1 part-time; includes 14 minority (2 African Americans, 8 Asian Americans or Pacific Islanders, 3 Hispanic Americans, 1 Native American), 15 international. 202 applicants, 23% accepted, 16 enrolled. In 2001, 4 master's, 8 doctorates awarded. Terminal master's awarded for partial completion of doctoral program.

Degree requirements: For master's, thesis optional; for doctorate, thesis/dissertation. *Median time to degree:* Master's–1.8 years full-time; doctorate–6.4 years full-time.
Application deadline: For fall admission, 8/30. Applications are processed on a rolling basis. *Application fee:* $50 ($55 for international students).
Expenses: Tuition: Full-time $26,526.
Financial support: In 2001–02, 14 fellowships with full tuition reimbursements (averaging $20,820 per year), 53 research assistantships with partial tuition reimbursements (averaging $20,160 per year), 5 teaching assistantships with full tuition reimbursements were awarded. Career-related internships or fieldwork, Federal Work-Study, institutionally sponsored loans, and scholarships/grants also available. Financial award application deadline: 1/15; financial award applicants required to submit FAFSA.
Faculty research: Materials design and polymers, biotechnology, biomedical engineering, fluid mechanics and transport, catalysis and reaction engineering environmental-bioengineering. *Total annual research expenditures:* $4.5 million.
Dr. William Miller, Chair, 847-491-2890, *Fax:* 847-491-3728, *E-mail:* wmiller@northwestern.edu.
Application contact: Chris Jurczyk, Admissions Contact, 847-491-2773, *Fax:* 847-491-3728, *E-mail:* c-jurczyk@northwestern.edu. *Web site:* http://www.chem-eng.northwestern.edu/

■ THE OHIO STATE UNIVERSITY

Graduate School, College of Engineering, Department of Chemical Engineering, Columbus, OH 43210

AWARDS MS, PhD.

Degree requirements: For master's and doctorate, thesis/dissertation.
Entrance requirements: For master's and doctorate, GRE General Test, GRE Subject Test (chemistry or physics) for international students.

■ OHIO UNIVERSITY

Graduate Studies, Russ College of Engineering and Technology, Department of Chemical Engineering, Athens, OH 45701-2979

AWARDS MS, PhD. Part-time programs available.

Faculty: 8 full-time (1 woman), 3 part-time/adjunct (0 women).
Students: 29 full-time (6 women), 4 part-time (1 woman), 28 international. Average age 25. 103 applicants, 73% accepted, 13 enrolled. In 2001, 6 master's, 5 doctorates awarded. Terminal master's awarded for partial completion of doctoral program.
Degree requirements: For master's, thesis; for doctorate, thesis/dissertation, qualifying exams, comprehensive exam.

Ohio University (continued)
Median time to degree: Master's–2 years full-time; doctorate–3.5 years full-time.
Entrance requirements: For master's and doctorate, GRE General Test, TOEFL. *Application deadline:* For fall admission, 3/1 (priority date). Applications are processed on a rolling basis. *Application fee:* $30. Electronic applications accepted.
Expenses: Tuition, state resident: full-time $6,585. Tuition, nonresident: full-time $12,254.
Financial support: In 2001–02, 4 fellowships with full tuition reimbursements (averaging $16,000 per year), 15 research assistantships with full tuition reimbursements (averaging $14,000 per year), 5 teaching assistantships with full tuition reimbursements (averaging $13,000 per year) were awarded. Institutionally sponsored loans also available. Financial award application deadline: 3/15.
Faculty research: Corrosion and multiphase flow, biochemical engineering, thin film materials, air pollution modeling and control, biomedical engineering. *Total annual research expenditures:* $1.2 million.
Dr. Michael E. Prudich, Chairman, 740-593-1501, *Fax:* 740-593-0873, *E-mail:* prudich@ohio.edu.
Application contact: Dr. Tingyue Gu, Graduate Chairman, 740-593-1499, *Fax:* 740-593-0873, *E-mail:* gu@ohio.edu. *Web site:* http://www.ent.ohiou.edu/che/

■ OKLAHOMA STATE UNIVERSITY

Graduate College, College of Engineering, Architecture and Technology, School of Chemical Engineering, Stillwater, OK 74078
AWARDS M En, MS, PhD.

Faculty: 9 full-time (1 woman), 1 part-time/adjunct (0 women).
Students: 21 full-time (4 women), 16 part-time (3 women); includes 1 minority (Native American), 21 international. Average age 27. 50 applicants, 68% accepted. In 2001, 4 master's, 4 doctorates awarded.
Degree requirements: For master's, thesis or alternative; for doctorate, thesis/dissertation.
Entrance requirements: For master's and doctorate, GRE, TOEFL. *Application deadline:* For fall admission, 7/1 (priority date). *Application fee:* $25.
Expenses: Tuition, state resident: part-time $92 per credit hour. Tuition, nonresident: part-time $297 per credit hour. Required fees: $21 per credit hour. $14 per semester. One-time fee: $20. Tuition and fees vary according to course load.
Financial support: In 2001–02, 27 research assistantships (averaging $16,170 per year), 1 teaching assistantship (averaging $16,800 per year) were awarded. Career-related internships or fieldwork, Federal Work-Study, and tuition waivers

(partial) also available. Support available to part-time students. Financial award application deadline: 3/1.
Dr. Russell Rhinehart, Head, 405-744-5280.

■ OREGON STATE UNIVERSITY

Graduate School, College of Engineering, Department of Chemical Engineering, Corvallis, OR 97331
AWARDS MAIS, MS, PhD. Part-time programs available.

Faculty: 7 full-time (0 women).
Students: 15 full-time (3 women), 5 part-time; includes 2 minority (both Asian Americans or Pacific Islanders), 13 international. Average age 28. In 2001, 6 master's, 2 doctorates awarded. Terminal master's awarded for partial completion of doctoral program.
Degree requirements: For master's, thesis or alternative; for doctorate, thesis/dissertation.
Entrance requirements: For master's and doctorate, TOEFL, minimum GPA of 3.0 in last 90 hours. *Application deadline:* For fall admission, 3/1. Applications are processed on a rolling basis. *Application fee:* $50.
Expenses: Tuition, area resident: Full-time $15,933. Tuition, state resident: full-time $28,937.
Financial support: Research assistantships, teaching assistantships, career-related internships or fieldwork, Federal Work-Study, and institutionally sponsored loans available. Support available to part-time students. Financial award application deadline: 2/1.
Faculty research: Fluidization, mass transfer, chemical reactor design, combustion and gasification, polymers.
Dr. Carol M. McConica, Head, 541-737-2496, *Fax:* 541-737-4600, *E-mail:* carol.mcconica@orst.edu.
Application contact: Dawn M. Belveal, Secretary, 541-737-4791, *Fax:* 541-737-2182, *E-mail:* belveadm@che.orst.edu. *Web site:* http://www.che.orst.edu/

■ THE PENNSYLVANIA STATE UNIVERSITY UNIVERSITY PARK CAMPUS

Graduate School, College of Engineering, Department of Chemical Engineering, State College, University Park, PA 16802-1503
AWARDS MS, PhD.

Students: 43 full-time (18 women), 15 part-time (1 woman). In 2001, 10 master's, 6 doctorates awarded.
Degree requirements: For master's and doctorate, thesis/dissertation.
Entrance requirements: For master's and doctorate, GRE General Test. *Application fee:* $45.
Expenses: Tuition, state resident: full-time $7,882; part-time $333 per credit. Tuition,

nonresident: full-time $16,142; part-time $673 per credit. Required fees: $124 per semester.
Dr. Henry C. Foley, Head, 814-865-2574.

■ POLYTECHNIC UNIVERSITY, BROOKLYN CAMPUS

Department of Chemical Engineering, Chemistry and Materials Science, Major in Chemical Engineering, Brooklyn, NY 11201-2990
AWARDS MS, PhD. Part-time and evening/weekend programs available.

Degree requirements: For master's and doctorate, thesis/dissertation.
Entrance requirements: For master's, GRE General Test, BS in chemical engineering; for doctorate, GRE General Test. Electronic applications accepted.
Faculty research: Plasma polymerization, crystallization of organic compounds, dipolar relaxations in reactive polymers.

■ POLYTECHNIC UNIVERSITY, LONG ISLAND GRADUATE CENTER

Graduate Programs, Department of Chemical Engineering, Chemistry and Material Science, Major in Chemical Engineering, Melville, NY 11747
AWARDS MS, PhD.

Degree requirements: For master's, thesis (for some programs); for doctorate, thesis/dissertation.

■ POLYTECHNIC UNIVERSITY, WESTCHESTER GRADUATE CENTER

Graduate Programs, Department of Chemical Engineering, Chemistry, and Materials Science, Major in Chemical Engineering, Hawthorne, NY 10532-1507
AWARDS MS.

■ PRINCETON UNIVERSITY

Graduate School, School of Engineering and Applied Science, Department of Chemical Engineering, Princeton, NJ 08544-1019
AWARDS Applied and computational mathematics (PhD); chemical engineering (M Eng, MSE, PhD); plasma science and technology (MSE, PhD); polymer sciences and materials (MSE, PhD).

Degree requirements: For master's, thesis; for doctorate, thesis/dissertation, general exam.
Entrance requirements: For master's and doctorate, GRE General Test, GRE Subject Test, TOEFL.

■ PURDUE UNIVERSITY

Graduate School, Schools of Engineering, School of Chemical Engineering, West Lafayette, IN 47907

AWARDS MS, PhD.

Faculty: 22 full-time (2 women), 3 part-time/adjunct (0 women).
Students: 103 full-time (19 women), 3 part-time (1 woman); includes 6 minority (1 African American, 3 Asian Americans or Pacific Islanders, 2 Hispanic Americans), 66 international. Average age 25. 193 applicants, 12% accepted. In 2001, 8 master's, 8 doctorates awarded.
Degree requirements: For master's and doctorate, thesis/dissertation.
Entrance requirements: For master's and doctorate, TOEFL. *Application deadline:* For fall admission, 1/15 (priority date); for spring admission, 11/1 (priority date). Applications are processed on a rolling basis. *Application fee:* $30. Electronic applications accepted.
Expenses: Tuition, state resident: full-time $4,164; part-time $149 per credit hour. Tuition, nonresident: full-time $13,872; part-time $458 per credit hour. Tuition and fees vary according to campus/location and program.
Financial support: In 2001–02, 22 fellowships with partial tuition reimbursements (averaging $15,000 per year), 87 research assistantships with partial tuition reimbursements (averaging $17,500 per year), 24 teaching assistantships with partial tuition reimbursements (averaging $17,500 per year) were awarded. Career-related internships or fieldwork also available. Support available to part-time students. Financial award applicants required to submit FAFSA.
Faculty research: Biochemical and biomedical processes, polymer materials, interfacial and surface phenomena, applied thermodynamics, process systems engineering. *Total annual research expenditures:* $3.9 million.
Dr. G. V. Reklaitis, Head, 765-494-4075, *Fax:* 765-494-0805, *E-mail:* reklaiti@ ecn.purdue.edu.
Application contact: Linda Hawkins, Graduate Administrator, 765-494-4057, *Fax:* 765-494-0805, *E-mail:* linda@ ecn.purdue.edu.

■ RENSSELAER POLYTECHNIC INSTITUTE

Graduate School, School of Engineering, Howard P. Isermann Department of Chemical Engineering, Troy, NY 12180-3590

AWARDS M Eng, MS, D Eng, PhD. Part-time programs available.

Faculty: 11 full-time (0 women), 3 part-time/adjunct (0 women).
Students: 65 full-time (13 women), 2 part-time (1 woman); includes 2 minority (1 Asian American or Pacific Islander, 1 Hispanic American), 55 international. Average age 24. 154 applicants, 29% accepted. In 2001, 5 master's, 15 doctorates awarded. Terminal master's awarded for partial completion of doctoral program.
Degree requirements: For master's, thesis (for some programs); for doctorate, thesis/dissertation. *Median time to degree:* Doctorate–5.5 years full-time.
Entrance requirements: For master's and doctorate, GRE, TOEFL. *Application deadline:* For fall admission, 1/15 (priority date). Applications are processed on a rolling basis. *Application fee:* $45. Electronic applications accepted.
Expenses: Tuition: Full-time $26,400; part-time $1,320 per credit hour. Required fees: $1,437.
Financial support: In 2001–02, 58 students received support, including 11 fellowships with full tuition reimbursements available (averaging $17,000 per year), 37 research assistantships with full tuition reimbursements available (averaging $17,000 per year), 10 teaching assistantships with full tuition reimbursements available (averaging $17,000 per year); institutionally sponsored loans and scholarships/grants also available. Financial award application deadline: 2/1.
Faculty research: Biocatalysis, bioseparations, polymers, microelectronics, high-temperature kinetics, advanced materials, interfacial phenomena. *Total annual research expenditures:* $390,000.
Dr. Jonathan Dordick, Chair, 518-276-2899, *Fax:* 518-276-2207, *E-mail:* dordick@rpi.edu.
Application contact: Dr. B. Wayne Bequette, Admissions Counselor, 518-276-6929, *Fax:* 518-276-4030, *E-mail:* bockea@ rpi.edu. *Web site:* http://www.rpi.edu/

Find an in-depth description at www.petersons.com/gradchannel.

■ RICE UNIVERSITY

Graduate Programs, George R. Brown School of Engineering, Department of Chemical Engineering, Houston, TX 77251-1892

AWARDS M Ch E, MS, PhD. Part-time programs available.

Faculty: 14 full-time (1 woman).
Students: 48 full-time (20 women); includes 5 minority (4 Asian Americans or Pacific Islanders, 1 Hispanic American), 29 international. Average age 24. 163 applicants, 6% accepted. In 2001, 2 master's, 6 doctorates awarded.
Degree requirements: For master's, thesis (for some programs); for doctorate, thesis/dissertation.
Entrance requirements: For master's and doctorate, GRE General Test, TOEFL, minimum GPA of 3.0. *Application deadline:* For fall admission, 1/15 (priority date). Applications are processed on a rolling basis. *Application fee:* $25.
Expenses: Tuition: Full-time $17,300. Required fees: $250.
Financial support: In 2001–02, 14 fellowships (averaging $19,000 per year), 31 research assistantships (averaging $19,000 per year) were awarded. Tuition waivers (full) also available.
Faculty research: Thermodynamics, phase equilibria, rheology, fluid mechanics, polymers, biomedical engineering, interfacial phenomena, process control, petroleum engineering, reaction engineering and catalysis, biomaterials, metabolic engineering.
Dr. Kyriacos Zygourakis, Chair, 713-348-4902, *Fax:* 713-348-5478, *E-mail:* ceng@ rice.edu.
Application contact: Graduate Admissions Committee, 713-527-4902, *E-mail:* cega@ rice.edu. *Web site:* http://www.ruf.rice.edu/ ~che/

Find an in-depth description at www.petersons.com/gradchannel.

■ ROSE-HULMAN INSTITUTE OF TECHNOLOGY

Faculty of Engineering and Applied Sciences, Department of Chemical Engineering, Terre Haute, IN 47803-3920

AWARDS MS. Part-time programs available.

Faculty: 8 full-time (1 woman), 2 part-time/adjunct (0 women).
Students: 7 full-time (3 women), 1 part-time, 1 international. Average age 24. 7 applicants, 71% accepted, 2 enrolled. In 2001, 3 degrees awarded.
Degree requirements: For master's, thesis.
Entrance requirements: For master's, GRE, TOEFL, minimum GPA of 3.0. *Application deadline:* For fall admission, 2/1 (priority date). Applications are processed on a rolling basis. *Application fee:* $0.
Expenses: Tuition: Full-time $21,792; part-time $615 per credit hour. Required fees: $405.
Financial support: In 2001–02, 7 students received support; fellowships with full and partial tuition reimbursements available, research assistantships with full and partial tuition reimbursements available, institutionally sponsored loans, scholarships/grants, and tuition waivers (full and partial) available. Financial award application deadline: 2/1.
Faculty research: Emulsification and emulsion stability, fermentation technology, sorption of NOx and SOx, adsorption and adsorption-based separations, process control. *Total annual research expenditures:* $1.4 million.
Dr. Hossein Hariri, Chairman, 812-877-8292, *Fax:* 812-877-3198, *E-mail:* hossein.hariri@rose-hulman.edu.
Application contact: Dr. Daniel J. Moore, Interim Associate Dean of the Faculty, 812-877-8110, *Fax:* 812-877-8061, *E-mail:* daniel.j.moore@rose-hulman.edu.

■ RUTGERS, THE STATE UNIVERSITY OF NEW JERSEY, NEW BRUNSWICK

Graduate School, Program in Chemical and Biochemical Engineering, New Brunswick, NJ 08901-1281

AWARDS MS, PhD. Part-time and evening/weekend programs available. Terminal master's awarded for partial completion of doctoral program.

Degree requirements: For master's, thesis or alternative; for doctorate, thesis/dissertation.
Entrance requirements: For master's, GRE General Test, TOEFL; for doctorate, GRE General Test.
Faculty research: Biotechnology, environmental engineering, statistical thermodynamics, polymers, pharmaceutical engineering. *Web site:* http://sol.rutgers.edu/

■ SAN JOSE STATE UNIVERSITY

Graduate Studies, College of Engineering, Department of Chemical Engineering and Materials Engineering, Program in Chemical Engineering, San Jose, CA 95192-0001

AWARDS MS.

Faculty: 3 full-time (0 women), 2 part-time/adjunct (0 women).
Students: 6 full-time (2 women), 36 part-time (15 women); includes 23 minority (1 African American, 20 Asian Americans or Pacific Islanders, 2 Hispanic Americans), 8 international. 30 applicants, 57% accepted. In 2001, 5 degrees awarded.
Degree requirements: For master's, thesis or alternative.
Application deadline: 6/29; for spring admission, 11/30. Applications are processed on a rolling basis.
Application fee: $59. Electronic applications accepted.
Expenses: Tuition, nonresident: part-time $246 per unit. Required fees: $678 per semester. Tuition and fees vary according to course load.
Financial support: Applicants required to submit FAFSA.
Application contact: Dr. Melanie McNeil, Coordinator, 408-924-3873.

■ SOUTH DAKOTA SCHOOL OF MINES AND TECHNOLOGY

Graduate Division, Department of Chemistry and Chemical Engineering, Rapid City, SD 57701-3995

AWARDS MS. Part-time programs available.

Degree requirements: For master's, thesis.
Entrance requirements: For master's, TOEFL, TWE. Electronic applications accepted.

Faculty research: Incineration chemistry, environmental chemistry, polymer surface chemistry.

■ SOUTH DAKOTA SCHOOL OF MINES AND TECHNOLOGY

Graduate Division, Division of Material Engineering and Science, Doctoral Program in Materials Engineering and Science, Rapid City, SD 57701-3995

AWARDS Chemical engineering (PhD); chemistry (PhD); civil engineering (PhD); electrical engineering (PhD); mechanical engineering (PhD); metallurgical engineering (PhD); physics (PhD). Part-time programs available.

Degree requirements: For doctorate, thesis/dissertation.
Entrance requirements: For doctorate, TOEFL, TWE, minimum graduate GPA of 3.0. Electronic applications accepted.
Faculty research: Thermophysical properties of solids, development of multiphase materials and composites, concrete technology, electronic polymer materials.

Find an in-depth description at www.petersons.com/gradchannel.

■ STANFORD UNIVERSITY

School of Engineering, Department of Chemical Engineering, Stanford, CA 94305-9991

AWARDS MS, PhD, Eng.

Faculty: 13 full-time (3 women).
Students: 96 full-time (30 women), 10 part-time (2 women); includes 35 minority (4 African Americans, 29 Asian Americans or Pacific Islanders, 2 Hispanic Americans), 34 international. Average age 25. 255 applicants, 26% accepted. In 2001, 18 master's, 7 doctorates awarded. Terminal master's awarded for partial completion of doctoral program.
Degree requirements: For doctorate and Eng, thesis/dissertation.
Entrance requirements: For master's, doctorate, and Eng, GRE General Test, TOEFL. *Application deadline:* For fall admission, 1/15. *Application fee:* $65 ($80 for international students). Electronic applications accepted.
Curtis W. Frank, Chairman, 650-723-4573, *Fax:* 650-723-9780, *E-mail:* curt@chemeng.stanford.edu.
Application contact: Graduate Admissions Coordinator, 650-723-1302. *Web site:* http://chemeng.stanford.edu/

■ STEVENS INSTITUTE OF TECHNOLOGY

Graduate School, Charles V. Schaefer Jr. School of Engineering, Department of Chemical Engineering, Hoboken, NJ 07030

AWARDS Analysis of polymer processing methods (Certificate); biochemical engineering

(M Eng, PhD, Engr); fundamentals of modern chemical engineering (Certificate); polymer engineering (M Eng, PhD, Engr); polymer processing (Certificate); process control (M Eng, PhD, Engr); process engineering (M Eng, PhD, Certificate, Engr). Part-time and evening/weekend programs available. Postbaccalaureate distance learning degree programs offered (no on-campus study). Terminal master's awarded for partial completion of doctoral program.

Degree requirements: For master's, thesis or alternative; for doctorate, one foreign language, thesis/dissertation; for other advanced degree, project or thesis.
Entrance requirements: For master's and doctorate, TOEFL. Electronic applications accepted.
Expenses: Tuition: Full-time $13,950; part-time $775 per credit. Required fees: $180. One-time fee: $180 part-time. Full-time tuition and fees vary according to degree level and program.
Faculty research: Biochemical reaction engineering, polymerization engineering, reactor design, biochemical process control and synthesis.

■ SYRACUSE UNIVERSITY

Graduate School, L. C. Smith College of Engineering and Computer Science, Department of Chemical Engineering and Materials Sciences, Program in Chemical Engineering, Syracuse, NY 13244-0003

AWARDS MS, PhD.

Students: 20 full-time (4 women), 4 part-time. Average age 29. In 2001, 13 master's, 12 doctorates awarded.
Degree requirements: For master's and doctorate, thesis/dissertation.
Entrance requirements: For master's and doctorate, GRE General Test, GRE Subject Test. *Application deadline:* Applications are processed on a rolling basis.
Expenses: Tuition: Full-time $15,528; part-time $647 per credit. Required fees: $420; $38 per term. Tuition and fees vary according to program.
Financial support: Fellowships, research assistantships, teaching assistantships, Federal Work-Study and tuition waivers (partial) available. Financial award application deadline: 1/10.
Faculty research: Fluid particle technology, water desalination and renovation, membrane technology.
Dr. George Martin, Chair, 315-443-4467, *Fax:* 315-443-1243, *E-mail:* gcmartin@syr.edu.
Application contact: Dr. John Heydweiller, Information Contact, 315-443-4468, *Fax:* 315-443-1243, *E-mail:* jcheydwe@esc.syr.edu. *Web site:* http://www.ees.syr.edu/

Find an in-depth description at www.petersons.com/gradchannel.

■ TENNESSEE TECHNOLOGICAL UNIVERSITY

Graduate School, College of Engineering, Department of Chemical Engineering, Cookeville, TN 38505

AWARDS MS, PhD. Part-time programs available.

Faculty: 8 full-time (0 women).
Students: 22 full-time (2 women), 2 part-time (1 woman); includes 23 Asian Americans or Pacific Islanders. Average age 26. 92 applicants, 37% accepted. In 2001, 10 degrees awarded.
Degree requirements: For master's, thesis; for doctorate, one foreign language, thesis/dissertation.
Entrance requirements: For master's, GRE General Test, TOEFL; for doctorate, GRE Subject Test, TOEFL, minimum GPA of 3.5. *Application deadline:* For fall admission, 3/1 (priority date); for spring admission, 8/1. *Application fee:* $25 ($30 for international students). Electronic applications accepted.
Expenses: Tuition, state resident: full-time $4,000; part-time $215 per hour. Tuition, nonresident: full-time $10,500; part-time $495 per hour. Required fees: $1,971 per semester.
Financial support: In 2001–02, 10 research assistantships (averaging $7,000 per year), 3 teaching assistantships (averaging $5,433 per year) were awarded. Fellowships, career-related internships or fieldwork also available. Financial award application deadline: 4/1.
Faculty research: Biochemical conversion, insulation, fuel reprocessing.
Dr. Clayton P. Kerr, Interim Chairperson, 931-372-3297, *Fax:* 931-372-6372.
Application contact: Dr. Francis O. Otuonye, Associate Vice President for Research and Graduate Studies, 931-372-3233, *Fax:* 931-372-3497, *E-mail:* fotuonye@tntech.edu.

■ TEXAS A&M UNIVERSITY

College of Engineering, Department of Chemical Engineering, College Station, TX 77843

AWARDS M Eng, MS, PhD.

Faculty: 19 full-time (3 women), 5 part-time/adjunct (1 woman).
Students: 103 full-time (27 women), 6 part-time (1 woman); includes 5 minority (1 African American, 2 Asian Americans or Pacific Islanders, 2 Hispanic Americans), 87 international. Average age 27. 280 applicants, 23% accepted, 23 enrolled. In 2001, 12 master's, 14 doctorates awarded. Terminal master's awarded for partial completion of doctoral program.
Degree requirements: For master's, thesis (MS); for doctorate, thesis/dissertation.
Entrance requirements: For master's and doctorate, GRE General Test, TOEFL. *Application deadline:* For fall admission, 3/1

(priority date); for spring admission, 10/1. Applications are processed on a rolling basis. *Application fee:* $50 ($75 for international students). Electronic applications accepted.
Expenses: Tuition, state resident: full-time $11,872. Tuition, nonresident: full-time $17,892.
Financial support: In 2001–02, 5 fellowships with full tuition reimbursements (averaging $16,632 per year), 59 research assistantships with full tuition reimbursements (averaging $16,957 per year), 32 teaching assistantships with full tuition reimbursements (averaging $17,603 per year) were awarded. Career-related internships or fieldwork, scholarships/grants, and tuition waivers (full) also available. Financial award application deadline: 3/31; financial award applicants required to submit FAFSA.
Faculty research: Reaction engineering, interface phenomena, environmental applications, biochemical engineering, polymers. *Total annual research expenditures:* $4 million.
Dr. Rayford G. Anthony, Head, 979-845-3361.
Application contact: Towanna H. Mann, Staff Assistant, 979-845-3364, *Fax:* 979-845-6446, *E-mail:* towanna@tamu.edu. *Web site:* http://www.chen.tamu.edu/chen/

■ TEXAS A&M UNIVERSITY–KINGSVILLE

College of Graduate Studies, College of Engineering, Department of Chemical Engineering and Natural Gas Engineering, Program in Chemical Engineering, Kingsville, TX 78363

AWARDS ME, MS. Part-time and evening/weekend programs available.

Students: 18 full-time (3 women), 5 part-time; includes 1 minority (Hispanic American), 21 international. Average age 25. In 2001, 11 degrees awarded.
Degree requirements: For master's, thesis or alternative, comprehensive exam.
Entrance requirements: For master's, GRE General Test, TOEFL, minimum GPA of 3.0. *Application deadline:* For fall admission, 6/1; for spring admission, 11/15. Applications are processed on a rolling basis. *Application fee:* $15 ($25 for international students).
Expenses: Tuition, state resident: part-time $42 per hour. Tuition, nonresident: part-time $253 per hour. Required fees: $56 per hour. One-time fee: $46 part-time. Tuition and fees vary according to program.
Financial support: Fellowships, Federal Work-Study, institutionally sponsored loans, and tuition waivers (partial) available. Financial award application deadline: 5/15.
Faculty research: Process control, error detection and reconciliation, fluid mechanics, handling of solids.

Dr. William Heenan, Coordinator, Department of Chemical Engineering and Natural Gas Engineering, 361-593-2001, *Fax:* 361-593-2106.

■ TEXAS TECH UNIVERSITY

Graduate School, College of Engineering, Department of Chemical Engineering, Lubbock, TX 79409

AWARDS MS Ch E, PhD. Part-time programs available.

Faculty: 11 full-time (2 women), 1 part-time/adjunct (0 women).
Students: 32 full-time (6 women), 2 part-time, 25 international. Average age 28. 52 applicants, 33% accepted, 10 enrolled. In 2001, 2 degrees awarded.
Degree requirements: For master's and doctorate, thesis/dissertation.
Entrance requirements: For master's and doctorate, GRE General Test, minimum GPA of 3.0. *Application deadline:* Applications are processed on a rolling basis. *Application fee:* $25 ($50 for international students). Electronic applications accepted.
Expenses: Tuition, state resident: full-time $1,926; part-time $107 per credit hour. Tuition, nonresident: full-time $5,724; part-time $318 per credit hour. Required fees: $779; $737 per year. Tuition and fees vary according to course level, course load and program.
Financial support: In 2001–02, 24 research assistantships with tuition reimbursements (averaging $12,930 per year), 5 teaching assistantships with partial tuition reimbursements (averaging $10,400 per year) were awarded. Fellowships, Federal Work-Study and institutionally sponsored loans also available. Support available to part-time students. Financial award application deadline: 5/1; financial award applicants required to submit FAFSA.
Faculty research: Cotton fiber use for aquatic crude oil spills, chemical process control, hazardous and toxic waste. *Total annual research expenditures:* $1.5 million.
Dr. Greg McKenna, Chair, 806-742-3553, *Fax:* 806-742-3552.
Application contact: Graduate Adviser, 806-742-3553, *Fax:* 806-742-3552. *Web site:* http://www.che.ttu.edu/che/

■ TUFTS UNIVERSITY

Division of Graduate and Continuing Studies and Research, Graduate School of Arts and Sciences, School of Engineering, Department of Chemical and Biological Engineering, Medford, MA 02155

AWARDS ME, MS, PhD. Part-time programs available.

Faculty: 11 full-time, 2 part-time/adjunct.
Students: 43 (20 women); includes 4 minority (3 Asian Americans or Pacific Islanders, 1 Hispanic American) 15 international. 42 applicants, 38% accepted.

Tufts University (continued)

In 2001, 8 degrees awarded. Terminal master's awarded for partial completion of doctoral program.

Degree requirements: For master's, thesis (for some programs); for doctorate, thesis/dissertation.

Entrance requirements: For master's and doctorate, GRE General Test, TOEFL. *Application deadline:* For fall admission, 2/15; for spring admission, 10/15. Applications are processed on a rolling basis. *Application fee:* $50. Electronic applications accepted.

Expenses: Tuition: Full-time $26,853. Full-time tuition and fees vary according to program.

Financial support: Research assistantships with full and partial tuition reimbursements, teaching assistantships with full and partial tuition reimbursements, Federal Work-Study, scholarships/grants, and tuition waivers (partial) available. Financial award application deadline: 2/15; financial award applicants required to submit FAFSA.

Eliana DeBernardez-Clark, Chair, 617-627-2573.

Application contact: Maria Flytzani-Stephanopoulas, Head, 617-627-3900, *Fax:* 617-627-3991, *E-mail:* chemstudent@infonet.tufts.edu. *Web site:* http://www.tufts.edu/chemical/

■ **TULANE UNIVERSITY**

School of Engineering, Department of Chemical Engineering, New Orleans, LA 70118-5669

AWARDS MS, MSE, PhD, Sc D. MS and PhD offered through the Graduate School.

Degree requirements: For master's, thesis optional; for doctorate, thesis/dissertation.

Entrance requirements: For master's and doctorate, GRE General Test, TOEFL, minimum B average in undergraduate course work.

Expenses: Tuition: Full-time $24,675. Required fees: $2,210.

Faculty research: Interfacial phenomena catalysis, electrochemical engineering, environmental science.

■ **UNIVERSITY AT BUFFALO, THE STATE UNIVERSITY OF NEW YORK**

Graduate School, School of Engineering and Applied Sciences, Department of Chemical Engineering, Buffalo, NY 14260

AWARDS M Eng, MS, PhD. Part-time programs available.

Faculty: 13 full-time (0 women), 5 part-time/adjunct (0 women).
Students: 55 full-time (12 women), 5 part-time (1 woman); includes 5 minority (3 African Americans, 1 Asian American or

Pacific Islander, 1 Hispanic American), 46 international. Average age 23. 193 applicants, 22% accepted. In 2001, 8 master's, 6 doctorates awarded.

Degree requirements: For master's, thesis (for some programs); for doctorate, thesis/dissertation.

Entrance requirements: For master's and doctorate, GRE General Test, TOEFL. *Application deadline:* For fall admission, 2/1 (priority date); for spring admission, 10/1 (priority date). Applications are processed on a rolling basis. *Application fee:* $35.

Expenses: Tuition, state resident: full-time $6,118. Tuition, nonresident: full-time $9,434.

Financial support: In 2001–02, 28 students received support, including 5 fellowships with full tuition reimbursements available (averaging $15,000 per year), 21 research assistantships with full tuition reimbursements available (averaging $12,000 per year), 14 teaching assistantships with full tuition reimbursements available (averaging $10,740 per year); career-related internships or fieldwork, Federal Work-Study, institutionally sponsored loans, tuition waivers (full and partial), and unspecified assistantships also available. Support available to part-time students. Financial award application deadline: 2/28; financial award applicants required to submit FAFSA.

Faculty research: Transport, polymers, materials, biochemical engineering, catalysis. *Total annual research expenditures:* $1.2 million.

Dr. Carl R. F. Lund, Chairman, 716-645-2911 Ext. 2211, *Fax:* 716-645-3822, *E-mail:* lund@eng.buffalo.edu.

Application contact: Dr. T. J. Mountziaris, Graduate Committee Chair, 716-645-2911 Ext. 2212, *Fax:* 716-645-3822, *E-mail:* tjm@eng.buffalo.edu. *Web site:* http://www.eng.buffalo.edu/dept/ce/index.html

Find an in-depth description at www.petersons.com/gradchannel.

■ **THE UNIVERSITY OF AKRON**

Graduate School, College of Engineering, Department of Chemical Engineering, Akron, OH 44325-0001

AWARDS MS, PhD. Part-time and evening/weekend programs available.

Faculty: 9 full-time (2 women).
Students: 28 full-time (2 women), 8 part-time (2 women); includes 1 minority (Asian American or Pacific Islander), 28 international. Average age 26. 21 applicants, 81% accepted, 6 enrolled. In 2001, 8 degrees awarded.

Degree requirements: For master's, thesis optional; for doctorate, one foreign language, thesis/dissertation, candidacy exam, qualifying exam.

Entrance requirements: For master's, GRE General Test, TOEFL, minimum GPA of 2.75; for doctorate, GRE General Test, TOEFL. *Application deadline:* For fall

admission, 3/1. Applications are processed on a rolling basis. *Application fee:* $40 ($50 for international students).

Expenses: Tuition, state resident: full-time $6,562; part-time $219 per credit. Tuition, nonresident: full-time $9,027; part-time $383 per credit. Required fees: $272; $11 per credit. Tuition and fees vary according to course load.

Financial support: In 2001–02, 20 research assistantships with full tuition reimbursements, 16 teaching assistantships with full tuition reimbursements were awarded. Fellowships with full tuition reimbursements, career-related internships or fieldwork and scholarships/grants also available. Financial award application deadline: 3/1.

Faculty research: Reactor design, catalysis, synthetic fuels, transport phenomena, process engineering.

Dr. Steven S. Chuang, Chair, 330-972-6993, *E-mail:* schuang@uakron.edu. *Web site:* http://www.ecgf.uakron.edu/~chem/index.html

---

■ **THE UNIVERSITY OF ALABAMA**

Graduate School, College of Engineering, Department of Chemical Engineering, Tuscaloosa, AL 35487

AWARDS MS Ch E, PhD. Part-time and evening/weekend programs available.

Faculty: 11 full-time (1 woman).
Students: 19 full-time (4 women), 2 part-time, 18 international. Average age 27. 67 applicants, 9% accepted, 5 enrolled. In 2001, 7 master's, 2 doctorates awarded.

Degree requirements: For master's, thesis or alternative; for doctorate, thesis/dissertation.

Entrance requirements: For master's, GRE General Test or minimum GPA of 3.0 in last 60 hours; for doctorate, GRE General Test or minimum GPA of 3.0. *Application deadline:* For fall admission, 7/1 (priority date); for spring admission, 11/1 (priority date). Applications are processed on a rolling basis. *Application fee:* $25. Electronic applications accepted.

Expenses: Tuition, state resident: full-time $3,292; part-time $183 per credit hour. Tuition, nonresident: full-time $8,912; part-time $495 per credit hour. Tuition and fees vary according to course load, campus/location and program.

Financial support: In 2001–02, 19 research assistantships with full tuition reimbursements (averaging $15,500 per year), teaching assistantships with full tuition reimbursements (averaging $15,500 per year) were awarded. Fellowships with full tuition reimbursements, Federal Work-Study also available. Financial award application deadline: 5/15.

Faculty research: Global environmental change, magnetic tape, process modeling, pollution prevention, polymeric materials. *Total annual research expenditures:* $3.1 million.

Dr. Gary C. April, Head, 205-348-6452, *Fax:* 205-348-7558, *E-mail:* gcapril@coe.eng.ua.edu.
Application contact: Dr. John Wiest, Information Contact, 205-348-1727, *Fax:* 205-348-7558, *E-mail:* jwiest@coe.eng.ua.edu. *Web site:* http://www.eng.ua.edu/~chedept/

■ THE UNIVERSITY OF ALABAMA IN HUNTSVILLE

School of Graduate Studies, College of Engineering, Department of Chemical and Materials Engineering, Huntsville, AL 35899

AWARDS Biotechnology science and engineering (PhD); chemical engineering (MSE). Part-time and evening/weekend programs available.

Faculty: 4 full-time (0 women).
Students: 16 full-time (6 women), 1 part-time; includes 2 minority (1 African American, 1 Asian American or Pacific Islander), 11 international. Average age 25. 72 applicants, 21% accepted, 9 enrolled. In 2001, 6 degrees awarded.
Degree requirements: For master's, thesis or alternative, oral and written exams, comprehensive exam, registration; for doctorate, thesis/dissertation, comprehensive exam, registration.
Entrance requirements: For master's, GRE General Test, appropriate bachelor's degree, minimum GPA of 3.0. *Application deadline:* For fall admission, 7/24 (priority date); for spring admission, 11/15 (priority date). Applications are processed on a rolling basis. *Application fee:* $35.
Expenses: Tuition, area resident: Part-time $175 per hour. Tuition, state resident: full-time $4,408. Tuition, nonresident: full-time $9,054; part-time $361 per hour.
Financial support: In 2001–02, 11 students received support, including 1 fellowship with full and partial tuition reimbursement available (averaging $10,800 per year), 6 research assistantships with full and partial tuition reimbursements available (averaging $9,424 per year), 4 teaching assistantships with full and partial tuition reimbursements available (averaging $9,150 per year); career-related internships or fieldwork, Federal Work-Study, institutionally sponsored loans, scholarships/grants, health care benefits, and tuition waivers (full and partial) also available. Support available to part-time students. Financial award application deadline: 4/1; financial award applicants required to submit FAFSA.
Faculty research: Turbulence modeling, computational fluid dynamics, microgravity processing, multiphase transport, blood materials transport. *Total annual research expenditures:* $265,040.
Dr. Ramon Cerro, Chair, 256-824-6810, *Fax:* 256-824-6839, *E-mail:* rlc@eb.uah.edu. *Web site:* http://www.eb-p5.eb.uah.edu/che/

■ THE UNIVERSITY OF ARIZONA

Graduate College, College of Engineering and Mines, Department of Chemical and Environmental Engineering, Tucson, AZ 85721

AWARDS Chemical engineering (MS, PhD); environmental engineering (MS, PhD). Part-time programs available.

Faculty: 14.
Students: 53 full-time (16 women), 10 part-time (3 women); includes 8 minority (1 Asian American or Pacific Islander, 5 Hispanic Americans, 2 Native Americans), 31 international. Average age 29. 168 applicants, 15% accepted, 14 enrolled. In 2001, 8 master's, 2 doctorates awarded.
Degree requirements: For master's, thesis; for doctorate, thesis/dissertation, departmental qualifying exams, comprehensive exam.
Entrance requirements: For master's and doctorate, TOEFL, minimum GPA of 3.0. *Application deadline:* For fall admission, 3/1. Applications are processed on a rolling basis. *Application fee:* $45.
Expenses: Tuition, state resident: full-time $2,490; part-time $436 per unit. Tuition, nonresident: full-time $10,300; part-time $436 per unit. Full-time tuition and fees vary according to degree level and program.
Financial support: Fellowships, research assistantships, teaching assistantships, institutionally sponsored loans and scholarships/grants available. Financial award application deadline: 6/1.
Faculty research: Energy and environment–hazardous waste incineration, fossil fuel combustion, processing high-purity gases and liquids, aerosol reactor theory, pharmacokinetics.
Dr. Jost O.L. Wendt, Head, 520-621-2591.
Application contact: Rosemary A. Myers, Graduate Coordinator, 520-621-6044, *Fax:* 520-621-6048, *E-mail:* rmyers@engr.arizona.edu. *Web site:* http://www.che.arizona.edu

■ UNIVERSITY OF ARKANSAS

Graduate School, College of Engineering, Department of Chemical Engineering, Fayetteville, AR 72701-1201

AWARDS MS Ch E, MSE, PhD.

Students: 21 full-time (9 women), 2 part-time (1 woman); includes 2 minority (1 Asian American or Pacific Islander, 1 Hispanic American), 15 international. 14 applicants, 86% accepted. In 2001, 8 master's, 2 doctorates awarded.
Degree requirements: For master's, thesis optional; for doctorate, one foreign language, thesis/dissertation.
Application fee: $40 ($50 for international students).
Expenses: Tuition, state resident: full-time $3,553; part-time $197 per credit. Tuition, nonresident: full-time $8,411; part-time

$467 per credit. Required fees: $42 per credit. Tuition and fees vary according to course load and program.
Financial support: In 2001–02, 3 research assistantships, 18 teaching assistantships were awarded. Fellowships, career-related internships or fieldwork and Federal Work-Study also available. Support available to part-time students. Financial award application deadline: 4/1; financial award applicants required to submit FAFSA.
Dr. Tom Spicer, Chair, 479-575-4951.
Application contact: Reed Welker, Graduate Coordinator, *E-mail:* jrw@engr.uark.edu.

■ UNIVERSITY OF CALIFORNIA, BERKELEY

Graduate Division, College of Chemistry, Department of Chemical Engineering, Berkeley, CA 94720-1500

AWARDS MS, PhD.

Degree requirements: For master's, thesis; for doctorate, thesis/dissertation, qualifying exam.
Entrance requirements: For master's and doctorate, GRE General Test, TOEFL, minimum GPA of 3.0.
Expenses: Tuition, nonresident: full-time $10,704. Required fees: $4,349.
Faculty research: Biochemical engineering, electrochemical engineering, electronic materials, heterogeneous catalysis and reaction engineering, complex fluids, molecular theory and simulation, environmental engineering. *Web site:* http://www.cchem.berkeley.edu/mailform.html

■ UNIVERSITY OF CALIFORNIA, DAVIS

Graduate Studies, College of Engineering, Program in Chemical Engineering and Materials Science, Davis, CA 95616

AWARDS Chemical engineering (MS, PhD); materials science (MS, PhD, Certificate).

Faculty: 12 full-time (3 women), 4 part-time/adjunct (1 woman).
Students: 63 full-time (22 women); includes 16 minority (11 Asian Americans or Pacific Islanders, 5 Hispanic Americans), 18 international. Average age 28. 143 applicants, 27% accepted, 13 enrolled. In 2001, 2 master's, 15 doctorates awarded. Terminal master's awarded for partial completion of doctoral program.
Degree requirements: For master's and doctorate, thesis/dissertation.
Entrance requirements: For master's, GRE General Test, minimum GPA of 3.0; for doctorate, GRE General Test, TOEFL, minimum GPA of 3.0. *Application deadline:* For fall admission, 1/15 (priority date). *Application fee:* $60. Electronic applications accepted.

University of California, Davis (continued)
Expenses: Tuition, state resident: full-time $4,831. Tuition, nonresident: full-time $15,725.
Financial support: In 2001–02, 57 students received support, including 12 fellowships with full and partial tuition reimbursements available (averaging $5,344 per year), 51 research assistantships with full and partial tuition reimbursements available (averaging $9,585 per year), 9 teaching assistantships with partial tuition reimbursements available (averaging $10,019 per year); Federal Work-Study, institutionally sponsored loans, and tuition waivers (full and partial) also available. Financial award application deadline: 1/15; financial award applicants required to submit FAFSA.
Faculty research: Transport phenomena, colloid science, catalysis, biotechnology, materials.
Subhash H. Risbud, Chair, 530-752-5132, *E-mail:* shrisbud@ucdavis.edu.
Application contact: Archietta Johnson, Graduate Administrative Assistant, 530-752-2504, *Fax:* 530-752-1031, *E-mail:* arcjohnson@ucdavis.edu. *Web site:* http://www.chms.ucdavis.edu/

■ UNIVERSITY OF CALIFORNIA, IRVINE

Office of Research and Graduate Studies, School of Engineering, Department of Chemical and Biochemical Engineering and Materials Science, Irvine, CA 92697

AWARDS Biomedical engineering (MS, PhD); chemical and biochemical engineering (MS, PhD). Part-time programs available.

Faculty: 12.
Students: 54 full-time (14 women), 1 part-time; includes 14 minority (1 African American, 12 Asian Americans or Pacific Islanders, 1 Hispanic American), 23 international. 133 applicants, 37% accepted, 24 enrolled. In 2001, 5 master's, 4 doctorates awarded. Terminal master's awarded for partial completion of doctoral program.
Degree requirements: For doctorate, thesis/dissertation.
Entrance requirements: For master's, GRE General Test, minimum GPA of 3.0; for doctorate, GRE General Test. *Application deadline:* For fall and spring admission, 1/15 (priority date); for winter admission, 10/15 (priority date). Applications are processed on a rolling basis. *Application fee:* $60. Electronic applications accepted.
Expenses: Tuition, nonresident: full-time $10,704. Required fees: $8,396. Tuition and fees vary according to course load, program and student level.
Financial support: In 2001–02, 10 fellowships with tuition reimbursements (averaging $1,250 per year), research assistantships with tuition reimbursements (averaging $1,120 per year), 7 teaching

assistantships with tuition reimbursements (averaging $1,480 per year) were awarded. Institutionally sponsored loans also available. Financial award application deadline: 3/2; financial award applicants required to submit FAFSA.
Faculty research: Bioreactors, recombinant cells, separation operations. *Total annual research expenditures:* $2.2 million.
Dr. Enrique J. Lavernia, Chair, 949-824-8277, *Fax:* 949-824-2541, *E-mail:* lavernia@uci.edu.
Application contact: Nancy Carter-Fields, Graduate Coordinator, 949-824-9250, *Fax:* 949-824-2541, *E-mail:* nvcarter@uci.edu. *Web site:* http://www.eng.uci.edu/cbe/

Find an in-depth description at www.petersons.com/gradchannel.

■ UNIVERSITY OF CALIFORNIA, LOS ANGELES

Graduate Division, School of Engineering and Applied Science, Department of Chemical Engineering, Los Angeles, CA 90095

AWARDS MS, PhD.

Faculty: 11 full-time, 3 part-time/adjunct.
Students: 57 full-time (14 women); includes 20 minority (1 African American, 18 Asian Americans or Pacific Islanders, 1 Hispanic American), 26 international. 151 applicants, 28% accepted, 20 enrolled. In 2001, 7 master's, 11 doctorates awarded.
Degree requirements: For master's, thesis; for doctorate, thesis/dissertation, qualifying exams.
Entrance requirements: For master's, GRE General Test, minimum GPA of 3.0; for doctorate, GRE General Test, minimum GPA of 3.25. *Application deadline:* For fall admission, 1/15; for spring admission, 12/15. *Application fee:* $60. Electronic applications accepted.
Expenses: Tuition, nonresident: full-time $10,244. Required fees: $3,609. Full-time tuition and fees vary according to program.
Financial support: In 2001–02, 29 fellowships, 37 research assistantships, 25 teaching assistantships were awarded. Federal Work-Study, institutionally sponsored loans, and tuition waivers (full and partial) also available. Financial award application deadline: 1/15; financial award applicants required to submit FAFSA.
Dr. Selim Senkan, Chair, 310-206-4106.
Application contact: Bridget Mendibles, Student Affairs Officer, 310-825-9063, *Fax:* 310-206-4107, *E-mail:* bridgetm@ea.ucla.edu. *Web site:* http://www.chemeng.ucla.edu/

■ UNIVERSITY OF CALIFORNIA, RIVERSIDE

Graduate Division, Department of Chemical and Environmental Engineering, Riverside, CA 92521-0102

AWARDS MS, PhD.

Faculty: 8 full-time (0 women), 8 part-time/adjunct (2 women).
Students: 18 full-time (4 women), 1 part-time; includes 1 minority (Asian American or Pacific Islander), 10 international. Average age 27. 34 applicants, 59% accepted. In 2001, 1 master's awarded.
Degree requirements: For doctorate, thesis/dissertation, English language proficiency qualifying exams.
Entrance requirements: For master's and doctorate, GRE General Test, TOEFL, minimum GPA of 3.5 for fellowships/teaching assistantships, 3.2 overall. *Application deadline:* For fall admission, 5/1; for winter admission, 9/1; for spring admission, 12/1. Applications are processed on a rolling basis. *Application fee:* $40. Electronic applications accepted.
Expenses: Tuition, state resident: full-time $5,001. Tuition, nonresident: full-time $15,897.
Financial support: In 2001–02, 2 students received support, including 2 teaching assistantships with partial tuition reimbursements available (averaging $7,000 per year) Financial award application deadline: 1/5; financial award applicants required to submit FAFSA.
Faculty research: Bioprocessing, biodegradation, bioremediation, water wastewater treatment, biosensors and biodetoxification, transport emissions. *Total annual research expenditures:* $395,171.
Dr. Ashok Mulchandani, Chair, 909-787-2423, *Fax:* 909-787-2425.
Application contact: Laura Ibarra, Graduate Student Affairs Office, 909-787-2484, *Fax:* 909-787-2425, *E-mail:* gradcee@engr.ucr.edu. *Web site:* http://www.engr.ucr.edu

Find an in-depth description at www.petersons.com/gradchannel.

■ UNIVERSITY OF CALIFORNIA, SAN DIEGO

Graduate Studies and Research, Department of Chemical Engineering, La Jolla, CA 92093

AWARDS MS, PhD. Part-time programs available.

Faculty: 23.
Students: 10 (3 women); includes 4 minority (all Asian Americans or Pacific Islanders) 2 international. 30 applicants, 30% accepted, 5 enrolled.
Degree requirements: For master's and doctorate, thesis/dissertation.
Entrance requirements: For master's and doctorate, GRE General Test. *Application*

deadline: For fall admission, 1/19. *Application fee:* $40. Electronic applications accepted.
Expenses: Tuition, nonresident: full-time $10,434. Required fees: $4,883.
Financial support: In 2001–02, 3 fellowships with full tuition reimbursements (averaging $15,000 per year), 1 research assistantship with full tuition reimbursement (averaging $15,000 per year), teaching assistantships with partial tuition reimbursements (averaging $13,000 per year) were awarded. Scholarships/grants also available. Financial award application deadline: 1/31; financial award applicants required to submit FAFSA.
Faculty research: Semiconductor and composite materials processing, biochemical processing, electrochemistry and catalysis.
Jan B Talbot, Director, 858-534-4387.
Application contact: Graduate Coordinator, 858-534-4387. *Web site:* http://www.ames.ucsd.edu/

Find an in-depth description at www.petersons.com/gradchannel.

■ UNIVERSITY OF CALIFORNIA, SANTA BARBARA

Graduate Division, College of Engineering, Department of Chemical Engineering, Santa Barbara, CA 93106

AWARDS MS, PhD. Terminal master's awarded for partial completion of doctoral program.

Degree requirements: For master's, thesis or alternative; for doctorate, thesis/dissertation.
Entrance requirements: For master's and doctorate, GRE General Test, TOEFL. Electronic applications accepted.
Faculty research: Macromolecules, surfaces and catalysis, process control, inorganic materials, transport. *Web site:* http://www.chemengr.ucsb.edu/

■ UNIVERSITY OF CINCINNATI

Division of Research and Advanced Studies, College of Engineering, Department of Chemical Engineering, Cincinnati, OH 45221

AWARDS MS, PhD. Part-time and evening/weekend programs available.

Faculty: 13 full-time.
Students: 41 full-time (8 women), 2 part-time. Terminal master's awarded for partial completion of doctoral program.
Degree requirements: For master's and doctorate, thesis/dissertation.
Entrance requirements: For master's and doctorate, GRE General Test, TOEFL. *Application deadline:* For fall admission, 2/1 (priority date). *Application fee:* $40. Electronic applications accepted.
Expenses: Tuition, state resident: part-time $2,698 per quarter. Tuition, nonresident: part-time $4,977 per quarter.

Financial support: Fellowships, career-related internships or fieldwork, tuition waivers (full), and unspecified assistantships available. Financial award application deadline: 2/1.
Faculty research: Process synthesis, aerosol processes, clean coal technology, membrane technology. *Total annual research expenditures:* $978,550.
Dr. Joel Fried, Head, 513-556-2767, *Fax:* 513-556-3473, *E-mail:* joel.fried@uc.edu.
Application contact: Jerry Lin, Graduate Program Director, 513-556-2769, *Fax:* 513-556-3473, *E-mail:* jerry.yue-sheng.lin@uc.edu. *Web site:* http://www.chemical.uc.edu/

■ UNIVERSITY OF COLORADO AT BOULDER

Graduate School, College of Engineering and Applied Science, Department of Chemical Engineering, Boulder, CO 80309

AWARDS ME, MS, PhD. Part-time programs available.

Faculty: 16 full-time (2 women).
Students: 51 full-time (20 women), 14 part-time (4 women); includes 5 minority (3 Asian Americans or Pacific Islanders, 2 Hispanic Americans), 15 international. Average age 26. 36 applicants, 89% accepted. In 2001, 7 master's, 8 doctorates awarded. Terminal master's awarded for partial completion of doctoral program.
Degree requirements: For master's, thesis/dissertation, comprehensive exam; for doctorate, thesis/dissertation.
Entrance requirements: For master's, minimum undergraduate GPA of 3.0. *Application deadline:* For fall admission, 3/1 (priority date). Applications are processed on a rolling basis. *Application fee:* $50 ($60 for international students). Electronic applications accepted.
Expenses: Tuition, state resident: full-time $3,474. Tuition, nonresident: full-time $16,624.
Financial support: In 2001–02, 10 fellowships (averaging $1,725 per year), 41 research assistantships (averaging $12,070 per year), 3 teaching assistantships (averaging $20,000 per year) were awarded. Career-related internships or fieldwork, scholarships/grants, traineeships, and tuition waivers (full) also available.
Faculty research: Bioengineering and biotechnology, ceramic materials, fluid dynamics and fluid-article technology, heterogeneous catalysis, interfacial and surface phenomena. *Total annual research expenditures:* $3.9 million.
Robert Davis, Patten Professor and Chair, 303-492-7314, *Fax:* 303-492-4341, *E-mail:* robert.davis@colorado.edu.
Application contact: Marilyn Anseth, Graduate Program Assistant, 303-375-1975, *Fax:* 303-492-4341, *E-mail:* marilyn.anseth@colorado.edu. *Web site:* http://colorado.EDU/che

■ UNIVERSITY OF CONNECTICUT

Graduate School, School of Engineering, Field of Chemical Engineering, Storrs, CT 06269

AWARDS MS, PhD. Terminal master's awarded for partial completion of doctoral program.

Degree requirements: For master's, thesis or alternative; for doctorate, thesis/dissertation.
Entrance requirements: For master's and doctorate, GRE General Test.
Faculty research: Catalysis, electrochemicals, polymers.

■ UNIVERSITY OF CONNECTICUT

Graduate School, School of Engineering, Field of Material Science, Polymer Program, Storrs, CT 06269

AWARDS Chemical engineering (MS, PhD); chemistry (MS, PhD); polymer science (MS, PhD). Part-time programs available.

Faculty: 14 full-time (1 woman), 6 part-time/adjunct (0 women).
Students: 46 full-time (7 women), 3 part-time; includes 2 minority (both Asian Americans or Pacific Islanders), 40 international. Average age 27. 95 applicants, 17% accepted, 11 enrolled. In 2001, 2 master's, 6 doctorates awarded. Terminal master's awarded for partial completion of doctoral program.
Degree requirements: For master's, one foreign language, thesis (for some programs); for doctorate, one foreign language, thesis/dissertation. *Median time to degree:* Master's–2.75 years full-time; doctorate–5 years full-time.
Entrance requirements: For master's, GRE, TOEFL; for doctorate, GRE General Test, TOEFL. *Application deadline:* For fall admission, 4/1 (priority date); for spring admission, 11/1 (priority date). Applications are processed on a rolling basis. *Application fee:* $40 ($45 for international students). Electronic applications accepted.
Financial support: In 2001–02, 43 research assistantships with tuition reimbursements (averaging $21,480 per year) were awarded; fellowships with tuition reimbursements, career-related internships or fieldwork, scholarships/grants, health care benefits, and unspecified assistantships also available. Financial award application deadline: 4/1.
Faculty research: Spectroscopy, photonics, rheology, processing polymer blends. *Total annual research expenditures:* $2.8 million.
Chong S. Sung, Director, 860-486-4630, *Fax:* 860-486-4745, *E-mail:* csung@uconnvm.uconn.edu.
Application contact: Barbara E. Garton, Graduate Coordinator, 860-486-4613, *Fax:* 860-486-4745, *E-mail:* grad@

University of Connecticut (continued)
mail.ims.uconn.edu. *Web site:* http://
www.ims.uconn.edu/polymer/index.htm
**Find an in-depth description at
www.petersons.com/gradchannel.**

■ UNIVERSITY OF DAYTON

**Graduate School, School of
Engineering, Department of Chemical
Engineering, Dayton, OH 45469-1300**

AWARDS MS Ch E. Part-time and evening/
weekend programs available.

Faculty: 7 full-time (1 woman).
Students: 12 full-time (1 woman), 5 part-
time (2 women); includes 2 minority (1
Asian American or Pacific Islander, 1
Hispanic American), 7 international. Average age 24. In 2001, 3 degrees awarded.
Degree requirements: For master's,
thesis optional.
Entrance requirements: For master's,
TOEFL. *Application deadline:* For fall
admission, 8/1 (priority date). Applications
are processed on a rolling basis. *Application
fee:* $30.
Expenses: Tuition: Full-time $5,436; part-
time $453 per credit hour. Required fees:
$50; $25 per term.
Financial support: In 2001–02, 5 research
assistantships with full tuition reimbursements (averaging $12,000 per year) were
awarded; institutionally sponsored loans
also available.
Faculty research: Process control, process
modeling, expert systems, materials
processing, agitation.
Dr. Tony Saliba, Chair, 937-229-2627,
E-mail: tsaliba@udayton.edu.
Application contact: Dr. Donald L.
Moon, Associate Dean, 937-229-2241, *Fax:*
937-229-2471, *E-mail:* dmoon@
notes.udayton.edu.

■ UNIVERSITY OF DELAWARE

**College of Engineering, Department of
Chemical Engineering, Newark, DE
19716**

AWARDS M Ch E, PhD. Part-time and
evening/weekend programs available.
Postbaccalaureate distance learning degree
programs offered (minimal on-campus study).

Faculty: 21 full-time (3 women), 31 part-
time/adjunct (0 women).
Students: 88 full-time (26 women), 4 part-
time (1 woman); includes 8 minority (1
African American, 1 Asian American or
Pacific Islander, 6 Hispanic Americans), 28
international. Average age 26. 308
applicants, 26% accepted, 25 enrolled. In
2001, 11 master's, 16 doctorates awarded.
Terminal master's awarded for partial
completion of doctoral program.
Degree requirements: For master's,
thesis (for some programs); for doctorate,
thesis/dissertation.
Entrance requirements: For master's and
doctorate, GRE General Test, TOEFL.
Application deadline: For fall admission,

3/15 (priority date). *Application fee:* $50.
Electronic applications accepted.
Expenses: Tuition, state resident: full-time
$4,770; part-time $265 per credit. Tuition,
nonresident: full-time $13,860; part-time
$770 per credit. Required fees: $414.
Financial support: In 2001–02, 92
students received support, including 85
research assistantships with full tuition
reimbursements available (averaging
$19,400 per year); fellowships with full
tuition reimbursements available, teaching
assistantships with full tuition reimbursements available, scholarships/grants also
available. Financial award application
deadline: 3/15; financial award applicants
required to submit FAFSA.
Faculty research: Biochemical/biomedical
engineer, thermodynamics, polymers/
composites, materials, catalysis/reactions,
colloid/interfaces, expert systems/process
control. *Total annual research expenditures:*
$5.3 million.
Dr. Mark A. Barteau, Chairman, 302-831-
8905, *Fax:* 302-831-8201, *E-mail:*
barteau@che.udel.edu.
Application contact: Dr. Norman J.
Wagner, Professor, 302-831-8079, *Fax:*
302-831-1048, *E-mail:* wagner@
che.udel.edu. *Web site:* http://
www.che.udel.edu/

■ UNIVERSITY OF DETROIT MERCY

**College of Engineering and Science,
Department of Chemical Engineering,
Detroit, MI 48219-0900**

AWARDS Chemical engineering (ME, DE);
polymer engineering (ME). Evening/weekend
programs available.

Faculty: 4 full-time (0 women).
Students: 1 full-time (0 women), 18 part-
time (1 woman); includes 2 minority (both
Asian Americans or Pacific Islanders), 13
international. Average age 28. In 2001, 6
degrees awarded.
Degree requirements: For doctorate,
thesis/dissertation.
Application deadline: For fall admission, 8/1
(priority date). Applications are processed
on a rolling basis. *Application fee:* $25 ($35
for international students).
Expenses: Tuition: Full-time $10,620;
part-time $590 per credit hour. Required
fees: $400. Tuition and fees vary according
to program.
Financial support: Career-related internships or fieldwork available.
Dr. Geoffrey Prentice, Chairman, 313-
993-1187.

■ UNIVERSITY OF FLORIDA

**Graduate School, College of
Engineering, Department of Chemical
Engineering, Gainesville, FL 32611**

AWARDS ME, MS, PhD, Engr.

Degree requirements: For master's and
Engr, thesis optional; for doctorate, thesis/
dissertation.

Entrance requirements: For master's and
doctorate, GRE General Test, TOEFL,
minimum GPA of 3.0; for Engr, GRE
General Test. Electronic applications
accepted.
Expenses: Tuition, state resident: part-
time $164 per hour. Tuition, nonresident:
part-time $571 per hour. Tuition and fees
vary according to course level and
program.
Faculty research: Microelectronics,
polymeric and biochemical materials,
applied control theory, electrochemical and
surface sciences. *Web site:* http://
www.che.ufl.edu/CHEl/

**Find an in-depth description at
www.petersons.com/gradchannel.**

■ UNIVERSITY OF HOUSTON

**Cullen College of Engineering,
Department of Chemical Engineering,
Houston, TX 77204**

AWARDS M Ch E, MS Ch E, PhD. Part-time
and evening/weekend programs available.

Faculty: 9 full-time (0 women), 8 part-
time/adjunct (0 women).
Students: 63 full-time (15 women), 31
part-time (7 women); includes 14 minority
(2 African Americans, 8 Asian Americans
or Pacific Islanders, 4 Hispanic
Americans), 51 international. Average age
29. 323 applicants, 5% accepted. In 2001,
20 master's, 7 doctorates awarded.
Terminal master's awarded for partial
completion of doctoral program.
Degree requirements: For master's,
thesis (for some programs); for doctorate,
thesis/dissertation, departmental qualifying
exam.
Entrance requirements: For master's and
doctorate, GRE General Test, TOEFL.
Application deadline: For fall admission,
2/15 (priority date). Applications are
processed on a rolling basis. *Application fee:*
$25 ($75 for international students).
Expenses: Tuition, state resident: full-time
$1,512. Tuition, nonresident: full-time
$5,310. Required fees: $1,308. Tuition and
fees vary according to program.
Financial support: In 2001–02, 54
students received support, including 7 fellowships with partial tuition reimbursements available (averaging $16,567 per
year), 53 research assistantships with
partial tuition reimbursements available
(averaging $15,696 per year), 15 teaching
assistantships with partial tuition
reimbursements available (averaging
$15,696 per year); Federal Work-Study
also available. Financial award application
deadline: 2/15.
Faculty research: Biochemical engineering, electronic materials, chemical reaction
engineering, two-phase flow. *Total annual
research expenditures:* $1.5 million.
Dr. Michael Harold, Chairman, 713-743-
4304, *Fax:* 713-743-4323, *E-mail:*
mharold@uh.edu.

Application contact: Rosalind Walker, Graduate Analyst, 713-743-4311, *Fax:* 713-743-4323, *E-mail:* rwalker@uh.edu. *Web site:* http://www.egr.uh.edu/departments/chcc/welcome.html

■ **UNIVERSITY OF IDAHO**

College of Graduate Studies, College of Engineering, Department of Chemical Engineering, Moscow, ID 83844-2282

AWARDS M Engr, MS, PhD.

Faculty: 6 full-time (0 women), 1 part-time/adjunct (0 women).
Students: 7 full-time (2 women), 6 part-time (3 women), 1 international. 20 applicants, 5% accepted. In 2001, 7 master's awarded.
Degree requirements: For master's, thesis; for doctorate, one foreign language, thesis/dissertation.
Entrance requirements: For master's, GRE, minimum GPA of 2.8; for doctorate, GRE, minimum undergraduate GPA of 2.8, 3.0 graduate. *Application deadline:* For fall admission, 8/1; for spring admission, 12/15. *Application fee:* $35 ($45 for international students).
Expenses: Tuition, state resident: full-time $1,613. Tuition, nonresident: full-time $3,000.
Financial support: In 2001–02, 4 research assistantships (averaging $8,966 per year), 3 teaching assistantships (averaging $3,414 per year) were awarded. Fellowships Financial award application deadline: 2/15.
Faculty research: Geothermal energy utilization, alcohol production from agriculture waste material, energy conservation in pulp and paper mills.
Dr. Wudneh Admassu, Chair, 208-885-8918. *Web site:* http://www.uidaho.edu/che/
Find an in-depth description at www.petersons.com/gradchannel.

■ **UNIVERSITY OF ILLINOIS AT CHICAGO**

Graduate College, College of Engineering, Department of Chemical Engineering, Chicago, IL 60607-7128

AWARDS MS, PhD.

Faculty: 9 full-time (0 women).
Students: 35 full-time (9 women), 18 part-time (2 women); includes 3 minority (all Hispanic Americans), 44 international. Average age 26. 131 applicants, 24% accepted, 10 enrolled. In 2001, 4 master's, 3 doctorates awarded.
Degree requirements: For master's, thesis or project; for doctorate, thesis/dissertation, departmental qualifying exam.
Entrance requirements: For master's and doctorate, GRE General Test, TOEFL, minimum GPA of 3.75 on a 5.0 scale. *Application deadline:* For fall admission, 6/1; for spring admission, 11/1. *Application fee:* $40 ($50 for international students).

Expenses: Tuition, state resident: full-time $3,060. Tuition, nonresident: full-time $6,688.
Financial support: In 2001–02, 29 students received support; fellowships with full tuition reimbursements available, research assistantships with full tuition reimbursements available, teaching assistantships with full tuition reimbursements available, Federal Work-Study and tuition waivers (full) available. Financial award application deadline: 3/1; financial award applicants required to submit FAFSA.
Faculty research: Multiphase flows, interfacial transport, heterogeneous catalysis, coal technology, molecular and static thermodynamics.
Dr. John H. Kiefer, Acting Head, 312-996-3424, *Fax:* 312-996-0808.
Application contact: John R. Regalbuto, Director of Graduate Studies, 312-996-0288, *Fax:* 312-996-0808, *E-mail:* jrr@uic.edu.

■ **UNIVERSITY OF ILLINOIS AT URBANA–CHAMPAIGN**

Graduate College, College of Liberal Arts and Sciences, Department of Chemical Engineering, Champaign, IL 61820

AWARDS MS, PhD.

Faculty: 13 full-time.
Students: 84 full-time (21 women); includes 9 minority (all Asian Americans or Pacific Islanders), 40 international. Average age 23. 247 applicants, 8% accepted. In 2001, 18 master's, 9 doctorates awarded.
Degree requirements: For master's, thesis; for doctorate, thesis/dissertation, departmental qualifying exam.
Entrance requirements: For master's, minimum GPA of 3.0. *Application deadline:* For fall admission, 2/15. Applications are processed on a rolling basis. *Application fee:* $40 ($50 for international students). Electronic applications accepted.
Expenses: Tuition, state resident: part-time $3,227 per degree program. Tuition, nonresident: part-time $7,169 per degree program. Tuition and fees vary according to program.
Financial support: In 2001–02, 3 fellowships, 65 research assistantships, 10 teaching assistantships were awarded. Financial award application deadline: 2/15.
Charles F. Zukoski, Head, 217-244-9214, *Fax:* 217-333-5052, *E-mail:* czukoski@uiuc.edu.
Application contact: Kim Johnson, Administrative Secretary, 217-244-9214, *Fax:* 217-333-5052, *E-mail:* kljohns@uiuc.edu. *Web site:* http://www.scs.uiuc.edu/chem_eng/

■ **THE UNIVERSITY OF IOWA**

Graduate College, College of Engineering, Department of Chemical and Biochemical Engineering, Iowa City, IA 52242-1316

AWARDS MS, PhD. Part-time programs available.

Faculty: 9 full-time (2 women), 4 part-time/adjunct (0 women).
Students: 21 full-time (7 women), 19 part-time (7 women); includes 3 minority (1 African American, 1 Asian American or Pacific Islander, 1 Hispanic American), 25 international. Average age 27. 93 applicants, 27% accepted, 9 enrolled. In 2001, 5 master's, 2 doctorates awarded.
Degree requirements: For master's, thesis (for some programs), comprehensive exam (for some programs), registration; for doctorate, thesis/dissertation, comprehensive exam, registration.
Entrance requirements: For master's and doctorate, GRE, TOEFL, minimum undergraduate GPA of 3.0. *Application deadline:* For fall admission, 2/1 (priority date); for spring admission, 10/1 (priority date). Applications are processed on a rolling basis. *Application fee:* $30 ($50 for international students). Electronic applications accepted.
Expenses: Tuition, state resident: full-time $3,702; part-time $206 per semester hour. Tuition, nonresident: full-time $11,924; part-time $206 per semester hour. Required fees: $101 per semester. Tuition and fees vary according to course load and program.
Financial support: In 2001–02, 34 students received support, including 6 fellowships (averaging $20,000 per year), 33 research assistantships with tuition reimbursements available (averaging $20,000 per year), 9 teaching assistantships (averaging $20,000 per year); health care benefits and unspecified assistantships also available. Financial award applicants required to submit FAFSA.
Faculty research: Photopolymerization, regional atmospheric modeling, biomaterials, medical engineering, cellular engineering. *Total annual research expenditures:* $3.1 million.
Dr. Alec Scranton, Departmental Executive Officer, 319-335-1414, *Fax:* 319-335-1415, *E-mail:* alec-scranton@uiowa.edu.
Application contact: Linda Wheatley, Secretary, 319-335-1400, *Fax:* 319-335-1415, *E-mail:* chemeng@engineering.uiowa.edu. *Web site:* http://www.cbe.engineering.uiowa.edu

■ **UNIVERSITY OF KANSAS**

Graduate School, School of Engineering, Department of Chemical and Petroleum Engineering, Lawrence, KS 66045

AWARDS Chemical engineering (MS); chemical/petroleum engineering (PhD);

University of Kansas (continued)
petroleum engineering (MS). Part-time programs available.

Faculty: 15.
Students: 30 full-time (10 women), 11 part-time (5 women); includes 1 minority (Asian American or Pacific Islander), 37 international. Average age 29. 21 applicants, 95% accepted, 10 enrolled. In 2001, 9 master's, 4 doctorates awarded.
Degree requirements: For master's, thesis (for some programs), exam; for doctorate, thesis/dissertation, qualifying exams, comprehensive exam.
Entrance requirements: For master's, GRE General Test, TOEFL, minimum GPA of 3.0; for doctorate, GRE General Test, TOEFL, minimum GPA of 3.5. *Application deadline:* For fall admission, 5/1 (priority date); for spring admission, 9/1 (priority date). Applications are processed on a rolling basis. *Application fee:* $40.
Expenses: Tuition, state resident: full-time $2,722; part-time $113 per credit. Tuition, nonresident: full-time $8,586; part-time $358 per credit. Required fees: $551; $46 per credit. Tuition and fees vary according to campus/location, program and reciprocity agreements.
Financial support: In 2001–02, 32 research assistantships with partial tuition reimbursements (averaging $9,737 per year), 12 teaching assistantships with full and partial tuition reimbursements (averaging $11,678 per year) were awarded. Fellowships, Federal Work-Study also available. Financial award application deadline: 1/31.
Faculty research: Enhanced oil recovery, catalysis and kinetics, electrochemical engineering, biochemical engineering, semiconductor materials processing.
Bala Subramaniam, Chairperson, 785-864-4965, *Fax:* 785-864-4967.
Application contact: Graduate Advisor, 785-864-4965, *Fax:* 785-864-4967, *E-mail:* cpeinfo@ku.edu. *Web site:* http://www.engr.ku.edu/cpe/

■ UNIVERSITY OF KENTUCKY

Graduate School, Graduate School Programs from the College of Engineering, Program in Chemical Engineering, Lexington, KY 40506-0032

AWARDS MS Ch E, PhD.

Faculty: 23 full-time (4 women).
Students: 29 full-time (7 women), 3 part-time; includes 3 minority (all Asian Americans or Pacific Islanders), 20 international. 68 applicants, 29% accepted. In 2001, 4 master's, 4 doctorates awarded.
Degree requirements: For master's, thesis optional; for doctorate, thesis/dissertation, comprehensive exam.
Entrance requirements: For master's, GRE General Test, minimum undergraduate GPA of 2.5; for doctorate, GRE General Test, minimum graduate GPA of 3.0. *Application deadline:* For fall admission,

7/19. Applications are processed on a rolling basis. *Application fee:* $30 ($35 for international students).
Expenses: Tuition, state resident: full-time $4,075; part-time $213 per credit hour. Tuition, nonresident: full-time $11,295; part-time $614 per credit hour.
Financial support: In 2001–02, 2 fellowships, 18 research assistantships, 6 teaching assistantships were awarded. Federal Work-Study and institutionally sponsored loans also available. Support available to part-time students.
Faculty research: Aerosol physics and chemistry, biocellular engineering fuel science, poly and membrane science.
Dr. D. Bhattacharyya, Director of Graduate Studies, 859-257-2794, *Fax:* 859-323-1929, *E-mail:* db@engr.uky.edu.
Application contact: Dr. Jeannine Blackwell, Associate Dean, 859-257-4905, *Fax:* 859-323-1928.

■ UNIVERSITY OF LOUISIANA AT LAFAYETTE

Graduate School, College of Engineering, Department of Chemical Engineering, Lafayette, LA 70504

AWARDS MSE. Evening/weekend programs available.

Faculty: 7 full-time (0 women).
Students: 27 full-time (5 women), (all international). 66 applicants, 42% accepted, 9 enrolled. In 2001, 6 degrees awarded.
Degree requirements: For master's, thesis or alternative, comprehensive exam.
Entrance requirements: For master's, GRE General Test, BS in chemical engineering, minimum GPA of 2.85. *Application deadline:* For fall admission, 5/15. *Application fee:* $20 ($30 for international students).
Expenses: Tuition, state resident: full-time $2,317; part-time $79 per credit. Tuition, nonresident: full-time $8,882; part-time $369 per credit. International tuition: $9,018 full-time.
Financial support: In 2001–02, 6 research assistantships with full tuition reimbursements (averaging $5,500 per year) were awarded; Federal Work-Study and tuition waivers (full and partial) also available. Financial award application deadline: 5/1.
Faculty research: Corrosion, transport phenomena and thermodynamics in the oil and gas industry.
Dr. James D. Garber, Head, 337-482-6562.
Application contact: Dr. Devesh Misra, Graduate Coordinator, 337-482-6430.

■ UNIVERSITY OF LOUISVILLE

Graduate School, Speed Scientific School, Department of Chemical Engineering, Louisville, KY 40292-0001

AWARDS M Eng, MS, PhD.

Students: 45 full-time (19 women), 21 part-time (7 women); includes 12 minority (3 African Americans, 5 Asian Americans or Pacific Islanders, 4 Hispanic Americans), 22 international. Average age 27. In 2001, 12 degrees awarded.
Degree requirements: For master's and doctorate, thesis/dissertation.
Entrance requirements: For master's and doctorate, GRE General Test. *Application deadline:* Applications are processed on a rolling basis. *Application fee:* $25.
Expenses: Tuition, state resident: full-time $4,134. Tuition, nonresident: full-time $11,486.
Financial support: In 2001–02, 5 fellowships with full tuition reimbursements (averaging $18,000 per year), 11 research assistantships with full tuition reimbursements (averaging $13,663 per year), 6 teaching assistantships with full tuition reimbursements (averaging $12,600 per year) were awarded.
Dr. Thomas L. Starr, Chair, 502-852-6347, *Fax:* 502-852-6355, *E-mail:* tlstar01@louisville.edu.

■ UNIVERSITY OF MAINE

Graduate School, College of Engineering, Department of Chemical and Biological Engineering, Program in Chemical Engineering, Orono, ME 04469

AWARDS MS, PhD. Part-time programs available.

Students: 20 full-time (2 women), 4 part-time (1 woman), 14 international. 31 applicants, 26% accepted, 4 enrolled. In 2001, 5 master's, 4 doctorates awarded. Terminal master's awarded for partial completion of doctoral program.
Degree requirements: For master's and doctorate, thesis/dissertation.
Entrance requirements: For master's and doctorate, GRE General Test, TOEFL. *Application deadline:* For fall admission, 2/1 (priority date). Applications are processed on a rolling basis. *Application fee:* $50. Electronic applications accepted.
Expenses: Tuition, state resident: full-time $3,780; part-time $210 per credit hour. Tuition, nonresident: full-time $10,782; part-time $599 per credit hour. Required fees: $9.5 per credit hour. $32 per semester. Tuition and fees vary according to reciprocity agreements.
Financial support: In 2001–02, 21 research assistantships with tuition reimbursements (averaging $14,500 per year), 3 teaching assistantships with tuition reimbursements (averaging $14,500 per year) were awarded. Federal Work-Study and tuition waivers (full and partial) also available. Financial award application deadline: 3/1.
Dr. Doug Bousfield, Coordinator, 207-581-2300, *Fax:* 207-581-2323.
Application contact: Scott G. Delcourt, Director of the Graduate School, 207-581-3218, *Fax:* 207-581-3232, *E-mail:*

graduate@maine.edu. *Web site:* http://www.umaine.edu/graduate

■ UNIVERSITY OF MARYLAND, BALTIMORE COUNTY

Graduate School, College of Engineering, Department of Chemical and Biochemical Engineering, Baltimore, MD 21250-5398

AWARDS MS, PhD.

Entrance requirements: For master's, GRE General Test, minimum GPA of 3.0; for doctorate, GRE General Test, GRE Subject Test, TOEFL, minimum GPA of 3.0.
Faculty research: Bioengineering, mammalian cell culture, protein purification, adsorptive separation.

Find an in-depth description at www.petersons.com/gradchannel.

■ UNIVERSITY OF MARYLAND, COLLEGE PARK

Graduate Studies and Research, A. James Clark School of Engineering, Department of Chemical Engineering, College Park, MD 20742

AWARDS M Eng, MS, PhD. Part-time and evening/weekend programs available.

Faculty: 14 full-time (2 women), 8 part-time/adjunct (2 women).
Students: 44 full-time (14 women), 13 part-time (5 women); includes 13 minority (4 African Americans, 7 Asian Americans or Pacific Islanders, 2 Hispanic Americans), 36 international. 165 applicants, 13% accepted, 9 enrolled. In 2001, 15 master's, 11 doctorates awarded.
Degree requirements: For master's, thesis optional; for doctorate, variable foreign language requirement, thesis/dissertation, exam, oral presentation.
Entrance requirements: For master's and doctorate, GRE General Test, TOEFL, minimum GPA of 3.0. *Application deadline:* For fall admission, 5/1; for spring admission, 12/1. Applications are processed on a rolling basis. *Application fee:* $50 ($70 for international students). Electronic applications accepted.
Expenses: Tuition, state resident: part-time $289 per credit hour. Tuition, nonresident: part-time $448 per credit hour. One-time fee: $436 part-time. Full-time tuition and fees vary according to course load, campus/location and program.
Financial support: In 2001–02, 2 fellowships with full tuition reimbursements (averaging $13,982 per year), 6 research assistantships with tuition reimbursements (averaging $17,820 per year), 22 teaching assistantships with tuition reimbursements (averaging $19,916 per year) were awarded. Federal Work-Study and scholarships/grants also available. Support

available to part-time students. Financial award applicants required to submit FAFSA.
Faculty research: Applied polymer science, biochemical engineering, process systems, thermal properties, aerosol nanoparticle technology.
Dr. Timothy Barbari, Chairman, 301-405-2983, *Fax:* 301-405-0523.
Application contact: Trudy Lindsey, Director, Graduate Admissions and Records, 301-405-6991, *Fax:* 301-314-9305, *E-mail:* grschool@deans.umd.edu.

■ UNIVERSITY OF MARYLAND, COLLEGE PARK

Graduate Studies and Research, A. James Clark School of Engineering, Professional Program in Engineering, College Park, MD 20742

AWARDS Aerospace engineering (M Eng); chemical engineering (M Eng); civil engineering (M Eng); electrical engineering (M Eng); fire protection engineering (M Eng); materials science and engineering (M Eng); mechanical engineering (M Eng); reliability engineering (M Eng). Systems engineering (M Eng). Part-time and evening/weekend programs available. Postbaccalaureate distance learning degree programs offered.

Faculty: 11 part-time/adjunct (0 women).
Students: 19 full-time (4 women), 144 part-time (31 women); includes 41 minority (17 African Americans, 18 Asian Americans or Pacific Islanders, 6 Hispanic Americans), 27 international. 71 applicants, 80% accepted, 50 enrolled. In 2001, 64 degrees awarded.
Application deadline: For fall admission, 8/15; for spring admission, 1/10. Applications are processed on a rolling basis.
Application fee: $50 ($70 for international students). Electronic applications accepted.
Expenses: Tuition, state resident: part-time $289 per credit hour. Tuition, nonresident: part-time $448 per credit hour. One-time fee: $436 part-time. Full-time tuition and fees vary according to course load, campus/location and program.
Financial support: In 2001–02, 1 research assistantship with tuition reimbursement (averaging $20,655 per year), 5 teaching assistantships with tuition reimbursements (averaging $11,114 per year) were awarded. Fellowships, Federal Work-Study and scholarships/grants also available. Support available to part-time students. Financial award applicants required to submit FAFSA.
Dr. George Syrmos, Acting Director, 301-405-5256, *Fax:* 301-314-9477.
Application contact: Trudy Lindsey, Director, Graduate Admissions and Records, 301-405-6991, *Fax:* 301-314-9305, *E-mail:* grschool@deans.umd.edu.

■ UNIVERSITY OF MASSACHUSETTS AMHERST

Graduate School, College of Engineering, Department of Chemical Engineering, Amherst, MA 01003

AWARDS MS, PhD. Part-time programs available.

Faculty: 21 full-time (4 women).
Students: 51 full-time (11 women), 4 part-time (2 women); includes 5 minority (3 Asian Americans or Pacific Islanders, 2 Hispanic Americans), 34 international. Average age 26. 165 applicants, 18% accepted. In 2001, 5 master's, 9 doctorates awarded. Terminal master's awarded for partial completion of doctoral program.
Degree requirements: For master's, thesis; for doctorate, one foreign language, thesis/dissertation.
Entrance requirements: For master's and doctorate, GRE General Test. *Application deadline:* For fall admission, 2/1 (priority date). Applications are processed on a rolling basis. *Application fee:* $40 ($50 for international students).
Expenses: Tuition, state resident: full-time $1,980; part-time $110 per credit. Tuition, nonresident: full-time $7,456; part-time $414 per credit. Required fees: $4,112. One-time fee: $115 full-time.
Financial support: In 2001–02, 2 fellowships with full tuition reimbursements (averaging $14,500 per year), 61 research assistantships with full tuition reimbursements (averaging $16,326 per year), 6 teaching assistantships with full tuition reimbursements (averaging $4,620 per year) were awarded. Career-related internships or fieldwork, Federal Work-Study, scholarships/grants, traineeships, and unspecified assistantships also available. Support available to part-time students. Financial award application deadline: 2/1.
Dr. Michael Malone, Head, 413-545-2359, *Fax:* 413-545-1647, *E-mail:* mmalone@ecs.umass.edu.

■ UNIVERSITY OF MASSACHUSETTS LOWELL

Graduate School, James B. Francis College of Engineering, Department of Chemical Engineering, Lowell, MA 01854-2881

AWARDS MS Eng. Part-time programs available.

Entrance requirements: For master's, GRE General Test. Electronic applications accepted.

■ UNIVERSITY OF MICHIGAN

Horace H. Rackham School of Graduate Studies, College of Engineering, Department of Chemical Engineering, Ann Arbor, MI 48109

AWARDS MSE, PhD, Ch E. Part-time programs available. Postbaccalaureate

University of Michigan (continued)
distance learning degree programs offered (no on-campus study).

Faculty: 18 full-time (2 women), 3 part-time/adjunct (1 woman).
Students: 95 full-time (30 women), 7 part-time (2 women); includes 20 minority (9 African Americans, 7 Asian Americans or Pacific Islanders, 4 Hispanic Americans), 46 international. Average age 26. 262 applicants, 27% accepted. In 2001, 26 master's, 11 doctorates awarded. Terminal master's awarded for partial completion of doctoral program.
Degree requirements: For doctorate, oral defense of dissertation, preliminary exams. *Median time to degree:* Master's–2 years full-time; doctorate–5 years full-time.
Entrance requirements: For master's and doctorate, GRE General Test. *Application deadline:* For fall admission, 1/15 (priority date); for winter admission, 10/15 (priority date). *Application fee:* $55. Electronic applications accepted.
Financial support: In 2001–02, 13 fellowships with full tuition reimbursements (averaging $20,000 per year), 50 research assistantships with full tuition reimbursements (averaging $20,000 per year), 12 teaching assistantships with full and partial tuition reimbursements (averaging $11,300 per year) were awarded.
Faculty research: Biochemical, fluid mechanics, polymers, catalysis, reaction engineering. *Total annual research expenditures:* $4.4 million.
Dr. Ronald G. Larson, Chair, 734-764-2383, *Fax:* 734-763-0459, *E-mail:* hamlins@engin.umich.edu.
Application contact: Melissa Bower, Department Office, 734-764-2383, *Fax:* 734-763-0459, *E-mail:* rdhd@umich.edu. *Web site:* http://www.engin.edu/dept/cheme/

■ **UNIVERSITY OF MINNESOTA, TWIN CITIES CAMPUS**

Graduate School, Institute of Technology, Department of Chemical Engineering and Materials Science, Program in Chemical Engineering, Minneapolis, MN 55455-0132

AWARDS M Ch E, MS Ch E, PhD. Part-time programs available. Terminal master's awarded for partial completion of doctoral program.

Degree requirements: For master's and doctorate, thesis/dissertation.
Entrance requirements: For master's and doctorate, GRE General Test.
Expenses: Tuition, state resident: full-time $2,932; part-time $489 per credit. Tuition, nonresident: full-time $5,758; part-time $960 per credit. Part-time tuition and fees vary according to course load, program and reciprocity agreements.
Faculty research: Chemical kinetics, reaction engineering and modeling, gas and

membrane separation processes, biochemical engineering, nonequilibrium statistical mechanics. *Web site:* http://www.cems.umn.edu/

■ **UNIVERSITY OF MISSOURI–COLUMBIA**

Graduate School, College of Engineering, Department of Chemical Engineering, Columbia, MO 65211

AWARDS MS, PhD.

Faculty: 12 full-time (1 woman).
Students: 14 full-time (3 women), 5 part-time (1 woman); includes 2 minority (both Asian Americans or Pacific Islanders), 7 international. 26 applicants, 23% accepted. In 2001, 7 master's, 5 doctorates awarded.
Degree requirements: For master's and doctorate, thesis/dissertation.
Entrance requirements: For master's and doctorate, GRE General Test, TOEFL, minimum GPA of 3.0. *Application deadline:* Applications are processed on a rolling basis. *Application fee:* $25 ($50 for international students).
Expenses: Tuition, state resident: part-time $179 per credit hour. Tuition, nonresident: part-time $539 per credit hour. Required fees: $122 per semester. Tuition and fees vary according to program.
Financial support: Research assistantships, teaching assistantships, institutionally sponsored loans available.
Dr. David Retzloff, Director of Graduate Studies, 573-882-4036, *E-mail:* retzloffd@missouri.edu. *Web site:* http://www.engineering.missouri.edu/chemical.htm

■ **UNIVERSITY OF MISSOURI–ROLLA**

Graduate School, School of Engineering, Department of Chemical Engineering, Rolla, MO 65409-0910

AWARDS MS, PhD. Part-time and evening/weekend programs available. Terminal master's awarded for partial completion of doctoral program.

Degree requirements: For master's and doctorate, thesis/dissertation.
Entrance requirements: For master's and doctorate, minimum GPA of 3.0.
Faculty research: Polymers, reaction engineering, bioengineering, mixing, physical properties.

■ **UNIVERSITY OF NEBRASKA–LINCOLN**

Graduate College, College of Engineering and Technology, Department of Chemical Engineering, Lincoln, NE 68588

AWARDS Chemical engineering (MS); engineering (PhD).
Faculty: 10.

Students: 11 (4 women) (all international). Average age 26. 27 applicants, 19% accepted, 2 enrolled. In 2001, 7 degrees awarded.
Degree requirements: For master's, thesis/dissertation; for doctorate, thesis/dissertation, comprehensive exam.
Entrance requirements: For master's and doctorate, GRE General Test, TOEFL. *Application deadline:* For fall admission, 3/1 (priority date). Applications are processed on a rolling basis. *Application fee:* $35. Electronic applications accepted.
Expenses: Tuition, state resident: full-time $2,412; part-time $134 per credit. Tuition, nonresident: full-time $6,223; part-time $346 per credit. Tuition and fees vary according to course load.
Financial support: In 2001–02, 9 research assistantships, 5 teaching assistantships were awarded. Fellowships, Federal Work-Study also available. Support available to part-time students. Financial award application deadline: 2/15.
Faculty research: Fermentation, radioactive waste remediation, chemical fuels from renewable feedstocks.
Dr. Delmar Timm, Acting Chair, 402-472-2750, *Fax:* 402-472-6989. *Web site:* http://che.unl.edu/

■ **UNIVERSITY OF NEVADA, RENO**

Graduate School, Mackay School of Mines, Department of Chemical Engineering, Reno, NV 89557

AWARDS MS, PhD.

Faculty: 6.
Students: 16 full-time (5 women); includes 1 minority (Hispanic American), 13 international. Average age 26. In 2001, 2 degrees awarded.
Degree requirements: For master's, thesis optional; for doctorate, thesis/dissertation.
Entrance requirements: For master's, TOEFL, minimum GPA of 2.75; for doctorate, TOEFL, minimum GPA of 3.0. *Application deadline:* For fall admission, 3/15; for spring admission, 10/1. *Application fee:* $40.
Expenses: Tuition, state resident: full-time $2,067; part-time $108 per credit. Tuition, nonresident: full-time $9,282; part-time $109 per credit. Required fees: $57 per semester. Tuition and fees vary according to course load.
Financial support: Research assistantships, teaching assistantships available. Financial award application deadline: 3/1.
Dr. Wallace Whiting, Graduate Program Director, 775-784-4307, *E-mail:* wwhiting@unr.edu.

■ UNIVERSITY OF NEW HAMPSHIRE

Graduate School, College of Engineering and Physical Sciences, Department of Chemical Engineering, Durham, NH 03824

AWARDS MS, PhD.

Faculty: 8 full-time.
Students: 4 full-time (2 women), 2 part-time (both women). Average age 29. 16 applicants, 94% accepted, 2 enrolled. In 2001, 1 degree awarded.
Degree requirements: For master's and doctorate, thesis/dissertation.
Application deadline: For fall admission, 4/1 (priority date); for winter admission, 12/1 (priority date). Applications are processed on a rolling basis. *Application fee:* $50. Electronic applications accepted.
Expenses: Tuition, state resident: full-time $6,300; part-time $350 per credit. Tuition, nonresident: full-time $15,720; part-time $643 per credit. Required fees: $560; $280 per term. One-time fee: $15 part-time. Tuition and fees vary according to course load.
Financial support: In 2001–02, 3 teaching assistantships were awarded; research assistantships, Federal Work-Study, scholarships/grants, and tuition waivers (full and partial) also available. Support available to part-time students. Financial award application deadline: 2/15.
Dr. Stephen S. T. Fan, Chairperson, 603-862-3656, *E-mail:* sstf@cisnnix.unh.edu. *Web site:* http://www.unh.edu/chemical-engineering/

■ UNIVERSITY OF NEW MEXICO

Graduate School, School of Engineering, Department of Chemical and Nuclear Engineering, Program in Chemical Engineering, Albuquerque, NM 87131-2039

AWARDS MS.

Faculty: 8 full-time (2 women), 7 part-time/adjunct (0 women).
Students: 33 full-time (6 women), 10 part-time (5 women); includes 7 minority (1 Asian American or Pacific Islander, 6 Hispanic Americans), 23 international. Average age 31. In 2001, 7 master's awarded.
Entrance requirements: For master's, GRE General Test, minimum GPA of 3.0.
Application deadline: For fall admission, 7/15; for spring admission, 11/10. *Application fee:* $40.
Expenses: Tuition, state resident: full-time $2,771; part-time $115 per credit hour. Tuition, nonresident: full-time $11,207; part-time $467 per credit hour. Required fees: $570; $24 per credit hour. Part-time tuition and fees vary according to course load and program.
Financial support: In 2001–02, 1 fellowship (averaging $9,000 per year), 38 research assistantships with tuition reimbursements (averaging $15,600 per year) were awarded. Health care benefits also available. Financial award application deadline: 3/1; financial award applicants required to submit FAFSA.
Faculty research: Nanostructures, microsystems, molecular self-assembly, catalysis and interfaces, colloidal transport. Dr. Abhaya K. Datye, Professor, 505-277-0477, *Fax:* 505-277-5433, *E-mail:* datye@unm.edu.
Application contact: Mercy M. Salazar, Information Contact, 505-277-5431, *Fax:* 505-277-5433, *E-mail:* mercy@unm.edu. *Web site:* http://www.chne.unm.edu/home01/ChEindex.htm/

■ UNIVERSITY OF NORTH DAKOTA

Graduate School, School of Engineering and Mines, Department of Chemical Engineering, Grand Forks, ND 58202

AWARDS M Engr, MS. Part-time programs available.

Faculty: 4 full-time (0 women).
Students: 3 full-time (1 woman), 2 part-time (1 woman). 14 applicants, 57% accepted, 2 enrolled. In 2001, 4 degrees awarded.
Degree requirements: For master's, thesis or alternative, final comprehensive exam.
Entrance requirements: For master's, GRE General Test, TOEFL, minimum GPA of 3.0 (MS), 2.5 (M Engr). *Application deadline:* For fall admission, 3/1 (priority date); for spring admission, 10/15 (priority date). Applications are processed on a rolling basis. *Application fee:* $30.
Expenses: Tuition, state resident: full-time $3,298. Tuition, nonresident: full-time $7,998.
Financial support: In 2001–02, 4 research assistantships with full tuition reimbursements (averaging $9,500 per year), 5 teaching assistantships with full tuition reimbursements (averaging $9,500 per year) were awarded. Fellowships, career-related internships or fieldwork, Federal Work-Study, institutionally sponsored loans, scholarships/grants, tuition waivers (full and partial), and unspecified assistantships also available. Support available to part-time students. Financial award application deadline: 3/15; financial award applicants required to submit FAFSA.
Faculty research: Catalysis, fluid flow and heat transfer, application of fractals, modeling and simulation, reaction engineering.
Dr. Rashid Hasan, Director, 701-777-3798, *Fax:* 701-777-4838, *E-mail:* rashid_hasan@mail.und.nodak.edu. *Web site:* http://www.und.edu/sem/html/chemical_engineering.html

■ UNIVERSITY OF NOTRE DAME

Graduate School, College of Engineering, Department of Chemical Engineering, Notre Dame, IN 46556

AWARDS MS, PhD.

Faculty: 16 full-time (2 women).
Students: 58 full-time (16 women), 1 (woman) part-time; includes 2 minority (both African Americans), 31 international. 134 applicants, 26% accepted, 14 enrolled. In 2001, 5 master's, 6 doctorates awarded.
Degree requirements: For master's and doctorate, thesis/dissertation, comprehensive exam. *Median time to degree:* Doctorate–6.3 years full-time.
Entrance requirements: For master's, GRE General Test, TOEFL; for doctorate, GRE General Test, GRE Subject Test (strongly recommended), TOEFL. *Application deadline:* For fall admission, 2/1; for spring admission, 11/15. *Application fee:* $50. Electronic applications accepted.
Expenses: Tuition: Full-time $24,220; part-time $1,346 per credit hour. Required fees: $155.
Financial support: In 2001–02, 59 students received support, including 15 fellowships with full tuition reimbursements available (averaging $18,000 per year), 26 research assistantships with full tuition reimbursements available (averaging $14,500 per year), 16 teaching assistantships with full tuition reimbursements available (averaging $14,500 per year); tuition waivers (full) also available. Financial award application deadline: 2/1.
Faculty research: Biomolecular engineering, engineering for minimizing environmental impact, advanced materials, nano engineering, catalysis and reaction engineering. *Total annual research expenditures:* $1.7 million.
Dr. Mark J. McCready, Chair, 574-631-5580, *E-mail:* chegdept.1@nd.edu.
Application contact: Marty Nemeth, Information Contact, 800-528-9487, *Fax:* 574-631-8366, *E-mail:* nemeth.1@nd.edu. *Web site:* http://www.nd.edu/~chegdept/

■ UNIVERSITY OF OKLAHOMA

Graduate College, College of Engineering, School of Chemical Engineering and Materials Science, Norman, OK 73019-0390

AWARDS Chemical engineering (MS, PhD). Part-time programs available.

Faculty: 15 full-time (0 women), 2 part-time/adjunct (0 women).
Students: 40 full-time (12 women), 7 part-time; includes 4 minority (1 African American, 2 Asian Americans or Pacific Islanders, 1 Hispanic American), 31 international. 22 applicants, 82% accepted, 12 enrolled. In 2001, 9 master's, 8 doctorates awarded.
Degree requirements: For master's, thesis, oral exams; for doctorate, thesis/dissertation, oral exam, qualifying exams.

University of Oklahoma (continued)

Entrance requirements: For master's and doctorate, TOEFL, minimum GPA of 3.0. *Application deadline:* For fall admission, 6/1 (priority date). Applications are processed on a rolling basis. *Application fee:* $25 ($50 for international students).

Expenses: Tuition, state resident: full-time $2,208; part-time $92 per credit hour. Tuition, nonresident: part-time $297 per credit hour. Tuition and fees vary according to course level, course load and program.

Financial support: In 2001–02, 37 research assistantships with partial tuition reimbursements (averaging $13,284 per year), 2 teaching assistantships with partial tuition reimbursements (averaging $8,739 per year) were awarded. Fellowships, tuition waivers (partial) and unspecified assistantships also available. Financial award application deadline: 8/1; financial award applicants required to submit FAFSA.

Faculty research: Catalysis, surface science, bioengineering, polymers, energy. *Total annual research expenditures:* $1.2 million.

Dr. Lance Lobban, Director, 405-325-5811, *Fax:* 405-325-5813, *E-mail:* llobban@ou.edu.

Application contact: Donna King, Graduate Program Secretary, 405-325-5811, *Fax:* 405-325-5813, *E-mail:* chegrad@ou.edu.

■ UNIVERSITY OF PENNSYLVANIA

School of Engineering and Applied Science, Department of Chemical Engineering, Philadelphia, PA 19104

AWARDS MSE, PhD, MSE/MBA. Part-time programs available. Terminal master's awarded for partial completion of doctoral program.

Degree requirements: For doctorate, thesis/dissertation.

Entrance requirements: For master's and doctorate, TOEFL.

Faculty research: Biochemical engineering, surface and interfacial phenomena, process and design control, zeolites, molecular dynamics. *Web site:* http://www.seas.upenn.edu/che/

■ UNIVERSITY OF PITTSBURGH

School of Engineering, Department of Chemical and Petroleum Engineering, Pittsburgh, PA 15260

AWARDS Chemical engineering (MS Ch E, PhD); petroleum engineering (MSPE). Part-time and evening/weekend programs available.

Faculty: 13 full-time (2 women), 6 part-time/adjunct (0 women).

Students: 43 full-time (8 women), 7 part-time (3 women); includes 2 minority (1 African American, 1 Asian American or Pacific Islander), 32 international. 200

applicants, 14% accepted, 14 enrolled. In 2001, 11 master's, 9 doctorates awarded.

Degree requirements: For master's, thesis; for doctorate, thesis/dissertation, final oral exams, comprehensive exam.

Entrance requirements: For master's and doctorate, GRE General Test, TOEFL, minimum QPA of 3.2. *Application deadline:* For fall admission, 8/1 (priority date); for spring admission, 12/1 (priority date). Applications are processed on a rolling basis. *Application fee:* $40.

Financial support: In 2001–02, 41 students received support, including 1 fellowship with full tuition reimbursement available (averaging $19,000 per year), 40 research assistantships with full tuition reimbursements available (averaging $19,392 per year); teaching assistantships with full tuition reimbursements available, scholarships/grants, traineeships, and tuition waivers (full and partial) also available. Financial award application deadline: 2/15.

Faculty research: Biotechnology, polymers, catalysis, energy and environment, computational modeling. *Total annual research expenditures:* $4.6 million.

Dr. Eric Beckman, Chairman, 412-624-9631, *Fax:* 412-624-9639, *E-mail:* beckman@pitt.edu.

Application contact: William Federspiel, Associate Professor and Grad Coordinator, 412-624-9499, *Fax:* 412-624-9639, *E-mail:* federspiel@engrng.pitt.edu. *Web site:* http://www.engrng.pitt.edu/~chewww/

■ UNIVERSITY OF PUERTO RICO, MAYAGÜEZ CAMPUS

Graduate Studies, College of Engineering, Department of Chemical Engineering, Mayagüez, PR 00681-9000

AWARDS M Ch E, MS. Part-time programs available.

Degree requirements: For master's, thesis, comprehensive exam.

Entrance requirements: For master's, minimum GPA of 2.5, proficiency in English and Spanish.

Faculty research: Process simulation and optimization, air and water pollution control, mass transport, biochemical engineering.

■ UNIVERSITY OF RHODE ISLAND

Graduate School, College of Engineering, Department of Chemical Engineering, Kingston, RI 02881

AWARDS MS, PhD.

Students: In 2001, 4 master's, 1 doctorate awarded.

Application deadline: For fall admission, 4/15 (priority date). Applications are processed on a rolling basis. *Application fee:* $35.

Expenses: Tuition, state resident: full-time $3,756; part-time $209 per credit. Tuition, nonresident: full-time $10,774; part-time $599 per credit. Required fees: $1,586; $76 per credit. $76 per credit. One-time fee: $60 full-time.

Dr. Richard Brown, Chairman, 401-874-2655.

■ UNIVERSITY OF ROCHESTER

The College, School of Engineering and Applied Sciences, Department of Chemical Engineering, Rochester, NY 14627-0250

AWARDS MS, PhD. Part-time programs available.

Faculty: 5.

Students: 13 full-time (4 women), 4 part-time (3 women); includes 1 minority (African American), 12 international. 184 applicants, 8% accepted, 8 enrolled. In 2001, 4 master's, 3 doctorates awarded. Terminal master's awarded for partial completion of doctoral program.

Degree requirements: For master's, comprehensive exam; for doctorate, thesis/dissertation, preliminary and oral exams.

Entrance requirements: For master's and doctorate, GRE, TOEFL. *Application deadline:* For fall admission, 2/1. *Application fee:* $25.

Expenses: Tuition: Part-time $755 per credit hour.

Financial support: Fellowships, research assistantships, teaching assistantships, tuition waivers (full and partial) available. Financial award application deadline: 2/1. Shaw-Horng Chen, Chair, 585-275-4041.

Application contact: Mary Ellen Felten, Graduate Program Secretary, 585-275-4042.

■ UNIVERSITY OF SOUTH ALABAMA

Graduate School, College of Engineering, Department of Chemical Engineering, Mobile, AL 36688-0002

AWARDS MS Ch E.

Faculty: 5 full-time (0 women).

Students: 40 full-time (6 women), 15 part-time (3 women); includes 3 minority (2 African Americans, 1 Asian American or Pacific Islander), 45 international. 52 applicants, 81% accepted. In 2001, 8 degrees awarded.

Degree requirements: For master's, project or thesis.

Entrance requirements: For master's, GRE General Test, BS in engineering, minimum GPA of 3.0. *Application deadline:* For fall admission, 9/1 (priority date). Applications are processed on a rolling basis. *Application fee:* $25.

Expenses: Tuition, state resident: full-time $3,048. Tuition, nonresident: full-time $6,096. Required fees: $320.

Financial support: In 2001–02, 1 research assistantship was awarded; career-related internships or fieldwork and institutionally sponsored loans also available. Support available to part-time students. Financial award application deadline: 4/1.
Dr. B. Keith Harrison, Chair, 334-460-6160.
Application contact: Dr. Russell M. Hayes, Director of Graduate Studies, 334-460-6117.

■ UNIVERSITY OF SOUTH CAROLINA

The Graduate School, College of Engineering and Information Technology, Department of Chemical Engineering, Columbia, SC 29208

AWARDS ME, MS, PhD. Part-time and evening/weekend programs available. Postbaccalaureate distance learning degree programs offered (minimal on-campus study).

Faculty: 16 full-time (1 woman).
Students: 59 full-time (21 women), 13 part-time (3 women); includes 51 minority (4 African Americans, 43 Asian Americans or Pacific Islanders, 4 Hispanic Americans). Average age 25. 154 applicants, 19% accepted. In 2001, 5 master's, 9 doctorates awarded.
Degree requirements: For master's, thesis (for some programs); for doctorate, thesis/dissertation.
Entrance requirements: For master's and doctorate, GRE General Test, TOEFL. *Application deadline:* For fall admission, 3/1 (priority date); for spring admission, 11/1. Applications are processed on a rolling basis. *Application fee:* $40. Electronic applications accepted.
Expenses: Tuition, state resident: full-time $4,434. Tuition, nonresident: full-time $9,854. Tuition and fees vary according to program.
Financial support: In 2001–02, 61 research assistantships with partial tuition reimbursements (averaging $20,100 per year) were awarded; fellowships, teaching assistantships with partial tuition reimbursements, career-related internships or fieldwork and institutionally sponsored loans also available.
Faculty research: Rheology, liquid and supercritical extractions, electrochemistry, corrosion, heterogeneous and homogeneous catalysis. *Total annual research expenditures:* $4.2 million.
Dr. Michael A. Matthews, Interim Chair and Associate Professor, 803-777-4181, *Fax:* 803-777-8265, *E-mail:* matthews@engr.sc.edu.
Application contact: Kay P. Dorrell, Administrative Assistant, 803-777-1261, *Fax:* 803-777-8265, *E-mail:* dorrellk@engr.sc.edu. *Web site:* http://www.che.sc.edu/

■ UNIVERSITY OF SOUTHERN CALIFORNIA

Graduate School, School of Engineering, Department of Chemical Engineering, Los Angeles, CA 90089

AWARDS MS, PhD, Engr. Part-time programs available. Terminal master's awarded for partial completion of doctoral program.

Degree requirements: For doctorate, thesis/dissertation.
Entrance requirements: For master's, doctorate, and Engr, GRE General Test.
Expenses: Tuition: Full-time $25,060; part-time $844 per unit. Required fees: $473.
Faculty research: Statistical mechanics, molecular simulation, porous media, polymer science and engineering, reaction engineering and catalysis.

■ UNIVERSITY OF SOUTH FLORIDA

College of Graduate Studies, College of Engineering, Department of Chemical Engineering, Tampa, FL 33620-9951

AWARDS M Ch E, ME, MS, MS Ch E, PhD. Part-time programs available.

Faculty: 10 full-time (0 women).
Students: 31 full-time (7 women), 7 part-time (1 woman); includes 5 minority (2 African Americans, 3 Hispanic Americans), 20 international. Average age 28. 95 applicants, 67% accepted, 8 enrolled. In 2001, 6 master's, 2 doctorates awarded. Terminal master's awarded for partial completion of doctoral program.
Degree requirements: For master's, thesis (for some programs); for doctorate, thesis/dissertation, 2 tools of research as specified by dissertation committee.
Entrance requirements: For master's, GRE General Test, minimum GPA of 3.0 during previous 2 years; for doctorate, GRE General Test. *Application deadline:* For fall admission, 6/1; for spring admission, 10/15. *Application fee:* $20. Electronic applications accepted.
Expenses: Tuition, state resident: part-time $166 per credit hour. Tuition, nonresident: part-time $573 per credit hour. Required fees: $17 per term.
Financial support: Fellowships with full tuition reimbursements, research assistantships with full tuition reimbursements, teaching assistantships with full tuition reimbursements, career-related internships or fieldwork, Federal Work-Study, institutionally sponsored loans, and tuition waivers (partial) available. Support available to part-time students. Financial award applicants required to submit FAFSA.
Faculty research: Process design and control, sensor development and identification, biomedical engineering, polymer characterization and synthesis, supercritical fluid technology. *Total annual research expenditures:* $319,748.

Babu Joseph, Chairperson, 813-974-0692, *Fax:* 813-974-3651.
Application contact: A. K. Sunol, Coordinator, 813-974-3997, *Fax:* 813-974-3651, *E-mail:* sunol@eng.usf.edu. *Web site:* http://www.eng.usf.edu/CE/chemeng.html

■ THE UNIVERSITY OF TENNESSEE

Graduate School, College of Engineering, Department of Chemical Engineering, Knoxville, TN 37996

AWARDS MS, PhD.

Faculty: 13 full-time (1 woman), 1 part-time/adjunct (0 women).
Students: 22 full-time (4 women), 11 part-time (3 women); includes 1 minority (African American), 14 international. 71 applicants, 25% accepted. In 2001, 9 master's, 3 doctorates awarded.
Degree requirements: For master's, thesis or alternative; for doctorate, thesis/dissertation.
Entrance requirements: For master's and doctorate, GRE General Test, TOEFL, minimum GPA of 2.7. *Application deadline:* For fall admission, 2/1 (priority date). Applications are processed on a rolling basis. *Application fee:* $35. Electronic applications accepted.
Expenses: Tuition, state resident: full-time $4,280; part-time $233 per hour. Tuition, nonresident: full-time $12,066; part-time $666 per hour. Tuition and fees vary according to program.
Financial support: In 2001–02, 11 research assistantships, 10 teaching assistantships were awarded. Fellowships, career-related internships or fieldwork, Federal Work-Study, institutionally sponsored loans, and unspecified assistantships also available. Financial award application deadline: 2/1; financial award applicants required to submit FAFSA.
Dr. John R. Collier, Head, 865-974-2421, *Fax:* 865-974-7076, *E-mail:* collier@utk.edu.
Application contact: Dr. Paul Frymier, Graduate Representative, 865-974-4961, *E-mail:* pdf@utk.edu.

■ THE UNIVERSITY OF TENNESSEE SPACE INSTITUTE

Graduate Programs, Program in Chemical Engineering, Tullahoma, TN 37388-9700

AWARDS MS.

Faculty: 1 full-time (0 women).
Students: 3 full-time (1 woman), 1 part-time, 2 international. In 2001, 1 degree awarded.
Degree requirements: For master's, thesis.
Application deadline: Applications are processed on a rolling basis. *Application fee:* $35.
Expenses: Tuition, state resident: full-time $4,730; part-time $208 per semester hour.

The University of Tennessee Space Institute (continued)

Tuition, nonresident: full-time $15,028; part-time $627 per semester hour. Required fees: $10 per semester hour. One-time fee: $35.
Financial support: Fellowships with full and partial tuition reimbursements, research assistantships with full tuition reimbursements, Federal Work-Study available. Financial award applicants required to submit FAFSA.
Dr. Atul Sheth, Degree Program Chairman, 931-393-7427, *Fax:* 931-393-7201, *E-mail:* asheth@utsi.edu.
Application contact: Dr. Alfonso Pujol, Assistant Vice President and Dean for Student Affairs, 931-393-7432, *Fax:* 931-393-7346, *E-mail:* apujol@utsi.edu.

■ THE UNIVERSITY OF TEXAS AT AUSTIN

Graduate School, College of Engineering, Department of Chemical Engineering, Austin, TX 78712-1111

AWARDS MSE, PhD.

Students: 119 full-time (25 women), 25 part-time; includes 10 minority (2 African Americans, 7 Asian Americans or Pacific Islanders, 1 Hispanic American), 40 international. Average age 25. 350 applicants, 19% accepted. In 2001, 18 master's, 17 doctorates awarded.
Entrance requirements: For master's and doctorate, GRE General Test. *Application deadline:* For fall admission, 2/1; for spring admission, 10/1. *Application fee:* $50 ($75 for international students). Electronic applications accepted.
Expenses: Tuition, state resident: full-time $3,159. Tuition, nonresident: full-time $6,957. Tuition and fees vary according to program.
Financial support: In 2001–02, 116 students received support, including 1 fellowship with full tuition reimbursement available (averaging $16,500 per year), 113 research assistantships with full tuition reimbursements available (averaging $16,500 per year), 3 teaching assistantships with full tuition reimbursements available (averaging $16,500 per year) Financial award application deadline: 2/1.
John G. Ekerdt, Chairman, 512-471-4689.
Application contact: Gary Rochelle, Graduate Adviser, 512-471-6991, *Fax:* 512-475-7824, *E-mail:* t@che.utexas.edu.

■ UNIVERSITY OF TOLEDO

Graduate School, College of Engineering, Department of Chemical and Environmental Engineering, Toledo, OH 43606-3398

AWARDS Chemical engineering (MS); engineering sciences (PhD). Part-time and evening/weekend programs available.
Faculty: 12 full-time (3 women).

Students: 38 full-time (6 women), 5 part-time (2 women); includes 2 minority (1 African American, 1 Asian American or Pacific Islander), 29 international. Average age 27. 110 applicants, 20% accepted. In 2001, 15 master's, 6 doctorates awarded.
Degree requirements: For master's, thesis optional; for doctorate, thesis/dissertation.
Entrance requirements: For master's, GRE General Test, TOEFL, minimum GPA of 2.7; for doctorate, GRE General Test, TOEFL, minimum GPA of 3.3. *Application deadline:* For fall admission, 5/31 (priority date). Applications are processed on a rolling basis. *Application fee:* $30. Electronic applications accepted.
Expenses: Tuition, state resident: full-time $7,278; part-time $303 per hour. Tuition, nonresident: full-time $15,731; part-time $699 per hour. Required fees: $43 per hour.
Financial support: In 2001–02, 20 research assistantships with full tuition reimbursements, 21 teaching assistantships with full tuition reimbursements were awarded. Fellowships, Federal Work-Study, scholarships/grants, tuition waivers (full), and unspecified assistantships also available. Financial award application deadline: 4/1.
Faculty research: Biomedical and environmental chemical engineering, polymers, applied computing, membranes. *Total annual research expenditures:* $2.2 million.
Dr. Steven E. LeBlanc, Chairman, 419-530-8080, *Fax:* 419-530-8086.
Application contact: Dr. Arun Nadarajah, Graduate Director, 419-530-8031, *Fax:* 419-530-8086, *E-mail:* anadaraj@eng.utoledo.edu. *Web site:* http://www.che.utoledo.edu/

Find an in-depth description at www.petersons.com/gradchannel.

■ UNIVERSITY OF TULSA

Graduate School, College of Business Administration and College of Engineering and Natural Sciences, Department of Engineering and Technology Management, Tulsa, OK 74104-3189

AWARDS Chemical engineering (METM); computer science (METM); electrical engineering (METM); geological science (METM); mathematics (METM); mechanical engineering (METM); petroleum engineering (METM). Part-time and evening/weekend programs available.
Students: 2 full-time (1 woman), 1 part-time, 2 international. Average age 26. 3 applicants, 100% accepted, 1 enrolled. In 2001, 2 degrees awarded.
Entrance requirements: For master's, GRE General Test, TOEFL. *Application deadline:* Applications are processed on a rolling basis. *Application fee:* $30. Electronic applications accepted.

Expenses: Tuition: Full-time $9,540; part-time $530 per credit hour. Required fees: $80. One-time fee: $230 full-time.
Financial support: Fellowships, research assistantships, teaching assistantships, Federal Work-Study, scholarships/grants, tuition waivers (partial), and unspecified assistantships available. Support available to part-time students. Financial award application deadline: 2/1; financial award applicants required to submit FAFSA.
Application contact: Information Contact, *E-mail:* graduate-business@utulsa.edu. *Web site:* http://www.cba.utulsa.edu/academic.asp#graduate_studies/

■ UNIVERSITY OF TULSA

Graduate School, College of Engineering and Natural Sciences, Department of Chemical Engineering, Tulsa, OK 74104-3189

AWARDS ME, MSE, PhD. Part-time programs available.

Faculty: 8 full-time (2 women).
Students: 20 full-time (6 women), 10 part-time (3 women); includes 1 minority (African American), 22 international. Average age 28. 39 applicants, 77% accepted, 11 enrolled. In 2001, 5 master's, 1 doctorate awarded.
Degree requirements: For master's, thesis optional; for doctorate, thesis/dissertation, comprehensive exam.
Entrance requirements: For master's and doctorate, GRE General Test, TOEFL. *Application deadline:* Applications are processed on a rolling basis. *Application fee:* $30. Electronic applications accepted.
Expenses: Tuition: Full-time $9,540; part-time $530 per credit hour. Required fees: $80. One-time fee: $230 full-time.
Financial support: In 2001–02, 8 research assistantships with full and partial tuition reimbursements (averaging $9,500 per year), 6 teaching assistantships with full and partial tuition reimbursements (averaging $7,400 per year) were awarded. Fellowships, career-related internships or fieldwork, Federal Work-Study, scholarships/grants, tuition waivers (partial), and unspecified assistantships also available. Support available to part-time students. Financial award application deadline: 2/1; financial award applicants required to submit FAFSA.
Faculty research: Refinery design, enhanced hydrocarbon recovery, fluid rheology, phase equilibria, fluid mechanics. *Total annual research expenditures:* $1.4 million.
Dr. Geoffrey Price, Chairperson, 918-631-2575, *E-mail:* geoffrey-price@utulsa.edu.
Application contact: Dr. Charles Sheppard, Adviser, 918-631-2644, *Fax:* 918-631-3268, *E-mail:* grad@utulsa.edu. *Web site:* http://www.ce.utulsa.edu/Graduates/index.html/

UNIVERSITY OF UTAH

Graduate School, College of Engineering, Department of Chemical and Fuels Engineering, Salt Lake City, UT 84112-1107

AWARDS Chemical and fuels engineering (M Phil, ME, MS, PhD); chemical engineering (M Phil, ME, MS, PhD); environmental engineering (ME, MS, PhD). Part-time programs available.

Faculty: 10 full-time (2 women), 6 part-time/adjunct (0 women).
Students: 47 full-time (7 women), 10 part-time (2 women); includes 18 minority (all Asian Americans or Pacific Islanders), 15 international. Average age 28. 84 applicants, 18% accepted. In 2001, 2 master's, 3 doctorates awarded.
Entrance requirements: For master's and doctorate, GRE, TOEFL, minimum GPA of 3.0. *Application deadline:* 7/1. *Application fee:* $40 ($60 for international students).
Expenses: Tuition, state resident: part-time $320 per semester hour. Tuition, nonresident: part-time $1,135 per semester hour. Required fees: $143 per semester hour. Tuition and fees vary according to course load, degree level and program.
Financial support: Fellowships, research assistantships, teaching assistantships available. Financial award applicants required to submit FAFSA.
Faculty research: Computer-aided process synthesis and design, combustion of solid and liquid fossil fuels, oxygen mass transport in biochemical reactors.
Terry Ring, Chair, 801-581-6915, *Fax:* 801-585-9291, *E-mail:* t.ring@m.cc.utah.edu.
Application contact: Grant Smith, Advisor, 801-581-6915, *Fax:* 801-585-9291, *E-mail:* gsmith@geoffrey.emro.utah.edu.

UNIVERSITY OF VIRGINIA

School of Engineering and Applied Science, Department of Chemical Engineering, Charlottesville, VA 22903

AWARDS ME, MS, PhD. Postbaccalaureate distance learning degree programs offered (no on-campus study).

Faculty: 11 full-time (1 woman), 1 part-time/adjunct (0 women).
Students: 46 full-time (16 women), 3 part-time; includes 6 minority (1 African American, 3 Asian Americans or Pacific Islanders, 2 Hispanic Americans), 18 international. Average age 25. 94 applicants, 43% accepted, 16 enrolled. In 2001, 8 master's, 3 doctorates awarded.
Degree requirements: For master's, thesis (for some programs); for doctorate, thesis/dissertation, comprehensive exam.
Entrance requirements: For master's and doctorate, GRE General Test. *Application deadline:* For fall admission, 8/1; for spring admission, 12/1. Applications are processed on a rolling basis. *Application fee:* $40. Electronic applications accepted.
Expenses: Tuition, state resident: full-time $3,988. Tuition, nonresident: full-time $17,078. Required fees: $1,190.
Financial support: Fellowships available. Financial award application deadline: 2/1; financial award applicants required to submit FAFSA.
Faculty research: Fluid mechanics, heat and mass transfer, chemical reactor analysis and engineering, biochemical engineering and biotechnology.
John P. O'Connell, Chairman, 434-924-7778.
Application contact: Matthew Neurock, Associate Professor, 434-924-6248, *E-mail:* mntn@virginia.edu. *Web site:* http://www.che.virginia.edu/

UNIVERSITY OF WASHINGTON

Graduate School, College of Engineering, Department of Chemical Engineering, Seattle, WA 98195

AWARDS MS Ch E, PhD.

Faculty: 17 full-time (2 women), 4 part-time/adjunct (1 woman).
Students: 75 full-time (24 women), 1 part-time; includes 8 minority (2 African Americans, 6 Asian Americans or Pacific Islanders), 33 international. Average age 24. 85 applicants, 52% accepted, 14 enrolled. In 2001, 8 master's, 8 doctorates awarded. Terminal master's awarded for partial completion of doctoral program.
Degree requirements: For master's, thesis or alternative; for doctorate, thesis/dissertation.
Entrance requirements: For master's and doctorate, GRE, TOEFL, minimum GPA of 3.0. *Application deadline:* For fall admission, 1/15 (priority date). Applications are processed on a rolling basis. *Application fee:* $50. Electronic applications accepted.
Expenses: Tuition, state resident: full-time $5,539. Tuition, nonresident: full-time $14,376. Required fees: $390. Tuition and fees vary according to course load and program.
Financial support: In 2001–02, 13 fellowships with full tuition reimbursements (averaging $19,800 per year), 47 research assistantships with full tuition reimbursements (averaging $19,800 per year), 13 teaching assistantships with full tuition reimbursements (averaging $19,800 per year) were awarded. Career-related internships or fieldwork, Federal Work-Study, and health care benefits also available. Financial award application deadline: 1/15.
Faculty research: Materials and interfacial phenomena, biochemical engineering and bioengineering, information and process techonology, environmental technology. *Total annual research expenditures:* $4.1 million.
Dr. Eric M. Stuve, Chair, 206-543-2250.
Application contact: Graduate Admissions Coordinator, 206-543-2252, *Fax:* 206-543-3778, *E-mail:* grad.admissions@cheme.washington.edu. *Web site:* http://depts.washington.edu/chemeng/

UNIVERSITY OF WISCONSIN–MADISON

Graduate School, College of Engineering, Department of Chemical Engineering, Madison, WI 53706-1380

AWARDS MS, PhD.

Faculty: 17 full-time (1 woman), 2 part-time/adjunct (0 women).
Students: 105 full-time (28 women); includes 9 minority (1 African American, 4 Asian Americans or Pacific Islanders, 4 Hispanic Americans), 43 international. 273 applicants, 26% accepted, 18 enrolled. In 2001, 8 master's, 13 doctorates awarded. Terminal master's awarded for partial completion of doctoral program.
Degree requirements: For master's, thesis or alternative; for doctorate, thesis/dissertation, comprehensive exam. *Median time to degree:* Master's–1.8 years full-time; doctorate–5.3 years full-time.
Entrance requirements: For master's and doctorate, GRE General Test. *Application deadline:* For fall admission, 1/15; for spring admission, 10/15. *Application fee:* $45. Electronic applications accepted.
Expenses: Tuition, state resident: full-time $7,361; part-time $399 per credit. Tuition, nonresident: full-time $20,499; part-time $1,282 per credit. Required fees: $34 per credit. Full-time tuition and fees vary according to course load, program, reciprocity agreements and student level.
Financial support: In 2001–02, 105 students received support, including fellowships with full tuition reimbursements available (averaging $21,500 per year), research assistantships with full tuition reimbursements available (averaging $19,000 per year), 37 teaching assistantships with full tuition reimbursements available (averaging $21,300 per year); traineeships and health care benefits also available. Financial award application deadline: 1/15.
Faculty research: Biotechnology, nanotechnology, systems, modeling and control, atomic and molecular modeling, complex fluids and multiscale modeling. *Total annual research expenditures:* $7.7 million.
Prof. James B. Rawlings, Chair, 608-262-1092, *Fax:* 608-262-5434.
Application contact: Donna M. Bell, Graduate Coordinator, 608-263-3138, *Fax:* 608-262-5434, *E-mail:* gradoffice@che.wisc.edu. *Web site:* http://www.engr.wisc.edu/che/

UNIVERSITY OF WYOMING

Graduate School, College of Engineering, Department of Chemical and Petroleum Engineering, Program in Chemical Engineering, Laramie, WY 82071

AWARDS MS, PhD.

Faculty: 9 full-time (0 women), 3 part-time/adjunct (0 women).

University of Wyoming (continued)
Students: 11 full-time (3 women), 5 part-time (1 woman), 9 international. 9 applicants, 100% accepted. In 2001, 2 degrees awarded. Terminal master's awarded for partial completion of doctoral program.
Degree requirements: For master's and doctorate, thesis/dissertation.
Entrance requirements: For master's and doctorate, GRE General Test, TOEFL, minimum GPA of 3.0. *Application deadline:* For fall admission, 4/15 (priority date). Applications are processed on a rolling basis. *Application fee:* $40. Electronic applications accepted.
Expenses: Tuition, state resident: full-time $2,895; part-time $161 per credit hour. Tuition, nonresident: full-time $8,367; part-time $465 per credit hour. Required fees: $491; $10 per credit hour. $2 per credit hour. Tuition and fees vary according to course load and program.
Financial support: In 2001–02, 10 research assistantships with full tuition reimbursements (averaging $13,000 per year), 6 teaching assistantships with full tuition reimbursements (averaging $12,000 per year) were awarded. Career-related internships or fieldwork, Federal Work-Study, and institutionally sponsored loans also available. Financial award application deadline: 4/15.
Faculty research: Microwave reactor systems, synthetic fuels, fluidization, coal combustion/gasification, flue-gas cleanup. *Total annual research expenditures:* $700,000. Dr. Maciej Radosz, Head, 307-766-2500, *Fax:* 307-766-6777, *E-mail:* radosz@uwyo.edu.
Application contact: Dr. David Bell, Graduate Student Coordinator, 307-766-5769, *Fax:* 307-766-6777, *E-mail:* chpe.info@uwyo.edu. *Web site:* http://wwweng.uwyo.edu

■ VANDERBILT UNIVERSITY

School of Engineering, Department of Chemical Engineering, Nashville, TN 37240-1001

AWARDS M Eng, MS, PhD. MS and PhD offered through the Graduate School. Part-time programs available.

Faculty: 11 full-time (1 woman).
Students: 28 full-time (9 women); includes 3 minority (all Asian Americans or Pacific Islanders), 16 international. Average age 23. 43 applicants, 30% accepted, 6 enrolled. In 2001, 5 master's, 2 doctorates awarded.
Degree requirements: For master's and doctorate, thesis/dissertation. *Median time to degree:* Master's–2 years full-time; doctorate–4.5 years full-time.
Entrance requirements: For master's and doctorate, GRE General Test, TOEFL. *Application deadline:* For fall admission, 1/15; for spring admission, 11/1. *Application fee:* $40. Electronic applications accepted.

Expenses: Tuition: Full-time $28,350.
Financial support: In 2001–02, 1 fellowship with tuition reimbursement (averaging $5,000 per year), 21 research assistantships with tuition reimbursements (averaging $17,400 per year), 7 teaching assistantships with tuition reimbursements (averaging $17,400 per year) were awarded. Federal Work-Study, institutionally sponsored loans, and tuition waivers (partial) also available. Support available to part-time students. Financial award application deadline: 1/15; financial award applicants required to submit CSS PROFILE or FAFSA.
Faculty research: Adsorption and surface chemistry; biochemical engineering and biotechnology; chemical reaction engineering, environment, materials, and process modeling and control; chemical reaction kinetics, thermodynamics. *Total annual research expenditures:* $1.3 million.
Dr. M. Douglas LeVan, Chair, 615-322-2441, *Fax:* 615-343-7451, *E-mail:* m.douglas.levan@vanderbilt.edu.
Application contact: Dr. G. Kane Jennings, Director of Graduate Studies, 615-322-2441, *Fax:* 615-343-7951, *E-mail:* jenningk@vuse.vanderbilt.edu. *Web site:* http://www.vuse.vanderbilt.edu/~cheinfo/

■ VILLANOVA UNIVERSITY

College of Engineering, Department of Chemical Engineering, Villanova, PA 19085-1699

AWARDS M Ch E. Part-time and evening/weekend programs available.

Faculty: 8 full-time (1 woman), 1 part-time/adjunct (0 women).
Students: 6 full-time (1 woman), 34 part-time (11 women); includes 5 minority (3 African Americans, 2 Asian Americans or Pacific Islanders), 4 international. Average age 26. 18 applicants, 83% accepted, 10 enrolled. In 2001, 10 degrees awarded.
Degree requirements: For master's, thesis optional.
Entrance requirements: For master's, GRE General Test (for applicants with degrees from foreign universities), B Ch E, minimum GPA of 3.0. *Application deadline:* For fall admission, 8/1 (priority date); for spring admission, 12/1 (priority date). Applications are processed on a rolling basis. *Application fee:* $40.
Expenses: Tuition: Part-time $340 per credit. One-time fee: $115 full-time. Tuition and fees vary according to program.
Financial support: In 2001–02, 5 students received support, including 5 teaching assistantships with tuition reimbursements available (averaging $10,265 per year); research assistantships, Federal Work-Study and tuition waivers (partial) also available. Financial award application deadline: 3/15.
Faculty research: Heat transfer, advanced materials, chemical vapor deposition,

pyrolysis and combustion chemistry, industrial waste treatment.
Dr. C. Michael Kelly, Chairperson, 610-519-4950, *E-mail:* c.michael.kelly@villanova.edu. *Web site:* http://www.engineering.villanova.edu/chem/index.html

■ VIRGINIA POLYTECHNIC INSTITUTE AND STATE UNIVERSITY

Graduate School, College of Engineering, Department of Chemical Engineering, Blacksburg, VA 24061

AWARDS MS, PhD.

Faculty: 13 full-time (2 women).
Students: 47 full-time (12 women), 5 part-time (2 women); includes 17 minority (1 African American, 16 Asian Americans or Pacific Islanders). Average age 25. 169 applicants, 15% accepted. In 2001, 8 master's, 5 doctorates awarded. Terminal master's awarded for partial completion of doctoral program.
Degree requirements: For master's and doctorate, thesis/dissertation. *Median time to degree:* Master's–2 years full-time; doctorate–4 years full-time.
Entrance requirements: For master's and doctorate, GRE, TOEFL. *Application deadline:* For fall admission, 1/15 (priority date). Applications are processed on a rolling basis. *Application fee:* $45. Electronic applications accepted.
Expenses: Tuition, state resident: part-time $241 per hour. Tuition, nonresident: part-time $406 per hour. Tuition and fees vary according to program.
Financial support: In 2001–02, 1 fellowship with full tuition reimbursement (averaging $8,000 per year), 31 research assistantships with full tuition reimbursements (averaging $18,549 per year), 12 teaching assistantships with full tuition reimbursements (averaging $18,549 per year) were awarded. Unspecified assistantships also available. Financial award application deadline: 4/1.
Faculty research: Polymers, characterization, and rheological properties. Synthesis and characterization of zeolite catalysts; affinity separations of biologically-produced materials; high vacuum surface science of single crystal metal oxides; innovative techniques for the removal of and/or deactivation of organic waste materials from soils.
Dr. Erdogan Kiran, Head, 540-231-4213, *Fax:* 540-231-5022, *E-mail:* ekiran@vt.edu.
Application contact: Diane S. Cannaday, Graduate Secretary, 540-231-5771, *E-mail:* dianec@vt.edu. *Web site:* http://www.che.vt.edu

■ WASHINGTON STATE UNIVERSITY

Graduate School, College of Engineering and Architecture, Department of Chemical Engineering, Pullman, WA 99164

AWARDS MS, PhD.

Faculty: 9 full-time (1 woman).
Students: 22 full-time (5 women), 3 part-time; includes 1 minority (Hispanic American), 11 international. 63 applicants, 24% accepted. In 2001, 5 master's, 3 doctorates awarded. Terminal master's awarded for partial completion of doctoral program.
Degree requirements: For master's, thesis, oral exam; for doctorate, one foreign language, thesis/dissertation, oral exam. *Median time to degree:* Master's–2 years full-time; doctorate–5 years full-time.
Entrance requirements: For master's and doctorate, TOEFL, minimum GPA of 3.0. *Application deadline:* For fall admission, 3/1 (priority date). Applications are processed on a rolling basis. *Application fee:* $35.
Expenses: Tuition, state resident: full-time $6,088; part-time $304 per semester. Tuition, nonresident: full-time $14,918; part-time $746 per semester. Tuition and fees vary according to program.
Financial support: In 2001–02, 11 research assistantships with full and partial tuition reimbursements, 4 teaching assistantships with full and partial tuition reimbursements were awarded. Fellowships, career-related internships or fieldwork, Federal Work-Study, institutionally sponsored loans, tuition waivers (partial), and teaching associateships also available. Financial award application deadline: 4/1; financial award applicants required to submit FAFSA.
Faculty research: Bioprocessing, kinetics and catalysis, hazardous waste remediation. *Total annual research expenditures:* $793,948.
Dr. Richard Zollars, Chair, 509-335-4332, *Fax:* 509-335-4806, *E-mail:* rzollars@ che.wsu.edu.
Application contact: Diana Thornton, Secretary Supervisor, 509-335-4332, *Fax:* 509-335-4806, *E-mail:* thorntd@ che.wsu.edu. *Web site:* http:// www.che.wsu.edu/

■ WASHINGTON UNIVERSITY IN ST. LOUIS

Henry Edwin Sever Graduate School of Engineering and Applied Science, Department of Chemical Engineering, St. Louis, MO 63130-4899

AWARDS Chemical engineering (MS, D Sc); environmental engineering (MS, D Sc); materials science and engineering (MS); materials science engineering (D Sc). Part-time programs available.

Faculty: 11 full-time (0 women), 2 part-time/adjunct (0 women).

Students: 34 full-time (5 women), 9 part-time (6 women), 34 international. Average age 25. 122 applicants, 19% accepted, 7 enrolled. In 2001, 3 master's, 7 doctorates awarded. Terminal master's awarded for partial completion of doctoral program.
Degree requirements: For master's, thesis optional; for doctorate, thesis/ dissertation, preliminary exam, qualifying exam. *Median time to degree:* Master's–1.8 years full-time; doctorate–4.1 years full-time.
Entrance requirements: For master's and doctorate, GRE, minimum B average during final 2 years. *Application deadline:* For fall admission, 2/1 (priority date). Applications are processed on a rolling basis. *Application fee:* $20. Electronic applications accepted.
Expenses: Tuition: Full-time $26,900.
Financial support: In 2001–02, 30 research assistantships with full tuition reimbursements were awarded; fellowships with full tuition reimbursements, career-related internships or fieldwork, Federal Work-Study, and institutionally sponsored loans also available. Financial award application deadline: 2/1.
Faculty research: Reaction engineering, materials processing, catalysis, process control, air pollution control. *Total annual research expenditures:* $2.4 million.
Dr. M. P. Dudukovic, Chairman, 314-935-6021, *Fax:* 314-935-4832, *E-mail:* dudu@ poly1.che.wustl.edu.
Application contact: Rose Baxter, Graduate Coordinator, 314-935-6070, *Fax:* 314-935-7211, *E-mail:* chedept@che.wustl.edu. *Web site:* http://www.che.wustl.edu/

■ WAYNE STATE UNIVERSITY

Graduate School, College of Engineering, Department of Chemical Engineering and Materials Science, Program in Chemical Engineering, Detroit, MI 48202

AWARDS MS, PhD.

Students: 59. In 2001, 11 master's, 5 doctorates awarded.
Degree requirements: For master's, thesis optional; for doctorate, thesis/ dissertation.
Application deadline: For fall admission, 7/1 (priority date); for spring admission, 3/15. Applications are processed on a rolling basis. *Application fee:* $20 ($30 for international students). Electronic applications accepted.
Expenses: Tuition, state resident: full-time $3,764. Tuition and fees vary according to degree level and program.
Faculty research: Environmental management, biochemical engineering, supercritical technology, polymer process catalysis. *Total annual research expenditures:* $500,000.
Application contact: Dr. Yinlun Huang, Graduate Director, 313-577-3800, *E-mail:* yhuang@che.eng.wayne.edu.

■ WESTERN MICHIGAN UNIVERSITY

Graduate College, College of Engineering and Applied Sciences, Department of Paper and Printing Science and Engineering, Kalamazoo, MI 49008-5202

AWARDS MS, PhD.

Faculty: 11 full-time (2 women).
Students: 22 full-time (3 women), 5 part-time (4 women); includes 1 minority (Asian American or Pacific Islander), 22 international. 34 applicants, 59% accepted, 12 enrolled. In 2001, 7 degrees awarded.
Degree requirements: For master's, thesis optional; for doctorate, one foreign language, thesis/dissertation, comprehensive exam.
Entrance requirements: For master's, minimum GPA of 3.0. *Application deadline:* For fall admission, 2/15 (priority date). Applications are processed on a rolling basis. *Application fee:* $25.
Expenses: Tuition, state resident: part-time $186 per credit hour. Tuition, nonresident: part-time $442 per credit hour. Required fees: $602. One-time fee: $132 part-time. Tuition and fees vary according to course load.
Financial support: Fellowships, research assistantships, teaching assistantships, Federal Work-Study available. Financial award application deadline: 2/15; financial award applicants required to submit FAFSA.
Faculty research: Fiber recycling, paper machine wet end operations, paper coating.
Dr. Said AbuBakr, Chairperson, 616-387-2775.
Application contact: Admissions and Orientation, 616-387-2000, *Fax:* 616-387-2355.

■ WEST VIRGINIA UNIVERSITY

College of Engineering and Mineral Resources, Department of Chemical Engineering, Morgantown, WV 26506

AWARDS Chemical engineering (MS Ch E, PhD); engineering (MSE). Part-time programs available.

Faculty: 13 full-time (0 women).
Students: 18 full-time (3 women), 9 part-time (3 women); includes 3 minority (2 Asian Americans or Pacific Islanders, 1 Hispanic American), 17 international. Average age 26. 242 applicants, 26% accepted. In 2001, 7 master's, 3 doctorates awarded. Terminal master's awarded for partial completion of doctoral program.
Degree requirements: For master's, thesis/dissertation; for doctorate, thesis/ dissertation, comprehensive exam.
Entrance requirements: For master's and doctorate, TOEFL, minimum GPA of 3.0. *Application deadline:* For fall admission, 3/1 (priority date); for spring admission, 10/1.

West Virginia University (continued)
Applications are processed on a rolling basis. *Application fee:* $45.
Expenses: Tuition, state resident: full-time $2,791. Tuition, nonresident: full-time $8,659. Required fees: $1,002. Tuition and fees vary according to program.
Financial support: In 2001–02, 20 students received support, including 17 research assistantships, 1 teaching assistantship; fellowships, career-related internships or fieldwork, Federal Work-Study, institutionally sponsored loans, and tuition waivers (full and partial) also available. Financial award application deadline: 2/1; financial award applicants required to submit FAFSA.
Faculty research: Fluidization, bioengineering, catalysis, coal gasification, coal liquefaction, polymer processing, materials engineering. *Total annual research expenditures:* $900,000.
Dr. Dady Dadyburjor, Chair, 304-293-2411 Ext. 2424, *Fax:* 304-293-4139, *E-mail:* dady.dadyburjor@mail.wvu.edu.
Application contact: Richard Turton, Graduate Admissions, 304-293-2111 Ext. 2415, *Fax:* 304-293-4139, *E-mail:* richard.turton@mail.wvu.edu. *Web site:* http://www.cemr.wvu.edu/~wwwche/index.html

■ WIDENER UNIVERSITY

School of Engineering, Program in Chemical Engineering, Chester, PA 19013-5792

AWARDS ME, ME/MBA. Part-time and evening/weekend programs available.

Degree requirements: For master's, thesis optional.
Entrance requirements: For master's, GMAT (ME/MBA).
Expenses: Tuition: Part-time $500 per credit. Required fees: $25 per semester.

Faculty research: Biotechnology, environmental engineering, computational fluid mechanics, reaction kinetics, process design.

■ WORCESTER POLYTECHNIC INSTITUTE

Graduate Studies, Department of Chemical Engineering, Worcester, MA 01609-2280

AWARDS MS, PhD.

Faculty: 10 full-time (2 women).
Students: 28 full-time (5 women), 3 part-time (1 woman), 22 international. 126 applicants, 39% accepted, 14 enrolled. In 2001, 4 master's, 3 doctorates awarded. Terminal master's awarded for partial completion of doctoral program.
Degree requirements: For doctorate, thesis/dissertation.
Entrance requirements: For master's and doctorate, GRE General Test (non-native speakers of English), TOEFL. *Application deadline:* For fall admission, 2/1 (priority date); for spring admission, 10/15 (priority date). Applications are processed on a rolling basis. *Application fee:* $60. Electronic applications accepted.
Expenses: Tuition: Part-time $796 per credit. Required fees: $20; $752 per credit. One-time fee: $30 full-time.
Financial support: In 2001–02, 27 students received support, including 6 fellowships with full and partial tuition reimbursements available (averaging $13,667 per year), 12 research assistantships with full tuition reimbursements available (averaging $17,256 per year), 12 teaching assistantships with full tuition reimbursements available (averaging $12,942 per year); career-related internships or fieldwork, institutionally sponsored loans, and scholarships/grants also available. Financial award application deadline: 2/15; financial award applicants required to submit FAFSA.

Faculty research: Biochemical engineering, biomedical engineering, environmental engineering, advanced materials processing, catalysis and reaction engineering. *Total annual research expenditures:* $1.2 million.
Dr. Ravindra Datta, Head, 508-831-5250, *Fax:* 508-831-5853, *E-mail:* rdatta@wpi.edu.
Application contact: Dr. Barbara Wyslouzil, Graduate Coordinator, 508-831-5493, *Fax:* 508-831-5853, *E-mail:* barbaraw@wpi.edu. *Web site:* http://www.wpi.edu/Acacemics/Depts/ChemEng/
Find an in-depth description at www.petersons.com/gradchannel.

■ YALE UNIVERSITY

Graduate School of Arts and Sciences, Programs in Engineering and Applied Science, Department of Chemical Engineering, New Haven, CT 06520

AWARDS MS, PhD. Terminal master's awarded for partial completion of doctoral program.

Degree requirements: For doctorate, thesis/dissertation, exam.
Entrance requirements: For master's and doctorate, GRE General Test, TOEFL.

■ YOUNGSTOWN STATE UNIVERSITY

Graduate School, William Rayen College of Engineering, Department of Civil, Chemical, and Environmental Engineering, Youngstown, OH 44555-0001

AWARDS MSE. Part-time and evening/weekend programs available.

Degree requirements: For master's, thesis optional.
Entrance requirements: For master's, TOEFL, minimum GPA of 2.75 in field.
Faculty research: Structural mechanics, water quality modeling, surface and ground water hydrology, physical and chemical processes in aquatic systems.

Civil and Environmental Engineering

CIVIL ENGINEERING

■ ARIZONA STATE UNIVERSITY

Graduate College, College of Engineering and Applied Sciences, Department of Civil and Environmental Engineering, Tempe, AZ 85287

AWARDS Civil engineering (MS, MSE, PhD).

Degree requirements: For master's, thesis or alternative; for doctorate, thesis/dissertation.
Entrance requirements: For master's and doctorate, GRE General Test (recommended).
Faculty research: Environmental/sanitary engineering, geotechnical/soil mechanics, structures, transportation, water resources/hydraulics.

■ AUBURN UNIVERSITY

Graduate School, College of Engineering, Department of Civil Engineering, Auburn University, AL 36849

AWARDS Construction engineering and management (MCE, MS, PhD); environmental engineering (MCE, MS, PhD); geotechnical/materials engineering (MCE, MS, PhD); hydraulics/hydrology (MCE, MS, PhD); Structural engineering (MCE, MS, PhD); transportation engineering (MCE, MS, PhD). Part-time programs available.

Faculty: 18 full-time (1 woman).
Students: 34 full-time (12 women), 25 part-time (9 women); includes 3 minority (all African Americans), 15 international. 74 applicants, 39% accepted. In 2001, 16 master's, 1 doctorate awarded.
Degree requirements: For master's, project (MCE), thesis (MS); for doctorate, thesis/dissertation, comprehensive exam.
Entrance requirements: For master's and doctorate, GRE General Test. *Application deadline:* For fall admission, 7/7; for spring admission, 11/24. Applications are processed on a rolling basis. *Application fee:* $25 ($50 for international students). Electronic applications accepted.
Financial support: Fellowships, research assistantships, teaching assistantships, Federal Work-Study available. Support available to part-time students. Financial award application deadline: 3/15.
Dr. Joseph F. Judkins, Head, 334-844-4320.
Application contact: Dr. John F. Pritchett, Dean of the Graduate School, 334-844-4700, *E-mail:* hatchlb@mail.auburn.edu.

■ BOISE STATE UNIVERSITY

Graduate College, College of Engineering, Program in Civil Engineering, Boise, ID 83725-0399

AWARDS MS. Part-time and evening/weekend programs available.

Degree requirements: For master's, thesis.
Entrance requirements: For master's, GRE General Test, TOEFL, minimum GPA of 3.0. Electronic applications accepted.

■ BRADLEY UNIVERSITY

Graduate School, College of Engineering and Technology, Department of Civil Engineering and Construction, Peoria, IL 61625-0002

AWARDS MSCE. Part-time and evening/weekend programs available.

Students: 8 full-time, 25 part-time. 83 applicants, 75% accepted. In 2001, 9 degrees awarded.
Degree requirements: For master's, comprehensive exam.
Entrance requirements: For master's, TOEFL, minimum GPA of 3.0. *Application deadline:* For fall admission, 7/1 (priority date); for spring admission, 11/1. Applications are processed on a rolling basis. *Application fee:* $40 ($50 for international students).
Expenses: Tuition: Part-time $7,615 per semester. Tuition and fees vary according to course load.
Financial support: In 2001–02, 8 research assistantships with full and partial tuition reimbursements were awarded; teaching assistantships, scholarships/grants and tuition waivers (partial) also available. Financial award application deadline: 3/1.
Dr. Amir Al-Khafaji, Chairperson, 309-677-2942.
Application contact: Dr. Robert Fuessle, Graduate Adviser, 309-677-2778.

■ BRIGHAM YOUNG UNIVERSITY

Graduate Studies, College of Engineering and Technology, Department of Civil and Environmental Engineering, Provo, UT 84602-1001

AWARDS Civil engineering (MS, PhD).

Faculty: 18 full-time (0 women), 6 part-time/adjunct (1 woman).
Students: 40 full-time (3 women), 21 part-time (2 women); includes 3 minority (1 Asian American or Pacific Islander, 2 Hispanic Americans), 4 international. Average age 27. 41 applicants, 68% accepted, 28 enrolled. In 2001, 38 degrees awarded.
Degree requirements: For master's, thesis (for some programs); for doctorate, thesis/dissertation, comprehensive exam.
Entrance requirements: For master's, GRE General Test, GRE Subject Test, minimum GPA of 3.0 in last 60 hours for international applicants; for doctorate, GRE General Test, GRE Subject Test, minimum graduate GPA of 3.3. *Application deadline:* For fall admission, 5/15; for winter admission, 9/15; for spring admission, 2/15. Applications are processed on a rolling basis. *Application fee:* $50. Electronic applications accepted.
Expenses: Tuition: Full-time $3,860; part-time $214 per hour.
Financial support: In 2001–02, 58 students received support, including 38 research assistantships (averaging $2,400 per year), 26 teaching assistantships (averaging $2,400 per year); fellowships, career-related internships or fieldwork and scholarships/grants also available. Support available to part-time students. Financial award application deadline: 3/15.
Faculty research: Computer graphics, liquefaction, wastewater treatment, hazardous waste management, contaminant transport, transportation. *Total annual research expenditures:* $1.2 million.
Dr. A. Woodruff Miller, Chair, 801-422-2811, *Fax:* 801-422-0159, *E-mail:* wood_miller@byu.edu. *Web site:* http://www.et.byu.edu/ce/

■ BUCKNELL UNIVERSITY

Graduate Studies, College of Engineering, Department of Civil and Environmental Engineering, Lewisburg, PA 17837

AWARDS MS, MSCE. Part-time programs available.

Faculty: 10 full-time (0 women).
Students: 6 full-time (1 woman), 3 international.
Degree requirements: For master's, thesis.
Entrance requirements: For master's, GRE General Test, GRE Subject Test, TOEFL, minimum GPA of 2.8. *Application deadline:* For fall admission, 6/1 (priority date); for spring admission, 12/1 (priority date). Applications are processed on a rolling basis. *Application fee:* $25.
Expenses: Tuition: Part-time $2,875 per course.
Financial support: In 2001–02, 6 students received support. Unspecified assistantships available. Financial award application deadline: 3/1.
Faculty research: Pile foundations, rehabilitation of bridges, deep-shaft biological-waste treatment, precast concrete structures.

Bucknell University (continued)
Dr. Jai B. Kim, Head, 570-577-1112. *Web site:* http://www.bucknell.edu/

■ CALIFORNIA INSTITUTE OF TECHNOLOGY

Division of Engineering and Applied Science, Option in Civil Engineering, Pasadena, CA 91125-0001

AWARDS MS, PhD.

Faculty: 4 full-time (0 women).
Students: 13 full-time (3 women); includes 3 minority (2 Asian Americans or Pacific Islanders, 1 Hispanic American), 6 international. 85 applicants, 7% accepted, 4 enrolled. In 2001, 1 degree awarded.
Degree requirements: For doctorate, thesis/dissertation.
Application deadline: For fall admission, 1/15. *Application fee:* $0.
Financial support: In 2001–02, 3 fellowships, 2 research assistantships, 7 teaching assistantships were awarded.
Faculty research: Earthquake engineering, soil mechanics, finite-element analysis, hydraulics, coastal engineering.
Dr. John Hall, Executive Officer, 626-395-4160.

■ CALIFORNIA POLYTECHNIC STATE UNIVERSITY, SAN LUIS OBISPO

College of Engineering, Department of Civil and Environmental Engineering, San Luis Obispo, CA 93407

AWARDS MS, MCRP/MS. Part-time programs available.

Faculty: 17 full-time (1 woman), 11 part-time/adjunct (3 women).
Students: 8 full-time (2 women), 4 part-time. 12 applicants, 42% accepted, 4 enrolled. In 2001, 4 degrees awarded.
Degree requirements: For master's, thesis or alternative.
Entrance requirements: For master's, GRE General Test, minimum GPA of 3.0 in last 90 quarter units. *Application deadline:* For fall admission, 5/31 (priority date); for spring admission, 12/31. Applications are processed on a rolling basis. *Application fee:* $55. Electronic applications accepted.
Expenses: Tuition, nonresident: part-time $164 per unit. One-time fee: $2,153 part-time.
Financial support: Fellowships, research assistantships, teaching assistantships, career-related internships or fieldwork available. Financial award application deadline: 3/2; financial award applicants required to submit FAFSA.
Faculty research: Soils, structures, transportation, traffic, environmental protection, biomediation.
Dr. Robert Lang, Chair, 805-756-2947, *Fax:* 805-756-6330, *E-mail:* rlang@calpoly.edu.

Application contact: Dr. Eric P. Kasper, Professor, 805-756-1422, *Fax:* 805-756-6330, *E-mail:* ekasper@calpoly.edu. *Web site:* http://www.calpoly.edu/~ceenve/

■ CALIFORNIA STATE UNIVERSITY, FRESNO

Division of Graduate Studies, College of Engineering and Computer Science, Department of Civil Engineering, Fresno, CA 93740-8027

AWARDS MS. Part-time and evening/weekend programs available.

Faculty: 10 full-time (0 women).
Students: 4 full-time (3 women), 10 part-time (2 women); includes 4 minority (2 Asian Americans or Pacific Islanders, 2 Hispanic Americans), 3 international. Average age 31. 19 applicants, 58% accepted, 6 enrolled. In 2001, 7 degrees awarded.
Degree requirements: For master's, thesis or alternative. *Median time to degree:* Master's–2.5 years full-time, 3.5 years part-time.
Entrance requirements: For master's, GRE General Test, TOEFL, minimum GPA of 2.75. *Application deadline:* For fall admission, 8/1 (priority date); for spring admission, 12/1. Applications are processed on a rolling basis. *Application fee:* $55. Electronic applications accepted.
Expenses: Tuition, nonresident: part-time $246 per unit. Required fees: $605 per semester. Tuition and fees vary according to course load.
Financial support: Career-related internships or fieldwork, Federal Work-Study, and scholarships/grants available. Financial award application deadline: 3/1; financial award applicants required to submit FAFSA.
Faculty research: Surveying, water damage, instrumentation equipment, agricultural drainage, aerial triangulation, dairy manure particles.
Dr. Mohamad A. Yousef, Chair, 559-278-2889, *Fax:* 559-278-7071.
Application contact: Dr. Jesus Larralde-Muro, Graduate Program Coordinator, 559-278-2566, *E-mail:* jesus_larralde-muro@csufresno.edu.

■ CALIFORNIA STATE UNIVERSITY, FULLERTON

Graduate Studies, College of Engineering and Computer Science, Department of Civil Engineering and Engineering Mechanics, Fullerton, CA 92834-9480

AWARDS MS.

Faculty: 7 full-time (0 women), 8 part-time/adjunct.
Students: 10 full-time (2 women), 19 part-time (5 women); includes 15 minority (2 African Americans, 11 Asian Americans or Pacific Islanders, 2 Hispanic Americans), 5 international. Average age 32. 27

applicants, 48% accepted, 6 enrolled. In 2001, 7 degrees awarded.
Degree requirements: For master's, project or thesis.
Entrance requirements: For master's, minimum undergraduate GPA of 2.5. *Application fee:* $55.
Expenses: Tuition, nonresident: part-time $246 per unit. Required fees: $964.
Financial support: Career-related internships or fieldwork, Federal Work-Study, institutionally sponsored loans, and scholarships/grants available. Support available to part-time students. Financial award application deadline: 3/1.
Faculty research: Soil-structure interaction, finite-element analysis, computer-aided analysis and design.
Dr. Chandra Putcha, Head, 714-278-3012.

■ CALIFORNIA STATE UNIVERSITY, LONG BEACH

Graduate Studies, College of Engineering, Department of Civil Engineering, Long Beach, CA 90840

AWARDS MSCE, MSE, CE. Part-time programs available.

Faculty: 12 full-time (1 woman), 8 part-time/adjunct (0 women).
Students: 18 full-time (0 women), 64 part-time (10 women); includes 25 minority (17 Asian Americans or Pacific Islanders, 8 Hispanic Americans), 15 international. Average age 31. 48 applicants, 58% accepted. In 2001, 26 degrees awarded.
Degree requirements: For master's, comprehensive exam or thesis.
Entrance requirements: For master's, TOEFL. *Application deadline:* For fall admission, 8/1; for spring admission, 12/1. *Application fee:* $55. Electronic applications accepted.
Financial support: Career-related internships or fieldwork, Federal Work-Study, institutionally sponsored loans, scholarships/grants, and unspecified assistantships available. Financial award application deadline: 3/2.
Faculty research: Soils, hydraulics, seismic structures, composite metals, computer-aided manufacturing.
Dr. Steve Tsai, Chairman, 562-985-5118, *Fax:* 562-985-2380, *E-mail:* stsai@engr.csulb.edu.
Application contact: Dr. Peter Cowan, Graduate Adviser, 562-985-5135, *Fax:* 562-985-2380, *E-mail:* cowan@engr.csulb.edu.

■ CALIFORNIA STATE UNIVERSITY, LOS ANGELES

Graduate Studies, College of Engineering, Computer Science, and Technology, Department of Civil Engineering, Los Angeles, CA 90032-8530

AWARDS MS. Part-time and evening/weekend programs available.

Faculty: 9 full-time, 2 part-time/adjunct.

Students: 15 full-time (0 women), 31 part-time (10 women); includes 24 minority (1 African American, 14 Asian Americans or Pacific Islanders, 9 Hispanic Americans), 14 international. In 2001, 11 degrees awarded.
Degree requirements: For master's, comprehensive exam or thesis.
Entrance requirements: For master's, TOEFL, GRE or minimum GPA of 2.4. *Application deadline:* For fall admission, 6/30; for spring admission, 2/1. Applications are processed on a rolling basis. *Application fee:* $55.
Expenses: Tuition, nonresident: part-time $164 per unit.
Financial support: Federal Work-Study available. Support available to part-time students. Financial award application deadline: 3/1.
Faculty research: Structure, hydraulics, hydrology, soil mechanics.
Dr. Young Kim, Chair, 323-343-4450.

■ CALIFORNIA STATE UNIVERSITY, NORTHRIDGE

Graduate Studies, College of Engineering and Computer Science, Department of Civil and Manufacturing Engineering, Northridge, CA 91330

AWARDS Applied mechanics (MSE); civil engineering (MS); engineering and computer science (MS); engineering management (MS); industrial engineering (MS); materials engineering (MS); mechanical engineering (MS), including aerospace engineering, applied engineering, machine design, mechanical engineering, structural engineering, thermofluids; mechanics (MS). Part-time and evening/weekend programs available.

Faculty: 14 full-time, 2 part-time/adjunct.
Students: 25 full-time (4 women), 72 part-time (9 women). Average age 31. 64 applicants, 77% accepted, 22 enrolled. In 2001, 34 degrees awarded.
Degree requirements: For master's, thesis.
Entrance requirements: For master's, GRE General Test, TOEFL, minimum GPA of 2.5. *Application deadline:* For fall admission, 11/30. *Application fee:* $55.
Expenses: Tuition, nonresident: part-time $631 per semester. Required fees: $246 per unit.
Financial support: Teaching assistantships available. Financial award application deadline: 3/1.
Faculty research: Composite study.
Dr. Stephen Gadomski, Chair, 818-677-2166.
Application contact: Dr. Ileana Costa, Graduate Coordinator, 818-677-3299.

■ CALIFORNIA STATE UNIVERSITY, SACRAMENTO

Graduate Studies, College of Engineering and Computer Science, Department of Civil Engineering, Sacramento, CA 95819-6048

AWARDS MS. Part-time and evening/weekend programs available.

Students: 12 full-time (3 women), 40 part-time (6 women); includes 10 minority (1 African American, 6 Asian Americans or Pacific Islanders, 3 Hispanic Americans), 9 international.
Degree requirements: For master's, thesis or alternative, writing proficiency exam.
Entrance requirements: For master's, TOEFL. *Application deadline:* For fall admission, 4/15; for spring admission, 11/1. *Application fee:* $55.
Expenses: Tuition, state resident: full-time $1,965; part-time $668 per semester. Tuition, nonresident: part-time $246 per unit.
Financial support: Research assistantships, teaching assistantships, career-related internships or fieldwork and Federal Work-Study available. Support available to part-time students. Financial award application deadline: 3/1.
Dr. Joan Al Kazily, Chair, 916-278-6982.

■ CARNEGIE MELLON UNIVERSITY

Carnegie Institute of Technology, Department of Civil and Environmental Engineering, Pittsburgh, PA 15213-3891

AWARDS Civil engineering (MS, PhD); civil engineering and industrial management (MS); civil engineering and robotics (PhD); civil engineering/bioengineering (PhD); civil engineering/engineering and public policy (MS, PhD). Part-time programs available. Terminal master's awarded for partial completion of doctoral program.

Degree requirements: For master's, thesis (for some programs); for doctorate, thesis/dissertation, qualifying exam.
Entrance requirements: For master's and doctorate, GRE General Test, TOEFL.
Faculty research: Computer-aided engineering and management, structured and computational machines, civil systems. *Web site:* http://www.ce.cmu.edu/

Find an in-depth description at www.petersons.com/gradchannel.

■ CASE WESTERN RESERVE UNIVERSITY

School of Graduate Studies, The Case School of Engineering, Department of Civil Engineering, Cleveland, OH 44106

AWARDS Civil engineering (MS, PhD); engineering mechanics (MS). Part-time

programs available. Postbaccalaureate distance learning degree programs offered (minimal on-campus study).
Faculty: 10 full-time (1 woman), 6 part-time/adjunct (2 women).
Students: 13 full-time (3 women), 7 part-time (3 women), 14 international. Average age 24. 149 applicants, 52% accepted, 4 enrolled. In 2001, 6 master's, 2 doctorates awarded.
Degree requirements: For master's, thesis (for some programs); for doctorate, thesis/dissertation, qualifying exam, teaching experience.
Entrance requirements: For master's, TOEFL; for doctorate, GRE, TOEFL. *Application deadline:* For fall admission, 8/1 (priority date); for spring admission, 1/1. *Application fee:* $25.
Financial support: In 2001–02, 8 fellowships with full and partial tuition reimbursements (averaging $16,200 per year), 6 research assistantships with full and partial tuition reimbursements (averaging $16,200 per year) were awarded. Institutionally sponsored loans also available. Financial award application deadline: 8/1; financial award applicants required to submit FAFSA.
Faculty research: Environmental engineering. Structural engineering; geotechnical engineering; engineering mechanics. *Total annual research expenditures:* $684,122.
Dr. Robert L. Mullen, Chairman, 216-368-2427, *Fax:* 216-368-5229, *E-mail:* rlm@po.cwru.edu.
Application contact: Kathleen Ballou, Secretary, 216-368-2950, *Fax:* 216-368-5229, *E-mail:* kad4@po.cwru.edu. *Web site:* http://ecivwww.cwru.edu/civil/

■ THE CATHOLIC UNIVERSITY OF AMERICA

School of Engineering, Department of Civil Engineering, Washington, DC 20064

AWARDS Civil engineering (MCE, D Engr); construction management (MCE, MS Engr); environmental engineering (MCE, MS Engr); geotechnical engineering (MCE). Structures and structural mechanics (MCE). Part-time and evening/weekend programs available.

Faculty: 6 full-time (0 women), 5 part-time/adjunct (2 women).
Students: 5 full-time (1 woman), 14 part-time (2 women); includes 5 minority (4 African Americans, 1 Asian American or Pacific Islander), 10 international. Average age 32. 18 applicants, 50% accepted, 2 enrolled. In 2001, 15 master's, 1 doctorate awarded.
Degree requirements: For master's, thesis optional; for doctorate, thesis/dissertation, qualifying exams, comprehensive exam.
Entrance requirements: For master's, TOEFL, minimum GPA of 3.0; for doctorate, TOEFL, minimum GPA of 3.5.

The Catholic University of America (continued)

Application deadline: For fall admission, 8/1 (priority date); for spring admission, 12/1. Applications are processed on a rolling basis. *Application fee:* $55. Electronic applications accepted.

Expenses: Tuition: Full-time $20,050; part-time $770 per credit. Required fees: $430 per term. Tuition and fees vary according to program.

Financial support: Research assistantships, teaching assistantships, career-related internships or fieldwork, Federal Work-Study, institutionally sponsored loans, and tuition waivers (full and partial) available. Support available to part-time students. Financial award application deadline: 2/1.

Faculty research: Wave propagation, geophysical fluid mechanics.

Dr. Timothy W. Kao, Chair, 202-319-5164, *Fax:* 202-319-4499, *E-mail:* kao@cua.edu. *Web site:* http://www.ee.cua.edu/programs/civil/

■ CITY COLLEGE OF THE CITY UNIVERSITY OF NEW YORK

Graduate School, School of Engineering, Department of Civil Engineering, New York, NY 10031-9198

AWARDS ME, MS, PhD. Part-time programs available.

Students: 81. In 2001, 19 degrees awarded.

Degree requirements: For master's, thesis optional; for doctorate, one foreign language, thesis/dissertation, comprehensive exam.

Entrance requirements: For master's, TOEFL; for doctorate, GRE General Test, TOEFL. *Application deadline:* Applications are processed on a rolling basis. *Application fee:* $40.

Expenses: Tuition, state resident: part-time $185 per credit. Tuition, nonresident: part-time $320 per credit. Required fees: $43 per term.

Faculty research: Earthquake engineering, transportation systems, groundwater, environmental systems, highway systems.

John Filos, Chairman, 212-650-8010. **Application contact:** Graduate Admissions Office, 212-650-6977.

■ CLARKSON UNIVERSITY

Graduate School, School of Engineering, Department of Civil and Environmental Engineering, Potsdam, NY 13699

AWARDS Civil and environmental engineering (PhD); civil engineering (ME, MS). Part-time programs available.

Faculty: 15 full-time (4 women), 4 part-time/adjunct (0 women).

Students: 39 full-time (13 women), 22 international. Average age 27. 103 applicants, 61% accepted. In 2001, 13 master's, 2 doctorates awarded.

Degree requirements: For master's, thesis; for doctorate, thesis/dissertation, departmental qualifying exam. *Median time to degree:* Master's–1.5 years full-time; doctorate–6.5 years full-time.

Entrance requirements: For master's, GRE, TOEFL. *Application deadline:* For fall admission, 5/15 (priority date); for spring admission, 10/15 (priority date). Applications are processed on a rolling basis. *Application fee:* $25 ($35 for international students).

Expenses: Tuition: Part-time $714 per credit. Required fees: $108 per semester.

Financial support: In 2001–02, 36 students received support, including 7 fellowships (averaging $20,000 per year), 22 research assistantships (averaging $17,000 per year), 7 teaching assistantships (averaging $17,000 per year). Scholarships/grants and tuition waivers (partial) also available.

Faculty research: Granular flows, water treatment, environmental systems, geotechnical structural dynamics, fluid dynamics. *Total annual research expenditures:* $2.5 million.

Dr. Thomas C. Young, Chairman, 315-268-4430, *Fax:* 315-268-7985, *E-mail:* young@clarkson.edu.

Application contact: Donna Brockway, Assistant to Dean/Foreign Student Advisor, 315-268-6447, *Fax:* 315-268-7994, *E-mail:* brockway@clarkson.edu.

■ CLEMSON UNIVERSITY

Graduate School, College of Engineering and Science, Department of Civil Engineering, Clemson, SC 29634

AWARDS M Engr, MS, PhD. Part-time programs available.

Students: 63 full-time (19 women), 6 part-time (1 woman); includes 2 minority (1 African American, 1 Hispanic American), 29 international. Average age 24. 134 applicants, 70% accepted, 18 enrolled. In 2001, 23 master's, 1 doctorate awarded.

Degree requirements: For master's, thesis or alternative, oral exam, seminar; for doctorate, thesis/dissertation, oral exam, seminar.

Entrance requirements: For master's and doctorate, GRE General Test, TOEFL, minimum GPA of 3.0. *Application deadline:* For fall admission, 6/1. *Application fee:* $40.

Expenses: Tuition, state resident: full-time $5,310. Tuition, nonresident: full-time $11,284.

Financial support: Fellowships, research assistantships, teaching assistantships available. Financial award application deadline: 2/15; financial award applicants required to submit FAFSA.

Faculty research: Applied fluid mechanics, construction materials, project management, structural engineering.

Dr. Russell H. Brown, Chair, 864-656-3002, *Fax:* 864-656-2670, *E-mail:* russel.brown@eng.clemson.edu.

Application contact: Nadim Aziz, Graduate Program Coordinator, 864-656-3321, *Fax:* 864-656-2670, *E-mail:* aziz@eng.clemson.edu. *Web site:* http://www.eng.clemson.edu/

■ CLEVELAND STATE UNIVERSITY

College of Graduate Studies, Fenn College of Engineering, Department of Civil and Environmental Engineering, Cleveland, OH 44115

AWARDS Civil engineering (MS, D Eng), including environmental engineering (D Eng), mechanical engineering (D Eng), structures engineering (D Eng); engineering mechanics (MS); environmental engineering (MS). Part-time programs available.

Faculty: 10 full-time (1 woman).

Students: 6 full-time (1 woman), 33 part-time (9 women); includes 3 minority (1 African American, 2 Hispanic Americans), 22 international. Average age 29. 62 applicants, 73% accepted. In 2001, 9 master's, 1 doctorate awarded.

Degree requirements: For master's, thesis (for some programs), project or thesis; for doctorate, thesis/dissertation, candidacy and qualifying exams.

Entrance requirements: For master's, GRE General Test, GRE Subject Test, TOEFL, minimum GPA of 2.75; for doctorate, GRE General Test, GRE Subject Test, TOEFL, minimum GPA of 3.25. *Application deadline:* For fall admission, 7/15 (priority date). Applications are processed on a rolling basis. *Application fee:* $25.

Expenses: Tuition, state resident: full-time $6,838; part-time $263 per credit hour. Tuition, nonresident: full-time $13,526; part-time $520 per credit hour.

Financial support: In 2001–02, 3 research assistantships, 6 teaching assistantships were awarded. Career-related internships or fieldwork and unspecified assistantships also available. Financial award application deadline: 9/1.

Faculty research: Environmental engineering, solid-waste disposal, composite materials, nonlinear buckling, constitutive modeling.

Dr. Paul Bosela, Chairperson, 216-687-2190, *Fax:* 216-687-9280. *Web site:* http://www.csuohio.edu/civileng/

■ COLORADO STATE UNIVERSITY

Graduate School, College of Engineering, Department of Civil Engineering, Fort Collins, CO 80523-0015

AWARDS Bioresource and agricultural engineering (MS); bioresource and agriculture engineering (PhD); environmental engineering (MS, PhD); hydraulics and wind engineering (MS, PhD). Structural and geotechnical engineering (MS, PhD); water resources planning and management (MS, PhD); water resources, hydrologic and environmental sciences (MS, PhD). Part-time programs available.

Faculty: 37 full-time (2 women).
Students: 56 full-time (7 women), 99 part-time (21 women); includes 10 minority (7 Asian Americans or Pacific Islanders, 3 Hispanic Americans), 59 international. Average age 33. 228 applicants, 62% accepted, 39 enrolled. In 2001, 19 master's, 6 doctorates awarded. Terminal master's awarded for partial completion of doctoral program.
Degree requirements: For master's, thesis or alternative; for doctorate, thesis/dissertation.
Entrance requirements: For master's and doctorate, GRE General Test, TOEFL, minimum GPA of 3.0. *Application deadline:* For fall admission, 3/1 (priority date); for spring admission, 8/1 (priority date). Applications are processed on a rolling basis. *Application fee:* $30. Electronic applications accepted.
Expenses: Tuition, state resident: full-time $2,880; part-time $160 per credit. Tuition, nonresident: full-time $11,412; part-time $634 per credit. Required fees: $750; $34 per credit.
Financial support: In 2001–02, 2 fellowships, 26 research assistantships (averaging $16,950 per year), 11 teaching assistantships (averaging $12,713 per year) were awarded. Federal Work-Study, institutionally sponsored loans, and traineeships also available.
Faculty research: Hydraulics, hydrology, water resources, infrastructure, environmental engineering. *Total annual research expenditures:* $5.4 million.
Sandra Woods, Head, 970-491-5049, *Fax:* 970-491-7727, *E-mail:* woods@engr.colostate.edu.
Application contact: Laurie Howard, Student Adviser, 970-491-5844, *Fax:* 970-491-7727, *E-mail:* lhoward@engr.colostate.edu. *Web site:* http://www.engr.colostate.edu/depts/ce/

■ COLUMBIA UNIVERSITY

Fu Foundation School of Engineering and Applied Science, Department of Civil Engineering and Engineering Mechanics, New York, NY 10027

AWARDS Civil engineering (MS, Eng Sc D, PhD, Engr); mechanics (MS, Eng Sc D, PhD, Engr). Part-time programs available.

Faculty: 11 full-time (0 women), 8 part-time/adjunct (0 women).
Students: 25 full-time (2 women), 23 part-time (3 women); includes 18 minority (15 Asian Americans or Pacific Islanders, 3 Hispanic Americans), 18 international. Average age 27. 168 applicants, 23% accepted, 16 enrolled. In 2001, 3 master's, 13 doctorates awarded. Terminal master's awarded for partial completion of doctoral program.

Degree requirements: For doctorate, thesis/dissertation, qualifying exam. *Median time to degree:* Master's–1 year full-time; doctorate–2.5 years full-time.
Entrance requirements: For master's, doctorate, and Engr, GRE General Test, TOEFL. *Application deadline:* For fall admission, 1/5; for spring admission, 10/1. *Application fee:* $55. Electronic applications accepted.
Expenses: Tuition: Full-time $27,528. Required fees: $1,638.
Financial support: In 2001–02, 16 students received support, including 3 fellowships with full tuition reimbursements available (averaging $23,000 per year), 6 research assistantships with full tuition reimbursements available (averaging $22,000 per year), 7 teaching assistantships with full tuition reimbursements available (averaging $22,000 per year); Federal Work-Study, scholarships/grants, and health care benefits also available. Financial award application deadline: 1/5; financial award applicants required to submit FAFSA.
Faculty research: Structural deterioration and control, structural materials, multihazard and risk assessment, geoenvironmental engineering, construction engineering. *Total annual research expenditures:* $720,000.
Rimas Vaicaitis, Chairman, 212-854-2396, *Fax:* 212-854-6267, *E-mail:* rimas@civil.columbia.edu.
Application contact: Carolyn Waldo, Administrative Assistant, 212-854-3143, *Fax:* 212-854-6267, *E-mail:* clw1@columbia.edu. *Web site:* http://www.civil.columbia.edu/

■ CORNELL UNIVERSITY

Graduate School, Graduate Fields of Engineering, Field of Civil and Environmental Engineering, Ithaca, NY 14853-0001

AWARDS Environmental engineering (M Eng, MS, PhD); environmental fluid mechanics and hydrology (M Eng, MS, PhD); environmental systems engineering (M Eng, MS, PhD); geotechnical engineering (M Eng, MS, PhD); remote sensing (M Eng, MS, PhD). Structural engineering (M Eng, MS, PhD); transportation engineering (M Eng, MS, PhD); water resource systems (M Eng, MS, PhD).

Faculty: 33 full-time.
Students: 131 full-time (35 women); includes 17 minority (1 African American, 9 Asian Americans or Pacific Islanders, 7 Hispanic Americans), 61 international. 515 applicants, 55% accepted. In 2001, 64 master's, 14 doctorates awarded. Terminal master's awarded for partial completion of doctoral program.
Degree requirements: For master's, thesis (MS); for doctorate, thesis/dissertation.

Entrance requirements: For master's and doctorate, GRE General Test (recommended), TOEFL, 2 letters of recommendation. *Application deadline:* For fall admission, 1/15 (priority date). *Application fee:* $65. Electronic applications accepted.
Expenses: Tuition: Full-time $25,970. Required fees: $50.
Financial support: In 2001–02, 71 students received support, including 24 fellowships with full tuition reimbursements available, 28 research assistantships with full tuition reimbursements available, 19 teaching assistantships with full tuition reimbursements available; institutionally sponsored loans, scholarships/grants, tuition waivers (full and partial), and unspecified assistantships also available. Financial award applicants required to submit FAFSA.
Faculty research: Environmental engineering, geotechnical engineering remote sensing, environmental fluid mechanics and hydrology, structural engineering.
Application contact: Graduate Field Assistant, 607-255-7560, *E-mail:* cee_grad@cornell.edu. *Web site:* http://www.gradschool.cornell.edu/grad/fields_1/cee.html

Find an in-depth description at www.petersons.com/gradchannel.

■ DREXEL UNIVERSITY

Graduate School, College of Engineering, Department of Civil and Architectural Engineering, Program in Civil Engineering, Philadelphia, PA 19104-2875

AWARDS MS, PhD. Part-time and evening/weekend programs available.

Faculty: 19 full-time (3 women), 6 part-time/adjunct (1 woman).
Students: 5 full-time (1 woman), 54 part-time (12 women); includes 1 minority (African American), 25 international. Average age 30. 49 applicants, 71% accepted, 10 enrolled. In 2001, 15 master's, 4 doctorates awarded.
Degree requirements: For master's, thesis optional; for doctorate, thesis/dissertation.
Entrance requirements: For master's, TOEFL, minimum GPA of 3.0; for doctorate, TOEFL, minimum GPA of 3.5, MS in civil engineering. *Application deadline:* For fall admission, 8/21. Applications are processed on a rolling basis. *Application fee:* $50. Electronic applications accepted.
Expenses: Tuition: Full-time $20,088; part-time $558 per credit. Required fees: $78 per term. One-time fee: $200. Tuition and fees vary according to course load, degree level and program.
Financial support: Research assistantships, teaching assistantships, career-related internships or fieldwork, Federal Work-Study, institutionally sponsored loans, tuition waivers (partial), and unspecified

Drexel University (continued)
assistantships available. Financial award
application deadline: 2/1.
Application contact: Director of Graduate Admissions, 215-895-6700, *Fax:* 215-895-5939, *E-mail:* enroll@drexel.edu.

■ DUKE UNIVERSITY

Graduate School, School of Engineering, Department of Civil and Environmental Engineering, Durham, NC 27708-0586

AWARDS Civil and environmental engineering (MS, PhD); environmental engineering (MS, PhD). Part-time programs available.

Faculty: 16 full-time, 3 part-time/adjunct.
Students: 35 full-time (10 women). 111 applicants, 25% accepted, 17 enrolled. In 2001, 6 master's, 3 doctorates awarded. Terminal master's awarded for partial completion of doctoral program.
Degree requirements: For doctorate, thesis/dissertation.
Entrance requirements: For master's and doctorate, GRE General Test. *Application deadline:* For fall admission, 12/31; for spring admission, 11/1. *Application fee:* $75.
Expenses: Tuition: Full-time $24,600.
Financial support: Fellowships, research assistantships, Federal Work-Study available. Financial award application deadline: 12/31.
Tomasz Hueckel, Director of Graduate Studies, 919-660-5218, *Fax:* 919-660-5219, *E-mail:* watkins@mail.duke.edu. *Web site:* http://www.cee.egr.duke.edu/
Find an in-depth description at www.petersons.com/gradchannel.

■ FLORIDA AGRICULTURAL AND MECHANICAL UNIVERSITY

Division of Graduate Studies, Research, and Continuing Education, FAMU-FSU College of Engineering, Department of Civil Engineering, Tallahassee, FL 32307-3200

AWARDS Civil engineering (MS, PhD); environmental engineering (MS, PhD).

Entrance requirements: For master's, GRE General Test, minimum GPA of 3.0.
Find an in-depth description at www.petersons.com/gradchannel.

■ FLORIDA ATLANTIC UNIVERSITY

College of Engineering, Department of Civil Engineering, Boca Raton, FL 33431-0991

AWARDS MS. Part-time and evening/weekend programs available.

Faculty: 5 full-time (0 women), 2 part-time/adjunct (0 women).
Students: 9 full-time (5 women), 9 part-time (2 women); includes 2 minority (both

Hispanic Americans), 5 international. Average age 32. 19 applicants, 58% accepted, 6 enrolled. In 2001, 7 degrees awarded.
Degree requirements: For master's, thesis (for some programs).
Entrance requirements: For master's, GRE General Test, TOEFL, minimum GPA of 3.0. *Application deadline:* For fall admission, 3/1 (priority date); for spring admission, 7/1. Applications are processed on a rolling basis. *Application fee:* $20.
Expenses: Tuition, state resident: full-time $3,098; part-time $172 per credit. Tuition, nonresident: full-time $10,427; part-time $579 per credit.
Financial support: In 2001–02, 5 students received support, including 4 research assistantships with full tuition reimbursements available (averaging $15,000 per year), 1 teaching assistantship with full tuition reimbursement available (averaging $15,000 per year); career-related internships or fieldwork, Federal Work-Study, scholarships/grants, tuition waivers (full), and unspecified assistantships also available. Financial award applicants required to submit FAFSA.
Faculty research: Structures, geotechnical engineering, environmental and water resources engineering, transportation engineering, materials. *Total annual research expenditures:* $250,000.
Dr. Stephan J. Nix, Chair and Professor, 561-297-0466, *Fax:* 561-297-0493, *E-mail:* snix@fau.edu. *Web site:* http://www.civil.fau.edu/

■ FLORIDA ATLANTIC UNIVERSITY

College of Engineering, Department of Ocean Engineering, Boca Raton, FL 33431-0991

AWARDS Civil engineering (MS); ocean engineering (MS, PhD). Part-time and evening/weekend programs available.

Faculty: 17 full-time (0 women), 5 part-time/adjunct (0 women).
Students: 40 full-time (10 women), 7 part-time; includes 4 minority (2 African Americans, 2 Hispanic Americans), 29 international. Average age 27. 55 applicants, 82% accepted, 25 enrolled. In 2001, 27 degrees awarded. Terminal master's awarded for partial completion of doctoral program.
Degree requirements: For master's, thesis optional; for doctorate, thesis/dissertation, qualifying exam.
Entrance requirements: For master's and doctorate, GRE General Test, TOEFL, minimum GPA of 3.0. *Application deadline:* For fall admission, 3/1 (priority date); for spring admission, 7/1. Applications are processed on a rolling basis. *Application fee:* $20.
Expenses: Tuition, state resident: full-time $3,098; part-time $172 per credit. Tuition, nonresident: full-time $10,427; part-time $579 per credit.

Financial support: Research assistantships, career-related internships or fieldwork, Federal Work-Study, scholarships/grants, tuition waivers (full), and unspecified assistantships available. Financial award applicants required to submit FAFSA.
Faculty research: Marine materials and corrosion, ocean structures, marine vehicles, acoustics and vibrations, hydrodynamics, coastal engineering. *Total annual research expenditures:* $4 million.
Dr. Stewart E. Glegg, Chairman, 561-297-3430, *Fax:* 561-297-3885, *E-mail:* glegg@oe.fau.edu.
Application contact: Patricia Capozziello, Graduate Admissions Coordinator, 561-297-2694, *Fax:* 561-297-2659, *E-mail:* capozzie@fau.edu. *Web site:* http://www.oe.fau.edu/

■ FLORIDA INSTITUTE OF TECHNOLOGY

Graduate Programs, College of Engineering, Civil Engineering Department, Melbourne, FL 32901-6975

AWARDS MS, PhD. Part-time programs available.

Faculty: 5 full-time (0 women), 2 part-time/adjunct (0 women).
Students: 10 full-time (1 woman), 13 part-time (5 women); includes 1 minority (African American), 17 international. Average age 29. 77 applicants, 62% accepted. In 2001, 2 degrees awarded.
Degree requirements: For master's, thesis optional; for doctorate, thesis/dissertation, comprehensive exam.
Entrance requirements: For master's, minimum GPA of 3.0, 1 year of undergraduate study in civil engineering; for doctorate, minimum GPA of 3.2, resumé. *Application deadline:* Applications are processed on a rolling basis. *Application fee:* $50. Electronic applications accepted.
Expenses: Tuition: Part-time $650 per credit.
Financial support: In 2001–02, 7 students received support, including 4 research assistantships with full and partial tuition reimbursements available (averaging $10,161 per year), 3 teaching assistantships with full and partial tuition reimbursements available (averaging $7,022 per year); career-related internships or fieldwork and tuition remissions also available. Financial award application deadline: 3/1; financial award applicants required to submit FAFSA.
Faculty research: Groundwater and surface water modeling, pavements, waste materials, *in situ* soil testing, fiber optic sensors. *Total annual research expenditures:* $202,000.
Dr. Ashok Pandit, Department Head, 321-674-7151, *Fax:* 321-768-7565, *E-mail:* apandit@fit.edu.
Application contact: Carolyn P. Farrior, Director of Graduate Admissions, 321-674-7118, *Fax:* 321-723-9468, *E-mail:*

cfarrior@fit.edu. *Web site:* http://www.fit.edu/

Find an in-depth description at www.petersons.com/gradchannel.

■ FLORIDA INTERNATIONAL UNIVERSITY

College of Engineering, Department of Civil and Environmental Engineering, Program in Civil Engineering, Miami, FL 33199

AWARDS MS, PhD. Part-time and evening/weekend programs available.

Students: 31 full-time (8 women), 32 part-time (10 women); includes 25 minority (2 African Americans, 3 Asian Americans or Pacific Islanders, 20 Hispanic Americans), 28 international. Average age 32. 91 applicants, 60% accepted, 22 enrolled. In 2001, 17 master's, 3 doctorates awarded.
Degree requirements: For master's, thesis optional; for doctorate, thesis/dissertation.
Entrance requirements: For master's, GRE General Test, TOEFL, bachelor's degree in related field; for doctorate, GRE General Test, TOEFL, minimum graduate GPA of 3.3. *Application deadline:* For fall admission, 4/1 (priority date); for spring admission, 10/1. Applications are processed on a rolling basis. *Application fee:* $20.
Expenses: Tuition, state resident: full-time $2,916; part-time $162 per credit hour. Tuition, nonresident: full-time $10,245; part-time $569 per credit hour. Required fees: $168 per term.
Dr. David Shen, Chairperson, Department of Civil and Environmental Engineering, 305-348-2824, *Fax:* 305-348-2802, *E-mail:* shen@eng.fiu.edu.

■ FLORIDA STATE UNIVERSITY

Graduate Studies, FAMU/FSU College of Engineering, Department of Civil Engineering, Tallahassee, FL 32306

AWARDS Civil engineering (MS, PhD); environmental engineering (MS, PhD). Part-time programs available.

Degree requirements: For master's, thesis optional; for doctorate, thesis/dissertation.
Entrance requirements: For master's, GRE General Test, TOEFL, BS in engineering or related field, minimum GPA of 3.0; for doctorate, Master's degree in engineering or related field, minimum GPA of 3.0.
Expenses: Tuition, state resident: part-time $163 per credit hour. Tuition, nonresident: part-time $570 per credit hour. Tuition and fees vary according to program.
Faculty research: Tidal hydraulics, temperature effects on bridge girders, codes for coastal construction, field performance of pine bridges, river basin management, transportation pavement

design, soil dynamics, structural analysis. *Web site:* http://www.eng.fsu.edu/

Find an in-depth description at www.petersons.com/gradchannel.

■ THE GEORGE WASHINGTON UNIVERSITY

School of Engineering and Applied Science, Department of Civil and Environmental Engineering, Washington, DC 20052

AWARDS MS, D Sc, App Sc, Engr. Part-time and evening/weekend programs available.

Faculty: 8 full-time (1 woman), 5 part-time/adjunct (1 woman).
Students: 29 full-time (4 women), 31 part-time (10 women); includes 12 minority (3 African Americans, 4 Asian Americans or Pacific Islanders, 5 Hispanic Americans), 30 international. Average age 32. 51 applicants, 98% accepted. In 2001, 14 master's, 1 doctorate awarded.
Degree requirements: For master's, thesis optional; for doctorate, thesis/dissertation, final and qualifying exams.
Entrance requirements: For master's, TOEFL or George Washington University English as a Foreign Language Test, appropriate bachelor's degree, minimum GPA of 3.0; for doctorate, TOEFL or George Washington University English as a Foreign Language Test, appropriate bachelor's or master's degree, minimum GPA of 3.4, GRE required if highest earned degree is BS; for other advanced degree, TOEFL or George Washington University English as a Foreign Language Test, appropriate master's degree, minimum GPA of 3.0. *Application deadline:* For fall admission, 3/1 (priority date); for spring admission, 10/1. Applications are processed on a rolling basis. *Application fee:* $55.
Expenses: Tuition: Part-time $810 per credit. Required fees: $1 per credit.
Financial support: In 2001–02, 9 fellowships with tuition reimbursements (averaging $10,000 per year), 5 teaching assistantships with tuition reimbursements (averaging $1,600 per year) were awarded. Research assistantships, career-related internships or fieldwork, Federal Work-Study, and institutionally sponsored loans also available. Financial award application deadline: 3/1; financial award applicants required to submit FAFSA.
Faculty research: Computer-integrated manufacturing, materials engineering, electronic materials, fatigue and fracture, reliability.
Dr. William Roper, Chair, 202-994-4901, *E-mail:* wroper@seas.gwu.edu.
Application contact: Howard M. Davis, Manager, Office of Admissions and Student Records, 202-994-6158, *Fax:* 202-994-0909, *E-mail:* data:adms@

seas.gwu.edu. *Web site:* http://www.gwu.edu/~gradinfo/

Find an in-depth description at www.petersons.com/gradchannel.

■ GEORGIA INSTITUTE OF TECHNOLOGY

Graduate Studies and Research, College of Engineering, School of Civil and Environmental Engineering, Program in Civil Engineering, Atlanta, GA 30332-0001

AWARDS Biomedical engineering (MS Bio E); civil engineering (MS, MSCE, PhD). Part-time programs available. Terminal master's awarded for partial completion of doctoral program.

Degree requirements: For doctorate, thesis/dissertation.
Entrance requirements: For master's, GRE, TOEFL, minimum GPA of 3.0; for doctorate, GRE, TOEFL, minimum GPA of 3.2.
Faculty research: Structural analysis, fluid mechanics, geotechnical engineering, construction management, transportation engineering. *Web site:* http://www.ce.gatech.edu/

■ GRADUATE SCHOOL AND UNIVERSITY CENTER OF THE CITY UNIVERSITY OF NEW YORK

Graduate Studies, Program in Engineering, New York, NY 10016-4039

AWARDS Chemical engineering (PhD); civil engineering (PhD); electrical engineering (PhD); mechanical engineering (PhD).

Faculty: 68 full-time (1 woman).
Students: 125 full-time (28 women), 6 part-time (1 woman); includes 13 minority (9 African Americans, 2 Asian Americans or Pacific Islanders, 2 Hispanic Americans), 95 international. Average age 32. 205 applicants, 63% accepted, 26 enrolled. In 2001, 22 degrees awarded.
Degree requirements: For doctorate, thesis/dissertation.
Entrance requirements: For doctorate, GRE General Test. *Application deadline:* For fall admission, 4/15. *Application fee:* $40.
Expenses: Tuition, state resident: part-time $245 per credit. Tuition, nonresident: part-time $425 per credit. Required fees: $72 per semester.
Financial support: In 2001–02, 67 students received support, including 64 fellowships; research assistantships, teaching assistantships, Federal Work-Study, institutionally sponsored loans, and tuition waivers (full and partial) also available. Financial award application deadline: 2/1; financial award applicants required to submit FAFSA.

Graduate School and University Center of the City University of New York (continued)
Dr. Mumtaz Kassir, Acting Executive Officer, 212-650-8031, *Fax:* 212-650-8029, *E-mail:* kassir@ce-mail.engr.ccny.cuny.edu.
Find an in-depth description at www.petersons.com/gradchannel.

■ HOWARD UNIVERSITY

College of Engineering, Architecture, and Computer Sciences, School of Engineering and Computer Science, Department of Civil Engineering, Washington, DC 20059-0002

AWARDS M Eng. Offered through the Graduate School of Arts and Sciences.

Students: Average age 27. In 2001, 5 degrees awarded.
Degree requirements: For master's, thesis (for some programs).
Entrance requirements: For master's, GRE General Test, TOEFL, minimum GPA of 3.0, bachelor's degree in engineering or related field. *Application deadline:* For fall admission, 4/1; for spring admission, 11/1. *Application fee:* $45. Electronic applications accepted.
Financial support: In 2001–02, 13 research assistantships with full tuition reimbursements, 4 teaching assistantships with full tuition reimbursements were awarded. Financial award application deadline: 4/1.
Faculty research: Modeling of concrete, structures, transportation planning, structural analysis, environmental and water resources.
Dr. Errol C. Noel, Chair, 202-806-6570, *Fax:* 202-806-5271, *E-mail:* enoel@howard.edu. *Web site:* http://www.howard.edu/

■ ILLINOIS INSTITUTE OF TECHNOLOGY

Graduate College, Armour College of Engineering and Sciences, Department of Civil and Architectural Engineering, Chicago, IL 60616-3793

AWARDS M Geoenv E, M Trans E, MCEM, MGE, MPW, MS, MSE, PhD. Part-time and evening/weekend programs available.

Faculty: 9 full-time (0 women), 7 part-time/adjunct (0 women).
Students: 42 full-time (6 women), 57 part-time (7 women); includes 10 minority (2 African Americans, 7 Asian Americans or Pacific Islanders, 1 Hispanic American), 69 international. Average age 29. 180 applicants, 64% accepted. In 2001, 22 master's, 3 doctorates awarded. Terminal master's awarded for partial completion of doctoral program.
Degree requirements: For master's, thesis (for some programs), comprehensive exam; for doctorate, thesis/dissertation, comprehensive exam.

Entrance requirements: For master's and doctorate, GRE General Test, TOEFL, minimum undergraduate GPA of 3.0. *Application deadline:* For fall admission, 7/1; for spring admission, 11/1. Applications are processed on a rolling basis. *Application fee:* $30. Electronic applications accepted.
Expenses: Tuition: Part-time $590 per credit hour.
Financial support: In 2001–02, 10 teaching assistantships were awarded; Federal Work-Study, institutionally sponsored loans, scholarships/grants, and unspecified assistantships also available. Support available to part-time students. Financial award application deadline: 3/1; financial award applicants required to submit FAFSA.
Faculty research: Structural faligue, behavior of steel-reinforced concrete structures, soil-structure interaction, geosynthetics. *Total annual research expenditures:* $3,988.
Dr. J. Mohammadi, Chairman, 312-567-3540, *Fax:* 312-567-3519, *E-mail:* mohammadi@iit.edu.
Application contact: Dr. Ali Cinar, Dean of Graduate College, 312-567-3637, *Fax:* 312-567-7517, *E-mail:* gradstu@iit.edu. *Web site:* http://www.iit.edu/~ce/

■ IOWA STATE UNIVERSITY OF SCIENCE AND TECHNOLOGY

Graduate College, College of Engineering, Department of Civil and Construction Engineering, Ames, IA 50011

AWARDS Civil engineering (MS, PhD), including civil engineering materials, construction engineering and management, environmental engineering, geometronics, geotechnical engineering, structural engineering, transportation engineering.

Faculty: 32 full-time, 5 part-time/adjunct.
Students: 55 full-time (9 women), 39 part-time (6 women); includes 1 minority (African American), 40 international. 256 applicants, 23% accepted, 21 enrolled. In 2001, 27 master's, 4 doctorates awarded.
Degree requirements: For master's, thesis or alternative; for doctorate, thesis/dissertation. *Median time to degree:* Master's–2 years full-time; doctorate–3.3 years full-time.
Entrance requirements: For master's and doctorate, GRE General Test (international applicants), TOEFL or IELTS. *Application deadline:* For fall admission, 3/1 (priority date); for spring admission, 10/1 (priority date). *Application fee:* $20 ($50 for international students). Electronic applications accepted.
Expenses: Tuition, state resident: full-time $1,851. Tuition, nonresident: full-time $5,449. Tuition and fees vary according to program.
Financial support: In 2001–02, 44 research assistantships with partial tuition reimbursements (averaging $12,963 per year), 5 teaching assistantships with partial

tuition reimbursements (averaging $11,756 per year) were awarded. Fellowships, scholarships/grants, health care benefits, and unspecified assistantships also available.
Dr. Lowell F. Greimann, Chair, 515-294-2140, *E-mail:* cceinfo@iastate.edu.
Application contact: Dr. Edward Kannel, Director of Graduate Education, 515-294-2861, *E-mail:* cceinfo@iastate.edu. *Web site:* http://www1.eng.iastate.edu/coe/grad.asp/

■ JOHNS HOPKINS UNIVERSITY

G. W. C. Whiting School of Engineering, Department of Civil Engineering, Baltimore, MD 21218-2699

AWARDS MCE, MSE, PhD. Part-time and evening/weekend programs available.

Faculty: 7 full-time (2 women), 4 part-time/adjunct (0 women).
Students: 34 full-time (5 women), 25 international. Average age 27. 96 applicants, 30% accepted, 16 enrolled. In 2001, 14 master's, 7 doctorates awarded. Terminal master's awarded for partial completion of doctoral program.
Degree requirements: For master's, thesis; for doctorate, thesis/dissertation, oral exam.
Entrance requirements: For master's and doctorate, GRE General Test, TOEFL. *Application deadline:* For fall admission, 2/1. *Application fee:* $0. Electronic applications accepted.
Expenses: Tuition: Full-time $27,390.
Financial support: In 2001–02, 4 fellowships (averaging $14,400 per year), 23 research assistantships (averaging $14,958 per year), 8 teaching assistantships (averaging $12,825 per year) were awarded. Federal Work-Study, institutionally sponsored loans, scholarships/grants, and unspecified assistantships also available. Financial award application deadline: 2/1.
Faculty research: Geotechnical engineering, structural engineering, structural mechanics, geomechanics, probabilistic modeling. *Total annual research expenditures:* $1.2 million.
Prof. Nicholas P. Jones, Chair, 410-516-7874, *Fax:* 410-516-7473, *E-mail:* nick@jhu.edu. *Web site:* http://www.ce.jhu.edu/

■ KANSAS STATE UNIVERSITY

Graduate School, College of Engineering, Department of Civil Engineering, Manhattan, KS 66506

AWARDS MS, PhD. Postbaccalaureate distance learning degree programs offered (no on-campus study).

Faculty: 15 full-time (0 women).
Students: 34 full-time (8 women), 21 part-time (2 women); includes 2 minority (1 Asian American or Pacific Islander, 1 Hispanic American), 33 international. 105 applicants, 73% accepted, 18 enrolled. In 2001, 9 master's, 7 doctorates awarded.

Degree requirements: For master's, thesis or alternative; for doctorate, thesis/dissertation.

Entrance requirements: For master's, GRE General Test, TOEFL, bachelor's degree in civil engineering or previous course work in civil engineering; for doctorate, GRE General Test, TOEFL. *Application deadline:* For fall admission, 2/1 (priority date); for spring admission, 9/1 (priority date). Applications are processed on a rolling basis. *Application fee:* $0 ($25 for international students). Electronic applications accepted.

Expenses: Tuition, state resident: part-time $113 per credit hour. Tuition, nonresident: part-time $358 per credit hour.

Financial support: In 2001–02, 30 research assistantships with partial tuition reimbursements (averaging $9,000 per year), 1 teaching assistantship with partial tuition reimbursement (averaging $7,000 per year) were awarded. Fellowships with partial tuition reimbursements, institutionally sponsored loans, scholarships/grants, and tuition waivers also available. Support available to part-time students. Financial award application deadline: 3/1; financial award applicants required to submit FAFSA.

Faculty research: Hydrology and hydraulic engineering, environmental engineering, soil mechanics and geotechnical engineering, structural engineering, transport and materials engineering. *Total annual research expenditures:* $1.6 million.
Dr. Lakshmi N. Reddi, Head, 785-532-5862, *Fax:* 785-532-7717, *E-mail:* danita@ksu.edu.

Application contact: Hani Melhem, Graduate Program Director, 785-532-5862, *Fax:* 785-532-7717, *E-mail:* danita@ksu.edu. *Web site:* http://www.engg.ksu.edu/CEDPT/home.html/

■ LAMAR UNIVERSITY

College of Graduate Studies, College of Engineering, Department of Civil Engineering, Program in Civil Engineering, Beaumont, TX 77710

AWARDS ME, MES, DE. Part-time programs available.

Faculty: 5 full-time (0 women).
Students: 19 full-time (0 women), (all international). Average age 26. 111 applicants, 60% accepted. In 2001, 19 degrees awarded.
Degree requirements: For master's, thesis optional; for doctorate, thesis/dissertation.
Entrance requirements: For master's and doctorate, GRE General Test, TOEFL. *Application deadline:* For fall admission, 5/15 (priority date); for spring admission, 10/1 (priority date). Applications are processed on a rolling basis. *Application fee:* $25 ($50 for international students).

Expenses: Tuition, state resident: full-time $1,114. Tuition, nonresident: full-time $3,670.

Financial support: In 2001–02, 6 fellowships with tuition reimbursements (averaging $1,000 per year), 5 research assistantships with partial tuition reimbursements (averaging $6,000 per year), 2 teaching assistantships (averaging $7,200 per year) were awarded. Tuition waivers (partial) also available. Financial award application deadline: 4/1.

Faculty research: Construction productivity, lake/reservoir hydrodynamics, geotechnical soil stabilization, environmental remediations, air quality. *Total annual research expenditures:* $200,000.
Dr. Enno Koehn, Chair, 409-880-8759, *Fax:* 409-880-8121, *E-mail:* koehneu@hal.lamar.edu.

Application contact: Sandy Drane, Coordinator of Graduate Admissions, 409-880-8356, *Fax:* 409-880-8414, *E-mail:* gradmissions@hal.lamar.edu.

■ LAWRENCE TECHNOLOGICAL UNIVERSITY

College of Engineering, Southfield, MI 48075-1058

AWARDS Automotive engineering (MAE); civil engineering (MCE); electrical and computer engineering (MS); manufacturing systems (MEMS, DE). Part-time and evening/weekend programs available.

Faculty: 27 full-time (2 women), 11 part-time/adjunct (1 woman).
Students: Average age 32. 133 applicants, 38 enrolled. In 2001, 43 degrees awarded. *Application deadline:* For fall admission, 8/1 (priority date); for winter admission, 12/1 (priority date); for spring admission, 5/1. Applications are processed on a rolling basis. *Application fee:* $50. Electronic applications accepted.
Expenses: Tuition: Part-time $460 per credit hour.
Financial support: Institutionally sponsored loans available. Support available to part-time students. Financial award application deadline: 3/1; financial award applicants required to submit FAFSA.
Faculty research: Advanced composite materials in bridges, strengthening existing bridges with carbon and glass fiber sheets, development of drive shafts using composite materials. *Total annual research expenditures:* $150,000.
Dr. Laird Johnston, Dean, 248-204-2500, *Fax:* 248-204-2509, *E-mail:* lejohnston@ltu.edu.

Application contact: Jane Rohrback, Interim Director of Admissions, 248-204-3160, *Fax:* 248-204-3188, *E-mail:* admission@ltu.edu.

■ LEHIGH UNIVERSITY

P.C. Rossin College of Engineering and Applied Science, Department of Civil and Environmental Engineering, Bethlehem, PA 18015-3094

AWARDS M Eng, MS, PhD. Part-time programs available.

Faculty: 17 full-time (1 woman), 1 part-time/adjunct (0 women).
Students: 54 full-time (13 women), 7 part-time (2 women); includes 11 minority (4 African Americans, 7 Hispanic Americans), 23 international. Average age 24. 123 applicants, 80% accepted, 12 enrolled. In 2001, 16 master's, 3 doctorates awarded. Terminal master's awarded for partial completion of doctoral program.
Degree requirements: For master's, thesis optional; for doctorate, thesis/dissertation. *Median time to degree:* Master's–2 years full-time; doctorate–4.7 years full-time.
Entrance requirements: For master's and doctorate, GRE General Test, TOEFL. *Application deadline:* For fall admission, 7/15; for spring admission, 12/1. Applications are processed on a rolling basis. *Application fee:* $50.
Expenses: Tuition: Part-time $468 per credit hour. Required fees: $200; $100 per semester. Tuition and fees vary according to program.
Financial support: In 2001–02, 44 students received support, including 7 fellowships (averaging $1,400 per year), 33 research assistantships (averaging $1,500 per year), 4 teaching assistantships (averaging $1,450 per year); tuition waivers (partial) also available. Financial award application deadline: 1/15.
Faculty research: Structural and geotechnical engineering, water resources and coastal engineering. *Total annual research expenditures:* $6.4 million.
Dr. Arup K. SenGupta, Chairman, 610-758-3538, *Fax:* 610-758-6405, *E-mail:* aks0@lehigh.edu.

Application contact: Prisca Vidanage, Graduate Coordinator, 610-758-3530, *Fax:* 610-758-6405, *E-mail:* pmv1@lehigh.edu. *Web site:* http://www.lehigh.edu/~incee/incee.html

Find an in-depth description at www.petersons.com/gradchannel.

■ LOUISIANA STATE UNIVERSITY AND AGRICULTURAL AND MECHANICAL COLLEGE

Graduate School, College of Engineering, Department of Civil and Environmental Engineering, Baton Rouge, LA 70803

AWARDS Environmental engineering (MSCE, PhD); geotechnical engineering (MSCE, PhD). Structural engineering and mechanics (MSCE, PhD); transportation engineering (MSCE, PhD); water resources (MSCE, PhD). Part-time programs available.

Louisiana State University and Agricultural and Mechanical College (continued)

Faculty: 30 full-time (1 woman).
Students: 78 full-time (19 women), 26 part-time (11 women); includes 4 minority (2 African Americans, 1 Hispanic American, 1 Native American), 67 international. Average age 29. 133 applicants, 41% accepted, 22 enrolled. In 2001, 15 master's, 7 doctorates awarded.
Degree requirements: For master's, thesis optional; for doctorate, one foreign language, thesis/dissertation.
Entrance requirements: For master's and doctorate, GRE General Test, TOEFL, minimum GPA of 3.0. *Application deadline:* For fall admission, 1/25 (priority date). Applications are processed on a rolling basis. *Application fee:* $25.
Expenses: Tuition, state resident: full-time $2,551. Tuition, nonresident: full-time $5,551. Required fees: $854. Part-time tuition and fees vary according to course load.
Financial support: In 2001–02, 5 fellowships (averaging $15,800 per year), 51 research assistantships with partial tuition reimbursements (averaging $12,089 per year), 2 teaching assistantships with partial tuition reimbursements (averaging $12,500 per year) were awarded. Career-related internships or fieldwork, institutionally sponsored loans, and scholarships/grants also available. Financial award application deadline: 3/1; financial award applicants required to submit FAFSA.
Faculty research: Solid waste management, electrokinetics, composite structures, transportation planning, river mechanics. *Total annual research expenditures:* $1.7 million.
Dr. George Z. Voyiadjis, Interim Chair/Boyd Professor, 225-578-8668, *Fax:* 225-578-8652, *E-mail:* cegzv@lsu.edu. *Web site:* http://www.ce.lsu.edu/

■ LOUISIANA TECH UNIVERSITY

Graduate School, College of Engineering and Science, Department of Civil Engineering, Ruston, LA 71272

AWARDS MS, D Eng. Part-time programs available. Terminal master's awarded for partial completion of doctoral program.

Degree requirements: For master's, thesis or alternative; for doctorate, thesis/dissertation.
Entrance requirements: For master's, GRE General Test, TOEFL, minimum GPA of 3.0 in last 60 hours; for doctorate, TOEFL, minimum graduate GPA of 3.25 (with MS) or GRE General Test.
Faculty research: Environmental engineering, trenchless excavation construction, structural mechanics, transportation materials and planning, water quality modeling.

■ LOYOLA MARYMOUNT UNIVERSITY

Graduate Division, College of Science and Engineering, Department of Civil Engineering and Environmental Science, Programs in Civil Engineering, Los Angeles, CA 90045-2659

AWARDS MS, MSE. Part-time and evening/weekend programs available.

Students: 6 full-time (2 women), 11 part-time (2 women); includes 7 minority (1 African American, 5 Asian Americans or Pacific Islanders, 1 Hispanic American), 1 international. 6 applicants, 67% accepted, 3 enrolled. In 2001, 11 degrees awarded.
Degree requirements: For master's, comprehensive exam.
Entrance requirements: For master's, TOEFL. *Application deadline:* Applications are processed on a rolling basis. *Application fee:* $45. Electronic applications accepted.
Expenses: Tuition: Part-time $612 per credit hour. Required fees: $86 per term. Tuition and fees vary according to program.
Financial support: In 2001–02, 6 students received support. Scholarships/grants and laboratory assistantships available. Support available to part-time students. Financial award application deadline: 7/1; financial award applicants required to submit FAFSA. *Web site:* http://www.lmu.edu/acad/gd/graddiv.htm

■ MANHATTAN COLLEGE

Graduate Division, School of Engineering, Civil Engineering Program, Riverdale, NY 10471

AWARDS MS. Part-time and evening/weekend programs available.

Entrance requirements: For master's, GRE, TOEFL, minimum GPA of 3.0.
Faculty research: Compressible-inclusion function for geofoams used with rigid walls under static loading, validation of sediment criteria.

■ MARQUETTE UNIVERSITY

Graduate School, College of Engineering, Department of Civil and Environmental Engineering, Milwaukee, WI 53201-1881

AWARDS Construction and public works management (MS, PhD); environmental/water resources engineering (MS, PhD). Structural/geotechnical engineering (MS, PhD); transportational planning and engineering (MS, PhD). Part-time and evening/weekend programs available.

Faculty: 12 full-time (0 women), 1 part-time/adjunct (0 women).
Students: 20 full-time (8 women), 24 part-time (3 women); includes 2 minority (1 Asian American or Pacific Islander, 1 Hispanic American), 13 international.

Average age 30. 57 applicants, 53% accepted, 9 enrolled. In 2001, 9 degrees awarded. Terminal master's awarded for partial completion of doctoral program.
Degree requirements: For master's, thesis or alternative, comprehensive exam; for doctorate, thesis/dissertation. *Median time to degree:* Master's–2 years full-time, 3 years part-time.
Entrance requirements: For master's, TOEFL; for doctorate, GRE General Test, TOEFL. *Application deadline:* For fall admission, 6/1 (priority date). Applications are processed on a rolling basis. *Application fee:* $40. Electronic applications accepted.
Expenses: Tuition: Full-time $10,170; part-time $445 per credit hour. Tuition and fees vary according to course load.
Financial support: In 2001–02, 18 students received support, including 3 fellowships with tuition reimbursements available, 1 research assistantship with tuition reimbursement available (averaging $10,600 per year), 4 teaching assistantships with tuition reimbursements available (averaging $10,200 per year); Federal Work-Study, institutionally sponsored loans, scholarships/grants, and tuition waivers (full and partial) also available. Support available to part-time students. Financial award application deadline: 2/15.
Faculty research: Highway safety, highway performance, and intelligent transportation systems. Surface mount technology; watershed management. *Total annual research expenditures:* $860,000.
Dr. Thomas H. Wenzel, Chair, 414-288-7030, *Fax:* 414-288-7521.

Find an in-depth description at www.petersons.com/gradchannel.

■ MASSACHUSETTS INSTITUTE OF TECHNOLOGY

School of Engineering, Department of Civil and Environmental Engineering, Cambridge, MA 02139-4307

AWARDS M Eng, SM, PhD, Sc D, CE, EE.

Faculty: 39 full-time (5 women).
Students: 269 full-time (70 women), 5 part-time; includes 23 minority (2 African Americans, 12 Asian Americans or Pacific Islanders, 9 Hispanic Americans), 169 international. Average age 23. 760 applicants, 40% accepted, 116 enrolled. In 2001, 112 master's, 21 doctorates awarded.
Degree requirements: For master's, thesis/dissertation; for doctorate, thesis/dissertation, comprehensive exam.
Entrance requirements: For master's and doctorate, GRE General Test, TOEFL. *Application deadline:* For fall admission, 1/15; for spring admission, 11/1. *Application fee:* $60. Electronic applications accepted.
Expenses: Tuition: Full-time $26,960. Full-time tuition and fees vary according to program.
Financial support: In 2001–02, 242 students received support, including 55

fellowships, 123 research assistantships, 35 teaching assistantships; career-related internships or fieldwork, Federal Work-Study, institutionally sponsored loans, scholarships/grants, health care benefits, and unspecified assistantships also available. Financial award application deadline: 1/15; financial award applicants required to submit FAFSA.

Faculty research: Environmental chemistry and biology, environmental fluid dynamics and hydrodynamics, geoenvironment and geotechnology, surface and groundwater hydrology, materials and structures. *Total annual research expenditures:* $9.7 million. Chiang C. Mei, Acting Head, 617-253-7101, *Fax:* 617-258-6775.

Application contact: Patricia Maguire, Graduate Admissions Coordinator, 617-253-7119, *Fax:* 617-258-6775, *E-mail:* ceed@mit.edu. *Web site:* http://web.mit.edu/civenv/

■ MCNEESE STATE UNIVERSITY

Graduate School, College of Engineering and Technology, Lake Charles, LA 70609

AWARDS Chemical engineering (M Eng); civil engineering (M Eng); electrical engineering (M Eng); mechanical engineering (M Eng). Part-time and evening/weekend programs available.

Faculty: 14 full-time (1 woman).
Students: 24 full-time (5 women), 5 part-time; includes 1 minority (Asian American or Pacific Islander), 23 international. In 2001, 5 degrees awarded.
Degree requirements: For master's, thesis or alternative.
Entrance requirements: For master's, GRE General Test, TOEFL, minimum undergraduate GPA of 3.0. *Application deadline:* For fall admission, 7/15 (priority date). Applications are processed on a rolling basis. *Application fee:* $20 ($30 for international students).
Expenses: Tuition, state resident: part-time $1,208 per semester. Tuition, nonresident: part-time $4,378 per semester.
Financial support: Federal Work-Study available. Support available to part-time students. Financial award application deadline: 5/1.
Dr. O. C. Karkalits, Dean, 337-475-5875, *Fax:* 337-475-5237, *E-mail:* ckarkal@mail.mcneese.edu.
Application contact: Dr. Jay O. Uppot, Director of Graduate Studies, 337-475-5874, *Fax:* 37-475-5286, *E-mail:* juppot@mail.mcneese.edu.

■ MICHIGAN STATE UNIVERSITY

Graduate School, College of Engineering, Department of Civil and Environmental Engineering, East Lansing, MI 48824

AWARDS Civil engineering (MS, PhD); civil engineering-environmental toxicology (PhD); civil engineering-urban studies (MS); environmental engineering (MS, PhD); environmental engineering-environmental toxicology (PhD). Part-time programs available.

Faculty: 19 full-time (2 women).
Students: 57 full-time (13 women), 38 part-time (9 women); includes 14 minority (3 African Americans, 4 Asian Americans or Pacific Islanders, 7 Hispanic Americans), 59 international. Average age 28. 258 applicants, 25% accepted. In 2001, 37 master's, 7 doctorates awarded. Terminal master's awarded for partial completion of doctoral program.
Degree requirements: For doctorate, thesis/dissertation.
Entrance requirements: For master's, GRE, TOEFL, minimum GPA of 3.0; for doctorate, GRE, TOEFL, minimum GPA of 3.0, MS. *Application deadline:* For fall admission, 5/31; for spring admission, 10/31. Applications are processed on a rolling basis. *Application fee:* $30 ($40 for international students). Electronic applications accepted.
Expenses: Tuition, state resident: part-time $244 per credit hour. Tuition, nonresident: part-time $494 per credit hour. Required fees: $268 per semester. Tuition and fees vary according to course load, degree level and program.
Financial support: In 2001–02, 33 fellowships (averaging $4,530 per year), 41 research assistantships (averaging $13,655 per year), 10 teaching assistantships with tuition reimbursements (averaging $13,130 per year) were awarded. Financial award application deadline: 2/15; financial award applicants required to submit FAFSA.
Faculty research: Highway safety, hazardous waste management, pavement research, concrete materials, waste water treatment. *Total annual research expenditures:* $1.6 million.
Dr. R. Harichandran, Chair, 517-355-5107, *Fax:* 517-432-1827, *E-mail:* cee@egr.msu.edu.
Application contact: Rick Lyles, Graduate Coordinator, 517-355-5107, *Fax:* 517-432-1827. *Web site:* http://www.egr.msu.edu/cee/

■ MICHIGAN TECHNOLOGICAL UNIVERSITY

Graduate School, College of Engineering, Department of Civil and Environmental Engineering, Program in Civil Engineering, Houghton, MI 49931-1295

AWARDS ME, MS, PhD. Part-time programs available.

Degree requirements: For doctorate, thesis/dissertation.
Entrance requirements: For master's and doctorate, GRE General Test, TOEFL. Electronic applications accepted. *Web site:* http://www.civil.mtu.edu/

Find an in-depth description at www.petersons.com/gradchannel.

■ MISSISSIPPI STATE UNIVERSITY

College of Engineering, Department of Civil Engineering, Mississippi State, MS 39762

AWARDS MS, PhD. Part-time programs available. Postbaccalaureate distance learning degree programs offered (no on-campus study).

Faculty: 11 full-time (0 women), 45 part-time/adjunct (1 woman).
Students: 9 full-time (3 women), 13 part-time (1 woman); includes 4 minority (all African Americans), 2 international. Average age 27. 6 applicants, 83% accepted. In 2001, 10 master's awarded.
Degree requirements: For master's, thesis (for some programs); for doctorate, thesis/dissertation. *Median time to degree:* Master's–1 year full-time, 6 years part-time; doctorate–5 years full-time.
Entrance requirements: For master's, GRE General Test, TOEFL, minimum GPA of 2.75. *Application deadline:* For fall admission, 7/1; for spring admission, 11/1. Applications are processed on a rolling basis. *Application fee:* $25 for international students.
Expenses: Tuition, state resident: full-time $3,586; part-time $150 per credit hour. Tuition, nonresident: full-time $8,128; part-time $339 per credit hour. Tuition and fees vary according to course load and campus/location.
Financial support: In 2001–02, 15 research assistantships with full tuition reimbursements (averaging $6,700 per year), 4 teaching assistantships with full tuition reimbursements (averaging $18,450 per year) were awarded. Fellowships with full tuition reimbursements, Federal Work-Study, institutionally sponsored loans, and unspecified assistantships also available. Financial award applicants required to submit FAFSA.
Faculty research: Transportation, water modeling, construction materials, structures. *Total annual research expenditures:* $981,116.

Mississippi State University (continued)
Dr. Thomas Dale White, Head, 662-325-3050, *Fax:* 662-325-7189, *E-mail:* tdwhite@engr.msstate.edu.
Application contact: Jerry B. Inmon, Director of Admissions, 662-325-2224, *Fax:* 662-325-7360, *E-mail:* admit@admissions.msstate.edu. *Web site:* http://www.msstate.edu/

■ **MONTANA STATE UNIVERSITY–BOZEMAN**

College of Graduate Studies, College of Engineering, Department of Civil Engineering, Bozeman, MT 59717

AWARDS Engineering (PhD). Part-time programs available.

Students: 32 full-time (6 women), 11 part-time (3 women), 1 international. Average age 28. 31 applicants, 68% accepted, 15 enrolled.
Degree requirements: For doctorate, thesis/dissertation.
Entrance requirements: For doctorate, GRE General Test, TOEFL, minimum GPA of 3.0. *Application deadline:* For fall admission, 7/1; for spring admission, 11/15. Applications are processed on a rolling basis. *Application fee:* $50. Electronic applications accepted.
Expenses: Tuition, state resident: full-time $3,894; part-time $198 per credit. Tuition, nonresident: full-time $10,661; part-time $480 per credit. International tuition: $10,811 full-time. Tuition and fees vary according to course load and program.
Financial support: In 2001–02, 15 students received support, including research assistantships with full and partial tuition reimbursements available (averaging $10,000 per year), teaching assistantships with full and partial tuition reimbursements available (averaging $8,000 per year); career-related internships or fieldwork, Federal Work-Study, scholarships/grants, tuition waivers (full and partial), and unspecified assistantships also available. Financial award application deadline: 3/1; financial award applicants required to submit FAFSA.
Faculty research: Structural engineering, solid engineering, construction engineering and management, environmental engineering, water resources engineering. *Total annual research expenditures:* $795,375.
Dr. Joel Cahoon, Interim Head, 406-994-2111, *Fax:* 406-994-6105, *E-mail:* cedept@ce.montana.edu. *Web site:* http://www.coe.montana.edu/ce/

■ **NEW JERSEY INSTITUTE OF TECHNOLOGY**

Office of Graduate Studies, Department of Civil and Environmental Engineering, Program in Civil Engineering, Newark, NJ 07102

AWARDS MS, PhD. Part-time and evening/weekend programs available.

Students: 27 full-time (1 woman), 60 part-time (9 women); includes 17 minority (4 African Americans, 5 Asian Americans or Pacific Islanders, 8 Hispanic Americans), 29 international. Average age 31. 100 applicants, 67% accepted, 25 enrolled. In 2001, 19 master's, 4 doctorates awarded. Terminal master's awarded for partial completion of doctoral program.
Degree requirements: For doctorate, thesis/dissertation, residency.
Entrance requirements: For master's and doctorate, GRE General Test. *Application deadline:* For fall admission, 6/5 (priority date); for spring admission, 10/15. Applications are processed on a rolling basis. *Application fee:* $50. Electronic applications accepted.
Expenses: Tuition, state resident: full-time $7,812; part-time $434 per credit. Tuition, nonresident: full-time $10,746; part-time $597 per credit. Required fees: $47 per credit. $76 per semester.
Financial support: Fellowships with full and partial tuition reimbursements, research assistantships with full and partial tuition reimbursements, teaching assistantships with full and partial tuition reimbursements, career-related internships or fieldwork, Federal Work-Study, institutionally sponsored loans, and unspecified assistantships available. Financial award application deadline: 3/15.
Application contact: Kathryn Kelly, Director of Admissions, 973-596-3300, *Fax:* 973-596-3461, *E-mail:* admissions@njit.edu. *Web site:* http://www.njit.edu/

■ **NEW MEXICO STATE UNIVERSITY**

Graduate School, College of Engineering, Department of Civil and Geological Engineering, Las Cruces, NM 88003-8001

AWARDS Civil engineering (MSCE, PhD); environmental engineering (MS Env E). Part-time programs available.

Faculty: 15 full-time (1 woman), 2 part-time/adjunct (0 women).
Students: 32 full-time (8 women), 16 part-time (5 women); includes 12 minority (1 Asian American or Pacific Islander, 10 Hispanic Americans, 1 Native American), 19 international. Average age 30. 39 applicants, 74% accepted, 12 enrolled. In 2001, 7 master's, 3 doctorates awarded.
Degree requirements: For master's, thesis (for some programs); for doctorate, thesis/dissertation.
Entrance requirements: For doctorate, BS in engineering, minimum GPA of 3.0. *Application deadline:* For fall admission, 7/1 (priority date); for spring admission, 11/1. Applications are processed on a rolling basis. *Application fee:* $15 ($35 for international students). Electronic applications accepted.
Expenses: Tuition, state resident: full-time $3,234; part-time $135 per credit. Tuition,

nonresident: full-time $9,420; part-time $428 per credit. Required fees: $858.
Financial support: In 2001–02, 13 research assistantships, 17 teaching assistantships were awarded. Fellowships, career-related internships or fieldwork and Federal Work-Study also available. Support available to part-time students. Financial award application deadline: 3/1.
Faculty research: Structural inspection, evaluation and testing, transportation engineering, hydraulics/hydrology, geotechnical engineering.
Dr. Ricardo B. Jacquez, Interim Head, 505-646-3801, *E-mail:* rjaquez@nmsu.edu. *Web site:* http://cagesun.nmsu.edu/

■ **NORTH CAROLINA AGRICULTURAL AND TECHNICAL STATE UNIVERSITY**

Graduate School, College of Engineering, Department of Architectural, Agricultural, Civil and Environmental Engineering, Greensboro, NC 27411

AWARDS MSAE, MSCE, MSE. Part-time programs available.

Faculty: 14 full-time (1 woman), 4 part-time/adjunct (0 women).
Students: 28 full-time (10 women), 10 part-time (4 women), 12 international. Average age 24. 22 applicants, 41% accepted. In 2001, 4 degrees awarded.
Degree requirements: For master's, thesis defense.
Entrance requirements: For master's, GRE General Test, GRE Subject Test (recommended), TOEFL (MSCE). *Application deadline:* For fall admission, 7/1; for spring admission, 1/9. Applications are processed on a rolling basis. *Application fee:* $35.
Financial support: In 2001–02, 1 fellowship (averaging $12,000 per year), 3 research assistantships (averaging $12,000 per year), 2 teaching assistantships (averaging $10,000 per year) were awarded. Career-related internships or fieldwork and unspecified assistantships also available.
Faculty research: Lightning, indoor air quality, material behavior HVAC controls, structural masonry systems. *Total annual research expenditures:* $800,000.
Dr. Peter Rojeski, Chairperson, 336-344-7575, *Fax:* 336-344-7126.
Application contact: Dr. W. Mark McGinley, Graduate Coordinator, 336-334-7575, *Fax:* 336-334-7126, *E-mail:* mcginley@garfield.ncat.edu.

■ **NORTH CAROLINA STATE UNIVERSITY**

Graduate School, College of Engineering, Department of Civil Engineering, Raleigh, NC 27695

AWARDS MCE, MS, PhD. Part-time programs available.

Faculty: 40 full-time (2 women), 25 part-time/adjunct (0 women).
Students: 140 full-time (29 women), 63 part-time (4 women); includes 17 minority (8 African Americans, 6 Asian Americans or Pacific Islanders, 3 Hispanic Americans), 86 international. Average age 29. 450 applicants, 26% accepted. In 2001, 56 master's, 14 doctorates awarded.
Degree requirements: For master's, thesis (for some programs), oral exams; for doctorate, thesis/dissertation, oral exams.
Entrance requirements: For master's, GRE General Test, TOEFL, minimum B average in major; for doctorate, GRE General Test, TOEFL. *Application fee:* $45.
Expenses: Tuition, state resident: full-time $1,748. Tuition, nonresident: full-time $6,904.
Financial support: In 2001–02, 6 fellowships (averaging $7,600 per year), 83 research assistantships (averaging $6,498 per year), 25 teaching assistantships (averaging $6,687 per year) were awarded. Federal Work-Study also available. Financial award application deadline: 3/1.
Faculty research: Materials. Systems environmental, geotechnical, structural, transportation and water rescue engineering. *Total annual research expenditures:* $6.3 million.
Dr. E. Downey Brill, Head, 919-515-2331, *Fax:* 919-515-7908, *E-mail:* brill@ eos.ncsu.edu.
Application contact: Dr. David W. Johnston, Director of Graduate Programs, 919-515-7412, *Fax:* 919-515-7908, *E-mail:* johnston@eos.ncsu.edu. *Web site:* http:// www.cc.ncsu.edu/

■ NORTH DAKOTA STATE UNIVERSITY

The Graduate School, College of Engineering and Architecture, Department of Civil Engineering, Fargo, ND 58105

AWARDS Civil engineering (MS); environmental engineering (MS); natural resource management (MS). Part-time programs available. Postbaccalaureate distance learning degree programs offered (minimal on-campus study).

Faculty: 8 full-time (1 woman), 4 part-time/adjunct (0 women).
Students: 15 full-time (2 women); includes 7 minority (all Asian Americans or Pacific Islanders). Average age 22. 20 applicants, 75% accepted. In 2001, 2 degrees awarded.
Degree requirements: For master's, thesis or alternative.
Entrance requirements: For master's, TOEFL. *Application deadline:* For fall admission, 7/1 (priority date). Applications are processed on a rolling basis. *Application fee:* $35.
Expenses: Tuition, state resident: part-time $124 per credit. Tuition, nonresident: part-time $325 per credit. Required fees: $22 per credit. Tuition and fees vary according to reciprocity agreements.

Financial support: In 2001–02, 4 research assistantships with full tuition reimbursements (averaging $3,740 per year), 9 teaching assistantships with full tuition reimbursements (averaging $1,870 per year) were awarded. Fellowships with full tuition reimbursements, career-related internships or fieldwork, Federal Work-Study, and institutionally sponsored loans also available. Support available to part-time students. Financial award application deadline: 4/15.
Faculty research: Wastewater, hydrology, structures, transportation, solid waste. *Total annual research expenditures:* $150,000.
G. Padmanabhan, Chair, 701-231-7043, *Fax:* 701-231-6185, *E-mail:* g.padmanabhan@ndsu.nodak.edu. *Web site:* http://www.ndsu.nodak.edu/

■ NORTHEASTERN UNIVERSITY

College of Engineering, Department of Civil and Environmental Engineering, Boston, MA 02115-5096

AWARDS MS, PhD. Part-time programs available.

Faculty: 12 full-time (1 woman), 1 part-time/adjunct (0 women).
Students: 41 full-time (8 women), 67 part-time (10 women); includes 1 minority (Hispanic American), 34 international. Average age 25. 133 applicants, 76% accepted, 32 enrolled.
Degree requirements: For master's, thesis optional; for doctorate, thesis/dissertation, departmental qualifying exam. *Median time to degree:* Master's–2 years full-time, 5.5 years part-time.
Entrance requirements: For master's and doctorate, GRE General Test. *Application deadline:* For fall admission, 2/15 (priority date). Applications are processed on a rolling basis. *Application fee:* $50. Electronic applications accepted.
Expenses: Tuition: Part-time $535 per credit hour. Required fees: $56. Tuition and fees vary according to program.
Financial support: In 2001–02, 30 students received support, including 1 fellowship, 10 research assistantships with full tuition reimbursements available (averaging $13,560 per year), 13 teaching assistantships with full tuition reimbursements available (averaging $13,560 per year); career-related internships or fieldwork, Federal Work-Study, scholarships/grants, tuition waivers (full), and unspecified assistantships also available. Support available to part-time students. Financial award application deadline: 2/15; financial award applicants required to submit FAFSA.
Faculty research: Earthquake engineering, geotechnical and geoenvironmental engineering, structural engineering, transportation engineering. *Total annual research expenditures:* $913,755.
Dr. Peter Furth, Acting Chairman, 617-373-2444, *Fax:* 617-373-4419.

Application contact: Stephen L. Gibson, Associate Director, 617-373-2711, *Fax:* 617-373-2501, *E-mail:* grad-eng@ coe.neu.edu. *Web site:* http:// www.coe.neu.edu/

■ NORTHWESTERN UNIVERSITY

McCormick School of Engineering and Applied Science, Department of Civil and Environmental Engineering, Evanston, IL 60208

AWARDS Environmental engineering and science (MS, PhD); geotechnical engineering (MS, PhD); mechanics of materials and solids (MS, PhD); project management (MPM). Structural engineering and materials (MS, PhD); theoretical and applied mechanics (MS, PhD); transportation systems analysis and planning (MS, PhD). MS and PhD admissions and degrees offered through The Graduate School. Part-time programs available.

Faculty: 26 full-time (3 women), 9 part-time/adjunct (2 women).
Students: 80 full-time (32 women), 1 part-time; includes 2 Asian Americans or Pacific Islanders, 1 Hispanic American, 38 international. 282 applicants, 7% accepted. In 2001, 20 master's, 14 doctorates awarded. Terminal master's awarded for partial completion of doctoral program.
Degree requirements: For master's, thesis (for some programs); for doctorate, thesis/dissertation.
Application deadline: For fall admission, 8/1. *Application fee:* $50 ($55 for international students). Electronic applications accepted.
Expenses: Tuition: Full-time $26,526.
Financial support: In 2001–02, 10 fellowships with full tuition reimbursements (averaging $13,338 per year), 66 research assistantships with partial tuition reimbursements (averaging $18,000 per year), 7 teaching assistantships with full tuition reimbursements (averaging $13,329 per year) were awarded. Career-related internships or fieldwork, institutionally sponsored loans, and scholarships/grants also available. Financial award application deadline: 1/15; financial award applicants required to submit FAFSA.
Faculty research: Environmental engineering and science, geotechnics, mechanics of materials and solids, structural engineering and materials, transportation systems analysis and planning. *Total annual research expenditures:* $8.4 million.
Joseph L. Schofer, Chair, 847-491-3257, *Fax:* 847-491-4011, *E-mail:* j-schofer@ northwestern.edu.
Application contact: Janet Soule, Academic Coordinator, 847-491-3176, *Fax:* 847-491-4011, *E-mail:* civil-info@ northwestern.edu. *Web site:* http:// www.civil.northwestern.edu/

Find an in-depth description at www.petersons.com/gradchannel.

■ THE OHIO STATE UNIVERSITY

Graduate School, College of Engineering, Program in Civil Engineering, Columbus, OH 43210

AWARDS MS, PhD.

Degree requirements: For master's, thesis optional; for doctorate, thesis/dissertation.

Entrance requirements: For master's and doctorate, GRE General Test, TOEFL.

■ OHIO UNIVERSITY

Graduate Studies, Russ College of Engineering and Technology, Department of Civil Engineering, Athens, OH 45701-2979

AWARDS Geotechnical and environmental engineering (MS); water resources and structures (MS).

Faculty: 11 full-time (1 woman).
Students: 19 full-time (4 women), 6 part-time (2 women), 18 international. Average age 28. 52 applicants, 71% accepted, 11 enrolled. In 2001, 7 degrees awarded.
Degree requirements: For master's, thesis optional.
Entrance requirements: For master's, minimum GPA of 3.0. *Application deadline:* For fall admission, 5/1 (priority date). Applications are processed on a rolling basis. *Application fee:* $30.
Expenses: Tuition, state resident: full-time $6,585. Tuition, nonresident: full-time $12,254.
Financial support: In 2001–02, 1 fellowship (averaging $15,000 per year), 12 research assistantships (averaging $12,000 per year), 6 teaching assistantships (averaging $6,000 per year) were awarded. Federal Work-Study, institutionally sponsored loans, and tuition waivers (full and partial) also available. Financial award application deadline: 3/15.
Faculty research: Soil-structure interaction, solid waste management, pipes, pavements, noise pollution, mine reclamation, drought analysis. *Total annual research expenditures:* $1.2 million.
Dr. Gayle Mitchell, Chair, 740-593-1465, *Fax:* 740-593-0625, *E-mail:* gmitchell@ bobcat.ent.ohiou.edu.
Application contact: Dr. Shad Sargand, Graduate Chair, 740-593-1467, *Fax:* 740-593-0625, *E-mail:* ssargand@ bobcat.ent.ohiou.edu. *Web site:* http://webce.ent.ohiou.edu/

■ OKLAHOMA STATE UNIVERSITY

Graduate College, College of Engineering, Architecture and Technology, School of Civil and Environmental Engineering, Stillwater, OK 74078

AWARDS Civil engineering (M En, MS, PhD); environmental engineering (M En, MS, PhD).

Faculty: 14 full-time (1 woman), 1 part-time/adjunct (0 women).
Students: 33 full-time (2 women), 32 part-time (1 woman); includes 8 minority (2 African Americans, 1 Asian American or Pacific Islander, 3 Hispanic Americans, 2 Native Americans), 32 international. Average age 30. 130 applicants, 68% accepted. In 2001, 23 master's, 2 doctorates awarded.
Degree requirements: For master's, thesis or alternative; for doctorate, thesis/dissertation.
Entrance requirements: For master's and doctorate, TOEFL. *Application deadline:* For fall admission, 7/1 (priority date). *Application fee:* $25.
Expenses: Tuition, state resident: part-time $92 per credit hour. Tuition, nonresident: part-time $297 per credit hour. Required fees: $21 per credit hour. $14 per semester. One-time fee: $20. Tuition and fees vary according to course load.
Financial support: In 2001–02, 27 students received support, including 9 research assistantships (averaging $8,480 per year), 9 teaching assistantships (averaging $6,667 per year); career-related internships or fieldwork, Federal Work-Study, and tuition waivers (partial) also available. Support available to part-time students. Financial award application deadline: 3/1.
Dr. Gosman Gilbert, Head, 405-744-5190.

■ OLD DOMINION UNIVERSITY

College of Engineering and Technology, Program in Civil Engineering, Norfolk, VA 23529

AWARDS ME, MS, PhD. Part-time and evening/weekend programs available. Postbaccalaureate distance learning degree programs offered (minimal on-campus study).

Faculty: 10 full-time (2 women), 2 part-time/adjunct (0 women).
Students: 12 full-time (0 women), 26 part-time (5 women); includes 6 minority (all African Americans), 17 international. Average age 32. 61 applicants, 97% accepted, 27 enrolled. In 2001, 4 master's, 1 doctorate awarded.
Degree requirements: For master's, thesis optional; for doctorate, thesis/dissertation, candidacy exam. *Median time to degree:* Master's–1 year full-time, 3 years part-time.
Entrance requirements: For master's, minimum GPA of 3.0, GRE or BS; for doctorate, minimum GPA of 3.5, GRE or MS. *Application deadline:* For fall admission, 7/1; for spring admission, 10/1. Applications are processed on a rolling basis. *Application fee:* $30. Electronic applications accepted.
Expenses: Tuition, state resident: part-time $202 per credit. Tuition, nonresident: part-time $534 per credit. Required fees: $76 per semester.
Financial support: In 2001–02, 1 fellowship (averaging $5,000 per year), 7

research assistantships with full and partial tuition reimbursements (averaging $7,752 per year), 2 teaching assistantships with full and partial tuition reimbursements (averaging $9,292 per year) were awarded. Career-related internships or fieldwork, scholarships/grants, tuition waivers (partial), and unspecified assistantships also available. Support available to part-time students. Financial award application deadline: 3/15.
Faculty research: Structural engineering, coastal engineering, environmental engineering, geotechnical engineering, water resources. *Total annual research expenditures:* $592,000.
Dr. Isao Ishibashi, Graduate Program Director, 757-683-4641, *Fax:* 757-683-5354, *E-mail:* cegpd@odu.edu. *Web site:* http://cee.odu.edu/

■ OREGON STATE UNIVERSITY

Graduate School, College of Engineering, Department of Civil, Construction, and Environmental Engineering, Corvallis, OR 97331

AWARDS Civil engineering (MAIS, MS, PhD); ocean engineering (M Oc E). Part-time programs available.

Faculty: 21 full-time (1 woman), 1 (woman) part-time/adjunct.
Students: 60 full-time (14 women), 8 part-time (2 women); includes 5 minority (1 African American, 1 Asian American or Pacific Islander, 2 Hispanic Americans, 1 Native American), 32 international. Average age 29. In 2001, 24 master's, 1 doctorate awarded. Terminal master's awarded for partial completion of doctoral program.
Degree requirements: For master's, thesis or alternative; for doctorate, one foreign language, thesis/dissertation.
Entrance requirements: For master's, GRE General Test, TOEFL, minimum GPA of 3.0 in last 90 hours (3.5 for MS); for doctorate, GRE General Test, TOEFL, minimum GPA of 3.0 in last 90 hours of undergraduate course work. *Application deadline:* For fall admission, 3/1 (priority date). Applications are processed on a rolling basis. *Application fee:* $50.
Expenses: Tuition, area resident: Full-time $15,933. Tuition, state resident: full-time $28,937.
Financial support: Fellowships, research assistantships, teaching assistantships, career-related internships or fieldwork and institutionally sponsored loans available. Support available to part-time students. Financial award application deadline: 2/1.
Faculty research: Hazardous waste management, carbon cycling, wave forces on structures, pavement design, seismic analysis.
Kenneth J. Williamson, Head, 541-737-6836, *E-mail:* kenneth.williamson@ orst.edu.

Application contact: Linda A. Rowe, Office Manager, 541-737-6149, *Fax:* 541-737-3052, *E-mail:* linda.rowe@orst.edu. *Web site:* http://www.ccee.orst.edu/

■ **THE PENNSYLVANIA STATE UNIVERSITY UNIVERSITY PARK CAMPUS**

Graduate School, College of Engineering, Department of Civil and Environmental Engineering, Program in Civil Engineering, State College, University Park, PA 16802-1503

AWARDS M Eng, MS, PhD.

Students: 82 full-time (13 women), 39 part-time (6 women). In 2001, 22 master's, 3 doctorates awarded.
Degree requirements: For master's, final paper (M Eng), oral exam and thesis (MS); for doctorate, one foreign language, thesis/dissertation, oral exams, comprehensive exam.
Entrance requirements: For master's and doctorate, GRE General Test, BS in engineering. *Application fee:* $45.
Expenses: Tuition, state resident: full-time $7,882; part-time $333 per credit. Tuition, nonresident: full-time $16,142; part-time $673 per credit. Required fees: $124 per semester.
Brian A. Dempsey, Head, 814-865-1226.

■ **POLYTECHNIC UNIVERSITY, BROOKLYN CAMPUS**

Department of Civil and Environmental Engineering, Major in Civil Engineering, Brooklyn, NY 11201-2990

AWARDS MS, PhD. Part-time and evening/weekend programs available.

Degree requirements: For master's, thesis or alternative; for doctorate, thesis/dissertation.
Entrance requirements: For doctorate, qualifying exam, MS in civil engineering. Electronic applications accepted.

■ **POLYTECHNIC UNIVERSITY, LONG ISLAND GRADUATE CENTER**

Graduate Programs, Department of Civil and Environmental Engineering, Major in Civil Engineering, Melville, NY 11747

AWARDS MS, PhD.

Degree requirements: For master's, thesis (for some programs); for doctorate, thesis/dissertation.
Electronic applications accepted.

■ **POLYTECHNIC UNIVERSITY OF PUERTO RICO**

Graduate Programs, Hato Rey, PR 00919

AWARDS Business administration (MBA); civil engineering (MCE); competitive manufacturing (MMC); engineering management (MEM); environmental protection management (MEPM); manufacturing engineering (MME).

■ **POLYTECHNIC UNIVERSITY, WESTCHESTER GRADUATE CENTER**

Graduate Programs, Department of Civil and Environmental Engineering, Major in Civil Engineering, Hawthorne, NY 10532-1507

AWARDS MS, PhD.

Degree requirements: For master's, thesis or alternative; for doctorate, thesis/dissertation.
Electronic applications accepted.

■ **PORTLAND STATE UNIVERSITY**

Graduate Studies, College of Engineering and Computer Science, Department of Civil Engineering, Portland, OR 97207-0751

AWARDS MS, PhD. Part-time and evening/weekend programs available.

Faculty: 8 full-time (1 woman), 2 part-time/adjunct (0 women).
Students: 9 full-time (2 women), 20 part-time (3 women); includes 5 minority (2 Asian Americans or Pacific Islanders, 2 Hispanic Americans, 1 Native American), 3 international. Average age 31. 27 applicants, 67% accepted. In 2001, 11 degrees awarded.
Degree requirements: For doctorate, one foreign language, thesis/dissertation, oral and written exams.
Entrance requirements: For master's, TOEFL, minimum GPA of 3.0 in upper-division course work or 2.75 overall, BS in civil engineering or allied field; for doctorate, GRE General Test, GRE Subject Test, minimum GPA of 3.0 in upper-division course work. *Application deadline:* For fall admission, 4/1; for spring admission, 11/1. Applications are processed on a rolling basis. *Application fee:* $50.
Financial support: In 2001–02, 3 research assistantships with tuition reimbursements (averaging $4,939 per year) were awarded; teaching assistantships with full tuition reimbursements, career-related internships or fieldwork, Federal Work-Study, and institutionally sponsored loans also available. Support available to part-time students. Financial award application deadline: 3/1; financial award applicants required to submit FAFSA.
Faculty research: Structures, water resources, geotechnical engineering,

environmental engineering, transportation. *Total annual research expenditures:* $402,774.
Dr. Franz Rad, Head, 503-725-4282, *Fax:* 503-725-4298.
Application contact: Information Contact, 503-725-4244, *Fax:* 503-725-4298, *E-mail:* cedept@eas.pdx.edu. *Web site:* http://www.ce.pdx.edu/

Find an in-depth description at www.petersons.com/gradchannel.

■ **PORTLAND STATE UNIVERSITY**

Graduate Studies, College of Engineering and Computer Science, Systems Science Program, Portland, OR 97207-0751

AWARDS Systems science/anthropology (PhD). Systems science/business administration (PhD). Systems science/civil engineering (PhD). Systems science/economics (PhD). Systems science/engineering management (PhD). Systems science/general (PhD). Systems science/mathematical sciences (PhD). Systems science/mechanical engineering (PhD). Systems science/psychology (PhD). Systems science/sociology (PhD).

Faculty: 4 full-time (0 women).
Students: 47 full-time (19 women), 32 part-time (10 women); includes 9 minority (4 Asian Americans or Pacific Islanders, 3 Hispanic Americans, 2 Native Americans), 15 international. Average age 36. 52 applicants, 38% accepted. In 2001, 8 degrees awarded.
Degree requirements: For doctorate, variable foreign language requirement, thesis/dissertation.
Entrance requirements: For doctorate, GMAT, GRE General Test, TOEFL, minimum undergraduate GPA of 3.0. *Application deadline:* For fall admission, 2/1; for spring admission, 11/1. *Application fee:* $50.
Financial support: In 2001–02, 1 research assistantship with full tuition reimbursement (averaging $6,839 per year) was awarded; teaching assistantships with full tuition reimbursements, career-related internships or fieldwork, Federal Work-Study, and institutionally sponsored loans also available. Support available to part-time students. Financial award application deadline: 3/1; financial award applicants required to submit FAFSA.
Faculty research: Systems theory and methodology, artificial intelligence neural networks, information theory, nonlinear dynamics/chaos, modeling and simulation. *Total annual research expenditures:* $106,413.
Dr. Nancy Perrin, Director, 503-725-4960, *E-mail:* perrinn@pdx.edu.
Application contact: Dawn Kuenle, Coordinator, 503-725-4960, *E-mail:* dawn@sysc.pdx.edu. *Web site:* http://www.sysc.pdx.edu/

■ PRINCETON UNIVERSITY

Graduate School, School of Engineering and Applied Science, Department of Civil and Environmental Engineering, Princeton, NJ 08544-1019

AWARDS Environmental engineering and water resources (PhD); mechanics, materials, and structures (M Eng, MSE, PhD). Statistics and operations research (MSE, PhD); transportation systems (MSE, PhD).

Degree requirements: For master's and doctorate, thesis/dissertation.

Entrance requirements: For master's and doctorate, GRE General Test, GRE Subject Test.

Find an in-depth description at www.petersons.com/gradchannel.

■ PURDUE UNIVERSITY

Graduate School, Schools of Engineering, School of Civil Engineering, West Lafayette, IN 47907

AWARDS MS, MSCE, MSE, PhD. Part-time programs available.

Faculty: 55 full-time (4 women), 8 part-time/adjunct (1 woman).
Students: 225 full-time (40 women), 41 part-time (7 women); includes 23 minority (6 African Americans, 10 Asian Americans or Pacific Islanders, 7 Hispanic Americans), 153 international. Average age 28. 619 applicants, 53% accepted. In 2001, 83 master's, 15 doctorates awarded. Terminal master's awarded for partial completion of doctoral program.
Degree requirements: For master's, thesis (for some programs); for doctorate, thesis/dissertation.
Entrance requirements: For master's and doctorate, GRE General Test, TOEFL. *Application deadline:* For fall admission, 1/1 (priority date); for spring admission, 9/15. Applications are processed on a rolling basis. *Application fee:* $30. Electronic applications accepted.
Expenses: Tuition, state resident: full-time $4,164; part-time $149 per credit hour. Tuition, nonresident: full-time $13,872; part-time $458 per credit hour. Tuition and fees vary according to campus/location and program.
Financial support: In 2001–02, 160 students received support, including 12 fellowships, 96 research assistantships, 52 teaching assistantships Support available to part-time students. Financial award application deadline: 6/30; financial award applicants required to submit FAFSA.
Faculty research: Environmental and hydraulic engineering, geotechnical and materials engineering, structural engineering, construction engineering, infrastructure and transportation systems engineering.
Dr. F. L. Mannering, Head, 765-494-2159.
Application contact: Marcie Duffin, Graduate Secretary, 765-494-2156, *Fax:* 765-494-0395, *E-mail:* cegrad@purdue.edu. *Web site:* http://www.purdue.edu/CE/grad

■ RENSSELAER POLYTECHNIC INSTITUTE

Graduate School, School of Engineering, Department of Civil and Environmental Engineering, Program in Civil Engineering, Troy, NY 12180-3590

AWARDS Geotechnical engineering (M Eng, MS, D Eng, PhD); mechanics of composite materials and structures (M Eng, MS, D Eng, PhD). Structural engineering (M Eng, MS, D Eng, PhD); transportation engineering (M Eng, MS, D Eng, PhD). Part-time programs available.

Faculty: 9 full-time (0 women), 4 part-time/adjunct (1 woman).
Students: 28 full-time (8 women), 6 part-time; includes 1 minority (Asian American or Pacific Islander), 15 international. Average age 24. 105 applicants, 40% accepted. In 2001, 8 master's, 2 doctorates awarded.
Degree requirements: For master's, thesis (for some programs); for doctorate, thesis/dissertation.
Entrance requirements: For master's and doctorate, GRE, TOEFL. *Application deadline:* For fall admission, 1/15 (priority date). Applications are processed on a rolling basis. *Application fee:* $45. Electronic applications accepted.
Expenses: Tuition: Full-time $26,400; part-time $1,320 per credit hour. Required fees: $1,437.
Financial support: In 2001–02, 18 students received support, including 3 fellowships, 5 research assistantships with full and partial tuition reimbursements available, 10 teaching assistantships with full tuition reimbursements available; career-related internships or fieldwork and institutionally sponsored loans also available. Financial award application deadline: 2/1.
Faculty research: Computational mechanics, earthquake engineering, geo-environmental engineering. *Total annual research expenditures:* $1.7 million.
Dr. George List, Department Chair, 518-276-6362, *Fax:* 518-276-4833, *E-mail:* listg@rpi.edu.
Application contact: Jo Ann Grega, Admissions Assistant, 518-276-6679, *Fax:* 518-276-4833, *E-mail:* gregaj2@rpi.edu. *Web site:* http://www.rpi.edu/dept/civil/htm

Find an in-depth description at www.petersons.com/gradchannel.

■ RICE UNIVERSITY

Graduate Programs, George R. Brown School of Engineering, Department of Civil and Environmental Engineering, Houston, TX 77251-1892

AWARDS Civil engineering (MCE, MS, PhD).

Faculty: 7 full-time (0 women), 14 part-time/adjunct (0 women).
Students: 19 full-time (3 women), 15 international. Average age 23. 77 applicants, 36% accepted, 8 enrolled. In 2001, 5 degrees awarded. Terminal master's awarded for partial completion of doctoral program.
Degree requirements: For master's, thesis (for some programs); for doctorate, thesis/dissertation.
Entrance requirements: For master's and doctorate, GRE General Test, TOEFL, minimum GPA of 3.0. *Application deadline:* For fall admission, 2/1 (priority date); for spring admission, 11/1. *Application fee:* $25. Electronic applications accepted.
Expenses: Tuition: Full-time $17,300. Required fees: $250.
Financial support: In 2001–02, 2 fellowships with full tuition reimbursements, 3 research assistantships with full tuition reimbursements were awarded.
Faculty research: Structural dynamics, probabilistic studies in dynamics, fatigue, reinforced concrete experimental research.
Dr. Joe Hughes, Chair, 713-348-5903, *Fax:* 713-348-5203, *E-mail:* hughes@rice.edu.
Application contact: Martha M. Thywissen, Coordinator, Graduate Admissions, 713-348-2353, *Fax:* 713-348-5268, *E-mail:* gradadm@civil.rice.edu.

■ RUTGERS, THE STATE UNIVERSITY OF NEW JERSEY, NEW BRUNSWICK

Graduate School, Program in Civil and Environmental Engineering, New Brunswick, NJ 08901-1281

AWARDS MS, PhD. Part-time and evening/weekend programs available. Terminal master's awarded for partial completion of doctoral program.

Degree requirements: For master's, thesis or alternative; for doctorate, thesis/dissertation.
Entrance requirements: For master's and doctorate, GRE General Test.
Faculty research: Structural mechanics, soil mechanics, environmental geotechnology, water resources, computational mechanics. *Web site:* http://www.liveng.rutgers.edu/

■ SAINT MARTIN'S COLLEGE

Graduate Programs, Program in Civil Engineering, Lacey, WA 98503-7500

AWARDS). Part-time and evening/weekend programs available.

Faculty: 3 full-time (0 women), 2 part-time/adjunct (0 women).
Students: 14; includes 3 minority (2 Asian Americans or Pacific Islanders, 1 Hispanic American). Average age 27. 10 applicants, 80% accepted, 8 enrolled.
Degree requirements: For master's, thesis optional.
Entrance requirements: For master's, minimum 2.8 GPA, BS in civil engineering

or BS in other engineering/science with completion of calculus, differential equations, physics, chemistry. *Application deadline:* For fall admission, 6/30 (priority date); for spring admission, 9/30 (priority date). Applications are processed on a rolling basis. *Application fee:* $35.
Expenses: Tuition: Part-time $519 per credit hour. Required fees: $180; $90 per semester. One-time fee: $125 full-time.
Financial support: In 2001–02, 2 students received support. Scholarships/grants and tuition waivers (partial) available. Support available to part-time students. Financial award application deadline: 2/5.
Faculty research: Transportation engineering, metal fatigue and fracture, environmental engineering.
Dr. Chun K. Seong, Director, 360-438-4318, *Fax:* 360-438-4548, *E-mail:* cseong@stmartin.edu.
Application contact: Jeannette Banter, Information Contact, 360-438-4320, *Fax:* 360-438-4548, *E-mail:* jbanter@stmartin.edu. *Web site:* http://www.stmartin.edu/engineering/mce/

■ SAN DIEGO STATE UNIVERSITY

Graduate and Research Affairs, College of Engineering, Department of Civil and Environmental Engineering, San Diego, CA 92182

AWARDS Civil engineering (MS). Part-time and evening/weekend programs available.

Degree requirements: For master's, thesis optional.
Entrance requirements: For master's, GRE General Test, TOEFL.
Faculty research: Hydraulics, hydrology, transportation, smart material, concrete material.

■ SAN JOSE STATE UNIVERSITY

Graduate Studies, College of Engineering, Department of Civil Engineering and Applied Mechanics, San Jose, CA 95192-0001

AWARDS Civil and environmental engineering (MS).

Faculty: 15 full-time (2 women), 9 part-time/adjunct (0 women).
Students: 22 full-time (11 women), 47 part-time (15 women); includes 37 minority (2 African Americans, 28 Asian Americans or Pacific Islanders, 6 Hispanic Americans, 1 Native American), 8 international. Average age 30. 53 applicants, 79% accepted. In 2001, 35 degrees awarded.
Degree requirements: For master's, thesis or alternative.
Entrance requirements: For master's, minimum GPA of 2.7. *Application deadline:* For fall admission, 6/29; for spring admission, 11/30. Applications are processed on a rolling basis. *Application fee:* $59. Electronic applications accepted.

Expenses: Tuition, nonresident: part-time $246 per unit. Required fees: $678 per semester. Tuition and fees vary according to course load.
Financial support: Applicants required to submit FAFSA.
Dick Desautel, Acting Chair, 408-924-3900, *Fax:* 408-924-4004.
Application contact: Dr. Rhea Williamson, Graduate Adviser, 408-924-3849.

■ SANTA CLARA UNIVERSITY

School of Engineering, Department of Civil Engineering, Santa Clara, CA 95053

AWARDS MSCE. Part-time and evening/weekend programs available.

Students: 1 (woman) full-time, 4 part-time (1 woman); includes 2 minority (1 Asian American or Pacific Islander, 1 Hispanic American), 1 international. Average age 27. 7 applicants, 43% accepted.
Degree requirements: For master's, thesis or alternative.
Entrance requirements: For master's, GRE General Test, TOEFL, minimum GPA of 2.75. *Application deadline:* For fall admission, 6/1; for spring admission, 1/1. Applications are processed on a rolling basis. *Application fee:* $45 ($55 for international students). Electronic applications accepted.
Expenses: Tuition: Part-time $320 per unit. Tuition and fees vary according to class time, degree level, program and student level.
Financial support: Research assistantships, teaching assistantships, Federal Work-Study and scholarships/grants available. Support available to part-time students. Financial award application deadline: 3/1; financial award applicants required to submit FAFSA. *Total annual research expenditures:* $1,988.
Dr. Sukhmander Singh, Chair, 408-554-4061.
Application contact: Tina Samms, Assistant Director of Graduate Admissions, 408-554-4313, *Fax:* 408-554-5474, *E-mail:* engr-grad@scu.edu.

■ SOUTH DAKOTA SCHOOL OF MINES AND TECHNOLOGY

Graduate Division, Department of Civil and Environmental Engineering, Rapid City, SD 57701-3995

AWARDS Civil engineering (MS). Part-time programs available.

Entrance requirements: For master's, TOEFL, TWE. Electronic applications accepted.
Faculty research: Concrete technology, environmental and sanitation engineering, water resources engineering, composite materials, geotechnical engineering.

■ SOUTH DAKOTA SCHOOL OF MINES AND TECHNOLOGY

Graduate Division, Division of Material Engineering and Science, Doctoral Program in Materials Engineering and Science, Rapid City, SD 57701-3995

AWARDS Chemical engineering (PhD); chemistry (PhD); civil engineering (PhD); electrical engineering (PhD); mechanical engineering (PhD); metallurgical engineering (PhD); physics (PhD). Part-time programs available.

Degree requirements: For doctorate, thesis/dissertation.
Entrance requirements: For doctorate, TOEFL, TWE, minimum graduate GPA of 3.0. Electronic applications accepted.
Faculty research: Thermophysical properties of solids, development of multiphase materials and composites, concrete technology, electronic polymer materials.
Find an in-depth description at www.petersons.com/gradchannel.

■ SOUTH DAKOTA STATE UNIVERSITY

Graduate School, College of Engineering, Department of Civil and Environmental Engineering, Brookings, SD 57007

AWARDS Engineering (MS), including civil engineering, environmental engineering.

Degree requirements: For master's, thesis, oral exam.
Entrance requirements: For master's, TOEFL.
Faculty research: Groundwater modeling, biological wastewater treatment, corrosion control, highway materials, traffic analysis.

■ SOUTHERN ILLINOIS UNIVERSITY CARBONDALE

Graduate School, College of Engineering, Department of Civil Engineering and Mechanics, Carbondale, IL 62901-6806

AWARDS MS.

Faculty: 10 full-time (1 woman).
Students: 13 full-time (2 women), 19 part-time (3 women); includes 2 minority (1 African American, 1 Asian American or Pacific Islander), 7 international. Average age 26. 11 applicants, 55% accepted. In 2001, 17 degrees awarded.
Degree requirements: For master's, thesis, comprehensive exam.
Entrance requirements: For master's, TOEFL, minimum GPA of 2.7. *Application deadline:* Applications are processed on a rolling basis. *Application fee:* $20.
Expenses: Tuition, state resident: full-time $3,794; part-time $154 per hour. Tuition, nonresident: full-time $6,566; part-time $308 per hour. Required fees: $277 per hour.

Southern Illinois University Carbondale (continued)

Financial support: In 2001–02, 21 students received support, including 5 research assistantships with full tuition reimbursements available, 9 teaching assistantships with full tuition reimbursements available; fellowships with full tuition reimbursements available, Federal Work-Study, institutionally sponsored loans, and tuition waivers (full) also available. Support available to part-time students. Financial award application deadline: 7/1.

Faculty research: Composite materials, wastewater treatment, solid waste disposal, slurry transport, geotechnical engineering. *Total annual research expenditures:* $230,856. Dr. Bruce DeVantier, Interim Chair, 618-453-7819.

Find an in-depth description at www.petersons.com/gradchannel.

■ **SOUTHERN ILLINOIS UNIVERSITY EDWARDSVILLE**

Graduate Studies and Research, School of Engineering, Department of Civil Engineering, Edwardsville, IL 62026-0001

AWARDS MS. Part-time programs available.

Students: 15 full-time (3 women), 32 part-time (7 women); includes 2 minority (both African Americans), 16 international. Average age 33. 60 applicants, 52% accepted, 11 enrolled. In 2001, 13 degrees awarded.
Degree requirements: For master's, thesis or research paper, final exam. *Median time to degree:* Master's–2.5 years full-time, 4 years part-time.
Entrance requirements: For master's, TOEFL, minimum undergraduate GPA of 2.75 in science, math, and engineering courses. *Application deadline:* For fall admission, 7/20; for spring admission, 12/7. *Application fee:* $25.
Expenses: Tuition, state resident: full-time $2,712; part-time $113 per credit hour. Tuition, nonresident: full-time $5,424; part-time $226 per credit hour. Required fees: $250; $125 per term. $125 per term. Tuition and fees vary according to course load, campus/location and reciprocity agreements.
Financial support: In 2001–02, 2 research assistantships with full tuition reimbursements, 10 teaching assistantships with full tuition reimbursements were awarded. Fellowships with full tuition reimbursements, career-related internships or fieldwork, Federal Work-Study, institutionally sponsored loans, traineeships, and unspecified assistantships also available. Support available to part-time students. Financial award application deadline: 3/1; financial award applicants required to submit FAFSA.
Dr. Nader Panahshahi, Chair, 618-650-2533, *E-mail:* npanash@siue.edu.

Application contact: Dr. Susan Morgan, Director, 618-650-5014, *E-mail:* smorgan@siue.edu.

■ **SOUTHERN METHODIST UNIVERSITY**

School of Engineering, Department of Environmental and Civil Engineering, Dallas, TX 75275

AWARDS Applied science (MS, PhD); civil engineering (MS); environmental engineering (MS); envrionmental systems management (MS). Part-time and evening/weekend programs available. Postbaccalaureate distance learning degree programs offered.

Students: 2 full-time (1 woman), 26 part-time (9 women); includes 12 minority (6 African Americans, 2 Asian Americans or Pacific Islanders, 4 Hispanic Americans). In 2001, 23 degrees awarded. Terminal master's awarded for partial completion of doctoral program.
Degree requirements: For master's, thesis optional; for doctorate, thesis/dissertation, oral and written qualifying exams.
Entrance requirements: For master's, GRE General Test, TOEFL, minimum GPA of 3.0 in last 2 years; bachelor's degree in engineering, mathematics, or sciences; for doctorate, bachelor's degree in related field. *Application deadline:* For fall admission, 7/1; for spring admission, 11/15. Applications are processed on a rolling basis. *Application fee:* $50.
Expenses: Tuition: Part-time $285 per credit hour.
Dr. Edward Forest, Head, 214-768-2280, *Fax:* 214-768-3845, *E-mail:* eforest@seas.smu.edu.
Application contact: Marc Valerin, Associate Director of Graduate Admissions, 214-768-3484, *E-mail:* valerin@seas.smu.edu.

Find an in-depth description at www.petersons.com/gradchannel.

■ **STANFORD UNIVERSITY**

School of Engineering, Department of Civil and Environmental Engineering, Stanford, CA 94305-9991

AWARDS MS, PhD, Eng.

Faculty: 28 full-time (3 women).
Students: 213 full-time (83 women), 40 part-time (19 women); includes 47 minority (7 African Americans, 21 Asian Americans or Pacific Islanders, 17 Hispanic Americans, 2 Native Americans), 110 international. Average age 27. 476 applicants, 47% accepted. In 2001, 122 master's, 12 doctorates awarded. Terminal master's awarded for partial completion of doctoral program.
Degree requirements: For doctorate and Eng, thesis/dissertation, qualifying exam.
Entrance requirements: For master's, doctorate, and Eng, GRE General Test, TOEFL. *Application deadline:* For fall

admission, 1/5. *Application fee:* $65 ($80 for international students). Electronic applications accepted.
Clyde B. Tatum, Chair, 650-723-3921, *Fax:* 650-725-8662, *E-mail:* tatumce@stanford.edu.
Application contact: Graduate Admissions Coordinator, 650-725-2387. *Web site:* http://www-ce.stanford.edu/

■ **STEVENS INSTITUTE OF TECHNOLOGY**

Graduate School, Charles V. Schaefer Jr. School of Engineering, Department of Civil, Environmental, and Ocean Engineering, Program in Civil Engineering, Hoboken, NJ 07030

AWARDS Coastal and ocean engineering (M Eng, PhD, Engr); construction accounting/estimating (Certificate); construction engineering (M Eng, PhD, Certificate, Engr); construction law/disputes (Certificate); construction/quality management (Certificate); geotechnical engineering (Certificate); geotechnical/geoenvironmental engineering (M Eng, PhD, Engr). Structures (M Eng, PhD, Engr).

Degree requirements: For master's, thesis optional; for doctorate, variable foreign language requirement, thesis/dissertation; for other advanced degree, project or thesis.
Entrance requirements: For master's, TOEFL; for doctorate, GRE, TOEFL. Electronic applications accepted.
Expenses: Tuition: Full-time $13,950; part-time $775 per credit. Required fees: $180. One-time fee: $180 part-time. Full-time tuition and fees vary according to degree level and program.

■ **SYRACUSE UNIVERSITY**

Graduate School, L. C. Smith College of Engineering and Computer Science, Department of Civil and Environmental Engineering, Syracuse, NY 13244-0003

AWARDS Civil engineering (MS, PhD); environmental engineering (MS); environmental engineering science (MS); hydrogeology (MS).

Faculty: 9 full-time (2 women), 2 part-time/adjunct (0 women).
Students: 26 full-time (7 women), 7 part-time (1 woman), 24 international. Average age 28. In 2001, 6 master's, 1 doctorate awarded.
Degree requirements: For doctorate, thesis/dissertation.
Entrance requirements: For master's and doctorate, GRE General Test, GRE Subject Test. *Application deadline:* Applications are processed on a rolling basis. *Application fee:* $50.
Expenses: Tuition: Full-time $15,528; part-time $647 per credit. Required fees: $420; $38 per term. Tuition and fees vary according to program.

Financial support: In 2001–02, 3 fellowships with full tuition reimbursements (averaging $13,680 per year), 20 research assistantships with full tuition reimbursements (averaging $11,000 per year), 9 teaching assistantships with full tuition reimbursements (averaging $11,000 per year) were awarded. Federal Work-Study and tuition waivers (partial) also available. Financial award application deadline: 1/10.
Faculty research: Fate and transport of pollutants, methods for characterization and remediation of hazardous wastes, response of eco-systems to disturbances, water quality and engineering. *Total annual research expenditures:* $1.5 million.
Dr. Charles T. Driscoll, Chair, 315-443-3434, *Fax:* 315-443-1243, *E-mail:* cdriscol@syr.edu.
Application contact: Ruth Dewey, Graduate Coordinator, 315-443-2558, *Fax:* 315-443-1243, *E-mail:* rrdewey@syr.edu.

Find an in-depth description at www.petersons.com/gradchannel.

■ TEMPLE UNIVERSITY

Graduate School, College of Science and Technology, College of Engineering, Program in Civil and Environmental Engineering, Philadelphia, PA 19122-6096

AWARDS MSE. Part-time programs available.

Degree requirements: For master's, thesis optional.
Entrance requirements: For master's, GRE General Test, TOEFL.
Expenses: Tuition, state resident: full-time $8,487; part-time $369 per credit hour. Tuition, nonresident: full-time $12,282; part-time $534 per credit hour. Required fees: $350. Tuition and fees vary according to course load, program and reciprocity agreements.
Faculty research: Prestressed masonry structure, recycling processes and products, finite element analysis of highways and runways. *Web site:* http://www.eng.temple.edu/

■ TENNESSEE TECHNOLOGICAL UNIVERSITY

Graduate School, College of Engineering, Department of Civil Engineering, Cookeville, TN 38505

AWARDS MS, PhD. Part-time programs available.

Faculty: 17 full-time (0 women).
Students: 17 full-time (1 woman), 5 part-time (1 woman); includes 7 minority (all Asian Americans or Pacific Islanders). Average age 27. 62 applicants, 79% accepted. In 2001, 6 degrees awarded.
Degree requirements: For master's, thesis; for doctorate, one foreign language, thesis/dissertation.
Entrance requirements: For master's, GRE General Test, TOEFL; for doctorate, GRE Subject Test, TOEFL, minimum

GPA of 3.5. *Application deadline:* For fall admission, 3/1 (priority date); for spring admission, 8/1. *Application fee:* $25 ($30 for international students). Electronic applications accepted.
Expenses: Tuition, state resident: full-time $4,000; part-time $215 per hour. Tuition, nonresident: full-time $10,500; part-time $495 per hour. Required fees: $1,971 per semester.
Financial support: In 2001–02, 12 research assistantships (averaging $8,227 per year), 3 teaching assistantships (averaging $7,200 per year) were awarded. Career-related internships or fieldwork also available. Financial award application deadline: 4/1.
Faculty research: Environmental engineering, transportation, structural engineering, water resources.
Dr. Nader Ghafoori, Chairperson, 931-372-3454, *Fax:* 931-372-6352, *E-mail:* nghafoori@tntech.edu.
Application contact: Dr. Francis O. Otuonye, Associate Vice President for Research and Graduate Studies, 931-372-3233, *Fax:* 931-372-3497, *E-mail:* fotuonye@tntech.edu.

■ TEXAS A&M UNIVERSITY

College of Engineering, Department of Civil Engineering, College Station, TX 77843

AWARDS Construction engineering and project management (M Eng, MS, D Eng, PhD); engineering mechanics (M Eng, MS, PhD); environmental engineering (M Eng, MS, D Eng, PhD); geotechnical engineering (M Eng, MS, D Eng, PhD); hydraulic engineering (M Eng, MS, PhD); hydrology (M Eng, MS, PhD); materials engineering (M Eng, MS, D Eng, PhD); ocean engineering (M Eng, MS, D Eng, PhD); public works engineering and management (M Eng, MS, PhD). Structural engineering and structural mechanics (M Eng, MS, D Eng, PhD); transportation engineering (M Eng, MS, D Eng, PhD); water resources engineering (M Eng, MS, D Eng, PhD). Part-time programs available.

Faculty: 59 full-time (4 women), 7 part-time/adjunct (2 women).
Students: 270. Average age 29. 375 applicants, 57% accepted, 68 enrolled. In 2001, 75 master's, 14 doctorates awarded.
Degree requirements: For master's, thesis (MS); for doctorate, dissertation (PhD), internship (D Eng).
Entrance requirements: For master's and doctorate, GRE General Test, TOEFL. *Application deadline:* Applications are processed on a rolling basis. *Application fee:* $50 ($75 for international students). Electronic applications accepted.
Expenses: Tuition, state resident: full-time $11,872. Tuition, nonresident: full-time $17,892.
Financial support: In 2001–02, 175 students received support, including 20 fellowships (averaging $4,000 per year), 112 research assistantships (averaging

$1,000 per year), 43 teaching assistantships (averaging $1,000 per year); career-related internships or fieldwork and institutionally sponsored loans also available. Financial award application deadline: 4/15; financial award applicants required to submit FAFSA. *Total annual research expenditures:* $7 million.
Dr. John M. Niedzwecki, Head, 979-845-7435, *Fax:* 979-862-2800, *E-mail:* ce-grad@tamu.edu.
Application contact: Dr. Peter B. Keating, Graduate Advisor, 979-845-2498, *Fax:* 979-862-2800, *E-mail:* ce-grad@tamu.edu. *Web site:* http://www.civil.tamu.edu/

Find an in-depth description at www.petersons.com/gradchannel.

■ TEXAS A&M UNIVERSITY–KINGSVILLE

College of Graduate Studies, College of Engineering, Department of Civil Engineering, Kingsville, TX 78363

AWARDS ME, MS. Part-time and evening/weekend programs available.

Faculty: 2 full-time (0 women).
Students: 12 full-time (0 women), 6 part-time; includes 3 minority (all Hispanic Americans), 15 international. Average age 26. In 2001, 1 degree awarded.
Degree requirements: For master's, thesis or alternative, comprehensive exam.
Entrance requirements: For master's, GRE General Test, TOEFL. *Application deadline:* For fall admission, 6/1; for spring admission, 11/15. Applications are processed on a rolling basis. *Application fee:* $15 ($25 for international students).
Expenses: Tuition, state resident: part-time $42 per hour. Tuition, nonresident: part-time $253 per hour. Required fees: $56 per hour. One-time fee: $46 part-time. Tuition and fees vary according to program.
Financial support: Fellowships, research assistantships, teaching assistantships, career-related internships or fieldwork and institutionally sponsored loans available. Financial award application deadline: 5/15.
Faculty research: Geotechnical engineering, structural mechanics, structural design, transportation engineering.
Application contact: Dr. Pat Leelani, Head.

■ TEXAS TECH UNIVERSITY

Graduate School, College of Engineering, Department of Civil Engineering, Lubbock, TX 79409

AWARDS Civil engineering (MSCE, PhD); environmental engineering (M Env E); environmental technology and management (MSETM). Part-time programs available.

Faculty: 19 full-time (0 women), 2 part-time/adjunct (0 women).
Students: 52 full-time (11 women), 15 part-time (5 women); includes 4 minority

Texas Tech University (continued)
(all Hispanic Americans), 34 international. Average age 28. 67 applicants, 54% accepted. In 2001, 26 master's, 7 doctorates awarded.
Degree requirements: For master's and doctorate, thesis/dissertation.
Entrance requirements: For master's and doctorate, GRE General Test, minimum GPA of 3.0. *Application deadline:* Applications are processed on a rolling basis. *Application fee:* $25 ($50 for international students). Electronic applications accepted.
Expenses: Tuition, state resident: full-time $1,926; part-time $107 per credit hour. Tuition, nonresident: full-time $5,724; part-time $318 per credit hour. Required fees: $779; $737 per year. Tuition and fees vary according to course level, course load and program.
Financial support: In 2001–02, 38 research assistantships with partial tuition reimbursements (averaging $9,144 per year), 4 teaching assistantships with partial tuition reimbursements (averaging $9,855 per year) were awarded. Federal Work-Study and institutionally sponsored loans also available. Support available to part-time students. Financial award application deadline: 5/1; financial award applicants required to submit FAFSA.
Faculty research: Wind load/engineering on structures, fluid mechanics, structural dynamics, water resource management. *Total annual research expenditures:* $3.2 million.
Dr. James R. McDonald, Chairman, 806-742-3523, *Fax:* 806-742-3488.
Application contact: Graduate Adviser, 806-742-3523, *Fax:* 806-742-3488. *Web site:* http://www.ce.ttu.edu/
Find an in-depth description at www.petersons.com/gradchannel.

■ **TUFTS UNIVERSITY**

Division of Graduate and Continuing Studies and Research, Graduate School of Arts and Sciences, School of Engineering, Department of Civil and Environmental Engineering, Medford, MA 02155

AWARDS Civil engineering (MS, PhD), including geotechnical engineering, structural engineering; environmental engineering (MS, PhD), including environmental engineering and environmental sciences, environmental geotechnology, environmental health, environmental science and management, hazardous materials management, water resources engineering. Part-time programs available.
Faculty: 13 full-time, 10 part-time/adjunct.
Students: 58 (29 women); includes 4 minority (2 African Americans, 2 Asian Americans or Pacific Islanders) 4 international. 53 applicants, 75% accepted. In 2001, 36 master's, 1 doctorate awarded.

Terminal master's awarded for partial completion of doctoral program.
Degree requirements: For master's, thesis or alternative; for doctorate, thesis/dissertation.
Entrance requirements: For master's and doctorate, GRE General Test, TOEFL. *Application deadline:* For fall admission, 2/15; for spring admission, 10/15. Applications are processed on a rolling basis. *Application fee:* $50. Electronic applications accepted.
Expenses: Tuition: Full-time $26,853. Full-time tuition and fees vary according to program.
Financial support: Research assistantships with full and partial tuition reimbursements, teaching assistantships with full and partial tuition reimbursements, Federal Work-Study, scholarships/grants, and tuition waivers (partial) available. Support available to part-time students. Financial award application deadline: 2/15; financial award applicants required to submit FAFSA.
Dr. Stephen Levine, Chair, 617-627-3211, *Fax:* 617-627-3994.
Application contact: Linfield Brown, Head, 617-627-3211, *Fax:* 617-627-3994. *Web site:* http://www.ase.tufts.edu/cee/

■ **TULANE UNIVERSITY**

School of Engineering, Department of Civil and Environmental Engineering, New Orleans, LA 70118-5669

AWARDS MS, MSE, PhD, Sc D. MS and PhD offered through the Graduate School. Part-time programs available.

Degree requirements: For master's, thesis; for doctorate, 2 foreign languages, thesis/dissertation.
Entrance requirements: For master's and doctorate, GRE General Test, TOEFL, minimum B average in undergraduate course work.
Expenses: Tuition: Full-time $24,675. Required fees: $2,210.

■ **UNIVERSITY AT BUFFALO, THE STATE UNIVERSITY OF NEW YORK**

Graduate School, School of Engineering and Applied Sciences, Department of Civil, Structural, and Environmental Engineering, Buffalo, NY 14260

AWARDS Civil engineering (M Eng, MS, PhD); engineering science (MS). Part-time programs available. Postbaccalaureate distance learning degree programs offered (minimal on-campus study).
Faculty: 22 full-time (0 women), 5 part-time/adjunct (0 women).
Students: 88 full-time (18 women), 50 part-time (9 women); includes 5 minority (2 African Americans, 3 Asian Americans or Pacific Islanders), 88 international.

Average age 27. 285 applicants, 31% accepted. In 2001, 42 master's, 13 doctorates awarded. Terminal master's awarded for partial completion of doctoral program.
Degree requirements: For master's, project or thesis; for doctorate, thesis/dissertation.
Entrance requirements: For master's and doctorate, GRE General Test, TOEFL. *Application deadline:* For fall admission, 1/15 (priority date); for spring admission, 10/1. Applications are processed on a rolling basis. *Application fee:* $35. Electronic applications accepted.
Expenses: Tuition, state resident: full-time $6,118. Tuition, nonresident: full-time $9,434.
Financial support: In 2001–02, 6 fellowships with full tuition reimbursements (averaging $14,700 per year), 58 research assistantships with full tuition reimbursements (averaging $11,400 per year), 27 teaching assistantships with full tuition reimbursements (averaging $11,400 per year) were awarded. Career-related internships or fieldwork, Federal Work-Study, institutionally sponsored loans, scholarships/grants, tuition waivers (full and partial), and unspecified assistantships also available. Support available to part-time students. Financial award application deadline: 1/15; financial award applicants required to submit FAFSA.
Faculty research: Earthquake protection, environmental engineering and fluid mechanics, structural dynamics, geomechanics. *Total annual research expenditures:* $1.5 million.
Dr. Michael C. Constantinou, Chairman, 716-645-2114 Ext. 2446, *Fax:* 716-645-3733, *E-mail:* constonl@eng.buffalo.edu.
Application contact: Dr. T. T. Soong, Director of Graduate Admissions, 716-645-2114 Ext. 2424, *Fax:* 716-645-3667, *E-mail:* dhm1@eng.buffalo.edu. *Web site:* http://www.civil.buffalo.edu/
Find an in-depth description at www.petersons.com/gradchannel.

■ **THE UNIVERSITY OF AKRON**

Graduate School, College of Engineering, Department of Civil Engineering, Akron, OH 44325-0001

AWARDS MS, PhD. Evening/weekend programs available.
Faculty: 11 full-time (1 woman), 9 part-time/adjunct (0 women).
Students: 21 full-time (4 women), 12 part-time (1 woman); includes 1 minority (Hispanic American), 17 international. Average age 29. 24 applicants, 88% accepted, 7 enrolled. In 2001, 24 degrees awarded.
Degree requirements: For master's, thesis optional; for doctorate, thesis/dissertation, candidacy exam, qualifying exam.
Entrance requirements: For master's, TOEFL, minimum GPA of 2.75; for doctorate, GRE, TOEFL. *Application*

deadline: For fall admission, 3/1. Applications are processed on a rolling basis. *Application fee:* $40 ($50 for international students).

Expenses: Tuition, state resident: full-time $6,562; part-time $219 per credit. Tuition, nonresident: full-time $9,027; part-time $383 per credit. Required fees: $272; $11 per credit. Tuition and fees vary according to course load.

Financial support: In 2001–02, 7 research assistantships with full tuition reimbursements, 23 teaching assistantships with full tuition reimbursements were awarded. Fellowships with full tuition reimbursements, career-related internships or fieldwork and Federal Work-Study also available. Financial award application deadline: 3/1.

Faculty research: Development of constitutive relations and numerical analysis of nonlinear problems in structural mechanics, computer modeling of large-scale water supply networks.
Dr. Wieslaw K. Binienda, Interim Chair, 330-972-6693, *E-mail:* wbinienda@uakron.edu. *Web site:* http://www.ecgf.uakron.edu/~civil/index.html

■ THE UNIVERSITY OF ALABAMA

Graduate School, College of Engineering, Department of Civil and Environmental Engineering, Tuscaloosa, AL 35487

AWARDS Civil engineering (MSCE, PhD); environmental engineering (MSE). Part-time programs available. Postbaccalaureate distance learning degree programs offered (no on-campus study).

Faculty: 12 full-time (1 woman), 2 part-time/adjunct (0 women).
Students: 36 full-time (6 women), 17 part-time; includes 2 minority (both African Americans), 30 international. Average age 29. 96 applicants, 39% accepted, 17 enrolled. In 2001, 8 master's, 3 doctorates awarded. Terminal master's awarded for partial completion of doctoral program.
Degree requirements: For master's, thesis or alternative; for doctorate, one foreign language, thesis/dissertation.
Entrance requirements: For master's and doctorate, GRE General Test, minimum GPA of 3.0 in last 60 hours. *Application deadline:* For fall admission, 7/6. Applications are processed on a rolling basis. *Application fee:* $25.
Expenses: Tuition, state resident: full-time $3,292; part-time $183 per credit hour. Tuition, nonresident: full-time $8,912; part-time $495 per credit hour. Tuition and fees vary according to course load, campus/location and program.
Financial support: In 2001–02, 19 research assistantships with full tuition reimbursements (averaging $1,000 per year) were awarded; fellowships, teaching assistantships, Federal Work-Study and institutionally sponsored loans also available.

Faculty research: Experimental structures, modeling of structures, bridge management systems, geotechnological engineering, environmental remediation. *Total annual research expenditures:* $5.6 million.
Dr. Michael H. Triche, Professor, Drummond Chair and Interim Head, 205-348-5834, *Fax:* 205-348-0783, *E-mail:* mtriche@coe.eng.ua.edu.

■ THE UNIVERSITY OF ALABAMA AT BIRMINGHAM

Graduate School, School of Engineering, Department of Civil and Environmental Engineering, Birmingham, AL 35294

AWARDS MSCE, PhD. Evening/weekend programs available.

Students: 23 full-time (7 women), 12 part-time; includes 4 minority (2 African Americans, 2 Asian Americans or Pacific Islanders), 14 international. 58 applicants, 78% accepted. In 2001, 12 master's, 1 doctorate awarded.
Degree requirements: For master's, thesis (for some programs); for doctorate, thesis/dissertation.
Entrance requirements: For master's, GRE General Test, BS in engineering, physical sciences, life sciences, or mathematics; for doctorate, GRE General Test, TOEFL, BS or MS in engineering or related field, minimum undergraduate GPA of 3.0. *Application deadline:* Applications are processed on a rolling basis. *Application fee:* $35 ($60 for international students). Electronic applications accepted.
Expenses: Tuition, state resident: full-time $3,058. Tuition, nonresident: full-time $5,746. Tuition and fees vary according to course load, degree level and program.
Financial support: In 2001–02, 2 fellowships with full tuition reimbursements (averaging $9,500 per year), 11 research assistantships (averaging $1,229 per year) were awarded.
Dr. Fouad H. Fouad, Chair, 205-934-8430, *Fax:* 205-934-9855, *E-mail:* ffouad@uab.edu. *Web site:* http://www.eng.uab.edu/cee/

■ THE UNIVERSITY OF ALABAMA IN HUNTSVILLE

School of Graduate Studies, College of Engineering, Department of Civil and Environmental Engineering, Huntsville, AL 35899

AWARDS MSE. Part-time and evening/weekend programs available.

Faculty: 4 full-time (0 women).
Students: 16 full-time (4 women), 8 part-time (2 women); includes 2 minority (1 African American, 1 Native American), 11 international. Average age 29. 33 applicants, 82% accepted, 13 enrolled. In 2001, 9 degrees awarded.

Degree requirements: For master's, thesis or alternative, oral and written exams, comprehensive exam, registration.
Entrance requirements: For master's, GRE General Test, BSE, minimum GPA of 3.0. *Application deadline:* For fall admission, 7/24 (priority date); for spring admission, 11/15 (priority date). Applications are processed on a rolling basis. *Application fee:* $35.
Expenses: Tuition, area resident: Part-time $175 per hour. Tuition, state resident: full-time $4,408. Tuition, nonresident: full-time $9,054; part-time $361 per hour.
Financial support: In 2001–02, 12 research assistantships with full and partial tuition reimbursements (averaging $8,433 per year), 2 teaching assistantships with full and partial tuition reimbursements (averaging $2,800 per year) were awarded. Fellowships with full and partial tuition reimbursements, career-related internships or fieldwork, Federal Work-Study, institutionally sponsored loans, scholarships/grants, health care benefits, tuition waivers (full and partial), and unspecified assistantships also available. Support available to part-time students. Financial award application deadline: 4/1; financial award applicants required to submit FAFSA.
Faculty research: Hydrologic modeling, orbital debris impact, hydrogeology, environmental engineering, water quality control. *Total annual research expenditures:* $486,685.
Dr. Vijaya Gopu, Chair, 256-824-6854, *Fax:* 256-824-6724, *E-mail:* vgopu@cee.uah.edu. *Web site:* http://www.eb-p5.eb.uah.edu/cce/

■ UNIVERSITY OF ALASKA ANCHORAGE

School of Engineering, Program in Civil Engineering, Anchorage, AK 99508-8060

AWARDS MCE, MS. Part-time and evening/weekend programs available.

Entrance requirements: For master's, GRE General Test, bachelor's degree in engineering.
Faculty research: Structural engineering, engineering education, astronomical observations related to engineering.

■ UNIVERSITY OF ALASKA FAIRBANKS

Graduate School, College of Science, Engineering and Mathematics, Department of Civil and Environmental Engineering, Fairbanks, AK 99775-7480

AWARDS Arctic engineering (MS); civil engineering (MCE, MS); environmental quality engineering (MS); environmental quality science (MS).

Faculty: 15 full-time (2 women), 5 part-time/adjunct (1 woman).

University of Alaska Fairbanks (continued)

Students: 17 full-time (9 women), 15 part-time (5 women), 9 international. Average age 31. 31 applicants, 58% accepted, 13 enrolled. In 2001, 7 degrees awarded. **Degree requirements:** For master's, thesis or alternative, comprehensive exam. **Entrance requirements:** For master's, GRE General Test, TOEFL. *Application deadline:* For fall admission, 4/1; for spring admission, 11/1. Applications are processed on a rolling basis. *Application fee:* $35. **Expenses:** Tuition, state resident: full-time $4,272; part-time $178 per credit. Tuition, nonresident: full-time $8,328; part-time $347 per credit. Required fees: $960; $60 per term. Part-time tuition and fees vary according to course load. **Financial support:** In 2001–02, fellowships with tuition reimbursements (averaging $10,000 per year); research assistantships with tuition reimbursements, teaching assistantships with tuition reimbursements, Federal Work-Study and scholarships/grants also available. **Faculty research:** Soils, structures, culvert thawing with solar power, pavement drainage, contaminant hydrogeology. Dr. Robert Carlson, Head, 907-474-7241.

■ **THE UNIVERSITY OF ARIZONA**

Graduate College, College of Engineering and Mines, Department of Civil Engineering and Engineering Mechanics, Program in Civil Engineering, Tucson, AZ 85721

AWARDS MS, PhD. Part-time programs available.

Faculty: 15 full-time, 2 part-time/adjunct. **Students:** 26 full-time (4 women), 6 part-time (1 woman); includes 2 minority (1 African American, 1 Asian American or Pacific Islander), 24 international. Average age 30. 58 applicants, 57% accepted, 6 enrolled. In 2001, 6 master's, 5 doctorates awarded. **Degree requirements:** For master's, thesis; for doctorate, thesis/dissertation, departmental qualifying exam. **Entrance requirements:** For master's, TOEFL, minimum GPA of 3.0; for doctorate, TOEFL, minimum GPA of 3.5. *Application deadline:* For fall admission, 8/1. Applications are processed on a rolling basis. *Application fee:* $45. **Expenses:** Tuition, state resident: full-time $2,490; part-time $436 per unit. Tuition, nonresident: full-time $10,300; part-time $436 per unit. Full-time tuition and fees vary according to degree level and program. **Financial support:** Fellowships, research assistantships, teaching assistantships, institutionally sponsored loans available. Financial award application deadline: 4/6. **Faculty research:** Soil-structure interaction, water resources, waste disposal, concrete and steel structures.

Dr. Juan B. Valdes, Department Head, 520-621-2266, *E-mail:* jvaldes@u.arizona.edu. **Application contact:** Olivia Hanson, Graduate Coordinator, 520-621-2266, *Fax:* 520-621-2550, *E-mail:* ceem@engr.arizona.edu. *Web site:* http://w3.arizona.edu/~civil/

■ **UNIVERSITY OF ARKANSAS**

Graduate School, College of Engineering, Department of Civil Engineering, Program in Civil Engineering, Fayetteville, AR 72701-1201

AWARDS MSCE, MSE, PhD.

Students: 12 full-time (1 woman), 15 part-time (3 women); includes 1 minority (Native American), 15 international. 9 applicants, 100% accepted. In 2001, 12 master's, 12 doctorates awarded. **Degree requirements:** For master's, thesis optional; for doctorate, one foreign language, thesis/dissertation. *Application fee:* $40 ($50 for international students). **Expenses:** Tuition, state resident: full-time $3,553; part-time $197 per credit. Tuition, nonresident: full-time $8,411; part-time $467 per credit. Required fees: $42 per credit. Tuition and fees vary according to course load and program. **Financial support:** Research assistantships, teaching assistantships, career-related internships or fieldwork and Federal Work-Study available. Support available to part-time students. Financial award application deadline: 4/1; financial award applicants required to submit FAFSA. Dr. Robert Elliott, Chair, Department of Civil Engineering, 479-575-4954.

■ **UNIVERSITY OF CALIFORNIA, BERKELEY**

Graduate Division, College of Engineering, Department of Civil and Environmental Engineering, Berkeley, CA 94720-1500

AWARDS Construction engineering and management (M Eng, MS, D Eng, PhD); environmental quality and environmental water resources engineering (M Eng, MS, D Eng, PhD); geotechnical engineering (M Eng, MS, D Eng, PhD). Structural engineering, mechanics and materials (M Eng, MS, D Eng, PhD); transportation engineering (M Eng, MS, D Eng, PhD).

Degree requirements: For master's, comprehensive exam or thesis (MS); for doctorate, thesis/dissertation, qualifying exam. **Entrance requirements:** For master's, GRE General Test, minimum GPA of 3.0; for doctorate, GRE General Test, minimum GPA of 3.5.

Expenses: Tuition, nonresident: full-time $10,704. Required fees: $4,349.

Find an in-depth description at www.petersons.com/gradchannel.

■ **UNIVERSITY OF CALIFORNIA, DAVIS**

Graduate Studies, College of Engineering, Program in Civil and Environmental Engineering, Davis, CA 95616

AWARDS M Engr, MS, D Engr, PhD, Certificate, M Engr/MBA. Part-time programs available.

Faculty: 35 full-time (5 women), 12 part-time/adjunct (2 women). **Students:** 120 full-time (39 women), 1 part-time; includes 12 minority (9 Asian Americans or Pacific Islanders, 2 Hispanic Americans, 1 Native American), 51 international. Average age 30. 282 applicants, 71% accepted, 40 enrolled. In 2001, 35 master's, 14 doctorates awarded. **Degree requirements:** For doctorate, thesis/dissertation. **Entrance requirements:** For master's, GRE General Test, minimum GPA of 3.0; for doctorate, GRE, minimum graduate GPA of 3.5. *Application deadline:* For fall admission, 1/15 (priority date). Applications are processed on a rolling basis. *Application fee:* $60. Electronic applications accepted. **Expenses:** Tuition, state resident: full-time $4,831. Tuition, nonresident: full-time $15,725. **Financial support:** In 2001–02, 92 students received support, including 40 fellowships with full and partial tuition reimbursements available (averaging $5,761 per year), 58 research assistantships with full and partial tuition reimbursements available (averaging $10,721 per year), 21 teaching assistantships with partial tuition reimbursements available (averaging $10,541 per year); career-related internships or fieldwork, Federal Work-Study, institutionally sponsored loans, and tuition waivers (full and partial) also available. Support available to part-time students. Financial award application deadline: 1/15; financial award applicants required to submit FAFSA. **Faculty research:** Environmental water resources, transportation, structural mechanics, structural engineering, geotechnical engineering. Debbie A. Niemeier, Chairperson, 530-752-8918, *E-mail:* dniemeier@ucdavis.edu. **Application contact:** Kathy LaGiusa, Administrative Assistant, 530-752-1441, *Fax:* 530-752-7872, *E-mail:* klagiusa@ucdavis.edu. *Web site:* http://cee.engr.ucdavis.edu/

■ UNIVERSITY OF CALIFORNIA, IRVINE

Office of Research and Graduate Studies, School of Engineering, Department of Civil and Environmental Engineering, Irvine, CA 92697

AWARDS Civil engineering (MS, PhD); environmental engineering (MS, PhD). Part-time programs available.

Faculty: 15.
Students: 47 full-time (7 women), 10 part-time (2 women); includes 9 minority (7 Asian Americans or Pacific Islanders, 2 Hispanic Americans), 20 international. 100 applicants, 43% accepted, 20 enrolled. In 2001, 16 master's, 8 doctorates awarded. Terminal master's awarded for partial completion of doctoral program.
Degree requirements: For doctorate, thesis/dissertation.
Entrance requirements: For master's, GRE General Test, minimum GPA of 3.0; for doctorate, GRE General Test. *Application deadline:* For fall and spring admission, 1/15 (priority date); for winter admission, 10/15 (priority date). Applications are processed on a rolling basis. *Application fee:* $60. Electronic applications accepted.
Expenses: Tuition, nonresident: full-time $10,704. Required fees: $8,396. Tuition and fees vary according to course load, program and student level.
Financial support: In 2001–02, 9 fellowships (averaging $1,250 per year), 24 research assistantships (averaging $1,120 per year), 6 teaching assistantships (averaging $1,480 per year) were awarded. Institutionally sponsored loans and tuition waivers (full and partial) also available. Financial award application deadline: 3/2; financial award applicants required to submit FAFSA.
Faculty research: Structural mechanics, earthquake and reliability engineering, geotechnical engineering, transportation planning and urban systems. *Total annual research expenditures:* $1.4 million.
Dr. Masanobu Shinozuka, Chair, 949-824-4515, *Fax:* 949-824-3672.
Application contact: Lucien Finley, Administrative Assistant, 949-824-2120, *Fax:* 949-824-2117, *E-mail:* lfinley@ uci.edu. *Web site:* http://www.eng.uci.edu/
Find an in-depth description at www.petersons.com/gradchannel.

■ UNIVERSITY OF CALIFORNIA, LOS ANGELES

Graduate Division, School of Engineering and Applied Science, Department of Civil and Environmental Engineering, Los Angeles, CA 90095

AWARDS Environmental engineering (MS, PhD); geotechnical engineering (MS, PhD). Structures (MS, PhD), including structural mechanics and earthquake engineering; water resource systems engineering (MS, PhD).

Faculty: 14 full-time, 11 part-time/adjunct.
Students: 96 full-time (28 women); includes 23 minority (1 African American, 17 Asian Americans or Pacific Islanders, 5 Hispanic Americans), 45 international. 216 applicants, 60% accepted, 34 enrolled. In 2001, 34 master's, 9 doctorates awarded.
Degree requirements: For master's, comprehensive exam or thesis; for doctorate, thesis/dissertation, qualifying exams.
Entrance requirements: For master's, GRE General Test, minimum GPA of 3.0; for doctorate, GRE General Test, minimum GPA of 3.25. *Application deadline:* For fall admission, 1/15; for spring admission, 12/1. *Application fee:* $60. Electronic applications accepted.
Expenses: Tuition, nonresident: full-time $10,244. Required fees: $3,609. Full-time tuition and fees vary according to program.
Financial support: In 2001–02, 39 fellowships, 50 research assistantships, 31 teaching assistantships were awarded. Federal Work-Study, institutionally sponsored loans, and tuition waivers (full and partial) also available. Financial award application deadline: 1/15; financial award applicants required to submit FAFSA.
Dr. Jiann-Wen Ju, Chair, 310-206-1751.
Application contact: Deeona Columbia, Graduate Affairs Officer, 310-825-1851, *Fax:* 310-206-2222, *E-mail:* deeona@ ea.ucla.edu. *Web site:* http:// www.cee.ucla.edu
Find an in-depth description at www.petersons.com/gradchannel.

■ UNIVERSITY OF CENTRAL FLORIDA

College of Engineering and Computer Sciences, Department of Civil and Environmental Engineering, Program in Civil Engineering, Orlando, FL 32816

AWARDS Civil engineering (MS, MSCE, PhD); geotechnical engineering (Certificate). Structural engineering (Certificate). Surface water modeling (Certificate); transportation engineering (Certificate). Part-time and evening/weekend programs available.

Faculty: 19 full-time (1 woman), 12 part-time/adjunct (0 women).
Students: 17 full-time (4 women), 37 part-time (7 women); includes 10 minority (1 African American, 2 Asian Americans or Pacific Islanders, 7 Hispanic Americans), 16 international. Average age 30. 84 applicants, 62% accepted, 16 enrolled. In 2001, 1 master's, 1 doctorate awarded.
Degree requirements: For master's, thesis or alternative; for doctorate, thesis/ dissertation, departmental qualifying exam, candidacy exam.
Entrance requirements: For master's, GRE General Test, TOEFL, minimum GPA of 3.0 in last 60 hours; for doctorate, GRE General Test, TOEFL, minimum

GPA of 3.5 in last 60 hours. *Application deadline:* For fall admission, 7/15 (priority date); for spring admission, 12/15 (priority date). *Application fee:* $20. Electronic applications accepted.
Expenses: Tuition, state resident: part-time $162 per hour. Tuition, nonresident: part-time $569 per hour.
Financial support: In 2001–02, 13 fellowships with partial tuition reimbursements (averaging $2,115 per year), 73 research assistantships with partial tuition reimbursements (averaging $3,846 per year), 13 teaching assistantships with partial tuition reimbursements (averaging $2,732 per year) were awarded. Career-related internships or fieldwork, Federal Work-Study, institutionally sponsored loans, tuition waivers (partial), and unspecified assistantships also available. Financial award application deadline: 3/1; financial award applicants required to submit FAFSA.
Application contact: Dr. Roger L. Wayson, Coordinator, 407-823-2841, *E-mail:* wayson@pegasus.cc.ucf.edu. *Web site:* http://www.ucf.edu/

■ UNIVERSITY OF CINCINNATI

Division of Research and Advanced Studies, College of Engineering, Department of Civil and Environmental Engineering, Program in Civil Engineering, Cincinnati, OH 45221

AWARDS MS, PhD.

Students: 53 full-time (10 women), 6 part-time (1 woman), 38 international. In 2001, 10 master's, 2 doctorates awarded.
Degree requirements: For master's, project or thesis; for doctorate, one foreign language, thesis/dissertation.
Entrance requirements: For master's and doctorate, GRE General Test, TOEFL. *Application deadline:* For fall admission, 2/1 (priority date). *Application fee:* $40. Electronic applications accepted.
Expenses: Tuition, state resident: part-time $2,698 per quarter. Tuition, nonresident: part-time $4,977 per quarter.
Financial support: Fellowships, career-related internships or fieldwork, tuition waivers (partial), and unspecified assistantships available. Financial award application deadline: 2/1.
Faculty research: Soil mechanics and foundations, structures, transportation, water resources systems and hydraulics.
Application contact: Dr. Steven Buchberger, Graduate Program Director, 513-556-3681, *Fax:* 513-556-2599, *E-mail:* steven.buchberger@uc.edu. *Web site:* http:// www.cee.uc.edu/

■ UNIVERSITY OF COLORADO AT BOULDER

Graduate School, College of Engineering and Applied Science, Department of Civil, Environmental, and Architectural Engineering, Boulder, CO 80309

AWARDS Building systems (MS, PhD); construction engineering and management (MS, PhD); environmental engineering (MS, PhD); geoenvironmental engineering (MS, PhD); geotechnical engineering (MS, PhD). Structural engineering (MS, PhD); water resource engineering (MS, PhD).

Faculty: 37 full-time (2 women).
Students: 167 full-time (49 women), 44 part-time (12 women); includes 14 minority (1 African American, 4 Asian Americans or Pacific Islanders, 9 Hispanic Americans), 88 international. Average age 30. 280 applicants, 59% accepted. In 2001, 59 master's, 13 doctorates awarded.
Degree requirements: For master's, thesis or alternative, comprehensive exam; for doctorate, thesis/dissertation.
Entrance requirements: For master's, GRE General Test, minimum undergraduate GPA of 3.0. *Application deadline:* For fall admission, 4/30; for spring admission, 10/31. *Application fee:* $50 ($60 for international students).
Expenses: Tuition, state resident: full-time $3,474. Tuition, nonresident: full-time $16,624.
Financial support: In 2001–02, 19 fellowships (averaging $5,252 per year), 45 research assistantships (averaging $15,638 per year), 14 teaching assistantships (averaging $13,821 per year) were awarded. Financial award application deadline: 2/15.
Faculty research: Building systems engineering, construction engineering and management, environmental engineering, geoenvironmental engineering, geotechnical engineering. *Total annual research expenditures:* $8.3 million.
Hon-Yim Ko, Chair, 303-492-6716, *Fax:* 303-492-7317, *E-mail:* ko@spot.colorado.edu.
Application contact: Jan Demay, Graduate Secretary, 303-492-7316, *Fax:* 303-492-7317, *E-mail:* demay@spot.colorado.edu. *Web site:* http://www.civil.colorado.edu/

■ UNIVERSITY OF COLORADO AT DENVER

Graduate School, College of Engineering and Applied Science, Department of Civil Engineering, Denver, CO 80217-3364

AWARDS MS, PhD. Part-time and evening/weekend programs available.

Faculty: 12 full-time (3 women).
Students: 13 full-time (0 women), 81 part-time (20 women); includes 13 minority (2 African Americans, 6 Asian Americans or Pacific Islanders, 5 Hispanic Americans), 8 international. Average age 31. 34 applicants, 62% accepted, 15 enrolled. In 2001, 19 master's, 2 doctorates awarded.
Degree requirements: For master's, thesis or alternative; for doctorate, one foreign language, thesis/dissertation.
Entrance requirements: For master's and doctorate, GRE. *Application deadline:* For fall admission, 6/1; for spring admission, 10/1. Applications are processed on a rolling basis. *Application fee:* $50 ($60 for international students). Electronic applications accepted.
Expenses: Tuition, state resident: full-time $3,284; part-time $198 per credit hour. Tuition, nonresident: full-time $13,380; part-time $802 per credit hour. Required fees: $444; $222 per semester.
Financial support: Research assistantships, teaching assistantships, career-related internships or fieldwork and Federal Work-Study available. Financial award application deadline: 3/1; financial award applicants required to submit FAFSA. *Total annual research expenditures:* $492,823.
Bruce Janson, Chair, 303-556-2831, *Fax:* 303-556-2368, *E-mail:* bjanson@carbon.cudenver.edu.
Application contact: Dawn Arge, Program Assistant, 303-556-2871, *Fax:* 303-556-2368, *E-mail:* darge@carbon.cudenver.edu. *Web site:* http://carbon.cudenver.edu/public/engineer/cedept.html

■ UNIVERSITY OF CONNECTICUT

Graduate School, School of Engineering, Field of Civil Engineering, Storrs, CT 06269

AWARDS MS, PhD. Terminal master's awarded for partial completion of doctoral program.

Degree requirements: For master's, thesis or alternative; for doctorate, thesis/dissertation.
Entrance requirements: For master's and doctorate, GRE General Test.
Faculty research: Structures, environmental and transportation engineering.

■ UNIVERSITY OF DAYTON

Graduate School, School of Engineering, Department of Civil Engineering, Dayton, OH 45469-1300

AWARDS Engineering mechanics (MSEM); environmental engineering (MSCE). Soil mechanics (MSCE). Structural engineering (MSCE); transport engineering (MSCE). Part-time programs available.

Faculty: 8 full-time (0 women), 2 part-time/adjunct (0 women).
Students: 8 full-time (6 women), 7 part-time (4 women), 6 international. In 2001, 2 degrees awarded.
Degree requirements: For master's, thesis or alternative.

Entrance requirements: For master's, TOEFL. *Application deadline:* For fall admission, 8/1. Applications are processed on a rolling basis. *Application fee:* $30.
Expenses: Tuition: Full-time $5,436; part-time $453 per credit hour. Required fees: $50; $25 per term.
Financial support: In 2001–02, 5 research assistantships with full tuition reimbursements (averaging $12,000 per year), 2 teaching assistantships with full tuition reimbursements (averaging $10,000 per year) were awarded. Institutionally sponsored loans also available.
Faculty research: Tire/soil interaction, tilt-up structures, viscoelastic response of restraint systems, composite materials.
Dr. Joseph E. Saliba, Chairperson, 937-229-3847, *E-mail:* jsaliba@engr.udayton.edu.
Application contact: Dr. Donald L. Moon, Associate Dean, 937-229-2241, *Fax:* 937-229-2471, *E-mail:* dmoon@notes.udayton.edu.

■ UNIVERSITY OF DELAWARE

College of Engineering, Department of Civil and Environmental Engineering, Newark, DE 19716

AWARDS Environmental engineering (MAS, MCE, PhD); geotechnical engineering (MAS, MCE, PhD); ocean engineering (MAS, MCE, PhD); railroad engineering (MAS, MCE, PhD). Structural engineering (MAS, MCE, PhD); transportation engineering (MAS, MCE, PhD); water resource engineering (MAS, MCE, PhD). Part-time programs available. Terminal master's awarded for partial completion of doctoral program.

Degree requirements: For master's and doctorate, thesis/dissertation.
Entrance requirements: For master's and doctorate, GRE General Test, TOEFL.
Expenses: Tuition, state resident: full-time $4,770; part-time $265 per credit. Tuition, nonresident: full-time $13,860; part-time $770 per credit. Required fees: $414.
Faculty research: Structural engineering and mechanics; transportation engineering; ocean engineering. Soil mechanics and foundation; water resources and environmental engineering. *Web site:* http://www.ce.udel.edu

Find an in-depth description at www.petersons.com/gradchannel.

■ UNIVERSITY OF DETROIT MERCY

College of Engineering and Science, Department of Civil and Environmental Engineering, Detroit, MI 48219-0900

AWARDS ME. Evening/weekend programs available.

Faculty: 5 full-time (1 woman).
Students: 1 full-time (0 women), 3 part-time, 3 international. Average age 28. *Application deadline:* For fall admission, 8/1 (priority date). Applications are processed

on a rolling basis. *Application fee:* $30 ($50 for international students).
Expenses: Tuition: Full-time $10,620; part-time $590 per credit hour. Required fees: $400. Tuition and fees vary according to program.
Financial support: Career-related internships or fieldwork available.
Faculty research: Geotechnical engineering.
Dr. Utpal Dutta, Chairman, 313-993-1040, *Fax:* 313-993-1187, *E-mail:* duttau@udmercy.edu.

■ UNIVERSITY OF FLORIDA

Graduate School, College of Engineering, Department of Civil and Coastal Engineering, Program in Civil Engineering, Gainesville, FL 32611

AWARDS MCE, ME, MS, PhD, Engr. Part-time programs available.

Degree requirements: For master's and Engr, thesis optional; for doctorate, 2 foreign languages, thesis/dissertation.
Entrance requirements: For master's and doctorate, GRE General Test, TOEFL, minimum GPA of 3.0; for Engr, GRE General Test. Electronic applications accepted.
Expenses: Tuition, state resident: part-time $164 per hour. Tuition, nonresident: part-time $571 per hour. Tuition and fees vary according to course level and program.
Faculty research: Structures, materials, hydrology, public works, surveying and mapping. *Web site:* http://www.ce.ufl.edu/

■ UNIVERSITY OF FLORIDA

Graduate School, College of Engineering, Department of Civil and Coastal Engineering, Program in Coastal and Oceanographic Engineering, Gainesville, FL 32611

AWARDS ME, MS, PhD, Engr.

Degree requirements: For master's and Engr, thesis optional; for doctorate, thesis/dissertation.
Entrance requirements: For master's and doctorate, GRE General Test, TOEFL, minimum GPA of 3.0; for Engr, GRE General Test. Electronic applications accepted.
Expenses: Tuition, state resident: part-time $164 per hour. Tuition, nonresident: part-time $571 per hour. Tuition and fees vary according to course level and program.
Faculty research: Coastal processes, ocean process, coastal structures, ocean structure, wave forces. *Web site:* http://www.coastal.ufl.edu/

■ UNIVERSITY OF HAWAII AT MANOA

Graduate Division, College of Engineering, Department of Civil Engineering, Honolulu, HI 96822

AWARDS MS, PhD. Part-time programs available.

Faculty: 24 full-time (1 woman).
Students: 41 full-time (13 women), 20 part-time (6 women); includes 32 Asian Americans or Pacific Islanders, 1 Hispanic American. Average age 29. 52 applicants, 77% accepted, 22 enrolled. In 2001, 9 degrees awarded.
Degree requirements: For master's, exams, thesis optional; for doctorate, thesis/dissertation, exams. *Median time to degree:* Master's–2 years full-time.
Entrance requirements: For master's and doctorate, GRE General Test. *Application deadline:* For fall admission, 3/1; for spring admission, 9/1. Applications are processed on a rolling basis. *Application fee:* $25 ($50 for international students).
Expenses: Tuition, state resident: full-time $2,160; part-time $1,980 per year. Tuition, nonresident: full-time $5,190; part-time $4,829 per year.
Financial support: In 2001–02, 31 students received support, including 21 research assistantships (averaging $15,103 per year), 3 teaching assistantships (averaging $13,134 per year); career-related internships or fieldwork, Federal Work-Study, and tuition waivers (full and partial) also available.
Faculty research: Structures, transportation, environmental engineering, geotechnical engineering, construction. *Total annual research expenditures:* $800,000.
Dr. Edmond Cheng, Chairperson, 808-956-7550.
Application contact: Panagiotis Prevedouros, Graduate Chairperson, 808-956-9698, *Fax:* 808-956-5014, *E-mail:* pdp@hawaii.edu. *Web site:* http://www.eng.hawaii.edu/CE/home.html

■ UNIVERSITY OF HOUSTON

Cullen College of Engineering, Department of Civil and Environmental Engineering, Houston, TX 77204

AWARDS MCE, MS Env E, MSCE, PhD. Part-time and evening/weekend programs available.

Faculty: 14 full-time (2 women), 2 part-time/adjunct (0 women).
Students: 27 full-time (4 women), 44 part-time (9 women); includes 14 minority (2 African Americans, 7 Asian Americans or Pacific Islanders, 5 Hispanic Americans), 28 international. Average age 29. 65 applicants, 42% accepted. In 2001, 11 master's, 5 doctorates awarded. Terminal master's awarded for partial completion of doctoral program.

Degree requirements: For master's, thesis (for some programs); for doctorate, thesis/dissertation, departmental qualifying exam.
Entrance requirements: For master's and doctorate, GRE General Test, TOEFL. *Application deadline:* For fall admission, 7/3 (priority date); for spring admission, 12/4. Applications are processed on a rolling basis. *Application fee:* $25 ($75 for international students).
Expenses: Tuition, state resident: full-time $1,512. Tuition, nonresident: full-time $5,310. Required fees: $1,308. Tuition and fees vary according to program.
Financial support: In 2001–02, 56 research assistantships with partial tuition reimbursements (averaging $14,400 per year), 10 teaching assistantships with partial tuition reimbursements (averaging $13,000 per year) were awarded. Career-related internships or fieldwork and Federal Work-Study also available. Financial award application deadline: 4/1.
Faculty research: Structural engineering and construction materials, geotechnical engineering and deep foundation, hydraulic engineering and wave mechanics, water and soil treatment. *Total annual research expenditures:* $1.5 million.
Dr. Cumaraswamy Vipulanandan, Chairperson, 713-743-4250, *Fax:* 713-743-4260.
Application contact: Charlene Holliday, Graduate Analyst, 713-743-4254, *Fax:* 713-743-4260, *E-mail:* wholliday@uh.edu. *Web site:* http://www.egr.uh.edu/cive/

Find an in-depth description at www.petersons.com/gradchannel.

■ UNIVERSITY OF IDAHO

College of Graduate Studies, College of Engineering, Department of Civil Engineering, Moscow, ID 83844-2282
AWARDS M Engr, MS, PhD.

Faculty: 12 full-time (0 women).
Students: 19 full-time (5 women), 36 part-time (7 women); includes 4 minority (1 African American, 3 Asian Americans or Pacific Islanders), 15 international. 71 applicants, 62% accepted. In 2001, 5 master's, 1 doctorate awarded.
Degree requirements: For master's and doctorate, thesis/dissertation.
Entrance requirements: For master's, minimum GPA of 2.8; for doctorate, minimum undergraduate GPA of 2.8, 3.0 graduate. *Application deadline:* For fall admission, 8/1; for spring admission, 12/15. *Application fee:* $35 ($45 for international students).
Expenses: Tuition, state resident: full-time $1,613. Tuition, nonresident: full-time $3,000.
Financial support: In 2001–02, 1 research assistantship (averaging $6,843 per year), 4 teaching assistantships (averaging $4,642 per year) were awarded. Fellowships, career-related internships or fieldwork also

University of Idaho (continued)
available. Financial award application deadline: 2/15.
Faculty research: Water resources, structural engineering, soil mechanics, materials science. *Web site:* http://www.uidaho.edu/engr/cedept/

Find an in-depth description at www.petersons.com/gradchannel.

■ UNIVERSITY OF ILLINOIS AT CHICAGO

Graduate College, College of Engineering, Department of Civil and Materials Engineering, Chicago, IL 60607-7128

AWARDS MS, PhD. Evening/weekend programs available.

Faculty: 13 full-time (0 women), 2 part-time/adjunct (0 women).
Students: 43 full-time (11 women), 47 part-time (10 women); includes 10 minority (4 African Americans, 4 Asian Americans or Pacific Islanders, 2 Hispanic Americans), 37 international. Average age 30. 152 applicants, 38% accepted, 30 enrolled. In 2001, 23 master's, 4 doctorates awarded.
Degree requirements: For master's, thesis (for some programs); for doctorate, thesis/dissertation, preliminary and qualifying exams.
Entrance requirements: For master's and doctorate, GRE General Test, TOEFL, minimum GPA of 4.0 on a 5.0 scale.
Application deadline: For fall admission, 6/1; for spring admission, 11/1. Applications are processed on a rolling basis. *Application fee:* $40 ($50 for international students). Electronic applications accepted.
Expenses: Tuition, state resident: full-time $3,060. Tuition, nonresident: full-time $6,688.
Financial support: In 2001–02, 27 students received support; fellowships with full tuition reimbursements available, research assistantships with full tuition reimbursements available, teaching assistantships with full tuition reimbursements available, Federal Work-Study and tuition waivers (full) available. Financial award application deadline: 3/1; financial award applicants required to submit FAFSA.
Faculty research: Transportation and geotechnical engineering, damage and anisotropic behavior, steel processing.
Dr. Ming Wang, Director of Graduate Studies, 312-996-3432, *E-mail:* mlwang@uic.edu.
Application contact: Rachel L. Morrow, Graduate Program Coordinator, 312-996-3411, *E-mail:* rlmorrow@uic.edu.

Find an in-depth description at www.petersons.com/gradchannel.

■ UNIVERSITY OF ILLINOIS AT URBANA–CHAMPAIGN

Graduate College, College of Engineering, Department of Civil and Environmental Engineering, Champaign, IL 61820

AWARDS Civil engineering (MS, PhD); environmental engineering and environmental science (MS, PhD), including environmental engineering, environmental science.

Faculty: 49 full-time, 2 part-time/adjunct.
Students: 367 full-time (86 women); includes 19 minority (3 African Americans, 5 Asian Americans or Pacific Islanders, 10 Hispanic Americans, 1 Native American), 206 international. 838 applicants, 18% accepted. In 2001, 90 master's, 30 doctorates awarded.
Degree requirements: For master's, thesis or alternative; for doctorate, thesis/dissertation.
Application deadline: Applications are processed on a rolling basis. *Application fee:* $40 ($50 for international students). Electronic applications accepted.
Expenses: Tuition, state resident: part-time $3,227 per degree program. Tuition, nonresident: part-time $7,169 per degree program. Tuition and fees vary according to program.
Financial support: In 2001–02, 24 fellowships, 179 research assistantships, 42 teaching assistantships were awarded. Tuition waivers (full and partial) also available. Financial award application deadline: 2/15.
Dr. Neil M. Hawkins, Interim Head, 217-333-3815, *Fax:* 217-333-9464, *E-mail:* nmhawkin@uiuc.edu.
Application contact: Mary Pearson, Administrative Secretary, 217-333-3811, *Fax:* 217-333-9464, *E-mail:* mkpearson@uiuc.edu. *Web site:* http://www.cee.ce.uiuc.edu

Find an in-depth description at www.petersons.com/gradchannel.

■ THE UNIVERSITY OF IOWA

Graduate College, College of Engineering, Department of Civil and Environmental Engineering, Iowa City, IA 52242-1316

AWARDS MS, PhD. Part-time programs available.

Faculty: 22 full-time (2 women), 1 part-time/adjunct (0 women).
Students: 47 full-time (15 women), 35 part-time (4 women); includes 2 minority (1 African American, 1 Asian American or Pacific Islander), 44 international. Average age 28. 198 applicants, 56% accepted, 21 enrolled. In 2001, 10 master's, 5 doctorates awarded. Terminal master's awarded for partial completion of doctoral program.
Degree requirements: For master's, exam, thesis optional; for doctorate, thesis/dissertation, exam, comprehensive exam.
Entrance requirements: For master's and doctorate, TOEFL. *Application deadline:*

For fall admission, 4/15 (priority date); for spring admission, 10/1 (priority date). Applications are processed on a rolling basis. *Application fee:* $30 ($50 for international students). Electronic applications accepted.
Expenses: Tuition, state resident: full-time $3,702; part-time $206 per semester hour. Tuition, nonresident: full-time $11,924; part-time $206 per semester hour. Required fees: $101 per semester. Tuition and fees vary according to course load and program.
Financial support: In 2001–02, 72 students received support, including 1 fellowship (averaging $17,989 per year), 16 research assistantships (averaging $17,989 per year), 17 teaching assistantships (averaging $14,718 per year); career-related internships or fieldwork, Federal Work-Study, scholarships/grants, traineeships, health care benefits, and unspecified assistantships also available. Support available to part-time students. Financial award application deadline: 2/1; financial award applicants required to submit FAFSA.
Faculty research: Bioremediation, optimal design of structures, environmental hydraulics, road paving systems, water quality. *Total annual research expenditures:* $6.2 million.
Dr. Robert Ettema, Departmental Executive Officer, 319-384-0596, *Fax:* 319-335-5660, *E-mail:* robert-ettema@uiowa.edu.
Application contact: Judy Holland, Secretary, 319-335-5647, *Fax:* 319-335-5660, *E-mail:* cee@engineering.uiowa.edu. *Web site:* http://www.cee.engineering.uiowa.edu/

■ UNIVERSITY OF KANSAS

Graduate School, School of Engineering, Department of Civil, Environmental, and Architectural Engineering, Lawrence, KS 66045

AWARDS Architectural engineering (MS); civil engineering (MCE, MS, DE, PhD); construction management (MCM); environmental engineering (MS, PhD); environmental science (MS, PhD); water resources engineering (MS); water resources science (MS).

Faculty: 27.
Students: 38 full-time (11 women), 97 part-time (20 women); includes 12 minority (4 African Americans, 3 Asian Americans or Pacific Islanders, 4 Hispanic Americans, 1 Native American), 37 international. Average age 32. 105 applicants, 31% accepted, 19 enrolled. In 2001, 32 master's, 4 doctorates awarded.
Degree requirements: For master's, thesis or alternative, exam; for doctorate, thesis/dissertation, comprehensive exam.
Entrance requirements: For master's, GRE, Michigan English Language Assessment Battery, TOEFL, minimum GPA of 3.0; for doctorate, GRE, Michigan English Language Assessment Battery, TOEFL, minimum GPA of 3.5. *Application deadline:*

Applications are processed on a rolling basis. *Application fee:* $40.
Expenses: Tuition, state resident: full-time $2,722; part-time $113 per credit. Tuition, nonresident: full-time $8,586; part-time $358 per credit. Required fees: $551; $46 per credit. Tuition and fees vary according to campus/location, program and reciprocity agreements.
Financial support: In 2001–02, 21 research assistantships with partial tuition reimbursements (averaging $10,367 per year), 6 teaching assistantships with full and partial tuition reimbursements (averaging $8,615 per year) were awarded. Fellowships, career-related internships or fieldwork also available.
Faculty research: Structures (fracture mechanics), transportation, environmental health.
Steve L. McCabe, Chair, 785-864-3766.
Application contact: David Parr, Graduate Director, *E-mail:* aparr@engr.ukans.edu. *Web site:* http://www.ceae.ku.edu/

■ UNIVERSITY OF KENTUCKY

Graduate School, Graduate School Programs from the College of Engineering, Program in Civil Engineering, Lexington, KY 40506-0032

AWARDS MCE, MSCE, PhD.

Faculty: 24 full-time (2 women).
Students: 37 full-time (15 women), 18 part-time (2 women); includes 1 minority (Asian American or Pacific Islander), 20 international. 52 applicants, 69% accepted. In 2001, 30 master's, 1 doctorate awarded.
Degree requirements: For master's, thesis optional; for doctorate, thesis/dissertation, comprehensive exam.
Entrance requirements: For master's, GRE General Test, minimum GPA of 2.8; for doctorate, GRE General Test, minimum graduate GPA of 3.0. *Application deadline:* For fall admission, 7/19. Applications are processed on a rolling basis. *Application fee:* $30 ($35 for international students).
Expenses: Tuition, state resident: full-time $4,075; part-time $213 per credit hour. Tuition, nonresident: full-time $11,295; part-time $614 per credit hour.
Financial support: In 2001–02, 7 fellowships, 14 research assistantships, 7 teaching assistantships were awarded. Federal Work-Study and institutionally sponsored loans also available. Support available to part-time students. Financial award application deadline: 2/1.
Faculty research: Geotechnical engineering, structures, construction engineering and management, environmental engineering and water resources, transportation and materials. *Total annual research expenditures:* $259,278.
Dr. Kamyar Mahboub, Director of Graduate Studies, 859-257-4279, *Fax:* 859-257-4404.

Application contact: Dr. Jeannine Blackwell, Associate Dean, 859-257-4905, *Fax:* 859-323-1928.

■ UNIVERSITY OF LOUISIANA AT LAFAYETTE

Graduate School, College of Engineering, Department of Civil Engineering, Lafayette, LA 70504

AWARDS MSE. Evening/weekend programs available.

Faculty: 6 full-time (1 woman).
Students: 13 full-time (3 women), 5 part-time (1 woman), 15 international. 42 applicants, 40% accepted, 4 enrolled. In 2001, 7 degrees awarded.
Degree requirements: For master's, thesis or alternative, comprehensive exam.
Entrance requirements: For master's, GRE General Test, BS in civil engineering, minimum GPA of 2.85. *Application deadline:* For fall admission, 5/15. *Application fee:* $20 ($30 for international students).
Expenses: Tuition, state resident: full-time $2,317; part-time $79 per credit. Tuition, nonresident: full-time $8,882; part-time $369 per credit. International tuition: $9,018 full-time.
Financial support: In 2001–02, 3 research assistantships with full tuition reimbursements (averaging $5,500 per year) were awarded; Federal Work-Study and tuition waivers (full and partial) also available. Financial award application deadline: 5/1.
Faculty research: Structural mechanics, computer-aided design, environmental engineering.
Dr. Robert Wang, Head, 337-482-6511.
Application contact: Dr. Xiaoduan Sun, Graduate Coordinator, 337-482-6514.

■ UNIVERSITY OF LOUISVILLE

Graduate School, Speed Scientific School, Department of Civil and Environmental Engineering, Louisville, KY 40292-0001

AWARDS M Eng, MS, PhD.

Students: 24 full-time (9 women), 45 part-time (8 women); includes 2 minority (both African Americans), 4 international. Average age 29. In 2001, 29 master's, 1 doctorate awarded.
Degree requirements: For master's and doctorate, thesis/dissertation.
Entrance requirements: For master's and doctorate, GRE General Test. *Application deadline:* Applications are processed on a rolling basis. *Application fee:* $25.
Expenses: Tuition, state resident: full-time $4,134. Tuition, nonresident: full-time $11,486.
Financial support: In 2001–02, 1 research assistantship with full tuition reimbursement (averaging $12,000 per year), 5 teaching assistantships with full tuition reimbursements (averaging $16,800 per year) were awarded.

Dr. Louis F. Cohn, Chair, 502-852-6276, *Fax:* 502-852-8851, *E-mail:* cohn@louisville.edu.

■ UNIVERSITY OF MAINE

Graduate School, College of Engineering, Department of Civil and Environmental Engineering, Orono, ME 04469

AWARDS Civil engineering (MS, PhD), including environmental engineering, geotechnical engineering, structural engineering.

Faculty: 11 full-time (0 women).
Students: 18 full-time (7 women), 8 part-time; includes 3 minority (2 Hispanic Americans, 1 Native American), 10 international. 21 applicants, 43% accepted, 4 enrolled. In 2001, 11 degrees awarded.
Degree requirements: For doctorate, thesis/dissertation.
Entrance requirements: For master's and doctorate, GRE General Test, TOEFL. *Application deadline:* For fall admission, 2/1 (priority date). Applications are processed on a rolling basis. *Application fee:* $50. Electronic applications accepted.
Expenses: Tuition, state resident: full-time $3,780; part-time $210 per credit hour. Tuition, nonresident: full-time $10,782; part-time $599 per credit hour. Required fees: $9.5 per credit hour. $32 per semester. Tuition and fees vary according to reciprocity agreements.
Financial support: In 2001–02, 15 research assistantships with tuition reimbursements (averaging $16,900 per year), 3 teaching assistantships with tuition reimbursements (averaging $15,000 per year) were awarded. Federal Work-Study, institutionally sponsored loans, scholarships/grants, and tuition waivers (full and partial) also available. Financial award application deadline: 3/1.
Dr. Dana Humphrey, Chair, 207-581-2170, *Fax:* 207-581-3888.
Application contact: Scott G. Delcourt, Director of the Graduate School, 207-581-3218, *Fax:* 207-581-3232, *E-mail:* graduate@maine.edu. *Web site:* http://www.umaine.edu/graduate/

■ UNIVERSITY OF MAINE

Graduate School, College of Engineering, Department of Spatial Information Science and Engineering, Orono, ME 04469

AWARDS MS, PhD.

Students: 36 full-time (9 women), 10 part-time (2 women), 18 international. Average age 25. 49 applicants, 55% accepted, 14 enrolled. In 2001, 5 master's, 2 doctorates awarded.
Degree requirements: For master's, thesis (for some programs); for doctorate, thesis/dissertation.
Entrance requirements: For master's and doctorate, GRE General Test, TOEFL. *Application deadline:* For fall admission, 2/1

University of Maine (continued)
(priority date). Applications are processed on a rolling basis. *Application fee:* $50. Electronic applications accepted.
Expenses: Tuition, state resident: full-time $3,780; part-time $210 per credit hour. Tuition, nonresident: full-time $10,782; part-time $599 per credit hour. Required fees: $9.5 per credit hour. $32 per semester. Tuition and fees vary according to reciprocity agreements.
Financial support: In 2001–02, 26 research assistantships with tuition reimbursements (averaging $16,800 per year), 3 teaching assistantships with tuition reimbursements (averaging $12,000 per year) were awarded. Federal Work-Study, institutionally sponsored loans, and tuition waivers (full and partial) also available. Financial award application deadline: 3/1.
Faculty research: Geographic information systems, analytical photogrammetry, geodesy, global positioning systems, remote sensing.
Dr. Mary Kate Beard-Tisdale, Chair, 207-581-2188, *Fax:* 207-581-2206.
Application contact: Scott G. Delcourt, Director of the Graduate School, 207-581-3218, *Fax:* 207-581-3232, *E-mail:* graduate@maine.edu. *Web site:* http://www.umaine.edu/graduate/

■ UNIVERSITY OF MARYLAND, COLLEGE PARK

Graduate Studies and Research, A. James Clark School of Engineering, Department of Civil and Environmental Engineering, College Park, MD 20742

AWARDS M Eng, MS, PhD. Part-time and evening/weekend programs available. Postbaccalaureate distance learning degree programs offered.

Faculty: 43 full-time (6 women), 17 part-time/adjunct (4 women).
Students: 93 full-time (16 women), 80 part-time (19 women); includes 19 minority (10 African Americans, 4 Asian Americans or Pacific Islanders, 5 Hispanic Americans), 85 international. 305 applicants, 31% accepted, 52 enrolled. In 2001, 28 master's, 8 doctorates awarded.
Degree requirements: For master's, thesis or alternative; for doctorate, thesis/dissertation, qualifying exam.
Entrance requirements: For master's and doctorate, GRE General Test, minimum GPA of 3.0. *Application deadline:* For fall admission, 5/1; for spring admission, 8/1. Applications are processed on a rolling basis. *Application fee:* $50 ($70 for international students). Electronic applications accepted.
Expenses: Tuition, state resident: part-time $289 per credit hour. Tuition, nonresident: part-time $448 per credit hour. One-time fee: $436 part-time. Full-time tuition and fees vary according to course load, campus/location and program.

Financial support: In 2001–02, 9 fellowships with full tuition reimbursements (averaging $12,516 per year), 41 research assistantships with tuition reimbursements (averaging $16,012 per year), 14 teaching assistantships with tuition reimbursements (averaging $14,025 per year) were awarded. Federal Work-Study and scholarships/grants also available. Support available to part-time students. Financial award applicants required to submit FAFSA.
Faculty research: Transportation and urban systems, environmental engineering, geotechnical engineering, construction engineering and management, hydraulics, remote sensing, soil mechanics.
Dr. Gregory Baecher, Chairman, 301-405-1972, *Fax:* 301-405-2585.
Application contact: Trudy Lindsey, Director, Graduate Admissions and Records, 301-405-6991, *Fax:* 301-314-9305, *E-mail:* grschool@deans.umd.edu.
Find an in-depth description at www.petersons.com/gradchannel.

■ UNIVERSITY OF MARYLAND, COLLEGE PARK

Graduate Studies and Research, A. James Clark School of Engineering, Professional Program in Engineering, College Park, MD 20742

AWARDS Aerospace engineering (M Eng); chemical engineering (M Eng); civil engineering (M Eng); electrical engineering (M Eng); fire protection engineering (M Eng); materials science and engineering (M Eng); mechanical engineering (M Eng); reliability engineering (M Eng). Systems engineering (M Eng). Part-time and evening/weekend programs available. Postbaccalaureate distance learning degree programs offered.

Faculty: 11 part-time/adjunct (0 women).
Students: 19 full-time (4 women), 144 part-time (31 women); includes 41 minority (17 African Americans, 18 Asian Americans or Pacific Islanders, 6 Hispanic Americans), 27 international. 71 applicants, 80% accepted, 50 enrolled. In 2001, 64 degrees awarded.
Application deadline: For fall admission, 8/15; for spring admission, 1/10. Applications are processed on a rolling basis. *Application fee:* $50 ($70 for international students). Electronic applications accepted.
Expenses: Tuition, state resident: part-time $289 per credit hour. Tuition, nonresident: part-time $448 per credit hour. One-time fee: $436 part-time. Full-time tuition and fees vary according to course load, campus/location and program.
Financial support: In 2001–02, 1 research assistantship with tuition reimbursement (averaging $20,655 per year), 5 teaching assistantships with tuition reimbursement (averaging $11,114 per year) were awarded. Fellowships, Federal Work-Study and scholarships/grants also available. Support available to part-time students.

Financial award applicants required to submit FAFSA.
Dr. George Syrmos, Acting Director, 301-405-5256, *Fax:* 301-314-9477.
Application contact: Trudy Lindsey, Director, Graduate Admissions and Records, 301-405-6991, *Fax:* 301-314-9305, *E-mail:* grschool@deans.umd.edu.

■ UNIVERSITY OF MASSACHUSETTS AMHERST

Graduate School, College of Engineering, Department of Civil Engineering, Program in Civil Engineering, Amherst, MA 01003

AWARDS MS, PhD. Part-time programs available.

Faculty: 23 full-time (5 women).
Students: 41 full-time (15 women), 11 part-time (4 women); includes 1 minority (Hispanic American), 17 international. Average age 27. 131 applicants, 24% accepted. In 2001, 11 master's, 4 doctorates awarded. Terminal master's awarded for partial completion of doctoral program.
Degree requirements: For master's, thesis or alternative; for doctorate, thesis/dissertation.
Entrance requirements: For master's and doctorate, GRE General Test. *Application deadline:* For fall admission, 2/1 (priority date); for spring admission, 10/1. Applications are processed on a rolling basis. *Application fee:* $40 ($50 for international students).
Expenses: Tuition, state resident: full-time $1,980; part-time $110 per credit. Tuition, nonresident: full-time $7,456; part-time $414 per credit. Required fees: $4,112. One-time fee: $115 full-time.
Financial support: In 2001–02, 81 fellowships with full tuition reimbursements (averaging $10,376 per year), 77 research assistantships with full tuition reimbursements (averaging $10,224 per year), 10 teaching assistantships with full tuition reimbursements (averaging $5,326 per year) were awarded. Career-related internships or fieldwork, Federal Work-Study, scholarships/grants, traineeships, and unspecified assistantships also available. Support available to part-time students. Financial award application deadline: 2/1.
Carlton Ho, Director, 413-545-0685, *Fax:* 413-545-2840, *E-mail:* ho@ecs.umass.edu.

■ UNIVERSITY OF MASSACHUSETTS LOWELL

Graduate School, James B. Francis College of Engineering, Department of Civil Engineering, Lowell, MA 01854-2881

AWARDS Civil engineering (MS Eng); environmental studies (MS Eng). Part-time programs available.

Degree requirements: For master's, thesis optional.

Entrance requirements: For master's, GRE General Test.
Faculty research: Bridge design, traffic control, groundwater remediation, pile capacity.

THE UNIVERSITY OF MEMPHIS

Graduate School, Herff College of Engineering, Department of Civil Engineering, Memphis, TN 38152

AWARDS Civil engineering (PhD); environmental engineering (MS); foundation engineering (MS). Structural engineering (MS); transportation engineering (MS); water resources engineering (MS).

Faculty: 12 full-time (0 women), 1 part-time/adjunct (0 women).
Students: 14 full-time (5 women), 7 part-time (1 woman), 10 international. Average age 32. 36 applicants, 56% accepted. In 2001, 5 degrees awarded.
Degree requirements: For master's, thesis or alternative, comprehensive exam; for doctorate, thesis/dissertation.
Entrance requirements: For master's, GRE General Test or MAT, minimum undergraduate GPA of 2.5. *Application deadline:* For fall admission, 8/1; for spring admission, 12/1. *Application fee:* $25 ($100 for international students).
Expenses: Tuition, state resident: full-time $2,026. Tuition, nonresident: full-time $4,528.
Financial support: In 2001–02, 1 fellowship with full tuition reimbursement, 13 research assistantships with full tuition reimbursements were awarded. Career-related internships or fieldwork also available.
Faculty research: Structural response to earthquakes, pavement design, water quality, bridge scour, intelligent transportation systems. *Total annual research expenditures:* $1.2 million.
Dr. Martin E. Lipinski, Chairman, 901-678-3279.
Application contact: Dr. Shahram Pezeshk, Coordinator of Graduate Studies, 901-678-4727.

UNIVERSITY OF MIAMI

Graduate School, College of Engineering, Department of Civil, Architectural, and Environmental Engineering, Coral Gables, FL 33124

AWARDS Architectural engineering (MSAE); civil engineering (MSCE, DA, PhD). Part-time and evening/weekend programs available.

Faculty: 11 full-time (1 woman).
Students: 18 full-time (6 women), 2 part-time; includes 15 minority (5 African Americans, 8 Asian Americans or Pacific Islanders, 2 Hispanic Americans). Average age 29. 42 applicants, 45% accepted. In 2001, 3 master's, 2 doctorates awarded.
Degree requirements: For master's, thesis (for some programs); for doctorate, thesis/dissertation, oral and qualifying exams.

Entrance requirements: For master's and doctorate, GRE General Test, TOEFL, minimum GPA of 3.0. *Application deadline:* For fall admission, 2/1 (priority date); for spring admission, 10/1 (priority date). Applications are processed on a rolling basis. *Application fee:* $50. Electronic applications accepted.
Expenses: Tuition: Part-time $960 per credit hour. Required fees: $85 per semester. Tuition and fees vary according to program.
Financial support: Fellowships with tuition reimbursements, research assistantships with tuition reimbursements, teaching assistantships with tuition reimbursements, institutionally sponsored loans and tuition waivers (partial) available.
Faculty research: Wastewater treatment, water management, structural reliability, structural dynamics, wind engineering, water resources.
Dr. David A. Chin, Chairman, 305-284-3391, *Fax:* 305-284-3492, *E-mail:* dchin@miami.edu.
Application contact: Dr. Helena M. Solo-Gabriele, Adviser, 305-284-3391, *Fax:* 305-284-3492, *E-mail:* hmsolo@miami.edu. *Web site:* http://www.eng.miami.edu/~caegrad

UNIVERSITY OF MICHIGAN

Horace H. Rackham School of Graduate Studies, College of Engineering, Department of Civil and Environmental Engineering, Ann Arbor, MI 48109

AWARDS Civil engineering (MSE, PhD, CE); construction engineering and management (MSE); environmental engineering (MSE, PhD).

Faculty: 26 full-time (2 women), 2 part-time/adjunct (0 women).
Students: 142 full-time (39 women), 15 part-time (3 women); includes 11 minority (3 African Americans, 4 Asian Americans or Pacific Islanders, 4 Hispanic Americans), 96 international. Average age 27. 452 applicants, 52% accepted. In 2001, 51 master's, 13 doctorates awarded.
Degree requirements: For doctorate, oral defense of dissertation, preliminary and written exams.
Entrance requirements: For master's, GRE General Test; for doctorate, GRE General Test, master's degree. *Application deadline:* For fall admission, 2/8. Applications are processed on a rolling basis. *Application fee:* $55. Electronic applications accepted.
Financial support: In 2001–02, 109 students received support, including fellowships (averaging $20,200 per year), research assistantships (averaging $20,200 per year), teaching assistantships (averaging $12,783 per year); institutionally sponsored loans and tuition waivers (partial) also available. Financial award application deadline: 3/15.
Faculty research: Earthquake engineering, environmental and water resources

engineering, geotechnical engineering, hydraulics and hydrologic engineering, structural engineering. *Total annual research expenditures:* $9.5 million.
Nikolaos D. Katopodes, Chair, 734-764-3674, *Fax:* 734-764-4292, *E-mail:* ndk@umich.edu.
Application contact: Janet Lineer, Student Advisor, 734-764-8495, *Fax:* 734-763-2275, *E-mail:* janetl@umich.edu. *Web site:* http://www.engin.umich.edu/dept/cee/

UNIVERSITY OF MICHIGAN

Horace H. Rackham School of Graduate Studies, College of Engineering, Department of Naval Architecture and Marine Engineering, Ann Arbor, MI 48109

AWARDS Concurrent marine design (M Eng); naval architecture and marine engineering (MS, MSE, PhD, Mar Eng, Nav Arch). Part-time programs available.

Faculty: 12 full-time (2 women), 9 part-time/adjunct (0 women).
Students: 51 full-time (5 women), 4 part-time; includes 3 minority (2 Asian Americans or Pacific Islanders, 1 Hispanic American), 35 international. Average age 28. 75 applicants, 80% accepted, 50 enrolled. In 2001, 21 master's, 6 doctorates awarded. Terminal master's awarded for partial completion of doctoral program.
Degree requirements: For master's, thesis (for some programs); for doctorate, thesis/dissertation, oral defense of dissertation, preliminary exams (written and oral); for other advanced degree, thesis, oral defense of thesis, comprehensive exam.
Entrance requirements: For master's, GRE General Test (financial award applicants only); TOEFL or Michigan English Language Assessment Battery; for doctorate, GRE General Test, master's degree; for other advanced degree, GRE General Test. *Application deadline:* For fall admission, 2/1. Applications are processed on a rolling basis. *Application fee:* $55. Electronic applications accepted.
Financial support: In 2001–02, 17 students received support, including 3 fellowships with full tuition reimbursements available (averaging $12,832 per year), 15 research assistantships with full tuition reimbursements available (averaging $10,972 per year), 2 teaching assistantships with full tuition reimbursements available (averaging $10,972 per year); career-related internships or fieldwork, Federal Work-Study, institutionally sponsored loans, scholarships/grants, and unspecified assistantships also available. Financial award application deadline: 2/1.
Faculty research: Marine mechanics including hydrodynamics, structures, marine environmental engineering, marine design analysis, concurrent marine design. *Total annual research expenditures:* $5.3 million.

University of Michigan (continued)
Dr. Michael M. Bernitsas, Chair, 734-936-7636, *Fax:* 734-936-8820, *E-mail:* kdrake@engin.umich.edu.
Application contact: Sandra Schippers Miller, Graduate Program Coordinator, 734-936-0566, *Fax:* 734-936-8820, *E-mail:* sschippe@engin.umich.edu. *Web site:* http://www.engin.umich.edu/dept/name

■ UNIVERSITY OF MINNESOTA, TWIN CITIES CAMPUS

Graduate School, Institute of Technology, Department of Civil Engineering, Minneapolis, MN 55455-0213

AWARDS Civil engineering (MCE, MS, PhD); geological engineering (M Geo E, MS, PhD). Part-time programs available.

Degree requirements: For master's, thesis optional; for doctorate, thesis/dissertation.
Entrance requirements: For master's and doctorate, GRE General Test, TOEFL.
Expenses: Tuition, state resident: full-time $2,932; part-time $489 per credit. Tuition, nonresident: full-time $5,758; part-time $960 per credit. Part-time tuition and fees vary according to course load, program and reciprocity agreements.
Faculty research: Environmental engineering, rock mechanics, water resources, structural engineering, transportation. *Web site:* http://www.ce.umn.edu/

■ UNIVERSITY OF MISSOURI–COLUMBIA

Graduate School, College of Engineering, Department of Civil and Environmental Engineering, Columbia, MO 65211

AWARDS Civil engineering (MS, PhD); environmental engineering (MS, PhD); geotechnical engineering (MS, PhD). Structural engineering (MS, PhD); transportation and highway engineering (MS); water resources (MS, PhD).

Faculty: 20 full-time (2 women), 1 part-time/adjunct (0 women).
Students: 28 full-time (6 women), 14 part-time (3 women); includes 4 minority (all Hispanic Americans), 23 international. 74 applicants, 43% accepted. In 2001, 19 master's, 1 doctorate awarded.
Degree requirements: For master's, report or thesis; for doctorate, thesis/dissertation.
Entrance requirements: For master's and doctorate, GRE General Test, TOEFL. *Application deadline:* For fall admission, 3/15 (priority date); for winter admission, 10/15 (priority date). *Application fee:* $25 ($50 for international students).
Expenses: Tuition, state resident: part-time $179 per credit hour. Tuition, nonresident: part-time $539 per credit

hour. Required fees: $122 per semester. Tuition and fees vary according to program.
Financial support: Research assistantships, teaching assistantships, institutionally sponsored loans available.
Dr. Mark Virkler, Director of Graduate Studies, 573-882-7434, *E-mail:* virklerm@missouri.edu. *Web site:* http://www.engineering.missouri.edu/civil.htm

■ UNIVERSITY OF MISSOURI–ROLLA

Graduate School, School of Engineering, Department of Civil Engineering, Program in Civil Engineering, Rolla, MO 65409-0910

AWARDS MS, PhD.

Degree requirements: For master's, thesis or alternative; for doctorate, thesis/dissertation.
Entrance requirements: For master's and doctorate, GRE General Test, TOEFL, minimum GPA of 3.0. Electronic applications accepted.

■ UNIVERSITY OF NEBRASKA–LINCOLN

Graduate College, College of Engineering and Technology, Department of Civil Engineering, Lincoln, NE 68588

AWARDS Civil engineering (MS); engineering (PhD).

Faculty: 21.
Students: 25 (6 women); includes 1 minority (African American) 3 international. Average age 28. 40 applicants, 58% accepted, 3 enrolled. In 2001, 14 degrees awarded.
Degree requirements: For master's, thesis optional; for doctorate, thesis/dissertation, comprehensive exam.
Entrance requirements: For master's and doctorate, GRE General Test, TOEFL. *Application deadline:* For fall admission, 4/15; for spring admission, 10/15. *Application fee:* $35. Electronic applications accepted.
Expenses: Tuition, state resident: full-time $2,412; part-time $134 per credit. Tuition, nonresident: full-time $6,223; part-time $346 per credit. Tuition and fees vary according to course load.
Financial support: In 2001–02, 20 research assistantships, 7 teaching assistantships were awarded. Fellowships, Federal Work-Study also available. Support available to part-time students. Financial award application deadline: 2/15.
Faculty research: Water resources engineering, sediment transport, steel bridge systems, highway safety.
Dr. Raymond Moore, Chair, 402-472-2371, *Fax:* 402-472-8934. *Web site:* http://www.civil.unl.edu/

■ UNIVERSITY OF NEVADA, LAS VEGAS

Graduate College, Howard R. Hughes College of Engineering, Department of Civil and Environmental Engineering, Las Vegas, NV 89154-9900

AWARDS MSE, PhD. Part-time programs available.

Faculty: 25 full-time (2 women).
Students: 23 full-time (4 women), 45 part-time (15 women); includes 12 minority (3 African Americans, 7 Asian Americans or Pacific Islanders, 2 Hispanic Americans), 23 international. 39 applicants, 54% accepted, 13 enrolled. In 2001, 8 master's, 1 doctorate awarded.
Degree requirements: For master's, thesis (for some programs), comprehensive exam (for some programs); for doctorate, thesis/dissertation, comprehensive exam. *Median time to degree:* Doctorate–5 years full-time.
Entrance requirements: For master's, minimum GPA of 3.0; for doctorate, GRE General Test, minimum GPA of 3.2. *Application deadline:* For fall admission, 6/15; for spring admission, 11/15. Applications are processed on a rolling basis. *Application fee:* $40 ($55 for international students).
Expenses: Tuition, state resident: full-time $1,926; part-time $107 per credit. Tuition, nonresident: full-time $9,376; part-time $220 per credit. Tuition and fees vary according to course load.
Financial support: In 2001–02, 15 research assistantships with full and partial tuition reimbursements (averaging $7,813 per year), 11 teaching assistantships with partial tuition reimbursements (averaging $10,000 per year) were awarded. Financial award application deadline: 3/1.
Dr. David James, Chair, 702-895-3701, *Fax:* 702-895-3936, *E-mail:* ce-info@ce.unlv.edu.
Application contact: Graduate College Admissions Evaluator, 702-895-3320, *Fax:* 702-895-4180, *E-mail:* gradcollege@ccmail.nevada.edu. *Web site:* http://www.ce.unlv.edu/

■ UNIVERSITY OF NEVADA, RENO

Graduate School, College of Engineering, Department of Civil Engineering, Reno, NV 89557

AWARDS MS, PhD.

Faculty: 11 full-time (1 woman).
Students: 48 full-time (10 women), 17 part-time (1 woman); includes 7 minority (5 Asian Americans or Pacific Islanders, 2 Hispanic Americans), 38 international. Average age 31. In 2001, 17 master's, 3 doctorates awarded. Terminal master's awarded for partial completion of doctoral program.

Degree requirements: For master's, thesis optional; for doctorate, thesis/dissertation.
Entrance requirements: For master's, TOEFL, minimum GPA of 2.75; for doctorate, TOEFL, minimum GPA of 3.0. *Application deadline:* For fall admission, 4/15 (priority date); for spring admission, 10/15. Applications are processed on a rolling basis. *Application fee:* $40.
Expenses: Tuition, state resident: full-time $2,067; part-time $108 per credit. Tuition, nonresident: full-time $9,282; part-time $109 per credit. Required fees: $57 per semester. Tuition and fees vary according to course load.
Financial support: In 2001–02, 32 research assistantships, 8 teaching assistantships were awarded. Federal Work-Study and institutionally sponsored loans also available. Financial award application deadline: 3/1.
Dr. Ahmad Itani, Graduate Program Director, 775-784-4379, *E-mail:* itani@scs.unr.edu.

■ UNIVERSITY OF NEW HAMPSHIRE

Graduate School, College of Engineering and Physical Sciences, Department of Civil Engineering, Durham, NH 03824

AWARDS MS, PhD. Part-time programs available.

Faculty: 13 full-time.
Students: 16 full-time (6 women), 32 part-time (13 women), 9 international. Average age 29. 38 applicants, 89% accepted, 10 enrolled. In 2001, 8 master's, 1 doctorate awarded.
Degree requirements: For master's, thesis or alternative; for doctorate, thesis/dissertation.
Entrance requirements: For master's and doctorate, GRE. *Application deadline:* For fall admission, 4/1 (priority date); for winter admission, 12/1 (priority date). Applications are processed on a rolling basis. *Application fee:* $50.
Expenses: Tuition, state resident: full-time $6,300; part-time $350 per credit. Tuition, nonresident: full-time $15,720; part-time $643 per credit. Required fees: $560; $280 per term. One-time fee: $15 part-time. Tuition and fees vary according to course load.
Financial support: In 2001–02, 18 research assistantships, 10 teaching assistantships were awarded. Fellowships, Federal Work-Study, scholarships/grants, and tuition waivers (full and partial) also available. Support available to part-time students. Financial award application deadline: 2/15.
Faculty research: Environmental, structural materials, geotechnical engineering, water resources, systems analysis.
Dr. Jean Benoit, Chairperson, 603-862-1419, *E-mail:* jbenoit@cisunix.edu.

Application contact: Dr. Thomas Ballestero, Graduate Coordinator, 603-862-1405, *E-mail:* tom.ballestero@unh.edu. *Web site:* http://www.unh.edu/civil-engineering/index.html

■ UNIVERSITY OF NEW MEXICO

Graduate School, School of Engineering, Department of Civil Engineering, Albuquerque, NM 87131-2039

AWARDS Civil engineering (MS); engineering (PhD). Part-time programs available.

Faculty: 14 full-time (2 women), 7 part-time/adjunct (0 women).
Students: 37 full-time (9 women), 36 part-time (10 women); includes 12 minority (1 Asian American or Pacific Islander, 8 Hispanic Americans, 3 Native Americans), 22 international. Average age 33. In 2001, 16 master's, 2 doctorates awarded.
Degree requirements: For master's, thesis (for some programs); for doctorate, thesis/dissertation.
Entrance requirements: For master's and doctorate, GRE General Test, minimum GPA of 3.0. *Application deadline:* For fall admission, 7/15; for spring admission, 11/10. *Application fee:* $40.
Expenses: Tuition, state resident: full-time $2,771; part-time $115 per credit hour. Tuition, nonresident: full-time $11,207; part-time $467 per credit hour. Required fees: $570; $24 per credit hour. Part-time tuition and fees vary according to course load and program.
Financial support: In 2001–02, 24 students received support, including 15 research assistantships with full and partial tuition reimbursements available (averaging $11,594 per year), 1 teaching assistantship with full tuition reimbursement available (averaging $5,000 per year). Scholarships/grants, health care benefits, and unspecified assistantships also available. Support available to part-time students. Financial award application deadline: 3/1; financial award applicants required to submit FAFSA.
Faculty research: Construction, environmental engineering, geotechnical engineering, structural engineering, transportation. *Total annual research expenditures:* $994,165.
Dr. Timothy J. Ward, Chair, 505-277-2722, *Fax:* 505-277-1988, *E-mail:* tjward@unm.edu.
Application contact: Gerri C. Hopkins, Administrative Assistant II, 505-277-6633, *Fax:* 505-277-1988, *E-mail:* ghopkins@unm.edu. *Web site:* http://www.unm.edu/~civil/

■ UNIVERSITY OF NEW ORLEANS

Graduate School, College of Engineering, Concentration in Civil Engineering, New Orleans, LA 70148

AWARDS MS. Part-time and evening/weekend programs available.

Faculty: 6 full-time (1 woman), 1 part-time/adjunct (0 women).
Students: 22 full-time (10 women), 24 part-time (9 women); includes 4 minority (1 African American, 1 Asian American or Pacific Islander, 1 Hispanic American, 1 Native American), 26 international. Average age 27. 55 applicants, 42% accepted, 7 enrolled. In 2001, 14 degrees awarded.
Degree requirements: For master's, thesis optional.
Entrance requirements: For master's, GRE General Test, minimum GPA of 3.0. *Application deadline:* For fall admission, 7/1 (priority date); for spring admission, 11/15 (priority date). Applications are processed on a rolling basis. *Application fee:* $20. Electronic applications accepted.
Expenses: Tuition, state resident: full-time $2,748; part-time $435 per credit. Tuition, nonresident: full-time $9,792; part-time $1,773 per credit.
Financial support: Applicants required to submit FAFSA.
Faculty research: Dynamic analysis for pile capacity, soil stabilization, groundwater modeling and aquifer remediation, potable water studies, water quality modeling.
Dr. Kenneth L. McManis, Chairman, 504-280-6271, *Fax:* 504-280-5586, *E-mail:* kmcmannis@uno.edu.
Application contact: Dr. Mike Folse, Graduate Coordinator, 504-280-7268, *Fax:* 504-280-5586, *E-mail:* mfolse@uno.edu.

■ UNIVERSITY OF NEW ORLEANS

Graduate School, College of Engineering, Concentration in Naval Architecture and Marine Engineering, New Orleans, LA 70148

AWARDS MS. Part-time and evening/weekend programs available.

Faculty: 2 full-time (0 women).
Students: 6 full-time (1 woman), 6 part-time; includes 2 minority (1 Asian American or Pacific Islander, 1 Hispanic American), 3 international. Average age 28. 28 applicants, 32% accepted, 2 enrolled. In 2001, 5 degrees awarded.
Degree requirements: For master's, thesis optional.
Entrance requirements: For master's, GRE General Test, minimum GPA of 3.0. *Application deadline:* For fall admission, 7/1 (priority date); for spring admission, 11/15. Applications are processed on a rolling basis. *Application fee:* $20. Electronic applications accepted.

University of New Orleans (continued)
Expenses: Tuition, state resident: full-time $2,748; part-time $435 per credit. Tuition, nonresident: full-time $9,792; part-time $1,773 per credit.
Financial support: Research assistantships, teaching assistantships, institutionally sponsored loans available. Financial award applicants required to submit FAFSA.
Faculty research: Ship structures, hydrodynamics, computer-aided ship design.
Dr. Bahadir Inozu, Chairman, 504-280-7180.
Application contact: Dr. William Vorus, Graduate Coordinator, 504-280-7181, *Fax:* 504-280-5542, *E-mail:* wvorus@uno.edu.

■ THE UNIVERSITY OF NORTH CAROLINA AT CHARLOTTE

Graduate School, The William States Lee College of Engineering, Department of Civil Engineering, Charlotte, NC 28223-0001

AWARDS MSCE. Part-time and evening/weekend programs available.

Faculty: 10 full-time (1 woman), 5 part-time/adjunct (0 women).
Students: 17 full-time (1 woman), 25 part-time (5 women); includes 6 minority (4 African Americans, 1 Asian American or Pacific Islander, 1 Hispanic American), 9 international. Average age 29. 39 applicants, 92% accepted, 15 enrolled. In 2001, 8 degrees awarded.
Degree requirements: For master's, thesis or project.
Entrance requirements: For master's, GRE General Test, minimum GPA of 3.0 in undergraduate major, 2.75 overall. *Application deadline:* For fall admission, 7/15; for spring admission, 11/15. Applications are processed on a rolling basis. *Application fee:* $35. Electronic applications accepted.
Expenses: Tuition, state resident: full-time $1,483; part-time $371 per year. Tuition, nonresident: full-time $9,850; part-time $2,463 per year. Required fees: $1,043; $277 per year. Tuition and fees vary according to course load.
Financial support: In 2001–02, 6 research assistantships, 6 teaching assistantships were awarded. Fellowships, career-related internships or fieldwork, Federal Work-Study, institutionally sponsored loans, scholarships/grants, and unspecified assistantships also available. Support available to part-time students. Financial award application deadline: 4/1; financial award applicants required to submit FAFSA.
Faculty research: Structural composite materials. Storm water systems; natural and man-made disaster reduction engineering; older drivers and nighttime driving. Soil contamination and transport.
Dr. David T. Young, Acting Chair, 704-687-2304, *Fax:* 704-687-2352, *E-mail:* dyoung@email.uncc.edu.

Application contact: Kathy Barringer, Director of Graduate Admissions, 704-687-3366, *Fax:* 704-687-3279, *E-mail:* gradadm@email.uncc.edu. *Web site:* http://www.uncc.edu/gradmiss/

■ UNIVERSITY OF NORTH DAKOTA

Graduate School, School of Engineering and Mines, Department of Civil Engineering, Grand Forks, ND 58202

AWARDS Civil engineering (M Engr). Sanitary engineering (M Engr), including soils and structures engineering, surface mining engineering. Part-time programs available.

Faculty: 6 full-time (0 women).
Students: 6 full-time (1 woman), 3 part-time. 2 applicants, 100% accepted, 0 enrolled. In 2001, 6 degrees awarded.
Degree requirements: For master's, thesis or alternative, final comprehensive exam.
Entrance requirements: For master's, GRE General Test, TOEFL, minimum GPA of 2.5. *Application deadline:* For fall admission, 3/1 (priority date); for spring admission, 10/15 (priority date). Applications are processed on a rolling basis. *Application fee:* $30.
Expenses: Tuition, state resident: full-time $3,298. Tuition, nonresident: full-time $7,998.
Financial support: In 2001–02, 4 students received support, including 4 teaching assistantships with full tuition reimbursements available (averaging $9,500 per year); fellowships, research assistantships, career-related internships or fieldwork, Federal Work-Study, institutionally sponsored loans, scholarships/grants, and tuition waivers (full and partial) also available. Support available to part-time students. Financial award application deadline: 3/15; financial award applicants required to submit FAFSA.
Faculty research: Soil-structures, environmental-water resources.
Dr. Charles J. Moretti, Chairperson, 701-777-5150, *Fax:* 701-777-4838, *E-mail:* charles_moretti@mail.und.nodak.edu. *Web site:* http://www.und.edu/dept/sem/html/civil_engineering.html

■ UNIVERSITY OF NOTRE DAME

Graduate School, College of Engineering, Department of Civil Engineering and Geological Sciences, Notre Dame, IN 46556

AWARDS Bioengineering (MS); civil engineering (MS); civil engineering and geological sciences (PhD); environmental engineering (MS); geological sciences (MS).

Faculty: 15 full-time (1 woman).
Students: 42 full-time (16 women), 4 part-time (1 woman); includes 3 minority (1 African American, 1 Asian American or Pacific Islander, 1 Hispanic American), 13

international. 118 applicants, 19% accepted, 12 enrolled. In 2001, 5 master's, 3 doctorates awarded. Terminal master's awarded for partial completion of doctoral program.
Degree requirements: For master's, comprehensive exam; for doctorate, thesis/dissertation. *Median time to degree:* Doctorate–5.5 years full-time.
Entrance requirements: For master's and doctorate, GRE General Test, TOEFL. *Application deadline:* For fall admission, 2/1 (priority date); for spring admission, 10/15. Applications are processed on a rolling basis. *Application fee:* $50. Electronic applications accepted.
Expenses: Tuition: Full-time $24,220; part-time $1,346 per credit hour. Required fees: $155.
Financial support: In 2001–02, 46 students received support, including 7 fellowships with full tuition reimbursements available (averaging $18,000 per year), 16 research assistantships with full tuition reimbursements available (averaging $12,800 per year), 17 teaching assistantships with full tuition reimbursements available (averaging $12,800 per year); tuition waivers (full) also available. Financial award application deadline: 2/1.
Faculty research: Structural analysis, finite-element methods, environmental modeling, biological-waste treatment, petrology, environmental geology, geochemistry. *Total annual research expenditures:* $1.4 million.
Dr. Peter C. Burns, Director of Graduate Studies, 574-631-5380, *Fax:* 574-631-9236, *E-mail:* cegeos@nd.edu.
Application contact: Dr. Terrence J. Akai, Director of Graduate Admissions, 574-631-7706, *Fax:* 574-631-4183, *E-mail:* gradad@nd.edu. *Web site:* http://www.nd.edu/~gradsch/degreeprograms/Engineering/CE/CEMenu.html

■ UNIVERSITY OF OKLAHOMA

Graduate College, College of Engineering, School of Civil Engineering and Environmental Science, Program in Civil Engineering, Norman, OK 73019-0390

AWARDS Civil engineering (PhD); environmental engineering (MS); geotechnical engineering (MS). Structures (MS); transportation (MS). Part-time programs available.

Students: 36 full-time (3 women), 18 part-time (2 women); includes 4 minority (2 Asian Americans or Pacific Islanders, 1 Hispanic American, 1 Native American), 35 international. 46 applicants, 85% accepted, 9 enrolled. In 2001, 17 degrees awarded. Terminal master's awarded for partial completion of doctoral program.
Degree requirements: For master's, oral exams; for doctorate, thesis/dissertation, oral and qualifying exams.
Entrance requirements: For master's, minimum GPA of 3.0; for doctorate,

minimum graduate GPA of 3.5. *Application deadline:* For fall admission, 4/1 (priority date). Applications are processed on a rolling basis. *Application fee:* $25 ($50 for international students).

Expenses: Tuition, state resident: full-time $2,208; part-time $92 per credit hour. Tuition, nonresident: part-time $297 per credit hour. Tuition and fees vary according to course level, course load and program.

Financial support: In 2001–02, 7 students received support; research assistantships with partial tuition reimbursements available, teaching assistantships with full and partial tuition reimbursements available, scholarships/grants available. Financial award application deadline: 3/1; financial award applicants required to submit FAFSA.

Application contact: Susan Williams, Graduate Programs Specialist, 405-325-2344, *Fax:* 405-325-4217, *E-mail:* srwilliams@ou.edu.

■ **UNIVERSITY OF PITTSBURGH**

School of Engineering, Department of Civil and Environmental Engineering, Pittsburgh, PA 15260

AWARDS MSCEE, PhD. Part-time and evening/weekend programs available.

Faculty: 13 full-time (0 women), 4 part-time/adjunct (0 women).
Students: 38 full-time (8 women), 56 part-time (7 women); includes 3 minority (1 African American, 2 Asian Americans or Pacific Islanders), 29 international. 79 applicants, 71% accepted, 21 enrolled. In 2001, 9 master's, 4 doctorates awarded. Terminal master's awarded for partial completion of doctoral program.
Degree requirements: For master's, thesis optional; for doctorate, thesis/dissertation, final oral exams, comprehensive exam.
Entrance requirements: For master's and doctorate, TOEFL, minimum QPA of 3.0. *Application deadline:* For fall admission, 8/1 (priority date); for spring admission, 12/1 (priority date). Applications are processed on a rolling basis. *Application fee:* $40.
Financial support: In 2001–02, 23 students received support, including 10 research assistantships with full tuition reimbursements available (averaging $16,980 per year), 13 teaching assistantships with full tuition reimbursements available (averaging $17,976 per year); fellowships with tuition reimbursements available, scholarships/grants, traineeships, and tuition waivers (full and partial) also available. Financial award application deadline: 2/15.
Faculty research: Environmental and water resources, structures and infrastructures, construction management. *Total annual research expenditures:* $930,452.
Dr. Rafael G. Quimpo, Chairman, 412-624-9870, *Fax:* 412-624-0135, *E-mail:* quimpo@civ.pitt.edu.

Application contact: Attila A. Sooky, Academic Coordinator, 412-624-9869, *Fax:* 412-624-0135, *E-mail:* sooky@civ.pitt.edu. *Web site:* http://www.engrng.pitt.edu/~civwww/

■ **UNIVERSITY OF PUERTO RICO, MAYAGÜEZ CAMPUS**

Graduate Studies, College of Engineering, Department of Civil Engineering, Mayagüez, PR 00681-9000

AWARDS MCE, MS, PhD. Part-time programs available.

Degree requirements: For master's, thesis (MS); for doctorate, one foreign language, thesis/dissertation.
Entrance requirements: For master's and doctorate, minimum GPA of 2.5, proficiency in English and Spanish.
Faculty research: Structural design, concrete structure, finite elements, dynamic analysis, transportation, soils.

■ **UNIVERSITY OF RHODE ISLAND**

Graduate School, College of Engineering, Department of Civil and Environmental Engineering, Kingston, RI 02881

AWARDS Environmental engineering (MS, PhD); geotechnical engineering (MS, PhD). Structural engineering (MS, PhD); transportation engineering (MS, PhD).

Students: In 2001, 10 master's, 2 doctorates awarded.
Entrance requirements: For master's and doctorate, GRE. *Application deadline:* For fall admission, 4/15 (priority date). Applications are processed on a rolling basis. *Application fee:* $35.
Expenses: Tuition, state resident: full-time $3,756; part-time $209 per credit. Tuition, nonresident: full-time $10,774; part-time $599 per credit. Required fees: $1,586; $76 per credit. $76 per credit. One-time fee: $60 full-time.
Dr. George Tsiatas, Chairman, 401-874-2692.

■ **UNIVERSITY OF SOUTH CAROLINA**

The Graduate School, College of Engineering and Information Technology, Department of Civil and Environmental Engineering, SC 29208

AWARDS Civil engineering (ME, MS, PhD). Part-time and evening/weekend programs available. Postbaccalaureate distance learning degree programs offered (minimal on-campus study).

Faculty: 15 full-time (3 women).
Students: 29 full-time (8 women), 33 part-time (4 women); includes 27 minority (2

African Americans, 24 Asian Americans or Pacific Islanders, 1 Hispanic American). Average age 34. 49 applicants, 49% accepted. In 2001, 12 degrees awarded.
Degree requirements: For master's, thesis (for some programs); for doctorate, thesis/dissertation.
Entrance requirements: For master's and doctorate, GRE General Test, TOEFL. *Application deadline:* For fall admission, 6/28 (priority date); for spring admission, 11/30. Applications are processed on a rolling basis. *Application fee:* $40. Electronic applications accepted.
Expenses: Tuition, state resident: full-time $4,434. Tuition, nonresident: full-time $9,854. Tuition and fees vary according to program.
Financial support: In 2001–02, fellowships (averaging $16,800 per year), 57 research assistantships with partial tuition reimbursements (averaging $16,000 per year), 7 teaching assistantships with partial tuition reimbursements (averaging $16,000 per year) were awarded. Career-related internships or fieldwork also available.
Faculty research: Pavement evaluation, mathematical modeling, cable-guyed towers, *in situ* bioremediation, groundwater hydraulics. *Total annual research expenditures:* $1.4 million.
Dr. M. Hanif Chaudhry, Chair, 803-777-3652, *Fax:* 803-777-0670, *E-mail:* chaudhry@engr.sc.edu.
Application contact: Kelly McIntyre, Administrative Assistant, 803-777-9482, *Fax:* 803-777-0670, *E-mail:* mcintyrk@engr.sc.edu. *Web site:* http://www.ce.sc.edu/

■ **UNIVERSITY OF SOUTHERN CALIFORNIA**

Graduate School, School of Engineering, Department of Civil Engineering, Program in Civil Engineering, Los Angeles, CA 90089

AWARDS MS, PhD, Engr.

Degree requirements: For master's, thesis optional; for doctorate, thesis/dissertation.
Entrance requirements: For master's, doctorate, and Engr, GRE General Test.
Expenses: Tuition: Full-time $25,060; part-time $844 per unit. Required fees: $473.

Find an in-depth description at www.petersons.com/gradchannel.

■ **UNIVERSITY OF SOUTH FLORIDA**

College of Graduate Studies, College of Engineering, Department of Civil and Environmental Engineering, Tampa, FL 33620-9951

AWARDS Civil engineering (MCE, MSCE, PhD); engineering (ME, MSE). Part-time programs available.

University of South Florida (continued)
Faculty: 19 full-time (2 women), 3 part-time/adjunct (0 women).
Students: 43 full-time (8 women), 52 part-time (9 women); includes 15 minority (1 African American, 6 Asian Americans or Pacific Islanders, 7 Hispanic Americans, 1 Native American), 30 international. Average age 32. 87 applicants, 56% accepted, 14 enrolled. In 2001, 21 master's, 6 doctorates awarded. Terminal master's awarded for partial completion of doctoral program.
Degree requirements: For master's, thesis (for some programs); for doctorate, thesis/dissertation, 2 tools of research as specified by dissertation committee.
Entrance requirements: For master's, GRE General Test, minimum GPA of 3.0 during previous 2 years; for doctorate, GRE General Test. *Application deadline:* For fall admission, 6/1; for spring admission, 10/15. *Application fee:* $20. Electronic applications accepted.
Expenses: Tuition, state resident: part-time $166 per credit hour. Tuition, nonresident: part-time $573 per credit hour. Required fees: $17 per term.
Financial support: In 2001–02, 2 fellowships with tuition reimbursements (averaging $13,500 per year), 47 research assistantships with partial tuition reimbursements (averaging $13,000 per year), 12 teaching assistantships with partial tuition reimbursements (averaging $13,500 per year) were awarded. Unspecified assistantships also available. Financial award application deadline: 4/1.
Faculty research: Water resources, structures and materials, transportation, geotechnical engineering, mechanics, pavement. *Total annual research expenditures:* $2 million.
Dr. W. C. Carpenter, Chairperson, 813-974-2275, *Fax:* 813-974-2957, *E-mail:* carpente@eng.usf.edu.
Application contact: Prof. Ram M. Pendyala, 813-974-1084, *Fax:* 813-974-5927, *E-mail:* pendyala@eng.usf.edu. *Web site:* http://www.eng.usf.edu/civ/

■ THE UNIVERSITY OF TENNESSEE

Graduate School, College of Engineering, Department of Civil and Environmental Engineering, Program in Civil Engineering, Knoxville, TN 37996

AWARDS MS, PhD. Part-time programs available. Postbaccalaureate distance learning degree programs offered (minimal on-campus study).

Students: 44 full-time (14 women), 27 part-time (7 women); includes 3 minority (1 African American, 1 Asian American or Pacific Islander, 1 Hispanic American), 13 international. 76 applicants, 49% accepted. In 2001, 33 master's, 5 doctorates awarded.

Degree requirements: For master's, thesis or alternative; for doctorate, thesis/dissertation.
Entrance requirements: For master's and doctorate, TOEFL, minimum GPA of 2.7. *Application deadline:* For fall admission, 2/1 (priority date). Applications are processed on a rolling basis. *Application fee:* $35. Electronic applications accepted.
Expenses: Tuition, state resident: full-time $4,280; part-time $233 per hour. Tuition, nonresident: full-time $12,066; part-time $666 per hour. Tuition and fees vary according to program.
Financial support: Application deadline: 2/1.
Dr. Gregory D. Reed, Head, Department of Civil and Environmental Engineering, 865-974-2503, *Fax:* 865-974-2669, *E-mail:* gdreed@utk.edu.

■ THE UNIVERSITY OF TEXAS AT ARLINGTON

Graduate School, College of Engineering, Department of Civil and Environmental Engineering, Arlington, TX 76019

AWARDS M Engr, MS, PhD. Part-time and evening/weekend programs available. Postbaccalaureate distance learning degree programs offered (minimal on-campus study).

Faculty: 13 full-time (0 women), 1 part-time/adjunct (0 women).
Students: 60 full-time (13 women), 51 part-time (13 women); includes 13 minority (2 African Americans, 6 Asian Americans or Pacific Islanders, 4 Hispanic Americans, 1 Native American), 62 international. 104 applicants, 96% accepted, 31 enrolled. In 2001, 23 master's, 3 doctorates awarded. Terminal master's awarded for partial completion of doctoral program.
Degree requirements: For master's, oral and written exams, thesis optional; for doctorate, one foreign language.
Entrance requirements: For master's, GRE General Test, TOEFL, minimum GPA of 3.0 in last 60 hours of undergraduate course work; for doctorate, GRE General Test, TOEFL, minimum graduate GPA of 3.5. *Application deadline:* For fall admission, 6/16. Applications are processed on a rolling basis. *Application fee:* $25 ($50 for international students).
Expenses: Tuition, area resident: Full-time $2,268. Tuition, nonresident: full-time $6,264. Required fees: $839. Tuition and fees vary according to course load.
Financial support: In 2001–02, 29 fellowships with partial tuition reimbursements (averaging $1,000 per year), 30 research assistantships with partial tuition reimbursements (averaging $750 per year), 14 teaching assistantships with partial tuition reimbursements (averaging $750 per year) were awarded. Federal Work-Study, scholarships/grants, and tuition waivers (partial) also available. Financial

award application deadline: 6/1; financial award applicants required to submit FAFSA.
Dr. Siamak A. Ardekani, Interim Chair, 817-272-5055, *Fax:* 817-272-2630, *E-mail:* ardekani@uta.edu.
Application contact: Dr. Ernest C. Crosby, Graduate Adviser, 817-272-3500, *Fax:* 817-272-2630, *E-mail:* ecrosby@uta.edu. *Web site:* http://www.ce.uta.edu/

■ THE UNIVERSITY OF TEXAS AT AUSTIN

Graduate School, College of Engineering, Department of Civil Engineering, Austin, TX 78712-1111

AWARDS Civil engineering (MSE, PhD); environmental and water resources engineering (MSE).

Students: 314 full-time (82 women), 41 part-time (12 women); includes 28 minority (7 African Americans, 9 Asian Americans or Pacific Islanders, 12 Hispanic Americans), 196 international. 700 applicants, 34% accepted. In 2001, 103 master's, 24 doctorates awarded.
Degree requirements: For doctorate, thesis/dissertation.
Entrance requirements: For master's and doctorate, GRE General Test. *Application deadline:* For fall admission, 1/15 (priority date); for spring admission, 9/1 (priority date). Applications are processed on a rolling basis. *Application fee:* $50 ($75 for international students). Electronic applications accepted.
Expenses: Tuition, state resident: full-time $3,159. Tuition, nonresident: full-time $6,957. Tuition and fees vary according to program.
Financial support: Fellowships, research assistantships, teaching assistantships available. Financial award application deadline: 2/1.
Dr. Gerald E. Speitel, Chairman, 512-471-4921, *E-mail:* speitel@mail.utexas.edu.
Application contact: Kathy Rose, Graduate Coordinator, 512-471-4921, *Fax:* 512-471-0592, *E-mail:* kros@mail.utexas.edu. *Web site:* http://www.ce.utexas.edu/

■ THE UNIVERSITY OF TEXAS AT EL PASO

Graduate School, College of Engineering, Department of Civil Engineering, El Paso, TX 79968-0001

AWARDS Civil engineering (MS); environmental engineering (MEENE, MSENE). Part-time and evening/weekend programs available.

Students: 52 (11 women); includes 14 minority (1 Asian American or Pacific Islander, 13 Hispanic Americans) 7 international. Average age 34. 16 applicants, 100% accepted. In 2001, 78 degrees awarded.
Degree requirements: For master's, thesis optional.

Entrance requirements: For master's, GRE General Test, TOEFL, minimum GPA of 3.0. *Application deadline:* For fall admission, 7/1 (priority date); for spring admission, 11/1 (priority date). Applications are processed on a rolling basis. *Application fee:* $15 ($65 for international students). Electronic applications accepted. **Expenses:** Tuition, state resident: full-time $2,450. Tuition, nonresident: full-time $6,000. **Financial support:** In 2001–02, research assistantships with partial tuition reimbursements (averaging $21,125 per year), teaching assistantships with partial tuition reimbursements (averaging $16,900 per year) were awarded. Fellowships with partial tuition reimbursements, career-related internships or fieldwork, Federal Work-Study, institutionally sponsored loans, scholarships/grants, tuition waivers (partial), and stipends also available. Financial award application deadline: 3/15; financial award applicants required to submit FAFSA. **Faculty research:** On-site wastewater treatment systems, wastewater reuse, disinfection by-product control, water resources, membrane filtration. Dr. Carlos M. Ferregut, Chairperson, 915-747-6921, *Fax:* 915-747-8037, *E-mail:* ferregut@miners.utep.edu. **Application contact:** Dr. Charles H. Ambler, Dean of the Graduate School, 915-747-5491 Ext. 7886, *Fax:* 915-747-5788, *E-mail:* cambler@miners.utep.edu.

■ THE UNIVERSITY OF TEXAS AT SAN ANTONIO

College of Engineering, Department of Civil and Environmental Engineering, San Antonio, TX 78249-0617

AWARDS Civil engineering (MSCE). Part-time and evening/weekend programs available.

Faculty: 5 full-time (0 women), 2 part-time/adjunct (0 women). **Students:** 12 full-time (5 women), 32 part-time (7 women); includes 14 minority (2 Asian Americans or Pacific Islanders, 12 Hispanic Americans), 6 international. 19 applicants, 95% accepted, 12 enrolled. In 2001, 8 degrees awarded. **Degree requirements:** For master's, thesis optional. **Entrance requirements:** For master's, GRE General Test, 3.0 on last 60 hours of undergraduate degree. *Application deadline:* For fall admission, 7/1; for spring admission, 12/1. **Expenses:** Tuition, state resident: full-time $2,268; part-time $126 per credit hour. Tuition, nonresident: full-time $6,066; part-time $337 per credit hour. Required fees: $781. Tuition and fees vary according to course load. **Financial support:** Research assistantships, teaching assistantships, career-related internships or fieldwork and institutionally sponsored loans available. Support available to part-time students. Financial award

application deadline: 3/31. *Total annual research expenditures:* $122,340. Dr. Alberto Arroyo, Chair, 210-458-5510.

■ UNIVERSITY OF TOLEDO

Graduate School, College of Engineering, Department of Civil Engineering, Toledo, OH 43606-3398

AWARDS Civil engineering (MS); engineering sciences (PhD). Part-time programs available.

Faculty: 12 full-time (2 women). **Students:** 15 full-time (1 woman), 24 part-time (3 women), 32 international. Average age 25. 125 applicants, 48% accepted. In 2001, 34 master's, 1 doctorate awarded. Terminal master's awarded for partial completion of doctoral program. **Degree requirements:** For master's, thesis or alternative; for doctorate, thesis/ dissertation. **Entrance requirements:** For master's, GRE General Test, TOEFL, minimum GPA of 2.7; for doctorate, GRE General Test, TOEFL. *Application deadline:* For fall admission, 5/31 (priority date). Applications are processed on a rolling basis. *Application fee:* $30. Electronic applications accepted. **Expenses:** Tuition, state resident: full-time $7,278; part-time $303 per hour. Tuition, nonresident: full-time $15,731; part-time $699 per hour. Required fees: $43 per hour. **Financial support:** In 2001–02, 1 fellowship with full tuition reimbursement, 9 research assistantships with full tuition reimbursements, 31 teaching assistantships with full tuition reimbursements were awarded. Federal Work-Study, scholarships/grants, tuition waivers (full), and unspecified assistantships also available. Support available to part-time students. Financial award application deadline: 4/1. **Faculty research:** Environmental modeling, soil/pavement interaction, structural mechanics, earthquakes, transportation engineering. *Total annual research expenditures:* $517,604. Dr. Brian Randolph, Chair, 419-530-8115, *Fax:* 419-530-8116. **Application contact:** Patrice McClelland, Academic Program Coordinator, 419-530-8114, *Fax:* 419-530-8116, *E-mail:* pmmclel@utnet.utoledo.edu. *Web site:* http://eng.utoledo.edu/civil/

Find an in-depth description at www.petersons.com/gradchannel.

■ UNIVERSITY OF UTAH

Graduate School, College of Engineering, Department of Civil and Environmental Engineering, Salt Lake City, UT 84112-1107

AWARDS Civil engineering (ME, MS, PhD); environmental engineering (ME, MS, PhD); nuclear engineering (ME, MS, PhD).

Faculty: 12 full-time (2 women).

Students: 50 full-time (8 women), 35 part-time (5 women); includes 22 minority (18 Asian Americans or Pacific Islanders, 3 Hispanic Americans, 1 Native American), 8 international. Average age 32. 106 applicants, 72% accepted. In 2001, 11 master's, 3 doctorates awarded. Terminal master's awarded for partial completion of doctoral program. **Degree requirements:** For master's, project (ME), thesis (MS); for doctorate, thesis/dissertation, departmental qualifying exam. **Entrance requirements:** For master's and doctorate, GRE General Test, TOEFL, minimum GPA of 3.0. *Application deadline:* For fall admission, 7/1. *Application fee:* $40 ($60 for international students). **Expenses:** Tuition, state resident: part-time $320 per semester hour. Tuition, nonresident: part-time $1,135 per semester hour. Required fees: $143 per semester hour. Tuition and fees vary according to course load, degree level and program. **Financial support:** Research assistantships, teaching assistantships available. Support available to part-time students. Financial award applicants required to submit FAFSA. **Faculty research:** Wastewater treatment, structural engineering, structural mechanics, hydraulics, composite materials. Dr. Lawrence D. Reaveley, Chair, 801-581-6931, *Fax:* 801-585-5477, *E-mail:* reaveley@civil.utah.edu. **Application contact:** Andy Hong, Advisor, 801-581-6931, *Fax:* 801-585-5477, *E-mail:* hong@civil.utah.edu. *Web site:* http://www.coe.utah.edu/

■ UNIVERSITY OF VERMONT

Graduate College, College of Engineering and Mathematics, Department of Civil and Environmental Engineering, Burlington, VT 05405

AWARDS MS, PhD.

Degree requirements: For master's, thesis or alternative; for doctorate, thesis/dissertation. **Entrance requirements:** For master's and doctorate, GRE General Test, TOEFL. **Expenses:** Tuition, state resident: part-time $335 per credit. Tuition, nonresident: part-time $838 per credit.

Find an in-depth description at www.petersons.com/gradchannel.

■ UNIVERSITY OF VIRGINIA

School of Engineering and Applied Science, Department of Civil Engineering, Charlottesville, VA 22903

AWARDS Applied mechanics (MAM, MS); environmental engineering (ME, MS, PhD), including environmental engineering, water resources. Structural mechanics (ME, MS, PhD); transportation engineering and management (ME, MS, PhD). Part-time programs

University of Virginia (continued)
available. Postbaccalaureate distance learning degree programs offered (no on-campus study).

Faculty: 17 full-time (3 women).
Students: 67 full-time (23 women); includes 2 minority (both African Americans), 30 international. Average age 28. 195 applicants, 18% accepted. In 2001, 13 master's, 5 doctorates awarded. Terminal master's awarded for partial completion of doctoral program.
Degree requirements: For doctorate, thesis/dissertation, comprehensive exam.
Entrance requirements: For master's and doctorate, GRE General Test. *Application deadline:* For fall admission, 2/1 (priority date); for spring admission, 8/1 (priority date). Applications are processed on a rolling basis. *Application fee:* $40. Electronic applications accepted.
Expenses: Tuition, state resident: full-time $3,988. Tuition, nonresident: full-time $17,078. Required fees: $1,190.
Financial support: In 2001–02, 58 students received support, including 9 fellowships with full tuition reimbursements available (averaging $17,000 per year), 42 research assistantships with full tuition reimbursements available (averaging $17,000 per year), 7 teaching assistantships with full tuition reimbursements available (averaging $17,000 per year) Financial award application deadline: 2/1.
Faculty research: Groundwater, surface water, traffic engineering, composite materials. *Total annual research expenditures:* $3.5 million.
Michael J. Demetsky, Professor, 434-924-6362, *Fax:* 434-982-2951, *E-mail:* mjd@virginia.edu.
Application contact: Dr. James A. Smith, Director of Graduate Studies, 434-924-7464, *Fax:* 434-982-2951, *E-mail:* civil@virginia.edu. *Web site:* http://www.cs.virginia.edu/~civil/

■ **UNIVERSITY OF WASHINGTON**

Graduate School, College of Engineering, Department of Civil and Environmental Engineering, Seattle, WA 98195

AWARDS Environmental engineering (MS, MSCE, MSE, PhD); hydraulic engineering (MSCE, MSE, PhD). Structural and geotechnical engineering and mechanics (MS, MSCE, MSE, PhD); transportation and construction engineering (MS, MSCE, MSE, PhD).

Faculty: 31 full-time (4 women), 26 part-time/adjunct (1 woman).
Students: 153 full-time (54 women), 42 part-time (13 women); includes 25 minority (2 African Americans, 19 Asian Americans or Pacific Islanders, 3 Hispanic Americans, 1 Native American), 34 international. Average age 29. 339 applicants, 60% accepted, 59 enrolled. In 2001, 71 master's, 11 doctorates awarded.

Terminal master's awarded for partial completion of doctoral program.
Degree requirements: For master's, thesis (for some programs); for doctorate, thesis/dissertation, comprehensive exam. *Median time to degree:* Doctorate–3.5 years full-time.
Entrance requirements: For master's, GRE General Test, TOEFL, minimum GPA of 3.0; for doctorate, GRE, TOEFL, minimum GPA of 3.5. *Application deadline:* For fall admission, 2/1 (priority date). Applications are processed on a rolling basis. *Application fee:* $50. Electronic applications accepted.
Expenses: Tuition, state resident: full-time $5,539. Tuition, nonresident: full-time $14,376. Required fees: $390. Tuition and fees vary according to course load and program.
Financial support: In 2001–02, 110 students received support, including 22 fellowships with partial tuition reimbursements available, 70 research assistantships with full tuition reimbursements available, 22 teaching assistantships with full tuition reimbursements available; career-related internships or fieldwork and scholarships/grants also available. Financial award application deadline: 2/1.
Faculty research: Water resources, hydrology, construction, environmental structures, geotechnical transportation. *Total annual research expenditures:* $3.7 million.
Prof. G. Scott Rutherford, Chair, 206-543-2390.
Application contact: Marcia Buck, Graduate Adviser, 206-543-2574, *E-mail:* cesendme@u.washington.edu. *Web site:* http://www.ce.washington.edu/grad_p.htm

■ **UNIVERSITY OF WISCONSIN–MADISON**

Graduate School, College of Engineering, Department of Civil and Environmental Engineering, Madison, WI 53706-1380

AWARDS MS, PhD. Part-time programs available.

Faculty: 30 full-time (1 woman), 3 part-time/adjunct (0 women).
Students: 131 full-time (29 women), 31 part-time (4 women). Average age 25. 266 applicants, 51% accepted, 25 enrolled. In 2001, 33 master's, 12 doctorates awarded. Terminal master's awarded for partial completion of doctoral program.
Degree requirements: For master's, thesis or alternative; for doctorate, thesis/dissertation, preliminary exam and qualifying exams.
Entrance requirements: For master's and doctorate, TOEFL, minimum GPA of 3.0 for last 60 credits. *Application deadline:* For fall admission, 6/30 (priority date); for spring admission, 11/15. Applications are processed on a rolling basis. *Application fee:* $45. Electronic applications accepted.

Expenses: Tuition, state resident: full-time $7,361; part-time $399 per credit. Tuition, nonresident: full-time $20,499; part-time $1,282 per credit. Required fees: $34 per credit. Full-time tuition and fees vary according to course load, program, reciprocity agreements and student level.
Financial support: In 2001–02, 126 students received support, including 11 fellowships with full tuition reimbursements available (averaging $16,350 per year), 77 research assistantships with full tuition reimbursements available (averaging $16,350 per year), 16 teaching assistantships with full tuition reimbursements available (averaging $6,982 per year); Federal Work-Study also available. Support available to part-time students. Financial award application deadline: 12/15.
Faculty research: Environmental geotechnics and soil mechanics, design and analysis of structures, traffic engineering and intelligent transport systems, industrial pollution control, hydrological monitoring. *Total annual research expenditures:* $6.5 million.
Erhard F. Joeres, Chair, 608-262-3542, *Fax:* 608-262-5199, *E-mail:* cee@engr.wisc.edu.
Application contact: Kathy Monroe, Student Services Coordinator, 608-262-5198, *Fax:* 608-262-5199, *E-mail:* kmonroe@engr.wisc.edu. *Web site:* http://www.engr.wisc.edu/cee/

■ **UNIVERSITY OF WYOMING**

Graduate School, College of Engineering, Department of Civil and Architectural Engineering, Program in Civil Engineering, Laramie, WY 82071

AWARDS MS, PhD. Part-time programs available.

Faculty: 14 full-time (1 woman).
Students: 16 full-time (5 women), 8 part-time (1 woman), 2 international. 16 applicants, 94% accepted. In 2001, 10 master's, 1 doctorate awarded. Terminal master's awarded for partial completion of doctoral program.
Degree requirements: For master's, thesis; for doctorate, variable foreign language requirement, thesis/dissertation.
Entrance requirements: For master's and doctorate, GRE General Test, TOEFL, minimum GPA of 3.0. *Application deadline:* For fall admission, 5/1; for spring admission, 9/1. Applications are processed on a rolling basis. *Application fee:* $40. Electronic applications accepted.
Expenses: Tuition, state resident: full-time $2,895; part-time $161 per credit hour. Tuition, nonresident: full-time $8,367; part-time $465 per credit hour. Required fees: $491; $10 per credit hour. $2 per credit hour. Tuition and fees vary according to course load and program.
Financial support: In 2001–02, 2 fellowships (averaging $4,000 per year), research

assistantships with full tuition reimbursements (averaging $8,667 per year), 7 teaching assistantships with full tuition reimbursements (averaging $8,667 per year) were awarded. Financial award application deadline: 3/1.

Faculty research: Structures, water, resources, geotechnical, transportation, architectural.

Dr. Charles Dolan, Head, 307-766-5255.

Application contact: Heather D. Warren, Graduate Coordinator, 307-766-5446, *Fax:* 307-766-2221, *E-mail:* hwarren@uwyo.edu. *Web site:* http://wwweng.uwyo.edu/ce.html

■ UTAH STATE UNIVERSITY

School of Graduate Studies, College of Engineering, Department of Civil and Environmental Engineering, Logan, UT 84322

AWARDS ME, MS, PhD, CE.

Faculty: 31 full-time (1 woman).
Students: 61 full-time (10 women), 30 part-time (2 women); includes 4 minority (2 Asian Americans or Pacific Islanders, 2 Native Americans), 49 international. Average age 28. 151 applicants, 69% accepted. In 2001, 25 master's, 2 doctorates awarded.
Degree requirements: For master's, thesis (for some programs); for doctorate, thesis/dissertation.
Entrance requirements: For master's and doctorate, GRE General Test, TOEFL, minimum GPA of 3.0. *Application deadline:* For fall admission, 6/15 (priority date); for spring admission, 10/15. Applications are processed on a rolling basis. *Application fee:* $40.
Expenses: Tuition, state resident: full-time $1,693. Tuition, nonresident: full-time $4,233. Required fees: $501. Tuition and fees vary according to program.
Financial support: In 2001–02, 2 fellowships with partial tuition reimbursements (averaging $12,000 per year), 49 research assistantships with partial tuition reimbursements (averaging $1,000 per year) were awarded. Teaching assistantships with partial tuition reimbursements, career-related internships or fieldwork, Federal Work-Study, and institutionally sponsored loans also available. Support available to part-time students. Financial award application deadline: 3/31.
Faculty research: Hazardous waste treatment, large space structures, river basin management, earthquake engineering, environmental impact.
Loren R. Anderson, Head, 435-797-2938, *Fax:* 435-797-1185.
Application contact: Becky Hansen, Staff Assistant IV, 435-797-2938, *Fax:* 435-797-1185, *E-mail:* beckyjh@cc.usu.edu. *Web site:* http://www.engineering.usu.edu/Departments/cee/

■ VANDERBILT UNIVERSITY

School of Engineering, Department of Civil and Environmental Engineering, Program in Civil Engineering, Nashville, TN 37240-1001

AWARDS M Eng, MS, PhD. MS and PhD offered through the Graduate School. Part-time programs available.

Faculty: 9 full-time (1 woman).
Students: 28 full-time (8 women); includes 12 minority (2 African Americans, 10 Asian Americans or Pacific Islanders). Average age 26. 31 applicants, 39% accepted, 8 enrolled. In 2001, 2 master's, 1 doctorate awarded. Terminal master's awarded for partial completion of doctoral program.
Degree requirements: For master's and doctorate, thesis/dissertation.
Entrance requirements: For master's and doctorate, GRE General Test. *Application deadline:* For fall admission, 1/15; for spring admission, 11/1. Applications are processed on a rolling basis. *Application fee:* $40.
Expenses: Tuition: Full-time $28,350.
Financial support: In 2001–02, 20 students received support, including 6 fellowships with full tuition reimbursements available (averaging $18,500 per year), 16 research assistantships with full tuition reimbursements available (averaging $19,600 per year), 6 teaching assistantships with full tuition reimbursements available (averaging $15,600 per year); institutionally sponsored loans and tuition waivers (full and partial) also available. Financial award application deadline: 1/15.
Faculty research: Structural mechanics, finite element analysis, urban transportation, hazardous material transport.
Application contact: Dr. Sankaran Mahadevan, Director of Graduate Studies, 615-322-3040, *Fax:* 615-322-3365, *E-mail:* sankaran.mahadevan@vanderbilt.edu. *Web site:* http://www.cee.vanderbilt.edu/

Find an in-depth description at www.petersons.com/gradchannel.

■ VILLANOVA UNIVERSITY

College of Engineering, Department of Civil and Environmental Engineering, Program in Civil Engineering, Villanova, PA 19085-1699

AWARDS MCE. Part-time and evening/weekend programs available.

Faculty: 11 full-time (1 woman), 8 part-time/adjunct (0 women).
Students: 10 full-time (1 woman), 42 part-time (5 women); includes 4 minority (all Hispanic Americans), 3 international. Average age 25. 22 applicants, 100% accepted. In 2001, 11 degrees awarded.
Degree requirements: For master's, thesis optional.
Entrance requirements: For master's, GRE General Test (for applicants with degrees from foreign universities),

minimum GPA of 3.0. *Application deadline:* For fall admission, 8/1 (priority date); for spring admission, 12/1. Applications are processed on a rolling basis. *Application fee:* $40. Electronic applications accepted.
Expenses: Tuition: Part-time $340 per credit. One-time fee: $115 full-time. Tuition and fees vary according to program.
Financial support: Teaching assistantships, Federal Work-Study, scholarships/grants, and tuition waivers (full and partial) available. Support available to part-time students. Financial award application deadline: 4/15.
Faculty research: Bridge inspection, environment maintenance, economy and risk.
Dr. Ronald A. Chadderton, Chairman, Department of Civil and Environmental Engineering, 610-519-4960, *Fax:* 610-519-6754.

■ VIRGINIA POLYTECHNIC INSTITUTE AND STATE UNIVERSITY

Graduate School, College of Engineering, Department of Civil and Environmental Engineering, Department of Civil Engineering, Blacksburg, VA 24061

AWARDS M Eng, MS, PhD.

Faculty: 44 full-time (3 women), 6 part-time/adjunct (0 women).
Students: 139 full-time (31 women), 117 part-time (32 women); includes 23 minority (10 African Americans, 10 Asian Americans or Pacific Islanders, 3 Hispanic Americans), 62 international. 354 applicants, 61% accepted. In 2001, 62 master's, 9 doctorates awarded.
Degree requirements: For master's, thesis (for some programs); for doctorate, thesis/dissertation.
Entrance requirements: For master's and doctorate, GRE, TOEFL. *Application deadline:* For fall admission, 12/1 (priority date). Applications are processed on a rolling basis. *Application fee:* $45. Electronic applications accepted.
Expenses: Tuition, state resident: part-time $241 per hour. Tuition, nonresident: part-time $406 per hour. Tuition and fees vary according to program.
Financial support: In 2001–02, 5 fellowships with full tuition reimbursements (averaging $25,000 per year), 26 research assistantships with full tuition reimbursements (averaging $17,350 per year), 19 teaching assistantships with full tuition reimbursements (averaging $14,500 per year) were awarded. Unspecified assistantships also available. Financial award application deadline: 4/1.
Dr. Bill Knocke, Head, Department of Civil and Environmental Engineering, 540-231-6637, *E-mail:* knocke@vt.edu.

Find an in-depth description at www.petersons.com/gradchannel.

■ WASHINGTON STATE UNIVERSITY

Graduate School, College of Engineering and Architecture, Department of Civil and Environmental Engineering, Program in Civil Engineering, Pullman, WA 99164

AWARDS MS, PhD.

Faculty: 24 full-time (1 woman), 6 part-time/adjunct (0 women).
Students: 57 full-time (15 women), 1 part-time; includes 1 Asian American or Pacific Islander, 1 Hispanic American, 24 international. Average age 23. 54 applicants, 56% accepted. In 2001, 24 master's, 5 doctorates awarded. Terminal master's awarded for partial completion of doctoral program.
Degree requirements: For master's, oral exam, thesis optional; for doctorate, thesis/dissertation, oral exam, written exam.
Entrance requirements: For master's and doctorate, GRE General Test, minimum GPA of 3.0. *Application deadline:* For fall admission, 3/1 (priority date); for spring admission, 10/1. Applications are processed on a rolling basis. *Application fee:* $35. Electronic applications accepted.
Expenses: Tuition, state resident: full-time $6,088; part-time $304 per semester. Tuition, nonresident: full-time $14,918; part-time $746 per semester. Tuition and fees vary according to program.
Financial support: In 2001–02, 3 fellowships (averaging $15,000 per year), 35 research assistantships with full and partial tuition reimbursements (averaging $14,403 per year), 11 teaching assistantships with full and partial tuition reimbursements (averaging $14,403 per year) were awarded. Career-related internships or fieldwork, Federal Work-Study, and institutionally sponsored loans also available. Financial award application deadline: 4/1; financial award applicants required to submit FAFSA.
Faculty research: Environmental geotechnical, hydraulics transportation, structures, wood. *Total annual research expenditures:* $4.3 million.
Application contact: Maureen Clausen, Secretary Senior, 509-335-2576, *Fax:* 509-335-7632, *E-mail:* mclausen@wsu.edu. *Web site:* http://www.ce.wsu.edu/

■ WASHINGTON UNIVERSITY IN ST. LOUIS

Henry Edwin Sever Graduate School of Engineering and Applied Science, Sever Institute of Technology, Department of Civil Engineering, St. Louis, MO 63130-4899

AWARDS Civil engineering (MSCE); construction engineering (MCE); construction management (MCM). Structural engineering (MSE, D Sc); transportation and urban systems engineering (D Sc). Part-time and evening/weekend programs available. Terminal

master's awarded for partial completion of doctoral program.
Degree requirements: For master's, thesis optional; for doctorate, thesis/dissertation, departmental qualifying exam.
Expenses: Tuition: Full-time $26,900.
Faculty research: Composites, earthquake, reinforced concrete steel. *Web site:* http://www.cive.wustl.edu/cive/

■ WAYNE STATE UNIVERSITY

Graduate School, College of Engineering, Department of Civil and Environmental Engineering, Detroit, MI 48202

AWARDS MS, PhD.

Faculty: 10 full-time.
Students: 130. 184 applicants, 43% accepted, 35 enrolled. In 2001, 26 master's, 5 doctorates awarded.
Degree requirements: For master's, thesis optional; for doctorate, thesis/dissertation.
Application deadline: For fall admission, 7/1 (priority date); for spring admission, 3/15. Applications are processed on a rolling basis. *Application fee:* $20 ($30 for international students). Electronic applications accepted.
Expenses: Tuition, state resident: full-time $3,764. Tuition and fees vary according to degree level and program.
Financial support: In 2001–02, 1 fellowship, 19 research assistantships, 5 teaching assistantships were awarded. Career-related internships or fieldwork and tuition waivers (partial) also available.
Faculty research: Environmental geotechnics, bridge engineering, seismic analysis, construction safety, mass transit. *Total annual research expenditures:* $485,000.
Dr. Mumtaz Usmen, Chairperson, 313-577-3789, *Fax:* 313-577-3881, *E-mail:* musmen@ce.eng.wayne.edu.

■ WEST VIRGINIA UNIVERSITY

College of Engineering and Mineral Resources, Department of Civil and Environmental Engineering, Morgantown, WV 26506

AWARDS Civil engineering (MSCE, MSE, PhD). Part-time programs available.

Faculty: 15 full-time (0 women).
Students: 36 full-time (9 women), 9 part-time (2 women), 23 international. Average age 24. 286 applicants, 75% accepted. In 2001, 15 master's, 2 doctorates awarded.
Degree requirements: For master's, thesis/dissertation; for doctorate, thesis/dissertation, comprehensive exam.
Entrance requirements: For master's, TOEFL, minimum GPA of 3.0; for doctorate, GRE (international applicants), TOEFL, minimum GPA of 3.0. *Application deadline:* For fall admission, 7/1 (priority date); for spring admission, 12/1. Applications are processed on a rolling basis. *Application fee:* $45.

Expenses: Tuition, state resident: full-time $2,791. Tuition, nonresident: full-time $8,659. Required fees: $1,002. Tuition and fees vary according to program.
Financial support: In 2001–02, 23 research assistantships, 3 teaching assistantships were awarded. Fellowships, career-related internships or fieldwork, Federal Work-Study, institutionally sponsored loans, and tuition waivers (full and partial) also available. Financial award application deadline: 2/1; financial award applicants required to submit FAFSA.
Faculty research: Environmental and hydrotechnical structural composites, bridge innovation and rehabilitation, transport, soil mechanics, geoenvironmental engineering. *Total annual research expenditures:* $2.5 million.
Dr. David R. Martinelli, Chair, 304-293-3031 Ext. 2616, *Fax:* 304-293-7109, *E-mail:* david.martinelli@mail.wvu.edu.
Application contact: Udaya Halabe, Graduate Program Coordinator, 304-293-3031 Ext. 2617, *Fax:* 304-293-7109, *E-mail:* udaya.halabe@mail.wvu.edu. *Web site:* http://www.cemr.wvu.edu/~wwwce/cee_4.0.html

■ WIDENER UNIVERSITY

School of Engineering, Program in Civil Engineering, Chester, PA 19013-5792

AWARDS ME, ME/MBA. Part-time and evening/weekend programs available.

Degree requirements: For master's, thesis optional.
Entrance requirements: For master's, GMAT (ME/MBA).
Expenses: Tuition: Part-time $500 per credit. Required fees: $25 per semester.
Faculty research: Environmental engineering, laws and water supply, structural analysis and design.

■ WOODS HOLE OCEANOGRAPHIC INSTITUTE

Joint Program with Massachusetts Institute of Technology in Oceanography/Applied Ocean Science and Engineering, Woods Hole, MA 02543

AWARDS Applied ocean sciences (PhD); biological oceanography (PhD, Sc D); chemical oceanography (PhD, Sc D); civil and environmental and oceanographic engineering (PhD); electrical and oceanographic engineering (PhD); geochemistry (PhD); geophysics (PhD); marine biology (PhD); marine geochemistry (PhD, Sc D); marine geology (PhD, Sc D); marine geophysics (PhD); mechanical and oceanographic engineering (PhD); ocean engineering (PhD); oceanographic engineering (M Eng, MS, PhD, Sc D, Eng); paleoceanography (PhD); physical oceanography (PhD, Sc D). MS, PhD, and Sc D offered jointly with Woods Hole Oceanographic Institution.

Faculty: 185 full-time (60 women).
Students: 119 full-time (59 women); includes 4 minority (2 African Americans, 2 Asian Americans or Pacific Islanders), 27 international. Average age 27. 125 applicants, 30% accepted, 24 enrolled. In 2001, 10 master's, 11 doctorates awarded. Terminal master's awarded for partial completion of doctoral program.
Degree requirements: For master's and Eng, thesis (for some programs); for doctorate, thesis/dissertation. *Median time to degree:* Master's–2.9 years full-time; doctorate–5.8 years full-time.
Entrance requirements: For master's, GRE General Test; for doctorate, GRE General Test, GRE Subject Test. *Application deadline:* For fall admission, 1/15 (priority date). *Application fee:* $60. Electronic applications accepted.
Expenses: Tuition: Full-time $26,960. Full-time tuition and fees vary according to program.
Financial support: In 2001–02, 13 fellowships (averaging $35,948 per year), 69 research assistantships (averaging $35,948 per year) were awarded. Teaching assistantships, institutionally sponsored loans, health care benefits, and unspecified assistantships also available. Financial award application deadline: 1/15.
Prof. Paola Rizzoli, Director, 617-253-2451, *E-mail:* rizzoli@mit.edu.
Application contact: Ronni Schwartz, Administrator, 617-253-7544, *Fax:* 617-253-9784, *E-mail:* mspiggy@mit.edu. *Web site:* http://www.whoi.edu/education/graduate/jp.html
Find an in-depth description at www.petersons.com/gradchannel.

■ WORCESTER POLYTECHNIC INSTITUTE

Graduate Studies, Department of Civil and Environmental Engineering, Worcester, MA 01609-2280

AWARDS M Eng, MS, PhD, Advanced Certificate, Certificate. Part-time and evening/weekend programs available.
Postbaccalaureate distance learning degree programs offered (minimal on-campus study).
Faculty: 15 full-time (1 woman), 3 part-time/adjunct (0 women).
Students: 19 full-time (6 women), 32 part-time (10 women); includes 2 minority (1 Asian American or Pacific Islander, 1 Hispanic American), 10 international. 62 applicants, 56% accepted, 17 enrolled. In 2001, 14 degrees awarded.
Degree requirements: For master's, thesis optional; for doctorate, thesis/dissertation.
Entrance requirements: For master's and doctorate, TOEFL. *Application deadline:* For fall admission, 2/1 (priority date); for spring admission, 10/15 (priority date). Applications are processed on a rolling basis. *Application fee:* $60. Electronic applications accepted.

Expenses: Tuition: Part-time $796 per credit. Required fees: $20; $752 per credit. One-time fee: $30 full-time.
Financial support: In 2001–02, 17 students received support, including 4 research assistantships with full tuition reimbursements available (averaging $17,256 per year), 8 teaching assistantships with full tuition reimbursements available (averaging $12,942 per year); fellowships, career-related internships or fieldwork, institutionally sponsored loans, and scholarships/grants also available. Financial award application deadline: 2/15; financial award applicants required to submit FAFSA.
Faculty research: Structural and environmental engineering, asphalt technology, highway safety, construction project management. *Total annual research expenditures:* $1.1 million.
Dr. Fred L. Hart, Head, 508-831-5530, *Fax:* 508-831-5808, *E-mail:* flhart@wpi.edu.
Application contact: Dr. James O'Shaughnessy, Graduate Coordinator, 508-831-5309, *Fax:* 508-831-5808, *E-mail:* jco@wpi.edu. *Web site:* http://www.wpi.edu/Academics/Depts/CEE/

■ YOUNGSTOWN STATE UNIVERSITY

Graduate School, William Rayen College of Engineering, Department of Civil, Chemical, and Environmental Engineering, Youngstown, OH 44555-0001

AWARDS MSE. Part-time and evening/weekend programs available.
Degree requirements: For master's, thesis optional.
Entrance requirements: For master's, TOEFL, minimum GPA of 2.75 in field.
Faculty research: Structural mechanics, water quality modeling, surface and ground water hydrology, physical and chemical processes in aquatic systems.

CONSTRUCTION ENGINEERING AND MANAGEMENT

■ ARIZONA STATE UNIVERSITY

Graduate College, College of Engineering and Applied Sciences, Del E. Webb School of Construction, Tempe, AZ 85287

AWARDS MS.

Entrance requirements: For master's, GRE General Test (recommended), TOEFL, minimum GPA of 3.0.
Faculty research: Roof performance, green building, use of waste and recycled materials, international construction alliances, water supply services.

■ AUBURN UNIVERSITY

Graduate School, College of Architecture, Design, and Construction, Department of Building Science, Auburn University, AL 36849

AWARDS Building science (MBS); construction management (MBS).

Faculty: 11 full-time (2 women).
Students: 13 full-time (0 women), 2 part-time, 1 international. 13 applicants, 85% accepted. In 2001, 5 degrees awarded.
Entrance requirements: For master's, GRE General Test. *Application deadline:* For fall admission, 7/17; for spring admission, 11/24. Applications are processed on a rolling basis. *Application fee:* $25 ($50 for international students). Electronic applications accepted.
Financial support: Application deadline: 3/15.
John D. Murphy, Head, 334-844-4518.
Application contact: Dr. John F. Pritchett, Dean of the Graduate School, 334-844-4700, *E-mail:* hatchlb@mail.auburn.edu. *Web site:* http://www.bsc.auburn.edu/

■ AUBURN UNIVERSITY

Graduate School, College of Engineering, Department of Civil Engineering, Auburn University, AL 36849

AWARDS Construction engineering and management (MCE, MS, PhD); environmental engineering (MCE, MS, PhD); geotechnical/materials engineering (MCE, MS, PhD); hydraulics/hydrology (MCE, MS, PhD). Structural engineering (MCE, MS, PhD); transportation engineering (MCE, MS, PhD). Part-time programs available.

Faculty: 18 full-time (1 woman).
Students: 34 full-time (12 women), 25 part-time (9 women); includes 3 minority (all African Americans), 15 international. 74 applicants, 39% accepted. In 2001, 16 master's, 1 doctorate awarded.
Degree requirements: For master's, project (MCE), thesis (MS); for doctorate, thesis/dissertation, comprehensive exam.
Entrance requirements: For master's and doctorate, GRE General Test. *Application deadline:* For fall admission, 7/7; for spring admission, 11/24. Applications are processed on a rolling basis. *Application fee:* $25 ($50 for international students). Electronic applications accepted.
Financial support: Fellowships, research assistantships, teaching assistantships, Federal Work-Study available. Support available to part-time students. Financial award application deadline: 3/15.
Dr. Joseph F. Judkins, Head, 334-844-4320.
Application contact: Dr. John F. Pritchett, Dean of the Graduate School, 334-844-4700, *E-mail:* hatchlb@mail.auburn.edu.

■ BRADLEY UNIVERSITY

Graduate School, College of Engineering and Technology, Department of Civil Engineering and Construction, Peoria, IL 61625-0002

AWARDS MSCE. Part-time and evening/weekend programs available.

Students: 8 full-time, 25 part-time. 83 applicants, 75% accepted. In 2001, 9 degrees awarded.
Degree requirements: For master's, comprehensive exam.
Entrance requirements: For master's, TOEFL, minimum GPA of 3.0. *Application deadline:* For fall admission, 7/1 (priority date); for spring admission, 11/1. Applications are processed on a rolling basis. *Application fee:* $40 ($50 for international students).
Expenses: Tuition: Part-time $7,615 per semester. Tuition and fees vary according to course load.
Financial support: In 2001–02, 8 research assistantships with full and partial tuition reimbursements were awarded; teaching assistantships, scholarships/grants and tuition waivers (partial) also available. Financial award application deadline: 3/1. Dr. Amir Al-Khafaji, Chairperson, 309-677-2942.
Application contact: Dr. Robert Fuessle, Graduate Adviser, 309-677-2778.

■ THE CATHOLIC UNIVERSITY OF AMERICA

School of Engineering, Department of Civil Engineering, Program in Construction Management, Washington, DC 20064

AWARDS MCE, MS Engr.

Students: 2 full-time (0 women), 2 part-time (1 woman); includes 1 minority (African American), 1 international. Average age 34. 5 applicants, 40% accepted, 0 enrolled. In 2001, 3 degrees awarded.
Degree requirements: For master's, thesis optional.
Entrance requirements: For master's, minimum GPA of 3.0. *Application deadline:* For fall admission, 8/1 (priority date); for spring admission, 12/1. Applications are processed on a rolling basis. *Application fee:* $55. Electronic applications accepted.
Expenses: Tuition: Full-time $20,050; part-time $770 per credit. Required fees: $430 per term. Tuition and fees vary according to program.
Financial support: Research assistantships, teaching assistantships, career-related internships or fieldwork, Federal Work-Study, institutionally sponsored loans, and tuition waivers (full and partial) available. Support available to part-time students. Financial award application deadline: 2/1. Dr. Timothy W. Kao, Chair, Department of Civil Engineering, 202-319-5164, *Fax:* 202-319-4499, *E-mail:* kao@cua.edu.

■ CENTRAL CONNECTICUT STATE UNIVERSITY

School of Graduate Studies, School of Technology, Department of Construction Management, Technology Management, New Britain, CT 06050-4010

AWARDS MS. Part-time and evening/weekend programs available.

Students: 7 full-time (2 women), 51 part-time (14 women); includes 8 minority (5 African Americans, 1 Asian American or Pacific Islander, 2 Hispanic Americans). Average age 35. 20 applicants, 85% accepted. In 2001, 19 degrees awarded.
Degree requirements: For master's, comprehensive exam.
Entrance requirements: For master's, TOEFL, minimum GPA of 2.7. *Application deadline:* For fall admission, 8/10 (priority date); for spring admission, 12/10. Applications are processed on a rolling basis. *Application fee:* $40.
Expenses: Tuition, state resident: full-time $2,772; part-time $245 per credit. Tuition, nonresident: full-time $7,726; part-time $245 per credit. Required fees: $2,102. Tuition and fees vary according to course level and degree level.
Financial support: Research assistantships, Federal Work-Study available. Financial award application deadline: 3/15; financial award applicants required to submit FAFSA.
Faculty research: All aspects of middle management, technical supervision in the workplace.
Dr. Paul Resetarits, Coordinator, 860-832-1831.

■ CLEMSON UNIVERSITY

Graduate School, College of Architecture, Arts, and Humanities, Department of Construction Science and Management, Clemson, SC 29634

AWARDS MCSM. Part-time programs available.

Students: 5 full-time (0 women), 12 part-time (2 women), 2 international. Average age 26. 25 applicants, 40% accepted, 1 enrolled.
Application deadline: For fall admission, 6/1. *Application fee:* $40.
Expenses: Tuition, state resident: full-time $5,310. Tuition, nonresident: full-time $11,284.
Financial support: Research assistantships, teaching assistantships available. Financial award applicants required to submit FAFSA.
Faculty research: Computer applications, employer incentive programs, artificial intelligence, productivity improvement, financial management.
Jose R. Caban, Chair, 864-656-3898, *Fax:* 864-656-1810, *E-mail:* c547196@clemson.edu.

Application contact: Christine Piper, Graduate Coordinator, 864-656-7581, *E-mail:* cpiper@clemson.edu. *Web site:* http://hubcap.clemson.edu/aah/csm/index.html

■ COLORADO STATE UNIVERSITY

Graduate School, College of Applied Human Sciences, Department of Manufacturing Technology and Construction Management, Fort Collins, CO 80523-0015

AWARDS Automotive pollution control (MS); construction management (MS); historic preservation (MS); industrial technology management (MS); technology education and training (MS); technology of industry (PhD). Part-time and evening/weekend programs available.

Faculty: 11 full-time (0 women).
Students: 16 full-time (5 women), 27 part-time (10 women); includes 2 minority (1 African American, 1 Hispanic American), 1 international. Average age 31. 57 applicants, 98% accepted, 9 enrolled. Terminal master's awarded for partial completion of doctoral program.
Degree requirements: For master's, thesis (for some programs); for doctorate, thesis/dissertation.
Entrance requirements: For master's and doctorate, GRE General Test, TOEFL. *Application deadline:* For fall admission, 4/1 (priority date); for spring admission, 9/1 (priority date). Applications are processed on a rolling basis. *Application fee:* $30. Electronic applications accepted.
Expenses: Tuition, state resident: full-time $2,880; part-time $160 per credit. Tuition, nonresident: full-time $11,412; part-time $634 per credit. Required fees: $750; $34 per credit.
Financial support: In 2001–02, 1 fellowship with full tuition reimbursement (averaging $12,960 per year), 3 research assistantships with full tuition reimbursements (averaging $9,720 per year), 8 teaching assistantships with full tuition reimbursements (averaging $9,720 per year) were awarded. Career-related internships or fieldwork, Federal Work-Study, and traineeships also available.
Faculty research: Construction processes, historical preservation, sustainability, technology education. *Total annual research expenditures:* $800,000.
Dr. Larry Grosse, Head, 970-491-7958, *Fax:* 970-491-2473, *E-mail:* drfire107@mindspring.com.
Application contact: Becky Bell, Graduate Liaison, 970-491-7355, *Fax:* 970-491-2473, *E-mail:* becky.bell@cahs.colostate.edu. *Web site:* http://www.cahs.colostate.edu/DIS/

■ FLORIDA INTERNATIONAL UNIVERSITY

College of Engineering, Department of Construction Management, Miami, FL 33199

AWARDS MS. Part-time and evening/weekend programs available.

Faculty: 6 full-time (0 women).
Students: 18 full-time (3 women), 45 part-time (9 women); includes 28 minority (6 African Americans, 22 Hispanic Americans), 12 international. 58 applicants, 48% accepted, 14 enrolled. In 2001, 24 degrees awarded.
Degree requirements: For master's, thesis optional.
Entrance requirements: For master's, GRE General Test, TOEFL. *Application deadline:* For fall admission, 4/1 (priority date); for spring admission, 10/1. Applications are processed on a rolling basis. *Application fee:* $20.
Expenses: Tuition, state resident: full-time $2,916; part-time $162 per credit hour. Tuition, nonresident: full-time $10,245; part-time $569 per credit hour. Required fees: $168 per term.
John Dye, Chairperson, 305-348-3172, *Fax:* 305-348-2766, *E-mail:* dyej@fiu.edu.

■ GEORGIA INSTITUTE OF TECHNOLOGY

Graduate Studies and Research, College of Engineering, School of Civil and Environmental Engineering, Program in Construction Management, Atlanta, GA 30332-0001

AWARDS MS, MSCE, PhD. Part-time programs available. Terminal master's awarded for partial completion of doctoral program.

Degree requirements: For doctorate, thesis/dissertation.
Entrance requirements: For master's, GRE General Test, TOEFL, minimum GPA of 3.0; for doctorate, GRE General Test, TOEFL, minimum GPA of 3.2.
Faculty research: Automation and robotics, risk management, design/construction integration, sustaining technologies, infrastructure rehabilitation.

■ IOWA STATE UNIVERSITY OF SCIENCE AND TECHNOLOGY

Graduate College, College of Engineering, Department of Civil and Construction Engineering, Ames, IA 50011

AWARDS Civil engineering (MS, PhD), including civil engineering materials, construction engineering and management, environmental engineering, geometronics, geotechnical engineering, structural engineering, transportation engineering.

Faculty: 32 full-time, 5 part-time/adjunct.

Students: 55 full-time (9 women), 39 part-time (6 women); includes 1 minority (African American), 40 international. 256 applicants, 23% accepted, 21 enrolled. In 2001, 27 master's, 4 doctorates awarded.
Degree requirements: For master's, thesis or alternative; for doctorate, thesis/dissertation. *Median time to degree:* Master's–2 years full-time; doctorate–3.3 years full-time.
Entrance requirements: For master's and doctorate, GRE General Test (international applicants), TOEFL or IELTS. *Application deadline:* For fall admission, 3/1 (priority date); for spring admission, 10/1 (priority date). *Application fee:* $20 ($50 for international students). Electronic applications accepted.
Expenses: Tuition, state resident: full-time $1,851. Tuition, nonresident: full-time $5,449. Tuition and fees vary according to program.
Financial support: In 2001–02, 44 research assistantships with partial tuition reimbursements (averaging $12,963 per year), 5 teaching assistantships with partial tuition reimbursements (averaging $11,756 per year) were awarded. Fellowships, scholarships/grants, health care benefits, and unspecified assistantships also available.
Dr. Lowell F. Greimann, Chair, 515-294-2140, *E-mail:* cceinfo@iastate.edu.
Application contact: Dr. Edward Kannel, Director of Graduate Education, 515-294-2861, *E-mail:* cceinfo@iastate.edu. *Web site:* http://www1.eng.iastate.edu/coe/grad.asp/

■ MARQUETTE UNIVERSITY

Graduate School, College of Engineering, Department of Civil and Environmental Engineering, Milwaukee, WI 53201-1881

AWARDS Construction and public works management (MS, PhD); environmental/water resources engineering (MS, PhD). Structural/geotechnical engineering (MS, PhD); transportational planning and engineering (MS, PhD). Part-time and evening/weekend programs available.

Faculty: 12 full-time (0 women), 1 part-time/adjunct (0 women).
Students: 20 full-time (8 women), 24 part-time (3 women); includes 2 minority (1 Asian American or Pacific Islander, 1 Hispanic American), 13 international. Average age 30. 57 applicants, 53% accepted, 9 enrolled. In 2001, 9 degrees awarded. Terminal master's awarded for partial completion of doctoral program.
Degree requirements: For master's, thesis or alternative, comprehensive exam; for doctorate, thesis/dissertation. *Median time to degree:* Master's–2 years full-time, 3 years part-time.
Entrance requirements: For master's, TOEFL; for doctorate, GRE General Test, TOEFL. *Application deadline:* For fall admission, 6/1 (priority date). Applications

are processed on a rolling basis. *Application fee:* $40. Electronic applications accepted.
Expenses: Tuition: Full-time $10,170; part-time $445 per credit hour. Tuition and fees vary according to course load.
Financial support: In 2001–02, 18 students received support, including 3 fellowships with tuition reimbursements available, 1 research assistantship with tuition reimbursement available (averaging $10,600 per year), 4 teaching assistantships with tuition reimbursements available (averaging $10,200 per year); Federal Work-Study, institutionally sponsored loans, scholarships/grants, and tuition waivers (full and partial) also available. Support available to part-time students. Financial award application deadline: 2/15.
Faculty research: Highway safety, highway performance, and intelligent transportation systems. Surface mount technology; watershed management. *Total annual research expenditures:* $860,000.
Dr. Thomas H. Wenzel, Chair, 414-288-7030, *Fax:* 414-288-7521.

Find an in-depth description at www.petersons.com/gradchannel.

■ MICHIGAN STATE UNIVERSITY

Graduate School, College of Agriculture and Natural Resources and College of Engineering, Department of Agricultural Engineering, Program in Building Construction Management, East Lansing, MI 48824

AWARDS MS.

Students: 25 full-time. Average age 25.
Entrance requirements: For master's, GRE General Test. *Application deadline:* For fall admission, 3/1; for spring admission, 8/15. Applications are processed on a rolling basis. *Application fee:* $30 ($40 for international students). Electronic applications accepted.
Expenses: Tuition, state resident: part-time $244 per credit hour. Tuition, nonresident: part-time $494 per credit hour. Required fees: $268 per semester. Tuition and fees vary according to course load, degree level and program.
Financial support: Applicants required to submit FAFSA.
Dr. Robert VonBernuth, Director, 517-432-2096.
Application contact: Information Contact, 517-353-4455, *Fax:* 517-355-7711, *E-mail:* cmgrad@msu.edu. *Web site:* http://www.canr.msu.edu/cm

■ OREGON STATE UNIVERSITY

Graduate School, College of Engineering, Department of Civil, Construction, and Environmental Engineering, Corvallis, OR 97331

AWARDS Civil engineering (MAIS, MS, PhD); ocean engineering (M Oc E). Part-time programs available.

Oregon State University (continued)
Faculty: 21 full-time (1 woman), 1 (woman) part-time/adjunct.
Students: 60 full-time (14 women), 8 part-time (2 women); includes 5 minority (1 African American, 1 Asian American or Pacific Islander, 2 Hispanic Americans, 1 Native American), 32 international. Average age 29. In 2001, 24 master's, 1 doctorate awarded. Terminal master's awarded for partial completion of doctoral program.
Degree requirements: For master's, thesis or alternative; for doctorate, one foreign language, thesis/dissertation.
Entrance requirements: For master's, GRE General Test, TOEFL, minimum GPA of 3.0 in last 90 hours (3.5 for MS); for doctorate, GRE General Test, TOEFL, minimum GPA of 3.0 in last 90 hours of undergraduate course work. *Application deadline:* For fall admission, 3/1 (priority date). Applications are processed on a rolling basis. *Application fee:* $50.
Expenses: Tuition, area resident: Full-time $15,933. Tuition, state resident: full-time $28,937.
Financial support: Fellowships, research assistantships, teaching assistantships, career-related internships or fieldwork and institutionally sponsored loans available. Support available to part-time students. Financial award application deadline: 2/1.
Faculty research: Hazardous waste management, carbon cycling, wave forces on structures, pavement design, seismic analysis.
Kenneth J. Williamson, Head, 541-737-6836, *E-mail:* kenneth.williamson@orst.edu.
Application contact: Linda A. Rowe, Office Manager, 541-737-6149, *Fax:* 541-737-3052, *E-mail:* linda.rowe@orst.edu. *Web site:* http://www.ccee.orst.edu/

■ **SOUTHERN POLYTECHNIC STATE UNIVERSITY**

School of Architecture, Civil Engineering Technology and Construction, Program in Construction, Marietta, GA 30060-2896

AWARDS MS. Part-time and evening/weekend programs available.

Faculty: 5 part-time/adjunct (0 women).
Students: 13 full-time (1 woman), 17 part-time (4 women); includes 8 minority (5 African Americans, 2 Asian Americans or Pacific Islanders, 1 Hispanic American), 7 international. Average age 34. In 2001, 17 degrees awarded.
Degree requirements: For master's, thesis.
Entrance requirements: For master's, GMAT or GRE, letters of recommendation (3), minimum GPA of 2.75. *Application deadline:* For fall admission, 7/15 (priority date); for spring admission, 12/1. Applications are processed on a rolling basis. *Application fee:* $20. Electronic applications accepted.

Expenses: Tuition, state resident: full-time $1,746; part-time $97 per credit. Tuition, nonresident: full-time $6,966; part-time $387 per credit. Required fees: $221 per term.
Financial support: Teaching assistantships, career-related internships or fieldwork, Federal Work-Study, scholarships/grants, and unspecified assistantships available. Support available to part-time students. Financial award application deadline: 5/1; financial award applicants required to submit FAFSA.
Dr. Khalid Siddiqi, Head, 770-528-7221, *Fax:* 770-528-4966, *E-mail:* ksiggiqi@spsu.edu.
Application contact: Virginia A. Head, Director of Admissions, 770-528-7281, *Fax:* 770-528-7292, *E-mail:* vhead@spsu.edu. *Web site:* http://www.cnst.spsu.edu

■ **STATE UNIVERSITY OF NEW YORK COLLEGE OF ENVIRONMENTAL SCIENCE AND FORESTRY**

Faculty of Construction Management and Wood Products Engineering, Syracuse, NY 13210-2779

AWARDS Environmental and resources engineering (MPS, MS, PhD).

Faculty: 8 full-time (0 women), 1 (woman) part-time/adjunct.
Students: 7 full-time (1 woman), 15 part-time (3 women), 8 international. Average age 36. 4 applicants, 100% accepted, 4 enrolled. In 2001, 3 master's, 3 doctorates awarded.
Degree requirements: For master's, thesis (for some programs), registration; for doctorate, thesis/dissertation, comprehensive exam, registration.
Entrance requirements: For master's and doctorate, GRE General Test, minimum GPA of 3.0. *Application deadline:* For fall admission, 2/1 (priority date); for spring admission, 11/1 (priority date). Applications are processed on a rolling basis. *Application fee:* $50.
Expenses: Tuition, area resident: Part-time $213 per credit hour. Tuition, state resident: full-time $5,100. Tuition, nonresident: full-time $8,416; part-time $351 per credit hour. Required fees: $250. One-time fee: $43 full-time.
Financial support: In 2001–02, 8 students received support, including 2 fellowships with full tuition reimbursements available (averaging $8,817 per year), 3 research assistantships with full tuition reimbursements available (averaging $9,000 per year), 3 teaching assistantships with full tuition reimbursements available (averaging $8,817 per year); career-related internships or fieldwork, Federal Work-Study, institutionally sponsored loans, scholarships/grants, health care benefits, and unspecified assistantships also available. Financial award applicants required

to submit FAFSA. *Total annual research expenditures:* $67,860.
Dr. George H. Kyanka, Chair, 315-470-6835, *Fax:* 315-470-6879.
Application contact: Dr. Robert H. Frey, Dean, Instruction and Graduate Studies, 315-470-6599, *Fax:* 315-470-6879, *E-mail:* esfgrad@esf.edu. *Web site:* http://www.esf.edu/faculty/wpe/

■ **STEVENS INSTITUTE OF TECHNOLOGY**

Graduate School, Wesley J. Howe School of Technology Management, Program in Construction Management, Hoboken, NJ 07030

AWARDS MS. Offered in cooperation with the Department of Civil, Environmental, and Ocean Engineering.

Degree requirements: For master's, thesis optional.
Entrance requirements: For master's, GMAT, GRE, TOEFL. Electronic applications accepted.
Expenses: Tuition: Full-time $13,950; part-time $775 per credit. Required fees: $180. One-time fee: $180 part-time. Full-time tuition and fees vary according to degree level and program.

■ **TEXAS A&M UNIVERSITY**

College of Architecture, Department of Construction Science, College Station, TX 77843

AWARDS Construction management (MS).

Faculty: 18 full-time (1 woman), 4 part-time/adjunct (1 woman).
Students: 28 full-time (4 women), 6 part-time; includes 15 minority (13 Asian Americans or Pacific Islanders, 2 Hispanic Americans). Average age 30. 29 applicants, 41% accepted. In 2001, 16 degrees awarded.
Degree requirements: For master's, comprehensive exam. *Median time to degree:* Master's–1.5 years full-time, 2.5 years part-time.
Entrance requirements: For master's, GRE General Test, TOEFL. *Application deadline:* For fall admission, 4/1 (priority date); for winter admission, 1/1 (priority date); for spring admission, 9/1 (priority date). Applications are processed on a rolling basis. *Application fee:* $50 ($75 for international students). Electronic applications accepted.
Expenses: Tuition, state resident: full-time $11,872. Tuition, nonresident: full-time $17,892.
Financial support: In 2001–02, 16 fellowships with partial tuition reimbursements (averaging $1,000 per year), 8 research assistantships with partial tuition reimbursements (averaging $9,000 per year), 2 teaching assistantships with partial tuition reimbursements (averaging $9,000 per year) were awarded. Financial award

application deadline: 4/1; financial award applicants required to submit FAFSA.
Faculty research: Fire safety, housing foundations, construction project management, quality management. *Total annual research expenditures:* $300,000.
Dr. James C. Smith, Head, 979-845-1017, *Fax:* 979-862-1572, *E-mail:* jsmith@archone.tamu.edu.
Application contact: Dr. Charles Graham, Coordinator, 979-845-0216, *Fax:* 979-862-1572, *E-mail:* cwgraham@archone.tamu.edu. *Web site:* http://archnt2.tamu.edu/cosc/

■ TEXAS A&M UNIVERSITY

College of Engineering, Department of Civil Engineering, Program in Construction Engineering and Project Management, College Station, TX 77843

AWARDS M Eng, MS, D Eng, PhD. D Eng offered through the College of Engineering.

Students: 31.
Degree requirements: For master's, thesis (MS); for doctorate, dissertation (PhD), internship (D Eng).
Entrance requirements: For master's and doctorate, GRE General Test, TOEFL. *Application fee:* $50 ($75 for international students).
Expenses: Tuition, state resident: full-time $11,872. Tuition, nonresident: full-time $17,892.
Financial support: Fellowships, research assistantships, teaching assistantships available. Financial award application deadline: 4/15; financial award applicants required to submit FAFSA.
Faculty research: Engineering management aspects of major engineered construction projects from concept formulation through start-up.
Dr. Paul N. Roschke, Head, 979-845-4414, *Fax:* 979-862-2800, *E-mail:* ce-grad@tamu.edu.
Application contact: Dr. Donald A. Maxwell, Information Contact, 979-845-2498, *Fax:* 979-862-2800, *E-mail:* ce-grad@tamu.edu. *Web site:* http://www.civil.tamu.edu/

■ UNIVERSITY OF CALIFORNIA, BERKELEY

Graduate Division, College of Engineering, Department of Civil and Environmental Engineering, Berkeley, CA 94720-1500

AWARDS Construction engineering and management (M Eng, MS, D Eng, PhD); environmental quality and environmental water resources engineering (M Eng, MS, D Eng, PhD); geotechnical engineering (M Eng, MS, D Eng, PhD). Structural engineering, mechanics and materials (M Eng, MS, D Eng, PhD); transportation engineering (M Eng, MS, D Eng, PhD).

Degree requirements: For master's, comprehensive exam or thesis (MS); for doctorate, thesis/dissertation, qualifying exam.
Entrance requirements: For master's, GRE General Test, minimum GPA of 3.0; for doctorate, GRE General Test, minimum GPA of 3.5.
Expenses: Tuition, nonresident: full-time $10,704. Required fees: $4,349.
Find an in-depth description at www.petersons.com/gradchannel.

■ UNIVERSITY OF COLORADO AT BOULDER

Graduate School, College of Engineering and Applied Science, Department of Civil, Environmental, and Architectural Engineering, Boulder, CO 80309

AWARDS Building systems (MS, PhD); construction engineering and management (MS, PhD); environmental engineering (MS, PhD); geoenvironmental engineering (MS, PhD); geotechnical engineering (MS, PhD). Structural engineering (MS, PhD); water resource engineering (MS, PhD).

Faculty: 37 full-time (2 women).
Students: 167 full-time (49 women), 44 part-time (12 women); includes 14 minority (1 African American, 4 Asian Americans or Pacific Islanders, 9 Hispanic Americans), 88 international. Average age 30. 280 applicants, 59% accepted. In 2001, 59 master's, 13 doctorates awarded.
Degree requirements: For master's, thesis or alternative, comprehensive exam; for doctorate, thesis/dissertation.
Entrance requirements: For master's, GRE General Test, minimum undergraduate GPA of 3.0. *Application deadline:* For fall admission, 4/30; for spring admission, 10/31. *Application fee:* $50 ($60 for international students).
Expenses: Tuition, state resident: full-time $3,474. Tuition, nonresident: full-time $16,624.
Financial support: In 2001–02, 19 fellowships (averaging $5,252 per year), 45 research assistantships (averaging $15,638 per year), 14 teaching assistantships (averaging $13,821 per year) were awarded. Financial award application deadline: 2/15.
Faculty research: Building systems engineering, construction engineering and management, environmental engineering, geoenvironmental engineering, geotechnical engineering. *Total annual research expenditures:* $8.3 million.
Hon-Yim Ko, Chair, 303-492-6716, *Fax:* 303-492-7317, *E-mail:* ko@spot.colorado.edu.
Application contact: Jan Demay, Graduate Secretary, 303-492-7316, *Fax:* 303-492-7317, *E-mail:* demay@spot.colorado.edu. *Web site:* http://www.civil.colorado.edu/

■ UNIVERSITY OF DENVER

Daniels College of Business, School of Real Estate and Construction Management, Denver, CO 80208

AWARDS Real estate (MBA). Part-time programs available.

Faculty: 4 full-time (0 women).
Students: 1 (woman). Average age 27. In 2001, 3 degrees awarded.
Entrance requirements: For master's, GMAT. *Application deadline:* For fall admission, 5/1 (priority date); for spring admission, 1/1. Applications are processed on a rolling basis. *Application fee:* $50.
Expenses: Tuition: Full-time $21,456.
Financial support: In 2001–02, 1 teaching assistantship with full and partial tuition reimbursement (averaging $6,201 per year) was awarded; research assistantships with full and partial tuition reimbursements, career-related internships or fieldwork, Federal Work-Study, institutionally sponsored loans, and scholarships/grants also available. Support available to part-time students. Financial award application deadline: 2/15; financial award applicants required to submit FAFSA.
Dr. Mark Levine, Director, 303-871-2142.
Application contact: Celeste Fredrico, Executive Director, Student Services, 303-871-3379, *Fax:* 303-871-4466, *E-mail:* dcb@du.edu.

■ UNIVERSITY OF FLORIDA

Graduate School, College of Design, Construction and Planning, M. E. Rinker, Sr. School of Building Construction, Gainesville, FL 32611

AWARDS MBC, MICM, MSBC. Part-time programs available.

Degree requirements: For master's, thesis/dissertation.
Entrance requirements: For master's, GRE General Test, minimum GPA of 3.0. Electronic applications accepted.
Expenses: Tuition, state resident: part-time $164 per hour. Tuition, nonresident: part-time $571 per hour. Tuition and fees vary according to course level and program.
Faculty research: Safety, affordable housing, construction management, environmental issues, sustainable construction, information technology. *Web site:* http://bcn.ufl.edu/

■ UNIVERSITY OF HOUSTON

College of Technology, Houston, TX 77204

AWARDS Construction management (MT); manufacturing systems (MT); microcomputer systems (MT); occupational technology (MSOT). Part-time and evening/weekend programs available.

Faculty: 11 full-time (5 women), 13 part-time/adjunct (4 women).

University of Houston (continued)

Students: 36 full-time (17 women), 60 part-time (21 women); includes 28 minority (16 African Americans, 4 Asian Americans or Pacific Islanders, 8 Hispanic Americans), 17 international. Average age 35. 33 applicants, 82% accepted. In 2001, 25 degrees awarded.
Entrance requirements: For master's, GMAT, GRE, or MAT (MSOT); GRE (MT), minimum GPA of 3.0 in last 60 hours. *Application deadline:* For fall admission, 7/1; for spring admission, 11/1. *Application fee:* $35 ($110 for international students).
Expenses: Tuition, state resident: full-time $1,512. Tuition, nonresident: full-time $5,310. Required fees: $1,308. Tuition and fees vary according to program.
Financial support: Fellowships, research assistantships, teaching assistantships, career-related internships or fieldwork, Federal Work-Study, and institutionally sponsored loans available. Support available to part-time students.
Faculty research: Educational delivery systems, technical curriculum development, computer-integrated manufacturing, neural networks. *Total annual research expenditures:* $354,283.
Uma G. Gupta, Dean, 713-743-4032, *Fax:* 713-743-4032.
Application contact: Holly Rosenthal, Graduate Academic Adviser, 713-743-4098, *Fax:* 713-743-4032, *E-mail:* hrosenthal@uh.edu. *Web site:* http://www.tech.uh.edu/

■ UNIVERSITY OF KANSAS

Graduate School, School of Engineering, Department of Civil, Environmental, and Architectural Engineering, Lawrence, KS 66045

AWARDS Architectural engineering (MS); civil engineering (MCE, MS, DE, PhD); construction management (MCM); environmental engineering (MS, PhD); environmental science (MS, PhD); water resources engineering (MS); water resources science (MS).

Faculty: 27.
Students: 38 full-time (11 women), 97 part-time (20 women); includes 12 minority (4 African Americans, 3 Asian Americans or Pacific Islanders, 4 Hispanic Americans, 1 Native American), 37 international. Average age 32. 105 applicants, 31% accepted, 19 enrolled. In 2001, 32 master's, 4 doctorates awarded.
Degree requirements: For master's, thesis or alternative, exam; for doctorate, thesis/dissertation, comprehensive exam.
Entrance requirements: For master's, GRE, Michigan English Language Assessment Battery, TOEFL, minimum GPA of 3.0; for doctorate, GRE, Michigan English Language Assessment Battery, TOEFL, minimum GPA of 3.5. *Application deadline:* Applications are processed on a rolling basis. *Application fee:* $40.

Expenses: Tuition, state resident: full-time $2,722; part-time $113 per credit. Tuition, nonresident: full-time $8,586; part-time $358 per credit. Required fees: $551; $46 per credit. Tuition and fees vary according to campus/location, program and reciprocity agreements.
Financial support: In 2001–02, 21 research assistantships with partial tuition reimbursements (averaging $10,367 per year), 6 teaching assistantships with full and partial tuition reimbursements (averaging $8,615 per year) were awarded. Fellowships, career-related internships or fieldwork also available.
Faculty research: Structures (fracture mechanics), transportation, environmental health.
Steve L. McCabe, Chair, 785-864-3766.
Application contact: David Parr, Graduate Director, *E-mail:* aparr@engr.ukans.edu. *Web site:* http://www.ceae.ku.edu/

■ UNIVERSITY OF MICHIGAN

Horace H. Rackham School of Graduate Studies, College of Engineering, Department of Civil and Environmental Engineering, Ann Arbor, MI 48109

AWARDS Civil engineering (MSE, PhD, CE); construction engineering and management (MSE); environmental engineering (MSE, PhD).

Faculty: 26 full-time (2 women), 2 part-time/adjunct (0 women).
Students: 142 full-time (39 women), 15 part-time (3 women); includes 11 minority (3 African Americans, 4 Asian Americans or Pacific Islanders, 4 Hispanic Americans), 96 international. Average age 27. 452 applicants, 52% accepted. In 2001, 51 master's, 13 doctorates awarded.
Degree requirements: For doctorate, oral defense of dissertation, preliminary and written exams.
Entrance requirements: For master's, GRE General Test; for doctorate, GRE General Test, master's degree. *Application deadline:* For fall admission, 2/8. Applications are processed on a rolling basis. *Application fee:* $55. Electronic applications accepted.
Financial support: In 2001–02, 109 students received support, including fellowships (averaging $20,200 per year), research assistantships (averaging $20,200 per year), teaching assistantships (averaging $12,783 per year); institutionally sponsored loans and tuition waivers (partial) also available. Financial award application deadline: 3/15.
Faculty research: Earthquake engineering, environmental and water resources engineering, geotechnical engineering, hydraulics and hydrologic engineering, structural engineering. *Total annual research expenditures:* $9.5 million.

Nikolaos D. Katopodes, Chair, 734-764-3674, *Fax:* 734-764-4292, *E-mail:* ndk@umich.edu.
Application contact: Janet Lineer, Student Advisor, 734-764-8495, *Fax:* 734-763-2275, *E-mail:* janetl@umich.edu. *Web site:* http://www.engin.umich.edu/dept/cee/

■ UNIVERSITY OF MISSOURI–ROLLA

Graduate School, School of Engineering, Department of Civil Engineering, Program in Construction Engineering, Rolla, MO 65409-0910

AWARDS MS, DE, PhD.

Degree requirements: For master's, thesis or alternative; for doctorate, thesis/dissertation.
Entrance requirements: For master's and doctorate, GRE General Test, TOEFL, minimum GPA of 3.0.

■ UNIVERSITY OF SOUTHERN CALIFORNIA

Graduate School, School of Engineering, Department of Civil Engineering, Program in Construction Engineering, Los Angeles, CA 90089

AWARDS MS.

Degree requirements: For master's, thesis optional.
Entrance requirements: For master's, GRE General Test.
Expenses: Tuition: Full-time $25,060; part-time $844 per unit. Required fees: $473.

■ UNIVERSITY OF SOUTHERN CALIFORNIA

Graduate School, School of Engineering, Department of Civil Engineering, Program in Construction Management, Los Angeles, CA 90089

AWARDS MCM.

Degree requirements: For master's, thesis optional.
Entrance requirements: For master's, GRE General Test.
Expenses: Tuition: Full-time $25,060; part-time $844 per unit. Required fees: $473.

Find an in-depth description at www.petersons.com/gradchannel.

■ UNIVERSITY OF WASHINGTON

Graduate School, College of Architecture and Urban Planning, Department of Construction Management, Seattle, WA 98195

AWARDS MS, MSCM. Part-time and evening/weekend programs available.

Faculty: 6 full-time (0 women), 3 part-time/adjunct (0 women).

Students: 21 full-time (3 women), 41 part-time (7 women); includes 2 minority (both African Americans), 10 international. Average age 34. 30 applicants, 50% accepted, 11 enrolled. In 2001, 13 degrees awarded.
Degree requirements: For master's, thesis or alternative. *Median time to degree:* Master's–1.5 years full-time, 2.5 years part-time.
Entrance requirements: For master's, GRE General Test, TOEFL, minimum GPA of 3.0. *Application deadline:* For fall admission, 7/1; for winter admission, 11/1; for spring admission, 2/1. Applications are processed on a rolling basis. *Application fee:* $50. Electronic applications accepted.
Expenses: Tuition, state resident: full-time $5,539. Tuition, nonresident: full-time $14,376. Required fees: $390. Tuition and fees vary according to course load and program.
Financial support: Application deadline: 2/15.
Faculty research: Business practices, delivery methods, materials, productivity. *Total annual research expenditures:* $30,000. Dr. Saeed Daniali, Chair, 206-685-1764, *Fax:* 206-685-1976, *E-mail:* sdaniali@u.washington.edu.
Application contact: Dr. John E. Schaufelberger, Graduate Coordinator, 206-685-4440, *Fax:* 206-685-1976, *E-mail:* jesbcon@u.washington.edu. *Web site:* http://depts.washington.edu/

■ UNIVERSITY OF WASHINGTON

Graduate School, College of Engineering, Department of Civil and Environmental Engineering, Seattle, WA 98195

AWARDS Environmental engineering (MS, MSCE, MSE, PhD); hydraulic engineering (MSCE, MSE, PhD). Structural and geotechnical engineering and mechanics (MS, MSCE, MSE, PhD); transportation and construction engineering (MS, MSCE, MSE, PhD).

Faculty: 31 full-time (4 women), 26 part-time/adjunct (1 woman).
Students: 153 full-time (54 women), 42 part-time (13 women); includes 25 minority (2 African Americans, 19 Asian Americans or Pacific Islanders, 3 Hispanic Americans, 1 Native American), 34 international. Average age 29. 339 applicants, 60% accepted, 59 enrolled. In 2001, 71 master's, 11 doctorates awarded. Terminal master's awarded for partial completion of doctoral program.
Degree requirements: For master's, thesis (for some programs); for doctorate, thesis/dissertation, comprehensive exam. *Median time to degree:* Doctorate–3.5 years full-time.
Entrance requirements: For master's, GRE General Test, TOEFL, minimum GPA of 3.0; for doctorate, GRE, TOEFL, minimum GPA of 3.5. *Application deadline:* For fall admission, 2/1 (priority date). Applications are processed on a rolling

basis. *Application fee:* $50. Electronic applications accepted.
Expenses: Tuition, state resident: full-time $5,539. Tuition, nonresident: full-time $14,376. Required fees: $390. Tuition and fees vary according to course load and program.
Financial support: In 2001–02, 110 students received support, including 22 fellowships with partial tuition reimbursements available, 70 research assistantships with full tuition reimbursements available, 22 teaching assistantships with full tuition reimbursements available; career-related internships or fieldwork and scholarships/grants also available. Financial award application deadline: 2/1.
Faculty research: Water resources, hydrology, construction, environmental structures, geotechnical transportation. *Total annual research expenditures:* $3.7 million.
Prof. G. Scott Rutherford, Chair, 206-543-2390.
Application contact: Marcia Buck, Graduate Adviser, 206-543-2574, *E-mail:* cesendme@u.washington.edu. *Web site:* http://www.ce.washington.edu/grad_p.htm

■ WASHINGTON UNIVERSITY IN ST. LOUIS

Henry Edwin Sever Graduate School of Engineering and Applied Science, Sever Institute of Technology, Department of Civil Engineering, Program in Construction Engineering, St. Louis, MO 63130-4899

AWARDS MCE.

Degree requirements: For master's, thesis optional.
Expenses: Tuition: Full-time $26,900. *Web site:* http://www.cive.wustl.edu/cive/

■ WASHINGTON UNIVERSITY IN ST. LOUIS

Henry Edwin Sever Graduate School of Engineering and Applied Science, Sever Institute of Technology, Department of Civil Engineering, Program in Construction Management, St. Louis, MO 63130-4899

AWARDS MCM, M Arch/MCM.

Degree requirements: For master's, thesis optional.
Expenses: Tuition: Full-time $26,900. *Web site:* http://www.cive.wustl.edu/cive/

■ WESTERN MICHIGAN UNIVERSITY

Graduate College, College of Engineering and Applied Sciences, Department of Construction Engineering, Materials Engineering and Industrial Design, Program in Construction Management, Kalamazoo, MI 49008-5202

AWARDS MS.

Faculty: 7 full-time (2 women).
Students: 24 full-time (6 women), 3 part-time; includes 1 minority (African American), 23 international. 43 applicants, 60% accepted, 13 enrolled.
Degree requirements: For master's, thesis optional.
Entrance requirements: For master's, minimum GPA of 3.0. *Application deadline:* For fall admission, 2/15 (priority date). Applications are processed on a rolling basis. *Application fee:* $25.
Expenses: Tuition, state resident: part-time $186 per credit hour. Tuition, nonresident: part-time $442 per credit hour. Required fees: $602. One-time fee: $132 part-time. Tuition and fees vary according to course load.
Financial support: Application deadline: 2/15.
Application contact: Admissions and Orientation, 616-387-2000, *Fax:* 616-387-2355.

ENVIRONMENTAL ENGINEERING

■ AIR FORCE INSTITUTE OF TECHNOLOGY

School of Engineering and Management, Department of Systems and Engineering Management, Dayton, OH 45433-7765

AWARDS Environmental and engineering management (MS); information resource management (MS). Systems acquisition management (MS). Part-time programs available.

Degree requirements: For master's, thesis.
Entrance requirements: For master's, GRE, GMAT, minimum GPA of 3.0. *Web site:* http://en.afit.edu/env/

■ AUBURN UNIVERSITY

Graduate School, College of Engineering, Department of Civil Engineering, Auburn University, AL 36849

AWARDS Construction engineering and management (MCE, MS, PhD); environmental engineering (MCE, MS, PhD); geotechnical/materials engineering (MCE, MS, PhD); hydraulics/hydrology (MCE, MS, PhD).

Auburn University (continued)
Structural engineering (MCE, MS, PhD); transportation engineering (MCE, MS, PhD). Part-time programs available.

Faculty: 18 full-time (1 woman).
Students: 34 full-time (12 women), 25 part-time (9 women); includes 3 minority (all African Americans), 15 international. 74 applicants, 39% accepted. In 2001, 16 master's, 1 doctorate awarded.
Degree requirements: For master's, project (MCE), thesis (MS); for doctorate, thesis/dissertation, comprehensive exam.
Entrance requirements: For master's and doctorate, GRE General Test. *Application deadline:* For fall admission, 7/7; for spring admission, 11/24. Applications are processed on a rolling basis. *Application fee:* $25 ($50 for international students). Electronic applications accepted.
Financial support: Fellowships, research assistantships, teaching assistantships, Federal Work-Study available. Support available to part-time students. Financial award application deadline: 3/15.
Dr. Joseph F. Judkins, Head, 334-844-4320.
Application contact: Dr. John F. Pritchett, Dean of the Graduate School, 334-844-4700, *E-mail:* hatchlb@mail.auburn.edu.

■ CALIFORNIA INSTITUTE OF TECHNOLOGY

Division of Engineering and Applied Science, Option in Environmental Science and Engineering, Pasadena, CA 91125-0001

AWARDS MS, PhD.

Faculty: 7 full-time (1 woman).
Students: 30 full-time (13 women); includes 6 minority (2 African Americans, 2 Asian Americans or Pacific Islanders, 2 Hispanic Americans), 8 international. 69 applicants, 20% accepted, 6 enrolled. In 2001, 5 master's, 9 doctorates awarded.
Degree requirements: For doctorate, thesis/dissertation.
Application deadline: For fall admission, 1/15. *Application fee:* $0. Electronic applications accepted.
Financial support: In 2001–02, 8 fellowships, 13 research assistantships, 4 teaching assistantships were awarded.
Faculty research: Chemistry of natural waters, physics and chemistry of particulates, fluid mechanics of the natural environment, pollutant formation and control, environmental modeling systems.
Dr. Michael Hoffmann, Executive Officer, 626-395-4391.

■ CALIFORNIA POLYTECHNIC STATE UNIVERSITY, SAN LUIS OBISPO

College of Engineering, Department of Civil and Environmental Engineering, San Luis Obispo, CA 93407

AWARDS MS, MCRP/MS. Part-time programs available.

Faculty: 17 full-time (1 woman), 11 part-time/adjunct (3 women).
Students: 8 full-time (2 women), 4 part-time. 12 applicants, 42% accepted, 4 enrolled. In 2001, 4 degrees awarded.
Degree requirements: For master's, thesis or alternative.
Entrance requirements: For master's, GRE General Test, minimum GPA of 3.0 in last 90 quarter units. *Application deadline:* For fall admission, 5/31 (priority date); for spring admission, 12/31. Applications are processed on a rolling basis. *Application fee:* $55. Electronic applications accepted.
Expenses: Tuition, nonresident: part-time $164 per unit. One-time fee: $2,153 part-time.
Financial support: Fellowships, research assistantships, teaching assistantships, career-related internships or fieldwork available. Financial award application deadline: 3/2; financial award applicants required to submit FAFSA.
Faculty research: Soils, structures, transportation, traffic, environmental protection, biomediation.
Dr. Robert Lang, Chair, 805-756-2947, *Fax:* 805-756-6330, *E-mail:* rlang@calpoly.edu.
Application contact: Dr. Eric P. Kasper, Professor, 805-756-1422, *Fax:* 805-756-6330, *E-mail:* ekasper@calpoly.edu. *Web site:* http://www.calpoly.edu/~ceenve/

■ CARNEGIE MELLON UNIVERSITY

Carnegie Institute of Technology, Department of Civil and Environmental Engineering, Pittsburgh, PA 15213-3891

AWARDS Civil engineering (MS, PhD); civil engineering and industrial management (MS); civil engineering and robotics (PhD); civil engineering/bioengineering (PhD); civil engineering/engineering and public policy (MS, PhD). Part-time programs available. Terminal master's awarded for partial completion of doctoral program.

Degree requirements: For master's, thesis (for some programs); for doctorate, thesis/dissertation, qualifying exam.
Entrance requirements: For master's and doctorate, GRE General Test, TOEFL.
Faculty research: Computer-aided engineering and management, structured and computational machines, civil systems.
Web site: http://www.ce.cmu.edu/

Find an in-depth description at www.petersons.com/gradchannel.

■ CARNEGIE MELLON UNIVERSITY

Graduate School of Industrial Administration, Pittsburgh, PA 15213-3891

AWARDS Accounting (PhD); algorithms, combinatorics, and optimization (MS, PhD); business management and software engineering (MBMSE); civil engineering and industrial management (MS); computational finance (MSCF); economics (MS, PhD); electronic commerce (MS); environmental engineering and management (MEEM); finance (PhD); financial economics (PhD); industrial administration (MBA), including administration and public management; information systems (PhD); management of manufacturing and automation (MOM, PhD), including industrial administration (PhD), manufacturing (MOM); marketing (PhD); mathematical finance (PhD); operations research (PhD); organizational behavior and theory (PhD); political economy (PhD); production and operations management (PhD); public policy and management (MS, MSED). Software engineering and business management (MS). Part-time programs available. Terminal master's awarded for partial completion of doctoral program.

Degree requirements: For doctorate, thesis/dissertation.
Entrance requirements: For master's, GMAT, TOEFL.
Expenses: Contact institution. *Web site:* http://www.gsia.cmu.edu/

■ THE CATHOLIC UNIVERSITY OF AMERICA

School of Engineering, Department of Civil Engineering, Program in Environmental Engineering, Washington, DC 20064

AWARDS MCE, MS Engr.

Students: 2 applicants, 0% accepted.
Degree requirements: For master's, thesis optional.
Entrance requirements: For master's, minimum GPA of 3.0. *Application deadline:* For fall admission, 8/1 (priority date); for spring admission, 12/1. Applications are processed on a rolling basis. *Application fee:* $55. Electronic applications accepted.
Expenses: Tuition: Full-time $20,050; part-time $770 per credit. Required fees: $430 per term. Tuition and fees vary according to program.
Financial support: Application deadline: 2/1.
Dr. Timothy W. Kao, Chair, Department of Civil Engineering, 202-319-5164, *Fax:* 202-319-4499, *E-mail:* kao@cua.edu.

■ CLARKSON UNIVERSITY

Graduate School, School of Engineering, Department of Civil and Environmental Engineering, Potsdam, NY 13699

AWARDS Civil and environmental engineering (PhD); civil engineering (ME, MS). Part-time programs available.

Faculty: 15 full-time (4 women), 4 part-time/adjunct (0 women).
Students: 39 full-time (13 women), 22 international. Average age 27. 103 applicants, 61% accepted. In 2001, 13 master's, 2 doctorates awarded.
Degree requirements: For master's, thesis; for doctorate, thesis/dissertation, departmental qualifying exam. *Median time to degree:* Master's–1.5 years full-time; doctorate–6.5 years full-time.
Entrance requirements: For master's, GRE, TOEFL. *Application deadline:* For fall admission, 5/15 (priority date); for spring admission, 10/15 (priority date). Applications are processed on a rolling basis. *Application fee:* $25 ($35 for international students).
Expenses: Tuition: Part-time $714 per credit. Required fees: $108 per semester.
Financial support: In 2001–02, 36 students received support, including 7 fellowships (averaging $20,000 per year), 22 research assistantships (averaging $17,000 per year), 7 teaching assistantships (averaging $17,000 per year). Scholarships/grants and tuition waivers (partial) also available.
Faculty research: Granular flows, water treatment, environmental systems, geotechnical structural dynamics, fluid dynamics. *Total annual research expenditures:* $2.5 million.
Dr. Thomas C. Young, Chairman, 315-268-4430, *Fax:* 315-268-7985, *E-mail:* young@clarkson.edu.
Application contact: Donna Brockway, Assistant to Dean/Foreign Student Advisor, 315-268-6447, *Fax:* 315-268-7994, *E-mail:* brockway@clarkson.edu.

■ CLEMSON UNIVERSITY

Graduate School, College of Engineering and Science, Department of Environmental Engineering and Science, Clemson, SC 29634

AWARDS M Engr, MS, PhD.

Students: 54 full-time (28 women), 12 part-time (3 women); includes 4 minority (all African Americans), 27 international. Average age 24. 104 applicants, 50% accepted, 16 enrolled. In 2001, 17 master's, 2 doctorates awarded.
Degree requirements: For master's and doctorate, thesis/dissertation.
Entrance requirements: For master's and doctorate, GRE General Test, TOEFL, minimum GPA of 3.0. *Application deadline:* For fall admission, 3/1 (priority date). *Application fee:* $40.

Expenses: Tuition, state resident: full-time $5,310. Tuition, nonresident: full-time $11,284.
Financial support: Fellowships, research assistantships, teaching assistantships, institutionally sponsored loans and unspecified assistantships available. Financial award applicants required to submit FAFSA.
Faculty research: Water and air pollution control, hazardous waste and environmental management, environmental chemistry and biology, containment transport modeling, risk assessment.
Dr. Cindy M. Lee, Coordinator, 864-656-1006, *Fax:* 864-656-0672, *E-mail:* lc@clemson.edu.
Application contact: Pamela S. Fjeld, Student Services, 864-656-1010, *Fax:* 864-656-0672, *E-mail:* hpamela@ces.clemson.edu. *Web site:* http://www.grad.clemson.edu/catalog/es3.htm

■ CLEVELAND STATE UNIVERSITY

College of Graduate Studies, Fenn College of Engineering, Department of Civil and Environmental Engineering, Cleveland, OH 44115

AWARDS Civil engineering (MS, D Eng), including environmental engineering (D Eng), mechanical engineering (D Eng), structures engineering (D Eng); engineering mechanics (MS); environmental engineering (MS). Part-time programs available.

Faculty: 10 full-time (1 woman).
Students: 6 full-time (1 woman), 33 part-time (9 women); includes 3 minority (1 African American, 2 Hispanic Americans), 22 international. Average age 29. 62 applicants, 73% accepted. In 2001, 9 master's, 1 doctorate awarded.
Degree requirements: For master's, thesis (for some programs), project or thesis; for doctorate, thesis/dissertation, candidacy and qualifying exams.
Entrance requirements: For master's, GRE General Test, GRE Subject Test, TOEFL, minimum GPA of 2.75; for doctorate, GRE General Test, GRE Subject Test, TOEFL, minimum GPA of 3.25. *Application deadline:* For fall admission, 7/15 (priority date). Applications are processed on a rolling basis. *Application fee:* $25.
Expenses: Tuition, state resident: full-time $6,838; part-time $263 per credit hour. Tuition, nonresident: full-time $13,526; part-time $520 per credit hour.
Financial support: In 2001–02, 3 research assistantships, 6 teaching assistantships were awarded. Career-related internships or fieldwork and unspecified assistantships also available. Financial award application deadline: 9/1.
Faculty research: Environmental engineering, solid-waste disposal, composite materials, nonlinear buckling, constitutive modeling.

Dr. Paul Bosela, Chairperson, 216-687-2190, *Fax:* 216-687-9280. *Web site:* http://www.csuohio.edu/civileng/

■ COLORADO SCHOOL OF MINES

Graduate School, Division of Environmental Science and Engineering, Golden, CO 80401-1887

AWARDS MS, PhD. Part-time programs available.

Faculty: 8 full-time (1 woman), 8 part-time/adjunct (1 woman).
Students: 42 full-time (22 women), 30 part-time (15 women); includes 3 minority (1 Asian American or Pacific Islander, 2 Hispanic Americans), 21 international. 63 applicants, 79% accepted, 27 enrolled. In 2001, 18 master's, 3 doctorates awarded.
Degree requirements: For master's, thesis (for some programs); for doctorate, thesis/dissertation, comprehensive exam. *Median time to degree:* Master's–2 years full-time; doctorate–4 years full-time.
Entrance requirements: For master's and doctorate, GRE General Test. *Application deadline:* For fall admission, 12/1 (priority date); for spring admission, 5/1 (priority date). Applications are processed on a rolling basis. *Application fee:* $40. Electronic applications accepted.
Expenses: Tuition, state resident: full-time $4,940; part-time $246 per credit. Tuition, nonresident: full-time $16,070; part-time $803 per credit. Required fees: $341 per semester.
Financial support: In 2001–02, 56 students received support, including 7 fellowships (averaging $2,818 per year), 23 research assistantships (averaging $3,880 per year), 24 teaching assistantships (averaging $4,738 per year); unspecified assistantships also available. Support available to part-time students. Financial award applicants required to submit FAFSA.
Faculty research: Treatment of water and wastes, environmental law–policy and practice, natural environment systems, hazardous waste management, environmental data analysis. *Total annual research expenditures:* $505,431.
Dr. Robert Seigrist, Head, 303-384-2158, *Fax:* 303-273-3413, *E-mail:* rseigris@mines.edu.
Application contact: Juanita Chuven, Administrative Assistant, 303-273-3427, *Fax:* 303-273-3413, *E-mail:* jchuven@mines.edu. *Web site:* http://www.mines.edu/academic/envsci/

■ COLORADO STATE UNIVERSITY

Graduate School, College of Engineering, Department of Civil Engineering, Fort Collins, CO 80523-0015

AWARDS Bioresource and agricultural engineering (MS); bioresource and agriculture

Colorado State University (continued)
engineering (PhD); environmental engineering (MS, PhD); hydraulics and wind engineering (MS, PhD). Structural and geotechnical engineering (MS, PhD); water resources planning and management (MS, PhD); water resources, hydrologic and environmental sciences (MS, PhD). Part-time programs available.

Faculty: 37 full-time (2 women).
Students: 56 full-time (7 women), 99 part-time (21 women); includes 10 minority (7 Asian Americans or Pacific Islanders, 3 Hispanic Americans), 59 international. Average age 33. 228 applicants, 62% accepted, 39 enrolled. In 2001, 19 master's, 6 doctorates awarded. Terminal master's awarded for partial completion of doctoral program.
Degree requirements: For master's, thesis or alternative; for doctorate, thesis/dissertation.
Entrance requirements: For master's and doctorate, GRE General Test, TOEFL, minimum GPA of 3.0. *Application deadline:* For fall admission, 3/1 (priority date); for spring admission, 8/1 (priority date). Applications are processed on a rolling basis. *Application fee:* $30. Electronic applications accepted.
Expenses: Tuition, state resident: full-time $2,880; part-time $160 per credit. Tuition, nonresident: full-time $11,412; part-time $634 per credit. Required fees: $750; $34 per credit.
Financial support: In 2001–02, 2 fellowships, 26 research assistantships (averaging $16,950 per year), 11 teaching assistantships (averaging $12,713 per year) were awarded. Federal Work-Study, institutionally sponsored loans, and traineeships also available.
Faculty research: Hydraulics, hydrology, water resources, infrastructure, environmental engineering. *Total annual research expenditures:* $5.4 million.
Sandra Woods, Head, 970-491-5049, *Fax:* 970-491-7727, *E-mail:* woods@ engr.colostate.edu.
Application contact: Laurie Howard, Student Adviser, 970-491-5844, *Fax:* 970-491-7727, *E-mail:* lhoward@ engr.colostate.edu. *Web site:* http:// www.engr.colostate.edu/depts/ce/

■ COLORADO STATE UNIVERSITY

Graduate School, College of Engineering, Department of Mechanical Engineering, Fort Collins, CO 80523-0015

AWARDS Bioengineering (MS, PhD); energy and environmental engineering (MS, PhD); energy conversion (MS, PhD); engineering management (MS); heat and mass transfer (MS, PhD); industrial and manufacturing systems engineering (MS, PhD); mechanical

engineering (MS, PhD); mechanics and materials (MS, PhD). Part-time programs available.

Faculty: 17 full-time (2 women).
Students: 36 full-time (6 women), 63 part-time (11 women); includes 5 minority (2 Asian Americans or Pacific Islanders, 2 Hispanic Americans, 1 Native American), 22 international. Average age 32. 234 applicants, 83% accepted, 32 enrolled. In 2001, 10 master's, 3 doctorates awarded. Terminal master's awarded for partial completion of doctoral program.
Degree requirements: For doctorate, thesis/dissertation.
Entrance requirements: For master's and doctorate, GRE General Test, TOEFL, minimum GPA of 3.0. *Application deadline:* For fall admission, 2/1 (priority date). Applications are processed on a rolling basis. *Application fee:* $30. Electronic applications accepted.
Expenses: Tuition, state resident: full-time $2,880; part-time $160 per credit. Tuition, nonresident: full-time $11,412; part-time $634 per credit. Required fees: $750; $34 per credit.
Financial support: In 2001–02, 2 fellowships, 15 research assistantships (averaging $15,792 per year), 14 teaching assistantships (averaging $11,844 per year) were awarded. Traineeships also available.
Faculty research: Space propulsion, controls and systems, engineering and materials. *Total annual research expenditures:* $2.1 million.
Dr. Allan T. Kirkpatrick, Head, 970-491-6559, *Fax:* 970-491-3827, *E-mail:* allan@ engr.colostate.edu. *Web site:* http:// www.engr.colostate.edu/depts/me/ index.html

■ COLUMBIA UNIVERSITY

Fu Foundation School of Engineering and Applied Science, Department of Earth and Environmental Engineering, Program in Earth Resources Engineering, New York, NY 10027

AWARDS MS, PhD. Part-time programs available.

Faculty: 8 full-time (0 women), 4 part-time/adjunct (1 woman).
Students: 8 full-time (5 women); includes 6 minority (all Asian Americans or Pacific Islanders), 2 international. Average age 21. In 2001, 5 degrees awarded.
Degree requirements: For doctorate, thesis/dissertation, qualifying exam.
Entrance requirements: For master's and doctorate, GRE General Test, TOEFL. *Application deadline:* For fall admission, 2/15; for spring admission, 10/1. *Application fee:* $55. Electronic applications accepted.
Expenses: Tuition: Full-time $27,528. Required fees: $1,638.
Financial support: Federal Work-Study available. Financial award application deadline: 1/5; financial award applicants required to submit FAFSA.

Faculty research: Industrial ecology, waste treatment and recycling, water resources, environmental remediation, hazardous waste disposal.
Dr. Peter Schlosser, Chairman, 212-854-0306, *Fax:* 212-854-7081, *E-mail:* ps10@ columbia.edu.
Application contact: Jaime Bradstreet, Student Coordinator, 212-854-2905, *Fax:* 212-854-7081, *E-mail:* jlb2001@ columbia.edu. *Web site:* http:// www.seas.columbia.edu/columbia/ departments/Krumb/

■ CORNELL UNIVERSITY

Graduate School, Graduate Fields of Engineering, Field of Civil and Environmental Engineering, Ithaca, NY 14853-0001

AWARDS Environmental engineering (M Eng, MS, PhD); environmental fluid mechanics and hydrology (M Eng, MS, PhD); environmental systems engineering (M Eng, MS, PhD); geotechnical engineering (M Eng, MS, PhD); remote sensing (M Eng, MS, PhD). Structural engineering (M Eng, MS, PhD); transportation engineering (M Eng, MS, PhD); water resource systems (M Eng, MS, PhD).

Faculty: 33 full-time.
Students: 131 full-time (35 women); includes 17 minority (1 African American, 9 Asian Americans or Pacific Islanders, 7 Hispanic Americans), 61 international. 515 applicants, 55% accepted. In 2001, 64 master's, 14 doctorates awarded. Terminal master's awarded for partial completion of doctoral program.
Degree requirements: For master's, thesis (MS); for doctorate, thesis/dissertation.
Entrance requirements: For master's and doctorate, GRE General Test (recommended), TOEFL, 2 letters of recommendation. *Application deadline:* For fall admission, 1/15 (priority date). *Application fee:* $65. Electronic applications accepted.
Expenses: Tuition: Full-time $25,970. Required fees: $50.
Financial support: In 2001–02, 71 students received support, including 24 fellowships with full tuition reimbursements available, 28 research assistantships with full tuition reimbursements available, 19 teaching assistantships with full tuition reimbursements available; institutionally sponsored loans, scholarships/grants, tuition waivers (full and partial), and unspecified assistantships also available. Financial award applicants required to submit FAFSA.
Faculty research: Environmental engineering, geotechnical engineering remote sensing, environmental fluid mechanics and hydrology, structural engineering.
Application contact: Graduate Field Assistant, 607-255-7560, *E-mail:* cee_

grad@cornell.edu. *Web site:* http://www.gradschool.cornell.edu/grad/fields_1/cee.html

Find an in-depth description at www.petersons.com/gradchannel.

■ **DARTMOUTH COLLEGE**

Thayer School of Engineering, Program in Environmental Engineering, Hanover, NH 03755

AWARDS MS, PhD.

Degree requirements: For master's, thesis; for doctorate, thesis/dissertation, candidacy oral exam.
Entrance requirements: For master's and doctorate, GRE General Test. *Application deadline:* For fall admission, 1/1 (priority date). *Application fee:* $40 ($50 for international students).
Expenses: Tuition: Full-time $26,425.
Financial support: Career-related internships or fieldwork, Federal Work-Study, institutionally sponsored loans, and tuition waivers (full and partial) available. Financial award application deadline: 1/15.
Faculty research: Environmental fluid mechanics, large-scale environmental simulation, water resources, physical oceanography, sustainable resource utilization. *Total annual research expenditures:* $800,000.
Application contact: Candace S. Potter, Graduate Admissions Administrator, 603-646-3844, *Fax:* 603-646-1620, *E-mail:* candace.potter@dartmouth.edu. *Web site:* http://engineering.dartmouth.edu/

■ **DREXEL UNIVERSITY**

Graduate School, School of Environmental Science, Engineering and Policy, Program in Environmental Engineering, Philadelphia, PA 19104-2875

AWARDS MS, PhD. Part-time and evening/weekend programs available.

Faculty: 10 full-time (3 women), 5 part-time/adjunct (1 woman).
Students: 2 full-time (1 woman), 26 part-time (11 women); includes 4 minority (1 African American, 2 Asian Americans or Pacific Islanders, 1 Hispanic American), 5 international. Average age 31. 23 applicants, 74% accepted, 5 enrolled. In 2001, 6 master's, 3 doctorates awarded. Terminal master's awarded for partial completion of doctoral program.
Degree requirements: For master's, thesis optional; for doctorate, thesis/dissertation.
Application deadline: For fall admission, 8/21. Applications are processed on a rolling basis. *Application fee:* $50. Electronic applications accepted.
Expenses: Tuition: Full-time $20,088; part-time $558 per credit. Required fees: $78 per term. One-time fee: $200. Tuition and fees vary according to course load, degree level and program.

Financial support: Research assistantships, teaching assistantships, career-related internships or fieldwork and unspecified assistantships available. Financial award application deadline: 2/1.
Application contact: Director of Graduate Admissions, 215-895-6700, *Fax:* 215-895-5939, *E-mail:* enroll@drexel.edu.

■ **DUKE UNIVERSITY**

Graduate School, School of Engineering, Department of Civil and Environmental Engineering, Durham, NC 27708-0586

AWARDS Civil and environmental engineering (MS, PhD); environmental engineering (MS, PhD). Part-time programs available.

Faculty: 16 full-time, 3 part-time/adjunct.
Students: 35 full-time (10 women). 111 applicants, 25% accepted, 17 enrolled. In 2001, 6 master's, 3 doctorates awarded. Terminal master's awarded for partial completion of doctoral program.
Degree requirements: For doctorate, thesis/dissertation.
Entrance requirements: For master's and doctorate, GRE General Test. *Application deadline:* For fall admission, 12/31; for spring admission, 11/1. *Application fee:* $75.
Expenses: Tuition: Full-time $24,600.
Financial support: Fellowships, research assistantships, Federal Work-Study available. Financial award application deadline: 12/31.
Tomasz Hueckel, Director of Graduate Studies, 919-660-5218, *Fax:* 919-660-5219, *E-mail:* watkins@mail.duke.edu. *Web site:* http://www.cee.egr.duke.edu/

Find an in-depth description at www.petersons.com/gradchannel.

■ **FLORIDA AGRICULTURAL AND MECHANICAL UNIVERSITY**

Division of Graduate Studies, Research, and Continuing Education, FAMU-FSU College of Engineering, Department of Civil Engineering, Tallahassee, FL 32307-3200

AWARDS Civil engineering (MS, PhD); environmental engineering (MS, PhD).

Entrance requirements: For master's, GRE General Test, minimum GPA of 3.0.

Find an in-depth description at www.petersons.com/gradchannel.

■ **FLORIDA INTERNATIONAL UNIVERSITY**

College of Engineering, Department of Civil and Environmental Engineering, Program in Environmental and Urban Systems, Miami, FL 33199

AWARDS MS. Part-time and evening/weekend programs available.

Students: 1 (woman) full-time, 1 (woman) part-time; includes 1 minority (African

American). Average age 38. 2 applicants, 50% accepted, 0 enrolled. In 2001, 1 degree awarded.
Degree requirements: For master's, thesis.
Entrance requirements: For master's, GRE General Test, TOEFL, bachelor's degree in related field. *Application deadline:* For fall admission, 4/1 (priority date); for spring admission, 10/1. Applications are processed on a rolling basis. *Application fee:* $20.
Expenses: Tuition, state resident: full-time $2,916; part-time $162 per credit hour. Tuition, nonresident: full-time $10,245; part-time $569 per credit hour. Required fees: $168 per term.
Faculty research: Water and wastewater treatment, housing systems.
Dr. David Shen, Chairperson, Department of Civil and Environmental Engineering, 305-348-2824, *Fax:* 305-348-2802, *E-mail:* shen@eng.fiu.edu.

■ **FLORIDA INTERNATIONAL UNIVERSITY**

College of Engineering, Department of Civil and Environmental Engineering, Program in Environmental Engineering, Miami, FL 33199

AWARDS MS. Part-time and evening/weekend programs available.

Students: 12 full-time (2 women), 7 part-time (3 women); includes 5 minority (2 African Americans, 3 Hispanic Americans), 9 international. Average age 32. 31 applicants, 58% accepted, 6 enrolled. In 2001, 12 degrees awarded.
Degree requirements: For master's, thesis optional.
Entrance requirements: For master's, GRE General Test, TOEFL, bachelor's degree in related field. *Application deadline:* For fall admission, 4/1 (priority date); for spring admission, 10/1. Applications are processed on a rolling basis. *Application fee:* $20.
Expenses: Tuition, state resident: full-time $2,916; part-time $162 per credit hour. Tuition, nonresident: full-time $10,245; part-time $569 per credit hour. Required fees: $168 per term.
Dr. David Shen, Chairperson, Department of Civil and Environmental Engineering, 305-348-2824, *Fax:* 305-348-2802, *E-mail:* shen@eng.fiu.edu.

■ **FLORIDA STATE UNIVERSITY**

Graduate Studies, FAMU/FSU College of Engineering, Department of Civil Engineering, Tallahassee, FL 32306

AWARDS Civil engineering (MS, PhD); environmental engineering (MS, PhD). Part-time programs available.

Degree requirements: For master's, thesis optional; for doctorate, thesis/dissertation.

Florida State University (continued)

Entrance requirements: For master's, GRE General Test, TOEFL, BS in engineering or related field, minimum GPA of 3.0; for doctorate, Master's degree in engineering or related field, minimum GPA of 3.0.

Expenses: Tuition, state resident: part-time $163 per credit hour. Tuition, nonresident: part-time $570 per credit hour. Tuition and fees vary according to program.

Faculty research: Tidal hydraulics, temperature effects on bridge girders, codes for coastal construction, field performance of pine bridges, river basin management, transportation pavement design, soil dynamics, structural analysis. *Web site:* http://www.eng.fsu.edu/

Find an in-depth description at www.petersons.com/gradchannel.

■ THE GEORGE WASHINGTON UNIVERSITY

School of Engineering and Applied Science, Department of Civil and Environmental Engineering, Washington, DC 20052

AWARDS MS, D Sc, App Sc, Engr. Part-time and evening/weekend programs available.

Faculty: 8 full-time (1 woman), 5 part-time/adjunct (1 woman).
Students: 29 full-time (4 women), 31 part-time (10 women); includes 12 minority (3 African Americans, 4 Asian Americans or Pacific Islanders, 5 Hispanic Americans), 30 international. Average age 32. 51 applicants, 98% accepted. In 2001, 14 master's, 1 doctorate awarded.
Degree requirements: For master's, thesis optional; for doctorate, thesis/dissertation, final and qualifying exams.
Entrance requirements: For master's, TOEFL or George Washington University English as a Foreign Language Test, appropriate bachelor's degree, minimum GPA of 3.0; for doctorate, TOEFL or George Washington University English as a Foreign Language Test, appropriate bachelor's or master's degree, minimum GPA of 3.4, GRE required if highest earned degree is BS; for other advanced degree, TOEFL or George Washington University English as a Foreign Language Test, appropriate master's degree, minimum GPA of 3.0. *Application deadline:* For fall admission, 3/1 (priority date); for spring admission, 10/1. Applications are processed on a rolling basis. *Application fee:* $55.
Expenses: Tuition: Part-time $810 per credit. Required fees: $1 per credit.
Financial support: In 2001–02, 9 fellowships with tuition reimbursements (averaging $10,000 per year), 5 teaching assistantships with tuition reimbursements (averaging $1,600 per year) were awarded. Research assistantships, career-related internships or fieldwork, Federal Work-Study, and institutionally sponsored loans also available. Financial award application deadline: 3/1; financial award applicants required to submit FAFSA.
Faculty research: Computer-integrated manufacturing, materials engineering, electronic materials, fatigue and fracture, reliability.
Dr. William Roper, Chair, 202-994-4901, *E-mail:* wroper@seas.gwu.edu.
Application contact: Howard M. Davis, Manager, Office of Admissions and Student Records, 202-994-6158, *Fax:* 202-994-0909, *E-mail:* data:adms@ seas.gwu.edu. *Web site:* http:// www.gwu.edu/~gradinfo/

Find an in-depth description at www.petersons.com/gradchannel.

■ GEORGIA INSTITUTE OF TECHNOLOGY

Graduate Studies and Research, College of Engineering, School of Civil and Environmental Engineering, Program in Environmental Engineering, Atlanta, GA 30332-0001

AWARDS MS, MS Env E, PhD. Part-time programs available. Postbaccalaureate distance learning degree programs offered (no on-campus study).

Degree requirements: For master's, research report or thesis; for doctorate, thesis/dissertation.
Entrance requirements: For master's and doctorate, GRE, TOEFL, minimum GPA of 3.2.
Faculty research: Advanced microbiology of water and wastes, industrial waste treatment and disposal, air pollution measurements and control.

■ HARVARD UNIVERSITY

School of Public Health, Department of Environmental Health, Boston, MA 02115-6096

AWARDS Environmental epidemiology (SM, DPH, SD); environmental health (SM); environmental science and engineering (SM, SD); occupational health (MOH, SM, DPH, SD); physiology (SD). Part-time programs available.

Faculty: 24 full-time (4 women), 30 part-time/adjunct (4 women).
Students: Average age 32. In 2001, 10 degrees awarded.
Degree requirements: For doctorate, thesis/dissertation, qualifying exam.
Entrance requirements: For master's and doctorate, GRE, TOEFL. *Application deadline:* For fall admission, 12/15. *Application fee:* $60. Electronic applications accepted.
Expenses: Tuition: Full-time $23,370. Required fees: $816. Full-time tuition and fees vary according to program and student level.
Financial support: Fellowships, research assistantships, teaching assistantships, career-related internships or fieldwork, Federal Work-Study, scholarships/grants, traineeships, tuition waivers (partial), and unspecified assistantships available. Support available to part-time students. Financial award application deadline: 2/12; financial award applicants required to submit FAFSA.
Faculty research: Industrial hygiene and occupational safety, population genetics, indoor and outdoor air pollution, cell and molecular biology of the lungs, infectious diseases.
Dr. Joseph D. Brain, Chairman, 617-432-1272, *Fax:* 617-277-2382, *E-mail:* fmarsh@ hsph.harvard.edu.
Application contact: Vincent W. James, Director of Admissions, 617-432-1031, *Fax:* 617-432-2009, *E-mail:* admisofc@ hsph.harvard.edu.

Find an in-depth description at www.petersons.com/gradchannel.

■ IDAHO STATE UNIVERSITY

Office of Graduate Studies, College of Engineering, Pocatello, ID 83209

AWARDS Engineering and applied science (PhD); engineering structures and mechanics (MS); environmental engineering (MS); measurement and control engineering (MS); nuclear science and engineering (MS); waste management and environmental science (MS). Part-time programs available.

Faculty: 13 full-time (0 women), 1 part-time/adjunct (0 women).
Students: 34 full-time (8 women), 18 part-time (1 woman); includes 7 minority (1 African American, 5 Asian Americans or Pacific Islanders, 1 Hispanic American), 15 international. Average age 34. In 2001, 12 master's, 1 doctorate awarded.
Degree requirements: For master's and doctorate, thesis/dissertation.
Entrance requirements: For master's and doctorate, GRE General Test, TOEFL. *Application deadline:* For fall admission, 7/1 (priority date); for spring admission, 12/1. Applications are processed on a rolling basis. *Application fee:* $35.
Expenses: Tuition, area resident: Full-time $3,432. Tuition, state resident: part-time $172 per credit. Tuition, nonresident: full-time $10,196; part-time $262 per credit. International tuition: $9,672 full-time. Part-time tuition and fees vary according to course load, program and reciprocity agreements.
Financial support: In 2001–02, 7 research assistantships with full and partial tuition reimbursements (averaging $10,740 per year), 16 teaching assistantships with full and partial tuition reimbursements (averaging $6,775 per year) were awarded. Federal Work-Study and institutionally sponsored loans also available. Support available to part-time students. Financial award application deadline: 2/15.

Faculty research: Isotope separation, control technology, two-phase flow, photosonolysis, criticality calculations. *Total annual research expenditures:* $293,915.
Dr. Jay Kunze, Dean, 208-282-2902, *Fax:* 208-282-4538. *Web site:* http://www.coe.isu.edu/engrg/

■ ILLINOIS INSTITUTE OF TECHNOLOGY

Graduate College, Armour College of Engineering and Sciences, Department of Chemical and Environmental Engineering, Environmental Engineering Division, Chicago, IL 60616-3793

AWARDS M Env E, MS, PhD. Part-time and evening/weekend programs available.

Faculty: 5 full-time (1 woman), 3 part-time/adjunct (0 women).
Students: 14 full-time (4 women), 31 part-time (11 women); includes 1 minority (Asian American or Pacific Islander), 24 international. Average age 31. 91 applicants, 63% accepted. In 2001, 6 master's, 2 doctorates awarded. Terminal master's awarded for partial completion of doctoral program.
Degree requirements: For master's, thesis (for some programs), comprehensive exam; for doctorate, thesis/dissertation, comprehensive exam.
Entrance requirements: For master's and doctorate, GRE General Test, TOEFL, minimum undergraduate GPA of 3.0. *Application deadline:* For fall admission, 7/1; for spring admission, 11/1. Applications are processed on a rolling basis. *Application fee:* $30. Electronic applications accepted.
Expenses: Tuition: Part-time $590 per credit hour.
Financial support: In 2001–02, 5 research assistantships, 5 teaching assistantships were awarded. Fellowships, Federal Work-Study, institutionally sponsored loans, scholarships/grants, and unspecified assistantships also available. Support available to part-time students. Financial award application deadline: 3/1; financial award applicants required to submit FAFSA.
Faculty research: Bioremediation, industrial wastewater control, water supply and quality, hazardous waste treatment, air pollution control.
Application contact: Dr. Ali Cinar, Dean of Graduate College, 312-567-3637, *Fax:* 312-567-7517, *E-mail:* gradstu@iit.edu. *Web site:* http://www.chee.iit.edu/grad/grad.htm

■ IOWA STATE UNIVERSITY OF SCIENCE AND TECHNOLOGY

Graduate College, College of Engineering, Department of Civil and Construction Engineering, Ames, IA 50011

AWARDS Civil engineering (MS, PhD), including civil engineering materials, construction engineering and management, environmental engineering, geometronics, geotechnical engineering, structural engineering, transportation engineering.

Faculty: 32 full-time, 5 part-time/adjunct.
Students: 55 full-time (9 women), 39 part-time (6 women); includes 1 minority (African American), 40 international. 256 applicants, 23% accepted, 21 enrolled. In 2001, 27 master's, 4 doctorates awarded.
Degree requirements: For master's, thesis or alternative; for doctorate, thesis/dissertation. *Median time to degree:* Master's–2 years full-time; doctorate–3.3 years full-time.
Entrance requirements: For master's and doctorate, GRE General Test (international applicants), TOEFL or IELTS. *Application deadline:* For fall admission, 3/1 (priority date); for spring admission, 10/1 (priority date). *Application fee:* $20 ($50 for international students). Electronic applications accepted.
Expenses: Tuition, state resident: full-time $1,851. Tuition, nonresident: full-time $5,449. Tuition and fees vary according to program.
Financial support: In 2001–02, 44 research assistantships with partial tuition reimbursements (averaging $12,963 per year), 5 teaching assistantships with partial tuition reimbursements (averaging $11,756 per year) were awarded. Fellowships, scholarships/grants, health care benefits, and unspecified assistantships also available.
Dr. Lowell F. Greimann, Chair, 515-294-2140, *E-mail:* cceinfo@iastate.edu.
Application contact: Dr. Edward Kannel, Director of Graduate Education, 515-294-2861, *E-mail:* cceinfo@iastate.edu. *Web site:* http://www1.eng.iastate.edu/coe/grad.asp/

■ JOHNS HOPKINS UNIVERSITY

G. W. C. Whiting School of Engineering, Department of Geography and Environmental Engineering, Baltimore, MD 21218-2699

AWARDS MA, MS, MSE, PhD.

Faculty: 15 full-time (3 women), 4 part-time/adjunct (0 women).
Students: 71 full-time (32 women); includes 8 minority (3 African Americans, 3 Asian Americans or Pacific Islanders, 2 Hispanic Americans), 24 international. Average age 29. 202 applicants, 33% accepted, 23 enrolled. In 2001, 17 master's, 2 doctorates awarded. Terminal master's awarded for partial completion of doctoral program.
Degree requirements: For master's, thesis (for some programs), one year full-time residency; for doctorate, thesis/dissertation, oral exam.
Entrance requirements: For master's and doctorate, GRE General Test, TOEFL. *Application deadline:* For fall admission, 1/15 (priority date). Applications are processed on a rolling basis. *Application fee:* $0. Electronic applications accepted.
Expenses: Tuition: Full-time $27,390.
Financial support: In 2001–02, 70 students received support, including 14 fellowships with full tuition reimbursements available (averaging $18,000 per year), 25 research assistantships with full tuition reimbursements available (averaging $17,400 per year), 5 teaching assistantships with full tuition reimbursements available (averaging $19,680 per year); Federal Work-Study, institutionally sponsored loans, scholarships/grants, tuition waivers (partial), and unspecified assistantships also available. Financial award application deadline: 2/1.
Faculty research: Environmental engineering; environmental chemistry; water resources engineering. Systems analysis and economics for public decision making; geomorphology, hydrology and ecology. *Total annual research expenditures:* $1.9 million.
Dr. Marc B. Parlange, Chair, 410-516-6537, *Fax:* 410-516-8996, *E-mail:* mbparlange@jhu.edu.
Application contact: Dr. Edward J. Bouwer, Admissions Coordinator, 410-516-6042, *Fax:* 410-516-8996, *E-mail:* dogee@jhu.edu. *Web site:* http://www.jhu.edu/~dogee/

■ JOHNS HOPKINS UNIVERSITY

School of Public Health, Department of Environmental Health Sciences, Division of Environmental Health Engineering, Baltimore, MD 21218-2699

AWARDS MHS, Sc M, Dr PH, PhD, Sc D.

Faculty: 6 full-time, 15 part-time/adjunct.
Students: 22 (8 women). 24 applicants, 21% accepted. In 2001, 5 master's, 2 doctorates awarded.
Degree requirements: For master's, thesis (for some programs), registration; for doctorate, thesis/dissertation, 1 year full-time residency, oral and written exams.
Entrance requirements: For master's and doctorate, GRE General Test, TOEFL. *Application deadline:* For fall admission, 2/1 (priority date). Applications are processed on a rolling basis. *Application fee:* $60. Electronic applications accepted.
Expenses: Tuition: Full-time $27,390.
Financial support: Fellowships, research assistantships, teaching assistantships, Federal Work-Study, institutionally sponsored loans, and scholarships/grants available. Support available to part-time students. Financial award application deadline: 4/15; financial award applicants required to submit FAFSA.
Faculty research: Industrial hygiene and safety, biofluid mechanics, environmental microbiology, aerosol science, microbiological water hazards.
Dr. Patrick Breysse, Director, 410-955-3608, *E-mail:* pbreysse@jhsph.edu.

Johns Hopkins University (continued)
Application contact: Kay Castleberry, Senior Academic Coordinator, 410-955-2212, *Fax:* 410-955-0617, *E-mail:* kcastleb@jhsph.edu.

■ LAMAR UNIVERSITY

College of Graduate Studies, College of Engineering, Department of Civil Engineering, Program in Environmental Engineering, Beaumont, TX 77710

AWARDS MS. Part-time programs available.

Faculty: 5 full-time (0 women).
Students: 14 full-time (0 women), 13 international. Average age 26. 60 applicants, 53% accepted. In 2001, 7 degrees awarded.
Degree requirements: For master's, thesis optional.
Entrance requirements: For master's, GRE General Test, TOEFL. *Application deadline:* For fall admission, 5/15 (priority date); for spring admission, 10/1 (priority date). Applications are processed on a rolling basis. *Application fee:* $25 ($50 for international students).
Expenses: Tuition, state resident: full-time $1,114. Tuition, nonresident: full-time $3,670.
Financial support: In 2001–02, 1 fellowship with tuition reimbursement (averaging $1,000 per year), research assistantships with partial tuition reimbursements (averaging $6,000 per year), teaching assistantships (averaging $7,200 per year) were awarded. Tuition waivers (partial) also available. Financial award application deadline: 4/1.
Faculty research: Reservoir hydrodynamics, geotechnical soil stabilization, environmental remediations, construction productivity, air quality. *Total annual research expenditures:* $75,000.
Dr. Enno Koehn, Chair, 409-880-8759, *Fax:* 409-880-8121, *E-mail:* koehneu@hal.lamar.edu.
Application contact: Sandy Drane, Coordinator of Graduate Admissions, 409-880-8356, *Fax:* 409-880-8414, *E-mail:* gradmissions@hal.lamar.edu.

■ LEHIGH UNIVERSITY

P.C. Rossin College of Engineering and Applied Science, Department of Civil and Environmental Engineering, Bethlehem, PA 18015-3094

AWARDS M Eng, MS, PhD. Part-time programs available.

Faculty: 17 full-time (1 woman), 1 part-time/adjunct (0 women).
Students: 54 full-time (13 women), 7 part-time (2 women); includes 11 minority (4 African Americans, 7 Hispanic Americans), 23 international. Average age 24. 123 applicants, 80% accepted, 12 enrolled. In 2001, 16 master's, 3 doctorates awarded.

Terminal master's awarded for partial completion of doctoral program.
Degree requirements: For master's, thesis optional; for doctorate, thesis/dissertation. *Median time to degree:* Master's–2 years full-time; doctorate–4.7 years full-time.
Entrance requirements: For master's and doctorate, GRE General Test, TOEFL. *Application deadline:* For fall admission, 7/15; for spring admission, 12/1. Applications are processed on a rolling basis. *Application fee:* $50.
Expenses: Tuition: Part-time $468 per credit hour. Required fees: $200; $100 per semester. Tuition and fees vary according to program.
Financial support: In 2001–02, 44 students received support, including 7 fellowships (averaging $1,400 per year), 33 research assistantships (averaging $1,500 per year), 4 teaching assistantships (averaging $1,450 per year); tuition waivers (partial) also available. Financial award application deadline: 1/15.
Faculty research: Structural and geotechnical engineering, water resources and coastal engineering. *Total annual research expenditures:* $6.4 million.
Dr. Arup K. SenGupta, Chairman, 610-758-3538, *Fax:* 610-758-6405, *E-mail:* aks0@lehigh.edu.
Application contact: Prisca Vidanage, Graduate Coordinator, 610-758-3530, *Fax:* 610-758-6405, *E-mail:* pmv1@lehigh.edu. *Web site:* http://www.lehigh.edu/~incee/incee.html

Find an in-depth description at www.petersons.com/gradchannel.

■ LOUISIANA STATE UNIVERSITY AND AGRICULTURAL AND MECHANICAL COLLEGE

Graduate School, College of Engineering, Department of Civil and Environmental Engineering, Baton Rouge, LA 70803

AWARDS Environmental engineering (MSCE, PhD); geotechnical engineering (MSCE, PhD). Structural engineering and mechanics (MSCE, PhD); transportation engineering (MSCE, PhD); water resources (MSCE, PhD). Part-time programs available.

Faculty: 30 full-time (1 woman).
Students: 78 full-time (19 women), 26 part-time (11 women); includes 4 minority (2 African Americans, 1 Hispanic American, 1 Native American), 67 international. Average age 29. 133 applicants, 41% accepted, 22 enrolled. In 2001, 15 master's, 7 doctorates awarded.
Degree requirements: For master's, thesis optional; for doctorate, one foreign language, thesis/dissertation.
Entrance requirements: For master's and doctorate, GRE General Test, TOEFL, minimum GPA of 3.0. *Application deadline:* For fall admission, 1/25 (priority date).

Applications are processed on a rolling basis. *Application fee:* $25.
Expenses: Tuition, state resident: full-time $2,551. Tuition, nonresident: full-time $5,551. Required fees: $854. Part-time tuition and fees vary according to course load.
Financial support: In 2001–02, 5 fellowships (averaging $15,800 per year), 51 research assistantships with partial tuition reimbursements (averaging $12,089 per year), 2 teaching assistantships with partial tuition reimbursements (averaging $12,500 per year) were awarded. Career-related internships or fieldwork, institutionally sponsored loans, and scholarships/grants also available. Financial award application deadline: 3/1; financial award applicants required to submit FAFSA.
Faculty research: Solid waste management, electrokinetics, composite structures, transportation planning, river mechanics. *Total annual research expenditures:* $1.7 million.
Dr. George Z. Voyiadjis, Interim Chair/Boyd Professor, 225-578-8668, *Fax:* 225-578-8652, *E-mail:* cegzv@lsu.edu. *Web site:* http://www.ce.lsu.edu/

■ MANHATTAN COLLEGE

Graduate Division, School of Engineering, Program in Environmental Engineering, Riverdale, NY 10471

AWARDS ME, MS. Part-time and evening/weekend programs available.

Degree requirements: For master's, thesis or alternative.
Entrance requirements: For master's, GRE, TOEFL, minimum GPA of 3.0.

■ MARQUETTE UNIVERSITY

Graduate School, College of Engineering, Department of Civil and Environmental Engineering, Milwaukee, WI 53201-1881

AWARDS Construction and public works management (MS, PhD); environmental/water resources engineering (MS, PhD). Structural/geotechnical engineering (MS, PhD); transportational planning and engineering (MS, PhD). Part-time and evening/weekend programs available.

Faculty: 12 full-time (0 women), 1 part-time/adjunct (0 women).
Students: 20 full-time (8 women), 24 part-time (3 women); includes 2 minority (1 Asian American or Pacific Islander, 1 Hispanic American), 13 international. Average age 30. 57 applicants, 53% accepted, 9 enrolled. In 2001, 9 degrees awarded. Terminal master's awarded for partial completion of doctoral program.
Degree requirements: For master's, thesis or alternative, comprehensive exam; for doctorate, thesis/dissertation. *Median time to degree:* Master's–2 years full-time, 3 years part-time.

Entrance requirements: For master's, TOEFL; for doctorate, GRE General Test, TOEFL. *Application deadline:* For fall admission, 6/1 (priority date). Applications are processed on a rolling basis. *Application fee:* $40. Electronic applications accepted.
Expenses: Tuition: Full-time $10,170; part-time $445 per credit hour. Tuition and fees vary according to course load.
Financial support: In 2001–02, 18 students received support, including 3 fellowships with tuition reimbursements available, 1 research assistantship with tuition reimbursement available (averaging $10,600 per year), 4 teaching assistantships with tuition reimbursements available (averaging $10,200 per year); Federal Work-Study, institutionally sponsored loans, scholarships/grants, and tuition waivers (full and partial) also available. Support available to part-time students. Financial award application deadline: 2/15.
Faculty research: Highway safety, highway performance, and intelligent transportation systems. Surface mount technology; watershed management. *Total annual research expenditures:* $860,000.
Dr. Thomas H. Wenzel, Chair, 414-288-7030, *Fax:* 414-288-7521.

Find an in-depth description at www.petersons.com/gradchannel.

■ MASSACHUSETTS INSTITUTE OF TECHNOLOGY

School of Engineering, Department of Civil and Environmental Engineering, Cambridge, MA 02139-4307

AWARDS M Eng, SM, PhD, Sc D, CE, EE.

Faculty: 39 full-time (5 women).
Students: 269 full-time (70 women), 5 part-time; includes 23 minority (2 African Americans, 12 Asian Americans or Pacific Islanders, 9 Hispanic Americans), 169 international. Average age 23. 760 applicants, 40% accepted, 116 enrolled. In 2001, 112 master's, 21 doctorates awarded.
Degree requirements: For master's, thesis/dissertation; for doctorate, thesis/dissertation, comprehensive exam.
Entrance requirements: For master's and doctorate, GRE General Test, TOEFL. *Application deadline:* For fall admission, 1/15; for spring admission, 11/1. *Application fee:* $60. Electronic applications accepted.
Expenses: Tuition: Full-time $26,960. Full-time tuition and fees vary according to program.
Financial support: In 2001–02, 242 students received support, including 55 fellowships, 123 research assistantships, 35 teaching assistantships; career-related internships or fieldwork, Federal Work-Study, institutionally sponsored loans, scholarships/grants, health care benefits, and unspecified assistantships also available. Financial award application deadline: 1/15; financial award applicants required to submit FAFSA.

Faculty research: Environmental chemistry and biology, environmental fluid dynamics and hydrodynamics, geoenvironment and geotechnology, surface and groundwater hydrology, materials and structures. *Total annual research expenditures:* $9.7 million.
Chiang C. Mei, Acting Head, 617-253-7101, *Fax:* 617-258-6775.
Application contact: Patricia Maguire, Graduate Admissions Coordinator, 617-253-7119, *Fax:* 617-258-6775, *E-mail:* ceed@mit.edu. *Web site:* http://web.mit.edu/civenv/

■ MICHIGAN STATE UNIVERSITY

Graduate School, College of Engineering, Department of Civil and Environmental Engineering, East Lansing, MI 48824

AWARDS Civil engineering (MS, PhD); civil engineering-environmental toxicology (PhD); civil engineering-urban studies (MS); environmental engineering (MS, PhD); environmental engineering-environmental toxicology (PhD). Part-time programs available.

Faculty: 19 full-time (2 women).
Students: 57 full-time (13 women), 38 part-time (9 women); includes 14 minority (3 African Americans, 4 Asian Americans or Pacific Islanders, 7 Hispanic Americans), 59 international. Average age 28. 258 applicants, 25% accepted. In 2001, 37 master's, 7 doctorates awarded. Terminal master's awarded for partial completion of doctoral program.
Degree requirements: For doctorate, thesis/dissertation.
Entrance requirements: For master's, GRE, TOEFL, minimum GPA of 3.0; for doctorate, GRE, TOEFL, minimum GPA of 3.0, MS. *Application deadline:* For fall admission, 5/31; for spring admission, 10/31. Applications are processed on a rolling basis. *Application fee:* $30 ($40 for international students). Electronic applications accepted.
Expenses: Tuition, state resident: part-time $244 per credit hour. Tuition, nonresident: part-time $494 per credit hour. Required fees: $268 per semester. Tuition and fees vary according to course load, degree level and program.
Financial support: In 2001–02, 33 fellowships (averaging $4,530 per year), 41 research assistantships (averaging $13,655 per year), 10 teaching assistantships with tuition reimbursements (averaging $13,130 per year) were awarded. Financial award application deadline: 2/15; financial award applicants required to submit FAFSA.
Faculty research: Highway safety, hazardous waste management, pavement research, concrete materials, waste water treatment. *Total annual research expenditures:* $1.6 million.
Dr. R. Harichandran, Chair, 517-355-5107, *Fax:* 517-432-1827, *E-mail:* cee@egr.msu.edu.

Application contact: Rick Lyles, Graduate Coordinator, 517-355-5107, *Fax:* 517-432-1827. *Web site:* http://www.egr.msu.edu/cee/

■ MICHIGAN TECHNOLOGICAL UNIVERSITY

Graduate School, College of Engineering, Department of Civil and Environmental Engineering, Program in Environmental Engineering, Houghton, MI 49931-1295

AWARDS ME, MS, PhD. Part-time programs available.

Degree requirements: For doctorate, thesis/dissertation.
Entrance requirements: For master's and doctorate, GRE General Test, TOEFL. Electronic applications accepted. *Web site:* http://www.civil.mtu.edu/

Find an in-depth description at www.petersons.com/gradchannel.

■ MICHIGAN TECHNOLOGICAL UNIVERSITY

Graduate School, College of Engineering, Department of Civil and Environmental Engineering, Program in Environmental Engineering Science, Houghton, MI 49931-1295

AWARDS MS. Part-time programs available.

Electronic applications accepted.

■ MILWAUKEE SCHOOL OF ENGINEERING

Department of Architectural Engineering and Building Construction, Milwaukee, WI 53202-3109

AWARDS Environmental engineering (MS). Structural engineering (MS). Part-time and evening/weekend programs available.

Faculty: 2 full-time (1 woman), 11 part-time/adjunct (0 women).
Students: 2 full-time (0 women), 25 part-time (6 women). Average age 25. 18 applicants, 61% accepted, 2 enrolled. In 2001, 8 degrees awarded.
Degree requirements: For master's, thesis or alternative, design project.
Entrance requirements: For master's, GRE General Test or GMAT, letters of recommendation (2), BS in architectural, civil or structural engineering or related field. *Application deadline:* Applications are processed on a rolling basis. *Application fee:* $35. Electronic applications accepted.
Expenses: Tuition: Part-time $440 per credit. Tuition and fees vary according to course load.
Financial support: In 2001–02, 3 students received support, including 2 research assistantships; career-related internships or fieldwork also available. Support available

Milwaukee School of Engineering (continued)
to part-time students. Financial award applicants required to submit FAFSA. **Faculty research:** Steel. *Total annual research expenditures:* $90,000.
Matt Fuchs, Chairman, 414-277-7302, *Fax:* 414-277-7479, *E-mail:* fuchs@ msoe.edu.
Application contact: Paul Borens, Admissions Director, 800-332-6763, *Fax:* 414-277-7475, *E-mail:* borens@msoe.edu. *Web site:* http://msoe.edu/

■ MONTANA TECH OF THE UNIVERSITY OF MONTANA

Graduate School, Environmental Engineering Program, Butte, MT 59701-8997

AWARDS MS. Part-time programs available.

Faculty: 7 full-time (1 woman).
Students: 8 full-time (2 women), 2 part-time; includes 2 minority (1 Asian American or Pacific Islander, 1 Hispanic American). 17 applicants, 47% accepted, 4 enrolled. In 2001, 10 degrees awarded.
Degree requirements: For master's, thesis, registration.
Entrance requirements: For master's, GRE General Test, TOEFL, minimum GPA of 3.0. *Application deadline:* For fall admission, 4/1 (priority date); for spring admission, 10/1 (priority date). Applications are processed on a rolling basis. *Application fee:* $30.
Expenses: Tuition, state resident: full-time $3,717; part-time $196 per credit. Tuition, nonresident: full-time $11,770; part-time $324 per credit.
Financial support: In 2001–02, 8 students received support, including 3 research assistantships with full tuition reimbursements available (averaging $8,000 per year), 4 teaching assistantships with partial tuition reimbursements available (averaging $5,525 per year); career-related internships or fieldwork, institutionally sponsored loans, and tuition waivers (full and partial) also available. Financial award application deadline: 4/1; financial award applicants required to submit FAFSA.
Faculty research: Air diffusion, modeling, air pollution control, wetlands, water pollution control, bioremediation. *Total annual research expenditures:* $436,834.
Dr. Kumar Ganesan, Department Head, 406-496-4239, *Fax:* 406-496-4650, *E-mail:* kganesan@mtech.edu.
Application contact: Cindy Dunstan, Administrator, Graduate School, 406-496-4304, *Fax:* 406-496-4334, *E-mail:* cdunstan@mtech.edu. *Web site:* http://www.mtech.edu/

■ NEW JERSEY INSTITUTE OF TECHNOLOGY

Office of Graduate Studies, Department of Civil and Environmental Engineering, Program in Environmental Engineering, Newark, NJ 07102

AWARDS MS, PhD. Part-time and evening/weekend programs available.

Students: 14 full-time (6 women), 9 part-time (2 women); includes 5 minority (4 Asian Americans or Pacific Islanders, 1 Hispanic American), 15 international. Average age 29. 77 applicants, 51% accepted, 9 enrolled. In 2001, 10 master's, 2 doctorates awarded. Terminal master's awarded for partial completion of doctoral program.
Degree requirements: For master's, thesis or alternative; for doctorate, thesis/dissertation, residency.
Entrance requirements: For master's, GRE General Test; for doctorate, GRE General Test, minimum graduate GPA of 3.5. *Application deadline:* For fall admission, 6/5 (priority date); for spring admission, 10/15. Applications are processed on a rolling basis. *Application fee:* $50. Electronic applications accepted.
Expenses: Tuition, state resident: full-time $7,812; part-time $434 per credit. Tuition, nonresident: full-time $10,746; part-time $597 per credit. Required fees: $47 per credit. $76 per semester.
Financial support: Fellowships with full and partial tuition reimbursements, research assistantships with full and partial tuition reimbursements, teaching assistantships with full and partial tuition reimbursements, career-related internships or fieldwork, Federal Work-Study, institutionally sponsored loans, and unspecified assistantships available. Financial award application deadline: 3/15.
Faculty research: Water resources engineering, solid and hazardous waste management. *Total annual research expenditures:* $7 million.
Application contact: Kathryn Kelly, Director of Admissions, 973-596-3300, *Fax:* 973-596-3461, *E-mail:* admissions@ njit.edu. *Web site:* http://www.njit.edu/

■ NEW MEXICO INSTITUTE OF MINING AND TECHNOLOGY

Graduate Studies, Department of Environmental Engineering, Socorro, NM 87801

AWARDS Environmental engineering (MS), including air quality engineering and science, hazardous waste engineering, water quality engineering and science.

Faculty: 5 full-time (1 woman).
Students: 9 full-time (1 woman), 1 part-time; includes 2 minority (both Hispanic Americans), 6 international. Average age 25. 15 applicants, 60% accepted, 5 enrolled. In 2001, 3 degrees awarded.

Degree requirements: For master's, thesis.
Entrance requirements: For master's, GRE General Test, TOEFL. *Application deadline:* For fall admission, 3/1 (priority date); for spring admission, 6/1. Applications are processed on a rolling basis. *Application fee:* $16 ($30 for international students).
Expenses: Tuition, state resident: part-time $1,084 per semester. Tuition, nonresident: part-time $4,367 per semester. Required fees: $429 per semester.
Financial support: In 2001–02, 3 research assistantships (averaging $13,505 per year), 2 teaching assistantships with full and partial tuition reimbursements (averaging $12,714 per year) were awarded. Fellowships, Federal Work-Study and institutionally sponsored loans also available. Financial award application deadline: 3/1; financial award applicants required to submit CSS PROFILE or FAFSA.
Faculty research: Rock mechanics, geological engineering, mining problems, blasting, shock waves.
Dr. Clinton P. Richardson, Chair, 505-835-5346, *Fax:* 505-835-5252.
Application contact: Dr. David B. Johnson, Dean of Graduate Studies, 505-835-5513, *Fax:* 505-835-5476, *E-mail:* graduate@nmt.edu. *Web site:* http://www.nmt.edu/~mining/default.htm

■ NEW MEXICO STATE UNIVERSITY

Graduate School, College of Engineering, Department of Civil and Geological Engineering, Las Cruces, NM 88003-8001

AWARDS Civil engineering (MSCE, PhD); environmental engineering (MS Env E). Part-time programs available.

Faculty: 15 full-time (1 woman), 2 part-time/adjunct (0 women).
Students: 32 full-time (8 women), 16 part-time (5 women); includes 12 minority (1 Asian American or Pacific Islander, 10 Hispanic Americans, 1 Native American), 19 international. Average age 30. 39 applicants, 74% accepted, 12 enrolled. In 2001, 7 master's, 3 doctorates awarded.
Degree requirements: For master's, thesis (for some programs); for doctorate, thesis/dissertation.
Entrance requirements: For doctorate, BS in engineering, minimum GPA of 3.0. *Application deadline:* For fall admission, 7/1 (priority date); for spring admission, 11/1. Applications are processed on a rolling basis. *Application fee:* $15 ($35 for international students). Electronic applications accepted.
Expenses: Tuition, state resident: full-time $3,234; part-time $135 per credit. Tuition, nonresident: full-time $9,420; part-time $428 per credit. Required fees: $858.
Financial support: In 2001–02, 13 research assistantships, 17 teaching

assistantships were awarded. Fellowships, career-related internships or fieldwork and Federal Work-Study also available. Support available to part-time students. Financial award application deadline: 3/1.
Faculty research: Structural inspection, evaluation and testing, transportation engineering, hydraulics/hydrology, geotechnical engineering.
Dr. Ricardo B. Jacquez, Interim Head, 505-646-3801, *E-mail:* rjaquez@nmsu.edu. *Web site:* http://cagesun.nmsu.edu/

■ **NEW YORK INSTITUTE OF TECHNOLOGY**

Graduate Division, School of Engineering and Technology, Program in Environmental Technology, Old Westbury, NY 11568-8000

AWARDS MS. Part-time and evening/weekend programs available.

Students: 9 full-time (5 women), 38 part-time (8 women); includes 6 minority (2 African Americans, 4 Asian Americans or Pacific Islanders), 9 international. Average age 26. 27 applicants, 78% accepted, 12 enrolled. In 2001, 20 degrees awarded.
Degree requirements: For master's, thesis or alternative.
Entrance requirements: For master's, minimum QPA of 2.85. *Application deadline:* For fall admission, 7/1 (priority date); for spring admission, 12/1 (priority date). Applications are processed on a rolling basis. *Application fee:* $50. Electronic applications accepted.
Expenses: Tuition: Part-time $545 per credit. Tuition and fees vary according to course load, degree level, program and student level.
Financial support: In 2001–02, 1 research assistantship with partial tuition reimbursement was awarded; fellowships, career-related internships or fieldwork, institutionally sponsored loans, tuition waivers (full and partial), and unspecified assistantships also available. Support available to part-time students. Financial award applicants required to submit FAFSA.
Faculty research: Develop and test methodology to assess health risks and environmental impacts from separate sanitary sewage; introduction of technology innovation, including GIS.
Stanley Greenwald, Chair, 516-686-7969.
Application contact: Jacquelyn Nealon, Dean of Admissions and Financial Aid, 516-686-7925, *Fax:* 516-686-7613, *E-mail:* jnealon@nyit.edu.

■ **NORTH CAROLINA AGRICULTURAL AND TECHNICAL STATE UNIVERSITY**

Graduate School, College of Engineering, Department of Architectural, Agricultural, Civil and Environmental Engineering, Greensboro, NC 27411

AWARDS MSAE, MSCE, MSE. Part-time programs available.

Faculty: 14 full-time (1 woman), 4 part-time/adjunct (0 women).
Students: 28 full-time (10 women), 10 part-time (4 women), 12 international. Average age 24. 22 applicants, 41% accepted. In 2001, 4 degrees awarded.
Degree requirements: For master's, thesis defense.
Entrance requirements: For master's, GRE General Test, GRE Subject Test (recommended), TOEFL (MSCE). *Application deadline:* For fall admission, 7/1; for spring admission, 1/9. Applications are processed on a rolling basis. *Application fee:* $35.
Financial support: In 2001–02, 1 fellowship (averaging $12,000 per year), 3 research assistantships (averaging $12,000 per year), 2 teaching assistantships (averaging $10,000 per year) were awarded. Career-related internships or fieldwork and unspecified assistantships also available.
Faculty research: Lightning, indoor air quality, material behavior HVAC controls, structural masonry systems. *Total annual research expenditures:* $800,000.
Dr. Peter Rojeski, Chairperson, 336-344-7575, *Fax:* 336-344-7126.
Application contact: Dr. W. Mark McGinley, Graduate Coordinator, 336-334-7575, *Fax:* 336-334-7126, *E-mail:* mcginley@garfield.ncat.edu.

■ **NORTH DAKOTA STATE UNIVERSITY**

The Graduate School, College of Engineering and Architecture, Department of Civil Engineering, Fargo, ND 58105

AWARDS Civil engineering (MS); environmental engineering (MS); natural resource management (MS). Part-time programs available. Postbaccalaureate distance learning degree programs offered (minimal on-campus study).

Faculty: 8 full-time (1 woman), 4 part-time/adjunct (0 women).
Students: 15 full-time (2 women); includes 7 minority (all Asian Americans or Pacific Islanders). Average age 22. 20 applicants, 75% accepted. In 2001, 2 degrees awarded.
Degree requirements: For master's, thesis or alternative.
Entrance requirements: For master's, TOEFL. *Application deadline:* For fall

admission, 7/1 (priority date). Applications are processed on a rolling basis. *Application fee:* $35.
Expenses: Tuition, state resident: part-time $124 per credit. Tuition, nonresident: part-time $325 per credit. Required fees: $22 per credit. Tuition and fees vary according to reciprocity agreements.
Financial support: In 2001–02, 4 research assistantships with full tuition reimbursements (averaging $3,740 per year), 9 teaching assistantships with full tuition reimbursements (averaging $1,870 per year) were awarded. Fellowships with full tuition reimbursements, career-related internships or fieldwork, Federal Work-Study, and institutionally sponsored loans also available. Support available to part-time students. Financial award application deadline: 4/15.
Faculty research: Wastewater, hydrology, structures, transportation, solid waste. *Total annual research expenditures:* $150,000.
G. Padmanabhan, Chair, 701-231-7043, *Fax:* 701-231-6185, *E-mail:* g.padmanabhan@ndsu.nodak.edu. *Web site:* http://www.ndsu.nodak.edu/

■ **NORTHEASTERN UNIVERSITY**

College of Engineering, Department of Civil and Environmental Engineering, Boston, MA 02115-5096

AWARDS MS, PhD. Part-time programs available.

Faculty: 12 full-time (1 woman), 1 part-time/adjunct (0 women).
Students: 41 full-time (8 women), 67 part-time (10 women); includes 1 minority (Hispanic American), 34 international. Average age 25. 133 applicants, 76% accepted, 32 enrolled.
Degree requirements: For master's, thesis optional; for doctorate, thesis/dissertation, departmental qualifying exam. *Median time to degree:* Master's–2 years full-time, 5.5 years part-time.
Entrance requirements: For master's and doctorate, GRE General Test. *Application deadline:* For fall admission, 2/15 (priority date). Applications are processed on a rolling basis. *Application fee:* $50. Electronic applications accepted.
Expenses: Tuition: Part-time $535 per credit hour. Required fees: $56. Tuition and fees vary according to program.
Financial support: In 2001–02, 30 students received support, including 1 fellowship, 10 research assistantships with full tuition reimbursements available (averaging $13,560 per year), 13 teaching assistantships with full tuition reimbursements available (averaging $13,560 per year); career-related internships or fieldwork, Federal Work-Study, scholarships/grants, tuition waivers (full), and unspecified assistantships also available. Support available to part-time students. Financial award application deadline: 2/15; financial award applicants required to submit FAFSA.

Northeastern University (continued)
Faculty research: Earthquake engineering, geotechnical and geoenvironmental engineering, structural engineering, transportation engineering. *Total annual research expenditures:* $913,755.
Dr. Peter Furth, Acting Chairman, 617-373-2444, *Fax:* 617-373-4419.
Application contact: Stephen L. Gibson, Associate Director, 617-373-2711, *Fax:* 617-373-2501, *E-mail:* grad-eng@coe.neu.edu. *Web site:* http://www.coe.neu.edu/

■ NORTHWESTERN UNIVERSITY

McCormick School of Engineering and Applied Science, Department of Civil and Environmental Engineering, Evanston, IL 60208

AWARDS Environmental engineering and science (MS, PhD); geotechnical engineering (MS, PhD); mechanics of materials and solids (MS, PhD); project management (MPM). Structural engineering and materials (MS, PhD); theoretical and applied mechanics (MS, PhD); transportation systems analysis and planning (MS, PhD). MS and PhD admissions and degrees offered through The Graduate School. Part-time programs available.

Faculty: 26 full-time (3 women), 9 part-time/adjunct (2 women).
Students: 80 full-time (32 women), 1 part-time; includes 2 Asian Americans or Pacific Islanders, 1 Hispanic American, 38 international. 282 applicants, 7% accepted. In 2001, 20 master's, 14 doctorates awarded. Terminal master's awarded for partial completion of doctoral program.
Degree requirements: For master's, thesis (for some programs); for doctorate, thesis/dissertation.
Application deadline: For fall admission, 8/1. *Application fee:* $50 ($55 for international students). Electronic applications accepted.
Expenses: Tuition: Full-time $26,526.
Financial support: In 2001–02, 10 fellowships with full tuition reimbursements (averaging $13,338 per year), 66 research assistantships with partial tuition reimbursements (averaging $18,000 per year), 7 teaching assistantships with full tuition reimbursements (averaging $13,329 per year) were awarded. Career-related internships or fieldwork, institutionally sponsored loans, and scholarships/grants also available. Financial award application deadline: 1/15; financial award applicants required to submit FAFSA.
Faculty research: Environmental engineering and science; geotechnics, mechanics of materials and solids, structural engineering and materials, transportation systems analysis and planning. *Total annual research expenditures:* $8.4 million.
Joseph L. Schofer, Chair, 847-491-3257, *Fax:* 847-491-4011, *E-mail:* j-schofer@northwestern.edu.
Application contact: Janet Soule, Academic Coordinator, 847-491-3176, *Fax:*

847-491-4011, *E-mail:* civil-info@northwestern.edu. *Web site:* http://www.civil.northwestern.edu/

Find an in-depth description at www.petersons.com/gradchannel.

■ OGI SCHOOL OF SCIENCE & ENGINEERING AT OREGON HEALTH & SCIENCE UNIVERSITY

Graduate Studies, Department of Environmental Science and Engineering, Beaverton, OR 97006-8921

AWARDS Ecosystem management and restoration (MS); environmental information technology (PhD); environmental science (MS, PhD); environmental science and engineering (MS, PhD); environmental systems management (MS). Part-time programs available.

Faculty: 8 full-time (1 woman).
Students: 17 full-time (5 women), 2 part-time. Average age 28. 41 applicants, 73% accepted. In 2001, 16 master's, 2 doctorates awarded. Terminal master's awarded for partial completion of doctoral program.
Degree requirements: For master's, thesis optional; for doctorate, oral defense of dissertation.
Entrance requirements: For master's and doctorate, GRE General Test, TOEFL. *Application fee:* $50. Electronic applications accepted.
Expenses: Tuition: Full-time $4,905; part-time $545 per credit hour. Required fees: $466.
Financial support: In 2001–02, 5 research assistantships with full and partial tuition reimbursements were awarded; fellowships, teaching assistantships, Federal Work-Study and scholarships/grants also available. Financial award application deadline: 2/15.
Faculty research: Air and water science, hydrogeology, estuarine and coastal modeling, environmental microbiology, contaminant transport. *Total annual research expenditures:* $3.2 million.
Dr. Antonio M. Baptista, Head, 503-748-1147, *Fax:* 503-748-1273, *E-mail:* baptista@ccalmr.ogi.edu.
Application contact: Therese Young, 800-748-1247, *E-mail:* tyoung@ese.ogi.edu. *Web site:* http://www.ese.ogi.edu/

Find an in-depth description at www.petersons.com/gradchannel.

■ OHIO UNIVERSITY

Graduate Studies, Russ College of Engineering and Technology, Department of Civil Engineering, Athens, OH 45701-2979

AWARDS Geotechnical and environmental engineering (MS); water resources and structures (MS).

Faculty: 11 full-time (1 woman).

Students: 19 full-time (4 women), 6 part-time (2 women), 18 international. Average age 28. 52 applicants, 71% accepted, 11 enrolled. In 2001, 7 degrees awarded.
Degree requirements: For master's, thesis optional.
Entrance requirements: For master's, minimum GPA of 3.0. *Application deadline:* For fall admission, 5/1 (priority date). Applications are processed on a rolling basis. *Application fee:* $30.
Expenses: Tuition, state resident: full-time $6,585. Tuition, nonresident: full-time $12,254.
Financial support: In 2001–02, 1 fellowship (averaging $15,000 per year), 12 research assistantships (averaging $12,000 per year), 6 teaching assistantships (averaging $6,000 per year) were awarded. Federal Work-Study, institutionally sponsored loans, and tuition waivers (full and partial) also available. Financial award application deadline: 3/15.
Faculty research: Soil-structure interaction, solid waste management, pipes, pavements, noise pollution, mine reclamation, drought analysis. *Total annual research expenditures:* $1.2 million.
Dr. Gayle Mitchell, Chair, 740-593-1465, *Fax:* 740-593-0625, *E-mail:* gmitchell@bobcat.ent.ohiou.edu.
Application contact: Dr. Shad Sargand, Graduate Chair, 740-593-1467, *Fax:* 740-593-0625, *E-mail:* ssargand@bobcat.ent.ohiou.edu. *Web site:* http://webce.ent.ohiou.edu/

■ OHIO UNIVERSITY

Graduate Studies, Russ College of Engineering and Technology, Integrated Engineering Program, Athens, OH 45701-2979

AWARDS Geotechnical and environmental engineering (PhD); intelligent systems (PhD); materials processing (PhD).

Faculty: 39 full-time (1 woman).
Students: 16 full-time (1 woman), 8 part-time (1 woman), 21 international. 34 applicants, 88% accepted. In 2001, 3 degrees awarded.
Degree requirements: For doctorate, thesis/dissertation, comprehensive exam.
Entrance requirements: For doctorate, GRE General Test, MS in engineering or related field. *Application deadline:* For fall admission, 3/15. Applications are processed on a rolling basis. *Application fee:* $30.
Expenses: Tuition, state resident: full-time $6,585. Tuition, nonresident: full-time $12,254.
Financial support: In 2001–02, 3 fellowships with full tuition reimbursements (averaging $10,500 per year), 3 research assistantships with full tuition reimbursements (averaging $10,500 per year) were awarded. Federal Work-Study, institutionally sponsored loans, and tuition waivers (full) also available. Financial award application deadline: 3/15.

Faculty research: Material processing, expert systems, environmental geotechnical manufacturing. *Total annual research expenditures:* $1.5 million.
Dr. Jerrel Mitchell, Associate Dean for Research and Graduate Studies, 740-593-1482, *E-mail:* mitchell@ bobcat.ent.ohiou.edu.

Find an in-depth description at www.petersons.com/gradchannel.

■ OKLAHOMA STATE UNIVERSITY

Graduate College, College of Engineering, Architecture and Technology, School of Civil and Environmental Engineering, Stillwater, OK 74078

AWARDS Civil engineering (M En, MS, PhD); environmental engineering (M En, MS, PhD).

Faculty: 14 full-time (1 woman), 1 part-time/adjunct (0 women).
Students: 33 full-time (2 women), 32 part-time (1 woman); includes 8 minority (2 African Americans, 1 Asian American or Pacific Islander, 3 Hispanic Americans, 2 Native Americans), 32 international. Average age 30. 130 applicants, 68% accepted. In 2001, 23 master's, 2 doctorates awarded.
Degree requirements: For master's, thesis or alternative; for doctorate, thesis/dissertation.
Entrance requirements: For master's and doctorate, TOEFL. *Application deadline:* For fall admission, 7/1 (priority date). *Application fee:* $25.
Expenses: Tuition, state resident: part-time $92 per credit hour. Tuition, nonresident: part-time $297 per credit hour. Required fees: $21 per credit hour. $14 per semester. One-time fee: $20. Tuition and fees vary according to course load.
Financial support: In 2001–02, 27 students received support, including 9 research assistantships (averaging $8,480 per year), 9 teaching assistantships (averaging $6,667 per year); career-related internships or fieldwork, Federal Work-Study, and tuition waivers (partial) also available. Support available to part-time students. Financial award application deadline: 3/1.
Dr. Gosman Gilbert, Head, 405-744-5190.

■ OLD DOMINION UNIVERSITY

College of Engineering and Technology, Program in Environmental Engineering, Norfolk, VA 23529

AWARDS ME, MS, PhD. Part-time and evening/weekend programs available. Postbaccalaureate distance learning degree programs offered (minimal on-campus study).

Faculty: 10 full-time (2 women), 2 part-time/adjunct (0 women).
Students: 10 full-time (4 women), 30 part-time (10 women); includes 4 minority (2

Asian Americans or Pacific Islanders, 2 Hispanic Americans), 20 international. Average age 28. 62 applicants, 97% accepted, 20 enrolled. In 2001, 10 master's, 1 doctorate awarded.
Degree requirements: For master's, thesis optional; for doctorate, thesis/dissertation, candidacy exam.
Application deadline: For fall admission, 7/1; for spring admission, 10/1. Applications are processed on a rolling basis. *Application fee:* $30. Electronic applications accepted.
Expenses: Tuition, state resident: part-time $202 per credit. Tuition, nonresident: part-time $534 per credit. Required fees: $76 per semester.
Financial support: In 2001–02, 1 fellowship with partial tuition reimbursement (averaging $5,000 per year), 6 research assistantships with full and partial tuition reimbursements (averaging $7,618 per year), 3 teaching assistantships with full and partial tuition reimbursements (averaging $6,666 per year) were awarded. Career-related internships or fieldwork, scholarships/grants, tuition waivers, and unspecified assistantships also available. Support available to part-time students. Financial award application deadline: 3/15.
Faculty research: Aquatic chemistry, physiochemical treatment, waste water treatment, hazardous waste treatment, environmental microbiology, water quality modeling.
Dr. Isao Ishibashi, Graduate Program Director, 757-683-4641, *Fax:* 757-683-5354, *E-mail:* cegpd@odu.edu. *Web site:* http://cee.odu.edu/

■ OREGON STATE UNIVERSITY

Graduate School, College of Engineering, Department of Civil, Construction, and Environmental Engineering, Corvallis, OR 97331

AWARDS Civil engineering (MAIS, MS, PhD); ocean engineering (M Oc E). Part-time programs available.

Faculty: 21 full-time (1 woman), 1 (woman) part-time/adjunct.
Students: 60 full-time (14 women), 8 part-time (2 women); includes 5 minority (1 African American, 1 Asian American or Pacific Islander, 2 Hispanic Americans, 1 Native American), 32 international. Average age 29. In 2001, 24 master's, 1 doctorate awarded. Terminal master's awarded for partial completion of doctoral program.
Degree requirements: For master's, thesis or alternative; for doctorate, one foreign language, thesis/dissertation.
Entrance requirements: For master's, GRE General Test, TOEFL, minimum GPA of 3.0 in last 90 hours (3.5 for MS); for doctorate, GRE General Test, TOEFL, minimum GPA of 3.0 in last 90 hours of undergraduate course work.
Application deadline: For fall admission, 3/1 (priority date). Applications are processed on a rolling basis. *Application fee:* $50.

Expenses: Tuition, area resident: Full-time $15,933. Tuition, state resident: full-time $28,937.
Financial support: Fellowships, research assistantships, teaching assistantships, career-related internships or fieldwork and institutionally sponsored loans available. Support available to part-time students. Financial award application deadline: 2/1.
Faculty research: Hazardous waste management, carbon cycling, wave forces on structures, pavement design, seismic analysis.
Kenneth J. Williamson, Head, 541-737-6836, *E-mail:* kenneth.williamson@ orst.edu.

Application contact: Linda A. Rowe, Office Manager, 541-737-6149, *Fax:* 541-737-3052, *E-mail:* linda.rowe@orst.edu. *Web site:* http://www.ccee.orst.edu/

■ OREGON STATE UNIVERSITY

Graduate School, College of Forestry, Department of Forest Engineering, Corvallis, OR 97331

AWARDS MAIS, MF, MS, PhD. Part-time programs available.

Faculty: 12 full-time (0 women).
Students: 16 full-time (8 women), 2 part-time (1 woman), 4 international. Average age 28. In 2001, 3 degrees awarded.
Degree requirements: For master's and doctorate, thesis/dissertation.
Entrance requirements: For master's and doctorate, GRE General Test, TOEFL, minimum GPA of 3.0 in last 90 hours.
Application deadline: For fall admission, 3/1. Applications are processed on a rolling basis. *Application fee:* $50.
Expenses: Tuition, area resident: Full-time $15,933. Tuition, state resident: full-time $28,937.
Financial support: Fellowships, research assistantships, career-related internships or fieldwork, Federal Work-Study, and institutionally sponsored loans available. Support available to part-time students. Financial award application deadline: 2/1.
Faculty research: Timber harvesting systems, forest hydrology, slope stability, impacts of harvesting on soil and water, training of logging labor force.
Dr. Steven D. Teschs, Head, 541-737-4952, *Fax:* 541-737-4316, *E-mail:* teschs@ for.orst.edu.

Application contact: Rayetta Beall, Office Manager, 541-737-1345, *Fax:* 541-737-4316, *E-mail:* rayetta.beall@orst.edu. *Web site:* http://www.cof.orst.edu/cof/fe/

■ THE PENNSYLVANIA STATE UNIVERSITY HARRISBURG CAMPUS OF THE CAPITAL COLLEGE

Graduate Center, School of Science, Engineering and Technology, Program in Environmental Pollution Control, Middletown, PA 17057-4898

AWARDS M Eng, MEPC, MS. Evening/weekend programs available.

Students: 13 full-time (7 women), 26 part-time (7 women). Average age 33. In 2001, 2 degrees awarded.

Degree requirements: For master's, thesis.

Entrance requirements: For master's, GRE General Test, TOEFL, minimum GPA of 2.75. *Application deadline:* For fall admission, 7/26. *Application fee:* $50.

Expenses: Tuition, state resident: full-time $7,882; part-time $333 per credit. Tuition, nonresident: full-time $14,384; part-time $600 per credit.

Dr. Charles Cole, Interim Coordinator, 717-948-6358.

■ THE PENNSYLVANIA STATE UNIVERSITY UNIVERSITY PARK CAMPUS

Graduate School, College of Earth and Mineral Sciences, Department of Energy and Geo-Environmental Engineering, Program in Geo-Environmental Engineering, State College, University Park, PA 16802-1503

AWARDS MS, PhD.

Students: 9 full-time (0 women), 1 part-time.

Degree requirements: For doctorate, thesis/dissertation.

Entrance requirements: For doctorate, GRE General Test, TOEFL. *Application fee:* $45.

Expenses: Tuition, state resident: full-time $7,882; part-time $333 per credit. Tuition, nonresident: full-time $16,142; part-time $673 per credit. Required fees: $124 per semester.

Financial support: Application deadline: 12/31.

Derek Elsworth, Graduate Program Chair, 814-863-1343.

■ THE PENNSYLVANIA STATE UNIVERSITY UNIVERSITY PARK CAMPUS

Graduate School, College of Engineering, Department of Civil and Environmental Engineering, Program in Environmental Engineering, State College, University Park, PA 16802-1503

AWARDS M Eng, MS, PhD.

Students: 22 full-time (9 women), 9 part-time (2 women). In 2001, 12 master's, 2 doctorates awarded.

Degree requirements: For master's, final paper (M Eng), oral exam and thesis (MS); for doctorate, one foreign language, thesis/dissertation, oral exams, comprehensive exam.

Entrance requirements: For master's and doctorate, GRE General Test, BS in engineering. *Application fee:* $45.

Expenses: Tuition, state resident: full-time $7,882; part-time $333 per credit. Tuition, nonresident: full-time $16,142; part-time $673 per credit. Required fees: $124 per semester.

Financial support: Fellowships, research assistantships, teaching assistantships available.

Faculty research: Physical, chemical, and biological treatment processes; reclamation and treatment of hazardous and toxic wastes. Subsoil transport of pollutants.
Brian A. Dempsey, Head, 814-865-1226.

■ POLYTECHNIC UNIVERSITY, BROOKLYN CAMPUS

Department of Civil and Environmental Engineering, Major in Environmental Engineering, Brooklyn, NY 11201-2990

AWARDS MS. Part-time and evening/weekend programs available.

Degree requirements: For master's, thesis or alternative.
Electronic applications accepted.

■ POLYTECHNIC UNIVERSITY, LONG ISLAND GRADUATE CENTER

Graduate Programs, Department of Civil and Environmental Engineering, Major in Environmental Engineering, Melville, NY 11747

AWARDS MS.
Electronic applications accepted.

■ POLYTECHNIC UNIVERSITY, WESTCHESTER GRADUATE CENTER

Graduate Programs, Department of Civil and Environmental Engineering, Major in Environmental Engineering, Hawthorne, NY 10532-1507

AWARDS MS.

Degree requirements: For master's, thesis (for some programs).
Electronic applications accepted.

■ PRINCETON UNIVERSITY

Graduate School, Department of Geosciences, Princeton, NJ 08544-1019

AWARDS Atmospheric and oceanic sciences (PhD); environmental engineering and water

resources (PhD); geological and geophysical sciences (PhD).

Degree requirements: For doctorate, one foreign language, thesis/dissertation.
Entrance requirements: For doctorate, GRE General Test, GRE Subject Test.

■ PRINCETON UNIVERSITY

Graduate School, School of Engineering and Applied Science, Department of Civil and Environmental Engineering and Department of Geosciences, Program in Environmental Engineering and Water Resources, Princeton, NJ 08544-1019

AWARDS PhD.

Degree requirements: For doctorate, one foreign language, thesis/dissertation.
Entrance requirements: For doctorate, GRE General Test, GRE Subject Test.

Find an in-depth description at www.petersons.com/gradchannel.

■ RENSSELAER POLYTECHNIC INSTITUTE

Graduate School, School of Engineering, Department of Civil and Environmental Engineering, Program in Environmental Engineering, Troy, NY 12180-3590

AWARDS M Eng, MS, D Eng, PhD. Part-time programs available.

Faculty: 5 full-time (1 woman), 2 part-time/adjunct (0 women).

Students: 17 full-time, 6 part-time; includes 4 minority (1 African American, 2 Asian Americans or Pacific Islanders, 1 Hispanic American), 9 international. 65 applicants, 35% accepted. In 2001, 5 master's, 1 doctorate awarded.

Degree requirements: For master's, thesis (for some programs); for doctorate, thesis/dissertation.

Entrance requirements: For master's and doctorate, GRE, TOEFL. *Application deadline:* For fall admission, 1/15 (priority date). Applications are processed on a rolling basis. *Application fee:* $45. Electronic applications accepted.

Expenses: Tuition: Full-time $26,400; part-time $1,320 per credit hour. Required fees: $1,437.

Financial support: In 2001–02, 11 students received support, including 6 research assistantships with full and partial tuition reimbursements available, 5 teaching assistantships with partial tuition reimbursements available; fellowships, career-related internships or fieldwork, institutionally sponsored loans, and tuition waivers (full and partial) also available. Financial award application deadline: 2/1.

Faculty research: Water treatment and membrane processes, sediment decontamination, bioremediation of hazardous wastes, environmental

chemistry, mathematical modeling. *Total annual research expenditures:* $250,000.
Dr. George List, Department Chair, 518-276-6362, *Fax:* 518-276-4833, *E-mail:* listg@rpi.edu.
Application contact: Nicole Gulley-Hughes, Administrative Secretary, 518-276-2993, *Fax:* 518-276-2095, *E-mail:* guilyn@rpi.edu. *Web site:* http://www.cee.rpi.edu/

Find an in-depth description at www.petersons.com/gradchannel.

■ RICE UNIVERSITY

Graduate Programs, George R. Brown School of Engineering, Department of Environmental Science and Engineering, Houston, TX 77251-1892

AWARDS Environmental engineering (MEE, MES, MS, PhD); environmental science (MEE, MES, MS, PhD). Part-time programs available.

Faculty: 6 full-time (0 women), 5 part-time/adjunct (0 women).
Students: 22 full-time (14 women), 1 part-time; includes 7 minority (1 African American, 3 Asian Americans or Pacific Islanders, 3 Hispanic Americans), 7 international. Average age 23. 50 applicants, 12% accepted, 5 enrolled. In 2001, 7 master's, 1 doctorate awarded.
Degree requirements: For master's, thesis (for some programs); for doctorate, thesis/dissertation.
Entrance requirements: For master's and doctorate, GRE General Test, GRE Subject Test, TOEFL, minimum GPA of 3.25. *Application deadline:* For fall admission, 2/1 (priority date); for spring admission, 11/1. Applications are processed on a rolling basis. *Application fee:* $25. Electronic applications accepted.
Expenses: Tuition: Full-time $17,300. Required fees: $250.
Financial support: In 2001–02, 4 fellowships with full tuition reimbursements (averaging $16,000 per year), 18 research assistantships with full and partial tuition reimbursements (averaging $16,000 per year) were awarded. Scholarships/grants and traineeships also available.
Faculty research: Biology and chemistry of groundwater, pollutant fate in groundwater systems, water quality monitoring, urban storm water runoff, urban air quality. *Total annual research expenditures:* $1.1 million.
Dr. Joe Hughes, Chair, 713-348-5903, *Fax:* 713-348-5203, *E-mail:* hughes@rice.edu.
Application contact: Emily J.P. Hall, Department Coordinator, 713-348-4951, *Fax:* 713-348-5203, *E-mail:* envi@rice.edu. *Web site:* http://dacnet.rice.edu/depts/envi/

■ ROSE-HULMAN INSTITUTE OF TECHNOLOGY

Faculty of Engineering and Applied Sciences, Program in Environmental Engineering, Terre Haute, IN 47803-3920

AWARDS MS. Part-time programs available.

Faculty: 6 full-time (1 woman).
Students: 1 (woman) full-time, 2 part-time (1 woman), 1 international. Average age 23. 5 applicants, 80% accepted, 1 enrolled. In 2001, 2 degrees awarded.
Degree requirements: For master's, thesis.
Entrance requirements: For master's, GRE, TOEFL, minimum GPA of 3.0. *Application deadline:* For fall admission, 2/1 (priority date). Applications are processed on a rolling basis. *Application fee:* $0.
Expenses: Tuition: Full-time $21,792; part-time $615 per credit hour. Required fees: $405.
Financial support: In 2001–02, 2 students received support; fellowships with full and partial tuition reimbursements available, research assistantships with full and partial tuition reimbursements available, institutionally sponsored loans, scholarships/grants, and tuition waivers (full and partial) available. Financial award application deadline: 2/1.
Faculty research: Urban stormwater management, groundwater and surface water models, solid and hazardous waste, risk and decision analysis. *Total annual research expenditures:* $4,000.
Sharon A. Jones, Advisor, 812-877-8279, *Fax:* 812-877-3198, *E-mail:* sharon.jones@rose-hulman.edu.
Application contact: Dr. Daniel J. Moore, Interim Associate Dean of the Faculty, 812-877-8110, *Fax:* 812-877-8061, *E-mail:* daniel.j.moore@rose-hulman.edu.

■ RUTGERS, THE STATE UNIVERSITY OF NEW JERSEY, NEW BRUNSWICK

Graduate School, Program in Civil and Environmental Engineering, New Brunswick, NJ 08901-1281

AWARDS MS, PhD. Part-time and evening/weekend programs available. Terminal master's awarded for partial completion of doctoral program.

Degree requirements: For master's, thesis or alternative; for doctorate, thesis/dissertation.
Entrance requirements: For master's and doctorate, GRE General Test.
Faculty research: Structural mechanics, soil mechanics, environmental geotechnology, water resources, computational mechanics. *Web site:* http://www.liveng.rutgers.edu/

■ SAN JOSE STATE UNIVERSITY

Graduate Studies, College of Engineering, Department of Civil Engineering and Applied Mechanics, San Jose, CA 95192-0001

AWARDS Civil and environmental engineering (MS).

Faculty: 15 full-time (2 women), 9 part-time/adjunct (0 women).
Students: 22 full-time (11 women), 47 part-time (15 women); includes 37 minority (2 African Americans, 28 Asian Americans or Pacific Islanders, 6 Hispanic Americans, 1 Native American), 8 international. Average age 30. 53 applicants, 79% accepted. In 2001, 35 degrees awarded.
Degree requirements: For master's, thesis or alternative.
Entrance requirements: For master's, minimum GPA of 2.7. *Application deadline:* For fall admission, 6/29; for spring admission, 11/30. Applications are processed on a rolling basis. *Application fee:* $59. Electronic applications accepted.
Expenses: Tuition, nonresident: part-time $246 per unit. Required fees: $678 per semester. Tuition and fees vary according to course load.
Financial support: Applicants required to submit FAFSA.
Dick Desautel, Acting Chair, 408-924-3900, *Fax:* 408-924-4004.
Application contact: Dr. Rhea Williamson, Graduate Adviser, 408-924-3849.

■ SOUTH DAKOTA STATE UNIVERSITY

Graduate School, College of Engineering, Department of Civil and Environmental Engineering, Brookings, SD 57007

AWARDS Engineering (MS), including civil engineering, environmental engineering.

Degree requirements: For master's, thesis, oral exam.
Entrance requirements: For master's, TOEFL.
Faculty research: Groundwater modeling, biological wastewater treatment, corrosion control, highway materials, traffic analysis.

■ SOUTHERN METHODIST UNIVERSITY

School of Engineering, Department of Environmental and Civil Engineering, Dallas, TX 75275

AWARDS Applied science (MS, PhD); civil engineering (MS); environmental engineering (MS); environmental systems management (MS). Part-time and evening/weekend programs available. Postbaccalaureate distance learning degree programs offered.

Students: 2 full-time (1 woman), 26 part-time (9 women); includes 12 minority (6

Southern Methodist University (continued)
African Americans, 2 Asian Americans or Pacific Islanders, 4 Hispanic Americans). In 2001, 23 degrees awarded. Terminal master's awarded for partial completion of doctoral program.

Degree requirements: For master's, thesis optional; for doctorate, thesis/ dissertation, oral and written qualifying exams.

Entrance requirements: For master's, GRE General Test, TOEFL, minimum GPA of 3.0 in last 2 years; bachelor's degree in engineering, mathematics, or sciences; for doctorate, bachelor's degree in related field. *Application deadline:* For fall admission, 7/1; for spring admission, 11/15. Applications are processed on a rolling basis. *Application fee:* $50.

Expenses: Tuition: Part-time $285 per credit hour.

Dr. Edward Forest, Head, 214-768-2280, *Fax:* 214-768-3845, *E-mail:* eforest@ seas.smu.edu.

Application contact: Marc Valerin, Associate Director of Graduate Admissions, 214-768-3484, *E-mail:* valerin@ seas.smu.edu.

Find an in-depth description at www.petersons.com/gradchannel.

■ STANFORD UNIVERSITY

School of Engineering, Department of Civil and Environmental Engineering, Stanford, CA 94305-9991

AWARDS MS, PhD, Eng.

Faculty: 28 full-time (3 women).
Students: 213 full-time (83 women), 40 part-time (19 women); includes 47 minority (7 African Americans, 21 Asian Americans or Pacific Islanders, 17 Hispanic Americans, 2 Native Americans), 110 international. Average age 27. 476 applicants, 47% accepted. In 2001, 122 master's, 12 doctorates awarded. Terminal master's awarded for partial completion of doctoral program.

Degree requirements: For doctorate and Eng, thesis/dissertation, qualifying exam.

Entrance requirements: For master's, doctorate, and Eng, GRE General Test, TOEFL. *Application deadline:* For fall admission, 1/5. *Application fee:* $65 ($80 for international students). Electronic applications accepted.

Clyde B. Tatum, Chair, 650-723-3921, *Fax:* 650-725-8662, *E-mail:* tatumce@ stanford.edu.

Application contact: Graduate Admissions Coordinator, 650-725-2387. *Web site:* http://www-ce.stanford.edu/

■ STATE UNIVERSITY OF NEW YORK COLLEGE OF ENVIRONMENTAL SCIENCE AND FORESTRY

Faculty of Construction Management and Wood Products Engineering, Syracuse, NY 13210-2779

AWARDS Environmental and resources engineering (MPS, MS, PhD).

Faculty: 8 full-time (0 women), 1 (woman) part-time/adjunct.
Students: 7 full-time (1 woman), 15 part-time (3 women), 8 international. Average age 36. 4 applicants, 100% accepted, 4 enrolled. In 2001, 3 master's, 3 doctorates awarded.

Degree requirements: For master's, thesis (for some programs), registration; for doctorate, thesis/dissertation, comprehensive exam, registration.

Entrance requirements: For master's and doctorate, GRE General Test, minimum GPA of 3.0. *Application deadline:* For fall admission, 2/1 (priority date); for spring admission, 11/1 (priority date). Applications are processed on a rolling basis. *Application fee:* $50.

Expenses: Tuition, area resident: Part-time $213 per credit hour. Tuition, state resident: full-time $5,100. Tuition, nonresident: full-time $8,416; part-time $351 per credit hour. Required fees: $250. One-time fee: $43 full-time.

Financial support: In 2001–02, 8 students received support, including 2 fellowships with full tuition reimbursements available (averaging $8,817 per year), 3 research assistantships with full tuition reimbursements available (averaging $9,000 per year), 3 teaching assistantships with full tuition reimbursements available (averaging $8,817 per year); career-related internships or fieldwork, Federal Work-Study, institutionally sponsored loans, scholarships/grants, health care benefits, and unspecified assistantships also available. Financial award applicants required to submit FAFSA. *Total annual research expenditures:* $67,860.

Dr. George H. Kyanka, Chair, 315-470-6835, *Fax:* 315-470-6879.

Application contact: Dr. Robert H. Frey, Dean, Instruction and Graduate Studies, 315-470-6599, *Fax:* 315-470-6879, *E-mail:* esfgrad@esf.edu. *Web site:* http://www.esf.edu/faculty/wpe/

■ STATE UNIVERSITY OF NEW YORK COLLEGE OF ENVIRONMENTAL SCIENCE AND FORESTRY

Faculty of Environmental Resources and Forest Engineering, Syracuse, NY 13210-2779

AWARDS Environmental and resources engineering (MPS, MS, PhD).

Faculty: 7 full-time (1 woman).
Students: 15 full-time (5 women), 48 part-time (12 women); includes 3 minority (1 African American, 2 Asian Americans or Pacific Islanders), 8 international. Average age 33. 31 applicants, 71% accepted, 12 enrolled. In 2001, 6 degrees awarded.

Degree requirements: For master's, thesis (for some programs), registration; for doctorate, thesis/dissertation, comprehensive exam, registration.

Entrance requirements: For master's and doctorate, GRE General Test, minimum GPA of 3.0. *Application deadline:* For fall admission, 2/1 (priority date); for spring admission, 11/1. Applications are processed on a rolling basis. *Application fee:* $50.

Expenses: Tuition, area resident: Part-time $213 per credit hour. Tuition, state resident: full-time $5,100. Tuition, nonresident: full-time $8,416; part-time $351 per credit hour. Required fees: $250. One-time fee: $43 full-time.

Financial support: In 2001–02, 20 students received support, including 3 fellowships with full and partial tuition reimbursements available (averaging $8,817 per year), 12 research assistantships with full and partial tuition reimbursements available (averaging $9,000 per year), 5 teaching assistantships with full and partial tuition reimbursements available (averaging $8,817 per year); Federal Work-Study, institutionally sponsored loans, scholarships/grants, health care benefits, and unspecified assistantships also available. Financial award applicants required to submit FAFSA.

Faculty research: Forest engineering, paper science and engineering, wood products engineering. *Total annual research expenditures:* $2.9 million.

Dr. James M. Hassett, Chairperson, 315-470-6633, *Fax:* 315-470-6958, *E-mail:* jhassett@esf.edu.

Application contact: Dr. Robert H. Frey, Dean, Instruction and Graduate Studies, 315-470-6599, *Fax:* 315-470-6978, *E-mail:* esfgrad@esf.edu. *Web site:* http://www.esf.edu/faculty/feg/

■ STATE UNIVERSITY OF NEW YORK COLLEGE OF ENVIRONMENTAL SCIENCE AND FORESTRY

Faculty of Paper Science and Engineering, Syracuse, NY 13210-2779

AWARDS Environmental and resources engineering (MS); environmental and resources engineering (PhD).

Faculty: 7 full-time (0 women).
Students: 7 full-time (3 women), 7 part-time (3 women), 11 international. 10 applicants, 80% accepted, 2 enrolled. In 2001, 2 degrees awarded.

Degree requirements: For master's, thesis/dissertation, registration; for doctorate, thesis/dissertation, comprehensive exam, registration.

Entrance requirements: For master's and doctorate, GRE General Test, minimum GPA of 3.0. *Application deadline:* For fall admission, 2/1 (priority date); for spring admission, 11/1 (priority date). Applications are processed on a rolling basis. *Application fee:* $50.

Expenses: Tuition, area resident: Part-time $213 per credit hour. Tuition, state resident: full-time $5,100. Tuition, nonresident: full-time $8,416; part-time $351 per credit hour. Required fees: $250. One-time fee: $43 full-time.

Financial support: In 2001–02, 12 students received support, including 2 fellowships with full tuition reimbursements available (averaging $8,817 per year), 8 research assistantships with full tuition reimbursements available (averaging $10,000 per year), 2 teaching assistantships with full tuition reimbursements available (averaging $8,817 per year); career-related internships or fieldwork, Federal Work-Study, institutionally sponsored loans, scholarships/grants, health care benefits, and unspecified assistantships also available. Support available to part-time students. Financial award applicants required to submit FAFSA. *Total annual research expenditures:* $885,627.
Dr. Thomas E. Amidon, Chair, 315-470-6524, *Fax:* 315-470-6945, *E-mail:* teamidon@syr.edu.

Application contact: Dr. Robert H. Frey, Dean, Instruction and Graduate Studies, 315-470-6599, *Fax:* 315-470-6978, *E-mail:* esfgrad@esf.edu. *Web site:* http://www.esf.edu/pse/

■ STEVENS INSTITUTE OF TECHNOLOGY

Graduate School, Charles V. Schaefer Jr. School of Engineering, Department of Civil, Environmental, and Ocean Engineering, Program in Environmental Engineering, Hoboken, NJ 07030

AWARDS Environmental compatibility in engineering (Certificate); environmental process (M Eng, PhD, Certificate); groundwater and soil pollution control (M Eng, PhD, Certificate); inland and coastal environmental hydrodynamics (M Eng, PhD, Certificate); water quality (Certificate).

Degree requirements: For master's, thesis optional; for doctorate, variable foreign language requirement, thesis/dissertation; for Certificate, project or thesis.

Entrance requirements: For master's, TOEFL; for doctorate, GRE, TOEFL. Electronic applications accepted.

Expenses: Tuition: Full-time $13,950; part-time $775 per credit. Required fees: $180. One-time fee: $180 part-time. Full-time tuition and fees vary according to degree level and program.

■ SYRACUSE UNIVERSITY

Graduate School, L. C. Smith College of Engineering and Computer Science, Department of Civil and Environmental Engineering, Syracuse, NY 13244-0003

AWARDS Civil engineering (MS, PhD); environmental engineering (MS); environmental engineering science (MS); hydrogeology (MS).

Faculty: 9 full-time (2 women), 2 part-time/adjunct (0 women).
Students: 26 full-time (7 women), 7 part-time (1 woman), 24 international. Average age 28. In 2001, 6 master's, 1 doctorate awarded.
Degree requirements: For doctorate, thesis/dissertation.
Entrance requirements: For master's and doctorate, GRE General Test, GRE Subject Test. *Application deadline:* Applications are processed on a rolling basis. *Application fee:* $50.
Expenses: Tuition: Full-time $15,528; part-time $647 per credit. Required fees: $420; $38 per term. Tuition and fees vary according to program.
Financial support: In 2001–02, 3 fellowships with full tuition reimbursements (averaging $13,680 per year), 20 research assistantships with full tuition reimbursements (averaging $11,000 per year), 9 teaching assistantships with full tuition reimbursements (averaging $11,000 per year) were awarded. Federal Work-Study and tuition waivers (partial) also available. Financial award application deadline: 1/10.
Faculty research: Fate and transport of pollutants, methods for characterization and remediation of hazardous wastes, response of eco-systems to disturbances, water quality and engineering. *Total annual research expenditures:* $1.5 million.
Dr. Charles T. Driscoll, Chair, 315-443-3434, *Fax:* 315-443-1243, *E-mail:* cdriscol@syr.edu.

Application contact: Ruth Dewey, Graduate Coordinator, 315-443-2558, *Fax:* 315-443-1243, *E-mail:* rrdewey@syr.edu.

Find an in-depth description at www.petersons.com/gradchannel.

■ TEMPLE UNIVERSITY

Graduate School, College of Science and Technology, College of Engineering, Program in Civil and Environmental Engineering, Philadelphia, PA 19122-6096

AWARDS MSE. Part-time programs available.

Degree requirements: For master's, thesis optional.
Entrance requirements: For master's, GRE General Test, TOEFL.
Expenses: Tuition, state resident: full-time $8,487; part-time $369 per credit hour. Tuition, nonresident: full-time $12,282; part-time $534 per credit hour. Required fees: $350. Tuition and fees vary according

to course load, program and reciprocity agreements.
Faculty research: Prestressed masonry structure, recycling processes and products, finite element analysis of highways and runways. *Web site:* http://www.eng.temple.edu/

■ TEXAS A&M UNIVERSITY

College of Engineering, Department of Civil Engineering, Program in Environmental Engineering, College Station, TX 77843

AWARDS M Eng, MS, D Eng, PhD. D Eng offered through the College of Engineering.

Students: 42.
Degree requirements: For master's, thesis (MS); for doctorate, dissertation (PhD), internship (D Eng).
Entrance requirements: For master's and doctorate, GRE General Test, TOEFL. *Application fee:* $50 ($75 for international students).
Expenses: Tuition, state resident: full-time $11,872. Tuition, nonresident: full-time $17,892.
Financial support: Fellowships, research assistantships, teaching assistantships available. Financial award application deadline: 4/15; financial award applicants required to submit FAFSA.
Faculty research: Prediction and control of environmental consequences, water resources, air resources, liquid and solid waste control technology, public health and sanitation.
Dr. Ralph A. Wurbs, Head, 979-845-3011, *Fax:* 979-862-2800, *E-mail:* ce-grad@tamu.edu.

Application contact: Dr. Roy W. Hann, Information Contact, 979-845-2498, *Fax:* 979-862-2800, *E-mail:* ce-grad@tamu.edu. *Web site:* http://www.civil.tamu.edu/

■ TEXAS A&M UNIVERSITY– KINGSVILLE

College of Graduate Studies, College of Engineering, Department of Environmental Engineering, Kingsville, TX 78363

AWARDS ME, MS. Part-time and evening/weekend programs available.

Faculty: 4 full-time (0 women).
Students: 17 full-time (4 women), 21 part-time (3 women); includes 9 minority (all Hispanic Americans), 25 international. Average age 29. In 2001, 14 degrees awarded.
Degree requirements: For master's, thesis, comprehensive exam.
Entrance requirements: For master's, GRE General Test, TOEFL, bachelor's degree in engineering or physical science, minimum undergraduate GPA of 2.7. *Application deadline:* For fall admission, 6/1; for spring admission, 11/15. *Application fee:* $15 ($25 for international students).

Texas A&M University–Kingsville (continued)

Expenses: Tuition, state resident: part-time $42 per hour. Tuition, nonresident: part-time $253 per hour. Required fees: $56 per hour. One-time fee: $46 part-time. Tuition and fees vary according to program.
Financial support: Fellowships, research assistantships, teaching assistantships, career-related internships or fieldwork, institutionally sponsored loans, and unspecified assistantships available. Financial award application deadline: 5/15.
Faculty research: Biodegradation of hazardous waste, air modeling, toxicology and industrial hygiene, water waste treating.
Dr. Andrew Ernest, Coordinator, 361-593-3046.

Find an in-depth description at www.petersons.com/gradchannel.

■ **TEXAS TECH UNIVERSITY**

Graduate School, College of Engineering, Department of Civil Engineering, Lubbock, TX 79409
AWARDS Civil engineering (MSCE, PhD); environmental engineering (M Env E); environmental technology and management (MSETM). Part-time programs available.
Faculty: 19 full-time (0 women), 2 part-time/adjunct (0 women).
Students: 52 full-time (11 women), 15 part-time (5 women); includes 4 minority (all Hispanic Americans), 34 international. Average age 28. 67 applicants, 54% accepted. In 2001, 26 master's, 7 doctorates awarded.
Degree requirements: For master's and doctorate, thesis/dissertation.
Entrance requirements: For master's and doctorate, GRE General Test, minimum GPA of 3.0. *Application deadline:* Applications are processed on a rolling basis. *Application fee:* $25 ($50 for international students). Electronic applications accepted.
Expenses: Tuition, state resident: full-time $1,926; part-time $107 per credit hour. Tuition, nonresident: full-time $5,724; part-time $318 per credit hour. Required fees: $779; $737 per year. Tuition and fees vary according to course level, course load and program.
Financial support: In 2001–02, 38 research assistantships with partial tuition reimbursements (averaging $9,144 per year), 4 teaching assistantships with partial tuition reimbursements (averaging $9,855 per year) were awarded. Federal Work-Study and institutionally sponsored loans also available. Support available to part-time students. Financial award application deadline: 5/1; financial award applicants required to submit FAFSA.
Faculty research: Wind load/engineering on structures, fluid mechanics, structural dynamics, water resource management. *Total annual research expenditures:* $3.2 million.

Dr. James R. McDonald, Chairman, 806-742-3523, *Fax:* 806-742-3488.
Application contact: Graduate Adviser, 806-742-3523, *Fax:* 806-742-3488. *Web site:* http://www.ce.ttu.edu/

Find an in-depth description at www.petersons.com/gradchannel.

■ **TUFTS UNIVERSITY**

Division of Graduate and Continuing Studies and Research, Graduate School of Arts and Sciences, School of Engineering, Department of Civil and Environmental Engineering, Medford, MA 02155
AWARDS Civil engineering (MS, PhD), including geotechnical engineering, structural engineering; environmental engineering (MS, PhD), including environmental engineering and environmental sciences, environmental geotechnology, environmental health, environmental science and management, hazardous materials management, water resources engineering. Part-time programs available.
Faculty: 13 full-time, 10 part-time/adjunct.
Students: 58 (29 women); includes 4 minority (2 African Americans, 2 Asian Americans or Pacific Islanders) 4 international. 53 applicants, 75% accepted. In 2001, 36 master's, 1 doctorate awarded. Terminal master's awarded for partial completion of doctoral program.
Degree requirements: For master's, thesis or alternative; for doctorate, thesis/dissertation.
Entrance requirements: For master's and doctorate, GRE General Test, TOEFL. *Application deadline:* For fall admission, 2/15; for spring admission, 10/15. Applications are processed on a rolling basis. *Application fee:* $50. Electronic applications accepted.
Expenses: Tuition: Full-time $26,853. Full-time tuition and fees vary according to program.
Financial support: Research assistantships with full and partial tuition reimbursements, teaching assistantships with full and partial tuition reimbursements, Federal Work-Study, scholarships/grants, and tuition waivers (partial) available. Support available to part-time students. Financial award application deadline: 2/15; financial award applicants required to submit FAFSA.
Dr. Stephen Levine, Chair, 617-627-3211, *Fax:* 617-627-3994.
Application contact: Linfield Brown, Head, 617-627-3211, *Fax:* 617-627-3994. *Web site:* http://www.ase.tufts.edu/cee/

■ **TULANE UNIVERSITY**

School of Engineering, Department of Civil and Environmental Engineering, New Orleans, LA 70118-5669
AWARDS MS, MSE, PhD, Sc D. MS and PhD offered through the Graduate School. Part-time programs available.
Degree requirements: For master's, thesis; for doctorate, 2 foreign languages, thesis/dissertation.
Entrance requirements: For master's and doctorate, GRE General Test, TOEFL, minimum B average in undergraduate course work.
Expenses: Tuition: Full-time $24,675. Required fees: $2,210.

■ **UNIVERSITY AT BUFFALO, THE STATE UNIVERSITY OF NEW YORK**

Graduate School, School of Engineering and Applied Sciences, Department of Civil, Structural, and Environmental Engineering, Buffalo, NY 14260
AWARDS Civil engineering (M Eng, MS, PhD); engineering science (MS). Part-time programs available. Postbaccalaureate distance learning degree programs offered (minimal on-campus study).
Faculty: 22 full-time (0 women), 5 part-time/adjunct (0 women).
Students: 88 full-time (18 women), 50 part-time (9 women); includes 5 minority (2 African Americans, 3 Asian Americans or Pacific Islanders), 88 international. Average age 27. 285 applicants, 31% accepted. In 2001, 42 master's, 13 doctorates awarded. Terminal master's awarded for partial completion of doctoral program.
Degree requirements: For master's, project or thesis; for doctorate, thesis/dissertation.
Entrance requirements: For master's and doctorate, GRE General Test, TOEFL. *Application deadline:* For fall admission, 1/15 (priority date); for spring admission, 10/1. Applications are processed on a rolling basis. *Application fee:* $35. Electronic applications accepted.
Expenses: Tuition, state resident: full-time $6,118. Tuition, nonresident: full-time $9,434.
Financial support: In 2001–02, 6 fellowships with full tuition reimbursements (averaging $14,700 per year), 58 research assistantships with full tuition reimbursements (averaging $11,400 per year), 27 teaching assistantships with full tuition reimbursements (averaging $11,400 per year) were awarded. Career-related internships or fieldwork, Federal Work-Study, institutionally sponsored loans, scholarships/grants, tuition waivers (full and partial), and unspecified assistantships also available. Support available to part-time students. Financial award application

deadline: 1/15; financial award applicants required to submit FAFSA.

Faculty research: Earthquake protection, environmental engineering and fluid mechanics, structural dynamics, geomechanics. *Total annual research expenditures:* $1.5 million.

Dr. Michael C. Constantinou, Chairman, 716-645-2114 Ext. 2446, *Fax:* 716-645-3733, *E-mail:* constonl@eng.buffalo.edu.

Application contact: Dr. T. T. Soong, Director of Graduate Admissions, 716-645-2114 Ext. 2424, *Fax:* 716-645-3667, *E-mail:* dhm1@eng.buffalo.edu. *Web site:* http://www.civil.buffalo.edu/

Find an in-depth description at www.petersons.com/gradchannel.

■ THE UNIVERSITY OF ALABAMA

Graduate School, College of Engineering, Department of Civil and Environmental Engineering, Tuscaloosa, AL 35487

AWARDS Civil engineering (MSCE, PhD); environmental engineering (MSE). Part-time programs available. Postbaccalaureate distance learning degree programs offered (no on-campus study).

Faculty: 12 full-time (1 woman), 2 part-time/adjunct (0 women).

Students: 36 full-time (6 women), 17 part-time; includes 2 minority (both African Americans), 30 international. Average age 29. 96 applicants, 39% accepted, 17 enrolled. In 2001, 8 master's, 3 doctorates awarded. Terminal master's awarded for partial completion of doctoral program.

Degree requirements: For master's, thesis or alternative; for doctorate, one foreign language, thesis/dissertation.

Entrance requirements: For master's and doctorate, GRE General Test, minimum GPA of 3.0 in last 60 hours. *Application deadline:* For fall admission, 7/6. Applications are processed on a rolling basis. *Application fee:* $25.

Expenses: Tuition, state resident: full-time $3,292; part-time $183 per credit hour. Tuition, nonresident: full-time $8,912; part-time $495 per credit hour. Tuition and fees vary according to course load, campus/location and program.

Financial support: In 2001–02, 19 research assistantships with full tuition reimbursements (averaging $1,000 per year) were awarded; fellowships, teaching assistantships, Federal Work-Study and institutionally sponsored loans also available.

Faculty research: Experimental structures, modeling of structures, bridge management systems, geotechnological engineering, environmental remediation. *Total annual research expenditures:* $5.6 million.

Dr. Michael H. Triche, Professor, Drummond Chair and Interim Head, 205-348-5834, *Fax:* 205-348-0783, *E-mail:* mtriche@coe.eng.ua.edu.

■ THE UNIVERSITY OF ALABAMA AT BIRMINGHAM

Graduate School, School of Engineering, Department of Civil and Environmental Engineering, Birmingham, AL 35294

AWARDS MSCE, PhD. Evening/weekend programs available.

Students: 23 full-time (7 women), 12 part-time; includes 4 minority (2 African Americans, 2 Asian Americans or Pacific Islanders), 14 international. 58 applicants, 78% accepted. In 2001, 12 master's, 1 doctorate awarded.

Degree requirements: For master's, thesis (for some programs); for doctorate, thesis/dissertation.

Entrance requirements: For master's, GRE General Test, BS in engineering, physical sciences, life sciences, or mathematics; for doctorate, GRE General Test, TOEFL, BS or MS in engineering or related field, minimum undergraduate GPA of 3.0. *Application deadline:* Applications are processed on a rolling basis. *Application fee:* $35 ($60 for international students). Electronic applications accepted.

Expenses: Tuition, state resident: full-time $3,058. Tuition, nonresident: full-time $5,746. Tuition and fees vary according to course load, degree level and program.

Financial support: In 2001–02, 2 fellowships with full tuition reimbursements (averaging $9,500 per year), 11 research assistantships (averaging $1,229 per year) were awarded.

Dr. Fouad H. Fouad, Chair, 205-934-8430, *Fax:* 205-934-9855, *E-mail:* ffouad@uab.edu. *Web site:* http://www.eng.uab.edu/cee/

■ THE UNIVERSITY OF ALABAMA IN HUNTSVILLE

School of Graduate Studies, College of Engineering, Department of Civil and Environmental Engineering, Huntsville, AL 35899

AWARDS MSE. Part-time and evening/weekend programs available.

Faculty: 4 full-time (0 women).

Students: 16 full-time (4 women), 8 part-time (2 women); includes 2 minority (1 African American, 1 Native American), 11 international. Average age 29. 33 applicants, 82% accepted, 13 enrolled. In 2001, 9 degrees awarded.

Degree requirements: For master's, thesis or alternative, oral and written exams, comprehensive exam, registration.

Entrance requirements: For master's, GRE General Test, BSE, minimum GPA of 3.0. *Application deadline:* For fall admission, 7/24 (priority date); for spring admission, 11/15 (priority date). Applications are processed on a rolling basis. *Application fee:* $35.

Expenses: Tuition, area resident: Part-time $175 per hour. Tuition, state resident:

full-time $4,408. Tuition, nonresident: full-time $9,054; part-time $361 per hour.

Financial support: In 2001–02, 12 research assistantships with full and partial tuition reimbursements (averaging $8,433 per year), 2 teaching assistantships with full and partial tuition reimbursements (averaging $2,800 per year) were awarded. Fellowships with full and partial tuition reimbursements, career-related internships or fieldwork, Federal Work-Study, institutionally sponsored loans, scholarships/grants, health care benefits, tuition waivers (full and partial), and unspecified assistantships also available. Support available to part-time students. Financial award application deadline: 4/1; financial award applicants required to submit FAFSA.

Faculty research: Hydrologic modeling, orbital debris impact, hydrogeology, environmental engineering, water quality control. *Total annual research expenditures:* $486,685.

Dr. Vijaya Gopu, Chair, 256-824-6854, *Fax:* 256-824-6724, *E-mail:* vgopu@cee.uah.edu. *Web site:* http://www.eb-p5.eb.uah.edu/cce/

■ UNIVERSITY OF ALASKA FAIRBANKS

Graduate School, College of Science, Engineering and Mathematics, Department of Civil and Environmental Engineering, Fairbanks, AK 99775-7480

AWARDS Arctic engineering (MS); civil engineering (MCE, MS); environmental quality engineering (MS); environmental quality science (MS).

Faculty: 15 full-time (2 women), 5 part-time/adjunct (1 woman).

Students: 17 full-time (9 women), 15 part-time (5 women), 9 international. Average age 31. 31 applicants, 58% accepted, 13 enrolled. In 2001, 7 degrees awarded.

Degree requirements: For master's, thesis or alternative, comprehensive exam.

Entrance requirements: For master's, GRE General Test, TOEFL. *Application deadline:* For fall admission, 4/1; for spring admission, 11/1. Applications are processed on a rolling basis. *Application fee:* $35.

Expenses: Tuition, state resident: full-time $4,272; part-time $178 per credit. Tuition, nonresident: full-time $8,328; part-time $347 per credit. Required fees: $960; $60 per term. Part-time tuition and fees vary according to course load.

Financial support: In 2001–02, fellowships with tuition reimbursements (averaging $10,000 per year); research assistantships with tuition reimbursements, teaching assistantships with tuition reimbursements, Federal Work-Study and scholarships/grants also available.

Faculty research: Soils, structures, culvert thawing with solar power, pavement drainage, contaminant hydrogeology.

University of Alaska Fairbanks (continued)
Dr. Robert Carlson, Head, 907-474-7241.

■ THE UNIVERSITY OF ARIZONA

Graduate College, College of Engineering and Mines, Department of Chemical and Environmental Engineering, Tucson, AZ 85721

AWARDS Chemical engineering (MS, PhD); environmental engineering (MS, PhD). Part-time programs available.

Faculty: 14.
Students: 53 full-time (16 women), 10 part-time (3 women); includes 8 minority (1 Asian American or Pacific Islander, 5 Hispanic Americans, 2 Native Americans), 31 international. Average age 29. 168 applicants, 15% accepted, 14 enrolled. In 2001, 8 master's, 2 doctorates awarded.
Degree requirements: For master's, thesis; for doctorate, thesis/dissertation, departmental qualifying exams, comprehensive exam.
Entrance requirements: For master's and doctorate, TOEFL, minimum GPA of 3.0. *Application deadline:* For fall admission, 3/1. Applications are processed on a rolling basis. *Application fee:* $45.
Expenses: Tuition, state resident: full-time $2,490; part-time $436 per unit. Tuition, nonresident: full-time $10,300; part-time $436 per unit. Full-time tuition and fees vary according to degree level and program.
Financial support: Fellowships, research assistantships, teaching assistantships, institutionally sponsored loans and scholarships/grants available. Financial award application deadline: 6/1.
Faculty research: Energy and environment–hazardous waste incineration, fossil fuel combustion, processing high-purity gases and liquids, aerosol reactor theory, pharmacokinetics.
Dr. Jost O.L. Wendt, Head, 520-621-2591.
Application contact: Rosemary A. Myers, Graduate Coordinator, 520-621-6044, *Fax:* 520-621-6048, *E-mail:* rmyers@engr.arizona.edu. *Web site:* http://www.che.arizona.edu

■ UNIVERSITY OF ARKANSAS

Graduate School, College of Engineering, Department of Civil Engineering, Program in Environmental Engineering, Fayetteville, AR 72701-1201

AWARDS MS En E, MSE.

Students: 5 full-time (1 woman), 2 part-time (1 woman), 4 international. 2 applicants, 100% accepted.
Degree requirements: For master's, thesis optional.
Application fee: $40 ($50 for international students).
Expenses: Tuition, state resident: full-time $3,553; part-time $197 per credit. Tuition,

nonresident: full-time $8,411; part-time $467 per credit. Required fees: $42 per credit. Tuition and fees vary according to course load and program.
Financial support: Career-related internships or fieldwork and Federal Work-Study available. Support available to part-time students. Financial award application deadline: 4/1; financial award applicants required to submit FAFSA.
Dr. Robert Elliott, Chair, Department of Civil Engineering, 479-575-4954.

■ UNIVERSITY OF CALIFORNIA, BERKELEY

Graduate Division, College of Engineering, Department of Civil and Environmental Engineering, Berkeley, CA 94720-1500

AWARDS Construction engineering and management (M Eng, MS, D Eng, PhD); environmental quality and environmental water resources engineering (M Eng, MS, D Eng, PhD); geotechnical engineering (M Eng, MS, D Eng, PhD). Structural engineering, mechanics and materials (M Eng, MS, D Eng, PhD); transportation engineering (M Eng, MS, D Eng, PhD).

Degree requirements: For master's, comprehensive exam or thesis (MS); for doctorate, thesis/dissertation, qualifying exam.
Entrance requirements: For master's, GRE General Test, minimum GPA of 3.0; for doctorate, GRE General Test, minimum GPA of 3.5.
Expenses: Tuition, nonresident: full-time $10,704. Required fees: $4,349.

Find an in-depth description at www.petersons.com/gradchannel.

■ UNIVERSITY OF CALIFORNIA, DAVIS

Graduate Studies, College of Engineering, Program in Civil and Environmental Engineering, Davis, CA 95616

AWARDS M Engr, MS, D Engr, PhD, Certificate, M Engr/MBA. Part-time programs available.

Faculty: 35 full-time (5 women), 12 part-time/adjunct (2 women).
Students: 120 full-time (39 women), 1 part-time; includes 12 minority (9 Asian Americans or Pacific Islanders, 2 Hispanic Americans, 1 Native American), 51 international. Average age 30. 282 applicants, 71% accepted, 40 enrolled. In 2001, 35 master's, 14 doctorates awarded.
Degree requirements: For doctorate, thesis/dissertation.
Entrance requirements: For master's, GRE General Test, minimum GPA of 3.0; for doctorate, GRE, minimum graduate GPA of 3.5. *Application deadline:* For fall

admission, 1/15 (priority date). Applications are processed on a rolling basis.
Application fee: $60. Electronic applications accepted.
Expenses: Tuition, state resident: full-time $4,831. Tuition, nonresident: full-time $15,725.
Financial support: In 2001–02, 92 students received support, including 40 fellowships with full and partial tuition reimbursements available (averaging $5,761 per year), 58 research assistantships with full and partial tuition reimbursements available (averaging $10,721 per year), 21 teaching assistantships with partial tuition reimbursements available (averaging $10,541 per year); career-related internships or fieldwork, Federal Work-Study, institutionally sponsored loans, and tuition waivers (full and partial) also available. Support available to part-time students. Financial award application deadline: 1/15; financial award applicants required to submit FAFSA.
Faculty research: Environmental water resources, transportation, structural mechanics, structural engineering, geotechnical engineering.
Debbie A. Niemeier, Chairperson, 530-752-8918, *E-mail:* dniemeier@ucdavis.edu.
Application contact: Kathy LaGiusa, Administrative Assistant, 530-752-1441, *Fax:* 530-752-7872, *E-mail:* klagiusa@ucdavis.edu. *Web site:* http://cee.engr.ucdavis.edu/

■ UNIVERSITY OF CALIFORNIA, LOS ANGELES

Graduate Division, School of Engineering and Applied Science, Department of Civil and Environmental Engineering, Los Angeles, CA 90095

AWARDS Environmental engineering (MS, PhD); geotechnical engineering (MS, PhD). Structures (MS, PhD), including structural mechanics and earthquake engineering; water resource systems engineering (MS, PhD).

Faculty: 14 full-time, 11 part-time/adjunct.
Students: 96 full-time (28 women); includes 23 minority (1 African American, 17 Asian Americans or Pacific Islanders, 5 Hispanic Americans), 45 international. 216 applicants, 60% accepted, 34 enrolled. In 2001, 34 master's, 9 doctorates awarded.
Degree requirements: For master's, comprehensive exam or thesis; for doctorate, thesis/dissertation, qualifying exams.
Entrance requirements: For master's, GRE General Test, minimum GPA of 3.0; for doctorate, GRE General Test, minimum GPA of 3.25. *Application deadline:* For fall admission, 1/15; for spring admission, 12/1. *Application fee:* $60. Electronic applications accepted.
Expenses: Tuition, nonresident: full-time $10,244. Required fees: $3,609. Full-time tuition and fees vary according to program.

Financial support: In 2001–02, 39 fellowships, 50 research assistantships, 31 teaching assistantships were awarded. Federal Work-Study, institutionally sponsored loans, and tuition waivers (full and partial) also available. Financial award application deadline: 1/15; financial award applicants required to submit FAFSA.
Dr. Jiann-Wen Ju, Chair, 310-206-1751. **Application contact:** Deeona Columbia, Graduate Affairs Officer, 310-825-1851, *Fax:* 310-206-2222, *E-mail:* deeona@ea.ucla.edu. *Web site:* http://www.cee.ucla.edu

Find an in-depth description at www.petersons.com/gradchannel.

■ **UNIVERSITY OF CALIFORNIA, LOS ANGELES**

Graduate Division, School of Public Health, Program in Environmental Science and Engineering, Los Angeles, CA 90095

AWARDS D Env.

Students: 41 full-time (20 women); includes 4 minority (1 African American, 2 Asian Americans or Pacific Islanders, 1 Hispanic American), 9 international. 11 applicants, 36% accepted, 4 enrolled. In 2001, 8 degrees awarded.
Degree requirements: For doctorate, thesis/dissertation, oral and written qualifying exams.
Entrance requirements: For doctorate, GRE General Test, minimum undergraduate GPA of 3.0, master's degree or equivalent in a natural science, engineering, or public health. *Application deadline:* For fall admission, 12/15. *Application fee:* $60. Electronic applications accepted.
Expenses: Tuition, nonresident: full-time $10,244. Required fees: $3,609. Full-time tuition and fees vary according to program.
Financial support: In 2001–02, 32 students received support, including 26 fellowships, 16 research assistantships, 1 teaching assistantship; institutionally sponsored loans, scholarships/grants, and tuition waivers (full and partial) also available. Financial award application deadline: 3/1.
Faculty research: Toxic and hazardous substances, air and water pollution, risk assessment/management, water resources, marine science.
Dr. Richard F. Ambrose, Director, 310-825-9901.
Application contact: Departmental Office, 310-825-9901, *E-mail:* app_ese@admin.ph.ucla.edu.

Find an in-depth description at www.petersons.com/gradchannel.

■ **UNIVERSITY OF CALIFORNIA, RIVERSIDE**

Graduate Division, Department of Chemical and Environmental Engineering, Riverside, CA 92521-0102

AWARDS MS, PhD.

Faculty: 8 full-time (0 women), 8 part-time/adjunct (2 women).
Students: 18 full-time (4 women), 1 part-time; includes 1 minority (Asian American or Pacific Islander), 10 international. Average age 27. 34 applicants, 59% accepted. In 2001, 1 master's awarded.
Degree requirements: For doctorate, thesis/dissertation, English language proficiency qualifying exams.
Entrance requirements: For master's and doctorate, GRE General Test, TOEFL, minimum GPA of 3.5 for fellowships/teaching assistantships, 3.2 overall. *Application deadline:* For fall admission, 5/1; for winter admission, 9/1; for spring admission, 12/1. Applications are processed on a rolling basis. *Application fee:* $40. Electronic applications accepted.
Expenses: Tuition, state resident: full-time $5,001. Tuition, nonresident: full-time $15,897.
Financial support: In 2001–02, 2 students received support, including 2 teaching assistantships with partial tuition reimbursements available (averaging $7,000 per year) Financial award application deadline: 1/5; financial award applicants required to submit FAFSA.
Faculty research: Bioprocessing, biodegradation, bioremediation, water wastewater treatment, biosensors and biodetoxification, transport emissions. *Total annual research expenditures:* $395,171.
Dr. Ashok Mulchandani, Chair, 909-787-2423, *Fax:* 909-787-2425.
Application contact: Laura Ibarra, Graduate Student Affairs Office, 909-787-2484, *Fax:* 909-787-2425, *E-mail:* gradcee@engr.ucr.edu. *Web site:* http://www.engr.ucr.edu

Find an in-depth description at www.petersons.com/gradchannel.

■ **UNIVERSITY OF CALIFORNIA, SANTA BARBARA**

Graduate Division, College of Engineering, Department of Mechanical and Environmental Engineering, Santa Barbara, CA 93106

AWARDS MS, PhD.

Degree requirements: For master's, thesis or alternative, project; for doctorate, thesis/dissertation.
Entrance requirements: For master's and doctorate, GRE General Test, TOEFL. Electronic applications accepted.
Faculty research: Dynamic systems, control, and robotics; environmental ocean and risk/safety engineering. Solid mechanics, materials, and structures; thermofluid sciences; computational science. *Web site:* http://www.me.ucsb.edu/

Find an in-depth description at www.petersons.com/gradchannel.

■ **UNIVERSITY OF CENTRAL FLORIDA**

College of Engineering and Computer Sciences, Department of Civil and Environmental Engineering, Program in Environmental Engineering, Orlando, FL 32816

AWARDS Air pollution control (Certificate); drinking water treatment (Certificate); environmental engineering (MS, MS Env E, PhD); hazardous waste management (Certificate); wastewater treatment (Certificate). Part-time and evening/weekend programs available.

Faculty: 19 full-time (1 woman), 12 part-time/adjunct (0 women).
Students: 33 full-time (6 women), 19 part-time (7 women); includes 4 minority (1 African American, 2 Asian Americans or Pacific Islanders, 1 Hispanic American), 26 international. Average age 28. 81 applicants, 74% accepted, 23 enrolled. In 2001, 5 master's, 1 doctorate awarded.
Degree requirements: For master's, thesis or alternative; for doctorate, thesis/dissertation, departmental qualifying exam, candidacy exam.
Entrance requirements: For master's, GRE General Test, TOEFL, minimum GPA of 3.0 in last 60 hours; for doctorate, GRE General Test, TOEFL, minimum GPA of 3.5 in last 60 hours, interview. *Application deadline:* For fall admission, 7/15 (priority date); for spring admission, 12/15 (priority date). *Application fee:* $20. Electronic applications accepted.
Expenses: Tuition, state resident: part-time $162 per hour. Tuition, nonresident: part-time $569 per hour.
Financial support: In 2001–02, 13 fellowships with partial tuition reimbursements (averaging $2,644 per year), 86 research assistantships with partial tuition reimbursements (averaging $3,300 per year), 5 teaching assistantships with partial tuition reimbursements (averaging $4,700 per year) were awarded. Career-related internships or fieldwork, Federal Work-Study, institutionally sponsored loans, tuition waivers (partial), and unspecified assistantships also available. Financial award application deadline: 3/1; financial award applicants required to submit FAFSA.
Application contact: Dr. Roger L. Wayson, Coordinator, 407-823-2841, *E-mail:* wayson@pegasus.cc.ucf.edu. *Web site:* http://www.ucf.edu/

■ UNIVERSITY OF CINCINNATI

Division of Research and Advanced Studies, College of Engineering, Department of Civil and Environmental Engineering, Program in Environmental Engineering, Cincinnati, OH 45221

AWARDS MS, PhD.

Students: 67 full-time (24 women), 2 part-time (1 woman), 54 international. In 2001, 10 master's, 5 doctorates awarded.
Degree requirements: For master's, project or thesis; for doctorate, one foreign language, thesis/dissertation.
Entrance requirements: For master's and doctorate, GRE General Test, TOEFL. *Application deadline:* For fall admission, 2/1 (priority date). *Application fee:* $40. Electronic applications accepted.
Expenses: Tuition, state resident: part-time $2,698 per quarter. Tuition, nonresident: part-time $4,977 per quarter.
Financial support: Fellowships, career-related internships or fieldwork, tuition waivers (full), and unspecified assistantships available. Financial award application deadline: 2/1.
Faculty research: Environmental microbiology, solid-waste management, air pollution control, water pollution control, aerosols.
Application contact: Dr. Steven Buchberger, Graduate Program Director, 513-556-3681, *Fax:* 513-556-2599, *E-mail:* steven.buchberger@uc.edu. *Web site:* http://www.cee.uc.edu/

■ UNIVERSITY OF CINCINNATI

Division of Research and Advanced Studies, College of Medicine, Graduate Programs in Medicine, Department of Environmental Health, Cincinnati, OH 45267

AWARDS Environmental and industrial hygiene (MS); environmental and occupational medicine (MS); environmental health (PhD); environmental hygiene science and engineering (MS, PhD); epidemiology and biostatistics (MS); occupational safety (MS); toxicology (MS, PhD).

Faculty: 20 full-time.
Students: 90 full-time (39 women), 49 part-time (27 women); includes 18 minority (10 African Americans, 7 Asian Americans or Pacific Islanders, 1 Hispanic American), 50 international. 120 applicants, 44% accepted. In 2001, 20 master's, 7 doctorates awarded. Terminal master's awarded for partial completion of doctoral program.
Degree requirements: For master's, thesis; for doctorate, thesis/dissertation, qualifying exam.
Entrance requirements: For master's, GRE General Test, TOEFL, bachelor's degree in science; for doctorate, GRE General Test, TOEFL. *Application deadline:* For fall admission, 3/1 (priority date).

Applications are processed on a rolling basis. *Application fee:* $30. Electronic applications accepted.
Expenses: Tuition, state resident: part-time $2,698 per quarter. Tuition, nonresident: part-time $4,977 per quarter.
Financial support: Research assistantships with full tuition reimbursements, teaching assistantships with full tuition reimbursements, career-related internships or fieldwork, tuition waivers (partial), and unspecified assistantships available. Financial award application deadline: 5/1.
Faculty research: Carcinogens and mutagenesis, pulmonary studies, reproduction and development. *Total annual research expenditures:* $15.1 million.
Dr. Marshall W. Anderson, Chairman, 513-558-5701, *Fax:* 513-558-4397, *E-mail:* marshall.anderson@uc.edu.
Application contact: Stephanie W. Starkey, Graduate Program Coordinator, 513-558-5704, *Fax:* 513-558-5457, *E-mail:* stephanie.starkey@uc.edu. *Web site:* http://www.med.uc.edu/

Find an in-depth description at www.petersons.com/gradchannel.

■ UNIVERSITY OF COLORADO AT BOULDER

Graduate School, College of Engineering and Applied Science, Department of Civil, Environmental, and Architectural Engineering, Boulder, CO 80309

AWARDS Building systems (MS, PhD); construction engineering and management (MS, PhD); environmental engineering (MS, PhD); geoenvironmental engineering (MS, PhD); geotechnical engineering (MS, PhD); Structural engineering (MS, PhD); water resource engineering (MS, PhD).

Faculty: 37 full-time (2 women).
Students: 167 full-time (49 women), 44 part-time (12 women); includes 14 minority (1 African American, 4 Asian Americans or Pacific Islanders, 9 Hispanic Americans), 88 international. Average age 30. 280 applicants, 59% accepted. In 2001, 59 master's, 13 doctorates awarded.
Degree requirements: For master's, thesis or alternative, comprehensive exam; for doctorate, thesis/dissertation.
Entrance requirements: For master's, GRE General Test, minimum undergraduate GPA of 3.0. *Application deadline:* For fall admission, 4/30; for spring admission, 10/31. *Application fee:* $50 ($60 for international students).
Expenses: Tuition, state resident: full-time $3,474. Tuition, nonresident: full-time $16,624.
Financial support: In 2001–02, 19 fellowships (averaging $5,252 per year), 45 research assistantships (averaging $15,638 per year), 14 teaching assistantships (averaging $13,821 per year) were awarded. Financial award application deadline: 2/15.

Faculty research: Building systems engineering, construction engineering and management, environmental engineering, geoenvironmental engineering, geotechnical engineering. *Total annual research expenditures:* $8.3 million.
Hon-Yim Ko, Chair, 303-492-6716, *Fax:* 303-492-7317, *E-mail:* ko@spot.colorado.edu.
Application contact: Jan Demay, Graduate Secretary, 303-492-7316, *Fax:* 303-492-7317, *E-mail:* demay@spot.colorado.edu. *Web site:* http://www.civil.colorado.edu/

■ UNIVERSITY OF CONNECTICUT

Graduate School, School of Engineering, Field of Environmental Engineering, Storrs, CT 06269

AWARDS MS, PhD.

Degree requirements: For doctorate, thesis/dissertation.

■ UNIVERSITY OF DAYTON

Graduate School, School of Engineering, Department of Civil Engineering, Dayton, OH 45469-1300

AWARDS Engineering mechanics (MSEM); environmental engineering (MSCE). Soil mechanics (MSCE). Structural engineering (MSCE); transport engineering (MSCE). Part-time programs available.

Faculty: 8 full-time (0 women), 2 part-time/adjunct (0 women).
Students: 8 full-time (6 women), 7 part-time (4 women), 6 international. In 2001, 2 degrees awarded.
Degree requirements: For master's, thesis or alternative.
Entrance requirements: For master's, TOEFL. *Application deadline:* For fall admission, 8/1. Applications are processed on a rolling basis. *Application fee:* $30.
Expenses: Tuition: Full-time $5,436; part-time $453 per credit hour. Required fees: $50; $25 per term.
Financial support: In 2001–02, 5 research assistantships with full tuition reimbursements (averaging $12,000 per year), 2 teaching assistantships with full tuition reimbursements (averaging $10,000 per year) were awarded. Institutionally sponsored loans also available.
Faculty research: Tire/soil interaction, tilt-up structures, viscoelastic response of restraint systems, composite materials.
Dr. Joseph E. Saliba, Chairperson, 937-229-3847, *E-mail:* jsaliba@engr.udayton.edu.
Application contact: Dr. Donald L. Moon, Associate Dean, 937-229-2241, *Fax:* 937-229-2471, *E-mail:* dmoon@notes.udayton.edu.

■ UNIVERSITY OF DELAWARE

College of Engineering, Department of Civil and Environmental Engineering, Program in Environmental Engineering, Newark, DE 19716

AWARDS MAS, MCE, PhD.

Degree requirements: For master's and doctorate, thesis/dissertation.
Entrance requirements: For master's and doctorate, GRE General Test, TOEFL.
Expenses: Tuition, state resident: full-time $4,770; part-time $265 per credit. Tuition, nonresident: full-time $13,860; part-time $770 per credit. Required fees: $414.
Faculty research: Transport phenomena, treatment of hazardous wastes, groundwater hydrology, water and wastewater treatment, contaminant removal from water and soil.

Find an in-depth description at www.petersons.com/gradchannel.

■ UNIVERSITY OF DETROIT MERCY

College of Engineering and Science, Department of Civil and Environmental Engineering, Detroit, MI 48219-0900

AWARDS ME. Evening/weekend programs available.

Faculty: 5 full-time (1 woman).
Students: 1 full-time (0 women), 3 part-time, 3 international. Average age 28. *Application deadline:* For fall admission, 8/1 (priority date). Applications are processed on a rolling basis. *Application fee:* $30 ($50 for international students).
Expenses: Tuition: Full-time $10,620; part-time $590 per credit hour. Required fees: $400. Tuition and fees vary according to program.
Financial support: Career-related internships or fieldwork available.
Faculty research: Geotechnical engineering.
Dr. Utpal Dutta, Chairman, 313-993-1040, *Fax:* 313-993-1187, *E-mail:* duttau@udmercy.edu.

■ UNIVERSITY OF FLORIDA

Graduate School, College of Engineering, Department of Environmental Engineering Sciences, Gainesville, FL 32611

AWARDS ME, MS, PhD, Engr. Terminal master's awarded for partial completion of doctoral program.

Degree requirements: For master's and Engr, project or thesis; for doctorate, thesis/dissertation.
Entrance requirements: For master's and doctorate, GRE General Test, TOEFL, minimum GPA of 3.0; for Engr, GRE General Test, TOEFL. Electronic applications accepted.

Expenses: Tuition, state resident: part-time $164 per hour. Tuition, nonresident: part-time $571 per hour. Tuition and fees vary according to course level and program.
Faculty research: Air pollution, potable water supply system, water pollution control, hazardous waste, aquatic ecology and chemistry. *Web site:* http://www.ees.ufl.edu/

■ UNIVERSITY OF HOUSTON

Cullen College of Engineering, Department of Civil and Environmental Engineering, Houston, TX 77204

AWARDS MCE, MS Env E, MSCE, PhD. Part-time and evening/weekend programs available.

Faculty: 14 full-time (2 women), 2 part-time/adjunct (0 women).
Students: 27 full-time (4 women), 44 part-time (9 women); includes 14 minority (2 African Americans, 7 Asian Americans or Pacific Islanders, 5 Hispanic Americans), 28 international. Average age 29. 65 applicants, 42% accepted. In 2001, 11 master's, 5 doctorates awarded. Terminal master's awarded for partial completion of doctoral program.
Degree requirements: For master's, thesis (for some programs); for doctorate, thesis/dissertation, departmental qualifying exam.
Entrance requirements: For master's and doctorate, GRE General Test, TOEFL. *Application deadline:* For fall admission, 7/3 (priority date); for spring admission, 12/4. Applications are processed on a rolling basis. *Application fee:* $25 ($75 for international students).
Expenses: Tuition, state resident: full-time $1,512. Tuition, nonresident: full-time $5,310. Required fees: $1,308. Tuition and fees vary according to program.
Financial support: In 2001–02, 56 research assistantships with partial tuition reimbursements (averaging $14,400 per year), 10 teaching assistantships with partial tuition reimbursements (averaging $13,000 per year) were awarded. Career-related internships or fieldwork and Federal Work-Study also available. Financial award application deadline: 4/1.
Faculty research: Structural engineering and construction materials, geotechnical engineering and deep foundation, hydraulic engineering and wave mechanics, water and soil treatment. *Total annual research expenditures:* $1.5 million.
Dr. Cumaraswamy Vipulanandan, Chairperson, 713-743-4250, *Fax:* 713-743-4260.
Application contact: Charlene Holliday, Graduate Analyst, 713-743-4254, *Fax:* 713-743-4260, *E-mail:* wholliday@uh.edu. *Web site:* http://www.egr.uh.edu/cive/

Find an in-depth description at www.petersons.com/gradchannel.

■ UNIVERSITY OF HOUSTON

Cullen College of Engineering, Department of Mechanical Engineering, Houston, TX 77204

AWARDS Aerospace engineering (MS, PhD); biomedical engineering (MS); computer and systems engineering (MS, PhD); environmental engineering (MS, PhD); materials engineering (MS, PhD); mechanical engineering (MME, MSME); petroleum engineering (MS). Part-time and evening/weekend programs available.

Faculty: 16 full-time (0 women), 1 part-time/adjunct (0 women).
Students: 34 full-time (4 women), 26 part-time (2 women); includes 7 minority (3 Asian Americans or Pacific Islanders, 4 Hispanic Americans), 32 international. Average age 28. 114 applicants, 64% accepted. In 2001, 20 master's, 3 doctorates awarded. Terminal master's awarded for partial completion of doctoral program.
Degree requirements: For master's, thesis (for some programs); for doctorate, thesis/dissertation, departmental qualifying exam.
Entrance requirements: For master's and doctorate, GRE General Test, TOEFL. *Application deadline:* For fall admission, 7/3 (priority date); for spring admission, 12/4. Applications are processed on a rolling basis. *Application fee:* $25 ($75 for international students).
Expenses: Tuition, state resident: full-time $1,512. Tuition, nonresident: full-time $5,310. Required fees: $1,308. Tuition and fees vary according to program.
Financial support: In 2001–02, 20 research assistantships (averaging $14,400 per year), 13 teaching assistantships (averaging $14,400 per year) were awarded. Fellowships, career-related internships or fieldwork and Federal Work-Study also available. Financial award application deadline: 2/15.
Faculty research: Experimental and computational turbulence, composites, rheology, phase change/heat transfer, characterization of superconducting materials. *Total annual research expenditures:* $396,172.
Dr. Lewis T. Wheeler, Interim Chair, 713-743-4500, *Fax:* 713-743-4503.
Application contact: Susan Sanderson-Clobe, Graduate Admissions Analyst, 713-743-4505, *Fax:* 713-743-4503, *E-mail:* megrad@uh.edu. *Web site:* http://www.mc.uh.edu

Find an in-depth description at www.petersons.com/gradchannel.

■ UNIVERSITY OF IDAHO

College of Graduate Studies, College of Engineering, Program in Environmental Engineering, Moscow, ID 83844-2282

AWARDS M Engr, MS.

University of Idaho (continued)
Students: 4 full-time (3 women), 1 (woman) part-time, 2 international. 13 applicants, 23% accepted. In 2001, 1 degree awarded.
Application deadline: For fall admission, 8/1; for spring admission, 12/15. Applications are processed on a rolling basis. *Application fee:* $35 ($45 for international students).
Expenses: Tuition, state resident: full-time $1,613. Tuition, nonresident: full-time $3,000.

■ UNIVERSITY OF ILLINOIS AT URBANA–CHAMPAIGN

Graduate College, College of Engineering, Department of Civil and Environmental Engineering, Champaign, IL 61820

AWARDS Civil engineering (MS, PhD); environmental engineering and environmental science (MS, PhD), including environmental engineering, environmental science.

Faculty: 49 full-time, 2 part-time/adjunct.
Students: 367 full-time (86 women); includes 19 minority (3 African Americans, 5 Asian Americans or Pacific Islanders, 10 Hispanic Americans, 1 Native American), 206 international. 838 applicants, 18% accepted. In 2001, 90 master's, 30 doctorates awarded.
Degree requirements: For master's, thesis or alternative; for doctorate, thesis/dissertation.
Application deadline: Applications are processed on a rolling basis. *Application fee:* $40 ($50 for international students). Electronic applications accepted.
Expenses: Tuition, state resident: part-time $3,227 per degree program. Tuition, nonresident: part-time $7,169 per degree program. Tuition and fees vary according to program.
Financial support: In 2001–02, 24 fellowships, 179 research assistantships, 42 teaching assistantships were awarded. Tuition waivers (full and partial) also available. Financial award application deadline: 2/15. Dr. Neil M. Hawkins, Interim Head, 217-333-3815, *Fax:* 217-333-9464, *E-mail:* nmhawkin@uiuc.edu.
Application contact: Mary Pearson, Administrative Secretary, 217-333-3811, *Fax:* 217-333-9464, *E-mail:* mkpearson@uiuc.edu. *Web site:* http://www.cee.ce.uiuc.edu

Find an in-depth description at www.petersons.com/gradchannel.

■ THE UNIVERSITY OF IOWA

Graduate College, College of Engineering, Department of Civil and Environmental Engineering, Iowa City, IA 52242-1316

AWARDS MS, PhD. Part-time programs available.

Faculty: 22 full-time (2 women), 1 part-time/adjunct (0 women).

Students: 47 full-time (15 women), 35 part-time (4 women); includes 2 minority (1 African American, 1 Asian American or Pacific Islander), 44 international. Average age 28. 198 applicants, 56% accepted, 21 enrolled. In 2001, 10 master's, 5 doctorates awarded. Terminal master's awarded for partial completion of doctoral program.
Degree requirements: For master's, exam, thesis optional; for doctorate, thesis/dissertation, exam, comprehensive exam.
Entrance requirements: For master's and doctorate, TOEFL. *Application deadline:* For fall admission, 4/15 (priority date); for spring admission, 10/1 (priority date). Applications are processed on a rolling basis. *Application fee:* $30 ($50 for international students). Electronic applications accepted.
Expenses: Tuition, state resident: full-time $3,702; part-time $206 per semester hour. Tuition, nonresident: full-time $11,924; part-time $206 per semester hour. Required fees: $101 per semester. Tuition and fees vary according to course load and program.
Financial support: In 2001–02, 72 students received support, including 1 fellowship (averaging $17,989 per year), 16 research assistantships (averaging $17,989 per year), 17 teaching assistantships (averaging $14,718 per year); career-related internships or fieldwork, Federal Work-Study, scholarships/grants, traineeships, health care benefits, and unspecified assistantships also available. Support available to part-time students. Financial award application deadline: 2/1; financial award applicants required to submit FAFSA.
Faculty research: Bioremediation, optimal design of structures, environmental hydraulics, road paving systems, water quality. *Total annual research expenditures:* $6.2 million.
Dr. Robert Ettema, Departmental Executive Officer, 319-384-0596, *Fax:* 319-335-5660, *E-mail:* robert-ettema@uiowa.edu.
Application contact: Judy Holland, Secretary, 319-335-5647, *Fax:* 319-335-5660, *E-mail:* cee@engineering.uiowa.edu. *Web site:* http://www.cee.engineering.uiowa.edu/

■ UNIVERSITY OF KANSAS

Graduate School, School of Engineering, Department of Civil, Environmental, and Architectural Engineering, Lawrence, KS 66045

AWARDS Architectural engineering (MS); civil engineering (MCE, MS, DE, PhD); construction management (MCM); environmental engineering (MS, PhD); environmental science (MS, PhD); water resources engineering (MS); water resources science (MS).

Faculty: 27.
Students: 38 full-time (11 women), 97 part-time (20 women); includes 12 minority (4 African Americans, 3 Asian Americans or Pacific Islanders, 4 Hispanic Americans, 1 Native American), 37 international. Average age 32. 105 applicants, 31% accepted, 19 enrolled. In 2001, 32 master's, 4 doctorates awarded.
Degree requirements: For master's, thesis or alternative, exam; for doctorate, thesis/dissertation, comprehensive exam.
Entrance requirements: For master's, GRE, Michigan English Language Assessment Battery, TOEFL, minimum GPA of 3.0; for doctorate, GRE, Michigan English Language Assessment Battery, TOEFL, minimum GPA of 3.5. *Application deadline:* Applications are processed on a rolling basis. *Application fee:* $40.
Expenses: Tuition, state resident: full-time $2,722; part-time $113 per credit. Tuition, nonresident: full-time $8,586; part-time $358 per credit. Required fees: $551; $46 per credit. Tuition and fees vary according to campus/location, program and reciprocity agreements.
Financial support: In 2001–02, 21 research assistantships with partial tuition reimbursements (averaging $10,367 per year), 6 teaching assistantships with full and partial tuition reimbursements (averaging $8,615 per year) were awarded. Fellowships, career-related internships or fieldwork also available.
Faculty research: Structures (fracture mechanics), transportation, environmental health.
Steve L. McCabe, Chair, 785-864-3766.
Application contact: David Parr, Graduate Director, *E-mail:* aparr@engr.ukans.edu. *Web site:* http://www.ceae.ku.edu/

■ UNIVERSITY OF LOUISVILLE

Graduate School, Speed Scientific School, Department of Civil and Environmental Engineering, Louisville, KY 40292-0001

AWARDS M Eng, MS, PhD.

Students: 24 full-time (9 women), 45 part-time (8 women); includes 2 minority (both African Americans), 4 international. Average age 29. In 2001, 29 master's, 1 doctorate awarded.
Degree requirements: For master's and doctorate, thesis/dissertation.
Entrance requirements: For master's and doctorate, GRE General Test. *Application deadline:* Applications are processed on a rolling basis. *Application fee:* $25.
Expenses: Tuition, state resident: full-time $4,134. Tuition, nonresident: full-time $11,486.
Financial support: In 2001–02, 1 research assistantship with full tuition reimbursement (averaging $12,000 per year), 5 teaching assistantships with full tuition reimbursements (averaging $16,800 per year) were awarded.
Dr. Louis F. Cohn, Chair, 502-852-6276, *Fax:* 502-852-8851, *E-mail:* cohn@louisville.edu.

■ UNIVERSITY OF MAINE

Graduate School, College of Engineering, Department of Civil and Environmental Engineering, Orono, ME 04469

AWARDS Civil engineering (MS, PhD), including environmental engineering, geotechnical engineering, structural engineering.

Faculty: 11 full-time (0 women).
Students: 18 full-time (7 women), 8 part-time; includes 3 minority (2 Hispanic Americans, 1 Native American), 10 international. 21 applicants, 43% accepted, 4 enrolled. In 2001, 11 degrees awarded.
Degree requirements: For doctorate, thesis/dissertation.
Entrance requirements: For master's and doctorate, GRE General Test, TOEFL. *Application deadline:* For fall admission, 2/1 (priority date). Applications are processed on a rolling basis. *Application fee:* $50. Electronic applications accepted.
Expenses: Tuition, state resident: full-time $3,780; part-time $210 per credit hour. Tuition, nonresident: full-time $10,782; part-time $599 per credit hour. Required fees: $9.5 per credit hour. $32 per semester. Tuition and fees vary according to reciprocity agreements.
Financial support: In 2001–02, 15 research assistantships with tuition reimbursements (averaging $16,900 per year), 3 teaching assistantships with tuition reimbursements (averaging $15,000 per year) were awarded. Federal Work-Study, institutionally sponsored loans, scholarships/grants, and tuition waivers (full and partial) also available. Financial award application deadline: 3/1.
Dr. Dana Humphrey, Chair, 207-581-2170, *Fax:* 207-581-3888.
Application contact: Scott G. Delcourt, Director of the Graduate School, 207-581-3218, *Fax:* 207-581-3232, *E-mail:* graduate@maine.edu. *Web site:* http://www.umaine.edu/graduate/

■ UNIVERSITY OF MARYLAND, COLLEGE PARK

Graduate Studies and Research, A. James Clark School of Engineering, Department of Civil and Environmental Engineering, College Park, MD 20742

AWARDS M Eng, MS, PhD. Part-time and evening/weekend programs available. Postbaccalaureate distance learning degree programs offered.

Faculty: 43 full-time (6 women), 17 part-time/adjunct (4 women).
Students: 93 full-time (16 women), 80 part-time (19 women); includes 19 minority (10 African Americans, 4 Asian Americans or Pacific Islanders, 5 Hispanic Americans, 85 international. 305 applicants, 31% accepted, 52 enrolled. In 2001, 28 master's, 8 doctorates awarded.

Degree requirements: For master's, thesis or alternative; for doctorate, thesis/dissertation, qualifying exam.
Entrance requirements: For master's and doctorate, GRE General Test, minimum GPA of 3.0. *Application deadline:* For fall admission, 5/1; for spring admission, 8/1. Applications are processed on a rolling basis. *Application fee:* $50 ($70 for international students). Electronic applications accepted.
Expenses: Tuition, state resident: part-time $289 per credit hour. Tuition, nonresident: part-time $448 per credit hour. One-time fee: $436 part-time. Full-time tuition and fees vary according to course load, campus/location and program.
Financial support: In 2001–02, 9 fellowships with full tuition reimbursements (averaging $12,516 per year), 41 research assistantships with tuition reimbursements (averaging $16,012 per year), 14 teaching assistantships with tuition reimbursements (averaging $14,025 per year) were awarded. Federal Work-Study and scholarships/grants also available. Support available to part-time students. Financial award applicants required to submit FAFSA.
Faculty research: Transportation and urban systems, environmental engineering, geotechnical engineering, construction engineering and management, hydraulics, remote sensing, soil mechanics.
Dr. Gregory Baecher, Chairman, 301-405-1972, *Fax:* 301-405-2585.
Application contact: Trudy Lindsey, Director, Graduate Admissions and Records, 301-405-6991, *Fax:* 301-314-9305, *E-mail:* grschool@deans.umd.edu.
Find an in-depth description at www.petersons.com/gradchannel.

■ UNIVERSITY OF MARYLAND, COLLEGE PARK

Graduate Studies and Research, College of Agriculture and Natural Resources, Department of Biological Resources Engineering, College Park, MD 20742

AWARDS MS, PhD.

Faculty: 16 full-time (2 women), 3 part-time/adjunct (1 woman).
Students: 31 full-time (18 women), 19 part-time (8 women); includes 8 minority (5 African Americans, 3 Asian Americans or Pacific Islanders), 17 international. 39 applicants, 56% accepted, 11 enrolled. In 2001, 1 degree awarded.
Degree requirements: For master's, thesis optional; for doctorate, thesis/dissertation.
Entrance requirements: For master's, GRE General Test, minimum GPA of 3.0. *Application deadline:* For fall admission, 6/1 (priority date); for spring admission, 10/1. Applications are processed on a rolling basis. *Application fee:* $50 ($70 for

international students). Electronic applications accepted.
Expenses: Tuition, state resident: part-time $289 per credit hour. Tuition, nonresident: part-time $448 per credit hour. One-time fee: $436 part-time. Full-time tuition and fees vary according to course load, campus/location and program.
Financial support: In 2001–02, 2 fellowships with full tuition reimbursements (averaging $9,771 per year), 17 research assistantships with tuition reimbursements (averaging $15,399 per year), 5 teaching assistantships with tuition reimbursements (averaging $15,588 per year) were awarded. Career-related internships or fieldwork also available. Financial award applicants required to submit FAFSA.
Faculty research: Engineering aspects of production; harvesting, processing, and marketing of terrestrial and aquatic food and fiber.
Dr. Frederick Wheaton, Chairman, 301-405-1193, *Fax:* 301-314-9023.
Application contact: Trudy Lindsey, Director, Graduate Admissions and Records, 301-405-6991, *Fax:* 301-314-9305, *E-mail:* grschool@deans.umd.edu.
Find an in-depth description at www.petersons.com/gradchannel.

■ UNIVERSITY OF MASSACHUSETTS AMHERST

Graduate School, College of Engineering, Department of Civil Engineering, Program in Environmental Engineering, Amherst, MA 01003

AWARDS MS. Part-time programs available.

Students: 19 full-time (12 women), 4 part-time (2 women); includes 2 minority (1 Asian American or Pacific Islander, 1 Native American), 4 international. Average age 24. 31 applicants, 55% accepted. In 2001, 8 degrees awarded.
Degree requirements: For master's, thesis or alternative.
Entrance requirements: For master's, GRE General Test. *Application deadline:* For fall admission, 2/1 (priority date); for spring admission, 10/1. Applications are processed on a rolling basis. *Application fee:* $40 ($50 for international students).
Expenses: Tuition, state resident: full-time $1,980; part-time $110 per credit. Tuition, nonresident: full-time $7,456; part-time $414 per credit. Required fees: $4,112. One-time fee: $115 full-time.
Financial support: Fellowships with full tuition reimbursements, research assistantships with full tuition reimbursements, teaching assistantships with full tuition reimbursements, career-related internships or fieldwork, Federal Work-Study, scholarships/grants, traineeships, and unspecified assistantships available. Support available to part-time students. Financial award application deadline: 2/1.

University of Massachusetts Amherst (continued)

David Ahlfeld, Head, 413-545-0685, *Fax:* 413-545-0964, *E-mail:* ahlfeld@ ecs.umass.edu.

■ UNIVERSITY OF MASSACHUSETTS LOWELL

Graduate School, James B. Francis College of Engineering, Department of Civil Engineering and College of Arts and Sciences, Program in Environmental Studies, Lowell, MA 01854-2881

AWARDS MS Eng. Part-time programs available.

Degree requirements: For master's, thesis optional.

Entrance requirements: For master's, GRE General Test.

Faculty research: Remote sensing of air pollutants, atmospheric deposition of toxic metals, contaminant transport in groundwater, soil remediation.

■ THE UNIVERSITY OF MEMPHIS

Graduate School, Herff College of Engineering, Department of Civil Engineering, Memphis, TN 38152

AWARDS Civil engineering (PhD); environmental engineering (MS); foundation engineering (MS). Structural engineering (MS); transportation engineering (MS); water resources engineering (MS).

Faculty: 12 full-time (0 women), 1 part-time/adjunct (0 women).

Students: 14 full-time (5 women), 7 part-time (1 woman), 10 international. Average age 32. 36 applicants, 56% accepted. In 2001, 5 degrees awarded.

Degree requirements: For master's, thesis or alternative, comprehensive exam; for doctorate, thesis/dissertation.

Entrance requirements: For master's, GRE General Test or MAT, minimum undergraduate GPA of 2.5. *Application deadline:* For fall admission, 8/1; for spring admission, 12/1. *Application fee:* $25 ($100 for international students).

Expenses: Tuition, state resident: full-time $2,026. Tuition, nonresident: full-time $4,528.

Financial support: In 2001–02, 1 fellowship with full tuition reimbursement, 13 research assistantships with full tuition reimbursements were awarded. Career-related internships or fieldwork also available.

Faculty research: Structural response to earthquakes, pavement design, water quality, bridge scour, intelligent transportation systems. *Total annual research expenditures:* $1.2 million.

Dr. Martin E. Lipinski, Chairman, 901-678-3279.

Application contact: Dr. Shahram Pezeshk, Coordinator of Graduate Studies, 901-678-4727.

■ UNIVERSITY OF MICHIGAN

Horace H. Rackham School of Graduate Studies, College of Engineering, Department of Civil and Environmental Engineering, Ann Arbor, MI 48109

AWARDS Civil engineering (MSE, PhD, CE); construction engineering and management (MSE); environmental engineering (MSE, PhD).

Faculty: 26 full-time (2 women), 2 part-time/adjunct (0 women).

Students: 142 full-time (39 women), 15 part-time (3 women); includes 11 minority (3 African Americans, 4 Asian Americans or Pacific Islanders, 4 Hispanic Americans), 96 international. Average age 27. 452 applicants, 52% accepted. In 2001, 51 master's, 13 doctorates awarded.

Degree requirements: For doctorate, oral defense of dissertation, preliminary and written exams.

Entrance requirements: For master's, GRE General Test; for doctorate, GRE General Test, master's degree. *Application deadline:* For fall admission, 2/8. Applications are processed on a rolling basis. *Application fee:* $55. Electronic applications accepted.

Financial support: In 2001–02, 109 students received support, including fellowships (averaging $20,200 per year), research assistantships (averaging $20,200 per year), teaching assistantships (averaging $12,783 per year); institutionally sponsored loans and tuition waivers (partial) also available. Financial award application deadline: 3/15.

Faculty research: Earthquake engineering, environmental and water resources engineering, geotechnical engineering, hydraulics and hydrologic engineering, structural engineering. *Total annual research expenditures:* $9.5 million.

Nikolaos D. Katopodes, Chair, 734-764-3674, *Fax:* 734-764-4292, *E-mail:* ndk@ umich.edu.

Application contact: Janet Lineer, Student Advisor, 734-764-8495, *Fax:* 734-763-2275, *E-mail:* janetl@umich.edu. *Web site:* http://www.engin.umich.edu/dept/cee/

■ UNIVERSITY OF MISSOURI–COLUMBIA

Graduate School, College of Engineering, Department of Civil and Environmental Engineering, Columbia, MO 65211

AWARDS Civil engineering (MS, PhD); environmental engineering (MS, PhD); geotechnical engineering (MS, PhD). Structural engineering (MS, PhD); transportation and highway engineering (MS); water resources (MS, PhD).

Faculty: 20 full-time (2 women), 1 part-time/adjunct (0 women).

Students: 28 full-time (6 women), 14 part-time (3 women); includes 4 minority (all

Hispanic Americans), 23 international. 74 applicants, 43% accepted. In 2001, 19 master's, 1 doctorate awarded.

Degree requirements: For master's, report or thesis; for doctorate, thesis/dissertation.

Entrance requirements: For master's and doctorate, GRE General Test, TOEFL. *Application deadline:* For fall admission, 3/15 (priority date); for winter admission, 10/15 (priority date). *Application fee:* $25 ($50 for international students).

Expenses: Tuition, state resident: part-time $179 per credit hour. Tuition, nonresident: part-time $539 per credit hour. Required fees: $122 per semester. Tuition and fees vary according to program.

Financial support: Research assistantships, teaching assistantships, institutionally sponsored loans available.

Dr. Mark Virkler, Director of Graduate Studies, 573-882-7434, *E-mail:* virklerm@ missouri.edu. *Web site:* http://www.engineering.missouri.edu/civil.htm

■ UNIVERSITY OF MISSOURI–ROLLA

Graduate School, School of Engineering, Department of Civil Engineering, Program in Environmental Engineering, Rolla, MO 65409-0910

AWARDS MS.

Degree requirements: For master's, thesis or alternative.

Entrance requirements: For master's, GRE General Test, TOEFL, minimum GPA of 3.0.

Faculty research: Hazardous waste treatment, groundwater remediation, air pollution control, advanced oxidation, phytoremediation.

■ UNIVERSITY OF MISSOURI–ROLLA

Graduate School, School of Engineering, Department of Civil Engineering, Program in Sanitary Engineering and Environmental Health, Rolla, MO 65409-0910

AWARDS MS, DE, PhD.

Degree requirements: For master's, thesis or alternative; for doctorate, thesis/dissertation.

Entrance requirements: For master's and doctorate, GRE General Test, TOEFL, minimum GPA of 3.0.

■ UNIVERSITY OF NEBRASKA–LINCOLN

Graduate College, College of Engineering and Technology, Interdepartmental Area of Environmental Engineering, Lincoln, NE 68588

AWARDS Engineering (PhD); environmental engineering (MS).

Faculty: 3.
Students: 10 (2 women) 2 international. Average age 29. 14 applicants, 21% accepted, 0 enrolled. In 2001, 7 degrees awarded.
Degree requirements: For master's, thesis optional; for doctorate, thesis/dissertation, comprehensive exam.
Entrance requirements: For master's and doctorate, GRE General Test, TOEFL. *Application deadline:* For fall admission, 4/15; for spring admission, 10/15. *Application fee:* $35. Electronic applications accepted.
Expenses: Tuition, state resident: full-time $2,412; part-time $134 per credit. Tuition, nonresident: full-time $6,223; part-time $346 per credit. Tuition and fees vary according to course load.
Financial support: In 2001–02, 4 research assistantships were awarded; fellowships Financial award application deadline: 2/15.
Faculty research: Wastewater engineering, hazardous waste management, solid waste management, groundwater engineering.
Dr. Mohamed F. Dahab, Graduate Committee Chair, 402-472-5020. *Web site:* http://www.bse.unl.edu/Grad/EnvEng.htm

■ UNIVERSITY OF NEVADA, LAS VEGAS

Graduate College, Howard R. Hughes College of Engineering, Department of Civil and Environmental Engineering, Las Vegas, NV 89154-9900

AWARDS MSE, PhD. Part-time programs available.

Faculty: 25 full-time (2 women).
Students: 23 full-time (4 women), 45 part-time (15 women); includes 12 minority (3 African Americans, 7 Asian Americans or Pacific Islanders, 2 Hispanic Americans), 23 international. 39 applicants, 54% accepted, 13 enrolled. In 2001, 8 master's, 1 doctorate awarded.
Degree requirements: For master's, thesis (for some programs), comprehensive exam (for some programs); for doctorate, thesis/dissertation, comprehensive exam. *Median time to degree:* Doctorate–5 years full-time.
Entrance requirements: For master's, minimum GPA of 3.0; for doctorate, GRE General Test, minimum GPA of 3.2. *Application deadline:* For fall admission,

6/15; for spring admission, 11/15. Applications are processed on a rolling basis. *Application fee:* $40 ($55 for international students).
Expenses: Tuition, state resident: full-time $1,926; part-time $107 per credit. Tuition, nonresident: full-time $9,376; part-time $220 per credit. Tuition and fees vary according to course load.
Financial support: In 2001–02, 15 research assistantships with full and partial tuition reimbursements (averaging $7,813 per year), 11 teaching assistantships with partial tuition reimbursements (averaging $10,000 per year) were awarded. Financial award application deadline: 3/1.
Dr. David James, Chair, 702-895-3701, *Fax:* 702-895-3936, *E-mail:* ce-info@ce.unlv.edu.
Application contact: Graduate College Admissions Evaluator, 702-895-3320, *Fax:* 702-895-4180, *E-mail:* gradcollege@ccmail.nevada.edu. *Web site:* http://www.ce.unlv.edu/

■ UNIVERSITY OF NEW HAVEN

Graduate School, School of Engineering and Applied Science, Program in Environmental Engineering, West Haven, CT 06516-1916

AWARDS Civil engineering design (Certificate); environmental engineering (MS). Part-time and evening/weekend programs available.

Students: 4 full-time (2 women), 17 part-time (3 women); includes 1 minority (African American), 1 international. In 2001, 5 degrees awarded.
Degree requirements: For master's, thesis or alternative.
Entrance requirements: For master's, bachelor's degree in engineering. *Application deadline:* Applications are processed on a rolling basis. *Application fee:* $50.
Expenses: Tuition: Full-time $12,015; part-time $445 per credit hour. Required fees: $30. One-time fee: $100 full-time.
Financial support: Federal Work-Study available. Support available to part-time students. Financial award application deadline: 5/1; financial award applicants required to submit FAFSA.
Dr. Agamemnon D. Koutsospyros, Coordinator, 203-932-7398.

■ THE UNIVERSITY OF NORTH CAROLINA AT CHAPEL HILL

Graduate School, School of Public Health, Department of Environmental Sciences and Engineering, Chapel Hill, NC 27599

AWARDS Air, radiation and industrial hygiene (MPH, MS, MSEE, MSPH, PhD); aquatic and atmospheric sciences (MPH, MS, MSPH, PhD); environmental engineering (MPH, MS, MSEE, MSPH, PhD); environmental health sciences (MPH, MS, MSPH, PhD);

environmental management and policy (MPH, MS, MSPH, PhD).

Faculty: 36 full-time (5 women), 35 part-time/adjunct.
Students: 138 full-time (64 women); includes 45 minority (10 African Americans, 32 Asian Americans or Pacific Islanders, 3 Hispanic Americans). Average age 26. 245 applicants, 45% accepted, 39 enrolled. In 2001, 24 master's, 14 doctorates awarded. Terminal master's awarded for partial completion of doctoral program.
Degree requirements: For master's, thesis (for some programs), research paper, comprehensive exam; for doctorate, thesis/dissertation, comprehensive exam. *Median time to degree:* Master's–2 years full-time; doctorate–4 years full-time.
Entrance requirements: For master's and doctorate, GRE General Test, minimum GPA of 3.0. *Application deadline:* For fall admission, 1/1 (priority date); for spring admission, 9/15. Applications are processed on a rolling basis. *Application fee:* $60. Electronic applications accepted.
Expenses: Tuition, state resident: full-time $2,864. Tuition, nonresident: full-time $12,030.
Financial support: In 2001–02, 120 students received support, including 44 fellowships with tuition reimbursements available (averaging $17,230 per year), 63 research assistantships with tuition reimbursements available (averaging $16,264 per year), 13 teaching assistantships with tuition reimbursements available (averaging $11,120 per year); career-related internships or fieldwork, Federal Work-Study, and traineeships also available. Support available to part-time students. Financial award application deadline: 1/1; financial award applicants required to submit FAFSA.
Faculty research: Air, radiation and industrial hygiene, aquatic and atmospheric sciences, environmental health sciences, environmental management and policy, water resources engineering. *Total annual research expenditures:* $7.7 million.
Dr. Cass T. Miller, Chair, 919-966-1024, *Fax:* 919-966-7911, *E-mail:* casey_miller@unc.edu.
Application contact: Jack Whaley, Assistant Registrar, 919-966-3844, *Fax:* 919-966-7911, *E-mail:* whaleyj@email.unc.edu. *Web site:* http://www.sph.unc.edu/envr/

■ UNIVERSITY OF NOTRE DAME

Graduate School, College of Engineering, Department of Civil Engineering and Geological Sciences, Notre Dame, IN 46556

AWARDS Bioengineering (MS); civil engineering (MS); civil engineering and geological sciences (PhD); environmental engineering (MS); geological sciences (MS).

Faculty: 15 full-time (1 woman).
Students: 42 full-time (16 women), 4 part-time (1 woman); includes 3 minority (1

University of Notre Dame (continued)
African American, 1 Asian American or Pacific Islander, 1 Hispanic American), 13 international. 118 applicants, 19% accepted, 12 enrolled. In 2001, 5 master's, 3 doctorates awarded. Terminal master's awarded for partial completion of doctoral program.
Degree requirements: For master's, comprehensive exam; for doctorate, thesis/dissertation. *Median time to degree:* Doctorate–5.5 years full-time.
Entrance requirements: For master's and doctorate, GRE General Test, TOEFL. *Application deadline:* For fall admission, 2/1 (priority date); for spring admission, 10/15. Applications are processed on a rolling basis. *Application fee:* $50. Electronic applications accepted.
Expenses: Tuition: Full-time $24,220; part-time $1,346 per credit hour. Required fees: $155.
Financial support: In 2001–02, 46 students received support, including 7 fellowships with full tuition reimbursements available (averaging $18,000 per year), 16 research assistantships with full tuition reimbursements available (averaging $12,800 per year), 17 teaching assistantships with full tuition reimbursements available (averaging $12,800 per year); tuition waivers (full) also available. Financial award application deadline: 2/1.
Faculty research: Structural analysis, finite-element methods, environmental modeling, biological-waste treatment, petrology, environmental geology, geochemistry. *Total annual research expenditures:* $1.4 million.
Dr. Peter C. Burns, Director of Graduate Studies, 574-631-5380, *Fax:* 574-631-9236, *E-mail:* cegeos@nd.edu.
Application contact: Dr. Terrence J. Akai, Director of Graduate Admissions, 574-631-7706, *Fax:* 574-631-4183, *E-mail:* gradad@nd.edu. *Web site:* http://www.nd.edu/~gradsch/degreeprograms/Engineering/CE/CEMenu.html

■ UNIVERSITY OF OKLAHOMA

Graduate College, College of Engineering, School of Civil Engineering and Environmental Science, Program in Civil Engineering, Norman, OK 73019-0390

AWARDS Civil engineering (PhD); environmental engineering (MS); geotechnical engineering (MS). Structures (MS); transportation (MS). Part-time programs available.

Students: 36 full-time (3 women), 18 part-time (2 women); includes 4 minority (2 Asian Americans or Pacific Islanders, 1 Hispanic American, 1 Native American), 35 international. 46 applicants, 85% accepted, 9 enrolled. In 2001, 17 degrees awarded. Terminal master's awarded for partial completion of doctoral program.

Degree requirements: For master's, oral exams; for doctorate, thesis/dissertation, oral and qualifying exams.
Entrance requirements: For master's, minimum GPA of 3.0; for doctorate, minimum graduate GPA of 3.5. *Application deadline:* For fall admission, 4/1 (priority date). Applications are processed on a rolling basis. *Application fee:* $25 ($50 for international students).
Expenses: Tuition, state resident: full-time $2,208; part-time $92 per credit hour. Tuition, nonresident: part-time $297 per credit hour. Tuition and fees vary according to course level, course load and program.
Financial support: In 2001–02, 7 students received support; research assistantships with partial tuition reimbursements available, teaching assistantships with full and partial tuition reimbursements available, scholarships/grants available. Financial award application deadline: 3/1; financial award applicants required to submit FAFSA.
Application contact: Susan Williams, Graduate Programs Specialist, 405-325-2344, *Fax:* 405-325-4217, *E-mail:* srwilliams@ou.edu.

■ UNIVERSITY OF PENNSYLVANIA

School of Engineering and Applied Science, Department of Systems Engineering, Philadelphia, PA 19104

AWARDS Environmental resources engineering (MSE); environmental/resources engineering (PhD); systems engineering (MSE, PhD); technology and public policy (MSE, PhD); transportation (MSE, PhD). Part-time programs available.

Faculty: 11 full-time (0 women), 3 part-time/adjunct (0 women).
Students: 38 full-time (10 women), 21 part-time (5 women); includes 39 minority (4 African Americans, 33 Asian Americans or Pacific Islanders, 2 Hispanic Americans). Terminal master's awarded for partial completion of doctoral program.
Degree requirements: For doctorate, one foreign language, thesis/dissertation.
Entrance requirements: For master's and doctorate, TOEFL. *Application deadline:* For fall admission, 1/2 (priority date). Applications are processed on a rolling basis. *Application fee:* $65. Electronic applications accepted.
Financial support: Fellowships, research assistantships, teaching assistantships, scholarships/grants available.
Faculty research: Systems methodology, operations research, decision sciences, telecommunication systems, logistics, transportation systems, manufacturing systems, infrastructure systems.
Dr. John D. Keenan, Chair, 215-898-5710, *Fax:* 215-898-5020, *E-mail:* keenan@seas.upenn.edu.
Application contact: Dr. Tony E. Smith, Graduate Group Chair, 215-898-9647,

Fax: 215-898-5020, *E-mail:* tesmith@seas.upenn.edu. *Web site:* http://www.seas.upenn.edu/ese

Find an in-depth description at www.petersons.com/gradchannel.

■ UNIVERSITY OF PITTSBURGH

School of Engineering, Department of Civil and Environmental Engineering, Pittsburgh, PA 15260

AWARDS MSCEE, PhD. Part-time and evening/weekend programs available.

Faculty: 13 full-time (0 women), 4 part-time/adjunct (0 women).
Students: 38 full-time (8 women), 56 part-time (7 women); includes 3 minority (1 African American, 2 Asian Americans or Pacific Islanders), 29 international. 79 applicants, 71% accepted, 21 enrolled. In 2001, 9 master's, 4 doctorates awarded. Terminal master's awarded for partial completion of doctoral program.
Degree requirements: For master's, thesis optional; for doctorate, thesis/dissertation, final oral exams, comprehensive exam.
Entrance requirements: For master's and doctorate, TOEFL, minimum QPA of 3.0. *Application deadline:* For fall admission, 8/1 (priority date); for spring admission, 12/1 (priority date). Applications are processed on a rolling basis. *Application fee:* $40.
Financial support: In 2001–02, 23 students received support, including 10 research assistantships with full tuition reimbursements available (averaging $16,980 per year), 13 teaching assistantships with full tuition reimbursements available (averaging $17,976 per year); fellowships with tuition reimbursements available, scholarships/grants, traineeships, and tuition waivers (full and partial) also available. Financial award application deadline: 2/15.
Faculty research: Environmental and water resources, structures and infrastructures, construction management. *Total annual research expenditures:* $930,452.
Dr. Rafael G. Quimpo, Chairman, 412-624-9870, *Fax:* 412-624-0135, *E-mail:* quimpo@civ.pitt.edu.
Application contact: Attila A. Sooky, Academic Coordinator, 412-624-9869, *Fax:* 412-624-0135, *E-mail:* sooky@civ.pitt.edu. *Web site:* http://www.engrng.pitt.edu/~civwww/

■ UNIVERSITY OF RHODE ISLAND

Graduate School, College of Engineering, Department of Civil and Environmental Engineering, Kingston, RI 02881

AWARDS Environmental engineering (MS, PhD); geotechnical engineering (MS, PhD). Structural engineering (MS, PhD); transportation engineering (MS, PhD).

Students: In 2001, 10 master's, 2 doctorates awarded.
Entrance requirements: For master's and doctorate, GRE. *Application deadline:* For fall admission, 4/15 (priority date). Applications are processed on a rolling basis. *Application fee:* $35.
Expenses: Tuition, state resident: full-time $3,756; part-time $209 per credit. Tuition, nonresident: full-time $10,774; part-time $599 per credit. Required fees: $1,586; $76 per credit. $76 per credit. One-time fee: $60 full-time.
Dr. George Tsiatas, Chairman, 401-874-2692.

■ UNIVERSITY OF SOUTHERN CALIFORNIA

Graduate School, School of Engineering, Department of Civil Engineering, Program in Environmental Engineering, Los Angeles, CA 90089
AWARDS MS, PhD.

Degree requirements: For master's, thesis optional; for doctorate, thesis/dissertation.
Entrance requirements: For master's and doctorate, GRE General Test, GRE Subject Test.
Expenses: Tuition: Full-time $25,060; part-time $844 per unit. Required fees: $473.
Faculty research: Environmental quality management.
Find an in-depth description at www.petersons.com/gradchannel.

■ UNIVERSITY OF SOUTH FLORIDA

College of Graduate Studies, College of Engineering, Department of Civil and Environmental Engineering, Tampa, FL 33620-9951
AWARDS Civil engineering (MCE, MSCE, PhD); engineering (ME, MSE). Part-time programs available.

Faculty: 19 full-time (2 women), 3 part-time/adjunct (0 women).
Students: 43 full-time (8 women), 52 part-time (9 women); includes 15 minority (1 African American, 6 Asian Americans or Pacific Islanders, 7 Hispanic Americans, 1 Native American), 30 international. Average age 32. 87 applicants, 56% accepted, 14 enrolled. In 2001, 21 master's, 6 doctorates awarded. Terminal master's awarded for partial completion of doctoral program.
Degree requirements: For master's, thesis (for some programs); for doctorate, thesis/dissertation, 2 tools of research as specified by dissertation committee.
Entrance requirements: For master's, GRE General Test, minimum GPA of 3.0 during previous 2 years; for doctorate, GRE General Test. *Application deadline:*

For fall admission, 6/1; for spring admission, 10/15. *Application fee:* $20. Electronic applications accepted.
Expenses: Tuition, state resident: part-time $166 per credit hour. Tuition, nonresident: part-time $573 per credit hour. Required fees: $17 per term.
Financial support: In 2001–02, 2 fellowships with tuition reimbursements (averaging $13,500 per year), 47 research assistantships with partial tuition reimbursements (averaging $13,000 per year), 12 teaching assistantships with partial tuition reimbursements (averaging $13,500 per year) were awarded. Unspecified assistantships also available. Financial award application deadline: 4/1.
Faculty research: Water resources, structures and materials, transportation, geotechnical engineering, mechanics, pavement. *Total annual research expenditures:* $2 million.
Dr. W. C. Carpenter, Chairperson, 813-974-2275, *Fax:* 813-974-2957, *E-mail:* carpente@eng.usf.edu.
Application contact: Prof. Ram M. Pendyala, 813-974-1084, *Fax:* 813-974-5927, *E-mail:* pendyala@eng.usf.edu. *Web site:* http://www.eng.usf.edu/civ/

■ THE UNIVERSITY OF TENNESSEE

Graduate School, College of Engineering, Department of Civil and Environmental Engineering, Program in Environmental Engineering, Knoxville, TN 37996

AWARDS MS. Part-time programs available. Postbaccalaureate distance learning degree programs offered (minimal on-campus study).

Students: 11 full-time (4 women), 22 part-time (3 women); includes 1 minority (African American), 9 international. 29 applicants, 48% accepted. In 2001, 12 degrees awarded.
Degree requirements: For master's, thesis or alternative.
Entrance requirements: For master's, TOEFL, minimum GPA of 2.7. *Application deadline:* For fall admission, 2/1 (priority date). Applications are processed on a rolling basis. *Application fee:* $35. Electronic applications accepted.
Expenses: Tuition, state resident: full-time $4,280; part-time $233 per hour. Tuition, nonresident: full-time $12,066; part-time $666 per hour. Tuition and fees vary according to program.
Financial support: Application deadline: 2/1.
Dr. Gregory D. Reed, Head, Department of Civil and Environmental Engineering, 865-974-2503, *Fax:* 865-974-2669, *E-mail:* gdreed@utk.edu.

■ THE UNIVERSITY OF TEXAS AT ARLINGTON

Graduate School, College of Engineering, Department of Civil and Environmental Engineering, Arlington, TX 76019

AWARDS M Engr, MS, PhD. Part-time and evening/weekend programs available. Postbaccalaureate distance learning degree programs offered (minimal on-campus study).

Faculty: 13 full-time (0 women), 1 part-time/adjunct (0 women).
Students: 60 full-time (13 women), 51 part-time (13 women); includes 13 minority (2 African Americans, 6 Asian Americans or Pacific Islanders, 4 Hispanic Americans, 1 Native American), 62 international. 104 applicants, 96% accepted, 31 enrolled. In 2001, 23 master's, 3 doctorates awarded. Terminal master's awarded for partial completion of doctoral program.
Degree requirements: For master's, oral and written exams, thesis optional; for doctorate, one foreign language.
Entrance requirements: For master's, GRE General Test, TOEFL, minimum GPA of 3.0 in last 60 hours of undergraduate course work; for doctorate, GRE General Test, TOEFL, minimum graduate GPA of 3.5. *Application deadline:* For fall admission, 6/16. Applications are processed on a rolling basis. *Application fee:* $25 ($50 for international students).
Expenses: Tuition, area resident: Full-time $2,268. Tuition, nonresident: full-time $6,264. Required fees: $839. Tuition and fees vary according to course load.
Financial support: In 2001–02, 29 fellowships with partial tuition reimbursements (averaging $1,000 per year), 30 research assistantships with partial tuition reimbursements (averaging $750 per year), 14 teaching assistantships with partial tuition reimbursements (averaging $750 per year) were awarded. Federal Work-Study, scholarships/grants, and tuition waivers (partial) also available. Financial award application deadline: 6/1; financial award applicants required to submit FAFSA.
Dr. Siamak A. Ardekani, Interim Chair, 817-272-5055, *Fax:* 817-272-2630, *E-mail:* ardekani@uta.edu.
Application contact: Dr. Ernest C. Crosby, Graduate Adviser, 817-272-3500, *Fax:* 817-272-2630, *E-mail:* ecrosby@uta.edu. *Web site:* http://www.ce.uta.edu/

■ THE UNIVERSITY OF TEXAS AT ARLINGTON

Graduate School, Program in Environmental Science and Engineering, Arlington, TX 76019
AWARDS MS, PhD.

Students: 5 full-time (1 woman), 6 part-time (1 woman); includes 1 minority (Hispanic American), 5 international. 7

The University of Texas at Arlington (continued)

applicants, 86% accepted, 1 enrolled. In 2001, 2 master's awarded.

Degree requirements: For master's, oral defense of thesis, thesis optional; for doctorate, thesis/dissertation, oral defense of thesis.

Entrance requirements: For master's, GRE General Test, TOEFL, minimum GPA of 3.0; for doctorate, GRE General Test, TOEFL, minimum graduate GPA of 3.5. *Application deadline:* For fall admission, 6/16. Applications are processed on a rolling basis. *Application fee:* $25 ($50 for international students). Electronic applications accepted.

Expenses: Tuition, area resident: Full-time $2,268. Tuition, nonresident: full-time $6,264. Required fees: $839. Tuition and fees vary according to course load.

Financial support: In 2001–02, 4 fellowships (averaging $1,000 per year), 2 research assistantships (averaging $15,500 per year) were awarded. Institutionally sponsored loans also available. Financial award application deadline: 6/1; financial award applicants required to submit FAFSA.

Dr. Robert McMahon, Associate Dean, 817-272-2492, *Fax:* 817-272-2628, *E-mail:* mcmahon@uta.edu.

Application contact: Dr. Andrew P. Kruzic, Graduate Advisor, 817-272-3822, *Fax:* 817-272-2630, *E-mail:* kruzic@uta.edu.

■ THE UNIVERSITY OF TEXAS AT AUSTIN

Graduate School, College of Engineering, Department of Civil Engineering, Program in Environmental and Water Resources Engineering, Austin, TX 78712-1111

AWARDS MSE.

Students: 29 (17 women); includes 1 minority (Hispanic American) 8 international. 82 applicants, 48% accepted, 14 enrolled. In 2001, 16 degrees awarded.

Entrance requirements: For master's, GRE General Test. *Application deadline:* For fall admission, 1/15 (priority date); for spring admission, 9/1 (priority date). Applications are processed on a rolling basis. *Application fee:* $50 ($75 for international students). Electronic applications accepted.

Expenses: Tuition, state resident: full-time $3,159. Tuition, nonresident: full-time $6,957. Tuition and fees vary according to program.

Financial support: Fellowships, research assistantships, teaching assistantships available. Financial award application deadline: 2/1.

Lynn E. Katz, Graduate Adviser, 512-471-4244.

Application contact: Kathy Rose, Graduate Coordinator, 512-471-4921, *Fax:* 512-471-0592, *E-mail:* krose@mail.utexas.edu.

■ THE UNIVERSITY OF TEXAS AT EL PASO

Graduate School, College of Engineering, Department of Civil Engineering, El Paso, TX 79968-0001

AWARDS Civil engineering (MS); environmental engineering (MEENE, MSENE). Part-time and evening/weekend programs available.

Students: 52 (11 women); includes 14 minority (1 Asian American or Pacific Islander, 13 Hispanic Americans) 7 international. Average age 34. 16 applicants, 100% accepted. In 2001, 78 degrees awarded.

Degree requirements: For master's, thesis optional.

Entrance requirements: For master's, GRE General Test, TOEFL, minimum GPA of 3.0. *Application deadline:* For fall admission, 7/1 (priority date); for spring admission, 11/1 (priority date). Applications are processed on a rolling basis. *Application fee:* $15 ($65 for international students). Electronic applications accepted.

Expenses: Tuition, state resident: full-time $2,450. Tuition, nonresident: full-time $6,000.

Financial support: In 2001–02, research assistantships with partial tuition reimbursements (averaging $21,125 per year), teaching assistantships with partial tuition reimbursements (averaging $16,900 per year) were awarded. Fellowships with partial tuition reimbursements, career-related internships or fieldwork, Federal Work-Study, institutionally sponsored loans, scholarships/grants, tuition waivers (partial), and stipends also available. Financial award application deadline: 3/15; financial award applicants required to submit FAFSA.

Faculty research: On-site wastewater treatment systems, wastewater reuse, disinfection by-product control, water resources, membrane filtration.

Dr. Carlos M. Ferregut, Chairperson, 915-747-6921, *Fax:* 915-747-8037, *E-mail:* ferregut@miners.utep.edu.

Application contact: Dr. Charles H. Ambler, Dean of the Graduate School, 915-747-5491 Ext. 7886, *Fax:* 915-747-5788, *E-mail:* cambler@miners.utep.edu.

■ THE UNIVERSITY OF TEXAS AT EL PASO

Graduate School, Interdisciplinary Program in Environmental Science and Engineering, El Paso, TX 79968-0001

AWARDS PhD. Part-time and evening/weekend programs available.

Students: 50 (17 women); includes 14 minority (2 African Americans, 2 Asian Americans or Pacific Islanders, 10 Hispanic Americans) 13 international. Average age 34. In 2001, 1 degree awarded.

Degree requirements: For doctorate, thesis/dissertation.

Entrance requirements: For doctorate, GRE General Test, TOEFL, minimum GPA of 3.0. *Application deadline:* For fall admission, 7/1; for spring admission, 11/1. Applications are processed on a rolling basis. *Application fee:* $15 ($65 for international students).

Expenses: Tuition, state resident: full-time $2,450. Tuition, nonresident: full-time $6,000.

Financial support: In 2001–02, research assistantships with partial tuition reimbursements (averaging $22,500 per year), teaching assistantships with partial tuition reimbursements (averaging $18,000 per year) were awarded. Fellowships with partial tuition reimbursements, Federal Work-Study, institutionally sponsored loans, scholarships/grants, and tuition waivers (partial) also available. Financial award application deadline: 3/15; financial award applicants required to submit FAFSA.

Dr. Jorge Gardea-Torredey, Chairperson, 915-747-5701, *Fax:* 915-747-5748, *E-mail:* jgardea@utep.edu.

Application contact: Dr. Charles H. Ambler, Dean of the Graduate School, 915-747-5491 Ext. 7886, *Fax:* 915-747-5788, *E-mail:* cambler@miners.utep.edu.

■ UNIVERSITY OF UTAH

Graduate School, College of Engineering, Department of Chemical and Fuels Engineering, Salt Lake City, UT 84112-1107

AWARDS Chemical and fuels engineering (M Phil, ME, MS, PhD); chemical engineering (M Phil, ME, MS, PhD); environmental engineering (ME, MS, PhD). Part-time programs available.

Faculty: 10 full-time (2 women), 6 part-time/adjunct (0 women).

Students: 47 full-time (7 women), 10 part-time (2 women); includes 18 minority (all Asian Americans or Pacific Islanders), 15 international. Average age 28. 84 applicants, 18% accepted. In 2001, 2 master's, 3 doctorates awarded.

Entrance requirements: For master's and doctorate, GRE, TOEFL, minimum GPA of 3.0. *Application deadline:* For fall admission, 7/1. *Application fee:* $40 ($60 for international students).

Expenses: Tuition, state resident: part-time $320 per semester hour. Tuition, nonresident: part-time $1,135 per semester hour. Required fees: $143 per semester hour. Tuition and fees vary according to course load, degree level and program.

Financial support: Fellowships, research assistantships, teaching assistantships available. Financial award applicants required to submit FAFSA.

Faculty research: Computer-aided process synthesis and design, combustion of solid and liquid fossil fuels, oxygen mass transport in biochemical reactors.

Terry Ring, Chair, 801-581-6915, *Fax:* 801-585-9291, *E-mail:* t.ring@m.cc.utah.edu.
Application contact: Grant Smith, Advisor, 801-581-6915, *Fax:* 801-585-9291, *E-mail:* gsmith@geoffrey.emro.utah.edu.

■ UNIVERSITY OF UTAH

Graduate School, College of Engineering, Department of Civil and Environmental Engineering, Salt Lake City, UT 84112-1107

AWARDS Civil engineering (ME, MS, PhD); environmental engineering (ME, MS, PhD); nuclear engineering (ME, MS, PhD).

Faculty: 12 full-time (2 women).
Students: 50 full-time (8 women), 35 part-time (5 women); includes 22 minority (18 Asian Americans or Pacific Islanders, 3 Hispanic Americans, 1 Native American), 8 international. Average age 32. 106 applicants, 72% accepted. In 2001, 11 master's, 3 doctorates awarded. Terminal master's awarded for partial completion of doctoral program.
Degree requirements: For master's, project (ME), thesis (MS); for doctorate, thesis/dissertation, departmental qualifying exam.
Entrance requirements: For master's and doctorate, GRE General Test, TOEFL, minimum GPA of 3.0. *Application deadline:* For fall admission, 7/1. *Application fee:* $40 ($60 for international students).
Expenses: Tuition, state resident: part-time $320 per semester hour. Tuition, nonresident: part-time $1,135 per semester hour. Required fees: $143 per semester hour. Tuition and fees vary according to course load, degree level and program.
Financial support: Research assistantships, teaching assistantships available. Support available to part-time students. Financial award applicants required to submit FAFSA.
Faculty research: Wastewater treatment, structural engineering, structural mechanics, hydraulics, composite materials.
Dr. Lawrence D. Reaveley, Chair, 801-581-6931, *Fax:* 801-585-5477, *E-mail:* reaveley@civil.utah.edu.
Application contact: Andy Hong, Advisor, 801-581-6931, *Fax:* 801-585-5477, *E-mail:* hong@civil.utah.edu. *Web site:* http://www.coe.utah.edu/

■ UNIVERSITY OF UTAH

Graduate School, College of Engineering, Department of Mechanical Engineering, Salt Lake City, UT 84112-1107

AWARDS Environmental engineering (ME, MS, PhD); mechanical engineering (ME, MS, PhD). Part-time programs available.

Faculty: 16 full-time (1 woman).
Students: 64 full-time (6 women), 51 part-time (4 women); includes 34 minority (3 African Americans, 26 Asian Americans or

Pacific Islanders, 4 Hispanic Americans, 1 Native American), 19 international. Average age 29. 169 applicants, 55% accepted. In 2001, 22 master's, 9 doctorates awarded. Terminal master's awarded for partial completion of doctoral program.
Degree requirements: For doctorate, thesis/dissertation, comprehensive exam.
Entrance requirements: For master's, GRE General Test, TOEFL, minimum GPA of 3.0; for doctorate, GRE, TOEFL, minimum GPA of 3.0. *Application deadline:* For fall admission, 7/1. *Application fee:* $40 ($60 for international students).
Expenses: Tuition, state resident: part-time $320 per semester hour. Tuition, nonresident: part-time $1,135 per semester hour. Required fees: $143 per semester hour. Tuition and fees vary according to course load, degree level and program.
Financial support: Fellowships, research assistantships, teaching assistantships, institutionally sponsored loans available. Financial award applicants required to submit FAFSA.
Faculty research: Thermal science, heat transfer, design fatigue, automated manufacturing, robotics.
Dr. Robert B. Roemer, Chair, 801-581-6441, *Fax:* 801-585-9826, *E-mail:* roemer@me.mech.utah.edu.
Application contact: Dr. Joseph C. Klewicki, Director of Graduate Studies, 801-581-7934, *Fax:* 801-585-9826, *E-mail:* klewicki@me.mech.utah.edu. *Web site:* http://www.coe.utah.edu/

■ UNIVERSITY OF VIRGINIA

School of Engineering and Applied Science, Department of Civil Engineering, Program in Environmental Engineering, Charlottesville, VA 22903

AWARDS Environmental engineering (ME, MS, PhD); water resources (ME, MS, PhD). Part-time programs available.

Faculty: 6 full-time (3 women).
Students: 26 full-time (11 women); includes 2 minority (both African Americans), 12 international. Average age 29. 62 applicants, 19% accepted, 8 enrolled. In 2001, 9 master's, 2 doctorates awarded. Terminal master's awarded for partial completion of doctoral program.
Degree requirements: For master's, thesis (for some programs); for doctorate, thesis/dissertation, comprehensive exam.
Entrance requirements: For master's and doctorate, GRE General Test. *Application deadline:* For fall admission, 2/1 (priority date); for spring admission, 8/1 (priority date). Applications are processed on a rolling basis. *Application fee:* $40. Electronic applications accepted.
Expenses: Tuition, state resident: full-time $3,988. Tuition, nonresident: full-time $17,078. Required fees: $1,190.
Financial support: In 2001–02, 20 students received support, including 4 fellowships with full tuition reimbursements

available (averaging $17,000 per year), 16 research assistantships with full tuition reimbursements available (averaging $17,000 per year), 4 teaching assistantships with full tuition reimbursements available (averaging $17,000 per year) Financial award application deadline: 2/1.
Faculty research: Stormwater management, nonpoint pollution control, water quality modeling, estuarine and coastal water quality management, groundwater flow and transport.
Dr. Shaw L. Yu, Professor, 434-924-6377, *Fax:* 434-982-2951, *E-mail:* sly@virginia.edu.

■ UNIVERSITY OF WASHINGTON

Graduate School, College of Engineering, Department of Civil and Environmental Engineering, Seattle, WA 98195

AWARDS Environmental engineering (MS, MSCE, MSE, PhD); hydraulic engineering (MSCE, MSE, PhD). Structural and geotechnical engineering and mechanics (MS, MSCE, MSE, PhD); transportation and construction engineering (MS, MSCE, MSE, PhD).

Faculty: 31 full-time (4 women), 26 part-time/adjunct (1 woman).
Students: 153 full-time (54 women), 42 part-time (13 women); includes 25 minority (2 African Americans, 19 Asian Americans or Pacific Islanders, 3 Hispanic Americans, 1 Native American), 34 international. Average age 29. 339 applicants, 60% accepted, 59 enrolled. In 2001, 71 master's, 11 doctorates awarded. Terminal master's awarded for partial completion of doctoral program.
Degree requirements: For master's, thesis (for some programs); for doctorate, thesis/dissertation, comprehensive exam. *Median time to degree:* Doctorate–3.5 years full-time.
Entrance requirements: For master's, GRE General Test, TOEFL, minimum GPA of 3.0; for doctorate, GRE, TOEFL, minimum GPA of 3.5. *Application deadline:* For fall admission, 2/1 (priority date). Applications are processed on a rolling basis. *Application fee:* $50. Electronic applications accepted.
Expenses: Tuition, state resident: full-time $5,539. Tuition, nonresident: full-time $14,376. Required fees: $390. Tuition and fees vary according to course load and program.
Financial support: In 2001–02, 110 students received support, including 22 fellowships with partial tuition reimbursements available, 70 research assistantships with full tuition reimbursements available, 22 teaching assistantships with full tuition reimbursements available; career-related internships or fieldwork and scholarships/grants also available. Financial award application deadline: 2/1.
Faculty research: Water resources, hydrology, construction, environmental

University of Washington (continued)
structures, geotechnical transportation. *Total annual research expenditures:* $3.7 million.
Prof. G. Scott Rutherford, Chair, 206-543-2390.
Application contact: Marcia Buck, Graduate Adviser, 206-543-2574, *E-mail:* cesendme@u.washington.edu. *Web site:* http://www.ce.washington.edu/grad_p.htm

■ UNIVERSITY OF WISCONSIN–MADISON

Graduate School, College of Engineering, Department of Civil and Environmental Engineering, Madison, WI 53706-1380

AWARDS MS, PhD. Part-time programs available.

Faculty: 30 full-time (1 woman), 3 part-time/adjunct (0 women).
Students: 131 full-time (29 women), 31 part-time (4 women). Average age 25. 266 applicants, 51% accepted, 25 enrolled. In 2001, 33 master's, 12 doctorates awarded. Terminal master's awarded for partial completion of doctoral program.
Degree requirements: For master's, thesis or alternative; for doctorate, thesis/dissertation, preliminary exam and qualifying exams.
Entrance requirements: For master's and doctorate, TOEFL, minimum GPA of 3.0 for last 60 credits. *Application deadline:* For fall admission, 6/30 (priority date); for spring admission, 11/15. Applications are processed on a rolling basis. *Application fee:* $45. Electronic applications accepted.
Expenses: Tuition, state resident: full-time $7,361; part-time $399 per credit. Tuition, nonresident: full-time $20,499; part-time $1,282 per credit. Required fees: $34 per credit. Full-time tuition and fees vary according to course load, program, reciprocity agreements and student level.
Financial support: In 2001–02, 126 students received support, including 11 fellowships with full tuition reimbursements available (averaging $16,350 per year), 77 research assistantships with full tuition reimbursements available (averaging $16,350 per year), 16 teaching assistantships with full tuition reimbursements available (averaging $6,982 per year); Federal Work-Study also available. Support available to part-time students. Financial award application deadline: 12/15.
Faculty research: Environmental geotechnics and soil mechanics, design and analysis of structures, traffic engineering and intelligent transport systems, industrial pollution control, hydrological monitoring. *Total annual research expenditures:* $6.5 million.
Erhard F. Joeres, Chair, 608-262-3542, *Fax:* 608-262-5199, *E-mail:* cee@engr.wisc.edu.

Application contact: Kathy Monroe, Student Services Coordinator, 608-262-5198, *Fax:* 608-262-5199, *E-mail:* kmonroe@engr.wisc.edu. *Web site:* http://www.engr.wisc.edu/cee/

■ UNIVERSITY OF WYOMING

Graduate School, College of Engineering, Department of Chemical and Petroleum Engineering, Laramie, WY 82071

AWARDS Chemical engineering (MS, PhD); environmental engineering (MS); petroleum engineering (MS, PhD).

Faculty: 6 full-time (0 women), 3 part-time/adjunct (0 women).
Students: 17 full-time (3 women), 6 part-time (1 woman), 16 international. 12 applicants, 100% accepted. In 2001, 3 degrees awarded.
Entrance requirements: For master's, GRE General Test, minimum GPA of 3.0; for doctorate, GRE General Test, TOEFL, minimum GPA of 3.0. *Application deadline:* For fall admission, 4/15 (priority date). Applications are processed on a rolling basis. *Application fee:* $40. Electronic applications accepted.
Expenses: Tuition, state resident: full-time $2,895; part-time $161 per credit hour. Tuition, nonresident: full-time $8,367; part-time $465 per credit hour. Required fees: $491; $10 per credit hour. $2 per credit hour. Tuition and fees vary according to course load and program.
Financial support: In 2001–02, 10 research assistantships with full tuition reimbursements (averaging $13,000 per year), 6 teaching assistantships with full tuition reimbursements (averaging $12,000 per year) were awarded. Career-related internships or fieldwork, Federal Work-Study, and institutionally sponsored loans also available. Financial award application deadline: 4/15.
Faculty research: Microwave reactor, synthetic fuels, fluidization, coal combustion/gasification, flue-gas cleanup.
Dr. Maciej Radosz, Head, 307-766-4923, *Fax:* 307-766-6777, *E-mail:* radosz@uwyo.edu.
Application contact: Dr. David Bell, Graduate Student Coordinator, 307-766-5769, *Fax:* 307-766-6777, *E-mail:* chpe.info@uwyo.edu. *Web site:* http://wwweng.uwyo.edu/

■ UNIVERSITY OF WYOMING

Graduate School, College of Engineering, Department of Civil and Architectural Engineering and Department of Chemical and Petroleum Engineering, Program in Environmental Engineering, Laramie, WY 82071

AWARDS MS. Part-time programs available.
Faculty: 6.

Students: 7 full-time (3 women), 2 part-time, 1 international. 6 applicants, 100% accepted. In 2001, 1 degree awarded.
Degree requirements: For master's, thesis optional.
Entrance requirements: For master's, GRE General Test, TOEFL, minimum GPA of 3.0. *Application deadline:* For fall admission, 5/1 (priority date); for spring admission, 9/1. Applications are processed on a rolling basis. *Application fee:* $40. Electronic applications accepted.
Expenses: Tuition, state resident: full-time $2,895; part-time $161 per credit hour. Tuition, nonresident: full-time $8,367; part-time $465 per credit hour. Required fees: $491; $10 per credit hour. $2 per credit hour. Tuition and fees vary according to course load and program.
Financial support: In 2001–02, 2 research assistantships with full tuition reimbursements (averaging $8,667 per year), 2 teaching assistantships with full tuition reimbursements (averaging $8,667 per year) were awarded. Fellowships, career-related internships or fieldwork, Federal Work-Study, and institutionally sponsored loans also available. Financial award application deadline: 3/1.
Faculty research: Water and waste water, solid and hazardous waste management, air pollution control, flue-gas cleanup.
Dr. Marge Bedessem, Chair, 307-766-5286, *Fax:* 307-766-2221, *E-mail:* bedessem@uwyo.edu.
Application contact: Heather D. Warren, Graduate Coordinator, 307-766-5446, *Fax:* 307-766-2221, *E-mail:* hwarren@uwyo.edu. *Web site:* http://wwweng.uwyo.edu/env.html

■ UTAH STATE UNIVERSITY

School of Graduate Studies, College of Engineering, Department of Civil and Environmental Engineering, Logan, UT 84322

AWARDS ME, MS, PhD, CE.

Faculty: 31 full-time (1 woman).
Students: 61 full-time (10 women), 30 part-time (2 women); includes 4 minority (2 Asian Americans or Pacific Islanders, 2 Native Americans), 49 international. Average age 28. 151 applicants, 69% accepted. In 2001, 25 master's, 2 doctorates awarded.
Degree requirements: For master's, thesis (for some programs); for doctorate, thesis/dissertation.
Entrance requirements: For master's and doctorate, GRE General Test, TOEFL, minimum GPA of 3.0. *Application deadline:* For fall admission, 6/15 (priority date); for spring admission, 10/15. Applications are processed on a rolling basis. *Application fee:* $40.
Expenses: Tuition, state resident: full-time $1,693. Tuition, nonresident: full-time $4,233. Required fees: $501. Tuition and fees vary according to program.
Financial support: In 2001–02, 2 fellowships with partial tuition reimbursements

(averaging $12,000 per year), 49 research assistantships with partial tuition reimbursements (averaging $1,000 per year) were awarded. Teaching assistantships with partial tuition reimbursements, career-related internships or fieldwork, Federal Work-Study, and institutionally sponsored loans also available. Support available to part-time students. Financial award application deadline: 3/31.

Faculty research: Hazardous waste treatment, large space structures, river basin management, earthquake engineering, environmental impact.

Loren R. Anderson, Head, 435-797-2938, *Fax:* 435-797-1185.

Application contact: Becky Hansen, Staff Assistant IV, 435-797-2938, *Fax:* 435-797-1185, *E-mail:* beckyjh@cc.usu.edu. *Web site:* http://www.engineering.usu.edu/Departments/cee/

■ VANDERBILT UNIVERSITY

School of Engineering, Department of Civil and Environmental Engineering, Program in Environmental Engineering, Nashville, TN 37240-1001

AWARDS M Eng, MS, PhD. MS and PhD offered through the Graduate School. Part-time programs available.

Faculty: 6 full-time (1 woman), 1 part-time/adjunct (0 women).
Students: 18 full-time (10 women), 1 part-time; includes 12 minority (11 Asian Americans or Pacific Islanders, 1 Hispanic American). Average age 27. 35 applicants, 23% accepted, 6 enrolled. In 2001, 1 master's, 1 doctorate awarded. Terminal master's awarded for partial completion of doctoral program.
Degree requirements: For master's, thesis or alternative; for doctorate, thesis/dissertation.
Entrance requirements: For master's and doctorate, GRE General Test. *Application deadline:* For fall admission, 1/15; for spring admission, 11/1. Applications are processed on a rolling basis. *Application fee:* $40.
Expenses: Tuition: Full-time $28,350.
Financial support: In 2001–02, 2 fellowships with full tuition reimbursements (averaging $11,500 per year), 10 research assistantships with full tuition reimbursements (averaging $15,540 per year), 7 teaching assistantships with full tuition reimbursements (averaging $14,500 per year) were awarded. Career-related internships or fieldwork, institutionally sponsored loans, and tuition waivers (full and partial) also available. Financial award application deadline: 1/15.
Faculty research: Waste treatment, hazardous waste management, chemical waste treatment, water quality.
Application contact: Dr. David S. Kosson, Chair, 615-322-2697, *Fax:* 615-322-3365, *E-mail:* david.kosson@

vanderbilt.edu. *Web site:* http://www.cee.vanderbilt.edu

Find an in-depth description at www.petersons.com/gradchannel.

■ VILLANOVA UNIVERSITY

College of Engineering, Department of Civil and Environmental Engineering, Program in Water Resources and Environmental Engineering, Villanova, PA 19085-1699

AWARDS MSWREE. Part-time and evening/weekend programs available.

Faculty: 5 full-time (0 women), 5 part-time/adjunct (0 women).
Students: 3 full-time (2 women), 8 part-time (5 women); includes 1 minority (Asian American or Pacific Islander), 3 international. Average age 25. 13 applicants, 92% accepted. In 2001, 9 degrees awarded.
Degree requirements: For master's, thesis optional.
Entrance requirements: For master's, GRE General Test (for applicants with degrees from foreign universities), BCE or bachelor's degree in science or related engineering field, minimum GPA of 3.0. *Application deadline:* For fall admission, 8/1 (priority date); for spring admission, 12/1. Applications are processed on a rolling basis. *Application fee:* $40. Electronic applications accepted.
Expenses: Tuition: Part-time $340 per credit. One-time fee: $115 full-time. Tuition and fees vary according to program.
Financial support: Federal Work-Study and tuition waivers (full and partial) available. Support available to part-time students. Financial award application deadline: 4/15.
Faculty research: Photocatalytic decontamination and disinfection of water, urban storm water wetlands, economy and risk, removal and destruction of organic acids in water, sludge treatment.
Dr. Ronald A. Chadderton, Chairman, Department of Civil and Environmental Engineering, 610-519-4960, *Fax:* 610-519-6754.

■ VIRGINIA POLYTECHNIC INSTITUTE AND STATE UNIVERSITY

Graduate School, College of Engineering, Department of Civil and Environmental Engineering, Program in Environmental Engineering, Blacksburg, VA 24061

AWARDS MS. Part-time programs available. Postbaccalaureate distance learning degree programs offered (no on-campus study).

Faculty: 11 full-time (2 women).
Students: 24 full-time (6 women); includes 12 minority (3 African Americans, 7 Asian Americans or Pacific Islanders, 2 Hispanic

Americans). Average age 23. In 2001, 14 degrees awarded.
Degree requirements: For master's, thesis.
Entrance requirements: For master's, GRE General Test, TOEFL. *Application deadline:* For fall admission, 12/1 (priority date); for spring admission, 10/1. Applications are processed on a rolling basis. *Application fee:* $45. Electronic applications accepted.
Expenses: Tuition, state resident: part-time $241 per hour. Tuition, nonresident: part-time $406 per hour. Tuition and fees vary according to program.
Financial support: In 2001–02, research assistantships with full and partial tuition reimbursements (averaging $14,500 per year), teaching assistantships with full and partial tuition reimbursements (averaging $14,500 per year) were awarded. Fellowships with full tuition reimbursements Financial award application deadline: 4/1.
Faculty research: Optimization of water treatment process, industrial waste water treatment, taste and odor issues, applied aquatic chemistry, air pollution control technology.
Dr. Marc Edwards, Coordinator, 540-231-7236, *Fax:* 540-231-7916, *E-mail:* edwardsm@vt.edu.
Application contact: Betty P. Wingate, Administrative and Program Specialist III, 540-231-6131, *Fax:* 540-231-7916, *E-mail:* bwingate@vt.edu.

Find an in-depth description at www.petersons.com/gradchannel.

■ VIRGINIA POLYTECHNIC INSTITUTE AND STATE UNIVERSITY

Graduate School, College of Engineering, Department of Civil and Environmental Engineering, Program in Environmental Sciences and Engineering, Blacksburg, VA 24061

AWARDS MS. Part-time programs available. Postbaccalaureate distance learning degree programs offered (no on-campus study).

Faculty: 10 full-time (2 women).
Students: 9 full-time (6 women); includes 2 minority (both Asian Americans or Pacific Islanders). Average age 23. 50 applicants, 20% accepted. In 2001, 3 degrees awarded.
Degree requirements: For master's, thesis.
Entrance requirements: For master's, GRE General Test, TOEFL. *Application deadline:* For fall admission, 12/1 (priority date); for spring admission, 10/1 (priority date). Applications are processed on a rolling basis. *Application fee:* $45. Electronic applications accepted.
Expenses: Tuition, state resident: part-time $241 per hour. Tuition, nonresident: part-time $406 per hour. Tuition and fees vary according to program.

Virginia Polytechnic Institute and State University (continued)

Financial support: Fellowships with full and partial tuition reimbursements, research assistantships with full and partial tuition reimbursements, teaching assistantships with full and partial tuition reimbursements, unspecified assistantships available. Financial award application deadline: 4/1.

Faculty research: Biological wastewater treatment, surface chemistry of metal oxides, air quality modeling, environmental toxicology.

Dr. Marc Edwards, Coordinator, 540-231-7236, *Fax:* 540-231-7916, *E-mail:* edwardsm@vt.edu.

Application contact: Betty P. Wingate, Administrative and Program Specialist III, 540-231-6131, *Fax:* 540-231-7916, *E-mail:* bwingate@vt.edu.

Find an in-depth description at www.petersons.com/gradchannel.

■ **WASHINGTON STATE UNIVERSITY**

Graduate School, College of Engineering and Architecture, Department of Civil and Environmental Engineering, Program in Environmental Engineering, Pullman, WA 99164

AWARDS MS.

Faculty: 24 full-time (1 woman), 6 part-time/adjunct (0 women).
Students: 11 full-time (5 women); includes 1 minority (Native American), 3 international. Average age 25. 28 applicants, 32% accepted. In 2001, 14 degrees awarded.
Degree requirements: For master's, oral exam, thesis optional.
Entrance requirements: For master's, GRE General Test, minimum GPA of 3.0. *Application deadline:* For fall admission, 3/1 (priority date); for spring admission, 10/1. Applications are processed on a rolling basis. *Application fee:* $35. Electronic applications accepted.
Expenses: Tuition, state resident: full-time $6,088; part-time $304 per semester. Tuition, nonresident: full-time $14,918; part-time $746 per semester. Tuition and fees vary according to program.
Financial support: In 2001–02, fellowships (averaging $15,000 per year), 5 research assistantships with full and partial tuition reimbursements (averaging $14,000 per year), 3 teaching assistantships with full and partial tuition reimbursements (averaging $14,000 per year) were awarded. Career-related internships or fieldwork, Federal Work-Study, and institutionally sponsored loans also available. Financial award application deadline: 4/1; financial award applicants required to submit FAFSA.

Faculty research: Air quality, hazardous waste, soil and ground water contamination, acid precipitation, global climate. *Total annual research expenditures:* $4.3 million.
Application contact: Maureen Clausen, Secretary Senior, 509-335-2576, *Fax:* 509-335-7632, *E-mail:* mclausen@wsu.edu. *Web site:* http://www.ce.wsu.edu/

■ **WAYNE STATE UNIVERSITY**

Graduate School, College of Engineering, Department of Civil and Environmental Engineering, Detroit, MI 48202

AWARDS MS, PhD.

Faculty: 10 full-time.
Students: 130. 184 applicants, 43% accepted, 35 enrolled. In 2001, 26 master's, 5 doctorates awarded.
Degree requirements: For master's, thesis optional; for doctorate, thesis/dissertation.
Application deadline: For fall admission, 7/1 (priority date); for spring admission, 3/15. Applications are processed on a rolling basis. *Application fee:* $20 ($30 for international students). Electronic applications accepted.
Expenses: Tuition, state resident: full-time $3,764. Tuition and fees vary according to degree level and program.
Financial support: In 2001–02, 1 fellowship, 19 research assistantships, 5 teaching assistantships were awarded. Career-related internships or fieldwork and tuition waivers (partial) also available.
Faculty research: Environmental geotechnics, bridge engineering, seismic analysis, construction safety, mass transit. *Total annual research expenditures:* $485,000.
Dr. Mumtaz Usmen, Chairperson, 313-577-3789, *Fax:* 313-577-3881, *E-mail:* musmen@ce.eng.wayne.edu.

■ **WEST VIRGINIA UNIVERSITY**

College of Engineering and Mineral Resources, Department of Civil and Environmental Engineering, Morgantown, WV 26506

AWARDS Civil engineering (MSCE, MSE, PhD). Part-time programs available.

Faculty: 15 full-time (0 women).
Students: 36 full-time (9 women), 9 part-time (2 women), 23 international. Average age 24. 286 applicants, 75% accepted. In 2001, 15 master's, 2 doctorates awarded.
Degree requirements: For master's, thesis/dissertation; for doctorate, thesis/dissertation, comprehensive exam.
Entrance requirements: For master's, TOEFL, minimum GPA of 3.0; for doctorate, GRE (international applicants), TOEFL, minimum GPA of 3.0. *Application deadline:* For fall admission, 7/1 (priority date); for spring admission, 12/1. Applications are processed on a rolling basis. *Application fee:* $45.

Expenses: Tuition, state resident: full-time $2,791. Tuition, nonresident: full-time $8,659. Required fees: $1,002. Tuition and fees vary according to program.
Financial support: In 2001–02, 23 research assistantships, 3 teaching assistantships were awarded. Fellowships, career-related internships or fieldwork, Federal Work-Study, institutionally sponsored loans, and tuition waivers (full and partial) also available. Financial award application deadline: 2/1; financial award applicants required to submit FAFSA.
Faculty research: Environmental and hydrotechnical structural composites, bridge innovation and rehabilitation, transport, soil mechanics, geoenvironmental engineering. *Total annual research expenditures:* $2.5 million.
Dr. David R. Martinelli, Chair, 304-293-3031 Ext. 2616, *Fax:* 304-293-7109, *E-mail:* david.martinelli@mail.wvu.edu.
Application contact: Udaya Halabe, Graduate Program Coordinator, 304-293-3031 Ext. 2617, *Fax:* 304-293-7109, *E-mail:* udaya.halabe@mail.wvu.edu. *Web site:* http://www.cemr.wvu.edu/~wwwce/cee_4.0.html

■ **WORCESTER POLYTECHNIC INSTITUTE**

Graduate Studies, Department of Civil and Environmental Engineering, Worcester, MA 01609-2280

AWARDS M Eng, MS, PhD, Advanced Certificate, Certificate. Part-time and evening/weekend programs available.
Postbaccalaureate distance learning degree programs offered (minimal on-campus study).

Faculty: 15 full-time (1 woman), 3 part-time/adjunct (0 women).
Students: 19 full-time (6 women), 32 part-time (10 women); includes 2 minority (1 Asian American or Pacific Islander, 1 Hispanic American), 10 international. 62 applicants, 56% accepted, 17 enrolled. In 2001, 14 degrees awarded.
Degree requirements: For master's, thesis optional; for doctorate, thesis/dissertation.
Entrance requirements: For master's and doctorate, TOEFL. *Application deadline:* For fall admission, 2/1 (priority date); for spring admission, 10/15 (priority date). Applications are processed on a rolling basis. *Application fee:* $60. Electronic applications accepted.
Expenses: Tuition: Part-time $796 per credit. Required fees: $20; $752 per credit. One-time fee: $30 full-time.
Financial support: In 2001–02, 17 students received support, including 4 research assistantships with full tuition reimbursements available (averaging $17,256 per year), 8 teaching assistantships with full tuition reimbursements available (averaging $12,942 per year); fellowships, career-related internships or fieldwork, institutionally sponsored loans, and scholarships/grants also available. Financial

award application deadline: 2/15; financial award applicants required to submit FAFSA.
Faculty research: Structural and environmental engineering, asphalt technology, highway safety, construction project management. *Total annual research expenditures:* $1.1 million.
Dr. Fred L. Hart, Head, 508-831-5530, *Fax:* 508-831-5808, *E-mail:* flhart@wpi.edu.
Application contact: Dr. James O'Shaughnessy, Graduate Coordinator, 508-831-5309, *Fax:* 508-831-5808, *E-mail:* jco@wpi.edu. *Web site:* http://www.wpi.edu/Academics/Depts/CEE/

■ YOUNGSTOWN STATE UNIVERSITY

Graduate School, William Rayen College of Engineering, Department of Civil, Chemical, and Environmental Engineering, Youngstown, OH 44555-0001

AWARDS MSE. Part-time and evening/weekend programs available.

Degree requirements: For master's, thesis optional.
Entrance requirements: For master's, TOEFL, minimum GPA of 2.75 in field.
Faculty research: Structural mechanics, water quality modeling, surface and ground water hydrology, physical and chemical processes in aquatic systems.

FIRE PROTECTION ENGINEERING

■ ANNA MARIA COLLEGE

Graduate Division, Program in Fire Science and Administration, Paxton, MA 01612

AWARDS Fire science (MA).

Faculty: 1 part-time/adjunct (0 women).
Students: 2 full-time (0 women), 19 part-time (2 women). Average age 40.
Degree requirements: For master's, internship, research project.
Entrance requirements: For master's, minimum GPA of 2.7, resumé. *Application deadline:* For fall admission, 3/1 (priority date); for spring admission, 11/1 (priority date). Applications are processed on a rolling basis. *Application fee:* $30. Electronic applications accepted.
Expenses: Tuition: Part-time $900 per course.
Financial support: Institutionally sponsored loans available.
Brian Duggan, Director, 508-849-3337, *Fax:* 508-849-3343, *E-mail:* bduggan@annamaria.edu.
Application contact: Eva Eaton, Director of Admissions for Graduate Programs and the Department of Professional Studies,

508-849-3488, *Fax:* 508-849-3362, *E-mail:* eveaton@annamaria.edu.

■ UNIVERSITY OF MARYLAND, COLLEGE PARK

Graduate Studies and Research, A. James Clark School of Engineering, Department of Fire Protection Engineering, College Park, MD 20742

AWARDS M Eng, MS. Part-time and evening/weekend programs available.

Faculty: 7 full-time (0 women), 6 part-time/adjunct (1 woman).
Students: 15 full-time (5 women), 10 part-time (4 women); includes 2 minority (both Asian Americans or Pacific Islanders), 9 international. Average age 26. 30 applicants, 50% accepted, 12 enrolled. In 2001, 10 degrees awarded.
Degree requirements: For master's, thesis optional.
Entrance requirements: For master's, GRE General Test, minimum GPA of 3.0, BS in any engineering or physical science area. *Application deadline:* For fall admission, 8/1; for spring admission, 11/1. Applications are processed on a rolling basis. *Application fee:* $50 ($70 for international students). Electronic applications accepted.
Expenses: Tuition, state resident: part-time $289 per credit hour. Tuition, nonresident: part-time $448 per credit hour. One-time fee: $436 part-time. Full-time tuition and fees vary according to course load, campus/location and program.
Financial support: In 2001–02, 10 research assistantships with tuition reimbursements (averaging $12,319 per year), 3 teaching assistantships with tuition reimbursements (averaging $12,601 per year) were awarded. Fellowships, career-related internships or fieldwork, Federal Work-Study, institutionally sponsored loans, and scholarships/grants also available. Financial award application deadline: 2/1; financial award applicants required to submit FAFSA.
Faculty research: Fire and thermal degradation of materials, fire modeling, fire dynamics, smoke detection and management, fire resistance.
Dr. Marino Dimarzo, Chair, 301-405-5257, *Fax:* 301-405-9383, *E-mail:* ss60@eng.umd.edu.
Application contact: Dr. James A. Milke, Graduate Director, 301-405-3995, *Fax:* 301-405-9383, *E-mail:* milke@eng.umd.edu. *Web site:* http://www.enfp.umd.edu/

■ UNIVERSITY OF MARYLAND, COLLEGE PARK

Graduate Studies and Research, A. James Clark School of Engineering, Professional Program in Engineering, College Park, MD 20742

AWARDS Aerospace engineering (M Eng); chemical engineering (M Eng); civil engineering (M Eng); electrical engineering (M Eng); fire protection engineering (M Eng); materials science and engineering (M Eng); mechanical engineering (M Eng); reliability engineering (M Eng). Systems engineering (M Eng). Part-time and evening/weekend programs available. Postbaccalaureate distance learning degree programs offered.

Faculty: 11 part-time/adjunct (0 women).
Students: 19 full-time (4 women), 144 part-time (31 women); includes 41 minority (17 African Americans, 18 Asian Americans or Pacific Islanders, 6 Hispanic Americans), 27 international. 71 applicants, 80% accepted, 50 enrolled. In 2001, 64 degrees awarded.
Application deadline: For fall admission, 8/15; for spring admission, 1/10. Applications are processed on a rolling basis. *Application fee:* $50 ($70 for international students). Electronic applications accepted.
Expenses: Tuition, state resident: part-time $289 per credit hour. Tuition, nonresident: part-time $448 per credit hour. One-time fee: $436 part-time. Full-time tuition and fees vary according to course load, campus/location and program.
Financial support: In 2001–02, 1 research assistantship with tuition reimbursement (averaging $20,655 per year), 5 teaching assistantships with tuition reimbursements (averaging $11,114 per year) were awarded. Fellowships, Federal Work-Study and scholarships/grants also available. Support available to part-time students. Financial award applicants required to submit FAFSA.
Dr. George Syrmos, Acting Director, 301-405-5256, *Fax:* 301-314-9477.
Application contact: Trudy Lindsey, Director, Graduate Admissions and Records, 301-405-6991, *Fax:* 301-314-9305, *E-mail:* grschool@deans.umd.edu.

■ UNIVERSITY OF NEW HAVEN

Graduate School, School of Public Safety and Professional Studies, Program in Fire Science, West Haven, CT 06516-1916

AWARDS MS.

Students: 2 full-time (0 women), 17 part-time (1 woman), 2 international. In 2001, 7 degrees awarded.
Degree requirements: For master's, thesis or alternative.
Application deadline: Applications are processed on a rolling basis. *Application fee:* $50.

University of New Haven (continued)
Expenses: Tuition: Full-time $12,015; part-time $445 per credit hour. Required fees: $30. One-time fee: $100 full-time.
Financial support: Career-related internships or fieldwork and Federal Work-Study available. Support available to part-time students. Financial award application deadline: 5/1; financial award applicants required to submit FAFSA.
Robert Massicotte, Director, 203-932-7424.

■ **WORCESTER POLYTECHNIC INSTITUTE**

Graduate Studies, Department of Fire Protection Engineering, Worcester, MA 01609-2280

AWARDS MS, PhD, Advanced Certificate, Certificate. Part-time and evening/weekend programs available. Postbaccalaureate distance learning degree programs offered (no on-campus study).

Faculty: 4 full-time (0 women), 1 part-time/adjunct (0 women).
Students: 45 full-time (4 women), 30 part-time (7 women); includes 2 minority (both Asian Americans or Pacific Islanders), 22 international. 72 applicants, 79% accepted, 24 enrolled. In 2001, 24 master's, 2 doctorates awarded.
Degree requirements: For doctorate, thesis/dissertation.
Entrance requirements: For master's, TOEFL, BS in engineering or physical sciences; for doctorate, TOEFL. *Application deadline:* For fall admission, 2/1 (priority date); for spring admission, 10/15 (priority date). Applications are processed on a rolling basis. *Application fee:* $60. Electronic applications accepted.
Expenses: Tuition: Part-time $796 per credit. Required fees: $20; $752 per credit. One-time fee: $30 full-time.
Financial support: In 2001–02, 12 students received support, including 2 fellowships with full tuition reimbursements available (averaging $14,928 per year), 4 research assistantships with full tuition reimbursements available (averaging $17,256 per year), 2 teaching assistantships with full tuition reimbursements available (averaging $12,942 per year); career-related internships or fieldwork, institutionally sponsored loans, and scholarships/grants also available. Financial award application deadline: 2/15; financial award applicants required to submit FAFSA.
Faculty research: Computer fire modeling, fire dynamics and material evaluation, structural systems and fire safety, explosions, risk assessment and regulatory reform. *Total annual research expenditures:* $459,768.
Dr. David A. Lucht, Head, 508-831-5593, *Fax:* 508-831-5680, *E-mail:* dalucht@ wpi.edu.

Application contact: Dr. Nicholas A. Dembsey, Graduate Coordinator, 508-831-5771, *Fax:* 508-831-5680, *E-mail:* nadembsey@wpi.edu. *Web site:* http:// www.wpi.edu/Academics/Depts/Fire/

GEOTECHNICAL ENGINEERING

■ **AUBURN UNIVERSITY**

Graduate School, College of Engineering, Department of Civil Engineering, Auburn University, AL 36849

AWARDS Construction engineering and management (MCE, MS, PhD); environmental engineering (MCE, MS, PhD); geotechnical/materials engineering (MCE, MS, PhD); hydraulics/hydrology (MCE, MS, PhD); Structural engineering (MCE, MS, PhD); transportation engineering (MCE, MS, PhD). Part-time programs available.

Faculty: 18 full-time (1 woman).
Students: 34 full-time (12 women), 25 part-time (9 women); includes 3 minority (all African Americans), 15 international. 74 applicants, 39% accepted. In 2001, 16 master's, 1 doctorate awarded.
Degree requirements: For master's, project (MCE), thesis (MS); for doctorate, thesis/dissertation, comprehensive exam.
Entrance requirements: For master's and doctorate, GRE General Test. *Application deadline:* For fall admission, 7/7; for spring admission, 11/24. Applications are processed on a rolling basis. *Application fee:* $25 ($50 for international students). Electronic applications accepted.
Financial support: Fellowships, research assistantships, teaching assistantships, Federal Work-Study available. Support available to part-time students. Financial award application deadline: 3/15.
Dr. Joseph F. Judkins, Head, 334-844-4320.
Application contact: Dr. John F. Pritchett, Dean of the Graduate School, 334-844-4700, *E-mail:* hatchlb@ mail.auburn.edu.

■ **THE CATHOLIC UNIVERSITY OF AMERICA**

School of Engineering, Department of Civil Engineering, Washington, DC 20064

AWARDS Civil engineering (MCE, D Engr); construction management (MCE, MS Engr); environmental engineering (MCE, MS Engr); geotechnical engineering (MCE). Structures and structural mechanics (MCE). Part-time and evening/weekend programs available.

Faculty: 6 full-time (0 women), 5 part-time/adjunct (2 women).
Students: 5 full-time (1 woman), 14 part-time (2 women); includes 5 minority (4

African Americans, 1 Asian American or Pacific Islander), 10 international. Average age 32. 18 applicants, 50% accepted, 2 enrolled. In 2001, 15 master's, 1 doctorate awarded.
Degree requirements: For master's, thesis optional; for doctorate, thesis/dissertation, qualifying exams, comprehensive exam.
Entrance requirements: For master's, TOEFL, minimum GPA of 3.0; for doctorate, TOEFL, minimum GPA of 3.5. *Application deadline:* For fall admission, 8/1 (priority date); for spring admission, 12/1. Applications are processed on a rolling basis. *Application fee:* $55. Electronic applications accepted.
Expenses: Tuition: Full-time $20,050; part-time $770 per credit. Required fees: $430 per term. Tuition and fees vary according to program.
Financial support: Research assistantships, teaching assistantships, career-related internships or fieldwork, Federal Work-Study, institutionally sponsored loans, and tuition waivers (full and partial) available. Support available to part-time students. Financial award application deadline: 2/1.
Faculty research: Wave propagation, geophysical fluid mechanics.
Dr. Timothy W. Kao, Chair, 202-319-5164, *Fax:* 202-319-4499, *E-mail:* kao@ cua.edu. *Web site:* http://www.ee.cua.edu/ programs/civil/

■ **COLORADO STATE UNIVERSITY**

Graduate School, College of Engineering, Department of Civil Engineering, Fort Collins, CO 80523-0015

AWARDS Bioresource and agricultural engineering (MS); bioresource and agriculture engineering (PhD); environmental engineering (MS, PhD); hydraulics and wind engineering (MS, PhD). Structural and geotechnical engineering (MS, PhD); water resources planning and management (MS, PhD); water resources, hydrologic and environmental sciences (MS, PhD). Part-time programs available.

Faculty: 37 full-time (2 women).
Students: 56 full-time (7 women), 99 part-time (21 women); includes 10 minority (7 Asian Americans or Pacific Islanders, 3 Hispanic Americans), 59 international. Average age 33. 228 applicants, 62% accepted, 39 enrolled. In 2001, 19 master's, 6 doctorates awarded. Terminal master's awarded for partial completion of doctoral program.
Degree requirements: For master's, thesis or alternative; for doctorate, thesis/dissertation.
Entrance requirements: For master's and doctorate, GRE General Test, TOEFL, minimum GPA of 3.0. *Application deadline:* For fall admission, 3/1 (priority date); for spring admission, 8/1 (priority date).

Applications are processed on a rolling basis. *Application fee:* $30. Electronic applications accepted.
Expenses: Tuition, state resident: full-time $2,880; part-time $160 per credit. Tuition, nonresident: full-time $11,412; part-time $634 per credit. Required fees: $750; $34 per credit.
Financial support: In 2001–02, 2 fellowships, 26 research assistantships (averaging $16,950 per year), 11 teaching assistantships (averaging $12,713 per year) were awarded. Federal Work-Study, institutionally sponsored loans, and traineeships also available.
Faculty research: Hydraulics, hydrology, water resources, infrastructure, environmental engineering. *Total annual research expenditures:* $5.4 million.
Sandra Woods, Head, 970-491-5049, *Fax:* 970-491-7727, *E-mail:* woods@ engr.colostate.edu.
Application contact: Laurie Howard, Student Adviser, 970-491-5844, *Fax:* 970-491-7727, *E-mail:* lhoward@ engr.colostate.edu. *Web site:* http://www.engr.colostate.edu/depts/ce/

■ CORNELL UNIVERSITY

Graduate School, Graduate Fields of Engineering, Field of Civil and Environmental Engineering, Ithaca, NY 14853-0001

AWARDS Environmental engineering (M Eng, MS, PhD); environmental fluid mechanics and hydrology (M Eng, MS, PhD); environmental systems engineering (M Eng, MS, PhD); geotechnical engineering (M Eng, MS, PhD); remote sensing (M Eng, MS, PhD). Structural engineering (M Eng, MS, PhD); transportation engineering (M Eng, MS, PhD); water resource systems (M Eng, MS, PhD).

Faculty: 33 full-time.
Students: 131 full-time (35 women); includes 17 minority (1 African American, 9 Asian Americans or Pacific Islanders, 7 Hispanic Americans), 61 international. 515 applicants, 55% accepted. In 2001, 64 master's, 14 doctorates awarded. Terminal master's awarded for partial completion of doctoral program.
Degree requirements: For master's, thesis (MS); for doctorate, thesis/dissertation.
Entrance requirements: For master's and doctorate, GRE General Test (recommended), TOEFL, 2 letters of recommendation. *Application deadline:* For fall admission, 1/15 (priority date). *Application fee:* $65. Electronic applications accepted.
Expenses: Tuition: Full-time $25,970. Required fees: $50.
Financial support: In 2001–02, 71 students received support, including 24 fellowships with full tuition reimbursements available, 28 research assistantships with full tuition reimbursements available, 19 teaching assistantships with full tuition reimbursements available; institutionally sponsored loans, scholarships/grants,

tuition waivers (full and partial), and unspecified assistantships also available. Financial award applicants required to submit FAFSA.
Faculty research: Environmental engineering, geotechnical engineering remote sensing, environmental fluid mechanics and hydrology, structural engineering.
Application contact: Graduate Field Assistant, 607-255-7560, *E-mail:* cee_grad@cornell.edu. *Web site:* http://www.gradschool.cornell.edu/grad/fields_1/cee.html

Find an in-depth description at www.petersons.com/gradchannel.

■ IOWA STATE UNIVERSITY OF SCIENCE AND TECHNOLOGY

Graduate College, College of Engineering, Department of Civil and Construction Engineering, Ames, IA 50011

AWARDS Civil engineering (MS, PhD), including civil engineering materials, construction engineering and management, environmental engineering, geometronics, geotechnical engineering, structural engineering, transportation engineering.

Faculty: 32 full-time, 5 part-time/adjunct.
Students: 55 full-time (9 women), 39 part-time (6 women); includes 1 minority (African American), 40 international. 256 applicants, 23% accepted, 21 enrolled. In 2001, 27 master's, 4 doctorates awarded.
Degree requirements: For master's, thesis or alternative; for doctorate, thesis/dissertation. *Median time to degree:* Master's–2 years full-time; doctorate–3.3 years full-time.
Entrance requirements: For master's and doctorate, GRE General Test (international applicants), TOEFL or IELTS. *Application deadline:* For fall admission, 3/1 (priority date); for spring admission, 10/1 (priority date). *Application fee:* $20 ($50 for international students). Electronic applications accepted.
Expenses: Tuition, state resident: full-time $1,851. Tuition, nonresident: full-time $5,449. Tuition and fees vary according to program.
Financial support: In 2001–02, 44 research assistantships with partial tuition reimbursements (averaging $12,963 per year), 5 teaching assistantships with partial tuition reimbursements (averaging $11,756 per year) were awarded. Fellowships, scholarships/grants, health care benefits, and unspecified assistantships also available.
Dr. Lowell F. Greimann, Chair, 515-294-2140, *E-mail:* cceinfo@iastate.edu.
Application contact: Dr. Edward Kannel, Director of Graduate Education, 515-294-2861, *E-mail:* cceinfo@iastate.edu. *Web site:* http://www1.eng.iastate.edu/coe/grad.asp/

■ LOUISIANA STATE UNIVERSITY AND AGRICULTURAL AND MECHANICAL COLLEGE

Graduate School, College of Engineering, Department of Civil and Environmental Engineering, Baton Rouge, LA 70803

AWARDS Environmental engineering (MSCE, PhD); geotechnical engineering (MSCE, PhD). Structural engineering and mechanics (MSCE, PhD); transportation engineering (MSCE, PhD); water resources (MSCE, PhD). Part-time programs available.

Faculty: 30 full-time (1 woman).
Students: 78 full-time (19 women), 26 part-time (11 women); includes 4 minority (2 African Americans, 1 Hispanic American, 1 Native American), 67 international. Average age 29. 133 applicants, 41% accepted, 22 enrolled. In 2001, 15 master's, 7 doctorates awarded.
Degree requirements: For master's, thesis optional; for doctorate, one foreign language, thesis/dissertation.
Entrance requirements: For master's and doctorate, GRE General Test, TOEFL, minimum GPA of 3.0. *Application deadline:* For fall admission, 1/25 (priority date). Applications are processed on a rolling basis. *Application fee:* $25.
Expenses: Tuition, state resident: full-time $2,551. Tuition, nonresident: full-time $5,551. Required fees: $854. Part-time tuition and fees vary according to course load.
Financial support: In 2001–02, 5 fellowships (averaging $15,800 per year), 51 research assistantships with partial tuition reimbursements (averaging $12,089 per year), 2 teaching assistantships with partial tuition reimbursements (averaging $12,500 per year) were awarded. Career-related internships or fieldwork, institutionally sponsored loans, and scholarships/grants also available. Financial award application deadline: 3/1; financial award applicants required to submit FAFSA.
Faculty research: Solid waste management, electrokinetics, composite structures, transportation planning, river mechanics. *Total annual research expenditures:* $1.7 million.
Dr. George Z. Voyiadjis, Interim Chair/Boyd Professor, 225-578-8668, *Fax:* 225-578-8652, *E-mail:* cegzv@lsu.edu. *Web site:* http://www.ce.lsu.edu/

■ MARQUETTE UNIVERSITY

Graduate School, College of Engineering, Department of Civil and Environmental Engineering, Milwaukee, WI 53201-1881

AWARDS Construction and public works management (MS, PhD); environmental/water resources engineering (MS, PhD). Structural/geotechnical engineering (MS, PhD); transportational planning and engineering

Marquette University (continued)
(MS, PhD). Part-time and evening/weekend programs available.

Faculty: 12 full-time (0 women), 1 part-time/adjunct (0 women).
Students: 20 full-time (8 women), 24 part-time (3 women); includes 2 minority (1 Asian American or Pacific Islander, 1 Hispanic American), 13 international. Average age 30. 57 applicants, 53% accepted, 9 enrolled. In 2001, 9 degrees awarded. Terminal master's awarded for partial completion of doctoral program.
Degree requirements: For master's, thesis or alternative, comprehensive exam; for doctorate, thesis/dissertation. *Median time to degree:* Master's–2 years full-time, 3 years part-time.
Entrance requirements: For master's, TOEFL; for doctorate, GRE General Test, TOEFL. *Application deadline:* For fall admission, 6/1 (priority date). Applications are processed on a rolling basis. *Application fee:* $40. Electronic applications accepted.
Expenses: Tuition: Full-time $10,170; part-time $445 per credit hour. Tuition and fees vary according to course load.
Financial support: In 2001–02, 18 students received support, including 3 fellowships with tuition reimbursements available, 1 research assistantship with tuition reimbursement available (averaging $10,600 per year), 4 teaching assistantships with tuition reimbursements available (averaging $10,200 per year); Federal Work-Study, institutionally sponsored loans, scholarships/grants, and tuition waivers (full and partial) also available. Support available to part-time students. Financial award application deadline: 2/15.
Faculty research: Highway safety, highway performance, and intelligent transportation systems. Surface mount technology; watershed management. *Total annual research expenditures:* $860,000.
Dr. Thomas H. Wenzel, Chair, 414-288-7030, *Fax:* 414-288-7521.

Find an in-depth description at www.petersons.com/gradchannel.

■ MICHIGAN TECHNOLOGICAL UNIVERSITY

Graduate School, College of Engineering, Department of Geology, Geophysics and Geological Engineering, Program in Geotechnical Engineering, Houghton, MI 49931-1295

AWARDS PhD. Part-time programs available.

Degree requirements: For doctorate, thesis/dissertation.
Electronic applications accepted.

■ NORTHWESTERN UNIVERSITY

McCormick School of Engineering and Applied Science, Department of Civil and Environmental Engineering, Evanston, IL 60208

AWARDS Environmental engineering and science (MS, PhD); geotechnical engineering (MS, PhD); mechanics of materials and solids (MS, PhD); project management (MPM). Structural engineering and materials (MS, PhD); theoretical and applied mechanics (MS, PhD); transportation systems analysis and planning (MS, PhD). MS and PhD admissions and degrees offered through The Graduate School. Part-time programs available.

Faculty: 26 full-time (3 women), 9 part-time/adjunct (2 women).
Students: 80 full-time (32 women), 1 part-time; includes 2 Asian Americans or Pacific Islanders, 1 Hispanic American, 38 international. 282 applicants, 7% accepted. In 2001, 20 master's, 14 doctorates awarded. Terminal master's awarded for partial completion of doctoral program.
Degree requirements: For master's, thesis (for some programs); for doctorate, thesis/dissertation.
Application deadline: For fall admission, 8/1. *Application fee:* $50 ($55 for international students). Electronic applications accepted.
Expenses: Tuition: Full-time $26,526.
Financial support: In 2001–02, 10 fellowships with full tuition reimbursements (averaging $13,338 per year), 66 research assistantships with partial tuition reimbursements (averaging $18,000 per year), 7 teaching assistantships with full tuition reimbursements (averaging $13,329 per year) were awarded. Career-related internships or fieldwork, institutionally sponsored loans, and scholarships/grants also available. Financial award application deadline: 1/15; financial award applicants required to submit FAFSA.
Faculty research: Environmental engineering and science, geotechnics, mechanics of materials and solids, structural engineering and materials, transportation systems analysis and planning. *Total annual research expenditures:* $8.4 million.
Joseph L. Schofer, Chair, 847-491-3257, *Fax:* 847-491-4011, *E-mail:* j-schofer@northwestern.edu.
Application contact: Janet Soule, Academic Coordinator, 847-491-3176, *Fax:* 847-491-4011, *E-mail:* civil-info@northwestern.edu. *Web site:* http://www.civil.northwestern.edu/

Find an in-depth description at www.petersons.com/gradchannel.

■ OHIO UNIVERSITY

Graduate Studies, Russ College of Engineering and Technology, Department of Civil Engineering, Athens, OH 45701-2979

AWARDS Geotechnical and environmental engineering (MS); water resources and structures (MS).
Faculty: 11 full-time (1 woman).
Students: 19 full-time (4 women), 6 part-time (2 women), 18 international. Average age 28. 52 applicants, 71% accepted, 11 enrolled. In 2001, 7 degrees awarded.
Degree requirements: For master's, thesis optional.
Entrance requirements: For master's, minimum GPA of 3.0. *Application deadline:* For fall admission, 5/1 (priority date). Applications are processed on a rolling basis. *Application fee:* $30.
Expenses: Tuition, state resident: full-time $6,585. Tuition, nonresident: full-time $12,254.
Financial support: In 2001–02, 1 fellowship (averaging $15,000 per year), 12 research assistantships (averaging $12,000 per year), 6 teaching assistantships (averaging $6,000 per year) were awarded. Federal Work-Study, institutionally sponsored loans, and tuition waivers (full and partial) also available. Financial award application deadline: 3/15.
Faculty research: Soil-structure interaction, solid waste management, pipes, pavements, noise pollution, mine reclamation, drought analysis. *Total annual research expenditures:* $1.2 million.
Dr. Gayle Mitchell, Chair, 740-593-1465, *Fax:* 740-593-0625, *E-mail:* gmitchell@bobcat.ent.ohiou.edu.
Application contact: Dr. Shad Sargand, Graduate Chair, 740-593-1467, *Fax:* 740-593-0625, *E-mail:* ssargand@bobcat.ent.ohiou.edu. *Web site:* http://webce.ent.ohiou.edu/

■ OHIO UNIVERSITY

Graduate Studies, Russ College of Engineering and Technology, Integrated Engineering Program, Athens, OH 45701-2979

AWARDS Geotechnical and environmental engineering (PhD); intelligent systems (PhD); materials processing (PhD).
Faculty: 39 full-time (1 woman).
Students: 16 full-time (1 woman), 8 part-time (1 woman), 21 international. 34 applicants, 88% accepted. In 2001, 3 degrees awarded.
Degree requirements: For doctorate, thesis/dissertation, comprehensive exam.
Entrance requirements: For doctorate, GRE General Test, MS in engineering or related field. *Application deadline:* For fall admission, 3/15. Applications are processed on a rolling basis. *Application fee:* $30.
Expenses: Tuition, state resident: full-time $6,585. Tuition, nonresident: full-time $12,254.

Financial support: In 2001–02, 3 fellowships with full tuition reimbursements (averaging $10,500 per year), 3 research assistantships with full tuition reimbursements (averaging $10,500 per year) were awarded. Federal Work-Study, institutionally sponsored loans, and tuition waivers (full) also available. Financial award application deadline: 3/15.
Faculty research: Material processing, expert systems, environmental geotechnical manufacturing. *Total annual research expenditures:* $1.5 million.
Dr. Jerrel Mitchell, Associate Dean for Research and Graduate Studies, 740-593-1482, *E-mail:* mitchell@ bobcat.ent.ohiou.edu.

Find an in-depth description at www.petersons.com/gradchannel.

■ THE PENNSYLVANIA STATE UNIVERSITY UNIVERSITY PARK CAMPUS

Graduate School, College of Earth and Mineral Sciences, Department of Energy and Geo-Environmental Engineering, Program in Geo-Environmental Engineering, State College, University Park, PA 16802-1503

AWARDS MS, PhD.
Students: 9 full-time (0 women), 1 part-time.
Degree requirements: For doctorate, thesis/dissertation.
Entrance requirements: For doctorate, GRE General Test, TOEFL. *Application fee:* $45.
Expenses: Tuition, state resident: full-time $7,882; part-time $333 per credit. Tuition, nonresident: full-time $16,142; part-time $673 per credit. Required fees: $124 per semester.
Financial support: Application deadline: 12/31.
Derek Elsworth, Graduate Program Chair, 814-863-1343.

■ RENSSELAER POLYTECHNIC INSTITUTE

Graduate School, School of Engineering, Department of Civil and Environmental Engineering, Program in Civil Engineering, Troy, NY 12180-3590

AWARDS Geotechnical engineering (M Eng, MS, D Eng, PhD); mechanics of composite materials and structures (M Eng, MS, D Eng, PhD). Structural engineering (M Eng, MS, D Eng, PhD); transportation engineering (M Eng, MS, D Eng, PhD). Part-time programs available.
Faculty: 9 full-time (0 women), 4 part-time/adjunct (1 woman).
Students: 28 full-time (8 women), 6 part-time; includes 1 minority (Asian American

or Pacific Islander), 15 international. Average age 24. 105 applicants, 40% accepted. In 2001, 8 master's, 2 doctorates awarded.
Degree requirements: For master's, thesis (for some programs); for doctorate, thesis/dissertation.
Entrance requirements: For master's and doctorate, GRE, TOEFL. *Application deadline:* For fall admission, 1/15 (priority date). Applications are processed on a rolling basis. *Application fee:* $45. Electronic applications accepted.
Expenses: Tuition: Full-time $26,400; part-time $1,320 per credit hour. Required fees: $1,437.
Financial support: In 2001–02, 18 students received support, including 3 fellowships, 5 research assistantships with full and partial tuition reimbursements available, 10 teaching assistantships with full tuition reimbursements available; career-related internships or fieldwork and institutionally sponsored loans also available. Financial award application deadline: 2/1.
Faculty research: Computational mechanics, earthquake engineering, geo-environmental engineering. *Total annual research expenditures:* $1.7 million.
Dr. George List, Department Chair, 518-276-6362, *Fax:* 518-276-4833, *E-mail:* listg@rpi.edu.
Application contact: Jo Ann Grega, Admissions Assistant, 518-276-6679, *Fax:* 518-276-4833, *E-mail:* gregaj2@rpi.edu. *Web site:* http://www.rpi.edu/dept/civil/htm

Find an in-depth description at www.petersons.com/gradchannel.

■ TEXAS A&M UNIVERSITY

College of Engineering, Department of Civil Engineering, Program in Geotechnical Engineering, College Station, TX 77843

AWARDS M Eng, MS, D Eng, PhD. D Eng offered through the College of Engineering.

Students: 25.
Degree requirements: For master's, thesis (MS); for doctorate, dissertation (PhD); internship (D Eng).
Entrance requirements: For master's and doctorate, GRE General Test, TOEFL. *Application fee:* $50 ($75 for international students).
Expenses: Tuition, state resident: full-time $11,872. Tuition, nonresident: full-time $17,892.
Financial support: Fellowships, research assistantships, teaching assistantships available. Financial award application deadline: 4/15; financial award applicants required to submit FAFSA.
Faculty research: Classical geotechnical engineering, marine geotechnical engineering with soil dynamics.
Dr. Paul N. Roschke, Head, 979-845-4414, *Fax:* 979-862-2800, *E-mail:* ce-grad@tamu.edu.

Application contact: Dr. Jean-Louis M. Briaud, Information Contact, 979-845-2498, *Fax:* 979-862-2800, *E-mail:* ce-grad@tamu.edu. *Web site:* http://www.civil.tamu.edu/

■ TUFTS UNIVERSITY

Division of Graduate and Continuing Studies and Research, Graduate School of Arts and Sciences, School of Engineering, Department of Civil and Environmental Engineering, Medford, MA 02155

AWARDS Civil engineering (MS, PhD), including geotechnical engineering, structural engineering; environmental engineering (MS, PhD), including environmental engineering and environmental sciences, environmental geotechnology, environmental health, environmental science and management, hazardous materials management, water resources engineering. Part-time programs available.

Faculty: 13 full-time, 10 part-time/adjunct.
Students: 58 (29 women); includes 4 minority (2 African Americans, 2 Asian Americans or Pacific Islanders) 4 international. 53 applicants, 75% accepted. In 2001, 36 master's, 1 doctorate awarded. Terminal master's awarded for partial completion of doctoral program.
Degree requirements: For master's, thesis or alternative; for doctorate, thesis/dissertation.
Entrance requirements: For master's and doctorate, GRE General Test, TOEFL. *Application deadline:* For fall admission, 2/15; for spring admission, 10/15. Applications are processed on a rolling basis. *Application fee:* $50. Electronic applications accepted.
Expenses: Tuition: Full-time $26,853. Full-time tuition and fees vary according to program.
Financial support: Research assistantships with full and partial tuition reimbursements, teaching assistantships with full and partial tuition reimbursements, Federal Work-Study, scholarships/grants, and tuition waivers (partial) available. Support available to part-time students. Financial award application deadline: 2/15; financial award applicants required to submit FAFSA.
Dr. Stephen Levine, Chair, 617-627-3211, *Fax:* 617-627-3994.
Application contact: Linfield Brown, Head, 617-627-3211, *Fax:* 617-627-3994. *Web site:* http://www.ase.tufts.edu/cee/

■ UNIVERSITY OF CALIFORNIA, BERKELEY

Graduate Division, College of Engineering, Department of Civil and Environmental Engineering, Berkeley, CA 94720-1500

AWARDS Construction engineering and management (M Eng, MS, D Eng, PhD); environmental quality and environmental water resources engineering (M Eng, MS, D Eng, PhD); geotechnical engineering (M Eng, MS, D Eng, PhD). Structural engineering, mechanics and materials (M Eng, MS, D Eng, PhD); transportation engineering (M Eng, MS, D Eng, PhD).

Degree requirements: For master's, comprehensive exam or thesis (MS); for doctorate, thesis/dissertation, qualifying exam.

Entrance requirements: For master's, GRE General Test, minimum GPA of 3.0; for doctorate, GRE General Test, minimum GPA of 3.5.

Expenses: Tuition, nonresident: full-time $10,704. Required fees: $4,349.

Find an in-depth description at www.petersons.com/gradchannel.

■ UNIVERSITY OF CALIFORNIA, LOS ANGELES

Graduate Division, School of Engineering and Applied Science, Department of Civil and Environmental Engineering, Los Angeles, CA 90095

AWARDS Environmental engineering (MS, PhD); geotechnical engineering (MS, PhD). Structures (MS, PhD), including structural mechanics and earthquake engineering; water resource systems engineering (MS, PhD).

Faculty: 14 full-time, 11 part-time/adjunct.
Students: 96 full-time (28 women); includes 23 minority (1 African American, 17 Asian Americans or Pacific Islanders, 5 Hispanic Americans), 45 international. 216 applicants, 60% accepted, 34 enrolled. In 2001, 34 master's, 9 doctorates awarded.
Degree requirements: For master's, comprehensive exam or thesis; for doctorate, thesis/dissertation, qualifying exams.
Entrance requirements: For master's, GRE General Test, minimum GPA of 3.0; for doctorate, GRE General Test, minimum GPA of 3.25. *Application deadline:* For fall admission, 1/15; for spring admission, 12/1. *Application fee:* $60. Electronic applications accepted.
Expenses: Tuition, nonresident: full-time $10,244. Required fees: $3,609. Full-time tuition and fees vary according to program.
Financial support: In 2001–02, 39 fellowships, 50 research assistantships, 31 teaching assistantships were awarded. Federal Work-Study, institutionally sponsored loans, and tuition waivers (full and partial) also available. Financial award application

deadline: 1/15; financial award applicants required to submit FAFSA.
Dr. Jiann-Wen Ju, Chair, 310-206-1751.
Application contact: Deeona Columbia, Graduate Affairs Officer, 310-825-1851, *Fax:* 310-206-2222, *E-mail:* deeona@ea.ucla.edu. *Web site:* http://www.cee.ucla.edu

Find an in-depth description at www.petersons.com/gradchannel.

■ UNIVERSITY OF CENTRAL FLORIDA

College of Engineering and Computer Sciences, Department of Civil and Environmental Engineering, Program in Civil Engineering, Orlando, FL 32816

AWARDS Civil engineering (MS, MSCE, PhD); geotechnical engineering (Certificate). Structural engineering (Certificate). Surface water modeling (Certificate); transportation engineering (Certificate). Part-time and evening/weekend programs available.

Faculty: 19 full-time (1 woman), 12 part-time/adjunct (0 women).
Students: 17 full-time (4 women), 37 part-time (7 women); includes 10 minority (1 African American, 2 Asian Americans or Pacific Islanders, 7 Hispanic Americans), 16 international. Average age 30. 84 applicants, 62% accepted, 16 enrolled. In 2001, 1 master's, 1 doctorate awarded.
Degree requirements: For master's, thesis or alternative; for doctorate, thesis/dissertation, departmental qualifying exam, candidacy exam.
Entrance requirements: For master's, GRE General Test, TOEFL, minimum GPA of 3.0 in last 60 hours; for doctorate, GRE General Test, TOEFL, minimum GPA of 3.5 in last 60 hours. *Application deadline:* For fall admission, 7/15 (priority date); for spring admission, 12/15 (priority date). *Application fee:* $20. Electronic applications accepted.
Expenses: Tuition, state resident: part-time $162 per hour. Tuition, nonresident: part-time $569 per hour.
Financial support: In 2001–02, 13 fellowships with partial tuition reimbursements (averaging $2,115 per year), 73 research assistantships with partial tuition reimbursements (averaging $3,846 per year), 13 teaching assistantships with partial tuition reimbursements (averaging $2,732 per year) were awarded. Career-related internships or fieldwork, Federal Work-Study, institutionally sponsored loans, tuition waivers (partial), and unspecified assistantships also available. Financial award application deadline: 3/1; financial award applicants required to submit FAFSA.
Application contact: Dr. Roger L. Wayson, Coordinator, 407-823-2841, *E-mail:* wayson@pegasus.cc.ucf.edu. *Web site:* http://www.ucf.edu/

■ UNIVERSITY OF COLORADO AT BOULDER

Graduate School, College of Engineering and Applied Science, Department of Civil, Environmental, and Architectural Engineering, Boulder, CO 80309

AWARDS Building systems (MS, PhD); construction engineering and management (MS, PhD); environmental engineering (MS, PhD); geoenvironmental engineering (MS, PhD); geotechnical engineering (MS, PhD). Structural engineering (MS, PhD); water resource engineering (MS, PhD).

Faculty: 37 full-time (2 women).
Students: 167 full-time (49 women), 44 part-time (12 women); includes 14 minority (1 African American, 4 Asian Americans or Pacific Islanders, 9 Hispanic Americans), 88 international. Average age 30. 280 applicants, 59% accepted. In 2001, 59 master's, 13 doctorates awarded.
Degree requirements: For master's, thesis or alternative, comprehensive exam; for doctorate, thesis/dissertation.
Entrance requirements: For master's, GRE General Test, minimum undergraduate GPA of 3.0. *Application deadline:* For fall admission, 4/30; for spring admission, 10/31. *Application fee:* $50 ($60 for international students).
Expenses: Tuition, state resident: full-time $3,474. Tuition, nonresident: full-time $16,624.
Financial support: In 2001–02, 19 fellowships (averaging $5,252 per year), 45 research assistantships (averaging $15,638 per year), 14 teaching assistantships (averaging $13,821 per year) were awarded. Financial award application deadline: 2/15.
Faculty research: Building systems engineering, construction engineering and management, environmental engineering, geoenvironmental engineering, geotechnical engineering. *Total annual research expenditures:* $8.3 million.
Hon-Yim Ko, Chair, 303-492-6716, *Fax:* 303-492-7317, *E-mail:* ko@spot.colorado.edu.
Application contact: Jan Demay, Graduate Secretary, 303-492-7316, *Fax:* 303-492-7317, *E-mail:* demay@spot.colorado.edu. *Web site:* http://www.civil.colorado.edu/

■ UNIVERSITY OF DELAWARE

College of Engineering, Department of Civil and Environmental Engineering, Program in Geotechnical Engineering, Newark, DE 19716

AWARDS MAS, MCE, PhD. Terminal master's awarded for partial completion of doctoral program.

Degree requirements: For master's and doctorate, thesis/dissertation.
Entrance requirements: For master's and doctorate, GRE General Test, TOEFL.

Expenses: Tuition, state resident: full-time $4,770; part-time $265 per credit. Tuition, nonresident: full-time $13,860; part-time $770 per credit. Required fees: $414.
Faculty research: Computational mechanics, behavior of composite soil structures subjected to seismic loadings, three dimensional stability analysis of inhomogeneous slopes.
Find an in-depth description at www.petersons.com/gradchannel.

■ UNIVERSITY OF ILLINOIS AT CHICAGO

Graduate College, College of Liberal Arts and Sciences, Department of Earth and Environmental Sciences, Program in Geotechnical Engineering and Geosciences, Chicago, IL 60607-7128

AWARDS PhD.

Faculty: 9 full-time (2 women).
Students: 2 full-time (1 woman), 1 part-time. Average age 30. 4 applicants, 0% accepted. In 2001, 1 degree awarded.
Degree requirements: For doctorate, thesis/dissertation.
Entrance requirements: For doctorate, GRE General Test, TOEFL, minimum GPA of 3.75 on a 5.0 scale. *Application deadline:* For fall admission, 6/1; for spring admission, 11/1. Applications are processed on a rolling basis. *Application fee:* $40 ($50 for international students). Electronic applications accepted.
Expenses: Tuition, state resident: full-time $3,060. Tuition, nonresident: full-time $6,688.
Financial support: In 2001–02, 3 students received support; fellowships with full tuition reimbursements available, research assistantships with full tuition reimbursements available, teaching assistantships with full tuition reimbursements available, Federal Work-Study and tuition waivers (full) available. Financial award application deadline: 3/1; financial award applicants required to submit FAFSA.
Application contact: Martin Flower, Graduate Director, 312-996-9662.

■ UNIVERSITY OF MAINE

Graduate School, College of Engineering, Department of Civil and Environmental Engineering, Orono, ME 04469

AWARDS Civil engineering (MS, PhD), including environmental engineering, geotechnical engineering, structural engineering.

Faculty: 11 full-time (0 women).
Students: 18 full-time (7 women), 8 part-time; includes 3 minority (2 Hispanic Americans, 1 Native American), 10 international. 21 applicants, 43% accepted, 4 enrolled. In 2001, 11 degrees awarded.
Degree requirements: For doctorate, thesis/dissertation.

Entrance requirements: For master's and doctorate, GRE General Test, TOEFL. *Application deadline:* For fall admission, 2/1 (priority date). Applications are processed on a rolling basis. *Application fee:* $50. Electronic applications accepted.
Expenses: Tuition, state resident: full-time $3,780; part-time $210 per credit hour. Tuition, nonresident: full-time $10,782; part-time $599 per credit hour. Required fees: $9.5 per credit hour. $32 per semester. Tuition and fees vary according to reciprocity agreements.
Financial support: In 2001–02, 15 research assistantships with tuition reimbursements (averaging $16,900 per year), 3 teaching assistantships with tuition reimbursements (averaging $15,000 per year) were awarded. Federal Work-Study, institutionally sponsored loans, scholarships/grants, and tuition waivers (full and partial) also available. Financial award application deadline: 3/1.
Dr. Dana Humphrey, Chair, 207-581-2170, *Fax:* 207-581-3888.
Application contact: Scott G. Delcourt, Director of the Graduate School, 207-581-3218, *Fax:* 207-581-3232, *E-mail:* graduate@maine.edu. *Web site:* http://www.umaine.edu/graduate/

■ UNIVERSITY OF MISSOURI–COLUMBIA

Graduate School, College of Engineering, Department of Civil and Environmental Engineering, Columbia, MO 65211

AWARDS Civil engineering (MS, PhD); environmental engineering (MS, PhD); geotechnical engineering (MS, PhD). Structural engineering (MS, PhD); transportation and highway engineering (MS); water resources (MS, PhD).

Faculty: 20 full-time (2 women), 1 part-time/adjunct (0 women).
Students: 28 full-time (6 women), 14 part-time (3 women); includes 4 minority (all Hispanic Americans), 23 international. 74 applicants, 43% accepted. In 2001, 19 master's, 1 doctorate awarded.
Degree requirements: For master's, report or thesis; for doctorate, thesis/dissertation.
Entrance requirements: For master's and doctorate, GRE General Test, TOEFL. *Application deadline:* For fall admission, 3/15 (priority date); for winter admission, 10/15 (priority date). *Application fee:* $25 ($50 for international students).
Expenses: Tuition, state resident: part-time $179 per credit hour. Tuition, nonresident: part-time $539 per credit hour. Required fees: $122 per semester. Tuition and fees vary according to program.
Financial support: Research assistantships, teaching assistantships, institutionally sponsored loans available.
Dr. Mark Virkler, Director of Graduate Studies, 573-882-7434, *E-mail:* virklerm@

missouri.edu. *Web site:* http://www.engineering.missouri.edu/civil.htm

■ UNIVERSITY OF MISSOURI–ROLLA

Graduate School, School of Engineering, Department of Civil Engineering, Program in Geotechnical Engineering, Rolla, MO 65409-0910

AWARDS MS, DE, PhD.

Degree requirements: For master's, thesis or alternative; for doctorate, thesis/dissertation.
Entrance requirements: For master's and doctorate, GRE General Test, TOEFL, minimum GPA of 3.0.

■ UNIVERSITY OF OKLAHOMA

Graduate College, College of Engineering, School of Civil Engineering and Environmental Science, Program in Civil Engineering, Norman, OK 73019-0390

AWARDS Civil engineering (PhD); environmental engineering (MS); geotechnical engineering (MS). Structures (MS); transportation (MS). Part-time programs available.

Students: 36 full-time (3 women), 18 part-time (2 women); includes 4 minority (2 Asian Americans or Pacific Islanders, 1 Hispanic American, 1 Native American), 35 international. 46 applicants, 85% accepted, 9 enrolled. In 2001, 17 degrees awarded. Terminal master's awarded for partial completion of doctoral program.
Degree requirements: For master's, oral exams; for doctorate, thesis/dissertation, oral and qualifying exams.
Entrance requirements: For master's, minimum GPA of 3.0; for doctorate, minimum graduate GPA of 3.5. *Application deadline:* For fall admission, 4/1 (priority date). Applications are processed on a rolling basis. *Application fee:* $25 ($50 for international students).
Expenses: Tuition, state resident: full-time $2,208; part-time $92 per credit hour. Tuition, nonresident: part-time $297 per credit hour. Tuition and fees vary according to course level, course load and program.
Financial support: In 2001–02, 7 students received support; research assistantships with partial tuition reimbursements available, teaching assistantships with full and partial tuition reimbursements available, scholarships/grants available. Financial award application deadline: 3/1; financial award applicants required to submit FAFSA.
Application contact: Susan Williams, Graduate Programs Specialist, 405-325-2344, *Fax:* 405-325-4217, *E-mail:* srwilliams@ou.edu.

■ UNIVERSITY OF RHODE ISLAND

Graduate School, College of Engineering, Department of Civil and Environmental Engineering, Program in Geotechnical Engineering, Kingston, RI 02881

AWARDS MS, PhD.

Application deadline: For fall admission, 4/15 (priority date). Applications are processed on a rolling basis. *Application fee:* $35.

Expenses: Tuition, state resident: full-time $3,756; part-time $209 per credit. Tuition, nonresident: full-time $10,774; part-time $599 per credit. Required fees: $1,586; $76 per credit. $76 per credit. One-time fee: $60 full-time.

Dr. George Tsiatas, Chairman, Department of Civil and Environmental Engineering, 401-874-2692.

■ UNIVERSITY OF SOUTHERN CALIFORNIA

Graduate School, School of Engineering, Department of Civil Engineering, Program in Soil Mechanics and Foundations, Los Angeles, CA 90089

AWARDS MS.

Degree requirements: For master's, thesis optional.

Entrance requirements: For master's, GRE General Test.

Expenses: Tuition: Full-time $25,060; part-time $844 per unit. Required fees: $473.

■ THE UNIVERSITY OF TEXAS AT AUSTIN

Graduate School, College of Engineering, Department of Petroleum and Geosystems Engineering, Austin, TX 78712-1111

AWARDS Energy and mineral resources (MA, MS); petroleum and geosystems engineering (MSE, PhD). Evening/weekend programs available. Postbaccalaureate distance learning degree programs offered (no on-campus study).

Faculty: 15 full-time (1 woman), 3 part-time/adjunct (1 woman).

Students: 80 full-time (16 women), 7 part-time (1 woman); includes 4 minority (1 African American, 2 Asian Americans or Pacific Islanders, 1 Hispanic American), 74 international. 69 applicants, 51% accepted. In 2001, 25 master's, 6 doctorates awarded.

Entrance requirements: For master's and doctorate, GRE General Test. *Application deadline:* For fall admission, 2/1 (priority date); for spring admission, 10/1. Applications are processed on a rolling basis. *Application fee:* $50 ($75 for international students). Electronic applications accepted.

Expenses: Tuition, state resident: full-time $3,159. Tuition, nonresident: full-time $6,957. Tuition and fees vary according to program.

Financial support: Fellowships, research assistantships, teaching assistantships available. Financial award application deadline: 2/1.

Dr. Mukul M. Sharma, Chairman, 512-471-3161, *Fax:* 512-471-9605, *E-mail:* msharma@mail.utexas.edu.

Application contact: Dr. Kamy Sepehrnoori, Graduate Adviser, 512-471-0231, *Fax:* 512-471-9605, *E-mail:* pge_gradoffice@mail.utexas.edu. *Web site:* http://www.utexas.edu/coe/pge/

■ UNIVERSITY OF WASHINGTON

Graduate School, College of Engineering, Department of Civil and Environmental Engineering, Seattle, WA 98195

AWARDS Environmental engineering (MS, MSCE, MSE, PhD); hydraulic engineering (MSCE, MSE, PhD). Structural and geotechnical engineering and mechanics (MS, MSCE, MSE, PhD); transportation and construction engineering (MS, MSCE, MSE, PhD).

Faculty: 31 full-time (4 women), 26 part-time/adjunct (1 woman).

Students: 153 full-time (54 women), 42 part-time (13 women); includes 25 minority (2 African Americans, 19 Asian Americans or Pacific Islanders, 3 Hispanic Americans, 1 Native American), 34 international. Average age 29. 339 applicants, 60% accepted, 59 enrolled. In 2001, 71 master's, 11 doctorates awarded. Terminal master's awarded for partial completion of doctoral program.

Degree requirements: For master's, thesis (for some programs); for doctorate, thesis/dissertation, comprehensive exam. *Median time to degree:* Doctorate–3.5 years full-time.

Entrance requirements: For master's, GRE General Test, TOEFL, minimum GPA of 3.0; for doctorate, GRE, TOEFL, minimum GPA of 3.5. *Application deadline:* For fall admission, 2/1 (priority date). Applications are processed on a rolling basis. *Application fee:* $50. Electronic applications accepted.

Expenses: Tuition, state resident: full-time $5,539. Tuition, nonresident: full-time $14,376. Required fees: $390. Tuition and fees vary according to course load and program.

Financial support: In 2001–02, 110 students received support, including 22 fellowships with partial tuition reimbursements available, 70 research assistantships with full tuition reimbursements available, 22 teaching assistantships with full tuition reimbursements available; career-related internships or fieldwork and scholarships/grants also available. Financial award application deadline: 2/1.

Faculty research: Water resources, hydrology, construction, environmental structures, geotechnical transportation. *Total annual research expenditures:* $3.7 million.

Prof. G. Scott Rutherford, Chair, 206-543-2390.

Application contact: Marcia Buck, Graduate Adviser, 206-543-2574, *E-mail:* cesendme@u.washington.edu. *Web site:* http://www.ce.washington.edu/grad_p.htm

HAZARDOUS MATERIALS MANAGEMENT

■ COLORADO STATE UNIVERSITY

College of Veterinary Medicine and Biomedical Sciences and Graduate School, Graduate Programs in Veterinary Medicine and Biomedical Sciences, Department of Radiological Health Sciences, Fort Collins, CO 80523-0015

AWARDS Cellular and molecular biology (MS, PhD); health physics (MS, PhD); mammalian radiobiology (MS, PhD); nuclear-waste management (MS); radiobiology (MS); radioecology (MS, PhD); radiology (MS, PhD); veterinary radiology (MS, PhD).

Faculty: 18 full-time (5 women).

Students: 14 full-time (4 women), 10 part-time (2 women), 5 international. Average age 35. 10 applicants, 90% accepted, 3 enrolled. In 2001, 2 master's, 1 doctorate awarded.

Degree requirements: For master's and doctorate, thesis/dissertation.

Entrance requirements: For master's and doctorate, GRE General Test, TOEFL. *Application deadline:* For fall admission, 2/1 (priority date). Applications are processed on a rolling basis. *Application fee:* $30. Electronic applications accepted.

Expenses: Tuition, state resident: full-time $2,880; part-time $160 per credit. Tuition, nonresident: full-time $11,412; part-time $634 per credit. Required fees: $750; $34 per credit.

Financial support: In 2001–02, 2 fellowships with full tuition reimbursements (averaging $10,000 per year), 4 research assistantships with full tuition reimbursements (averaging $15,000 per year) were awarded. Teaching assistantships, career-related internships or fieldwork, Federal Work-Study, and traineeships also available.

Faculty research: Radiation therapy; cell, molecular, and tissue mechanisms in radiation biology; diagnostic radiology; radiation dose measurements; dose calculations. *Total annual research expenditures:* $1.7 million.

Dr. F. Ward Whicker, Interim Chairman, 970-491-5222, *Fax:* 970-491-0623, *E-mail:* ward.whicker@colostate.edu.
Application contact: Julie A. Asmus, Administrative Assistant, 970-491-5222, *Fax:* 970-491-0623, *E-mail:* julie.asmus@colostate.edu. *Web site:* http://www.colostate.edu/Depts/RHS/

■ IDAHO STATE UNIVERSITY

Office of Graduate Studies, College of Engineering, Pocatello, ID 83209

AWARDS Engineering and applied science (PhD); engineering structures and mechanics (MS); environmental engineering (MS); measurement and control engineering (MS); nuclear science and engineering (MS); waste management and environmental science (MS). Part-time programs available.

Faculty: 13 full-time (0 women), 1 part-time/adjunct (0 women).
Students: 34 full-time (8 women), 18 part-time (1 woman); includes 7 minority (1 African American, 5 Asian Americans or Pacific Islanders, 1 Hispanic American), 15 international. Average age 34. In 2001, 12 master's, 1 doctorate awarded.
Degree requirements: For master's and doctorate, thesis/dissertation.
Entrance requirements: For master's and doctorate, GRE General Test, TOEFL. *Application deadline:* For fall admission, 7/1 (priority date); for spring admission, 12/1. Applications are processed on a rolling basis. *Application fee:* $35.
Expenses: Tuition, area resident: Full-time $3,432. Tuition, state resident: part-time $172 per credit. Tuition, nonresident: full-time $10,196; part-time $262 per credit. International tuition: $9,672 full-time. Part-time tuition and fees vary according to course load, program and reciprocity agreements.
Financial support: In 2001–02, 7 research assistantships with full and partial tuition reimbursements (averaging $10,740 per year), 16 teaching assistantships with full and partial tuition reimbursements (averaging $6,775 per year) were awarded. Federal Work-Study and institutionally sponsored loans also available. Support available to part-time students. Financial award application deadline: 2/15.
Faculty research: Isotope separation, control technology, two-phase flow, photosonolysis, criticality calculations. *Total annual research expenditures:* $293,915.
Dr. Jay Kunze, Dean, 208-282-2902, *Fax:* 208-282-4538. *Web site:* http://www.coe.isu.edu/engrg/

■ IDAHO STATE UNIVERSITY

Office of Graduate Studies, Department of Interdisciplinary Studies, Pocatello, ID 83209

AWARDS Biology (MNS); chemistry (MNS); general interdisciplinary (M Ed, MA); geology (MNS); mathematics (MNS); physics (MNS); waste management and environmental science (MS).

Faculty: 2 full-time (0 women).
Students: 12 full-time (5 women), 14 part-time (8 women), 1 international. Average age 36. In 2001, 7 degrees awarded.
Entrance requirements: For master's, GRE General Test. *Application fee:* $35.
Expenses: Tuition, area resident: Full-time $3,432. Tuition, state resident: part-time $172 per credit. Tuition, nonresident: full-time $10,196; part-time $262 per credit. International tuition: $9,672 full-time. Part-time tuition and fees vary according to course load, program and reciprocity agreements.
Financial support: In 2001–02, 1 research assistantship (averaging $10,997 per year), 3 teaching assistantships (averaging $8,117 per year) were awarded.
Dr. Paul Tate, Dean, Office of Graduate Studies, 208-282-2150, *Fax:* 208-282-4847, *E-mail:* graddean@isu.edu.

■ NEW MEXICO INSTITUTE OF MINING AND TECHNOLOGY

Graduate Studies, Department of Environmental Engineering, Socorro, NM 87801

AWARDS Environmental engineering (MS), including air quality engineering and science, hazardous waste engineering, water quality engineering and science.

Faculty: 5 full-time (1 woman).
Students: 9 full-time (1 woman), 1 part-time; includes 2 minority (both Hispanic Americans), 6 international. Average age 25. 15 applicants, 60% accepted, 5 enrolled. In 2001, 3 degrees awarded.
Degree requirements: For master's, thesis.
Entrance requirements: For master's, GRE General Test, TOEFL. *Application deadline:* For fall admission, 3/1 (priority date); for spring admission, 6/1. Applications are processed on a rolling basis. *Application fee:* $16 ($30 for international students).
Expenses: Tuition, state resident: part-time $1,084 per semester. Tuition, nonresident: part-time $4,367 per semester. Required fees: $429 per semester.
Financial support: In 2001–02, 3 research assistantships (averaging $13,505 per year), 2 teaching assistantships with full and partial tuition reimbursements (averaging $12,714 per year) were awarded. Fellowships, Federal Work-Study and institutionally sponsored loans also available. Financial award application deadline: 3/1; financial award applicants required to submit CSS PROFILE or FAFSA.
Faculty research: Rock mechanics, geological engineering, mining problems, blasting, shock waves.
Dr. Clinton P. Richardson, Chair, 505-835-5346, *Fax:* 505-835-5252.

Application contact: Dr. David B. Johnson, Dean of Graduate Studies, 505-835-5513, *Fax:* 505-835-5476, *E-mail:* graduate@nmt.edu. *Web site:* http://www.nmt.edu/~mining/default.htm

■ RUTGERS, THE STATE UNIVERSITY OF NEW JERSEY, NEW BRUNSWICK

Graduate School, Program in Environmental Sciences, New Brunswick, NJ 08901-1281

AWARDS Air resources (MS, PhD); aquatic biology (MS, PhD); aquatic chemistry (MS, PhD); chemistry and physics of aerosol and hydrosol systems (MS, PhD); environmental chemistry (MS, PhD); environmental microbiology (MS, PhD); environmental toxicology (MS, PhD); exposure assessment (PhD); water and wastewater treatment (MS, PhD); water resources (MS, PhD). Part-time and evening/weekend programs available.

Students: Average age 26. 122 applicants, 39% accepted. In 2001, 10 master's, 7 doctorates awarded. Terminal master's awarded for partial completion of doctoral program.
Degree requirements: For master's, thesis or alternative, oral final exam; for doctorate, thesis defense, qualifying exam.
Entrance requirements: For master's and doctorate, GRE General Test, TOEFL. *Application deadline:* For fall admission, 3/1; for spring admission, 11/1. Applications are processed on a rolling basis. *Application fee:* $50.
Financial support: In 2001–02, 38 research assistantships with full tuition reimbursements (averaging $15,600 per year), 9 teaching assistantships with full tuition reimbursements (averaging $13,800 per year) were awarded. Fellowships, career-related internships or fieldwork and Federal Work-Study also available. Financial award application deadline: 1/15; financial award applicants required to submit FAFSA.
Faculty research: Atmospheric sciences; biological waste treatment; contaminant fate and transport; exposure assessment; air, soil and water quality.
Dr. Peter F. Strom, Director, 732-932-8078, *Fax:* 732-932-8644, *E-mail:* strom@aesop.rutgers.edu.
Application contact: Paul J. Lioy, Graduate Admissions Committee, 732-932-0150, *Fax:* 732-445-0116, *E-mail:* plioy@eohsi.rutgers.edu. *Web site:* http://www.envsci.edu/

■ STONY BROOK UNIVERSITY, STATE UNIVERSITY OF NEW YORK

School of Professional Development and Continuing Studies, Stony Brook, NY 11794

AWARDS Art and philosophy (Certificate); biology 7-12 (MAT); chemistry-grade 7-12 (MAT); coaching (Certificate); computer integrated engineering (Certificate); cultural studies (Certificate); earth science-grade 7-12 (MAT); educational computing (Certificate); English-grade 7-12 (MAT); environmental/occupational health and safety (Certificate); French-grade 7-12 (MAT); German-grade 7-12 (MAT); human resource management (Certificate); industrial management (Certificate); information systems management (Certificate); Italian-grade 7-12 (MAT); liberal studies (MA); liberal studies online (MA); Long Island regional studies (Certificate); oceanic science (Certificate); operation research (Certificate); physics-grade 7-12 (MAT); Russian-grade 7-12 (MAT). School administration and supervision (Certificate). School district administration (Certificate). Social science and the professions (MPS), including labor management, public affairs, waste management. Social studies 7-12 (MAT); waste management (Certificate); women's studies (Certificate). Part-time and evening/weekend programs available. Postbaccalaureate distance learning degree programs offered.

Faculty: 1 full-time, 101 part-time/adjunct.
Students: 240 full-time (133 women), 1,307 part-time (868 women); includes 101 minority (43 African Americans, 13 Asian Americans or Pacific Islanders, 43 Hispanic Americans, 2 Native Americans), 9 international. Average age 28. In 2001, 478 master's, 157 other advanced degrees awarded.
Degree requirements: For master's, one foreign language, thesis or alternative. *Application deadline:* Applications are processed on a rolling basis. *Application fee:* $50.
Expenses: Tuition, state resident: full-time $5,100; part-time $213 per credit. Tuition, nonresident: full-time $8,416; part-time $351 per credit. Required fees: $496.
Financial support: In 2001–02, 1 fellowship, 7 teaching assistantships were awarded. Research assistantships, career-related internships or fieldwork also available. Support available to part-time students.
Dr. Paul J. Edelson, Dean, 631-632-7052, *Fax:* 631-632-9046, *E-mail:* paul.edelson@sunysb.edu.
Application contact: Sandra Romansky, Director of Admissions and Advisement, 631-632-7050, *Fax:* 631-632-9046, *E-mail:* sandra.romansky@sunysb.edu. *Web site:* http://www.sunysb.edu/spd/

■ UNIVERSITY OF CENTRAL FLORIDA

College of Engineering and Computer Sciences, Department of Civil and Environmental Engineering, Program in Environmental Engineering, Orlando, FL 32816

AWARDS Air pollution control (Certificate); drinking water treatment (Certificate); environmental engineering (MS, MS Env E, PhD); hazardous waste management (Certificate); wastewater treatment (Certificate). Part-time and evening/weekend programs available.

Faculty: 19 full-time (1 woman), 12 part-time/adjunct (0 women).
Students: 33 full-time (6 women), 19 part-time (7 women); includes 4 minority (1 African American, 2 Asian Americans or Pacific Islanders, 1 Hispanic American), 26 international. Average age 28. 81 applicants, 74% accepted, 23 enrolled. In 2001, 5 master's, 1 doctorate awarded.
Degree requirements: For master's, thesis or alternative; for doctorate, thesis/dissertation, departmental qualifying exam, candidacy exam.
Entrance requirements: For master's, GRE General Test, TOEFL, minimum GPA of 3.0 in last 60 hours; for doctorate, GRE General Test, TOEFL, minimum GPA of 3.5 in last 60 hours, interview. *Application deadline:* For fall admission, 7/15 (priority date); for spring admission, 12/15 (priority date). *Application fee:* $20. Electronic applications accepted.
Expenses: Tuition, state resident: part-time $162 per hour. Tuition, nonresident: part-time $569 per hour.
Financial support: In 2001–02, 13 fellowships with partial tuition reimbursements (averaging $2,644 per year), 86 research assistantships with partial tuition reimbursements (averaging $3,300 per year), 5 teaching assistantships with partial tuition reimbursements (averaging $4,700 per year) were awarded. Career-related internships or fieldwork, Federal Work-Study, institutionally sponsored loans, tuition waivers (partial), and unspecified assistantships also available. Financial award application deadline: 3/1; financial award applicants required to submit FAFSA.
Application contact: Dr. Roger L. Wayson, Coordinator, 407-823-2841, *E-mail:* wayson@pegasus.cc.ucf.edu. *Web site:* http://www.ucf.edu/

■ UNIVERSITY OF IDAHO

College of Graduate Studies, College of Letters and Science, Program in Interdisciplinary Studies, Program in Waste Management, Moscow, ID 83844-2282

AWARDS MS.

Degree requirements: For master's, thesis.

Entrance requirements: For master's, GRE, minimum GPA of 2.8. *Application deadline:* For fall admission, 8/1; for spring admission, 12/15. *Application fee:* $35 ($45 for international students).
Expenses: Tuition, state resident: full-time $1,613. Tuition, nonresident: full-time $3,000.
Financial support: Application deadline: 2/15.
Dr. Roger P. Wallins, Associate Dean, Program in Interdisciplinary Studies, 208-885-6243, *Fax:* 208-885-6198, *E-mail:* uigrad@uidaho.edu.

■ UNIVERSITY OF OKLAHOMA

Graduate College, College of Engineering, School of Civil Engineering and Environmental Science, Program in Environmental Science, Norman, OK 73019-0390

AWARDS Air (M Env Sc); environmental science (PhD); groundwater management (M Env Sc); hazardous solid waste (M Env Sc); occupational safety and health (M Env Sc); process design (M Env Sc); water quality resources (M Env Sc). Part-time programs available.

Students: 13 full-time (9 women), 7 part-time (4 women); includes 4 minority (1 African American, 1 Asian American or Pacific Islander, 1 Hispanic American, 1 Native American), 5 international. 23 applicants, 65% accepted, 6 enrolled. In 2001, 4 master's, 1 doctorate awarded. Terminal master's awarded for partial completion of doctoral program.
Degree requirements: For master's, oral exams; for doctorate, thesis/dissertation, oral, and qualifying exams, comprehensive exam.
Entrance requirements: For master's, minimum GPA of 3.0; for doctorate, minimum graduate GPA of 3.5. *Application deadline:* For fall admission, 4/1 (priority date). Applications are processed on a rolling basis. *Application fee:* $25 ($50 for international students).
Expenses: Tuition, state resident: full-time $2,208; part-time $92 per credit hour. Tuition, nonresident: part-time $297 per credit hour. Tuition and fees vary according to course level, course load and program.
Financial support: In 2001–02, 8 students received support; fellowships, research assistantships with partial tuition reimbursements available, teaching assistantships with partial tuition reimbursements available, scholarships/grants available. Financial award application deadline: 3/1; financial award applicants required to submit FAFSA.
Application contact: Susan Williams, Graduate Programs Specialist, 405-325-2344, *Fax:* 405-325-4217, *E-mail:* srwilliams@ou.edu.

■ UNIVERSITY OF SOUTH CAROLINA

The Graduate School, Norman J. Arnold School of Public Health, Department of Environmental Health Sciences, Program in Hazardous Materials Management, Columbia, SC 29208

AWARDS MPH, MSPH, PhD.

Degree requirements: For master's, thesis (for some programs), practicum (MPH), comprehensive exam; for doctorate, one foreign language, thesis/dissertation, comprehensive exam.
Entrance requirements: For master's and doctorate, GRE. *Application deadline:* For fall admission, 7/1; for spring admission, 11/1. Applications are processed on a rolling basis. *Application fee:* $35. Electronic applications accepted.
Expenses: Tuition, state resident: full-time $4,434. Tuition, nonresident: full-time $9,854. Tuition and fees vary according to program.
Faculty research: Environmental/human health protection; use and disposal of hazardous materials. Site safety; exposure assessment; migration, fate and transformation of materials.
Application contact: Dr. Edward Oswald, Graduate Director, 803-777-6994, *Fax:* 803-777-3391, *E-mail:* eoswald@ sph.sc.edu.

HYDRAULICS

■ AUBURN UNIVERSITY

Graduate School, College of Engineering, Department of Civil Engineering, Auburn University, AL 36849

AWARDS Construction engineering and management (MCE, MS, PhD); environmental engineering (MCE, MS, PhD); geotechnical/materials engineering (MCE, MS, PhD); hydraulics/hydrology (MCE, MS, PhD). Structural engineering (MCE, MS, PhD); transportation engineering (MCE, MS, PhD). Part-time programs available.

Faculty: 18 full-time (1 woman).
Students: 34 full-time (12 women), 25 part-time (9 women); includes 3 minority (all African Americans), 15 international. 74 applicants, 39% accepted. In 2001, 16 master's, 1 doctorate awarded.
Degree requirements: For master's, project (MCE), thesis (MS); for doctorate, thesis/dissertation, comprehensive exam.
Entrance requirements: For master's and doctorate, GRE General Test. *Application deadline:* For fall admission, 7/7; for spring admission, 11/24. Applications are processed on a rolling basis. *Application fee:* $25 ($50 for international students). Electronic applications accepted.

Financial support: Fellowships, research assistantships, teaching assistantships, Federal Work-Study available. Support available to part-time students. Financial award application deadline: 3/15.
Dr. Joseph F. Judkins, Head, 334-844-4320.
Application contact: Dr. John F. Pritchett, Dean of the Graduate School, 334-844-4700, *E-mail:* hatchlb@ mail.auburn.edu.

■ COLORADO STATE UNIVERSITY

Graduate School, College of Engineering, Department of Civil Engineering, Fort Collins, CO 80523-0015

AWARDS Bioresource and agricultural engineering (MS); bioresource and agriculture engineering (PhD); environmental engineering (MS, PhD); hydraulics and wind engineering (MS, PhD). Structural and geotechnical engineering (MS, PhD); water resources planning and management (MS, PhD); water resources, hydrologic and environmental sciences (MS, PhD). Part-time programs available.

Faculty: 37 full-time (2 women).
Students: 56 full-time (7 women), 99 part-time (21 women); includes 10 minority (7 Asian Americans or Pacific Islanders, 3 Hispanic Americans), 59 international. Average age 33. 228 applicants, 62% accepted, 39 enrolled. In 2001, 19 master's, 6 doctorates awarded. Terminal master's awarded for partial completion of doctoral program.
Degree requirements: For master's, thesis or alternative; for doctorate, thesis/dissertation.
Entrance requirements: For master's and doctorate, GRE General Test, TOEFL, minimum GPA of 3.0. *Application deadline:* For fall admission, 3/1 (priority date); for spring admission, 8/1 (priority date). Applications are processed on a rolling basis. *Application fee:* $30. Electronic applications accepted.
Expenses: Tuition, state resident: full-time $2,880; part-time $160 per credit. Tuition, nonresident: full-time $11,412; part-time $634 per credit. Required fees: $750; $34 per credit.
Financial support: In 2001–02, 2 fellowships, 26 research assistantships (averaging $16,950 per year), 11 teaching assistantships (averaging $12,713 per year) were awarded. Federal Work-Study, institutionally sponsored loans, and traineeships also available.
Faculty research: Hydraulics, hydrology, water resources, infrastructure, environmental engineering. *Total annual research expenditures:* $5.4 million.
Sandra Woods, Head, 970-491-5049, *Fax:* 970-491-7727, *E-mail:* woods@ engr.colostate.edu.

Application contact: Laurie Howard, Student Adviser, 970-491-5844, *Fax:* 970-491-7727, *E-mail:* lhoward@ engr.colostate.edu. *Web site:* http://www.engr.colostate.edu/depts/ce/

■ TEXAS A&M UNIVERSITY

College of Engineering, Department of Civil Engineering, College Station, TX 77843

AWARDS Construction engineering and project management (M Eng, MS, D Eng, PhD); engineering mechanics (M Eng, MS, PhD); environmental engineering (M Eng, MS, D Eng, PhD); geotechnical engineering (M Eng, MS, D Eng, PhD); hydraulic engineering (M Eng, MS, PhD); hydrology (M Eng, MS, PhD); materials engineering (M Eng, MS, D Eng, PhD); ocean engineering (M Eng, MS, D Eng, PhD); public works engineering and management (M Eng, MS, PhD). Structural engineering and structural mechanics (M Eng, MS, D Eng, PhD); transportation engineering (M Eng, MS, D Eng, PhD); water resources engineering (M Eng, MS, D Eng, PhD). Part-time programs available.

Faculty: 59 full-time (4 women), 7 part-time/adjunct (2 women).
Students: 270. Average age 29. 375 applicants, 57% accepted, 68 enrolled. In 2001, 75 master's, 14 doctorates awarded.
Degree requirements: For master's, thesis (MS); for doctorate, dissertation (PhD), internship (D Eng).
Entrance requirements: For master's and doctorate, GRE General Test, TOEFL. *Application deadline:* Applications are processed on a rolling basis. *Application fee:* $50 ($75 for international students). Electronic applications accepted.
Expenses: Tuition, state resident: full-time $11,872. Tuition, nonresident: full-time $17,892.
Financial support: In 2001–02, 175 students received support, including 20 fellowships (averaging $4,000 per year), 112 research assistantships (averaging $1,000 per year), 43 teaching assistantships (averaging $1,000 per year); career-related internships or fieldwork and institutionally sponsored loans also available. Financial award application deadline: 4/15; financial award applicants required to submit FAFSA. *Total annual research expenditures:* $7 million.
Dr. John M. Niedzwecki, Head, 979-845-7435, *Fax:* 979-862-2800, *E-mail:* ce-grad@tamu.edu.
Application contact: Dr. Peter B. Keating, Graduate Advisor, 979-845-2498, *Fax:* 979-862-2800, *E-mail:* ce-grad@ tamu.edu. *Web site:* http://www.civil.tamu.edu/

Find an in-depth description at www.petersons.com/gradchannel.

■ UNIVERSITY OF MISSOURI–ROLLA

Graduate School, School of Engineering, Department of Civil Engineering, Program in Hydrology and Hydraulic Engineering, Rolla, MO 65409-0910

AWARDS MS, DE, PhD.

Degree requirements: For master's, thesis or alternative; for doctorate, thesis/dissertation.

Entrance requirements: For master's and doctorate, GRE General Test, TOEFL, minimum GPA of 3.0.

■ UNIVERSITY OF WASHINGTON

Graduate School, College of Engineering, Department of Civil and Environmental Engineering, Seattle, WA 98195

AWARDS Environmental engineering (MS, MSCE, MSE, PhD); hydraulic engineering (MSCE, MSE, PhD). Structural and geotechnical engineering and mechanics (MS, MSCE, MSE, PhD); transportation and construction engineering (MS, MSCE, MSE, PhD).

Faculty: 31 full-time (4 women), 26 part-time/adjunct (1 woman).
Students: 153 full-time (54 women), 42 part-time (13 women); includes 25 minority (2 African Americans, 19 Asian Americans or Pacific Islanders, 3 Hispanic Americans, 1 Native American), 34 international. Average age 29. 339 applicants, 60% accepted, 59 enrolled. In 2001, 71 master's, 11 doctorates awarded. Terminal master's awarded for partial completion of doctoral program.
Degree requirements: For master's, thesis (for some programs); for doctorate, thesis/dissertation, comprehensive exam. *Median time to degree:* Doctorate–3.5 years full-time.
Entrance requirements: For master's, GRE General Test, TOEFL, minimum GPA of 3.0; for doctorate, GRE, TOEFL, minimum GPA of 3.5. *Application deadline:* For fall admission, 2/1 (priority date). Applications are processed on a rolling basis. *Application fee:* $50. Electronic applications accepted.
Expenses: Tuition, state resident: full-time $5,539. Tuition, nonresident: full-time $14,376. Required fees: $390. Tuition and fees vary according to course load and program.
Financial support: In 2001–02, 110 students received support, including 22 fellowships with partial tuition reimbursements available, 70 research assistantships with full tuition reimbursements available, 22 teaching assistantships with full tuition reimbursements available; career-related internships or fieldwork and scholarships/grants also available. Financial award application deadline: 2/1.

Faculty research: Water resources, hydrology, construction, environmental structures, geotechnical transportation. *Total annual research expenditures:* $3.7 million.
Prof. G. Scott Rutherford, Chair, 206-543-2390.
Application contact: Marcia Buck, Graduate Adviser, 206-543-2574, *E-mail:* cesendme@u.washington.edu. *Web site:* http://www.ce.washington.edu/grad_p.htm

STRUCTURAL ENGINEERING

■ AUBURN UNIVERSITY

Graduate School, College of Engineering, Department of Civil Engineering, Auburn University, AL 36849

AWARDS Construction engineering and management (MCE, MS, PhD); environmental engineering (MCE, MS, PhD); geotechnical/materials engineering (MCE, MS, PhD); hydraulics/hydrology (MCE, MS, PhD); structural engineering (MCE, MS, PhD); transportation engineering (MCE, MS, PhD). Part-time programs available.

Faculty: 18 full-time (1 woman).
Students: 34 full-time (12 women), 25 part-time (9 women); includes 3 minority (all African Americans), 15 international. 74 applicants, 39% accepted. In 2001, 16 master's, 1 doctorate awarded.
Degree requirements: For master's, project (MCE), thesis (MS); for doctorate, thesis/dissertation, comprehensive exam.
Entrance requirements: For master's and doctorate, GRE General Test. *Application deadline:* For fall admission, 7/7; for spring admission, 11/24. Applications are processed on a rolling basis. *Application fee:* $25 ($50 for international students). Electronic applications accepted.
Financial support: Fellowships, research assistantships, teaching assistantships, Federal Work-Study available. Support available to part-time students. Financial award application deadline: 3/15.
Dr. Joseph F. Judkins, Head, 334-844-4320.
Application contact: Dr. John F. Pritchett, Dean of the Graduate School, 334-844-4700, *E-mail:* hatchlb@mail.auburn.edu.

■ CALIFORNIA STATE UNIVERSITY, NORTHRIDGE

Graduate Studies, College of Engineering and Computer Science, Department of Civil and Manufacturing Engineering, Northridge, CA 91330

AWARDS Applied mechanics (MSE); civil engineering (MS); engineering and computer science (MS); engineering management (MS); industrial engineering (MS); materials

engineering (MS); mechanical engineering (MS), including aerospace engineering, applied engineering, machine design, mechanical engineering, structural engineering, thermofluids; mechanics (MS). Part-time and evening/weekend programs available.

Faculty: 14 full-time, 2 part-time/adjunct.
Students: 25 full-time (4 women), 72 part-time (9 women). Average age 31. 64 applicants, 77% accepted, 22 enrolled. In 2001, 34 degrees awarded.
Degree requirements: For master's, thesis.
Entrance requirements: For master's, GRE General Test, TOEFL, minimum GPA of 2.5. *Application deadline:* For fall admission, 11/30. *Application fee:* $55.
Expenses: Tuition, nonresident: part-time $631 per semester. Required fees: $246 per unit.
Financial support: Teaching assistantships available. Financial award application deadline: 3/1.
Faculty research: Composite study.
Dr. Stephen Gadomski, Chair, 818-677-2166.
Application contact: Dr. Ileana Costa, Graduate Coordinator, 818-677-3299.

■ CALIFORNIA STATE UNIVERSITY, NORTHRIDGE

Graduate Studies, College of Engineering and Computer Science, Department of Civil and Manufacturing Engineering, Department of Mechanical Engineering, Northridge, CA 91330

AWARDS Aerospace engineering (MS); applied engineering (MS); machine design (MS); mechanical engineering (MS). Structural engineering (MS); thermofluids (MS). Part-time and evening/weekend programs available.

Faculty: 8 full-time, 2 part-time/adjunct.
Students: 6 full-time (0 women), 42 part-time (6 women); includes 19 minority (14 Asian Americans or Pacific Islanders, 4 Hispanic Americans, 1 Native American), 3 international. Average age 34. 24 applicants, 79% accepted, 6 enrolled. In 2001, 4 degrees awarded.
Degree requirements: For master's, thesis or alternative.
Entrance requirements: For master's, GRE General Test, TOEFL, minimum GPA of 2.5. *Application deadline:* For fall admission, 11/30. *Application fee:* $55.
Expenses: Tuition, nonresident: part-time $631 per semester. Required fees: $246 per unit.
Financial support: Application deadline: 3/1.
Dr. Sidney H. Schwartz, Chair, 818-677-2187.
Application contact: Dr. Tom Mincer, Graduate Coordinator, 818-677-2007.

◾ THE CATHOLIC UNIVERSITY OF AMERICA

School of Engineering, Department of Civil Engineering, Washington, DC 20064

AWARDS Civil engineering (MCE, D Engr); construction management (MCE, MS Engr); environmental engineering (MCE, MS Engr); geotechnical engineering (MCE). Structures and structural mechanics (MCE). Part-time and evening/weekend programs available.

Faculty: 6 full-time (0 women), 5 part-time/adjunct (2 women).
Students: 5 full-time (1 woman), 14 part-time (2 women); includes 5 minority (4 African Americans, 1 Asian American or Pacific Islander), 10 international. Average age 32. 18 applicants, 50% accepted, 2 enrolled. In 2001, 15 master's, 1 doctorate awarded.
Degree requirements: For master's, thesis optional; for doctorate, thesis/dissertation, qualifying exams, comprehensive exam.
Entrance requirements: For master's, TOEFL, minimum GPA of 3.0; for doctorate, TOEFL, minimum GPA of 3.5. *Application deadline:* For fall admission, 8/1 (priority date); for spring admission, 12/1. Applications are processed on a rolling basis. *Application fee:* $55. Electronic applications accepted.
Expenses: Tuition: Full-time $20,050; part-time $770 per credit. Required fees: $430 per term. Tuition and fees vary according to program.
Financial support: Research assistantships, teaching assistantships, career-related internships or fieldwork, Federal Work-Study, institutionally sponsored loans, and tuition waivers (full and partial) available. Support available to part-time students. Financial award application deadline: 2/1.
Faculty research: Wave propagation, geophysical fluid mechanics.
Dr. Timothy W. Kao, Chair, 202-319-5164, *Fax:* 202-319-4499, *E-mail:* kao@cua.edu. *Web site:* http://www.ee.cua.edu/programs/civil/

◾ CLEVELAND STATE UNIVERSITY

College of Graduate Studies, Fenn College of Engineering, Department of Civil and Environmental Engineering, Cleveland, OH 44115

AWARDS Civil engineering (MS, D Eng), including environmental engineering (D Eng), mechanical engineering (D Eng), structures engineering (D Eng); engineering mechanics (MS); environmental engineering (MS). Part-time programs available.

Faculty: 10 full-time (1 woman).
Students: 6 full-time (1 woman), 33 part-time (9 women); includes 3 minority (1 African American, 2 Hispanic Americans), 22 international. Average age 29. 62

applicants, 73% accepted. In 2001, 9 master's, 1 doctorate awarded.
Degree requirements: For master's, thesis (for some programs), project or thesis; for doctorate, thesis/dissertation, candidacy and qualifying exams.
Entrance requirements: For master's, GRE General Test, GRE Subject Test, TOEFL, minimum GPA of 2.75; for doctorate, GRE General Test, GRE Subject Test, TOEFL, minimum GPA of 3.25. *Application deadline:* For fall admission, 7/15 (priority date). Applications are processed on a rolling basis. *Application fee:* $25.
Expenses: Tuition, state resident: full-time $6,838; part-time $263 per credit hour. Tuition, nonresident: full-time $13,526; part-time $520 per credit hour.
Financial support: In 2001–02, 3 research assistantships, 6 teaching assistantships were awarded. Career-related internships or fieldwork and unspecified assistantships also available. Financial award application deadline: 9/1.
Faculty research: Environmental engineering, solid-waste disposal, composite materials, nonlinear buckling, constitutive modeling.
Dr. Paul Bosela, Chairperson, 216-687-2190, *Fax:* 216-687-9280. *Web site:* http://www.csuohio.edu/civileng/

◾ COLORADO STATE UNIVERSITY

Graduate School, College of Engineering, Department of Civil Engineering, Fort Collins, CO 80523-0015

AWARDS Bioresource and agricultural engineering (MS); bioresource and agriculture engineering (PhD); environmental engineering (MS, PhD); hydraulics and wind engineering (MS, PhD). Structural and geotechnical engineering (MS, PhD); water resources planning and management (MS, PhD); water resources, hydrologic and environmental sciences (MS, PhD). Part-time programs available.

Faculty: 37 full-time (2 women).
Students: 56 full-time (7 women), 99 part-time (21 women); includes 10 minority (7 Asian Americans or Pacific Islanders, 3 Hispanic Americans), 59 international. Average age 33. 228 applicants, 62% accepted, 39 enrolled. In 2001, 19 master's, 6 doctorates awarded. Terminal master's awarded for partial completion of doctoral program.
Degree requirements: For master's, thesis or alternative; for doctorate, thesis/dissertation.
Entrance requirements: For master's and doctorate, GRE General Test, TOEFL, minimum GPA of 3.0. *Application deadline:* For fall admission, 3/1 (priority date); for spring admission, 8/1 (priority date). Applications are processed on a rolling

basis. *Application fee:* $30. Electronic applications accepted.
Expenses: Tuition, state resident: full-time $2,880; part-time $160 per credit. Tuition, nonresident: full-time $11,412; part-time $634 per credit. Required fees: $750; $34 per credit.
Financial support: In 2001–02, 2 fellowships, 26 research assistantships (averaging $16,950 per year), 11 teaching assistantships (averaging $12,713 per year) were awarded. Federal Work-Study, institutionally sponsored loans, and traineeships also available.
Faculty research: Hydraulics, hydrology, water resources, infrastructure, environmental engineering. *Total annual research expenditures:* $5.4 million.
Sandra Woods, Head, 970-491-5049, *Fax:* 970-491-7727, *E-mail:* woods@engr.colostate.edu.
Application contact: Laurie Howard, Student Adviser, 970-491-5844, *Fax:* 970-491-7727, *E-mail:* lhoward@engr.colostate.edu. *Web site:* http://www.engr.colostate.edu/depts/ce/

◾ CORNELL UNIVERSITY

Graduate School, Graduate Fields of Engineering, Field of Civil and Environmental Engineering, Ithaca, NY 14853-0001

AWARDS Environmental engineering (M Eng, MS, PhD); environmental fluid mechanics and hydrology (M Eng, MS, PhD); environmental systems engineering (M Eng, MS, PhD); geotechnical engineering (M Eng, MS, PhD); remote sensing (M Eng, MS, PhD). Structural engineering (M Eng, MS, PhD); transportation engineering (M Eng, MS, PhD); water resource systems (M Eng, MS, PhD).

Faculty: 33 full-time.
Students: 131 full-time (35 women); includes 17 minority (1 African American, 9 Asian Americans or Pacific Islanders, 7 Hispanic Americans), 61 international. 515 applicants, 55% accepted. In 2001, 64 master's, 14 doctorates awarded. Terminal master's awarded for partial completion of doctoral program.
Degree requirements: For master's, thesis (MS); for doctorate, thesis/dissertation.
Entrance requirements: For master's and doctorate, GRE General Test (recommended), TOEFL, 2 letters of recommendation. *Application deadline:* For fall admission, 1/15 (priority date). *Application fee:* $65. Electronic applications accepted.
Expenses: Tuition: Full-time $25,970. Required fees: $50.
Financial support: In 2001–02, 71 students received support, including 24 fellowships with full tuition reimbursements available, 28 research assistantships with full tuition reimbursements available, 19 teaching assistantships with full tuition reimbursements available; institutionally sponsored loans, scholarships/grants, tuition waivers (full and partial), and

Cornell University (continued)
unspecified assistantships also available.
Financial award applicants required to
submit FAFSA.
Faculty research: Environmental
engineering, geotechnical engineering
remote sensing, environmental fluid
mechanics and hydrology, structural
engineering.
Application contact: Graduate Field
Assistant, 607-255-7560, *E-mail:* cee_
grad@cornell.edu. *Web site:* http://
www.gradschool.cornell.edu/grad/fields_1/
cee.html

**Find an in-depth description at
www.petersons.com/gradchannel.**

■ IOWA STATE UNIVERSITY OF SCIENCE AND TECHNOLOGY

**Graduate College, College of
Engineering, Department of Civil and
Construction Engineering, Ames, IA
50011**

AWARDS Civil engineering (MS, PhD), including civil engineering materials, construction
engineering and management, environmental
engineering, geometronics, geotechnical
engineering, structural engineering,
transportation engineering.

Faculty: 32 full-time, 5 part-time/adjunct.
Students: 55 full-time (9 women), 39 part-
time (6 women); includes 1 minority
(African American), 40 international. 256
applicants, 23% accepted, 21 enrolled. In
2001, 27 master's, 4 doctorates awarded.
Degree requirements: For master's,
thesis or alternative; for doctorate, thesis/
dissertation. *Median time to degree:*
Master's–2 years full-time; doctorate–3.3
years full-time.
Entrance requirements: For master's and
doctorate, GRE General Test
(international applicants), TOEFL or
IELTS. *Application deadline:* For fall admission, 3/1 (priority date); for spring admission, 10/1 (priority date). *Application fee:*
$20 ($50 for international students).
Electronic applications accepted.
Expenses: Tuition, state resident: full-time
$1,851. Tuition, nonresident: full-time
$5,449. Tuition and fees vary according to
program.
Financial support: In 2001–02, 44
research assistantships with partial tuition
reimbursements (averaging $12,963 per
year), 5 teaching assistantships with partial
tuition reimbursements (averaging $11,756
per year) were awarded. Fellowships,
scholarships/grants, health care benefits,
and unspecified assistantships also available.
Dr. Lowell F. Greimann, Chair, 515-294-
2140, *E-mail:* cceinfo@iastate.edu.
Application contact: Dr. Edward Kannel,
Director of Graduate Education, 515-294-
2861, *E-mail:* cceinfo@iastate.edu. *Web site:*
http://www1.eng.iastate.edu/coe/grad.asp/

■ LOUISIANA STATE UNIVERSITY AND AGRICULTURAL AND MECHANICAL COLLEGE

**Graduate School, College of
Engineering, Department of Civil and
Environmental Engineering, Baton
Rouge, LA 70803**

AWARDS Environmental engineering (MSCE,
PhD); geotechnical engineering (MSCE, PhD).
Structural engineering and mechanics (MSCE,
PhD); transportation engineering (MSCE,
PhD); water resources (MSCE, PhD). Part-
time programs available.

Faculty: 30 full-time (1 woman).
Students: 78 full-time (19 women), 26
part-time (11 women); includes 4 minority
(2 African Americans, 1 Hispanic
American, 1 Native American), 67
international. Average age 29. 133
applicants, 41% accepted, 22 enrolled. In
2001, 15 master's, 7 doctorates awarded.
Degree requirements: For master's,
thesis optional; for doctorate, one foreign
language, thesis/dissertation.
Entrance requirements: For master's and
doctorate, GRE General Test, TOEFL,
minimum GPA of 3.0. *Application deadline:*
For fall admission, 1/25 (priority date).
Applications are processed on a rolling
basis. *Application fee:* $25.
Expenses: Tuition, state resident: full-time
$2,551. Tuition, nonresident: full-time
$5,551. Required fees: $854. Part-time
tuition and fees vary according to course
load.
Financial support: In 2001–02, 5 fellowships (averaging $15,800 per year), 51
research assistantships with partial tuition
reimbursements (averaging $12,089 per
year), 2 teaching assistantships with partial
tuition reimbursements (averaging $12,500
per year) were awarded. Career-related
internships or fieldwork, institutionally
sponsored loans, and scholarships/grants
also available. Financial award application
deadline: 3/1; financial award applicants
required to submit FAFSA.
Faculty research: Solid waste management, electrokinetics, composite structures,
transportation planning, river mechanics.
Total annual research expenditures: $1.7 mil-
lion.
Dr. George Z. Voyiadjis, Interim Chair/
Boyd Professor, 225-578-8668, *Fax:* 225-
578-8652, *E-mail:* cegzv@lsu.edu. *Web site:*
http://www.ce.lsu.edu/

■ MARQUETTE UNIVERSITY

**Graduate School, College of
Engineering, Department of Civil and
Environmental Engineering,
Milwaukee, WI 53201-1881**

AWARDS Construction and public works
management (MS, PhD); environmental/water
resources engineering (MS, PhD). Structural/
geotechnical engineering (MS, PhD);
transportational planning and engineering

(MS, PhD). Part-time and evening/weekend
programs available.

Faculty: 12 full-time (0 women), 1 part-
time/adjunct (0 women).
Students: 20 full-time (8 women), 24 part-
time (3 women); includes 2 minority (1
Asian American or Pacific Islander, 1
Hispanic American), 13 international.
Average age 30. 57 applicants, 53%
accepted, 9 enrolled. In 2001, 9 degrees
awarded. Terminal master's awarded for
partial completion of doctoral program.
Degree requirements: For master's,
thesis or alternative, comprehensive exam;
for doctorate, thesis/dissertation. *Median
time to degree:* Master's–2 years full-time, 3
years part-time.
Entrance requirements: For master's,
TOEFL; for doctorate, GRE General
Test, TOEFL. *Application deadline:* For fall
admission, 6/1 (priority date). Applications
are processed on a rolling basis. *Application
fee:* $40. Electronic applications accepted.
Expenses: Tuition: Full-time $10,170;
part-time $445 per credit hour. Tuition
and fees vary according to course load.
Financial support: In 2001–02, 18
students received support, including 3 fellowships with tuition reimbursements
available, 1 research assistantship with
tuition reimbursement available (averaging
$10,600 per year), 4 teaching assistantships
with tuition reimbursements available
(averaging $10,200 per year); Federal
Work-Study, institutionally sponsored
loans, scholarships/grants, and tuition
waivers (full and partial) also available.
Support available to part-time students.
Financial award application deadline: 2/15.
Faculty research: Highway safety,
highway performance, and intelligent
transportation systems. Surface mount
technology; watershed management. *Total
annual research expenditures:* $860,000.
Dr. Thomas H. Wenzel, Chair, 414-288-
7030, *Fax:* 414-288-7521.

**Find an in-depth description at
www.petersons.com/gradchannel.**

■ MICHIGAN TECHNOLOGICAL UNIVERSITY

**Graduate School, College of
Engineering, Department of Civil and
Environmental Engineering, Program
in Structural Engineering, Houghton,
MI 49931-1295**

AWARDS PhD.

Degree requirements: For doctorate,
thesis/dissertation.
Electronic applications accepted.

■ MILWAUKEE SCHOOL OF ENGINEERING

Department of Architectural Engineering and Building Construction, Milwaukee, WI 53202-3109

AWARDS Environmental engineering (MS). Structural engineering (MS). Part-time and evening/weekend programs available.

Faculty: 2 full-time (1 woman), 11 part-time/adjunct (0 women).
Students: 2 full-time (0 women), 25 part-time (6 women). Average age 25. 18 applicants, 61% accepted, 2 enrolled. In 2001, 8 degrees awarded.
Degree requirements: For master's, thesis or alternative, design project.
Entrance requirements: For master's, GRE General Test or GMAT, letters of recommendation (2), BS in architectural, civil or structural engineering or related field. *Application deadline:* Applications are processed on a rolling basis. *Application fee:* $35. Electronic applications accepted.
Expenses: Tuition: Part-time $440 per credit. Tuition and fees vary according to course load.
Financial support: In 2001–02, 3 students received support, including 2 research assistantships; career-related internships or fieldwork also available. Support available to part-time students. Financial award applicants required to submit FAFSA.
Faculty research: Steel. *Total annual research expenditures:* $90,000.
Matt Fuchs, Chairman, 414-277-7302, *Fax:* 414-277-7479, *E-mail:* fuchs@msoe.edu.
Application contact: Paul Borens, Admissions Director, 800-332-6763, *Fax:* 414-277-7475, *E-mail:* borens@msoe.edu. *Web site:* http://msoe.edu/

■ NORTHWESTERN UNIVERSITY

McCormick School of Engineering and Applied Science, Department of Civil and Environmental Engineering, Evanston, IL 60208

AWARDS Environmental engineering and science (MS, PhD); geotechnical engineering (MS, PhD); mechanics of materials and solids (MS, PhD); project management (MPM). Structural engineering and materials (MS, PhD); theoretical and applied mechanics (MS, PhD); transportation systems analysis and planning (MS, PhD). MS and PhD admissions and degrees offered through The Graduate School. Part-time programs available.

Faculty: 26 full-time (3 women), 9 part-time/adjunct (2 women).
Students: 80 full-time (32 women), 1 part-time; includes 2 Asian Americans or Pacific Islanders, 1 Hispanic American, 38 international. 282 applicants, 7% accepted. In 2001, 20 master's, 14 doctorates awarded. Terminal master's awarded for partial completion of doctoral program.
Degree requirements: For master's, thesis (for some programs); for doctorate, thesis/dissertation.
Application deadline: For fall admission, 8/1. *Application fee:* $50 ($55 for international students). Electronic applications accepted.
Expenses: Tuition: Full-time $26,526.
Financial support: In 2001–02, 10 fellowships with full tuition reimbursements (averaging $13,338 per year), 66 research assistantships with partial tuition reimbursements (averaging $18,000 per year), 7 teaching assistantships with full tuition reimbursements (averaging $13,329 per year) were awarded. Career-related internships or fieldwork, institutionally sponsored loans, and scholarships/grants also available. Financial award application deadline: 1/15; financial award applicants required to submit FAFSA.
Faculty research: Environmental engineering and science, geotechnics, mechanics of materials and solids, structural engineering and materials, transportation systems analysis and planning. *Total annual research expenditures:* $8.4 million.
Joseph L. Schofer, Chair, 847-491-3257, *Fax:* 847-491-4011, *E-mail:* j-schofer@northwestern.edu.
Application contact: Janet Soule, Academic Coordinator, 847-491-3176, *Fax:* 847-491-4011, *E-mail:* civil-info@northwestern.edu. *Web site:* http://www.civil.northwestern.edu/

Find an in-depth description at www.petersons.com/gradchannel.

■ OHIO UNIVERSITY

Graduate Studies, Russ College of Engineering and Technology, Department of Civil Engineering, Athens, OH 45701-2979

AWARDS Geotechnical and environmental engineering (MS); water resources and structures (MS).

Faculty: 11 full-time (1 woman).
Students: 19 full-time (4 women), 6 part-time (2 women), 18 international. Average age 28. 52 applicants, 71% accepted, 11 enrolled. In 2001, 7 degrees awarded.
Degree requirements: For master's, thesis optional.
Entrance requirements: For master's, minimum GPA of 3.0. *Application deadline:* For fall admission, 5/1 (priority date). Applications are processed on a rolling basis. *Application fee:* $30.
Expenses: Tuition, state resident: full-time $6,585. Tuition, nonresident: full-time $12,254.
Financial support: In 2001–02, 1 fellowship (averaging $15,000 per year), 12 research assistantships (averaging $12,000 per year), 6 teaching assistantships (averaging $6,000 per year) were awarded. Federal Work-Study, institutionally sponsored loans, and tuition waivers (full and partial) also available. Financial award application deadline: 3/15.

Faculty research: Soil-structure interaction, solid waste management, pipes, pavements, noise pollution, mine reclamation, drought analysis. *Total annual research expenditures:* $1.2 million.
Dr. Gayle Mitchell, Chair, 740-593-1465, *Fax:* 740-593-0625, *E-mail:* gmitchell@bobcat.ent.ohiou.edu.
Application contact: Dr. Shad Sargand, Graduate Chair, 740-593-1467, *Fax:* 740-593-0625, *E-mail:* ssargand@bobcat.ent.ohiou.edu. *Web site:* http://webce.ent.ohiou.edu/

■ THE PENNSYLVANIA STATE UNIVERSITY UNIVERSITY PARK CAMPUS

Graduate School, College of Engineering, Department of Civil and Environmental Engineering, State College, University Park, PA 16802-1503

AWARDS Civil engineering (M Eng, MS, PhD); environmental engineering (M Eng, MS, PhD). Structural engineering (M Eng, MS, PhD); transportation and highway engineering (M Eng, MS, PhD); water resources engineering (M Eng, MS, PhD).

Students: 102 full-time (26 women), 37 part-time (5 women).
Degree requirements: For master's, final paper (M Eng), oral exam and thesis (MS); for doctorate, one foreign language, thesis/dissertation, oral exams, comprehensive exam.
Entrance requirements: For master's and doctorate, GRE General Test. *Application fee:* $45.
Expenses: Tuition, state resident: full-time $7,882; part-time $333 per credit. Tuition, nonresident: full-time $16,142; part-time $673 per credit. Required fees: $124 per semester.
Financial support: Fellowships, research assistantships, teaching assistantships available.
Faculty research: Construction engineering and management; materials and pavements; geotechnical engineering; hydraulics, hydrology, and water resource systems. Structures.
Dr. Andrew Scanlon, Head, 814-863-3084.

■ PRINCETON UNIVERSITY

Graduate School, School of Engineering and Applied Science, Department of Civil and Environmental Engineering, Program in Mechanics, Materials, and Structures, Princeton, NJ 08544-1019

AWARDS M Eng, MSE, PhD.

Degree requirements: For master's and doctorate, thesis/dissertation.

Find an in-depth description at www.petersons.com/gradchannel.

■ RENSSELAER POLYTECHNIC INSTITUTE

Graduate School, School of Engineering, Department of Civil and Environmental Engineering, Program in Civil Engineering, Troy, NY 12180-3590

AWARDS Geotechnical engineering (M Eng, MS, D Eng, PhD); mechanics of composite materials and structures (M Eng, MS, D Eng, PhD). Structural engineering (M Eng, MS, D Eng, PhD); transportation engineering (M Eng, MS, D Eng, PhD). Part-time programs available.

Faculty: 9 full-time (0 women), 4 part-time/adjunct (1 woman).

Students: 28 full-time (8 women), 6 part-time; includes 1 minority (Asian American or Pacific Islander), 15 international. Average age 24. 105 applicants, 40% accepted. In 2001, 8 master's, 2 doctorates awarded.

Degree requirements: For master's, thesis (for some programs); for doctorate, thesis/dissertation.

Entrance requirements: For master's and doctorate, GRE, TOEFL. *Application deadline:* For fall admission, 1/15 (priority date). Applications are processed on a rolling basis. *Application fee:* $45. Electronic applications accepted.

Expenses: Tuition: Full-time $26,400; part-time $1,320 per credit hour. Required fees: $1,437.

Financial support: In 2001–02, 18 students received support, including 3 fellowships, 5 research assistantships with full and partial tuition reimbursements available, 10 teaching assistantships with full tuition reimbursements available; career-related internships or fieldwork and institutionally sponsored loans also available. Financial award application deadline: 2/1.

Faculty research: Computational mechanics, earthquake engineering, geo-environmental engineering. *Total annual research expenditures:* $1.7 million.

Dr. George List, Department Chair, 518-276-6362, *Fax:* 518-276-4833, *E-mail:* listg@rpi.edu.

Application contact: Jo Ann Grega, Admissions Assistant, 518-276-6679, *Fax:* 518-276-4833, *E-mail:* gregaj2@rpi.edu. *Web site:* http://www.rpi.edu/dept/civil/htm

Find an in-depth description at www.petersons.com/gradchannel.

■ TEXAS A&M UNIVERSITY

College of Engineering, Department of Civil Engineering, Program in Structural Engineering and Structural Mechanics, College Station, TX 77843

AWARDS M Eng, MS, D Eng, PhD. D Eng offered through the College of Engineering.

Students: 44.

Degree requirements: For master's, thesis (MS); for doctorate, dissertation (PhD), internship (D Eng).

Entrance requirements: For master's and doctorate, GRE General Test, TOEFL. *Application fee:* $50 ($75 for international students).

Expenses: Tuition, state resident: full-time $11,872. Tuition, nonresident: full-time $17,892.

Financial support: Fellowships, research assistantships, teaching assistantships available. Financial award application deadline: 4/15; financial award applicants required to submit FAFSA.

Faculty research: Analysis and design of bridges, buildings, and offshore structures; dynamic loads and structural behavior. Structural reliability; computer-aided design.

Dr. Paul N. Roschke, Head, 979-845-4414, *Fax:* 979-862-2800, *E-mail:* ce-grad@tamu.edu.

Application contact: Dr. Gary T. Fry, Information Contact, 979-845-2498, *Fax:* 979-862-2800, *E-mail:* ce-grad@tamu.edu. *Web site:* http://www.civil.tamu.edu/

■ TUFTS UNIVERSITY

Division of Graduate and Continuing Studies and Research, Graduate School of Arts and Sciences, School of Engineering, Department of Civil and Environmental Engineering, Medford, MA 02155

AWARDS Civil engineering (MS, PhD), including geotechnical engineering, structural engineering; environmental engineering (MS, PhD), including environmental engineering and environmental sciences, environmental geotechnology, environmental health, environmental science and management, hazardous materials management, water resources engineering. Part-time programs available.

Faculty: 13 full-time, 10 part-time/adjunct.

Students: 58 (29 women); includes 4 minority (2 African Americans, 2 Asian Americans or Pacific Islanders) 4 international. 53 applicants, 75% accepted. In 2001, 36 master's, 1 doctorate awarded. Terminal master's awarded for partial completion of doctoral program.

Degree requirements: For master's, thesis or alternative; for doctorate, thesis/dissertation.

Entrance requirements: For master's and doctorate, GRE General Test, TOEFL. *Application deadline:* For fall admission, 2/15; for spring admission, 10/15. Applications are processed on a rolling basis. *Application fee:* $50. Electronic applications accepted.

Expenses: Tuition: Full-time $26,853. Full-time tuition and fees vary according to program.

Financial support: Research assistantships with full and partial tuition reimbursements, teaching assistantships with full and partial tuition reimbursements, Federal Work-Study, scholarships/grants, and tuition waivers (partial) available. Support available to part-time students. Financial award application deadline: 2/15; financial award applicants required to submit FAFSA.

Dr. Stephen Levine, Chair, 617-627-3211, *Fax:* 617-627-3994.

Application contact: Linfield Brown, Head, 617-627-3211, *Fax:* 617-627-3994. *Web site:* http://www.ase.tufts.edu/cee/

■ UNIVERSITY AT BUFFALO, THE STATE UNIVERSITY OF NEW YORK

Graduate School, School of Engineering and Applied Sciences, Department of Civil, Structural, and Environmental Engineering, Buffalo, NY 14260

AWARDS Civil engineering (M Eng, MS, PhD); engineering science (MS). Part-time programs available. Postbaccalaureate distance learning degree programs offered (minimal on-campus study).

Faculty: 22 full-time (0 women), 5 part-time/adjunct (0 women).

Students: 88 full-time (18 women), 50 part-time (9 women); includes 5 minority (2 African Americans, 3 Asian Americans or Pacific Islanders), 88 international. Average age 27. 285 applicants, 31% accepted. In 2001, 42 master's, 13 doctorates awarded. Terminal master's awarded for partial completion of doctoral program.

Degree requirements: For master's, project or thesis; for doctorate, thesis/dissertation.

Entrance requirements: For master's and doctorate, GRE General Test, TOEFL. *Application deadline:* For fall admission, 1/15 (priority date); for spring admission, 10/1. Applications are processed on a rolling basis. *Application fee:* $35. Electronic applications accepted.

Expenses: Tuition, state resident: full-time $6,118. Tuition, nonresident: full-time $9,434.

Financial support: In 2001–02, 6 fellowships with full tuition reimbursements (averaging $14,700 per year), 58 research assistantships with full tuition reimbursements (averaging $11,400 per year), 27 teaching assistantships with full tuition reimbursements (averaging $11,400 per year) were awarded. Career-related internships or fieldwork, Federal Work-Study, institutionally sponsored loans, scholarships/grants, tuition waivers (full and partial), and unspecified assistantships also available. Support available to part-time students. Financial award application deadline: 1/15; financial award applicants required to submit FAFSA.

Faculty research: Earthquake protection, environmental engineering and fluid mechanics, structural dynamics, geomechanics. *Total annual research expenditures:* $1.5 million.

Dr. Michael C. Constantinou, Chairman, 716-645-2114 Ext. 2446, *Fax:* 716-645-3733, *E-mail:* constonl@eng.buffalo.edu. **Application contact:** Dr. T. T. Soong, Director of Graduate Admissions, 716-645-2114 Ext. 2424, *Fax:* 716-645-3667, *E-mail:* dhm1@eng.buffalo.edu. *Web site:* http://www.civil.buffalo.edu/

Find an in-depth description at www.petersons.com/gradchannel.

■ UNIVERSITY OF CALIFORNIA, BERKELEY

Graduate Division, College of Engineering, Department of Civil and Environmental Engineering, Berkeley, CA 94720-1500

AWARDS Construction engineering and management (M Eng, MS, D Eng, PhD); environmental quality and environmental water resources engineering (M Eng, MS, D Eng, PhD); geotechnical engineering (M Eng, MS, D Eng, PhD). Structural engineering, mechanics and materials (M Eng, MS, D Eng, PhD); transportation engineering (M Eng, MS, D Eng, PhD).

Degree requirements: For master's, comprehensive exam or thesis (MS); for doctorate, thesis/dissertation, qualifying exam.
Entrance requirements: For master's, GRE General Test, minimum GPA of 3.0; for doctorate, GRE General Test, minimum GPA of 3.5.
Expenses: Tuition, nonresident: full-time $10,704. Required fees: $4,349.

Find an in-depth description at www.petersons.com/gradchannel.

■ UNIVERSITY OF CALIFORNIA, LOS ANGELES

Graduate Division, School of Engineering and Applied Science, Department of Civil and Environmental Engineering, Los Angeles, CA 90095

AWARDS Environmental engineering (MS, PhD); geotechnical engineering (MS, PhD). Structures (MS, PhD), including structural mechanics and earthquake engineering; water resource systems engineering (MS, PhD).

Faculty: 14 full-time, 11 part-time/adjunct.
Students: 96 full-time (28 women); includes 23 minority (1 African American, 17 Asian Americans or Pacific Islanders, 5 Hispanic Americans), 45 international. 216 applicants, 60% accepted, 34 enrolled. In 2001, 34 master's, 9 doctorates awarded.
Degree requirements: For master's, comprehensive exam or thesis; for doctorate, thesis/dissertation, qualifying exams.
Entrance requirements: For master's, GRE General Test, minimum GPA of 3.0; for doctorate, GRE General Test, minimum GPA of 3.25. *Application deadline:*

For fall admission, 1/15; for spring admission, 12/1. *Application fee:* $60. Electronic applications accepted.
Expenses: Tuition, nonresident: full-time $10,244. Required fees: $3,609. Full-time tuition and fees vary according to program.
Financial support: In 2001–02, 39 fellowships, 50 research assistantships, 31 teaching assistantships were awarded. Federal Work-Study, institutionally sponsored loans, and tuition waivers (full and partial) also available. Financial award application deadline: 1/15; financial award applicants required to submit FAFSA.
Dr. Jiann-Wen Ju, Chair, 310-206-1751. **Application contact:** Deeona Columbia, Graduate Affairs Officer, 310-825-1851, *Fax:* 310-206-2222, *E-mail:* deeona@ea.ucla.edu. *Web site:* http://www.cee.ucla.edu

Find an in-depth description at www.petersons.com/gradchannel.

■ UNIVERSITY OF CALIFORNIA, SAN DIEGO

Graduate Studies and Research, Department of Structural Engineering, La Jolla, CA 92093

AWARDS MS, PhD. Part-time programs available.

Students: 57 (9 women). 137 applicants, 49% accepted, 23 enrolled. In 2001, 11 master's, 2 doctorates awarded.
Degree requirements: For master's, comprehensive exam or thesis; for doctorate, thesis/dissertation, qualifying exam.
Entrance requirements: For master's and doctorate, GRE General Test, TOEFL, minimum GPA of 3.0. *Application deadline:* For fall admission, 5/31. *Application fee:* $40.
Expenses: Tuition, nonresident: full-time $10,434. Required fees: $4,883.
Financial support: In 2001–02, fellowships with full tuition reimbursements (averaging $15,000 per year), research assistantships with full tuition reimbursements (averaging $15,000 per year), teaching assistantships with partial tuition reimbursements (averaging $13,000 per year) were awarded. Scholarships/grants also available. Financial award application deadline: 1/31; financial award applicants required to submit FAFSA.
Faculty research: Advanced large-scale civil, mechanical, and aerospace structures. Dr. Yistasp M Karbhari, Chair, 858-882-5212, *Fax:* 858-534-1730, *E-mail:* l. **Application contact:** Linda Floyd, AMES Graduate Student Affairs, 858-822-1421, *Fax:* 858-534-1310, *E-mail:* lfloyd@ucsd.edu. *Web site:* http://www-ames.ucsd.edu/

Find an in-depth description at www.petersons.com/gradchannel.

■ UNIVERSITY OF CENTRAL FLORIDA

College of Engineering and Computer Sciences, Department of Civil and Environmental Engineering, Program in Civil Engineering, Orlando, FL 32816

AWARDS Civil engineering (MS, MSCE, PhD); geotechnical engineering (Certificate). Structural engineering (Certificate). Surface water modeling (Certificate); transportation engineering (Certificate). Part-time and evening/weekend programs available.

Faculty: 19 full-time (1 woman), 12 part-time/adjunct (0 women).
Students: 17 full-time (4 women), 37 part-time (7 women); includes 10 minority (1 African American, 2 Asian Americans or Pacific Islanders, 7 Hispanic Americans), 16 international. Average age 30. 84 applicants, 62% accepted, 16 enrolled. In 2001, 1 master's, 1 doctorate awarded.
Degree requirements: For master's, thesis or alternative; for doctorate, thesis/dissertation, departmental qualifying exam, candidacy exam.
Entrance requirements: For master's, GRE General Test, TOEFL, minimum GPA of 3.0 in last 60 hours; for doctorate, GRE General Test, TOEFL, minimum GPA of 3.5 in last 60 hours. *Application deadline:* For fall admission, 7/15 (priority date); for spring admission, 12/15 (priority date). *Application fee:* $20. Electronic applications accepted.
Expenses: Tuition, state resident: part-time $162 per hour. Tuition, nonresident: part-time $569 per hour.
Financial support: In 2001–02, 13 fellowships with partial tuition reimbursements (averaging $2,115 per year), 73 research assistantships with partial tuition reimbursements (averaging $3,846 per year), 13 teaching assistantships with partial tuition reimbursements (averaging $2,732 per year) were awarded. Career-related internships or fieldwork, Federal Work-Study, institutionally sponsored loans, tuition waivers (partial), and unspecified assistantships also available. Financial award application deadline: 3/1; financial award applicants required to submit FAFSA.
Application contact: Dr. Roger L. Wayson, Coordinator, 407-823-2841, *E-mail:* wayson@pegasus.cc.ucf.edu. *Web site:* http://www.ucf.edu/

■ UNIVERSITY OF COLORADO AT BOULDER

Graduate School, College of Engineering and Applied Science, Department of Civil, Environmental, and Architectural Engineering, Boulder, CO 80309

AWARDS Building systems (MS, PhD); construction engineering and management (MS, PhD); environmental engineering (MS,

University of Colorado at Boulder (continued)
PhD); geoenvironmental engineering (MS, PhD); geotechnical engineering (MS, PhD). Structural engineering (MS, PhD); water resource engineering (MS, PhD).

Faculty: 37 full-time (2 women).
Students: 167 full-time (49 women), 44 part-time (12 women); includes 14 minority (1 African American, 4 Asian Americans or Pacific Islanders, 9 Hispanic Americans), 88 international. Average age 30. 280 applicants, 59% accepted. In 2001, 59 master's, 13 doctorates awarded.
Degree requirements: For master's, thesis or alternative, comprehensive exam; for doctorate, thesis/dissertation.
Entrance requirements: For master's, GRE General Test, minimum undergraduate GPA of 3.0. *Application deadline:* For fall admission, 4/30; for spring admission, 10/31. *Application fee:* $50 ($60 for international students).
Expenses: Tuition, state resident: full-time $3,474. Tuition, nonresident: full-time $16,624.
Financial support: In 2001–02, 19 fellowships (averaging $5,252 per year), 45 research assistantships (averaging $15,638 per year), 14 teaching assistantships (averaging $13,821 per year) were awarded. Financial award application deadline: 2/15.
Faculty research: Building systems engineering, construction engineering and management, environmental engineering, geoenvironmental engineering, geotechnical engineering. *Total annual research expenditures:* $8.3 million.
Hon-Yim Ko, Chair, 303-492-6716, *Fax:* 303-492-7317, *E-mail:* ko@spot.colorado.edu.
Application contact: Jan Demay, Graduate Secretary, 303-492-7316, *Fax:* 303-492-7317, *E-mail:* demay@spot.colorado.edu. *Web site:* http://www.civil.colorado.edu/

■ UNIVERSITY OF DAYTON

Graduate School, School of Engineering, Department of Civil Engineering, Dayton, OH 45469-1300

AWARDS Engineering mechanics (MSEM); environmental engineering (MSCE). Soil mechanics (MSCE). Structural engineering (MSCE); transport engineering (MSCE). Part-time programs available.

Faculty: 8 full-time (0 women), 2 part-time/adjunct (0 women).
Students: 8 full-time (6 women), 7 part-time (4 women), 6 international. In 2001, 2 degrees awarded.
Degree requirements: For master's, thesis or alternative.
Entrance requirements: For master's, TOEFL. *Application deadline:* For fall admission, 8/1. Applications are processed on a rolling basis. *Application fee:* $30.
Expenses: Tuition: Full-time $5,436; part-time $453 per credit hour. Required fees: $50; $25 per term.

Financial support: In 2001–02, 5 research assistantships with full tuition reimbursements (averaging $12,000 per year), 2 teaching assistantships with full tuition reimbursements (averaging $10,000 per year) were awarded. Institutionally sponsored loans also available.
Faculty research: Tire/soil interaction, tilt-up structures, viscoelastic response of restraint systems, composite materials.
Dr. Joseph E. Saliba, Chairperson, 937-229-3847, *E-mail:* jsaliba@engr.udayton.edu.
Application contact: Dr. Donald L. Moon, Associate Dean, 937-229-2241, *Fax:* 937-229-2471, *E-mail:* dmoon@notes.udayton.edu.

■ UNIVERSITY OF DELAWARE

College of Engineering, Department of Civil and Environmental Engineering, Program in Structural Engineering, Newark, DE 19716

AWARDS MAS, MCE, PhD. Terminal master's awarded for partial completion of doctoral program.

Degree requirements: For master's and doctorate, thesis/dissertation.
Entrance requirements: For master's and doctorate, GRE General Test, TOEFL.
Expenses: Tuition, state resident: full-time $4,770; part-time $265 per credit. Tuition, nonresident: full-time $13,860; part-time $770 per credit. Required fees: $414.
Faculty research: Structural dynamics, analytical and numerical methods in structural mechanics and geomechanics, analysis of geomaterials, ice mechanics, structural stability.

Find an in-depth description at www.petersons.com/gradchannel.

■ UNIVERSITY OF MAINE

Graduate School, College of Engineering, Department of Civil and Environmental Engineering, Orono, ME 04469

AWARDS Civil engineering (MS, PhD), including environmental engineering, geotechnical engineering, structural engineering.

Faculty: 11 full-time (0 women).
Students: 18 full-time (7 women), 8 part-time; includes 3 minority (2 Hispanic Americans, 1 Native American), 10 international. 21 applicants, 43% accepted, 4 enrolled. In 2001, 11 degrees awarded.
Degree requirements: For doctorate, thesis/dissertation.
Entrance requirements: For master's and doctorate, GRE General Test, TOEFL. *Application deadline:* For fall admission, 2/1 (priority date). Applications are processed on a rolling basis. *Application fee:* $50. Electronic applications accepted.
Expenses: Tuition, state resident: full-time $3,780; part-time $210 per credit hour. Tuition, nonresident: full-time $10,782; part-time $599 per credit hour. Required

fees: $9.5 per credit hour. $32 per semester. Tuition and fees vary according to reciprocity agreements.
Financial support: In 2001–02, 15 research assistantships with tuition reimbursements (averaging $16,900 per year), 3 teaching assistantships with tuition reimbursements (averaging $15,000 per year) were awarded. Federal Work-Study, institutionally sponsored loans, scholarships/grants, and tuition waivers (full and partial) also available. Financial award application deadline: 3/1.
Dr. Dana Humphrey, Chair, 207-581-2170, *Fax:* 207-581-3888.
Application contact: Scott G. Delcourt, Director of the Graduate School, 207-581-3218, *Fax:* 207-581-3232, *E-mail:* graduate@maine.edu. *Web site:* http://www.umaine.edu/graduate/

■ THE UNIVERSITY OF MEMPHIS

Graduate School, Herff College of Engineering, Department of Civil Engineering, Memphis, TN 38152

AWARDS Civil engineering (PhD); environmental engineering (MS); foundation engineering (MS). Structural engineering (MS); transportation engineering (MS); water resources engineering (MS).

Faculty: 12 full-time (0 women), 1 part-time/adjunct (0 women).
Students: 14 full-time (5 women), 7 part-time (1 woman), 10 international. Average age 32. 36 applicants, 56% accepted. In 2001, 5 degrees awarded.
Degree requirements: For master's, thesis or alternative, comprehensive exam; for doctorate, thesis/dissertation.
Entrance requirements: For master's, GRE General Test or MAT, minimum undergraduate GPA of 2.5. *Application deadline:* For fall admission, 8/1; for spring admission, 12/1. *Application fee:* $25 ($100 for international students).
Expenses: Tuition, state resident: full-time $2,026. Tuition, nonresident: full-time $4,528.
Financial support: In 2001–02, 1 fellowship with full tuition reimbursement, 13 research assistantships with full tuition reimbursements were awarded. Career-related internships or fieldwork also available.
Faculty research: Structural response to earthquakes, pavement design, water quality, bridge scour, intelligent transportation systems. *Total annual research expenditures:* $1.2 million.
Dr. Martin E. Lipinski, Chairman, 901-678-3279.
Application contact: Dr. Shahram Pezeshk, Coordinator of Graduate Studies, 901-678-4727.

UNIVERSITY OF MISSOURI–COLUMBIA

Graduate School, College of Engineering, Department of Civil and Environmental Engineering, Columbia, MO 65211

AWARDS Civil engineering (MS, PhD); environmental engineering (MS, PhD); geotechnical engineering (MS, PhD). Structural engineering (MS, PhD); transportation and highway engineering (MS); water resources (MS, PhD).

Faculty: 20 full-time (2 women), 1 part-time/adjunct (0 women).

Students: 28 full-time (6 women), 14 part-time (3 women); includes 4 minority (all Hispanic Americans), 23 international. 74 applicants, 43% accepted. In 2001, 19 master's, 1 doctorate awarded.

Degree requirements: For master's, report or thesis; for doctorate, thesis/dissertation.

Entrance requirements: For master's and doctorate, GRE General Test, TOEFL. *Application deadline:* For fall admission, 3/15 (priority date); for winter admission, 10/15 (priority date). *Application fee:* $25 ($50 for international students).

Expenses: Tuition, state resident: part-time $179 per credit hour. Tuition, nonresident: part-time $539 per credit hour. Required fees: $122 per semester. Tuition and fees vary according to program.

Financial support: Research assistantships, teaching assistantships, institutionally sponsored loans available.

Dr. Mark Virkler, Director of Graduate Studies, 573-882-7434, *E-mail:* virklerm@missouri.edu. *Web site:* http://www.engineering.missouri.edu/civil.htm

UNIVERSITY OF MISSOURI–ROLLA

Graduate School, School of Engineering, Department of Civil Engineering, Program in Structural Analysis and Design, Rolla, MO 65409-0910

AWARDS MS, DE, PhD.

Degree requirements: For master's, thesis or alternative; for doctorate, thesis/dissertation.

Entrance requirements: For master's and doctorate, GRE General Test, TOEFL, minimum GPA of 3.0.

UNIVERSITY OF MISSOURI–ROLLA

Graduate School, School of Engineering, Department of Civil Engineering, Program in Structural Materials, Rolla, MO 65409-0910

AWARDS MS.

Degree requirements: For master's, thesis or alternative.

Entrance requirements: For master's, GRE General Test, TOEFL, minimum GPA of 3.0.

UNIVERSITY OF MISSOURI–ROLLA

Graduate School, School of Engineering, Department of Civil Engineering, Program in Structural Methods, Rolla, MO 65409-0910

AWARDS DE, PhD.

Degree requirements: For doctorate, thesis/dissertation.

Entrance requirements: For doctorate, GRE General Test, TOEFL, minimum GPA of 3.0.

UNIVERSITY OF NORTH DAKOTA

Graduate School, School of Engineering and Mines, Department of Civil Engineering, Grand Forks, ND 58202

AWARDS Civil engineering (M Engr). Sanitary engineering (M Engr), including soils and structures engineering, surface mining engineering. Part-time programs available.

Faculty: 6 full-time (0 women).

Students: 6 full-time (1 woman), 3 part-time. 2 applicants, 100% accepted, 0 enrolled. In 2001, 6 degrees awarded.

Degree requirements: For master's, thesis or alternative, final comprehensive exam.

Entrance requirements: For master's, GRE General Test, TOEFL, minimum GPA of 2.5. *Application deadline:* For fall admission, 3/1 (priority date); for spring admission, 10/15 (priority date). Applications are processed on a rolling basis. *Application fee:* $30.

Expenses: Tuition, state resident: full-time $3,298. Tuition, nonresident: full-time $7,998.

Financial support: In 2001–02, 4 students received support, including 4 teaching assistantships with full tuition reimbursements available (averaging $9,500 per year); fellowships, research assistantships, career-related internships or fieldwork, Federal Work-Study, institutionally sponsored loans, scholarships/grants, and tuition waivers (full and partial) also available. Support available to part-time students. Financial award application deadline: 3/15; financial award applicants required to submit FAFSA.

Faculty research: Soil-structures, environmental-water resources.

Dr. Charles J. Moretti, Chairperson, 701-777-5150, *Fax:* 701-777-4838, *E-mail:* charles_moretti@mail.und.nodak.edu. *Web site:* http://www.und.edu/dept/sem/html/civil_engineering.html

UNIVERSITY OF OKLAHOMA

Graduate College, College of Engineering, School of Civil Engineering and Environmental Science, Program in Civil Engineering, Norman, OK 73019-0390

AWARDS Civil engineering (PhD); environmental engineering (MS); geotechnical engineering (MS). Structures (MS); transportation (MS). Part-time programs available.

Students: 36 full-time (3 women), 18 part-time (2 women); includes 4 minority (2 Asian Americans or Pacific Islanders, 1 Hispanic American, 1 Native American), 35 international. 46 applicants, 85% accepted, 9 enrolled. In 2001, 17 degrees awarded. Terminal master's awarded for partial completion of doctoral program.

Degree requirements: For master's, oral exams; for doctorate, thesis/dissertation, oral and qualifying exams.

Entrance requirements: For master's, minimum GPA of 3.0; for doctorate, minimum graduate GPA of 3.5. *Application deadline:* For fall admission, 4/1 (priority date). Applications are processed on a rolling basis. *Application fee:* $25 ($50 for international students).

Expenses: Tuition, state resident: full-time $2,208; part-time $92 per credit hour. Tuition, nonresident: part-time $297 per credit hour. Tuition and fees vary according to course level, course load and program.

Financial support: In 2001–02, 7 students received support; research assistantships with partial tuition reimbursements available, teaching assistantships with full and partial tuition reimbursements available, scholarships/grants available. Financial award application deadline: 3/1; financial award applicants required to submit FAFSA.

Application contact: Susan Williams, Graduate Programs Specialist, 405-325-2344, *Fax:* 405-325-4217, *E-mail:* srwilliams@ou.edu.

UNIVERSITY OF RHODE ISLAND

Graduate School, College of Engineering, Department of Civil and Environmental Engineering, Program in Structural Engineering, Kingston, RI 02881

AWARDS MS, PhD.

Application deadline: For fall admission, 4/15 (priority date). Applications are processed on a rolling basis. *Application fee:* $35.

Expenses: Tuition, state resident: full-time $3,756; part-time $209 per credit. Tuition, nonresident: full-time $10,774; part-time $599 per credit. Required fees: $1,586; $76 per credit. $76 per credit. One-time fee: $60 full-time.

University of Rhode Island (continued)
Dr. George Tsiatas, Chairman, Department of Civil and Environmental Engineering, 401-874-2692.

■ UNIVERSITY OF SOUTHERN CALIFORNIA

Graduate School, School of Engineering, Department of Civil Engineering, Program in Structural Engineering, Los Angeles, CA 90089
AWARDS MS.

Degree requirements: For master's, thesis optional.
Entrance requirements: For master's, GRE General Test.
Expenses: Tuition: Full-time $25,060; part-time $844 per unit. Required fees: $473.

■ UNIVERSITY OF SOUTHERN CALIFORNIA

Graduate School, School of Engineering, Department of Civil Engineering, Program in Structural Mechanics, Los Angeles, CA 90089
AWARDS MS.

Degree requirements: For master's, thesis optional.
Entrance requirements: For master's, GRE General Test.
Expenses: Tuition: Full-time $25,060; part-time $844 per unit. Required fees: $473.

■ UNIVERSITY OF VIRGINIA

School of Engineering and Applied Science, Department of Civil Engineering, Program in Structural Mechanics, Charlottesville, VA 22903
AWARDS ME, MS, PhD. Part-time programs available. Postbaccalaureate distance learning degree programs offered (no on-campus study).

Faculty: 5 full-time (0 women).
Students: 10 full-time (3 women), 4 international. Average age 26. 80 applicants, 13% accepted, 4 enrolled. In 2001, 3 master's, 1 doctorate awarded. Terminal master's awarded for partial completion of doctoral program.
Degree requirements: For master's, thesis (for some programs); for doctorate, thesis/dissertation, comprehensive exam.
Entrance requirements: For master's and doctorate, GRE General Test. *Application deadline:* For fall admission, 2/1 (priority date); for spring admission, 8/1 (priority date). Applications are processed on a rolling basis. *Application fee:* $40. Electronic applications accepted.
Expenses: Tuition, state resident: full-time $3,988. Tuition, nonresident: full-time $17,078. Required fees: $1,190.
Financial support: In 2001–02, 4 fellowships with full tuition reimbursements

(averaging $17,000 per year), 4 research assistantships with full tuition reimbursements (averaging $17,000 per year), 4 teaching assistantships with full tuition reimbursements (averaging $17,000 per year) were awarded. Financial award application deadline: 2/1.
Faculty research: Dynamic structural response, computational mechanics, probabilistic methods, mechanics and design of composites, computer-aided design. *Total annual research expenditures:* $700,000.
Dr. Thomas T. Baber, Associate Professor, 434-924-7464, *Fax:* 434-982-2951, *E-mail:* ttb@virginia.edu. *Web site:* http://www.cs.virginia.edu/~civil/

■ UNIVERSITY OF WASHINGTON

Graduate School, College of Engineering, Department of Civil and Environmental Engineering, Seattle, WA 98195
AWARDS Environmental engineering (MS, MSCE, MSE, PhD); hydraulic engineering (MSCE, MSE, PhD). Structural and geotechnical engineering and mechanics (MS, MSCE, MSE, PhD); transportation and construction engineering (MS, MSCE, MSE, PhD).

Faculty: 31 full-time (4 women), 26 part-time/adjunct (1 woman).
Students: 153 full-time (54 women), 42 part-time (13 women); includes 25 minority (2 African Americans, 19 Asian Americans or Pacific Islanders, 3 Hispanic Americans, 1 Native American), 34 international. Average age 29. 339 applicants, 60% accepted, 59 enrolled. In 2001, 71 master's, 11 doctorates awarded. Terminal master's awarded for partial completion of doctoral program.
Degree requirements: For master's, thesis (for some programs); for doctorate, thesis/dissertation, comprehensive exam. *Median time to degree:* Doctorate–3.5 years full-time.
Entrance requirements: For master's, GRE General Test, TOEFL, minimum GPA of 3.0; for doctorate, GRE, TOEFL, minimum GPA of 3.5. *Application deadline:* For fall admission, 2/1 (priority date). Applications are processed on a rolling basis. *Application fee:* $50. Electronic applications accepted.
Expenses: Tuition, state resident: full-time $5,539. Tuition, nonresident: full-time $14,376. Required fees: $390. Tuition and fees vary according to course load and program.
Financial support: In 2001–02, 110 students received support, including 22 fellowships with partial tuition reimbursements available, 70 research assistantships with full tuition reimbursements available, 22 teaching assistantships with full tuition reimbursements available; career-related internships or fieldwork and scholarships/grants also available. Financial award application deadline: 2/1.

Faculty research: Water resources, hydrology, construction, environmental structures, geotechnical transportation. *Total annual research expenditures:* $3.7 million.
Prof. G. Scott Rutherford, Chair, 206-543-2390.
Application contact: Marcia Buck, Graduate Adviser, 206-543-2574, *E-mail:* cesendme@u.washington.edu. *Web site:* http://www.ce.washington.edu/grad_p.htm

■ WASHINGTON UNIVERSITY IN ST. LOUIS

Henry Edwin Sever Graduate School of Engineering and Applied Science, Sever Institute of Technology, Department of Civil Engineering, Program in Structural Engineering, St. Louis, MO 63130-4899
AWARDS MSE, D Sc.

Degree requirements: For master's, thesis optional; for doctorate, variable foreign language requirement, thesis/dissertation, departmental qualifying exam.
Expenses: Tuition: Full-time $26,900. *Web site:* http://www.cive.wustl.edu/cive/

SURVEYING SCIENCE AND ENGINEERING

■ THE OHIO STATE UNIVERSITY

Graduate School, College of Engineering, Program in Geodetic Science and Surveying, Columbus, OH 43210
AWARDS MS, PhD.

Degree requirements: For master's, thesis optional; for doctorate, thesis/dissertation.
Faculty research: Photogrammetry, cartography, geodesy, land information systems.

TRANSPORTATION AND HIGHWAY ENGINEERING

■ AUBURN UNIVERSITY

Graduate School, College of Engineering, Department of Civil Engineering, Auburn University, AL 36849
AWARDS Construction engineering and management (MCE, MS, PhD); environmental engineering (MCE, MS, PhD); geotechnical/materials engineering (MCE, MS, PhD); hydraulics/hydrology (MCE, MS, PhD). Structural engineering (MCE, MS, PhD); transportation engineering (MCE, MS, PhD). Part-time programs available.

Faculty: 18 full-time (1 woman).
Students: 34 full-time (12 women), 25 part-time (9 women); includes 3 minority (all African Americans), 15 international. 74 applicants, 39% accepted. In 2001, 16 master's, 1 doctorate awarded.
Degree requirements: For master's, project (MCE), thesis (MS); for doctorate, thesis/dissertation, comprehensive exam.
Entrance requirements: For master's and doctorate, GRE General Test. *Application deadline:* For fall admission, 7/7; for spring admission, 11/24. Applications are processed on a rolling basis. *Application fee:* $25 ($50 for international students). Electronic applications accepted.
Financial support: Fellowships, research assistantships, teaching assistantships, Federal Work-Study available. Support available to part-time students. Financial award application deadline: 3/15.
Dr. Joseph F. Judkins, Head, 334-844-4320.
Application contact: Dr. John F. Pritchett, Dean of the Graduate School, 334-844-4700, *E-mail:* hatchlb@mail.auburn.edu.

■ CORNELL UNIVERSITY

Graduate School, Graduate Fields of Engineering, Field of Civil and Environmental Engineering, Ithaca, NY 14853-0001

AWARDS Environmental engineering (M Eng, MS, PhD); environmental fluid mechanics and hydrology (M Eng, MS, PhD); environmental systems engineering (M Eng, MS, PhD); geotechnical engineering (M Eng, MS, PhD); remote sensing (M Eng, MS, PhD). Structural engineering (M Eng, MS, PhD); transportation engineering (M Eng, MS, PhD); water resource systems (M Eng, MS, PhD).

Faculty: 33 full-time.
Students: 131 full-time (35 women); includes 17 minority (1 African American, 9 Asian Americans or Pacific Islanders, 7 Hispanic Americans), 61 international. 515 applicants, 15% accepted. In 2001, 64 master's, 14 doctorates awarded. Terminal master's awarded for partial completion of doctoral program.
Degree requirements: For master's, thesis (MS); for doctorate, thesis/dissertation.
Entrance requirements: For master's and doctorate, GRE General Test (recommended), TOEFL, 2 letters of recommendation. *Application deadline:* For fall admission, 1/15 (priority date). *Application fee:* $65. Electronic applications accepted.
Expenses: Tuition: Full-time $25,970. Required fees: $50.
Financial support: In 2001–02, 71 students received support, including 24 fellowships with full tuition reimbursements available, 28 research assistantships with full tuition reimbursements available, 19 teaching assistantships with full tuition reimbursements available; institutionally sponsored loans, scholarships/grants,

tuition waivers (full and partial), and unspecified assistantships also available. Financial award applicants required to submit FAFSA.
Faculty research: Environmental engineering, geotechnical engineering remote sensing, environmental fluid mechanics and hydrology, structural engineering.
Application contact: Graduate Field Assistant, 607-255-7560, *E-mail:* cee_grad@cornell.edu. *Web site:* http://www.gradschool.cornell.edu/grad/fields_1/cee.html

Find an in-depth description at www.petersons.com/gradchannel.

■ IOWA STATE UNIVERSITY OF SCIENCE AND TECHNOLOGY

Graduate College, College of Engineering, Department of Civil and Construction Engineering, Ames, IA 50011

AWARDS Civil engineering (MS, PhD), including civil engineering materials, construction engineering and management, environmental engineering, geometronics, geotechnical engineering, structural engineering, transportation engineering.

Faculty: 32 full-time, 5 part-time/adjunct.
Students: 55 full-time (9 women), 39 part-time (6 women); includes 1 minority (African American), 40 international. 256 applicants, 23% accepted, 21 enrolled. In 2001, 27 master's, 4 doctorates awarded.
Degree requirements: For master's, thesis or alternative; for doctorate, thesis/dissertation. *Median time to degree:* Master's–2 years full-time; doctorate–3.3 years full-time.
Entrance requirements: For master's and doctorate, GRE General Test (international applicants), TOEFL or IELTS. *Application deadline:* For fall admission, 3/1 (priority date); for spring admission, 10/1 (priority date). *Application fee:* $20 ($50 for international students). Electronic applications accepted.
Expenses: Tuition, state resident: full-time $1,851. Tuition, nonresident: full-time $5,449. Tuition and fees vary according to program.
Financial support: In 2001–02, 44 research assistantships with partial tuition reimbursements (averaging $12,963 per year), 5 teaching assistantships with partial tuition reimbursements (averaging $11,756 per year) were awarded. Fellowships, scholarships/grants, health care benefits, and unspecified assistantships also available.
Dr. Lowell F. Greimann, Chair, 515-294-2140, *E-mail:* cceinfo@iastate.edu.
Application contact: Dr. Edward Kannel, Director of Graduate Education, 515-294-2861, *E-mail:* cceinfo@iastate.edu. *Web site:* http://www1.eng.iastate.edu/coe/grad.asp/

■ LOUISIANA STATE UNIVERSITY AND AGRICULTURAL AND MECHANICAL COLLEGE

Graduate School, College of Engineering, Department of Civil and Environmental Engineering, Baton Rouge, LA 70803

AWARDS Environmental engineering (MSCE, PhD); geotechnical engineering (MSCE, PhD). Structural engineering and mechanics (MSCE, PhD); transportation engineering (MSCE, PhD); water resources (MSCE, PhD). Part-time programs available.

Faculty: 30 full-time (1 woman).
Students: 78 full-time (19 women), 26 part-time (11 women); includes 4 minority (2 African Americans, 1 Hispanic American, 1 Native American), 67 international. Average age 29. 133 applicants, 41% accepted, 22 enrolled. In 2001, 15 master's, 7 doctorates awarded.
Degree requirements: For master's, thesis optional; for doctorate, one foreign language, thesis/dissertation.
Entrance requirements: For master's and doctorate, GRE General Test, TOEFL, minimum GPA of 3.0. *Application deadline:* For fall admission, 1/25 (priority date). Applications are processed on a rolling basis. *Application fee:* $25.
Expenses: Tuition, state resident: full-time $2,551. Tuition, nonresident: full-time $5,551. Required fees: $854. Part-time tuition and fees vary according to course load.
Financial support: In 2001–02, 5 fellowships (averaging $15,800 per year), 51 research assistantships with partial tuition reimbursements (averaging $12,089 per year), 2 teaching assistantships with partial tuition reimbursements (averaging $12,500 per year) were awarded. Career-related internships or fieldwork, institutionally sponsored loans, and scholarships/grants also available. Financial award application deadline: 3/1; financial award applicants required to submit FAFSA.
Faculty research: Solid waste management, electrokinetics, composite structures, transportation planning, river mechanics. *Total annual research expenditures:* $1.7 million.
Dr. George Z. Voyiadjis, Interim Chair/Boyd Professor, 225-578-8668, *Fax:* 225-578-8652, *E-mail:* cegzv@lsu.edu. *Web site:* http://www.ce.lsu.edu/

■ MARQUETTE UNIVERSITY

Graduate School, College of Engineering, Department of Civil and Environmental Engineering, Milwaukee, WI 53201-1881

AWARDS Construction and public works management (MS, PhD); environmental/water resources engineering (MS, PhD). Structural/geotechnical engineering (MS, PhD); transportational planning and engineering

Marquette University (continued)
(MS, PhD). Part-time and evening/weekend programs available.

Faculty: 12 full-time (0 women), 1 part-time/adjunct (0 women).
Students: 20 full-time (8 women), 24 part-time (3 women); includes 2 minority (1 Asian American or Pacific Islander, 1 Hispanic American), 13 international. Average age 30. 57 applicants, 53% accepted, 9 enrolled. In 2001, 9 degrees awarded. Terminal master's awarded for partial completion of doctoral program.
Degree requirements: For master's, thesis or alternative, comprehensive exam; for doctorate, thesis/dissertation. *Median time to degree:* Master's–2 years full-time, 3 years part-time.
Entrance requirements: For master's, TOEFL; for doctorate, GRE General Test, TOEFL. *Application deadline:* For fall admission, 6/1 (priority date). Applications are processed on a rolling basis. *Application fee:* $40. Electronic applications accepted.
Expenses: Tuition: Full-time $10,170; part-time $445 per credit hour. Tuition and fees vary according to course load.
Financial support: In 2001–02, 18 students received support, including 3 fellowships with tuition reimbursements available, 1 research assistantship with tuition reimbursement available (averaging $10,600 per year), 4 teaching assistantships with tuition reimbursements available (averaging $10,200 per year); Federal Work-Study, institutionally sponsored loans, scholarships/grants, and tuition waivers (full and partial) also available. Support available to part-time students. Financial award application deadline: 2/15.
Faculty research: Highway safety, highway performance, and intelligent transportation systems. Surface mount technology; watershed management. *Total annual research expenditures:* $860,000.
Dr. Thomas H. Wenzel, Chair, 414-288-7030, *Fax:* 414-288-7521.

Find an in-depth description at www.petersons.com/gradchannel.

■ **MASSACHUSETTS INSTITUTE OF TECHNOLOGY**

School of Engineering, Engineering Systems Division, Center for Transportation Studies, Cambridge, MA 02139-4307

AWARDS Logistics (M Eng); transportation (MST, PhD).

Degree requirements: For master's, thesis/dissertation; for doctorate, thesis/dissertation, comprehensive exam.
Entrance requirements: For master's, GRE General Test (or GMAT for logistics), TOEFL; for doctorate, GRE General Test, TOEFL. *Application deadline:* For fall admission, 1/15; for spring admission, 11/1. *Application fee:* $60. Electronic applications accepted.

Financial support: Fellowships, research assistantships, teaching assistantships, Federal Work-Study, institutionally sponsored loans, scholarships/grants, health care benefits, and unspecified assistantships available. Financial award applicants required to submit FAFSA. *Total annual research expenditures:* $1.6 million.
Yossi Sheffi, Director, 617-253-5316, *Fax:* 617-253-4560, *E-mail:* sheffi@mit.edu.
Application contact: Sara Goplin, Admissions Coordinator, 617-253-8069, *Fax:* 617-253-4560, *E-mail:* sarag@mit.edu. *Web site:* http://web.mit.edu/cts/www/

Find an in-depth description at www.petersons.com/gradchannel.

■ **NEW JERSEY INSTITUTE OF TECHNOLOGY**

Office of Graduate Studies, Department of Civil and Environmental Engineering, Interdisciplinary Program in Transportation, Newark, NJ 07102

AWARDS MS, PhD. Part-time and evening/weekend programs available.

Faculty: 2 full-time (0 women).
Students: 17 full-time (6 women), 22 part-time (3 women); includes 5 minority (1 African American, 2 Asian Americans or Pacific Islanders, 1 Hispanic American, 1 Native American), 12 international. Average age 33. 57 applicants, 63% accepted, 13 enrolled. In 2001, 17 master's, 1 doctorate awarded. Terminal master's awarded for partial completion of doctoral program.
Degree requirements: For master's, thesis or alternative; for doctorate, thesis/dissertation, residency.
Entrance requirements: For master's, GRE General Test; for doctorate, GRE General Test, minimum graduate GPA of 3.5. *Application deadline:* For fall admission, 6/5 (priority date); for spring admission, 10/15. Applications are processed on a rolling basis. *Application fee:* $50. Electronic applications accepted.
Expenses: Tuition, state resident: full-time $7,812; part-time $434 per credit. Tuition, nonresident: full-time $10,746; part-time $597 per credit. Required fees: $47 per credit. $76 per semester.
Financial support: Fellowships with full and partial tuition reimbursements, research assistantships with full and partial tuition reimbursements, teaching assistantships with full and partial tuition reimbursements, career-related internships or fieldwork, Federal Work-Study, institutionally sponsored loans, and unspecified assistantships available. Financial award application deadline: 3/15.
Faculty research: Transportation planning, administration, and policy; intelligent vehicle highway systems; bridge maintenance. *Total annual research expenditures:* $4.8 million.

Dr. Athanassios K. Bladikas, Director, 973-596-3653, *E-mail:* athanassios.bladikas@njit.edu.
Application contact: Kathryn Kelly, Director of Admissions, 973-596-3300, *Fax:* 973-596-3461, *E-mail:* admissions@njit.edu. *Web site:* http://www.njit.edu/

■ **NORTHWESTERN UNIVERSITY**

McCormick School of Engineering and Applied Science, Department of Civil and Environmental Engineering, Evanston, IL 60208

AWARDS Environmental engineering and science (MS, PhD); geotechnical engineering (MS, PhD); mechanics of materials and solids (MS, PhD); project management (MPM). Structural engineering and materials (MS, PhD); theoretical and applied mechanics (MS, PhD); transportation systems analysis and planning (MS, PhD). MS and PhD admissions and degrees offered through The Graduate School. Part-time programs available.

Faculty: 26 full-time (3 women), 9 part-time/adjunct (2 women).
Students: 80 full-time (32 women), 1 part-time; includes 2 Asian Americans or Pacific Islanders, 1 Hispanic American, 38 international. 282 applicants, 7% accepted. In 2001, 20 master's, 14 doctorates awarded. Terminal master's awarded for partial completion of doctoral program.
Degree requirements: For master's, thesis (for some programs); for doctorate, thesis/dissertation.
Application deadline: For fall admission, 8/1. *Application fee:* $50 ($55 for international students). Electronic applications accepted.
Expenses: Tuition: Full-time $26,526.
Financial support: In 2001–02, 10 fellowships with full tuition reimbursements (averaging $13,338 per year), 66 research assistantships with partial tuition reimbursements (averaging $18,000 per year), 7 teaching assistantships with full tuition reimbursements (averaging $13,329 per year) were awarded. Career-related internships or fieldwork, institutionally sponsored loans, and scholarships/grants also available. Financial award application deadline: 1/15; financial award applicants required to submit FAFSA.
Faculty research: Environmental engineering and science, geotechnics, mechanics of materials and solids, structural engineering and materials, transportation systems analysis and planning. *Total annual research expenditures:* $8.4 million.
Joseph L. Schofer, Chair, 847-491-3257, *Fax:* 847-491-4011, *E-mail:* j-schofer@northwestern.edu.
Application contact: Janet Soule, Academic Coordinator, 847-491-3176, *Fax:* 847-491-4011, *E-mail:* civil-info@northwestern.edu. *Web site:* http://www.civil.northwestern.edu/

Find an in-depth description at www.petersons.com/gradchannel.

■ THE PENNSYLVANIA STATE UNIVERSITY UNIVERSITY PARK CAMPUS

Graduate School, College of Engineering, Department of Civil and Environmental Engineering, State College, University Park, PA 16802-1503

AWARDS Civil engineering (M Eng, MS, PhD); environmental engineering (M Eng, MS, PhD). Structural engineering (M Eng, MS, PhD); transportation and highway engineering (M Eng, MS, PhD); water resources engineering (M Eng, MS, PhD).

Students: 102 full-time (26 women), 37 part-time (5 women).
Degree requirements: For master's, final paper (M Eng), oral exam and thesis (MS); for doctorate, one foreign language, thesis/dissertation, oral exams, comprehensive exam.
Entrance requirements: For master's and doctorate, GRE General Test. *Application fee:* $45.
Expenses: Tuition, state resident: full-time $7,882; part-time $333 per credit. Tuition, nonresident: full-time $16,142; part-time $673 per credit. Required fees: $124 per semester.
Financial support: Fellowships, research assistantships, teaching assistantships available.
Faculty research: Construction engineering and management; materials and pavements; geotechnical engineering; hydraulics, hydrology, and water resource systems. Structures.
Dr. Andrew Scanlon, Head, 814-863-3084.

■ POLYTECHNIC UNIVERSITY, BROOKLYN CAMPUS

Department of Civil and Environmental Engineering, Major in Transportation Planning and Engineering, Brooklyn, NY 11201-2990

AWARDS MS. Part-time and evening/weekend programs available.

Degree requirements: For master's, thesis or alternative.
Electronic applications accepted.

■ POLYTECHNIC UNIVERSITY, LONG ISLAND GRADUATE CENTER

Graduate Programs, Department of Civil and Environmental Engineering, Major in Transportation Planning and Engineering, Melville, NY 11747

AWARDS MS.

Degree requirements: For master's, thesis (for some programs).
Electronic applications accepted.

■ PRINCETON UNIVERSITY

Graduate School, School of Engineering and Applied Science, Department of Civil and Environmental Engineering, Program in Transportation Systems, Princeton, NJ 08544-1019

AWARDS MSE, PhD.

Degree requirements: For master's and doctorate, thesis/dissertation.
Entrance requirements: For master's and doctorate, GRE General Test, GRE Subject Test.

■ RENSSELAER POLYTECHNIC INSTITUTE

Graduate School, School of Engineering, Department of Civil and Environmental Engineering, Program in Civil Engineering, Troy, NY 12180-3590

AWARDS Geotechnical engineering (M Eng, MS, D Eng, PhD); mechanics of composite materials and structures (M Eng, MS, D Eng, PhD). Structural engineering (M Eng, MS, D Eng, PhD); transportation engineering (M Eng, MS, D Eng, PhD). Part-time programs available.

Faculty: 9 full-time (0 women), 4 part-time/adjunct (1 woman).
Students: 28 full-time (8 women), 6 part-time; includes 1 minority (Asian American or Pacific Islander), 15 international. Average age 24. 105 applicants, 40% accepted. In 2001, 8 master's, 2 doctorates awarded.
Degree requirements: For master's, thesis (for some programs); for doctorate, thesis/dissertation.
Entrance requirements: For master's and doctorate, GRE, TOEFL. *Application deadline:* For fall admission, 1/15 (priority date). Applications are processed on a rolling basis. *Application fee:* $45. Electronic applications accepted.
Expenses: Tuition: Full-time $26,400; part-time $1,320 per credit hour. Required fees: $1,437.
Financial support: In 2001–02, 18 students received support, including 3 fellowships, 5 research assistantships with full and partial tuition reimbursements available, 10 teaching assistantships with full tuition reimbursements available; career-related internships or fieldwork and institutionally sponsored loans also available. Financial award application deadline: 2/1.
Faculty research: Computational mechanics, earthquake engineering, geo-environmental engineering. *Total annual research expenditures:* $1.7 million.
Dr. George List, Department Chair, 518-276-6362, *Fax:* 518-276-4833, *E-mail:* listg@rpi.edu.
Application contact: Jo Ann Grega, Admissions Assistant, 518-276-6679, *Fax:* 518-276-4833, *E-mail:* gregaj2@rpi.edu.
Web site: http://www.rpi.edu/dept/civil/htm

Find an in-depth description at www.petersons.com/gradchannel.

■ RENSSELAER POLYTECHNIC INSTITUTE

Graduate School, School of Engineering, Department of Civil and Environmental Engineering, Program in Transportation Engineering, Troy, NY 12180-3590

AWARDS M Eng, MS, D Eng, PhD, MBA/M Eng. Part-time programs available.

Faculty: 9 full-time (0 women), 4 part-time/adjunct (1 woman).
Students: 2 full-time (0 women), 1 part-time, 2 international. 22 applicants, 14% accepted.
Degree requirements: For master's, thesis (for some programs); for doctorate, thesis/dissertation.
Entrance requirements: For master's and doctorate, GRE, TOEFL. *Application deadline:* For fall admission, 1/15 (priority date). Applications are processed on a rolling basis. *Application fee:* $45. Electronic applications accepted.
Expenses: Tuition: Full-time $26,400; part-time $1,320 per credit hour. Required fees: $1,437.
Financial support: Fellowships, research assistantships, teaching assistantships, institutionally sponsored loans available. Financial award application deadline: 2/1.
Faculty research: Intelligent transportation systems, routing algorithms, dynamic network management, user behavior.
Application contact: Jo Ann Grega, Admissions Assistant, 518-276-6679, *Fax:* 518-276-4833, *E-mail:* gregaj2@rpi.edu.
Web site: http://www.cee.rpi.edu/

Find an in-depth description at www.petersons.com/gradchannel.

■ TEXAS A&M UNIVERSITY

College of Engineering, Department of Civil Engineering, Program in Transportation Engineering, College Station, TX 77843

AWARDS M Eng, MS, D Eng, PhD. D Eng offered through the College of Engineering.

Students: 40.
Degree requirements: For master's, thesis (MS); for doctorate, dissertation (PhD), internship (D Eng).
Entrance requirements: For master's and doctorate, GRE General Test, TOEFL. *Application fee:* $50 ($75 for international students).
Expenses: Tuition, state resident: full-time $11,872. Tuition, nonresident: full-time $17,892.
Financial support: Fellowships, research assistantships, teaching assistantships available. Financial award application deadline:

Texas A&M University (continued)
4/15; financial award applicants required to submit FAFSA.

Faculty research: Design and operation of transportation facilities and systems, intelligent transportation systems.

Dr. Dallas N. Little, Head, 979-845-1737, *Fax:* 979-862-2800, *E-mail:* ce-grad@tamu.edu.

Application contact: Dr. Laurence R. Rilett, Information Contact, 979-845-2498, *Fax:* 979-862-2800, *E-mail:* ce-grad@tamu.edu. *Web site:* http://www.civil.tamu.edu/

■ TEXAS SOUTHERN UNIVERSITY

Graduate School, School of Science and Technology, Program in Transportation, Houston, TX 77004-4584

AWARDS MS. Part-time and evening/weekend programs available.

Faculty: 3 full-time (1 woman), 3 part-time/adjunct (0 women).
Students: 20 full-time (4 women), 13 part-time (3 women); includes 25 minority (20 African Americans, 5 Asian Americans or Pacific Islanders), 7 international. Average age 26. In 2001, 12 degrees awarded.
Degree requirements: For master's, thesis optional.
Entrance requirements: For master's, GRE General Test, TOEFL, minimum GPA of 2.5. *Application deadline:* For fall admission, 7/15 (priority date); for spring admission, 11/15. Applications are processed on a rolling basis. *Application fee:* $35 ($75 for international students).
Expenses: Tuition, state resident: full-time $1,188. Tuition, nonresident: full-time $4,644. Required fees: $900. Tuition and fees vary according to degree level.
Financial support: In 2001–02, 15 students received support, including 3 fellowships with partial tuition reimbursements available (averaging $15,000 per year), 5 research assistantships (averaging $12,000 per year); teaching assistantships, career-related internships or fieldwork, Federal Work-Study, institutionally sponsored loans, scholarships/grants, and unspecified assistantships also available. Financial award application deadline: 5/1.
Faculty research: Highway traffic operations, transportation and policy planning, air quality in transportation, transportation modeling. *Total annual research expenditures:* $500,000.

Dr. Lei Yu, Chair, 713-313-7282, *Fax:* 713-313-1856, *E-mail:* yu_lx@tsu.edu. *Web site:* http://lltechnology.tsu.edu/tra

■ UNIVERSITY OF ARKANSAS

Graduate School, College of Engineering, Department of Civil Engineering, Program in Transportation Engineering, Fayetteville, AR 72701-1201

AWARDS MSE, MSTE.

Students: 2 full-time (0 women); both minorities (both Hispanic Americans). 1 applicant, 100% accepted. In 2001, 1 degree awarded.
Degree requirements: For master's, thesis optional.
Application fee: $40 ($50 for international students).
Expenses: Tuition, state resident: full-time $3,553; part-time $197 per credit. Tuition, nonresident: full-time $8,411; part-time $467 per credit. Required fees: $42 per credit. Tuition and fees vary according to course load and program.
Financial support: Application deadline: 4/1.

Dr. Robert Elliott, Chair, Department of Civil Engineering, 479-575-4954.

■ UNIVERSITY OF CALIFORNIA, BERKELEY

Graduate Division, College of Engineering, Department of Civil and Environmental Engineering, Berkeley, CA 94720-1500

AWARDS Construction engineering and management (M Eng, MS, D Eng, PhD); environmental quality and environmental water resources engineering (M Eng, MS, D Eng, PhD); geotechnical engineering (M Eng, MS, D Eng, PhD). Structural engineering, mechanics and materials (M Eng, MS, D Eng, PhD); transportation engineering (M Eng, MS, D Eng, PhD).

Degree requirements: For master's, comprehensive exam or thesis (MS); for doctorate, thesis/dissertation, qualifying exam.
Entrance requirements: For master's, GRE General Test, minimum GPA of 3.0; for doctorate, GRE General Test, minimum GPA of 3.5.
Expenses: Tuition, nonresident: full-time $10,704. Required fees: $4,349.

Find an in-depth description at www.petersons.com/gradchannel.

■ UNIVERSITY OF CALIFORNIA, DAVIS

Graduate Studies, College of Engineering, Graduate Group in Transportation Technology and Policy, Davis, CA 95616

AWARDS MS, PhD.

Faculty: 29 full-time (4 women).
Students: 16 full-time (3 women); includes 1 minority (Hispanic American), 4 international. Average age 32. 28

applicants, 82% accepted, 8 enrolled. In 2001, 4 master's, 2 doctorates awarded.
Degree requirements: For doctorate, thesis/dissertation.
Entrance requirements: For master's, GRE General Test, minimum GPA of 3.0; for doctorate, GRE General Test, minimum GPA of 3.5. *Application deadline:* For fall admission, 1/15 (priority date). *Application fee:* $60. Electronic applications accepted.
Expenses: Tuition, state resident: full-time $4,831. Tuition, nonresident: full-time $15,725.
Financial support: In 2001–02, 16 students received support, including 14 fellowships with full and partial tuition reimbursements available (averaging $6,406 per year), 4 research assistantships with full and partial tuition reimbursements available (averaging $9,808 per year), 2 teaching assistantships with partial tuition reimbursements available (averaging $10,608 per year); career-related internships or fieldwork, Federal Work-Study, institutionally sponsored loans, scholarships/grants, and tuition waivers (full and partial) also available. Financial award application deadline: 1/15; financial award applicants required to submit FAFSA.

Patricia Makhtarian, Chair, 530-752-2062, *E-mail:* itsgraduate@ucdavis.edu.
Application contact: Joan Tolentino, Administrative Assistant, 530-752-0247, *Fax:* 530-752-6572, *E-mail:* jstolentino@ucdavis.edu. *Web site:* http://www.its.ucdavis.edu

Find an in-depth description at www.petersons.com/gradchannel.

■ UNIVERSITY OF CALIFORNIA, IRVINE

Office of Research and Graduate Studies, School of Social Sciences, Program in Transportation Science, Irvine, CA 92697

AWARDS MA, PhD.

Students: 4 full-time (3 women), 1 international. 3 applicants, 67% accepted, 1 enrolled.
Application deadline: For fall and spring admission, 1/15; for winter admission, 10/15.
Expenses: Tuition, nonresident: full-time $10,704. Required fees: $8,396. Tuition and fees vary according to course load, program and student level.

Michael McNally, Director, 949-824-8462, *Fax:* 949-824-8305.
Application contact: Ivonne Maldonado, Graduate Counselor, 949-824-7352, *Fax:* 949-824-3548, *E-mail:* immaldon@uci.edu. *Web site:* http://www.its.uci.edu/

■ UNIVERSITY OF CENTRAL FLORIDA

College of Engineering and Computer Sciences, Department of Civil and Environmental Engineering, Program in Civil Engineering, Orlando, FL 32816

AWARDS Civil engineering (MS, MSCE, PhD); geotechnical engineering (Certificate). Structural engineering (Certificate). Surface water modeling (Certificate); transportation engineering (Certificate). Part-time and evening/weekend programs available.

Faculty: 19 full-time (1 woman), 12 part-time/adjunct (0 women).
Students: 17 full-time (4 women), 37 part-time (7 women); includes 10 minority (1 African American, 2 Asian Americans or Pacific Islanders, 7 Hispanic Americans), 16 international. Average age 30. 84 applicants, 62% accepted, 16 enrolled. In 2001, 1 master's, 1 doctorate awarded.
Degree requirements: For master's, thesis or alternative; for doctorate, thesis/dissertation, departmental qualifying exam, candidacy exam.
Entrance requirements: For master's, GRE General Test, TOEFL, minimum GPA of 3.0 in last 60 hours; for doctorate, GRE General Test, TOEFL, minimum GPA of 3.5 in last 60 hours. *Application deadline:* For fall admission, 7/15 (priority date); for spring admission, 12/15 (priority date). *Application fee:* $20. Electronic applications accepted.
Expenses: Tuition, state resident: part-time $162 per hour. Tuition, nonresident: part-time $569 per hour.
Financial support: In 2001–02, 13 fellowships with partial tuition reimbursements (averaging $2,115 per year), 73 research assistantships with partial tuition reimbursements (averaging $3,846 per year), 13 teaching assistantships with partial tuition reimbursements (averaging $2,732 per year) were awarded. Career-related internships or fieldwork, Federal Work-Study, institutionally sponsored loans, tuition waivers (partial), and unspecified assistantships also available. Financial award application deadline: 3/1; financial award applicants required to submit FAFSA.
Application contact: Dr. Roger L. Wayson, Coordinator, 407-823-2841, *E-mail:* wayson@pegasus.cc.ucf.edu. *Web site:* http://www.ucf.edu/

■ UNIVERSITY OF DAYTON

Graduate School, School of Engineering, Department of Civil Engineering, Dayton, OH 45469-1300

AWARDS Engineering mechanics (MSEM); environmental engineering (MSCE). Soil mechanics (MSCE). Structural engineering (MSCE); transport engineering (MSCE). Part-time programs available.

Faculty: 8 full-time (0 women), 2 part-time/adjunct (0 women).
Students: 8 full-time (6 women), 7 part-time (4 women), 6 international. In 2001, 2 degrees awarded.
Degree requirements: For master's, thesis or alternative.
Entrance requirements: For master's, TOEFL. *Application deadline:* For fall admission, 8/1. Applications are processed on a rolling basis. *Application fee:* $30.
Expenses: Tuition: Full-time $5,436; part-time $453 per credit hour. Required fees: $50; $25 per term.
Financial support: In 2001–02, 5 research assistantships with full tuition reimbursements (averaging $12,000 per year), 2 teaching assistantships with full tuition reimbursements (averaging $10,000 per year) were awarded. Institutionally sponsored loans also available.
Faculty research: Tire/soil interaction, tilt-up structures, viscoelastic response of restraint systems, composite materials. Dr. Joseph E. Saliba, Chairperson, 937-229-3847, *E-mail:* jsaliba@ engr.udayton.edu.
Application contact: Dr. Donald L. Moon, Associate Dean, 937-229-2241, *Fax:* 937-229-2471, *E-mail:* dmoon@ notes.udayton.edu.

■ UNIVERSITY OF DELAWARE

College of Engineering, Department of Civil and Environmental Engineering, Program in Railroad Engineering, Newark, DE 19716

AWARDS MAS, MCE, PhD. Terminal master's awarded for partial completion of doctoral program.

Degree requirements: For master's and doctorate, thesis/dissertation.
Entrance requirements: For master's and doctorate, GRE General Test, TOEFL.
Expenses: Tuition, state resident: full-time $4,770; part-time $265 per credit. Tuition, nonresident: full-time $13,860; part-time $770 per credit. Required fees: $414.
Faculty research: Railway analyses.
Find an in-depth description at www.petersons.com/gradchannel.

■ UNIVERSITY OF DELAWARE

College of Engineering, Department of Civil and Environmental Engineering, Program in Transportation Engineering, Newark, DE 19716

AWARDS MAS, MCE, PhD. Terminal master's awarded for partial completion of doctoral program.

Degree requirements: For master's and doctorate, thesis/dissertation.
Entrance requirements: For master's and doctorate, GRE General Test, TOEFL.
Expenses: Tuition, state resident: full-time $4,770; part-time $265 per credit. Tuition, nonresident: full-time $13,860; part-time $770 per credit. Required fees: $414.

Faculty research: Traffic operations and highway traffic management, public transportation systems, highway maintenance planning, properties of pavement structure, analyses of impact of highway construction on wetlands regions.
Find an in-depth description at www.petersons.com/gradchannel.

■ THE UNIVERSITY OF MEMPHIS

Graduate School, Herff College of Engineering, Department of Civil Engineering, Memphis, TN 38152

AWARDS Civil engineering (PhD); environmental engineering (MS); foundation engineering (MS). Structural engineering (MS); transportation engineering (MS); water resources engineering (MS).

Faculty: 12 full-time (0 women), 1 part-time/adjunct (0 women).
Students: 14 full-time (5 women), 7 part-time (1 woman), 10 international. Average age 32. 36 applicants, 56% accepted. In 2001, 5 degrees awarded.
Degree requirements: For master's, thesis or alternative, comprehensive exam; for doctorate, thesis/dissertation.
Entrance requirements: For master's, GRE General Test or MAT, minimum undergraduate GPA of 2.5. *Application deadline:* For fall admission, 8/1; for spring admission, 12/1. *Application fee:* $25 ($100 for international students).
Expenses: Tuition, state resident: full-time $2,026. Tuition, nonresident: full-time $4,528.
Financial support: In 2001–02, 1 fellowship with full tuition reimbursement, 13 research assistantships with full tuition reimbursements were awarded. Career-related internships or fieldwork also available.
Faculty research: Structural response to earthquakes, pavement design, water quality, bridge scour, intelligent transportation systems. *Total annual research expenditures:* $1.2 million.
Dr. Martin E. Lipinski, Chairman, 901-678-3279.
Application contact: Dr. Shahram Pezeshk, Coordinator of Graduate Studies, 901-678-4727.

■ UNIVERSITY OF MISSOURI– COLUMBIA

Graduate School, College of Engineering, Department of Civil and Environmental Engineering, Columbia, MO 65211

AWARDS Civil engineering (MS, PhD); environmental engineering (MS, PhD); geotechnical engineering (MS, PhD). Structural engineering (MS, PhD); transportation and highway engineering (MS); water resources (MS, PhD).

Faculty: 20 full-time (2 women), 1 part-time/adjunct (0 women).

University of Missouri–Columbia (continued)

Students: 28 full-time (6 women), 14 part-time (3 women); includes 4 minority (all Hispanic Americans), 23 international. 74 applicants, 43% accepted. In 2001, 19 master's, 1 doctorate awarded.
Degree requirements: For master's, report or thesis; for doctorate, thesis/dissertation.
Entrance requirements: For master's and doctorate, GRE General Test, TOEFL. *Application deadline:* For fall admission, 3/15 (priority date); for winter admission, 10/15 (priority date). *Application fee:* $25 ($50 for international students).
Expenses: Tuition, state resident: part-time $179 per credit hour. Tuition, nonresident: part-time $539 per credit hour. Required fees: $122 per semester. Tuition and fees vary according to program.
Financial support: Research assistantships, teaching assistantships, institutionally sponsored loans available.
Dr. Mark Virkler, Director of Graduate Studies, 573-882-7434, *E-mail:* virklerm@missouri.edu. *Web site:* http://www.engineering.missouri.edu/civil.htm

■ UNIVERSITY OF OKLAHOMA

Graduate College, College of Engineering, School of Civil Engineering and Environmental Science, Program in Civil Engineering, Norman, OK 73019-0390

AWARDS Civil engineering (PhD); environmental engineering (MS); geotechnical engineering (MS). Structures (MS); transportation (MS). Part-time programs available.

Students: 36 full-time (3 women), 18 part-time (2 women); includes 4 minority (2 Asian Americans or Pacific Islanders, 1 Hispanic American, 1 Native American), 35 international. 46 applicants, 85% accepted, 9 enrolled. In 2001, 17 degrees awarded. Terminal master's awarded for partial completion of doctoral program.
Degree requirements: For master's, oral exams; for doctorate, thesis/dissertation, oral and qualifying exams.
Entrance requirements: For master's, minimum GPA of 3.0; for doctorate, minimum graduate GPA of 3.5. *Application deadline:* For fall admission, 4/1 (priority date). Applications are processed on a rolling basis. *Application fee:* $25 ($50 for international students).
Expenses: Tuition, state resident: full-time $2,208; part-time $92 per credit hour. Tuition, nonresident: part-time $297 per credit hour. Tuition and fees vary according to course level, course load and program.
Financial support: In 2001–02, 7 students received support; research assistantships with partial tuition reimbursements available, teaching assistantships with full and partial tuition reimbursements available,

scholarships/grants available. Financial award application deadline: 3/1; financial award applicants required to submit FAFSA.
Application contact: Susan Williams, Graduate Programs Specialist, 405-325-2344, *Fax:* 405-325-4217, *E-mail:* srwilliams@ou.edu.

■ UNIVERSITY OF PENNSYLVANIA

School of Engineering and Applied Science, Department of Systems Engineering, Philadelphia, PA 19104

AWARDS Environmental resources engineering (MSE); environmental/resources engineering (PhD). Systems engineering (MSE, PhD); technology and public policy (MSE, PhD); transportation (MSE, PhD). Part-time programs available.

Faculty: 11 full-time (0 women), 3 part-time/adjunct (0 women).
Students: 38 full-time (10 women), 21 part-time (5 women); includes 39 minority (4 African Americans, 33 Asian Americans or Pacific Islanders, 2 Hispanic Americans). Terminal master's awarded for partial completion of doctoral program.
Degree requirements: For doctorate, one foreign language, thesis/dissertation.
Entrance requirements: For master's and doctorate, TOEFL. *Application deadline:* For fall admission, 1/2 (priority date). Applications are processed on a rolling basis. *Application fee:* $65. Electronic applications accepted.
Financial support: Fellowships, research assistantships, teaching assistantships, scholarships/grants available.
Faculty research: Systems methodology, operations research, decision sciences, telecommunication systems, logistics, transportation systems, manufacturing systems, infrastructure systems.
Dr. John D. Keenan, Chair, 215-898-5710, *Fax:* 215-898-5020, *E-mail:* keenan@seas.upenn.edu.
Application contact: Dr. Tony E. Smith, Graduate Group Chair, 215-898-9647, *Fax:* 215-898-5020, *E-mail:* tesmith@seas.upenn.edu. *Web site:* http://www.seas.upenn.edu/ese

Find an in-depth description at www.petersons.com/gradchannel.

■ UNIVERSITY OF RHODE ISLAND

Graduate School, College of Engineering, Department of Civil and Environmental Engineering, Program in Transportation Engineering, Kingston, RI 02881

AWARDS MS, PhD.
Application deadline: For fall admission, 4/15 (priority date). Applications are processed on a rolling basis. *Application fee:* $35.

Expenses: Tuition, state resident: full-time $3,756; part-time $209 per credit. Tuition, nonresident: full-time $10,774; part-time $599 per credit. Required fees: $1,586; $76 per credit. $76 per credit. One-time fee: $60 full-time.
Dr. George Tsiatas, Chairman, Department of Civil and Environmental Engineering, 401-874-2692.

■ UNIVERSITY OF SOUTHERN CALIFORNIA

Graduate School, School of Engineering, Department of Civil Engineering, Program in Transportation Engineering, Los Angeles, CA 90089

AWARDS MS.

Degree requirements: For master's, thesis optional.
Entrance requirements: For master's, GRE General Test.
Expenses: Tuition: Full-time $25,060; part-time $844 per unit. Required fees: $473.

■ UNIVERSITY OF VIRGINIA

School of Engineering and Applied Science, Department of Civil Engineering, Program in Transportation Engineering and Management, Charlottesville, VA 22903

AWARDS ME, MS, PhD. Part-time programs available.

Faculty: 5 full-time (0 women).
Students: 23 full-time (5 women). Average age 27. 60 applicants, 28% accepted, 12 enrolled. In 2001, 6 master's, 1 doctorate awarded. Terminal master's awarded for partial completion of doctoral program.
Degree requirements: For master's, thesis (for some programs); for doctorate, thesis/dissertation, comprehensive exam.
Entrance requirements: For master's and doctorate, GRE General Test. *Application deadline:* For fall admission, 2/1 (priority date); for spring admission, 8/1 (priority date). Applications are processed on a rolling basis. *Application fee:* $40. Electronic applications accepted.
Expenses: Tuition, state resident: full-time $3,988. Tuition, nonresident: full-time $17,078. Required fees: $1,190.
Financial support: In 2001–02, 20 students received support, including 20 research assistantships with full tuition reimbursements available (averaging $17,000 per year); fellowships, teaching assistantships Financial award application deadline: 2/1.
Faculty research: Intermodal freight planning, highway safety, land use/air quality, intelligent transportation systems, artificial intelligence applications. *Total annual research expenditures:* $1.6 million.

Dr. Lester A. Hobl, Professor, 434-924-7464, *Fax:* 434-982-2951, *E-mail:* lah@virginia.edu.

■ UNIVERSITY OF WASHINGTON

Graduate School, College of Engineering, Department of Civil and Environmental Engineering, Seattle, WA 98195

AWARDS Environmental engineering (MS, MSCE, MSE, PhD); hydraulic engineering (MSCE, MSE, PhD). Structural and geotechnical engineering and mechanics (MS, MSCE, MSE, PhD); transportation and construction engineering (MS, MSCE, MSE, PhD).

Faculty: 31 full-time (4 women), 26 part-time/adjunct (1 woman).
Students: 153 full-time (54 women), 42 part-time (13 women); includes 25 minority (2 African Americans, 19 Asian Americans or Pacific Islanders, 3 Hispanic Americans, 1 Native American), 34 international. Average age 29. 339 applicants, 60% accepted, 59 enrolled. In 2001, 71 master's, 11 doctorates awarded. Terminal master's awarded for partial completion of doctoral program.
Degree requirements: For master's, thesis (for some programs); for doctorate, thesis/dissertation, comprehensive exam. *Median time to degree:* Doctorate–3.5 years full-time.
Entrance requirements: For master's, GRE General Test, TOEFL, minimum GPA of 3.0; for doctorate, GRE, TOEFL, minimum GPA of 3.5. *Application deadline:* For fall admission, 2/1 (priority date). Applications are processed on a rolling basis. *Application fee:* $50. Electronic applications accepted.
Expenses: Tuition, state resident: full-time $5,539. Tuition, nonresident: full-time $14,376. Required fees: $390. Tuition and fees vary according to course load and program.
Financial support: In 2001–02, 110 students received support, including 22 fellowships with partial tuition reimbursements available, 70 research assistantships with full tuition reimbursements available, 22 teaching assistantships with full tuition reimbursements available; career-related internships or fieldwork and scholarships/grants also available. Financial award application deadline: 2/1.
Faculty research: Water resources, hydrology, construction, environmental structures, geotechnical transportation. *Total annual research expenditures:* $3.7 million.
Prof. G. Scott Rutherford, Chair, 206-543-2390.
Application contact: Marcia Buck, Graduate Adviser, 206-543-2574, *E-mail:* cesendme@u.washington.edu. *Web site:* http://www.ce.washington.edu/grad_p.htm

■ VILLANOVA UNIVERSITY

College of Engineering, Department of Civil and Environmental Engineering, Program in Transportation Engineering, Villanova, PA 19085-1699

AWARDS MSTE. Part-time and evening/weekend programs available.

Faculty: 2 full-time (0 women), 2 part-time/adjunct (0 women).
Students: 1 (woman) full-time, 6 part-time (2 women). Average age 25. 7 applicants, 100% accepted.
Degree requirements: For master's, thesis optional.
Entrance requirements: For master's, GRE General Test (for applicants with degrees from foreign universities), minimum GPA of 3.0, BCE or bachelor's degree in science, business, or related engineering field. *Application deadline:* For fall admission, 8/1 (priority date); for spring admission, 12/1. Applications are processed on a rolling basis. *Application fee:* $40. Electronic applications accepted.
Expenses: Tuition: Part-time $340 per credit. One-time fee: $115 full-time. Tuition and fees vary according to program.
Financial support: Federal Work-Study and tuition waivers (full and partial) available. Support available to part-time students. Financial award application deadline: 4/15.
Faculty research: Simulation of unsignalized intersections, services to the elderly and disabled, recycling of secondary materials into hot mix asphalt concrete pavements.
Dr. Ronald A. Chadderton, Chairman, Department of Civil and Environmental Engineering, 610-519-4960, *Fax:* 610-519-6754.

■ WASHINGTON UNIVERSITY IN ST. LOUIS

Henry Edwin Sever Graduate School of Engineering and Applied Science, Sever Institute of Technology, Department of Civil Engineering, Program in Transportation and Urban Systems Engineering, St. Louis, MO 63130-4899

AWARDS D Sc.

Degree requirements: For doctorate, variable foreign language requirement, thesis/dissertation, departmental qualifying exam.
Expenses: Tuition: Full-time $26,900. *Web site:* http://www.cive.wustl.edu/cive/

WATER RESOURCES ENGINEERING

■ CALIFORNIA POLYTECHNIC STATE UNIVERSITY, SAN LUIS OBISPO

College of Engineering, Program in Engineering, San Luis Obispo, CA 93407

AWARDS Biochemical engineering (MS); industrial engineering (MS); integrated technology management (MS); materials engineering (MS); water engineering (MS), including bioengineering, biomedical engineering, manufacturing engineering.

Faculty: 98 full-time (8 women), 82 part-time/adjunct (14 women).
Students: 20 full-time (4 women), 9 part-time (1 woman). 25 applicants, 68% accepted, 15 enrolled. In 2001, 22 degrees awarded.
Entrance requirements: For master's, GRE General Test, minimum GPA of 2.5 in last 90 quarter units. *Application fee:* $55.
Expenses: Tuition, nonresident: part-time $164 per unit. One-time fee: $2,153 part-time.
Financial support: Application deadline: 3/2.
Dr. Peter Y. Lee, Dean, 805-756-2131, *Fax:* 805-756-6503, *E-mail:* plee@calpoly.edu.
Application contact: Dr. Daniel W. Walsh, Associate Dean, 805-756-2131, *Fax:* 805-756-6503, *E-mail:* dwalsh@calpoly.edu. *Web site:* http://www.synner.ceng.calpoly.edu/

■ CORNELL UNIVERSITY

Graduate School, Graduate Fields of Engineering, Field of Civil and Environmental Engineering, Ithaca, NY 14853-0001

AWARDS Environmental engineering (M Eng, MS, PhD); environmental fluid mechanics and hydrology (M Eng, MS, PhD); environmental systems engineering (M Eng, MS, PhD); geotechnical engineering (M Eng, MS, PhD); remote sensing (M Eng, MS, PhD). Structural engineering (M Eng, MS, PhD); transportation engineering (M Eng, MS, PhD); water resource systems (M Eng, MS, PhD).

Faculty: 33 full-time.
Students: 131 full-time (35 women); includes 17 minority (1 African American, 9 Asian Americans or Pacific Islanders, 7 Hispanic Americans), 61 international. 515 applicants, 55% accepted. In 2001, 64 master's, 14 doctorates awarded. Terminal master's awarded for partial completion of doctoral program.
Degree requirements: For master's, thesis (MS); for doctorate, thesis/dissertation.

Cornell University (continued)

Entrance requirements: For master's and doctorate, GRE General Test (recommended), TOEFL, 2 letters of recommendation. *Application deadline:* For fall admission, 1/15 (priority date). *Application fee:* $65. Electronic applications accepted.
Expenses: Tuition: Full-time $25,970. Required fees: $50.
Financial support: In 2001–02, 71 students received support, including 24 fellowships with full tuition reimbursements available, 28 research assistantships with full tuition reimbursements available, 19 teaching assistantships with full tuition reimbursements available; institutionally sponsored loans, scholarships/grants, tuition waivers (full and partial), and unspecified assistantships also available. Financial award applicants required to submit FAFSA.
Faculty research: Environmental engineering, geotechnical engineering remote sensing, environmental fluid mechanics and hydrology, structural engineering.
Application contact: Graduate Field Assistant, 607-255-7560, *E-mail:* cee_grad@cornell.edu. *Web site:* http://www.gradschool.cornell.edu/grad/fields_1/cee.html

Find an in-depth description at www.petersons.com/gradchannel.

■ **LOUISIANA STATE UNIVERSITY AND AGRICULTURAL AND MECHANICAL COLLEGE**

Graduate School, College of Engineering, Department of Civil and Environmental Engineering, Baton Rouge, LA 70803

AWARDS Environmental engineering (MSCE, PhD); geotechnical engineering (MSCE, PhD). Structural engineering and mechanics (MSCE, PhD); transportation engineering (MSCE, PhD); water resources (MSCE, PhD). Part-time programs available.

Faculty: 30 full-time (1 woman).
Students: 78 full-time (19 women), 26 part-time (11 women); includes 4 minority (2 African Americans, 1 Hispanic American, 1 Native American), 67 international. Average age 29. 133 applicants, 41% accepted, 22 enrolled. In 2001, 15 master's, 7 doctorates awarded.
Degree requirements: For master's, thesis optional; for doctorate, one foreign language, thesis/dissertation.
Entrance requirements: For master's and doctorate, GRE General Test, TOEFL, minimum GPA of 3.0. *Application deadline:* For fall admission, 1/25 (priority date). Applications are processed on a rolling basis. *Application fee:* $25.
Expenses: Tuition, state resident: full-time $2,551. Tuition, nonresident: full-time $5,551. Required fees: $854. Part-time tuition and fees vary according to course load.

Financial support: In 2001–02, 5 fellowships (averaging $15,800 per year), 51 research assistantships with partial tuition reimbursements (averaging $12,089 per year), 2 teaching assistantships with partial tuition reimbursements (averaging $12,500 per year) were awarded. Career-related internships or fieldwork, institutionally sponsored loans, and scholarships/grants also available. Financial award application deadline: 3/1; financial award applicants required to submit FAFSA.
Faculty research: Solid waste management, electrokinetics, composite structures, transportation planning, river mechanics. *Total annual research expenditures:* $1.7 million.
Dr. George Z. Voyiadjis, Interim Chair/Boyd Professor, 225-578-8668, *Fax:* 225-578-8652, *E-mail:* cegzv@lsu.edu. *Web site:* http://www.ce.lsu.edu/

■ **MARQUETTE UNIVERSITY**

Graduate School, College of Engineering, Department of Civil and Environmental Engineering, Milwaukee, WI 53201-1881

AWARDS Construction and public works management (MS, PhD); environmental/water resources engineering (MS, PhD). Structural/geotechnical engineering (MS, PhD); transportational planning and engineering (MS, PhD). Part-time and evening/weekend programs available.

Faculty: 12 full-time (0 women), 1 part-time/adjunct (0 women).
Students: 20 full-time (8 women), 24 part-time (3 women); includes 2 minority (1 Asian American or Pacific Islander, 1 Hispanic American), 13 international. Average age 30. 57 applicants, 53% accepted, 9 enrolled. In 2001, 9 degrees awarded. Terminal master's awarded for partial completion of doctoral program.
Degree requirements: For master's, thesis or alternative, comprehensive exam; for doctorate, thesis/dissertation. *Median time to degree:* Master's–2 years full-time, 3 years part-time.
Entrance requirements: For master's, TOEFL; for doctorate, GRE General Test, TOEFL. *Application deadline:* For fall admission, 6/1 (priority date). Applications are processed on a rolling basis. *Application fee:* $40. Electronic applications accepted.
Expenses: Tuition: Full-time $10,170; part-time $445 per credit hour. Tuition and fees vary according to course load.
Financial support: In 2001–02, 18 students received support, including 3 fellowships with tuition reimbursements available, 1 research assistantship with tuition reimbursement available (averaging $10,600 per year), 4 teaching assistantships with tuition reimbursements available (averaging $10,200 per year); Federal Work-Study, institutionally sponsored loans, scholarships/grants, and tuition waivers (full and partial) also available.

Support available to part-time students. Financial award application deadline: 2/15.
Faculty research: Highway safety, highway performance, and intelligent transportation systems. Surface mount technology; watershed management. *Total annual research expenditures:* $860,000.
Dr. Thomas H. Wenzel, Chair, 414-288-7030, *Fax:* 414-288-7521.

Find an in-depth description at www.petersons.com/gradchannel.

■ **NEW MEXICO INSTITUTE OF MINING AND TECHNOLOGY**

Graduate Studies, Department of Environmental Engineering, Socorro, NM 87801

AWARDS Environmental engineering (MS), including air quality engineering and science, hazardous waste engineering, water quality engineering and science.

Faculty: 5 full-time (1 woman).
Students: 9 full-time (1 woman), 1 part-time; includes 2 minority (both Hispanic Americans), 6 international. Average age 25. 15 applicants, 60% accepted, 5 enrolled. In 2001, 3 degrees awarded.
Degree requirements: For master's, thesis.
Entrance requirements: For master's, GRE General Test, TOEFL. *Application deadline:* For fall admission, 3/1 (priority date); for spring admission, 6/1. Applications are processed on a rolling basis. *Application fee:* $16 ($30 for international students).
Expenses: Tuition, state resident: part-time $1,084 per semester. Tuition, nonresident: part-time $4,367 per semester. Required fees: $429 per semester.
Financial support: In 2001–02, 3 research assistantships (averaging $13,505 per year), 2 teaching assistantships with full and partial tuition reimbursements (averaging $12,714 per year) were awarded. Fellowships, Federal Work-Study and institutionally sponsored loans also available. Financial award application deadline: 3/1; financial award applicants required to submit CSS PROFILE or FAFSA.
Faculty research: Rock mechanics, geological engineering, mining problems, blasting, shock waves.
Dr. Clinton P. Richardson, Chair, 505-835-5346, *Fax:* 505-835-5252.
Application contact: Dr. David B. Johnson, Dean of Graduate Studies, 505-835-5513, *Fax:* 505-835-5476, *E-mail:* graduate@nmt.edu. *Web site:* http://www.nmt.edu/~mining/default.htm

◼ OHIO UNIVERSITY

Graduate Studies, Russ College of Engineering and Technology, Department of Civil Engineering, Athens, OH 45701-2979

AWARDS Geotechnical and environmental engineering (MS); water resources and structures (MS).

Faculty: 11 full-time (1 woman).
Students: 19 full-time (4 women), 6 part-time (2 women), 18 international. Average age 28. 52 applicants, 71% accepted, 11 enrolled. In 2001, 7 degrees awarded.
Degree requirements: For master's, thesis optional.
Entrance requirements: For master's, minimum GPA of 3.0. *Application deadline:* For fall admission, 5/1 (priority date). Applications are processed on a rolling basis. *Application fee:* $30.
Expenses: Tuition, state resident: full-time $6,585. Tuition, nonresident: full-time $12,254.
Financial support: In 2001–02, 1 fellowship (averaging $15,000 per year), 12 research assistantships (averaging $12,000 per year), 6 teaching assistantships (averaging $6,000 per year) were awarded. Federal Work-Study, institutionally sponsored loans, and tuition waivers (full and partial) also available. Financial award application deadline: 3/15.
Faculty research: Soil-structure interaction, solid waste management, pipes, pavements, noise pollution, mine reclamation, drought analysis. *Total annual research expenditures:* $1.2 million.
Dr. Gayle Mitchell, Chair, 740-593-1465, *Fax:* 740-593-0625, *E-mail:* gmitchell@ bobcat.ent.ohiou.edu.
Application contact: Dr. Shad Sargand, Graduate Chair, 740-593-1467, *Fax:* 740-593-0625, *E-mail:* ssargand@ bobcat.ent.ohiou.edu. *Web site:* http:// webce.ent.ohiou.edu/

◼ OREGON STATE UNIVERSITY

Graduate School, College of Engineering, Department of Bioengineering, Corvallis, OR 97331

AWARDS M Agr, MAIS, MS, PhD.

Students: 22 full-time (11 women), 2 part-time, 10 international. Average age 31. In 2001, 3 master's, 3 doctorates awarded. Terminal master's awarded for partial completion of doctoral program.
Degree requirements: For master's, thesis or alternative; for doctorate, thesis/dissertation.
Entrance requirements: For master's and doctorate, TOEFL, minimum GPA of 3.0 in last 90 hours. *Application deadline:* For fall admission, 3/1. Applications are processed on a rolling basis. *Application fee:* $50.
Expenses: Contact institution.
Financial support: Fellowships, research assistantships, teaching assistantships, Federal Work-Study and institutionally

sponsored loans available. Support available to part-time students. Financial award application deadline: 2/1.
Faculty research: Bioengineering, water resources engineering, food engineering, cell culture and fermentation, vadose zone transport, regional hydrology modeling, bioseparations, post-harvest processing, biomedical engineering, nonpoint pollution abatement, drug formulation and delivery, waste management, stochastic hydrology, biological modeling.
Dr. James A. Moore, Head, 541-737-6299, *Fax:* 541-737-2082, *E-mail:* mooreja@ engr.orst.edu. *Web site:* http:// www.bioe.orst.edu/

◼ THE PENNSYLVANIA STATE UNIVERSITY UNIVERSITY PARK CAMPUS

Graduate School, College of Engineering, Department of Civil and Environmental Engineering, State College, University Park, PA 16802-1503

AWARDS Civil engineering (M Eng, MS, PhD); environmental engineering (M Eng, MS, PhD). Structural engineering (M Eng, MS, PhD); transportation and highway engineering (M Eng, MS, PhD); water resources engineering (M Eng, MS, PhD).

Students: 102 full-time (26 women), 37 part-time (5 women).
Degree requirements: For master's, final paper (M Eng), oral exam and thesis (MS); for doctorate, one foreign language, thesis/dissertation, oral exams, comprehensive exam.
Entrance requirements: For master's and doctorate, GRE General Test. *Application fee:* $45.
Expenses: Tuition, state resident: full-time $7,882; part-time $333 per credit. Tuition, nonresident: full-time $16,142; part-time $673 per credit. Required fees: $124 per semester.
Financial support: Fellowships, research assistantships, teaching assistantships available.
Faculty research: Construction engineering and management; materials and pavements; geotechnical engineering; hydraulics, hydrology, and water resource systems. Structures.
Dr. Andrew Scanlon, Head, 814-863-3084.

◼ PRINCETON UNIVERSITY

Graduate School, Department of Geosciences, Princeton, NJ 08544-1019

AWARDS Atmospheric and oceanic sciences (PhD); environmental engineering and water resources (PhD); geological and geophysical sciences (PhD).

Degree requirements: For doctorate, one foreign language, thesis/dissertation.
Entrance requirements: For doctorate, GRE General Test, GRE Subject Test.

◼ PRINCETON UNIVERSITY

Graduate School, School of Engineering and Applied Science, Department of Civil and Environmental Engineering and Department of Geosciences, Program in Environmental Engineering and Water Resources, Princeton, NJ 08544-1019

AWARDS PhD.

Degree requirements: For doctorate, one foreign language, thesis/dissertation.
Entrance requirements: For doctorate, GRE General Test, GRE Subject Test.

Find an in-depth description at www.petersons.com/gradchannel.

◼ TEXAS A&M UNIVERSITY

College of Engineering, Department of Civil Engineering, Program in Water Resources Engineering, College Station, TX 77843

AWARDS M Eng, MS, D Eng, PhD. D Eng offered through the College of Engineering.

Students: 20.
Degree requirements: For master's, thesis (MS); for doctorate, dissertation (PhD), internship (D Eng).
Entrance requirements: For master's and doctorate, GRE General Test, TOEFL. *Application fee:* $50 ($75 for international students).
Expenses: Tuition, state resident: full-time $11,872. Tuition, nonresident: full-time $17,892.
Financial support: Fellowships, research assistantships, teaching assistantships available. Financial award application deadline: 4/15; financial award applicants required to submit FAFSA.
Faculty research: Water resources development, planning, and management; water resources system engineering, hydrology, and hydraulics; groundwater systems analysis.
Dr. Ralph A. Wurbs, Head, 979-845-3011, *Fax:* 979-862-2800, *E-mail:* ce-grad@ tamu.edu.
Application contact: Dr. Anthony T. Cahill, Information Contact, 979-845-2498, *Fax:* 979-862-2800, *E-mail:* ce-grad@tamu.edu. *Web site:* http:// www.civil.tamu.edu/

◼ TUFTS UNIVERSITY

Division of Graduate and Continuing Studies and Research, Graduate School of Arts and Sciences, School of Engineering, Department of Civil and Environmental Engineering, Medford, MA 02155

AWARDS Civil engineering (MS, PhD), including geotechnical engineering, structural engineering; environmental engineering (MS, PhD), including environmental engineering and environmental sciences, environmental geotechnology, environmental health,

Tufts University (continued)
environmental science and management, hazardous materials management, water resources engineering. Part-time programs available.

Faculty: 13 full-time, 10 part-time/ adjunct.
Students: 58 (29 women); includes 4 minority (2 African Americans, 2 Asian Americans or Pacific Islanders) 4 international. 53 applicants, 75% accepted. In 2001, 36 master's, 1 doctorate awarded. Terminal master's awarded for partial completion of doctoral program.
Degree requirements: For master's, thesis or alternative; for doctorate, thesis/ dissertation.
Entrance requirements: For master's and doctorate, GRE General Test, TOEFL. *Application deadline:* For fall admission, 2/15; for spring admission, 10/15. Applications are processed on a rolling basis. *Application fee:* $50. Electronic applications accepted.
Expenses: Tuition: Full-time $26,853. Full-time tuition and fees vary according to program.
Financial support: Research assistantships with full and partial tuition reimbursements, teaching assistantships with full and partial tuition reimbursements, Federal Work-Study, scholarships/grants, and tuition waivers (partial) available. Support available to part-time students. Financial award application deadline: 2/15; financial award applicants required to submit FAFSA.
Dr. Stephen Levine, Chair, 617-627-3211, *Fax:* 617-627-3994.
Application contact: Linfield Brown, Head, 617-627-3211, *Fax:* 617-627-3994. *Web site:* http://www.ase.tufts.edu/cee/

■ **UNIVERSITY OF CALIFORNIA, BERKELEY**

Graduate Division, College of Engineering, Department of Civil and Environmental Engineering, Berkeley, CA 94720-1500

AWARDS Construction engineering and management (M Eng, MS, D Eng, PhD); environmental quality and environmental water resources engineering (M Eng, MS, D Eng, PhD); geotechnical engineering (M Eng, MS, D Eng, PhD). Structural engineering, mechanics and materials (M Eng, MS, D Eng, PhD); transportation engineering (M Eng, MS, D Eng, PhD).

Degree requirements: For master's, comprehensive exam or thesis (MS); for doctorate, thesis/dissertation, qualifying exam.
Entrance requirements: For master's, GRE General Test, minimum GPA of 3.0; for doctorate, GRE General Test, minimum GPA of 3.5.

Expenses: Tuition, nonresident: full-time $10,704. Required fees: $4,349.
Find an in-depth description at www.petersons.com/gradchannel.

■ **UNIVERSITY OF CALIFORNIA, LOS ANGELES**

Graduate Division, School of Engineering and Applied Science, Department of Civil and Environmental Engineering, Los Angeles, CA 90095

AWARDS Environmental engineering (MS, PhD); geotechnical engineering (MS, PhD). Structures (MS, PhD), including structural mechanics and earthquake engineering; water resource systems engineering (MS, PhD).

Faculty: 14 full-time, 11 part-time/ adjunct.
Students: 96 full-time (28 women); includes 23 minority (1 African American, 17 Asian Americans or Pacific Islanders, 5 Hispanic Americans), 45 international. 216 applicants, 60% accepted, 34 enrolled. In 2001, 34 master's, 9 doctorates awarded.
Degree requirements: For master's, comprehensive exam or thesis; for doctorate, thesis/dissertation, qualifying exams.
Entrance requirements: For master's, GRE General Test, minimum GPA of 3.0; for doctorate, GRE General Test, minimum GPA of 3.25. *Application deadline:* For fall admission, 1/15; for spring admission, 12/1. *Application fee:* $60. Electronic applications accepted.
Expenses: Tuition, nonresident: full-time $10,244. Required fees: $3,609. Full-time tuition and fees vary according to program.
Financial support: In 2001–02, 39 fellowships, 50 research assistantships, 31 teaching assistantships were awarded. Federal Work-Study, institutionally sponsored loans, and tuition waivers (full and partial) also available. Financial award application deadline: 1/15; financial award applicants required to submit FAFSA.
Dr. Jiann-Wen Ju, Chair, 310-206-1751.
Application contact: Deeona Columbia, Graduate Affairs Officer, 310-825-1851, *Fax:* 310-206-2222, *E-mail:* deeona@ ea.ucla.edu. *Web site:* http:// www.cee.ucla.edu

Find an in-depth description at www.petersons.com/gradchannel.

■ **UNIVERSITY OF CENTRAL FLORIDA**

College of Engineering and Computer Sciences, Department of Civil and Environmental Engineering, Program in Environmental Engineering, Orlando, FL 32816

AWARDS Air pollution control (Certificate); drinking water treatment (Certificate); environmental engineering (MS, MS Env E, PhD); hazardous waste management (Certificate); wastewater treatment

(Certificate). Part-time and evening/weekend programs available.

Faculty: 19 full-time (1 woman), 12 part-time/adjunct (0 women).
Students: 33 full-time (6 women), 19 part-time (7 women); includes 4 minority (1 African American, 2 Asian Americans or Pacific Islanders, 1 Hispanic American), 26 international. Average age 28. 81 applicants, 74% accepted, 23 enrolled. In 2001, 5 master's, 1 doctorate awarded.
Degree requirements: For master's, thesis or alternative; for doctorate, thesis/ dissertation, departmental qualifying exam, candidacy exam.
Entrance requirements: For master's, GRE General Test, TOEFL, minimum GPA of 3.0 in last 60 hours; for doctorate, GRE General Test, TOEFL, minimum GPA of 3.5 in last 60 hours, interview. *Application deadline:* For fall admission, 7/15 (priority date); for spring admission, 12/15 (priority date). *Application fee:* $20. Electronic applications accepted.
Expenses: Tuition, state resident: part-time $162 per hour. Tuition, nonresident: part-time $569 per hour.
Financial support: In 2001–02, 13 fellowships with partial tuition reimbursements (averaging $2,644 per year), 86 research assistantships with partial tuition reimbursements (averaging $3,300 per year), 5 teaching assistantships with partial tuition reimbursements (averaging $4,700 per year) were awarded. Career-related internships or fieldwork, Federal Work-Study, institutionally sponsored loans, tuition waivers (partial), and unspecified assistantships also available. Financial award application deadline: 3/1; financial award applicants required to submit FAFSA.
Application contact: Dr. Roger L. Wayson, Coordinator, 407-823-2841, *E-mail:* wayson@pegasus.cc.ucf.edu. *Web site:* http://www.ucf.edu/

■ **UNIVERSITY OF COLORADO AT BOULDER**

Graduate School, College of Engineering and Applied Science, Department of Civil, Environmental, and Architectural Engineering, Boulder, CO 80309

AWARDS Building systems (MS, PhD); construction engineering and management (MS, PhD); environmental engineering (MS, PhD); geoenvironmental engineering (MS, PhD); geotechnical engineering (MS, PhD). Structural engineering (MS, PhD); water resource engineering (MS, PhD).

Faculty: 37 full-time (2 women).
Students: 167 full-time (49 women), 44 part-time (12 women); includes 14 minority (1 African American, 4 Asian Americans or Pacific Islanders, 9 Hispanic Americans), 88 international. Average age 30. 280 applicants, 59% accepted. In 2001, 59 master's, 13 doctorates awarded.

Degree requirements: For master's, thesis or alternative, comprehensive exam; for doctorate, thesis/dissertation.

Entrance requirements: For master's, GRE General Test, minimum undergraduate GPA of 3.0. *Application deadline:* For fall admission, 4/30; for spring admission, 10/31. *Application fee:* $50 ($60 for international students).

Expenses: Tuition, state resident: full-time $3,474. Tuition, nonresident: full-time $16,624.

Financial support: In 2001–02, 19 fellowships (averaging $5,252 per year), 45 research assistantships (averaging $15,638 per year), 14 teaching assistantships (averaging $13,821 per year) were awarded. Financial award application deadline: 2/15.

Faculty research: Building systems engineering, construction engineering and management, environmental engineering, geoenvironmental engineering, geotechnical engineering. *Total annual research expenditures:* $8.3 million.
Hon-Yim Ko, Chair, 303-492-6716, *Fax:* 303-492-7317, *E-mail:* ko@spot.colorado.edu.

Application contact: Jan Demay, Graduate Secretary, 303-492-7316, *Fax:* 303-492-7317, *E-mail:* demay@spot.colorado.edu. *Web site:* http://www.civil.colorado.edu/

■ UNIVERSITY OF DELAWARE

College of Engineering, Department of Civil and Environmental Engineering, Program in Water Resource Engineering, Newark, DE 19716

AWARDS MAS, MCE, PhD. Terminal master's awarded for partial completion of doctoral program.

Degree requirements: For master's and doctorate, thesis/dissertation.

Entrance requirements: For master's and doctorate, GRE General Test, TOEFL.

Expenses: Tuition, state resident: full-time $4,770; part-time $265 per credit. Tuition, nonresident: full-time $13,860; part-time $770 per credit. Required fees: $414.

Faculty research: Computer program for groundwater modeling, *in situ* stress determination by microhydraulic fracturing, stochastic groundwater flow modeling, poroelasticity in rock mechanics.

Find an in-depth description at www.petersons.com/gradchannel.

■ UNIVERSITY OF KANSAS

Graduate School, School of Engineering, Department of Civil, Environmental, and Architectural Engineering, Lawrence, KS 66045

AWARDS Architectural engineering (MS); civil engineering (MCE, MS, DE, PhD); construction management (MCM); environmental engineering (MS, PhD); environmental science (MS, PhD); water resources engineering (MS); water resources science (MS).

Faculty: 27.

Students: 38 full-time (11 women), 97 part-time (20 women); includes 12 minority (4 African Americans, 3 Asian Americans or Pacific Islanders, 4 Hispanic Americans, 1 Native American), 37 international. Average age 32. 105 applicants, 31% accepted, 19 enrolled. In 2001, 32 master's, 4 doctorates awarded.

Degree requirements: For master's, thesis or alternative, exam; for doctorate, thesis/dissertation, comprehensive exam.

Entrance requirements: For master's, GRE, Michigan English Language Assessment Battery, TOEFL, minimum GPA of 3.0; for doctorate, GRE, Michigan English Language Assessment Battery, TOEFL, minimum GPA of 3.5. *Application deadline:* Applications are processed on a rolling basis. *Application fee:* $40.

Expenses: Tuition, state resident: full-time $2,722; part-time $113 per credit. Tuition, nonresident: full-time $8,586; part-time $358 per credit. Required fees: $551; $46 per credit. Tuition and fees vary according to campus/location, program and reciprocity agreements.

Financial support: In 2001–02, 21 research assistantships with partial tuition reimbursements (averaging $10,367 per year), 6 teaching assistantships with full and partial tuition reimbursements (averaging $8,615 per year) were awarded. Fellowships, career-related internships or fieldwork also available.

Faculty research: Structures (fracture mechanics), transportation, environmental health.
Steve L. McCabe, Chair, 785-864-3766.

Application contact: David Parr, Graduate Director, *E-mail:* aparr@ engr.ukans.edu. *Web site:* http://www.ceae.ku.edu/

■ UNIVERSITY OF MARYLAND, COLLEGE PARK

Graduate Studies and Research, College of Agriculture and Natural Resources, Department of Biological Resources Engineering, College Park, MD 20742

AWARDS MS, PhD.

Faculty: 16 full-time (2 women), 3 part-time/adjunct (1 woman).

Students: 31 full-time (18 women), 19 part-time (8 women); includes 8 minority (5 African Americans, 3 Asian Americans or Pacific Islanders), 17 international. 39 applicants, 56% accepted, 11 enrolled. In 2001, 1 degree awarded.

Degree requirements: For master's, thesis optional; for doctorate, thesis/dissertation.

Entrance requirements: For master's, GRE General Test, minimum GPA of 3.0. *Application deadline:* For fall admission, 6/1 (priority date); for spring admission, 10/1. Applications are processed on a rolling basis. *Application fee:* $50 ($70 for

international students). Electronic applications accepted.

Expenses: Tuition, state resident: part-time $289 per credit hour. Tuition, nonresident: part-time $448 per credit hour. One-time fee: $436 part-time. Full-time tuition and fees vary according to course load, campus/location and program.

Financial support: In 2001–02, 2 fellowships with full tuition reimbursements (averaging $9,771 per year), 17 research assistantships with tuition reimbursements (averaging $15,399 per year), 5 teaching assistantships with tuition reimbursements (averaging $15,588 per year) were awarded. Career-related internships or fieldwork also available. Financial award applicants required to submit FAFSA.

Faculty research: Engineering aspects of production; harvesting, processing, and marketing of terrestrial and aquatic food and fiber.
Dr. Frederick Wheaton, Chairman, 301-405-1193, *Fax:* 301-314-9023.

Application contact: Trudy Lindsey, Director, Graduate Admissions and Records, 301-405-6991, *Fax:* 301-314-9305, *E-mail:* grschool@deans.umd.edu.

Find an in-depth description at www.petersons.com/gradchannel.

■ THE UNIVERSITY OF MEMPHIS

Graduate School, Herff College of Engineering, Department of Civil Engineering, Memphis, TN 38152

AWARDS Civil engineering (PhD); environmental engineering (MS); foundation engineering (MS). Structural engineering (MS); transportation engineering (MS); water resources engineering (MS).

Faculty: 12 full-time (0 women), 1 part-time/adjunct (0 women).

Students: 14 full-time (5 women), 7 part-time (1 woman), 10 international. Average age 32. 36 applicants, 56% accepted. In 2001, 5 degrees awarded.

Degree requirements: For master's, thesis or alternative, comprehensive exam; for doctorate, thesis/dissertation.

Entrance requirements: For master's, GRE General Test or MAT, minimum undergraduate GPA of 2.5. *Application deadline:* For fall admission, 8/1; for spring admission, 12/1. *Application fee:* $25 ($100 for international students).

Expenses: Tuition, state resident: full-time $2,026. Tuition, nonresident: full-time $4,528.

Financial support: In 2001–02, 1 fellowship with full tuition reimbursement, 13 research assistantships with full tuition reimbursements were awarded. Career-related internships or fieldwork also available.

Faculty research: Structural response to earthquakes, pavement design, water quality, bridge scour, intelligent transportation systems. *Total annual research expenditures:* $1.2 million.

The University of Memphis (continued)
Dr. Martin E. Lipinski, Chairman, 901-678-3279.
Application contact: Dr. Shahram Pezeshk, Coordinator of Graduate Studies, 901-678-4727.

■ UNIVERSITY OF MISSOURI–COLUMBIA

Graduate School, College of Engineering, Department of Civil and Environmental Engineering, Columbia, MO 65211

AWARDS Civil engineering (MS, PhD); environmental engineering (MS, PhD); geotechnical engineering (MS, PhD). Structural engineering (MS, PhD); transportation and highway engineering (MS); water resources (MS, PhD).

Faculty: 20 full-time (2 women), 1 part-time/adjunct (0 women).
Students: 28 full-time (6 women), 14 part-time (3 women); includes 4 minority (all Hispanic Americans), 23 international. 74 applicants, 43% accepted. In 2001, 19 master's, 1 doctorate awarded.
Degree requirements: For master's, report or thesis; for doctorate, thesis/dissertation.
Entrance requirements: For master's and doctorate, GRE General Test, TOEFL. *Application deadline:* For fall admission, 3/15 (priority date); for winter admission, 10/15 (priority date). *Application fee:* $25 ($50 for international students).
Expenses: Tuition, state resident: part-time $179 per credit hour. Tuition, nonresident: part-time $539 per credit hour. Required fees: $122 per semester. Tuition and fees vary according to program.
Financial support: Research assistantships, teaching assistantships, institutionally sponsored loans available.
Dr. Mark Virkler, Director of Graduate Studies, 573-882-7434, *E-mail:* virklerm@missouri.edu. *Web site:* http://www.engineering.missouri.edu/civil.htm

■ UNIVERSITY OF SOUTHERN CALIFORNIA

Graduate School, School of Engineering, Department of Civil Engineering, Program in Water Resources, Los Angeles, CA 90089

AWARDS MS.

Degree requirements: For master's, thesis optional.
Entrance requirements: For master's, GRE General Test.
Expenses: Tuition: Full-time $25,060; part-time $844 per unit. Required fees: $473.

■ THE UNIVERSITY OF TEXAS AT AUSTIN

Graduate School, College of Engineering, Department of Civil Engineering, Program in Environmental and Water Resources Engineering, Austin, TX 78712-1111

AWARDS MSE.

Students: 29 (17 women); includes 1 minority (Hispanic American) 8 international. 82 applicants, 48% accepted, 14 enrolled. In 2001, 16 degrees awarded.
Entrance requirements: For master's, GRE General Test. *Application deadline:* For fall admission, 1/15 (priority date); for spring admission, 9/1 (priority date). Applications are processed on a rolling basis. *Application fee:* $50 ($75 for international students). Electronic applications accepted.
Expenses: Tuition, state resident: full-time $3,159. Tuition, nonresident: full-time $6,957. Tuition and fees vary according to program.
Financial support: Fellowships, research assistantships, teaching assistantships available. Financial award application deadline: 2/1.
Lynn E. Katz, Graduate Adviser, 512-471-4244.
Application contact: Kathy Rose, Graduate Coordinator, 512-471-4921, *Fax:* 512-471-0592, *E-mail:* krose@mail.utexas.edu.

■ UNIVERSITY OF VIRGINIA

School of Engineering and Applied Science, Department of Civil Engineering, Program in Environmental Engineering, Charlottesville, VA 22903

AWARDS Environmental engineering (ME, MS, PhD); water resources (ME, MS, PhD). Part-time programs available.

Faculty: 6 full-time (3 women).
Students: 26 full-time (11 women); includes 2 minority (both African Americans), 12 international. Average age 29. 62 applicants, 19% accepted, 8 enrolled. In 2001, 9 master's, 2 doctorates awarded. Terminal master's awarded for partial completion of doctoral program.
Degree requirements: For master's, thesis (for some programs); for doctorate, thesis/dissertation, comprehensive exam.
Entrance requirements: For master's and doctorate, GRE General Test. *Application deadline:* For fall admission, 2/1 (priority date); for spring admission, 8/1 (priority date). Applications are processed on a rolling basis. *Application fee:* $40. Electronic applications accepted.
Expenses: Tuition, state resident: full-time $3,988. Tuition, nonresident: full-time $17,078. Required fees: $1,190.
Financial support: In 2001–02, 20 students received support, including 4 fellowships with full tuition reimbursements available (averaging $17,000 per year), 16

research assistantships with full tuition reimbursements available (averaging $17,000 per year), 4 teaching assistantships with full tuition reimbursements available (averaging $17,000 per year) Financial award application deadline: 2/1.
Faculty research: Stormwater management, nonpoint pollution control, water quality modeling, estuarine and coastal water quality management, groundwater flow and transport.
Dr. Shaw L. Yu, Professor, 434-924-6377, *Fax:* 434-982-2951, *E-mail:* sly@virginia.edu.

■ UTAH STATE UNIVERSITY

School of Graduate Studies, College of Engineering, Department of Biological and Irrigation Engineering, Logan, UT 84322

AWARDS Biological and agricultural engineering (MS, PhD); irrigation engineering (MS, PhD). Part-time programs available.

Faculty: 10 full-time (0 women).
Students: 27 full-time (5 women), 12 part-time (1 woman); includes 3 minority (1 African American, 2 Hispanic Americans), 30 international. Average age 28. 22 applicants, 59% accepted. In 2001, 10 master's, 3 doctorates awarded. Terminal master's awarded for partial completion of doctoral program.
Degree requirements: For master's, thesis (for some programs); for doctorate, thesis/dissertation.
Entrance requirements: For master's and doctorate, GRE General Test, TOEFL, minimum GPA of 3.0. *Application deadline:* For fall admission, 6/15 (priority date); for spring admission, 10/15. Applications are processed on a rolling basis. *Application fee:* $40.
Expenses: Tuition, state resident: full-time $1,693. Tuition, nonresident: full-time $4,233. Required fees: $501. Tuition and fees vary according to program.
Financial support: In 2001–02, 15 fellowships with partial tuition reimbursements, 15 research assistantships with partial tuition reimbursements, 2 teaching assistantships with partial tuition reimbursements were awarded. Tuition waivers (partial) also available. Support available to part-time students.
Faculty research: Surge flow, on-farm water management, crop-water yield modeling, drainage, groundwater modeling.
Wynn Walker, Head, 435-797-2788, *Fax:* 435-797-1248, *E-mail:* wynnwalk@cc.usu.edu.
Application contact: Lyman Willardson, Graduate Adviser, 435-797-2789, *Fax:* 435-797-1248, *E-mail:* fath8@cc.usu.edu. *Web site:* http://www.engineering.usu.edu/bie/

■ VILLANOVA UNIVERSITY

College of Engineering, Department of Civil and Environmental Engineering, Program in Water Resources and Environmental Engineering, Villanova, PA 19085-1699

AWARDS MSWREE. Part-time and evening/weekend programs available.

Faculty: 5 full-time (0 women), 5 part-time/adjunct (0 women).
Students: 3 full-time (2 women), 8 part-time (5 women); includes 1 minority (Asian American or Pacific Islander), 3 international. Average age 25. 13 applicants, 92% accepted. In 2001, 9 degrees awarded.
Degree requirements: For master's, thesis optional.
Entrance requirements: For master's, GRE General Test (for applicants with degrees from foreign universities), BCE or bachelor's degree in science or related engineering field, minimum GPA of 3.0. *Application deadline:* For fall admission, 8/1 (priority date); for spring admission, 12/1. Applications are processed on a rolling basis. *Application fee:* $40. Electronic applications accepted.
Expenses: Tuition: Part-time $340 per credit. One-time fee: $115 full-time. Tuition and fees vary according to program.
Financial support: Federal Work-Study and tuition waivers (full and partial) available. Support available to part-time

students. Financial award application deadline: 4/15.
Faculty research: Photocatalytic decontamination and disinfection of water, urban storm water wetlands, economy and risk, removal and destruction of organic acids in water, sludge treatment.
Dr. Ronald A. Chadderton, Chairman, Department of Civil and Environmental Engineering, 610-519-4960, *Fax:* 610-519-6754.

■ VIRGINIA POLYTECHNIC INSTITUTE AND STATE UNIVERSITY

Graduate School, College of Engineering, Department of Biological Systems Engineering, Blacksburg, VA 24061

AWARDS Bio-process engineering (M Eng, MS, PhD); food engineering (M Eng, MS, PhD); land and water engineering (M Eng, MS, PhD); nonpoint source pollution control (M Eng, MS, PhD); watershed engineering (M Eng, MS, PhD); wood engineering (M Eng, MS, PhD).

Faculty: 12 full-time (0 women), 8 part-time/adjunct (0 women).
Students: 24 full-time (13 women), 5 part-time; includes 1 minority (Asian American or Pacific Islander), 10 international. Average age 25. 19 applicants, 58% accepted. In 2001, 3 master's, 1 doctorate awarded.

Degree requirements: For master's and doctorate, thesis/dissertation. *Median time to degree:* Master's–2 years full-time; doctorate–3 years full-time.
Entrance requirements: For master's and doctorate, GRE General Test, TOEFL. *Application deadline:* For fall admission, 12/1 (priority date); for spring admission, 9/1 (priority date). Applications are processed on a rolling basis. *Application fee:* $45. Electronic applications accepted.
Expenses: Tuition, state resident: part-time $241 per hour. Tuition, nonresident: part-time $406 per hour. Tuition and fees vary according to program.
Financial support: In 2001–02, 4 fellowships with full tuition reimbursements (averaging $17,000 per year), 7 research assistantships with full tuition reimbursements (averaging $16,500 per year), 2 teaching assistantships with full tuition reimbursements (averaging $16,500 per year) were awarded. Career-related internships or fieldwork, institutionally sponsored loans, tuition waivers (full and partial), and unspecified assistantships also available. Support available to part-time students. Financial award application deadline: 4/1.
Faculty research: Soil and water engineering, alternative energy sources for agriculture and agricultural mechanization. *Total annual research expenditures:* $800,000.
Dr. John V. Perumpral, Head, 540-231-6615, *E-mail:* perump@vt.edu.
Application contact: Dr. S. Mostaghimi, Chairman, 540-231-7605, *E-mail:* smostagh@vt.edu. *Web site:* http://www.bse.vt.edu/

Electrical and Computer Engineering

COMPUTER ENGINEERING

■ AIR FORCE INSTITUTE OF TECHNOLOGY

School of Engineering and Management, Department of Electrical and Computer Engineering, Dayton, OH 45433-7765

AWARDS Computer engineering (MS, PhD); computer systems/science (MS); electrical engineering (MS, PhD); electro-optics (MS, PhD). Part-time programs available.

Degree requirements: For master's and doctorate, thesis/dissertation.
Entrance requirements: For master's and doctorate, GRE General Test, minimum GPA of 3.0, U.S. citizenship.
Faculty research: Remote sensing, information survivability, microelectronics, computer networks, artificial intelligence. *Web site:* http://en.afit.edu/bng/

■ ARIZONA STATE UNIVERSITY EAST

College of Technology and Applied Sciences, Department of Electronics and Computer Engineering Technology, Mesa, AZ 85212

AWARDS MS. Part-time and evening/weekend programs available.

Faculty: 6 full-time (1 woman), 1 part-time/adjunct (0 women).
Students: 68 full-time (26 women), 57 part-time (22 women); includes 17 minority (3 African Americans, 12 Asian Americans or Pacific Islanders, 2 Hispanic Americans), 85 international. Average age 31. 103 applicants, 65% accepted, 36 enrolled. In 2001, 29 degrees awarded.
Degree requirements: For master's, thesis or applied project and oral defense. *Median time to degree:* Master's–1.6 years full-time, 2 years part-time.
Entrance requirements: For master's, GRE, TOEFL. *Application deadline:*

Applications are processed on a rolling basis. *Application fee:* $45. Electronic applications accepted.
Expenses: Tuition, state resident: full-time $2,412; part-time $126 per credit hour. Tuition, nonresident: full-time $10,278; part-time $428 per credit hour. Required fees: $26. Tuition and fees vary according to course load.
Financial support: In 2001–02, 46 students received support, including 11 research assistantships with partial tuition reimbursements available (averaging $6,693 per year), 11 teaching assistantships with partial tuition reimbursements available (averaging $4,534 per year); career-related internships or fieldwork, Federal Work-Study, scholarships/grants, tuition waivers (full and partial), and unspecified assistantships also available. Support available to part-time students. Financial award application deadline: 3/1; financial award applicants required to submit FAFSA.

Arizona State University East (continued)
Faculty research: Systems, circuit applications and hardware design. *Total annual research expenditures:* $716,685.
Dr. Timothy Lindquist, Chair, 480-727-2783, *Fax:* 480-727-1723, *E-mail:* timothy.lindquist@asu.edu.

■ AUBURN UNIVERSITY

Graduate School, College of Engineering, Department of Electrical and Computer Engineering, Auburn University, AL 36849

AWARDS MEE, MS, PhD. Part-time programs available.

Faculty: 26 full-time (1 woman).
Students: 36 full-time (5 women), 29 part-time (2 women); includes 2 minority (1 African American, 1 Hispanic American), 38 international. 145 applicants, 38% accepted. In 2001, 14 master's, 6 doctorates awarded.
Degree requirements: For master's, thesis (for some programs), comprehensive exam; for doctorate, thesis/dissertation.
Entrance requirements: For master's and doctorate, GRE General Test, GRE Subject Test. *Application deadline:* For fall admission, 7/7; for spring admission, 11/24. Applications are processed on a rolling basis. *Application fee:* $25 ($50 for international students). Electronic applications accepted.
Financial support: Fellowships, research assistantships, teaching assistantships, Federal Work-Study available. Support available to part-time students. Financial award application deadline: 3/15.
Faculty research: Power systems, energy conversion, electronics, electromagnetics, digital systems.
Dr. J. David Irwin, Head, 334-844-1800.
Application contact: Dr. John F. Pritchett, Dean of the Graduate School, 334-844-4700, *E-mail:* hatchlb@mail.auburn.edu. *Web site:* http://www.eng.auburn.edu/department/ee/

■ BOISE STATE UNIVERSITY

Graduate College, College of Engineering, Program in Computer Engineering, Boise, ID 83725-0399

AWARDS MS. Part-time and evening/weekend programs available.

Degree requirements: For master's, thesis.
Entrance requirements: For master's, GRE General Test, TOEFL, minimum GPA of 3.0. Electronic applications accepted.

■ BOSTON UNIVERSITY

College of Engineering, Department of Electrical and Computer Engineering, Boston, MA 02215

AWARDS Computer engineering (PhD); computer systems engineering (MS); electrical engineering (MS, PhD). Systems engineering (PhD). Part-time programs available.

Faculty: 39 full-time (3 women), 3 part-time/adjunct (0 women).
Students: 110 full-time (25 women), 28 part-time (9 women); includes 9 minority (4 African Americans, 4 Asian Americans or Pacific Islanders, 1 Hispanic American), 72 international. Average age 29. 662 applicants, 19% accepted, 39 enrolled. In 2001, 39 master's, 7 doctorates awarded. Terminal master's awarded for partial completion of doctoral program.
Degree requirements: For master's, thesis optional; for doctorate, thesis/dissertation, comprehensive exam.
Entrance requirements: For master's and doctorate, GRE General Test, TOEFL. *Application deadline:* For fall admission, 4/1; for spring admission, 10/1. Applications are processed on a rolling basis. *Application fee:* $60. Electronic applications accepted.
Expenses: Tuition: Full-time $25,872; part-time $340 per credit. Required fees: $40 per semester. Part-time tuition and fees vary according to class time, course level and program.
Financial support: In 2001–02, 83 students received support, including 5 fellowships with full tuition reimbursements available (averaging $15,500 per year), 40 research assistantships with full tuition reimbursements available (averaging $13,500 per year), 19 teaching assistantships with full tuition reimbursements available (averaging $13,500 per year); career-related internships or fieldwork, Federal Work-Study, institutionally sponsored loans, and scholarships/grants also available. Financial award application deadline: 1/15; financial award applicants required to submit FAFSA.
Faculty research: Computer networks, computer reliability, photonics, signal and image processing, solid state materials, subsurface imaging. *Total annual research expenditures:* $9.5 million.
Dr. Bahaa Saleh, Chairman, 617-353-7176, *Fax:* 617-353-6440.
Application contact: Cheryl Kelley, Director of Graduate Programs, 617-353-9760, *Fax:* 617-353-0259, *E-mail:* enggrad@bu.edu. *Web site:* http://www.eng.bu.edu/grad/

Find an in-depth description at www.petersons.com/gradchannel.

■ CALIFORNIA STATE UNIVERSITY, LONG BEACH

Graduate Studies, College of Engineering, Department of Computer Engineering and Computer Science, Long Beach, CA 90840

AWARDS Computer engineering (MS); computer science (MS). Part-time programs available.

Faculty: 17 full-time (3 women), 8 part-time/adjunct (0 women).
Students: 71 full-time (27 women), 140 part-time (47 women); includes 89 minority (2 African Americans, 80 Asian Americans or Pacific Islanders, 7 Hispanic Americans), 76 international. Average age 33. 261 applicants, 11% accepted. In 2001, 62 degrees awarded.
Degree requirements: For master's, thesis or alternative.
Entrance requirements: For master's, TOEFL. *Application deadline:* For fall admission, 8/1; for spring admission, 12/1. *Application fee:* $55. Electronic applications accepted.
Financial support: Teaching assistantships, Federal Work-Study, institutionally sponsored loans, scholarships/grants, and unspecified assistantships available. Financial award application deadline: 3/2.
Faculty research: Artificial intelligence, software engineering, computer simulation and modeling, user-interface design, networking.
Dr. Sandra Cynar, Chair, 562-985-4285, *Fax:* 562-985-7561, *E-mail:* cynar@csulb.edu.
Application contact: Dr. Dar Liu, Graduate Adviser, 562-985-1594, *Fax:* 562-985-7561, *E-mail:* liu@csulb.edu.

■ CALIFORNIA STATE UNIVERSITY, NORTHRIDGE

Graduate Studies, College of Engineering and Computer Science, Department of Electrical and Computer Engineering, Northridge, CA 91330

AWARDS Biomedical engineering (MS); communications/radar engineering (MS); control engineering (MS); digital/computer engineering (MS); electronics engineering (MS); microwave/antenna engineering (MS). Part-time and evening/weekend programs available.

Faculty: 19 full-time, 6 part-time/adjunct.
Students: 31 full-time (3 women), 81 part-time (9 women); includes 30 minority (1 African American, 21 Asian Americans or Pacific Islanders, 8 Hispanic Americans), 32 international. Average age 33. 77 applicants, 73% accepted, 19 enrolled. In 2001, 22 degrees awarded.
Degree requirements: For master's, thesis or alternative.
Entrance requirements: For master's, GRE General Test, TOEFL, minimum

GPA of 2.5. *Application deadline:* For fall admission, 11/30. *Application fee:* $55.
Expenses: Tuition, nonresident: part-time $631 per semester. Required fees: $246 per unit.
Financial support: Application deadline: 3/1.
Faculty research: Reflector antenna study, radome study.
Dr. Nagwa Bekir, Chair, 818-677-2190.
Application contact: Nagi El Naga, Graduate Coordinator, 818-677-2180.

■ CARNEGIE MELLON UNIVERSITY

Carnegie Institute of Technology, Department of Electrical and Computer Engineering, Pittsburgh, PA 15213-3891

AWARDS Biomedical engineering (MS, PhD); electrical and computer engineering (MS, PhD). Part-time programs available.

Degree requirements: For master's, thesis; for doctorate, thesis/dissertation, qualifying exam, teaching experience.
Entrance requirements: For master's and doctorate, GRE General Test, TOEFL.
Faculty research: Computer-aided design, solid-state devices, VLSI, processing, robotics and controls, signal processing, data systems storage. *Web site:* http://www.ece.cmu.edu/

Find an in-depth description at www.petersons.com/gradchannel.

■ CASE WESTERN RESERVE UNIVERSITY

School of Graduate Studies, The Case School of Engineering, Department of Electrical Engineering and Computer Science, Cleveland, OH 44106

AWARDS Computer engineering (MS, PhD); computing and information science (MS, PhD); electrical engineering (MS, PhD). Systems and control engineering (MS, PhD). Part-time and evening/weekend programs available. Postbaccalaureate distance learning degree programs offered (minimal on-campus study).

Faculty: 29 full-time (2 women), 15 part-time/adjunct (1 woman).
Students: 61 full-time (17 women), 72 part-time (6 women); includes 8 minority (3 African Americans, 5 Asian Americans or Pacific Islanders), 85 international. Average age 25. 843 applicants, 16% accepted, 27 enrolled. In 2001, 33 master's, 16 doctorates awarded. Terminal master's awarded for partial completion of doctoral program.
Degree requirements: For master's, thesis; for doctorate, thesis/dissertation, qualifying exam, teaching experience.
Entrance requirements: For master's and doctorate, GRE General Test, TOEFL.
Application deadline: For fall admission, 2/1;

for spring admission, 11/1. Applications are processed on a rolling basis. *Application fee:* $25.
Financial support: In 2001–02, 34 fellowships with full and partial tuition reimbursements (averaging $15,240 per year), 22 research assistantships with full and partial tuition reimbursements (averaging $14,220 per year) were awarded. Career-related internships or fieldwork, Federal Work-Study, and institutionally sponsored loans also available. Support available to part-time students. Financial award application deadline: 3/1; financial award applicants required to submit FAFSA.
Faculty research: Computational biology and biorobotics; HEHS and solid state, VSLI system design and testing; databases, software engineering, computer systems. Systems optimization, planning and decision making; digital signal processing, control and filtering theory. *Total annual research expenditures:* $3.2 million.
Dr. B. Ross Barmish, Chairman, 216-368-2833, *Fax:* 216-368-6888, *E-mail:* brb8@po.cwru.edu.
Application contact: Elizabethanne M. Fuller, Department Assistant, 216-368-4080, *Fax:* 216-368-2668, *E-mail:* emf4@po.cwru.edu. *Web site:* http://eecs.cwru.edu/

■ CLARKSON UNIVERSITY

Graduate School, School of Engineering, Department of Electrical and Computer Engineering, Potsdam, NY 13699

AWARDS Computer engineering (ME, MS); electrical and computer engineering (PhD); electrical engineering (ME, MS). Part-time programs available.

Faculty: 13 full-time (2 women).
Students: 23 full-time (7 women), 17 international. Average age 26. 283 applicants, 55% accepted. In 2001, 18 master's awarded.
Degree requirements: For master's, thesis; for doctorate, thesis/dissertation, departmental qualifying exam. *Median time to degree:* Master's–1.5 years full-time.
Entrance requirements: For master's, GRE, TOEFL. *Application deadline:* For fall admission, 5/15 (priority date); for spring admission, 10/15 (priority date). Applications are processed on a rolling basis. *Application fee:* $25 ($35 for international students).
Expenses: Tuition: Part-time $714 per credit. Required fees: $108 per semester.
Financial support: In 2001–02, 8 students received support, including fellowships (averaging $20,000 per year), 2 research assistantships (averaging $17,000 per year), 6 teaching assistantships (averaging $17,000 per year). Scholarships/grants and tuition waivers (partial) also available.
Faculty research: Robotics, electrical machines, electrical circuits, dielectric liquids, controls, power systems. *Total annual research expenditures:* $324,885.

Dr. Thomas H. Ortmeyer, Chair, 315-268-6511, *Fax:* 315-268-7994.
Application contact: Donna Brockway, Assistant to Dean/Foreign Student Advisor, 315-268-6447, *Fax:* 315-268-7994, *E-mail:* brockway@clarkson.edu.

■ CLEMSON UNIVERSITY

Graduate School, College of Engineering and Science, Department of Electrical and Computer Engineering, Program in Computer Engineering, Clemson, SC 29634

AWARDS MS, PhD.

Students: 32 full-time (3 women), 2 part-time (1 woman), 19 international. 160 applicants, 31% accepted, 15 enrolled. In 2001, 18 master's, 3 doctorates awarded.
Degree requirements: For master's, thesis or alternative; for doctorate, thesis/dissertation, departmental qualifying exam.
Entrance requirements: For master's and doctorate, GRE General Test, TOEFL. *Application deadline:* For fall admission, 6/1. *Application fee:* $40.
Expenses: Tuition, state resident: full-time $5,310. Tuition, nonresident: full-time $11,284.
Financial support: Fellowships, research assistantships, teaching assistantships, career-related internships or fieldwork available. Financial award applicants required to submit FAFSA.
Faculty research: Interface applications, software development, multisystem communications, artificial intelligence, robotics.
Dr. Ernest Baxa, Coordinator, 864-656-5900, *Fax:* 864-656-5910, *E-mail:* ece-grad-program@clemson.edu. *Web site:* http://ece.clemson.edu/

■ CLEVELAND STATE UNIVERSITY

College of Graduate Studies, Fenn College of Engineering, Department of Electrical and Computer Engineering, Cleveland, OH 44115

AWARDS MS, D Eng. Part-time programs available.

Degree requirements: For master's, thesis or extra course work; for doctorate, thesis/dissertation, candidacy and qualifying exams.
Entrance requirements: For master's, GRE General Test, TOEFL, minimum GPA of 3.0; for doctorate, GRE General Test, TOEFL, minimum GPA of 3.5.
Expenses: Tuition, state resident: full-time $6,838; part-time $263 per credit hour. Tuition, nonresident: full-time $13,526; part-time $520 per credit hour.
Faculty research: Computer networks, knowledge-based control systems, artificial intelligence, electromagnetic interference, semiconducting materials for solar cell digital communications. *Web site:* http://csaxp.csuohio.edu/electrical/index.html

■ COLORADO STATE UNIVERSITY

Graduate School, College of Engineering, Department of Electrical and Computer Engineering, Fort Collins, CO 80523-0015

AWARDS M Eng, MS, PhD. Part-time programs available. Postbaccalaureate distance learning degree programs offered (no on-campus study).

Faculty: 19 full-time (1 woman).
Students: 48 full-time (6 women), 104 part-time (14 women); includes 8 minority (5 Asian Americans or Pacific Islanders, 2 Hispanic Americans, 1 Native American), 113 international. Average age 28. 413 applicants, 53% accepted, 57 enrolled. In 2001, 15 master's, 1 doctorate awarded. Terminal master's awarded for partial completion of doctoral program.
Degree requirements: For master's, thesis (for some programs), final exam; for doctorate, thesis/dissertation, qualifying, preliminary, and final exams.
Entrance requirements: For master's, GRE General Test, TOEFL, minimum GPA of 3.0; for doctorate, GRE General Test, TOEFL, minimum GPA of 3.5. *Application deadline:* For fall admission, 2/15 (priority date); for spring admission, 7/15 (priority date). Applications are processed on a rolling basis. *Application fee:* $30. Electronic applications accepted.
Expenses: Tuition, state resident: full-time $2,880; part-time $160 per credit. Tuition, nonresident: full-time $11,412; part-time $634 per credit. Required fees: $750; $34 per credit.
Financial support: In 2001–02, 4 fellowships, 33 research assistantships (averaging $15,060 per year), 4 teaching assistantships (averaging $11,295 per year) were awarded. Career-related internships or fieldwork, Federal Work-Study, institutionally sponsored loans, and traineeships also available.
Faculty research: Communications, optoelectronics, controls and robotics, computer engineering, signal image processing. *Total annual research expenditures:* $3.2 million.
Dr. Derek L. Lile, Head, 970-491-6600, *Fax:* 970-491-2249, *E-mail:* lile@ engr.colostate.edu.
Application contact: Elizabeth L. Wadman, Graduate Coordinator, 970-491-6600, *Fax:* 970-491-6706, *E-mail:* ewadman@engr.colostate.edu. *Web site:* http://www.engr.colostate.edu/depts/ee/index.html

■ COLORADO TECHNICAL UNIVERSITY

Graduate Studies, Program in Computer Engineering, Colorado Springs, CO 80907-3896

AWARDS MSCE. Part-time and evening/weekend programs available.

Faculty: 3 full-time (1 woman), 9 part-time/adjunct (1 woman).
Students: 2 full-time (0 women). Average age 38. 2 applicants, 50% accepted, 1 enrolled. In 2001, 4 degrees awarded.
Degree requirements: For master's, thesis or alternative. *Median time to degree:* Master's–2 years full-time, 3 years part-time.
Application deadline: For fall admission, 10/2; for winter admission, 1/3; for spring admission, 4/3. Applications are processed on a rolling basis. *Application fee:* $100.
Expenses: Tuition: Full-time $6,960; part-time $290 per credit. Required fees: $40 per quarter. One-time fee: $100. Tuition and fees vary according to course load and degree level.
Financial support: Career-related internships or fieldwork and Federal Work-Study available. Financial award applicants required to submit FAFSA.
Alex Dwelis, Dean, 719-590-6791, *Fax:* 719-598-3740, *E-mail:* adwelis@ coloradotech.edu.
Application contact: Judy Galante, Graduate Admissions, 719-590-6720, *Fax:* 719-598-3740, *E-mail:* jgalante@ coloradotech.edu. *Web site:* http://www.coloradotech.edu/

■ CORNELL UNIVERSITY

Graduate School, Graduate Fields of Engineering, Field of Electrical Engineering, Ithaca, NY 14853-0001

AWARDS Computer engineering (M Eng, PhD); electrical engineering (M Eng, PhD); electrical systems (M Eng, PhD); electrophysics (M Eng, PhD).

Faculty: 45 full-time.
Students: 250 full-time (30 women); includes 43 minority (2 African Americans, 37 Asian Americans or Pacific Islanders, 3 Hispanic Americans, 1 Native American), 160 international. 850 applicants, 32% accepted. In 2001, 87 master's, 20 doctorates awarded. Terminal master's awarded for partial completion of doctoral program.
Degree requirements: For doctorate, thesis/dissertation.
Entrance requirements: For master's, GRE General Test, TOEFL, preapplication if currently enrolled at a non-US college or university, 2 letters of recommendation; for doctorate, GRE General Test, TOEFL, preapplication if currently enrolled at a non-US college or university, 3 letters of recommendation. *Application deadline:* For fall admission, 1/15. *Application fee:* $65. Electronic applications accepted.
Expenses: Tuition: Full-time $25,970. Required fees: $50.
Financial support: In 2001–02, 141 students received support, including 22 fellowships with full tuition reimbursements available, 75 research assistantships with full tuition reimbursements available, 44 teaching assistantships with full tuition reimbursements available; institutionally

sponsored loans, scholarships/grants, tuition waivers (full and partial), and unspecified assistantships also available. Financial award applicants required to submit FAFSA.
Faculty research: Communications; information theory. Signal processing, and power control; computer engineering; microelectromechanical systems and nanotechnology.
Application contact: Graduate Field Assistant, 607-255-4304, *E-mail:* meng@ ee.cornell.edu; ms-phd@ee.cornell.edu. *Web site:* http://www.gradschool.cornell.edu/grad/fields_1/elec-engr.html

Find an in-depth description at www.petersons.com/gradchannel.

■ DARTMOUTH COLLEGE

Thayer School of Engineering, Program in Computer Engineering, Hanover, NH 03755

AWARDS MS, PhD.

Degree requirements: For master's, thesis; for doctorate, thesis/dissertation, candidacy oral exam.
Entrance requirements: For master's and doctorate, GRE General Test. *Application deadline:* For fall admission, 1/1 (priority date). *Application fee:* $40 ($50 for international students).
Expenses: Tuition: Full-time $26,425.
Financial support: Fellowships, research assistantships, teaching assistantships, career-related internships or fieldwork, Federal Work-Study, institutionally sponsored loans, and tuition waivers (full and partial) available. Financial award application deadline: 1/15.
Faculty research: Networking and communications, computer architecture, mobile agents, parallel and distributed computing, simulation and performance analysis, VLSI design and testing. *Total annual research expenditures:* $2.5 million.
Application contact: Candace S. Potter, Graduate Admissions Administrator, 603-646-3844, *Fax:* 603-646-1620, *E-mail:* candace.potter@dartmouth.edu. *Web site:* http://engineering.dartmouth.edu/

■ DREXEL UNIVERSITY

Graduate School, College of Engineering, Department of Electrical and Computer Engineering, Program in Computer Engineering, Philadelphia, PA 19104-2875

AWARDS MS. Part-time and evening/weekend programs available.

Faculty: 32 full-time (4 women), 3 part-time/adjunct (0 women).
Students: 6 full-time (1 woman), 9 part-time, 12 international. Average age 25. 21 applicants, 48% accepted, 2 enrolled. In 2001, 2 degrees awarded.
Degree requirements: For master's, thesis (for some programs).

Application deadline: For fall admission, 8/21. Applications are processed on a rolling basis. *Application fee:* $50. Electronic applications accepted.

Expenses: Tuition: Full-time $20,088; part-time $558 per credit. Required fees: $78 per term. One-time fee: $200. Tuition and fees vary according to course load, degree level and program.

Financial support: Career-related internships or fieldwork and unspecified assistantships available. Financial award application deadline: 2/1.

Application contact: Director of Graduate Admissions, 215-895-6700, *Fax:* 215-895-5939, *E-mail:* enroll@drexel.edu.

■ **DUKE UNIVERSITY**

Graduate School, School of Engineering, Department of Electrical and Computer Engineering, Durham, NC 27708-0586

AWARDS MS, PhD. Part-time programs available.

Faculty: 22 full-time, 7 part-time/adjunct.
Students: 93 full-time (22 women); includes 5 minority (4 Asian Americans or Pacific Islanders, 1 Hispanic American), 74 international. 241 applicants, 20% accepted, 28 enrolled. In 2001, 17 master's, 11 doctorates awarded. Terminal master's awarded for partial completion of doctoral program.
Degree requirements: For doctorate, thesis/dissertation.
Entrance requirements: For master's and doctorate, GRE General Test. *Application deadline:* For fall admission, 12/31; for spring admission, 11/1. *Application fee:* $75.
Expenses: Tuition: Full-time $24,600.
Financial support: Fellowships, research assistantships, Federal Work-Study available. Financial award application deadline: 12/31.
Peter Marinos, Director of Graduate Studies, 919-660-5245, *Fax:* 919-660-5293, *E-mail:* joyce@ee.duke.edu. *Web site:* http://www.ee.duke.edu/

Find an in-depth description at www.petersons.com/gradchannel.

■ **FAIRLEIGH DICKINSON UNIVERSITY, METROPOLITAN CAMPUS**

University College: Arts, Sciences, and Professional Studies, School of Engineering and Engineering Technology, Program in Computer Engineering, Teaneck, NJ 07666-1914

AWARDS MS.

Students: 15 full-time (1 woman), 3 part-time (1 woman), 15 international. Average age 25. 42 applicants, 93% accepted, 9 enrolled.
Application deadline: Applications are processed on a rolling basis. *Application fee:* $40.

Expenses: Tuition: Full-time $11,484; part-time $638 per credit. Required fees: $420; $97.
Dr. Alfredo Tan, Director, School of Engineering and Engineering Technology, 201-692-2347, *Fax:* 201-692-2130, *E-mail:* tan@fdu.edu.

■ **FLORIDA ATLANTIC UNIVERSITY**

College of Engineering, Department of Computer Science and Engineering, Program in Computer Engineering, Boca Raton, FL 33431-0991

AWARDS MS, PhD. Part-time and evening/weekend programs available.

Faculty: 11 full-time (1 woman).
Students: 34 full-time (9 women), 20 part-time (6 women); includes 11 minority (1 African American, 8 Asian Americans or Pacific Islanders, 2 Hispanic Americans), 37 international. Average age 31. 35 applicants, 63% accepted, 9 enrolled. In 2001, 26 master's, 1 doctorate awarded. Terminal master's awarded for partial completion of doctoral program.
Degree requirements: For master's, thesis optional; for doctorate, thesis/dissertation, qualifying exam.
Entrance requirements: For master's, GRE General Test, TOEFL, minimum GPA of 3.0; for doctorate, TOEFL, minimum GPA of 3.5, Masters Degree. *Application deadline:* For fall admission, 4/10 (priority date); for spring admission, 10/1. Applications are processed on a rolling basis. *Application fee:* $20.
Expenses: Tuition, state resident: full-time $3,098; part-time $172 per credit. Tuition, nonresident: full-time $10,427; part-time $579 per credit.
Financial support: In 2001–02, 18 research assistantships with partial tuition reimbursements (averaging $10,090 per year), 8 teaching assistantships with full tuition reimbursements (averaging $11,936 per year) were awarded. Fellowships, career-related internships or fieldwork, Federal Work-Study, and unspecified assistantships also available. Support available to part-time students. Financial award application deadline: 4/1; financial award applicants required to submit FAFSA.
Faculty research: VLSI and neural networks, data communications, fault tolerance, data security, parallel systems.
Application contact: Donna Rubinoff, Graduate Admissions Coordinator, 561-297-3855, *Fax:* 561-297-2800, *E-mail:* donna@cse.fau.edu. *Web site:* http://www.fau.edu/

■ **FLORIDA INSTITUTE OF TECHNOLOGY**

Graduate Programs, College of Engineering, Electrical and Computer Engineering Department, Melbourne, FL 32901-6975

AWARDS Computer engineering (MS, PhD); electrical engineering (MS, PhD). Part-time and evening/weekend programs available.

Faculty: 15 full-time (0 women), 7 part-time/adjunct (0 women).
Students: 25 full-time (4 women), 97 part-time (12 women); includes 19 minority (4 African Americans, 9 Asian Americans or Pacific Islanders, 6 Hispanic Americans), 48 international. Average age 31. 331 applicants, 46% accepted. In 2001, 27 master's, 2 doctorates awarded. Terminal master's awarded for partial completion of doctoral program.
Degree requirements: For doctorate, thesis/dissertation, comprehensive exam.
Entrance requirements: For master's, minimum GPA of 3.0; for doctorate, minimum GPA of 3.2. *Application deadline:* Applications are processed on a rolling basis. *Application fee:* $50. Electronic applications accepted.
Expenses: Tuition: Part-time $650 per credit.
Financial support: In 2001–02, 22 students received support, including 5 research assistantships with full and partial tuition reimbursements available (averaging $9,264 per year), 17 teaching assistantships with full and partial tuition reimbursements available (averaging $8,938 per year); tuition remissions also available. Financial award application deadline: 3/1; financial award applicants required to submit FAFSA.
Faculty research: Electro-optics, electromagnetics, microelectronics, communications, computer architecture, neural networks. *Total annual research expenditures:* $658,000.
Dr. Joseph Wheeler, Department Head, 321-674-8060, *Fax:* 321-674-8192, *E-mail:* jwheeler@fit.edu.
Application contact: Carolyn P. Farrior, Director of Graduate Admissions, 321-674-7118, *Fax:* 321-723-9468, *E-mail:* cfarrior@fit.edu. *Web site:* http://www.fit.edu/

Find an in-depth description at www.petersons.com/gradchannel.

■ **FLORIDA INTERNATIONAL UNIVERSITY**

College of Engineering, Department of Electrical Engineering, Program in Computer Engineering, Miami, FL 33199

AWARDS MS. Part-time and evening/weekend programs available.

Students: 28 full-time (4 women), 22 part-time (2 women); includes 19 minority (1

Florida International University
(continued)
African American, 18 Hispanic Americans),
27 international. Average age 30. 65
applicants, 40% accepted, 10 enrolled. In
2001, 5 degrees awarded.
Degree requirements: For master's,
thesis optional.
Entrance requirements: For master's,
GRE General Test, TOEFL. *Application
deadline:* For fall admission, 4/1 (priority
date); for spring admission, 10/1. Applications are processed on a rolling basis.
Application fee: $20.
Expenses: Tuition, state resident: full-time
$2,916; part-time $162 per credit hour.
Tuition, nonresident: full-time $10,245;
part-time $569 per credit hour. Required
fees: $168 per term.
Dr. Kang Yen, Acting Chairperson,
Department of Electrical Engineering,
305-348-2807, *Fax:* 305-348-3707, *E-mail:*
yenk@fiu.edu.

■ GEORGE MASON UNIVERSITY

**School of Information Technology and
Engineering, Department of Electrical
and Computer Engineering, Fairfax,
VA 22030-4444**

AWARDS Electrical and computer engineering
(PhD); electrical engineering (MS). Part-time
and evening/weekend programs available.

Faculty: 23 full-time (2 women), 13 part-
time/adjunct (3 women).
Students: 42 full-time (7 women), 201
part-time (34 women); includes 60 minority (13 African Americans, 37 Asian
Americans or Pacific Islanders, 10
Hispanic Americans), 76 international.
Average age 31. 177 applicants, 84%
accepted. In 2001, 20 master's, 2 doctorates awarded.
Degree requirements: For master's,
thesis optional; for doctorate, thesis/
dissertation, comprehensive oral and written exams.
Entrance requirements: For master's,
GMAT or GRE General Test, TOEFL,
bachelor's degree in electrical engineering
or related field, minimum GPA of 3.0 in
last 60 hours. *Application deadline:* For fall
admission, 5/1; for spring admission, 11/1.
Application fee: $30. Electronic applications
accepted.
Expenses: Tuition, state resident: full-time
$3,168; part-time $132 per credit hour.
Tuition, nonresident: full-time $11,280;
part-time $470 per credit hour. Required
fees: $1,416; $59 per credit hour.
Financial support: Fellowships, research
assistantships, teaching assistantships,
career-related internships or fieldwork and
Federal Work-Study available. Support
available to part-time students. Financial
award application deadline: 3/1; financial
award applicants required to submit
FAFSA.
Faculty research: Communication
networks, signal processing, system failure

diagnosis, multiprocessors, material
processing using microwave energy.
Dr. Andre Manitius, Chairperson, 703-
993-1569, *Fax:* 703-993-1601, *E-mail:*
ece@gmu.edu. *Web site:* http://
ece.gmu.edu/

■ THE GEORGE WASHINGTON UNIVERSITY

**School of Engineering and Applied
Science, Department of Electrical and
Computer Engineering, Washington,
DC 20052**

AWARDS MS, D Sc, App Sc, Engr, MEM/MS.
Part-time and evening/weekend programs
available.

Faculty: 21 full-time (2 women), 10 part-
time/adjunct (0 women).
Students: 107 full-time (12 women), 172
part-time (38 women); includes 58 minority (20 African Americans, 30 Asian
Americans or Pacific Islanders, 7 Hispanic
Americans, 1 Native American), 118
international. Average age 32. 300
applicants, 95% accepted. In 2001, 90
master's, 6 doctorates, 2 other advanced
degrees awarded.
Degree requirements: For master's,
thesis optional; for doctorate and other
advanced degree, dissertation defense,
qualifying exam.
Entrance requirements: For master's,
TOEFL or George Washington University
English as a Foreign Language Test,
appropriate bachelor's degree, minimum
GPA of 3.0; for doctorate, TOEFL or
George Washington University English as
a Foreign Language Test, appropriate
bachelor's or master's degree, minimum
GPA of 3.3, GRE required if highest
earned degree is BS; for other advanced
degree, TOEFL or George Washington
University English as a Foreign Language
Test, appropriate master's degree,
minimum GPA of 3.0. *Application deadline:*
For fall admission, 3/1 (priority date); for
spring admission, 10/1. Applications are
processed on a rolling basis. *Application fee:*
$55.
Expenses: Tuition: Part-time $810 per
credit. Required fees: $1 per credit.
Financial support: In 2001–02, 15 fellowships with tuition reimbursements (averaging $5,300 per year), 17 teaching
assistantships with tuition reimbursements
(averaging $5,200 per year) were awarded.
Research assistantships, career-related
internships or fieldwork and institutionally
sponsored loans also available. Financial
award application deadline: 3/1; financial
award applicants required to submit
FAFSA.
Faculty research: Computer graphics,
multimedia systems.
Dr. Branimir Vojcic, Chair, 202-994-4874,
Fax: 202-994-0227, *E-mail:* eecs@
seas.gwu.edu.
Application contact: Howard M. Davis,
Manager, Office of Admissions and

Student Records, 202-994-6158, *Fax:* 202-
994-0909, *E-mail:* data:adms@
seas.gwu.edu. *Web site:* http://
www.gwu.edu/~gradinfo/

**Find an in-depth description at
www.petersons.com/gradchannel.**

■ GEORGIA INSTITUTE OF TECHNOLOGY

**Graduate Studies and Research,
College of Engineering, School of
Electrical and Computer Engineering,
Atlanta, GA 30332-0001**

AWARDS MS, MSEE, PhD. Part-time
programs available. Postbaccalaureate
distance learning degree programs offered.
Terminal master's awarded for partial completion of doctoral program.

Degree requirements: For master's,
thesis optional; for doctorate, thesis/
dissertation.
Entrance requirements: For master's,
GRE General Test, TOEFL, minimum
GPA of 3.0; for doctorate, GRE General
Test, TOEFL, minimum GPA of 3.5.
Faculty research: Telecommunications,
computer systems, microelectronics, opti-
cal engineering, digital signal processing.
Web site: http://www.ee.gatech.edu/

**Find an in-depth description at
www.petersons.com/gradchannel.**

■ ILLINOIS INSTITUTE OF TECHNOLOGY

**Graduate College, Armour College of
Engineering and Sciences,
Department of Electrical and
Computer Engineering, Chicago, IL
60616-3793**

AWARDS Computer systems engineering
(MS); electrical and computer engineering
(MECE); electrical engineering (MS, PhD);
manufacturing engineering (MME, MS). Part-
time and evening/weekend programs available.

Faculty: 20 full-time (2 women), 7 part-
time/adjunct (0 women).
Students: 157 full-time (26 women), 212
part-time (21 women); includes 34 minority (4 African Americans, 21 Asian
Americans or Pacific Islanders, 9 Hispanic
Americans), 259 international. Average age
27. 1,295 applicants, 52% accepted. In
2001, 93 master's, 8 doctorates awarded.
Terminal master's awarded for partial
completion of doctoral program.
Degree requirements: For master's,
thesis (for some programs), comprehensive
exam; for doctorate, thesis/dissertation,
comprehensive exam.
Entrance requirements: For master's and
doctorate, GRE General Test, TOEFL,
minimum undergraduate GPA of 3.0.
Application deadline: For fall admission, 7/1;
for spring admission, 12/1. Applications
are processed on a rolling basis. *Application
fee:* $30. Electronic applications accepted.

Expenses: Tuition: Part-time $590 per credit hour.
Financial support: In 2001–02, 13 research assistantships, 19 teaching assistantships were awarded. Federal Work-Study, institutionally sponsored loans, scholarships/grants, and unspecified assistantships also available. Support available to part-time students. Financial award application deadline: 3/1; financial award applicants required to submit FAFSA.
Faculty research: Computer system design, photonics, biomedical engineering, power systems analysis, communications theory. *Total annual research expenditures:* $585,216.
Dr. Thomas Wong, Interim Chairman, 312-567-5786, *Fax:* 312-567-8976, *E-mail:* wong@iit.edu.
Application contact: Dr. Ali Cinar, Dean of Graduate College, 312-567-3637, *Fax:* 312-567-7517, *E-mail:* gradstu@iit.edu. *Web site:* http://www.ece.iit.edu/

■ INDIANA STATE UNIVERSITY

School of Graduate Studies, School of Technology, Department of Electronics and Computer Technology, Terre Haute, IN 47809-1401

AWARDS MA, MS.

Degree requirements: For master's, thesis.
Entrance requirements: For master's, TOEFL, bachelor's degree in industrial technology or related field, minimum undergraduate GPA of 2.5. Electronic applications accepted.

■ INTERNATIONAL TECHNOLOGICAL UNIVERSITY

Program in Computer Engineering, Santa Clara, CA 95050

AWARDS MSCE.

Faculty: 1 full-time (0 women), 15 part-time/adjunct (3 women).
Students: 7 full-time (1 woman), 2 part-time (1 woman). In 2001, 3 degrees awarded.
Degree requirements: For master's, thesis or alternative.
Entrance requirements: For master's, TOEFL, 3 semesters of calculus, minimum GPA of 2.5. *Application deadline:* For fall admission, 8/31 (priority date); for winter admission, 12/31 (priority date); for spring admission, 3/30 (priority date). *Application fee:* $30 ($80 for international students).
Expenses: Tuition: Full-time $6,800; part-time $425 per unit.
Faculty research: Computer networking management, digital systems, embedded system design.
Dr. Russell Quong, Chairman of Computer Engineering, 408-556-9010, *Fax:* 408-556-9012.

Application contact: Dr. Chun-Mou Peng, Director of Research and Development Center, 408-556-9010, *Fax:* 408-556-9212, *E-mail:* chunmou@itu.edu. *Web site:* http://www.itu.edu/

■ IOWA STATE UNIVERSITY OF SCIENCE AND TECHNOLOGY

Graduate College, College of Engineering, Department of Electrical and Computer Engineering, Ames, IA 50011

AWARDS Computer engineering (MS, PhD); electrical engineering (MS, PhD).

Faculty: 41 full-time, 7 part-time/adjunct.
Students: 193 full-time (34 women), 70 part-time (14 women); includes 9 minority (5 African Americans, 3 Asian Americans or Pacific Islanders, 1 Hispanic American), 179 international. 833 applicants, 11% accepted, 59 enrolled. In 2001, 64 master's, 20 doctorates awarded.
Degree requirements: For master's, thesis or alternative; for doctorate, thesis/dissertation. *Median time to degree:* Master's–2.3 years full-time; doctorate–4.5 years full-time.
Entrance requirements: For master's and doctorate, GRE General Test, TOEFL or IELTS. *Application deadline:* For fall admission, 1/15 (priority date); for spring admission, 9/15. *Application fee:* $20 ($50 for international students). Electronic applications accepted.
Expenses: Tuition, state resident: full-time $1,851. Tuition, nonresident: full-time $5,449. Tuition and fees vary according to program.
Financial support: In 2001–02, 146 research assistantships with partial tuition reimbursements (averaging $13,060 per year), 48 teaching assistantships with partial tuition reimbursements (averaging $12,208 per year) were awarded. Fellowships, scholarships/grants, health care benefits, and unspecified assistantships also available.
Dr. S. S. Venkata, Chair, 515-294-2667, *E-mail:* ecegrad@ee.iastate.edu.
Application contact: Dr. Vijay Vittal, Director of Graduate Education, 515-294-2667, *E-mail:* ecegrad@ee.iastate.edu. *Web site:* http://www.eng.iastate.edu/coe/grad.asp/

■ JOHNS HOPKINS UNIVERSITY

G. W. C. Whiting School of Engineering, Department of Electrical and Computer Engineering, Baltimore, MD 21218-2699

AWARDS MSE, PhD. Part-time programs available.

Faculty: 17 full-time (0 women), 8 part-time/adjunct (0 women).
Students: 73 full-time (17 women), 13 part-time (2 women); includes 4 minority (1 Asian American or Pacific Islander, 3 Hispanic Americans), 52 international.

Average age 28. 388 applicants, 17% accepted, 29 enrolled. In 2001, 34 master's, 8 doctorates awarded. Terminal master's awarded for partial completion of doctoral program.
Degree requirements: For doctorate, thesis/dissertation, oral exam.
Entrance requirements: For master's and doctorate, GRE General Test, TOEFL. *Application deadline:* For fall admission, 1/15. Applications are processed on a rolling basis. *Application fee:* $0. Electronic applications accepted.
Expenses: Tuition: Full-time $27,390.
Financial support: In 2001–02, 86 students received support, including 2 fellowships with full tuition reimbursements available (averaging $16,000 per year), 50 research assistantships with full tuition reimbursements available (averaging $16,000 per year), 20 teaching assistantships with full tuition reimbursements available (averaging $16,000 per year); Federal Work-Study, institutionally sponsored loans, scholarships/grants, and unspecified assistantships also available. Financial award application deadline: 1/1.
Faculty research: Computer engineering, systems and control, speech and image processing, quantum electronics, analog and digital VLSI sensors and devices. *Total annual research expenditures:* $2 million.
Dr. Gerard G. L. Meyer, Chair, 410-516-7003, *Fax:* 410-516-5566, *E-mail:* gglmeyer@jhu.edu.
Application contact: Gail M. O'Connor, Academic Coordinator II, 410-516-4808, *Fax:* 410-516-5566, *E-mail:* ecegrad@jhu.edu. *Web site:* http://www.ece.jhu.edu/

Find an in-depth description at www.petersons.com/gradchannel.

■ KANSAS STATE UNIVERSITY

Graduate School, College of Engineering, Department of Electrical and Computer Engineering, Manhattan, KS 66506

AWARDS Bioengineering (MS, PhD); communications (MS, PhD); computer engineering (MS, PhD); control systems (MS, PhD); electric energy systems (MS, PhD); instrumentation (MS, PhD). Signal processing (MS, PhD). Postbaccalaureate distance learning degree programs offered (no on-campus study).

Faculty: 22 full-time (3 women).
Students: 34 full-time (8 women), 15 part-time (1 woman); includes 1 minority (Hispanic American), 23 international. 325 applicants, 8% accepted, 16 enrolled. In 2001, 15 master's, 4 doctorates awarded.
Degree requirements: For master's, thesis or alternative, final exam; for doctorate, thesis/dissertation, preliminary exams.
Entrance requirements: For master's, GRE General Test, TOEFL, bachelor's degree in electrical engineering or computer science; minimum GPA of 3.0; for doctorate, GRE General Test,

Kansas State University (continued)
TOEFL. *Application deadline:* For fall admission, 3/1; for spring admission, 9/1. Applications are processed on a rolling basis. *Application fee:* $0 ($25 for international students). Electronic applications accepted.

Expenses: Tuition, state resident: part-time $113 per credit hour. Tuition, nonresident: part-time $358 per credit hour.

Financial support: In 2001–02, 17 research assistantships with partial tuition reimbursements (averaging $9,900 per year), 7 teaching assistantships with full tuition reimbursements (averaging $9,900 per year) were awarded. Career-related internships or fieldwork, institutionally sponsored loans, and scholarships/grants also available. Support available to part-time students. Financial award application deadline: 3/1; financial award applicants required to submit FAFSA.

Faculty research: Communications systems and signal processing, real-time embedded systems, integrated circuits and devices, bioengineering, power systems. *Total annual research expenditures:* $1.3 million.

Dr. David Soldan, Head, 785-532-5600, *Fax:* 785-532-1188, *E-mail:* grad@eece.ksu.edu.

Application contact: Anil Pahwa, Graduate Program Director, 785-532-5600, *Fax:* 785-532-1188, *E-mail:* pahw@ksu.edu. *Web site:* http://www.eece.ksu.edu/

■ LAWRENCE TECHNOLOGICAL UNIVERSITY

College of Engineering, Southfield, MI 48075-1058

AWARDS Automotive engineering (MAE); civil engineering (MCE); electrical and computer engineering (MS); manufacturing systems (MEMS, DE). Part-time and evening/weekend programs available.

Faculty: 27 full-time (2 women), 11 part-time/adjunct (1 woman).

Students: Average age 32. 133 applicants, 38 enrolled. In 2001, 43 degrees awarded. *Application deadline:* For fall admission, 8/1 (priority date); for winter admission, 12/1 (priority date); for spring admission, 5/1. Applications are processed on a rolling basis. *Application fee:* $50. Electronic applications accepted.

Expenses: Tuition: Part-time $460 per credit hour.

Financial support: Institutionally sponsored loans available. Support available to part-time students. Financial award application deadline: 3/1; financial award applicants required to submit FAFSA.

Faculty research: Advanced composite materials in bridges, strengthening existing bridges with carbon and glass fiber sheets, development of drive shafts using composite materials. *Total annual research expenditures:* $150,000.

Dr. Laird Johnston, Dean, 248-204-2500, *Fax:* 248-204-2509, *E-mail:* lejohnston@ltu.edu.

Application contact: Jane Rohrback, Interim Director of Admissions, 248-204-3160, *Fax:* 248-204-3188, *E-mail:* admission@ltu.edu.

■ LEHIGH UNIVERSITY

P.C. Rossin College of Engineering and Applied Science, Department of Electrical and Computer Engineering, Program in Computer Engineering, Bethlehem, PA 18015-3094

AWARDS MS. Part-time programs available.

Faculty: 2 full-time (0 women).
Students: 12 full-time (0 women), 7 part-time; includes 5 minority (all Asian Americans or Pacific Islanders), 3 international. Average age 24. 41 applicants, 20% accepted. In 2001, 3 degrees awarded.

Degree requirements: For master's, oral presentation of thesis. *Median time to degree:* Master's–2 years full-time.

Entrance requirements: For master's, GRE General Test, TOEFL, minimum GPA of 3.0. *Application deadline:* For fall admission, 4/15; for spring admission, 11/1. Applications are processed on a rolling basis. *Application fee:* $50. Electronic applications accepted.

Expenses: Tuition: Part-time $468 per credit hour. Required fees: $200; $100 per semester. Tuition and fees vary according to program.

Financial support: In 2001–02, 1 fellowship with full tuition reimbursement (averaging $15,000 per year), 5 research assistantships with full tuition reimbursements (averaging $11,700 per year), 2 teaching assistantships with full tuition reimbursements (averaging $12,330 per year) were awarded. Financial award application deadline: 1/15.

Application contact: Anne Nierer, Graduate Coordinator, 610-758-4072, *Fax:* 610-758-6279, *E-mail:* aln3@lehigh.edu. *Web site:* http://www.eecs.lehigh.edu/

Find an in-depth description at www.petersons.com/gradchannel.

■ LOUISIANA STATE UNIVERSITY AND AGRICULTURAL AND MECHANICAL COLLEGE

Graduate School, College of Engineering, Department of Electrical and Computer Engineering, Baton Rouge, LA 70803

AWARDS MSEE, PhD.

Faculty: 18 full-time (0 women).
Students: 67 full-time (17 women), 11 part-time (2 women); includes 1 minority (Asian American or Pacific Islander), 68 international. Average age 26. 261 applicants, 39% accepted, 26 enrolled. In 2001, 30 master's, 2 doctorates awarded.

Terminal master's awarded for partial completion of doctoral program.

Degree requirements: For master's, thesis optional; for doctorate, thesis/dissertation.

Entrance requirements: For master's, GRE General Test, TOEFL, minimum GPA of 3.0; for doctorate, GRE General Test, TOEFL, minimum GPA of 3.5. *Application deadline:* For fall admission, 1/25 (priority date). Applications are processed on a rolling basis. *Application fee:* $25.

Expenses: Tuition, state resident: full-time $2,551. Tuition, nonresident: full-time $5,551. Required fees: $854. Part-time tuition and fees vary according to course load.

Financial support: In 2001–02, 13 research assistantships with partial tuition reimbursements (averaging $12,850 per year), 29 teaching assistantships with partial tuition reimbursements (averaging $12,112 per year) were awarded. Fellowships, institutionally sponsored loans and unspecified assistantships also available. Financial award application deadline: 2/28; financial award applicants required to submit FAFSA.

Faculty research: Electronics, power engineering, systems and signal processing, communications. *Total annual research expenditures:* $708,704.

Dr. Alan H. Marshak, Chair, 225-578-5243, *Fax:* 225-578-5200, *E-mail:* amarsh5@lsu.edu.

Application contact: Dr. Jorge L. Aravena, Graduate Adviser, 225-578-5478, *Fax:* 225-578-5200, *E-mail:* eearav@lsu.edu. *Web site:* http://www.ee.lsu.edu/

Find an in-depth description at www.petersons.com/gradchannel.

■ MANHATTAN COLLEGE

Graduate Division, School of Engineering, Program in Computer Engineering, Riverdale, NY 10471

AWARDS MS. Part-time and evening/weekend programs available.

Degree requirements: For master's, thesis or alternative.

Entrance requirements: For master's, GRE, TOEFL, minimum GPA of 3.0.

■ MARQUETTE UNIVERSITY

Graduate School, College of Engineering, Department of Electrical and Computer Engineering, Milwaukee, WI 53201-1881

AWARDS Computing (MS); electrical engineering (MS, PhD). Part-time and evening/weekend programs available.

Faculty: 4 full-time (2 women), 2 part-time/adjunct (0 women).
Students: 37 full-time (8 women), 67 part-time (12 women); includes 12 minority (6 African Americans, 5 Asian Americans or Pacific Islanders, 1 Hispanic American), 41

international. Average age 25. 83 applicants, 42% accepted. In 2001, 11 master's, 2 doctorates awarded. Terminal master's awarded for partial completion of doctoral program.

Degree requirements: For master's, thesis optional; for doctorate, dissertation defense, qualifying exam.

Entrance requirements: For master's, TOEFL, GRE General Test or minimum GPA of 3.0; for doctorate, GRE General Test, TOEFL. *Application deadline:* For fall admission, 7/15 (priority date); for spring admission, 11/15. Applications are processed on a rolling basis. *Application fee:* $40. Electronic applications accepted.

Expenses: Tuition: Full-time $10,170; part-time $445 per credit hour. Tuition and fees vary according to course load.

Financial support: In 2001–02, 16 students received support, including 6 fellowships with full tuition reimbursements available (averaging $18,000 per year), 7 research assistantships with full tuition reimbursements available (averaging $12,000 per year), 14 teaching assistantships with full tuition reimbursements available (averaging $10,025 per year); Federal Work-Study, institutionally sponsored loans, and scholarships/grants also available. Financial award application deadline: 2/15.

Faculty research: Electric machines, drives, and controls; applied solid-state electronics; computers and signal processing; microwaves and antennas. Solid state devices and acoustic wave sensors. *Total annual research expenditures:* $750,000.

Dr. Edwin E. Yaz, Chair, 414-288-6820, *Fax:* 414-288-5579, *E-mail:* edwin.yaz@ marquette.edu.

Application contact: Dr. Fabien J. Josse, Director of Graduate Studies, 414-288-6789, *Fax:* 414-288-5579, *E-mail:* fabien.josse@marquette.edu. *Web site:* http://www.eng.mu.edu/departments/eece/

Find an in-depth description at www.petersons.com/gradchannel.

■ MICHIGAN STATE UNIVERSITY

Graduate School, College of Engineering, Department of Electrical and Computer Engineering, East Lansing, MI 48824

AWARDS MS, PhD.

Faculty: 25.

Students: 107 full-time (18 women), 62 part-time (13 women); includes 37 minority (14 African Americans, 11 Asian Americans or Pacific Islanders, 12 Hispanic Americans), 97 international. Average age 26. 852 applicants, 16% accepted. In 2001, 67 master's, 10 doctorates awarded.

Degree requirements: For master's, exit exam, thesis optional; for doctorate, thesis/dissertation, qualifying exams, comprehensive exam.

Entrance requirements: For master's and doctorate, GRE General Test, TOEFL.

Application deadline: Applications are processed on a rolling basis. *Application fee:* $30 ($40 for international students). Electronic applications accepted.

Expenses: Tuition, state resident: part-time $244 per credit hour. Tuition, nonresident: part-time $494 per credit hour. Required fees: $268 per semester. Tuition and fees vary according to course load, degree level and program.

Financial support: In 2001–02, 53 fellowships (averaging $3,861 per year), 40 research assistantships with tuition reimbursements (averaging $13,811 per year), 28 teaching assistantships with tuition reimbursements (averaging $12,896 per year) were awarded. Financial award applicants required to submit FAFSA.

Faculty research: Computer-aided engineering, electromagnetics, robotics. *Total annual research expenditures:* $1.4 million.

Dr. Satish Udpa, Interim Chair, 517-355-5066, *Fax:* 517-353-1980.

Application contact: Graduate Coordinator, 517-353-6773, *E-mail:* ece_mailbox@ egr.msu.edu. *Web site:* http://www.egr.msu.edu/ece/

■ MICHIGAN TECHNOLOGICAL UNIVERSITY

Graduate School, College of Engineering, Department of Electrical and Computer Engineering, Program in Computational Science and Engineering, Houghton, MI 49931-1295

AWARDS PhD. Part-time programs available.

Degree requirements: For doctorate, thesis/dissertation.

Electronic applications accepted.

Find an in-depth description at www.petersons.com/gradchannel.

■ MISSISSIPPI STATE UNIVERSITY

College of Engineering, Department of Electrical and Computer Engineering, Mississippi State, MS 39762

AWARDS Computer engineering (MS, PhD); electrical engineering (MS, PhD). Part-time programs available. Postbaccalaureate distance learning degree programs offered (minimal on-campus study).

Faculty: 24 full-time (3 women), 3 part-time/adjunct (0 women).

Students: 132 full-time (17 women), 50 part-time (8 women); includes 10 minority (4 African Americans, 4 Asian Americans or Pacific Islanders, 1 Hispanic American, 1 Native American), 136 international. Average age 26. 399 applicants, 80% accepted, 50 enrolled. In 2001, 38 master's, 2 doctorates awarded. Terminal master's awarded for partial completion of doctoral program.

Degree requirements: For master's, thesis optional; for doctorate, thesis/

dissertation, comprehensive oral and written exam, comprehensive exam, registration.

Entrance requirements: For master's, GRE General Test, TOEFL, minimum Undergraduate GPA of 3.00; for doctorate, GRE, TOEFL, minimum graduate GPA of 3.5. *Application deadline:* For fall admission, 7/1; for spring admission, 11/1. Applications are processed on a rolling basis. *Application fee:* $25 for international students. Electronic applications accepted.

Expenses: Tuition, state resident: full-time $3,586; part-time $150 per credit hour. Tuition, nonresident: full-time $8,128; part-time $339 per credit hour. Tuition and fees vary according to course load and campus/location.

Financial support: In 2001–02, 6 fellowships (averaging $5,000 per year), 35 research assistantships with full tuition reimbursements (averaging $12,000 per year), 23 teaching assistantships with full tuition reimbursements (averaging $12,000 per year) were awarded. Federal Work-Study, institutionally sponsored loans, scholarships/grants, and unspecified assistantships also available. Financial award application deadline: 4/1; financial award applicants required to submit FAFSA.

Faculty research: Digital computing, power, controls, communication systems, microelectronics. *Total annual research expenditures:* $7.1 million.

Dr. G. Marshall Molen, Head, 662-325-3912, *Fax:* 662-325-2298, *E-mail:* molen@ ece.msstate.edu.

Application contact: Jerry B. Inmon, Director of Admissions, 662-325-2224, *Fax:* 662-325-7360, *E-mail:* admit@ admissions.msstate.edu. *Web site:* http://www.ece.msstate.edu/

Find an in-depth description at www.petersons.com/gradchannel.

■ NATIONAL TECHNOLOGICAL UNIVERSITY

Programs in Engineering, Fort Collins, CO 80526-1842

AWARDS Chemical engineering (MS); computer engineering (MS); computer science (MS); electrical engineering (MS); engineering management (MS); environmental systems management (MS); management of technology (MS); manufacturing systems engineering (MS); materials science and engineering (MS); mechanical engineering (MS); microelectronics and semiconductor engineering (MS). Software engineering (MS). Special majors (MS). Systems engineering (MS). Part-time programs available. Postbaccalaureate distance learning degree programs offered (no on-campus study).

Students: In 2001, 114 degrees awarded.

Degree requirements: For master's, comprehensive exam.

Entrance requirements: For master's, BS in engineering or related field; 2.9

National Technological University (continued)

minimum GPA. *Application deadline:* Applications are processed on a rolling basis. *Application fee:* $50. Electronic applications accepted.

Expenses: Tuition: Part-time $660 per credit hour. Part-time tuition and fees vary according to course load, campus/location and program.

Dr. Andre Vacroux, President, 970-495-6400, *Fax:* 970-484-0668, *E-mail:* andre@ntu.edu.

Application contact: Rhonda Bonham, Admissions Officer, 970-495-6400, *Fax:* 970-498-0601, *E-mail:* rhonda@ntu.edu. *Web site:* http://www.ntu.edu/

■ NAVAL POSTGRADUATE SCHOOL

Graduate Programs, Department of Electrical and Computer Engineering, Monterey, CA 93943

AWARDS MS, PhD, Eng. Program only open to commissioned officers of the United States and friendly nations and selected United States federal civilian employees. Part-time programs available. Postbaccalaureate distance learning degree programs offered (minimal on-campus study).

Degree requirements: For master's and Eng, thesis; for doctorate, one foreign language, thesis/dissertation.

■ NEW JERSEY INSTITUTE OF TECHNOLOGY

Office of Graduate Studies, Department of Electrical and Computer Engineering, Program in Computer Engineering, Newark, NJ 07102

AWARDS MS, PhD. Part-time and evening/weekend programs available.

Students: 65 full-time (14 women), 41 part-time (7 women); includes 31 minority (8 African Americans, 19 Asian Americans or Pacific Islanders, 4 Hispanic Americans), 58 international. Average age 28. 233 applicants, 54% accepted, 38 enrolled. In 2001, 42 degrees awarded. Terminal master's awarded for partial completion of doctoral program.

Degree requirements: For master's, thesis, residency.

Entrance requirements: For master's, GRE General Test; for doctorate, GRE General Test, minimum graduate GPA of 3.5. *Application deadline:* For fall admission, 6/5; for spring admission, 10/15. Applications are processed on a rolling basis. *Application fee:* $50. Electronic applications accepted.

Expenses: Tuition, state resident: full-time $7,812; part-time $434 per credit. Tuition, nonresident: full-time $10,746; part-time $597 per credit. Required fees: $47 per credit. $76 per semester.

Financial support: Fellowships with full and partial tuition reimbursements, research assistantships with full and partial tuition reimbursements, teaching assistantships with full and partial tuition reimbursements, career-related internships or fieldwork, Federal Work-Study, institutionally sponsored loans, and unspecified assistantships available. Financial award application deadline: 3/15.

Application contact: Kathryn Kelly, Director of Admissions, 973-596-3300, *Fax:* 973-596-3461, *E-mail:* admissions@njit.edu. *Web site:* http://www.njit.edu/

■ NEW JERSEY INSTITUTE OF TECHNOLOGY

Office of Graduate Studies, Department of Electrical and Computer Engineering, Program in Internet Engineering, Newark, NJ 07102

AWARDS MS. Part-time and evening/weekend programs available.

Students: 9 applicants, 56% accepted, 3 enrolled.

Entrance requirements: For master's, GRE General Test. *Application deadline:* For fall admission, 6/5 (priority date); for spring admission, 10/15. Applications are processed on a rolling basis. *Application fee:* $50. Electronic applications accepted.

Expenses: Tuition, state resident: full-time $7,812; part-time $434 per credit. Tuition, nonresident: full-time $10,746; part-time $597 per credit. Required fees: $47 per credit. $76 per semester.

Financial support: Fellowships with full and partial tuition reimbursements, research assistantships with full and partial tuition reimbursements, teaching assistantships with full and partial tuition reimbursements, career-related internships or fieldwork, Federal Work-Study, institutionally sponsored loans, and unspecified assistantships available. Financial award application deadline: 3/15.

Application contact: Kathryn Kelly, Director of Admissions, 973-596-3300, *Fax:* 973-596-3461, *E-mail:* admissions@njit.edu. *Web site:* http://www.njit.edu/

■ NEW MEXICO STATE UNIVERSITY

Graduate School, College of Engineering, Klipsch School of Electrical and Computer Engineering, Las Cruces, NM 88003-8001

AWARDS MSEE, PhD. Part-time programs available.

Faculty: 21 full-time (0 women), 3 part-time/adjunct (0 women).

Students: 81 full-time (13 women), 52 part-time (5 women); includes 24 minority (1 African American, 2 Asian Americans or Pacific Islanders, 19 Hispanic Americans, 2 Native Americans), 76 international. Average age 29. 168 applicants, 79% accepted,

37 enrolled. In 2001, 20 master's, 6 doctorates awarded.

Degree requirements: For master's, thesis (for some programs); for doctorate, 2 foreign languages, thesis/dissertation, comprehensive exam.

Entrance requirements: For master's, GRE, minimum GPA of 3.0; for doctorate, departmental qualifying exam, minimum GPA of 3.0. *Application deadline:* For fall admission, 7/1 (priority date); for spring admission, 11/1. Applications are processed on a rolling basis. *Application fee:* $15 ($35 for international students). Electronic applications accepted.

Expenses: Tuition, state resident: full-time $3,234; part-time $135 per credit. Tuition, nonresident: full-time $9,420; part-time $428 per credit. Required fees: $858.

Financial support: In 2001–02, 60 students received support, including 25 research assistantships with partial tuition reimbursements available, 33 teaching assistantships with partial tuition reimbursements available; fellowships, career-related internships or fieldwork, Federal Work-Study, and unspecified assistantships also available. Support available to part-time students. Financial award application deadline: 3/1.

Faculty research: Software engineering, high performance computing, telemetering and space telecommunications, computational electromagnetics.

Dr. Steven P. Castillo, Head, 505-646-3115, *Fax:* 505-646-1435, *E-mail:* scastill@nmsu.edu.

Application contact: Dr. Javin M. Taylor, Associate Department Head, 505-646-3115, *Fax:* 505-646-1435, *E-mail:* jtaylor@nmsu.edu. *Web site:* http://gauss.nmsu.edu:8000/

■ NEW YORK INSTITUTE OF TECHNOLOGY

Graduate Division, School of Engineering and Technology, Program in Electrical Engineering and Computer Engineering, Old Westbury, NY 11568-8000

AWARDS MS. Part-time and evening/weekend programs available.

Students: 32 full-time (2 women), 28 part-time; includes 15 minority (6 African Americans, 8 Asian Americans or Pacific Islanders, 1 Hispanic American), 23 international. Average age 30. 91 applicants, 64% accepted, 16 enrolled. In 2001, 16 degrees awarded.

Degree requirements: For master's, project.

Entrance requirements: For master's, GRE General Test, TOEFL, BS in electrical engineering or related field, minimum QPA of 2.85. *Application deadline:* For fall admission, 7/1 (priority date); for spring admission, 12/1 (priority date). Applications are processed on a rolling basis. *Application fee:* $50. Electronic applications accepted.

Expenses: Tuition: Part-time $545 per credit. Tuition and fees vary according to course load, degree level, program and student level.

Financial support: In 2001–02, 3 research assistantships with partial tuition reimbursements were awarded; fellowships, institutionally sponsored loans, tuition waivers (full and partial), and unspecified assistantships also available. Support available to part-time students. Financial award applicants required to submit FAFSA.

Faculty research: Computer networks, control theory, light waves and optics, robotics, signal processing.

Dr. Ayat Jafari, Chair, 516-686-7523, *E-mail:* ajafari@nyit.edu.

Application contact: Jacquelyn Nealon, Dean of Admissions and Financial Aid, 516-686-7925, *Fax:* 516-686-7613, *E-mail:* jnealon@nyit.edu.

■ NORTH CAROLINA STATE UNIVERSITY

Graduate School, College of Engineering, Department of Electrical and Computer Engineering, Program in Computer Engineering, Raleigh, NC 27695

AWARDS MS, PhD.

Faculty: 50 full-time (3 women), 41 part-time/adjunct (3 women).

Students: 139 full-time (35 women), 52 part-time (6 women); includes 27 minority (5 African Americans, 19 Asian Americans or Pacific Islanders, 2 Hispanic Americans, 1 Native American), 110 international. Average age 27. 201 applicants, 54% accepted. In 2001, 64 master's, 5 doctorates awarded.

Application fee: $45.

Expenses: Tuition, state resident: full-time $1,748. Tuition, nonresident: full-time $6,904.

Financial support: In 2001–02, 2 fellowships (averaging $5,274 per year), 26 research assistantships (averaging $5,756 per year), 34 teaching assistantships (averaging $5,215 per year) were awarded. *Total annual research expenditures:* $14.7 million.

Dr. Winser E. Alexander, Director of Graduate Programs, 919-515-5091, *Fax:* 919-515-5601, *E-mail:* jbrisen@eos.ncsu.edu.

■ NORTH DAKOTA STATE UNIVERSITY

The Graduate School, College of Engineering and Architecture, Department of Electrical and Computer Engineering, Fargo, ND 58105

AWARDS MS.

Faculty: 16 full-time (1 woman), 2 part-time/adjunct (0 women).

Students: 6 full-time (2 women), 13 part-time, 13 international. Average age 28. 31

applicants, 71% accepted. In 2001, 3 degrees awarded.

Degree requirements: For master's, thesis or alternative.

Entrance requirements: For master's, TOEFL. *Application deadline:* For fall admission, 3/1 (priority date). Applications are processed on a rolling basis. *Application fee:* $35.

Expenses: Tuition, state resident: part-time $124 per credit. Tuition, nonresident: part-time $325 per credit. Required fees: $22 per credit. Tuition and fees vary according to reciprocity agreements.

Financial support: In 2001–02, 2 fellowships with tuition reimbursements (averaging $25,000 per year), research assistantships with tuition reimbursements (averaging $8,100 per year), teaching assistantships with tuition reimbursements (averaging $8,100 per year) were awarded. Career-related internships or fieldwork, Federal Work-Study, institutionally sponsored loans, and tuition waivers (full) also available. Financial award application deadline: 4/15.

Faculty research: Computers, power and control systems, microwaves, communications and signal processing, bioengineering. *Total annual research expenditures:* $599,000.

Dr. Daniel L. Ewert, Chair, 701-231-7608, *Fax:* 701-231-8677, *E-mail:* dan.ewert@ndsu.nodak.edu.

■ NORTHEASTERN UNIVERSITY

College of Engineering, Computer Systems Engineering Program, Boston, MA 02115-5096

AWARDS MS. Part-time programs available.

Students: 40 full-time (15 women), 36 part-time (3 women); includes 11 minority (3 African Americans, 8 Asian Americans or Pacific Islanders), 39 international. Average age 25. 67 applicants, 69% accepted, 12 enrolled. In 2001, 20 degrees awarded.

Degree requirements: For master's, thesis optional. *Median time to degree:* Master's–2.5 years full-time, 4.5 years part-time.

Entrance requirements: For master's, GRE General Test. *Application deadline:* For fall admission, 2/15 (priority date). Applications are processed on a rolling basis. *Application fee:* $50. Electronic applications accepted.

Expenses: Tuition: Part-time $535 per credit hour. Required fees: $56. Tuition and fees vary according to program.

Financial support: In 2001–02, 17 students received support, including 3 research assistantships with full tuition reimbursements available (averaging $13,560 per year), 6 teaching assistantships with full tuition reimbursements available (averaging $13,560 per year); fellowships, career-related internships or fieldwork, Federal Work-Study, scholarships/grants, tuition waivers (full), and unspecified

assistantships also available. Support available to part-time students. Financial award application deadline: 2/15; financial award applicants required to submit FAFSA.

Faculty research: Engineering software design, CAD/CAM, virtual environments.

Application contact: Stephen L. Gibson, Associate Director, 617-373-2711, *Fax:* 617-373-2501, *E-mail:* grad-eng@coe.neu.edu. *Web site:* http://www.coe.neu.edu/

■ NORTHEASTERN UNIVERSITY

College of Engineering, Department of Electrical and Computer Engineering, Boston, MA 02115-5096

AWARDS MS, PhD. Part-time programs available.

Faculty: 34 full-time (2 women), 8 part-time/adjunct (0 women).

Students: 132 full-time (27 women), 133 part-time (17 women); includes 29 minority (5 African Americans, 20 Asian Americans or Pacific Islanders, 4 Hispanic Americans), 130 international. Average age 25. 606 applicants, 35% accepted, 67 enrolled. In 2001, 52 master's, 11 doctorates awarded.

Degree requirements: For master's, thesis optional; for doctorate, thesis/dissertation, departmental qualifying exam. *Median time to degree:* Master's–3.5 years full-time, 6 years part-time; doctorate–5.5 years full-time.

Entrance requirements: For master's and doctorate, GRE General Test. *Application deadline:* For fall admission, 2/15 (priority date). Applications are processed on a rolling basis. *Application fee:* $50.

Expenses: Tuition: Part-time $535 per credit hour. Required fees: $56. Tuition and fees vary according to program.

Financial support: In 2001–02, 107 students received support, including 3 fellowships, 66 research assistantships with full tuition reimbursements available (averaging $13,560 per year), 32 teaching assistantships with full tuition reimbursements available (averaging $13,560 per year); career-related internships or fieldwork, Federal Work-Study, scholarships/grants, tuition waivers (full), and unspecified assistantships also available. Support available to part-time students. Financial award application deadline: 2/15; financial award applicants required to submit FAFSA.

Faculty research: Digital communications, signal processing and sensor data fusion, control systems, plasma science, sensing and imaging. *Total annual research expenditures:* $8.6 million.

Dr. Fabrizio Lombardi, Chairman, 617-373-4159, *Fax:* 617-373-8970.

Application contact: Stephen L. Gibson, Associate Director, 617-373-2711, *Fax:* 617-373-2501, *E-mail:* grad-eng@

Northeastern University (continued)
coe.neu.edu. *Web site:* http://
www.coe.neu.edu/
**Find an in-depth description at
www.petersons.com/gradchannel.**

■ NORTHWESTERN POLYTECHNIC UNIVERSITY

**School of Engineering, Fremont, CA
94539-7482**

AWARDS Computer science (MS); computer systems engineering (MS); electrical engineering (MS). Part-time and evening/weekend programs available.

Faculty: 7 full-time (0 women), 53 part-time/adjunct (4 women).
Students: 239 full-time (119 women), 210 part-time (108 women). Average age 30. 132 applicants, 55% accepted. In 2001, 148 degrees awarded.
Degree requirements: For master's, thesis optional.
Entrance requirements: For master's, TOEFL, minimum GPA of 2.0. *Application deadline:* For fall admission, 8/12 (priority date); for spring admission, 2/11 (priority date). Applications are processed on a rolling basis. *Application fee:* $50 ($75 for international students).
Expenses: Tuition: Full-time $8,100; part-time $450 per unit. Required fees: $45; $15 per term.
Financial support: In 2001–02, 160 teaching assistantships with full and partial tuition reimbursements (averaging $1,000 per year) were awarded; career-related internships or fieldwork and unspecified assistantships also available.
Faculty research: Computer networking; database design; internet technology. Software engineering; digital signal processing.
Dr. Pochang Hsu, Dean, 510-657-5911, *Fax:* 510-657-8975, *E-mail:* npuadm@npu.edu.
Application contact: Jack Xie, Director of Admissions, 510-657-5913, *Fax:* 510-657-8975, *E-mail:* jack@npu.edu. *Web site:* http://www.npu.edu/engineeringindex.htm

■ NORTHWESTERN UNIVERSITY

McCormick School of Engineering and Applied Science, Department of Electrical and Computer Engineering, Evanston, IL 60208

AWARDS Electrical and computer engineering (MS, PhD); electronic materials (MS, PhD, Certificate); information technology (MIT). MS and PhD admissions and degrees offered through The Graduate School. Part-time programs available.

Faculty: 30 full-time (3 women), 7 part-time/adjunct (0 women).
Students: 95 full-time (15 women), 15 part-time (2 women); includes 10 minority (1 African American, 7 Asian Americans or Pacific Islanders, 2 Hispanic Americans),

76 international. 639 applicants, 5% accepted, 24 enrolled. In 2001, 29 master's, 22 doctorates awarded. Terminal master's awarded for partial completion of doctoral program.
Degree requirements: For master's, thesis or project; for doctorate, thesis/dissertation.
Application deadline: For fall admission, 6/1. Applications are processed on a rolling basis. *Application fee:* $50 ($55 for international students).
Expenses: Tuition: Full-time $26,526.
Financial support: In 2001–02, 104 students received support, including 10 fellowships with full tuition reimbursements available (averaging $14,238 per year), 61 research assistantships with partial tuition reimbursements available (averaging $21,000 per year), 33 teaching assistantships with full tuition reimbursements available (averaging $12,843 per year); career-related internships or fieldwork, Federal Work-Study, institutionally sponsored loans, and scholarships/grants also available. Financial award application deadline: 1/15; financial award applicants required to submit FAFSA.
Faculty research: Solid-state engineering networks and communications, optical systems, parallel and distributed computing, VLSI design and computer-aided design. *Total annual research expenditures:* $8.3 million.
Abraham Haddad, Chair, 847-491-3641, *Fax:* 847-491-4455.
Application contact: Peter Scheuermann, Admission Officer, 847-491-7141, *Fax:* 847-491-4455, *E-mail:* peters@ece.northwestern.edu. *Web site:* http://www.ece.northwestern.edu/
**Find an in-depth description at
www.petersons.com/gradchannel.**

■ OAKLAND UNIVERSITY

Graduate Study and Lifelong Learning, School of Engineering and Computer Science, Program in Computer Science and Engineering, Rochester, MI 48309-4401

AWARDS Computer science (MS); embedded systems (MS). Software engineering (MS). Part-time and evening/weekend programs available.

Faculty: 15 full-time (2 women).
Students: 83 full-time (33 women), 98 part-time (35 women); includes 26 minority (2 African Americans, 24 Asian Americans or Pacific Islanders), 77 international. Average age 33. 135 applicants, 81% accepted. In 2001, 56 degrees awarded.
Entrance requirements: For master's, minimum GPA of 3.0 for unconditional admission. *Application deadline:* For fall admission, 8/1 (priority date); for winter admission, 12/1 (priority date); for spring admission, 4/1 (priority date). Applications are processed on a rolling basis. *Application fee:* $30. Electronic applications accepted.

Expenses: Tuition, state resident: full-time $5,904; part-time $246 per credit hour. Tuition, nonresident: full-time $12,192; part-time $508 per credit hour. Required fees: $472; $236 per term.
Financial support: Federal Work-Study, institutionally sponsored loans, and tuition waivers (full) available. Financial award application deadline: 3/1; financial award applicants required to submit FAFSA.
Dr. Ishwar K. Sethi, Chair, 248-370-2820.

■ OAKLAND UNIVERSITY

Graduate Study and Lifelong Learning, School of Engineering and Computer Science, Program in Electrical and Computer Engineering, Rochester, MI 48309-4401

AWARDS MS. Part-time and evening/weekend programs available.

Faculty: 6 full-time (1 woman), 1 part-time/adjunct (0 women).
Students: 31 full-time (8 women), 54 part-time (10 women); includes 11 minority (4 African Americans, 6 Asian Americans or Pacific Islanders, 1 Native American), 26 international. Average age 29. 65 applicants, 74% accepted. In 2001, 16 degrees awarded.
Entrance requirements: For master's, minimum GPA of 3.0 for unconditional admission. *Application deadline:* For fall admission, 8/1 (priority date); for winter admission, 12/1 (priority date); for spring admission, 4/1 (priority date). Applications are processed on a rolling basis. *Application fee:* $30. Electronic applications accepted.
Expenses: Tuition, state resident: full-time $5,904; part-time $246 per credit hour. Tuition, nonresident: full-time $12,192; part-time $508 per credit hour. Required fees: $472; $236 per term.
Financial support: Federal Work-Study, institutionally sponsored loans, and tuition waivers (full) available. Financial award application deadline: 3/1; financial award applicants required to submit FAFSA.
Dr. Naim A. Kheir, Chair, 248-370-2177.

■ OGI SCHOOL OF SCIENCE & ENGINEERING AT OREGON HEALTH & SCIENCE UNIVERSITY

Graduate Studies, Department of Computer Science and Engineering, Beaverton, OR 97006-8921

AWARDS Computational finance (MS, Certificate); computer science and engineering (MS, PhD). Part-time and evening/weekend programs available.

Faculty: 20 full-time (2 women), 28 part-time/adjunct (3 women).
Students: 47 full-time, 124 part-time. Average age 31. 279 applicants, 51% accepted. In 2001, 35 master's, 3 doctorates awarded. Terminal master's awarded for partial completion of doctoral program.

Degree requirements: For master's, thesis optional; for doctorate, oral defense of dissertation.
Entrance requirements: For master's and doctorate, GRE General Test, TOEFL. *Application deadline:* For fall admission, 3/1 (priority date). Applications are processed on a rolling basis. *Application fee:* $50. Electronic applications accepted.
Expenses: Tuition: Full-time $4,905; part-time $545 per credit hour. Required fees: $466.
Financial support: In 2001–02, 41 students received support, including 39 research assistantships with full and partial tuition reimbursements available, 3 teaching assistantships; fellowships, scholarships/grants also available. Financial award application deadline: 3/1.
Faculty research: Computer systems architecture, intelligent and interactive systems, programming models and systems, theory of computation. *Total annual research expenditures:* $6.8 million. Dr. James Hook, Head, 503-748-1169, *E-mail:* hook@cse.ogi.edu.
Application contact: Shirley Kapsch, Enrollment Manager, 503-748-1255, *Fax:* 503-748-1285, *E-mail:* kapsch@cse.ogi.edu. *Web site:* http://www.cse.ogi.edu/

Find an in-depth description at www.petersons.com/gradchannel.

■ OGI SCHOOL OF SCIENCE & ENGINEERING AT OREGON HEALTH & SCIENCE UNIVERSITY

Graduate Studies, Department of Electrical and Computer Engineering, Beaverton, OR 97006-8921

AWARDS Computer engineering (MS, PhD); electrical engineering (MS, PhD). Part-time programs available.

Faculty: 23 full-time (2 women), 31 part-time/adjunct (0 women).
Students: 54 full-time (19 women), 75 part-time (23 women). Average age 29. 184 applicants, 97% accepted. In 2001, 25 master's, 2 doctorates awarded. Terminal master's awarded for partial completion of doctoral program.
Degree requirements: For master's, thesis optional; for doctorate, oral defense of dissertation.
Entrance requirements: For master's, TOEFL; for doctorate, GRE General Test, GRE Subject Test, TOEFL. *Application deadline:* For fall admission, 3/1 (priority date). Applications are processed on a rolling basis. *Application fee:* $50. Electronic applications accepted.
Expenses: Tuition: Full-time $4,905; part-time $545 per credit hour. Required fees: $466.
Financial support: In 2001–02, 20 students received support, including 19 research assistantships with full and partial tuition reimbursements available; fellowships, Federal Work-Study also available. Financial award application deadline: 3/1.

Faculty research: Semiconductor materials, microwave circuits, atmospheric optics, surface physics, electron and ion optics. *Total annual research expenditures:* $3.5 million.
John Carruthers, Head, 503-748-1616, *Fax:* 503-748-1406.
Application contact: Barbara Olsen, Enrollment Manager, 503-748-1418, *Fax:* 503-748-1406, *E-mail:* bolsen@ece.ogi.edu. *Web site:* http://www.eeap.ogi.edu/

Find an in-depth description at www.petersons.com/gradchannel.

■ OKLAHOMA STATE UNIVERSITY

Graduate College, College of Engineering, Architecture and Technology, School of Electrical and Computer Engineering, Stillwater, OK 74078

AWARDS M En, MS, PhD.

Faculty: 24 full-time (0 women), 5 part-time/adjunct (0 women).
Students: 149 full-time (32 women), 68 part-time (8 women); includes 9 minority (3 African Americans, 3 Asian Americans or Pacific Islanders, 1 Hispanic American, 2 Native Americans), 170 international. Average age 27. 371 applicants, 57% accepted. In 2001, 33 master's, 2 doctorates awarded.
Degree requirements: For master's, thesis or alternative; for doctorate, thesis/dissertation.
Entrance requirements: For master's and doctorate, TOEFL. *Application deadline:* For fall admission, 7/1 (priority date). *Application fee:* $25.
Expenses: Tuition, state resident: part-time $92 per credit hour. Tuition, nonresident: part-time $297 per credit hour. Required fees: $21 per credit hour. $14 per semester. One-time fee: $20. Tuition and fees vary according to course load.
Financial support: In 2001–02, 33 research assistantships (averaging $11,304 per year), 47 teaching assistantships (averaging $7,442 per year) were awarded. Career-related internships or fieldwork, Federal Work-Study, and tuition waivers (partial) also available. Support available to part-time students. Financial award application deadline: 3/1.
Dr. Michael A. Soderstrand, Head, 405-744-5151.

Find an in-depth description at www.petersons.com/gradchannel.

■ OLD DOMINION UNIVERSITY

College of Engineering and Technology, Program in Computer Engineering, Norfolk, VA 23529

AWARDS ME, MS.

Faculty: 17 full-time (1 woman), 5 part-time/adjunct (0 women).

Students: 10 full-time (1 woman), 11 part-time (3 women); includes 4 minority (2 African Americans, 2 Asian Americans or Pacific Islanders), 11 international. Average age 28. 24 applicants, 29% accepted, 3 enrolled. In 2001, 3 degrees awarded.
Degree requirements: For master's, thesis (for some programs), comprehensive exam (for some programs), registration.
Entrance requirements: For master's, minimum GPA of 3.0. *Application deadline:* For fall admission, 7/1; for spring admission, 10/1. Applications are processed on a rolling basis. *Application fee:* $30. Electronic applications accepted.
Expenses: Tuition, state resident: part-time $202 per credit. Tuition, nonresident: part-time $534 per credit. Required fees: $76 per semester.
Financial support: In 2001–02, 3 fellowships with full tuition reimbursements (averaging $15,333 per year), 6 research assistantships with partial tuition reimbursements (averaging $12,000 per year), 2 teaching assistantships with partial tuition reimbursements (averaging $12,000 per year) were awarded. Career-related internships or fieldwork, Federal Work-Study, scholarships/grants, and unspecified assistantships also available. Financial award application deadline: 2/15; financial award applicants required to submit FAFSA.
Faculty research: Neural network architecture, pattern recognition, modeling and simulation. *Total annual research expenditures:* $2 million.
Dr. Amin N. Dharamsi, Graduate Program Director, 757-683-3741, *Fax:* 757-683-3220, *E-mail:* ecegpd@odu.edu. *Web site:* http://www.ece.odu.edu/

■ OLD DOMINION UNIVERSITY

College of Engineering and Technology, Program in Electrical and Computer Engineering, Norfolk, VA 23529

AWARDS Electrical engineering and computer engineering (PhD). Part-time programs available. Postbaccalaureate distance learning degree programs offered (minimal on-campus study).

Faculty: 17 full-time (1 woman), 5 part-time/adjunct (0 women).
Students: 25 full-time (5 women), 13 part-time (3 women); includes 3 minority (1 African American, 2 Asian Americans or Pacific Islanders), 33 international. Average age 30. 23 applicants, 96% accepted, 5 enrolled. In 2001, 5 degrees awarded.
Degree requirements: For doctorate, thesis/dissertation, candidacy exam, diagnostic exam.
Entrance requirements: For doctorate, GRE, TOEFL. *Application deadline:* For fall admission, 7/1; for spring admission, 10/1. Applications are processed on a rolling basis. *Application fee:* $30. Electronic applications accepted.

Old Dominion University (continued)

Expenses: Tuition, state resident: part-time $202 per credit. Tuition, nonresident: part-time $534 per credit. Required fees: $76 per semester.

Financial support: In 2001–02, 3 fellowships (averaging $19,333 per year), 12 research assistantships with tuition reimbursements (averaging $15,000 per year), 7 teaching assistantships with tuition reimbursements (averaging $15,000 per year) were awarded. Career-related internships or fieldwork, scholarships/grants, and tuition waivers (partial) also available. Support available to part-time students. Financial award application deadline: 2/15; financial award applicants required to submit FAFSA.

Faculty research: Digital signal processing, control engineering, gaseous electronics, ultrafast (femtosecom) laser applications, interaction of fields with living organisms, modeling and simulation. *Total annual research expenditures:* $2 million.

Dr. Amin N. Dharamsi, Graduate Program Director, 757-683-3741, *Fax:* 757-683-3220, *E-mail:* ecegpd@odu.edu. *Web site:* http://www.ee.odu.edu/

■ THE PENNSYLVANIA STATE UNIVERSITY UNIVERSITY PARK CAMPUS

Graduate School, College of Engineering, Department of Computer Science and Engineering, State College, University Park, PA 16802-1503

AWARDS M Eng, MS, PhD.

Students: 110 full-time (27 women), 50 part-time (16 women). In 2001, 47 master's, 10 doctorates awarded.

Degree requirements: For doctorate, thesis/dissertation.

Entrance requirements: For master's and doctorate, GRE General Test. *Application fee:* $45.

Expenses: Tuition, state resident: full-time $7,882; part-time $333 per credit. Tuition, nonresident: full-time $16,142; part-time $673 per credit. Required fees: $124 per semester.

Raj Acharya, Head, 814-865-9505.

Find an in-depth description at www.petersons.com/gradchannel.

■ POLYTECHNIC UNIVERSITY, BROOKLYN CAMPUS

Department of Electrical Engineering, Major in Computer Engineering, Brooklyn, NY 11201-2990

AWARDS MS.

Degree requirements: For master's, thesis optional.

Entrance requirements: For master's, BS in electrical engineering.

■ POLYTECHNIC UNIVERSITY, LONG ISLAND GRADUATE CENTER

Graduate Programs, Department of Electrical Engineering, Major in Computer Engineering, Melville, NY 11747

AWARDS MS.

Degree requirements: For master's, thesis (for some programs). Electronic applications accepted.

■ POLYTECHNIC UNIVERSITY, WESTCHESTER GRADUATE CENTER

Graduate Programs, Department of Electrical Engineering, Major in Computer Engineering, Hawthorne, NY 10532-1507

AWARDS MS.

Electronic applications accepted.

■ PORTLAND STATE UNIVERSITY

Graduate Studies, College of Engineering and Computer Science, Department of Electrical and Computer Engineering, Portland, OR 97207-0751

AWARDS MS, PhD. Part-time and evening/weekend programs available.

Faculty: 14 full-time (1 woman).

Students: 35 full-time (7 women), 59 part-time (12 women); includes 11 minority (8 Asian Americans or Pacific Islanders, 2 Hispanic Americans, 1 Native American), 47 international. Average age 31. 82 applicants, 73% accepted. In 2001, 42 master's, 2 doctorates awarded.

Degree requirements: For master's, variable foreign language requirement, thesis or alternative, oral exam; for doctorate, one foreign language, thesis/dissertation, oral and written exams.

Entrance requirements: For master's, TOEFL, minimum GPA of 3.0 in upper-division course work or 2.75 overall; for doctorate, GRE General Test, GRE Subject Test, minimum GPA of 3.0 in upper-division course work. *Application deadline:* For fall admission, 3/1 (priority date); for spring admission, 11/1. Applications are processed on a rolling basis. *Application fee:* $50.

Financial support: In 2001–02, 2 research assistantships with full tuition reimbursements (averaging $7,653 per year), 2 teaching assistantships with full tuition reimbursements (averaging $9,620 per year) were awarded. Career-related internships or fieldwork, Federal Work-Study, and institutionally sponsored loans also available. Support available to part-time students. Financial award application

deadline: 3/1; financial award applicants required to submit FAFSA.

Faculty research: Optics and laser systems, design automation, VLSI design, computer systems, power electronics. *Total annual research expenditures:* $242,094.

Dr. Doug Hall, Interim Chair, 503-725-3806, *Fax:* 503-725-3807.

Application contact: Dr. Y. C. Jenq, Coordinator, 503-725-3806, *Fax:* 503-725-3807, *E-mail:* jenq@ee.pdx.edu. *Web site:* http://www.ee.pdx.edu/

Find an in-depth description at www.petersons.com/gradchannel.

■ PRINCETON UNIVERSITY

Graduate School, School of Engineering and Applied Science, Department of Electrical Engineering, Princeton, NJ 08544-1019

AWARDS Computer engineering (PhD); electrical engineering (M Eng); electronic materials and devices (PhD); information sciences and systems (PhD); optoelectronics (PhD). Part-time programs available.

Degree requirements: For doctorate, thesis/dissertation.

Entrance requirements: For master's and doctorate, GRE General Test, TOEFL. Electronic applications accepted.

Faculty research: Nanostructures, computer architecture, multimedia. *Web site:* http://www.princeton.edu/

■ PURDUE UNIVERSITY

Graduate School, Schools of Engineering, School of Electrical and Computer Engineering, West Lafayette, IN 47907

AWARDS Biomedical engineering (MS Bm E, PhD); computer engineering (MS, PhD); electrical engineering (MS, PhD). Part-time programs available. Postbaccalaureate distance learning degree programs offered (no on-campus study).

Faculty: 63 full-time (5 women), 10 part-time/adjunct (0 women).

Students: 355 full-time (46 women), 109 part-time (22 women); includes 27 minority (5 African Americans, 17 Asian Americans or Pacific Islanders, 5 Hispanic Americans), 353 international. Average age 27. 1,506 applicants, 27% accepted. In 2001, 123 master's, 38 doctorates awarded.

Degree requirements: For master's, thesis optional; for doctorate, thesis/dissertation.

Entrance requirements: For master's and doctorate, GRE General Test, TOEFL. *Application deadline:* For fall admission, 1/15 (priority date); for spring admission, 9/1. Applications are processed on a rolling basis. *Application fee:* $30. Electronic applications accepted.

Expenses: Tuition, state resident: full-time $4,164; part-time $149 per credit hour. Tuition, nonresident: full-time $13,872; part-time $458 per credit hour. Tuition and fees vary according to campus/location and program.

Financial support: In 2001–02, 305 students received support, including 28 fellowships with partial tuition reimbursements available (averaging $16,200 per year), 179 research assistantships with partial tuition reimbursements available (averaging $15,000 per year), 98 teaching assistantships with partial tuition reimbursements available (averaging $11,900 per year) Financial award application deadline: 1/5.

Faculty research: Biomedical communications and signal processing, solid-state materials and devices fields and optics, automatic controls, energy sources and systems, VLSI and circuit design. *Total annual research expenditures:* $13.9 million. Dr. W. K. Fuchs, Head, 765-494-3539, *Fax:* 765-494-3544, *E-mail:* fuchs@purdue.edu.

Application contact: Dr. A. M. Weiner, Director of Admissions, 765-494-3392, *Fax:* 765-494-3393, *E-mail:* ecegrad@ecn.purdue.edu. *Web site:* http://www.ece.purdue.edu/ECE/

Find an in-depth description at www.petersons.com/gradchannel.

■ **RENSSELAER AT HARTFORD**

Department of Engineering, Program in Computer and Systems Engineering, Hartford, CT 06120-2991

AWARDS ME.

Students: 18 applicants, 44% accepted, 6 enrolled.

Expenses: Tuition: Full-time $11,700; part-time $650 per credit.

James McKim, Chair, 860-548-2455, *E-mail:* jcm@rh.edu.

Application contact: Rebecca Danchak, Director of Admissions, 860-548-2420, *Fax:* 860-548-7823, *E-mail:* rdanchak@rh.edu.

■ **RENSSELAER POLYTECHNIC INSTITUTE**

Graduate School, School of Engineering, Department of Electrical, Computer, and Systems Engineering, Program in Computer and Systems Engineering, Troy, NY 12180-3590

AWARDS M Eng, MS, D Eng, PhD, MBA/M Eng. Part-time programs available.

Faculty: 31 full-time (1 woman).

Students: 27 full-time (5 women), 9 part-time (2 women). 154 applicants, 29% accepted. In 2001, 25 master's, 4 doctorates awarded. Terminal master's awarded for partial completion of doctoral program.

Degree requirements: For master's, thesis (for some programs); for doctorate, thesis/dissertation.

Entrance requirements: For master's and doctorate, GRE, TOEFL. *Application deadline:* For fall admission, 1/15; for spring admission, 10/1. Applications are

processed on a rolling basis. *Application fee:* $45. Electronic applications accepted.

Expenses: Tuition: Full-time $26,400; part-time $1,320 per credit hour. Required fees: $1,437.

Financial support: Fellowships, research assistantships, teaching assistantships, career-related internships or fieldwork and institutionally sponsored loans available. Financial award application deadline: 2/1.

Faculty research: Multimedia via ATM, mobile robotics, thermophotovoltaic devices, microelectronic interconnections, agile manufacturing. *Total annual research expenditures:* $7 million.

Application contact: Ann Bruno, Manager of Student Services and Graduate Enrollment, 518-276-2554, *Fax:* 518-276-2433, *E-mail:* bruno@ecse.rpi.edu. *Web site:* http://www.ecse.rpi.edu/

Find an in-depth description at www.petersons.com/gradchannel.

■ **RICE UNIVERSITY**

Graduate Programs, George R. Brown School of Engineering, Department of Computer Science, Houston, TX 77251-1892

AWARDS Computer science (MCS, MS, PhD); computer science in bioinformatics (MCS).

Faculty: 15 full-time (2 women), 9 part-time/adjunct (0 women).

Students: 61 full-time (6 women), 6 part-time; includes 8 minority (7 Asian Americans or Pacific Islanders, 1 Hispanic American), 41 international. 506 applicants, 10% accepted, 24 enrolled. In 2001, 12 master's, 5 doctorates awarded. Terminal master's awarded for partial completion of doctoral program.

Degree requirements: For master's, thesis (for some programs), registration; for doctorate, thesis/dissertation, qualifying exam, teaching assistant, PhD proposal defense. *Median time to degree:* Doctorate–6.4 years full-time.

Entrance requirements: For master's and doctorate, GRE General Test, GRE Subject Test, TOEFL, minimum GPA of 3.0. *Application deadline:* For fall admission, 2/1 (priority date); for spring admission, 10/15. Applications are processed on a rolling basis. *Application fee:* $25. Electronic applications accepted.

Expenses: Tuition: Full-time $17,300. Required fees: $250.

Financial support: In 2001–02, 17 fellowships with tuition reimbursements (averaging $22,667 per year), 30 research assistantships with tuition reimbursements (averaging $22,667 per year), 1 teaching assistantship with tuition reimbursement (averaging $23,667 per year) were awarded. Financial award application deadline: 2/1; financial award applicants required to submit FAFSA.

Faculty research: Operating systems, distributed systems, programming languages, algorithms, automatic program

testing. *Total annual research expenditures:* $10.5 million.

Moshe Y. Vardi, Chairman, 713-527-4834.

Application contact: Melissa Cisneros, Staff Assistant, 713-348-4834, *Fax:* 713-348-5930, *E-mail:* mcisnero@rice.edu. *Web site:* http://www.cs.rice.edu/

Find an in-depth description at www.petersons.com/gradchannel.

■ **RICE UNIVERSITY**

Graduate Programs, George R. Brown School of Engineering, Department of Electrical and Computer Engineering, Houston, TX 77251-1892

AWARDS Bioengineering (MS, PhD); circuits, controls, and communication systems (MS, PhD); computer science and engineering (MS, PhD); electrical engineering (MEE); lasers, microwaves, and solid-state electronics (MS, PhD). Part-time programs available.

Faculty: 20 full-time (2 women), 4 part-time/adjunct (0 women).

Students: 98 full-time (18 women), 8 part-time (2 women); includes 6 minority (1 African American, 3 Asian Americans or Pacific Islanders, 2 Hispanic Americans), 72 international. 337 applicants, 19% accepted, 34 enrolled. In 2001, 12 master's, 9 doctorates awarded.

Degree requirements: For master's, thesis (for some programs); for doctorate, thesis/dissertation.

Entrance requirements: For master's and doctorate, GRE General Test, GRE Subject Test, TOEFL, minimum GPA of 3.0. *Application deadline:* For fall admission, 2/1; for spring admission, 11/1. Applications are processed on a rolling basis. *Application fee:* $25.

Expenses: Tuition: Full-time $17,300. Required fees: $250.

Financial support: In 2001–02, 29 fellowships with tuition reimbursements, 60 research assistantships with tuition reimbursements, 2 teaching assistantships with tuition reimbursements were awarded. Federal Work-Study also available.

Faculty research: Physical electronics, systems, computer engineering, bioengineering. *Total annual research expenditures:* $4.5 million.

Don H. Johnson, Chairman, 713-348-4020.

Application contact: Bea Sparks, Information Contact, 713-348-4020, *E-mail:* elec@rice.edu. *Web site:* http://www.ece.rice.edu/

■ **ROCHESTER INSTITUTE OF TECHNOLOGY**

Graduate Enrollment Services, College of Engineering, Department of Computer Engineering, Rochester, NY 14623-5698

AWARDS MS.

Students: 6 full-time (1 woman), 4 part-time (1 woman); includes 1 minority (Asian American or Pacific Islander), 6

Rochester Institute of Technology (continued)

international. 44 applicants, 73% accepted, 7 enrolled. In 2001, 5 degrees awarded.
Entrance requirements: For master's, TOEFL, minimum GPA of 3.0. *Application deadline:* For fall admission, 3/1 (priority date). Applications are processed on a rolling basis. *Application fee:* $50.
Expenses: Tuition: Full-time $20,928; part-time $587 per hour. Required fees: $162. Tuition and fees vary according to program.
Dr. Andreas Savakis, Head, 585-475-2987, *E-mail:* axseec@rit.edu.

■ RUTGERS, THE STATE UNIVERSITY OF NEW JERSEY, NEW BRUNSWICK

Graduate School, Program in Electrical and Computer Engineering, New Brunswick, NJ 08901-1281

AWARDS Communications and solid-state electronics (MS, PhD); computer engineering (MS, PhD); control systems (MS, PhD); digital signal processing (MS, PhD). Part-time programs available. Terminal master's awarded for partial completion of doctoral program.

Degree requirements: For master's, thesis or alternative; for doctorate, thesis/dissertation.
Entrance requirements: For master's and doctorate, GRE General Test. Electronic applications accepted.
Faculty research: Communication and information processing, wireless information networks, micro-vacuum devices, machine vision, VLSI design. *Web site:* http://www.ece.rutgers.edu/
Find an in-depth description at www.petersons.com/gradchannel.

■ ST. MARY'S UNIVERSITY OF SAN ANTONIO

Graduate School, Department of Engineering, Program in Electrical Engineering, San Antonio, TX 78228-8507

AWARDS Electrical /computer engineering (MS); electrical engineering (MS).

Faculty: 6 full-time, 3 part-time/adjunct.
Students: 4 full-time (0 women), 12 part-time (2 women); includes 5 minority (2 Asian Americans or Pacific Islanders, 3 Hispanic Americans), 3 international. Average age 25. In 2001, 2 degrees awarded.
Degree requirements: For master's, thesis.
Entrance requirements: For master's, GRE General Test. *Application deadline:* Applications are processed on a rolling basis. *Application fee:* $15. Electronic applications accepted.
Expenses: Tuition: Full-time $8,190; part-time $455 per credit hour. Required fees: $375.

Financial support: Teaching assistantships, Federal Work-Study available. Financial award application deadline: 2/15; financial award applicants required to submit FAFSA.
Faculty research: Image processing, control, communication, artificial intelligence, robotics.
Dr. Djaffer Ibaroudene, Advisor.

■ SAN JOSE STATE UNIVERSITY

Graduate Studies, College of Engineering, Department of Computer, Information and Systems Engineering, Program in Computer Engineering, San Jose, CA 95192-0001

AWARDS Computer engineering (MS); computer software (MS); computerized robots and computer applications (MS); microprocessors and microcomputers (MS).

Faculty: 5 full-time (0 women), 12 part-time/adjunct (1 woman).
Students: 62 full-time (36 women), 124 part-time (45 women); includes 119 minority (4 African Americans, 115 Asian Americans or Pacific Islanders), 33 international. Average age 28. 236 applicants, 39% accepted. In 2001, 53 degrees awarded.
Degree requirements: For master's, thesis, comprehensive exam.
Entrance requirements: For master's, GRE General Test, BS in computer science or 24 credits in related area. *Application deadline:* For fall admission, 6/29; for spring admission, 11/30. Applications are processed on a rolling basis. *Application fee:* $59. Electronic applications accepted.
Expenses: Tuition, nonresident: part-time $246 per unit. Required fees: $678 per semester. Tuition and fees vary according to course load.
Financial support: Teaching assistantships, career-related internships or fieldwork, Federal Work-Study, and institutionally sponsored loans available. Support available to part-time students. Financial award application deadline: 5/1; financial award applicants required to submit FAFSA.
Faculty research: Robotics, database management systems, computer networks.
Application contact: Dr. Haluk Ozemek, Coordinator, 408-924-4100.

■ SANTA CLARA UNIVERSITY

School of Engineering, Department of Computer Science and Engineering, Santa Clara, CA 95053

AWARDS Computer science and engineering (MSCSE, PhD); high performance computing (Certificate). Software engineering (MS, Certificate). Part-time and evening/weekend programs available.

Students: 90 full-time (52 women), 144 part-time (62 women); includes 54 minority (3 African Americans, 51 Asian Americans or Pacific Islanders), 148

international. Average age 28. 233 applicants, 44% accepted. In 2001, 103 degrees awarded.
Degree requirements: For master's, thesis or alternative; for doctorate and Certificate, thesis/dissertation.
Entrance requirements: For master's, GRE General Test, TOEFL, minimum GPA of 2.75; for doctorate, GRE General Test, GRE Subject Test, TOEFL, master's degree or equivalent; for Certificate, master's degree, published paper. *Application deadline:* For fall admission, 6/1; for spring admission, 1/1. Applications are processed on a rolling basis. *Application fee:* $45 ($55 for international students). Electronic applications accepted.
Expenses: Tuition: Part-time $320 per unit. Tuition and fees vary according to class time, degree level, program and student level.
Financial support: Fellowships, research assistantships, teaching assistantships, Federal Work-Study available. Support available to part-time students. Financial award application deadline: 3/1; financial award applicants required to submit FAFSA. *Total annual research expenditures:* $13,156.
Dr. Daniel W. Lewis, Chair, 408-554-5281.
Application contact: Tina Samms, Assistant Director of Graduate Admissions, 408-554-4313, *Fax:* 408-554-5474, *E-mail:* engr-grad@scu.edu.

■ SOUTHERN METHODIST UNIVERSITY

School of Engineering, Department of Computer Science and Engineering, Dallas, TX 75275

AWARDS Computer engineering (MS Cp E, PhD); computer science (MS, PhD); engineering management (MSEM, DE); operations research (MS, PhD). Software engineering (MS). Part-time and evening/weekend programs available. Postbaccalaureate distance learning degree programs offered (no on-campus study).

Faculty: 9 full-time (3 women).
Students: 53 full-time (15 women), 163 part-time (37 women); includes 73 minority (16 African Americans, 43 Asian Americans or Pacific Islanders, 14 Hispanic Americans), 49 international. Average age 32. 307 applicants, 78% accepted. In 2001, 59 master's, 4 doctorates awarded. Terminal master's awarded for partial completion of doctoral program.
Degree requirements: For master's, thesis optional; for doctorate, thesis/dissertation, oral and written qualifying exams, oral final exam (PhD).
Entrance requirements: For master's, GRE General Test, TOEFL, minimum GPA of 3.0 in last 2 years; bachelor's degree in engineering, mathematics, or sciences; for doctorate, preliminary counseling exam (PhD), minimum GPA of

3.0, bachelor's degree in related field, MA (DE). *Application deadline:* For fall admission, 7/1 (priority date); for spring admission, 11/15. Applications are processed on a rolling basis. *Application fee:* $50.
Expenses: Tuition: Part-time $285 per credit hour.
Financial support: In 2001–02, 14 research assistantships with full tuition reimbursements (averaging $15,000 per year), 11 teaching assistantships with full tuition reimbursements (averaging $9,000 per year) were awarded. Financial award applicants required to submit FAFSA.
Faculty research: Trusted and high performance network computing, software engineering and management, knowledge engineering and management, computer arithmetic. *Total annual research expenditures:* $126,192.
Hesham El-Rewini, Head, 214-768-3278.
Application contact: Jim Dees, Director, Student Administration, 214-768-1456, *Fax:* 214-768-3845, *E-mail:* jdees@engr.smu.edu. *Web site:* http://www.seas.sm.edu/cse/
Find an in-depth description at www.petersons.com/gradchannel.

■ **SOUTHERN POLYTECHNIC STATE UNIVERSITY**

School of Engineering Technology and Management, Program in Electrical and Computer Engineering Technology, Marietta, GA 30060-2896

AWARDS Engineering technology (MS). Part-time and evening/weekend programs available.

Faculty: 2 part-time/adjunct (0 women).
Students: 1 full-time (0 women), 23 part-time (3 women); includes 7 minority (4 African Americans, 3 Asian Americans or Pacific Islanders), 9 international. Average age 32. In 2001, 2 degrees awarded.
Degree requirements: For master's, thesis.
Entrance requirements: For master's, GRE General Test, 3 letters of recommendation. *Application deadline:* For fall admission, 7/15 (priority date); for spring admission, 12/1. Applications are processed on a rolling basis. *Application fee:* $20. Electronic applications accepted.
Expenses: Tuition, state resident: full-time $1,746; part-time $97 per credit. Tuition, nonresident: full-time $6,966; part-time $387 per credit. Required fees: $221 per term.
Financial support: Teaching assistantships, career-related internships or fieldwork, Federal Work-Study, scholarships/grants, and unspecified assistantships available. Support available to part-time students. Financial award application deadline: 5/1; financial award applicants required to submit FAFSA.
Kim Davis, Head, 770-528-7246, *Fax:* 770-528-7285, *E-mail:* kdavis0@spsu.edu.

Application contact: Virginia A. Head, Director of Admissions, 770-528-7281, *Fax:* 770-528-7292, *E-mail:* vhead@spsu.edu. *Web site:* http://ecet.spsu.edu/

■ **STATE UNIVERSITY OF NEW YORK AT NEW PALTZ**

Graduate School, School of Physical Sciences and Engineering, Department of Electrical and Computer Engineering, New Paltz, NY 12561

AWARDS MS.

Application deadline: For fall admission, 3/15 (priority date). Applications are processed on a rolling basis. *Application fee:* $50.
Expenses: Tuition, state resident: full-time $5,100; part-time $213 per credit. Tuition, nonresident: full-time $8,416; part-time $351 per credit. Required fees: $624; $21 per credit. $60 per semester.
Dr. Ghader Eftekhari, Chair, 845-257-3722.

■ **STEVENS INSTITUTE OF TECHNOLOGY**

Graduate School, Charles V. Schaefer Jr. School of Engineering, Department of Electrical and Computer Engineering, Program in Computer Engineering, Hoboken, NJ 07030

AWARDS Computer and communications security (Certificate); computer and information engineering (M Eng, PhD, Engr); computer architecture and digital system design (M Eng, PhD, Engr); digital systems and VLSI design (Certificate); image and signal processing (M Eng, PhD, Engr); information networks (Certificate); robotics and automation (M Eng, PhD, Engr). Software engineering (M Eng, PhD, Engr). Part-time and evening/weekend programs available. Terminal master's awarded for partial completion of doctoral program.

Degree requirements: For doctorate, thesis/dissertation.
Entrance requirements: For master's and doctorate, GRE, TOEFL; for other advanced degree, GRE. Electronic applications accepted.
Expenses: Tuition: Full-time $13,950; part-time $775 per credit. Required fees: $180. One-time fee: $180 part-time. Full-time tuition and fees vary according to degree level and program.

■ **STONY BROOK UNIVERSITY, STATE UNIVERSITY OF NEW YORK**

Graduate School, College of Engineering and Applied Sciences, Department of Electrical and Computer Engineering, Stony Brook, NY 11794

AWARDS MS, PhD. Evening/weekend programs available.

Faculty: 22 full-time (3 women), 1 part-time/adjunct (0 women).
Students: 89 full-time (17 women), 48 part-time (10 women); includes 13 minority (3 African Americans, 8 Asian Americans or Pacific Islanders, 2 Hispanic Americans), 104 international. 401 applicants, 68% accepted. In 2001, 23 master's, 5 doctorates awarded.
Degree requirements: For master's, thesis or alternative; for doctorate, thesis/dissertation, comprehensive exam.
Entrance requirements: For master's and doctorate, GRE General Test, TOEFL. *Application deadline:* For fall admission, 1/15. *Application fee:* $50.
Expenses: Tuition, state resident: full-time $5,100; part-time $213 per credit. Tuition, nonresident: full-time $8,416; part-time $351 per credit. Required fees: $496.
Financial support: In 2001–02, 27 research assistantships, 36 teaching assistantships were awarded.
Faculty research: System science, solid-state electronics, computer engineering. *Total annual research expenditures:* $3 million.
Dr. Serge Luryi, Chairman, 631-632-8420.
Application contact: Dr. Chi-Tsong Chen, Director, 631-632-8400, *Fax:* 631-632-8494, *E-mail:* ctchen@sbee.sunysb.edu. *Web site:* http://www.ee.sunysb.edu/
Find an in-depth description at www.petersons.com/gradchannel.

■ **SYRACUSE UNIVERSITY**

Graduate School, L. C. Smith College of Engineering and Computer Science, Department of Electrical Engineering and Computer Science, Program in Computer Engineering, Syracuse, NY 13244-0003

AWARDS MS, PhD, CE.

Students: 157 full-time (20 women), 52 part-time (7 women); includes 6 minority (all Asian Americans or Pacific Islanders), 149 international. Average age 29. In 2001, 166 master's, 43 doctorates awarded.
Degree requirements: For doctorate, thesis/dissertation.
Entrance requirements: For master's and doctorate, GRE General Test, GRE Subject Test. *Application deadline:* Applications are processed on a rolling basis. *Application fee:* $50.
Expenses: Tuition: Full-time $15,528; part-time $647 per credit. Required fees:

Syracuse University (continued)
$420; $38 per term. Tuition and fees vary according to program.
Financial support: Fellowships, research assistantships, teaching assistantships, Federal Work-Study and tuition waivers (partial) available. Financial award application deadline: 1/10.
Faculty research: Hardware, software, computer applications.
Dr. Garth Foster, Chair, 315-443-4375, *Fax:* 315-443-2583, *E-mail:* gfoster@ syr.edu.
Application contact: Barbara Hazard, Information Contact, 315-443-2655, *Fax:* 315-443-2583, *E-mail:* bahazard@syr.edu. *Web site:* http://www.ecs.syr.edu/
Find an in-depth description at www.petersons.com/gradchannel.

■ TEMPLE UNIVERSITY

Graduate School, College of Science and Technology, College of Engineering, Program in Electrical and Computer Engineering, Philadelphia, PA 19122-6096

AWARDS MSE. Part-time and evening/weekend programs available.

Degree requirements: For master's, thesis optional.
Entrance requirements: For master's, GRE General Test, TOEFL.
Expenses: Tuition, state resident: full-time $8,487; part-time $369 per credit hour. Tuition, nonresident: full-time $12,282; part-time $534 per credit hour. Required fees: $350. Tuition and fees vary according to course load, program and reciprocity agreements.
Faculty research: Computer engineering, intelligent control, microprocessors, digital processing, neutral networks. *Web site:* http://www.eng.temple.edu/

■ TEXAS A&M UNIVERSITY

College of Engineering, Department of Computer Science, College Station, TX 77843

AWARDS Computer engineering (MCE, MS, PhD); computer science (MCS, MS, PhD). Part-time programs available.

Faculty: 39.
Students: 263 (59 women). Average age 28.
Degree requirements: For master's, thesis (MS); for doctorate, thesis/dissertation.
Entrance requirements: For master's and doctorate, GRE General Test, TOEFL. *Application deadline:* For fall admission, 5/1 (priority date). *Application fee:* $50 ($75 for international students).
Expenses: Tuition, state resident: full-time $11,872. Tuition, nonresident: full-time $17,892.

Financial support: Fellowships with full tuition reimbursements, research assistantships, teaching assistantships available. Financial award application deadline: 3/1.
Faculty research: Software development, numerical applications and controls, data structures.
Dr. Jennifer Welch, Interim Head, 979-845-5534, *Fax:* 979-847-8578, *E-mail:* csdept@cs.tamu.edu.
Application contact: Dr. S. Bart Childs, Graduate Advisor, 979-845-8981, *E-mail:* grad-advisor@cs.tamu.edu. *Web site:* http:// www.cs.tamu.edu/
Find an in-depth description at www.petersons.com/gradchannel.

■ THE UNIVERSITY OF ALABAMA AT BIRMINGHAM

Graduate School, School of Engineering, Department of Electrical and Computer Engineering, Birmingham, AL 35294

AWARDS MSEE, PhD. Evening/weekend programs available.

Students: 38 full-time (2 women), 81 part-time (16 women); includes 10 minority (9 African Americans, 1 Asian American or Pacific Islander), 68 international. 308 applicants, 78% accepted. In 2001, 15 degrees awarded.
Degree requirements: For master's, thesis or alternative; for doctorate, thesis/dissertation.
Entrance requirements: For master's, GRE General Test, BSEE. *Application deadline:* Applications are processed on a rolling basis. *Application fee:* $35 ($60 for international students). Electronic applications accepted.
Expenses: Tuition, state resident: full-time $3,058. Tuition, nonresident: full-time $5,746. Tuition and fees vary according to course load, degree level and program.
Financial support: In 2001–02, 1 student received support, including 1 research assistantship with full tuition reimbursement available (averaging $9,500 per year); tuition waivers (full and partial) also available.
Dr. Gregg L. Vaughn, Chair, 205-934-8440, *Fax:* 205-975-3337, *E-mail:* gvaughn@uab.edu. *Web site:* http:// www.eng.uab.edu/ece/

■ THE UNIVERSITY OF ALABAMA IN HUNTSVILLE

School of Graduate Studies, College of Engineering, Department of Electrical and Computer Engineering, Huntsville, AL 35899

AWARDS Computer engineering (PhD); electrical and computer engineering (MSE); electrical engineering (PhD); optical science and engineering (PhD). Part-time and evening/weekend programs available.

Faculty: 23 full-time (3 women), 3 part-time/adjunct (0 women).
Students: 85 full-time (11 women), 87 part-time (16 women); includes 17 minority (6 African Americans, 10 Asian Americans or Pacific Islanders, 1 Hispanic American), 59 international. Average age 30. 254 applicants, 45% accepted, 58 enrolled. In 2001, 40 master's, 7 doctorates awarded.
Degree requirements: For master's, thesis or alternative, oral and written exams, comprehensive exam, registration; for doctorate, thesis/dissertation, oral and written exams, comprehensive exam, registration.
Entrance requirements: For master's, GRE General Test, appropriate bachelor's degree, minimum GPA of 3.0; for doctorate, GRE General Test, minimum GPA of 3.0. *Application deadline:* For fall admission, 7/24 (priority date); for spring admission, 11/15 (priority date). Applications are processed on a rolling basis. *Application fee:* $35.
Expenses: Tuition, area resident: Part-time $175 per hour. Tuition, state resident: full-time $4,408. Tuition, nonresident: full-time $9,054; part-time $361 per hour.
Financial support: In 2001–02, 57 students received support, including 2 fellowships with full and partial tuition reimbursements available (averaging $14,100 per year), 27 research assistantships with full and partial tuition reimbursements available (averaging $9,172 per year), 27 teaching assistantships with full and partial tuition reimbursements available (averaging $7,331 per year); career-related internships or fieldwork, Federal Work-Study, institutionally sponsored loans, scholarships/grants, health care benefits, tuition waivers (full and partial), and unspecified assistantships also available. Support available to part-time students. Financial award application deadline: 4/1; financial award applicants required to submit FAFSA.
Faculty research: Optical signal processing, electromagnetics, photonics, nonlinear waves, computer architecture. *Total annual research expenditures:* $698,764.
Dr. Reza Adhami, Chair, 256-824-6316, *Fax:* 256-824-6803, *E-mail:* adhami@ eb.uah.edu. *Web site:* http://www.eb-p5.eb.uah.edu/ece/
Find an in-depth description at www.petersons.com/gradchannel.

■ THE UNIVERSITY OF ARIZONA

Graduate College, College of Engineering and Mines, Department of Electrical and Computer Engineering, Tucson, AZ 85721

AWARDS M Eng, MS, PhD. Part-time programs available.

Faculty: 64.
Students: 204 full-time (35 women), 75 part-time (11 women); includes 22 minority (2 African Americans, 13 Asian

Americans or Pacific Islanders, 7 Hispanic Americans), 190 international. Average age 29. 615 applicants, 43% accepted, 84 enrolled. In 2001, 36 master's, 9 doctorates awarded.

Degree requirements: For master's, thesis (for some programs); for doctorate, thesis/dissertation.

Entrance requirements: For master's and doctorate, GRE General Test, TOEFL. *Application deadline:* For fall admission, 6/15. Applications are processed on a rolling basis. *Application fee:* $45.

Expenses: Tuition, state resident: full-time $2,490; part-time $436 per unit. Tuition, nonresident: full-time $10,300; part-time $436 per unit. Full-time tuition and fees vary according to degree level and program.

Financial support: Fellowships, research assistantships, teaching assistantships, institutionally sponsored loans and scholarships/grants available. Financial award application deadline: 3/15.

Faculty research: Communication systems, control systems, signal processing, computer-aided logic.
Dr. John A Reagan, Head, 520-621-6193.
Application contact: Tami J Whelan, Graduate Academic Adviser, SR, 520-621-6195, *Fax:* 520-621-8076, *E-mail:* whelan@ ece.arizona.edu. *Web site:* http:// www.ece.arizona.edu

Find an in-depth description at www.petersons.com/gradchannel.

■ UNIVERSITY OF ARKANSAS

Graduate School, College of Engineering, Department of Computer Systems Engineering, Fayetteville, AR 72701-1201

AWARDS MSCSE, MSE, PhD.

Students: 22 full-time (7 women), 8 part-time (3 women); includes 6 minority (2 African Americans, 4 Asian Americans or Pacific Islanders, 18 international. 39 applicants, 54% accepted. In 2001, 7 degrees awarded.

Degree requirements: For master's, thesis optional; for doctorate, one foreign language, thesis/dissertation.
Application fee: $40 ($50 for international students).

Expenses: Tuition, state resident: full-time $3,553; part-time $197 per credit. Tuition, nonresident: full-time $8,411; part-time $467 per credit. Required fees: $42 per credit. Tuition and fees vary according to course load and program.

Financial support: In 2001–02, 7 research assistantships, 25 teaching assistantships were awarded. Career-related internships or fieldwork and Federal Work-Study also available. Support available to part-time students. Financial award application deadline: 4/1; financial award applicants required to submit FAFSA.
Aicha Elshabini, Chair, 479-575-6427.

Application contact: Dr. Ron Skeith, Graduate Coordinator, *E-mail:* grad-info@ engr.uark.edu.

■ UNIVERSITY OF BRIDGEPORT

School of Engineering, Department of Computer Science and Engineering, Bridgeport, CT 06601

AWARDS Computer engineering (MS); computer science (MS).

Faculty: 6 full-time (0 women), 5 part-time/adjunct (0 women).
Students: 127 full-time (30 women), 319 part-time (119 women); includes 2 African Americans, 27 Asian Americans or Pacific Islanders, 1 Native American, 404 international. Average age 30. 626 applicants, 69% accepted, 71 enrolled. In 2001, 109 degrees awarded.
Degree requirements: For master's, thesis optional.
Entrance requirements: For master's, TOEFL. *Application deadline:* For fall admission, 8/1 (priority date); for spring admission, 12/1 (priority date). Applications are processed on a rolling basis. *Application fee:* $25 ($35 for international students). Electronic applications accepted.
Expenses: Tuition: Part-time $385 per credit hour. Required fees: $50 per term. Tuition and fees vary according to degree level and program.
Financial support: In 2001–02, 58 students received support; research assistantships, teaching assistantships, career-related internships or fieldwork, Federal Work-Study, institutionally sponsored loans, and tuition waivers (partial) available. Support available to part-time students. Financial award application deadline: 6/1; financial award applicants required to submit FAFSA.
Dr. Stephen F. Grodzinsky, Chairman, 203-576-4145, *Fax:* 203-576-4766, *E-mail:* grodzinsky@bridgeport.edu.

Find an in-depth description at www.petersons.com/gradchannel.

■ UNIVERSITY OF CALIFORNIA, DAVIS

Graduate Studies, College of Engineering, Program in Electrical and Computer Engineering, Davis, CA 95616

AWARDS MS, PhD.

Faculty: 36.
Students: 154 full-time (28 women), 3 part-time; includes 36 minority (4 African Americans, 31 Asian Americans or Pacific Islanders, 1 Hispanic American), 55 international. Average age 28. 719 applicants, 15% accepted, 41 enrolled. In 2001, 22 master's, 11 doctorates awarded. Terminal master's awarded for partial completion of doctoral program.
Degree requirements: For master's, thesis optional; for doctorate, preliminary and qualifying exams, thesis defense.

Entrance requirements: For master's, GRE General Test, minimum GPA of 3.2; for doctorate, GRE, minimum graduate GPA of 3.5. *Application deadline:* For fall admission, 2/15. *Application fee:* $60. Electronic applications accepted.
Expenses: Tuition, state resident: full-time $4,831. Tuition, nonresident: full-time $15,725.
Financial support: In 2001–02, 105 students received support, including 47 fellowships with full and partial tuition reimbursements available (averaging $6,793 per year), 74 research assistantships with full and partial tuition reimbursements available (averaging $8,984 per year), 35 teaching assistantships with partial tuition reimbursements available (averaging $11,234 per year); Federal Work-Study, scholarships/grants, and tuition waivers (full and partial) also available. Financial award application deadline: 1/15; financial award applicants required to submit FAFSA.
Andre Knoessen, Chairperson, 530-752-2455, *E-mail:* knoessen@ece.ucdavis.edu.
Application contact: Anita Morales, Graduate Staff Assistant, 530-752-8251, *Fax:* 530-752-9217, *E-mail:* morales@ ece.ucdavis.edu. *Web site:* http:// www.ece.ucdavis.edu/grads/

■ UNIVERSITY OF CALIFORNIA, IRVINE

Office of Research and Graduate Studies, School of Engineering, Department of Electrical and Computer Engineering, Irvine, CA 92697

AWARDS Computer networks and distributed computing (MS, PhD); computer systems and software (MS, PhD); electrical engineering (MS, PhD). Part-time programs available.

Faculty: 27.
Students: 139 full-time (26 women), 28 part-time (1 woman); includes 42 minority (39 Asian Americans or Pacific Islanders, 3 Hispanic Americans), 84 international. 542 applicants, 31% accepted, 80 enrolled. In 2001, 23 master's, 3 doctorates awarded. Terminal master's awarded for partial completion of doctoral program.
Degree requirements: For doctorate, thesis/dissertation.
Entrance requirements: For master's, GRE General Test, minimum GPA of 3.0; for doctorate, GRE General Test. *Application deadline:* For fall and spring admission, 1/15 (priority date); for winter admission, 10/15 (priority date). Applications are processed on a rolling basis. *Application fee:* $60. Electronic applications accepted.
Expenses: Tuition, nonresident: full-time $10,704. Required fees: $8,396. Tuition and fees vary according to course load, program and student level.
Financial support: In 2001–02, 12 fellowships (averaging $1,250 per year), 36 research assistantships (averaging $1,120

University of California, Irvine (continued)
per year), 13 teaching assistantships (averaging $1,480 per year) were awarded. Institutionally sponsored loans and tuition waivers (full and partial) also available. Financial award application deadline: 3/2; financial award applicants required to submit FAFSA.
Faculty research: Optical and solid-state devices, systems and signal processing. *Total annual research expenditures:* $2.2 million.
Dr. Nader Bagherzadeh, Chair, 949-824-5689, *Fax:* 949-824-3779.
Application contact: Ronnie A. Gran, Graduate Admissions Coordinator, 949-824-5489, *Fax:* 949-824-1853, *E-mail:* ragran@uci.edu. *Web site:* http://www.eng.uci.edu/
Find an in-depth description at www.petersons.com/gradchannel.

■ UNIVERSITY OF CALIFORNIA, SAN DIEGO

Graduate Studies and Research, Department of Computer Science and Engineering, La Jolla, CA 92093
AWARDS Computer engineering (MS, PhD); computer science (MS, PhD).
Faculty: 18.
Students: 207 (44 women). 1,086 applicants, 16% accepted, 72 enrolled. In 2001, 44 master's, 12 doctorates awarded.
Degree requirements: For doctorate, thesis/dissertation.
Entrance requirements: For master's and doctorate, GRE General Test. *Application deadline:* For fall admission, 1/8. *Application fee:* $40. Electronic applications accepted.
Expenses: Tuition, nonresident: full-time $10,434. Required fees: $4,883.
Faculty research: Analysis of algorithms, combinatorial algorithms, discrete optimization.
Mohan Paturi, Chair, 858-534-1126, *Fax:* 858-534-7029, *E-mail:* paturi@cs.ucsd.edu.
Application contact: Graduate Coordinator, 858-534-6005.
Find an in-depth description at www.petersons.com/gradchannel.

■ UNIVERSITY OF CALIFORNIA, SAN DIEGO

Graduate Studies and Research, Department of Electrical and Computer Engineering, La Jolla, CA 92093
AWARDS Applied ocean science (MS, PhD); applied physics (MS, PhD); communication theory and systems (MS, PhD); computer engineering (MS, PhD); electrical engineering (M Eng); electronic circuits and systems (MS, PhD); intelligent systems, robotics and control (MS, PhD); photonics (MS, PhD). Signal and image processing (MS, PhD).
Faculty: 35.

Students: 334 (44 women). 1,149 applicants, 20% accepted, 114 enrolled. In 2001, 51 master's, 12 doctorates awarded.
Entrance requirements: For master's and doctorate, GRE General Test. *Application deadline:* For fall admission, 1/12. *Application fee:* $40. Electronic applications accepted.
Expenses: Tuition, nonresident: full-time $10,434. Required fees: $4,883.
Charles Tu, Chair.
Application contact: Graduate Coordinator, 858-534-6606.

■ UNIVERSITY OF CALIFORNIA, SAN DIEGO

Graduate Studies and Research, Interdisciplinary Program in Cognitive Science, La Jolla, CA 92093
AWARDS Cognitive science/anthropology (PhD); cognitive science/communication (PhD); cognitive science/computer science and engineering (PhD); cognitive science/linguistics (PhD); cognitive science/neuroscience (PhD); cognitive science/philosophy (PhD); cognitive science/psychology (PhD); cognitive science/sociology (PhD). Admissions through affiliated departments.
Faculty: 57 full-time (12 women).
Students: 8 full-time (4 women). Average age 26. 2 applicants. In 2001, 2 degrees awarded.
Degree requirements: For doctorate, thesis/dissertation.
Entrance requirements: For doctorate, GRE General Test. *Application deadline:* Applications are processed on a rolling basis. *Application fee:* $0.
Expenses: Tuition, nonresident: full-time $10,434. Required fees: $4,883.
Faculty research: Cognition, neurobiology of cognition, artificial intelligence, neural networks, psycholinguistics.
Gary Cottrell, Director, 858-534-7141, *Fax:* 858-534-1128, *E-mail:* gcottrell@ucsd.edu.
Application contact: Graduate Coordinator, 858-534-7141, *Fax:* 858-534-1128, *E-mail:* gradinfo@cogsci.ucsd.edu. *Web site:* http://cogsci.ucsd.edu/CURRENT/Cog-interdisciplinary.html

■ UNIVERSITY OF CALIFORNIA, SANTA BARBARA

Graduate Division, College of Engineering, Department of Electrical and Computer Engineering, Santa Barbara, CA 93106
AWARDS MS, PhD.
Degree requirements: For master's, thesis or alternative; for doctorate, thesis/dissertation.
Entrance requirements: For master's and doctorate, GRE General Test, TOEFL. Electronic applications accepted.
Faculty research: Solid-state device theory, physics of solid-state materials,

computer architecture. *Web site:* http://www.ece.ucsb.edu/

■ UNIVERSITY OF CALIFORNIA, SANTA CRUZ

Division of Graduate Studies, School of Engineering, Program in Computer Engineering, Santa Cruz, CA 95064
AWARDS MS, PhD.
Faculty: 12 full-time.
Students: 101 full-time (26 women); includes 22 minority (1 African American, 21 Asian Americans or Pacific Islanders), 60 international. 282 applicants, 45% accepted. In 2001, 17 master's, 8 doctorates awarded.
Degree requirements: For doctorate, one foreign language, thesis/dissertation, oral exams, comprehensive exam. *Median time to degree:* Doctorate–2 years full-time.
Entrance requirements: For master's and doctorate, GRE General Test, GRE Subject Test. *Application deadline:* For fall admission, 2/1. *Application fee:* $40.
Expenses: Tuition: Full-time $19,857.
Financial support: Fellowships, research assistantships, teaching assistantships, career-related internships or fieldwork, Federal Work-Study, and institutionally sponsored loans available. Financial award application deadline: 2/1.
Faculty research: Computer-aided design of digital systems.
Dr. Joel Ferguson, Chairperson, 831-459-4172.
Application contact: Carol Mullane, Graduate Assistant, 831-459-2576, *E-mail:* jodi@cse.ucsc.edu. *Web site:* http://www.ucsc.edu/
Find an in-depth description at www.petersons.com/gradchannel.

■ UNIVERSITY OF CENTRAL FLORIDA

College of Engineering and Computer Sciences, School of Electrical Engineering and Computer Science, Department of Computer Engineering, Orlando, FL 32816
AWARDS MS Cp E, PhD, Certificate. Part-time and evening/weekend programs available.
Faculty: 11 full-time (1 woman), 2 part-time/adjunct (0 women).
Students: 57 full-time (15 women), 64 part-time (20 women); includes 39 minority (3 African Americans, 29 Asian Americans or Pacific Islanders, 7 Hispanic Americans), 47 international. Average age 29. 127 applicants, 66% accepted, 33 enrolled. In 2001, 36 master's, 5 doctorates awarded.
Degree requirements: For master's, thesis or alternative; for doctorate, thesis/dissertation, departmental qualifying exam, candidacy exam.
Entrance requirements: For master's, GRE General Test, TOEFL, minimum

GPA of 3.0 in last 60 hours; for doctorate, GRE General Test, TOEFL, minimum GPA of 3.5 in last 60 hours. *Application deadline:* For fall admission, 7/15 (priority date); for spring admission, 12/1 (priority date). *Application fee:* $20. Electronic applications accepted.
Expenses: Tuition, state resident: part-time $162 per hour. Tuition, nonresident: part-time $569 per hour.
Financial support: In 2001–02, 21 fellowships (averaging $3,752 per year), 138 research assistantships (averaging $3,066 per year), 49 teaching assistantships (averaging $2,020 per year) were awarded. Tuition waivers (partial) also available.
Application contact: Dr. Christian S. Bauer, Coordinator, 407-823-2236, *E-mail:* csb@engr.ucf.edu.

■ UNIVERSITY OF CINCINNATI

Division of Research and Advanced Studies, College of Engineering, Department of Electrical and Computer Engineering and Computer Science, Program in Computer Engineering, Cincinnati, OH 45221
AWARDS MS.

Degree requirements: For master's, thesis, registration.
Entrance requirements: For master's, GRE General Test, TOEFL. *Application deadline:* For fall admission, 2/1 (priority date). *Application fee:* $40.
Expenses: Tuition, state resident: part-time $2,698 per quarter. Tuition, nonresident: part-time $4,977 per quarter.
Financial support: Fellowships, tuition waivers (full) and unspecified assistantships available. Financial award application deadline: 2/1.
Faculty research: Digital signal processing, large-scale systems, picture processing.
Application contact: Dieter Schmidt, Graduate Program Director, 513-556-1816, *Fax:* 513-556-7326, *E-mail:* dieter.schmidt@uc.edu. *Web site:* http://www.ececs.uc.edu/

Find an in-depth description at www.petersons.com/gradchannel.

■ UNIVERSITY OF CINCINNATI

Division of Research and Advanced Studies, College of Engineering, Department of Electrical and Computer Engineering and Computer Science, Program in Computer Science and Engineering, Cincinnati, OH 45221

AWARDS PhD.

Degree requirements: For doctorate, thesis/dissertation, registration.
Entrance requirements: For doctorate, GRE General Test, TOEFL. *Application deadline:* For fall admission, 2/1 (priority date). *Application fee:* $40.

Expenses: Tuition, state resident: part-time $2,698 per quarter. Tuition, nonresident: part-time $4,977 per quarter.
Financial support: Fellowships, tuition waivers (full) and unspecified assistantships available. Financial award application deadline: 2/1.
Application contact: Dieter Schmidt, Graduate Program Director, 513-556-1816, *Fax:* 513-556-7326, *E-mail:* dieter.schmidt@uc.edu. *Web site:* http://www.ececs.uc.edu/

Find an in-depth description at www.petersons.com/gradchannel.

■ UNIVERSITY OF COLORADO AT BOULDER

Graduate School, College of Engineering and Applied Science, Department of Electrical and Computer Engineering, Boulder, CO 80309

AWARDS Electrical engineering (ME, MS, PhD), including computer engineering. Part-time programs available. Postbaccalaureate distance learning degree programs offered (no on-campus study).

Faculty: 31 full-time (4 women).
Students: 159 full-time (25 women), 45 part-time (4 women); includes 16 minority (2 African Americans, 9 Asian Americans or Pacific Islanders, 5 Hispanic Americans), 103 international. Average age 28. 328 applicants, 46% accepted. In 2001, 47 master's, 14 doctorates awarded. Terminal master's awarded for partial completion of doctoral program.
Degree requirements: For master's, thesis or alternative; for doctorate, one foreign language, thesis/dissertation, departmental qualifying exam.
Entrance requirements: For master's, GRE General Test, minimum undergraduate GPA of 3.0; for doctorate, GRE General Test, minimum undergraduate GPA of 3.5. *Application deadline:* For fall admission, 3/1 (priority date). Applications are processed on a rolling basis. *Application fee:* $50 ($60 for international students).
Expenses: Tuition, state resident: full-time $3,474. Tuition, nonresident: full-time $16,624.
Financial support: In 2001–02, 14 fellowships (averaging $5,813 per year), 26 research assistantships (averaging $19,344 per year), 18 teaching assistantships (averaging $12,675 per year) were awarded. Career-related internships or fieldwork, scholarships/grants, and tuition waivers (full) also available. Financial award application deadline: 1/15.
Faculty research: Biomedical engineering, cognitive disabilities, control systems, digital signal processing communications, electromagnetic waves. *Total annual research expenditures:* $5.3 million.
Renjeng Su, Chair, 303-492-3511, *Fax:* 303-492-2758, *E-mail:* sur@boulder.colorado.edu.

Application contact: Adam Sadoff, Graduate Program Assistant, 303-375-0490, *Fax:* 303-492-2758, *E-mail:* adam.sadoff@colorado.edu. *Web site:* http://ece-www.colorado.edu/

■ UNIVERSITY OF COLORADO AT COLORADO SPRINGS

Graduate School, College of Engineering and Applied Science, Department of Electrical and Computer Engineering, Colorado Springs, CO 80933-7150

AWARDS Electrical engineering (MS, PhD). Part-time and evening/weekend programs available.

Faculty: 10 full-time (0 women), 3 part-time/adjunct (0 women).
Students: 44 full-time (8 women), 47 part-time (4 women); includes 15 minority (1 African American, 10 Asian Americans or Pacific Islanders, 4 Hispanic Americans), 8 international. Average age 33. In 2001, 8 master's, 1 doctorate awarded.
Degree requirements: For master's, thesis (for some programs); for doctorate, thesis/dissertation, comprehensive exam.
Entrance requirements: For master's, GRE General Test, TOEFL, minimum GPA of 3.0, B.S. in electrical engineering or previous course work in electrical engineering; for doctorate, GRE General Test, TOEFL, minimum GPA of 3.3. *Application fee:* $60 ($75 for international students).
Expenses: Tuition, state resident: full-time $2,900; part-time $174 per credit. Tuition, nonresident: full-time $9,961; part-time $591 per credit. Required fees: $14 per credit. $141 per semester. Tuition and fees vary according to course load, program and student level.
Financial support: Fellowships, research assistantships, teaching assistantships, career-related internships or fieldwork and Federal Work-Study available.
Faculty research: Integrated ferroelectric devices; applied electromagnetics; digital/mixed-signal circuit design, test and design for testability. Signal processing for communications and controls.
Dr. Rodger Ziemer, Chairman, 719-262-3350, *Fax:* 719-262-3589, *E-mail:* ziemer@eas.uccs.edu.
Application contact: Ruth Ann Nelson, Academic Adviser, 719-262-3351, *Fax:* 719-262-3589, *E-mail:* rnelson@eas.uccs.edu. *Web site:* http://ece.uccs.edu/

■ UNIVERSITY OF DAYTON

Graduate School, School of Engineering, Department of Electrical and Computer Engineering, Dayton, OH 45469-1300

AWARDS MSEE, DE, PhD. Part-time and evening/weekend programs available.

Faculty: 16 full-time (0 women), 4 part-time/adjunct (0 women).

University of Dayton (continued)

Students: 42 full-time (4 women), 26 part-time (6 women); includes 9 minority (3 African Americans, 2 Asian Americans or Pacific Islanders, 4 Hispanic Americans), 27 international. Average age 24. In 2001, 14 master's, 11 doctorates awarded.
Degree requirements: For master's, thesis optional; for doctorate, variable foreign language requirement, thesis/dissertation, departmental qualifying exam.
Entrance requirements: For master's, TOEFL. *Application deadline:* For fall admission, 8/1. Applications are processed on a rolling basis. *Application fee:* $30.
Expenses: Tuition: Full-time $5,436; part-time $453 per credit hour. Required fees: $50; $25 per term.
Financial support: In 2001–02, 15 students received support, including 14 research assistantships with full tuition reimbursements available (averaging $12,000 per year), 3 teaching assistantships with full tuition reimbursements available (averaging $12,000 per year); institutionally sponsored loans also available. Financial award application deadline: 5/1.
Faculty research: Analog and signal processing, electromagnetics, electro-optics, digital computer architectures.
Dr. Partha Banerjee, Chair, 937-229-3611, *E-mail:* p.banerjee@notes.udayton.edu.
Application contact: Dr. Donald L. Moon, Associate Dean, 937-229-2241, *Fax:* 937-229-2471, *E-mail:* dmoon@notes.udayton.edu.

■ UNIVERSITY OF DENVER

Graduate Studies, Faculty of Natural Sciences, Mathematics and Engineering, Department of Engineering, Denver, CO 80208

AWARDS Computer science and engineering (MS); electrical engineering (MS); management and general engineering (MSMGEN); materials science (PhD); mechanical engineering (MS). Part-time and evening/weekend programs available.

Faculty: 13 full-time (2 women), 3 part-time/adjunct (0 women).
Students: 17 (6 women) 11 international. 50 applicants, 62% accepted. In 2001, 11 degrees awarded. Terminal master's awarded for partial completion of doctoral program.
Degree requirements: For master's, thesis (for some programs); for doctorate, thesis/dissertation.
Entrance requirements: For master's and doctorate, GRE General Test, TOEFL, TSE. *Application deadline:* Applications are processed on a rolling basis. *Application fee:* $45.
Expenses: Tuition: Full-time $21,456.
Financial support: In 2001–02, 11 students received support, including 6 research assistantships with full and partial tuition reimbursements available (averaging $9,999 per year), 7 teaching assistantships with full and partial tuition

reimbursements available (averaging $10,782 per year); fellowships with full and partial tuition reimbursements available, career-related internships or fieldwork, Federal Work-Study, institutionally sponsored loans, and scholarships/grants also available. Financial award application deadline: 3/1; financial award applicants required to submit FAFSA.
Faculty research: Microelectrics, digital signal processing, robotics, speech recognition, microwaves, aerosols, x-ray analysis, acoustic emissions. *Total annual research expenditures:* $1 million.
Dr. James C. Wilson, Chair, 303-871-2102.
Application contact: Susie Montoya, Assistant to Chair, 303-871-2102. *Web site:* http://littlebird.engr.du.edu/

■ UNIVERSITY OF FLORIDA

Graduate School, College of Engineering, Department of Electrical and Computer Engineering, Gainesville, FL 32611

AWARDS ME, MS, PhD, Engr. Part-time programs available.

Faculty: 64.
Students: 325 full-time (47 women), 78 part-time (7 women); includes 37 minority (5 African Americans, 15 Asian Americans or Pacific Islanders, 16 Hispanic Americans, 1 Native American), 280 international. Average age 23. 1,352 applicants, 53% accepted. In 2001, 117 master's, 19 doctorates awarded. Terminal master's awarded for partial completion of doctoral program.
Degree requirements: For master's, thesis optional; for doctorate, thesis/dissertation, comprehensive exam, registration. *Median time to degree:* Master's–2 years full-time, 4 years part-time; doctorate–4 years full-time, 7 years part-time.
Entrance requirements: For master's, GRE General Test, TOEFL, minimum GPA of 3.0; for doctorate, GRE General Test, TOEFL, minimum GPA of 3.5; for Engr, GRE General Test. *Application deadline:* For fall admission, 2/1 (priority date); for spring admission, 7/1 (priority date). Applications are processed on a rolling basis. *Application fee:* $20. Electronic applications accepted.
Expenses: Tuition, state resident: part-time $164 per hour. Tuition, nonresident: part-time $571 per hour. Tuition and fees vary according to course level and program.
Financial support: In 2001–02, 41 fellowships, 141 research assistantships, 45 teaching assistantships were awarded. Unspecified assistantships also available. Financial award application deadline: 4/15.
Faculty research: Communications, electronics, digital signal processing, computer engineering.

Dr. Martin A. Uman, Chair, 352-392-0913, *Fax:* 352-392-8671, *E-mail:* uman@ece.ufl.edu.
Application contact: Dr. Jacob Hammer, Graduate Coordinator, 352-392-4934, *Fax:* 352-392-8671, *E-mail:* hammer@graduate.ece.ufl.edu. *Web site:* http://www.ece.ufl.edu/

Find an in-depth description at www.petersons.com/gradchannel.

■ UNIVERSITY OF FLORIDA

Graduate School, Graduate Engineering and Research Center (GERC), Gainesville, FL 32611

AWARDS Aerospace engineering (ME, MS, PhD, Engr); electrical and computer engineering (ME, MS, PhD, Engr); engineering mechanics (ME, MS, PhD, Engr); industrial and systems engineering (ME, MS, PhD, Engr). Part-time programs available. Postbaccalaureate distance learning degree programs offered. Terminal master's awarded for partial completion of doctoral program.

Degree requirements: For master's, thesis optional; for doctorate and Engr, thesis/dissertation.
Entrance requirements: For master's, GRE General Test, TOEFL, minimum GPA of 3.0; for doctorate, GRE General Test, written and oral qualifying exams, TOEFL, minimum GPA of 3.0, master's degree in engineering; for Engr, GRE General Test, TOEFL, minimum GPA of 3.0, master's degree in engineering. Electronic applications accepted.
Expenses: Contact institution.
Faculty research: Aerodynamics, terradynamics, and propulsion; composite materials and stress analysis; optical processing of microwave signals and photonics; holography, radar, and communications. System and signal theory; digital signal processing. *Web site:* http://www.gerc.eng.ufl.edu/

■ UNIVERSITY OF HOUSTON

Cullen College of Engineering, Department of Mechanical Engineering, Houston, TX 77204

AWARDS Aerospace engineering (MS, PhD); biomedical engineering (MS); computer and systems engineering (MS, PhD); environmental engineering (MS, PhD); materials engineering (MS, PhD); mechanical engineering (MME, MSME); petroleum engineering (MS). Part-time and evening/weekend programs available.

Faculty: 16 full-time (0 women), 1 part-time/adjunct (0 women).
Students: 34 full-time (4 women), 26 part-time (2 women); includes 7 minority (3 Asian Americans or Pacific Islanders, 4 Hispanic Americans), 32 international. Average age 28. 114 applicants, 64% accepted. In 2001, 20 master's, 3 doctorates awarded. Terminal master's awarded for partial completion of doctoral program.

Degree requirements: For master's, thesis (for some programs); for doctorate, thesis/dissertation, departmental qualifying exam.
Entrance requirements: For master's and doctorate, GRE General Test, TOEFL. *Application deadline:* For fall admission, 7/3 (priority date); for spring admission, 12/4. Applications are processed on a rolling basis. *Application fee:* $25 ($75 for international students).
Expenses: Tuition, state resident: full-time $1,512. Tuition, nonresident: full-time $5,310. Required fees: $1,308. Tuition and fees vary according to program.
Financial support: In 2001–02, 20 research assistantships (averaging $14,400 per year), 13 teaching assistantships (averaging $14,400 per year) were awarded. Fellowships, career-related internships or fieldwork and Federal Work-Study also available. Financial award application deadline: 2/15.
Faculty research: Experimental and computational turbulence, composites, rheology, phase change/heat transfer, characterization of superconducting materials. *Total annual research expenditures:* $396,172.
Dr. Lewis T. Wheeler, Interim Chair, 713-743-4500, *Fax:* 713-743-4503.
Application contact: Susan Sanderson-Clobe, Graduate Admissions Analyst, 713-743-4505, *Fax:* 713-743-4503, *E-mail:* megrad@uh.edu. *Web site:* http://www.mc.uh.edu
Find an in-depth description at www.petersons.com/gradchannel.

■ UNIVERSITY OF HOUSTON–CLEAR LAKE

School of Natural and Applied Sciences, Program in Computer Engineering, Houston, TX 77058-1098

AWARDS MS. Part-time and evening/weekend programs available.

Students: 34; includes 9 minority (5 Asian Americans or Pacific Islanders, 4 Hispanic Americans), 13 international. Average age 30. In 2001, 8 degrees awarded.
Entrance requirements: For master's, GRE General Test. *Application deadline:* For fall admission, 8/1; for spring admission, 12/1. Applications are processed on a rolling basis. *Application fee:* $30 ($70 for international students).
Expenses: Tuition, state resident: full-time $2,016; part-time $84 per credit hour. Tuition, nonresident: full-time $6,072; part-time $253 per credit hour. Tuition and fees vary according to course load.
Financial support: Research assistantships, teaching assistantships, career-related internships or fieldwork, Federal Work-Study, institutionally sponsored loans, and scholarships/grants available. Support available to part-time students. Financial award application deadline: 5/1.

Dr. Tom Harman, Chair, 281-283-3850, *Fax:* 281-283-3703, *E-mail:* harman@cl.uh.edu.
Application contact: Dr. Robert Ferebee, Associate Dean, 281-283-3700, *Fax:* 281-283-3707, *E-mail:* ferebee@cl.uh.edu.

■ UNIVERSITY OF IDAHO

College of Graduate Studies, College of Engineering, Department of Electrical and Computer Engineering, Moscow, ID 83844-2282

AWARDS Computer engineering (M Engr, MS); electrical engineering (M Engr, MS, PhD).

Faculty: 15 full-time (0 women), 3 part-time/adjunct (1 woman).
Students: 29 full-time (7 women), 75 part-time (2 women); includes 11 minority (9 Asian Americans or Pacific Islanders, 2 Hispanic Americans), 38 international. 118 applicants, 69% accepted. In 2001, 17 master's, 1 doctorate awarded.
Degree requirements: For master's and doctorate, thesis/dissertation.
Entrance requirements: For master's, minimum GPA of 2.8; for doctorate, minimum undergraduate GPA of 2.8, 3.0 graduate. *Application deadline:* For fall admission, 8/1; for spring admission, 12/15. *Application fee:* $35 ($45 for international students).
Expenses: Tuition, state resident: full-time $1,613. Tuition, nonresident: full-time $3,000.
Financial support: In 2001–02, 5 research assistantships, 8 teaching assistantships (averaging $4,638 per year) were awarded. Fellowships, career-related internships or fieldwork and Federal Work-Study also available. Financial award application deadline: 2/15.
Faculty research: Digital systems, energy systems.
Dr. Joseph Feeley, Head, 208-885-2783. *Web site:* http://www.ee.uidaho.edu/
Find an in-depth description at www.petersons.com/gradchannel.

■ UNIVERSITY OF ILLINOIS AT CHICAGO

Graduate College, College of Engineering, Department of Electrical Engineering and Computer Science, Program in Computer Science, Chicago, IL 60607-7128

AWARDS MS, PhD. Evening/weekend programs available.

Students: 134 full-time (28 women), 107 part-time (22 women); includes 19 minority (7 African Americans, 12 Asian Americans or Pacific Islanders), 178 international. Average age 26. 791 applicants, 13% accepted, 51 enrolled.
Degree requirements: For master's, thesis or alternative; for doctorate, thesis/dissertation, departmental qualifying exam.

Entrance requirements: For master's, TOEFL, BS in related field, minimum GPA of 3.75 on a 5.0 scale; for doctorate, GRE General Test, TOEFL, minimum GPA of 3.75 on a 5.0 scale, MS in related field. *Application deadline:* For fall admission, 6/7; for spring admission, 11/1. *Application fee:* $40 ($50 for international students).
Expenses: Tuition, state resident: full-time $3,060. Tuition, nonresident: full-time $6,688.
Financial support: In 2001–02, 127 students received support; fellowships, research assistantships, teaching assistantships, tuition waivers (full) available. Ugo Buy, Head, 313-996-8679.
Find an in-depth description at www.petersons.com/gradchannel.

■ UNIVERSITY OF ILLINOIS AT URBANA–CHAMPAIGN

Graduate College, College of Engineering, Department of Electrical and Computer Engineering, Champaign, IL 61820

AWARDS Computer engineering (MS, PhD); electrical engineering (MS, PhD).

Faculty: 82 full-time, 5 part-time/adjunct.
Students: 475 full-time (55 women); includes 68 minority (2 African Americans, 61 Asian Americans or Pacific Islanders, 4 Hispanic Americans, 1 Native American), 244 international. 1,437 applicants, 19% accepted. In 2001, 88 master's, 55 doctorates awarded.
Degree requirements: For master's and doctorate, thesis/dissertation.
Entrance requirements: For master's, GRE, minimum GPA of 3.0. *Application deadline:* For fall admission, 1/15. Applications are processed on a rolling basis. *Application fee:* $40 ($50 for international students). Electronic applications accepted.
Expenses: Tuition, state resident: part-time $3,227 per degree program. Tuition, nonresident: part-time $7,169 per degree program. Tuition and fees vary according to program.
Financial support: In 2001–02, 30 fellowships, 277 research assistantships, 94 teaching assistantships were awarded. Tuition waivers (full and partial) also available. Financial award application deadline: 1/15. Richard E. Blahut, Head, 217-333-2301, *Fax:* 217-244-7075, *E-mail:* blahut@uiuc.edu.
Application contact: W. R. Perkins, Administrative Clerk, 217-333-0207, *Fax:* 217-244-7075, *E-mail:* wperkins@uiuc.edu. *Web site:* http://www.ece.uiuc.edu/
Find an in-depth description at www.petersons.com/gradchannel.

■ THE UNIVERSITY OF IOWA

Graduate College, College of Engineering, Department of Electrical and Computer Engineering, Iowa City, IA 52242-1316

AWARDS MS, PhD. Part-time programs available.

Faculty: 16 full-time (0 women), 2 part-time/adjunct (0 women).
Students: 51 full-time (5 women), 25 part-time (7 women); includes 3 minority (all Asian Americans or Pacific Islanders), 50 international. Average age 27. 245 applicants, 34% accepted, 34 enrolled. In 2001, 18 degrees awarded.
Degree requirements: For master's, thesis, PhD qualifying exam, comprehensive exam, registration; for doctorate, thesis/dissertation, comprehensive exam, registration. *Median time to degree:* Master's–2.5 years full-time, 4.5 years part-time.
Entrance requirements: For master's and doctorate, TOEFL, GRE. *Application deadline:* For fall admission, 4/15 (priority date); for spring admission, 12/1 (priority date). Applications are processed on a rolling basis. *Application fee:* $30 ($50 for international students). Electronic applications accepted.
Expenses: Tuition, state resident: full-time $3,702; part-time $206 per semester hour. Tuition, nonresident: full-time $11,924; part-time $206 per semester hour. Required fees: $101 per semester. Tuition and fees vary according to course load and program.
Financial support: In 2001–02, 52 students received support, including 29 research assistantships with partial tuition reimbursements available (averaging $14,718 per year), 23 teaching assistantships with partial tuition reimbursements available (averaging $14,718 per year); fellowships, scholarships/grants, health care benefits, and unspecified assistantships also available. Financial award application deadline: 2/1; financial award applicants required to submit FAFSA.
Faculty research: Quantitative medical image processing, bioinformatics, design and testing of very large scale integrated circuits, wireless communication, photonics. *Total annual research expenditures:* $3.8 million.
Dr. Jon G. Kuhl, Departmental Executive Officer, 319-335-5958, *Fax:* 319-335-6028, *E-mail:* jon-kuhl@uiowa.edu.
Application contact: Kim Sherwood, Secretary, 319-335-5197, *Fax:* 319-335-6028, *E-mail:* ece@engineering.uiowa.edu. *Web site:* http:// www.ece.engineering.uiowa.edu/

■ UNIVERSITY OF KANSAS

Graduate School, School of Engineering, Department of Electrical Engineering and Computer Science, Program in Computer Engineering, Lawrence, KS 66045

AWARDS MS.

Students: 43 full-time (3 women), 7 part-time (1 woman); includes 1 minority (Asian American or Pacific Islander), 39 international. Average age 23. 116 applicants, 34% accepted, 16 enrolled. In 2001, 29 degrees awarded.
Entrance requirements: For master's, GRE, TOEFL. *Application deadline:* For fall admission, 3/1 (priority date); for spring admission, 10/1. Applications are processed on a rolling basis. *Application fee:* $40.
Expenses: Tuition, state resident: full-time $2,722; part-time $113 per credit. Tuition, nonresident: full-time $8,586; part-time $358 per credit. Required fees: $551; $46 per credit. Tuition and fees vary according to campus/location, program and reciprocity agreements.
Financial support: Research assistantships with partial tuition reimbursements, teaching assistantships with full and partial tuition reimbursements available.
Application contact: John M. Gauch, Graduate Director, 785-864-4487, *Fax:* 785-864-3226, *E-mail:* grad_admissions@ eecs.ku.edu.

■ UNIVERSITY OF LOUISIANA AT LAFAYETTE

Graduate School, College of Engineering, Center for Advanced Computer Studies, Lafayette, LA 70504

AWARDS Computer engineering (MS, PhD); computer science (MS, PhD). Part-time programs available.

Faculty: 24 full-time (1 woman).
Students: 137 full-time (23 women), 34 part-time (8 women); includes 2 minority (1 Asian American or Pacific Islander, 1 Hispanic American), 153 international. 502 applicants, 57% accepted, 54 enrolled. In 2001, 73 master's, 6 doctorates awarded. Terminal master's awarded for partial completion of doctoral program.
Degree requirements: For master's, thesis or alternative; for doctorate, thesis/dissertation, final oral exam.
Entrance requirements: For master's, GRE General Test, TOEFL, minimum GPA of 2.75; for doctorate, GRE General Test, TOEFL, minimum GPA of 3.0. *Application deadline:* For fall admission, 5/15. *Application fee:* $20 ($30 for international students).
Expenses: Tuition, state resident: full-time $2,317; part-time $79 per credit. Tuition, nonresident: full-time $8,882; part-time $369 per credit. International tuition: $9,018 full-time.

Financial support: In 2001–02, 5 fellowships with full tuition reimbursements (averaging $13,900 per year), 34 research assistantships with full tuition reimbursements (averaging $6,868 per year), 23 teaching assistantships with full tuition reimbursements (averaging $6,868 per year) were awarded. Federal Work-Study and tuition waivers (full) also available. Financial award application deadline: 3/1. Dr. Magdy A. Bayoumi, Chair, 337-482-6147.
Application contact: Dr. William Edwards, Graduate Coordinator, 337-482-6338.
Find an in-depth description at www.petersons.com/gradchannel.

■ UNIVERSITY OF LOUISIANA AT LAFAYETTE

Graduate School, College of Engineering, Department of Electrical and Computer Engineering, Lafayette, LA 70504

AWARDS Computer engineering (MS, PhD); telecommunications (MSTC).

Faculty: 5 full-time (1 woman).
Students: 78 full-time (19 women), 25 part-time (4 women); includes 5 minority (4 African Americans, 1 Asian American or Pacific Islander), 80 international. 308 applicants, 59% accepted, 38 enrolled. In 2001, 30 master's, 5 doctorates awarded.
Degree requirements: For master's, thesis or alternative.
Entrance requirements: For master's, GRE General Test, minimum GPA of 2.75. *Application deadline:* For fall admission, 5/15. *Application fee:* $20 ($30 for international students).
Expenses: Tuition, state resident: full-time $2,317; part-time $79 per credit. Tuition, nonresident: full-time $8,882; part-time $369 per credit. International tuition: $9,018 full-time.
Financial support: Federal Work-Study and tuition waivers (partial) available. Financial award application deadline: 5/1. Dr. Robert Henry, Head, 337-482-6568.
Application contact: Dr. George Thomas, Graduate Coordinator, 337-482-5365.

■ UNIVERSITY OF LOUISVILLE

Graduate School, Speed Scientific School, Department of Computer Engineering and Computer Science, Program in Computer Engineering and Computer Science, Louisville, KY 40292-0001

AWARDS M Eng, MS.

Students: 15 full-time (2 women), 37 part-time (9 women); includes 13 minority (2 African Americans, 10 Asian Americans or Pacific Islanders, 1 Hispanic American), 1 international. Average age 28. In 2001, 10 degrees awarded.
Degree requirements: For master's, thesis.

Entrance requirements: For master's, GRE General Test. *Application deadline:* Applications are processed on a rolling basis. *Application fee:* $25.
Expenses: Tuition, state resident: full-time $4,134. Tuition, nonresident: full-time $11,486.
Dr. Khaled A. Kamel, Chair, Department of Computer Engineering and Computer Science, 502-852-6304.

■ UNIVERSITY OF LOUISVILLE

Graduate School, Speed Scientific School, Department of Computer Engineering and Computer Science, Program in Computer Science and Engineering, Louisville, KY 40292-0001

AWARDS PhD.

Students: 32 full-time (5 women), 4 part-time; includes 2 minority (both Asian Americans or Pacific Islanders), 27 international. Average age 29. In 2001, 2 degrees awarded.
Degree requirements: For doctorate, thesis/dissertation.
Entrance requirements: For doctorate, GRE General Test. *Application deadline:* Applications are processed on a rolling basis. *Application fee:* $25.
Expenses: Tuition, state resident: full-time $4,134. Tuition, nonresident: full-time $11,486.
Dr. Peter Aronhime, Director.

■ UNIVERSITY OF LOUISVILLE

Graduate School, Speed Scientific School, Department of Electrical and Computer Engineering, Louisville, KY 40292-0001

AWARDS M Eng, MS.

Students: 35 full-time (6 women), 64 part-time (8 women); includes 9 minority (4 African Americans, 2 Asian Americans or Pacific Islanders, 2 Hispanic Americans, 1 Native American), 31 international. Average age 29. In 2001, 18 degrees awarded.
Degree requirements: For master's, thesis.
Entrance requirements: For master's, GRE General Test, minimum GPA of 2.75. *Application deadline:* Applications are processed on a rolling basis. *Application fee:* $25. Electronic applications accepted.
Expenses: Tuition, state resident: full-time $4,134. Tuition, nonresident: full-time $11,486.
Financial support: In 2001–02, 3 fellowships with full tuition reimbursements (averaging $18,000 per year), 18 research assistantships with full tuition reimbursements (averaging $15,072 per year), 6 teaching assistantships with full tuition reimbursements (averaging $15,252 per year) were awarded.
Darrel L. Chenoweth, Chair, 502-852-6289, *Fax:* 502-852-8851, *E-mail:* dlchen01@gwise.louisville.edu.

Application contact: Joyce M. Hack, Administrative Assistant, 502-852-7517, *Fax:* 502-852-8851, *E-mail:* jmhack01@gwise.louisville.edu.

■ UNIVERSITY OF MAINE

Graduate School, College of Engineering, Department of Electrical and Computer Engineering, Orono, ME 04469

AWARDS Computer engineering (MS); electrical engineering (MS, PhD). Part-time programs available.

Students: 14 full-time (1 woman), 7 part-time, 6 international. Average age 25. 32 applicants, 53% accepted, 4 enrolled. In 2001, 5 master's awarded.
Degree requirements: For master's, thesis (for some programs); for doctorate, thesis/dissertation.
Entrance requirements: For master's and doctorate, GRE General Test, TOEFL. *Application deadline:* For fall admission, 2/1 (priority date). Applications are processed on a rolling basis. *Application fee:* $50. Electronic applications accepted.
Expenses: Tuition, state resident: full-time $3,780; part-time $210 per credit hour. Tuition, nonresident: full-time $10,782; part-time $599 per credit hour. Required fees: $9.5 per credit hour. $32 per semester. Tuition and fees vary according to reciprocity agreements.
Financial support: In 2001–02, 13 research assistantships with tuition reimbursements (averaging $14,280 per year), 2 teaching assistantships with tuition reimbursements (averaging $10,200 per year) were awarded. Federal Work-Study, institutionally sponsored loans, and tuition waivers (full and partial) also available. Financial award application deadline: 3/1.
Dr. James Patton, Chair, 207-581-2223, *Fax:* 201-581-2220.
Application contact: Scott G. Delcourt, Director of the Graduate School, 207-581-3218, *Fax:* 207-581-3232, *E-mail:* graduate@maine.edu. *Web site:* http://www.umaine.edu/graduate/

■ UNIVERSITY OF MARYLAND, COLLEGE PARK

Graduate Studies and Research, A. James Clark School of Engineering, Department of Electrical and Computer Engineering, College Park, MD 20742

AWARDS Electrical and computer engineering (M Eng, MS, PhD); electrical engineering (MS, PhD); telecommunications (MS). Part-time and evening/weekend programs available. Postbaccalaureate distance learning degree programs offered.

Faculty: 73 full-time (9 women), 15 part-time/adjunct (0 women).
Students: 361 full-time (64 women), 170 part-time (38 women); includes 44 minority (18 African Americans, 24 Asian

Americans or Pacific Islanders, 2 Hispanic Americans), 403 international. 1,430 applicants, 20% accepted, 154 enrolled. In 2001, 82 master's, 32 doctorates awarded.
Degree requirements: For master's, thesis or alternative; for doctorate, thesis/dissertation, oral exam, qualifying exam.
Entrance requirements: For master's and doctorate, GRE General Test, minimum GPA of 3.0. *Application deadline:* For spring admission, 12/1. Applications are processed on a rolling basis. *Application fee:* $50 ($70 for international students). Electronic applications accepted.
Expenses: Tuition, state resident: part-time $289 per credit hour. Tuition, nonresident: part-time $448 per credit hour. One-time fee: $436 part-time. Full-time tuition and fees vary according to course load, campus/location and program.
Financial support: In 2001–02, 16 fellowships with full tuition reimbursements (averaging $11,621 per year), 72 research assistantships with tuition reimbursements (averaging $12,422 per year), 65 teaching assistantships with tuition reimbursements (averaging $11,377 per year) were awarded. Career-related internships or fieldwork also available. Financial award applicants required to submit FAFSA.
Faculty research: Communications and control, electrophysics, micro-electronics.
Dr. Steven Marcus, Acting Chair, 301-405-3683.
Application contact: Trudy Lindsey, Director, Graduate Admissions and Records, 301-405-6991, *Fax:* 301-314-9305, *E-mail:* grschool@deans.umd.edu.

Find an in-depth description at www.petersons.com/gradchannel.

■ UNIVERSITY OF MASSACHUSETTS AMHERST

Graduate School, College of Engineering, Department of Electrical and Computer Engineering, Amherst, MA 01003

AWARDS MS, PhD. Part-time and evening/weekend programs available.

Faculty: 31 full-time (1 woman).
Students: 82 full-time (16 women), 114 part-time (14 women); includes 13 minority (2 African Americans, 8 Asian Americans or Pacific Islanders, 2 Hispanic Americans, 1 Native American), 139 international. Average age 27. 872 applicants, 14% accepted. In 2001, 50 master's, 8 doctorates awarded. Terminal master's awarded for partial completion of doctoral program.
Degree requirements: For doctorate, thesis/dissertation.
Entrance requirements: For master's and doctorate, GRE General Test. *Application deadline:* For fall admission, 1/15 (priority date); for spring admission, 10/1. Applications are processed on a rolling basis. *Application fee:* $40 ($50 for international students).

University of Massachusetts Amherst (continued)

Expenses: Tuition, state resident: full-time $1,980; part-time $110 per credit. Tuition, nonresident: full-time $7,456; part-time $414 per credit. Required fees: $4,112. One-time fee: $115 full-time.

Financial support: In 2001–02, 8 fellowships with full tuition reimbursements (averaging $5,608 per year), 112 research assistantships with full tuition reimbursements (averaging $9,657 per year), 49 teaching assistantships with full tuition reimbursements (averaging $5,517 per year) were awarded. Career-related internships or fieldwork, Federal Work-Study, scholarships/grants, traineeships, and unspecified assistantships also available. Support available to part-time students. Financial award application deadline: 1/5.
Dr. Seshu B. Desu, Head, 413-545-0962, *Fax:* 413-545-4611, *E-mail:* sdesu@ ecs.umass.edu.

Application contact: Dr. Donald E. Scott, Chair, Admissions Committee, 413-545-0937, *Fax:* 413-545-4611, *E-mail:* scott@ ecs.umass.edu.

■ UNIVERSITY OF MASSACHUSETTS DARTMOUTH

Graduate School, College of Engineering, Department of Electrical and Computer Engineering, North Dartmouth, MA 02747-2300

AWARDS Computer engineering (MS, Certificate); electrical engineering (MS, PhD, Certificate). Part-time programs available.

Faculty: 21 full-time (2 women), 3 part-time/adjunct (0 women).
Students: 57 full-time (10 women), 34 part-time (8 women); includes 1 minority (Hispanic American), 73 international. Average age 26. 236 applicants, 72% accepted, 27 enrolled. In 2001, 13 master's, 3 doctorates awarded.
Degree requirements: For master's, thesis or alternative, culminating project or thesis; for doctorate, thesis/dissertation, comprehensive exam.
Entrance requirements: For master's, GRE General Test, TOEFL, minimum undergraduate GPA of 3.0. *Application deadline:* For fall admission, 2/1 (priority date); for spring admission, 11/1 (priority date). Applications are processed on a rolling basis. *Application fee:* $25 ($45 for international students).
Expenses: Tuition, state resident: full-time $2,071; part-time $86 per credit. Tuition, nonresident: full-time $8,099; part-time $337 per credit. Part-time tuition and fees vary according to course load and reciprocity agreements.
Financial support: In 2001–02, 38 research assistantships with full tuition reimbursements (averaging $6,706 per year), 15 teaching assistantships with full tuition reimbursements (averaging $6,783 per year) were awarded. Federal Work-Study and unspecified assistantships also

available. Support available to part-time students. Financial award application deadline: 3/1; financial award applicants required to submit FAFSA.
Faculty research: Marine mammal acoustics, acoustic motion accelerometers, instrumentation for monitoring/control wastewater treatment, acoustics for pollution detection, acoustic correlates of speech intelligibility. *Total annual research expenditures:* $854,000.
Dr. Paul Fortier, Director, 508-999-8544, *Fax:* 508-999-8489, *E-mail:* pfortier@ umassd.edu.
Application contact: Maria E. Lomba, Graduate Admissions Officer, 508-999-8604, *Fax:* 508-999-8183, *E-mail:* graduate@umassd.edu.

■ UNIVERSITY OF MASSACHUSETTS LOWELL

Graduate School, James B. Francis College of Engineering, Department of Electrical Engineering, Program in Computer Engineering, Lowell, MA 01854-2881

AWARDS MS Eng, D Eng.

Degree requirements: For master's, thesis optional; for doctorate, 2 foreign languages, thesis/dissertation.
Entrance requirements: For master's and doctorate, GRE General Test.

■ THE UNIVERSITY OF MEMPHIS

Graduate School, Herff College of Engineering, Department of Electrical Engineering, Memphis, TN 38152

AWARDS Automatic control systems (MS); biomedical systems (MS); communications and propagation systems (MS); electrical engineering (PhD); engineering computer systems (MS).

Degree requirements: For master's, thesis or alternative, comprehensive exam.
Entrance requirements: For master's, GRE General Test or MAT, minimum undergraduate GPA of 2.5.
Expenses: Tuition, state resident: full-time $2,026. Tuition, nonresident: full-time $4,528.
Faculty research: Ventricular arrhythmias, cerebral palsy, automatic computer troubleshooting, noninvasive monitoring of gastric motor functions.

■ UNIVERSITY OF MIAMI

Graduate School, College of Engineering, Department of Electrical and Computer Engineering, Coral Gables, FL 33124

AWARDS MSECE, PhD. Part-time programs available.

Faculty: 23 full-time (2 women).
Students: 40 full-time (6 women), 6 part-time (2 women); includes 28 minority (3 African Americans, 15 Asian Americans or

Pacific Islanders, 10 Hispanic Americans). Average age 25. 141 applicants, 45% accepted. In 2001, 10 master's, 7 doctorates awarded.
Degree requirements: For master's, thesis optional; for doctorate, thesis/dissertation, comprehensive exam.
Entrance requirements: For master's, GRE General Test, TOEFL, minimum GPA of 3.0; for doctorate, GRE General Test, TOEFL, minimum undergraduate GPA of 3.3, 3.5 graduate. *Application deadline:* Applications are processed on a rolling basis. *Application fee:* $50. Electronic applications accepted.
Expenses: Tuition: Part-time $960 per credit hour. Required fees: $85 per semester. Tuition and fees vary according to program.
Financial support: In 2001–02, 3 fellowships with full tuition reimbursements, 3 research assistantships with full tuition reimbursements, 16 teaching assistantships with full tuition reimbursements were awarded. Career-related internships or fieldwork, Federal Work-Study, institutionally sponsored loans, scholarships/grants, and unspecified assistantships also available. Support available to part-time students. Financial award application deadline: 2/1.
Faculty research: Computer network, image processing, database systems, digital signal processing, machine intelligence, information systems. *Total annual research expenditures:* $252,439.
Dr. James W. Modestino, Chairman, 305-284-3291, *Fax:* 305-284-4044, *E-mail:* jmodestino@miami.edu.
Application contact: Dr. Kamal Premaratne, Graduate Adviser, 305-284-3291, *Fax:* 305-284-4044, *E-mail:* kamal@ miami.edu. *Web site:* http:// www.eng.miami.edu/

■ UNIVERSITY OF MICHIGAN

Horace H. Rackham School of Graduate Studies, College of Engineering, Department of Electrical Engineering and Computer Science, Division of Computer Science and Engineering, Ann Arbor, MI 48109

AWARDS MS, MSE, PhD.

Faculty: 40 full-time (4 women), 2 part-time/adjunct (0 women).
Students: 221 full-time (33 women), 11 part-time (2 women); includes 28 minority (3 African Americans, 23 Asian Americans or Pacific Islanders, 1 Hispanic American, 1 Native American), 95 international. Average age 25. 1,230 applicants, 24% accepted. In 2001, 60 master's, 13 doctorates awarded. Terminal master's awarded for partial completion of doctoral program.
Degree requirements: For doctorate, thesis/dissertation, oral defense of dissertation, preliminary exams.
Entrance requirements: For master's and doctorate, GRE General Test, TOEFL. *Application deadline:* For fall admission, 5/1.

Applications are processed on a rolling basis. *Application fee:* $55. Electronic applications accepted.
Financial support: In 2001–02, 171 students received support, including 30 fellowships with full tuition reimbursements available (averaging $20,220 per year), 100 research assistantships with full tuition reimbursements available (averaging $20,220 per year), 41 teaching assistantships with full tuition reimbursements available (averaging $18,880 per year); health care benefits also available. Financial award application deadline: 1/15.
Faculty research: Intelligent systems, hardware systems, software systems, theory of computation, VLSI. *Total annual research expenditures:* $10.4 million.
Dr. John E. Laird, Chair, 734-764-2390, *Fax:* 734-763-1503, *E-mail:* admit@eecs.umich.edu.
Application contact: Dawn Freysinger, Student Services Associate, 734-764-2390, *Fax:* 734-763-1503, *E-mail:* admit@eecs.umich.edu. *Web site:* http://www.eecs.umich.edu/

■ UNIVERSITY OF MICHIGAN–DEARBORN

College of Engineering and Computer Science, Department of Electrical and Computer Engineering, Dearborn, MI 48128-1491

AWARDS Computer engineering (MSE); electrical engineering (MSE). Part-time programs available.

Faculty: 11 full-time (1 woman), 10 part-time/adjunct (1 woman).
Students: 6 full-time (0 women), 120 part-time (12 women); includes 30 minority (2 African Americans, 22 Asian Americans or Pacific Islanders, 6 Hispanic Americans). Average age 29. 108 applicants, 44% accepted. In 2001, 28 degrees awarded.
Degree requirements: For master's, thesis optional.
Entrance requirements: For master's, bachelor's degree in electrical and computer engineering or equivalent, minimum GPA of 3.0. *Application deadline:* For fall admission, 8/1; for winter admission, 12/1; for spring admission, 4/1. Applications are processed on a rolling basis. *Application fee:* $55.
Expenses: Tuition, state resident: part-time $300 per credit hour. Tuition, nonresident: part-time $756 per credit hour. Required fees: $90 per semester. Tuition and fees vary according to course level, course load and program.
Financial support: In 2001–02, 9 research assistantships were awarded; fellowships, teaching assistantships, Federal Work-Study also available. Financial award application deadline: 4/1; financial award applicants required to submit FAFSA.
Faculty research: Process control, fuzzy systems design, machine vision image processing and pattern recognition.

Dr. M. Shridhar, Chair, 313-593-5420, *Fax:* 313-593-9967, *E-mail:* shridhar@engin.umd.umich.edu.
Application contact: Graduate Secretary, 313-593-5420, *Fax:* 313-593-9967. *Web site:* http://www.engin.umd.umich.edu/

■ UNIVERSITY OF MINNESOTA, TWIN CITIES CAMPUS

Graduate School, Institute of Technology, Department of Electrical and Computer Engineering, Minneapolis, MN 55455-0213

AWARDS MEE, MSEE, PhD. Part-time programs available.

Degree requirements: For master's, thesis or alternative; for doctorate, thesis/dissertation.
Entrance requirements: For master's and doctorate, TOEFL.
Expenses: Tuition, state resident: full-time $2,932; part-time $489 per credit. Tuition, nonresident: full-time $5,758; part-time $960 per credit. Part-time tuition and fees vary according to course load, program and reciprocity agreements.
Faculty research: Signal processing, microelectronics, computers, controls, power electronics. *Web site:* http://www.ece.umn.edu/

Find an in-depth description at www.petersons.com/gradchannel.

■ UNIVERSITY OF MINNESOTA, TWIN CITIES CAMPUS

Graduate School, Institute of Technology, Program in Computer Engineering, Minneapolis, MN 55455-0213

AWARDS M Comp E, MS. Part-time programs available. Postbaccalaureate distance learning degree programs offered (no on-campus study).

Degree requirements: For master's, thesis or alternative.
Entrance requirements: For master's, TOEFL.
Expenses: Tuition, state resident: full-time $2,932; part-time $489 per credit. Tuition, nonresident: full-time $5,758; part-time $960 per credit. Part-time tuition and fees vary according to course load, program and reciprocity agreements.
Faculty research: Computer networks, parallel computing, software engineering, VLSI and CAI, databases. *Web site:* http://www.compengr.umn.edu/

Find an in-depth description at www.petersons.com/gradchannel.

■ UNIVERSITY OF MISSOURI–COLUMBIA

Graduate School, College of Engineering, Department of Computer Engineering and Computer Science, Columbia, MO 65211

AWARDS MS, PhD. Part-time programs available.

Faculty: 16 full-time (3 women).
Students: 53 full-time (21 women), 45 part-time (11 women); includes 6 minority (1 African American, 4 Asian Americans or Pacific Islanders, 1 Hispanic American), 74 international. 32 applicants, 47% accepted. In 2001, 22 master's, 3 doctorates awarded.
Degree requirements: For doctorate, thesis/dissertation.
Entrance requirements: For master's, GRE General Test, minimum GPA of 3.0; for doctorate, GRE General Test, TOEFL. *Application deadline:* For fall admission, 4/15 (priority date); for winter admission, 9/15 (priority date). Applications are processed on a rolling basis. *Application fee:* $25 ($50 for international students).
Expenses: Tuition, state resident: part-time $179 per credit hour. Tuition, nonresident: part-time $539 per credit hour. Required fees: $122 per semester. Tuition and fees vary according to program.
Financial support: Research assistantships, teaching assistantships, institutionally sponsored loans available.
Dr. Hongchi Shi, Director of Graduate Studies, 573-882-3088, *E-mail:* shih@cecs.missouri.edu. *Web site:* http://www.engineering.missouri.edu/computer.htm

■ UNIVERSITY OF MISSOURI–ROLLA

Graduate School, School of Engineering, Department of Electrical and Computer Engineering, Program in Computer Engineering, Rolla, MO 65409-0910

AWARDS MS, DE, PhD. Part-time and evening/weekend programs available. Terminal master's awarded for partial completion of doctoral program.

Degree requirements: For master's, thesis or alternative; for doctorate, thesis/dissertation, departmental qualifying exam.
Entrance requirements: For master's and doctorate, GRE General Test, TOEFL. Electronic applications accepted.

■ UNIVERSITY OF NEBRASKA–LINCOLN

Graduate College, College of Arts and Sciences and College of Engineering and Technology, Department of Computer Science and Engineering, Lincoln, NE 68588

AWARDS Computer engineering (PhD); computer science (MS, PhD).

Faculty: 18.
Students: 138 (34 women); includes 1 minority (Asian American or Pacific Islander) 120 international. Average age 31. 339 applicants, 36% accepted, 58 enrolled. In 2001, 21 master's, 3 doctorates awarded.
Degree requirements: For master's, thesis optional; for doctorate, thesis/dissertation, comprehensive exam.
Entrance requirements: For master's and doctorate, GRE General Test, TOEFL. *Application deadline:* For fall admission, 3/1; for spring admission, 10/1. *Application fee:* $35. Electronic applications accepted.
Expenses: Tuition, state resident: full-time $2,412; part-time $134 per credit. Tuition, nonresident: full-time $6,223; part-time $346 per credit. Tuition and fees vary according to course load.
Financial support: In 2001–02, 1 fellowship, 53 research assistantships, 33 teaching assistantships were awarded. Federal Work-Study, health care benefits, and unspecified assistantships also available. Support available to part-time students. Financial award application deadline: 1/15.
Faculty research: Software engineering, geo- and bio-informatics, scientific computation, secure communication.
Dr. Richard Sincovec, Chair, 402-472-2401, *Fax:* 402-472-7767.
Application contact: Dr. Hong Jiang, Graduate Committee Chair. *Web site:* http://www.cse.unl.edu

Find an in-depth description at www.petersons.com/gradchannel.

■ UNIVERSITY OF NEVADA, LAS VEGAS

Graduate College, Howard R. Hughes College of Engineering, Department of Electrical and Computer Engineering, Las Vegas, NV 89154-9900

AWARDS MSE, PhD. Part-time programs available.

Faculty: 14 full-time (0 women).
Students: 15 full-time (3 women), 3 part-time; includes 1 minority (Asian American or Pacific Islander), 12 international. 27 applicants, 41% accepted, 7 enrolled. In 2001, 10 master's, 1 doctorate awarded.
Degree requirements: For master's, thesis (for some programs), project, comprehensive exam; for doctorate, thesis/dissertation, comprehensive exam. *Median time to degree:* Doctorate–4 years full-time.

Entrance requirements: For master's, bachelor's degree in electrical engineering or related field, GRE General Test or minimum GPA of 3.0; for doctorate, GRE General Test, minimum GPA of 3.2. *Application deadline:* For fall admission, 6/15; for spring admission, 11/15. Applications are processed on a rolling basis. *Application fee:* $40 ($55 for international students).
Expenses: Tuition, state resident: full-time $1,926; part-time $107 per credit. Tuition, nonresident: full-time $9,376; part-time $220 per credit. Tuition and fees vary according to course load.
Financial support: In 2001–02, 5 research assistantships with full and partial tuition reimbursements (averaging $7,500 per year), 13 teaching assistantships with partial tuition reimbursements (averaging $11,000 per year) were awarded. Tuition waivers (full) also available. Financial award application deadline: 3/1.
Dr. Rama Venket, Chair, 702-895-4184.
Application contact: Graduate College Admissions Evaluator, 702-895-3320, *Fax:* 702-895-4180, *E-mail:* gradcollege@ccmail.nevada.edu. *Web site:* http://www.egr.unlv.edu/

■ UNIVERSITY OF NEVADA, RENO

Graduate School, College of Engineering, Program in Computer Engineering, Reno, NV 89557

AWARDS MS, PhD.

Faculty: 4.
Students: 13 full-time (3 women), 3 part-time, 13 international. Average age 30. In 2001, 5 degrees awarded.
Entrance requirements: For master's, GRE General Test, TOEFL, minimum GPA of 2.75; for doctorate, GRE General Test, TOEFL, minimum GPA of 3.0. *Application deadline:* For fall admission, 3/1 (priority date). *Application fee:* $40.
Expenses: Tuition, state resident: full-time $2,067; part-time $108 per credit. Tuition, nonresident: full-time $9,282; part-time $109 per credit. Required fees: $57 per semester. Tuition and fees vary according to course load.
Financial support: Research assistantships, teaching assistantships available.
Dr. Sushil Louis, Program Director and Chair, 775-784-4313, *Fax:* 775-784-1877, *E-mail:* looney@cs.unr.edu.

■ UNIVERSITY OF NEW MEXICO

Graduate School, School of Engineering, Department of Electrical and Computer Engineering, Albuquerque, NM 87131-2039

AWARDS Electrical engineering (MS); engineering (PhD); optical sciences (PhD). MEME offered through the Manufacturing Engineering Program. Part-time and evening/weekend programs available.

Faculty: 41 full-time (2 women), 23 part-time/adjunct (3 women).
Students: 121 full-time (28 women), 49 part-time (6 women); includes 26 minority (2 African Americans, 11 Asian Americans or Pacific Islanders, 11 Hispanic Americans, 2 Native Americans), 100 international. Average age 31. In 2001, 34 master's, 6 doctorates awarded.
Degree requirements: For master's, thesis (for some programs); for doctorate, thesis/dissertation.
Entrance requirements: For master's, GRE General Test, minimum GPA of 3.0; for doctorate, GRE General Test, minimum GPA of 3.5. *Application deadline:* For fall admission, 7/30; for spring admission, 11/30. *Application fee:* $40.
Expenses: Tuition, state resident: full-time $2,771; part-time $115 per credit hour. Tuition, nonresident: full-time $11,207; part-time $467 per credit hour. Required fees: $570; $24 per credit hour. Part-time tuition and fees vary according to course load and program.
Financial support: In 2001–02, 68 students received support, including 1 fellowship with full tuition reimbursement available (averaging $9,000 per year), 51 research assistantships with full tuition reimbursements available (averaging $13,908 per year), 63 teaching assistantships with full tuition reimbursements available (averaging $11,528 per year). Scholarships/grants, health care benefits, and unspecified assistantships also available. Financial award application deadline: 3/1; financial award applicants required to submit FAFSA.
Faculty research: Applied electromagnetics, high performance computing, wireless communications, optoelectronics, control systems. *Total annual research expenditures:* $843,280.
Dr. Christos Christodoulou, Chair, 505-277-2436, *Fax:* 505-277-1439, *E-mail:* christos@eece.unm.edu.
Application contact: Heather N. Shinn, Administrative Assistant I, 505-277-2600, *Fax:* 505-277-1439, *E-mail:* hshinn@unm.edu. *Web site:* http://www.eece.unm.edu/

Find an in-depth description at www.petersons.com/gradchannel.

■ THE UNIVERSITY OF NORTH CAROLINA AT CHARLOTTE

Graduate School, The William States Lee College of Engineering, Department of Electrical and Computer Engineering, Charlotte, NC 28223-0001

AWARDS MSEE, PhD. Part-time and evening/weekend programs available.

Faculty: 12 full-time (0 women), 4 part-time/adjunct (0 women).
Students: 64 full-time (15 women), 50 part-time (8 women); includes 11 minority (9 African Americans, 2 Asian Americans

or Pacific Islanders), 63 international. Average age 27. 246 applicants, 65% accepted, 34 enrolled. In 2001, 20 master's, 3 doctorates awarded.
Degree requirements: For master's, thesis or project.
Entrance requirements: For master's, GRE General Test, minimum GPA of 3.0 in undergraduate major, 2.75 overall. *Application deadline:* For fall admission, 7/15; for spring admission, 11/15. Applications are processed on a rolling basis. *Application fee:* $35. Electronic applications accepted.
Expenses: Tuition, state resident: full-time $1,483; part-time $371 per year. Tuition, nonresident: full-time $9,850; part-time $2,463 per year. Required fees: $1,043; $277 per year. Tuition and fees vary according to course load.
Financial support: In 2001–02, 21 research assistantships, 24 teaching assistantships were awarded. Fellowships, career-related internships or fieldwork, Federal Work-Study, institutionally sponsored loans, scholarships/grants, and unspecified assistantships also available. Support available to part-time students. Financial award application deadline: 4/1; financial award applicants required to submit FAFSA.
Faculty research: Integrated circuits self test; control systems; optoelectronics/microelectronics devices and systems; communications; computer engineering.
Dr. Farid M. Tranjan, Chair, 704-687-2302, *Fax:* 704-687-2352, *E-mail:* tranjan@email.uncc.edu.
Application contact: Kathy Barringer, Director of Graduate Admissions, 704-687-3366, *Fax:* 704-687-3279, *E-mail:* gradadm@email.uncc.edu. *Web site:* http://www.uncc.edu/gradmiss/

■ UNIVERSITY OF NOTRE DAME

Graduate School, College of Engineering, Department of Computer Science and Engineering, Notre Dame, IN 46556

AWARDS MS, PhD. Part-time programs available.
Faculty: 14 full-time (1 woman), 2 part-time/adjunct (0 women).
Students: 51 full-time (15 women), 2 part-time; includes 8 minority (3 African Americans, 3 Asian Americans or Pacific Islanders, 1 Hispanic American, 1 Native American), 26 international. 133 applicants, 21% accepted, 13 enrolled. In 2001, 6 master's, 1 doctorate awarded. Terminal master's awarded for partial completion of doctoral program.
Degree requirements: For master's, comprehensive exam; for doctorate, thesis/dissertation. *Median time to degree:* Doctorate–4 years full-time.
Entrance requirements: For master's and doctorate, GRE General Test, TOEFL. *Application deadline:* For fall admission, 2/1 (priority date); for spring admission, 10/1.

Applications are processed on a rolling basis. *Application fee:* $50. Electronic applications accepted.
Expenses: Tuition: Full-time $24,220; part-time $1,346 per credit hour. Required fees: $155.
Financial support: In 2001–02, 51 students received support, including 9 fellowships with full tuition reimbursements available (averaging $16,000 per year), 13 research assistantships with full tuition reimbursements available (averaging $13,700 per year), 18 teaching assistantships with full tuition reimbursements available (averaging $13,700 per year); tuition waivers (full) also available. Financial award application deadline: 2/1.
Faculty research: Parallel architectures, VLSI design, VLSI CAD, parallel and distributed computing, operating systems. *Total annual research expenditures:* $1.1 million.
Dr. Kevin W. Bowyer, Chair, 574-631-8320, *Fax:* 574-631-9260, *E-mail:* cse@cse.nd.edu.
Application contact: Dr. Terrence J. Akai, Director of Graduate Admissions, 574-631-7706, *Fax:* 574-631-4183, *E-mail:* gradad@nd.edu. *Web site:* http://www.cse.nd.edu/

Find an in-depth description at www.petersons.com/gradchannel.

■ UNIVERSITY OF OKLAHOMA

Graduate College, College of Engineering, School of Electrical and Computer Engineering, Norman, OK 73019-0390

AWARDS MS, PhD.
Faculty: 14 full-time (1 woman).
Students: 81 full-time (15 women), 42 part-time (9 women); includes 9 minority (2 African Americans, 4 Asian Americans or Pacific Islanders, 1 Hispanic American, 2 Native Americans), 92 international. 90 applicants, 79% accepted, 25 enrolled. In 2001, 19 master's, 4 doctorates awarded. Terminal master's awarded for partial completion of doctoral program.
Degree requirements: For master's, thesis, oral exam; for doctorate, thesis/dissertation, general exam, oral exam, qualifying exam.
Entrance requirements: For master's and doctorate, GRE General Test, TOEFL. *Application deadline:* For fall admission, 4/1 (priority date); for spring admission, 9/1 (priority date). Applications are processed on a rolling basis. *Application fee:* $25 ($50 for international students).
Expenses: Tuition, state resident: full-time $2,208; part-time $92 per credit hour. Tuition, nonresident: part-time $297 per credit hour. Tuition and fees vary according to course level, course load and program.
Financial support: In 2001–02, 31 research assistantships with partial tuition reimbursements (averaging $9,371 per year), 22 teaching assistantships with

partial tuition reimbursements (averaging $9,345 per year) were awarded. Fellowships, career-related internships or fieldwork, Federal Work-Study, scholarships/grants, and unspecified assistantships also available. Financial award application deadline: 4/15; financial award applicants required to submit FAFSA.
Faculty research: Signal and image processing, bioengineering, electric energy, telecommunication and systems, solid state laser services and systems. *Total annual research expenditures:* $1.8 million.
Gerald E. Crain, Director, 405-325-4721, *Fax:* 405-325-7066, *E-mail:* crain@ou.edu.
Application contact: Sam Lee, Graduate Program Assistant, 405-325-4285, *Fax:* 405-325-7066, *E-mail:* samlee@ou.edu.

■ UNIVERSITY OF PUERTO RICO, MAYAGÜEZ CAMPUS

Graduate Studies, College of Engineering, Department of Electrical Engineering, Mayagüez, PR 00681-9000

AWARDS Computer engineering (M Co E, MS); electrical engineering (MEE, MS). Part-time programs available.
Degree requirements: For master's, thesis, comprehensive exam.
Entrance requirements: For master's, minimum GPA of 2.5, proficiency in English and Spanish.
Faculty research: Microcomputer interfacing, control systems, power systems, electronics.

■ UNIVERSITY OF RHODE ISLAND

Graduate School, College of Engineering, Department of Electrical and Computer Engineering, Kingston, RI 02881

AWARDS MS, PhD. Part-time programs available.
Students: In 2001, 21 master's, 4 doctorates awarded.
Degree requirements: For master's, thesis or alternative; for doctorate, thesis/dissertation, comprehensive exam.
Entrance requirements: For master's and doctorate, GRE General Test, TOEFL. *Application deadline:* For fall admission, 4/15. Applications are processed on a rolling basis. *Application fee:* $25.
Expenses: Tuition, state resident: full-time $3,756; part-time $209 per credit. Tuition, nonresident: full-time $10,774; part-time $599 per credit. Required fees: $1,586; $76 per credit. $76 per credit. One-time fee: $60 full-time.
Financial support: In 2001–02, 33 students received support.
Faculty research: Digital signal processing, computer engineering, VLSI, fiber optics and materials, communication and control systems, biomedical engineering.

University of Rhode Island (continued)
Dr. Richard Vaccaro, Chairman, 401-874-2505.
Application contact: Director of Graduate Studies, 401-874-2506.

■ UNIVERSITY OF ROCHESTER

The College, School of Engineering and Applied Sciences, Department of Electrical and Computer Engineering, Rochester, NY 14627-0250

AWARDS MS, PhD.

Faculty: 16.
Students: 64 full-time (10 women), 7 part-time; includes 5 minority (2 African Americans, 3 Asian Americans or Pacific Islanders, 48 international. 298 applicants, 7% accepted, 19 enrolled. In 2001, 13 master's, 7 doctorates awarded. Terminal master's awarded for partial completion of doctoral program.
Degree requirements: For master's, comprehensive exam; for doctorate, thesis/dissertation, preliminary and oral exams.
Entrance requirements: For master's and doctorate, GRE, TOEFL. *Application deadline:* For fall admission, 2/1. *Application fee:* $25.
Expenses: Tuition: Part-time $755 per credit hour.
Financial support: Fellowships, research assistantships, teaching assistantships, tuition waivers (full and partial) available. Financial award application deadline: 2/1. Philippe Fauchet, Chair, 585-275-4054.
Application contact: Yana Shikhman, Graduate Program Secretary, 585-275-4054.
Find an in-depth description at www.petersons.com/gradchannel.

■ UNIVERSITY OF SOUTH CAROLINA

The Graduate School, College of Engineering and Information Technology, Department of Computer Science and Engineering, Columbia, SC 29208

AWARDS Computer science and engineering (ME, MS, PhD). Software engineering (MS). Part-time and evening/weekend programs available. Postbaccalaureate distance learning degree programs offered (minimal on-campus study).

Faculty: 20 full-time (3 women).
Students: 136 full-time (26 women), 41 part-time (10 women); includes 149 minority (5 African Americans, 143 Asian Americans or Pacific Islanders, 1 Hispanic American). Average age 27. 399 applicants, 48% accepted. In 2001, 126 master's, 2 doctorates awarded.
Degree requirements: For master's, thesis (for some programs), registration; for doctorate, thesis/dissertation, comprehensive exam, registration.
Entrance requirements: For master's and doctorate, GRE General Test, TOEFL.

Application deadline: For fall admission, 3/1 (priority date); for spring admission, 10/1. *Application fee:* $35. Electronic applications accepted.
Expenses: Tuition, state resident: full-time $4,434. Tuition, nonresident: full-time $9,854. Tuition and fees vary according to program.
Financial support: In 2001–02, 5 fellowships (averaging $9,600 per year), 29 research assistantships with partial tuition reimbursements (averaging $15,000 per year), 24 teaching assistantships with partial tuition reimbursements (averaging $13,000 per year) were awarded. Career-related internships or fieldwork also available.
Faculty research: Computer security and computer vision, artificial intelligence, multiagent systems, conceptual modeling. *Total annual research expenditures:* $1.3 million.
Dr. Duncan A. Buell, Professor and Chair, 803-777-2880, *Fax:* 803-777-3767, *E-mail:* buell@cse.sc.edu.
Application contact: Jewel Rogers, Administrative Assistant, 803-777-7849, *Fax:* 803-777-3767, *E-mail:* jewel@engr.sc.edu. *Web site:* http://www.cse.sc.edu/

■ UNIVERSITY OF SOUTHERN CALIFORNIA

Graduate School, School of Engineering, Department of Computer Science, Los Angeles, CA 90089

AWARDS Computer networks (MS); computer science (MS, PhD); multimedia and creative technologies (MS); robotics and automation (MS). Software engineering (MS). Part-time programs available. Postbaccalaureate distance learning degree programs offered. Terminal master's awarded for partial completion of doctoral program.

Degree requirements: For doctorate, thesis/dissertation.
Entrance requirements: For master's and doctorate, GRE General Test.
Expenses: Tuition: Full-time $25,060; part-time $844 per unit. Required fees: $473.
Faculty research: Neural computation, molecular composition, multi-media and virtual reality, databases.

■ UNIVERSITY OF SOUTHERN CALIFORNIA

Graduate School, School of Engineering, Department of Electrical Engineering, Program in Computer Engineering, Los Angeles, CA 90089

AWARDS MS, PhD.

Degree requirements: For master's, thesis optional; for doctorate, thesis/dissertation.
Entrance requirements: For master's and doctorate, GRE General Test.

Expenses: Tuition: Full-time $25,060; part-time $844 per unit. Required fees: $473.

Find an in-depth description at www.petersons.com/gradchannel.

■ UNIVERSITY OF SOUTHERN CALIFORNIA

Graduate School, School of Engineering, Department of Electrical Engineering and Department of Computer Science, Program in Computer Networks, Los Angeles, CA 90089

AWARDS MS.

Degree requirements: For master's, thesis optional.
Entrance requirements: For master's, GRE General Test.
Expenses: Tuition: Full-time $25,060; part-time $844 per unit. Required fees: $473.

Find an in-depth description at www.petersons.com/gradchannel.

■ UNIVERSITY OF SOUTH FLORIDA

College of Graduate Studies, College of Engineering, Department of Computer Science and Engineering, Tampa, FL 33620-9951

AWARDS Computer engineering (M Cp E, MS Cp E); computer science (MCS, MSCS); computer science and engineering (PhD). Part-time programs available.

Faculty: 19 full-time (2 women).
Students: 109 full-time (32 women), 33 part-time (6 women); includes 20 minority (2 African Americans, 14 Asian Americans or Pacific Islanders, 4 Hispanic Americans, 85 international. Average age 30. 648 applicants, 26% accepted, 53 enrolled. In 2001, 4 master's, 4 doctorates awarded. Terminal master's awarded for partial completion of doctoral program.
Degree requirements: For doctorate, thesis/dissertation, 2 tools of research as specified by dissertation committee.
Entrance requirements: For master's, GRE General Test, minimum GPA of 3.0 during previous 2 years; for doctorate, GRE General Test. *Application deadline:* For fall admission, 6/1; for spring admission, 10/15. *Application fee:* $20. Electronic applications accepted.
Expenses: Tuition, state resident: part-time $166 per credit hour. Tuition, nonresident: part-time $573 per credit hour. Required fees: $17 per term.
Financial support: Fellowships with full tuition reimbursements, research assistantships with full tuition reimbursements, teaching assistantships with full tuition reimbursements, career-related internships or fieldwork, Federal Work-Study,

institutionally sponsored loans, and tuition waivers (partial) available. Support available to part-time students. Financial award applicants required to submit FAFSA.
Faculty research: Computer vision, databases, VLSI design and test, networks, artificial intelligence. *Total annual research expenditures:* $1.2 million.
Dr. Abe Kandel, Chairperson, 813-974-3652, *Fax:* 813-974-5456, *E-mail:* kandel@csee.usf.edu.
Application contact: Dr. Dmitry B. Goldgof, Graduate Director, 813-974-3033, *Fax:* 813-974-5456, *E-mail:* msphd@csee.usf.edu. *Web site:* http://www.csee.usf.edu/

Find an in-depth description at www.petersons.com/gradchannel.

■ THE UNIVERSITY OF TEXAS AT ARLINGTON

Graduate School, College of Engineering, Department of Computer Science and Engineering, Arlington, TX 76019

AWARDS M Engr, M Sw En, MCS, MS, PhD. Part-time and evening/weekend programs available. Postbaccalaureate distance learning degree programs offered.

Faculty: 16 full-time (2 women), 3 part-time/adjunct (0 women).
Students: 320 full-time (73 women), 141 part-time (28 women); includes 44 minority (1 African American, 39 Asian Americans or Pacific Islanders, 4 Hispanic Americans), 371 international. 845 applicants, 62% accepted, 124 enrolled. In 2001, 111 master's, 5 doctorates awarded.
Degree requirements: For master's, thesis optional; for doctorate, thesis/dissertation, comprehensive exam.
Entrance requirements: For master's, GRE General Test, TOEFL, minimum GPA of 3.2; for doctorate, GRE General Test, TOEFL, minimum GPA of 3.5. *Application deadline:* For fall admission, 6/16. Applications are processed on a rolling basis. *Application fee:* $25 ($50 for international students).
Expenses: Tuition, area resident: Full-time $2,268. Tuition, nonresident: full-time $6,264. Required fees: $839. Tuition and fees vary according to course load.
Financial support: In 2001–02, 23 fellowships (averaging $1,000 per year), 80 teaching assistantships (averaging $12,000 per year) were awarded. Research assistantships, career-related internships or fieldwork, scholarships/grants, and tuition waivers (partial) also available. Financial award application deadline: 6/1; financial award applicants required to submit FAFSA.
Dr. Behrooz A. Shirazi, Chairman, 817-272-3065, *Fax:* 817-272-3784, *E-mail:* shirazi@uta.edu.

Application contact: Dr. Ramesh Yerraballi, Graduate Adviser, 817-272-5128, *Fax:* 817-272-3784, *E-mail:* ramesh@uta.edu. *Web site:* http://www.cse.uta.edu/

Find an in-depth description at www.petersons.com/gradchannel.

■ THE UNIVERSITY OF TEXAS AT AUSTIN

Graduate School, College of Engineering, Department of Electrical and Computer Engineering, Austin, TX 78712-1111

AWARDS MSE, PhD. Part-time programs available.

Faculty: 65 full-time (5 women), 12 part-time/adjunct (1 woman).
Students: 396 full-time (59 women), 169 part-time (16 women); includes 63 minority (5 African Americans, 42 Asian Americans or Pacific Islanders, 15 Hispanic Americans, 1 Native American), 336 international.
Entrance requirements: For master's, GRE General Test, minimum GPA of 3.3 in upper-division course work; for doctorate, GRE General Test. *Application deadline:* For fall admission, 1/2. Applications are processed on a rolling basis. *Application fee:* $50 ($75 for international students). Electronic applications accepted.
Expenses: Tuition, state resident: full-time $3,159. Tuition, nonresident: full-time $6,957. Tuition and fees vary according to program.
Financial support: Fellowships, research assistantships, teaching assistantships available. Financial award application deadline: 1/2.

Application contact: Dr. Anthony P. Ambler, Chairman, 512-475-6153, *Fax:* 512-471-5532, *E-mail:* ambler@ece.utexas.edu. *Web site:* http://www.ece.utexas.edu.

Find an in-depth description at www.petersons.com/gradchannel.

■ THE UNIVERSITY OF TEXAS AT EL PASO

Graduate School, College of Engineering, Department of Electrical and Computer Engineering, El Paso, TX 79968-0001

AWARDS Computer engineering (MS, PhD); computer science (PhD); electrical engineering (MS, PhD). Part-time and evening/weekend programs available.

Students: 94 (23 women); includes 22 minority (1 African American, 1 Asian American or Pacific Islander, 20 Hispanic Americans) 20 international. Average age 34. 17 applicants, 100% accepted. In 2001, 24 master's, 1 doctorate awarded.
Degree requirements: For master's, thesis optional; for doctorate, thesis/dissertation.

Entrance requirements: For master's, GRE General Test, TOEFL, minimum GPA of 3.0; for doctorate, GRE General Test, TOEFL, qualifying exam, minimum graduate GPA of 3.0. *Application deadline:* For fall admission, 7/1 (priority date); for spring admission, 11/1 (priority date). Applications are processed on a rolling basis. *Application fee:* $15 ($65 for international students). Electronic applications accepted.
Expenses: Tuition, state resident: full-time $2,450. Tuition, nonresident: full-time $6,000.
Financial support: In 2001–02, 60 students received support, including research assistantships with partial tuition reimbursements available (averaging $22,375 per year), teaching assistantships with partial tuition reimbursements available (averaging $17,900 per year); fellowships with partial tuition reimbursements available, Federal Work-Study, institutionally sponsored loans, scholarships/grants, and tuition waivers (partial) also available. Financial award application deadline: 3/15; financial award applicants required to submit FAFSA.
Faculty research: Signal and image processing, computer architecture, fiber optics, computational electromagnetics, electronic displays and thin films.
Dr. Mehdi Shadaram, Chairperson, 915-747-5470, *Fax:* 915-747-7871, *E-mail:* shadaram@miners.utep.edu.
Application contact: Dr. Charles H. Ambler, Dean of the Graduate School, 915-747-5491 Ext. 7886, *Fax:* 915-747-5788, *E-mail:* cambler@miners.utep.edu.

■ UNIVERSITY OF VIRGINIA

School of Engineering and Applied Science, Department of Electrical and Computer Engineering, Charlottesville, VA 22903

AWARDS ME, MS, PhD. Postbaccalaureate distance learning degree programs offered (no on-campus study).

Faculty: 23 full-time (3 women), 2 part-time/adjunct (0 women).
Students: 104 full-time (18 women), 9 part-time (1 woman); includes 5 minority (1 African American, 3 Asian Americans or Pacific Islanders, 1 Hispanic American), 73 international. Average age 27. 407 applicants, 11% accepted, 29 enrolled. In 2001, 8 master's, 3 doctorates awarded.
Degree requirements: For master's, thesis (MS); for doctorate, thesis/dissertation, comprehensive exam.
Entrance requirements: For master's and doctorate, GRE General Test. *Application deadline:* For fall admission, 8/1; for spring admission, 12/1. *Application fee:* $40. Electronic applications accepted.
Expenses: Tuition, state resident: full-time $3,988. Tuition, nonresident: full-time $17,078. Required fees: $1,190.
Financial support: Fellowships available. Financial award application deadline: 2/1;

University of Virginia (continued)
financial award applicants required to submit FAFSA.
James H. Aylor, Chairman, 434-924-6100, *Fax:* 434-924-8818.
Application contact: Kathryn Thornton, Assistant Dean, 434-924-3897, *Fax:* 434-982-2214, *E-mail:* inquiry@cs.virginia.edu. *Web site:* http://www.ee.virginia.edu/
Find an in-depth description at www.petersons.com/gradchannel.

■ VILLANOVA UNIVERSITY

College of Engineering, Department of Electrical and Computer Engineering, Program in Computer Engineering, Villanova, PA 19085-1699

AWARDS MSCE. Part-time and evening/weekend programs available.

Faculty: 8 full-time (1 woman), 5 part-time/adjunct (0 women).
Students: 20 full-time (4 women), 11 part-time (2 women); includes 1 minority (Asian American or Pacific Islander), 18 international. Average age 27. 45 applicants, 42% accepted, 15 enrolled. In 2001, 6 degrees awarded.
Degree requirements: For master's, thesis optional. *Median time to degree:* Master's–2 years full-time, 4 years part-time.
Entrance requirements: For master's, GRE General Test (for applicants with degrees from foreign universities), TOEFL, BEE, minimum GPA of 3.0. *Application deadline:* For fall admission, 8/1 (priority date); for spring admission, 12/1. Applications are processed on a rolling basis. *Application fee:* $40.
Expenses: Tuition: Part-time $340 per credit. One-time fee: $115 full-time. Tuition and fees vary according to program.
Financial support: In 2001–02, 15 students received support, including 8 teaching assistantships with full tuition reimbursements available (averaging $10,265 per year); research assistantships, scholarships/grants and tuition waivers (full and partial) also available. Financial award application deadline: 3/15.
Faculty research: Expert systems, computer vision, neural networks, image processing, computer architectures.
Dr. S. S. Rao, Chairman, Department of Electrical and Computer Engineering, 610-519-4971, *Fax:* 610-519-4436, *E-mail:* rao@ee.vill.edu. *Web site:* http://www.ece.vill.edu/
Find an in-depth description at www.petersons.com/gradchannel.

■ VIRGINIA POLYTECHNIC INSTITUTE AND STATE UNIVERSITY

Graduate School, College of Engineering, Department of Electrical and Computer Engineering, Blacksburg, VA 24061

AWARDS Computer engineering (MS, PhD); electrical engineering (MS, PhD). Part-time programs available.

Faculty: 67 full-time (2 women).
Students: 408 full-time (56 women), 161 part-time (22 women); includes 57 minority (14 African Americans, 32 Asian Americans or Pacific Islanders, 10 Hispanic Americans, 1 Native American), 317 international. Average age 24. 1,361 applicants, 30% accepted, 134 enrolled. In 2001, 112 master's, 29 doctorates awarded.
Degree requirements: For master's, thesis optional; for doctorate, thesis/dissertation.
Entrance requirements: For master's and doctorate, GRE General Test, TOEFL. *Application deadline:* For fall admission, 1/15 (priority date); for spring admission, 10/1 (priority date). Applications are processed on a rolling basis. *Application fee:* $45. Electronic applications accepted.
Expenses: Tuition, state resident: part-time $241 per hour. Tuition, nonresident: part-time $406 per hour. Tuition and fees vary according to program.
Financial support: In 2001–02, 17 fellowships with full tuition reimbursements (averaging $19,000 per year), 213 research assistantships with full tuition reimbursements (averaging $17,700 per year), 59 teaching assistantships with full tuition reimbursements (averaging $13,275 per year) were awarded. Career-related internships or fieldwork and unspecified assistantships also available. Financial award application deadline: 1/15.
Faculty research: Electromagnetics, controls, electronics, power, communications. *Total annual research expenditures:* $20 million.
Dr. Robert J. Trew, Department Head, 540-231-6646, *E-mail:* trew@vt.edu.
Application contact: Cynthia B. Hopkins, Graduate Counselor, 540-231-8393, *Fax:* 540-231-3362, *E-mail:* hopkins@vt.edu. *Web site:* http://www.ece.vt.edu/
Find an in-depth description at www.petersons.com/gradchannel.

■ WAYNE STATE UNIVERSITY

Graduate School, College of Engineering, Department of Electrical and Computer Engineering, Program in Computer Engineering, Detroit, MI 48202

AWARDS MS, PhD.

Students: 239. In 2001, 117 master's, 2 doctorates awarded.

Degree requirements: For master's, thesis optional; for doctorate, thesis/dissertation.
Application deadline: For fall admission, 7/1 (priority date); for spring admission, 3/15. Applications are processed on a rolling basis. *Application fee:* $20 ($30 for international students). Electronic applications accepted.
Expenses: Tuition, state resident: full-time $3,764. Tuition and fees vary according to degree level and program.
Financial support: Application deadline: 3/16.
Faculty research: Neural networks, parallel processing, pattern recognition, VLSI, computer architecture.
Application contact: Pepe Siy, Graduate Director, 313-577-3841, *Fax:* 313-577-1101, *E-mail:* psiy@ece.eng.wayne.edu.

■ WAYNE STATE UNIVERSITY

Graduate School, College of Engineering, Interdisciplinary Program in Electronics and Computer Control Systems, Detroit, MI 48202

AWARDS MS.

Students: 16. In 2001, 77 degrees awarded.
Degree requirements: For master's, thesis optional.
Application deadline: For fall admission, 7/1 (priority date); for spring admission, 3/15. Applications are processed on a rolling basis. *Application fee:* $20 ($30 for international students). Electronic applications accepted.
Expenses: Tuition, state resident: full-time $3,764. Tuition and fees vary according to degree level and program.
Pepe Siy, Graduate Director, 313-577-3841, *Fax:* 313-577-1101, *E-mail:* psiy@ece.eng.wayne.edu.

■ WESTERN MICHIGAN UNIVERSITY

Graduate College, College of Engineering and Applied Sciences, Department of Electrical Engineering and Computer Engineering, Kalamazoo, MI 49008-5202

AWARDS Computer engineering (MSE, PhD); electrical engineering (MSE, PhD). Part-time programs available.

Faculty: 15 full-time (2 women).
Students: 146 full-time (24 women), 9 part-time; includes 2 minority (both Asian Americans or Pacific Islanders), 151 international. 342 applicants, 80% accepted, 67 enrolled. In 2001, 23 degrees awarded.
Degree requirements: For master's, thesis optional.
Entrance requirements: For master's, minimum GPA of 3.0. *Application deadline:* For fall admission, 2/15 (priority date). Applications are processed on a rolling basis. *Application fee:* $25.

Expenses: Tuition, state resident: part-time $186 per credit hour. Tuition, nonresident: part-time $442 per credit hour. Required fees: $602. One-time fee: $132 part-time. Tuition and fees vary according to course load.
Financial support: Fellowships, research assistantships, teaching assistantships, career-related internships or fieldwork and Federal Work-Study available. Financial award application deadline: 2/15; financial award applicants required to submit FAFSA.
Faculty research: Fiber optics, computer architecture, bioelectromagnetics, acoustics.
Dr. S. Hossein Mousavinezhad, Chair, 616-387-4057.
Application contact: Admissions and Orientation, 616-387-2000, *Fax:* 616-387-2355.

■ **WESTERN NEW ENGLAND COLLEGE**

School of Engineering, Department of Electrical Engineering, Springfield, MA 01119-2654

AWARDS Computer and engineering information systems (MSEE); computer engineering (MSEE). Part-time and evening/weekend programs available.

Faculty: 7 full-time (0 women).
Students: Average age 29. 3 applicants, 0% accepted. In 2001, 4 degrees awarded.
Degree requirements: For master's, thesis optional.
Entrance requirements: For master's, GRE, bachelor's degree in engineering or related field. *Application deadline:* Applications are processed on a rolling basis. *Application fee:* $30.
Expenses: Tuition: Part-time $429 per credit. Required fees: $9 per credit. $20 per semester.
Financial support: Teaching assistantships available. Support available to part-time students. Financial award application deadline: 4/1; financial award applicants required to submit FAFSA.
Faculty research: Superconductors, microwave cooking, computer voice output, digital filters, computer engineering.
Dr. James J. Moriarty, Chair, 413-782-1491 Ext. 1725, *E-mail:* jmoriart@wnec.edu.
Application contact: Dr. Janet Castleman, Director of Continuing Education, 413-782-1750, *Fax:* 413-782-1779, *E-mail:* jcastlem@wnec.edu.

■ **WEST VIRGINIA UNIVERSITY**

College of Engineering and Mineral Resources, Lane Department of Computer Science and Electrical Engineering, Program in Computer Engineering, Morgantown, WV 26506

AWARDS PhD.

Students: 25 applicants, 60% accepted. In 2001, 1 degree awarded.
Degree requirements: For doctorate, thesis/dissertation, comprehensive exam.
Entrance requirements: For doctorate, GRE General Test, TOEFL, minimum GPA of 3.0. *Application deadline:* For fall admission, 7/1 (priority date). Applications are processed on a rolling basis. *Application fee:* $45.
Expenses: Tuition, state resident: full-time $2,791. Tuition, nonresident: full-time $8,659. Required fees: $1,002. Tuition and fees vary according to program.
Financial support: Fellowships, research assistantships, teaching assistantships, Federal Work-Study, institutionally sponsored loans, and tuition waivers (full and partial) available. Financial award application deadline: 2/1; financial award applicants required to submit FAFSA.
Faculty research: Software engineering, microprocessor applications, microelectronic systems, fault tolerance, advanced computer architectures and networks, neural networks.
Application contact: Dr. Wils L. Cooley, Graduate Coordinator, 304-293-0405 Ext. 2527, *Fax:* 304-293-8602, *E-mail:* wils.cooley@mail.wvu.edu.

■ **WIDENER UNIVERSITY**

School of Engineering, Program in Computer and Software Engineering, Chester, PA 19013-5792

AWARDS ME, ME/MBA. Part-time and evening/weekend programs available.

Degree requirements: For master's, thesis optional.
Entrance requirements: For master's, GMAT (ME/MBA).
Expenses: Tuition: Part-time $500 per credit. Required fees: $25 per semester.
Faculty research: Computer and software engineering, computer network fault-tolerant computing, and optical computing.

■ **WORCESTER POLYTECHNIC INSTITUTE**

Graduate Studies, Department of Electrical and Computer Engineering, Worcester, MA 01609-2280

AWARDS Electrical and computer engineering (MS, PhD, Advanced Certificate, Certificate); power systems engineering (MS, PhD). Part-time and evening/weekend programs available.

Faculty: 23 full-time (1 woman), 7 part-time/adjunct (0 women).
Students: 42 full-time (4 women), 39 part-time (8 women); includes 12 minority (2 African Americans, 7 Asian Americans or Pacific Islanders, 3 Hispanic Americans), 34 international. 209 applicants, 46% accepted, 32 enrolled. In 2001, 26 master's, 3 doctorates awarded. Terminal

master's awarded for partial completion of doctoral program.
Degree requirements: For master's, thesis optional; for doctorate, thesis/dissertation.
Entrance requirements: For master's and doctorate, TOEFL. *Application deadline:* For fall admission, 2/1 (priority date); for spring admission, 10/15 (priority date). Applications are processed on a rolling basis. *Application fee:* $60. Electronic applications accepted.
Expenses: Tuition: Part-time $796 per credit. Required fees: $20; $752 per credit. One-time fee: $30 full-time.
Financial support: In 2001–02, 37 students received support, including 1 fellowship with full and partial tuition reimbursement available (averaging $12,951 per year), 15 research assistantships with full tuition reimbursements available (averaging $17,256 per year), 15 teaching assistantships with full tuition reimbursements available (averaging $12,942 per year); career-related internships or fieldwork, institutionally sponsored loans, and scholarships/grants also available. Financial award application deadline: 2/15; financial award applicants required to submit FAFSA.
Faculty research: Analog and mixed signal IC design, cryptography and data security, power systems and power electronics, computer networking, image processing and visualization. *Total annual research expenditures:* $1.2 million.
Dr. John A. Orr, Head, 508-831-5231, *Fax:* 508-831-5491, *E-mail:* orr@wpi.edu.
Application contact: Dr. Fred J. Looft, Graduate Coordinator, 508-831-5231, *Fax:* 508-831-5491, *E-mail:* fjlooft@wpi.edu.
Web site: http://ee.wpi.edu/

■ **WRIGHT STATE UNIVERSITY**

School of Graduate Studies, College of Engineering and Computer Science, Department of Computer Science and Engineering, Computer Engineering Program, Dayton, OH 45435

AWARDS MSCE.

Students: 35 full-time (10 women), 7 part-time; includes 3 minority (1 African American, 2 Asian Americans or Pacific Islanders), 29 international. 77 applicants, 65% accepted. In 2001, 27 degrees awarded.
Degree requirements: For master's, thesis optional.
Entrance requirements: For master's, GRE General Test, TOEFL, minimum GPA of 3.0 in major, 2.7 overall. *Application fee:* $25.
Expenses: Tuition, state resident: full-time $7,161; part-time $225 per quarter hour. Tuition, nonresident: full-time $12,324; part-time $385 per quarter hour. Tuition and fees vary according to course load, degree level and program.

Wright State University (continued)

Financial support: Fellowships, research assistantships, teaching assistantships available. Support available to part-time students. Financial award application deadline: 3/31; financial award applicants required to submit FAFSA.

Faculty research: Networking and digital communications, parallel and concurrent computing, robotics and control, computer vision, optical computing.

Application contact: Dr. Jay E. Dejongh, Graduate Program Director, 937-775-5136, *Fax:* 937-775-5133, *E-mail:* jay.dejongh@wright.edu.

Find an in-depth description at www.petersons.com/gradchannel.

■ WRIGHT STATE UNIVERSITY

School of Graduate Studies, College of Engineering and Computer Science, Department of Computer Science and Engineering, Program in Computer Science and Engineering, Dayton, OH 45435

AWARDS PhD.

Students: 21 full-time (3 women), 5 part-time, 16 international. 34 applicants, 68% accepted.

Degree requirements: For doctorate, thesis/dissertation, candidacy and general exams.

Entrance requirements: For doctorate, GRE General Test, TOEFL, minimum GPA of 3.3. *Application fee:* $25.

Expenses: Tuition, state resident: full-time $7,161; part-time $225 per quarter hour. Tuition, nonresident: full-time $12,324; part-time $385 per quarter hour. Tuition and fees vary according to course load, degree level and program.

Financial support: Application deadline: 3/31.

Dr. Nikolas G. Bourbakis, Director, 937-775-5138, *Fax:* 937-775-5133, *E-mail:* nikolas.bourbakis@wright.edu.

ELECTRICAL ENGINEERING

■ AIR FORCE INSTITUTE OF TECHNOLOGY

School of Engineering and Management, Department of Electrical and Computer Engineering, Dayton, OH 45433-7765

AWARDS Computer engineering (MS, PhD); computer systems/science (MS); electrical engineering (MS, PhD); electro-optics (MS, PhD). Part-time programs available.

Degree requirements: For master's and doctorate, thesis/dissertation.

Entrance requirements: For master's and doctorate, GRE General Test, minimum GPA of 3.0, U.S. citizenship.

Faculty research: Remote sensing, information survivability, microelectronics, computer networks, artificial intelligence. *Web site:* http://en.afit.edu/bng/

■ ALFRED UNIVERSITY

Graduate School, Program in Electrical Engineering, Alfred, NY 14802-1205

AWARDS MS. Part-time programs available.

Students: 8 full-time (1 woman), 3 part-time (1 woman). 33 applicants, 52% accepted. In 2001, 2 degrees awarded.

Degree requirements: For master's, thesis.

Entrance requirements: For master's, TOEFL. *Application deadline:* Applications are processed on a rolling basis. *Application fee:* $50. Electronic applications accepted.

Expenses: Tuition: Full-time $23,554. Required fees: $698. One-time fee: $116 part-time. Full-time tuition and fees vary according to program.

Financial support: Research assistantships, tuition waivers (full and partial) and unspecified assistantships available. Financial award applicants required to submit FAFSA.

Dr. James Lancaster, Director, 607-871-2130, *E-mail:* flancaster@alfred.edu.

Application contact: Cathleen R. Johnson, Coordinator of Graduate Admissions, 607-871-2141, *Fax:* 607-871-2198, *E-mail:* johnsonc@alfred.edu. *Web site:* http://www.alfred.edu/

■ ARIZONA STATE UNIVERSITY

Graduate College, College of Engineering and Applied Sciences, Department of Electrical Engineering, Tempe, AZ 85287

AWARDS MS, MSE, PhD.

Degree requirements: For master's, thesis or alternative; for doctorate, thesis/dissertation.

Entrance requirements: For master's and doctorate, GRE General Test (recommended), TOEFL.

Faculty research: Solid-state electronics, computer applications, power systems, communications. *Web site:* http://www.eas.asu.edu:7001/

Find an in-depth description at www.petersons.com/gradchannel.

■ ARIZONA STATE UNIVERSITY EAST

College of Technology and Applied Sciences, Department of Electronics and Computer Engineering Technology, Mesa, AZ 85212

AWARDS MS. Part-time and evening/weekend programs available.

Faculty: 6 full-time (1 woman), 1 part-time/adjunct (0 women).

Students: 68 full-time (26 women), 57 part-time (22 women); includes 17 minority (3 African Americans, 12 Asian Americans or Pacific Islanders, 2 Hispanic Americans), 85 international. Average age 31. 103 applicants, 65% accepted, 36 enrolled. In 2001, 29 degrees awarded.

Degree requirements: For master's, thesis or applied project and oral defense. *Median time to degree:* Master's–1.6 years full-time, 2 years part-time.

Entrance requirements: For master's, GRE, TOEFL. *Application deadline:* Applications are processed on a rolling basis. *Application fee:* $45. Electronic applications accepted.

Expenses: Tuition, state resident: full-time $2,412; part-time $126 per credit hour. Tuition, nonresident: full-time $10,278; part-time $428 per credit hour. Required fees: $26. Tuition and fees vary according to course load.

Financial support: In 2001–02, 46 students received support, including 11 research assistantships with partial tuition reimbursements available (averaging $6,693 per year), 11 teaching assistantships with partial tuition reimbursements available (averaging $4,534 per year); career-related internships or fieldwork, Federal Work-Study, scholarships/grants, tuition waivers (full and partial), and unspecified assistantships also available. Support available to part-time students. Financial award application deadline: 3/1; financial award applicants required to submit FAFSA.

Faculty research: Systems, circuit applications and hardware design. *Total annual research expenditures:* $716,685.

Dr. Timothy Lindquist, Chair, 480-727-2783, *Fax:* 480-727-1723, *E-mail:* timothy.lindquist@asu.edu.

■ AUBURN UNIVERSITY

Graduate School, College of Engineering, Department of Electrical and Computer Engineering, Auburn University, AL 36849

AWARDS MEE, MS, PhD. Part-time programs available.

Faculty: 26 full-time (1 woman).

Students: 36 full-time (5 women), 29 part-time (2 women); includes 2 minority (1 African American, 1 Hispanic American), 38 international. 145 applicants, 38% accepted. In 2001, 14 master's, 6 doctorates awarded.

Degree requirements: For master's, thesis (for some programs), comprehensive exam; for doctorate, thesis/dissertation.

Entrance requirements: For master's and doctorate, GRE General Test, GRE Subject Test. *Application deadline:* For fall admission, 7/7; for spring admission, 11/24. Applications are processed on a rolling basis. *Application fee:* $25 ($50 for international students). Electronic applications accepted.

Financial support: Fellowships, research assistantships, teaching assistantships,

Federal Work-Study available. Support available to part-time students. Financial award application deadline: 3/15.
Faculty research: Power systems, energy conversion, electronics, electromagnetics, digital systems.
Dr. J. David Irwin, Head, 334-844-1800.
Application contact: Dr. John F. Pritchett, Dean of the Graduate School, 334-844-4700, *E-mail:* hatchlb@ mail.auburn.edu. *Web site:* http:// www.eng.auburn.edu/department/ee/

■ BOISE STATE UNIVERSITY

Graduate College, College of Engineering, Program in Electrical Engineering, Boise, ID 83725-0399

AWARDS MS. Part-time and evening/weekend programs available.

Degree requirements: For master's, thesis.
Entrance requirements: For master's, GRE General Test, TOEFL, minimum GPA of 3.0. Electronic applications accepted.

■ BOSTON UNIVERSITY

College of Engineering, Department of Electrical and Computer Engineering, Boston, MA 02215

AWARDS Computer engineering (PhD); computer systems engineering (MS); electrical engineering (MS, PhD). Systems engineering (PhD). Part-time programs available.

Faculty: 39 full-time (3 women), 3 part-time/adjunct (0 women).
Students: 110 full-time (25 women), 28 part-time (9 women); includes 9 minority (4 African Americans, 4 Asian Americans or Pacific Islanders, 1 Hispanic American), 72 international. Average age 29. 662 applicants, 19% accepted, 39 enrolled. In 2001, 39 master's, 7 doctorates awarded. Terminal master's awarded for partial completion of doctoral program.
Degree requirements: For master's, thesis optional; for doctorate, thesis/dissertation, comprehensive exam.
Entrance requirements: For master's and doctorate, GRE General Test, TOEFL. *Application deadline:* For fall admission, 4/1; for spring admission, 10/1. Applications are processed on a rolling basis. *Application fee:* $60. Electronic applications accepted.
Expenses: Tuition: Full-time $25,872; part-time $340 per credit. Required fees: $40 per semester. Part-time tuition and fees vary according to class time, course level and program.
Financial support: In 2001–02, 83 students received support, including 5 fellowships with full tuition reimbursements available (averaging $15,500 per year), 40 research assistantships with full tuition reimbursements available (averaging $13,500 per year), 19 teaching assistantships with full tuition reimbursements available (averaging $13,500 per year); career-related internships or fieldwork,

Federal Work-Study, institutionally sponsored loans, and scholarships/grants also available. Financial award application deadline: 1/15; financial award applicants required to submit FAFSA.
Faculty research: Computer networks, computer reliability, photonics, signal and image processing, solid state materials, subsurface imaging. *Total annual research expenditures:* $9.5 million.
Dr. Bahaa Saleh, Chairman, 617-353-7176, *Fax:* 617-353-6440.
Application contact: Cheryl Kelley, Director of Graduate Programs, 617-353-9760, *Fax:* 617-353-0259, *E-mail:* enggrad@bu.edu. *Web site:* http:// www.eng.bu.edu/grad/

Find an in-depth description at www.petersons.com/gradchannel.

■ BRADLEY UNIVERSITY

Graduate School, College of Engineering and Technology, Department of Electrical Engineering, Peoria, IL 61625-0002

AWARDS MSEE. Part-time and evening/weekend programs available.

Students: 10 full-time, 20 part-time. 138 applicants, 59% accepted. In 2001, 10 degrees awarded.
Degree requirements: For master's, comprehensive exam.
Entrance requirements: For master's, GRE, TOEFL, minimum GPA of 3.0. *Application deadline:* For fall admission, 7/1 (priority date); for spring admission, 11/1. Applications are processed on a rolling basis. *Application fee:* $40 ($50 for international students).
Expenses: Tuition: Part-time $7,615 per semester. Tuition and fees vary according to course load.
Financial support: In 2001–02, 9 research assistantships with full and partial tuition reimbursements were awarded; teaching assistantships, scholarships/grants and tuition waivers (partial) also available. Financial award application deadline: 3/1.
Dr. Brian Huggins, Chairperson, 309-677-2732.
Application contact: Dr. Prasad Shastry, Graduate Adviser, 309-677-2133.

■ BRIGHAM YOUNG UNIVERSITY

Graduate Studies, College of Engineering and Technology, Department of Electrical and Computer Engineering, Provo, UT 84602-1001

AWARDS Electrical engineering (MS); engineering (PhD). Part-time programs available.

Faculty: 22 full-time (0 women).
Students: 48 full-time (6 women), 28 part-time; includes 1 minority (Asian American or Pacific Islander), 10 international. Average age 26. 58 applicants, 38% accepted,

18 enrolled. In 2001, 26 master's, 2 doctorates awarded.
Degree requirements: For master's, thesis optional; for doctorate, thesis/dissertation, comprehensive exam, registration. *Median time to degree:* Master's–2 years full-time, 3.5 years part-time; doctorate–4 years full-time, 5.5 years part-time.
Entrance requirements: For master's, GRE General Test (international applicants and U.S. applicants from non-ABET-accredited institutions), TOEFL, minimum GPA of 3.0 in last 60 hours; for doctorate, GRE General Test (international applicants and U.S. applicants from non-ABET-accredited institutions), TOEFL, minimum GPA of 3.4 in last 60 hours. *Application deadline:* For fall admission, 2/15; for winter admission, 9/15. *Application fee:* $50. Electronic applications accepted.
Expenses: Tuition: Full-time $3,860; part-time $214 per hour.
Financial support: In 2001–02, 3 fellowships, 45 research assistantships, 5 teaching assistantships were awarded. Scholarships/grants and tuition waivers (full and partial) also available. Financial award application deadline: 2/15.
Faculty research: Microwave remote sensing, reconfigurable computing, VLSI design tools, microelectronics circuit design and fabrication, digital signal processing, intelligent multi-agent control. *Total annual research expenditures:* $2.5 million.
Dr. Richard L. Frost, Chair, 801-422-4012, *Fax:* 801-422-0201, *E-mail:* rickf@ ee.byu.edu.
Application contact: Ann Tanner, Department Advisement Assistant, 801-422-4013, *Fax:* 801-422-0201, *E-mail:* grad@ ee.byu.edu. *Web site:* http:// www.ee.byu.edu/

■ BROWN UNIVERSITY

Graduate School, Division of Engineering, Program in Electrical Sciences, Providence, RI 02912

AWARDS Sc M, PhD.

Degree requirements: For doctorate, thesis/dissertation, preliminary exam.

■ BUCKNELL UNIVERSITY

Graduate Studies, College of Engineering, Department of Electrical Engineering, Lewisburg, PA 17837

AWARDS MS, MSEE. Part-time programs available.

Faculty: 7 full-time (1 woman).
Students: 5 full-time (1 woman), 3 international.
Degree requirements: For master's, thesis.
Entrance requirements: For master's, GRE General Test, GRE Subject Test, TOEFL, minimum GPA of 2.8. *Application deadline:* For fall admission, 6/1 (priority

Bucknell University (continued)
date); for spring admission, 12/1 (priority date). Applications are processed on a rolling basis. *Application fee:* $25.
Expenses: Tuition: Part-time $2,875 per course.
Financial support: Unspecified assistantships available. Financial award application deadline: 3/1.
Dr. Edward Mastascusa, Head, 570-577-1234. *Web site:* http://www.bucknell.edu/

■ CALIFORNIA INSTITUTE OF TECHNOLOGY

Division of Engineering and Applied Science, Option in Electrical Engineering, Pasadena, CA 91125-0001

AWARDS MS, PhD.

Faculty: 14 full-time (1 woman).
Students: 104 full-time (13 women); includes 11 minority (1 African American, 7 Asian Americans or Pacific Islanders, 3 Hispanic Americans), 78 international. 652 applicants, 9% accepted, 28 enrolled. In 2001, 30 master's, 17 doctorates awarded.
Degree requirements: For doctorate, thesis/dissertation.
Application deadline: For fall admission, 1/15. *Application fee:* $0. Electronic applications accepted.
Financial support: In 2001–02, 23 fellowships, 49 research assistantships, 22 teaching assistantships were awarded.
Faculty research: Solid-state electronics, power electronics, communications, controls, submillimeter-wave integrated circuits.

■ CALIFORNIA POLYTECHNIC STATE UNIVERSITY, SAN LUIS OBISPO

College of Engineering, Department of Electrical Engineering, San Luis Obispo, CA 93407

AWARDS MS. Part-time programs available.

Faculty: 15 full-time (0 women).
Students: 19 full-time (2 women), 12 part-time (4 women). 21 applicants, 57% accepted, 11 enrolled. In 2001, 6 degrees awarded.
Degree requirements: For master's, thesis or alternative.
Entrance requirements: For master's, GRE General Test, GRE Subject Test, minimum GPA of 3.0 in last 90 quarter units. *Application deadline:* For fall admission, 5/31 (priority date); for spring admission, 12/31. Applications are processed on a rolling basis. *Application fee:* $55.
Expenses: Tuition, nonresident: part-time $164 per unit. One-time fee: $2,153 part-time.
Financial support: In 2001–02, 6 fellowships, 7 research assistantships, 8 teaching assistantships were awarded. Career-related internships or fieldwork also available.

Financial award application deadline: 3/2; financial award applicants required to submit FAFSA.
Faculty research: Communications, systems analysis, control systems, electronic devices, microprocessors.
Dr. Martin Kaliski, Chair, 805-756-2781, *Fax:* 805-756-1458, *E-mail:* mkaliski@calpoly.edu.
Application contact: Dr. Donley Winger, Coordinator, 805-756-1462, *Fax:* 805-756-1458, *E-mail:* dwinger@calpoly.edu. *Web site:* http://www.ee.calpoly.edu/

■ CALIFORNIA STATE POLYTECHNIC UNIVERSITY, POMONA

Academic Affairs, College of Engineering, Pomona, CA 91768-2557

AWARDS Electrical engineering (MSEE); engineering (MSE). Part-time programs available.

Faculty: 106 full-time (15 women), 34 part-time/adjunct (1 woman).
Students: 48 full-time (10 women), 101 part-time (11 women); includes 66 minority (57 Asian Americans or Pacific Islanders, 9 Hispanic Americans), 34 international. Average age 28. 133 applicants, 68% accepted. In 2001, 49 degrees awarded.
Degree requirements: For master's, thesis or comprehensive exam.
Entrance requirements: For master's, TOEFL, GRE General Test or minimum GPA of 3.0 in upper-level course work. *Application deadline:* For fall admission, 5/1 (priority date); for winter admission, 10/15 (priority date); for spring admission, 1/2 (priority date). Applications are processed on a rolling basis. *Application fee:* $55. Electronic applications accepted.
Expenses: Tuition, nonresident: part-time $164 per unit. Required fees: $1,850.
Financial support: In 2001–02, 1 fellowship, 6 research assistantships, 5 teaching assistantships were awarded. Career-related internships or fieldwork, Federal Work-Study, institutionally sponsored loans, and unspecified assistantships also available. Support available to part-time students. Financial award application deadline: 3/2; financial award applicants required to submit FAFSA.
Faculty research: Aerospace; alternative vehicles; communications, computers, and controls; engineering management. *Total annual research expenditures:* $650,000.
Dr. Ed Hohmann, Dean, 909-869-2472, *Fax:* 909-869-4370, *E-mail:* echohmann@csupomona.edu.
Application contact: Dr. Rajan Chandra, Director, 909-869-2476, *Fax:* 909-869-4687, *E-mail:* rmchandra@csupomona.edu. *Web site:* http://www.csupomona.edu/~engineering/

■ CALIFORNIA STATE UNIVERSITY, CHICO

Graduate School, College of Engineering, Computer Science, and Technology, Department of Electrical Engineering, Chico, CA 95929-0722

AWARDS MS.

Students: 12 full-time, 4 part-time; includes 9 minority (8 Asian Americans or Pacific Islanders, 1 Hispanic American). 45 applicants, 76% accepted, 11 enrolled. In 2001, 3 degrees awarded.
Degree requirements: For master's, thesis or alternative, oral exam.
Entrance requirements: For master's, GRE General Test. *Application deadline:* For fall admission, 4/1; for spring admission, 10/1. Applications are processed on a rolling basis. *Application fee:* $55. Electronic applications accepted.
Expenses: Tuition, state resident: full-time $2,148. Tuition, nonresident: full-time $6,576.
Financial support: Fellowships, teaching assistantships available.
Dr. Larry Wear, Chair, 530-898-5343.

■ CALIFORNIA STATE UNIVERSITY, FRESNO

Division of Graduate Studies, College of Engineering and Computer Science, Program in Electrical Engineering, Fresno, CA 93740-8027

AWARDS MS. Offered at Edwards Air Force Base. Part-time and evening/weekend programs available.

Faculty: 6 full-time (0 women).
Students: 6 full-time (1 woman), 5 part-time; includes 2 minority (1 African American, 1 Asian American or Pacific Islander), 5 international. Average age 31. 23 applicants, 65% accepted, 3 enrolled. In 2001, 3 degrees awarded.
Degree requirements: For master's, thesis or alternative. *Median time to degree:* Master's–2.5 years full-time, 3.5 years part-time.
Entrance requirements: For master's, GRE General Test, TOEFL, minimum GPA of 2.7. *Application deadline:* For fall admission, 8/1 (priority date); for spring admission, 12/1. Applications are processed on a rolling basis. *Application fee:* $55. Electronic applications accepted.
Expenses: Tuition, nonresident: part-time $246 per unit. Required fees: $605 per semester. Tuition and fees vary according to course load.
Financial support: Application deadline: 3/1;
Faculty research: Research in electromagnetic devices.
Dr. Nagy Bengiamin, Head, 559-278-6297, *Fax:* 559-278-6297, *E-mail:* nagy_bengiamin@esufresno.edu.
Application contact: James W. Smolka, Coordinator, 661-258-5936.

■ CALIFORNIA STATE UNIVERSITY, FULLERTON

Graduate Studies, College of Engineering and Computer Science, Department of Electrical Engineering, Fullerton, CA 92834-9480

AWARDS MS. Part-time programs available.

Faculty: 13 full-time (2 women), 2 part-time/adjunct.
Students: 33 full-time (8 women), 45 part-time (8 women); includes 36 minority (1 African American, 30 Asian Americans or Pacific Islanders, 5 Hispanic Americans), 28 international. Average age 30. 88 applicants, 55% accepted, 22 enrolled. In 2001, 25 degrees awarded.
Degree requirements: For master's, project or thesis.
Entrance requirements: For master's, GRE General Test, GRE Subject Test, minimum undergraduate GPA of 2.5, 3.0 graduate. *Application fee:* $55.
Expenses: Tuition, nonresident: part-time $246 per unit. Required fees: $964.
Financial support: Career-related internships or fieldwork, Federal Work-Study, institutionally sponsored loans, and scholarships/grants available. Support available to part-time students. Financial award application deadline: 3/1.
Dr. David Cheng, Head, 714-278-3013.

■ CALIFORNIA STATE UNIVERSITY, LONG BEACH

Graduate Studies, College of Engineering, Department of Electrical Engineering, Long Beach, CA 90840

AWARDS MSE, MSEE. Part-time programs available.

Faculty: 24 full-time (0 women), 6 part-time/adjunct (0 women).
Students: 37 full-time (3 women), 75 part-time (9 women); includes 56 minority (7 African Americans, 38 Asian Americans or Pacific Islanders, 11 Hispanic Americans), 35 international. Average age 32. 107 applicants, 67% accepted. In 2001, 26 degrees awarded.
Degree requirements: For master's, comprehensive exam or thesis.
Entrance requirements: For master's, TOEFL. *Application deadline:* For fall admission, 8/1; for spring admission, 12/1. *Application fee:* $55. Electronic applications accepted.
Financial support: Teaching assistantships, career-related internships or fieldwork, Federal Work-Study, institutionally sponsored loans, scholarships/grants, and unspecified assistantships available. Financial award application deadline: 3/2.
Faculty research: Health care systems, IC, VLSI, communications, CAD/CAM.
Dr. Fumio Hamano, Chair, 562-985-5102, *Fax:* 562-985-5327.
Application contact: Dr. Michael Singh-Chelian, Graduate Adviser, 562-985-1516,

Fax: 562-985-5327, *E-mail:* mchelian@engr.csulb.edu.

■ CALIFORNIA STATE UNIVERSITY, LOS ANGELES

Graduate Studies, College of Engineering, Computer Science, and Technology, Department of Electrical and Computer Engineering, Los Angeles, CA 90032-8530

AWARDS Electrical engineering (MS). Part-time and evening/weekend programs available.

Faculty: 9 full-time, 3 part-time/adjunct.
Students: 20 full-time (6 women), 73 part-time (8 women); includes 46 minority (3 African Americans, 28 Asian Americans or Pacific Islanders, 15 Hispanic Americans), 37 international. In 2001, 24 degrees awarded.
Degree requirements: For master's, comprehensive exam or thesis.
Entrance requirements: For master's, GRE General Test, GRE Subject Test, TOEFL. *Application deadline:* For fall admission, 6/30; for spring admission, 2/1. Applications are processed on a rolling basis. *Application fee:* $55.
Expenses: Tuition, nonresident: part-time $164 per unit.
Financial support: Federal Work-Study available. Support available to part-time students. Financial award application deadline: 3/1.
Dr. Helen Boussalis, Chair, 323-343-4470.

■ CALIFORNIA STATE UNIVERSITY, NORTHRIDGE

Graduate Studies, College of Engineering and Computer Science, Department of Electrical and Computer Engineering, Northridge, CA 91330

AWARDS Biomedical engineering (MS); communications/radar engineering (MS); control engineering (MS); digital/computer engineering (MS); electronics engineering (MS); microwave/antenna engineering (MS). Part-time and evening/weekend programs available.

Faculty: 19 full-time, 6 part-time/adjunct.
Students: 31 full-time (3 women), 81 part-time (9 women); includes 30 minority (1 African American, 21 Asian Americans or Pacific Islanders, 8 Hispanic Americans), 32 international. Average age 33. 77 applicants, 73% accepted, 19 enrolled. In 2001, 22 degrees awarded.
Degree requirements: For master's, thesis or alternative.
Entrance requirements: For master's, GRE General Test, TOEFL, minimum GPA of 2.5. *Application deadline:* For fall admission, 11/30. *Application fee:* $55.
Expenses: Tuition, nonresident: part-time $631 per semester. Required fees: $246 per unit.

Financial support: Application deadline: 3/1.
Faculty research: Reflector antenna study, radome study.
Dr. Nagwa Bekir, Chair, 818-677-2190.
Application contact: Nagi El Naga, Graduate Coordinator, 818-677-2180.

■ CALIFORNIA STATE UNIVERSITY, SACRAMENTO

Graduate Studies, College of Engineering and Computer Science, Department of Electrical and Electronic Engineering, Sacramento, CA 95819-6048

AWARDS Electrical engineering (MS). Part-time and evening/weekend programs available.

Students: 73 full-time (11 women), 54 part-time (7 women); includes 17 minority (1 African American, 13 Asian Americans or Pacific Islanders, 3 Hispanic Americans), 90 international.
Degree requirements: For master's, writing proficiency exam.
Entrance requirements: For master's, TOEFL. *Application deadline:* For fall admission, 4/15; for spring admission, 11/1. *Application fee:* $55.
Expenses: Tuition, state resident: full-time $1,965; part-time $668 per semester. Tuition, nonresident: part-time $246 per unit.
Financial support: Research assistantships, teaching assistantships, career-related internships or fieldwork and Federal Work-Study available. Support available to part-time students. Financial award application deadline: 3/1.
Dr. S. K. Ramesh, Chair, 916-278-6873.
Application contact: Dr. John Oldenburg, Graduate Coordinator, 916-278-6873.

■ CAPITOL COLLEGE

Graduate Programs, Laurel, MD 20708-9759

AWARDS Computer science (MS); electrical engineering (MS); electronic commerce management (MS); information and telecommunications systems management (MS); information architecture (MS); network security (MS). Part-time and evening/weekend programs available. Postbaccalaureate distance learning degree programs offered (no on-campus study).

Faculty: 3 full-time (0 women), 34 part-time/adjunct (4 women).
Students: 6 full-time (3 women), 625 part-time (175 women). Average age 35. 400 applicants, 75% accepted, 275 enrolled. In 2001, 52 degrees awarded. *Median time to degree:* Master's–2 years part-time.
Entrance requirements: For master's, GRE General Test and TOEFL (for international students), minimum GPA of 2.5. *Application deadline:* For fall admission, 7/1 (priority date); for winter admission, 12/1 (priority date); for spring admission,

Capitol College (continued)
3/1 (priority date). Applications are processed on a rolling basis. *Application fee:* $100 for international students. Electronic applications accepted.
Expenses: Tuition: Part-time $354 per credit.
Financial support: In 2001–02, 2 students received support. Available to part-time students. Applicants required to submit FAFSA.
Pat Smit, Dean of Academics, 301-369-2800 Ext. 3044, *Fax:* 301-953-3876, *E-mail:* gradschool@capitol-college.edu.
Application contact: Ken Crockett, Director of Graduate Admissions, 301-369-2800 Ext. 3026, *Fax:* 301-953-3876, *E-mail:* gradschool@capitol-college.edu.
Web site: http://www.capitol-college.edu/

■ CARNEGIE MELLON UNIVERSITY

Carnegie Institute of Technology, Department of Electrical and Computer Engineering, Pittsburgh, PA 15213-3891

AWARDS Biomedical engineering (MS, PhD); electrical and computer engineering (MS, PhD). Part-time programs available.

Degree requirements: For master's, thesis; for doctorate, thesis/dissertation, qualifying exam, teaching experience.
Entrance requirements: For master's and doctorate, GRE General Test, TOEFL.
Faculty research: Computer-aided design, solid-state devices, VLSI, processing, robotics and controls, signal processing, data systems storage. *Web site:* http://www.ece.cmu.edu/

Find an in-depth description at www.petersons.com/gradchannel.

■ CASE WESTERN RESERVE UNIVERSITY

School of Graduate Studies, The Case School of Engineering, Department of Electrical Engineering and Computer Science, Cleveland, OH 44106

AWARDS Computer engineering (MS, PhD); computing and information science (MS, PhD); electrical engineering (MS, PhD). Systems and control engineering (MS, PhD). Part-time and evening/weekend programs available. Postbaccalaureate distance learning degree programs offered (minimal on-campus study).
Faculty: 29 full-time (2 women), 15 part-time/adjunct (1 woman).
Students: 61 full-time (17 women), 72 part-time (6 women); includes 8 minority (3 African Americans, 5 Asian Americans or Pacific Islanders), 85 international. Average age 25. 843 applicants, 16% accepted, 27 enrolled. In 2001, 33 master's, 16 doctorates awarded. Terminal master's awarded for partial completion of doctoral program.

Degree requirements: For master's, thesis; for doctorate, thesis/dissertation, qualifying exam, teaching experience.
Entrance requirements: For master's and doctorate, GRE General Test, TOEFL. *Application deadline:* For fall admission, 2/1; for spring admission, 11/1. Applications are processed on a rolling basis. *Application fee:* $25.
Financial support: In 2001–02, 34 fellowships with full and partial tuition reimbursements (averaging $15,240 per year), 22 research assistantships with full and partial tuition reimbursements (averaging $14,220 per year) were awarded. Career-related internships or fieldwork, Federal Work-Study, and institutionally sponsored loans also available. Support available to part-time students. Financial award application deadline: 3/1; financial award applicants required to submit FAFSA.
Faculty research: Computational biology and biorobotics; HEHS and solid state, VSLI system design and testing; databases, software engineering, computer systems. Systems optimization, planning and decision making; digital signal processing, control and filtering theory. *Total annual research expenditures:* $3.2 million.
Dr. B. Ross Barmish, Chairman, 216-368-2833, *Fax:* 216-368-6888, *E-mail:* brb8@po.cwru.edu.
Application contact: Elizabethanne M. Fuller, Department Assistant, 216-368-4080, *Fax:* 216-368-2668, *E-mail:* emf4@po.cwru.edu. *Web site:* http://eecs.cwru.edu/

■ THE CATHOLIC UNIVERSITY OF AMERICA

School of Engineering, Department of Electrical Engineering and Computer Science, Washington, DC 20064

AWARDS MEE, MS Engr, MSCS, D Engr, PhD. Part-time and evening/weekend programs available.

Faculty: 8 full-time (0 women), 3 part-time/adjunct (0 women).
Students: 6 full-time (1 woman), 31 part-time (4 women); includes 4 minority (1 African American, 1 Asian American or Pacific Islander, 2 Hispanic Americans), 17 international. Average age 33. 64 applicants, 69% accepted, 10 enrolled. In 2001, 6 master's, 2 doctorates awarded.
Degree requirements: For master's, thesis optional; for doctorate, thesis/dissertation, oral exams, comprehensive exam.
Entrance requirements: For master's, TOEFL, minimum GPA of 3.0; for doctorate, TOEFL, minimum GPA of 3.4. *Application deadline:* For fall admission, 8/1 (priority date); for spring admission, 12/1. Applications are processed on a rolling basis. *Application fee:* $55. Electronic applications accepted.
Expenses: Tuition: Full-time $20,050; part-time $770 per credit. Required fees:

$430 per term. Tuition and fees vary according to program.
Financial support: Research assistantships, career-related internships or fieldwork, Federal Work-Study, institutionally sponsored loans, tuition waivers (full and partial), and unspecified assistantships available. Support available to part-time students. Financial award application deadline: 2/1.
Faculty research: Signal and image processing, computer communications, robotics, intelligent controls, bioelectromagnetics, properties of materials.
Dr. Nader Namazi, Chair, 202-319-5193.

■ CITY COLLEGE OF THE CITY UNIVERSITY OF NEW YORK

Graduate School, School of Engineering, Department of Electrical Engineering, New York, NY 10031-9198

AWARDS ME, MS, PhD. Part-time programs available.

Students: 50. In 2001, 18 degrees awarded.
Degree requirements: For master's, thesis optional; for doctorate, one foreign language, thesis/dissertation, comprehensive exam.
Entrance requirements: For master's, TOEFL; for doctorate, GRE General Test, TOEFL. *Application deadline:* Applications are processed on a rolling basis. *Application fee:* $40.
Expenses: Tuition, state resident: part-time $185 per credit. Tuition, nonresident: part-time $320 per credit. Required fees: $43 per term.
Financial support: Fellowships, research assistantships, Federal Work-Study and tuition waivers (full and partial) available. Support available to part-time students. Financial award application deadline: 5/1.
Faculty research: Optical electronics, microwaves, communication, signal processing, control systems.
Fred Thau, Chairman, 212-690-7250.
Application contact: Graduate Admissions Office, 212-650-6977.

■ CLARKSON UNIVERSITY

Graduate School, School of Engineering, Department of Electrical and Computer Engineering, Potsdam, NY 13699

AWARDS Computer engineering (ME, MS); electrical and computer engineering (PhD); electrical engineering (ME, MS). Part-time programs available.

Faculty: 13 full-time (2 women).
Students: 23 full-time (7 women), 17 international. Average age 26. 283 applicants, 55% accepted. In 2001, 18 master's awarded.
Degree requirements: For master's, thesis; for doctorate, thesis/dissertation,

departmental qualifying exam. *Median time to degree:* Master's–1.5 years full-time.
Entrance requirements: For master's, GRE, TOEFL. *Application deadline:* For fall admission, 5/15 (priority date); for spring admission, 10/15 (priority date). Applications are processed on a rolling basis. *Application fee:* $25 ($35 for international students).
Expenses: Tuition: Part-time $714 per credit. Required fees: $108 per semester.
Financial support: In 2001–02, 8 students received support, including fellowships (averaging $20,000 per year), 2 research assistantships (averaging $17,000 per year), 6 teaching assistantships (averaging $17,000 per year). Scholarships/grants and tuition waivers (partial) also available.
Faculty research: Robotics, electrical machines, electrical circuits, dielectric liquids, controls, power systems. *Total annual research expenditures:* $324,885.
Dr. Thomas H. Ortmeyer, Chair, 315-268-6511, *Fax:* 315-268-7994.
Application contact: Donna Brockway, Assistant to Dean/Foreign Student Advisor, 315-268-6447, *Fax:* 315-268-7994, *E-mail:* brockway@clarkson.edu.

■ CLEMSON UNIVERSITY

Graduate School, College of Engineering and Science, Department of Electrical and Computer Engineering, Program in Electrical Engineering, Clemson, SC 29634

AWARDS M Engr, MS, PhD.

Students: 113 full-time (15 women), 16 part-time (2 women); includes 7 minority (3 African Americans, 4 Asian Americans or Pacific Islanders), 89 international. 586 applicants, 40% accepted, 48 enrolled. In 2001, 36 master's, 5 doctorates awarded.
Degree requirements: For master's, thesis or alternative; for doctorate, thesis/dissertation, departmental qualifying exam.
Entrance requirements: For master's, GRE General Test (MS), TOEFL; for doctorate, GRE General Test, TOEFL. *Application deadline:* For fall admission, 6/1. *Application fee:* $40.
Expenses: Tuition, state resident: full-time $5,310. Tuition, nonresident: full-time $11,284.
Financial support: Fellowships, research assistantships, teaching assistantships, career-related internships or fieldwork available. Financial award applicants required to submit FAFSA.
Faculty research: Microelectronics, robotics, signal processing/communications, power systems, control.
Dr. Ernest Baxa, Coordinator, 864-656-5900, *Fax:* 864-656-5910, *E-mail:* ece-grad-program@clemson.edu. *Web site:* http://ece.clemson.edu/

■ CLEVELAND STATE UNIVERSITY

College of Graduate Studies, Fenn College of Engineering, Department of Electrical and Computer Engineering, Cleveland, OH 44115

AWARDS MS, D Eng. Part-time programs available.

Degree requirements: For master's, thesis or extra course work; for doctorate, thesis/dissertation, candidacy and qualifying exams.
Entrance requirements: For master's, GRE General Test, TOEFL, minimum GPA of 3.0; for doctorate, GRE General Test, TOEFL, minimum GPA of 3.5.
Expenses: Tuition, state resident: full-time $6,838; part-time $263 per credit hour. Tuition, nonresident: full-time $13,526; part-time $520 per credit hour.
Faculty research: Computer networks, knowledge-based control systems, artificial intelligence, electromagnetic interference, semiconducting materials for solar cell digital communications. *Web site:* http://csaxp.csuohio.edu/electrical/index.html

■ COLORADO STATE UNIVERSITY

Graduate School, College of Engineering, Department of Electrical and Computer Engineering, Fort Collins, CO 80523-0015

AWARDS M Eng, MS, PhD. Part-time programs available. Postbaccalaureate distance learning degree programs offered (no on-campus study).

Faculty: 19 full-time (1 woman).
Students: 48 full-time (6 women), 104 part-time (14 women); includes 8 minority (5 Asian Americans or Pacific Islanders, 2 Hispanic Americans, 1 Native American), 113 international. Average age 28. 413 applicants, 53% accepted, 57 enrolled. In 2001, 15 master's, 1 doctorate awarded. Terminal master's awarded for partial completion of doctoral program.
Degree requirements: For master's, thesis (for some programs), final exam; for doctorate, thesis/dissertation, qualifying, preliminary, and final exams.
Entrance requirements: For master's, GRE General Test, TOEFL, minimum GPA of 3.0; for doctorate, GRE General Test, TOEFL, minimum GPA of 3.5. *Application deadline:* For fall admission, 2/15 (priority date); for spring admission, 7/15 (priority date). Applications are processed on a rolling basis. *Application fee:* $30. Electronic applications accepted.
Expenses: Tuition, state resident: full-time $2,880; part-time $160 per credit. Tuition, nonresident: full-time $11,412; part-time $634 per credit. Required fees: $750; $34 per credit.
Financial support: In 2001–02, 4 fellowships, 33 research assistantships (averaging $15,060 per year), 4 teaching assistantships

(averaging $11,295 per year) were awarded. Career-related internships or fieldwork, Federal Work-Study, institutionally sponsored loans, and traineeships also available.
Faculty research: Communications, optoelectronics, controls and robotics, computer engineering, signal image processing. *Total annual research expenditures:* $3.2 million.
Dr. Derek L. Lile, Head, 970-491-6600, *Fax:* 970-491-2249, *E-mail:* lile@engr.colostate.edu.
Application contact: Elizabeth L. Wadman, Graduate Coordinator, 970-491-6600, *Fax:* 970-491-6706, *E-mail:* ewadman@engr.colostate.edu. *Web site:* http://www.engr.colostate.edu/depts/ee/index.html

■ COLORADO TECHNICAL UNIVERSITY

Graduate Studies, Program in Electrical Engineering, Colorado Springs, CO 80907-3896

AWARDS Communication systems (MSEE); electronic systems (MSEE). Part-time and evening/weekend programs available.

Faculty: 3 full-time (1 woman), 9 part-time/adjunct (1 woman).
Students: 7 full-time (0 women), 1 part-time; includes 4 minority (1 African American, 2 Asian Americans or Pacific Islanders, 1 Hispanic American). Average age 38. 3 applicants, 67% accepted, 2 enrolled. In 2001, 5 degrees awarded.
Degree requirements: For master's, thesis or alternative. *Median time to degree:* Master's–2 years full-time, 3 years part-time.
Application deadline: For fall admission, 10/2; for winter admission, 1/3; for spring admission, 4/3. Applications are processed on a rolling basis. *Application fee:* $100.
Expenses: Tuition: Full-time $6,960; part-time $290 per credit. Required fees: $40 per quarter. One-time fee: $100. Tuition and fees vary according to course load and degree level.
Financial support: Career-related internships or fieldwork and Federal Work-Study available. Financial award applicants required to submit FAFSA.
Faculty research: Electronic systems design, communication systems design.
Alex Dwelis, Dean, 719-590-6791, *Fax:* 719-598-3740, *E-mail:* adwelis@coloradotech.edu.
Application contact: Judy Galante, Graduate Admissions, 719-590-6720, *Fax:* 719-598-3740, *E-mail:* jgalante@coloradotech.edu. *Web site:* http://www.coloradotech.edu/

■ COLUMBIA UNIVERSITY

Fu Foundation School of Engineering and Applied Science, Department of Electrical Engineering, New York, NY 10027

AWARDS Electrical engineering (MS, Eng Sc D, PhD, EE). Solid state science and engineering (MS, Eng Sc D, PhD); telecommunications (MS). PhD offered through the Graduate School of Arts and Sciences. Part-time programs available. Postbaccalaureate distance learning degree programs offered (no on-campus study).

Faculty: 20 full-time (0 women), 13 part-time/adjunct (1 woman).
Students: 136 full-time (20 women), 87 part-time (11 women); includes 30 minority (2 African Americans, 28 Asian Americans or Pacific Islanders), 136 international. Average age 23. 882 applicants, 27% accepted, 53 enrolled. In 2001, 59 master's, 8 doctorates awarded. Terminal master's awarded for partial completion of doctoral program.
Degree requirements: For doctorate, thesis/dissertation, qualifying exam.
Entrance requirements: For master's and doctorate, GRE General Test, TOEFL. *Application deadline:* For fall admission, 1/5; for spring admission, 10/1. *Application fee:* $55. Electronic applications accepted.
Expenses: Tuition: Full-time $27,528. Required fees: $1,638.
Financial support: In 2001–02, 2 fellowships (averaging $19,800 per year), 49 research assistantships with full tuition reimbursements (averaging $20,550 per year), 17 teaching assistantships with full tuition reimbursements (averaging $20,550 per year) were awarded. Federal Work-Study and readerships, preceptorships also available. Financial award application deadline: 1/5; financial award applicants required to submit FAFSA.
Faculty research: Communications/networking, signal/image processing, microelectronic circuits/VLSI design, microelectronic devices/optoelectronics/electromagnetics/plasma physics. *Total annual research expenditures:* $6.5 million. Prof. Charles Zukowski, Chairman, 212-854-5019, *Fax:* 212-932-9421, *E-mail:* caz@ee.columbia.edu.
Application contact: Marlene Mansfield, Student Coordinator, 212-854-3104, *Fax:* 212-932-9421, *E-mail:* mansfield@ee.columbia.edu. *Web site:* http://www.ee.columbia.edu/

Find an in-depth description at www.petersons.com/gradchannel.

■ CORNELL UNIVERSITY

Graduate School, Graduate Fields of Engineering, Field of Electrical Engineering, Ithaca, NY 14853-0001

AWARDS Computer engineering (M Eng, PhD); electrical engineering (M Eng, PhD); electrical systems (M Eng, PhD); electrophysics (M Eng, PhD).

Faculty: 45 full-time.
Students: 250 full-time (30 women); includes 43 minority (2 African Americans, 37 Asian Americans or Pacific Islanders, 3 Hispanic Americans, 1 Native American), 160 international. 850 applicants, 32% accepted. In 2001, 87 master's, 20 doctorates awarded. Terminal master's awarded for partial completion of doctoral program.
Degree requirements: For doctorate, thesis/dissertation.
Entrance requirements: For master's, GRE General Test, TOEFL, preapplication if currently enrolled at a non-US college or university, 2 letters of recommendation; for doctorate, GRE General Test, TOEFL, preapplication if currently enrolled at a non-US college or university, 3 letters of recommendation. *Application deadline:* For fall admission, 1/15. *Application fee:* $65. Electronic applications accepted.
Expenses: Tuition: Full-time $25,970. Required fees: $50.
Financial support: In 2001–02, 141 students received support, including 22 fellowships with full tuition reimbursements available, 75 research assistantships with full tuition reimbursements available, 44 teaching assistantships with full tuition reimbursements available; institutionally sponsored loans, scholarships/grants, tuition waivers (full and partial), and unspecified assistantships also available. Financial award applicants required to submit FAFSA.
Faculty research: Communications; information theory. Signal processing, and power control; computer engineering; microelectromechanical systems and nanotechnology.
Application contact: Graduate Field Assistant, 607-255-4304, *E-mail:* meng@ee.cornell.edu; ms-phd@ee.cornell.edu. *Web site:* http://www.gradschool.cornell.edu/grad/fields_1/elec-engr.html

Find an in-depth description at www.petersons.com/gradchannel.

■ DARTMOUTH COLLEGE

Thayer School of Engineering, Program in Electrical Engineering, Hanover, NH 03755

AWARDS MS, PhD.

Degree requirements: For master's, thesis; for doctorate, thesis/dissertation, candidacy oral exam.
Entrance requirements: For master's and doctorate, GRE General Test. *Application deadline:* For fall admission, 1/1 (priority date). *Application fee:* $40 ($50 for international students).
Expenses: Tuition: Full-time $26,425.
Financial support: Career-related internships or fieldwork, Federal Work-Study, institutionally sponsored loans, and tuition waivers (full and partial) available. Financial award application deadline: 1/15.

Faculty research: Power electronics and microengineering, signal/image processing and communications, optics, lasers and optoelectronics, electromagnetic fields. *Total annual research expenditures:* $2.5 million.
Application contact: Candace S. Potter, Graduate Admissions Administrator, 603-646-3844, *Fax:* 603-646-1620, *E-mail:* candace.potter@dartmouth.edu. *Web site:* http://engineering.dartmouth.edu/

■ DREXEL UNIVERSITY

Graduate School, College of Engineering, Department of Electrical and Computer Engineering, Program in Electrical Engineering, Philadelphia, PA 19104-2875

AWARDS MSEE, PhD. Part-time and evening/weekend programs available.

Faculty: 32 full-time (4 women), 3 part-time/adjunct (0 women).
Students: 39 full-time (11 women), 85 part-time (12 women); includes 9 minority (1 African American, 6 Asian Americans or Pacific Islanders, 2 Hispanic Americans), 69 international. Average age 27. 472 applicants, 65% accepted, 19 enrolled. In 2001, 25 master's, 3 doctorates awarded. Terminal master's awarded for partial completion of doctoral program.
Degree requirements: For master's, thesis (for some programs); for doctorate, thesis/dissertation.
Application deadline: For fall admission, 8/21. Applications are processed on a rolling basis. *Application fee:* $50. Electronic applications accepted.
Expenses: Tuition: Full-time $20,088; part-time $558 per credit. Required fees: $78 per term. One-time fee: $200. Tuition and fees vary according to course load, degree level and program.
Financial support: Research assistantships, teaching assistantships, career-related internships or fieldwork and unspecified assistantships available. Financial award application deadline: 2/1.
Application contact: Director of Graduate Admissions, 215-895-6700, *Fax:* 215-895-5939, *E-mail:* enroll@drexel.edu.

■ DUKE UNIVERSITY

Graduate School, School of Engineering, Department of Electrical and Computer Engineering, Durham, NC 27708-0586

AWARDS MS, PhD. Part-time programs available.

Faculty: 22 full-time, 7 part-time/adjunct.
Students: 93 full-time (22 women); includes 5 minority (4 Asian Americans or Pacific Islanders, 1 Hispanic American), 74 international. 241 applicants, 20% accepted, 28 enrolled. In 2001, 17 master's, 11 doctorates awarded. Terminal master's awarded for partial completion of doctoral program.

Degree requirements: For doctorate, thesis/dissertation.

Entrance requirements: For master's and doctorate, GRE General Test. *Application deadline:* For fall admission, 12/31; for spring admission, 11/1. *Application fee:* $75.

Expenses: Tuition: Full-time $24,600.

Financial support: Fellowships, research assistantships, Federal Work-Study available. Financial award application deadline: 12/31.

Peter Marinos, Director of Graduate Studies, 919-660-5245, *Fax:* 919-660-5293, *E-mail:* joyce@ee.duke.edu. *Web site:* http://www.ee.duke.edu/

Find an in-depth description at www.petersons.com/gradchannel.

■ **FAIRLEIGH DICKINSON UNIVERSITY, METROPOLITAN CAMPUS**

University College: Arts, Sciences, and Professional Studies, School of Engineering and Engineering Technology, Program in Electrical Engineering, Teaneck, NJ 07666-1914

AWARDS MSEE.

Students: 70 full-time (7 women), 13 part-time (2 women); includes 5 minority (1 African American, 3 Asian Americans or Pacific Islanders, 1 Hispanic American), 71 international. Average age 26. 258 applicants, 86% accepted, 41 enrolled. In 2001, 10 degrees awarded.

Entrance requirements: For master's, GRE General Test. *Application deadline:* Applications are processed on a rolling basis. *Application fee:* $40.

Expenses: Tuition: Full-time $11,484; part-time $638 per credit. Required fees: $420; $97.

Dr. Alfredo Tan, Director, School of Engineering and Engineering Technology, 201-692-2347, *Fax:* 201-692-2130, *E-mail:* tan@fdu.edu.

■ **FLORIDA AGRICULTURAL AND MECHANICAL UNIVERSITY**

Division of Graduate Studies, Research, and Continuing Education, FAMU-FSU College of Engineering, Department of Electrical Engineering, Tallahassee, FL 32307-3200

AWARDS MS, PhD.

Entrance requirements: For master's, GRE General Test, minimum GPA of 3.0.

■ **FLORIDA ATLANTIC UNIVERSITY**

College of Engineering, Department of Electrical Engineering, Boca Raton, FL 33431-0991

AWARDS MS, PhD. Part-time and evening/weekend programs available.

Postbaccalaureate distance learning degree programs offered (minimal on-campus study).

Faculty: 18 full-time (3 women), 2 part-time/adjunct (0 women).

Students: 22 full-time (2 women), 32 part-time (2 women); includes 12 minority (4 African Americans, 2 Asian Americans or Pacific Islanders, 6 Hispanic Americans), 27 international. Average age 31. 133 applicants, 69% accepted, 11 enrolled. In 2001, 12 master's, 9 doctorates awarded. Terminal master's awarded for partial completion of doctoral program.

Degree requirements: For master's, thesis optional; for doctorate, thesis/dissertation, qualifying exam.

Entrance requirements: For master's and doctorate, GRE General Test, TOEFL, minimum GPA of 3.0. *Application deadline:* For fall admission, 4/10 (priority date); for spring admission, 10/1. Applications are processed on a rolling basis. *Application fee:* $20.

Expenses: Tuition, state resident: full-time $3,098; part-time $172 per credit. Tuition, nonresident: full-time $10,427; part-time $579 per credit.

Financial support: In 2001–02, 8 research assistantships with full and partial tuition reimbursements (averaging $2,436 per year), 12 teaching assistantships with full and partial tuition reimbursements (averaging $5,929 per year) were awarded. Fellowships, career-related internships or fieldwork, Federal Work-Study, and unspecified assistantships also available. Support available to part-time students. Financial award application deadline: 4/1; financial award applicants required to submit FAFSA.

Faculty research: Telecommunications, signal processing, imaging systems, electromagnetics, controls. *Total annual research expenditures:* $1.7 million.

Dr. Salvatore D. Morgera, Chairman, 561-297-3412, *Fax:* 561-297-2336, *E-mail:* smorgera@fau.edu.

Application contact: Marilyn Russo, Graduate Admissions Coordinator, 561-297-2694, *Fax:* 561-297-2659, *E-mail:* mrusso@fau.edu. *Web site:* http://www.ee.fau.edu/

■ **FLORIDA INSTITUTE OF TECHNOLOGY**

Graduate Programs, College of Engineering, Electrical and Computer Engineering Department, Melbourne, FL 32901-6975

AWARDS Computer engineering (MS, PhD); electrical engineering (MS, PhD). Part-time and evening/weekend programs available.

Faculty: 15 full-time (0 women), 7 part-time/adjunct (0 women).

Students: 25 full-time (4 women), 97 part-time (12 women); includes 19 minority (4 African Americans, 9 Asian Americans or Pacific Islanders, 6 Hispanic Americans), 48 international. Average age 31. 331

applicants, 46% accepted. In 2001, 27 master's, 2 doctorates awarded. Terminal master's awarded for partial completion of doctoral program.

Degree requirements: For doctorate, thesis/dissertation, comprehensive exam.

Entrance requirements: For master's, minimum GPA of 3.0; for doctorate, minimum GPA of 3.2. *Application deadline:* Applications are processed on a rolling basis. *Application fee:* $50. Electronic applications accepted.

Expenses: Tuition: Part-time $650 per credit.

Financial support: In 2001–02, 22 students received support, including 5 research assistantships with full and partial tuition reimbursements available (averaging $9,264 per year), 17 teaching assistantships with full and partial tuition reimbursements available (averaging $8,938 per year); tuition remissions also available. Financial award application deadline: 3/1; financial award applicants required to submit FAFSA.

Faculty research: Electro-optics, electromagnetics, microelectronics, communications, computer architecture, neural networks. *Total annual research expenditures:* $658,000.

Dr. Joseph Wheeler, Department Head, 321-674-8060, *Fax:* 321-674-8192, *E-mail:* jwheeler@fit.edu.

Application contact: Carolyn P. Farrior, Director of Graduate Admissions, 321-674-7118, *Fax:* 321-723-9468, *E-mail:* cfarrior@fit.edu. *Web site:* http://www.fit.edu/

Find an in-depth description at www.petersons.com/gradchannel.

■ **FLORIDA INSTITUTE OF TECHNOLOGY**

Graduate Programs, School of Extended Graduate Studies, Melbourne, FL 32901-6975

AWARDS Acquisition and contract management (MS, MSM, PMBA); aerospace engineering (MS); business administration (PMBA); computer information systems (MS); computer science (MS); ebusiness (MSM); electrical engineering (MS); engineering management (MS); health management (MS); human resource management (MSM, PMBA); human resources management (MS); information systems (MSM, PMBA); logistics management (MS, MSM); management (MS); material acquisition management (MS); mechanical engineering (MS); operations research (MS); project management (MS), including information systems, operations research; public administration (MPA). Software engineering (MS). Space systems (MS). Space systems management (MS). Systems management (MS), including information systems, operations research; transportation management (MSM). Part-time and evening/weekend programs available.

Florida Institute of Technology (continued)
Postbaccalaureate distance learning degree programs offered (no on-campus study).

Faculty: 10 full-time (2 women), 131 part-time/adjunct (15 women).
Students: 57 full-time (29 women), 1,198 part-time (455 women); includes 277 minority (183 African Americans, 38 Asian Americans or Pacific Islanders, 51 Hispanic Americans, 5 Native Americans), 16 international. Average age 37. 299 applicants, 42% accepted. In 2001, 434 degrees awarded.
Entrance requirements: For master's, minimum GPA of 3.0. *Application deadline:* Applications are processed on a rolling basis. *Application fee:* $50. Electronic applications accepted.
Expenses: Tuition: Part-time $650 per credit.
Financial support: Institutionally sponsored loans available. Financial award application deadline: 3/1; financial award applicants required to submit FAFSA.
Dr. Ronald L. Marshall, Dean, School of Extended Graduate Studies, 321-674-8880.
Application contact: Carolyn P. Farrior, Director of Graduate Admissions, 321-674-7118, *Fax:* 321-723-9468, *E-mail:* cfarrior@fit.edu. *Web site:* http://www.segs.fit.edu/

■ FLORIDA INTERNATIONAL UNIVERSITY

College of Engineering, Department of Electrical Engineering, Program in Electrical Engineering, Miami, FL 33199

AWARDS MS, PhD. Part-time and evening/weekend programs available.

Students: 45 full-time (6 women), 25 part-time (2 women); includes 22 minority (2 African Americans, 20 Hispanic Americans), 43 international. Average age 32. 214 applicants, 29% accepted, 12 enrolled. In 2001, 7 master's, 1 doctorate awarded.
Degree requirements: For master's, thesis optional; for doctorate, thesis/dissertation.
Entrance requirements: For master's, GRE General Test, TOEFL; for doctorate, GRE General Test, TOEFL, minimum graduate GPA of 3.3. *Application deadline:* For fall admission, 4/1 (priority date); for spring admission, 10/1. Applications are processed on a rolling basis. *Application fee:* $20.
Expenses: Tuition, state resident: full-time $2,916; part-time $162 per credit hour. Tuition, nonresident: full-time $10,245; part-time $569 per credit hour. Required fees: $168 per term.
Dr. Kang Yen, Acting Chairperson, Department of Electrical Engineering, 305-348-2807, *Fax:* 305-348-3707, *E-mail:* yenk@fiu.edu.

■ FLORIDA STATE UNIVERSITY

Graduate Studies, FAMU/FSU College of Engineering, Department of Electrical Engineering, Tallahassee, FL 32306

AWARDS MS, PhD. Part-time programs available.

Degree requirements: For master's, thesis; for doctorate, thesis/dissertation, preliminary exam, qualifying exam.
Entrance requirements: For master's, GRE General Test, TOEFL, minimum GPA of 3.0, BS in electrical engineering; for doctorate, GRE General Test, TOEFL, minimum graduate GPA of 3.5, MS in electrical engineering.
Expenses: Tuition, state resident: part-time $163 per credit hour. Tuition, nonresident: part-time $570 per credit hour. Tuition and fees vary according to program.
Faculty research: Electromagnetics, digital signal processing, computer systems, image processing, laser optics.
Web site: http://www.eng.fsu.edu/

■ GANNON UNIVERSITY

School of Graduate Studies, College of Sciences, Engineering, and Health Sciences, School of Engineering and Computer Science, Program in Engineering, Erie, PA 16541-0001

AWARDS Electrical engineering (MS); embedded software engineering (MS); mechanical engineering (MS). Part-time and evening/weekend programs available.

Degree requirements: For master's, thesis or alternative, comprehensive exam.
Entrance requirements: For master's, GRE Subject Test, bachelor's degree in engineering, minimum QPA of 2.5. *Web site:* http://www.gannon.edu/

■ GEORGE MASON UNIVERSITY

School of Information Technology and Engineering, Department of Electrical and Computer Engineering, Fairfax, VA 22030-4444

AWARDS Electrical and computer engineering (PhD); electrical engineering (MS). Part-time and evening/weekend programs available.

Faculty: 23 full-time (2 women), 13 part-time/adjunct (3 women).
Students: 42 full-time (7 women), 201 part-time (34 women); includes 60 minority (13 African Americans, 37 Asian Americans or Pacific Islanders, 10 Hispanic Americans), 76 international. Average age 31. 177 applicants, 84% accepted. In 2001, 20 master's, 2 doctorates awarded.
Degree requirements: For master's, thesis optional; for doctorate, thesis/dissertation, comprehensive oral and written exams.
Entrance requirements: For master's, GMAT or GRE General Test, TOEFL,

bachelor's degree in electrical engineering or related field, minimum GPA of 3.0 in last 60 hours. *Application deadline:* For fall admission, 5/1; for spring admission, 11/1. *Application fee:* $30. Electronic applications accepted.
Expenses: Tuition, state resident: full-time $3,168; part-time $132 per credit hour. Tuition, nonresident: full-time $11,280; part-time $470 per credit hour. Required fees: $1,416; $59 per credit hour.
Financial support: Fellowships, research assistantships, teaching assistantships, career-related internships or fieldwork and Federal Work-Study available. Support available to part-time students. Financial award application deadline: 3/1; financial award applicants required to submit FAFSA.
Faculty research: Communication networks, signal processing, system failure diagnosis, multiprocessors, material processing using microwave energy.
Dr. Andre Manitius, Chairperson, 703-993-1569, *Fax:* 703-993-1601, *E-mail:* ece@gmu.edu. *Web site:* http://ece.gmu.edu/

■ THE GEORGE WASHINGTON UNIVERSITY

School of Engineering and Applied Science, Department of Electrical and Computer Engineering, Washington, DC 20052

AWARDS MS, D Sc, App Sc, Engr, MEM/MS. Part-time and evening/weekend programs available.

Faculty: 21 full-time (2 women), 10 part-time/adjunct (0 women).
Students: 107 full-time (12 women), 172 part-time (38 women); includes 58 minority (20 African Americans, 30 Asian Americans or Pacific Islanders, 7 Hispanic Americans, 1 Native American), 118 international. Average age 32. 300 applicants, 95% accepted. In 2001, 90 master's, 6 doctorates, 2 other advanced degrees awarded.
Degree requirements: For master's, thesis optional; for doctorate and other advanced degree, dissertation defense, qualifying exam.
Entrance requirements: For master's, TOEFL or George Washington University English as a Foreign Language Test, appropriate bachelor's degree, minimum GPA of 3.0; for doctorate, TOEFL or George Washington University English as a Foreign Language Test, appropriate bachelor's or master's degree, minimum GPA of 3.3, GRE required if highest earned degree is BS; for other advanced degree, TOEFL or George Washington University English as a Foreign Language Test, appropriate master's degree, minimum GPA of 3.0. *Application deadline:* For fall admission, 3/1 (priority date); for spring admission, 10/1. Applications are processed on a rolling basis. *Application fee:* $55.

Expenses: Tuition: Part-time $810 per credit. Required fees: $1 per credit.
Financial support: In 2001–02, 15 fellowships with tuition reimbursements (averaging $5,300 per year), 17 teaching assistantships with tuition reimbursements (averaging $5,200 per year) were awarded. Research assistantships, career-related internships or fieldwork and institutionally sponsored loans also available. Financial award application deadline: 3/1; financial award applicants required to submit FAFSA.
Faculty research: Computer graphics, multimedia systems.
Dr. Branimir Vojcic, Chair, 202-994-4874, *Fax:* 202-994-0227, *E-mail:* eecs@ seas.gwu.edu.
Application contact: Howard M. Davis, Manager, Office of Admissions and Student Records, 202-994-6158, *Fax:* 202-994-0909, *E-mail:* data:adms@ seas.gwu.edu. *Web site:* http:// www.gwu.edu/~gradinfo/
Find an in-depth description at www.petersons.com/gradchannel.

■ GEORGIA INSTITUTE OF TECHNOLOGY

Graduate Studies and Research, College of Engineering, School of Electrical and Computer Engineering, Atlanta, GA 30332-0001

AWARDS MS, MSEE, PhD. Part-time programs available. Postbaccalaureate distance learning degree programs offered. Terminal master's awarded for partial completion of doctoral program.

Degree requirements: For master's, thesis optional; for doctorate, thesis/dissertation.
Entrance requirements: For master's, GRE General Test, TOEFL, minimum GPA of 3.0; for doctorate, GRE General Test, TOEFL, minimum GPA of 3.5.
Faculty research: Telecommunications, computer systems, microelectronics, optical engineering, digital signal processing. *Web site:* http://www.ee.gatech.edu/
Find an in-depth description at www.petersons.com/gradchannel.

■ GRADUATE SCHOOL AND UNIVERSITY CENTER OF THE CITY UNIVERSITY OF NEW YORK

Graduate Studies, Program in Engineering, New York, NY 10016-4039

AWARDS Chemical engineering (PhD); civil engineering (PhD); electrical engineering (PhD); mechanical engineering (PhD).
Faculty: 68 full-time (1 woman).
Students: 125 full-time (28 women), 6 part-time (1 woman); includes 13 minority (9 African Americans, 2 Asian Americans or Pacific Islanders, 2 Hispanic Americans), 95 international. Average age

32. 205 applicants, 63% accepted, 26 enrolled. In 2001, 22 degrees awarded.
Degree requirements: For doctorate, thesis/dissertation.
Entrance requirements: For doctorate, GRE General Test. *Application deadline:* For fall admission, 4/15. *Application fee:* $40.
Expenses: Tuition, state resident: part-time $245 per credit. Tuition, nonresident: part-time $425 per credit. Required fees: $72 per semester.
Financial support: In 2001–02, 67 students received support, including 64 fellowships; research assistantships, teaching assistantships, Federal Work-Study, institutionally sponsored loans, and tuition waivers (full and partial) also available. Financial award application deadline: 2/1; financial award applicants required to submit FAFSA.
Dr. Mumtaz Kassir, Acting Executive Officer, 212-650-8031, *Fax:* 212-650-8029, *E-mail:* kassir@ce-mail.engr.ccny.cuny.edu.
Find an in-depth description at www.petersons.com/gradchannel.

■ HOWARD UNIVERSITY

College of Engineering, Architecture, and Computer Sciences, School of Engineering and Computer Science, Department of Electrical Engineering, Washington, DC 20059-0002

AWARDS M Eng, PhD. Offered through the Graduate School of Arts and Sciences. Part-time programs available.

Students: Average age 25. In 2001, 3 master's, 3 doctorates awarded.
Degree requirements: For master's, thesis (for some programs), qualifying exam; for doctorate, thesis/dissertation, preliminary exam.
Entrance requirements: For master's, GRE General Test, TOEFL, bachelor's degree in electrical engineering, minimum GPA of 3.0; for doctorate, GRE General Test, TOEFL, minimum GPA of 3.0. *Application deadline:* For fall admission, 4/1; for spring admission, 11/1. *Application fee:* $45. Electronic applications accepted.
Financial support: In 2001–02, 15 research assistantships with full tuition reimbursements, 2 teaching assistantships with full tuition reimbursements were awarded. Fellowships with full tuition reimbursements, career-related internships or fieldwork, institutionally sponsored loans, and scholarships/grants also available. Financial award application deadline: 4/1.
Faculty research: Solid-state electronics, antennas and microwaves, communications and signal processing, controls and power systems, applied electromagnetics.
Dr. Mohamed E. Chouikha, Chair, 202-806-6585, *Fax:* 202-806-5288, *E-mail:*

cm@scs.howard.edu. *Web site:* http:// www.howard.edu/
Find an in-depth description at www.petersons.com/gradchannel.

■ ILLINOIS INSTITUTE OF TECHNOLOGY

Graduate College, Armour College of Engineering and Sciences, Department of Electrical and Computer Engineering, Chicago, IL 60616-3793

AWARDS Computer systems engineering (MS); electrical and computer engineering (MECE); electrical engineering (MS, PhD); manufacturing engineering (MME, MS). Part-time and evening/weekend programs available.

Faculty: 20 full-time (2 women), 7 part-time/adjunct (0 women).
Students: 157 full-time (26 women), 212 part-time (21 women); includes 34 minority (4 African Americans, 21 Asian Americans or Pacific Islanders, 9 Hispanic Americans), 259 international. Average age 27. 1,295 applicants, 52% accepted. In 2001, 93 master's, 8 doctorates awarded. Terminal master's awarded for partial completion of doctoral program.
Degree requirements: For master's, thesis (for some programs), comprehensive exam; for doctorate, thesis/dissertation, comprehensive exam.
Entrance requirements: For master's and doctorate, GRE General Test, TOEFL, minimum undergraduate GPA of 3.0. *Application deadline:* For fall admission, 7/1; for spring admission, 12/1. Applications are processed on a rolling basis. *Application fee:* $30. Electronic applications accepted.
Expenses: Tuition: Part-time $590 per credit hour.
Financial support: In 2001–02, 13 research assistantships, 19 teaching assistantships were awarded. Federal Work-Study, institutionally sponsored loans, scholarships/grants, and unspecified assistantships also available. Support available to part-time students. Financial award application deadline: 3/1; financial award applicants required to submit FAFSA.
Faculty research: Computer system design, photonics, biomedical engineering, power systems analysis, communications theory. *Total annual research expenditures:* $585,216.
Dr. Thomas Wong, Interim Chairman, 312-567-5786, *Fax:* 312-567-8976, *E-mail:* wong@iit.edu.
Application contact: Dr. Ali Cinar, Dean of Graduate College, 312-567-3637, *Fax:* 312-567-7517, *E-mail:* gradstu@iit.edu. *Web site:* http://www.ece.iit.edu/

■ INDIANA UNIVERSITY–PURDUE UNIVERSITY INDIANAPOLIS

School of Engineering and Technology, Department of Electrical Engineering, Indianapolis, IN 46202-2896

AWARDS Biomedical engineering (MS Bm E, PhD); electrical engineering (MSEE). Part-time and evening/weekend programs available.

Students: 25 full-time (7 women), 34 part-time (10 women); includes 4 minority (2 African Americans, 2 Asian Americans or Pacific Islanders), 40 international. Average age 27. In 2001, 9 degrees awarded.
Degree requirements: For master's, thesis optional.
Entrance requirements: For master's, GRE, TOEFL, minimum B average. *Application deadline:* For fall admission, 7/1. *Application fee:* $45 ($55 for international students).
Expenses: Tuition, state resident: full-time $4,480; part-time $187 per credit. Tuition, nonresident: full-time $12,926; part-time $539 per credit. Required fees: $177.
Financial support: In 2001–02, research assistantships with full and partial tuition reimbursements (averaging $13,000 per year); fellowships with tuition reimbursements, Federal Work-Study, institutionally sponsored loans, and tuition waivers (full and partial) also available. Financial award application deadline: 3/1.
Faculty research: Control and automation, signal processing, robotics, medical imaging, neural networks. *Total annual research expenditures:* $172,654.
Dr. Edward Berbari, Chair, 317-274-9721, *Fax:* 317-274-4493.
Application contact: Valerie Lim, Graduate Program, 317-278-4960, *Fax:* 317-278-1671, *E-mail:* grad@engr.iupui.edu. *Web site:* http://www.engr.iupui.edu/ee/

■ INTERNATIONAL TECHNOLOGICAL UNIVERSITY

Program in Electrical Engineering, Santa Clara, CA 95050

AWARDS MSEE. Part-time and evening/weekend programs available.

Faculty: 3 full-time (0 women), 9 part-time/adjunct (1 woman).
Students: 9 full-time (1 woman), 8 part-time (1 woman). In 2001, 1 degree awarded.
Degree requirements: For master's, thesis or alternative.
Entrance requirements: For master's, TOEFL, 3 semesters of calculus, minimum GPA of 2.5. *Application deadline:* For fall admission, 8/31 (priority date); for winter admission, 12/31 (priority date); for spring admission, 3/30 (priority date). *Application fee:* $30 ($80 for international students).
Expenses: Tuition: Full-time $6,800; part-time $425 per unit.

Faculty research: VLSI design, digital systems, routing and optimization theory. Wai-kai Chen, Vice President, 408-556-9010, *Fax:* 408-556-2012.
Application contact: Dr. Chun-Mou Peng, Director of Research and Development Center, 408-556-9010, *Fax:* 408-556-9212, *E-mail:* chunmou@itu.edu.

■ IOWA STATE UNIVERSITY OF SCIENCE AND TECHNOLOGY

Graduate College, College of Engineering, Department of Electrical and Computer Engineering, Ames, IA 50011

AWARDS Computer engineering (MS, PhD); electrical engineering (MS, PhD).

Faculty: 41 full-time, 7 part-time/adjunct.
Students: 193 full-time (34 women), 70 part-time (14 women); includes 9 minority (5 African Americans, 3 Asian Americans or Pacific Islanders, 1 Hispanic American), 179 international. 833 applicants, 11% accepted, 59 enrolled. In 2001, 64 master's, 20 doctorates awarded.
Degree requirements: For master's, thesis or alternative; for doctorate, thesis/dissertation. *Median time to degree:* Master's–2.3 years full-time; doctorate–4.5 years full-time.
Entrance requirements: For master's and doctorate, GRE General Test, TOEFL or IELTS. *Application deadline:* For fall admission, 1/15 (priority date); for spring admission, 9/15. *Application fee:* $20 ($50 for international students). Electronic applications accepted.
Expenses: Tuition, state resident: full-time $1,851. Tuition, nonresident: full-time $5,449. Tuition and fees vary according to program.
Financial support: In 2001–02, 146 research assistantships with partial tuition reimbursements (averaging $13,060 per year), 48 teaching assistantships with partial tuition reimbursements (averaging $12,208 per year) were awarded. Fellowships, scholarships/grants, health care benefits, and unspecified assistantships also available.
Dr. S. S. Venkata, Chair, 515-294-2667, *E-mail:* ecegrad@ee.iastate.edu.
Application contact: Dr. Vijay Vittal, Director of Graduate Education, 515-294-2667, *E-mail:* ecegrad@ee.iastate.edu. *Web site:* http://www.eng.iastate.edu/coe/grad.asp/

■ JOHNS HOPKINS UNIVERSITY

G. W. C. Whiting School of Engineering, Department of Electrical and Computer Engineering, Baltimore, MD 21218-2699

AWARDS MSE, PhD. Part-time programs available.

Faculty: 17 full-time (0 women), 8 part-time/adjunct (0 women).

Students: 73 full-time (17 women), 13 part-time (2 women); includes 4 minority (1 Asian American or Pacific Islander, 3 Hispanic Americans), 52 international. Average age 28. 388 applicants, 17% accepted, 29 enrolled. In 2001, 34 master's, 8 doctorates awarded. Terminal master's awarded for partial completion of doctoral program.
Degree requirements: For doctorate, thesis/dissertation, oral exam.
Entrance requirements: For master's and doctorate, GRE General Test, TOEFL. *Application deadline:* For fall admission, 1/15. Applications are processed on a rolling basis. *Application fee:* $0. Electronic applications accepted.
Expenses: Tuition: Full-time $27,390.
Financial support: In 2001–02, 86 students received support, including 2 fellowships with full tuition reimbursements available (averaging $16,000 per year), 50 research assistantships with full tuition reimbursements available (averaging $16,000 per year), 20 teaching assistantships with full tuition reimbursements available (averaging $16,000 per year); Federal Work-Study, institutionally sponsored loans, scholarships/grants, and unspecified assistantships also available. Financial award application deadline: 1/1.
Faculty research: Computer engineering, systems and control, speech and image processing, quantum electronics, analog and digital VLSI sensors and devices. *Total annual research expenditures:* $2 million.
Dr. Gerard G. L. Meyer, Chair, 410-516-7003, *Fax:* 410-516-5566, *E-mail:* gglmeyer@jhu.edu.
Application contact: Gail M. O'Connor, Academic Coordinator II, 410-516-4808, *Fax:* 410-516-5566, *E-mail:* ecegrad@jhu.edu. *Web site:* http://www.ece.jhu.edu/

Find an in-depth description at www.petersons.com/gradchannel.

■ KANSAS STATE UNIVERSITY

Graduate School, College of Engineering, Department of Electrical and Computer Engineering, Manhattan, KS 66506

AWARDS Bioengineering (MS, PhD); communications (MS, PhD); computer engineering (MS, PhD); control systems (MS, PhD); electric energy systems (MS, PhD); instrumentation (MS, PhD). Signal processing (MS, PhD). Postbaccalaureate distance learning degree programs offered (no on-campus study).

Faculty: 22 full-time (3 women).
Students: 34 full-time (8 women), 15 part-time (1 woman); includes 1 minority (Hispanic American), 23 international. 325 applicants, 8% accepted, 16 enrolled. In 2001, 15 master's, 4 doctorates awarded.
Degree requirements: For master's, thesis or alternative, final exam; for doctorate, thesis/dissertation, preliminary exams.

Peterson's ■ *Graduate Programs in Engineering and Computer Science 2004*

Entrance requirements: For master's, GRE General Test, TOEFL, bachelor's degree in electrical engineering or computer science; minimum GPA of 3.0; for doctorate, GRE General Test, TOEFL. *Application deadline:* For fall admission, 3/1; for spring admission, 9/1. Applications are processed on a rolling basis. *Application fee:* $0 ($25 for international students). Electronic applications accepted.
Expenses: Tuition, state resident: part-time $113 per credit hour. Tuition, nonresident: part-time $358 per credit hour.
Financial support: In 2001–02, 17 research assistantships with partial tuition reimbursements (averaging $9,900 per year), 7 teaching assistantships with full tuition reimbursements (averaging $9,900 per year) were awarded. Career-related internships or fieldwork, institutionally sponsored loans, and scholarships/grants also available. Support available to part-time students. Financial award application deadline: 3/1; financial award applicants required to submit FAFSA.
Faculty research: Communications systems and signal processing, real-time embedded systems, integrated circuits and devices, bioengineering, power systems. *Total annual research expenditures:* $1.3 million.
Dr. David Soldan, Head, 785-532-5600, *Fax:* 785-532-1188, *E-mail:* grad@eece.ksu.edu.
Application contact: Anil Pahwa, Graduate Program Director, 785-532-5600, *Fax:* 785-532-1188, *E-mail:* pahw@ksu.edu. *Web site:* http://www.eece.ksu.edu/

■ LAMAR UNIVERSITY

College of Graduate Studies, College of Engineering, Department of Electrical Engineering, Beaumont, TX 77710

AWARDS ME, MES, DE. Part-time programs available.

Faculty: 6 full-time (1 woman), 1 part-time/adjunct (0 women).
Students: 27 full-time (5 women), 4 part-time (1 woman), 29 international. Average age 26. 145 applicants, 52% accepted. In 2001, 6 master's, 3 doctorates awarded.
Degree requirements: For master's, thesis (for some programs); for doctorate, thesis/dissertation.
Entrance requirements: For master's and doctorate, GRE General Test, TOEFL. *Application deadline:* For fall admission, 5/15 (priority date); for spring admission, 10/1 (priority date). Applications are processed on a rolling basis. *Application fee:* $25 ($50 for international students).
Expenses: Tuition, state resident: full-time $1,114. Tuition, nonresident: full-time $3,670.
Financial support: In 2001–02, 2 fellowships with partial tuition reimbursements (averaging $6,000 per year), 1 research

assistantship with partial tuition reimbursement (averaging $6,000 per year), 3 teaching assistantships with partial tuition reimbursements (averaging $4,500 per year) were awarded. Tuition waivers (partial) also available. Financial award application deadline: 4/1.
Faculty research: Fiber optics, virtual instrumentation, field programmable logic device research, controls. *Total annual research expenditures:* $85,000.
Dr. Bernard Maxum, Chair, 409-880-8746, *Fax:* 409-880-8121, *E-mail:* maxumbj@hal.lamar.edu. *Web site:* http://hal.lamar.edu/~eece/

■ LAWRENCE TECHNOLOGICAL UNIVERSITY

College of Engineering, Southfield, MI 48075-1058

AWARDS Automotive engineering (MAE); civil engineering (MCE); electrical and computer engineering (MS); manufacturing systems (MEMS, DE). Part-time and evening/weekend programs available.

Faculty: 27 full-time (2 women), 11 part-time/adjunct (1 woman).
Students: Average age 32. 133 applicants, 38 enrolled. In 2001, 43 degrees awarded. *Application deadline:* For fall admission, 8/1 (priority date); for winter admission, 12/1 (priority date); for spring admission, 5/1. Applications are processed on a rolling basis. *Application fee:* $50. Electronic applications accepted.
Expenses: Tuition: Part-time $460 per credit hour.
Financial support: Institutionally sponsored loans available. Support available to part-time students. Financial award application deadline: 3/1; financial award applicants required to submit FAFSA.
Faculty research: Advanced composite materials in bridges, strengthening existing bridges with carbon and glass fiber sheets, development of drive shafts using composite materials. *Total annual research expenditures:* $150,000.
Dr. Laird Johnston, Dean, 248-204-2500, *Fax:* 248-204-2509, *E-mail:* lejohnston@ltu.edu.
Application contact: Jane Rohrback, Interim Director of Admissions, 248-204-3160, *Fax:* 248-204-3188, *E-mail:* admission@ltu.edu.

■ LEHIGH UNIVERSITY

P.C. Rossin College of Engineering and Applied Science, Department of Electrical and Computer Engineering, Program in Electrical Engineering, Bethlehem, PA 18015-3094

AWARDS M Eng, MS, PhD. Part-time programs available.

Faculty: 15 full-time (1 woman), 2 part-time/adjunct (0 women).
Students: 58 full-time (10 women), 25 part-time (2 women); includes 12 minority

(3 African Americans, 9 Asian Americans or Pacific Islanders), 45 international. Average age 24. 320 applicants, 19% accepted, 36 enrolled. In 2001, 11 master's, 10 doctorates awarded.
Degree requirements: For master's, oral presentation of thesis; for doctorate, thesis/dissertation, qualifying, general, and oral exams.
Entrance requirements: For master's, GRE General Test, TOEFL, minimum GPA of 3.0; for doctorate, GRE General Test, TOEFL, MS, minimum GPA of 3.25. *Application deadline:* For fall admission, 4/15; for spring admission, 11/1. Applications are processed on a rolling basis. *Application fee:* $50. Electronic applications accepted.
Expenses: Tuition: Part-time $468 per credit hour. Required fees: $200; $100 per semester. Tuition and fees vary according to program.
Financial support: In 2001–02, 3 fellowships with full tuition reimbursements (averaging $15,000 per year), 5 research assistantships with full tuition reimbursements (averaging $11,700 per year), 8 teaching assistantships with full tuition reimbursements (averaging $12,330 per year) were awarded. Financial award application deadline: 1/15.
Application contact: Anne Nierer, Graduate Coordinator, 610-758-4072, *Fax:* 610-758-6279, *E-mail:* aln3@lehigh.edu. *Web site:* http://www.eecs.lehigh.edu/

Find an in-depth description at www.petersons.com/gradchannel.

■ LOUISIANA STATE UNIVERSITY AND AGRICULTURAL AND MECHANICAL COLLEGE

Graduate School, College of Engineering, Department of Electrical and Computer Engineering, Baton Rouge, LA 70803

AWARDS MSEE, PhD.

Faculty: 18 full-time (0 women).
Students: 67 full-time (17 women), 11 part-time (2 women); includes 1 minority (Asian American or Pacific Islander), 68 international. Average age 26. 261 applicants, 39% accepted, 26 enrolled. In 2001, 30 master's, 2 doctorates awarded. Terminal master's awarded for partial completion of doctoral program.
Degree requirements: For master's, thesis optional; for doctorate, thesis/dissertation.
Entrance requirements: For master's, GRE General Test, TOEFL, minimum GPA of 3.0; for doctorate, GRE General Test, TOEFL, minimum GPA of 3.5. *Application deadline:* For fall admission, 1/25 (priority date). Applications are processed on a rolling basis. *Application fee:* $25.
Expenses: Tuition, state resident: full-time $2,551. Tuition, nonresident: full-time

Louisiana State University and Agricultural and Mechanical College (continued)

$5,551. Required fees: $854. Part-time tuition and fees vary according to course load.

Financial support: In 2001–02, 13 research assistantships with partial tuition reimbursements (averaging $12,850 per year), 29 teaching assistantships with partial tuition reimbursements (averaging $12,112 per year) were awarded. Fellowships, institutionally sponsored loans and unspecified assistantships also available. Financial award application deadline: 2/28; financial award applicants required to submit FAFSA.

Faculty research: Electronics, power engineering, systems and signal processing, communications. *Total annual research expenditures:* $708,704.

Dr. Alan H. Marshak, Chair, 225-578-5243, *Fax:* 225-578-5200, *E-mail:* amarsh5@lsu.edu.

Application contact: Dr. Jorge L. Aravena, Graduate Adviser, 225-578-5478, *Fax:* 225-578-5200, *E-mail:* eearav@lsu.edu. *Web site:* http://www.ee.lsu.edu/

Find an in-depth description at www.petersons.com/gradchannel.

■ LOUISIANA TECH UNIVERSITY

Graduate School, College of Engineering and Science, Department of Electrical Engineering, Ruston, LA 71272

AWARDS MS, D Eng. Part-time programs available. Terminal master's awarded for partial completion of doctoral program.

Degree requirements: For master's and doctorate, thesis/dissertation.

Entrance requirements: For master's, GRE General Test, TOEFL, minimum GPA of 3.0 in last 60 hours; for doctorate, TOEFL, minimum graduate GPA of 3.25 (with MS) or GRE General Test.

Faculty research: Communications, computers and microprocessors, electrical and power systems, pattern recognition, robotics.

■ LOYOLA MARYMOUNT UNIVERSITY

Graduate Division, College of Science and Engineering, Department of Electrical Engineering and Computer Science, Program in Electrical Engineering, Los Angeles, CA 90045-2659

AWARDS MSE. Part-time and evening/weekend programs available.

Students: 5 full-time (2 women), 5 part-time; includes 4 minority (3 Asian Americans or Pacific Islanders, 1 Hispanic American), 5 international. 16 applicants, 63% accepted, 3 enrolled. In 2001, 8 degrees awarded.

Degree requirements: For master's, research seminar.

Entrance requirements: For master's, TOEFL. *Application deadline:* Applications are processed on a rolling basis. *Application fee:* $45. Electronic applications accepted.

Expenses: Tuition: Part-time $612 per credit hour. Required fees: $86 per term. Tuition and fees vary according to program.

Financial support: In 2001–02, 2 students received support. Scholarships/grants available. Support available to part-time students. Financial award application deadline: 7/1; financial award applicants required to submit FAFSA. *Web site:* http://www.lmu.edu/acad/gd/graddiv.htm

■ MANHATTAN COLLEGE

Graduate Division, School of Engineering, Program in Electrical Engineering, Riverdale, NY 10471

AWARDS MS. Part-time and evening/weekend programs available.

Degree requirements: For master's, thesis or alternative.

Entrance requirements: For master's, GRE, TOEFL, minimum GPA of 3.0.

Faculty research: Multimedia tools, neural networks, robotic control systems, magnetic resonance imaging, telemedicine, computer-based instruction.

■ MARQUETTE UNIVERSITY

Graduate School, College of Engineering, Department of Electrical and Computer Engineering, Milwaukee, WI 53201-1881

AWARDS Computing (MS); electrical engineering (MS, PhD). Part-time and evening/weekend programs available.

Faculty: 4 full-time (2 women), 2 part-time/adjunct (0 women).

Students: 37 full-time (8 women), 67 part-time (12 women); includes 12 minority (6 African Americans, 5 Asian Americans or Pacific Islanders, 1 Hispanic American), 41 international. Average age 25. 83 applicants, 42% accepted. In 2001, 11 master's, 2 doctorates awarded. Terminal master's awarded for partial completion of doctoral program.

Degree requirements: For master's, thesis optional; for doctorate, dissertation defense, qualifying exam.

Entrance requirements: For master's, TOEFL, GRE General Test or minimum GPA of 3.0; for doctorate, GRE General Test, TOEFL. *Application deadline:* For fall admission, 7/15 (priority date); for spring admission, 11/15. Applications are processed on a rolling basis. *Application fee:* $40. Electronic applications accepted.

Expenses: Tuition: Full-time $10,170; part-time $445 per credit hour. Tuition and fees vary according to course load.

Financial support: In 2001–02, 16 students received support, including 6 fellowships with full tuition reimbursements

available (averaging $18,000 per year), 7 research assistantships with full tuition reimbursements available (averaging $12,000 per year), 14 teaching assistantships with full tuition reimbursements available (averaging $10,025 per year); Federal Work-Study, institutionally sponsored loans, and scholarships/grants also available. Financial award application deadline: 2/15.

Faculty research: Electric machines, drives, and controls; applied solid-state electronics; computers and signal processing; microwaves and antennas. Solid state devices and acoustic wave sensors. *Total annual research expenditures:* $750,000.

Dr. Edwin E. Yaz, Chair, 414-288-6820, *Fax:* 414-288-5579, *E-mail:* edwin.yaz@marquette.edu.

Application contact: Dr. Fabien J. Josse, Director of Graduate Studies, 414-288-6789, *Fax:* 414-288-5579, *E-mail:* fabien.josse@marquette.edu. *Web site:* http://www.eng.mu.edu/departments/eece/

Find an in-depth description at www.petersons.com/gradchannel.

■ MASSACHUSETTS INSTITUTE OF TECHNOLOGY

School of Engineering, Department of Electrical Engineering and Computer Science, Cambridge, MA 02139-4307

AWARDS Computer science (EE); electrical engineering (EE); electrical engineering and computer science (M Eng, SM, PhD, Sc D).

Faculty: 111 full-time (11 women), 2 part-time/adjunct (0 women).

Students: 853 full-time (170 women), 3 part-time (1 woman); includes 220 minority (22 African Americans, 180 Asian Americans or Pacific Islanders, 15 Hispanic Americans, 3 Native Americans), 238 international. Average age 22. 2,491 applicants, 21% accepted, 306 enrolled. In 2001, 314 master's, 73 doctorates awarded. Terminal master's awarded for partial completion of doctoral program.

Degree requirements: For master's, thesis/dissertation; for doctorate, thesis/dissertation, comprehensive exam.

Entrance requirements: For master's and doctorate, TOEFL. *Application deadline:* For fall admission, 1/1. *Application fee:* $60. Electronic applications accepted.

Expenses: Tuition: Full-time $26,960. Full-time tuition and fees vary according to program.

Financial support: In 2001–02, 781 students received support, including 163 fellowships, 594 research assistantships, 123 teaching assistantships; career-related internships or fieldwork, Federal Work-Study, institutionally sponsored loans, scholarships/grants, health care benefits, and unspecified assistantships also available. Financial award applicants required to submit FAFSA.

Faculty research: Modem control and system theory, radio astronomy,

knowledge-based application systems, artificial intelligence, electrohydrodynamics. *Total annual research expenditures:* $50.5 million.
Dr. John V. Guttag, Head, 617-253-4001, *Fax:* 617-258-7354, *E-mail:* guttag@eecs.mit.edu.
Application contact: Peggy Carney, Administrator, 617-253-4603, *Fax:* 617-258-7354, *E-mail:* grad-ap@eecs.mit.edu. *Web site:* http://www.eecs.mit.edu/

■ MCNEESE STATE UNIVERSITY

Graduate School, College of Engineering and Technology, Lake Charles, LA 70609

AWARDS Chemical engineering (M Eng); civil engineering (M Eng); electrical engineering (M Eng); mechanical engineering (M Eng). Part-time and evening/weekend programs available.

Faculty: 14 full-time (1 woman).
Students: 24 full-time (5 women), 5 part-time; includes 1 minority (Asian American or Pacific Islander), 23 international. In 2001, 5 degrees awarded.
Degree requirements: For master's, thesis or alternative.
Entrance requirements: For master's, GRE General Test, TOEFL, minimum undergraduate GPA of 3.0. *Application deadline:* For fall admission, 7/15 (priority date). Applications are processed on a rolling basis. *Application fee:* $20 ($30 for international students).
Expenses: Tuition, state resident: part-time $1,208 per semester. Tuition, nonresident: part-time $4,378 per semester.
Financial support: Federal Work-Study available. Support available to part-time students. Financial award application deadline: 5/1.
Dr. O. C. Karkalits, Dean, 337-475-5875, *Fax:* 337-475-5237, *E-mail:* ckarkal@mail.mcneese.edu.
Application contact: Dr. Jay O. Uppot, Director of Graduate Studies, 337-475-5874, *Fax:* 37-475-5286, *E-mail:* juppot@mail.mcneese.edu.

■ MERCER UNIVERSITY

Graduate Studies, Macon Campus, School of Engineering, Macon, GA 31207-0003

AWARDS Biomedical engineering (MSE); electrical engineering (MSE); engineering management (MSE); mechanical engineering (MSE). Software engineering (MSE). Software systems (MS); technical communications management (MS); technical management (MS). Part-time and evening/weekend programs available.

Faculty: 10 full-time (1 woman), 5 part-time/adjunct (1 woman).
Students: 3 full-time (2 women), 104 part-time (31 women); includes 19 minority (13 African Americans, 6 Asian Americans or

Pacific Islanders), 5 international. Average age 36. 31 applicants, 97% accepted, 27 enrolled. In 2001, 32 degrees awarded.
Degree requirements: For master's, thesis or alternative, registration.
Entrance requirements: For master's, GRE, minimum undergraduate GPA of 3.0. *Application deadline:* For fall admission, 7/1; for spring admission, 11/15. Applications are processed on a rolling basis. *Application fee:* $35 ($50 for international students).
Expenses: Contact institution.
Financial support: Federal Work-Study available.
Dr. M. Dayne Aldridge, Dean, 478-301-2459, *Fax:* 478-301-5593, *E-mail:* aldridge_md@mercer.edu.
Application contact: Kathy Olivier, Graduate Administrative Coordinator, 478-301-2196, *E-mail:* olivier_kk@mercer.edu. *Web site:* http://www.mercer.edu/engineer.htm

■ MICHIGAN STATE UNIVERSITY

Graduate School, College of Engineering, Department of Electrical and Computer Engineering, East Lansing, MI 48824

AWARDS MS, PhD.

Faculty: 25.
Students: 107 full-time (18 women), 62 part-time (13 women); includes 37 minority (14 African Americans, 11 Asian Americans or Pacific Islanders, 12 Hispanic Americans), 97 international. Average age 26. 852 applicants, 16% accepted. In 2001, 67 master's, 10 doctorates awarded.
Degree requirements: For master's, exit exam, thesis optional; for doctorate, thesis/dissertation, qualifying exams, comprehensive exam.
Entrance requirements: For master's and doctorate, GRE General Test, TOEFL. *Application deadline:* Applications are processed on a rolling basis. *Application fee:* $30 ($40 for international students). Electronic applications accepted.
Expenses: Tuition, state resident: part-time $244 per credit hour. Tuition, nonresident: part-time $494 per credit hour. Required fees: $268 per semester. Tuition and fees vary according to course load, degree level and program.
Financial support: In 2001–02, 53 fellowships (averaging $3,861 per year), 40 research assistantships with tuition reimbursements (averaging $13,811 per year), 28 teaching assistantships with tuition reimbursements (averaging $12,896 per year) were awarded. Financial award applicants required to submit FAFSA.
Faculty research: Computer-aided engineering, electromagnetics, robotics. *Total annual research expenditures:* $1.4 million.
Dr. Satish Udpa, Interim Chair, 517-355-5066, *Fax:* 517-353-1980.

Application contact: Graduate Coordinator, 517-353-6773, *E-mail:* ece_mailbox@egr.msu.edu. *Web site:* http://www.egr.msu.edu/ece/

■ MICHIGAN TECHNOLOGICAL UNIVERSITY

Graduate School, College of Engineering, Department of Electrical and Computer Engineering, Program in Electrical Engineering, Houghton, MI 49931-1295

AWARDS ME, MS, PhD. Part-time programs available.

Degree requirements: For master's, thesis or alternative; for doctorate, thesis/dissertation.
Electronic applications accepted.

Find an in-depth description at www.petersons.com/gradchannel.

■ MINNESOTA STATE UNIVERSITY, MANKATO

College of Graduate Studies, College of Science, Engineering and Technology, Program in Electrical Engineering and Electronic Engineering Technology, Mankato, MN 56001

AWARDS MSE.

Faculty: 9 full-time (0 women).
Students: 15 full-time (2 women), 2 part-time. Average age 31. In 2001, 3 degrees awarded.
Degree requirements: For master's, thesis, comprehensive exam.
Entrance requirements: For master's, GRE General Test, minimum GPA of 3.0 during previous 2 years. *Application deadline:* For fall admission, 7/9 (priority date); for spring admission, 11/27. Applications are processed on a rolling basis. *Application fee:* $20.
Expenses: Tuition, state resident: full-time $3,253; part-time $157 per credit. Tuition, nonresident: full-time $4,893; part-time $248 per credit. Required fees: $24 per credit. Tuition and fees vary according to reciprocity agreements.
Financial support: Research assistantships with full tuition reimbursements, teaching assistantships with full tuition reimbursements available. Financial award application deadline: 3/15.
Dr. T. Hendrickson, Chairman, 507-389-6536.
Application contact: Joni Roberts, Admissions Coordinator, 507-389-5244, *Fax:* 507-389-5974, *E-mail:* grad@mankato.msus.edu. *Web site:* http://www.ee.mankato.msus.edu/

■ MISSISSIPPI STATE UNIVERSITY

College of Engineering, Department of Electrical and Computer Engineering, Mississippi State, MS 39762

AWARDS Computer engineering (MS, PhD); electrical engineering (MS, PhD). Part-time programs available. Postbaccalaureate distance learning degree programs offered (minimal on-campus study).

Faculty: 24 full-time (3 women), 3 part-time/adjunct (0 women).
Students: 132 full-time (17 women), 50 part-time (8 women); includes 10 minority (4 African Americans, 4 Asian Americans or Pacific Islanders, 1 Hispanic American, 1 Native American), 136 international. Average age 26. 399 applicants, 80% accepted, 50 enrolled. In 2001, 38 master's, 2 doctorates awarded. Terminal master's awarded for partial completion of doctoral program.
Degree requirements: For master's, thesis optional; for doctorate, thesis/dissertation, comprehensive oral and written exam, comprehensive exam, registration.
Entrance requirements: For master's, GRE General Test, TOEFL, minimum Undergraduate GPA of 3.00; for doctorate, GRE, TOEFL, minimum graduate GPA of 3.5. *Application deadline:* For fall admission, 7/1; for spring admission, 11/1. Applications are processed on a rolling basis. *Application fee:* $25 for international students. Electronic applications accepted.
Expenses: Tuition, state resident: full-time $3,586; part-time $150 per credit hour. Tuition, nonresident: full-time $8,128; part-time $339 per credit hour. Tuition and fees vary according to course load and campus/location.
Financial support: In 2001–02, 6 fellowships (averaging $5,000 per year), 35 research assistantships with full tuition reimbursements (averaging $12,000 per year), 23 teaching assistantships with full tuition reimbursements (averaging $12,000 per year) were awarded. Federal Work-Study, institutionally sponsored loans, scholarships/grants, and unspecified assistantships also available. Financial award application deadline: 4/1; financial award applicants required to submit FAFSA.
Faculty research: Digital computing, power, controls, communication systems, microelectronics. *Total annual research expenditures:* $7.1 million.
Dr. G. Marshall Molen, Head, 662-325-3912, *Fax:* 662-325-2298, *E-mail:* molen@ece.msstate.edu.
Application contact: Jerry B. Inmon, Director of Admissions, 662-325-2224, *Fax:* 662-325-7360, *E-mail:* admit@admissions.msstate.edu. *Web site:* http://www.ece.msstate.edu/

Find an in-depth description at www.petersons.com/gradchannel.

■ MONTANA STATE UNIVERSITY–BOZEMAN

College of Graduate Studies, College of Engineering, Department of Electrical and Computer Engineering, Bozeman, MT 59717

AWARDS Electrical engineering (MS); engineering (PhD). Part-time programs available.

Students: 15 full-time (3 women), 8 part-time (1 woman), 10 international. Average age 26. 28 applicants, 64% accepted, 11 enrolled. In 2001, 2 degrees awarded.
Degree requirements: For master's, thesis or alternative; for doctorate, thesis/dissertation.
Entrance requirements: For master's and doctorate, GRE General Test, TOEFL, minimum GPA of 3.0. *Application deadline:* For fall admission, 6/15; for spring admission, 11/1. Applications are processed on a rolling basis. *Application fee:* $50. Electronic applications accepted.
Expenses: Tuition, state resident: full-time $3,894; part-time $198 per credit. Tuition, nonresident: full-time $10,661; part-time $480 per credit. International tuition: $10,811 full-time. Tuition and fees vary according to course load and program.
Financial support: Career-related internships or fieldwork, Federal Work-Study, and scholarships/grants available. Financial award application deadline: 3/1; financial award applicants required to submit FAFSA.
Faculty research: Fiber optics, fuel cells, signal processing, real time systems, speech recognition. *Total annual research expenditures:* $410,367.
Dr. James Peterson, Head, 406-994-2505, *Fax:* 406-994-5958, *E-mail:* eedept@ee.montana.edu. *Web site:* http://www.coe.montana.edu/ee/

■ NATIONAL TECHNOLOGICAL UNIVERSITY

Programs in Engineering, Fort Collins, CO 80526-1842

AWARDS Chemical engineering (MS); computer engineering (MS); computer science (MS); electrical engineering (MS); engineering management (MS); environmental systems management (MS); management of technology (MS); manufacturing systems engineering (MS); materials science and engineering (MS); mechanical engineering (MS); microelectronics and semiconductor engineering (MS); Software engineering (MS). Special majors (MS). Systems engineering (MS). Part-time programs available. Postbaccalaureate distance learning degree programs offered (no on-campus study).

Students: In 2001, 114 degrees awarded.
Degree requirements: For master's, comprehensive exam.
Entrance requirements: For master's, BS in engineering or related field; 2.9 minimum GPA. *Application deadline:* Applications are processed on a rolling basis. *Application fee:* $50. Electronic applications accepted.
Expenses: Tuition: Part-time $660 per credit hour. Part-time tuition and fees vary according to course load, campus/location and program.
Dr. Andre Vacroux, President, 970-495-6400, *Fax:* 970-484-0668, *E-mail:* andre@ntu.edu.
Application contact: Rhonda Bonham, Admissions Officer, 970-495-6400, *Fax:* 970-498-0601, *E-mail:* rhonda@ntu.edu. *Web site:* http://www.ntu.edu/

■ NAVAL POSTGRADUATE SCHOOL

Graduate Programs, Department of Electrical and Computer Engineering, Monterey, CA 93943

AWARDS MS, PhD, Eng. Program only open to commissioned officers of the United States and friendly nations and selected United States federal civilian employees. Part-time programs available. Postbaccalaureate distance learning degree programs offered (minimal on-campus study).

Degree requirements: For master's and Eng, thesis; for doctorate, one foreign language, thesis/dissertation.

■ NEW JERSEY INSTITUTE OF TECHNOLOGY

Office of Graduate Studies, Department of Electrical and Computer Engineering, Program in Electrical Engineering, Newark, NJ 07102

AWARDS MS, PhD. Part-time and evening/weekend programs available.

Students: 164 full-time (31 women), 137 part-time (13 women); includes 65 minority (21 African Americans, 30 Asian Americans or Pacific Islanders, 14 Hispanic Americans), 173 international. Average age 29. 679 applicants, 54% accepted, 79 enrolled. In 2001, 42 master's, 19 doctorates awarded.
Degree requirements: For doctorate, thesis/dissertation, residency.
Entrance requirements: For master's, GRE General Test; for doctorate, GRE General Test, minimum graduate GPA of 3.5. *Application deadline:* For fall admission, 6/5 (priority date); for spring admission, 10/15. Applications are processed on a rolling basis. *Application fee:* $50. Electronic applications accepted.
Expenses: Tuition, state resident: full-time $7,812; part-time $434 per credit. Tuition, nonresident: full-time $10,746; part-time $597 per credit. Required fees: $47 per credit. $76 per semester.
Financial support: Fellowships with full and partial tuition reimbursements, research assistantships with full and partial

tuition reimbursements, teaching assistant-ships with full and partial tuition reimbursements, career-related internships or fieldwork, Federal Work-Study, institutionally sponsored loans, and unspecified assistantships available. Financial award application deadline: 3/15. **Application contact:** Kathryn Kelly, Director of Admissions, 973-596-3300, *Fax:* 973-596-3461, *E-mail:* admissions@njit.edu. *Web site:* http://www.njit.edu/

■ NEW MEXICO STATE UNIVERSITY

Graduate School, College of Engineering, Klipsch School of Electrical and Computer Engineering, Las Cruces, NM 88003-8001

AWARDS MSEE, PhD. Part-time programs available.

Faculty: 21 full-time (0 women), 3 part-time/adjunct (0 women).
Students: 81 full-time (13 women), 52 part-time (5 women); includes 24 minority (1 African American, 2 Asian Americans or Pacific Islanders, 19 Hispanic Americans, 2 Native Americans), 76 international. Average age 29. 168 applicants, 79% accepted, 37 enrolled. In 2001, 20 master's, 6 doctorates awarded.
Degree requirements: For master's, thesis (for some programs); for doctorate, 2 foreign languages, thesis/dissertation, comprehensive exam.
Entrance requirements: For master's, GRE, minimum GPA of 3.0; for doctorate, departmental qualifying exam, minimum GPA of 3.0. *Application deadline:* For fall admission, 7/1 (priority date); for spring admission, 11/1. Applications are processed on a rolling basis. *Application fee:* $15 ($35 for international students). Electronic applications accepted.
Expenses: Tuition, state resident: full-time $3,234; part-time $135 per credit. Tuition, nonresident: full-time $9,420; part-time $428 per credit. Required fees: $858.
Financial support: In 2001–02, 60 students received support, including 25 research assistantships with partial tuition reimbursements available, 33 teaching assistantships with partial tuition reimbursements available; fellowships, career-related internships or fieldwork, Federal Work-Study, and unspecified assistantships also available. Support available to part-time students. Financial award application deadline: 3/1.
Faculty research: Software engineering, high performance computing, telemetering and space telecommunications, computational electromagnetics.
Dr. Steven P. Castillo, Head, 505-646-3115, *Fax:* 505-646-1435, *E-mail:* scastill@nmsu.edu.
Application contact: Dr. Javin M. Taylor, Associate Department Head, 505-646-3115, *Fax:* 505-646-1435, *E-mail:* jtaylor@nmsu.edu. *Web site:* http://gauss.nmsu.edu:8000/

■ NEW YORK INSTITUTE OF TECHNOLOGY

Graduate Division, School of Engineering and Technology, Program in Electrical Engineering and Computer Engineering, Old Westbury, NY 11568-8000

AWARDS MS. Part-time and evening/weekend programs available.

Students: 32 full-time (2 women), 28 part-time; includes 15 minority (6 African Americans, 8 Asian Americans or Pacific Islanders, 1 Hispanic American), 23 international. Average age 30. 91 applicants, 64% accepted, 16 enrolled. In 2001, 16 degrees awarded.
Degree requirements: For master's, project.
Entrance requirements: For master's, GRE General Test, TOEFL, BS in electrical engineering or related field, minimum QPA of 2.85. *Application deadline:* For fall admission, 7/1 (priority date); for spring admission, 12/1 (priority date). Applications are processed on a rolling basis. *Application fee:* $50. Electronic applications accepted.
Expenses: Tuition: Part-time $545 per credit. Tuition and fees vary according to course load, degree level, program and student level.
Financial support: In 2001–02, 3 research assistantships with partial tuition reimbursements were awarded; fellowships, institutionally sponsored loans, tuition waivers (full and partial), and unspecified assistantships also available. Support available to part-time students. Financial award applicants required to submit FAFSA.
Faculty research: Computer networks, control theory, light waves and optics, robotics, signal processing.
Dr. Ayat Jafari, Chair, 516-686-7523, *E-mail:* ajafari@nyit.edu.
Application contact: Jacquelyn Nealon, Dean of Admissions and Financial Aid, 516-686-7925, *Fax:* 516-686-7613, *E-mail:* jnealon@nyit.edu.

■ NORTH CAROLINA AGRICULTURAL AND TECHNICAL STATE UNIVERSITY

Graduate School, College of Engineering, Department of Electrical Engineering, Greensboro, NC 27411

AWARDS MSEE, PhD. Part-time programs available.

Faculty: 16 full-time (1 woman), 1 part-time/adjunct (0 women).
Students: 74 full-time (20 women), 8 part-time (1 woman); includes 32 minority (29 African Americans, 2 Asian Americans or Pacific Islanders, 1 Hispanic American), 37 international. Average age 23. 64 applicants, 63% accepted. In 2001, 12 master's, 2 doctorates awarded.

Degree requirements: For master's, project, thesis defense; for doctorate, thesis/dissertation.
Entrance requirements: For master's, GRE General Test, GRE Subject Test, minimum GPA of 2.8; for doctorate, GRE General Test, minimum GPA of 3.0. *Application deadline:* For fall admission, 7/1; for spring admission, 1/9. Applications are processed on a rolling basis. *Application fee:* $35.
Financial support: In 2001–02, 59 students received support, including 10 fellowships with tuition reimbursements available (averaging $16,000 per year), 20 research assistantships with partial tuition reimbursements available (averaging $14,000 per year), 15 teaching assistantships with partial tuition reimbursements available (averaging $12,000 per year); institutionally sponsored loans, scholarships/grants, and tuition waivers (partial) also available. Financial award application deadline: 3/30.
Faculty research: Semiconductor compounds, VLSI design, image processing, optical systems and devices, fault-tolerant computing. *Total annual research expenditures:* $1.9 million.
Dr. John C. Kelly, Interim Chairperson, 336-334-7760 Ext. 210, *Fax:* 336-334-7716, *E-mail:* jck@ncat.edu.
Application contact: Dr. Chung Yu, Graduate Coordinator, 336-334-7760 Ext. 211, *Fax:* 336-334-7716, *E-mail:* yu@genesis.ncat.edu.

■ NORTH CAROLINA STATE UNIVERSITY

Graduate School, College of Engineering, Department of Electrical and Computer Engineering, Program in Electrical Engineering, Raleigh, NC 27695

AWARDS MS, PhD.

Faculty: 50 full-time (3 women), 41 part-time/adjunct (3 women).
Students: 266 full-time (50 women), 82 part-time (8 women); includes 24 minority (12 African Americans, 10 Asian Americans or Pacific Islanders, 2 Hispanic Americans), 229 international. Average age 28. 777 applicants, 41% accepted. In 2001, 37 master's, 14 doctorates awarded.
Application fee: $45.
Expenses: Tuition, state resident: full-time $1,748. Tuition, nonresident: full-time $6,904.
Financial support: In 2001–02, 7 fellowships (averaging $7,386 per year), 96 research assistantships (averaging $5,862 per year), 68 teaching assistantships (averaging $5,198 per year) were awarded.
Faculty research: Microwave devices, solid state, power and control systems, wireless communications.
Dr. Winser E. Alexander, Director of Graduate Programs, 919-515-5091, *Fax:* 919-515-5601, *E-mail:* jbrisen@eos.ncsu.edu.

■ NORTH DAKOTA STATE UNIVERSITY

The Graduate School, College of Engineering and Architecture, Department of Electrical and Computer Engineering, Fargo, ND 58105

AWARDS MS.

Faculty: 16 full-time (1 woman), 2 part-time/adjunct (0 women).

Students: 6 full-time (2 women), 13 part-time, 13 international. Average age 28. 31 applicants, 71% accepted. In 2001, 3 degrees awarded.

Degree requirements: For master's, thesis or alternative.

Entrance requirements: For master's, TOEFL. *Application deadline:* For fall admission, 3/1 (priority date). Applications are processed on a rolling basis. *Application fee:* $35.

Expenses: Tuition, state resident: part-time $124 per credit. Tuition, nonresident: part-time $325 per credit. Required fees: $22 per credit. Tuition and fees vary according to reciprocity agreements.

Financial support: In 2001–02, 2 fellowships with tuition reimbursements (averaging $25,000 per year), research assistantships with tuition reimbursements (averaging $8,100 per year), teaching assistantships with tuition reimbursements (averaging $8,100 per year) were awarded. Career-related internships or fieldwork, Federal Work-Study, institutionally sponsored loans, and tuition waivers (full) also available. Financial award application deadline: 4/15.

Faculty research: Computers, power and control systems, microwaves, communications and signal processing, bioengineering. *Total annual research expenditures:* $599,000.

Dr. Daniel L. Ewert, Chair, 701-231-7608, *Fax:* 701-231-8677, *E-mail:* dan.ewert@ndsu.nodak.edu.

■ NORTHEASTERN UNIVERSITY

College of Engineering, Department of Electrical and Computer Engineering, Boston, MA 02115-5096

AWARDS MS, PhD. Part-time programs available.

Faculty: 34 full-time (2 women), 8 part-time/adjunct (0 women).

Students: 132 full-time (27 women), 133 part-time (17 women); includes 29 minority (5 African Americans, 20 Asian Americans or Pacific Islanders, 4 Hispanic Americans), 130 international. Average age 25. 606 applicants, 35% accepted, 67 enrolled. In 2001, 52 master's, 11 doctorates awarded.

Degree requirements: For master's, thesis optional; for doctorate, thesis/dissertation, departmental qualifying exam. *Median time to degree:* Master's–3.5 years

full-time, 6 years part-time; doctorate–5.5 years full-time.

Entrance requirements: For master's and doctorate, GRE General Test. *Application deadline:* For fall admission, 2/15 (priority date). Applications are processed on a rolling basis. *Application fee:* $50.

Expenses: Tuition: Part-time $535 per credit hour. Required fees: $56. Tuition and fees vary according to program.

Financial support: In 2001–02, 107 students received support, including 3 fellowships, 66 research assistantships with full tuition reimbursements available (averaging $13,560 per year), 32 teaching assistantships with full tuition reimbursements available (averaging $13,560 per year); career-related internships or fieldwork, Federal Work-Study, scholarships/grants, tuition waivers (full), and unspecified assistantships also available. Support available to part-time students. Financial award application deadline: 2/15; financial award applicants required to submit FAFSA.

Faculty research: Digital communications, signal processing and sensor data fusion, control systems, plasma science, sensing and imaging. *Total annual research expenditures:* $8.6 million.

Dr. Fabrizio Lombardi, Chairman, 617-373-4159, *Fax:* 617-373-8970.

Application contact: Stephen L. Gibson, Associate Director, 617-373-2711, *Fax:* 617-373-2501, *E-mail:* grad-eng@coe.neu.edu. *Web site:* http://www.coe.neu.edu/

Find an in-depth description at www.petersons.com/gradchannel.

■ NORTHERN ILLINOIS UNIVERSITY

Graduate School, College of Engineering and Engineering Technology, Department of Electrical Engineering, De Kalb, IL 60115-2854

AWARDS MS. Part-time and evening/weekend programs available.

Faculty: 11 full-time (0 women).

Students: 56 full-time (18 women), 27 part-time (4 women); includes 7 minority (all Asian Americans or Pacific Islanders), 64 international. Average age 25. 252 applicants, 50% accepted, 41 enrolled. In 2001, 10 degrees awarded.

Degree requirements: For master's, thesis optional.

Entrance requirements: For master's, GRE General Test, TOEFL, minimum GPA of 2.75. *Application deadline:* For fall admission, 6/1; for spring admission, 11/1. Applications are processed on a rolling basis. *Application fee:* $30.

Expenses: Tuition, state resident: full-time $5,124; part-time $148 per credit hour. Tuition, nonresident: full-time $8,666; part-time $295 per credit hour. Required fees: $51 per term.

Financial support: In 2001–02, 2 research assistantships with full tuition reimbursements, 13 teaching assistantships with full tuition reimbursements were awarded. Fellowships with full tuition reimbursements, career-related internships or fieldwork, Federal Work-Study, tuition waivers (full), and unspecified assistantships also available. Support available to part-time students.

Dr. Vincent McGinn, Chair, 815-753-9962, *Fax:* 815-753-1289.

■ NORTHWESTERN POLYTECHNIC UNIVERSITY

School of Engineering, Fremont, CA 94539-7482

AWARDS Computer science (MS); computer systems engineering (MS); electrical engineering (MS). Part-time and evening/weekend programs available.

Faculty: 7 full-time (0 women), 53 part-time/adjunct (4 women).

Students: 239 full-time (119 women), 210 part-time (108 women). Average age 30. 132 applicants, 55% accepted. In 2001, 148 degrees awarded.

Degree requirements: For master's, thesis optional.

Entrance requirements: For master's, TOEFL, minimum GPA of 2.0. *Application deadline:* For fall admission, 8/12 (priority date); for spring admission, 2/11 (priority date). Applications are processed on a rolling basis. *Application fee:* $50 ($75 for international students).

Expenses: Tuition: Full-time $8,100; part-time $450 per unit. Required fees: $45; $15 per term.

Financial support: In 2001–02, 160 teaching assistantships with full and partial tuition reimbursements (averaging $1,000 per year) were awarded; career-related internships or fieldwork and unspecified assistantships also available.

Faculty research: Computer networking; database design; internet technology. Software engineering; digital signal processing.

Dr. Pochang Hsu, Dean, 510-657-5911, *Fax:* 510-657-8975, *E-mail:* npuadm@npu.edu.

Application contact: Jack Xie, Director of Admissions, 510-657-5913, *Fax:* 510-657-8975, *E-mail:* jack@npu.edu. *Web site:* http://www.npu.edu/engineeringindex.htm

■ NORTHWESTERN UNIVERSITY

McCormick School of Engineering and Applied Science, Department of Electrical and Computer Engineering, Evanston, IL 60208

AWARDS Electrical and computer engineering (MS, PhD); electronic materials (MS, PhD, Certificate); information technology (MIT). MS and PhD admissions and degrees offered through The Graduate School. Part-time programs available.

Faculty: 30 full-time (3 women), 7 part-time/adjunct (0 women).
Students: 95 full-time (15 women), 15 part-time (2 women); includes 10 minority (1 African American, 7 Asian Americans or Pacific Islanders, 2 Hispanic Americans), 76 international. 639 applicants, 5% accepted, 24 enrolled. In 2001, 29 master's, 22 doctorates awarded. Terminal master's awarded for partial completion of doctoral program.
Degree requirements: For master's, thesis or project; for doctorate, thesis/dissertation.
Application deadline: For fall admission, 6/1. Applications are processed on a rolling basis. *Application fee:* $50 ($55 for international students).
Expenses: Tuition: Full-time $26,526.
Financial support: In 2001–02, 104 students received support, including 10 fellowships with full tuition reimbursements available (averaging $14,238 per year), 61 research assistantships with partial tuition reimbursements available (averaging $21,000 per year), 33 teaching assistantships with full tuition reimbursements available (averaging $12,843 per year); career-related internships or fieldwork, Federal Work-Study, institutionally sponsored loans, and scholarships/grants also available. Financial award application deadline: 1/15; financial award applicants required to submit FAFSA.
Faculty research: Solid-state engineering networks and communications, optical systems, parallel and distributed computing, VLSI design and computer-aided design. *Total annual research expenditures:* $8.3 million.
Abraham Haddad, Chair, 847-491-3641, *Fax:* 847-491-4455.
Application contact: Peter Scheuermann, Admission Officer, 847-491-7141, *Fax:* 847-491-4455, *E-mail:* peters@ ece.northwestern.edu. *Web site:* http:// www.ece.northwestern.edu/

Find an in-depth description at www.petersons.com/gradchannel.

■ OAKLAND UNIVERSITY

Graduate Study and Lifelong Learning, School of Engineering and Computer Science, Program in Electrical and Computer Engineering, Rochester, MI 48309-4401

AWARDS MS. Part-time and evening/weekend programs available.

Faculty: 6 full-time (1 woman), 1 part-time/adjunct (0 women).
Students: 31 full-time (8 women), 54 part-time (10 women); includes 11 minority (4 African Americans, 6 Asian Americans or Pacific Islanders, 1 Native American), 26 international. Average age 29. 65 applicants, 74% accepted. In 2001, 16 degrees awarded.
Entrance requirements: For master's, minimum GPA of 3.0 for unconditional admission. *Application deadline:* For fall

admission, 8/1 (priority date); for winter admission, 12/1 (priority date); for spring admission, 4/1 (priority date). Applications are processed on a rolling basis. *Application fee:* $30. Electronic applications accepted.
Expenses: Tuition, state resident: full-time $5,904; part-time $246 per credit hour. Tuition, nonresident: full-time $12,192; part-time $508 per credit hour. Required fees: $472; $236 per term.
Financial support: Federal Work-Study, institutionally sponsored loans, and tuition waivers (full) available. Financial award application deadline: 3/1; financial award applicants required to submit FAFSA.
Dr. Naim A. Kheir, Chair, 248-370-2177.

■ OGI SCHOOL OF SCIENCE & ENGINEERING AT OREGON HEALTH & SCIENCE UNIVERSITY

Graduate Studies, Department of Electrical and Computer Engineering, Beaverton, OR 97006-8921

AWARDS Computer engineering (MS, PhD); electrical engineering (MS, PhD). Part-time programs available.

Faculty: 23 full-time (2 women), 31 part-time/adjunct (0 women).
Students: 54 full-time (19 women), 75 part-time (23 women). Average age 29. 184 applicants, 97% accepted. In 2001, 25 master's, 2 doctorates awarded. Terminal master's awarded for partial completion of doctoral program.
Degree requirements: For master's, thesis optional; for doctorate, oral defense of dissertation.
Entrance requirements: For master's, TOEFL; for doctorate, GRE General Test, GRE Subject Test, TOEFL. *Application deadline:* For fall admission, 3/1 (priority date). Applications are processed on a rolling basis. *Application fee:* $50. Electronic applications accepted.
Expenses: Tuition: Full-time $4,905; part-time $545 per credit hour. Required fees: $466.
Financial support: In 2001–02, 20 students received support, including 19 research assistantships with full and partial tuition reimbursements available; fellowships, Federal Work-Study also available. Financial award application deadline: 3/1.
Faculty research: Semiconductor materials, microwave circuits, atmospheric optics, surface physics, electron and ion optics. *Total annual research expenditures:* $3.5 million.
John Carruthers, Head, 503-748-1616, *Fax:* 503-748-1406.
Application contact: Barbara Olsen, Enrollment Manager, 503-748-1418, *Fax:* 503-748-1406, *E-mail:* bolsen@ece.ogi.edu. *Web site:* http://www.eeap.ogi.edu/

Find an in-depth description at www.petersons.com/gradchannel.

■ THE OHIO STATE UNIVERSITY

Graduate School, College of Engineering, Department of Electrical Engineering, Columbus, OH 43210

AWARDS MS, PhD. Part-time programs available.

Faculty: 49 full-time (3 women), 20 part-time/adjunct (0 women).
Students: 292 full-time (41 women), 24 part-time (5 women). 1,517 applicants, 11% accepted. In 2001, 57 master's, 18 doctorates awarded. Terminal master's awarded for partial completion of doctoral program.
Degree requirements: For master's, thesis optional; for doctorate, thesis/dissertation.
Entrance requirements: For master's, TOEFL, GRE General Test, or minimum GPA of 3.2; for doctorate, TOEFL, GRE General Test, or minimum GPA of 3.5. *Application deadline:* For fall admission, 8/15. Applications are processed on a rolling basis. *Application fee:* $30 ($40 for international students).
Financial support: In 2001–02, 25 fellowships with full tuition reimbursements (averaging $18,000 per year), 100 research assistantships with full tuition reimbursements (averaging $18,000 per year), 30 teaching assistantships with full tuition reimbursements (averaging $15,000 per year) were awarded. Career-related internships or fieldwork, Federal Work-Study, institutionally sponsored loans, scholarships/grants, traineeships, health care benefits, and unspecified assistantships also available. Support available to part-time students. *Total annual research expenditures:* $13 million.
Dr. Yuan F. Zheng, Chair, 614-292-2572, *Fax:* 614-292-7596, *E-mail:* zheng.5@ osu.edu.
Application contact: Dr. Fusun Ozguner, Graduate Studies Committee Chair, 614-292-1357, *Fax:* 614-292-7596, *E-mail:* ozguner.2@osu.edu. *Web site:* http:// eewww.eng.ohio-state.edu/

Find an in-depth description at www.petersons.com/gradchannel.

■ OHIO UNIVERSITY

Graduate Studies, Russ College of Engineering and Technology, School of Electrical Engineering and Computer Science, Athens, OH 45701-2979

AWARDS Computer science (MS); electrical engineering (MS, PhD).

Faculty: 31 full-time (2 women), 10 part-time/adjunct (3 women).
Students: 95 full-time (19 women), 28 part-time (9 women); includes 5 minority (1 African American, 4 Asian Americans or Pacific Islanders), 98 international. 549 applicants, 51% accepted, 43 enrolled. In 2001, 16 master's, 4 doctorates awarded.

Ohio University (continued)

Degree requirements: For master's, thesis; for doctorate, thesis/dissertation, qualifying exams, comprehensive exam. *Median time to degree:* Master's–3 years full-time; doctorate–5 years full-time. **Entrance requirements:** For master's, GRE, BSEE, minimum GPA of 3.0; for doctorate, GRE, MSEE, minimum GPA of 3.0. *Application fee:* $30.
Expenses: Tuition, state resident: full-time $6,585. Tuition, nonresident: full-time $12,254.
Financial support: In 2001–02, 11 fellowships with full tuition reimbursements (averaging $14,000 per year), 5 research assistantships with full tuition reimbursements (averaging $12,000 per year), 5 teaching assistantships with full tuition reimbursements (averaging $10,500 per year) were awarded. Federal Work-Study and institutionally sponsored loans also available.
Faculty research: Avionics, networking/communications, intelligent distribution, real-time computing, control systems, optical properties of semiconductors. *Total annual research expenditures:* $9 million.
Application contact: Dr. David M. Chelberg, Graduate Chair, 740-593-1922, *Fax:* 740-593-0007, *E-mail:* chelberg@ohio.edu. *Web site:* http://webeers.ent.ohiou.edu

Find an in-depth description at www.petersons.com/gradchannel.

■ **OKLAHOMA STATE UNIVERSITY**

Graduate College, College of Engineering, Architecture and Technology, School of Electrical and Computer Engineering, Stillwater, OK 74078

AWARDS M En, MS, PhD.

Faculty: 24 full-time (0 women), 5 part-time/adjunct (0 women).
Students: 149 full-time (32 women), 68 part-time (8 women); includes 9 minority (3 African Americans, 3 Asian Americans or Pacific Islanders, 1 Hispanic American, 2 Native Americans), 170 international. Average age 27. 371 applicants, 57% accepted. In 2001, 33 master's, 2 doctorates awarded.
Degree requirements: For master's, thesis or alternative; for doctorate, thesis/dissertation.
Entrance requirements: For master's and doctorate, TOEFL. *Application deadline:* For fall admission, 7/1 (priority date). *Application fee:* $25.
Expenses: Tuition, state resident: part-time $92 per credit hour. Tuition, nonresident: part-time $297 per credit hour. Required fees: $21 per credit hour. $14 per semester. One-time fee: $20. Tuition and fees vary according to course load.

Financial support: In 2001–02, 33 research assistantships (averaging $11,304 per year), 47 teaching assistantships (averaging $7,442 per year) were awarded. Career-related internships or fieldwork, Federal Work-Study, and tuition waivers (partial) also available. Support available to part-time students. Financial award application deadline: 3/1.
Dr. Michael A. Soderstrand, Head, 405-744-5151.

Find an in-depth description at www.petersons.com/gradchannel.

■ **OLD DOMINION UNIVERSITY**

College of Engineering and Technology, Program in Electrical and Computer Engineering, Norfolk, VA 23529

AWARDS Electrical engineering and computer engineering (PhD). Part-time programs available. Postbaccalaureate distance learning degree programs offered (minimal on-campus study).

Faculty: 17 full-time (1 woman), 5 part-time/adjunct (0 women).
Students: 25 full-time (5 women), 13 part-time (3 women); includes 3 minority (1 African American, 2 Asian Americans or Pacific Islanders), 33 international. Average age 30. 23 applicants, 96% accepted, 5 enrolled. In 2001, 5 degrees awarded.
Degree requirements: For doctorate, thesis/dissertation, candidacy exam, diagnostic exam.
Entrance requirements: For doctorate, GRE, TOEFL. *Application deadline:* For fall admission, 7/1; for spring admission, 10/1. Applications are processed on a rolling basis. *Application fee:* $30. Electronic applications accepted.
Expenses: Tuition, state resident: part-time $202 per credit. Tuition, nonresident: part-time $534 per credit. Required fees: $76 per semester.
Financial support: In 2001–02, 3 fellowships (averaging $19,333 per year), 12 research assistantships with tuition reimbursements (averaging $15,000 per year), 7 teaching assistantships with tuition reimbursements (averaging $15,000 per year) were awarded. Career-related internships or fieldwork, scholarships/grants, and tuition waivers (partial) also available. Support available to part-time students. Financial award application deadline: 2/15; financial award applicants required to submit FAFSA.
Faculty research: Digital signal processing, control engineering, gaseous electronics, ultrafast (femtosecom) laser applications, interaction of fields with living organisms, modeling and simulation. *Total annual research expenditures:* $2 million.
Dr. Amin N. Dharamsi, Graduate Program Director, 757-683-3741, *Fax:* 757-683-3220, *E-mail:* ecegpd@odu.edu. *Web site:* http://www.ee.odu.edu/

■ **OLD DOMINION UNIVERSITY**

College of Engineering and Technology, Program in Electrical Engineering, Norfolk, VA 23529

AWARDS ME, MS.

Faculty: 17 full-time (1 woman), 5 part-time/adjunct (0 women).
Students: 18 full-time (3 women), 22 part-time (7 women); includes 3 minority (2 African Americans, 1 Asian American or Pacific Islander), 29 international. Average age 26. 159 applicants, 48% accepted, 10 enrolled. In 2001, 12 degrees awarded.
Degree requirements: For master's, thesis (for some programs), comprehensive exam (for some programs), registration.
Entrance requirements: For master's, minimum GPA of 3.0. *Application deadline:* For fall admission, 7/1; for spring admission, 10/1. Applications are processed on a rolling basis. *Application fee:* $30. Electronic applications accepted.
Expenses: Tuition, state resident: part-time $202 per credit. Tuition, nonresident: part-time $534 per credit. Required fees: $76 per semester.
Financial support: In 2001–02, 2 fellowships with full tuition reimbursements (averaging $20,000 per year), 5 research assistantships with partial tuition reimbursements (averaging $12,000 per year), 3 teaching assistantships with partial tuition reimbursements (averaging $12,000 per year) were awarded. Career-related internships or fieldwork, Federal Work-Study, scholarships/grants, and unspecified assistantships also available. Financial award application deadline: 2/15.
Faculty research: Digital signal processing, bioelectrics, laser interaction with matter, control engineering, micro and nano electronics. *Total annual research expenditures:* $2 million.
Dr. Amin N. Dharamsi, Graduate Program Director, 757-683-3741, *Fax:* 757-683-3220, *E-mail:* ecegpd@odu.edu. *Web site:* http://www.ece.odu.edu/

■ **THE PENNSYLVANIA STATE UNIVERSITY HARRISBURG CAMPUS OF THE CAPITAL COLLEGE**

Graduate Center, School of Science, Engineering and Technology, Program in Electrical Engineering, Middletown, PA 17057-4898

AWARDS M Eng.

Students: In 2001, 1 degree awarded.
Degree requirements: For master's, thesis.
Application deadline: For fall admission, 7/26. *Application fee:* $45.
Expenses: Tuition, state resident: full-time $7,882; part-time $333 per credit. Tuition, nonresident: full-time $14,384; part-time $600 per credit.
Dr. Jerry Shoup, Chair, 717-948-6114.

■ THE PENNSYLVANIA STATE UNIVERSITY UNIVERSITY PARK CAMPUS

Graduate School, College of Engineering, Department of Electrical Engineering, State College, University Park, PA 16802-1503

AWARDS M Eng, MS, PhD.

Students: 192 full-time (25 women), 48 part-time (3 women). In 2001, 93 master's, 22 doctorates awarded.
Degree requirements: For doctorate, thesis/dissertation.
Entrance requirements: For master's and doctorate, GRE General Test. *Application fee:* $45.
Expenses: Tuition, state resident: full-time $7,882; part-time $333 per credit. Tuition, nonresident: full-time $16,142; part-time $673 per credit. Required fees: $124 per semester.
Dr. W. Kenneth Jenkins, Head, 814-863-7295.
Application contact: Dr. James W. Robinson, Chair, 814-863-7295.

■ POLYTECHNIC UNIVERSITY, BROOKLYN CAMPUS

Department of Electrical Engineering, Major in Electrical Engineering, Brooklyn, NY 11201-2990

AWARDS MS, PhD. Part-time and evening/weekend programs available.

Degree requirements: For master's, thesis optional; for doctorate, thesis/dissertation.
Entrance requirements: For master's, BS in electrical engineering; for doctorate, qualifying exam, MS in electrical engineering. Electronic applications accepted.
Find an in-depth description at www.petersons.com/gradchannel.

■ POLYTECHNIC UNIVERSITY, LONG ISLAND GRADUATE CENTER

Graduate Programs, Department of Electrical Engineering, Major in Electrical Engineering, Melville, NY 11747

AWARDS MS, PhD.

Degree requirements: For master's, thesis (for some programs); for doctorate, thesis/dissertation.
Electronic applications accepted.

■ POLYTECHNIC UNIVERSITY, WESTCHESTER GRADUATE CENTER

Graduate Programs, Department of Electrical Engineering, Major in Electrical Engineering, Hawthorne, NY 10532-1507

AWARDS MS, PhD.

Degree requirements: For master's, thesis (for some programs); for doctorate, thesis/dissertation.
Electronic applications accepted.

■ PORTLAND STATE UNIVERSITY

Graduate Studies, College of Engineering and Computer Science, Department of Electrical and Computer Engineering, Portland, OR 97207-0751

AWARDS MS, PhD. Part-time and evening/weekend programs available.

Faculty: 14 full-time (1 woman).
Students: 35 full-time (7 women), 59 part-time (12 women); includes 11 minority (8 Asian Americans or Pacific Islanders, 2 Hispanic Americans, 1 Native American), 47 international. Average age 31. 82 applicants, 73% accepted. In 2001, 42 master's, 2 doctorates awarded.
Degree requirements: For master's, variable foreign language requirement, thesis or alternative, oral exam; for doctorate, one foreign language, thesis/dissertation, oral and written exams.
Entrance requirements: For master's, TOEFL, minimum GPA of 3.0 in upper-division course work or 2.75 overall; for doctorate, GRE General Test, GRE Subject Test, minimum GPA of 3.0 in upper-division course work. *Application deadline:* For fall admission, 3/1 (priority date); for spring admission, 11/1. Applications are processed on a rolling basis. *Application fee:* $50.
Financial support: In 2001–02, 2 research assistantships with full tuition reimbursements (averaging $7,653 per year), 2 teaching assistantships with full tuition reimbursements (averaging $9,620 per year) were awarded. Career-related internships or fieldwork, Federal Work-Study, and institutionally sponsored loans also available. Support available to part-time students. Financial award application deadline: 3/1; financial award applicants required to submit FAFSA.
Faculty research: Optics and laser systems, design automation, VLSI design, computer systems, power electronics. *Total annual research expenditures:* $242,094.
Dr. Doug Hall, Interim Chair, 503-725-3806, *Fax:* 503-725-3807.

Application contact: Dr. Y. C. Jenq, Coordinator, 503-725-3806, *Fax:* 503-725-3807, *E-mail:* jenq@ee.pdx.edu. *Web site:* http://www.ee.pdx.edu/
Find an in-depth description at www.petersons.com/gradchannel.

■ PRINCETON UNIVERSITY

Graduate School, School of Engineering and Applied Science, Department of Electrical Engineering, Princeton, NJ 08544-1019

AWARDS Computer engineering (PhD); electrical engineering (M Eng); electronic materials and devices (PhD); information sciences and systems (PhD); optoelectronics (PhD). Part-time programs available.

Degree requirements: For doctorate, thesis/dissertation.
Entrance requirements: For master's and doctorate, GRE General Test, TOEFL. Electronic applications accepted.
Faculty research: Nanostructures, computer architecture, multimedia. *Web site:* http://www.princeton.edu/

■ PURDUE UNIVERSITY

Graduate School, Schools of Engineering, School of Electrical and Computer Engineering, West Lafayette, IN 47907

AWARDS Biomedical engineering (MS Bm E, PhD); computer engineering (MS, PhD); electrical engineering (MS, PhD). Part-time programs available. Postbaccalaureate distance learning degree programs offered (no on-campus study).

Faculty: 63 full-time (5 women), 10 part-time/adjunct (0 women).
Students: 355 full-time (46 women), 109 part-time (22 women); includes 27 minority (5 African Americans, 17 Asian Americans or Pacific Islanders, 5 Hispanic Americans), 353 international. Average age 27. 1,506 applicants, 27% accepted. In 2001, 123 master's, 38 doctorates awarded.
Degree requirements: For master's, thesis optional; for doctorate, thesis/dissertation.
Entrance requirements: For master's and doctorate, GRE General Test, TOEFL. *Application deadline:* For fall admission, 1/15 (priority date); for spring admission, 9/1. Applications are processed on a rolling basis. *Application fee:* $30. Electronic applications accepted.
Expenses: Tuition, state resident: full-time $4,164; part-time $149 per credit hour. Tuition, nonresident: full-time $13,872; part-time $458 per credit hour. Tuition and fees vary according to campus/location and program.
Financial support: In 2001–02, 305 students received support, including 28 fellowships with partial tuition reimbursements available (averaging $16,200 per year), 179 research assistantships with partial tuition reimbursements available

Purdue University (continued)
(averaging $15,000 per year), 98 teaching assistantships with partial tuition reimbursements available (averaging $11,900 per year) Financial award application deadline: 1/5.
Faculty research: Biomedical communications and signal processing, solid-state materials and devices fields and optics, automatic controls, energy sources and systems, VLSI and circuit design. *Total annual research expenditures:* $13.9 million.
Dr. W. K. Fuchs, Head, 765-494-3539, *Fax:* 765-494-3544, *E-mail:* fuchs@purdue.edu.
Application contact: Dr. A. M. Weiner, Director of Admissions, 765-494-3392, *Fax:* 765-494-3393, *E-mail:* ecegrad@ecn.purdue.edu. *Web site:* http://www.ece.purdue.edu/ECE/
Find an in-depth description at www.petersons.com/gradchannel.

■ **RENSSELAER AT HARTFORD**

Department of Engineering, Program in Electrical Engineering, Hartford, CT 06120-2991

AWARDS MS. Part-time and evening/weekend programs available.

Faculty: 2 full-time (0 women), 5 part-time/adjunct (0 women).
Students: Average age 31. 10 applicants, 50% accepted, 5 enrolled. In 2001, 6 degrees awarded.
Degree requirements: For master's, seminar, thesis optional.
Entrance requirements: For master's, TOEFL. *Application deadline:* For fall admission, 8/6 (priority date). Applications are processed on a rolling basis. *Application fee:* $45.
Expenses: Tuition: Full-time $11,700; part-time $650 per credit.
Financial support: Research assistantships, tuition waivers (full and partial) and unspecified assistantships available. Support available to part-time students. Financial award applicants required to submit FAFSA.
Application contact: Rebecca Danchak, Director of Admissions, 860-548-2420, *Fax:* 860-548-7823, *E-mail:* rdanchak@rh.edu.

■ **RENSSELAER POLYTECHNIC INSTITUTE**

Graduate School, School of Engineering, Department of Electrical, Computer, and Systems Engineering, Program in Electrical Engineering, Troy, NY 12180-3590

AWARDS M Eng, MS, D Eng, PhD, MBA/M Eng. Part-time programs available. Postbaccalaureate distance learning degree programs offered (no on-campus study).

Faculty: 31 full-time (1 woman).
Students: 111 full-time (13 women), 39 part-time (2 women); includes 9 minority

(4 African Americans, 5 Asian Americans or Pacific Islanders), 87 international. 571 applicants, 34% accepted. In 2001, 28 master's, 4 doctorates awarded. Terminal master's awarded for partial completion of doctoral program.
Degree requirements: For master's, thesis (for some programs); for doctorate, thesis/dissertation.
Entrance requirements: For master's and doctorate, GRE, TOEFL. *Application deadline:* For fall admission, 1/15; for spring admission, 10/1. Applications are processed on a rolling basis. *Application fee:* $45. Electronic applications accepted.
Expenses: Tuition: Full-time $26,400; part-time $1,320 per credit hour. Required fees: $1,437.
Financial support: In 2001–02, 4 fellowships, 64 research assistantships, 20 teaching assistantships were awarded. Career-related internships or fieldwork and institutionally sponsored loans also available. Financial award application deadline: 2/1.
Faculty research: Networking and multimedia via ATM, thermophotovoltaic devices, microelectronic interconnections, agile manufacturing, mobile robotics. *Total annual research expenditures:* $2.4 million.
Application contact: Ann Bruno, Manager of Student Services and Graduate Enrollment, 518-276-2554, *Fax:* 518-276-2433, *E-mail:* bruno@ecse.rpi.edu. *Web site:* http://www.ecse.rpi.edu/
Find an in-depth description at www.petersons.com/gradchannel.

■ **RICE UNIVERSITY**

Graduate Programs, George R. Brown School of Engineering, Department of Electrical and Computer Engineering, Houston, TX 77251-1892

AWARDS Bioengineering (MS, PhD); circuits, controls, and communication systems (MS, PhD); computer science and engineering (MS, PhD); electrical engineering (MEE); lasers, microwaves, and solid-state electronics (MS, PhD). Part-time programs available.

Faculty: 20 full-time (2 women), 4 part-time/adjunct (0 women).
Students: 98 full-time (18 women), 8 part-time (2 women); includes 6 minority (1 African American, 3 Asian Americans or Pacific Islanders, 2 Hispanic Americans), 72 international. 337 applicants, 19% accepted, 34 enrolled. In 2001, 12 master's, 9 doctorates awarded.
Degree requirements: For master's, thesis (for some programs); for doctorate, thesis/dissertation.
Entrance requirements: For master's and doctorate, GRE General Test, GRE Subject Test, TOEFL, minimum GPA of 3.0. *Application deadline:* For fall admission, 2/1; for spring admission, 11/1. Applications are processed on a rolling basis. *Application fee:* $25.
Expenses: Tuition: Full-time $17,300. Required fees: $250.

Financial support: In 2001–02, 29 fellowships with tuition reimbursements, 60 research assistantships with tuition reimbursements, 2 teaching assistantships with tuition reimbursements were awarded. Federal Work-Study also available.
Faculty research: Physical electronics, systems, computer engineering, bioengineering. *Total annual research expenditures:* $4.5 million.
Don H. Johnson, Chairman, 713-348-4020.
Application contact: Bea Sparks, Information Contact, 713-348-4020, *E-mail:* elec@rice.edu. *Web site:* http://www.ece.rice.edu/

■ **ROCHESTER INSTITUTE OF TECHNOLOGY**

Graduate Enrollment Services, College of Engineering, Department of Electrical Engineering, Rochester, NY 14623-5698

AWARDS MSEE.

Students: 17 full-time (5 women), 28 part-time (3 women); includes 1 minority (Asian American or Pacific Islander), 22 international. 209 applicants, 56% accepted, 21 enrolled. In 2001, 24 degrees awarded.
Degree requirements: For master's, thesis optional.
Entrance requirements: For master's, TOEFL, minimum GPA of 3.0. *Application deadline:* For fall admission, 3/1 (priority date). Applications are processed on a rolling basis. *Application fee:* $50.
Expenses: Tuition: Full-time $20,928; part-time $587 per hour. Required fees: $162. Tuition and fees vary according to program.
Financial support: Research assistantships available.
Faculty research: Integrated optics, control systems, digital signal processing, robotic vision.
Dr. Swaminathan Madhu, Head, 585-475-2165, *E-mail:* snmeee1@rit.edu.

■ **ROCHESTER INSTITUTE OF TECHNOLOGY**

Graduate Enrollment Services, College of Engineering, Department of Microelectronic Engineering, Rochester, NY 14623-5698

AWARDS ME, MS.

Students: 14 full-time (4 women), 7 part-time; includes 4 minority (1 African American, 3 Asian Americans or Pacific Islanders), 9 international. 20 applicants, 70% accepted, 9 enrolled. In 2001, 2 degrees awarded.
Entrance requirements: For master's, TOEFL, minimum GPA of 3.0. *Application deadline:* For fall admission, 3/1 (priority date). Applications are processed on a rolling basis. *Application fee:* $50.

Expenses: Tuition: Full-time $20,928; part-time $587 per hour. Required fees: $162. Tuition and fees vary according to program.

Financial support: Fellowships, research assistantships, teaching assistantships, career-related internships or fieldwork, Federal Work-Study, and institutionally sponsored loans available. Support available to part-time students.

Faculty research: Semiconductor device fabrication, lithography, materials, gallium arsenide.

Dr. Santosh Kurinec, Director, 585-4765-2927, *E-mail:* skkeme@rit.edu.

Application contact: Dr. Richard Reeve, Associate Dean, 585-475-5382, *E-mail:* nrreie@rit.edu.

■ ROSE-HULMAN INSTITUTE OF TECHNOLOGY

Faculty of Engineering and Applied Sciences, Department of Electrical and Computer Engineering, Terre Haute, IN 47803-3920

AWARDS Electrical engineering (MS). Part-time programs available. Postbaccalaureate distance learning degree programs offered (minimal on-campus study).

Faculty: 16 full-time (1 woman), 1 (woman) part-time/adjunct.

Students: 9 full-time (3 women), 16 part-time (1 woman); includes 2 minority (both Asian Americans or Pacific Islanders), 10 international. Average age 27. 20 applicants, 65% accepted, 5 enrolled. In 2001, 9 degrees awarded.

Degree requirements: For master's, thesis.

Entrance requirements: For master's, GRE, TOEFL, minimum GPA of 3.0. *Application deadline:* For fall admission, 2/1 (priority date). Applications are processed on a rolling basis. *Application fee:* $0.

Expenses: Tuition: Full-time $21,792; part-time $615 per credit hour. Required fees: $405.

Financial support: In 2001–02, 10 students received support; fellowships with full and partial tuition reimbursements available, research assistantships with full and partial tuition reimbursements available, institutionally sponsored loans, scholarships/grants, and tuition waivers (full and partial) available. Financial award application deadline: 2/1.

Faculty research: Wireless systems, VLSI design, aerial robotics, power system dynamics and control, image and speech processing. *Total annual research expenditures:* $4.1 million.

Dr. Frederick Berry, Chairman, 812-877-8105, *Fax:* 812-877-8895, *E-mail:* frederick.berry@rose-hulman.edu.

Application contact: Dr. Daniel J. Moore, Interim Associate Dean of the Faculty, 812-877-8110, *Fax:* 812-877-8061, *E-mail:* daniel.j.moore@rose-hulman.edu.

■ RUTGERS, THE STATE UNIVERSITY OF NEW JERSEY, NEW BRUNSWICK

Graduate School, Program in Electrical and Computer Engineering, New Brunswick, NJ 08901-1281

AWARDS Communications and solid-state electronics (MS, PhD); computer engineering (MS, PhD); control systems (MS, PhD); digital signal processing (MS, PhD). Part-time programs available. Terminal master's awarded for partial completion of doctoral program.

Degree requirements: For master's, thesis or alternative; for doctorate, thesis/dissertation.

Entrance requirements: For master's and doctorate, GRE General Test. Electronic applications accepted.

Faculty research: Communication and information processing, wireless information networks, micro-vacuum devices, machine vision, VLSI design. *Web site:* http://www.ece.rutgers.edu/

Find an in-depth description at www.petersons.com/gradchannel.

■ ST. CLOUD STATE UNIVERSITY

School of Graduate Studies, College of Science and Engineering, Department of Electrical Engineering, St. Cloud, MN 56301-4498

AWARDS MS.

Faculty: 8 full-time (2 women).

Students: 4 full-time (0 women); all minorities (all Asian Americans or Pacific Islanders). 18 applicants, 11% accepted.

Degree requirements: For master's, thesis or alternative.

Entrance requirements: For master's, GRE General Test, minimum GPA of 2.75. *Application deadline:* Applications are processed on a rolling basis. *Application fee:* $35.

Expenses: Tuition, state resident: part-time $156 per credit. Tuition, nonresident: part-time $244 per credit. Required fees: $20 per credit.

Financial support: Unspecified assistantships available.

Yi Zheng, Department Chairperson, 320-255-3252, *Fax:* 320-654-5127, *E-mail:* eedept@stcloudstate.edu.

Application contact: Lindalou Krueger, Graduate Studies Office, 320-255-2113, *Fax:* 320-654-5371, *E-mail:* lekrueger@stcloudstate.edu.

■ ST. MARY'S UNIVERSITY OF SAN ANTONIO

Graduate School, Department of Engineering, Program in Electrical Engineering, San Antonio, TX 78228-8507

AWARDS Electrical /computer engineering (MS); electrical engineering (MS).

Faculty: 6 full-time, 3 part-time/adjunct.

Students: 4 full-time (0 women), 12 part-time (2 women); includes 5 minority (2 Asian Americans or Pacific Islanders, 3 Hispanic Americans), 3 international. Average age 25. In 2001, 2 degrees awarded.

Degree requirements: For master's, thesis.

Entrance requirements: For master's, GRE General Test. *Application deadline:* Applications are processed on a rolling basis. *Application fee:* $15. Electronic applications accepted.

Expenses: Tuition: Full-time $8,190; part-time $455 per credit hour. Required fees: $375.

Financial support: Teaching assistantships, Federal Work-Study available. Financial award application deadline: 2/15; financial award applicants required to submit FAFSA.

Faculty research: Image processing, control, communication, artificial intelligence, robotics.

Dr. Djaffer Ibaroudene, Advisor.

■ SAN DIEGO STATE UNIVERSITY

Graduate and Research Affairs, College of Engineering, Department of Electrical and Computer Engineering, San Diego, CA 92182

AWARDS Electrical engineering (MS). Evening/weekend programs available.

Entrance requirements: For master's, GRE General Test, TOEFL.

Faculty research: Ultra-high speed integral circuits and systems, naval command control and ocean surveillance, signal processing and analysis.

■ SAN JOSE STATE UNIVERSITY

Graduate Studies, College of Engineering, Department of Electrical Engineering, San Jose, CA 95192-0001

AWARDS MS.

Faculty: 15 full-time (2 women), 27 part-time/adjunct (4 women).

Students: 73 full-time (31 women), 194 part-time (28 women); includes 188 minority (3 African Americans, 180 Asian Americans or Pacific Islanders, 5 Hispanic Americans), 35 international. Average age 30. 219 applicants, 54% accepted. In 2001, 64 degrees awarded.

Degree requirements: For master's, thesis.

Entrance requirements: For master's, GRE General Test, minimum GPA of 3.0. *Application deadline:* For fall admission, 6/29; for spring admission, 11/30. Applications are processed on a rolling basis. *Application fee:* $59. Electronic applications accepted.

Expenses: Tuition, nonresident: part-time $246 per unit. Required fees: $678 per semester. Tuition and fees vary according to course load.

San Jose State University (continued)
Financial support: Applicants required to submit FAFSA.
Dr. Belle Wei, Chair, 408-924-3881, *Fax:* 408-924-3925.
Application contact: Dr. Rangaiya Rao, Graduate Coordinator, 408-924-3914.

■ SANTA CLARA UNIVERSITY

School of Engineering, Department of Electrical Engineering, Santa Clara, CA 95053

AWARDS ASIC design and test (Certificate); data storage technologies (Certificate); electrical engineering (MSEE, PhD, Engineer). Part-time and evening/weekend programs available.

Students: 30 full-time (8 women), 130 part-time (20 women); includes 60 minority (2 African Americans, 54 Asian Americans or Pacific Islanders, 4 Hispanic Americans), 57 international. Average age 30. 122 applicants, 43% accepted. In 2001, 39 master's, 1 doctorate, 1 other advanced degree awarded.
Degree requirements: For master's, thesis or alternative; for doctorate and other advanced degree, thesis/dissertation.
Entrance requirements: For master's, GRE General Test, TOEFL, minimum GPA of 2.75; for doctorate, GRE General Test, GRE Subject Test, TOEFL, master's degree or equivalent; for other advanced degree, master's degree, published paper. *Application deadline:* For fall admission, 6/1; for spring admission, 1/1. Applications are processed on a rolling basis. *Application fee:* $45 ($55 for international students). Electronic applications accepted.
Expenses: Tuition: Part-time $320 per unit. Tuition and fees vary according to class time, degree level, program and student level.
Financial support: Fellowships, research assistantships, teaching assistantships, Federal Work-Study and institutionally sponsored loans available. Support available to part-time students. Financial award application deadline: 3/1; financial award applicants required to submit FAFSA. *Total annual research expenditures:* $41,764.
Dr. Sally Wood, Chair, 408-554-6867.
Application contact: Tina Samms, Assistant Director of Graduate Admissions, 408-554-4313, *Fax:* 408-554-5474, *E-mail:* engr-grad@scu.edu.

■ SOUTH DAKOTA SCHOOL OF MINES AND TECHNOLOGY

Graduate Division, Department of Electrical Engineering and Computer Engineering, Rapid City, SD 57701-3995

AWARDS MS. Part-time programs available.

Degree requirements: For master's, thesis.

Entrance requirements: For master's, GRE (non-accredited school graduates), TOEFL, TWE. Electronic applications accepted.
Faculty research: Semiconductors, systems, digital systems, computers, superconductivity.

■ SOUTH DAKOTA SCHOOL OF MINES AND TECHNOLOGY

Graduate Division, Division of Material Engineering and Science, Doctoral Program in Materials Engineering and Science, Rapid City, SD 57701-3995

AWARDS Chemical engineering (PhD); chemistry (PhD); civil engineering (PhD); electrical engineering (PhD); mechanical engineering (PhD); metallurgical engineering (PhD); physics (PhD). Part-time programs available.

Degree requirements: For doctorate, thesis/dissertation.
Entrance requirements: For doctorate, TOEFL, TWE, minimum graduate GPA of 3.0. Electronic applications accepted.
Faculty research: Thermophysical properties of solids, development of multiphase materials and composites, concrete technology, electronic polymer materials.

Find an in-depth description at www.petersons.com/gradchannel.

■ SOUTH DAKOTA STATE UNIVERSITY

Graduate School, College of Engineering, Department of Electrical Engineering, Brookings, SD 57007

AWARDS MS.

Degree requirements: For master's, thesis, oral exam.
Entrance requirements: For master's, TOEFL.
Faculty research: Image processing, electromagnetics communications, power systems, electrical materials and sensors.

■ SOUTHERN ILLINOIS UNIVERSITY CARBONDALE

Graduate School, College of Engineering, Department of Electrical Engineering, Carbondale, IL 62901-6806

AWARDS MS.

Faculty: 15 full-time (1 woman), 1 part-time/adjunct (0 women).
Students: 78 full-time (17 women), 34 part-time (11 women); includes 8 minority (4 African Americans, 4 Asian Americans or Pacific Islanders), 93 international. 143 applicants, 46% accepted. In 2001, 26 degrees awarded.
Degree requirements: For master's, thesis, comprehensive exam.
Entrance requirements: For master's, TOEFL, minimum GPA of 2.7. *Application*

deadline: Applications are processed on a rolling basis. *Application fee:* $20.
Expenses: Tuition, state resident: full-time $3,794; part-time $154 per hour. Tuition, nonresident: full-time $6,566; part-time $308 per hour. Required fees: $277 per hour.
Financial support: In 2001–02, 21 students received support, including 6 research assistantships with full tuition reimbursements available; fellowships with full tuition reimbursements available, teaching assistantships with full tuition reimbursements available, Federal Work-Study, institutionally sponsored loans, and tuition waivers (full) also available. Support available to part-time students. Financial award application deadline: 1/15.
Faculty research: Circuits and power systems, communications and signal processing, controls and systems, electromagnetics and optics, electronics instrumentation and bioengineering. *Total annual research expenditures:* $254,257.
Dr. Glafkos D. Galanos, Chair, 618-536-2364.

Find an in-depth description at www.petersons.com/gradchannel.

■ SOUTHERN ILLINOIS UNIVERSITY CARBONDALE

Graduate School, College of Engineering, Program in Engineering Sciences, Carbondale, IL 62901-6806

AWARDS Electrical systems (PhD); fossil energy (PhD); mechanics (PhD).

Faculty: 55 full-time (3 women), 3 part-time/adjunct (0 women).
Students: 22 full-time (3 women), 18 part-time (4 women); includes 2 minority (1 African American, 1 Asian American or Pacific Islander), 30 international. 31 applicants, 19% accepted. In 2001, 3 degrees awarded.
Degree requirements: For doctorate, thesis/dissertation.
Entrance requirements: For doctorate, GRE General Test, TOEFL, minimum GPA of 3.5. *Application fee:* $20.
Expenses: Tuition, state resident: full-time $3,794; part-time $154 per hour. Tuition, nonresident: full-time $6,566; part-time $308 per hour. Required fees: $277 per hour.
Financial support: In 2001–02, 13 students received support; fellowships with full tuition reimbursements available, research assistantships with full tuition reimbursements available, teaching assistantships with full tuition reimbursements available, Federal Work-Study, institutionally sponsored loans, and tuition waivers (full) available. Support available to part-time students.
Dr. Hasan Sevim, Interim Chairperson, 618-536-6637, *Fax:* 618-453-4235.

■ SOUTHERN ILLINOIS UNIVERSITY EDWARDSVILLE

Graduate Studies and Research, School of Engineering, Department of Electrical Engineering, Edwardsville, IL 62026-0001

AWARDS MS. Part-time programs available.

Students: 71 full-time (11 women), 55 part-time (7 women); includes 5 minority (1 African American, 4 Asian Americans or Pacific Islanders), 96 international. Average age 33. 96 applicants, 65% accepted, 29 enrolled. In 2001, 45 degrees awarded.
Degree requirements: For master's, thesis or research paper, final exam. *Median time to degree:* Master's–2.5 years full-time, 4 years part-time.
Entrance requirements: For master's, TOEFL, minimum undergraduate GPA of 2.75 in engineering, mathematics, and science courses. *Application deadline:* For fall admission, 7/20; for spring admission, 12/7. *Application fee:* $25.
Expenses: Tuition, state resident: full-time $2,712; part-time $113 per credit hour. Tuition, nonresident: full-time $5,424; part-time $226 per credit hour. Required fees: $250; $125 per term. $125 per term. Tuition and fees vary according to course load, campus/location and reciprocity agreements.
Financial support: In 2001–02, 8 research assistantships with full tuition reimbursements, 10 teaching assistantships with full tuition reimbursements were awarded. Fellowships with full tuition reimbursements, career-related internships or fieldwork, Federal Work-Study, institutionally sponsored loans, traineeships, and unspecified assistantships also available. Support available to part-time students. Financial award application deadline: 3/1; financial award applicants required to submit FAFSA.
Dr. Oktay Alkin, Chair, 618-650-2524.
Application contact: Dr. Jen-Shiun Chen, Program Director, 618-650-2524, *E-mail:* jchen@siue.edu.

■ SOUTHERN METHODIST UNIVERSITY

School of Engineering, Department of Electrical Engineering, Dallas, TX 75275

AWARDS Electrical engineering (MSEE, PhD); telecommunications (MS). Part-time and evening/weekend programs available. Postbaccalaureate distance learning degree programs offered (no on-campus study).

Faculty: 18 full-time (1 woman).
Students: 98 full-time (21 women), 272 part-time (49 women); includes 114 minority (20 African Americans, 76 Asian Americans or Pacific Islanders, 18 Hispanic Americans), 91 international. Average age 33. 370 applicants, 49%

accepted. In 2001, 96 master's, 6 doctorates awarded. Terminal master's awarded for partial completion of doctoral program.
Degree requirements: For master's, thesis optional; for doctorate, thesis/dissertation, oral and written qualifying exams, oral final exam.
Entrance requirements: For master's, GRE General Test, TOEFL, minimum GPA of 3.0 in last 2 years; bachelor's degree in engineering, mathematics, or sciences; for doctorate, preliminary counseling exam, minimum GPA of 3.0, bachelor's degree in related field. *Application deadline:* For fall admission, 7/1 (priority date); for spring admission, 11/15. Applications are processed on a rolling basis. *Application fee:* $50.
Expenses: Tuition: Part-time $285 per credit hour.
Financial support: In 2001–02, 19 research assistantships (averaging $15,000 per year), 3 teaching assistantships (averaging $9,000 per year) were awarded. Institutionally sponsored loans and tuition waivers (full) also available. Financial award applicants required to submit FAFSA.
Faculty research: Mobile communications, optical and millimeter wave communications, solid state devices and materials, digital signal processing.
Mandyam Srinath, Head, 214-768-3114, *Fax:* 214-768-3573.
Application contact: Jim Dees, Director, Student Administration, 214-768-1456, *Fax:* 214-768-3845, *E-mail:* jdees@engr.smu.edu. *Web site:* http://www.seas.smu.edu/ee/

Find an in-depth description at www.petersons.com/gradchannel.

■ SOUTHERN POLYTECHNIC STATE UNIVERSITY

School of Engineering Technology and Management, Program in Electrical and Computer Engineering Technology, Marietta, GA 30060-2896

AWARDS Engineering technology (MS). Part-time and evening/weekend programs available.

Faculty: 2 part-time/adjunct (0 women).
Students: 1 full-time (0 women), 23 part-time (3 women); includes 7 minority (4 African Americans, 3 Asian Americans or Pacific Islanders), 9 international. Average age 32. In 2001, 2 degrees awarded.
Degree requirements: For master's, thesis.
Entrance requirements: For master's, GRE General Test, 3 letters of recommendation. *Application deadline:* For fall admission, 7/15 (priority date); for spring admission, 12/1. Applications are processed on a rolling basis. *Application fee:* $20. Electronic applications accepted.
Expenses: Tuition, state resident: full-time $1,746; part-time $97 per credit. Tuition,

nonresident: full-time $6,966; part-time $387 per credit. Required fees: $221 per term.
Financial support: Teaching assistantships, career-related internships or fieldwork, Federal Work-Study, scholarships/grants, and unspecified assistantships available. Support available to part-time students. Financial award application deadline: 5/1; financial award applicants required to submit FAFSA.
Kim Davis, Head, 770-528-7246, *Fax:* 770-528-7285, *E-mail:* kdavis0@spsu.edu.
Application contact: Virginia A. Head, Director of Admissions, 770-528-7281, *Fax:* 770-528-7292, *E-mail:* vhead@spsu.edu. *Web site:* http://ecet.spsu.edu/

■ STANFORD UNIVERSITY

School of Engineering, Department of Electrical Engineering, Stanford, CA 94305-9991

AWARDS MS, PhD, Eng.

Faculty: 49 full-time (2 women).
Students: 677 full-time (103 women), 182 part-time (26 women); includes 139 minority (10 African Americans, 116 Asian Americans or Pacific Islanders, 12 Hispanic Americans, 1 Native American), 486 international. Average age 26. 1,180 applicants, 37% accepted. In 2001, 241 master's, 61 doctorates awarded. Terminal master's awarded for partial completion of doctoral program.
Degree requirements: For doctorate and Eng, thesis/dissertation.
Entrance requirements: For master's, doctorate, and Eng, GRE General Test, TOEFL. *Application deadline:* For fall admission, 12/15. *Application fee:* $65 ($80 for international students). Electronic applications accepted.
Bruce A. Wooley, Chair, 650-725-3710, *Fax:* 650-725-3383, *E-mail:* wooley@par.stanford.edu.
Application contact: Director of Graduate Admissions, 650-723-3931. *Web site:* http://www.ee.stanford.edu/

■ STANFORD UNIVERSITY

School of Engineering, Department of Management Science and Engineering, Stanford, CA 94305-9991

AWARDS Management science and engineering (MS, PhD); management science and engineering and electrical engineering (MS); manufacturing systems engineering (MS).

Faculty: 31 full-time (5 women).
Students: 301 full-time (77 women), 82 part-time (18 women); includes 59 minority (5 African Americans, 48 Asian Americans or Pacific Islanders, 6 Hispanic Americans), 226 international. Average age 27. 484 applicants, 38% accepted. In 2001, 187 master's, 28 doctorates awarded. Terminal master's awarded for partial completion of doctoral program.
Degree requirements: For doctorate, thesis/dissertation, qualification procedure.

Stanford University (continued)

Entrance requirements: For master's and doctorate, GRE General Test, TOEFL. *Application deadline:* For fall admission, 2/1. *Application fee:* $65 ($80 for international students). Electronic applications accepted. M. Elisabeth Paté-Cornell, Chair, 650-723-3823 Ext. ', *Fax:* 650-725-8799, *E-mail:* mep@stanford.edu.

Application contact: Graduate Admissions Coordinator, 650-723-4094, *Fax:* 650-723-1614. *Web site:* http://www.stanford.edu/dept/MSandE/.

Find an in-depth description at www.petersons.com/gradchannel.

■ STATE UNIVERSITY OF NEW YORK AT BINGHAMTON

Graduate School, Thomas J. Watson School of Engineering and Applied Science, Department of Electrical Engineering, Binghamton, NY 13902-6000

AWARDS M Eng, MS, PhD. Part-time and evening/weekend programs available.

Faculty: 11 full-time (1 woman), 3 part-time/adjunct (0 women).
Students: 51 full-time (7 women), 73 part-time (15 women); includes 19 minority (6 African Americans, 12 Asian Americans or Pacific Islanders, 1 Hispanic American), 54 international. Average age 30. 263 applicants, 44% accepted, 28 enrolled. In 2001, 28 master's, 1 doctorate awarded.
Degree requirements: For master's, thesis or alternative; for doctorate, thesis/dissertation.
Entrance requirements: For master's and doctorate, GRE General Test, GRE Subject Test, TOEFL. *Application deadline:* For fall admission, 4/15 (priority date); for spring admission, 11/1. Applications are processed on a rolling basis. Electronic applications accepted.
Expenses: Tuition, state resident: full-time $5,100; part-time $213 per credit. Tuition, nonresident: full-time $8,416; part-time $351 per credit. Required fees: $811.
Financial support: In 2001–02, 32 students received support, including 2 fellowships with full and partial tuition reimbursements available (averaging $5,422 per year), 16 research assistantships with full tuition reimbursements available (averaging $6,590 per year), 15 teaching assistantships with full tuition reimbursements available (averaging $7,653 per year); career-related internships or fieldwork, Federal Work-Study, institutionally sponsored loans, tuition waivers (full and partial), and unspecified assistantships also available. Support available to part-time students. Financial award application deadline: 2/15.
Dr. Richard Plumb, Chairperson, 609-777-4856.

■ STATE UNIVERSITY OF NEW YORK AT NEW PALTZ

Graduate School, School of Physical Sciences and Engineering, Department of Electrical and Computer Engineering, New Paltz, NY 12561

AWARDS MS.

Application deadline: For fall admission, 3/15 (priority date). Applications are processed on a rolling basis. *Application fee:* $50.
Expenses: Tuition, state resident: full-time $5,100; part-time $213 per credit. Tuition, nonresident: full-time $8,416; part-time $351 per credit. Required fees: $624; $21 per credit. $60 per semester.
Dr. Ghader Eftekhari, Chair, 845-257-3722.

■ STEVENS INSTITUTE OF TECHNOLOGY

Graduate School, Charles V. Schaefer Jr. School of Engineering, Department of Electrical and Computer Engineering, Program in Electrical Engineering, Hoboken, NJ 07030

AWARDS Computer architecture and digital system design (M Eng, PhD, Engr); robotics/control/instrumentation (M Eng, PhD, Engr). Signal and image processing (M Eng, PhD, Engr); telecommunications engineering (M Eng, PhD, Engr); telecommunications management (MS, PhD, Certificate). MS, PhD, and Certificate offered in cooperation with the Program in Telecommunications Management.

Degree requirements: For master's, thesis optional; for doctorate, variable foreign language requirement, thesis/dissertation.
Entrance requirements: For master's and doctorate, GRE, TOEFL; for other advanced degree, GRE. Electronic applications accepted.
Expenses: Tuition: Full-time $13,950; part-time $775 per credit. Required fees: $180. One-time fee: $180 part-time. Full-time tuition and fees vary according to degree level and program.

■ STONY BROOK UNIVERSITY, STATE UNIVERSITY OF NEW YORK

Graduate School, College of Engineering and Applied Sciences, Department of Electrical and Computer Engineering, Stony Brook, NY 11794

AWARDS MS, PhD. Evening/weekend programs available.

Faculty: 22 full-time (3 women), 1 part-time/adjunct (0 women).
Students: 89 full-time (17 women), 48 part-time (10 women); includes 13 minority (3 African Americans, 8 Asian Americans or Pacific Islanders, 2 Hispanic Americans), 104 international. 401 applicants, 68% accepted. In 2001, 23 master's, 5 doctorates awarded.
Degree requirements: For master's, thesis or alternative; for doctorate, thesis/dissertation, comprehensive exam.
Entrance requirements: For master's and doctorate, GRE General Test, TOEFL. *Application deadline:* For fall admission, 1/15. *Application fee:* $50.
Expenses: Tuition, state resident: full-time $5,100; part-time $213 per credit. Tuition, nonresident: full-time $8,416; part-time $351 per credit. Required fees: $496.
Financial support: In 2001–02, 27 research assistantships, 36 teaching assistantships were awarded.
Faculty research: System science, solid-state electronics, computer engineering. *Total annual research expenditures:* $3 million.
Dr. Serge Luryi, Chairman, 631-632-8420.
Application contact: Dr. Chi-Tsong Chen, Director, 631-632-8400, *Fax:* 631-632-8494, *E-mail:* ctchen@sbee.sunysb.edu. *Web site:* http://www.ee.sunysb.edu/

Find an in-depth description at www.petersons.com/gradchannel.

■ SYRACUSE UNIVERSITY

Graduate School, L. C. Smith College of Engineering and Computer Science, Department of Electrical Engineering and Computer Science, Program in Electrical Engineering, Syracuse, NY 13244-0003

AWARDS MS, PhD, EE.

Students: 98 full-time (9 women), 49 part-time (4 women); includes 3 minority (1 African American, 2 Asian Americans or Pacific Islanders), 88 international. Average age 29. In 2001, 80 master's, 67 doctorates awarded.
Degree requirements: For doctorate, thesis/dissertation.
Entrance requirements: For master's and doctorate, GRE General Test, GRE Subject Test. *Application deadline:* Applications are processed on a rolling basis. *Application fee:* $50.
Expenses: Tuition: Full-time $15,528; part-time $647 per credit. Required fees: $420; $38 per term. Tuition and fees vary according to program.
Financial support: Fellowships, research assistantships, teaching assistantships, Federal Work-Study available. Financial award application deadline: 1/10.
Faculty research: Electromagnetics, electronic devices, systems.
Dr. Can Isik, Graduate Head, 315-443-1125, *Fax:* 315-443-2583, *E-mail:* cisik@syr.edu.
Application contact: Barbara Hazard, Information Contact, 315-443-2655, *Fax:*

315-443-2583, *E-mail:* bahazard@syr.edu. *Web site:* http://www.ecs.syr.edu/

Find an in-depth description at www.petersons.com/gradchannel.

■ **TEMPLE UNIVERSITY**

Graduate School, College of Science and Technology, College of Engineering, Program in Electrical and Computer Engineering, Philadelphia, PA 19122-6096

AWARDS MSE. Part-time and evening/weekend programs available.

Degree requirements: For master's, thesis optional.
Entrance requirements: For master's, GRE General Test, TOEFL.
Expenses: Tuition, state resident: full-time $8,487; part-time $369 per credit hour. Tuition, nonresident: full-time $12,282; part-time $534 per credit hour. Required fees: $350. Tuition and fees vary according to course load, program and reciprocity agreements.
Faculty research: Computer engineering, intelligent control, microprocessors, digital processing, neutral networks. *Web site:* http://www.eng.temple.edu/

■ **TENNESSEE TECHNOLOGICAL UNIVERSITY**

Graduate School, College of Engineering, Department of Electrical Engineering, Cookeville, TN 38505

AWARDS MS, PhD. Part-time programs available.

Faculty: 19 full-time (0 women).
Students: 29 full-time (5 women), 10 part-time (3 women); includes 33 minority (3 African Americans, 30 Asian Americans or Pacific Islanders). Average age 27. 373 applicants, 38% accepted. In 2001, 13 degrees awarded.
Degree requirements: For master's, thesis; for doctorate, one foreign language, thesis/dissertation.
Entrance requirements: For master's, GRE General Test, TOEFL; for doctorate, GRE Subject Test, TOEFL, minimum GPA of 3.5. *Application deadline:* For fall admission, 3/1 (priority date); for spring admission, 8/1. *Application fee:* $25 ($30 for international students). Electronic applications accepted.
Expenses: Tuition, state resident: full-time $4,000; part-time $215 per hour. Tuition, nonresident: full-time $10,500; part-time $495 per hour. Required fees: $1,971 per semester.
Financial support: In 2001–02, fellowships (averaging $8,000 per year), 15 research assistantships (averaging $7,650 per year), 14 teaching assistantships (averaging $7,500 per year) were awarded. Career-related internships or fieldwork also available. Financial award application deadline: 4/1.

Faculty research: Control, digital, and power systems.
Dr. P. K. Rajan, Chairperson, 931-372-3397, *Fax:* 931-372-3436, *E-mail:* pkrajan@tntech.edu.
Application contact: Dr. Francis O. Otuonye, Associate Vice President for Research and Graduate Studies, 931-372-3233, *Fax:* 931-372-3497, *E-mail:* fotuonye@tntech.edu.

■ **TEXAS A&M UNIVERSITY**

College of Engineering, Department of Electrical Engineering, College Station, TX 77843

AWARDS M Eng, MS, PhD.

Faculty: 68.
Students: 323 (42 women). Average age 28.
Degree requirements: For master's, thesis (MS); for doctorate, dissertation (PhD).
Entrance requirements: For master's and doctorate, GRE General Test, TOEFL. *Application fee:* $50 ($75 for international students).
Expenses: Tuition, state resident: full-time $11,872. Tuition, nonresident: full-time $17,892.
Financial support: Fellowships, research assistantships, teaching assistantships, career-related internships or fieldwork available. Financial award application deadline: 4/1; financial award applicants required to submit FAFSA.
Faculty research: Solid-state, electric power systems, and communications engineering.
Dr. Chanan Singh, Head, 979-845-7441.
Application contact: Graduate Advisor, 979-845-7441.

Find an in-depth description at www.petersons.com/gradchannel.

■ **TEXAS A&M UNIVERSITY– KINGSVILLE**

College of Graduate Studies, College of Engineering, Department of Electrical Engineering and Computer Science, Program in Electrical Engineering, Kingsville, TX 78363

AWARDS ME, MS.

Students: 41 full-time (7 women), 17 part-time (3 women); includes 6 minority (1 African American, 1 Asian American or Pacific Islander, 4 Hispanic Americans), 52 international. Average age 25. In 2001, 19 degrees awarded.
Degree requirements: For master's, thesis or alternative, comprehensive exam.
Entrance requirements: For master's, GRE General Test, TOEFL, minimum GPA of 3.0. *Application deadline:* For fall admission, 6/1; for spring admission, 11/15. Applications are processed on a rolling basis. *Application fee:* $15 ($25 for international students).

Expenses: Tuition, state resident: part-time $42 per hour. Tuition, nonresident: part-time $253 per hour. Required fees: $56 per hour. One-time fee: $46 part-time. Tuition and fees vary according to program.
Financial support: Application deadline: 5/15.
Dr. Rajab Challoo, Coordinator, 361-593-2001.
Application contact: H. D. Gorakhpurwalla, Graduate Coordinator, 361-593-2004.

■ **TEXAS TECH UNIVERSITY**

Graduate School, College of Engineering, Department of Electrical and Computer Engineering, Lubbock, TX 79409

AWARDS MSEE, PhD. Part-time programs available.

Faculty: 17 full-time (2 women).
Students: 85 full-time (6 women), 22 part-time (6 women); includes 5 minority (1 African American, 1 Asian American or Pacific Islander, 3 Hispanic Americans), 75 international. Average age 25. 329 applicants, 15% accepted, 26 enrolled. In 2001, 24 degrees awarded.
Degree requirements: For master's and doctorate, thesis/dissertation.
Entrance requirements: For master's and doctorate, GRE General Test, minimum GPA of 3.0. *Application deadline:* Applications are processed on a rolling basis. *Application fee:* $25 ($50 for international students). Electronic applications accepted.
Expenses: Tuition, state resident: full-time $1,926; part-time $107 per credit hour. Tuition, nonresident: full-time $5,724; part-time $318 per credit hour. Required fees: $779; $737 per year. Tuition and fees vary according to course level, course load and program.
Financial support: In 2001–02, 67 research assistantships with partial tuition reimbursements (averaging $9,435 per year) were awarded; fellowships, teaching assistantships with partial tuition reimbursements, Federal Work-Study and institutionally sponsored loans also available. Support available to part-time students. Financial award application deadline: 5/1; financial award applicants required to submit FAFSA.
Faculty research: High-voltage space power, accuracy enhancement in optical computing, computer vision in image processing. *Total annual research expenditures:* $3.5 million.
Dr. Jon G. Bredeson, Chair, 806-742-3533, *Fax:* 806-742-1245.
Application contact: Graduate Adviser, 806-742-3533, *Fax:* 806-742-1245.

■ TUFTS UNIVERSITY

Division of Graduate and Continuing Studies and Research, Graduate and Professional Studies, Microwave and Wireless Engineering Program, Medford, MA 02155

AWARDS Certificate. Part-time and evening/weekend programs available.

Students: Average age 47. In 2001, 2 degrees awarded.
Application deadline: For fall admission, 8/15 (priority date); for spring admission, 12/12 (priority date). Applications are processed on a rolling basis. *Application fee:* $50. Electronic applications accepted.
Expenses: Tuition: Full-time $26,853. Full-time tuition and fees vary according to program.
Financial support: Available to part-time students. Application deadline: 5/1.
Alida Poirier, Assistant Director, 617-627-3395, *Fax:* 617-627-3016, *E-mail:* pcs@ase.tufts.edu.
Application contact: Information Contact, 617-627-3395, *Fax:* 617-627-3016, *E-mail:* pcs@ase.tufts.edu. *Web site:* http://ase.tufts.edu/gradstudy

■ TUFTS UNIVERSITY

Division of Graduate and Continuing Studies and Research, Graduate School of Arts and Sciences, School of Engineering, Department of Electrical Engineering and Computer Science, Medford, MA 02155

AWARDS Computer science (MS, PhD); electrical engineering (MS, PhD). Part-time programs available.

Faculty: 17 full-time, 5 part-time/adjunct.
Students: 123 (37 women); includes 16 minority (1 African American, 10 Asian Americans or Pacific Islanders, 4 Hispanic Americans, 1 Native American) 43 international. 154 applicants, 49% accepted. In 2001, 30 master's, 2 doctorates awarded. Terminal master's awarded for partial completion of doctoral program.
Degree requirements: For master's, thesis or alternative; for doctorate, thesis/dissertation.
Entrance requirements: For master's and doctorate, GRE General Test, TOEFL. *Application deadline:* For fall admission, 3/1; for spring admission, 10/15. Applications are processed on a rolling basis. *Application fee:* $50. Electronic applications accepted.
Expenses: Tuition: Full-time $26,853. Full-time tuition and fees vary according to program.
Financial support: Research assistantships with full and partial tuition reimbursements, teaching assistantships with full and partial tuition reimbursements, Federal Work-Study, scholarships/grants, and tuition waivers (partial) available. Financial award application deadline: 2/15; financial award applicants required to submit FAFSA.

Jim Schmolze, Chair, 617-627-3217, *Fax:* 617-627-3220.
Application contact: Anselm Blumer, Information Contact, 617-623-3217, *Fax:* 617-627-3220, *E-mail:* webmaster@eecs.tufts.edu. *Web site:* http://www.cs.tufts.edu/

■ TULANE UNIVERSITY

School of Engineering, Department of Electrical Engineering, New Orleans, LA 70118-5669

AWARDS MS, MSE, PhD, Sc D. MS and PhD offered through the Graduate School. Part-time programs available. Terminal master's awarded for partial completion of doctoral program.

Degree requirements: For master's and doctorate, thesis/dissertation.
Entrance requirements: For master's and doctorate, GRE General Test, TOEFL, minimum B average in undergraduate course work.
Expenses: Tuition: Full-time $24,675. Required fees: $2,210.
Faculty research: Control systems, digital signal processing, image processing, power systems.

■ TUSKEGEE UNIVERSITY

Graduate Programs, College of Engineering, Architecture and Physical Sciences, Department of Electrical Engineering, Tuskegee, AL 36088

AWARDS MSEE.

Faculty: 8 full-time (0 women).
Students: 17 full-time (2 women), 4 part-time (1 woman); includes 9 minority (8 African Americans, 1 Asian American or Pacific Islander), 9 international. Average age 24. In 2001, 10 degrees awarded.
Degree requirements: For master's, thesis or alternative.
Entrance requirements: For master's, GRE General Test, GRE Subject Test. *Application deadline:* For fall admission, 7/15. Applications are processed on a rolling basis. *Application fee:* $25 ($35 for international students).
Expenses: Tuition: Full-time $5,163; part-time $612 per credit hour.
Financial support: Fellowships, research assistantships, teaching assistantships, career-related internships or fieldwork, Federal Work-Study, and institutionally sponsored loans available. Support available to part-time students. Financial award application deadline: 4/15.
Faculty research: Photovoltaic insulation, automatic guidance and control, wind energy.
Dr. Sammie Giles, Director, 334-727-8298.

■ UNION COLLEGE

Center for Graduate Education and Special Programs, Division of Engineering and Computer Science, Department of Electrical and Computer Engineering, Schenectady, NY 12308-2311

AWARDS Electrical engineering (MS).

Students: 5 full-time (1 woman), 7 part-time (3 women); includes 1 minority (African American), 3 international. Average age 29. 5 applicants, 100% accepted, 3 enrolled. In 2001, 9 degrees awarded.
Degree requirements: For master's, departmental qualifying exams.
Entrance requirements: For master's, minimum GPA of 3.0. *Application deadline:* Applications are processed on a rolling basis. *Application fee:* $50.
Expenses: Tuition: Part-time $1,620 per course.
Financial support: Health care benefits available.
Dr. Ekram Hassib, Chair, 518-388-6272.
Application contact: Rhonda Sheehan, Coordinator of Recruiting and Admissions, 518-388-6238, *Fax:* 518-388-6754, *E-mail:* sheehanr@union.edu. *Web site:* http://www.engineering.union.edu

■ UNIVERSITY AT BUFFALO, THE STATE UNIVERSITY OF NEW YORK

Graduate School, School of Engineering and Applied Sciences, Department of Electrical Engineering, Buffalo, NY 14260

AWARDS M Eng, MS, PhD. Part-time programs available.

Faculty: 18 full-time (1 woman), 5 part-time/adjunct (1 woman).
Students: 98 full-time (17 women), 28 part-time (6 women); includes 15 minority (4 African Americans, 10 Asian Americans or Pacific Islanders, 1 Native American), 86 international. Average age 24. 645 applicants, 54% accepted. In 2001, 33 master's, 8 doctorates awarded. Terminal master's awarded for partial completion of doctoral program.
Degree requirements: For master's, project or thesis; for doctorate, thesis/dissertation.
Entrance requirements: For master's and doctorate, GRE General Test, TOEFL. *Application deadline:* For fall admission, 12/31 (priority date); for spring admission, 10/1. Applications are processed on a rolling basis. *Application fee:* $35. Electronic applications accepted.
Expenses: Tuition, state resident: full-time $6,118. Tuition, nonresident: full-time $9,434.
Financial support: In 2001–02, 57 students received support, including 5 fellowships with full tuition reimbursements available (averaging $8,200 per year), 25 research assistantships with full tuition

reimbursements available (averaging $10,000 per year), 18 teaching assistant-ships with full tuition reimbursements available (averaging $10,360 per year); career-related internships or fieldwork, Federal Work-Study, institutionally sponsored loans, tuition waivers (full and partial), and unspecified assistantships also available. Financial award application deadline: 2/1; financial award applicants required to submit FAFSA.

Faculty research: High power electronics and plasmas, electronic materials signal and image processing, photonics and communications, optics. *Total annual research expenditures:* $2.3 million.

Dr. Dennis P. Malone, Interim Chairman, 716-645-3115 Ext. 1137, *Fax:* 716-645-3656.

Application contact: Dr. Donald Givone, Director of Graduate Admissions, 716-345-3115 Ext. 2129, *Fax:* 716-645-3656, *E-mail:* eegradapply@eng.buffalo.edu. *Web site:* http://www.ee.buffalo.edu/

Find an in-depth description at www.petersons.com/gradchannel.

■ THE UNIVERSITY OF AKRON

Graduate School, College of Engineering, Department of Electrical Engineering, Akron, OH 44325-0001

AWARDS MS, PhD. Evening/weekend programs available.

Faculty: 13 full-time (1 woman), 1 part-time/adjunct (0 women).

Students: 18 full-time (7 women), 11 part-time (2 women); includes 1 minority (Asian American or Pacific Islander), 16 international. Average age 30. 23 applicants, 91% accepted, 8 enrolled. In 2001, 6 degrees awarded.

Degree requirements: For master's, oral comprehensive exam or thesis; for doctorate, one foreign language, thesis/dissertation, candidacy exam, qualifying exam.

Entrance requirements: For master's, TOEFL, minimum GPA of 2.75; for doctorate, GRE, TOEFL. *Application deadline:* For fall admission, 3/1. Applications are processed on a rolling basis. *Application fee:* $40 ($50 for international students).

Expenses: Tuition, state resident: full-time $6,562; part-time $219 per credit. Tuition, nonresident: full-time $9,027; part-time $383 per credit. Required fees: $272; $11 per credit. Tuition and fees vary according to course load.

Financial support: In 2001–02, 6 research assistantships with full tuition reimbursements, 18 teaching assistantships with full tuition reimbursements were awarded. Fellowships with full tuition reimbursements, career-related internships or fieldwork and tuition waivers (full) also available. Financial award application deadline: 3/1.

Faculty research: Signal processing, digital control systems, computer interfacing, nondestructive testing.

Dr. Jose De Abreu-Garcia, Interim Chair, 330-972-6209. *Web site:* http://www.ecgf.uakron.edu/~elec/index.html

■ THE UNIVERSITY OF ALABAMA

Graduate School, College of Engineering, Department of Electrical Engineering, Tuscaloosa, AL 35487

AWARDS MSEE, PhD.

Faculty: 13 full-time (0 women), 1 part-time/adjunct (0 women).

Students: 35 full-time (4 women), 13 part-time (1 woman); includes 3 minority (2 African Americans, 1 Native American), 29 international. Average age 29. 177 applicants, 11% accepted, 13 enrolled. In 2001, 7 master's, 3 doctorates awarded.

Degree requirements: For master's, thesis or alternative; for doctorate, one foreign language, thesis/dissertation.

Entrance requirements: For master's and doctorate, GRE General Test, minimum GPA of 3.0 in last 60 hours. *Application deadline:* For fall admission, 7/6. Applications are processed on a rolling basis. *Application fee:* $25.

Expenses: Tuition, state resident: full-time $3,292; part-time $183 per credit hour. Tuition, nonresident: full-time $8,912; part-time $495 per credit hour. Tuition and fees vary according to course load, campus/location and program.

Financial support: In 2001–02, 25 students received support, including 3 research assistantships, 16 teaching assistantships; fellowships, Federal Work-Study also available.

Faculty research: Computer engineering, microelectronics, power systems, electromagnetics, control systems. *Total annual research expenditures:* $234,140.

Dr. Lloyd A. Morley, Head, 205-348-0672, *Fax:* 205-348-6959, *E-mail:* lmorley@coe.eng.ua.edu.

■ THE UNIVERSITY OF ALABAMA AT BIRMINGHAM

Graduate School, School of Engineering, Department of Electrical and Computer Engineering, Birmingham, AL 35294

AWARDS MSEE, PhD. Evening/weekend programs available.

Students: 38 full-time (2 women), 81 part-time (16 women); includes 10 minority (9 African Americans, 1 Asian American or Pacific Islander), 68 international. 308 applicants, 78% accepted. In 2001, 15 degrees awarded.

Degree requirements: For master's, thesis or alternative; for doctorate, thesis/dissertation.

Entrance requirements: For master's, GRE General Test, BSEE. *Application deadline:* Applications are processed on a rolling basis. *Application fee:* $35 ($60 for international students). Electronic applications accepted.

Expenses: Tuition, state resident: full-time $3,058. Tuition, nonresident: full-time $5,746. Tuition and fees vary according to course load, degree level and program.

Financial support: In 2001–02, 1 student received support, including 1 research assistantship with full tuition reimbursement available (averaging $9,500 per year); tuition waivers (full and partial) also available.

Dr. Gregg L. Vaughn, Chair, 205-934-8440, *Fax:* 205-975-3337, *E-mail:* gvaughn@uab.edu. *Web site:* http://www.eng.uab.edu/ece/

■ THE UNIVERSITY OF ALABAMA IN HUNTSVILLE

School of Graduate Studies, College of Engineering, Department of Electrical and Computer Engineering, Huntsville, AL 35899

AWARDS Computer engineering (PhD); electrical and computer engineering (MSE); electrical engineering (PhD); optical science and engineering (PhD). Part-time and evening/weekend programs available.

Faculty: 23 full-time (3 women), 3 part-time/adjunct (0 women).

Students: 85 full-time (11 women), 87 part-time (16 women); includes 17 minority (6 African Americans, 10 Asian Americans or Pacific Islanders, 1 Hispanic American), 59 international. Average age 30. 254 applicants, 45% accepted, 58 enrolled. In 2001, 40 master's, 7 doctorates awarded.

Degree requirements: For master's, thesis or alternative, oral and written exams, comprehensive exam, registration; for doctorate, thesis/dissertation, oral and written exams, comprehensive exam, registration.

Entrance requirements: For master's, GRE General Test, appropriate bachelor's degree, minimum GPA of 3.0; for doctorate, GRE General Test, minimum GPA of 3.0. *Application deadline:* For fall admission, 7/24 (priority date); for spring admission, 11/15 (priority date). Applications are processed on a rolling basis. *Application fee:* $35.

Expenses: Tuition, area resident: Part-time $175 per hour. Tuition, state resident: full-time $4,408. Tuition, nonresident: full-time $9,054; part-time $361 per hour.

Financial support: In 2001–02, 57 students received support, including 2 fellowships with full and partial tuition reimbursements available (averaging $14,100 per year), 27 research assistantships with full and partial tuition reimbursements available (averaging $9,172 per year), 27 teaching assistantships with full and partial tuition reimbursements available (averaging $7,331 per year); career-related internships or fieldwork, Federal Work-Study, institutionally sponsored loans, scholarships/grants, health care benefits, tuition waivers (full

The University of Alabama in Huntsville (continued)

and partial), and unspecified assistantships also available. Support available to part-time students. Financial award application deadline: 4/1; financial award applicants required to submit FAFSA.

Faculty research: Optical signal processing, electromagnetics, photonics, nonlinear waves, computer architecture. *Total annual research expenditures:* $698,764.

Dr. Reza Adhami, Chair, 256-824-6316, *Fax:* 256-824-6803, *E-mail:* adhami@eb.uah.edu. *Web site:* http://www.eb-p5.eb.uah.edu/ece/

Find an in-depth description at www.petersons.com/gradchannel.

■ UNIVERSITY OF ALASKA FAIRBANKS

Graduate School, College of Science, Engineering and Mathematics, Department of Electrical Engineering, Fairbanks, AK 99775-7480

AWARDS MEE, MS.

Faculty: 6 full-time (0 women).
Students: 13 full-time (0 women), 4 part-time (3 women); includes 2 minority (1 Asian American or Pacific Islander, 1 Hispanic American), 9 international. Average age 30. 10 applicants, 50% accepted, 3 enrolled. In 2001, 7 degrees awarded.
Degree requirements: For master's, thesis or alternative, comprehensive exam.
Entrance requirements: For master's, GRE General Test, TOEFL. *Application deadline:* For fall admission, 4/1; for spring admission, 11/1. Applications are processed on a rolling basis. *Application fee:* $35.
Expenses: Tuition, state resident: full-time $4,272; part-time $178 per credit. Tuition, nonresident: full-time $8,328; part-time $347 per credit. Required fees: $960; $60 per term. Part-time tuition and fees vary according to course load.
Financial support: In 2001–02, fellowships (averaging $10,000 per year); research assistantships, teaching assistantships, career-related internships or fieldwork, Federal Work-Study, and scholarships/grants also available.
Faculty research: Geomagnetically-induced currents in power lines, telecommunications, electromagnetic wave propagation, laser radar systems, alternative energy systems.
Dr. Charles Mayer, Chair, 907-474-7137.

■ THE UNIVERSITY OF ARIZONA

Graduate College, College of Engineering and Mines, Department of Electrical and Computer Engineering, Tucson, AZ 85721

AWARDS M Eng, MS, PhD. Part-time programs available.
Faculty: 64.

Students: 204 full-time (35 women), 75 part-time (11 women); includes 22 minority (2 African Americans, 13 Asian Americans or Pacific Islanders, 7 Hispanic Americans), 190 international. Average age 29. 615 applicants, 43% accepted, 84 enrolled. In 2001, 36 master's, 9 doctorates awarded.
Degree requirements: For master's, thesis (for some programs); for doctorate, thesis/dissertation.
Entrance requirements: For master's and doctorate, GRE General Test, TOEFL. *Application deadline:* For fall admission, 6/15. Applications are processed on a rolling basis. *Application fee:* $45.
Expenses: Tuition, state resident: full-time $2,490; part-time $436 per unit. Tuition, nonresident: full-time $10,300; part-time $436 per unit. Full-time tuition and fees vary according to degree level and program.
Financial support: Fellowships, research assistantships, teaching assistantships, institutionally sponsored loans and scholarships/grants available. Financial award application deadline: 3/15.
Faculty research: Communication systems, control systems, signal processing, computer-aided logic.
Dr. John A Reagan, Head, 520-621-6193.
Application contact: Tami J Whelan, Graduate Academic Adviser, SR, 520-621-6195, *Fax:* 520-621-8076, *E-mail:* whelan@ece.arizona.edu. *Web site:* http://www.ece.arizona.edu

Find an in-depth description at www.petersons.com/gradchannel.

■ UNIVERSITY OF ARKANSAS

Graduate School, College of Engineering, Department of Electrical Engineering, Program in Electrical Engineering, Fayetteville, AR 72701-1201

AWARDS MSEE, PhD.

Students: 59 full-time (6 women), 20 part-time (1 woman); includes 5 minority (all Asian Americans or Pacific Islanders), 55 international. 57 applicants, 61% accepted. In 2001, 21 master's, 1 doctorate awarded. *Application fee:* $40 ($50 for international students).
Expenses: Tuition, state resident: full-time $3,553; part-time $197 per credit. Tuition, nonresident: full-time $8,411; part-time $467 per credit. Required fees: $42 per credit. Tuition and fees vary according to course load and program.
Financial support: Application deadline: 4/1.
Dr. J. S. Charlton, Head, 479-575-6048.

■ UNIVERSITY OF BRIDGEPORT

School of Engineering, Department of Electrical Engineering, Bridgeport, CT 06601

AWARDS MS.

Faculty: 2 full-time (0 women), 1 part-time/adjunct (0 women).
Students: 58 full-time (5 women), 11 part-time (2 women), 68 international. Average age 24. 296 applicants, 90% accepted, 43 enrolled. In 2001, 9 degrees awarded.
Degree requirements: For master's, thesis optional.
Entrance requirements: For master's, TOEFL. *Application deadline:* For fall admission, 8/1 (priority date); for spring admission, 12/1 (priority date). Applications are processed on a rolling basis. *Application fee:* $25 ($35 for international students). Electronic applications accepted.
Expenses: Tuition: Part-time $385 per credit hour. Required fees: $50 per term. Tuition and fees vary according to degree level and program.
Financial support: In 2001–02, 12 students received support; research assistantships, teaching assistantships, career-related internships or fieldwork, Federal Work-Study, institutionally sponsored loans, and tuition waivers (partial) available. Support available to part-time students. Financial award application deadline: 6/1; financial award applicants required to submit FAFSA.
Dr. Lawrence Hmurcik, Chairman, 203-576-4296, *Fax:* 203-576-4105, *E-mail:* mnurcik@bridgeport.edu.

■ UNIVERSITY OF CALIFORNIA, BERKELEY

Graduate Division, College of Engineering, Department of Electrical Engineering and Computer Sciences, Berkeley, CA 94720-1500

AWARDS Computer science (MS, PhD); electrical engineering (M Eng, MS, D Eng, PhD).

Degree requirements: For master's, comprehensive exam or thesis (MS); for doctorate, thesis/dissertation, qualifying exam.
Entrance requirements: For master's and doctorate, GRE General Test, TOEFL, minimum GPA of 3.0.
Expenses: Tuition, nonresident: full-time $10,704. Required fees: $4,349.

■ UNIVERSITY OF CALIFORNIA, DAVIS

Graduate Studies, College of Engineering, Program in Electrical and Computer Engineering, Davis, CA 95616

AWARDS MS, PhD.

Faculty: 36.
Students: 154 full-time (28 women), 3 part-time; includes 36 minority (4 African Americans, 31 Asian Americans or Pacific Islanders, 1 Hispanic American), 55 international. Average age 28. 719 applicants, 15% accepted, 41 enrolled. In 2001, 22 master's, 11 doctorates awarded.

Terminal master's awarded for partial completion of doctoral program.

Degree requirements: For master's, thesis optional; for doctorate, preliminary and qualifying exams, thesis defense.

Entrance requirements: For master's, GRE General Test, minimum GPA of 3.2; for doctorate, GRE, minimum graduate GPA of 3.5. *Application deadline:* For fall admission, 2/15. *Application fee:* $60. Electronic applications accepted.

Expenses: Tuition, state resident: full-time $4,831. Tuition, nonresident: full-time $15,725.

Financial support: In 2001–02, 105 students received support, including 47 fellowships with full and partial tuition reimbursements available (averaging $6,793 per year), 74 research assistantships with full and partial tuition reimbursements available (averaging $8,984 per year), 35 teaching assistantships with partial tuition reimbursements available (averaging $11,234 per year); Federal Work-Study, scholarships/grants, and tuition waivers (full and partial) also available. Financial award application deadline: 1/15; financial award applicants required to submit FAFSA.
Andre Knoessen, Chairperson, 530-752-2455, *E-mail:* knoessen@ece.ucdavis.edu.
Application contact: Anita Morales, Graduate Staff Assistant, 530-752-8251, *Fax:* 530-752-9217, *E-mail:* morales@ ece.ucdavis.edu. *Web site:* http:// www.ece.ucdavis.edu/grads/

■ UNIVERSITY OF CALIFORNIA, IRVINE

Office of Research and Graduate Studies, School of Engineering, Department of Electrical and Computer Engineering, Irvine, CA 92697

AWARDS Computer networks and distributed computing (MS, PhD); computer systems and software (MS, PhD); electrical engineering (MS, PhD). Part-time programs available.

Faculty: 27.
Students: 139 full-time (26 women), 28 part-time (1 woman); includes 42 minority (39 Asian Americans or Pacific Islanders, 3 Hispanic Americans), 84 international. 542 applicants, 31% accepted, 80 enrolled. In 2001, 23 master's, 3 doctorates awarded. Terminal master's awarded for partial completion of doctoral program.

Degree requirements: For doctorate, thesis/dissertation.

Entrance requirements: For master's, GRE General Test, minimum GPA of 3.0; for doctorate, GRE General Test. *Application deadline:* For fall and spring admission, 1/15 (priority date); for winter admission, 10/15 (priority date). Applications are processed on a rolling basis. *Application fee:* $60. Electronic applications accepted.

Expenses: Tuition, nonresident: full-time $10,704. Required fees: $8,396. Tuition

and fees vary according to course load, program and student level.

Financial support: In 2001–02, 12 fellowships (averaging $1,250 per year), 36 research assistantships (averaging $1,120 per year), 13 teaching assistantships (averaging $1,480 per year) were awarded. Institutionally sponsored loans and tuition waivers (full and partial) also available. Financial award application deadline: 3/2; financial award applicants required to submit FAFSA.

Faculty research: Optical and solid-state devices, systems and signal processing. *Total annual research expenditures:* $2.2 million.
Dr. Nader Bagherzadeh, Chair, 949-824-5689, *Fax:* 949-824-3779.

Application contact: Ronnie A. Gran, Graduate Admissions Coordinator, 949-824-5489, *Fax:* 949-824-1853, *E-mail:* ragran@uci.edu. *Web site:* http:// www.eng.uci.edu/

Find an in-depth description at www.petersons.com/gradchannel.

■ UNIVERSITY OF CALIFORNIA, LOS ANGELES

Graduate Division, School of Engineering and Applied Science, Department of Electrical Engineering, Los Angeles, CA 90095

AWARDS Electrical engineering (MS, PhD); operations research (MS, PhD).

Faculty: 42 full-time, 33 part-time/ adjunct.
Students: 409 full-time (53 women); includes 115 minority (1 African American, 106 Asian Americans or Pacific Islanders, 8 Hispanic Americans), 218 international. 1,314 applicants, 28% accepted, 130 enrolled. In 2001, 75 master's, 28 doctorates awarded.

Degree requirements: For master's, comprehensive exam or thesis; for doctorate, thesis/dissertation, qualifying exams.

Entrance requirements: For master's, GRE General Test, minimum GPA of 3.0; for doctorate, GRE General Test, minimum GPA of 3.25. *Application deadline:* For fall admission, 1/15. *Application fee:* $60. Electronic applications accepted.

Expenses: Tuition, nonresident: full-time $10,244. Required fees: $3,609. Full-time tuition and fees vary according to program.

Financial support: In 2001–02, 58 fellowships, 203 research assistantships, 133 teaching assistantships were awarded. Career-related internships or fieldwork, Federal Work-Study, institutionally sponsored loans, and tuition waivers (full and partial) also available. Financial award application deadline: 1/15; financial award applicants required to submit FAFSA.
Dr. Yahya Rahmat-Samii, Chair, 310-206-3847.

Application contact: Sharron Bryant, Student Affairs Officer, 310-825-9383,

E-mail: sharron@ea.ucla.edu. *Web site:* http://www.ee.ucla.edu/i

■ UNIVERSITY OF CALIFORNIA, RIVERSIDE

Graduate Division, Department of Electrical Engineering, Riverside, CA 92521-0102

AWARDS MS, PhD.

Faculty: 10 full-time (1 woman).
Students: 46 full-time (11 women); includes 1 minority (Asian American or Pacific Islander), 41 international. Average age 27. 114 applicants, 43% accepted. In 2001, 4 master's awarded.

Degree requirements: For doctorate, thesis/dissertation, qualifying exams, English language proficiency.

Entrance requirements: For master's and doctorate, GRE General Test, TOEFL, minimum GPA of 3.2. *Application deadline:* For fall admission, 5/1; for spring admission, 12/1. Applications are processed on a rolling basis. *Application fee:* $40.

Expenses: Tuition, state resident: full-time $5,001. Tuition, nonresident: full-time $15,897.

Financial support: In 2001–02, teaching assistantships (averaging $14,000 per year) Financial award application deadline: 2/1.

Faculty research: Solid state devices, integrated circuits, signal processing, control systems, robotics, visualization and intelligent systems, automatic target and object recognition, machine learning and image understanding, perception-based navigation, virtual reality and computer vision.
Dr. Ilya Dumer, Graduate Adviser, 909-787-2924, *E-mail:* ilya.dumer@ucr.edu.
Application contact: Laura Ibarra, Graduate Student Affairs Assistant, 909-787-2484, *Fax:* 909-787-2425, *E-mail:* grad-adm@ee.ucr.edu. *Web site:* http:// www.ee.ucr.edu/grad/index.html

Find an in-depth description at www.petersons.com/gradchannel.

■ UNIVERSITY OF CALIFORNIA, SAN DIEGO

Graduate Studies and Research, Department of Electrical and Computer Engineering, La Jolla, CA 92093

AWARDS Applied ocean science (MS, PhD); applied physics (MS, PhD); communication theory and systems (MS, PhD); computer engineering (MS, PhD); electrical engineering (M Eng); electronic circuits and systems (MS, PhD); intelligent systems, robotics and control (MS, PhD); photonics (MS, PhD). Signal and image processing (MS, PhD).

Faculty: 35.
Students: 334 (44 women). 1,149 applicants, 20% accepted, 114 enrolled. In 2001, 51 master's, 12 doctorates awarded.

University of California, San Diego (continued)

Entrance requirements: For master's and doctorate, GRE General Test. *Application deadline:* For fall admission, 1/12. *Application fee:* $40. Electronic applications accepted.

Expenses: Tuition, nonresident: full-time $10,434. Required fees: $4,883. Charles Tu, Chair.

Application contact: Graduate Coordinator, 858-534-6606.

■ UNIVERSITY OF CALIFORNIA, SANTA BARBARA

Graduate Division, College of Engineering, Department of Electrical and Computer Engineering, Santa Barbara, CA 93106

AWARDS MS, PhD.

Degree requirements: For master's, thesis or alternative; for doctorate, thesis/dissertation.

Entrance requirements: For master's and doctorate, GRE General Test, TOEFL. Electronic applications accepted.

Faculty research: Solid-state device theory, physics of solid-state materials, computer architecture. *Web site:* http://www.ece.ucsb.edu/

■ UNIVERSITY OF CALIFORNIA, SANTA CRUZ

Division of Graduate Studies, School of Engineering, Department of Electrical Engineering, Santa Cruz, CA 95064

AWARDS MS, PhD. The graduate program is in the approval process and we anticipate approval in time for admission of EE graduate students by Autumn, 2002. Students wishing to apply for EE graduate study at UCSC should apply to Computer Engineering, noting that they intend to transfer to EE.

Entrance requirements: For master's, TOEFL, GRE General Test; for doctorate, TOEFL, GRE General Test. *Application deadline:* For fall admission, 1/15. *Application fee:* $40. Electronic applications accepted.

Expenses: Tuition: Full-time $19,857. John Vesecky, Professor and Chair, *E-mail:* vesecky@cse.ucsc.edu.

Application contact: Carol Mullane, Graduate Assistant, 831-459-2576, *E-mail:* jodi@cse.ucsc.edu.

Find an in-depth description at www.petersons.com/gradchannel.

■ UNIVERSITY OF CINCINNATI

Division of Research and Advanced Studies, College of Engineering, Department of Electrical and Computer Engineering and Computer Science, Program in Electrical Engineering, Cincinnati, OH 45221

AWARDS MS, PhD.

Degree requirements: For master's and doctorate, thesis/dissertation, registration.

Entrance requirements: For master's and doctorate, GRE General Test, TOEFL. *Application deadline:* For fall admission, 2/1 (priority date). *Application fee:* $40.

Expenses: Tuition, state resident: part-time $2,698 per quarter. Tuition, nonresident: part-time $4,977 per quarter.

Financial support: Fellowships, tuition waivers (full) and unspecified assistantships available. Support available to part-time students. Financial award application deadline: 2/1.

Faculty research: Integrated circuits and optical devices, charge-coupled devices, photosensitive devices.

Application contact: Dieter Schmidt, Graduate Program Director, 513-556-1816, *Fax:* 513-556-7326, *E-mail:* dieter.schmidt@uc.edu. *Web site:* http://www.ececs.uc.edu/

Find an in-depth description at www.petersons.com/gradchannel.

■ UNIVERSITY OF COLORADO AT BOULDER

Graduate School, College of Engineering and Applied Science, Department of Electrical and Computer Engineering, Boulder, CO 80309

AWARDS Electrical engineering (ME, MS, PhD), including computer engineering. Part-time programs available. Postbaccalaureate distance learning degree programs offered (no on-campus study).

Faculty: 31 full-time (4 women).

Students: 159 full-time (25 women), 45 part-time (4 women); includes 16 minority (2 African Americans, 9 Asian Americans or Pacific Islanders, 5 Hispanic Americans), 103 international. Average age 28. 328 applicants, 46% accepted. In 2001, 47 master's, 14 doctorates awarded. Terminal master's awarded for partial completion of doctoral program.

Degree requirements: For master's, thesis or alternative; for doctorate, one foreign language, thesis/dissertation, departmental qualifying exam.

Entrance requirements: For master's, GRE General Test, minimum undergraduate GPA of 3.0; for doctorate, GRE General Test, minimum undergraduate GPA of 3.5. *Application deadline:* For fall admission, 3/1 (priority date). Applications are processed on a rolling basis. *Application fee:* $50 ($60 for international students).

Expenses: Tuition, state resident: full-time $3,474. Tuition, nonresident: full-time $16,624.

Financial support: In 2001–02, 14 fellowships (averaging $5,813 per year), 26 research assistantships (averaging $19,344 per year), 18 teaching assistantships (averaging $12,675 per year) were awarded. Career-related internships or fieldwork, scholarships/grants, and tuition waivers (full) also available. Financial award application deadline: 1/15.

Faculty research: Biomedical engineering, cognitive disabilities, control systems, digital signal processing communications, electromagnetic waves. *Total annual research expenditures:* $5.3 million. Renjeng Su, Chair, 303-492-3511, *Fax:* 303-492-2758, *E-mail:* sur@boulder.colorado.edu.

Application contact: Adam Sadoff, Graduate Program Assistant, 303-375-0490, *Fax:* 303-492-2758, *E-mail:* adam.sadoff@colorado.edu. *Web site:* http://ece-www.colorado.edu/

■ UNIVERSITY OF COLORADO AT COLORADO SPRINGS

Graduate School, College of Engineering and Applied Science, Department of Electrical and Computer Engineering, Colorado Springs, CO 80933-7150

AWARDS Electrical engineering (MS, PhD). Part-time and evening/weekend programs available.

Faculty: 10 full-time (0 women), 3 part-time/adjunct (0 women).

Students: 44 full-time (8 women), 47 part-time (4 women); includes 15 minority (1 African American, 10 Asian Americans or Pacific Islanders, 4 Hispanic Americans), 8 international. Average age 33. In 2001, 8 master's, 1 doctorate awarded.

Degree requirements: For master's, thesis (for some programs); for doctorate, thesis/dissertation, comprehensive exam.

Entrance requirements: For master's, GRE General Test, TOEFL, minimum GPA of 3.0, B.S. in electrical engineering or previous course work in electrical engineering; for doctorate, GRE General Test, TOEFL, minimum GPA of 3.3. *Application fee:* $60 ($75 for international students).

Expenses: Tuition, state resident: full-time $2,900; part-time $174 per credit. Tuition, nonresident: full-time $9,961; part-time $591 per credit. Required fees: $14 per credit. $141 per semester. Tuition and fees vary according to course load, program and student level.

Financial support: Fellowships, research assistantships, teaching assistantships, career-related internships or fieldwork and Federal Work-Study available.

Faculty research: Integrated ferroelectric devices; applied electromagnetics; digital/mixed-signal circuit design, test and design

for testability. Signal processing for communications and controls.
Dr. Rodger Ziemer, Chairman, 719-262-3350, *Fax:* 719-262-3589, *E-mail:* ziemer@eas.uccs.edu.
Application contact: Ruth Ann Nelson, Academic Adviser, 719-262-3351, *Fax:* 719-262-3589, *E-mail:* rnelson@eas.uccs.edu. *Web site:* http://ece.uccs.edu/

■ UNIVERSITY OF COLORADO AT DENVER

Graduate School, College of Engineering and Applied Science, Department of Electrical Engineering, Denver, CO 80217-3364

AWARDS MS. Part-time and evening/weekend programs available.

Faculty: 8 full-time (2 women).
Students: 3 full-time (0 women), 25 part-time (3 women); includes 12 minority (3 African Americans, 7 Asian Americans or Pacific Islanders, 2 Hispanic Americans), 3 international. Average age 32. 34 applicants, 71% accepted, 8 enrolled. In 2001, 9 degrees awarded.
Degree requirements: For master's, thesis or alternative.
Entrance requirements: For master's, GRE. *Application deadline:* For fall admission, 3/15; for spring admission, 9/15. Applications are processed on a rolling basis. *Application fee:* $50 ($60 for international students). Electronic applications accepted.
Expenses: Tuition, state resident: full-time $3,284; part-time $198 per credit hour. Tuition, nonresident: full-time $13,380; part-time $802 per credit hour. Required fees: $444; $222 per semester.
Financial support: Research assistantships, teaching assistantships, career-related internships or fieldwork and Federal Work-Study available. Financial award application deadline: 3/1; financial award applicants required to submit FAFSA. *Total annual research expenditures:* $44,927.
Application contact: Judith Stalnaker, Associate Dean, 303-556-8405, *Fax:* 303-556-2368, *E-mail:* judy.stalnaker@cudenver.edu. *Web site:* http://carbon.cudenver.edu/public/engineer/eedept.html

■ UNIVERSITY OF CONNECTICUT

Graduate School, School of Engineering, Field of Electrical and Systems Engineering, Storrs, CT 06269

AWARDS Biological engineering (MS); control and communication systems (MS, PhD); electromagnetics and physical electronics (MS, PhD). Terminal master's awarded for partial completion of doctoral program.

Degree requirements: For master's, thesis or alternative; for doctorate, thesis/dissertation.

Entrance requirements: For master's and doctorate, GRE General Test, TOEFL.

■ UNIVERSITY OF DAYTON

Graduate School, School of Engineering, Department of Electrical and Computer Engineering, Dayton, OH 45469-1300

AWARDS MSEE, DE, PhD. Part-time and evening/weekend programs available.

Faculty: 16 full-time (0 women), 4 part-time/adjunct (0 women).
Students: 42 full-time (4 women), 26 part-time (6 women); includes 9 minority (3 African Americans, 2 Asian Americans or Pacific Islanders, 4 Hispanic Americans), 27 international. Average age 24. In 2001, 14 master's, 11 doctorates awarded.
Degree requirements: For master's, thesis optional; for doctorate, variable foreign language requirement, thesis/dissertation, departmental qualifying exam.
Entrance requirements: For master's, TOEFL. *Application deadline:* For fall admission, 8/1. Applications are processed on a rolling basis. *Application fee:* $30.
Expenses: Tuition: Full-time $5,436; part-time $453 per credit hour. Required fees: $50; $25 per term.
Financial support: In 2001–02, 15 students received support, including 14 research assistantships with full tuition reimbursements available (averaging $12,000 per year), 3 teaching assistantships with full tuition reimbursements available (averaging $12,000 per year); institutionally sponsored loans also available. Financial award application deadline: 5/1.
Faculty research: Analog and signal processing, electromagnetics, electro-optics, digital computer architectures.
Dr. Partha Banerjee, Chair, 937-229-3611, *E-mail:* p.banerjee@notes.udayton.edu.
Application contact: Dr. Donald L. Moon, Associate Dean, 937-229-2241, *Fax:* 937-229-2471, *E-mail:* dmoon@notes.udayton.edu.

■ UNIVERSITY OF DELAWARE

College of Engineering, Department of Electrical and Computer Engineering, Newark, DE 19716

AWARDS MEE, PhD. Part-time programs available. Postbaccalaureate distance learning degree programs offered (no on-campus study).

Faculty: 20 full-time (0 women), 9 part-time/adjunct (0 women).
Students: 100 full-time (19 women), 16 part-time (2 women); includes 5 minority (2 African Americans, 3 Asian Americans or Pacific Islanders), 90 international. Average age 27. 497 applicants, 14% accepted, 46 enrolled. In 2001, 16 master's, 4 doctorates awarded. Terminal master's awarded for partial completion of doctoral program.

Degree requirements: For master's, thesis optional; for doctorate, thesis/dissertation.

Entrance requirements: For master's, GRE General Test, TOEFL; for doctorate, GRE General Test, TOEFL, qualifying exam. *Application deadline:* For fall admission, 7/1; for spring admission, 12/1. Applications are processed on a rolling basis. *Application fee:* $50. Electronic applications accepted.
Expenses: Tuition, state resident: full-time $4,770; part-time $265 per credit. Tuition, nonresident: full-time $13,860; part-time $770 per credit. Required fees: $414.
Financial support: In 2001–02, 82 students received support, including 2 fellowships with full tuition reimbursements available (averaging $13,500 per year), 66 research assistantships with full tuition reimbursements available (averaging $13,500 per year), 14 teaching assistantships with full tuition reimbursements available (averaging $13,500 per year); Federal Work-Study, institutionally sponsored loans, and unspecified assistantships also available. Financial award application deadline: 3/1.
Faculty research: Signal and image processing, communications, devices and materials, optoelectronics, computer engineering. *Total annual research expenditures:* $6.1 million.
Dr. Gonzalo R. Arce, Chairman, 302-831-8030 Ext. 3142, *Fax:* 302-831-4316, *E-mail:* arce@ee.udel.edu.
Application contact: Dr. Kenneth Barner, Chair, Graduate Committee, 302-831-8031, *Fax:* 302-831-6937, *E-mail:* barner@ee.udel.edu. *Web site:* http://www.ee.udel.edu/

■ UNIVERSITY OF DENVER

Graduate Studies, Faculty of Natural Sciences, Mathematics and Engineering, Department of Engineering, Denver, CO 80208

AWARDS Computer science and engineering (MS); electrical engineering (MS); management and general engineering (MSMGEN); materials science (PhD); mechanical engineering (MS). Part-time and evening/weekend programs available.

Faculty: 13 full-time (2 women), 3 part-time/adjunct (0 women).
Students: 17 (6 women) 11 international. 50 applicants, 62% accepted. In 2001, 11 degrees awarded. Terminal master's awarded for partial completion of doctoral program.
Degree requirements: For master's, thesis (for some programs); for doctorate, thesis/dissertation.
Entrance requirements: For master's and doctorate, GRE General Test, TOEFL, TSE. *Application deadline:* Applications are processed on a rolling basis. *Application fee:* $45.
Expenses: Tuition: Full-time $21,456.

University of Denver (continued)
Financial support: In 2001–02, 11 students received support, including 6 research assistantships with full and partial tuition reimbursements available (averaging $9,999 per year), 7 teaching assistantships with full and partial tuition reimbursements available (averaging $10,782 per year); fellowships with full and partial tuition reimbursements available, career-related internships or fieldwork, Federal Work-Study, institutionally sponsored loans, and scholarships/grants also available. Financial award application deadline: 3/1; financial award applicants required to submit FAFSA.
Faculty research: Microelectrics, digital signal processing, robotics, speech recognition, microwaves, aerosols, x-ray analysis, acoustic emissions. *Total annual research expenditures:* $1 million.
Dr. James C. Wilson, Chair, 303-871-2102.
Application contact: Susie Montoya, Assistant to Chair, 303-871-2102. *Web site:* http://littlebird.engr.du.edu/

■ **UNIVERSITY OF DETROIT MERCY**

College of Engineering and Science, Department of Electrical and Computer Engineering, Detroit, MI 48219-0900

AWARDS ME, DE. Evening/weekend programs available.

Faculty: 6 full-time (1 woman).
Students: 5 full-time (0 women), 27 part-time (6 women); includes 2 minority (1 African American, 1 Asian American or Pacific Islander), 18 international. Average age 27. In 2001, 5 master's, 1 doctorate awarded.
Degree requirements: For doctorate, thesis/dissertation.
Application deadline: For fall admission, 8/1 (priority date). Applications are processed on a rolling basis. *Application fee:* $30 ($50 for international students).
Expenses: Tuition: Full-time $10,620; part-time $590 per credit hour. Required fees: $400. Tuition and fees vary according to program.
Financial support: Career-related internships or fieldwork available.
Faculty research: Electromagnetics, computer architecture, systems.
Dr. Nizar Al-Holou, Chairperson, 313-993-3365, *Fax:* 313-993-1187, *E-mail:* alholoun@udmercy.edu.

■ **UNIVERSITY OF FLORIDA**

Graduate School, College of Engineering, Department of Electrical and Computer Engineering, Gainesville, FL 32611

AWARDS ME, MS, PhD, Engr. Part-time programs available.
Faculty: 64.

Students: 325 full-time (47 women), 78 part-time (7 women); includes 37 minority (5 African Americans, 15 Asian Americans or Pacific Islanders, 16 Hispanic Americans, 1 Native American), 280 international. Average age 23. 1,352 applicants, 53% accepted. In 2001, 117 master's, 19 doctorates awarded. Terminal master's awarded for partial completion of doctoral program.
Degree requirements: For master's, thesis optional; for doctorate, thesis/dissertation, comprehensive exam, registration. *Median time to degree:* Master's–2 years full-time, 4 years part-time; doctorate–4 years full-time, 7 years part-time.
Entrance requirements: For master's, GRE General Test, TOEFL, minimum GPA of 3.0; for doctorate, GRE General Test, TOEFL, minimum GPA of 3.5; for Engr, GRE General Test. *Application deadline:* For fall admission, 2/1 (priority date); for spring admission, 7/1 (priority date). Applications are processed on a rolling basis. *Application fee:* $20. Electronic applications accepted.
Expenses: Tuition, state resident: part-time $164 per hour. Tuition, nonresident: part-time $571 per hour. Tuition and fees vary according to course level and program.
Financial support: In 2001–02, 41 fellowships, 141 research assistantships, 45 teaching assistantships were awarded. Unspecified assistantships also available. Financial award application deadline: 4/15.
Faculty research: Communications, electronics, digital signal processing, computer engineering.
Dr. Martin A. Uman, Chair, 352-392-0913, *Fax:* 352-392-8671, *E-mail:* uman@ece.ufl.edu.
Application contact: Dr. Jacob Hammer, Graduate Coordinator, 352-392-4934, *Fax:* 352-392-8671, *E-mail:* hammer@graduate.ece.ufl.edu. *Web site:* http://www.ece.ufl.edu/

Find an in-depth description at www.petersons.com/gradchannel.

■ **UNIVERSITY OF FLORIDA**

Graduate School, Graduate Engineering and Research Center (GERC), Gainesville, FL 32611

AWARDS Aerospace engineering (ME, MS, PhD, Engr); electrical and computer engineering (ME, MS, PhD, Engr); engineering mechanics (ME, MS, PhD, Engr); industrial and systems engineering (ME, MS, PhD, Engr). Part-time programs available. Postbaccalaureate distance learning degree programs offered. Terminal master's awarded for partial completion of doctoral program.
Degree requirements: For master's, thesis optional; for doctorate and Engr, thesis/dissertation.
Entrance requirements: For master's, GRE General Test, TOEFL, minimum GPA of 3.0; for doctorate, GRE General

Test, written and oral qualifying exams, TOEFL, minimum GPA of 3.0, master's degree in engineering; for Engr, GRE General Test, TOEFL, minimum GPA of 3.0, master's degree in engineering. Electronic applications accepted.
Expenses: Contact institution.
Faculty research: Aerodynamics, terradynamics, and propulsion; composite materials and stress analysis; optical processing of microwave signals and photonics; holography, radar, and communications. System and signal theory; digital signal processing. *Web site:* http://www.gerc.eng.ufl.edu/

■ **UNIVERSITY OF HAWAII AT MANOA**

Graduate Division, College of Engineering, Department of Electrical Engineering, Honolulu, HI 96822

AWARDS MS, PhD.

Faculty: 21 full-time (2 women), 1 part-time/adjunct (0 women).
Students: 45 full-time (6 women), 21 part-time (3 women); includes 20 Asian Americans or Pacific Islanders, 1 Hispanic American. Average age 28. 61 applicants, 44% accepted, 11 enrolled. In 2001, 16 master's, 1 doctorate awarded.
Degree requirements: For master's, thesis; for doctorate, one foreign language, thesis/dissertation, exams. *Median time to degree:* Master's–2 years full-time; doctorate–5 years full-time.
Entrance requirements: For master's, TOEFL; for doctorate, GRE General Test, GRE Subject Test, TOEFL. *Application deadline:* For fall admission, 3/1 (priority date); for spring admission, 8/1. Applications are processed on a rolling basis. *Application fee:* $25 ($50 for international students).
Expenses: Tuition, state resident: full-time $2,160; part-time $1,980 per year. Tuition, nonresident: full-time $5,190; part-time $4,829 per year.
Financial support: In 2001–02, 24 research assistantships (averaging $15,166 per year), 4 teaching assistantships (averaging $13,526 per year) were awarded. Tuition waivers (full and partial) also available.
Faculty research: Computers and artificial intelligence, communication and networking, control theory, physical electronics, VLSI design, micromillimeter waves. *Total annual research expenditures:* $2 million.
Dr. Kazutoshi Najita, Chairperson, 808-956-7586, *Fax:* 808-956-3427, *E-mail:* najita@spectra.eng.hawaii.edu.
Application contact: Dr. Vinod Malhotra, Graduate Field Chairperson, 808-956-7609, *Fax:* 808-956-3427, *E-mail:* vinod@spectra.eng.hawaii.edu.

■ UNIVERSITY OF HOUSTON

Cullen College of Engineering, Department of Electrical and Computer Engineering, Houston, TX 77204

AWARDS MEE, MSEE, PhD. Part-time and evening/weekend programs available.

Faculty: 25 full-time (2 women), 3 part-time/adjunct (0 women).
Students: 144 full-time (41 women), 61 part-time (9 women); includes 36 minority (8 African Americans, 22 Asian Americans or Pacific Islanders, 6 Hispanic Americans), 128 international. Average age 29. 208 applicants, 58% accepted. In 2001, 53 master's, 3 doctorates awarded. Terminal master's awarded for partial completion of doctoral program.
Degree requirements: For master's, thesis (for some programs); for doctorate, thesis/dissertation, departmental qualifying exam.
Entrance requirements: For master's and doctorate, GRE General Test, TOEFL. *Application deadline:* For fall admission, 2/1; for spring admission, 10/1. Applications are processed on a rolling basis. *Application fee:* $25 ($75 for international students).
Expenses: Tuition, state resident: full-time $1,512. Tuition, nonresident: full-time $5,310. Required fees: $1,308. Tuition and fees vary according to program.
Financial support: In 2001–02, 93 research assistantships with partial tuition reimbursements (averaging $1,237 per year), 51 teaching assistantships with partial tuition reimbursements (averaging $946 per year) were awarded. Career-related internships or fieldwork, Federal Work-Study, institutionally sponsored loans, and tuition waivers (partial) also available. Financial award application deadline: 7/1.
Faculty research: Applied electromagnetics and microelectronics, signal and image processing, biomedical engineering, geophysical applications, control engineering. *Total annual research expenditures:* $2.7 million.
Dr. Frank J. Claydon, Chairman, 713-743-4440, *Fax:* 713-743-4444, *E-mail:* fclaydon@uh.edu.
Application contact: Mytrang Baccam, Graduate Analyst, 713-743-4402, *Fax:* 713-743-4444, *E-mail:* ece_grad_admit@uh.edu. *Web site:* http://www.egr.uh.edu/ece/

■ UNIVERSITY OF IDAHO

College of Graduate Studies, College of Engineering, Department of Electrical and Computer Engineering, Moscow, ID 83844-2282

AWARDS Computer engineering (M Engr, MS); electrical engineering (M Engr, MS, PhD).

Faculty: 15 full-time (0 women), 3 part-time/adjunct (1 woman).
Students: 29 full-time (7 women), 75 part-time (2 women); includes 11 minority (9 Asian Americans or Pacific Islanders, 2 Hispanic Americans), 38 international. 118 applicants, 69% accepted. In 2001, 17 master's, 1 doctorate awarded.
Degree requirements: For master's and doctorate, thesis/dissertation.
Entrance requirements: For master's, minimum GPA of 2.8; for doctorate, minimum undergraduate GPA of 2.8, 3.0 graduate. *Application deadline:* For fall admission, 8/1; for spring admission, 12/15. *Application fee:* $35 ($45 for international students).
Expenses: Tuition, state resident: full-time $1,613. Tuition, nonresident: full-time $3,000.
Financial support: In 2001–02, 5 research assistantships, 8 teaching assistantships (averaging $4,638 per year) were awarded. Fellowships, career-related internships or fieldwork and Federal Work-Study also available. Financial award application deadline: 2/15.
Faculty research: Digital systems, energy systems.
Dr. Joseph Feeley, Head, 208-885-2783. *Web site:* http://www.ee.uidaho.edu/
Find an in-depth description at www.petersons.com/gradchannel.

■ UNIVERSITY OF ILLINOIS AT CHICAGO

Graduate College, College of Engineering, Department of Electrical Engineering and Computer Science, Program in Electrical Engineering, Chicago, IL 60607-7128

AWARDS MS, PhD. Evening/weekend programs available.

Students: 135 full-time (39 women), 99 part-time (17 women); includes 25 minority (3 African Americans, 19 Asian Americans or Pacific Islanders, 3 Hispanic Americans), 174 international. Average age 27.
Degree requirements: For master's, thesis or alternative; for doctorate, thesis/dissertation, departmental qualifying exam.
Entrance requirements: For master's, TOEFL, minimum GPA of 3.75 on a 5.0 scale, BS in related field; for doctorate, GRE General Test, TOEFL, minimum GPA of 3.75 on a 5.0 scale, MS in related field. *Application deadline:* For fall admission, 6/7; for spring admission, 11/1. *Application fee:* $40 ($50 for international students).
Expenses: Tuition, state resident: full-time $3,060. Tuition, nonresident: full-time $6,688.
Financial support: In 2001–02, 132 students received support; fellowships, research assistantships, teaching assistantships, tuition waivers (full) available.
Sharad Laxpati, Head, 312-996-8679.
Find an in-depth description at www.petersons.com/gradchannel.

■ UNIVERSITY OF ILLINOIS AT URBANA–CHAMPAIGN

Graduate College, College of Engineering, Department of Electrical and Computer Engineering, Champaign, IL 61820

AWARDS Computer engineering (MS, PhD); electrical engineering (MS, PhD).

Faculty: 82 full-time, 5 part-time/adjunct.
Students: 475 full-time (55 women); includes 68 minority (2 African Americans, 61 Asian Americans or Pacific Islanders, 4 Hispanic Americans, 1 Native American), 244 international. 1,437 applicants, 19% accepted. In 2001, 88 master's, 55 doctorates awarded.
Degree requirements: For master's and doctorate, thesis/dissertation.
Entrance requirements: For master's, GRE, minimum GPA of 3.0. *Application deadline:* For fall admission, 1/15. Applications are processed on a rolling basis. *Application fee:* $40 ($50 for international students). Electronic applications accepted.
Expenses: Tuition, state resident: part-time $3,227 per degree program. Tuition, nonresident: part-time $7,169 per degree program. Tuition and fees vary according to program.
Financial support: In 2001–02, 30 fellowships, 277 research assistantships, 94 teaching assistantships were awarded. Tuition waivers (full and partial) also available. Financial award application deadline: 1/15.
Richard E. Blahut, Head, 217-333-2301, *Fax:* 217-244-7075, *E-mail:* blahut@uiuc.edu.
Application contact: W. R. Perkins, Administrative Clerk, 217-333-0207, *Fax:* 217-244-7075, *E-mail:* wperkins@uiuc.edu. *Web site:* http://www.ece.uiuc.edu/
Find an in-depth description at www.petersons.com/gradchannel.

■ THE UNIVERSITY OF IOWA

Graduate College, College of Engineering, Department of Electrical and Computer Engineering, Iowa City, IA 52242-1316

AWARDS MS, PhD. Part-time programs available.

Faculty: 16 full-time (0 women), 2 part-time/adjunct (0 women).
Students: 51 full-time (5 women), 25 part-time (7 women); includes 3 minority (all Asian Americans or Pacific Islanders), 50 international. Average age 27. 245 applicants, 34% accepted, 34 enrolled. In 2001, 18 degrees awarded.
Degree requirements: For master's, thesis, PhD qualifying exam, comprehensive exam, registration; for doctorate, thesis/dissertation, comprehensive exam, registration. *Median time to degree:* Master's–2.5 years full-time, 4.5 years part-time.
Entrance requirements: For master's and doctorate, TOEFL, GRE. *Application*

The University of Iowa (continued)
deadline: For fall admission, 4/15 (priority date); for spring admission, 12/1 (priority date). Applications are processed on a rolling basis. *Application fee:* $30 ($50 for international students). Electronic applications accepted.
Expenses: Tuition, state resident: full-time $3,702; part-time $206 per semester hour. Tuition, nonresident: full-time $11,924; part-time $206 per semester hour. Required fees: $101 per semester. Tuition and fees vary according to course load and program.
Financial support: In 2001–02, 52 students received support, including 29 research assistantships with partial tuition reimbursements available (averaging $14,718 per year), 23 teaching assistantships with partial tuition reimbursements available (averaging $14,718 per year); fellowships, scholarships/grants, health care benefits, and unspecified assistantships also available. Financial award application deadline: 2/1; financial award applicants required to submit FAFSA.
Faculty research: Quantitative medical image processing, bioinformatics, design and testing of very large scale integrated circuits, wireless communication, photonics. *Total annual research expenditures:* $3.8 million.
Dr. Jon G. Kuhl, Departmental Executive Officer, 319-335-5958, *Fax:* 319-335-6028, *E-mail:* jon-kuhl@uiowa.edu.
Application contact: Kim Sherwood, Secretary, 319-335-5197, *Fax:* 319-335-6028, *E-mail:* ece@engineering.uiowa.edu. *Web site:* http://www.ece.engineering.uiowa.edu/

■ UNIVERSITY OF KANSAS

Graduate School, School of Engineering, Department of Electrical Engineering and Computer Science, Program in Electrical Engineering, Lawrence, KS 66045

AWARDS MS, DE, PhD.

Students: 55 full-time (6 women), 28 part-time (2 women); includes 1 minority (Asian American or Pacific Islander), 60 international. Average age 26. 305 applicants, 24% accepted, 30 enrolled. In 2001, 13 master's, 1 doctorate awarded. Terminal master's awarded for partial completion of doctoral program.
Degree requirements: For master's, exam, thesis optional; for doctorate, one foreign language, thesis/dissertation, qualifying exams, comprehensive exam.
Entrance requirements: For master's, GRE, TOEFL, minimum GPA of 3.0; for doctorate, GRE, TOEFL, minimum GPA of 3.5. *Application deadline:* For fall admission, 3/1 (priority date); for spring admission, 10/1. Applications are processed on a rolling basis. *Application fee:* $40.
Expenses: Tuition, state resident: full-time $2,722; part-time $113 per credit. Tuition, nonresident: full-time $8,586; part-time

$358 per credit. Required fees: $551; $46 per credit. Tuition and fees vary according to campus/location, program and reciprocity agreements.
Financial support: Fellowships, research assistantships with partial tuition reimbursements, teaching assistantships with full and partial tuition reimbursements, career-related internships or fieldwork available.
Application contact: John M. Gauch, Graduate Director, 785-864-4487, *Fax:* 785-864-3226, *E-mail:* grad_admissions@eecs.ku.edu.

■ UNIVERSITY OF KENTUCKY

Graduate School, Graduate School Programs from the College of Engineering, Program in Electrical Engineering, Lexington, KY 40506-0032

AWARDS MSEE, PhD.

Faculty: 28 full-time (2 women).
Students: 72 full-time (11 women), 19 part-time (2 women); includes 2 minority (1 Asian American or Pacific Islander, 1 Hispanic American), 71 international. 202 applicants, 72% accepted. In 2001, 25 master's, 2 doctorates awarded.
Degree requirements: For master's, thesis optional; for doctorate, one foreign language, thesis/dissertation, comprehensive exam.
Entrance requirements: For master's, GRE General Test, minimum undergraduate GPA of 3.0; for doctorate, GRE General Test, minimum graduate GPA of 3.0. *Application deadline:* For fall admission, 7/19. Applications are processed on a rolling basis. *Application fee:* $30 ($35 for international students).
Expenses: Tuition, state resident: full-time $4,075; part-time $213 per credit hour. Tuition, nonresident: full-time $11,295; part-time $614 per credit hour.
Financial support: In 2001–02, 3 fellowships, 28 research assistantships, 15 teaching assistantships were awarded. Federal Work-Study and institutionally sponsored loans also available. Support available to part-time students. Financial award application deadline: 3/1.
Faculty research: Signal processing, systems, and control; electromagnetic field theory; power electronics and machines; computer engineering and VLSI; materials and devices. *Total annual research expenditures:* $1.5 million.
Dr. William Smith, Director of Graduate Studies, 859-257-1009, *Fax:* 859-257-3092, *E-mail:* bsmith@engr.uky.edu.
Application contact: Dr. Jeannine Blackwell, Associate Dean, 859-257-4905, *Fax:* 859-323-1928.

■ UNIVERSITY OF LOUISVILLE

Graduate School, Speed Scientific School, Department of Electrical and Computer Engineering, Louisville, KY 40292-0001

AWARDS M Eng, MS.

Students: 35 full-time (6 women), 64 part-time (8 women); includes 9 minority (4 African Americans, 2 Asian Americans or Pacific Islanders, 2 Hispanic Americans, 1 Native American), 31 international. Average age 29. In 2001, 18 degrees awarded.
Degree requirements: For master's, thesis.
Entrance requirements: For master's, GRE General Test, minimum GPA of 2.75. *Application deadline:* Applications are processed on a rolling basis. *Application fee:* $25. Electronic applications accepted.
Expenses: Tuition, state resident: full-time $4,134. Tuition, nonresident: full-time $11,486.
Financial support: In 2001–02, 3 fellowships with full tuition reimbursements (averaging $18,000 per year), 18 research assistantships with full tuition reimbursements (averaging $15,072 per year), 6 teaching assistantships with full tuition reimbursements (averaging $15,252 per year) were awarded.
Darrel L. Chenoweth, Chair, 502-852-6289, *Fax:* 502-852-8851, *E-mail:* dlchen01@gwise.louisville.edu.
Application contact: Joyce M. Hack, Administrative Assistant, 502-852-7517, *Fax:* 502-852-8851, *E-mail:* jmhack01@gwise.louisville.edu.

■ UNIVERSITY OF MAINE

Graduate School, College of Engineering, Department of Electrical and Computer Engineering, Orono, ME 04469

AWARDS Computer engineering (MS); electrical engineering (MS, PhD). Part-time programs available.

Students: 14 full-time (1 woman), 7 part-time, 6 international. Average age 25. 32 applicants, 53% accepted, 4 enrolled. In 2001, 5 master's awarded.
Degree requirements: For master's, thesis (for some programs); for doctorate, thesis/dissertation.
Entrance requirements: For master's and doctorate, GRE General Test, TOEFL. *Application deadline:* For fall admission, 2/1 (priority date). Applications are processed on a rolling basis. *Application fee:* $50. Electronic applications accepted.
Expenses: Tuition, state resident: full-time $3,780; part-time $210 per credit hour. Tuition, nonresident: full-time $10,782; part-time $599 per credit hour. Required fees: $9.5 per credit hour. $32 per semester. Tuition and fees vary according to reciprocity agreements.
Financial support: In 2001–02, 13 research assistantships with tuition reimbursements (averaging $14,280 per

year), 2 teaching assistantships with tuition reimbursements (averaging $10,200 per year) were awarded. Federal Work-Study, institutionally sponsored loans, and tuition waivers (full and partial) also available. Financial award application deadline: 3/1. Dr. James Patton, Chair, 207-581-2223, *Fax:* 201-581-2220.
Application contact: Scott G. Delcourt, Director of the Graduate School, 207-581-3218, *Fax:* 207-581-3232, *E-mail:* graduate@maine.edu. *Web site:* http://www.umaine.edu/graduate/

■ UNIVERSITY OF MARYLAND, BALTIMORE COUNTY

Graduate School, College of Engineering, Department of Computer Science and Electrical Engineering, Program in Electrical Engineering, Baltimore, MD 21250-5398

AWARDS MS, PhD.

Degree requirements: For doctorate, thesis/dissertation.
Entrance requirements: For master's and doctorate, GRE General Test.
Faculty research: Integrated optics and optoelectronics, light propagation, communications and signal processing, medical imaging, semiconductor lasers.

■ UNIVERSITY OF MARYLAND, COLLEGE PARK

Graduate Studies and Research, A. James Clark School of Engineering, Department of Electrical and Computer Engineering, College Park, MD 20742

AWARDS Electrical and computer engineering (M Eng, MS, PhD); electrical engineering (MS, PhD); telecommunications (MS). Part-time and evening/weekend programs available. Postbaccalaureate distance learning degree programs offered.

Faculty: 73 full-time (9 women), 15 part-time/adjunct (0 women).
Students: 361 full-time (64 women), 170 part-time (38 women); includes 44 minority (18 African Americans, 24 Asian Americans or Pacific Islanders, 2 Hispanic Americans), 403 international. 1,430 applicants, 20% accepted, 154 enrolled. In 2001, 82 master's, 32 doctorates awarded.
Degree requirements: For master's, thesis or alternative; for doctorate, thesis/dissertation, oral exam, qualifying exam.
Entrance requirements: For master's and doctorate, GRE General Test, minimum GPA of 3.0. *Application deadline:* For spring admission, 12/1. Applications are processed on a rolling basis. *Application fee:* $50 ($70 for international students). Electronic applications accepted.
Expenses: Tuition, state resident: part-time $289 per credit hour. Tuition, nonresident: part-time $448 per credit

hour. One-time fee: $436 part-time. Full-time tuition and fees vary according to course load, campus/location and program.
Financial support: In 2001–02, 16 fellowships with full tuition reimbursements (averaging $11,621 per year), 72 research assistantships with tuition reimbursements (averaging $12,422 per year), 65 teaching assistantships with tuition reimbursements (averaging $11,377 per year) were awarded. Career-related internships or fieldwork also available. Financial award applicants required to submit FAFSA.
Faculty research: Communications and control, electrophysics, micro-electronics. Dr. Steven Marcus, Acting Chair, 301-405-3683.
Application contact: Trudy Lindsey, Director, Graduate Admissions and Records, 301-405-6991, *Fax:* 301-314-9305, *E-mail:* grschool@deans.umd.edu.
Find an in-depth description at www.petersons.com/gradchannel.

■ UNIVERSITY OF MARYLAND, COLLEGE PARK

Graduate Studies and Research, A. James Clark School of Engineering, Professional Program in Engineering, College Park, MD 20742

AWARDS Aerospace engineering (M Eng); chemical engineering (M Eng); civil engineering (M Eng); electrical engineering (M Eng); fire protection engineering (M Eng); materials science and engineering (M Eng); mechanical engineering (M Eng); reliability engineering (M Eng). Systems engineering (M Eng). Part-time and evening/weekend programs available. Postbaccalaureate distance learning degree programs offered.

Faculty: 11 part-time/adjunct (0 women).
Students: 19 full-time (4 women), 144 part-time (31 women); includes 41 minority (17 African Americans, 18 Asian Americans or Pacific Islanders, 6 Hispanic Americans), 27 international. 71 applicants, 80% accepted, 50 enrolled. In 2001, 64 degrees awarded.
Application deadline: For fall admission, 8/15; for spring admission, 1/10. Applications are processed on a rolling basis.
Application fee: $50 ($70 for international students). Electronic applications accepted.
Expenses: Tuition, state resident: part-time $289 per credit hour. Tuition, nonresident: part-time $448 per credit hour. One-time fee: $436 part-time. Full-time tuition and fees vary according to course load, campus/location and program.
Financial support: In 2001–02, 1 research assistantship with tuition reimbursement (averaging $20,655 per year), 5 teaching assistantships with tuition reimbursements (averaging $11,114 per year) were awarded. Fellowships, Federal Work-Study and scholarships/grants also available. Support available to part-time students. Financial award applicants required to submit FAFSA.

Dr. George Syrmos, Acting Director, 301-405-5256, *Fax:* 301-314-9477.
Application contact: Trudy Lindsey, Director, Graduate Admissions and Records, 301-405-6991, *Fax:* 301-314-9305, *E-mail:* grschool@deans.umd.edu.

■ UNIVERSITY OF MASSACHUSETTS AMHERST

Graduate School, College of Engineering, Department of Electrical and Computer Engineering, Amherst, MA 01003

AWARDS MS, PhD. Part-time and evening/weekend programs available.

Faculty: 31 full-time (1 woman).
Students: 82 full-time (16 women), 114 part-time (14 women); includes 13 minority (2 African Americans, 8 Asian Americans or Pacific Islanders, 2 Hispanic Americans, 1 Native American), 139 international. Average age 27. 872 applicants, 14% accepted. In 2001, 50 master's, 8 doctorates awarded. Terminal master's awarded for partial completion of doctoral program.
Degree requirements: For doctorate, thesis/dissertation.
Entrance requirements: For master's and doctorate, GRE General Test. *Application deadline:* For fall admission, 1/15 (priority date); for spring admission, 10/1. Applications are processed on a rolling basis.
Application fee: $40 ($50 for international students).
Expenses: Tuition, state resident: full-time $1,980; part-time $110 per credit. Tuition, nonresident: full-time $7,456; part-time $414 per credit. Required fees: $4,112. One-time fee: $115 full-time.
Financial support: In 2001–02, 8 fellowships with full tuition reimbursements (averaging $5,608 per year), 112 research assistantships with full tuition reimbursements (averaging $9,657 per year), 49 teaching assistantships with full tuition reimbursements (averaging $5,517 per year) were awarded. Career-related internships or fieldwork, Federal Work-Study, scholarships/grants, traineeships, and unspecified assistantships also available. Support available to part-time students. Financial award application deadline: 1/5. Dr. Seshu B. Desu, Head, 413-545-0962, *Fax:* 413-545-4611, *E-mail:* sdesu@ecs.umass.edu.
Application contact: Dr. Donald E. Scott, Chair, Admissions Committee, 413-545-0937, *Fax:* 413-545-4611, *E-mail:* scott@ecs.umass.edu.

■ UNIVERSITY OF MASSACHUSETTS DARTMOUTH

Graduate School, College of Engineering, Department of Electrical and Computer Engineering, North Dartmouth, MA 02747-2300

AWARDS Computer engineering (MS, Certificate); electrical engineering (MS, PhD, Certificate). Part-time programs available.

Faculty: 21 full-time (2 women), 3 part-time/adjunct (0 women).
Students: 57 full-time (10 women), 34 part-time (8 women); includes 1 minority (Hispanic American), 73 international. Average age 26. 236 applicants, 72% accepted. In 2001, 13 master's, 3 doctorates awarded.
Degree requirements: For master's, thesis or alternative, culminating project or thesis; for doctorate, thesis/dissertation, comprehensive exam.
Entrance requirements: For master's, GRE General Test, TOEFL, minimum undergraduate GPA of 3.0. *Application deadline:* For fall admission, 2/1 (priority date); for spring admission, 11/1 (priority date). Applications are processed on a rolling basis. *Application fee:* $25 ($45 for international students).
Expenses: Tuition, state resident: full-time $2,071; part-time $86 per credit. Tuition, nonresident: full-time $8,099; part-time $337 per credit. Part-time tuition and fees vary according to course load and reciprocity agreements.
Financial support: In 2001–02, 38 research assistantships with full tuition reimbursements (averaging $6,706 per year), 15 teaching assistantships with full tuition reimbursements (averaging $6,783 per year) were awarded. Federal Work-Study and unspecified assistantships also available. Support available to part-time students. Financial award application deadline: 3/1; financial award applicants required to submit FAFSA.
Faculty research: Marine mammal acoustics, acoustic motion accelerometers, instrumentation for monitoring/control wastewater treatment, acoustics for pollution detection, acoustic correlates of speech intelligibility. *Total annual research expenditures:* $854,000.
Dr. Paul Fortier, Director, 508-999-8544, *Fax:* 508-999-8489, *E-mail:* pfortier@umassd.edu.
Application contact: Maria E. Lomba, Graduate Admissions Officer, 508-999-8604, *Fax:* 508-999-8183, *E-mail:* graduate@umassd.edu.

■ UNIVERSITY OF MASSACHUSETTS LOWELL

Graduate School, James B. Francis College of Engineering, Department of Electrical Engineering, Program in Electrical Engineering, Lowell, MA 01854-2881

AWARDS MS Eng, D Eng. Part-time and evening/weekend programs available. Terminal master's awarded for partial completion of doctoral program.

Degree requirements: For master's, thesis; for doctorate, 2 foreign languages, thesis/dissertation.
Entrance requirements: For master's and doctorate, GRE General Test.

■ THE UNIVERSITY OF MEMPHIS

Graduate School, Herff College of Engineering, Department of Electrical Engineering, Memphis, TN 38152

AWARDS Automatic control systems (MS); biomedical systems (MS); communications and propagation systems (MS); electrical engineering (PhD); engineering computer systems (MS).

Degree requirements: For master's, thesis or alternative, comprehensive exam.
Entrance requirements: For master's, GRE General Test or MAT, minimum undergraduate GPA of 2.5.
Expenses: Tuition, state resident: full-time $2,026. Tuition, nonresident: full-time $4,528.
Faculty research: Ventricular arrhythmias, cerebral palsy, automatic computer troubleshooting, noninvasive monitoring of gastric motor functions.

■ UNIVERSITY OF MIAMI

Graduate School, College of Engineering, Department of Electrical and Computer Engineering, Coral Gables, FL 33124

AWARDS MSECE, PhD. Part-time programs available.

Faculty: 23 full-time (2 women).
Students: 40 full-time (6 women), 6 part-time (2 women); includes 28 minority (3 African Americans, 15 Asian Americans or Pacific Islanders, 10 Hispanic Americans). Average age 25. 141 applicants, 45% accepted. In 2001, 10 master's, 7 doctorates awarded.
Degree requirements: For master's, thesis optional; for doctorate, thesis/dissertation, comprehensive exam.
Entrance requirements: For master's, GRE General Test, TOEFL, minimum GPA of 3.0; for doctorate, GRE General Test, TOEFL, minimum undergraduate GPA of 3.3, 3.5 graduate. *Application deadline:* Applications are processed on a rolling basis. *Application fee:* $50. Electronic applications accepted.
Expenses: Tuition: Part-time $960 per credit hour. Required fees: $85 per semester. Tuition and fees vary according to program.
Financial support: In 2001–02, 3 fellowships with full tuition reimbursements, 3 research assistantships with full tuition reimbursements, 16 teaching assistantships with full tuition reimbursements were awarded. Career-related internships or fieldwork, Federal Work-Study, institutionally sponsored loans, scholarships/grants, and unspecified assistantships also available. Support available to part-time students. Financial award application deadline: 2/1.
Faculty research: Computer network, image processing, database systems, digital signal processing, machine intelligence, information systems. *Total annual research expenditures:* $252,439.
Dr. James W. Modestino, Chairman, 305-284-3291, *Fax:* 305-284-4044, *E-mail:* jmodestino@miami.edu.
Application contact: Dr. Kamal Premaratne, Graduate Adviser, 305-284-3291, *Fax:* 305-284-4044, *E-mail:* kamal@miami.edu. *Web site:* http://www.eng.miami.edu/

■ UNIVERSITY OF MICHIGAN

Horace H. Rackham School of Graduate Studies, College of Engineering, Department of Electrical Engineering and Computer Science, Division of Electrical and Computer Engineering, Ann Arbor, MI 48109

AWARDS MS, MSE, PhD.

Faculty: 41 full-time (3 women), 2 part-time/adjunct (0 women).
Students: 393 full-time (57 women), 8 part-time; includes 35 minority (3 African Americans, 28 Asian Americans or Pacific Islanders, 3 Hispanic Americans, 1 Native American), 253 international. Average age 26. 1,366 applicants, 38% accepted. In 2001, 104 master's, 41 doctorates awarded. Terminal master's awarded for partial completion of doctoral program.
Degree requirements: For doctorate, thesis/dissertation, oral defense of dissertation, preliminary exams.
Entrance requirements: For master's, GRE General Test, TOEFL; for doctorate, GRE General Test, TOEFL, master's degree. *Application deadline:* Applications are processed on a rolling basis. *Application fee:* $55. Electronic applications accepted.
Financial support: In 2001–02, 286 students received support, including 47 fellowships with full tuition reimbursements available (averaging $20,220 per year), 197 research assistantships with full tuition reimbursements available (averaging $20,220 per year), 41 teaching assistantships with full tuition reimbursements available (averaging $18,880 per year) Financial award application deadline: 1/15.
Faculty research: Applied electromagnetics, solid-state electronics, optical sciences, VLSI, circuits and

microsystems. *Total annual research expenditures:* $22.2 million.
Application contact: Beth Stalnaker, Student Service Associate, 734-764-2390, *Fax:* 734-763-1503, *E-mail:* admit@eecs.umich.edu. *Web site:* http://www.eecs.umich.edu/

■ UNIVERSITY OF MICHIGAN–DEARBORN

College of Engineering and Computer Science, Department of Electrical and Computer Engineering, Dearborn, MI 48128-1491

AWARDS Computer engineering (MSE); electrical engineering (MSE). Part-time programs available.

Faculty: 11 full-time (1 woman), 10 part-time/adjunct (1 woman).
Students: 6 full-time (0 women), 120 part-time (12 women); includes 30 minority (2 African Americans, 22 Asian Americans or Pacific Islanders, 6 Hispanic Americans). Average age 29. 108 applicants, 44% accepted. In 2001, 28 degrees awarded.
Degree requirements: For master's, thesis optional.
Entrance requirements: For master's, bachelor's degree in electrical and computer engineering or equivalent, minimum GPA of 3.0. *Application deadline:* For fall admission, 8/1; for winter admission, 12/1; for spring admission, 4/1. Applications are processed on a rolling basis. *Application fee:* $55.
Expenses: Tuition, state resident: part-time $300 per credit hour. Tuition, nonresident: part-time $756 per credit hour. Required fees: $90 per semester. Tuition and fees vary according to course level, course load and program.
Financial support: In 2001–02, 9 research assistantships were awarded; fellowships, teaching assistantships, Federal Work-Study also available. Financial award application deadline: 4/1; financial award applicants required to submit FAFSA.
Faculty research: Process control, fuzzy systems design, machine vision image processing and pattern recognition.
Dr. M. Shridhar, Chair, 313-593-5420, *Fax:* 313-593-9967, *E-mail:* shridhar@engin.umd.umich.edu.
Application contact: Graduate Secretary, 313-593-5420, *Fax:* 313-593-9967. *Web site:* http://www.engin.umd.umich.edu/

■ UNIVERSITY OF MINNESOTA, TWIN CITIES CAMPUS

Graduate School, Institute of Technology, Department of Electrical and Computer Engineering, Minneapolis, MN 55455-0213

AWARDS MEE, MSEE, PhD. Part-time programs available.

Degree requirements: For master's, thesis or alternative; for doctorate, thesis/dissertation.

Entrance requirements: For master's and doctorate, TOEFL.
Expenses: Tuition, state resident: full-time $2,932; part-time $489 per credit. Tuition, nonresident: full-time $5,758; part-time $960 per credit. Part-time tuition and fees vary according to course load, program and reciprocity agreements.
Faculty research: Signal processing, microelectronics, computers, controls, power electronics. *Web site:* http://www.ece.umn.edu/

Find an in-depth description at www.petersons.com/gradchannel.

■ UNIVERSITY OF MISSOURI–COLUMBIA

Graduate School, College of Engineering, Department of Electrical and Computer Engineering, Columbia, MO 65211

AWARDS MS, PhD.

Faculty: 23 full-time (0 women).
Students: 44 full-time (8 women), 30 part-time (4 women); includes 1 minority (African American), 65 international. 45 applicants, 36% accepted. In 2001, 16 master's, 6 doctorates awarded.
Degree requirements: For master's, thesis or alternative; for doctorate, thesis/dissertation.
Entrance requirements: For master's, GRE General Test, TOEFL, minimum GPA of 3.0; for doctorate, GRE General Test, GRE Subject Test, TOEFL, minimum GPA of 3.0. *Application deadline:* For fall admission, 2/15 (priority date). Applications are processed on a rolling basis. *Application fee:* $25 ($50 for international students).
Expenses: Tuition, state resident: part-time $179 per credit hour. Tuition, nonresident: part-time $539 per credit hour. Required fees: $122 per semester. Tuition and fees vary according to program.
Financial support: Research assistantships, teaching assistantships, institutionally sponsored loans available.
Dr. Kenneth Unklesbay, Chair, 573-882-2781, *Fax:* 573-882-0397, *E-mail:* unk@ece.missouri.edu. *Web site:* http://www.engineering.missouri.edu/electrical.htm

Find an in-depth description at www.petersons.com/gradchannel.

■ UNIVERSITY OF MISSOURI–ROLLA

Graduate School, School of Engineering, Department of Electrical and Computer Engineering, Program in Electrical Engineering, Rolla, MO 65409-0910

AWARDS MS, DE, PhD. Part-time and evening/weekend programs available. Terminal

master's awarded for partial completion of doctoral program.

Degree requirements: For master's, thesis or alternative; for doctorate, thesis/dissertation, departmental qualifying exam.
Entrance requirements: For master's and doctorate, GRE General Test, TOEFL. Electronic applications accepted.

■ UNIVERSITY OF NEBRASKA–LINCOLN

Graduate College, College of Engineering and Technology, Department of Electrical Engineering, Lincoln, NE 68588

AWARDS Electrical engineering (MS); engineering (PhD).

Faculty: 25.
Students: 31 (3 women); includes 3 minority (1 African American, 1 Asian American or Pacific Islander, 1 Hispanic American) 13 international. Average age 27. 96 applicants, 11% accepted, 9 enrolled. In 2001, 16 degrees awarded.
Degree requirements: For master's, thesis optional; for doctorate, thesis/dissertation, comprehensive exam.
Entrance requirements: For master's and doctorate, GRE General Test, TOEFL. *Application deadline:* For fall admission, 4/15; for spring admission, 10/15. *Application fee:* $35. Electronic applications accepted.
Expenses: Tuition, state resident: full-time $2,412; part-time $134 per credit. Tuition, nonresident: full-time $6,223; part-time $346 per credit. Tuition and fees vary according to course load.
Financial support: In 2001–02, 34 research assistantships, 5 teaching assistantships were awarded. Fellowships, Federal Work-Study, health care benefits, and unspecified assistantships also available. Support available to part-time students. Financial award application deadline: 2/15.
Faculty research: Electromagnetics, communications, biomedical digital signal processing, electrical breakdown of gases, optical properties of microelectronic materials.
Dr. John Boye, Interim Chair, 402-472-3771, *Fax:* 402-472-4732. *Web site:* http://www.engr.unl.edu/ee/html/

Find an in-depth description at www.petersons.com/gradchannel.

■ UNIVERSITY OF NEVADA, LAS VEGAS

Graduate College, Howard R. Hughes College of Engineering, Department of Electrical and Computer Engineering, Las Vegas, NV 89154-9900

AWARDS MSE, PhD. Part-time programs available.

Faculty: 14 full-time (0 women).

University of Nevada, Las Vegas (continued)

Students: 15 full-time (3 women), 3 part-time; includes 1 minority (Asian American or Pacific Islander), 12 international. 27 applicants, 41% accepted, 11 enrolled. In 2001, 10 master's, 1 doctorate awarded.
Degree requirements: For master's, thesis (for some programs), project, comprehensive exam; for doctorate, thesis/dissertation, comprehensive exam. *Median time to degree:* Doctorate–4 years full-time.
Entrance requirements: For master's, bachelor's degree in electrical engineering or related field, GRE General Test or minimum GPA of 3.0; for doctorate, GRE General Test, minimum GPA of 3.2. *Application deadline:* For fall admission, 6/15; for spring admission, 11/15. Applications are processed on a rolling basis. *Application fee:* $40 ($55 for international students).
Expenses: Tuition, state resident: full-time $1,926; part-time $107 per credit. Tuition, nonresident: full-time $9,376; part-time $220 per credit. Tuition and fees vary according to course load.
Financial support: In 2001–02, 5 research assistantships with full and partial tuition reimbursements (averaging $7,500 per year), 13 teaching assistantships with partial tuition reimbursements (averaging $11,000 per year) were awarded. Tuition waivers (full) also available. Financial award application deadline: 3/1.
Dr. Rama Venket, Chair, 702-895-4184.
Application contact: Graduate College Admissions Evaluator, 702-895-3320, *Fax:* 702-895-4180, *E-mail:* gradcollege@ccmail.nevada.edu. *Web site:* http://www.egr.unlv.edu/

■ UNIVERSITY OF NEVADA, RENO

Graduate School, College of Engineering, Department of Electrical Engineering, Reno, NV 89557

AWARDS MS, PhD.
Faculty: 12.
Students: 27 full-time (4 women), 7 part-time; includes 3 minority (2 Asian Americans or Pacific Islanders, 1 Hispanic American), 18 international. Average age 29. In 2001, 7 degrees awarded. Terminal master's awarded for partial completion of doctoral program.
Degree requirements: For master's, thesis optional; for doctorate, thesis/dissertation.
Entrance requirements: For master's, GRE General Test, TOEFL, minimum GPA of 2.75; for doctorate, GRE General Test, TOEFL, minimum GPA of 3.0. *Application deadline:* For fall admission, 3/1 (priority date). Applications are processed on a rolling basis. *Application fee:* $40.
Expenses: Tuition, state resident: full-time $2,067; part-time $108 per credit. Tuition, nonresident: full-time $9,282; part-time $109 per credit. Required fees: $57 per semester. Tuition and fees vary according to course load.
Financial support: In 2001–02, 1 research assistantship, 7 teaching assistantships were awarded. Fellowships, Federal Work-Study, institutionally sponsored loans, and tuition waivers (full) also available. Financial award application deadline: 3/1.
Dr. John Kleppe, Graduate Program Director, 775-784-6944, *E-mail:* kleppe@ee.unr.edu.

■ UNIVERSITY OF NEW HAMPSHIRE

Graduate School, College of Engineering and Physical Sciences, Department of Electrical and Computer Engineering, Durham, NH 03824

AWARDS Electrical engineering (MS, PhD). Part-time and evening/weekend programs available.

Faculty: 15 full-time.
Students: 20 full-time (6 women), 38 part-time (4 women); includes 5 minority (all Asian Americans or Pacific Islanders), 26 international. Average age 30. 61 applicants, 72% accepted, 17 enrolled. In 2001, 10 degrees awarded.
Degree requirements: For master's, thesis or alternative; for doctorate, thesis/dissertation.
Entrance requirements: For master's, GRE for non-U.S. university bachelor's degree; for doctorate, GRE for non-U.S. universities. *Application deadline:* For fall admission, 4/1 (priority date); for winter admission, 12/1 (priority date). Applications are processed on a rolling basis. *Application fee:* $50. Electronic applications accepted.
Expenses: Tuition, state resident: full-time $6,300; part-time $350 per credit. Tuition, nonresident: full-time $15,720; part-time $643 per credit. Required fees: $560; $280 per term. One-time fee: $15 part-time. Tuition and fees vary according to course load.
Financial support: In 2001–02, 24 research assistantships, 8 teaching assistantships were awarded. Federal Work-Study, scholarships/grants, and tuition waivers (full and partial) also available. Support available to part-time students. Financial award application deadline: 2/15.
Faculty research: Biomedical engineering, communications systems and information theory, digital systems, illumination engineering.
John LaCourse, Chairperson, 603-862-1324, *E-mail:* lacourse@cisunix.unh.edu. *Web site:* http://www.ece.unh.edu/

■ UNIVERSITY OF NEW HAVEN

Graduate School, School of Engineering and Applied Science, Program in Electrical Engineering, West Haven, CT 06516-1916

AWARDS MSEE. Part-time and evening/weekend programs available.

Students: 5 full-time (1 woman), 32 part-time (2 women); includes 2 minority (both Asian Americans or Pacific Islanders), 14 international. In 2001, 11 degrees awarded.
Degree requirements: For master's, thesis or alternative.
Entrance requirements: For master's, bachelor's degree in electrical engineering. *Application deadline:* Applications are processed on a rolling basis. *Application fee:* $50.
Expenses: Tuition: Full-time $12,015; part-time $445 per credit hour. Required fees: $30. One-time fee: $100 full-time.
Financial support: Federal Work-Study available. Support available to part-time students. Financial award application deadline: 5/1; financial award applicants required to submit FAFSA.
Dr. Bijan Karimi, Coordinator, 203-932-7164.

■ UNIVERSITY OF NEW MEXICO

Graduate School, School of Engineering, Department of Electrical and Computer Engineering, Albuquerque, NM 87131-2039

AWARDS Electrical engineering (MS); engineering (PhD); optical sciences (PhD). MEME offered through the Manufacturing Engineering Program. Part-time and evening/weekend programs available.

Faculty: 41 full-time (2 women), 23 part-time/adjunct (3 women).
Students: 121 full-time (28 women), 49 part-time (6 women); includes 26 minority (2 African Americans, 11 Asian Americans or Pacific Islanders, 11 Hispanic Americans, 2 Native Americans), 100 international. Average age 31. In 2001, 34 master's, 6 doctorates awarded.
Degree requirements: For master's, thesis (for some programs); for doctorate, thesis/dissertation.
Entrance requirements: For master's, GRE General Test, minimum GPA of 3.0; for doctorate, GRE General Test, minimum GPA of 3.5. *Application deadline:* For fall admission, 7/30; for spring admission, 11/30. *Application fee:* $40.
Expenses: Tuition, state resident: full-time $2,771; part-time $115 per credit hour. Tuition, nonresident: full-time $11,207; part-time $467 per credit hour. Required fees: $570; $24 per credit hour. Part-time tuition and fees vary according to course load and program.
Financial support: In 2001–02, 68 students received support, including 1 fellowship with full tuition reimbursement available (averaging $9,000 per year), 51 research assistantships with full tuition

reimbursements available (averaging $13,908 per year), 63 teaching assistantships with full tuition reimbursements available (averaging $11,528 per year). Scholarships/grants, health care benefits, and unspecified assistantships also available. Financial award application deadline: 3/1; financial award applicants required to submit FAFSA.
Faculty research: Applied electromagnetics, high performance computing, wireless communications, optoelectronics, control systems. *Total annual research expenditures:* $843,280.
Dr. Christos Christodoulou, Chair, 505-277-2436, *Fax:* 505-277-1439, *E-mail:* christos@eece.unm.edu.
Application contact: Heather N. Shinn, Administrative Assistant I, 505-277-2600, *Fax:* 505-277-1439, *E-mail:* hshinn@unm.edu. *Web site:* http://www.eece.unm.edu/
Find an in-depth description at www.petersons.com/gradchannel.

■ UNIVERSITY OF NEW ORLEANS

Graduate School, College of Engineering, Concentration in Electrical Engineering, New Orleans, LA 70148

AWARDS MS.

Faculty: 2 full-time (1 woman), 2 part-time/adjunct (0 women).
Students: 20 full-time (5 women), 10 part-time (2 women); includes 4 minority (1 African American, 2 Asian Americans or Pacific Islanders, 1 Hispanic American), 16 international. Average age 26. 162 applicants, 43% accepted, 11 enrolled. In 2001, 7 degrees awarded.
Degree requirements: For master's, thesis optional.
Entrance requirements: For master's, GRE General Test, minimum GPA of 3.0. *Application deadline:* For fall admission, 7/1 (priority date); for spring admission, 11/15 (priority date). Applications are processed on a rolling basis. *Application fee:* $20. Electronic applications accepted.
Expenses: Tuition, state resident: full-time $2,748; part-time $435 per credit. Tuition, nonresident: full-time $9,792; part-time $1,773 per credit.
Financial support: Research assistantships, teaching assistantships available. Financial award applicants required to submit FAFSA.
Faculty research: Optics, ellipsometry, power systems, power-harmonics, optimal controls.
Dr. Russell Trahan, Chairman, 504-280-6176, *Fax:* 504-286-3950, *E-mail:* rtrahan@uno.edu.
Application contact: Dr. Xiao-Rong Li, Graduate Coordinator, 504-280-7416, *Fax:* 504-286-3950, *E-mail:* xli@uno.edu.

■ THE UNIVERSITY OF NORTH CAROLINA AT CHARLOTTE

Graduate School, The William States Lee College of Engineering, Department of Electrical and Computer Engineering, Charlotte, NC 28223-0001

AWARDS MSEE, PhD. Part-time and evening/weekend programs available.

Faculty: 12 full-time (0 women), 4 part-time/adjunct (0 women).
Students: 64 full-time (15 women), 50 part-time (8 women); includes 11 minority (9 African Americans, 2 Asian Americans or Pacific Islanders), 63 international. Average age 27. 246 applicants, 65% accepted, 34 enrolled. In 2001, 20 master's, 3 doctorates awarded.
Degree requirements: For master's, thesis or project.
Entrance requirements: For master's, GRE General Test, GPA of 3.0 in undergraduate major, 2.75 overall. *Application deadline:* For fall admission, 7/15; for spring admission, 11/15. Applications are processed on a rolling basis. *Application fee:* $35. Electronic applications accepted.
Expenses: Tuition, state resident: full-time $1,483; part-time $371 per year. Tuition, nonresident: full-time $9,850; part-time $2,463 per year. Required fees: $1,043; $277 per year. Tuition and fees vary according to course load.
Financial support: In 2001–02, 21 research assistantships, 24 teaching assistantships were awarded. Fellowships, career-related internships or fieldwork, Federal Work-Study, institutionally sponsored loans, scholarships/grants, and unspecified assistantships also available. Support available to part-time students. Financial award application deadline: 4/1; financial award applicants required to submit FAFSA.
Faculty research: Integrated circuits self test; control systems; optoelectronics/microelectronics devices and systems; communications; computer engineering.
Dr. Farid M. Tranjan, Chair, 704-687-2302, *Fax:* 704-687-2352, *E-mail:* tranjan@email.uncc.edu.
Application contact: Kathy Barringer, Director of Graduate Admissions, 704-687-3366, *Fax:* 704-687-3279, *E-mail:* gradadm@email.uncc.edu. *Web site:* http://www.uncc.edu/gradmiss/

■ UNIVERSITY OF NORTH DAKOTA

Graduate School, School of Engineering and Mines, Department of Electrical Engineering, Grand Forks, ND 58202

AWARDS M Engr, MS. Part-time programs available.

Faculty: 5 full-time (0 women).

Students: 1 full-time (0 women), 7 part-time. 19 applicants, 95% accepted, 2 enrolled.
Degree requirements: For master's, thesis or alternative, final comprehensive exam.
Entrance requirements: For master's, GRE General Test, TOEFL, minimum GPA of 3.0 (MS), 2.5 (M Engr). *Application deadline:* For fall admission, 3/1 (priority date); for spring admission, 10/15 (priority date). Applications are processed on a rolling basis. *Application fee:* $30.
Expenses: Tuition, state resident: full-time $3,298. Tuition, nonresident: full-time $7,998.
Financial support: In 2001–02, 4 students received support, including 1 research assistantship with full tuition reimbursement available (averaging $9,500 per year), 3 teaching assistantships with full tuition reimbursements available (averaging $9,500 per year); fellowships, Federal Work-Study, institutionally sponsored loans, and tuition waivers (full and partial) also available. Financial award application deadline: 3/15.
Faculty research: Controls and robotics, signal processing, energy conversion, microwaves, computer engineering.
Dr. David L. Heckmann, Chairperson, 701-777-4433, *Fax:* 701-777-4838, *E-mail:* david_heckmann@mail.und.nodak.edu. *Web site:* http://www.und.nodak.edu/dept/sem/electric.eng/

■ UNIVERSITY OF NOTRE DAME

Graduate School, College of Engineering, Department of Electrical Engineering, Notre Dame, IN 46556

AWARDS MS, PhD. Part-time programs available.

Faculty: 24 full-time (0 women), 2 part-time/adjunct (0 women).
Students: 95 full-time (22 women); includes 3 minority (1 Asian American or Pacific Islander, 1 Hispanic American, 1 Native American), 80 international. 294 applicants, 21% accepted, 34 enrolled. In 2001, 20 master's, 3 doctorates awarded. Terminal master's awarded for partial completion of doctoral program.
Degree requirements: For master's, comprehensive exam; for doctorate, thesis/dissertation. *Median time to degree:* Doctorate–5.3 years full-time.
Entrance requirements: For master's and doctorate, GRE General Test, TOEFL. *Application deadline:* For fall admission, 2/1 (priority date); for spring admission, 11/1. Applications are processed on a rolling basis. *Application fee:* $50. Electronic applications accepted.
Expenses: Tuition: Full-time $24,220; part-time $1,346 per credit hour. Required fees: $155.
Financial support: In 2001–02, 94 students received support, including 12 fellowships with full tuition reimbursements available (averaging $18,000 per

University of Notre Dame (continued)
year), 49 research assistantships with full tuition reimbursements available (averaging $13,100 per year), 20 teaching assistantships with full tuition reimbursements available (averaging $13,100 per year). Scholarships/grants and tuition waivers (full) also available. Financial award application deadline: 2/1.
Faculty research: Electronic properties of materials and devices, signal and imaging processing, communication theory, control theory and applications, optoelectronics. *Total annual research expenditures:* $4.2 million.
Dr. Thomas E. Fuja, Director of Graduate Studies, 574-631-4647, *Fax:* 574-631-4393, *E-mail:* e.grad@nd.edu.
Application contact: Dr. Terrence J. Akai, Director of Graduate Admissions, 574-631-7706, *Fax:* 574-631-4183, *E-mail:* gradad@nd.edu. *Web site:* http://www.nd.edu/~ee/

Find an in-depth description at www.petersons.com/gradchannel.

■ **UNIVERSITY OF OKLAHOMA**

Graduate College, College of Engineering, School of Electrical and Computer Engineering, Norman, OK 73019-0390

AWARDS MS, PhD.

Faculty: 14 full-time (1 woman).
Students: 81 full-time (15 women), 42 part-time (9 women); includes 9 minority (2 African Americans, 4 Asian Americans or Pacific Islanders, 1 Hispanic American, 2 Native Americans), 92 international. 90 applicants, 79% accepted, 25 enrolled. In 2001, 19 master's, 4 doctorates awarded. Terminal master's awarded for partial completion of doctoral program.
Degree requirements: For master's, thesis, oral exam; for doctorate, thesis/dissertation, general exam, oral exam, qualifying exam.
Entrance requirements: For master's and doctorate, GRE General Test, TOEFL. *Application deadline:* For fall admission, 4/1 (priority date); for spring admission, 9/1 (priority date). Applications are processed on a rolling basis. *Application fee:* $25 ($50 for international students).
Expenses: Tuition, state resident: full-time $2,208; part-time $92 per credit hour. Tuition, nonresident: part-time $297 per credit hour. Tuition and fees vary according to course level, course load and program.
Financial support: In 2001–02, 31 research assistantships with partial tuition reimbursements (averaging $9,371 per year), 22 teaching assistantships with partial tuition reimbursements (averaging $9,345 per year) were awarded. Fellowships, career-related internships or fieldwork, Federal Work-Study, scholarships/grants, and unspecified assistantships also available. Financial

award application deadline: 4/15; financial award applicants required to submit FAFSA.
Faculty research: Signal and image processing, bioengineering, electric energy, telecommunication and systems, solid state laser services and systems. *Total annual research expenditures:* $1.8 million.
Gerald E. Crain, Director, 405-325-4721, *Fax:* 405-325-7066, *E-mail:* crain@ou.edu.
Application contact: Sam Lee, Graduate Program Assistant, 405-325-4285, *Fax:* 405-325-7066, *E-mail:* samlee@ou.edu.

■ **UNIVERSITY OF PENNSYLVANIA**

School of Engineering and Applied Science, Department of Electrical Engineering, Philadelphia, PA 19104

AWARDS MSE, PhD. Part-time programs available.

Faculty: 32 full-time, 23 part-time/adjunct.
Students: 5. 235 applicants, 14% accepted. In 2001, 4 master's, 3 doctorates awarded. Terminal master's awarded for partial completion of doctoral program.
Degree requirements: For master's, thesis optional; for doctorate, thesis/dissertation, comprehensive exam.
Entrance requirements: For master's and doctorate, TOEFL, GRE General Test. *Application deadline:* For fall admission, 12/15; for spring admission, 11/15. Applications are processed on a rolling basis. *Application fee:* $65. Electronic applications accepted.
Financial support: In 2001–02, 6 fellowships with full tuition reimbursements (averaging $20,000 per year), 10 research assistantships with full tuition reimbursements (averaging $20,000 per year), teaching assistantships with full tuition reimbursements (averaging $20,000 per year) were awarded. Institutionally sponsored loans also available. Financial award application deadline: 1/2.
Faculty research: Electro-optics, microwave and millimeter-wave optics, solid-state and chemical electronics, electromagnetic propagation, telecommunications.
Dr. George E. Pappas, Graduate Group Chair, 215-898-9780, *Fax:* 215-573-2068, *E-mail:* pappas@ee.upenn.edu.
Application contact: Shelley Brown, Assistant to Graduate Group Chair, 215-898-9390, *Fax:* 215-573-2068, *E-mail:* shelley@seas.upenn.edu. *Web site:* http://www.seas.upenn.edu/es

Find an in-depth description at www.petersons.com/gradchannel.

■ **UNIVERSITY OF PITTSBURGH**

School of Engineering, Department of Electrical Engineering, Pittsburgh, PA 15260

AWARDS MSEE, PhD. Part-time and evening/weekend programs available.

Faculty: 19 full-time (0 women), 4 part-time/adjunct (0 women).
Students: 66 full-time (15 women), 51 part-time (2 women); includes 11 minority (4 African Americans, 7 Asian Americans or Pacific Islanders), 50 international. 341 applicants, 54% accepted, 35 enrolled. In 2001, 26 master's, 11 doctorates awarded. Terminal master's awarded for partial completion of doctoral program.
Degree requirements: For master's, thesis optional; for doctorate, thesis/dissertation, final oral exams, comprehensive exam.
Entrance requirements: For master's and doctorate, GRE General Test, TOEFL, minimum QPA of 3.0. *Application deadline:* For fall admission, 8/1 (priority date); for spring admission, 12/1 (priority date). Applications are processed on a rolling basis. *Application fee:* $40.
Financial support: In 2001–02, 47 students received support, including 1 fellowship with full tuition reimbursement available (averaging $18,000 per year), 29 research assistantships with full tuition reimbursements available (averaging $17,676 per year), 17 teaching assistantships with full tuition reimbursements available (averaging $18,180 per year). Scholarships/grants and tuition waivers (full and partial) also available. Financial award application deadline: 2/15.
Faculty research: Computer engineering, image processing, signal processing, electro-optic devices, controls/power. *Total annual research expenditures:* $3.2 million.
Dr. Joel Falk, Chairman, 412-624-8000, *Fax:* 412-624-8003, *E-mail:* falk@pitt.edu.
Application contact: John Boston, Graduate Coordinator, 412-624-3244, *Fax:* 412-624-8003, *E-mail:* bbn@pitt.edu. *Web site:* http://www.ee.pitt.edu/~eewww/

Find an in-depth description at www.petersons.com/gradchannel.

■ **UNIVERSITY OF PUERTO RICO, MAYAGÜEZ CAMPUS**

Graduate Studies, College of Engineering, Department of Electrical Engineering, Mayagüez, PR 00681-9000

AWARDS Computer engineering (M Co E, MS); electrical engineering (MEE, MS). Part-time programs available.

Degree requirements: For master's, thesis, comprehensive exam.
Entrance requirements: For master's, minimum GPA of 2.5, proficiency in English and Spanish.
Faculty research: Microcomputer interfacing, control systems, power systems, electronics.

■ UNIVERSITY OF RHODE ISLAND

Graduate School, College of Engineering, Department of Electrical and Computer Engineering, Kingston, RI 02881

AWARDS MS, PhD. Part-time programs available.

Students: In 2001, 21 master's, 4 doctorates awarded.
Degree requirements: For master's, thesis or alternative; for doctorate, thesis/dissertation, comprehensive exam.
Entrance requirements: For master's and doctorate, GRE General Test, TOEFL. *Application deadline:* For fall admission, 4/15. Applications are processed on a rolling basis. *Application fee:* $25.
Expenses: Tuition, state resident: full-time $3,756; part-time $209 per credit. Tuition, nonresident: full-time $10,774; part-time $599 per credit. Required fees: $1,586; $76 per credit. $76 per credit. One-time fee: $60 full-time.
Financial support: In 2001–02, 33 students received support.
Faculty research: Digital signal processing, computer engineering, VLSI, fiber optics and materials, communication and control systems, biomedical engineering. Dr. Richard Vaccaro, Chairman, 401-874-2505.
Application contact: Director of Graduate Studies, 401-874-2506.

■ UNIVERSITY OF ROCHESTER

The College, School of Engineering and Applied Sciences, Department of Electrical and Computer Engineering, Rochester, NY 14627-0250

AWARDS MS, PhD.

Faculty: 16.
Students: 64 full-time (10 women), 7 part-time; includes 5 minority (2 African Americans, 3 Asian Americans or Pacific Islanders), 48 international. 298 applicants, 7% accepted, 19 enrolled. In 2001, 13 master's, 7 doctorates awarded. Terminal master's awarded for partial completion of doctoral program.
Degree requirements: For master's, comprehensive exam; for doctorate, thesis/dissertation, preliminary and oral exams.
Entrance requirements: For master's and doctorate, GRE, TOEFL. *Application deadline:* For fall admission, 2/1. *Application fee:* $25.
Expenses: Tuition: Part-time $755 per credit hour.
Financial support: Fellowships, research assistantships, teaching assistantships, tuition waivers (full and partial) available. Financial award application deadline: 2/1. Philippe Fauchet, Chair, 585-275-4054.

Application contact: Yana Shikhman, Graduate Program Secretary, 585-275-4054.

Find an in-depth description at www.petersons.com/gradchannel.

■ UNIVERSITY OF SOUTH ALABAMA

Graduate School, College of Engineering, Department of Computer and Electrical Engineering, Mobile, AL 36688-0002

AWARDS MSEE. Part-time programs available.

Faculty: 9 full-time (0 women).
Students: 34 full-time (5 women), 12 part-time, 42 international. 88 applicants, 59% accepted. In 2001, 8 degrees awarded.
Degree requirements: For master's, project or thesis.
Entrance requirements: For master's, GRE General Test, BS in engineering, minimum GPA of 3.0. *Application deadline:* For fall admission, 9/1 (priority date). Applications are processed on a rolling basis. *Application fee:* $25.
Expenses: Tuition, state resident: full-time $3,048. Tuition, nonresident: full-time $6,096. Required fees: $320.
Financial support: In 2001–02, 1 research assistantship was awarded; career-related internships or fieldwork and institutionally sponsored loans also available. Support available to part-time students. Financial award application deadline: 4/1. Dr. Mohammed Alam, Chair, 334-460-6117.

■ UNIVERSITY OF SOUTH CAROLINA

The Graduate School, College of Engineering and Information Technology, Department of Electrical Engineering, Columbia, SC 29208

AWARDS ME, MS, PhD. Part-time and evening/weekend programs available. Postbaccalaureate distance learning degree programs offered.

Faculty: 17 full-time (0 women), 1 (woman) part-time/adjunct.
Students: 67 full-time (16 women), 18 part-time; includes 71 minority (3 African Americans, 68 Asian Americans or Pacific Islanders). Average age 30. 139 applicants, 80% accepted. In 2001, 8 master's, 7 doctorates awarded.
Degree requirements: For master's, thesis (for some programs); for doctorate, thesis/dissertation.
Entrance requirements: For master's and doctorate, GRE General Test, TOEFL. *Application deadline:* For fall admission, 3/1 (priority date); for spring admission, 11/1. Applications are processed on a rolling basis. *Application fee:* $40. Electronic applications accepted.

Expenses: Tuition, state resident: full-time $4,434. Tuition, nonresident: full-time $9,854. Tuition and fees vary according to program.
Financial support: In 2001–02, research assistantships with partial tuition reimbursements (averaging $16,000 per year), teaching assistantships with partial tuition reimbursements (averaging $16,000 per year) were awarded. Fellowships, career-related internships or fieldwork also available.
Faculty research: Machine intelligence and robotics, VLSI design, computer design, high-voltage and pulsed-power electronics, electromagnetic field theory. *Total annual research expenditures:* $7.8 million.
Dr. Asif Khan, Chair, 803-777-5174, *Fax:* 803-777-8045, *E-mail:* asif@engr.sc.edu.
Application contact: Kathey Lorick, Administrative Assistant, 803-777-7362, *Fax:* 803-777-8045, *E-mail:* klorick@ engr.sc.edu. *Web site:* http:// www.ece.sc.edu/

■ UNIVERSITY OF SOUTHERN CALIFORNIA

Graduate School, School of Engineering, Department of Electrical Engineering, Program in Electrical Engineering, Los Angeles, CA 90089

AWARDS MS, PhD, Engr.

Degree requirements: For master's, thesis optional; for doctorate, thesis/dissertation.
Entrance requirements: For master's, doctorate, and Engr, GRE General Test.
Expenses: Tuition: Full-time $25,060; part-time $844 per unit. Required fees: $473.

Find an in-depth description at www.petersons.com/gradchannel.

■ UNIVERSITY OF SOUTH FLORIDA

College of Graduate Studies, College of Engineering, Department of Electrical Engineering, Tampa, FL 33620-9951

AWARDS ME, MSEE, PhD. Part-time programs available.

Faculty: 16 full-time (0 women), 1 part-time/adjunct (0 women).
Students: 155 full-time (38 women), 73 part-time (10 women); includes 28 minority (6 African Americans, 16 Asian Americans or Pacific Islanders, 6 Hispanic Americans), 150 international. Average age 31. 442 applicants, 54% accepted, 76 enrolled. In 2001, 40 master's, 2 doctorates awarded. Terminal master's awarded for partial completion of doctoral program.
Degree requirements: For master's, thesis or alternative; for doctorate, thesis/dissertation, 2 tools of research as specified by dissertation committee.

University of South Florida (continued)
Entrance requirements: For master's, GRE General Test, minimum GPA of 3.0 during previous 2 years; for doctorate, GRE General Test. *Application deadline:* For fall admission, 6/1; for spring admission, 10/15. *Application fee:* $20. Electronic applications accepted.
Expenses: Tuition, state resident: part-time $166 per credit hour. Tuition, nonresident: part-time $573 per credit hour. Required fees: $17 per term.
Financial support: Fellowships with full tuition reimbursements, research assistantships with full tuition reimbursements, teaching assistantships with full tuition reimbursements, career-related internships or fieldwork, Federal Work-Study, institutionally sponsored loans, and tuition waivers (partial) available. Support available to part-time students. Financial award applicants required to submit FAFSA.
Faculty research: Controls, including system parameter identification; design and modeling; microwave and hybrid circuits. *Total annual research expenditures:* $1.2 million.
Dr. E. K. Stefanakos, Chairperson, 813-974-2369, *Fax:* 813-974-5250, *E-mail:* stefanak@eng.usf.edu.
Application contact: Dr. Kenneth A. Buckle, Graduate Coordinator, 813-974-4772, *Fax:* 813-974-5250, *E-mail:* buckle@eng.usf.edu. *Web site:* http://www.eng.usf.edu
Find an in-depth description at www.petersons.com/gradchannel.

■ **THE UNIVERSITY OF TENNESSEE**

Graduate School, College of Engineering, Department of Electrical Engineering, Knoxville, TN 37996

AWARDS MS, PhD. Part-time programs available.

Faculty: 26 full-time (0 women), 4 part-time/adjunct (0 women).
Students: 58 full-time (8 women), 27 part-time (6 women); includes 2 minority (1 African American, 1 Asian American or Pacific Islander), 51 international. Average age 33. 210 applicants, 62% accepted. In 2001, 10 master's, 3 doctorates awarded.
Degree requirements: For master's, thesis or alternative; for doctorate, thesis/dissertation.
Entrance requirements: For master's, TOEFL, minimum GPA of 2.7; for doctorate, GRE General Test, TOEFL, minimum GPA of 2.7. *Application deadline:* For fall admission, 2/1 (priority date). Applications are processed on a rolling basis. *Application fee:* $35. Electronic applications accepted.
Expenses: Tuition, state resident: full-time $4,280; part-time $233 per hour. Tuition, nonresident: full-time $12,066; part-time $666 per hour. Tuition and fees vary according to program.

Financial support: In 2001–02, 2 fellowships, 29 research assistantships, 10 teaching assistantships were awarded. Career-related internships or fieldwork, Federal Work-Study, institutionally sponsored loans, and unspecified assistantships also available. Financial award application deadline: 2/1; financial award applicants required to submit FAFSA.
Dr. W. T. Snyder, Head, 865-974-3461, *Fax:* 865-974-5483.

■ **THE UNIVERSITY OF TENNESSEE SPACE INSTITUTE**

Graduate Programs, Program in Electrical Engineering, Tullahoma, TN 37388-9700

AWARDS MS, PhD.

Faculty: 4 full-time (0 women), 1 part-time/adjunct (0 women).
Students: 4 full-time (1 woman), 2 part-time, 4 international. 5 applicants, 80% accepted, 1 enrolled. In 2001, 2 degrees awarded.
Degree requirements: For master's, thesis (for some programs); for doctorate, one foreign language, thesis/dissertation. *Application deadline:* Applications are processed on a rolling basis. *Application fee:* $35.
Expenses: Tuition, state resident: full-time $4,730; part-time $208 per semester hour. Tuition, nonresident: full-time $15,028; part-time $627 per semester hour. Required fees: $10 per semester hour. One-time fee: $35.
Financial support: Fellowships, research assistantships, career-related internships or fieldwork, Federal Work-Study, and tuition waivers (full and partial) available. Financial award applicants required to submit FAFSA.
Dr. Roy Joseph, Degree Program Chairman, 931-393-7457, *Fax:* 931-454-2271, *E-mail:* rjoseph@utsi.edu.
Application contact: Dr. Alfonso Pujol, Assistant Vice President and Dean for Student Affairs, 931-393-7432, *Fax:* 931-393-7346, *E-mail:* apujol@utsi.edu.

■ **THE UNIVERSITY OF TEXAS AT ARLINGTON**

Graduate School, College of Engineering, Department of Electrical Engineering, Arlington, TX 76019

AWARDS M Engr, MS, PhD. Part-time and evening/weekend programs available. Postbaccalaureate distance learning degree programs offered (no on-campus study).

Faculty: 22 full-time (0 women), 3 part-time/adjunct (1 woman).
Students: 363 full-time (65 women), 110 part-time (17 women); includes 41 minority (1 African American, 36 Asian Americans or Pacific Islanders, 3 Hispanic Americans, 1 Native American), 392 international. 770 applicants, 86% accepted, 159 enrolled. In 2001, 70

master's, 7 doctorates awarded. Terminal master's awarded for partial completion of doctoral program.
Degree requirements: For master's, thesis optional; for doctorate, thesis/dissertation, research potential assessment, comprehensive exam.
Entrance requirements: For master's, GRE General Test, TOEFL, minimum GPA of 3.0; for doctorate, GRE General Test, TOEFL, minimum GPA of 3.5. *Application deadline:* For fall admission, 6/16. Applications are processed on a rolling basis. *Application fee:* $25 ($50 for international students).
Expenses: Tuition, area resident: Full-time $2,268. Tuition, nonresident: full-time $6,264. Required fees: $839. Tuition and fees vary according to course load.
Financial support: In 2001–02, 22 fellowships (averaging $1,000 per year), 74 research assistantships (averaging $10,400 per year), 1 teaching assistantship (averaging $9,600 per year) were awarded. Federal Work-Study, institutionally sponsored loans, scholarships/grants, and unspecified assistantships also available. Financial award application deadline: 6/1; financial award applicants required to submit FAFSA.
Dr. Raymond Shoults, Chair, 817-272-2672, *Fax:* 817-272-2253, *E-mail:* shoults@uta.edu.
Application contact: Dr. Adrian Fung, Graduate Adviser, 817-272-2671, *Fax:* 817-272-2253, *E-mail:* eefung@uta.edu.
Find an in-depth description at www.petersons.com/gradchannel.

■ **THE UNIVERSITY OF TEXAS AT AUSTIN**

Graduate School, College of Engineering, Department of Electrical and Computer Engineering, Austin, TX 78712-1111

AWARDS MSE, PhD. Part-time programs available.

Faculty: 65 full-time (5 women), 12 part-time/adjunct (1 woman).
Students: 396 full-time (59 women), 169 part-time (16 women); includes 63 minority (5 African Americans, 42 Asian Americans or Pacific Islanders, 15 Hispanic Americans, 1 Native American), 336 international.
Entrance requirements: For master's, GRE General Test, minimum GPA of 3.3 in upper-division course work; for doctorate, GRE General Test. *Application deadline:* For fall admission, 1/2. Applications are processed on a rolling basis. *Application fee:* $50 ($75 for international students). Electronic applications accepted.
Expenses: Tuition, state resident: full-time $3,159. Tuition, nonresident: full-time $6,957. Tuition and fees vary according to program.

Financial support: Fellowships, research assistantships, teaching assistantships available. Financial award application deadline: 1/2.

Application contact: Dr. Anthony P. Ambler, Chairman, 512-475-6153, *Fax:* 512-471-5532, *E-mail:* ambler@ ece.utexas.edu. *Web site:* http:// www.ece.utexas.edu/

Find an in-depth description at www.petersons.com/gradchannel.

■ **THE UNIVERSITY OF TEXAS AT DALLAS**

Erik Jonsson School of Engineering and Computer Science, Programs in Electrical Engineering, Richardson, TX 75083-0688

AWARDS Electrical engineering (MSEE, PhD); microelectronics (MSEE); telecommunications (MSEE, MSTE). Part-time and evening/ weekend programs available.

Faculty: 26 full-time (1 woman), 5 part-time/adjunct (1 woman).
Students: 195 full-time (38 women), 126 part-time (18 women); includes 52 minority (6 African Americans, 38 Asian Americans or Pacific Islanders, 8 Hispanic Americans), 212 international. Average age 28. 950 applicants, 29% accepted. In 2001, 68 master's, 7 doctorates awarded.
Degree requirements: For master's, thesis or major design project; for doctorate, thesis/dissertation.
Entrance requirements: For master's, GRE General Test, TOEFL, minimum GPA of 3.0 in related bachelor's degree; for doctorate, GRE General Test, TOEFL, minimum GPA of 3.5. *Application deadline:* For fall admission, 7/15; for spring admission, 11/15. Applications are processed on a rolling basis. *Application fee:* $25 ($75 for international students). Electronic applications accepted.
Expenses: Tuition, state resident: full-time $1,440; part-time $84 per credit. Tuition, nonresident: full-time $5,310; part-time $295 per credit. Required fees: $1,835; $87 per credit. $138 per term.
Financial support: In 2001–02, 4 fellowships (averaging $3,000 per year), 40 research assistantships with full tuition reimbursements (averaging $5,288 per year), 35 teaching assistantships with full tuition reimbursements (averaging $5,256 per year) were awarded. Federal Work-Study, institutionally sponsored loans, and scholarships/grants also available. Support available to part-time students. Financial award application deadline: 4/30; financial award applicants required to submit FAFSA.
Faculty research: Communications and signal processing, solid-state devices and circuits, digital systems, optical devices, materials and systems, lasers and photonics.

Dr. Gerry Burnham, Head, 972-883-6755, *Fax:* 972-883-2710, *E-mail:* burnham@ utdallas.edu.
Application contact: Kathy Gribble, Secretary, 972-883-2649, *Fax:* 972-883-2710, *E-mail:* ee-grad-info@utdallas.edu. *Web site:* http://www.utdallas.edu/dept/ee/

■ **THE UNIVERSITY OF TEXAS AT EL PASO**

Graduate School, College of Engineering, Department of Electrical and Computer Engineering, El Paso, TX 79968-0001

AWARDS Computer engineering (MS, PhD); computer science (PhD); electrical engineering (MS, PhD). Part-time and evening/ weekend programs available.

Students: 94 (23 women); includes 22 minority (1 African American, 1 Asian American or Pacific Islander, 20 Hispanic Americans) 20 international. Average age 34. 17 applicants, 100% accepted. In 2001, 24 master's, 1 doctorate awarded.
Degree requirements: For master's, thesis optional; for doctorate, thesis/dissertation.
Entrance requirements: For master's, GRE General Test, TOEFL, minimum GPA of 3.0; for doctorate, GRE General Test, TOEFL, qualifying exam, minimum graduate GPA of 3.0. *Application deadline:* For fall admission, 7/1 (priority date); for spring admission, 11/1 (priority date). Applications are processed on a rolling basis. *Application fee:* $15 ($65 for international students). Electronic applications accepted.
Expenses: Tuition, state resident: full-time $2,450. Tuition, nonresident: full-time $6,000.
Financial support: In 2001–02, 60 students received support, including research assistantships with partial tuition reimbursements available (averaging $22,375 per year), teaching assistantships with partial tuition reimbursements available (averaging $17,900 per year); fellowships with partial tuition reimbursements available, Federal Work-Study, institutionally sponsored loans, scholarships/grants, and tuition waivers (partial) also available. Financial award application deadline: 3/15; financial award applicants required to submit FAFSA.
Faculty research: Signal and image processing, computer architecture, fiber optics, computational electromagnetics, electronic displays and thin films.
Dr. Mehdi Shadaram, Chairperson, 915-747-5470, *Fax:* 915-747-7871, *E-mail:* shadaram@miners.utep.edu.
Application contact: Dr. Charles H. Ambler, Dean of the Graduate School, 915-747-5491 Ext. 7886, *Fax:* 915-747-5788, *E-mail:* cambler@miners.utep.edu.

■ **THE UNIVERSITY OF TEXAS AT SAN ANTONIO**

College of Engineering, Department of Electrical and Computer Engineering, San Antonio, TX 78249-0617

AWARDS Electrical engineering (MSEE). Part-time and evening/weekend programs available.

Faculty: 9 full-time (1 woman).
Students: 32 full-time (5 women), 25 part-time (1 woman); includes 10 minority (1 African American, 3 Asian Americans or Pacific Islanders, 6 Hispanic Americans), 35 international. Average age 28. 57 applicants, 91% accepted, 26 enrolled. In 2001, 11 degrees awarded.
Degree requirements: For master's, thesis optional.
Entrance requirements: For master's, GRE General Test, minimum GPA of 3.0 in last 60 hours of undergraduate degree. *Application deadline:* For fall admission, 7/1; for spring admission, 12/1.
Expenses: Tuition, state resident: full-time $2,268; part-time $126 per credit hour. Tuition, nonresident: full-time $6,066; part-time $337 per credit hour. Required fees: $781. Tuition and fees vary according to course load.
Financial support: Research assistantships, teaching assistantships, career-related internships or fieldwork and institutionally sponsored loans available. Support available to part-time students. Financial award application deadline: 3/31. *Total annual research expenditures:* $42,903.
Dr. Parimal Patel, Chair, 210-458-5568.

■ **UNIVERSITY OF TOLEDO**

Graduate School, College of Engineering, Department of Electrical Engineering and Computer Science, Toledo, OH 43606-3398

AWARDS Computer science (MS); electrical engineering (MS); engineering sciences (PhD). Part-time and evening/weekend programs available.

Faculty: 22 full-time (2 women).
Students: 53 full-time (5 women), 149 part-time (23 women); includes 2 minority (both African Americans), 183 international. Average age 25. 945 applicants, 22% accepted. In 2001, 71 master's, 1 doctorate awarded.
Degree requirements: For master's, thesis or alternative; for doctorate, thesis/dissertation.
Entrance requirements: For master's, GRE General Test, TOEFL, minimum GPA of 2.7; for doctorate, GRE General Test, TOEFL. *Application deadline:* For fall admission, 5/31 (priority date). Applications are processed on a rolling basis. *Application fee:* $30. Electronic applications accepted.
Expenses: Tuition, state resident: full-time $7,278; part-time $303 per hour. Tuition,

University of Toledo (continued)
nonresident: full-time $15,731; part-time $699 per hour. Required fees: $43 per hour.

Financial support: In 2001–02, 182 students received support, including 19 research assistantships with full tuition reimbursements available, 28 teaching assistantships with full tuition reimbursements available; fellowships with full tuition reimbursements available, Federal Work-Study, scholarships/grants, and tuition waivers (full) also available. Support available to part-time students. Financial award application deadline: 4/1.

Faculty research: Power electronics, digital television, satellite communications, computer networks, fault-tolerant computing, weather and intelligent transportation. *Total annual research expenditures:* $8,495. Dr. Demetrios Kazakos, Interim Chairman, 419-530-8140.

Application contact: Ezzatollah Salari, Director of Graduate Program, 419-530-8148, *Fax:* 419-530-8146, *E-mail:* esalari@uoft2.utoledo.edu. *Web site:* http://www.eecs.utoledo.edu/

Find an in-depth description at www.petersons.com/gradchannel.

■ **UNIVERSITY OF TULSA**

Graduate School, College of Business Administration and College of Engineering and Natural Sciences, Department of Engineering and Technology Management, Tulsa, OK 74104-3189

AWARDS Chemical engineering (METM); computer science (METM); electrical engineering (METM); geological science (METM); mathematics (METM); mechanical engineering (METM); petroleum engineering (METM). Part-time and evening/weekend programs available.

Students: 2 full-time (1 woman), 1 part-time, 2 international. Average age 26. 3 applicants, 100% accepted, 1 enrolled. In 2001, 2 degrees awarded.

Entrance requirements: For master's, GRE General Test, TOEFL. *Application deadline:* Applications are processed on a rolling basis. *Application fee:* $30. Electronic applications accepted.

Expenses: Tuition: Full-time $9,540; part-time $530 per credit hour. Required fees: $80. One-time fee: $230 full-time.

Financial support: Fellowships, research assistantships, teaching assistantships, Federal Work-Study, scholarships/grants, tuition waivers (partial), and unspecified assistantships available. Support available to part-time students. Financial award application deadline: 2/1; financial award applicants required to submit FAFSA.

Application contact: Information Contact, *E-mail:* graduate-business@utulsa.edu. *Web site:* http://www.cba.utulsa.edu/academic.asp#graduate_studies/

■ **UNIVERSITY OF TULSA**

Graduate School, College of Engineering and Natural Sciences, Department of Electrical Engineering, Tulsa, OK 74104-3189

AWARDS ME, MSE. Part-time programs available.

Faculty: 7 full-time (0 women).
Students: 30 full-time (3 women), 4 part-time (1 woman), (all international). Average age 26. 64 applicants, 88% accepted, 18 enrolled. In 2001, 2 degrees awarded.
Degree requirements: For master's, thesis (for some programs), design report (ME), thesis (MS), comprehensive exam (for some programs).
Entrance requirements: For master's, GRE General Test, TOEFL. *Application deadline:* Applications are processed on a rolling basis. *Application fee:* $30. Electronic applications accepted.
Expenses: Tuition: Full-time $9,540; part-time $530 per credit hour. Required fees: $80. One-time fee: $230 full-time.
Financial support: In 2001–02, 8 research assistantships with full and partial tuition reimbursements (averaging $8,100 per year), 4 teaching assistantships with full and partial tuition reimbursements (averaging $7,200 per year) were awarded. Fellowships, career-related internships or fieldwork, Federal Work-Study, scholarships/grants, tuition waivers (partial), and unspecified assistantships also available. Support available to part-time students. Financial award application deadline: 2/1; financial award applicants required to submit FAFSA.
Faculty research: Simulation, linear and digital electronics, VLSI microprocessors, radar scattering, computer-aided design. *Total annual research expenditures:* $215,742. Dr. Gerald R. Kane, Chairperson, 918-631-3270.
Application contact: Dr. Heng-Ming Tai, Adviser, 918-631-3271, *Fax:* 918-631-3344, *E-mail:* grad@utulsa.edu. *Web site:* http://www.ee.utulsa.edu/

■ **UNIVERSITY OF UTAH**

Graduate School, College of Engineering, Department of Electrical Engineering, Salt Lake City, UT 84112-1107

AWARDS M Phil, ME, MS, PhD, EE. Part-time programs available.

Faculty: 13 full-time (3 women), 1 part-time/adjunct (0 women).
Students: 67 full-time (11 women), 33 part-time (10 women); includes 43 minority (1 African American, 39 Asian Americans or Pacific Islanders, 2 Hispanic Americans, 1 Native American), 30 international. Average age 27. 341 applicants, 41% accepted. In 2001, 10 master's, 2 doctorates awarded. Terminal master's awarded for partial completion of doctoral program.

Degree requirements: For master's, thesis (for some programs), comprehensive exam (MS); for doctorate, thesis/dissertation, comprehensive exam.
Entrance requirements: For master's and doctorate, GRE, TOEFL, minimum GPA of 3.0. *Application deadline:* For fall admission, 2/1. *Application fee:* $40 ($60 for international students).
Expenses: Tuition, state resident: part-time $320 per semester hour. Tuition, nonresident: part-time $1,135 per semester hour. Required fees: $143 per semester hour. Tuition and fees vary according to course load, degree level and program.
Financial support: Fellowships, research assistantships, teaching assistantships, Federal Work-Study and institutionally sponsored loans available. Financial award application deadline: 2/1; financial award applicants required to submit FAFSA.
Faculty research: Semiconductors, VLSI design, control systems, electromagnetics and applied optics, communication theory and digital signal processing.
Dr. John V. Mathews, Chair, 801-581-6941, *Fax:* 801-581-5281, *E-mail:* mathews@ee.utah.edu.
Application contact: Dr. Marian Swenson, Advisor, 801-581-8590, *Fax:* 801-581-5281, *E-mail:* swenson@ee.utah.edu. *Web site:* http://www.coe.utah.edu/

■ **UNIVERSITY OF VERMONT**

Graduate College, College of Engineering and Mathematics, Department of Computer Science and Electrical Engineering, Program in Electrical Engineering, Burlington, VT 05405

AWARDS MS, PhD.

Degree requirements: For master's, thesis or alternative; for doctorate, one foreign language, thesis/dissertation.
Entrance requirements: For master's and doctorate, TOEFL.
Expenses: Tuition, state resident: part-time $335 per credit. Tuition, nonresident: part-time $838 per credit.

Find an in-depth description at www.petersons.com/gradchannel.

■ **UNIVERSITY OF VIRGINIA**

School of Engineering and Applied Science, Department of Electrical and Computer Engineering, Charlottesville, VA 22903

AWARDS ME, MS, PhD. Postbaccalaureate distance learning degree programs offered (no on-campus study).

Faculty: 23 full-time (3 women), 2 part-time/adjunct (0 women).
Students: 104 full-time (18 women), 9 part-time (1 woman); includes 5 minority (1 African American, 3 Asian Americans or Pacific Islanders, 1 Hispanic American), 73 international. Average age 27. 407

applicants, 11% accepted, 29 enrolled. In 2001, 8 master's, 3 doctorates awarded. **Degree requirements:** For master's, thesis (MS); for doctorate, thesis/dissertation, comprehensive exam. **Entrance requirements:** For master's and doctorate, GRE General Test. *Application deadline:* For fall admission, 8/1; for spring admission, 12/1. *Application fee:* $40. Electronic applications accepted. **Expenses:** Tuition, state resident: full-time $3,988. Tuition, nonresident: full-time $17,078. Required fees: $1,190. **Financial support:** Fellowships available. Financial award application deadline: 2/1; financial award applicants required to submit FAFSA. James H. Aylor, Chairman, 434-924-6100, *Fax:* 434-924-8818. **Application contact:** Kathryn Thornton, Assistant Dean, 434-924-3897, *Fax:* 434-982-2214, *E-mail:* inquiry@cs.virginia.edu. *Web site:* http://www.ee.virginia.edu/

Find an in-depth description at www.petersons.com/gradchannel.

■ **UNIVERSITY OF WASHINGTON**

Graduate School, College of Engineering, Department of Electrical Engineering, Seattle, WA 98195

AWARDS MSEE, PhD.

Faculty: 39 full-time (3 women), 13 part-time/adjunct (1 woman). **Students:** 282 (52 women); includes 37 minority (1 African American, 30 Asian Americans or Pacific Islanders, 3 Hispanic Americans, 3 Native Americans) 140 international. 358 applicants, 48% accepted, 70 enrolled. In 2001, 53 master's, 26 doctorates awarded. **Degree requirements:** For master's, thesis optional; for doctorate, thesis/dissertation. **Entrance requirements:** For master's, GRE General Test, TOEFL, minimum GPA of 3.0; for doctorate, GRE General Test, TOEFL, MS, minimum GPA of 3.0. *Application deadline:* For fall admission, 1/15. *Application fee:* $45. **Expenses:** Tuition, state resident: full-time $5,539. Tuition, nonresident: full-time $14,376. Required fees: $390. Tuition and fees vary according to course load and program. **Financial support:** Fellowships, research assistantships, teaching assistantships, career-related internships or fieldwork, Federal Work-Study, and institutionally sponsored loans available. Financial award application deadline: 2/1. **Faculty research:** Controls and robotics, communications and signal processing, electromagnetics, optics and acoustics, electronic devices and photonics. Dr. Howard J. Chizeck, Chair, 206-543-6515, *Fax:* 206-543-3842, *E-mail:* chizeck@ee.washington.edu. **Application contact:** Prof. Bruce Darling, Graduate Coordinator, 206-543-4703,

E-mail: darling@ee.washington.edu. *Web site:* http://www.ee.washington.edu/

Find an in-depth description at www.petersons.com/gradchannel.

■ **UNIVERSITY OF WISCONSIN–MADISON**

Graduate School, College of Engineering, Department of Electrical and Computer Engineering, Madison, WI 53706-1380

AWARDS Electrical engineering (MS, PhD). Part-time programs available. Postbaccalaureate distance learning degree programs offered (minimal on-campus study).

Faculty: 40 full-time (2 women). **Students:** 249 full-time (23 women), 43 part-time (4 women); includes 14 minority (3 African Americans, 9 Asian Americans or Pacific Islanders, 2 Hispanic Americans), 199 international. Average age 27. 752 applicants, 58% accepted. In 2001, 48 master's, 11 doctorates awarded. Terminal master's awarded for partial completion of doctoral program. **Degree requirements:** For master's, thesis or alternative; for doctorate, thesis/dissertation, exam. **Entrance requirements:** For master's and doctorate, GRE General Test, TOEFL. *Application deadline:* For fall admission, 3/1; for spring admission, 9/30. Applications are processed on a rolling basis. *Application fee:* $45. Electronic applications accepted. **Expenses:** Tuition, state resident: full-time $7,361; part-time $399 per credit. Tuition, nonresident: full-time $20,499; part-time $1,282 per credit. Required fees: $34 per credit. Full-time tuition and fees vary according to course load, program, reciprocity agreements and student level. **Financial support:** In 2001–02, 173 students received support, including 18 fellowships with full tuition reimbursements available (averaging $10,300 per year), 143 research assistantships with full tuition reimbursements available (averaging $15,800 per year), 48 teaching assistantships with full tuition reimbursements available; career-related internships or fieldwork, Federal Work-Study, and institutionally sponsored loans also available. Support available to part-time students. Financial award application deadline: 12/1. **Faculty research:** Microelectronics, computer architecture, power electronics and systems, communications, signal processing. *Total annual research expenditures:* $12.1 million. W. Nicholas Hitchon, Chair, *Fax:* 608-262-1267, *E-mail:* hitchon@engr.wisc.edu. **Application contact:** Graduate Secretary, *Fax:* 608-262-1267, *E-mail:* gradscty@ece.wisc.edu. *Web site:* http://www.engr.wisc.edu/ece/

■ **UNIVERSITY OF WYOMING**

Graduate School, College of Engineering, Department of Electrical and Computer Engineering, Laramie, WY 82071

AWARDS Electrical engineering (MS, PhD). Part-time programs available.

Faculty: 12 full-time (1 woman), 1 part-time/adjunct (0 women). **Students:** 28 full-time (9 women), 9 part-time; includes 1 minority (Hispanic American), 21 international. 56 applicants, 18% accepted. In 2001, 15 master's, 1 doctorate awarded. **Degree requirements:** For master's and doctorate, thesis/dissertation. **Entrance requirements:** For master's, GRE General Test, TOEFL, minimum undergraduate GPA of 3.0; for doctorate, GRE General Test, TOEFL, minimum GPA of 3.0. *Application deadline:* For fall admission, 3/1 (priority date); for spring admission, 9/1 (priority date). Applications are processed on a rolling basis. *Application fee:* $40. Electronic applications accepted. **Expenses:** Tuition, state resident: full-time $2,895; part-time $161 per credit hour. Tuition, nonresident: full-time $8,367; part-time $465 per credit hour. Required fees: $491; $10 per credit hour. $2 per credit hour. Tuition and fees vary according to course load and program. **Financial support:** In 2001–02, 10 research assistantships with full tuition reimbursements (averaging $9,500 per year), 15 teaching assistantships with full tuition reimbursements (averaging $8,667 per year) were awarded. Financial award application deadline: 3/1. **Faculty research:** Robotics and controls, signal and speech processing, power electronics, power systems, fuzzy and neural systems, instrumentation. *Total annual research expenditures:* $855,000. Dr. John W. Steadman, Head, 307-766-2240, *Fax:* 307-766-2248, *E-mail:* ece.info@uwyo.edu. **Application contact:** Dr. Suresh Muk Nahallipatna, Graduate Coordinator, 307-766-3174, *Fax:* 307-766-2248, *E-mail:* eceinfo@uwyo.edu. *Web site:* http://wwweng.uwyo.edu/electrical/

■ **UTAH STATE UNIVERSITY**

School of Graduate Studies, College of Engineering, Department of Electrical and Computer Engineering, Logan, UT 84322

AWARDS Electrical engineering (ME, MS, PhD, EE). Part-time programs available.

Faculty: 17 full-time (2 women), 2 part-time/adjunct (0 women). **Students:** 55 full-time (6 women), 40 part-time (3 women), 56 international. Average age 26. 301 applicants, 42% accepted. In 2001, 25 master's, 2 doctorates awarded. **Degree requirements:** For master's, thesis (for some programs); for doctorate, thesis/dissertation.

Utah State University (continued)

Entrance requirements: For master's and doctorate, GRE General Test, TOEFL, minimum GPA of 3.0. *Application deadline:* For fall admission, 1/15 (priority date); for spring admission, 10/15. *Application fee:* $40.

Expenses: Tuition, state resident: full-time $1,693. Tuition, nonresident: full-time $4,233. Required fees: $501. Tuition and fees vary according to program.

Financial support: In 2001–02, 2 fellowships with partial tuition reimbursements (averaging $11,000 per year), 50 research assistantships with partial tuition reimbursements (averaging $7,000 per year), 4 teaching assistantships with partial tuition reimbursements (averaging $4,000 per year) were awarded. Federal Work-Study and institutionally sponsored loans also available.

Faculty research: Parallel processing, networking, control systems, digital signal processing, communications, real time systems. *Total annual research expenditures:* $3 million.

Randy L. Haupt, Head, 435-797-2840, *Fax:* 435-797-3054, *E-mail:* randy.haupt@ece.usu.edu. *Web site:* http://www.engineering.usu.edu/

■ VANDERBILT UNIVERSITY

School of Engineering, Department of Electrical Engineering and Computer Science, Program in Electrical Engineering, Nashville, TN 37240-1001

AWARDS M Eng, MS, PhD. MS and PhD offered through the Graduate School. Part-time programs available.

Faculty: 25 full-time (0 women).
Students: 95 full-time (23 women), 6 part-time; includes 8 minority (6 African Americans, 1 Asian American or Pacific Islander, 1 Hispanic American), 66 international. Average age 28. 155 applicants, 19% accepted, 26 enrolled. In 2001, 23 master's, 7 doctorates awarded. Terminal master's awarded for partial completion of doctoral program.

Degree requirements: For master's, thesis/dissertation; for doctorate, thesis/dissertation, comprehensive exam.

Entrance requirements: For master's and doctorate, GRE General Test, TOEFL, 3 letters of recommendation. *Application deadline:* For fall admission, 1/15; for spring admission, 11/1. *Application fee:* $40. Electronic applications accepted.

Expenses: Tuition: Full-time $28,350.
Financial support: In 2001–02, 87 students received support, including 15 fellowships with full and partial tuition reimbursements available (averaging $5,000 per year), 45 research assistantships with full tuition reimbursements available (averaging $21,187 per year), 27 teaching assistantships with full tuition reimbursements available (averaging $12,274 per year); institutionally sponsored loans, scholarships/grants, health care benefits,

and tuition waivers (full and partial) also available. Financial award application deadline: 1/15.

Faculty research: Robotics microelectronics, signal and image processing, VLSI, solid-state sensors. *Total annual research expenditures:* $8.5 million.

Application contact: Dr. Francis Wells, Director of Graduate Studies, 615-343-7549, *Fax:* 615-322-0677, *E-mail:* eegradapp@vuse.vanderbilt.edu. *Web site:* http://www.eecs.vuse.vanderbilt.edu/

■ VILLANOVA UNIVERSITY

College of Engineering, Department of Electrical and Computer Engineering, Program in Electrical Engineering, Villanova, PA 19085-1699

AWARDS MSEE. Part-time and evening/weekend programs available.

Faculty: 13 full-time (0 women), 2 part-time/adjunct (0 women).
Students: 25 full-time (8 women), 30 part-time (3 women); includes 5 minority (all Asian Americans or Pacific Islanders), 23 international. Average age 27. 80 applicants, 40% accepted, 13 enrolled. In 2001, 20 degrees awarded.

Degree requirements: For master's, thesis optional. *Median time to degree:* Master's–2 years full-time, 4 years part-time.

Entrance requirements: For master's, GRE General Test (for applicants with degrees from foreign universities), TOEFL, BEE, minimum GPA of 3.0. *Application deadline:* For fall admission, 8/1 (priority date); for spring admission, 12/1. Applications are processed on a rolling basis. *Application fee:* $40.

Expenses: Tuition: Part-time $340 per credit. One-time fee: $115 full-time. Tuition and fees vary according to program.

Financial support: In 2001–02, 11 students received support, including 5 research assistantships with full tuition reimbursements available, 5 teaching assistantships with full tuition reimbursements available (averaging $10,265 per year); Federal Work-Study and scholarships/grants also available. Financial award application deadline: 3/15.

Faculty research: Signal processing, communications, antennas, devices.

Dr. S. S. Rao, Chairman, Department of Electrical and Computer Engineering, 610-519-4971, *Fax:* 610-519-4436, *E-mail:* rao@ee.vill.edu. *Web site:* http://www.ece.vill.edu/

Find an in-depth description at www.petersons.com/gradchannel.

■ VIRGINIA POLYTECHNIC INSTITUTE AND STATE UNIVERSITY

Graduate School, College of Engineering, Department of Electrical and Computer Engineering, Blacksburg, VA 24061

AWARDS Computer engineering (MS, PhD); electrical engineering (MS, PhD). Part-time programs available.

Faculty: 67 full-time (2 women).
Students: 408 full-time (56 women), 161 part-time (22 women); includes 57 minority (14 African Americans, 32 Asian Americans or Pacific Islanders, 10 Hispanic Americans, 1 Native American), 317 international. Average age 24. 1,361 applicants, 30% accepted, 134 enrolled. In 2001, 112 master's, 29 doctorates awarded.

Degree requirements: For master's, thesis optional; for doctorate, thesis/dissertation.

Entrance requirements: For master's and doctorate, GRE General Test, TOEFL. *Application deadline:* For fall admission, 1/15 (priority date); for spring admission, 10/1 (priority date). Applications are processed on a rolling basis. *Application fee:* $45. Electronic applications accepted.

Expenses: Tuition, state resident: part-time $241 per hour. Tuition, nonresident: part-time $406 per hour. Tuition and fees vary according to program.

Financial support: In 2001–02, 17 fellowships with full tuition reimbursements (averaging $19,000 per year), 213 research assistantships with full tuition reimbursements (averaging $17,700 per year), 59 teaching assistantships with full tuition reimbursements (averaging $13,275 per year) were awarded. Career-related internships or fieldwork and unspecified assistantships also available. Financial award application deadline: 1/15.

Faculty research: Electromagnetics, controls, electronics, power, communications. *Total annual research expenditures:* $20 million.

Dr. Robert J. Trew, Department Head, 540-231-6646, *E-mail:* trew@vt.edu.
Application contact: Cynthia B. Hopkins, Graduate Counselor, 540-231-8393, *Fax:* 540-231-3362, *E-mail:* hopkins@vt.edu. *Web site:* http://www.ece.vt.edu/

Find an in-depth description at www.petersons.com/gradchannel.

■ WASHINGTON STATE UNIVERSITY

Graduate School, College of Engineering and Architecture, School of Electrical Engineering and Computer Science, Program in Electrical Engineering, Pullman, WA 99164

AWARDS MS, PhD.

Faculty: 18 full-time (1 woman), 3 part-time/adjunct (0 women).
Students: 44 full-time (10 women), 7 part-time; includes 1 minority (Hispanic American), 43 international. In 2001, 28 master's, 4 doctorates awarded.
Degree requirements: For master's, thesis, oral exam; for doctorate, thesis/dissertation, oral exam, qualifying exam, preliminary exam, oral defense of dissertation.
Entrance requirements: For master's and doctorate, GRE General Test, TOEFL, minimum GPA of 3.0. *Application deadline:* For fall admission, 3/1 (priority date). Applications are processed on a rolling basis. *Application fee:* $35.
Expenses: Tuition, state resident: full-time $6,088; part-time $304 per semester. Tuition, nonresident: full-time $14,918; part-time $746 per semester. Tuition and fees vary according to program.
Financial support: In 2001–02, fellowships with full tuition reimbursements (averaging $15,000 per year), 32 research assistantships with full tuition reimbursements (averaging $10,500 per year), 28 teaching assistantships with full tuition reimbursements (averaging $10,500 per year) were awarded. Career-related internships or fieldwork, Federal Work-Study, institutionally sponsored loans, and tuition waivers (partial) also available. Financial award application deadline: 4/1; financial award applicants required to submit FAFSA.
Faculty research: Energy and power systems, microelectronics, electrophysics controls, systems telecommunications. *Total annual research expenditures:* $3.3 million.
Dr. Thomas R. Fischer, Director, 509-335-8148, *Fax:* 509-335-3818.
Application contact: Dr. Ali Saberi, Graduate Coordinator, 509-335-5222, *Fax:* 509-335-3818, *E-mail:* saberi@eecs.wsu.edu. *Web site:* http://www.eecs.wsu.edu

■ WASHINGTON STATE UNIVERSITY SPOKANE

Graduate Programs, Program in Electrical Engineering, Spokane, WA 99201-3899

AWARDS MS.

■ WASHINGTON UNIVERSITY IN ST. LOUIS

Henry Edwin Sever Graduate School of Engineering and Applied Science, Department of Electrical Engineering, St. Louis, MO 63130-4899

AWARDS MSEE, D Sc. Part-time programs available.

Faculty: 16 full-time (2 women), 15 part-time/adjunct (1 woman).
Students: 41 full-time (8 women), 22 part-time (2 women); includes 10 minority (1 African American, 9 Asian Americans or

Pacific Islanders), 26 international. Average age 26. 248 applicants, 20% accepted, 19 enrolled. In 2001, 17 master's, 4 doctorates awarded. Terminal master's awarded for partial completion of doctoral program.
Degree requirements: For master's, thesis optional; for doctorate, thesis/dissertation, departmental qualifying exam.
Entrance requirements: For master's, minimum GPA of 3.0 during previous 2 years. *Application deadline:* For fall admission, 8/18 (priority date); for spring admission, 1/10 (priority date). Applications are processed on a rolling basis. *Application fee:* $40. Electronic applications accepted.
Expenses: Tuition: Full-time $26,900.
Financial support: In 2001–02, 42 students received support, including 6 fellowships with full tuition reimbursements available (averaging $14,070 per year), 17 research assistantships with full tuition reimbursements available (averaging $19,500 per year); Federal Work-Study and institutionally sponsored loans also available. Financial award application deadline: 2/1; financial award applicants required to submit FAFSA.
Faculty research: Applied physics, signal and image processing, computer engineering, telecommunications, biomedical engineering. *Total annual research expenditures:* $1.2 million.
Dr. Barry Spielman, Chairman, 314-935-5565, *Fax:* 314-935-7500, *E-mail:* bes@ee.wustl.edu.
Application contact: Graduate Admissions, 314-935-6138, *Fax:* 314-935-7500, *E-mail:* eeadmin@ee.wustl.edu. *Web site:* http://www.ee.wustl.edu/ee/

■ WAYNE STATE UNIVERSITY

Graduate School, College of Engineering, Department of Electrical and Computer Engineering, Program in Electrical Engineering, Detroit, MI 48202

AWARDS MS, PhD.

Students: 197. In 2001, 24 master's, 5 doctorates awarded.
Degree requirements: For master's, thesis optional; for doctorate, thesis/dissertation.
Application deadline: For fall admission, 7/1 (priority date); for spring admission, 3/15. Applications are processed on a rolling basis. *Application fee:* $20 ($30 for international students). Electronic applications accepted.
Expenses: Tuition, state resident: full-time $3,764. Tuition and fees vary according to degree level and program.
Financial support: Application deadline: 3/16.
Faculty research: Biomedical systems, control systems, solid state materials, optical materials, hybrid vehicle.
Application contact: Pepe Siy, Graduate Director, 313-577-3841, *Fax:* 313-577-1101, *E-mail:* psiy@ece.eng.wayne.edu.

■ WAYNE STATE UNIVERSITY

Graduate School, College of Engineering, Interdisciplinary Program in Electronics and Computer Control Systems, Detroit, MI 48202

AWARDS MS.

Students: 16. In 2001, 77 degrees awarded.
Degree requirements: For master's, thesis optional.
Application deadline: For fall admission, 7/1 (priority date); for spring admission, 3/15. Applications are processed on a rolling basis. *Application fee:* $20 ($30 for international students). Electronic applications accepted.
Expenses: Tuition, state resident: full-time $3,764. Tuition and fees vary according to degree level and program.
Pepe Siy, Graduate Director, 313-577-3841, *Fax:* 313-577-1101, *E-mail:* psiy@ece.eng.wayne.edu.

■ WESTERN MICHIGAN UNIVERSITY

Graduate College, College of Engineering and Applied Sciences, Department of Electrical Engineering and Computer Engineering, Kalamazoo, MI 49008-5202

AWARDS Computer engineering (MSE, PhD); electrical engineering (MSE, PhD). Part-time programs available.

Faculty: 15 full-time (2 women).
Students: 146 full-time (24 women), 9 part-time; includes 2 minority (both Asian Americans or Pacific Islanders), 151 international. 342 applicants, 80% accepted, 67 enrolled. In 2001, 23 degrees awarded.
Degree requirements: For master's, thesis optional.
Entrance requirements: For master's, minimum GPA of 3.0. *Application deadline:* For fall admission, 2/15 (priority date). Applications are processed on a rolling basis. *Application fee:* $25.
Expenses: Tuition, state resident: part-time $186 per credit hour. Tuition, nonresident: part-time $442 per credit hour. Required fees: $602. One-time fee: $132 part-time. Tuition and fees vary according to course load.
Financial support: Fellowships, research assistantships, teaching assistantships, career-related internships or fieldwork and Federal Work-Study available. Financial award application deadline: 2/15; financial award applicants required to submit FAFSA.
Faculty research: Fiber optics, computer architecture, bioelectromagnetics, acoustics.
Dr. S. Hossein Mousavinezhad, Chair, 616-387-4057.
Application contact: Admissions and Orientation, 616-387-2000, *Fax:* 616-387-2355.

■ WESTERN NEW ENGLAND COLLEGE

School of Engineering, Department of Electrical Engineering, Springfield, MA 01119-2654

AWARDS Computer and engineering information systems (MSEE); computer engineering (MSEE). Part-time and evening/weekend programs available.

Faculty: 7 full-time (0 women).
Students: Average age 29. 3 applicants, 0% accepted. In 2001, 4 degrees awarded.
Degree requirements: For master's, thesis optional.
Entrance requirements: For master's, GRE, bachelor's degree in engineering or related field. *Application deadline:* Applications are processed on a rolling basis. *Application fee:* $30.
Expenses: Tuition: Part-time $429 per credit. Required fees: $9 per credit. $20 per semester.
Financial support: Teaching assistantships available. Support available to part-time students. Financial award application deadline: 4/1; financial award applicants required to submit FAFSA.
Faculty research: Superconductors, microwave cooking, computer voice output, digital filters, computer engineering.
Dr. James J. Moriarty, Chair, 413-782-1491 Ext. 1725, *E-mail:* jmoriart@wnec.edu.
Application contact: Dr. Janet Castleman, Director of Continuing Education, 413-782-1750, *Fax:* 413-782-1779, *E-mail:* jcastlem@wnec.edu.

■ WEST VIRGINIA UNIVERSITY

College of Engineering and Mineral Resources, Lane Department of Computer Science and Electrical Engineering, Program in Electrical Engineering, Morgantown, WV 26506

AWARDS Electrical engineering (MSEE, PhD); engineering (MSE).

Students: 66 full-time (14 women), 11 part-time (2 women); includes 1 minority (Asian American or Pacific Islander), 59 international. Average age 24. 195 applicants, 66% accepted. In 2001, 28 master's, 2 doctorates awarded. Terminal master's awarded for partial completion of doctoral program.
Degree requirements: For master's, thesis or alternative; for doctorate, thesis/dissertation, comprehensive exam.
Entrance requirements: For master's and doctorate, GRE General Test, TOEFL, minimum GPA of 3.0. *Application deadline:* For fall admission, 7/1 (priority date). Applications are processed on a rolling basis. *Application fee:* $45.
Expenses: Tuition, state resident: full-time $2,791. Tuition, nonresident: full-time $8,659. Required fees: $1,002. Tuition and fees vary according to program.

Financial support: In 2001–02, 15 research assistantships, 23 teaching assistantships were awarded. Fellowships, Federal Work-Study, institutionally sponsored loans, tuition waivers (full and partial), and graduate administrative assistantships also available. Financial award application deadline: 2/1; financial award applicants required to submit FAFSA.
Faculty research: Power and control systems, communications and signal processing, electromechanical systems, microelectronics and photonics. *Total annual research expenditures:* $1.2 million.
Application contact: Dr. Wils L. Cooley, Graduate Coordinator, 304-293-0405 Ext. 2527, *Fax:* 304-293-8602, *E-mail:* wils.cooley@mail.wvu.edu. *Web site:* http://www.csee.wvu.edu/students/grad/msphdee.htm

■ WICHITA STATE UNIVERSITY

Graduate School, College of Engineering, Department of Electrical Engineering, Wichita, KS 67260

AWARDS MS, PhD. Part-time and evening/weekend programs available.

Faculty: 9 full-time (0 women), 2 part-time/adjunct (0 women).
Students: 163 full-time (19 women), 116 part-time (11 women); includes 29 minority (1 African American, 25 Asian Americans or Pacific Islanders, 3 Hispanic Americans), 214 international. Average age 27. 388 applicants, 64% accepted, 70 enrolled. In 2001, 36 master's, 5 doctorates awarded.
Degree requirements: For master's, thesis or alternative, oral exam; for doctorate, one foreign language, thesis/dissertation, comprehensive exam.
Entrance requirements: For master's and doctorate, GRE, TOEFL. *Application deadline:* For fall admission, 7/1 (priority date); for spring admission, 1/1. Applications are processed on a rolling basis. *Application fee:* $25 ($40 for international students). Electronic applications accepted.
Expenses: Tuition, state resident: full-time $1,888; part-time $105 per credit. Tuition, nonresident: full-time $6,129; part-time $341 per credit. Required fees: $345; $19 per credit. $17 per semester. Tuition and fees vary according to course load and program.
Financial support: In 2001–02, 19 research assistantships (averaging $3,122 per year), 6 teaching assistantships with full tuition reimbursements (averaging $4,400 per year) were awarded. Fellowships, Federal Work-Study, institutionally sponsored loans, and unspecified assistantships also available. Financial award application deadline: 4/1; financial award applicants required to submit FAFSA.
Faculty research: Rehabilitation engineering, control systems, power systems, digital systems, communications/signal processing.

Dr. Edwin Sawan, Chairperson, 316-978-5431, *Fax:* 316-978-3307, *E-mail:* edwin.sawan@wichita.edu. *Web site:* http://www.wichita.edu/

■ WIDENER UNIVERSITY

School of Engineering, Program in Electrical/Telecommunication Engineering, Chester, PA 19013-5792

AWARDS ME, ME/MBA. Part-time and evening/weekend programs available.

Degree requirements: For master's, thesis optional.
Entrance requirements: For master's, GMAT (ME/MBA).
Expenses: Tuition: Part-time $500 per credit. Required fees: $25 per semester.
Faculty research: Signal and image processing, electromagnetics, telecommunications and computer network.

■ WILKES UNIVERSITY

College of Arts, Sciences, and Professional Studies, Department of Engineering and Physics, Wilkes-Barre, PA 18766-0002

AWARDS Electrical engineering (MSEE); physics (MS Ed).

Students: 5 full-time (2 women), 5 part-time, 5 international. Average age 25. In 2001, 10 degrees awarded.
Degree requirements: For master's, thesis or alternative.
Entrance requirements: For master's, GRE. *Application deadline:* Applications are processed on a rolling basis. *Application fee:* $30.
Expenses: Tuition: Full-time $14,304; part-time $596 per credit hour. Required fees: $312; $13 per credit hour. Tuition and fees vary according to program.
Financial support: Application deadline: 2/28.
Dr. Roger Maxwell, Chairman, 570-408-4810, *Fax:* 570-408-7880, *E-mail:* rmaxwell@wilkes.edu.

■ WOODS HOLE OCEANOGRAPHIC INSTITUTE

Joint Program with Massachusetts Institute of Technology in Oceanography/Applied Ocean Science and Engineering, Woods Hole, MA 02543

AWARDS Applied ocean sciences (PhD); biological oceanography (PhD, Sc D); chemical oceanography (PhD, Sc D); civil and environmental and oceanographic engineering (PhD); electrical and oceanographic engineering (PhD); geochemistry (PhD); geophysics (PhD); marine biology (PhD); marine geochemistry (PhD, Sc D); marine geology (PhD, Sc D); marine geophysics (PhD); mechanical and oceanographic engineering (PhD); ocean engineering (PhD); oceanographic engineering (M Eng, MS, PhD,

Sc D, Eng); paleoceanography (PhD); physical oceanography (PhD, Sc D). MS, PhD, and Sc D offered jointly with Woods Hole Oceanographic Institution.

Faculty: 185 full-time (60 women).

Students: 119 full-time (59 women); includes 4 minority (2 African Americans, 2 Asian Americans or Pacific Islanders), 27 international. Average age 27. 125 applicants, 30% accepted, 24 enrolled. In 2001, 10 master's, 11 doctorates awarded. Terminal master's awarded for partial completion of doctoral program.

Degree requirements: For master's and Eng, thesis (for some programs); for doctorate, thesis/dissertation. *Median time to degree:* Master's–2.9 years full-time; doctorate–5.8 years full-time.

Entrance requirements: For master's, GRE General Test; for doctorate, GRE General Test, GRE Subject Test. *Application deadline:* For fall admission, 1/15 (priority date). *Application fee:* $60. Electronic applications accepted.

Expenses: Tuition: Full-time $26,960. Full-time tuition and fees vary according to program.

Financial support: In 2001–02, 13 fellowships (averaging $35,948 per year), 69 research assistantships (averaging $35,948 per year) were awarded. Teaching assistantships, institutionally sponsored loans, health care benefits, and unspecified assistantships also available. Financial award application deadline: 1/15.

Prof. Paola Rizzoli, Director, 617-253-2451, *E-mail:* rizzoli@mit.edu.

Application contact: Ronni Schwartz, Administrator, 617-253-7544, *Fax:* 617-253-9784, *E-mail:* mspiggy@mit.edu. *Web site:* http://www.whoi.edu/education/graduate/jp.html

Find an in-depth description at www.petersons.com/gradchannel.

■ WORCESTER POLYTECHNIC INSTITUTE

Graduate Studies, Department of Electrical and Computer Engineering, Worcester, MA 01609-2280

AWARDS Electrical and computer engineering (MS, PhD, Advanced Certificate, Certificate); power systems engineering (MS, PhD). Part-time and evening/weekend programs available.

Faculty: 23 full-time (1 woman), 7 part-time/adjunct (0 women).

Students: 42 full-time (4 women), 39 part-time (8 women); includes 12 minority (2 African Americans, 7 Asian Americans or Pacific Islanders, 3 Hispanic Americans), 34 international. 209 applicants, 46%

accepted, 32 enrolled. In 2001, 26 master's, 3 doctorates awarded. Terminal master's awarded for partial completion of doctoral program.

Degree requirements: For master's, thesis optional; for doctorate, thesis/dissertation.

Entrance requirements: For master's and doctorate, TOEFL. *Application deadline:* For fall admission, 2/1 (priority date); for spring admission, 10/15 (priority date). Applications are processed on a rolling basis. *Application fee:* $60. Electronic applications accepted.

Expenses: Tuition: Part-time $796 per credit. Required fees: $20; $752 per credit. One-time fee: $30 full-time.

Financial support: In 2001–02, 37 students received support, including 1 fellowship with full and partial tuition reimbursement available (averaging $12,951 per year), 15 research assistantships with full tuition reimbursements available (averaging $17,256 per year), 15 teaching assistantships with full tuition reimbursements available (averaging $12,942 per year); career-related internships or fieldwork, institutionally sponsored loans, and scholarships/grants also available. Financial award application deadline: 2/15; financial award applicants required to submit FAFSA.

Faculty research: Analog and mixed signal IC design, cryptography and data security, power systems and power electronics, computer networking, image processing and visualization. *Total annual research expenditures:* $1.2 million.

Dr. John A. Orr, Head, 508-831-5231, *Fax:* 508-831-5491, *E-mail:* orr@wpi.edu.

Application contact: Dr. Fred J. Looft, Graduate Coordinator, 508-831-5231, *Fax:* 508-831-5491, *E-mail:* fjlooft@wpi.edu. *Web site:* http://ee.wpi.edu/

■ WRIGHT STATE UNIVERSITY

School of Graduate Studies, College of Engineering and Computer Science, Programs in Engineering, Program in Electrical Engineering, Dayton, OH 45435

AWARDS MSE. Part-time and evening/weekend programs available.

Students: 83 full-time (9 women), 40 part-time (3 women); includes 8 minority (3 African Americans, 5 Asian Americans or Pacific Islanders), 82 international. Average age 27. 273 applicants, 95% accepted. In 2001, 61 degrees awarded.

Degree requirements: For master's, thesis or course option alternative.

Entrance requirements: For master's, TOEFL. *Application deadline:* Applications are processed on a rolling basis. *Application fee:* $25.

Expenses: Tuition, state resident: full-time $7,161; part-time $225 per quarter hour. Tuition, nonresident: full-time $12,324; part-time $385 per quarter hour. Tuition and fees vary according to course load, degree level and program.

Financial support: Fellowships, research assistantships, teaching assistantships, unspecified assistantships available. Support available to part-time students. Financial award application deadline: 3/1; financial award applicants required to submit FAFSA.

Faculty research: Robotics, circuit design, power electronics, image processing, communication systems.

Dr. Fred D. Garber, Chair, 937-775-5037, *Fax:* 937-775-5009, *E-mail:* fred.garber@wright.edu.

Application contact: Dr. Lang Hong, Graduate Program Director, 937-775-5037, *Fax:* 937-775-5009, *E-mail:* lang.hong@wright.edu.

■ YALE UNIVERSITY

Graduate School of Arts and Sciences, Programs in Engineering and Applied Science, Department of Electrical Engineering, New Haven, CT 06520

AWARDS MS, PhD. Terminal master's awarded for partial completion of doctoral program.

Degree requirements: For doctorate, thesis/dissertation, exam.

Entrance requirements: For master's and doctorate, GRE General Test, TOEFL.

Find an in-depth description at www.petersons.com/gradchannel.

■ YOUNGSTOWN STATE UNIVERSITY

Graduate School, William Rayen College of Engineering, Department of Electrical Engineering, Youngstown, OH 44555-0001

AWARDS MSE. Part-time and evening/weekend programs available.

Degree requirements: For master's, thesis optional.

Entrance requirements: For master's, TOEFL, minimum GPA of 2.75 in field.

Faculty research: Computer-aided design, power systems, electromagnetic energy conversion, sensors, control systems.

Energy and Power Engineering

ENERGY AND POWER ENGINEERING

■ NEW YORK INSTITUTE OF TECHNOLOGY

Graduate Division, School of Engineering and Technology, Program in Energy Management, Old Westbury, NY 11568-8000

AWARDS Energy management (MS); energy technology (Advanced Certificate); environmental management (Advanced Certificate); facilities management (Advanced Certificate). Part-time and evening/weekend programs available. Postbaccalaureate distance learning degree programs offered.

Students: 8 full-time (2 women), 64 part-time (6 women); includes 15 minority (6 African Americans, 4 Asian Americans or Pacific Islanders, 5 Hispanic Americans), 9 international. Average age 37. 26 applicants, 73% accepted, 8 enrolled. In 2001, 17 degrees awarded.
Degree requirements: For master's, thesis or alternative, comprehensive exam.
Entrance requirements: For master's, minimum QPA of 2.85. *Application deadline:* For fall admission, 7/1 (priority date); for spring admission, 12/1 (priority date). Applications are processed on a rolling basis. *Application fee:* $50. Electronic applications accepted.
Expenses: Tuition: Part-time $545 per credit. Tuition and fees vary according to course load, degree level, program and student level.
Financial support: In 2001–02, 1 research assistantship with partial tuition reimbursement was awarded; fellowships, institutionally sponsored loans, tuition waivers (full and partial), and unspecified assistantships also available. Support available to part-time students. Financial award applicants required to submit FAFSA.
Dr. Robert Amundsen, Director, 516-686-7578.
Application contact: Jacquelyn Nealon, Dean of Admissions and Financial Aid, 516-686-7925, *Fax:* 516-686-7613, *E-mail:* jnealon@nyit.edu.

■ RENSSELAER POLYTECHNIC INSTITUTE

Graduate School, School of Engineering, Department of Electric Power Engineering, Troy, NY 12180-3590

AWARDS M Eng, MS, D Eng, PhD, MBA/M Eng. Part-time and evening/weekend programs available. Postbaccalaureate

distance learning degree programs offered (no on-campus study).
Faculty: 4 full-time (0 women), 2 part-time/adjunct (0 women).
Students: 47 full-time (7 women), 9 part-time (1 woman); includes 4 minority (2 African Americans, 2 Hispanic Americans), 37 international. Average age 22. 79 applicants, 58% accepted, 21 enrolled. In 2001, 19 master's, 4 doctorates awarded. Terminal master's awarded for partial completion of doctoral program.
Degree requirements: For master's, thesis (for some programs); for doctorate, thesis/dissertation.
Entrance requirements: For master's and doctorate, TOEFL. *Application deadline:* For fall admission, 1/15 (priority date). Applications are processed on a rolling basis. *Application fee:* $45. Electronic applications accepted.
Expenses: Tuition: Full-time $26,400; part-time $1,320 per credit hour. Required fees: $1,437.
Financial support: In 2001–02, 18 students received support, including fellowships with full tuition reimbursements available (averaging $21,000 per year), 9 research assistantships with full and partial tuition reimbursements available (averaging $12,000 per year), 9 teaching assistantships with full and partial tuition reimbursements available (averaging $11,700 per year); career-related internships or fieldwork and institutionally sponsored loans also available. Financial award application deadline: 2/1.
Faculty research: Power switching technology, electric and magnetic field computation, power system analysis and optimization, semiconductor power electronic and motor control systems, electrical transients in power systems. *Total annual research expenditures:* $410,000.
Dr. J. Keith Nelson, Chair, 518-276-6328, *Fax:* 518-276-6226.
Application contact: Roselaine Carignan, Admissions Assistant, 518-276-6329, *Fax:* 518-276-6226, *E-mail:* carigr@rpi.edu. *Web site:* http://www.rpi.edu/dept/epe/www/

Find an in-depth description at www.petersons.com/gradchannel.

■ SOUTHERN ILLINOIS UNIVERSITY CARBONDALE

Graduate School, College of Engineering, Program in Engineering Sciences, Carbondale, IL 62901-6806

AWARDS Electrical systems (PhD); fossil energy (PhD); mechanics (PhD).

Faculty: 55 full-time (3 women), 3 part-time/adjunct (0 women).
Students: 22 full-time (3 women), 18 part-time (4 women); includes 2 minority (1

African American, 1 Asian American or Pacific Islander), 30 international. 31 applicants, 19% accepted. In 2001, 3 degrees awarded.
Degree requirements: For doctorate, thesis/dissertation.
Entrance requirements: For doctorate, GRE General Test, TOEFL, minimum GPA of 3.5. *Application fee:* $20.
Expenses: Tuition, state resident: full-time $3,794; part-time $154 per hour. Tuition, nonresident: full-time $6,566; part-time $308 per hour. Required fees: $277 per hour.
Financial support: In 2001–02, 13 students received support; fellowships with full tuition reimbursements available, research assistantships with full tuition reimbursements available, teaching assistantships with full tuition reimbursements available, Federal Work-Study, institutionally sponsored loans, and tuition waivers (full) available. Support available to part-time students.
Dr. Hasan Sevim, Interim Chairperson, 618-536-6637, *Fax:* 618-453-4235.

■ UNIVERSITY OF MASSACHUSETTS LOWELL

Graduate School, College of Arts and Sciences, Department of Physics and Applied Physics, Program in Energy Engineering, Lowell, MA 01854-2881

AWARDS PhD.

Degree requirements: For doctorate, 2 foreign languages, thesis/dissertation.
Entrance requirements: For doctorate, GRE General Test.

■ UNIVERSITY OF MASSACHUSETTS LOWELL

Graduate School, James B. Francis College of Engineering, Department of Energy Engineering, Lowell, MA 01854-2881

AWARDS MS Eng.

Degree requirements: For master's, thesis optional.
Entrance requirements: For master's, GRE General Test.

■ THE UNIVERSITY OF MEMPHIS

Graduate School, Herff College of Engineering, Department of Mechanical Engineering, Memphis, TN 38152

AWARDS Design and mechanical engineering (MS); energy systems (MS); mechanical engineering (PhD); mechanical systems (MS); power systems (MS). Part-time programs available. Terminal master's awarded for partial completion of doctoral program.

Degree requirements: For master's and doctorate, thesis/dissertation, comprehensive exam.
Entrance requirements: For master's, GRE General Test, BS in mechanical engineering, minimum undergraduate GPA of 3.0.
Expenses: Tuition, state resident: full-time $2,026. Tuition, nonresident: full-time $4,528.
Faculty research: Computational fluid dynamics, fracture mechanics, computational mechanics, composites, phase change. *Web site:* http://www.memphis.edu/

■ UNIVERSITY OF NORTH DAKOTA

Graduate School, School of Engineering and Mines, Program in Energy Engineering, Grand Forks, ND 58202

AWARDS PhD.

Faculty: 8 full-time (0 women).
Students: 1 full-time (0 women), 7 part-time (1 woman). 9 applicants, 100% accepted, 3 enrolled. In 2001, 2 degrees awarded.
Degree requirements: For doctorate, thesis/dissertation, final exam, comprehensive exam.
Entrance requirements: For doctorate, TOEFL, minimum GPA of 3.5. *Application deadline:* For fall admission, 3/1 (priority date); for spring admission, 10/15 (priority date). Applications are processed on a rolling basis. *Application fee:* $30.
Expenses: Tuition, state resident: full-time $3,298. Tuition, nonresident: full-time $7,998.
Financial support: In 2001–02, 2 students received support, including 2 research assistantships (averaging $10,500 per year); fellowships, career-related internships or fieldwork, Federal Work-Study, institutionally sponsored loans, scholarships/grants, and tuition waivers (full and partial) also available. Support available to part-time students. Financial award application deadline: 3/15; financial award applicants required to submit FAFSA.
Faculty research: Combustion science, energy conversion, power transmission, environmental engineering.
Dr. Michael D. Mann, Director, 701-777-3852, *Fax:* 701-777-4838, *E-mail:* mike_mann@mail.und.nodak.edu. *Web site:* http://www.und.nodak.edu/dept/sem/energy.eng/

■ WORCESTER POLYTECHNIC INSTITUTE

Graduate Studies, Department of Electrical and Computer Engineering, Worcester, MA 01609-2280

AWARDS Electrical and computer engineering (MS, PhD, Advanced Certificate, Certificate); power systems engineering (MS, PhD). Part-time and evening/weekend programs available.

Faculty: 23 full-time (1 woman), 7 part-time/adjunct (0 women).
Students: 42 full-time (4 women), 39 part-time (8 women); includes 12 minority (2 African Americans, 7 Asian Americans or Pacific Islanders, 3 Hispanic Americans), 34 international. 209 applicants, 46% accepted, 32 enrolled. In 2001, 26 master's, 3 doctorates awarded. Terminal master's awarded for partial completion of doctoral program.
Degree requirements: For master's, thesis optional; for doctorate, thesis/dissertation.
Entrance requirements: For master's and doctorate, TOEFL. *Application deadline:* For fall admission, 2/1 (priority date); for spring admission, 10/15 (priority date). Applications are processed on a rolling basis. *Application fee:* $60. Electronic applications accepted.
Expenses: Tuition: Part-time $796 per credit. Required fees: $20; $752 per credit. One-time fee: $30 full-time.
Financial support: In 2001–02, 37 students received support, including 1 fellowship with full and partial tuition reimbursement available (averaging $12,951 per year), 15 research assistantships with full tuition reimbursements available (averaging $17,256 per year), 15 teaching assistantships with full tuition reimbursements available (averaging $12,942 per year); career-related internships or fieldwork, institutionally sponsored loans, and scholarships/grants also available. Financial award application deadline: 2/15; financial award applicants required to submit FAFSA.
Faculty research: Analog and mixed signal IC design, cryptography and data security, power systems and power electronics, computer networking, image processing and visualization. *Total annual research expenditures:* $1.2 million.
Dr. John A. Orr, Head, 508-831-5231, *Fax:* 508-831-5491, *E-mail:* orr@wpi.edu.
Application contact: Dr. Fred J. Looft, Graduate Coordinator, 508-831-5231, *Fax:* 508-831-5491, *E-mail:* fjlooft@wpi.edu. *Web site:* http://ee.wpi.edu/

NUCLEAR ENGINEERING

■ AIR FORCE INSTITUTE OF TECHNOLOGY

School of Engineering and Management, Department of Engineering Physics, Dayton, OH 45433-7765

AWARDS Applied physics (MS, PhD); electro-optics (MS, PhD); environmental science (MS, PhD); materials science (MS, PhD); meteorology (MS); nuclear engineering (MS, PhD). Part-time programs available.

Degree requirements: For master's and doctorate, thesis/dissertation.
Entrance requirements: For master's and doctorate, GRE General Test, minimum GPA of 3.0, U.S. citizenship.
Faculty research: High-energy lasers, space physics, nuclear weapon effects, semiconductor physics. *Web site:* http://en.afit.edu/bnp/

Find an in-depth description at www.petersons.com/gradchannel.

■ CORNELL UNIVERSITY

Graduate School, Graduate Fields of Engineering, Field of Nuclear Science and Engineering, Ithaca, NY 14853-0001

AWARDS Nuclear engineering (M Eng, MS, PhD); nuclear science (MS, PhD).

Faculty: 8 full-time.
Students: 3 full-time (0 women), 1 international. 15 applicants, 7% accepted. In 2001, 1 degree awarded. Terminal master's awarded for partial completion of doctoral program.
Degree requirements: For master's, thesis (MS); for doctorate, thesis/dissertation.
Entrance requirements: For master's and doctorate, GRE General Test (recommended), TOEFL, 3 letters of recommendation. *Application deadline:* For fall admission, 1/15 (priority date). *Application fee:* $65. Electronic applications accepted.
Expenses: Tuition: Full-time $25,970. Required fees: $50.
Financial support: In 2001–02, 2 students received support, including 1 research assistantship with full tuition reimbursement available, 1 teaching assistantship with full tuition reimbursement available; fellowships with full tuition reimbursements available, institutionally sponsored loans, scholarships/grants, tuition waivers (full and partial), and unspecified assistantships also available. Financial award applicants required to submit FAFSA.
Faculty research: Nuclear fuel recycling, severe accident analysis, nuclear fuel cycle economics, plasma physics, fusion reactor technology.

Cornell University (continued)
Application contact: Graduate Field Assistant, 607-255-3480, *Fax:* 607-255-9147, *E-mail:* ward_lab-mailbox@cornell.edu. *Web site:* http://www.gradschool.cornell.edu/grad/fields_1/nucl-sci.html

■ GEORGIA INSTITUTE OF TECHNOLOGY

Graduate Studies and Research, College of Engineering, George W. Woodruff School of Mechanical Engineering, Nuclear Engineering and Health Physics Programs, Atlanta, GA 30332-0001

AWARDS Health physics (MSHP); nuclear engineering (MSNE, PhD). Part-time programs available. Terminal master's awarded for partial completion of doctoral program.

Degree requirements: For master's, thesis optional; for doctorate, thesis/dissertation, exams.
Entrance requirements: For master's and doctorate, GRE General Test (recommended), TOEFL.
Faculty research: Reactor engineering and systems, radiation technology, nuclear materials, environmental engineering, plasma physics.

■ IDAHO STATE UNIVERSITY

Office of Graduate Studies, College of Engineering, Pocatello, ID 83209

AWARDS Engineering and applied science (PhD); engineering structures and mechanics (MS); environmental engineering (MS); measurement and control engineering (MS); nuclear science and engineering (MS); waste management and environmental science (MS). Part-time programs available.

Faculty: 13 full-time (0 women), 1 part-time/adjunct (0 women).
Students: 34 full-time (8 women), 18 part-time (1 woman); includes 7 minority (1 African American, 5 Asian Americans or Pacific Islanders, 1 Hispanic American), 15 international. Average age 34. In 2001, 12 master's, 1 doctorate awarded.
Degree requirements: For master's and doctorate, thesis/dissertation.
Entrance requirements: For master's and doctorate, GRE General Test, TOEFL. *Application deadline:* For fall admission, 7/1 (priority date); for spring admission, 12/1. Applications are processed on a rolling basis. *Application fee:* $35.
Expenses: Tuition, area resident: Full-time $3,432. Tuition, state resident: part-time $172 per credit. Tuition, nonresident: full-time $10,196; part-time $262 per credit. International tuition: $9,672 full-time. Part-time tuition and fees vary according to course load, program and reciprocity agreements.
Financial support: In 2001–02, 7 research assistantships with full and partial tuition

reimbursements (averaging $10,740 per year), 16 teaching assistantships with full and partial tuition reimbursements (averaging $6,775 per year) were awarded. Federal Work-Study and institutionally sponsored loans also available. Support available to part-time students. Financial award application deadline: 2/15.
Faculty research: Isotope separation, control technology, two-phase flow, photosonolysis, criticality calculations. *Total annual research expenditures:* $293,915.
Dr. Jay Kunze, 208-282-2902, *Fax:* 208-282-4538. *Web site:* http://www.coe.isu.edu/engrg/

■ KANSAS STATE UNIVERSITY

Graduate School, College of Engineering, Department of Mechanical Engineering, Manhattan, KS 66506

AWARDS Engineering (PhD); mechanical engineering (MS); nuclear engineering (MS).

Faculty: 23 full-time (1 woman).
Students: 39 full-time (5 women), 11 part-time, 27 international. 169 applicants, 8% accepted, 13 enrolled. In 2001, 9 degrees awarded.
Degree requirements: For master's, thesis or alternative; for doctorate, thesis/dissertation, comprehensive exam.
Entrance requirements: For master's, GRE General Test, TOEFL, minimum GPA of 3.0 in physics, mathematics, and chemistry; for doctorate, GRE General Test, TOEFL, master's degree in mechanical engineering. *Application deadline:* For fall admission, 3/1; for spring admission, 9/1. Applications are processed on a rolling basis. *Application fee:* $0 ($25 for international students). Electronic applications accepted.
Expenses: Tuition, state resident: part-time $113 per credit hour. Tuition, nonresident: part-time $358 per credit hour.
Financial support: In 2001–02, 35 research assistantships (averaging $9,000 per year), 3 teaching assistantships with full tuition reimbursements (averaging $9,000 per year) were awarded. Career-related internships or fieldwork, Federal Work-Study, institutionally sponsored loans, and scholarships/grants also available. Support available to part-time students. Financial award application deadline: 3/1; financial award applicants required to submit FAFSA.
Faculty research: Holographic particle velocimetry, optical measurements, thermal sciences, heat transfer, machine design. *Total annual research expenditures:* $4.1 million.
Mohammad Hosni, Head, 785-532-2283, *Fax:* 785-532-7057.
Application contact: Sameer Madanshetty, Graduate Program Coordinator, 785-532-5610, *Fax:* 785-532-7057, *E-mail:* dgs@ksume.me.ksu.edu. *Web site:* http://www.mne.ksu.edu/

■ MASSACHUSETTS INSTITUTE OF TECHNOLOGY

School of Engineering, Department of Nuclear Engineering, Cambridge, MA 02139-4307

AWARDS Nuclear engineering (SM, PhD, Sc D, NE); nuclear systems engineering (M Eng); radiological health and industrial radiation engineering (M Eng); radiological sciences (PhD, Sc D).

Faculty: 16 full-time (1 woman).
Students: 107 full-time (26 women); includes 9 minority (2 African Americans, 4 Asian Americans or Pacific Islanders, 3 Hispanic Americans), 56 international. Average age 25. 79 applicants, 46% accepted, 19 enrolled. In 2001, 17 master's, 20 doctorates awarded.
Degree requirements: For master's, thesis/dissertation; for doctorate, thesis/dissertation, comprehensive exam.
Entrance requirements: For master's and doctorate, GRE General Test, TOEFL. *Application deadline:* For fall admission, 1/15 (priority date); for spring admission, 11/1. *Application fee:* $60. Electronic applications accepted.
Expenses: Tuition: Full-time $26,960. Full-time tuition and fees vary according to program.
Financial support: In 2001–02, 101 students received support, including 12 fellowships, 76 research assistantships, 11 teaching assistantships; career-related internships or fieldwork, Federal Work-Study, institutionally sponsored loans, scholarships/grants, health care benefits, and unspecified assistantships also available. Financial award application deadline: 2/15; financial award applicants required to submit FAFSA.
Faculty research: Reactor engineering, reactor safety analysis, nuclear materials engineering, applied plasma physics, applied radiation physics. *Total annual research expenditures:* $21.4 million.
Dr. Jeffrey P. Freidberg, Head, 617-253-8670, *Fax:* 617-258-7437, *E-mail:* jpfreid@mit.edu.
Application contact: Clare Egan, Graduate Office Administrator, 617-253-3814, *Fax:* 617-258-7437, *E-mail:* cegan@mit.edu. *Web site:* http://web.mit.edu/Ned/www/

Find an in-depth description at www.petersons.com/gradchannel.

■ NORTH CAROLINA STATE UNIVERSITY

Graduate School, College of Engineering, Department of Nuclear Engineering, Raleigh, NC 27695

AWARDS MNE, MS, PhD.

Faculty: 12 full-time (0 women), 10 part-time/adjunct (0 women).
Students: 26 full-time (4 women), 3 part-time; includes 2 minority (1 Asian

American or Pacific Islander, 1 Hispanic American), 16 international. Average age 28. 49 applicants, 39% accepted. In 2001, 9 master's, 2 doctorates awarded.

Degree requirements: For master's, thesis (for some programs); for doctorate, thesis/dissertation.

Entrance requirements: For master's, bachelor's degree in engineering or GRE; for doctorate, engineering degree or GRE. *Application fee:* $45.

Expenses: Tuition, state resident: full-time $1,748. Tuition, nonresident: full-time $6,904.

Financial support: In 2001–02, 1 fellowship (averaging $8,858 per year), 21 research assistantships (averaging $5,749 per year), 3 teaching assistantships (averaging $7,566 per year) were awarded. Career-related internships or fieldwork, institutionally sponsored loans, and traineeships also available.

Faculty research: Reactor analysis methods, computational fluid models, nuclear materials, radiation measurements, plasma technology. *Total annual research expenditures:* $2.2 million.
Dr. Paul J. Turinsky, Head, 919-515-5098, *Fax:* 919-515-5115, *E-mail:* turinsky@eos.ncsu.edu.

Application contact: Dr. Man-Sung Yim, Director of Graduate Programs, 919-515-1466, *Fax:* 919-515-5115, *E-mail:* yim@eos.ncsu.edu. *Web site:* http://www.ne.ncsu.edu/

Find an in-depth description at www.petersons.com/gradchannel.

■ THE OHIO STATE UNIVERSITY

Graduate School, College of Engineering, Department of Mechanical Engineering, Program in Nuclear Engineering, Columbus, OH 43210

AWARDS MS, PhD.

Degree requirements: For master's, thesis optional; for doctorate, thesis/dissertation.

Entrance requirements: For master's and doctorate, GRE General Test, TOEFL.

■ OREGON STATE UNIVERSITY

Graduate School, College of Engineering, Department of Nuclear Engineering and Radiation Health Physics, Corvallis, OR 97331

AWARDS Nuclear engineering (MS, PhD); radiation health physics (MS, PhD). Part-time programs available.

Faculty: 10 full-time (1 woman).
Students: 23 full-time (5 women), 3 part-time; includes 1 minority (Asian American or Pacific Islander), 5 international. Average age 31. In 2001, 10 master's, 5 doctorates awarded. Terminal master's awarded for partial completion of doctoral program.
Degree requirements: For master's and doctorate, thesis/dissertation.

Entrance requirements: For master's and doctorate, GRE General Test, TOEFL, minimum GPA of 3.0 in last 90 hours. *Application deadline:* For fall admission, 6/15. Applications are processed on a rolling basis. *Application fee:* $50.
Expenses: Tuition, area resident: Full-time $15,933. Tuition, state resident: full-time $28,937.
Financial support: Fellowships, research assistantships, teaching assistantships, institutionally sponsored loans available. Support available to part-time students. Financial award application deadline: 2/1.
Faculty research: Reactor thermal hydraulics and safety, applications of radiation and nuclear techniques, computational methods development, environmental transport of radioactive materials.
Dr. Andrew C. Klein, Head, 541-737-2343, *Fax:* 541-737-0480, *E-mail:* kleina@ne.orst.edu.
Application contact: Dr. Todd S. Palmer, Coordinator, 541-737-2343, *Fax:* 541-737-0480, *E-mail:* nuc_engr@ne.orst.edu. *Web site:* http://www.ne.orst.edu/

Find an in-depth description at www.petersons.com/gradchannel.

■ THE PENNSYLVANIA STATE UNIVERSITY UNIVERSITY PARK CAMPUS

Graduate School, College of Engineering, Department of Mechanical and Nuclear Engineering, Program in Nuclear Engineering, State College, University Park, PA 16802-1503

AWARDS M Eng, MS, PhD.

Students: 26 full-time (8 women), 12 part-time (2 women). In 2001, 8 master's, 4 doctorates awarded.
Expenses: Tuition, state resident: full-time $7,882; part-time $333 per credit. Tuition, nonresident: full-time $16,142; part-time $673 per credit. Required fees: $124 per semester.
Dr. Arthur T. Motta, Graduate Officer, 814-863-6384.

■ PURDUE UNIVERSITY

Graduate School, Schools of Engineering, School of Nuclear Engineering, West Lafayette, IN 47907

AWARDS MS, MSNE, PhD. Part-time programs available.

Faculty: 8 full-time (0 women), 2 part-time/adjunct (0 women).
Students: 30 full-time (1 woman), 5 part-time (1 woman); includes 1 minority (Hispanic American), 20 international. Average age 27. 68 applicants, 16% accepted. In 2001, 9 master's, 4 doctorates awarded. Terminal master's awarded for partial completion of doctoral program.

Degree requirements: For master's, thesis or alternative; for doctorate, thesis/dissertation.
Entrance requirements: For master's and doctorate, TOEFL, minimum GPA of 3.0. *Application deadline:* For fall admission, 12/31 (priority date); for spring admission, 8/15 (priority date). Applications are processed on a rolling basis. *Application fee:* $30. Electronic applications accepted.
Expenses: Tuition, state resident: full-time $4,164; part-time $149 per credit hour. Tuition, nonresident: full-time $13,872; part-time $458 per credit hour. Tuition and fees vary according to campus/location and program.
Financial support: In 2001–02, 6 fellowships with full tuition reimbursements (averaging $15,000 per year), 27 research assistantships with full tuition reimbursements (averaging $15,600 per year) were awarded. Teaching assistantships with full tuition reimbursements Support available to part-time students. Financial award application deadline: 5/1; financial award applicants required to submit FAFSA.
Faculty research: Nuclear reactor safety, thermal hydraulics, fusion technology, reactor materials, reactor physics. *Total annual research expenditures:* $3.5 million.
Dr. L. H. Tsoukalas, Head, 765-494-5742, *Fax:* 765-494-9570.
Application contact: Dr. C. K. Choi, Graduate Chairman, 765-494-6789, *Fax:* 765-494-9570, *E-mail:* choi@ecn.purdue.edu. *Web site:* http://ne.www.ecn.purdue.edu/NE/

■ TEXAS A&M UNIVERSITY

College of Engineering, Department of Nuclear Engineering, College Station, TX 77843

AWARDS Health physics/radiological health (MS), including health physics, industrial hygiene, safety engineering; nuclear engineering (M Eng, MS, PhD).

Faculty: 47.
Students: 69 (19 women). Average age 28.
Degree requirements: For master's, thesis or alternative; for doctorate, thesis/dissertation, departmental qualifying exams.
Entrance requirements: For master's and doctorate, GRE General Test, TOEFL. *Application fee:* $50 ($75 for international students).
Expenses: Tuition, state resident: full-time $11,872. Tuition, nonresident: full-time $17,892.
Financial support: Fellowships, research assistantships, teaching assistantships, career-related internships or fieldwork available. Financial award application deadline: 4/1; financial award applicants required to submit FAFSA.
Dr. Alan E. Waltar, Head, 979-845-4161.

Texas A&M University (continued)
Application contact: Dr. Yassin A. Hassan, Graduate Coordinator, 979-845-7090.

Find an in-depth description at www.petersons.com/gradchannel.

■ THE UNIVERSITY OF ARIZONA

Graduate College, College of Engineering and Mines, Department of Nuclear and Energy Engineering, Tucson, AZ 85721

AWARDS Nuclear engineering (MS, PhD). Part-time programs available.

Degree requirements: For master's and doctorate, thesis/dissertation.
Entrance requirements: For master's, TOEFL, minimum GPA of 3.0; for doctorate, TOEFL.
Expenses: Tuition, state resident: full-time $2,490; part-time $436 per unit. Tuition, nonresident: full-time $10,300; part-time $436 per unit. Full-time tuition and fees vary according to degree level and program.
Faculty research: Nuclear safety, waste management, energy resources, dynamics and control.

■ UNIVERSITY OF CALIFORNIA, BERKELEY

Graduate Division, College of Engineering, Department of Nuclear Engineering, Berkeley, CA 94720-1500

AWARDS M Eng, MS, PhD.

Degree requirements: For master's, project or thesis; for doctorate, thesis/dissertation, oral exam.
Entrance requirements: For master's and doctorate, GRE General Test, TOEFL, minimum GPA of 3.0.
Expenses: Tuition, nonresident: full-time $10,704. Required fees: $4,349.
Faculty research: Applied nuclear reactions and instrumentation, fission reactor engineering, fusion reactor technology, nuclear waste and materials management, radiation protection and environmental effects. *Web site:* http://www.nuc.berkeley.edu

■ UNIVERSITY OF CINCINNATI

Division of Research and Advanced Studies, College of Engineering, Department of Mechanical, Industrial and Nuclear Engineering, Program in Nuclear Engineering, Cincinnati, OH 45221

AWARDS MS, PhD. Part-time programs available. Terminal master's awarded for partial completion of doctoral program.

Degree requirements: For master's, project or thesis; for doctorate, thesis/dissertation.
Entrance requirements: For master's and doctorate, GRE General Test, TOEFL.

Application deadline: For fall admission, 2/1 (priority date). *Application fee:* $40. Electronic applications accepted.
Expenses: Tuition, state resident: part-time $2,698 per quarter. Tuition, nonresident: part-time $4,977 per quarter.
Financial support: Fellowships, career-related internships or fieldwork, tuition waivers (partial), and unspecified assistantships available. Financial award application deadline: 2/1.
Faculty research: Nuclear fission reactor engineering, reduction and fusion effects, health and medical physics, radiological assessment.
Application contact: Dr. Henry Spitz, Graduate Program Director, 513-556-2003, *Fax:* 513-556-3390, *E-mail:* henry.spitz@uc.edu. *Web site:* http://www.min.uc.edu/

■ UNIVERSITY OF FLORIDA

Graduate School, College of Engineering, Department of Nuclear and Radiological Engineering, Gainesville, FL 32611

AWARDS Biomedical engineering (ME, MS, PhD, Certificate, Engr); engineering physics (ME, MS, PhD, Engr); health physics (MS, PhD); medical physics (MS, PhD); nuclear engineering sciences (ME, PhD, Engr); nuclear sciences engineering (MS).

Degree requirements: For master's and doctorate, one foreign language, thesis/dissertation; for other advanced degree, thesis optional.
Entrance requirements: For master's and doctorate, GRE General Test, TOEFL, minimum GPA of 3.0; for other advanced degree, GRE General Test. Electronic applications accepted.
Expenses: Tuition, state resident: part-time $164 per hour. Tuition, nonresident: part-time $571 per hour. Tuition and fees vary according to course level and program.
Faculty research: Robotics, Florida radon mitigation, nuclear space power, radioactive waste management, internal dosimetry. *Web site:* http://www.nucegn.ufl.edu/

■ UNIVERSITY OF IDAHO

College of Graduate Studies, College of Engineering, Department of Mechanical Engineering, Program in Nuclear Engineering, Moscow, ID 83844-2282

AWARDS M Engr, MS, PhD.

Degree requirements: For master's, thesis or alternative; for doctorate, thesis/dissertation.
Entrance requirements: For master's, TOEFL, minimum GPA of 2.8; for doctorate, TOEFL, minimum undergraduate GPA of 2.8, 3.0 graduate. *Application deadline:* For fall admission, 8/1; for spring admission, 12/15. *Application fee:* $35 ($45 for international students).

Expenses: Tuition, state resident: full-time $1,613. Tuition, nonresident: full-time $3,000.
Financial support: Application deadline: 2/15.
Application contact: Dr. Alan G. Stephens, Director, 208-526-4907, *Fax:* 208-526-4970, *E-mail:* drislorr@is.is.isu.edu.

■ UNIVERSITY OF ILLINOIS AT URBANA–CHAMPAIGN

Graduate College, College of Engineering, Department of Nuclear, Plasma, and Radiological Engineering, Champaign, IL 61820

AWARDS Health physics (MS, PhD); nuclear engineering (MS, PhD).

Faculty: 9 full-time, 2 part-time/adjunct.
Students: 41 full-time (7 women); includes 5 minority (3 Asian Americans or Pacific Islanders, 2 Hispanic Americans), 25 international. 50 applicants, 26% accepted. In 2001, 12 master's, 13 doctorates awarded.
Degree requirements: For master's and doctorate, thesis/dissertation.
Application deadline: For fall admission, 2/15 (priority date). Applications are processed on a rolling basis. *Application fee:* $40 ($50 for international students). Electronic applications accepted.
Expenses: Tuition, state resident: part-time $3,227 per degree program. Tuition, nonresident: part-time $7,169 per degree program. Tuition and fees vary according to program.
Financial support: In 2001–02, 22 research assistantships, 11 teaching assistantships were awarded. Fellowships Financial award application deadline: 2/15. James F. Stubbins, Head, 217-333-6474, *Fax:* 217-333-2906, *E-mail:* jstubbin@uiuc.edu.
Application contact: Jeffrey Farlow-Cornell, Coordinator, 217-244-5382, *Fax:* 217-333-2906, *E-mail:* jfarlow@uiuc.edu. *Web site:* http://www.ne.uiuc.edu/

Find an in-depth description at www.petersons.com/gradchannel.

■ UNIVERSITY OF MARYLAND, COLLEGE PARK

Graduate Studies and Research, A. James Clark School of Engineering, Department of Materials and Nuclear Engineering, Nuclear Engineering Program, College Park, MD 20742

AWARDS ME, MS, PhD. Part-time and evening/weekend programs available. Postbaccalaureate distance learning degree programs offered.

Students: 8 full-time (0 women), 3 part-time (2 women); includes 3 minority (1 African American, 1 Asian American or Pacific Islander, 1 Hispanic American), 3 international. 23 applicants, 30% accepted,

3 enrolled. In 2001, 3 master's, 2 doctorates awarded.
Degree requirements: For master's, thesis optional; for doctorate, variable foreign language requirement, thesis/dissertation, oral exam.
Entrance requirements: For master's and doctorate, GRE General Test, TOEFL, minimum GPA of 3.0. *Application deadline:* For fall admission, 8/1; for spring admission, 12/1. Applications are processed on a rolling basis. *Application fee:* $50 ($70 for international students). Electronic applications accepted.
Expenses: Tuition, state resident: part-time $289 per credit hour. Tuition, nonresident: part-time $448 per credit hour. One-time fee: $436 part-time. Full-time tuition and fees vary according to course load, campus/location and program.
Financial support: Fellowships, research assistantships, teaching assistantships, tuition waivers (full) available. Financial award applicants required to submit FAFSA.
Faculty research: Reliability and risk assessment, heat transfer and two-phase flow, reactor safety analysis, nuclear reactor, radiation/polymers.
Dr. Luther Wolf, Associate Chair and Contact, 301-405-0042, *Fax:* 301-314-2029.
Application contact: Trudy Lindsey, Director, Graduate Admissions and Records, 301-405-6991, *Fax:* 301-314-9305, *E-mail:* grschool@deans.umd.edu.

■ UNIVERSITY OF MICHIGAN
Horace H. Rackham School of Graduate Studies, College of Engineering, Department of Nuclear Engineering and Radiological Sciences, Ann Arbor, MI 48109

AWARDS Nuclear engineering (Nuc E); nuclear engineering and radiological sciences (PhD); nuclear science (MS, PhD).

Faculty: 16 full-time (1 woman), 6 part-time/adjunct (1 woman).
Students: 68 full-time (21 women), 2 part-time (1 woman); includes 7 minority (1 African American, 3 Asian Americans or Pacific Islanders, 3 Hispanic Americans), 25 international. Average age 26. 80 applicants, 61% accepted, 24 enrolled. In 2001, 20 master's, 6 doctorates awarded. Terminal master's awarded for partial completion of doctoral program.
Degree requirements: For master's, thesis optional; for doctorate, thesis/dissertation, oral defense of dissertation, preliminary exams. *Median time to degree:* Master's–1.5 years full-time; doctorate–5 years full-time.
Entrance requirements: For master's and doctorate, GRE General Test. *Application deadline:* For fall admission, 2/1 (priority date). Applications are processed on a rolling basis. *Application fee:* $55. Electronic applications accepted.

Financial support: In 2001–02, 24 fellowships with full tuition reimbursements (averaging $22,000 per year), 44 research assistantships with full tuition reimbursements (averaging $22,000 per year), 3 teaching assistantships with full tuition reimbursements (averaging $18,624 per year) were awarded. Career-related internships or fieldwork, Federal Work-Study, institutionally sponsored loans, scholarships/grants, traineeships, health care benefits, and unspecified assistantships also available. Financial award application deadline: 4/15.
Faculty research: Reactor physics and engineering, instrumentation and measurement, nuclear materials, plasma physics and fusion, medical physics. *Total annual research expenditures:* $8.1 million.
Dr. John C. Lee, Chair, 734-764-4260, *Fax:* 734-763-4540, *E-mail:* jcl@umich.edu.
Application contact: Peggy Jo Gramer, Student Services Associate, 734-615-8810, *Fax:* 734-763-4540, *E-mail:* pjgramer@umich.edu. *Web site:* http://www.ners.engin.umich.edu/~nuclear/
Find an in-depth description at www.petersons.com/gradchannel.

■ UNIVERSITY OF MISSOURI–COLUMBIA
Graduate School, College of Engineering, Nuclear Engineering Program, Columbia, MO 65211

AWARDS Nuclear engineering (MS, PhD), including health physics (MS), medical physics (MS), nuclear engineering (MS).

Faculty: 7 full-time (2 women).
Students: 20 full-time (6 women), 12 part-time (4 women); includes 7 minority (1 Asian American or Pacific Islander, 6 Hispanic Americans), 10 international. 9 applicants, 78% accepted. In 2001, 4 master's, 6 doctorates awarded.
Degree requirements: For master's, research project; for doctorate, thesis/dissertation.
Entrance requirements: For master's and doctorate, GRE General Test, TOEFL. *Application deadline:* For fall admission, 3/15 (priority date). *Application fee:* $25 ($50 for international students).
Expenses: Tuition, state resident: part-time $179 per credit hour. Tuition, nonresident: part-time $539 per credit hour. Required fees: $122 per semester. Tuition and fees vary according to program.
Financial support: In 2001–02, 6 fellowships were awarded; research assistantships, teaching assistantships, institutionally sponsored loans also available.
Dr. Tushar Ghosh, Director of Graduate Studies, 573-882-9736, *E-mail:* ghosht@missouri.edu. *Web site:* http://www.engineering.missouri.edu/nuclear.htm

■ UNIVERSITY OF MISSOURI–ROLLA
Graduate School, School of Mines and Metallurgy, Department of Nuclear Engineering, Rolla, MO 65409-0910

AWARDS MS, DE, PhD. Part-time programs available.

Degree requirements: For master's and doctorate, thesis/dissertation.
Entrance requirements: For master's, GRE General Test, TOEFL, minimum GPA of 3.0 in last 4 semesters; for doctorate, GRE General Test, TOEFL. Electronic applications accepted.
Faculty research: Radiation transport, reactor safety, materials research, probabilistic risk assessment, reactor diagnostics.

■ UNIVERSITY OF NEW MEXICO
Graduate School, School of Engineering, Department of Chemical and Nuclear Engineering, Program in Nuclear Engineering, Albuquerque, NM 87131-2039

AWARDS MS.

Faculty: 5 full-time (0 women), 2 part-time/adjunct (0 women).
Students: 10 full-time (2 women), 21 part-time (3 women); includes 5 minority (all Hispanic Americans), 6 international. Average age 38. In 2001, 7 master's awarded.
Entrance requirements: For master's, GRE General Test, minimum GPA of 3.0. *Application deadline:* For fall admission, 7/15; for spring admission, 11/10. *Application fee:* $40.
Expenses: Tuition, state resident: full-time $2,771; part-time $115 per credit hour. Tuition, nonresident: full-time $11,207; part-time $467 per credit hour. Required fees: $570; $24 per credit hour. Part-time tuition and fees vary according to course load and program.
Financial support: In 2001–02, 5 students received support, including 1 fellowship (averaging $9,000 per year), 2 research assistantships with tuition reimbursements available (averaging $18,000 per year); health care benefits also available. Financial award application deadline: 3/1.
Faculty research: Plasma science, fusion technology, space power, thermal hydraulics, radiation diagnostics.
Application contact: Mercy M. Salazar, Administrative Assistant II, 505-277-5431, *Fax:* 505-277-5433, *E-mail:* mercy@unm.edu. *Web site:* http://www-chne.unm.edu/home01/NEindex.htm/

■ THE UNIVERSITY OF TENNESSEE

Graduate School, College of Engineering, Department of Nuclear Engineering, Knoxville, TN 37996

AWARDS Nuclear engineering (MS, PhD), including radiological engineering (MS). Part-time programs available.

Faculty: 11 full-time (1 woman), 2 part-time/adjunct (0 women).
Students: 28 full-time (5 women), 14 part-time (3 women); includes 2 minority (1 African American, 1 Asian American or Pacific Islander), 8 international. 43 applicants, 53% accepted. In 2001, 3 master's, 6 doctorates awarded.
Degree requirements: For master's, thesis or alternative; for doctorate, thesis/dissertation.
Entrance requirements: For master's and doctorate, GRE General Test, TOEFL, minimum GPA of 2.7. *Application deadline:* For fall admission, 2/1 (priority date). Applications are processed on a rolling basis. *Application fee:* $35. Electronic applications accepted.
Expenses: Tuition, state resident: full-time $4,280; part-time $233 per hour. Tuition, nonresident: full-time $12,066; part-time $666 per hour. Tuition and fees vary according to program.
Financial support: In 2001–02, 2 fellowships, 22 research assistantships, 1 teaching assistantship were awarded. Career-related internships or fieldwork, Federal Work-Study, institutionally sponsored loans, and unspecified assistantships also available. Financial award application deadline: 2/1; financial award applicants required to submit FAFSA.
Dr. H. L. Dodds, Head, 865-974-2525, *Fax:* 865-974-0668, *E-mail:* hdj@utk.edu.

■ UNIVERSITY OF UTAH

Graduate School, College of Engineering, Department of Civil and Environmental Engineering, Program in Nuclear Engineering, Salt Lake City, UT 84112-1107

AWARDS ME, MS, PhD.

Students: 4 full-time (1 woman), 2 part-time; includes 1 minority (Asian American or Pacific Islander), 1 international. Average age 30. Terminal master's awarded for partial completion of doctoral program.
Degree requirements: For master's, special project (ME), thesis (MS); for doctorate, thesis/dissertation, comprehensive exam.

Entrance requirements: For master's, GRE General Test, TOEFL, minimum GPA of 3.0; for doctorate, GRE, TOEFL, minimum GPA of 3.0. *Application deadline:* For fall admission, 7/1. *Application fee:* $40 ($60 for international students).
Expenses: Tuition, state resident: part-time $320 per semester hour. Tuition, nonresident: part-time $1,135 per semester hour. Required fees: $143 per semester hour. Tuition and fees vary according to course load, degree level and program.
Financial support: Fellowships available. Financial award applicants required to submit FAFSA.
Dr. David M. Slaughter, Chair, 801-581-8304, *E-mail:* slaughter@nuclear.utah.edu.
Application contact: Melinda Krahenbuhl, Advisor, 801-581-8304, *E-mail:* mpk@nuclear.utah.edu. *Web site:* http://www.coe.utah.edu/

■ UNIVERSITY OF VIRGINIA

School of Engineering and Applied Science, Program in Nuclear Engineering, Charlottesville, VA 22903

AWARDS ME, MS, PhD. Part-time programs available.

Faculty: 4 full-time (0 women).
Students: 2 full-time (0 women). Average age 44. 1 applicant, 100% accepted. In 2001, 1 master's, 1 doctorate awarded. Terminal master's awarded for partial completion of doctoral program.
Degree requirements: For master's, thesis (MS); for doctorate, thesis/dissertation, comprehensive exam.
Entrance requirements: For master's and doctorate, GRE General Test, TOEFL. *Application deadline:* For fall admission, 8/1 (priority date); for spring admission, 12/1. Applications are processed on a rolling basis. *Application fee:* $40. Electronic applications accepted.
Expenses: Tuition, state resident: full-time $3,988. Tuition, nonresident: full-time $17,078. Required fees: $1,190.
Financial support: Fellowships, research assistantships, teaching assistantships available. Financial award application deadline: 2/1; financial award applicants required to submit FAFSA.
Faculty research: Reactor design, nuclear reactor safety, radio isotope usage, radiation damage studies, neutron radiography.
Joseph A.C. Humprey, Chair, 434-924-7422, *Fax:* 434-982-2037, *E-mail:* mae-adm@virginia.edu.
Application contact: Kathryn Thornton, Assistant Dean, 434-924-3897, *Fax:* 434-982-2214, *E-mail:* inquiry@cs.virginia.edu. *Web site:* http://www.mane.virginia.edu/

■ UNIVERSITY OF WISCONSIN–MADISON

Graduate School, College of Engineering, Department of Engineering Physics, Madison, WI 53706-1380

AWARDS Engineering mechanics (MS, PhD); nuclear engineering and engineering physics (MS, PhD). Part-time programs available. Postbaccalaureate distance learning degree programs offered (minimal on-campus study).

Faculty: 24 full-time (2 women), 4 part-time/adjunct (0 women).
Students: 62 full-time (8 women), 2 part-time. Average age 25. 125 applicants, 20% accepted. In 2001, 12 master's, 9 doctorates awarded. Terminal master's awarded for partial completion of doctoral program.
Degree requirements: For master's, thesis optional; for doctorate, thesis/dissertation.
Entrance requirements: For master's and doctorate, GRE General Test, minimum GPA of 3.0 in last 60 hours, appropriate bachelor's degree. *Application deadline:* For fall admission, 1/15 (priority date). Applications are processed on a rolling basis. *Application fee:* $45. Electronic applications accepted.
Expenses: Tuition, state resident: full-time $7,361; part-time $399 per credit. Tuition, nonresident: full-time $20,499; part-time $1,282 per credit. Required fees: $34 per credit. Full-time tuition and fees vary according to course load, program, reciprocity agreements and student level.
Financial support: In 2001–02, 47 students received support, including 4 fellowships with full tuition reimbursements available (averaging $17,400 per year), 34 research assistantships with full tuition reimbursements available (averaging $15,792 per year), 9 teaching assistantships with full tuition reimbursements available (averaging $15,800 per year); career-related internships or fieldwork, Federal Work-Study, and institutionally sponsored loans also available. Support available to part-time students. Financial award application deadline: 1/15.
Faculty research: Fission reactor engineering and safety, plasma physics and fusion technology, plasma processing and ion implantation, applied superconductivity and cryogenics, engineering mechanics and astronautics. *Total annual research expenditures:* $6.5 million.
Dr. Michael L. Corradini, Chair, 608-263-1646, *Fax:* 608-263-7451, *E-mail:* corradini@engr.wisc.edu. *Web site:* http://www.engr.wisc.edu/ep/

Find an in-depth description at www.petersons.com/gradchannel.

Engineering Design

ENGINEERING DESIGN

■ THE CATHOLIC UNIVERSITY OF AMERICA

School of Engineering, Department of Mechanical Engineering, Washington, DC 20064

AWARDS Design (D Engr, PhD); design and robotics (MME, D Engr, PhD); fluid mechanics and thermal science (MME, D Engr, PhD); mechanical design (MME); ocean and structural acoustics (MME, MS Engr, PhD). Part-time and evening/weekend programs available.

Faculty: 6 full-time (1 woman).
Students: 7 full-time (0 women), 16 part-time (3 women); includes 4 minority (2 African Americans, 2 Asian Americans or Pacific Islanders), 8 international. Average age 34. 14 applicants, 36% accepted, 2 enrolled. In 2001, 3 master's, 3 doctorates awarded.
Degree requirements: For master's, thesis optional; for doctorate, thesis/dissertation, oral exams, comprehensive exam.
Entrance requirements: For master's, minimum GPA of 3.0; for doctorate, minimum GPA of 3.5. *Application deadline:* For fall admission, 8/1 (priority date); for spring admission, 12/1. Applications are processed on a rolling basis. *Application fee:* $55. Electronic applications accepted.
Expenses: Tuition: Full-time $20,050; part-time $770 per credit. Required fees: $430 per term. Tuition and fees vary according to program.
Financial support: Research assistantships, teaching assistantships, career-related internships or fieldwork, Federal Work-Study, institutionally sponsored loans, and tuition waivers (full and partial) available. Support available to part-time students. Financial award application deadline: 2/1.
Faculty research: Automated engineering.
Dr. Ji Steven Brown, Chair, 202-319-5170.

■ KETTERING UNIVERSITY

Graduate School, Mechanical Engineering Department, Flint, MI 48504-4898

AWARDS Automotive systems (MS Eng); manufacturing (MS Eng); mechanical cognate (MS Eng); mechanical design (MS Eng). Part-time and evening/weekend programs available. Postbaccalaureate distance learning degree programs offered (no on-campus study).

Faculty: 15 full-time (0 women).
Students: 6 full-time (1 woman), 88 part-time (12 women); includes 8 minority (7

African Americans, 1 Native American), 43 international. 163 applicants, 87% accepted. In 2001, 18 degrees awarded.
Degree requirements: For master's, thesis (for some programs), registration. *Median time to degree:* Master's–3 years full-time, 6 years part-time.
Application deadline: For fall admission, 7/15. Applications are processed on a rolling basis. *Application fee:* $0. Electronic applications accepted.
Expenses: Tuition: Full-time $8,370; part-time $465 per credit.
Financial support: Fellowships with full tuition reimbursements, research assistantships with full tuition reimbursements, teaching assistantships with full tuition reimbursements, Federal Work-Study, scholarships/grants, and tuition waivers (partial) available. Support available to part-time students. Financial award application deadline: 7/15; financial award applicants required to submit CSS PROFILE or FAFSA.
Dr. K. Joel Berry, Head, 810-762-7833, *Fax:* 810-762-7860, *E-mail:* jberry@kettering.edu.
Application contact: Betty L. Bedore, Coordinator of Publicity, 810-762-7494, *Fax:* 810-762-9935, *E-mail:* bbedore@kettering.edu. *Web site:* http://www.kettering.edu/

■ ROCHESTER INSTITUTE OF TECHNOLOGY

Graduate Enrollment Services, College of Engineering, Department of Design, Development and Manufacturing, Rochester, NY 14623-5698

AWARDS Product development (MS).

Students: In 2001, 24 degrees awarded.
Application deadline: For fall admission, 3/1 (priority date). Applications are processed on a rolling basis. *Application fee:* $50.
Expenses: Tuition: Full-time $20,928; part-time $587 per hour. Required fees: $162. Tuition and fees vary according to program.
Mark Smith, Director, 585-475-7102, *E-mail:* mpdmail@rit.edu.

■ STANFORD UNIVERSITY

School of Engineering, Department of Mechanical Engineering, Program in Product Design, Stanford, CA 94305-9991

AWARDS MS.

Entrance requirements: For master's, GRE General Test, TOEFL. *Application deadline:* For fall admission, 1/15. *Application fee:* $65 ($80 for international students). Electronic applications accepted.

Application contact: Admissions Office, 650-723-3148.
Find an in-depth description at www.petersons.com/gradchannel.

■ UNIVERSITY OF CENTRAL FLORIDA

College of Engineering and Computer Sciences, Department of Industrial Engineering and Management Systems, Orlando, FL 32816

AWARDS Applied operations research (Certificate); computer-integrated manufacturing (MS); design for usability (Certificate); engineering management (MS); industrial engineering (MSIE); industrial engineering and management systems (PhD); industrial ergonomics and safety (Certificate); operations research (MS); product assurance engineering (MS); project engineering (Certificate); quality assurance (Certificate). Simulation systems (MS). Systems simulations for engineers (Certificate); training simulation (Certificate). Part-time and evening/weekend programs available.

Faculty: 20 full-time (4 women), 8 part-time/adjunct (1 woman).
Students: 92 full-time (19 women), 182 part-time (49 women); includes 66 minority (18 African Americans, 10 Asian Americans or Pacific Islanders, 35 Hispanic Americans, 3 Native Americans), 57 international. Average age 32. 231 applicants, 84% accepted, 85 enrolled. In 2001, 3 master's, 9 doctorates awarded.
Degree requirements: For master's, thesis; for doctorate, thesis/dissertation, departmental qualifying exam, candidacy exam.
Entrance requirements: For master's, GRE General Test, TOEFL, minimum GPA of 3.0 in last 60 hours; for doctorate, TOEFL, minimum GPA of 3.5 in last 60 hours. *Application deadline:* For fall admission, 7/15 (priority date); for spring admission, 12/1 (priority date). *Application fee:* $20. Electronic applications accepted.
Expenses: Tuition, state resident: part-time $162 per hour. Tuition, nonresident: part-time $569 per hour.
Financial support: In 2001–02, 23 fellowships with partial tuition reimbursements (averaging $3,272 per year), 131 research assistantships with partial tuition reimbursements (averaging $3,125 per year), 24 teaching assistantships with partial tuition reimbursements (averaging $3,823 per year) were awarded. Career-related internships or fieldwork, Federal Work-Study, institutionally sponsored loans, tuition waivers (partial), and unspecified assistantships also available. Financial award application deadline: 3/1;

University of Central Florida (continued)
financial award applicants required to submit FAFSA.
Dr. Charles Reily, Chair, 407-823-2204, *E-mail:* creily@mail.ucf.edu.
Application contact: Dr. Linda Malone, Coordinator, 407-823-2204, *E-mail:* malone@mail.ucf.edu. *Web site:* http://www.ucf.edu/

Find an in-depth description at www.petersons.com/gradchannel.

■ UNIVERSITY OF ILLINOIS AT URBANA–CHAMPAIGN

Graduate College, College of Engineering, Department of General Engineering, Champaign, IL 61820

AWARDS Systems engineering and engineering design (MS), including general engineering.

Faculty: 20 full-time (5 women), 2 part-time/adjunct (0 women).
Students: 31 full-time (4 women); includes 3 minority (1 Asian American or Pacific Islander, 2 Hispanic Americans), 20 international. 41 applicants, 32% accepted. In 2001, 9 degrees awarded.

Entrance requirements: For master's, GRE, minimum GPA of 3.0. *Application deadline:* For fall admission, 2/1. Applications are processed on a rolling basis. *Application fee:* $40 ($50 for international students). Electronic applications accepted.
Expenses: Tuition, state resident: part-time $3,227 per degree program. Tuition, nonresident: part-time $7,169 per degree program. Tuition and fees vary according to program.
Financial support: In 2001–02, 1 fellowship, 17 research assistantships, 9 teaching assistantships were awarded. Scholarships/grants also available. Financial award application deadline: 2/15.
Dr. Harry E. Cook, Head, 217-333-2730, *Fax:* 217-244-5705, *E-mail:* h-cook3@uiuc.edu.
Application contact: Donna J. Eiskamp, Administrative Aide, 217-333-2730, *Fax:* 217-244-5705, *E-mail:* deiskamp@uiuc.edu. *Web site:* http://www.ge.uiuc.edu/

Find an in-depth description at www.petersons.com/gradchannel.

■ UNIVERSITY OF NEW HAVEN

Graduate School, School of Engineering and Applied Science, Program in Environmental Engineering, West Haven, CT 06516-1916

AWARDS Civil engineering design (Certificate); environmental engineering (MS). Part-time and evening/weekend programs available.

Students: 4 full-time (2 women), 17 part-time (3 women); includes 1 minority (African American), 1 international. In 2001, 5 degrees awarded.
Degree requirements: For master's, thesis or alternative.
Entrance requirements: For master's, bachelor's degree in engineering. *Application deadline:* Applications are processed on a rolling basis. *Application fee:* $50.
Expenses: Tuition: Full-time $12,015; part-time $445 per credit hour. Required fees: $30. One-time fee: $100 full-time.
Financial support: Federal Work-Study available. Support available to part-time students. Financial award application deadline: 5/1; financial award applicants required to submit FAFSA.
Dr. Agamemnon D. Koutsospyros, Coordinator, 203-932-7398.

Engineering Physics

ENGINEERING PHYSICS

■ AIR FORCE INSTITUTE OF TECHNOLOGY

School of Engineering and Management, Department of Engineering Physics, Dayton, OH 45433-7765

AWARDS Applied physics (MS, PhD); electro-optics (MS, PhD); environmental science (MS, PhD); materials science (MS, PhD); meteorology (MS); nuclear engineering (MS, PhD). Part-time programs available.

Degree requirements: For master's and doctorate, thesis/dissertation.
Entrance requirements: For master's and doctorate, GRE General Test, minimum GPA of 3.0, U.S. citizenship.
Faculty research: High-energy lasers, space physics, nuclear weapon effects, semiconductor physics. *Web site:* http://en.afit.edu/bnp/

Find an in-depth description at www.petersons.com/gradchannel.

■ CORNELL UNIVERSITY

Graduate School, Graduate Fields of Engineering, Field of Applied Physics, Ithaca, NY 14853-0001

AWARDS Applied physics (PhD); engineering physics (M Eng, PhD).

Faculty: 40 full-time.
Students: 62 full-time (11 women); includes 9 minority (1 African American, 5 Asian Americans or Pacific Islanders, 2 Hispanic Americans, 1 Native American), 22 international. 98 applicants, 48% accepted. In 2001, 20 master's, 7 doctorates awarded. Terminal master's awarded for partial completion of doctoral program.
Degree requirements: For doctorate, thesis/dissertation, written exams.
Entrance requirements: For master's, GRE General Test, TOEFL, 3 letters of recommendation; for doctorate, GRE General Test, GRE Subject Test (physics), TOEFL, 3 letters of recommendation. *Application deadline:* For fall admission, 1/15. *Application fee:* $65. Electronic applications accepted.
Expenses: Tuition: Full-time $25,970. Required fees: $50.
Financial support: In 2001–02, 55 students received support, including 6 fellowships with full tuition reimbursements available, 38 research assistantships with full tuition reimbursements available, 11 teaching assistantships with full tuition reimbursements available; institutionally sponsored loans, scholarships/grants, tuition waivers (full and partial), and unspecified assistantships also available.
Faculty research: Quantum and nonlinear optics, plasma physics, solid state physics, condensed matter physics and nanotechnology, condensed matter physics.
Application contact: Graduate Field Assistant, 607-255-0638, *E-mail:* aep_info@cornell.edu. *Web site:* http://www.gradschool.cornell.edu/grad/fields_1/app-phys.html

■ GEORGE MASON UNIVERSITY

College of Arts and Sciences, Department of Physics, Fairfax, VA 22030-4444

AWARDS Applied and engineering physics (MS).

Faculty: 16 full-time (7 women), 10 part-time/adjunct (2 women).
Students: 2 full-time (1 woman), 7 part-time (2 women). Average age 34. 10 applicants, 30% accepted, 2 enrolled. In 2001, 3 degrees awarded.
Degree requirements: For master's, thesis optional.
Entrance requirements: For master's, minimum GPA of 2.75 in last 60 hours.

Application deadline: For fall admission, 5/1; for spring admission, 11/1. *Application fee:* $30. Electronic applications accepted.

Expenses: Tuition, state resident: full-time $3,168; part-time $132 per credit hour. Tuition, nonresident: full-time $11,280; part-time $470 per credit hour. Required fees: $1,416; $59 per credit hour.

Financial support: Research assistantships, teaching assistantships available. Support available to part-time students. Financial award application deadline: 3/1; financial award applicants required to submit FAFSA.

Maria Dworzecka, Chairman, 703-993-1280, *Fax:* 703-993-1269, *E-mail:* mdworzecka@gmu.edu.

Application contact: Dr. Paul So, Information Contact, 703-993-1280, *E-mail:* physics@gmu.edu. *Web site:* http://www.physics.gmu.edu/program/graduate.html

■ MICHIGAN TECHNOLOGICAL UNIVERSITY

Graduate School, College of Engineering, Program in Engineering Physics, Houghton, MI 49931-1295

AWARDS PhD.

Entrance requirements: For doctorate, GRE, TOEFL. Electronic applications accepted.

Financial support: Fellowships, research assistantships, teaching assistantships available.

Ravi Pandey, Department Chair.

Application contact: 906-487-2086, *Fax:* 906-487-2933, *E-mail:* physics@mtu.edu. *Web site:* http://www.phy.mtu.edu/Engphys/program.html

Find an in-depth description at www.petersons.com/gradchannel.

■ POLYTECHNIC UNIVERSITY, LONG ISLAND GRADUATE CENTER

Graduate Programs, Department of Electrical Engineering, Major in Electrophysics, Melville, NY 11747

AWARDS MS.

Degree requirements: For master's, thesis (for some programs). Electronic applications accepted.

■ POLYTECHNIC UNIVERSITY, WESTCHESTER GRADUATE CENTER

Graduate Programs, Department of Electrical Engineering, Major in Electrophysics, Hawthorne, NY 10532-1507

AWARDS MS.

Degree requirements: For master's, thesis (for some programs). Electronic applications accepted.

■ RENSSELAER POLYTECHNIC INSTITUTE

Graduate School, School of Engineering, Department of Mechanical, Aerospace, and Nuclear Engineering, Program in Engineering Physics, Troy, NY 12180-3590

AWARDS M Eng, MS, D Eng, PhD. Part-time programs available.

Faculty: 6 full-time (0 women), 1 part-time/adjunct (0 women).

Students: 5 full-time (0 women), 1 part-time; includes 3 minority (1 African American, 2 Asian Americans or Pacific Islanders), 1 international. 8 applicants, 50% accepted, 2 enrolled. Terminal master's awarded for partial completion of doctoral program.

Degree requirements: For master's, thesis (for some programs); for doctorate, thesis/dissertation.

Entrance requirements: For master's and doctorate, TOEFL, GRE. *Application deadline:* For fall admission, 1/15 (priority date); for spring admission, 10/15 (priority date). Applications are processed on a rolling basis. *Application fee:* $45. Electronic applications accepted.

Expenses: Tuition: Full-time $26,400; part-time $1,320 per credit hour. Required fees: $1,437.

Financial support: In 2001–02, 3 research assistantships with full and partial tuition reimbursements (averaging $12,000 per year), 1 teaching assistantship with full and partial tuition reimbursement (averaging $12,000 per year) were awarded. Fellowships, career-related internships or fieldwork, institutionally sponsored loans, and tuition waivers (full and partial) also available. Financial award application deadline: 2/1.

Faculty research: Nuclear data management, multiphase flow and heat transfer, environmental and operational health physics, fusion reactor engineering and safety, radiation destruction of hazardous chemicals. *Total annual research expenditures:* $844,828.

Dr. Don Steiner, Program Director and Institute Professor, 518-276-4016, *Fax:* 518-276-3055, *E-mail:* steind@rpi.edu.

Application contact: Pamela Zepf, Administrative Secretary, 518-276-6402, *Fax:* 518-276-3055, *E-mail:* zepfp@rpi.edu. *Web site:* http://www.rpi.edu/dept/mane/

Find an in-depth description at www.petersons.com/gradchannel.

■ STEVENS INSTITUTE OF TECHNOLOGY

Graduate School, School of Applied Sciences and Liberal Arts, Department of Physics and Engineering Physics, Hoboken, NJ 07030

AWARDS Applied optics (Certificate); engineering physics (M Eng), including engineering optics, engineering physics; physics (MS, PhD). Surface physics (Certificate). Part-time and evening/weekend programs available. Terminal master's awarded for partial completion of doctoral program.

Degree requirements: For master's, thesis optional; for doctorate, thesis/dissertation.

Entrance requirements: For master's and doctorate, GRE, TOEFL. Electronic applications accepted.

Faculty research: Laser spectroscopy, physical kinetics, semiconductor-device physics, condensed-matter theory. *Web site:* http://attila.stevens-tech.edu/physics/

■ UNIVERSITY OF CALIFORNIA, SAN DIEGO

Graduate Studies and Research, Department of Mechanical and Aerospace Engineering, Program in Engineering Physics, La Jolla, CA 92093

AWARDS MS, PhD. Part-time programs available.

Degree requirements: For master's, comprehensive exam or thesis; for doctorate, thesis/dissertation, qualifying exam.

Entrance requirements: For master's and doctorate, GRE General Test, TOEFL, minimum GPA of 3.0.

Expenses: Tuition, nonresident: full-time $10,434. Required fees: $4,883.

Faculty research: Combustion engineering, environmental mechanics, magnetic recording, materials processing, computational fluid dynamics. *Web site:* http://www-ames.ucsd.edu/

Find an in-depth description at www.petersons.com/gradchannel.

■ UNIVERSITY OF FLORIDA

Graduate School, College of Engineering, Department of Nuclear and Radiological Engineering, Gainesville, FL 32611

AWARDS Biomedical engineering (ME, MS, PhD, Certificate, Engr); engineering physics (ME, MS, PhD, Engr); health physics (MS, PhD); medical physics (MS, PhD); nuclear engineering sciences (ME, PhD, Engr); nuclear sciences engineering (MS).

Degree requirements: For master's and doctorate, one foreign language, thesis/dissertation; for other advanced degree, thesis optional.

Entrance requirements: For master's and doctorate, GRE General Test, TOEFL, minimum GPA of 3.0; for other advanced degree, GRE General Test. Electronic applications accepted.

Expenses: Tuition, state resident: part-time $164 per hour. Tuition, nonresident: part-time $571 per hour. Tuition and fees vary according to course level and program.

University of Florida (continued)
Faculty research: Robotics, Florida radon mitigation, nuclear space power, radioactive waste management, internal dosimetry. *Web site:* http://www.nucegn.ufl.edu/

■ UNIVERSITY OF MAINE

Graduate School, College of Liberal Arts and Sciences, Department of Physics and Astronomy, Program in Engineering Physics, Orono, ME 04469

AWARDS M Eng.

Faculty: 17 full-time, 1 part-time/adjunct.
Degree requirements: For master's, thesis or alternative.
Entrance requirements: For master's, GRE General Test, GRE Subject Test, TOEFL. *Application deadline:* For fall admission, 2/1 (priority date); for spring admission, 10/15. Applications are processed on a rolling basis. *Application fee:* $50.
Expenses: Tuition, state resident: full-time $3,780; part-time $210 per credit hour. Tuition, nonresident: full-time $10,782; part-time $599 per credit hour. Required fees: $9.5 per credit hour. $32 per semester. Tuition and fees vary according to reciprocity agreements.
Financial support: Fellowships, teaching assistantships available. Financial award application deadline: 3/1.
Application contact: Scott G. Delcourt, Director of the Graduate School, 207-581-3218, *Fax:* 207-581-3232, *E-mail:* graduate@maine.edu. *Web site:* http://www.umaine.edu/graduate/

■ UNIVERSITY OF OKLAHOMA

Graduate College, College of Engineering, Program in Engineering Physics, Norman, OK 73019-0390

AWARDS MS, PhD. Part-time and evening/weekend programs available.

Students: 2 full-time (0 women), 1 part-time, 1 international. In 2001, 3 degrees awarded. Terminal master's awarded for partial completion of doctoral program.
Degree requirements: For master's, thesis or alternative, departmental qualifying exam; for doctorate, thesis/dissertation, comprehensive, departmental qualifying, oral, and written exams, comprehensive exam.
Entrance requirements: For master's and doctorate, GRE General Test, GRE Subject Test (physics), TOEFL, previous course work in physics. *Application deadline:* For fall admission, 3/1 (priority date); for spring admission, 10/1. Applications are processed on a rolling basis. *Application fee:* $25.
Expenses: Tuition, state resident: full-time $2,208; part-time $92 per credit hour. Tuition, nonresident: part-time $297 per credit hour. Tuition and fees vary according to course level, course load and program.

Financial support: In 2001–02, 1 student received support, including 1 research assistantship with partial tuition reimbursement available (averaging $14,284 per year), 1 teaching assistantship with partial tuition reimbursement available (averaging $13,781 per year); Federal Work-Study and tuition waivers (full) also available. Financial award application deadline: 3/1; financial award applicants required to submit FAFSA.
Faculty research: Atomic, molecular and chemical physics; high energy physics. Solid state and applied physics.
Mike Santos, Chair, 405-325-3961.
Application contact: Clarissa Dobrinski, Graduate Coordinator, 405-325-3961 Ext. 36127, *Fax:* 405-325-7557, *E-mail:* clarissa@mail.nhn.ou.edu.

■ UNIVERSITY OF SOUTH FLORIDA

College of Graduate Studies, College of Arts and Sciences, Department of Physics, Tampa, FL 33620-9951

AWARDS Engineering science/physics (PhD); physics (MA). Part-time programs available.

Faculty: 15 full-time (0 women), 1 part-time/adjunct (0 women).
Students: 25 full-time (4 women), 7 part-time (3 women); includes 1 minority (African American), 8 international. Average age 26. 17 applicants, 71% accepted, 9 enrolled. In 2001, 2 degrees awarded.
Degree requirements: For master's, thesis optional; for doctorate, 2 foreign languages, thesis/dissertation.
Entrance requirements: For master's, GRE General Test, minimum GPA of 3.0 in last 60 hours; for doctorate, GRE General Test, minimum graduate GPA of 3.2. *Application deadline:* For fall admission, 6/1 (priority date); for spring admission, 10/1. Applications are processed on a rolling basis. *Application fee:* $20. Electronic applications accepted.
Expenses: Tuition, state resident: part-time $166 per credit hour. Tuition, nonresident: part-time $573 per credit hour. Required fees: $17 per term.
Financial support: Fellowships, research assistantships with full tuition reimbursements, teaching assistantships with full tuition reimbursements, Federal Work-Study, institutionally sponsored loans, and scholarships/grants available. Support available to part-time students. Financial award applicants required to submit FAFSA.
Faculty research: Laser, medical, and solid-state physics. *Total annual research expenditures:* $535,934.
R. S. Chang, Chairperson, 813-974-2871, *Fax:* 813-974-5813, *E-mail:* chang@chuma.cas.usf.edu.
Application contact: Dr. Pritish Mukherjee, Director, 813-974-5230, *Fax:* 813-974-5813, *E-mail:* pritish@chuma.cas.usf.edu. *Web site:* http://www.cas.usf.edu/physics/

■ UNIVERSITY OF VERMONT

Graduate College, College of Arts and Sciences, Department of Physics, Program in Engineering Physics, Burlington, VT 05405

AWARDS MS.

Entrance requirements: For master's, GRE General Test, TOEFL.
Expenses: Tuition, state resident: part-time $335 per credit. Tuition, nonresident: part-time $838 per credit.

■ UNIVERSITY OF VIRGINIA

School of Engineering and Applied Science, Department of Materials Science and Engineering, Program in Engineering Physics, Charlottesville, VA 22903

AWARDS MEP, MS, PhD.

Faculty: 22 full-time (1 woman).
Students: 30 full-time (5 women), 3 part-time (1 woman); includes 5 minority (2 African Americans, 2 Asian Americans or Pacific Islanders, 1 Hispanic American), 10 international. Average age 28. 27 applicants, 74% accepted, 8 enrolled. In 2001, 1 degree awarded.
Degree requirements: For master's, comprehensive exam; for doctorate, thesis/dissertation, comprehensive exam.
Entrance requirements: For master's and doctorate, GRE General Test. *Application deadline:* For fall admission, 8/1; for spring admission, 12/1. Applications are processed on a rolling basis. *Application fee:* $40. Electronic applications accepted.
Expenses: Tuition, state resident: full-time $3,988. Tuition, nonresident: full-time $17,078. Required fees: $1,190.
Financial support: Fellowships available. Financial award application deadline: 2/1; financial award applicants required to submit FAFSA.
Faculty research: Continuum and rarefied gas dynamics, ultracentrifuge isotope enrichment, solid-state physics, atmospheric physics, atomic collisions.
Application contact: Kathryn Thornton, Assistant Dean, 434-924-3897, *Fax:* 434-982-2214, *E-mail:* inquiry@cs.virginia.edu.

■ UNIVERSITY OF WISCONSIN–MADISON

Graduate School, College of Engineering, Department of Engineering Physics, Madison, WI 53706-1380

AWARDS Engineering mechanics (MS, PhD); nuclear engineering and engineering physics (MS, PhD). Part-time programs available. Postbaccalaureate distance learning degree programs offered (minimal on-campus study).

Faculty: 24 full-time (2 women), 4 part-time/adjunct (0 women).
Students: 62 full-time (8 women), 2 part-time. Average age 25. 125 applicants, 20%

accepted. In 2001, 12 master's, 9 doctorates awarded. Terminal master's awarded for partial completion of doctoral program.
Degree requirements: For master's, thesis optional; for doctorate, thesis/dissertation.
Entrance requirements: For master's and doctorate, GRE General Test, minimum GPA of 3.0 in last 60 hours, appropriate bachelor's degree. *Application deadline:* For fall admission, 1/15 (priority date). Applications are processed on a rolling basis. *Application fee:* $45. Electronic applications accepted.
Expenses: Tuition, state resident: full-time $7,361; part-time $399 per credit. Tuition, nonresident: full-time $20,499; part-time $1,282 per credit. Required fees: $34 per credit. Full-time tuition and fees vary according to course load, program, reciprocity agreements and student level.

Financial support: In 2001–02, 47 students received support, including 4 fellowships with full tuition reimbursements available (averaging $17,400 per year), 34 research assistantships with full tuition reimbursements available (averaging $15,792 per year), 9 teaching assistantships with full tuition reimbursements available (averaging $15,800 per year); career-related internships or fieldwork, Federal Work-Study, and institutionally sponsored loans also available. Support available to part-time students. Financial award application deadline: 1/15.
Faculty research: Fission reactor engineering and safety, plasma physics and fusion technology, plasma processing and ion implantation, applied superconductivity and cryogenics, engineering mechanics and astronautics. *Total annual research expenditures:* $6.5 million.

Dr. Michael L. Corradini, Chair, 608-263-1646, *Fax:* 608-263-7451, *E-mail:* corradini@engr.wisc.edu. *Web site:* http://www.engr.wisc.edu/ep/
Find an in-depth description at www.petersons.com/gradchannel.

■ YALE UNIVERSITY
Graduate School of Arts and Sciences, Programs in Engineering and Applied Science, Department of Applied Physics, New Haven, CT 06520
AWARDS MS, PhD. Terminal master's awarded for partial completion of doctoral program.
Degree requirements: For doctorate, thesis/dissertation, area exam.
Entrance requirements: For master's and doctorate, GRE General Test, TOEFL.

Geological, Mineral/Mining, and Petroleum Engineering

GEOLOGICAL ENGINEERING

■ ARIZONA STATE UNIVERSITY
Graduate College, College of Liberal Arts and Sciences, Department of Geology, Tempe, AZ 85287
AWARDS Geological engineering (MS, PhD); natural science (MNS).
Degree requirements: For master's, thesis or alternative; for doctorate, thesis/dissertation.
Entrance requirements: For master's and doctorate, GRE.
Faculty research: Mechanics and deposits of volcanic eruptions, possible controls on global climate, electron microprobe studies of ore minerals.

■ COLORADO SCHOOL OF MINES
Graduate School, Department of Geology and Geological Engineering, Golden, CO 80401-1887
AWARDS Engineering geology (Diploma); exploration geosciences (Diploma); geochemistry (MS, PhD); geological engineering (ME, MS, PhD, Diploma); geology (MS, PhD); hydrogeology (Diploma). Part-time programs available.
Faculty: 27 full-time (5 women), 23 part-time/adjunct (0 women).

Students: 59 full-time (24 women), 39 part-time (8 women); includes 4 minority (1 African American, 1 Asian American or Pacific Islander, 1 Hispanic American, 1 Native American), 31 international. 93 applicants, 76% accepted, 20 enrolled. In 2001, 22 master's, 3 doctorates awarded.
Degree requirements: For master's, thesis/dissertation; for doctorate, thesis/dissertation, comprehensive exam. *Median time to degree:* Master's–2 years full-time; doctorate–4 years full-time.
Entrance requirements: For master's and doctorate, GRE General Test; for Diploma, GRE General Test, minimum GPA of 3.0. *Application deadline:* For fall admission, 12/1 (priority date); for spring admission, 5/1 (priority date). Applications are processed on a rolling basis. *Application fee:* $40. Electronic applications accepted.
Expenses: Tuition, state resident: full-time $4,940; part-time $246 per credit. Tuition, nonresident: full-time $16,070; part-time $803 per credit. Required fees: $341 per semester.
Financial support: In 2001–02, 54 students received support, including 5 fellowships (averaging $3,729 per year), 29 research assistantships (averaging $5,087 per year), 34 teaching assistantships (averaging $4,561 per year); unspecified assistantships also available. Support available to part-time students. Financial award applicants required to submit FAFSA.
Faculty research: Predictive sediment modeling, petrophysics, aquifer-contaminant flow modeling, water-rock

interactions, geotechnical engineering. *Total annual research expenditures:* $1.2 million.
Dr. Murray W. Hitzman, Head, 303-273-2127, *E-mail:* mhitzman@mines.edu.
Application contact: Marilyn Schwinger, Administrative Assistant, 303-273-3800, *Fax:* 303-273-3859, *E-mail:* mschwing@mines.edu. *Web site:* http://www.mines.edu/academic/geology/

■ COLORADO SCHOOL OF MINES
Graduate School, Department of Geophysics, Golden, CO 80401-1887
AWARDS Geophysical engineering (ME, MS, PhD); geophysics (MS, PhD, Diploma). Part-time programs available.
Faculty: 11 full-time (0 women), 6 part-time/adjunct (0 women).
Students: 51 full-time (14 women), 7 part-time; includes 1 minority (Hispanic American); 34 international. 43 applicants, 74% accepted, 11 enrolled. In 2001, 7 master's, 6 doctorates awarded.
Degree requirements: For master's, thesis; for doctorate, one foreign language, thesis/dissertation, oral exams, comprehensive exam. *Median time to degree:* Master's–2 years full-time; doctorate–4 years full-time.
Entrance requirements: For master's, doctorate, and Diploma, GRE General Test. *Application deadline:* For fall admission, 12/1; for spring admission, 5/1. Applications are processed on a rolling

Colorado School of Mines (continued)
basis. *Application fee:* $40. Electronic applications accepted.
Expenses: Tuition, state resident: full-time $4,940; part-time $246 per credit. Tuition, nonresident: full-time $16,070; part-time $803 per credit. Required fees: $341 per semester.
Financial support: In 2001–02, 28 fellowships (averaging $3,859 per year), 37 research assistantships (averaging $7,902 per year), 65 teaching assistantships (averaging $4,997 per year) were awarded. Unspecified assistantships also available. Support available to part-time students. Financial award applicants required to submit FAFSA.
Faculty research: Seismic exploration, gravity and geomagnetic fields, electrical mapping and sounding, bore hole measurements, environmental physics. *Total annual research expenditures:* $1.3 million.
Dr. Terence K. Young, Acting Head, 303-273-3454, *E-mail:* tkyoung@mine.edu.
Application contact: Sara Summers, Program Assistant, 303-273-3935, *Fax:* 303-273-3478, *E-mail:* ssummers@mines.edu. *Web site:* http://www.geophysics.mines.edu/

■ COLUMBIA UNIVERSITY

Fu Foundation School of Engineering and Applied Science, Department of Earth and Environmental Engineering, Program in Earth Resources Engineering, New York, NY 10027

AWARDS MS, PhD. Part-time programs available.

Faculty: 8 full-time (0 women), 4 part-time/adjunct (1 woman).
Students: 8 full-time (5 women); includes 6 minority (all Asian Americans or Pacific Islanders), 2 international. Average age 21. In 2001, 5 degrees awarded.
Degree requirements: For doctorate, thesis/dissertation, qualifying exam.
Entrance requirements: For master's and doctorate, GRE General Test, TOEFL. *Application deadline:* For fall admission, 2/15; for spring admission, 10/1. *Application fee:* $55. Electronic applications accepted.
Expenses: Tuition: Full-time $27,528. Required fees: $1,638.
Financial support: Federal Work-Study available. Financial award application deadline: 1/5; financial award applicants required to submit FAFSA.
Faculty research: Industrial ecology, waste treatment and recycling, water resources, environmental remediation, hazardous waste disposal.
Dr. Peter Schlosser, Chairman, 212-854-0306, *Fax:* 212-854-7081, *E-mail:* ps10@columbia.edu.
Application contact: Jaime Bradstreet, Student Coordinator, 212-854-2905, *Fax:* 212-854-7081, *E-mail:* jlb2001@columbia.edu. *Web site:* http://

www.seas.columbia.edu/columbia/departments/Krumb/

■ DREXEL UNIVERSITY

Graduate School, College of Engineering, Department of Civil and Architectural Engineering, Program in Engineering Geology, Philadelphia, PA 19104-2875

AWARDS MS.

Faculty: 2 full-time (0 women).
Students: Average age 29. In 2001, 3 degrees awarded.
Degree requirements: For master's, thesis optional.
Entrance requirements: For master's, TOEFL, BS in geology, civil engineering, or equivalent; minimum GPA of 3.0. *Application deadline:* For fall admission, 8/21. Applications are processed on a rolling basis. *Application fee:* $50. Electronic applications accepted.
Expenses: Tuition: Full-time $20,088; part-time $558 per credit. Required fees: $78 per term. One-time fee: $200. Tuition and fees vary according to course load, degree level and program.
Financial support: Research assistantships, teaching assistantships, unspecified assistantships available. Financial award application deadline: 2/1.
Dr. Edward Doheny, Director, 215-895-2344.
Application contact: Director of Graduate Admissions, 215-895-6700, *Fax:* 215-895-5939, *E-mail:* enroll@drexel.edu.

■ MICHIGAN STATE UNIVERSITY

Graduate School, College of Engineering, Department of Chemical Engineering and Materials Science, East Lansing, MI 48824

AWARDS Chemical engineering (MS, PhD), including environmental toxicology (PhD); engineering mechanics (MS, PhD); materials science and engineering (MS, PhD); mechanics (PhD); metallurgy (MS, PhD). Part-time programs available.

Faculty: 22.
Students: 41 full-time (10 women), 5 part-time (1 woman); includes 9 minority (2 African Americans, 4 Asian Americans or Pacific Islanders, 3 Hispanic Americans), 21 international. Average age 26. 99 applicants, 14% accepted. In 2001, 8 master's, 6 doctorates awarded. Terminal master's awarded for partial completion of doctoral program.
Degree requirements: For doctorate, thesis/dissertation.
Entrance requirements: For master's, GRE, TOEFL, minimum GPA of 3.0; for doctorate, GRE, TOEFL. *Application deadline:* For fall admission, 1/15 (priority date); for spring admission, 11/1. Applications are processed on a rolling basis. *Application fee:* $30 ($40 for international students). Electronic applications accepted.

Expenses: Tuition, state resident: part-time $244 per credit hour. Tuition, nonresident: part-time $494 per credit hour. Required fees: $268 per semester. Tuition and fees vary according to course load, degree level and program.
Financial support: In 2001–02, 26 fellowships with tuition reimbursements (averaging $3,950 per year), 49 research assistantships with tuition reimbursements (averaging $14,052 per year), 19 teaching assistantships with tuition reimbursements (averaging $12,741 per year) were awarded. Financial award applicants required to submit FAFSA.
Faculty research: Agricultural bioprocessing, impact resistance of thermoplastic composite materials, durability of polymer composites. *Total annual research expenditures:* $989,316.
Dr. Martin Hawley, Interim Chair, 517-355-5135, *Fax:* 517-353-9842.
Application contact: Information Contact, 517-355-5135, *Fax:* 517-432-1105, *E-mail:* chems@egr.msu.edu. *Web site:* http://www.chems.msu.edu/

■ MICHIGAN TECHNOLOGICAL UNIVERSITY

Graduate School, College of Engineering, Department of Geology, Geophysics and Geological Engineering, Program in Geological Engineering, Houghton, MI 49931-1295

AWARDS MS, PhD. Part-time programs available.

Degree requirements: For master's, thesis.
Entrance requirements: For master's, GRE General Test, TOEFL. Electronic applications accepted. *Web site:* http://www.geo.mtu.edu/

Find an in-depth description at www.petersons.com/gradchannel.

■ MONTANA TECH OF THE UNIVERSITY OF MONTANA

Graduate School, Geoscience Program, Butte, MT 59701-8997

AWARDS Geochemistry (MS); geological engineering (MS); geology (MS); geophysical engineering (MS); hydrogeological engineering (MS); hydrogeology (MS); mineral economics (MS). Part-time programs available.

Faculty: 8 full-time (1 woman).
Students: 12 full-time (5 women), 5 part-time (3 women); includes 1 minority (Hispanic American). 13 applicants, 62% accepted, 6 enrolled. In 2001, 7 degrees awarded.
Degree requirements: For master's, thesis (for some programs), registration.
Entrance requirements: For master's, GRE General Test, TOEFL, minimum GPA of 3.0. *Application deadline:* For fall admission, 4/1 (priority date); for spring

admission, 10/1 (priority date). Applications are processed on a rolling basis. *Application fee:* $30.

Expenses: Tuition, state resident: full-time $3,717; part-time $196 per credit. Tuition, nonresident: full-time $11,770; part-time $324 per credit.

Financial support: In 2001–02, 13 students received support, including 4 research assistantships with partial tuition reimbursements available (averaging $8,600 per year), 7 teaching assistantships with partial tuition reimbursements available (averaging $5,343 per year); career-related internships or fieldwork, institutionally sponsored loans, and tuition waivers (full and partial) also available. Financial award application deadline: 4/1; financial award applicants required to submit FAFSA.

Faculty research: Water resource development, seismic processing, petroleum reservoir characterization, environmental geochemistry, molecular modeling, magmatic and hydrothermal ore deposits. *Total annual research expenditures:* $293,854.

Dr. Diane Wolfgram, Department Head, 406-496-4353, *Fax:* 406-496-4260, *E-mail:* dwolfgram@mtech.edu.

Application contact: Cindy Dunstan, Administrator, Graduate School, 406-496-4304, *Fax:* 406-496-4334, *E-mail:* cdunstan@mtech.edu. *Web site:* http://www.mtech.edu/

■ SOUTH DAKOTA SCHOOL OF MINES AND TECHNOLOGY

Graduate Division, Department of Geology and Geological Engineering, Rapid City, SD 57701-3995

AWARDS Geology and geological engineering (MS, PhD); paleontology (MS). Part-time programs available.

Degree requirements: For master's and doctorate, thesis/dissertation.

Entrance requirements: For master's and doctorate, GRE General Test, GRE Subject Test, TOEFL, TWE. Electronic applications accepted.

Faculty research: Contaminants in soil, nitrate leaching, environmental changes, fracture formations, greenhouse effect.

■ UNIVERSITY OF ALASKA FAIRBANKS

Graduate School, School of Mineral Engineering, Department of Mining and Geological Engineering, Fairbanks, AK 99775-7480

AWARDS Geological engineering (MS, EM); mining engineering (MS, EM).

Faculty: 9 full-time (0 women).

Students: 4 full-time (0 women), 3 international. Average age 25. 8 applicants, 63% accepted, 3 enrolled. In 2001, 1 degree awarded.

Degree requirements: For master's, thesis, comprehensive exam.

Entrance requirements: For master's, GRE General Test, TOEFL. *Application deadline:* For fall admission, 4/1; for spring admission, 11/1. Applications are processed on a rolling basis. *Application fee:* $35.

Expenses: Tuition, state resident: full-time $4,272; part-time $178 per credit. Tuition, nonresident: full-time $8,328; part-time $347 per credit. Required fees: $960; $60 per term. Part-time tuition and fees vary according to course load.

Financial support: In 2001–02, fellowships with tuition reimbursements (averaging $10,000 per year); research assistantships with tuition reimbursements, career-related internships or fieldwork, Federal Work-Study, and scholarships/grants also available.

Faculty research: Underground mining in permafrost.

Dr. Paul Metz, Head, 907-474-5120.

■ THE UNIVERSITY OF ARIZONA

Graduate College, College of Engineering and Mines, Department of Mining, Geological and Geophysical Engineering, Program in Geological and Geophysical Engineering, Tucson, AZ 85721

AWARDS MS, PhD. Part-time programs available. Postbaccalaureate distance learning degree programs offered (minimal on-campus study).

Faculty: 3 full-time (1 woman), 6 part-time/adjunct (0 women).

Students: 16 full-time (4 women), 3 part-time; includes 1 minority (Native American), 10 international. Average age 30. 14 applicants, 79% accepted. In 2001, 7 degrees awarded.

Degree requirements: For master's and doctorate, thesis/dissertation. *Median time to degree:* Master's–3 years full-time.

Entrance requirements: For master's and doctorate, GRE General Test, TOEFL. *Application deadline:* For fall admission, 2/1; for spring admission, 10/1. Applications are processed on a rolling basis. *Application fee:* $45.

Expenses: Tuition, state resident: full-time $2,490; part-time $436 per unit. Tuition, nonresident: full-time $10,300; part-time $436 per unit. Full-time tuition and fees vary according to degree level and program.

Financial support: In 2001–02, 6 students received support, including fellowships (averaging $15,000 per year), research assistantships with partial tuition reimbursements available (averaging $12,861 per year), teaching assistantships with partial tuition reimbursements available (averaging $13,569 per year); institutionally sponsored loans, scholarships/grants, health care benefits, tuition waivers (partial), and unspecified assistantships also available. Financial award application deadline: 4/1.

Faculty research: High-resolution subsurface imaging, monitoring subsurface contamination, neural networks, remote sensing. *Total annual research expenditures:* $470,463.

Dr. Mary M Poulton, Head, 520-621-6063, *Fax:* 520-621-6063, *E-mail:* mpoulton@u.arizona.edu.

Application contact: Elsie Nonaka, Graduate Adviser, 520-621-3006, *Fax:* 520-621-8330, *E-mail:* nonakae@email.arizona.edu.

Find an in-depth description at www.petersons.com/gradchannel.

■ UNIVERSITY OF CALIFORNIA, BERKELEY

Graduate Division, College of Engineering, Department of Materials Science and Mineral Engineering, Program in Engineering Geoscience, Berkeley, CA 94720-1500

AWARDS M Eng, MS, D Eng, PhD.

Degree requirements: For master's, comprehensive exam or thesis (MS); for doctorate, thesis/dissertation, qualifying exam.

Entrance requirements: For master's and doctorate, GRE General Test, minimum GPA of 3.0.

Expenses: Tuition, nonresident: full-time $10,704. Required fees: $4,349.

■ UNIVERSITY OF IDAHO

College of Graduate Studies, College of Mines and Earth Resources, Department of Materials, Metallurgical, Mining, and Geological Engineering, Program in Geological Engineering, Moscow, ID 83844-2282

AWARDS MS.

Students: 3 full-time (1 woman), 9 part-time (1 woman); includes 2 minority (1 Asian American or Pacific Islander, 1 Native American). In 2001, 2 degrees awarded.

Degree requirements: For master's, one foreign language, thesis.

Entrance requirements: For master's, minimum GPA of 2.8. *Application deadline:* For fall admission, 8/1; for spring admission, 12/15. *Application fee:* $35 ($45 for international students).

Expenses: Tuition, state resident: full-time $1,613. Tuition, nonresident: full-time $3,000.

Financial support: Application deadline: 2/15.

Dr. Sam Froes, Head, Department of Materials, Metallurgical, Mining, and Geological Engineering, 208-885-6769.

■ UNIVERSITY OF MINNESOTA, TWIN CITIES CAMPUS

Graduate School, Institute of Technology, Department of Civil Engineering, Minneapolis, MN 55455-0213

AWARDS Civil engineering (MCE, MS, PhD); geological engineering (M Geo E, MS, PhD). Part-time programs available.

Degree requirements: For master's, thesis optional; for doctorate, thesis/dissertation.
Entrance requirements: For master's and doctorate, GRE General Test, TOEFL.
Expenses: Tuition, state resident: full-time $2,932; part-time $489 per credit. Tuition, nonresident: full-time $5,758; part-time $960 per credit. Part-time tuition and fees vary according to course load, program and reciprocity agreements.
Faculty research: Environmental engineering, rock mechanics, water resources, structural engineering, transportation. *Web site:* http://www.ce.umn.edu/

■ UNIVERSITY OF MISSOURI–ROLLA

Graduate School, School of Mines and Metallurgy, Department of Geological and Petroleum Engineering, Program in Geological Engineering, Rolla, MO 65409-0910

AWARDS MS, DE, PhD. Part-time programs available.

Degree requirements: For doctorate, thesis/dissertation.
Entrance requirements: For master's, GRE General Test, TOEFL, minimum GPA of 3.0 in last 4 semesters; for doctorate, GRE General Test, TOEFL. Electronic applications accepted.
Faculty research: Groundwater hydrology, hazardous waste management remote sensing and geographic information systems, geostatistics, geotechnical site selection.

■ UNIVERSITY OF NEVADA, RENO

Graduate School, Mackay School of Mines, Department of Geological Sciences, Reno, NV 89557

AWARDS Geochemistry (MS, PhD); geological engineering (MS, Geol E); geology (MS, PhD); geophysics (MS, PhD).
Faculty: 37.
Students: 45 full-time (11 women), 13 part-time (1 woman); includes 4 minority (2 Asian Americans or Pacific Islanders, 1 Hispanic American, 1 Native American), 10 international. Average age 33. In 2001, 10 master's, 2 doctorates awarded.
Degree requirements: For master's, thesis optional; for doctorate, one foreign language, thesis/dissertation.

Entrance requirements: For master's, GRE General Test, GRE Subject Test, TOEFL, minimum GPA of 2.75; for doctorate, GRE General Test, GRE Subject Test, TOEFL, minimum GPA of 3.0. *Application deadline:* For fall admission, 2/15 (priority date); for spring admission, 9/15. Applications are processed on a rolling basis. *Application fee:* $40.
Expenses: Tuition, state resident: full-time $2,067; part-time $108 per credit. Tuition, nonresident: full-time $9,282; part-time $109 per credit. Required fees: $57 per semester. Tuition and fees vary according to course load.
Financial support: In 2001–02, 17 research assistantships, 8 teaching assistantships were awarded. Institutionally sponsored loans and tuition waivers (full) also available. Financial award application deadline: 3/1.
Faculty research: Hydrothermal ore deposits, metamorphic and igneous petrogenesis, sedimentary rock record of earth history, field and petrographic investigation of magnetism, rock fracture mechanics.
Dr. Robert Karlin, Graduate Program Director, 775-784-1770.

■ UNIVERSITY OF OKLAHOMA

Graduate College, College of Engineering, School of Petroleum and Geological Engineering, Norman, OK 73019-0390

AWARDS Natural gas engineering and management (MS); petroleum and geological engineering (MS, PhD). Part-time and evening/weekend programs available. Postbaccalaureate distance learning degree programs offered (no on-campus study).
Faculty: 10 full-time (0 women).
Students: 49 full-time (4 women), 43 part-time (1 woman); includes 1 minority (Hispanic American), 63 international. 53 applicants, 85% accepted, 17 enrolled. In 2001, 25 master's, 3 doctorates awarded.
Degree requirements: For master's, thesis optional; for doctorate, one foreign language, thesis/dissertation, qualifying exam.
Entrance requirements: For master's and doctorate, GRE, TOEFL. *Application deadline:* For fall admission, 6/1 (priority date); for spring admission, 11/1. Applications are processed on a rolling basis. *Application fee:* $25 ($50 for international students).
Expenses: Tuition, state resident: full-time $2,208; part-time $92 per credit hour. Tuition, nonresident: part-time $297 per credit hour. Tuition and fees vary according to course level, course load and program.
Financial support: In 2001–02, 31 research assistantships with partial tuition reimbursements (averaging $9,006 per year), 7 teaching assistantships with partial tuition reimbursements (averaging $9,181 per year) were awarded. Career-related

internships or fieldwork and tuition waivers (full and partial) also available. Financial award application deadline: 4/15; financial award applicants required to submit FAFSA.
Faculty research: Wellbone stability, drilling and production operations, reservoir management, reservoir characterization techniques, coiled tubing, well stimulation, fluid rheology. *Total annual research expenditures:* $733,427.
Dr. Subhash Shah, Interim Director, 405-325-2921, *Fax:* 405-325-7477.
Application contact: Dr. Djebbar Tiab, Graduate Liaison, 405-325-2921, *Fax:* 405-325-7477, *E-mail:* dtiab@ou.edu.

■ UNIVERSITY OF UTAH

Graduate School, College of Mines and Earth Sciences, Department of Geology and Geophysics, Program in Geological Engineering, Salt Lake City, UT 84112-1107

AWARDS ME, MS, PhD. Terminal master's awarded for partial completion of doctoral program.

Degree requirements: For master's, thesis, qualifying exam; for doctorate, one foreign language, thesis/dissertation.
Entrance requirements: For master's and doctorate, GRE General Test, TOEFL, minimum GPA of 3.25. *Application deadline:* For fall admission, 1/15. *Application fee:* $40 ($60 for international students).
Expenses: Tuition, state resident: part-time $320 per semester hour. Tuition, nonresident: part-time $1,135 per semester hour. Required fees: $143 per semester hour. Tuition and fees vary according to course load, degree level and program.
Financial support: Fellowships with full tuition reimbursements, research assistantships with full tuition reimbursements, teaching assistantships with full tuition reimbursements, institutionally sponsored loans available. Financial award application deadline: 2/15.
Faculty research: Electrical methods, mineral exploration, geothermal resources, groundwater.
Application contact: Kim Atwater, Academic Coordinator, 801-581-6553, *Fax:* 801-581-7065, *E-mail:* katwater@mines.utah.edu. *Web site:* http://www.mines.utah.edu/geo

■ UNIVERSITY OF WISCONSIN–MADISON

Graduate School, College of Engineering, Geological Engineering Program, Madison, WI 53706-1380

AWARDS MS, PhD. Part-time programs available.

Faculty: 17 full-time (3 women), 1 part-time/adjunct (0 women).
Students: 16 full-time (4 women), 1 (woman) part-time. Average age 25. In 2001, 2 master's awarded.

Degree requirements: For doctorate, thesis/dissertation. *Median time to degree:* Master's–4 years part-time; doctorate–6 years part-time.
Entrance requirements: For master's and doctorate, GRE, TOEFL. *Application deadline:* For fall admission, 1/1; for spring admission, 10/15 (priority date). Applications are processed on a rolling basis. *Application fee:* $45. Electronic applications accepted.
Expenses: Tuition, state resident: full-time $7,361; part-time $399 per credit. Tuition, nonresident: full-time $20,499; part-time $1,282 per credit. Required fees: $34 per credit. Full-time tuition and fees vary according to course load, program, reciprocity agreements and student level.
Financial support: In 2001–02, 17 students received support, including fellowships with partial tuition reimbursements available (averaging $15,960 per year), 8 research assistantships with partial tuition reimbursements available (averaging $15,792 per year), 2 teaching assistantships with partial tuition reimbursements available (averaging $10,170 per year). Scholarships/grants and traineeships also available. Financial award application deadline: 1/1.
Faculty research: Constitute models for geomaterials, rock fracture, *in situ* stress determination, environmental geotechnics, site remediation. *Total annual research expenditures:* $1.2 million.
David M. Mickelson, Chair, 608-262-3491, *Fax:* 608-263-2453, *E-mail:* mickelson@geology.wisc.edu.
Application contact: Lynn D. Maertz, Program Assistant 3, 608-262-3491, *Fax:* 608-263-2453, *E-mail:* maertz@engr.wisc.edu. *Web site:* http://www.eng.wisc.edu/interd/gep/

MINERAL/MINING ENGINEERING

■ COLORADO SCHOOL OF MINES

Graduate School, Department of Mining Engineering, Golden, CO 80401-1887

AWARDS ME, MS, PhD. Part-time programs available.
Faculty: 7 full-time (0 women), 3 part-time/adjunct (0 women).
Students: 20 full-time (0 women), 14 part-time (1 woman), 23 international. 38 applicants, 92% accepted, 13 enrolled. In 2001, 9 master's, 4 doctorates awarded.
Degree requirements: For master's, thesis (for some programs); for doctorate, one foreign language, thesis/dissertation, comprehensive exam. *Median time to degree:* Master's–2 years full-time; doctorate–4 years full-time.

Entrance requirements: For master's and doctorate, GRE General Test. *Application deadline:* For fall admission, 12/1 (priority date); for spring admission, 5/1 (priority date). Applications are processed on a rolling basis. *Application fee:* $40. Electronic applications accepted.
Expenses: Tuition, state resident: full-time $4,940; part-time $246 per credit. Tuition, nonresident: full-time $16,070; part-time $803 per credit. Required fees: $341 per semester.
Financial support: In 2001–02, 18 students received support, including 7 fellowships (averaging $6,506 per year), 3 research assistantships (averaging $10,143 per year), 13 teaching assistantships (averaging $2,662 per year); unspecified assistantships also available. Support available to part-time students. Financial award applicants required to submit FAFSA.
Faculty research: Mine evaluation and planning, geostatistics, mining robotics, water jet cutting, rock mechanics. *Total annual research expenditures:* $7,808.
Dr. Tibor Rozgonyi, Head, 303-273-3701, *E-mail:* trozgony@mines.edu.
Application contact: Shannon Mann, Program Assistant, 303-273-3701, *E-mail:* smann@mines.edu. *Web site:* http://www.mines.edu/academic/mining

■ COLUMBIA UNIVERSITY

Fu Foundation School of Engineering and Applied Science, Department of Applied Physics and Applied Mathematics, Program in Minerals Engineering and Materials Science, New York, NY 10027

AWARDS Eng Sc D, PhD, Engr. Part-time programs available.
Faculty: 10 full-time (2 women), 4 part-time/adjunct (1 woman).
Students: 21 full-time (6 women), 6 part-time (2 women); includes 16 minority (2 African Americans, 13 Asian Americans or Pacific Islanders, 1 Hispanic American). Average age 23. 75 applicants, 39% accepted. In 2001, 4 degrees awarded.
Degree requirements: For doctorate, one foreign language, thesis/dissertation, qualifying exam.
Entrance requirements: For doctorate and Engr, GRE General Test, TOEFL. *Application fee:* $55. Electronic applications accepted.
Expenses: Tuition: Full-time $27,528. Required fees: $1,638.
Financial support: In 2001–02, 7 fellowships with partial tuition reimbursements (averaging $15,000 per year), 5 research assistantships with full tuition reimbursements (averaging $18,000 per year), 2 teaching assistantships with partial tuition reimbursements (averaging $10,000 per year) were awarded. Federal Work-Study, institutionally sponsored loans, and scholarships/grants also available. Financial

award application deadline: 1/5; financial award applicants required to submit FAFSA.
Faculty research: Comminution, mineral processing, flotation and flocculation, transport phenomena in heterogeneous reactions, extractive metallurgy, electrochemistry. *Total annual research expenditures:* $1.1 million.
Prof. James S. Im, Professor of Material Sciences, 212-854-8341, *Fax:* 212-854-8257, *E-mail:* ji12@columbia.edu.
Application contact: Marlene Arbo, Department Administrator, 212-854-4458, *Fax:* 212-854-8257, *E-mail:* mja2@columbia.edu. *Web site:* http://www.seas.columbia.edu/columbia/departments/Krumb

■ COLUMBIA UNIVERSITY

Fu Foundation School of Engineering and Applied Science, Department of Earth and Environmental Engineering, New York, NY 10027

AWARDS Earth resources engineering (MS, PhD); minerals engineering and materials science (Eng Sc D, PhD, Engr). Part-time programs available. Postbaccalaureate distance learning degree programs offered.

Faculty: 8 full-time (0 women), 4 part-time/adjunct (1 woman).
Students: 29 full-time (11 women), 6 part-time (2 women); includes 1 minority (Asian American or Pacific Islander), 23 international. Average age 23. 40 applicants, 45% accepted, 10 enrolled. In 2001, 5 master's, 4 doctorates awarded. Terminal master's awarded for partial completion of doctoral program.
Degree requirements: For master's, thesis; for doctorate, thesis/dissertation, qualifying exam.
Entrance requirements: For master's, doctorate, and Engr, GRE General Test, TOEFL. *Application deadline:* For fall admission, 1/5; for spring admission, 10/1. *Application fee:* $55. Electronic applications accepted.
Expenses: Tuition: Full-time $27,528. Required fees: $1,638.
Financial support: In 2001–02, 18 fellowships with partial tuition reimbursements (averaging $15,000 per year), 5 research assistantships with full tuition reimbursements (averaging $18,000 per year), 4 teaching assistantships with partial tuition reimbursements (averaging $10,000 per year) were awarded. Career-related internships or fieldwork, Federal Work-Study, and scholarships/grants also available. Support available to part-time students. Financial award application deadline: 1/5; financial award applicants required to submit FAFSA. *Total annual research expenditures:* $1.1 million.
Dr. Peter Schlosser, Chairman, 212-854-0306, *Fax:* 212-854-7081, *E-mail:* ps10@columbia.edu.
Application contact: Jaime Bradstreet, Student Coordinator, 212-854-2905, *Fax:*

Columbia University (continued)
212-854-7081, *E-mail:* jlb2001@
columbia.edu. *Web site:* http://
www.seas.columbia.edu/columbia/
department/krumb/

■ MICHIGAN TECHNOLOGICAL UNIVERSITY

Graduate School, College of Engineering, Department of Mining and Materials Processing Engineering, Houghton, MI 49931-1295

AWARDS Mining engineering (MS, PhD). Part-time programs available.

Degree requirements: For master's, thesis or alternative; for doctorate, thesis/dissertation.
Entrance requirements: For master's and doctorate, TOEFL, BS in engineering or science. Electronic applications accepted.
Faculty research: Rock mechanics and fragmentation, recycling and recovery of secondary materials, tunneling and underground construction, hydrometallurgy, mineral processing. *Web site:* http://www.mg.mtu.edu/

Find an in-depth description at www.petersons.com/gradchannel.

■ MONTANA TECH OF THE UNIVERSITY OF MONTANA

Graduate School, Metallurgical/Mineral Processing Engineering Programs, Butte, MT 59701-8997

AWARDS MS. Part-time programs available.

Faculty: 5 full-time (0 women).
Students: 7 full-time (1 woman), 2 part-time (1 woman). 5 applicants, 60% accepted, 2 enrolled. In 2001, 5 degrees awarded.
Degree requirements: For master's, thesis optional.
Entrance requirements: For master's, GRE General Test, TOEFL, minimum GPA of 3.0. *Application deadline:* For fall admission, 4/1 (priority date); for spring admission, 10/1 (priority date). Applications are processed on a rolling basis. *Application fee:* $30.
Expenses: Tuition, state resident: full-time $3,717; part-time $196 per credit. Tuition, nonresident: full-time $11,770; part-time $324 per credit.
Financial support: In 2001–02, 6 students received support, including 1 research assistantship with partial tuition reimbursement available (averaging $8,000 per year), 5 teaching assistantships with partial tuition reimbursements available (averaging $5,100 per year); career-related internships or fieldwork, institutionally sponsored loans, and tuition waivers (full and partial) also available. Financial award application deadline: 4/1; financial award applicants required to submit FAFSA.
Faculty research: Stabilizing hazardous waste, decontamination of metals by melt refining, ultraviolet enhancement of stabilization reactions. *Total annual research expenditures:* $68,516.
Dr. Courtney Young, Department Head, 406-496-4158, *Fax:* 406-496-4664, *E-mail:* cyoung@mtech.edu.
Application contact: Cindy Dunstan, Administrator, Graduate School, 406-496-4304, *Fax:* 406-496-4334, *E-mail:* cdunstan@mtech.edu. *Web site:* http://www.mtech.edu/

■ MONTANA TECH OF THE UNIVERSITY OF MONTANA

Graduate School, Mining Engineering Program, Butte, MT 59701-8997

AWARDS MS. Part-time programs available.

Faculty: 4 full-time (1 woman).
Students: 2 full-time (0 women). 6 applicants, 83% accepted, 1 enrolled. In 2001, 12 degrees awarded.
Degree requirements: For master's, thesis optional.
Entrance requirements: For master's, GRE General Test, TOEFL, minimum GPA of 3.0. *Application deadline:* For fall admission, 4/1 (priority date); for spring admission, 10/1 (priority date). Applications are processed on a rolling basis. *Application fee:* $30.
Expenses: Tuition, state resident: full-time $3,717; part-time $196 per credit. Tuition, nonresident: full-time $11,770; part-time $324 per credit.
Financial support: In 2001–02, 2 students received support, including 1 teaching assistantship with partial tuition reimbursement available (averaging $6,800 per year); career-related internships or fieldwork, institutionally sponsored loans, and tuition waivers (full and partial) also available. Financial award application deadline: 4/1; financial award applicants required to submit FAFSA.
Faculty research: Geostatistics, geomechanics, mine planning, economic models, equipment selection. *Total annual research expenditures:* $17,246.
Dr. H. Peter Knudsen, Dean, School of Mines, 406-496-4395, *Fax:* 406-496-4260, *E-mail:* hknudsen@mtech.edu.
Application contact: Cindy Dunstan, Administrator, Graduate School, 406-496-4304, *Fax:* 406-496-4334, *E-mail:* cdunstan@mtech.edu. *Web site:* http://www.mtech.edu/

■ THE PENNSYLVANIA STATE UNIVERSITY UNIVERSITY PARK CAMPUS

Graduate School, College of Earth and Mineral Sciences, Department of Energy and Geo-Environmental Engineering, Program in Mineral Processing, State College, University Park, PA 16802-1503

AWARDS MS, PhD.

Students: 3 full-time (0 women), 3 part-time (1 woman).
Degree requirements: For master's and doctorate, thesis/dissertation.
Entrance requirements: For master's and doctorate, GRE General Test, TOEFL. *Application fee:* $45.
Expenses: Tuition, state resident: full-time $7,882; part-time $333 per credit. Tuition, nonresident: full-time $16,142; part-time $673 per credit. Required fees: $124 per semester.
Financial support: Application deadline: 12/31.
Subhash Chander, Graduate Program Chair, 814-863-1640.

■ THE PENNSYLVANIA STATE UNIVERSITY UNIVERSITY PARK CAMPUS

Graduate School, College of Earth and Mineral Sciences, Department of Energy and Geo-Environmental Engineering, Program in Mining Engineering, State College, University Park, PA 16802-1503

AWARDS M Eng, MS, PhD.

Students: 4 full-time (0 women). In 2001, 3 degrees awarded.
Degree requirements: For doctorate, thesis/dissertation.
Entrance requirements: For master's and doctorate, GRE General Test, TOEFL. *Application fee:* $45.
Expenses: Tuition, state resident: full-time $7,882; part-time $333 per credit. Tuition, nonresident: full-time $16,142; part-time $673 per credit. Required fees: $124 per semester.
Financial support: Application deadline: 12/31.
Marek Mrugala, Graduate Program Chair, 814-863-7598.

■ SOUTHERN ILLINOIS UNIVERSITY CARBONDALE

Graduate School, College of Engineering, Department of Mining Engineering, Carbondale, IL 62901-6806

AWARDS MS.

Faculty: 3 full-time (0 women), 1 part-time/adjunct (0 women).
Students: 7 full-time (0 women), 5 part-time, 9 international. Average age 25. 7 applicants, 57% accepted. In 2001, 2 degrees awarded.
Degree requirements: For master's, thesis, comprehensive exam.
Entrance requirements: For master's, TOEFL, minimum GPA of 2.7. *Application deadline:* Applications are processed on a rolling basis. *Application fee:* $20.
Expenses: Tuition, state resident: full-time $3,794; part-time $154 per hour. Tuition,

nonresident: full-time $6,566; part-time $308 per hour. Required fees: $277 per hour.
Financial support: In 2001–02, 8 students received support; fellowships with full tuition reimbursements available, research assistantships with full tuition reimbursements available, teaching assistantships with full tuition reimbursements available, Federal Work-Study, institutionally sponsored loans, and tuition waivers (full) available. Support available to part-time students. Financial award application deadline: 3/1.
Faculty research: Rock mechanics and ground control, mine subsidence, mine systems analysis, fine coal cleaning, surface mine reclamation. *Total annual research expenditures:* $1.7 million.
Dr. Sutya Harpalani, Interim Chairperson, 618-536-6637, *Fax:* 618-453-4235.

Find an in-depth description at www.petersons.com/gradchannel.

■ UNIVERSITY OF ALASKA FAIRBANKS

Graduate School, School of Mineral Engineering, Department of Mining and Geological Engineering, Fairbanks, AK 99775-7480

AWARDS Geological engineering (MS, EM); mining engineering (MS, EM).

Faculty: 9 full-time (0 women).
Students: 4 full-time (0 women), 3 international. Average age 25. 8 applicants, 63% accepted, 3 enrolled. In 2001, 1 degree awarded.
Degree requirements: For master's, thesis, comprehensive exam.
Entrance requirements: For master's, GRE General Test, TOEFL. *Application deadline:* For fall admission, 4/1; for spring admission, 11/1. Applications are processed on a rolling basis. *Application fee:* $35.
Expenses: Tuition, state resident: full-time $4,272; part-time $178 per credit. Tuition, nonresident: full-time $8,328; part-time $347 per credit. Required fees: $960; $60 per term. Part-time tuition and fees vary according to course load.
Financial support: In 2001–02, fellowships with tuition reimbursements (averaging $10,000 per year); research assistantships with tuition reimbursements, career-related internships or fieldwork, Federal Work-Study, and scholarships/grants also available.
Faculty research: Underground mining in permafrost.
Dr. Paul Metz, Head, 907-474-5120.

■ UNIVERSITY OF ALASKA FAIRBANKS

Graduate School, School of Mineral Engineering, Program in Mineral Preparation Engineering, Fairbanks, AK 99775-7480

AWARDS MS.

Degree requirements: For master's, thesis, comprehensive exam.
Entrance requirements: For master's, GRE General Test, TOEFL. *Application deadline:* For fall admission, 4/1; for spring admission, 11/1. Applications are processed on a rolling basis. *Application fee:* $35.
Expenses: Tuition, state resident: full-time $4,272; part-time $178 per credit. Tuition, nonresident: full-time $8,328; part-time $347 per credit. Required fees: $960; $60 per term. Part-time tuition and fees vary according to course load.
Financial support: In 2001–02, fellowships with tuition reimbursements (averaging $10,000 per year); research assistantships with tuition reimbursements, career-related internships or fieldwork also available.
Faculty research: Washability of coal, microbial mining, mineral leaching.
Dr. Sukumar Bandopadhyay, Head, School of Mineral Engineering, 907-474-7366.

■ THE UNIVERSITY OF ARIZONA

Graduate College, College of Engineering and Mines, Department of Mining, Geological and Geophysical Engineering, Program in Mining Engineering, Tucson, AZ 85721

AWARDS MS, PhD. Part-time programs available. Postbaccalaureate distance learning degree programs offered (minimal on-campus study).

Faculty: 3 full-time (0 women), 6 part-time/adjunct (0 women).
Students: 1 full-time (0 women), 1 (woman) part-time, (both international). Average age 33. 10 applicants, 50% accepted. In 2001, 1 degree awarded.
Degree requirements: For master's and doctorate, thesis/dissertation.
Entrance requirements: For master's and doctorate, GRE General Test, TOEFL. *Application deadline:* For fall admission, 2/1; for spring admission, 10/1. Applications are processed on a rolling basis. *Application fee:* $45.
Expenses: Tuition, state resident: full-time $2,490; part-time $436 per unit. Tuition, nonresident: full-time $10,300; part-time $436 per unit. Full-time tuition and fees vary according to degree level and program.
Financial support: In 2001–02, 2 students received support, including fellowships (averaging $15,000 per year), research assistantships with partial tuition reimbursements available (averaging $12,861 per year), teaching assistantships with partial tuition reimbursements available (averaging $13,569 per year); institutionally sponsored loans, scholarships/grants, health care benefits, tuition waivers (partial), and unspecified assistantships also available. Financial award application deadline: 4/1.
Faculty research: Mine system design, in-site leaching, fluid flow in rocks,

geostatistics, rock mechanics. *Total annual research expenditures:* $470,463.
Dr. Mary M Poulton, Head, 520-621-6063, *Fax:* 520-621-6063, *E-mail:* mpoulton@u.arizona.edu.
Application contact: Elsie Nonaka, Graduate Adviser, 520-621-3006, *Fax:* 621-8330, *E-mail:* nonakae@email.arizona.edu.

Find an in-depth description at www.petersons.com/gradchannel.

■ UNIVERSITY OF CALIFORNIA, BERKELEY

Graduate Division, College of Engineering, Department of Materials Science and Mineral Engineering, Berkeley, CA 94720-1500

AWARDS Ceramic sciences and engineering (M Eng, MS, D Eng, PhD); engineering geoscience (M Eng, MS, D Eng, PhD); materials engineering (M Eng, MS, D Eng, PhD); mineral engineering (M Eng, MS, D Eng, PhD); petroleum engineering (M Eng, MS, D Eng, PhD); physical metallurgy (M Eng, MS, D Eng, PhD).

Degree requirements: For master's, comprehensive exam or thesis (MS); for doctorate, thesis/dissertation, qualifying exam.
Entrance requirements: For master's and doctorate, GRE General Test, minimum GPA of 3.0.
Expenses: Tuition, nonresident: full-time $10,704. Required fees: $4,349.

■ UNIVERSITY OF IDAHO

College of Graduate Studies, College of Mines and Earth Resources, Department of Materials, Metallurgical, Mining, and Geological Engineering, Programs in Mining Engineering, Moscow, ID 83844-2282

AWARDS Metallurgical engineering (MS, PhD); mining engineering (MS, PhD).

Degree requirements: For doctorate, one foreign language, thesis/dissertation.
Entrance requirements: For master's, minimum GPA of 2.8; for doctorate, minimum undergraduate GPA of 2.8, 3.0 graduate. *Application deadline:* For fall admission, 8/1; for spring admission, 12/15. *Application fee:* $35 ($45 for international students).
Expenses: Tuition, state resident: full-time $1,613. Tuition, nonresident: full-time $3,000.
Financial support: Career-related internships or fieldwork available. Financial award application deadline: 2/15.
Dr. Sam Froes, Head, Department of Materials, Metallurgical, Mining, and Geological Engineering, 208-885-6769.

■ UNIVERSITY OF KENTUCKY

Graduate School, Graduate School Programs from the College of Engineering, Program in Mining Engineering, Lexington, KY 40506-0032

AWARDS MME, MS Min, PhD.

Faculty: 12 full-time (0 women).
Students: 10 full-time (1 woman), 1 part-time, 7 international. 9 applicants, 33% accepted. In 2001, 1 degree awarded.
Degree requirements: For master's, thesis optional; for doctorate, one foreign language, thesis/dissertation, comprehensive exam.
Entrance requirements: For master's, GRE General Test, minimum undergraduate GPA of 2.5; for doctorate, GRE General Test, minimum graduate GPA of 3.0. *Application deadline:* For fall admission, 7/19; for spring admission, 12/5. Applications are processed on a rolling basis. *Application fee:* $30 ($35 for international students).
Expenses: Tuition, state resident: full-time $4,075; part-time $213 per credit hour. Tuition, nonresident: full-time $11,295; part-time $614 per credit hour.
Financial support: In 2001–02, 11 students received support, including 9 research assistantships, 1 teaching assistantship; fellowships, career-related internships or fieldwork, Federal Work-Study, and institutionally sponsored loans also available. Support available to part-time students.
Faculty research: Benefication of fine and ultrafine particles, operation research in mining and mineral processing, land reclamation. *Total annual research expenditures:* $219,330.
Dr. Ricky Honaker, Director of Graduate Studies, 859-257-1108, *Fax:* 859-323-1962, *E-mail:* rhonaker@engr.uky.edu.
Application contact: Dr. Jeannine Blackwell, Associate Dean, 859-257-4905, *Fax:* 859-323-1928.

■ UNIVERSITY OF MISSOURI–ROLLA

Graduate School, School of Mines and Metallurgy, Department of Mining Engineering, Rolla, MO 65409-0910

AWARDS MS, DE, PhD. Part-time programs available.

Degree requirements: For master's and doctorate, thesis/dissertation.
Entrance requirements: For master's, GRE General Test, TOEFL, minimum GPA of 3.0 in last 4 semesters; for doctorate, GRE General Test, TOEFL.
Faculty research: Rock mechanics, coal preparation, explosives engineering, mine land reclamation, health and safety.

■ UNIVERSITY OF NEVADA, RENO

Graduate School, Mackay School of Mines, Department of Mining Engineering, Reno, NV 89557

AWARDS MS, EM.

Faculty: 6.
Students: 5 full-time (0 women), 2 international. Average age 33. In 2001, 2 degrees awarded.
Degree requirements: For master's, thesis (for some programs).
Entrance requirements: For master's, GRE, TOEFL, minimum GPA of 2.75. *Application deadline:* For fall admission, 4/5 (priority date); for spring admission, 10/15. Applications are processed on a rolling basis. *Application fee:* $40.
Expenses: Tuition, state resident: full-time $2,067; part-time $108 per credit. Tuition, nonresident: full-time $9,282; part-time $109 per credit. Required fees: $57 per semester. Tuition and fees vary according to course load.
Financial support: In 2001–02, 3 research assistantships, 2 teaching assistantships were awarded. Financial award application deadline: 3/1.
Dr. Pierre Mousset-Jones, Graduate Program Director, *E-mail:* mousset@mines.unr.edu.

■ UNIVERSITY OF NORTH DAKOTA

Graduate School, School of Engineering and Mines, Department of Civil Engineering, Grand Forks, ND 58202

AWARDS Civil engineering (M Engr). Sanitary engineering (M Engr), including soils and structures engineering, surface mining engineering. Part-time programs available.

Faculty: 6 full-time (0 women).
Students: 6 full-time (1 woman), 3 part-time. 2 applicants, 100% accepted, 0 enrolled. In 2001, 6 degrees awarded.
Degree requirements: For master's, thesis or alternative, final comprehensive exam.
Entrance requirements: For master's, GRE General Test, TOEFL, minimum GPA of 2.5. *Application deadline:* For fall admission, 3/1 (priority date); for spring admission, 10/15 (priority date). Applications are processed on a rolling basis. *Application fee:* $30.
Expenses: Tuition, state resident: full-time $3,298. Tuition, nonresident: full-time $7,998.
Financial support: In 2001–02, 4 students received support, including 4 teaching assistantships with full tuition reimbursements available (averaging $9,500 per year); fellowships, research assistantships, career-related internships or fieldwork, Federal Work-Study, institutionally sponsored loans, scholarships/grants, and

tuition waivers (full and partial) also available. Support available to part-time students. Financial award application deadline: 3/15; financial award applicants required to submit FAFSA.
Faculty research: Soil-structures, environmental-water resources.
Dr. Charles J. Moretti, Chairperson, 701-777-5150, *Fax:* 701-777-4838, *E-mail:* charles_moretti@mail.und.nodak.edu. *Web site:* http://www.und.edu/dept/sem/html/civil_engineering.html

■ THE UNIVERSITY OF TEXAS AT AUSTIN

Graduate School, College of Engineering, Department of Petroleum and Geosystems Engineering, Program in Energy and Mineral Resources, Austin, TX 78712-1111

AWARDS MA, MS.

Faculty: 2 full-time (0 women).
Students: 13 full-time (3 women), 12 international. Average age 30. 7 applicants, 43% accepted.
Degree requirements: For master's, thesis, seminar.
Entrance requirements: For master's, GRE General Test, TOEFL. *Application deadline:* For fall admission, 4/30 (priority date). Applications are processed on a rolling basis. *Application fee:* $50 ($75 for international students). Electronic applications accepted.
Expenses: Tuition, state resident: full-time $3,159. Tuition, nonresident: full-time $6,957. Tuition and fees vary according to program.
Dr. Willem C. J. vanRensburg, Graduate Adviser, 512-471-3248, *Fax:* 512-471-9605, *E-mail:* willem_vanrensburg@pe.utexas.edu.
Application contact: Julia Casarez, Graduate Coordinator, 512-471-3247, *Fax:* 512-471-9605, *E-mail:* julia_casarez@mail.utexas.edu. *Web site:* http://www.pe.utexas.edu/dept/academic.emr/

■ UNIVERSITY OF UTAH

Graduate School, College of Mines and Earth Sciences, Department of Mining Engineering, Salt Lake City, UT 84112-1107

AWARDS ME, MS, PhD.

Faculty: 5 full-time (0 women).
Students: 7 full-time (1 woman), 2 part-time; includes 1 minority (African American), 3 international. Average age 29. 6 applicants, 67% accepted. In 2001, 2 degrees awarded.
Degree requirements: For master's, comprehensive exam (ME), thesis (MS); for doctorate, one foreign language, thesis/dissertation.
Entrance requirements: For master's and doctorate, GRE General Test, TOEFL. *Application deadline:* For fall admission, 7/1. *Application fee:* $40 ($60 for international students).

Expenses: Tuition, state resident: part-time $320 per semester hour. Tuition, nonresident: part-time $1,135 per semester hour. Required fees: $143 per semester hour. Tuition and fees vary according to course load, degree level and program.
Financial support: Fellowships, research assistantships, teaching assistantships, career-related internships or fieldwork and institutionally sponsored loans available. Support available to part-time students. Financial award application deadline: 2/15.
Faculty research: Mineral economics, rock mechanics, mine ventilation, computer economics, slope stability.
Dr. M. Kim McCarter, Chair, 801-581-7198, *Fax:* 801-585-5410, *E-mail:* mkmccart@mines.utah.edu.
Application contact: Judy Hancey, Administrative Assistant, 801-581-7198, *E-mail:* jhancey@mines.utah.edu.

■ VIRGINIA POLYTECHNIC INSTITUTE AND STATE UNIVERSITY

Graduate School, College of Engineering, Department of Mining and Minerals Engineering, Blacksburg, VA 24061

AWARDS M Eng, MS, PhD.

Faculty: 7 full-time (0 women), 3 part-time/adjunct (0 women).
Students: 14 full-time (1 woman); includes 1 minority (African American), 4 international. Average age 22. 6 applicants, 0% accepted. In 2001, 2 degrees awarded.
Degree requirements: For master's, thesis.
Entrance requirements: For master's and doctorate, GRE, TOEFL. *Application deadline:* For fall admission, 12/1 (priority date). Applications are processed on a rolling basis. *Application fee:* $45. Electronic applications accepted.
Expenses: Tuition, state resident: part-time $241 per hour. Tuition, nonresident: part-time $406 per hour. Tuition and fees vary according to program.
Financial support: In 2001–02, 5 research assistantships with full tuition reimbursements (averaging $11,637 per year), 7 teaching assistantships with full tuition reimbursements (averaging $11,637 per year) were awarded. Fellowships, career-related internships or fieldwork and unspecified assistantships also available. Financial award application deadline: 4/1.
Faculty research: Sensor development, slope stability, rock fracture, mechanics, ground control, environmental remediation.
Dr. M. Karmis, Head, 540-231-6671, *E-mail:* mkarmis@vt.edu.

■ WEST VIRGINIA UNIVERSITY

College of Engineering and Mineral Resources, Department of Mining Engineering, Morgantown, WV 26506

AWARDS MS Min E, PhD. Part-time programs available.

Faculty: 4 full-time (1 woman).
Students: 7 full-time (1 woman), 4 part-time, 7 international. Average age 36. 12 applicants, 67% accepted. In 2001, 1 degree awarded.
Degree requirements: For master's, thesis/dissertation; for doctorate, thesis/dissertation, comprehensive exam.
Entrance requirements: For master's, TOEFL, minimum GPA of 3.0; for doctorate, GRE General Test, TOEFL, MS in mineral engineering, minimum GPA of 3.5. *Application deadline:* For fall admission, 8/15 (priority date); for spring admission, 12/31. *Application fee:* $45.
Expenses: Tuition, state resident: full-time $2,791. Tuition, nonresident: full-time $8,659. Required fees: $1,002. Tuition and fees vary according to program.
Financial support: In 2001–02, 3 research assistantships, 2 teaching assistantships were awarded. Career-related internships or fieldwork, Federal Work-Study, institutionally sponsored loans, and tuition waivers (full and partial) also available. Financial award application deadline: 2/1; financial award applicants required to submit FAFSA.
Faculty research: Surface subsidence, mine ventilation, longwall mining, computer applications, respirable mine dust, mineral/coal processing. *Total annual research expenditures:* $150,000.
Dr. Syd S. Peng, Chair, 304-293-7680 Ext. 3301, *Fax:* 304-293-5780, *E-mail:* syd.peng@mail.wvu.edu. *Web site:* http://www.wvu.edu/~minegin/

PETROLEUM ENGINEERING

■ COLORADO SCHOOL OF MINES

Graduate School, Department of Petroleum Engineering, Golden, CO 80401-1887

AWARDS ME, MS, PhD. Part-time programs available.

Faculty: 8 full-time (1 woman), 2 part-time/adjunct (0 women).
Students: 41 full-time (5 women), 6 part-time; includes 3 minority (1 African American, 1 Hispanic American, 1 Native American), 39 international. 74 applicants, 92% accepted, 17 enrolled. In 2001, 10 master's, 7 doctorates awarded.
Degree requirements: For master's, thesis (for some programs); for doctorate, one foreign language, thesis/dissertation, comprehensive exam. *Median time to degree:*

Master's–2 years full-time; doctorate–4 years full-time.
Entrance requirements: For master's and doctorate, GRE General Test. *Application deadline:* For fall admission, 12/1 (priority date); for spring admission, 5/1 (priority date). Applications are processed on a rolling basis. *Application fee:* $40. Electronic applications accepted.
Expenses: Tuition, state resident: full-time $4,940; part-time $246 per credit. Tuition, nonresident: full-time $16,070; part-time $803 per credit. Required fees: $341 per semester.
Financial support: In 2001–02, 27 fellowships (averaging $6,083 per year), 3 research assistantships (averaging $12,609 per year), 10 teaching assistantships (averaging $6,644 per year) were awarded. Career-related internships or fieldwork, institutionally sponsored loans, and unspecified assistantships also available. Financial award applicants required to submit FAFSA.
Faculty research: Dynamic rock mechanics, deflagration theory, geostatistics, geochemistry, petrophysics. *Total annual research expenditures:* $40,061.
Dr. Craig W. Van Kirk, Head, 303-273-3749, *E-mail:* cvankirk@mines.edu.
Application contact: Chris Cardwell, Administrative Assistant, 303-273-3740, *Fax:* 303-273-3189, *E-mail:* ccardwel@mines.edu. *Web site:* http://www.mines.edu/academic/petroleum/

■ LOUISIANA STATE UNIVERSITY AND AGRICULTURAL AND MECHANICAL COLLEGE

Graduate School, College of Engineering, Department of Petroleum Engineering, Baton Rouge, LA 70803

AWARDS MS Pet E, PhD.

Faculty: 7 full-time (0 women).
Students: 19 full-time (3 women), 6 part-time, 20 international. Average age 31. 42 applicants, 21% accepted, 5 enrolled. In 2001, 9 degrees awarded.
Degree requirements: For master's, thesis or alternative; for doctorate, thesis/dissertation, exam.
Entrance requirements: For master's and doctorate, GRE General Test, minimum GPA of 3.0. *Application deadline:* For fall admission, 1/25 (priority date). Applications are processed on a rolling basis. *Application fee:* $25.
Expenses: Tuition, state resident: full-time $2,551. Tuition, nonresident: full-time $5,551. Required fees: $854. Part-time tuition and fees vary according to course load.
Financial support: In 2001–02, 14 research assistantships with partial tuition reimbursements (averaging $12,071 per year) were awarded; fellowships, teaching assistantships with partial tuition reimbursements, institutionally sponsored

Louisiana State University and Agricultural and Mechanical College (continued)
loans also available. Financial award applicants required to submit FAFSA.
Faculty research: Enhanced oil and gas recovery, well control and blowout prevention, formation evaluation, environmental control. *Total annual research expenditures:* $704,504.
Dr. Z. Bassiouni, Chair, 225-578-5215, *Fax:* 225-578-6039, *E-mail:* pezab@lsu.edu.
Application contact: Dr. Andrew Wojtanowicz, Graduate Adviser, 225-578-5215, *Fax:* 225-578-6039, *E-mail:* awojtan@lsu.edu. *Web site:* http://www.eng.lsu.edu/

■ MONTANA TECH OF THE UNIVERSITY OF MONTANA

Graduate School, Petroleum Engineering Program, Butte, MT 59701-8997

AWARDS MS. Part-time and evening/weekend programs available.

Faculty: 4 full-time (1 woman).
Students: 3 full-time (1 woman), 1 part-time. 9 applicants, 22% accepted, 1 enrolled. In 2001, 3 degrees awarded.
Degree requirements: For master's, thesis optional.
Entrance requirements: For master's, GRE General Test, TOEFL, minimum GPA of 3.0. *Application deadline:* For fall admission, 4/1 (priority date); for spring admission, 10/1 (priority date). Applications are processed on a rolling basis. *Application fee:* $30.
Expenses: Tuition, state resident: full-time $3,717; part-time $196 per credit. Tuition, nonresident: full-time $11,770; part-time $324 per credit.
Financial support: In 2001–02, 3 students received support, including 3 teaching assistantships with partial tuition reimbursements available (averaging $5,667 per year); career-related internships or fieldwork, institutionally sponsored loans, and tuition waivers (full and partial) also available. Financial award application deadline: 4/1; financial award applicants required to submit FAFSA.
Faculty research: Reservoir characterization, simulation, near well bore problems, PVT, environmental waste. *Total annual research expenditures:* $58,795.
Dr. Tarek Ahmed, Department Head, 406-496-4259, *Fax:* 406-496-4417, *E-mail:* tahmed@mtech.edu.
Application contact: Cindy Dunstan, Administrator, Graduate School, 406-496-4304, *Fax:* 406-496-4334, *E-mail:* cdunstan@mtech.edu. *Web site:* http://www.mtech.edu/

■ NEW MEXICO INSTITUTE OF MINING AND TECHNOLOGY

Graduate Studies, Department of Petroleum Engineering, Socorro, NM 87801

AWARDS MS, PhD.

Faculty: 8 full-time (0 women), 14 part-time/adjunct (1 woman).
Students: 31 full-time (4 women), 27 international. Average age 24. 50 applicants, 46% accepted, 12 enrolled. In 2001, 10 master's, 1 doctorate awarded.
Degree requirements: For master's and doctorate, thesis/dissertation.
Entrance requirements: For master's, GRE General Test, TOEFL; for doctorate, GRE General Test, GRE Subject Test, TOEFL. *Application deadline:* For fall admission, 3/1 (priority date); for spring admission, 6/1. Applications are processed on a rolling basis. *Application fee:* $16 ($30 for international students).
Expenses: Tuition, state resident: part-time $1,084 per semester. Tuition, nonresident: part-time $4,367 per semester. Required fees: $429 per semester.
Financial support: In 2001–02, 24 research assistantships (averaging $13,505 per year), 4 teaching assistantships with full and partial tuition reimbursements (averaging $12,714 per year) were awarded. Fellowships, Federal Work-Study and institutionally sponsored loans also available. Financial award application deadline: 3/1; financial award applicants required to submit CSS PROFILE or FAFSA.
Faculty research: Reservoir simulation, oil recovery processes, drilling and production.
Dr. Tom Engler, Chairman, 505-835-5412, *Fax:* 505-835-5207, *E-mail:* engler@nmt.edu.
Application contact: Dr. David B. Johnson, Dean of Graduate Studies, 505-835-5513, *Fax:* 505-835-5476, *E-mail:* graduate@nmt.edu. *Web site:* http://www.nmt.edu/~petro/

■ THE PENNSYLVANIA STATE UNIVERSITY UNIVERSITY PARK CAMPUS

Graduate School, College of Earth and Mineral Sciences, Department of Energy and Geo-Environmental Engineering, Program in Petroleum and Natural Gas Engineering, State College, University Park, PA 16802-1503

AWARDS MS, PhD.

Students: 17 full-time (3 women), 4 part-time. In 2001, 4 master's, 3 doctorates awarded.
Degree requirements: For master's, thesis; for doctorate, one foreign language, thesis/dissertation.

Entrance requirements: For master's and doctorate, GRE General Test, TOEFL. *Application fee:* $45.
Expenses: Tuition, state resident: full-time $7,882; part-time $333 per credit. Tuition, nonresident: full-time $16,142; part-time $673 per credit. Required fees: $124 per semester.
Financial support: Application deadline: 12/31.
Michael Adewumi, Graduate Program Officer, 814-863-2816.

■ STANFORD UNIVERSITY

School of Earth Sciences, Department of Petroleum Engineering, Stanford, CA 94305-9991

AWARDS MS, PhD, Eng.

Faculty: 8 full-time (0 women).
Students: 50 full-time (12 women), 2 part-time; includes 1 minority (Asian American or Pacific Islander), 46 international. Average age 27. 48 applicants, 44% accepted. In 2001, 20 master's, 7 doctorates awarded. Terminal master's awarded for partial completion of doctoral program.
Degree requirements: For doctorate and Eng, thesis/dissertation.
Entrance requirements: For master's, doctorate, and Eng, GRE General Test, TOEFL. *Application deadline:* For fall admission, 1/15. *Application fee:* $65 ($80 for international students). Electronic applications accepted.
Roland Horne, Chair, 650-723-9595, *Fax:* 650-725-2099, *E-mail:* horne@pangea.stanford.edu.
Application contact: 650-723-8314. *Web site:* http://ekofisk.stanford.edu/pe.html

■ TEXAS A&M UNIVERSITY

College of Engineering, Harold Vance Department of Petroleum Engineering, College Station, TX 77843

AWARDS M Eng, MS, D Eng, PhD. Part-time programs available. Postbaccalaureate distance learning degree programs offered (no on-campus study).

Faculty: 31.
Students: 163 (22 women). Average age 30.
Degree requirements: For master's, thesis, thesis (MS); for doctorate, thesis/dissertation, dissertation (PhD).
Entrance requirements: For master's and doctorate, GRE General Test, TOEFL. *Application deadline:* Applications are processed on a rolling basis. *Application fee:* $50 ($75 for international students). Electronic applications accepted.
Expenses: Tuition, state resident: full-time $11,872. Tuition, nonresident: full-time $17,892.
Financial support: Fellowships, research assistantships, teaching assistantships, career-related internships or fieldwork and tuition waivers (partial) available. Financial

award application deadline: 3/1; financial award applicants required to submit FAFSA.

Faculty research: Drilling and well stimulation, well completions and well performance, reservoir modeling and reservoir description, reservoir simulation, improved/enhanced recovery. *Total annual research expenditures:* $1.8 million.
Dr. Charles H. Bowman, Head, 979-845-2241, *Fax:* 979-845-1307, *E-mail:* bauman@spindletop.tamu.edu.
Application contact: Dr. Thomas A. Blasingame, Graduate Advisor, 979-847-9095, *Fax:* 979-845-1307, *E-mail:* t-blasingame@spindletop.tamu.edu. *Web site:* http://pumpjack.tamu.edu/

Find an in-depth description at www.petersons.com/gradchannel.

■ TEXAS A&M UNIVERSITY–KINGSVILLE

College of Graduate Studies, College of Engineering, Department of Chemical Engineering and Natural Gas Engineering, Program in Natural Gas Engineering, Kingsville, TX 78363

AWARDS ME, MS.

Students: 13 full-time (1 woman), 7 part-time, (all international). Average age 25. In 2001, 9 degrees awarded.
Degree requirements: For master's, thesis or alternative, comprehensive exam.
Entrance requirements: For master's, GRE General Test, TOEFL, minimum GPA of 3.0. *Application deadline:* For fall admission, 6/1; for spring admission, 11/15. Applications are processed on a rolling basis. *Application fee:* $15 ($25 for international students).
Expenses: Tuition, state resident: part-time $42 per hour. Tuition, nonresident: part-time $253 per hour. Required fees: $56 per hour. One-time fee: $46 part-time. Tuition and fees vary according to program.
Financial support: Fellowships, research assistantships, Federal Work-Study, institutionally sponsored loans, and tuition waivers (partial) available. Financial award application deadline: 5/15.
Faculty research: Gas processing, coal gasification and liquefaction, enhanced oil recovery, gas measurement, unconventional gas recovery.
Dr. Faleh Al-Sadoon, Coordinator, 361-593-2002.

■ TEXAS TECH UNIVERSITY

Graduate School, College of Engineering, Department of Petroleum Engineering, Lubbock, TX 79409

AWARDS MS Pet E, PhD. Part-time programs available.
Faculty: 6 full-time (0 women).
Students: 12 full-time (2 women), 1 part-time, 12 international. Average age 29. 29

applicants, 52% accepted, 2 enrolled. In 2001, 7 degrees awarded.
Degree requirements: For master's, thesis or alternative.
Entrance requirements: For master's, GRE General Test, minimum GPA of 3.0. *Application deadline:* Applications are processed on a rolling basis. *Application fee:* $25 ($50 for international students). Electronic applications accepted.
Expenses: Tuition, state resident: full-time $1,926; part-time $107 per credit hour. Tuition, nonresident: full-time $5,724; part-time $318 per credit hour. Required fees: $779; $737 per year. Tuition and fees vary according to course level, course load and program.
Financial support: In 2001–02, 11 research assistantships with partial tuition reimbursements (averaging $10,897 per year) were awarded; fellowships, teaching assistantships with partial tuition reimbursements, career-related internships or fieldwork, Federal Work-Study, and institutionally sponsored loans also available. Support available to part-time students. Financial award application deadline: 5/1; financial award applicants required to submit FAFSA.
Faculty research: In new test well: test current methods and develop new methods of artificial lift; test current models and develop improved multiphase flow correlations; production optimization studies; artificial lift systems optimization; gas well-de-watering techniques. *Total annual research expenditures:* $257,510.
Dr. James F. Lea, Chair, 806-742-3573, *Fax:* 806-742-3502.
Application contact: Graduate Adviser, 806-742-3573, *Fax:* 806-742-3502. *Web site:* http://www.pe.ttu.edu/

■ UNIVERSITY OF ALASKA FAIRBANKS

Graduate School, School of Mineral Engineering, Department of Petroleum Engineering, Fairbanks, AK 99775-7480

AWARDS MS.

Faculty: 6 full-time (0 women), 1 part-time/adjunct (0 women).
Students: 5 full-time (0 women), 1 part-time, 4 international. Average age 33. 15 applicants, 33% accepted, 2 enrolled. In 2001, 2 degrees awarded.
Degree requirements: For master's, thesis, comprehensive exam.
Entrance requirements: For master's, GRE General Test, TOEFL. *Application deadline:* For fall admission, 4/1; for spring admission, 11/1. Applications are processed on a rolling basis. *Application fee:* $35.
Expenses: Tuition, state resident: full-time $4,272; part-time $178 per credit. Tuition, nonresident: full-time $8,328; part-time $347 per credit. Required fees: $960; $60 per term. Part-time tuition and fees vary according to course load.

Financial support: In 2001–02, fellowships with tuition reimbursements (averaging $10,000 per year); research assistantships with tuition reimbursements, teaching assistantships with tuition reimbursements, career-related internships or fieldwork, Federal Work-Study, and scholarships/grants also available.
Faculty research: Characterization of oil and gas.
Godwin Chukwu, Head, 907-474-7730.

■ UNIVERSITY OF CALIFORNIA, BERKELEY

Graduate Division, College of Engineering, Department of Materials Science and Mineral Engineering, Program in Petroleum Engineering, Berkeley, CA 94720-1500

AWARDS M Eng, MS, D Eng, PhD.

Degree requirements: For master's, comprehensive exam or thesis (MS); for doctorate, thesis/dissertation, qualifying exam.
Entrance requirements: For master's and doctorate, GRE General Test, minimum GPA of 3.0.
Expenses: Tuition, nonresident: full-time $10,704. Required fees: $4,349.

■ UNIVERSITY OF HOUSTON

Cullen College of Engineering, Department of Mechanical Engineering, Houston, TX 77204

AWARDS Aerospace engineering (MS, PhD); biomedical engineering (MS); computer and systems engineering (MS, PhD); environmental engineering (MS, PhD); materials engineering (MS, PhD); mechanical engineering (MME, MSME); petroleum engineering (MS). Part-time and evening/weekend programs available.

Faculty: 16 full-time (0 women), 1 part-time/adjunct (0 women).
Students: 34 full-time (4 women), 26 part-time (2 women); includes 7 minority (3 Asian Americans or Pacific Islanders, 4 Hispanic Americans), 32 international. Average age 28. 114 applicants, 64% accepted. In 2001, 20 master's, 3 doctorates awarded. Terminal master's awarded for partial completion of doctoral program.
Degree requirements: For master's, thesis (for some programs); for doctorate, thesis/dissertation, departmental qualifying exam.
Entrance requirements: For master's and doctorate, GRE General Test, TOEFL. *Application deadline:* For fall admission, 7/3 (priority date); for spring admission, 12/4. Applications are processed on a rolling basis. *Application fee:* $25 ($75 for international students).
Expenses: Tuition, state resident: full-time $1,512. Tuition, nonresident: full-time $5,310. Required fees: $1,308. Tuition and fees vary according to program.

University of Houston (continued)

Financial support: In 2001–02, 20 research assistantships (averaging $14,400 per year), 13 teaching assistantships (averaging $14,400 per year) were awarded. Fellowships, career-related internships or fieldwork and Federal Work-Study also available. Financial award application deadline: 2/15.

Faculty research: Experimental and computational turbulence, composites, rheology, phase change/heat transfer, characterization of superconducting materials. *Total annual research expenditures:* $396,172.

Dr. Lewis T. Wheeler, Interim Chair, 713-743-4500, *Fax:* 713-743-4503.

Application contact: Susan Sanderson-Clobe, Graduate Admissions Analyst, 713-743-4505, *Fax:* 713-743-4503, *E-mail:* megrad@uh.edu. *Web site:* http://www.mc.uh.edu

Find an in-depth description at www.petersons.com/gradchannel.

■ **UNIVERSITY OF KANSAS**

Graduate School, School of Engineering, Department of Chemical and Petroleum Engineering, Lawrence, KS 66045

AWARDS Chemical engineering (MS); chemical/petroleum engineering (PhD); petroleum engineering (MS). Part-time programs available.

Faculty: 15.

Students: 30 full-time (10 women), 11 part-time (5 women); includes 1 minority (Asian American or Pacific Islander), 37 international. Average age 29. 21 applicants, 95% accepted, 10 enrolled. In 2001, 9 master's, 4 doctorates awarded.

Degree requirements: For master's, thesis (for some programs), exam; for doctorate, thesis/dissertation, qualifying exams, comprehensive exam.

Entrance requirements: For master's, GRE General Test, TOEFL, minimum GPA of 3.0; for doctorate, GRE General Test, TOEFL, minimum GPA of 3.5. *Application deadline:* For fall admission, 5/1 (priority date); for spring admission, 9/1 (priority date). Applications are processed on a rolling basis. *Application fee:* $40.

Expenses: Tuition, state resident: full-time $2,722; part-time $113 per credit. Tuition, nonresident: full-time $8,586; part-time $358 per credit. Required fees: $551; $46 per credit. Tuition and fees vary according to campus/location, program and reciprocity agreements.

Financial support: In 2001–02, 32 research assistantships with partial tuition reimbursements (averaging $9,737 per year), 12 teaching assistantships with full and partial tuition reimbursements (averaging $11,678 per year) were awarded. Fellowships, Federal Work-Study also available. Financial award application deadline: 1/31.

Faculty research: Enhanced oil recovery, catalysis and kinetics, electrochemical engineering, biochemical engineering, semiconductor materials processing. Bala Subramaniam, Chairperson, 785-864-4965, *Fax:* 785-864-4967.

Application contact: Graduate Advisor, 785-864-4965, *Fax:* 785-864-4967, *E-mail:* cpeinfo@ku.edu. *Web site:* http://www.engr.ku.edu/cpe/

■ **UNIVERSITY OF LOUISIANA AT LAFAYETTE**

Graduate School, College of Engineering, Department of Petroleum Engineering, Lafayette, LA 70504

AWARDS MSE. Evening/weekend programs available.

Faculty: 3 full-time (0 women).

Degree requirements: For master's, thesis or alternative, comprehensive exam.

Entrance requirements: For master's, GRE General Test, minimum GPA of 2.85. *Application deadline:* For fall admission, 5/15. *Application fee:* $20 ($30 for international students).

Expenses: Tuition, state resident: full-time $2,317; part-time $79 per credit. Tuition, nonresident: full-time $8,882; part-time $369 per credit. International tuition: $9,018 full-time.

Financial support: Federal Work-Study and tuition waivers (full and partial) available. Financial award application deadline: 5/1.

Dr. Ali Ghalambor, Head, 337-482-6517.

■ **UNIVERSITY OF MISSOURI– ROLLA**

Graduate School, School of Mines and Metallurgy, Department of Geological and Petroleum Engineering, Program in Petroleum Engineering, Rolla, MO 65409-0910

AWARDS MS, DE, PhD. Part-time programs available.

Degree requirements: For doctorate, thesis/dissertation.

Entrance requirements: For master's, GRE General Test, TOEFL, minimum GPA of 3.0 in last 4 semesters; for doctorate, GRE General Test, TOEFL. Electronic applications accepted.

Faculty research: Oil recovery, drilling systems, petroleum reservoir, formation evaluation, core analysis/interpretation.

■ **UNIVERSITY OF OKLAHOMA**

Graduate College, College of Engineering, School of Petroleum and Geological Engineering, Norman, OK 73019-0390

AWARDS Natural gas engineering and management (MS); petroleum and geological engineering (MS, PhD). Part-time and evening/weekend programs available.

Postbaccalaureate distance learning degree programs offered (no on-campus study).

Faculty: 10 full-time (0 women).

Students: 49 full-time (4 women), 43 part-time (1 woman); includes 1 minority (Hispanic American), 63 international. 53 applicants, 85% accepted, 17 enrolled. In 2001, 25 master's, 3 doctorates awarded.

Degree requirements: For master's, thesis optional; for doctorate, one foreign language, thesis/dissertation, qualifying exam.

Entrance requirements: For master's and doctorate, GRE, TOEFL. *Application deadline:* For fall admission, 6/1 (priority date); for spring admission, 11/1. Applications are processed on a rolling basis. *Application fee:* $25 ($50 for international students).

Expenses: Tuition, state resident: full-time $2,208; part-time $92 per credit hour. Tuition, nonresident: part-time $297 per credit hour. Tuition and fees vary according to course level, course load and program.

Financial support: In 2001–02, 31 research assistantships with partial tuition reimbursements (averaging $9,006 per year), 7 teaching assistantships with partial tuition reimbursements (averaging $9,181 per year) were awarded. Career-related internships or fieldwork and tuition waivers (full and partial) also available. Financial award application deadline: 4/15; financial award applicants required to submit FAFSA.

Faculty research: Wellbone stability, drilling and production operations, reservoir management, reservoir characterization techniques, coiled tubing, well stimulation, fluid rheology. *Total annual research expenditures:* $733,427.

Dr. Subhash Shah, Interim Director, 405-325-2921, *Fax:* 405-325-7477.

Application contact: Dr. Djebbar Tiab, Graduate Liaison, 405-325-2921, *Fax:* 405-325-7477, *E-mail:* dtiab@ou.edu.

■ **UNIVERSITY OF PITTSBURGH**

School of Engineering, Department of Chemical and Petroleum Engineering, Pittsburgh, PA 15260

AWARDS Chemical engineering (MS Ch E, PhD); petroleum engineering (MSPE). Part-time and evening/weekend programs available.

Faculty: 13 full-time (2 women), 6 part-time/adjunct (0 women).

Students: 43 full-time (8 women), 7 part-time (3 women); includes 2 minority (1 African American, 1 Asian American or Pacific Islander), 32 international. 200 applicants, 14% accepted, 14 enrolled. In 2001, 11 master's, 9 doctorates awarded.

Degree requirements: For master's, thesis; for doctorate, thesis/dissertation, final oral exams, comprehensive exam.

Entrance requirements: For master's and doctorate, GRE General Test, TOEFL, minimum QPA of 3.2. *Application deadline:*

For fall admission, 8/1 (priority date); for spring admission, 12/1 (priority date). Applications are processed on a rolling basis. *Application fee:* $40.
Financial support: In 2001–02, 41 students received support, including 1 fellowship with full tuition reimbursement available (averaging $19,000 per year), 40 research assistantships with full tuition reimbursements available (averaging $19,392 per year); teaching assistantships with full tuition reimbursements available, scholarships/grants, traineeships, and tuition waivers (full and partial) also available. Financial award application deadline: 2/15.
Faculty research: Biotechnology, polymers, catalysis, energy and environment, computational modeling. *Total annual research expenditures:* $4.6 million.
Dr. Eric Beckman, Chairman, 412-624-9631, *Fax:* 412-624-9639, *E-mail:* beckman@pitt.edu.
Application contact: William Federspiel, Associate Professor and Grad Coordinator, 412-624-9499, *Fax:* 412-624-9639, *E-mail:* federspiel@engrng.pitt.edu. *Web site:* http://www.engrng.pitt.edu/~chewww/

■ UNIVERSITY OF SOUTHERN CALIFORNIA

Graduate School, School of Engineering, Department of Petroleum Engineering, Los Angeles, CA 90089
AWARDS MS, PhD, Engr.

Degree requirements: For master's, thesis optional; for doctorate, thesis/dissertation.
Entrance requirements: For master's, doctorate, and Engr, GRE General Test, GRE Subject Test.
Expenses: Tuition: Full-time $25,060; part-time $844 per unit. Required fees: $473.

■ THE UNIVERSITY OF TEXAS AT AUSTIN

Graduate School, College of Engineering, Department of Petroleum and Geosystems Engineering, Austin, TX 78712-1111

AWARDS Energy and mineral resources (MA, MS); petroleum and geosystems engineering (MSE, PhD). Evening/weekend programs available. Postbaccalaureate distance learning degree programs offered (no on-campus study).
Faculty: 15 full-time (1 woman), 3 part-time/adjunct (1 woman).
Students: 80 full-time (16 women), 7 part-time (1 woman); includes 4 minority (1 African American, 2 Asian Americans or Pacific Islanders, 1 Hispanic American), 74 international. 69 applicants, 51% accepted. In 2001, 25 master's, 6 doctorates awarded.
Entrance requirements: For master's and doctorate, GRE General Test. *Application*

deadline: For fall admission, 2/1 (priority date); for spring admission, 10/1. Applications are processed on a rolling basis.
Application fee: $50 ($75 for international students). Electronic applications accepted.
Expenses: Tuition, state resident: full-time $3,159. Tuition, nonresident: full-time $6,957. Tuition and fees vary according to program.
Financial support: Fellowships, research assistantships, teaching assistantships available. Financial award application deadline: 2/1.
Dr. Mukul M. Sharma, Chairman, 512-471-3161, *Fax:* 512-471-9605, *E-mail:* msharma@mail.utexas.edu.
Application contact: Dr. Kamy Sepehrnoori, Graduate Adviser, 512-471-0231, *Fax:* 512-471-9605, *E-mail:* pge_gradoffice@mail.utexas.edu. *Web site:* http://www.utexas.edu/coe/pge/

■ UNIVERSITY OF TULSA

Graduate School, College of Business Administration and College of Engineering and Natural Sciences, Department of Engineering and Technology Management, Tulsa, OK 74104-3189

AWARDS Chemical engineering (METM); computer science (METM); electrical engineering (METM); geological science (METM); mathematics (METM); mechanical engineering (METM); petroleum engineering (METM). Part-time and evening/weekend programs available.

Students: 2 full-time (1 woman), 1 part-time, 2 international. Average age 26. 3 applicants, 100% accepted, 1 enrolled. In 2001, 2 degrees awarded.
Entrance requirements: For master's, GRE General Test, TOEFL. *Application deadline:* Applications are processed on a rolling basis. *Application fee:* $30. Electronic applications accepted.
Expenses: Tuition: Full-time $9,540; part-time $530 per credit hour. Required fees: $80. One-time fee: $230 full-time.
Financial support: Fellowships, research assistantships, teaching assistantships, Federal Work-Study, scholarships/grants, tuition waivers (partial), and unspecified assistantships available. Support available to part-time students. Financial award application deadline: 2/1; financial award applicants required to submit FAFSA.
Application contact: Information Contact, *E-mail:* graduate-business@utulsa.edu. *Web site:* http://www.cba.utulsa.edu/academic.asp#graduate_studies/

■ UNIVERSITY OF TULSA

Graduate School, College of Engineering and Natural Sciences, Department of Petroleum Engineering, Tulsa, OK 74104-3189

AWARDS ME, MSE, PhD. Part-time programs available.

Faculty: 8 full-time (0 women).
Students: 43 full-time (5 women), 18 part-time (2 women); includes 1 minority (Hispanic American), 58 international. Average age 29. 67 applicants, 57% accepted, 15 enrolled. In 2001, 10 master's, 5 doctorates awarded.
Degree requirements: For master's, thesis (MSE), thesis optional; for doctorate, one foreign language, thesis/dissertation, comprehensive exam.
Entrance requirements: For master's and doctorate, GRE General Test, TOEFL. *Application deadline:* Applications are processed on a rolling basis. *Application fee:* $30. Electronic applications accepted.
Expenses: Tuition: Full-time $9,540; part-time $530 per credit hour. Required fees: $80. One-time fee: $230 full-time.
Financial support: In 2001–02, 3 fellowships with partial tuition reimbursements (averaging $5,500 per year), 20 research assistantships with full and partial tuition reimbursements (averaging $9,100 per year), 5 teaching assistantships with full and partial tuition reimbursements (averaging $7,900 per year) were awarded. Career-related internships or fieldwork, Federal Work-Study, scholarships/grants, tuition waivers (partial), and unspecified assistantships also available. Support available to part-time students. Financial award application deadline: 2/1; financial award applicants required to submit FAFSA.
Faculty research: Drilling, artificial lift, reservoir simulation, reservoir characterization, well testing. *Total annual research expenditures:* $8.7 million.
Dr. Dean Oliver, Chairperson, 918-631-3035, *Fax:* 915-631-2059, *E-mail:* dean-oliver@utulsa.edu.
Application contact: Dr. Albert C. Reynolds, Adviser, 918-631-3043, *Fax:* 918-631-2059, *E-mail:* grad@utulsa.edu. *Web site:* http://www.pe.utulsa.edu/

■ UNIVERSITY OF UTAH

Graduate School, College of Engineering, Department of Chemical and Fuels Engineering, Salt Lake City, UT 84112-1107

AWARDS Chemical and fuels engineering (M Phil, ME, MS, PhD); chemical engineering (M Phil, ME, MS, PhD); environmental engineering (ME, MS, PhD). Part-time programs available.

Faculty: 10 full-time (2 women), 6 part-time/adjunct (0 women).
Students: 47 full-time (7 women), 10 part-time (2 women); includes 18 minority (all Asian Americans or Pacific Islanders), 15 international. Average age 28. 84 applicants, 18% accepted. In 2001, 2 master's, 3 doctorates awarded.
Entrance requirements: For master's and doctorate, GRE, TOEFL, minimum GPA of 3.0. *Application deadline:* For fall admission, 7/1. *Application fee:* $40 ($60 for international students).

University of Utah (continued)

Expenses: Tuition, state resident: part-time $320 per semester hour. Tuition, nonresident: part-time $1,135 per semester hour. Required fees: $143 per semester hour. Tuition and fees vary according to course load, degree level and program.
Financial support: Fellowships, research assistantships, teaching assistantships available. Financial award applicants required to submit FAFSA.
Faculty research: Computer-aided process synthesis and design, combustion of solid and liquid fossil fuels, oxygen mass transport in biochemical reactors.
Terry Ring, Chair, 801-581-6915, *Fax:* 801-585-9291, *E-mail:* t.ring@m.cc.utah.edu.
Application contact: Grant Smith, Advisor, 801-581-6915, *Fax:* 801-585-9291, *E-mail:* gsmith@geoffrey.emro.utah.edu.

■ **UNIVERSITY OF WYOMING**

Graduate School, College of Engineering, Department of Chemical and Petroleum Engineering, Program in Petroleum Engineering, Laramie, WY 82071

AWARDS MS, PhD.

Faculty: 3 full-time (0 women).
Students: 6 full-time (0 women), 1 part-time, (all international). 3 applicants, 100% accepted. In 2001, 1 degree awarded. Terminal master's awarded for partial completion of doctoral program.
Degree requirements: For master's and doctorate, thesis/dissertation.
Entrance requirements: For master's and doctorate, GRE General Test, TOEFL,

minimum GPA of 3.0. *Application deadline:* For fall admission, 4/15 (priority date). Applications are processed on a rolling basis. *Application fee:* $40. Electronic applications accepted.
Expenses: Tuition, state resident: full-time $2,895; part-time $161 per credit hour. Tuition, nonresident: full-time $8,367; part-time $465 per credit hour. Required fees: $491; $10 per credit hour. $2 per credit hour. Tuition and fees vary according to course load and program.
Financial support: In 2001–02, research assistantships with full tuition reimbursements (averaging $13,000 per year), teaching assistantships with full tuition reimbursements (averaging $12,000 per year) were awarded. Career-related internships or fieldwork, Federal Work-Study, and institutionally sponsored loans also available. Financial award application deadline: 4/15.
Faculty research: Oil recovery methods, oil production, coal bed methane. *Total annual research expenditures:* $300,000.
Dr. Maciej Radosz, Head, 307-766-2500, *Fax:* 307-766-6777, *E-mail:* radosz@uwyo.edu.
Application contact: Dr. David Bell, Graduate Student Coordinator, 307-766-5769, *Fax:* 307-766-6777, *E-mail:* chpe.info@uwyo.edu. *Web site:* http://wwweng.uwyo.edu/

■ **WEST VIRGINIA UNIVERSITY**

College of Engineering and Mineral Resources, Department of Petroleum and Natural Gas Engineering, Morgantown, WV 26506

AWARDS MSPNGE, PhD. Part-time programs available.

Faculty: 5 full-time (0 women).
Students: 9 full-time (0 women), 3 part-time; includes 1 minority (Asian American or Pacific Islander), 9 international. Average age 28. 20 applicants, 75% accepted. In 2001, 8 degrees awarded.
Degree requirements: For master's, thesis.
Entrance requirements: For master's, TOEFL, minimum GPA of 3.0, BS or equivalent in petroleum or natural gas engineering. *Application deadline:* For fall admission, 8/15 (priority date); for spring admission, 12/31. *Application fee:* $45.
Expenses: Tuition, state resident: full-time $2,791. Tuition, nonresident: full-time $8,659. Required fees: $1,002. Tuition and fees vary according to program.
Financial support: In 2001–02, 5 research assistantships, 1 teaching assistantship were awarded. Career-related internships or fieldwork, Federal Work-Study, institutionally sponsored loans, and tuition waivers (full and partial) also available. Financial award application deadline: 2/1; financial award applicants required to submit FAFSA.
Faculty research: Gas reservoir engineering, well logging, environment artificial intelligence. *Total annual research expenditures:* $200,000.
Dr. Samuel Ameri, Chair, 304-293-7682 Ext. 3401, *Fax:* 304-293-5708, *E-mail:* samuel.ameri@mail.wvu.edu. *Web site:* http://www.cemr.wvu.edu/~wwwpnge

Industrial Engineering

AUTOMOTIVE ENGINEERING

■ **COLORADO STATE UNIVERSITY**

Graduate School, College of Applied Human Sciences, Department of Manufacturing Technology and Construction Management, Fort Collins, CO 80523-0015

AWARDS Automotive pollution control (MS); construction management (MS); historic preservation (MS); industrial technology management (MS); technology education and training (MS); technology of industry (PhD). Part-time and evening/weekend programs available.

Faculty: 11 full-time (0 women).

Students: 16 full-time (5 women), 27 part-time (10 women); includes 2 minority (1 African American, 1 Hispanic American), 1 international. Average age 31. 57 applicants, 98% accepted, 9 enrolled. Terminal master's awarded for partial completion of doctoral program.
Degree requirements: For master's, thesis (for some programs); for doctorate, thesis/dissertation.
Entrance requirements: For master's and doctorate, GRE General Test, TOEFL. *Application deadline:* For fall admission, 4/1 (priority date); for spring admission, 9/1 (priority date). Applications are processed on a rolling basis. *Application fee:* $30. Electronic applications accepted.
Expenses: Tuition, state resident: full-time $2,880; part-time $160 per credit. Tuition, nonresident: full-time $11,412; part-time $634 per credit. Required fees: $750; $34 per credit.

Financial support: In 2001–02, 1 fellowship with full tuition reimbursement (averaging $12,960 per year), 3 research assistantships with full tuition reimbursements (averaging $9,720 per year), 8 teaching assistantships with full tuition reimbursements (averaging $9,720 per year) were awarded. Career-related internships or fieldwork, Federal Work-Study, and traineeships also available.
Faculty research: Construction processes, historical preservation, sustainability, technology education. *Total annual research expenditures:* $800,000.
Dr. Larry Grosse, Head, 970-491-7958, *Fax:* 970-491-2473, *E-mail:* drfire107@mindspring.com.
Application contact: Becky Bell, Graduate Liaison, 970-491-7355, *Fax:* 970-491-2473, *E-mail:* becky.bell@cahs.colostate.edu. *Web site:* http://www.cahs.colostate.edu/DIS/

■ KETTERING UNIVERSITY

Graduate School, Mechanical Engineering Department, Flint, MI 48504-4898

AWARDS Automotive systems (MS Eng); manufacturing (MS Eng); mechanical cognate (MS Eng); mechanical design (MS Eng). Part-time and evening/weekend programs available. Postbaccalaureate distance learning degree programs offered (no on-campus study).

Faculty: 15 full-time (0 women).
Students: 6 full-time (1 woman), 88 part-time (12 women); includes 8 minority (7 African Americans, 1 Native American), 43 international. 163 applicants, 87% accepted. In 2001, 18 degrees awarded.
Degree requirements: For master's, thesis (for some programs), registration. *Median time to degree:* Master's–3 years full-time, 6 years part-time.
Application deadline: For fall admission, 7/15. Applications are processed on a rolling basis. *Application fee:* $0. Electronic applications accepted.
Expenses: Tuition: Full-time $8,370; part-time $465 per credit.
Financial support: Fellowships with full tuition reimbursements, research assistantships with full tuition reimbursements, teaching assistantships with full tuition reimbursements, Federal Work-Study, scholarships/grants, and tuition waivers (partial) available. Support available to part-time students. Financial award application deadline: 7/15; financial award applicants required to submit CSS PROFILE or FAFSA.
Dr. K. Joel Berry, Head, 810-762-7833, *Fax:* 810-762-7860, *E-mail:* jberry@kettering.edu.
Application contact: Betty L. Bedore, Coordinator of Publicity, 810-762-7494, *Fax:* 810-762-9935, *E-mail:* bbedore@kettering.edu. *Web site:* http://www.kettering.edu/

■ LAWRENCE TECHNOLOGICAL UNIVERSITY

College of Engineering, Southfield, MI 48075-1058

AWARDS Automotive engineering (MAE); civil engineering (MCE); electrical and computer engineering (MS); manufacturing systems (MEMS, DE). Part-time and evening/weekend programs available.

Faculty: 27 full-time (2 women), 11 part-time/adjunct (1 woman).
Students: Average age 32. 133 applicants, 38 enrolled. In 2001, 43 degrees awarded.
Application deadline: For fall admission, 8/1 (priority date); for winter admission, 12/1 (priority date); for spring admission, 5/1. Applications are processed on a rolling basis. *Application fee:* $50. Electronic applications accepted.
Expenses: Tuition: Part-time $460 per credit hour.

Financial support: Institutionally sponsored loans available. Support available to part-time students. Financial award application deadline: 3/1; financial award applicants required to submit FAFSA.
Faculty research: Advanced composite materials in bridges, strengthening existing bridges with carbon and glass fiber sheets, development of drive shafts using composite materials. *Total annual research expenditures:* $150,000.
Dr. Laird Johnston, Dean, 248-204-2500, *Fax:* 248-204-2509, *E-mail:* lejohnston@ltu.edu.
Application contact: Jane Rohrback, Interim Director of Admissions, 248-204-3160, *Fax:* 248-204-3188, *E-mail:* admission@ltu.edu.

■ UNIVERSITY OF DETROIT MERCY

College of Engineering and Science, Department of Mechanical Engineering, Detroit, MI 48219-0900

AWARDS Automotive engineering (DE); manufacturing engineering (DE); mechanical engineering (ME, DE). Evening/weekend programs available.

Faculty: 8 full-time (1 woman).
Students: 5 full-time (0 women), 28 part-time (3 women); includes 1 minority (Asian American or Pacific Islander), 23 international. Average age 31. In 2001, 12 degrees awarded.
Degree requirements: For doctorate, thesis/dissertation.
Application deadline: For fall admission, 8/1 (priority date). Applications are processed on a rolling basis. *Application fee:* $30 ($50 for international students).
Expenses: Tuition: Full-time $10,620; part-time $590 per credit hour. Required fees: $400. Tuition and fees vary according to program.
Faculty research: CAD/CAM.
Mark Schumak, Chairman, 313-993-3370, *Fax:* 313-993-1187, *E-mail:* schumamr@udmercy.edu.

■ UNIVERSITY OF MICHIGAN

Horace H. Rackham School of Graduate Studies, College of Engineering, Program in Automotive Engineering, Ann Arbor, MI 48109

AWARDS M Eng.

Faculty: 4 full-time (0 women), 2 part-time/adjunct (0 women).
Students: 16 full-time (2 women), 64 part-time (5 women); includes 9 minority (2 African Americans, 3 Asian Americans or Pacific Islanders, 3 Hispanic Americans, 1 Native American), 4 international. Average age 28. 40 applicants, 75% accepted, 20 enrolled. In 2001, 40 degrees awarded.
Degree requirements: For master's, registration. *Median time to degree:* Master's–1 year full-time, 2.5 years part-time.

Application deadline: For fall admission, 7/15 (priority date); for winter admission, 10/15 (priority date); for spring admission, 1/15 (priority date). Applications are processed on a rolling basis. *Application fee:* $55. Electronic applications accepted.
Financial support: In 2001–02, 1 fellowship (averaging $3,000 per year), 1 teaching assistantship with tuition reimbursement (averaging $6,726 per year) were awarded. Financial award applicants required to submit FAFSA.
Prof. Huei Peng, Director, 734-763-1134, *Fax:* 734-647-0079, *E-mail:* hpeng@umich.edu.
Application contact: Henia Kamil, Program Manager, 734-763-1134, *Fax:* 734-647-0079, *E-mail:* autoeng@umich.edu. *Web site:* http://ott-outreach.engin.umich.edu/automotive-engineering/auto.html

■ UNIVERSITY OF MICHIGAN–DEARBORN

College of Engineering and Computer Science, Interdisciplinary Programs, Program in Automotive Systems Engineering, Dearborn, MI 48128-1491

AWARDS MSE. Part-time and evening/weekend programs available.

Faculty: 1 full-time (0 women).
Students: 10 full-time (3 women), 65 part-time (6 women). Average age 29. 47 applicants, 60% accepted, 21 enrolled. In 2001, 20 degrees awarded.
Degree requirements: For master's, thesis optional.
Entrance requirements: For master's, TOEFL, bachelor's degree in applied mathematics, computer science, engineering, or physical science; minimum GPA of 3.0. *Application deadline:* For fall admission, 8/1 (priority date); for winter admission, 12/1 (priority date); for spring admission, 4/1. Applications are processed on a rolling basis. *Application fee:* $55. Electronic applications accepted.
Expenses: Tuition, state resident: part-time $300 per credit hour. Tuition, nonresident: part-time $756 per credit hour. Required fees: $90 per semester. Tuition and fees vary according to course level, course load and program.
Financial support: In 2001–02, 2 fellowships with full tuition reimbursements, 4 research assistantships with full tuition reimbursements were awarded. Financial award application deadline: 4/1; financial award applicants required to submit FAFSA.
Application contact: Sherry Boyd, Administrative Assistant I, 313-593-5582, *Fax:* 313-593-5386, *E-mail:* idpgrad@umd.umich.edu. *Web site:* http://www.engin.umd.umich.edu/

INDUSTRIAL/ MANAGEMENT ENGINEERING

■ ARIZONA STATE UNIVERSITY

Graduate College, College of Engineering and Applied Sciences, Department of Industrial Engineering, Tempe, AZ 85287

AWARDS MS, MSE, PhD, MSE/MIMOT.

Degree requirements: For master's, thesis or alternative; for doctorate, thesis/ dissertation.
Entrance requirements: For master's, GRE General Test (recommended), minimum GPA of 3.0; for doctorate, GRE General Test (recommended), minimum GPA of 3.5.
Faculty research: Computer-aided manufacturing, human factors, productivity improvement, computer-integrated manufacturing, operations research.

■ AUBURN UNIVERSITY

Graduate School, College of Engineering, Department of Industrial and Systems Engineering, Auburn University, AL 36849

AWARDS MIE, MS, PhD. Part-time programs available.

Faculty: 7 full-time (1 woman).
Students: 25 full-time (7 women), 30 part-time (9 women); includes 6 minority (2 African Americans, 1 Asian American or Pacific Islander, 2 Hispanic Americans, 1 Native American), 15 international. 113 applicants, 41% accepted. In 2001, 6 master's, 2 doctorates awarded.
Degree requirements: For master's, design project (MIE), thesis (MS); for doctorate, thesis/dissertation.
Entrance requirements: For master's and doctorate, GRE General Test. *Application deadline:* For fall admission, 7/7; for spring admission, 11/24. Applications are processed on a rolling basis. *Application fee:* $25 ($50 for international students).
Financial support: Fellowships, research assistantships, teaching assistantships, Federal Work-Study available. Support available to part-time students. Financial award application deadline: 3/15.
Dr. Alice E. Smith, Chair, 334-844-1401.
Application contact: Dr. John F. Pritchett, Dean of the Graduate School, 334-844-4700, *E-mail:* hatchlb@ mail.auburn.edu. *Web site:* http:// www.eng.auburn.edu/department/ie

■ BRADLEY UNIVERSITY

Graduate School, College of Engineering and Technology, Department of Industrial and Manufacturing Engineering and Technology, Peoria, IL 61625-0002

AWARDS MSIE, MSMFE. Part-time and evening/weekend programs available.

Students: 13 full-time, 33 part-time. 92 applicants, 79% accepted. In 2001, 23 degrees awarded.
Degree requirements: For master's, project.
Entrance requirements: For master's, TOEFL, minimum GPA of 3.0. *Application deadline:* For fall admission, 7/1 (priority date); for spring admission, 11/1. Applications are processed on a rolling basis. *Application fee:* $40 ($50 for international students).
Expenses: Tuition: Part-time $7,615 per semester. Tuition and fees vary according to course load.
Financial support: In 2001–02, 5 research assistantships with full and partial tuition reimbursements were awarded. Scholarships/grants and tuition waivers (partial) also available. Financial award application deadline: 3/1.
Dr. Joseph Emanuel, Chairperson, 309-677-2742.
Application contact: Dr. Fred Tayyari, Graduate Adviser, 309-677-2748.

■ CALIFORNIA POLYTECHNIC STATE UNIVERSITY, SAN LUIS OBISPO

College of Engineering, Program in Engineering, San Luis Obispo, CA 93407

AWARDS Biochemical engineering (MS); industrial engineering (MS); integrated technology management (MS); materials engineering (MS); water engineering (MS), including bioengineering, biomedical engineering, manufacturing engineering.

Faculty: 98 full-time (8 women), 82 part-time/adjunct (14 women).
Students: 20 full-time (4 women), 9 part-time (1 woman). 25 applicants, 68% accepted, 15 enrolled. In 2001, 22 degrees awarded.
Entrance requirements: For master's, GRE General Test, minimum GPA of 2.5 in last 90 quarter units. *Application fee:* $55.
Expenses: Tuition, nonresident: part-time $164 per unit. One-time fee: $2,153 part-time.
Financial support: Application deadline: 3/2.
Dr. Peter Y. Lee, Dean, 805-756-2131, *Fax:* 805-756-6503, *E-mail:* plee@ calpoly.edu.
Application contact: Dr. Daniel W. Walsh, Associate Dean, 805-756-2131, *Fax:* 805-756-6503, *E-mail:* dwalsh@ calpoly.edu. *Web site:* http:// www.synner.ceng.calpoly.edu/

■ CALIFORNIA STATE UNIVERSITY, FRESNO

Division of Graduate Studies, College of Agricultural Sciences and Technology, Department of Industrial Technology, Fresno, CA 93740-8027

AWARDS MS. Part-time and evening/weekend programs available.

Faculty: 7.
Students: 13 full-time (2 women), 12 part-time (1 woman); includes 7 minority (2 Asian Americans or Pacific Islanders, 5 Hispanic Americans), 7 international. Average age 31. 17 applicants, 82% accepted, 5 enrolled. In 2001, 3 degrees awarded.
Degree requirements: For master's, thesis or alternative. *Median time to degree:* Master's–2.5 years full-time, 3.5 years part-time.
Entrance requirements: For master's, GRE General Test, TOEFL, minimum GPA of 2.5. *Application deadline:* For fall admission, 6/1 (priority date); for spring admission, 11/1. Applications are processed on a rolling basis. *Application fee:* $55. Electronic applications accepted.
Expenses: Tuition, nonresident: part-time $246 per unit. Required fees: $605 per semester. Tuition and fees vary according to course load.
Financial support: Career-related internships or fieldwork, Federal Work-Study, and scholarships/grants available. Support available to part-time students. Financial award application deadline: 3/1; financial award applicants required to submit FAFSA.
Faculty research: Fuels/pollution, energy, computer integrative manufacturing.
Dr. Tony Au, Chair, 559-278-2145, *Fax:* 559-278-5081, *E-mail:* tony_au@ csufresno.edu.
Application contact: Dr. Gary Paqlierani, Graduate Coordinator, 559-278-2145, *Fax:* 559-278-5081, *E-mail:* gary_paqlierani@ csufresno.edu.

■ CALIFORNIA STATE UNIVERSITY, NORTHRIDGE

Graduate Studies, College of Engineering and Computer Science, Department of Civil and Manufacturing Engineering, Northridge, CA 91330

AWARDS Applied mechanics (MSE); civil engineering (MS); engineering and computer science (MS); engineering management (MS); industrial engineering (MS); materials engineering (MS); mechanical engineering (MS), including aerospace engineering, applied engineering, machine design, mechanical engineering, structural engineering, thermofluids; mechanics (MS). Part-time and evening/weekend programs available.

Faculty: 14 full-time, 2 part-time/adjunct.
Students: 25 full-time (4 women), 72 part-time (9 women). Average age 31. 64

applicants, 77% accepted, 22 enrolled. In 2001, 34 degrees awarded.

Degree requirements: For master's, thesis.

Entrance requirements: For master's, GRE General Test, TOEFL, minimum GPA of 2.5. *Application deadline:* For fall admission, 11/30. *Application fee:* $55.

Expenses: Tuition, nonresident: part-time $631 per semester. Required fees: $246 per unit.

Financial support: Teaching assistantships available. Financial award application deadline: 3/1.

Faculty research: Composite study. Dr. Stephen Gadomski, Chair, 818-677-2166.

Application contact: Dr. Ileana Costa, Graduate Coordinator, 818-677-3299.

■ CENTRAL MISSOURI STATE UNIVERSITY

School of Graduate Studies, College of Applied Sciences and Technology, Department of Manufacturing and Construction, Warrensburg, MO 64093

AWARDS Industrial management (MS); industrial technology (MS). Part-time programs available.

Faculty: 5 full-time (0 women), 1 part-time/adjunct (0 women).

Students: 13 full-time (1 woman), 24 part-time (5 women); includes 1 minority (African American), 12 international. Average age 32. 18 applicants, 67% accepted. In 2001, 12 degrees awarded.

Degree requirements: For master's, comprehensive exam.

Entrance requirements: For master's, minimum GPA of 2.5; previous course work in mathematics, science, and technology. *Application deadline:* Applications are processed on a rolling basis. *Application fee:* $25 ($50 for international students).

Expenses: Tuition, area resident: Full-time $4,200; part-time $175 per credit hour. Tuition, nonresident: full-time $8,352; part-time $348 per credit hour.

Financial support: In 2001–02, 3 research assistantships with full tuition reimbursements (averaging $3,917 per year), 9 teaching assistantships with full and partial tuition reimbursements (averaging $6,900 per year) were awarded. Federal Work-Study, scholarships/grants, unspecified assistantships, and laboratory assistantships also available. Support available to part-time students. Financial award application deadline: 3/1; financial award applicants required to submit FAFSA.

Faculty research: Industrial management, industrial production, training, manufacturing technologies, internet instruction. *Total annual research expenditures:* $100,000.

Dr. John Sutton, Coordinator, 660-543-4439, *Fax:* 660-543-4578, *E-mail:* sutton@cmsu1.cmsu.edu. *Web site:* http://www.cmsu.edu/

■ CENTRAL MISSOURI STATE UNIVERSITY

School of Graduate Studies, College of Applied Sciences and Technology, Department of Safety Science Technology, Warrensburg, MO 64093

AWARDS Human services/public services (Ed S); industrial hygiene (MS); industrial safety management (MS); occupational safety management (MS); public services administration (MS). Safety management (MS). Secondary education/safety education (MSE). Security (MS); transportation safety (MS). Part-time programs available.

Faculty: 7 full-time (2 women), 3 part-time/adjunct (0 women).

Students: 7 full-time (4 women), 39 part-time (15 women); includes 5 minority (4 Hispanic Americans, 1 Native American). Average age 37. 20 applicants, 75% accepted. In 2001, 40 degrees awarded.

Degree requirements: For master's, comprehensive exam (MS), comprehensive exam or thesis (MSE).

Entrance requirements: For master's, GRE General Test, minimum GPA of 2.5, 15 hours in related area (MS); minimum GPA of 2.75, teaching certificate (MSE); for Ed S, master's degree in related field. *Application deadline:* Applications are processed on a rolling basis. *Application fee:* $25 ($50 for international students).

Expenses: Tuition, area resident: Full-time $4,200; part-time $175 per credit hour. Tuition, nonresident: full-time $8,352; part-time $348 per credit hour.

Financial support: In 2001–02, 2 research assistantships with full and partial tuition reimbursements (averaging $8,000 per year), 9 teaching assistantships (averaging $4,000 per year) were awarded. Federal Work-Study, scholarships/grants, unspecified assistantships, and administrative and laboratory assistantships also available. Support available to part-time students. Financial award application deadline: 3/1; financial award applicants required to submit FAFSA.

Faculty research: Hazard assessment, crisis and disaster, ergonomics, fire science, safety management. *Total annual research expenditures:* $2,000.

Larry Womble, Interim Chair, 660-543-8764, *Fax:* 660-543-8142, *E-mail:* womble@cmsu1.cmsu.edu. *Web site:* http://www.cmsu.edu/

■ CENTRAL WASHINGTON UNIVERSITY

Graduate Studies and Research, College of Education and Professional Studies, Department of Industrial and Engineering Technology, Ellensburg, WA 98926-7463

AWARDS Engineering technology (MS). Part-time programs available.

Faculty: 8 full-time (0 women).

Students: 3 full-time (1 woman), 27 part-time (2 women); includes 8 minority (3 African Americans, 3 Asian Americans or Pacific Islanders, 1 Hispanic American, 1 Native American), 1 international. 20 applicants, 85% accepted, 14 enrolled.

Degree requirements: For master's, thesis or alternative.

Entrance requirements: For master's, minimum GPA of 3.0. *Application deadline:* For fall admission, 4/1 (priority date); for winter admission, 10/1; for spring admission, 1/1. Applications are processed on a rolling basis. *Application fee:* $35.

Expenses: Tuition, state resident: full-time $4,848; part-time $162 per credit. Tuition, nonresident: full-time $14,772; part-time $492 per credit. Required fees: $324.

Financial support: In 2001–02, 1 research assistantship with partial tuition reimbursement (averaging $7,120 per year), 1 teaching assistantship with partial tuition reimbursement (averaging $7,120 per year) were awarded. Career-related internships or fieldwork and Federal Work-Study also available.

Dr. Walter Kaminski, Chair, 509-963-1756.

Application contact: Barbara Sisko, Office Assistant, Graduate Studies and Research, 509-963-3103, *Fax:* 509-963-1799, *E-mail:* masters@cwu.edu.

■ CLEMSON UNIVERSITY

Graduate School, College of Engineering and Science, Department of Industrial Engineering, Clemson, SC 29634

AWARDS MS, PhD. Part-time programs available.

Students: 57 full-time (12 women), 12 part-time (2 women), 62 international. Average age 25. 211 applicants, 57% accepted, 25 enrolled. In 2001, 39 master's, 5 doctorates awarded. Terminal master's awarded for partial completion of doctoral program.

Degree requirements: For master's, thesis or alternative; for doctorate, thesis/dissertation.

Entrance requirements: For master's and doctorate, GRE General Test, TOEFL. *Application deadline:* For fall admission, 6/1. Applications are processed on a rolling basis. *Application fee:* $40.

Expenses: Tuition, state resident: full-time $5,310. Tuition, nonresident: full-time $11,284.

Financial support: Fellowships, research assistantships, teaching assistantships, career-related internships or fieldwork available. Financial award applicants required to submit FAFSA.

Faculty research: Computer-integrated manufacturing, human-computer interaction, ergonomics, quality engineering. *Total annual research expenditures:* $292,665.

Dr. Delbert L. Kimbler, Chair, 864-656-4716, *Fax:* 864-656-0795, *E-mail:* del.kimbler@ces.clemson.edu.

Clemson University (continued)
Application contact: Dr. William Ferrell, Coordinator, 864-656-2724, *Fax:* 864-656-0795, *E-mail:* fwillia@ces.clemson.edu. *Web site:* http://ie.eng.clemson.edu/

■ CLEVELAND STATE UNIVERSITY

College of Graduate Studies, Fenn College of Engineering, Department of Industrial and Manufacturing Engineering, Cleveland, OH 44115

AWARDS Engineering (D Eng); industrial engineering (MS). Part-time programs available.

Faculty: 5 full-time (0 women).
Students: 3 full-time (0 women), 51 part-time (8 women); includes 2 minority (both Hispanic Americans), 29 international. Average age 31. 64 applicants, 69% accepted. In 2001, 9 master's, 1 doctorate awarded. Terminal master's awarded for partial completion of doctoral program.
Degree requirements: For master's, project or thesis; for doctorate, thesis/dissertation, candidacy and qualifying exams.
Entrance requirements: For master's, GRE General Test, TOEFL, minimum GPA of 2.75; for doctorate, GRE General Test, TOEFL, minimum GPA of 3.25. *Application deadline:* For fall admission, 7/15 (priority date). Applications are processed on a rolling basis. *Application fee:* $25.
Expenses: Tuition, state resident: full-time $6,838; part-time $263 per credit hour. Tuition, nonresident: full-time $13,526; part-time $520 per credit hour.
Financial support: In 2001–02, 4 research assistantships, 1 teaching assistantship were awarded. Fellowships, career-related internships or fieldwork, institutionally sponsored loans, and unspecified assistantships also available. Support available to part-time students.
Faculty research: Modeling of manufacturing systems, statistical process control, computerized production planning and facilities design, cellular manufacturing, artificial intelligence and sensors.
Dr. Joseph A. Svestka, Chairperson, 216-687-4662, *Fax:* 216-687-9330, *E-mail:* j.svestka@csuohio.edu.
Application contact: Shirley A. Love, Administrative Coordinator, 216-523-7250, *Fax:* 216-687-9330, *E-mail:* s.love@csuohio.edu. *Web site:* http://csaxp.csuohio.edu/industrial/

■ COLORADO STATE UNIVERSITY

Graduate School, College of Engineering, Department of Mechanical Engineering, Fort Collins, CO 80523-0015

AWARDS Bioengineering (MS, PhD); energy and environmental engineering (MS, PhD);

energy conversion (MS, PhD); engineering management (MS); heat and mass transfer (MS, PhD); industrial and manufacturing systems engineering (MS, PhD); mechanical engineering (MS, PhD); mechanics and materials (MS, PhD). Part-time programs available.

Faculty: 17 full-time (2 women).
Students: 36 full-time (6 women), 63 part-time (11 women); includes 5 minority (2 Asian Americans or Pacific Islanders, 2 Hispanic Americans, 1 Native American), 22 international. Average age 32. 234 applicants, 83% accepted, 32 enrolled. In 2001, 10 master's, 3 doctorates awarded. Terminal master's awarded for partial completion of doctoral program.
Degree requirements: For doctorate, thesis/dissertation.
Entrance requirements: For master's and doctorate, GRE General Test, TOEFL, minimum GPA of 3.0. *Application deadline:* For fall admission, 2/1 (priority date). Applications are processed on a rolling basis. *Application fee:* $30. Electronic applications accepted.
Expenses: Tuition, state resident: full-time $2,880; part-time $160 per credit. Tuition, nonresident: full-time $11,412; part-time $634 per credit. Required fees: $750; $34 per credit.
Financial support: In 2001–02, 2 fellowships, 15 research assistantships (averaging $15,792 per year), 14 teaching assistantships (averaging $11,844 per year) were awarded. Traineeships also available.
Faculty research: Space propulsion, controls and systems, engineering and materials. *Total annual research expenditures:* $2.1 million.
Dr. Allan T. Kirkpatrick, Head, 970-491-6559, *Fax:* 970-491-3827, *E-mail:* allan@engr.colostate.edu. *Web site:* http://www.engr.colostate.edu/depts/me/index.html

■ COLUMBIA UNIVERSITY

Fu Foundation School of Engineering and Applied Science, Department of Industrial Engineering and Operations Research, New York, NY 10027

AWARDS Financial engineering (MS); industrial engineering (MS, Eng Sc D, PhD, Engr); operations research (MS, Eng Sc D, PhD). Part-time and evening/weekend programs available. Postbaccalaureate distance learning degree programs offered (no on-campus study).

Faculty: 16 full-time (0 women), 10 part-time/adjunct (0 women).
Students: 91 full-time (31 women), 69 part-time (21 women); includes 9 minority (8 Asian Americans or Pacific Islanders, 1 Native American), 125 international. Average age 26. 482 applicants, 46% accepted, 72 enrolled. In 2001, 76 master's, 4 doctorates awarded. Terminal master's awarded for partial completion of doctoral program.

Degree requirements: For doctorate, thesis/dissertation, oral and written qualifying exams.
Entrance requirements: For master's, doctorate, and Engr, GRE General Test, TOEFL. *Application deadline:* For fall admission, 1/5; for spring admission, 10/1. *Application fee:* $55. Electronic applications accepted.
Expenses: Tuition: Full-time $27,528. Required fees: $1,638.
Financial support: In 2001–02, 2 fellowships (averaging $5,000 per year), 12 research assistantships with full tuition reimbursements (averaging $19,200 per year), 12 teaching assistantships with full tuition reimbursements (averaging $19,200 per year) were awarded. Federal Work-Study also available. Financial award application deadline: 1/5; financial award applicants required to submit FAFSA.
Faculty research: Discrete event stochastic systems, optimization, productions planning and scheduling, inventory control, yield management, simulation, mathematical programming, combinatorial optimization, queuing, financial engineering. *Total annual research expenditures:* $682,685.
Dr. Donald Goldfarb, Chairman, 212-854-8011, *Fax:* 212-854-8103, *E-mail:* gold@ieor.columbia.edu.
Application contact: Nathaniel C. Farrell, Program Coordinator, 212-854-4351, *Fax:* 212-854-8103, *E-mail:* nat@ieor.columbia.edu. *Web site:* http://www.ieor.columbia.edu/

Find an in-depth description at www.petersons.com/gradchannel.

■ CORNELL UNIVERSITY

Graduate School, Graduate Fields of Engineering, Field of Operations Research and Industrial Engineering, Ithaca, NY 14853-0001

AWARDS Applied probability and statistics (PhD); manufacturing systems engineering (PhD); mathematical programming (PhD); operations research and industrial engineering (M Eng).

Faculty: 28 full-time.
Students: 109 full-time (19 women); includes 17 minority (1 African American, 15 Asian Americans or Pacific Islanders, 1 Hispanic American), 66 international. 380 applicants, 53% accepted. In 2001, 87 master's, 4 doctorates awarded. Terminal master's awarded for partial completion of doctoral program.
Degree requirements: For doctorate, thesis/dissertation.
Entrance requirements: For master's and doctorate, GRE General Test, TOEFL, 3 letters of recommendation. *Application deadline:* For fall admission, 1/15 (priority date). *Application fee:* $65. Electronic applications accepted.
Expenses: Tuition: Full-time $25,970. Required fees: $50.

Financial support: In 2001–02, 41 students received support, including 13 fellowships with full tuition reimbursements available, 8 research assistantships with full tuition reimbursements available, 20 teaching assistantships with full tuition reimbursements available; institutionally sponsored loans, scholarships/grants, tuition waivers (full and partial), and unspecified assistantships also available. Financial award applicants required to submit FAFSA.

Faculty research: Mathematical programming and combinatorial optimization, statistics, stochastic processes, mathematical finance, simulation, manufacturing.

Application contact: Graduate Field Assistant, 607-255-9128, *E-mail:* orphd@cornell.edu. *Web site:* http://www.gradschool.cornell.edu/grad/fields_1/oper-res.html

Find an in-depth description at www.petersons.com/gradchannel.

■ EAST CAROLINA UNIVERSITY

Graduate School, School of Industry and Technology, Department of Industrial Technology, Greenville, NC 27858-4353

AWARDS MS.

Faculty: 8 full-time (0 women), 1 part-time/adjunct (0 women).

Students: 12 full-time (0 women), 65 part-time (12 women); includes 6 minority (5 African Americans, 1 Hispanic American). Average age 35. 27 applicants, 74% accepted. In 2001, 11 degrees awarded.

Entrance requirements: For master's, GRE General Test or MAT. *Application deadline:* For fall admission, 6/1 (priority date). Applications are processed on a rolling basis. *Application fee:* $45.

Expenses: Tuition, state resident: full-time $2,636. Tuition, nonresident: full-time $11,365.

Financial support: Application deadline: 6/1.

Dr. Charles Coddington, Director of Graduate Studies, 252-328-6012, *E-mail:* sitgradprog@mail.ecu.edu.

Application contact: Bonnie Eshelman, Information Contact, 252-328-6013, *Fax:* 252-328-4250, *E-mail:* eshelmanb@mail.ecu.edu.

■ EASTERN KENTUCKY UNIVERSITY

The Graduate School, College of Business and Technology, Department of Technology, Program in Industrial Technology, Richmond, KY 40475-3102

AWARDS MS. Part-time programs available.

Faculty: 2 full-time (0 women), 1 part-time/adjunct (0 women).

Students: 2 full-time (1 woman), 29 part-time (3 women); includes 7 minority (6

African Americans, 1 Hispanic American), 1 international. In 2001, 26 degrees awarded.

Entrance requirements: For master's, GRE General Test, minimum GPA of 2.5. *Application fee:* $0.

Expenses: Tuition, state resident: full-time $1,468; part-time $165 per credit hour. Tuition, nonresident: full-time $4,034; part-time $450 per credit hour.

Financial support: Research assistantships, teaching assistantships, Federal Work-Study available. Support available to part-time students.

Faculty research: Quality control, dental implants, manufacturing technology.

William E. Davis, Chair, 859-622-3232.

■ EASTERN MICHIGAN UNIVERSITY

Graduate School, College of Technology, Department of Industrial Technology, Program in Industrial Technology, Ypsilanti, MI 48197

AWARDS MS.

Degree requirements: For master's, thesis optional.

Entrance requirements: For master's, TOEFL. *Application deadline:* For fall admission, 5/15; for spring admission, 3/15. Applications are processed on a rolling basis. *Application fee:* $30.

Expenses: Tuition, state resident: part-time $285 per credit hour. Tuition, nonresident: part-time $510 per credit hour.

Financial support: Available to part-time students. Application deadline: 3/15.

Dr. Victoria Gotts, Coordinator, 734-487-2040.

■ FLORIDA AGRICULTURAL AND MECHANICAL UNIVERSITY

Division of Graduate Studies, Research, and Continuing Education, FAMU-FSU College of Engineering, Department of Industrial Engineering, Tallahassee, FL 32307-3200

AWARDS MS.

Entrance requirements: For master's, GRE General Test, minimum GPA of 3.0.

■ FLORIDA INTERNATIONAL UNIVERSITY

College of Engineering, Department of Industrial Engineering, Miami, FL 33199

AWARDS MS. Part-time and evening/weekend programs available.

Faculty: 7 full-time (1 woman).

Students: 54 full-time (11 women), 76 part-time (26 women); includes 53 minority (5 African Americans, 3 Asian Americans or Pacific Islanders, 45 Hispanic Americans), 63 international.

Average age 29. 121 applicants, 50% accepted, 24 enrolled. In 2001, 29 degrees awarded.

Entrance requirements: For master's, GRE General Test, TOEFL. *Application deadline:* For fall admission, 4/1 (priority date); for spring admission, 10/1. Applications are processed on a rolling basis. *Application fee:* $20.

Expenses: Tuition, state resident: full-time $2,916; part-time $162 per credit hour. Tuition, nonresident: full-time $10,245; part-time $569 per credit hour. Required fees: $168 per term.

Dr. Shih-Ming Lee, Chairperson, 305-348-2256, *Fax:* 305-348-3721, *E-mail:* leet@eng.fiu.edu.

■ FLORIDA STATE UNIVERSITY

Graduate Studies, FAMU/FSU College of Engineering, Department of Industrial Engineering, Tallahassee, FL 32306

AWARDS MS, PhD.

Degree requirements: For master's, thesis; for doctorate, thesis/dissertation, preliminary exam, qualifying exam.

Entrance requirements: For master's, GRE General Test, minimum GPA of 3.0; for doctorate, GRE General Test, minimum GPA of 3.0 (without MS in industrial engineering), 3.4 (with MS in industrial engineering).

Expenses: Tuition, state resident: part-time $163 per credit hour. Tuition, nonresident: part-time $570 per credit hour. Tuition and fees vary according to program.

Faculty research: Precision manufacturing, composite manufacturing, green manufacturing, applied optimization, simulation. *Web site:* http://chaos.eng.fsu.edu/ie/

■ GEORGIA INSTITUTE OF TECHNOLOGY

Graduate Studies and Research, College of Engineering, School of Industrial and Systems Engineering, Program in Industrial and Systems Engineering, Atlanta, GA 30332-0001

AWARDS Algorithms, combinatorics, and optimization (PhD); industrial and systems engineering (PhD); industrial engineering (MS, MSIE). Statistics (MS Stat). Part-time programs available. Terminal master's awarded for partial completion of doctoral program.

Degree requirements: For master's, thesis optional; for doctorate, thesis/dissertation.

Entrance requirements: For master's and doctorate, GRE General Test, TOEFL, minimum GPA of 3.0. Electronic applications accepted.

Faculty research: Computer-integrated manufacturing systems, materials handling

Georgia Institute of Technology (continued) systems, production and distribution. *Web site:* http://www.isye.gatech.edu/

Find an in-depth description at www.petersons.com/gradchannel.

■ ILLINOIS STATE UNIVERSITY

Graduate School, College of Applied Science and Technology, Department of Technology, Normal, IL 61790-2200

AWARDS MS.

Faculty: 8 full-time (1 woman).
Students: 8 full-time (2 women), 21 part-time (3 women); includes 4 minority (2 African Americans, 2 Asian Americans or Pacific Islanders), 3 international. 13 applicants, 85% accepted. In 2001, 10 degrees awarded.
Degree requirements: For master's, thesis or alternative.
Entrance requirements: For master's, GRE General Test, minimum GPA of 2.8. *Application deadline:* Applications are processed on a rolling basis. *Application fee:* $30.
Expenses: Tuition, state resident: full-time $2,691; part-time $112 per credit hour. Tuition, nonresident: full-time $5,880; part-time $245 per credit hour. Required fees: $1,146; $48 per credit hour.
Financial support: In 2001–02, 6 teaching assistantships (averaging $7,425 per year) were awarded; research assistantships, tuition waivers (full) and unspecified assistantships also available. Financial award application deadline: 4/1.
Faculty research: Technical assistance for education-to-careers and tech prep programming, Illinois Manufacturing Extension Center. *Total annual research expenditures:* $397,183.
Dr. Rodney Custer, Chairperson, 309-438-3661. *Web site:* http://www.cast.ilstu.edu/tec/

■ INDIANA STATE UNIVERSITY

School of Graduate Studies, School of Technology, Program in Industrial Technology, Terre Haute, IN 47809-1401

AWARDS MA, MS.

Degree requirements: For master's, thesis optional.
Entrance requirements: For master's, TOEFL, bachelor's degree in industrial technology or related field, minimum undergraduate GPA of 2.5. Electronic applications accepted.

■ IOWA STATE UNIVERSITY OF SCIENCE AND TECHNOLOGY

Graduate College, College of Engineering, Department of Industrial and Manufacturing Systems Engineering, Ames, IA 50011

AWARDS Industrial engineering (MS, PhD); operations research (MS).

Faculty: 16 full-time.
Students: 35 full-time (5 women), 30 part-time (3 women), 62 international. 205 applicants, 42% accepted, 11 enrolled. In 2001, 12 master's, 3 doctorates awarded.
Degree requirements: For master's, thesis or alternative; for doctorate, thesis/dissertation. *Median time to degree:* Master's–2.7 years full-time; doctorate–4.3 years full-time.
Entrance requirements: For master's, GRE General Test, TOEFL or IELTS; for doctorate, GRE General Test, TOEFL, or IELTS. *Application deadline:* For fall admission, 3/1 (priority date); for spring admission, 10/1 (priority date). *Application fee:* $20 ($50 for international students). Electronic applications accepted.
Expenses: Tuition, state resident: full-time $1,851. Tuition, nonresident: full-time $5,449. Tuition and fees vary according to program.
Financial support: In 2001–02, 21 research assistantships with partial tuition reimbursements (averaging $10,714 per year), 24 teaching assistantships with partial tuition reimbursements (averaging $13,000 per year) were awarded. Fellowships, scholarships/grants, health care benefits, and unspecified assistantships also available.
Faculty research: Economic modeling, valuation techniques, robotics, digital controls, systems reliability.
Dr. Patrick Patterson, Chair, 515-294-1682, *Fax:* 515-294-3524, *E-mail:* ppatters@iastate.edu.
Application contact: Dr. John Jackman, Director of Graduate Studies, 515-294-0126. *Web site:* http://www.eng.iastate.edu/coe/grad.asp/

■ KANSAS STATE UNIVERSITY

Graduate School, College of Engineering, Department of Industrial and Manufacturing Systems Engineering, Manhattan, KS 66506

AWARDS Engineering management (MEM); industrial and manufacturing systems engineering (PhD); industrial engineering (MS); operations research (MS). Part-time programs available. Postbaccalaureate distance learning degree programs offered.

Faculty: 11 full-time (1 woman).
Students: 30 full-time (7 women), 24 part-time (2 women), 31 international. 201 applicants, 49% accepted, 19 enrolled. In 2001, 5 master's, 1 doctorate awarded.
Degree requirements: For master's, thesis or alternative; for doctorate, thesis/dissertation.
Entrance requirements: For master's, GRE General Test, TOEFL, bachelor's degree in engineering, mathematics, or physical science; for doctorate, GRE General Test, TOEFL, master's degree in engineering or industrial manufacturing. *Application deadline:* For fall admission, 3/1 (priority date); for spring admission, 9/1. Applications are processed on a rolling

basis. *Application fee:* $0 ($25 for international students). Electronic applications accepted.
Expenses: Tuition, state resident: part-time $113 per credit hour. Tuition, nonresident: part-time $358 per credit hour.
Financial support: In 2001–02, 18 research assistantships with partial tuition reimbursements (averaging $9,000 per year), 2 teaching assistantships with full tuition reimbursements (averaging $9,000 per year) were awarded. Federal Work-Study, institutionally sponsored loans, and scholarships/grants also available. Support available to part-time students. Financial award application deadline: 3/1; financial award applicants required to submit FAFSA.
Faculty research: Manufacturing engineering, operations research, engineering management, quality engineering, ergonomics. *Total annual research expenditures:* $1.7 million.
Dr. Bradley Kramer, Head, 785-532-5606, *Fax:* 785-532-7810, *E-mail:* bradleyk@ksu.edu.
Application contact: E. Stanley Lee, Graduate Program Director, 785-532-5606, *Fax:* 785-532-7810, *E-mail:* eslee@ksu.edu. *Web site:* http://cheetah.imse.ksu.edu/

■ LAMAR UNIVERSITY

College of Graduate Studies, College of Engineering, Department of Industrial Engineering, Program in Industrial Engineering, Beaumont, TX 77710

AWARDS ME, MES, DE.

Faculty: 4 full-time (0 women).
Students: 34 full-time (2 women), 3 part-time, 36 international. Average age 25. 135 applicants, 54% accepted. In 2001, 21 degrees awarded.
Degree requirements: For master's, thesis (for some programs); for doctorate, thesis/dissertation.
Entrance requirements: For master's and doctorate, GRE General Test, TOEFL. *Application deadline:* For fall admission, 5/15 (priority date); for spring admission, 10/1 (priority date). Applications are processed on a rolling basis. *Application fee:* $25 ($50 for international students).
Expenses: Tuition, state resident: full-time $1,114. Tuition, nonresident: full-time $3,670.
Financial support: In 2001–02, 2 fellowships with partial tuition reimbursements, 1 research assistantship with partial tuition reimbursement, 2 teaching assistantships with partial tuition reimbursements were awarded. Financial award application deadline: 4/1.
Faculty research: Total quality management, CAD/CAM/CIM, scheduling. *Total annual research expenditures:* $31,000.
Dr. Victor Zaloom, Chair, 409-880-8804, *Fax:* 409-880-8121.

Application contact: Dr. Hsing-Wei Chu, Professor, 409-880-8804, *Fax:* 409-880-8121.

■ LEHIGH UNIVERSITY

P.C. Rossin College of Engineering and Applied Science, Department of Industrial and Systems Engineering, Bethlehem, PA 18015-3094

AWARDS Industrial engineering (M Eng, MS, PhD); management science (MS); quality engineering (MS). Part-time and evening/weekend programs available. Postbaccalaureate distance learning degree programs offered (no on-campus study).

Faculty: 13 full-time (0 women), 2 part-time/adjunct (0 women).
Students: 46 full-time (11 women), 23 part-time (5 women); includes 7 minority (2 African Americans, 5 Hispanic Americans), 27 international. 101 applicants, 39% accepted, 23 enrolled. In 2001, 22 master's, 4 doctorates awarded.
Degree requirements: For doctorate, thesis/dissertation.
Entrance requirements: For master's and doctorate, GRE General Test, TOEFL, minimum GPA of 2.75. *Application deadline:* For fall admission, 7/15; for spring admission, 12/1. Applications are processed on a rolling basis. *Application fee:* $50.
Expenses: Tuition: Part-time $468 per credit hour. Required fees: $200; $100 per semester. Tuition and fees vary according to program.
Financial support: In 2001–02, 12 fellowships with full and partial tuition reimbursements (averaging $13,300 per year), 13 research assistantships with full and partial tuition reimbursements (averaging $14,400 per year), 7 teaching assistantships with full and partial tuition reimbursements (averaging $12,000 per year) were awarded. Career-related internships or fieldwork, scholarships/grants, tuition waivers (full and partial), and unspecified assistantships also available. Financial award application deadline: 1/15.
Faculty research: Manufacturing systems and processes, operations research and applied statistics, information systems and technologies, quality engineering, logistics and supply chain. *Total annual research expenditures:* $3.5 million.
Dr. S. David Wu, Chairman and Professor, 610-758-4050, *Fax:* 610-758-4886, *E-mail:* sdw1@lehigh.edu.
Application contact: Rita R. Frey, Graduate Coordinator, 610-758-4051, *Fax:* 610-758-4886, *E-mail:* inime@lehigh.edu. *Web site:* http://www.lehigh.edu/inime/inime.html

Find an in-depth description at www.petersons.com/gradchannel.

■ LOUISIANA STATE UNIVERSITY AND AGRICULTURAL AND MECHANICAL COLLEGE

Graduate School, College of Engineering, Department of Industrial and Manufacturing Systems Engineering, Baton Rouge, LA 70803

AWARDS Engineering science (PhD); industrial engineering (MSIE).

Faculty: 8 full-time (0 women).
Students: 14 full-time (1 woman), 4 part-time, 17 international. Average age 26. 101 applicants, 44% accepted, 7 enrolled. In 2001, 7 degrees awarded. Terminal master's awarded for partial completion of doctoral program.
Degree requirements: For master's and doctorate, thesis/dissertation.
Entrance requirements: For master's and doctorate, GRE General Test, minimum GPA of 3.0. *Application deadline:* For fall admission, 1/25 (priority date). Applications are processed on a rolling basis. *Application fee:* $25.
Expenses: Tuition, state resident: full-time $2,551. Tuition, nonresident: full-time $5,551. Required fees: $854. Part-time tuition and fees vary according to course load.
Financial support: In 2001–02, 1 student received support; fellowships, research assistantships with partial tuition reimbursements available, teaching assistantships with partial tuition reimbursements available, institutionally sponsored loans and unspecified assistantships available. Financial award application deadline: 5/1; financial award applicants required to submit FAFSA.
Faculty research: Ergonomics/human factors engineering, industrial hygiene, production systems, operations research, manufacturing engineering and maintenance. *Total annual research expenditures:* $76,608.
Dr. Thomas Ray, Interim Chair, 225-578-5369, *Fax:* 225-578-5109, *E-mail:* tray@lsu.edu.
Application contact: Dr. F. Aghazadeh, Graduate Adviser, 225-578-5112, *E-mail:* aghazadeh@lsu.edu. *Web site:* http://www.imse.lsu.edu

■ LOUISIANA TECH UNIVERSITY

Graduate School, College of Engineering and Science, Department of Mechanical and Industrial Engineering, Ruston, LA 71272

AWARDS Industrial engineering (MS, D Eng); manufacturing systems engineering (MS); mechanical engineering (MS, D Eng); operations research (MS). Part-time programs available. Terminal master's awarded for partial completion of doctoral program.

Degree requirements: For master's and doctorate, thesis/dissertation.
Entrance requirements: For master's, GRE General Test, TOEFL, minimum

GPA of 3.0 in last 60 hours; for doctorate, TOEFL, minimum graduate GPA of 3.25 (with MS) or GRE General Test.
Faculty research: Engineering management, facilities planning, thermodynamics, automated manufacturing, micromanufacturing.

■ LOYOLA MARYMOUNT UNIVERSITY

Graduate Division, College of Science and Engineering, Department of Mechanical Engineering, Program in Engineering and Production Management, Los Angeles, CA 90045-2659

AWARDS MS. Part-time and evening/weekend programs available.

Students: 14 full-time (3 women), 9 part-time (1 woman); includes 9 minority (1 African American, 4 Asian Americans or Pacific Islanders, 4 Hispanic Americans), 2 international. 12 applicants, 75% accepted, 7 enrolled. In 2001, 6 degrees awarded.
Degree requirements: For master's, thesis or alternative, project.
Entrance requirements: For master's, GMAT or GRE General Test, TOEFL. *Application deadline:* Applications are processed on a rolling basis. *Application fee:* $45. Electronic applications accepted.
Expenses: Contact institution.
Financial support: In 2001–02, 6 students received support; research assistantships, Federal Work-Study, scholarships/grants, and laboratory assistantships available. Support available to part-time students. Financial award application deadline: 7/1; financial award applicants required to submit FAFSA. *Web site:* http://www.lmu.edu/acad/gd/graddiv.htm

■ MISSISSIPPI STATE UNIVERSITY

College of Engineering, Department of Industrial Engineering, Mississippi State, MS 39762

AWARDS MS, PhD. Part-time programs available. Postbaccalaureate distance learning degree programs offered (no on-campus study).

Faculty: 8 full-time (1 woman).
Students: 20 full-time (5 women), 6 part-time (3 women); includes 2 minority (both African Americans), 14 international. Average age 27. 144 applicants, 43% accepted, 13 enrolled. In 2001, 7 degrees awarded.
Degree requirements: For master's, thesis (for some programs), comprehensive oral or written exam, comprehensive exam (for some programs); for doctorate, thesis/dissertation, candidacy exam.
Entrance requirements: For master's, GRE General Test, TOEFL, minimum GPA of 3.00; for doctorate, GRE General Test, TOEFL, minimum GPA of 3.30. *Application deadline:* For fall admission, 7/1;

Mississippi State University (continued)
for spring admission, 11/1. Applications are processed on a rolling basis. *Application fee:* $25 for international students.
Expenses: Tuition, state resident: full-time $3,586; part-time $150 per credit hour. Tuition, nonresident: full-time $8,128; part-time $339 per credit hour. Tuition and fees vary according to course load and campus/location.
Financial support: In 2001–02, 2 fellowships with full tuition reimbursements, 15 research assistantships with full tuition reimbursements, 3 teaching assistantships with full tuition reimbursements were awarded. Federal Work-Study and institutionally sponsored loans also available. Financial award applicants required to submit FAFSA.
Faculty research: Operations research, ergonomics, production systems, management systems, transportation. *Total annual research expenditures:* $524,125.
Dr. Larry G. Brown, Head, 662-325-3865, *Fax:* 662-325-7618, *E-mail:* brown@engr.msstate.edu.
Application contact: Dr. Stanley F. Bullington, Graduate Coordinator, 662-325-7621, *Fax:* 662-325-7618, *E-mail:* bullington@ie.msstate.edu. *Web site:* http://www.msstate.edu/

■ MONTANA STATE UNIVERSITY–BOZEMAN

College of Graduate Studies, College of Engineering, Department of Mechanical and Industrial Engineering, Bozeman, MT 59717

AWARDS Engineering (PhD); industrial and management engineering (MS); mechanical engineering (MS). Part-time programs available.

Students: 22 full-time (4 women), 11 part-time (2 women); includes 1 minority (Asian American or Pacific Islander), 16 international. Average age 26. 58 applicants, 91% accepted, 14 enrolled. In 2001, 15 degrees awarded.
Degree requirements: For master's, thesis or alternative; for doctorate, thesis/dissertation, qualifying exam, supporting course area, comprehensive exam.
Entrance requirements: For master's, GRE General Test, TOEFL, TSE, minimum GPA of 3.0; for doctorate, GRE General Test, TOEFL, minimum undergraduate GPA of 3.0, minimum graduate GPA of 3.0. *Application deadline:* For fall admission, 7/21; for spring admission, 11/15. Applications are processed on a rolling basis. *Application fee:* $50. Electronic applications accepted.
Expenses: Tuition, state resident: full-time $3,894; part-time $198 per credit. Tuition, nonresident: full-time $10,661; part-time $480 per credit. International tuition: $10,811 full-time. Tuition and fees vary according to course load and program.

Financial support: In 2001–02, 21 research assistantships with full and partial tuition reimbursements (averaging $17,050 per year), 29 teaching assistantships with full and partial tuition reimbursements (averaging $8,658 per year) were awarded. Health care benefits and unspecified assistantships also available. Support available to part-time students. Financial award application deadline: 3/1; financial award applicants required to submit FAFSA.
Faculty research: Design representation in synthesis process, composites and smart materials, software for pulse detonation engines, HVAC, damage and failure criteria for advanced composites. *Total annual research expenditures:* $1.2 million.
Dr. Vic Cundy, Head, 406-994-2203, *Fax:* 406-994-6292, *E-mail:* vcundy@me.montana.edu. *Web site:* http://www.coe.montana.edu/mie/

■ MONTANA TECH OF THE UNIVERSITY OF MONTANA

Graduate School, Project Engineering and Management Program, Butte, MT 59701-8997

AWARDS MPEM. Part-time and evening/weekend programs available. Postbaccalaureate distance learning degree programs offered (no on-campus study).

Faculty: 3 full-time (0 women).
Students: 2 applicants, 100% accepted, 2 enrolled. In 2001, 2 degrees awarded.
Degree requirements: For master's, comprehensive exam, registration.
Entrance requirements: For master's, GRE General Test, TOEFL, minimum GPA of 3.0. *Application deadline:* For fall admission, 4/1 (priority date); for spring admission, 10/1 (priority date). Applications are processed on a rolling basis. *Application fee:* $30.
Expenses: Tuition, state resident: full-time $3,717; part-time $196 per credit. Tuition, nonresident: full-time $11,770; part-time $324 per credit.
Financial support: Application deadline: 4/1.
Dr. Kumar Ganesan, Director, 406-496-4239, *Fax:* 406-496-4650, *E-mail:* kganesan@mtech.edu.
Application contact: Cindy Dunstan, Administrator, Graduate School, 406-496-4304, *Fax:* 406-496-4334, *E-mail:* cdunstan@mtech.edu.

■ NEW JERSEY INSTITUTE OF TECHNOLOGY

Office of Graduate Studies, Department of Industrial and Manufacturing Engineering, Program in Industrial/Manufacturing Engineering, Newark, NJ 07102

AWARDS MS, PhD. Part-time and evening/weekend programs available.

Students: 30 full-time (2 women), 27 part-time (3 women); includes 7 minority (2

African Americans, 3 Asian Americans or Pacific Islanders, 2 Hispanic Americans), 34 international. Average age 27. 202 applicants, 59% accepted, 12 enrolled. In 2001, 25 master's, 2 doctorates awarded. Terminal master's awarded for partial completion of doctoral program.
Degree requirements: For master's, thesis or alternative; for doctorate, thesis/dissertation.
Entrance requirements: For master's, GRE General Test; for doctorate, GRE General Test, minimum graduate GPA of 3.5. *Application deadline:* For fall admission, 6/5 (priority date); for spring admission, 10/15. Applications are processed on a rolling basis. *Application fee:* $50. Electronic applications accepted.
Expenses: Tuition, state resident: full-time $7,812; part-time $434 per credit. Tuition, nonresident: full-time $10,746; part-time $597 per credit. Required fees: $47 per credit. $76 per semester.
Financial support: Fellowships with full and partial tuition reimbursements, research assistantships with full and partial tuition reimbursements, teaching assistantships with full and partial tuition reimbursements, career-related internships or fieldwork, Federal Work-Study, institutionally sponsored loans, and unspecified assistantships available. Financial award application deadline: 3/15.
Faculty research: Knowledge based systems, CAS/CAM simulation and interface, expert systems. *Total annual research expenditures:* $100,000.
Dr. George Abdou, Director, 973-596-3651, *Fax:* 973-596-3652, *E-mail:* george.abdou@njit.edu.
Application contact: Kathryn Kelly, Director of Admissions, 973-596-3300, *Fax:* 973-596-3461, *E-mail:* admissions@njit.edu. *Web site:* http://www.njit.edu/

■ NEW MEXICO STATE UNIVERSITY

Graduate School, College of Engineering, Department of Industrial Engineering, Las Cruces, NM 88003-8001

AWARDS MSIE, PhD. Part-time programs available. Postbaccalaureate distance learning degree programs offered (no on-campus study).

Faculty: 5 full-time (0 women), 2 part-time/adjunct (both women).
Students: 30 full-time (11 women), 20 part-time (8 women); includes 12 minority (1 African American, 1 Asian American or Pacific Islander, 10 Hispanic Americans), 20 international. Average age 35. 45 applicants, 80% accepted, 16 enrolled. In 2001, 58 degrees awarded.
Degree requirements: For master's, thesis optional; for doctorate, thesis/dissertation.
Entrance requirements: For doctorate, qualifying exam. *Application deadline:* For fall admission, 7/1 (priority date); for

spring admission, 11/1. Applications are processed on a rolling basis. *Application fee:* $15 ($35 for international students). Electronic applications accepted.

Expenses: Tuition, state resident: full-time $3,234; part-time $135 per credit. Tuition, nonresident: full-time $9,420; part-time $428 per credit. Required fees: $858.

Financial support: In 2001–02, 8 research assistantships, 6 teaching assistantships were awarded. Career-related internships or fieldwork, Federal Work-Study, and unspecified assistantships also available. Support available to part-time students. Financial award application deadline: 3/1.

Faculty research: Quality control, reliability, operations research, economic analysis, manufacturing systems.

Dr. Edward Pines, Head, 505-646-4923, *Fax:* 505-646-2976, *E-mail:* epines@ nmsu.edu.

Application contact: Adela Castro, Departmental Secretary, 505-646-4923, *Fax:* 505-646-2976, *E-mail:* acastro@ nmsu.edu. *Web site:* http://www.nmsu.edu/ Academic_Progs/Colleges/Engineering/IE/ public_html

■ NORTH CAROLINA AGRICULTURAL AND TECHNICAL STATE UNIVERSITY

Graduate School, College of Engineering, Department of Industrial and Systems Engineering, Greensboro, NC 27411

AWARDS MSISE, PhD. Part-time programs available.

Faculty: 9 full-time (0 women), 1 part-time/adjunct (0 women).

Students: 50 full-time (24 women), 7 part-time (3 women); includes 43 minority (42 African Americans, 1 Hispanic American), 10 international. Average age 25. 32 applicants, 81% accepted. In 2001, 10 degrees awarded.

Degree requirements: For master's, thesis, project; for doctorate, thesis/ dissertation.

Entrance requirements: For master's, GRE General Test (recommended); for doctorate, GRE General Test. *Application deadline:* For fall admission, 7/1; for spring admission, 1/9. Applications are processed on a rolling basis. *Application fee:* $35.

Financial support: In 2001–02, 3 fellowships with full tuition reimbursements, 24 research assistantships with partial tuition reimbursements, 8 teaching assistantships with partial tuition reimbursements were awarded.

Faculty research: Human-machine systems engineering, management systems engineering, operations research and systems analysis, production systems engineering. *Total annual research expenditures:* $24,000.

Dr. Eui H. Park, Chairperson, 336-334-7780, *Fax:* 336-334-7729, *E-mail:* park@ ncat.edu.

Application contact: Dr. Bala Ram, Graduate Coordinator, 336-334-7780, *Fax:* 336-334-7729, *E-mail:* ram@ncat.edu. *Web site:* http://www.eng.ncat.edu:80/niedept/

■ NORTH CAROLINA STATE UNIVERSITY

Graduate School, College of Engineering, Department of Industrial Engineering, Raleigh, NC 27695

AWARDS MIE, MSIE, PhD. Part-time programs available.

Faculty: 22 full-time (1 woman), 8 part-time/adjunct (0 women).

Students: 64 full-time (22 women), 13 part-time (6 women); includes 4 minority (3 African Americans, 1 Native American), 52 international. Average age 28. 245 applicants, 24% accepted. In 2001, 16 master's, 8 doctorates awarded. Terminal master's awarded for partial completion of doctoral program.

Degree requirements: For master's, thesis (for some programs); for doctorate, thesis/dissertation.

Entrance requirements: For master's, GRE General Test, TOEFL, minimum GPA of 3.0; for doctorate, GRE General Test, TOEFL. *Application deadline:* For fall admission, 6/25; for spring admission, 11/25. Applications are processed on a rolling basis. *Application fee:* $45.

Expenses: Tuition, state resident: full-time $1,748. Tuition, nonresident: full-time $6,904.

Financial support: In 2001–02, 4 fellowships (averaging $6,578 per year), 21 research assistantships (averaging $4,976 per year), 17 teaching assistantships (averaging $5,804 per year) were awarded. Career-related internships or fieldwork and institutionally sponsored loans also available. Financial award application deadline: 3/1.

Faculty research: Computer-integrated manufacturing production, scheduling, industrial ergonomics, simulation and modeling. *Total annual research expenditures:* $4.4 million.

Dr. James R. Wilson, Head, 919-515-2362, *Fax:* 919-515-5281, *E-mail:* jwilson@ eos.ncsu.edu.

Application contact: Dr. Shu Cherng Fang, Director of Graduate Programs, 919-515-2192, *Fax:* 919-515-1908, *E-mail:* fang@ros.ncsu.edu. *Web site:* http:// www.ie.ncsu.edu/

■ NORTH CAROLINA STATE UNIVERSITY

Graduate School, College of Management, Program in Management, Raleigh, NC 27695

AWARDS Biotechnology (MS); computer science (MS); engineering (MS); forest resources management (MS); general business (MS); management information systems (MS); operations research (MS). Statistics

(MS); telecommunications systems engineering (MS); textile management (MS); total quality management (MS). Part-time programs available.

Faculty: 14 full-time (6 women), 3 part-time/adjunct (0 women).

Students: 60 full-time (18 women), 138 part-time (47 women); includes 27 minority (12 African Americans, 13 Asian Americans or Pacific Islanders, 2 Hispanic Americans), 17 international. Average age 32. 225 applicants, 44% accepted. In 2001, 67 degrees awarded.

Entrance requirements: For master's, GMAT or GRE, TOEFL, minimum undergraduate GPA of 3.0. *Application deadline:* For fall admission, 6/25; for spring admission, 11/25. Applications are processed on a rolling basis. *Application fee:* $45.

Expenses: Tuition, state resident: full-time $1,748. Tuition, nonresident: full-time $6,904.

Financial support: In 2001–02, fellowships (averaging $3,551 per year), 32 teaching assistantships (averaging $3,027 per year) were awarded. Research assistantships Financial award application deadline: 3/1.

Faculty research: Manufacturing strategy, information systems, technology commercialization, managing research and development, historical stock returns. *Total annual research expenditures:* $69,089.

Dr. Stephen G. Allen, Head, 919-515-5584, *Fax:* 919-515-5073, *E-mail:* steve_ allen@ncsu.edu. *Web site:* http:// www.mgt.ncsu.edu/facdep/bizmgmt/ bizman.html

■ NORTH DAKOTA STATE UNIVERSITY

The Graduate School, College of Engineering and Architecture, Department of Industrial and Manufacturing Engineering, Fargo, ND 58105

AWARDS Industrial engineering and management (MS). Part-time programs available.

Faculty: 8 full-time (1 woman).

Students: 10 full-time (1 woman), 1 part-time; includes 8 minority (all Asian Americans or Pacific Islanders). Average age 26. 18 applicants, 100% accepted, 4 enrolled. In 2001, 1 degree awarded.

Degree requirements: For master's, thesis. *Median time to degree:* Master's–3 years full-time.

Entrance requirements: For master's, GRE General Test, TOEFL. *Application deadline:* For fall admission, 6/1; for spring admission, 10/1. Applications are processed on a rolling basis. *Application fee:* $35.

Expenses: Tuition, state resident: part-time $124 per credit. Tuition, nonresident: part-time $325 per credit. Required fees: $22 per credit. Tuition and fees vary according to reciprocity agreements.

North Dakota State University (continued)
Financial support: In 2001–02, 10 students received support, including 10 research assistantships with tuition reimbursements available; teaching assistantships with tuition reimbursements available, Federal Work-Study, institutionally sponsored loans, scholarships/grants, and unspecified assistantships also available. Financial award application deadline: 4/15.
Faculty research: Automation, engineering economy, artificial intelligence, human factors engineering, production and inventory control.
Dr. David L. Wells, Chair, 701-231-7283, *Fax:* 701-231-7195, *E-mail:* david_l_wells@ndsu.nodak.edu.

■ NORTHEASTERN UNIVERSITY

College of Engineering, Department of Mechanical, Industrial, and Manufacturing Engineering, Boston, MA 02115-5096
AWARDS Engineering management (MS); industrial engineering (MS, PhD); mechanical engineering (MS, PhD); operations research (MS). Part-time programs available.

Faculty: 26 full-time (1 woman), 5 part-time/adjunct (1 woman).
Students: 97 full-time (22 women), 80 part-time (10 women); includes 32 minority (6 African Americans, 7 Asian Americans or Pacific Islanders, 19 Hispanic Americans), 77 international. Average age 25. 262 applicants, 53% accepted, 57 enrolled. In 2001, 46 master's, 6 doctorates awarded.
Degree requirements: For master's, thesis (for some programs), registration; for doctorate, one foreign language, thesis/dissertation, departmental qualifying exam.
Entrance requirements: For master's and doctorate, GRE General Test. *Application deadline:* For fall admission, 2/15 (priority date). Applications are processed on a rolling basis. *Application fee:* $50. Electronic applications accepted.
Expenses: Tuition: Part-time $535 per credit hour. Required fees: $56. Tuition and fees vary according to program.
Financial support: In 2001–02, 61 students received support, including 1 fellowship, 24 research assistantships with full tuition reimbursements available (averaging $13,560 per year), 26 teaching assistantships with full tuition reimbursements available (averaging $13,560 per year); career-related internships or fieldwork, Federal Work-Study, scholarships/grants, tuition waivers (full), and unspecified assistantships also available. Support available to part-time students. Financial award application deadline: 2/15; financial award applicants required to submit FAFSA.
Faculty research: Dry sliding instabilities, droplet deposition, helical hydraulic turbines, combustion, manufacturing

systems. *Total annual research expenditures:* $1.8 million.
Dr. John W. Cipolla, Chairman, 617-373-3810, *Fax:* 617-373-2921.
Application contact: Stephen L. Gibson, Associate Director, 617-373-2711, *Fax:* 617-373-2501, *E-mail:* grad-eng@coe.neu.edu.

Find an in-depth description at www.petersons.com/gradchannel.

■ NORTHERN ILLINOIS UNIVERSITY

Graduate School, College of Engineering and Engineering Technology, Department of Industrial Engineering, De Kalb, IL 60115-2854
AWARDS MS. Part-time programs available.

Faculty: 3 full-time (0 women), 1 part-time/adjunct (0 women).
Students: 11 full-time (0 women), 10 part-time (1 woman), 14 international. Average age 25. 93 applicants, 33% accepted, 3 enrolled. In 2001, 4 degrees awarded.
Degree requirements: For master's, thesis optional.
Entrance requirements: For master's, GRE General Test, TOEFL, minimum GPA of 2.75. *Application deadline:* For fall admission, 6/1; for spring admission, 11/1. Applications are processed on a rolling basis. *Application fee:* $30.
Expenses: Tuition, state resident: full-time $5,124; part-time $148 per credit hour. Tuition, nonresident: full-time $8,666; part-time $295 per credit hour. Required fees: $51 per term.
Financial support: In 2001–02, 9 teaching assistantships were awarded; fellowships, research assistantships, Federal Work-Study, tuition waivers (full), and unspecified assistantships also available. Support available to part-time students.

■ NORTHWESTERN UNIVERSITY

McCormick School of Engineering and Applied Science, Department of Industrial Engineering and Management Sciences, Evanston, IL 60208
AWARDS Engineering management (MEM); industrial engineering and management science (MS, PhD); operations research (MS, PhD). MS and PhD admissions and degrees offered through The Graduate School.

Faculty: 17 full-time (2 women), 7 part-time/adjunct (0 women).
Students: 40 full-time (12 women); includes 1 minority (Asian American or Pacific Islander), 33 international. Average age 23. 230 applicants, 17% accepted, 12 enrolled. In 2001, 9 master's, 8 doctorates awarded. Terminal master's awarded for partial completion of doctoral program.
Degree requirements: For master's, comprehensive exam; for doctorate, thesis/dissertation, comprehensive exam. *Median*

time to degree: Master's–1 year full-time; doctorate–4.5 years full-time.
Application deadline: For fall admission, 8/30; for winter admission, 11/27; for spring admission, 2/19. Applications are processed on a rolling basis. *Application fee:* $50 ($55 for international students). Electronic applications accepted.
Expenses: Tuition: Full-time $26,526.
Financial support: In 2001–02, 29 students received support, including 7 fellowships with full tuition reimbursements available (averaging $16,000 per year), 14 research assistantships with full tuition reimbursements available (averaging $19,962 per year), 8 teaching assistantships with full tuition reimbursements available (averaging $16,000 per year); career-related internships or fieldwork, Federal Work-Study, institutionally sponsored loans, scholarships/grants, and tuition waivers (full) also available. Financial award application deadline: 1/15; financial award applicants required to submit FAFSA.
Faculty research: Production, logistics, optimization, simulation, statistics. *Total annual research expenditures:* $900,000.
Ajit Tamhane, Chair, 847-491-3577, *Fax:* 847-491-8005, *E-mail:* tamhane@iems.northwestern.edu.
Application contact: Lesley Perry, Graduate Program Coordinator, 847-491-4394, *Fax:* 847-491-8005, *E-mail:* lperry@iems.northwestern.edu. *Web site:* http://www.iems.northwestern.edu/

Find an in-depth description at www.petersons.com/gradchannel.

■ THE OHIO STATE UNIVERSITY

Graduate School, College of Engineering, Program in Industrial and Systems Engineering, Columbus, OH 43210
AWARDS MS, PhD.

Degree requirements: For master's, thesis optional; for doctorate, thesis/dissertation.
Entrance requirements: For master's and doctorate, GRE General Test.

■ OHIO UNIVERSITY

Graduate Studies, Russ College of Engineering and Technology, Department of Industrial and Manufacturing Systems Engineering, Athens, OH 45701-2979
AWARDS MS.

Faculty: 8 full-time (0 women), 2 part-time/adjunct (1 woman).
Students: 30 full-time (6 women), 12 part-time (1 woman); includes 2 minority (1 African American, 1 Asian American or Pacific Islander), 34 international. Average age 24. 99 applicants, 78% accepted, 17 enrolled. In 2001, 20 degrees awarded.
Degree requirements: For master's, research project, thesis optional.

Entrance requirements: For master's, GRE General Test. *Application deadline:* For fall admission, 3/1 (priority date). Applications are processed on a rolling basis. *Application fee:* $30.
Expenses: Tuition, state resident: full-time $6,585. Tuition, nonresident: full-time $12,254.
Financial support: In 2001–02, 1 fellowship with full tuition reimbursement, 12 research assistantships with full tuition reimbursements, 7 teaching assistantships with full tuition reimbursements were awarded. Federal Work-Study, institutionally sponsored loans, and tuition waivers (full) also available. Financial award application deadline: 3/1.
Faculty research: MIS, distribution systems, or MFG systems. *Total annual research expenditures:* $350,000.
Dr. Charles M. Parks, Chairman, 740-593-1540, *Fax:* 740-593-0778, *E-mail:* cparks@bobcat.ent.ohiou.edu.
Application contact: Dr. David Koonce, Graduate Chairman, 740-593-1550, *Fax:* 740-593-0778, *E-mail:* imsegrad@ohio.edu. *Web site:* http://webise.ent.ohiou.edu/

■ OKLAHOMA STATE UNIVERSITY

Graduate College, College of Engineering, Architecture and Technology, School of Industrial Engineering and Management, Stillwater, OK 74078

AWARDS M En, MIE Mgmt, MS, PhD.
Faculty: 13 full-time (2 women), 1 part-time/adjunct (0 women).
Students: 90 full-time (9 women), 156 part-time (22 women); includes 16 minority (3 African Americans, 5 Asian Americans or Pacific Islanders, 4 Hispanic Americans, 4 Native Americans), 100 international. Average age 31. 348 applicants, 86% accepted. In 2001, 45 master's, 1 doctorate awarded.
Degree requirements: For master's, creative component or thesis; for doctorate, thesis/dissertation.
Entrance requirements: For master's and doctorate, TOEFL. *Application deadline:* For fall admission, 7/1 (priority date). *Application fee:* $25.
Expenses: Tuition, state resident: part-time $92 per credit hour. Tuition, nonresident: part-time $297 per credit hour. Required fees: $21 per credit hour. $14 per semester. One-time fee: $20. Tuition and fees vary according to course load.
Financial support: In 2001–02, 36 students received support, including 25 research assistantships (averaging $7,468 per year), 20 teaching assistantships (averaging $5,983 per year); career-related internships or fieldwork, Federal Work-Study, and tuition waivers (partial) also available. Support available to part-time students. Financial award application deadline: 3/1.

Dr. William J. Kolarik, Head, 405-744-6055.

■ OREGON STATE UNIVERSITY

Graduate School, College of Engineering, Department of Industrial and Manufacturing Engineering, Corvallis, OR 97331

AWARDS Industrial engineering (MAIS, MS, PhD); manufacturing engineering (M Eng). Part-time programs available.
Postbaccalaureate distance learning degree programs offered (minimal on-campus study).
Faculty: 8 full-time (2 women).
Students: 40 full-time (11 women), 10 part-time (1 woman); includes 2 minority (both Asian Americans or Pacific Islanders), 44 international. Average age 28. In 2001, 5 master's, 2 doctorates awarded.
Degree requirements: For master's, thesis or alternative; for doctorate, thesis/dissertation.
Entrance requirements: For master's, TOEFL, placement exam, minimum GPA of 3.0 in last 90 hours; for doctorate, GRE, TOEFL, placement exam, minimum GPA of 3.0 in last 90 hours. *Application deadline:* Applications are processed on a rolling basis. *Application fee:* $50.
Expenses: Tuition, area resident: Full-time $15,933. Tuition, state resident: full-time $28,937.
Financial support: Fellowships, research assistantships, teaching assistantships, institutionally sponsored loans and instructorships available. Support available to part-time students. Financial award application deadline: 2/1.
Faculty research: Computer-integrated manufacturing, human factors, robotics, decision support systems, simulation modeling and analysis.
Richard E. Billo, Head, 541-737-2365, *Fax:* 541-737-5241, *E-mail:* richard.billo@orst.edu.
Application contact: Dr. Suat Tanaydin, Graduate Committee Chair, 541-737-2875, *Fax:* 541-737-5241, *E-mail:* tanaydin@engr.orst.edu. *Web site:* http://www.ie.orst.edu/

■ THE PENNSYLVANIA STATE UNIVERSITY UNIVERSITY PARK CAMPUS

Graduate School, College of Engineering, Department of Industrial and Manufacturing Engineering, Program in Industrial Engineering, State College, University Park, PA 16802-1503

AWARDS M Eng, MS, PhD.
Students: 104 full-time (13 women), 14 part-time (2 women). In 2001, 18 master's, 9 doctorates awarded.
Degree requirements: For master's, thesis; for doctorate, one foreign language, thesis/dissertation.

Entrance requirements: For master's and doctorate, GRE General Test. *Application fee:* $45.
Expenses: Tuition, state resident: full-time $7,882; part-time $333 per credit. Tuition, nonresident: full-time $16,142; part-time $673 per credit. Required fees: $124 per semester.
Dr. Jose Ventura, Graduate Advisor, 814-865-3841.

■ POLYTECHNIC UNIVERSITY, BROOKLYN CAMPUS

Department of Mechanical, Aerospace and Manufacturing Engineering, Major in Industrial Engineering, Brooklyn, NY 11201-2990

AWARDS MS.

Entrance requirements: For master's, BE or BS in engineering, physics, chemistry, mathematical sciences, or biological sciences or MBA. Electronic applications accepted.

■ POLYTECHNIC UNIVERSITY, LONG ISLAND GRADUATE CENTER

Graduate Programs, Department of Mechanical, Aerospace and Manufacturing Engineering, Major in Industrial Engineering, Melville, NY 11747

AWARDS MS.

Electronic applications accepted.

■ POLYTECHNIC UNIVERSITY, WESTCHESTER GRADUATE CENTER

Graduate Programs, Department of Mechanical, Aerospace and Manufacturing Engineering, Major in Industrial Engineering, Hawthorne, NY 10532-1507

AWARDS MS.

Electronic applications accepted.

■ PURDUE UNIVERSITY

Graduate School, Schools of Engineering, School of Industrial Engineering, West Lafayette, IN 47907

AWARDS Human factors in industrial engineering (MS, MSIE, PhD); manufacturing engineering (MS, MSIE, PhD); operations research (MS, MSIE, PhD). Systems engineering (MS, MSIE, PhD). Part-time programs available.

Faculty: 23 full-time (2 women), 4 part-time/adjunct (0 women).
Students: 117 full-time (24 women), 19 part-time (6 women); includes 6 minority (4 African Americans, 2 Hispanic Americans), 108 international. Average age 28. 370 applicants, 44% accepted. In 2001,

Purdue University (continued)
51 master's, 11 doctorates awarded.
Terminal master's awarded for partial
completion of doctoral program.
Degree requirements: For master's,
thesis optional; for doctorate, thesis/
dissertation.
Entrance requirements: For master's,
GRE General Test, TOEFL, minimum
GPA of 3.0; for doctorate, GRE General
Test, TOEFL, MS thesis. *Application
deadline:* For fall admission, 3/15; for
spring admission, 9/1. *Application fee:* $30.
Electronic applications accepted.
Expenses: Tuition, state resident: full-time
$4,164; part-time $149 per credit hour.
Tuition, nonresident: full-time $13,872;
part-time $458 per credit hour. Tuition
and fees vary according to campus/location
and program.
Financial support: In 2001–02, 78
students received support, including 3 fellowships with full tuition reimbursements
available (averaging $13,070 per year), 29
research assistantships with full tuition
reimbursements available (averaging
$12,720 per year), 46 teaching assistant-
ships with full tuition reimbursements
available (averaging $10,600 per year) Sup-
port available to part-time students.
Financial award application deadline: 3/15;
financial award applicants required to
submit FAFSA.
Faculty research: Precision manufacturing
process, computer-aided manufacturing,
computer-aided process planning,
knowledge-based systems, combinatorics.
Total annual research expenditures: $1.8 mil-
lion.
Dr. Dennis Engi, Head, 765-494-5444,
Fax: 765-494-1299, *E-mail:* engi@
ecn.purdue.edu.
Application contact: Dr. J. W. Barany,
Associate Head, 765-494-5406, *Fax:* 765-
494-1299, *E-mail:* jwb@ecn.purdue.edu.
Web site: http://ie.www.ecn.purdue.edu/

■ RENSSELAER POLYTECHNIC INSTITUTE

**Graduate School, School of
Engineering, Department of Decision
Sciences and Engineering Systems,
Program in Industrial and
Management Engineering, Troy, NY
12180-3590**

AWARDS M Eng, MS, MBA/M Eng. Part-time
and evening/weekend programs available.
Postbaccalaureate distance learning degree
programs offered (no on-campus study).

Faculty: 16 full-time (1 woman), 3 part-
time/adjunct (2 women).
Students: 31 full-time (10 women), 13
part-time (2 women); includes 7 minority
(3 African Americans, 2 Asian Americans
or Pacific Islanders, 2 Hispanic
Americans), 29 international. 87 applicants,
52% accepted, 23 enrolled. In 2001, 19
degrees awarded.

Degree requirements: For master's,
thesis (for some programs).
Entrance requirements: For master's,
GRE General Test, TOEFL. *Application
deadline:* For fall admission, 1/15 (priority
date). Applications are processed on a rolling basis. *Application fee:* $35. Electronic
applications accepted.
Expenses: Tuition: Full-time $26,400;
part-time $1,320 per credit hour. Required
fees: $1,437.
Financial support: In 2001–02, 3 fellowships (averaging $11,956 per year), 4
research assistantships with full tuition
reimbursements (averaging $12,620 per
year), 8 teaching assistantships with full
tuition reimbursements (averaging $12,620
per year) were awarded. Career-related
internships or fieldwork and institutionally
sponsored loans also available. Financial
award application deadline: 1/15.
Faculty research: Manufacturing, MIS,
statistical consulting, education/services,
production/logistics/inventory. *Total annual
research expenditures:* $1 million.
Application contact: Lee Vilardi, Graduate Coordinator, 518-276-6681, *Fax:* 518-
276-8227, *E-mail:* dsesgr@rpi.edu. *Web site:*
http://www.rpi.edu/

**Find an in-depth description at
www.petersons.com/gradchannel.**

■ ROCHESTER INSTITUTE OF TECHNOLOGY

**Graduate Enrollment Services, College
of Engineering, Department of
Industrial and Manufacturing
Engineering, Rochester, NY 14623-
5698**

AWARDS Engineering management (ME);
industrial engineering (ME); manufacturing
engineering (ME). Systems engineering (ME).

Students: 6 full-time (0 women), 19 part-
time (6 women); includes 4 minority (2
African Americans, 2 Hispanic Americans),
10 international. 105 applicants, 51%
accepted, 8 enrolled. In 2001, 14 degrees
awarded.
Degree requirements: For master's,
internship.
Entrance requirements: For master's,
TOEFL, minimum GPA of 3.0. *Application
deadline:* For fall admission, 3/1 (priority
date). Applications are processed on a rolling basis. *Application fee:* $50.
Expenses: Tuition: Full-time $20,928;
part-time $587 per hour. Required fees:
$162. Tuition and fees vary according to
program.
Financial support: Research assistantships,
career-related internships or fieldwork and
tuition waivers (partial) available.
Faculty research: Safety, manufacturing
(CAM), simulation.
Dr. Jacqueline Mozrall, Head, 585-475-
7142, *E-mail:* jrmeie@rit.edu.

■ RUTGERS, THE STATE UNIVERSITY OF NEW JERSEY, NEW BRUNSWICK

**Graduate School, Program in
Industrial and Systems Engineering,
New Brunswick, NJ 08901-1281**

AWARDS Industrial and systems engineering
(MS, PhD); manufacturing systems (MS);
quality and reliability engineering (MS). Part-
time and evening/weekend programs available. Terminal master's awarded for partial
completion of doctoral program.

Degree requirements: For master's,
thesis or alternative; for doctorate, thesis/
dissertation.
Entrance requirements: For master's and
doctorate, GRE General Test, TOEFL.
Faculty research: Production and
manufacturing systems, quality and reliability engineering, systems engineering
and aviation safety. *Web site:* http://
coewww.rutgers.edu/~ie/

■ ST. MARY'S UNIVERSITY OF SAN ANTONIO

**Graduate School, Department of
Engineering, Program in Industrial
Engineering, San Antonio, TX 78228-
8507**

AWARDS Engineering computer applications
(MS); engineering management (MS);
industrial engineering (MS); operations
research (MS).

Faculty: 6 full-time, 3 part-time/adjunct.
Students: 4 full-time (1 woman), 6 part-
time (2 women); includes 1 minority
(Hispanic American), 3 international. Aver-
age age 25. In 2001, 5 degrees awarded.
Degree requirements: For master's,
thesis.
Entrance requirements: For master's,
GRE General Test, BS in science or
engineering. *Application deadline:* Applications are processed on a rolling basis.
Application fee: $15. Electronic applications
accepted.
Expenses: Tuition: Full-time $8,190; part-
time $455 per credit hour. Required fees:
$375.
Financial support: Teaching assistantships, Federal Work-Study available.
Financial award application deadline: 2/15;
financial award applicants required to
submit FAFSA.
Faculty research: Robotics, artificial intelligence, manufacturing engineering.
Dr. Rafael Moras, Chairperson, 210-436-
3305, *E-mail:* moras@stmarytx.edu.

■ SOUTH DAKOTA STATE UNIVERSITY

**Graduate School, College of
Engineering, Industrial Management
Program, Brookings, SD 57007**
AWARDS MS.

Degree requirements: For master's, thesis, oral exam.

Entrance requirements: For master's, TOEFL.

Faculty research: Query, language development, statistical process control, foreign business plans.

■ SOUTHERN POLYTECHNIC STATE UNIVERSITY

School of Engineering Technology and Management, Program in Industrial Engineering Technology, Marietta, GA 30060-2896

AWARDS Quality assurance (MS). Part-time and evening/weekend programs available. Postbaccalaureate distance learning degree programs offered (minimal on-campus study).

Faculty: 7 part-time/adjunct (1 woman).

Students: 4 full-time (3 women), 81 part-time (20 women); includes 29 minority (21 African Americans, 4 Asian Americans or Pacific Islanders, 4 Hispanic Americans), 4 international. Average age 39. In 2001, 18 degrees awarded.

Degree requirements: For master's, thesis.

Entrance requirements: For master's, GRE, 2 years full-time experience in field, letters of recommendation (3), minimum GPA of 2.7. *Application deadline:* For fall admission, 7/15 (priority date); for spring admission, 12/1. Applications are processed on a rolling basis. *Application fee:* $20. Electronic applications accepted.

Expenses: Tuition, state resident: full-time $1,746; part-time $97 per credit. Tuition, nonresident: full-time $6,966; part-time $387 per credit. Required fees: $221 per term.

Financial support: Teaching assistantships, career-related internships or fieldwork, Federal Work-Study, scholarships/grants, and unspecified assistantships available. Support available to part-time students. Financial award application deadline: 5/1; financial award applicants required to submit FAFSA.

Dr. Patricia Carden, Head, 770-528-7243, *Fax:* 770-528-4991, *E-mail:* pcarden@spsu.edu.

Application contact: Virginia A. Head, Director of Admissions, 770-528-7281, *Fax:* 770-528-7292, *E-mail:* vhead@spsu.edu. *Web site:* http://www.iet.spsu.edu/

■ SOUTHWEST TEXAS STATE UNIVERSITY

Graduate School, College of Science, Department of Technology, Program in Industrial Technology, San Marcos, TX 78666

AWARDS MST. Part-time and evening/weekend programs available.

Faculty: 3 full-time (0 women).

Students: 5 full-time (1 woman), 12 part-time (3 women); includes 5 minority (1

African American, 1 Asian American or Pacific Islander, 3 Hispanic Americans), 3 international. Average age 35. 9 applicants, 78% accepted, 4 enrolled. In 2001, 5 degrees awarded.

Degree requirements: For master's, thesis optional.

Entrance requirements: For master's, GRE General Test, TOEFL, minimum GPA of 2.75 in last 60 hours. *Application deadline:* For fall admission, 6/15 (priority date); for spring admission, 10/15 (priority date). Applications are processed on a rolling basis. *Application fee:* $40 ($90 for international students).

Expenses: Tuition, state resident: full-time $1,512; part-time $84 per credit hour. Tuition, nonresident: full-time $5,310; part-time $295 per credit hour. Required fees: $864; $29 per credit hour. $195 per term. Full-time tuition and fees vary according to course load.

Financial support: Research assistantships, teaching assistantships, career-related internships or fieldwork, Federal Work-Study, and institutionally sponsored loans available. Support available to part-time students. Financial award application deadline: 4/1; financial award applicants required to submit FAFSA.

Dr. Andy Batey, Graduate Adviser, 512-245-2137, *Fax:* 512-245-3052, *E-mail:* ab08@swt.edu. *Web site:* http://www.swt.edu/

■ STANFORD UNIVERSITY

School of Engineering, Department of Management Science and Engineering, Stanford, CA 94305-9991

AWARDS Management science and engineering (MS, PhD); management science and engineering and electrical engineering (MS); manufacturing systems engineering (MS).

Faculty: 31 full-time (5 women).

Students: 301 full-time (77 women), 82 part-time (18 women); includes 59 minority (5 African Americans, 48 Asian Americans or Pacific Islanders, 6 Hispanic Americans), 226 international. Average age 27. 484 applicants, 38% accepted. In 2001, 187 master's, 28 doctorates awarded. Terminal master's awarded for partial completion of doctoral program.

Degree requirements: For doctorate, thesis/dissertation, qualification procedure.

Entrance requirements: For master's and doctorate, GRE General Test, TOEFL. *Application deadline:* For fall admission, 2/1. *Application fee:* $65 ($80 for international students). Electronic applications accepted.

M. Elisabeth Paté-Cornell, Chair, 650-723-3823 Ext. ', *Fax:* 650-725-8799, *E-mail:* mep@stanford.edu.

Application contact: Graduate Admissions Coordinator, 650-723-4094, *Fax:* 650-723-1614. *Web site:* http://www.stanford.edu/dept/MSandE/

Find an in-depth description at www.petersons.com/gradchannel.

■ STATE UNIVERSITY OF NEW YORK AT BINGHAMTON

Graduate School, Thomas J. Watson School of Engineering and Applied Science, Department of Systems Science and Industrial Engineering, Binghamton, NY 13902-6000

AWARDS M Eng, MS, MSAT, PhD. Part-time and evening/weekend programs available.

Faculty: 10 full-time (3 women), 4 part-time/adjunct (0 women).

Students: 80 full-time (8 women), 41 part-time (7 women); includes 5 minority (1 African American, 4 Asian Americans or Pacific Islanders), 80 international. Average age 29. 200 applicants, 54% accepted, 21 enrolled. In 2001, 24 master's, 2 doctorates awarded. Terminal master's awarded for partial completion of doctoral program.

Degree requirements: For master's, thesis or alternative; for doctorate, thesis/dissertation.

Entrance requirements: For master's and doctorate, GRE General Test, GRE Subject Test, TOEFL. *Application deadline:* For fall admission, 4/15 (priority date); for spring admission, 11/1. Applications are processed on a rolling basis. Electronic applications accepted.

Expenses: Tuition, state resident: full-time $5,100; part-time $213 per credit. Tuition, nonresident: full-time $8,416; part-time $351 per credit. Required fees: $811.

Financial support: In 2001–02, 58 students received support, including 1 fellowship with full tuition reimbursement available (averaging $7,500 per year), 42 research assistantships with full tuition reimbursements available (averaging $5,621 per year), 15 teaching assistantships with full tuition reimbursements available (averaging $6,457 per year); career-related internships or fieldwork, Federal Work-Study, institutionally sponsored loans, tuition waivers (full and partial), and unspecified assistantships also available. Support available to part-time students. Financial award application deadline: 2/15.

Faculty research: Problem restructuring, protein modeling.

Dr. Robert Emerson, Chair, 607-777-6509.

■ STATE UNIVERSITY OF NEW YORK COLLEGE AT BUFFALO

Graduate Studies and Research, Faculty of Applied Science and Education, Department of Technology, Program in Industrial Technology, Buffalo, NY 14222-1095

AWARDS MS.

Students: 1 full-time (0 women), 29 part-time; includes 4 minority (3 African Americans, 1 Asian American or Pacific Islander). Average age 36. 12 applicants, 83% accepted. In 2001, 6 degrees awarded.

Degree requirements: For master's, thesis or project.

State University of New York College at Buffalo (continued)

Entrance requirements: For master's, minimum GPA of 2.5 in last 60 hours, New York teaching certificate. *Application deadline:* For fall admission, 5/1 (priority date); for spring admission, 10/1 (priority date). *Application fee:* $50.

Expenses: Tuition, state resident: full-time $5,100; part-time $226 per credit hour. Tuition, nonresident: full-time $8,416; part-time $351 per credit hour.

Financial support: Fellowships available. Financial award application deadline: 3/1. Dr. John Earshen, Coordinator, 716-878-4305, *Fax:* 716-878-3033, *E-mail:* earshejj@buffalostate.edu.

■ STONY BROOK UNIVERSITY, STATE UNIVERSITY OF NEW YORK

Graduate School, College of Engineering and Applied Sciences, Department of Technology and Society, Program in Industrial Management, Stony Brook, NY 11794

AWARDS MS.

Expenses: Tuition, state resident: full-time $5,100; part-time $213 per credit. Tuition, nonresident: full-time $8,416; part-time $351 per credit. Required fees: $496.

Find an in-depth description at www.petersons.com/gradchannel.

■ TENNESSEE TECHNOLOGICAL UNIVERSITY

Graduate School, College of Engineering, Department of Industrial Engineering, Cookeville, TN 38505

AWARDS MS, PhD. Part-time programs available.

Faculty: 7 full-time (0 women).

Students: 3 full-time (0 women), 4 part-time (1 woman); includes 6 minority (all Asian Americans or Pacific Islanders). Average age 26. 129 applicants, 46% accepted. In 2001, 6 degrees awarded.

Degree requirements: For master's, thesis; for doctorate, one foreign language, thesis/dissertation.

Entrance requirements: For master's, GRE General Test, TOEFL; for doctorate, GRE Subject Test, TOEFL, minimum GPA of 3.5. *Application deadline:* For fall admission, 3/1 (priority date); for spring admission, 8/1. *Application fee:* $25 ($30 for international students). Electronic applications accepted.

Expenses: Tuition, state resident: full-time $4,000; part-time $215 per hour. Tuition, nonresident: full-time $10,500; part-time $495 per hour. Required fees: $1,971 per semester.

Financial support: In 2001–02, 2 research assistantships (averaging $5,400 per year) were awarded; fellowships, teaching assistantships, career-related internships or fieldwork also available. Financial award application deadline: 4/1.

Faculty research: Economic analysis, manufacturing systems, quality control. Dr. Jessica Matson, Chairperson, 931-372-3466, *Fax:* 931-372-6352.

Application contact: Dr. Francis O. Otuonye, Associate Vice President for Research and Graduate Studies, 931-372-3233, *Fax:* 931-372-3497, *E-mail:* fotuonye@tntech.edu.

■ TEXAS A&M UNIVERSITY

College of Engineering, Department of Industrial Engineering, College Station, TX 77843

AWARDS M Eng, MS, D Eng, PhD. Part-time programs available. Postbaccalaureate distance learning degree programs offered (no on-campus study).

Faculty: 20 full-time (2 women), 1 part-time/adjunct (0 women).

Students: 171 full-time (22 women), 38 part-time (4 women); includes 4 minority (2 African Americans, 1 Asian American or Pacific Islander, 1 Hispanic American), 194 international. Average age 28. 471 applicants, 44% accepted, 70 enrolled. In 2001, 55 master's, 7 doctorates awarded.

Degree requirements: For master's, thesis optional; for doctorate, thesis/dissertation, dissertation (PhD), comprehensive exam.

Entrance requirements: For master's and doctorate, GRE General Test, TOEFL. *Application deadline:* For fall admission, 3/1 (priority date); for spring admission, 7/1 (priority date). Applications are processed on a rolling basis. *Application fee:* $50 ($75 for international students). Electronic applications accepted.

Expenses: Tuition, state resident: full-time $11,872. Tuition, nonresident: full-time $17,892.

Financial support: In 2001–02, fellowships with partial tuition reimbursements (averaging $12,000 per year), 24 research assistantships with partial tuition reimbursements (averaging $12,000 per year), 17 teaching assistantships with partial tuition reimbursements (averaging $12,000 per year) were awarded. Career-related internships or fieldwork, scholarships/grants, health care benefits, and unspecified assistantships also available. Financial award application deadline: 2/1.

Faculty research: Manufacturing systems, computer integration, operations research, logistics, simulation. *Total annual research expenditures:* $1.4 million. Dr. Bryan L. Deuermeyer, Interim Head, 979-845-5535, *Fax:* 979-847-9005, *E-mail:* b-deuermeyer@tamu.edu.

Application contact: Dr. Richard M. Feldman, Graduate Advisor, 979-845-5536, *Fax:* 979-458-4299, *E-mail:* richf@tamu.edu.

■ TEXAS A&M UNIVERSITY–COMMERCE

Graduate School, College of Business and Technology, Department of Industrial and Engineering Technology, Commerce, TX 75429-3011

AWARDS Industry and technology (MS). Part-time programs available.

Faculty: 3 full-time (0 women), 1 part-time/adjunct (0 women).

Students: 14 full-time (1 woman), 19 part-time (1 woman); includes 7 minority (5 African Americans, 1 Asian American or Pacific Islander, 1 Hispanic American), 12 international. Average age 36. 8 applicants, 88% accepted. In 2001, 17 degrees awarded.

Degree requirements: For master's, thesis (for some programs), comprehensive exam.

Entrance requirements: For master's, GMAT, GRE General Test. *Application deadline:* For fall admission, 6/1 (priority date); for spring admission, 11/1 (priority date). Applications are processed on a rolling basis. *Application fee:* $0 ($25 for international students). Electronic applications accepted.

Expenses: Tuition, state resident: full-time $2,221. International tuition: $7,285 full-time.

Financial support: In 2001–02, research assistantships (averaging $7,875 per year), teaching assistantships (averaging $7,875 per year) were awarded. Federal Work-Study, institutionally sponsored loans, and scholarships/grants also available. Financial award application deadline: 5/1; financial award applicants required to submit FAFSA.

Faculty research: Environmental science, engineering microelectronics, natural sciences. *Total annual research expenditures:* $128,781. Dr. Jerry D. Parish, Graduate Admissions Adviser, 903-886-5167, *Fax:* 903-886-5165, *E-mail:* jerry_parish@tamu-commerce.edu.

Application contact: Tammi Higginbotham, Graduate Admissions Adviser, 843-886-5167, *Fax:* 843-886-5165, *E-mail:* tammi_higginbotham@tamu-commerce.edu. *Web site:* http://www.tamu-commerce.edu/cobt/iet/index.html

■ TEXAS A&M UNIVERSITY–KINGSVILLE

College of Graduate Studies, College of Engineering, Department of Mechanical and Industrial Engineering, Program in Industrial Engineering, Kingsville, TX 78363

AWARDS ME, MS.

Students: 19 full-time (2 women), 14 part-time (1 woman); includes 5 minority (2 Asian Americans or Pacific Islanders, 3

Hispanic Americans), 26 international. Average age 26. In 2001, 10 degrees awarded.
Degree requirements: For master's, thesis or alternative, comprehensive exam.
Entrance requirements: For master's, GRE General Test, TOEFL, minimum GPA of 3.0. *Application deadline:* For fall admission, 6/1; for spring admission, 11/15. Applications are processed on a rolling basis. *Application fee:* $15 ($25 for international students).
Expenses: Tuition, state resident: part-time $42 per hour. Tuition, nonresident: part-time $253 per hour. Required fees: $56 per hour. One-time fee: $46 part-time. Tuition and fees vary according to program.
Financial support: Fellowships available. Financial award application deadline: 5/15.
Faculty research: Robotics and automation, neural networks and fuzzy logic, systems engineering/simulation modeling, integrated manufacturing and production systems.
Application contact: Dr. Hayder Abdul Razzak, Coordinator, 361-593-2001.

■ TEXAS TECH UNIVERSITY

Graduate School, College of Engineering, Department of Industrial Engineering, Lubbock, TX 79409

AWARDS Industrial engineering (MSIE, PhD). Systems and engineering management (MSSEM). Part-time programs available.

Faculty: 6 full-time (0 women), 1 part-time/adjunct (0 women).
Students: 50 full-time (11 women), 10 part-time (1 woman); includes 5 minority (1 African American, 1 Asian American or Pacific Islander, 3 Hispanic Americans), 42 international. Average age 29. 133 applicants, 47% accepted, 16 enrolled. In 2001, 11 master's, 3 doctorates awarded.
Degree requirements: For master's and doctorate, thesis/dissertation.
Entrance requirements: For master's and doctorate, GRE General Test, minimum GPA of 3.0. *Application deadline:* Applications are processed on a rolling basis. *Application fee:* $25 ($50 for international students). Electronic applications accepted.
Expenses: Tuition, state resident: full-time $1,926; part-time $107 per credit hour. Tuition, nonresident: full-time $5,724; part-time $318 per credit hour. Required fees: $779; $737 per year. Tuition and fees vary according to course level, course load and program.
Financial support: In 2001–02, 25 students received support, including 15 research assistantships with partial tuition reimbursements available (averaging $8,670 per year), 6 teaching assistantships with partial tuition reimbursements available (averaging $7,575 per year); fellowships, Federal Work-Study and institutionally sponsored loans also available. Support available to part-time students. Financial award application

deadline: 5/1; financial award applicants required to submit FAFSA.
Faculty research: Knowledge and engineering management, environmentally conscious manufacturing, biomechanical simulation, aviation security. *Total annual research expenditures:* $223,554.
Dr. Milton Smith, Chair, 806-742-3543, *Fax:* 806-742-3411, *E-mail:* jlsmith@coe.ttu.edu.
Application contact: Graduate Adviser, 806-742-3543, *Fax:* 806-742-3411. *Web site:* http://www.ie.ttu.edu

■ UNIVERSITY AT BUFFALO, THE STATE UNIVERSITY OF NEW YORK

Graduate School, School of Engineering and Applied Sciences, Department of Industrial Engineering, Buffalo, NY 14260

AWARDS M Eng, MS, PhD. Part-time programs available. Postbaccalaureate distance learning degree programs offered (minimal on-campus study).

Faculty: 13 full-time (1 woman), 5 part-time/adjunct (0 women).
Students: 73 full-time (10 women), 41 part-time (10 women); includes 5 minority (1 African American, 1 Asian American or Pacific Islander, 2 Hispanic Americans, 1 Native American), 73 international. Average age 26. 314 applicants, 47% accepted, 38 enrolled. In 2001, 40 master's, 6 doctorates awarded. Terminal master's awarded for partial completion of doctoral program.
Degree requirements: For master's, thesis or alternative, comprehensive exam (for some programs); for doctorate, thesis/dissertation.
Entrance requirements: For master's and doctorate, GRE General Test, TOEFL. *Application deadline:* For fall admission, 2/1 (priority date); for spring admission, 8/1. Applications are processed on a rolling basis. *Application fee:* $35. Electronic applications accepted.
Expenses: Tuition, state resident: full-time $6,118. Tuition, nonresident: full-time $9,434.
Financial support: In 2001–02, 39 students received support, including 5 fellowships with full tuition reimbursements available, 26 research assistantships with full tuition reimbursements available (averaging $11,429 per year), 14 teaching assistantships with full tuition reimbursements available (averaging $11,429 per year); Federal Work-Study, institutionally sponsored loans, tuition waivers (full and partial), and unspecified assistantships also available. Financial award application deadline: 2/1; financial award applicants required to submit FAFSA.
Faculty research: Ergonomics, operations research, production systems. *Total annual research expenditures:* $750,000.

Dr. Rajan Batta, Chairman, 716-645-2357 Ext. 2110, *Fax:* 716-645-3302, *E-mail:* indgrad@ubvms.cc.buffalo.edu.
Application contact: Colin Drury, Director of Graduate Studies, 716-645-2357 Ext. 2117, *Fax:* 716-645-3302, *E-mail:* iegrad@eng.buffalo.edu. *Web site:* http://www.eng.buffalo.edu/departments/ie/index.html

Find an in-depth description at www.petersons.com/gradchannel.

■ THE UNIVERSITY OF ALABAMA

Graduate School, College of Engineering, Department of Industrial Engineering, Tuscaloosa, AL 35487

AWARDS MSE, MSIE. Postbaccalaureate distance learning degree programs offered.

Faculty: 8 full-time (0 women).
Students: 28 full-time (4 women), 10 part-time, 35 international. Average age 25. 84 applicants, 38% accepted, 6 enrolled. In 2001, 7 degrees awarded.
Degree requirements: For master's, thesis or alternative.
Entrance requirements: For master's, GRE General Test, minimum GPA of 3.0 in last 60 hours. *Application deadline:* For fall admission, 7/6. Applications are processed on a rolling basis. *Application fee:* $25. Electronic applications accepted.
Expenses: Tuition, state resident: full-time $3,292; part-time $183 per credit hour. Tuition, nonresident: full-time $8,912; part-time $495 per credit hour. Tuition and fees vary according to course load, campus/location and program.
Financial support: In 2001–02, 19 students received support, including 2 fellowships (averaging $10,000 per year), 4 research assistantships (averaging $8,000 per year), 10 teaching assistantships (averaging $8,000 per year); Federal Work-Study and institutionally sponsored loans also available. Financial award application deadline: 2/15.
Faculty research: Systems engineering and operations research, human factors engineering, manufacturing engineering, quality engineering. *Total annual research expenditures:* $258,052.
Dr. Robert P. Davis, Head, 205-348-7160, *Fax:* 205-348-7160.
Application contact: Teresa A. McGhee, Secretary, 205-348-7160, *Fax:* 205-348-7162, *E-mail:* tmcghee@coe.eng.ua.edu. *Web site:* http://www.ie.eng.ua.edu/

■ THE UNIVERSITY OF ALABAMA IN HUNTSVILLE

School of Graduate Studies, College of Engineering, Department of Industrial and Systems Engineering/Engineering Management, Huntsville, AL 35899

AWARDS Industrial engineering (MSE, PhD); operations research (MSOR). Part-time and evening/weekend programs available.

The University of Alabama in Huntsville (continued)

Postbaccalaureate distance learning degree programs offered (no on-campus study).

Faculty: 10 full-time (2 women), 1 part-time/adjunct (0 women).
Students: 22 full-time (5 women), 143 part-time (36 women); includes 21 minority (14 African Americans, 5 Asian Americans or Pacific Islanders, 1 Hispanic American, 1 Native American), 10 international. Average age 39. 124 applicants, 54% accepted, 27 enrolled. In 2001, 20 master's, 3 doctorates awarded.
Degree requirements: For master's, thesis or alternative, oral and written exams, comprehensive exam, registration; for doctorate, thesis/dissertation, oral and written exams, comprehensive exam, registration.
Entrance requirements: For master's and doctorate, GRE General Test, minimum GPA of 3.0. *Application deadline:* For fall admission, 7/24 (priority date); for spring admission, 11/15 (priority date). Applications are processed on a rolling basis. *Application fee:* $35.
Expenses: Tuition, area resident: Part-time $175 per hour. Tuition, state resident: full-time $4,408. Tuition, nonresident: full-time $9,054; part-time $361 per hour.
Financial support: In 2001–02, 7 students received support, including 6 teaching assistantships with full and partial tuition reimbursements available (averaging $6,879 per year); fellowships with full and partial tuition reimbursements available, research assistantships with full and partial tuition reimbursements available, career-related internships or fieldwork, Federal Work-Study, institutionally sponsored loans, scholarships/grants, health care benefits, tuition waivers (full and partial), and unspecified assistantships also available. Support available to part-time students. Financial award application deadline: 4/1; financial award applicants required to submit FAFSA.
Faculty research: Simulation, manufacturing systems, system ergonomics, logistics. *Total annual research expenditures:* $104,684.
Dr. James Swain, Chair, 256-824-6749, *Fax:* 256-824-6608, *E-mail:* jswain@ise.email.uah. *Web site:* http://www.eb-p5.eb.uah.edu/ise/

■ THE UNIVERSITY OF ARIZONA

Graduate College, College of Engineering and Mines, Department of Systems and Industrial Engineering, Program in Industrial Engineering, Tucson, AZ 85721

AWARDS MS. Part-time programs available.

Students: 32 full-time (6 women), 2 part-time. Average age 26. 64 applicants, 73% accepted, 16 enrolled. In 2001, 11 degrees awarded.
Entrance requirements: For master's, GRE General Test, TOEFL, minimum GPA of 3.0. *Application deadline:* For fall

admission, 7/1. Applications are processed on a rolling basis. *Application fee:* $45.
Expenses: Tuition, state resident: full-time $2,490; part-time $436 per unit. Tuition, nonresident: full-time $10,300; part-time $436 per unit. Full-time tuition and fees vary according to degree level and program.
Financial support: Fellowships, research assistantships, teaching assistantships, institutionally sponsored loans and scholarships/grants available.
Faculty research: Operations research, manufacturing systems, quality and reliability, statistical/engineering design.
Application contact: Celia Stenzel, Graduate Secretary, 520-621-6551, *Fax:* 520-621-6555.

■ THE UNIVERSITY OF ARIZONA

Graduate College, College of Engineering and Mines, Department of Systems and Industrial Engineering, Program in Systems and Industrial Engineering, Tucson, AZ 85721

AWARDS PhD.

Students: 32 full-time (3 women), 6 part-time (1 woman); includes 1 minority (Native American), 31 international. Average age 30. 41 applicants, 85% accepted, 11 enrolled. In 2001, 1 degree awarded.
Degree requirements: For doctorate, thesis/dissertation.
Entrance requirements: For doctorate, GRE General Test, TOEFL, minimum GPA of 3.0. *Application deadline:* For fall admission, 7/1. *Application fee:* $45.
Expenses: Tuition, state resident: full-time $2,490; part-time $436 per unit. Tuition, nonresident: full-time $10,300; part-time $436 per unit. Full-time tuition and fees vary according to degree level and program.
Application contact: Celia Stenzel, Graduate Secretary, 520-621-6551, *Fax:* 520-621-6555.

■ UNIVERSITY OF ARKANSAS

Graduate School, College of Engineering, Department of Industrial Engineering, Program in Industrial Engineering, Fayetteville, AR 72701-1201

AWARDS MSE, MSIE, PhD.

Students: 29 full-time (4 women), 5 part-time (1 woman); includes 3 minority (2 Asian Americans or Pacific Islanders, 1 Hispanic American), 21 international. 78 applicants, 97% accepted. In 2001, 20 degrees awarded.
Degree requirements: For master's, thesis optional; for doctorate, one foreign language, thesis/dissertation.
Application fee: $40 ($50 for international students).
Expenses: Tuition, state resident: full-time $3,553; part-time $197 per credit. Tuition, nonresident: full-time $8,411; part-time

$467 per credit. Required fees: $42 per credit. Tuition and fees vary according to course load and program.
Financial support: Research assistantships, teaching assistantships, career-related internships or fieldwork and Federal Work-Study available. Support available to part-time students. Financial award application deadline: 4/1; financial award applicants required to submit FAFSA.
Dr. John English, Interim Chair, Department of Industrial Engineering, 479-575-3157.

■ UNIVERSITY OF CALIFORNIA, BERKELEY

Graduate Division, College of Engineering, Department of Industrial Engineering and Operations Research, Berkeley, CA 94720-1500

AWARDS M Eng, MS, D Eng, PhD.

Degree requirements: For master's, comprehensive exam or thesis (MS); for doctorate, thesis/dissertation, qualifying exam.
Entrance requirements: For master's and doctorate, GRE General Test, minimum GPA of 3.0.
Expenses: Tuition, nonresident: full-time $10,704. Required fees: $4,349.
Faculty research: Mathematical programming, robotics and manufacturing, linear and nonlinear optimization, production planning and scheduling, queuing theory.
Web site: http://www.ieor.berkeley.edu/
Find an in-depth description at www.petersons.com/gradchannel.

■ UNIVERSITY OF CENTRAL FLORIDA

College of Engineering and Computer Sciences, Department of Industrial Engineering and Management Systems, Orlando, FL 32816

AWARDS Applied operations research (Certificate); computer-integrated manufacturing (MS); design for usability (Certificate); engineering management (MS); industrial engineering (MSIE); industrial engineering and management systems (PhD); industrial ergonomics and safety (Certificate); operations research (MS); product assurance engineering (MS); project engineering (Certificate); quality assurance (Certificate). Simulation systems (MS). Systems simulations for engineers (Certificate); training simulation (Certificate). Part-time and evening/weekend programs available.

Faculty: 20 full-time (4 women), 8 part-time/adjunct (1 woman).
Students: 92 full-time (19 women), 182 part-time (49 women); includes 66 minority (18 African Americans, 10 Asian Americans or Pacific Islanders, 35 Hispanic Americans, 3 Native Americans), 57 international. Average age 32. 231

applicants, 84% accepted, 85 enrolled. In 2001, 3 master's, 9 doctorates awarded.
Degree requirements: For master's, thesis; for doctorate, thesis/dissertation, departmental qualifying exam, candidacy exam.
Entrance requirements: For master's, GRE General Test, TOEFL, minimum GPA of 3.0 in last 60 hours; for doctorate, TOEFL, minimum GPA of 3.5 in last 60 hours. *Application deadline:* For fall admission, 7/15 (priority date); for spring admission, 12/1 (priority date). *Application fee:* $20. Electronic applications accepted.
Expenses: Tuition, state resident: part-time $162 per hour. Tuition, nonresident: part-time $569 per hour.
Financial support: In 2001–02, 23 fellowships with partial tuition reimbursements (averaging $3,272 per year), 131 research assistantships with partial tuition reimbursements (averaging $3,125 per year), 24 teaching assistantships with partial tuition reimbursements (averaging $3,823 per year) were awarded. Career-related internships or fieldwork, Federal Work-Study, institutionally sponsored loans, tuition waivers (partial), and unspecified assistantships also available. Financial award application deadline: 3/1; financial award applicants required to submit FAFSA.
Dr. Charles Reily, Chair, 407-823-2204, *E-mail:* creilly@mail.ucf.edu.
Application contact: Dr. Linda Malone, Coordinator, 407-823-2204, *E-mail:* malone@mail.ucf.edu. *Web site:* http://www.ucf.edu/

Find an in-depth description at www.petersons.com/gradchannel.

■ UNIVERSITY OF CINCINNATI

Division of Research and Advanced Studies, College of Engineering, Department of Mechanical, Industrial and Nuclear Engineering, Program in Industrial Engineering, Cincinnati, OH 45221

AWARDS MS, PhD, MBA/MS. Part-time and evening/weekend programs available.

Degree requirements: For master's, oral exam, thesis defense; for doctorate, variable foreign language requirement, thesis/dissertation, oral exam.
Entrance requirements: For master's and doctorate, GRE General Test, TOEFL, TSE. *Application deadline:* For fall admission, 2/1 (priority date). *Application fee:* $40. Electronic applications accepted.
Expenses: Tuition, state resident: part-time $2,698 per quarter. Tuition, nonresident: part-time $4,977 per quarter.
Financial support: Fellowships, career-related internships or fieldwork, tuition waivers (partial), and unspecified assistantships available. Financial award application deadline: 2/1.
Faculty research: Operations research, engineering administration, safety.

Application contact: Dr. Ash Genaidy, Graduate Program Director, 513-556-6299, *Fax:* 513-556-3390. *Web site:* http://www.min.uc.edu/

■ UNIVERSITY OF DAYTON

Graduate School, School of Engineering, Program in Management Science, Dayton, OH 45469-1300

AWARDS MSMS. Part-time and evening/weekend programs available.

Faculty: 5 full-time (0 women), 6 part-time/adjunct (1 woman).
Students: 28 full-time (4 women), 21 part-time (3 women); includes 8 minority (4 African Americans, 1 Asian American or Pacific Islander, 3 Hispanic Americans), 3 international. Average age 28. In 2001, 14 degrees awarded.
Entrance requirements: For master's, GRE General Test, TOEFL. *Application deadline:* For fall admission, 8/1. *Application fee:* $30.
Expenses: Tuition: Full-time $5,436; part-time $453 per credit hour. Required fees: $50; $25 per term.
Financial support: Research assistantships, teaching assistantships available.
Faculty research: Artificial intelligence, program management, reliability, simulation modeling.
Dr. Edward F. Mykytka, Chairman, 937-229-2238, *Fax:* 937-229-2756, *E-mail:* emykytka@notes.udayton.edu.
Application contact: Dr. Donald L. Moon, Associate Dean, 937-229-2241, *Fax:* 937-229-2471, *E-mail:* dmoon@notes.udayton.edu.

■ UNIVERSITY OF FLORIDA

Graduate School, College of Engineering, Department of Industrial and Systems Engineering, Gainesville, FL 32611

AWARDS Engineering management (ME, MS); facilities layout decision support systems energy (PhD); health systems (ME, MS); industrial engineering (PhD, Engr); manufacturing systems engineering (ME, MS, PhD, Certificate); operations research (ME, MS, PhD, Engr); production planning and control engineering management (PhD); quality and reliability assurance (ME, MS). Systems engineering (PhD, Engr).

Degree requirements: For master's, core exam, thesis optional; for doctorate, thesis/dissertation, comprehensive exam.
Entrance requirements: For master's and doctorate, GRE General Test, TOEFL, minimum GPA of 3.0; for other advanced degree, GRE General Test. Electronic applications accepted.
Expenses: Tuition, state resident: part-time $164 per hour. Tuition, nonresident: part-time $571 per hour. Tuition and fees

vary according to course level and program. *Web site:* http://www.ise.ufl.edu/

Find an in-depth description at www.petersons.com/gradchannel.

■ UNIVERSITY OF FLORIDA

Graduate School, Graduate Engineering and Research Center (GERC), Gainesville, FL 32611

AWARDS Aerospace engineering (ME, MS, PhD, Engr); electrical and computer engineering (ME, MS, PhD, Engr); engineering mechanics (ME, MS, PhD, Engr); industrial and systems engineering (ME, MS, PhD, Engr). Part-time programs available. Postbaccalaureate distance learning degree programs offered. Terminal master's awarded for partial completion of doctoral program.

Degree requirements: For master's, thesis optional; for doctorate and Engr, thesis/dissertation.
Entrance requirements: For master's, GRE General Test, TOEFL, minimum GPA of 3.0; for doctorate, GRE General Test, written and oral qualifying exams, TOEFL, minimum GPA of 3.0, master's degree in engineering; for Engr, GRE General Test, TOEFL, minimum GPA of 3.0, master's degree in engineering. Electronic applications accepted.
Expenses: Contact institution.
Faculty research: Aerodynamics, terradynamics, and propulsion; composite materials and stress analysis; optical processing of microwave signals and photonics; holography, radar, and communications. System and signal theory; digital signal processing. *Web site:* http://www.gerc.eng.ufl.edu/

■ UNIVERSITY OF HOUSTON

Cullen College of Engineering, Department of Industrial Engineering, Houston, TX 77204

AWARDS MIE, MSIE, PhD, MBA/MIE. Part-time and evening/weekend programs available.

Faculty: 9 full-time (1 woman).
Students: 58 full-time (5 women), 39 part-time (14 women); includes 16 minority (4 African Americans, 4 Asian Americans or Pacific Islanders, 8 Hispanic Americans), 57 international. Average age 28. 115 applicants, 45% accepted. In 2001, 16 master's, 4 doctorates awarded. Terminal master's awarded for partial completion of doctoral program.
Degree requirements: For master's, thesis (for some programs); for doctorate, thesis/dissertation, departmental qualifying exam.
Entrance requirements: For master's and doctorate, GRE General Test, TOEFL. *Application deadline:* For fall admission, 7/1 (priority date); for spring admission, 11/1. Applications are processed on a rolling basis. *Application fee:* $25 ($75 for international students).

University of Houston (continued)

Expenses: Tuition, state resident: full-time $1,512. Tuition, nonresident: full-time $5,310. Required fees: $1,308. Tuition and fees vary according to program.

Financial support: In 2001–02, 3 fellowships, 8 research assistantships, 25 teaching assistantships were awarded. Career-related internships or fieldwork, Federal Work-Study, and institutionally sponsored loans also available. Financial award application deadline: 7/1.

Faculty research: CAD/CAM, artificial intelligence, applied operations research, engineering management, human factors and safety. *Total annual research expenditures:* $515,497.

Dr. Hamid R. Parsaei, Chairman, 713-743-4180, *Fax:* 713-743-4190, *E-mail:* parsaei@uh.edu.

Application contact: Mary Patronella, Information Contact, 713-743-4188, *Fax:* 713-743-4190, *E-mail:* inde8qo@uh.edu. *Web site:* http://www.egr.uh.edu/ie/

■ **UNIVERSITY OF ILLINOIS AT CHICAGO**

Graduate College, College of Engineering, Department of Mechanical Engineering, Program in Industrial Engineering and Operations Research, Chicago, IL 60607-7128

AWARDS PhD.

Students: 6 full-time (3 women), 2 part-time (1 woman), 7 international. Average age 31. 17 applicants, 29% accepted, 4 enrolled. In 2001, 3 degrees awarded.

Degree requirements: For doctorate, thesis/dissertation.

Entrance requirements: For doctorate, GRE General Test, TOEFL, minimum GPA of 3.75 on a 5.0 scale. *Application deadline:* For fall admission, 6/1; for spring admission, 11/1. Applications are processed on a rolling basis. *Application fee:* $40 ($50 for international students). Electronic applications accepted.

Expenses: Tuition, state resident: full-time $3,060. Tuition, nonresident: full-time $6,688.

Financial support: In 2001–02, 6 students received support; fellowships with full tuition reimbursements available, research assistantships with full tuition reimbursements available, teaching assistantships with full tuition reimbursements available, Federal Work-Study and tuition waivers (full) available. Financial award application deadline: 3/1; financial award applicants required to submit FAFSA.

Application contact: Mun Young Choi, Director of Graduate Studies.

Find an in-depth description at www.petersons.com/gradchannel.

■ **UNIVERSITY OF ILLINOIS AT URBANA–CHAMPAIGN**

Graduate College, College of Engineering, Department of Mechanical and Industrial Engineering, Champaign, IL 61820

AWARDS Industrial engineering (MS, PhD); mechanical engineering (MS, PhD).

Faculty: 43 full-time.

Students: 240 full-time (20 women); includes 22 minority (4 African Americans, 14 Asian Americans or Pacific Islanders, 4 Hispanic Americans), 135 international. 778 applicants, 12% accepted. In 2001, 70 master's, 29 doctorates awarded. Terminal master's awarded for partial completion of doctoral program.

Degree requirements: For master's, thesis, non-thesis available by petition; for doctorate, thesis/dissertation.

Entrance requirements: For master's, GRE General Test, TOEFL, minimum GPA of 3.25; for doctorate, GRE General Test, TOEFL. *Application deadline:* For fall admission, 2/15; for spring admission, 10/1. Applications are processed on a rolling basis. *Application fee:* $40 ($50 for international students).

Expenses: Tuition, state resident: part-time $3,227 per degree program. Tuition, nonresident: part-time $7,169 per degree program. Tuition and fees vary according to program.

Financial support: In 2001–02, 9 fellowships, 168 research assistantships, 37 teaching assistantships were awarded. Federal Work-Study, institutionally sponsored loans, and tuition waivers (full and partial) also available. Financial award application deadline: 3/1.

Faculty research: Combustion and propulsion, design methodology, dynamic systems and controls, energy transfer, materials behavior and processing, manufacturing systems operations, management. *Total annual research expenditures:* $8 million.

Dr. Richard O. Buckius, Head, 217-333-1079, *Fax:* 217-244-6534, *E-mail:* buckius@uiuc.edu.

Application contact: Karen Bryan, Administrative Secretary, 217-244-4539, *Fax:* 217-244-6534, *E-mail:* k-bryan@uiuc.edu. *Web site:* http://www.mie.uiuc.edu/academic-programs/

Find an in-depth description at www.petersons.com/gradchannel.

■ **THE UNIVERSITY OF IOWA**

Graduate College, College of Engineering, Department of Industrial Engineering, Iowa City, IA 52242-1316

AWARDS Engineering design and manufacturing (MS, PhD); ergonomics (MS, PhD); information and engineering management (MS, PhD); operations research (MS, PhD); quality engineering (MS, PhD).

Faculty: 7 full-time, 1 part-time/adjunct.

Students: 37 full-time (13 women), 24 international. Average age 27. 115 applicants, 50% accepted, 6 enrolled. In 2001, 12 master's, 3 doctorates awarded.

Degree requirements: For master's, exam, thesis optional; for doctorate, thesis/dissertation, final defense exam, comprehensive exam, registration. *Median time to degree:* Master's–2 years full-time; doctorate–4 years full-time.

Entrance requirements: For master's and doctorate, GRE General Test, TOEFL. *Application deadline:* For fall admission, 4/15; for winter admission, 10/1; for spring admission, 3/1. Applications are processed on a rolling basis. *Application fee:* $30 ($50 for international students). Electronic applications accepted.

Expenses: Tuition, state resident: full-time $3,702; part-time $206 per semester hour. Tuition, nonresident: full-time $11,924; part-time $206 per semester hour. Required fees: $101 per semester. Tuition and fees vary according to course load and program.

Financial support: In 2001–02, fellowships with tuition reimbursements (averaging $14,764 per year), 16 research assistantships (averaging $14,764 per year), 6 teaching assistantships (averaging $14,764 per year) were awarded. Career-related internships or fieldwork, scholarships/grants, and unspecified assistantships also available. Support available to part-time students. Financial award applicants required to submit FAFSA.

Faculty research: Informatics, industrial robotics, operations research, human-computer interfaces, human factors (ergonomics). *Total annual research expenditures:* $752,000.

Dr. Jeffrey S. Marshall, Departmental Executive Officer, 319-335-5817, *Fax:* 319-335-5669, *E-mail:* jeffrey-marshall@uiowa.edu.

Application contact: Sue Mulder, Secretary, 319-335-5939, *Fax:* 319-335-5669, *E-mail:* indeng@engineering.uiowa.edu. *Web site:* http://www.mie.engineering.uiowa.edu

■ **UNIVERSITY OF LOUISVILLE**

Graduate School, Speed Scientific School, Department of Industrial Engineering, Program in Industrial Engineering, Louisville, KY 40292-0001

AWARDS M Eng, PhD.

Students: 44 full-time (13 women), 54 part-time (14 women); includes 8 minority (5 African Americans, 3 Asian Americans or Pacific Islanders), 50 international. In 2001, 17 master's, 1 doctorate awarded.

Expenses: Tuition, state resident: full-time $4,134. Tuition, nonresident: full-time $11,486.

Application contact: Nancy D. White, Executive Secretary, 502-852-6342, *Fax:* 502-852-5633, *E-mail:* ndwhit01@gwise.louisville.edu.

■ UNIVERSITY OF MASSACHUSETTS AMHERST

Graduate School, College of Engineering, Department of Mechanical and Industrial Engineering, Program in Industrial Engineering and Operations Research, Amherst, MA 01003-2210

AWARDS MS, PhD.

Students: 14 full-time (4 women), 21 part-time (4 women); includes 1 minority (Asian American or Pacific Islander), 25 international. Average age 29. 175 applicants, 19% accepted. In 2001, 4 master's, 4 doctorates awarded.
Degree requirements: For master's, project; for doctorate, thesis/dissertation.
Entrance requirements: For master's and doctorate, GRE General Test. *Application deadline:* For fall admission, 2/1 (priority date). Applications are processed on a rolling basis. *Application fee:* $40 ($50 for international students).
Expenses: Tuition, state resident: full-time $1,980; part-time $110 per credit. Tuition, nonresident: full-time $7,456; part-time $414 per credit. Required fees: $4,112. One-time fee: $115 full-time.
Financial support: Fellowships with full tuition reimbursements, research assistantships with full tuition reimbursements, teaching assistantships with full tuition reimbursements, career-related internships or fieldwork, Federal Work-Study, scholarships/grants, traineeships, and unspecified assistantships available. Support available to part-time students. Financial award application deadline: 2/1. Dr. Ian Grosse, Director, 413-545-2505, *Fax:* 413-545-1027. *Web site:* http://www.ecs.umass.edu/MIE/

■ UNIVERSITY OF MASSACHUSETTS LOWELL

Graduate School, James B. Francis College of Engineering, Department of Work Environment, Lowell, MA 01854-2881

AWARDS MS, Sc D. Terminal master's awarded for partial completion of doctoral program.

Degree requirements: For master's and doctorate, thesis/dissertation.
Entrance requirements: For master's and doctorate, GRE General Test.
Faculty research: Ergonomics, industrial hygiene, epidemiology, work environment policy, toxic use reduction.

■ THE UNIVERSITY OF MEMPHIS

Graduate School, Herff College of Engineering, Program in Industrial and Systems Engineering, Memphis, TN 38152

AWARDS MS. Part-time programs available.

Degree requirements: For master's, thesis or alternative, comprehensive exam.
Entrance requirements: For master's, GRE General Test or MAT, minimum undergraduate GPA of 3.0.
Expenses: Tuition, state resident: full-time $2,026. Tuition, nonresident: full-time $4,528.
Faculty research: Integer programming, ergonomics, scheduling. *Web site:* http://www.inse.memphis.edu/

■ UNIVERSITY OF MIAMI

Graduate School, College of Engineering, Department of Industrial Engineering, Coral Gables, FL 33124

AWARDS Environmental health and safety (MS, MSEVH, MSOES), including environmental health and safety (MS, MSEVH), occupational ergonomics and safety (MSOES); ergonomics (PhD); industrial engineering (MSIE, PhD); management of technology (MS).

Faculty: 9 full-time (0 women), 3 part-time/adjunct (1 woman).
Students: 54 full-time (10 women); includes 16 minority (14 African Americans, 2 Hispanic Americans), 7 international. Average age 28. 79 applicants, 75% accepted. In 2001, 25 master's, 5 doctorates awarded.
Degree requirements: For master's, thesis (for some programs); for doctorate, thesis/dissertation.
Entrance requirements: For master's and doctorate, GRE General Test, TOEFL, minimum GPA of 3.0. *Application deadline:* For fall admission, 5/1 (priority date). Applications are processed on a rolling basis. *Application fee:* $50.
Expenses: Tuition: Part-time $960 per credit hour. Required fees: $85 per semester. Tuition and fees vary according to program.
Financial support: In 2001–02, 4 fellowships, 5 research assistantships, 4 teaching assistantships were awarded. Federal Work-Study also available. Financial award application deadline: 3/1; financial award applicants required to submit FAFSA.
Faculty research: Logistics, supply chain management, industrial applications of biomechanics and ergonomics, technology management, back pain, aging, operations research, manufacturing, safety, human reliability, energy assessment. *Total annual research expenditures:* $235,000.
Dr. Shihab S. Asfour, Chair, 305-284-2344, *Fax:* 305-284-4040, *E-mail:* sasfour@miami.edu.
Application contact: Dr. Eleftherios Iakovou, Associate Professor, Graduate Director, 305-284-2344, *Fax:* 305-284-4040. *Web site:* http://www.eng.miami.edu/

■ UNIVERSITY OF MICHIGAN

Horace H. Rackham School of Graduate Studies, College of Engineering, Department of Industrial and Operations Engineering, Ann Arbor, MI 48109

AWARDS MS, MSE, PhD, IOE, MBA/MS, MBA/MSE, MHSA/MS. Part-time programs available. Terminal master's awarded for partial completion of doctoral program.

Degree requirements: For doctorate, oral defense of dissertation, preliminary exams, qualifying exam.
Entrance requirements: For master's, GRE General Test, TOEFL, minimum GPA of 3.2; for doctorate, GRE General Test, TOEFL, minimum GPA of 3.5. Electronic applications accepted.
Faculty research: Optimization and stochastic processes, human performance and ergonomics, engineering management, quality engineering, production manufacturing. *Web site:* http://ioe.engin.umich.edu

■ UNIVERSITY OF MICHIGAN–DEARBORN

College of Engineering and Computer Science, Department of Industrial and Systems Engineering, Dearborn, MI 48128-1491

AWARDS Engineering management (MS); industrial and systems engineering (MSE); information systems and technology (MS). Part-time and evening/weekend programs available.

Faculty: 12 full-time (0 women), 8 part-time/adjunct (2 women).
Students: 7 full-time (2 women), 239 part-time (61 women); includes 45 minority (7 African Americans, 26 Asian Americans or Pacific Islanders, 12 Hispanic Americans). Average age 31. 107 applicants, 91% accepted. In 2001, 78 degrees awarded.
Degree requirements: For master's, thesis optional.
Entrance requirements: For master's, bachelor's degree in applied mathematics, computer science, engineering, or physical science; minimum GPA of 3.0. *Application deadline:* For fall admission, 8/1 (priority date); for winter admission, 12/1 (priority date); for spring admission, 4/1. Applications are processed on a rolling basis. *Application fee:* $55.
Expenses: Tuition, state resident: part-time $300 per credit hour. Tuition, nonresident: part-time $756 per credit hour. Required fees: $90 per semester. Tuition and fees vary according to course level, course load and program.
Financial support: Fellowships, research assistantships, teaching assistantships, Federal Work-Study available. Financial award application deadline: 4/1; financial award applicants required to submit FAFSA.

University of Michigan–Dearborn (continued)

Faculty research: Health care systems, databases, human factors, machine diagnostics, precision machining.
Dr. S. K. Kachhal, Chair, 313-593-5361, *Fax:* 313-593-3692.
Application contact: Shelly A. Harris, Graduate Secretary, 313-593-5361, *Fax:* 313-593-3692, *E-mail:* saharris@engin.umd.umich.edu. *Web site:* http://www.engin.umd.umich.edu/

■ UNIVERSITY OF MINNESOTA, TWIN CITIES CAMPUS

Graduate School, Institute of Technology, Department of Mechanical Engineering, Program in Industrial Engineering, Minneapolis, MN 55455-0213

AWARDS MSIE, PhD. Part-time programs available.

Degree requirements: For doctorate, thesis/dissertation.
Entrance requirements: For master's, GRE General Test, minimum GPA of 3.0; for doctorate, GRE General Test.
Expenses: Tuition, state resident: full-time $2,932; part-time $489 per credit. Tuition, nonresident: full-time $5,758; part-time $960 per credit. Part-time tuition and fees vary according to course load, program and reciprocity agreements. *Web site:* http://www.me.umn.edu/
Find an in-depth description at www.petersons.com/gradchannel.

■ UNIVERSITY OF MISSOURI–COLUMBIA

Graduate School, College of Engineering, Department of Industrial and Manufacturing Systems Engineering, Columbia, MO 65211

AWARDS MS, PhD.

Faculty: 7 full-time (0 women).
Students: 18 full-time (3 women), 7 part-time; includes 3 minority (all African Americans), 21 international. 31 applicants, 48% accepted. In 2001, 8 master's, 6 doctorates awarded.
Degree requirements: For master's, thesis or alternative; for doctorate, thesis/dissertation.
Entrance requirements: For master's and doctorate, GRE General Test, TOEFL, minimum GPA of 3.0. *Application deadline:* For fall admission, 5/1 (priority date). Applications are processed on a rolling basis. *Application fee:* $25 ($50 for international students).
Expenses: Tuition, state resident: part-time $179 per credit hour. Tuition, nonresident: part-time $539 per credit hour. Required fees: $122 per semester. Tuition and fees vary according to program.

Financial support: Research assistantships, teaching assistantships, institutionally sponsored loans available.
Dr. Jose Zayas-Castro, Director of Graduate Studies, 573-882-9567, *E-mail:* zayascastroj@missouri.edu. *Web site:* http://www.engineering.missouri.edu/industrial.htm

■ UNIVERSITY OF NEBRASKA–LINCOLN

Graduate College, College of Engineering and Technology, Department of Industrial and Management Systems Engineering, Lincoln, NE 68588

AWARDS Engineering (PhD); industrial and management systems engineering (MS). Postbaccalaureate distance learning degree programs offered.

Faculty: 16.
Students: 48 (14 women); includes 3 minority (1 Asian American or Pacific Islander, 2 Hispanic Americans) 34 international. Average age 32. 136 applicants, 43% accepted, 15 enrolled. In 2001, 12 degrees awarded.
Degree requirements: For master's, thesis optional; for doctorate, thesis/dissertation, comprehensive exam.
Entrance requirements: For master's and doctorate, GRE General Test, TOEFL. *Application deadline:* For fall admission, 3/1 (priority date). Applications are processed on a rolling basis. *Application fee:* $35. Electronic applications accepted.
Expenses: Tuition, state resident: full-time $2,412; part-time $134 per credit. Tuition, nonresident: full-time $6,223; part-time $346 per credit. Tuition and fees vary according to course load.
Financial support: In 2001–02, 12 research assistantships, 3 teaching assistantships were awarded. Fellowships, Federal Work-Study, health care benefits, and unspecified assistantships also available. Support available to part-time students. Financial award application deadline: 2/15.
Faculty research: Ergonomics, occupational safety, quality control, industrial packaging, facility design.
Dr. Michael W. Riley, Chair, 402-472-3495. *Web site:* http://www.engr.unl.edu/ie/

■ UNIVERSITY OF NEW HAVEN

Graduate School, School of Engineering and Applied Science, Program in Industrial Engineering, West Haven, CT 06516-1916

AWARDS Industrial engineering (MSIE); logistics (Certificate). Part-time and evening/weekend programs available.

Students: 6 full-time (2 women), 11 part-time (2 women); includes 2 minority (1 African American, 1 Hispanic American), 12 international. In 2001, 9 degrees awarded.

Degree requirements: For master's, thesis or alternative.
Entrance requirements: For master's, bachelor's degree in engineering. *Application deadline:* Applications are processed on a rolling basis. *Application fee:* $50.
Expenses: Tuition: Full-time $12,015; part-time $445 per credit hour. Required fees: $30. One-time fee: $100 full-time.
Financial support: Federal Work-Study available. Support available to part-time students. Financial award application deadline: 5/1; financial award applicants required to submit FAFSA.
Dr. Ronald Wentworth, Coordinator, 203-932-7434.

■ UNIVERSITY OF OKLAHOMA

Graduate College, College of Engineering, School of Industrial Engineering, Norman, OK 73019-0390

AWARDS MS, PhD.

Faculty: 8 full-time (3 women), 1 part-time/adjunct (0 women).
Students: 55 full-time (9 women), 16 part-time (2 women); includes 3 minority (1 Asian American or Pacific Islander, 2 Hispanic Americans), 53 international. 83 applicants, 90% accepted, 18 enrolled. In 2001, 17 master's, 3 doctorates awarded.
Degree requirements: For master's, thesis optional; for doctorate, thesis/dissertation, qualifying exam.
Entrance requirements: For master's and doctorate, TOEFL. *Application deadline:* For fall admission, 6/1 (priority date). Applications are processed on a rolling basis. *Application fee:* $25 ($50 for international students).
Expenses: Tuition, state resident: full-time $2,208; part-time $92 per credit hour. Tuition, nonresident: part-time $297 per credit hour. Tuition and fees vary according to course level, course load and program.
Financial support: In 2001–02, 3 fellowships (averaging $5,000 per year), 10 research assistantships with partial tuition reimbursements (averaging $9,379 per year), 17 teaching assistantships with partial tuition reimbursements (averaging $10,324 per year) were awarded. Career-related internships or fieldwork, Federal Work-Study, scholarships/grants, tuition waivers (partial), and unspecified assistantships also available. Support available to part-time students. Financial award application deadline: 5/1; financial award applicants required to submit FAFSA.
Faculty research: Engineering education, quality engineering, interaction of cell phones with hearing aids and pacemakers, human information processing, physical ergonomics and safety. *Total annual research expenditures:* $1.1 million.
Pakize Simin Pulat, Director, 405-325-3721, *Fax:* 405-325-7555, *E-mail:* pulat@ou.edu.

Application contact: Dr. Shivakuman Raman, Graduate Liaison, 405-325-3721, *Fax:* 405-325-7555, *E-mail:* raman@ou.edu.

■ UNIVERSITY OF PITTSBURGH

School of Engineering, Department of Industrial Engineering, Pittsburgh, PA 15260

AWARDS MSIE, PhD. Part-time and evening/weekend programs available.

Faculty: 11 full-time (2 women), 2 part-time/adjunct (0 women).
Students: 35 full-time (6 women), 36 part-time (8 women); includes 5 minority (2 African Americans, 1 Asian American or Pacific Islander, 2 Hispanic Americans), 31 international. 141 applicants, 56% accepted, 21 enrolled. In 2001, 31 master's, 6 doctorates awarded. Terminal master's awarded for partial completion of doctoral program.
Degree requirements: For master's, thesis optional; for doctorate, thesis/dissertation, final oral exams, comprehensive exam.
Entrance requirements: For master's and doctorate, GRE General Test, TOEFL, minimum QPA of 3.0. *Application deadline:* For fall admission, 8/1 (priority date); for spring admission, 12/1 (priority date). Applications are processed on a rolling basis. *Application fee:* $40.
Financial support: In 2001–02, 19 students received support, including 2 fellowships with full tuition reimbursements available (averaging $21,672 per year), 12 research assistantships with full tuition reimbursements available (averaging $17,244 per year), 5 teaching assistantships with full tuition reimbursements available (averaging $18,408 per year). Scholarships/grants and tuition waivers (full and partial) also available. Financial award application deadline: 2/15.
Faculty research: Operations research, engineering management, computational intelligence, manufacturing, information systems. *Total annual research expenditures:* $1.9 million.
Dr. Harvey Wolfe, Chairman, 412-624-9830, *Fax:* 412-624-9831, *E-mail:* hwolfe@engrng.pitt.edu.
Application contact: Dr. Jayant Rajgopal, Graduate Coordinator, 412-624-9840, *Fax:* 412-624-9831, *E-mail:* rajgopal@engrng.pitt.edu.

■ UNIVERSITY OF PUERTO RICO, MAYAGÜEZ CAMPUS

Graduate Studies, College of Engineering, Department of Industrial Engineering, Mayagüez, PR 00681-9000

AWARDS MMSE. Part-time programs available.

Degree requirements: For master's, thesis, project, comprehensive exam.

Entrance requirements: For master's, minimum GPA of 2.5, proficiency in English and Spanish.
Faculty research: Quality control operations research.

■ UNIVERSITY OF RHODE ISLAND

Graduate School, College of Engineering, Department of Industrial and Manufacturing Engineering, Program in Industrial Engineering, Kingston, RI 02881

AWARDS MS.

Application deadline: For fall admission, 4/15 (priority date). Applications are processed on a rolling basis. *Application fee:* $35.
Expenses: Tuition, state resident: full-time $3,756; part-time $209 per credit. Tuition, nonresident: full-time $10,774; part-time $599 per credit. Required fees: $1,586; $76 per credit. $76 per credit. One-time fee: $60 full-time.
Application contact: Graduate Program Director, 401-874-2455.

■ UNIVERSITY OF SOUTHERN CALIFORNIA

Graduate School, School of Engineering, Department of Industrial and Systems Engineering, Program in Industrial and Systems Engineering, Los Angeles, CA 90089

AWARDS MS, PhD, Engr, MBA/MS.

Degree requirements: For master's, thesis optional; for doctorate, thesis/dissertation.
Entrance requirements: For master's, doctorate, and Engr, GRE General Test.
Expenses: Tuition: Full-time $25,060; part-time $844 per unit. Required fees: $473.
Faculty research: Work organization and high-tech manufacturing.

■ UNIVERSITY OF SOUTHERN COLORADO

College of Education, Engineering and Professional Studies, Program in Industrial and Systems Engineering, Pueblo, CO 81001-4901

AWARDS MS. Part-time and evening/weekend programs available.

Faculty: 3 full-time (1 woman), 1 part-time/adjunct (0 women).
Students: 16 full-time (4 women), 18 part-time (3 women); includes 5 minority (1 African American, 3 Hispanic Americans, 1 Native American), 20 international. Average age 29. 23 applicants, 74% accepted. In 2001, 13 degrees awarded.
Degree requirements: For master's, thesis optional. *Median time to degree:* Master's–1.5 years full-time, 3.5 years part-time.

Entrance requirements: For master's, GRE General Test, TOEFL. *Application deadline:* For fall admission, 7/19 (priority date); for spring admission, 11/30 (priority date). *Application fee:* $35.
Expenses: Tuition, state resident: full-time $1,746; part-time $97 per credit. Tuition, nonresident: full-time $8,298; part-time $461 per credit. Required fees: $445; $97 per credit. $582 per semester. Tuition and fees vary according to course load.
Financial support: In 2001–02, 1 fellowship (averaging $17,000 per year), 1 research assistantship with partial tuition reimbursement (averaging $13,000 per year), 3 teaching assistantships with partial tuition reimbursements (averaging $8,000 per year) were awarded. Career-related internships or fieldwork, Federal Work-Study, institutionally sponsored loans, and scholarships/grants also available. Financial award application deadline: 3/1; financial award applicants required to submit FAFSA.
Faculty research: Computer-integrated manufacturing, reliability, economic development, design of experiments, scheduling. *Total annual research expenditures:* $178,000.
Dr. Jane M. Fraser, Chair, 719-549-2036, *Fax:* 719-549-2519, *E-mail:* jfraser@uscolo.edu.
Application contact: Dr. Huseyin Sarper, Graduate Coordinator, 719-549-2889, *Fax:* 719-549-2519, *E-mail:* sarper@uscolo.edu. *Web site:* http://www.ceeps.edu/engin/index.html

■ UNIVERSITY OF SOUTH FLORIDA

College of Graduate Studies, College of Engineering, Department of Industrial and Management Systems Engineering, Tampa, FL 33620-9951

AWARDS Engineering management (ME, MIE, MSIE); engineering science (PhD); industrial engineering (ME, MIE, MSIE, PhD). Part-time programs available. Postbaccalaureate distance learning degree programs offered (minimal on-campus study).

Faculty: 10 full-time (0 women).
Students: 54 full-time (14 women), 66 part-time (13 women); includes 14 minority (3 African Americans, 1 Asian American or Pacific Islander, 10 Hispanic Americans), 58 international. Average age 35. 187 applicants, 64% accepted, 32 enrolled. In 2001, 12 degrees awarded. Terminal master's awarded for partial completion of doctoral program.
Degree requirements: For master's, thesis (for some programs); for doctorate, thesis/dissertation, 2 tools of research as specified by dissertation committee.
Entrance requirements: For master's, GRE General Test, minimum GPA of 3.0 during previous 2 years; for doctorate, GRE General Test. *Application deadline:*

University of South Florida (continued)
For fall admission, 6/1; for spring admission, 10/15. *Application fee:* $20. Electronic applications accepted.
Expenses: Tuition, state resident: part-time $166 per credit hour. Tuition, nonresident: part-time $573 per credit hour. Required fees: $17 per term.
Financial support: Fellowships with full tuition reimbursements, research assistantships with full tuition reimbursements, teaching assistantships with full tuition reimbursements, career-related internships or fieldwork, Federal Work-Study, institutionally sponsored loans, and tuition waivers (partial) available. Support available to part-time students. Financial award application deadline: 3/31; financial award applicants required to submit FAFSA.
Faculty research: Quality control, optimization techniques, stochastic processes, computer automated manufacturing. *Total annual research expenditures:* $229,700.
Application contact: Dr. William Miller, Graduate Director, 813-974-5584, *Fax:* 813-974-5953, *E-mail:* miller@eng.usf.edu. *Web site:* http://www.eng.usf.edu/IE/industrial.html

■ **THE UNIVERSITY OF TENNESSEE**

Graduate School, College of Engineering, Department of Industrial Engineering, Knoxville, TN 37996

AWARDS Engineering management (MS); manufacturing systems engineering (MS); product development and manufacturing (MS); traditional industrial engineering (MS). Part-time programs available.
Postbaccalaureate distance learning degree programs offered (no on-campus study).

Faculty: 10 full-time (1 woman).
Students: 21 full-time (6 women), 70 part-time (15 women); includes 6 minority (4 African Americans, 2 Asian Americans or Pacific Islanders), 13 international. 56 applicants, 50% accepted. In 2001, 50 degrees awarded.
Degree requirements: For master's, thesis or alternative.
Entrance requirements: For master's, GRE General Test, TOEFL, minimum GPA of 2.7. *Application deadline:* For fall admission, 2/1 (priority date). Applications are processed on a rolling basis. *Application fee:* $35. Electronic applications accepted.
Expenses: Tuition, state resident: full-time $4,280; part-time $233 per hour. Tuition, nonresident: full-time $12,066; part-time $666 per hour. Tuition and fees vary according to program.
Financial support: In 2001–02, 1 fellowship, 5 research assistantships, 5 teaching assistantships were awarded. Career-related internships or fieldwork, Federal Work-Study, institutionally sponsored loans, and unspecified assistantships also available. Financial award application deadline: 2/1;

financial award applicants required to submit FAFSA.
Dr. Adedeji B. Badiru, Head, 865-974-3333, *Fax:* 865-974-0588, *E-mail:* abadiru@utk.edu.
Application contact: Dr. Denise Jackson, Graduate Representative, *E-mail:* djackson@utk.edu.

■ **THE UNIVERSITY OF TENNESSEE**

Graduate School, College of Engineering, Department of Mechanical and Aerospace Engineering and Engineering Science, Program in Engineering Science, Knoxville, TN 37996

AWARDS Applied artificial intelligence (MS); biomedical engineering (MS, PhD); composite materials (MS, PhD); computational mechanics (MS, PhD); engineering science (MS, PhD); fluid mechanics (MS, PhD); industrial engineering (PhD); optical engineering (MS, PhD); product development and manufacturing (MS). Solid mechanics (MS, PhD). Part-time programs available.

Students: 25 full-time (5 women), 16 part-time (2 women); includes 6 minority (2 African Americans, 2 Asian Americans or Pacific Islanders, 1 Hispanic American, 1 Native American), 9 international. 20 applicants, 70% accepted. In 2001, 6 master's, 6 doctorates awarded.
Degree requirements: For master's, thesis or alternative; for doctorate, thesis/dissertation.
Entrance requirements: For master's and doctorate, TOEFL, minimum GPA of 2.7. *Application deadline:* For fall admission, 2/1 (priority date). Applications are processed on a rolling basis. *Application fee:* $35. Electronic applications accepted.
Expenses: Tuition, state resident: full-time $4,280; part-time $233 per hour. Tuition, nonresident: full-time $12,066; part-time $666 per hour. Tuition and fees vary according to program.
Financial support: Career-related internships or fieldwork, Federal Work-Study, and institutionally sponsored loans available. Financial award application deadline: 2/1; financial award applicants required to submit FAFSA.
Application contact: Dr. Majid Keyhani, Graduate Representative, 865-974-4795, *E-mail:* keyhani@utk.edu.

■ **THE UNIVERSITY OF TEXAS AT ARLINGTON**

Graduate School, College of Engineering, Department of Industrial and Manufacturing Systems Engineering, Arlington, TX 76019

AWARDS M Engr, MS, PhD. Part-time and evening/weekend programs available.
Postbaccalaureate distance learning degree programs offered (no on-campus study).

Faculty: 8 full-time (2 women), 1 part-time/adjunct (0 women).
Students: 109 full-time (15 women), 37 part-time (7 women); includes 6 minority (3 African Americans, 3 Asian Americans or Pacific Islanders), 127 international. 279 applicants, 94% accepted, 54 enrolled. In 2001, 22 degrees awarded.
Degree requirements: For master's, thesis optional; for doctorate, thesis/dissertation, comprehensive exam.
Entrance requirements: For master's and doctorate, GRE General Test, TOEFL, minimum GPA of 3.0. *Application deadline:* For fall admission, 6/16. Applications are processed on a rolling basis. *Application fee:* $25 ($50 for international students).
Expenses: Tuition, area resident: Full-time $2,268. Tuition, nonresident: full-time $6,264. Required fees: $839. Tuition and fees vary according to course load.
Financial support: In 2001–02, 8 fellowships (averaging $1,000 per year), 15 research assistantships (averaging $8,400 per year), 15 teaching assistantships (averaging $9,000 per year) were awarded. Career-related internships or fieldwork, Federal Work-Study, institutionally sponsored loans, scholarships/grants, tuition waivers (partial), and unspecified assistantships also available. Financial award application deadline: 6/1; financial award applicants required to submit FAFSA.
Dr. Donald R. Liles, Chair, 817-272-3092, *Fax:* 817-272-3406, *E-mail:* dliles@uta.edu.
Application contact: Dr. Bill Corley, Graduate Adviser, 817-272-3159, *Fax:* 817-272-3406, *E-mail:* hwcorley@exchange.uta.edu.

■ **THE UNIVERSITY OF TEXAS AT AUSTIN**

Graduate School, College of Engineering, Department of Mechanical Engineering, Program in Operations Research and Industrial Engineering, Austin, TX 78712-1111

AWARDS MSE, PhD.

Students: 75 full-time (13 women), 10 part-time (3 women); includes 4 minority (2 African Americans, 2 Asian Americans or Pacific Islanders), 62 international. 193 applicants, 45% accepted. In 2001, 15 master's, 2 doctorates awarded.
Entrance requirements: For master's, GRE General Test, TOEFL; for doctorate, GRE General Test. *Application fee:* $50 ($75 for international students).
Expenses: Tuition, state resident: full-time $3,159. Tuition, nonresident: full-time $6,957. Tuition and fees vary according to program.
Financial support: Fellowships, research assistantships, teaching assistantships available. Financial award application deadline: 2/1.
Application contact: Dr. J. Wesley Barnes, Graduate Advisor, 512-471-3083, *Fax:* 512-471-8727.

■ THE UNIVERSITY OF TEXAS AT EL PASO

Graduate School, College of Engineering, Department of Mechanical and Industrial Engineering, Program in Industrial Engineering, El Paso, TX 79968-0001

AWARDS MS. Part-time and evening/weekend programs available.

Students: 29 (8 women); includes 6 minority (all Hispanic Americans) 11 international. Average age 34. 3 applicants, 100% accepted. In 2001, 9 degrees awarded.
Degree requirements: For master's, thesis optional.
Entrance requirements: For master's, GRE General Test, TOEFL, minimum GPA of 3.0 in major. *Application deadline:* For fall admission, 7/1 (priority date); for spring admission, 11/1 (priority date). Applications are processed on a rolling basis. *Application fee:* $15 ($65 for international students). Electronic applications accepted.
Expenses: Tuition, state resident: full-time $2,450. Tuition, nonresident: full-time $6,000.
Financial support: In 2001–02, research assistantships with partial tuition reimbursements (averaging $21,125 per year), teaching assistantships with partial tuition reimbursements (averaging $16,900 per year) were awarded. Fellowships with partial tuition reimbursements, Federal Work-Study, institutionally sponsored loans, scholarships/grants, and tuition waivers (partial) also available. Financial award application deadline: 3/15; financial award applicants required to submit FAFSA.
Faculty research: Computer vision, automated inspection, simulation and modeling.
Dr. Luis Contreras, Graduate Adviser, 915-747-5450, *Fax:* 915-747-5019, *E-mail:* lrcontreras@utep.edu.
Application contact: Dr. Charles H. Ambler, Dean of the Graduate School, 915-747-5491 Ext. 7886, *Fax:* 915-747-5788, *E-mail:* cambler@miners.utep.edu.

■ UNIVERSITY OF TOLEDO

Graduate School, College of Engineering, Department of Mechanical, Industrial, and Manufacturing Engineering, Toledo, OH 43606-3398

AWARDS Engineering sciences (PhD); industrial engineering (MS); mechanical engineering (MS). Part-time programs available. Postbaccalaureate distance learning degree programs offered (minimal on-campus study).

Faculty: 23 full-time (1 woman).
Students: 121 full-time (26 women), 76 part-time (6 women); includes 2 minority (both African Americans), 158 international. Average age 27. 673 applicants, 25% accepted. In 2001, 67 master's, 2 doctorates awarded.
Degree requirements: For master's, thesis optional; for doctorate, thesis/dissertation.
Entrance requirements: For master's, GRE General Test, TOEFL, minimum GPA of 2.7; for doctorate, GRE General Test, TOEFL, minimum GPA of 3.3. *Application deadline:* For fall admission, 5/31 (priority date). Applications are processed on a rolling basis. *Application fee:* $30. Electronic applications accepted.
Expenses: Tuition, state resident: full-time $7,278; part-time $303 per hour. Tuition, nonresident: full-time $15,731; part-time $699 per hour. Required fees: $43 per hour.
Financial support: In 2001–02, 188 students received support, including 1 fellowship with full tuition reimbursement available, 61 research assistantships with full tuition reimbursements available, 43 teaching assistantships with full tuition reimbursements available; Federal Work-Study, scholarships/grants, tuition waivers (full), and unspecified assistantships also available. Financial award application deadline: 4/1.
Faculty research: Computational and experimental thermal sciences, manufacturing process and systems, mechanics, materials, design, quality and management engineering systems. *Total annual research expenditures:* $2.7 million.
Dr. Abdollah A. Afjeh, Interim Chairman, 419-530-8210, *Fax:* 419-539-8214, *E-mail:* aafjch@eng.utoledo.edu.
Application contact: Dr. M. Samir Hefzy, Director of Graduate Program, 419-530-8234, *Fax:* 419-530-8206, *E-mail:* mhefzy@eng.utoledo.edu. *Web site:* http://www-mime.eng.utoledo.edu/

Find an in-depth description at www.petersons.com/gradchannel.

■ UNIVERSITY OF WASHINGTON

Graduate School, College of Engineering, Industrial Engineering Program, Seattle, WA 98195

AWARDS MSIE, PhD. Part-time programs available.

Faculty: 7 full-time (3 women), 13 part-time/adjunct (3 women).
Students: 43 full-time (18 women); includes 26 minority (all Asian Americans or Pacific Islanders). Average age 29. 100 applicants, 20% accepted, 13 enrolled. In 2001, 9 master's, 1 doctorate awarded. Terminal master's awarded for partial completion of doctoral program.
Degree requirements: For master's, thesis optional; for doctorate, thesis/dissertation.
Entrance requirements: For master's and doctorate, GRE General Test. *Application deadline:* For fall admission, 2/1 (priority date); for spring admission, 2/1. Applications are processed on a rolling basis. *Application fee:* $50. Electronic applications accepted.
Expenses: Tuition, state resident: full-time $5,539. Tuition, nonresident: full-time $14,376. Required fees: $390. Tuition and fees vary according to course load and program.
Financial support: In 2001–02, 22 students received support, including 1 fellowship (averaging $5,929 per year), 21 teaching assistantships with full tuition reimbursements available (averaging $15,120 per year); career-related internships or fieldwork, scholarships/grants, and traineeships also available. Financial award application deadline: 2/1.
Faculty research: Manufacturing, operations research, supply chain systems, human interface technology, quality control. *Total annual research expenditures:* $3.8 million.
Tony C. Woo, Director, 206-543-1541, *Fax:* 206-685-3072, *E-mail:* twoo@u.washington.edu.
Application contact: DJ Miller, Academic Counselor, 206-543-5041, *Fax:* 206-685-3072, *E-mail:* mrmiller@u.washington.edu. *Web site:* http://www.depts.washington.edu/ie

■ UNIVERSITY OF WISCONSIN–MADISON

Graduate School, College of Engineering, Department of Industrial Engineering, Madison, WI 53706-1380

AWARDS MS, PhD. Part-time programs available.

Faculty: 15 full-time (4 women), 1 (woman) part-time/adjunct.
Students: 130 full-time (38 women), 8 part-time (2 women); includes 7 minority (1 African American, 4 Asian Americans or Pacific Islanders, 2 Hispanic Americans), 106 international. 284 applicants, 51% accepted. In 2001, 28 master's, 7 doctorates awarded. Terminal master's awarded for partial completion of doctoral program.
Degree requirements: For master's, thesis optional; for doctorate, thesis/dissertation.
Entrance requirements: For master's, GRE General Test, minimum GPA of 3.0; for doctorate, GRE General Test, minimum GPA of 3.5. *Application deadline:* For fall admission, 4/1 (priority date); for spring admission, 10/1 (priority date). Applications are processed on a rolling basis. *Application fee:* $45. Electronic applications accepted.
Expenses: Tuition, state resident: full-time $7,361; part-time $399 per credit. Tuition, nonresident: full-time $20,499; part-time $1,282 per credit. Required fees: $34 per credit. Full-time tuition and fees vary according to course load, program, reciprocity agreements and student level.

University of Wisconsin–Madison (continued)

Financial support: In 2001–02, 92 students received support, including 3 fellowships with full tuition reimbursements available (averaging $18,293 per year), 35 research assistantships with full tuition reimbursements available (averaging $14,770 per year), 30 teaching assistantships with full tuition reimbursements available (averaging $9,489 per year); career-related internships or fieldwork, Federal Work-Study, and unspecified assistantships also available. Financial award application deadline: 12/1.
Faculty research: Human factors, manufacturing and production systems, quality, health systems, decision sciences/operations research. *Total annual research expenditures:* $10.1 million.
Prof. Harold J. Steudel, Chair, 608-262-9927, *Fax:* 608-262-8454, *E-mail:* steudel@engr.wisc.edu.
Application contact: Lisa A. Zovar, Student Status Examiner II, 608-263-3955, *Fax:* 608-262-8454, *E-mail:* lzovar@engr.wisc.edu. *Web site:* http://www.engr.wisc.edu/ie/

■ VIRGINIA POLYTECHNIC INSTITUTE AND STATE UNIVERSITY

Graduate School, College of Engineering, Department of Industrial and Systems Engineering, Program in Industrial Engineering, Blacksburg, VA 24061

AWARDS M Eng, MS, PhD.

Degree requirements: For master's and doctorate, thesis/dissertation.
Entrance requirements: For master's, TOEFL; for doctorate, TOEFL, minimum GPA of 3.0. *Application deadline:* For fall admission, 12/1 (priority date). Applications are processed on a rolling basis. *Application fee:* $45. Electronic applications accepted.
Expenses: Tuition, state resident: part-time $241 per hour. Tuition, nonresident: part-time $406 per hour. Tuition and fees vary according to program.
Financial support: Application deadline: 4/1.
Application contact: Lovedia S. Cole, Graduate Secretary, 540-231-5586, *Fax:* 540-231-3322, *E-mail:* lovediac@vt.edu.

■ WAYNE STATE UNIVERSITY

Graduate School, College of Engineering, Department of Industrial and Manufacturing Engineering, Program in Industrial Engineering, Detroit, MI 48202

AWARDS MS, PhD.

Students: 148. In 2001, 18 master's, 6 doctorates awarded.

Degree requirements: For master's, thesis optional; for doctorate, thesis/dissertation.
Entrance requirements: For master's, minimum undergraduate GPA of 2.8; for doctorate, minimum graduate GPA of 3.5. *Application deadline:* For fall admission, 7/1 (priority date); for spring admission, 3/15. Applications are processed on a rolling basis. *Application fee:* $20 ($30 for international students). Electronic applications accepted.
Expenses: Tuition, state resident: full-time $3,764. Tuition and fees vary according to degree level and program.
Financial support: Fellowships, research assistantships, teaching assistantships, career-related internships or fieldwork available.
Faculty research: Reliability and quality, technology management, manufacturing systems, operations research, concurrent engineering.
Application contact: Olugbenga Mejabi, Graduate Director, 313-577-3134, *E-mail:* mejabi@mie.eng.wayne.edu.

■ WESTERN CAROLINA UNIVERSITY

Graduate School, College of Applied Science, Department of Engineering Technology, Cullowhee, NC 28723

AWARDS MS. Part-time and evening/weekend programs available.

Faculty: 4 full-time (0 women).
Students: 3 full-time (0 women), 2 part-time. 3 applicants, 67% accepted, 2 enrolled. In 2001, 3 degrees awarded.
Degree requirements: For master's, comprehensive exam.
Entrance requirements: For master's, GRE General Test. *Application deadline:* For fall admission, 5/1 (priority date); for spring admission, 10/1 (priority date). Applications are processed on a rolling basis. *Application fee:* $35.
Expenses: Tuition, state resident: full-time $1,072. Tuition, nonresident: full-time $8,704. Required fees: $1,171.
Financial support: In 2001–02, 3 students received support, including 1 research assistantship with full and partial tuition reimbursement available (averaging $2,500 per year), 2 teaching assistantships (averaging $5,004 per year); fellowships, Federal Work-Study, institutionally sponsored loans, and scholarships/grants also available. Financial award application deadline: 3/15; financial award applicants required to submit FAFSA.
Dr. Duane Dunlap, Head, 828-227-7272, *E-mail:* ddunlap@email.wcu.edu.
Application contact: Josie Bewsey, Assistant to the Dean, 828-227-7398, *Fax:* 828-227-7480, *E-mail:* jbewsey@email.wcu.edu. *Web site:* http://et.wcu.edu

■ WESTERN MICHIGAN UNIVERSITY

Graduate College, College of Engineering and Applied Sciences, Department of Industrial and Manufacturing Engineering, Program in Industrial Engineering, Kalamazoo, MI 49008-5202

AWARDS MSE.

Faculty: 25 full-time (3 women).
Students: 67 full-time (7 women), 10 part-time (2 women); includes 4 minority (3 African Americans, 1 Asian American or Pacific Islander), 62 international. 191 applicants, 61% accepted, 33 enrolled. In 2001, 13 degrees awarded.
Entrance requirements: For master's, minimum GPA of 3.0. *Application deadline:* For fall admission, 2/15 (priority date). Applications are processed on a rolling basis. *Application fee:* $25.
Expenses: Tuition, state resident: part-time $186 per credit hour. Tuition, nonresident: part-time $442 per credit hour. Required fees: $602. One-time fee: $132 part-time. Tuition and fees vary according to course load.
Financial support: Application deadline: 2/15.
Application contact: Admissions and Orientation, 616-387-2000, *Fax:* 616-387-2355.

■ WESTERN NEW ENGLAND COLLEGE

School of Engineering, Department of Industrial and Manufacturing Engineering, Springfield, MA 01119-2654

AWARDS Production management (MSEM). Part-time and evening/weekend programs available.

Faculty: 4 full-time (0 women), 2 part-time/adjunct (0 women).
Students: Average age 29. 3 applicants, 67% accepted. In 2001, 6 degrees awarded.
Degree requirements: For master's, thesis optional.
Entrance requirements: For master's, GRE, bachelor's degree in engineering or related field. *Application deadline:* Applications are processed on a rolling basis. *Application fee:* $30.
Expenses: Tuition: Part-time $429 per credit. Required fees: $9 per credit. $20 per semester.
Financial support: Teaching assistantships available. Support available to part-time students. Financial award application deadline: 4/1; financial award applicants required to submit FAFSA.
Faculty research: Project scheduling, flexible manufacturing systems, facility layout, energy management.
Dr. Eric W. Haffner, Chair, 413-782-1272, *E-mail:* ehaffner@wnec.edu.

Application contact: Dr. Janet Castleman, Director of Continuing Education, 413-782-1750, *Fax:* 413-782-1779, *E-mail:* jcastlem@wnec.edu.

■ WEST VIRGINIA UNIVERSITY

College of Engineering and Mineral Resources, Department of Industrial and Management Systems Engineering, Program in Industrial Engineering, Morgantown, WV 26506

AWARDS Engineering (MSE); industrial engineering (MSIE, PhD). Part-time programs available.

Students: 42 full-time (7 women), 4 part-time, 40 international. Average age 24. 90 applicants, 79% accepted. In 2001, 17 master's, 3 doctorates awarded.
Degree requirements: For master's, thesis or alternative; for doctorate, thesis/dissertation, comprehensive exam.
Entrance requirements: For master's, GRE General Test, TOEFL, minimum GPA of 3.0; for doctorate; GRE General Test, TOEFL, minimum GPA of 3.5. *Application deadline:* For fall admission, 6/15 (priority date). Applications are processed on a rolling basis. *Application fee:* $45.
Expenses: Tuition, state resident: full-time $2,791. Tuition, nonresident: full-time $8,659. Required fees: $1,002. Tuition and fees vary according to program.
Financial support: In 2001–02, 20 research assistantships, 7 teaching assistantships were awarded. Fellowships, Federal Work-Study, institutionally sponsored loans, and tuition waivers (full and partial) also available. Financial award application deadline: 4/1; financial award applicants required to submit FAFSA.
Faculty research: Production planning and control, quality control, robotics and CIMS, ergonomics, castings.
Application contact: Dr. Wafik H. Iskander, Graduate Program Coordinator, 304-293-4607 Ext. 3710, *Fax:* 304-293-4970, *E-mail:* wafik.iskander@mail.wvu.edu.

■ WICHITA STATE UNIVERSITY

Graduate School, College of Engineering, Department of Industrial and Manufacturing Engineering, Wichita, KS 67260

AWARDS MEM, MS, PhD. Part-time programs available.

Faculty: 9 full-time (0 women).
Students: 85 full-time (3 women), 76 part-time (16 women); includes 8 minority (3 African Americans, 3 Asian Americans or Pacific Islanders, 2 Hispanic Americans), 120 international. Average age 29. 218 applicants, 78% accepted, 44 enrolled. In 2001, 26 degrees awarded.
Degree requirements: For master's, thesis optional; for doctorate, one foreign language, thesis/dissertation, comprehensive exam.

Entrance requirements: For master's, GRE, TOEFL; for doctorate, GRE General Test, TOEFL. *Application deadline:* For fall admission, 7/1 (priority date); for spring admission, 1/1. Applications are processed on a rolling basis. *Application fee:* $25 ($40 for international students). Electronic applications accepted.
Expenses: Tuition, state resident: full-time $1,888; part-time $105 per credit. Tuition, nonresident: full-time $6,129; part-time $341 per credit. Required fees: $345; $19 per credit. $17 per semester. Tuition and fees vary according to course load and program.
Financial support: In 2001–02, 47 research assistantships (averaging $4,673 per year), 12 teaching assistantships with full tuition reimbursements (averaging $4,108 per year) were awarded. Fellowships, Federal Work-Study, institutionally sponsored loans, and unspecified assistantships also available. Support available to part-time students. Financial award application deadline: 4/1; financial award applicants required to submit FAFSA.
Faculty research: Ergonomics, rehabilitation, operations research, reverse engineering, assembly design/planning.
Dr. Abu Masud, Chairperson, 316-978-3425, *Fax:* 316-978-3742, *E-mail:* abu.masud@wichita.edu. *Web site:* http://www.wichita.edu/

■ YOUNGSTOWN STATE UNIVERSITY

Graduate School, William Rayen College of Engineering, Department of Mechanical and Industrial Engineering, Youngstown, OH 44555-0001

AWARDS MSE. Part-time and evening/weekend programs available.

Degree requirements: For master's, thesis optional.
Entrance requirements: For master's, TOEFL, minimum GPA of 2.75 in field.
Faculty research: Kinematics and dynamics of machines, computational and experimental heat transfer, machine controls and mechanical design.

MANUFACTURING ENGINEERING

■ ARIZONA STATE UNIVERSITY EAST

College of Technology and Applied Sciences, Department of Manufacturing and Aeronautical Engineering Technology, Mesa, AZ 85212

AWARDS MS. Part-time and evening/weekend programs available.

Faculty: 6 full-time (0 women), 1 part-time/adjunct (0 women).
Students: 8 full-time (0 women), 8 part-time (1 woman); includes 1 minority (Hispanic American), 6 international. Average age 29. 16 applicants, 56% accepted, 4 enrolled. In 2001, 5 degrees awarded.
Degree requirements: For master's, thesis or applied project and oral defense. *Median time to degree:* Master's–2.5 years part-time.
Entrance requirements: For master's, GRE Subject Test (science and mathematics), TOEFL. *Application deadline:* Applications are processed on a rolling basis. *Application fee:* $45. Electronic applications accepted.
Expenses: Tuition, state resident: full-time $2,412; part-time $126 per credit hour. Tuition, nonresident: full-time $10,278; part-time $428 per credit hour. Required fees: $26. Tuition and fees vary according to course load.
Financial support: In 2001–02, 9 students received support, including 5 research assistantships with partial tuition reimbursements available (averaging $3,325 per year); teaching assistantships, career-related internships or fieldwork, Federal Work-Study, scholarships/grants, tuition waivers (full and partial), and unspecified assistantships also available. Support available to part-time students. Financial award application deadline: 3/1; financial award applicants required to submit FAFSA.
Faculty research: Manufacturing modeling and simulation. Semiconductor fabrication process; "smart" materials (composite materials, hydrogen generation, optimization of turbine engines, and machinability and manufacturing processes design). *Total annual research expenditures:* $55,051.
Dr. Scott Danielson, Chair, 480-727-1185, *Fax:* 480-727-1549, *E-mail:* scottda@asu.edu.

■ BOSTON UNIVERSITY

College of Engineering, Department of Manufacturing Engineering, Boston, MA 02215

AWARDS MS, PhD, MBA/MS. Part-time programs available. Postbaccalaureate distance learning degree programs offered (no on-campus study).

Faculty: 21 full-time (2 women), 6 part-time/adjunct (0 women).
Students: 54 full-time (7 women), 15 part-time (4 women); includes 3 minority (2 Asian Americans or Pacific Islanders, 1 Hispanic American), 43 international. Average age 27. 95 applicants, 41% accepted; 23 enrolled. In 2001, 27 master's, 4 doctorates awarded. Terminal master's awarded for partial completion of doctoral program.
Degree requirements: For master's, thesis optional; for doctorate, thesis/dissertation, comprehensive exam.

Boston University (continued)

Entrance requirements: For master's and doctorate, GRE General Test or GMAT Test, TOEFL. *Application deadline:* For fall admission, 4/1; for spring admission, 10/1. Applications are processed on a rolling basis. *Application fee:* $60. Electronic applications accepted.

Expenses: Tuition: Full-time $25,872; part-time $340 per credit. Required fees: $40 per semester. Part-time tuition and fees vary according to class time, course level and program.

Financial support: In 2001–02, 38 students received support, including 5 fellowships with full tuition reimbursements available (averaging $15,500 per year), 17 research assistantships with full tuition reimbursements available (averaging $13,500 per year), 8 teaching assistantships with full tuition reimbursements available (averaging $13,500 per year); career-related internships or fieldwork, Federal Work-Study, institutionally sponsored loans, and scholarships/grants also available. Financial award application deadline: 1/15; financial award applicants required to submit FAFSA.

Faculty research: Automation, environment-friendly manufacturing, micro-electro mechanical systems, process control, systems engineering. *Total annual research expenditures:* $5.6 million.

Dr. Thomas Bifano, Chairman, 617-353-6373.

Application contact: Cheryl Kelley, Director of Graduate Programs, 617-353-9760, *Fax:* 617-353-0259, *E-mail:* enggrad@bu.edu. *Web site:* http://www.bu.edu/eng/grad/

Find an in-depth description at www.petersons.com/gradchannel.

■ BOWLING GREEN STATE UNIVERSITY

Graduate College, College of Technology, Department of Technology Systems, Bowling Green, OH 43403

AWARDS Manufacturing technology (MIT). Part-time programs available.

Faculty: 10.

Students: 10 full-time (1 woman), 12 part-time (1 woman); includes 1 minority (African American), 6 international. Average age 31. 12 applicants, 67% accepted, 5 enrolled. In 2001, 2 degrees awarded.

Degree requirements: For master's, thesis or alternative.

Entrance requirements: For master's, GRE General Test, TOEFL, minimum GPA of 3.0. *Application deadline:* For fall admission, 3/1. *Application fee:* $30. Electronic applications accepted.

Expenses: Tuition, state resident: full-time $7,376; part-time $342 per credit hour. Tuition, nonresident: full-time $13,628; part-time $640 per credit hour.

Financial support: Research assistantships with full tuition reimbursements, teaching assistantships with full tuition reimbursements, career-related internships or fieldwork, Federal Work-Study, institutionally sponsored loans, tuition waivers (full and partial), and unspecified assistantships available. Financial award applicants required to submit FAFSA.

Dr. Thomas Andrews, Chair, 419-372-2439.

Application contact: Dr. Donna Trautmen, Graduate Coordinator, 419-372-7575.

■ BRADLEY UNIVERSITY

Graduate School, College of Engineering and Technology, Department of Industrial and Manufacturing Engineering and Technology, Peoria, IL 61625-0002

AWARDS MSIE, MSMFE. Part-time and evening/weekend programs available.

Students: 13 full-time, 33 part-time. 92 applicants, 79% accepted. In 2001, 23 degrees awarded.

Degree requirements: For master's, project.

Entrance requirements: For master's, TOEFL, minimum GPA of 3.0. *Application deadline:* For fall admission, 7/1 (priority date); for spring admission, 11/1. Applications are processed on a rolling basis. *Application fee:* $40 ($50 for international students).

Expenses: Tuition: Part-time $7,615 per semester. Tuition and fees vary according to course load.

Financial support: In 2001–02, 5 research assistantships with full and partial tuition reimbursements were awarded. Scholarships/grants and tuition waivers (partial) also available. Financial award application deadline: 3/1.

Dr. Joseph Emanuel, Chairperson, 309-677-2742.

Application contact: Dr. Fred Tayyari, Graduate Adviser, 309-677-2748.

■ BRIGHAM YOUNG UNIVERSITY

Graduate Studies, College of Engineering and Technology, School of Technology, Provo, UT 84602-1001

AWARDS Engineering technology (MS); technology teacher education (MS).

Faculty: 24 full-time (0 women).

Students: 11 full-time (0 women), 13 part-time; includes 1 minority (Asian American or Pacific Islander), 4 international. Average age 25. 15 applicants, 73% accepted. In 2001, 11 degrees awarded.

Degree requirements: For master's, thesis (for some programs).

Entrance requirements: For master's, GRE General Test, minimum GPA of 3.0 in last 60 hours. *Application deadline:* For fall admission, 2/28. *Application fee:* $50. Electronic applications accepted.

Expenses: Tuition: Full-time $3,860; part-time $214 per hour.

Financial support: In 2001–02, 18 students received support; fellowships, research assistantships, teaching assistantships, career-related internships or fieldwork available. Financial award application deadline: 3/15.

Faculty research: Composites, plasma treatment, geometric modeling, robotics, manufacturing control, product design.

Thomas L. Erekson, Director, 801-378-6300, *Fax:* 801-378-7575, *E-mail:* erekson@byu.edu.

Application contact: Graduate Coordinator, 801-378-6300, *Fax:* 801-378-7575, *E-mail:* ralowe@byu.edu. *Web site:* http://www.et.byu.edu/abet-sot/

■ CALIFORNIA POLYTECHNIC STATE UNIVERSITY, SAN LUIS OBISPO

College of Engineering, Program in Engineering, San Luis Obispo, CA 93407

AWARDS Biochemical engineering (MS); industrial engineering (MS); integrated technology management (MS); materials engineering (MS); water engineering (MS), including bioengineering, biomedical engineering, manufacturing engineering.

Faculty: 98 full-time (8 women), 82 part-time/adjunct (14 women).

Students: 20 full-time (4 women), 9 part-time (1 woman). 25 applicants, 68% accepted, 15 enrolled. In 2001, 22 degrees awarded.

Entrance requirements: For master's, GRE General Test, minimum GPA of 2.5 in last 90 quarter units. *Application fee:* $55.

Expenses: Tuition, nonresident: part-time $164 per unit. One-time fee: $2,153 part-time.

Financial support: Application deadline: 3/2.

Dr. Peter Y. Lee, Dean, 805-756-2131, *Fax:* 805-756-6503, *E-mail:* plee@calpoly.edu.

Application contact: Dr. Daniel W. Walsh, Associate Dean, 805-756-2131, *Fax:* 805-756-6503, *E-mail:* dwalsh@calpoly.edu. *Web site:* http://www.synner.ceng.calpoly.edu/

■ COLORADO STATE UNIVERSITY

Graduate School, College of Engineering, Department of Mechanical Engineering, Fort Collins, CO 80523-0015

AWARDS Bioengineering (MS, PhD); energy and environmental engineering (MS, PhD); energy conversion (MS, PhD); engineering management (MS); heat and mass transfer (MS, PhD); industrial and manufacturing systems engineering (MS, PhD); mechanical engineering (MS, PhD); mechanics and materials (MS, PhD). Part-time programs available.

Faculty: 17 full-time (2 women).
Students: 36 full-time (6 women), 63 part-time (11 women); includes 5 minority (2 Asian Americans or Pacific Islanders, 2 Hispanic Americans, 1 Native American), 22 international. Average age 32. 234 applicants, 83% accepted, 32 enrolled. In 2001, 10 master's, 3 doctorates awarded. Terminal master's awarded for partial completion of doctoral program.
Degree requirements: For doctorate, thesis/dissertation.
Entrance requirements: For master's and doctorate, GRE General Test, TOEFL, minimum GPA of 3.0. *Application deadline:* For fall admission, 2/1 (priority date). Applications are processed on a rolling basis. *Application fee:* $30. Electronic applications accepted.
Expenses: Tuition, state resident: full-time $2,880; part-time $160 per credit. Tuition, nonresident: full-time $11,412; part-time $634 per credit. Required fees: $750; $34 per credit.
Financial support: In 2001–02, 2 fellowships, 15 research assistantships (averaging $15,792 per year), 14 teaching assistantships (averaging $11,844 per year) were awarded. Traineeships also available.
Faculty research: Space propulsion, controls and systems, engineering and materials. *Total annual research expenditures:* $2.1 million.
Dr. Allan T. Kirkpatrick, Head, 970-491-6559, *Fax:* 970-491-3827, *E-mail:* allan@engr.colostate.edu. *Web site:* http://www.engr.colostate.edu/depts/me/index.html

■ CORNELL UNIVERSITY

Graduate School, Graduate Fields of Engineering, Field of Operations Research and Industrial Engineering, Ithaca, NY 14853-0001

AWARDS Applied probability and statistics (PhD); manufacturing systems engineering (PhD); mathematical programming (PhD); operations research and industrial engineering (M Eng).

Faculty: 28 full-time.
Students: 109 full-time (19 women); includes 17 minority (1 African American, 15 Asian Americans or Pacific Islanders, 1 Hispanic American), 66 international. 380 applicants, 53% accepted. In 2001, 87 master's, 4 doctorates awarded. Terminal master's awarded for partial completion of doctoral program.
Degree requirements: For doctorate, thesis/dissertation.
Entrance requirements: For master's and doctorate, GRE General Test, TOEFL, 3 letters of recommendation. *Application deadline:* For fall admission, 1/15 (priority date). *Application fee:* $65. Electronic applications accepted.

Expenses: Tuition: Full-time $25,970. Required fees: $50.
Financial support: In 2001–02, 41 students received support, including 13 fellowships with full tuition reimbursements available, 8 research assistantships with full tuition reimbursements available, 20 teaching assistantships with full tuition reimbursements available; institutionally sponsored loans, scholarships/grants, tuition waivers (full and partial), and unspecified assistantships also available. Financial award applicants required to submit FAFSA.
Faculty research: Mathematical programming and combinatorial optimization, statistics, stochastic processes, mathematical finance, simulation, manufacturing.
Application contact: Graduate Field Assistant, 607-255-9128, *E-mail:* orphd@cornell.edu. *Web site:* http://www.gradschool.cornell.edu/grad/fields_1/oper-res.html

Find an in-depth description at www.petersons.com/gradchannel.

■ DREXEL UNIVERSITY

Graduate School, College of Engineering, Mechanical Engineering and Mechanics Department, Philadelphia, PA 19104-2875

AWARDS Manufacturing engineering (MS, PhD); mechanical engineering and mechanics (MS, PhD). Part-time and evening/weekend programs available.

Faculty: 22 full-time (0 women), 1 part-time/adjunct (0 women).
Students: 19 full-time (2 women), 69 part-time (7 women); includes 15 minority (4 African Americans, 8 Asian Americans or Pacific Islanders, 2 Hispanic Americans, 1 Native American), 32 international. Average age 30. 124 applicants, 88% accepted, 14 enrolled. In 2001, 20 master's, 2 doctorates awarded. Terminal master's awarded for partial completion of doctoral program.
Degree requirements: For master's, thesis optional; for doctorate, thesis/dissertation.
Entrance requirements: For master's, TOEFL, minimum GPA of 3.0, BS in engineering or science; for doctorate, TOEFL, minimum GPA of 3.5, MS in engineering or science. *Application deadline:* For fall admission, 8/21. Applications are processed on a rolling basis. *Application fee:* $50. Electronic applications accepted.
Expenses: Tuition: Full-time $20,088; part-time $558 per credit. Required fees: $78 per term. One-time fee: $200. Tuition and fees vary according to course load, degree level and program.
Financial support: Research assistantships, teaching assistantships, unspecified assistantships available. Financial award application deadline: 2/1.

Faculty research: Composites, dynamic systems and control, combustion and fuels, biomechanics, mechanics and thermal fluid sciences.
Dr. Mun Young Choi, Acting Head, 215-895-2284, *Fax:* 215-895-1478, *E-mail:* mem@drexel.edu.
Application contact: Director of Graduate Admissions, 215-895-6700, *Fax:* 215-895-5939, *E-mail:* enroll@drexel.edu.

Find an in-depth description at www.petersons.com/gradchannel.

■ EASTERN KENTUCKY UNIVERSITY

The Graduate School, College of Business and Technology, Department of Technology, Richmond, KY 40475-3102

AWARDS Industrial education (MS), including industrial training, technology education, vocational administration; industrial technology (MS). Part-time and evening/weekend programs available.

Faculty: 7 full-time (0 women), 1 part-time/adjunct (0 women).
Students: 3 full-time (1 woman), 99 part-time (29 women); includes 7 minority (6 African Americans, 1 Hispanic American), 1 international. 50 applicants, 70% accepted. In 2001, 31 degrees awarded.
Entrance requirements: For master's, GRE General Test, minimum GPA of 2.5. *Application fee:* $0.
Expenses: Tuition, state resident: full-time $1,468; part-time $165 per credit hour. Tuition, nonresident: full-time $4,034; part-time $450 per credit hour.
Financial support: In 2001–02, 2 students received support; research assistantships, teaching assistantships, Federal Work-Study available. Support available to part-time students.
Faculty research: Lunar excavation, computer networking, integrating academic and vocational education.
William E. Davis, Chair, 859-622-3232. *Web site:* http://157.89.19.144/TEC/homepage.htm

■ EAST TENNESSEE STATE UNIVERSITY

School of Graduate Studies, College of Applied Science and Technology, Department of Technology, Johnson City, TN 37614

AWARDS Engineering technology (MS); industrial arts/technology education (MS). Part-time programs available.

Faculty: 10 full-time (1 woman).
Students: 38 full-time (8 women), 23 part-time (3 women); includes 4 minority (1 African American, 3 Asian Americans or Pacific Islanders), 4 international. Average age 32. In 2001, 30 degrees awarded.
Degree requirements: For master's, thesis or alternative, final oral exam.

East Tennessee State University (continued)

Entrance requirements: For master's, TOEFL, bachelor's degree in technical or related area, minimum GPA of 3.0. *Application deadline:* For fall admission, 7/15 (priority date); for spring admission, 11/15. Applications are processed on a rolling basis. *Application fee:* $25 ($35 for international students).
Expenses: Tuition, state resident: part-time $181 per hour. Tuition, nonresident: part-time $270 per hour. Required fees: $220 per term.
Financial support: Research assistantships with full tuition reimbursements, teaching assistantships with full tuition reimbursements, career-related internships or fieldwork and Federal Work-Study available. Support available to part-time students. Financial award application deadline: 7/1; financial award applicants required to submit FAFSA.
Faculty research: Computer-integrated manufacturing, technology education, CAD/CAM, organizational change. *Total annual research expenditures:* $39,024.
Dr. Keith V. Johnson, Chair, 423-439-7813, *Fax:* 423-439-7750, *E-mail:* johnsonk@etsu.edu. *Web site:* http://www.etsu.edu/

■ FLORIDA ATLANTIC UNIVERSITY

College of Engineering, Department of Mechanical Engineering, Program in Manufacturing Systems Engineering, Boca Raton, FL 33431-0991

AWARDS MS. Part-time and evening/weekend programs available.
Faculty: 3 full-time (0 women).
Students: 3 full-time (2 women), 5 part-time (1 woman), 4 international. Average age 36. 6 applicants, 67% accepted, 2 enrolled. In 2001, 2 degrees awarded.
Degree requirements: For master's, thesis optional.
Entrance requirements: For master's, GRE General Test, TOEFL, minimum GPA of 3.0. *Application deadline:* For fall admission, 4/10 (priority date); for spring admission, 10/1. Applications are processed on a rolling basis. *Application fee:* $20.
Expenses: Tuition, state resident: full-time $3,098; part-time $172 per credit. Tuition, nonresident: full-time $10,427; part-time $579 per credit.
Financial support: Research assistantships, teaching assistantships, career-related internships or fieldwork and Federal Work-Study available. Support available to part-time students. Financial award application deadline: 4/1; financial award applicants required to submit FAFSA.
Faculty research: Packaging, materials handling, design for manufacture, robotics, automation.
Application contact: Patricia Capozziello, Graduate Admissions Coordinator, 561-297-2694, *Fax:* 561-297-2659, *E-mail:*

capozzie@fau.edu. *Web site:* http://www.me.fau.edu/

■ GRAND VALLEY STATE UNIVERSITY

Science and Mathematics Division, Seymour and Esther Padnos School of Engineering, Allendale, MI 49401-9403

AWARDS Manufacturing engineering (MSE); manufacturing operations (MSE); mechanical engineering (MSE). Part-time programs available.
Faculty: 10 full-time (1 woman), 3 part-time/adjunct (1 woman).
Students: 5 full-time (1 woman), 42 part-time (7 women); includes 4 minority (1 African American, 2 Asian Americans or Pacific Islanders, 1 Hispanic American), 2 international. Average age 31. 37 applicants, 57% accepted, 15 enrolled. In 2001, 2 degrees awarded.
Degree requirements: For master's, project. *Median time to degree:* Master's–3 years part-time.
Entrance requirements: For master's, engineering degree with minimum GPA of 3.0. *Application deadline:* Applications are processed on a rolling basis. *Application fee:* $20.
Expenses: Tuition, state resident: part-time $202 per credit hour. Tuition, nonresident: part-time $437 per credit hour.
Financial support: In 2001–02, 2 research assistantships with full tuition reimbursements (averaging $11,000 per year), 3 teaching assistantships with full tuition reimbursements (averaging $8,000 per year) were awarded. Career-related internships or fieldwork, Federal Work-Study, institutionally sponsored loans, scholarships/grants, and unspecified assistantships also available.
Faculty research: Digital signal processing, computer aided design, computer aided manufacturing, manufacturing simulation, biomechanics. *Total annual research expenditures:* $300,000.
Dr. Paul Plotkowski, Director, 616-771-6750, *Fax:* 616-336-7215, *E-mail:* plotkowp@gvsu.edu.
Application contact: Dr. Hugh Jack, Graduate Coordinator, 616-771-6750, *Fax:* 616-336-7215, *E-mail:* jackh@gvsu.edu. *Web site:* http://www.engineer.gvsu.edu/

■ ILLINOIS INSTITUTE OF TECHNOLOGY

Graduate College, Armour College of Engineering and Sciences, Department of Electrical and Computer Engineering, Chicago, IL 60616-3793

AWARDS Computer systems engineering (MS); electrical and computer engineering (MECE); electrical engineering (MS, PhD);

manufacturing engineering (MME, MS). Part-time and evening/weekend programs available.
Faculty: 20 full-time (2 women), 7 part-time/adjunct (0 women).
Students: 157 full-time (26 women), 212 part-time (21 women); includes 34 minority (4 African Americans, 21 Asian Americans or Pacific Islanders, 9 Hispanic Americans), 259 international. Average age 27. 1,295 applicants, 52% accepted. In 2001, 93 master's, 8 doctorates awarded. Terminal master's awarded for partial completion of doctoral program.
Degree requirements: For master's, thesis (for some programs), comprehensive exam; for doctorate, thesis/dissertation, comprehensive exam.
Entrance requirements: For master's and doctorate, GRE General Test, TOEFL, minimum undergraduate GPA of 3.0. *Application deadline:* For fall admission, 7/1; for spring admission, 12/1. Applications are processed on a rolling basis. *Application fee:* $30. Electronic applications accepted.
Expenses: Tuition: Part-time $590 per credit hour.
Financial support: In 2001–02, 13 research assistantships, 19 teaching assistantships were awarded. Federal Work-Study, institutionally sponsored loans, scholarships/grants, and unspecified assistantships also available. Support available to part-time students. Financial award application deadline: 3/1; financial award applicants required to submit FAFSA.
Faculty research: Computer system design, photonics, biomedical engineering, power systems analysis, communications theory. *Total annual research expenditures:* $585,216.
Dr. Thomas Wong, Interim Chairman, 312-567-5786, *Fax:* 312-567-8976, *E-mail:* wong@iit.edu.
Application contact: Dr. Ali Cinar, Dean of Graduate College, 312-567-3637, *Fax:* 312-567-7517, *E-mail:* gradstu@iit.edu. *Web site:* http://www.ece.iit.edu/

■ ILLINOIS INSTITUTE OF TECHNOLOGY

Graduate College, Armour College of Engineering and Sciences, Department of Mechanical, Materials and Aerospace Engineering, Chicago, IL 60616-3793

AWARDS Manufacturing engineering (MME, MS); mechanical and aerospace engineering (MMAE, MS, PhD); metallurgical and materials engineering (MMME, MS, PhD). Part-time programs available.
Faculty: 25 full-time (3 women), 11 part-time/adjunct (0 women).
Students: 74 full-time (11 women), 72 part-time (3 women); includes 11 minority (1 African American, 8 Asian Americans or Pacific Islanders, 2 Hispanic Americans), 102 international. Average age 27. 606 applicants, 40% accepted. In 2001, 40

master's, 2 doctorates awarded. Terminal master's awarded for partial completion of doctoral program.

Degree requirements: For master's, thesis (for some programs), comprehensive exam; for doctorate, thesis/dissertation, comprehensive exam.

Entrance requirements: For master's and doctorate, GRE General Test, TOEFL, minimum undergraduate GPA of 3.0. *Application deadline:* For fall admission, 7/1; for spring admission, 11/1. Applications are processed on a rolling basis. *Application fee:* $30. Electronic applications accepted.

Expenses: Tuition: Part-time $590 per credit hour.

Financial support: In 2001–02, 1 fellowship, 15 research assistantships, 11 teaching assistantships were awarded. Federal Work-Study, institutionally sponsored loans, scholarships/grants, and unspecified assistantships also available. Support available to part-time students. Financial award application deadline: 3/1; financial award applicants required to submit FAFSA.

Faculty research: Computer-integrated manufacturing, mechanics of solids, biomechanics, fluid dynamics, railroad engineering. *Total annual research expenditures:* $988,318.

Dr. Jamal Yagoobi, Chair, 312-567-3239, *Fax:* 312-567-7230, *E-mail:* yagoobi@iit.edu.

Application contact: Dr. Ali Cinar, Dean of Graduate College, 312-567-3637, *Fax:* 312-567-7517, *E-mail:* gradstu@iit.edu. *Web site:* http://www.mmae.iit.edu/

■ KANSAS STATE UNIVERSITY

Graduate School, College of Engineering, Department of Industrial and Manufacturing Systems Engineering, Manhattan, KS 66506

AWARDS Engineering management (MEM); industrial and manufacturing systems engineering (PhD); industrial engineering (MS); operations research (MS). Part-time programs available. Postbaccalaureate distance learning degree programs offered.

Faculty: 11 full-time (1 woman).
Students: 30 full-time (7 women), 24 part-time (2 women), 31 international. 201 applicants, 49% accepted, 19 enrolled. In 2001, 5 master's, 1 doctorate awarded.
Degree requirements: For master's, thesis or alternative; for doctorate, thesis/dissertation.
Entrance requirements: For master's, GRE General Test, TOEFL, bachelor's degree in engineering, mathematics, or physical science; for doctorate, GRE General Test, TOEFL, master's degree in engineering or industrial manufacturing. *Application deadline:* For fall admission, 3/1 (priority date); for spring admission, 9/1. Applications are processed on a rolling basis. *Application fee:* $0 ($25 for international students). Electronic applications accepted.

Expenses: Tuition, state resident: part-time $113 per credit hour. Tuition, nonresident: part-time $358 per credit hour.
Financial support: In 2001–02, 18 research assistantships with partial tuition reimbursements (averaging $9,000 per year), 2 teaching assistantships with full tuition reimbursements (averaging $9,000 per year) were awarded. Federal Work-Study, institutionally sponsored loans, and scholarships/grants also available. Support available to part-time students. Financial award application deadline: 3/1; financial award applicants required to submit FAFSA.

Faculty research: Manufacturing engineering, operations research, engineering management, quality engineering, ergonomics. *Total annual research expenditures:* $1.7 million.

Dr. Bradley Kramer, Head, 785-532-5606, *Fax:* 785-532-7810, *E-mail:* bradleyk@ksu.edu.

Application contact: E. Stanley Lee, Graduate Program Director, 785-532-5606, *Fax:* 785-532-7810, *E-mail:* eslee@ksu.edu. *Web site:* http://cheetah.imse.ksu.edu/

■ KETTERING UNIVERSITY

Graduate School, Industrial and Manufacturing Engineering and Business Department, Flint, MI 48504-4898

AWARDS Manufacturing management (MSMM, MSMO); manufacturing systems engineering (MS Eng); operations management (MSOM). Part-time and evening/weekend programs available. Postbaccalaureate distance learning degree programs offered (no on-campus study).

Faculty: 20 full-time (5 women).
Students: 3 full-time (1 woman), 579 part-time (168 women); includes 80 minority (56 African Americans, 13 Asian Americans or Pacific Islanders, 11 Hispanic Americans), 12 international. 157 applicants, 100% accepted. In 2001, 176 degrees awarded.
Degree requirements: For master's, thesis (for some programs), registration. *Median time to degree:* Master's–3 years full-time, 6 years part-time. *Application deadline:* For fall admission, 7/15. Applications are processed on a rolling basis. *Application fee:* $0. Electronic applications accepted.
Expenses: Tuition: Full-time $8,370; part-time $465 per credit.
Financial support: Fellowships with full tuition reimbursements, research assistantships with full tuition reimbursements, teaching assistantships with full tuition reimbursements, Federal Work-Study, scholarships/grants, and tuition waivers (partial) available. Support available to part-time students. Financial award application deadline: 7/15; financial award

applicants required to submit CSS PROFILE or FAFSA.

Dr. David W. Poock, Head, 810-762-7959, *Fax:* 810-762-9924, *E-mail:* dpoock@kettering.edu.

Application contact: Betty L. Bedore, Coordinator of Publicity, 810-762-7494, *Fax:* 810-762-9935, *E-mail:* bbedore@kettering.edu. *Web site:* http://www.kettering.edu/

■ KETTERING UNIVERSITY

Graduate School, Mechanical Engineering Department, Flint, MI 48504-4898

AWARDS Automotive systems (MS Eng); manufacturing (MS Eng); mechanical cognate (MS Eng); mechanical design (MS Eng). Part-time and evening/weekend programs available. Postbaccalaureate distance learning degree programs offered (no on-campus study).

Faculty: 15 full-time (0 women).
Students: 6 full-time (1 woman), 88 part-time (12 women); includes 8 minority (7 African Americans, 1 Native American), 43 international. 163 applicants, 87% accepted. In 2001, 18 degrees awarded.
Degree requirements: For master's, thesis (for some programs), registration. *Median time to degree:* Master's–3 years full-time, 6 years part-time. *Application deadline:* For fall admission, 7/15. Applications are processed on a rolling basis. *Application fee:* $0. Electronic applications accepted.
Expenses: Tuition: Full-time $8,370; part-time $465 per credit.
Financial support: Fellowships with full tuition reimbursements, research assistantships with full tuition reimbursements, teaching assistantships with full tuition reimbursements, Federal Work-Study, scholarships/grants, and tuition waivers (partial) available. Support available to part-time students. Financial award application deadline: 7/15; financial award applicants required to submit CSS PROFILE or FAFSA.

Dr. K. Joel Berry, Head, 810-762-7833, *Fax:* 810-762-7860, *E-mail:* jberry@kettering.edu.

Application contact: Betty L. Bedore, Coordinator of Publicity, 810-762-7494, *Fax:* 810-762-9935, *E-mail:* bbedore@kettering.edu. *Web site:* http://www.kettering.edu/

■ LAWRENCE TECHNOLOGICAL UNIVERSITY

College of Engineering, Southfield, MI 48075-1058

AWARDS Automotive engineering (MAE); civil engineering (MCE); electrical and computer engineering (MS); manufacturing systems (MEMS, DE). Part-time and evening/weekend programs available.

Lawrence Technological University (continued)

Faculty: 27 full-time (2 women), 11 part-time/adjunct (1 woman).
Students: Average age 32. 133 applicants, 38 enrolled. In 2001, 43 degrees awarded. *Application deadline:* For fall admission, 8/1 (priority date); for winter admission, 12/1 (priority date); for spring admission, 5/1. Applications are processed on a rolling basis. *Application fee:* $50. Electronic applications accepted.
Expenses: Tuition: Part-time $460 per credit hour.
Financial support: Institutionally sponsored loans available. Support available to part-time students. Financial award application deadline: 3/1; financial award applicants required to submit FAFSA.
Faculty research: Advanced composite materials in bridges, strengthening existing bridges with carbon and glass fiber sheets, development of drive shafts using composite materials. *Total annual research expenditures:* $150,000.
Dr. Laird Johnston, Dean, 248-204-2500, *Fax:* 248-204-2509, *E-mail:* lejohnston@ltu.edu.
Application contact: Jane Rohrback, Interim Director of Admissions, 248-204-3160, *Fax:* 248-204-3188, *E-mail:* admission@ltu.edu.

■ **LEHIGH UNIVERSITY**

P.C. Rossin College of Engineering and Applied Science, Program in Manufacturing Systems Engineering, Bethlehem, PA 18015-3094

AWARDS MS. Part-time and evening/weekend programs available.

Faculty: 4 full-time (0 women).
Students: Average age 38. 6 applicants, 83% accepted, 2 enrolled. In 2001, 9 degrees awarded.
Degree requirements: For master's, project or thesis. *Median time to degree:* Master's–1 year full-time, 2 years part-time.
Entrance requirements: For master's, GRE General Test, TOEFL, minimum GPA of 2.75. *Application deadline:* For fall admission, 7/15; for spring admission, 12/1. Applications are processed on a rolling basis. *Application fee:* $50. Electronic applications accepted.
Expenses: Tuition: Part-time $468 per credit hour. Required fees: $200; $100 per semester. Tuition and fees vary according to program.
Financial support: Fellowships, research assistantships, career-related internships or fieldwork and tuition waivers (full and partial) available. Financial award application deadline: 1/15.
Faculty research: Manufacturing systems design, development, and implementation, accounting and management, agile/lean systems and supply chain issues.

Dr. Keith M. Gardiner, Director, 610-758-5070, *Fax:* 610-758-6527, *E-mail:* kg03@lehigh.edu.
Application contact: Carolyn C. Jones, Graduate Coordinator, 610-758-5157, *Fax:* 610-758-6527, *E-mail:* ccj1@lehigh.edu. *Web site:* http://www.lehigh.edu/~inmse/gradprogram/

■ **LOUISIANA TECH UNIVERSITY**

Graduate School, College of Engineering and Science, Department of Mechanical and Industrial Engineering, Ruston, LA 71272

AWARDS Industrial engineering (MS, D Eng); manufacturing systems engineering (MS); mechanical engineering (MS, D Eng); operations research (MS). Part-time programs available. Terminal master's awarded for partial completion of doctoral program.

Degree requirements: For master's and doctorate, thesis/dissertation.
Entrance requirements: For master's, GRE General Test, TOEFL, minimum GPA of 3.0 in last 60 hours; for doctorate, TOEFL, minimum graduate GPA of 3.25 (with MS) or GRE General Test.
Faculty research: Engineering management, facilities planning, thermodynamics, automated manufacturing, micromanufacturing.

■ **MARQUETTE UNIVERSITY**

Graduate School, College of Engineering, Department of Mechanical and Industrial Engineering, Milwaukee, WI 53201-1881

AWARDS Engineering management (MS); mechanical engineering (MS, PhD), including manufacturing systems engineering. Part-time and evening/weekend programs available.

Faculty: 13 full-time (0 women), 9 part-time/adjunct (0 women).
Students: 26 full-time (4 women), 50 part-time (2 women); includes 1 minority (Native American), 28 international. Average age 27. 75 applicants, 73% accepted. In 2001, 6 master's, 3 doctorates awarded. Terminal master's awarded for partial completion of doctoral program.
Degree requirements: For master's, thesis; for doctorate, thesis/dissertation, qualifying exam.
Entrance requirements: For master's and doctorate, GRE General Test, TOEFL, minimum GPA of 3.0. *Application deadline:* For fall admission, 8/1 (priority date); for spring admission, 1/1 (priority date). Applications are processed on a rolling basis. *Application fee:* $40. Electronic applications accepted.
Expenses: Tuition: Full-time $10,170; part-time $445 per credit hour. Tuition and fees vary according to course load.
Financial support: In 2001–02, 13 students received support, including fellowships with tuition reimbursements

available (averaging $10,190 per year), 1 research assistantship with tuition reimbursement available (averaging $10,835 per year), 7 teaching assistantships with tuition reimbursements available (averaging $10,835 per year); Federal Work-Study, institutionally sponsored loans, scholarships/grants, and tuition waivers (full and partial) also available. Support available to part-time students. Financial award application deadline: 2/15.
Faculty research: Computer-integrated manufacturing, energy conversion, simulation modeling and optimization, applied mechanics, metallurgy. *Total annual research expenditures:* $250,000.
Dr. Kyle Kim, Chair, 414-288-7259, *Fax:* 414-288-7790, *E-mail:* kyle.kim@marquette.edu.
Application contact: Dr. Robert J. Stango, Director of Graduate Studies, 414-288-6972, *Fax:* 414-288-7790, *E-mail:* robert.stango@marquette.edu. *Web site:* http://www.eng.mu.edu/~meen/index.html

Find an in-depth description at www.petersons.com/gradchannel.

■ **MASSACHUSETTS INSTITUTE OF TECHNOLOGY**

School of Engineering, Engineering Systems Division, Leaders for Manufacturing Program, Cambridge, MA 02139-4307

AWARDS SM/MBA, SM/SM.

Application deadline: For fall admission, 1/15. Electronic applications accepted.
Financial support: Fellowships, career-related internships or fieldwork, Federal Work-Study, institutionally sponsored loans, scholarships/grants, health care benefits, and unspecified assistantships available. Financial award application deadline: 1/15; financial award applicants required to submit FAFSA.
Faculty research: Scheduling logistics, product life cycle, variation reduction, product development, manufacturing operations.
Paul A. Lagace, Co-Director, 617-253-3628, *E-mail:* pal@mit.edu.
Application contact: Sarah Shohet, Admissions and Career Placement Coordinator, 617-253-1662, *Fax:* 617-253-1462, *E-mail:* lfmsdm@mit.edu. *Web site:* http://lfmsdm.mit.edu/lfm

■ **MICHIGAN STATE UNIVERSITY**

Graduate School, College of Agriculture and Natural Resources, School of Packaging, East Lansing, MI 48824

AWARDS MS, PhD. Part-time programs available.

Faculty: 11.
Students: 27 full-time (8 women), 25 part-time (11 women); includes 7 minority (2 African Americans, 4 Asian Americans or Pacific Islanders, 1 Hispanic American), 39

international. Average age 29. 33 applicants, 76% accepted. In 2001, 10 master's, 1 doctorate awarded.

Degree requirements: For master's and doctorate, thesis/dissertation.

Entrance requirements: For master's, GRE General Test, minimum GPA of 3.0; previous course work in calculus, chemistry, and physics; for doctorate, GRE General Test, MS, minimum GPA of 3.4. *Application deadline:* For fall admission, 12/1. Applications are processed on a rolling basis. *Application fee:* $30 ($40 for international students). Electronic applications accepted.

Expenses: Tuition, state resident: part-time $244 per credit hour. Tuition, nonresident: part-time $494 per credit hour. Required fees: $268 per semester. Tuition and fees vary according to course load, degree level and program.

Financial support: In 2001–02, 13 fellowships (averaging $1,781 per year), 9 research assistantships with tuition reimbursements (averaging $11,056 per year), 10 teaching assistantships with tuition reimbursements (averaging $10,819 per year) were awarded. Federal Work-Study and tuition waivers (partial) also available. Support available to part-time students. Financial award applicants required to submit FAFSA.

Faculty research: Barrier packaging–food and health care, physical–protection packaging, ergonomics, environmental management. *Total annual research expenditures:* $341,907.

Dr. Bruce Harte, Director, 517-355-9580, *Fax:* 517-353-8999.

Application contact: 517-353-5143, *Fax:* 517-353-8999. *Web site:* http://www.mus.edu/~sop/

■ MINNESOTA STATE UNIVERSITY, MANKATO

College of Graduate Studies, College of Science, Engineering and Technology, Department of Manufacturing, Mankato, MN 56001

AWARDS MS.

Faculty: 4 full-time (0 women).

Students: 2 full-time (0 women), 3 part-time. Average age 30. In 2001, 6 degrees awarded.

Degree requirements: For master's, thesis, comprehensive exam.

Entrance requirements: For master's, minimum GPA of 3.0 during previous 2 years. *Application deadline:* For fall admission, 7/9 (priority date); for spring admission, 11/27. Applications are processed on a rolling basis. *Application fee:* $20.

Expenses: Tuition, state resident: full-time $3,253; part-time $157 per credit. Tuition, nonresident: full-time $4,893; part-time $248 per credit. Required fees: $24 per credit. Tuition and fees vary according to reciprocity agreements.

Financial support: Research assistantships with full tuition reimbursements, teaching

assistantships with full tuition reimbursements available. Financial award application deadline: 3/15; financial award applicants required to submit FAFSA. Kirk Ready, Chairperson, 507-389-6383.

Application contact: Joni Roberts, Admissions Coordinator, 507-389-5244, *Fax:* 507-389-5974, *E-mail:* grad@mankato.msus.edu.

■ NATIONAL TECHNOLOGICAL UNIVERSITY

Programs in Engineering, Fort Collins, CO 80526-1842

AWARDS Chemical engineering (MS); computer engineering (MS); computer science (MS); electrical engineering (MS); engineering management (MS); environmental systems management (MS); management of technology (MS); manufacturing systems engineering (MS); materials science and engineering (MS); mechanical engineering (MS); microelectronics and semiconductor engineering (MS). Software engineering (MS). Special majors (MS). Systems engineering (MS). Part-time programs available. Postbaccalaureate distance learning degree programs offered (no on-campus study).

Students: In 2001, 114 degrees awarded.

Degree requirements: For master's, comprehensive exam.

Entrance requirements: For master's, BS in engineering or related field; 2.9 minimum GPA. *Application deadline:* Applications are processed on a rolling basis. *Application fee:* $50. Electronic applications accepted.

Expenses: Tuition: Part-time $660 per credit hour. Part-time tuition and fees vary according to course load, campus/location and program.

Dr. Andre Vacroux, President, 970-495-6400, *Fax:* 970-484-0668, *E-mail:* andre@ntu.edu.

Application contact: Rhonda Bonham, Admissions Officer, 970-495-6400, *Fax:* 970-498-0601, *E-mail:* rhonda@ntu.edu. *Web site:* http://www.ntu.edu/

■ NEW JERSEY INSTITUTE OF TECHNOLOGY

Office of Graduate Studies, Department of Industrial and Manufacturing Engineering, Program in Industrial/Manufacturing Engineering, Newark, NJ 07102

AWARDS MS, PhD. Part-time and evening/weekend programs available.

Students: 30 full-time (2 women), 27 part-time (3 women); includes 7 minority (2 African Americans, 3 Asian Americans or Pacific Islanders, 2 Hispanic Americans), 34 international. Average age 27. 202 applicants, 59% accepted, 12 enrolled. In 2001, 25 master's, 2 doctorates awarded. Terminal master's awarded for partial completion of doctoral program.

Degree requirements: For master's, thesis or alternative; for doctorate, thesis/dissertation.

Entrance requirements: For master's, GRE General Test; for doctorate, GRE General Test, minimum graduate GPA of 3.5. *Application deadline:* For fall admission, 6/5 (priority date); for spring admission, 10/15. Applications are processed on a rolling basis. *Application fee:* $50. Electronic applications accepted.

Expenses: Tuition, state resident: full-time $7,812; part-time $434 per credit. Tuition, nonresident: full-time $10,746; part-time $597 per credit. Required fees: $47 per credit. $76 per semester.

Financial support: Fellowships with full and partial tuition reimbursements, research assistantships with full and partial tuition reimbursements, teaching assistantships with full and partial tuition reimbursements, career-related internships or fieldwork, Federal Work-Study, institutionally sponsored loans, and unspecified assistantships available. Financial award application deadline: 3/15.

Faculty research: Knowledge based systems, CAS/CAM simulation and interface, expert systems. *Total annual research expenditures:* $100,000.

Dr. George Abdou, Director, 973-596-3651, *Fax:* 973-596-3652, *E-mail:* george.abdou@njit.edu.

Application contact: Kathryn Kelly, Director of Admissions, 973-596-3300, *Fax:* 973-596-3461, *E-mail:* admissions@njit.edu. *Web site:* http://www.njit.edu/

■ NORTH CAROLINA STATE UNIVERSITY

Graduate School, College of Engineering, Department of Integrated Manufacturing Systems Engineering, Raleigh, NC 27695

AWARDS MIMS. Part-time programs available.

Faculty: 35 full-time (2 women), 10 part-time/adjunct (0 women).

Students: 25 full-time (5 women), 8 part-time (2 women); includes 4 minority (3 African Americans, 1 Native American), 1 international. Average age 28. 38 applicants, 37% accepted. In 2001, 17 degrees awarded.

Degree requirements: For master's, thesis or alternative.

Entrance requirements: For master's, TOEFL. *Application deadline:* For fall admission, 6/25; for spring admission, 11/25. Applications are processed on a rolling basis. *Application fee:* $45.

Expenses: Tuition, state resident: full-time $1,748. Tuition, nonresident: full-time $6,904.

Financial support: In 2001–02, fellowships (averaging $2,301 per year), 19 research assistantships (averaging $6,023 per year) were awarded. Teaching

North Carolina State University (continued)

assistantships, career-related internships or fieldwork and scholarships/grants also available.

Faculty research: Mechatronics, manufacturing systems modeling, systems integration product and process engineering.

Dr. Larry M. Silverberg, Director of Graduate Programs, 919-515-5282, *Fax:* 919-515-1675, *E-mail:* silver@eos.ncsu.edu. *Web site:* http://www.imse.ncsu.edu/

■ NORTH DAKOTA STATE UNIVERSITY

The Graduate School, College of Engineering and Architecture, Department of Industrial and Manufacturing Engineering, Fargo, ND 58105

AWARDS Industrial engineering and management (MS). Part-time programs available.

Faculty: 8 full-time (1 woman).
Students: 10 full-time (1 woman), 1 part-time; includes 8 minority (all Asian Americans or Pacific Islanders). Average age 26. 18 applicants, 100% accepted, 4 enrolled. In 2001, 1 degree awarded.
Degree requirements: For master's, thesis. *Median time to degree:* Master's–3 years full-time.
Entrance requirements: For master's, GRE General Test, TOEFL. *Application deadline:* For fall admission, 6/1; for spring admission, 10/1. Applications are processed on a rolling basis. *Application fee:* $35.
Expenses: Tuition, state resident: part-time $124 per credit. Tuition, nonresident: part-time $325 per credit. Required fees: $22 per credit. Tuition and fees vary according to reciprocity agreements.
Financial support: In 2001–02, 10 students received support, including 10 research assistantships with tuition reimbursements available; teaching assistantships with tuition reimbursements available, Federal Work-Study, institutionally sponsored loans, scholarships/grants, and unspecified assistantships also available. Financial award application deadline: 4/15.
Faculty research: Automation, engineering economy, artificial intelligence, human factors engineering, production and inventory control.
Dr. David L. Wells, Chair, 701-231-7283, *Fax:* 701-231-7195, *E-mail:* david_l_wells@ndsu.nodak.edu.

■ NORTHEASTERN UNIVERSITY

College of Engineering, Department of Mechanical, Industrial, and Manufacturing Engineering, Boston, MA 02115-5096

AWARDS Engineering management (MS); industrial engineering (MS, PhD); mechanical engineering (MS, PhD); operations research (MS). Part-time programs available.

Faculty: 26 full-time (1 woman), 5 part-time/adjunct (1 woman).
Students: 97 full-time (22 women), 80 part-time (10 women); includes 32 minority (6 African Americans, 7 Asian Americans or Pacific Islanders, 19 Hispanic Americans), 77 international. Average age 25. 262 applicants, 53% accepted, 57 enrolled. In 2001, 46 master's, 6 doctorates awarded.
Degree requirements: For master's, thesis (for some programs), registration; for doctorate, one foreign language, thesis/dissertation, departmental qualifying exam.
Entrance requirements: For master's and doctorate, GRE General Test. *Application deadline:* For fall admission, 2/15 (priority date). Applications are processed on a rolling basis. *Application fee:* $50. Electronic applications accepted.
Expenses: Tuition: Part-time $535 per credit hour. Required fees: $56. Tuition and fees vary according to program.
Financial support: In 2001–02, 61 students received support, including 1 fellowship, 24 research assistantships with full tuition reimbursements available (averaging $13,560 per year), 26 teaching assistantships with full tuition reimbursements available (averaging $13,560 per year); career-related internships or fieldwork, Federal Work-Study, scholarships/grants, tuition waivers (full), and unspecified assistantships also available. Support available to part-time students. Financial award application deadline: 2/15; financial award applicants required to submit FAFSA.
Faculty research: Dry sliding instabilities, droplet deposition, helical hydraulic turbines, combustion, manufacturing systems. *Total annual research expenditures:* $1.8 million.
Dr. John W. Cipolla, Chairman, 617-373-3810, *Fax:* 617-373-2921.
Application contact: Stephen L. Gibson, Associate Director, 617-373-2711, *Fax:* 617-373-2501, *E-mail:* grad-eng@coe.neu.edu.

Find an in-depth description at www.petersons.com/gradchannel.

■ NORTHWESTERN UNIVERSITY

McCormick School of Engineering and Applied Science, Department of Mechanical Engineering, Program in Manufacturing Engineering, Evanston, IL 60208

AWARDS MME. Part-time programs available.
Faculty: 23 full-time (3 women), 7 part-time/adjunct (0 women).
Students: 2 applicants, 100% accepted. In 2001, 2 degrees awarded.
Application deadline: For fall admission, 8/30. Applications are processed on a rolling basis. *Application fee:* $25.
Expenses: Tuition: Full-time $26,526.

Financial support: Institutionally sponsored loans available. Financial award application deadline: 1/15; financial award applicants required to submit FAFSA. *Total annual research expenditures:* $50,000.
Henry Stoll, Director, 847-467-2676, *E-mail:* hstoll@northwestern.edu.
Application contact: Pat Dyess, Admission Contact, 847-491-7190, *Fax:* 847-491-3915, *E-mail:* j-dyess@northwestern.edu. *Web site:* http://www.mech.northwestern.edu/

■ OHIO UNIVERSITY

Graduate Studies, Russ College of Engineering and Technology, Department of Mechanical Engineering, Athens, OH 45701-2979

AWARDS Manufacturing engineering (MS); mechanical engineering (MS, PhD), including CAD/CAM (MS), manufacturing (MS), mechanical systems (MS), technology management (MS), thermal systems (MS).

Faculty: 10 full-time (0 women).
Students: 48 full-time (4 women), 20 part-time (3 women); includes 3 minority (2 African Americans, 1 Asian American or Pacific Islander), 51 international. 144 applicants, 63% accepted, 25 enrolled. In 2001, 34 degrees awarded.
Degree requirements: For master's and doctorate, thesis/dissertation.
Entrance requirements: For master's, BS in engineering or science, minimum GPA of 2.8; for doctorate, GRE. *Application deadline:* For fall admission, 3/15 (priority date). Applications are processed on a rolling basis. *Application fee:* $30.
Expenses: Tuition, state resident: full-time $6,585. Tuition, nonresident: full-time $12,254.
Financial support: In 2001–02, 41 students received support, including 9 research assistantships with tuition reimbursements available, 14 teaching assistantships with tuition reimbursements available; fellowships with tuition reimbursements available, career-related internships or fieldwork, Federal Work-Study, institutionally sponsored loans, tuition waivers (full and partial), and unspecified assistantships also available. Financial award application deadline: 3/15.
Faculty research: Machine design, controls, aerodynamics, thermal manufacturing, robotics process modeling, air pollution, combustion.
Dr. Jay S. Gunasekara, Chairman, 740-593-0563, *Fax:* 740-593-0476, *E-mail:* gsekera@bobcat.ent.ohiou.edu.
Application contact: Dr. M. Khairul Alam, Graduate Chairman, 740-593-1598, *Fax:* 740-593-0476, *E-mail:* agrawal@bobcat.ent.ohiou.edu. *Web site:* http://www.ent.ohiou.edu/

■ OKLAHOMA STATE UNIVERSITY

Graduate College, College of Engineering, Architecture and Technology, School of Industrial Engineering and Management, Interdisciplinary Master of Manufacturing Systems Engineering Program, Stillwater, OK 74078

AWARDS M En.

Faculty: 5 full-time (0 women), 1 part-time/adjunct (0 women).
Students: 1 full-time (0 women), 136 part-time (15 women); includes 9 minority (3 African Americans, 3 Asian Americans or Pacific Islanders, 3 Hispanic Americans), 3 international. Average age 36. 39 applicants, 97% accepted. In 2001, 9 degrees awarded.
Degree requirements: For master's, creative component or thesis.
Entrance requirements: For master's, TOEFL. *Application deadline:* For fall admission, 7/1 (priority date). *Application fee:* $25.
Expenses: Tuition, state resident: part-time $92 per credit hour. Tuition, nonresident: part-time $297 per credit hour. Required fees: $21 per credit hour. $14 per semester. One-time fee: $20. Tuition and fees vary according to course load.
Financial support: Research assistantships, teaching assistantships, career-related internships or fieldwork, Federal Work-Study, and tuition waivers (partial) available. Support available to part-time students. Financial award application deadline: 3/1.
Faculty research: Integrated manufacturing systems, engineering practice in management, hardware aspects.
John W. Nazemetz, Director, 405-744-6055.

■ OLD DOMINION UNIVERSITY

College of Engineering and Technology, Program in Mechanical Engineering, Norfolk, VA 23529

AWARDS Design manufacturing (ME); engineering mechanics (ME, MS, PhD); mechanical engineering (ME, MS, PhD). Part-time and evening/weekend programs available. Postbaccalaureate distance learning degree programs offered (no on-campus study).

Faculty: 13 full-time (0 women).
Students: 46 full-time (4 women), 58 part-time (4 women). Average age 28. 154 applicants, 90% accepted. In 2001, 32 master's, 2 doctorates awarded.
Degree requirements: For master's, thesis optional; for doctorate, thesis/dissertation, candidacy exam.
Entrance requirements: For master's, GRE, TOEFL, minimum GPA of 3.0; for doctorate, GRE, TOEFL. *Application deadline:* For fall admission, 7/1; for spring

admission, 10/1. Applications are processed on a rolling basis. *Application fee:* $30. Electronic applications accepted.
Expenses: Tuition, state resident: part-time $202 per credit. Tuition, nonresident: part-time $534 per credit. Required fees: $76 per semester.
Financial support: In 2001–02, 61 students received support, including 2 fellowships (averaging $10,000 per year), 40 research assistantships with tuition reimbursements available (averaging $8,433 per year); teaching assistantships, career-related internships or fieldwork, institutionally sponsored loans, scholarships/grants, and tuition waivers (partial) also available. Support available to part-time students. Financial award application deadline: 2/15; financial award applicants required to submit FAFSA.
Faculty research: Computational applied mechanics, manufacturing, experimental stress analysis, systems dynamics and control, mechanical design, computational fluid dynamics, optimization. *Total annual research expenditures:* $1.5 million.
Dr. Jen-Kuang Huang, Graduate Program Director, 757-683-6363, *Fax:* 757-683-5344, *E-mail:* megpd@odu.edu. *Web site:* http://www.mem.odu.edu/

■ OREGON STATE UNIVERSITY

Graduate School, College of Engineering, Department of Industrial and Manufacturing Engineering, Corvallis, OR 97331

AWARDS Industrial engineering (MAIS, MS, PhD); manufacturing engineering (M Eng). Part-time programs available. Postbaccalaureate distance learning degree programs offered (minimal on-campus study).

Faculty: 8 full-time (2 women).
Students: 40 full-time (11 women), 10 part-time (1 woman); includes 2 minority (both Asian Americans or Pacific Islanders), 44 international. Average age 28. In 2001, 5 master's, 2 doctorates awarded.
Degree requirements: For master's, thesis or alternative; for doctorate, thesis/dissertation.
Entrance requirements: For master's, TOEFL, placement exam, minimum GPA of 3.0 in last 90 hours; for doctorate, GRE, TOEFL, placement exam, minimum GPA of 3.0 in last 90 hours. *Application deadline:* Applications are processed on a rolling basis. *Application fee:* $50.
Expenses: Tuition, area resident: Full-time $15,933. Tuition, state resident: full-time $28,937.
Financial support: Fellowships, research assistantships, teaching assistantships, institutionally sponsored loans and instructorships available. Support available to part-time students. Financial award application deadline: 2/1.
Faculty research: Computer-integrated manufacturing, human factors, robotics, decision support systems, simulation modeling and analysis.

Richard E. Billo, Head, 541-737-2365, *Fax:* 541-737-5241, *E-mail:* richard.billo@orst.edu.
Application contact: Dr. Suat Tanaydin, Graduate Committee Chair, 541-737-2875, *Fax:* 541-737-5241, *E-mail:* tanaydin@engr.orst.edu. *Web site:* http://www.ie.orst.edu/

■ THE PENNSYLVANIA STATE UNIVERSITY UNIVERSITY PARK CAMPUS

Graduate School, College of Engineering, Department of Industrial and Manufacturing Engineering, Program in Manufacturing Engineering, State College, University Park, PA 16802-1503

AWARDS M Eng.

Students: 1 full-time (0 women), 1 (woman) part-time.
Degree requirements: For master's, thesis.
Entrance requirements: For master's, GRE General Test. *Application fee:* $45.
Expenses: Tuition, state resident: full-time $7,882; part-time $333 per credit. Tuition, nonresident: full-time $16,142; part-time $673 per credit. Required fees: $124 per semester.
Dr. Jose Ventura, Graduate Advisor, 814-865-3841.

■ POLYTECHNIC UNIVERSITY, BROOKLYN CAMPUS

Department of Mechanical, Aerospace and Manufacturing Engineering, Major in Manufacturing Engineering, Brooklyn, NY 11201-2990

AWARDS MS.

Entrance requirements: For master's, BE or BS in engineering, physics, chemistry, mathematical sciences, or biological sciences or MBA. Electronic applications accepted.

■ POLYTECHNIC UNIVERSITY, LONG ISLAND GRADUATE CENTER

Graduate Programs, Department of Mechanical, Aerospace and Manufacturing Engineering, Major in Manufacturing Engineering, Melville, NY 11747

AWARDS MS.

Electronic applications accepted.

■ POLYTECHNIC UNIVERSITY OF PUERTO RICO

Graduate Programs, Hato Rey, PR 00919

AWARDS Business administration (MBA); civil engineering (MCE); competitive manufacturing

Polytechnic University of Puerto Rico (continued)
(MMC); engineering management (MEM); environmental protection management (MEPM); manufacturing engineering (MME).

■ POLYTECHNIC UNIVERSITY, WESTCHESTER GRADUATE CENTER

Graduate Programs, Department of Mechanical, Aerospace and Manufacturing Engineering, Major in Manufacturing Engineering, Hawthorne, NY 10532-1507

AWARDS MS.

Electronic applications accepted.

■ PORTLAND STATE UNIVERSITY

Graduate Studies, College of Engineering and Computer Science, Program in Manufacturing Engineering, Portland, OR 97207-0751

AWARDS ME. Part-time and evening/weekend programs available.

Students: 1 full-time (0 women), 3 part-time (1 woman). Average age 34. 5 applicants, 40% accepted. In 2001, 1 degree awarded.
Entrance requirements: For master's, TOEFL, minimum GPA of 3.0 in upper-division course work or 2.75 overall. *Application deadline:* For fall admission, 4/1 (priority date); for spring admission, 11/1. Applications are processed on a rolling basis. *Application fee:* $50.
Financial support: Research assistantships, teaching assistantships, career-related internships or fieldwork, Federal Work-Study, and institutionally sponsored loans available. Support available to part-time students. Financial award application deadline: 3/1; financial award applicants required to submit FAFSA.
Faculty research: Quality assurance, concurrent engineering, production scheduling and control, manufacturing automation.
Dr. Graig Spolek, Head, 503-725-4631, *Fax:* 503-725-4298, *E-mail:* graig@eas.pdx.edu.
Application contact: David Turcic, Coordinator, 503-725-4631, *Fax:* 503-725-4298, *E-mail:* davet@eas.pdx.edu.

■ PURDUE UNIVERSITY

Graduate School, Schools of Engineering, School of Industrial Engineering, West Lafayette, IN 47907

AWARDS Human factors in industrial engineering (MS, MSIE, PhD); manufacturing engineering (MS, MSIE, PhD); operations research (MS, MSIE, PhD). Systems engineering (MS, MSIE, PhD). Part-time programs available.

Faculty: 23 full-time (2 women), 4 part-time/adjunct (0 women).
Students: 117 full-time (24 women), 19 part-time (6 women); includes 6 minority (4 African Americans, 2 Hispanic Americans), 108 international. Average age 28. 370 applicants, 44% accepted. In 2001, 51 master's, 11 doctorates awarded. Terminal master's awarded for partial completion of doctoral program.
Degree requirements: For master's, thesis optional; for doctorate, thesis/dissertation.
Entrance requirements: For master's, GRE General Test, TOEFL, minimum GPA of 3.0; for doctorate, GRE General Test, TOEFL, MS thesis. *Application deadline:* For fall admission, 3/15; for spring admission, 9/1. *Application fee:* $30. Electronic applications accepted.
Expenses: Tuition, state resident: full-time $4,164; part-time $149 per credit hour. Tuition, nonresident: full-time $13,872; part-time $458 per credit hour. Tuition and fees vary according to campus/location and program.
Financial support: In 2001–02, 78 students received support, including 3 fellowships with full tuition reimbursements available (averaging $13,070 per year), 29 research assistantships with full tuition reimbursements available (averaging $12,720 per year), 46 teaching assistantships with full tuition reimbursements available (averaging $10,600 per year) Support available to part-time students. Financial award application deadline: 3/15; financial award applicants required to submit FAFSA.
Faculty research: Precision manufacturing process, computer-aided manufacturing, computer-aided process planning, knowledge-based systems, combinatorics. *Total annual research expenditures:* $1.8 million.
Dr. Dennis Engi, Head, 765-494-5444, *Fax:* 765-494-1299, *E-mail:* engi@ecn.purdue.edu.
Application contact: Dr. J. W. Barany, Associate Head, 765-494-5406, *Fax:* 765-494-1299, *E-mail:* jwb@ecn.purdue.edu. *Web site:* http://ie.www.ecn.purdue.edu/

■ RENSSELAER POLYTECHNIC INSTITUTE

Graduate School, School of Engineering, Department of Decision Sciences and Engineering Systems, Program in Manufacturing Systems Engineering, Troy, NY 12180-3590

AWARDS M Eng, MS, MBA/M Eng. Part-time and evening/weekend programs available.

Faculty: 16 full-time (1 woman), 3 part-time/adjunct (2 women).
Students: 2 full-time (0 women), 2 part-time (1 woman), 2 international. 18 applicants, 33% accepted, 4 enrolled. In 2001, 3 degrees awarded.
Degree requirements: For master's, thesis (for some programs).

Entrance requirements: For master's, GRE General Test, TOEFL. *Application deadline:* For fall admission, 1/15 (priority date). Applications are processed on a rolling basis. *Application fee:* $45. Electronic applications accepted.
Expenses: Tuition: Full-time $26,400; part-time $1,320 per credit hour. Required fees: $1,437.
Financial support: Fellowships, research assistantships, teaching assistantships, career-related internships or fieldwork and institutionally sponsored loans available. Financial award application deadline: 1/15.
Faculty research: Information systems, statistical consulting, education/services, production/logistics/inventory. *Total annual research expenditures:* $1 million.
Application contact: Lee Vilardi, Graduate Coordinator, 518-276-6681, *Fax:* 518-276-8227, *E-mail:* dsesgr@rpi.edu. *Web site:* http://www.rpi.edu/

Find an in-depth description at www.petersons.com/gradchannel.

■ ROCHESTER INSTITUTE OF TECHNOLOGY

Graduate Enrollment Services, College of Applied Science and Technology, Department of Manufacturing and Mechanical Engineering Technology, Program in Computer Integrated Manufacturing, Rochester, NY 14623-5698

AWARDS MS.

Students: 24 full-time (0 women), 27 part-time; includes 2 minority (both African Americans), 34 international. 46 applicants, 91% accepted, 28 enrolled. In 2001, 13 degrees awarded.
Degree requirements: For master's, thesis.
Entrance requirements: For master's, minimum GPA of 3.0. *Application deadline:* For fall admission, 3/1 (priority date). Applications are processed on a rolling basis. *Application fee:* $50.
Expenses: Tuition: Full-time $20,928; part-time $587 per hour. Required fees: $162. Tuition and fees vary according to program.
Financial support: Unspecified assistantships available.
Manian Ramkumar, Chair, 585-475-7024, *E-mail:* smrmet@rit.edu.

■ ROCHESTER INSTITUTE OF TECHNOLOGY

Graduate Enrollment Services, College of Applied Science and Technology, Department of Packaging Science, Rochester, NY 14623-5698

AWARDS MS.

Students: 7 full-time (3 women), 3 part-time, 4 international. 4 applicants, 100% accepted, 3 enrolled. In 2001, 23 degrees awarded.

Degree requirements: For master's, thesis.
Entrance requirements: For master's, minimum GPA of 3.0. *Application deadline:* For fall admission, 3/1 (priority date). Applications are processed on a rolling basis. *Application fee:* $50.
Expenses: Tuition: Full-time $20,928; part-time $587 per hour. Required fees: $162. Tuition and fees vary according to program.
Financial support: Research assistantships available.
Dr. Daniel Goodwin, Program Chair, 585-475-5557, *E-mail:* dlgipk@rit.edu.

ROCHESTER INSTITUTE OF TECHNOLOGY

Graduate Enrollment Services, College of Engineering, Department of Design, Development and Manufacturing, Rochester, NY 14623-5698

AWARDS Product development (MS).

Students: In 2001, 24 degrees awarded. *Application deadline:* For fall admission, 3/1 (priority date). Applications are processed on a rolling basis. *Application fee:* $50.
Expenses: Tuition: Full-time $20,928; part-time $587 per hour. Required fees: $162. Tuition and fees vary according to program.
Mark Smith, Director, 585-475-7102, *E-mail:* mpdmail@rit.edu.

ROCHESTER INSTITUTE OF TECHNOLOGY

Graduate Enrollment Services, College of Engineering, Department of Industrial and Manufacturing Engineering, Rochester, NY 14623-5698

AWARDS Engineering management (ME); industrial engineering (ME); manufacturing engineering (ME). Systems engineering (ME).

Students: 6 full-time (0 women), 19 part-time (6 women); includes 4 minority (2 African Americans, 2 Hispanic Americans), 10 international. 105 applicants, 51% accepted, 8 enrolled. In 2001, 14 degrees awarded.
Degree requirements: For master's, internship.
Entrance requirements: For master's, TOEFL, minimum GPA of 3.0. *Application deadline:* For fall admission, 3/1 (priority date). Applications are processed on a rolling basis. *Application fee:* $50.
Expenses: Tuition: Full-time $20,928; part-time $587 per hour. Required fees: $162. Tuition and fees vary according to program.
Financial support: Research assistantships, career-related internships or fieldwork or tuition waivers (partial) available.
Faculty research: Safety, manufacturing (CAM), simulation.
Dr. Jacqueline Mozrall, Head, 585-475-7142, *E-mail:* jrmeie@rit.edu.

SOUTHERN ILLINOIS UNIVERSITY CARBONDALE

Graduate School, College of Engineering, Department of Technology, Carbondale, IL 62901-6806

AWARDS Manufacturing systems (MS).

Faculty: 11 full-time (1 woman).
Students: 13 full-time (0 women), 20 part-time (5 women); includes 6 minority (4 African Americans, 2 Asian Americans or Pacific Islanders), 6 international. Average age 25. 17 applicants, 59% accepted. In 2001, 5 degrees awarded.
Degree requirements: For master's, thesis, comprehensive exam.
Entrance requirements: For master's, TOEFL, minimum GPA of 2.7. *Application deadline:* Applications are processed on a rolling basis. *Application fee:* $20.
Expenses: Tuition, state resident: full-time $3,794; part-time $154 per hour. Tuition, nonresident: full-time $6,566; part-time $308 per hour. Required fees: $277 per hour.
Financial support: In 2001–02, 15 students received support, including 1 fellowship with full tuition reimbursement available, 3 research assistantships with full tuition reimbursements available, 9 teaching assistantships with full tuition reimbursements available; tuition waivers (full) also available. Financial award application deadline: 7/1.
Faculty research: Computer-aided manufacturing, robotics, quality assurance. *Total annual research expenditures:* $205,198.
Dr. Ron Marusurz, Interim Chair, 618-536-3396.
Application contact: Robert R. Ferketich, Director, 618-536-3396.

Find an in-depth description at www.petersons.com/gradchannel.

SOUTHERN METHODIST UNIVERSITY

School of Engineering, Department of Mechanical Engineering, Dallas, TX 75275

AWARDS Manufacturing systems management (MS); mechanical engineering (MSME, PhD). Part-time and evening/weekend programs available. Postbaccalaureate distance learning degree programs offered (no on-campus study).

Faculty: 10 full-time (0 women).
Students: 25 full-time (4 women), 30 part-time; includes 9 minority (3 African Americans, 4 Asian Americans or Pacific Islanders, 2 Hispanic Americans), 18 international. Average age 32. 103 applicants, 97% accepted. In 2001, 14 master's, 3 doctorates awarded. Terminal master's awarded for partial completion of doctoral program.
Degree requirements: For master's, thesis optional; for doctorate, thesis/

dissertation, oral and written qualifying exams, oral final exam.
Entrance requirements: For master's, GRE General Test, TOEFL, minimum GPA of 3.0 in last 2 years; bachelor's degree in engineering, mathematics, or sciences; for doctorate, preliminary counseling exam, minimum graduate GPA of 3.0, bachelor's degree in related field. *Application deadline:* For fall admission, 7/1 (priority date); for spring admission, 11/15. Applications are processed on a rolling basis. *Application fee:* $50.
Expenses: Tuition: Part-time $285 per credit hour.
Financial support: In 2001–02, 12 research assistantships (averaging $15,000 per year), 6 teaching assistantships (averaging $9,000 per year) were awarded. Federal Work-Study, institutionally sponsored loans, and tuition waivers (full and partial) also available. Financial award applicants required to submit FAFSA.
Faculty research: Design, systems, and controls; thermal and fluid sciences. *Total annual research expenditures:* $1.3 million.
Yildirim Hurmuzlu, Head, 214-768-3498, *Fax:* 214-768-1473.
Application contact: Jim Dees, Director, Student Administration, 214-768-1456, *Fax:* 214-768-3845, *E-mail:* jdees@engr.smu.edu. *Web site:* http://www.seas.smu.edu/me/

Find an in-depth description at www.petersons.com/gradchannel.

STANFORD UNIVERSITY

School of Engineering, Department of Management Science and Engineering, Stanford, CA 94305-9991

AWARDS Management science and engineering (MS, PhD); management science and engineering and electrical engineering (MS); manufacturing systems engineering (MS).

Faculty: 31 full-time (5 women).
Students: 301 full-time (77 women), 82 part-time (18 women); includes 59 minority (5 African Americans, 48 Asian Americans or Pacific Islanders, 6 Hispanic Americans), 226 international. Average age 27. 484 applicants, 38% accepted. In 2001, 187 master's, 28 doctorates awarded. Terminal master's awarded for partial completion of doctoral program.
Degree requirements: For doctorate, thesis/dissertation, qualification procedure.
Entrance requirements: For master's and doctorate, GRE General Test, TOEFL. *Application deadline:* For fall admission, 2/1. *Application fee:* $65 ($80 for international students). Electronic applications accepted.
M. Elisabeth Paté-Cornell, Chair, 650-723-3823 Ext. ', *Fax:* 650-725-8799, *E-mail:* mep@stanford.edu.
Application contact: Graduate Admissions Coordinator, 650-723-4094, *Fax:* 650-723-1614. *Web site:* http://www.stanford.edu/dept/MSandE/

Find an in-depth description at www.petersons.com/gradchannel.

■ STANFORD UNIVERSITY

School of Engineering, Department of Mechanical Engineering, Program in Manufacturing Systems Engineering, Stanford, CA 94305-9991

AWARDS MS, MBA/MS.

Entrance requirements: For master's, GMAT, GRE General Test, TOEFL. *Application deadline:* For fall admission, 1/14. *Application fee:* $65 ($80 for international students). Electronic applications accepted.
Application contact: Admissions Office, 650-723-3148.

■ SYRACUSE UNIVERSITY

Graduate School, L. C. Smith College of Engineering and Computer Science, Program in Manufacturing Engineering, Syracuse, NY 13244-0003

AWARDS MS.

Students: 9 full-time (2 women), 7 part-time (1 woman), 10 international. Average age 31. In 2001, 16 degrees awarded.
Entrance requirements: For master's, GRE General Test, GRE Subject Test. *Application deadline:* Applications are processed on a rolling basis. *Application fee:* $50.
Expenses: Tuition: Full-time $15,528; part-time $647 per credit. Required fees: $420; $38 per term. Tuition and fees vary according to program.
Financial support: Fellowships, research assistantships, teaching assistantships, Federal Work-Study and tuition waivers (partial) available. Financial award application deadline: 1/10.
Dr. Uptal Roy, Graduate Director, 315-443-2592, *Fax:* 315-443-9099, *E-mail:* uroy@syr.edu.
Application contact: Kathy Datthyn-Madigan, Information Contact, 315-443-4367, *Fax:* 315-443-9099, *E-mail:* kjdatthy@ecs.syr.edu. *Web site:* http://www.ecs.syr.edu/
Find an in-depth description at www.petersons.com/gradchannel.

■ TUFTS UNIVERSITY

Division of Graduate and Continuing Studies and Research, Graduate and Professional Studies, Manufacturing Engineering Program, Medford, MA 02155

AWARDS Certificate. Part-time and evening/weekend programs available.

Students: Average age 39. In 2001, 3 degrees awarded.
Application deadline: For fall admission, 8/15 (priority date); for spring admission, 12/12 (priority date). Applications are processed on a rolling basis. *Application fee:* $50. Electronic applications accepted.
Expenses: Tuition: Full-time $26,853. Full-time tuition and fees vary according to program.

Financial support: Available to part-time students. Application deadline: 5/1.
Alida Poirier, Assistant Director, 617-627-3395, *Fax:* 617-627-3016, *E-mail:* pcs@ase.tufts.edu.
Application contact: Information Contact, 617-627-3395, *Fax:* 617-627-3016, *E-mail:* pcs@ase.tufts.edu. *Web site:* http://ase.tufts.edu/gradstudy

■ UNIVERSITY OF CALIFORNIA, LOS ANGELES

Graduate Division, School of Engineering and Applied Science, Department of Mechanical and Aerospace Engineering, Program in Manufacturing Engineering, Los Angeles, CA 90095

AWARDS MS.

Students: 2 full-time (0 women), 1 international. 11 applicants, 18% accepted, 0 enrolled. In 2001, 1 degree awarded.
Degree requirements: For master's, comprehensive exam or thesis.
Entrance requirements: For master's, GRE General Test, GRE Subject Test (international applicants), minimum GPA of 3.0. *Application deadline:* For fall admission, 1/5; for spring admission, 12/31. *Application fee:* $60. Electronic applications accepted.
Expenses: Tuition, nonresident: full-time $10,244. Required fees: $3,609. Full-time tuition and fees vary according to program.
Financial support: In 2001–02, 2 research assistantships, 3 teaching assistantships were awarded. Fellowships, Federal Work-Study, institutionally sponsored loans, and tuition waivers (full and partial) also available. Financial award application deadline: 1/5; financial award applicants required to submit FAFSA.
Application contact: Dr. Angie Castillo, Student Affairs Officer, 310-825-7793, *Fax:* 310-206-4830, *E-mail:* angie@ea.ucla.edu.

■ UNIVERSITY OF CENTRAL FLORIDA

College of Engineering and Computer Sciences, Department of Industrial Engineering and Management Systems, Orlando, FL 32816

AWARDS Applied operations research (Certificate); computer-integrated manufacturing (MS); design for usability (Certificate); engineering management (MS); industrial engineering (MSIE); industrial engineering and management systems (PhD); industrial ergonomics and safety (Certificate); operations research (MS); product assurance engineering (MS); project engineering (Certificate); quality assurance (Certificate). Simulation systems (MS). Systems simulation for engineers (Certificate); training

simulation (Certificate). Part-time and evening/weekend programs available.

Faculty: 20 full-time (4 women), 8 part-time/adjunct (1 woman).
Students: 92 full-time (19 women), 182 part-time (49 women); includes 66 minority (18 African Americans, 10 Asian Americans or Pacific Islanders, 35 Hispanic Americans, 3 Native Americans), 57 international. Average age 32. 231 applicants, 84% accepted, 85 enrolled. In 2001, 3 master's, 9 doctorates awarded.
Degree requirements: For master's, thesis; for doctorate, thesis/dissertation, departmental qualifying exam, candidacy exam.
Entrance requirements: For master's, GRE General Test, TOEFL, minimum GPA of 3.0 in last 60 hours; for doctorate, TOEFL, minimum GPA of 3.5 in last 60 hours. *Application deadline:* For fall admission, 7/15 (priority date); for spring admission, 12/1 (priority date). *Application fee:* $20. Electronic applications accepted.
Expenses: Tuition, state resident: part-time $162 per hour. Tuition, nonresident: part-time $569 per hour.
Financial support: In 2001–02, 23 fellowships with partial tuition reimbursements (averaging $3,272 per year), 131 research assistantships with partial tuition reimbursements (averaging $3,125 per year), 24 teaching assistantships with partial tuition reimbursements (averaging $3,823 per year) were awarded. Career-related internships or fieldwork, Federal Work-Study, institutionally sponsored loans, tuition waivers (partial), and unspecified assistantships also available. Financial award application deadline: 3/1; financial award applicants required to submit FAFSA.
Dr. Charles Reily, Chair, 407-823-2204, *E-mail:* creilly@mail.ucf.edu.
Application contact: Dr. Linda Malone, Coordinator, 407-823-2204, *E-mail:* malone@mail.ucf.edu. *Web site:* http://www.ucf.edu/
Find an in-depth description at www.petersons.com/gradchannel.

■ UNIVERSITY OF COLORADO AT COLORADO SPRINGS

Graduate School, College of Engineering and Applied Science, Department of Mechanical and Aerospace Engineering, Colorado Springs, CO 80933-7150

AWARDS Engineering management (ME); information operations (ME); manufacturing (ME); mechanical engineering (MS). Software engineering (ME). Space operations (ME). Part-time and evening/weekend programs available.

Faculty: 7 full-time (0 women), 5 part-time/adjunct (3 women).
Students: 16 full-time (3 women), 14 part-time (1 woman); includes 1 minority (Asian American or Pacific Islander), 1

international. Average age 35. In 2001, 26 degrees awarded.
Degree requirements: For master's, thesis optional.
Entrance requirements: For master's, GRE General Test, TOEFL, bachelor's degree in engineering or related degree, minimum GPA of 3.0. *Application deadline:* For fall admission, 7/15; for spring admission, 12/10. Applications are processed on a rolling basis. *Application fee:* $60 ($75 for international students).
Expenses: Tuition, state resident: full-time $2,900; part-time $174 per credit. Tuition, nonresident: full-time $9,961; part-time $591 per credit. Required fees: $14 per credit. $141 per semester. Tuition and fees vary according to course load, program and student level.
Faculty research: Neural networks, artificial intelligence, robust control, space operations, space propulsion.
Dr. Peter Gorder, Chair, 719-262-3168, *Fax:* 719-262-3589, *E-mail:* pgorder@ eas.uccs.edu.
Application contact: Siew Nylund, Academic Adviser, 719-262-3243, *Fax:* 719-262-3042, *E-mail:* snylund@uccs.edu. *Web site:* http://mepo-b.uccs.edu/ newsletter.html

■ UNIVERSITY OF DETROIT MERCY

College of Engineering and Science, Department of Mechanical Engineering, Detroit, MI 48219-0900
AWARDS Automotive engineering (DE); manufacturing engineering (DE); mechanical engineering (ME, DE). Evening/weekend programs available.

Faculty: 8 full-time (1 woman).
Students: 5 full-time (0 women), 28 part-time (3 women); includes 1 minority (Asian American or Pacific Islander), 23 international. Average age 31. In 2001, 12 degrees awarded.
Degree requirements: For doctorate, thesis/dissertation.
Application deadline: For fall admission, 8/1 (priority date). Applications are processed on a rolling basis. *Application fee:* $30 ($50 for international students).
Expenses: Tuition: Full-time $10,620; part-time $590 per credit hour. Required fees: $400. Tuition and fees vary according to program.
Faculty research: CAD/CAM.
Mark Schumak, Chairman, 313-993-3370, *Fax:* 313-993-1187, *E-mail:* schumamr@ udmercy.edu.

■ UNIVERSITY OF FLORIDA

Graduate School, College of Engineering, Department of Industrial and Systems Engineering, Program in Manufacturing Systems Engineering, Gainesville, FL 32611
AWARDS ME, MS, PhD, Certificate. Offered in cooperation with the Departments of

Aerospace Engineering, Mechanics, and Engineering Science; Computer and Information Sciences; Electrical Engineering; Industrial and Systems Engineering; Materials Science and Engineering; and Mechanical Engineering.

Degree requirements: For master's, core exam, project or thesis; for doctorate, thesis/dissertation, comprehensive exam.
Entrance requirements: For master's and doctorate, GRE General Test, TOEFL, minimum GPA of 3.0; for Certificate, GRE General Test. Electronic applications accepted.
Expenses: Tuition, state resident: part-time $164 per hour. Tuition, nonresident: part-time $571 per hour. Tuition and fees vary according to course level and program.
Find an in-depth description at www.petersons.com/gradchannel.

■ UNIVERSITY OF HOUSTON

College of Technology, Houston, TX 77204
AWARDS Construction management (MT); manufacturing systems (MT); microcomputer systems (MT); occupational technology (MSOT). Part-time and evening/weekend programs available.

Faculty: 11 full-time (5 women), 13 part-time/adjunct (4 women).
Students: 36 full-time (17 women), 60 part-time (21 women); includes 28 minority (16 African Americans, 4 Asian Americans or Pacific Islanders, 8 Hispanic Americans), 17 international. Average age 35. 33 applicants, 82% accepted. In 2001, 25 degrees awarded.
Entrance requirements: For master's, GMAT, GRE, or MAT (MSOT); GRE (MT), minimum GPA of 3.0 in last 60 hours. *Application deadline:* For fall admission, 7/1; for spring admission, 11/1. *Application fee:* $35 ($110 for international students).
Expenses: Tuition, state resident: full-time $1,512. Tuition, nonresident: full-time $5,310. Required fees: $1,308. Tuition and fees vary according to program.
Financial support: Fellowships, research assistantships, teaching assistantships, career-related internships or fieldwork, Federal Work-Study, and institutionally sponsored loans available. Support available to part-time students.
Faculty research: Educational delivery systems, technical curriculum development, computer-integrated manufacturing, neural networks. *Total annual research expenditures:* $354,283.
Uma G. Gupta, Dean, 713-743-4032, *Fax:* 713-743-4032.
Application contact: Holly Rosenthal, Graduate Academic Adviser, 713-743-4098, *Fax:* 713-743-4032, *E-mail:* hrosenthal@uh.edu. *Web site:* http:// www.tech.uh.edu/

■ THE UNIVERSITY OF IOWA

Graduate College, College of Engineering, Department of Industrial Engineering, Iowa City, IA 52242-1316
AWARDS Engineering design and manufacturing (MS, PhD); ergonomics (MS, PhD); information and engineering management (MS, PhD); operations research (MS, PhD); quality engineering (MS, PhD).

Faculty: 7 full-time, 1 part-time/adjunct.
Students: 37 full-time (13 women), 24 international. Average age 27. 115 applicants, 50% accepted, 6 enrolled. In 2001, 12 master's, 3 doctorates awarded.
Degree requirements: For master's, exam, thesis optional; for doctorate, thesis/ dissertation, final defense exam, comprehensive exam, registration. *Median time to degree:* Master's–2 years full-time; doctorate–4 years full-time.
Entrance requirements: For master's and doctorate, GRE General Test, TOEFL. *Application deadline:* For fall admission, 4/15; for winter admission, 10/1; for spring admission, 3/1. Applications are processed on a rolling basis. *Application fee:* $30 ($50 for international students). Electronic applications accepted.
Expenses: Tuition, state resident: full-time $3,702; part-time $206 per semester hour. Tuition, nonresident: full-time $11,924; part-time $206 per semester hour. Required fees: $101 per semester. Tuition and fees vary according to course load and program.
Financial support: In 2001–02, fellowships with tuition reimbursements (averaging $14,764 per year), 16 research assistantships (averaging $14,764 per year), 6 teaching assistantships (averaging $14,764 per year) were awarded. Career-related internships or fieldwork, scholarships/grants, and unspecified assistantships also available. Support available to part-time students. Financial award applicants required to submit FAFSA.
Faculty research: Informatics, industrial robotics, operations research, human-computer interfaces, human factors (ergonomics). *Total annual research expenditures:* $752,000.
Dr. Jeffrey S. Marshall, Departmental Executive Officer, 319-335-5817, *Fax:* 319-335-5669, *E-mail:* jeffrey-marshall@ uiowa.edu.
Application contact: Sue Mulder, Secretary, 319-335-5939, *Fax:* 319-335-5669, *E-mail:* indeng@ engineering.uiowa.edu. *Web site:* http:// www.mie.engineering.uiowa.edu

■ UNIVERSITY OF KENTUCKY

Graduate School, Graduate School Programs from the College of Engineering, Program in Manufacturing Systems Engineering, Lexington, KY 40506-0032
AWARDS MSMSE.

University of Kentucky (continued)

Students: 21 full-time (1 woman), 4 part-time, 17 international. 75 applicants, 59% accepted. In 2001, 2 degrees awarded.

Degree requirements: For master's, comprehensive exam.

Entrance requirements: For master's, GRE General Test. *Application deadline:* For fall admission, 7/19. Applications are processed on a rolling basis. *Application fee:* $30 ($35 for international students).

Expenses: Tuition, state resident: full-time $4,075; part-time $213 per credit hour. Tuition, nonresident: full-time $11,295; part-time $614 per credit hour.

Financial support: In 2001–02, 11 research assistantships were awarded.

Faculty research: Manufacturing processes and equipment, manufacturing systems and control, computer-aided design and manufacturing, automation in manufacturing, electric manufacturing and packaging.

Dr. Larry Holloway, Director of Graduate Studies, 859-257-6262 Ext. 203, *Fax:* 859-323-1035, *E-mail:* dgs-mts@engr.uky.edu.

Application contact: Dr. Jeannine Blackwell, Associate Dean, 859-257-4905, *Fax:* 859-323-1928.

■ UNIVERSITY OF MARYLAND, COLLEGE PARK

Graduate Studies and Research, A. James Clark School of Engineering, Department of Mechanical Engineering, College Park, MD 20742

AWARDS Electronic packaging and reliability (MS, PhD); manufacturing and design (MS, PhD); mechanics and materials (MS, PhD); thermal and fluid sciences (MS, PhD). Part-time and evening/weekend programs available. Postbaccalaureate distance learning degree programs offered.

Faculty: 69 full-time (6 women), 15 part-time/adjunct (2 women).

Students: 142 full-time (18 women), 67 part-time (5 women); includes 13 minority (5 African Americans, 6 Asian Americans or Pacific Islanders, 2 Hispanic Americans), 134 international. 519 applicants, 14% accepted, 40 enrolled. In 2001, 49 master's, 21 doctorates awarded.

Degree requirements: For master's, thesis optional; for doctorate, thesis/dissertation, qualifying exam.

Entrance requirements: For master's and doctorate, GRE General Test, minimum GPA of 3.0. *Application deadline:* For fall admission, 8/1; for spring admission, 12/1. Applications are processed on a rolling basis. *Application fee:* $50 ($70 for international students). Electronic applications accepted.

Expenses: Tuition, state resident: part-time $289 per credit hour. Tuition, nonresident: part-time $448 per credit hour. One-time fee: $436 part-time. Full-time tuition and fees vary according to course load, campus/location and program.

Financial support: In 2001–02, 5 fellowships with full tuition reimbursements (averaging $4,406 per year), 123 research assistantships with tuition reimbursements (averaging $14,539 per year), 36 teaching assistantships with tuition reimbursements (averaging $11,663 per year) were awarded. Federal Work-Study and scholarships/grants also available. Support available to part-time students. Financial award applicants required to submit FAFSA.

Faculty research: Decomposition-based design, powder metallurgy, injection molding, kinematic synthesis, electronic packaging, dynamic deformation and fracture, turbulent flow.

Dr. Avi Bar-Cohen, Chairman, 301-405-5294, *Fax:* 301-314-9477.

Application contact: Dr. James M. Wallace, Graduate Director, 301-405-4216.

■ UNIVERSITY OF MASSACHUSETTS AMHERST

Graduate School, College of Engineering, Department of Mechanical and Industrial Engineering, Program in Manufacturing Engineering, Amherst, MA 01003

AWARDS MS.

Students: Average age 24. 24 applicants, 4% accepted. In 2001, 1 degree awarded.

Entrance requirements: For master's, GRE General Test. *Application deadline:* For fall admission, 2/1 (priority date); for spring admission, 10/1. Applications are processed on a rolling basis. *Application fee:* $40 ($50 for international students).

Expenses: Tuition, state resident: full-time $1,980; part-time $110 per credit. Tuition, nonresident: full-time $7,456; part-time $414 per credit. Required fees: $4,112. One-time fee: $115 full-time.

Financial support: Fellowships with full tuition reimbursements, research assistantships with full tuition reimbursements, teaching assistantships with full tuition reimbursements, career-related internships or fieldwork, Federal Work-Study, scholarships/grants, traineeships, and unspecified assistantships available. Support available to part-time students. Financial award application deadline: 2/1.

Dr. Ian Grosse, Director, 413-545-2505, *Fax:* 413-545-1027.

■ THE UNIVERSITY OF MEMPHIS

Graduate School, Herff College of Engineering, Department of Engineering Technology, Memphis, TN 38152

AWARDS Architectural technology (MS); electronics engineering technology (MS); manufacturing engineering technology (MS). Part-time and evening/weekend programs available.

Faculty: 7 full-time (1 woman), 3 part-time/adjunct (1 woman).

Students: 76 full-time (15 women), 6 part-time (1 woman), 77 international. Average age 28. 25 applicants, 68% accepted. In 2001, 26 degrees awarded.

Degree requirements: For master's, thesis optional.

Entrance requirements: For master's, GRE General Test, minimum undergraduate GPA of 2.5. *Application deadline:* For fall admission, 8/1; for spring admission, 12/1. Applications are processed on a rolling basis. *Application fee:* $25 ($50 for international students). Electronic applications accepted.

Expenses: Tuition, state resident: full-time $2,026. Tuition, nonresident: full-time $4,528.

Financial support: In 2001–02, 56 research assistantships with full tuition reimbursements (averaging $1,700 per year) were awarded; career-related internships or fieldwork also available. Financial award application deadline: 9/1.

Faculty research: Teacher education services-technology education; flexible manufacturing control systems; embedded, dedicated, and real-time computer systems; network, Internet, and web-based programming; analog and digital electronic communication systems. *Total annual research expenditures:* $68,205.

Ronald L. Day, Chairman, 901-678-2238, *Fax:* 901-678-5145, *E-mail:* rday@memphis.edu.

Application contact: Dr. Dean L. Smith, Coordinator of Graduate Studies, 901-678-3300, *Fax:* 901-678-5145, *E-mail:* dlsmith@memphis.edu. *Web site:* http://www.people.memphis.edu/~engtech/grad.htm

■ UNIVERSITY OF MICHIGAN

Horace H. Rackham School of Graduate Studies, College of Engineering, Program in Manufacturing, Ann Arbor, MI 48109

AWARDS M Eng, D Eng, MBA/M Eng. Part-time programs available. Postbaccalaureate distance learning degree programs offered (no on-campus study).

Faculty: 1 full-time (0 women), 2 part-time/adjunct (0 women).

Students: 35 full-time (6 women), 60 part-time (14 women); includes 15 minority (6 African Americans, 5 Asian Americans or Pacific Islanders, 4 Hispanic Americans), 41 international. Average age 30. 65 applicants, 72% accepted. In 2001, 19 master's, 1 doctorate awarded. Terminal master's awarded for partial completion of doctoral program.

Degree requirements: For master's, team project; for doctorate, thesis/dissertation, preliminary and qualifying exams. *Median time to degree:* Master's–1 year full-time, 2.5 years part-time; doctorate–4 years full-time.

Entrance requirements: For doctorate, GRE General Test. *Application deadline:* For fall admission, 7/15 (priority date); for winter admission, 10/15 (priority date); for spring admission, 1/15 (priority date). Applications are processed on a rolling basis. *Application fee:* $55. Electronic applications accepted.
Financial support: In 2001–02, 2 students received support, including 2 fellowships with full and partial tuition reimbursements available, 2 teaching assistantships with full tuition reimbursements available (averaging $12,852 per year); research assistantships, career-related internships or fieldwork and institutionally sponsored loans also available. Financial award application deadline: 2/1; financial award applicants required to submit FAFSA. Prof. Jack Shixin Hu, Director, 734-764-3312, *Fax:* 734-647-0079, *E-mail:* pim@engin.umich.edu.
Application contact: Henia Kamil, Administrative Associate, 734-763-0480, *Fax:* 734-647-0079, *E-mail:* hek@umich.edu. *Web site:* http://www.engin.umich.edu/prog/pim/

■ UNIVERSITY OF MICHIGAN–DEARBORN

College of Engineering and Computer Science, Interdisciplinary Programs, Program in Manufacturing Systems Engineering, Dearborn, MI 48128-1491
AWARDS MSE, D Eng. Part-time and evening/weekend programs available.
Faculty: 1 full-time (0 women).
Students: 8 full-time (1 woman), 38 part-time (8 women); includes 10 minority (4 African Americans, 5 Asian Americans or Pacific Islanders, 1 Hispanic American). Average age 30. 20 applicants, 75% accepted, 15 enrolled. In 2001, 16 degrees awarded.
Degree requirements: For master's, thesis optional.
Entrance requirements: For master's, TOEFL, bachelor's degree in applied mathematics, computer science, engineering, or physical science; minimum GPA of 3.0. *Application deadline:* For fall admission, 8/1 (priority date); for winter admission, 12/1 (priority date); for spring admission, 4/1. Applications are processed on a rolling basis. *Application fee:* $55. Electronic applications accepted.
Expenses: Tuition, state resident: part-time $300 per credit hour. Tuition, nonresident: part-time $756 per credit hour. Required fees: $90 per semester. Tuition and fees vary according to course level, course load and program.
Financial support: In 2001–02, 3 research assistantships with full tuition reimbursements were awarded. Financial award application deadline: 4/1; financial award applicants required to submit FAFSA.
Faculty research: Toolwear metrology, paper handling, grinding wheel imbalance, machine mission.

Application contact: Sherry Boyd, Administrative Assistant I, 313-593-5582, *Fax:* 313-593-5386, *E-mail:* idpgrad@umd.umich.edu. *Web site:* http://www.engin.umd.umich.edu

■ UNIVERSITY OF MISSOURI–COLUMBIA

Graduate School, College of Engineering, Department of Industrial and Manufacturing Systems Engineering, Columbia, MO 65211
AWARDS MS, PhD.
Faculty: 7 full-time (0 women).
Students: 18 full-time (3 women), 7 part-time; includes 3 minority (all African Americans), 21 international. 31 applicants, 48% accepted. In 2001, 8 master's, 6 doctorates awarded.
Degree requirements: For master's, thesis or alternative; for doctorate, thesis/dissertation.
Entrance requirements: For master's and doctorate, GRE General Test, TOEFL, minimum GPA of 3.0. *Application deadline:* For fall admission, 5/1 (priority date). Applications are processed on a rolling basis. *Application fee:* $25 ($50 for international students).
Expenses: Tuition, state resident: part-time $179 per credit hour. Tuition, nonresident: part-time $539 per credit hour. Required fees: $122 per semester. Tuition and fees vary according to program.
Financial support: Research assistantships, teaching assistantships, institutionally sponsored loans available.
Dr. Jose Zayas-Castro, Director of Graduate Studies, 573-882-9567, *E-mail:* zayascastroj@missouri.edu. *Web site:* http://www.engineering.missouri.edu/industrial.htm

■ UNIVERSITY OF MISSOURI–ROLLA

Graduate School, School of Engineering, Program in Manufacturing Engineering, Rolla, MO 65409-0910
AWARDS M Eng, MS.

■ UNIVERSITY OF NEBRASKA–LINCOLN

Graduate College, College of Engineering and Technology, Interdepartmental Area of Manufacturing Systems Engineering, Lincoln, NE 68588
AWARDS Engineering (PhD); manufacturing systems engineering (MS). Postbaccalaureate distance learning degree programs offered.
Students: 17 (3 women) 12 international. Average age 28. 24 applicants, 54% accepted, 4 enrolled. In 2001, 6 degrees awarded.

Degree requirements: For master's, thesis optional; for doctorate, thesis/dissertation, comprehensive exam.
Entrance requirements: For master's and doctorate, GRE General Test, TOEFL. *Application deadline:* For fall admission, 3/1 (priority date). Applications are processed on a rolling basis. *Application fee:* $35. Electronic applications accepted.
Expenses: Tuition, state resident: full-time $2,412; part-time $134 per credit. Tuition, nonresident: full-time $6,223; part-time $346 per credit. Tuition and fees vary according to course load.
Financial support: In 2001–02, 6 research assistantships were awarded; fellowships, teaching assistantships, Federal Work-Study also available. Support available to part-time students. Financial award application deadline: 2/15.
Faculty research: Design and control of manufacturing systems; non-traditional manufacturing processes.
Dr. Robert Williams, Graduate Committee Chair, 402-472-3495. *Web site:* http://www.engr.unl.edu/ie/manufacturing/html/

■ UNIVERSITY OF NEW MEXICO

Graduate School, School of Engineering, Manufacturing Engineering Program, Albuquerque, NM 87131-2039
AWARDS MEME. Program supports concentration in manufacturing engineering available in the MS programs in mechanical engineering and electrical engineering and computer engineering. Part-time programs available.
Faculty: 1 part-time/adjunct (0 women).
Students: 7 full-time (0 women), 5 part-time (1 woman); includes 1 minority (Hispanic American), 4 international. Average age 34. In 2001, 2 degrees awarded.
Entrance requirements: For master's, GRE General Test, minimum GPA of 3.0. *Application deadline:* For fall admission, 6/30; for spring admission, 11/15. *Application fee:* $40.
Expenses: Tuition, state resident: full-time $2,771; part-time $115 per credit hour. Tuition, nonresident: full-time $11,207; part-time $467 per credit hour. Required fees: $570; $24 per credit hour. Part-time tuition and fees vary according to course load and program.
Financial support: In 2001–02, 1 fellowship (averaging $10,000 per year), 6 research assistantships with full tuition reimbursements (averaging $20,150 per year) were awarded. Career-related internships or fieldwork and health care benefits also available. Financial award application deadline: 3/1; financial award applicants required to submit FAFSA.
Faculty research: Robotics and automation control, microsystems, semiconductor manufacturing, cross training and operations, metrology. *Total annual research expenditures:* $679,837.

University of New Mexico (continued)
Dr. John E. Wood, Director, 505-277-1420, *Fax:* 505-277-1281, *E-mail:* wood@me.unm.edu.
Application contact: Information Contact, 505-277-7150, *Fax:* 505-277-1281, *E-mail:* wood@me.unm.edu.
Find an in-depth description at www.petersons.com/gradchannel.

■ UNIVERSITY OF PITTSBURGH

School of Engineering, Program in Manufacturing Systems Engineering, Pittsburgh, PA 15260

AWARDS MSMfSE. Part-time and evening/weekend programs available. Postbaccalaureate distance learning degree programs offered (no on-campus study).

Degree requirements: For master's, thesis, internship or project.
Entrance requirements: For master's, GRE General Test, TOEFL.
Faculty research: Manufacturing information systems, manufacturing process simulation, product design methods. *Web site:* http://www.pitt.edu/~pittie/

■ UNIVERSITY OF RHODE ISLAND

Graduate School, College of Engineering, Department of Industrial and Manufacturing Engineering, Program in Manufacturing Engineering, Kingston, RI 02881

AWARDS MS.

Application deadline: For fall admission, 4/15 (priority date). Applications are processed on a rolling basis. *Application fee:* $35.
Expenses: Tuition, state resident: full-time $3,756; part-time $209 per credit. Tuition, nonresident: full-time $10,774; part-time $599 per credit. Required fees: $1,586; $76 per credit. $76 per credit. One-time fee: $60 full-time.
Application contact: Graduate Program Director, 401-874-2455.

■ UNIVERSITY OF ST. THOMAS

Graduate Studies, Graduate School of Applied Science and Engineering, Program in Engineering and Technology Management, St. Paul, MN 55105-1096

AWARDS Engineering and technology management (Certificate); manufacturing systems (MS); manufacturing systems engineering (MMSE); technology management (MS). Part-time and evening/weekend programs available.
Faculty: 3 full-time (0 women), 32 part-time/adjunct (1 woman).
Students: 2 full-time (0 women), 219 part-time (39 women); includes 23 minority (10 African Americans, 9 Asian Americans or Pacific Islanders, 3 Hispanic Americans, 1

Native American), 6 international. Average age 34. 60 applicants, 97% accepted. In 2001, 29 master's, 5 other advanced degrees awarded.
Degree requirements: For master's, thesis (for some programs).
Application deadline: For fall admission, 8/1 (priority date); for spring admission, 1/1 (priority date). Applications are processed on a rolling basis. *Application fee:* $30. Electronic applications accepted.
Expenses: Tuition: Part-time $401 per credit. Tuition and fees vary according to degree level and program.
Financial support: In 2001–02, 6 students received support; fellowships, research assistantships, institutionally sponsored loans and scholarships/grants available. Support available to part-time students. Financial award application deadline: 4/1; financial award applicants required to submit FAFSA.
Ron Bennett, Director, 651-962-5750, *Fax:* 651-962-6419, *E-mail:* rjbennett@stthomas.edu.
Application contact: Marlene L. Houliston, Student Services Coordinator, 651-962-5750, *Fax:* 651-962-6419, *E-mail:* technology@stthomas.edu. *Web site:* http://www.stthomas.edu/technology/

■ UNIVERSITY OF SOUTHERN CALIFORNIA

Graduate School, School of Engineering, Department of Industrial and Systems Engineering, Program in Manufacturing Engineering, Los Angeles, CA 90089

AWARDS MS.

Degree requirements: For master's, thesis optional.
Entrance requirements: For master's, GRE General Test.
Expenses: Tuition: Full-time $25,060; part-time $844 per unit. Required fees: $473.
Faculty research: Transportation systems, rapid prototyping.
Find an in-depth description at www.petersons.com/gradchannel.

■ UNIVERSITY OF SOUTHERN MAINE

School of Applied Science, Engineering, and Technology, Department of Technology, Portland, ME 04104-9300

AWARDS Manufacturing systems (MS).

Expenses: Tuition, state resident: part-time $200 per credit. Tuition, nonresident: part-time $560 per credit. *Web site:* http://www.usm.maine.edu/tech/

■ THE UNIVERSITY OF TENNESSEE

Graduate School, College of Engineering, Department of Industrial Engineering, Knoxville, TN 37996

AWARDS Engineering management (MS); manufacturing systems engineering (MS); product development and manufacturing (MS); traditional industrial engineering (MS). Part-time programs available. Postbaccalaureate distance learning degree programs offered (no on-campus study).

Faculty: 10 full-time (1 woman).
Students: 21 full-time (6 women), 70 part-time (15 women); includes 6 minority (4 African Americans, 2 Asian Americans or Pacific Islanders), 13 international. 56 applicants, 50% accepted. In 2001, 50 degrees awarded.
Degree requirements: For master's, thesis or alternative.
Entrance requirements: For master's, GRE General Test, TOEFL, minimum GPA of 2.7. *Application deadline:* For fall admission, 2/1 (priority date). Applications are processed on a rolling basis. *Application fee:* $35. Electronic applications accepted.
Expenses: Tuition, state resident: full-time $4,280; part-time $233 per hour. Tuition, nonresident: full-time $12,066; part-time $666 per hour. Tuition and fees vary according to program.
Financial support: In 2001–02, 1 fellowship, 5 research assistantships, 5 teaching assistantships were awarded. Career-related internships or fieldwork, Federal Work-Study, institutionally sponsored loans, and unspecified assistantships also available. Financial award application deadline: 2/1; financial award applicants required to submit FAFSA.
Dr. Adedeji B. Badiru, Head, 865-974-3333, *Fax:* 865-974-0588, *E-mail:* abadiru@utk.edu.
Application contact: Dr. Denise Jackson, Graduate Representative, *E-mail:* djackson@utk.edu.

■ THE UNIVERSITY OF TENNESSEE

Graduate School, College of Engineering, Department of Mechanical and Aerospace Engineering and Engineering Science, Program in Engineering Science, Knoxville, TN 37996

AWARDS Applied artificial intelligence (MS); biomedical engineering (MS, PhD); composite materials (MS, PhD); computational mechanics (MS, PhD); engineering science (MS, PhD); fluid mechanics (MS, PhD); industrial engineering (PhD); optical engineering (MS, PhD); product development and manufacturing (MS). Solid mechanics (MS, PhD). Part-time programs available.

Students: 25 full-time (5 women), 16 part-time (2 women); includes 6 minority (2

African Americans, 2 Asian Americans or Pacific Islanders, 1 Hispanic American, 1 Native American), 9 international. 20 applicants, 70% accepted. In 2001, 6 master's, 6 doctorates awarded.
Degree requirements: For master's, thesis or alternative; for doctorate, thesis/dissertation.
Entrance requirements: For master's and doctorate, TOEFL, minimum GPA of 2.7. *Application deadline:* For fall admission, 2/1 (priority date). Applications are processed on a rolling basis. *Application fee:* $35. Electronic applications accepted.
Expenses: Tuition, state resident: full-time $4,280; part-time $233 per hour. Tuition, nonresident: full-time $12,066; part-time $666 per hour. Tuition and fees vary according to program.
Financial support: Career-related internships or fieldwork, Federal Work-Study, and institutionally sponsored loans available. Financial award application deadline: 2/1; financial award applicants required to submit FAFSA.
Application contact: Dr. Majid Keyhani, Graduate Representative, 865-974-4795, *E-mail:* keyhani@utk.edu.

■ **THE UNIVERSITY OF TEXAS AT AUSTIN**

Graduate School, College of Engineering, Department of Mechanical Engineering, Austin, TX 78712-1111

AWARDS Manufacturing systems engineering (MSE); mechanical engineering (MSE, PhD); operations research and industrial engineering (MSE, PhD).

Students: 162 full-time (14 women), 45 part-time (7 women); includes 11 minority (4 African Americans, 7 Hispanic Americans), 109 international. 501 applicants, 43% accepted. In 2001, 35 master's, 16 doctorates awarded.
Entrance requirements: For master's, GRE General Test, TOEFL; for doctorate, GRE General Test. *Application fee:* $50 ($75 for international students).
Expenses: Tuition, state resident: full-time $3,159. Tuition, nonresident: full-time $6,957. Tuition and fees vary according to program.
Financial support: Fellowships, research assistantships, teaching assistantships available. Financial award application deadline: 2/1.
Dr. Joseph J. Beaman, Chairman, 512-471-3058, *Fax:* 512-471-8727.
Application contact: Dr. David G. Bogard, Graduate Advisor, 512-471-3128, *Fax:* 512-471-8727.

■ **THE UNIVERSITY OF TEXAS AT AUSTIN**

Graduate School, College of Engineering, Program in Manufacturing Systems Engineering, Austin, TX 78712-1111

AWARDS MSE, MBA/MSE.

Faculty: 69 full-time (7 women), 1 part-time/adjunct (0 women).
Students: 62 full-time (6 women), 8 part-time; includes 4 minority (3 Asian Americans or Pacific Islanders, 1 Hispanic American), 19 international. 76 applicants, 71% accepted. In 2001, 15 degrees awarded.
Entrance requirements: For master's, GRE General Test. *Application fee:* $50 ($75 for international students).
Expenses: Tuition, state resident: full-time $3,159. Tuition, nonresident: full-time $6,957. Tuition and fees vary according to program.
Financial support: In 2001–02, 15 students received support, including 1 fellowship; research assistantships, teaching assistantships, career-related internships or fieldwork also available. Financial award application deadline: 2/1; financial award applicants required to submit FAFSA.
Joel Barlow, Director, 512-471-1271.
Application contact: Michael Bryant, Graduate Adviser, 512-471-3610. *Web site:* http://www.me.utexas.edu/~bryant/mfg

■ **THE UNIVERSITY OF TEXAS AT EL PASO**

Graduate School, College of Engineering, Department of Mechanical and Industrial Engineering, Program in Manufacturing Engineering, El Paso, TX 79968-0001

AWARDS MS. Part-time and evening/weekend programs available.

Students: 26 (4 women); includes 10 minority (all Hispanic Americans) 15 international. Average age 34. 10 applicants, 100% accepted. In 2001, 6 degrees awarded.
Degree requirements: For master's, thesis optional.
Entrance requirements: For master's, GRE General Test, TOEFL, minimum GPA of 3.0 in major. *Application deadline:* For fall admission, 7/1 (priority date); for spring admission, 11/1 (priority date). Applications are processed on a rolling basis. *Application fee:* $15 ($65 for international students). Electronic applications accepted.
Expenses: Tuition, state resident: full-time $2,450. Tuition, nonresident: full-time $6,000.
Financial support: In 2001–02, research assistantships with partial tuition reimbursements (averaging $21,125 per year), teaching assistantships with partial tuition reimbursements (averaging $16,900

per year) were awarded. Fellowships with partial tuition reimbursements, Federal Work-Study, institutionally sponsored loans, scholarships/grants, and tuition waivers (partial) also available. Financial award application deadline: 3/15.
Dr. Rafael Gutierrez, Graduate Adviser, 915-747-5450, *Fax:* 915-747-5019, *E-mail:* rsgutier@utep.edu.
Application contact: Dr. Charles H. Ambler, Dean of the Graduate School, 915-747-5491 Ext. 7886, *Fax:* 915-747-5788, *E-mail:* cambler@miners.utep.edu.

■ **UNIVERSITY OF WISCONSIN–MADISON**

Graduate School, College of Engineering, Manufacturing Systems Engineering Program, Madison, WI 53706-1380

AWARDS MS. Part-time programs available. Postbaccalaureate distance learning degree programs offered (minimal on-campus study).

Faculty: 46 part-time/adjunct (7 women).
Students: 37 full-time (3 women), 16 part-time (1 woman); includes 3 minority (1 African American, 1 Asian American or Pacific Islander, 1 Hispanic American), 25 international. Average age 27. 135 applicants, 27% accepted, 25 enrolled. In 2001, 17 degrees awarded.
Degree requirements: For master's, thesis (for some programs), independent research projects. *Median time to degree:* Master's–2 years full-time, 2.5 years part-time.
Entrance requirements: For master's, GRE General Test, TOEFL. *Application deadline:* For fall admission, 6/15 (priority date); for spring admission, 10/31 (priority date). Applications are processed on a rolling basis. *Application fee:* $45. Electronic applications accepted.
Expenses: Tuition, state resident: full-time $7,361; part-time $399 per credit. Tuition, nonresident: full-time $20,499; part-time $1,282 per credit. Required fees: $34 per credit. Full-time tuition and fees vary according to course load, program, reciprocity agreements and student level.
Financial support: In 2001–02, 15 students received support, including 3 fellowships with tuition reimbursements available, 2 research assistantships with tuition reimbursements available (averaging $23,688 per year); career-related internships or fieldwork, Federal Work-Study, institutionally sponsored loans, and unspecified assistantships also available.
Faculty research: CAD/CAM, rapid prototyping, lead time reduction, quick response manufacturing. *Total annual research expenditures:* $250,000.
Rajan Suri, Director, 608-262-0921, *Fax:* 608-265-4017, *E-mail:* suri@engr.wisc.edu.
Application contact: Kurt J. Zimmerman, Assistant Director, 608-262-0921, *Fax:*

University of Wisconsin–Madison (continued)

608-265-4017, *E-mail:* mse@engr.wisc.edu. *Web site:* http://www.engr.wisc.edu/msep/

Find an in-depth description at www.petersons.com/gradchannel.

■ VILLANOVA UNIVERSITY

College of Engineering, Department of Mechanical Engineering, Villanova, PA 19085-1699

AWARDS Composite engineering (Certificate); machinery dynamics (Certificate); manufacturing (Certificate); mechanical engineering (MME); thermofluid systems (Certificate). Part-time and evening/weekend programs available. Postbaccalaureate distance learning degree programs offered (no on-campus study).

Faculty: 11 full-time (1 woman), 1 part-time/adjunct (0 women).
Students: 15 full-time (2 women), 27 part-time (1 woman); includes 8 minority (1 African American, 7 Asian Americans or Pacific Islanders). Average age 27. 16 applicants, 81% accepted, 6 enrolled. In 2001, 9 degrees awarded.
Degree requirements: For master's, thesis (for some programs).
Entrance requirements: For master's, GRE General Test (applicants with degrees from foreign universities), TOEFL, BME, minimum GPA of 3.0. *Application deadline:* For fall admission, 7/1 (priority date); for spring admission, 11/1. Applications are processed on a rolling basis. *Application fee:* $40. Electronic applications accepted.
Expenses: Tuition: Part-time $340 per credit. One-time fee: $115 full-time. Tuition and fees vary according to program.
Financial support: In 2001–02, 5 research assistantships with full tuition reimbursements (averaging $10,400 per year), 6 teaching assistantships with full tuition reimbursements (averaging $10,265 per year) were awarded. Federal Work-Study and tuition waivers (full) also available. Financial award application deadline: 3/15.
Faculty research: Composite materials, power plant systems, fluid mechanics, automated manufacturing, dynamic analysis.
Dr. Gerard F. Jones, Chairperson, 610-519-4980, *Fax:* 610-519-7312, *E-mail:* gerard.jones@villanova.edu.
Application contact: 800-338-7927, *Fax:* 610-519-6450. *Web site:* http://www.engineering.villanova.edu/me/index.html

Find an in-depth description at www.petersons.com/gradchannel.

■ WAYNE STATE UNIVERSITY

Graduate School, College of Engineering, Department of Industrial and Manufacturing Engineering, Program in Manufacturing Engineering, Detroit, MI 48202

AWARDS MS.

Students: 54. In 2001, 27 degrees awarded.
Degree requirements: For master's, thesis optional.
Entrance requirements: For master's, minimum undergraduate GPA of 2.8. *Application deadline:* For fall admission, 7/1 (priority date); for spring admission, 3/15. Applications are processed on a rolling basis. *Application fee:* $20 ($30 for international students).
Expenses: Tuition, state resident: full-time $3,764. Tuition and fees vary according to degree level and program.
Financial support: Fellowships, research assistantships, teaching assistantships, career-related internships or fieldwork available.
Faculty research: Design for manufacturing, machine tools, manufacturing processes, material selection for manufacturing, manufacturing systems.
Application contact: Olugbenga Mejabi, Graduate Director, 313-577-3134, *E-mail:* mejabi@mie.eng.wayne.edu.

■ WESTERN MICHIGAN UNIVERSITY

Graduate College, College of Engineering and Applied Sciences, Department of Industrial and Manufacturing Engineering, Program in Manufacturing Engineering, Kalamazoo, MI 49008-5202

AWARDS MS.

Faculty: 25 full-time (3 women).
Students: 18 full-time (0 women), 10 part-time; includes 4 minority (1 African American, 2 Asian Americans or Pacific Islanders, 1 Hispanic American), 20 international. 20 applicants, 55% accepted, 4 enrolled. In 2001, 4 degrees awarded.
Entrance requirements: For master's, GRE General Test, minimum GPA of 3.0. *Application deadline:* For fall admission, 2/15 (priority date). Applications are processed on a rolling basis. *Application fee:* $25.
Expenses: Tuition, state resident: part-time $186 per credit hour. Tuition, nonresident: part-time $442 per credit hour. Required fees: $602. One-time fee: $132 part-time. Tuition and fees vary according to course load.
Financial support: Application deadline: 2/15.
Application contact: Admissions and Orientation, 616-387-2000, *Fax:* 616-387-2355.

■ WESTERN NEW ENGLAND COLLEGE

School of Engineering, Department of Industrial and Manufacturing Engineering, Springfield, MA 01119-2654

AWARDS Production management (MSEM). Part-time and evening/weekend programs available.

Faculty: 4 full-time (0 women), 2 part-time/adjunct (0 women).
Students: Average age 29. 3 applicants, 67% accepted. In 2001, 6 degrees awarded.
Degree requirements: For master's, thesis optional.
Entrance requirements: For master's, GRE, bachelor's degree in engineering or related field. *Application deadline:* Applications are processed on a rolling basis. *Application fee:* $30.
Expenses: Tuition: Part-time $429 per credit. Required fees: $9 per credit. $20 per semester.
Financial support: Teaching assistantships available. Support available to part-time students. Financial award application deadline: 4/1; financial award applicants required to submit FAFSA.
Faculty research: Project scheduling, flexible manufacturing systems, facility layout, energy management.
Dr. Eric W. Haffner, Chair, 413-782-1272, *E-mail:* ehaffner@wnec.edu.
Application contact: Dr. Janet Castleman, Director of Continuing Education, 413-782-1750, *Fax:* 413-782-1779, *E-mail:* jcastlem@wnec.edu.

■ WICHITA STATE UNIVERSITY

Graduate School, College of Engineering, Department of Industrial and Manufacturing Engineering, Wichita, KS 67260

AWARDS MEM, MS, PhD. Part-time programs available.

Faculty: 9 full-time (0 women).
Students: 85 full-time (3 women), 76 part-time (16 women); includes 8 minority (3 African Americans, 3 Asian Americans or Pacific Islanders, 2 Hispanic Americans), 120 international. Average age 29. 218 applicants, 78% accepted, 44 enrolled. In 2001, 26 degrees awarded.
Degree requirements: For master's, thesis optional; for doctorate, one foreign language, thesis/dissertation, comprehensive exam.
Entrance requirements: For master's, GRE, TOEFL; for doctorate, GRE General Test, TOEFL. *Application deadline:* For fall admission, 7/1 (priority date); for spring admission, 1/1. Applications are processed on a rolling basis. *Application fee:* $25 ($40 for international students). Electronic applications accepted.
Expenses: Tuition, state resident: full-time $1,888; part-time $105 per credit. Tuition, nonresident: full-time $6,129; part-time

$341 per credit. Required fees: $345; $19 per credit. $17 per semester. Tuition and fees vary according to course load and program.
Financial support: In 2001–02, 47 research assistantships (averaging $4,673 per year), 12 teaching assistantships with full tuition reimbursements (averaging $4,108 per year) were awarded. Fellowships, Federal Work-Study, institutionally sponsored loans, and unspecified assistantships also available. Support available to part-time students. Financial award application deadline: 4/1; financial award applicants required to submit FAFSA.
Faculty research: Ergonomics, rehabilitation, operations research, reverse engineering, assembly design/planning.
Dr. Abu Masud, Chairperson, 316-978-3425, *Fax:* 316-978-3742, *E-mail:* abu.masud@wichita.edu. *Web site:* http://www.wichita.edu/

■ WORCESTER POLYTECHNIC INSTITUTE

Graduate Studies, Program in Manufacturing Engineering, Worcester, MA 01609-2280

AWARDS MS, PhD, Certificate. Part-time and evening/weekend programs available.

Faculty: 3 full-time (0 women), 1 part-time/adjunct (0 women).
Students: 16 full-time (2 women), 15 part-time; includes 4 minority (all African Americans), 14 international. 37 applicants, 76% accepted, 6 enrolled. In 2001, 5 degrees awarded.
Degree requirements: For master's, thesis; for doctorate, thesis/dissertation, research proposal, comprehensive exam.
Entrance requirements: For master's and doctorate, TOEFL. *Application deadline:* For fall admission, 2/1 (priority date); for spring admission, 10/15 (priority date). Applications are processed on a rolling basis. *Application fee:* $60. Electronic applications accepted.
Expenses: Tuition: Part-time $796 per credit. Required fees: $20; $752 per credit. One-time fee: $30 full-time.
Financial support: In 2001–02, 11 research assistantships with full tuition reimbursements (averaging $17,256 per year), 2 teaching assistantships with full tuition reimbursements (averaging $12,942 per year) were awarded. Fellowships with full tuition reimbursements, career-related internships or fieldwork, institutionally sponsored loans, and scholarships/grants also available. Financial award application deadline: 2/15; financial award applicants required to submit FAFSA.
Faculty research: Design for manufacturability, intelligent control engineering, traditional and non-traditional machining, computer integration and control of manufacturing, manufacturing management engineering. *Total annual research expenditures:* $305,932.

Dr. Christopher Brown, Director, 508-831-5627, *Fax:* 508-831-5680, *E-mail:* brown@@wpi.edu.
Application contact: Susan Milkman, Graduate Secretary, 508-831-6288, *Fax:* 508-831-5178, *E-mail:* smilkman@wpi.edu. *Web site:* http://guinness.wpi.edu/~mfe/

RELIABILITY ENGINEERING

■ THE UNIVERSITY OF ARIZONA

Graduate College, College of Engineering and Mines, Department of Systems and Industrial Engineering, Program in Reliability and Quality Engineering, Tucson, AZ 85721

AWARDS MS.

Students: 5 full-time (0 women), 1 international. Average age 40. 3 applicants, 100% accepted, 2 enrolled. In 2001, 3 degrees awarded.
Entrance requirements: For master's, GRE General Test, TOEFL, minimum GPA of 3.0. *Application deadline:* For fall admission, 7/1. Applications are processed on a rolling basis. *Application fee:* $45.
Expenses: Tuition, state resident: full-time $2,490; part-time $436 per unit. Tuition, nonresident: full-time $10,300; part-time $436 per unit. Full-time tuition and fees vary according to degree level and program.
Financial support: Fellowships, research assistantships, teaching assistantships available.
Application contact: Celia Stenzel, Graduate Secretary, 520-621-6551, *Fax:* 520-621-6555.

■ UNIVERSITY OF MARYLAND, COLLEGE PARK

Graduate Studies and Research, A. James Clark School of Engineering, Department of Materials and Nuclear Engineering, Reliability Engineering Program, College Park, MD 20742

AWARDS M Eng, MS, PhD. Part-time and evening/weekend programs available. Postbaccalaureate distance learning degree programs offered.

Students: 22 full-time (6 women), 31 part-time (7 women); includes 4 minority (1 African American, 3 Hispanic Americans), 24 international. 44 applicants, 43% accepted, 17 enrolled. In 2001, 26 master's, 3 doctorates awarded.
Degree requirements: For master's, thesis optional; for doctorate, thesis/dissertation, oral exam.
Entrance requirements: For master's and doctorate, GRE General Test, TOEFL, minimum GPA of 3.0. *Application deadline:* For fall admission, 8/1; for spring admission, 12/1. Applications are processed on a

rolling basis. *Application fee:* $50 ($70 for international students). Electronic applications accepted.
Expenses: Tuition, state resident: part-time $289 per credit hour. Tuition, nonresident: part-time $448 per credit hour. One-time fee: $436 part-time. Full-time tuition and fees vary according to course load, campus/location and program.
Financial support: Fellowships, research assistantships, teaching assistantships, career-related internships or fieldwork available. Financial award applicants required to submit FAFSA.
Faculty research: Electron linear acceleration, x-ray and imaging.
Dr. Carol Smidts, Associate Professor, 301-405-7299, *Fax:* 301-314-2029.
Application contact: Information, 301-405-7299.

Find an in-depth description at www.petersons.com/gradchannel.

■ UNIVERSITY OF MARYLAND, COLLEGE PARK

Graduate Studies and Research, A. James Clark School of Engineering, Professional Program in Engineering, College Park, MD 20742

AWARDS Aerospace engineering (M Eng); chemical engineering (M Eng); civil engineering (M Eng); electrical engineering (M Eng); fire protection engineering (M Eng); materials science and engineering (M Eng); mechanical engineering (M Eng); reliability engineering (M Eng). Systems engineering (M Eng). Part-time and evening/weekend programs available. Postbaccalaureate distance learning degree programs offered.

Faculty: 11 part-time/adjunct (0 women).
Students: 19 full-time (4 women), 144 part-time (31 women); includes 41 minority (17 African Americans, 18 Asian Americans or Pacific Islanders, 6 Hispanic Americans), 27 international. 71 applicants, 80% accepted, 50 enrolled. In 2001, 64 degrees awarded.
Application deadline: For fall admission, 8/15; for spring admission, 1/10. Applications are processed on a rolling basis. *Application fee:* $50 ($70 for international students). Electronic applications accepted.
Expenses: Tuition, state resident: part-time $289 per credit hour. Tuition, nonresident: part-time $448 per credit hour. One-time fee: $436 part-time. Full-time tuition and fees vary according to course load, campus/location and program.
Financial support: In 2001–02, 1 research assistantship with tuition reimbursement (averaging $20,655 per year), 5 teaching assistantships with tuition reimbursements (averaging $11,114 per year) were awarded. Fellowships, Federal Work-Study and scholarships/grants also available. Support available to part-time students. Financial award applicants required to submit FAFSA.

University of Maryland, College Park (continued)
Dr. George Syrmos, Acting Director, 301-405-5256, *Fax:* 301-314-9477.
Application contact: Trudy Lindsey, Director, Graduate Admissions and Records, 301-405-6991, *Fax:* 301-314-9305, *E-mail:* grschool@deans.umd.edu.

SAFETY ENGINEERING

■ CENTRAL MISSOURI STATE UNIVERSITY

School of Graduate Studies, College of Applied Sciences and Technology, Department of Safety Science Technology, Warrensburg, MO 64093

AWARDS Human services/public services (Ed S); industrial hygiene (MS); industrial safety management (MS); occupational safety management (MS); public services administration (MS). Safety management (MS). Secondary education/safety education (MSE). Security (MS); transportation safety (MS). Part-time programs available.

Faculty: 7 full-time (2 women), 3 part-time/adjunct (0 women).
Students: 7 full-time (4 women), 39 part-time (15 women); includes 5 minority (4 Hispanic Americans, 1 Native American). Average age 37. 20 applicants, 75% accepted. In 2001, 40 degrees awarded.
Degree requirements: For master's, comprehensive exam (MS), comprehensive exam or thesis (MSE).
Entrance requirements: For master's, GRE General Test, minimum GPA of 2.5, 15 hours in related area (MS); minimum GPA of 2.75, teaching certificate (MSE); for Ed S, master's degree in related field. *Application deadline:* Applications are processed on a rolling basis. *Application fee:* $25 ($50 for international students).
Expenses: Tuition, area resident: Full-time $4,200; part-time $175 per credit hour. Tuition, nonresident: full-time $8,352; part-time $348 per credit hour.
Financial support: In 2001–02, 2 research assistantships with full and partial tuition reimbursements (averaging $8,000 per year), 9 teaching assistantships (averaging $4,000 per year) were awarded. Federal Work-Study, scholarships/grants, unspecified assistantships, and administrative and laboratory assistantships also available. Support available to part-time students. Financial award application deadline: 3/1; financial award applicants required to submit FAFSA.
Faculty research: Hazard assessment, crisis and disaster, ergonomics, fire science, safety management. *Total annual research expenditures:* $2,000.
Larry Womble, Interim Chair, 660-543-8764, *Fax:* 660-543-8142, *E-mail:* womble@cmsu1.cmsu.edu. *Web site:* http://www.cmsu.edu/

■ MURRAY STATE UNIVERSITY

College of Health Sciences and Human Services, Department of Occupational Safety and Health, Murray, KY 42071-0009

AWARDS MS. Part-time programs available.

Students: 27 full-time (9 women), 20 part-time (4 women), 3 international. 11 applicants, 100% accepted.
Entrance requirements: For master's, GRE General Test, TOEFL. *Application deadline:* Applications are processed on a rolling basis. *Application fee:* $25.
Expenses: Tuition, state resident: full-time $1,440; part-time $169 per hour. Tuition, nonresident: full-time $4,004; part-time $450 per hour.
Financial support: Research assistantships, teaching assistantships, Federal Work-Study available. Financial award application deadline: 4/1.
Dr. Bassam Atieh, Graduate Coordinator, 270-762-6652, *Fax:* 270-762-3630, *E-mail:* bassam.atieh@murraystate.edu.

■ NEW JERSEY INSTITUTE OF TECHNOLOGY

Office of Graduate Studies, Department of Industrial and Manufacturing Engineering, Program in Occupational Safety and Health Engineering, Newark, NJ 07102

AWARDS MS. Part-time and evening/weekend programs available.

Students: 3 full-time (all women), 13 part-time (3 women); includes 8 minority (3 African Americans, 3 Asian Americans or Pacific Islanders, 2 Hispanic Americans). Average age 30. 15 applicants, 60% accepted, 4 enrolled. In 2001, 4 degrees awarded. Terminal master's awarded for partial completion of doctoral program.
Degree requirements: For master's, thesis or alternative.
Entrance requirements: For master's, GRE General Test. *Application deadline:* For fall admission, 6/5 (priority date); for spring admission, 10/15. Applications are processed on a rolling basis. *Application fee:* $50. Electronic applications accepted.
Expenses: Tuition, state resident: full-time $7,812; part-time $434 per credit. Tuition, nonresident: full-time $10,746; part-time $597 per credit. Required fees: $47 per credit. $76 per semester.
Financial support: Fellowships with full and partial tuition reimbursements, research assistantships with full and partial tuition reimbursements, teaching assistantships with full and partial tuition reimbursements, career-related internships or fieldwork, Federal Work-Study, institutionally sponsored loans, and unspecified assistantships available. Financial award application deadline: 3/15.
Faculty research: Human factors engineering, manufacturing systems, materials, manufacturing automation and

computer integration. *Total annual research expenditures:* $200,000.
Application contact: Kathryn Kelly, Director of Admissions, 973-596-3300, *Fax:* 973-596-3461, *E-mail:* admissions@njit.edu. *Web site:* http://www.njit.edu/

■ TEXAS A&M UNIVERSITY

College of Engineering, Department of Nuclear Engineering, Program in Health Physics/Radiological Health, College Station, TX 77843

AWARDS Health physics (MS); industrial hygiene (MS). Safety engineering (MS).

Students: Average age 33.
Degree requirements: For master's, thesis or alternative.
Entrance requirements: For master's, GRE General Test, TOEFL. *Application fee:* $50 ($75 for international students).
Expenses: Tuition, state resident: full-time $11,872. Tuition, nonresident: full-time $17,892.
Financial support: Fellowships, research assistantships, teaching assistantships available. Financial award application deadline: 4/1; financial award applicants required to submit FAFSA.
Application contact: Dr. Yassin A. Hassan, Graduate Coordinator, 979-845-7090.

■ UNIVERSITY OF MINNESOTA, DULUTH

Graduate School, College of Science and Engineering, Department of Industrial Engineering, Duluth, MN 55812-2496

AWARDS Engineering management (MS); environmental health and safety (MEHS). Part-time programs available. Postbaccalaureate distance learning degree programs offered (minimal on-campus study).

Faculty: 5 full-time (1 woman), 5 part-time/adjunct (0 women).
Students: 26 full-time (13 women), 21 part-time (2 women), 1 international. Average age 27. 28 applicants, 89% accepted, 25 enrolled. In 2001, 26 degrees awarded.
Degree requirements: For master's, capstone design project (MS), field project (MEHS).
Entrance requirements: For master's, interview (MEHS). *Application deadline:* For fall admission, 7/15; for spring admission, 5/1. *Application fee:* $50 ($55 for international students).
Expenses: Tuition, state resident: full-time $2,932; part-time $489 per credit. Tuition, nonresident: full-time $5,758; part-time $960 per credit. Tuition and fees vary according to course load.
Financial support: In 2001–02, 2 students received support, including 2 research assistantships with full tuition reimbursements available (averaging $11,000 per year); lab attendantship also available.

Faculty research: Transportation, ergonomics, industrial hygiene, toxicology, supply chain management. *Total annual research expenditures:* $40,000.
Dr. David A. Wyrick, Director of Graduate Studies, 218-726-7184, *Fax:* 218-726-8596, *E-mail:* dwyrick@d.umn.edu.
Application contact: Pat Wollack, Executive Secretary, 218-726-8117, *Fax:* 218-726-8581, *E-mail:* msem@d.umn.edu. *Web site:* http://ie.d.umn.edu/

■ UNIVERSITY OF WISCONSIN–STOUT

Graduate School, College of Technology, Engineering, and Management, Program in Risk Control, Menomonie, WI 54751

AWARDS MS. Part-time programs available.

Students: 20 full-time (5 women), 14 part-time (3 women); includes 3 minority (2 Hispanic Americans, 1 Native American). 14 applicants, 100% accepted, 12 enrolled. In 2001, 13 degrees awarded.
Degree requirements: For master's, thesis.
Application deadline: For fall admission, 6/1 (priority date); for spring admission, 12/1 (priority date). Applications are processed on a rolling basis. *Application fee:* $45.
Expenses: Tuition, state resident: full-time $4,915. Tuition, nonresident: full-time $12,553.
Financial support: In 2001–02, 5 research assistantships were awarded; teaching assistantships, Federal Work-Study and tuition waivers (full and partial) also available. Support available to part-time students. Financial award application deadline: 4/1; financial award applicants required to submit FAFSA.
Dr. Elbert Sorrell, Director, 715-232-2630, *E-mail:* sorrelle@uwstout.edu.
Application contact: Anne E. Johnson, Graduate Student Evaluator, 715-232-1322, *Fax:* 715-232-2413, *E-mail:* johnsona@uwstout.edu.

■ WEST VIRGINIA UNIVERSITY

College of Engineering and Mineral Resources, Department of Industrial and Management Systems Engineering, Program in Occupational Hygiene and Occupational Safety, Morgantown, WV 26506

AWARDS MS. Part-time programs available.

Students: 16 full-time (5 women), 18 part-time (6 women); includes 3 minority (1 African American, 1 Asian American or Pacific Islander, 1 Hispanic American), 2 international. Average age 31. In 2001, 30 degrees awarded.
Degree requirements: For master's, thesis or alternative.
Entrance requirements: For master's, TOEFL, minimum GPA of 2.75. *Application deadline:* For fall admission, 6/15 (priority date); for spring admission, 11/1.

Applications are processed on a rolling basis. *Application fee:* $45.
Expenses: Tuition, state resident: full-time $2,791. Tuition, nonresident: full-time $8,659. Required fees: $1,002. Tuition and fees vary according to program.
Financial support: In 2001–02, 10 research assistantships, 1 teaching assistantship were awarded. Fellowships, career-related internships or fieldwork, Federal Work-Study, institutionally sponsored loans, and tuition waivers (full and partial) also available. Financial award application deadline: 4/1; financial award applicants required to submit FAFSA.
Faculty research: Ergonomics, industrial hygiene, human factors engineering, back injuries. *Total annual research expenditures:* $258,000.
Dr. Warren R. Myers, Chair, 304-293-4607 Ext. 3716, *E-mail:* warren.myers@mail.wvu.edu. *Web site:* http://www.cemr.wvu.edu/%7ewwwohos/

■ WEST VIRGINIA UNIVERSITY

College of Engineering and Mineral Resources, Department of Industrial and Management Systems Engineering, Program in Safety and Environmental Management, Morgantown, WV 26506

AWARDS Safety management (MS).

Students: 36 full-time (7 women), 40 part-time (15 women); includes 2 minority (1 African American, 1 Asian American or Pacific Islander), 2 international. Average age 29. In 2001, 40 degrees awarded.
Expenses: Tuition, state resident: full-time $2,791. Tuition, nonresident: full-time $8,659. Required fees: $1,002. Tuition and fees vary according to program.
Financial support: In 2001–02, 11 research assistantships, 1 teaching assistantship were awarded.
Gary L. Winn, Program Coordinator, 304-293-2742 Ext. 3744, *E-mail:* gawinn@mail.wvu.edu.

SYSTEMS ENGINEERING

■ AIR FORCE INSTITUTE OF TECHNOLOGY

School of Engineering and Management, Department of Aeronautics and Astronautics, Dayton, OH 45433-7765

AWARDS Aeronautical engineering (MS, PhD); astronautical engineering (MS, PhD); materials science (MS, PhD). Space operations (MS). Systems engineering (MS). Part-time programs available.

Degree requirements: For master's and doctorate, thesis/dissertation.

Entrance requirements: For master's and doctorate, GRE General Test, minimum GPA of 3.0, U.S. citizenship.
Faculty research: Computational fluid dynamics, experimental aerodynamics, computational structural mechanics, experimental structural mechanics, aircraft and spacecraft stability and control. *Web site:* http://en.afit.edu/bny

■ AUBURN UNIVERSITY

Graduate School, College of Engineering, Department of Industrial and Systems Engineering, Auburn University, AL 36849

AWARDS MIE, MS, PhD. Part-time programs available.

Faculty: 7 full-time (1 woman).
Students: 25 full-time (7 women), 30 part-time (9 women); includes 6 minority (2 African Americans, 1 Asian American or Pacific Islander, 2 Hispanic Americans, 1 Native American), 15 international. 113 applicants, 41% accepted. In 2001, 6 master's, 2 doctorates awarded.
Degree requirements: For master's, design project (MIE), thesis (MS); for doctorate, thesis/dissertation.
Entrance requirements: For master's and doctorate, GRE General Test. *Application deadline:* For fall admission, 7/7; for spring admission, 11/24. Applications are processed on a rolling basis. *Application fee:* $25 ($50 for international students).
Financial support: Fellowships, research assistantships, teaching assistantships, Federal Work-Study available. Support available to part-time students. Financial award application deadline: 3/15.
Dr. Alice E. Smith, Chair, 334-844-1401.
Application contact: Dr. John F. Pritchett, Dean of the Graduate School, 334-844-4700, *E-mail:* hatchlb@mail.auburn.edu. *Web site:* http://www.eng.auburn.edu/department/ie

■ BOSTON UNIVERSITY

College of Engineering, Department of Electrical and Computer Engineering, Boston, MA 02215

AWARDS Computer engineering (PhD); computer systems engineering (MS); electrical engineering (MS, PhD). Systems engineering (PhD). Part-time programs available.

Faculty: 39 full-time (3 women), 3 part-time/adjunct (0 women).
Students: 110 full-time (25 women), 28 part-time (9 women); includes 9 minority (4 African Americans, 4 Asian Americans or Pacific Islanders, 1 Hispanic American), 72 international. Average age 29. 662 applicants, 19% accepted, 39 enrolled. In 2001, 39 master's, 7 doctorates awarded. Terminal master's awarded for partial completion of doctoral program.
Degree requirements: For master's, thesis optional; for doctorate, thesis/dissertation, comprehensive exam.

Boston University (continued)
Entrance requirements: For master's and doctorate, GRE General Test, TOEFL. *Application deadline:* For fall admission, 4/1; for spring admission, 10/1. Applications are processed on a rolling basis. *Application fee:* $60. Electronic applications accepted.
Expenses: Tuition: Full-time $25,872; part-time $340 per credit. Required fees: $40 per semester. Part-time tuition and fees vary according to class time, course level and program.
Financial support: In 2001–02, 83 students received support, including 5 fellowships with full tuition reimbursements available (averaging $15,500 per year), 40 research assistantships with full tuition reimbursements available (averaging $13,500 per year), 19 teaching assistantships with full tuition reimbursements available (averaging $13,500 per year); career-related internships or fieldwork, Federal Work-Study, institutionally sponsored loans, and scholarships/grants also available. Financial award application deadline: 1/15; financial award applicants required to submit FAFSA.
Faculty research: Computer networks, computer reliability, photonics, signal and image processing, solid state materials, subsurface imaging. *Total annual research expenditures:* $9.5 million.
Dr. Bahaa Saleh, Chairman, 617-353-7176, *Fax:* 617-353-6440.
Application contact: Cheryl Kelley, Director of Graduate Programs, 617-353-9760, *Fax:* 617-353-0259, *E-mail:* enggrad@bu.edu. *Web site:* http://www.eng.bu.edu/grad/
Find an in-depth description at www.petersons.com/gradchannel.

■ CALIFORNIA INSTITUTE OF TECHNOLOGY

Division of Engineering and Applied Science, Option in Control and Dynamical Systems, Pasadena, CA 91125-0001

AWARDS MS, PhD.

Faculty: 2 full-time (0 women).
Students: 23 full-time (4 women); includes 3 minority (1 Asian American or Pacific Islander, 2 Hispanic Americans), 13 international. 75 applicants, 7% accepted, 3 enrolled. In 2001, 1 master's, 1 doctorate awarded.
Degree requirements: For doctorate, thesis/dissertation.
Application deadline: For fall admission, 1/15. *Application fee:* $0.
Financial support: In 2001–02, 7 fellowships, 12 research assistantships, 5 teaching assistantships were awarded.
Faculty research: Robustness, multivariable and nonlinear systems, optimal control, decentralized control, modeling and system identification for robust control.

Dr. Jerrold Marsden, Option Representative, 626-395-6460.

■ CALIFORNIA STATE UNIVERSITY, FULLERTON

Graduate Studies, College of Engineering and Computer Science, Division of Engineering, Fullerton, CA 92834-9480

AWARDS Engineering science (MS). Systems engineering (MS). Part-time programs available.

Students: Average age 29. 3 applicants, 67% accepted, 0 enrolled. In 2001, 1 degree awarded.
Degree requirements: For master's, project or thesis.
Entrance requirements: For master's, minimum undergraduate GPA of 2.5. *Application fee:* $55.
Expenses: Tuition, nonresident: part-time $246 per unit. Required fees: $964.
Financial support: Career-related internships or fieldwork, Federal Work-Study, institutionally sponsored loans, and scholarships/grants available. Support available to part-time students. Financial award application deadline: 3/1.
Dr. Jesa Kreiner, Chair, 714-278-3362.

■ CAPITOL COLLEGE

Graduate Programs, Laurel, MD 20708-9759

AWARDS Computer science (MS); electrical engineering (MS); electronic commerce management (MS); information and telecommunications systems management (MS); information architecture (MS); network security (MS). Part-time and evening/weekend programs available. Postbaccalaureate distance learning degree programs offered (no on-campus study).

Faculty: 3 full-time (0 women), 34 part-time/adjunct (4 women).
Students: 6 full-time (3 women), 625 part-time (175 women). Average age 35. 400 applicants, 75% accepted, 275 enrolled. In 2001, 52 degrees awarded. *Median time to degree:* Master's–2 years part-time.
Entrance requirements: For master's, GRE General Test and TOEFL (for international students), minimum GPA of 2.5. *Application deadline:* For fall admission, 7/1 (priority date); for winter admission, 12/1 (priority date); for spring admission, 3/1 (priority date). Applications are processed on a rolling basis. *Application fee:* $100 for international students. Electronic applications accepted.
Expenses: Tuition: Part-time $354 per credit.
Financial support: In 2001–02, 2 students received support. Available to part-time students. Applicants required to submit FAFSA.
Pat Smit, Dean of Academics, 301-369-2800 Ext. 3044, *Fax:* 301-953-3876, *E-mail:* gradschool@capitol-college.edu.

Application contact: Ken Crockett, Director of Graduate Admissions, 301-369-2800 Ext. 3026, *Fax:* 301-953-3876, *E-mail:* gradschool@capitol-college.edu. *Web site:* http://www.capitol-college.edu/

■ CASE WESTERN RESERVE UNIVERSITY

School of Graduate Studies, The Case School of Engineering, Department of Electrical Engineering and Computer Science, Cleveland, OH 44106

AWARDS Computer engineering (MS, PhD); computing and information science (MS, PhD); electrical engineering (MS, PhD). Systems and control engineering (MS, PhD). Part-time and evening/weekend programs available. Postbaccalaureate distance learning degree programs offered (minimal on-campus study).

Faculty: 29 full-time (2 women), 15 part-time/adjunct (1 woman).
Students: 61 full-time (17 women), 72 part-time (6 women); includes 8 minority (3 African Americans, 5 Asian Americans or Pacific Islanders), 85 international. Average age 25. 843 applicants, 16% accepted, 27 enrolled. In 2001, 33 master's, 16 doctorates awarded. Terminal master's awarded for partial completion of doctoral program.
Degree requirements: For master's, thesis; for doctorate, thesis/dissertation, qualifying exam, teaching experience.
Entrance requirements: For master's and doctorate, GRE General Test, TOEFL. *Application deadline:* For fall admission, 2/1; for spring admission, 11/1. Applications are processed on a rolling basis. *Application fee:* $25.
Financial support: In 2001–02, 34 fellowships with full and partial tuition reimbursements (averaging $15,240 per year), 22 research assistantships with full and partial tuition reimbursements (averaging $14,220 per year) were awarded. Career-related internships or fieldwork, Federal Work-Study, and institutionally sponsored loans also available. Support available to part-time students. Financial award application deadline: 3/1; financial award applicants required to submit FAFSA.
Faculty research: Computational biology and biorobotics; HEHS and solid state, VSLI system design and testing; databases, software engineering, computer systems. Systems optimization, planning and decision making; digital signal processing, control and filtering theory. *Total annual research expenditures:* $3.2 million.
Dr. B. Ross Barmish, Chairman, 216-368-2833, *Fax:* 216-368-6888, *E-mail:* brb8@po.cwru.edu.
Application contact: Elizabethanne M. Fuller, Department Assistant, 216-368-4080, *Fax:* 216-368-2668, *E-mail:* emf4@po.cwru.edu. *Web site:* http://eecs.cwru.edu/

■ COLORADO SCHOOL OF MINES

Graduate School, Division of Engineering, Golden, CO 80401-1887

AWARDS Engineering systems (ME, MS, PhD). Part-time programs available.

Faculty: 33 full-time (3 women), 19 part-time/adjunct (4 women).
Students: 51 full-time (11 women), 11 part-time (1 woman); includes 3 minority (1 Asian American or Pacific Islander, 1 Hispanic American, 1 Native American), 16 international. 56 applicants, 82% accepted, 10 enrolled. In 2001, 11 master's, 4 doctorates awarded.
Degree requirements: For master's, thesis; for doctorate, one foreign language, thesis/dissertation, comprehensive exam. *Median time to degree:* Master's–2 years full-time; doctorate–4 years full-time.
Entrance requirements: For master's and doctorate, GRE General Test. *Application deadline:* For fall admission, 12/1 (priority date); for spring admission, 5/1 (priority date). Applications are processed on a rolling basis. *Application fee:* $40. Electronic applications accepted.
Expenses: Tuition, state resident: full-time $4,940; part-time $246 per credit. Tuition, nonresident: full-time $16,070; part-time $803 per credit. Required fees: $341 per semester.
Financial support: In 2001–02, 4 fellowships (averaging $4,875 per year), 71 research assistantships (averaging $4,606 per year), 42 teaching assistantships (averaging $6,091 per year) were awarded. Federal Work-Study and unspecified assistantships also available. Financial award applicants required to submit FAFSA.
Faculty research: Geotechnical engineering, offshore mechanics, analytical design, process simulation, health monitoring. *Total annual research expenditures:* $936,455.
Dr. Joan Gosink, Head, 303-273-3650, *Fax:* 303-273-3602, *E-mail:* jgosink@mines.edu.
Application contact: Leslie Urioste, Information Contact, 303-384-2394, *Fax:* 303-273-3278, *E-mail:* lurioste@mines.edu. *Web site:* http://www.mines.edu/academic/eng/

■ CORNELL UNIVERSITY

Graduate School, Graduate Fields of Engineering, Field of Systems Engineering, Ithaca, NY 14853-0001

AWARDS M Eng.

Faculty: 15 full-time.
Students: 18 full-time (4 women); includes 4 minority (2 African Americans, 2 Asian Americans or Pacific Islanders), 1 international. 17 applicants, 100% accepted.
Degree requirements: For master's, thesis.
Application fee: $65.

Expenses: Tuition: Full-time $25,970. Required fees: $50.
Financial support: In 2001–02, 16 students received support, including 15 fellowships with full and partial tuition reimbursements available, 1 research assistantship with full and partial tuition reimbursement available; teaching assistantships with full and partial tuition reimbursements available, institutionally sponsored loans, scholarships/grants, tuition waivers (full and partial), and unspecified assistantships also available. Financial award applicants required to submit FAFSA.
Faculty research: Space systems, systems engineering of mechanical and aerospace systems, multi-echelon inventory theory, math modeling of complex systems, chain supply integration.
Application contact: Graduate Field Assistant, 607-255-7757, *E-mail:* systemseng@cornell.edu.

■ EMBRY-RIDDLE AERONAUTICAL UNIVERSITY

Daytona Beach Campus Graduate Program, Department of Human Factors and Systems, Daytona Beach, FL 32114-3900

AWARDS Human factors engineering (MSHFS). Systems engineering (MSHFS). Part-time and evening/weekend programs available.

Faculty: 7 full-time (3 women).
Students: 15 full-time (8 women), 29 part-time (17 women); includes 7 minority (4 African Americans, 3 Hispanic Americans), 10 international. Average age 29. 26 applicants, 73% accepted, 14 enrolled. In 2001, 8 degrees awarded.
Degree requirements: For master's, thesis, practicum, qualifying oral exam.
Entrance requirements: For master's, TOEFL, minimum GPA of 2.5. *Application deadline:* For fall admission, 8/1 (priority date); for spring admission, 12/1 (priority date). Applications are processed on a rolling basis. *Application fee:* $30 ($50 for international students).
Expenses: Tuition: Full-time $13,140; part-time $730 per credit. Required fees: $250; $250 per year. $125 per semester. Tuition and fees vary according to program.
Financial support: In 2001–02, 13 students received support, including 1 research assistantship with partial tuition reimbursement available (averaging $8,100 per year), 2 teaching assistantships with partial tuition reimbursements available (averaging $8,100 per year); fellowships with partial tuition reimbursements available, career-related internships or fieldwork and unspecified assistantships also available. Financial award application deadline: 4/15; financial award applicants required to submit FAFSA.

Faculty research: Future mission concepts. *Total annual research expenditures:* $8,774.
Dr. John Wise, Program Coordinator, 386-226-6384, *Fax:* 386-226-7050, *E-mail:* wise@erau.edu.
Application contact: Christine Castetter, Graduate Admissions, 800-388-3728, *Fax:* 386-226-7111, *E-mail:* gradmit@erau.edu.
Find an in-depth description at www.petersons.com/gradchannel.

■ FLORIDA ATLANTIC UNIVERSITY

College of Engineering, Department of Mechanical Engineering, Program in Manufacturing Systems Engineering, Boca Raton, FL 33431-0991

AWARDS MS. Part-time and evening/weekend programs available.

Faculty: 3 full-time (0 women).
Students: 3 full-time (2 women), 5 part-time (1 woman), 4 international. Average age 36. 6 applicants, 67% accepted, 2 enrolled. In 2001, 2 degrees awarded.
Degree requirements: For master's, thesis optional.
Entrance requirements: For master's, GRE General Test, TOEFL, minimum GPA of 3.0. *Application deadline:* For fall admission, 4/10 (priority date); for spring admission, 10/1. Applications are processed on a rolling basis. *Application fee:* $20.
Expenses: Tuition, state resident: full-time $3,098; part-time $172 per credit. Tuition, nonresident: full-time $10,427; part-time $579 per credit.
Financial support: Research assistantships, teaching assistantships, career-related internships or fieldwork and Federal Work-Study available. Support available to part-time students. Financial award application deadline: 4/1; financial award applicants required to submit FAFSA.
Faculty research: Packaging, materials handling, design for manufacture, robotics, automation.
Application contact: Patricia Capozziello, Graduate Admissions Coordinator, 561-297-2694, *Fax:* 561-297-2659, *E-mail:* capozzie@fau.edu. *Web site:* http://www.me.fau.edu/

■ GEORGE MASON UNIVERSITY

School of Information Technology and Engineering, Department of Systems Engineering and Operations Research, Fairfax, VA 22030-4444

AWARDS Operations research and management science (MS). Systems engineering (MS). Part-time and evening/weekend programs available.

Faculty: 13 full-time (3 women), 4 part-time/adjunct (1 woman).
Students: 29 full-time (9 women), 208 part-time (48 women); includes 63 minority (24 African Americans, 30 Asian Americans or Pacific Islanders, 9 Hispanic

George Mason University (continued)
Americans), 20 international. Average age 35. 122 applicants, 84% accepted. In 2001, 44 degrees awarded.
Degree requirements: For master's, thesis optional.
Entrance requirements: For master's, GRE General Test, TOEFL, minimum GPA of 3.0 in last 60 hours. *Application deadline:* For fall admission, 5/1; for spring admission, 11/1. *Application fee:* $30. Electronic applications accepted.
Expenses: Tuition, state resident: full-time $3,168; part-time $132 per credit hour. Tuition, nonresident: full-time $11,280; part-time $470 per credit hour. Required fees: $1,416; $59 per credit hour.
Financial support: Fellowships, research assistantships, teaching assistantships, career-related internships or fieldwork and Federal Work-Study available. Support available to part-time students. Financial award application deadline: 3/1; financial award applicants required to submit FAFSA.
Faculty research: Requirements engineering, signal processing, systems architecture, data fusion.
Dr. Karla L. Hoffman, Chairman, 703-993-1670, *Fax:* 703-993-1521, *E-mail:* seor@gmu.edu. *Web site:* http://www.gmu.edu/departments/seor/

■ **THE GEORGE WASHINGTON UNIVERSITY**
School of Engineering and Applied Science, Department of Engineering Management and Systems Engineering, Washington, DC 20052
AWARDS MEM, MS, D Sc, App Sc, Engr, MEM/MS. Part-time and evening/weekend programs available.
Faculty: 20 full-time (3 women), 44 part-time/adjunct (3 women).
Students: 154 full-time (43 women), 635 part-time (197 women); includes 167 minority (90 African Americans, 46 Asian Americans or Pacific Islanders, 27 Hispanic Americans, 4 Native Americans), 176 international. Average age 36. 264 applicants, 90% accepted. In 2001, 173 master's, 28 doctorates, 6 other advanced degrees awarded.
Degree requirements: For master's, thesis optional; for doctorate, one foreign language, thesis/dissertation, final and qualifying exams; for other advanced degree, professional project.
Entrance requirements: For master's, TOEFL or George Washington University English as a Foreign Language Test, appropriate bachelor's degree; for doctorate, TOEFL or George Washington University English as a Foreign Language Test, appropriate master's degree, minimum GPA of 3.5; for other advanced degree, TOEFL or George Washington University English as a Foreign Language Test, appropriate master's degree,

minimum GPA of 3.5, GRE required if highest earned degree is BS. *Application deadline:* For fall admission, 3/1; for spring admission, 10/1. Applications are processed on a rolling basis. *Application fee:* $50.
Expenses: Tuition: Part-time $810 per credit. Required fees: $1 per credit.
Financial support: In 2001–02, 10 fellowships with tuition reimbursements (averaging $3,900 per year), 4 research assistantships, 9 teaching assistantships with tuition reimbursements (averaging $2,500 per year) were awarded. Career-related internships or fieldwork and institutionally sponsored loans also available. Financial award application deadline: 3/1; financial award applicants required to submit FAFSA.
Faculty research: Artificial intelligence and expert systems, human factors engineering and systems analysis. *Total annual research expenditures:* $421,800.
Dr. Thomas Mazzuchi, Chair, 202-994-0558, *E-mail:* mazzuchi@seas.gwu.edu.
Application contact: Howard M. Davis, Manager, Office of Admissions and Student Records, 202-994-6158, *Fax:* 202-994-0909, *E-mail:* data:adms@seas.gwu.edu. *Web site:* http://www.gwu.edu/~gradinfo/

Find an in-depth description at www.petersons.com/gradchannel.

■ **GEORGIA INSTITUTE OF TECHNOLOGY**
Graduate Studies and Research, College of Engineering, School of Industrial and Systems Engineering, Program in Industrial and Systems Engineering, Atlanta, GA 30332-0001
AWARDS Algorithms, combinatorics, and optimization (PhD); industrial and systems engineering (PhD); industrial engineering (MS, MSIE). Statistics (MS Stat). Part-time programs available. Terminal master's awarded for partial completion of doctoral program.
Degree requirements: For master's, thesis optional; for doctorate, thesis/dissertation.
Entrance requirements: For master's and doctorate, GRE General Test, TOEFL, minimum GPA of 3.0. Electronic applications accepted.
Faculty research: Computer-integrated manufacturing systems, materials handling systems, production and distribution. *Web site:* http://www.isye.gatech.edu/

Find an in-depth description at www.petersons.com/gradchannel.

■ **IOWA STATE UNIVERSITY OF SCIENCE AND TECHNOLOGY**
Graduate College, Interdisciplinary Programs, Program in Systems Engineering, Ames, IA 50011
AWARDS M Eng.

Students: 3 full-time (0 women), 59 part-time (10 women); includes 3 minority (1 African American, 2 Asian Americans or Pacific Islanders), 5 international. 12 applicants, 75% accepted, 8 enrolled. In 2001, 11 degrees awarded. *Median time to degree:* Master's–3.7 years full-time. *Application deadline:* For fall admission, 3/1 (priority date); for spring admission, 10/1. Applications are processed on a rolling basis. *Application fee:* $20 ($50 for international students). Electronic applications accepted.
Expenses: Tuition, state resident: full-time $1,851. Tuition, nonresident: full-time $5,449. Tuition and fees vary according to program.
Financial support: In 2001–02, 1 research assistantship (averaging $16,056 per year), 1 teaching assistantship (averaging $12,150 per year) were awarded. Scholarships/grants, health care benefits, and unspecified assistantships also available.
Dr. Douglas D. Gemmill, Supervisory Committee Chair, 515-294-8731, *Fax:* 515-294-3524, *E-mail:* syseng@iastate.edu. *Web site:* http://www.eng.iastate.edu/ede/systems.html

■ **LEHIGH UNIVERSITY**
P.C. Rossin College of Engineering and Applied Science, Program in Manufacturing Systems Engineering, Bethlehem, PA 18015-3094
AWARDS MS. Part-time and evening/weekend programs available.
Faculty: 4 full-time (0 women).
Students: Average age 38. 6 applicants, 83% accepted, 2 enrolled. In 2001, 9 degrees awarded.
Degree requirements: For master's, project or thesis. *Median time to degree:* Master's–1 year full-time, 2 years part-time.
Entrance requirements: For master's, GRE General Test, TOEFL, minimum GPA of 2.75. *Application deadline:* For fall admission, 7/15; for spring admission, 12/1. Applications are processed on a rolling basis. *Application fee:* $50. Electronic applications accepted.
Expenses: Tuition: Part-time $468 per credit hour. Required fees: $200; $100 per semester. Tuition and fees vary according to program.
Financial support: Fellowships, research assistantships, career-related internships or fieldwork and tuition waivers (full and partial) available. Financial award application deadline: 1/15.
Faculty research: Manufacturing systems design, development, and implementation, accounting and management, agile/lean systems and supply chain issues.
Dr. Keith M. Gardiner, Director, 610-758-5070, *Fax:* 610-758-6527, *E-mail:* kg03@lehigh.edu.
Application contact: Carolyn C. Jones, Graduate Coordinator, 610-758-5157, *Fax:* 610-758-6527, *E-mail:* ccj1@lehigh.edu.

Web site: http://www.lehigh.edu/~inmse/gradprogram/

■ LOUISIANA STATE UNIVERSITY IN SHREVEPORT

College of Sciences, Shreveport, LA 71115-2399

AWARDS Systems technology (MST). Part-time and evening/weekend programs available.

Degree requirements: For master's, comprehensive exam.
Entrance requirements: For master's, GRE General Test.
Expenses: Tuition, area resident: Full-time $1,890; part-time $105 per credit. Tuition, nonresident: full-time $6,000; part-time $175 per credit. Required fees: $220; $55 per credit.
Faculty research: Graphics, software quality, programming languages, tutoring systems. *Web site:* http://www.lsus.edu/

■ MASSACHUSETTS INSTITUTE OF TECHNOLOGY

School of Engineering, Engineering Systems Division, System Design and Management Program, Cambridge, MA 02139-4307

AWARDS Engineering and management (SM).

Students: 74 full-time (10 women); includes 3 minority (all Asian Americans or Pacific Islanders), 9 international. Average age 31. In 2001, 49 degrees awarded.
Degree requirements: For master's, thesis.
Entrance requirements: For master's, GRE General Test or GMAT, TOEFL, MS in engineering (or equivalent) and 3 years of experience or BS in engineering (or hard science) and 5 years of experience. *Application deadline:* For winter admission, 8/15. *Application fee:* $60. Electronic applications accepted.
Expenses: Contact institution.
Financial support: Research assistantships, teaching assistantships, career-related internships or fieldwork, Federal Work-Study, institutionally sponsored loans, scholarships/grants, health care benefits, and unspecified assistantships available. Financial award applicants required to submit FAFSA.
Paul A. Lagace, Co-Director, 617-253-3628, *E-mail:* pal@mit.edu.
Application contact: Sarah Shohet, Admissions and Career Placement Coordinator, 617-253-1662, *Fax:* 617-253-1462, *E-mail:* lfmsdm@mit.edu. *Web site:* http://lfmsdm.mit.edu/sdm

■ NATIONAL TECHNOLOGICAL UNIVERSITY

Programs in Engineering, Fort Collins, CO 80526-1842

AWARDS Chemical engineering (MS); computer engineering (MS); computer science (MS); electrical engineering (MS); engineering management (MS); environmental systems management (MS); management of technology (MS); manufacturing systems engineering (MS); materials science and engineering (MS); mechanical engineering (MS); microelectronics and semiconductor engineering (MS). Software engineering (MS). Special majors (MS). Systems engineering (MS). Part-time programs available. Postbaccalaureate distance learning degree programs offered (no on-campus study).
Students: In 2001, 114 degrees awarded.
Degree requirements: For master's, comprehensive exam.
Entrance requirements: For master's, BS in engineering or related field; 2.9 minimum GPA. *Application deadline:* Applications are processed on a rolling basis. *Application fee:* $50. Electronic applications accepted.
Expenses: Tuition: Part-time $660 per credit hour. Part-time tuition and fees vary according to course load, campus/location and program.
Dr. Andre Vacroux, President, 970-495-6400, *Fax:* 970-484-0668, *E-mail:* andre@ntu.edu.
Application contact: Rhonda Bonham, Admissions Officer, 970-495-6400, *Fax:* 970-498-0601, *E-mail:* rhonda@ntu.edu. *Web site:* http://www.ntu.edu/

■ NAVAL POSTGRADUATE SCHOOL

Graduate Programs, Program in Systems Engineering and Integration, Monterey, CA 93943

AWARDS MS. Program only open to commissioned officers of the United States and friendly nations and selected United States federal civilian employees. Part-time programs available.

Degree requirements: For master's, thesis.

■ NORTH CAROLINA AGRICULTURAL AND TECHNICAL STATE UNIVERSITY

Graduate School, College of Engineering, Department of Industrial and Systems Engineering, Greensboro, NC 27411

AWARDS MSISE, PhD. Part-time programs available.

Faculty: 9 full-time (0 women), 1 part-time/adjunct (0 women).
Students: 50 full-time (24 women), 7 part-time (3 women); includes 43 minority (42

African Americans, 1 Hispanic American), 10 international. Average age 25. 32 applicants, 81% accepted. In 2001, 10 degrees awarded.
Degree requirements: For master's, thesis, project; for doctorate, thesis/dissertation.
Entrance requirements: For master's, GRE General Test (recommended); for doctorate, GRE General Test. *Application deadline:* For fall admission, 7/1; for spring admission, 1/9. Applications are processed on a rolling basis. *Application fee:* $35.
Financial support: In 2001–02, 3 fellowships with full tuition reimbursements, 24 research assistantships with partial tuition reimbursements, 8 teaching assistantships with partial tuition reimbursements were awarded.
Faculty research: Human-machine systems engineering, management systems engineering, operations research and systems analysis, production systems engineering. *Total annual research expenditures:* $24,000.
Dr. Eui H. Park, Chairperson, 336-334-7780, *Fax:* 336-334-7729, *E-mail:* park@ncat.edu.
Application contact: Dr. Bala Ram, Graduate Coordinator, 336-334-7780, *Fax:* 336-334-7729, *E-mail:* ram@ncat.edu. *Web site:* http://www.eng.ncat.edu:80/niedept/

■ NORTHEASTERN UNIVERSITY

College of Engineering, Computer Systems Engineering Program, Boston, MA 02115-5096

AWARDS MS. Part-time programs available.

Students: 40 full-time (15 women), 36 part-time (3 women); includes 11 minority (3 African Americans, 8 Asian Americans or Pacific Islanders), 39 international. Average age 25. 67 applicants, 69% accepted, 12 enrolled. In 2001, 20 degrees awarded.
Degree requirements: For master's, thesis optional. *Median time to degree:* Master's–2.5 years full-time, 4.5 years part-time.
Entrance requirements: For master's, GRE General Test. *Application deadline:* For fall admission, 2/15 (priority date). Applications are processed on a rolling basis. *Application fee:* $50. Electronic applications accepted.
Expenses: Tuition: Part-time $535 per credit hour. Required fees: $56. Tuition and fees vary according to program.
Financial support: In 2001–02, 17 students received support, including 3 research assistantships with full tuition reimbursements available (averaging $13,560 per year), 6 teaching assistantships with full tuition reimbursements available (averaging $13,560 per year); fellowships, career-related internships or fieldwork, Federal Work-Study, scholarships/grants, tuition waivers (full), and unspecified assistantships also available. Support available to part-time students. Financial award

Northeastern University (continued)
application deadline: 2/15; financial award applicants required to submit FAFSA.
Faculty research: Engineering software design, CAD/CAM, virtual environments.
Application contact: Stephen L. Gibson, Associate Director, 617-373-2711, *Fax:* 617-373-2501, *E-mail:* grad-eng@coe.neu.edu. *Web site:* http://www.coe.neu.edu/

■ OAKLAND UNIVERSITY

Graduate Study and Lifelong Learning, School of Engineering and Computer Science, Program in Systems Engineering, Rochester, MI 48309-4401

AWARDS MS, PhD.

Faculty: 7 full-time (0 women), 1 part-time/adjunct (0 women).
Students: 59 full-time (14 women), 59 part-time (7 women); includes 26 minority (4 African Americans, 21 Asian Americans or Pacific Islanders, 1 Hispanic American), 31 international. Average age 34. 41 applicants, 88% accepted. In 2001, 14 master's, 8 doctorates awarded.
Degree requirements: For doctorate, thesis/dissertation.
Entrance requirements: For master's and doctorate, minimum GPA of 3.0 for unconditional admission. *Application deadline:* For fall admission, 8/1 (priority date); for winter admission, 12/1 (priority date); for spring admission, 4/1 (priority date). Applications are processed on a rolling basis. *Application fee:* $30. Electronic applications accepted.
Expenses: Tuition, state resident: full-time $5,904; part-time $246 per credit hour. Tuition, nonresident: full-time $12,192; part-time $508 per credit hour. Required fees: $472; $236 per term.
Financial support: Federal Work-Study, institutionally sponsored loans, and tuition waivers (full) available. Financial award application deadline: 3/1; financial award applicants required to submit FAFSA.
Dr. Naim A. Kheir, Chair, 248-370-2177.

■ THE OHIO STATE UNIVERSITY

Graduate School, College of Engineering, Program in Industrial and Systems Engineering, Columbus, OH 43210

AWARDS MS, PhD.

Degree requirements: For master's, thesis optional; for doctorate, thesis/dissertation.
Entrance requirements: For master's and doctorate, GRE General Test.

■ OHIO UNIVERSITY

Graduate Studies, Russ College of Engineering and Technology, Department of Industrial and Manufacturing Systems Engineering, Athens, OH 45701-2979

AWARDS MS.

Faculty: 8 full-time (0 women), 2 part-time/adjunct (1 woman).
Students: 30 full-time (6 women), 12 part-time (1 woman); includes 2 minority (1 African American, 1 Asian American or Pacific Islander), 34 international. Average age 24. 99 applicants, 78% accepted, 17 enrolled. In 2001, 20 degrees awarded.
Degree requirements: For master's, research project, thesis optional.
Entrance requirements: For master's, GRE General Test. *Application deadline:* For fall admission, 3/1 (priority date). Applications are processed on a rolling basis. *Application fee:* $30.
Expenses: Tuition, state resident: full-time $6,585. Tuition, nonresident: full-time $12,254.
Financial support: In 2001–02, 1 fellowship with full tuition reimbursement, 12 research assistantships with full tuition reimbursements, 7 teaching assistantships with full tuition reimbursements were awarded. Federal Work-Study, institutionally sponsored loans, and tuition waivers (full) also available. Financial award application deadline: 3/1.
Faculty research: MIS, distribution systems, or MFG systems. *Total annual research expenditures:* $350,000.
Dr. Charles M. Parks, Chairman, 740-593-1540, *Fax:* 740-593-0778, *E-mail:* cparks@bobcat.ent.ohiou.edu.
Application contact: Dr. David Koonce, Graduate Chairman, 740-593-1550, *Fax:* 740-593-0778, *E-mail:* imsegrad@ohio.edu. *Web site:* http://webise.ent.ohiou.edu/

■ OKLAHOMA STATE UNIVERSITY

Graduate College, College of Engineering, Architecture and Technology, School of Industrial Engineering and Management, Interdisciplinary Master of Manufacturing Systems Engineering Program, Stillwater, OK 74078

AWARDS M En.

Faculty: 5 full-time (0 women), 1 part-time/adjunct (0 women).
Students: 1 full-time (0 women), 136 part-time (15 women); includes 9 minority (3 African Americans, 3 Asian Americans or Pacific Islanders, 3 Hispanic Americans), 3 international. Average age 36. 39 applicants, 97% accepted. In 2001, 9 degrees awarded.
Degree requirements: For master's, creative component or thesis.
Entrance requirements: For master's, TOEFL. *Application deadline:* For fall admission, 7/1 (priority date). *Application fee:* $25.
Expenses: Tuition, state resident: part-time $92 per credit hour. Tuition, nonresident: part-time $297 per credit hour. Required fees: $21 per credit hour.

$14 per semester. One-time fee: $20. Tuition and fees vary according to course load.
Financial support: Research assistantships, teaching assistantships, career-related internships or fieldwork, Federal Work-Study, and tuition waivers (partial) available. Support available to part-time students. Financial award application deadline: 3/1.
Faculty research: Integrated manufacturing systems, engineering practice in management, hardware aspects.
John W. Nazemetz, Director, 405-744-6055.

■ THE PENNSYLVANIA STATE UNIVERSITY GREAT VALLEY CAMPUS

Graduate Studies and Continuing Education, School of Graduate Professional Studies, Department of Engineering and Information Science, Program in Systems Engineering, Malvern, PA 19355-1488

AWARDS M Eng.

Students: 2 full-time (0 women), 53 part-time (4 women). In 2001, 34 degrees awarded.
Application fee: $45.
Expenses: Tuition, state resident: part-time $415 per credit. Tuition, nonresident: part-time $680 per credit. Tuition and fees vary according to program.
Application contact: 610-648-3242, *Fax:* 610-889-1334.

■ POLYTECHNIC UNIVERSITY, BROOKLYN CAMPUS

Department of Electrical Engineering, Major in Systems Engineering, Brooklyn, NY 11201-2990

AWARDS MS. Part-time and evening/weekend programs available.

Degree requirements: For master's, thesis optional.
Entrance requirements: For master's, BS in electrical engineering. Electronic applications accepted.

Find an in-depth description at www.petersons.com/gradchannel.

■ POLYTECHNIC UNIVERSITY, LONG ISLAND GRADUATE CENTER

Graduate Programs, Department of Electrical Engineering, Major in Systems Engineering, Melville, NY 11747

AWARDS MS.

Electronic applications accepted.

■ POLYTECHNIC UNIVERSITY, WESTCHESTER GRADUATE CENTER

Graduate Programs, Department of Electrical Engineering, Major in Systems Engineering, Hawthorne, NY 10532-1507

AWARDS MS.

Degree requirements: For master's, thesis (for some programs). Electronic applications accepted.

■ PORTLAND STATE UNIVERSITY

Graduate Studies, College of Engineering and Computer Science, Program in Systems Engineering, Portland, OR 97207-0751

AWARDS Systems engineering (M Eng). Systems engineering fundamentals (Certificate). Postbaccalaureate distance learning degree programs offered (no on-campus study).

Students: 4 full-time, 7 part-time.
Entrance requirements: For master's, 3 years of responsible engineering experience and bachelor's degree in engineering with minimum undergraduate GPA of 3.0 in upper division courses; or minimum graduate GPA of 3.0 for minimum of 12 graduate-level credits. *Application deadline:* Applications are processed on a rolling basis. *Application fee:* $50.
Dr. Herman Migliore, Director, 503-725-4262, *Fax:* 503-725-4298, *E-mail:* herm@cecs.pdx.edu.
Application contact: Marcia Fischer, Director of Enrollment, 503-725-4289, *Fax:* 503-725-4298. *E-mail:* fischerm@eas.pdx.edu. *Web site:* http://www.cecs.pdx.edu/Systems/

Find an in-depth description at www.petersons.com/gradchannel.

■ PURDUE UNIVERSITY

Graduate School, Schools of Engineering, School of Industrial Engineering, West Lafayette, IN 47907

AWARDS Human factors in industrial engineering (MS, MSIE, PhD); manufacturing engineering (MS, MSIE, PhD); operations research (MS, MSIE, PhD). Systems engineering (MS, MSIE, PhD). Part-time programs available.

Faculty: 23 full-time (2 women), 4 part-time/adjunct (0 women).
Students: 117 full-time (24 women), 19 part-time (6 women); includes 6 minority (4 African Americans, 2 Hispanic Americans), 108 international. Average age 28. 370 applicants, 44% accepted. In 2001, 51 master's, 11 doctorates awarded. Terminal master's awarded for partial completion of doctoral program.

Degree requirements: For master's, thesis optional; for doctorate, thesis/dissertation.
Entrance requirements: For master's, GRE General Test, TOEFL, minimum GPA of 3.0; for doctorate, GRE General Test, TOEFL, MS thesis. *Application deadline:* For fall admission, 3/15; for spring admission, 9/1. *Application fee:* $30. Electronic applications accepted.
Expenses: Tuition, state resident: full-time $4,164; part-time $149 per credit hour. Tuition, nonresident: full-time $13,872; part-time $458 per credit hour. Tuition and fees vary according to campus/location and program.
Financial support: In 2001–02, 78 students received support, including 3 fellowships with full tuition reimbursements available (averaging $13,070 per year), 29 research assistantships with full tuition reimbursements available (averaging $12,720 per year), 46 teaching assistantships with full tuition reimbursements available (averaging $10,600 per year) Support available to part-time students. Financial award application deadline: 3/15; financial award applicants required to submit FAFSA.
Faculty research: Precision manufacturing process, computer-aided manufacturing, computer-aided process planning, knowledge-based systems, combinatorics. *Total annual research expenditures:* $1.8 million.
Dr. Dennis Engi, Head, 765-494-5444, *Fax:* 765-494-1299, *E-mail:* engi@ecn.purdue.edu.
Application contact: Dr. J. W. Barany, Associate Head, 765-494-5406, *Fax:* 765-494-1299, *E-mail:* jwb@ecn.purdue.edu. *Web site:* http://ie.www.ecn.purdue.edu/

■ RENSSELAER POLYTECHNIC INSTITUTE

Graduate School, School of Engineering, Department of Decision Sciences and Engineering Systems, Troy, NY 12180-3590

AWARDS Decision sciences and engineering systems (PhD), including industrial and management engineering, manufacturing systems engineering, operations research and statistics; industrial and management engineering (M Eng, MS); manufacturing systems engineering (M Eng, MS); operations research and statistics (M Eng, MS). Part-time and evening/weekend programs available. Postbaccalaureate distance learning degree programs offered (no on-campus study).

Faculty: 16 full-time (1 woman), 3 part-time/adjunct (2 women).
Students: 82 full-time (22 women), 29 part-time (6 women); includes 9 minority (5 African Americans, 2 Asian Americans or Pacific Islanders, 2 Hispanic Americans), 67 international. 282 applicants, 38% accepted, 50 enrolled. In 2001, 30 master's, 4 doctorates awarded.

Terminal master's awarded for partial completion of doctoral program.
Degree requirements: For doctorate, thesis/dissertation.
Entrance requirements: For master's and doctorate, GRE General Test, TOEFL. *Application deadline:* For fall admission, 1/15 (priority date). Applications are processed on a rolling basis. *Application fee:* $45. Electronic applications accepted.
Expenses: Tuition: Full-time $26,400; part-time $1,320 per credit hour. Required fees: $1,437.
Financial support: In 2001–02, 4 fellowships with full tuition reimbursements (averaging $12,800 per year), 17 research assistantships with full tuition reimbursements (averaging $12,620 per year), 19 teaching assistantships with full tuition reimbursements (averaging $12,620 per year) were awarded. Career-related internships or fieldwork and institutionally sponsored loans also available. Financial award application deadline: 1/15.
Faculty research: Decision support systems, simulation and modeling, statistical methods/computing, operations research, services/manufacturing applications. *Total annual research expenditures:* $1 million.
Dr. James M. Tien, Chair, 518-276-2773, *Fax:* 518-276-8227, *E-mail:* dsesgr@rpi.edu.
Application contact: Lee Vilardi, Graduate Coordinator, 518-276-6681, *Fax:* 518-276-8227, *E-mail:* dsesgr@rpi.edu. *Web site:* http://www.rpi.edu/dept/dses/www/homepage.html

Find an in-depth description at www.petersons.com/gradchannel.

■ RENSSELAER POLYTECHNIC INSTITUTE

Graduate School, School of Engineering, Department of Electrical, Computer, and Systems Engineering, Program in Computer and Systems Engineering, Troy, NY 12180-3590

AWARDS M Eng, MS, D Eng, PhD, MBA/M Eng. Part-time programs available.

Faculty: 31 full-time (1 woman).
Students: 27 full-time (5 women), 9 part-time (2 women). 154 applicants, 29% accepted. In 2001, 25 master's, 4 doctorates awarded. Terminal master's awarded for partial completion of doctoral program.
Degree requirements: For master's, thesis (for some programs); for doctorate, thesis/dissertation.
Entrance requirements: For master's and doctorate, GRE, TOEFL. *Application deadline:* For fall admission, 1/15; for spring admission, 10/1. Applications are processed on a rolling basis. *Application fee:* $45. Electronic applications accepted.
Expenses: Tuition: Full-time $26,400; part-time $1,320 per credit hour. Required fees: $1,437.

Rensselaer Polytechnic Institute (continued)
Financial support: Fellowships, research assistantships, teaching assistantships, career-related internships or fieldwork and institutionally sponsored loans available. Financial award application deadline: 2/1.
Faculty research: Multimedia via ATM, mobile robotics, thermophotovoltaic devices, microelectronic interconnections, agile manufacturing. *Total annual research expenditures:* $7 million.
Application contact: Ann Bruno, Manager of Student Services and Graduate Enrollment, 518-276-2554, *Fax:* 518-276-2433, *E-mail:* bruno@ecse.rpi.edu. *Web site:* http://www.ecse.rpi.edu/

Find an in-depth description at www.petersons.com/gradchannel.

■ ROCHESTER INSTITUTE OF TECHNOLOGY

Graduate Enrollment Services, College of Engineering, Department of Design, Development and Manufacturing, Program in Product Development, Rochester, NY 14623-5698

AWARDS MS.

Students: In 2001, 24 degrees awarded.
Entrance requirements: For master's, undergraduate degree in engineering or related field, minimum GPA of 3.0, 5 years experience in product development. *Application fee:* $50.
Expenses: Contact institution.
Mark Smith, Director, Department of Design, Development and Manufacturing, 585-475-7102, *E-mail:* mpdmail@rit.edu.

Find an in-depth description at www.petersons.com/gradchannel.

■ ROCHESTER INSTITUTE OF TECHNOLOGY

Graduate Enrollment Services, College of Engineering, Department of Industrial and Manufacturing Engineering, Rochester, NY 14623-5698

AWARDS Engineering management (ME); industrial engineering (ME); manufacturing engineering (ME). Systems engineering (ME).

Students: 6 full-time (0 women), 19 part-time (6 women); includes 4 minority (2 African Americans, 2 Hispanic Americans), 10 international. 105 applicants, 51% accepted, 8 enrolled. In 2001, 14 degrees awarded.
Degree requirements: For master's, internship.
Entrance requirements: For master's, TOEFL, minimum GPA of 3.0. *Application deadline:* For fall admission, 3/1 (priority date). Applications are processed on a rolling basis. *Application fee:* $50.

Expenses: Tuition: Full-time $20,928; part-time $587 per hour. Required fees: $162. Tuition and fees vary according to program.
Financial support: Research assistantships, career-related internships or fieldwork and tuition waivers (partial) available.
Faculty research: Safety, manufacturing (CAM), simulation.
Dr. Jacqueline Mozrall, Head, 585-475-7142, *E-mail:* jrmeie@rit.edu.

■ RUTGERS, THE STATE UNIVERSITY OF NEW JERSEY, NEW BRUNSWICK

Graduate School, Program in Industrial and Systems Engineering, New Brunswick, NJ 08901-1281

AWARDS Industrial and systems engineering (MS, PhD); manufacturing systems (MS); quality and reliability engineering (MS). Part-time and evening/weekend programs available. Terminal master's awarded for partial completion of doctoral program.

Degree requirements: For master's, thesis or alternative; for doctorate, thesis/dissertation.
Entrance requirements: For master's and doctorate, GRE General Test, TOEFL.
Faculty research: Production and manufacturing systems, quality and reliability engineering, systems engineering and aviation safety. *Web site:* http://coewww.rutgers.edu/~ie/

■ SAN JOSE STATE UNIVERSITY

Graduate Studies, College of Engineering, Department of Computer, Information and Systems Engineering, Program in Information and Systems Engineering, San Jose, CA 95192-0001

AWARDS MS. Part-time programs available.

Faculty: 5 full-time (0 women), 9 part-time/adjunct (1 woman).
Students: 21 full-time (7 women), 20 part-time (5 women); includes 15 minority (1 African American, 11 Asian Americans or Pacific Islanders, 3 Hispanic Americans), 19 international. Average age 28. 17 applicants, 53% accepted. In 2001, 9 degrees awarded.
Degree requirements: For master's, comprehensive exam.
Entrance requirements: For master's, minimum GPA of 3.0. *Application deadline:* For fall admission, 6/29; for spring admission, 11/30. Applications are processed on a rolling basis. *Application fee:* $59. Electronic applications accepted.
Expenses: Tuition, nonresident: part-time $246 per unit. Required fees: $678 per semester. Tuition and fees vary according to course load.
Financial support: Federal Work-Study available. Financial award applicants required to submit FAFSA.
Application contact: Dr. Louis Freund, Graduate Coordinator, 408-924-3890.

■ SOUTHERN METHODIST UNIVERSITY

School of Engineering, Department of Engineering Management, Information and Systems, Dallas, TX 75275

AWARDS Applied science (MS); engineering management (MSEM, DE); operations research (MS, PhD). Systems engineering (MS). Part-time and evening/weekend programs available. Postbaccalaureate distance learning degree programs offered.

Faculty: 6 full-time (1 woman).
Students: 10 full-time (1 woman), 100 part-time (22 women); includes 29 minority (6 African Americans, 11 Asian Americans or Pacific Islanders, 10 Hispanic Americans, 2 Native Americans), 10 international. 55 applicants, 78% accepted. In 2001, 25 master's, 5 doctorates awarded. Terminal master's awarded for partial completion of doctoral program.
Degree requirements: For master's, thesis optional; for doctorate, thesis/dissertation, oral and written qualifying exams.
Entrance requirements: For master's, GRE General, TOEFL, minimum GPA of 3.0 in last 2 years; bachelor's degree in engineering, mathematics, or sciences; for doctorate, bachelor's degree in related field. *Application deadline:* For fall admission, 7/1; for spring admission, 11/15. Applications are processed on a rolling basis. *Application fee:* $50.
Expenses: Tuition: Part-time $285 per credit hour.
Faculty research: Telecommunications, decision systems, information engineering, operations research, software.
Richard S. Barr, Chair, 214-768-2605, *E-mail:* emis@engr.smu.edu.
Application contact: Marc Valerin, Associate Director of Graduate Admissions, 214-768-3484, *E-mail:* valerin@seas.smu.edu.

Find an in-depth description at www.petersons.com/gradchannel.

■ STANFORD UNIVERSITY

School of Engineering, Department of Mechanical Engineering, Program in Manufacturing Systems Engineering, Stanford, CA 94305-9991

AWARDS MS, MBA/MS.

Entrance requirements: For master's, GMAT, GRE General Test, TOEFL. *Application deadline:* For fall admission, 1/14. *Application fee:* $65 ($80 for international students). Electronic applications accepted.
Application contact: Admissions Office, 650-723-3148.

■ TEXAS TECH UNIVERSITY

Graduate School, College of Engineering, Department of Industrial Engineering, Lubbock, TX 79409

AWARDS Industrial engineering (MSIE, PhD). Systems and engineering management (MSSEM). Part-time programs available.

Faculty: 6 full-time (0 women), 1 part-time/adjunct (0 women).
Students: 50 full-time (11 women), 10 part-time (1 woman); includes 5 minority (1 African American, 1 Asian American or Pacific Islander, 3 Hispanic Americans), 42 international. Average age 29. 133 applicants, 47% accepted, 16 enrolled. In 2001, 11 master's, 3 doctorates awarded.
Degree requirements: For master's and doctorate, thesis/dissertation.
Entrance requirements: For master's and doctorate, GRE General Test, minimum GPA of 3.0. *Application deadline:* Applications are processed on a rolling basis. *Application fee:* $25 ($50 for international students). Electronic applications accepted.
Expenses: Tuition, state resident: full-time $1,926; part-time $107 per credit hour. Tuition, nonresident: full-time $5,724; part-time $318 per credit hour. Required fees: $779; $737 per year. Tuition and fees vary according to course level, course load and program.
Financial support: In 2001–02, 25 students received support, including 15 research assistantships with partial tuition reimbursements available (averaging $8,670 per year), 6 teaching assistantships with partial tuition reimbursements available (averaging $7,575 per year); fellowships, Federal Work-Study and institutionally sponsored loans also available. Support available to part-time students. Financial award application deadline: 5/1; financial award applicants required to submit FAFSA.
Faculty research: Knowledge and engineering management, environmentally conscious manufacturing, biomechanical simulation, aviation security. *Total annual research expenditures:* $223,554.
Dr. Milton Smith, Chair, 806-742-3543, *Fax:* 806-742-3411, *E-mail:* jlsmith@coe.ttu.edu.
Application contact: Graduate Adviser, 806-742-3543, *Fax:* 806-742-3411. *Web site:* http://www.ie.ttu.edu

■ THE UNIVERSITY OF ARIZONA

Graduate College, College of Engineering and Mines, Department of Systems and Industrial Engineering, Program in Systems and Industrial Engineering, Tucson, AZ 85721

AWARDS PhD.

Students: 32 full-time (3 women), 6 part-time (1 woman); includes 1 minority (Native American), 31 international. Average age 30. 41 applicants, 85% accepted, 11 enrolled. In 2001, 1 degree awarded.

Degree requirements: For doctorate, thesis/dissertation.
Entrance requirements: For doctorate, GRE General Test, TOEFL, minimum GPA of 3.0. *Application deadline:* For fall admission, 7/1. *Application fee:* $45.
Expenses: Tuition, state resident: full-time $2,490; part-time $436 per unit. Tuition, nonresident: full-time $10,300; part-time $436 per unit. Full-time tuition and fees vary according to degree level and program.
Application contact: Celia Stenzel, Graduate Secretary, 520-621-6551, *Fax:* 520-621-6555.

■ THE UNIVERSITY OF ARIZONA

Graduate College, College of Engineering and Mines, Department of Systems and Industrial Engineering, Program in Systems Engineering, Tucson, AZ 85721

AWARDS MS. Part-time programs available.

Students: 28 full-time (12 women), 1 (woman) part-time; includes 8 minority (1 African American, 3 Asian Americans or Pacific Islanders, 4 Hispanic Americans), 12 international. Average age 29. 28 applicants, 68% accepted, 9 enrolled. In 2001, 6 degrees awarded.
Entrance requirements: For master's, GRE General Test, TOEFL, minimum GPA of 3.0. *Application deadline:* For fall admission, 7/1. Applications are processed on a rolling basis. *Application fee:* $45.
Expenses: Tuition, state resident: full-time $2,490; part-time $436 per unit. Tuition, nonresident: full-time $10,300; part-time $436 per unit. Full-time tuition and fees vary according to degree level and program.
Financial support: Fellowships, research assistantships, teaching assistantships, institutionally sponsored loans and scholarships/grants available.
Faculty research: Man/machine systems, optimal control, algorithmic probability.
Application contact: Celia Stenzel, Graduate Secretary, 520-621-6551, *Fax:* 520-621-6555.

■ UNIVERSITY OF CENTRAL FLORIDA

College of Engineering and Computer Sciences, Department of Industrial Engineering and Management Systems, Orlando, FL 32816

AWARDS Applied operations research (Certificate); computer-integrated manufacturing (MS); design for usability (Certificate); engineering management (MS); industrial engineering (MSIE); industrial engineering and management systems (PhD); industrial ergonomics and safety (Certificate); operations research (MS); product assurance engineering (MS); project engineering (Certificate); quality assurance (Certificate);

simulation systems (MS). Systems simulations for engineers (Certificate); training simulation (Certificate). Part-time and evening/weekend programs available.

Faculty: 20 full-time (4 women), 8 part-time/adjunct (1 woman).
Students: 92 full-time (19 women), 182 part-time (49 women); includes 66 minority (18 African Americans, 10 Asian Americans or Pacific Islanders, 35 Hispanic Americans, 3 Native Americans), 57 international. Average age 32. 231 applicants, 84% accepted, 85 enrolled. In 2001, 3 master's, 9 doctorates awarded.
Degree requirements: For master's, thesis; for doctorate, thesis/dissertation, departmental qualifying exam, candidacy exam.
Entrance requirements: For master's, GRE General Test, TOEFL, minimum GPA of 3.0 in last 60 hours; for doctorate, TOEFL, minimum GPA of 3.5 in last 60 hours. *Application deadline:* For fall admission, 7/15 (priority date); for spring admission, 12/1 (priority date). *Application fee:* $20. Electronic applications accepted.
Expenses: Tuition, state resident: part-time $162 per hour. Tuition, nonresident: part-time $569 per hour.
Financial support: In 2001–02, 23 fellowships with partial tuition reimbursements (averaging $3,272 per year), 131 research assistantships with partial tuition reimbursements (averaging $3,125 per year), 24 teaching assistantships with partial tuition reimbursements (averaging $3,823 per year) were awarded. Career-related internships or fieldwork, Federal Work-Study, institutionally sponsored loans, tuition waivers (partial), and unspecified assistantships also available. Financial award application deadline: 3/1; financial award applicants required to submit FAFSA.
Dr. Charles Reily, Chair, 407-823-2204, *E-mail:* creilly@mail.ucf.edu.
Application contact: Dr. Linda Malone, Coordinator, 407-823-2204, *E-mail:* malone@mail.ucf.edu. *Web site:* http://www.ucf.edu/

Find an in-depth description at www.petersons.com/gradchannel.

■ UNIVERSITY OF CONNECTICUT

Graduate School, School of Engineering, Field of Electrical and Systems Engineering, Storrs, CT 06269

AWARDS Biological engineering (MS); control and communication systems (MS, PhD); electromagnetics and physical electronics (MS, PhD). Terminal master's awarded for partial completion of doctoral program.

Degree requirements: For master's, thesis or alternative; for doctorate, thesis/dissertation.
Entrance requirements: For master's and doctorate, GRE General Test, TOEFL.

■ UNIVERSITY OF FLORIDA

Graduate School, College of Engineering, Department of Industrial and Systems Engineering, Gainesville, FL 32611

AWARDS Engineering management (ME, MS); facilities layout decision support systems energy (PhD); health systems (ME, MS); industrial engineering (PhD, Engr); manufacturing systems engineering (ME, MS, PhD, Certificate); operations research (ME, MS, PhD, Engr); production planning and control engineering management (PhD); quality and reliability assurance (ME, MS). Systems engineering (PhD, Engr).

Degree requirements: For master's, core exam, thesis optional; for doctorate, thesis/dissertation, comprehensive exam.
Entrance requirements: For master's and doctorate, GRE General Test, TOEFL, minimum GPA of 3.0; for other advanced degree, GRE General Test. Electronic applications accepted.
Expenses: Tuition, state resident: part-time $164 per hour. Tuition, nonresident: part-time $571 per hour. Tuition and fees vary according to course level and program. *Web site:* http://www.ise.ufl.edu/

Find an in-depth description at www.petersons.com/gradchannel.

■ UNIVERSITY OF FLORIDA

Graduate School, Graduate Engineering and Research Center (GERC), Gainesville, FL 32611

AWARDS Aerospace engineering (ME, MS, PhD, Engr); electrical and computer engineering (ME, MS, PhD, Engr); engineering mechanics (ME, MS, PhD, Engr); industrial and systems engineering (ME, MS, PhD, Engr). Part-time programs available. Postbaccalaureate distance learning degree programs offered. Terminal master's awarded for partial completion of doctoral program.

Degree requirements: For master's, thesis optional; for doctorate and Engr, thesis/dissertation.
Entrance requirements: For master's, GRE General Test, TOEFL, minimum GPA of 3.0; for doctorate, GRE General Test, written and oral qualifying exams, TOEFL, minimum GPA of 3.0, master's degree in engineering; for Engr, GRE General Test, TOEFL, minimum GPA of 3.0, master's degree in engineering. Electronic applications accepted.
Expenses: Contact institution.
Faculty research: Aerodynamics, terradynamics, and propulsion; composite materials and stress analysis; optical processing of microwave signals and photonics; holography, radar, and communications. System and signal theory; digital signal processing. *Web site:* http://www.gerc.eng.ufl.edu/

■ UNIVERSITY OF HOUSTON

Cullen College of Engineering, Department of Mechanical Engineering, Houston, TX 77204

AWARDS Aerospace engineering (MS, PhD); biomedical engineering (MS); computer and systems engineering (MS, PhD); environmental engineering (MS, PhD); materials engineering (MS, PhD); mechanical engineering (MME, MSME); petroleum engineering (MS). Part-time and evening/weekend programs available.
Faculty: 16 full-time (0 women), 1 part-time/adjunct (0 women).
Students: 34 full-time (4 women), 26 part-time (2 women); includes 7 minority (3 Asian Americans or Pacific Islanders, 4 Hispanic Americans), 32 international. Average age 28. 114 applicants, 64% accepted. In 2001, 20 master's, 3 doctorates awarded. Terminal master's awarded for partial completion of doctoral program.
Degree requirements: For master's, thesis (for some programs); for doctorate, thesis/dissertation, departmental qualifying exam.
Entrance requirements: For master's and doctorate, GRE General Test, TOEFL. *Application deadline:* For fall admission, 7/3 (priority date); for spring admission, 12/4. Applications are processed on a rolling basis. *Application fee:* $25 ($75 for international students).
Expenses: Tuition, state resident: full-time $1,512. Tuition, nonresident: full-time $5,310. Required fees: $1,308. Tuition and fees vary according to program.
Financial support: In 2001–02, 20 research assistantships (averaging $14,400 per year), 13 teaching assistantships (averaging $14,400 per year) were awarded. Fellowships, career-related internships or fieldwork and Federal Work-Study also available. Financial award application deadline: 2/15.
Faculty research: Experimental and computational turbulence, composites, rheology, phase change/heat transfer, characterization of superconducting materials. *Total annual research expenditures:* $396,172.
Dr. Lewis T. Wheeler, Interim Chair, 713-743-4500, *Fax:* 713-743-4503.
Application contact: Susan Sanderson-Clobe, Graduate Admissions Analyst, 713-743-4505, *Fax:* 713-743-4503, *E-mail:* megrad@uh.edu. *Web site:* http://www.mc.uh.edu

Find an in-depth description at www.petersons.com/gradchannel.

■ UNIVERSITY OF IDAHO

College of Graduate Studies, College of Engineering, Department of Mechanical Engineering, Program in Systems Engineering, Moscow, ID 83844-2282

AWARDS M Engr.

Degree requirements: For master's, thesis or alternative.
Application deadline: For fall admission, 8/1; for spring admission, 12/15. *Application fee:* $35 ($45 for international students).
Expenses: Tuition, state resident: full-time $1,613. Tuition, nonresident: full-time $3,000.
Financial support: Application deadline: 2/15.

■ UNIVERSITY OF ILLINOIS AT URBANA–CHAMPAIGN

Graduate College, College of Engineering, Department of General Engineering, Champaign, IL 61820

AWARDS Systems engineering and engineering design (MS), including general engineering.

Faculty: 20 full-time (5 women), 2 part-time/adjunct (0 women).
Students: 31 full-time (4 women); includes 3 minority (1 Asian American or Pacific Islander, 2 Hispanic Americans), 20 international. 41 applicants, 32% accepted. In 2001, 9 degrees awarded.
Entrance requirements: For master's, GRE, minimum GPA of 3.0. *Application deadline:* For fall admission, 2/1. Applications are processed on a rolling basis. *Application fee:* $40 ($50 for international students). Electronic applications accepted.
Expenses: Tuition, state resident: part-time $3,227 per degree program. Tuition, nonresident: part-time $7,169 per degree program. Tuition and fees vary according to program.
Financial support: In 2001–02, 1 fellowship, 17 research assistantships, 9 teaching assistantships were awarded. Scholarships/grants also available. Financial award application deadline: 2/15.
Dr. Harry E. Cook, Head, 217-333-2730, *Fax:* 217-244-5705, *E-mail:* h-cook3@uiuc.edu.
Application contact: Donna J. Eiskamp, Administrative Aide, 217-333-2730, *Fax:* 217-244-5705, *E-mail:* deiskamp@uiuc.edu. *Web site:* http://www.ge.uiuc.edu/

Find an in-depth description at www.petersons.com/gradchannel.

■ UNIVERSITY OF MARYLAND, COLLEGE PARK

Graduate Studies and Research, A. James Clark School of Engineering, Professional Program in Engineering, College Park, MD 20742

AWARDS Aerospace engineering (M Eng); chemical engineering (M Eng); civil engineering (M Eng); electrical engineering (M Eng); fire protection engineering (M Eng); materials science and engineering (M Eng); mechanical engineering (M Eng); reliability engineering (M Eng). Systems engineering (M Eng). Part-time and evening/weekend programs available. Postbaccalaureate distance learning degree programs offered.

Faculty: 11 part-time/adjunct (0 women).
Students: 19 full-time (4 women), 144 part-time (31 women); includes 41 minority (17 African Americans, 18 Asian Americans or Pacific Islanders, 6 Hispanic Americans), 27 international. 71 applicants, 80% accepted, 50 enrolled. In 2001, 64 degrees awarded.
Application deadline: For fall admission, 8/15; for spring admission, 1/10. Applications are processed on a rolling basis. *Application fee:* $50 ($70 for international students). Electronic applications accepted.
Expenses: Tuition, state resident: part-time $289 per credit hour. Tuition, nonresident: part-time $448 per credit hour. One-time fee: $436 part-time. Full-time tuition and fees vary according to course load, campus/location and program.
Financial support: In 2001–02, 1 research assistantship with tuition reimbursement (averaging $20,655 per year), 5 teaching assistantships with tuition reimbursements (averaging $11,114 per year) were awarded. Fellowships, Federal Work-Study and scholarships/grants also available. Support available to part-time students. Financial award applicants required to submit FAFSA.
Dr. George Syrmos, Acting Director, 301-405-5256, *Fax:* 301-314-9477.
Application contact: Trudy Lindsey, Director, Graduate Admissions and Records, 301-405-6991, *Fax:* 301-314-9305, *E-mail:* grschool@deans.umd.edu.

■ UNIVERSITY OF MARYLAND, COLLEGE PARK

Graduate Studies and Research, A. James Clark School of Engineering, Systems Engineering Program, College Park, MD 20742

AWARDS M Eng, MS. Part-time and evening/weekend programs available.

Faculty: 20 full-time (4 women), 2 part-time/adjunct (0 women).
Students: 21 full-time (2 women), 6 part-time (1 woman); includes 3 minority (2 Asian Americans or Pacific Islanders, 1 Native American), 19 international. 77 applicants, 13% accepted, 4 enrolled. In 2001, 8 degrees awarded.
Degree requirements: For master's, thesis optional.
Entrance requirements: For master's, GRE General Test, minimum GPA of 3.0. *Application deadline:* For fall admission, 3/1; for spring admission, 10/1. Applications are processed on a rolling basis. *Application fee:* $50 ($70 for international students). Electronic applications accepted.
Expenses: Tuition, state resident: part-time $289 per credit hour. Tuition, nonresident: part-time $448 per credit hour. One-time fee: $436 part-time. Full-time tuition and fees vary according to course load, campus/location and program.
Financial support: In 2001–02, 124 research assistantships with tuition reimbursements (averaging $12,935 per

year), 1 teaching assistantship with tuition reimbursement (averaging $12,703 per year) were awarded. Fellowships with tuition reimbursements, Federal Work-Study and scholarships/grants also available. Support available to part-time students. Financial award applicants required to submit FAFSA.
Faculty research: Automation, computer, information, manufacturing, and process systems.
Application contact: Trudy Lindsey, Director, Graduate Admissions and Records, 301-405-6991, *Fax:* 301-314-9305, *E-mail:* grschool@deans.umd.edu.

■ UNIVERSITY OF MASSACHUSETTS LOWELL

Graduate School, James B. Francis College of Engineering, Department of Electrical Engineering, Program in Systems Engineering, Lowell, MA 01854-2881

AWARDS MS Eng, D Eng. Part-time programs available.

Degree requirements: For master's, thesis optional; for doctorate, 2 foreign languages, thesis/dissertation.
Entrance requirements: For master's and doctorate, GRE General Test.

■ THE UNIVERSITY OF MEMPHIS

Graduate School, Herff College of Engineering, Program in Industrial and Systems Engineering, Memphis, TN 38152

AWARDS MS. Part-time programs available.

Degree requirements: For master's, thesis or alternative, comprehensive exam.
Entrance requirements: For master's, GRE General Test or MAT, minimum undergraduate GPA of 3.0.
Expenses: Tuition, state resident: full-time $2,026. Tuition, nonresident: full-time $4,528.
Faculty research: Integer programming, ergonomics, scheduling. *Web site:* http://www.inse.memphis.edu/

■ UNIVERSITY OF MICHIGAN

Horace H. Rackham School of Graduate Studies, College of Engineering, Department of Electrical Engineering and Computer Science, Division of Systems Science and Engineering, Ann Arbor, MI 48109

AWARDS MS, MSE, PhD. Terminal master's awarded for partial completion of doctoral program.

Degree requirements: For doctorate, thesis/dissertation, oral defense of dissertation, preliminary exams.
Entrance requirements: For master's, GRE General Test, TOEFL; for doctorate, GRE General Test, TOEFL, master's degree. Electronic applications accepted.

Faculty research: Control, communications, signal processing. *Web site:* http://www.eecs.umich.edu/

■ UNIVERSITY OF MICHIGAN

Horace H. Rackham School of Graduate Studies, College of Engineering, Program in Integrated Microsystems, Ann Arbor, MI 48109

AWARDS M Eng.

Yogesh B. Gianchandani, Director.
Application contact: Information Contact, 734-763-0480, *Fax:* 734-647-0079, *E-mail:* intermicros@engin.umich.edu. *Web site:* http://www.wimserc.org/

Find an in-depth description at www.petersons.com/gradchannel.

■ UNIVERSITY OF MICHIGAN–DEARBORN

College of Engineering and Computer Science, Department of Industrial and Systems Engineering, Dearborn, MI 48128-1491

AWARDS Engineering management (MS); industrial and systems engineering (MSE); information systems and technology (MS). Part-time and evening/weekend programs available.

Faculty: 12 full-time (0 women), 8 part-time/adjunct (2 women).
Students: 7 full-time (2 women), 239 part-time (61 women); includes 45 minority (7 African Americans, 26 Asian Americans or Pacific Islanders, 12 Hispanic Americans). Average age 31. 107 applicants, 91% accepted. In 2001, 78 degrees awarded.
Degree requirements: For master's, thesis optional.
Entrance requirements: For master's, bachelor's degree in applied mathematics, computer science, engineering, or physical science; minimum GPA of 3.0. *Application deadline:* For fall admission, 8/1 (priority date); for winter admission, 12/1 (priority date); for spring admission, 4/1. Applications are processed on a rolling basis. *Application fee:* $55.
Expenses: Tuition, state resident: part-time $300 per credit hour. Tuition, nonresident: part-time $756 per credit hour. Required fees: $90 per semester. Tuition and fees vary according to course level, course load and program.
Financial support: Fellowships, research assistantships, teaching assistantships, Federal Work-Study available. Financial award deadline: 4/1; financial award applicants required to submit FAFSA.
Faculty research: Health care systems, databases, human factors, machine diagnostics, precision machining.
Dr. S. K. Kachhal, Chair, 313-593-5361, *Fax:* 313-593-3692.
Application contact: Shelly A. Harris, Graduate Secretary, 313-593-5361, *Fax:*

University of Michigan–Dearborn (continued)
313-593-3692, *E-mail:* saharris@engin.umd.umich.edu. *Web site:* http://www.engin.umd.umich.edu/

■ UNIVERSITY OF MINNESOTA, TWIN CITIES CAMPUS

Graduate School, Institute of Technology, Center for the Development of Technological Leadership, Program in Infrastructure Systems Engineering, Minneapolis, MN 55455-0213

AWARDS MS. Part-time and evening/weekend programs available.

Faculty: 12.
Students: 31 (2 women); includes 3 minority (all African Americans). Average age 36. 17 applicants, 82% accepted. In 2001, 13 degrees awarded.
Degree requirements: For master's, capstone project.
Entrance requirements: For master's, minimum of one year of work experience in related field, undergraduate degree in civil engineering or related field, minimum GPA of 3.0. *Application deadline:* For fall admission, 10/15 (priority date). Applications are processed on a rolling basis. *Application fee:* $50 ($55 for international students). Electronic applications accepted.
Expenses: Contact institution.
Financial support: Scholarships/grants available. Support available to part-time students. Financial award applicants required to submit FAFSA.
Faculty research: Water distribution, pavement maintenance and management, traffic management systems, infrastructure systems maintenance and management.
Dr. Vaughan Voller, Director of Graduate Studies, 612-625-0764, *Fax:* 612-626-7750, *E-mail:* volle001@tc.umn.edu.
Application contact: Shelli Burns, Admissions, 612-624-4380, *Fax:* 612-624-7510, *E-mail:* shelli@cdtl.umn.edu. *Web site:* http://www.cdtl.umn.edu/

■ UNIVERSITY OF MISSOURI–ROLLA

Graduate School, School of Engineering, Program in Systems Engineering, Rolla, MO 65409-0910

AWARDS MS.

Entrance requirements: For master's, GRE General Test, TOEFL, minimum GPA of 3.0. Electronic applications accepted.

■ UNIVERSITY OF PENNSYLVANIA

School of Engineering and Applied Science, Department of Systems Engineering, Philadelphia, PA 19104

AWARDS Environmental resources engineering (MSE); environmental/resources engineering (PhD). Systems engineering (MSE, PhD); technology and public policy (MSE, PhD); transportation (MSE, PhD). Part-time programs available.

Faculty: 11 full-time (0 women), 3 part-time/adjunct (0 women).
Students: 38 full-time (10 women), 21 part-time (5 women); includes 39 minority (4 African Americans, 33 Asian Americans or Pacific Islanders, 2 Hispanic Americans). Terminal master's awarded for partial completion of doctoral program.
Degree requirements: For doctorate, one foreign language, thesis/dissertation.
Entrance requirements: For master's and doctorate, TOEFL. *Application deadline:* For fall admission, 1/2 (priority date). Applications are processed on a rolling basis. *Application fee:* $65. Electronic applications accepted.
Financial support: Fellowships, research assistantships, teaching assistantships, scholarships/grants available.
Faculty research: Systems methodology, operations research, decision sciences, telecommunication systems, logistics, transportation systems, manufacturing systems, infrastructure systems.
Dr. John D. Keenan, Chair, 215-898-5710, *Fax:* 215-898-5020, *E-mail:* keenan@seas.upenn.edu.
Application contact: Dr. Tony E. Smith, Graduate Group Chair, 215-898-9647, *Fax:* 215-898-5020, *E-mail:* tesmith@seas.upenn.edu. *Web site:* http://www.seas.upenn.edu/ese

Find an in-depth description at www.petersons.com/gradchannel.

■ UNIVERSITY OF PITTSBURGH

School of Engineering, Program in Manufacturing Systems Engineering, Pittsburgh, PA 15260

AWARDS MSMfSE. Part-time and evening/weekend programs available. Postbaccalaureate distance learning degree programs offered (no on-campus study).

Degree requirements: For master's, thesis, internship or project.
Entrance requirements: For master's, GRE General Test, TOEFL.
Faculty research: Manufacturing information systems, manufacturing process simulation, product design methods. *Web site:* http://www.pitt.edu/~pittie/

■ UNIVERSITY OF RHODE ISLAND

Graduate School, College of Engineering, Department of Mechanical Engineering and Applied Mechanics, Program in Design/Systems, Kingston, RI 02881

AWARDS MS, PhD.

Entrance requirements: For master's and doctorate, GRE General Test (international applicants). *Application fee:* $25.
Expenses: Tuition, state resident: full-time $3,756; part-time $209 per credit. Tuition, nonresident: full-time $10,774; part-time $599 per credit. Required fees: $1,586; $76 per credit. $76 per credit. One-time fee: $60 full-time.

■ UNIVERSITY OF ST. THOMAS

Graduate Studies, Graduate School of Applied Science and Engineering, Program in Engineering and Technology Management, St. Paul, MN 55105-1096

AWARDS Engineering and technology management (Certificate); manufacturing systems (MS); manufacturing systems engineering (MMSE); technology management (MS). Part-time and evening/weekend programs available.

Faculty: 3 full-time (0 women), 32 part-time/adjunct (1 woman).
Students: 2 full-time (0 women), 219 part-time (39 women); includes 23 minority (10 African Americans, 9 Asian Americans or Pacific Islanders, 3 Hispanic Americans, 1 Native American), 6 international. Average age 34. 60 applicants, 97% accepted. In 2001, 29 master's, 5 other advanced degrees awarded.
Degree requirements: For master's, thesis (for some programs).
Application deadline: For fall admission, 8/1 (priority date); for spring admission, 1/1 (priority date). Applications are processed on a rolling basis. *Application fee:* $30. Electronic applications accepted.
Expenses: Tuition: Part-time $401 per credit. Tuition and fees vary according to degree level and program.
Financial support: In 2001–02, 6 students received support; fellowships, research assistantships, institutionally sponsored loans and scholarships/grants available. Support available to part-time students. Financial award application deadline: 4/1; financial award applicants required to submit FAFSA.
Ron Bennett, Director, 651-962-5750, *Fax:* 651-962-6419, *E-mail:* rjbennett@stthomas.edu.
Application contact: Marlene L. Houliston, Student Services Coordinator, 651-962-5750, *Fax:* 651-962-6419, *E-mail:* technology@stthomas.edu. *Web site:* http://www.stthomas.edu/technology/

■ UNIVERSITY OF SOUTHERN CALIFORNIA

Graduate School, School of Engineering, Department of Electrical Engineering, Program in Systems Architecture and Engineering, Los Angeles, CA 90089

AWARDS MS.

Degree requirements: For master's, thesis optional.
Entrance requirements: For master's, GRE General Test.
Expenses: Tuition: Full-time $25,060; part-time $844 per unit. Required fees: $473.

Find an in-depth description at www.petersons.com/gradchannel.

■ UNIVERSITY OF SOUTHERN CALIFORNIA

Graduate School, School of Engineering, Department of Electrical Engineering, Program in VLSI Design, Los Angeles, CA 90089

AWARDS MS.

Degree requirements: For master's, thesis optional.
Entrance requirements: For master's, GRE General Test.
Expenses: Tuition: Full-time $25,060; part-time $844 per unit. Required fees: $473.

Find an in-depth description at www.petersons.com/gradchannel.

■ UNIVERSITY OF SOUTHERN CALIFORNIA

Graduate School, School of Engineering, Department of Industrial and Systems Engineering, Program in Industrial and Systems Engineering, Los Angeles, CA 90089

AWARDS MS, PhD, Engr, MBA/MS.

Degree requirements: For master's, thesis optional; for doctorate, thesis/dissertation.
Entrance requirements: For master's, doctorate, and Engr, GRE General Test.
Expenses: Tuition: Full-time $25,060; part-time $844 per unit. Required fees: $473.
Faculty research: Work organization and high-tech manufacturing.

■ UNIVERSITY OF SOUTHERN COLORADO

College of Education, Engineering and Professional Studies, Program in Industrial and Systems Engineering, Pueblo, CO 81001-4901

AWARDS MS. Part-time and evening/weekend programs available.

Faculty: 3 full-time (1 woman), 1 part-time/adjunct (0 women).
Students: 16 full-time (4 women), 18 part-time (3 women); includes 5 minority (1 African American, 3 Hispanic Americans, 1 Native American), 20 international. Average age 29. 23 applicants, 74% accepted. In 2001, 13 degrees awarded.
Degree requirements: For master's, thesis optional. *Median time to degree:* Master's–1.5 years full-time, 3.5 years part-time.
Entrance requirements: For master's, GRE General Test, TOEFL. *Application deadline:* For fall admission, 7/19 (priority date); for spring admission, 11/30 (priority date). *Application fee:* $35.
Expenses: Tuition, state resident: full-time $1,746; part-time $97 per credit. Tuition, nonresident: full-time $8,298; part-time $461 per credit. Required fees: $445; $97 per credit. $582 per semester. Tuition and fees vary according to course load.
Financial support: In 2001–02, 1 fellowship (averaging $17,000 per year), 1 research assistantship with partial tuition reimbursement (averaging $13,000 per year), 3 teaching assistantships with partial tuition reimbursements (averaging $8,000 per year) were awarded. Career-related internships or fieldwork, Federal Work-Study, institutionally sponsored loans, and scholarships/grants also available. Financial award application deadline: 3/1; financial award applicants required to submit FAFSA.
Faculty research: Computer-integrated manufacturing, reliability, economic development, design of experiments, scheduling. *Total annual research expenditures:* $178,000.
Dr. Jane M. Fraser, Chair, 719-549-2036, *Fax:* 719-549-2519, *E-mail:* jfraser@uscolo.edu.
Application contact: Dr. Huseyin Sarper, Graduate Coordinator, 719-549-2889, *Fax:* 719-549-2519, *E-mail:* sarper@uscolo.edu. *Web site:* http://www.ceeps.edu/engin/index.html

■ UNIVERSITY OF VIRGINIA

School of Engineering and Applied Science, Department of Systems Engineering, Charlottesville, VA 22903

AWARDS ME, MS, PhD, ME/MBA. Postbaccalaureate distance learning degree programs offered (no on-campus study).

Faculty: 16 full-time (2 women), 1 part-time/adjunct (0 women).
Students: 69 full-time (15 women), 7 part-time (1 woman); includes 6 minority (2 African Americans, 4 Asian Americans or Pacific Islanders), 25 international. Average age 30. 107 applicants, 47% accepted, 20 enrolled. In 2001, 41 master's, 3 doctorates awarded.
Degree requirements: For doctorate, thesis/dissertation, comprehensive exam.
Entrance requirements: For master's and doctorate, GRE General Test. *Application*

deadline: For fall admission, 8/1; for spring admission, 12/1. Applications are processed on a rolling basis. *Application fee:* $40. Electronic applications accepted.
Expenses: Tuition, state resident: full-time $3,988. Tuition, nonresident: full-time $17,078. Required fees: $1,190.
Financial support: Fellowships available. Financial award application deadline: 2/1; financial award applicants required to submit FAFSA.
Faculty research: Operations research. Systems methodology and design. Systems management, decision, and control.
Donald E. Brown, Chairman, 434-924-5393, *Fax:* 434-982-2972.
Application contact: Kathryn Thornton, Assistant Dean, 434-924-3897, *Fax:* 434-982-2214, *E-mail:* inquiry@cs.virginia.edu. *Web site:* http://www.sys.virginia.edu/

Find an in-depth description at www.petersons.com/gradchannel.

■ UNIVERSITY OF WEST FLORIDA

College of Arts and Sciences: Sciences, Department of Computer Science, Pensacola, FL 32514-5750

AWARDS Computer science (MS). Systems and control engineering (MS). Part-time and evening/weekend programs available.

Faculty: 7 full-time (2 women), 1 part-time/adjunct (0 women).
Students: 19 full-time (5 women), 42 part-time (14 women); includes 14 minority (3 African Americans, 6 Asian Americans or Pacific Islanders, 4 Hispanic Americans, 1 Native American), 6 international. Average age 34. 61 applicants, 31% accepted, 9 enrolled. In 2001, 38 degrees awarded.
Degree requirements: For master's, thesis optional.
Entrance requirements: For master's, GRE General Test. *Application deadline:* For fall admission, 6/30; for spring admission, 11/1. Applications are processed on a rolling basis. *Application fee:* $20.
Expenses: Tuition, state resident: full-time $3,995; part-time $166 per credit hour. Tuition, nonresident: full-time $13,766; part-time $574 per credit hour. Tuition and fees vary according to campus/location.
Financial support: Fellowships, research assistantships available.
Dr. Mohsen Guizani, Chairperson, 850-474-2542.

■ VIRGINIA POLYTECHNIC INSTITUTE AND STATE UNIVERSITY

Graduate School, College of Engineering, Program in Systems Engineering, Blacksburg, VA 24061

AWARDS M Eng, MS. Part-time and evening/weekend programs available.

Faculty: 5 full-time (0 women).

Virginia Polytechnic Institute and State University (continued)

Students: Average age 29. 14 applicants, 50% accepted. In 2001, 34 degrees awarded.

Degree requirements: For master's, thesis or alternative.

Entrance requirements: For master's, GRE General Test, TOEFL. *Application deadline:* For fall admission, 12/1 (priority date). Applications are processed on a rolling basis. *Application fee:* $45. Electronic applications accepted.

Expenses: Tuition, state resident: part-time $241 per hour. Tuition, nonresident: part-time $406 per hour. Tuition and fees vary according to program.

Financial support: Application deadline: 4/1.

Dr. H. Kurstedt, Chairman, 540-231-5458, *E-mail:* hak@vt.edu.

■ WASHINGTON UNIVERSITY IN ST. LOUIS

Henry Edwin Sever Graduate School of Engineering and Applied Science, Sever Institute of Technology, Department of Civil Engineering, Program in Transportation and Urban Systems Engineering, St. Louis, MO 63130-4899

AWARDS D Sc.

Degree requirements: For doctorate, variable foreign language requirement, thesis/dissertation, departmental qualifying exam.

Expenses: Tuition: Full-time $26,900. *Web site:* http://www.cive.wustl.edu/cive/

■ WEST VIRGINIA UNIVERSITY INSTITUTE OF TECHNOLOGY

College of Engineering, Program in Control Systems Engineering, Montgomery, WV 25136

AWARDS MS. Part-time programs available.

Faculty: 10 full-time (1 woman).

Students: 20 full-time (5 women), 1 part-time, 20 international. Average age 24. 35 applicants, 77% accepted. In 2001, 2 degrees awarded.

Degree requirements: For master's, thesis or alternative, fieldwork.

Entrance requirements: For master's, GRE General Test, TOEFL, minimum GPA of 3.0. *Application deadline:* For fall admission, 3/15 (priority date). Applications are processed on a rolling basis. *Application fee:* $10.

Expenses: Tuition, state resident: full-time $3,248; part-time $180 per credit. Tuition, nonresident: full-time $7,852; part-time $436 per credit.

Financial support: In 2001–02, 21 teaching assistantships with full tuition reimbursements (averaging $4,000 per year) were awarded; career-related internships or fieldwork, Federal Work-Study, and institutionally sponsored loans also available. Financial award application deadline: 3/15.

Faculty research: Process control.

Application contact: Robert P. Scholl, Registrar, 304-442-3167, *Fax:* 304-442-3097, *E-mail:* rscholl@wvutech.edu. *Web site:* http://wvit.wvnet.edu/

Management of Engineering and Technology

ENERGY MANAGEMENT AND POLICY

■ BOSTON UNIVERSITY

Graduate School of Arts and Sciences, Program in Energy and Environmental Studies, Boston, MA 02215

AWARDS Energy and environmental analysis (MA); environmental remote sensing and geographic information systems (MA); international relations and enivronmental policy (MA).

Students: 10 full-time (7 women), 3 part-time (2 women); includes 1 minority (Hispanic American), 1 international. Average age 26. 110 applicants, 58% accepted, 20 enrolled.

Degree requirements: For master's, one foreign language, comprehensive exam, registration, research paper.

Entrance requirements: For master's, GRE General Test, TOEFL, 2 letters of recommendation. *Application deadline:* For fall admission, 7/1; for spring admission, 11/15. *Application fee:* $60.

Expenses: Tuition: Full-time $25,872; part-time $340 per credit. Required fees: $40 per semester. Part-time tuition and fees vary according to class time, course level and program.

Financial support: In 2001–02, 8 students received support, including 3 research assistantships; fellowships, career-related internships or fieldwork and Federal Work-Study also available. Support available to part-time students. Financial award application deadline: 1/15; financial award applicants required to submit FAFSA. Cutler J. Cleveland, Director, 617-353-7552, *Fax:* 617-353-5986, *E-mail:* cutler@bu.edu.

Application contact: Alpana Roy, Administrative Assistant, 617-353-3083, *Fax:* 617-353-5986, *E-mail:* alpana@bu.edu. *Web site:* http://www.bu.edu//CEES/

■ NEW YORK INSTITUTE OF TECHNOLOGY

Graduate Division, School of Engineering and Technology, Program in Energy Management, Old Westbury, NY 11568-8000

AWARDS Energy management (MS); energy technology (Advanced Certificate); environmental management (Advanced Certificate); facilities management (Advanced Certificate). Part-time and evening/weekend programs available. Postbaccalaureate distance learning degree programs offered.

Students: 8 full-time (2 women), 64 part-time (6 women); includes 15 minority (6 African Americans, 4 Asian Americans or Pacific Islanders, 5 Hispanic Americans), 9 international. Average age 37. 26 applicants, 73% accepted, 8 enrolled. In 2001, 17 degrees awarded.

Degree requirements: For master's, thesis or alternative, comprehensive exam.

Entrance requirements: For master's, minimum QPA of 2.85. *Application deadline:* For fall admission, 7/1 (priority date); for spring admission, 12/1 (priority date). Applications are processed on a rolling basis. *Application fee:* $50. Electronic applications accepted.

Expenses: Tuition: Part-time $545 per credit. Tuition and fees vary according to course load, degree level, program and student level.

Financial support: In 2001–02, 1 research assistantship with partial tuition reimbursement was awarded; fellowships, institutionally sponsored loans, tuition waivers (full and partial), and unspecified assistantships also available. Support available to part-time students. Financial award applicants required to submit FAFSA. Dr. Robert Amundsen, Director, 516-686-7578.

Application contact: Jacquelyn Nealon, Dean of Admissions and Financial Aid, 516-686-7925, *Fax:* 516-686-7613, *E-mail:* jnealon@nyit.edu.

■ UNIVERSITY OF CALIFORNIA, BERKELEY

Graduate Division, Group in Energy and Resources, Berkeley, CA 94720-1500

AWARDS MA, MS, PhD.

Degree requirements: For master's, project or thesis; for doctorate, one foreign language, thesis/dissertation, qualifying exam.
Entrance requirements: For master's and doctorate, GRE General Test, minimum GPA of 3.0.
Expenses: Tuition, nonresident: full-time $10,704. Required fees: $4,349.
Faculty research: Technical, economic, environmental, and institutional aspects of energy conservation in residential and commercial buildings; international patterns of energy use; renewable energy sources and barriers to their potential contribution to energy supplies; assessment of conventional and nonconventional valuation of energy and environmental resources pricing.

ENGINEERING MANAGEMENT

■ AIR FORCE INSTITUTE OF TECHNOLOGY

School of Engineering and Management, Department of Systems and Engineering Management, Dayton, OH 45433-7765

AWARDS Environmental and engineering management (MS); information resource management (MS). Systems acquisition management (MS). Part-time programs available.

Degree requirements: For master's, thesis.
Entrance requirements: For master's, GRE, GMAT, minimum GPA of 3.0. *Web site:* http://en.afit.edu/env/

■ CALIFORNIA POLYTECHNIC STATE UNIVERSITY, SAN LUIS OBISPO

College of Engineering and Orfalea College of Business, Engineering Management Program, San Luis Obispo, CA 93407

AWARDS MBA/MS.

Students: 7 full-time (0 women), 2 part-time. 11 applicants, 36% accepted, 3 enrolled.
Application deadline: For fall admission, 7/1. Applications are processed on a rolling basis. *Application fee:* $55.
Expenses: Tuition, nonresident: part-time $164 per unit. One-time fee: $2,153 part-time.

Financial support: Fellowships, research assistantships, teaching assistantships, career-related internships or fieldwork, Federal Work-Study, and institutionally sponsored loans available. Financial award application deadline: 3/2; financial award applicants required to submit FAFSA.
Don White, Professor, 805-756-2418, *Fax:* 805-756-5439, *E-mail:* dewhite@oboe.calpoly.edu.
Application contact: Dr. David Peach, Director, Graduate Management Program, 805-756-7187, *Fax:* 805-756-0110, *E-mail:* dpeach@calpoly.edu. *Web site:* http://www.cob.calpoly.edu/cob/grad/page8.html

■ CALIFORNIA STATE UNIVERSITY, NORTHRIDGE

Graduate Studies, College of Engineering and Computer Science, Department of Civil and Manufacturing Engineering, Northridge, CA 91330

AWARDS Applied mechanics (MSE); civil engineering (MS); engineering and computer science (MS); engineering management (MS); industrial engineering (MS); materials engineering (MS); mechanical engineering (MS), including aerospace engineering, applied engineering, machine design, mechanical engineering, structural engineering, thermofluids; mechanics (MS). Part-time and evening/weekend programs available.

Faculty: 14 full-time, 2 part-time/adjunct.
Students: 25 full-time (4 women), 72 part-time (9 women). Average age 31. 64 applicants, 77% accepted, 22 enrolled. In 2001, 34 degrees awarded.
Degree requirements: For master's, thesis.
Entrance requirements: For master's, GRE General Test, TOEFL, minimum GPA of 2.5. *Application deadline:* For fall admission, 11/30. *Application fee:* $55.
Expenses: Tuition, nonresident: part-time $631 per semester. Required fees: $246 per unit.
Financial support: Teaching assistantships available. Financial award application deadline: 3/1.
Faculty research: Composite study.
Dr. Stephen Gadomski, Chair, 818-677-2166.
Application contact: Dr. Ileana Costa, Graduate Coordinator, 818-677-3299.

■ THE CATHOLIC UNIVERSITY OF AMERICA

School of Engineering, Program in Engineering Management, Washington, DC 20064

AWARDS MS Engr. Part-time and evening/weekend programs available.

Faculty: 6 part-time/adjunct (0 women).
Students: 1 full-time (0 women), 16 part-time (3 women); includes 2 minority (1 African American, 1 Asian American or Pacific Islander), 2 international. Average age 34. 9 applicants, 56% accepted, 2 enrolled. In 2001, 16 degrees awarded.
Application deadline: For fall admission, 8/15 (priority date); for spring admission, 12/10. Applications are processed on a rolling basis. *Application fee:* $55. Electronic applications accepted.
Expenses: Tuition: Full-time $20,050; part-time $770 per credit. Required fees: $430 per term. Tuition and fees vary according to program.
Financial support: Federal Work-Study, institutionally sponsored loans, and tuition waivers (full) available. Support available to part-time students. Financial award application deadline: 2/1.
Donald Purcell, Director, 202-319-5191, *Fax:* 202-319-4499.

■ CLARKSON UNIVERSITY

Graduate School, Interdisciplinary Studies, Program in Engineering and Management, Potsdam, NY 13699

AWARDS Engineering and manufacturing management (MS). Part-time and evening/weekend programs available.

Students: Average age 35. 5 applicants, 100% accepted. In 2001, 8 degrees awarded. *Median time to degree:* Master's–2 years full-time, 4 years part-time.
Entrance requirements: For master's, TOEFL. *Application deadline:* For fall admission, 5/15 (priority date); for spring admission, 10/15 (priority date). Applications are processed on a rolling basis. *Application fee:* $25 ($35 for international students).
Expenses: Tuition: Part-time $714 per credit. Required fees: $108 per semester.
Financial support: Fellowships, research assistantships, teaching assistantships available.
Dr. Farzad Mahmoodi, Director, Engineering and Management Program, 315-268-4281, *Fax:* 315-268-3810, *E-mail:* mahmoodi@clarkson.edu.

■ COLORADO SCHOOL OF MINES

Graduate School, Division of Economics and Business, Golden, CO 80401-1887

AWARDS Engineering and technology management (MS); mineral economics (MS, PhD). Part-time programs available.

Faculty: 13 full-time (2 women), 13 part-time/adjunct (5 women).
Students: 58 full-time (11 women), 27 part-time (5 women); includes 6 minority (2 African Americans, 2 Asian Americans or Pacific Islanders, 2 Hispanic Americans), 37 international. 114 applicants, 94% accepted, 30 enrolled. In 2001, 31 master's, 2 doctorates awarded.
Degree requirements: For doctorate, thesis/dissertation, comprehensive exam. *Median time to degree:* Master's–2 years full-time; doctorate–4 years full-time.

Colorado School of Mines (continued)

Entrance requirements: For master's and doctorate, GRE General Test. *Application deadline:* For fall admission, 12/1 (priority date); for spring admission, 5/1 (priority date). Applications are processed on a rolling basis. *Application fee:* $40. Electronic applications accepted.
Expenses: Tuition, state resident: full-time $4,940; part-time $246 per credit. Tuition, nonresident: full-time $16,070; part-time $803 per credit. Required fees: $341 per semester.
Financial support: In 2001–02, 32 students received support, including 5 fellowships (averaging $6,471 per year), 4 research assistantships (averaging $7,793 per year), 31 teaching assistantships (averaging $5,232 per year); unspecified assistantships also available. Support available to part-time students. Financial award applicants required to submit FAFSA.
Faculty research: International trade, resource and environmental economics, energy economics, operations research. *Total annual research expenditures:* $45,408.
Dr. Roderick G. Eggert, Head, 303-273-3981, *Fax:* 303-273-3416, *E-mail:* reggert@mines.edu.
Application contact: Kathleen A. Feighny, Administrative Faculty, 303-273-3979, *Fax:* 303-273-3416, *E-mail:* kfeighny@mines.edu. *Web site:* http://www.mines.edu/academic/econbus/

■ COLORADO STATE UNIVERSITY

Graduate School, College of Engineering, Department of Mechanical Engineering, Fort Collins, CO 80523-0015

AWARDS Bioengineering (MS, PhD); energy and environmental engineering (MS, PhD); energy conversion (MS, PhD); engineering management (MS); heat and mass transfer (MS, PhD); industrial and manufacturing systems engineering (MS, PhD); mechanical engineering (MS, PhD); mechanics and materials (MS, PhD). Part-time programs available.

Faculty: 17 full-time (2 women).
Students: 36 full-time (6 women), 63 part-time (11 women); includes 5 minority (2 Asian Americans or Pacific Islanders, 2 Hispanic Americans, 1 Native American), 22 international. Average age 32. 234 applicants, 83% accepted, 32 enrolled. In 2001, 10 master's, 3 doctorates awarded. Terminal master's awarded for partial completion of doctoral program.
Degree requirements: For doctorate, thesis/dissertation.
Entrance requirements: For master's and doctorate, GRE General Test, TOEFL, minimum GPA of 3.0. *Application deadline:* For fall admission, 2/1 (priority date). Applications are processed on a rolling basis. *Application fee:* $30. Electronic applications accepted.

Expenses: Tuition, state resident: full-time $2,880; part-time $160 per credit. Tuition, nonresident: full-time $11,412; part-time $634 per credit. Required fees: $750; $34 per credit.
Financial support: In 2001–02, 2 fellowships, 15 research assistantships (averaging $15,792 per year), 14 teaching assistantships (averaging $11,844 per year) were awarded. Traineeships also available.
Faculty research: Space propulsion, controls and systems, engineering and materials. *Total annual research expenditures:* $2.1 million.
Dr. Allan T. Kirkpatrick, Head, 970-491-6559, *Fax:* 970-491-3827, *E-mail:* allan@engr.colostate.edu. *Web site:* http://www.engr.colostate.edu/depts/me/index.html

■ DALLAS BAPTIST UNIVERSITY

College of Business, Business Administration Program, Dallas, TX 75211-9299

AWARDS Accounting (MBA); E. business (MBA); finance (MBA); health care management (MBA); international business (MBA); management (MBA); management information systems (MBA); marketing (MBA); technology and engineering management (MBA). Part-time and evening/weekend programs available. Postbaccalaureate distance learning degree programs offered (no on-campus study).

Faculty: 14 full-time (5 women), 31 part-time/adjunct (10 women).
Students: 388 (187 women). 196 applicants, 66% accepted, 54 enrolled. In 2001, 86 degrees awarded.
Entrance requirements: For master's, GMAT, TOEFL, minimum GPA of 3.0. *Application deadline:* Applications are processed on a rolling basis. *Application fee:* $25. Electronic applications accepted.
Expenses: Tuition: Full-time $6,030; part-time $335 per credit.
Financial support: Career-related internships or fieldwork, Federal Work-Study, institutionally sponsored loans, scholarships/grants, and tuition waivers (full and partial) available. Support available to part-time students.
Faculty research: Sports management, services marketing, retailing, strategic management, financial planning/investments.
Barbara Sleeper, Director of MBA Program, 214-333-5280, *Fax:* 214-333-5579, *E-mail:* graduate@dbu.edu.
Application contact: Sarah R. Brancaccio, Director of Graduate Programs, 214-333-5243, *Fax:* 214-333-5579, *E-mail:* graduate@dbu.edu. *Web site:* http://www.dbu.edu

■ DARTMOUTH COLLEGE

Thayer School of Engineering, Program in Engineering Management, Hanover, NH 03755

AWARDS MEM, MBA/MEM.

Degree requirements: For master's, design experience.
Entrance requirements: For master's, GRE General Test. *Application deadline:* For fall admission, 1/1 (priority date). Applications are processed on a rolling basis. *Application fee:* $40 ($50 for international students).
Expenses: Tuition: Full-time $26,425.
Financial support: Fellowships, teaching assistantships, career-related internships or fieldwork, Federal Work-Study, institutionally sponsored loans, and tuition waivers (full and partial) available. Financial award application deadline: 1/15; financial award applicants required to submit CSS PROFILE.
Application contact: Candace S. Potter, Graduate Admissions Administrator, 603-646-3844, *Fax:* 603-646-1620, *E-mail:* candace.potter@dartmouth.edu. *Web site:* http://engineering.dartmouth.edu/

■ DREXEL UNIVERSITY

Graduate School, College of Engineering, Program in Engineering Management, Philadelphia, PA 19104-2875

AWARDS MS, PhD. All classes held in evening. Part-time and evening/weekend programs available. Postbaccalaureate distance learning degree programs offered (no on-campus study).

Faculty: 3 part-time/adjunct (0 women).
Students: 4 full-time (2 women), 70 part-time (16 women); includes 11 minority (4 African Americans, 4 Asian Americans or Pacific Islanders, 3 Hispanic Americans), 4 international. Average age 32. 21 applicants, 81% accepted, 13 enrolled. In 2001, 32 degrees awarded.
Degree requirements: For master's, thesis optional; for doctorate, thesis/dissertation.
Entrance requirements: For master's, TOEFL, minimum GPA of 3.0; for doctorate, TOEFL. *Application deadline:* For fall admission, 8/21. Applications are processed on a rolling basis. *Application fee:* $50. Electronic applications accepted.
Expenses: Tuition: Full-time $20,088; part-time $558 per credit. Required fees: $78 per term. One-time fee: $200. Tuition and fees vary according to course load, degree level and program.
Financial support: Application deadline: 2/1.
Faculty research: Quality, operations research and management, ergonomics, applied statistics.
Dr. Steve Smith, Director, 215-895-5809.
Application contact: Director of Graduate Admissions, 215-895-6700, *Fax:* 215-895-5939, *E-mail:* enroll@drexel.edu.

■ DUKE UNIVERSITY

Graduate School, School of Engineering, Program in Engineering Management, Durham, NC 27708-0586

AWARDS MEM.

Entrance requirements: For master's, GRE General Test. *Application deadline:* For fall admission, 12/31; for spring admission, 11/1. *Application fee:* $75.
Expenses: Tuition: Full-time $24,600.
Financial support: Application deadline: 12/31.
F. Hadley Cocks, Head, 919-660-5455, *Fax:* 919-660-5456, *E-mail:* memp@mems.egr.duke.edu.

Find an in-depth description at www.petersons.com/gradchannel.

■ FLORIDA INSTITUTE OF TECHNOLOGY

Graduate Programs, College of Engineering, Engineering Management Program, Melbourne, FL 32901-6975

AWARDS MS. Part-time and evening/weekend programs available.

Faculty: 2 full-time (0 women), 2 part-time/adjunct (0 women).
Students: 9 full-time (0 women), 23 part-time (4 women); includes 4 minority (1 African American, 3 Hispanic Americans), 10 international. Average age 29. 45 applicants, 58% accepted. In 2001, 14 degrees awarded.
Degree requirements: For master's, thesis optional.
Entrance requirements: For master's, GRE General Test, BS in engineering, minimum GPA of 3.0. *Application deadline:* Applications are processed on a rolling basis. *Application fee:* $50. Electronic applications accepted.
Expenses: Tuition: Part-time $650 per credit.
Financial support: In 2001–02, 4 students received support, including 3 research assistantships with full and partial tuition reimbursements available (averaging $8,337 per year), 1 teaching assistantship with full and partial tuition reimbursement available (averaging $7,600 per year); career-related internships or fieldwork and tuition remissions also available. Financial award application deadline: 3/1; financial award applicants required to submit FAFSA.
Faculty research: System/software engineering, simulation and analytical modeling, project management, multimedia tools, quality. *Total annual research expenditures:* $15,000.
Dr. Muzaffar A. Shaikh, Program Director, 321-674-7345, *Fax:* 321-674-8192, *E-mail:* mshaikh@fit.edu.
Application contact: Carolyn P. Farrior, Director of Graduate Admissions, 321-674-7118, *Fax:* 321-723-9468, *E-mail:*

cfarrior@fit.edu. *Web site:* http://www.fit.edu/

Find an in-depth description at www.petersons.com/gradchannel.

■ FLORIDA INSTITUTE OF TECHNOLOGY

Graduate Programs, School of Extended Graduate Studies, Melbourne, FL 32901-6975

AWARDS Acquisition and contract management (MS, MSM, PMBA); aerospace engineering (MS); business administration (PMBA); computer information systems (MS); computer science (MS); ebusiness (MSM); electrical engineering (MS); engineering management (MS); health management (MS); human resource management (MSM, PMBA); human resources management (MS); information systems (MSM, PMBA); logistics management (MS, MSM); management (MS); material acquisition management (MS); mechanical engineering (MS); operations research (MS); project management (MS), including information systems, operations research; public administration (MPA). Software engineering (MS). Space systems (MS). Space systems management (MS). Systems management (MS), including information systems, operations research; transportation management (MSM). Part-time and evening/weekend programs available. Postbaccalaureate distance learning degree programs offered (no on-campus study).

Faculty: 10 full-time (2 women), 131 part-time/adjunct (15 women).
Students: 57 full-time (29 women), 1,198 part-time (455 women); includes 277 minority (183 African Americans, 38 Asian Americans or Pacific Islanders, 51 Hispanic Americans, 5 Native Americans), 16 international. Average age 37. 299 applicants, 42% accepted. In 2001, 434 degrees awarded.
Entrance requirements: For master's, minimum GPA of 3.0. *Application deadline:* Applications are processed on a rolling basis. *Application fee:* $50. Electronic applications accepted.
Expenses: Tuition: Part-time $650 per credit.
Financial support: Institutionally sponsored loans available. Financial award application deadline: 3/1; financial award applicants required to submit FAFSA.
Dr. Ronald L. Marshall, Dean, School of Extended Graduate Studies, 321-674-8880.
Application contact: Carolyn P. Farrior, Director of Graduate Admissions, 321-674-7118, *Fax:* 321-723-9468, *E-mail:* cfarrior@fit.edu. *Web site:* http://www.segs.fit.edu/

■ THE GEORGE WASHINGTON UNIVERSITY

School of Engineering and Applied Science, Department of Engineering Management and Systems Engineering, Washington, DC 20052

AWARDS MEM, MS, D Sc, App Sc, Engr, MEM/MS. Part-time and evening/weekend programs available.

Faculty: 20 full-time (3 women), 44 part-time/adjunct (3 women).
Students: 154 full-time (43 women), 635 part-time (197 women); includes 167 minority (90 African Americans, 46 Asian Americans or Pacific Islanders, 27 Hispanic Americans, 4 Native Americans), 176 international. Average age 36. 264 applicants, 90% accepted. In 2001, 173 master's, 28 doctorates, 6 other advanced degrees awarded.
Degree requirements: For master's, thesis optional; for doctorate, one foreign language, thesis/dissertation, final and qualifying exams; for other advanced degree, professional project.
Entrance requirements: For master's, TOEFL or George Washington University English as a Foreign Language Test, appropriate bachelor's degree; for doctorate, TOEFL or George Washington University English as a Foreign Language Test, appropriate master's degree, minimum GPA of 3.5; for other advanced degree, TOEFL or George Washington University English as a Foreign Language Test, appropriate master's degree, minimum GPA of 3.5, GRE required if highest earned degree is BS. *Application deadline:* For fall admission, 3/1; for spring admission, 10/1. Applications are processed on a rolling basis. *Application fee:* $50.
Expenses: Tuition: Part-time $810 per credit. Required fees: $1 per credit.
Financial support: In 2001–02, 10 fellowships with tuition reimbursements (averaging $3,900 per year), 4 research assistantships, 9 teaching assistantships with tuition reimbursements (averaging $2,500 per year) were awarded. Career-related internships or fieldwork and institutionally sponsored loans also available. Financial award application deadline: 3/1; financial award applicants required to submit FAFSA.
Faculty research: Artificial intelligence and expert systems, human factors engineering and systems analysis. *Total annual research expenditures:* $421,800.
Dr. Thomas Mazzuchi, Chair, 202-994-0558, *E-mail:* mazzuchi@seas.gwu.edu.
Application contact: Howard M. Davis, Manager, Office of Admissions and Student Records, 202-994-6158, *Fax:* 202-994-0909, *E-mail:* data:adms@seas.gwu.edu. *Web site:* http://www.gwu.edu/~gradinfo/

Find an in-depth description at www.petersons.com/gradchannel.

■ KANSAS STATE UNIVERSITY

Graduate School, College of Engineering, Department of Industrial and Manufacturing Systems Engineering, Manhattan, KS 66506

AWARDS Engineering management (MEM); industrial and manufacturing systems engineering (PhD); industrial engineering (MS); operations research (MS). Part-time programs available. Postbaccalaureate distance learning degree programs offered.

Faculty: 11 full-time (1 woman).
Students: 30 full-time (7 women), 24 part-time (2 women), 31 international. 201 applicants, 49% accepted, 19 enrolled. In 2001, 5 master's, 1 doctorate awarded.
Degree requirements: For master's, thesis or alternative; for doctorate, thesis/dissertation.
Entrance requirements: For master's, GRE General Test, TOEFL, bachelor's degree in engineering, mathematics, or physical science; for doctorate, GRE General Test, TOEFL, master's degree in engineering or industrial manufacturing. *Application deadline:* For fall admission, 3/1 (priority date); for spring admission, 9/1. Applications are processed on a rolling basis. *Application fee:* $0 ($25 for international students). Electronic applications accepted.
Expenses: Tuition, state resident: part-time $113 per credit hour. Tuition, nonresident: part-time $358 per credit hour.
Financial support: In 2001–02, 18 research assistantships with partial tuition reimbursements (averaging $9,000 per year), 2 teaching assistantships with full tuition reimbursements (averaging $9,000 per year) were awarded. Federal Work-Study, institutionally sponsored loans, and scholarships/grants also available. Support available to part-time students. Financial award application deadline: 3/1; financial award applicants required to submit FAFSA.
Faculty research: Manufacturing engineering, operations research, engineering management, quality engineering, ergonomics. *Total annual research expenditures:* $1.7 million.
Dr. Bradley Kramer, Head, 785-532-5606, *Fax:* 785-532-7810, *E-mail:* bradleyk@ksu.edu.
Application contact: E. Stanley Lee, Graduate Program Director, 785-532-5606, *Fax:* 785-532-7810, *E-mail:* eslee@ksu.edu. *Web site:* http://cheetah.imse.ksu.edu/

■ LAMAR UNIVERSITY

College of Graduate Studies, College of Engineering, Department of Industrial Engineering, Program in Engineering Management, Beaumont, TX 77710

AWARDS MEM.

Faculty: 4 full-time (0 women).
Students: 3 full-time (0 women), 4 part-time (3 women); includes 1 minority (African American), 2 international. Average age 27. 13 applicants, 46% accepted. In 2001, 8 degrees awarded.
Degree requirements: For master's, thesis or alternative.
Entrance requirements: For master's, GRE General Test, TOEFL, 5 years of work experience, minimum GPA of 2.5 or 3.0 on last 60 hours of undergraduate course work. *Application deadline:* For fall admission, 5/15 (priority date); for spring admission, 10/1 (priority date). Applications are processed on a rolling basis. *Application fee:* $25 ($50 for international students).
Expenses: Tuition, state resident: full-time $1,114. Tuition, nonresident: full-time $3,670.
Financial support: Fellowships with partial tuition reimbursements, research assistantships with partial tuition reimbursements, teaching assistantships with partial tuition reimbursements available. Financial award application deadline: 4/1.
Faculty research: Total quality management, ergonomics and safety.
Dr. Victor Zaloom, Chair, 409-880-8804, *Fax:* 409-880-8121.
Application contact: Dr. Hsing-Wei Chu, Professor, 409-880-8804, *Fax:* 409-880-8121. *Web site:* http://dept.lamar.edu/industrial/

■ LONG ISLAND UNIVERSITY, C.W. POST CAMPUS

College of Information and Computer Science, Department of Computer Science/Management Engineering, Brookville, NY 11548-1300

AWARDS Computer science education (MS); information systems (MS); management engineering (MS). Part-time and evening/weekend programs available.

Faculty: 11 full-time (3 women), 7 part-time/adjunct (0 women).
Students: 41 full-time (16 women), 100 part-time (38 women). 96 applicants, 90% accepted, 42 enrolled. In 2001, 31 degrees awarded.
Degree requirements: For master's, thesis or alternative, comprehensive exam.
Entrance requirements: For master's, bachelor's degree in science, mathematics, or engineering; minimum GPA of 2.5. *Application deadline:* Applications are processed on a rolling basis. *Application fee:* $30. Electronic applications accepted.
Expenses: Tuition: Full-time $10,296; part-time $572 per credit. Required fees: $380; $190 per semester.
Financial support: Career-related internships or fieldwork, Federal Work-Study, institutionally sponsored loans, unspecified assistantships, and management engineering prize available. Support available to part-time students. Financial award

application deadline: 5/15; financial award applicants required to submit CSS PROFILE or FAFSA.
Faculty research: Inductive music learning, re-engineering business process, technology and ethics.
Dr. Susan Fife-Dorchak, Chair, 516-299-2293, *E-mail:* susan.dorchak@liu.edu.
Application contact: Christopher Malinowski, Director of Graduate Programs, 516-299-2663, *E-mail:* cmalinow@liu.edu. *Web site:* http://www.liu.edu/postlas/

■ LOYOLA MARYMOUNT UNIVERSITY

Graduate Division, College of Science and Engineering, Department of Mechanical Engineering, Program in Engineering and Production Management, Los Angeles, CA 90045-2659

AWARDS MS. Part-time and evening/weekend programs available.

Students: 14 full-time (3 women), 9 part-time (1 woman); includes 9 minority (1 African American, 4 Asian Americans or Pacific Islanders, 4 Hispanic Americans), 2 international. 12 applicants, 75% accepted, 7 enrolled. In 2001, 6 degrees awarded.
Degree requirements: For master's, thesis or alternative, project.
Entrance requirements: For master's, GMAT or GRE General Test, TOEFL. *Application deadline:* Applications are processed on a rolling basis. *Application fee:* $45. Electronic applications accepted.
Expenses: Contact institution.
Financial support: In 2001–02, 6 students received support; research assistantships, Federal Work-Study, scholarships/grants, and laboratory assistantships available. Support available to part-time students. Financial award application deadline: 7/1; financial award applicants required to submit FAFSA. *Web site:* http://www.lmu.edu/acad/gd/graddiv.htm

■ MARQUETTE UNIVERSITY

Graduate School, College of Engineering, Department of Mechanical and Industrial Engineering, Milwaukee, WI 53201-1881

AWARDS Engineering management (MS); mechanical engineering (MS, PhD), including manufacturing systems engineering. Part-time and evening/weekend programs available.

Faculty: 13 full-time (0 women), 9 part-time/adjunct (0 women).
Students: 26 full-time (4 women), 50 part-time (2 women); includes 1 minority (Native American), 28 international. Average age 27. 75 applicants, 73% accepted. In 2001, 6 master's, 3 doctorates awarded. Terminal master's awarded for partial completion of doctoral program.

Degree requirements: For master's, thesis; for doctorate, thesis/dissertation, qualifying exam.
Entrance requirements: For master's and doctorate, GRE General Test, TOEFL, minimum GPA of 3.0. *Application deadline:* For fall admission, 8/1 (priority date); for spring admission, 1/1 (priority date). Applications are processed on a rolling basis. *Application fee:* $40. Electronic applications accepted.
Expenses: Tuition: Full-time $10,170; part-time $445 per credit hour. Tuition and fees vary according to course load.
Financial support: In 2001–02, 13 students received support, including fellowships with tuition reimbursements available (averaging $10,190 per year), 1 research assistantship with tuition reimbursement available (averaging $10,835 per year), 7 teaching assistantships with tuition reimbursements available (averaging $10,835 per year); Federal Work-Study, institutionally sponsored loans, scholarships/grants, and tuition waivers (full and partial) also available. Support available to part-time students. Financial award application deadline: 2/15.
Faculty research: Computer-integrated manufacturing, energy conversion, simulation modeling and optimization, applied mechanics, metallurgy. *Total annual research expenditures:* $250,000.
Dr. Kyle Kim, Chair, 414-288-7259, *Fax:* 414-288-7790, *E-mail:* kyle.kim@marquette.edu.
Application contact: Dr. Robert J. Stango, Director of Graduate Studies, 414-288-6972, *Fax:* 414-288-7790, *E-mail:* robert.stango@marquette.edu. *Web site:* http://www.eng.mu.edu/~meen/index.html
Find an in-depth description at www.petersons.com/gradchannel.

■ MASSACHUSETTS INSTITUTE OF TECHNOLOGY

School of Engineering, Engineering Systems Division, System Design and Management Program, Cambridge, MA 02139-4307

AWARDS Engineering and management (SM).

Students: 74 full-time (10 women); includes 3 minority (all Asian Americans or Pacific Islanders), 9 international. Average age 31. In 2001, 49 degrees awarded.
Degree requirements: For master's, thesis.
Entrance requirements: For master's, GRE General Test or GMAT, TOEFL, MS in engineering (or equivalent) and 3 years of experience or BS in engineering (or hard science) and 5 years of experience. *Application deadline:* For winter admission, 8/15. *Application fee:* $60. Electronic applications accepted.
Expenses: Contact institution.
Financial support: Research assistantships, teaching assistantships, career-related internships or fieldwork, Federal Work-Study, institutionally sponsored loans, scholarships/grants, health care benefits, and unspecified assistantships available. Financial award applicants required to submit FAFSA.
Paul A. Lagace, Co-Director, 617-253-3628, *E-mail:* pal@mit.edu.
Application contact: Sarah Shohet, Admissions and Career Placement Coordinator, 617-253-1662, *Fax:* 617-253-1462, *E-mail:* lfmsdm@mit.edu. *Web site:* http://lfmsdm.mit.edu/sdm

■ MERCER UNIVERSITY

Graduate Studies, Macon Campus, School of Engineering, Macon, GA 31207-0003

AWARDS Biomedical engineering (MSE); electrical engineering (MSE); engineering management (MSE); mechanical engineering (MSE). Software engineering (MSE). Software systems (MS); technical communications management (MS); technical management (MS). Part-time and evening/weekend programs available.

Faculty: 10 full-time (1 woman), 5 part-time/adjunct (1 woman).
Students: 3 full-time (2 women), 104 part-time (31 women); includes 19 minority (13 African Americans, 6 Asian Americans or Pacific Islanders), 5 international. Average age 36. 31 applicants, 97% accepted, 27 enrolled. In 2001, 32 degrees awarded.
Degree requirements: For master's, thesis or alternative, registration.
Entrance requirements: For master's, GRE, minimum undergraduate GPA of 3.0. *Application deadline:* For fall admission, 7/1; for spring admission, 11/15. Applications are processed on a rolling basis. *Application fee:* $35 ($50 for international students).
Expenses: Contact institution.
Financial support: Federal Work-Study available.
Dr. M. Dayne Aldridge, Dean, 478-301-2459, *Fax:* 478-301-5593, *E-mail:* aldridge_md@mercer.edu.
Application contact: Kathy Olivier, Graduate Administrative Coordinator, 478-301-2196, *E-mail:* olivier_kk@mercer.edu. *Web site:* http://www.mercer.edu/engineer.htm

■ MILWAUKEE SCHOOL OF ENGINEERING

School of Business, Milwaukee, WI 53202-3109

AWARDS Engineering management (MS); medical informatics (MS). Part-time and evening/weekend programs available.

Faculty: 4 full-time (1 woman), 27 part-time/adjunct (2 women).
Students: 9 full-time (4 women), 230 part-time (48 women); includes 9 minority (5 African Americans, 4 Asian Americans or Pacific Islanders), 4 international. Average age 25. 80 applicants, 60% accepted, 31 enrolled.
Degree requirements: For master's, thesis or alternative, thesis defense or capstone project, comprehensive exam, registration.
Entrance requirements: For master's, GMAT or GRE General Test or MCAT, BS in engineering, science, business or related fields; letters of recommendation. *Application deadline:* Applications are processed on a rolling basis. *Application fee:* $35. Electronic applications accepted.
Expenses: Tuition: Part-time $440 per credit. Tuition and fees vary according to course load.
Financial support: In 2001–02, 10 students received support. Career-related internships or fieldwork available. Support available to part-time students. Financial award applicants required to submit FAFSA.
Joseph Papp, Chairman, 414-277-7352, *Fax:* 414-277-7479, *E-mail:* papp@msoe.edu.
Application contact: Paul Borens, Admissions Director, 800-332-6763, *Fax:* 414-277-7475, *E-mail:* borens@msoe.edu. *Web site:* http://www.msoe.edu/

■ NATIONAL TECHNOLOGICAL UNIVERSITY

Programs in Engineering, Fort Collins, CO 80526-1842

AWARDS Chemical engineering (MS); computer engineering (MS); computer science (MS); electrical engineering (MS); engineering management (MS); environmental systems management (MS); management of technology (MS); manufacturing systems engineering (MS); materials science and engineering (MS); mechanical engineering (MS); microelectronics and semiconductor engineering (MS). Software engineering (MS). Special majors (MS). Systems engineering (MS). Part-time programs available. Postbaccalaureate distance learning degree programs offered (no on-campus study).

Students: In 2001, 114 degrees awarded.
Degree requirements: For master's, comprehensive exam.
Entrance requirements: For master's, BS in engineering or related field; 2.9 minimum GPA. *Application deadline:* Applications are processed on a rolling basis. *Application fee:* $50. Electronic applications accepted.
Expenses: Tuition: Part-time $660 per credit hour. Part-time tuition and fees vary according to course load, campus/location and program.
Dr. Andre Vacroux, President, 970-495-6400, *Fax:* 970-484-0668, *E-mail:* andre@ntu.edu.
Application contact: Rhonda Bonham, Admissions Officer, 970-495-6400, *Fax:* 970-498-0601, *E-mail:* rhonda@ntu.edu. *Web site:* http://www.ntu.edu/

■ NEW JERSEY INSTITUTE OF TECHNOLOGY

Office of Graduate Studies, Department of Industrial and Manufacturing Engineering, Program in Engineering Management, Newark, NJ 07102

AWARDS MS. Part-time and evening/weekend programs available.

Faculty: 15 full-time (1 woman), 13 part-time/adjunct (2 women).
Students: 13 full-time (0 women), 131 part-time (18 women); includes 47 minority (25 African Americans, 9 Asian Americans or Pacific Islanders, 13 Hispanic Americans), 11 international. Average age 34. 90 applicants, 59% accepted, 32 enrolled. In 2001, 47 degrees awarded. Terminal master's awarded for partial completion of doctoral program.
Degree requirements: For master's, thesis or alternative.
Entrance requirements: For master's, GRE General Test. *Application deadline:* For fall admission, 6/5 (priority date); for spring admission, 10/15. Applications are processed on a rolling basis. *Application fee:* $50. Electronic applications accepted.
Expenses: Tuition, state resident: full-time $7,812; part-time $434 per credit. Tuition, nonresident: full-time $10,746; part-time $597 per credit. Required fees: $47 per credit. $76 per semester.
Financial support: Fellowships with full and partial tuition reimbursements, research assistantships with full and partial tuition reimbursements, teaching assistantships with full and partial tuition reimbursements, career-related internships or fieldwork, Federal Work-Study, institutionally sponsored loans, and unspecified assistantships available. Financial award application deadline: 3/15. *Total annual research expenditures:* $1.6 million.
Dr. Carl Wolf, Director, 973-596-3657, *Fax:* 973-596-2316, *E-mail:* carl.wolf@njit.edu.
Application contact: Kathryn Kelly, Director of Admissions, 973-596-3300, *Fax:* 973-596-3461, *E-mail:* admissions@njit.edu. *Web site:* http://www.njit.edu/

■ NORTHEASTERN UNIVERSITY

College of Engineering, Department of Mechanical, Industrial, and Manufacturing Engineering, Boston, MA 02115-5096

AWARDS Engineering management (MS); industrial engineering (MS, PhD); mechanical engineering (MS, PhD); operations research (MS). Part-time programs available.

Faculty: 26 full-time (1 woman), 5 part-time/adjunct (1 woman).
Students: 97 full-time (22 women), 80 part-time (10 women); includes 32 minority (6 African Americans, 7 Asian Americans or Pacific Islanders, 19

Hispanic Americans), 77 international. Average age 25. 262 applicants, 53% accepted, 57 enrolled. In 2001, 46 master's, 6 doctorates awarded.
Degree requirements: For master's, thesis (for some programs), registration; for doctorate, one foreign language, thesis/dissertation, departmental qualifying exam.
Entrance requirements: For master's and doctorate, GRE General Test. *Application deadline:* For fall admission, 2/15 (priority date). Applications are processed on a rolling basis. *Application fee:* $50. Electronic applications accepted.
Expenses: Tuition: Part-time $535 per credit hour. Required fees: $56. Tuition and fees vary according to program.
Financial support: In 2001–02, 61 students received support, including 1 fellowship, 24 research assistantships with full tuition reimbursements available (averaging $13,560 per year), 26 teaching assistantships with full tuition reimbursements available (averaging $13,560 per year); career-related internships or fieldwork, Federal Work-Study, scholarships/grants, tuition waivers (full), and unspecified assistantships also available. Support available to part-time students. Financial award application deadline: 2/15; financial award applicants required to submit FAFSA.
Faculty research: Dry sliding instabilities, droplet deposition, helical hydraulic turbines, combustion, manufacturing systems. *Total annual research expenditures:* $1.8 million.
Dr. John W. Cipolla, Chairman, 617-373-3810, *Fax:* 617-373-2921.
Application contact: Stephen L. Gibson, Associate Director, 617-373-2711, *Fax:* 617-373-2501, *E-mail:* grad-eng@coe.neu.edu.

Find an in-depth description at www.petersons.com/gradchannel.

■ NORTHWESTERN UNIVERSITY

McCormick School of Engineering and Applied Science, Department of Industrial Engineering and Management Sciences, Program in Engineering Management, Evanston, IL 60208

AWARDS MEM. Part-time and evening/weekend programs available.

Faculty: 8 full-time (0 women), 9 part-time/adjunct (1 woman).
Students: 1 (woman) full-time, 92 part-time (14 women); includes 23 minority (2 African Americans, 17 Asian Americans or Pacific Islanders, 4 Hispanic Americans), 15 international. Average age 34. 91 applicants, 74% accepted. In 2001, 31 degrees awarded.
Entrance requirements: For master's, TOEFL, 3 years of work experience. *Application deadline:* For fall admission, 8/30 (priority date); for winter admission, 11/30 (priority date); for spring admission, 2/28 (priority date). Applications are

processed on a rolling basis. *Application fee:* $30. Electronic applications accepted.
Expenses: Tuition: Full-time $26,526.
Financial support: Institutionally sponsored loans available. Financial award application deadline: 12/31; financial award applicants required to submit FAFSA.
Faculty research: Computer simulation, stochastic processes, network flow theory, logistics, statistics, production system design.
Barry L. Nelson, Director.
Application contact: Dianne Kessler, Assistant Director, 847-491-2281, *E-mail:* mem@iems.nwu.edu. *Web site:* http://www.mem.nwu.edu/

Find an in-depth description at www.petersons.com/gradchannel.

■ OAKLAND UNIVERSITY

Graduate Study and Lifelong Learning, School of Engineering and Computer Science, Program in Engineering Management, Rochester, MI 48309-4401

AWARDS MS.

Students: 23 full-time (5 women), 92 part-time (14 women); includes 9 minority (2 African Americans, 7 Asian Americans or Pacific Islanders), 14 international. Average age 30. 45 applicants, 84% accepted. In 2001, 40 degrees awarded.
Application deadline: For fall admission, 8/1 (priority date); for winter admission, 12/1 (priority date); for spring admission, 4/1 (priority date). Applications are processed on a rolling basis. *Application fee:* $30. Electronic applications accepted.
Expenses: Tuition, state resident: full-time $5,904; part-time $246 per credit hour. Tuition, nonresident: full-time $12,192; part-time $508 per credit hour. Required fees: $472; $236 per term.
Financial support: Federal Work-Study, institutionally sponsored loans, and tuition waivers (full) available. Financial award application deadline: 3/1; financial award applicants required to submit FAFSA.
Dr. Naim A. Kheir, Chair, 248-370-2177.

■ OHIO UNIVERSITY

Graduate Studies, Russ College of Engineering and Technology, Department of Mechanical Engineering, Athens, OH 45701-2979

AWARDS Manufacturing engineering (MS); mechanical engineering (MS, PhD), including CAD/CAM (MS), manufacturing (MS), mechanical systems (MS), technology management (MS), thermal systems (MS).

Faculty: 10 full-time (0 women).
Students: 48 full-time (4 women), 20 part-time (3 women); includes 3 minority (2 African Americans, 1 Asian American or Pacific Islander), 51 international. 144 applicants, 63% accepted, 25 enrolled. In 2001, 34 degrees awarded.

Degree requirements: For master's and doctorate, thesis/dissertation.
Entrance requirements: For master's, BS in engineering or science, minimum GPA of 2.8; for doctorate, GRE. *Application deadline:* For fall admission, 3/15 (priority date). Applications are processed on a rolling basis. *Application fee:* $30.
Expenses: Tuition, state resident: full-time $6,585. Tuition, nonresident: full-time $12,254.
Financial support: In 2001–02, 41 students received support, including 9 research assistantships with tuition reimbursements available, 14 teaching assistantships with tuition reimbursements available; fellowships with tuition reimbursements available, career-related internships or fieldwork, Federal Work-Study, institutionally sponsored loans, tuition waivers (full and partial), and unspecified assistantships also available. Financial award application deadline: 3/15.
Faculty research: Machine design, controls, aerodynamics, thermal manufacturing, robotics process modeling, air pollution, combustion.
Dr. Jay S. Gunasekara, Chairman, 740-593-0563, *Fax:* 740-593-0476, *E-mail:* gsekera@bobcat.ent.ohiou.edu.
Application contact: Dr. M. Khairul Alam, Graduate Chairman, 740-593-1598, *Fax:* 740-593-0476, *E-mail:* agrawal@bobcat.ent.ohiou.edu. *Web site:* http://www.ent.ohiou.edu/

■ OLD DOMINION UNIVERSITY
College of Engineering and Technology, Program in Engineering Management, Norfolk, VA 23529

AWARDS Engineering management (MEM, MS, PhD). Part-time and evening/weekend programs available. Postbaccalaureate distance learning degree programs offered (no on-campus study).

Faculty: 7 full-time (1 woman), 1 part-time/adjunct (0 women).
Students: Average age 33. 74 applicants, 91% accepted. In 2001, 32 degrees awarded.
Degree requirements: For master's, project, thesis optional; for doctorate, thesis/dissertation, candidacy exam.
Entrance requirements: For master's, GRE, TOEFL, minimum GPA of 3.0; for doctorate, GRE, TOEFL. *Application deadline:* For fall admission, 7/1; for spring admission, 10/1. Applications are processed on a rolling basis. *Application fee:* $30. Electronic applications accepted.
Expenses: Tuition, state resident: part-time $202 per credit. Tuition, nonresident: part-time $534 per credit. Required fees: $76 per semester.
Financial support: In 2001–02, research assistantships with tuition reimbursements (averaging $10,844 per year); fellowships, teaching assistantships, career-related internships or fieldwork, scholarships/grants, and tuition waivers (partial) also

available. Support available to part-time students. Financial award application deadline: 2/15; financial award applicants required to submit FAFSA.
Faculty research: Project management, systems engineering, modeling and simulation, virtual collaborative environments, multidisciplinary designs, cost estimation. *Total annual research expenditures:* $248,703.
Dr. Charles Keating, Graduate Program Director, 757-683-5753, *Fax:* 757-683-5640, *E-mail:* enmagpd@odu.edu. *Web site:* http://www.odu.edu/engr/enma

■ THE PENNSYLVANIA STATE UNIVERSITY UNIVERSITY PARK CAMPUS
Graduate School, College of Earth and Mineral Sciences, Department of Energy and Geo-Environmental Engineering, Program in Mineral Engineering Management, State College, University Park, PA 16802-1503

AWARDS M Eng.

Degree requirements: For master's, thesis.
Application fee: $45.
Expenses: Tuition, state resident: full-time $7,882; part-time $333 per credit. Tuition, nonresident: full-time $16,142; part-time $673 per credit. Required fees: $124 per semester.
Financial support: Application deadline: 12/31.
R. V. Ramani, Head, 814-863-1617.

■ POINT PARK COLLEGE
Department of Natural Science and Engineering Technology, Pittsburgh, PA 15222-1984

AWARDS Engineering management (MS).

Faculty: 3 full-time, 1 part-time/adjunct.
Students: Average age 38. 20 applicants, 75% accepted, 13 enrolled.
Entrance requirements: For master's, minimum QPA of 2.75, 2 letters of recommendation, B's in Engineering Technology or a related field. *Application deadline:* Applications are processed on a rolling basis. Electronic applications accepted.
Expenses: Tuition: Full-time $7,290; part-time $405 per credit. Required fees: $270; $15 per credit.
Financial support: Career-related internships or fieldwork and scholarships/grants available. Support available to part-time students. Financial award applicants required to submit FAFSA.
Walter Zalot, Director, 412-392-3897, *Fax:* 412-392-3962, *E-mail:* wzalot@ppc.edu.
Application contact: Debbie Bateman, Associate Director, 412-392-3433, *Fax:* 412-392-6164, *E-mail:* dbateman@ppc.edu.

■ POLYTECHNIC UNIVERSITY OF PUERTO RICO
Graduate Programs, Hato Rey, PR 00919

AWARDS Business administration (MBA); civil engineering (MCE); competitive manufacturing (MMC); engineering management (MEM); environmental protection management (MEPM); manufacturing engineering (MME).

■ PORTLAND STATE UNIVERSITY
Graduate Studies, College of Engineering and Computer Science, Department of Engineering and Technology Management, Portland, OR 97207-0751

AWARDS M Eng, MS, PhD. Part-time and evening/weekend programs available.

Faculty: 3 full-time (0 women), 3 part-time/adjunct (0 women).
Students: 23 full-time (7 women), 31 part-time (7 women); includes 5 minority (2 African Americans, 2 Asian Americans or Pacific Islanders, 1 Hispanic American), 34 international. Average age 30. 30 applicants, 77% accepted. In 2001, 17 degrees awarded.
Degree requirements: For master's, thesis optional; for doctorate, one foreign language, thesis/dissertation, oral and written exams.
Entrance requirements: For master's, TOEFL, minimum GPA of 3.0 in upper-division course work or 2.75 overall; for doctorate, GRE General Test, GRE Subject Test, TOEFL, minimum GPA of 3.0 in upper-division course work. *Application deadline:* For fall admission, 4/1 (priority date); for spring admission, 11/1. Applications are processed on a rolling basis. *Application fee:* $50.
Financial support: In 2001–02, 7 research assistantships with full tuition reimbursements (averaging $3,275 per year), 4 teaching assistantships with full tuition reimbursements (averaging $3,402 per year) were awarded. Career-related internships or fieldwork, Federal Work-Study, and institutionally sponsored loans also available. Support available to part-time students. Financial award application deadline: 3/1; financial award applicants required to submit FAFSA.
Faculty research: Scheduling, hierarchical decision modeling, operations research, knowledge-based information systems. *Total annual research expenditures:* $60,342.
Dr. Dundar Kocaoglu, Director, 503-725-4660, *Fax:* 503-725-4667, *E-mail:* kocaoglu@emp.pdx.edu.
Application contact: Mary E. Wiltse, Coordinator, 503-725-4660, *Fax:* 503-725-4667, *E-mail:* maryw@emp.pdx.edu. *Web site:* http://www.emp.pdx.edu/

Find an in-depth description at www.petersons.com/gradchannel.

■ PORTLAND STATE UNIVERSITY

Graduate Studies, College of Engineering and Computer Science, Systems Science Program, Portland, OR 97207-0751

AWARDS Systems science/anthropology (PhD). Systems science/business administration (PhD). Systems science/civil engineering (PhD). Systems science/economics (PhD). Systems science/engineering management (PhD). Systems science/general (PhD). Systems science/mathematical sciences (PhD). Systems science/mechanical engineering (PhD). Systems science/psychology (PhD). Systems science/sociology (PhD).

Faculty: 4 full-time (0 women).
Students: 47 full-time (19 women), 32 part-time (10 women); includes 9 minority (4 Asian Americans or Pacific Islanders, 3 Hispanic Americans, 2 Native Americans), 15 international. Average age 36. 52 applicants, 38% accepted. In 2001, 8 degrees awarded.
Degree requirements: For doctorate, variable foreign language requirement, thesis/dissertation.
Entrance requirements: For doctorate, GMAT, GRE General Test, TOEFL, minimum undergraduate GPA of 3.0. *Application deadline:* For fall admission, 2/1; for spring admission, 11/1. *Application fee:* $50.
Financial support: In 2001–02, 1 research assistantship with full tuition reimbursement (averaging $6,839 per year) was awarded; teaching assistantships with full tuition reimbursements, career-related internships or fieldwork, Federal Work-Study, and institutionally sponsored loans also available. Support available to part-time students. Financial award application deadline: 3/1; financial award applicants required to submit FAFSA.
Faculty research: Systems theory and methodology, artificial intelligence neural networks, information theory, nonlinear dynamics/chaos, modeling and simulation. *Total annual research expenditures:* $106,413.
Dr. Nancy Perrin, Director, 503-725-4960, *E-mail:* perrinn@pdx.edu.
Application contact: Dawn Kuenle, Coordinator, 503-725-4960, *E-mail:* dawn@sysc.pdx.edu. *Web site:* http://www.sysc.pdx.edu/

■ RENSSELAER POLYTECHNIC INSTITUTE

Graduate School, Lally School of Management and Technology, Troy, NY 12180-3590

AWARDS MBA, MS, PhD, JD/MBA, MBA/M Eng, MBA/MS. Part-time and evening/weekend programs available. Postbaccalaureate distance learning degree programs offered (no on-campus study).

Faculty: 41 full-time (6 women), 2 part-time/adjunct (0 women).
Students: 404 full-time (62 women), 1,230 part-time (383 women); includes 139 minority (37 African Americans, 68 Asian Americans or Pacific Islanders, 33 Hispanic Americans, 1 Native American), 95 international. Average age 32. 659 applicants, 68% accepted, 274 enrolled. In 2001, 692 master's, 3 doctorates awarded.
Degree requirements: For doctorate, thesis/dissertation.
Entrance requirements: For master's, GMAT, TOEFL, 3 letters of recommendation, resumé; for doctorate, GMAT or GRE General Test, TOEFL. *Application deadline:* For fall admission, 1/15 (priority date); for spring admission, 11/1 (priority date). Applications are processed on a rolling basis. *Application fee:* $45. Electronic applications accepted.
Expenses: Tuition: Full-time $26,400; part-time $1,320 per credit hour. Required fees: $1,437.
Financial support: In 2001–02, 104 students received support; fellowships, research assistantships, teaching assistantships, career-related internships or fieldwork, institutionally sponsored loans, scholarships/grants, and tuition waivers (full and partial) available. Financial award application deadline: 1/15.
Faculty research: Entrepreneurship, operations management, product development, information systems, finance.
Dr. Robert A. Baron, Interim Dean, 518-276-6586, *Fax:* 518-276-2665, *E-mail:* lallymba@rpi.edu.
Application contact: Michele Martens, Manager of Enrollment Services, 518-276-6586, *Fax:* 518-276-2665, *E-mail:* martem@rpi.edu. *Web site:* http://lallymba.mgmt.rpi.edu/

Find an in-depth description at www.petersons.com/gradchannel.

■ ROBERT MORRIS UNIVERSITY

Graduate Studies, Program in Engineering Management, Moon Township, PA 15108-1189

AWARDS MS. Part-time and evening/weekend programs available.

Faculty: 3 full-time (0 women).
Application deadline: For fall admission, 8/1 (priority date); for spring admission, 11/30 (priority date). Applications are processed on a rolling basis. *Application fee:* $35. Electronic applications accepted.
Expenses: Contact institution.
Financial support: Federal Work-Study, institutionally sponsored loans, and unspecified assistantships available. Financial award application deadline: 5/1; financial award applicants required to submit FAFSA.
Dr. John C. Hayward, Department Head, 412-262-8485, *Fax:* 412-262-8494, *E-mail:* hayward@rmu.edu.

Application contact: Kellie Laurenzi, Director of Enrollment Services, 800-762-0097, *Fax:* 412-299-2425, *E-mail:* laurenzi@rmu.edu. *Web site:* http://www.rmu.edu/

■ ROCHESTER INSTITUTE OF TECHNOLOGY

Graduate Enrollment Services, College of Engineering, Department of Design, Development and Manufacturing, Program in Product Development, Rochester, NY 14623-5698

AWARDS MS.

Students: In 2001, 24 degrees awarded.
Entrance requirements: For master's, undergraduate degree in engineering or related field, minimum GPA of 3.0, 5 years experience in product development. *Application fee:* $50.
Expenses: Contact institution.
Mark Smith, Director, Department of Design, Development and Manufacturing, 585-475-7102, *E-mail:* mpdmail@rit.edu.

Find an in-depth description at www.petersons.com/gradchannel.

■ ROCHESTER INSTITUTE OF TECHNOLOGY

Graduate Enrollment Services, College of Engineering, Department of Industrial and Manufacturing Engineering, Rochester, NY 14623-5698

AWARDS Engineering management (ME); industrial engineering (ME); manufacturing engineering (ME). Systems engineering (ME).

Students: 6 full-time (0 women), 19 part-time (6 women); includes 4 minority (2 African Americans, 2 Hispanic Americans), 10 international. 105 applicants, 51% accepted, 8 enrolled. In 2001, 14 degrees awarded.
Degree requirements: For master's, internship.
Entrance requirements: For master's, TOEFL, minimum GPA of 3.0. *Application deadline:* For fall admission, 3/1 (priority date). Applications are processed on a rolling basis. *Application fee:* $50.
Expenses: Tuition: Full-time $20,928; part-time $587 per hour. Required fees: $162. Tuition and fees vary according to program.
Financial support: Research assistantships, career-related internships or fieldwork and tuition waivers (partial) available.
Faculty research: Safety, manufacturing (CAM), simulation.
Dr. Jacqueline Mozrall, Head, 585-475-7142, *E-mail:* jrmeie@rit.edu.

■ ROSE-HULMAN INSTITUTE OF TECHNOLOGY

Faculty of Engineering and Applied Sciences, Program in Engineering Management, Terre Haute, IN 47803-3920

AWARDS MS. Part-time and evening/weekend programs available. Postbaccalaureate distance learning degree programs offered (minimal on-campus study).

Faculty: 2 full-time (0 women), 1 part-time/adjunct (0 women).
Students: 7 full-time (0 women), 74 part-time (7 women). Average age 31. 24 applicants, 88% accepted, 2 enrolled. In 2001, 5 degrees awarded.
Degree requirements: For master's, integrated project.
Entrance requirements: For master's, GRE, TOEFL, minimum GPA of 3.0. *Application deadline:* For fall admission, 2/1 (priority date). Applications are processed on a rolling basis. *Application fee:* $0.
Expenses: Tuition: Full-time $21,792; part-time $615 per credit hour. Required fees: $405.
Financial support: In 2001–02, 8 students received support; fellowships with full and partial tuition reimbursements available available. Financial award application deadline: 2/1.
Faculty research: Entrepreneurship, managerial economics, impact assessment, marketing, management of technology.
Dr. Thomas W. Mason, Director, 812-877-8155, *Fax:* 812-877-3198, *E-mail:* thomas.mason@rose-hulman.edu.
Application contact: Dr. Daniel J. Moore, Interim Associate Dean of the Faculty, 812-877-8110, *Fax:* 812-877-8061, *E-mail:* daniel.j.moore@rose-hulman.edu.

■ SAINT MARTIN'S COLLEGE

Graduate Programs, Program in Engineering Management, Lacey, WA 98503-7500

AWARDS M Eng Mgt. Part-time and evening/weekend programs available.

Faculty: 5 full-time (0 women), 5 part-time/adjunct (0 women).
Students: Average age 30. 28 applicants, 68% accepted, 13 enrolled. In 2001, 9 degrees awarded.
Degree requirements: For master's, thesis optional. *Median time to degree:* Master's–1.2 years full-time, 2 years part-time.
Entrance requirements: For master's, TOEFL, minimum GPA of 3.0 or professional engineer license. *Application deadline:* For fall admission, 8/1 (priority date); for spring admission, 12/1 (priority date). Applications are processed on a rolling basis. *Application fee:* $35.
Expenses: Tuition: Part-time $519 per credit hour. Required fees: $180; $90 per semester. One-time fee: $125 full-time.

Financial support: In 2001–02, 2 students received support; research assistantships, Federal Work-Study available. Support available to part-time students. Financial award application deadline: 3/1; financial award applicants required to submit FAFSA.
Faculty research: Highway safety management, transportation, hydraulics, database structure. *Total annual research expenditures:* $77,000.
Dr. Donald E. Stout, Director, 360-438-4587, *Fax:* 360-438-4522, *E-mail:* dstout@stmartin.edu.
Application contact: Jeannette Banter, Information Contact, 360-438-4320, *Fax:* 360-438-4548, *E-mail:* jbanter@stmartin.edu. *Web site:* http://www.stmartin.edu/engineering/mem

■ ST. MARY'S UNIVERSITY OF SAN ANTONIO

Graduate School, Department of Engineering, Program in Engineering Systems Management, San Antonio, TX 78228-8507

AWARDS MS. Part-time programs available. Postbaccalaureate distance learning degree programs offered (no on-campus study).

Faculty: 6 full-time, 3 part-time/adjunct.
Students: 1 (woman) full-time, 15 part-time (3 women); includes 8 minority (1 African American, 7 Hispanic Americans). In 2001, 9 degrees awarded.
Entrance requirements: For master's, GRE or GMAT. *Application deadline:* Applications are processed on a rolling basis. Electronic applications accepted.
Expenses: Tuition: Full-time $8,190; part-time $455 per credit hour. Required fees: $375.
Financial support: Application deadline: 2/15.
Dr. Rafael Moras, Chairperson, 210-436-3305, *E-mail:* moras@stmarytx.edu.

■ ST. MARY'S UNIVERSITY OF SAN ANTONIO

Graduate School, Department of Engineering, Program in Industrial Engineering, San Antonio, TX 78228-8507

AWARDS Engineering computer applications (MS); engineering management (MS); industrial engineering (MS); operations research (MS).

Faculty: 6 full-time, 3 part-time/adjunct.
Students: 4 full-time (1 woman), 6 part-time (2 women); includes 1 minority (Hispanic American), 3 international. Average age 25. In 2001, 5 degrees awarded.
Degree requirements: For master's, thesis.
Entrance requirements: For master's, GRE General Test, BS in science or

engineering. *Application deadline:* Applications are processed on a rolling basis. *Application fee:* $15. Electronic applications accepted.
Expenses: Tuition: Full-time $8,190; part-time $455 per credit hour. Required fees: $375.
Financial support: Teaching assistantships, Federal Work-Study available. Financial award application deadline: 2/15; financial award applicants required to submit FAFSA.
Faculty research: Robotics, artificial intelligence, manufacturing engineering.
Dr. Rafael Moras, Chairperson, 210-436-3305, *E-mail:* moras@stmarytx.edu.

■ SANTA CLARA UNIVERSITY

School of Engineering, Program in Engineering Management, Santa Clara, CA 95053

AWARDS MSE Mgt. Part-time and evening/weekend programs available.

Students: 15 full-time (4 women), 139 part-time (26 women); includes 76 minority (3 African Americans, 66 Asian Americans or Pacific Islanders, 7 Hispanic Americans), 38 international. Average age 32. 42 applicants, 86% accepted. In 2001, 50 degrees awarded.
Degree requirements: For master's, thesis or alternative.
Entrance requirements: For master's, GRE General Test, TOEFL, minimum GPA of 2.75. *Application deadline:* For fall admission, 6/1; for spring admission, 1/1. Applications are processed on a rolling basis. *Application fee:* $45 ($55 for international students). Electronic applications accepted.
Expenses: Tuition: Part-time $320 per unit. Tuition and fees vary according to class time, degree level, program and student level.
Financial support: Fellowships, research assistantships, teaching assistantships, Federal Work-Study and institutionally sponsored loans available. Support available to part-time students. Financial award application deadline: 3/1; financial award applicants required to submit FAFSA.
Dr. Robert J. Parden, Chair, 408-554-4061.
Application contact: Tina Samms, Assistant Director of Graduate Admissions, 408-554-4313, *Fax:* 408-554-5474, *E-mail:* engr-grad@scu.edu.

■ SOUTHERN METHODIST UNIVERSITY

School of Engineering, Department of Computer Science and Engineering, Dallas, TX 75275

AWARDS Computer engineering (MS Cp E, PhD); computer science (MS, PhD); engineering management (MSEM, DE); operations research (MS, PhD). Software engineering (MS). Part-time and evening/weekend

Southern Methodist University (continued) programs available. Postbaccalaureate distance learning degree programs offered (no on-campus study).

Faculty: 9 full-time (3 women).
Students: 53 full-time (15 women), 163 part-time (37 women); includes 73 minority (16 African Americans, 43 Asian Americans or Pacific Islanders, 14 Hispanic Americans), 49 international. Average age 32. 307 applicants, 78% accepted. In 2001, 59 master's, 4 doctorates awarded. Terminal master's awarded for partial completion of doctoral program.
Degree requirements: For master's, thesis optional; for doctorate, thesis/dissertation, oral and written qualifying exams, oral final exam (PhD).
Entrance requirements: For master's, GRE General Test, TOEFL, minimum GPA of 3.0 in last 2 years; bachelor's degree in engineering, mathematics, or sciences; for doctorate, preliminary counseling exam (PhD), minimum GPA of 3.0, bachelor's degree in related field, MA (DE). *Application deadline:* For fall admission, 7/1 (priority date); for spring admission, 11/15. Applications are processed on a rolling basis. *Application fee:* $50.
Expenses: Tuition: Part-time $285 per credit hour.
Financial support: In 2001–02, 14 research assistantships with full tuition reimbursements (averaging $15,000 per year), 11 teaching assistantships with full tuition reimbursements (averaging $9,000 per year) were awarded. Financial award applicants required to submit FAFSA.
Faculty research: Trusted and high performance network computing, software engineering and management, knowledge engineering and management, computer arithmetic. *Total annual research expenditures:* $126,192.
Hesham El-Rewini, Head, 214-768-3278.
Application contact: Jim Dees, Director, Student Administration, 214-768-1456, *Fax:* 214-768-3845, *E-mail:* jdees@ engr.smu.edu. *Web site:* http:// www.seas.sm.edu/cse/

Find an in-depth description at www.petersons.com/gradchannel.

■ **SOUTHERN METHODIST UNIVERSITY**

School of Engineering, Department of Engineering Management, Information and Systems, Dallas, TX 75275

AWARDS Applied science (MS); engineering management (MSEM, DE); operations research (MS, PhD). Systems engineering (MS). Part-time and evening/weekend programs available. Postbaccalaureate distance learning degree programs offered.

Faculty: 6 full-time (1 woman).
Students: 10 full-time (1 woman), 100 part-time (22 women); includes 29 minority (6 African Americans, 11 Asian Americans or Pacific Islanders, 10

Hispanic Americans, 2 Native Americans), 10 international. 55 applicants, 78% accepted. In 2001, 25 master's, 5 doctorates awarded. Terminal master's awarded for partial completion of doctoral program.
Degree requirements: For master's, thesis optional; for doctorate, thesis/dissertation, oral and written qualifying exams.
Entrance requirements: For master's, GRE General, TOEFL, minimum GPA of 3.0 in last 2 years; bachelor's degree in engineering, mathematics, or sciences; for doctorate, bachelor's degree in related field. *Application deadline:* For fall admission, 7/1; for spring admission, 11/15. Applications are processed on a rolling basis. *Application fee:* $50.
Expenses: Tuition: Part-time $285 per credit hour.
Faculty research: Telecommunications, decision systems, information engineering, operations research, software.
Richard S. Barr, Chair, 214-768-2605, *E-mail:* emis@engr.smu.edu.
Application contact: Marc Valerin, Associate Director of Graduate Admissions, 214-768-3484, *E-mail:* valerin@ seas.smu.edu.

Find an in-depth description at www.petersons.com/gradchannel.

■ **STANFORD UNIVERSITY**

School of Engineering, Department of Management Science and Engineering, Stanford, CA 94305-9991

AWARDS Management science and engineering (MS, PhD); management science and engineering and electrical engineering (MS); manufacturing systems engineering (MS).

Faculty: 31 full-time (5 women).
Students: 301 full-time (77 women), 82 part-time (18 women); includes 59 minority (5 African Americans, 48 Asian Americans or Pacific Islanders, 6 Hispanic Americans), 226 international. Average age 27. 484 applicants, 38% accepted. In 2001, 187 master's, 28 doctorates awarded. Terminal master's awarded for partial completion of doctoral program.
Degree requirements: For doctorate, thesis/dissertation, qualification procedure.
Entrance requirements: For master's and doctorate, GRE General Test, TOEFL. *Application deadline:* For fall admission, 2/1. *Application fee:* $65 ($80 for international students). Electronic applications accepted.
M. Elisabeth Paté-Cornell, Chair, 650-723-3823 Ext. ', *Fax:* 650-725-8799, *E-mail:* mep@stanford.edu.
Application contact: Graduate Admissions Coordinator, 650-723-4094, *Fax:* 650-723-1614. *Web site:* http://www.stanford.edu/ dept/MSandE/

Find an in-depth description at www.petersons.com/gradchannel.

■ **SYRACUSE UNIVERSITY**

Graduate School, L. C. Smith College of Engineering and Computer Science, Program in Engineering Management, Syracuse, NY 13244-0003

AWARDS MS.

Students: Average age 33. In 2001, 22 degrees awarded.
Entrance requirements: For master's, GRE General Test, GRE Subject Test. *Application deadline:* Applications are processed on a rolling basis. *Application fee:* $50.
Expenses: Tuition: Full-time $15,528; part-time $647 per credit. Required fees: $420; $38 per term. Tuition and fees vary according to program.
Financial support: Application deadline: 1/10.
Thomas Vedder, Head, 315-443-2132, *Fax:* 315-443-9099, *E-mail:* tduedder@ syr.edu.
Application contact: Kathy Datthyn-Madigan, Information Contact, 315-443-4367, *Fax:* 315-443-9099, *E-mail:* kjdatthy@ecs.syr.edu. *Web site:* http:// www.ecs.syr.edu/

■ **TEXAS TECH UNIVERSITY**

Graduate School, College of Engineering, Department of Industrial Engineering, Lubbock, TX 79409

AWARDS Industrial engineering (MSIE, PhD). Systems and engineering management (MSSEM). Part-time programs available.

Faculty: 6 full-time (0 women), 1 part-time/adjunct (0 women).
Students: 50 full-time (11 women), 10 part-time (1 woman); includes 5 minority (1 African American, 1 Asian American or Pacific Islander, 3 Hispanic Americans), 42 international. Average age 29. 133 applicants, 47% accepted, 16 enrolled. In 2001, 11 master's, 3 doctorates awarded.
Degree requirements: For master's and doctorate, thesis/dissertation.
Entrance requirements: For master's and doctorate, GRE General Test, minimum GPA of 3.0. *Application deadline:* Applications are processed on a rolling basis. *Application fee:* $25 ($50 for international students). Electronic applications accepted.
Expenses: Tuition, state resident: full-time $1,926; part-time $107 per credit hour. Tuition, nonresident: full-time $5,724; part-time $318 per credit hour. Required fees: $779; $737 per year. Tuition and fees vary according to course level, course load and program.
Financial support: In 2001–02, 25 students received support, including 15 research assistantships with partial tuition reimbursements available (averaging $8,670 per year), 6 teaching assistantships with partial tuition reimbursements available (averaging $7,575 per year); fellowships, Federal Work-Study and institutionally sponsored loans also available. Support available to part-time

students. Financial award application deadline: 5/1; financial award applicants required to submit FAFSA.

Faculty research: Knowledge and engineering management, environmentally conscious manufacturing, biomechanical simulation, aviation security. *Total annual research expenditures:* $223,554.

Dr. Milton Smith, Chair, 806-742-3543, *Fax:* 806-742-3411, *E-mail:* jlsmith@ coe.ttu.edu.

Application contact: Graduate Adviser, 806-742-3543, *Fax:* 806-742-3411. *Web site:* http://www.ie.ttu.edu

■ TUFTS UNIVERSITY

Division of Graduate and Continuing Studies and Research, Graduate School of Arts and Sciences, School of Engineering, The Gordon Institute, Medford, MA 02155

AWARDS MSEM. Part-time programs available.

Faculty: 10 full-time, 5 part-time/adjunct.
Students: 76 (15 women) 11 international. 32 applicants, 100% accepted. In 2001, 22 degrees awarded.
Entrance requirements: For master's, TOEFL. *Application deadline:* For fall admission, 5/1 (priority date). Applications are processed on a rolling basis. *Application fee:* $0.
Expenses: Contact institution.
Financial support: Application deadline: 2/15.

Edward N. Aqua, Director, 617-627-3111, *Fax:* 617-627-3180, *E-mail:* eaqua@ emerald.tufts.edu. *Web site:* http:// gordon.tufts.edu/index.html

■ THE UNIVERSITY OF AKRON

Graduate School, College of Engineering, Program in Engineering (Management Specialization), Akron, OH 44325-0001

AWARDS MS.

Students: 1 (woman) full-time, 20 part-time (4 women); includes 1 minority (Hispanic American). Average age 30. 2 applicants, 100% accepted, 2 enrolled.
Degree requirements: For master's, engineering report.
Entrance requirements: For master's, TOEFL. *Application deadline:* Applications are processed on a rolling basis. *Application fee:* $40 ($50 for international students).
Expenses: Tuition, state resident: full-time $6,562; part-time $219 per credit. Tuition, nonresident: full-time $9,027; part-time $383 per credit. Required fees: $272; $11 per credit. Tuition and fees vary according to course load.
Financial support: Application deadline: 3/1.

Dr. Subramaniya Hariharan, Head, 330-972-6580.

■ UNIVERSITY OF ALASKA ANCHORAGE

School of Engineering, Program in Engineering Management, Anchorage, AK 99508-8060

AWARDS MS. Part-time and evening/weekend programs available.

Entrance requirements: For master's, GRE General Test, BS in engineering or science, work experience in engineering or science.
Faculty research: Engineering economy, long-range forecasting, multicriteria design making, project management process and training.

■ UNIVERSITY OF ALASKA ANCHORAGE

School of Engineering, Program in Science Management, Anchorage, AK 99508-8060

AWARDS MS. Part-time and evening/weekend programs available.

Entrance requirements: For master's, GRE General Test, BS in engineering or scientific field.
Faculty research: Engineering economy, long-range forecasting, multicriteria decision making, project management process and training.

■ UNIVERSITY OF CENTRAL FLORIDA

College of Engineering and Computer Sciences, Department of Industrial Engineering and Management Systems, Orlando, FL 32816

AWARDS Applied operations research (Certificate); computer-integrated manufacturing (MS); design for usability (Certificate); engineering management (MS); industrial engineering (MSIE); industrial engineering and management systems (PhD); industrial ergonomics and safety (Certificate); operations research (MS); product assurance engineering (MS); project engineering (Certificate); quality assurance (Certificate). Simulation systems (MS). Systems simulations for engineers (Certificate); training simulation (Certificate). Part-time and evening/weekend programs available.

Faculty: 20 full-time (4 women), 8 part-time/adjunct (1 woman).
Students: 92 full-time (19 women), 182 part-time (49 women); includes 66 minority (18 African Americans, 10 Asian Americans or Pacific Islanders, 35 Hispanic Americans, 3 Native Americans), 57 international. Average age 32. 231 applicants, 84% accepted, 85 enrolled. In 2001, 3 master's, 9 doctorates awarded.
Degree requirements: For master's, thesis; for doctorate, thesis/dissertation, departmental qualifying exam, candidacy exam.

Entrance requirements: For master's, GRE General Test, TOEFL, minimum GPA of 3.0 in last 60 hours; for doctorate, TOEFL, minimum GPA of 3.5 in last 60 hours. *Application deadline:* For fall admission, 7/15 (priority date); for spring admission, 12/1 (priority date). *Application fee:* $20. Electronic applications accepted.
Expenses: Tuition, state resident: part-time $162 per hour. Tuition, nonresident: part-time $569 per hour.
Financial support: In 2001–02, 23 fellowships with partial tuition reimbursements (averaging $3,272 per year), 131 research assistantships with partial tuition reimbursements (averaging $3,125 per year), 24 teaching assistantships with partial tuition reimbursements (averaging $3,823 per year) were awarded. Career-related internships or fieldwork, Federal Work-Study, institutionally sponsored loans, tuition waivers (partial), and unspecified assistantships also available. Financial award application deadline: 3/1; financial award applicants required to submit FAFSA.

Dr. Charles Reily, Chair, 407-823-2204, *E-mail:* creily@mail.ucf.edu.
Application contact: Dr. Linda Malone, Coordinator, 407-823-2204, *E-mail:* malone@mail.ucf.edu. *Web site:* http:// www.ucf.edu/

Find an in-depth description at www.petersons.com/gradchannel.

■ UNIVERSITY OF COLORADO AT BOULDER

Graduate School, College of Engineering and Applied Science, Engineering Management Program, Boulder, CO 80309

AWARDS ME.

Faculty: 1 (woman) full-time.
Students: 3 full-time (0 women), 2 part-time; includes 1 minority (Asian American or Pacific Islander). Average age 32. 14 applicants, 50% accepted. In 2001, 17 degrees awarded.
Application fee: $50 ($60 for international students).
Expenses: Tuition, state resident: full-time $3,474. Tuition, nonresident: full-time $16,624. *Total annual research expenditures:* $96,037.

Dr. William Daughton, Director.
Application contact: Bonnee Basso, Graduate Program Assistant, 303-492-2570, *Fax:* 303-492-5987, *E-mail:* bonnee.basso@colorado.edu.

■ UNIVERSITY OF COLORADO AT COLORADO SPRINGS

Graduate School, College of Engineering and Applied Science, Department of Mechanical and Aerospace Engineering, Colorado Springs, CO 80933-7150

AWARDS Engineering management (ME); information operations (ME); manufacturing (ME); mechanical engineering (MS). Software engineering (ME). Space operations (ME). Part-time and evening/weekend programs available.

Faculty: 7 full-time (0 women), 5 part-time/adjunct (3 women).
Students: 16 full-time (3 women), 14 part-time (1 woman); includes 1 minority (Asian American or Pacific Islander), 1 international. Average age 35. In 2001, 26 degrees awarded.
Degree requirements: For master's, thesis optional.
Entrance requirements: For master's, GRE General Test, TOEFL, bachelor's degree in engineering or related degree, minimum GPA of 3.0. *Application deadline:* For fall admission, 7/15; for spring admission, 12/10. Applications are processed on a rolling basis. *Application fee:* $60 ($75 for international students).
Expenses: Tuition, state resident: full-time $2,900; part-time $174 per credit. Tuition, nonresident: full-time $9,961; part-time $591 per credit. Required fees: $14 per credit. $141 per semester. Tuition and fees vary according to course load, program and student level.
Faculty research: Neural networks, artificial intelligence, robust control, space operations, space propulsion.
Dr. Peter Gorder, Chair, 719-262-3168, *Fax:* 719-262-3589, *E-mail:* pgorder@eas.uccs.edu.
Application contact: Siew Nylund, Academic Adviser, 719-262-3243, *Fax:* 719-262-3042, *E-mail:* snylund@uccs.edu. *Web site:* http://mepo-b.uccs.edu/newsletter.html

■ UNIVERSITY OF DAYTON

Graduate School, School of Engineering, Program in Engineering Management, Dayton, OH 45469-1300

AWARDS MSEM. Part-time and evening/weekend programs available.

Faculty: 5 full-time (0 women), 6 part-time/adjunct (1 woman).
Students: 40 full-time (12 women), 34 part-time (6 women); includes 10 minority (6 African Americans, 3 Asian Americans or Pacific Islanders, 1 Hispanic American), 11 international. Average age 26. In 2001, 30 degrees awarded.
Entrance requirements: For master's, GRE General Test, TOEFL. *Application deadline:* For fall admission, 8/1. *Application fee:* $30.

Expenses: Tuition: Full-time $5,436; part-time $453 per credit hour. Required fees: $50; $25 per term.
Financial support: In 2001–02, 1 teaching assistantship (averaging $10,500 per year) was awarded; research assistantships with partial tuition reimbursements
Faculty research: Artificial intelligence, program management.
Dr. Edward F. Mykytka, Chairman, 937-229-2238, *Fax:* 937-229-2756, *E-mail:* emykytka@notes.udayton.edu.
Application contact: Dr. Donald L. Moon, Associate Dean, 937-229-2241, *Fax:* 937-229-2471, *E-mail:* dmoon@notes.udayton.edu.

■ UNIVERSITY OF DENVER

Daniels College of Business, General Business Administration Program, Denver, CO 80208

AWARDS Business administration (MBA); education management (MSM); health care management (MSM); management and communications (MSMC); management and general engineering (MSMGEN); management and telecommunications (MSMC); public health management (MSM). Sports management (MSM). Part-time and evening/weekend programs available.

Faculty: 76.
Students: 363 (128 women); includes 24 minority (3 African Americans, 7 Asian Americans or Pacific Islanders, 12 Hispanic Americans, 2 Native Americans) 48 international. Average age 28. 386 applicants, 77% accepted. In 2001, 247 degrees awarded.
Entrance requirements: For master's, GMAT, LSAT (JD/MBA). *Application deadline:* For fall admission, 5/1 (priority date); for spring admission, 1/1. Applications are processed on a rolling basis. *Application fee:* $50.
Expenses: Tuition: Full-time $21,456.
Financial support: In 2001–02, 91 students received support, including 8 teaching assistantships with full and partial tuition reimbursements available (averaging $6,273 per year); research assistantships with full and partial tuition reimbursements available, career-related internships or fieldwork, Federal Work-Study, institutionally sponsored loans, and scholarships/grants also available. Support available to part-time students. Financial award application deadline: 2/15; financial award applicants required to submit FAFSA.
Faculty research: International business, privatization, alternative energy models, balancing economic growth in emerging economies.
Dr. Tom Howard, Director, 303-871-4402.
Application contact: Becca Cannon, Executive Director, Student Services, 303-871-3421, *Fax:* 303-871-4466, *E-mail:* dcb@du.edu.

■ UNIVERSITY OF DETROIT MERCY

College of Engineering and Science, Program in Engineering Management, Detroit, MI 48219-0900

AWARDS M Eng Mgt. Evening/weekend programs available.

Students: 1 (woman) full-time, 67 part-time (7 women); includes 9 minority (3 African Americans, 2 Asian Americans or Pacific Islanders, 3 Hispanic Americans, 1 Native American), 5 international. Average age 31. In 2001, 12 degrees awarded.
Degree requirements: For master's, thesis or alternative.
Application deadline: For fall admission, 8/1 (priority date). Applications are processed on a rolling basis. *Application fee:* $30 ($50 for international students).
Expenses: Tuition: Full-time $10,620; part-time $590 per credit hour. Required fees: $400. Tuition and fees vary according to program.
Dr. Richard Snydes, Head, 313-993-3334, *Fax:* 313-993-1187, *E-mail:* clayvc@udmercy.edu.

■ UNIVERSITY OF FLORIDA

Graduate School, College of Engineering, Department of Industrial and Systems Engineering, Gainesville, FL 32611

AWARDS Engineering management (ME, MS); facilities layout decision support systems energy (PhD); health systems (ME, MS); industrial engineering (PhD, Engr); manufacturing systems engineering (ME, MS, PhD, Certificate); operations research (ME, MS, PhD, Engr); production planning and control engineering management (PhD); quality and reliability assurance (ME, MS). Systems engineering (PhD, Engr).

Degree requirements: For master's, core exam, thesis optional; for doctorate, thesis/dissertation, comprehensive exam.
Entrance requirements: For master's and doctorate, GRE General Test, TOEFL, minimum GPA of 3.0; for other advanced degree, GRE General Test. Electronic applications accepted.
Expenses: Tuition, state resident: part-time $164 per hour. Tuition, nonresident: part-time $571 per hour. Tuition and fees vary according to course level and program. *Web site:* http://www.ise.ufl.edu/

Find an in-depth description at www.petersons.com/gradchannel.

■ UNIVERSITY OF KANSAS

Graduate School, School of Engineering, Department of Engineering Management, Lawrence, KS 66045

AWARDS MS. Part-time and evening/weekend programs available.
Faculty: 5.

Students: Average age 34. 32 applicants, 59% accepted, 15 enrolled. In 2001, 27 degrees awarded.
Degree requirements: For master's, exam.
Entrance requirements: For master's, Michigan English Language Assessment Battery, TOEFL, minimum GPA of 3.0, 2 years of industrial experience. *Application deadline:* Applications are processed on a rolling basis. *Application fee:* $40.
Expenses: Tuition, state resident: full-time $2,722; part-time $113 per credit. Tuition, nonresident: full-time $8,586; part-time $358 per credit. Required fees: $551; $46 per credit. Tuition and fees vary according to campus/location, program and reciprocity agreements.
Financial support: Fellowships, teaching assistantships available.
Robert Zerwekh, Director, 785-897-8560, *Fax:* 785-897-8682, *E-mail:* emgt@ku.edu. *Web site:* http://emgt.ku.edu/

■ **UNIVERSITY OF LOUISIANA AT LAFAYETTE**

Graduate School, College of Engineering, Department of Engineering and Technology Management, Lafayette, LA 70504

AWARDS MSET. Part-time and evening/weekend programs available.

Faculty: 3 full-time (0 women).
Students: 10 full-time (3 women), 15 part-time (2 women); includes 1 minority (African American), 7 international. 20 applicants, 85% accepted, 7 enrolled. In 2001, 4 degrees awarded.
Degree requirements: For master's, thesis or alternative, comprehensive exam.
Entrance requirements: For master's, GRE General Test, minimum GPA of 2.85. *Application deadline:* For fall admission, 5/15. *Application fee:* $20 ($30 for international students).
Expenses: Tuition, state resident: full-time $2,317; part-time $79 per credit. Tuition, nonresident: full-time $8,882; part-time $369 per credit. International tuition: $9,018 full-time.
Financial support: In 2001–02, 1 research assistantship with full tuition reimbursement (averaging $5,500 per year) was awarded; teaching assistantships, Federal Work-Study and tuition waivers (full and partial) also available. Financial award application deadline: 5/1.
Faculty research: Mathematical programming, production management forecasting.
Dr. Thomas Davies, Head, 337-482-5737.
Application contact: Dr. Jim Lee, Graduate Coordinator, 337-482-5354.

■ **UNIVERSITY OF LOUISVILLE**

Graduate School, Speed Scientific School, Department of Industrial Engineering, Program in Engineering Management, Louisville, KY 40292-0001

AWARDS M Eng.

Students: 33 full-time (3 women), 27 part-time (4 women); includes 1 minority (Hispanic American), 48 international. In 2001, 64 degrees awarded.
Expenses: Tuition, state resident: full-time $4,134. Tuition, nonresident: full-time $11,486.
Application contact: Nancy D. White, Executive Secretary, 502-852-6342, *Fax:* 502-852-5633, *E-mail:* ndwhit01@ gwise.louisville.edu.

■ **UNIVERSITY OF MARYLAND, BALTIMORE COUNTY**

Graduate School, College of Engineering, Engineering Management Program, Baltimore, MD 21250-5398

AWARDS MS. Part-time and evening/weekend programs available.

Degree requirements: For master's, thesis optional.
Entrance requirements: For master's, GRE General Test, minimum GPA of 3.0. Electronic applications accepted.
Faculty research: Regulatory engineering, systems, environmental engineering.

■ **UNIVERSITY OF MASSACHUSETTS AMHERST**

Graduate School, College of Engineering, Department of Mechanical and Industrial Engineering, Program in Engineering Management, Amherst, MA 01003

AWARDS MS.

Students: Average age 37. 8 applicants, 63% accepted. In 2001, 10 degrees awarded.
Entrance requirements: For master's, GRE General Test. *Application deadline:* For fall admission, 2/1 (priority date); for spring admission, 10/1. Applications are processed on a rolling basis. *Application fee:* $40 ($50 for international students).
Expenses: Tuition, state resident: full-time $1,980; part-time $110 per credit. Tuition, nonresident: full-time $7,456; part-time $414 per credit. Required fees: $4,112. One-time fee: $115 full-time.
Financial support: Fellowships with full tuition reimbursements, research assistantships with full tuition reimbursements, teaching assistantships with full tuition reimbursements, career-related internships or fieldwork, Federal Work-Study, scholarships/grants, traineeships, and unspecified assistantships available. Support available to part-time students. Financial award application deadline: 2/1.

Dr. Ian Grosse, Director, 413-545-2505, *Fax:* 413-545-1027.

■ **UNIVERSITY OF MICHIGAN–DEARBORN**

College of Engineering and Computer Science, Department of Industrial and Systems Engineering, Dearborn, MI 48128-1491

AWARDS Engineering management (MS); industrial and systems engineering (MSE); information systems and technology (MS). Part-time and evening/weekend programs available.

Faculty: 12 full-time (0 women), 8 part-time/adjunct (2 women).
Students: 7 full-time (2 women), 239 part-time (61 women); includes 45 minority (7 African Americans, 26 Asian Americans or Pacific Islanders, 12 Hispanic Americans). Average age 31. 107 applicants, 91% accepted. In 2001, 78 degrees awarded.
Degree requirements: For master's, thesis optional.
Entrance requirements: For master's, bachelor's degree in applied mathematics, computer science, engineering, or physical science; minimum GPA of 3.0. *Application deadline:* For fall admission, 8/1 (priority date); for winter admission, 12/1 (priority date); for spring admission, 4/1. Applications are processed on a rolling basis. *Application fee:* $55.
Expenses: Tuition, state resident: part-time $300 per credit hour. Tuition, nonresident: part-time $756 per credit hour. Required fees: $90 per semester. Tuition and fees vary according to course level, course load and program.
Financial support: Fellowships, research assistantships, teaching assistantships, Federal Work-Study available. Financial award application deadline: 4/1; financial award applicants required to submit FAFSA.
Faculty research: Health care systems, databases, human factors, machine diagnostics, precision machining.
Dr. S. K. Kachhal, Chair, 313-593-5361, *Fax:* 313-593-3692.
Application contact: Shelly A. Harris, Graduate Secretary, 313-593-5361, *Fax:* 313-593-3692, *E-mail:* saharris@ engin.umd.umich.edu. *Web site:* http:// www.engin.umd.umich.edu/

■ **UNIVERSITY OF MINNESOTA, DULUTH**

Graduate School, College of Science and Engineering, Department of Industrial Engineering, Duluth, MN 55812-2496

AWARDS Engineering management (MS); environmental health and safety (MEHS). Part-time programs available. Postbaccalaureate distance learning degree programs offered (minimal on-campus study).

University of Minnesota, Duluth (continued)

Faculty: 5 full-time (1 woman), 5 part-time/adjunct (0 women).
Students: 26 full-time (13 women), 21 part-time (2 women), 1 international. Average age 27. 28 applicants, 89% accepted, 25 enrolled. In 2001, 26 degrees awarded.
Degree requirements: For master's, capstone design project (MS), field project (MEHS).
Entrance requirements: For master's, interview (MEHS). *Application deadline:* For fall admission, 7/15; for spring admission, 5/1. *Application fee:* $50 ($55 for international students).
Expenses: Tuition, state resident: full-time $2,932; part-time $489 per credit. Tuition, nonresident: full-time $5,758; part-time $960 per credit. Tuition and fees vary according to course load.
Financial support: In 2001–02, 2 students received support, including 2 research assistantships with full tuition reimbursements available (averaging $11,000 per year); lab attendantship also available.
Faculty research: Transportation, ergonomics, industrial hygiene, toxicology, supply chain management. *Total annual research expenditures:* $40,000.
Dr. David A. Wyrick, Director of Graduate Studies, 218-726-7184, *Fax:* 218-726-8596, *E-mail:* dwyrick@d.umn.edu.
Application contact: Pat Wollack, Executive Secretary, 218-726-8117, *Fax:* 218-726-8581, *E-mail:* msem@d.umn.edu. *Web site:* http://ie.d.umn.edu/

■ UNIVERSITY OF MISSOURI–ROLLA

Graduate School, School of Engineering, Department of Engineering Management, Rolla, MO 65409-0910

AWARDS MS, PhD. Part-time and evening/weekend programs available. Terminal master's awarded for partial completion of doctoral program.

Degree requirements: For master's, comprehensive exam or thesis; for doctorate, thesis/dissertation.
Entrance requirements: For master's and doctorate, GRE General Test, TOEFL. Electronic applications accepted.
Faculty research: Intelligent manufacturing, MIS, total quality management, packaging, management of technology.

■ UNIVERSITY OF NEW ORLEANS

Graduate School, College of Engineering, Program in Engineering Management, New Orleans, LA 70148
AWARDS MS, Certificate.

Faculty: 1 full-time (0 women), 1 part-time/adjunct (0 women).

Students: 7 full-time (3 women), 32 part-time (10 women); includes 7 minority (1 African American, 4 Hispanic Americans, 2 Native Americans), 6 international. Average age 31. 29 applicants, 55% accepted, 8 enrolled. In 2001, 9 degrees awarded.
Degree requirements: For master's, thesis optional.
Entrance requirements: For master's, GRE General Test, minimum GPA of 3.0. *Application deadline:* For fall admission, 7/1 (priority date); for spring admission, 11/15 (priority date). Applications are processed on a rolling basis. *Application fee:* $20. Electronic applications accepted.
Expenses: Tuition, state resident: full-time $2,748; part-time $435 per credit. Tuition, nonresident: full-time $9,792; part-time $1,773 per credit.
Financial support: Fellowships, research assistantships, institutionally sponsored loans available. Financial award applicants required to submit FAFSA.
Will Lannes, Director, 504-280-7122, *E-mail:* wlannes@uno.edu.

■ THE UNIVERSITY OF NORTH CAROLINA AT CHARLOTTE

Graduate School, The William States Lee College of Engineering, Program in Engineering Management, Charlotte, NC 28223-0001

AWARDS MS. Part-time and evening/weekend programs available.

Students: 3 full-time (2 women), 19 part-time (4 women); includes 3 minority (1 African American, 2 Asian Americans or Pacific Islanders), 1 international. Average age 33. 17 applicants, 82% accepted, 9 enrolled. In 2001, 1 degree awarded. *Application deadline:* For fall admission, 7/15; for spring admission, 11/15. Applications are processed on a rolling basis. *Application fee:* $35. Electronic applications accepted.
Expenses: Tuition, state resident: full-time $1,483; part-time $371 per credit. Tuition, nonresident: full-time $9,850; part-time $2,463 per year. Required fees: $1,043; $277 per year. Tuition and fees vary according to course load.
Financial support: Fellowships, research assistantships, teaching assistantships, career-related internships or fieldwork, Federal Work-Study, institutionally sponsored loans, scholarships/grants, and unspecified assistantships available. Support available to part-time students. Financial award application deadline: 4/1; financial award applicants required to submit FAFSA.
Dr. S. Gary Teng, Director, 704-687-3989, *Fax:* 704-687-2352, *E-mail:* sgteng@email.uncc.edu.
Application contact: Kathy Barringer, Director of Graduate Admissions, 704-687-3366, *Fax:* 704-687-3279, *E-mail:* gradadm@email.uncc.edu. *Web site:* http://www.uncc.edu/gradmiss/

■ UNIVERSITY OF OKLAHOMA

Graduate College, College of Engineering, School of Petroleum and Geological Engineering, Program in Natural Gas Engineering and Management, Norman, OK 73019-0390
AWARDS MS.

Students: 1.
Degree requirements: For master's, industrial type team project or thesis. *Median time to degree:* Master's–2 years full-time.
Entrance requirements: For master's, GMAT or GRE, TOEFL, bachelor's degree in engineering, letter of recommendation, minimum GPA of 3.0 during final 60 hours of undergraduate course work. *Application deadline:* For fall admission, 6/1 (priority date); for spring admission, 11/1. Applications are processed on a rolling basis. *Application fee:* $25 ($50 for international students).
Expenses: Tuition, state resident: full-time $2,208; part-time $92 per credit hour. Tuition, nonresident: part-time $297 per credit hour. Tuition and fees vary according to course level, course load and program.
Financial support: Application deadline: 4/15.
Application contact: Shawn Love, Coordinator, 405-325-6799, *E-mail:* shawnlove@ou.edu.

■ UNIVERSITY OF ST. THOMAS

Graduate Studies, Graduate School of Applied Science and Engineering, Program in Engineering and Technology Management, St. Paul, MN 55105-1096

AWARDS Engineering and technology management (Certificate); manufacturing systems (MS); manufacturing systems engineering (MMSE); technology management (MS). Part-time and evening/weekend programs available.

Faculty: 3 full-time (0 women), 32 part-time/adjunct (1 woman).
Students: 2 full-time (0 women), 219 part-time (39 women); includes 23 minority (10 African Americans, 9 Asian Americans or Pacific Islanders, 3 Hispanic Americans, 1 Native American), 6 international. Average age 34. 60 applicants, 97% accepted. In 2001, 29 master's, 5 other advanced degrees awarded.
Degree requirements: For master's, thesis (for some programs). *Application deadline:* For fall admission, 8/1 (priority date); for spring admission, 1/1 (priority date). Applications are processed on a rolling basis. *Application fee:* $30. Electronic applications accepted.
Expenses: Tuition: Part-time $401 per credit. Tuition and fees vary according to degree level and program.
Financial support: In 2001–02, 6 students received support; fellowships, research

assistantships, institutionally sponsored loans and scholarships/grants available. Support available to part-time students. Financial award application deadline: 4/1; financial award applicants required to submit FAFSA.
Ron Bennett, Director, 651-962-5750, *Fax:* 651-962-6419, *E-mail:* rjbennett@ stthomas.edu.
Application contact: Marlene L. Houliston, Student Services Coordinator, 651-962-5750, *Fax:* 651-962-6419, *E-mail:* technology@stthomas.edu. *Web site:* http://www.stthomas.edu/technology/

■ UNIVERSITY OF SOUTHERN CALIFORNIA

Graduate School, School of Engineering, Department of Industrial and Systems Engineering, Program in Engineering Management, Los Angeles, CA 90089
AWARDS MS.

Degree requirements: For master's, thesis optional.
Entrance requirements: For master's, GRE General Test.
Expenses: Tuition: Full-time $25,060; part-time $844 per unit. Required fees: $473.

■ UNIVERSITY OF SOUTH FLORIDA

College of Graduate Studies, College of Engineering, Department of Industrial and Management Systems Engineering, Tampa, FL 33620-9951
AWARDS Engineering management (ME, MIE, MSIE); engineering science (PhD); industrial engineering (ME, MIE, MSIE, PhD). Part-time programs available. Postbaccalaureate distance learning degree programs offered (minimal on-campus study).

Faculty: 10 full-time (0 women).
Students: 54 full-time (14 women), 66 part-time (18 women); includes 14 minority (3 African Americans, 1 Asian American or Pacific Islander, 10 Hispanic Americans), 58 international. Average age 35. 187 applicants, 64% accepted, 32 enrolled. In 2001, 12 degrees awarded. Terminal master's awarded for partial completion of doctoral program.
Degree requirements: For master's, thesis (for some programs); for doctorate, thesis/dissertation, 2 tools of research as specified by dissertation committee.
Entrance requirements: For master's, GRE General Test, minimum GPA of 3.0 during previous 2 years; for doctorate, GRE General Test. *Application deadline:* For fall admission, 6/1; for spring admission, 10/15. *Application fee:* $20. Electronic applications accepted.
Expenses: Tuition, state resident: part-time $166 per credit hour. Tuition, nonresident: part-time $573 per credit hour. Required fees: $17 per term.

Financial support: Fellowships with full tuition reimbursements, research assistantships with full tuition reimbursements, teaching assistantships with full tuition reimbursements, career-related internships or fieldwork, Federal Work-Study, institutionally sponsored loans, and tuition waivers (partial) available. Support available to part-time students. Financial award application deadline: 3/31; financial award applicants required to submit FAFSA.
Faculty research: Quality control, optimization techniques, stochastic processes, computer automated manufacturing. *Total annual research expenditures:* $229,700.
Application contact: Dr. William Miller, Graduate Director, 813-974-5584, *Fax:* 813-974-5953, *E-mail:* miller@eng.usf.edu. *Web site:* http://www.eng.usf.edu/IE/industrial.html

■ THE UNIVERSITY OF TENNESSEE

Graduate School, College of Engineering, Department of Industrial Engineering, Knoxville, TN 37996
AWARDS Engineering management (MS); manufacturing systems engineering (MS); product development and manufacturing (MS); traditional industrial engineering (MS). Part-time programs available. Postbaccalaureate distance learning degree programs offered (no on-campus study).

Faculty: 10 full-time (1 woman).
Students: 21 full-time (6 women), 70 part-time (15 women); includes 6 minority (4 African Americans, 2 Asian Americans or Pacific Islanders), 13 international. 56 applicants, 50% accepted. In 2001, 50 degrees awarded.
Degree requirements: For master's, thesis or alternative.
Entrance requirements: For master's, GRE General Test, TOEFL, minimum GPA of 2.7. *Application deadline:* For fall admission, 2/1 (priority date). Applications are processed on a rolling basis. *Application fee:* $35. Electronic applications accepted.
Expenses: Tuition, state resident: full-time $4,280; part-time $233 per hour. Tuition, nonresident: full-time $12,066; part-time $666 per hour. Tuition and fees vary according to program.
Financial support: In 2001–02, 1 fellowship, 5 research assistantships, 5 teaching assistantships were awarded. Career-related internships or fieldwork, Federal Work-Study, institutionally sponsored loans, and unspecified assistantships also available. Financial award application deadline: 2/1; financial award applicants required to submit FAFSA.
Dr. Adedeji B. Badiru, Head, 865-974-3333, *Fax:* 865-974-0588, *E-mail:* abadiru@utk.edu.
Application contact: Dr. Denise Jackson, Graduate Representative, *E-mail:* djackson@utk.edu.

■ THE UNIVERSITY OF TENNESSEE AT CHATTANOOGA

Graduate Division, College of Engineering and Computer Sciences, Program in Engineering Management, Chattanooga, TN 37403-2598
AWARDS MS.

Faculty: 4 full-time (2 women).
Students: 1 full-time (0 women), 19 part-time; includes 3 minority (all African Americans), 1 international. Average age 38. 9 applicants, 89% accepted, 6 enrolled. In 2001, 2 degrees awarded.
Degree requirements: For master's, thesis.
Entrance requirements: For master's, GRE General Test. *Application deadline:* For fall admission, 8/1 (priority date); for spring admission, 12/1 (priority date). Applications are processed on a rolling basis. *Application fee:* $25.
Expenses: Tuition, state resident: full-time $3,752; part-time $228 per hour. Tuition, nonresident: full-time $10,282; part-time $565 per hour.
Financial support: Fellowships, research assistantships available. Financial award application deadline: 4/1; financial award applicants required to submit FAFSA.
Dr. Edward H. McMahon, Director, 423-425-4771, *Fax:* 423-425-5229, *E-mail:* ed-mcmahon@utc.edu.
Application contact: Dr. Deborah E. Arfken, Dean of Graduate Studies, 865-425-1740, *Fax:* 865-425-5223, *E-mail:* deborah-arfken@utc.edu. *Web site:* http://www.utc.edu/

■ THE UNIVERSITY OF TENNESSEE SPACE INSTITUTE

Graduate Programs, Program in Industrial Engineering (Engineering Management), Tullahoma, TN 37388-9700
AWARDS Engineering management (MS).

Faculty: 3 full-time (0 women).
Students: 2 full-time (1 woman), 44 part-time (8 women), 3 international. 11 applicants, 82% accepted, 9 enrolled. In 2001, 18 degrees awarded.
Degree requirements: For master's, thesis (for some programs).
Application deadline: Applications are processed on a rolling basis. *Application fee:* $35.
Expenses: Tuition, state resident: full-time $4,730; part-time $208 per semester hour. Tuition, nonresident: full-time $15,028; part-time $627 per semester hour. Required fees: $10 per semester hour. One-time fee: $35.
Financial support: Fellowships with full and partial tuition reimbursements, research assistantships with full tuition reimbursements, career-related internships or fieldwork, Federal Work-Study, and tuition waivers (full and partial) available.

The University of Tennessee Space Institute (continued)

Financial award applicants required to submit FAFSA.

Dr. Max Hailey, Degree Program Chairman, 931-393-7378, *Fax:* 931-393-7201, *E-mail:* mhailey@utsi.edu.

Application contact: Dr. Alfonso Pujol, Assistant Vice President and Dean for Student Affairs, 931-393-7432, *Fax:* 931-393-7346, *E-mail:* apujol@utsi.edu.

■ UNIVERSITY OF TULSA

Graduate School, College of Business Administration and College of Engineering and Natural Sciences, Department of Engineering and Technology Management, Tulsa, OK 74104-3189

AWARDS Chemical engineering (METM); computer science (METM); electrical engineering (METM); geological science (METM); mathematics (METM); mechanical engineering (METM); petroleum engineering (METM). Part-time and evening/weekend programs available.

Students: 2 full-time (1 woman), 1 part-time, 2 international. Average age 26. 3 applicants, 100% accepted, 1 enrolled. In 2001, 2 degrees awarded.
Entrance requirements: For master's, GRE General Test, TOEFL. *Application deadline:* Applications are processed on a rolling basis. *Application fee:* $30. Electronic applications accepted.
Expenses: Tuition: Full-time $9,540; part-time $530 per credit hour. Required fees: $80. One-time fee: $230 full-time.
Financial support: Fellowships, research assistantships, teaching assistantships, Federal Work-Study, scholarships/grants, tuition waivers (partial), and unspecified assistantships available. Support available to part-time students. Financial award application deadline: 2/1; financial award applicants required to submit FAFSA.
Application contact: Information Contact, *E-mail:* graduate-business@utulsa.edu. *Web site:* http://www.cba.utulsa.edu/academic.asp#graduate_studies/

■ VIRGINIA POLYTECHNIC INSTITUTE AND STATE UNIVERSITY

Graduate School, College of Engineering, Department of Industrial and Systems Engineering, Program in Engineering Administration, Blacksburg, VA 24061

AWARDS MEA.

Degree requirements: For master's, thesis.
Entrance requirements: For master's, TOEFL. *Application deadline:* For fall

admission, 12/1 (priority date). Applications are processed on a rolling basis. *Application fee:* $45. Electronic applications accepted.
Expenses: Tuition, state resident: part-time $241 per hour. Tuition, nonresident: part-time $406 per hour. Tuition and fees vary according to program.
Financial support: Application deadline: 4/1.

■ WASHINGTON STATE UNIVERSITY SPOKANE

Graduate Programs, Program in Engineering Management, Spokane, WA 99201-3899

AWARDS MEM.

■ WAYNE STATE UNIVERSITY

Graduate School, College of Engineering, Department of Industrial and Manufacturing Engineering, Program in Engineering Management, Detroit, MI 48202

AWARDS MS.

Students: 85. In 2001, 24 degrees awarded.
Degree requirements: For master's, thesis optional.
Entrance requirements: For master's, minimum undergraduate GPA of 2.8. *Application deadline:* For fall admission, 7/1 (priority date); for spring admission, 3/15. Applications are processed on a rolling basis. *Application fee:* $20 ($30 for international students). Electronic applications accepted.
Expenses: Tuition, state resident: full-time $3,764. Tuition and fees vary according to degree level and program.
Financial support: In 2001–02, 20 students received support, including 15 research assistantships, 5 teaching assistantships; fellowships, career-related internships or fieldwork and tuition waivers (full) also available.
Faculty research: Technology and change management, quality/reliability, manufacturing systems/infrastructure.

■ WESTERN MICHIGAN UNIVERSITY

Graduate College, College of Engineering and Applied Sciences, Department of Industrial and Manufacturing Engineering, Program in Engineering Management, Kalamazoo, MI 49008-5202

AWARDS MS.

Faculty: 25 full-time (3 women).
Students: 10 full-time (3 women), 48 part-time (8 women); includes 6 minority (2 African Americans, 1 Asian American or Pacific Islander, 3 Hispanic Americans), 2 international. 27 applicants, 67% accepted, 6 enrolled. In 2001, 35 degrees awarded.

Entrance requirements: For master's, minimum GPA of 3.0. *Application deadline:* For fall admission, 2/15 (priority date). Applications are processed on a rolling basis. *Application fee:* $25.
Expenses: Tuition, state resident: part-time $186 per credit hour. Tuition, nonresident: part-time $442 per credit hour. Required fees: $602. One-time fee: $132 part-time. Tuition and fees vary according to course load.
Financial support: Application deadline: 2/15.
Application contact: Paula J. Boodt, Admissions and Orientation, 616-387-2000, *Fax:* 616-387-2355, *E-mail:* paula.boodt@wmich.edu.

■ WIDENER UNIVERSITY

School of Engineering, Program in Engineering Management, Chester, PA 19013-5792

AWARDS ME.

Degree requirements: For master's, thesis optional.
Expenses: Tuition: Part-time $500 per credit. Required fees: $25 per semester.

ERGONOMICS AND HUMAN FACTORS

■ BENTLEY COLLEGE

The Elkin B. McCallum Graduate School of Business, Program in Human Factors in Information Design, Waltham, MA 02452-4705

AWARDS MSHFID. Part-time and evening/weekend programs available.

Faculty: 6 full-time (1 woman), 4 part-time/adjunct (1 woman).
Students: 3 full-time (1 woman), 47 part-time (30 women); includes 1 minority (African American). Average age 34.
Entrance requirements: For master's, GMAT or GRE, TOEFL. *Application deadline:* For fall admission, 6/1 (priority date); for spring admission, 11/1 (priority date). Applications are processed on a rolling basis. *Application fee:* $50. Electronic applications accepted.
Expenses: Tuition: Full-time $18,640; part-time $777 per credit. Required fees: $100.
Financial support: Research assistantships, career-related internships or fieldwork, Federal Work-Study, and unspecified assistantships available. Support available to part-time students. Financial award application deadline: 4/15; financial award applicants required to submit CSS PROFILE or FAFSA.
Dr. William Gribbons, Director, 781-891-2926.

Application contact: Debbie K. Love, Senior Associate Director of Graduate Admissions, 781-891-2108, *Fax:* 781-891-2464.

■ THE CATHOLIC UNIVERSITY OF AMERICA

School of Arts and Sciences, Department of Psychology, Program in Human Factors, Washington, DC 20064

AWARDS MA. Part-time programs available.

Students: 2 full-time (1 woman), 1 (woman) part-time. Average age 26. 6 applicants, 67% accepted, 1 enrolled.
Degree requirements: For master's, thesis, comprehensive exam.
Entrance requirements: For master's, GRE General Test, TOEFL. *Application deadline:* For fall admission, 8/1 (priority date); for spring admission, 12/1. Applications are processed on a rolling basis. *Application fee:* $55. Electronic applications accepted.
Expenses: Tuition: Full-time $20,050; part-time $770 per credit. Required fees: $430 per term. Tuition and fees vary according to program.
Financial support: Fellowships, research assistantships, career-related internships or fieldwork, Federal Work-Study, institutionally sponsored loans, scholarships/grants, and tuition waivers (full and partial) available. Support available to part-time students. Financial award application deadline: 2/1.
Faculty research: Human factors of automation, cognitive aging, pattern perception, applied memory, human-computer interaction.
Dr. Lene Jensen, Director, 202-319-5750.

■ CLEMSON UNIVERSITY

Graduate School, College of Business and Behavioral Science, Department of Psychology, Clemson, SC 29634

AWARDS Applied psychology (MS); human factors (MS); industrial/organizational psychology (PhD).

Students: 29 full-time (17 women), 8 part-time (4 women); includes 2 minority (1 African American, 1 Asian American or Pacific Islander). 170 applicants, 6% accepted, 9 enrolled. In 2001, 4 degrees awarded.
Degree requirements: For master's, thesis, internship; for doctorate, thesis/dissertation.
Entrance requirements: For master's, GRE General Test, TOEFL, 18 hours in psychology; for doctorate, GRE General Test, TOEFL. *Application deadline:* For fall admission, 3/15. *Application fee:* $40.
Expenses: Tuition, state resident: full-time $5,310. Tuition, nonresident: full-time $11,284.
Financial support: Application deadline: 3/15.

Dr. Christopher Pagano, Coordinator, 864-656-4984, *E-mail:* cpagano@clemson.edu.

■ CORNELL UNIVERSITY

Graduate School, Graduate Fields of Human Ecology, Field of Design and Environmental Analysis, Ithaca, NY 14853-0001

AWARDS Applied research in human-environment relations (MS); facilities planning and management (MS); housing and design (MS); human factors and ergonomics (MS); human-environment relations (MS); interior design (MA).

Faculty: 11 full-time.
Students: 22 full-time (17 women); includes 2 minority (both Asian Americans or Pacific Islanders), 12 international. 46 applicants, 61% accepted. In 2001, 14 degrees awarded.
Degree requirements: For master's, thesis.
Entrance requirements: For master's, GRE General Test, TOEFL, portfolio or slides of recent work, bachelors degree in interior design, architecture or related design discipline, 2 letters of recommendation. *Application deadline:* For fall admission, 2/1. *Application fee:* $65. Electronic applications accepted.
Expenses: Tuition: Full-time $25,970. Required fees: $50.
Financial support: In 2001–02, 15 students received support, including 1 fellowship with full tuition reimbursement available, 14 teaching assistantships with full tuition reimbursements available; research assistantships with full tuition reimbursements available, institutionally sponsored loans, scholarships/grants, tuition waivers (full and partial), and unspecified assistantships also available. Financial award applicants required to submit FAFSA.
Faculty research: Facility planning and management, environmental psychology, housing, interior design, ergonomics and human factors.
Application contact: Graduate Field Assistant, 607-255-2168, *Fax:* 607-255-0305, *E-mail:* bjr6@cornell.edu. *Web site:* http://www.gradschool.cornell.edu/grad/fields_1/dea.html

■ EMBRY-RIDDLE AERONAUTICAL UNIVERSITY

Daytona Beach Campus Graduate Program, Department of Human Factors and Systems, Daytona Beach, FL 32114-3900

AWARDS Human factors engineering (MSHFS). Systems engineering (MSHFS). Part-time and evening/weekend programs available.

Faculty: 7 full-time (3 women).
Students: 15 full-time (8 women), 29 part-time (17 women); includes 7 minority (4

African Americans, 3 Hispanic Americans), 10 international. Average age 29. 26 applicants, 73% accepted, 14 enrolled. In 2001, 8 degrees awarded.
Degree requirements: For master's, thesis, practicum, qualifying oral exam.
Entrance requirements: For master's, TOEFL, minimum GPA of 2.5. *Application deadline:* For fall admission, 8/1 (priority date); for spring admission, 12/1 (priority date). Applications are processed on a rolling basis. *Application fee:* $30 ($50 for international students).
Expenses: Tuition: Full-time $13,140; part-time $730 per credit. Required fees: $250; $250 per year. $125 per semester. Tuition and fees vary according to program.
Financial support: In 2001–02, 13 students received support, including 1 research assistantship with partial tuition reimbursement available (averaging $8,100 per year), 2 teaching assistantships with partial tuition reimbursements available (averaging $8,100 per year); fellowships with partial tuition reimbursements available, career-related internships or fieldwork and unspecified assistantships also available. Financial award application deadline: 4/15; financial award applicants required to submit FAFSA.
Faculty research: Future mission concepts. *Total annual research expenditures:* $8,774.
Dr. John Wise, Program Coordinator, 386-226-6384, *Fax:* 386-226-7050, *E-mail:* wise@erau.edu.
Application contact: Christine Castetter, Graduate Admissions, 800-388-3728, *Fax:* 386-226-7111, *E-mail:* gradmit@erau.edu.

Find an in-depth description at www.petersons.com/gradchannel.

■ FLORIDA INSTITUTE OF TECHNOLOGY

Graduate Programs, School of Aeronautics, Melbourne, FL 32901-6975

AWARDS Airport development and management (MSA); applied aviation safety (MSA); aviation human factors (MS). Part-time and evening/weekend programs available.

Faculty: 6 full-time (1 woman).
Students: 9 full-time (5 women), 8 part-time (4 women); includes 3 minority (1 African American, 2 Hispanic Americans), 8 international. Average age 26. 26 applicants, 65% accepted. In 2001, 4 degrees awarded.
Degree requirements: For master's, thesis.
Entrance requirements: For master's, GRE General Test or GRE Subject Test, minimum undergraduate GPA of 3.0. *Application deadline:* For fall admission, 8/1; for spring admission, 12/1. Applications are processed on a rolling basis. *Application fee:* $50. Electronic applications accepted.

Florida Institute of Technology (continued)
Expenses: Tuition: Part-time $650 per credit.
Financial support: In 2001–02, 1 student received support, including 1 teaching assistantship with full and partial tuition reimbursement available (averaging $6,840 per year); research assistantships with full and partial tuition reimbursements available, career-related internships or fieldwork, institutionally sponsored loans, unspecified assistantships, and tuition remissions also available. Financial award application deadline: 3/1.
Faculty research: Aircraft cockpit design; medical human factors; operating room human factors; hypobaric chamber operations and effects; aviation professional education. *Total annual research expenditures:* $157,100.
Dr. Nathaniel Villaire, Chairman of Graduate Studies, 321-674-8120, *Fax:* 321-674-8059, *E-mail:* villaire@fit.edu.
Application contact: Carolyn P. Farrior, Director of Graduate Admissions, 321-674-7118, *Fax:* 321-723-9468, *E-mail:* cfarrior@fit.edu. *Web site:* http://www.fit.edu/soa/

Find an in-depth description at www.petersons.com/gradchannel.

■ NEW YORK UNIVERSITY

Graduate School of Arts and Science, Nelson Institute of Environmental Medicine, New York, NY 10012-1019
AWARDS Environmental health sciences (MS, PhD), including environmental health sciences (MS), ergonomics and biomechanics (PhD), occupational biomechanics (PhD). Part-time programs available.
Faculty: 26 full-time (7 women).
Students: 30 full-time (15 women), 17 part-time (8 women); includes 5 minority (1 African American, 3 Asian Americans or Pacific Islanders, 1 Hispanic American), 17 international. Average age 26. 69 applicants, 55% accepted, 23 enrolled. In 2001, 5 master's, 4 doctorates awarded. Terminal master's awarded for partial completion of doctoral program.
Degree requirements: For master's, thesis or alternative; for doctorate, one foreign language, thesis/dissertation, oral and written exams.
Entrance requirements: For master's and doctorate, GRE General Test, GRE Subject Test, TOEFL, minimum GPA of 3.0; bachelor's degree in biological, physical, or engineering science. *Application deadline:* For fall admission, 2/1. *Application fee:* $60.
Expenses: Tuition: Full-time $19,536; part-time $814 per credit. Required fees: $1,330; $38 per credit. Tuition and fees vary according to course load and program.
Financial support: Fellowships with tuition reimbursements, teaching assistantships with tuition reimbursements, career-related internships or fieldwork, Federal

Work-Study, and institutionally sponsored loans available. Financial award application deadline: 2/1; financial award applicants required to submit FAFSA.
Faculty research: Epidemiology and biostatistics, molecular toxicology/carcinogenesis, toxicology, exposure assessment and health effects, ergonomics and biomechanics.
Dr. Max Costa, Director, 845-731-3661, *Fax:* 914-351-3317.
Application contact: Jerry Solomon, Director of Graduate Studies, 845-731-3661, *Fax:* 914-351-3317, *E-mail:* ehs@env.med.nyu.edu. *Web site:* http://www.niem.med.nyu.edu/gradprog/

Find an in-depth description at www.petersons.com/gradchannel.

■ PURDUE UNIVERSITY

Graduate School, Schools of Engineering, School of Industrial Engineering, West Lafayette, IN 47907
AWARDS Human factors in industrial engineering (MS, MSIE, PhD); manufacturing engineering (MS, MSIE, PhD); operations research (MS, MSIE, PhD). Systems engineering (MS, MSIE, PhD). Part-time programs available.
Faculty: 23 full-time (2 women), 4 part-time/adjunct (0 women).
Students: 117 full-time (24 women), 19 part-time (6 women); includes 6 minority (4 African Americans, 2 Hispanic Americans), 108 international. Average age 28. 370 applicants, 44% accepted. In 2001, 51 master's, 11 doctorates awarded. Terminal master's awarded for partial completion of doctoral program.
Degree requirements: For master's, thesis optional; for doctorate, thesis/dissertation.
Entrance requirements: For master's, GRE General Test, TOEFL, minimum GPA of 3.0; for doctorate, GRE General Test, TOEFL, MS thesis. *Application deadline:* For fall admission, 3/15; for spring admission, 9/1. *Application fee:* $30. Electronic applications accepted.
Expenses: Tuition, state resident: full-time $4,164; part-time $149 per credit hour. Tuition, nonresident: full-time $13,872; part-time $458 per credit hour. Tuition and fees vary according to campus/location and program.
Financial support: In 2001–02, 78 students received support, including 3 fellowships with full tuition reimbursements available (averaging $13,070 per year), 29 research assistantships with full tuition reimbursements available (averaging $12,720 per year), 46 teaching assistantships with full tuition reimbursements available (averaging $10,600 per year) Support available to part-time students. Financial award application deadline: 3/15; financial award applicants required to submit FAFSA.
Faculty research: Precision manufacturing process, computer-aided manufacturing,

computer-aided process planning, knowledge-based systems, combinatorics. *Total annual research expenditures:* $1.8 million.
Dr. Dennis Engi, Head, 765-494-5444, *Fax:* 765-494-1299, *E-mail:* engi@ecn.purdue.edu.
Application contact: Dr. J. W. Barany, Associate Head, 765-494-5406, *Fax:* 765-494-1299, *E-mail:* jwb@ecn.purdue.edu. *Web site:* http://ie.www.ecn.purdue.edu/

■ RENSSELAER POLYTECHNIC INSTITUTE

Graduate School, School of Humanities and Social Sciences, Department of Cognitive Science, Program in Psychology, Troy, NY 12180-3590
AWARDS Human factors (MS); industrial-organizational psychology (MS). Part-time programs available.
Faculty: 7 full-time (0 women), 4 part-time/adjunct (0 women).
Students: 27 full-time (10 women), 3 part-time (1 woman); includes 3 minority (1 African American, 2 Asian Americans or Pacific Islanders), 2 international. Average age 22. 23 applicants, 74% accepted. In 2001, 4 degrees awarded.
Degree requirements: For master's, thesis.
Entrance requirements: For master's, GRE General Test, GRE Subject Test, TOEFL. *Application deadline:* For fall admission, 1/15 (priority date). Applications are processed on a rolling basis. *Application fee:* $45. Electronic applications accepted.
Expenses: Tuition: Full-time $26,400; part-time $1,320 per credit hour. Required fees: $1,437.
Financial support: In 2001–02, 1 fellowship with full tuition reimbursement (averaging $10,000 per year), 12 teaching assistantships with partial tuition reimbursements (averaging $4,000 per year) were awarded. Research assistantships, career-related internships or fieldwork, institutionally sponsored loans, scholarships/grants, and tuition waivers (partial) also available. Financial award application deadline: 2/1.
Faculty research: Cognitive psychology. *Web site:* http://www.rpi.edu/

Find an in-depth description at www.petersons.com/gradchannel.

■ SAN JOSE STATE UNIVERSITY

Graduate Studies, Graduate Studies Program, Program in Human Factors/Ergonomics, San Jose, CA 95192-0001
AWARDS MS. Part-time programs available.
Faculty: 7.
Students: 6 full-time (1 woman), 32 part-time (22 women); includes 9 minority (8 Asian Americans or Pacific Islanders, 1

Hispanic American), 3 international. Average age 33. 18 applicants, 72% accepted. In 2001, 4 degrees awarded.

Entrance requirements: For master's, minimum GPA of 3.0, previous course work in basic statistics. *Application deadline:* For fall admission, 6/29; for spring admission, 11/30. Applications are processed on a rolling basis. *Application fee:* $59. Electronic applications accepted.

Expenses: Tuition, nonresident: part-time $246 per unit. Required fees: $678 per semester. Tuition and fees vary according to course load.

Financial support: Applicants required to submit FAFSA.

Faculty research: Ergonomic design and engineering, occupational therapy.

Kevin Corker, Graduate Advisor, 408-924-3988.

■ TUFTS UNIVERSITY

Division of Graduate and Continuing Studies and Research, Graduate School of Arts and Sciences, School of Engineering, Department of Mechanical Engineering, Medford, MA 02155

AWARDS Human factors (MS); mechanical engineering (ME, MS, PhD). Part-time programs available.

Faculty: 13 full-time, 2 part-time/adjunct.
Students: 71 (12 women); includes 12 minority (8 Asian Americans or Pacific Islanders, 4 Hispanic Americans) 16 international. 36 applicants, 78% accepted. In 2001, 15 master's, 2 doctorates awarded. Terminal master's awarded for partial completion of doctoral program.
Degree requirements: For master's and doctorate, thesis/dissertation.
Entrance requirements: For master's and doctorate, GRE General Test, TOEFL. *Application deadline:* For fall admission, 2/15; for spring admission, 10/15. Applications are processed on a rolling basis. *Application fee:* $50. Electronic applications accepted.
Expenses: Tuition: Full-time $26,853. Full-time tuition and fees vary according to program.
Financial support: Research assistantships with full and partial tuition reimbursements, teaching assistantships with full and partial tuition reimbursements, Federal Work-Study, scholarships/grants, and tuition waivers (partial) available. Financial award application deadline: 2/15; financial award applicants required to submit FAFSA.

April Saigal, Chair, 617-627-3239, *Fax:* 617-627-3058, *E-mail:* meinfo@tufts.edu.
Application contact: Robert Greif, Head, 617-627-3239, *Fax:* 617-627-3058, *E-mail:* meinfo@tufts.edu. *Web site:* http://ase.tufts.edu/mechanical/

■ UNIVERSITY OF CENTRAL FLORIDA

College of Engineering and Computer Sciences, Department of Industrial Engineering and Management Systems, Orlando, FL 32816

AWARDS Applied operations research (Certificate); computer-integrated manufacturing (MS); design for usability (Certificate); engineering management (MS); industrial engineering (MSIE); industrial engineering and management systems (PhD); industrial ergonomics and safety (Certificate); operations research (MS); product assurance engineering (MS); project engineering (Certificate); quality assurance (Certificate). Simulation systems (MS). Systems simulations for engineers (Certificate); training simulation (Certificate). Part-time and evening/weekend programs available.

Faculty: 20 full-time (4 women), 8 part-time/adjunct (1 woman).
Students: 92 full-time (19 women), 182 part-time (49 women); includes 66 minority (18 African Americans, 10 Asian Americans or Pacific Islanders, 35 Hispanic Americans, 3 Native Americans), 57 international. Average age 32. 231 applicants, 84% accepted, 85 enrolled. In 2001, 3 master's, 9 doctorates awarded.
Degree requirements: For master's, thesis; for doctorate, thesis/dissertation, departmental qualifying exam, candidacy exam.
Entrance requirements: For master's, GRE General Test, TOEFL, minimum GPA of 3.0 in last 60 hours; for doctorate, TOEFL, minimum GPA of 3.5 in last 60 hours. *Application deadline:* For fall admission, 7/15 (priority date); for spring admission, 12/1 (priority date). *Application fee:* $20. Electronic applications accepted.
Expenses: Tuition, state resident: part-time $162 per hour. Tuition, nonresident: part-time $569 per hour.
Financial support: In 2001–02, 23 fellowships with partial tuition reimbursements (averaging $3,272 per year), 131 research assistantships with partial tuition reimbursements (averaging $3,125 per year), 24 teaching assistantships with partial tuition reimbursements (averaging $3,823 per year) were awarded. Career-related internships or fieldwork, Federal Work-Study, institutionally sponsored loans, tuition waivers (partial), and unspecified assistantships also available. Financial award application deadline: 3/1; financial award applicants required to submit FAFSA.

Dr. Charles Reily, Chair, 407-823-2204, *E-mail:* creilly@mail.ucf.edu.
Application contact: Dr. Linda Malone, Coordinator, 407-823-2204, *E-mail:* malone@mail.ucf.edu. *Web site:* http://www.ucf.edu/

Find an in-depth description at www.petersons.com/gradchannel.

■ THE UNIVERSITY OF IOWA

Graduate College, College of Engineering, Department of Industrial Engineering, Iowa City, IA 52242-1316

AWARDS Engineering design and manufacturing (MS, PhD); ergonomics (MS, PhD); information and engineering management (MS, PhD); operations research (MS, PhD); quality engineering (MS, PhD).

Faculty: 7 full-time, 1 part-time/adjunct.
Students: 37 full-time (13 women), 24 international. Average age 27. 115 applicants, 50% accepted, 6 enrolled. In 2001, 12 master's, 3 doctorates awarded.
Degree requirements: For master's, exam, thesis optional; for doctorate, thesis/dissertation, final defense exam, comprehensive exam, registration. *Median time to degree:* Master's–2 years full-time; doctorate–4 years full-time.
Entrance requirements: For master's and doctorate, GRE General Test, TOEFL. *Application deadline:* For fall admission, 4/15; for winter admission, 10/1; for spring admission, 3/1. Applications are processed on a rolling basis. *Application fee:* $30 ($50 for international students). Electronic applications accepted.
Expenses: Tuition, state resident: full-time $3,702; part-time $206 per semester hour. Tuition, nonresident: full-time $11,924; part-time $206 per semester hour. Required fees: $101 per semester. Tuition and fees vary according to course load and program.
Financial support: In 2001–02, fellowships with tuition reimbursements (averaging $14,764 per year), 16 research assistantships (averaging $14,764 per year), 6 teaching assistantships (averaging $14,764 per year) were awarded. Career-related internships or fieldwork, scholarships/grants, and unspecified assistantships also available. Support available to part-time students. Financial award applicants required to submit FAFSA.
Faculty research: Informatics, industrial robotics, operations research, human-computer interfaces, human factors (ergonomics). *Total annual research expenditures:* $752,000.

Dr. Jeffrey S. Marshall, Departmental Executive Officer, 319-335-5817, *Fax:* 319-335-5669, *E-mail:* jeffrey-marshall@uiowa.edu.
Application contact: Sue Mulder, Secretary, 319-335-5939, *Fax:* 319-335-5669, *E-mail:* indeng@engineering.uiowa.edu. *Web site:* http://www.mie.engineering.uiowa.edu

■ UNIVERSITY OF MIAMI

Graduate School, College of Engineering, Department of Industrial Engineering, Coral Gables, FL 33124

AWARDS Environmental health and safety (MS, MSEVH, MSOES), including environmental health and safety (MS, MSEVH), occupational ergonomics and safety

University of Miami (continued)
(MSOES); ergonomics (PhD); industrial engineering (MSIE, PhD); management of technology (MS).

Faculty: 9 full-time (0 women), 3 part-time/adjunct (1 woman).
Students: 54 full-time (10 women); includes 16 minority (14 African Americans, 2 Hispanic Americans), 7 international. Average age 28. 79 applicants, 75% accepted. In 2001, 25 master's, 5 doctorates awarded.
Degree requirements: For master's, thesis (for some programs); for doctorate, thesis/dissertation.
Entrance requirements: For master's and doctorate, GRE General Test, TOEFL, minimum GPA of 3.0. *Application deadline:* For fall admission, 5/1 (priority date). Applications are processed on a rolling basis. *Application fee:* $50.
Expenses: Tuition: Part-time $960 per credit hour. Required fees: $85 per semester. Tuition and fees vary according to program.
Financial support: In 2001–02, 4 fellowships, 5 research assistantships, 4 teaching assistantships were awarded. Federal Work-Study also available. Financial award application deadline: 3/1; financial award applicants required to submit FAFSA.
Faculty research: Logistics, supply chain management, industrial applications of biomechanics and ergonomics, technology management, back pain, aging, operations research, manufacturing, safety, human reliability, energy assessment. *Total annual research expenditures:* $235,000.
Dr. Shihab S. Asfour, Chair, 305-284-2344, *Fax:* 305-284-4040, *E-mail:* sasfour@miami.edu.
Application contact: Dr. Eleftherios Iakovou, Associate Professor, Graduate Director, 305-284-2344, *Fax:* 305-284-4040. *Web site:* http://www.eng.miami.edu/.

■ WRIGHT STATE UNIVERSITY

School of Graduate Studies, College of Science and Mathematics, Department of Psychology, Program in Human Factors and Industrial/Organizational Psychology, Dayton, OH 45435

AWARDS MS, PhD.

Degree requirements: For master's and doctorate, thesis/dissertation.
Expenses: Tuition, state resident: full-time $7,161; part-time $225 per quarter hour. Tuition, nonresident: full-time $12,324; part-time $385 per quarter hour. Tuition and fees vary according to course load, degree level and program.
Dr. John M. Flach, Director, 937-775-2391, *Fax:* 937-775-3347, *E-mail:* john.flach@wright.edu.

MANAGEMENT OF TECHNOLOGY

■ AIR FORCE INSTITUTE OF TECHNOLOGY

School of Engineering and Management, Department of Operational Sciences, Dayton, OH 45433-7765

AWARDS Logistics management (MS); operations research (MS, PhD). Space operations (MS). Part-time programs available.

Degree requirements: For master's and doctorate, thesis/dissertation.
Entrance requirements: For doctorate, GRE General Test, minimum GPA of 3.0, must be U.S. citizen.
Faculty research: Optimization, simulation, combat modeling and analysis, reliability and maintainability, resource scheduling. *Web site:* http://en.afit.edu/ens/

■ ALLIANT INTERNATIONAL UNIVERSITY

United States International College of Business, San Francisco, CA 94109

AWARDS Business administration (MBA); information and technology management (DBA); international business (MIBA, DBA), including finance (DBA), marketing (DBA). Strategic business (DBA). Part-time and evening/weekend programs available.

Faculty: 14 full-time (5 women), 14 part-time/adjunct (6 women).
Students: 205. Terminal master's awarded for partial completion of doctoral program.
Degree requirements: For doctorate, thesis/dissertation.
Entrance requirements: For master's, GMAT, minimum GPA of 3.0; for doctorate, GMAT, minimum GPA of 3.3. *Application deadline:* For fall admission, 8/1 (priority date); for winter admission, 12/1 (priority date); for spring admission, 3/1 (priority date). Applications are processed on a rolling basis. *Application fee:* $40. Electronic applications accepted.
Expenses: Tuition: Part-time $397 per credit hour. Tuition and fees vary according to degree level, campus/location and program.
Financial support: Research assistantships, teaching assistantships, career-related internships or fieldwork, Federal Work-Study, institutionally sponsored loans, scholarships/grants, and tuition waivers (partial) available. Support available to part-time students. Financial award applicants required to submit FAFSA.
Faculty research: Cross-cultural management.
Dr. Mink H. Stavenga, Dean, 858-635-4695, *Fax:* 858-635-4528, *E-mail:* mstaveng@alliant.edu. *Web site:* http://www.alliant.edu

■ BENTLEY COLLEGE

The Elkin B. McCallum Graduate School of Business, Part-Time MBA Program, Waltham, MA 02452-4705

AWARDS Accountancy (MBA); advanced accountancy (MBA); business administration (Advanced Certificate); business communication (MBA); business data analysis (MBA, Certificate); business economics (MBA); business ethics (MBA, Certificate); e-business (MBA, Certificate); entrepreneurial studies (MBA); finance (MBA); international business (MBA); management (MBA); management information systems (MBA); management of technology (MBA); marketing (MBA); operations management (MBA); taxation (MBA). Part-time and evening/weekend programs available.

Faculty: 243 full-time (82 women), 179 part-time/adjunct (79 women).
Students: Average age 30. In 2001, 290 degrees awarded.
Entrance requirements: For master's, GMAT, TOEFL; for other advanced degree, MBA (Advanced Certificate). *Application deadline:* For fall admission, 6/1 (priority date); for spring admission, 11/1. Applications are processed on a rolling basis. *Application fee:* $50. Electronic applications accepted.
Expenses: Tuition: Full-time $18,640; part-time $777 per credit. Required fees: $100.
Financial support: In 2001–02, 182 students received support, including 32 research assistantships; career-related internships or fieldwork, Federal Work-Study, and unspecified assistantships also available. Support available to part-time students. Financial award application deadline: 4/15; financial award applicants required to submit CSS PROFILE or FAFSA.
Faculty research: Information technology for high-performance teams, electronic commerce, mergers and acquisitions, workforce diversity, accounting profession.
Dr. Judith B. Kamm, Director, 781-891-3433, *Fax:* 781-891-2464.
Application contact: Paul Vaccaro, Director of Graduate Admissions, 781-891-2108, *Fax:* 781-891-2464, *E-mail:* pvaccaro@bentley.edu.

Find an in-depth description at www.petersons.com/gradchannel.

■ BOSTON UNIVERSITY

Metropolitan College, Program in Administrative Studies, Boston, MA 02215

AWARDS Electronic commerce (MSAS); financial economics (MSAS); innovation and technology (MSAS); multinational commerce (MSAS). Part-time and evening/weekend programs available.

Faculty: 7 full-time (2 women), 25 part-time/adjunct (5 women).

Students: 105 full-time (39 women), 204 part-time (85 women); includes 32 minority (6 African Americans, 17 Asian Americans or Pacific Islanders, 8 Hispanic Americans, 1 Native American), 122 international. Average age 31.
Degree requirements: For master's, thesis optional.
Entrance requirements: For master's, TOEFL, 1 year of work experience. *Application deadline:* Applications are processed on a rolling basis. *Application fee:* $60.
Expenses: Tuition: Full-time $25,872; part-time $340 per credit. Required fees: $40 per semester. Part-time tuition and fees vary according to class time, course level and program.
Financial support: In 2001–02, 10 students received support; research assistantships, career-related internships or fieldwork and Federal Work-Study available.
Faculty research: International business, innovative process.
Dr. Kip Becker, Chairman, *E-mail:* adminsc@bu.edu.
Application contact: Department of Administrative Sciences, 617-353-3016, *Fax:* 617-353-6840, *E-mail:* adminsc@bu.edu. *Web site:* http://www.bu.edu/met/programs
Find an in-depth description at www.petersons.com/gradchannel.

■ BRIGHAM YOUNG UNIVERSITY

Graduate Studies, College of Engineering and Technology, School of Technology, Provo, UT 84602-1001

AWARDS Engineering technology (MS); technology teacher education (MS).

Faculty: 24 full-time (0 women).
Students: 11 full-time (0 women), 13 part-time; includes 1 minority (Asian American or Pacific Islander), 4 international. Average age 25. 15 applicants, 73% accepted. In 2001, 11 degrees awarded.
Degree requirements: For master's, thesis (for some programs).
Entrance requirements: For master's, GRE General Test, minimum GPA of 3.0 in last 60 hours. *Application deadline:* For fall admission, 2/28. *Application fee:* $50. Electronic applications accepted.
Expenses: Tuition: Full-time $3,860; part-time $214 per hour.
Financial support: In 2001–02, 18 students received support; fellowships, research assistantships, teaching assistantships, career-related internships or fieldwork available. Financial award application deadline: 3/15.
Faculty research: Composites, plasma treatment, geometric modeling, robotics, manufacturing control, product design.
Thomas L. Erekson, Director, 801-378-6300, *Fax:* 801-378-7575, *E-mail:* erekson@byu.edu.
Application contact: Graduate Coordinator, 801-378-6300, *Fax:* 801-378-7575,

E-mail: ralowe@byu.edu. *Web site:* http://www.et.byu.edu/abet-sot/

■ CALIFORNIA POLYTECHNIC STATE UNIVERSITY, SAN LUIS OBISPO

College of Engineering, Program in Engineering, San Luis Obispo, CA 93407

AWARDS Biochemical engineering (MS); industrial engineering (MS); integrated technology management (MS); materials engineering (MS); water engineering (MS), including bioengineering, biomedical engineering, manufacturing engineering.

Faculty: 98 full-time (8 women), 82 part-time/adjunct (14 women).
Students: 20 full-time (4 women), 9 part-time (1 woman). 25 applicants, 68% accepted, 15 enrolled. In 2001, 22 degrees awarded.
Entrance requirements: For master's, GRE General Test, minimum GPA of 2.5 in last 90 quarter units. *Application fee:* $55.
Expenses: Tuition, nonresident: part-time $164 per unit. One-time fee: $2,153 part-time.
Financial support: Application deadline: 3/2.
Dr. Peter Y. Lee, Dean, 805-756-2131, *Fax:* 805-756-6503, *E-mail:* plee@calpoly.edu.
Application contact: Dr. Daniel W. Walsh, Associate Dean, 805-756-2131, *Fax:* 805-756-6503, *E-mail:* dwalsh@calpoly.edu. *Web site:* http://www.synner.ceng.calpoly.edu/

■ CARLOW COLLEGE

Division of Management, Pittsburgh, PA 15213-3165

AWARDS Management and technology (MS). Part-time and evening/weekend programs available.

Faculty: 4 full-time (3 women), 3 part-time/adjunct (1 woman).
Students: 2 full-time (both women), 66 part-time (57 women); includes 15 minority (all African Americans). Average age 38. 25 applicants, 92% accepted, 18 enrolled. In 2001, 6 degrees awarded.
Degree requirements: For master's, strategic planning II, capstone experience.
Entrance requirements: For master's, interview, minimum GPA of 3.0, 2 years of professional experience, resumé. *Application deadline:* For fall admission, 6/15 (priority date); for spring admission, 11/15 (priority date). Applications are processed on a rolling basis. *Application fee:* $35.
Expenses: Tuition: Part-time $444 per credit. Required fees: $27 per credit.
Financial support: In 2001–02, 11 students received support. Federal Work-Study and scholarships/grants available. Support available to part-time students. Financial award application deadline: 4/3.

Faculty research: Learning styles and distance learning, women and distance learning, women and organizational behavior.
Dr. Mary Rothenberger, Chair, 412-578-6181, *Fax:* 412-587-6367, *E-mail:* mrothenberger@carlow.edu.
Application contact: Maggie Golofski, Secretary, Graduate Studies, 412-578-8764, *Fax:* 412-578-8822, *E-mail:* mgolofski@carlow.edu. *Web site:* http://www.carlow.edu/

■ CARNEGIE MELLON UNIVERSITY

Graduate School of Industrial Administration, Program in Management of Manufacturing and Automation, Pittsburgh, PA 15213-3891

AWARDS Industrial administration (PhD); manufacturing (MOM).

Degree requirements: For doctorate, thesis/dissertation.
Entrance requirements: For master's, GMAT. *Web site:* http://www.gsia.cmu.edu/

■ CENTRAL CONNECTICUT STATE UNIVERSITY

School of Graduate Studies, School of Technology, Department of Construction Management, Technology Management, New Britain, CT 06050-4010

AWARDS MS. Part-time and evening/weekend programs available.

Students: 7 full-time (2 women), 51 part-time (14 women); includes 8 minority (5 African Americans, 1 Asian American or Pacific Islander, 2 Hispanic Americans). Average age 35. 20 applicants, 85% accepted. In 2001, 19 degrees awarded.
Degree requirements: For master's, comprehensive exam.
Entrance requirements: For master's, TOEFL, minimum GPA of 2.7. *Application deadline:* For fall admission, 8/10 (priority date); for spring admission, 12/10. Applications are processed on a rolling basis. *Application fee:* $40.
Expenses: Tuition, state resident: full-time $2,772; part-time $245 per credit. Tuition, nonresident: full-time $7,726; part-time $245 per credit. Required fees: $2,102. Tuition and fees vary according to course level and degree level.
Financial support: Research assistantships, Federal Work-Study available. Financial award application deadline: 3/15; financial award applicants required to submit FAFSA.
Faculty research: All aspects of middle management, technical supervision in the workplace.
Dr. Paul Resetarits, Coordinator, 860-832-1831.

■ CHAMPLAIN COLLEGE

Program in Managing Innovation and Information Technology, Burlington, VT 05402-0670

AWARDS MS.

Entrance requirements: For master's, at least 2 years experience or equivalent demonstrable competencies in a business environment.

Find an in-depth description at www.petersons.com/gradchannel.

■ COLORADO SCHOOL OF MINES

Graduate School, Division of Economics and Business, Golden, CO 80401-1887

AWARDS Engineering and technology management (MS); mineral economics (MS, PhD). Part-time programs available.

Faculty: 13 full-time (2 women), 13 part-time/adjunct (5 women).
Students: 58 full-time (11 women), 27 part-time (5 women); includes 6 minority (2 African Americans, 2 Asian Americans or Pacific Islanders, 2 Hispanic Americans), 37 international. 114 applicants, 94% accepted, 30 enrolled. In 2001, 31 master's, 2 doctorates awarded.
Degree requirements: For doctorate, thesis/dissertation, comprehensive exam. *Median time to degree:* Master's–2 years full-time; doctorate–4 years full-time.
Entrance requirements: For master's and doctorate, GRE General Test. *Application deadline:* For fall admission, 12/1 (priority date); for spring admission, 5/1 (priority date). Applications are processed on a rolling basis. *Application fee:* $40. Electronic applications accepted.
Expenses: Tuition, state resident: full-time $4,940; part-time $246 per credit. Tuition, nonresident: full-time $16,070; part-time $803 per credit. Required fees: $341 per semester.
Financial support: In 2001–02, 32 students received support, including 5 fellowships (averaging $6,471 per year), 4 research assistantships (averaging $7,793 per year), 31 teaching assistantships (averaging $5,232 per year); unspecified assistantships also available. Support available to part-time students. Financial award applicants required to submit FAFSA.
Faculty research: International trade, resource and environmental economics, energy economics, operations research. *Total annual research expenditures:* $45,408.
Dr. Roderick G. Eggert, Head, 303-273-3981, *Fax:* 303-273-3416, *E-mail:* reggert@mines.edu.
Application contact: Kathleen A. Feighny, Administrative Faculty, 303-273-3979, *Fax:* 303-273-3416, *E-mail:* kfeighny@mines.edu. *Web site:* http://www.mines.edu/academic/econbus/

■ COLORADO STATE UNIVERSITY

Graduate School, College of Applied Human Sciences, Department of Manufacturing Technology and Construction Management, Fort Collins, CO 80523-0015

AWARDS Automotive pollution control (MS); construction management (MS); historic preservation (MS); industrial technology management (MS); technology education and training (MS); technology of industry (PhD). Part-time and evening/weekend programs available.

Faculty: 11 full-time (0 women).
Students: 16 full-time (5 women), 27 part-time (10 women); includes 2 minority (1 African American, 1 Hispanic American), 1 international. Average age 31. 57 applicants, 98% accepted, 9 enrolled. Terminal master's awarded for partial completion of doctoral program.
Degree requirements: For master's, thesis (for some programs); for doctorate, thesis/dissertation.
Entrance requirements: For master's and doctorate, GRE General Test, TOEFL. *Application deadline:* For fall admission, 4/1 (priority date); for spring admission, 9/1 (priority date). Applications are processed on a rolling basis. *Application fee:* $30. Electronic applications accepted.
Expenses: Tuition, state resident: full-time $2,880; part-time $160 per credit. Tuition, nonresident: full-time $11,412; part-time $634 per credit. Required fees: $750; $34 per credit.
Financial support: In 2001–02, 1 fellowship with full tuition reimbursement (averaging $12,960 per year), 3 research assistantships with full tuition reimbursements (averaging $9,720 per year), 8 teaching assistantships with full tuition reimbursements (averaging $9,720 per year) were awarded. Career-related internships or fieldwork, Federal Work-Study, and traineeships also available.
Faculty research: Construction processes, historical preservation, sustainability, technology education. *Total annual research expenditures:* $800,000.
Dr. Larry Grosse, Head, 970-491-7958, *Fax:* 970-491-2473, *E-mail:* drfire107@mindspring.com.
Application contact: Becky Bell, Graduate Liaison, 970-491-7355, *Fax:* 970-491-2473, *E-mail:* becky.bell@cahs.colostate.edu. *Web site:* http://www.cahs.colostate.edu/DIS/

■ DALLAS BAPTIST UNIVERSITY

College of Business, Business Administration Program, Dallas, TX 75211-9299

AWARDS Accounting (MBA); E. business (MBA); finance (MBA); health care management (MBA); international business (MBA); management (MBA); management information systems (MBA); marketing (MBA); technology

and engineering management (MBA). Part-time and evening/weekend programs available. Postbaccalaureate distance learning degree programs offered (no on-campus study).

Faculty: 14 full-time (5 women), 31 part-time/adjunct (10 women).
Students: 388 (187 women). 196 applicants, 66% accepted, 54 enrolled. In 2001, 86 degrees awarded.
Entrance requirements: For master's, GMAT, TOEFL, minimum GPA of 3.0. *Application deadline:* Applications are processed on a rolling basis. *Application fee:* $25. Electronic applications accepted.
Expenses: Tuition: Full-time $6,030; part-time $335 per credit.
Financial support: Career-related internships or fieldwork, Federal Work-Study, institutionally sponsored loans, scholarships/grants, and tuition waivers (full and partial) available. Support available to part-time students.
Faculty research: Sports management, services marketing, retailing, strategic management, financial planning/investments.
Barbara Sleeper, Director of MBA Program, 214-333-5280, *Fax:* 214-333-5579, *E-mail:* graduate@dbu.edu.
Application contact: Sarah R. Brancaccio, Director of Graduate Programs, 214-333-5243, *Fax:* 214-333-5579, *E-mail:* graduate@dbu.edu. *Web site:* http://www.dbu.edu

■ EMBRY-RIDDLE AERONAUTICAL UNIVERSITY, EXTENDED CAMPUS

Graduate Resident Centers, Program in Technical Management, Daytona Beach, FL 32114-3900

AWARDS MSTM. Part-time and evening/weekend programs available. Postbaccalaureate distance learning degree programs offered.

Faculty: 4 full-time (0 women), 10 part-time/adjunct (4 women).
Students: 21 full-time (7 women), 159 part-time (42 women); includes 32 minority (18 African Americans, 5 Asian Americans or Pacific Islanders, 7 Hispanic Americans, 2 Native Americans), 1 international. Average age 39. 59 applicants, 88% accepted, 11 enrolled. In 2001, 156 degrees awarded.
Degree requirements: For master's, thesis optional.
Entrance requirements: For master's, GMAT. *Application deadline:* Applications are processed on a rolling basis. *Application fee:* $30 ($50 for international students). Electronic applications accepted.
Expenses: Tuition: Full-time $5,880; part-time $245 per credit.
Dr. Wayne Harsha, Program Chair, 512-659-0801, *E-mail:* harshaw@erau.edu.

Application contact: Pam Thomas, Director of Admissions and Records, 386-226-6910, *Fax:* 386-226-6984, *E-mail:* ecinfo@erau.edu.

Find an in-depth description at www.petersons.com/gradchannel.

■ FAIRFIELD UNIVERSITY

School of Engineering, Fairfield, CT 06824

AWARDS Management of technology (MS). Software engineering (MS). Part-time and evening/weekend programs available.

Faculty: 2 full-time (0 women), 16 part-time/adjunct (2 women).
Students: 9 full-time (2 women), 215 part-time (43 women); includes 35 minority (8 African Americans, 21 Asian Americans or Pacific Islanders, 6 Hispanic Americans), 39 international. 53 applicants, 100% accepted, 42 enrolled. In 2001, 47 degrees awarded.
Degree requirements: For master's, thesis, final exam.
Entrance requirements: For master's, interview, minimum GPA of 2.8. *Application deadline:* For fall admission, 6/30 (priority date). Applications are processed on a rolling basis. *Application fee:* $55.
Expenses: Contact institution.
Financial support: Tuition waivers (partial) available. Financial award applicants required to submit FAFSA.
Faculty research: Vehicle dynamics, image processing, digital signal processing, modeling, multimedia.
Dr. Evangelos Hadjimichael, Dean, 203-254-4000 Ext. 4147, *Fax:* 203-254-4013, *E-mail:* hadjm@fair1.fairfield.edu.
Application contact: Dr. Richard G. Weber, Associate Dean, 203-254-4000 Ext. 4147, *Fax:* 203-254-4013, *E-mail:* rweber@fair1.fairfield.edu. *Web site:* http://www.fairfield.edu/

Find an in-depth description at www.petersons.com/gradchannel.

■ GEORGE MASON UNIVERSITY

School of Management, Program in Technology Management, Fairfax, VA 22030-4444

AWARDS MS.

Faculty: 56 full-time (21 women), 36 part-time/adjunct (7 women).
Students: Average age 34. In 2001, 17 degrees awarded.
Entrance requirements: For master's, GMAT, TOEFL. *Application deadline:* For fall admission, 5/1; for spring admission, 11/1. Applications are processed on a rolling basis. *Application fee:* $30. Electronic applications accepted.
Expenses: Tuition, state resident: full-time $3,168; part-time $132 per credit hour. Tuition, nonresident: full-time $11,280; part-time $470 per credit hour. Required fees: $1,416; $59 per credit hour.

Financial support: Application deadline: 3/1.
Dr. Andres Fortino, Director, 703-993-1872, *Fax:* 703-993-1867, *E-mail:* masonmba@som.gmu.edu. *Web site:* http://www.som.gmu.edu/

■ GEORGE MASON UNIVERSITY

School of Public Policy, Program in Public Policy, Fairfax, VA 22030-4444

AWARDS MSNPS, PhD. Terminal master's awarded for partial completion of doctoral program.

Degree requirements: For master's, thesis or alternative; for doctorate, thesis/dissertation, comprehensive exam.
Entrance requirements: For master's, minimum GPA of 3.0 in last 60 hours; for doctorate, GMAT or GRE General Test, minimum GPA of 3.0 in last 60 hours, resumé, sample of written work.
Expenses: Tuition, state resident: full-time $3,168; part-time $132 per credit hour. Tuition, nonresident: full-time $11,280; part-time $470 per credit hour. Required fees: $1,416; $59 per credit hour. *Web site:* http://www.gmu.edu/departments/tipp

Find an in-depth description at www.petersons.com/gradchannel.

■ GEORGE MASON UNIVERSITY

School of Public Policy, Program in Social and Organizational Learning, Fairfax, VA 22030-4444

AWARDS Organizational learning (MSNPS).

Degree requirements: For master's, thesis or alternative.
Entrance requirements: For master's, minimum GPA of 3.0 in last 60 hours.
Expenses: Tuition, state resident: full-time $3,168; part-time $132 per credit hour. Tuition, nonresident: full-time $11,280; part-time $470 per credit hour. Required fees: $1,416; $59 per credit hour.

■ THE GEORGE WASHINGTON UNIVERSITY

School of Business and Public Management, Full Time MBA Program, Department of Management Science, Washington, DC 20052

AWARDS Human resources management (MBA); information systems management (MBA); logistics, operations, and materials management (MBA); management and organizations (PhD); management decision making (MBA, PhD); management information systems technology (MSIST); management of science, technology, and innovation (MBA); organizational behavior and development (MBA); project management (MS). Part-time and evening/weekend programs available.

Faculty: 33 full-time (2 women), 26 part-time/adjunct (5 women).
Students: 191 full-time (80 women), 561 part-time (225 women); includes 178

minority (74 African Americans, 81 Asian Americans or Pacific Islanders, 22 Hispanic Americans, 1 Native American), 138 international. Average age 34. 512 applicants, 66% accepted. In 2001, 326 master's, 7 doctorates awarded.
Degree requirements: For doctorate, thesis/dissertation.
Entrance requirements: For master's, GMAT, TOEFL; for doctorate, GMAT or GRE, TOEFL. *Application deadline:* For fall admission, 4/1 (priority date); for spring admission, 10/1. Applications are processed on a rolling basis. *Application fee:* $55.
Expenses: Tuition: Part-time $810 per credit. Required fees: $1 per credit.
Financial support: In 2001–02, 46 fellowships (averaging $2,500 per year), 42 teaching assistantships (averaging $3,200 per year) were awarded. Career-related internships or fieldwork, Federal Work-Study, and institutionally sponsored loans also available. Financial award application deadline: 4/1.
Faculty research: Artificial intelligence, technological entrepreneurship, expert systems, strategic planning/management. Dr. Erik K. Winslow, Chair, 202-994-6447.
Application contact: David Toomer, Director Enrollment Management, 202-994-6584, *Fax:* 202-994-6382. *Web site:* http://www.gwu.edu/~gradinfo/

■ GEORGIA INSTITUTE OF TECHNOLOGY

Graduate Studies and Research, Dupree College of Management, Program in Management of Technology, Atlanta, GA 30332-0001

AWARDS MSMOT. Part-time and evening/weekend programs available.

Degree requirements: For master's, study abroad.
Entrance requirements: For master's, GMAT, TOEFL, 5 years of professional work experience. Electronic applications accepted.
Expenses: Contact institution.
Faculty research: Innovation management, technology analysis, operations management. *Web site:* http://www.iac.gatech.edu/~mot/mot.html

■ IDAHO STATE UNIVERSITY

Office of Graduate Studies, College of Technology, Department of Human Resource Training and Development, Pocatello, ID 83209

AWARDS Industrial training management (M Ed); training and development (MTD); vocational program management (M Ed).

Faculty: 4 full-time (0 women).
Students: 27 full-time (15 women), 56 part-time (31 women); includes 6 minority (1 African American, 4 Hispanic

Idaho State University (continued)
Americans, 1 Native American), 3 international. In 2001, 20 degrees awarded. *Application fee:* $35.
Expenses: Tuition, area resident: Full-time $3,432. Tuition, state resident: part-time $172 per credit. Tuition, nonresident: full-time $10,196; part-time $262 per credit. International tuition: $9,672 full-time. Part-time tuition and fees vary according to course load, program and reciprocity agreements.
Financial support: In 2001–02, 1 teaching assistantship with full and partial tuition reimbursement (averaging $8,117 per year) was awarded *Total annual research expenditures:* $1.9 million.
Dr. Robert Croker, Chair, 208-282-2884.

■ **ILLINOIS INSTITUTE OF TECHNOLOGY**
Stuart Graduate School of Business, Program in Operations and Technology Management, Chicago, IL 60616-3793
AWARDS MS. Part-time and evening/weekend programs available.
Students: Average age 37. 22 applicants, 77% accepted. In 2001, 10 degrees awarded.
Entrance requirements: For master's, GMAT or GRE, TOEFL. *Application deadline:* For fall admission, 8/1; for spring admission, 4/15. Applications are processed on a rolling basis. *Application fee:* $50. Electronic applications accepted.
Expenses: Tuition: Part-time $590 per credit hour.
Financial support: Institutionally sponsored loans, scholarships/grants, and unspecified assistantships available. Support available to part-time students. Financial award applicants required to submit FAFSA.
Kenneth Gibson, Director, 312-906-6557, *Fax:* 312-906-6549, *E-mail:* gibson@itt.edu.
Application contact: Lynn Miller, Director, Admission, 312-906-6544, *Fax:* 312-906-6549, *E-mail:* degrees@stuart.itt.edu.

■ **IONA COLLEGE**
Hagan School of Business, Department of Information and Decision Technology Management, New Rochelle, NY 10801-1890
AWARDS MBA, PMC. Part-time and evening/weekend programs available.
Faculty: 6 full-time (0 women), 2 part-time/adjunct (both women).
Students: 2 full-time (1 woman), 25 part-time (9 women); includes 2 minority (1 Asian American or Pacific Islander, 1 Hispanic American). Average age 29. In 2001, 17 master's, 1 other advanced degree awarded.

Entrance requirements: For master's and PMC, GMAT. *Application deadline:* Applications are processed on a rolling basis. *Application fee:* $50.
Expenses: Tuition: Part-time $525 per credit.
Financial support: Tuition waivers (partial) and unspecified assistantships available. Support available to part-time students.
Faculty research: Fuzzy sets, risk management, computer security, competence set analysis, investment strategies.
Dr. Donald Moscato, Chairman, 914-633-2555.
Application contact: Tara Feller, Director of MBA Admissions, 914-633-2288, *Fax:* 914-633-2012, *E-mail:* tfeller@iona.edu. *Web site:* http://www.iona.edu.hagan/

■ **JONES INTERNATIONAL UNIVERSITY**
Graduate School of Business and e-Learning, Englewood, CO 80112
AWARDS Business communication (MA, MBA); electric commerce (MBA); entrepreneurship (MBA); global enterprise management (MBA); health care management (MBA); information technology management (MBA); negotiation and conflict management (MBA); project management (MBA). Program offered through the Internet only. Postbaccalaureate distance learning degree programs offered (no on-campus study).
Degree requirements: For master's, one foreign language.
Expenses: Tuition: Part-time $925 per course. *Web site:* http://www.jonesinternational.edu/
Find an in-depth description at www.petersons.com/gradchannel.

■ **LA SALLE UNIVERSITY**
Business Administration Program, Philadelphia, PA 19141-1199
AWARDS Business administration (MBA, Certificate); global management of technology (MS). Part-time and evening/weekend programs available.
Faculty: 27 full-time (7 women), 15 part-time/adjunct (1 woman).
Students: 69 full-time (19 women), 504 part-time (208 women); includes 63 minority (38 African Americans, 14 Asian Americans or Pacific Islanders, 9 Hispanic Americans, 2 Native Americans), 2 international. Average age 33. 285 applicants, 59% accepted, 110 enrolled. In 2001, 211 degrees awarded.
Entrance requirements: For master's, GMAT, TOEFL; for Certificate, MBA. *Application deadline:* For fall admission, 8/30 (priority date); for spring admission, 1/10. Applications are processed on a rolling basis. *Application fee:* $30. Electronic applications accepted.
Expenses: Contact institution.

Financial support: In 2001–02, 10 students received support. Career-related internships or fieldwork and scholarships/grants available. Financial award application deadline: 8/15.
Faculty research: Small business development, unemployment insurance costs, nonprofit business, transfer pricing, forecasting.
Joseph Y. Ugras, Associate Dean, 215-951-1057, *Fax:* 215-951-1886, *E-mail:* ugras@lasalle.edu.
Application contact: Paul J. Reilly, Director of Marketing/Graduate Enrollment, 215-951-1946, *Fax:* 215-951-1886, *E-mail:* reilly@lasalle.edu. *Web site:* http://www.lasalle.edu/mba.htm

■ **LA SALLE UNIVERSITY**
School of Arts and Sciences, Program in Computer Information Science, Philadelphia, PA 19141-1199
AWARDS Computer information science (MS); information technology leadership (MS). Part-time and evening/weekend programs available.
Faculty: 8 full-time (3 women), 2 part-time/adjunct (0 women).
Students: 1 full-time (0 women), 87 part-time (31 women); includes 12 minority (5 African Americans, 7 Asian Americans or Pacific Islanders), 3 international. Average age 35. 44 applicants, 27% accepted, 11 enrolled. In 2001, 24 degrees awarded.
Entrance requirements: For master's, GRE or MAT, 18 undergraduate credits in computer science, professional experience. *Application deadline:* Applications are processed on a rolling basis. *Application fee:* $30.
Expenses: Contact institution.
Financial support: Institutionally sponsored loans and scholarships/grants available. Support available to part-time students. Financial award application deadline: 7/15; financial award applicants required to submit FAFSA.
Faculty research: Human-computer interaction, networks, technology trends, databases, groupware.
Dr. Linda Elliot, Director, 215-951-1133, *Fax:* 215-951-1805, *E-mail:* macis@lasalle.edu. *Web site:* http://www.lasalle.edu/academ/grad/

■ **MARQUETTE UNIVERSITY**
Graduate School, College of Engineering, Department of Biomedical Engineering, Milwaukee, WI 53201-1881
AWARDS Bioinstrumentation/computers (MS, PhD); biomechanics/biomaterials (MS, PhD); functional imaging (PhD); healthcare technologies management (MS). Systems physiology (MS, PhD). Part-time and evening/weekend programs available.
Faculty: 16 full-time (2 women), 39 part-time/adjunct (6 women).

Students: 41 full-time (13 women), 25 part-time (6 women); includes 7 minority (6 Asian Americans or Pacific Islanders, 1 Hispanic American), 8 international. 61 applicants, 75% accepted. In 2001, 12 master's, 1 doctorate awarded. Terminal master's awarded for partial completion of doctoral program.
Degree requirements: For master's, thesis, comprehensive exam; for doctorate, dissertation defense, qualifying exam.
Entrance requirements: For master's and doctorate, GRE General Test, TOEFL. *Application deadline:* For fall admission, 2/15 (priority date); for spring admission, 11/15 (priority date). Applications are processed on a rolling basis. *Application fee:* $40. Electronic applications accepted.
Expenses: Tuition: Full-time $10,170; part-time $445 per credit hour. Tuition and fees vary according to course load.
Financial support: In 2001–02, 12 fellowships with full tuition reimbursements, 14 research assistantships with full tuition reimbursements, 6 teaching assistantships with full tuition reimbursements were awarded. Scholarships/grants also available. Financial award application deadline: 2/15.
Faculty research: Cell and organ physiology, signal processing, gait analysis, orthopedic rehabilitation engineering, telemedicine. *Total annual research expenditures:* $3.6 million.
Dr. John M. Winters, Chair, 414-288-3375, *Fax:* 414-288-7938, *E-mail:* jack.winters@marquette.edu.
Application contact: Brigid J. Lagerman, Assistant Chair, 414-288-7856, *Fax:* 414-288-7938, *E-mail:* brigid.lagerman@marquette.edu. *Web site:* http://www.eng.mu.edu/bien/

Find an in-depth description at www.petersons.com/gradchannel.

■ MARSHALL UNIVERSITY

Graduate College, College of Information, Technology and Engineering, Division of Information Systems and Technology Management, Program in Technology Management, Huntington, WV 25755

AWARDS MS. Part-time and evening/weekend programs available.

Students: 4 full-time (0 women), 30 part-time (7 women); includes 2 minority (1 African American, 1 Native American), 2 international. Average age 40. In 2001, 12 degrees awarded.
Degree requirements: For master's, final project, oral exam.
Entrance requirements: For master's, GRE General Test or GMAT, minimum undergraduate GPA of 2.5.
Expenses: Tuition, state resident: part-time $147 per credit. Tuition, nonresident: part-time $468 per credit. Tuition and fees vary according to campus/location and reciprocity agreements.
Financial support: Tuition waivers (full) available. Support available to part-time

students. Financial award application deadline: 8/1; financial award applicants required to submit FAFSA.
Dr. Bernard Gillispie, Director, 304-696-6007, *E-mail:* gillespb@marshall.edu.
Application contact: Ken O'Neal, Assistant Vice President, Adult Student Services, 304-746-2500 Ext. 1907, *Fax:* 304-746-1902, *E-mail:* oneal@marshall.edu.

■ MERCER UNIVERSITY

Graduate Studies, Cecil B. Day Campus, Stetson School of Business and Economics, Macon, GA 31207-0003

AWARDS Business administration (MBA, XMBA); health care management (MS); technology management (MS). Part-time and evening/weekend programs available.

Faculty: 24 full-time (8 women), 7 part-time/adjunct (1 woman).
Students: 229 full-time (111 women), 224 part-time (110 women); includes 167 minority (135 African Americans, 23 Asian Americans or Pacific Islanders, 9 Hispanic Americans), 69 international. Average age 31. 193 applicants, 87% accepted, 121 enrolled. In 2001, 175 degrees awarded.
Degree requirements: For master's, oral exam (health care management).
Entrance requirements: For master's, GMAT. *Application deadline:* For fall admission, 7/1 (priority date); for spring admission, 11/1 (priority date). Applications are processed on a rolling basis. *Application fee:* $35 ($50 for international students).
Expenses: Tuition: Part-time $228 per credit hour. Tuition and fees vary according to degree level, campus/location and program.
Financial support: Federal Work-Study available.
Faculty research: Entrepreneurship, market studies, international business strategy, financial analysis.
Dr. W. Carl Joiner, Dean, 478-301-2832, *Fax:* 478-301-2635, *E-mail:* joiner_wc@mercer.edu.
Application contact: Dr. Argy S, Russell, Director, 678-547-6417, *Fax:* 678-547-6367, *E-mail:* russell_a@mercer.edu. *Web site:* http://www.mercer.edu/ssbe/

■ MERCER UNIVERSITY

Graduate Studies, Macon Campus, School of Engineering, Macon, GA 31207-0003

AWARDS Biomedical engineering (MSE); electrical engineering (MSE); engineering management (MSE); mechanical engineering (MSE). Software engineering (MSE). Software systems (MS); technical communications management (MS); technical management (MS). Part-time and evening/weekend programs available.

Faculty: 10 full-time (1 woman), 5 part-time/adjunct (1 woman).

Students: 3 full-time (2 women), 104 part-time (31 women); includes 19 minority (13 African Americans, 6 Asian Americans or Pacific Islanders), 5 international. Average age 36. 31 applicants, 97% accepted, 27 enrolled. In 2001, 32 degrees awarded.
Degree requirements: For master's, thesis or alternative, registration.
Entrance requirements: For master's, GRE, minimum undergraduate GPA of 3.0. *Application deadline:* For fall admission, 7/1; for spring admission, 11/15. Applications are processed on a rolling basis. *Application fee:* $35 ($50 for international students).
Expenses: Contact institution.
Financial support: Federal Work-Study available.
Dr. M. Dayne Aldridge, Dean, 478-301-2459, *Fax:* 478-301-5593, *E-mail:* aldridge_md@mercer.edu.
Application contact: Kathy Olivier, Graduate Administrative Coordinator, 478-301-2196, *E-mail:* olivier_kk@mercer.edu. *Web site:* http://www.mercer.edu/engineer.htm

■ MURRAY STATE UNIVERSITY

College of Science, Engineering and Technology, Department of Industrial and Engineering Technology, Murray, KY 42071-0009

AWARDS Management of technology (MS). Part-time programs available.

Students: 52 full-time (21 women), 36 part-time (9 women); includes 13 minority (7 African Americans, 1 Asian American or Pacific Islander, 5 Hispanic Americans), 40 international. 35 applicants, 100% accepted. In 2001, 40 degrees awarded.
Entrance requirements: For master's, GRE General Test, TOEFL. *Application deadline:* Applications are processed on a rolling basis. *Application fee:* $25.
Expenses: Tuition, state resident: full-time $1,440; part-time $169 per hour. Tuition, nonresident: full-time $4,004; part-time $450 per hour.
Financial support: Research assistantships, teaching assistantships, Federal Work-Study available. Financial award application deadline: 4/1.
Dr. Dan Claiborne, Chairman, 270-762-6910, *Fax:* 270-762-6916, *E-mail:* danny.claiborne@murraystate.edu.

■ NATIONAL TECHNOLOGICAL UNIVERSITY

Programs in Engineering, Fort Collins, CO 80526-1842

AWARDS Chemical engineering (MS); computer engineering (MS); computer science (MS); electrical engineering (MS); engineering management (MS); environmental systems management (MS); management of technology (MS); manufacturing systems engineering (MS); materials science and engineering (MS); mechanical engineering

National Technological University (continued)

(MS); microelectronics and semiconductor engineering (MS). Software engineering (MS). Special majors (MS). Systems engineering (MS). Part-time programs available. Postbaccalaureate distance learning degree programs offered (no on-campus study).

Students: In 2001, 114 degrees awarded. **Degree requirements:** For master's, comprehensive exam. **Entrance requirements:** For master's, BS in engineering or related field; 2.9 minimum GPA. *Application deadline:* Applications are processed on a rolling basis. *Application fee:* $50. Electronic applications accepted. **Expenses:** Tuition: Part-time $660 per credit hour. Part-time tuition and fees vary according to course load, campus/location and program.
Dr. Andre Vacroux, President, 970-495-6400, *Fax:* 970-484-0668, *E-mail:* andre@ntu.edu.
Application contact: Rhonda Bonham, Admissions Officer, 970-495-6400, *Fax:* 970-498-0601, *E-mail:* rhonda@ntu.edu. *Web site:* http://www.ntu.edu/

■ NATIONAL UNIVERSITY

Academic Affairs, School of Business and Technology, Department of Technology, La Jolla, CA 92037-1011

AWARDS Biotechnology (MBA); electronic commerce (MBA, MS); environmental management (MBA). Software engineering (MS). Space commerce (MBA); technology management (MBA, MS); telecommunications systems management (MS). Part-time and evening/weekend programs available. Postbaccalaureate distance learning degree programs offered (minimal on-campus study).

Faculty: 9 full-time (0 women), 148 part-time/adjunct (20 women).
Students: 349 full-time (108 women), 130 part-time (44 women); includes 145 minority (45 African Americans, 76 Asian Americans or Pacific Islanders, 21 Hispanic Americans, 3 Native Americans), 138 international. 82 applicants, 100% accepted. In 2001, 250 degrees awarded. **Entrance requirements:** For master's, interview, minimum GPA of 2.5. *Application deadline:* Applications are processed on a rolling basis. *Application fee:* $60 ($100 for international students). **Expenses:** Tuition: Part-time $221 per quarter hour. **Financial support:** Institutionally sponsored loans, scholarships/grants, and tuition waivers (full and partial) available. Support available to part-time students. Financial award application deadline: 5/1; financial award applicants required to submit FAFSA.
Dr. Leonid Preiser, Chair, 858-642-8425, *Fax:* 858-642-8716, *E-mail:* lpreiser@nu.edu.

Application contact: Nancy Rohland, Director of Enrollment Management, 858-642-8180, *Fax:* 858-642-8710, *E-mail:* advisor@nu.edu. *Web site:* http://www.nu.edu/

■ NEW JERSEY INSTITUTE OF TECHNOLOGY

Office of Graduate Studies, School of Management, Program in Management of Technology, Newark, NJ 07102

AWARDS MS, PhD. Part-time and evening/weekend programs available.

Students: 53 full-time (20 women), 100 part-time (26 women); includes 35 minority (16 African Americans, 11 Asian Americans or Pacific Islanders, 8 Hispanic Americans), 24 international. Average age 34. 171 applicants, 47% accepted, 51 enrolled. In 2001, 33 degrees awarded. Terminal master's awarded for partial completion of doctoral program. **Degree requirements:** For master's, thesis optional; for doctorate, thesis/dissertation. **Entrance requirements:** For doctorate, GRE General Test, minimum GPA of 3.5. *Application deadline:* For fall admission, 6/5; for spring admission, 10/15. Applications are processed on a rolling basis. *Application fee:* $50. Electronic applications accepted. **Expenses:** Tuition, state resident: full-time $7,812; part-time $434 per credit. Tuition, nonresident: full-time $10,746; part-time $597 per credit. Required fees: $47 per credit. $76 per semester. **Financial support:** Fellowships with full and partial tuition reimbursements, research assistantships with full and partial tuition reimbursements, teaching assistantships with full and partial tuition reimbursements, career-related internships or fieldwork, Federal Work-Study, institutionally sponsored loans, and unspecified assistantships available. Financial award application deadline: 3/15; financial award applicants required to submit FAFSA.
Application contact: Kathryn Kelly, Director of Admissions, 973-596-3300, *Fax:* 973-596-3461, *E-mail:* admissions@njit.edu. *Web site:* http://www.njit.edu/

■ NEW YORK UNIVERSITY

The Steinhardt School of Education, Department of Culture and Communication, Program in Graphic Communications Management and Technology, New York, NY 10012-1019

AWARDS Administration and management of technology and industry oriented programs (MA, Ed D, PhD, Advanced Certificate); graphic communications management and technology (MA). Part-time and evening/weekend programs available.

Faculty: 2 full-time (1 woman).

Students: 29 full-time (19 women), 41 part-time (22 women); includes 13 minority (6 African Americans, 7 Asian Americans or Pacific Islanders). 32 applicants, 91% accepted, 19 enrolled. In 2001, 19 master's, 1 doctorate awarded. Terminal master's awarded for partial completion of doctoral program. **Degree requirements:** For master's, thesis (for some programs); for doctorate, thesis/dissertation. **Entrance requirements:** For master's, TOEFL; for doctorate, GRE General Test, TOEFL, interview. *Application deadline:* For fall admission, 2/1 (priority date); for spring admission, 12/1. Applications are processed on a rolling basis. *Application fee:* $40 ($60 for international students). **Expenses:** Tuition: Full-time $19,536; part-time $814 per credit. Required fees: $1,330; $38 per credit. Tuition and fees vary according to course load and program. **Financial support:** Career-related internships or fieldwork, Federal Work-Study, institutionally sponsored loans, scholarships/grants, and tuition waivers (partial) available. Support available to part-time students. Financial award application deadline: 3/1; financial award applicants required to submit FAFSA. **Faculty research:** Production operations management and marketing, human resources and quality management.
Gregory D'Amico, Director, 212-998-5126, *Fax:* 212-995-4046.
Application contact: 212-998-5030, *Fax:* 212-995-4328, *E-mail:* grad.admissions@nyu.edu.

■ NORTH CAROLINA AGRICULTURAL AND TECHNICAL STATE UNIVERSITY

Graduate School, School of Technology, Department of Manufacturing Systems, Greensboro, NC 27411

AWARDS Industrial technology (MS, MSIT). Safety and driver education (MS). Part-time and evening/weekend programs available.

Degree requirements: For master's, thesis or alternative, qualifying exam, comprehensive exam.
Entrance requirements: For master's, GRE General Test, minimum GPA of 3.0.

■ NORTH CAROLINA STATE UNIVERSITY

Graduate School, College of Textiles, Program in Textile Technology Management, Raleigh, NC 27695

AWARDS PhD.

Faculty: 24 full-time (1 woman), 6 part-time/adjunct (0 women).
Students: 17 full-time (13 women); includes 2 minority (1 African American, 1

Asian American or Pacific Islander), 8 international. Average age 33. 11 applicants, 27% accepted. In 2001, 5 degrees awarded.
Degree requirements: For doctorate, one foreign language, thesis/dissertation, cumulative exams.
Entrance requirements: For doctorate, GRE or GMAT. *Application fee:* $45.
Expenses: Tuition, state resident: full-time $1,748. Tuition, nonresident: full-time $6,904.
Financial support: In 2001–02, fellowships (averaging $6,806 per year), 10 research assistantships (averaging $5,268 per year) were awarded.
Dr. Charles D. Livengood, Associate Dean, 919-515-6643, *Fax:* 919-515-8578, *E-mail:* charles_livengood@ncsu.edu. *Web site:* http://www.tx.ncsu.edu/academic/graduate/programs.html

■ **NORTHERN KENTUCKY UNIVERSITY**

School of Graduate Programs, Program in Technology, Highland Heights, KY 41099

AWARDS MST.

Faculty: 7 full-time (2 women).
Students: 8 full-time (4 women), 25 part-time (9 women); includes 4 minority (3 African Americans, 1 Hispanic American), 5 international. Average age 36. In 2001, 8 degrees awarded.
Degree requirements: For master's, thesis optional.
Entrance requirements: For master's, GRE General Test. *Application deadline:* For fall admission, 8/15 (priority date); for spring admission, 10/15. Applications are processed on a rolling basis. *Application fee:* $25.
Expenses: Tuition, state resident: full-time $2,958; part-time $149 per credit hour. Tuition, nonresident: full-time $7,872; part-time $422 per credit hour.
Financial support: In 2001–02, 1 research assistantship was awarded; fellowships, career-related internships or fieldwork and institutionally sponsored loans also available.
Dr. Charles Pinder, Chairperson, 859-572-5441.
Application contact: Peg Griffin, Graduate Coordinator, 859-572-6364, *E-mail:* griffinp@nku.edu.

■ **OGI SCHOOL OF SCIENCE & ENGINEERING AT OREGON HEALTH & SCIENCE UNIVERSITY**

Graduate Studies, Department of Management in Science and Technology, Beaverton, OR 97006-8921

AWARDS Computational finance (Certificate); management in science and technology (MS). Part-time and evening/weekend programs available.

Faculty: 7 full-time (2 women), 29 part-time/adjunct (4 women).
Students: 6 full-time, 102 part-time. Average age 37. 19 applicants, 79% accepted. In 2001, 32 master's, 6 other advanced degrees awarded.
Entrance requirements: For master's, TOEFL. *Application deadline:* Applications are processed on a rolling basis. *Application fee:* $50. Electronic applications accepted.
Expenses: Tuition: Full-time $4,905; part-time $545 per credit hour. Required fees: $466.
Dr. Fred Young Phillips, Head, 503-748-1353, *Fax:* 503-748-1268, *E-mail:* fphillips@admin.ogi.edu.
Application contact: Victoria Tyler, Enrollment Manager, 503-748-1335, *Fax:* 503-748-1285, *E-mail:* vtyler@admin.ogi.edu. *Web site:* http://www.ogi.edu/MST/

Find an in-depth description at www.petersons.com/gradchannel.

■ **PACIFIC LUTHERAN UNIVERSITY**

Division of Graduate Studies, School of Business Administration and Management, Tacoma, WA 98447

AWARDS Business administration (MBA), including technology and innovation management. Part-time and evening/weekend programs available.

Faculty: 11 full-time (1 woman).
Students: 70 full-time (23 women), 38 part-time (14 women); includes 11 minority (3 African Americans, 7 Asian Americans or Pacific Islanders, 1 Hispanic American), 15 international. Average age 32. 60 applicants, 75% accepted, 45 enrolled. In 2001, 50 degrees awarded.
Entrance requirements: For master's, GMAT, TOEFL. *Application deadline:* Applications are processed on a rolling basis. *Application fee:* $35.
Expenses: Tuition: Full-time $13,296; part-time $554 per credit. Tuition and fees vary according to course load and program.
Financial support: Fellowships, research assistantships, career-related internships or fieldwork, Federal Work-Study, and scholarships/grants available. Financial award application deadline: 3/1.
Dr. Donald Bell, Dean, 253-535-7251.
Application contact: Catherine Pratt, Director, 253-535-7250, *E-mail:* prattca@plu.edu. *Web site:* http://www.plu.edu/~busa/mba

■ **PACIFIC STATES UNIVERSITY**

College of Business, Los Angeles, CA 90006

AWARDS Finance (MBA); international business (MBA); management of technology (MBA). Part-time and evening/weekend programs available.

Faculty: 3 full-time (0 women), 12 part-time/adjunct (0 women).
Students: 54 full-time (26 women); includes 52 Asian Americans or Pacific Islanders. Average age 25. 35 applicants, 100% accepted. In 2001, 40 degrees awarded.
Entrance requirements: For master's, TOEFL, minimum undergraduate GPA of 2.5 during last 90 hours. *Application deadline:* For fall admission, 8/15 (priority date); for winter admission, 10/15 (priority date); for spring admission, 1/15 (priority date). Applications are processed on a rolling basis. *Application fee:* $100. Electronic applications accepted.
Expenses: Tuition: Full-time $9,600. Required fees: $1,050.
Financial support: In 2001–02, 1 student received support; fellowships, research assistantships, teaching assistantships, scholarships/grants available. Financial award applicants required to submit FAFSA.
Dr. Kamol Somvichian, Director, 888-200-0383, *Fax:* 323-731-2383, *E-mail:* admission@psuca.edu.
Application contact: Mai A. Diep, Registrar, 888-200-0383, *Fax:* 323-731-7276, *E-mail:* admission@psuca.edu.

■ **PEPPERDINE UNIVERSITY**

The Graziado School of Business and Management, Culver City, CA 90230-7615

AWARDS Business (MBA), including business administration; executive business administration (MBAA); organizational development (MSOD); technology management (MSTM). Part-time and evening/weekend programs available.

Faculty: 78 full-time (14 women), 61 part-time/adjunct (15 women).
Students: 442 full-time (131 women), 1,360 part-time (551 women); includes 432 minority (84 African Americans, 216 Asian Americans or Pacific Islanders, 130 Hispanic Americans, 2 Native Americans), 54 international. Average age 35. 663 applicants, 68% accepted. In 2001, 740 degrees awarded.
Entrance requirements: For master's, GMAT or MAT. *Application deadline:* For fall admission, 6/28. Applications are processed on a rolling basis. *Application fee:* $45.
Expenses: Contact institution.
Financial support: Career-related internships or fieldwork, institutionally sponsored loans, scholarships/grants, and unspecified assistantships available. Support available to part-time students. Financial award applicants required to submit FAFSA.
Dr. William Larson, Interim Dean, 310-568-5500, *Fax:* 310-568-5766.
Application contact: Darrell Eriksen, Director of Career Development and Student Recruitment, 310-568-5790. *Web site:* http://www.bschool.pepperdine.edu/

■ POLYTECHNIC UNIVERSITY, BROOKLYN CAMPUS

Department of Management, Major in Management of Technology, Brooklyn, NY 11201-2990

AWARDS MS.

Degree requirements: For master's, thesis or alternative.
Entrance requirements: For master's, GMAT, minimum B average in undergraduate course work. Electronic applications accepted.

■ PORTLAND STATE UNIVERSITY

Graduate Studies, College of Engineering and Computer Science, Department of Engineering and Technology Management, Portland, OR 97207-0751

AWARDS M Eng, MS, PhD. Part-time and evening/weekend programs available.

Faculty: 3 full-time (0 women), 3 part-time/adjunct (0 women).
Students: 23 full-time (7 women), 31 part-time (7 women); includes 5 minority (2 African Americans, 2 Asian Americans or Pacific Islanders, 1 Hispanic American), 34 international. Average age 30. 30 applicants, 77% accepted. In 2001, 17 degrees awarded.
Degree requirements: For master's, thesis optional; for doctorate, one foreign language, thesis/dissertation, oral and written exams.
Entrance requirements: For master's, TOEFL, minimum GPA of 3.0 in upper-division course work or 2.75 overall; for doctorate, GRE General Test, GRE Subject Test, TOEFL, minimum GPA of 3.0 in upper-division course work. *Application deadline:* For fall admission, 4/1 (priority date); for spring admission, 11/1. Applications are processed on a rolling basis. *Application fee:* $50.
Financial support: In 2001–02, 7 research assistantships with full tuition reimbursements (averaging $3,275 per year), 4 teaching assistantships with full tuition reimbursements (averaging $3,402 per year) were awarded. Career-related internships or fieldwork, Federal Work-Study, and institutionally sponsored loans also available. Support available to part-time students. Financial award application deadline: 3/1; financial award applicants required to submit FAFSA.
Faculty research: Scheduling, hierarchical decision modeling, operations research, knowledge-based information systems. *Total annual research expenditures:* $60,342.
Dr. Dundar Kocaoglu, Director, 503-725-4660, *Fax:* 503-725-4667, *E-mail:* kocaoglu@emp.pdx.edu.

Application contact: Mary E. Wiltse, Coordinator, 503-725-4660, *Fax:* 503-725-4667, *E-mail:* maryw@emp.pdx.edu. *Web site:* http://www.emp.pdx.edu/
Find an in-depth description at www.petersons.com/gradchannel.

■ RENSSELAER POLYTECHNIC INSTITUTE

Graduate School, Lally School of Management and Technology, Program in Management and Technology, Troy, NY 12180-3590

AWARDS E-business (MBA, MS); environmental management and policy (MBA, MS); finance (MBA, MS); management (PhD); management information systems (MBA, MS); new product development and marketing (MBA); new production and operations research (MS); product development and marketing (MS); production and operations research (MBA); technological entrepreneurship (MBA, MS). Part-time and evening/weekend programs available. Postbaccalaureate distance learning degree programs offered (no on-campus study).
Faculty: 41 full-time (6 women), 2 part-time/adjunct (0 women).
Students: 388 full-time (54 women), 1,213 part-time (379 women); includes 139 minority (37 African Americans, 68 Asian Americans or Pacific Islanders, 33 Hispanic Americans, 1 Native American), 91 international. Average age 33. 628 applicants, 68% accepted, 268 enrolled. In 2001, 667 master's, 3 doctorates awarded.
Entrance requirements: For master's, GMAT, TOEFL, resumé, 3 letters of recommendation; for doctorate, GMAT or GRE General Test, TOEFL. *Application deadline:* For fall admission, 1/15 (priority date); for spring admission, 11/1 (priority date). Applications are processed on a rolling basis. *Application fee:* $45. Electronic applications accepted.
Expenses: Tuition: Full-time $26,400; part-time $1,320 per credit hour. Required fees: $1,437.
Financial support: In 2001–02, 89 students received support; fellowships, research assistantships, teaching assistantships, career-related internships or fieldwork, institutionally sponsored loans, scholarships/grants, and tuition waivers (full and partial) available. Financial award application deadline: 1/15; financial award applicants required to submit FAFSA.
Faculty research: Entrepreneurship, operations management, new product development and marketing, information systems, finance.
Dr. Richard Burke, Director MBA/MS Programs, 518-276-6586, *Fax:* 518-276-2665, *E-mail:* lallymba@rpi.edu.
Application contact: Zamiul Haque, Director, MBA/MS Admissions, 518-276-6586, *Fax:* 518-276-2665, *E-mail:* lallymba@rpi.edu. *Web site:* http://www.lallymba.mgmt.rpi.edu/

■ RHODE ISLAND COLLEGE

School of Graduate Studies, Center for Management and Technology, Department of Management and Technology, Providence, RI 02908-1991

AWARDS Industrial technology (MS).

Faculty: 6 full-time (3 women), 1 part-time/adjunct (0 women).
Students: Average age 34. In 2001, 8 degrees awarded.
Expenses: Tuition, state resident: full-time $3,060; part-time $170 per credit. Tuition, nonresident: full-time $6,390; part-time $355 per credit.
Dr. David Blanchette, Chairperson, 401-456-8036, *E-mail:* dblanchette@ric.edu.

■ SAGINAW VALLEY STATE UNIVERSITY

College of Science, Engineering, and Technology, Program in Technological Processes, University Center, MI 48710

AWARDS MS. Part-time and evening/weekend programs available.

Faculty: 7 full-time (0 women), 5 part-time/adjunct (1 woman).
Students: 19 full-time (7 women), 23 part-time (5 women); includes 5 minority (3 African Americans, 1 Asian American or Pacific Islander, 1 Hispanic American), 5 international. Average age 33. 20 applicants, 75% accepted, 6 enrolled. In 2001, 10 degrees awarded. *Median time to degree:* Master's–2.32 years full-time, 2.5 years part-time.
Entrance requirements: For master's, TOEFL, minimum GPA of 3.0. *Application deadline:* Applications are processed on a rolling basis. *Application fee:* $25.
Expenses: Tuition, state resident: full-time $2,263; part-time $189 per credit. Tuition, nonresident: full-time $4,480; part-time $373 per credit. Required fees: $201; $17 per credit.
Financial support: In 2001–02, 1 fellowship with partial tuition reimbursement, 1 research assistantship with full tuition reimbursement (averaging $2,500 per year) were awarded. Federal Work-Study also available. Support available to part-time students. Financial award application deadline: 4/1; financial award applicants required to submit FAFSA.
Faculty research: Materials, manufacturing processes, environmental remediation.
Dr. Brook Byan, Coordinator, 989-790-4489.
Application contact: Barb Sageman, Director, Graduate Admissions, 989-249-1696, *Fax:* 989-790-0180, *E-mail:* gradadm@svsu.edu. *Web site:* http://www.svsu.edu/gradadm/mtsp/index.html

■ ST. AMBROSE UNIVERSITY

College of Business, Program in Business Administration, Davenport, IA 52803-2898

AWARDS Business administration (DBA); management generalist (MBA); technical management (MBA). Part-time and evening/weekend programs available.

Faculty: 24 full-time (3 women), 21 part-time/adjunct (5 women).
Students: 117 full-time (48 women), 442 part-time (197 women); includes 32 minority (15 African Americans, 6 Asian Americans or Pacific Islanders, 11 Hispanic Americans), 15 international. Average age 36. 223 applicants, 97% accepted, 174 enrolled. In 2001, 148 master's awarded.
Degree requirements: For master's, thesis or alternative, capstone seminar, comprehensive exam (for some programs), registration; for doctorate, thesis/dissertation, oral and written exams, comprehensive exam, registration. *Median time to degree:* Master's–1.5 years full-time, 4 years part-time; doctorate–2.5 years full-time, 4.5 years part-time.
Entrance requirements: For master's, GMAT; for doctorate, GMAT, master's degree. *Application deadline:* For fall admission, 8/15 (priority date); for winter admission, 12/15; for spring admission, 1/1. Applications are processed on a rolling basis. *Application fee:* $25. Electronic applications accepted.
Expenses: Contact institution.
Financial support: In 2001–02, 415 students received support, including 17 research assistantships with partial tuition reimbursements available (averaging $2,736 per year); career-related internships or fieldwork, scholarships/grants, tuition waivers (partial), and unspecified assistantships also available. Support available to part-time students. Financial award application deadline: 3/15; financial award applicants required to submit FAFSA.
Dr. Frank Borst, Director, 563-333-6137, *Fax:* 563-333-6243, *E-mail:* fborst@sau.edu. *Web site:* http://www.sau.edu/mba

■ ST. AMBROSE UNIVERSITY

College of Human Services, Program in Information Technology Management, Davenport, IA 52803-2898

AWARDS MSITM. Part-time programs available.

Faculty: 2 full-time (0 women).
Students: 2 full-time (both women), 7 part-time (3 women). Average age 38. 7 applicants, 100% accepted, 7 enrolled.
Degree requirements: For master's, thesis (for some programs), practiums.
Entrance requirements: For master's, GRE or GMAT, minimum GPA of 2.8. *Application deadline:* For fall admission, 8/15 (priority date); for winter admission, 12/15 (priority date); for spring admission, 1/1 (priority date). *Application fee:* $25.
Financial support: In 2001–02, 3 students received support. Career-related internships or fieldwork and unspecified assistantships available. Financial award application deadline: 3/15; financial award applicants required to submit FAFSA.
Mark McGinn, Director, 563-333-6144.

■ SOUTH DAKOTA SCHOOL OF MINES AND TECHNOLOGY

Graduate Division, Program in Technology Management, Rapid City, SD 57701-3995

AWARDS MS. Part-time programs available.

Entrance requirements: For master's, GMAT, TOEFL, TWE. Electronic applications accepted.

■ SOUTHERN POLYTECHNIC STATE UNIVERSITY

School of Engineering Technology and Management, Program in Management, Marietta, GA 30060-2896

AWARDS MS. Part-time and evening/weekend programs available.

Faculty: 7 part-time/adjunct (1 woman).
Students: 14 full-time (8 women), 25 part-time (13 women); includes 12 minority (11 African Americans, 1 Hispanic American), 9 international. Average age 32. In 2001, 20 degrees awarded.
Degree requirements: For master's, thesis optional.
Entrance requirements: For master's, GMAT, letters of recommendation (3). *Application deadline:* For fall admission, 7/15 (priority date); for spring admission, 12/1. Applications are processed on a rolling basis. *Application fee:* $20. Electronic applications accepted.
Expenses: Tuition, state resident: full-time $1,746; part-time $97 per credit. Tuition, nonresident: full-time $6,966; part-time $387 per credit. Required fees: $221 per term.
Financial support: In 2001–02, 4 teaching assistantships with tuition reimbursements (averaging $2,500 per year) were awarded; career-related internships or fieldwork, Federal Work-Study, scholarships/grants, and unspecified assistantships also available. Support available to part-time students. Financial award application deadline: 5/1; financial award applicants required to submit FAFSA.
Dr. Mohammed Obeidat, Dean, 770-528-7440, *Fax:* 770-528-4967, *E-mail:* mobeidat@spsu.edu.
Application contact: Virginia A. Head, Director of Admissions, 770-528-7281, *Fax:* 770-528-7292, *E-mail:* vhead@spsu.edu. *Web site:* http://www2.spsu.edu/tmgt/

■ SOUTHWEST TEXAS STATE UNIVERSITY

Graduate School, College of Science, Department of Technology, San Marcos, TX 78666

AWARDS Industrial technology (MST). Part-time and evening/weekend programs available.

Faculty: 3 full-time (0 women).
Students: 5 full-time (1 woman), 12 part-time (3 women); includes 5 minority (1 African American, 1 Asian American or Pacific Islander, 3 Hispanic Americans), 3 international. Average age 35. 9 applicants, 78% accepted, 4 enrolled. In 2001, 5 degrees awarded.
Degree requirements: For master's, thesis optional.
Entrance requirements: For master's, GRE General Test, TOEFL, minimum GPA of 3.0 in last 60 hours. *Application deadline:* For fall admission, 6/15 (priority date); for spring admission, 10/15 (priority date). Applications are processed on a rolling basis. *Application fee:* $40 ($90 for international students).
Expenses: Tuition, state resident: full-time $1,512; part-time $84 per credit hour. Tuition, nonresident: full-time $5,310; part-time $295 per credit hour. Required fees: $864; $29 per credit hour. $195 per term. Full-time tuition and fees vary according to course load.
Financial support: In 2001–02, 4 teaching assistantships (averaging $9,383 per year) were awarded; research assistantships, career-related internships or fieldwork, Federal Work-Study, and institutionally sponsored loans also available. Support available to part-time students. Financial award application deadline: 4/1; financial award applicants required to submit FAFSA.
Faculty research: Rapid prototyping, casting technology, statistical process control, spatial abilities and gender.
Dr. Robert B. Habingreither, Chair, 512-245-2137, *Fax:* 512-245-3052, *E-mail:* rh03@swt.edu.
Application contact: Dr. Andy Batey, Graduate Adviser, 512-245-2137, *Fax:* 512-245-3052, *E-mail:* ab08@swt.edu. *Web site:* http://www.swt.edu/

■ STEVENS INSTITUTE OF TECHNOLOGY

Graduate School, Wesley J. Howe School of Technology Management, Program in Executive Master of Technology Management, Hoboken, NJ 07030

AWARDS EMTM. Part-time and evening/weekend programs available. Postbaccalaureate distance learning degree programs offered (minimal on-campus study).

Entrance requirements: For master's, GMAT, GRE, TOEFL. Electronic applications accepted.

Stevens Institute of Technology (continued)

Expenses: Tuition: Full-time $13,950; part-time $775 per credit. Required fees: $180. One-time fee: $180 part-time. Full-time tuition and fees vary according to degree level and program.

■ STEVENS INSTITUTE OF TECHNOLOGY

Graduate School, Wesley J. Howe School of Technology Management, Program in Technology Management, Hoboken, NJ 07030

AWARDS MS, MTM, PhD, Certificate. Part-time and evening/weekend programs available. Postbaccalaureate distance learning degree programs offered. Terminal master's awarded for partial completion of doctoral program.

Degree requirements: For doctorate, thesis/dissertation.
Entrance requirements: For master's and doctorate, GMAT, GRE, TOEFL. Electronic applications accepted.
Expenses: Contact institution.

■ STONY BROOK UNIVERSITY, STATE UNIVERSITY OF NEW YORK

Graduate School, College of Engineering and Applied Sciences, Department of Technology and Society, Stony Brook, NY 11794

AWARDS Educational computing (MS); environmental and waste management (MS); industrial management (MS); technological systems management (MS). Evening/weekend programs available.

Faculty: 8 full-time (1 woman), 8 part-time/adjunct (0 women).
Students: 13 full-time (9 women), 57 part-time (33 women); includes 5 minority (4 Asian Americans or Pacific Islanders, 1 Hispanic American), 8 international. 17 applicants, 29% accepted. In 2001, 33 degrees awarded.
Degree requirements: For master's, thesis.
Entrance requirements: For master's, GRE General Test, TOEFL. *Application deadline:* For fall admission, 1/15. *Application fee:* $50.
Expenses: Tuition, state resident: full-time $5,100; part-time $213 per credit. Tuition, nonresident: full-time $8,416; part-time $351 per credit. Required fees: $496.
Financial support: In 2001–02, 5 teaching assistantships were awarded; fellowships, research assistantships
Faculty research: Computer applications for technology and society issues. *Total annual research expenditures:* $1.7 million.
Dr. Thomas Liao, Director, 631-632-8770.
Application contact: Dr. Sheldon Reaven, Graduate Director, 631-632-8765, *Fax:* 631-632-7809, *E-mail:* sreaven@ccmail.sunysb.edu.

■ STONY BROOK UNIVERSITY, STATE UNIVERSITY OF NEW YORK

Graduate School, College of Engineering and Applied Sciences, W. Averell Harriman School for Management and Policy, Stony Brook, NY 11794

AWARDS Industrial management (Certificate); management and policy (MS); technology management (MBA, MS). Part-time and evening/weekend programs available.

Faculty: 10 full-time (1 woman), 27 part-time/adjunct (2 women).
Students: 85 full-time (48 women), 86 part-time (21 women); includes 14 minority (3 African Americans, 6 Asian Americans or Pacific Islanders, 5 Hispanic Americans), 127 international. 184 applicants, 46% accepted. In 2001, 73 degrees awarded.
Degree requirements: For master's, internship.
Entrance requirements: For master's, GMAT or GRE General Test, TOEFL. *Application deadline:* For fall admission, 1/15. *Application fee:* $50.
Expenses: Tuition, state resident: full-time $5,100; part-time $213 per credit. Tuition, nonresident: full-time $8,416; part-time $351 per credit. Required fees: $496.
Financial support: In 2001–02, 24 teaching assistantships were awarded; fellowships, research assistantships, career-related internships or fieldwork also available. Financial award application deadline: 4/1.
Faculty research: Economic development policies, entrepreneurship, decision support systems, worker-owned firms. *Total annual research expenditures:* $342,012.
Dr. Thomas Sexton, Director, 631-632-7180.
Application contact: Thomas Gjerde, Director of Graduate Studies, 631-632-7163. *Web site:* http://www.sunysb.edu/harriman/home.htm

Find an in-depth description at www.petersons.com/gradchannel.

■ TEXAS A&M UNIVERSITY–COMMERCE

Graduate School, College of Business and Technology, Department of Industrial and Engineering Technology, Commerce, TX 75429-3011

AWARDS Industry and technology (MS). Part-time programs available.

Faculty: 3 full-time (0 women), 1 part-time/adjunct (0 women).
Students: 14 full-time (1 woman), 19 part-time (1 woman); includes 7 minority (5 African Americans, 1 Asian American or Pacific Islander, 1 Hispanic American), 12 international. Average age 36. 8 applicants, 88% accepted. In 2001, 17 degrees awarded.
Degree requirements: For master's, thesis (for some programs), comprehensive exam.
Entrance requirements: For master's, GMAT, GRE General Test. *Application deadline:* For fall admission, 6/1 (priority date); for spring admission, 11/1 (priority date). Applications are processed on a rolling basis. *Application fee:* $0 ($25 for international students). Electronic applications accepted.
Expenses: Tuition, state resident: full-time $2,221. International tuition: $7,285 full-time.
Financial support: In 2001–02, research assistantships (averaging $7,875 per year), teaching assistantships (averaging $7,875 per year) were awarded. Federal Work-Study, institutionally sponsored loans, and scholarships/grants also available. Financial award application deadline: 5/1; financial award applicants required to submit FAFSA.
Faculty research: Environmental science, engineering microelectronics, natural sciences. *Total annual research expenditures:* $128,781.
Dr. Jerry D. Parish, Graduate Admissions Adviser, 903-886-5167, *Fax:* 903-886-5165, *E-mail:* jerry_parish@tamu-commerce.edu.
Application contact: Tammi Higginbotham, Graduate Admissions Adviser, 843-886-5167, *Fax:* 843-886-5165, *E-mail:* tammi_higginbotham@tamu-commerce.edu. *Web site:* http://www.tamu-commerce.edu/cobt/iet/index.html

■ UNIVERSITY OF ADVANCING TECHNOLOGY

Program in Technology, Tempe, AZ 85283-1042

AWARDS MS.

Faculty: 11 full-time (3 women), 3 part-time/adjunct (0 women).
Students: 16 full-time (2 women). Average age 25. In 2001, 3 degrees awarded. *Median time to degree:* Master's–1.5 years full-time.
Entrance requirements: For master's, project or thesis. *Application deadline:* For fall admission, 8/15 (priority date); for winter admission, 12/15 (priority date); for spring admission, 4/1 (priority date).
Expenses: Tuition: Full-time $4,824; part-time $402 per credit.
Faculty research: Artificial intelligence, fractals, organizational management.
Application contact: Information Contact, 800-658-5744, *Fax:* 602-383-8222.

■ THE UNIVERSITY OF AKRON

Graduate School, College of Business Administration, Department of Management, Program in Management of Technology, Akron, OH 44325-0001

AWARDS MBA.

Students: 2 full-time (0 women), 9 part-time (2 women). Average age 28. 11 applicants, 82% accepted, 8 enrolled. *Application deadline:* For fall admission, 8/15. *Application fee:* $40 ($50 for international students).
Expenses: Tuition, state resident: full-time $6,562; part-time $219 per credit. Tuition, nonresident: full-time $9,027; part-time $383 per credit. Required fees: $272; $11 per credit. Tuition and fees vary according to course load.
Financial support: Application deadline: 4/30.
Application contact: Dr. James Divoky, Director of Graduate Business Programs, 330-972-7032, *Fax:* 330-972-6588, *E-mail:* jdivoky@uakron.edu. *Web site:* http://www.uakron.edu/cba/mgmt/

■ UNIVERSITY OF BRIDGEPORT

School of Engineering, Department of Mechanical Engineering, Department of Technology Management, Bridgeport, CT 06601

AWARDS MS.

Faculty: 1 full-time (0 women), 5 part-time/adjunct (0 women).
Students: 16 full-time (1 woman), 4 part-time; includes 1 minority (African American), 17 international. Average age 27. 64 applicants, 89% accepted, 12 enrolled. In 2001, 20 degrees awarded.
Degree requirements: For master's, thesis optional.
Entrance requirements: For master's, TOEFL. *Application deadline:* For fall admission, 8/1 (priority date); for spring admission, 12/1 (priority date). Applications are processed on a rolling basis. *Application fee:* $25 ($35 for international students). Electronic applications accepted.
Expenses: Tuition: Part-time $385 per credit hour. Required fees: $50 per term. Tuition and fees vary according to degree level and program.
Financial support: In 2001–02, 3 students received support; fellowships, research assistantships, teaching assistantships, career-related internships or fieldwork, Federal Work-Study, institutionally sponsored loans, and tuition waivers (partial) available. Support available to part-time students. Financial award application deadline: 6/1; financial award applicants required to submit FAFSA.
Faculty research: CAD/CAM.
Dr. Paul Bauer, Coordinator, 203-576-4379, *Fax:* 203-576-4766, *E-mail:* bauer@bridgeport.edu.

■ UNIVERSITY OF COLORADO AT BOULDER

Leeds School of Business, Boulder, CO 80309

AWARDS Accounting (MS); business administration (MBA, PhD), including business administration, entrepreneurship (MBA),

operations management (MBA), real estate (MBA); business self designed (MBA); finance (MBA, PhD); marketing (MBA, PhD); organization management (MBA, PhD); taxation (MS); technology and innovation management (MBA). Part-time and evening/weekend programs available.

Faculty: 61 full-time (11 women).
Students: 234 full-time (70 women), 17 part-time (4 women); includes 27 minority (4 African Americans, 16 Asian Americans or Pacific Islanders, 6 Hispanic Americans, 1 Native American), 40 international. Average age 31. 182 applicants, 64% accepted. In 2001, 127 master's, 6 doctorates awarded.
Degree requirements: For doctorate, thesis/dissertation, research internship.
Entrance requirements: For master's and doctorate, GMAT. *Application deadline:* For fall admission, 3/1 (priority date). Applications are processed on a rolling basis. *Application fee:* $50 ($60 for international students). Electronic applications accepted.
Expenses: Contact institution.
Financial support: In 2001–02, 21 fellowships (averaging $3,931 per year), 9 research assistantships (averaging $23,035 per year), 12 teaching assistantships (averaging $21,181 per year) were awarded. Career-related internships or fieldwork, Federal Work-Study, scholarships/grants, and unspecified assistantships also available. Financial award application deadline: 3/1. *Total annual research expenditures:* $2 million.
Steven Manaster, Dean, 303-492-1809, *Fax:* 303-492-7676.
Application contact: Diane Dimeff, Assistant Director, Admissions, 303-492-3537, *Fax:* 303-492-1727, *E-mail:* busgrad@spot.colorado.edu. *Web site:* http://leeds.colorado.edu

Find an in-depth description at www.petersons.com/gradchannel.

■ UNIVERSITY OF DELAWARE

College of Business and Economics and Department of Electrical and Computer Engineering, Program in Information Systems and Technology Management, Newark, DE 19716

AWARDS MS. Part-time programs available.

Entrance requirements: For master's, GRE or GMAT, TOEFL, 3 letters of recommendations, resumé, minimum GPA of 2.75.
Expenses: Tuition, state resident: full-time $4,770; part-time $265 per credit. Tuition, nonresident: full-time $13,860; part-time $770 per credit. Required fees: $414. *Web site:* http://www.istm.udel.edu

■ UNIVERSITY OF DENVER

University College, Denver, CO 80208

AWARDS Applied communication (MSS); computer information systems (MCIS); environmental policy and management

(MEPM); healthcare systems (MHS); liberal studies (MLS); library and information services (MLIS); public health (MPH); technology management (MoTM); telecommunications (MTEL). Part-time and evening/weekend programs available. Postbaccalaureate distance learning degree programs offered (no on-campus study).

Faculty: 167 part-time/adjunct (52 women).
Students: 1,244 (618 women); includes 177 minority (65 African Americans, 53 Asian Americans or Pacific Islanders, 54 Hispanic Americans, 5 Native Americans) 76 international. 54 applicants, 85% accepted. In 2001, 274 degrees awarded.
Entrance requirements: For master's, minimum undergraduate GPA of 3.0. *Application deadline:* For fall admission, 7/15 (priority date); for winter admission, 10/14 (priority date); for spring admission, 2/10 (priority date). Applications are processed on a rolling basis. *Application fee:* $25.
Expenses: Contact institution.
Financial support: In 2001–02, 174 students received support. *Total annual research expenditures:* $59,206.
Mike Bloom, Dean, 303-871-3141.
Application contact: Cindy Kraft, Admission Coordinator, 303-871-3969, *Fax:* 303-871-3303. *Web site:* http://www.du.edu/ucol/

■ UNIVERSITY OF MARYLAND UNIVERSITY COLLEGE

Graduate School of Management and Technology, Program in Technology Management, Adelphi, MD 20783

AWARDS Exec MS, MS. Offered evenings and weekends only. Part-time and evening/weekend programs available. Postbaccalaureate distance learning degree programs offered (no on-campus study).

Students: 11 full-time (4 women), 443 part-time (165 women); includes 144 minority (100 African Americans, 26 Asian Americans or Pacific Islanders, 17 Hispanic Americans, 1 Native American), 26 international. 127 applicants, 99% accepted. In 2001, 83 degrees awarded.
Degree requirements: For master's, thesis or alternative.
Application deadline: Applications are processed on a rolling basis. *Application fee:* $50. Electronic applications accepted.
Expenses: Tuition, state resident: full-time $5,418; part-time $301 per credit hour. Tuition, nonresident: full-time $8,892; part-time $494 per credit hour.
Financial support: Federal Work-Study and scholarships/grants available. Support available to part-time students. Financial award application deadline: 6/1; financial award applicants required to submit FAFSA.
Dr. Robert Ouellette, Acting Chair, 301-985-7200, *Fax:* 301-985-4611, *E-mail:* rouellette@umuc.edu.

University of Maryland University College (continued)

Application contact: Coordinator, Graduate Admissions, 301-985-7155, *Fax:* 301-985-7175, *E-mail:* gradinfo@nova.umuc.edu. *Web site:* http://www.umuc.edu/prog/gsmt/tman.html

■ UNIVERSITY OF MIAMI

Graduate School, College of Engineering, Department of Industrial Engineering, Coral Gables, FL 33124

AWARDS Environmental health and safety (MS, MSEVH, MSOES), including environmental health and safety (MS, MSEVH), occupational ergonomics and safety (MSOES); ergonomics (PhD); industrial engineering (MSIE, PhD); management of technology (MS).

Faculty: 9 full-time (0 women), 3 part-time/adjunct (1 woman).
Students: 54 full-time (10 women); includes 16 minority (14 African Americans, 2 Hispanic Americans), 7 international. Average age 28. 79 applicants, 75% accepted. In 2001, 25 master's, 5 doctorates awarded.
Degree requirements: For master's, thesis (for some programs); for doctorate, thesis/dissertation.
Entrance requirements: For master's and doctorate, GRE General Test, TOEFL, minimum GPA of 3.0. *Application deadline:* For fall admission, 5/1 (priority date). Applications are processed on a rolling basis. *Application fee:* $50.
Expenses: Tuition: Part-time $960 per credit hour. Required fees: $85 per semester. Tuition and fees vary according to program.
Financial support: In 2001–02, 4 fellowships, 5 research assistantships, 4 teaching assistantships were awarded. Federal Work-Study also available. Financial award application deadline: 3/1; financial award applicants required to submit FAFSA.
Faculty research: Logistics, supply chain management, industrial applications of biomechanics and ergonomics, technology management, back pain, aging, operations research, manufacturing, safety, human reliability, energy assessment. *Total annual research expenditures:* $235,000.
Dr. Shihab S. Asfour, Chair, 305-284-2344, *Fax:* 305-284-4040, *E-mail:* sasfour@miami.edu.
Application contact: Dr. Eleftherios Iakovou, Associate Professor, Graduate Director, 305-284-2344, *Fax:* 305-284-4040. *Web site:* http://www.eng.miami.edu/

■ UNIVERSITY OF MINNESOTA, TWIN CITIES CAMPUS

Graduate School, Institute of Technology, Center for the Development of Technological Leadership, Program in Management of Technology, Minneapolis, MN 55455-0213

AWARDS MSMOT. Part-time and evening/weekend programs available.

Faculty: 24.
Students: 67 (7 women); includes 14 minority (2 African Americans, 10 Asian Americans or Pacific Islanders, 2 Hispanic Americans) 1 international. Average age 34. 60 applicants, 67% accepted. In 2001, 32 degrees awarded.
Degree requirements: For master's, thesis, capstone project.
Entrance requirements: For master's, 5 years of work experience in high-tech company, preferably in Twin Cities area; GMAT, GRE General Test, or minimum GPA of 3.0. *Application deadline:* For fall admission, 6/15 (priority date). Applications are processed on a rolling basis. *Application fee:* $50 ($55 for international students). Electronic applications accepted.
Expenses: Contact institution.
Financial support: Institutionally sponsored loans available. Support available to part-time students. Financial award applicants required to submit FAFSA.
Faculty research: Operations management, strategic management, technology foresight, marketing, business analysis.
Dr. Rias J. van Wyk, Director of Graduate Studies, 612-624-8296, *Fax:* 612-624-7510, *E-mail:* vanwyk@cdtl.umn.edu.
Application contact: Ann Bechtell, Admission Associate, 612-624-5747, *Fax:* 612-624-7510, *E-mail:* mot@cdtl.umn.edu. *Web site:* http://www.cdtl.umn.edu/cdtl_home.html

■ UNIVERSITY OF NEW HAVEN

Graduate School, School of Business, Program in Business Administration, West Haven, CT 06516-1916

AWARDS Accounting (MBA); business policy and strategy (MBA); finance (MBA); health care management (MBA); human resources management (MBA); international business (MBA); marketing (MBA); public relations (MBA). Sports management (MBA); technology management (MBA). Part-time and evening/weekend programs available.

Students: 91 full-time (51 women), 299 part-time (127 women); includes 32 minority (19 African Americans, 9 Asian Americans or Pacific Islanders, 3 Hispanic Americans, 1 Native American), 75 international. In 2001, 134 degrees awarded.
Degree requirements: For master's, thesis or alternative.

Entrance requirements: For master's, GMAT. *Application deadline:* Applications are processed on a rolling basis. *Application fee:* $50.
Expenses: Tuition: Full-time $12,015; part-time $445 per credit hour. Required fees: $30. One-time fee: $100 full-time.
Financial support: Federal Work-Study available. Support available to part-time students. Financial award application deadline: 5/1.
Charles Coleman, Chairman, 203-932-7375.

■ UNIVERSITY OF NEW MEXICO

Graduate School, Robert O. Anderson Graduate School of Management, Department of Organizational Studies, Albuquerque, NM 87131-2039

AWARDS Management of technology (MBA). Part-time and evening/weekend programs available.

Faculty: 16 full-time (7 women), 15 part-time/adjunct (5 women).
Entrance requirements: For master's, GMAT, TOEFL. *Application deadline:* For fall admission, 6/1 (priority date); for spring admission, 11/1 (priority date). Applications are processed on a rolling basis. *Application fee:* $40.
Expenses: Tuition, state resident: full-time $2,771; part-time $115 per credit hour. Tuition, nonresident: full-time $11,207; part-time $467 per credit hour. Required fees: $570; $24 per credit hour. Part-time tuition and fees vary according to course load and program.
Financial support: Fellowships, research assistantships, teaching assistantships, career-related internships or fieldwork, Federal Work-Study, scholarships/grants, health care benefits, and unspecified assistantships available.
Dr. Helen J. Muller, Chair, 505-277-7133, *Fax:* 505-277-7108, *E-mail:* muller@mgt.unm.edu.
Application contact: Loyola Chastain, MBA Manager, 505-277-3147, *Fax:* 505-277-9356, *E-mail:* chastain@mgt.unm.edu. *Web site:* http://asm.unm.edu/mot/

■ UNIVERSITY OF PENNSYLVANIA

School of Engineering and Applied Science, Executive Master's in Technology Management Program, Philadelphia, PA 19104

AWARDS Management of technology (MSE, AC). Cosponsor is the Wharton School of Business. Part-time and evening/weekend programs available. *Web site:* http://www.emtm.upenn.edu/

■ UNIVERSITY OF PHOENIX– BOSTON CAMPUS

College of Graduate Business and Management, Braintree, MA 02184-4949

AWARDS Administration (MBA); global management (MBA); technology management (MBA). Evening/weekend programs available. Postbaccalaureate distance learning degree programs offered (no on-campus study).

Entrance requirements: For master's, TOEFL, Comprehensive Cognitive Assessment, 3 years of work experience, minimum GPA of 2.5. *Application deadline:* Applications are processed on a rolling basis.
Expenses: Tuition: Full-time $10,560; part-time $440 per credit.
Financial support: Applicants required to submit FAFSA.
Dr. Brian Lindquist, Dean, 480-537-1221, *E-mail:* brian.lindquist@phoenix.edu. *Web site:* http://www.phoenix.edu

■ UNIVERSITY OF PHOENIX– COLORADO CAMPUS

College of Graduate Business and Management, Lone Tree, CO 80124-5453

AWARDS Business administration (MBA); e-business (MBA); organizational management (MAOM); technology management (MBA). Evening/weekend programs available. Postbaccalaureate distance learning degree programs offered (no on-campus study).
Students: 633 full-time. Average age 33. In 2001, 237 degrees awarded.
Degree requirements: For master's, thesis.
Entrance requirements: For master's, TOEFL, Comprehensive Cognitive Assessment, minimum undergraduate GPA of 2.5, 3 years work experience. *Application deadline:* Applications are processed on a rolling basis. *Application fee:* $85.
Expenses: Tuition: Full-time $7,788; part-time $325 per credit.
Financial support: Applicants required to submit FAFSA.
Dr. Brian Lindquist, Dean, 480-557-1221, *E-mail:* brian.lindquist@phoenix.edu. *Web site:* http://www.phoenix.edu

■ UNIVERSITY OF PHOENIX– FORT LAUDERDALE CAMPUS

College of Graduate Business and Management, Fort Lauderdale, FL 33324-1393

AWARDS Business administration (MBA); health care management (MBA); organizational management (MAOM); technology management (MBA). Evening/weekend programs available. Postbaccalaureate distance learning degree programs offered (no on-campus study).

Students: 309 full-time. Average age 35. In 2001, 65 degrees awarded.
Degree requirements: For master's, thesis or alternative.
Entrance requirements: For master's, TOEFL, Comprehensive Cognitive Assessment, minimum undergraduate GPA of 2.5, 3 years work experience. *Application deadline:* Applications are processed on a rolling basis. *Application fee:* $85.
Expenses: Tuition: Full-time $7,320; part-time $305 per credit.
Financial support: Applicants required to submit FAFSA.
Dr. Brian Lindquist, Dean, 480-557-1221, *E-mail:* brian.lindquist@phoenix.edu.
Application contact: Campus Information Center, 954-382-5303, *Fax:* 954-382-5304. *Web site:* http://www.phoenix.edu

■ UNIVERSITY OF PHOENIX– JACKSONVILLE CAMPUS

College of Graduate Business and Management, Jacksonville, FL 32216-0959

AWARDS Business administration (MBA); health care management (MBA); organizational management (MAOM); technology management (MBA). Evening/weekend programs available. Postbaccalaureate distance learning degree programs offered (no on-campus study).

Students: 343 full-time. Average age 35. In 2001, 65 degrees awarded.
Degree requirements: For master's, thesis or alternative.
Entrance requirements: For master's, TOEFL, Comprehensive Cognitive Assessment, minimum undergraduate GPA of 2.5, 3 years work experience. *Application deadline:* Applications are processed on a rolling basis. *Application fee:* $85.
Expenses: Tuition: Full-time $7,320; part-time $305 per credit.
Financial support: Applicants required to submit FAFSA.
Dr. Brian Lindquist, Dean, 480-557-1221, *E-mail:* brian.lindquist@phoenix.edu.
Application contact: 904-636-6645, *Fax:* 904-636-0998. *Web site:* http://www.phoenix.edu/

■ UNIVERSITY OF PHOENIX– LOUISIANA CAMPUS

College of Graduate Business and Management, Metairie, LA 70001-2082

AWARDS Business administration (MBA); e-business (MBA); health care management (MBA); organizational management (MAOM); technology management (MBA). Evening/weekend programs available.
Students: 549 full-time. Average age 34. In 2001, 113 degrees awarded.
Degree requirements: For master's, thesis or alternative.
Entrance requirements: For master's, TOEFL, Comprehensive Cognitive Assessment, minimum undergraduate GPA

of 2.5, 3 years work experience. *Application deadline:* Applications are processed on a rolling basis. *Application fee:* $85.
Expenses: Tuition: Full-time $6,552; part-time $273 per credit.
Financial support: Applicants required to submit FAFSA.
Dr. Brian Lindquist, Dean, 480-557-1221, *E-mail:* brian.lindquist@phoenix.edu.

■ UNIVERSITY OF PHOENIX– MARYLAND CAMPUS

College of Graduate Business and Management, Columbia, MD 21045-5424

AWARDS Business administration (MBA); global management (MBA); organizational management (MAOM); technology management (MBA). Evening/weekend programs available. Postbaccalaureate distance learning degree programs offered (no on-campus study).

Students: 321 full-time. Average age 35. In 2001, 6 degrees awarded.
Degree requirements: For master's, thesis or alternative.
Entrance requirements: For master's, TOEFL, Comprehensive Cognitive Assessment, minimum undergraduate GPA of 2.5, 3 years work experience. *Application deadline:* Applications are processed on a rolling basis. *Application fee:* $85.
Expenses: Tuition: Full-time $9,960; part-time $415 per credit.
Financial support: Applicants required to submit FAFSA.
Dr. Brian Lindquist, Dean, 480-557-1221, *E-mail:* brian.lindquist@phoenix.edu. *Web site:* http://www.phoenix.edu

■ UNIVERSITY OF PHOENIX– METRO DETROIT CAMPUS

College of Graduate Business and Management, Troy, MI 48098-2623

AWARDS Business administration (MBA); global management (MBA); health care management (MBA); organizational management (MAOM); technology management (MBA). Evening/weekend programs available. Postbaccalaureate distance learning degree programs offered (no on-campus study).

Students: 712 full-time. In 2001, 197 degrees awarded.
Degree requirements: For master's, thesis or alternative.
Entrance requirements: For master's, TOEFL, Comprehensive Cognitive Assessment, minimum undergraduate GPA of 2.5, 3 years work experience. *Application deadline:* Applications are processed on a rolling basis. *Application fee:* $85.
Expenses: Tuition: Full-time $9,120; part-time $380 per credit. Full-time tuition and fees vary according to program.
Financial support: Applicants required to submit FAFSA.

University of Phoenix–Metro Detroit Campus (continued)
Dr. Brian Lindquist, Dean, 480-557-1221, *E-mail:* brian.lindquist@phoenix.edu. *Web site:* http://www.phoenix.edu

■ UNIVERSITY OF PHOENIX–NEW MEXICO CAMPUS

College of Graduate Business and Management, Albuquerque, NM 87109-4645

AWARDS Business administration (MBA); global management (MBA); health care management (MBA); organizational management (MAOM); technology management (MBA). Evening/weekend programs available. Postbaccalaureate distance learning degree programs offered (no on-campus study).

Students: 699 full-time. In 2001, 290 degrees awarded.
Degree requirements: For master's, thesis or alternative.
Entrance requirements: For master's, Comprehensive Cognitive Assessment Test, TOEFL, 3 years of work experience, minimum undergraduate GPA of 2.5. *Application deadline:* Applications are processed on a rolling basis. *Application fee:* $85.
Expenses: Tuition: Full-time $7,336; part-time $306 per credit. Full-time tuition and fees vary according to program.
Financial support: Applicants required to submit FAFSA.
Dr. Brian Lindquist, Dean, 480-557-1221, *E-mail:* brian.lindquist@phoenix.edu. *Web site:* http://www.phoenix.edu

■ UNIVERSITY OF PHOENIX–NORTHERN CALIFORNIA CAMPUS

College of Graduate Business and Management, Pleasanton, CA 94588-3677

AWARDS Business administration (MBA); global management (MBA); health care management (MBA); organizational management (MAOM); technology management (MBA). Evening/weekend programs available. Postbaccalaureate distance learning degree programs offered (no on-campus study).

Students: 1,023 full-time. Average age 35. In 2001, 378 degrees awarded.
Degree requirements: For master's, thesis or alternative.
Entrance requirements: For master's, TOEFL, Comprehensive Cognitive Assessment, minimum undergraduate GPA of 2.5, 3 years of work experience. *Application deadline:* Applications are processed on a rolling basis. *Application fee:* $85.
Expenses: Tuition: Full-time $9,504; part-time $396 per credit.
Financial support: Applicants required to submit FAFSA.
Dr. Brian Lindquist, Dean, 408-557-1221, *E-mail:* brian.lindquist@phoenix.edu.

Application contact: 408-435-8500, *Fax:* 408-435-8250. *Web site:* http://www.phoenix.edu

■ UNIVERSITY OF PHOENIX–OREGON CAMPUS

College of Graduate Business and Management, Portland, OR 97223-8368

AWARDS Business administration (MBA); organizational management (MAOM); technology management (MBA). Evening/weekend programs available. Postbaccalaureate distance learning degree programs offered (no on-campus study).

Students: 239 full-time. Average age 36. In 2001, 86 degrees awarded.
Degree requirements: For master's, thesis or alternative.
Entrance requirements: For master's, TOEFL, Comprehensive Cognitive Assessment, minimum undergraduate GPA of 2.5, 3 years work experience. *Application deadline:* Applications are processed on a rolling basis. *Application fee:* $85.
Expenses: Tuition: Full-time $7,800; part-time $325 per credit.
Financial support: Applicants required to submit FAFSA.
Dr. Brian Lindquist, Dean, 480-557-1221, *E-mail:* brian.lindquist@phoenix.edu. *Web site:* http://www.phoenix.edu

■ UNIVERSITY OF PHOENIX–ORLANDO CAMPUS

College of Graduate Business and Management, Maitland, FL 32751

AWARDS Business administration (MBA); health care management (MBA); organizational management (MAOM); technology management (MBA). Evening/weekend programs available. Postbaccalaureate distance learning degree programs offered (no on-campus study).

Students: 349 full-time. Average age 35. In 2001, 114 degrees awarded.
Degree requirements: For master's, thesis or alternative.
Entrance requirements: For master's, TOEFL, Comprehensive Cognitive Assessment, minimum undergraduate GPA of 2.5, 3 years work experience. *Application deadline:* Applications are processed on a rolling basis. *Application fee:* $85.
Expenses: Tuition: Full-time $7,320; part-time $305 per credit.
Dr. Brian Lindquist, Dean, 480-557-1221, *E-mail:* brian.lindquist@phoenix.edu. *Web site:* http://www.phoenix.edu

■ UNIVERSITY OF PHOENIX–PHILADELPHIA CAMPUS

College of Graduate Business and Management, Wayne, PA 19087-2121

AWARDS Business administration (MBA); global management (MBA); technology management (MBA). Evening/weekend

programs available. Postbaccalaureate distance learning degree programs offered (no on-campus study).

Students: 303 full-time. Average age 35.
Degree requirements: For master's, thesis or alternative.
Entrance requirements: For master's, TOEFL, Comprehensive Cognitive Assessment, minimum undergraduate GPA of 2.5, 3 years work experience. *Application deadline:* Applications are processed on a rolling basis. *Application fee:* $85.
Expenses: Tuition: Full-time $8,040; part-time $335 per credit.
Financial support: Applicants required to submit FAFSA.
Dr. Brian Lindquist, Dean, 480-557-1221, *E-mail:* brian.lindquist@phoenix.edu.
Application contact: 610-984-0880, *Fax:* 610-989-0881. *Web site:* http://www.phoenix.edu

■ UNIVERSITY OF PHOENIX–PHOENIX CAMPUS

College of Graduate Business and Management, Phoenix, AZ 85040-1958

AWARDS Business administration (MBA); global management (MBA); health care management (MBA); organizational management (MAOM); technology management (MBA). Evening/weekend programs available. Postbaccalaureate distance learning degree programs offered (no on-campus study).

Students: 1,751 full-time. Average age 33. In 2001, 635 degrees awarded.
Degree requirements: For master's, thesis or alternative.
Entrance requirements: For master's, TOEFL, 3 years of work experience, comprehensive cognitive assessment, minimum undergraduate GPA of 2.5. *Application deadline:* Applications are processed on a rolling basis. *Application fee:* $85.
Expenses: Tuition: Full-time $7,680; part-time $320 per credit. Full-time tuition and fees vary according to campus/location and program.
Financial support: Applicants required to submit FAFSA.
Dr. Brian Lindquist, Dean, 480-557-1221, *E-mail:* brian.lindquist@apollogrp.edu.
Application contact: 602-966-7400. *Web site:* http://www.phoenix.edu

■ UNIVERSITY OF PHOENIX–PITTSBURGH CAMPUS

College of Graduate Business and Management, Pittsburgh, PA 15276

AWARDS Business administration (MBA); organizational management (MAOM); technology management (MBA). Evening/weekend programs available. Postbaccalaureate distance learning degree programs offered (no on-campus study).

Faculty: 7 full-time.
Students: 110 full-time.

Degree requirements: For master's, thesis or alternative.
Entrance requirements: For master's, TOEFL, comprehensive cognitive assessment (COCA), minimum undergraduate GPA of 2.5, 3 years work experience. *Application deadline:* Applications are processed on a rolling basis. *Application fee:* $85.
Financial support: Applicants required to submit FAFSA.
Dr. Brian Lindquist, Dean, 480-557-1221, *E-mail:* brian.lindquist@phoenix.edu.
Application contact: 412-747-9000, *Fax:* 412-747-0676. *Web site:* http://www.phoenix.edu

■ UNIVERSITY OF PHOENIX–SAN DIEGO CAMPUS

College of Graduate Business and Management, San Diego, CA 92130-2092

AWARDS Business administration (MBA); global management (MBA); health care management (MBA); organizational management (MAOM); technology management (MBA). Evening/weekend programs available. Postbaccalaureate distance learning degree programs offered (no on-campus study).

Students: 822 full-time. Average age 34. In 2001, 209 degrees awarded.
Degree requirements: For master's, thesis or alternative.
Application deadline: Applications are processed on a rolling basis. *Application fee:* $85.
Expenses: Tuition: Full-time $8,808; part-time $367 per credit.
Financial support: Applicants required to submit FAFSA.
Dr. Brian Lindquist, Dean, 480-557-1221, *E-mail:* brian.lindquist@phoenix.edu.
Application contact: Campus Information Center, 888-UOP-INFO.

■ UNIVERSITY OF PHOENIX–SOUTHERN ARIZONA CAMPUS

College of Graduate Business and Management, Tucson, AZ 85712

AWARDS Business administration (MBA); global management (MBA); health care management (MBA); organizational management (MAOM); technology management (MBA). Evening/weekend programs available. Postbaccalaureate distance learning degree programs offered (no on-campus study).

Students: 448 full-time. Average age 34. In 2001, 188 degrees awarded.
Degree requirements: For master's, thesis.
Entrance requirements: For master's, TOEFL, comprehensive cognitive assessment (COCA), minimum undergraduate GPA of 2.5, 3 years work experience. *Application deadline:* Applications are processed on a rolling basis. *Application fee:* $85.

Expenses: Tuition: Full-time $6,456; part-time $269 per credit.
Financial support: Applicants required to submit FAFSA.
Dr. Brian Lindquist, Dean, 480-557-1221, *E-mail:* brian.lindquist@phoenix.edu.
Application contact: 520-881-6512, *Fax:* 520-795-6177.

■ UNIVERSITY OF PHOENIX–SOUTHERN CALIFORNIA CAMPUS

College of Graduate Business and Management, Fountain Valley, CA 92708-6027

AWARDS Business administration (MBA); health care management (MBA); organizational management (MAOM); technology management (MBA). Evening/weekend programs available. Postbaccalaureate distance learning degree programs offered (no on-campus study).

Students: 1,415 full-time. Average age 35. In 2001, 413 degrees awarded.
Degree requirements: For master's, thesis or alternative.
Entrance requirements: For master's, TOEFL, minimum undergraduate GPA of 2.5, 3 years work experience, comprehensive cognitive assessment (COCA). *Application deadline:* Applications are processed on a rolling basis. *Application fee:* $85.
Expenses: Tuition: Full-time $9,696; part-time $404 per credit.
Financial support: Applicants required to submit FAFSA.
Dr. Brian Lindquist, Dean, 480-557-1221, *E-mail:* brian.lindquist@phoenix.edu.
Application contact: 714-378-1878, *Fax:* 714-378-5856.

■ UNIVERSITY OF PHOENIX–SOUTHERN COLORADO CAMPUS

College of Graduate Business and Management, Colorado Springs, CO 80919-2335

AWARDS Business administration (MBA); organizational management (MAOM); technology management (MBA). Evening/weekend programs available. Postbaccalaureate distance learning degree programs offered (no on-campus study).

Students: 130 full-time. Average age 34.
Degree requirements: For master's, thesis or alternative.
Entrance requirements: For master's, TOEFL, comprehensive cognitive assessment (COCA), minimum undergraduate GPA of 2.5, 3 years work experience. *Application deadline:* Applications are processed on a rolling basis. *Application fee:* $85.
Expenses: Tuition: Full-time $7,698; part-time $321 per credit. Full-time tuition and fees vary according to program.

Financial support: Applicants required to submit FAFSA.
Dr. Brian Lindquist, Dean, 480-557-1221, *E-mail:* brian.lindquist@phoenix.edu. *Web site:* http://www.phoenix.edu

■ UNIVERSITY OF PHOENIX–TAMPA CAMPUS

College of Graduate Business and Management, Tampa, FL 33637-1920

AWARDS Business administration (MBA); health care management (MBA); organizational management (MAOM); technology management (MBA). Evening/weekend programs available. Postbaccalaureate distance learning degree programs offered (no on-campus study).

Students: 409 full-time. Average age 35. In 2001, 97 degrees awarded.
Degree requirements: For master's, thesis or alternative.
Entrance requirements: For master's, TOEFL, comprehensive cognitive assessment (COCA), 3 years work experience, minimum undergraduate GPA of 2.5. *Application deadline:* Applications are processed on a rolling basis. *Application fee:* $85.
Expenses: Tuition: Full-time $7,320; part-time $305 per credit.
Financial support: Applicants required to submit FAFSA.
Dr. Brian Lindquist, Dean, 480-557-1221, *E-mail:* brian.lindquist@phoenix.edu.
Application contact: 813-626-7911, *Fax:* 813-630-9377.

■ UNIVERSITY OF PHOENIX–WASHINGTON CAMPUS

College of Graduate Business and Management, Seattle, WA 98188-7500

AWARDS Business administration (MBA); organizational management (MAOM); technology management (MBA). Evening/weekend programs available. Postbaccalaureate distance learning degree programs offered (no on-campus study).

Students: 356 full-time. Average age 33. In 2001, 75 degrees awarded.
Degree requirements: For master's, thesis or alternative.
Entrance requirements: For master's, TOEFL, comprehensive cognitive assessment (COCA), minimum undergraduate GPA of 2.5, 3 years work experience. *Application deadline:* Applications are processed on a rolling basis. *Application fee:* $85.
Expenses: Tuition: Full-time $7,848; part-time $327 per credit.
Financial support: Applicants required to submit FAFSA.
Dr. Brian Lindquist, Dean, 480-557-1221, *E-mail:* brian.lindquist@phoenix.edu.

■ UNIVERSITY OF PHOENIX–WEST MICHIGAN CAMPUS

College of Graduate Business and Management, Grand Rapids, MI 49544-1683

AWARDS Business administration (MBA); e-business (MBA); health care management (MBA); organizational management (MAOM); technology management (MBA). Evening/weekend programs available. Postbaccalaureate distance learning degree programs offered (no on-campus study).

Students: 68 full-time. Average age 34.
Degree requirements: For master's, thesis or alternative.
Entrance requirements: For master's, TOEFL, Comprehensive Cognitive Assessment, minimum undergraduate GPA of 2.5, 3 years work experience. *Application deadline:* Applications are processed on a rolling basis. *Application fee:* $85.
Expenses: Tuition: Full-time $9,120; part-time $380 per credit.
Financial support: Applicants required to submit FAFSA.
Dr. Brian Lindquist, Dean, 480-557-1221, *E-mail:* brian.lindquist@phoenix.edu. *Web site:* http://www.phoenix.edu

■ UNIVERSITY OF ST. THOMAS

Graduate Studies, Graduate School of Applied Science and Engineering, Program in Engineering and Technology Management, St. Paul, MN 55105-1096

AWARDS Engineering and technology management (Certificate); manufacturing systems (MS); manufacturing systems engineering (MMSE); technology management (MS). Part-time and evening/weekend programs available.

Faculty: 3 full-time (0 women), 32 part-time/adjunct (1 woman).
Students: 2 full-time (0 women), 219 part-time (39 women); includes 23 minority (10 African Americans, 9 Asian Americans or Pacific Islanders, 3 Hispanic Americans, 1 Native American, 6 international. Average age 34. 60 applicants, 97% accepted. In 2001, 29 master's, 5 other advanced degrees awarded.
Degree requirements: For master's, thesis (for some programs).
Application deadline: For fall admission, 8/1 (priority date); for spring admission, 1/1 (priority date). Applications are processed on a rolling basis. *Application fee:* $30. Electronic applications accepted.
Expenses: Tuition: Part-time $401 per credit. Tuition and fees vary according to degree level and program.
Financial support: In 2001–02, 6 students received support; fellowships, research assistantships, institutionally sponsored loans and scholarships/grants available. Support available to part-time students. Financial award application deadline: 4/1;

financial award applicants required to submit FAFSA.
Ron Bennett, Director, 651-962-5750, *Fax:* 651-962-6419, *E-mail:* rjbennett@stthomas.edu.
Application contact: Marlene L. Houliston, Student Services Coordinator, 651-962-5750, *Fax:* 651-962-6419, *E-mail:* technology@stthomas.edu. *Web site:* http://www.stthomas.edu/technology/

■ THE UNIVERSITY OF SCRANTON

Graduate School, Program in Business Administration, Scranton, PA 18510

AWARDS Accounting (MBA); enterprise management technology (MBA); finance (MBA); general business administration (MBA); international business (MBA); management information systems (MBA); marketing (MBA); operations management (MBA). Part-time and evening/weekend programs available.

Faculty: 37 full-time (9 women).
Students: 42 full-time (17 women), 72 part-time (31 women); includes 2 minority (both Asian Americans or Pacific Islanders), 40 international. Average age 29. 45 applicants, 87% accepted. In 2001, 44 degrees awarded.
Degree requirements: For master's, capstone experience.
Entrance requirements: For master's, GMAT, TOEFL, minimum GPA of 2.75. *Application deadline:* Applications are processed on a rolling basis. *Application fee:* $50.
Expenses: Tuition: Part-time $539 per credit. Required fees: $25 per term.
Financial support: In 2001–02, 15 students received support, including 13 teaching assistantships with full tuition reimbursements available (averaging $6,206 per year); career-related internships or fieldwork, Federal Work-Study, and teaching fellowships also available. Support available to part-time students. Financial award application deadline: 3/1.
Faculty research: Financial markets, strategic impact of total quality management, internal accounting controls, consumer preference, information systems and the Internet.
Dr. Wayne H. J. Cunningam, Director, 570-941-4043, *Fax:* 570-941-4342, *E-mail:* cunninghamw1@uofs.edu. *Web site:* http://www.academic.scranton.edu/department/MBA/

■ THE UNIVERSITY OF TAMPA

John H. Sykes College of Business, Tampa, FL 33606-1490

AWARDS Accounting (MBA); entrepreneurship (MBA); information systems management (MBA); international business (MBA);

management (MBA); management of technology (MSTIM). Part-time and evening/weekend programs available.

Faculty: 41 full-time (13 women).
Students: 116 full-time (50 women), 270 part-time (116 women); includes 56 minority (16 African Americans, 10 Asian Americans or Pacific Islanders, 29 Hispanic Americans, 1 Native American), 96 international. Average age 30. 191 applicants, 77% accepted, 98 enrolled. In 2001, 97 degrees awarded.
Entrance requirements: For master's, GMAT, TOEFL. *Application deadline:* For fall admission, 8/15 (priority date). Applications are processed on a rolling basis. *Application fee:* $35.
Expenses: Tuition: Full-time $6,048; part-time $336 per credit. Required fees: $35 per semester.
Financial support: Research assistantships with tuition reimbursements, career-related internships or fieldwork and unspecified assistantships available. Support available to part-time students. Financial award applicants required to submit FAFSA.
Faculty research: Industrial organization and antitrust, artificial intelligence, corporate quality, leadership, ethics, quality.
Dr. Joseph E. McCann, Dean and Co-Chief Academic Officer, 813-253-6211, *Fax:* 813-258-7408, *E-mail:* jmccan@ut.edu.
Application contact: Dr. Mary B. Prescott, Director of Graduate Programs, 813-253-6211, *Fax:* 813-259-5403, *E-mail:* mprescott@ut.edu. *Web site:* http://mba.ut.edu/

■ THE UNIVERSITY OF TEXAS AT ARLINGTON

Graduate School, Program in Management of Technology, Arlington, TX 76019

AWARDS MS. Part-time and evening/weekend programs available. Postbaccalaureate distance learning degree programs offered (no on-campus study).

Students: 4 full-time (2 women), 7 part-time (1 woman); includes 1 minority (Asian American or Pacific Islander), 3 international. 11 applicants, 73% accepted, 5 enrolled. In 2001, 3 degrees awarded.
Entrance requirements: For master's, GRE, TOEFL, 3 years of full time work experience, minimum GPA of 3.0. *Application deadline:* For fall admission, 6/16. *Application fee:* $25 ($50 for international students).
Expenses: Tuition, area resident: Full-time $2,268. Tuition, nonresident: full-time $6,264. Required fees: $839. Tuition and fees vary according to course load.
Financial support: Fellowships, research assistantships, teaching assistantships, career-related internships or fieldwork, Federal Work-Study, institutionally sponsored loans, scholarships/grants, and

unspecified assistantships available. Financial award application deadline: 6/1; financial award applicants required to submit FAFSA.

Dr. Donald R. Liles, Chair, 817-272-3092, *Fax:* 817-272-3406, *E-mail:* dliles@uta.edu. **Application contact:** Dr. Bill Corley, Graduate Advisor, 817-272-3159, *Fax:* 817-272-3406, *E-mail:* hwcorley@exchange.uta.edu.

■ UNIVERSITY OF TULSA

Graduate School, College of Business Administration and College of Engineering and Natural Sciences, Department of Engineering and Technology Management, Tulsa, OK 74104-3189

AWARDS Chemical engineering (METM); computer science (METM); electrical engineering (METM); geological science (METM); mathematics (METM); mechanical engineering (METM); petroleum engineering (METM). Part-time and evening/weekend programs available.

Students: 2 full-time (1 woman), 1 part-time, 2 international. Average age 26. 3 applicants, 100% accepted, 1 enrolled. In 2001, 2 degrees awarded.
Entrance requirements: For master's, GRE General Test, TOEFL. *Application deadline:* Applications are processed on a rolling basis. *Application fee:* $30. Electronic applications accepted.
Expenses: Tuition: Full-time $9,540; part-time $530 per credit hour. Required fees: $80. One-time fee: $230 full-time.
Financial support: Fellowships, research assistantships, teaching assistantships, Federal Work-Study, scholarships/grants, tuition waivers (partial), and unspecified assistantships available. Support available to part-time students. Financial award application deadline: 2/1; financial award applicants required to submit FAFSA.
Application contact: Information Contact, *E-mail:* graduate-business@utulsa.edu. *Web site:* http://www.cba.utulsa.edu/academic.asp#graduate_studies/

■ UNIVERSITY OF WISCONSIN–STOUT

Graduate School, College of Technology, Engineering, and Management, Program in Management Technology, Menomonie, WI 54751

AWARDS MS. Part-time programs available.

Students: 13 full-time (1 woman), 14 part-time (3 women); includes 2 minority (both Asian Americans or Pacific Islanders), 8 international. 25 applicants, 72% accepted, 15 enrolled. In 2001, 12 degrees awarded.
Degree requirements: For master's, thesis.
Application deadline: Applications are processed on a rolling basis. *Application fee:* $45.

Expenses: Tuition, state resident: full-time $4,915. Tuition, nonresident: full-time $12,553.
Financial support: In 2001–02, 5 research assistantships were awarded; teaching assistantships, Federal Work-Study and tuition waivers (full and partial) also available. Support available to part-time students. Financial award application deadline: 4/1; financial award applicants required to submit FAFSA.
Dr. Thomas Lackosen, Director, 715-232-1144, *E-mail:* lackosent@uwstout.edu.
Application contact: Anne E. Johnson, Graduate Student Evaluator, 715-232-1322, *Fax:* 715-232-2413, *E-mail:* johnsona@uwstout.edu.

■ VANDERBILT UNIVERSITY

School of Engineering, Management of Technology Program, Nashville, TN 37240-1001

AWARDS M Eng, MS, PhD. MS and PhD offered through the Graduate School. Part-time programs available.

Faculty: 7 full-time (0 women), 5 part-time/adjunct (1 woman).
Students: 23 full-time (3 women), 13 part-time (3 women); includes 4 minority (2 African Americans, 1 Asian American or Pacific Islander, 1 Hispanic American), 11 international. Average age 30. 35 applicants, 77% accepted, 17 enrolled. In 2001, 1 master's, 1 doctorate awarded.
Degree requirements: For master's, thesis; for doctorate, thesis/dissertation, qualifying and final exams, comprehensive exam. *Median time to degree:* Master's–2 years full-time, 3.5 years part-time; doctorate–4 years full-time.
Entrance requirements: For master's, GMAT or GRE General Test, undergraduate degree in engineering or science, minimum GPA of 3.0; for doctorate, GRE General Test or GMAT, undergraduate degree in engineering or science, minimum GPA of 3.0. *Application deadline:* For fall admission, 1/15; for spring admission, 11/1. *Application fee:* $40. Electronic applications accepted.
Expenses: Tuition: Full-time $28,350.
Financial support: In 2001–02, 7 students received support, including 4 research assistantships with full tuition reimbursements available (averaging $13,750 per year), 7 teaching assistantships with full tuition reimbursements available (averaging $12,085 per year); fellowships, career-related internships or fieldwork and tuition waivers (full and partial) also available. Financial award application deadline: 1/15; financial award applicants required to submit FAFSA.
Faculty research: Management of emerging technologies, strategic management of advanced technology, technology policy, electronic commerce and marketplaces (business-to-business), systems engineering

and project management of rapidly evolving technologies. *Total annual research expenditures:* $27,000.
Dr. William F. Mahaffey, Director, 615-322-3479, *Fax:* 615-322-7996, *E-mail:* william.r.maaffey@vanderbilt.edu. *Web site:* http://www.vuse.vanderbilt.edu/

■ VILLA JULIE COLLEGE

School of Graduate and Professional Studies, Stevenson, MD 21153

AWARDS Advanced Information Technologies (MS); Business and Technology Management (MS); E-Commerce (MS). Part-time and evening/weekend programs available.

Faculty: 6 full-time (1 woman), 6 part-time/adjunct (1 woman).
Students: Average age 35. In 2001, 18 degrees awarded.
Degree requirements: For master's, thesis.
Entrance requirements: For master's, GRE General Test. *Application deadline:* For fall admission, 8/1; for spring admission, 12/31. Applications are processed on a rolling basis. *Application fee:* $25.
Expenses: Tuition: Part-time $385 per credit. Required fees: $100 per semester. One-time fee: $25 part-time. Part-time tuition and fees vary according to degree level.
Dr. Jean Blosser, Dean, 410-653-6400, *Fax:* 410-653-6405, *E-mail:* masters@vjc.edu.
Application contact: Judith B. Snyder, Admissions and Enrollment Services, 410-653-6400, *Fax:* 410-653-6405, *E-mail:* jsnyder@atec.vjc.edu. *Web site:* http://www.atec.vjc.edu/

■ WASHINGTON STATE UNIVERSITY

Graduate School, College of Business and Economics, Department of Business Administration, Pullman, WA 99164

AWARDS Accounting and business law (M Acc); business administration (MBA, PhD); technology management (MTM).

Faculty: 38.
Students: 167 full-time (67 women), 10 part-time (3 women); includes 12 minority (4 African Americans, 3 Asian Americans or Pacific Islanders, 3 Hispanic Americans, 2 Native Americans), 74 international. Average age 28. 289 applicants, 42% accepted, 69 enrolled. In 2001, 120 master's, 12 doctorates awarded.
Degree requirements: For master's, final presentation; for doctorate, thesis/dissertation, oral, written exam. *Median time to degree:* Master's–1.5 years full-time; doctorate–4.5 years part-time.
Entrance requirements: For master's, GMAT, TOEFL, minimum TOEFL of 550, minimum GPA of 3.0; for doctorate, GMAT, minimum GPA of 3.0. *Application deadline:* For fall admission, 3/1 (priority

Washington State University (continued) date). Applications are processed on a rolling basis. *Application fee:* $35. Electronic applications accepted.

Expenses: Tuition, state resident: full-time $6,088; part-time $304 per semester. Tuition, nonresident: full-time $14,918; part-time $746 per semester. Tuition and fees vary according to program.

Financial support: In 2001–02, 6 research assistantships with full and partial tuition reimbursements (averaging $12,000 per year), 52 teaching assistantships with full and partial tuition reimbursements (averaging $12,000 per year) were awarded. Career-related internships or fieldwork, Federal Work-Study, institutionally sponsored loans, health care benefits, tuition waivers (partial), unspecified assistantships, and teaching associateships also available. Financial award application deadline: 4/1.

Dr. Val Miskin, Director, 509-335-7617, *Fax:* 509-335-4735, *E-mail:* mba@wsu.edu. *Web site:* http://www.cbe.wsu.edu/graduate/index.html/

■ **WASHINGTON STATE UNIVERSITY SPOKANE**

Graduate Programs, Program in Technology Management, Spokane, WA 99201-3899

AWARDS MTM.

OPERATIONS RESEARCH

■ **AIR FORCE INSTITUTE OF TECHNOLOGY**

School of Engineering and Management, Department of Operational Sciences, Dayton, OH 45433-7765

AWARDS Logistics management (MS); operations research (MS, PhD). Space operations (MS). Part-time programs available.

Degree requirements: For master's and doctorate, thesis/dissertation.

Entrance requirements: For doctorate, GRE General Test, minimum GPA of 3.0, must be U.S. citizen.

Faculty research: Optimization, simulation, combat modeling and analysis, reliability and maintainability, resource scheduling. *Web site:* http://en.afit.edu/ens/

■ **BERNARD M. BARUCH COLLEGE OF THE CITY UNIVERSITY OF NEW YORK**

Zicklin School of Business, Department of Statistics and Computer Information Systems, Program in Operations Research, New York, NY 10010-5585

AWARDS MBA, MS. Part-time and evening/weekend programs available.

Faculty: 4 full-time (1 woman).
Students: 10 full-time (0 women), 12 part-time (2 women). 25 applicants, 64% accepted, 7 enrolled.
Entrance requirements: For master's, GMAT, TOEFL, TWE. *Application deadline:* For fall admission, 4/30; for spring admission, 10/31. *Application fee:* $40.
Expenses: Tuition, state resident: full-time $4,350; part-time $185 per credit. Tuition, nonresident: full-time $7,600; part-time $320 per credit. Tuition and fees vary according to program.
Financial support: Fellowships, research assistantships, career-related internships or fieldwork and Federal Work-Study available. Financial award application deadline: 5/1; financial award applicants required to submit FAFSA.
Application contact: Frances Murphy, Office of Graduate Admissions, 646-312-1300, *Fax:* 646-312-1301, *E-mail:* zicklingradadmissions@baruch.cuny.edu.

■ **CALIFORNIA STATE UNIVERSITY, FULLERTON**

Graduate Studies, College of Business and Economics, Department of Information Systems and Decision Sciences, Fullerton, CA 92834-9480

AWARDS Management information systems (MS); management science (MBA, MS); operations research (MS). Statistics (MS). Part-time and evening/weekend programs available.

Faculty: 28 full-time (4 women), 18 part-time/adjunct.
Students: 58 full-time (30 women), 50 part-time (15 women); includes 33 minority (2 African Americans, 29 Asian Americans or Pacific Islanders, 1 Hispanic American, 1 Native American), 48 international. Average age 30. 120 applicants, 46% accepted, 33 enrolled. In 2001, 44 degrees awarded.
Degree requirements: For master's, project or thesis.
Entrance requirements: For master's, GMAT, minimum AACSB index of 950. *Application fee:* $55.
Expenses: Tuition, nonresident: part-time $246 per unit. Required fees: $964.
Financial support: Teaching assistantships, Federal Work-Study, institutionally sponsored loans, and scholarships/grants available. Support available to part-time

students. Financial award application deadline: 3/1.
Dr. Barry Pasternack, Chair, 714-278-2221.

■ **CALIFORNIA STATE UNIVERSITY, HAYWARD**

Academic Programs and Graduate Studies, School of Business and Economics, Department of Management and Finance, Option in Operations Research, Hayward, CA 94542-3000

AWARDS MBA.

Degree requirements: For master's, comprehensive exam or thesis.
Entrance requirements: For master's, GMAT, minimum GPA of 2.75. *Application deadline:* For fall admission, 6/15; for winter admission, 10/27; for spring admission, 1/5. *Application fee:* $55.
Expenses: Tuition, nonresident: part-time $164 per unit. Required fees: $405 per semester.
Financial support: Federal Work-Study and institutionally sponsored loans available. Support available to part-time students. Financial award application deadline: 3/1.
Dr. Alan Goldberg, Coordinator, 510-885-3304.
Application contact: Dr. Donna L. Wiley, Director of Graduate Programs, 510-885-3964.

■ **CARNEGIE MELLON UNIVERSITY**

Graduate School of Industrial Administration, Program in Operations Research, Pittsburgh, PA 15213-3891

AWARDS PhD.

Degree requirements: For doctorate, thesis/dissertation.
Entrance requirements: For doctorate, GMAT or GRE General Test. *Web site:* http://www.gsia.cmu.edu/

■ **CASE WESTERN RESERVE UNIVERSITY**

Weatherhead School of Management, Department of Operations, Cleveland, OH 44106

AWARDS Management (MS), including finance, information systems, marketing, operations management, operations research, quality management, supply chain; operations research (PhD). Part-time programs available.

Faculty: 11 full-time (1 woman).
Students: 19 full-time (1 woman), 7 part-time (4 women), 11 international. Average age 28. In 2001, 19 master's, 1 doctorate awarded.
Degree requirements: For doctorate, thesis/dissertation.
Entrance requirements: For master's, GMAT (MBA), GRE General Test (MS);

for doctorate, GMAT, GRE General Test. *Application deadline:* For fall admission, 4/15 (priority date). Applications are processed on a rolling basis. *Application fee:* $50.

Financial support: Tuition waivers (full and partial) available. Financial award application deadline: 5/1.

Faculty research: Mathematical finance, mathematical programming, scheduling, stochastic optimization, environmental/energy models.

Matthew J. Sobel, Chairman, 216-368-6003, *E-mail:* mjs13@po.cwru.edu.

Application contact: Christine L. Gill, Director of Marketing and Admissions, 216-368-3845, *Fax:* 216-368-4776, *E-mail:* clg3@po.cwru.edu.

Find an in-depth description at www.petersons.com/gradchannel.

■ CLAREMONT GRADUATE UNIVERSITY

Graduate Programs, Independent Programs, Department of Mathematics, Claremont, CA 91711-6160

AWARDS Computer science (PhD); engineering mathematics (PhD); financial engineering (MS); operations research and statistics (MA, MS); physical applied mathematics (MA, MS); pure mathematics (MA, MS, PhD). Scientific computing (MA, MS). Systems and control theory (MA, MS). Part-time programs available.

Faculty: 3 full-time (0 women), 1 part-time/adjunct (0 women).

Students: 28 full-time (8 women), 11 part-time; includes 11 minority (1 African American, 8 Asian Americans or Pacific Islanders, 2 Hispanic Americans), 8 international. Average age 38. In 2001, 4 master's, 2 doctorates awarded. Terminal master's awarded for partial completion of doctoral program.

Degree requirements: For doctorate, 2 foreign languages, thesis/dissertation.

Entrance requirements: For master's and doctorate, GRE General Test. *Application deadline:* For fall admission, 2/15 (priority date). Applications are processed on a rolling basis. *Application fee:* $50. Electronic applications accepted.

Expenses: Tuition: Full-time $22,984; part-time $1,000 per unit. Required fees: $160; $80 per semester.

Financial support: Fellowships, research assistantships, career-related internships or fieldwork, Federal Work-Study, institutionally sponsored loans, and tuition waivers (full and partial) available. Support available to part-time students. Financial award application deadline: 2/15; financial award applicants required to submit FAFSA.

John Angus, Chair, 909-621-8080, *Fax:* 909-607-9261, *E-mail:* john.angus@cgu.edu.

Application contact: Mary Solberg, Administrative Assistant, 909-621-8080,

Fax: 909-607-9261, *E-mail:* math@cgu.edu. *Web site:* http://www.cgu.edu/math/index.html

■ CLEMSON UNIVERSITY

Graduate School, College of Engineering and Science, Department of Mathematical Sciences, Clemson, SC 29634

AWARDS Applied and pure mathematics (MS, PhD); computational mathematics (MS, PhD); management science (PhD); operations research (MS, PhD). Statistics (MS, PhD). Part-time programs available.

Students: 58 full-time (23 women), 4 part-time (1 woman); includes 6 minority (4 African Americans, 2 Hispanic Americans), 23 international. Average age 29. 76 applicants, 66% accepted, 24 enrolled. In 2001, 11 master's, 4 doctorates awarded.

Degree requirements: For master's, final project, thesis optional; for doctorate, thesis/dissertation, qualifying exams.

Entrance requirements: For master's and doctorate, GRE General Test, TOEFL. *Application deadline:* For fall admission, 6/1. *Application fee:* $40.

Expenses: Tuition, state resident: full-time $5,310. Tuition, nonresident: full-time $11,284.

Financial support: Fellowships, research assistantships, teaching assistantships available. Financial award application deadline: 4/15; financial award applicants required to submit FAFSA.

Faculty research: Applied and computational analysis, discrete mathematics, mathematical programming statistics.

Chair, 864-656-3436, *Fax:* 864-656-5230, *E-mail:* mathsci@clemson.edu.

Application contact: Dr. Douglas Shier, Graduate Coordinator, 864-656-1100, *Fax:* 864-656-5230, *E-mail:* shierd@clemson.edu.

■ THE COLLEGE OF WILLIAM AND MARY

Faculty of Arts and Sciences, Department of Computer Science, Program in Computational Operations Research, Williamsburg, VA 23187-8795

AWARDS MS. Part-time programs available.

Degree requirements: For master's, research project, thesis optional.

Entrance requirements: For master's, GRE General Test, minimum GPA of 2.5. *Application deadline:* For fall admission, 3/1 (priority date); for spring admission, 11/1. Applications are processed on a rolling basis. *Application fee:* $30.

Expenses: Tuition, state resident: full-time $3,262; part-time $175 per credit hour. Tuition, nonresident: full-time $14,768; part-time $550 per credit hour. Required fees: $2,478.

Financial support: In 2001–02, 7 teaching assistantships with full tuition reimbursements (averaging $10,500 per year) were awarded. Scholarships/grants and tuition waivers (full) also available.

Faculty research: Metaheuristics, simulation, reliability, optimization, statistics. *Total annual research expenditures:* $50,000.

Dr. Rex Kincaid, Professor, 757-221-2038, *Fax:* 757-221-1717, *E-mail:* rxkinc@math.wm.edu.

Application contact: Vanessa Godwin, Administrative Director, 757-221-3455, *Fax:* 757-221-1717, *E-mail:* gradinfo@cs.wm.edu.

■ COLUMBIA UNIVERSITY

Fu Foundation School of Engineering and Applied Science, Department of Industrial Engineering and Operations Research, New York, NY 10027

AWARDS Financial engineering (MS); industrial engineering (MS, Eng Sc D, PhD, Engr); operations research (MS, Eng Sc D, PhD). Part-time and evening/weekend programs available. Postbaccalaureate distance learning degree programs offered (no on-campus study).

Faculty: 16 full-time (0 women), 10 part-time/adjunct (0 women).

Students: 91 full-time (31 women), 69 part-time (21 women); includes 9 minority (8 Asian Americans or Pacific Islanders, 1 Native American), 125 international. Average age 26. 482 applicants, 46% accepted, 72 enrolled. In 2001, 76 master's, 4 doctorates awarded. Terminal master's awarded for partial completion of doctoral program.

Degree requirements: For doctorate, thesis/dissertation, oral and written qualifying exams.

Entrance requirements: For master's, doctorate, and Engr, GRE General Test, TOEFL. *Application deadline:* For fall admission, 1/5; for spring admission, 10/1. *Application fee:* $55. Electronic applications accepted.

Expenses: Tuition: Full-time $27,528. Required fees: $1,638.

Financial support: In 2001–02, 2 fellowships (averaging $5,000 per year), 12 research assistantships with full tuition reimbursements (averaging $19,200 per year), 12 teaching assistantships with full tuition reimbursements (averaging $19,200 per year) were awarded. Federal Work-Study also available. Financial award application deadline: 1/5; financial award applicants required to submit FAFSA.

Faculty research: Discrete event stochastic systems, optimization, productions planning and scheduling, inventory control, yield management, simulation, mathematical programming, combinatorial optimization, queuing, financial engineering. *Total annual research expenditures:* $682,685.

Columbia University (continued)
Dr. Donald Goldfarb, Chairman, 212-854-8011, *Fax:* 212-854-8103, *E-mail:* gold@ieor.columbia.edu.
Application contact: Nathaniel C. Farrell, Program Coordinator, 212-854-4351, *Fax:* 212-854-8103, *E-mail:* nat@ieor.columbia.edu. *Web site:* http://www.ieor.columbia.edu/

Find an in-depth description at www.petersons.com/gradchannel.

■ CORNELL UNIVERSITY

Graduate School, Graduate Fields of Engineering, Field of Operations Research and Industrial Engineering, Ithaca, NY 14853-0001

AWARDS Applied probability and statistics (PhD); manufacturing systems engineering (PhD); mathematical programming (PhD); operations research and industrial engineering (M Eng).

Faculty: 28 full-time.
Students: 109 full-time (19 women); includes 17 minority (1 African American, 15 Asian Americans or Pacific Islanders, 1 Hispanic American), 66 international. 380 applicants, 53% accepted. In 2001, 87 master's, 4 doctorates awarded. Terminal master's awarded for partial completion of doctoral program.
Degree requirements: For doctorate, thesis/dissertation.
Entrance requirements: For master's and doctorate, GRE General Test, TOEFL, 3 letters of recommendation. *Application deadline:* For fall admission, 1/15 (priority date). *Application fee:* $65. Electronic applications accepted.
Expenses: Tuition: Full-time $25,970. Required fees: $50.
Financial support: In 2001–02, 41 students received support, including 13 fellowships with full tuition reimbursements available, 8 research assistantships with full tuition reimbursements available, 20 teaching assistantships with full tuition reimbursements available; institutionally sponsored loans, scholarships/grants, tuition waivers (full and partial), and unspecified assistantships also available. Financial award applicants required to submit FAFSA.
Faculty research: Mathematical programming and combinatorial optimization, statistics, stochastic processes, mathematical finance, simulation, manufacturing.
Application contact: Graduate Field Assistant, 607-255-9128, *E-mail:* orphd@cornell.edu. *Web site:* http://www.gradschool.cornell.edu/grad/fields_1/oper-res.html

Find an in-depth description at www.petersons.com/gradchannel.

■ FLORIDA INSTITUTE OF TECHNOLOGY

Graduate Programs, College of Science and Liberal Arts, Department of Mathematical Sciences, Melbourne, FL 32901-6975

AWARDS Applied mathematics (MS, PhD); operations research (MS, PhD). Part-time and evening/weekend programs available.

Faculty: 12 full-time (2 women), 2 part-time/adjunct (0 women).
Students: 12 full-time (5 women), 16 part-time (1 woman); includes 3 minority (1 African American, 2 Asian Americans or Pacific Islanders), 11 international. Average age 34. 54 applicants, 63% accepted. In 2001, 8 master's, 7 doctorates awarded. Terminal master's awarded for partial completion of doctoral program.
Degree requirements: For master's, thesis optional; for doctorate, thesis/dissertation, comprehensive exam.
Entrance requirements: For master's, minimum GPA of 3.0; for doctorate, minimum GPA of 3.2. *Application deadline:* Applications are processed on a rolling basis. *Application fee:* $50. Electronic applications accepted.
Expenses: Tuition: Part-time $650 per credit.
Financial support: In 2001–02, 12 students received support, including 12 teaching assistantships with full and partial tuition reimbursements available (averaging $9,310 per year); research assistantships with full and partial tuition reimbursements available, career-related internships or fieldwork and tuition remissions also available. Financial award application deadline: 3/1; financial award applicants required to submit FAFSA.
Faculty research: Real analysis, ODE, PDE, numerical analysis, statistics, data analysis, combinatorics, artificial intelligence, simulation. *Total annual research expenditures:* $20,000.
Dr. V. Lakshmikantham, Department Head, 321-674-8091, *Fax:* 321-674-7412, *E-mail:* lakshmik@winnie.fit.edu.
Application contact: Carolyn P. Farrior, Director of Graduate Admissions, 321-674-7118, *Fax:* 321-723-9468, *E-mail:* cfarrior@fit.edu. *Web site:* http://www.fit.edu/

■ FLORIDA INSTITUTE OF TECHNOLOGY

Graduate Programs, School of Extended Graduate Studies, Melbourne, FL 32901-6975

AWARDS Acquisition and contract management (MS, MSM, PMBA); aerospace engineering (MS); business administration (PMBA); computer information systems (MS); computer science (MS); ebusiness (MSM); electrical engineering (MS); engineering management (MS); health management (MS); human resource management (MSM, PMBA); human resources management (MS); information systems (MSM, PMBA); logistics management (MS, MSM); management (MS); material acquisition management (MS); mechanical engineering (MS); operations research (MS); project management (MS), including information systems, operations research; public administration (MPA). Software engineering (MS). Space systems (MS). Space systems management (MS). Systems management (MS), including information systems, operations research; transportation management (MSM). Part-time and evening/weekend programs available. Postbaccalaureate distance learning degree programs offered (no on-campus study).

Faculty: 10 full-time (2 women), 131 part-time/adjunct (15 women).
Students: 57 full-time (29 women), 1,198 part-time (455 women); includes 277 minority (183 African Americans, 38 Asian Americans or Pacific Islanders, 51 Hispanic Americans, 5 Native Americans), 16 international. Average age 37. 299 applicants, 42% accepted. In 2001, 434 degrees awarded.
Entrance requirements: For master's, minimum GPA of 3.0. *Application deadline:* Applications are processed on a rolling basis. *Application fee:* $50. Electronic applications accepted.
Expenses: Tuition: Part-time $650 per credit.
Financial support: Institutionally sponsored loans available. Financial award application deadline: 3/1; financial award applicants required to submit FAFSA.
Dr. Ronald L. Marshall, Dean, School of Extended Graduate Studies, 321-674-8880.
Application contact: Carolyn P. Farrior, Director of Graduate Admissions, 321-674-7118, *Fax:* 321-723-9468, *E-mail:* cfarrior@fit.edu. *Web site:* http://www.segs.fit.edu/

■ GEORGE MASON UNIVERSITY

School of Information Technology and Engineering, Department of Systems Engineering and Operations Research, Fairfax, VA 22030-4444

AWARDS Operations research and management science (MS). Systems engineering (MS). Part-time and evening/weekend programs available.

Faculty: 13 full-time (3 women), 4 part-time/adjunct (1 woman).
Students: 29 full-time (9 women), 208 part-time (48 women); includes 63 minority (24 African Americans, 30 Asian Americans or Pacific Islanders, 9 Hispanic Americans), 20 international. Average age 35. 122 applicants, 84% accepted. In 2001, 44 degrees awarded.
Degree requirements: For master's, thesis optional.
Entrance requirements: For master's, GRE General Test, TOEFL, minimum GPA of 3.0 in last 60 hours. *Application deadline:* For fall admission, 5/1; for spring

admission, 11/1. *Application fee:* $30. Electronic applications accepted.

Expenses: Tuition, state resident: full-time $3,168; part-time $132 per credit hour. Tuition, nonresident: full-time $11,280; part-time $470 per credit hour. Required fees: $1,416; $59 per credit hour.

Financial support: Fellowships, research assistantships, teaching assistantships, career-related internships or fieldwork and Federal Work-Study available. Support available to part-time students. Financial award application deadline: 3/1; financial award applicants required to submit FAFSA.

Faculty research: Requirements engineering, signal processing, systems architecture, data fusion.

Dr. Karla L. Hoffman, Chairman, 703-993-1670, *Fax:* 703-993-1521, *E-mail:* seor@gmu.edu. *Web site:* http://www.gmu.edu/departments/seor/

■ GEORGIA INSTITUTE OF TECHNOLOGY

Graduate Studies and Research, College of Engineering, School of Industrial and Systems Engineering, Program in Operations Research, Atlanta, GA 30332-0001

AWARDS MSOR. Part-time programs available.

Entrance requirements: For master's, GRE General Test, TOEFL, minimum GPA of 3.0. Electronic applications accepted.

Faculty research: Linear and nonlinear deterministic models in operations research, mathematical statistics, design of experiments. *Web site:* http://www.isye.gatech.edu/

Find an in-depth description at www.petersons.com/gradchannel.

■ GEORGIA STATE UNIVERSITY

J. Mack Robinson College of Business, Department of Management, Atlanta, GA 30303-3083

AWARDS Decision sciences (MBA, MS); entrepreneurship (MBA); management (MBA, MS, PhD); operations management (PhD). Part-time and evening/weekend programs available. Terminal master's awarded for partial completion of doctoral program.

Degree requirements: For doctorate, thesis/dissertation.

Entrance requirements: For master's and doctorate, GMAT, TOEFL. Electronic applications accepted.

■ IDAHO STATE UNIVERSITY

Office of Graduate Studies, College of Engineering, Pocatello, ID 83209

AWARDS Engineering and applied science (PhD); engineering structures and mechanics (MS); environmental engineering (MS);

measurement and control engineering (MS); nuclear science and engineering (MS); waste management and environmental science (MS). Part-time programs available.

Faculty: 13 full-time (0 women), 1 part-time/adjunct (0 women).

Students: 34 full-time (8 women), 18 part-time (1 woman); includes 7 minority (1 African American, 5 Asian Americans or Pacific Islanders, 1 Hispanic American), 15 international. Average age 34. In 2001, 12 master's, 1 doctorate awarded.

Degree requirements: For master's and doctorate, thesis/dissertation.

Entrance requirements: For master's and doctorate, GRE General Test, TOEFL. *Application deadline:* For fall admission, 7/1 (priority date); for spring admission, 12/1. Applications are processed on a rolling basis. *Application fee:* $35.

Expenses: Tuition, area resident: Full-time $3,432. Tuition, state resident: part-time $172 per credit. Tuition, nonresident: full-time $10,196; part-time $262 per credit. International tuition: $9,672 full-time. Part-time tuition and fees vary according to course load, program and reciprocity agreements.

Financial support: In 2001–02, 7 research assistantships with full and partial tuition reimbursements (averaging $10,740 per year), 16 teaching assistantships with full and partial tuition reimbursements (averaging $6,775 per year) were awarded. Federal Work-Study and institutionally sponsored loans also available. Support available to part-time students. Financial award application deadline: 2/15.

Faculty research: Isotope separation, control technology, two-phase flow, photosonolysis, criticality calculations. *Total annual research expenditures:* $293,915.

Dr. Jay Kunze, Dean, 208-282-2902, *Fax:* 208-282-4538. *Web site:* http://www.coe.isu.edu/engrg/

■ INDIANA UNIVERSITY–PURDUE UNIVERSITY FORT WAYNE

School of Arts and Sciences, Department of Mathematical Sciences, Fort Wayne, IN 46805-1499

AWARDS Applied mathematics (MS); mathematics (MS); operations research (MS). Part-time and evening/weekend programs available.

Faculty: 3 full-time (1 woman).

Students: 1 full-time (0 women), 12 part-time (4 women); includes 1 minority (Asian American or Pacific Islander). Average age 34. 8 applicants, 75% accepted, 6 enrolled. In 2001, 1 degree awarded.

Entrance requirements: For master's, minimum GPA of 3.0, major or minor in mathematics. *Application deadline:* For fall admission, 7/1 (priority date); for spring admission, 12/1. Applications are processed on a rolling basis. *Application fee:* $30.

Expenses: Tuition, state resident: full-time $2,845; part-time $158 per credit hour.

Tuition, nonresident: full-time $6,323; part-time $351 per credit hour. Required fees: $9 per credit hour. Tuition and fees vary according to course load.

Financial support: In 2001–02, teaching assistantships with partial tuition reimbursements (averaging $7,350 per year); Federal Work-Study, scholarships/grants, and unspecified assistantships also available. Support available to part-time students. Financial award application deadline: 3/1; financial award applicants required to submit FAFSA.

Faculty research: Graph theory, biostatistics, statistical design, mathematics education, partial differential equations.

Dr. David A. Legg, Chair, 260-481-6821, *Fax:* 260-481-6880, *E-mail:* legg@ipfw.edu.

Application contact: Dr. W. Douglas Weakley, Director of Graduate Studies, 260-481-6821, *Fax:* 260-481-6880, *E-mail:* weakley@ipfw.edu. *Web site:* http://www.ipfw.edu/math/

■ IOWA STATE UNIVERSITY OF SCIENCE AND TECHNOLOGY

Graduate College, College of Engineering, Department of Industrial and Manufacturing Systems Engineering, Ames, IA 50011

AWARDS Industrial engineering (MS, PhD); operations research (MS).

Faculty: 16 full-time.

Students: 35 full-time (5 women), 30 part-time (3 women), 62 international. 205 applicants, 42% accepted, 11 enrolled. In 2001, 12 master's, 3 doctorates awarded.

Degree requirements: For master's, thesis or alternative; for doctorate, thesis/dissertation. *Median time to degree:* Master's–2.7 years full-time; doctorate–4.3 years full-time.

Entrance requirements: For master's, GRE General Test, TOEFL or IELTS; for doctorate, GRE General Test, TOEFL, or IELTS. *Application deadline:* For fall admission, 3/1 (priority date); for spring admission, 10/1 (priority date). *Application fee:* $20 ($50 for international students). Electronic applications accepted.

Expenses: Tuition, state resident: full-time $1,851. Tuition, nonresident: full-time $5,449. Tuition and fees vary according to program.

Financial support: In 2001–02, 21 research assistantships with partial tuition reimbursements (averaging $10,714 per year), 24 teaching assistantships with partial tuition reimbursements (averaging $13,000 per year) were awarded. Fellowships, scholarships/grants, health care benefits, and unspecified assistantships also available.

Faculty research: Economic modeling, valuation techniques, robotics, digital controls, systems reliability.

Dr. Patrick Patterson, Chair, 515-294-1682, *Fax:* 515-294-3524, *E-mail:* ppatters@iastate.edu.

Iowa State University of Science and Technology (continued)

Application contact: Dr. John Jackman, Director of Graduate Studies, 515-294-0126. *Web site:* http://www.eng.iastate.edu/coe/grad.asp/

■ JOHNS HOPKINS UNIVERSITY

G. W. C. Whiting School of Engineering, Department of Mathematical Sciences, Baltimore, MD 21218-2699

AWARDS Discrete mathematics (MA, MSE, PhD); operations research/optimization/decision science (MA, MSE, PhD). Statistics/probability/stochastic processes (MA, MSE, PhD).

Faculty: 11 full-time (0 women), 3 part-time/adjunct (1 woman).
Students: 20 full-time (10 women), 3 part-time (1 woman); includes 1 minority (African American), 14 international. Average age 29. 70 applicants, 41% accepted, 7 enrolled. In 2001, 11 master's, 2 doctorates awarded. Terminal master's awarded for partial completion of doctoral program.
Degree requirements: For master's, thesis (for some programs); for doctorate, thesis/dissertation, oral exam.
Entrance requirements: For master's and doctorate, GRE General Test, GRE Subject Test, TOEFL. *Application deadline:* For fall admission, 1/15 (priority date). Applications are processed on a rolling basis. *Application fee:* $0. Electronic applications accepted.
Expenses: Tuition: Full-time $27,390.
Financial support: In 2001–02, 23 students received support, including 1 fellowship with full tuition reimbursement available (averaging $16,000 per year), 5 research assistantships with full tuition reimbursements available (averaging $14,247 per year), 13 teaching assistantships with full tuition reimbursements available (averaging $14,247 per year); Federal Work-Study, institutionally sponsored loans, tuition waivers (full), and unspecified assistantships also available. Financial award application deadline: 1/15.
Faculty research: Discrete mathematics, probability, optimization, statistics, operations research. *Total annual research expenditures:* $545,614.
Dr. Edward R. Scheinerman, Chair, 410-516-7210, *Fax:* 410-516-7459, *E-mail:* ers@jhu.edu.
Application contact: Kay Lutz, Graduate Coordinator, 410-516-7198, *Fax:* 410-516-7459, *E-mail:* lutz@jhu.edu. *Web site:* http://brutus.mts.jhu.edu/

■ KANSAS STATE UNIVERSITY

Graduate School, College of Engineering, Department of Industrial and Manufacturing Systems Engineering, Manhattan, KS 66506

AWARDS Engineering management (MEM); industrial and manufacturing systems engineering (PhD); industrial engineering (MS); operations research (MS). Part-time programs available. Postbaccalaureate distance learning degree programs offered.

Faculty: 11 full-time (1 woman).
Students: 30 full-time (7 women), 24 part-time (2 women), 31 international. 201 applicants, 49% accepted, 19 enrolled. In 2001, 5 master's, 1 doctorate awarded.
Degree requirements: For master's, thesis or alternative; for doctorate, thesis/dissertation.
Entrance requirements: For master's, GRE General Test, TOEFL, bachelor's degree in engineering, mathematics, or physical science; for doctorate, GRE General Test, TOEFL, master's degree in engineering or industrial manufacturing. *Application deadline:* For fall admission, 3/1 (priority date); for spring admission, 9/1. Applications are processed on a rolling basis. *Application fee:* $0 ($25 for international students). Electronic applications accepted.
Expenses: Tuition, state resident: part-time $113 per credit hour. Tuition, nonresident: part-time $358 per credit hour.
Financial support: In 2001–02, 18 research assistantships with partial tuition reimbursements (averaging $9,000 per year), 2 teaching assistantships with full tuition reimbursements (averaging $9,000 per year) were awarded. Federal Work-Study, institutionally sponsored loans, and scholarships/grants also available. Support available to part-time students. Financial award application deadline: 3/1; financial award applicants required to submit FAFSA.
Faculty research: Manufacturing engineering, operations research, engineering management, quality engineering, ergonomics. *Total annual research expenditures:* $1.7 million.
Dr. Bradley Kramer, Head, 785-532-5606, *Fax:* 785-532-7810, *E-mail:* bradleyk@ksu.edu.
Application contact: E. Stanley Lee, Graduate Program Director, 785-532-5606, *Fax:* 785-532-7810, *E-mail:* eslee@ksu.edu. *Web site:* http://cheetah.imse.ksu.edu/

■ KETTERING UNIVERSITY

Graduate School, Industrial and Manufacturing Engineering and Business Department, Flint, MI 48504-4898

AWARDS Manufacturing management (MSMM, MSMO); manufacturing systems engineering (MS Eng); operations management (MSOM). Part-time and evening/weekend programs available. Postbaccalaureate distance learning degree programs offered (no on-campus study).

Faculty: 20 full-time (5 women).
Students: 3 full-time (1 woman), 579 part-time (168 women); includes 80 minority (56 African Americans, 13 Asian Americans or Pacific Islanders, 11 Hispanic Americans), 12 international. 157 applicants, 100% accepted. In 2001, 176 degrees awarded.
Degree requirements: For master's, thesis (for some programs), registration. *Median time to degree:* Master's–3 years full-time, 6 years part-time. *Application deadline:* For fall admission, 7/15. Applications are processed on a rolling basis. *Application fee:* $0. Electronic applications accepted.
Expenses: Tuition: Full-time $8,370; part-time $465 per credit.
Financial support: Fellowships with full tuition reimbursements, research assistantships with full tuition reimbursements, teaching assistantships with full tuition reimbursements, Federal Work-Study, scholarships/grants, and tuition waivers (partial) available. Support available to part-time students. Financial award application deadline: 7/15; financial award applicants required to submit CSS PROFILE or FAFSA.
Dr. David W. Poock, Head, 810-762-7959, *Fax:* 810-762-9924, *E-mail:* dpoock@kettering.edu.
Application contact: Betty L. Bedore, Coordinator of Publicity, 810-762-7494, *Fax:* 810-762-9935, *E-mail:* bbedore@kettering.edu. *Web site:* http://www.kettering.edu/

■ LOUISIANA TECH UNIVERSITY

Graduate School, College of Engineering and Science, Department of Mechanical and Industrial Engineering, Ruston, LA 71272

AWARDS Industrial engineering (MS, D Eng); manufacturing systems engineering (MS); mechanical engineering (MS, D Eng); operations research (MS). Part-time programs available. Terminal master's awarded for partial completion of doctoral program.

Degree requirements: For master's and doctorate, thesis/dissertation.
Entrance requirements: For master's, GRE General Test, TOEFL, minimum GPA of 3.0 in last 60 hours; for doctorate, TOEFL, minimum graduate GPA of 3.25 (with MS) or GRE General Test.
Faculty research: Engineering management, facilities planning, thermodynamics, automated manufacturing, micromanufacturing.

■ MASSACHUSETTS INSTITUTE OF TECHNOLOGY

Operations Research Center, Cambridge, MA 02139-4307

AWARDS SM, PhD.

Faculty: 44 full-time (2 women).
Students: 47 full-time (14 women); includes 1 minority (African American), 25 international. Average age 22. 117 applicants, 20% accepted. In 2001, 10

master's, 4 doctorates awarded. Terminal master's awarded for partial completion of doctoral program.

Degree requirements: For master's, thesis; for doctorate, thesis/dissertation, qualifying exam, general exam.

Entrance requirements: For master's and doctorate, GRE General Test, TOEFL. *Application deadline:* For fall admission, 12/31. *Application fee:* $60. Electronic applications accepted.

Expenses: Tuition: Full-time $26,960. Full-time tuition and fees vary according to program.

Financial support: In 2001–02, 45 students received support, including 10 fellowships (averaging $14,670 per year), 29 research assistantships (averaging $14,670 per year), 6 teaching assistantships (averaging $14,670 per year); Federal Work-Study, institutionally sponsored loans, scholarships/grants, and tuition waivers also available. Financial award application deadline: 12/31.

Faculty research: Linear and nonlinear programming, combinatorial and network optimization, operations management, transportation, applied probabilistic systems.

Dr. James B. Orlin, Co-Director, 617-253-6606, *Fax:* 617-258-9214, *E-mail:* jorlin@mit.edu.

Application contact: Laura A. Rose, Admissions Coordinator, 617-253-9303, *Fax:* 617-258-9214, *E-mail:* lrose@mit.edu. *Web site:* http://web.mit.edu/orc/www

Find an in-depth description at www.petersons.com/gradchannel.

■ MIAMI UNIVERSITY

Graduate School, College of Arts and Sciences, Department of Mathematics and Statistics, Program in Mathematics, Oxford, OH 45056

AWARDS Mathematics (MA, MAT, MS); mathematics/operations research (MS). Part-time programs available.

Students: 26 full-time (14 women); includes 1 minority (Hispanic American), 1 international. 18 applicants, 94% accepted, 16 enrolled. In 2001, 10 degrees awarded.

Degree requirements: For master's, final exam.

Entrance requirements: For master's, minimum undergraduate GPA of 3.0 during previous 2 years or 2.75 overall. *Application deadline:* For fall admission, 3/1 (priority date); for spring admission, 12/1. Applications are processed on a rolling basis. *Application fee:* $35.

Expenses: Tuition, state resident: full-time $7,155; part-time $295 per semester hour. Tuition, nonresident: full-time $14,829; part-time $615 per semester hour. Tuition and fees vary according to degree level and campus/location.

Financial support: Fellowships, research assistantships, teaching assistantships, Federal Work-Study and tuition waivers

(full) available. Financial award application deadline: 3/1.

Application contact: Dr. Robert Schaefer, Director of Graduate Studies, 513-529-5818, *E-mail:* math@muohio.edu. *Web site:* http://www.muohio.edu/~gsrcwis/programs/teach-edu/med.html

■ MICHIGAN STATE UNIVERSITY

Graduate School, College of Natural Science, Department of Statistics and Probability, East Lansing, MI 48824

AWARDS Applied statistics (MS); computational statistics (MS); operations research-statistics (MS). Statistics (MA, MS, PhD). Part-time programs available.

Faculty: 16 full-time (2 women).

Students: 34 full-time (23 women), 15 part-time (6 women); includes 2 minority (1 Asian American or Pacific Islander, 1 Hispanic American), 41 international. Average age 28. 102 applicants, 33% accepted. In 2001, 10 master's, 4 doctorates awarded. Terminal master's awarded for partial completion of doctoral program.

Degree requirements: For doctorate, one foreign language, thesis/dissertation.

Entrance requirements: For master's and doctorate, GRE, TOEFL. *Application deadline:* For fall admission, 1/1 (priority date). Applications are processed on a rolling basis. *Application fee:* $30 ($40 for international students).

Expenses: Tuition, state resident: part-time $244 per credit hour. Tuition, nonresident: part-time $494 per credit hour. Required fees: $268 per semester. Tuition and fees vary according to course load, degree level and program.

Financial support: In 2001–02, 16 fellowships with tuition reimbursements (averaging $903 per year), 26 teaching assistantships with tuition reimbursements (averaging $11,463 per year) were awarded. Research assistantships Financial award application deadline: 1/1; financial award applicants required to submit FAFSA.

Faculty research: Weak convergence in statistical inference, stochastic approximation, nonparametrics, sequential procedures, stochastic processes. *Total annual research expenditures:* $85,808.

Dr. Habib Salehi, Chairman, 517-355-9589, *Fax:* 517-432-1405.

Application contact: Graduate Program Director, 517-355-9589. *Web site:* http://www.stt.msu.edu/

Find an in-depth description at www.petersons.com/gradchannel.

■ NAVAL POSTGRADUATE SCHOOL

Graduate Programs, Department of Operations Research, Monterey, CA 93943

AWARDS MS, PhD. Program only open to commissioned officers of the United States

and friendly nations and selected United States federal civilian employees. Part-time programs available.

Degree requirements: For master's, thesis; for doctorate, one foreign language, thesis/dissertation.

■ NEW MEXICO INSTITUTE OF MINING AND TECHNOLOGY

Graduate Studies, Department of Mathematics, Socorro, NM 87801

AWARDS Mathematics (MS); operations research (MS).

Faculty: 8 full-time (0 women), 3 part-time/adjunct (0 women).

Students: 8 full-time (0 women), 1 (woman) part-time; includes 1 minority (Hispanic American), 3 international. Average age 32. 10 applicants, 80% accepted, 3 enrolled. In 2001, 1 degree awarded.

Degree requirements: For master's, thesis optional.

Entrance requirements: For master's, GRE General Test, TOEFL. *Application deadline:* For fall admission, 3/1 (priority date); for spring admission, 6/1. Applications are processed on a rolling basis. *Application fee:* $16 ($30 for international students).

Expenses: Tuition, state resident: part-time $1,084 per semester. Tuition, nonresident: part-time $4,367 per semester. Required fees: $429 per semester.

Financial support: In 2001–02, 1 research assistantship (averaging $13,505 per year), 5 teaching assistantships with full and partial tuition reimbursements (averaging $12,714 per year) were awarded. Fellowships, Federal Work-Study and institutionally sponsored loans also available. Financial award application deadline: 3/1; financial award applicants required to submit CSS PROFILE or FAFSA.

Faculty research: Abstract algebra, applied analysis, probability and statistics, stochastic processes, combinatorics.

Brian Borchers, Chairman, 505-835-5393, *Fax:* 505-835-5813, *E-mail:* borchers@nmt.edu.

Application contact: Dr. David B. Johnson, Dean of Graduate Studies, 505-835-5513, *Fax:* 505-835-5476, *E-mail:* graduate@nmt.edu. *Web site:* http://www.nmt.edu/~math/

■ NEW YORK UNIVERSITY

Leonard N. Stern School of Business, Department of Statistics and Operations Research, New York, NY 10012-1019

AWARDS MBA, MS, PhD, APC.

Degree requirements: For doctorate, thesis/dissertation.

Entrance requirements: For master's, GMAT, TOEFL; for doctorate, GMAT. Electronic applications accepted.

New York University (continued)

Expenses: Tuition: Full-time $19,536; part-time $814 per credit. Required fees: $1,330; $38 per credit. Tuition and fees vary according to course load and program.

Faculty research: Time series analysis, computer intensive statistical methodologies, stochastic modeling of financial instruments, prediction and control theory, sampling theory.

■ NORTH CAROLINA STATE UNIVERSITY

Graduate School, College of Engineering, Program in Operations Research, Raleigh, NC 27695

AWARDS MOR, MS, PhD. Part-time programs available.

Faculty: 37 full-time (1 woman), 3 part-time/adjunct (0 women).

Students: 42 full-time (18 women), 3 part-time (1 woman); includes 6 minority (4 African Americans, 2 Hispanic Americans), 26 international. Average age 28. 60 applicants, 47% accepted. In 2001, 7 master's, 7 doctorates awarded.

Degree requirements: For master's, thesis (MS); for doctorate, thesis/dissertation, comprehensive oral and written exams.

Entrance requirements: For master's, GRE General Test, TOEFL, minimum GPA of 2.7; for doctorate, GRE General Test, TOEFL, minimum GPA of 3.0. *Application deadline:* For fall admission, 6/25; for spring admission, 11/25. Applications are processed on a rolling basis. *Application fee:* $45.

Expenses: Tuition, state resident: full-time $1,748. Tuition, nonresident: full-time $6,904.

Financial support: In 2001–02, 3 fellowships (averaging $7,739 per year), 10 research assistantships (averaging $6,317 per year), 16 teaching assistantships (averaging $6,333 per year) were awarded.

Faculty research: Queuing analysis, simulation, inventory theory, supply chain management.

Dr. Xiuli Chao, Director of Graduate Programs, 919-515-4472, *Fax:* 919-515-1908, *E-mail:* xchao@eos.ncsu.edu.

Application contact: Dr. Elmor L. Peterson, Director of Graduate Programs, 919-515-4859, *Fax:* 919-515-1908, *E-mail:* elpeters@eos.ncsu.edu. *Web site:* http://www.or.ncsv.edu/

■ NORTH CAROLINA STATE UNIVERSITY

Graduate School, College of Management, Program in Management, Raleigh, NC 27695

AWARDS Biotechnology (MS); computer science (MS); engineering (MS); forest resources management (MS); general business (MS); management information systems (MS); operations research (MS). Statistics (MS); telecommunications systems engineering (MS); textile management (MS); total quality management (MS). Part-time programs available.

Faculty: 14 full-time (6 women), 3 part-time/adjunct (0 women).

Students: 60 full-time (18 women), 138 part-time (47 women); includes 27 minority (12 African Americans, 13 Asian Americans or Pacific Islanders, 2 Hispanic Americans), 17 international. Average age 32. 225 applicants, 44% accepted. In 2001, 67 degrees awarded.

Entrance requirements: For master's, GMAT or GRE, TOEFL, minimum undergraduate GPA of 3.0. *Application deadline:* For fall admission, 6/25; for spring admission, 11/25. Applications are processed on a rolling basis. *Application fee:* $45.

Expenses: Tuition, state resident: full-time $1,748. Tuition, nonresident: full-time $6,904.

Financial support: In 2001–02, fellowships (averaging $3,551 per year), 32 teaching assistantships (averaging $3,027 per year) were awarded. Research assistantships Financial award application deadline: 3/1.

Faculty research: Manufacturing strategy, information systems, technology commercialization, managing research and development, historical stock returns. *Total annual research expenditures:* $69,089.

Dr. Stephen G. Allen, Head, 919-515-5584, *Fax:* 919-515-5073, *E-mail:* steve_allen@ncsu.edu. *Web site:* http://www.mgt.ncsu.edu/facdep/bizmgmt/bizman.html

■ NORTH DAKOTA STATE UNIVERSITY

The Graduate School, College of Science and Mathematics, Department of Computer Science, Fargo, ND 58105

AWARDS Computer science (MS, PhD); operations research (MS). Part-time programs available.

Faculty: 11 full-time (0 women), 5 part-time/adjunct (2 women).

Students: 95 full-time (25 women), 29 part-time (7 women); includes 90 minority (5 African Americans, 85 Asian Americans or Pacific Islanders). Average age 24. 113 applicants, 33% accepted. In 2001, 29 master's, 2 doctorates awarded.

Degree requirements: For master's, thesis optional; for doctorate, thesis/dissertation, qualifying exam.

Entrance requirements: For master's, TOEFL, minimum GPA of 3.0, BS in computer science or related field; for doctorate, TOEFL, minimum GPA of 3.25, MS in computer science or related field. *Application deadline:* For fall admission, 8/15 (priority date); for spring admission, 12/15 (priority date). *Application fee:* $35.

Expenses: Tuition, state resident: part-time $124 per credit. Tuition, nonresident: part-time $325 per credit. Required fees: $22 per credit. Tuition and fees vary according to reciprocity agreements.

Financial support: In 2001–02, 31 research assistantships with full tuition reimbursements (averaging $10,000 per year), 13 teaching assistantships with full tuition reimbursements (averaging $8,000 per year) were awarded. Career-related internships or fieldwork, Federal Work-Study, and institutionally sponsored loans also available. Financial award application deadline: 4/15.

Faculty research: Networking, software engineering, artificial intelligence, database, programming languages.

Dr. Kendall E. Nygard, Chair, 701-231-8562, *Fax:* 701-231-8255, *E-mail:* kendall_nygard@ndsu.nodak.edu.

Application contact: Mimi E. Monson, Secretary, 701-231-9460, *Fax:* 701-231-8255, *E-mail:* mimi_monson@ndsu.nodak.edu. *Web site:* http://www.cs.ndsu.nodak.edu

■ NORTHEASTERN UNIVERSITY

College of Engineering, Department of Mechanical, Industrial, and Manufacturing Engineering, Boston, MA 02115-5096

AWARDS Engineering management (MS); industrial engineering (MS, PhD); mechanical engineering (MS, PhD); operations research (MS). Part-time programs available.

Faculty: 26 full-time (1 woman), 5 part-time/adjunct (1 woman).

Students: 97 full-time (22 women), 80 part-time (10 women); includes 32 minority (6 African Americans, 7 Asian Americans or Pacific Islanders, 19 Hispanic Americans), 77 international. Average age 25. 262 applicants, 53% accepted, 57 enrolled. In 2001, 46 master's, 6 doctorates awarded.

Degree requirements: For master's, thesis (for some programs), registration; for doctorate, one foreign language, thesis/dissertation, departmental qualifying exam.

Entrance requirements: For master's and doctorate, GRE General Test. *Application deadline:* For fall admission, 2/15 (priority date). Applications are processed on a rolling basis. *Application fee:* $50. Electronic applications accepted.

Expenses: Tuition: Part-time $535 per credit hour. Required fees: $56. Tuition and fees vary according to program.

Financial support: In 2001–02, 61 students received support, including 1 fellowship, 24 research assistantships with full tuition reimbursements available (averaging $13,560 per year), 26 teaching assistantships with full tuition reimbursements available (averaging $13,560 per year); career-related internships or fieldwork, Federal Work-Study, scholarships/grants, tuition waivers (full), and unspecified assistantships also available. Support available to part-time students. Financial award application deadline: 2/15; financial award applicants required to submit FAFSA.

Faculty research: Dry sliding instabilities, droplet deposition, helical hydraulic turbines, combustion, manufacturing systems. *Total annual research expenditures:* $1.8 million.

Dr. John W. Cipolla, Chairman, 617-373-3810, *Fax:* 617-373-2921.

Application contact: Stephen L. Gibson, Associate Director, 617-373-2711, *Fax:* 617-373-2501, *E-mail:* grad-eng@ coe.neu.edu.

Find an in-depth description at www.petersons.com/gradchannel.

■ NORTHWESTERN UNIVERSITY

McCormick School of Engineering and Applied Science, Department of Industrial Engineering and Management Sciences, Evanston, IL 60208

AWARDS Engineering management (MEM); industrial engineering and management science (MS, PhD); operations research (MS, PhD). MS and PhD admissions and degrees offered through The Graduate School.

Faculty: 17 full-time (2 women), 7 part-time/adjunct (0 women).
Students: 40 full-time (12 women); includes 1 minority (Asian American or Pacific Islander), 33 international. Average age 23. 230 applicants, 17% accepted, 12 enrolled. In 2001, 9 master's, 8 doctorates awarded. Terminal master's awarded for partial completion of doctoral program.
Degree requirements: For master's, comprehensive exam; for doctorate, thesis/dissertation, comprehensive exam. *Median time to degree:* Master's–1 year full-time; doctorate–4.5 years full-time.
Application deadline: For fall admission, 8/30; for winter admission, 11/27; for spring admission, 2/19. Applications are processed on a rolling basis. *Application fee:* $50 ($55 for international students). Electronic applications accepted.
Expenses: Tuition: Full-time $26,526.
Financial support: In 2001–02, 29 students received support, including 7 fellowships with full tuition reimbursements available (averaging $16,000 per year), 14 research assistantships with full tuition reimbursements available (averaging $19,962 per year), 8 teaching assistantships with full tuition reimbursements available (averaging $16,000 per year); career-related internships or fieldwork, Federal Work-Study, institutionally sponsored loans, scholarships/grants, and tuition waivers (full) also available. Financial award application deadline: 1/15; financial award applicants required to submit FAFSA.
Faculty research: Production, logistics, optimization, simulation, statistics. *Total annual research expenditures:* $900,000.

Ajit Tamhane, Chair, 847-491-3577, *Fax:* 847-491-8005, *E-mail:* tamhane@ iems.northwestern.edu.
Application contact: Lesley Perry, Graduate Program Coordinator, 847-491-4394, *Fax:* 847-491-8005, *E-mail:* lperry@ iems.northwestern.edu. *Web site:* http://www.iems.northwestern.edu/

Find an in-depth description at www.petersons.com/gradchannel.

■ OLD DOMINION UNIVERSITY

College of Engineering and Technology, Program in Operations Research and System Analysis, Norfolk, VA 23529

AWARDS ME.

Students: 3 full-time (2 women), 7 part-time (2 women), 3 international. Average age 35. In 2001, 4 degrees awarded.
Expenses: Tuition, state resident: part-time $202 per credit. Tuition, nonresident: part-time $534 per credit. Required fees: $76 per semester.

Dr. Charles Keating, Graduate Program Director, 757-683-5753, *Fax:* 757-683-5640, *E-mail:* enmagpd@odu.edu. *Web site:* http://www.odu.edu/engr/enma/

■ OREGON STATE UNIVERSITY

Graduate School, College of Science, Department of Statistics, Corvallis, OR 97331

AWARDS Applied statistics (MA, MS, PhD); biometry (MA, MS, PhD); environmental statistics (MA, MS, PhD); mathematical statistics (MA, MS, PhD); operations research (MA, MAIS, MS); Statistics (M Agr, MA, MS, PhD). Part-time programs available.

Faculty: 10 full-time (3 women).
Students: 25 full-time (10 women); includes 1 minority (Hispanic American), 7 international. Average age 30. In 2001, 10 master's, 3 doctorates awarded.
Degree requirements: For master's, consulting experience; for doctorate, thesis/dissertation, consulting experience.
Entrance requirements: For master's and doctorate, TOEFL, minimum GPA of 3.0 in last 90 hours. *Application deadline:* For fall admission, 2/15. Applications are processed on a rolling basis. *Application fee:* $50.
Expenses: Tuition, area resident: Full-time $15,933. Tuition, state resident: full-time $28,937.
Financial support: In 2001–02, 8 research assistantships, 19 teaching assistantships were awarded. Federal Work-Study and institutionally sponsored loans also available. Financial award application deadline: 2/15.
Faculty research: Analysis of enumerative data, nonparametric statistics, asymptotics, experimental design, generalized regression models, linear model theory, reliability theory, survival analysis, wildlife and general survey methodology.

Dr. Robert T. Smythe, Chair, 541-737-3480, *Fax:* 541-737-3489, *E-mail:* symthe@ stat.orst.edu.
Application contact: Dr. Daniel W. Schafer, Director of Graduate Studies, 541-737-3366, *Fax:* 541-737-3489, *E-mail:* statoff@stat.orst.edu. *Web site:* http://www.orst.edu/dept/statistics/

Find an in-depth description at www.petersons.com/gradchannel.

■ PRINCETON UNIVERSITY

Graduate School, School of Engineering and Applied Science, Department of Civil and Environmental Engineering, Program in Statistics and Operations Research, Princeton, NJ 08544-1019

AWARDS MSE, PhD.

Degree requirements: For master's, thesis; for doctorate, thesis/dissertation, qualifying exam.
Entrance requirements: For master's, GRE General Test, GRE Subject Test, bachelor's degree in engineering or science; for doctorate, GRE General Test, GRE Subject Test.

■ PRINCETON UNIVERSITY

Graduate School, School of Engineering and Applied Science, Department of Operations Research and Financial Engineering, Princeton, NJ 08544-1019

AWARDS Financial engineering (M Eng); operations research and financial engineering (MSE, PhD). *Web site:* http://www.orfe.princeton.edu/

■ PURDUE UNIVERSITY

Graduate School, Schools of Engineering, School of Industrial Engineering, West Lafayette, IN 47907

AWARDS Human factors in industrial engineering (MS, MSIE, PhD); manufacturing engineering (MS, MSIE, PhD); operations research (MS, MSIE, PhD). Systems engineering (MS, MSIE, PhD). Part-time programs available.

Faculty: 23 full-time (2 women), 4 part-time/adjunct (0 women).
Students: 117 full-time (24 women), 19 part-time (6 women); includes 6 minority (4 African Americans, 2 Hispanic Americans), 108 international. Average age 28. 370 applicants, 44% accepted. In 2001, 51 master's, 11 doctorates awarded. Terminal master's awarded for partial completion of doctoral program.
Degree requirements: For master's, thesis optional; for doctorate, thesis/dissertation.
Entrance requirements: For master's, GRE General Test, TOEFL, minimum GPA of 3.0; for doctorate, GRE General Test, TOEFL, MS thesis. *Application deadline:* For fall admission, 3/15; for

Purdue University (continued)
spring admission, 9/1. *Application fee:* $30. Electronic applications accepted.
Expenses: Tuition, state resident: full-time $4,164; part-time $149 per credit hour. Tuition, nonresident: full-time $13,872; part-time $458 per credit hour. Tuition and fees vary according to campus/location and program.
Financial support: In 2001–02, 78 students received support, including 3 fellowships with full tuition reimbursements available (averaging $13,070 per year), 29 research assistantships with full tuition reimbursements available (averaging $12,720 per year), 46 teaching assistantships with full tuition reimbursements available (averaging $10,600 per year) Support available to part-time students. Financial award application deadline: 3/15; financial award applicants required to submit FAFSA.
Faculty research: Precision manufacturing process, computer-aided manufacturing, computer-aided process planning, knowledge-based systems, combinatorics. *Total annual research expenditures:* $1.8 million.
Dr. Dennis Engi, Head, 765-494-5444, *Fax:* 765-494-1299, *E-mail:* engi@ ecn.purdue.edu.
Application contact: Dr. J. W. Barany, Associate Head, 765-494-5406, *Fax:* 765-494-1299, *E-mail:* jwb@ecn.purdue.edu. *Web site:* http://ie.www.ecn.purdue.edu/

■ RENSSELAER POLYTECHNIC INSTITUTE

Graduate School, Lally School of Management and Technology, Program in Management and Technology, Troy, NY 12180-3590

AWARDS E-business (MBA, MS); environmental management and policy (MBA, MS); finance (MBA, MS); management (PhD); management information systems (MBA, MS); new product development and marketing (MBA); new production and operations research (MS); product development and marketing (MS); production and operations research (MBA); technological entrepreneurship (MBA, MS). Part-time and evening/weekend programs available.
Postbaccalaureate distance learning degree programs offered (no on-campus study).
Faculty: 41 full-time (6 women), 2 part-time/adjunct (0 women).
Students: 388 full-time (54 women), 1,213 part-time (379 women); includes 139 minority (37 African Americans, 68 Asian Americans or Pacific Islanders, 33 Hispanic Americans, 1 Native American), 91 international. Average age 33. 628 applicants, 68% accepted, 268 enrolled. In 2001, 667 master's, 3 doctorates awarded.
Entrance requirements: For master's, GMAT, TOEFL, resumé, 3 letters of recommendation; for doctorate, GMAT or GRE General Test, TOEFL. *Application*

deadline: For fall admission, 1/15 (priority date); for spring admission, 11/1 (priority date). Applications are processed on a rolling basis. *Application fee:* $45. Electronic applications accepted.
Expenses: Tuition: Full-time $26,400; part-time $1,320 per credit hour. Required fees: $1,437.
Financial support: In 2001–02, 89 students received support; fellowships, research assistantships, teaching assistantships, career-related internships or fieldwork, institutionally sponsored loans, scholarships/grants, and tuition waivers (full and partial) available. Financial award application deadline: 1/15; financial award applicants required to submit FAFSA.
Faculty research: Entrepreneurship, operations management, new product development and marketing, information systems, finance.
Dr. Richard Burke, Director MBA/MS Programs, 518-276-6586, *Fax:* 518-276-2665, *E-mail:* lallymba@rpi.edu.
Application contact: Zamiul Haque, Director, MBA/MS Admissions, 518-276-6586, *Fax:* 518-276-2665, *E-mail:* lallymba@rpi.edu. *Web site:* http://www.lallymba.mgmt.rpi.edu/

■ RENSSELAER POLYTECHNIC INSTITUTE

Graduate School, School of Engineering, Department of Decision Sciences and Engineering Systems, Program in Operations Research and Statistics, Troy, NY 12180-3590

AWARDS M Eng, MS, MBA/M Eng. Part-time programs available.
Faculty: 16 full-time (1 woman), 3 part-time/adjunct (2 women).
Students: 13 full-time (2 women), 9 international. 30 applicants, 70% accepted, 9 enrolled. In 2001, 8 degrees awarded.
Degree requirements: For master's, thesis (for some programs).
Entrance requirements: For master's, GRE General Test, TOEFL. *Application deadline:* For fall admission, 1/15 (priority date). Applications are processed on a rolling basis. *Application fee:* $45. Electronic applications accepted.
Expenses: Tuition: Full-time $26,400; part-time $1,320 per credit hour. Required fees: $1,437.
Financial support: In 2001–02, 5 fellowships with full tuition reimbursements (averaging $6,310 per year), 2 teaching assistantships with full tuition reimbursements (averaging $12,620 per year) were awarded. Research assistantships with full tuition reimbursements, career-related internships or fieldwork and institutionally sponsored loans also available. Financial award application deadline: 1/15.
Faculty research: Manufacturing, MIS, statistical consulting, education services, production, logistics, inventory. *Total annual research expenditures:* $1 million.

Application contact: Lee Vilardi, Graduate Coordinator, 518-276-6681, *Fax:* 518-276-8227, *E-mail:* dsesgr@rpi.edu. *Web site:* http://www.rpi.edu/

Find an in-depth description at www.petersons.com/gradchannel.

■ RUTGERS, THE STATE UNIVERSITY OF NEW JERSEY, NEW BRUNSWICK

Graduate School, Program in Operations Research, New Brunswick, NJ 08901-1281

AWARDS PhD. Part-time programs available.

Degree requirements: For doctorate, thesis/dissertation, qualifying exam.
Entrance requirements: For doctorate, GRE General Test, GRE Subject Test.
Faculty research: Mathematical programming, combinatorial optimization, graph theory, stochastic modeling, queuing theory. *Web site:* http://rutcor.rutgers.edu/

■ ST. MARY'S UNIVERSITY OF SAN ANTONIO

Graduate School, Department of Engineering, Program in Industrial Engineering, San Antonio, TX 78228-8507

AWARDS Engineering computer applications (MS); engineering management (MS); industrial engineering (MS); operations research (MS).

Faculty: 6 full-time, 3 part-time/adjunct.
Students: 4 full-time (1 woman), 6 part-time (2 women); includes 1 minority (Hispanic American), 3 international. Average age 25. In 2001, 5 degrees awarded.
Degree requirements: For master's, thesis.
Entrance requirements: For master's, GRE General Test, BS in science or engineering. *Application deadline:* Applications are processed on a rolling basis. *Application fee:* $15. Electronic applications accepted.
Expenses: Tuition: Full-time $8,190; part-time $455 per credit hour. Required fees: $375.
Financial support: Teaching assistantships, Federal Work-Study available. Financial award application deadline: 2/15; financial award applicants required to submit FAFSA.
Faculty research: Robotics, artificial intelligence, manufacturing engineering.
Dr. Rafael Moras, Chairperson, 210-436-3305, *E-mail:* moras@stmarytx.edu.

■ SOUTHERN METHODIST UNIVERSITY

School of Engineering, Department of Computer Science and Engineering, Dallas, TX 75275

AWARDS Computer engineering (MS Cp E, PhD); computer science (MS, PhD); engineering management (MSEM, DE); operations research (MS, PhD). Software engineering (MS). Part-time and evening/weekend programs available. Postbaccalaureate distance learning degree programs offered (no on-campus study).

Faculty: 9 full-time (3 women).
Students: 53 full-time (15 women), 163 part-time (37 women); includes 73 minority (16 African Americans, 43 Asian Americans or Pacific Islanders, 14 Hispanic Americans), 49 international. Average age 32. 307 applicants, 78% accepted. In 2001, 59 master's, 4 doctorates awarded. Terminal master's awarded for partial completion of doctoral program.
Degree requirements: For master's, thesis optional; for doctorate, thesis/ dissertation, oral and written qualifying exams, oral final exam (PhD).
Entrance requirements: For master's, GRE General Test, TOEFL, minimum GPA of 3.0 in last 2 years; bachelor's degree in engineering, mathematics, or sciences; for doctorate, preliminary counseling exam (PhD), minimum GPA of 3.0, bachelor's degree in related field, MA (DE). *Application deadline:* For fall admission, 7/1 (priority date); for spring admission, 11/15. Applications are processed on a rolling basis. *Application fee:* $50.
Expenses: Tuition: Part-time $285 per credit hour.
Financial support: In 2001–02, 14 research assistantships with full tuition reimbursements (averaging $15,000 per year), 11 teaching assistantships with full tuition reimbursements (averaging $9,000 per year) were awarded. Financial award applicants required to submit FAFSA.
Faculty research: Trusted and high performance network computing, software engineering and management, knowledge engineering and management, computer arithmetic. *Total annual research expenditures:* $126,192.
Hesham El-Rewini, Head, 214-768-3278.
Application contact: Jim Dees, Director, Student Administration, 214-768-1456, *Fax:* 214-768-3845, *E-mail:* jdees@ engr.smu.edu. *Web site:* http:// www.seas.sm.edu/cse/

Find an in-depth description at www.petersons.com/gradchannel.

■ SOUTHERN METHODIST UNIVERSITY

School of Engineering, Department of Engineering Management, Information and Systems, Dallas, TX 75275

AWARDS Applied science (MS); engineering management (MSEM, DE); operations research (MS, PhD). Systems engineering (MS). Part-time and evening/weekend programs available. Postbaccalaureate distance learning degree programs offered.

Faculty: 6 full-time (1 woman).
Students: 10 full-time (1 woman), 100 part-time (22 women); includes 29 minority (6 African Americans, 11 Asian Americans or Pacific Islanders, 10 Hispanic Americans, 2 Native Americans), 10 international. 55 applicants, 78% accepted. In 2001, 25 master's, 5 doctorates awarded. Terminal master's awarded for partial completion of doctoral program.
Degree requirements: For master's, thesis optional; for doctorate, thesis/ dissertation, oral and written qualifying exams.
Entrance requirements: For master's, GRE General, TOEFL, minimum GPA of 3.0 in last 2 years; bachelor's degree in engineering, mathematics, or sciences; for doctorate, bachelor's degree in related field. *Application deadline:* For fall admission, 7/1; for spring admission, 11/15. Applications are processed on a rolling basis. *Application fee:* $50.
Expenses: Tuition: Part-time $285 per credit hour.
Faculty research: Telecommunications, decision systems, information engineering, operations research, software.
Richard S. Barr, Chair, 214-768-2605, *E-mail:* emis@engr.smu.edu.
Application contact: Marc Valerin, Associate Director of Graduate Admissions, 214-768-3484, *E-mail:* valerin@ seas.smu.edu.

Find an in-depth description at www.petersons.com/gradchannel.

■ TEMPLE UNIVERSITY

Graduate School, Fox School of Business and Management, Doctoral Programs in Business, Philadelphia, PA 19122-6096

AWARDS Accounting (PhD); economics (PhD); finance (PhD); general and strategic management (PhD); healthcare management (PhD); human resource administration (PhD); international business administration (PhD); management information systems (PhD); management science/operations research (PhD); marketing (PhD); risk, insurance, and health-care management (PhD). Statistics (PhD); tourism (PhD).

Students: 140; includes 18 minority (5 African Americans, 11 Asian Americans or Pacific Islanders, 2 Hispanic Americans),

81 international. Average age 31. 771 applicants, 63% accepted.
Entrance requirements: For doctorate, GRE General Test, TOEFL, minimum GPA of 3.0. *Application deadline:* For fall admission, 1/15. Applications are processed on a rolling basis. *Application fee:* $40.
Natale Butto, Director of Graduate Admissions, 215-204-7678, *Fax:* 215-204-8300, *E-mail:* butto@sbm.temple.edu. *Web site:* http://www.sbm.temple.edu/

Find an in-depth description at www.petersons.com/gradchannel.

■ TEMPLE UNIVERSITY

Graduate School, Fox School of Business and Management, Masters Programs in Business, Philadelphia, PA 19122-6096

AWARDS Accounting (MBA, MS); actuarial science (MS); business administration (EMBA, MBA); e-business (MBA, MS); economics (MA, MBA); finance (MBA, MS); general and strategic management (MBA); healthcare financial management (MS); healthcare management (MBA); human resource administration (MBA, MS); international business administration (IMBA); management information systems (MBA, MS); management science/operations management (MS); management science/operations research (MBA); marketing (MBA, MS); risk management and insurance (MBA). Statistics (MBA, MS). EMBA offered in Philadelphia, PA, or Tokyo, Japan.

Students: Average age 31.
Entrance requirements: For master's, GMAT, TOEFL, minimum GPA of 3.0. *Application deadline:* For fall admission, 4/15; for spring admission, 9/30. Applications are processed on a rolling basis. *Application fee:* $40. Electronic applications accepted.
Natale Butto, Director of Graduate Admissions, 215-204-7678, *Fax:* 215-204-8300, *E-mail:* butto@sbm.temple.edu.

Find an in-depth description at www.petersons.com/gradchannel.

■ THE UNIVERSITY OF ALABAMA IN HUNTSVILLE

School of Graduate Studies, College of Engineering, Department of Industrial and Systems Engineering/ Engineering Management, Program in Operations Research, Huntsville, AL 35899

AWARDS MSOR. Part-time and evening/ weekend programs available.

Students: 2 full-time (0 women), 3 part-time (1 woman); includes 2 minority (both African Americans), 2 international. Average age 25. 9 applicants, 67% accepted, 4 enrolled. In 2001, 2 degrees awarded.
Degree requirements: For master's, thesis or alternative, oral and written exams, comprehensive exam, registration.

The University of Alabama in Huntsville (continued)

Entrance requirements: For master's, GRE General Test, minimum GPA of 3.0, 6 hours of applied or mathematical statistics and calculus. *Application deadline:* For fall admission, 7/24 (priority date); for spring admission, 11/15 (priority date). Applications are processed on a rolling basis. *Application fee:* $35.

Expenses: Tuition, area resident: Part-time $175 per hour. Tuition, state resident: full-time $4,408. Tuition, nonresident: full-time $9,054; part-time $361 per hour.

Financial support: Fellowships with full and partial tuition reimbursements, research assistantships with full and partial tuition reimbursements, teaching assistantships with full and partial tuition reimbursements, career-related internships or fieldwork, Federal Work-Study, institutionally sponsored loans, scholarships/grants, and tuition waivers (full and partial) available. Support available to part-time students. Financial award application deadline: 4/1; financial award applicants required to submit FAFSA.

Faculty research: Simulation, manufacturing systems, system ergonomics, logistics. Dr. James Swain, Chair, Department of Industrial and Systems Engineering/Engineering Management, 256-824-6749, *Fax:* 256-824-6608, *E-mail:* jswain@ise.email.uah.

■ UNIVERSITY OF ARKANSAS

Graduate School, College of Engineering, Department of Industrial Engineering, Program in Operations Research, Fayetteville, AR 72701-1201

AWARDS MSE, MSOR.

Students: In 2001, 2 degrees awarded.
Degree requirements: For master's, thesis optional.
Application fee: $40 ($50 for international students).
Expenses: Tuition, state resident: full-time $3,553; part-time $197 per credit. Tuition, nonresident: full-time $8,411; part-time $467 per credit. Required fees: $42 per credit. Tuition and fees vary according to course load and program.
Financial support: Career-related internships or fieldwork and Federal Work-Study available. Support available to part-time students. Financial award application deadline: 4/1; financial award applicants required to submit FAFSA.
Dr. John English, Interim Chair, Department of Industrial Engineering, 479-575-3157.

■ UNIVERSITY OF CALIFORNIA, BERKELEY

Graduate Division, College of Engineering, Department of Industrial Engineering and Operations Research, Berkeley, CA 94720-1500

AWARDS M Eng, MS, D Eng, PhD.

Degree requirements: For master's, comprehensive exam or thesis (MS); for doctorate, thesis/dissertation, qualifying exam.
Entrance requirements: For master's and doctorate, GRE General Test, minimum GPA of 3.0.
Expenses: Tuition, nonresident: full-time $10,704. Required fees: $4,349.
Faculty research: Mathematical programming, robotics and manufacturing, linear and nonlinear optimization, production planning and scheduling, queuing theory.
Web site: http://www.ieor.berkeley.edu/

Find an in-depth description at www.petersons.com/gradchannel.

■ UNIVERSITY OF CALIFORNIA, LOS ANGELES

Graduate Division, School of Engineering and Applied Science, Department of Electrical Engineering, Program in Operations Research, Los Angeles, CA 90095

AWARDS MS, PhD.

Degree requirements: For master's, comprehensive exam or thesis; for doctorate, thesis/dissertation, qualifying exams.
Entrance requirements: For master's, GRE General Test, minimum GPA of 3.0; for doctorate, GRE General Test, minimum GPA of 3.25. *Application deadline:* For fall admission, 1/15. *Application fee:* $60. Electronic applications accepted.
Expenses: Tuition, nonresident: full-time $10,244. Required fees: $3,609. Full-time tuition and fees vary according to program.
Financial support: Fellowships, research assistantships, teaching assistantships, career-related internships or fieldwork, Federal Work-Study, institutionally sponsored loans, and tuition waivers (full and partial) available. Financial award application deadline: 1/15; financial award applicants required to submit FAFSA.
Application contact: Sharron Bryant, Student Affairs Officer, 310-825-9383, *E-mail:* sharron@ea.ucla.edu.

■ UNIVERSITY OF CENTRAL FLORIDA

College of Engineering and Computer Sciences, Department of Industrial Engineering and Management Systems, Orlando, FL 32816

AWARDS Applied operations research (Certificate); computer-integrated manufacturing (MS); design for usability (Certificate); engineering management (MS); industrial engineering (MSIE); industrial engineering and management systems (PhD); industrial ergonomics and safety (Certificate); operations research (MS); product assurance engineering (MS); project engineering (Certificate); quality assurance (Certificate).

Simulation systems (MS). Systems simulations for engineers (Certificate); training simulation (Certificate). Part-time and evening/weekend programs available.

Faculty: 20 full-time (4 women), 8 part-time/adjunct (1 woman).
Students: 92 full-time (19 women), 182 part-time (49 women); includes 66 minority (18 African Americans, 10 Asian Americans or Pacific Islanders, 35 Hispanic Americans, 3 Native Americans), 57 international. Average age 32. 231 applicants, 84% accepted, 85 enrolled. In 2001, 3 master's, 9 doctorates awarded.
Degree requirements: For master's, thesis; for doctorate, thesis/dissertation, departmental qualifying exam, candidacy exam.
Entrance requirements: For master's, GRE General Test, TOEFL, minimum GPA of 3.0 in last 60 hours; for doctorate, TOEFL, minimum GPA of 3.5 in last 60 hours. *Application deadline:* For fall admission, 7/15 (priority date); for spring admission, 12/1 (priority date). *Application fee:* $20. Electronic applications accepted.
Expenses: Tuition, state resident: part-time $162 per hour. Tuition, nonresident: part-time $569 per hour.
Financial support: In 2001–02, 23 fellowships with partial tuition reimbursements (averaging $3,272 per year), 131 research assistantships with partial tuition reimbursements (averaging $3,125 per year), 24 teaching assistantships with partial tuition reimbursements (averaging $3,823 per year) were awarded. Career-related internships or fieldwork, Federal Work-Study, institutionally sponsored loans, tuition waivers (partial), and unspecified assistantships also available. Financial award application deadline: 3/1; financial award applicants required to submit FAFSA.
Dr. Charles Reily, Chair, 407-823-2204, *E-mail:* creilly@mail.ucf.edu.
Application contact: Dr. Linda Malone, Coordinator, 407-823-2204, *E-mail:* malone@mail.ucf.edu. *Web site:* http://www.ucf.edu/

Find an in-depth description at www.petersons.com/gradchannel.

■ UNIVERSITY OF DELAWARE

College of Agriculture and Natural Resources, Operations Research Program, Newark, DE 19716

AWARDS MS, PhD. Part-time programs available.

Faculty: 25 full-time (2 women).
Students: 13 full-time (5 women), 4 part-time (2 women); includes 1 minority (African American), 11 international. Average age 30. 40 applicants, 25% accepted, 6 enrolled. In 2001, 8 degrees awarded. Terminal master's awarded for partial completion of doctoral program.
Degree requirements: For master's, thesis, oral exam; for doctorate, thesis/dissertation, qualifying exam.

Entrance requirements: For master's, GRE General Test, TOEFL, TSE, letters of recommendation (3), program language/s, engineering calculus, transcripts; for doctorate, GRE General Test, TOEFL, TSE, letters of recommendation (3), program language/s, engineering calculus. *Application deadline:* For fall admission, 5/1; for spring admission, 12/1. Applications are processed on a rolling basis. *Application fee:* $50. Electronic applications accepted.
Expenses: Tuition, state resident: full-time $4,770; part-time $265 per credit. Tuition, nonresident: full-time $13,860; part-time $770 per credit. Required fees: $414.
Financial support: In 2001–02, 14 students received support, including 11 research assistantships with full tuition reimbursements available (averaging $12,350 per year); teaching assistantships, career-related internships or fieldwork and tuition waivers (full) also available. Financial award application deadline: 5/1.
Faculty research: Simulation and modeling-production scheduling and optimization, agricultural production and resource economics, transportation engineering, statistical quality control. *Total annual research expenditures:* $10,570. Dr. Palaniappa Krishnan, Chair, 302-831-6242, *Fax:* 302-831-6243, *E-mail:* baba@ udel.edu.
Application contact: Jean E. Zistl, Staff Assistant, 302-831-6242, *Fax:* 302-831-6243, *E-mail:* jeanz@udel.edu. *Web site:* http://www.udel.edu/or/

■ UNIVERSITY OF FLORIDA

Graduate School, College of Engineering, Department of Industrial and Systems Engineering, Gainesville, FL 32611

AWARDS Engineering management (ME, MS); facilities layout decision support systems energy (PhD); health systems (ME, MS); industrial engineering (PhD, Engr); manufacturing systems engineering (ME, MS, PhD, Certificate); operations research (ME, MS, PhD, Engr); production planning and control engineering management (PhD); quality and reliability assurance (ME, MS). Systems engineering (PhD, Engr).

Degree requirements: For master's, core exam, thesis optional; for doctorate, thesis/dissertation, comprehensive exam.
Entrance requirements: For master's and doctorate, GRE General Test, TOEFL, minimum GPA of 3.0; for other advanced degree, GRE General Test. Electronic applications accepted.
Expenses: Tuition, state resident: part-time $164 per hour. Tuition, nonresident: part-time $571 per hour. Tuition and fees vary according to course level and program. *Web site:* http://www.ise.ufl.edu/

Find an in-depth description at www.petersons.com/gradchannel.

■ UNIVERSITY OF ILLINOIS AT CHICAGO

Graduate College, College of Engineering, Department of Mechanical Engineering, Program in Industrial Engineering and Operations Research, Chicago, IL 60607-7128

AWARDS PhD.

Students: 6 full-time (3 women), 2 part-time (1 woman), 7 international. Average age 31. 17 applicants, 29% accepted, 4 enrolled. In 2001, 3 degrees awarded.
Degree requirements: For doctorate, thesis/dissertation.
Entrance requirements: For doctorate, GRE General Test, TOEFL, minimum GPA of 3.75 on a 5.0 scale. *Application deadline:* For fall admission, 6/1; for spring admission, 11/1. Applications are processed on a rolling basis. *Application fee:* $40 ($50 for international students). Electronic applications accepted.
Expenses: Tuition, state resident: full-time $3,060. Tuition, nonresident: full-time $6,688.
Financial support: In 2001–02, 6 students received support; fellowships with full tuition reimbursements available, research assistantships with full tuition reimbursements available, teaching assistantships with full tuition reimbursements available, Federal Work-Study and tuition waivers (full) available. Financial award application deadline: 3/1; financial award applicants required to submit FAFSA.
Application contact: Mun Young Choi, Director of Graduate Studies.

Find an in-depth description at www.petersons.com/gradchannel.

■ THE UNIVERSITY OF IOWA

Graduate College, College of Engineering, Department of Industrial Engineering, Iowa City, IA 52242-1316

AWARDS Engineering design and manufacturing (MS, PhD); ergonomics (MS, PhD); information and engineering management (MS, PhD); operations research (MS, PhD); quality engineering (MS, PhD).

Faculty: 7 full-time, 1 part-time/adjunct.
Students: 37 full-time (13 women), 24 international. Average age 27. 115 applicants, 50% accepted, 6 enrolled. In 2001, 12 master's, 3 doctorates awarded.
Degree requirements: For master's, exam, thesis optional; for doctorate, thesis/dissertation, final defense exam, comprehensive exam, registration. *Median time to degree:* Master's–2 years full-time; doctorate–4 years full-time.
Entrance requirements: For master's and doctorate, GRE General Test, TOEFL. *Application deadline:* For fall admission, 4/15; for winter admission, 10/1; for spring admission, 3/1. Applications are processed on a rolling basis. *Application fee:* $30 ($50 for international students). Electronic applications accepted.

Expenses: Tuition, state resident: full-time $3,702; part-time $206 per semester hour. Tuition, nonresident: full-time $11,924; part-time $206 per semester hour. Required fees: $101 per semester. Tuition and fees vary according to course load and program.
Financial support: In 2001–02, fellowships with tuition reimbursements (averaging $14,764 per year), 16 research assistantships (averaging $14,764 per year), 6 teaching assistantships (averaging $14,764 per year) were awarded. Career-related internships or fieldwork, scholarships/grants, and unspecified assistantships also available. Support available to part-time students. Financial award applicants required to submit FAFSA.
Faculty research: Informatics, industrial robotics, operations research, human-computer interfaces, human factors (ergonomics). *Total annual research expenditures:* $752,000.
Dr. Jeffrey S. Marshall, Departmental Executive Officer, 319-335-5817, *Fax:* 319-335-5669, *E-mail:* jeffrey-marshall@uiowa.edu.
Application contact: Sue Mulder, Secretary, 319-335-5939, *Fax:* 319-335-5669, *E-mail:* indeng@engineering.uiowa.edu. *Web site:* http://www.mie.engineering.uiowa.edu

■ UNIVERSITY OF MASSACHUSETTS AMHERST

Graduate School, College of Engineering, Department of Mechanical and Industrial Engineering, Program in Industrial Engineering and Operations Research, Amherst, MA 01003-2210

AWARDS MS, PhD.

Students: 14 full-time (4 women), 21 part-time (4 women); includes 1 minority (Asian American or Pacific Islander), 25 international. Average age 29. 175 applicants, 19% accepted. In 2001, 4 master's, 4 doctorates awarded.
Degree requirements: For master's, project; for doctorate, thesis/dissertation.
Entrance requirements: For master's and doctorate, GRE General Test. *Application deadline:* For fall admission, 2/1 (priority date). Applications are processed on a rolling basis. *Application fee:* $40 ($50 for international students).
Expenses: Tuition, state resident: full-time $1,980; part-time $110 per credit. Tuition, nonresident: full-time $7,456; part-time $414 per credit. Required fees: $4,112. One-time fee: $115 full-time.
Financial support: Fellowships with full tuition reimbursements, research assistantships with full tuition reimbursements, teaching assistantships with full tuition reimbursements, career-related internships or fieldwork, Federal Work-Study, scholarships/grants, traineeships, and

University of Massachusetts Amherst (continued)

unspecified assistantships available. Support available to part-time students. Financial award application deadline: 2/1. Dr. Ian Grosse, Director, 413-545-2505, *Fax:* 413-545-1027. *Web site:* http://www.ecs.umass.edu/MIE/

■ UNIVERSITY OF MIAMI

Graduate School, School of Business Administration, Department of Management Science, Coral Gables, FL 33124

AWARDS Management science (MS, PhD), including applied statistics (MS), operations research (MS). Part-time and evening/weekend programs available. Postbaccalaureate distance learning degree programs offered.

Faculty: 10 full-time (2 women).
Students: 2 full-time (1 woman), 3 part-time (1 woman); includes 2 minority (1 African American, 1 Asian American or Pacific Islander), 1 international. Average age 30. 8 applicants, 75% accepted. In 2001, 2 master's awarded. Terminal master's awarded for partial completion of doctoral program.
Degree requirements: For master's, thesis optional; for doctorate, thesis/dissertation, comprehensive exam. *Median time to degree:* Master's–1.5 years full-time, 3 years part-time.
Entrance requirements: For master's and doctorate, GRE General Test, TOEFL. *Application deadline:* For fall admission, 6/30 (priority date); for spring admission, 10/31. Applications are processed on a rolling basis. *Application fee:* $50.
Expenses: Tuition: Part-time $960 per credit hour. Required fees: $85 per semester. Tuition and fees vary according to program.
Financial support: In 2001–02, 3 students received support, including 3 teaching assistantships (averaging $3,000 per year); career-related internships or fieldwork and Federal Work-Study also available. Financial award application deadline: 3/1.
Faculty research: Mathematical programming, applied statistics, applied probability, logistics, statistical process control. *Total annual research expenditures:* $20,000.
Dr. Edward Baker, Chairman, 305-284-6595, *Fax:* 305-284-2321, *E-mail:* ebaker@miami.edu.
Application contact: Dr. Moshe Friedman, Director, 305-284-1970, *Fax:* 305-284-2321, *E-mail:* moshef@miami.edu. *Web site:* http://www.bus.miami.edu/~mas/

■ UNIVERSITY OF MICHIGAN

Horace H. Rackham School of Graduate Studies, College of Engineering, Department of Industrial and Operations Engineering, Ann Arbor, MI 48109

AWARDS MS, MSE, PhD, IOE, MBA/MS, MBA/MSE, MHSA/MS. Part-time programs available. Terminal master's awarded for partial completion of doctoral program.

Degree requirements: For doctorate, oral defense of dissertation, preliminary exams, qualifying exam.
Entrance requirements: For master's, GRE General Test, TOEFL, minimum GPA of 3.2; for doctorate, GRE General Test, TOEFL, minimum GPA of 3.5. Electronic applications accepted.
Faculty research: Optimization and stochastic processes, human performance and ergonomics, engineering management, quality engineering, production manufacturing. *Web site:* http://ioe.engin.umich.edu

■ UNIVERSITY OF NEW HAVEN

Graduate School, School of Engineering and Applied Science, Program in Operations Research, West Haven, CT 06516-1916

AWARDS MS. Part-time and evening/weekend programs available.

Students: 2 full-time (0 women), (both international). In 2001, 1 degree awarded.
Degree requirements: For master's, thesis or alternative.
Application deadline: Applications are processed on a rolling basis. *Application fee:* $50.
Expenses: Tuition: Full-time $12,015; part-time $445 per credit hour. Required fees: $30. One-time fee: $100 full-time.
Financial support: Federal Work-Study available. Support available to part-time students. Financial award application deadline: 5/1; financial award applicants required to submit FAFSA.
Dr. Ronald Wentworth, Coordinator, 203-932-7434.

■ THE UNIVERSITY OF NORTH CAROLINA AT CHAPEL HILL

Graduate School, College of Arts and Sciences, Department of Operations Research, Chapel Hill, NC 27599

AWARDS MS, PhD.

Degree requirements: For master's, comprehensive exam; for doctorate, thesis/dissertation, comprehensive exam.
Entrance requirements: For master's and doctorate, GRE General Test, minimum GPA of 3.0.
Expenses: Tuition, state resident: full-time $2,864. Tuition, nonresident: full-time $12,030. *Web site:* http://www.or.unc.edu/

■ UNIVERSITY OF SOUTHERN CALIFORNIA

Graduate School, School of Engineering, Department of Industrial and Systems Engineering, Program in Operations Research, Los Angeles, CA 90089

AWARDS MS.

Degree requirements: For master's, thesis optional.
Entrance requirements: For master's, GRE General Test.
Expenses: Tuition: Full-time $25,060; part-time $844 per unit. Required fees: $473.

■ THE UNIVERSITY OF TEXAS AT AUSTIN

Graduate School, College of Engineering, Department of Mechanical Engineering, Program in Operations Research and Industrial Engineering, Austin, TX 78712-1111

AWARDS MSE, PhD.

Students: 75 full-time (13 women), 10 part-time (3 women); includes 4 minority (2 African Americans, 2 Asian Americans or Pacific Islanders), 62 international. 193 applicants, 45% accepted. In 2001, 15 master's, 2 doctorates awarded.
Entrance requirements: For master's, GRE General Test, TOEFL; for doctorate, GRE General Test. *Application fee:* $50 ($75 for international students).
Expenses: Tuition, state resident: full-time $3,159. Tuition, nonresident: full-time $6,957. Tuition and fees vary according to program.
Financial support: Fellowships, research assistantships, teaching assistantships available. Financial award application deadline: 2/1.
Application contact: Dr. J. Wesley Barnes, Graduate Advisor, 512-471-3083, *Fax:* 512-471-8727.

■ VIRGINIA COMMONWEALTH UNIVERSITY

School of Graduate Studies, College of Humanities and Sciences, Department of Mathematical Sciences, Program in Operations Research, Richmond, VA 23284-9005

AWARDS MS.

Entrance requirements: For master's, GRE General Test, GRE Subject Test, TOEFL. *Application deadline:* For fall admission, 7/1; for spring admission, 11/15. Applications are processed on a rolling basis. *Application fee:* $30.
Expenses: Tuition, state resident: full-time $4,276; part-time $238 per credit. Tuition, nonresident: full-time $12,672; part-time $704 per credit. Required fees: $1,167; $43 per credit.

Application contact: Dr. James A. Ames, Program Head. *Web site:* http://www.mas.vcu.edu/

■ VIRGINIA POLYTECHNIC INSTITUTE AND STATE UNIVERSITY

Graduate School, College of Engineering, Department of Industrial and Systems Engineering, Program in Operations Research, Blacksburg, VA 24061

AWARDS M Eng, MS, PhD.

Degree requirements: For master's and doctorate, thesis/dissertation.
Entrance requirements: For master's, TOEFL; for doctorate, TOEFL, minimum GPA of 3.0. *Application deadline:* For fall admission, 12/1 (priority date). Applications are processed on a rolling basis. *Application fee:* $45. Electronic applications accepted.
Expenses: Tuition, state resident: part-time $241 per hour. Tuition, nonresident: part-time $406 per hour. Tuition and fees vary according to program.
Financial support: Application deadline: 4/1.
Application contact: Lovedia S. Cole, Graduate Secretary, 540-231-5586, *Fax:* 540-231-3322, *E-mail:* lovediac@vt.edu.

■ WAYNE STATE UNIVERSITY

Graduate School, College of Engineering, Department of Industrial and Manufacturing Engineering, Detroit, MI 48202

AWARDS Engineering management (MS); industrial engineering (MS, PhD); manufacturing engineering (MS); operations research (MS).

Faculty: 10 full-time.
Students: 287. 611 applicants, 47% accepted, 103 enrolled. In 2001, 69 master's, 6 doctorates awarded.
Degree requirements: For master's, thesis optional; for doctorate, thesis/dissertation.
Entrance requirements: For master's, minimum undergraduate GPA of 2.8; for doctorate, minimum graduate GPA of 3.5. *Application deadline:* For fall admission, 7/1 (priority date); for spring admission, 3/15. Applications are processed on a rolling basis. *Application fee:* $20 ($30 for international students). Electronic applications accepted.
Expenses: Tuition, state resident: full-time $3,764. Tuition and fees vary according to degree level and program.
Financial support: In 2001–02, 2 fellowships, 8 research assistantships, 6 teaching assistantships were awarded. Career-related internships or fieldwork and tuition waivers (full) also available.

Faculty research: Reliability and quality design for manufacturing, manufacturing systems and processes, composite materials.
Frank Plonka, Chairperson, 313-577-3821, *Fax:* 313-577-8833, *E-mail:* fplonka@mie.eng.wayne.edu.
Application contact: Olugbenga Mejabi, Graduate Director, 313-577-3134, *E-mail:* mejabi@mie.eng.wayne.edu.

■ WESTERN MICHIGAN UNIVERSITY

Graduate College, College of Engineering and Applied Sciences, Department of Industrial and Manufacturing Engineering, Program in Operations Research, Kalamazoo, MI 49008-5202

AWARDS MS.

Faculty: 25 full-time (3 women).
Students: 7 full-time (2 women), 2 part-time; includes 1 minority (African American), 7 international. 8 applicants, 75% accepted, 3 enrolled. In 2001, 2 degrees awarded.
Degree requirements: For master's, oral exams.
Entrance requirements: For master's, minimum GPA of 3.0. *Application deadline:* For fall admission, 2/15 (priority date). Applications are processed on a rolling basis. *Application fee:* $25.
Expenses: Tuition, state resident: part-time $186 per credit hour. Tuition, nonresident: part-time $442 per credit hour. Required fees: $602. One-time fee: $132 part-time. Tuition and fees vary according to course load.
Financial support: Fellowships, research assistantships, teaching assistantships, Federal Work-Study available. Financial award application deadline: 2/15; financial award applicants required to submit FAFSA.
Application contact: Admissions and Orientation, 616-387-2000, *Fax:* 616-387-2355.

TECHNOLOGY AND PUBLIC POLICY
···

■ CALIFORNIA STATE UNIVERSITY, LOS ANGELES

Graduate Studies, College of Engineering, Computer Science, and Technology, Department of Technology, Major in Industrial and Technical Studies, Los Angeles, CA 90032-8530

AWARDS MA.

Students: 14 full-time (7 women), 31 part-time (4 women); includes 17 minority (4 African Americans, 8 Asian Americans or Pacific Islanders, 4 Hispanic Americans, 1

Native American), 7 international. In 2001, 9 degrees awarded.
Degree requirements: For master's, project or thesis.
Entrance requirements: For master's, TOEFL, minimum GPA of 2.5. *Application deadline:* For fall admission, 6/30; for spring admission, 2/1. Applications are processed on a rolling basis. *Application fee:* $55.
Expenses: Tuition, nonresident: part-time $164 per unit.
Financial support: Application deadline: 3/1.
Faculty research: Instructional improvement, new applications.
Dr. Virgil Seaman, Chair, Department of Technology, 323-343-4550.

■ CARNEGIE MELLON UNIVERSITY

Carnegie Institute of Technology, Department of Civil and Environmental Engineering, Program in Civil Engineering/Engineering and Public Policy, Pittsburgh, PA 15213-3891

AWARDS MS, PhD.

Degree requirements: For master's, thesis; for doctorate, thesis/dissertation, qualifying exam.
Entrance requirements: For master's and doctorate, GRE General Test, TOEFL.

■ CARNEGIE MELLON UNIVERSITY

Carnegie Institute of Technology, Department of Engineering and Public Policy, Pittsburgh, PA 15213-3891

AWARDS MS, PhD.

Degree requirements: For doctorate, thesis/dissertation, qualifying exam.
Entrance requirements: For master's, GRE General Test, TOEFL; for doctorate, GRE General Test, TOEFL, BS in physical sciences or engineering.
Faculty research: Restructuring the electric power industry, economics of network-based information services, mathematical modeling of environmental systems, risk assessment and analysis. *Web site:* http://www.epp.cmu.edu/
Find an in-depth description at www.petersons.com/gradchannel.

■ COLORADO STATE UNIVERSITY

Graduate School, College of Applied Human Sciences, Department of Manufacturing Technology and Construction Management, Fort Collins, CO 80523-0015

AWARDS Automotive pollution control (MS); construction management (MS); historic preservation (MS); industrial technology management (MS); technology education and

Colorado State University (continued)
training (MS); technology of industry (PhD).
Part-time and evening/weekend programs
available.

Faculty: 11 full-time (0 women).
Students: 16 full-time (5 women), 27 part-time (10 women); includes 2 minority (1
African American, 1 Hispanic American), 1
international. Average age 31. 57
applicants, 98% accepted, 9 enrolled.
Terminal master's awarded for partial
completion of doctoral program.
Degree requirements: For master's,
thesis (for some programs); for doctorate,
thesis/dissertation.
Entrance requirements: For master's and
doctorate, GRE General Test, TOEFL.
Application deadline: For fall admission, 4/1
(priority date); for spring admission, 9/1
(priority date). Applications are processed
on a rolling basis. *Application fee:* $30.
Electronic applications accepted.
Expenses: Tuition, state resident: full-time
$2,880; part-time $160 per credit. Tuition,
nonresident: full-time $11,412; part-time
$634 per credit. Required fees: $750; $34
per credit.
Financial support: In 2001–02, 1 fellow-ship with full tuition reimbursement
(averaging $12,960 per year), 3 research
assistantships with full tuition reimburse-ments (averaging $9,720 per year), 8
teaching assistantships with full tuition
reimbursements (averaging $9,720 per
year) were awarded. Career-related intern-ships or fieldwork, Federal Work-Study,
and traineeships also available.
Faculty research: Construction processes,
historical preservation, sustainability,
technology education. *Total annual research
expenditures:* $800,000.
Dr. Larry Grosse, Head, 970-491-7958,
Fax: 970-491-2473, *E-mail:* drfire107@
mindspring.com.
Application contact: Becky Bell, Graduate
Liaison, 970-491-7355, *Fax:* 970-491-2473,
E-mail: becky.bell@cahs.colostate.edu. *Web
site:* http://www.cahs.colostate.edu/DIS/

■ EASTERN MICHIGAN UNIVERSITY

**Graduate School, College of
Technology, Department of
Interdisciplinary Technology, Program
in Liberal Studies in Technology,
Ypsilanti, MI 48197**

AWARDS MLS.

Degree requirements: For master's,
thesis optional.
Entrance requirements: For master's,
GRE General Test, TOEFL, minimum
GPA of 2.6. *Application deadline:* For fall
admission, 5/15; for spring admission,
3/15. Applications are processed on a roll-ing basis. *Application fee:* $30.
Expenses: Tuition, state resident: part-time $285 per credit hour. Tuition,
nonresident: part-time $510 per credit
hour.

Financial support: Fellowships, teaching
assistantships available. Support available
to part-time students. Financial award
application deadline: 3/15; financial award
applicants required to submit FAFSA.
Dr. Wayne Hanewicz, Coordinator, 734-487-1161.

■ GEORGE MASON UNIVERSITY

**School of Public Policy, Program in
Enterprise Engineering and Policy,
Fairfax, VA 22030-4444**

AWARDS MS.

Degree requirements: For master's,
thesis or alternative.
Entrance requirements: For master's,
minimum GPA of 3.0 in last 60 hours.
Expenses: Tuition, state resident: full-time
$3,168; part-time $132 per credit hour.
Tuition, nonresident: full-time $11,280;
part-time $470 per credit hour. Required
fees: $1,416; $59 per credit hour.

■ THE GEORGE WASHINGTON UNIVERSITY

**Elliott School of International Affairs,
Program in Science, Technology, and
Public Policy, Washington, DC 20052**

AWARDS MA, JD/MA, LL M/MA. Part-time
and evening/weekend programs available.

Students: 14 full-time (9 women), 8 part-time (2 women); includes 3 minority (1
African American, 1 Asian American or
Pacific Islander, 1 Hispanic American), 2
international. Average age 27. 35
applicants, 89% accepted. In 2001, 17
degrees awarded.
Degree requirements: For master's, one
foreign language.
Entrance requirements: For master's,
GRE General Test, TOEFL, minimum B
average. *Application deadline:* For fall admis-sion, 2/1; for spring admission, 11/1.
Application fee: $55. Electronic applications
accepted.
Expenses: Tuition: Part-time $810 per
credit. Required fees: $1 per credit.
Financial support: Fellowships with
tuition reimbursements, research assistant-ships with tuition reimbursements, career-related internships or fieldwork, Federal
Work-Study, institutionally sponsored
loans, and tuition waivers (full and partial)
available. Financial award application
deadline: 1/15; financial award applicants
required to submit FAFSA.
Faculty research: Science policy, space
policy, risk assessment, technology transfer,
energy policy.
Dr. Nicholas Vonortas, Director, 202-994-6458.
Application contact: Jeff V. Miles, Direc-tor of Graduate Admissions, 202-994-7050, *Fax:* 202-994-9537, *E-mail:*
esiagrad@gwu.edu. *Web site:* http://
www.gwu.edu/~elliott/

■ MASSACHUSETTS INSTITUTE OF TECHNOLOGY

**School of Engineering, Engineering
Systems Division, Technology and
Policy Program, Cambridge, MA
02139-4307**

AWARDS SM, PhD. Terminal master's
awarded for partial completion of doctoral
program.

Degree requirements: For master's,
thesis/dissertation; for doctorate, thesis/
dissertation, comprehensive exam.
Entrance requirements: For master's and
doctorate, GRE General Test, TOEFL.
Application deadline: For fall admission,
1/15; for spring admission, 11/15. *Applica-tion fee:* $60. Electronic applications
accepted.
Financial support: In 2001–02, 72
students received support; fellowships,
research assistantships, teaching assistant-ships, career-related internships or
fieldwork, Federal Work-Study, institution-ally sponsored loans, scholarships/grants,
health care benefits, tuition waivers
(partial), and unspecified assistantships
available. Financial award application
deadline: 3/15; financial award applicants
required to submit FAFSA.
Daniel Hastings, Director, 617-253-0906,
Fax: 617-258-0863, *E-mail:* hastings@
mit.edu.
Application contact: Sydney Miller,
Graduate Student Administrator, 617-452-3187, *Fax:* 617-253-7568. *Web site:* http://
web.mit.edu//tpp/www/

■ MASSACHUSETTS INSTITUTE OF TECHNOLOGY

**School of Humanities, Arts and Social
Sciences, Program in Science,
Technology, and Society, Cambridge,
MA 02139-4307**

AWARDS History and social study of science
and technology (PhD).

Faculty: 15 full-time (5 women).
Students: 21 full-time (8 women); includes
4 minority (3 Asian Americans or Pacific
Islanders, 1 Hispanic American), 2
international. Average age 29. 62
applicants, 8% accepted. In 2001, 5
degrees awarded.
Degree requirements: For doctorate, 2
foreign languages, thesis/dissertation.
Entrance requirements: For doctorate,
GRE General Test, TOEFL. *Application
deadline:* For fall admission, 1/15. *Applica-tion fee:* $60.
Expenses: Tuition: Full-time $26,960.
Full-time tuition and fees vary according
to program.
Financial support: In 2001–02, 21
students received support, including 17
fellowships (averaging $13,000 per year), 2
research assistantships, 6 teaching
assistantships (averaging $13,000 per year);
Federal Work-Study and institutionally

sponsored loans also available. Financial award application deadline: 1/15.

Faculty research: Cultural studies of science and technology.

Merritt Roe Smith, Director, 617-253-2564, *Fax:* 617-258-8118, *E-mail:* roesmith@mit.edu.

Application contact: Le Roy Stafford, Coordinator, 617-253-4085, *Fax:* 617-258-8118, *E-mail:* stsprogram@mit.edu. *Web site:* http://web.mit.edu/sts/

■ NORTHWESTERN UNIVERSITY

The Graduate School, Program in Telecommunications Science, Management, and Policy, Evanston, IL 60208

AWARDS Certificate.

Expenses: Tuition: Full-time $26,526. Rick Morris, Director, 847-467-1168, *Fax:* 847-467-1171.

■ RENSSELAER POLYTECHNIC INSTITUTE

Graduate School, School of Humanities and Social Sciences, Department of Science and Technology Studies, Troy, NY 12180-3590

AWARDS MS, PhD. Part-time programs available.

Faculty: 14 full-time (5 women), 3 part-time/adjunct (1 woman).

Students: 36 full-time (15 women), 7 part-time (3 women); includes 1 minority (Hispanic American), 13 international. Average age 26. 27 applicants, 70% accepted, 9 enrolled.

Degree requirements: For master's, thesis (for some programs); for doctorate, thesis/dissertation.

Entrance requirements: For master's and doctorate, GRE General Test, TOEFL. *Application deadline:* For fall admission, 1/15 (priority date). Applications are processed on a rolling basis. *Application fee:* $45. Electronic applications accepted.

Expenses: Tuition: Full-time $26,400; part-time $1,320 per credit hour. Required fees: $1,437.

Financial support: In 2001–02, 1 fellowship with full tuition reimbursement (averaging $15,000 per year), 7 research assistantships with full and partial tuition reimbursements (averaging $11,000 per year), 20 teaching assistantships with full and partial tuition reimbursements (averaging $11,000 per year) were awarded. Career-related internships or fieldwork, institutionally sponsored loans, and tuition waivers (partial) also available. Financial award application deadline: 2/1.

Faculty research: Communities and technology, social dimensions of IT and biotechnology, ethics and policy, design. *Total annual research expenditures:* $100,000.

Dr. David Hess, Chair, 518-276-6574, *Fax:* 518-276-2659, *E-mail:* hessd@rpi.edu.

Application contact: Dr. Linda Layne, Director of Graduate Studies, 518-276-6115, *Fax:* 518-276-2659, *E-mail:* laynel@rpi.edu. *Web site:* http://www.rpi.edu/dept/STS/

Find an in-depth description at www.petersons.com/gradchannel.

■ ROCHESTER INSTITUTE OF TECHNOLOGY

Graduate Enrollment Services, College of Liberal Arts, Department of Public Policy, Rochester, NY 14623-5698

AWARDS MS.

Students: 2 full-time (1 woman); includes 1 minority (African American). 1 applicant, 100% accepted, 1 enrolled. *Application deadline:* For fall admission, 3/1 (priority date). Applications are processed on a rolling basis. *Application fee:* $50. Electronic applications accepted.

Expenses: Tuition: Full-time $20,928; part-time $587 per hour. Required fees: $162. Tuition and fees vary according to program.

Ann M. Howard, Chair, 585-475-5104, *E-mail:* mahgsh@rit.edu.

■ ST. CLOUD STATE UNIVERSITY

School of Graduate Studies, College of Science and Engineering, Department of Environmental and Technological Studies, St. Cloud, MN 56301-4498

AWARDS MS.

Faculty: 11 full-time (3 women).

Students: 3 full-time (0 women), 4 part-time. 9 applicants, 100% accepted.

Degree requirements: For master's, thesis or alternative.

Entrance requirements: For master's, GRE General Test, minimum GPA of 2.75. *Application deadline:* Applications are processed on a rolling basis. *Application fee:* $35.

Expenses: Tuition, state resident: part-time $156 per credit. Tuition, nonresident: part-time $244 per credit. Required fees: $20 per credit.

Financial support: Federal Work-Study and unspecified assistantships available. Financial award application deadline: 3/1. Dr. Anthony Schwaller, Chairperson, 320-255-3235, *Fax:* 320-654-5122, *E-mail:* ets@stcloudstate.edu.

Application contact: Lindalou Krueger, Graduate Studies Office, 320-255-2113, *Fax:* 320-654-5371, *E-mail:* lekrueger@stcloudstate.edu.

■ UNIVERSITY OF MINNESOTA, TWIN CITIES CAMPUS

Graduate School, Hubert H. Humphrey Institute of Public Affairs, Program in Science, Technology, and Environmental Policy, Minneapolis, MN 55455-0213

AWARDS MS, JD/MS.

Degree requirements: For master's, thesis, internship or equivalent work experience.

Entrance requirements: For master's, GRE General Test, TOEFL, undergraduate training in the biological or physical sciences or engineering. Electronic applications accepted.

Expenses: Tuition, state resident: full-time $2,932; part-time $489 per credit. Tuition, nonresident: full-time $5,758; part-time $960 per credit. Part-time tuition and fees vary according to course load, program and reciprocity agreements.

Faculty research: Economics, history, philosophy, and politics of science and technology; organization and management of science and technology. *Web site:* http://www.hhh.umn.edu/

■ UNIVERSITY OF PENNSYLVANIA

School of Engineering and Applied Science, Department of Systems Engineering, Philadelphia, PA 19104

AWARDS Environmental resources engineering (MSE); environmental/resources engineering (PhD). Systems engineering (MSE, PhD); technology and public policy (MSE, PhD); transportation (MSE, PhD). Part-time programs available.

Faculty: 11 full-time (0 women), 3 part-time/adjunct (0 women).

Students: 38 full-time (10 women), 21 part-time (5 women); includes 39 minority (4 African Americans, 33 Asian Americans or Pacific Islanders, 2 Hispanic Americans). Terminal master's awarded for partial completion of doctoral program.

Degree requirements: For doctorate, one foreign language, thesis/dissertation.

Entrance requirements: For master's and doctorate, TOEFL. *Application deadline:* For fall admission, 1/2 (priority date). Applications are processed on a rolling basis. *Application fee:* $65. Electronic applications accepted.

Financial support: Fellowships, research assistantships, teaching assistantships, scholarships/grants available.

Faculty research: Systems methodology, operations research, decision sciences, telecommunication systems, logistics, transportation systems, manufacturing systems, infrastructure systems.

Dr. John D. Keenan, Chair, 215-898-5710, *Fax:* 215-898-5020, *E-mail:* keenan@seas.upenn.edu.

Application contact: Dr. Tony E. Smith, Graduate Group Chair, 215-898-9647,

University of Pennsylvania (continued)
Fax: 215-898-5020, *E-mail:* tesmith@
seas.upenn.edu. *Web site:* http://
www.seas.upenn.edu/ese

**Find an in-depth description at
www.petersons.com/gradchannel.**

■ THE UNIVERSITY OF TEXAS AT AUSTIN

**Graduate School, Program in Science
and Technology Commercialization,
Austin, TX 78712-1111**

AWARDS MS. Twelve month program, beginning in May, with classes held every other Friday and Saturday. Evening/weekend programs available. Postbaccalaureate distance learning degree programs offered (minimal on-campus study).

Faculty: 13 full-time (4 women).
Students: 50 full-time (12 women), 7 international. Average age 40. In 2001, 31 degrees awarded.
Degree requirements: For master's, year-long global teaming project.
Entrance requirements: For master's, GRE General Test, or GMAT. *Application deadline:* For spring admission, 2/15 (priority date). Applications are processed on a

rolling basis. *Application fee:* $50 ($75 for international students). Electronic applications accepted.
Expenses: Contact institution.
Financial support: In 2001–02, 17 students received support. Institutionally sponsored loans available. Financial award application deadline: 2/15; financial award applicants required to submit FAFSA.
Faculty research: Technology transfer, entrepreneurship, commercialization, research and development.
Dr. W. Bradley Zehner, Director, 512-475-8977, *Fax:* 512-475-8901.
Application contact: Program Coordinator, 512-475-8900, *Fax:* 512-475-8903, *E-mail:* exec.ms@icc.utexas.edu. *Web site:* http://www.ic2.org/msdegree/

■ WESTERN ILLINOIS UNIVERSITY

**School of Graduate Studies, College
of Business and Technology,
Department of Engineering
Technology, Macomb, IL 61455-1390**

AWARDS MS. Part-time programs available.

Faculty: 9 full-time (0 women).
Students: 16 full-time (5 women), 14 part-time (2 women); includes 2 minority (both

African Americans), 8 international. Average age 33. 17 applicants, 76% accepted. In 2001, 8 degrees awarded.
Degree requirements: For master's, thesis or alternative.
Application deadline: Applications are processed on a rolling basis. *Application fee:* $0 ($25 for international students). Electronic applications accepted.
Expenses: Tuition, state resident: part-time $108 per credit hour. Tuition, nonresident: part-time $216 per credit hour. Required fees: $33 per credit hour.
Financial support: In 2001–02, 8 students received support, including 8 research assistantships with full tuition reimbursements available (averaging $5,720 per year) Financial award applicants required to submit FAFSA.
Faculty research: Blended fuels training, production of *Illinois Journal of Technology*, occupational safety.
Dr. Thomas Bridge, Chairperson, 309-298-1091.
Application contact: Dr. Barbara Baily, Director of Graduate Studies, 309-298-1806, *Fax:* 309-298-2345, *E-mail:* gradoffice@wiu.edu. *Web site:* http://www.wiu.edu/

Materials Sciences and Engineering

CERAMIC SCIENCES AND ENGINEERING

■ ALFRED UNIVERSITY

**Graduate School, New York State
College of Ceramics, School of
Ceramic Engineering and Materials
Science, Alfred, NY 14802-1205**

AWARDS Biomedical materials engineering science (MS); ceramic engineering (MS); ceramics (PhD); glass science (MS, PhD); materials science (MS).

Students: 51 full-time (14 women), 10 part-time (2 women). Average age 24. 108 applicants, 25% accepted. In 2001, 16 master's, 5 doctorates awarded.
Degree requirements: For master's and doctorate, thesis/dissertation.
Entrance requirements: For master's and doctorate, TOEFL. *Application deadline:* Applications are processed on a rolling basis. *Application fee:* $50. Electronic applications accepted.
Expenses: Contact institution.
Financial support: Fellowships, research assistantships, teaching assistantships, tuition waivers (full and partial) available.

Financial award applicants required to submit FAFSA.
Faculty research: Fine-particle technology, x-ray diffraction, superconductivity, electronic materials.
Dr. Ronald S. Gordon, Dean, 607-871-2441, *E-mail:* gordon@alfred.edu.
Application contact: Cathleen R. Johnson, Coordinator of Graduate Admissions, 607-871-2141, *Fax:* 607-871-2198, *E-mail:* johnsonc@alfred.edu. *Web site:* http://www.alfred.edu/gradschool

**Find an in-depth description at
www.petersons.com/gradchannel.**

■ CASE WESTERN RESERVE UNIVERSITY

**School of Graduate Studies, The Case
School of Engineering, Department of
Materials Science and Engineering,
Cleveland, OH 44106**

AWARDS Ceramics and materials science (MS); materials science and engineering (MS, PhD). Part-time programs available. Postbaccalaureate distance learning degree programs offered (no on-campus study).

Faculty: 11 full-time (0 women), 13 part-time/adjunct (1 woman).

Students: 40 full-time (16 women), 22 part-time (3 women); includes 5 minority (all Asian Americans or Pacific Islanders), 39 international. Average age 24. 152 applicants, 91% accepted, 20 enrolled. In 2001, 12 master's, 3 doctorates awarded. Terminal master's awarded for partial completion of doctoral program.
Degree requirements: For master's, thesis (for some programs); for doctorate, thesis/dissertation, qualifying exam, teaching experience.
Entrance requirements: For master's, TOEFL; for doctorate, GRE, TOEFL. *Application deadline:* For fall admission, 2/15 (priority date); for spring admission, 9/15. Applications are processed on a rolling basis. *Application fee:* $25.
Financial support: In 2001–02, 35 fellowships with full and partial tuition reimbursements (averaging $16,200 per year), 15 research assistantships with full and partial tuition reimbursements (averaging $16,200 per year) were awarded. Financial award application deadline: 4/30; financial award applicants required to submit FAFSA.
Faculty research: Materials processing; mechanical behavior; coatings and thin films; materials performance. *Total annual research expenditures:* $4.2 million.

Dr. Gary M. Michal, Chairman, 216-368-5070, *Fax:* 216-368-4224, *E-mail:* emse@po.cwru.edu.
Application contact: Patsy Harris, Information Contact, 216-368-4230, *Fax:* 216-368-3209, *E-mail:* pah7@po.cwru.edu. *Web site:* http://vulcan.mse.cwru.edu/emse/

■ CLEMSON UNIVERSITY

Graduate School, College of Engineering and Science, Department of Ceramic and Materials Engineering, Clemson, SC 29634

AWARDS MS, PhD.

Students: 3 full-time (1 woman), 2 part-time (1 woman), 2 international. 18 applicants, 22% accepted, 0 enrolled. In 2001, 2 degrees awarded.
Degree requirements: For master's and doctorate, thesis/dissertation.
Entrance requirements: For master's and doctorate, GRE General Test, TOEFL. *Application deadline:* For fall admission, 6/1. *Application fee:* $40.
Expenses: Tuition, state resident: full-time $5,310. Tuition, nonresident: full-time $11,284.
Financial support: Fellowships, research assistantships, teaching assistantships, career-related internships or fieldwork available. Financial award application deadline: 5/1; financial award applicants required to submit FAFSA.
Faculty research: Ceramic processing, hazardous material mediation, ceramic and carbon fibers, ceramic matrix composites, electronic ceramic materials.
Dr. Gary Lickfield, Chair, 864-656-5964, *Fax:* 864-656-5973, *E-mail:* lgary@clemson.edu. *Web site:* http://www.ces.clemson.edu/cme/

■ GEORGIA INSTITUTE OF TECHNOLOGY

Graduate Studies and Research, College of Engineering, School of Materials Science and Engineering, Program in Ceramic Engineering, Atlanta, GA 30332-0001

AWARDS MSMSE, PhD. Terminal master's awarded for partial completion of doctoral program.

Degree requirements: For master's and doctorate, thesis/dissertation.
Entrance requirements: For master's and doctorate, GRE General Test, TOEFL. Electronic applications accepted.
Faculty research: Crystal growth, cathode materials refractories, superconductivity, thermodynamics.

■ THE PENNSYLVANIA STATE UNIVERSITY UNIVERSITY PARK CAMPUS

Graduate School, College of Earth and Mineral Sciences, Department of Materials Science and Engineering, State College, University Park, PA 16802-1503

AWARDS Ceramic science (MS, PhD); fuel science (MS, PhD); metals science and engineering (MS, PhD); polymer science (MS, PhD).

Students: 106 full-time (19 women), 10 part-time (3 women). In 2001, 25 master's, 16 doctorates awarded.
Entrance requirements: For master's and doctorate, GRE. *Application deadline:* For fall admission, 7/1. *Application fee:* $45.
Expenses: Tuition, state resident: full-time $7,882; part-time $333 per credit. Tuition, nonresident: full-time $16,142; part-time $673 per credit. Required fees: $124 per semester.
Financial support: Fellowships, unspecified assistantships available. Financial award application deadline: 2/28.
Gray L. Messing, Head, 814-865-2262.

■ RENSSELAER POLYTECHNIC INSTITUTE

Graduate School, School of Engineering, Department of Materials Science and Engineering, Troy, NY 12180-3590

AWARDS Ceramics and glass science (M Eng, MS, PhD); composites (M Eng, MS, PhD); electronic materials (M Eng, MS, PhD); metallurgy (M Eng, MS, PhD); polymers (M Eng, MS, PhD). Part-time and evening/weekend programs available.

Faculty: 15 full-time (1 woman), 5 part-time/adjunct (0 women).
Students: 56 full-time (15 women), 18 part-time (5 women), 35 international. Average age 24. 287 applicants, 11% accepted, 10 enrolled. In 2001, 11 master's, 5 doctorates awarded. Terminal master's awarded for partial completion of doctoral program.
Degree requirements: For master's, thesis (for some programs); for doctorate, thesis/dissertation. *Median time to degree:* Master's–2 years full-time, 5 years part-time; doctorate–5.5 years full-time, 8 years part-time.
Entrance requirements: For master's and doctorate, GRE, TOEFL. *Application deadline:* For fall admission, 1/15 (priority date). Applications are processed on a rolling basis. *Application fee:* $45. Electronic applications accepted.
Expenses: Tuition: Full-time $26,400; part-time $1,320 per credit hour. Required fees: $1,437.
Financial support: In 2001–02, 53 students received support, including 13 fellowships with full tuition reimbursements available (averaging $22,000 per year), 29 research assistantships with full tuition reimbursements available (averaging $16,800 per year), 11 teaching assistantships with full tuition reimbursements available (averaging $16,800 per year); career-related internships or fieldwork and institutionally sponsored loans also available. Financial award application deadline: 2/1.
Faculty research: Materials processing, nanostructural materials, materials for microelectronics, composite materials, materials theory. *Total annual research expenditures:* $4.1 million.
Dr. David J. Duquette, Chair, 518-276-6373, *Fax:* 518-276-8554.
Application contact: Dr. Roger Wright, Admissions Coordinator, 518-276-6372, *Fax:* 518-276-8554, *E-mail:* fowlen@rpi.edu. *Web site:* http://www.rpi.edu/dept/materials/

Find an in-depth description at www.petersons.com/gradchannel.

■ RUTGERS, THE STATE UNIVERSITY OF NEW JERSEY, NEW BRUNSWICK

Graduate School, Program in Ceramic and Materials Science and Engineering, New Brunswick, NJ 08901-1281

AWARDS MS, PhD. Part-time programs available.

Degree requirements: For master's and doctorate, thesis/dissertation.
Entrance requirements: For master's and doctorate, GRE General Test.
Faculty research: Ceramic processing, nanostructured materials, electrical and structural ceramics, fiber optics. *Web site:* http://www.rci.rutgers.edu/~mjohnm/

■ UNIVERSITY OF CALIFORNIA, BERKELEY

Graduate Division, College of Engineering, Department of Materials Science and Mineral Engineering, Program in Ceramic Sciences and Engineering, Berkeley, CA 94720-1500

AWARDS M Eng, MS, D Eng, PhD.

Degree requirements: For master's, comprehensive exam or thesis (MS); for doctorate, thesis/dissertation, qualifying exam.
Entrance requirements: For master's and doctorate, GRE General Test, minimum GPA of 3.0.
Expenses: Tuition, nonresident: full-time $10,704. Required fees: $4,349.

■ UNIVERSITY OF CALIFORNIA, LOS ANGELES

Graduate Division, School of Engineering and Applied Science, Department of Materials Science and Engineering, Program in Ceramics Engineering, Los Angeles, CA 90095

AWARDS MS, PhD.

Degree requirements: For master's, comprehensive exam or thesis; for doctorate, thesis/dissertation, qualifying exams.
Entrance requirements: For master's, GRE General Test, minimum GPA of 3.0; for doctorate, GRE General Test, minimum GPA of 3.25. *Application deadline:* For fall admission, 1/15; for spring admission, 12/31. *Application fee:* $60. Electronic applications accepted.
Expenses: Tuition, nonresident: full-time $10,244. Required fees: $3,609. Full-time tuition and fees vary according to program.
Financial support: Fellowships, research assistantships, teaching assistantships, Federal Work-Study, institutionally sponsored loans, and tuition waivers (full and partial) available. Financial award application deadline: 1/15; financial award applicants required to submit FAFSA.
Application contact: Paradee Chularee, Student Affairs Officer, 310-825-8913, *Fax:* 310-206-7353, *E-mail:* paradee@ea.ucla.edu.

■ UNIVERSITY OF CINCINNATI

Division of Research and Advanced Studies, College of Engineering, Department of Materials Science and Metallurgical Engineering, Cincinnati, OH 45221

AWARDS Ceramic science and engineering (MS, PhD); materials science and engineering (MS, PhD); metallurgical engineering (MS, PhD); polymer science and engineering (MS, PhD). Evening/weekend programs available.

Degree requirements: For master's, thesis optional; for doctorate, one foreign language, thesis/dissertation, oral English proficiency exam, comprehensive exam.
Entrance requirements: For master's and doctorate, GRE General Test, TOEFL, BS in related field, minimum undergraduate GPA of 3.0. *Application deadline:* For fall admission, 2/1 (priority date). Applications are processed on a rolling basis. *Application fee:* $40. Electronic applications accepted.
Expenses: Contact institution.
Financial support: Fellowships, research assistantships, teaching assistantships, career-related internships or fieldwork, tuition waivers (partial), and unspecified assistantships available. Financial award application deadline: 2/1. *Total annual research expenditures:* $1.6 million.
Dr. Narayanan Jayaraman, Head, 513-556-3112, *Fax:* 513-556-2569, *E-mail:* narayanan.jayaraman@uc.edu.

Application contact: Dr. F. James Boerio, Director of Graduate Studies, 513-556-3111, *Fax:* 513-556-2569, *E-mail:* f.james.boerio@uc.edu. *Web site:* http://www.mse.uc.edu/

■ UNIVERSITY OF FLORIDA

Graduate School, College of Engineering, Department of Materials Science and Engineering, Program in Ceramic Science and Engineering, Gainesville, FL 32611

AWARDS ME, MS, PhD, Engr.

Degree requirements: For master's and Engr, thesis optional; for doctorate, thesis/dissertation.
Entrance requirements: For master's and doctorate, GRE General Test, TOEFL, minimum GPA of 3.0; for Engr, GRE General Test.
Expenses: Tuition, state resident: part-time $164 per hour. Tuition, nonresident: part-time $571 per hour. Tuition and fees vary according to course level and program.

Find an in-depth description at www.petersons.com/gradchannel.

■ UNIVERSITY OF MISSOURI–ROLLA

Graduate School, School of Mines and Metallurgy, Department of Ceramic Engineering, Rolla, MO 65409-0910

AWARDS MS, PhD. Part-time programs available.

Degree requirements: For master's and doctorate, thesis/dissertation.
Entrance requirements: For master's, GRE General Test, TOEFL, minimum GPA of 3.0 in last 4 semesters; for doctorate, GRE General Test, TOEFL. Electronic applications accepted.
Faculty research: Composite sintering, refractory materials, glass structure and properties, dielectrics and ferroelectrics, surfaces and coatings.

ELECTRONIC MATERIALS

■ COLORADO SCHOOL OF MINES

Graduate School, Department of Metallurgical and Materials Engineering, Golden, CO 80401-1887

AWARDS Materials science (MS, PhD); metallurgical and materials engineering (ME, MS, PhD). Part-time programs available.

Faculty: 25 full-time (0 women), 1 part-time/adjunct (0 women).
Students: 69 full-time (23 women), 18 part-time (4 women); includes 8 minority (4 Asian Americans or Pacific Islanders, 4

Hispanic Americans), 27 international. 96 applicants, 40% accepted, 12 enrolled. In 2001, 9 master's, 5 doctorates awarded.
Degree requirements: For master's, thesis/dissertation; for doctorate, thesis/dissertation, comprehensive exam. *Median time to degree:* Master's–2 years full-time; doctorate–4 years full-time.
Entrance requirements: For master's and doctorate, GRE General Test. *Application deadline:* For fall admission, 12/1 (priority date); for spring admission, 5/1 (priority date). Applications are processed on a rolling basis. *Application fee:* $40. Electronic applications accepted.
Expenses: Tuition, state resident: full-time $4,940; part-time $246 per credit. Tuition, nonresident: full-time $16,070; part-time $803 per credit. Required fees: $341 per semester.
Financial support: In 2001–02, 26 fellowships (averaging $4,733 per year), 103 research assistantships (averaging $3,866 per year), 43 teaching assistantships (averaging $3,467 per year) were awarded. Unspecified assistantships also available. Support available to part-time students. Financial award applicants required to submit FAFSA.
Faculty research: Phase transformations, nonferrous alloy systems, pyrometallurgy, reactive metals, engineered materials. *Total annual research expenditures:* $141,430.
Dr. John J. Moore, Head, 303-273-3770, *Fax:* 303-273-3795, *E-mail:* jjmoore@mines.edu.
Application contact: Chaz Siler, Program Assistant I, 303-273-3660, *Fax:* 303-384-2189. *Web site:* http://met.mines.edu:3872/index.html

■ NORTHWESTERN UNIVERSITY

McCormick School of Engineering and Applied Science, Department of Electrical and Computer Engineering and Department of Materials Science and Engineering, Program in Electronic Materials, Evanston, IL 60208

AWARDS MS, PhD, Certificate. Part-time programs available.

Faculty: 11 full-time (1 woman). Terminal master's awarded for partial completion of doctoral program.
Degree requirements: For master's, thesis/dissertation; for doctorate, thesis/dissertation, comprehensive exam.
Expenses: Tuition: Full-time $26,526.
Financial support: Fellowships with tuition reimbursements, research assistantships with tuition reimbursements, teaching assistantships with tuition reimbursements available.
Faculty research: Electronic optical magnetic materials and devices.
Prof. Bruce W. Wessels, Director, 847-491-3219, *Fax:* 847-491-7820, *E-mail:* b-wessels@northwestern.edu.

■ NORTHWESTERN UNIVERSITY

McCormick School of Engineering and Applied Science, Department of Materials Science and Engineering, Evanston, IL 60208

AWARDS Electronic materials (Certificate); materials science and engineering (MS, PhD). Admissions and degrees offered through The Graduate School. Part-time programs available.

Faculty: 26 full-time (2 women).
Students: 109 full-time (25 women), 2 part-time (1 woman); includes 16 minority (2 African Americans, 10 Asian Americans or Pacific Islanders, 4 Hispanic Americans), 33 international. 263 applicants, 22% accepted, 24 enrolled. In 2001, 9 master's, 19 doctorates awarded. Terminal master's awarded for partial completion of doctoral program.
Degree requirements: For master's, oral thesis defense; for doctorate, oral defense of dissertation, preliminary evaluation, qualifying exam.
Application deadline: For fall admission, 1/15. Applications are processed on a rolling basis. *Application fee:* $60 ($75 for international students). Electronic applications accepted.
Expenses: Tuition: Full-time $26,526.
Financial support: In 2001–02, 28 fellowships with full tuition reimbursements (averaging $21,208 per year), 81 research assistantships with full tuition reimbursements (averaging $19,440 per year), teaching assistantships with full tuition reimbursements (averaging $19,440 per year) were awarded. Career-related internships or fieldwork and institutionally sponsored loans also available. Financial award application deadline: 1/15; financial award applicants required to submit FAFSA.
Faculty research: Metallurgy, ceramics, polymers, electronic materials, biomaterials. *Total annual research expenditures:* $9.9 million.
Katherine T. Faber, Chair, 847-491-3537, *Fax:* 847-491-7820.
Application contact: Jason Grocholski, Admissions Contact, 847-491-3587, *Fax:* 847-491-7820, *E-mail:* matsci@ northwestern.edu. *Web site:* http:// www.matsci.northwestern.edu/

■ PRINCETON UNIVERSITY

Graduate School, School of Engineering and Applied Science, Department of Electrical Engineering, Princeton, NJ 08544-1019

AWARDS Computer engineering (PhD); electrical engineering (M Eng); electronic materials and devices (PhD); information sciences and systems (PhD); optoelectronics (PhD). Part-time programs available.

Degree requirements: For doctorate, thesis/dissertation.

Entrance requirements: For master's and doctorate, GRE General Test, TOEFL. Electronic applications accepted.
Faculty research: Nanostructures, computer architecture, multimedia. *Web site:* http://www.princeton.edu/

■ UNIVERSITY OF ARKANSAS

Graduate School, Interdisciplinary Program in Microelectronics and Photonics, Fayetteville, AR 72701-1201

AWARDS MS, PhD.

Students: 29 full-time (4 women), 6 part-time (2 women); includes 7 minority (3 African Americans, 3 Asian Americans or Pacific Islanders, 1 Hispanic American), 18 international. 14 applicants, 93% accepted. In 2001, 4 degrees awarded.
Degree requirements: For doctorate, thesis/dissertation.
Application fee: $40 ($50 for international students).
Expenses: Tuition, state resident: full-time $3,553; part-time $197 per credit. Tuition, nonresident: full-time $8,411; part-time $467 per credit. Required fees: $42 per credit. Tuition and fees vary according to course load and program.
Financial support: In 2001–02, 6 fellowships, 17 research assistantships were awarded. Financial award application deadline: 4/1; financial award applicants required to submit FAFSA.
Ken Vickers, Head, 479-575-2875.

MATERIALS ENGINEERING

■ ARIZONA STATE UNIVERSITY

Graduate College, College of Engineering and Applied Sciences, Department of Chemical, Bio and Materials Engineering, Program in Materials Science and Engineering, Tempe, AZ 85287

AWARDS Engineering science (MS, MSE, PhD), including materials science and engineering.

Degree requirements: For doctorate, thesis/dissertation.
Entrance requirements: For master's and doctorate, GRE General Test.
Faculty research: Fluid dynamics, mechanics of solids and structures, structural dynamics, structural stability, nonlinear mechanics.

Find an in-depth description at www.petersons.com/gradchannel.

■ ARIZONA STATE UNIVERSITY

Graduate College, Interdisciplinary Program in Science and Engineering of Materials, Tempe, AZ 85287

AWARDS PhD.

Degree requirements: For doctorate, thesis/dissertation.
Entrance requirements: For doctorate, GRE.
Faculty research: Silicon and gallium arsenide, fabrication of ultra small solid state electronic devices, structure of free surfaces of crystalline solids, ion implantation on solids, effects of high pressures on solids.

Find an in-depth description at www.petersons.com/gradchannel.

■ AUBURN UNIVERSITY

Graduate School, College of Engineering, Department of Mechanical Engineering, Program in Materials Engineering, Auburn University, AL 36849

AWARDS M Mtl E, MS, PhD.

Faculty: 23 full-time (0 women).
Students: 10 full-time (2 women), 23 part-time (4 women); includes 3 minority (2 African Americans, 1 Asian American or Pacific Islander), 23 international. 35 applicants, 43% accepted. In 2001, 5 master's, 3 doctorates awarded.
Degree requirements: For master's, thesis (MS), oral exam; for doctorate, one foreign language, thesis/dissertation.
Entrance requirements: For master's and doctorate, GRE General Test. *Application deadline:* For fall admission, 7/7; for spring admission, 11/24. Applications are processed on a rolling basis. *Application fee:* $25 ($50 for international students). Electronic applications accepted.
Financial support: Fellowships, research assistantships, teaching assistantships, Federal Work-Study available. Support available to part-time students. Financial award application deadline: 3/15.
Faculty research: Smart materials.
Dr. Bryan Chin, Head, 334-844-3322.
Application contact: Dr. John F. Pritchett, Dean of the Graduate School, 334-844-4700, *E-mail:* hatchlb@ mail.auburn.edu.

■ CALIFORNIA STATE UNIVERSITY, NORTHRIDGE

Graduate Studies, College of Engineering and Computer Science, Department of Civil and Manufacturing Engineering, Northridge, CA 91330

AWARDS Applied mechanics (MSE); civil engineering (MS); engineering and computer science (MS); engineering management (MS); industrial engineering (MS); materials engineering (MS); mechanical engineering (MS), including aerospace engineering, applied engineering, machine design, mechanical engineering, structural engineering, thermofluids; mechanics (MS). Part-time and evening/weekend programs available.

Faculty: 14 full-time, 2 part-time/adjunct.
Students: 25 full-time (4 women), 72 part-time (9 women). Average age 31. 64

California State University, Northridge (continued)

applicants, 77% accepted, 22 enrolled. In 2001, 34 degrees awarded.

Degree requirements: For master's, thesis.

Entrance requirements: For master's, GRE General Test, TOEFL, minimum GPA of 2.5. *Application deadline:* For fall admission, 11/30. *Application fee:* $55.

Expenses: Tuition, nonresident: part-time $631 per semester. Required fees: $246 per unit.

Financial support: Teaching assistantships available. Financial award application deadline: 3/1.

Faculty research: Composite study. Dr. Stephen Gadomski, Chair, 818-677-2166.

Application contact: Dr. Ileana Costa, Graduate Coordinator, 818-677-3299.

■ CARNEGIE MELLON UNIVERSITY

Carnegie Institute of Technology, Department of Materials Science and Engineering, Pittsburgh, PA 15213-3891

AWARDS ME, MS, PhD. Part-time programs available. Terminal master's awarded for partial completion of doctoral program.

Degree requirements: For master's, exam; for doctorate, thesis/dissertation, qualifying exam.

Entrance requirements: For master's and doctorate, GRE General Test, TOEFL.

Faculty research: Materials characterization, process metallurgy, high strength alloys, growth kinetics, ceramics. *Web site:* http://neon.mems.cmu.edu/newfront.shtml

Find an in-depth description at www.petersons.com/gradchannel.

■ CASE WESTERN RESERVE UNIVERSITY

School of Graduate Studies, The Case School of Engineering, Department of Materials Science and Engineering, Cleveland, OH 44106

AWARDS Ceramics and materials science (MS); materials science and engineering (MS, PhD). Part-time programs available. Postbaccalaureate distance learning degree programs offered (no on-campus study).

Faculty: 11 full-time (0 women), 13 part-time/adjunct (1 woman).

Students: 40 full-time (16 women), 22 part-time (3 women); includes 5 minority (all Asian Americans or Pacific Islanders), 39 international. Average age 24. 152 applicants, 91% accepted, 20 enrolled. In 2001, 12 master's, 3 doctorates awarded. Terminal master's awarded for partial completion of doctoral program.

Degree requirements: For master's, thesis (for some programs); for doctorate,

thesis/dissertation, qualifying exam, teaching experience.

Entrance requirements: For master's, TOEFL; for doctorate, GRE, TOEFL. *Application deadline:* For fall admission, 2/15 (priority date); for spring admission, 9/15. Applications are processed on a rolling basis. *Application fee:* $25.

Financial support: In 2001–02, 35 fellowships with full and partial tuition reimbursements (averaging $16,200 per year), 15 research assistantships with full and partial tuition reimbursements (averaging $16,200 per year) were awarded. Financial award application deadline: 4/30; financial award applicants required to submit FAFSA.

Faculty research: Materials processing; mechanical behavior; coatings and thin films; materials performance. *Total annual research expenditures:* $4.2 million.
Dr. Gary M. Michal, Chairman, 216-368-5070, *Fax:* 216-368-4224, *E-mail:* emse@po.cwru.edu.

Application contact: Patsy Harris, Information Contact, 216-368-4230, *Fax:* 216-368-3209, *E-mail:* pah7@po.cwru.edu. *Web site:* http://vulcan.mse.cwru.edu/emse/

■ CLEMSON UNIVERSITY

Graduate School, College of Engineering and Science, Department of Ceramic and Materials Engineering, Clemson, SC 29634

AWARDS MS, PhD.

Students: 3 full-time (1 woman), 2 part-time (1 woman), 2 international. 18 applicants, 22% accepted, 0 enrolled. In 2001, 2 degrees awarded.

Degree requirements: For master's and doctorate, thesis/dissertation.

Entrance requirements: For master's and doctorate, GRE General Test, TOEFL. *Application deadline:* For fall admission, 6/1. *Application fee:* $40.

Expenses: Tuition, state resident: full-time $5,310. Tuition, nonresident: full-time $11,284.

Financial support: Fellowships, research assistantships, teaching assistantships, career-related internships or fieldwork available. Financial award application deadline: 5/1; financial award applicants required to submit FAFSA.

Faculty research: Ceramic processing, hazardous material mediation, ceramic and carbon fibers, ceramic matrix composites, electronic ceramic materials.
Dr. Gary Lickfeld, Chair, 864-656-5964, *Fax:* 864-656-5973, *E-mail:* lgary@clemson.edu. *Web site:* http://www.ces.clemson.edu/cme/

■ CLEMSON UNIVERSITY

Graduate School, College of Engineering and Science, Program in Materials Science and Engineering, Clemson, SC 29634

AWARDS MS, PhD. Part-time programs available.

Students: 31 full-time (9 women), 5 part-time (1 woman), 31 international. Average age 24. 113 applicants, 63% accepted, 9 enrolled. In 2001, 10 master's, 4 doctorates awarded. Terminal master's awarded for partial completion of doctoral program.

Degree requirements: For master's and doctorate, thesis/dissertation.

Entrance requirements: For master's and doctorate, GRE General Test, TOEFL. *Application deadline:* For fall admission, 2/15. Applications are processed on a rolling basis. *Application fee:* $40.

Expenses: Tuition, state resident: full-time $5,310. Tuition, nonresident: full-time $11,284.

Financial support: Research assistantships, career-related internships or fieldwork available. Financial award applicants required to submit FAFSA.

Faculty research: Composites, fibers, ceramics, metallurgy, biomaterials, semiconductors. *Total annual research expenditures:* $1.2 million.
Dr. R. Larry Dooley, Coordinator, 864-656-5562, *Fax:* 864-656-5910, *E-mail:* dooley@eng.clemson.edu. *Web site:* http://www.ces.clemson.edu/mse/MSE_GR.html

Find an in-depth description at www.petersons.com/gradchannel.

■ COLORADO SCHOOL OF MINES

Graduate School, Department of Metallurgical and Materials Engineering, Golden, CO 80401-1887

AWARDS Materials science (MS, PhD); metallurgical and materials engineering (ME, MS, PhD). Part-time programs available.

Faculty: 25 full-time (0 women), 1 part-time/adjunct (0 women).

Students: 69 full-time (23 women), 18 part-time (4 women); includes 8 minority (4 Asian Americans or Pacific Islanders, 4 Hispanic Americans), 27 international. 96 applicants, 40% accepted, 12 enrolled. In 2001, 9 master's, 5 doctorates awarded.

Degree requirements: For master's, thesis/dissertation; for doctorate, thesis/dissertation, comprehensive exam. *Median time to degree:* Master's–2 years full-time; doctorate–4 years full-time.

Entrance requirements: For master's and doctorate, GRE General Test. *Application deadline:* For fall admission, 12/1 (priority date); for spring admission, 5/1 (priority date). Applications are processed on a rolling basis. *Application fee:* $40. Electronic applications accepted.

Expenses: Tuition, state resident: full-time $4,940; part-time $246 per credit. Tuition,

nonresident: full-time $16,070; part-time $803 per credit. Required fees: $341 per semester.
Financial support: In 2001–02, 26 fellowships (averaging $4,733 per year), 103 research assistantships (averaging $3,866 per year), 43 teaching assistantships (averaging $3,467 per year) were awarded. Unspecified assistantships also available. Support available to part-time students. Financial award applicants required to submit FAFSA.
Faculty research: Phase transformations, nonferrous alloy systems, pyrometallurgy, reactive metals, engineered materials. *Total annual research expenditures:* $141,430.
Dr. John J. Moore, Head, 303-273-3770, *Fax:* 303-273-3795, *E-mail:* jjmoore@mines.edu.
Application contact: Chaz Siler, Program Assistant I, 303-273-3660, *Fax:* 303-384-2189. *Web site:* http://met.mines.edu:3872/index.html

■ **COLORADO STATE UNIVERSITY**

Graduate School, College of Engineering, Department of Mechanical Engineering, Fort Collins, CO 80523-0015

AWARDS Bioengineering (MS, PhD); energy and environmental engineering (MS, PhD); energy conversion (MS, PhD); engineering management (MS); heat and mass transfer (MS, PhD); industrial and manufacturing systems engineering (MS, PhD); mechanical engineering (MS, PhD); mechanics and materials (MS, PhD). Part-time programs available.

Faculty: 17 full-time (2 women).
Students: 36 full-time (6 women), 63 part-time (11 women); includes 5 minority (2 Asian Americans or Pacific Islanders, 2 Hispanic Americans, 1 Native American), 22 international. Average age 32. 234 applicants, 83% accepted, 32 enrolled. In 2001, 10 master's, 3 doctorates awarded. Terminal master's awarded for partial completion of doctoral program.
Degree requirements: For doctorate, thesis/dissertation.
Entrance requirements: For master's and doctorate, GRE General Test, TOEFL, minimum GPA of 3.0. *Application deadline:* For fall admission, 2/1 (priority date). Applications are processed on a rolling basis. *Application fee:* $30. Electronic applications accepted.
Expenses: Tuition, state resident: full-time $2,880; part-time $160 per credit. Tuition, nonresident: full-time $11,412; part-time $634 per credit. Required fees: $750; $34 per credit.
Financial support: In 2001–02, 2 fellowships, 15 research assistantships (averaging $15,792 per year), 14 teaching assistantships (averaging $11,844 per year) were awarded. Traineeships also available.

Faculty research: Space propulsion, controls and systems, engineering and materials. *Total annual research expenditures:* $2.1 million.
Dr. Allan T. Kirkpatrick, Head, 970-491-6559, *Fax:* 970-491-3827, *E-mail:* allan@engr.colostate.edu. *Web site:* http://www.engr.colostate.edu/depts/me/index.html

■ **COLUMBIA UNIVERSITY**

Fu Foundation School of Engineering and Applied Science, Department of Applied Physics and Applied Mathematics, Program in Materials Science and Engineering, New York, NY 10027

AWARDS MS, Eng Sc D, PhD. Part-time programs available. Postbaccalaureate distance learning degree programs offered (no on-campus study).

Faculty: 15 full-time (2 women), 2 part-time/adjunct (1 woman). Terminal master's awarded for partial completion of doctoral program.
Degree requirements: For doctorate, thesis/dissertation, qualifying exam.
Entrance requirements: For master's and doctorate, GRE General Test, TOEFL. *Application deadline:* For fall admission, 1/5; for spring admission, 10/1. *Application fee:* $55. Electronic applications accepted.
Expenses: Tuition: Full-time $27,528. Required fees: $1,638.
Financial support: In 2001–02, 4 fellowships with partial tuition reimbursements (averaging $18,500 per year), 4 research assistantships with full tuition reimbursements (averaging $18,500 per year), 2 teaching assistantships with partial tuition reimbursements (averaging $18,500 per year) were awarded. Federal Work-Study also available. Financial award application deadline: 1/5; financial award applicants required to submit FAFSA.
Faculty research: Thin films, inelasticity, plastic deformation, interstitial impurities, materials for fuel cells and corrosion. *Total annual research expenditures:* $824,000.
Prof. James S. Im, Professor of Material Sciences, 212-854-8341, *Fax:* 212-854-8257, *E-mail:* ji12@columbia.edu.
Application contact: Marlene Arbo, Department Administrator, 212-854-4458, *Fax:* 212-854-8257, *E-mail:* mja2@columbia.edu. *Web site:* http://www.columbia.edu/cu/matsci/

■ **CORNELL UNIVERSITY**

Graduate School, Graduate Fields of Engineering, Field of Materials Science and Engineering, Ithaca, NY 14853-0001

AWARDS Materials engineering (M Eng, PhD); materials science (M Eng, PhD).

Faculty: 30 full-time.
Students: 42 full-time (16 women); includes 3 minority (all Asian Americans or

Pacific Islanders), 28 international. 106 applicants, 26% accepted. In 2001, 12 master's, 6 doctorates awarded. Terminal master's awarded for partial completion of doctoral program.
Degree requirements: For doctorate, thesis/dissertation.
Entrance requirements: For master's and doctorate, GRE General Test, GRE Writing Test, pre-application required if undergraduate degree is from a non-US college/university, 3 letters of recommendation. *Application deadline:* For fall admission, 1/15 (priority date). *Application fee:* $65. Electronic applications accepted.
Expenses: Tuition: Full-time $25,970. Required fees: $50.
Financial support: In 2001–02, 6 fellowships with full tuition reimbursements, 31 research assistantships with full tuition reimbursements, 6 teaching assistantships with full tuition reimbursements were awarded. Institutionally sponsored loans, scholarships/grants, tuition waivers (full and partial), and unspecified assistantships also available. Financial award applicants required to submit FAFSA.
Faculty research: Ceramics, complex fluids, glass, metals, polymers semiconductors, biomaterials; electrical, magnetic, mechanical, optical, and structural properties; thin films, organic optoelectronics, nano-composites, organic-inorganic hybrids, biomedical sensors; materials synthesis and processing. Self-assembly and biomimetrics.
Application contact: Graduate Field Assistant, 607-255-9159, *E-mail:* matsci@cornell.edu. *Web site:* http://www.gradschool.cornell.edu/grad/fields_1/mat-sci.html

■ **DARTMOUTH COLLEGE**

Thayer School of Engineering, Program in Materials Sciences and Engineering, Hanover, NH 03755

AWARDS MS, PhD.

Degree requirements: For master's, thesis; for doctorate, thesis/dissertation, candidacy oral exam.
Entrance requirements: For master's and doctorate, GRE General Test. *Application deadline:* For fall admission, 1/1 (priority date). *Application fee:* $40 ($50 for international students).
Expenses: Tuition: Full-time $26,425.
Financial support: Fellowships, research assistantships, teaching assistantships, career-related internships or fieldwork, Federal Work-Study, institutionally sponsored loans, and tuition waivers (full and partial) available. Financial award application deadline: 1/15.
Faculty research: Microelectronic and magnetic materials, optical thin films, biomaterials and nanostructures, laser-material interactions, nano composites. *Total annual research expenditures:* $800,000.

Dartmouth College (continued)
Application contact: Candace S. Potter, Graduate Admissions Administrator, 603-646-3844, *Fax:* 603-646-1620, *E-mail:* candace.potter@dartmouth.edu. *Web site:* http://engineering.dartmouth.edu/

■ DREXEL UNIVERSITY

Graduate School, College of Engineering, Department of Materials Engineering, Philadelphia, PA 19104-2875

AWARDS MS, PhD. Part-time and evening/weekend programs available.

Faculty: 12 full-time (1 woman).
Students: 1 full-time (0 women), 38 part-time (10 women); includes 1 minority (Asian American or Pacific Islander), 19 international. Average age 29. 66 applicants, 67% accepted, 5 enrolled. In 2001, 6 master's, 4 doctorates awarded. Terminal master's awarded for partial completion of doctoral program.
Degree requirements: For master's, thesis or alternative; for doctorate, thesis/dissertation.
Entrance requirements: For master's, TOEFL, minimum GPA of 3.0; for doctorate, TOEFL, minimum GPA of 3.0, MS. *Application deadline:* For fall admission, 8/21. Applications are processed on a rolling basis. *Application fee:* $50. Electronic applications accepted.
Expenses: Tuition: Full-time $20,088; part-time $558 per credit. Required fees: $78 per term. One-time fee: $200. Tuition and fees vary according to course load, degree level and program.
Financial support: Research assistantships, teaching assistantships, career-related internships or fieldwork and unspecified assistantships available. Financial award application deadline: 2/1.
Faculty research: Composite science; polymer and biomedical engineering. Solidification; near net shape processing, including powder metallurgy.
Dr. Roger Doherty, Acting Head, 215-895-2330.
Application contact: Director of Graduate Admissions, 215-895-6700, *Fax:* 215-895-5939, *E-mail:* enroll@drexel.edu.

■ GEORGIA INSTITUTE OF TECHNOLOGY

Graduate Studies and Research, College of Engineering, School of Materials Science and Engineering, Atlanta, GA 30332-0001

AWARDS Biomedical engineering (MS Bio E); ceramic engineering (MSMSE, PhD); materials engineering (MS); metallurgy (MSMSE, PhD); polymers (MS Poly). Terminal master's awarded for partial completion of doctoral program.

Degree requirements: For doctorate, thesis/dissertation.

Entrance requirements: For master's and doctorate, GRE General Test, TOEFL. Electronic applications accepted.
Faculty research: Corrosion, composites, surface modifications, *in situ* oxide-metal composites.

■ ILLINOIS INSTITUTE OF TECHNOLOGY

Graduate College, Armour College of Engineering and Sciences, Department of Mechanical, Materials and Aerospace Engineering, Metallurgical and Materials Engineering Division, Chicago, IL 60616-3793

AWARDS MMME, MS, PhD. Part-time programs available.

Faculty: 8 full-time (1 woman), 3 part-time/adjunct (0 women).
Students: 8 full-time (1 woman), 14 part-time (1 woman); includes 4 minority (1 African American, 1 Asian American or Pacific Islander, 2 Hispanic Americans), 10 international. Average age 31. 67 applicants, 55% accepted. In 2001, 4 degrees awarded. Terminal master's awarded for partial completion of doctoral program.
Degree requirements: For master's, thesis (for some programs), comprehensive exam; for doctorate, thesis/dissertation, comprehensive exam.
Entrance requirements: For master's and doctorate, GRE General Test, TOEFL, minimum undergraduate GPA of 3.0. *Application deadline:* For fall admission, 7/1; for spring admission, 11/1. Applications are processed on a rolling basis. *Application fee:* $30. Electronic applications accepted.
Expenses: Tuition: Part-time $590 per credit hour.
Financial support: In 2001–02, 1 fellowship, 2 research assistantships, 1 teaching assistantship were awarded. Federal Work-Study, institutionally sponsored loans, scholarships/grants, and unspecified assistantships also available. Financial award application deadline: 3/1; financial award applicants required to submit FAFSA.
Faculty research: High-temperature materials, laser processing, fracture mechanics, powder metallurgy, alloy design.
Dr. John Kallend, Associate Chair, 312-567-3054, *Fax:* 312-567-8875, *E-mail:* kallend@iit.edu.
Application contact: Dr. Ali Cinar, Dean of Graduate College, 312-567-3637, *Fax:* 312-567-7517, *E-mail:* gradstu@iit.edu. *Web site:* http://www.mmae.iit.edu/

■ IOWA STATE UNIVERSITY OF SCIENCE AND TECHNOLOGY

Graduate College, College of Engineering and College of Liberal Arts and Sciences, Department of Materials Science and Engineering, Ames, IA 50011

AWARDS MS, PhD.

Faculty: 23 full-time, 3 part-time/adjunct.
Students: 49 full-time (11 women), 16 part-time (5 women); includes 1 minority (Asian American or Pacific Islander), 36 international. 133 applicants, 19% accepted, 12 enrolled. In 2001, 7 degrees awarded.
Degree requirements: For master's and doctorate, thesis/dissertation. *Median time to degree:* Master's–2.2 years full-time.
Entrance requirements: For master's and doctorate, GRE General Test (international applicants), TOEFL. *Application deadline:* For fall admission, 2/15 (priority date); for spring admission, 8/15 (priority date). *Application fee:* $20 ($50 for international students). Electronic applications accepted.
Expenses: Tuition, state resident: full-time $1,851. Tuition, nonresident: full-time $5,449. Tuition and fees vary according to program.
Financial support: In 2001–02, 45 research assistantships with partial tuition reimbursements (averaging $15,938 per year), 1 teaching assistantship with partial tuition reimbursement (averaging $13,114 per year) were awarded. Fellowships, scholarships/grants, health care benefits, and unspecified assistantships also available.
Dr. Mufit Akinc, Chair, 515-294-0738, *Fax:* 515-204-5444, *E-mail:* mse@iastate.edu.
Application contact: Dr. David Cann, Information Contact, 515-294-1214, *E-mail:* mse@iastate.edu. *Web site:* http://www1.eng.iastate.edu/coe/grad.asp/

■ JOHNS HOPKINS UNIVERSITY

G. W. C. Whiting School of Engineering, Department of Materials Science and Engineering, Baltimore, MD 21218-2699

AWARDS M Mat SE, MSE, PhD. Part-time and evening/weekend programs available.

Faculty: 10 full-time (1 woman), 6 part-time/adjunct (1 woman).
Students: 25 full-time (5 women), 3 part-time; includes 2 minority (1 Asian American or Pacific Islander, 1 Hispanic American), 13 international. Average age 30. 74 applicants, 18% accepted, 2 enrolled. In 2001, 6 degrees awarded. Terminal master's awarded for partial completion of doctoral program.
Degree requirements: For master's, thesis, cumulative exam; for doctorate, thesis/dissertation, cumulative and oral exam.

Entrance requirements: For master's and doctorate, GRE General Test, TOEFL. *Application deadline:* Applications are processed on a rolling basis. *Application fee:* $0. Electronic applications accepted.
Expenses: Tuition: Full-time $27,390.
Financial support: In 2001–02, 27 students received support, including 3 fellowships with full tuition reimbursements available (averaging $18,540 per year), 18 research assistantships with full tuition reimbursements available (averaging $18,540 per year), 6 teaching assistantships with full tuition reimbursements available (averaging $18,540 per year); Federal Work-Study, institutionally sponsored loans, tuition waivers (full), and unspecified assistantships also available. Financial award application deadline: 3/14.
Faculty research: Thin films, nanomaterials, biomaterials, materials processing, computational materials science. *Total annual research expenditures:* $1.6 million.
Dr. Peter C. Searson, Chair, 410-516-8774, *Fax:* 410-516-5293, *E-mail:* searson@jhu.edu.
Application contact: Dr. Robert C. Cammarata, Chair, Graduate Program, 410-516-8145, *Fax:* 410-516-5293, *E-mail:* dmse.admissions@jhu.edu. *Web site:* http://www.jhu.edu/~matsci/

Find an in-depth description at www.petersons.com/gradchannel.

■ LEHIGH UNIVERSITY

P.C. Rossin College of Engineering and Applied Science, Department of Materials Science and Engineering, Bethlehem, PA 18015-3094

AWARDS M Eng, MS, PhD. Part-time programs available.
Faculty: 13 full-time (1 woman), 2 part-time/adjunct (0 women).
Students: 41 full-time (7 women), 4 part-time; includes 9 minority (1 African American, 8 Asian Americans or Pacific Islanders), 4 international. 408 applicants, 4% accepted, 11 enrolled. In 2001, 8 master's, 8 doctorates awarded.
Degree requirements: For master's and doctorate, thesis/dissertation.
Entrance requirements: For master's and doctorate, GRE General Test, TOEFL, minimum GPA of 3.0. *Application deadline:* For fall admission, 2/15 (priority date); for spring admission, 10/1 (priority date). Applications are processed on a rolling basis. *Application fee:* $50.
Expenses: Tuition: Part-time $468 per credit hour. Required fees: $200; $100 per semester. Tuition and fees vary according to program.
Financial support: In 2001–02, 3 fellowships with full tuition reimbursements (averaging $17,400 per year), 36 research assistantships with full tuition reimbursements (averaging $17,700 per year) were awarded. Teaching assistantships, tuition

waivers (full) also available. Financial award application deadline: 1/15.
Faculty research: Metals, ceramics, crystals, polymers, fatigue crack propagation, electron microscopy. *Total annual research expenditures:* $5.1 million.
Dr. G. Slade Cargill, Chairperson, 610-758-4207, *Fax:* 610-758-4244, *E-mail:* gsc3@lehigh.edu.
Application contact: Maxine C. Mattie, Graduate Administrative Coordinator, 610-758-4222, *Fax:* 610-758-4244, *E-mail:* mcm1@lehigh.edu.

Find an in-depth description at www.petersons.com/gradchannel.

■ MASSACHUSETTS INSTITUTE OF TECHNOLOGY

School of Engineering, Department of Materials Science and Engineering, Cambridge, MA 02139-4307

AWARDS Materials engineering (Mat E); materials science and engineering (SM, PhD, Sc D); metallurgical engineering (Met E).
Faculty: 33 full-time (6 women).
Students: 179 full-time (52 women), 1 (woman) part-time; includes 21 minority (3 African Americans, 14 Asian Americans or Pacific Islanders, 4 Hispanic Americans), 77 international. Average age 23. 288 applicants, 36% accepted, 44 enrolled. In 2001, 30 master's, 29 doctorates awarded. Terminal master's awarded for partial completion of doctoral program.
Degree requirements: For master's and other advanced degree, thesis; for doctorate, thesis/dissertation, qualifying exams, comprehensive exam.
Entrance requirements: For master's and doctorate, GRE General Test, TOEFL. *Application deadline:* For fall admission, 1/15 (priority date); for spring admission, 11/1. *Application fee:* $60. Electronic applications accepted.
Expenses: Tuition: Full-time $26,960. Full-time tuition and fees vary according to program.
Financial support: In 2001–02, 173 students received support, including 42 fellowships, 138 research assistantships, 11 teaching assistantships; career-related internships or fieldwork, Federal Work-Study, institutionally sponsored loans, scholarships/grants, traineeships, health care benefits, and unspecified assistantships also available. Financial award application deadline: 1/1; financial award applicants required to submit FAFSA.
Faculty research: Photonic band gap materials, advanced spectroscopic and diffraction techniques, rapid solidification process, high-strength polymer materials, computer modeling of structures and processing. *Total annual research expenditures:* $15.5 million.
Subra Suresh, Head, 617-253-3320, *Fax:* 617-252-1773, *E-mail:* ssuresh@mit.edu.
Application contact: Kathleen R. Farrell, Student Administrator, 617-253-3302,

E-mail: krf@mit.edu. *Web site:* http://dmse.mit.edu/

■ MICHIGAN STATE UNIVERSITY

Graduate School, College of Engineering, Department of Chemical Engineering and Materials Science, East Lansing, MI 48824

AWARDS Chemical engineering (MS, PhD), including environmental toxicology (PhD); engineering mechanics (MS, PhD); materials science and engineering (MS, PhD); mechanics (PhD); metallurgy (MS, PhD). Part-time programs available.
Faculty: 22.
Students: 41 full-time (10 women), 5 part-time (1 woman); includes 9 minority (2 African Americans, 4 Asian Americans or Pacific Islanders, 3 Hispanic Americans), 21 international. Average age 26. 99 applicants, 14% accepted. In 2001, 8 master's, 6 doctorates awarded. Terminal master's awarded for partial completion of doctoral program.
Degree requirements: For doctorate, thesis/dissertation.
Entrance requirements: For master's, GRE, TOEFL, minimum GPA of 3.0; for doctorate, GRE, TOEFL. *Application deadline:* For fall admission, 1/15 (priority date); for spring admission, 11/1. Applications are processed on a rolling basis. *Application fee:* $30 ($40 for international students). Electronic applications accepted.
Expenses: Tuition, state resident: part-time $244 per credit hour. Tuition, nonresident: part-time $494 per credit hour. Required fees: $268 per semester. Tuition and fees vary according to course load, degree level and program.
Financial support: In 2001–02, 26 fellowships with tuition reimbursements (averaging $3,950 per year), 49 research assistantships with tuition reimbursements (averaging $14,052 per year), 19 teaching assistantships with tuition reimbursements (averaging $12,741 per year) were awarded. Financial award applicants required to submit FAFSA.
Faculty research: Agricultural bioprocessing, impact resistance of thermoplastic composite materials, durability of polymer composites. *Total annual research expenditures:* $989,316.
Dr. Martin Hawley, Interim Chair, 517-355-5135, *Fax:* 517-353-9842.
Application contact: Information Contact, 517-355-5135, *Fax:* 517-432-1105, *E-mail:* chems@egr.msu.edu. *Web site:* http://www.chems.msu.edu/

■ MICHIGAN TECHNOLOGICAL UNIVERSITY

Graduate School, College of Engineering, Department of Materials Science and Engineering, Houghton, MI 49931-1295

AWARDS MS, PhD. Part-time programs available.

Michigan Technological University (continued)

Degree requirements: For master's, thesis; for doctorate, thesis/dissertation, qualifying exam.
Entrance requirements: For master's and doctorate, GRE General Test, TOEFL. Electronic applications accepted.
Faculty research: Structure/property/processing relationships, microstructural characterization, alloy design, electronic/magnetic/photonic materials, materials and manufacturing processes. *Web site:* http://www.my.mtu.edu/

Find an in-depth description at www.petersons.com/gradchannel.

■ **NATIONAL TECHNOLOGICAL UNIVERSITY**

Programs in Engineering, Fort Collins, CO 80526-1842

AWARDS Chemical engineering (MS); computer engineering (MS); computer science (MS); electrical engineering (MS); engineering management (MS); environmental systems management (MS); management of technology (MS); manufacturing systems engineering (MS); materials science and engineering (MS); mechanical engineering (MS); microelectronics and semiconductor engineering (MS). Software engineering (MS). Special majors (MS). Systems engineering (MS). Part-time programs available. Postbaccalaureate distance learning degree programs offered (no on-campus study).

Students: In 2001, 114 degrees awarded.
Degree requirements: For master's, comprehensive exam.
Entrance requirements: For master's, BS in engineering or related field; 2.9 minimum GPA. *Application deadline:* Applications are processed on a rolling basis. *Application fee:* $50. Electronic applications accepted.
Expenses: Tuition: Part-time $660 per credit hour. Part-time tuition and fees vary according to course load, campus/location and program.
Dr. Andre Vacroux, President, 970-495-6400, *Fax:* 970-484-0668, *E-mail:* andre@ntu.edu.
Application contact: Rhonda Bonham, Admissions Officer, 970-495-6400, *Fax:* 970-498-0601, *E-mail:* rhonda@ntu.edu. *Web site:* http://www.ntu.edu/

■ **NEW JERSEY INSTITUTE OF TECHNOLOGY**

Office of Graduate Studies, Department of Physics, Program in Materials Science and Engineering, Newark, NJ 07102

AWARDS MS, PhD. Part-time and evening/weekend programs available.

Students: 26 full-time (2 women), 7 part-time (2 women); includes 7 minority (1 African American, 5 Asian Americans or Pacific Islanders, 1 Hispanic American), 24 international. Average age 30. 61 applicants, 69% accepted, 9 enrolled. In 2001, 4 master's, 1 doctorate awarded. Terminal master's awarded for partial completion of doctoral program.
Degree requirements: For master's and doctorate, thesis/dissertation.
Entrance requirements: For master's, GRE General Test; for doctorate, GRE General Test, minimum graduate GPA of 3.5. *Application deadline:* For fall admission, 6/5 (priority date); for spring admission, 10/15. Applications are processed on a rolling basis. *Application fee:* $50. Electronic applications accepted.
Expenses: Tuition, state resident: full-time $7,812; part-time $434 per credit. Tuition, nonresident: full-time $10,746; part-time $597 per credit. Required fees: $47 per credit. $76 per semester.
Financial support: Fellowships with full and partial tuition reimbursements, research assistantships with full and partial tuition reimbursements, teaching assistantships with full and partial tuition reimbursements, career-related internships or fieldwork, Federal Work-Study, institutionally sponsored loans, and unspecified assistantships available. Financial award application deadline: 3/15.
Application contact: Kathryn Kelly, Director of Admissions, 973-596-3300, *Fax:* 973-596-3461, *E-mail:* admissions@njit.edu. *Web site:* http://www.njit.edu/

■ **NEW MEXICO INSTITUTE OF MINING AND TECHNOLOGY**

Graduate Studies, Department of Materials Engineering, Socorro, NM 87801

AWARDS MS, PhD.

Faculty: 7 full-time (2 women), 5 part-time/adjunct (0 women).
Students: 26 full-time (4 women), 4 part-time; includes 3 minority (all Hispanic Americans), 15 international. Average age 25. 44 applicants, 50% accepted, 7 enrolled. In 2001, 10 master's, 2 doctorates awarded.
Degree requirements: For master's and doctorate, thesis/dissertation.
Entrance requirements: For master's, GRE General Test, TOEFL; for doctorate, GRE General Test, GRE Subject Test, TOEFL. *Application deadline:* For fall admission, 3/1 (priority date); for spring admission, 6/1. Applications are processed on a rolling basis. *Application fee:* $16 ($30 for international students).
Expenses: Tuition, state resident: part-time $1,084 per semester. Tuition, nonresident: part-time $4,367 per semester. Required fees: $429 per semester.
Financial support: In 2001–02, 17 research assistantships (averaging $13,505 per year), 3 teaching assistantships with full and partial tuition reimbursements (averaging $12,714 per year) were

awarded. Fellowships, Federal Work-Study and institutionally sponsored loans also available. Financial award application deadline: 3/1; financial award applicants required to submit CSS PROFILE or FAFSA.
Faculty research: Materials, metallurgy, ceramic working.
Dr. Gillian Bond, Chair, 505-835-5519, *Fax:* 505-835-5653, *E-mail:* gbond@nmt.edu.
Application contact: Dr. David B. Johnson, Dean of Graduate Studies, 505-835-5513, *Fax:* 505-835-5476, *E-mail:* graduate@nmt.edu. *Web site:* http://www.nmt.edu/~mtls/

■ **NORTH CAROLINA STATE UNIVERSITY**

Graduate School, College of Engineering, Department of Materials Science and Engineering, Raleigh, NC 27695

AWARDS MMSE, MS, PhD.

Faculty: 24 full-time (1 woman), 17 part-time/adjunct (0 women).
Students: 77 full-time (12 women), 8 part-time (2 women); includes 5 minority (1 African American, 2 Asian Americans or Pacific Islanders, 2 Hispanic Americans), 33 international. Average age 29. 180 applicants, 17% accepted. In 2001, 6 master's, 14 doctorates awarded.
Degree requirements: For master's and doctorate, thesis/dissertation.
Application deadline: For fall admission, 6/25. *Application fee:* $45.
Expenses: Tuition, state resident: full-time $1,748. Tuition, nonresident: full-time $6,904.
Financial support: In 2001–02, 4 fellowships (averaging $8,121 per year), 56 research assistantships (averaging $6,257 per year), 8 teaching assistantships (averaging $5,777 per year) were awarded.
Faculty research: Processing and properties of wide band gap semiconductors, ferroelectric thin-film materials, ductility of nanocrystalline materials, computational materials science, defects in silicon-based devices. *Total annual research expenditures:* $6.4 million.
Dr. J. Michael Rigsbee, Head, 919-515-3568, *Fax:* 919-515-7724, *E-mail:* mike_rigsbee@ncsu.edu.
Application contact: Dr. Ronald O. Scattergood, Director of Graduate Programs, 919-515-7843, *Fax:* 919-515-7724, *E-mail:* mte_gradprog@ncsu.edu. *Web site:* http://vims.ncsu.edu/matsci/

■ **NORTHWESTERN UNIVERSITY**

McCormick School of Engineering and Applied Science, Department of Materials Science and Engineering, Evanston, IL 60208

AWARDS Electronic materials (Certificate); materials science and engineering (MS, PhD).

Admissions and degrees offered through The Graduate School. Part-time programs available.

Faculty: 26 full-time (2 women).
Students: 109 full-time (25 women), 2 part-time (1 woman); includes 16 minority (2 African Americans, 10 Asian Americans or Pacific Islanders, 4 Hispanic Americans), 33 international. 263 applicants, 22% accepted, 24 enrolled. In 2001, 9 master's, 19 doctorates awarded. Terminal master's awarded for partial completion of doctoral program.
Degree requirements: For master's, oral thesis defense; for doctorate, oral defense of dissertation, preliminary evaluation, qualifying exam.
Application deadline: For fall admission, 1/15. Applications are processed on a rolling basis. *Application fee:* $60 ($75 for international students). Electronic applications accepted.
Expenses: Tuition: Full-time $26,526.
Financial support: In 2001–02, 28 fellowships with full tuition reimbursements (averaging $21,208 per year), 81 research assistantships with full tuition reimbursements (averaging $19,440 per year), teaching assistantships with full tuition reimbursements (averaging $19,440 per year) were awarded. Career-related internships or fieldwork and institutionally sponsored loans also available. Financial award application deadline: 1/15; financial award applicants required to submit FAFSA.
Faculty research: Metallurgy, ceramics, polymers, electronic materials, biomaterials. *Total annual research expenditures:* $9.9 million.
Katherine T. Faber, Chair, 847-491-3537, *Fax:* 847-491-7820.
Application contact: Jason Grocholski, Admissions Contact, 847-491-3587, *Fax:* 847-491-7820, *E-mail:* matsci@ northwestern.edu. *Web site:* http:// www.matsci.northwestern.edu/

■ THE OHIO STATE UNIVERSITY

Graduate School, College of Engineering, Department of Materials Science and Engineering, Columbus, OH 43210

AWARDS MS, PhD.

Degree requirements: For master's and doctorate, thesis/dissertation.
Entrance requirements: For master's and doctorate, GRE General Test (international applicants).
Faculty research: Computational materials modeling, biomaterials, metallurgy, ceramics, advanced alloys/composites. *Web site:* http://www.osu.edu/mse/

Find an in-depth description at www.petersons.com/gradchannel.

■ OLD DOMINION UNIVERSITY

College of Engineering and Technology, Program in Materials Science and Engineering, Norfolk, VA 23529

AWARDS ME, MS.

Faculty: 4 full-time (0 women), 2 part-time/adjunct (0 women).
Students: Average age 36. 12 applicants, 75% accepted. In 2001, 1 degree awarded.
Degree requirements: For master's, comprehensive exam.
Application deadline: For fall admission, 7/1; for spring admission, 10/1. Applications are processed on a rolling basis. *Application fee:* $30. Electronic applications accepted.
Expenses: Tuition, state resident: part-time $202 per credit. Tuition, nonresident: part-time $534 per credit. Required fees: $76 per semester. *Total annual research expenditures:* $1 million.
Dr. Mool Gupta, Graduate Program Director, 757-683-5645, *Fax:* 757-269-5644, *E-mail:* mgupta@odu.edu. *Web site:* http://www.arc.odu.edu/academics.htm

■ THE PENNSYLVANIA STATE UNIVERSITY UNIVERSITY PARK CAMPUS

Graduate School, College of Earth and Mineral Sciences, Department of Materials Science and Engineering, State College, University Park, PA 16802-1503

AWARDS Ceramic science (MS, PhD); fuel science (MS, PhD); metals science and engineering (MS, PhD); polymer science (MS, PhD).

Students: 106 full-time (19 women), 10 part-time (3 women). In 2001, 25 master's, 16 doctorates awarded.
Entrance requirements: For master's and doctorate, GRE. *Application deadline:* For fall admission, 7/1. *Application fee:* $45.
Expenses: Tuition, state resident: full-time $7,882; part-time $333 per credit. Tuition, nonresident: full-time $16,142; part-time $673 per credit. Required fees: $124 per semester.
Financial support: Fellowships, unspecified assistantships available. Financial award application deadline: 2/28.
Gray L. Messing, Head, 814-865-2262.

■ PURDUE UNIVERSITY

Graduate School, Schools of Engineering, School of Materials Engineering, West Lafayette, IN 47907

AWARDS Materials engineering (MS, MSE, PhD); metallurgical engineering (MS Met E). Part-time programs available.

Faculty: 11 full-time (1 woman), 4 part-time/adjunct (0 women).
Students: 25 full-time (4 women), 4 part-time (1 woman), 18 international. Average

age 26. 100 applicants, 21% accepted. In 2001, 6 master's, 4 doctorates awarded.
Degree requirements: For master's, thesis (for some programs); for doctorate, thesis/dissertation.
Entrance requirements: For master's and doctorate, TOEFL. *Application deadline:* For fall admission, 2/1 (priority date). *Application fee:* $30. Electronic applications accepted.
Expenses: Tuition, state resident: full-time $4,164; part-time $149 per credit hour. Tuition, nonresident: full-time $13,872; part-time $458 per credit hour. Tuition and fees vary according to campus/location and program.
Financial support: In 2001–02, 31 research assistantships with full tuition reimbursements (averaging $16,500 per year) were awarded; fellowships, teaching assistantships Support available to part-time students. Financial award applicants required to submit FAFSA.
Faculty research: Electronic behavior, mechanical behavior, thermodynamics, kinetics, phase transformations. *Total annual research expenditures:* $4.5 million.
Dr. A. H. King, Head, 765-494-4100, *Fax:* 765-494-1204, *E-mail:* alexking@ ecn.purdue.edu.
Application contact: Dr. K. J. Bowman, Graduate Committee Chair, 765-494-6316, *Fax:* 765-494-1204, *E-mail:* kbowman@ ecn.purdue.edu. *Web site:* http:// mse.www.ecn.purdue.edu/mse/

■ RENSSELAER POLYTECHNIC INSTITUTE

Graduate School, School of Engineering, Department of Materials Science and Engineering, Troy, NY 12180-3590

AWARDS Ceramics and glass science (M Eng, MS, PhD); composites (M Eng, MS, PhD); electronic materials (M Eng, MS, PhD); metallurgy (M Eng, MS, PhD); polymers (M Eng, MS, PhD). Part-time and evening/weekend programs available.

Faculty: 15 full-time (1 woman), 5 part-time/adjunct (0 women).
Students: 56 full-time (15 women), 18 part-time (5 women), 35 international. Average age 24. 287 applicants, 11% accepted, 10 enrolled. In 2001, 11 master's, 5 doctorates awarded. Terminal master's awarded for partial completion of doctoral program.
Degree requirements: For master's, thesis (for some programs); for doctorate, thesis/dissertation. *Median time to degree:* Master's–2 years full-time, 5 years part-time; doctorate–5.5 years full-time, 8 years part-time.
Entrance requirements: For master's and doctorate, GRE, TOEFL. *Application deadline:* For fall admission, 1/15 (priority date). Applications are processed on a rolling basis. *Application fee:* $45. Electronic applications accepted.

Rensselaer Polytechnic Institute (continued)

Expenses: Tuition: Full-time $26,400; part-time $1,320 per credit hour. Required fees: $1,437.

Financial support: In 2001–02, 53 students received support, including 13 fellowships with full tuition reimbursements available (averaging $22,000 per year), 29 research assistantships with full tuition reimbursements available (averaging $16,800 per year), 11 teaching assistantships with full tuition reimbursements available (averaging $16,800 per year); career-related internships or fieldwork and institutionally sponsored loans also available. Financial award application deadline: 2/1.

Faculty research: Materials processing, nanostructural materials, materials for microelectronics, composite materials, materials theory. *Total annual research expenditures:* $4.1 million.

Dr. David J. Duquette, Chair, 518-276-6373, *Fax:* 518-276-8554.

Application contact: Dr. Roger Wright, Admissions Coordinator, 518-276-6372, *Fax:* 518-276-8554, *E-mail:* fowlen@rpi.edu. *Web site:* http://www.rpi.edu/dept/materials/

Find an in-depth description at www.petersons.com/gradchannel.

■ **ROCHESTER INSTITUTE OF TECHNOLOGY**

Graduate Enrollment Services, College of Science, Center for Materials Science and Engineering, Rochester, NY 14623-5603

AWARDS MS. Part-time programs available.

Students: 8 full-time (3 women), 8 part-time (4 women); includes 2 minority (1 Asian American or Pacific Islander, 1 Hispanic American), 9 international. 40 applicants, 73% accepted, 7 enrolled. In 2001, 6 degrees awarded.

Degree requirements: For master's, thesis optional.

Entrance requirements: For master's, TOEFL, minimum GPA of 3.0. *Application deadline:* For fall admission, 3/1 (priority date). Applications are processed on a rolling basis. *Application fee:* $50.

Expenses: Tuition: Full-time $20,928; part-time $587 per hour. Required fees: $162. Tuition and fees vary according to program.

Financial support: Teaching assistantships, career-related internships or fieldwork, institutionally sponsored loans, and tuition waivers (partial) available. Support available to part-time students. Financial award application deadline: 7/29.

Faculty research: VUV modification of polymers, structure and morphology of sputtered copper films; MRI applications to materials problems.

Dr. K. S.V. Santhanam, Interim Director, 585-475-2920, *E-mail:* ksssch@rit.edu. *Web site:* http://www.rit.edu/~670www/

■ **SAN JOSE STATE UNIVERSITY**

Graduate Studies, College of Engineering, Department of Chemical Engineering and Materials Engineering, Program in Materials Engineering, San Jose, CA 95192-0001

AWARDS MS. Part-time programs available.

Faculty: 6 full-time (1 woman), 3 part-time/adjunct (0 women).

Students: Average age 33. 22 applicants, 64% accepted. In 2001, 6 degrees awarded.

Degree requirements: For master's, thesis or alternative.

Entrance requirements: For master's, GRE, TOEFL. *Application deadline:* For fall admission, 6/29; for spring admission, 11/30. Applications are processed on a rolling basis. *Application fee:* $59. Electronic applications accepted.

Expenses: Tuition, nonresident: part-time $246 per unit. Required fees: $678 per semester. Tuition and fees vary according to course load.

Financial support: In 2001–02, 3 teaching assistantships were awarded; career-related internships or fieldwork, Federal Work-Study, and institutionally sponsored loans also available. Support available to part-time students. Financial award applicants required to submit FAFSA.

Faculty research: Electronic materials, thin films, electron microscopy, fiber composites, polymeric materials.

Application contact: Dr. Guna Selvaduray, Graduate Coordinator, 408-924-3874.

■ **SOUTH DAKOTA SCHOOL OF MINES AND TECHNOLOGY**

Graduate Division, Division of Material Engineering and Science, Doctoral Program in Materials Engineering and Science, Rapid City, SD 57701-3995

AWARDS Chemical engineering (PhD); chemistry (PhD); civil engineering (PhD); electrical engineering (PhD); mechanical engineering (PhD); metallurgical engineering (PhD); physics (PhD). Part-time programs available.

Degree requirements: For doctorate, thesis/dissertation.

Entrance requirements: For doctorate, TOEFL, TWE, minimum graduate GPA of 3.0. Electronic applications accepted.

Faculty research: Thermophysical properties of solids, development of multiphase materials and composites, concrete technology, electronic polymer materials.

Find an in-depth description at www.petersons.com/gradchannel.

■ **SOUTH DAKOTA SCHOOL OF MINES AND TECHNOLOGY**

Graduate Division, Division of Material Engineering and Science, Master's Program in Materials Engineering and Science, Rapid City, SD 57701-3995

AWARDS Chemistry (MS); metallurgical engineering (MS); physics (MS).

Entrance requirements: For master's, TOEFL, TWE. Electronic applications accepted.

■ **STANFORD UNIVERSITY**

School of Engineering, Department of Materials Science and Engineering, Stanford, CA 94305-9991

AWARDS MS, PhD, Eng.

Faculty: 10 full-time (0 women).

Students: 110 full-time (31 women), 30 part-time (9 women); includes 34 minority (7 African Americans, 26 Asian Americans or Pacific Islanders, 1 Hispanic American), 60 international. Average age 27. 219 applicants, 37% accepted. In 2001, 43 master's, 12 doctorates awarded. Terminal master's awarded for partial completion of doctoral program.

Degree requirements: For doctorate and Eng, thesis/dissertation.

Entrance requirements: For master's, doctorate, and Eng, GRE General Test, TOEFL. *Application deadline:* For fall admission, 1/5. *Application fee:* $65 ($80 for international students). Electronic applications accepted.

Bruce M. Clemens, Chair, 650-725-7455, *Fax:* 650-725-4034, *E-mail:* clemens@sce.stanford.edu.

Application contact: Graduate Administrator, 650-725-2648. *Web site:* http://www-mse.stanford.edu/

■ **STEVENS INSTITUTE OF TECHNOLOGY**

Graduate School, Charles V. Schaefer Jr. School of Engineering, Department of Materials Science and Engineering, Hoboken, NJ 07030

AWARDS Materials engineering (M Eng, PhD); materials science (MS, PhD). Structural analysis of materials (Certificate). Surface modification of materials (Certificate). Part-time and evening/weekend programs available. Terminal master's awarded for partial completion of doctoral program.

Degree requirements: For master's, thesis optional; for doctorate, thesis/dissertation.

Entrance requirements: For master's and doctorate, TOEFL. Electronic applications accepted.

Expenses: Tuition: Full-time $13,950; part-time $775 per credit. Required fees: $180. One-time fee: $180 part-time. Full-time tuition and fees vary according to degree level and program.

Faculty research: Surface modification techniques, structure and surface analysis, corrosion, tribology, superconductor materials.

■ STONY BROOK UNIVERSITY, STATE UNIVERSITY OF NEW YORK

Graduate School, College of Engineering and Applied Sciences, Department of Materials Science and Engineering, Stony Brook, NY 11794

AWARDS MS, PhD.

Faculty: 11 full-time (2 women), 3 part-time/adjunct (0 women).
Students: 36 full-time (7 women), 20 part-time (5 women); includes 6 minority (1 African American, 3 Asian Americans or Pacific Islanders, 2 Hispanic Americans), 42 international. 65 applicants, 72% accepted. In 2001, 9 master's, 12 doctorates awarded.
Degree requirements: For master's, thesis or alternative; for doctorate, thesis/dissertation, comprehensive exam.
Entrance requirements: For master's and doctorate, GRE General Test, TOEFL, minimum undergraduate GPA of 3.0. *Application deadline:* For fall admission, 1/15. *Application fee:* $50.
Expenses: Tuition, state resident: full-time $5,100; part-time $213 per credit. Tuition, nonresident: full-time $8,416; part-time $351 per credit. Required fees: $496.
Financial support: In 2001–02, 1 fellowship, 22 research assistantships, 22 teaching assistantships were awarded.
Faculty research: Electronic materials, biomaterials, synchrotron topography. *Total annual research expenditures:* $3.9 million.
Dr. Michael Dudley, Chairman, 631-632-8484.
Application contact: Dr. Miriam Rafailovich, Director, 631-632-8484, *Fax:* 631-632-8052, *E-mail:* mrafailovich.nsf@ notes.cc.sunysb.edu. *Web site:* http:// dol1.eng.sunysb.edu/
Find an in-depth description at www.petersons.com/gradchannel.

■ TEXAS A&M UNIVERSITY

College of Engineering, Department of Civil Engineering, Program in Materials Engineering, College Station, TX 77843

AWARDS M Eng, MS, D Eng, PhD. D Eng offered through the College of Engineering.

Students: 28.
Degree requirements: For master's, thesis (MS); for doctorate, dissertation (PhD), internship (D Eng).
Entrance requirements: For master's and doctorate, GRE General Test, TOEFL. *Application fee:* $50 ($75 for international students).

Expenses: Tuition, state resident: full-time $11,872. Tuition, nonresident: full-time $17,892.
Financial support: Fellowships, research assistantships, teaching assistantships available. Financial award application deadline: 4/15; financial award applicants required to submit FAFSA.
Faculty research: Innovative design methods, pavement distress characterization, materials property, characterization and modeling recyclable materials.
Dr. Dallas N. Little, Head, 979-845-1737, *Fax:* 979-862-2800, *E-mail:* ce-grad@ tamu.edu.
Application contact: Dr. Amy L. Epps, Information Contact, 409-845-2498, *Fax:* 409-845-2800, *E-mail:* ce-grad@tamu.edu. *Web site:* http://www.civil.tamu.edu/

■ TUSKEGEE UNIVERSITY

Graduate Programs, College of Engineering, Architecture and Physical Sciences, Program in Material Science Engineering, Tuskegee, AL 36088

AWARDS PhD.

Students: 5 full-time (2 women), 7 part-time (5 women); includes 11 minority (all African Americans), 1 international. Average age 31.
Application deadline: For fall admission, 7/15. Applications are processed on a rolling basis. *Application fee:* $25 ($35 for international students).
Expenses: Tuition: Full-time $5,163; part-time $612 per credit hour.
Financial support: Application deadline: 4/15.
Dr. Shaik Jeelani, Head, 334-727-8375.

■ THE UNIVERSITY OF ALABAMA

Graduate School, College of Engineering, Department of Metallurgical and Materials Engineering, Tuscaloosa, AL 35487

AWARDS MS Met E, PhD.

Faculty: 8 full-time (1 woman).
Students: 25 full-time (3 women), 5 part-time; includes 2 minority (both African Americans), 23 international. Average age 28. 13 applicants, 54% accepted, 4 enrolled. In 2001, 8 master's, 4 doctorates awarded.
Degree requirements: For master's, thesis or alternative; for doctorate, one foreign language, thesis/dissertation.
Entrance requirements: For master's, GRE General Test, minimum GPA of 3.0 in last 60 hours. *Application deadline:* For fall admission, 7/1 (priority date). Applications are processed on a rolling basis. *Application fee:* $25. Electronic applications accepted.
Expenses: Tuition, state resident: full-time $3,292; part-time $183 per credit hour. Tuition, nonresident: full-time $8,912; part-time $495 per credit hour. Tuition

and fees vary according to course load, campus/location and program.
Financial support: In 2001–02, 3 fellowships, 14 research assistantships, 6 teaching assistantships were awarded. Federal Work-Study also available.
Faculty research: Metals casting and solidification, corrosion and alloy development, metal matrix composites, electronic and magnetic properties. *Total annual research expenditures:* $1.7 million.
Dr. Richard C. Bradt, Head, 205-348-1740, *Fax:* 205-348-2164, *E-mail:* rcbradt@ coe.eng.ua.edu.
Application contact: Dr. Garry W. Warren, Professor, 205-348-1740, *Fax:* 205-348-2164, *E-mail:* gwarren@ coe.eng.ua.edu. *Web site:* http:// www.eng.ua.edu/~mtedept/

■ THE UNIVERSITY OF ALABAMA AT BIRMINGHAM

Graduate School, School of Engineering, Department of Materials Science and Engineering, Program in Materials Engineering, Birmingham, AL 35294

AWARDS MS Mt E, PhD.

Students: 17 full-time (2 women), 3 part-time (1 woman); includes 4 minority (3 African Americans, 1 Asian American or Pacific Islander), 11 international. 64 applicants, 69% accepted. In 2001, 4 master's, 1 doctorate awarded.
Degree requirements: For master's, project/thesis; for doctorate, thesis/dissertation, comprehensive exam.
Entrance requirements: For master's and doctorate, GRE General Test, minimum B average. *Application deadline:* Applications are processed on a rolling basis. *Application fee:* $35 ($60 for international students). Electronic applications accepted.
Expenses: Tuition, state resident: full-time $3,058. Tuition, nonresident: full-time $5,746. Tuition and fees vary according to course load, degree level and program.
Financial support: In 2001–02, 10 fellowships with full and partial tuition reimbursements (averaging $12,500 per year), 8 research assistantships with full tuition reimbursements (averaging $12,500 per year) were awarded. Career-related internships or fieldwork, Federal Work-Study, and institutionally sponsored loans also available. Support available to part-time students.
Faculty research: Casting metallurgy, microgravity solidification, thin film techniques, ceramics/glass processing, biomedical materials processing.
Dr. J. Barry Andrews, Interim Chair, Department of Materials Science and Engineering, 205-934-8460, *Fax:* 205-934-8485, *E-mail:* barry@uab.edu. *Web site:* http://www.eng.uab.edu/mme/ mtegrams.htm/

■ THE UNIVERSITY OF ALABAMA IN HUNTSVILLE

School of Graduate Studies, College of Engineering, Department of Chemical and Materials Engineering, Huntsville, AL 35899

AWARDS Biotechnology science and engineering (PhD); chemical engineering (MSE). Part-time and evening/weekend programs available.

Faculty: 4 full-time (0 women).
Students: 16 full-time (6 women), 1 part-time; includes 2 minority (1 African American, 1 Asian American or Pacific Islander), 11 international. Average age 25. 72 applicants, 21% accepted, 9 enrolled. In 2001, 6 degrees awarded.
Degree requirements: For master's, thesis or alternative, oral and written exams, comprehensive exam, registration; for doctorate, thesis/dissertation, comprehensive exam, registration.
Entrance requirements: For master's, GRE General Test, appropriate bachelor's degree, minimum GPA of 3.0. *Application deadline:* For fall admission, 7/24 (priority date); for spring admission, 11/15 (priority date). Applications are processed on a rolling basis. *Application fee:* $35.
Expenses: Tuition, area resident: Part-time $175 per hour. Tuition, state resident: full-time $4,408. Tuition, nonresident: full-time $9,054; part-time $361 per hour.
Financial support: In 2001–02, 11 students received support, including 1 fellowship with full and partial tuition reimbursement available (averaging $10,800 per year), 6 research assistantships with full and partial tuition reimbursements available (averaging $9,424 per year), 4 teaching assistantships with full and partial tuition reimbursements available (averaging $9,150 per year); career-related internships or fieldwork, Federal Work-Study, institutionally sponsored loans, scholarships/grants, health care benefits, and tuition waivers (full and partial) also available. Support available to part-time students. Financial award application deadline: 4/1; financial award applicants required to submit FAFSA.
Faculty research: Turbulence modeling, computational fluid dynamics, microgravity processing, multiphase transport, blood materials transport. *Total annual research expenditures:* $265,040.
Dr. Ramon Cerro, Chair, 256-824-6810, *Fax:* 256-824-6839, *E-mail:* rlc@eb.uah.edu. *Web site:* http://www.eb-p5.eb.uah.edu/che/

■ THE UNIVERSITY OF ARIZONA

Graduate College, College of Engineering and Mines, Department of Materials Science and Engineering, Tucson, AZ 85721

AWARDS MS, PhD. Part-time programs available.

Faculty: 15 full-time (2 women), 2 part-time/adjunct (1 woman).
Students: 42 full-time (6 women), 12 part-time (3 women); includes 7 minority (5 Asian Americans or Pacific Islanders, 2 Hispanic Americans), 27 international. Average age 30. 68 applicants, 35% accepted, 15 enrolled. In 2001, 8 master's, 5 doctorates awarded.
Degree requirements: For master's, thesis (for some programs); for doctorate, thesis/dissertation, comprehensive exam.
Entrance requirements: For master's and doctorate, GRE, TOEFL. *Application deadline:* For fall admission, 5/15. Applications are processed on a rolling basis. *Application fee:* $45.
Expenses: Tuition, state resident: full-time $2,490; part-time $436 per unit. Tuition, nonresident: full-time $10,300; part-time $436 per unit. Full-time tuition and fees vary according to degree level and program.
Financial support: Fellowships with tuition reimbursements, research assistantships with tuition reimbursements, teaching assistantships with tuition reimbursements, institutionally sponsored loans and scholarships/grants available. Financial award application deadline: 12/31.
Faculty research: High-technology ceramics, optical materials, electronic materials, chemical metallurgy, science of materials.
Dr. Joseph H. Simmons, Head, 520-621-6070, *Fax:* 520-621-8059.
Application contact: Mary E Cromwell, Graduate Secretary, 520-621-6070, *Fax:* 520-621-8059, *E-mail:* msed@email.arizona.edu. *Web site:* http://www.mse.arizona.edu/

■ UNIVERSITY OF CALIFORNIA, BERKELEY

Graduate Division, College of Engineering, Department of Materials Science and Mineral Engineering, Berkeley, CA 94720-1500

AWARDS Ceramic sciences and engineering (M Eng, MS, D Eng, PhD); engineering geoscience (M Eng, MS, D Eng, PhD); materials engineering (M Eng, MS, D Eng, PhD); mineral engineering (M Eng, MS, D Eng, PhD); petroleum engineering (M Eng, MS, D Eng, PhD); physical metallurgy (M Eng, MS, D Eng, PhD).

Degree requirements: For master's, comprehensive exam or thesis (MS); for doctorate, thesis/dissertation, qualifying exam.
Entrance requirements: For master's and doctorate, GRE General Test, minimum GPA of 3.0.
Expenses: Tuition, nonresident: full-time $10,704. Required fees: $4,349.

■ UNIVERSITY OF CALIFORNIA, IRVINE

Office of Research and Graduate Studies, School of Engineering, Program in Materials Science and Engineering, Irvine, CA 92697

AWARDS Engineering (MS, PhD); material science (MS). Part-time programs available.

Faculty: 4.
Students: 44 full-time (12 women), 4 part-time; includes 12 minority (1 African American, 8 Asian Americans or Pacific Islanders, 3 Hispanic Americans), 18 international. 36 applicants, 72% accepted, 12 enrolled. In 2001, 7 master's, 1 doctorate awarded. Terminal master's awarded for partial completion of doctoral program.
Degree requirements: For doctorate, thesis/dissertation.
Entrance requirements: For master's, GRE General Test, minimum GPA of 3.0; for doctorate, GRE General Test. *Application deadline:* For fall and spring admission, 1/15 (priority date); for winter admission, 10/15 (priority date). Applications are processed on a rolling basis. *Application fee:* $60. Electronic applications accepted.
Expenses: Tuition, nonresident: full-time $10,704. Required fees: $8,396. Tuition and fees vary according to course load, program and student level.
Financial support: In 2001–02, fellowships with tuition reimbursements (averaging $1,250 per year), research assistantships with tuition reimbursements (averaging $1,120 per year), teaching assistantships with tuition reimbursements (averaging $1,480 per year) were awarded. Institutionally sponsored loans and tuition waivers (full and partial) also available. Financial award application deadline: 3/2; financial award applicants required to submit FAFSA.
Faculty research: Composite materials, solidification processing, sol-gel processing, microstructural characterization, deformation and damage processes in advanced materials.
Dr. Farghalli A. Mohamed, Director, 949-824-5807, *Fax:* 949-824-3440, *E-mail:* famohame@uci.edu.
Application contact: Gwen Donaldson, Admissions Assistant, 949-824-3562, *Fax:* 949-824-3440, *E-mail:* gmdonald@uci.edu. *Web site:* http://www.eng.uci.edu/
Find an in-depth description at www.petersons.com/gradchannel.

■ UNIVERSITY OF CALIFORNIA, LOS ANGELES

Graduate Division, School of Engineering and Applied Science, Department of Materials Science and Engineering, Los Angeles, CA 90095

AWARDS Ceramics engineering (MS, PhD); metallurgy (MS, PhD).

Faculty: 8 full-time, 4 part-time/adjunct.

Students: 58 full-time (14 women); includes 15 minority (1 African American, 13 Asian Americans or Pacific Islanders, 1 Hispanic American), 35 international. 81 applicants, 60% accepted, 13 enrolled. In 2001, 14 master's, 8 doctorates awarded.
Degree requirements: For master's, comprehensive exam or thesis; for doctorate, thesis/dissertation, qualifying exams.
Entrance requirements: For master's, GRE General Test, minimum GPA of 3.0; for doctorate, GRE General Test, minimum GPA of 3.25. *Application deadline:* For fall admission, 1/15; for spring admission, 12/31. *Application fee:* $60. Electronic applications accepted.
Expenses: Tuition, nonresident: full-time $10,244. Required fees: $3,609. Full-time tuition and fees vary according to program.
Financial support: In 2001–02, 25 fellowships, 55 research assistantships, 24 teaching assistantships were awarded. Federal Work-Study, institutionally sponsored loans, and tuition waivers (full and partial) also available. Financial award application deadline: 1/15; financial award applicants required to submit FAFSA.
Dr. King-Ning Tu, Chair, 310-206-4838.
Application contact: Paradee Chularee, Student Affairs Officer, 310-825-8913, *Fax:* 310-206-7353, *E-mail:* paradee@ea.ucla.edu. *Web site:* http://www.seas.ucla.edu/ms/

■ UNIVERSITY OF CALIFORNIA, SANTA BARBARA

Graduate Division, College of Engineering, Department of Materials, Santa Barbara, CA 93106

AWARDS MS, PhD.

Degree requirements: For master's and doctorate, thesis/dissertation.
Entrance requirements: For master's and doctorate, GRE General Test, TOEFL. Electronic applications accepted.
Faculty research: Electronically conducting polymer systems, growth and processing of advanced semiconductors, structure and properties of artificially structured materials–electronic packages and composites, fine structures by nonequilibrium solidification or advanced deposition techniques, sensors for intelligent control systems in materials processing. *Web site:* http://www.materials.ucsb.edu/

■ UNIVERSITY OF CENTRAL FLORIDA

College of Engineering and Computer Sciences, Department of Mechanical, Materials, and Aerospace Engineering, Program in Materials Science and Engineering, Orlando, FL 32816

AWARDS MSMSE, PhD.

Faculty: 19 full-time (1 woman), 5 part-time/adjunct (0 women).

Students: 28 full-time (5 women), 10 part-time (2 women); includes 9 minority (1 African American, 8 Asian Americans or Pacific Islanders), 21 international. Average age 28. 68 applicants, 75% accepted, 16 enrolled. In 2001, 8 master's, 1 doctorate awarded.
Degree requirements: For master's, thesis or alternative; for doctorate, thesis/dissertation, candidacy exam, departmental qualifying exam.
Application deadline: For fall admission, 7/15 (priority date); for spring admission, 12/1 (priority date). *Application fee:* $20. Electronic applications accepted.
Expenses: Tuition, state resident: part-time $162 per hour. Tuition, nonresident: part-time $569 per hour.
Financial support: In 2001–02, 9 fellowships (averaging $5,208 per year), 87 research assistantships (averaging $3,617 per year), 5 teaching assistantships (averaging $3,108 per year) were awarded.
Application contact: Dr. A. J. Kassab, Coordinator, 407-823-2416, *Fax:* 407-823-0208, *E-mail:* kassab@mail.ucf.edu.

Find an in-depth description at www.petersons.com/gradchannel.

■ UNIVERSITY OF CINCINNATI

Division of Research and Advanced Studies, College of Engineering, Department of Materials Science and Metallurgical Engineering, Program in Materials Science and Engineering, Cincinnati, OH 45221

AWARDS MS, PhD. Evening/weekend programs available.

Degree requirements: For master's, thesis optional; for doctorate, one foreign language, thesis/dissertation, oral English proficiency exam, comprehensive exam.
Entrance requirements: For master's and doctorate, GRE General Test, TOEFL, BS in related field, minimum undergraduate GPA of 3.0. *Application deadline:* For fall admission, 2/1 (priority date). *Application fee:* $40. Electronic applications accepted.
Expenses: Tuition, state resident: part-time $2,698 per quarter. Tuition, nonresident: part-time $4,977 per quarter.
Financial support: Fellowships, career-related internships or fieldwork, tuition waivers (partial), and unspecified assistantships available. Financial award application deadline: 2/1.
Faculty research: Polymer characterization, surface analysis, and adhesion; mechanical behavior of high-temperature materials; composites; electrochemistry of materials.
Application contact: Dr. F. James Boerio, Graduate Program Director, 513-556-3117, *Fax:* 513-556-2569, *E-mail:* r.j.roe@uc.edu. *Web site:* http://www.mse.uc.edu/

■ UNIVERSITY OF DAYTON

Graduate School, School of Engineering, Department of Materials Engineering, Dayton, OH 45469-1300

AWARDS MS Mat E, DE, PhD. Part-time and evening/weekend programs available.

Faculty: 1 full-time (0 women), 12 part-time/adjunct (1 woman).
Students: 32 full-time (9 women), 7 part-time (2 women); includes 3 minority (2 Asian Americans or Pacific Islanders, 1 Hispanic American), 4 international. Average age 26. In 2001, 8 master's, 2 doctorates awarded.
Degree requirements: For master's, thesis optional; for doctorate, variable foreign language requirement, thesis/dissertation, departmental qualifying exam.
Entrance requirements: For master's, TOEFL. *Application deadline:* For fall admission, 8/1. Applications are processed on a rolling basis. *Application fee:* $30.
Expenses: Tuition: Full-time $5,436; part-time $453 per credit hour. Required fees: $50; $25 per term.
Financial support: In 2001–02, 15 students received support, including 2 fellowships with full tuition reimbursements available (averaging $18,000 per year), 14 research assistantships with full tuition reimbursements available (averaging $13,500 per year); teaching assistantships, institutionally sponsored loans also available.
Dr. Daniel Eylon, Director, 937-229-2679, *E-mail:* deylon@udayton.edu.
Application contact: Dr. Donald L. Moon, Associate Dean, 937-229-2241, *Fax:* 937-229-2471, *E-mail:* dmoon@notes.udayton.edu.

■ UNIVERSITY OF DELAWARE

College of Engineering, Department of Materials Science and Engineering, Newark, DE 19716

AWARDS MMSE, PhD.

Faculty: 7 full-time (2 women).
Students: 48 full-time (17 women), 7 part-time (3 women); includes 5 minority (2 African Americans, 3 Asian Americans or Pacific Islanders), 29 international. Average age 28. 153 applicants, 16% accepted, 15 enrolled. In 2001, 7 master's, 2 doctorates awarded. Terminal master's awarded for partial completion of doctoral program.
Degree requirements: For master's and doctorate, thesis/dissertation.
Entrance requirements: For master's and doctorate, GRE General Test, TOEFL, letters of recommendation (3), minimum GPA of 3.2. *Application deadline:* For fall admission, 2/28 (priority date). Applications are processed on a rolling basis. *Application fee:* $50. Electronic applications accepted.
Expenses: Tuition, state resident: full-time $4,770; part-time $265 per credit. Tuition, nonresident: full-time $13,860; part-time $770 per credit. Required fees: $414.

University of Delaware (continued)

Financial support: In 2001–02, 45 students received support, including 3 fellowships with full tuition reimbursements available (averaging $22,600 per year), 35 research assistantships with full tuition reimbursements available (averaging $16,400 per year), 7 teaching assistantships with full tuition reimbursements available (averaging $16,396 per year); career-related internships or fieldwork and Federal Work-Study also available. Support available to part-time students. Financial award application deadline: 2/28.
Faculty research: Materials chemistry; biomolecular materials, biomimetics; polymers and composites; thinfilms, surfaces and interfaces; electronic and magnetic materials. *Total annual research expenditures:* $1.1 million.
Dr. John F. Rabolt, Chairman, 302-831-2062, *Fax:* 302-831-4545, *E-mail:* matsci@udel.edu.
Application contact: Dr. Jingguang G. Chen, Professor, 302-831-2062, *Fax:* 302-831-4545, *E-mail:* matsci@udel.edu. *Web site:* http://www.udel.edu/engg/DeptsPrgms/MatSciPrgm.html

■ UNIVERSITY OF FLORIDA

Graduate School, College of Engineering, Department of Materials Science and Engineering, Gainesville, FL 32611

AWARDS Ceramic science and engineering (ME, MS, PhD, Engr); materials science and engineering (ME, MS, PhD, Certificate, Engr); metallurgical and materials engineering (ME, MS, PhD, Engr); metallurgical engineering (ME, MS, PhD, Engr); polymer science and engineering (ME, MS, PhD, Engr).

Degree requirements: For master's and other advanced degree, thesis optional; for doctorate, thesis/dissertation.
Entrance requirements: For master's and doctorate, GRE General Test, TOEFL, minimum GPA of 3.0; for other advanced degree, GRE General Test. Electronic applications accepted.
Expenses: Tuition, state resident: part-time $164 per hour. Tuition, nonresident: part-time $571 per hour. Tuition and fees vary according to course level and program.
Faculty research: Polymeric materials, electronic materials, glass, biomaterials, composites. *Web site:* http://www.mse.ufl.edu/

Find an in-depth description at www.petersons.com/gradchannel.

■ UNIVERSITY OF HOUSTON

Cullen College of Engineering, Department of Mechanical Engineering, Houston, TX 77204

AWARDS Aerospace engineering (MS, PhD); biomedical engineering (MS); computer and systems engineering (MS, PhD);

environmental engineering (MS, PhD); materials engineering (MS, PhD); mechanical engineering (MME, MSME); petroleum engineering (MS). Part-time and evening/weekend programs available.

Faculty: 16 full-time (0 women), 1 part-time/adjunct (0 women).
Students: 34 full-time (4 women), 26 part-time (2 women); includes 7 minority (3 Asian Americans or Pacific Islanders, 4 Hispanic Americans), 32 international. Average age 28. 114 applicants, 64% accepted. In 2001, 20 master's, 3 doctorates awarded. Terminal master's awarded for partial completion of doctoral program.
Degree requirements: For master's, thesis (for some programs); for doctorate, thesis/dissertation, departmental qualifying exam.
Entrance requirements: For master's and doctorate, GRE General Test, TOEFL. *Application deadline:* For fall admission, 7/3 (priority date); for spring admission, 12/4. Applications are processed on a rolling basis. *Application fee:* $25 ($75 for international students).
Expenses: Tuition, state resident: full-time $1,512. Tuition, nonresident: full-time $5,310. Required fees: $1,308. Tuition and fees vary according to program.
Financial support: In 2001–02, 20 research assistantships (averaging $14,400 per year), 13 teaching assistantships (averaging $14,400 per year) were awarded. Fellowships, career-related internships or fieldwork and Federal Work-Study also available. Financial award application deadline: 2/15.
Faculty research: Experimental and computational turbulence, composites, rheology, phase change/heat transfer, characterization of superconducting materials. *Total annual research expenditures:* $396,172.
Dr. Lewis T. Wheeler, Interim Chair, 713-743-4500, *Fax:* 713-743-4503.
Application contact: Susan Sanderson-Clobe, Graduate Admissions Analyst, 713-743-4505, *Fax:* 713-743-4503, *E-mail:* megrad@uh.edu. *Web site:* http://www.mc.uh.edu

Find an in-depth description at www.petersons.com/gradchannel.

■ UNIVERSITY OF ILLINOIS AT CHICAGO

Graduate College, College of Engineering, Department of Civil and Materials Engineering, Chicago, IL 60607-7128

AWARDS MS, PhD. Evening/weekend programs available.

Faculty: 13 full-time (0 women), 2 part-time/adjunct (0 women).
Students: 43 full-time (11 women), 47 part-time (10 women); includes 10 minority (4 African Americans, 4 Asian Americans or Pacific Islanders, 2 Hispanic Americans), 37 international. Average age

30. 152 applicants, 38% accepted, 30 enrolled. In 2001, 23 master's, 4 doctorates awarded.
Degree requirements: For master's, thesis (for some programs); for doctorate, thesis/dissertation, preliminary and qualifying exams.
Entrance requirements: For master's and doctorate, GRE General Test, TOEFL, minimum GPA of 4.0 on a 5.0 scale. *Application deadline:* For fall admission, 6/1; for spring admission, 11/1. Applications are processed on a rolling basis. *Application fee:* $40 ($50 for international students). Electronic applications accepted.
Expenses: Tuition, state resident: full-time $3,060. Tuition, nonresident: full-time $6,688.
Financial support: In 2001–02, 27 students received support; fellowships with full tuition reimbursements available, research assistantships with full tuition reimbursements available, teaching assistantships with full tuition reimbursements available, Federal Work-Study and tuition waivers (full) available. Financial award application deadline: 3/1; financial award applicants required to submit FAFSA.
Faculty research: Transportation and geotechnical engineering, damage and anisotropic behavior, steel processing.
Dr. Ming Wang, Director of Graduate Studies, 312-996-3432, *E-mail:* mlwang@uic.edu.
Application contact: Rachel L. Morrow, Graduate Program Coordinator, 312-996-3411, *E-mail:* rlmorrow@uic.edu.

Find an in-depth description at www.petersons.com/gradchannel.

■ UNIVERSITY OF ILLINOIS AT URBANA–CHAMPAIGN

Graduate College, College of Engineering, Department of Materials Science and Engineering, Champaign, IL 61820

AWARDS MS, PhD.

Faculty: 28 full-time, 1 part-time/adjunct.
Students: 130 full-time (34 women); includes 11 minority (1 African American, 5 Asian Americans or Pacific Islanders, 4 Hispanic Americans, 1 Native American), 71 international. 315 applicants, 14% accepted. In 2001, 14 master's, 14 doctorates awarded.
Degree requirements: For master's, thesis; for doctorate, thesis/dissertation, departmental qualifying exam.
Entrance requirements: For master's and doctorate, GRE, minimum GPA of 3.0. *Application deadline:* Applications are processed on a rolling basis. *Application fee:* $40 ($50 for international students). Electronic applications accepted.
Expenses: Tuition, state resident: part-time $3,227 per degree program. Tuition, nonresident: part-time $7,169 per degree

program. Tuition and fees vary according to program.

Financial support: In 2001–02, 14 fellowships, 97 research assistantships, 7 teaching assistantships were awarded. Tuition waivers (full and partial) also available. Financial award application deadline: 2/15. John Weaver, Head, 217-333-1440, *Fax:* 217-333-2736, *E-mail:* jh-weaver@ uiuc.edu.

Application contact: Kathy Dysart, Administrative Secretary, 217-333-1440, *Fax:* 217-333-2736, *E-mail:* k-dysart@ uiuc.edu. *Web site:* http:// www.mse.uiuc.edu/

■ UNIVERSITY OF MARYLAND, COLLEGE PARK

Graduate Studies and Research, A. James Clark School of Engineering, Department of Materials and Nuclear Engineering, Materials Science and Engineering Program, College Park, MD 20742

AWARDS MS, PhD. Part-time and evening/ weekend programs available. Postbaccalaureate distance learning degree programs offered.

Students: 44 full-time (13 women), 12 part-time (5 women); includes 7 minority (5 African Americans, 1 Asian American or Pacific Islander, 1 Hispanic American), 36 international. 131 applicants, 34% accepted, 19 enrolled. In 2001, 7 master's, 11 doctorates awarded.

Degree requirements: For master's, thesis or alternative, research paper, comprehensive exam; for doctorate, variable foreign language requirement, thesis/ dissertation, oral exam.

Entrance requirements: For master's and doctorate, GRE General Test, TOEFL, minimum B+ average in undergraduate course work. *Application deadline:* For fall admission, 8/1; for spring admission, 12/1. Applications are processed on a rolling basis. *Application fee:* $50 ($70 for international students). Electronic applications accepted.

Expenses: Tuition, state resident: part-time $289 per credit hour. Tuition, nonresident: part-time $448 per credit hour. One-time fee: $436 part-time. Full-time tuition and fees vary according to course load, campus/location and program.

Financial support: Fellowships, research assistantships, teaching assistantships available. Financial award applicants required to submit FAFSA. Dr. Peter Kofinas, Head, 301-405-5221.

Application contact: Trudy Lindsey, Director, Graduate Admissions and Records, 301-405-6991, *Fax:* 301-314-9477, *E-mail:* grschool@deans.umd.edu.

■ UNIVERSITY OF MARYLAND, COLLEGE PARK

Graduate Studies and Research, A. James Clark School of Engineering, Department of Mechanical Engineering, College Park, MD 20742

AWARDS Electronic packaging and reliability (MS, PhD); manufacturing and design (MS, PhD); mechanics and materials (MS, PhD); thermal and fluid sciences (MS, PhD). Part-time and evening/weekend programs available. Postbaccalaureate distance learning degree programs offered.

Faculty: 69 full-time (6 women), 15 part-time/adjunct (2 women).

Students: 142 full-time (18 women), 67 part-time (5 women); includes 13 minority (5 African Americans, 6 Asian Americans or Pacific Islanders, 2 Hispanic Americans), 134 international. 519 applicants, 14% accepted, 40 enrolled. In 2001, 49 master's, 21 doctorates awarded.

Degree requirements: For master's, thesis optional; for doctorate, thesis/ dissertation, qualifying exam.

Entrance requirements: For master's and doctorate, GRE General Test, minimum GPA of 3.0. *Application deadline:* For fall admission, 8/1; for spring admission, 12/1. Applications are processed on a rolling basis. *Application fee:* $50 ($70 for international students). Electronic applications accepted.

Expenses: Tuition, state resident: part-time $289 per credit hour. Tuition, nonresident: part-time $448 per credit hour. One-time fee: $436 part-time. Full-time tuition and fees vary according to course load, campus/location and program.

Financial support: In 2001–02, 5 fellowships with full tuition reimbursements (averaging $4,406 per year), 123 research assistantships with tuition reimbursements (averaging $14,539 per year), 36 teaching assistantships with tuition reimbursements (averaging $11,663 per year) were awarded. Federal Work-Study and scholarships/grants also available. Support available to part-time students. Financial award applicants required to submit FAFSA.

Faculty research: Decomposition-based design, powder metallurgy, injection molding, kinematic synthesis, electronic packaging, dynamic deformation and fracture, turbulent flow. Dr. Avi Bar-Cohen, Chairman, 301-405-5294, *Fax:* 301-314-9477.

Application contact: Dr. James M. Wallace, Graduate Director, 301-405-4216.

■ UNIVERSITY OF MARYLAND, COLLEGE PARK

Graduate Studies and Research, A. James Clark School of Engineering, Professional Program in Engineering, College Park, MD 20742

AWARDS Aerospace engineering (M Eng); chemical engineering (M Eng); civil engineering (M Eng); electrical engineering (M Eng); fire protection engineering (M Eng); materials science and engineering (M Eng); mechanical engineering (M Eng); reliability engineering (M Eng). Systems engineering (M Eng). Part-time and evening/weekend programs available. Postbaccalaureate distance learning degree programs offered.

Faculty: 11 part-time/adjunct (0 women).

Students: 19 full-time (4 women), 144 part-time (31 women); includes 41 minority (17 African Americans, 18 Asian Americans or Pacific Islanders, 6 Hispanic Americans), 27 international. 71 applicants, 80% accepted, 50 enrolled. In 2001, 64 degrees awarded.

Application deadline: For fall admission, 8/15; for spring admission, 1/10. Applications are processed on a rolling basis. *Application fee:* $50 ($70 for international students). Electronic applications accepted.

Expenses: Tuition, state resident: part-time $289 per credit hour. Tuition, nonresident: part-time $448 per credit hour. One-time fee: $436 part-time. Full-time tuition and fees vary according to course load, campus/location and program.

Financial support: In 2001–02, 1 research assistantship with tuition reimbursement (averaging $20,655 per year), 5 teaching assistantships with tuition reimbursements (averaging $11,114 per year) were awarded. Fellowships, Federal Work-Study and scholarships/grants also available. Support available to part-time students. Financial award applicants required to submit FAFSA. Dr. George Syrmos, Acting Director, 301-405-5256, *Fax:* 301-314-9477.

Application contact: Trudy Lindsey, Director, Graduate Admissions and Records, 301-405-6991, *Fax:* 301-314-9305, *E-mail:* grschool@deans.umd.edu.

■ UNIVERSITY OF MICHIGAN

Horace H. Rackham School of Graduate Studies, College of Engineering, Department of Materials Science and Engineering, Ann Arbor, MI 48109

AWARDS MS, PhD. Part-time programs available.

Faculty: 24 full-time (5 women).

Students: 63 full-time (13 women), 5 part-time (4 women); includes 6 minority (1 African American, 3 Asian Americans or Pacific Islanders, 2 Hispanic Americans), 31 international. Average age 26. 280 applicants, 16% accepted, 22 enrolled. In 2001, 11 master's, 10 doctorates awarded.

University of Michigan (continued)

Degree requirements: For master's, thesis, oral defense of thesis; for doctorate, thesis/dissertation, oral defense of dissertation, written exam. *Median time to degree:* Master's–2 years full-time, 4 years part-time; doctorate–4 years full-time.

Entrance requirements: For master's, GRE General Test, TOEFL, minimum GPA of 3.0 in related field; for doctorate, GRE General Test, TOEFL, minimum GPA of 3.0 in related field, master's degree. *Application deadline:* For fall admission, 1/15. Applications are processed on a rolling basis. *Application fee:* $55. Electronic applications accepted.

Financial support: In 2001–02, 11 fellowships with full tuition reimbursements (averaging $20,202 per year), 43 research assistantships with full tuition reimbursements (averaging $20,202 per year), 6 teaching assistantships with full tuition reimbursements (averaging $12,783 per year) were awarded. Financial award application deadline: 1/15; financial award applicants required to submit FAFSA. *Total annual research expenditures:* $4 million. John Halloran, Chair, 734-763-2445, *Fax:* 734-763-4788, *E-mail:* peterjon@engin.umich.edu.

Application contact: Renee Hilgendorf, Graduate Program Assistant, 734-763-9790, *Fax:* 734-763-4788, *E-mail:* reneeh@umich.edu. *Web site:* http://msewww.engin.umich.edu/

Find an in-depth description at www.petersons.com/gradchannel.

■ **UNIVERSITY OF MINNESOTA, TWIN CITIES CAMPUS**

Graduate School, Institute of Technology, Department of Chemical Engineering and Materials Science, Program in Materials Science and Engineering, Minneapolis, MN 55455-0132

AWARDS M Mat SE, MS Mat SE, PhD. Part-time programs available. Terminal master's awarded for partial completion of doctoral program.

Degree requirements: For master's and doctorate, thesis/dissertation.
Entrance requirements: For master's and doctorate, GRE General Test.
Expenses: Tuition, state resident: full-time $2,932; part-time $489 per credit. Tuition, nonresident: full-time $5,758; part-time $960 per credit. Part-time tuition and fees vary according to course load, program and reciprocity agreements.
Faculty research: Fracture micromechanics, hydrogen embrittlement, polymer physics, microelectric materials, corrosion science. *Web site:* http://www.cems.umn.edu/

■ **UNIVERSITY OF NEBRASKA–LINCOLN**

Graduate College, College of Engineering and Technology, Department of Mechanical Engineering, Lincoln, NE 68588

AWARDS Engineering (PhD); mechanical engineering (MS), including materials science engineering.

Faculty: 21.
Students: 35 (2 women); includes 1 minority (Hispanic American) 22 international. Average age 28. 205 applicants, 30% accepted, 14 enrolled. In 2001, 7 degrees awarded.
Degree requirements: For master's, thesis optional; for doctorate, thesis/dissertation, comprehensive exam.
Entrance requirements: For master's and doctorate, GRE General Test, TOEFL. *Application deadline:* For fall admission, 3/1 (priority date). Applications are processed on a rolling basis. *Application fee:* $35. Electronic applications accepted.
Expenses: Tuition, state resident: full-time $2,412; part-time $134 per credit. Tuition, nonresident: full-time $6,223; part-time $346 per credit. Tuition and fees vary according to course load.
Financial support: In 2001–02, 15 research assistantships, 4 teaching assistantships were awarded. Fellowships, Federal Work-Study, health care benefits, and unspecified assistantships also available. Support available to part-time students. Financial award application deadline: 2/15.
Faculty research: Robotics for planetary exploration, vehicle crashworthiness, transient heat conduction, laser beam/particle interactions.
Dr. David Lou, Chair, 402-472-2375. *Web site:* http://www.engr.unl.edu/me/index.html/

Find an in-depth description at www.petersons.com/gradchannel.

■ **UNIVERSITY OF PENNSYLVANIA**

School of Engineering and Applied Science, Department of Materials Science and Engineering, Philadelphia, PA 19104

AWARDS MSE, PhD, MSE/MBA. Part-time programs available. Terminal master's awarded for partial completion of doctoral program.

Degree requirements: For master's and doctorate, thesis/dissertation.
Entrance requirements: For master's and doctorate, TOEFL. Electronic applications accepted.
Faculty research: Advanced metallic, ceramic, and polymeric materials for device applications; micromechanics and structure of interfaces; thin film electronic materials; physics and chemistry of solids.

Find an in-depth description at www.petersons.com/gradchannel.

■ **UNIVERSITY OF PITTSBURGH**

School of Engineering, Department of Materials Science and Engineering, Pittsburgh, PA 15260

AWARDS Materials science and engineering (MSMSE, PhD); metallurgical engineering (MS Met E, PhD). Part-time and evening/weekend programs available.

Faculty: 9 full-time (1 woman).
Students: 26 full-time (8 women), 10 part-time (2 women); includes 1 minority (African American), 16 international. 80 applicants, 6% accepted, 5 enrolled. In 2001, 6 master's, 2 doctorates awarded. Terminal master's awarded for partial completion of doctoral program.
Degree requirements: For master's, thesis (for some programs); for doctorate, thesis/dissertation, final oral exams, comprehensive exam.
Entrance requirements: For master's and doctorate, TOEFL, minimum QPA of 3.0. *Application deadline:* For fall admission, 8/1 (priority date); for spring admission, 12/1 (priority date). Applications are processed on a rolling basis. *Application fee:* $40.
Financial support: In 2001–02, 24 students received support, including 21 research assistantships with full tuition reimbursements available (averaging $18,492 per year), 3 teaching assistantships with full tuition reimbursements available (averaging $17,976 per year). Scholarships/grants and tuition waivers (full and partial) also available. Financial award application deadline: 2/15. *Total annual research expenditures:* $3.5 million.
Dr. William A. Soffa, Chairman, 412-624-9720, *Fax:* 412-624-8069, *E-mail:* wsoffa@pitt.edu.
Application contact: Pradeep P. Phule, Professor and Graduate Coordinator, 412-624-9736, *Fax:* 412-624-8069, *E-mail:* ppp@pitt.edu. *Web site:* http://www.engrng.pitt.edu/~msewww/

■ **UNIVERSITY OF SOUTHERN CALIFORNIA**

Graduate School, School of Engineering, Department of Materials Science and Engineering, Program in Materials Engineering, Los Angeles, CA 90089

AWARDS MS.

Degree requirements: For master's, thesis optional.
Entrance requirements: For master's, GRE General Test.
Expenses: Tuition: Full-time $25,060; part-time $844 per unit. Required fees: $473.

Find an in-depth description at www.petersons.com/gradchannel.

■ THE UNIVERSITY OF TENNESSEE

Graduate School, College of Engineering, Department of Materials Science and Engineering, Program in Materials Science and Engineering, Knoxville, TN 37996

AWARDS MS, PhD.

Students: 31 full-time (8 women), 13 part-time (3 women); includes 1 minority (African American), 23 international. 49 applicants, 63% accepted. In 2001, 6 master's, 1 doctorate awarded.

Degree requirements: For master's, thesis or alternative; for doctorate, thesis/dissertation.

Entrance requirements: For master's and doctorate, TOEFL, minimum GPA of 2.7. *Application deadline:* For fall admission, 2/1 (priority date). Applications are processed on a rolling basis. *Application fee:* $35. Electronic applications accepted.

Expenses: Tuition, state resident: full-time $4,280; part-time $233 per hour. Tuition, nonresident: full-time $12,066; part-time $666 per hour. Tuition and fees vary according to program.

Financial support: Application deadline: 2/1.

Dr. Patrick R. Taylor, Head, Department of Materials Science and Engineering, 865-974-5336, *Fax:* 865-974-4115, *E-mail:* prtaylor@utk.edu.

■ THE UNIVERSITY OF TEXAS AT ARLINGTON

Graduate School, College of Engineering, Department of Mechanical and Aerospace Engineering, Materials Science and Engineering Program, Arlington, TX 76019

AWARDS M Engr, MS, PhD. Part-time and evening/weekend programs available. Postbaccalaureate distance learning degree programs offered (minimal on-campus study).

Students: 17 full-time (3 women), 5 part-time; includes 2 minority (1 African American, 1 Asian American or Pacific Islander), 16 international. 32 applicants, 88% accepted, 5 enrolled. In 2001, 2 master's, 2 doctorates awarded. Terminal master's awarded for partial completion of doctoral program.

Degree requirements: For master's, thesis optional; for doctorate, thesis/dissertation, comprehensive exam.

Entrance requirements: For master's, GRE General Test, TOEFL, minimum GPA of 3.0; for doctorate, GRE General Test, TOEFL, minimum GPA of 3.5. *Application deadline:* For fall admission, 6/16. Applications are processed on a rolling basis. *Application fee:* $25 ($50 for international students).

Expenses: Tuition, area resident: Full-time $2,268. Tuition, nonresident: full-time $6,264. Required fees: $839. Tuition and fees vary according to course load.

Financial support: In 2001–02, 3 fellowships (averaging $1,000 per year), 11 research assistantships (averaging $15,000 per year), 5 teaching assistantships (averaging $15,000 per year) were awarded. Financial award application deadline: 6/1; financial award applicants required to submit FAFSA.

Dr. Ronald L. Elsenbaumer, Chair, 817-272-2559, *Fax:* 817-272-2538, *E-mail:* elsenbaumer@uta.edu.

Application contact: Dr. Pranesh B. Aswath, Graduate Adviser, 817-272-7108, *Fax:* 817-272-2538, *E-mail:* aswath@uta.edu. *Web site:* http://www.mse.uta.edu/

Find an in-depth description at www.petersons.com/gradchannel.

■ THE UNIVERSITY OF TEXAS AT AUSTIN

Graduate School, College of Engineering, Program in Materials Science and Engineering, Austin, TX 78712-1111

AWARDS MSE, PhD. Part-time programs available.

Degree requirements: For master's, thesis (for some programs); for doctorate, thesis/dissertation.

Entrance requirements: For master's and doctorate, GRE General Test. Electronic applications accepted.

Expenses: Tuition, state resident: full-time $3,159. Tuition, nonresident: full-time $6,957. Tuition and fees vary according to program.

Faculty research: Ceramics and glasses, microelectronic materials and processing, metal systems, nanostructures, polymers . *Web site:* http://www.utexas.edu/academic/tmi/

■ THE UNIVERSITY OF TEXAS AT EL PASO

Graduate School, Interdisciplinary Program in Materials Science and Engineering, El Paso, TX 79968-0001

AWARDS PhD. Part-time and evening/weekend programs available.

Students: 21 (8 women); includes 9 minority (1 African American, 6 Asian Americans or Pacific Islanders, 2 Hispanic Americans) 6 international. Average age 34. In 2001, 4 degrees awarded.

Degree requirements: For doctorate, thesis/dissertation.

Entrance requirements: For doctorate, GRE General Test, TOEFL, minimum GPA of 3.2. *Application deadline:* For fall admission, 7/1 (priority date); for spring admission, 11/1 (priority date). Applications are processed on a rolling basis. *Application fee:* $15 ($65 for international students). Electronic applications accepted.

Expenses: Tuition, state resident: full-time $2,450. Tuition, nonresident: full-time $6,000.

Financial support: In 2001–02, research assistantships with partial tuition reimbursements (averaging $22,500 per year), teaching assistantships with partial tuition reimbursements (averaging $1,800 per year) were awarded. Fellowships with partial tuition reimbursements, Federal Work-Study, institutionally sponsored loans, scholarships/grants, and tuition waivers (partial) also available. Financial award application deadline: 3/15; financial award applicants required to submit FAFSA.

Dr. Lawrence E. Murr, Director, 915-747-6664, *Fax:* 915-747-6601, *E-mail:* fekberg@utep.edu.

Application contact: Dr. Charles H. Ambler, Dean of the Graduate School, 915-747-5491 Ext. 7886, *Fax:* 915-747-5788, *E-mail:* cambler@miners.utep.edu.

■ UNIVERSITY OF UTAH

Graduate School, College of Engineering, Department of Materials Science and Engineering, Salt Lake City, UT 84112-1107

AWARDS ME, MS, PhD. Part-time programs available.

Faculty: 7 full-time (0 women), 2 part-time/adjunct (0 women).

Students: 21 full-time (3 women), 11 part-time (2 women); includes 16 minority (15 Asian Americans or Pacific Islanders, 1 Native American), 4 international. Average age 30. 77 applicants, 48% accepted. In 2001, 6 master's, 5 doctorates awarded. Terminal master's awarded for partial completion of doctoral program.

Degree requirements: For master's, thesis (MS); for doctorate, thesis/dissertation, exam.

Entrance requirements: For master's and doctorate, TOEFL, minimum GPA of 3.0. *Application deadline:* For fall admission, 5/1. *Application fee:* $40 ($60 for international students).

Expenses: Tuition, state resident: part-time $320 per semester hour. Tuition, nonresident: part-time $1,135 per semester hour. Required fees: $143 per semester hour. Tuition and fees vary according to course load, degree level and program.

Financial support: In 2001–02, 20 research assistantships with full tuition reimbursements (averaging $16,000 per year) were awarded; career-related internships or fieldwork and Federal Work-Study also available. Financial award application deadline: 3/1; financial award applicants required to submit FAFSA.

Faculty research: Solid oxide fuel cells, computational nanostructures, computational polymers, biomaterials, electronic materials. *Total annual research expenditures:* $4 million.

University of Utah (continued)
Anil V. Virkar, Chair, 801-581-6863, *Fax:* 801-581-4816, *E-mail:* anil.virkar@ m.cc.utah.edu.
Application contact: John A. Nairn, Director of Graduate Studies, 801-581-3413, *Fax:* 801-581-4816, *E-mail:* nairn@ m.ee.utah.edu. *Web site:* http:// www.coe.utah.edu/

■ UNIVERSITY OF WASHINGTON

Graduate School, College of Engineering, Department of Materials Science and Engineering, Seattle, WA 98195-2120

AWARDS Inter-engineering specialization in materials science and engineering (MS); materials science and engineering (MS, PhD); materials science and engineering nanotechnology (PhD). Part-time programs available. Postbaccalaureate distance learning degree programs offered (no on-campus study).

Faculty: 15 full-time (2 women), 8 part-time/adjunct (0 women).
Students: 40 full-time (14 women), 19 part-time (13 women); includes 10 minority (2 African Americans, 6 Asian Americans or Pacific Islanders, 2 Hispanic Americans), 18 international. 54 applicants, 33% accepted, 7 enrolled. In 2001, 9 master's, 3 doctorates awarded.
Degree requirements: For master's and doctorate, thesis/dissertation, comprehensive exam, registration. *Median time to degree:* Master's–2.4 years full-time, 5.25 years part-time; doctorate–3.5 years full-time, 8 years part-time.
Entrance requirements: For master's and doctorate, GRE General Test, TOEFL, minimum GPA of 3.0. *Application deadline:* For fall admission, 1/15 (priority date); for winter admission, 9/30 (priority date); for spring admission, 12/30 (priority date). Applications are processed on a rolling basis. *Application fee:* $50. Electronic applications accepted.
Expenses: Tuition, state resident: full-time $5,539. Tuition, nonresident: full-time $14,376. Required fees: $390. Tuition and fees vary according to course load and program.
Financial support: In 2001–02, 42 students received support, including 4 fellowships with full tuition reimbursements available (averaging $8,375 per year), 24 research assistantships with full tuition reimbursements available (averaging $13,465 per year), 11 teaching assistantships with full tuition reimbursements available (averaging $13,275 per year); career-related internships or fieldwork, Federal Work-Study, institutionally sponsored loans, scholarships/grants, unspecified assistantships, and stipend supplements also available. Financial award application deadline: 1/15.
Faculty research: Processing, characterization and properties of all classes of materials, research on ceramics,

composites, metals, polymers and semiconductors. *Total annual research expenditures:* $1.2 million.
Dr. Rajendra K. Bordia, Chair, 206-543-2600, *Fax:* 206-543-3100, *E-mail:* bordia@ u.washington.edu.
Application contact: Lara A. Davis, Academic Counselor, 206-616-6581, *Fax:* 206-543-3100, *E-mail:* mse@ u.washington.edu. *Web site:* http:// depts.washington.edu/mse/

■ VIRGINIA POLYTECHNIC INSTITUTE AND STATE UNIVERSITY

Graduate School, College of Engineering, Department of Materials Science and Engineering, Blacksburg, VA 24061

AWARDS M Eng, MS, PhD.

Students: 41 full-time (12 women), 2 part-time; includes 3 minority (1 Asian American or Pacific Islander, 1 Hispanic American, 1 Native American), 19 international. 116 applicants, 16% accepted. In 2001, 9 master's, 8 doctorates awarded.
Degree requirements: For master's, thesis.
Entrance requirements: For master's, TOEFL. *Application deadline:* For fall admission, 12/1 (priority date). Applications are processed on a rolling basis. *Application fee:* $45. Electronic applications accepted.
Expenses: Tuition, state resident: part-time $241 per hour. Tuition, nonresident: part-time $406 per hour. Tuition and fees vary according to program.
Financial support: In 2001–02, 3 research assistantships with full tuition reimbursements (averaging $12,063 per year), 5 teaching assistantships with full tuition reimbursements (averaging $12,063 per year) were awarded. Fellowships, unspecified assistantships also available. Financial award application deadline: 4/1.
Dr. David Clark, Head, 540-231-6640.
Application contact: Admissions Office, *E-mail:* msegrad@vt.edu. *Web site:* http:// www.mse.vt.edu

■ WASHINGTON STATE UNIVERSITY

Graduate School, College of Engineering and Architecture, School of Mechanical and Materials Engineering, Pullman, WA 99164

AWARDS Materials science (MS, PhD), including materials science (PhD), materials science and engineering (MS); mechanical engineering (MS, PhD).

Faculty: 34 full-time (2 women).
Students: 42 full-time (5 women), 5 part-time; includes 1 minority (Asian American

or Pacific Islander), 25 international. Average age 25. In 2001, 7 master's, 8 doctorates awarded.
Degree requirements: For master's, oral exam, thesis optional; for doctorate, thesis/ dissertation, oral exam.
Application deadline: For fall admission, 3/1 (priority date). Applications are processed on a rolling basis. *Application fee:* $35.
Expenses: Tuition, state resident: full-time $6,088; part-time $304 per semester. Tuition, nonresident: full-time $14,918; part-time $746 per semester. Tuition and fees vary according to program.
Financial support: In 2001–02, 14 research assistantships with full and partial tuition reimbursements, 19 teaching assistantships with full and partial tuition reimbursements were awarded. Fellowships, career-related internships or fieldwork, Federal Work-Study, institutionally sponsored loans, and teaching associateships also available. Financial award application deadline: 4/1; financial award applicants required to submit FAFSA. *Total annual research expenditures:* $1.3 million.
Dr. Belakavadi R. Ramaprian, Interim, 509-335-8654, *E-mail:* br_ramaprian@ wsu.edu.
Application contact: Lanni MacKenzie, Coordinator, 509-335-2727, *Fax:* 509-335-4662, *E-mail:* gradapp@mme.wsu.edu. *Web site:* http://www.mme.wsu.edu/

■ WASHINGTON STATE UNIVERSITY

Graduate School, College of Sciences and College of Engineering and Architecture, Program in Materials Science, Pullman, WA 99164

AWARDS Materials science (PhD); materials science and engineering (MS).

Faculty: 20 full-time (3 women), 1 part-time/adjunct (0 women).
Students: 10 full-time (1 woman), 3 international. Average age 25. In 2001, 2 degrees awarded.
Degree requirements: For master's, thesis, oral exam; for doctorate, thesis/ dissertation, oral exam, written exam.
Entrance requirements: For doctorate, minimum GPA of 3.0. *Application deadline:* For fall admission, 3/1 (priority date). Applications are processed on a rolling basis. *Application fee:* $35.
Expenses: Tuition, state resident: full-time $6,088; part-time $304 per semester. Tuition, nonresident: full-time $14,918; part-time $746 per semester. Tuition and fees vary according to program.
Financial support: In 2001–02, 2 research assistantships with full and partial tuition reimbursements, 1 teaching assistantship with full and partial tuition reimbursement were awarded. Fellowships, career-related internships or fieldwork, Federal Work-Study, institutionally sponsored loans, and teaching associateships also available. Financial award application deadline: 4/1.

Faculty research: Thin films, materials characterization, mechanical properties, materials processing, electrical and optical behavior.
Dr. Grant Norton, Chair, 509-835-4520. *Web site:* http://www.wsu.edu~matscipr/

■ WASHINGTON UNIVERSITY IN ST. LOUIS

Henry Edwin Sever Graduate School of Engineering and Applied Science, Department of Chemical Engineering, St. Louis, MO 63130-4899

AWARDS Chemical engineering (MS, D Sc); environmental engineering (MS, D Sc); materials science and engineering (MS); materials science engineering (D Sc). Part-time programs available.

Faculty: 11 full-time (0 women), 2 part-time/adjunct (0 women).
Students: 34 full-time (5 women), 9 part-time (6 women), 34 international. Average age 25. 122 applicants, 19% accepted, 7 enrolled. In 2001, 3 master's, 7 doctorates awarded. Terminal master's awarded for partial completion of doctoral program.
Degree requirements: For master's, thesis optional; for doctorate, thesis/dissertation, preliminary exam, qualifying exam. *Median time to degree:* Master's–1.8 years full-time; doctorate–4.1 years full-time.
Entrance requirements: For master's and doctorate, GRE, minimum B average during final 2 years. *Application deadline:* For fall admission, 2/1 (priority date). Applications are processed on a rolling basis. *Application fee:* $20. Electronic applications accepted.
Expenses: Tuition: Full-time $26,900.
Financial support: In 2001–02, 30 research assistantships with full tuition reimbursements were awarded; fellowships with full tuition reimbursements, career-related internships or fieldwork, Federal Work-Study, and institutionally sponsored loans also available. Financial award application deadline: 2/1.
Faculty research: Reaction engineering, materials processing, catalysis, process control, air pollution control. *Total annual research expenditures:* $2.4 million.
Dr. M. P. Dudukovic, Chairman, 314-935-6021, *Fax:* 314-935-4832, *E-mail:* dudu@poly1.che.wustl.edu.
Application contact: Rose Baxter, Graduate Coordinator, 314-935-6070, *Fax:* 314-935-7211, *E-mail:* chedept@che.wustl.edu. *Web site:* http://www.che.wustl.edu/

■ WAYNE STATE UNIVERSITY

Graduate School, College of Engineering, Department of Chemical Engineering and Materials Science, Program in Materials Science and Engineering, Detroit, MI 48202

AWARDS Materials science and engineering (MS, PhD); polymer engineering (Certificate). Part-time programs available.

Students: 18. In 2001, 6 master's, 1 doctorate awarded. Terminal master's awarded for partial completion of doctoral program.
Degree requirements: For master's, thesis optional; for doctorate, thesis/dissertation.
Application deadline: For fall admission, 7/1 (priority date); for spring admission, 3/15. Applications are processed on a rolling basis. *Application fee:* $20 ($30 for international students). Electronic applications accepted.
Expenses: Tuition, state resident: full-time $3,764. Tuition and fees vary according to degree level and program.
Financial support: Fellowships, research assistantships, teaching assistantships available. Financial award application deadline: 2/15.
Faculty research: Polymer science, rheology, fatigue in metals, metal matrix composites, ceramics. *Total annual research expenditures:* $300,000.
Application contact: Rangaramanujam Kannan, Graduate Director, 313-577-3800, *Fax:* 313-577-3810, *E-mail:* rkannan@che.eng.wayne.edu.

■ WESTERN MICHIGAN UNIVERSITY

Graduate College, College of Engineering and Applied Sciences, Department of Construction Engineering, Materials Engineering and Industrial Design, Program in Materials Science and Engineering, Kalamazoo, MI 49008-5202

AWARDS MS.

Faculty: 7 full-time (1 woman).
Students: 11 full-time (1 woman), 3 part-time (2 women), 12 international. In 2001, 2 degrees awarded.
Degree requirements: For master's, thesis optional.
Entrance requirements: For master's, minimum GPA of 3.0. *Application deadline:* For fall admission, 2/15 (priority date). Applications are processed on a rolling basis. *Application fee:* $25.
Expenses: Tuition, state resident: part-time $186 per credit hour. Tuition, nonresident: part-time $442 per credit hour. Required fees: $602. One-time fee: $132 part-time. Tuition and fees vary according to course load.
Financial support: Application deadline: 2/15.
Application contact: Admissions and Orientation, 616-387-2000, *Fax:* 616-387-2355.

■ WORCESTER POLYTECHNIC INSTITUTE

Graduate Studies, Program in Materials Science and Engineering, Worcester, MA 01609-2280

AWARDS MS, PhD, Certificate. Part-time and evening/weekend programs available.

Faculty: 7 full-time (2 women), 2 part-time/adjunct (1 woman).
Students: 15 full-time (4 women), 3 part-time (2 women), 9 international. 16 applicants, 69% accepted, 4 enrolled. In 2001, 10 master's, 2 doctorates awarded.
Degree requirements: For master's and doctorate, thesis/dissertation.
Entrance requirements: For master's and doctorate, TOEFL. *Application deadline:* For fall admission, 2/1 (priority date); for spring admission, 10/15 (priority date). Applications are processed on a rolling basis. *Application fee:* $60. Electronic applications accepted.
Expenses: Tuition: Part-time $796 per credit. Required fees: $20; $752 per credit. One-time fee: $30 full-time.
Financial support: In 2001–02, 11 students received support, including 1 fellowship (averaging $13,500 per year), 4 research assistantships with full tuition reimbursements available (averaging $17,256 per year), 3 teaching assistantships with full tuition reimbursements available (averaging $12,942 per year); career-related internships or fieldwork, institutionally sponsored loans, and scholarships/grants also available. Financial award application deadline: 2/15; financial award applicants required to submit FAFSA.
Faculty research: Physical metallurgy and ceramics, electron microscopy and x-ray diffraction analysis, polymer processing and properties, biomaterials, fracture mechanics/reliability analysis/corrosion. *Total annual research expenditures:* $138,539.
Dr. Richard D. Sisson, Director, 508-831-5335, *Fax:* 508-831-5178, *E-mail:* sisson@wpi.edu.
Application contact: Rita Shilarsky, Graduate Secretary, 508-831-5633, *Fax:* 508-831-5140, *E-mail:* rita@wpi.edu. *Web site:* http://guinness.upi.edu/~mte/

■ WRIGHT STATE UNIVERSITY

School of Graduate Studies, College of Engineering and Computer Science, Programs in Engineering, Program in Mechanical and Materials Engineering, Dayton, OH 45435

AWARDS Materials science and engineering (MSE); mechanical engineering (MSE).

Students: 32 full-time (1 woman), 21 part-time (3 women); includes 3 minority (1 African American, 1 Asian American or Pacific Islander, 1 Hispanic American), 22 international. Average age 29. 176 applicants, 56% accepted. In 2001, 10 degrees awarded.

Wright State University (continued)
Degree requirements: For master's, thesis or course option alternative.
Entrance requirements: For master's, TOEFL. *Application fee: $25.*
Expenses: Tuition, state resident: full-time $7,161; part-time $225 per quarter hour. Tuition, nonresident: full-time $12,324; part-time $385 per quarter hour. Tuition and fees vary according to course load, degree level and program.
Financial support: Fellowships, research assistantships, teaching assistantships, unspecified assistantships available. Support available to part-time students. Financial award application deadline: 3/15; financial award applicants required to submit FAFSA.
Dr. Richard J. Bethke, Chair, 937-775-5040, *Fax:* 937-775-5009, *E-mail:* richard.bethke@wright.edu.

MATERIALS SCIENCES

■ AIR FORCE INSTITUTE OF TECHNOLOGY

School of Engineering and Management, Department of Aeronautics and Astronautics, Dayton, OH 45433-7765

AWARDS Aeronautical engineering (MS, PhD); astronautical engineering (MS, PhD); materials science (MS, PhD). Space operations (MS). Systems engineering (MS). Part-time programs available.

Degree requirements: For master's and doctorate, thesis/dissertation.
Entrance requirements: For master's and doctorate, GRE General Test, minimum GPA of 3.0, U.S. citizenship.
Faculty research: Computational fluid dynamics, experimental aerodynamics, computational structural mechanics, experimental structural mechanics, aircraft and spacecraft stability and control. *Web site:* http://en.afit.edu/bny

■ AIR FORCE INSTITUTE OF TECHNOLOGY

School of Engineering and Management, Department of Engineering Physics, Dayton, OH 45433-7765

AWARDS Applied physics (MS, PhD); electro-optics (MS, PhD); environmental science (MS, PhD); materials science (MS, PhD); meteorology (MS); nuclear engineering (MS, PhD). Part-time programs available.

Degree requirements: For master's and doctorate, thesis/dissertation.
Entrance requirements: For master's and doctorate, GRE General Test, minimum GPA of 3.0, U.S. citizenship.
Faculty research: High-energy lasers, space physics, nuclear weapon effects,

semiconductor physics. *Web site:* http://en.afit.edu/bnp/
Find an in-depth description at www.petersons.com/gradchannel.

■ ALABAMA AGRICULTURAL AND MECHANICAL UNIVERSITY

School of Graduate Studies, School of Arts and Sciences, Department of Natural and Physical Sciences, Huntsville, AL 35811

AWARDS Biology (MS); physics (MS, PhD), including applied physics (PhD), materials science (PhD), optics (PhD), physics (MS). Part-time and evening/weekend programs available.

Faculty: 6 full-time (1 woman).
Students: 1 (woman) full-time, 19 part-time (6 women); includes 13 minority (12 African Americans, 1 Asian American or Pacific Islander), 3 international. In 2001, 4 master's, 4 doctorates awarded.
Degree requirements: For doctorate, thesis/dissertation.
Entrance requirements: For master's and doctorate, GRE General Test. *Application deadline:* For fall admission, 5/1. *Application fee:* $15 ($20 for international students).
Expenses: Tuition, state resident: full-time $1,380. Tuition, nonresident: full-time $2,500.
Financial support: In 2001–02, 1 fellowship with tuition reimbursement (averaging $18,000 per year), 5 research assistantships with tuition reimbursements (averaging $10,000 per year), 1 teaching assistantship with tuition reimbursement (averaging $10,000 per year) were awarded. Career-related internships or fieldwork and Federal Work-Study also available. Financial award application deadline: 4/1. *Total annual research expenditures:* $1.5 million.
Dr. R. V. Lal, Chair, 256-851-8148.

■ ALFRED UNIVERSITY

Graduate School, New York State College of Ceramics, School of Ceramic Engineering and Materials Science, Alfred, NY 14802-1205

AWARDS Biomedical materials engineering science (MS); ceramic engineering (MS); ceramics (PhD); glass science (MS, PhD); materials science (MS).

Students: 51 full-time (14 women), 10 part-time (2 women). Average age 24. 108 applicants, 25% accepted. In 2001, 16 master's, 5 doctorates awarded.
Degree requirements: For master's and doctorate, thesis/dissertation.
Entrance requirements: For master's and doctorate, TOEFL. *Application deadline:* Applications are processed on a rolling basis. *Application fee:* $50. Electronic applications accepted.
Expenses: Contact institution.
Financial support: Fellowships, research assistantships, teaching assistantships,

tuition waivers (full and partial) available. Financial award applicants required to submit FAFSA.
Faculty research: Fine-particle technology, x-ray diffraction, superconductivity, electronic materials.
Dr. Ronald S. Gordon, Dean, 607-871-2441, *E-mail:* gordon@alfred.edu.
Application contact: Cathleen R. Johnson, Coordinator of Graduate Admissions, 607-871-2141, *Fax:* 607-871-2198, *E-mail:* johnsonc@alfred.edu. *Web site:* http://www.alfred.edu/gradschool
Find an in-depth description at www.petersons.com/gradchannel.

■ ARIZONA STATE UNIVERSITY

Graduate College, College of Engineering and Applied Sciences, Department of Chemical, Bio and Materials Engineering, Program in Materials Science and Engineering, Tempe, AZ 85287

AWARDS Engineering science (MS, MSE, PhD), including materials science and engineering.

Degree requirements: For doctorate, thesis/dissertation.
Entrance requirements: For master's and doctorate, GRE General Test.
Faculty research: Fluid dynamics, mechanics of solids and structures, structural dynamics, structural stability, nonlinear mechanics.
Find an in-depth description at www.petersons.com/gradchannel.

■ ARIZONA STATE UNIVERSITY

Graduate College, Interdisciplinary Program in Science and Engineering of Materials, Tempe, AZ 85287

AWARDS PhD.

Degree requirements: For doctorate, thesis/dissertation.
Entrance requirements: For doctorate, GRE.
Faculty research: Silicon and gallium arsenide, fabrication of ultra small solid state electronic devices, structure of free surfaces of crystalline solids, ion implantation on solids, effects of high pressures on solids.
Find an in-depth description at www.petersons.com/gradchannel.

■ BROWN UNIVERSITY

Graduate School, Division of Engineering, Program in Materials Science, Providence, RI 02912

AWARDS Sc M, PhD.

Degree requirements: For doctorate, thesis/dissertation, preliminary exam.

■ CALIFORNIA INSTITUTE OF TECHNOLOGY

Division of Engineering and Applied Science, Option in Materials Science, Pasadena, CA 91125-0001

AWARDS MS, PhD.

Faculty: 4 full-time (1 woman).
Students: 36 full-time (8 women); includes 3 minority (1 African American, 2 Hispanic Americans), 12 international. 93 applicants, 19% accepted, 12 enrolled. In 2001, 5 master's, 6 doctorates awarded.
Degree requirements: For doctorate, thesis/dissertation.
Application deadline: For fall admission, 1/15. *Application fee:* $0.
Financial support: In 2001–02, 10 fellowships, 15 research assistantships, 3 teaching assistantships were awarded.
Faculty research: Mechanical properties, physical properties, kinetics of phase transformations, metastable phases, transmission electron microscopy.
Dr. Brent T. Fultz, Representative, 626-395-2170.

■ CALIFORNIA POLYTECHNIC STATE UNIVERSITY, SAN LUIS OBISPO

College of Engineering, Program in Engineering, San Luis Obispo, CA 93407

AWARDS Biochemical engineering (MS); industrial engineering (MS); integrated technology management (MS); materials engineering (MS); water engineering (MS), including bioengineering, biomedical engineering, manufacturing engineering.

Faculty: 98 full-time (8 women), 82 part-time/adjunct (14 women).
Students: 20 full-time (4 women), 9 part-time (1 woman). 25 applicants, 68% accepted, 15 enrolled. In 2001, 22 degrees awarded.
Entrance requirements: For master's, GRE General Test, minimum GPA of 2.5 in last 90 quarter units. *Application fee:* $55.
Expenses: Tuition, nonresident: part-time $164 per unit. One-time fee: $2,153 part-time.
Financial support: Application deadline: 3/2.
Dr. Peter Y. Lee, Dean, 805-756-2131, *Fax:* 805-756-6503, *E-mail:* plee@ calpoly.edu.
Application contact: Dr. Daniel W. Walsh, Associate Dean, 805-756-2131, *Fax:* 805-756-6503, *E-mail:* dwalsh@ calpoly.edu. *Web site:* http:// www.synner.ceng.calpoly.edu/

■ CARNEGIE MELLON UNIVERSITY

Carnegie Institute of Technology, Department of Materials Science and Engineering, Pittsburgh, PA 15213-3891

AWARDS ME, MS, PhD. Part-time programs available. Terminal master's awarded for partial completion of doctoral program.

Degree requirements: For master's, exam; for doctorate, thesis/dissertation, qualifying exam.
Entrance requirements: For master's and doctorate, GRE General Test, TOEFL.
Faculty research: Materials characterization, process metallurgy, high strength alloys, growth kinetics, ceramics. *Web site:* http://neon.mems.cmu.edu/newfront.shtml

Find an in-depth description at www.petersons.com/gradchannel.

■ CASE WESTERN RESERVE UNIVERSITY

School of Graduate Studies, The Case School of Engineering, Department of Materials Science and Engineering, Cleveland, OH 44106

AWARDS Ceramics and materials science (MS); materials science and engineering (MS, PhD). Part-time programs available. Postbaccalaureate distance learning degree programs offered (no on-campus study).

Faculty: 11 full-time (0 women), 13 part-time/adjunct (1 woman).
Students: 40 full-time (16 women), 22 part-time (3 women); includes 5 minority (all Asian Americans or Pacific Islanders), 39 international. Average age 24. 152 applicants, 91% accepted, 20 enrolled. In 2001, 12 master's, 3 doctorates awarded. Terminal master's awarded for partial completion of doctoral program.
Degree requirements: For master's, thesis (for some programs); for doctorate, thesis/dissertation, qualifying exam, teaching experience.
Entrance requirements: For master's, TOEFL; for doctorate, GRE, TOEFL.
Application deadline: For fall admission, 2/15 (priority date); for spring admission, 9/15. Applications are processed on a rolling basis. *Application fee:* $25.
Financial support: In 2001–02, 35 fellowships with full and partial tuition reimbursements (averaging $16,200 per year), 15 research assistantships with full and partial tuition reimbursements (averaging $16,200 per year) were awarded. Financial award application deadline: 4/30; financial award applicants required to submit FAFSA.
Faculty research: Materials processing; mechanical behavior; coatings and thin films; materials performance. *Total annual research expenditures:* $4.2 million.

Dr. Gary M. Michal, Chairman, 216-368-5070, *Fax:* 216-368-4224, *E-mail:* emse@ po.cwru.edu.
Application contact: Patsy Harris, Information Contact, 216-368-4230, *Fax:* 216-368-3209, *E-mail:* pah7@po.cwru.edu. *Web site:* http://vulcan.mse.cwru.edu/emse/

■ CLEMSON UNIVERSITY

Graduate School, College of Engineering and Science, Program in Materials Science and Engineering, Clemson, SC 29634

AWARDS MS, PhD. Part-time programs available.

Students: 31 full-time (9 women), 5 part-time (1 woman), 31 international. Average age 24. 113 applicants, 63% accepted, 9 enrolled. In 2001, 10 master's, 4 doctorates awarded. Terminal master's awarded for partial completion of doctoral program.
Degree requirements: For master's and doctorate, thesis/dissertation.
Entrance requirements: For master's and doctorate, GRE General Test, TOEFL.
Application deadline: For fall admission, 2/15. Applications are processed on a rolling basis. *Application fee:* $40.
Expenses: Tuition, state resident: full-time $5,310. Tuition, nonresident: full-time $11,284.
Financial support: Research assistantships, career-related internships or fieldwork available. Financial award applicants required to submit FAFSA.
Faculty research: Composites, fibers, ceramics, metallurgy, biomaterials, semiconductors. *Total annual research expenditures:* $1.2 million.
Dr. R. Larry Dooley, Coordinator, 864-656-5562, *Fax:* 864-656-5910, *E-mail:* dooley@eng.clemson.edu. *Web site:* http:// www.ces.clemson.edu/mse/MSE_GR.html

Find an in-depth description at www.petersons.com/gradchannel.

■ COLORADO SCHOOL OF MINES

Graduate School, Department of Metallurgical and Materials Engineering, Golden, CO 80401-1887

AWARDS Materials science (MS, PhD); metallurgical and materials engineering (ME, MS, PhD). Part-time programs available.

Faculty: 25 full-time (0 women), 1 part-time/adjunct (0 women).
Students: 69 full-time (23 women), 18 part-time (4 women); includes 8 minority (4 Asian Americans or Pacific Islanders, 4 Hispanic Americans), 27 international. 96 applicants, 40% accepted, 12 enrolled. In 2001, 9 master's, 5 doctorates awarded.
Degree requirements: For master's, thesis/dissertation; for doctorate, thesis/dissertation, comprehensive exam. *Median time to degree:* Master's–2 years full-time; doctorate–4 years full-time.

Colorado School of Mines (continued)

Entrance requirements: For master's and doctorate, GRE General Test. *Application deadline:* For fall admission, 12/1 (priority date); for spring admission, 5/1 (priority date). Applications are processed on a rolling basis. *Application fee:* $40. Electronic applications accepted.
Expenses: Tuition, state resident: full-time $4,940; part-time $246 per credit. Tuition, nonresident: full-time $16,070; part-time $803 per credit. Required fees: $341 per semester.
Financial support: In 2001–02, 26 fellowships (averaging $4,733 per year), 103 research assistantships (averaging $3,866 per year), 43 teaching assistantships (averaging $3,467 per year) were awarded. Unspecified assistantships also available. Support available to part-time students. Financial award applicants required to submit FAFSA.
Faculty research: Phase transformations, nonferrous alloy systems, pyrometallurgy, reactive metals, engineered materials. *Total annual research expenditures:* $141,430.
Dr. John J. Moore, Head, 303-273-3770, *Fax:* 303-273-3795, *E-mail:* jjmoore@ mines.edu.
Application contact: Chaz Siler, Program Assistant I, 303-273-3660, *Fax:* 303-384-2189. *Web site:* http://met.mines.edu:3872/ index.html

■ **COLORADO SCHOOL OF MINES**

Graduate School, Program in Materials Science, Golden, CO 80401-1887

AWARDS MS, PhD. Part-time programs available.

Students: 27 full-time (11 women), 6 part-time (2 women); includes 6 minority (2 Asian Americans or Pacific Islanders, 4 Hispanic Americans), 8 international. 40 applicants, 58% accepted, 3 enrolled. In 2001, 3 master's, 6 doctorates awarded.
Degree requirements: For master's, thesis/dissertation; for doctorate, thesis/ dissertation, comprehensive exam. *Median time to degree:* Master's–2 years full-time; doctorate–4 years full-time.
Entrance requirements: For master's and doctorate, GRE General Test. *Application deadline:* For fall admission, 12/1 (priority date); for spring admission, 5/1 (priority date). Applications are processed on a rolling basis. *Application fee:* $40. Electronic applications accepted.
Expenses: Tuition, state resident: full-time $4,940; part-time $246 per credit. Tuition, nonresident: full-time $16,070; part-time $803 per credit. Required fees: $341 per semester.
Financial support: In 2001–02, 14 fellowships (averaging $5,828 per year), 46 research assistantships (averaging $4,207 per year), 6 teaching assistantships (averaging $4,779 per year) were awarded. Unspecified assistantships also available.

Financial award applicants required to submit FAFSA.
Faculty research: Ceramics processing, solar and electronic materials, optical properties of surfaces and interfaces, materials synthesis, metal and alloy processing.
Dr. John J. Moore, Director, 303-273-3770, *Fax:* 303-273-3795, *E-mail:* jjmoore@mines.edu.
Application contact: Chaz Siler, Program Assistant I, 303-273-3660, *Fax:* 303-384-2189. *Web site:* http://met.mines.edu:3872/ index.html

■ **COLUMBIA UNIVERSITY**

Fu Foundation School of Engineering and Applied Science, Department of Applied Physics and Applied Mathematics, Program in Materials Science and Engineering, New York, NY 10027

AWARDS MS, Eng Sc D, PhD. Part-time programs available. Postbaccalaureate distance learning degree programs offered (no on-campus study).

Faculty: 15 full-time (2 women), 2 part-time/adjunct (1 woman). Terminal master's awarded for partial completion of doctoral program.
Degree requirements: For doctorate, thesis/dissertation, qualifying exam.
Entrance requirements: For master's and doctorate, GRE General Test, TOEFL. *Application deadline:* For fall admission, 1/5; for spring admission, 10/1. *Application fee:* $55. Electronic applications accepted.
Expenses: Tuition: Full-time $27,528. Required fees: $1,638.
Financial support: In 2001–02, 4 fellowships with partial tuition reimbursements (averaging $18,500 per year), 4 research assistantships with full tuition reimbursements (averaging $18,500 per year), 2 teaching assistantships with partial tuition reimbursements (averaging $18,500 per year) were awarded. Federal Work-Study also available. Financial award application deadline: 1/5; financial award applicants required to submit FAFSA.
Faculty research: Thin films, inelasticity, plastic deformation, interstitial impurities, materials for fuel cells and corrosion. *Total annual research expenditures:* $824,000.
Prof. James S. Im, Professor of Material Sciences, 212-854-8341, *Fax:* 212-854-8257, *E-mail:* ji12@columbia.edu.
Application contact: Marlene Arbo, Department Administrator, 212-854-4458, *Fax:* 212-854-8257, *E-mail:* mja2@ columbia.edu. *Web site:* http:// www.columbia.edu/cu/matsci/

■ **COLUMBIA UNIVERSITY**

Fu Foundation School of Engineering and Applied Science, Department of Applied Physics and Applied Mathematics, Program in Minerals Engineering and Materials Science, New York, NY 10027

AWARDS Eng Sc D, PhD, Engr. Part-time programs available.

Faculty: 10 full-time (2 women), 4 part-time/adjunct (1 woman).
Students: 21 full-time (6 women), 6 part-time (2 women); includes 16 minority (2 African Americans, 13 Asian Americans or Pacific Islanders, 1 Hispanic American). Average age 23. 75 applicants, 39% accepted. In 2001, 4 degrees awarded.
Degree requirements: For doctorate, one foreign language, thesis/dissertation, qualifying exam.
Entrance requirements: For doctorate and Engr, GRE General Test, TOEFL. *Application fee:* $55. Electronic applications accepted.
Expenses: Tuition: Full-time $27,528. Required fees: $1,638.
Financial support: In 2001–02, 7 fellowships with partial tuition reimbursements (averaging $15,000 per year), 5 research assistantships with full tuition reimbursements (averaging $18,000 per year), 2 teaching assistantships with partial tuition reimbursements (averaging $10,000 per year) were awarded. Federal Work-Study, institutionally sponsored loans, and scholarships/grants also available. Financial award application deadline: 1/5; financial award applicants required to submit FAFSA.
Faculty research: Comminution, mineral processing, flotation and flocculation, transport phenomena in heterogeneous reactions, extractive metallurgy, electrochemistry. *Total annual research expenditures:* $1.1 million.
Prof. James S. Im, Professor of Material Sciences, 212-854-8341, *Fax:* 212-854-8257, *E-mail:* ji12@columbia.edu.
Application contact: Marlene Arbo, Department Administrator, 212-854-4458, *Fax:* 212-854-8257, *E-mail:* mja2@ columbia.edu. *Web site:* http:// www.seas.columbia.edu/columbia/ departments/Krumb

■ **COLUMBIA UNIVERSITY**

Fu Foundation School of Engineering and Applied Science, Department of Earth and Environmental Engineering, New York, NY 10027

AWARDS Earth resources engineering (MS, PhD); minerals engineering and materials science (Eng Sc D, PhD, Engr). Part-time programs available. Postbaccalaureate distance learning degree programs offered.

Faculty: 8 full-time (0 women), 4 part-time/adjunct (1 woman).

Students: 29 full-time (11 women), 6 part-time (2 women); includes 1 minority (Asian American or Pacific Islander), 23 international. Average age 23. 40 applicants, 45% accepted, 10 enrolled. In 2001, 5 master's, 4 doctorates awarded. Terminal master's awarded for partial completion of doctoral program.
Degree requirements: For master's, thesis; for doctorate, thesis/dissertation, qualifying exam.
Entrance requirements: For master's, doctorate, and Engr, GRE General Test, TOEFL. *Application deadline:* For fall admission, 1/5; for spring admission, 10/1. *Application fee:* $55. Electronic applications accepted.
Expenses: Tuition: Full-time $27,528. Required fees: $1,638.
Financial support: In 2001–02, 18 fellowships with partial tuition reimbursements (averaging $15,000 per year), 5 research assistantships with full tuition reimbursements (averaging $18,000 per year), 4 teaching assistantships with partial tuition reimbursements (averaging $10,000 per year) were awarded. Career-related internships or fieldwork, Federal Work-Study, and scholarships/grants also available. Support available to part-time students. Financial award application deadline: 1/5; financial award applicants required to submit FAFSA. *Total annual research expenditures:* $1.1 million.
Dr. Peter Schlosser, Chairman, 212-854-0306, *Fax:* 212-854-7081, *E-mail:* ps10@columbia.edu.
Application contact: Jaime Bradstreet, Student Coordinator, 212-854-2905, *Fax:* 212-854-7081, *E-mail:* jlb2001@columbia.edu. *Web site:* http://www.seas.columbia.edu/columbia/department/krumb/

■ CORNELL UNIVERSITY

Graduate School, Graduate Fields of Engineering, Field of Materials Science and Engineering, Ithaca, NY 14853-0001

AWARDS Materials engineering (M Eng, PhD); materials science (M Eng, PhD).

Faculty: 30 full-time.
Students: 42 full-time (16 women); includes 3 minority (all Asian Americans or Pacific Islanders), 28 international. 106 applicants, 26% accepted. In 2001, 12 master's, 6 doctorates awarded. Terminal master's awarded for partial completion of doctoral program.
Degree requirements: For doctorate, thesis/dissertation.
Entrance requirements: For master's and doctorate, GRE General Test, GRE Writing Test, pre-application required if undergraduate degree is from a non-US college/university, 3 letters of recommendation. *Application deadline:* For fall admission, 1/15 (priority date). *Application fee:* $65. Electronic applications accepted.

Expenses: Tuition: Full-time $25,970. Required fees: $50.
Financial support: In 2001–02, 6 fellowships with full tuition reimbursements, 31 research assistantships with full tuition reimbursements, 6 teaching assistantships with full tuition reimbursements were awarded. Institutionally sponsored loans, scholarships/grants, tuition waivers (full and partial), and unspecified assistantships also available. Financial award applicants required to submit FAFSA.
Faculty research: Ceramics, complex fluids, glass, metals, polymers semiconductors, biomaterials; electrical, magnetic, mechanical, optical, and structural properties; thin films, organic optoelectronics, nano-composites, organic-inorganic hybrids, biomedical sensors; materials synthesis and processing. Self-assembly and biomimetrics.
Application contact: Graduate Field Assistant, 607-255-9159, *E-mail:* matsci@cornell.edu. *Web site:* http://www.gradschool.cornell.edu/grad/fields_1/mat-sci.html

■ DARTMOUTH COLLEGE

Thayer School of Engineering, Program in Materials Sciences and Engineering, Hanover, NH 03755
AWARDS MS, PhD.

Degree requirements: For master's, thesis; for doctorate, thesis/dissertation, candidacy oral exam.
Entrance requirements: For master's and doctorate, GRE General Test. *Application deadline:* For fall admission, 1/1 (priority date). *Application fee:* $40 ($50 for international students).
Expenses: Tuition: Full-time $26,425.
Financial support: Fellowships, research assistantships, teaching assistantships, career-related internships or fieldwork, Federal Work-Study, institutionally sponsored loans, and tuition waivers (full and partial) available. Financial award application deadline: 1/15.
Faculty research: Microelectronic and magnetic materials, optical thin films, biomaterials and nanostructures, laser-material interactions, nano composites. *Total annual research expenditures:* $800,000.
Application contact: Candace S. Potter, Graduate Admissions Administrator, 603-646-3844, *Fax:* 603-646-1620, *E-mail:* candace.potter@dartmouth.edu. *Web site:* http://engineering.dartmouth.edu/

■ DUKE UNIVERSITY

Graduate School, School of Engineering, Department of Mechanical Engineering and Materials Science, Durham, NC 27708-0586

AWARDS Materials science (MS, PhD); mechanical engineering (MS, PhD). Part-time programs available.

Faculty: 24 full-time, 4 part-time/adjunct.

Students: 44 full-time (4 women), 19 international. 146 applicants, 22% accepted, 9 enrolled. In 2001, 4 master's, 10 doctorates awarded. Terminal master's awarded for partial completion of doctoral program.
Degree requirements: For master's, thesis optional; for doctorate, thesis/dissertation.
Entrance requirements: For master's and doctorate, GRE General Test. *Application deadline:* For fall admission, 12/31; for spring admission, 11/1. *Application fee:* $75.
Expenses: Tuition: Full-time $24,600.
Financial support: Fellowships, research assistantships, teaching assistantships, Federal Work-Study available. Financial award application deadline: 12/31.
Laurens Howle, Director of Graduate Studies, 919-660-5308, *Fax:* 919-660-8963, *E-mail:* kmrogers@duke.edu. *Web site:* http://www.mems.egr.duke.html/

Find an in-depth description at www.petersons.com/gradchannel.

■ THE GEORGE WASHINGTON UNIVERSITY

Columbian College of Arts and Sciences, Department of Chemistry, Washington, DC 20052

AWARDS Analytical chemistry (MS, PhD); inorganic chemistry (MS, PhD); materials science (MS, PhD); organic chemistry (MS, PhD); physical chemistry (MS, PhD). Part-time and evening/weekend programs available.

Faculty: 6 full-time (0 women).
Students: 19 full-time (8 women), 8 part-time (5 women); includes 4 minority (1 African American, 2 Asian Americans or Pacific Islanders, 1 Hispanic American), 5 international. Average age 27. 53 applicants, 92% accepted. In 2001, 2 master's, 3 doctorates awarded. Terminal master's awarded for partial completion of doctoral program.
Degree requirements: For master's, thesis or alternative, comprehensive exam; for doctorate, thesis/dissertation, general exam.
Entrance requirements: For master's and doctorate, GRE General Test, interview, minimum GPA of 3.0. *Application fee:* $55.
Expenses: Tuition: Part-time $810 per credit. Required fees: $1 per credit.
Financial support: In 2001–02, 20 fellowships with tuition reimbursements (averaging $6,900 per year), 16 teaching assistantships with tuition reimbursements (averaging $3,500 per year) were awarded. Research assistantships, Federal Work-Study also available. Financial award application deadline: 2/1.
Dr. Michael King, Chair, 202-994-6488.
Application contact: Information Contact, *E-mail:* gwchem@www.gwu.edu. *Web site:* http://www.gwu.edu/~gradinfo/

■ IOWA STATE UNIVERSITY OF SCIENCE AND TECHNOLOGY

Graduate College, College of Engineering and College of Liberal Arts and Sciences, Department of Materials Science and Engineering, Ames, IA 50011

AWARDS MS, PhD.

Faculty: 23 full-time, 3 part-time/adjunct.
Students: 49 full-time (11 women), 16 part-time (5 women); includes 1 minority (Asian American or Pacific Islander), 36 international. 133 applicants, 19% accepted, 12 enrolled. In 2001, 7 degrees awarded.
Degree requirements: For master's and doctorate, thesis/dissertation. *Median time to degree:* Master's–2.2 years full-time.
Entrance requirements: For master's and doctorate, GRE General Test (international applicants), TOEFL. *Application deadline:* For fall admission, 2/15 (priority date); for spring admission, 8/15 (priority date). *Application fee:* $20 ($50 for international students). Electronic applications accepted.
Expenses: Tuition, state resident: full-time $1,851. Tuition, nonresident: full-time $5,449. Tuition and fees vary according to program.
Financial support: In 2001–02, 45 research assistantships with partial tuition reimbursements (averaging $15,938 per year), 1 teaching assistantship with partial tuition reimbursement (averaging $13,114 per year) were awarded. Fellowships, scholarships/grants, health care benefits, and unspecified assistantships also available.
Dr. Mufit Akinc, Chair, 515-294-0738, *Fax:* 515-204-5444, *E-mail:* mse@iastate.edu.
Application contact: Dr. David Cann, Information Contact, 515-294-1214, *E-mail:* mse@iastate.edu. *Web site:* http://www1.eng.iastate.edu/coe/grad.asp/

■ JACKSON STATE UNIVERSITY

Graduate School, School of Science and Technology, Department of Technology and Industrial Arts, Jackson, MS 39217

AWARDS Hazardous materials management (MS); industrial arts education (MS Ed). Part-time and evening/weekend programs available.

Degree requirements: For master's, thesis or alternative, comprehensive exam.
Entrance requirements: For master's, GRE General Test, TOEFL.

■ JOHNS HOPKINS UNIVERSITY

G. W. C. Whiting School of Engineering, Department of Materials Science and Engineering, Baltimore, MD 21218-2699

AWARDS M Mat SE, MSE, PhD. Part-time and evening/weekend programs available.

Faculty: 10 full-time (1 woman), 6 part-time/adjunct (1 woman).
Students: 25 full-time (5 women), 3 part-time; includes 2 minority (1 Asian American or Pacific Islander, 1 Hispanic American), 13 international. Average age 30. 74 applicants, 18% accepted, 2 enrolled. In 2001, 6 degrees awarded. Terminal master's awarded for partial completion of doctoral program.
Degree requirements: For master's, thesis, cumulative exam; for doctorate, thesis/dissertation, cumulative and oral exam.
Entrance requirements: For master's and doctorate, GRE General Test, TOEFL. *Application deadline:* Applications are processed on a rolling basis. *Application fee:* $0. Electronic applications accepted.
Expenses: Tuition: Full-time $27,390.
Financial support: In 2001–02, 27 students received support, including 3 fellowships with full tuition reimbursements available (averaging $18,540 per year), 18 research assistantships with full tuition reimbursements available (averaging $18,540 per year), 6 teaching assistantships with full tuition reimbursements available (averaging $18,540 per year); Federal Work-Study, institutionally sponsored loans, tuition waivers (full), and unspecified assistantships also available. Financial award application deadline: 3/14.
Faculty research: Thin films, nanomaterials, biomaterials, materials processing, computational materials science. *Total annual research expenditures:* $1.6 million.
Dr. Peter C. Searson, Chair, 410-516-8774, *Fax:* 410-516-5293, *E-mail:* searson@jhu.edu.
Application contact: Dr. Robert C. Cammarata, Chair, Graduate Program, 410-516-8145, *Fax:* 410-516-5293, *E-mail:* dmse.admissions@jhu.edu. *Web site:* http://www.jhu.edu/~matsci/

Find an in-depth description at www.petersons.com/gradchannel.

■ LEHIGH UNIVERSITY

P.C. Rossin College of Engineering and Applied Science, Department of Materials Science and Engineering, Bethlehem, PA 18015-3094

AWARDS M Eng, MS, PhD. Part-time programs available.

Faculty: 13 full-time (1 woman), 2 part-time/adjunct (0 women).
Students: 41 full-time (7 women), 4 part-time; includes 9 minority (1 African American, 8 Asian Americans or Pacific

Islanders), 4 international. 408 applicants, 4% accepted, 11 enrolled. In 2001, 8 master's, 8 doctorates awarded.
Degree requirements: For master's and doctorate, thesis/dissertation.
Entrance requirements: For master's and doctorate, GRE General Test, TOEFL, minimum GPA of 3.0. *Application deadline:* For fall admission, 2/15 (priority date); for spring admission, 10/1 (priority date). Applications are processed on a rolling basis. *Application fee:* $50.
Expenses: Tuition: Part-time $468 per credit hour. Required fees: $200; $100 per semester. Tuition and fees vary according to program.
Financial support: In 2001–02, 3 fellowships with full tuition reimbursements (averaging $17,400 per year), 36 research assistantships with full tuition reimbursements (averaging $17,700 per year) were awarded. Teaching assistantships, tuition waivers (full) also available. Financial award application deadline: 1/15.
Faculty research: Metals, ceramics, crystals, polymers, fatigue crack propagation, electron microscopy. *Total annual research expenditures:* $5.1 million.
Dr. G. Slade Cargill, Chairperson, 610-758-4207, *Fax:* 610-758-4244, *E-mail:* gsc3@lehigh.edu.
Application contact: Maxine C. Mattie, Graduate Administrative Coordinator, 610-758-4222, *Fax:* 610-758-4244, *E-mail:* mcm1@lehigh.edu.

Find an in-depth description at www.petersons.com/gradchannel.

■ MASSACHUSETTS INSTITUTE OF TECHNOLOGY

School of Engineering, Department of Materials Science and Engineering, Cambridge, MA 02139-4307

AWARDS Materials engineering (Mat E); materials science and engineering (SM, PhD, Sc D); metallurgical engineering (Met E).

Faculty: 33 full-time (6 women).
Students: 179 full-time (52 women), 1 (woman) part-time; includes 21 minority (3 African Americans, 14 Asian Americans or Pacific Islanders, 4 Hispanic Americans), 77 international. Average age 23. 288 applicants, 36% accepted, 44 enrolled. In 2001, 30 master's, 29 doctorates awarded. Terminal master's awarded for partial completion of doctoral program.
Degree requirements: For master's and other advanced degree, thesis; for doctorate, thesis/dissertation, qualifying exams, comprehensive exam.
Entrance requirements: For master's and doctorate, GRE General Test, TOEFL. *Application deadline:* For fall admission, 1/15 (priority date); for spring admission, 11/1. *Application fee:* $60. Electronic applications accepted.
Expenses: Tuition: Full-time $26,960. Full-time tuition and fees vary according to program.

Financial support: In 2001–02, 173 students received support, including 42 fellowships, 138 research assistantships, 11 teaching assistantships; career-related internships or fieldwork, Federal Work-Study, institutionally sponsored loans, scholarships/grants, traineeships, health care benefits, and unspecified assistantships also available. Financial award application deadline: 1/1; financial award applicants required to submit FAFSA.

Faculty research: Photonic band gap materials, advanced spectroscopic and diffraction techniques, rapid solidification process, high-strength polymer materials, computer modeling of structures and processing. *Total annual research expenditures:* $15.5 million.

Subra Suresh, Head, 617-253-3320, *Fax:* 617-252-1773, *E-mail:* ssuresh@mit.edu.

Application contact: Kathleen R. Farrell, Student Administrator, 617-253-3302, *E-mail:* krf@mit.edu. *Web site:* http://dmse.mit.edu/

■ MICHIGAN STATE UNIVERSITY

Graduate School, College of Engineering, Department of Chemical Engineering and Materials Science, East Lansing, MI 48824

AWARDS Chemical engineering (MS, PhD), including environmental toxicology (PhD); engineering mechanics (MS, PhD); materials science and engineering (MS, PhD); mechanics (PhD); metallurgy (MS, PhD). Part-time programs available.

Faculty: 22.

Students: 41 full-time (10 women), 5 part-time (1 woman); includes 9 minority (2 African Americans, 4 Asian Americans or Pacific Islanders, 3 Hispanic Americans), 21 international. Average age 26. 99 applicants, 14% accepted. In 2001, 8 master's, 6 doctorates awarded. Terminal master's awarded for partial completion of doctoral program.

Degree requirements: For doctorate, thesis/dissertation.

Entrance requirements: For master's, GRE, TOEFL, minimum GPA of 3.0; for doctorate, GRE, TOEFL. *Application deadline:* For fall admission, 1/15 (priority date); for spring admission, 11/1. Applications are processed on a rolling basis. *Application fee:* $30 ($40 for international students). Electronic applications accepted.

Expenses: Tuition, state resident: part-time $244 per credit hour. Tuition, nonresident: part-time $494 per credit hour. Required fees: $268 per semester. Tuition and fees vary according to course load, degree level and program.

Financial support: In 2001–02, 26 fellowships with tuition reimbursements (averaging $3,950 per year), 49 research assistantships with tuition reimbursements (averaging $14,052 per year), 19 teaching assistantships with tuition reimbursements (averaging $12,741 per year) were

awarded. Financial award applicants required to submit FAFSA.

Faculty research: Agricultural bioprocessing, impact resistance of thermoplastic composite materials, durability of polymer composites. *Total annual research expenditures:* $989,316.

Dr. Martin Hawley, Interim Chair, 517-355-5135, *Fax:* 517-353-9842.

Application contact: Information Contact, 517-355-5135, *Fax:* 517-432-1105, *E-mail:* chems@egr.msu.edu. *Web site:* http://www.chems.msu.edu/

■ NATIONAL TECHNOLOGICAL UNIVERSITY

Programs in Engineering, Fort Collins, CO 80526-1842

AWARDS Chemical engineering (MS); computer engineering (MS); computer science (MS); electrical engineering (MS); engineering management (MS); environmental systems management (MS); management of technology (MS); manufacturing systems engineering (MS); materials science and engineering (MS); mechanical engineering (MS); microelectronics and semiconductor engineering (MS). Software engineering (MS). Special majors (MS). Systems engineering (MS). Part-time programs available. Postbaccalaureate distance learning degree programs offered (no on-campus study).

Students: In 2001, 114 degrees awarded.

Degree requirements: For master's, comprehensive exam.

Entrance requirements: For master's, BS in engineering or related field; 2.9 minimum GPA. *Application deadline:* Applications are processed on a rolling basis. *Application fee:* $50. Electronic applications accepted.

Expenses: Tuition: Part-time $660 per credit hour. Part-time tuition and fees vary according to course load, campus/location and program.

Dr. Andre Vacroux, President, 970-495-6400, *Fax:* 970-484-0668, *E-mail:* andre@ntu.edu.

Application contact: Rhonda Bonham, Admissions Officer, 970-495-6400, *Fax:* 970-498-0601, *E-mail:* rhonda@ntu.edu. *Web site:* http://www.ntu.edu/

■ NEW JERSEY INSTITUTE OF TECHNOLOGY

Office of Graduate Studies, Department of Physics, Program in Materials Science and Engineering, Newark, NJ 07102

AWARDS MS, PhD. Part-time and evening/weekend programs available.

Students: 26 full-time (2 women), 7 part-time (2 women); includes 7 minority (1 African American, 5 Asian Americans or Pacific Islanders, 1 Hispanic American), 24 international. Average age 30. 61 applicants, 69% accepted, 9 enrolled. In

2001, 4 master's, 1 doctorate awarded. Terminal master's awarded for partial completion of doctoral program.

Degree requirements: For master's and doctorate, thesis/dissertation.

Entrance requirements: For master's, GRE General Test; for doctorate, GRE General Test, minimum graduate GPA of 3.5. *Application deadline:* For fall admission, 6/5 (priority date); for spring admission, 10/15. Applications are processed on a rolling basis. *Application fee:* $50. Electronic applications accepted.

Expenses: Tuition, state resident: full-time $7,812; part-time $434 per credit. Tuition, nonresident: full-time $10,746; part-time $597 per credit. Required fees: $47 per credit. $76 per semester.

Financial support: Fellowships with full and partial tuition reimbursements, research assistantships with full and partial tuition reimbursements, teaching assistantships with full and partial tuition reimbursements, career-related internships or fieldwork, Federal Work-Study, institutionally sponsored loans, and unspecified assistantships available. Financial award application deadline: 3/15.

Application contact: Kathryn Kelly, Director of Admissions, 973-596-3300, *Fax:* 973-596-3461, *E-mail:* admissions@njit.edu. *Web site:* http://www.njit.edu/

■ NORFOLK STATE UNIVERSITY

School of Graduate Studies, School of Science and Technology, Department of Chemistry, Norfolk, VA 23504

AWARDS Materials science (MS).

Expenses: Tuition, area resident: Part-time $197 per credit. Tuition, nonresident: part-time $503 per credit.

■ NORTH CAROLINA STATE UNIVERSITY

Graduate School, College of Engineering, Department of Materials Science and Engineering, Raleigh, NC 27695

AWARDS MMSE, MS, PhD.

Faculty: 24 full-time (1 woman), 17 part-time/adjunct (0 women).

Students: 77 full-time (12 women), 8 part-time (2 women); includes 5 minority (1 African American, 2 Asian Americans or Pacific Islanders, 2 Hispanic Americans), 33 international. Average age 29. 180 applicants, 17% accepted. In 2001, 6 master's, 14 doctorates awarded.

Degree requirements: For master's and doctorate, thesis/dissertation. *Application deadline:* For fall admission, 6/25. *Application fee:* $45.

Expenses: Tuition, state resident: full-time $1,748. Tuition, nonresident: full-time $6,904.

Financial support: In 2001–02, 4 fellowships (averaging $8,121 per year), 56 research assistantships (averaging $6,257

North Carolina State University (continued)

per year), 8 teaching assistantships (averaging $5,777 per year) were awarded.
Faculty research: Processing and properties of wide band gap semiconductors, ferroelectric thin-film materials, ductility of nanocrystalline materials, computational materials science, defects in silicon-based devices. *Total annual research expenditures:* $6.4 million.
Dr. J. Michael Rigsbee, Head, 919-515-3568, *Fax:* 919-515-7724, *E-mail:* mike_rigsbee@ncsu.edu.
Application contact: Dr. Ronald O. Scattergood, Director of Graduate Programs, 919-515-7843, *Fax:* 919-515-7724, *E-mail:* mte_gradprog@ncsu.edu. *Web site:* http://vims.ncsu.edu/matsci/

■ NORTHWESTERN UNIVERSITY

McCormick School of Engineering and Applied Science, Department of Civil and Environmental Engineering, Evanston, IL 60208

AWARDS Environmental engineering and science (MS, PhD); geotechnical engineering (MS, PhD); mechanics of materials and solids (MS, PhD); project management (MPM). Structural engineering and materials (MS, PhD); theoretical and applied mechanics (MS, PhD); transportation systems analysis and planning (MS, PhD). MS and PhD admissions and degrees offered through The Graduate School. Part-time programs available.

Faculty: 26 full-time (3 women), 9 part-time/adjunct (2 women).
Students: 80 full-time (32 women), 1 part-time; includes 2 Asian Americans or Pacific Islanders, 1 Hispanic American, 38 international. 282 applicants, 7% accepted. In 2001, 20 master's, 14 doctorates awarded. Terminal master's awarded for partial completion of doctoral program.
Degree requirements: For master's, thesis (for some programs); for doctorate, thesis/dissertation.
Application deadline: For fall admission, 8/1.
Application fee: $50 ($55 for international students). Electronic applications accepted.
Expenses: Tuition: Full-time $26,526.
Financial support: In 2001–02, 10 fellowships with full tuition reimbursements (averaging $13,338 per year), 66 research assistantships with partial tuition reimbursements (averaging $18,000 per year), 7 teaching assistantships with full tuition reimbursements (averaging $13,329 per year) were awarded. Career-related internships or fieldwork, institutionally sponsored loans, and scholarships/grants also available. Financial award application deadline: 1/15; financial award applicants required to submit FAFSA.
Faculty research: Environmental engineering and science, geotechnics, mechanics of materials and solids, structural engineering and materials,

transportation systems analysis and planning. *Total annual research expenditures:* $8.4 million.
Joseph L. Schofer, Chair, 847-491-3257, *Fax:* 847-491-4011, *E-mail:* j-schofer@northwestern.edu.
Application contact: Janet Soule, Academic Coordinator, 847-491-3176, *Fax:* 847-491-4011, *E-mail:* civil-info@northwestern.edu. *Web site:* http://www.civil.northwestern.edu/

Find an in-depth description at www.petersons.com/gradchannel.

■ NORTHWESTERN UNIVERSITY

McCormick School of Engineering and Applied Science, Department of Materials Science and Engineering, Evanston, IL 60208

AWARDS Electronic materials (Certificate); materials science and engineering (MS, PhD). Admissions and degrees offered through The Graduate School. Part-time programs available.

Faculty: 26 full-time (2 women).
Students: 109 full-time (25 women), 2 part-time (1 woman); includes 16 minority (2 African Americans, 10 Asian Americans or Pacific Islanders, 4 Hispanic Americans), 33 international. 263 applicants, 22% accepted, 24 enrolled. In 2001, 9 master's, 19 doctorates awarded. Terminal master's awarded for partial completion of doctoral program.
Degree requirements: For master's, oral thesis defense; for doctorate, oral defense of dissertation, preliminary evaluation, qualifying exam.
Application deadline: For fall admission, 1/15. Applications are processed on a rolling basis. *Application fee:* $60 ($75 for international students). Electronic applications accepted.
Expenses: Tuition: Full-time $26,526.
Financial support: In 2001–02, 28 fellowships with full tuition reimbursements (averaging $21,208 per year), 81 research assistantships with full tuition reimbursements (averaging $19,440 per year), teaching assistantships with full tuition reimbursements (averaging $19,440 per year) were awarded. Career-related internships or fieldwork and institutionally sponsored loans also available. Financial award application deadline: 1/15; financial award applicants required to submit FAFSA.
Faculty research: Metallurgy, ceramics, polymers, electronic materials, biomaterials. *Total annual research expenditures:* $9.9 million.
Katherine T. Faber, Chair, 847-491-3537, *Fax:* 847-491-7820.
Application contact: Jason Grocholski, Admissions Contact, 847-491-3587, *Fax:* 847-491-7820, *E-mail:* matsci@northwestern.edu. *Web site:* http://www.matsci.northwestern.edu/

■ THE OHIO STATE UNIVERSITY

Graduate School, College of Engineering, Department of Materials Science and Engineering, Columbus, OH 43210

AWARDS MS, PhD.

Degree requirements: For master's and doctorate, thesis/dissertation.
Entrance requirements: For master's and doctorate, GRE General Test (international applicants).
Faculty research: Computational materials modeling, biomaterials, metallurgy, ceramics, advanced alloys/composites. *Web site:* http://www.osu.edu/mse/

Find an in-depth description at www.petersons.com/gradchannel.

■ OHIO UNIVERSITY

Graduate Studies, Russ College of Engineering and Technology, Integrated Engineering Program, Athens, OH 45701-2979

AWARDS Geotechnical and environmental engineering (PhD); intelligent systems (PhD); materials processing (PhD).

Faculty: 39 full-time (1 woman).
Students: 16 full-time (1 woman), 8 part-time (1 woman), 21 international. 34 applicants, 88% accepted. In 2001, 3 degrees awarded.
Degree requirements: For doctorate, thesis/dissertation, comprehensive exam.
Entrance requirements: For doctorate, GRE General Test, MS in engineering or related field. *Application deadline:* For fall admission, 3/15. Applications are processed on a rolling basis. *Application fee:* $30.
Expenses: Tuition, state resident: full-time $6,585. Tuition, nonresident: full-time $12,254.
Financial support: In 2001–02, 3 fellowships with full tuition reimbursements (averaging $10,500 per year), 3 research assistantships with full tuition reimbursements (averaging $10,500 per year) were awarded. Federal Work-Study, institutionally sponsored loans, and tuition waivers (full) also available. Financial award application deadline: 3/15.
Faculty research: Material processing, expert systems, environmental geotechnical manufacturing. *Total annual research expenditures:* $1.5 million.
Dr. Jerrel Mitchell, Associate Dean for Research and Graduate Studies, 740-593-1482, *E-mail:* mitchell@bobcat.ent.ohiou.edu.

Find an in-depth description at www.petersons.com/gradchannel.

■ OLD DOMINION UNIVERSITY

College of Engineering and Technology, Program in Materials Science and Engineering, Norfolk, VA 23529

AWARDS ME, MS.

Faculty: 4 full-time (0 women), 2 part-time/adjunct (0 women).
Students: Average age 36. 12 applicants, 75% accepted. In 2001, 1 degree awarded.
Degree requirements: For master's, comprehensive exam.
Application deadline: For fall admission, 7/1; for spring admission, 10/1. Applications are processed on a rolling basis. *Application fee:* $30. Electronic applications accepted.
Expenses: Tuition, state resident: part-time $202 per credit. Tuition, nonresident: part-time $534 per credit. Required fees: $76 per semester. *Total annual research expenditures:* $1 million.
Dr. Mool Gupta, Graduate Program Director, 757-683-5645, *Fax:* 757-269-5644, *E-mail:* mgupta@odu.edu. *Web site:* http://www.arc.odu.edu/academics.htm

■ OREGON STATE UNIVERSITY

Graduate School, College of Engineering, Department of Mechanical Engineering, Program in Materials Science, Corvallis, OR 97331

AWARDS MAIS, MS.

Students: 5 full-time (1 woman), 1 part-time, 2 international. Average age 32. In 2001, 2 degrees awarded.
Degree requirements: For master's, thesis or alternative.
Entrance requirements: For master's, GRE General Test, TOEFL, minimum GPA of 3.0 in last 90 hours. *Application deadline:* For fall admission, 3/1. Applications are processed on a rolling basis. *Application fee:* $50.
Expenses: Tuition, area resident: Full-time $15,933. Tuition, state resident: full-time $28,937.
Financial support: Fellowships, research assistantships, teaching assistantships, Federal Work-Study and institutionally sponsored loans available. Support available to part-time students. Financial award application deadline: 2/1.
Dr. Michael E. Kassner, Director, 541-737-7023, *Fax:* 541-737-2600, *E-mail:* kassner@engr.orst.edu.
Application contact: Graduate Admissions Clerk, 541-737-3441, *Fax:* 541-737-2600.

■ THE PENNSYLVANIA STATE UNIVERSITY UNIVERSITY PARK CAMPUS

Graduate School, College of Earth and Mineral Sciences, Department of Materials Science and Engineering, State College, University Park, PA 16802-1503

AWARDS Ceramic science (MS, PhD); fuel science (MS, PhD); metals science and engineering (MS, PhD); polymer science (MS, PhD).

Students: 106 full-time (19 women), 10 part-time (3 women). In 2001, 25 master's, 16 doctorates awarded.

Entrance requirements: For master's and doctorate, GRE. *Application deadline:* For fall admission, 7/1. *Application fee:* $45.
Expenses: Tuition, state resident: full-time $7,882; part-time $333 per credit. Tuition, nonresident: full-time $16,142; part-time $673 per credit. Required fees: $124 per semester.
Financial support: Fellowships, unspecified assistantships available. Financial award application deadline: 2/28.
Gray L. Messing, Head, 814-865-2262.

■ THE PENNSYLVANIA STATE UNIVERSITY UNIVERSITY PARK CAMPUS

Graduate School, Intercollege Graduate Programs, Intercollege Graduate Program in Materials, State College, University Park, PA 16802-1503

AWARDS MS, PhD.

Students: 47 full-time (9 women), 10 part-time (3 women).
Entrance requirements: For master's and doctorate, GRE General Test. *Application fee:* $45.
Expenses: Tuition, state resident: full-time $7,882; part-time $333 per credit. Tuition, nonresident: full-time $16,142; part-time $673 per credit. Required fees: $124 per semester.
Dr. Barbara Shaw, Chair, 814-865-1451.

■ POLYTECHNIC UNIVERSITY, BROOKLYN CAMPUS

Department of Mechanical, Aerospace and Manufacturing Engineering, Major in Materials Science, Brooklyn, NY 11201-2990

AWARDS MS. Part-time and evening/weekend programs available.

Degree requirements: For master's, project or thesis.
Electronic applications accepted.
Faculty research: Studies of materials for aerospace, electronics, and energy-related applications; alloy hardening; deformation and fracture; phase transformations.

■ POLYTECHNIC UNIVERSITY, WESTCHESTER GRADUATE CENTER

Graduate Programs, Department of Mechanical, Aerospace and Manufacturing Engineering, Major in Materials Science, Hawthorne, NY 10532-1507

AWARDS MS.

Electronic applications accepted.

■ RENSSELAER POLYTECHNIC INSTITUTE

Graduate School, School of Engineering, Department of Materials Science and Engineering, Troy, NY 12180-3590

AWARDS Ceramics and glass science (M Eng, MS, PhD); composites (M Eng, MS, PhD); electronic materials (M Eng, MS, PhD); metallurgy (M Eng, MS, PhD); polymers (M Eng, MS, PhD). Part-time and evening/weekend programs available.

Faculty: 15 full-time (1 woman), 5 part-time/adjunct (0 women).
Students: 56 full-time (15 women), 18 part-time (5 women), 35 international. Average age 24. 287 applicants, 11% accepted, 10 enrolled. In 2001, 11 master's, 5 doctorates awarded. Terminal master's awarded for partial completion of doctoral program.
Degree requirements: For master's, thesis (for some programs); for doctorate, thesis/dissertation. *Median time to degree:* Master's–2 years full-time, 5 years part-time; doctorate–5.5 years full-time, 8 years part-time.
Entrance requirements: For master's and doctorate, GRE, TOEFL. *Application deadline:* For fall admission, 1/15 (priority date). Applications are processed on a rolling basis. *Application fee:* $45. Electronic applications accepted.
Expenses: Tuition: Full-time $26,400; part-time $1,320 per credit hour. Required fees: $1,437.
Financial support: In 2001–02, 53 students received support, including 13 fellowships with full tuition reimbursements available (averaging $22,000 per year), 29 research assistantships with full tuition reimbursements available (averaging $16,800 per year), 11 teaching assistantships with full tuition reimbursements available (averaging $16,800 per year); career-related internships or fieldwork and institutionally sponsored loans also available. Financial award application deadline: 2/1.
Faculty research: Materials processing, nanostructural materials, materials for microelectronics, composite materials, materials theory. *Total annual research expenditures:* $4.1 million.
Dr. David J. Duquette, Chair, 518-276-6373, *Fax:* 518-276-8554.
Application contact: Dr. Roger Wright, Admissions Coordinator, 518-276-6372, *Fax:* 518-276-8554, *E-mail:* fowlen@rpi.edu. *Web site:* http://www.rpi.edu/dept/materials/

Find an in-depth description at www.petersons.com/gradchannel.

■ RICE UNIVERSITY

Graduate Programs, George R. Brown School of Engineering, Department of Mechanical Engineering and Materials Science, Houston, TX 77251-1892

AWARDS Materials science (MMS, MS, PhD); mechanical engineering (MME, MS, PhD). Part-time programs available.

Faculty: 19 full-time (3 women), 7 part-time/adjunct (1 woman).

Students: 41 full-time (12 women), 8 part-time (1 woman); includes 8 minority (1 African American, 2 Asian Americans or Pacific Islanders, 3 Hispanic Americans, 2 Native Americans), 28 international. Average age 23. 183 applicants, 10% accepted, 17 enrolled. In 2001, 7 master's, 4 doctorates awarded. Terminal master's awarded for partial completion of doctoral program.

Degree requirements: For master's and doctorate, thesis/dissertation, comprehensive exam, registration. *Median time to degree:* Master's–3 years full-time; doctorate–4 years full-time.

Entrance requirements: For master's and doctorate, GRE General Test, TOEFL, minimum GPA of 3.0. *Application deadline:* For fall admission, 2/1 (priority date); for spring admission, 11/15 (priority date). Applications are processed on a rolling basis. *Application fee:* $25. Electronic applications accepted.

Expenses: Tuition: Full-time $17,300. Required fees: $250.

Financial support: In 2001–02, 37 students received support, including 18 fellowships with full tuition reimbursements available (averaging $12,600 per year), 16 research assistantships with full tuition reimbursements available (averaging $12,600 per year), 2 teaching assistantships with full tuition reimbursements available (averaging $12,600 per year). Financial award application deadline: 2/1.

Faculty research: Heat transfer, biomedical engineering, fluid dynamics, aeroastronautics, control systems/robotics, materials science. *Total annual research expenditures:* $1.4 million.

Tayfun Tezduyar, Chair, 713-348-4906, *Fax:* 713-348-5423.

Application contact: Judith E. Farhat, Graduate Coordinator, 713-348-3582, *Fax:* 713-348-5423, *E-mail:* gradcoord@mems.rice.edu. *Web site:* http://www.mems.rice.edu/

■ ROCHESTER INSTITUTE OF TECHNOLOGY

Graduate Enrollment Services, College of Science, Center for Materials Science and Engineering, Rochester, NY 14623-5603

AWARDS MS. Part-time programs available.

Students: 8 full-time (3 women), 8 part-time (4 women); includes 2 minority (1 Asian American or Pacific Islander, 1 Hispanic American), 9 international. 40

applicants, 73% accepted, 7 enrolled. In 2001, 6 degrees awarded.

Degree requirements: For master's, thesis optional.

Entrance requirements: For master's, TOEFL, minimum GPA of 3.0. *Application deadline:* For fall admission, 3/1 (priority date). Applications are processed on a rolling basis. *Application fee:* $50.

Expenses: Tuition: Full-time $20,928; part-time $587 per hour. Required fees: $162. Tuition and fees vary according to program.

Financial support: Teaching assistantships, career-related internships or fieldwork, institutionally sponsored loans, and tuition waivers (partial) available. Support available to part-time students. Financial award application deadline: 7/29.

Faculty research: VUV modification of polymers, stress and morphology of sputtered copper films, MRI applications to materials problems.

Dr. K. S.V. Santhanam, Interim Director, 585-475-2920, *E-mail:* ksssch@rit.edu. *Web site:* http://www.rit.edu/~670www/

■ RUTGERS, THE STATE UNIVERSITY OF NEW JERSEY, NEW BRUNSWICK

Graduate School, Program in Materials Science and Engineering, New Brunswick, NJ 08901-1281

AWARDS Physical metallurgy (MS, PhD); polymer science (MS, PhD). Part-time programs available. Terminal master's awarded for partial completion of doctoral program.

Degree requirements: For master's, thesis optional; for doctorate, thesis/dissertation.

Entrance requirements: For master's and doctorate, GRE General Test.

Faculty research: Nanostructured materials, electroactive polymers, phase transformation, polymeric properties.

■ SOUTH DAKOTA SCHOOL OF MINES AND TECHNOLOGY

Graduate Division, Division of Material Engineering and Science, Doctoral Program in Materials Engineering and Science, Rapid City, SD 57701-3995

AWARDS Chemical engineering (PhD); chemistry (PhD); civil engineering (PhD); electrical engineering (PhD); mechanical engineering (PhD); metallurgical engineering (PhD); physics (PhD). Part-time programs available.

Degree requirements: For doctorate, thesis/dissertation.

Entrance requirements: For doctorate, TOEFL, TWE, minimum graduate GPA of 3.0. Electronic applications accepted.

Faculty research: Thermophysical properties of solids, development of multiphase

materials and composites, concrete technology, electronic polymer materials.

Find an in-depth description at www.petersons.com/gradchannel.

■ SOUTH DAKOTA SCHOOL OF MINES AND TECHNOLOGY

Graduate Division, Division of Material Engineering and Science, Master's Program in Materials Engineering and Science, Rapid City, SD 57701-3995

AWARDS Chemistry (MS); metallurgical engineering (MS); physics (MS).

Entrance requirements: For master's, TOEFL, TWE. Electronic applications accepted.

■ SOUTHWEST MISSOURI STATE UNIVERSITY

Graduate College, College of Natural and Applied Sciences, Department of Physics, Astronomy, and Materials Science, Springfield, MO 65804-0094

AWARDS Materials science (MS). Part-time programs available.

Faculty: 13 full-time (1 woman).

Students: 6 full-time (0 women), 3 part-time (1 woman); includes 1 minority (African American), 5 international. In 2001, 1 degree awarded.

Degree requirements: For master's, thesis, comprehensive exam.

Entrance requirements: For master's, GRE General Test, minimum undergraduate GPA of 3.0. *Application deadline:* For fall admission, 8/5 (priority date); for spring admission, 12/20 (priority date). Applications are processed on a rolling basis. *Application fee:* $25. Electronic applications accepted.

Expenses: Tuition, state resident: full-time $2,286; part-time $127 per credit. Tuition, nonresident: full-time $4,572; part-time $254 per credit. Required fees: $151 per semester. Tuition and fees vary according to course level and program.

Financial support: In 2001–02, 4 research assistantships with full tuition reimbursements (averaging $6,150 per year), 4 teaching assistantships with full tuition reimbursements (averaging $8,200 per year) were awarded. Federal Work-Study, scholarships/grants, and unspecified assistantships also available. Financial award application deadline: 3/31.

Dr. Ryan Giedd, Head, 417-836-5131, *Fax:* 417-836-6934, *E-mail:* materialsscience@smsu.edu. *Web site:* http://www.smsu.edu/phys-astr/index html

■ STANFORD UNIVERSITY

School of Engineering, Department of Materials Science and Engineering, Stanford, CA 94305-9991

AWARDS MS, PhD, Eng.

Faculty: 10 full-time (0 women).

Students: 110 full-time (31 women), 30 part-time (9 women); includes 34 minority (7 African Americans, 26 Asian Americans or Pacific Islanders, 1 Hispanic American), 60 international. Average age 27. 219 applicants, 37% accepted. In 2001, 43 master's, 12 doctorates awarded. Terminal master's awarded for partial completion of doctoral program.

Degree requirements: For doctorate and Eng, thesis/dissertation.

Entrance requirements: For master's, doctorate, and Eng, GRE General Test, TOEFL. *Application deadline:* For fall admission, 1/5. *Application fee:* $65 ($80 for international students). Electronic applications accepted.

Bruce M. Clemens, Chair, 650-725-7455, *Fax:* 650-725-4034, *E-mail:* clemens@sce.stanford.edu.

Application contact: Graduate Administrator, 650-725-2648. *Web site:* http://www-mse.stanford.edu/

■ STEVENS INSTITUTE OF TECHNOLOGY

Graduate School, Charles V. Schaefer Jr. School of Engineering, Department of Materials Science and Engineering, Hoboken, NJ 07030

AWARDS Materials engineering (M Eng, PhD); materials science (MS, PhD). Structural analysis of materials (Certificate). Surface modification of materials (Certificate). Part-time and evening/weekend programs available. Terminal master's awarded for partial completion of doctoral program.

Degree requirements: For master's, thesis optional; for doctorate, thesis/dissertation.

Entrance requirements: For master's and doctorate, TOEFL. Electronic applications accepted.

Expenses: Tuition: Full-time $13,950; part-time $775 per credit. Required fees: $180. One-time fee: $180 part-time. Full-time tuition and fees vary according to degree level and program.

Faculty research: Surface modification techniques, structure and surface analysis, corrosion, tribology, superconductor materials.

■ STONY BROOK UNIVERSITY, STATE UNIVERSITY OF NEW YORK

Graduate School, College of Engineering and Applied Sciences, Department of Materials Science and Engineering, Stony Brook, NY 11794

AWARDS MS, PhD.

Faculty: 11 full-time (2 women), 3 part-time/adjunct (0 women).

Students: 36 full-time (7 women), 20 part-time (5 women); includes 6 minority (1 African American, 3 Asian Americans or Pacific Islanders, 2 Hispanic Americans),

42 international. 65 applicants, 72% accepted. In 2001, 9 master's, 12 doctorates awarded.

Degree requirements: For master's, thesis or alternative; for doctorate, thesis/dissertation, comprehensive exam.

Entrance requirements: For master's and doctorate, GRE General Test, TOEFL, minimum undergraduate GPA of 3.0. *Application deadline:* For fall admission, 1/15. *Application fee:* $50.

Expenses: Tuition, state resident: full-time $5,100; part-time $213 per credit. Tuition, nonresident: full-time $8,416; part-time $351 per credit. Required fees: $496.

Financial support: In 2001–02, 1 fellowship, 22 research assistantships, 22 teaching assistantships were awarded.

Faculty research: Electronic materials, biomaterials, synchrotron topography. *Total annual research expenditures:* $3.9 million.

Dr. Michael Dudley, Chairman, 631-632-8484.

Application contact: Dr. Miriam Rafailovich, Director, 631-632-8484, *Fax:* 631-632-8052, *E-mail:* mrafailovich.nsf@notes.cc.sunysb.edu. *Web site:* http://dol1.eng.sunysb.edu/

Find an in-depth description at www.petersons.com/gradchannel.

■ SYRACUSE UNIVERSITY

Graduate School, L. C. Smith College of Engineering and Computer Science, Department of Chemical Engineering and Materials Sciences, Syracuse, NY 13244-0003

AWARDS Chemical engineering (MS, PhD). Solid-state science and technology (MS, PhD).

Faculty: 7 full-time (1 woman), 4 part-time/adjunct (0 women).

Students: 21 full-time (5 women), 4 part-time; includes 2 minority (1 African American, 1 Asian American or Pacific Islander), 20 international. Average age 29. In 2001, 7 master's, 2 doctorates awarded.

Degree requirements: For doctorate, thesis/dissertation.

Entrance requirements: For master's and doctorate, GRE General Test, GRE Subject Test. *Application deadline:* Applications are processed on a rolling basis. *Application fee:* $50.

Expenses: Tuition: Full-time $15,528; part-time $647 per credit. Required fees: $420; $38 per term. Tuition and fees vary according to program.

Financial support: In 2001–02, 2 fellowships with full tuition reimbursements (averaging $13,680 per year), 2 research assistantships with full tuition reimbursements (averaging $11,000 per year), 4 teaching assistantships with full tuition reimbursements (averaging $11,000 per year) were awarded. Federal Work-Study and tuition waivers (partial) also available. Financial award application deadline: 1/10.

Faculty research: Adsorption, biochemical processes, chemical process stimulation

and optimization, hydrometallurgical chemical reactions. *Total annual research expenditures:* $359,507.

Dr. George Martin, Chair, 315-443-4467, *Fax:* 315-443-1243, *E-mail:* gcmartin@syr.edu.

Application contact: Dr. John Heydweiller, Information Contact, 315-443-4468, *Fax:* 315-443-1243, *E-mail:* jcheydwe@esc.syr.edu. *Web site:* http://www.ecs.syr.edu/

Find an in-depth description at www.petersons.com/gradchannel.

■ UNIVERSITY AT BUFFALO, THE STATE UNIVERSITY OF NEW YORK

Graduate School, School of Dental Medicine, Graduate Programs in Dental Medicine, Interdisciplinary Program in Biomaterials, Buffalo, NY 14260

AWARDS MS. Part-time programs available.

Faculty: 21 full-time (7 women), 61 part-time/adjunct (18 women).

Students: 5 full-time (1 woman), 2 part-time (1 woman), 5 international. Average age 26. 8 applicants, 25% accepted, 2 enrolled.

Degree requirements: For master's, thesis.

Entrance requirements: For master's, TOEFL. *Application deadline:* For fall admission, 3/1 (priority date); for spring admission, 9/1 (priority date). Applications are processed on a rolling basis. *Application fee:* $35. Electronic applications accepted.

Expenses: Tuition, state resident: full-time $6,118. Tuition, nonresident: full-time $9,434.

Financial support: In 2001–02, 6 students received support, including 6 research assistantships with full and partial tuition reimbursements available; Federal Work-Study, institutionally sponsored loans, scholarships/grants, and unspecified assistantships also available. Financial award application deadline: 2/1; financial award applicants required to submit FAFSA.

Faculty research: Bioengineering, surface science, bioadhesion, regulatory sterilization. *Total annual research expenditures:* $308,634.

Dr. Robert E. Baier, Director, 716-829-3560, *Fax:* 716-835-4872, *E-mail:* baier@acsu.buffalo.edu.

Application contact: Lois R. Karhinen, Assistant Registrar, 716-829-2839, *Fax:* 716-833-3517, *E-mail:* karhinen@acsu.buffalo.edu.

■ THE UNIVERSITY OF ALABAMA

Graduate School, and College of Engineering, and College of Arts and Sciences, Joint Materials Science PhD Program, Tuscaloosa, AL 35487

AWARDS PhD.

The University of Alabama (continued)

Students: 24 applicants, 33% accepted, 6 enrolled. In 2001, 2 degrees awarded.
Degree requirements: For doctorate, thesis/dissertation, comprehensive exam.
Entrance requirements: For doctorate, GRE General Test. *Application deadline:* For fall admission, 7/6. Applications are processed on a rolling basis. *Application fee:* $25.
Expenses: Tuition, state resident: full-time $3,292; part-time $183 per credit hour. Tuition, nonresident: full-time $8,912; part-time $495 per credit hour. Tuition and fees vary according to course load, campus/location and program.
Financial support: Research assistantships available. Financial award application deadline: 4/1.
Faculty research: Magnetic multilayers, metals casting, molecular electronics, conducting polymers, metals physics.
Dr. Chester Alexander, Campus Coordinator, 205-348-6837, *Fax:* 205-348-2346, *E-mail:* calexand@aalan.ua.edu.

■ THE UNIVERSITY OF ALABAMA AT BIRMINGHAM

Graduate School, School of Engineering, Department of Materials Science and Engineering, Joint Materials Science PhD Program, Birmingham, AL 35294

AWARDS PhD.

Students: 8 full-time (2 women); includes 1 minority (Asian American or Pacific Islander), 5 international. 36 applicants, 47% accepted. In 2001, 1 degree awarded.
Degree requirements: For doctorate, thesis/dissertation.
Entrance requirements: For doctorate, GRE General Test, minimum B average. *Application deadline:* For fall admission, 8/6. Applications are processed on a rolling basis. *Application fee:* $35 ($60 for international students). Electronic applications accepted.
Expenses: Tuition, state resident: full-time $3,058. Tuition, nonresident: full-time $5,746. Tuition and fees vary according to course load, degree level and program.
Financial support: In 2001–02, 4 fellowships with full and partial tuition reimbursements (averaging $12,500 per year), 1 research assistantship with full tuition reimbursement (averaging $12,500 per year) were awarded. Career-related internships or fieldwork, Federal Work-Study, and institutionally sponsored loans also available. Support available to part-time students. Financial award application deadline: 4/1.
Faculty research: Biocompatibility studies with biomaterials, microgravity solidification of proteins and metals, analysis of microelectronic materials, and thin film analysis using TEM.
Dr. J. Barry Andrews, Interim Chair, Department of Materials Science and Engineering, 205-934-8460, *Fax:* 205-934-8485, *E-mail:* barry@uab.edu. *Web site:* http://www.eng.uab.edu/mme/msgprogram.htm/

■ THE UNIVERSITY OF ALABAMA IN HUNTSVILLE

School of Graduate Studies, College of Science, Interdisciplinary Program in Materials Science, Huntsville, AL 35899

AWARDS MS, PhD. Part-time and evening/weekend programs available.

Faculty: 1 full-time (0 women).
Students: 15 full-time (6 women), 5 part-time (1 woman); includes 1 minority (African American), 11 international. Average age 33. 15 applicants, 73% accepted, 9 enrolled. In 2001, 1 master's, 4 doctorates awarded.
Degree requirements: For master's, thesis or alternative, comprehensive exam, registration; for doctorate, thesis/dissertation, oral and written exams, comprehensive exam, registration.
Entrance requirements: For doctorate, GRE General Test, bachelor's degree in engineering or physical science, minimum GPA of 3.0. *Application deadline:* For fall admission, 7/24 (priority date); for spring admission, 11/15 (priority date). Applications are processed on a rolling basis. *Application fee:* $35.
Expenses: Tuition, area resident: Part-time $175 per hour. Tuition, state resident: full-time $4,408. Tuition, nonresident: full-time $9,054; part-time $361 per hour.
Financial support: In 2001–02, 15 students received support, including 7 research assistantships with full and partial tuition reimbursements available (averaging $9,873 per year), 8 teaching assistantships with full and partial tuition reimbursements available (averaging $9,000 per year); fellowships with full and partial tuition reimbursements available, career-related internships or fieldwork, Federal Work-Study, institutionally sponsored loans, scholarships/grants, health care benefits, tuition waivers (full and partial), and unspecified assistantships also available. Support available to part-time students. Financial award application deadline: 4/1; financial award applicants required to submit FAFSA.
Faculty research: Materials structure and properties; materials processing; mechanical behavior; macromolecular materials; electronic, optical, and magnetic materials.
Dr. James Baird, Director, 256-824-6144, *Fax:* 256-824-6349. *Web site:* http://www.matsci.uah.edu/Materials/

■ THE UNIVERSITY OF ARIZONA

Graduate College, College of Engineering and Mines, Department of Materials Science and Engineering, Tucson, AZ 85721

AWARDS MS, PhD. Part-time programs available.

Faculty: 15 full-time (2 women), 2 part-time/adjunct (1 woman).
Students: 42 full-time (6 women), 12 part-time (3 women); includes 7 minority (5 Asian Americans or Pacific Islanders, 2 Hispanic Americans), 27 international. Average age 30. 68 applicants, 35% accepted, 15 enrolled. In 2001, 8 master's, 5 doctorates awarded.
Degree requirements: For master's, thesis (for some programs); for doctorate, thesis/dissertation, comprehensive exam.
Entrance requirements: For master's and doctorate, GRE, TOEFL. *Application deadline:* For fall admission, 5/15. Applications are processed on a rolling basis. *Application fee:* $45.
Expenses: Tuition, state resident: full-time $2,490; part-time $436 per unit. Tuition, nonresident: full-time $10,300; part-time $436 per unit. Full-time tuition and fees vary according to degree level and program.
Financial support: Fellowships with tuition reimbursements, research assistantships with tuition reimbursements, teaching assistantships with tuition reimbursements, institutionally sponsored loans and scholarships/grants available. Financial award application deadline: 12/31.
Faculty research: High-technology ceramics, optical materials, electronic materials, chemical metallurgy, science of materials.
Dr. Joseph H. Simmons, Head, 520-621-6070, *Fax:* 520-621-8059.
Application contact: Mary E Cromwell, Graduate Secretary, 520-621-6070, *Fax:* 520-621-8059, *E-mail:* msed@email.arizona.edu. *Web site:* http://www.mse.arizona.edu/

■ UNIVERSITY OF CALIFORNIA, BERKELEY

Graduate Division, College of Engineering, Department of Materials Science and Mineral Engineering, Berkeley, CA 94720-1500

AWARDS Ceramic sciences and engineering (M Eng, MS, D Eng, PhD); engineering geoscience (M Eng, MS, D Eng, PhD); materials engineering (M Eng, MS, D Eng, PhD); mineral engineering (M Eng, MS, D Eng, PhD); petroleum engineering (M Eng, MS, D Eng, PhD); physical metallurgy (M Eng, MS, D Eng, PhD).

Degree requirements: For master's, comprehensive exam or thesis (MS); for doctorate, thesis/dissertation, qualifying exam.

Entrance requirements: For master's and doctorate, GRE General Test, minimum GPA of 3.0.

Expenses: Tuition, nonresident: full-time $10,704. Required fees: $4,349.

■ UNIVERSITY OF CALIFORNIA, DAVIS

Graduate Studies, College of Engineering, Program in Chemical Engineering and Materials Science, Davis, CA 95616

AWARDS Chemical engineering (MS, PhD); materials science (MS, PhD, Certificate).

Faculty: 12 full-time (3 women), 4 part-time/adjunct (1 woman).

Students: 63 full-time (22 women); includes 16 minority (11 Asian Americans or Pacific Islanders, 5 Hispanic Americans), 18 international. Average age 28. 143 applicants, 27% accepted, 13 enrolled. In 2001, 2 master's, 15 doctorates awarded. Terminal master's awarded for partial completion of doctoral program.

Degree requirements: For master's and doctorate, thesis/dissertation.

Entrance requirements: For master's, GRE General Test, minimum GPA of 3.0; for doctorate, GRE General Test, TOEFL, minimum GPA of 3.0. *Application deadline:* For fall admission, 1/15 (priority date). *Application fee:* $60. Electronic applications accepted.

Expenses: Tuition, state resident: full-time $4,831. Tuition, nonresident: full-time $15,725.

Financial support: In 2001–02, 57 students received support, including 12 fellowships with full and partial tuition reimbursements available (averaging $5,344 per year), 51 research assistantships with full and partial tuition reimbursements available (averaging $9,585 per year), 9 teaching assistantships with partial tuition reimbursements available (averaging $10,019 per year); Federal Work-Study, institutionally sponsored loans, and tuition waivers (full and partial) also available. Financial award application deadline: 1/15; financial award applicants required to submit FAFSA.

Faculty research: Transport phenomena, colloid science, catalysis, biotechnology, materials.
Subhash H. Risbud, Chair, 530-752-5132, *E-mail:* shrisbud@ucdavis.edu.

Application contact: Archietta Johnson, Graduate Administrative Assistant, 530-752-2504, *Fax:* 530-752-1031, *E-mail:* arcjohnson@ucdavis.edu. *Web site:* http://www.chms.ucdavis.edu/

■ UNIVERSITY OF CALIFORNIA, IRVINE

Office of Research and Graduate Studies, School of Engineering, Program in Materials Science and Engineering, Irvine, CA 92697

AWARDS Engineering (MS, PhD); material science (MS). Part-time programs available.

Faculty: 4.

Students: 44 full-time (12 women), 4 part-time; includes 12 minority (1 African American, 8 Asian Americans or Pacific Islanders, 3 Hispanic Americans), 18 international. 36 applicants, 72% accepted, 12 enrolled. In 2001, 7 master's, 1 doctorate awarded. Terminal master's awarded for partial completion of doctoral program.

Degree requirements: For doctorate, thesis/dissertation.

Entrance requirements: For master's, GRE General Test, minimum GPA of 3.0; for doctorate, GRE General Test. *Application deadline:* For fall and spring admission, 1/15 (priority date); for winter admission, 10/15 (priority date). Applications are processed on a rolling basis. *Application fee:* $60. Electronic applications accepted.

Expenses: Tuition, nonresident: full-time $10,704. Required fees: $8,396. Tuition and fees vary according to course load, program and student level.

Financial support: In 2001–02, fellowships with tuition reimbursements (averaging $1,250 per year), research assistantships with tuition reimbursements (averaging $1,120 per year), teaching assistantships with tuition reimbursements (averaging $1,480 per year) were awarded. Institutionally sponsored loans and tuition waivers (full and partial) also available. Financial award application deadline: 3/2; financial award applicants required to submit FAFSA.

Faculty research: Composite materials, solidification processing, sol-gel processing, microstructural characterization, deformation and damage processes in advanced materials.
Dr. Farghalli A. Mohamed, Director, 949-824-5807, *Fax:* 949-824-3440, *E-mail:* famohame@uci.edu.

Application contact: Gwen Donaldson, Admissions Assistant, 949-824-3562, *Fax:* 949-824-3440, *E-mail:* gmdonald@uci.edu. *Web site:* http://www.eng.uci.edu/

Find an in-depth description at www.petersons.com/gradchannel.

■ UNIVERSITY OF CALIFORNIA, LOS ANGELES

Graduate Division, School of Engineering and Applied Science, Department of Materials Science and Engineering, Los Angeles, CA 90095

AWARDS Ceramics engineering (MS, PhD); metallurgy (MS, PhD).

Faculty: 8 full-time, 4 part-time/adjunct.

Students: 58 full-time (14 women); includes 15 minority (1 African American, 13 Asian Americans or Pacific Islanders, 1 Hispanic American), 35 international. 81 applicants, 60% accepted, 13 enrolled. In 2001, 14 master's, 8 doctorates awarded.

Degree requirements: For master's, comprehensive exam or thesis; for doctorate, thesis/dissertation, qualifying exams.

Entrance requirements: For master's, GRE General Test, minimum GPA of 3.0; for doctorate, GRE General Test, minimum GPA of 3.25. *Application deadline:* For fall admission, 1/15; for spring admission, 12/31. *Application fee:* $60. Electronic applications accepted.

Expenses: Tuition, nonresident: full-time $10,244. Required fees: $3,609. Full-time tuition and fees vary according to program.

Financial support: In 2001–02, 25 fellowships, 55 research assistantships, 24 teaching assistantships were awarded. Federal Work-Study, institutionally sponsored loans, and tuition waivers (full and partial) also available. Financial award application deadline: 1/15; financial award applicants required to submit FAFSA.
Dr. King-Ning Tu, Chair, 310-206-4838.

Application contact: Paradee Chularee, Student Affairs Officer, 310-825-8913, *Fax:* 310-206-7353, *E-mail:* paradee@ea.ucla.edu. *Web site:* http://www.seas.ucla.edu/ms/

■ UNIVERSITY OF CALIFORNIA, SAN DIEGO

Graduate Studies and Research, Materials Science and Engineering Program, La Jolla, CA 92093

AWARDS MS, PhD.

Faculty: 10.

Students: 35 (10 women). 142 applicants, 41% accepted, 8 enrolled. In 2001, 4 master's, 2 doctorates awarded.

Degree requirements: For doctorate, thesis/dissertation.

Entrance requirements: For master's and doctorate, GRE General Test, TOEFL, minimum GPA of 3.0. *Application deadline:* For fall admission, 1/18. *Application fee:* $40. Electronic applications accepted.

Expenses: Tuition, nonresident: full-time $10,434. Required fees: $4,883.

Financial support: Fellowships, research assistantships, traineeships available. Financial award application deadline: 1/15.
Vitali Nesterenko, Director.

Application contact: Graduate Coordinator, 858-534-7715.

■ UNIVERSITY OF CALIFORNIA, SANTA BARBARA

Graduate Division, College of Engineering, Department of Materials, Santa Barbara, CA 93106

AWARDS MS, PhD.

University of California, Santa Barbara (continued)

Degree requirements: For master's and doctorate, thesis/dissertation.

Entrance requirements: For master's and doctorate, GRE General Test, TOEFL. Electronic applications accepted.

Faculty research: Electronically conducting polymer systems, growth and processing of advanced semiconductors, structure and properties of artificially structured materials–electronic packages and composites, fine structures by nonequilibrium solidification or advanced deposition techniques, sensors for intelligent control systems in materials processing. *Web site:* http://www.materials.ucsb.edu/

■ **UNIVERSITY OF CENTRAL FLORIDA**

College of Engineering and Computer Sciences, Department of Mechanical, Materials, and Aerospace Engineering, Program in Materials Science and Engineering, Orlando, FL 32816

AWARDS MSMSE, PhD.

Faculty: 19 full-time (1 woman), 5 part-time/adjunct (0 women).

Students: 28 full-time (5 women), 10 part-time (2 women); includes 9 minority (1 African American, 8 Asian Americans or Pacific Islanders, 21 international. Average age 28. 68 applicants, 75% accepted, 16 enrolled. In 2001, 8 master's, 1 doctorate awarded.

Degree requirements: For master's, thesis or alternative; for doctorate, thesis/dissertation, candidacy exam, departmental qualifying exam.

Application deadline: For fall admission, 7/15 (priority date); for spring admission, 12/1 (priority date). *Application fee:* $20. Electronic applications accepted.

Expenses: Tuition, state resident: part-time $162 per hour. Tuition, nonresident: part-time $569 per hour.

Financial support: In 2001–02, 9 fellowships (averaging $5,208 per year), 87 research assistantships (averaging $3,617 per year), 5 teaching assistantships (averaging $3,108 per year) were awarded.

Application contact: Dr. A. J. Kassab, Coordinator, 407-823-2416, *Fax:* 407-823-0208, *E-mail:* kassab@mail.ucf.edu.

Find an in-depth description at www.petersons.com/gradchannel.

■ **UNIVERSITY OF CINCINNATI**

Division of Research and Advanced Studies, College of Engineering, Department of Materials Science and Metallurgical Engineering, Program in Materials Science and Engineering, Cincinnati, OH 45221

AWARDS MS, PhD. Evening/weekend programs available.

Degree requirements: For master's, thesis optional; for doctorate, one foreign language, thesis/dissertation, oral English proficiency exam, comprehensive exam.

Entrance requirements: For master's and doctorate, GRE General Test, TOEFL, BS in related field, minimum undergraduate GPA of 3.0. *Application deadline:* For fall admission, 2/1 (priority date). *Application fee:* $40. Electronic applications accepted.

Expenses: Tuition, state resident: part-time $2,698 per quarter. Tuition, nonresident: part-time $4,977 per quarter.

Financial support: Fellowships, career-related internships or fieldwork, tuition waivers (partial), and unspecified assistantships available. Financial award application deadline: 2/1.

Faculty research: Polymer characterization, surface analysis, and adhesion; mechanical behavior of high-temperature materials; composites; electrochemistry of materials.

Application contact: Dr. F. James Boerio, Graduate Program Director, 513-556-3117, *Fax:* 513-556-2569, *E-mail:* r.j.roe@uc.edu. *Web site:* http://www.mse.uc.edu/

■ **UNIVERSITY OF CONNECTICUT**

Graduate School, School of Engineering, Field of Material Science, Storrs, CT 06269

AWARDS MS, PhD.

Faculty: 33 full-time (5 women).

Students: 55 full-time (19 women), 59 part-time (25 women); includes 6 minority (2 African Americans, 3 Asian Americans or Pacific Islanders, 1 Hispanic American), 17 international. Average age 31. 16 applicants, 56% accepted. In 2001, 34 master's, 3 doctorates awarded.

Degree requirements: For doctorate, thesis/dissertation.

Entrance requirements: For master's and doctorate, GRE General Test, GRE Subject Test. *Application deadline:* For fall admission, 6/1 (priority date); for spring admission, 11/1. Applications are processed on a rolling basis. *Application fee:* $25.

Financial support: In 2001–02, 5 fellowships, 43 research assistantships, 3 teaching assistantships were awarded. Financial award application deadline: 2/15.

Dr. Bonnie Neumann, Dean, 570-422-3491, *Fax:* 570-422-3506, *E-mail:* bneumann@po-box.esu.edu.

Application contact: Theodore Z. Kattamis, Chairperson, 860-486-4718.

■ **UNIVERSITY OF DELAWARE**

College of Engineering, Department of Materials Science and Engineering, Newark, DE 19716

AWARDS MMSE, PhD.

Faculty: 7 full-time (2 women).

Students: 48 full-time (17 women), 7 part-time (3 women); includes 5 minority (2 African Americans, 3 Asian Americans or Pacific Islanders), 29 international. Average age 28. 153 applicants, 16% accepted, 15 enrolled. In 2001, 7 master's, 2 doctorates awarded. Terminal master's awarded for partial completion of doctoral program.

Degree requirements: For master's and doctorate, thesis/dissertation.

Entrance requirements: For master's and doctorate, GRE General Test, TOEFL, letters of recommendation (3), minimum GPA of 3.2. *Application deadline:* For fall admission, 2/28 (priority date). Applications are processed on a rolling basis. *Application fee:* $50. Electronic applications accepted.

Expenses: Tuition, state resident: full-time $4,770; part-time $265 per credit. Tuition, nonresident: full-time $13,860; part-time $770 per credit. Required fees: $414.

Financial support: In 2001–02, 45 students received support, including 3 fellowships with full tuition reimbursements available (averaging $22,600 per year), 35 research assistantships with full tuition reimbursements available (averaging $16,400 per year), 7 teaching assistantships with full tuition reimbursements available (averaging $16,396 per year); career-related internships or fieldwork and Federal Work-Study also available. Support available to part-time students. Financial award application deadline: 2/28.

Faculty research: Materials chemistry; biomolecular materials, biomimetics; polymers and composites; thinfilms, surfaces and interfaces; electronic and magnetic materials. *Total annual research expenditures:* $1.1 million.

Dr. John F. Rabolt, Chairman, 302-831-2062, *Fax:* 302-831-4545, *E-mail:* matsci@udel.edu.

Application contact: Dr. Jingguang G. Chen, Professor, 302-831-2062, *Fax:* 302-831-4545, *E-mail:* matsci@udel.edu. *Web site:* http://www.udel.edu/engg/DeptsPrgms/MatSciPrgm.html

■ **UNIVERSITY OF DENVER**

Graduate Studies, Faculty of Natural Sciences, Mathematics and Engineering, Department of Engineering, Denver, CO 80208

AWARDS Computer science and engineering (MS); electrical engineering (MS); management and general engineering (MSMGEN); materials science (PhD); mechanical engineering (MS). Part-time and evening/weekend programs available.

Faculty: 13 full-time (2 women), 3 part-time/adjunct (0 women).

Students: 17 (6 women) 11 international. 50 applicants, 62% accepted. In 2001, 11 degrees awarded. Terminal master's awarded for partial completion of doctoral program.

Degree requirements: For master's, thesis (for some programs); for doctorate, thesis/dissertation.

Entrance requirements: For master's and doctorate, GRE General Test, TOEFL,

TSE. *Application deadline:* Applications are processed on a rolling basis. *Application fee:* $45.

Expenses: Tuition: Full-time $21,456.
Financial support: In 2001–02, 11 students received support, including 6 research assistantships with full and partial tuition reimbursements available (averaging $9,999 per year), 7 teaching assistantships with full and partial tuition reimbursements available (averaging $10,782 per year); fellowships with full and partial tuition reimbursements available, career-related internships or fieldwork, Federal Work-Study, institutionally sponsored loans, and scholarships/grants also available. Financial award application deadline: 3/1; financial award applicants required to submit FAFSA.
Faculty research: Microelectrics, digital signal processing, robotics, speech recognition, microwaves, aerosols, x-ray analysis, acoustic emissions. *Total annual research expenditures:* $1 million.
Dr. James C. Wilson, Chair, 303-871-2102.
Application contact: Susie Montoya, Assistant to Chair, 303-871-2102. *Web site:* http://littlebird.engr.du.edu/

■ UNIVERSITY OF FLORIDA

Graduate School, College of Engineering, Department of Materials Science and Engineering, Gainesville, FL 32611

AWARDS Ceramic science and engineering (ME, MS, PhD, Engr); materials science and engineering (ME, MS, PhD, Certificate, Engr); metallurgical and materials engineering (ME, MS, PhD, Engr); metallurgical engineering (ME, MS, PhD, Engr); polymer science and engineering (ME, MS, PhD, Engr).

Degree requirements: For master's and other advanced degree, thesis optional; for doctorate, thesis/dissertation.
Entrance requirements: For master's and doctorate, GRE General Test, TOEFL, minimum GPA of 3.0; for other advanced degree, GRE General Test. Electronic applications accepted.
Expenses: Tuition, state resident: part-time $164 per hour. Tuition, nonresident: part-time $571 per hour. Tuition and fees vary according to course level and program.
Faculty research: Polymeric materials, electronic materials, glass, biomaterials, composites. *Web site:* http://www.mse.ufl.edu/

Find an in-depth description at www.petersons.com/gradchannel.

■ UNIVERSITY OF ILLINOIS AT URBANA–CHAMPAIGN

Graduate College, College of Engineering, Department of Materials Science and Engineering, Champaign, IL 61820

AWARDS MS, PhD.

Faculty: 28 full-time, 1 part-time/adjunct.
Students: 130 full-time (34 women); includes 11 minority (1 African American, 5 Asian Americans or Pacific Islanders, 4 Hispanic Americans, 1 Native American), 71 international. 315 applicants, 14% accepted. In 2001, 14 master's, 14 doctorates awarded.
Degree requirements: For master's, thesis; for doctorate, thesis/dissertation, departmental qualifying exam.
Entrance requirements: For master's and doctorate, GRE, minimum GPA of 3.0. *Application deadline:* Applications are processed on a rolling basis. *Application fee:* $40 ($50 for international students). Electronic applications accepted.
Expenses: Tuition, state resident: part-time $3,227 per degree program. Tuition, nonresident: part-time $7,169 per degree program. Tuition and fees vary according to program.
Financial support: In 2001–02, 14 fellowships, 97 research assistantships, 7 teaching assistantships were awarded. Tuition waivers (full and partial) also available. Financial award application deadline: 2/15.
John Weaver, Head, 217-333-1440, *Fax:* 217-333-2736, *E-mail:* jh-weaver@uiuc.edu.
Application contact: Kathy Dysart, Administrative Secretary, 217-333-1440, *Fax:* 217-333-2736, *E-mail:* k-dysart@uiuc.edu. *Web site:* http://www.mse.uiuc.edu/

■ UNIVERSITY OF KENTUCKY

Graduate School, Graduate School Programs from the College of Engineering, Program in Materials Science, Lexington, KY 40506-0032

AWARDS MSMAE, PhD.

Faculty: 8 full-time (4 women).
Students: 15 full-time (8 women), 6 part-time, 13 international. 58 applicants, 26% accepted. In 2001, 2 master's, 1 doctorate awarded.
Degree requirements: For master's, thesis optional; for doctorate, thesis/dissertation, comprehensive exam.
Entrance requirements: For master's, GRE General Test, minimum undergraduate GPA of 2.5; for doctorate, GRE General Test, minimum graduate GPA of 3.0. *Application deadline:* For fall admission, 7/19. Applications are processed on a rolling basis. *Application fee:* $30 ($35 for international students).
Expenses: Tuition, state resident: full-time $4,075; part-time $213 per credit hour.

Tuition, nonresident: full-time $11,295; part-time $614 per credit hour.
Financial support: In 2001–02, 2 fellowships, 8 research assistantships, 4 teaching assistantships were awarded. Federal Work-Study and institutionally sponsored loans also available.
Faculty research: Physical and mechanical metallurgy, computational material engineering, polymers and composites, high-temperature ceramics, powder metallurgy.
Dr. Phillip Reucroft, Director of Graduate Studies, 859-257-8723, *Fax:* 859-323-1929, *E-mail:* pjreuc1@pop.uky.edu.
Application contact: Dr. Jeannine Blackwell, Associate Dean, 859-257-4905, *Fax:* 859-323-1928.

■ UNIVERSITY OF MARYLAND, COLLEGE PARK

Graduate Studies and Research, A. James Clark School of Engineering, Department of Materials and Nuclear Engineering, Materials Science and Engineering Program, College Park, MD 20742

AWARDS MS, PhD. Part-time and evening/weekend programs available.
Postbaccalaureate distance learning degree programs offered.

Students: 44 full-time (13 women), 12 part-time (5 women); includes 7 minority (5 African Americans, 1 Asian American or Pacific Islander, 1 Hispanic American), 36 international. 131 applicants, 34% accepted, 19 enrolled. In 2001, 7 master's, 11 doctorates awarded.
Degree requirements: For master's, thesis or alternative, research paper, comprehensive exam; for doctorate, variable foreign language requirement, thesis/dissertation, oral exam.
Entrance requirements: For master's and doctorate, GRE General Test, TOEFL, minimum B+ average in undergraduate course work. *Application deadline:* For fall admission, 8/1; for spring admission, 12/1. Applications are processed on a rolling basis. *Application fee:* $50 ($70 for international students). Electronic applications accepted.
Expenses: Tuition, state resident: part-time $289 per credit hour. Tuition, nonresident: part-time $448 per credit hour. One-time fee: $436 part-time. Full-time tuition and fees vary according to course load, campus/location and program.
Financial support: Fellowships, research assistantships, teaching assistantships available. Financial award applicants required to submit FAFSA.
Dr. Peter Kofinas, Head, 301-405-5221.
Application contact: Trudy Lindsey, Director, Graduate Admissions and Records, 301-405-6991, *Fax:* 301-314-9305, *E-mail:* grschool@deans.umd.edu.

■ UNIVERSITY OF MARYLAND, COLLEGE PARK

Graduate Studies and Research, A. James Clark School of Engineering, Professional Program in Engineering, College Park, MD 20742

AWARDS Aerospace engineering (M Eng); chemical engineering (M Eng); civil engineering (M Eng); electrical engineering (M Eng); fire protection engineering (M Eng); materials science and engineering (M Eng); mechanical engineering (M Eng); reliability engineering (M Eng). Systems engineering (M Eng). Part-time and evening/weekend programs available. Postbaccalaureate distance learning degree programs offered.

Faculty: 11 part-time/adjunct (0 women).
Students: 19 full-time (4 women), 144 part-time (31 women); includes 41 minority (17 African Americans, 18 Asian Americans or Pacific Islanders, 6 Hispanic Americans), 27 international. 71 applicants, 80% accepted, 50 enrolled. In 2001, 64 degrees awarded.
Application deadline: For fall admission, 8/15; for spring admission, 1/10. Applications are processed on a rolling basis. *Application fee:* $50 ($70 for international students). Electronic applications accepted.
Expenses: Tuition, state resident: part-time $289 per credit hour. Tuition, nonresident: part-time $448 per credit hour. One-time fee: $436 part-time. Full-time tuition and fees vary according to course load, campus/location and program.
Financial support: In 2001–02, 1 research assistantship with tuition reimbursement (averaging $20,655 per year), 5 teaching assistantships with tuition reimbursements (averaging $11,114 per year) were awarded. Fellowships, Federal Work-Study and scholarships/grants also available. Support available to part-time students. Financial award applicants required to submit FAFSA.
Dr. George Syrmos, Acting Director, 301-405-5256, *Fax:* 301-314-9477.
Application contact: Trudy Lindsey, Director, Graduate Admissions and Records, 301-405-6991, *Fax:* 301-314-9305, *E-mail:* grschool@deans.umd.edu.

■ UNIVERSITY OF MICHIGAN

Horace H. Rackham School of Graduate Studies, College of Engineering, Department of Materials Science and Engineering, Ann Arbor, MI 48109

AWARDS MS, PhD. Part-time programs available.

Faculty: 24 full-time (5 women).
Students: 63 full-time (13 women), 5 part-time (4 women); includes 6 minority (1 African American, 3 Asian Americans or Pacific Islanders, 2 Hispanic Americans), 31 international. Average age 26. 280 applicants, 16% accepted, 22 enrolled. In 2001, 11 master's, 10 doctorates awarded.

Degree requirements: For master's, thesis, oral defense of thesis; for doctorate, thesis/dissertation, oral defense of dissertation, written exam. *Median time to degree:* Master's–2 years full-time, 4 years part-time; doctorate–4 years full-time.
Entrance requirements: For master's, GRE General Test, TOEFL, minimum GPA of 3.0 in related field; for doctorate, GRE General Test, TOEFL, minimum GPA of 3.0 in related field, master's degree. *Application deadline:* For fall admission, 1/15. Applications are processed on a rolling basis. *Application fee:* $55. Electronic applications accepted.
Financial support: In 2001–02, 11 fellowships with full tuition reimbursements (averaging $20,202 per year), 43 research assistantships with full tuition reimbursements (averaging $20,202 per year), 6 teaching assistantships with full tuition reimbursements (averaging $12,783 per year) were awarded. Financial award application deadline: 1/15; financial award applicants required to submit FAFSA. *Total annual research expenditures:* $4 million.
John Halloran, Chair, 734-763-2445, *Fax:* 734-763-4788, *E-mail:* peterjon@engin.umich.edu.
Application contact: Renee Hilgendorf, Graduate Program Assistant, 734-763-9790, *Fax:* 734-763-4788, *E-mail:* reneeh@umich.edu. *Web site:* http://msewww.engin.umich.edu/

Find an in-depth description at www.petersons.com/gradchannel.

■ UNIVERSITY OF MINNESOTA, TWIN CITIES CAMPUS

Graduate School, Institute of Technology, Department of Chemical Engineering and Materials Science, Program in Materials Science and Engineering, Minneapolis, MN 55455-0132

AWARDS M Mat SE, MS Mat SE, PhD. Part-time programs available. Terminal master's awarded for partial completion of doctoral program.

Degree requirements: For master's and doctorate, thesis/dissertation.
Entrance requirements: For master's and doctorate, GRE General Test.
Expenses: Tuition, state resident: full-time $2,932; part-time $489 per credit. Tuition, nonresident: full-time $5,758; part-time $960 per credit. Part-time tuition and fees vary according to course load, program and reciprocity agreements.
Faculty research: Fracture micromechanics, hydrogen embrittlement, polymer physics, microelectric materials, corrosion science. *Web site:* http://www.cems.umn.edu/

■ UNIVERSITY OF NEW HAMPSHIRE

Graduate School, College of Engineering and Physical Sciences, Program in Materials Science, Durham, NH 03824

AWARDS MS, PhD.

Faculty: 9.
Students: 2 full-time (0 women). Average age 28. 6 applicants, 100% accepted, 1 enrolled.
Degree requirements: For master's, thesis or alternative.
Entrance requirements: For master's, GRE. *Application deadline:* For fall admission, 4/1 (priority date); for winter admission, 12/1. Applications are processed on a rolling basis. *Application fee:* $50. Electronic applications accepted.
Expenses: Tuition, state resident: full-time $6,300; part-time $350 per credit. Tuition, nonresident: full-time $15,720; part-time $643 per credit. Required fees: $560; $280 per term. One-time fee: $15 part-time. Tuition and fees vary according to course load.
Financial support: In 2001–02, 4 research assistantships were awarded; Federal Work-Study, scholarships/grants, and tuition waivers (full and partial) also available. Support available to part-time students. Financial award application deadline: 2/15.
Dr. Todd Gross, Coordinator, 603-862-2445. *Web site:* http://www.unh.edu/materials-science/

■ THE UNIVERSITY OF NORTH CAROLINA AT CHAPEL HILL

Graduate School, Curriculum in Applied and Materials Science, Chapel Hill, NC 27599

AWARDS Materials science (MS, PhD).

Faculty: 31 full-time.
Students: 19 full-time (10 women); includes 15 minority (2 African Americans, 13 Asian Americans or Pacific Islanders), 1 international. Average age 23. 30 applicants, 43% accepted, 6 enrolled. In 2001, 1 master's, 2 doctorates awarded. Terminal master's awarded for partial completion of doctoral program.
Degree requirements: For doctorate, thesis/dissertation. *Median time to degree:* Master's–2 years full-time; doctorate–5 years full-time.
Entrance requirements: For master's, GRE General Test, minimum GPA of 3.0; for doctorate, GRE General Test. *Application deadline:* For fall and spring admission, 4/15 (priority date); for winter admission, 10/15. Applications are processed on a rolling basis. *Application fee:* $55. Electronic applications accepted.
Expenses: Tuition, state resident: full-time $2,864. Tuition, nonresident: full-time $12,030.

Financial support: In 2001–02, 13 students received support, including 10 research assistantships with full tuition reimbursements available (averaging $18,000 per year), 5 teaching assistantships with full tuition reimbursements available (averaging $13,950 per year). Scholarships/grants, tuition waivers (full), and unspecified assistantships also available. Financial award application deadline: 3/1.
Faculty research: Scanning tunneling microscopy, magnetic resonance, carbon nanotubes, thin films, biomaterials, nanomaterials, nanotechnology, polymeric materials, electronic and optic materials, tissue engineering.
Prof. Sean Washburn, Chair, 919-962-6293, *Fax:* 919-962-3341, *E-mail:* materials_science@unc.edu.
Application contact: Elizabeth F. Craig, Coordinator, 919-962-6293, *Fax:* 919-962-3341, *E-mail:* materials_science@unc.edu. *Web site:* http://www.unc.edu/depts/appl_sci/

■ UNIVERSITY OF NORTH TEXAS

Robert B. Toulouse School of Graduate Studies, College of Arts and Sciences, Department of Materials Science, Denton, TX 76203

AWARDS MS, PhD.

Faculty: 5 full-time (1 woman), 1 part-time/adjunct (0 women).
Students: 40. In 2001, 3 master's, 1 doctorate awarded.
Degree requirements: For doctorate, thesis/dissertation.
Entrance requirements: For master's and doctorate, GRE General Test. *Application deadline:* For fall admission, 7/17. *Application fee:* $25 ($50 for international students).
Expenses: Tuition, state resident: part-time $1,861 per hour. Tuition, nonresident: part-time $319 per hour. Required fees: $88; $21 per hour.
Dr. Bruce Gnade, Chair, 940-565-3260, *Fax:* 940-565-4824, *E-mail:* gnade@unt.edu.
Application contact: Dr. Witold Brostow, Graduate Adviser, 940-565-3260, *Fax:* 940-565-4824, *E-mail:* brostow@unt.edu.

■ UNIVERSITY OF PENNSYLVANIA

School of Engineering and Applied Science, Department of Materials Science and Engineering, Philadelphia, PA 19104

AWARDS MSE, PhD, MSE/MBA. Part-time programs available. Terminal master's awarded for partial completion of doctoral program.

Degree requirements: For master's and doctorate, thesis/dissertation.
Entrance requirements: For master's and doctorate, TOEFL. Electronic applications accepted.

Faculty research: Advanced metallic, ceramic, and polymeric materials for device applications; micromechanics and structure of interfaces; thin film electronic materials; physics and chemistry of solids.
Find an in-depth description at www.petersons.com/gradchannel.

■ UNIVERSITY OF PITTSBURGH

School of Engineering, Department of Materials Science and Engineering, Pittsburgh, PA 15260

AWARDS Materials science and engineering (MSMSE, PhD); metallurgical engineering (MS Met E, PhD). Part-time and evening/weekend programs available.

Faculty: 9 full-time (1 woman).
Students: 26 full-time (8 women), 10 part-time (2 women); includes 1 minority (African American), 16 international. 80 applicants, 6% accepted, 5 enrolled. In 2001, 6 master's, 2 doctorates awarded. Terminal master's awarded for partial completion of doctoral program.
Degree requirements: For master's, thesis (for some programs); for doctorate, thesis/dissertation, final oral exams, comprehensive exam.
Entrance requirements: For master's and doctorate, TOEFL, minimum QPA of 3.0. *Application deadline:* For fall admission, 8/1 (priority date); for spring admission, 12/1 (priority date). Applications are processed on a rolling basis. *Application fee:* $40.
Financial support: In 2001–02, 24 students received support, including 21 research assistantships with full tuition reimbursements available (averaging $18,492 per year), 3 teaching assistantships with full tuition reimbursements available (averaging $17,976 per year). Scholarships/grants and tuition waivers (full and partial) also available. Financial award application deadline: 2/15. *Total annual research expenditures:* $3.5 million.
Dr. William A. Soffa, Chairman, 412-624-9720, *Fax:* 412-624-8069, *E-mail:* wsoffa@pitt.edu.
Application contact: Pradeep P. Phule, Professor and Graduate Coordinator, 412-624-9736, *Fax:* 412-624-8069, *E-mail:* ppp@pitt.edu. *Web site:* http://www.engrng.pitt.edu/~msewww/

■ UNIVERSITY OF ROCHESTER

The College, School of Engineering and Applied Sciences, Program in Materials Science, Rochester, NY 14627-0250

AWARDS MS, PhD.

Students: 17 full-time (3 women), 4 part-time (2 women); includes 2 minority (both Hispanic Americans), 12 international. 99 applicants, 16% accepted, 5 enrolled. In 2001, 3 master's, 2 doctorates awarded. Terminal master's awarded for partial completion of doctoral program.

Degree requirements: For master's, thesis optional; for doctorate, thesis/dissertation, preliminary and qualifying exams.
Entrance requirements: For master's and doctorate, GRE, TOEFL. *Application deadline:* For fall admission, 2/1. *Application fee:* $25.
Expenses: Tuition: Part-time $755 per credit hour.
Financial support: Fellowships, research assistantships, teaching assistantships, tuition waivers (full and partial) available. Financial award application deadline: 2/1.
Dr. Paul Slattery, Interim Director, 585-275-6955.

■ UNIVERSITY OF SOUTHERN CALIFORNIA

Graduate School, School of Engineering, Department of Materials Science and Engineering, Program in Materials Science, Los Angeles, CA 90089

AWARDS MS, PhD, Engr.

Degree requirements: For master's, thesis optional; for doctorate, thesis/dissertation.
Entrance requirements: For master's, doctorate, and Engr, GRE General Test.
Expenses: Tuition: Full-time $25,060; part-time $844 per unit. Required fees: $473.

■ THE UNIVERSITY OF TENNESSEE

Graduate School, College of Engineering, Department of Materials Science and Engineering, Program in Materials Science and Engineering, Knoxville, TN 37996

AWARDS MS, PhD.

Students: 31 full-time (8 women), 13 part-time (3 women); includes 1 minority (African American), 23 international. 49 applicants, 63% accepted. In 2001, 6 master's, 1 doctorate awarded.
Degree requirements: For master's, thesis or alternative; for doctorate, thesis/dissertation.
Entrance requirements: For master's and doctorate, TOEFL, minimum GPA of 2.7. *Application deadline:* For fall admission, 2/1 (priority date). Applications are processed on a rolling basis. *Application fee:* $35. Electronic applications accepted.
Expenses: Tuition, state resident: full-time $4,280; part-time $233 per hour. Tuition, nonresident: full-time $12,066; part-time $666 per hour. Tuition and fees vary according to program.
Financial support: Application deadline: 2/1.
Dr. Patrick R. Taylor, Head, Department of Materials Science and Engineering, 865-974-5336, *Fax:* 865-974-4115, *E-mail:* prtaylor@utk.edu.

■ THE UNIVERSITY OF TENNESSEE

Graduate School, College of Engineering, Department of Mechanical and Aerospace Engineering and Engineering Science, Program in Engineering Science, Knoxville, TN 37996

AWARDS Applied artificial intelligence (MS); biomedical engineering (MS, PhD); composite materials (MS, PhD); computational mechanics (MS, PhD); engineering science (MS, PhD); fluid mechanics (MS, PhD); industrial engineering (PhD); optical engineering (MS, PhD); product development and manufacturing (MS). Solid mechanics (MS, PhD). Part-time programs available.

Students: 25 full-time (5 women), 16 part-time (2 women); includes 6 minority (2 African Americans, 2 Asian Americans or Pacific Islanders, 1 Hispanic American, 1 Native American), 9 international. 20 applicants, 70% accepted. In 2001, 6 master's, 6 doctorates awarded.
Degree requirements: For master's, thesis or alternative; for doctorate, thesis/dissertation.
Entrance requirements: For master's and doctorate, TOEFL, minimum GPA of 2.7. *Application deadline:* For fall admission, 2/1 (priority date). Applications are processed on a rolling basis. *Application fee:* $35. Electronic applications accepted.
Expenses: Tuition, state resident: full-time $4,280; part-time $233 per hour. Tuition, nonresident: full-time $12,066; part-time $666 per hour. Tuition and fees vary according to program.
Financial support: Career-related internships or fieldwork, Federal Work-Study, and institutionally sponsored loans available. Financial award application deadline: 2/1; financial award applicants required to submit FAFSA.
Application contact: Dr. Majid Keyhani, Graduate Representative, 865-974-4795, *E-mail:* keyhani@utk.edu.

■ THE UNIVERSITY OF TEXAS AT ARLINGTON

Graduate School, College of Engineering, Department of Mechanical and Aerospace Engineering, Materials Science and Engineering Program, Arlington, TX 76019

AWARDS M Engr, MS, PhD. Part-time and evening/weekend programs available. Postbaccalaureate distance learning degree programs offered (minimal on-campus study).

Students: 17 full-time (3 women), 5 part-time; includes 2 minority (1 African American, 1 Asian American or Pacific Islander), 16 international. 32 applicants, 88% accepted, 5 enrolled. In 2001, 2 master's, 2 doctorates awarded. Terminal

master's awarded for partial completion of doctoral program.
Degree requirements: For master's, thesis optional; for doctorate, thesis/dissertation, comprehensive exam.
Entrance requirements: For master's, GRE General Test, TOEFL, minimum GPA of 3.0; for doctorate, GRE General Test, TOEFL, minimum GPA of 3.5. *Application deadline:* For fall admission, 6/16. Applications are processed on a rolling basis. *Application fee:* $25 ($50 for international students).
Expenses: Tuition, area resident: Full-time $2,268. Tuition, nonresident: full-time $6,264. Required fees: $839. Tuition and fees vary according to course load.
Financial support: In 2001–02, 3 fellowships (averaging $1,000 per year), 11 research assistantships (averaging $15,000 per year), 5 teaching assistantships (averaging $15,000 per year) were awarded. Financial award application deadline: 6/1; financial award applicants required to submit FAFSA.
Dr. Ronald L. Elsenbaumer, Chair, 817-272-2559, *Fax:* 817-272-2538, *E-mail:* elsenbaumer@uta.edu.
Application contact: Dr. Pranesh B. Aswath, Graduate Adviser, 817-272-7108, *Fax:* 817-272-2538, *E-mail:* aswath@uta.edu. *Web site:* http://www.mse.uta.edu/
Find an in-depth description at www.petersons.com/gradchannel.

■ THE UNIVERSITY OF TEXAS AT AUSTIN

Graduate School, College of Engineering, Program in Materials Science and Engineering, Austin, TX 78712-1111

AWARDS MSE, PhD. Part-time programs available.

Degree requirements: For master's, thesis (for some programs); for doctorate, thesis/dissertation.
Entrance requirements: For master's and doctorate, GRE General Test. Electronic applications accepted.
Expenses: Tuition, state resident: full-time $3,159. Tuition, nonresident: full-time $6,957. Tuition and fees vary according to program.
Faculty research: Ceramics and glasses, microelectronic materials and processing, metal systems, nanostructures, polymers . *Web site:* http://www.utexas.edu/academic/tmi/

■ THE UNIVERSITY OF TEXAS AT EL PASO

Graduate School, Interdisciplinary Program in Materials Science and Engineering, El Paso, TX 79968-0001

AWARDS PhD. Part-time and evening/weekend programs available.

Students: 21 (8 women); includes 9 minority (1 African American, 6 Asian Americans or Pacific Islanders, 2 Hispanic Americans) 6 international. Average age 34. In 2001, 4 degrees awarded.
Degree requirements: For doctorate, thesis/dissertation.
Entrance requirements: For doctorate, GRE General Test, TOEFL, minimum GPA of 3.2. *Application deadline:* For fall admission, 7/1 (priority date); for spring admission, 11/1 (priority date). Applications are processed on a rolling basis. *Application fee:* $15 ($65 for international students). Electronic applications accepted.
Expenses: Tuition, state resident: full-time $2,450. Tuition, nonresident: full-time $6,000.
Financial support: In 2001–02, research assistantships with partial tuition reimbursements (averaging $22,500 per year), teaching assistantships with partial tuition reimbursements (averaging $1,800 per year) were awarded. Fellowships with partial tuition reimbursements, Federal Work-Study, institutionally sponsored loans, scholarships/grants, and tuition waivers (partial) also available. Financial award application deadline: 3/15; financial award applicants required to submit FAFSA.
Dr. Lawrence E. Murr, Director, 915-747-6664, *Fax:* 915-747-6601, *E-mail:* fekberg@utep.edu.
Application contact: Dr. Charles H. Ambler, Dean of the Graduate School, 915-747-5491 Ext. 7886, *Fax:* 915-747-5788, *E-mail:* cambler@miners.utep.edu.

■ UNIVERSITY OF UTAH

Graduate School, College of Engineering, Department of Materials Science and Engineering, Salt Lake City, UT 84112-1107

AWARDS ME, MS, PhD. Part-time programs available.

Faculty: 7 full-time (0 women), 2 part-time/adjunct (0 women).
Students: 21 full-time (3 women), 11 part-time (2 women); includes 16 minority (15 Asian Americans or Pacific Islanders, 1 Native American), 4 international. Average age 30. 77 applicants, 48% accepted. In 2001, 6 master's, 5 doctorates awarded. Terminal master's awarded for partial completion of doctoral program.
Degree requirements: For master's, thesis (MS); for doctorate, thesis/dissertation, exam.
Entrance requirements: For master's and doctorate, TOEFL, minimum GPA of 3.0. *Application deadline:* For fall admission, 5/1. *Application fee:* $40 ($60 for international students).
Expenses: Tuition, state resident: part-time $320 per semester hour. Tuition, nonresident: part-time $1,135 per semester hour. Required fees: $143 per semester hour. Tuition and fees vary according to course load, degree level and program.

Financial support: In 2001–02, 20 research assistantships with full tuition reimbursements (averaging $16,000 per year) were awarded; career-related internships or fieldwork and Federal Work-Study also available. Financial award application deadline: 3/1; financial award applicants required to submit FAFSA.
Faculty research: Solid oxide fuel cells, computational nanostructures, computational polymers, biomaterials, electronic materials. *Total annual research expenditures:* $4 million.
Anil V. Virkar, Chair, 801-581-6863, *Fax:* 801-581-4816, *E-mail:* anil.virkar@m.cc.utah.edu.
Application contact: John A. Nairn, Director of Graduate Studies, 801-581-3413, *Fax:* 801-581-4816, *E-mail:* nairn@m.ee.utah.edu. *Web site:* http://www.coe.utah.edu/

■ UNIVERSITY OF VERMONT

Graduate College, College of Engineering and Mathematics, Program in Materials Science, Burlington, VT 05405

AWARDS MS, PhD.

Degree requirements: For master's, thesis or alternative; for doctorate, thesis/dissertation.
Entrance requirements: For master's and doctorate, TOEFL.
Expenses: Tuition, state resident: part-time $335 per credit. Tuition, nonresident: part-time $838 per credit.
Find an in-depth description at www.petersons.com/gradchannel.

■ UNIVERSITY OF VIRGINIA

School of Engineering and Applied Science, Department of Materials Science and Engineering, Program in Materials Science, Charlottesville, VA 22903

AWARDS MMSE, MS, PhD. Postbaccalaureate distance learning degree programs offered (no on-campus study).

Faculty: 22 full-time (1 woman).
Students: 55 full-time (14 women), 2 part-time; includes 4 minority (1 African American, 2 Asian Americans or Pacific Islanders, 1 Hispanic American), 26 international. Average age 28. 75 applicants, 45% accepted, 15 enrolled. In 2001, 11 master's, 10 doctorates awarded.
Degree requirements: For master's, comprehensive exam; for doctorate, thesis/dissertation, comprehensive exam.
Entrance requirements: For master's and doctorate, GRE General Test. *Application deadline:* For fall admission, 8/1; for spring admission, 12/1. Applications are processed on a rolling basis. *Application fee:* $40. Electronic applications accepted.
Expenses: Tuition, state resident: full-time $3,988. Tuition, nonresident: full-time $17,078. Required fees: $1,190.

Financial support: Application deadline: 2/1.
Application contact: Kathryn Thornton, Assistant Dean, 434-924-3897, *Fax:* 434-982-2214, *E-mail:* inquiry@cs.virginia.edu.

■ UNIVERSITY OF WASHINGTON

Graduate School, College of Engineering, Department of Materials Science and Engineering, Seattle, WA 98195-2120

AWARDS Inter-engineering specialization in materials science and engineering (MS); materials science and engineering (MS, PhD); materials science and engineering nanotechnology (PhD). Part-time programs available. Postbaccalaureate distance learning degree programs offered (no on-campus study).

Faculty: 15 full-time (2 women), 8 part-time/adjunct (0 women).
Students: 40 full-time (14 women), 19 part-time (13 women); includes 10 minority (2 African Americans, 6 Asian Americans or Pacific Islanders, 2 Hispanic Americans), 18 international. 54 applicants, 33% accepted, 7 enrolled. In 2001, 9 master's, 3 doctorates awarded.
Degree requirements: For master's and doctorate, thesis/dissertation, comprehensive exam, registration. *Median time to degree:* Master's–2.4 years full-time, 5.25 years part-time; doctorate–3.5 years full-time, 8 years part-time.
Entrance requirements: For master's and doctorate, GRE General Test, TOEFL, minimum GPA of 3.0. *Application deadline:* For fall admission, 1/15 (priority date); for winter admission, 9/30 (priority date); for spring admission, 12/30 (priority date). Applications are processed on a rolling basis. *Application fee:* $50. Electronic applications accepted.
Expenses: Tuition, state resident: full-time $5,539. Tuition, nonresident: full-time $14,376. Required fees: $390. Tuition and fees vary according to course load and program.
Financial support: In 2001–02, 42 students received support, including 4 fellowships with full tuition reimbursements available (averaging $8,375 per year), 24 research assistantships with full tuition reimbursements available (averaging $13,465 per year), 11 teaching assistantships with full tuition reimbursements available (averaging $13,275 per year); career-related internships or fieldwork, Federal Work-Study, institutionally sponsored loans, scholarships/grants, unspecified assistantships, and stipend supplements also available. Financial award application deadline: 1/15.
Faculty research: Processing, characterization and properties of all classes of materials, research on ceramics, composites, metals, polymers and semiconductors. *Total annual research expenditures:* $1.2 million.

Dr. Rajendra K. Bordia, Chair, 206-543-2600, *Fax:* 206-543-3100, *E-mail:* bordia@u.washington.edu.
Application contact: Lara A. Davis, Academic Counselor, 206-616-6581, *Fax:* 206-543-3100, *E-mail:* mse@u.washington.edu. *Web site:* http://depts.washington.edu/mse/

■ UNIVERSITY OF WISCONSIN–MADISON

Graduate School, College of Engineering, Materials Science Program, Madison, WI 53706-1380

AWARDS MS, PhD. Part-time programs available.

Faculty: 45 full-time (6 women).
Students: 54 full-time (12 women), 2 part-time; includes 1 minority (African American), 26 international. Average age 29. 159 applicants, 48% accepted, 17 enrolled. In 2001, 3 master's, 4 doctorates awarded.
Degree requirements: For doctorate, thesis/dissertation.
Entrance requirements: For master's and doctorate, GRE General Test. *Application deadline:* For fall admission, 7/1 (priority date); for spring admission, 11/15 (priority date). Applications are processed on a rolling basis. *Application fee:* $45. Electronic applications accepted.
Expenses: Tuition, state resident: full-time $7,361; part-time $399 per credit. Tuition, nonresident: full-time $20,499; part-time $1,282 per credit. Required fees: $34 per credit. Full-time tuition and fees vary according to course load, program, reciprocity agreements and student level.
Financial support: In 2001–02, 6 fellowships with full tuition reimbursements (averaging $20,438 per year), 41 research assistantships with full tuition reimbursements (averaging $16,350 per year), 2 teaching assistantships with tuition reimbursements were awarded. Financial award application deadline: 1/15.
Faculty research: Superconductors, electronic materials, cast metals, vapor deposition, composites, surfaces, interfaces, x-ray lithography.
John H. Booske, Acting Director, 608-263-1795, *Fax:* 608-262-8353, *E-mail:* matsciad@engr.wisc.edu.
Application contact: Diana J. Rhoads, Program Assistant 4, 608-263-1795, *Fax:* 608-262-8353, *E-mail:* matsciad@engr.wisc.edu. *Web site:* http://www.engr.wisc.edu/interd/msp/

■ VANDERBILT UNIVERSITY

School of Engineering, Interdisciplinary Graduate Program in Materials Science, Nashville, TN 37240-1001

AWARDS M Eng, MS, PhD. Part-time programs available.

Vanderbilt University (continued)
Faculty: 37 full-time (2 women), 2 part-time/adjunct (0 women).
Students: 13 full-time (2 women), 1 part-time; includes 2 minority (1 Asian American or Pacific Islander, 1 Hispanic American), 9 international. Average age 28. 38 applicants, 21% accepted, 4 enrolled. In 2001, 4 degrees awarded. Terminal master's awarded for partial completion of doctoral program.
Degree requirements: For master's and doctorate, thesis/dissertation.
Entrance requirements: For master's and doctorate, GRE General Test. *Application deadline:* For fall admission, 1/15; for spring admission, 11/1. *Application fee:* $40. Electronic applications accepted.
Expenses: Tuition: Full-time $28,350.
Financial support: In 2001–02, 2 fellowships with tuition reimbursements (averaging $9,999 per year), 10 research assistantships with tuition reimbursements (averaging $15,900 per year), 7 teaching assistantships with tuition reimbursements (averaging $12,000 per year) were awarded. Institutionally sponsored loans and tuition waivers (partial) also available. Support available to part-time students. Financial award application deadline: 1/15.
Faculty research: Nanostructure materials, materials physics, surface and interface science, materials synthesis, biomaterials.
Dr. Robert J. Bayuzick, Director, 615-322-7047, *Fax:* 615-322-3202, *E-mail:* bayuzick@vuse.vanderbilt.edu.
Application contact: Sarah M. Ross, Administrative Assistant, 615-343-6868, *Fax:* 615-322-3202, *E-mail:* sarah.m.ross@vanderbilt.edu. *Web site:* http://www.ims.vanderbilt.edu/

■ VIRGINIA POLYTECHNIC INSTITUTE AND STATE UNIVERSITY

Graduate School, College of Engineering, Department of Materials Science and Engineering, Blacksburg, VA 24061

AWARDS M Eng, MS, PhD.

Students: 41 full-time (12 women), 2 part-time; includes 3 minority (1 Asian American or Pacific Islander, 1 Hispanic American, 1 Native American), 19 international. 116 applicants, 16% accepted. In 2001, 9 master's, 8 doctorates awarded.
Degree requirements: For master's, thesis.
Entrance requirements: For master's, TOEFL. *Application deadline:* For fall admission, 12/1 (priority date). Applications are processed on a rolling basis. *Application fee:* $45. Electronic applications accepted.
Expenses: Tuition, state resident: part-time $241 per hour. Tuition, nonresident: part-time $406 per hour. Tuition and fees vary according to program.

Financial support: In 2001–02, 3 research assistantships with full tuition reimbursements (averaging $12,063 per year), 5 teaching assistantships with full tuition reimbursements (averaging $12,063 per year) were awarded. Fellowships, unspecified assistantships also available. Financial award application deadline: 4/1.
Dr. David Clark, Head, 540-231-6640.
Application contact: Admissions Office, *E-mail:* msegrad@vt.edu. *Web site:* http://www.mse.vt.edu

■ WASHINGTON STATE UNIVERSITY

Graduate School, College of Engineering and Architecture, School of Mechanical and Materials Engineering, Pullman, WA 99164

AWARDS Materials science (MS, PhD), including materials science (PhD); materials science and engineering (MS); mechanical engineering (MS, PhD).

Faculty: 34 full-time (2 women).
Students: 42 full-time (5 women), 5 part-time; includes 1 minority (Asian American or Pacific Islander), 25 international. Average age 25. In 2001, 7 master's, 8 doctorates awarded.
Degree requirements: For master's, oral exam, thesis optional; for doctorate, thesis/dissertation, oral exam.
Application deadline: For fall admission, 3/1 (priority date). Applications are processed on a rolling basis. *Application fee:* $35.
Expenses: Tuition, state resident: full-time $6,088; part-time $304 per semester. Tuition, nonresident: full-time $14,918; part-time $746 per semester. Tuition and fees vary according to program.
Financial support: In 2001–02, 14 research assistantships with full and partial tuition reimbursements, 19 teaching assistantships with full and partial tuition reimbursements were awarded. Fellowships, career-related internships or fieldwork, Federal Work-Study, institutionally sponsored loans, and teaching associateships also available. Financial award application deadline: 4/1; financial award applicants required to submit FAFSA. *Total annual research expenditures:* $1.3 million.
Dr. Belakavadi R. Ramaprian, Interim, 509-335-8654, *E-mail:* br_ramaprian@wsu.edu.
Application contact: Lanni MacKenzie, Coordinator, 509-335-2727, *Fax:* 509-335-4662, *E-mail:* gradapp@mme.wsu.edu. *Web site:* http://www.mme.wsu.edu/

■ WASHINGTON STATE UNIVERSITY

Graduate School, College of Sciences, Department of Physics, Pullman, WA 99164

AWARDS Chemical physics (PhD); material science (MS, PhD); physics (MS, PhD).

Faculty: 19 full-time (2 women), 2 part-time/adjunct (1 woman).
Students: 41 full-time (7 women), 2 part-time (1 woman), 21 international. 56 applicants, 48% accepted, 16 enrolled. In 2001, 3 master's, 7 doctorates awarded. Terminal master's awarded for partial completion of doctoral program.
Degree requirements: For master's, thesis (for some programs), oral exam; for doctorate, thesis/dissertation, oral exam, written exam.
Entrance requirements: For master's and doctorate, GRE General Test, GRE Subject Test, minimum GPA of 3.0. *Application deadline:* For fall admission, 3/1 (priority date); for spring admission, 7/1 (priority date). Applications are processed on a rolling basis. *Application fee:* $35.
Expenses: Tuition, state resident: full-time $6,088; part-time $304 per semester. Tuition, nonresident: full-time $14,918; part-time $746 per semester. Tuition and fees vary according to program.
Financial support: In 2001–02, 20 research assistantships with full and partial tuition reimbursements (averaging $17,322 per year), 19 teaching assistantships with full and partial tuition reimbursements (averaging $17,322 per year) were awarded. Fellowships, Federal Work-Study and institutionally sponsored loans also available. Financial award application deadline: 3/1; financial award applicants required to submit FAFSA.
Faculty research: Linear and nonlinear acoustics and optics, shock wave dynamics, solid-state physics, surface physics, high-pressure and semi conductor physics. *Total annual research expenditures:* $2.4 million.
Dr. Michael Miller, Chair, 509-335-9532, *E-mail:* physics@wsu.edu.
Application contact: Sabreen Yamini Dodson, Graduate Coordinator, 509-335-9532, *Fax:* 509-335-7816, *E-mail:* sabreen@wsu.edu. *Web site:* http://www.physics.wsu.edu/

■ WASHINGTON STATE UNIVERSITY

Graduate School, College of Sciences and College of Engineering and Architecture, Program in Materials Science, Pullman, WA 99164

AWARDS Materials science (PhD); materials science and engineering (MS).

Faculty: 20 full-time (3 women), 1 part-time/adjunct (0 women).
Students: 10 full-time (1 woman), 3 international. Average age 25. In 2001, 2 degrees awarded.
Degree requirements: For master's, thesis, oral exam; for doctorate, thesis/dissertation, oral exam, written exam.
Entrance requirements: For doctorate, minimum GPA of 3.0. *Application deadline:* For fall admission, 3/1 (priority date). Applications are processed on a rolling basis. *Application fee:* $35.

Expenses: Tuition, state resident: full-time $6,088; part-time $304 per semester. Tuition, nonresident: full-time $14,918; part-time $746 per semester. Tuition and fees vary according to program.
Financial support: In 2001–02, 2 research assistantships with full and partial tuition reimbursements, 1 teaching assistantship with full and partial tuition reimbursement were awarded. Fellowships, career-related internships or fieldwork, Federal Work-Study, and institutionally sponsored loans, and teaching associateships also available. Financial award application deadline: 4/1.
Faculty research: Thin films, materials characterization, mechanical properties, materials processing, electrical and optical behavior.
Dr. Grant Norton, Chair, 509-835-4520. *Web site:* http://www.wsu.edu~matscipr/

■ WASHINGTON UNIVERSITY IN ST. LOUIS

Henry Edwin Sever Graduate School of Engineering and Applied Science, Department of Chemical Engineering, St. Louis, MO 63130-4899

AWARDS Chemical engineering (MS, D Sc); environmental engineering (MS, D Sc); materials science and engineering (MS); materials science engineering (D Sc). Part-time programs available.

Faculty: 11 full-time (0 women), 2 part-time/adjunct (0 women).
Students: 34 full-time (5 women), 9 part-time (6 women), 34 international. Average age 25. 122 applicants, 19% accepted, 7 enrolled. In 2001, 3 master's, 7 doctorates awarded. Terminal master's awarded for partial completion of doctoral program.
Degree requirements: For master's, thesis optional; for doctorate, thesis/dissertation, preliminary exam, qualifying exam. *Median time to degree:* Master's–1.8 years full-time; doctorate–4.1 years full-time.
Entrance requirements: For master's and doctorate, GRE, minimum B average during final 2 years. *Application deadline:* For fall admission, 2/1 (priority date). Applications are processed on a rolling basis. *Application fee:* $20. Electronic applications accepted.
Expenses: Tuition: Full-time $26,900.
Financial support: In 2001–02, 30 research assistantships with full tuition reimbursements were awarded; fellowships with full tuition reimbursements, career-related internships or fieldwork, Federal Work-Study, and institutionally sponsored loans also available. Financial award application deadline: 2/1.
Faculty research: Reaction engineering, materials processing, catalysis, process control, air pollution control. *Total annual research expenditures:* $2.4 million.
Dr. M. P. Dudukovic, Chairman, 314-935-6021, *Fax:* 314-935-4832, *E-mail:* dudu@poly1.che.wustl.edu.

Application contact: Rose Baxter, Graduate Coordinator, 314-935-6070, *Fax:* 314-935-7211, *E-mail:* chedept@che.wustl.edu. *Web site:* http://www.che.wustl.edu/

■ WAYNE STATE UNIVERSITY

Graduate School, College of Engineering, Department of Chemical Engineering and Materials Science, Program in Materials Science and Engineering, Detroit, MI 48202

AWARDS Materials science and engineering (MS, PhD); polymer engineering (Certificate). Part-time programs available.

Students: 18. In 2001, 6 master's, 1 doctorate awarded. Terminal master's awarded for partial completion of doctoral program.
Degree requirements: For master's, thesis optional; for doctorate, thesis/dissertation.
Application deadline: For fall admission, 7/1 (priority date); for spring admission, 3/15. Applications are processed on a rolling basis. *Application fee:* $20 ($30 for international students). Electronic applications accepted.
Expenses: Tuition, state resident: full-time $3,764. Tuition and fees vary according to degree level and program.
Financial support: Fellowships, research assistantships, teaching assistantships available. Financial award application deadline: 2/15.
Faculty research: Polymer science, rheology, fatigue in metals, metal matrix composites, ceramics. *Total annual research expenditures:* $300,000.
Application contact: Rangaramanujam Kannan, Graduate Director, 313-577-3800, *Fax:* 313-577-3810, *E-mail:* rkannan@che.eng.wayne.edu.

■ WESTERN MICHIGAN UNIVERSITY

Graduate College, College of Engineering and Applied Sciences, Department of Construction Engineering, Materials Engineering and Industrial Design, Program in Materials Science and Engineering, Kalamazoo, MI 49008-5202

AWARDS MS.

Faculty: 7 full-time (1 woman).
Students: 11 full-time (1 woman), 3 part-time (2 women), 12 international. In 2001, 2 degrees awarded.
Degree requirements: For master's, thesis optional.
Entrance requirements: For master's, minimum GPA of 3.0. *Application deadline:* For fall admission, 2/15 (priority date). Applications are processed on a rolling basis. *Application fee:* $25.
Expenses: Tuition, state resident: part-time $186 per credit hour. Tuition, nonresident: part-time $442 per credit hour. Required fees: $602. One-time fee:

$132 part-time. Tuition and fees vary according to course load.
Financial support: Application deadline: 2/15.
Application contact: Admissions and Orientation, 616-387-2000, *Fax:* 616-387-2355.

■ WORCESTER POLYTECHNIC INSTITUTE

Graduate Studies, Program in Materials Science and Engineering, Worcester, MA 01609-2280

AWARDS MS, PhD, Certificate. Part-time and evening/weekend programs available.

Faculty: 7 full-time (2 women), 2 part-time/adjunct (1 woman).
Students: 15 full-time (4 women), 3 part-time (2 women), 9 international. 16 applicants, 69% accepted, 4 enrolled. In 2001, 10 master's, 2 doctorates awarded.
Degree requirements: For master's and doctorate, thesis/dissertation.
Entrance requirements: For master's and doctorate, TOEFL. *Application deadline:* For fall admission, 2/1 (priority date); for spring admission, 10/15 (priority date). Applications are processed on a rolling basis. *Application fee:* $60. Electronic applications accepted.
Expenses: Tuition: Part-time $796 per credit. Required fees: $20; $752 per credit. One-time fee: $30 full-time.
Financial support: In 2001–02, 11 students received support, including 1 fellowship (averaging $13,500 per year), 4 research assistantships with full tuition reimbursements available (averaging $17,256 per year), 3 teaching assistantships with full tuition reimbursements available (averaging $12,942 per year); career-related internships or fieldwork, institutionally sponsored loans, and scholarships/grants also available. Financial award application deadline: 2/15; financial award applicants required to submit FAFSA.
Faculty research: Physical metallurgy and ceramics, electron microscopy and x-ray diffraction analysis, polymer processing and properties, biomaterials, fracture mechanics/reliability analysis/corrosion. *Total annual research expenditures:* $138,539.
Dr. Richard D. Sisson, Director, 508-831-5335, *Fax:* 508-831-5178, *E-mail:* sisson@wpi.edu.
Application contact: Rita Shilarsky, Graduate Secretary, 508-831-5633, *Fax:* 508-831-5140, *E-mail:* rita@wpi.edu. *Web site:* http://guinness.upi.edu/~mte/

■ WRIGHT STATE UNIVERSITY

School of Graduate Studies, College of Engineering and Computer Science, Programs in Engineering, Program in Mechanical and Materials Engineering, Dayton, OH 45435

AWARDS Materials science and engineering (MSE); mechanical engineering (MSE).

Wright State University (continued)

Students: 32 full-time (1 woman), 21 part-time (3 women); includes 3 minority (1 African American, 1 Asian American or Pacific Islander, 1 Hispanic American), 22 international. Average age 29. 176 applicants, 56% accepted. In 2001, 10 degrees awarded.
Degree requirements: For master's, thesis or course option alternative.
Entrance requirements: For master's, TOEFL. *Application fee:* $25.
Expenses: Tuition, state resident: full-time $7,161; part-time $225 per quarter hour. Tuition, nonresident: full-time $12,324; part-time $385 per quarter hour. Tuition and fees vary according to course load, degree level and program.
Financial support: Fellowships, research assistantships, teaching assistantships, unspecified assistantships available. Support available to part-time students. Financial award application deadline: 3/15; financial award applicants required to submit FAFSA.
Dr. Richard J. Bethke, Chair, 937-775-5040, *Fax:* 937-775-5009, *E-mail:* richard.bethke@wright.edu.

METALLURGICAL ENGINEERING AND METALLURGY

■ COLORADO SCHOOL OF MINES

Graduate School, Department of Metallurgical and Materials Engineering, Golden, CO 80401-1887

AWARDS Materials science (MS, PhD); metallurgical and materials engineering (ME, MS, PhD). Part-time programs available.

Faculty: 25 full-time (0 women), 1 part-time/adjunct (0 women).
Students: 69 full-time (23 women), 18 part-time (4 women); includes 8 minority (4 Asian Americans or Pacific Islanders, 4 Hispanic Americans), 27 international. 96 applicants, 40% accepted, 12 enrolled. In 2001, 9 master's, 5 doctorates awarded.
Degree requirements: For master's, thesis/dissertation; for doctorate, thesis/dissertation, comprehensive exam. *Median time to degree:* Master's–2 years full-time; doctorate–4 years full-time.
Entrance requirements: For master's and doctorate, GRE General Test. *Application deadline:* For fall admission, 12/1 (priority date); for spring admission, 5/1 (priority date). Applications are processed on a rolling basis. *Application fee:* $40. Electronic applications accepted.
Expenses: Tuition, state resident: full-time $4,940; part-time $246 per credit. Tuition, nonresident: full-time $16,070; part-time $803 per credit. Required fees: $341 per semester.

Financial support: In 2001–02, 26 fellowships (averaging $4,733 per year), 103 research assistantships (averaging $3,866 per year), 43 teaching assistantships (averaging $3,467 per year) were awarded. Unspecified assistantships also available. Support available to part-time students. Financial award applicants required to submit FAFSA.
Faculty research: Phase transformations, nonferrous alloy systems, pyrometallurgy, reactive metals, engineered materials. *Total annual research expenditures:* $141,430.
Dr. John J. Moore, Head, 303-273-3770, *Fax:* 303-273-3795, *E-mail:* jjmoore@mines.edu.
Application contact: Chaz Siler, Program Assistant I, 303-273-3660, *Fax:* 303-384-2189. *Web site:* http://met.mines.edu:3872/index.html

■ GEORGIA INSTITUTE OF TECHNOLOGY

Graduate Studies and Research, College of Engineering, School of Materials Science and Engineering, Program in Metallurgy, Atlanta, GA 30332-0001

AWARDS MSMSE, PhD. Terminal master's awarded for partial completion of doctoral program.

Degree requirements: For master's, thesis optional; for doctorate, thesis/dissertation.
Entrance requirements: For master's and doctorate, GRE General Test, TOEFL. Electronic applications accepted.
Faculty research: Surface science, corrosion, fracture and fatigue, surface modification, ion implantation and plating.

■ ILLINOIS INSTITUTE OF TECHNOLOGY

Graduate College, Armour College of Engineering and Sciences, Department of Mechanical, Materials and Aerospace Engineering, Metallurgical and Materials Engineering Division, Chicago, IL 60616-3793

AWARDS MMME, MS, PhD. Part-time programs available.

Faculty: 8 full-time (1 woman), 3 part-time/adjunct (0 women).
Students: 8 full-time (1 woman), 14 part-time (1 woman); includes 4 minority (1 African American, 1 Asian American or Pacific Islander, 2 Hispanic Americans), 10 international. Average age 31. 67 applicants, 55% accepted. In 2001, 4 degrees awarded. Terminal master's awarded for partial completion of doctoral program.
Degree requirements: For master's, thesis (for some programs), comprehensive exam; for doctorate, thesis/dissertation, comprehensive exam.

Entrance requirements: For master's and doctorate, GRE General Test, TOEFL, minimum undergraduate GPA of 3.0. *Application deadline:* For fall admission, 7/1; for spring admission, 11/1. Applications are processed on a rolling basis. *Application fee:* $30. Electronic applications accepted.
Expenses: Tuition: Part-time $590 per credit hour.
Financial support: In 2001–02, 1 fellowship, 2 research assistantships, 1 teaching assistantship were awarded. Federal Work-Study, institutionally sponsored loans, scholarships/grants, and unspecified assistantships also available. Financial award application deadline: 3/1; financial award applicants required to submit FAFSA.
Faculty research: High-temperature materials, laser processing, fracture mechanics, powder metallurgy, alloy design.
Dr. John Kallend, Associate Chair, 312-567-3054, *Fax:* 312-567-8875, *E-mail:* kallend@iit.edu.
Application contact: Dr. Ali Cinar, Dean of Graduate College, 312-567-3637, *Fax:* 312-567-7517, *E-mail:* gradstu@iit.edu. *Web site:* http://www.mmae.iit.edu/

■ MASSACHUSETTS INSTITUTE OF TECHNOLOGY

School of Engineering, Department of Materials Science and Engineering, Cambridge, MA 02139-4307

AWARDS Materials engineering (Mat E); materials science and engineering (SM, PhD, Sc D); metallurgical engineering (Met E).

Faculty: 33 full-time (6 women).
Students: 179 full-time (52 women), 1 (woman) part-time; includes 21 minority (3 African Americans, 14 Asian Americans or Pacific Islanders, 4 Hispanic Americans), 77 international. Average age 23. 288 applicants, 36% accepted, 44 enrolled. In 2001, 30 master's, 29 doctorates awarded. Terminal master's awarded for partial completion of doctoral program.
Degree requirements: For master's and other advanced degree, thesis; for doctorate, thesis/dissertation, qualifying exams, comprehensive exam.
Entrance requirements: For master's and doctorate, GRE General Test, TOEFL. *Application deadline:* For fall admission, 1/15 (priority date); for spring admission, 11/1. *Application fee:* $60. Electronic applications accepted.
Expenses: Tuition: Full-time $26,960. Full-time tuition and fees vary according to program.
Financial support: In 2001–02, 173 students received support, including 42 fellowships, 138 research assistantships, 11 teaching assistantships; career-related internships or fieldwork, Federal Work-Study, institutionally sponsored loans, scholarships/grants, traineeships, health care benefits, and unspecified assistantships also available. Financial award application

deadline: 1/1; financial award applicants required to submit FAFSA.

Faculty research: Photonic band gap materials, advanced spectroscopic and diffraction techniques, rapid solidification process, high-strength polymer materials, computer modeling of structures and processing. *Total annual research expenditures:* $15.5 million.

Subra Suresh, Head, 617-253-3320, *Fax:* 617-252-1773, *E-mail:* ssuresh@mit.edu.

Application contact: Kathleen R. Farrell, Student Administrator, 617-253-3302, *E-mail:* krf@mit.edu. *Web site:* http://dmse.mit.edu/

■ MICHIGAN STATE UNIVERSITY

Graduate School, College of Engineering, Department of Chemical Engineering and Materials Science, East Lansing, MI 48824

AWARDS Chemical engineering (MS, PhD), including environmental toxicology (PhD); engineering mechanics (MS, PhD); materials science and engineering (MS, PhD); mechanics (PhD); metallurgy (MS, PhD). Part-time programs available.

Faculty: 22.

Students: 41 full-time (10 women), 5 part-time (1 woman); includes 9 minority (2 African Americans, 4 Asian Americans or Pacific Islanders, 3 Hispanic Americans), 21 international. Average age 26. 99 applicants, 14% accepted. In 2001, 8 master's, 6 doctorates awarded. Terminal master's awarded for partial completion of doctoral program.

Degree requirements: For doctorate, thesis/dissertation.

Entrance requirements: For master's, GRE, TOEFL, minimum GPA of 3.0; for doctorate, GRE, TOEFL. *Application deadline:* For fall admission, 1/15 (priority date); for spring admission, 11/1. Applications are processed on a rolling basis. *Application fee:* $30 ($40 for international students). Electronic applications accepted.

Expenses: Tuition, state resident: part-time $244 per credit hour. Tuition, nonresident: part-time $494 per credit hour. Required fees: $268 per semester. Tuition and fees vary according to course load, degree level and program.

Financial support: In 2001–02, 26 fellowships with tuition reimbursements (averaging $3,950 per year), 49 research assistantships with tuition reimbursements (averaging $14,052 per year), 19 teaching assistantships with tuition reimbursements (averaging $12,741 per year) were awarded. Financial award applicants required to submit FAFSA.

Faculty research: Agricultural bioprocessing, impact resistance of thermoplastic composite materials, durability of polymer composites. *Total annual research expenditures:* $989,316.

Dr. Martin Hawley, Interim Chair, 517-355-5135, *Fax:* 517-353-9842.

Application contact: Information Contact, 517-355-5135, *Fax:* 517-432-1105, *E-mail:* chems@egr.msu.edu. *Web site:* http://www.chems.msu.edu/

■ MICHIGAN TECHNOLOGICAL UNIVERSITY

Graduate School, College of Engineering, Department of Materials Science and Engineering, Houghton, MI 49931-1295

AWARDS MS, PhD. Part-time programs available.

Degree requirements: For master's, thesis; for doctorate, thesis/dissertation, qualifying exam.

Entrance requirements: For master's and doctorate, GRE General Test, TOEFL. Electronic applications accepted.

Faculty research: Structure/property/processing relationships, microstructural characterization, alloy design, electronic/magnetic/photonic materials, materials and manufacturing processes. *Web site:* http://www.my.mtu.edu/

Find an in-depth description at www.petersons.com/gradchannel.

■ MONTANA TECH OF THE UNIVERSITY OF MONTANA

Graduate School, Metallurgical/Mineral Processing Engineering Programs, Butte, MT 59701-8997

AWARDS MS. Part-time programs available.

Faculty: 5 full-time (0 women).

Students: 7 full-time (1 woman), 2 part-time (1 woman). 5 applicants, 60% accepted, 2 enrolled. In 2001, 5 degrees awarded.

Degree requirements: For master's, thesis optional.

Entrance requirements: For master's, GRE General Test, TOEFL, minimum GPA of 3.0. *Application deadline:* For fall admission, 4/1 (priority date); for spring admission, 10/1 (priority date). Applications are processed on a rolling basis. *Application fee:* $30.

Expenses: Tuition, state resident: full-time $3,717; part-time $196 per credit. Tuition, nonresident: full-time $11,770; part-time $324 per credit.

Financial support: In 2001–02, 6 students received support, including 1 research assistantship with partial tuition reimbursement available (averaging $8,000 per year), 5 teaching assistantships with partial tuition reimbursements available (averaging $5,100 per year); career-related internships or fieldwork, institutionally sponsored loans, and tuition waivers (full and partial) also available. Financial award application deadline: 4/1; financial award applicants required to submit FAFSA.

Faculty research: Stabilizing hazardous waste, decontamination of metals by melt refining, ultraviolet enhancement of

stabilization reactions. *Total annual research expenditures:* $68,516.

Dr. Courtney Young, Department Head, 406-496-4158, *Fax:* 406-496-4664, *E-mail:* cyoung@mtech.edu.

Application contact: Cindy Dunstan, Administrator, Graduate School, 406-496-4304, *Fax:* 406-496-4334, *E-mail:* cdunstan@mtech.edu. *Web site:* http://www.mtech.edu/

■ THE OHIO STATE UNIVERSITY

Graduate School, College of Engineering, Program in Welding Engineering, Columbus, OH 43210

AWARDS MS, PhD.

Degree requirements: For master's, thesis optional; for doctorate, thesis/dissertation.

Entrance requirements: For master's and doctorate, GRE General Test.

■ THE PENNSYLVANIA STATE UNIVERSITY UNIVERSITY PARK CAMPUS

Graduate School, College of Earth and Mineral Sciences, Department of Materials Science and Engineering, State College, University Park, PA 16802-1503

AWARDS Ceramic science (MS, PhD); fuel science (MS, PhD); metals science and engineering (MS, PhD); polymer science (MS, PhD).

Students: 106 full-time (19 women), 10 part-time (3 women). In 2001, 25 master's, 16 doctorates awarded.

Entrance requirements: For master's and doctorate, GRE. *Application deadline:* For fall admission, 7/1. *Application fee:* $45.

Expenses: Tuition, state resident: full-time $7,882; part-time $333 per credit. Tuition, nonresident: full-time $16,142; part-time $673 per credit. Required fees: $124 per semester.

Financial support: Fellowships, unspecified assistantships available. Financial award application deadline: 2/28.

Gray L. Messing, Head, 814-865-2262.

■ PURDUE UNIVERSITY

Graduate School, Schools of Engineering, School of Materials Engineering, West Lafayette, IN 47907

AWARDS Materials engineering (MS, MSE, PhD); metallurgical engineering (MS Met E). Part-time programs available.

Faculty: 11 full-time (1 woman), 4 part-time/adjunct (0 women).

Students: 25 full-time (4 women), 4 part-time (1 woman), 18 international. Average age 26. 100 applicants, 21% accepted. In 2001, 6 master's, 4 doctorates awarded.

Degree requirements: For master's, thesis (for some programs); for doctorate, thesis/dissertation.

Purdue University (continued)

Entrance requirements: For master's and doctorate, TOEFL. *Application deadline:* For fall admission, 2/1 (priority date). *Application fee:* $30. Electronic applications accepted.

Expenses: Tuition, state resident: full-time $4,164; part-time $149 per credit hour. Tuition, nonresident: full-time $13,872; part-time $458 per credit hour. Tuition and fees vary according to campus/location and program.

Financial support: In 2001–02, 31 research assistantships with full tuition reimbursements (averaging $16,500 per year) were awarded; fellowships, teaching assistantships Support available to part-time students. Financial award applicants required to submit FAFSA.

Faculty research: Electronic behavior, mechanical behavior, thermodynamics, kinetics, phase transformations. *Total annual research expenditures:* $4.5 million.
Dr. A. H. King, Head, 765-494-4100, *Fax:* 765-494-1204, *E-mail:* alexking@ecn.purdue.edu.

Application contact: Dr. K. J. Bowman, Graduate Committee Chair, 765-494-6316, *Fax:* 765-494-1204, *E-mail:* kbowman@ecn.purdue.edu. *Web site:* http://mse.www.ecn.purdue.edu/mse/

■ RENSSELAER POLYTECHNIC INSTITUTE

Graduate School, School of Engineering, Department of Materials Science and Engineering, Troy, NY 12180-3590

AWARDS Ceramics and glass science (M Eng, MS, PhD); composites (M Eng, MS, PhD); electronic materials (M Eng, MS, PhD); metallurgy (M Eng, MS, PhD); polymers (M Eng, MS, PhD). Part-time and evening/weekend programs available.

Faculty: 15 full-time (1 woman), 5 part-time/adjunct (0 women).
Students: 56 full-time (15 women), 18 part-time (5 women), 35 international. Average age 24. 287 applicants, 11% accepted, 10 enrolled. In 2001, 11 master's, 5 doctorates awarded. Terminal master's awarded for partial completion of doctoral program.
Degree requirements: For master's, thesis (for some programs); for doctorate, thesis/dissertation. *Median time to degree:* Master's–2 years full-time, 5 years part-time; doctorate–5.5 years full-time, 8 years part-time.
Entrance requirements: For master's and doctorate, GRE, TOEFL. *Application deadline:* For fall admission, 1/15 (priority date). Applications are processed on a rolling basis. *Application fee:* $45. Electronic applications accepted.
Expenses: Tuition: Full-time $26,400; part-time $1,320 per credit hour. Required fees: $1,437.

Financial support: In 2001–02, 53 students received support, including 13 fellowships with full tuition reimbursements available (averaging $22,000 per year), 29 research assistantships with full tuition reimbursements available (averaging $16,800 per year), 11 teaching assistantships with full tuition reimbursements available (averaging $16,800 per year); career-related internships or fieldwork and institutionally sponsored loans also available. Financial award application deadline: 2/1.
Faculty research: Materials processing, nanostructural materials, materials for microelectronics, composite materials, materials theory. *Total annual research expenditures:* $4.1 million.
Dr. David J. Duquette, Chair, 518-276-6373, *Fax:* 518-276-8554.
Application contact: Dr. Roger Wright, Admissions Coordinator, 518-276-6372, *Fax:* 518-276-8554, *E-mail:* fowlen@rpi.edu. *Web site:* http://www.rpi.edu/dept/materials/

Find an in-depth description at www.petersons.com/gradchannel.

■ RUTGERS, THE STATE UNIVERSITY OF NEW JERSEY, NEW BRUNSWICK

Graduate School, Program in Materials Science and Engineering, New Brunswick, NJ 08901-1281

AWARDS Physical metallurgy (MS, PhD); polymer science (MS, PhD). Part-time programs available. Terminal master's awarded for partial completion of doctoral program.

Degree requirements: For master's, thesis optional; for doctorate, thesis/dissertation.
Entrance requirements: For master's and doctorate, GRE General Test.
Faculty research: Nanostructured materials, electroactive polymers, phase transformation, polymeric properties.

■ SOUTH DAKOTA SCHOOL OF MINES AND TECHNOLOGY

Graduate Division, Division of Material Engineering and Science, Doctoral Program in Materials Engineering and Science, Rapid City, SD 57701-3995

AWARDS Chemical engineering (PhD); chemistry (PhD); civil engineering (PhD); electrical engineering (PhD); mechanical engineering (PhD); metallurgical engineering (PhD); physics (PhD). Part-time programs available.

Degree requirements: For doctorate, thesis/dissertation.
Entrance requirements: For doctorate, TOEFL, TWE, minimum graduate GPA of 3.0. Electronic applications accepted.
Faculty research: Thermophysical properties of solids, development of multiphase

materials and composites, concrete technology, electronic polymer materials.

Find an in-depth description at www.petersons.com/gradchannel.

■ SOUTH DAKOTA SCHOOL OF MINES AND TECHNOLOGY

Graduate Division, Division of Material Engineering and Science, Master's Program in Materials Engineering and Science, Rapid City, SD 57701-3995

AWARDS Chemistry (MS); metallurgical engineering (MS); physics (MS).

Entrance requirements: For master's, TOEFL, TWE. Electronic applications accepted.

■ THE UNIVERSITY OF ALABAMA

Graduate School, College of Engineering, Department of Metallurgical and Materials Engineering, Tuscaloosa, AL 35487

AWARDS MS Met E, PhD.

Faculty: 8 full-time (1 woman).
Students: 25 full-time (3 women), 5 part-time; includes 2 minority (both African Americans), 23 international. Average age 28. 13 applicants, 54% accepted, 4 enrolled. In 2001, 8 master's, 4 doctorates awarded.
Degree requirements: For master's, thesis or alternative; for doctorate, one foreign language, thesis/dissertation.
Entrance requirements: For master's, GRE General Test, minimum GPA of 3.0 in last 60 hours. *Application deadline:* For fall admission, 7/1 (priority date). Applications are processed on a rolling basis. *Application fee:* $25. Electronic applications accepted.
Expenses: Tuition, state resident: full-time $3,292; part-time $183 per credit hour. Tuition, nonresident: full-time $8,912; part-time $495 per credit hour. Tuition and fees vary according to course load, campus/location and program.
Financial support: In 2001–02, 3 fellowships, 14 research assistantships, 6 teaching assistantships were awarded. Federal Work-Study also available.
Faculty research: Metals casting and solidification, corrosion and alloy development, metal matrix composites, electronic and magnetic properties. *Total annual research expenditures:* $1.7 million.
Dr. Richard C. Bradt, Head, 205-348-1740, *Fax:* 205-348-2164, *E-mail:* rcbradt@coe.eng.ua.edu.
Application contact: Dr. Garry W. Warren, Professor, 205-348-1740, *Fax:* 205-348-2164, *E-mail:* gwarren@coe.eng.ua.edu. *Web site:* http://www.eng.ua.edu/~mtedept/

■ THE UNIVERSITY OF ALABAMA AT BIRMINGHAM

Graduate School, School of Engineering, Department of Materials Science and Engineering, Birmingham, AL 35294

AWARDS Materials engineering (MS Mt E, PhD), including materials engineering (MS Mt E), materials/metallurgical engineering (PhD); materials science (PhD); mechanical engineering (MSME, PhD). Evening/weekend programs available.

Students: 25 full-time (4 women), 3 part-time (1 woman). 161 applicants, 62% accepted. In 2001, 8 master's, 1 doctorate awarded.
Degree requirements: For master's, project/thesis.
Entrance requirements: For master's, GRE General Test, minimum B average. *Application deadline:* Applications are processed on a rolling basis. *Application fee:* $35 ($60 for international students). Electronic applications accepted.
Expenses: Tuition, state resident: full-time $3,058. Tuition, nonresident: full-time $5,746. Tuition and fees vary according to course load, degree level and program.
Financial support: In 2001–02, 15 fellowships with full and partial tuition reimbursements, 14 research assistantships with full tuition reimbursements were awarded. Career-related internships or fieldwork, Federal Work-Study, and institutionally sponsored loans also available. Support available to part-time students.
Faculty research: Corrosion, casting metallurgy, powder metallurgy, welding metallurgy, glass/ceramics.
Dr. J. Barry Andrews, Interim Chair, 205-934-8460, *Fax:* 205-934-8485, *E-mail:* barry@uab.edu. *Web site:* http://www.eng.uab.edu/mme/

■ UNIVERSITY OF CALIFORNIA, BERKELEY

Graduate Division, College of Engineering, Department of Materials Science and Mineral Engineering, Program in Physical Metallurgy, Berkeley, CA 94720-1500

AWARDS M Eng, MS, D Eng, PhD.

Degree requirements: For master's, comprehensive exam or thesis (MS); for doctorate, thesis/dissertation, qualifying exam.
Entrance requirements: For master's and doctorate, GRE General Test, minimum GPA of 3.0.
Expenses: Tuition, nonresident: full-time $10,704. Required fees: $4,349.

■ UNIVERSITY OF CALIFORNIA, LOS ANGELES

Graduate Division, School of Engineering and Applied Science, Department of Materials Science and Engineering, Program in Metallurgy, Los Angeles, CA 90095

AWARDS MS, PhD.

Degree requirements: For master's, comprehensive exam or thesis; for doctorate, thesis/dissertation, qualifying exams.
Entrance requirements: For master's, GRE General Test, minimum GPA of 3.0; for doctorate, GRE General Test, minimum GPA of 3.25. *Application deadline:* For fall admission, 1/15; for spring admission, 12/31. *Application fee:* $60. Electronic applications accepted.
Expenses: Tuition, nonresident: full-time $10,244. Required fees: $3,609. Full-time tuition and fees vary according to program.
Financial support: Fellowships, research assistantships, teaching assistantships, Federal Work-Study, institutionally sponsored loans, and tuition waivers (full and partial) available. Financial award application deadline: 1/15; financial award applicants required to submit FAFSA.
Application contact: Paradee Chularee, Student Affairs Officer, 310-825-8913, *Fax:* 310-206-7353, *E-mail:* paradee@ea.ucla.edu.

■ UNIVERSITY OF CINCINNATI

Division of Research and Advanced Studies, College of Engineering, Department of Materials Science and Metallurgical Engineering, Program in Metallurgical Engineering, Cincinnati, OH 45221

AWARDS MS, PhD. Evening/weekend programs available.

Degree requirements: For master's, thesis optional; for doctorate, one foreign language, thesis/dissertation, oral English proficiency exam, comprehensive exam.
Entrance requirements: For master's and doctorate, GRE General Test, TOEFL, BS in related field, minimum undergraduate GPA of 3.0. *Application deadline:* For fall admission, 2/1 (priority date). *Application fee:* $40. Electronic applications accepted.
Expenses: Tuition, state resident: part-time $2,698 per quarter. Tuition, nonresident: part-time $4,977 per quarter.
Financial support: Fellowships, career-related internships or fieldwork, tuition waivers (partial), and unspecified assistantships available. Financial award application deadline: 2/1.
Faculty research: Polymer characterization, surface analysis, and adhesion; high-temperature coatings and physical chemistry of materials.

Application contact: Dr. F. James Boerio, Graduate Program Director, 513-556-3117, *Fax:* 513-556-2569, *E-mail:* r.j.roe@uc.edu. *Web site:* http://www.mse.uc.edu/

■ UNIVERSITY OF CONNECTICUT

Graduate School, School of Engineering, Field of Metallurgy, Storrs, CT 06269

AWARDS MS, PhD. Terminal master's awarded for partial completion of doctoral program.

Degree requirements: For master's, thesis or alternative; for doctorate, thesis/dissertation.
Entrance requirements: For master's and doctorate, GRE General Test, GRE Subject Test.
Faculty research: Microsegregation and coarsening, fatigue crack, electron-dislocation interaction.

■ UNIVERSITY OF FLORIDA

Graduate School, College of Engineering, Department of Materials Science and Engineering, Program in Metallurgical Engineering, Gainesville, FL 32611

AWARDS ME, MS, PhD, Engr.

Degree requirements: For master's and Engr, thesis optional; for doctorate, thesis/dissertation.
Entrance requirements: For master's and doctorate, GRE General Test, TOEFL, minimum GPA of 3.0; for Engr, GRE General Test.
Expenses: Tuition, state resident: part-time $164 per hour. Tuition, nonresident: part-time $571 per hour. Tuition and fees vary according to course level and program.
Find an in-depth description at www.petersons.com/gradchannel.

■ UNIVERSITY OF IDAHO

College of Graduate Studies, College of Mines and Earth Resources, Department of Materials, Metallurgical, Mining, and Geological Engineering, Program in Metallurgy, Moscow, ID 83844-2282

AWARDS MS.

Students: 6 full-time (0 women), 9 part-time (2 women), 6 international. In 2001, 7 degrees awarded.
Entrance requirements: For master's, minimum GPA of 2.8. *Application deadline:* For fall admission, 8/1; for spring admission, 12/15. *Application fee:* $35 ($45 for international students).
Expenses: Tuition, state resident: full-time $1,613. Tuition, nonresident: full-time $3,000.
Financial support: Application deadline: 2/15.

University of Idaho (continued)
Dr. Sam Froes, Head, Department of Materials, Metallurgical, Mining, and Geological Engineering, 208-885-6769.

■ UNIVERSITY OF IDAHO

College of Graduate Studies, College of Mines and Earth Resources, Department of Materials, Metallurgical, Mining, and Geological Engineering, Program in Mining Engineering: Metallurgy, Moscow, ID 83844-2282

AWARDS PhD.

Students: 7 full-time (0 women), 3 part-time, 8 international.
Degree requirements: For doctorate, one foreign language, thesis/dissertation.
Entrance requirements: For doctorate, minimum undergraduate GPA of 2.8, 3.0 graduate. *Application deadline:* For fall admission, 8/1; for spring admission, 12/15. *Application fee:* $35 ($45 for international students).
Expenses: Tuition, state resident: full-time $1,613. Tuition, nonresident: full-time $3,000.
Financial support: Application deadline: 2/15.
Dr. Sam Froes, Head, Department of Materials, Metallurgical, Mining, and Geological Engineering, 208-885-6769.

■ UNIVERSITY OF IDAHO

College of Graduate Studies, College of Mines and Earth Resources, Department of Materials, Metallurgical, Mining, and Geological Engineering, Programs in Metallurgy, Moscow, ID 83844-2282

AWARDS MS.

Degree requirements: For master's, thesis.
Entrance requirements: For master's, minimum GPA of 2.8. *Application deadline:* For fall admission, 8/1; for spring admission, 12/15. *Application fee:* $35 ($45 for international students).
Expenses: Tuition, state resident: full-time $1,613. Tuition, nonresident: full-time $3,000.
Financial support: Career-related internships or fieldwork available. Financial award application deadline: 2/15.
Faculty research: Critical metals, mineral preparation, hydrometallurgy, trace metals.
Dr. Sam Froes, Head, Department of Materials, Metallurgical, Mining, and Geological Engineering, 208-885-6769.

■ UNIVERSITY OF IDAHO

College of Graduate Studies, College of Mines and Earth Resources, Department of Materials, Metallurgical, Mining, and Geological Engineering, Programs in Mining Engineering, Moscow, ID 83844-2282

AWARDS Metallurgical engineering (MS, PhD); mining engineering (MS, PhD).

Degree requirements: For doctorate, one foreign language, thesis/dissertation.
Entrance requirements: For master's, minimum GPA of 2.8; for doctorate, minimum undergraduate GPA of 2.8, 3.0 graduate. *Application deadline:* For fall admission, 8/1; for spring admission, 12/15. *Application fee:* $35 ($45 for international students).
Expenses: Tuition, state resident: full-time $1,613. Tuition, nonresident: full-time $3,000.
Financial support: Career-related internships or fieldwork available. Financial award application deadline: 2/15.
Dr. Sam Froes, Head, Department of Materials, Metallurgical, Mining, and Geological Engineering, 208-885-6769.

■ UNIVERSITY OF MISSOURI–ROLLA

Graduate School, School of Mines and Metallurgy, Department of Metallurgical Engineering, Rolla, MO 65409-0910

AWARDS MS, PhD. Part-time programs available.

Degree requirements: For master's and doctorate, thesis/dissertation.
Entrance requirements: For master's, GRE General Test, TOEFL, minimum GPA of 3.0 in last 4 semesters; for doctorate, GRE General Test, TOEFL. Electronic applications accepted.
Faculty research: Pyrometallurgy, electrometallurgy, material processing, advanced materials development and defect characterization.

■ UNIVERSITY OF NEVADA, RENO

Graduate School, Mackay School of Mines, Department of Metallurgical Engineering, Reno, NV 89557

AWARDS MS, PhD, Met E.

Faculty: 2.
Students: 17 full-time (4 women), 2 part-time, 13 international. Average age 31. In 2001, 1 master's, 3 doctorates awarded. Terminal master's awarded for partial completion of doctoral program.
Degree requirements: For master's, thesis; for doctorate, one foreign language, thesis/dissertation.
Entrance requirements: For master's, GRE, TOEFL, minimum GPA of 2.75; for doctorate, GRE, TOEFL, minimum

GPA of 3.0. *Application deadline:* For fall admission, 3/15 (priority date). Applications are processed on a rolling basis. *Application fee:* $40.
Expenses: Tuition, state resident: full-time $2,067; part-time $108 per credit. Tuition, nonresident: full-time $9,282; part-time $109 per credit. Required fees: $57 per semester. Tuition and fees vary according to course load.
Financial support: Research assistantships, teaching assistantships, Federal Work-Study and institutionally sponsored loans available. Financial award application deadline: 3/1.
Faculty research: Hydrometallurgy, applied surface chemistry, mineral processing, mineral bioprocessing, ceramics.
Dr. Manoranjan Misra, Graduate Program Director, 775-784-1603.

■ UNIVERSITY OF PITTSBURGH

School of Engineering, Department of Materials Science and Engineering, Pittsburgh, PA 15260

AWARDS Materials science and engineering (MSMSE, PhD); metallurgical engineering (MS Met E, PhD). Part-time and evening/weekend programs available.

Faculty: 9 full-time (1 woman).
Students: 26 full-time (8 women), 10 part-time (2 women); includes 1 minority (African American), 16 international. 80 applicants, 6% accepted, 5 enrolled. In 2001, 6 master's, 2 doctorates awarded. Terminal master's awarded for partial completion of doctoral program.
Degree requirements: For master's, thesis (for some programs); for doctorate, thesis/dissertation, final oral exams, comprehensive exam.
Entrance requirements: For master's and doctorate, TOEFL, minimum QPA of 3.0. *Application deadline:* For fall admission, 8/1 (priority date); for spring admission, 12/1 (priority date). Applications are processed on a rolling basis. *Application fee:* $40.
Financial support: In 2001–02, 24 students received support, including 21 research assistantships with full tuition reimbursements available (averaging $18,492 per year), 3 teaching assistantships with full tuition reimbursements available (averaging $17,976 per year). Scholarships/grants and tuition waivers (full and partial) also available. Financial award application deadline: 2/15. *Total annual research expenditures:* $3.5 million.
Dr. William A. Soffa, Chairman, 412-624-9720, *Fax:* 412-624-8069, *E-mail:* wsoffa@pitt.edu.
Application contact: Pradeep P. Phule, Professor and Graduate Coordinator, 412-624-9736, *Fax:* 412-624-8069, *E-mail:* ppp@pitt.edu. *Web site:* http://www.engrng.pitt.edu/~msewww/

■ THE UNIVERSITY OF TENNESSEE SPACE INSTITUTE

Graduate Programs, Program in Metallurgical Engineering, Tullahoma, TN 37388-9700

AWARDS MS, PhD. Part-time programs available.

Faculty: 2 full-time (1 woman).
Students: 3 full-time (1 woman), 1 part-time, 2 international. 1 applicant, 100% accepted, 0 enrolled. In 2001, 1 degree awarded.
Degree requirements: For doctorate, one foreign language, thesis/dissertation. *Application deadline:* Applications are processed on a rolling basis. *Application fee:* $35.
Expenses: Tuition, state resident: full-time $4,730; part-time $208 per semester hour. Tuition, nonresident: full-time $15,028; part-time $627 per semester hour. Required fees: $10 per semester hour. One-time fee: $35.
Financial support: Fellowships with full tuition reimbursements, research assistantships with full tuition reimbursements, career-related internships or fieldwork and Federal Work-Study available.
Dr. Mary Helen McCay, Degree Program Chair, 931-393-7473, *Fax:* 931-454-2271, *E-mail:* mmccay@utsi.edu.
Application contact: Dr. Alfonso Pujol, Assistant Vice President and Dean for Student Affairs, 931-393-7432, *Fax:* 931-393-7346, *E-mail:* apujol@utsi.edu.

■ THE UNIVERSITY OF TEXAS AT EL PASO

Graduate School, College of Engineering, Department of Metallurgical and Materials Engineering, El Paso, TX 79968-0001

AWARDS Metallurgical engineering (MS). Part-time and evening/weekend programs available.

Students: 11 (2 women); includes 4 minority (all Hispanic Americans) 2 international. Average age 34. 6 applicants, 100% accepted. In 2001, 4 degrees awarded.
Degree requirements: For master's, thesis.
Entrance requirements: For master's, GRE General Test, TOEFL. *Application deadline:* For fall admission, 7/1 (priority date); for spring admission, 11/1 (priority date). Applications are processed on a rolling basis. *Application fee:* $15 ($65 for international students). Electronic applications accepted.
Expenses: Tuition, state resident: full-time $2,450. Tuition, nonresident: full-time $6,000.
Financial support: In 2001–02, research assistantships with partial tuition reimbursements (averaging $21,125 per year), teaching assistantships with partial tuition reimbursements (averaging $16,900

per year) were awarded. Fellowships with partial tuition reimbursements, career-related internships or fieldwork, Federal Work-Study, institutionally sponsored loans, scholarships/grants, and tuition waivers (partial) also available. Financial award application deadline: 3/15; financial award applicants required to submit FAFSA.
Dr. Lawrence E. Murr, Chairperson, 915-747-5468, *Fax:* 915-747-8036, *E-mail:* fekberg@utep.edu.
Application contact: Dr. Charles H. Ambler, Dean of the Graduate School, 915-747-5491 Ext. 7886, *Fax:* 915-747-5788, *E-mail:* cambler@miners.utep.edu.

■ UNIVERSITY OF UTAH

Graduate School, College of Mines and Earth Sciences, Department of Metallurgical Engineering, Salt Lake City, UT 84112-1107

AWARDS ME, MS, PhD. Part-time programs available.

Faculty: 8 full-time (1 woman), 1 part-time/adjunct (0 women).
Students: 25 full-time (4 women), 10 part-time (2 women); includes 21 minority (18 Asian Americans or Pacific Islanders, 3 Hispanic Americans), 8 international. Average age 32. In 2001, 4 master's, 3 doctorates awarded. Terminal master's awarded for partial completion of doctoral program.
Degree requirements: For master's, comprehensive exam (ME), thesis (MS); for doctorate, thesis/dissertation.
Entrance requirements: For master's and doctorate, GRE General Test, TOEFL, minimum GPA of 3.0. *Application deadline:* For fall admission, 7/1; for spring admission, 9/1 (priority date). Applications are processed on a rolling basis. *Application fee:* $40 ($60 for international students). Electronic applications accepted.
Expenses: Tuition, state resident: part-time $320 per semester hour. Tuition, nonresident: part-time $1,135 per semester hour. Required fees: $143 per semester hour. Tuition and fees vary according to course load, degree level and program.
Financial support: Fellowships with full and partial tuition reimbursements, research assistantships with full and partial tuition reimbursements, teaching assistantships with full and partial tuition reimbursements, institutionally sponsored loans available. Financial award application deadline: 2/15.
Faculty research: Physical metallurgy, mathematical modeling, mineral processing, thermodynamics, solvent extraction.
Dr. R. Peter King, Chair, 801-585-3113, *Fax:* 801-581-4937, *E-mail:* rpking@mines.utah.edu.
Application contact: Karen Haynes, Administrative Assistant, 801-581-6386, *Fax:* 801-581-4937, *E-mail:* khaynes@mines.utah.edu. *Web site:* http://www.mines.utah.edu/metallurgy/

■ UNIVERSITY OF WISCONSIN–MADISON

Graduate School, College of Engineering, Department of Materials Science and Engineering, Madison, WI 53706-1380

AWARDS Metallurgical engineering (MS, PhD).

Faculty: 14 full-time (1 woman).
Students: 15 full-time (2 women), 13 international. Average age 35. 19 applicants, 16% accepted. In 2001, 4 doctorates awarded.
Degree requirements: For master's and doctorate, thesis/dissertation.
Entrance requirements: For master's and doctorate, GRE General Test. *Application deadline:* For fall admission, 7/1 (priority date); for spring admission, 11/15 (priority date). Applications are processed on a rolling basis. *Application fee:* $45. Electronic applications accepted.
Expenses: Tuition, state resident: full-time $7,361; part-time $399 per credit. Tuition, nonresident: full-time $20,499; part-time $1,282 per credit. Required fees: $34 per credit. Full-time tuition and fees vary according to course load, program, reciprocity agreements and student level.
Financial support: Fellowships with tuition reimbursements, research assistantships with tuition reimbursements, teaching assistantships with tuition reimbursements available. Financial award application deadline: 1/15.
Faculty research: Superconductors, electronic materials, cast metals, ceramics, materials characterization. *Total annual research expenditures:* $8 million.
Sindo Kou, Chair, 608-262-1821, *Fax:* 608-262-8353, *E-mail:* matsciad@engr.wisc.edu.
Application contact: Diana J. Rhoads, Program Assistant 4, 608-263-1795, *Fax:* 608-262-8353, *E-mail:* matsciad@engr.wisc.edu. *Web site:* http://www.engr.wisc.edu/mse/grad

POLYMER SCIENCE AND ENGINEERING

■ CARNEGIE MELLON UNIVERSITY

Carnegie Institute of Technology, Department of Chemical Engineering and Department of Chemistry, Program in Colloids, Polymers and Surfaces, Pittsburgh, PA 15213-3891

AWARDS MS. Part-time and evening/weekend programs available.

Entrance requirements: For master's, GRE General Test, GRE Subject Test, TOEFL.
Faculty research: Surface phenomena, polymer rheology, solubilization

Carnegie Mellon University (continued)
phenomena, colloid transport phenomena, polymer synthesis. *Web site:* http://www.cheme.cmu.edu/

■ **CARNEGIE MELLON UNIVERSITY**

Mellon College of Science, Department of Chemistry, Pittsburgh, PA 15213-3891

AWARDS Chemical instrumentation (MS); chemistry (MS, PhD); colloids, polymers and surfaces (MS); polymer science (MS). Part-time programs available. Terminal master's awarded for partial completion of doctoral program.

Degree requirements: For doctorate, thesis/dissertation, departmental qualifying and oral exams, teaching experience.
Entrance requirements: For master's, GRE General Test; for doctorate, GRE General Test, GRE Subject Test, TOEFL. Electronic applications accepted.
Faculty research: Physical and theoretical chemistry, chemical synthesis, biophysical/bioinorganic chemistry. *Web site:* http://www.chem.cmu.edu/grad/

Find an in-depth description at www.petersons.com/gradchannel.

■ **CASE WESTERN RESERVE UNIVERSITY**

School of Graduate Studies, The Case School of Engineering, Department of Macromolecular Science and Engineering, Cleveland, OH 44106

AWARDS Macromolecular science (MS, PhD). Part-time programs available.

Faculty: 12 full-time (2 women), 8 part-time/adjunct (0 women).
Students: 51 full-time (17 women), 16 part-time (4 women); includes 6 minority (1 African American, 4 Asian Americans or Pacific Islanders, 1 Hispanic American), 47 international. Average age 24. 162 applicants, 9% accepted, 11 enrolled. In 2001, 6 master's, 6 doctorates awarded. Terminal master's awarded for partial completion of doctoral program.
Degree requirements: For master's, thesis; for doctorate, thesis/dissertation, qualifying exam, teaching experience.
Entrance requirements: For master's and doctorate, GRE General Test, TOEFL. *Application deadline:* For fall admission, 2/28 (priority date); for spring admission, 10/1 (priority date). Applications are processed on a rolling basis. *Application fee:* $25.
Financial support: In 2001–02, 14 fellowships with full tuition reimbursements (averaging $16,200 per year), 30 research assistantships with full and partial tuition reimbursements (averaging $16,200 per year) were awarded. Financial award applicants required to submit FAFSA.

Faculty research: Polymer synthesis; imaging of polymer materials; polymer rheology and polymer processing. Structure-property relationships; biomaterials. *Total annual research expenditures:* $3.3 million.
Dr. Alexander M. Jamieson, Chairman, 216-368-4172, *Fax:* 216-368-4202, *E-mail:* amj@po.cwru.edu.
Application contact: Diane Shedroff, Secretary, 216-368-4166, *Fax:* 216-368-4202, *E-mail:* dxs12@po.cwru.edu. *Web site:* http://www.scl.cwru.edu/cse/emac/

Find an in-depth description at www.petersons.com/gradchannel.

■ **CLEMSON UNIVERSITY**

Graduate School, College of Engineering and Science, Department of Textiles, Fiber and Polymer Science, Clemson, SC 29634

AWARDS MS, PhD. Part-time programs available.

Students: 30 full-time (11 women), 2 part-time, 27 international. 72 applicants, 49% accepted, 8 enrolled. In 2001, 5 master's, 1 doctorate awarded.
Degree requirements: For doctorate, thesis/dissertation.
Entrance requirements: For master's and doctorate, GRE General Test, TOEFL. *Application fee:* $40.
Expenses: Tuition, state resident: full-time $5,310. Tuition, nonresident: full-time $11,284.
Financial support: Fellowships, research assistantships, teaching assistantships, career-related internships or fieldwork, institutionally sponsored loans, and unspecified assistantships available. Financial award applicants required to submit FAFSA.
Dr. D. V. Rippy, Director, 864-656-3176, *Fax:* 864-656-5973, *E-mail:* rippyd@clemson.edu. *Web site:* http://www.eng.clemson.edu/textiles/Textiles.html

■ **CORNELL UNIVERSITY**

Graduate School, Graduate Fields of Engineering, Field of Chemical Engineering, Ithaca, NY 14853-0001

AWARDS Advanced materials processing (M Eng, MS, PhD); applied mathematics and computational methods (M Eng, MS, PhD); biochemical engineering (M Eng, MS, PhD); chemical reaction engineering (M Eng, MS, PhD); classical and statistical thermodynamics (M Eng, MS, PhD); fluid dynamics, rheology and biorheology (M Eng, MS, PhD); heat and mass transfer (M Eng, MS, PhD); kinetics and catalysis (M Eng, MS, PhD); polymers (M Eng, MS, PhD). Surface science (M Eng, MS, PhD).

Faculty: 18 full-time.
Students: 81 full-time (20 women); includes 12 minority (9 Asian Americans or Pacific Islanders, 3 Hispanic Americans), 44 international. 151

applicants, 50% accepted. In 2001, 17 master's, 6 doctorates awarded.
Degree requirements: For master's, thesis (MS); for doctorate, thesis/dissertation.
Entrance requirements: For master's and doctorate, GRE General Test, TOEFL, pre-application, 2 letters of recommendation. *Application deadline:* For fall admission, 1/15. *Application fee:* $65. Electronic applications accepted.
Expenses: Tuition: Full-time $25,970. Required fees: $50.
Financial support: In 2001–02, 64 students received support, including 19 fellowships with full tuition reimbursements available, 33 research assistantships with full tuition reimbursements available, 12 teaching assistantships with full tuition reimbursements available; institutionally sponsored loans, scholarships/grants, tuition waivers (full and partial), and unspecified assistantships also available. Financial award applicants required to submit FAFSA.
Faculty research: Biochemical and biomedical engineering, fluid dynamics, stability and rheology, surface science, kinetics and reactor design, electronics materials design and processing, polymer science and engineering.
Application contact: Graduate Field Assistant, 607-255-4550, *E-mail:* dgs@cheme.cornell.edu. *Web site:* http://www.gradschool.cornell.edu/grad/fields_1/chem-engr.html

■ **CORNELL UNIVERSITY**

Graduate School, Graduate Fields of Human Ecology, Field of Textiles, Ithaca, NY 14853-0001

AWARDS Apparel design (MA, MPS); fiber science (MS, PhD); polymer science (MS, PhD); textile science (MS, PhD).

Faculty: 12 full-time.
Students: 13 full-time (7 women), 12 international. 29 applicants, 34% accepted. In 2001, 4 degrees awarded.
Degree requirements: For master's, thesis (MA, MS), project paper (MPS); for doctorate, thesis/dissertation.
Entrance requirements: For master's, GRE General Test, TOEFL, 2 letters of recommendation, portfolio (functional apparel design); for doctorate, GRE General Test, TOEFL, 2 letters of recommendation. *Application deadline:* For fall admission, 3/1. *Application fee:* $65. Electronic applications accepted.
Expenses: Tuition: Full-time $25,970. Required fees: $50.
Financial support: In 2001–02, 12 students received support, including 2 fellowships with full tuition reimbursements available, 2 research assistantships with full tuition reimbursements available, 8 teaching assistantships with full tuition reimbursements available; institutionally sponsored loans, scholarships/grants, tuition waivers (full and partial), and

unspecified assistantships also available. Financial award applicants required to submit FAFSA.

Faculty research: High performance fibers and composites. Surface chemistry of fibers; geosynthetics; mechanics of fibrous assemblies/ biopolymers; biological tissue engineering, detergency, protective clothing.

Application contact: Graduate Field Assistant, 607-255-8065, *E-mail:* textiles_grad@cornell.edu. *Web site:* http://www.gradschool.cornell.edu/grad/fields_1/textiles.html

■ DEPAUL UNIVERSITY

College of Liberal Arts and Sciences, Department of Chemistry, Chicago, IL 60604-2287

AWARDS Biochemistry (MS); chemistry (MS); polymer chemistry and coating (MS). Part-time and evening/weekend programs available.

Faculty: 10 full-time (3 women), 4 part-time/adjunct (2 women).
Students: 6 full-time (3 women), 13 part-time (6 women); includes 3 minority (2 African Americans, 1 Hispanic American), 2 international. Average age 30. 12 applicants, 75% accepted. In 2001, 10 degrees awarded.
Degree requirements: For master's, thesis (for some programs), oral exam for selected programs. *Median time to degree:* Master's–2 years full-time, 3 years part-time.
Entrance requirements: For master's, BS in chemistry or equivalent. *Application deadline:* Applications are processed on a rolling basis. *Application fee:* $35. Electronic applications accepted.
Expenses: Tuition: Part-time $362 per credit hour. Tuition and fees vary according to program.
Financial support: In 2001–02, 6 teaching assistantships with tuition reimbursements (averaging $6,000 per year) were awarded. Financial award application deadline: 4/1.
Faculty research: Polymers, DNA sequencing, computational chemistry, water pollution, diffusion kinetics. *Total annual research expenditures:* $80,000.
Dr. Wendy S. Wolbach, Chair, 773-325-7420, *Fax:* 773-325-7421, *E-mail:* wwolbach@condor.depaul.edu.
Application contact: Marion Blackmon, Director of Graduate Admissions, 773-362-8880, *Fax:* 773-325-7311, *E-mail:* mblackmo@wppost.depaul.edu. *Web site:* http://www.depaul.edu/~alchemy/

■ EASTERN MICHIGAN UNIVERSITY

Graduate School, College of Technology, Department of Interdisciplinary Technology, Program in Polymer Technology, Ypsilanti, MI 48197

AWARDS MS.

Degree requirements: For master's, thesis optional.
Entrance requirements: For master's, GRE General Test, TOEFL, BS in chemistry, minimum GPA of 2.6. *Application deadline:* For fall admission, 5/15; for spring admission, 3/15. Applications are processed on a rolling basis. *Application fee:* $30.
Expenses: Tuition, state resident: part-time $285 per credit hour. Tuition, nonresident: part-time $510 per credit hour.
Financial support: Fellowships, teaching assistantships available. Support available to part-time students. Financial award application deadline: 3/15; financial award applicants required to submit FAFSA.
Dr. Jamil Baghdaci, Coordinator, 734-487-1235.

■ GEORGIA INSTITUTE OF TECHNOLOGY

Graduate Studies and Research, College of Engineering, Multidisciplinary Program in Polymers, Atlanta, GA 30332-0001

AWARDS MS Poly.

Degree requirements: For master's, thesis.
Entrance requirements: For master's, TOEFL, minimum GPA of 2.7.

■ LEHIGH UNIVERSITY

P.C. Rossin College of Engineering and Applied Science and College of Arts and Sciences, Center for Polymer Science and Engineering, Bethlehem, PA 18015-3094

AWARDS MS, PhD. Programs are interdisciplinary. Part-time and evening/weekend programs available. Postbaccalaureate distance learning degree programs offered (no on-campus study).

Faculty: 24 full-time (2 women).
Students: 20 full-time (7 women), 25 part-time (11 women); includes 20 minority (19 Asian Americans or Pacific Islanders, 1 Hispanic American). Average age 30. In 2001, 5 master's, 3 doctorates awarded. Terminal master's awarded for partial completion of doctoral program.
Degree requirements: For master's, thesis (for some programs), registration; for doctorate, thesis/dissertation, registration.
Entrance requirements: For master's and doctorate, GRE General Test, TOEFL. *Application deadline:* For fall admission, 7/15; for spring admission, 12/1. Applications are processed on a rolling basis. *Application fee:* $40.
Expenses: Tuition: Part-time $468 per credit hour. Required fees: $200; $100 per semester. Tuition and fees vary according to program.

Financial support: Fellowships, research assistantships, teaching assistantships available. Financial award application deadline: 1/15.
Faculty research: Polymer colloids, polymer coatings, blends and composites, polymer interfaces, emulsion polymer. *Total annual research expenditures:* $3 million.
Dr. Raymond A. Pearson, Director, 610-758-3857, *Fax:* 610-758-3526, *E-mail:* rp02@lehigh.edu.
Application contact: James E. Roberts, Chair, Polymer Education Committee, 610-758-4841, *Fax:* 610-758-6536, *E-mail:* jer1@lehigh.edu. *Web site:* http://www.lehighedu/nesd0/cpse/OCPSEHOM.htm

Find an in-depth description at www.petersons.com/gradchannel.

■ NORTH DAKOTA STATE UNIVERSITY

The Graduate School, College of Science and Mathematics, Department of Polymers and Coatings, Fargo, ND 58105

AWARDS MS, PhD. Part-time programs available. Terminal master's awarded for partial completion of doctoral program.

Degree requirements: For master's, thesis/dissertation, cumulative exams; for doctorate, thesis/dissertation, cumulative exams, comprehensive exam.
Entrance requirements: For master's, GRE General Test, TOEFL, BS in chemistry or chemical engineering; for doctorate, GRE Subject Test, TOEFL, BS in chemistry or chemical engineering.
Expenses: Tuition, state resident: part-time $124 per credit. Tuition, nonresident: part-time $325 per credit. Required fees: $22 per credit. Tuition and fees vary according to reciprocity agreements.
Faculty research: Spectroscopy of adhesion and interfaces, corrosion and electrochemistry, polymer synthesis, organic/inorganic coatings, carbohydrate polymers. *Web site:* http://www.ndsu.nodak.edu/ndsu/nupply/poly_coat/poly_coa.html

■ THE PENNSYLVANIA STATE UNIVERSITY UNIVERSITY PARK CAMPUS

Graduate School, College of Earth and Mineral Sciences, Department of Materials Science and Engineering, State College, PA 16802-1503

AWARDS Ceramic science (MS, PhD); fuel science (MS, PhD); metals science and engineering (MS, PhD); polymer science (MS, PhD).

Students: 106 full-time (19 women), 10 part-time (3 women). In 2001, 25 master's, 16 doctorates awarded.

The Pennsylvania State University University Park Campus (continued)

Entrance requirements: For master's and doctorate, GRE. *Application deadline:* For fall admission, 7/1. *Application fee:* $45.
Expenses: Tuition, state resident: full-time $7,882; part-time $333 per credit. Tuition, nonresident: full-time $16,142; part-time $673 per credit. Required fees: $124 per semester.
Financial support: Fellowships, unspecified assistantships available. Financial award application deadline: 2/28.
Gray L. Messing, Head, 814-865-2262.

■ POLYTECHNIC UNIVERSITY, BROOKLYN CAMPUS

Department of Chemical Engineering, Chemistry and Materials Science, Major in Polymer Science and Engineering, Brooklyn, NY 11201-2990
AWARDS MS.

Electronic applications accepted.

■ PRINCETON UNIVERSITY

Graduate School, Department of Chemistry and Department of Chemical Engineering, Program in Polymer Sciences and Materials, Princeton, NJ 08544-1019

AWARDS MSE, PhD.

Degree requirements: For master's, one foreign language, thesis; for doctorate, one foreign language, thesis/dissertation, cumulative and general exams.
Entrance requirements: For master's, GRE General Test; for doctorate, GRE General Test, GRE Subject Test.

■ PRINCETON UNIVERSITY

Graduate School, School of Engineering and Applied Science, Department of Chemical Engineering, Princeton, NJ 08544-1019

AWARDS Applied and computational mathematics (PhD); chemical engineering (M Eng, MSE, PhD); plasma science and technology (MSE, PhD); polymer sciences and materials (MSE, PhD).

Degree requirements: For master's, thesis; for doctorate, thesis/dissertation, general exam.
Entrance requirements: For master's and doctorate, GRE General Test, GRE Subject Test, TOEFL.

■ RENSSELAER POLYTECHNIC INSTITUTE

Graduate School, School of Engineering, Department of Materials Science and Engineering, Troy, NY 12180-3590

AWARDS Ceramics and glass science (M Eng, MS, PhD); composites (M Eng, MS, PhD);

electronic materials (M Eng, MS, PhD); metallurgy (M Eng, MS, PhD); polymers (M Eng, MS, PhD). Part-time and evening/weekend programs available.

Faculty: 15 full-time (1 woman), 5 part-time/adjunct (0 women).
Students: 56 full-time (15 women), 18 part-time (5 women), 35 international. Average age 24. 287 applicants, 11% accepted, 10 enrolled. In 2001, 11 master's, 5 doctorates awarded. Terminal master's awarded for partial completion of doctoral program.
Degree requirements: For master's, thesis (for some programs); for doctorate, thesis/dissertation. *Median time to degree:* Master's–2 years full-time, 5 years part-time; doctorate–5.5 years full-time, 8 years part-time.
Entrance requirements: For master's and doctorate, GRE, TOEFL. *Application deadline:* For fall admission, 1/15 (priority date). Applications are processed on a rolling basis. *Application fee:* $45. Electronic applications accepted.
Expenses: Tuition: Full-time $26,400; part-time $1,320 per credit hour. Required fees: $1,437.
Financial support: In 2001–02, 53 students received support, including 13 fellowships with full tuition reimbursements available (averaging $22,000 per year), 29 research assistantships with full tuition reimbursements available (averaging $16,800 per year), 11 teaching assistantships with full tuition reimbursements available (averaging $16,800 per year); career-related internships or fieldwork and institutionally sponsored loans also available. Financial award application deadline: 2/1.
Faculty research: Materials processing, nanostructural materials, materials for microelectronics, composite materials, materials theory. *Total annual research expenditures:* $4.1 million.
Dr. David J. Duquette, Chair, 518-276-6373, *Fax:* 518-276-8554.
Application contact: Dr. Roger Wright, Admissions Coordinator, 518-276-6372, *Fax:* 518-276-8554, *E-mail:* fowlen@rpi.edu. *Web site:* http://www.rpi.edu/dept/materials/

Find an in-depth description at www.petersons.com/gradchannel.

■ RUTGERS, THE STATE UNIVERSITY OF NEW JERSEY, NEW BRUNSWICK

Graduate School, Program in Materials Science and Engineering, New Brunswick, NJ 08901-1281

AWARDS Physical metallurgy (MS, PhD); polymer science (MS, PhD). Part-time programs available. Terminal master's awarded for partial completion of doctoral program.

Degree requirements: For master's, thesis optional; for doctorate, thesis/dissertation.
Entrance requirements: For master's and doctorate, GRE General Test.
Faculty research: Nanostructured materials, electroactive polymers, phase transformation, polymeric properties.

■ SAN JOSE STATE UNIVERSITY

Graduate Studies, College of Science, Department of Chemistry, San Jose, CA 95192-0001

AWARDS Analytical chemistry (MS); biochemistry (MS); chemistry (MA); inorganic chemistry (MS); organic chemistry (MS); physical chemistry (MS); polymer chemistry (MS); radiochemistry (MS). Part-time and evening/weekend programs available.

Faculty: 24 full-time (3 women), 5 part-time/adjunct (2 women).
Students: 3 full-time (2 women), 11 part-time (7 women); includes 3 Asian Americans or Pacific Islanders, 1 Hispanic American, 4 international. Average age 33. 24 applicants, 50% accepted. In 2001, 5 degrees awarded.
Degree requirements: For master's, thesis or alternative.
Entrance requirements: For master's, GRE, minimum B average. *Application deadline:* For fall admission, 6/29; for spring admission, 11/30. Applications are processed on a rolling basis. *Application fee:* $59. Electronic applications accepted.
Expenses: Tuition, nonresident: part-time $246 per unit. Required fees: $678 per semester. Tuition and fees vary according to course load.
Financial support: In 2001–02, 8 teaching assistantships were awarded; career-related internships or fieldwork, Federal Work-Study, and institutionally sponsored loans also available. Support available to part-time students. Financial award application deadline: 6/5; financial award applicants required to submit FAFSA.
Faculty research: Intercalated compounds, organic/biochemical reaction mechanisms, complexing agents in biochemistry, DNA repair, metabolic inhibitors.
Dr. Pamela Stacks, Chair, 408-924-5000, *Fax:* 408-924-4945.
Application contact: Dr. Roger Biringer, Graduate Adviser, 408-924-4961.

■ THE UNIVERSITY OF AKRON

Graduate School, College of Engineering, Program in Engineering (Polymer Specialization), Akron, OH 44325-0001

AWARDS MS.

Students: 2 full-time (0 women), 1 part-time; includes 1 minority (African American), 1 international. Average age 32. 1 applicant, 100% accepted, 1 enrolled.
Degree requirements: For master's, thesis.

Application fee: $40 ($50 for international students).

Expenses: Tuition, state resident: full-time $6,562; part-time $219 per credit. Tuition, nonresident: full-time $9,027; part-time $383 per credit. Required fees: $272; $11 per credit. Tuition and fees vary according to course load.

Dr. Subramaniya Hariharan, Head, 330-972-6580.

■ THE UNIVERSITY OF AKRON

Graduate School, College of Polymer Science and Polymer Engineering, Department of Polymer Engineering, Akron, OH 44325-0001

AWARDS MS, PhD. Part-time and evening/weekend programs available.

Faculty: 10 full-time (1 woman), 6 part-time/adjunct (0 women).
Students: 99 full-time (20 women), 4 part-time; includes 1 minority (Hispanic American), 96 international. Average age 29. 75 applicants, 84% accepted, 36 enrolled. In 2001, 14 master's, 19 doctorates awarded.
Degree requirements: For master's, thesis; for doctorate, one foreign language, thesis/dissertation, candidacy exam.
Entrance requirements: For master's, TOEFL, bachelor's degree in engineering or physical science, minimum GPA of 2.75; for doctorate, TOEFL. *Application deadline:* For fall admission, 8/15. Applications are processed on a rolling basis. *Application fee:* $40 ($50 for international students).
Expenses: Tuition, state resident: full-time $6,562; part-time $219 per credit. Tuition, nonresident: full-time $9,027; part-time $383 per credit. Required fees: $272; $11 per credit. Tuition and fees vary according to course load.
Financial support: In 2001–02, 84 research assistantships with full tuition reimbursements were awarded; fellowships with full tuition reimbursements, teaching assistantships with full tuition reimbursements, tuition waivers (full) and unspecified assistantships also available.
Faculty research: Experimental numerical simulation of polymer processing, high-performance engineering plastics rheology, polymer blends.
Dr. Lloyd Goettler, Chair, 330-972-7467.

■ THE UNIVERSITY OF AKRON

Graduate School, College of Polymer Science and Polymer Engineering, Department of Polymer Science, Akron, OH 44325-0001

AWARDS MS, PhD. Part-time and evening/weekend programs available.

Faculty: 19 full-time (1 woman), 3 part-time/adjunct (1 woman).
Students: 97 full-time (23 women), 20 part-time (7 women); includes 5 minority (2 African Americans, 3 Asian Americans

or Pacific Islanders), 61 international. Average age 29. 93 applicants, 39% accepted, 25 enrolled. In 2001, 6 master's, 21 doctorates awarded. Terminal master's awarded for partial completion of doctoral program.
Degree requirements: For master's, thesis; for doctorate, one foreign language, thesis/dissertation, cumulative exam, seminars.
Entrance requirements: For master's, TOEFL, minimum GPA of 2.75; for doctorate, TOEFL. *Application deadline:* For fall admission, 4/1. Applications are processed on a rolling basis. *Application fee:* $40 ($50 for international students).
Expenses: Tuition, state resident: full-time $6,562; part-time $219 per credit. Tuition, nonresident: full-time $9,027; part-time $383 per credit. Required fees: $272; $11 per credit. Tuition and fees vary according to course load.
Financial support: In 2001–02, 105 students received support, including 1 fellowship with full tuition reimbursement available, 89 research assistantships with full tuition reimbursements available; teaching assistantships with full tuition reimbursements available, scholarships/grants, tuition waivers (full), and research contracts also available. Financial award application deadline: 3/30.
Faculty research: Synthesis of polymers, structure of polymers, physical properties of polymers, engineering and technological properties of polymers, elastomers.
Dr. Stephen Cheng, Chair, 330-972-5147.

■ UNIVERSITY OF CINCINNATI

Division of Research and Advanced Studies, College of Engineering, Department of Materials Science and Metallurgical Engineering, Cincinnati, OH 45221

AWARDS Ceramic science and engineering (MS, PhD); materials science and engineering (MS, PhD); metallurgical engineering (MS, PhD); polymer science and engineering (MS, PhD). Evening/weekend programs available.

Degree requirements: For master's, thesis optional; for doctorate, one foreign language, thesis/dissertation, oral English proficiency exam, comprehensive exam.
Entrance requirements: For master's and doctorate, GRE General Test, TOEFL, BS in related field, minimum undergraduate GPA of 3.0. *Application deadline:* For fall admission, 2/1 (priority date). Applications are processed on a rolling basis. *Application fee:* $40. Electronic applications accepted.
Expenses: Contact institution.
Financial support: Fellowships, research assistantships, teaching assistantships, career-related internships or fieldwork, tuition waivers (partial), and unspecified assistantships available. Financial award application deadline: 2/1. *Total annual research expenditures:* $1.6 million.

Dr. Narayanan Jayaraman, Head, 513-556-3112, *Fax:* 513-556-2569, *E-mail:* narayanan.jayaraman@uc.edu.
Application contact: Dr. F. James Boerio, Director of Graduate Studies, 513-556-3111, *Fax:* 513-556-2569, *E-mail:* f.james.boerio@uc.edu. *Web site:* http://www.mse.uc.edu/

■ UNIVERSITY OF CONNECTICUT

Graduate School, School of Engineering, Field of Material Science, Polymer Program, Storrs, CT 06269

AWARDS Chemical engineering (MS, PhD); chemistry (MS, PhD); polymer science (MS, PhD). Part-time programs available.

Faculty: 14 full-time (1 woman), 6 part-time/adjunct (0 women).
Students: 46 full-time (7 women), 3 part-time; includes 2 minority (both Asian Americans or Pacific Islanders), 40 international. Average age 27. 95 applicants, 17% accepted, 11 enrolled. In 2001, 2 master's, 6 doctorates awarded. Terminal master's awarded for partial completion of doctoral program.
Degree requirements: For master's, one foreign language, thesis (for some programs); for doctorate, one foreign language, thesis/dissertation. *Median time to degree:* Master's–2.75 years full-time; doctorate–5 years full-time.
Entrance requirements: For master's, GRE, TOEFL; for doctorate, GRE General Test, TOEFL. *Application deadline:* For fall admission, 4/1 (priority date); for spring admission, 11/1 (priority date). Applications are processed on a rolling basis. *Application fee:* $40 ($45 for international students). Electronic applications accepted.
Financial support: In 2001–02, 43 research assistantships with tuition reimbursements (averaging $21,480 per year) were awarded; fellowships with tuition reimbursements, career-related internships or fieldwork, scholarships/grants, health care benefits, and unspecified assistantships also available. Financial award application deadline: 4/1.
Faculty research: Spectroscopy, photonics, rheology, processing polymer blends. *Total annual research expenditures:* $2.8 million.
Chong S. Sung, Director, 860-486-4630, *Fax:* 860-486-4745, *E-mail:* csung@uconnvm.uconn.edu.
Application contact: Barbara E. Garton, Graduate Coordinator, 860-486-4613, *Fax:* 860-486-4745, *E-mail:* grad@mail.ims.uconn.edu. *Web site:* http://www.ims.uconn.edu/polymer/index.htm

Find an in-depth description at www.petersons.com/gradchannel.

■ UNIVERSITY OF DETROIT MERCY

College of Engineering and Science, Department of Chemical Engineering, Detroit, MI 48219-0900

AWARDS Chemical engineering (ME, DE); polymer engineering (ME). Evening/weekend programs available.

Faculty: 4 full-time (0 women).
Students: 1 full-time (0 women), 18 part-time (1 woman); includes 2 minority (both Asian Americans or Pacific Islanders), 13 international. Average age 28. In 2001, 6 degrees awarded.
Degree requirements: For doctorate, thesis/dissertation.
Application deadline: For fall admission, 8/1 (priority date). Applications are processed on a rolling basis. *Application fee:* $25 ($35 for international students).
Expenses: Tuition: Full-time $10,620; part-time $590 per credit hour. Required fees: $400. Tuition and fees vary according to program.
Financial support: Career-related internships or fieldwork available.
Dr. Geoffrey Prentice, Chairman, 313-993-1187.

■ UNIVERSITY OF FLORIDA

Graduate School, College of Engineering, Department of Materials Science and Engineering, Program in Polymer Science and Engineering, Gainesville, FL 32611

AWARDS ME, MS, PhD, Engr.

Degree requirements: For master's and Engr, thesis optional; for doctorate, thesis/dissertation.
Entrance requirements: For master's and doctorate, GRE General Test, TOEFL, minimum GPA of 3.0; for Engr, GRE General Test.
Expenses: Tuition, state resident: part-time $164 per hour. Tuition, nonresident: part-time $571 per hour. Tuition and fees vary according to course level and program.
Find an in-depth description at www.petersons.com/gradchannel.

■ UNIVERSITY OF MASSACHUSETTS AMHERST

Graduate School, College of Natural Sciences and Mathematics, Department of Polymer Science and Engineering, Amherst, MA 01003

AWARDS MS, PhD. Part-time programs available.

Faculty: 14 full-time (0 women).
Students: 86 full-time (27 women), 9 part-time (5 women); includes 7 minority (2 African Americans, 5 Asian Americans or Pacific Islanders), 39 international. Average age 26. 192 applicants, 18% accepted. In 2001, 6 master's, 9 doctorates awarded.

Terminal master's awarded for partial completion of doctoral program.
Degree requirements: For doctorate, one foreign language, thesis/dissertation.
Entrance requirements: For master's and doctorate, GRE General Test. *Application deadline:* For fall admission, 2/1 (priority date). Applications are processed on a rolling basis. *Application fee:* $40 ($50 for international students).
Expenses: Tuition, state resident: full-time $1,980; part-time $110 per credit. Tuition, nonresident: full-time $7,456; part-time $414 per credit. Required fees: $4,112. One-time fee: $115 full-time.
Financial support: In 2001–02, 8 fellowships with full tuition reimbursements (averaging $14,875 per year), 78 research assistantships with full tuition reimbursements (averaging $14,261 per year), teaching assistantships with full tuition reimbursements (averaging $1,427 per year) were awarded. Career-related internships or fieldwork, Federal Work-Study, scholarships/grants, traineeships, and unspecified assistantships also available. Support available to part-time students. Financial award application deadline: 2/1.
Dr. Thomas McCarthy, Head, 413-577-1127, *Fax:* 413-545-0082, *E-mail:* tmccarthy@polysci.umass.edu.

Find an in-depth description at www.petersons.com/gradchannel.

■ UNIVERSITY OF MASSACHUSETTS LOWELL

Graduate School, College of Arts and Sciences, Department of Chemistry, Program in Polymer Sciences, Lowell, MA 01854-2881

AWARDS MS, PhD. Terminal master's awarded for partial completion of doctoral program.

Degree requirements: For master's, thesis; for doctorate, 2 foreign languages, thesis/dissertation.
Entrance requirements: For master's and doctorate, GRE General Test. Electronic applications accepted.

■ UNIVERSITY OF MASSACHUSETTS LOWELL

Graduate School, James B. Francis College of Engineering, Department of Plastics Engineering, Lowell, MA 01854-2881

AWARDS Chemistry (PhD), including polymer science/plastics engineering; plastics engineering (MS Eng, D Eng), including coatings and adhesives (MS Eng), composites (MS Eng), plastics processing (MS Eng), product design (MS Eng). Part-time programs available. Terminal master's awarded for partial completion of doctoral program.

Degree requirements: For master's, thesis; for doctorate, 2 foreign languages, thesis/dissertation.

Entrance requirements: For master's and doctorate, GRE General Test.

■ UNIVERSITY OF MICHIGAN

Horace H. Rackham School of Graduate Studies, College of Engineering, Program in Plastics Engineering, Ann Arbor, MI 48109

AWARDS M Eng.

Application deadline: For fall admission, 7/1; for winter admission, 9/30.
Application contact: Henia Kamil, Administrative Assistant, 734-763-0480, *Fax:* 734-647-0079, *E-mail:* plastics@engin.umich.edu.

■ UNIVERSITY OF MISSOURI–KANSAS CITY

College of Arts and Sciences, Department of Chemistry, Kansas City, MO 64110-2499

AWARDS Analytical chemistry (MS, PhD); inorganic chemistry (MS, PhD); organic chemistry (MS, PhD); physical chemistry (MS, PhD); polymer chemistry (MS, PhD). PhD offered through the School of Graduate Studies. Part-time and evening/weekend programs available.

Faculty: 11 full-time (1 woman), 1 part-time/adjunct (0 women).
Students: 3 full-time (1 woman), 4 part-time (1 woman); includes 1 minority (Hispanic American), 2 international. Average age 30. 56 applicants, 46% accepted. In 2001, 3 degrees awarded.
Degree requirements: For master's, thesis (for some programs); for doctorate, thesis/dissertation.
Entrance requirements: For master's, TOEFL, equivalent of American Chemical Society approved bachelor's degree in chemistry; for doctorate, GRE General Test, TWE, equivalent of American Chemical Society approved bachelor's degree in chemistry. *Application deadline:* For fall and spring admission, 4/15 (priority date); for winter admission, 10/15 (priority date). Applications are processed on a rolling basis. *Application fee:* $25.
Expenses: Tuition, state resident: part-time $233 per credit hour. Tuition, nonresident: part-time $623 per credit hour. Tuition and fees vary according to course load.
Financial support: In 2001–02, fellowships with partial tuition reimbursements (averaging $11,000 per year), 4 research assistantships with partial tuition reimbursements (averaging $14,340 per year), 15 teaching assistantships with partial tuition reimbursements (averaging $14,340 per year) were awarded. Federal Work-Study, institutionally sponsored loans, and scholarships/grants also available. Support available to part-time students. Financial award application deadline: 2/15.

Faculty research: Molecular spectroscopy, characterization and synthesis of materials and compounds, computational chemistry. *Total annual research expenditures:* $306,800. Dr. Jerry Jean, Chairperson, 816-235-2280, *Fax:* 816-235-5502, *E-mail:* jeany@umkc.edu.

Application contact: Dr. Kathleen Y. Kilway, Graduate Recruiting Committee, 816-235-2289, *Fax:* 816-235-5502, *E-mail:* kilwayk@umkc.edu. *Web site:* http://www.umkc.edu/chem/

Find an in-depth description at www.petersons.com/gradchannel.

■ UNIVERSITY OF SOUTHERN MISSISSIPPI

Graduate School, College of Science and Technology, Department of Polymer Science, Hattiesburg, MS 39406

AWARDS MS, PhD.

Faculty: 13 full-time (0 women), 1 part-time/adjunct (0 women).
Students: 61 full-time (11 women), 4 part-time (1 woman); includes 7 minority (1 African American, 6 Asian Americans or Pacific Islanders). Average age 26. 88 applicants, 19% accepted. In 2001, 1 master's, 15 doctorates awarded.
Degree requirements: For master's, thesis; for doctorate, 2 foreign languages, thesis/dissertation, original proposal, comprehensive exam.
Entrance requirements: For master's, GRE General Test, TOEFL, minimum GPA of 2.75; for doctorate, GRE General Test, TOEFL, minimum GPA of 3.0. *Application deadline:* For fall admission, 8/6 (priority date). Applications are processed on a rolling basis. *Application fee:* $0 ($25 for international students).
Expenses: Tuition, state resident: full-time $3,416; part-time $190 per credit hour. Tuition, nonresident: full-time $7,932; part-time $441 per credit hour.
Financial support: Fellowships, research assistantships, teaching assistantships available. Financial award application deadline: 3/15.
Faculty research: Water-soluble polymers; polymer composites; coatings. Solid-state, laser-initiated polymerization.
Dr. Douglas Wicks, Chair, 601-266-4868.

■ THE UNIVERSITY OF TENNESSEE

Graduate School, College of Engineering, Department of Materials Science and Engineering, Program in Polymer Engineering, Knoxville, TN 37996

AWARDS MS, PhD.

Students: 11 full-time (5 women), 10 part-time (5 women); includes 3 minority (all African Americans), 10 international. 73 applicants, 33% accepted. In 2001, 6 master's, 1 doctorate awarded.
Degree requirements: For master's, thesis or alternative; for doctorate, thesis/dissertation.
Entrance requirements: For master's and doctorate, TOEFL, minimum GPA of 2.7. *Application deadline:* For fall admission, 2/1 (priority date). Applications are processed on a rolling basis. *Application fee:* $35. Electronic applications accepted.
Expenses: Tuition, state resident: full-time $4,280; part-time $233 per hour. Tuition, nonresident: full-time $12,066; part-time $666 per hour. Tuition and fees vary according to program.
Financial support: Application deadline: 2/1.
Dr. Patrick R. Taylor, Head, Department of Materials Science and Engineering, 865-974-5336, *Fax:* 865-974-4115, *E-mail:* prtaylor@utk.edu.

■ UNIVERSITY OF WISCONSIN–MADISON

Graduate School, College of Engineering, Department of Mechanical Engineering, Madison, WI 53706-1380

AWARDS Mechanical engineering (MS, PhD); polymers (ME). Part-time programs available. Postbaccalaureate distance learning degree programs offered (no on-campus study).

Faculty: 33 full-time (3 women).
Students: 142 full-time (8 women), 21 part-time. Average age 23. 335 applicants, 22% accepted, 31 enrolled. In 2001, 35 master's, 22 doctorates awarded. Terminal master's awarded for partial completion of doctoral program.
Degree requirements: For master's, thesis optional; for doctorate, thesis/dissertation, qualifying exam, preliminary exam.
Entrance requirements: For master's, GRE, TOEFL, BS in mechanical engineering or related field, minimum GPA of 3.0 in last 60 hours; for doctorate, GRE, TOEFL, BS in mechanical engineering or related field, minimum undergraduate GPA of 3.0 in last 60 hours. *Application deadline:* Applications are processed on a rolling basis. *Application fee:* $45. Electronic applications accepted.
Expenses: Tuition, state resident: full-time $7,361; part-time $399 per credit. Tuition, nonresident: full-time $20,499; part-time $1,282 per credit. Required fees: $34 per credit. Full-time tuition and fees vary according to course load, program, reciprocity agreements and student level.

Financial support: In 2001–02, 5 fellowships with tuition reimbursements (averaging $17,940 per year), 94 research assistantships with tuition reimbursements (averaging $16,350 per year), 20 teaching assistantships with tuition reimbursements (averaging $6,593 per year) were awarded. Institutionally sponsored loans and scholarships/grants also available.
Faculty research: Dynamics, vibrations and acoustics, mechatronics, robotics and automation, design and manufacturing, materials processing, solar energy, combustion, fluids. *Total annual research expenditures:* $10.3 million.
Neil A. Duffie, Chair, 608-262-9457, *Fax:* 608-265-2316, *E-mail:* duffie@engr.wisc.edu.

Application contact: Linda S. Aaberg, Student Status Examiner, 608-262-0666, *Fax:* 608-265-2316, *E-mail:* aaberg@engr.wisc.edu. *Web site:* http://www.engr.wisc.edu/me/

Find an in-depth description at www.petersons.com/gradchannel.

■ WAYNE STATE UNIVERSITY

Graduate School, College of Engineering, Department of Chemical Engineering and Materials Science, Program in Materials Science and Engineering, Detroit, MI 48202

AWARDS Materials science and engineering (MS, PhD); polymer engineering (Certificate). Part-time programs available.

Students: 18. In 2001, 6 master's, 1 doctorate awarded. Terminal master's awarded for partial completion of doctoral program.
Degree requirements: For master's, thesis optional; for doctorate, thesis/dissertation.
Application deadline: For fall admission, 7/1 (priority date); for spring admission, 3/15. Applications are processed on a rolling basis. *Application fee:* $20 ($30 for international students). Electronic applications accepted.
Expenses: Tuition, state resident: full-time $3,764. Tuition and fees vary according to degree level and program.
Financial support: Fellowships, research assistantships, teaching assistantships available. Financial award application deadline: 2/15.
Faculty research: Polymer science, rheology, fatigue in metals, metal matrix composites, ceramics. *Total annual research expenditures:* $300,000.
Application contact: Rangaramanujam Kannan, Graduate Director, 313-577-3800, *Fax:* 313-577-3810, *E-mail:* rkannan@che.eng.wayne.edu.

Mechanical Engineering and Mechanics

MECHANICAL ENGINEERING

■ ALFRED UNIVERSITY

Graduate School, Program in Mechanical Engineering, Alfred, NY 14802-1205

AWARDS MS. Part-time programs available.

Students: 3 full-time (2 women). 16 applicants, 44% accepted.
Degree requirements: For master's, thesis.
Entrance requirements: For master's, TOEFL. *Application deadline:* Applications are processed on a rolling basis. *Application fee:* $50. Electronic applications accepted.
Expenses: Tuition: Full-time $23,554. Required fees: $698. One-time fee: $116 part-time. Full-time tuition and fees vary according to program.
Financial support: Research assistantships, tuition waivers (full and partial) and unspecified assistantships available. Financial award applicants required to submit FAFSA.
Dr. William F. Hahn, Chair, 602-871-2100, *E-mail:* fhahn@alfred.edu.
Application contact: Cathleen R. Johnson, Coordinator of Graduate Admissions, 607-871-2141, *Fax:* 607-871-2198, *E-mail:* johnsonc@alfred.edu. *Web site:* http://www.alfred.edu/

■ ARIZONA STATE UNIVERSITY

Graduate College, College of Engineering and Applied Sciences, Department of Mechanical and Aerospace Engineering, Tempe, AZ 85287

AWARDS Aerospace engineering (MS, MSE, PhD); engineering science (MS, MSE, PhD); mechanical engineering (MS, MSE, PhD).

Degree requirements: For master's, thesis or alternative; for doctorate, thesis/dissertation.
Entrance requirements: For master's and doctorate, GRE General Test.
Faculty research: Aerodynamics, fluid mechanics, propulsion and space power, advanced structures and materials, robotics and automation.

■ AUBURN UNIVERSITY

Graduate School, College of Engineering, Department of Mechanical Engineering, Auburn University, AL 36849

AWARDS Materials engineering (M Mtl E, MS, PhD); mechanical engineering (MME, MS, PhD). Part-time programs available.

Faculty: 23 full-time (0 women).
Students: 38 full-time (8 women), 56 part-time (10 women); includes 3 African Americans, 1 Asian American or Pacific Islander, 55 international. 93 applicants, 52% accepted. In 2001, 12 master's, 8 doctorates awarded.
Degree requirements: For master's, thesis (for some programs); for doctorate, one foreign language, thesis/dissertation.
Entrance requirements: For master's and doctorate, GRE General Test. *Application deadline:* For fall admission, 7/7; for spring admission, 11/24. Applications are processed on a rolling basis. *Application fee:* $25 ($50 for international students).
Financial support: Fellowships, research assistantships, teaching assistantships, Federal Work-Study available. Support available to part-time students. Financial award application deadline: 3/15.
Faculty research: Engineering mechanics, experimental mechanics, engineering design, engineering acoustics, engineering optics.
Dr. David Dyer, Chair, 334-844-4820.
Application contact: Dr. John F. Pritchett, Dean of the Graduate School, 334-844-4700, *E-mail:* hatchlb@mail.auburn.edu. *Web site:* http://www.eng.auburn.edu/department/me/

■ BOISE STATE UNIVERSITY

Graduate College, College of Engineering, Program in Mechanical Engineering, Boise, ID 83725-0399

AWARDS MS. Part-time and evening/weekend programs available.

Degree requirements: For master's, thesis.
Entrance requirements: For master's, GRE General Test, TOEFL, minimum GPA of 3.0. Electronic applications accepted.

■ BOSTON UNIVERSITY

College of Engineering, Department of Aerospace and Mechanical Engineering, Boston, MA 02215

AWARDS Aerospace engineering (MS, PhD); mechanical engineering (MS, PhD). Part-time programs available.

Faculty: 24 full-time (1 woman), 6 part-time/adjunct (0 women).
Students: 47 full-time (7 women), 6 part-time (1 woman), 31 international. Average age 27. 223 applicants, 17% accepted, 14 enrolled. In 2001, 9 master's, 4 doctorates awarded. Terminal master's awarded for partial completion of doctoral program.
Degree requirements: For master's, thesis optional; for doctorate, thesis/dissertation, comprehensive exam.

Entrance requirements: For master's and doctorate, GRE General Test, TOEFL. *Application deadline:* For fall admission, 4/1; for spring admission, 10/1. Applications are processed on a rolling basis. *Application fee:* $60. Electronic applications accepted.
Expenses: Tuition: Full-time $25,872; part-time $340 per credit. Required fees: $40 per semester. Part-time tuition and fees vary according to class time, course level and program.
Financial support: In 2001–02, 43 students received support, including 3 fellowships with full tuition reimbursements available (averaging $15,500 per year), 21 research assistantships with full tuition reimbursements available (averaging $13,500 per year), 12 teaching assistantships with full tuition reimbursements available (averaging $13,500 per year); career-related internships or fieldwork, Federal Work-Study, institutionally sponsored loans, and scholarships/grants also available. Financial award application deadline: 1/15; financial award applicants required to submit FAFSA.
Faculty research: Acoustics and vibrations, fluid mechanics, MEMS, nanotechnology, robotics. *Total annual research expenditures:* $2.1 million.
Dr. John Baillieul, Chairman, 617-353-9848, *Fax:* 617-353-5548.
Application contact: Cheryl Kelley, Director of Graduate Programs, 617-353-9760, *Fax:* 617-353-0259, *E-mail:* enggrad@bu.edu. *Web site:* http://www.bu.edu/eng/grad/

Find an in-depth description at www.petersons.com/gradchannel.

■ BRADLEY UNIVERSITY

Graduate School, College of Engineering and Technology, Department of Mechanical Engineering, Peoria, IL 61625-0002

AWARDS MSME. Part-time and evening/weekend programs available.

Students: 13 full-time, 34 part-time. 140 applicants, 81% accepted. In 2001, 27 degrees awarded.
Degree requirements: For master's, thesis optional.
Entrance requirements: For master's, TOEFL, minimum GPA of 3.0. *Application deadline:* For fall admission, 7/1 (priority date); for spring admission, 11/1. Applications are processed on a rolling basis. *Application fee:* $40 ($50 for international students).
Expenses: Tuition: Part-time $7,615 per semester. Tuition and fees vary according to course load.
Financial support: In 2001–02, 7 research assistantships with full and partial tuition

reimbursements were awarded; teaching assistantships, scholarships/grants and tuition waivers (partial) also available. Support available to part-time students. Financial award application deadline: 3/1.
Faculty research: Ground-coupled heat pumps, robotic end-effectors, power plant optimization.
Dr. Paul Mehta, Chairperson, 309-677-2754.

■ BRIGHAM YOUNG UNIVERSITY

Graduate Studies, College of Engineering and Technology, Department of Mechanical Engineering, Provo, UT 84602-1001
AWARDS MS, PhD, MBA/MS.

Faculty: 23 full-time (0 women).
Students: 44 full-time (2 women), 48 part-time (3 women). Average age 25. 42 applicants, 71% accepted. In 2001, 32 master's awarded.
Degree requirements: For doctorate, 2 foreign languages, thesis/dissertation. *Median time to degree:* Master's–2 years full-time, 3 years part-time; doctorate–3 years full-time, 5 years part-time.
Entrance requirements: For master's, GRE General Test, minimum GPA of 3.0 in last 60 hours; for doctorate, GRE General Test. *Application deadline:* For fall and spring admission, 2/15; for winter admission, 9/15. Applications are processed on a rolling basis. *Application fee:* $50. Electronic applications accepted.
Expenses: Tuition: Full-time $3,860; part-time $214 per hour.
Financial support: In 2001–02, 4 fellowships with partial tuition reimbursements (averaging $13,000 per year), 20 research assistantships with partial tuition reimbursements (averaging $10,000 per year), 48 teaching assistantships with partial tuition reimbursements (averaging $8,000 per year) were awarded. Scholarships/grants also available. Financial award application deadline: 2/15; financial award applicants required to submit FAFSA.
Faculty research: Combustion, composite materials, advanced design methods and optimization, electronics heat transfer, acoustic noise controls and robotics, manufacturing. *Total annual research expenditures:* $2.5 million.
Dr. Larry L. Howell, Chair, 801-422-2625, *Fax:* 801-422-5037, *E-mail:* @byu.edu.
Application contact: Dr. Brent L. Adams, Graduate Coordinator, 801-422-7124, *Fax:* 801-422-0516, *E-mail:* b_l_adams@byu.edu. *Web site:* http://www.byu.edu/me/

■ BROWN UNIVERSITY

Graduate School, Division of Engineering, Program in Mechanics of Solids and Structures, Providence, RI 02912
AWARDS Sc M, PhD.

Degree requirements: For doctorate, thesis/dissertation, preliminary exam.

■ BUCKNELL UNIVERSITY

Graduate Studies, College of Engineering, Department of Mechanical Engineering, Lewisburg, PA 17837
AWARDS MS, MSME. Part-time programs available.

Faculty: 10 full-time (1 woman).
Students: 5 full-time (1 woman), 1 part-time, 2 international.
Degree requirements: For master's, thesis.
Entrance requirements: For master's, GRE General Test, GRE Subject Test, TOEFL, minimum GPA of 2.8. *Application deadline:* For fall admission, 6/1 (priority date); for spring admission, 12/1 (priority date). Applications are processed on a rolling basis. *Application fee:* $25.
Expenses: Tuition: Part-time $2,875 per course.
Financial support: In 2001–02, 6 students received support. Unspecified assistantships available. Financial award application deadline: 3/1.
Faculty research: Heat pump performance, microprocessors in heat engine testing, computer-aided design.
Dr. David Cartwright, Head, 570-577-3193. *Web site:* http://www.bucknell.edu/

■ CALIFORNIA INSTITUTE OF TECHNOLOGY

Division of Engineering and Applied Science, Option in Mechanical Engineering, Pasadena, CA 91125-0001
AWARDS MS, PhD, Engr.

Faculty: 8 full-time (1 woman).
Students: 45 full-time (8 women); includes 5 minority (2 African Americans, 3 Asian Americans or Pacific Islanders), 22 international. 223 applicants, 21% accepted, 18 enrolled. In 2001, 13 master's, 6 doctorates awarded.
Degree requirements: For doctorate, thesis/dissertation.
Application deadline: For fall admission, 1/15. *Application fee:* $0.
Faculty research: Design, mechanics, thermal and fluids engineering, jet propulsion.
Dr. Erik Antonsson, Executive Officer, 626-395-3790.

■ CALIFORNIA STATE UNIVERSITY, CHICO

Graduate School, Interdisciplinary Programs, Chico, CA 95929-0722
AWARDS Applied mechanical engineering (MS); interdisciplinary studies (MS); interdispinary studies (MA). Simulation science (MS). Part-time programs available.

Students: 100 full-time, 116 part-time; includes 49 minority (3 African Americans, 30 Asian Americans or Pacific Islanders, 12 Hispanic Americans, 4 Native Americans). Average age 36. 21 applicants, 57% accepted, 12 enrolled. In 2001, 13 degrees awarded.
Degree requirements: For master's, thesis or alternative, oral exam.
Entrance requirements: For master's, GRE General Test or MAT, letters of recommendation (3). *Application deadline:* For fall admission, 4/1. Applications are processed on a rolling basis. *Application fee:* $55.
Expenses: Tuition, state resident: full-time $2,148. Tuition, nonresident: full-time $6,576.
Financial support: Fellowships, Federal Work-Study available. Support available to part-time students.
Dr. Jane Rysberg, Graduate Coordinator, 530-895-5178.

■ CALIFORNIA STATE UNIVERSITY, FRESNO

Division of Graduate Studies, College of Engineering and Computer Science, Program in Mechanical Engineering, Fresno, CA 93740-8027
AWARDS MS. Offered at Edwards Air Force Base.

Faculty: 3 full-time (0 women).
Students: 4 full-time (0 women), 7 part-time; includes 1 minority (Asian American or Pacific Islander), 3 international. Average age 31. 15 applicants, 67% accepted, 5 enrolled. In 2001, 3 degrees awarded.
Degree requirements: For master's, thesis or alternative. *Median time to degree:* Master's–2.5 years full-time, 3.5 years part-time.
Entrance requirements: For master's, GRE General Test, TOEFL, minimum GPA of 2.7. *Application deadline:* For fall admission, 8/1 (priority date); for spring admission, 12/1. Applications are processed on a rolling basis. *Application fee:* $55. Electronic applications accepted.
Expenses: Tuition, nonresident: part-time $246 per unit. Required fees: $605 per semester. Tuition and fees vary according to course load.
Financial support: Application deadline: 3/1;
Faculty research: Flowmeter calibration, digital camera calibration.
Dr. Satya Mahanty, Chair, 559-278-2368, *Fax:* 559-278-6759, *E-mail:* satya_mahanty@csufresno.edu.
Application contact: James W. Smolka, Coordinator, 661-258-5936.

■ CALIFORNIA STATE UNIVERSITY, FULLERTON

Graduate Studies, College of Engineering and Computer Science, Department of Mechanical Engineering, Fullerton, CA 92834-9480

AWARDS MS. Part-time programs available.

Faculty: 8 full-time (0 women), 7 part-time/adjunct.
Students: 4 full-time (0 women), 19 part-time (3 women); includes 8 minority (1 African American, 5 Asian Americans or Pacific Islanders, 2 Hispanic Americans), 5 international. Average age 31. 36 applicants, 44% accepted, 11 enrolled. In 2001, 12 degrees awarded.
Degree requirements: For master's, project or thesis.
Entrance requirements: For master's, minimum undergraduate GPA of 2.5. *Application fee:* $55.
Expenses: Tuition, nonresident: part-time $246 per unit. Required fees: $964.
Financial support: Career-related internships or fieldwork, Federal Work-Study, institutionally sponsored loans, and scholarships/grants available. Support available to part-time students. Financial award application deadline: 3/1.
Dr. Hossein Moini, Head, 714-278-3014.

■ CALIFORNIA STATE UNIVERSITY, LONG BEACH

Graduate Studies, College of Engineering, Department of Mechanical Engineering, Long Beach, CA 90840

AWARDS MSE, MSME. Part-time programs available.

Faculty: 18 full-time (1 woman), 14 part-time/adjunct (2 women).
Students: 15 full-time (1 woman), 62 part-time (5 women); includes 28 minority (5 African Americans, 16 Asian Americans or Pacific Islanders, 7 Hispanic Americans), 16 international. Average age 31. 52 applicants, 65% accepted. In 2001, 13 degrees awarded.
Degree requirements: For master's, thesis.
Entrance requirements: For master's, TOEFL. *Application deadline:* For fall admission, 8/1; for spring admission, 12/1. *Application fee:* $55. Electronic applications accepted.
Financial support: Career-related internships or fieldwork, Federal Work-Study, institutionally sponsored loans, scholarships/grants, and unspecified assistantships available. Financial award application deadline: 3/2.
Faculty research: Unsteady turbulent flows, solar energy, energy conversion, CAD/CAM, computer-assisted instruction.
Dr. Leonardo Perez y Perez, Chairman, 562-985-4407, *Fax:* 562-985-4408, *E-mail:* perez@engr.csulb.edu.

Application contact: Dr. Hamid Rahai, Graduate Coordinator, 562-985-5132, *Fax:* 562-985-4408, *E-mail:* rahai@engr.csulb.edu.

■ CALIFORNIA STATE UNIVERSITY, LOS ANGELES

Graduate Studies, College of Engineering, Computer Science, and Technology, Department of Mechanical Engineering, Los Angeles, CA 90032-8530

AWARDS MS. Part-time and evening/weekend programs available.

Faculty: 5 full-time, 5 part-time/adjunct.
Students: 4 full-time (0 women), 19 part-time (2 women); includes 13 minority (6 Asian Americans or Pacific Islanders, 7 Hispanic Americans), 5 international. In 2001, 11 degrees awarded.
Degree requirements: For master's, comprehensive exam or thesis.
Entrance requirements: For master's, TOEFL, minimum GPA of 2.75. *Application deadline:* For fall admission, 6/30; for spring admission, 2/1. Applications are processed on a rolling basis. *Application fee:* $55.
Expenses: Tuition, nonresident: part-time $164 per unit.
Financial support: Federal Work-Study available. Support available to part-time students. Financial award application deadline: 3/1.
Faculty research: Mechanical design, thermal systems, solar-powered vehicle.
Dr. Stephen Felszeghy, Chair, 323-343-4490.

■ CALIFORNIA STATE UNIVERSITY, NORTHRIDGE

Graduate Studies, College of Engineering and Computer Science, Department of Civil and Manufacturing Engineering, Northridge, CA 91330

AWARDS Applied mechanics (MSE); civil engineering (MS); engineering and computer science (MS); engineering management (MS); industrial engineering (MS); materials engineering (MS); mechanical engineering (MS), including aerospace engineering, applied engineering, machine design, mechanical engineering, structural engineering, thermofluids; mechanics (MS). Part-time and evening/weekend programs available.

Faculty: 14 full-time, 2 part-time/adjunct.
Students: 25 full-time (4 women), 72 part-time (9 women). Average age 31. 64 applicants, 77% accepted, 22 enrolled. In 2001, 34 degrees awarded.
Degree requirements: For master's, thesis.
Entrance requirements: For master's, GRE General Test, TOEFL, minimum GPA of 2.5. *Application deadline:* For fall admission, 11/30. *Application fee:* $55.

Expenses: Tuition, nonresident: part-time $631 per semester. Required fees: $246 per unit.
Financial support: Teaching assistantships available. Financial award application deadline: 3/1.
Faculty research: Composite study.
Dr. Stephen Gadomski, Chair, 818-677-2166.
Application contact: Dr. Ileana Costa, Graduate Coordinator, 818-677-3299.

■ CALIFORNIA STATE UNIVERSITY, NORTHRIDGE

Graduate Studies, College of Engineering and Computer Science, Department of Civil and Manufacturing Engineering, Department of Mechanical Engineering, Northridge, CA 91330

AWARDS Aerospace engineering (MS); applied engineering (MS); machine design (MS); mechanical engineering (MS). Structural engineering (MS); thermofluids (MS). Part-time and evening/weekend programs available.

Faculty: 8 full-time, 2 part-time/adjunct.
Students: 6 full-time (0 women), 42 part-time (6 women); includes 19 minority (14 Asian Americans or Pacific Islanders, 4 Hispanic Americans, 1 Native American), 3 international. Average age 34. 24 applicants, 79% accepted, 6 enrolled. In 2001, 4 degrees awarded.
Degree requirements: For master's, thesis or alternative.
Entrance requirements: For master's, GRE General Test, TOEFL, minimum GPA of 2.5. *Application deadline:* For fall admission, 11/30. *Application fee:* $55.
Expenses: Tuition, nonresident: part-time $631 per semester. Required fees: $246 per unit.
Financial support: Application deadline: 3/1.
Dr. Sidney H. Schwartz, Chair, 818-677-2187.
Application contact: Dr. Tom Mincer, Graduate Coordinator, 818-677-2007.

■ CALIFORNIA STATE UNIVERSITY, SACRAMENTO

Graduate Studies, College of Engineering and Computer Science, Department of Mechanical Engineering, Sacramento, CA 95819-6048

AWARDS MS. Evening/weekend programs available.

Students: 17 full-time (3 women), 20 part-time (2 women); includes 2 minority (both Asian Americans or Pacific Islanders), 17 international.
Degree requirements: For master's, thesis or alternative, writing proficiency exam.

Entrance requirements: For master's, TOEFL. *Application deadline:* For fall admission, 4/15; for spring admission, 11/1. *Application fee:* $55.
Expenses: Tuition, state resident: full-time $1,965; part-time $668 per semester. Tuition, nonresident: part-time $246 per unit.
Financial support: Research assistantships, teaching assistantships, career-related internships or fieldwork and Federal Work-Study available. Support available to part-time students. Financial award application deadline: 3/1.
Dr. Thinh Dinh Ngo, Chair, 916-278-6624.
Application contact: Dr. Estelle Eke, Graduate Coordinator, 916-278-6248.

■ CARNEGIE MELLON UNIVERSITY

Carnegie Institute of Technology, Department of Mechanical Engineering, Pittsburgh, PA 15213-3891

AWARDS ME, MS, PhD. Part-time and evening/weekend programs available. Terminal master's awarded for partial completion of doctoral program.

Degree requirements: For master's, thesis (for some programs); for doctorate, thesis/dissertation (for some programs), qualifying exam.
Entrance requirements: For master's and doctorate, GRE General Test, TOEFL.
Faculty research: Combustion, design, fluid, and thermal sciences; computational fluid dynamics; energy and environment. Solid mechanics. Systems and controls; materials and manufacturing. *Web site:* http://www.me.cmu.edu/

■ CASE WESTERN RESERVE UNIVERSITY

School of Graduate Studies, The Case School of Engineering, Department of Mechanical and Aerospace Engineering, Cleveland, OH 44106

AWARDS Aerospace engineering (MS, PhD); fluid and thermal engineering sciences (MS); fluid and thermal engineering sciences (PhD); mechanical engineering (MS, PhD). Part-time programs available. Postbaccalaureate distance learning degree programs offered (no on-campus study).

Faculty: 16 full-time (1 woman), 9 part-time/adjunct (1 woman).
Students: 34 full-time (4 women), 49 part-time (7 women); includes 7 minority (6 Asian Americans or Pacific Islanders, 1 Hispanic American), 31 international. Average age 24. 290 applicants, 21% accepted, 14 enrolled. In 2001, 19 master's, 9 doctorates awarded.
Degree requirements: For master's, thesis (for some programs); for doctorate,

thesis/dissertation, qualifying exam, teaching experience.
Entrance requirements: For master's, TOEFL; for doctorate, GRE, TOEFL. *Application deadline:* For fall admission, 7/1 (priority date). Applications are processed on a rolling basis. *Application fee:* $25.
Expenses: Contact institution.
Financial support: In 2001–02, 27 fellowships with full and partial tuition reimbursements (averaging $16,200 per year), 23 research assistantships with full and partial tuition reimbursements (averaging $16,200 per year) were awarded. Institutionally sponsored loans and tuition waivers (full and partial) also available. Financial award application deadline: 3/1; financial award applicants required to submit FAFSA.
Faculty research: Microgravity studies of combustion and fluid interfaces; molecular dynamics of transport processes; mechanical analysis of materials and biomaterials; machinery diagnostics and control; biorobotics; DPIV and LDV measurements in two-phase flows. *Total annual research expenditures:* $4.7 million.
Dr. Joseph M. Prahl, Chairman, 216-368-2941, *Fax:* 216-368-6445, *E-mail:* jmp@po.cwru.edu.
Application contact: Angelika Szakacs, Secretary, 216-368-5403, *Fax:* 216-368-3007, *E-mail:* mechgac@po.cwru.edu. *Web site:* http://www.scl.cwru.edu/cse/emae/

■ THE CATHOLIC UNIVERSITY OF AMERICA

School of Engineering, Department of Mechanical Engineering, Washington, DC 20064

AWARDS Design (D Engr, PhD); design and robotics (MME, D Engr, PhD); fluid mechanics and thermal science (MME, D Engr, PhD); mechanical design (MME); ocean and structural acoustics (MME, MS Engr, PhD). Part-time and evening/weekend programs available.

Faculty: 6 full-time (1 woman).
Students: 7 full-time (0 women), 16 part-time (3 women); includes 4 minority (2 African Americans, 2 Asian Americans or Pacific Islanders), 8 international. Average age 34. 14 applicants, 36% accepted, 2 enrolled. In 2001, 3 master's, 3 doctorates awarded.
Degree requirements: For master's, thesis optional; for doctorate, thesis/dissertation, oral exams, comprehensive exam.
Entrance requirements: For master's, minimum GPA of 3.0; for doctorate, minimum GPA of 3.5. *Application deadline:* For fall admission, 8/1 (priority date); for spring admission, 12/1. Applications are processed on a rolling basis. *Application fee:* $55. Electronic applications accepted.
Expenses: Tuition: Full-time $20,050; part-time $770 per credit. Required fees: $430 per term. Tuition and fees vary according to program.

Financial support: Research assistantships, teaching assistantships, career-related internships or fieldwork, Federal Work-Study, institutionally sponsored loans, and tuition waivers (full and partial) available. Support available to part-time students. Financial award application deadline: 2/1.
Faculty research: Automated engineering.
Dr. Ji Steven Brown, Chair, 202-319-5170.

■ CITY COLLEGE OF THE CITY UNIVERSITY OF NEW YORK

Graduate School, School of Engineering, Department of Mechanical Engineering, New York, NY 10031-9198

AWARDS ME, MS, PhD. Part-time programs available.

Students: 48. In 2001, 14 degrees awarded.
Degree requirements: For master's, thesis optional; for doctorate, one foreign language, thesis/dissertation, comprehensive exam.
Entrance requirements: For master's, TOEFL; for doctorate, GRE General Test, TOEFL. *Application deadline:* Applications are processed on a rolling basis. *Application fee:* $40.
Expenses: Tuition, state resident: part-time $185 per credit. Tuition, nonresident: part-time $320 per credit. Required fees: $43 per term.
Financial support: Fellowships, research assistantships, teaching assistantships, Federal Work-Study and tuition waivers (full and partial) available.
Faculty research: Bio-heat and mass transfer, bone mechanics, fracture mechanics, heat transfer in computer parts, mechanisms design.
Feridun Delale, Chairman, 212-650-5220.
Application contact: Graduate Admissions Office, 212-650-6977.

■ CLARKSON UNIVERSITY

Graduate School, School of Engineering, Department of Mechanical and Aeronautical Engineering, Potsdam, NY 13699

AWARDS Mechanical engineering (ME, MS, PhD). Part-time programs available.

Faculty: 19 full-time (2 women).
Students: 38 full-time (10 women); includes 2 minority (1 Asian American or Pacific Islander, 1 Hispanic American), 13 international. Average age 26. 169 applicants, 78% accepted. In 2001, 9 master's, 7 doctorates awarded.
Degree requirements: For master's, thesis; for doctorate, thesis/dissertation, departmental qualifying exam. *Median time to degree:* Master's–2.5 years full-time; doctorate–6.5 years full-time.
Entrance requirements: For master's, GRE, TOEFL. *Application deadline:* For fall admission, 5/15 (priority date); for spring admission, 10/15 (priority date).

Clarkson University (continued)

Applications are processed on a rolling basis. *Application fee:* $25 ($35 for international students).

Expenses: Tuition: Part-time $714 per credit. Required fees: $108 per semester.

Financial support: In 2001–02, 29 students received support, including 7 fellowships (averaging $20,000 per year), 12 research assistantships (averaging $17,000 per year), 10 teaching assistantships (averaging $17,000 per year). Scholarships/grants and tuition waivers (partial) also available.

Faculty research: Turbulent flow, controls, fracture mechanics, materials science, fluid mechanics. *Total annual research expenditures:* $891,518.

Dr. John Moosbrugger, Chairman, 315-268-4429, *E-mail:* moose@clarkson.edu.

Application contact: Donna Brockway, Assistant to Dean/Foreign Student Advisor, 315-268-6447, *Fax:* 315-268-7994, *E-mail:* brockway@clarkson.edu.

■ CLEMSON UNIVERSITY

Graduate School, College of Engineering and Science, Department of Mechanical Engineering, Program in Mechanical Engineering, Clemson, SC 29634

AWARDS MS, PhD.

Students: 68 full-time (9 women), 13 part-time (1 woman); includes 4 minority (2 African Americans, 2 Hispanic Americans), 39 international. Average age 28. 338 applicants, 41% accepted, 20 enrolled. In 2001, 32 master's, 3 doctorates awarded.

Degree requirements: For master's and doctorate, thesis/dissertation.

Entrance requirements: For master's and doctorate, GRE General Test, TOEFL. *Application deadline:* For fall admission, 6/1. Applications are processed on a rolling basis. *Application fee:* $40.

Expenses: Tuition, state resident: full-time $5,310. Tuition, nonresident: full-time $11,284.

Financial support: Applicants required to submit FAFSA.

Dr. Georges Fadel, Graduate Coordinator, 864-656-5620, *Fax:* 864-656-4435, *E-mail:* fgeorge@clemson.edu. *Web site:* http://www.eng.clemson.edu/~mechengr/ME.htm

■ CLEVELAND STATE UNIVERSITY

College of Graduate Studies, Fenn College of Engineering, Department of Civil and Environmental Engineering, Cleveland, OH 44115

AWARDS Civil engineering (MS, D Eng), including environmental engineering (D Eng), mechanical engineering (D Eng), structures engineering (D Eng); engineering mechanics (MS); environmental engineering (MS). Part-time programs available.

Faculty: 10 full-time (1 woman).

Students: 6 full-time (1 woman), 33 part-time (9 women); includes 3 minority (1 African American, 2 Hispanic Americans), 22 international. Average age 29. 62 applicants, 73% accepted. In 2001, 9 master's, 1 doctorate awarded.

Degree requirements: For master's, thesis (for some programs), project or thesis; for doctorate, thesis/dissertation, candidacy and qualifying exams.

Entrance requirements: For master's, GRE General Test, GRE Subject Test, TOEFL, minimum GPA of 2.75; for doctorate, GRE General Test, GRE Subject Test, TOEFL, minimum GPA of 3.25. *Application deadline:* 7/15 (priority date). Applications are processed on a rolling basis. *Application fee:* $25.

Expenses: Tuition, state resident: full-time $6,838; part-time $263 per credit hour. Tuition, nonresident: full-time $13,526; part-time $520 per credit hour.

Financial support: In 2001–02, 3 research assistantships, 6 teaching assistantships were awarded. Career-related internships or fieldwork and unspecified assistantships also available. Financial award application deadline: 9/1.

Faculty research: Environmental engineering, solid-waste disposal, composite materials, nonlinear buckling, constitutive modeling.

Dr. Paul Bosela, Chairperson, 216-687-2190, *Fax:* 216-687-9280. *Web site:* http://www.csuohio.edu/civileng/

■ CLEVELAND STATE UNIVERSITY

College of Graduate Studies, Fenn College of Engineering, Department of Mechanical Engineering, Cleveland, OH 44115

AWARDS MS, D Eng. Part-time programs available.

Faculty: 12 full-time (0 women).

Students: 4 full-time (0 women), 25 part-time (4 women); includes 2 minority (1 African American, 1 Asian American or Pacific Islander), 16 international. Average age 31. 118 applicants, 57% accepted, 32 enrolled. In 2001, 2 master's, 2 doctorates awarded.

Degree requirements: For master's, project or thesis, thesis optional; for doctorate, thesis/dissertation, candidacy and qualifying exams.

Entrance requirements: For master's, GRE General Test, GRE Subject Test, TOEFL, minimum GPA of 2.75; for doctorate, GRE General Test, GRE Subject Test, TOEFL, minimum GPA of 3.25. *Application deadline:* For fall admission, 7/15 (priority date); for spring admission, 12/15 (priority date). Applications are processed on a rolling basis. *Application fee:* $25.

Expenses: Tuition, state resident: full-time $6,838; part-time $263 per credit hour.

Tuition, nonresident: full-time $13,526; part-time $520 per credit hour.

Financial support: In 2001–02, 22 students received support, including 4 research assistantships (averaging $3,480 per year), 2 teaching assistantships (averaging $2,960 per year); career-related internships or fieldwork, Federal Work-Study, institutionally sponsored loans, and unspecified assistantships also available. Support available to part-time students.

Faculty research: Fluid piezoelectric sensors, laser-optical inspection simulation of forging and forming processes, multiphase flow and heat transfer, turbulent flows.

Dr. Mournir B. Ibrahim, Chair, 216-687-2580, *Fax:* 216-687-5375, *E-mail:* m.ibrahim@csuohio.edu. *Web site:* http://www.csuohio.edu/mce/mce.html

■ COLORADO STATE UNIVERSITY

Graduate School, College of Engineering, Department of Mechanical Engineering, Fort Collins, CO 80523-0015

AWARDS Bioengineering (MS, PhD); energy and environmental engineering (MS, PhD); energy conversion (MS, PhD); engineering management (MS); heat and mass transfer (MS, PhD); industrial and manufacturing systems engineering (MS, PhD); mechanical engineering (MS, PhD); mechanics and materials (MS, PhD). Part-time programs available.

Faculty: 17 full-time (2 women).

Students: 36 full-time (6 women), 63 part-time (11 women); includes 5 minority (2 Asian Americans or Pacific Islanders, 2 Hispanic Americans, 1 Native American), 22 international. Average age 32. 234 applicants, 83% accepted, 32 enrolled. In 2001, 10 master's, 3 doctorates awarded. Terminal master's awarded for partial completion of doctoral program.

Degree requirements: For doctorate, thesis/dissertation.

Entrance requirements: For master's and doctorate, GRE General Test, TOEFL, minimum GPA of 3.0. *Application deadline:* For fall admission, 2/1 (priority date). Applications are processed on a rolling basis. *Application fee:* $30. Electronic applications accepted.

Expenses: Tuition, state resident: full-time $2,880; part-time $160 per credit. Tuition, nonresident: full-time $11,412; part-time $634 per credit. Required fees: $750; $34 per credit.

Financial support: In 2001–02, 2 fellowships, 15 research assistantships (averaging $15,792 per year), 14 teaching assistantships (averaging $11,844 per year) were awarded. Traineeships also available.

Faculty research: Space propulsion, controls and systems, engineering and materials. *Total annual research expenditures:* $2.1 million.

Dr. Allan T. Kirkpatrick, Head, 970-491-6559, *Fax:* 970-491-3827, *E-mail:* allan@engr.colostate.edu. *Web site:* http://www.engr.colostate.edu/depts/me/index.html

■ COLUMBIA UNIVERSITY

Fu Foundation School of Engineering and Applied Science, Department of Mechanical Engineering, New York, NY 10027

AWARDS ME, MS, Eng Sc D, PhD. PhD offered through the Graduate School of Arts and Sciences. Part-time programs available.

Faculty: 10 full-time (0 women), 6 part-time/adjunct (0 women).
Students: 35 full-time (6 women), 13 part-time (2 women). Average age 24. 225 applicants, 29% accepted, 15 enrolled. In 2001, 12 master's, 16 doctorates awarded. Terminal master's awarded for partial completion of doctoral program.
Degree requirements: For doctorate, thesis/dissertation, qualifying exam.
Entrance requirements: For master's, GRE General Test, TOEFL, minimum GPA of 3.3; for doctorate, GRE General Test, TOEFL. *Application deadline:* For fall admission, 1/5; for spring admission, 10/1. *Application fee:* $55. Electronic applications accepted.
Expenses: Tuition: Full-time $27,528. Required fees: $1,638.
Financial support: In 2001–02, 25 students received support, including 3 fellowships (averaging $6,000 per year), 15 research assistantships with tuition reimbursements available (averaging $14,240 per year), 7 teaching assistantships with tuition reimbursements available (averaging $14,040 per year); career-related internships or fieldwork, Federal Work-Study, institutionally sponsored loans, scholarships/grants, health care benefits, unspecified assistantships, and research student support awards also available. Financial award application deadline: 1/5; financial award applicants required to submit FAFSA.
Faculty research: Heat transfer and fluid mechanics, control theory and robotics, kinematics and dynamics of mechanisms, manufacturing engineering, orthopedic biomechanics. *Total annual research expenditures:* $942,148.
Vijay Modi, Chairman, 212-854-2956, *Fax:* 212-854-3304, *E-mail:* modi@columbia.edu.
Application contact: Sandra Morris, Student Coordinator, 212-854-2966, *Fax:* 212-854-3304, *E-mail:* swm16@columbia.edu. *Web site:* http://www.columbia.edu/cu/mechanical/

■ CORNELL UNIVERSITY

Graduate School, Graduate Fields of Engineering, Field of Mechanical Engineering, Ithaca, NY 14853-0001

AWARDS Biomechanical engineering (M Eng, MS, PhD); combustion (M Eng, MS, PhD); energy and power systems (M Eng, MS, PhD); fluid mechanics (M Eng, MS, PhD); heat transfer (M Eng, MS, PhD); materials and manufacturing engineering (M Eng, MS, PhD); mechanical systems and design (M Eng, MS, PhD); multiphase flows (M Eng, MS, PhD).

Faculty: 31 full-time.
Students: 88 full-time (18 women); includes 14 minority (1 African American, 12 Asian Americans or Pacific Islanders, 1 Hispanic American), 43 international. 471 applicants, 24% accepted. In 2001, 31 master's, 5 doctorates awarded. Terminal master's awarded for partial completion of doctoral program.
Degree requirements: For master's, project (M Eng), thesis (MS); for doctorate, one foreign language, thesis/dissertation, 2 semesters of teaching experience.
Entrance requirements: For master's and doctorate, GRE General Test, TOEFL, 3 letters of recommendation. *Application deadline:* For fall admission, 1/15. *Application fee:* $65. Electronic applications accepted.
Expenses: Tuition: Full-time $25,970. Required fees: $50.
Financial support: In 2001–02, 47 students received support, including 16 fellowships with full tuition reimbursements available, 17 research assistantships with full tuition reimbursements available, 14 teaching assistantships with full tuition reimbursements available; institutionally sponsored loans, scholarships/grants, tuition waivers (full and partial), and unspecified assistantships also available. Financial award applicants required to submit FAFSA.
Faculty research: Combustion and heat transfer, fluid mechanics and CFD, system dynamics and control, biomechanics, manufacturing.
Application contact: Graduate Field Assistant, 607-255-5250, *E-mail:* maegrad@cornell.edu. *Web site:* http://www.gradschool.cornell.edu/grad/fields_1/mech-engr.html

■ DARTMOUTH COLLEGE

Thayer School of Engineering, Program in Mechanical Engineering, Hanover, NH 03755

AWARDS MS, PhD.

Degree requirements: For master's, thesis; for doctorate, thesis/dissertation, candidacy oral exam.
Entrance requirements: For master's and doctorate, GRE General Test. *Application deadline:* For fall admission, 1/1 (priority date). *Application fee:* $40 ($50 for international students).
Expenses: Tuition: Full-time $26,425.
Financial support: Fellowships, research assistantships, teaching assistantships, career-related internships or fieldwork, Federal Work-Study, institutionally sponsored loans, and tuition waivers (full and partial) available. Financial award application deadline: 1/15.
Faculty research: Solid mechanics and mechanical design, tribology, dynamics and control systems, thermal science and energy conversion, fluid mechanics and multi-phase flow. *Total annual research expenditures:* $800,000.
Application contact: Candace S. Potter, Graduate Admissions Administrator, 603-646-3844, *Fax:* 603-646-1620, *E-mail:* candace.potter@dartmouth.edu. *Web site:* http://engineering.dartmouth.edu/

■ DREXEL UNIVERSITY

Graduate School, College of Engineering, Mechanical Engineering and Mechanics Department, Philadelphia, PA 19104-2875

AWARDS Manufacturing engineering (MS, PhD); mechanical engineering and mechanics (MS, PhD). Part-time and evening/weekend programs available.

Faculty: 22 full-time (0 women), 1 part-time/adjunct (0 women).
Students: 19 full-time (2 women), 69 part-time (7 women); includes 15 minority (4 African Americans, 8 Asian Americans or Pacific Islanders, 2 Hispanic Americans, 1 Native American), 32 international. Average age 30. 124 applicants, 88% accepted, 14 enrolled. In 2001, 20 master's, 2 doctorates awarded. Terminal master's awarded for partial completion of doctoral program.
Degree requirements: For master's, thesis optional; for doctorate, thesis/dissertation.
Entrance requirements: For master's, TOEFL, minimum GPA of 3.0, BS in engineering or science; for doctorate, TOEFL, minimum GPA of 3.5, MS in engineering or science. *Application deadline:* For fall admission, 8/21. Applications are processed on a rolling basis. *Application fee:* $50. Electronic applications accepted.
Expenses: Tuition: Full-time $20,088; part-time $558 per credit. Required fees: $78 per term. One-time fee: $200. Tuition and fees vary according to course load, degree level and program.
Financial support: Research assistantships, teaching assistantships, unspecified assistantships available. Financial award application deadline: 2/1.
Faculty research: Composites, dynamic systems and control, combustion and fuels, biomechanics, mechanics and thermal fluid sciences.
Dr. Mun Young Choi, Acting Head, 215-895-2284, *Fax:* 215-895-1478, *E-mail:* mem@drexel.edu.

Drexel University (continued)

Application contact: Director of Graduate Admissions, 215-895-6700, *Fax:* 215-895-5939, *E-mail:* enroll@drexel.edu.

Find an in-depth description at www.petersons.com/gradchannel.

■ DUKE UNIVERSITY

Graduate School, School of Engineering, Department of Mechanical Engineering and Materials Science, Durham, NC 27708-0586

AWARDS Materials science (MS, PhD); mechanical engineering (MS, PhD). Part-time programs available.

Faculty: 24 full-time, 4 part-time/adjunct.
Students: 44 full-time (4 women), 19 international. 146 applicants, 22% accepted, 9 enrolled. In 2001, 4 master's, 10 doctorates awarded. Terminal master's awarded for partial completion of doctoral program.
Degree requirements: For master's, thesis optional; for doctorate, thesis/dissertation.
Entrance requirements: For master's and doctorate, GRE General Test. *Application deadline:* For fall admission, 12/31; for spring admission, 11/1. *Application fee:* $75.
Expenses: Tuition: Full-time $24,600.
Financial support: Fellowships, research assistantships, teaching assistantships, Federal Work-Study available. Financial award application deadline: 12/31.
Laurens Howle, Director of Graduate Studies, 919-660-5308, *Fax:* 919-660-8963, *E-mail:* kmrogers@duke.edu. *Web site:* http://www.mems.egr.duke.html/

Find an in-depth description at www.petersons.com/gradchannel.

■ FLORIDA AGRICULTURAL AND MECHANICAL UNIVERSITY

Division of Graduate Studies, Research, and Continuing Education, FAMU-FSU College of Engineering, Department of Mechanical Engineering, Tallahassee, FL 32307-3200

AWARDS MS, PhD.

Entrance requirements: For master's, GRE General Test, minimum GPA of 3.0.

Find an in-depth description at www.petersons.com/gradchannel.

■ FLORIDA ATLANTIC UNIVERSITY

College of Engineering, Department of Mechanical Engineering, Program in Mechanical Engineering, Boca Raton, FL 33431-0991

AWARDS MS, PhD. Part-time and evening/weekend programs available.

Faculty: 16 full-time (0 women).

Students: 9 full-time (1 woman), 8 part-time (1 woman); includes 2 minority (both Hispanic Americans), 12 international. Average age 29. 52 applicants, 73% accepted, 3 enrolled. In 2001, 10 master's, 1 doctorate awarded. Terminal master's awarded for partial completion of doctoral program.
Degree requirements: For master's, thesis optional; for doctorate, thesis/dissertation, qualifying exam.
Entrance requirements: For master's and doctorate, GRE General Test, TOEFL, minimum GPA of 3.0. *Application deadline:* For fall admission, 4/10 (priority date); for spring admission, 10/1. Applications are processed on a rolling basis. *Application fee:* $20.
Expenses: Tuition, state resident: full-time $3,098; part-time $172 per credit. Tuition, nonresident: full-time $10,427; part-time $579 per credit.
Financial support: Research assistantships, teaching assistantships, career-related internships or fieldwork available. Financial award application deadline: 4/1.
Faculty research: Fault detection and diagnostics, computational fluid mechanics, composite materials, two-phase flows, helicopter dynamics.
Application contact: Patricia Capozziello, Graduate Admissions Coordinator, 561-297-2694, *Fax:* 561-297-2659, *E-mail:* capozzie@fau.edu. *Web site:* http://me.fau.edu/

■ FLORIDA INSTITUTE OF TECHNOLOGY

Graduate Programs, College of Engineering, Mechanical and Aerospace Engineering Department, Melbourne, FL 32901-6975

AWARDS Aerospace engineering (MS, PhD); mechanical engineering (MS, PhD). Part-time programs available.

Faculty: 12 full-time (0 women), 2 part-time/adjunct (0 women).
Students: 14 full-time (3 women), 22 part-time (1 woman); includes 2 minority (both Hispanic Americans), 16 international. Average age 29. 146 applicants, 50% accepted. In 2001, 4 master's, 2 doctorates awarded.
Degree requirements: For master's, thesis optional; for doctorate, thesis/dissertation, comprehensive exam.
Entrance requirements: For master's, GRE General Test, GRE Subject Test, minimum GPA of 3.0; for doctorate, GRE General Test, minimum GPA of 3.2, resumé. *Application deadline:* Applications are processed on a rolling basis. *Application fee:* $50. Electronic applications accepted.
Expenses: Tuition: Part-time $650 per credit.
Financial support: In 2001–02, 15 students received support, including 5 research assistantships with full and partial

tuition reimbursements available (averaging $7,182 per year), 10 teaching assistantships with full and partial tuition reimbursements available (averaging $6,734 per year); career-related internships or fieldwork and tuition remissions also available. Financial award application deadline: 3/1; financial award applicants required to submit FAFSA.
Faculty research: Dynamic systems, robotics, and controls. Structures, solid mechanics, and materials; thermal-fluid sciences, optical tomography, composite/recycled materials. *Total annual research expenditures:* $338,000.
Dr. John J. Engblom, Department Head, 321-674-7132, *Fax:* 321-674-8813, *E-mail:* engblom@fit.edu.
Application contact: Carolyn P. Farrior, Director of Graduate Admissions, 321-674-7118, *Fax:* 321-723-9468, *E-mail:* cfarrior@fit.edu. *Web site:* http://www.fit.edu/

Find an in-depth description at www.petersons.com/gradchannel.

■ FLORIDA INSTITUTE OF TECHNOLOGY

Graduate Programs, School of Extended Graduate Studies, Melbourne, FL 32901-6975

AWARDS Acquisition and contract management (MS, MSM, PMBA); aerospace engineering (MS); business administration (PMBA); computer information systems (MS); computer science (MS); ebusiness (MSM); electrical engineering (MS); engineering management (MS); health management (MS); human resource management (MSM, PMBA); human resources management (MS); information systems (MSM, PMBA); logistics management (MS, MSM); management (MS); material acquisition management (MS); mechanical engineering (MS); operations research (MS); project management (MS), including information systems, operations research; public administration (MPA). Software engineering (MS). Space systems (MS). Space systems management (MS). Systems management (MS), including information systems, operations research; transportation management (MSM). Part-time and evening/weekend programs available. Postbaccalaureate distance learning degree programs offered (no on-campus study).

Faculty: 10 full-time (2 women), 131 part-time/adjunct (15 women).
Students: 57 full-time (29 women), 1,198 part-time (455 women); includes 277 minority (183 African Americans, 38 Asian Americans or Pacific Islanders, 51 Hispanic Americans, 5 Native Americans), 16 international. Average age 37. 299 applicants, 42% accepted. In 2001, 434 degrees awarded.
Entrance requirements: For master's, minimum GPA of 3.0. *Application deadline:* Applications are processed on a rolling

basis. *Application fee:* $50. Electronic applications accepted.

Expenses: Tuition: Part-time $650 per credit.

Financial support: Institutionally sponsored loans available. Financial award application deadline: 3/1; financial award applicants required to submit FAFSA. Dr. Ronald L. Marshall, Dean, School of Extended Graduate Studies, 321-674-8880.

Application contact: Carolyn P. Farrior, Director of Graduate Admissions, 321-674-7118, *Fax:* 321-723-9468, *E-mail:* cfarrior@fit.edu. *Web site:* http://www.segs.fit.edu/

■ FLORIDA INTERNATIONAL UNIVERSITY

College of Engineering, Department of Mechanical Engineering, Miami, FL 33199

AWARDS Biomedical engineering (MS); mechanical engineering (MS, PhD). Part-time and evening/weekend programs available.

Faculty: 12 full-time (1 woman).

Students: 55 full-time (6 women), 16 part-time (2 women); includes 17 minority (2 African Americans, 1 Asian American or Pacific Islander, 14 Hispanic Americans), 52 international. Average age 31. 176 applicants, 56% accepted, 37 enrolled. In 2001, 5 master's, 1 doctorate awarded.

Degree requirements: For doctorate, thesis/dissertation.

Entrance requirements: For master's and doctorate, GRE General Test, TOEFL. *Application deadline:* For fall admission, 4/1 (priority date); for spring admission, 10/1. Applications are processed on a rolling basis. *Application fee:* $20.

Expenses: Tuition, state resident: full-time $2,916; part-time $162 per credit hour. Tuition, nonresident: full-time $10,245; part-time $569 per credit hour. Required fees: $168 per term.

Dr. Norman Munroe, Chairperson, 305-348-2569, *Fax:* 305-348-1932, *E-mail:* munroen@fiu.edu.

■ FLORIDA STATE UNIVERSITY

Graduate Studies, FAMU/FSU College of Engineering, Department of Mechanical Engineering, Tallahassee, FL 32306

AWARDS MS, PhD. Part-time programs available. Postbaccalaureate distance learning degree programs offered (minimal on-campus study).

Faculty: 19 full-time (1 woman).

Students: 54 full-time (15 women); includes 42 minority (19 African Americans, 22 Asian Americans or Pacific Islanders, 1 Hispanic American). Average age 27. 86 applicants, 21% accepted, 14 enrolled. In 2001, 4 master's, 1 doctorate awarded.

Degree requirements: For master's, thesis or comprehensive exam, thesis

optional; for doctorate, thesis/dissertation, preliminary exam, qualifying exam. *Median time to degree:* Master's–2 years full-time; doctorate–4 years full-time.

Entrance requirements: For master's, GRE General Test, TOEFL, minimum GPA of 3.0 (U.S. applicants), 3.5 (international applicants); BS in mechanical engineering; for doctorate, GRE General Test, TOEFL, minimum graduate GPA of 3.5, MA (mechanical engineering), 3 units of directed research. *Application deadline:* For fall admission, 7/1; for spring admission, 11/1. Applications are processed on a rolling basis. *Application fee:* $20. Electronic applications accepted.

Expenses: Tuition, state resident: part-time $163 per credit hour. Tuition, nonresident: part-time $570 per credit hour. Tuition and fees vary according to program.

Financial support: In 2001–02, 54 students received support, including 1 fellowship, 28 research assistantships, 25 teaching assistantships; career-related internships or fieldwork, institutionally sponsored loans, and tuition waivers (full) also available. Financial award application deadline: 6/15.

Faculty research: Fluid mechanics, super plastic metal forming, superconducting composite materials, dynamics and controls, magnet design. *Total annual research expenditures:* $3 million.

Dr. E. Collins, Associate Chair for Graduate Studies, 850-410-6373, *Fax:* 850-410-6337.

Application contact: George Green, Graduate Administrator, 850-410-6330, *Fax:* 850-410-6337. *Web site:* http://www.eng.fsu.edu/

Find an in-depth description at www.petersons.com/gradchannel.

■ GANNON UNIVERSITY

School of Graduate Studies, College of Sciences, Engineering, and Health Sciences, School of Engineering and Computer Science, Program in Engineering, Erie, PA 16541-0001

AWARDS Electrical engineering (MS); embedded software engineering (MS); mechanical engineering (MS). Part-time and evening/weekend programs available.

Degree requirements: For master's, thesis or alternative, comprehensive exam.

Entrance requirements: For master's, GRE Subject Test, bachelor's degree in engineering, minimum QPA of 2.5. *Web site:* http://www.gannon.edu/

■ THE GEORGE WASHINGTON UNIVERSITY

School of Engineering and Applied Science, Department of Mechanical and Aerospace Engineering, Washington, DC 20052

AWARDS MS, D Sc, App Sc, Engr. Part-time and evening/weekend programs available.

Faculty: 12 full-time (1 woman), 13 part-time/adjunct (0 women).

Students: 46 full-time (8 women), 97 part-time (19 women); includes 17 minority (4 African Americans, 4 Asian Americans or Pacific Islanders, 9 Hispanic Americans), 37 international. Average age 29. 89 applicants, 97% accepted. In 2001, 28 master's, 2 doctorates awarded.

Degree requirements: For master's, thesis optional; for doctorate, thesis/dissertation, final and qualifying exams.

Entrance requirements: For master's, TOEFL or George Washington University English as a Foreign Language Test, appropriate bachelor's degree, minimum GPA of 3.0; for doctorate, TOEFL or George Washington University English as a Foreign Language Test, appropriate bachelor's or master's degree, minimum GPA of 3.4, GRE required if highest earned degree is BS; for other advanced degree, TOEFL or George Washington University English as a Foreign Language Test, appropriate master's degree, minimum GPA of 3.0. *Application deadline:* For fall admission, 3/1 (priority date); for spring admission, 10/1. Applications are processed on a rolling basis. *Application fee:* $55.

Expenses: Tuition: Part-time $810 per credit. Required fees: $1 per credit.

Financial support: In 2001–02, 7 fellowships with tuition reimbursements (averaging $3,900 per year), 8 teaching assistantships with tuition reimbursements (averaging $3,000 per year) were awarded. Research assistantships, career-related internships or fieldwork and institutionally sponsored loans also available. Financial award application deadline: 3/1; financial award applicants required to submit FAFSA.

Dr. Michael K. Myers, Chair, 202-994-6749, *Fax:* 202-994-0238, *E-mail:* mkmyers@seas.gwu.edu.

Application contact: Howard M. Davis, Manager, Office of Admissions and Student Records, 202-994-6158, *Fax:* 202-994-0909, *E-mail:* data:adms@seas.gwu.edu. *Web site:* http://www.gwu.edu/~gradinfo/

Find an in-depth description at www.petersons.com/gradchannel.

■ GEORGIA INSTITUTE OF TECHNOLOGY

Graduate Studies and Research, College of Engineering, George W. Woodruff School of Mechanical Engineering, Program in Mechanical Engineering, Atlanta, GA 30332-0001

AWARDS Biomedical engineering (MS Bio E); mechanical engineering (MS, MSME, PhD). Part-time programs available. Terminal master's awarded for partial completion of doctoral program.

Degree requirements: For master's, thesis optional; for doctorate, thesis/dissertation.
Entrance requirements: For master's and doctorate, GRE General Test (recommended), TOEFL.
Faculty research: Acoustics, automatic controls, CAD/CAM, fluid mechanics, lubrication.

■ GRADUATE SCHOOL AND UNIVERSITY CENTER OF THE CITY UNIVERSITY OF NEW YORK

Graduate Studies, Program in Engineering, New York, NY 10016-4039

AWARDS Chemical engineering (PhD); civil engineering (PhD); electrical engineering (PhD); mechanical engineering (PhD).

Faculty: 68 full-time (1 woman).
Students: 125 full-time (28 women), 6 part-time (1 woman); includes 13 minority (9 African Americans, 2 Asian Americans or Pacific Islanders, 2 Hispanic Americans), 95 international. Average age 32. 205 applicants, 63% accepted, 26 enrolled. In 2001, 22 degrees awarded.
Degree requirements: For doctorate, thesis/dissertation.
Entrance requirements: For doctorate, GRE General Test. *Application deadline:* For fall admission, 4/15. *Application fee:* $40.
Expenses: Tuition, state resident: part-time $245 per credit. Tuition, nonresident: part-time $425 per credit. Required fees: $72 per semester.
Financial support: In 2001–02, 67 students received support, including 64 fellowships; research assistantships, teaching assistantships, Federal Work-Study, institutionally sponsored loans, and tuition waivers (full and partial) also available. Financial award application deadline: 2/1; financial award applicants required to submit FAFSA.
Dr. Mumtaz Kassir, Acting Executive Officer, 212-650-8031, *Fax:* 212-650-8029, *E-mail:* kassir@ce-mail.engr.ccny.cuny.edu.

Find an in-depth description at www.petersons.com/gradchannel.

■ GRAND VALLEY STATE UNIVERSITY

Science and Mathematics Division, Seymour and Esther Padnos School of Engineering, Allendale, MI 49401-9403

AWARDS Manufacturing engineering (MSE); manufacturing operations (MSE); mechanical engineering (MSE). Part-time programs available.
Faculty: 10 full-time (1 woman), 3 part-time/adjunct (1 woman).
Students: 5 full-time (1 woman), 42 part-time (7 women); includes 4 minority (1 African American, 2 Asian Americans or Pacific Islanders, 1 Hispanic American), 2 international. Average age 31. 37 applicants, 57% accepted, 15 enrolled. In 2001, 2 degrees awarded.
Degree requirements: For master's, project. *Median time to degree:* Master's–3 years part-time.
Entrance requirements: For master's, engineering degree with minimum GPA of 3.0. *Application deadline:* Applications are processed on a rolling basis. *Application fee:* $20.
Expenses: Tuition, state resident: part-time $202 per credit hour. Tuition, nonresident: part-time $437 per credit hour.
Financial support: In 2001–02, 2 research assistantships with full tuition reimbursements (averaging $11,000 per year), 3 teaching assistantships with full tuition reimbursements (averaging $8,000 per year) were awarded. Career-related internships or fieldwork, Federal Work-Study, institutionally sponsored loans, scholarships/grants, and unspecified assistantships also available.
Faculty research: Digital signal processing, computer aided design, computer aided manufacturing, manufacturing simulation, biomechanics. *Total annual research expenditures:* $300,000.
Dr. Paul Plotkowski, Director, 616-771-6750, *Fax:* 616-336-7215, *E-mail:* plotkowp@gvsu.edu.
Application contact: Dr. Hugh Jack, Graduate Coordinator, 616-771-6750, *Fax:* 616-336-7215, *E-mail:* jackh@gvsu.edu. *Web site:* http://www.engineer.gvsu.edu/

■ HOWARD UNIVERSITY

College of Engineering, Architecture, and Computer Sciences, School of Engineering and Computer Science, Department of Mechanical Engineering, Washington, DC 20059-0002

AWARDS M Eng, PhD.
Students: 8. Average age 25. In 2001, 1 master's, 1 doctorate awarded.
Degree requirements: For master's, comprehensive exam; for doctorate, one foreign language, thesis/dissertation, 2 terms of residency.

Entrance requirements: For master's and doctorate, GRE General Test, TOEFL, minimum GPA of 3.0. *Application deadline:* For fall admission, 4/1 (priority date); for spring admission, 11/1. Applications are processed on a rolling basis. *Application fee:* $45. Electronic applications accepted.
Financial support: In 2001–02, 1 fellowship with full tuition reimbursement (averaging $14,400 per year), 3 research assistantships, 5 teaching assistantships with full tuition reimbursements were awarded. Institutionally sponsored loans, scholarships/grants, and tuition waivers (partial) also available. Financial award application deadline: 4/1; financial award applicants required to submit FAFSA.
Faculty research: The dynamics and control of large flexible space structures, optimization of space structures.
Dr. Lewis Thigpen, Chair, 202-806-6600, *Fax:* 202-806-5258, *E-mail:* lthigpen@scs.howard.edu. *Web site:* http://www.howard.edu/

Find an in-depth description at www.petersons.com/gradchannel.

■ ILLINOIS INSTITUTE OF TECHNOLOGY

Graduate College, Armour College of Engineering and Sciences, Department of Mechanical, Materials and Aerospace Engineering, Mechanical and Aerospace Engineering Division, Chicago, IL 60616-3793

AWARDS MMAE, MS, PhD. Part-time programs available.

Faculty: 17 full-time (2 women), 8 part-time/adjunct (0 women).
Students: 66 full-time (10 women), 58 part-time (2 women); includes 7 minority (all Asian Americans or Pacific Islanders), 92 international. Average age 28. 539 applicants, 39% accepted. In 2001, 36 master's, 2 doctorates awarded. Terminal master's awarded for partial completion of doctoral program.
Degree requirements: For master's, thesis (for some programs), comprehensive exam; for doctorate, thesis/dissertation, comprehensive exam.
Entrance requirements: For master's and doctorate, GRE General Test, TOEFL, minimum undergraduate GPA of 3.0. *Application deadline:* For fall admission, 7/1; for spring admission, 11/1. Applications are processed on a rolling basis. *Application fee:* $30. Electronic applications accepted.
Expenses: Tuition: Part-time $590 per credit hour.
Financial support: In 2001–02, 13 research assistantships, 10 teaching assistantships were awarded. Federal Work-Study, institutionally sponsored loans, scholarships/grants, and unspecified assistantships also available. Financial

award application deadline: 3/1; financial award applicants required to submit FAFSA.

Faculty research: Solid and structural mechanics, fluid dynamics, thermal sciences, transportation engineering, design and manufacturing.
Dr. Candace Wark, Associate Chair, Mechanical Engineering, 312-567-3209, *Fax:* 312-567-7230, *E-mail:* wark@iit.edu.
Application contact: Dr. Ali Cinar, Dean of Graduate College, 312-567-3637, *Fax:* 312-567-7517, *E-mail:* gradstu@iit.edu. *Web site:* http://www.mmae.iit.edu/

■ INDIANA UNIVERSITY–PURDUE UNIVERSITY INDIANAPOLIS

School of Engineering and Technology, Department of Mechanical Engineering, Indianapolis, IN 46202-2896

AWARDS Biomedical engineering (MS Bm E); mechanical engineering (MSME). Part-time programs available.

Students: 11 full-time (2 women), 18 part-time (2 women); includes 4 minority (1 Asian American or Pacific Islander, 1 Hispanic American, 2 Native Americans), 20 international. Average age 30. In 2001, 3 degrees awarded.
Degree requirements: For master's, thesis optional.
Entrance requirements: For master's, GRE, TOEFL, minimum B average. *Application deadline:* For fall admission, 7/1. *Application fee:* $45 ($55 for international students).
Expenses: Tuition, state resident: full-time $4,480; part-time $187 per credit. Tuition, nonresident: full-time $12,926; part-time $539 per credit. Required fees: $177.
Financial support: Fellowships with tuition reimbursements, research assistantships with full and partial tuition reimbursements, tuition waivers (full and partial) available. Financial award application deadline: 3/1.
Faculty research: Computational fluid dynamics, heat transfer, finite-element methods, composites, biomechanics.
Dr. Hasan Akay, Chairman, 317-274-9717, *Fax:* 317-274-9744.
Application contact: Valerie Lim, Graduate Program, 317-278-4960, *Fax:* 317-278-1671, *E-mail:* grad@engr.iupui.edu. *Web site:* http://www.engr.iupui.edu/me/

■ INSTITUTE OF PAPER SCIENCE AND TECHNOLOGY

Graduate Programs, Program in Mechanical Engineering, Atlanta, GA 30318-5794

AWARDS MS, PhD. Terminal master's awarded for partial completion of doctoral program.

Degree requirements: For master's, industrial experience, research project; for doctorate, thesis/dissertation.

Entrance requirements: For master's and doctorate, GRE, minimum GPA of 3.0. *Web site:* http://www.ipst.edu/

■ IOWA STATE UNIVERSITY OF SCIENCE AND TECHNOLOGY

Graduate College, College of Engineering, Department of Mechanical Engineering, Ames, IA 50011

AWARDS MS, PhD.

Faculty: 33 full-time.
Students: 57 full-time (7 women), 54 part-time (5 women); includes 5 minority (2 African Americans, 2 Asian Americans or Pacific Islanders, 1 Hispanic American), 45 international. 206 applicants, 19% accepted, 30 enrolled. In 2001, 17 master's, 8 doctorates awarded.
Degree requirements: For master's, thesis or alternative; for doctorate, thesis/dissertation. *Median time to degree:* Master's–2.2 years full-time; doctorate–4.3 years full-time.
Entrance requirements: For master's and doctorate, GRE General Test (international applicants), TOEFL or IELTS. *Application deadline:* For fall admission, 3/1 (priority date); for spring admission, 9/1 (priority date). *Application fee:* $20 ($50 for international students). Electronic applications accepted.
Expenses: Tuition, state resident: full-time $1,851. Tuition, nonresident: full-time $5,449. Tuition and fees vary according to program.
Financial support: In 2001–02, 53 research assistantships with partial tuition reimbursements (averaging $12,980 per year), 17 teaching assistantships with partial tuition reimbursements (averaging $12,660 per year) were awarded. Fellowships, scholarships/grants, health care benefits, and unspecified assistantships also available.
Dr. Warren R. DeVries, Chair, 515-294-1423, *Fax:* 515-294-3261, *E-mail:* megradinfo@iastate.edu.
Application contact: Dr. Judy M. Vance, Director of Graduate Education, 515-294-9474, *E-mail:* megradinfo@iastate.edu. *Web site:* http://www1.eng.iastate.edu/coe/grad.asp/

■ JOHNS HOPKINS UNIVERSITY

G. W. C. Whiting School of Engineering, Department of Mechanical Engineering, Baltimore, MD 21218-2699

AWARDS Mechanical engineering (MS, MSE, PhD), including mechanical engineering (MS), mechanics (MSE, PhD). Part-time programs available.

Faculty: 14 full-time (2 women), 6 part-time/adjunct (0 women).
Students: 49 full-time (10 women); includes 2 minority (1 African American, 1 Asian American or Pacific Islander), 36

international. Average age 28. 279 applicants, 10% accepted, 9 enrolled. In 2001, 9 master's, 5 doctorates awarded. Terminal master's awarded for partial completion of doctoral program.
Degree requirements: For master's, thesis (for some programs); for doctorate, thesis/dissertation, oral exam.
Entrance requirements: For master's and doctorate, GRE General Test, TOEFL. *Application deadline:* For fall admission, 1/15 (priority date). *Application fee:* $0. Electronic applications accepted.
Expenses: Tuition: Full-time $27,390.
Financial support: In 2001–02, 49 students received support, including 3 fellowships with full tuition reimbursements available (averaging $18,996 per year), 39 research assistantships with full tuition reimbursements available (averaging $18,996 per year); teaching assistantships, Federal Work-Study, institutionally sponsored loans, scholarships/grants, tuition waivers (full), and unspecified assistantships also available. Support available to part-time students. Financial award application deadline: 1/15.
Faculty research: Mechanical behavior of materials, robotics, heat and mass transfer, fluid mechanics, biomechanics. *Total annual research expenditures:* $4 million.
Dr. K. T. Ramesh, Chair, 410-516-7735, *Fax:* 410-516-7254, *E-mail:* ramesh@jhu.edu.
Application contact: Dr. Shiyi Chen, Chair, Graduate Admissions Committee, 410-516-7154, *Fax:* 410-516-7254, *E-mail:* megrad@titan.me.jhu.edu. *Web site:* http://www.me.jhu.edu/

Find an in-depth description at www.petersons.com/gradchannel.

■ KANSAS STATE UNIVERSITY

Graduate School, College of Engineering, Department of Mechanical Engineering, Manhattan, KS 66506

AWARDS Engineering (PhD); mechanical engineering (MS); nuclear engineering (MS).

Faculty: 23 full-time (1 woman).
Students: 39 full-time (5 women), 11 part-time, 27 international. 169 applicants, 8% accepted, 13 enrolled. In 2001, 9 degrees awarded.
Degree requirements: For master's, thesis or alternative; for doctorate, thesis/dissertation, comprehensive exam.
Entrance requirements: For master's, GRE General Test, TOEFL, minimum GPA of 3.0 in physics, mathematics, and chemistry; for doctorate, GRE General Test, TOEFL, master's degree in mechanical engineering. *Application deadline:* For fall admission, 3/1; for spring admission, 9/1. Applications are processed on a rolling basis. *Application fee:* $0 ($25 for international students). Electronic applications accepted.

Kansas State University (continued)

Expenses: Tuition, state resident: part-time $113 per credit hour. Tuition, nonresident: part-time $358 per credit hour.

Financial support: In 2001–02, 35 research assistantships (averaging $9,000 per year), 3 teaching assistantships with full tuition reimbursements (averaging $9,000 per year) were awarded. Career-related internships or fieldwork, Federal Work-Study, institutionally sponsored loans, and scholarships/grants also available. Support available to part-time students. Financial award application deadline: 3/1; financial award applicants required to submit FAFSA.

Faculty research: Holographic particle velocimetry, optical measurements, thermal sciences, heat transfer, machine design. *Total annual research expenditures:* $4.1 million.

Mohammad Hosni, Head, 785-532-2283, *Fax:* 785-532-7057.

Application contact: Sameer Madanshetty, Graduate Program Coordinator, 785-532-5610, *Fax:* 785-532-7057, *E-mail:* dgs@ksume.me.ksu.edu. *Web site:* http://www.mne.ksu.edu/

■ KETTERING UNIVERSITY

Graduate School, Mechanical Engineering Department, Flint, MI 48504-4898

AWARDS Automotive systems (MS Eng); manufacturing (MS Eng); mechanical cognate (MS Eng); mechanical design (MS Eng). Part-time and evening/weekend programs available. Postbaccalaureate distance learning degree programs offered (no on-campus study).

Faculty: 15 full-time (0 women).
Students: 6 full-time (1 woman), 88 part-time (12 women); includes 8 minority (7 African Americans, 1 Native American), 43 international. 163 applicants, 87% accepted. In 2001, 18 degrees awarded.
Degree requirements: For master's, thesis (for some programs), registration. *Median time to degree:* Master's–3 years full-time, 6 years part-time.
Application deadline: For fall admission, 7/15. Applications are processed on a rolling basis. *Application fee:* $0. Electronic applications accepted.
Expenses: Tuition: Full-time $8,370; part-time $465 per credit.
Financial support: Fellowships with full tuition reimbursements, research assistantships with full tuition reimbursements, teaching assistantships with full tuition reimbursements, Federal Work-Study, scholarships/grants, and tuition waivers (partial) available. Support available to part-time students. Financial award application deadline: 7/15; financial award applicants required to submit CSS PROFILE or FAFSA.

Dr. K. Joel Berry, Head, 810-762-7833, *Fax:* 810-762-7860, *E-mail:* jberry@kettering.edu.
Application contact: Betty L. Bedore, Coordinator of Publicity, 810-762-7494, *Fax:* 810-762-9935, *E-mail:* bbedore@kettering.edu. *Web site:* http://www.kettering.edu/

■ LAMAR UNIVERSITY

College of Graduate Studies, College of Engineering, Department of Mechanical Engineering, Beaumont, TX 77710

AWARDS ME, MES, DE. Part-time programs available.

Faculty: 5 full-time (0 women).
Students: 23 full-time (3 women), 6 part-time (2 women); includes 3 minority (all Asian Americans or Pacific Islanders), 22 international. Average age 26. 115 applicants, 55% accepted. In 2001, 12 master's, 1 doctorate awarded. Terminal master's awarded for partial completion of doctoral program.
Degree requirements: For master's, thesis (for some programs); for doctorate, thesis/dissertation.
Entrance requirements: For master's and doctorate, GRE General Test, TOEFL. *Application deadline:* For fall admission, 5/15 (priority date); for spring admission, 10/1 (priority date). Applications are processed on a rolling basis. *Application fee:* $25 ($50 for international students).
Expenses: Tuition, state resident: full-time $1,114. Tuition, nonresident: full-time $3,670.
Financial support: In 2001–02, 1 fellowship, 4 research assistantships, 5 teaching assistantships were awarded. Tuition waivers (partial) also available. Financial award application deadline: 4/1.
Faculty research: Aerospace systems, electrical power, robotics, solar energy, thermal control. *Total annual research expenditures:* $100,000.
Dr. Malur N. Srinivasan, Chair, 409-880-8094, *Fax:* 409-880-8121, *E-mail:* srinivasmn@hal.lamar.edu.

■ LEHIGH UNIVERSITY

P.C. Rossin College of Engineering and Applied Science, Department of Mechanical Engineering and Mechanics, Bethlehem, PA 18015-3094

AWARDS Applied mathematics (MS, PhD); mechanical engineering (M Eng, MS, PhD); mechanics (M Eng, MS, PhD). Part-time programs available.

Faculty: 28 full-time (0 women).
Students: 64 full-time (7 women), 7 part-time; includes 2 minority (1 African American, 1 Hispanic American), 39 international. 577 applicants, 31% accepted, 12 enrolled. In 2001, 14 master's, 5 doctorates awarded. Terminal master's awarded for partial completion of doctoral program.

Degree requirements: For master's and doctorate, thesis/dissertation.
Entrance requirements: For master's and doctorate, TOEFL. *Application deadline:* For fall admission, 7/15; for spring admission, 12/1. Applications are processed on a rolling basis. *Application fee:* $50.
Expenses: Tuition: Part-time $468 per credit hour. Required fees: $200; $100 per semester. Tuition and fees vary according to program.
Financial support: In 2001–02, 5 fellowships with full and partial tuition reimbursements (averaging $10,380 per year), 27 research assistantships with full and partial tuition reimbursements (averaging $14,475 per year), 8 teaching assistantships with full and partial tuition reimbursements (averaging $12,330 per year) were awarded. Financial award application deadline: 1/15.
Faculty research: Thermofluids, dynamic systems, CAD/CAM. *Total annual research expenditures:* $2.5 million.
Dr. Charles R. Smith, Chairman, 610-758-4102, *Fax:* 610-758-6224, *E-mail:* crs1@lehigh.edu.
Application contact: Donna Reiss, Graduate Coordinator, 610-758-4139, *Fax:* 610-758-6224, *E-mail:* dmr1@lehigh.edu. *Web site:* http://www.lehigh.edu/~inmem/

Find an in-depth description at www.petersons.com/gradchannel.

■ LOUISIANA STATE UNIVERSITY AND AGRICULTURAL AND MECHANICAL COLLEGE

Graduate School, College of Engineering, Department of Mechanical Engineering, Baton Rouge, LA 70803

AWARDS MSME, PhD. Part-time programs available.

Faculty: 20 full-time (0 women), 2 part-time/adjunct (0 women).
Students: 71 full-time (9 women), 11 part-time (2 women); includes 2 minority (both African Americans), 65 international. Average age 27. 139 applicants, 41% accepted, 24 enrolled. In 2001, 18 master's, 2 doctorates awarded. Terminal master's awarded for partial completion of doctoral program.
Degree requirements: For master's and doctorate, thesis/dissertation.
Entrance requirements: For master's and doctorate, GRE General Test, TOEFL, minimum GPA of 3.0. *Application deadline:* For fall admission, 1/25 (priority date). Applications are processed on a rolling basis. *Application fee:* $25.
Expenses: Tuition, state resident: full-time $2,551. Tuition, nonresident: full-time $5,551. Required fees: $854. Part-time tuition and fees vary according to course load.
Financial support: In 2001–02, 2 fellowships (averaging $26,250 per year), 32 research assistantships with partial tuition

reimbursements (averaging $13,560 per year), 29 teaching assistantships with partial tuition reimbursements (averaging $11,579 per year) were awarded. Institutionally sponsored loans, tuition waivers (full and partial), and unspecified assistantships also available. Financial award applicants required to submit FAFSA.

Faculty research: Computer-aided design, thermal and fluid sciences materials engineering, fluid mechanics, combustion and microsystems engineering. *Total annual research expenditures:* $3.2 million.
Dr. Glenn Sinclair, Chair, 225-578-5792, *Fax:* 225-578-5924, *E-mail:* sinclair@ me.lsu.edu.

Application contact: Dr. S. Acharya, Graduate Adviser, 225-578-5809, *Fax:* 225-578-5924, *E-mail:* acharya@lsu.edu. *Web site:* http://me.lsu.edu/

■ LOUISIANA TECH UNIVERSITY

Graduate School, College of Engineering and Science, Department of Mechanical and Industrial Engineering, Ruston, LA 71272

AWARDS Industrial engineering (MS, D Eng); manufacturing systems engineering (MS); mechanical engineering (MS, D Eng); operations research (MS). Part-time programs available. Terminal master's awarded for partial completion of doctoral program.

Degree requirements: For master's and doctorate, thesis/dissertation.
Entrance requirements: For master's, GRE General Test, TOEFL, minimum GPA of 3.0 in last 60 hours; for doctorate, TOEFL, minimum graduate GPA of 3.25 (with MS) or GRE General Test.
Faculty research: Engineering management, facilities planning, thermodynamics, automated manufacturing, micromanufacturing.

■ LOYOLA MARYMOUNT UNIVERSITY

Graduate Division, College of Science and Engineering, Department of Mechanical Engineering, Program in Mechanical Engineering, Los Angeles, CA 90045-2659

AWARDS MSE.

Students: 4 full-time (0 women), 3 part-time (1 woman); includes 3 minority (1 Asian American or Pacific Islander, 2 Hispanic Americans). 6 applicants, 67% accepted, 3 enrolled. In 2001, 6 degrees awarded.
Degree requirements: For master's, one foreign language.
Entrance requirements: For master's, TOEFL. *Application deadline:* Applications are processed on a rolling basis. *Application fee:* $45. Electronic applications accepted.

Expenses: Tuition: Part-time $612 per credit hour. Required fees: $86 per term. Tuition and fees vary according to program.
Financial support: In 2001–02, 2 students received support; research assistantships, Federal Work-Study, scholarships/grants, and laboratory assistantships available. Support available to part-time students. Financial award application deadline: 7/1; financial award applicants required to submit FAFSA. *Web site:* http://www.lmu.edu/acad/gd/graddiv.htm

■ MANHATTAN COLLEGE

Graduate Division, School of Engineering, Program in Mechanical Engineering, Riverdale, NY 10471

AWARDS MS. Part-time and evening/weekend programs available.

Degree requirements: For master's, thesis or alternative.
Entrance requirements: For master's, GRE, TOEFL, minimum GPA of 3.0.
Faculty research: Thermal analysis of rocket thrust chambers, stress analysis of torque transmission, quality of wood.

■ MARQUETTE UNIVERSITY

Graduate School, College of Engineering, Department of Mechanical and Industrial Engineering, Milwaukee, WI 53201-1881

AWARDS Engineering management (MS); mechanical engineering (MS, PhD), including manufacturing systems engineering. Part-time and evening/weekend programs available.

Faculty: 13 full-time (0 women), 9 part-time/adjunct (0 women).
Students: 26 full-time (4 women), 50 part-time (2 women); includes 1 minority (Native American), 28 international. Average age 27. 75 applicants, 73% accepted. In 2001, 6 master's, 3 doctorates awarded. Terminal master's awarded for partial completion of doctoral program.
Degree requirements: For master's, thesis; for doctorate, thesis/dissertation, qualifying exam.
Entrance requirements: For master's and doctorate, GRE General Test, TOEFL, minimum GPA of 3.0. *Application deadline:* For fall admission, 8/1 (priority date); for spring admission, 1/1 (priority date). Applications are processed on a rolling basis. *Application fee:* $40. Electronic applications accepted.
Expenses: Tuition: Full-time $10,170; part-time $445 per credit hour. Tuition and fees vary according to course load.
Financial support: In 2001–02, 13 students received support, including fellowships with tuition reimbursements available (averaging $10,190 per year), 1 research assistantship with tuition reimbursement available (averaging $10,835 per year), 7 teaching assistantships

with tuition reimbursements available (averaging $10,835 per year); Federal Work-Study, institutionally sponsored loans, scholarships/grants, and tuition waivers (full and partial) also available. Support available to part-time students. Financial award application deadline: 2/15.
Faculty research: Computer-integrated manufacturing, energy conversion, simulation modeling and optimization, applied mechanics, metallurgy. *Total annual research expenditures:* $250,000.
Dr. Kyle Kim, Chair, 414-288-7259, *Fax:* 414-288-7790, *E-mail:* kyle.kim@ marquette.edu.
Application contact: Dr. Robert J. Stango, Director of Graduate Studies, 414-288-6972, *Fax:* 414-288-7790, *E-mail:* robert.stango@marquette.edu. *Web site:* http://www.eng.mu.edu/~meen/index.html

Find an in-depth description at www.petersons.com/gradchannel.

■ MASSACHUSETTS INSTITUTE OF TECHNOLOGY

School of Engineering, Department of Mechanical Engineering, Cambridge, MA 02139-4307

AWARDS SM, PhD, Sc D, Mech E.

Faculty: 54 full-time (2 women).
Students: 348 full-time (60 women), 3 part-time (1 woman); includes 53 minority (15 African Americans, 31 Asian Americans or Pacific Islanders, 7 Hispanic Americans, 144 international. Average age 24. 641 applicants, 28% accepted, 100 enrolled. In 2001, 136 master's, 35 doctorates awarded. Terminal master's awarded for partial completion of doctoral program.
Degree requirements: For master's, thesis/dissertation; for doctorate, thesis/dissertation, comprehensive exam.
Entrance requirements: For master's and doctorate, GRE General Test, TOEFL. *Application deadline:* For fall admission, 12/15. *Application fee:* $60. Electronic applications accepted.
Expenses: Tuition: Full-time $26,960. Full-time tuition and fees vary according to program.
Financial support: In 2001–02, 338 students received support, including 91 fellowships, 235 research assistantships, 31 teaching assistantships; career-related internships or fieldwork, Federal Work-Study, institutionally sponsored loans, scholarships/grants, health care benefits, and unspecified assistantships also available. Financial award applicants required to submit FAFSA.
Faculty research: Systems and control, fluid and thermal sciences, mechanics and materials, design and manufacturing. *Total annual research expenditures:* $17.8 million.
Rohan Abeyaratne, Head, 617-253-0066, *Fax:* 617-258-6156, *E-mail:* rohan@ mit.edu.
Application contact: Leslie M. Regan, Graduate Programs Administrator, 617-253-2291, *Fax:* 617-258-5802, *E-mail:*

Massachusetts Institute of Technology (continued)
me-gradoffice@mit.edu. *Web site:* http://www-me.mit.edu/

■ MCNEESE STATE UNIVERSITY

Graduate School, College of Engineering and Technology, Lake Charles, LA 70609

AWARDS Chemical engineering (M Eng); civil engineering (M Eng); electrical engineering (M Eng); mechanical engineering (M Eng). Part-time and evening/weekend programs available.

Faculty: 14 full-time (1 woman).
Students: 24 full-time (5 women), 5 part-time; includes 1 minority (Asian American or Pacific Islander), 23 international. In 2001, 5 degrees awarded.
Degree requirements: For master's, thesis or alternative.
Entrance requirements: For master's, GRE General Test, TOEFL, minimum undergraduate GPA of 3.0. *Application deadline:* For fall admission, 7/15 (priority date). Applications are processed on a rolling basis. *Application fee:* $20 ($30 for international students).
Expenses: Tuition, state resident: part-time $1,208 per semester. Tuition, nonresident: part-time $4,378 per semester.
Financial support: Federal Work-Study available. Support available to part-time students. Financial award application deadline: 5/1.
Dr. O. C. Karkalits, Dean, 337-475-5875, *Fax:* 337-475-5237, *E-mail:* ckarkal@mail.mcneese.edu.
Application contact: Dr. Jay O. Uppot, Director of Graduate Studies, 337-475-5874, *Fax:* 37-475-5286, *E-mail:* juppot@mail.mcneese.edu.

■ MERCER UNIVERSITY

Graduate Studies, Macon Campus, School of Engineering, Macon, GA 31207-0003

AWARDS Biomedical engineering (MSE); electrical engineering (MSE); engineering management (MSE); mechanical engineering (MSE). Software engineering (MSE). Software systems (MS); technical communications management (MS); technical management (MS). Part-time and evening/weekend programs available.

Faculty: 10 full-time (1 woman), 5 part-time/adjunct (1 woman).
Students: 3 full-time (2 women), 104 part-time (31 women); includes 19 minority (13 African Americans, 6 Asian Americans or Pacific Islanders), 5 international. Average age 36. 31 applicants, 97% accepted, 27 enrolled. In 2001, 32 degrees awarded.
Degree requirements: For master's, thesis or alternative, registration.
Entrance requirements: For master's, GRE, minimum undergraduate GPA of

3.0. *Application deadline:* For fall admission, 7/1; for spring admission, 11/15. Applications are processed on a rolling basis. *Application fee:* $35 ($50 for international students).
Expenses: Contact institution.
Financial support: Federal Work-Study available.
Dr. M. Dayne Aldridge, Dean, 478-301-2459, *Fax:* 478-301-5593, *E-mail:* aldridge_md@mercer.edu.
Application contact: Kathy Olivier, Graduate Administrative Coordinator, 478-301-2196, *E-mail:* olivier_kk@mercer.edu. *Web site:* http://www.mercer.edu/engineer.htm

■ MICHIGAN STATE UNIVERSITY

Graduate School, College of Engineering, Department of Mechanical Engineering, East Lansing, MI 48824

AWARDS MS, PhD. Part-time programs available. Postbaccalaureate distance learning degree programs offered (minimal on-campus study).

Faculty: 33.
Students: 67 full-time (10 women), 23 part-time (3 women); includes 2 minority (1 Asian American or Pacific Islander, 1 Hispanic American), 63 international. Average age 27. 454 applicants, 10% accepted. In 2001, 21 master's, 7 doctorates awarded.
Degree requirements: For master's, thesis optional; for doctorate, thesis/dissertation.
Entrance requirements: For master's, GRE General Test, TOEFL, minimum GPA of 3.0; for doctorate, GRE General Test, TOEFL. *Application deadline:* Applications are processed on a rolling basis. *Application fee:* $30 ($40 for international students). Electronic applications accepted.
Expenses: Tuition, state resident: part-time $244 per credit hour. Tuition, nonresident: part-time $494 per credit hour. Required fees: $268 per semester. Tuition and fees vary according to course load, degree level and program.
Financial support: In 2001–02, 38 fellowships (averaging $1,854 per year), 24 research assistantships with tuition reimbursements (averaging $14,062 per year), 37 teaching assistantships with tuition reimbursements (averaging $13,212 per year) were awarded. Financial award applicants required to submit FAFSA.
Faculty research: Experimental fluid mechanics, nonlinear vibrations, control of ER fluids, flow diagnostics in IC engines, turbomachinery design. *Total annual research expenditures:* $3 million.
Dr. Ronald C. Rosenberg, Chairperson, 517-353-9861, *Fax:* 517-353-1750, *E-mail:* megradad@egr.msu.edu. *Web site:* http://www.egr.msu.edu/ME/

■ MICHIGAN TECHNOLOGICAL UNIVERSITY

Graduate School, College of Engineering, Department of Mechanical Engineering-Engineering Mechanics, Program in Mechanical Engineering, Houghton, MI 49931-1295

AWARDS Mechanical engineering (MS); mechanical engineering-engineering mechanics (PhD). Part-time programs available.

Degree requirements: For master's and doctorate, thesis/dissertation.
Entrance requirements: For master's and doctorate, GRE General Test, TOEFL. Electronic applications accepted. *Web site:* http://www.me.mtu.edu/

Find an in-depth description at www.petersons.com/gradchannel.

■ MINNESOTA STATE UNIVERSITY, MANKATO

College of Graduate Studies, College of Science, Engineering and Technology, Program in Mechanical Engineering, Mankato, MN 56001

AWARDS MS. Part-time programs available.

Faculty: 7 full-time (0 women).
Degree requirements: For master's, comprehensive exam.
Application deadline: For fall admission, 7/9 (priority date); for spring admission, 11/27. Applications are processed on a rolling basis. *Application fee:* $20.
Expenses: Tuition, state resident: full-time $3,253; part-time $157 per credit. Tuition, nonresident: full-time $4,893; part-time $248 per credit. Required fees: $24 per credit. Tuition and fees vary according to reciprocity agreements.
Financial support: Application deadline: 3/15.
Dr. S. Moaveni, Head, 507-389-6383.
Application contact: College of Grad Studies and Research, 507-389-2021, *Fax:* 507-379-5974, *E-mail:* grad@mnsu.edu.

■ MISSISSIPPI STATE UNIVERSITY

College of Engineering, Department of Mechanical Engineering, Mississippi State, MS 39762

AWARDS MS, PhD. Part-time programs available. Postbaccalaureate distance learning degree programs offered (minimal on-campus study).

Faculty: 18 full-time (2 women), 4 part-time/adjunct (0 women).
Students: 20 full-time (5 women), 4 part-time (1 woman); includes 6 minority (3 African Americans, 3 Asian Americans or Pacific Islanders), 10 international. Average age 25. 124 applicants, 17% accepted. In 2001, 10 degrees awarded.
Degree requirements: For master's, oral exam, thesis optional; for doctorate, thesis/

dissertation, qualifying exam, preliminary exam, dissertation defense.
Entrance requirements: For master's and doctorate, GRE General Test, TOEFL, minimum GPA of 2.75. *Application deadline:* For fall admission, 7/1; for spring admission, 11/1. Applications are processed on a rolling basis. *Application fee:* $25 for international students.
Expenses: Tuition, state resident: full-time $3,586; part-time $150 per credit hour. Tuition, nonresident: full-time $8,128; part-time $339 per credit hour. Tuition and fees vary according to course load and campus/location.
Financial support: In 2001–02, 4 fellowships (averaging $4,000 per year), 20 research assistantships with full tuition reimbursements (averaging $11,700 per year), teaching assistantships with full tuition reimbursements (averaging $13,200 per year) were awarded. Career-related internships or fieldwork, Federal Work-Study, and institutionally sponsored loans also available. Financial award applicants required to submit FAFSA.
Faculty research: Fatigue and fracture, heat transfer, fluid dynamics, CFD energy systems, manufacturing systems, materials. *Total annual research expenditures:* $1.7 million.
Dr. W. Glenn Steele, Head, 662-325-3260, *Fax:* 662-325-7223, *E-mail:* graduate@meng.msstate.edu.
Application contact: Jerry B. Inmon, Director of Admissions, 662-325-2224, *Fax:* 662-325-7360, *E-mail:* admit@admissions.msstate.edu. *Web site:* http://www.msstate.edu/

■ MONTANA STATE UNIVERSITY–BOZEMAN

College of Graduate Studies, College of Engineering, Department of Mechanical and Industrial Engineering, Bozeman, MT 59717

AWARDS Engineering (PhD); industrial and management engineering (MS); mechanical engineering (MS). Part-time programs available.

Students: 22 full-time (4 women), 11 part-time (2 women); includes 1 minority (Asian American or Pacific Islander), 16 international. Average age 26. 58 applicants, 91% accepted, 14 enrolled. In 2001, 15 degrees awarded.
Degree requirements: For master's, thesis or alternative; for doctorate, thesis/dissertation, qualifying exam, supporting course area, comprehensive exam.
Entrance requirements: For master's, GRE General Test, TOEFL, TSE, minimum GPA of 3.0; for doctorate, GRE General Test, TOEFL, minimum undergraduate GPA of 3.0, minimum graduate GPA of 3.0. *Application deadline:* For fall admission, 7/21; for spring admission, 11/15. Applications are processed on a rolling basis. *Application fee:* $50. Electronic applications accepted.

Expenses: Tuition, state resident: full-time $3,894; part-time $198 per credit. Tuition, nonresident: full-time $10,661; part-time $480 per credit. International tuition: $10,811 full-time. Tuition and fees vary according to course load and program.
Financial support: In 2001–02, 21 research assistantships with full and partial tuition reimbursements (averaging $17,050 per year), 29 teaching assistantships with full and partial tuition reimbursements (averaging $8,658 per year) were awarded. Health care benefits and unspecified assistantships also available. Support available to part-time students. Financial award application deadline: 3/1; financial award applicants required to submit FAFSA.
Faculty research: Design representation in synthesis process, composites and smart materials, software for pulse detonation engines, HVAC, damage and failure criteria for advanced composites. *Total annual research expenditures:* $1.2 million.
Dr. Vic Cundy, Head, 406-994-2203, *Fax:* 406-994-6292, *E-mail:* vcundy@me.montana.edu. *Web site:* http://www.coe.montana.edu/mie/

■ NATIONAL TECHNOLOGICAL UNIVERSITY

Programs in Engineering, Fort Collins, CO 80526-1842

AWARDS Chemical engineering (MS); computer engineering (MS); computer science (MS); electrical engineering (MS); engineering management (MS); environmental systems management (MS); management of technology (MS); manufacturing systems engineering (MS); materials science and engineering (MS); mechanical engineering (MS); microelectronics and semiconductor engineering (MS). Software engineering (MS). Special majors (MS). Systems engineering (MS). Part-time programs available. Postbaccalaureate distance learning degree programs offered (no on-campus study).

Students: In 2001, 114 degrees awarded.
Degree requirements: For master's, comprehensive exam.
Entrance requirements: For master's, BS in engineering or related field; 2.9 minimum GPA. *Application deadline:* Applications are processed on a rolling basis. *Application fee:* $50. Electronic applications accepted.
Expenses: Tuition: Part-time $660 per credit hour. Part-time tuition and fees vary according to course load, campus/location and program.
Dr. Andre Vacroux, President, 970-495-6400, *Fax:* 970-484-0668, *E-mail:* andre@ntu.edu.
Application contact: Rhonda Bonham, Admissions Officer, 970-495-6400, *Fax:* 970-498-0601, *E-mail:* rhonda@ntu.edu. *Web site:* http://www.ntu.edu/

■ NAVAL POSTGRADUATE SCHOOL

Graduate Programs, Department of Mechanical Engineering, Monterey, CA 93943

AWARDS MS, D Eng, PhD, Eng. Program only open to commissioned officers of the United States and friendly nations and selected United States federal civilian employees. Part-time programs available. Postbaccalaureate distance learning degree programs offered.

Degree requirements: For master's and Eng, thesis; for doctorate, one foreign language, thesis/dissertation.

■ NEW JERSEY INSTITUTE OF TECHNOLOGY

Office of Graduate Studies, Department of Mechanical Engineering, Newark, NJ 07102

AWARDS MS, PhD, Engineer. Part-time and evening/weekend programs available.

Faculty: 23 full-time (1 woman).
Students: 67 full-time (9 women), 22 part-time (3 women); includes 7 minority (2 Asian Americans or Pacific Islanders, 5 Hispanic Americans), 65 international. Average age 27. 296 applicants, 67% accepted, 37 enrolled. In 2001, 13 master's, 8 doctorates awarded.
Degree requirements: For doctorate, thesis/dissertation.
Entrance requirements: For master's, GRE General Test; for doctorate, GRE General Test, minimum graduate GPA of 3.5. *Application deadline:* For fall admission, 6/5 (priority date); for spring admission, 10/15. Applications are processed on a rolling basis. *Application fee:* $50. Electronic applications accepted.
Expenses: Tuition, state resident: full-time $7,812; part-time $434 per credit. Tuition, nonresident: full-time $10,746; part-time $597 per credit. Required fees: $47 per credit. $76 per semester.
Financial support: Fellowships with full and partial tuition reimbursements, research assistantships with full and partial tuition reimbursements, teaching assistantships with full and partial tuition reimbursements, career-related internships or fieldwork, Federal Work-Study, institutionally sponsored loans, and unspecified assistantships available. Financial award application deadline: 3/15.
Faculty research: Energy systems, structural mechanics, electromechanical systems.
Dr. Nadine Aubry, Chairperson, 973-596-3330, *E-mail:* nadine.n.aubry@njit.edu.
Application contact: Kathryn Kelly, Director of Admissions, 973-596-3300, *Fax:* 973-596-3461, *E-mail:* admissions@njit.edu. *Web site:* http://www.njit.edu/

■ NEW MEXICO STATE UNIVERSITY

Graduate School, College of Engineering, Department of Mechanical Engineering, Las Cruces, NM 88003-8001

AWARDS MSME, PhD. Postbaccalaureate distance learning degree programs offered (no on-campus study).

Faculty: 12 full-time (0 women), 3 part-time/adjunct (0 women).
Students: 22 full-time (1 woman), 11 part-time; includes 8 minority (1 Asian American or Pacific Islander, 6 Hispanic Americans, 1 Native American), 10 international. Average age 27. 48 applicants, 90% accepted, 3 enrolled. In 2001, 10 master's, 1 doctorate awarded.
Degree requirements: For master's, thesis (for some programs); for doctorate, thesis/dissertation, 2 research tools.
Entrance requirements: For master's, minimum GPA of 3.0; for doctorate, qualifying exam, minimum GPA of 3.0. *Application deadline:* For fall admission, 7/1 (priority date); for spring admission, 11/1. Applications are processed on a rolling basis. *Application fee:* $15 ($35 for international students). Electronic applications accepted.
Expenses: Tuition, state resident: full-time $3,234; part-time $135 per credit. Tuition, nonresident: full-time $9,420; part-time $428 per credit. Required fees: $858.
Financial support: In 2001–02, 5 research assistantships with partial tuition reimbursements, 16 teaching assistantships with partial tuition reimbursements were awarded. Fellowships with partial tuition reimbursements, career-related internships or fieldwork, Federal Work-Study, and scholarships/grants also available. Support available to part-time students. Financial award application deadline: 3/1.
Faculty research: Computational mechanics; robotics; CAD/CAM; control, dynamics, and solid mechanics; interconnection engineering, heat transfer, composites.
Dr. Bahram Nassersharif, Head, 505-646-3501, *Fax:* 505-646-6111, *E-mail:* bn@nmsu.edu. *Web site:* http://me.nmsu.edu/

■ NORTH CAROLINA AGRICULTURAL AND TECHNICAL STATE UNIVERSITY

Graduate School, College of Engineering, Department of Mechanical Engineering, Greensboro, NC 27411

AWARDS MSME, PhD. Part-time programs available.

Faculty: 17 full-time (1 woman), 8 part-time/adjunct (1 woman).
Students: 36 full-time (6 women), 9 part-time (3 women); includes 27 minority (all

African Americans), 12 international. Average age 26. 61 applicants, 87% accepted. In 2001, 7 master's, 3 doctorates awarded.
Degree requirements: For master's, dual exam, qualifying exam, thesis defense, thesis optional; for doctorate, thesis/dissertation.
Entrance requirements: For doctorate, GRE. *Application deadline:* For fall admission, 7/1 (priority date); for spring admission, 11/1 (priority date). Applications are processed on a rolling basis. *Application fee:* $35.
Financial support: Fellowships with full tuition reimbursements, research assistantships with partial tuition reimbursements, teaching assistantships, unspecified assistantships available.
Faculty research: Composites, smart materials and sensors, mechanical systems modeling and finite element analysis, computational fluid dynamics and engine research, design and manufacturing. *Total annual research expenditures:* $1.4 million.
Dr. William J. Craft, Chairperson, 336-334-7620, *Fax:* 336-334-7417, *E-mail:* craft@ncat.edu.
Application contact: Dr. Shih-Liang Wang, Graduate Coordinator, 336-334-7620, *Fax:* 336-334-7414, *E-mail:* wang@ncat.edu.

■ NORTH CAROLINA STATE UNIVERSITY

Graduate School, College of Engineering, Department of Mechanical and Aerospace Engineering, Program in Mechanical Engineering, Raleigh, NC 27695

AWARDS MME, MS, PhD. Part-time programs available.

Faculty: 38 full-time (3 women), 45 part-time/adjunct (1 woman).
Students: 68 full-time (8 women), 24 part-time; includes 5 minority (2 African Americans, 2 Asian Americans or Pacific Islanders, 1 Hispanic American), 39 international. Average age 29. 288 applicants, 15% accepted. In 2001, 25 master's, 8 doctorates awarded.
Degree requirements: For master's, thesis, oral exam; for doctorate, thesis/dissertation, oral and preliminary exams.
Entrance requirements: For master's and doctorate, GRE General Test. *Application deadline:* For fall admission, 7/15; for spring admission, 12/15. Applications are processed on a rolling basis. *Application fee:* $45.
Expenses: Tuition, state resident: full-time $1,748. Tuition, nonresident: full-time $6,904.
Financial support: In 2001–02, 3 fellowships (averaging $7,624 per year), 46 research assistantships (averaging $5,767 per year), 17 teaching assistantships (averaging $5,428 per year) were awarded. Career-related internships or fieldwork and institutionally sponsored loans also available.

Faculty research: Vibration and control, fluid dynamics, thermal sciences, structure and materials, aerodynamics acoustics.
Dr. Richard D. Gould, Director of Graduate Programs, 919-515-5236, *Fax:* 919-515-7968, *E-mail:* gould@eos.ncsu.edu.
Find an in-depth description at www.petersons.com/gradchannel.

■ NORTH DAKOTA STATE UNIVERSITY

The Graduate School, College of Engineering and Architecture, Department of Mechanical Engineering and Applied Mechanics, Fargo, ND 58105

AWARDS MS. Part-time and evening/weekend programs available.

Faculty: 13 full-time (0 women).
Students: 10 full-time (0 women), 7 part-time, 6 international. Average age 25. 9 applicants, 100% accepted, 6 enrolled. In 2001, 3 degrees awarded.
Degree requirements: For master's, thesis.
Entrance requirements: For master's, TOEFL, minimum GPA of 3.0. *Application deadline:* For fall admission, 7/1 (priority date); for spring admission, 12/1 (priority date). Applications are processed on a rolling basis. *Application fee:* $35.
Expenses: Tuition, state resident: part-time $124 per credit. Tuition, nonresident: part-time $325 per credit. Required fees: $22 per credit. Tuition and fees vary according to reciprocity agreements.
Financial support: In 2001–02, 9 students received support, including research assistantships with full tuition reimbursements available (averaging $9,000 per year), teaching assistantships with full tuition reimbursements available (averaging $9,000 per year); career-related internships or fieldwork, Federal Work-Study, and institutionally sponsored loans also available. Financial award application deadline: 2/15.
Faculty research: Thermodynamics, finite element analysis, automotive systems, robotics.
Dr. Robert V. Pieri, Chair, 701-231-8671, *Fax:* 701-231-8913, *E-mail:* robert.pieri@ndsu.nodak.edu.

■ NORTHEASTERN UNIVERSITY

College of Engineering, Department of Mechanical, Industrial, and Manufacturing Engineering, Boston, MA 02115-5096

AWARDS Engineering management (MS); industrial engineering (MS, PhD); mechanical engineering (MS, PhD); operations research (MS). Part-time programs available.

Faculty: 26 full-time (1 woman), 5 part-time/adjunct (1 woman).
Students: 97 full-time (22 women), 80 part-time (10 women); includes 32 minority (6 African Americans, 7 Asian

Americans or Pacific Islanders, 19 Hispanic Americans), 77 international. Average age 25. 262 applicants, 53% accepted, 57 enrolled. In 2001, 46 master's, 6 doctorates awarded.
Degree requirements: For master's, thesis (for some programs), registration; for doctorate, one foreign language, thesis/dissertation, departmental qualifying exam.
Entrance requirements: For master's and doctorate, GRE General Test. *Application deadline:* For fall admission, 2/15 (priority date). Applications are processed on a rolling basis. *Application fee:* $50. Electronic applications accepted.
Expenses: Tuition: Part-time $535 per credit hour. Required fees: $56. Tuition and fees vary according to program.
Financial support: In 2001–02, 61 students received support, including 1 fellowship, 24 research assistantships with full tuition reimbursements available (averaging $13,560 per year), 26 teaching assistantships with full tuition reimbursements available (averaging $13,560 per year); career-related internships or fieldwork, Federal Work-Study, scholarships/grants, tuition waivers (full), and unspecified assistantships also available. Support available to part-time students. Financial award application deadline: 2/15; financial award applicants required to submit FAFSA.
Faculty research: Dry sliding instabilities, droplet deposition, helical hydraulic turbines, combustion, manufacturing systems. *Total annual research expenditures:* $1.8 million.
Dr. John W. Cipolla, Chairman, 617-373-3810, *Fax:* 617-373-2921.
Application contact: Stephen L. Gibson, Associate Director, 617-373-2711, *Fax:* 617-373-2501, *E-mail:* grad-eng@coe.neu.edu.

Find an in-depth description at www.petersons.com/gradchannel.

■ NORTHERN ILLINOIS UNIVERSITY

Graduate School, College of Engineering and Engineering Technology, Department of Mechanical Engineering, De Kalb, IL 60115-2854

AWARDS MS. Part-time programs available.

Faculty: 9 full-time (0 women), 1 part-time/adjunct (0 women).
Students: 24 full-time (0 women), 14 part-time (1 woman); includes 1 minority (Asian American or Pacific Islander), 29 international. Average age 25. 117 applicants, 64% accepted, 20 enrolled. In 2001, 4 degrees awarded.
Degree requirements: For master's, thesis defense, thesis optional.
Entrance requirements: For master's, GRE General Test, TOEFL, minimum GPA of 2.75. *Application deadline:* For fall admission, 6/1; for spring admission, 11/1.

Applications are processed on a rolling basis. *Application fee:* $30.
Expenses: Tuition, state resident: full-time $5,124; part-time $148 per credit hour. Tuition, nonresident: full-time $8,666; part-time $295 per credit hour. Required fees: $51 per term.
Financial support: In 2001–02, 1 research assistantship with full tuition reimbursement, 11 teaching assistantships with full tuition reimbursements were awarded. Fellowships with full tuition reimbursements, Federal Work-Study, tuition waivers (full), and unspecified assistantships also available. Support available to part-time students.
Dr. Simon Song, Chair, 815-753-9980.

■ NORTHWESTERN UNIVERSITY

McCormick School of Engineering and Applied Science, Department of Mechanical Engineering, Evanston, IL 60208

AWARDS Manufacturing engineering (MME); mechanical engineering (MS, PhD). MS, PhD admissions and degrees offered through The Graduate School. Part-time programs available.

Faculty: 23 full-time (3 women), 7 part-time/adjunct (0 women).
Students: 84 full-time (10 women), 1 part-time; includes 4 minority (2 African Americans, 1 Asian American or Pacific Islander, 1 Hispanic American), 55 international. 204 applicants, 30% accepted. In 2001, 8 master's, 12 doctorates awarded. Terminal master's awarded for partial completion of doctoral program.
Degree requirements: For master's, thesis or alternative; for doctorate, thesis/dissertation. *Median time to degree:* Master's–1.5 years full-time; doctorate–4.5 years full-time.
Application deadline: For fall admission, 8/30. *Application fee:* $50 ($55 for international students). Electronic applications accepted.
Expenses: Tuition: Full-time $26,526.
Financial support: In 2001–02, 7 fellowships with full tuition reimbursements (averaging $12,438 per year), 35 research assistantships with partial tuition reimbursements (averaging $16,650 per year), 33 teaching assistantships with full tuition reimbursements (averaging $12,843 per year) were awarded. Career-related internships or fieldwork, Federal Work-Study, institutionally sponsored loans, and scholarships/grants also available. Financial award application deadline: 1/15; financial award applicants required to submit FAFSA.
Faculty research: Experimental, theoretical and computational mechanics of materials; fluid mechanics; manufacturing processes; robotics and control; microelectromechanical systems and nanotechnology. *Total annual research expenditures:* $4.8 million.

Brian Moran, Chair, 847-491-7470, *Fax:* 847-491-3915, *E-mail:* b-moran@northwestern.edu.
Application contact: Pat Dyess, Admission Contact, 847-491-7190, *Fax:* 847-491-3915, *E-mail:* j-dyess@northwestern.edu. *Web site:* http://www.mech.northwestern.edu/

Find an in-depth description at www.petersons.com/gradchannel.

■ OAKLAND UNIVERSITY

Graduate Study and Lifelong Learning, School of Engineering and Computer Science, Program in Mechanical Engineering, Rochester, MI 48309-4401

AWARDS MS. Part-time and evening/weekend programs available.

Faculty: 9 full-time (1 woman), 8 part-time/adjunct (0 women).
Students: 74 full-time (15 women), 75 part-time (10 women); includes 17 minority (5 African Americans, 7 Asian Americans or Pacific Islanders, 4 Hispanic Americans, 1 Native American), 19 international. Average age 27. 95 applicants, 82% accepted. In 2001, 47 degrees awarded.
Entrance requirements: For master's, minimum GPA of 3.0 for unconditional admission. *Application deadline:* For fall admission, 8/1 (priority date); for winter admission, 12/1 (priority date); for spring admission, 4/1 (priority date). Applications are processed on a rolling basis. *Application fee:* $30. Electronic applications accepted.
Expenses: Tuition, state resident: full-time $5,904; part-time $246 per credit hour. Tuition, nonresident: full-time $12,192; part-time $508 per credit hour. Required fees: $472; $236 per term.
Financial support: Federal Work-Study, institutionally sponsored loans, and tuition waivers (full) available. Financial award application deadline: 3/1; financial award applicants required to submit FAFSA.
Dr. Gary C. Barber, Chair, 248-370-2184.

■ THE OHIO STATE UNIVERSITY

Graduate School, College of Engineering, Department of Mechanical Engineering, Columbus, OH 43210

AWARDS Engineering mechanics (MS, PhD); mechanical engineering (MS, PhD); nuclear engineering (MS, PhD).

Degree requirements: For doctorate, thesis/dissertation.
Entrance requirements: For master's, GRE General Test or 3.3 GPA and engineering degree; for doctorate, GRE General Test or 3.75 GPA and engineering degree.

■ OHIO UNIVERSITY

Graduate Studies, Russ College of Engineering and Technology, Department of Mechanical Engineering, Athens, OH 45701-2979

AWARDS Manufacturing engineering (MS); mechanical engineering (MS, PhD), including CAD/CAM (MS), manufacturing (MS), mechanical systems (MS), technology management (MS), thermal systems (MS).

Faculty: 10 full-time (0 women).
Students: 48 full-time (4 women), 20 part-time (3 women); includes 3 minority (2 African Americans, 1 Asian American or Pacific Islander), 51 international. 144 applicants, 63% accepted, 25 enrolled. In 2001, 34 degrees awarded.
Degree requirements: For master's and doctorate, thesis/dissertation.
Entrance requirements: For master's, BS in engineering or science, minimum GPA of 2.8; for doctorate, GRE. *Application deadline:* For fall admission, 3/15 (priority date). Applications are processed on a rolling basis. *Application fee:* $30.
Expenses: Tuition, state resident: full-time $6,585. Tuition, nonresident: full-time $12,254.
Financial support: In 2001–02, 41 students received support, including 9 research assistantships with tuition reimbursements available, 14 teaching assistantships with tuition reimbursements available; fellowships with tuition reimbursements available, career-related internships or fieldwork, Federal Work-Study, institutionally sponsored loans, tuition waivers (full and partial), and unspecified assistantships also available. Financial award application deadline: 3/15.
Faculty research: Machine design, controls, aerodynamics, thermal manufacturing, robotics process modeling, air pollution, combustion.
Dr. Jay S. Gunasekara, Chairman, 740-593-0563, *Fax:* 740-593-0476, *E-mail:* gsekera@bobcat.ent.ohiou.edu.
Application contact: Dr. M. Khairul Alam, Graduate Chairman, 740-593-1598, *Fax:* 740-593-0476, *E-mail:* agrawal@bobcat.ent.ohiou.edu. *Web site:* http://www.ent.ohiou.edu/

■ OKLAHOMA STATE UNIVERSITY

Graduate College, College of Engineering, Architecture and Technology, School of Mechanical and Aerospace Engineering, Stillwater, OK 74078

AWARDS Mechanical engineering (M En, MS, PhD).

Faculty: 22 full-time (0 women), 2 part-time/adjunct (0 women).
Students: 63 full-time (5 women), 48 part-time (4 women); includes 6 minority (1 African American, 3 Asian Americans or Pacific Islanders, 1 Hispanic American, 1

Native American), 73 international. Average age 27. 229 applicants, 52% accepted. In 2001, 27 master's, 6 doctorates awarded.
Degree requirements: For master's, thesis or alternative; for doctorate, thesis/dissertation.
Entrance requirements: For master's and doctorate, TOEFL. *Application deadline:* For fall admission, 7/1 (priority date). *Application fee:* $25.
Expenses: Tuition, state resident: part-time $92 per credit hour. Tuition, nonresident: part-time $297 per credit hour. Required fees: $21 per credit hour. $14 per semester. One-time fee: $20. Tuition and fees vary according to course load.
Financial support: In 2001–02, 110 students received support, including 51 research assistantships (averaging $9,005 per year), 33 teaching assistantships (averaging $5,678 per year); career-related internships or fieldwork, Federal Work-Study, and tuition waivers (partial) also available. Support available to part-time students. Financial award application deadline: 3/1.
Dr. Lawrence L. Hoberock, Head, 405-744-5900.

■ OLD DOMINION UNIVERSITY

College of Engineering and Technology, Program in Engineering Mechanics (Aerospace Emphasis), Norfolk, VA 23529

AWARDS ME, MS, PhD.

Students: 2 full-time (0 women), 2 part-time, 1 international. Average age 32. In 2001, 1 master's, 2 doctorates awarded.
Expenses: Tuition, state resident: part-time $202 per credit. Tuition, nonresident: part-time $534 per credit. Required fees: $76 per semester.
Dr. Brett Newman, Graduate Program Director, 757-683-5860, *Fax:* 757-683-3200, *E-mail:* aeroinfo@aero.odu.edu. *Web site:* http://www.odu.edu/webroot/orgs/engr/aero.nsf

■ OLD DOMINION UNIVERSITY

College of Engineering and Technology, Program in Engineering Mechanics (Mechanical Emphasis), Norfolk, VA 23529

AWARDS ME, MS, PhD.

Students: 2 full-time (0 women); includes 1 minority (African American), 1 international. Average age 27. In 2001, 1 degree awarded.
Expenses: Tuition, state resident: part-time $202 per credit. Tuition, nonresident: part-time $534 per credit. Required fees: $76 per semester.
Dr. Jen-Kuang Huang, Graduate Program Director, 757-683-6363, *Fax:* 757-683-5344, *E-mail:* megpd@odu.edu. *Web site:* http://www.mem.odu.edu/

■ OLD DOMINION UNIVERSITY

College of Engineering and Technology, Program in Mechanical Engineering, Norfolk, VA 23529

AWARDS Design manufacturing (ME); engineering mechanics (ME, MS, PhD); mechanical engineering (ME, MS, PhD). Part-time and evening/weekend programs available. Postbaccalaureate distance learning degree programs offered (no on-campus study).

Faculty: 13 full-time (0 women).
Students: 46 full-time (4 women), 58 part-time (4 women). Average age 28. 154 applicants, 90% accepted. In 2001, 32 master's, 2 doctorates awarded.
Degree requirements: For master's, thesis optional; for doctorate, thesis/dissertation, candidacy exam.
Entrance requirements: For master's, GRE, TOEFL, minimum GPA of 3.0; for doctorate, GRE, TOEFL. *Application deadline:* For fall admission, 7/1; for spring admission, 10/1. Applications are processed on a rolling basis. *Application fee:* $30. Electronic applications accepted.
Expenses: Tuition, state resident: part-time $202 per credit. Tuition, nonresident: part-time $534 per credit. Required fees: $76 per semester.
Financial support: In 2001–02, 61 students received support, including 2 fellowships (averaging $10,000 per year), 40 research assistantships with tuition reimbursements available (averaging $8,433 per year); teaching assistantships, career-related internships or fieldwork, institutionally sponsored loans, scholarships/grants, and tuition waivers (partial) also available. Support available to part-time students. Financial award application deadline: 2/15; financial award applicants required to submit FAFSA.
Faculty research: Computational applied mechanics, manufacturing, experimental stress analysis, systems dynamics and control, mechanical design, computational fluid dynamics, optimization. *Total annual research expenditures:* $1.5 million.
Dr. Jen-Kuang Huang, Graduate Program Director, 757-683-6363, *Fax:* 757-683-5344, *E-mail:* megpd@odu.edu. *Web site:* http://www.mem.odu.edu/

■ OREGON STATE UNIVERSITY

Graduate School, College of Engineering, Department of Mechanical Engineering, Corvallis, OR 97331

AWARDS Materials science (MAIS, MS); mechanical engineering (MS, PhD).

Faculty: 16 full-time (2 women).
Students: 45 full-time (4 women), 2 part-time; includes 2 minority (both Asian Americans or Pacific Islanders), 27 international. Average age 29. In 2001, 12 master's, 3 doctorates awarded.

Degree requirements: For master's, thesis or alternative; for doctorate, thesis/dissertation.
Entrance requirements: For master's, GRE General Test, TOEFL, minimum GPA of 3.0 in last 90 hours; for doctorate, GRE General Test, GRE Subject Test, TOEFL, minimum GPA of 3.0 in last 90 hours. *Application deadline:* For fall admission, 3/1. Applications are processed on a rolling basis. *Application fee:* $50.
Expenses: Tuition, area resident: Full-time $15,933. Tuition, state resident: full-time $28,937.
Financial support: Fellowships, research assistantships, teaching assistantships, Federal Work-Study and institutionally sponsored loans available. Support available to part-time students. Financial award application deadline: 2/1.
Faculty research: Design, thermal fluid sciences, energy conversion, mechanics. Dr. Gordon M. Reistad, Head, 541-737-3441, *Fax:* 541-737-2600, *E-mail:* reistag@engr.orst.edu.
Application contact: Graduate Admissions Clerk, 541-737-3441, *Fax:* 541-737-2600. *Web site:* http://www.me.orst.edu/

■ THE PENNSYLVANIA STATE UNIVERSITY UNIVERSITY PARK CAMPUS

Graduate School, College of Engineering, Department of Mechanical and Nuclear Engineering, Program in Mechanical Engineering, State College, University Park, PA 16802-1503

AWARDS M Eng, MS, PhD.

Students: 147 full-time (18 women), 41 part-time (6 women). In 2001, 42 master's, 27 doctorates awarded.
Expenses: Tuition, state resident: full-time $7,882; part-time $333 per credit. Tuition, nonresident: full-time $16,142; part-time $673 per credit. Required fees: $124 per semester.
Dr. H. Joseph Sommer, Graduate Officer, 814-865-1345.

■ POLYTECHNIC UNIVERSITY, BROOKLYN CAMPUS

Department of Mechanical, Aerospace and Manufacturing Engineering, Major in Mechanical Engineering, Brooklyn, NY 11201-2990

AWARDS MS, PhD.

Entrance requirements: For master's, BE or BS in engineering, physics, chemistry, mathematical sciences, or biological sciences or MBA. Electronic applications accepted.

■ POLYTECHNIC UNIVERSITY, LONG ISLAND GRADUATE CENTER

Graduate Programs, Department of Mechanical, Aerospace and Manufacturing Engineering, Major in Mechanical Engineering, Melville, NY 11747

AWARDS MS, PhD.

Electronic applications accepted.

■ PORTLAND STATE UNIVERSITY

Graduate Studies, College of Engineering and Computer Science, Department of Mechanical Engineering, Portland, OR 97207-0751

AWARDS MS, PhD. Part-time and evening/weekend programs available.

Faculty: 11 full-time (0 women), 5 part-time/adjunct (2 women).
Students: 13 full-time (1 woman), 7 part-time; includes 1 minority (African American), 5 international. Average age 32. 23 applicants, 65% accepted. In 2001, 7 degrees awarded.
Degree requirements: For master's, thesis or alternative; for doctorate, one foreign language, thesis/dissertation, oral and written exams.
Entrance requirements: For master's, TOEFL, minimum GPA of 3.0 in upper-division course work or 2.75 overall; for doctorate, GRE General Test, GRE Subject Test, minimum GPA of 3.0 in upper-division course work. *Application deadline:* For fall admission, 4/1 (priority date); for spring admission, 11/1. Applications are processed on a rolling basis. *Application fee:* $50.
Financial support: In 2001–02, 1 research assistantship with full tuition reimbursement (averaging $10,827 per year) was awarded; teaching assistantships with full tuition reimbursements, Federal Work-Study and institutionally sponsored loans also available. Support available to part-time students. Financial award application deadline: 3/1; financial award applicants required to submit FAFSA.
Faculty research: Mechanical system modeling, indoor air quality, manufacturing process, computational fluid dynamics, building science. *Total annual research expenditures:* $333,506.
Dr. Graig Spolek, Head, 503-725-4631, *Fax:* 503-725-4298, *E-mail:* graig@eas.pdx.edu.
Application contact: Gerald Recktenwald, Coordinator, 503-725-4290, *Fax:* 503-725-4298, *E-mail:* gerry@me.pdx.edu. *Web site:* http://www.me.pdx.edu/
Find an in-depth description at www.petersons.com/gradchannel.

■ PORTLAND STATE UNIVERSITY

Graduate Studies, College of Engineering and Computer Science, Systems Science Program, Portland, OR 97207-0751

AWARDS Systems science/anthropology (PhD). Systems science/business administration (PhD). Systems science/civil engineering (PhD). Systems science/economics (PhD). Systems science/engineering management (PhD). Systems science/general (PhD). Systems science/mathematical sciences (PhD). Systems science/mechanical engineering (PhD). Systems science/psychology (PhD). Systems science/sociology (PhD).

Faculty: 4 full-time (0 women).
Students: 47 full-time (19 women), 32 part-time (10 women); includes 9 minority (4 Asian Americans or Pacific Islanders, 3 Hispanic Americans, 2 Native Americans), 15 international. Average age 36. 52 applicants, 38% accepted. In 2001, 8 degrees awarded.
Degree requirements: For doctorate, variable foreign language requirement, thesis/dissertation.
Entrance requirements: For doctorate, GMAT, GRE General Test, TOEFL, minimum undergraduate GPA of 3.0. *Application deadline:* For fall admission, 2/1; for spring admission, 11/1. *Application fee:* $50.
Financial support: In 2001–02, 1 research assistantship with full tuition reimbursement (averaging $6,839 per year) was awarded; teaching assistantships with full tuition reimbursements, career-related internships or fieldwork, Federal Work-Study, and institutionally sponsored loans also available. Support available to part-time students. Financial award application deadline: 3/1; financial award applicants required to submit FAFSA.
Faculty research: Systems theory and methodology, artificial intelligence neural networks, information theory, nonlinear dynamics/chaos, modeling and simulation. *Total annual research expenditures:* $106,413.
Dr. Nancy Perrin, Director, 503-725-4960, *E-mail:* perrinn@pdx.edu.
Application contact: Dawn Kuenle, Coordinator, 503-725-4960, *E-mail:* dawn@sysc.pdx.edu. *Web site:* http://www.sysc.pdx.edu/

■ PRINCETON UNIVERSITY

Graduate School, School of Engineering and Applied Science, Department of Mechanical and Aerospace Engineering, Princeton, NJ 08544-1019

AWARDS Applied physics (M Eng, MSE, PhD); computational methods (M Eng, MSE); dynamics and control systems (M Eng, MSE, PhD); energy and environmental policy (M Eng, MSE, PhD); energy conversion, propulsion, and combustion (M Eng, MSE,

Princeton University (continued)
PhD); flight science and technology (M Eng, MSE, PhD); fluid mechanics (M Eng, MSE, PhD).

Faculty: 26 full-time (2 women).
Students: 70 full-time (12 women), 42 international. Average age 26. 256 applicants, 18% accepted. In 2001, 8 master's, 9 doctorates awarded.
Degree requirements: For master's, thesis/dissertation; for doctorate, thesis/dissertation, comprehensive exam (for some programs).
Entrance requirements: For master's and doctorate, GRE General Test. *Application deadline:* For fall admission, 1/3. Electronic applications accepted.
Financial support: Fellowships, research assistantships, teaching assistantships, Federal Work-Study and institutionally sponsored loans available. Financial award application deadline: 1/3. *Total annual research expenditures:* $5.3 million.
Prof. Naomi Enrich Leonard, Director of Graduate Studies, 609-258-5129, *Fax:* 609-258-6109, *E-mail:* maegrad@princeton.edu.
Application contact: Jessica H. Buchanan, Graduate Administrator, 609-258-4683, *Fax:* 609-258-6109, *E-mail:* maegrad@ princeton.edu. *Web site:* http://www.princeton.edu/~mae/maegrad/index.html

Find an in-depth description at www.petersons.com/gradchannel.

■ **PURDUE UNIVERSITY**

Graduate School, Schools of Engineering, School of Mechanical Engineering, West Lafayette, IN 47907

AWARDS Biomedical engineering (MS Bm E, PhD); mechanical engineering (MS, MSE, MSME, PhD).

Faculty: 53 full-time (3 women), 2 part-time/adjunct (0 women).
Students: 311 full-time (28 women), 33 part-time (7 women); includes 15 minority (5 African Americans, 6 Asian Americans or Pacific Islanders, 4 Hispanic Americans), 210 international. Average age 23. 645 applicants, 33% accepted, 123 enrolled. In 2001, 88 master's, 18 doctorates awarded.
Degree requirements: For doctorate, thesis/dissertation.
Entrance requirements: For master's and doctorate, TOEFL. *Application fee:* $30. Electronic applications accepted.
Expenses: Tuition, state resident: full-time $4,164; part-time $149 per credit hour. Tuition, nonresident: full-time $13,872; part-time $458 per credit hour. Tuition and fees vary according to campus/location and program.
Financial support: In 2001–02, 209 students received support, including 23 fellowships with full tuition reimbursements available (averaging $18,450 per year), 140 research assistantships with full

tuition reimbursements available (averaging $18,900 per year), 46 teaching assistantships with full tuition reimbursements available (averaging $15,300 per year); career-related internships or fieldwork also available. Support available to part-time students. Financial award applicants required to submit FAFSA.
Faculty research: Design, manufacturing, thermal/fluid sciences, mechanics, electromechanical systems.
Dr. E. Dan Hirleman, Head, 765-494-5688.
Application contact: Susan K. Fisher, Graduate Administrator, 765-494-5729, *Fax:* 765-496-7534.

Find an in-depth description at www.petersons.com/gradchannel.

■ **RENSSELAER AT HARTFORD**

Department of Engineering, Program in Mechanical Engineering, Hartford, CT 06120-2991

AWARDS MS. Part-time and evening/weekend programs available.

Faculty: 2 full-time (0 women), 14 part-time/adjunct (0 women).
Students: Average age 31. 45 applicants, 69% accepted, 30 enrolled. In 2001, 4995 degrees awarded.
Degree requirements: For master's, seminar, thesis optional.
Entrance requirements: For master's, TOEFL. *Application deadline:* For fall admission, 8/6 (priority date). Applications are processed on a rolling basis. *Application fee:* $45.
Expenses: Tuition: Full-time $11,700; part-time $650 per credit.
Financial support: Research assistantships, tuition waivers (full and partial) and unspecified assistantships available. Financial award applicants required to submit FAFSA.
Application contact: Rebecca Danchak, Director of Admissions, 860-548-2420, *Fax:* 860-548-7823, *E-mail:* rdanchak@ rh.edu.

■ **RENSSELAER POLYTECHNIC INSTITUTE**

Graduate School, School of Engineering, Department of Mechanical, Aerospace, and Nuclear Engineering, Program in Mechanical Engineering, Troy, NY 12180-3590

AWARDS M Eng, MS, D Eng, PhD, MBA/M Eng. Part-time and evening/weekend programs available. Postbaccalaureate distance learning degree programs offered (no on-campus study).

Faculty: 29 full-time (2 women), 2 part-time/adjunct (0 women).
Students: 122 full-time (6 women), 54 part-time (8 women); includes 22 minority (2 African Americans, 15 Asian Americans or Pacific Islanders, 5 Hispanic Americans), 77 international. 272

applicants, 31% accepted. In 2001, 36 master's, 15 doctorates awarded.
Degree requirements: For master's, thesis (for some programs); for doctorate, thesis/dissertation.
Entrance requirements: For master's and doctorate, GRE, TOEFL. *Application deadline:* For fall admission, 1/15 (priority date). Applications are processed on a rolling basis. *Application fee:* $45. Electronic applications accepted.
Expenses: Tuition: Full-time $26,400; part-time $1,320 per credit hour. Required fees: $1,437.
Financial support: In 2001–02, 100 students received support; fellowships, research assistantships, teaching assistantships, career-related internships or fieldwork, institutionally sponsored loans, and tuition waivers (partial) available. Financial award application deadline: 2/1.
Faculty research: Tribology, advanced composite materials, energy and combustion systems, computer-aided and optimal design, manufacturing. *Total annual research expenditures:* $2.5 million.
Application contact: Dr. Kevin C. Craig, Director, 518-276-6620, *Fax:* 518-276-4860, *E-mail:* craigk@rpi.edu. *Web site:* http://www.rpi.edu/dept/meaem/

Find an in-depth description at www.petersons.com/gradchannel.

■ **RICE UNIVERSITY**

Graduate Programs, George R. Brown School of Engineering, Department of Mechanical Engineering and Materials Science, Houston, TX 77251-1892

AWARDS Materials science (MMS, MS, PhD); mechanical engineering (MME, MS, PhD). Part-time programs available.

Faculty: 19 full-time (3 women), 7 part-time/adjunct (1 woman).
Students: 41 full-time (12 women), 8 part-time (1 woman); includes 8 minority (1 African American, 2 Asian Americans or Pacific Islanders, 3 Hispanic Americans, 2 Native Americans), 28 international. Average age 23. 183 applicants, 10% accepted, 17 enrolled. In 2001, 7 master's, 4 doctorates awarded. Terminal master's awarded for partial completion of doctoral program.
Degree requirements: For master's and doctorate, thesis/dissertation, comprehensive exam, registration. *Median time to degree:* Master's–3 years full-time; doctorate–4 years full-time.
Entrance requirements: For master's and doctorate, GRE General Test, TOEFL, minimum GPA of 3.0. *Application deadline:* For fall admission, 2/1 (priority date); for spring admission, 11/15 (priority date). Applications are processed on a rolling basis. *Application fee:* $25. Electronic applications accepted.
Expenses: Tuition: Full-time $17,300. Required fees: $250.
Financial support: In 2001–02, 37 students received support, including 18

fellowships with full tuition reimbursements available (averaging $12,600 per year), 16 research assistantships with full tuition reimbursements available (averaging $12,600 per year), 2 teaching assistantships with full tuition reimbursements available (averaging $12,600 per year) Financial award application deadline: 2/1. **Faculty research:** Heat transfer, biomedical engineering, fluid dynamics, aero-astronautics, control systems/robotics, materials science. *Total annual research expenditures:* $1.4 million.
Tayfun Tezduyar, Chair, 713-348-4906, *Fax:* 713-348-5423.
Application contact: Judith E. Farhat, Graduate Coordinator, 713-348-3582, *Fax:* 713-348-5423, *E-mail:* gradcoord@mems.rice.edu. *Web site:* http://www.mems.rice.edu/

■ ROCHESTER INSTITUTE OF TECHNOLOGY

Graduate Enrollment Services, College of Engineering, Department of Mechanical Engineering, Rochester, NY 14623-5698

AWARDS MSME.

Students: 15 full-time (2 women), 25 part-time (2 women); includes 3 minority (2 Asian Americans or Pacific Islanders, 1 Hispanic American), 15 international. 122 applicants, 37% accepted, 14 enrolled. In 2001, 23 degrees awarded.
Degree requirements: For master's, thesis optional.
Entrance requirements: For master's, TOEFL, minimum GPA of 3.0. *Application deadline:* For fall admission, 3/1 (priority date). Applications are processed on a rolling basis. *Application fee:* $50.
Expenses: Tuition: Full-time $20,928; part-time $587 per hour. Required fees: $162. Tuition and fees vary according to program.
Financial support: Research assistantships, teaching assistantships available.
Dr. Edward Hensel, Head, 585-475-7684, *E-mail:* echeme@rit.edu.
Application contact: Dr. Richard Reeve, Associate Dean, 585-475-5382, *E-mail:* nrreie@rit.edu.

■ ROSE-HULMAN INSTITUTE OF TECHNOLOGY

Faculty of Engineering and Applied Sciences, Department of Mechanical Engineering, Terre Haute, IN 47803-3920

AWARDS MS. Part-time programs available. Postbaccalaureate distance learning degree programs offered (minimal on-campus study).

Faculty: 18 full-time (1 woman).
Students: 11 full-time (1 woman), 9 part-time; includes 1 minority (Asian American or Pacific Islander), 9 international. Average age 25. 14 applicants, 86% accepted, 7 enrolled. In 2001, 2 degrees awarded.

Degree requirements: For master's, thesis.
Entrance requirements: For master's, GRE, TOEFL, minimum GPA of 3.0. *Application deadline:* For fall admission, 2/1 (priority date). Applications are processed on a rolling basis. *Application fee:* $0.
Expenses: Tuition: Full-time $21,792; part-time $615 per credit hour. Required fees: $405.
Financial support: In 2001–02, 12 students received support; fellowships with full and partial tuition reimbursements available, research assistantships with full and partial tuition reimbursements available, institutionally sponsored loans, scholarships/grants, and tuition waivers (full and partial) available. Financial award application deadline: 2/1.
Faculty research: Dynamics of large flexible space structures, finite-element analysis, system simulation and optimization, mechanical design, fracture mechanics and fatigue. *Total annual research expenditures:* $5.6 million.
Dr. David J. Purdy, Chairman, 812-877-8320, *Fax:* 812-877-3198, *E-mail:* robert.steinhauser@rose-hulman.edu.
Application contact: Dr. Daniel J. Moore, Interim Associate Dean of the Faculty, 812-877-8110, *Fax:* 812-877-8061, *E-mail:* daniel.j.moore@rose-hulman.edu.

■ RUTGERS, THE STATE UNIVERSITY OF NEW JERSEY, NEW BRUNSWICK

Graduate School, Program in Mechanical and Aerospace Engineering, New Brunswick, NJ 08901-1281

AWARDS Computational fluid dynamics (MS, PhD); design and dynamics (MS, PhD); fluid mechanics (MS, PhD); heat transfer (MS, PhD). Solid mechanics (MS, PhD). Part-time and evening/weekend programs available.

Degree requirements: For master's, thesis (for some programs); for doctorate, thesis/dissertation.
Entrance requirements: For master's, GRE General Test, BS in mechanical/aerospace engineering or related field; for doctorate, GRE General Test, MS in mechanical/aerospace engineering or related field. *Web site:* http://cronos.rutgers.edu/~mechaero/

■ ST. CLOUD STATE UNIVERSITY

School of Graduate Studies, College of Science and Engineering, Program in Mechanical Engineering, St. Cloud, MN 56301-4498

AWARDS MS.

Degree requirements: For master's, thesis or alternative.
Entrance requirements: For master's, GRE General Test, minimum GPA of 2.75. *Application deadline:* Applications are processed on a rolling basis. *Application fee:* $35.
Expenses: Tuition, state resident: part-time $156 per credit. Tuition, nonresident: part-time $244 per credit. Required fees: $20 per credit.
Warren Yu, Coordinator, 320-255-3964.

■ SAINT LOUIS UNIVERSITY

Graduate School, Parks College of Engineering and Aviation, Department of Aerospace and Mechanical Engineering, St. Louis, MO 63103-2097

AWARDS Aerospace engineering (MS, MS(R)).

Faculty: 11 full-time (2 women), 8 part-time/adjunct (0 women).
Students: 8 full-time (3 women), 9 part-time; includes 1 minority (Hispanic American), 12 international. Average age 26. 5 applicants, 100% accepted, 4 enrolled. In 2001, 4 degrees awarded.
Degree requirements: For master's, thesis (for some programs), comprehensive exam.
Entrance requirements: For master's, GRE General Test. *Application deadline:* For fall admission, 7/1; for spring admission, 11/1. Applications are processed on a rolling basis. *Application fee:* $40.
Expenses: Tuition: Part-time $630 per credit hour.
Financial support: In 2001–02, 11 students received support, including 5 research assistantships with tuition reimbursements available, 4 teaching assistantships with tuition reimbursements available Financial award application deadline: 4/1; financial award applicants required to submit FAFSA.
Faculty research: Hypersonic vehicle design, high temperature lubrication, design optimization, research on free shear layer flows mechanical design methodology. *Total annual research expenditures:* $191,132.
Dr. Krishnaswamy Ravindra, Chairperson, 314-977-8331, *Fax:* 314-977-8403, *E-mail:* ravindrak@slu.edu.
Application contact: Dr. Marcia Buresch, Associate Dean of the Graduate School, 314-977-2240, *Fax:* 314-977-3943, *E-mail:* bureschm@slu.edu.

■ SAN DIEGO STATE UNIVERSITY

Graduate and Research Affairs, College of Engineering, Department of Mechanical Engineering, San Diego, CA 92182

AWARDS Engineering sciences and applied mechanics (PhD); mechanical engineering (MS). Evening/weekend programs available.

Degree requirements: For doctorate, thesis/dissertation.
Entrance requirements: For master's, GRE General Test, TOEFL.

San Diego State University (continued)
Faculty research: Energy analysis and diagnosis, seawater pump design, space-related research. *Web site:* http://www.kahuna.sdsu.edu/engineering/mechanical/

■ SAN JOSE STATE UNIVERSITY

Graduate Studies, College of Engineering, Department of Mechanical and Aerospace Engineering, Program in Mechanical Engineering, San Jose, CA 95192-0001

AWARDS MS. Part-time programs available.

Faculty: 11 full-time (0 women), 20 part-time/adjunct (1 woman).
Students: 5 full-time (0 women), 43 part-time (5 women); includes 29 minority (1 African American, 22 Asian Americans or Pacific Islanders, 5 Hispanic Americans, 1 Native American), 5 international. Average age 30. 45 applicants, 69% accepted. In 2001, 16 degrees awarded.
Degree requirements: For master's, thesis optional.
Entrance requirements: For master's, GRE, TOEFL, BS in mechanical engineering or equivalent. *Application deadline:* For fall admission, 6/29; for spring admission, 11/30. Applications are processed on a rolling basis. *Application fee:* $59. Electronic applications accepted.
Expenses: Tuition, nonresident: part-time $246 per unit. Required fees: $678 per semester. Tuition and fees vary according to course load.
Financial support: In 2001–02, 1 teaching assistantship was awarded. Financial award applicants required to submit FAFSA.
Faculty research: Gas dynamics, mechanics/vibrations, heat transfer, structural analysis, two-phase fluid flow.
Application contact: Dr. William Seto, Graduate Adviser, 408-924-3947.

■ SANTA CLARA UNIVERSITY

School of Engineering, Department of Mechanical Engineering, Santa Clara, CA 95053

AWARDS MSME, PhD, Engineer. Part-time and evening/weekend programs available.

Students: 7 full-time (1 woman), 30 part-time (3 women); includes 11 minority (8 Asian Americans or Pacific Islanders, 3 Hispanic Americans), 3 international. Average age 29. 32 applicants, 56% accepted. In 2001, 4 master's, 1 doctorate awarded.
Degree requirements: For master's, thesis or alternative; for doctorate and Engineer, thesis/dissertation.
Entrance requirements: For master's, GRE General Test, GRE Subject Test, TOEFL, minimum GPA of 2.75; for doctorate, GRE General Test, GRE Subject Test, TOEFL, master's degree or equivalent; for Engineer, master's degree, published paper. *Application deadline:* For fall admission, 6/1; for spring admission,

1/1. Applications are processed on a rolling basis. *Application fee:* $45 ($55 for international students). Electronic applications accepted.
Expenses: Tuition: Part-time $320 per unit. Tuition and fees vary according to class time, degree level, program and student level.
Financial support: Fellowships, research assistantships, teaching assistantships, Federal Work-Study and institutionally sponsored loans available. Support available to part-time students. Financial award application deadline: 3/1; financial award applicants required to submit FAFSA. *Total annual research expenditures:* $317,097. Dr. Timothy Hight, Chair, 408-554-4937.
Application contact: Tina Samms, Assistant Director of Graduate Admissions, 408-554-4313, *Fax:* 408-554-5474, *E-mail:* engr-grad@scu.edu.

■ SOUTH DAKOTA SCHOOL OF MINES AND TECHNOLOGY

Graduate Division, Department of Mechanical Engineering, Rapid City, SD 57701-3995

AWARDS MS. Part-time programs available.

Entrance requirements: For master's, TOEFL, TWE. Electronic applications accepted.
Faculty research: Advanced composite materials, robotics, computer-integrated manufacturing, enhanced heat transfer, dynamic systems controls.

■ SOUTH DAKOTA SCHOOL OF MINES AND TECHNOLOGY

Graduate Division, Division of Material Engineering and Science, Doctoral Program in Materials Engineering and Science, Rapid City, SD 57701-3995

AWARDS Chemical engineering (PhD); chemistry (PhD); civil engineering (PhD); electrical engineering (PhD); mechanical engineering (PhD); metallurgical engineering (PhD); physics (PhD). Part-time programs available.

Degree requirements: For doctorate, thesis/dissertation.
Entrance requirements: For doctorate, TOEFL, TWE, minimum graduate GPA of 3.0. Electronic applications accepted.
Faculty research: Thermophysical properties of solids, development of multiphase materials and composites, concrete technology, electronic polymer materials.

Find an in-depth description at www.petersons.com/gradchannel.

■ SOUTH DAKOTA STATE UNIVERSITY

Graduate School, College of Engineering, Department of Mechanical Engineering, Brookings, SD 57007

AWARDS MS.

Degree requirements: For master's, thesis, oral exam.
Entrance requirements: For master's, TOEFL.
Faculty research: Energy and system optimization, thermal transfer, mechanics of components, ground source heat pump, mechanical design.

■ SOUTHERN ILLINOIS UNIVERSITY CARBONDALE

Graduate School, College of Engineering, Department of Mechanical Engineering and Energy Processes, Carbondale, IL 62901-6806

AWARDS MS.

Faculty: 16 full-time (0 women), 1 part-time/adjunct (0 women).
Students: 36 full-time (3 women), 13 part-time (2 women); includes 7 minority (1 African American, 2 Asian Americans or Pacific Islanders, 1 Hispanic American, 3 Native Americans), 29 international. Average age 23. 73 applicants, 19% accepted. In 2001, 10 degrees awarded.
Degree requirements: For master's, thesis or alternative, comprehensive exam.
Entrance requirements: For master's, GRE General Test, TOEFL, minimum GPA of 2.7. *Application deadline:* For fall admission, 1/31. Applications are processed on a rolling basis. *Application fee:* $20.
Expenses: Tuition, state resident: full-time $3,794; part-time $154 per hour. Tuition, nonresident: full-time $6,566; part-time $308 per hour. Required fees: $277 per hour.
Financial support: In 2001–02, 34 students received support; fellowships with full tuition reimbursements available, research assistantships with full tuition reimbursements available, teaching assistantships with full tuition reimbursements available, Federal Work-Study and institutionally sponsored loans available. Support available to part-time students.
Faculty research: Coal conversion and processing, combustion, materials science and engineering, mechanical system dynamics. *Total annual research expenditures:* $1.4 million.
Dr. Suri Rajan, Acting Chair, 618-453-7010.

Find an in-depth description at www.petersons.com/gradchannel.

■ SOUTHERN ILLINOIS UNIVERSITY EDWARDSVILLE

Graduate Studies and Research, School of Engineering, Department of Mechanical Engineering, Edwardsville, IL 62026-0001

AWARDS MS. Part-time programs available.

Students: 25 full-time (3 women), 11 part-time (1 woman); includes 1 minority (Asian American or Pacific Islander), 29 international. Average age 33. 86 applicants, 62% accepted, 15 enrolled. In 2001, 3 degrees awarded.
Degree requirements: For master's, thesis or research paper, final exam. *Median time to degree:* Master's–2.5 years full-time, 4 years part-time.
Entrance requirements: For master's, TOEFL, minimum undergraduate GPA of 2.75 in mathematics, engineering, and science courses. *Application deadline:* For fall admission, 7/20; for spring admission, 12/7. *Application fee:* $25.
Expenses: Tuition, state resident: full-time $2,712; part-time $113 per credit hour. Tuition, nonresident: full-time $5,424; part-time $226 per credit hour. Required fees: $250; $125 per term. $125 per term. Tuition and fees vary according to course load, campus/location and reciprocity agreements.
Financial support: Fellowships with full tuition reimbursements, research assistantships with full tuition reimbursements, teaching assistantships with full tuition reimbursements, career-related internships or fieldwork, Federal Work-Study, institutionally sponsored loans, scholarships/grants, traineeships, and unspecified assistantships available. Support available to part-time students. Financial award application deadline: 3/1; financial award applicants required to submit FAFSA.
Dr. Nader Saniei, Chair, 618-650-2584, *E-mail:* nsaniei@siue.edu.
Application contact: Dr. Kegin Gu, Program Director, 618-650-2803, *E-mail:* kgu@siue.edu.

■ SOUTHERN METHODIST UNIVERSITY

School of Engineering, Department of Mechanical Engineering, Dallas, TX 75275

AWARDS Manufacturing systems management (MS); mechanical engineering (MSME, PhD). Part-time and evening/weekend programs available. Postbaccalaureate distance learning degree programs offered (no on-campus study).

Faculty: 10 full-time (0 women).
Students: 25 full-time (4 women), 30 part-time; includes 9 minority (3 African Americans, 4 Asian Americans or Pacific Islanders, 2 Hispanic Americans), 18 international. Average age 32. 103 applicants, 97% accepted. In 2001, 14

master's, 3 doctorates awarded. Terminal master's awarded for partial completion of doctoral program.
Degree requirements: For master's, thesis optional; for doctorate, thesis/dissertation, oral and written qualifying exams, oral final exam.
Entrance requirements: For master's, GRE General Test, TOEFL, minimum GPA of 3.0 in last 2 years; bachelor's degree in engineering, mathematics, or sciences; for doctorate, preliminary counseling exam, minimum graduate GPA of 3.0, bachelor's degree in related field. *Application deadline:* For fall admission, 7/1 (priority date); for spring admission, 11/15. Applications are processed on a rolling basis. *Application fee:* $50.
Expenses: Tuition: Part-time $285 per credit hour.
Financial support: In 2001–02, 12 research assistantships (averaging $15,000 per year), 6 teaching assistantships (averaging $9,000 per year) were awarded. Federal Work-Study, institutionally sponsored loans, and tuition waivers (full and partial) also available. Financial award applicants required to submit FAFSA.
Faculty research: Design, systems, and controls; thermal and fluid sciences. *Total annual research expenditures:* $1.3 million. Yildirim Hurmuzlu, Head, 214-768-3498, *Fax:* 214-768-1473.
Application contact: Jim Dees, Director, Student Administration, 214-768-1456, *Fax:* 214-768-3845, *E-mail:* jdees@engr.smu.edu. *Web site:* http://www.seas.smu.edu/me/

Find an in-depth description at www.petersons.com/gradchannel.

■ STANFORD UNIVERSITY

School of Engineering, Department of Mechanical Engineering, Stanford, CA 94305-9991

AWARDS Biomechanical engineering (MS); manufacturing systems engineering (MS); mechanical engineering (MS, PhD, Eng); product design (MS).

Faculty: 36 full-time (1 woman).
Students: 477 full-time (98 women), 91 part-time (15 women); includes 128 minority (24 African Americans, 76 Asian Americans or Pacific Islanders, 27 Hispanic Americans, 1 Native American), 161 international. Average age 27. 678 applicants, 53% accepted. In 2001, 175 master's, 30 doctorates awarded. Terminal master's awarded for partial completion of doctoral program.
Degree requirements: For doctorate and Eng, thesis/dissertation.
Entrance requirements: For master's, doctorate, and Eng, GRE General Test, TOEFL. *Application deadline:* For fall admission, 1/14. *Application fee:* $65 ($80 for international students). Electronic applications accepted.

Ronald Hanson, Chair, 650-723-1745, *Fax:* 650-725-4862, *E-mail:* hanson@cdr.stanford.edu.
Application contact: Admissions Office, 650-723-3148. *Web site:* http://cdr.stanford.edu/html/me/home.html

Find an in-depth description at www.petersons.com/gradchannel.

■ STATE UNIVERSITY OF NEW YORK AT BINGHAMTON

Graduate School, Thomas J. Watson School of Engineering and Applied Science, Department of Mechanical Engineering, Binghamton, NY 13902-6000

AWARDS M Eng, MS, PhD. Part-time and evening/weekend programs available.

Faculty: 13 full-time (0 women), 2 part-time/adjunct (0 women).
Students: 42 full-time (5 women), 21 part-time (2 women); includes 5 minority (3 African Americans, 2 Asian Americans or Pacific Islanders), 34 international. Average age 28. 117 applicants, 39% accepted, 16 enrolled. In 2001, 20 master's, 4 doctorates awarded.
Degree requirements: For master's, thesis or alternative; for doctorate, thesis/dissertation.
Entrance requirements: For master's and doctorate, GRE General Test, GRE Subject Test, TOEFL. *Application deadline:* For fall admission, 4/15 (priority date); for spring admission, 11/1. Applications are processed on a rolling basis. Electronic applications accepted.
Expenses: Tuition, state resident: full-time $5,100; part-time $213 per credit. Tuition, nonresident: full-time $8,416; part-time $351 per credit. Required fees: $811.
Financial support: In 2001–02, 42 students received support, including 33 research assistantships with full tuition reimbursements available (averaging $7,987 per year), 8 teaching assistantships with full tuition reimbursements available (averaging $9,279 per year); fellowships with full tuition reimbursements available, career-related internships or fieldwork, Federal Work-Study, institutionally sponsored loans, and unspecified assistantships also available. Support available to part-time students. Financial award application deadline: 2/15.
Dr. Ron Miles, Chairperson, 609-777-4747.

■ STEVENS INSTITUTE OF TECHNOLOGY

Graduate School, Charles V. Schaefer Jr. School of Engineering, Department of Mechanical Engineering, Hoboken, NJ 07030

AWARDS Advanced manufacturing (Certificate); air pollution technology (Certificate); building energy systems

Stevens Institute of Technology (continued) (Certificate); computational methods in fluid mechanics and heat transfer (Certificate); concurrent design management (M Eng); controls in aerospace and robotics (Certificate); design and production management (MS, Certificate); finite-element analysis (Certificate); integrated production design (Certificate); mechanical engineering (M Eng, PhD, Engr); mechanism design (Certificate); power generation (Certificate); robotics and control (Certificate). Stress analysis and design (Certificate); vibration and noise control (Certificate). MS and Certificate offered in cooperation with the Program in Design and Production Management; M Eng offered in cooperation with the Program in Concurrent Design Management. Part-time and evening/weekend programs available. Terminal master's awarded for partial completion of doctoral program.

Degree requirements: For master's, thesis optional; for doctorate, variable foreign language requirement, thesis/dissertation; for other advanced degree, project or thesis.
Entrance requirements: For master's, doctorate, and other advanced degree, TOEFL. Electronic applications accepted.
Expenses: Tuition: Full-time $13,950; part-time $775 per credit. Required fees: $180. One-time fee: $180 part-time. Full-time tuition and fees vary according to degree level and program.
Faculty research: Acoustics, incineration, CAD/CAM, computational fluid dynamics and heat transfer, robotics.

Find an in-depth description at www.petersons.com/gradchannel.

■ STONY BROOK UNIVERSITY, STATE UNIVERSITY OF NEW YORK

Graduate School, College of Engineering and Applied Sciences, Department of Mechanical Engineering, Stony Brook, NY 11794

AWARDS MS, PhD. Evening/weekend programs available.
Faculty: 17 full-time (1 woman), 1 part-time/adjunct (0 women).
Students: 48 full-time (11 women), 31 part-time (3 women); includes 9 minority (1 African American, 8 Asian Americans or Pacific Islanders), 53 international. 176 applicants, 19% accepted. In 2001, 8 master's, 3 doctorates awarded.
Degree requirements: For master's, thesis or alternative; for doctorate, thesis/dissertation, comprehensive exam.
Entrance requirements: For master's, GRE General Test, TOEFL, minimum GPA of 3.0; for doctorate, GRE General Test, TOEFL, minimum GPA of 3.5.
Application deadline: For fall admission, 1/15. *Application fee:* $50.
Expenses: Tuition, state resident: full-time $5,100; part-time $213 per credit. Tuition,

nonresident: full-time $8,416; part-time $351 per credit. Required fees: $496.
Financial support: In 2001–02, 1 fellowship, 28 research assistantships, 17 teaching assistantships were awarded.
Faculty research: Atmospheric sciences, thermal fluid sciences, solid mechanics.
Total annual research expenditures: $2.7 million.
Dr. Fu-Pen Chiang, Chairman, 631-632-8310.
Application contact: Dr. John Kincaid, Director, 631-632-8305, *Fax:* 631-632-8720, *E-mail:* jkincaid@ccmail.sunysb.edu. *Web site:* http://mech.eng.sunysb.edu/

Find an in-depth description at www.petersons.com/gradchannel.

■ STONY BROOK UNIVERSITY, STATE UNIVERSITY OF NEW YORK

School of Professional Development and Continuing Studies, Stony Brook, NY 11794

AWARDS Art and philosophy (Certificate); biology 7-12 (MAT); chemistry-grade 7-12 (MAT); coaching (Certificate); computer integrated engineering (Certificate); cultural studies (Certificate); earth science-grade 7-12 (MAT); educational computing (Certificate); English-grade 7-12 (MAT); environmental/occupational health and safety (Certificate); French-grade 7-12 (MAT); German-grade 7-12 (MAT); human resource management (Certificate); industrial management (Certificate); information systems management (Certificate); Italian-grade 7-12 (MAT); liberal studies (MA); liberal studies online (MA); Long Island regional studies (Certificate); oceanic science (Certificate); operation research (Certificate); physics-grade 7-12 (MAT); Russian-grade 7-12 (MAT). School administration and supervision (Certificate). School district administration (Certificate). Social science and the professions (MPS), including labor management, public affairs, waste management. Social studies 7-12 (MAT); waste management (Certificate); women's studies (Certificate). Part-time and evening/weekend programs available. Postbaccalaureate distance learning degree programs offered.
Faculty: 1 full-time, 101 part-time/adjunct.
Students: 240 full-time (133 women), 1,307 part-time (868 women); includes 101 minority (43 African Americans, 13 Asian Americans or Pacific Islanders, 43 Hispanic Americans, 2 Native Americans), 9 international. Average age 28. In 2001, 478 master's, 157 other advanced degrees awarded.
Degree requirements: For master's, one foreign language, thesis or alternative.
Application deadline: Applications are processed on a rolling basis. *Application fee:* $50.

Expenses: Tuition, state resident: full-time $5,100; part-time $213 per credit. Tuition, nonresident: full-time $8,416; part-time $351 per credit. Required fees: $496.
Financial support: In 2001–02, 1 fellowship, 7 teaching assistantships were awarded. Research assistantships, career-related internships or fieldwork also available. Support available to part-time students.
Dr. Paul J. Edelson, Dean, 631-632-7052, *Fax:* 631-632-9046, *E-mail:* paul.edelson@sunysb.edu.
Application contact: Sandra Romansky, Director of Admissions and Advisement, 631-632-7050, *Fax:* 631-632-9046, *E-mail:* sandra.romansky@sunysb.edu. *Web site:* http://www.sunysb.edu/spd/

■ SYRACUSE UNIVERSITY

Graduate School, L. C. Smith College of Engineering and Computer Science, Department of Mechanical and Aerospace Engineering, Program in Mechanical Engineering, Syracuse, NY 13244-0003

AWARDS MS.
Students: 2 full-time (0 women), 10 part-time (3 women), 8 international. Average age 31. In 2001, 12 degrees awarded.
Degree requirements: For master's, project or thesis.
Entrance requirements: For master's, GRE General Test, GRE Subject Test.
Application deadline: Applications are processed on a rolling basis. *Application fee:* $50.
Expenses: Tuition: Full-time $15,528; part-time $647 per credit. Required fees: $420; $38 per term. Tuition and fees vary according to program.
Financial support: Fellowships, research assistantships, teaching assistantships available. Financial award application deadline: 1/10.
Dr. Uptal Roy, Graduate Director, 315-443-2592, *Fax:* 315-443-9099, *E-mail:* uroy@syr.edu.
Application contact: Kathy Datthyn-Madigan, Information Contact, 315-443-4367, *Fax:* 315-443-9099, *E-mail:* kjdatthy@ecs.syr.edu. *Web site:* http://www.ecs.syr.edu/

Find an in-depth description at www.petersons.com/gradchannel.

■ TEMPLE UNIVERSITY

Graduate School, College of Science and Technology, College of Engineering, Program in Mechanical Engineering, Philadelphia, PA 19122-6096

AWARDS MSE. Part-time and evening/weekend programs available.

Degree requirements: For master's, thesis optional.

Entrance requirements: For master's, GRE General Test, TOEFL. Electronic applications accepted.
Expenses: Tuition, state resident: full-time $8,487; part-time $369 per credit hour. Tuition, nonresident: full-time $12,282; part-time $534 per credit hour. Required fees: $350. Tuition and fees vary according to course load, program and reciprocity agreements.
Faculty research: Rapid solidification by melt spinning, microfracture analysis of dental materials, failure detection methods. *Web site:* http://www.eng.temple.edu/

■ **TENNESSEE TECHNOLOGICAL UNIVERSITY**

Graduate School, College of Engineering, Department of Mechanical Engineering, Cookeville, TN 38505

AWARDS MS, PhD. Part-time programs available.

Faculty: 25 full-time (2 women).
Students: 38 full-time (3 women), 15 part-time (1 woman); includes 37 minority (1 African American, 36 Asian Americans or Pacific Islanders). Average age 28. 215 applicants, 55% accepted. In 2001, 22 degrees awarded.
Degree requirements: For master's, thesis; for doctorate, one foreign language, thesis/dissertation.
Entrance requirements: For master's, GRE General Test, TOEFL; for doctorate, GRE Subject Test, TOEFL, minimum GPA of 3.5. *Application deadline:* For fall admission, 3/1 (priority date); for spring admission, 8/1. *Application fee:* $25 ($30 for international students).
Expenses: Tuition, state resident: full-time $4,000; part-time $215 per hour. Tuition, nonresident: full-time $10,500; part-time $495 per hour. Required fees: $1,971 per semester.
Financial support: In 2001–02, 1 fellowship (averaging $10,000 per year), 30 research assistantships (averaging $8,190 per year), 6 teaching assistantships (averaging $6,711 per year) were awarded. Financial award application deadline: 4/1.
Faculty research: Energy-related systems, design, acoustics and acoustical systems. Dr. Dale A. Wilson, Chairperson, 931-372-3254, *Fax:* 931-372-6340.
Application contact: Dr. Francis O. Otuonye, Associate Vice President for Research and Graduate Studies, 931-372-3233, *Fax:* 931-372-3497, *E-mail:* fotuonye@tntech.edu.

■ **TEXAS A&M UNIVERSITY**

College of Engineering, Department of Mechanical Engineering, College Station, TX 77843

AWARDS M Eng, MS, D Eng, PhD.

Faculty: 52 full-time (1 woman), 4 part-time/adjunct (0 women).

Students: 288 full-time (9 women), 47 part-time (3 women); includes 22 minority (2 African Americans, 8 Asian Americans or Pacific Islanders, 12 Hispanic Americans), 261 international. Average age 24. 160 applicants, 86% accepted. In 2001, 38 master's, 22 doctorates awarded.
Degree requirements: For master's, thesis (MS); for doctorate, dissertation (PhD).
Entrance requirements: For master's, GRE General Test, TOEFL, minimum undergraduate GPA of 3.0; for doctorate, GRE General Test, TOEFL, minimum graduate GPA of 3.5. *Application deadline:* For fall admission, 2/1 (priority date); for spring admission, 11/1. Applications are processed on a rolling basis. *Application fee:* $50 ($75 for international students). Electronic applications accepted.
Expenses: Tuition, state resident: full-time $11,872. Tuition, nonresident: full-time $17,892.
Financial support: In 2001–02, 40 fellowships with partial tuition reimbursements (averaging $5,000 per year), 150 research assistantships with partial tuition reimbursements (averaging $14,000 per year), 75 teaching assistantships (averaging $14,000 per year) were awarded. Institutionally sponsored loans and health care benefits also available. Financial award application deadline: 3/1; financial award applicants required to submit FAFSA.
Faculty research: Thermal/fluid sciences, materials/manufacturing and controls systems. *Total annual research expenditures:* $7.1 million.
Dr. John Weese, Interim Head, 979-845-1251, *Fax:* 979-845-3081.
Application contact: Kim Moses, Academic Advisor, 409-845-1270, *Fax:* 409-845-3081, *E-mail:* kmoses@ menar.tamu.edu. *Web site:* http:// www.mengr.tamu.edu/

Find an in-depth description at www.petersons.com/gradchannel.

■ **TEXAS A&M UNIVERSITY– KINGSVILLE**

College of Graduate Studies, College of Engineering, Department of Mechanical and Industrial Engineering, Program in Mechanical Engineering, Kingsville, TX 78363

AWARDS ME, MS.

Students: 8 full-time (0 women), 7 part-time; includes 1 minority (Hispanic American), 12 international. Average age 30. In 2001, 2 degrees awarded.
Degree requirements: For master's, thesis or alternative, comprehensive exam.
Entrance requirements: For master's, GRE General Test, TOEFL, minimum GPA of 3.0. *Application deadline:* For fall admission, 6/1; for spring admission, 11/15. Applications are processed on a rolling basis. *Application fee:* $15 ($25 for international students).

Expenses: Tuition, state resident: part-time $42 per hour. Tuition, nonresident: part-time $253 per hour. Required fees: $56 per hour. One-time fee: $46 part-time. Tuition and fees vary according to program.
Financial support: Fellowships, research assistantships, teaching assistantships available. Financial award application deadline: 5/15.
Faculty research: Intelligent systems and controls; neural networks and fuzzy logic; robotics and automation; biomass, cogeneration, and enhanced heat transfer. Dr. Hayder Abdul Razzak, Coordinator, 361-593-2001.

■ **TEXAS TECH UNIVERSITY**

Graduate School, College of Engineering, Department of Mechanical Engineering, Lubbock, TX 79409

AWARDS MSME, PhD. Part-time programs available.

Faculty: 17 full-time (1 woman).
Students: 37 full-time (1 woman), 11 part-time; includes 1 minority (Native American), 32 international. Average age 27. 117 applicants, 35% accepted, 20 enrolled. In 2001, 12 master's, 4 doctorates awarded.
Degree requirements: For master's and doctorate, thesis/dissertation.
Entrance requirements: For master's and doctorate, GRE General Test, minimum GPA of 3.0. *Application deadline:* Applications are processed on a rolling basis. *Application fee:* $25 ($50 for international students). Electronic applications accepted.
Expenses: Tuition, state resident: full-time $1,926; part-time $107 per credit hour. Tuition, nonresident: full-time $5,724; part-time $318 per credit hour. Required fees: $779; $737 per year. Tuition and fees vary according to course level, course load and program.
Financial support: In 2001–02, 19 research assistantships with partial tuition reimbursements (averaging $10,316 per year), 9 teaching assistantships with partial tuition reimbursements (averaging $11,410 per year) were awarded. Fellowships, Federal Work-Study and institutionally sponsored loans also available. Support available to part-time students. Financial award application deadline: 5/1; financial award applicants required to submit FAFSA.
Faculty research: Aerodynamics of automobiles and parachutes, natural gas, methanol and electric fueled vehicles, optomechanics, lubrication. *Total annual research expenditures:* $280,438.
Dr. Thomas D. Burton, Chair, 806-742-3563, *Fax:* 806-742-3540, *E-mail:* tburton@coe.ttu.edu.
Application contact: Graduate Adviser, 806-742-3563, *Fax:* 806-742-3540. *Web site:* http://www.me.ttu.edu/

■ TUFTS UNIVERSITY

Division of Graduate and Continuing Studies and Research, Graduate School of Arts and Sciences, School of Engineering, Department of Mechanical Engineering, Medford, MA 02155

AWARDS Human factors (MS); mechanical engineering (ME, MS, PhD). Part-time programs available.

Faculty: 13 full-time, 2 part-time/adjunct.
Students: 71 (12 women); includes 12 minority (8 Asian Americans or Pacific Islanders, 4 Hispanic Americans) 16 international. 36 applicants, 78% accepted. In 2001, 15 master's, 2 doctorates awarded. Terminal master's awarded for partial completion of doctoral program.
Degree requirements: For master's and doctorate, thesis/dissertation.
Entrance requirements: For master's and doctorate, GRE General Test, TOEFL. *Application deadline:* For fall admission, 2/15; for spring admission, 10/15. Applications are processed on a rolling basis. *Application fee:* $50. Electronic applications accepted.
Expenses: Tuition: Full-time $26,853. Full-time tuition and fees vary according to program.
Financial support: Research assistantships with full and partial tuition reimbursements, teaching assistantships with full and partial tuition reimbursements, Federal Work-Study, scholarships/grants, and tuition waivers (partial) available. Financial award application deadline: 2/15; financial award applicants required to submit FAFSA.
April Saigal, Chair, 617-627-3239, *Fax:* 617-627-3058, *E-mail:* meinfo@tufts.edu.
Application contact: Robert Greif, Head, 617-627-3239, *Fax:* 617-627-3058, *E-mail:* meinfo@tufts.edu. *Web site:* http://ase.tufts.edu/mechanical/

■ TULANE UNIVERSITY

School of Engineering, Department of Mechanical Engineering, New Orleans, LA 70118-5669

AWARDS MS, MSE, PhD, Sc D. MS and PhD offered through the Graduate School. Part-time programs available. Terminal master's awarded for partial completion of doctoral program.

Degree requirements: For master's, thesis; for doctorate, 2 foreign languages, thesis/dissertation.
Entrance requirements: For master's and doctorate, GRE General Test, TOEFL, minimum B average in undergraduate course work.
Expenses: Tuition: Full-time $24,675. Required fees: $2,210.

Find an in-depth description at www.petersons.com/gradchannel.

■ TUSKEGEE UNIVERSITY

Graduate Programs, College of Engineering, Architecture and Physical Sciences, Department of Mechanical Engineering, Tuskegee, AL 36088

AWARDS MSME.

Faculty: 11 full-time (0 women).
Students: 11 full-time (2 women), 16 part-time (3 women); includes 11 minority (10 African Americans, 1 Asian American or Pacific Islander), 16 international. Average age 24. In 2001, 7 degrees awarded.
Degree requirements: For master's, thesis or alternative.
Entrance requirements: For master's, GRE General Test, GRE Subject Test. *Application deadline:* For fall admission, 7/15. Applications are processed on a rolling basis. *Application fee:* $25 ($35 for international students).
Expenses: Tuition: Full-time $5,163; part-time $612 per credit hour.
Financial support: Fellowships, research assistantships, teaching assistantships, career-related internships or fieldwork, Federal Work-Study, and institutionally sponsored loans available. Support available to part-time students. Financial award application deadline: 4/15.
Faculty research: Superalloys, fatigue and surface machinery, energy management, solar energy.
Dr. Pradosh Ray, Head, 334-727-8989.

■ UNION COLLEGE

Center for Graduate Education and Special Programs, Division of Engineering and Computer Science, Department of Mechanical Engineering, Schenectady, NY 12308-2311

AWARDS MS.

Students: 2 full-time (both women), 14 part-time. Average age 31. 1 applicant, 100% accepted, 1 enrolled. In 2001, 5 degrees awarded.
Degree requirements: For master's, one foreign language, comprehensive exam.
Entrance requirements: For master's, minimum GPA of 3.0. *Application deadline:* Applications are processed on a rolling basis. *Application fee:* $50.
Expenses: Contact institution.
Faculty research: Metal fatigue testing, energy-related projects and equipment.
Dr. Ann Anderson, Chair, 518-388-6537.
Application contact: Rhonda Sheehan, Coordinator of Recruiting and Admissions, 518-388-6238, *Fax:* 518-388-6754, *E-mail:* sheehanr@union.edu. *Web site:* http://www.engineering.union.edu

■ UNIVERSITY AT BUFFALO, THE STATE UNIVERSITY OF NEW YORK

Graduate School, School of Engineering and Applied Sciences, Department of Mechanical and Aerospace Engineering, Buffalo, NY 14260

AWARDS Aerospace engineering (M Eng, MS, PhD); mechanical engineering (M Eng, MS, PhD). Part-time programs available.

Faculty: 25 full-time (3 women), 3 part-time/adjunct (0 women).
Students: 150 full-time (7 women), 48 part-time (6 women); includes 7 minority (6 Asian Americans or Pacific Islanders, 1 Hispanic American), 136 international. Average age 24. 454 applicants, 48% accepted. In 2001, 48 master's, 17 doctorates awarded. Terminal master's awarded for partial completion of doctoral program.
Degree requirements: For master's, project, or thesis; for doctorate, thesis/dissertation.
Entrance requirements: For master's and doctorate, GRE General Test, GRE Subject Test, TOEFL. *Application deadline:* For fall admission, 2/1; for spring admission, 10/1. Applications are processed on a rolling basis. *Application fee:* $35.
Expenses: Tuition, state resident: full-time $6,118. Tuition, nonresident: full-time $9,434.
Financial support: In 2001–02, 70 students received support, including 3 fellowships with tuition reimbursements available, 41 research assistantships with tuition reimbursements available (averaging $12,500 per year), 29 teaching assistantships with tuition reimbursements available (averaging $10,740 per year); Federal Work-Study, institutionally sponsored loans, tuition waivers (full), and unspecified assistantships also available. Financial award application deadline: 2/1; financial award applicants required to submit FAFSA.
Faculty research: Fluid and thermal sciences, systems and design, mechanics and materials. *Total annual research expenditures:* $1.4 million.
Dr. Christina L. Bloebaum, Chair, 716-645-2593 Ext. 2231, *Fax:* 716-645-3875, *E-mail:* clb@eng.buffalo.edu.
Application contact: Dr. Dale B. Taulbee, Director of Graduate Studies, 716-645-2593 Ext. 2307, *Fax:* 716-645-3875, *E-mail:* trldale@eng.buffalo.edu. *Web site:* http://www.eng.buffalo.edu/dept/mae/

Find an in-depth description at www.petersons.com/gradchannel.

■ THE UNIVERSITY OF AKRON

Graduate School, College of Engineering, Department of Mechanical Engineering, Akron, OH 44325-0001

AWARDS MS, PhD. Part-time and evening/weekend programs available.

Faculty: 15 full-time (1 woman), 14 part-time/adjunct (0 women).

Students: 39 full-time (4 women), 30 part-time (3 women); includes 1 minority (Native American), 36 international. Average age 30. 45 applicants, 87% accepted, 12 enrolled. In 2001, 27 degrees awarded. Terminal master's awarded for partial completion of doctoral program.

Degree requirements: For master's, thesis optional; for doctorate, one foreign language, thesis/dissertation, candidacy exam, qualifying exam.

Entrance requirements: For master's, TOEFL, minimum GPA of 2.75; for doctorate, GRE, TOEFL. *Application deadline:* For fall admission, 4/1. Applications are processed on a rolling basis. *Application fee:* $40 ($50 for international students).

Expenses: Tuition, state resident: full-time $6,562; part-time $219 per credit. Tuition, nonresident: full-time $9,027; part-time $383 per credit. Required fees: $272; $11 per credit. Tuition and fees vary according to course load.

Financial support: In 2001–02, 62 students received support, including 14 research assistantships with full tuition reimbursements available, 27 teaching assistantships with full tuition reimbursements available; fellowships with full tuition reimbursements available, tuition waivers (full) also available. Financial award application deadline: 3/1.

Faculty research: Computational fluid dynamics system control, energy systems, heat transfer, solid mechanics.

Dr. Celal Batur, Chair, 330-972-7367, *E-mail:* batur@uakron.edu. *Web site:* http://www.ecgf.uakron.edu/~mech

■ THE UNIVERSITY OF ALABAMA

Graduate School, College of Engineering, Department of Mechanical Engineering, Tuscaloosa, AL 35487

AWARDS MSME, PhD. Part-time and evening/weekend programs available.

Faculty: 15 full-time (1 woman).

Students: 44 full-time (4 women), 12 part-time; includes 2 minority (1 Asian American or Pacific Islander, 1 Hispanic American), 38 international. Average age 26. 153 applicants, 25% accepted, 14 enrolled. In 2001, 11 master's, 3 doctorates awarded. Terminal master's awarded for partial completion of doctoral program.

Degree requirements: For master's, thesis or alternative; for doctorate, thesis/dissertation.

Entrance requirements: For master's and doctorate, GRE General Test, minimum GPA of 3.0 in last 60 hours. *Application deadline:* For fall admission, 7/6 (priority date). Applications are processed on a rolling basis. *Application fee:* $25.

Expenses: Tuition, state resident: full-time $3,292; part-time $183 per credit hour. Tuition, nonresident: full-time $8,912; part-time $495 per credit hour. Tuition and fees vary according to course load, campus/location and program.

Financial support: In 2001–02, 3 fellowships with tuition reimbursements (averaging $10,000 per year), 15 research assistantships with tuition reimbursements (averaging $10,000 per year), 15 teaching assistantships with tuition reimbursements (averaging $10,000 per year) were awarded. Career-related internships or fieldwork and Federal Work-Study also available. Financial award application deadline: 1/15.

Faculty research: Thermal/fluids, robotics, numerical modeling, energy conservation, manufacturing. *Total annual research expenditures:* $968,093.

Dr. Stuart R. Bell, Head, 205-348-1644, *Fax:* 205-348-6419, *E-mail:* sbell@coe.eng.ua.edu.

Application contact: Dr. Will Schreiber, Graduate Supervisor, 205-348-1650, *E-mail:* wschreiber@coe.eng.ua.edu.

■ THE UNIVERSITY OF ALABAMA AT BIRMINGHAM

Graduate School, School of Engineering, Department of Materials Science and Engineering, Department of Mechanical Engineering, Birmingham, AL 35294

AWARDS MSME, PhD.

Expenses: Tuition, state resident: full-time $3,058. Tuition, nonresident: full-time $5,746. Tuition and fees vary according to course load, degree level and program.

Dr. Ernest M. Stokely, Interim Chair, 205-934-8400.

■ THE UNIVERSITY OF ALABAMA AT BIRMINGHAM

Graduate School, School of Engineering, Department of Materials Science and Engineering, Program in Mechanical Engineering, Birmingham, AL 35294

AWARDS MSME, PhD. Evening/weekend programs available.

Students: 8 full-time (0 women), 7 part-time (1 woman); includes 3 minority (1 African American, 2 Asian Americans or Pacific Islanders), 6 international. 61 applicants, 64% accepted. In 2001, 4 degrees awarded.

Degree requirements: For master's, project/thesis.

Entrance requirements: For master's, GRE General Test, minimum B average.

Application deadline: Applications are processed on a rolling basis. *Application fee:* $35 ($60 for international students). Electronic applications accepted.

Expenses: Tuition, state resident: full-time $3,058. Tuition, nonresident: full-time $5,746. Tuition and fees vary according to course load, degree level and program.

Financial support: In 2001–02, 1 fellowship with full tuition reimbursement (averaging $12,500 per year), 5 research assistantships with full tuition reimbursements (averaging $12,500 per year) were awarded. Career-related internships or fieldwork, Federal Work-Study, and institutionally sponsored loans also available. Support available to part-time students.

Faculty research: Microfluid dynamics, rarefied gas dynamics, biofluid mechanics of the cardiovascular system, electro-optical diagnostic implementation.

Dr. J. Barry Andrews, Interim Chair, Department of Materials Science and Engineering, 205-934-8460, *Fax:* 205-934-8485, *E-mail:* barry@uab.edu. *Web site:* http://www.eng.uab.edu/mme/megprogram.htm/

■ THE UNIVERSITY OF ALABAMA IN HUNTSVILLE

School of Graduate Studies, College of Engineering, Department of Mechanical and Aerospace Engineering, Huntsville, AL 35899

AWARDS Aerospace engineering (MSE); mechanical engineering (MSE, PhD). Part-time and evening/weekend programs available.

Faculty: 15 full-time (0 women), 4 part-time/adjunct (0 women).

Students: 40 full-time (6 women), 29 part-time (6 women); includes 4 minority (2 Asian Americans or Pacific Islanders, 2 Hispanic Americans), 26 international. Average age 31. 91 applicants, 60% accepted, 21 enrolled. In 2001, 8 master's, 4 doctorates awarded.

Degree requirements: For master's, thesis or alternative, oral and written exams, comprehensive exam, registration; for doctorate, thesis/dissertation, oral and written exams, comprehensive exam, registration.

Entrance requirements: For master's, GRE General Test, BSE, minimum GPA of 3.0; for doctorate, GRE General Test, minimum GPA of 3.0. *Application deadline:* For fall admission, 7/24 (priority date); for spring admission, 11/15 (priority date). Applications are processed on a rolling basis. *Application fee:* $35.

Expenses: Tuition, area resident: Part-time $175 per hour. Tuition, state resident: full-time $4,408. Tuition, nonresident: full-time $9,054; part-time $361 per hour.

Financial support: In 2001–02, 29 students received support, including 21 research assistantships with full and partial

The University of Alabama in Huntsville (continued)

tuition reimbursements available (averaging $9,936 per year), 8 teaching assistantships with full and partial tuition reimbursements available (averaging $7,100 per year); fellowships with full and partial tuition reimbursements available, career-related internships or fieldwork, Federal Work-Study, institutionally sponsored loans, scholarships/grants, health care benefits, and tuition waivers (full and partial) also available. Support available to part-time students. Financial award application deadline: 4/1; financial award applicants required to submit FAFSA.
Faculty research: Combustion, fluid dynamics, solar energy, propulsion, laser diagnostics. *Total annual research expenditures:* $1.6 million.
Dr. Francis C. Wessling, Chair, 256-824-6469, *Fax:* 256-824-6758, *E-mail:* wesslif@eb.uah.edu. *Web site:* http://www.eb-p5.eb.uah.edu/mae/

■ UNIVERSITY OF ALASKA FAIRBANKS

Graduate School, College of Science, Engineering and Mathematics, Department of Mechanical Engineering, Fairbanks, AK 99775-7480

AWARDS MS.

Faculty: 7 full-time (1 woman), 2 part-time/adjunct (0 women).
Students: 12 full-time (2 women), 6 part-time (1 woman); includes 3 minority (1 African American, 2 Asian Americans or Pacific Islanders), 11 international. Average age 32. 13 applicants, 69% accepted, 6 enrolled. In 2001, 2 degrees awarded.
Degree requirements: For master's, thesis or alternative.
Entrance requirements: For master's, GRE General Test, TOEFL. *Application deadline:* For fall admission, 4/1; for spring admission, 11/1. Applications are processed on a rolling basis. *Application fee:* $35.
Expenses: Tuition, state resident: full-time $4,272; part-time $178 per credit. Tuition, nonresident: full-time $8,328; part-time $347 per credit. Required fees: $960; $60 per term. Part-time tuition and fees vary according to course load.
Financial support: In 2001–02, fellowships with tuition reimbursements (averaging $10,000 per year); research assistantships with tuition reimbursements, teaching assistantships with tuition reimbursements, Federal Work-Study and scholarships/grants also available.
Faculty research: Cold regions engineering, fluid mechanics, heat transfer, energy systems, vibrations.
Dr. Jonah Lee, Head, 907-474-7209.

■ THE UNIVERSITY OF ARIZONA

Graduate College, College of Engineering and Mines, Department of Aerospace and Mechanical Engineering, Program in Mechanical Engineering, Tucson, AZ 85721

AWARDS MS, PhD. Part-time programs available.

Degree requirements: For master's, thesis or alternative; for doctorate, one foreign language, thesis/dissertation.
Entrance requirements: For master's and doctorate, GRE General Test, GRE Subject Test, TOEFL, minimum GPA of 3.0.
Expenses: Tuition, state resident: full-time $2,490; part-time $436 per unit. Tuition, nonresident: full-time $10,300; part-time $436 per unit. Full-time tuition and fees vary according to degree level and program.
Faculty research: Fluid mechanics, structures, computer-aided design, stability and control, probabilistic design.
Find an in-depth description at www.petersons.com/gradchannel.

■ UNIVERSITY OF ARKANSAS

Graduate School, College of Engineering, Department of Mechanical Engineering, Fayetteville, AR 72701-1201

AWARDS MSE, MSME, PhD.

Students: 20 full-time (2 women), 9 part-time (1 woman); includes 3 minority (2 Asian Americans or Pacific Islanders, 1 Native American), 16 international. 23 applicants, 78% accepted. In 2001, 7 master's, 3 doctorates awarded.
Degree requirements: For master's, thesis optional; for doctorate, one foreign language, thesis/dissertation.
Application fee: $40 ($50 for international students).
Expenses: Tuition, state resident: full-time $3,553; part-time $197 per credit. Tuition, nonresident: full-time $8,411; part-time $467 per credit. Required fees: $42 per credit. Tuition and fees vary according to course load and program.
Financial support: In 2001–02, 11 research assistantships, 6 teaching assistantships were awarded. Career-related internships or fieldwork and Federal Work-Study also available. Support available to part-time students. Financial award application deadline: 4/1; financial award applicants required to submit FAFSA.
Dr. W. F. Schmidt, Head, 479-575-3153, *E-mail:* ned@engr.uark.edu.

■ UNIVERSITY OF BRIDGEPORT

School of Engineering, Department of Mechanical Engineering, Program in Mechanical Engineering, Bridgeport, CT 06601

AWARDS MS.

Faculty: 2 full-time (0 women), 4 part-time/adjunct (0 women).
Students: 62 full-time (7 women), 20 part-time (1 woman); includes 1 African American, 78 international. Average age 25. 223 applicants, 96% accepted, 33 enrolled. In 2001, 2 degrees awarded.
Degree requirements: For master's, thesis optional.
Entrance requirements: For master's, TOEFL. *Application deadline:* For fall admission, 8/1 (priority date); for spring admission, 12/1 (priority date). Applications are processed on a rolling basis. *Application fee:* $25 ($35 for international students). Electronic applications accepted.
Expenses: Tuition: Part-time $385 per credit hour. Required fees: $50 per term. Tuition and fees vary according to degree level and program.
Financial support: In 2001–02, 3 students received support; research assistantships, teaching assistantships, career-related internships or fieldwork, Federal Work-Study, and institutionally sponsored loans available. Support available to part-time students. Financial award application deadline: 6/1; financial award applicants required to submit FAFSA.
Faculty research: Heat transfer.
Dr. Tienko Ting, Chairman, Department of Mechanical Engineering, 203-576-4669, *Fax:* 203-576-4343, *E-mail:* ting@bridgeport.edu.

■ UNIVERSITY OF CALIFORNIA, BERKELEY

Graduate Division, College of Engineering, Department of Mechanical Engineering, Berkeley, CA 94720-1500

AWARDS M Eng, MS, D Eng, PhD.

Students: 302 full-time (46 women); includes 66 minority (8 African Americans, 35 Asian Americans or Pacific Islanders, 22 Hispanic Americans, 1 Native American), 134 international. 715 applicants, 33% accepted, 92 enrolled. In 2001, 60 master's, 49 doctorates awarded.
Degree requirements: For master's, comprehensive exam or thesis (MS); for doctorate, thesis/dissertation, preliminary and qualifying exams.
Entrance requirements: For master's and doctorate, GRE General Test, TOEFL, minimum GPA of 3.0. *Application deadline:* For fall admission, 12/14; for spring admission, 9/1. *Application fee:* $60.
Expenses: Tuition, nonresident: full-time $10,704. Required fees: $4,349.
Financial support: Fellowships available. Financial award application deadline: 1/2.
Dr. J. Karl Hedrick, Chair, 510-642-1339.
Application contact: Pat Giddings, Student Affairs Officer, 510-642-5084, *Fax:* 510-642-6163, *E-mail:* mech@

me.berkeley.edu. *Web site:* http://www.me.berkeley.edu/

Find an in-depth description at www.petersons.com/gradchannel.

■ UNIVERSITY OF CALIFORNIA, DAVIS

Graduate Studies, College of Engineering, Program in Mechanical and Aeronautical Engineering, Davis, CA 95616

AWARDS Aeronautical engineering (M Engr, MS, D Engr, PhD, Certificate); mechanical engineering (M Engr, MS, D Engr, PhD, Certificate).

Faculty: 29 full-time (1 woman).
Students: 106 full-time (18 women); includes 25 minority (3 African Americans, 20 Asian Americans or Pacific Islanders, 2 Hispanic Americans), 28 international. Average age 28. 234 applicants, 69% accepted, 38 enrolled. In 2001, 25 master's, 8 doctorates awarded.
Degree requirements: For master's, thesis optional; for doctorate, thesis/dissertation.
Entrance requirements: For master's and doctorate, GRE General Test, minimum GPA of 3.0. *Application deadline:* For fall admission, 3/15. *Application fee:* $60. Electronic applications accepted.
Expenses: Tuition, state resident: full-time $4,831. Tuition, nonresident: full-time $15,725.
Financial support: In 2001–02, 80 students received support, including 13 fellowships with full and partial tuition reimbursements available (averaging $2,246 per year), 53 research assistantships with full and partial tuition reimbursements available (averaging $9,707 per year), 20 teaching assistantships with partial tuition reimbursements available (averaging $9,897 per year); career-related internships or fieldwork, Federal Work-Study, institutionally sponsored loans, scholarships/grants, and tuition waivers (full and partial) also available. Financial award application deadline: 1/15; financial award applicants required to submit FAFSA.
Rida T. Farouki, Chairperson, 530-752-1779, *Fax:* 530-752-4158, *E-mail:* farouki@ucdavis.edu.
Application contact: Susan Fann, Academic Assistant, 530-752-0581, *Fax:* 530-752-4158, *E-mail:* sfann@ucdavis.edu. *Web site:* http://mae.ucdavis.edu/

■ UNIVERSITY OF CALIFORNIA, IRVINE

Office of Research and Graduate Studies, School of Engineering, Department of Mechanical and Aerospace Engineering, Irvine, CA 92697

AWARDS MS, PhD. Part-time programs available.

Students: 62 full-time (10 women), 14 part-time (3 women); includes 20 minority (16 Asian Americans or Pacific Islanders, 4 Hispanic Americans), 16 international. 180 applicants, 33% accepted, 19 enrolled. In 2001, 18 master's, 4 doctorates awarded. Terminal master's awarded for partial completion of doctoral program.
Degree requirements: For doctorate, thesis/dissertation.
Entrance requirements: For master's, GRE General Test, minimum GPA of 3.0; for doctorate, GRE General Test. *Application deadline:* For fall and spring admission, 1/15 (priority date); for winter admission, 10/15 (priority date). Applications are processed on a rolling basis. *Application fee:* $60. Electronic applications accepted.
Expenses: Tuition, nonresident: full-time $10,704. Required fees: $8,396. Tuition and fees vary according to course load, program and student level.
Financial support: In 2001–02, 14 fellowships with tuition reimbursements (averaging $1,250 per year), 24 research assistantships with tuition reimbursements (averaging $1,120 per year), 12 teaching assistantships with tuition reimbursements (averaging $1,480 per year) were awarded. Institutionally sponsored loans and tuition waivers (full and partial) also available. Financial award application deadline: 3/2; financial award applicants required to submit FAFSA.
Faculty research: Thermal and fluid sciences, combustion and propulsion, control systems, robotics. *Total annual research expenditures:* $3.5 million.
Dr. Said Elghobashi, Chair, 949-824-6131, *Fax:* 949-824-8585, *E-mail:* selghoba@uci.edu.
Application contact: Dorothy Miles, Graduate Coordinator, 949-824-5469, *Fax:* 949-824-8585, *E-mail:* djmiles@uci.edu. *Web site:* http://www.eng.uci.edu/

Find an in-depth description at www.petersons.com/gradchannel.

■ UNIVERSITY OF CALIFORNIA, LOS ANGELES

Graduate Division, School of Engineering and Applied Science, Department of Mechanical and Aerospace Engineering, Program in Mechanical Engineering, Los Angeles, CA 90095

AWARDS MS, PhD.

Students: 143 full-time (16 women); includes 38 minority (2 African Americans, 31 Asian Americans or Pacific Islanders, 5 Hispanic Americans), 71 international. 226 applicants, 45% accepted, 36 enrolled. In 2001, 14 master's, 14 doctorates awarded.
Degree requirements: For master's, comprehensive exam or thesis; for doctorate, thesis/dissertation, qualifying exams.
Entrance requirements: For master's, GRE General Test, GRE Subject Test (international applicants), minimum GPA

of 3.0; for doctorate, GRE General Test, GRE Subject Test (international applicants), minimum GPA of 3.25.
Application deadline: For fall admission, 1/5; for spring admission, 12/31. *Application fee:* $60. Electronic applications accepted.
Expenses: Tuition, nonresident: full-time $10,244. Required fees: $3,609. Full-time tuition and fees vary according to program.
Financial support: In 2001–02, 262 research assistantships, 42 teaching assistantships were awarded. Fellowships, Federal Work-Study, institutionally sponsored loans, and tuition waivers (full and partial) also available. Financial award application deadline: 1/5; financial award applicants required to submit FAFSA.
Application contact: Dr. Angie Castillo, Student Affairs Officer, 310-825-7793, *Fax:* 310-206-4830, *E-mail:* angie@ea.ucla.edu.

■ UNIVERSITY OF CALIFORNIA, SAN DIEGO

Graduate Studies and Research, Department of Mechanical and Aerospace Engineering, Program in Mechanical Engineering, La Jolla, CA 92093

AWARDS MS, PhD. Part-time programs available.

Degree requirements: For master's, comprehensive exam or thesis; for doctorate, thesis/dissertation, qualifying exam.
Entrance requirements: For master's and doctorate, GRE General Test, TOEFL, minimum GPA of 3.0.
Expenses: Tuition, nonresident: full-time $10,434. Required fees: $4,883.
Faculty research: Combustion engineering, environmental mechanics, magnetic recording, materials processing, computational fluid dynamics. *Web site:* http://www-ames.ucsd.edu/

Find an in-depth description at www.petersons.com/gradchannel.

■ UNIVERSITY OF CALIFORNIA, SANTA BARBARA

Graduate Division, College of Engineering, Department of Mechanical and Environmental Engineering, Santa Barbara, CA 93106

AWARDS MS, PhD.

Degree requirements: For master's, thesis or alternative, project; for doctorate, thesis/dissertation.
Entrance requirements: For master's and doctorate, GRE General Test, TOEFL. Electronic applications accepted.
Faculty research: Dynamic systems, control, and robotics; environmental ocean and risk/safety engineering. Solid mechanics, materials, and structures; thermofluid

University of California, Santa Barbara (continued)

sciences; computational science. *Web site:* http://www.me.ucsb.edu/

Find an in-depth description at www.petersons.com/gradchannel.

■ UNIVERSITY OF CENTRAL FLORIDA

College of Engineering and Computer Sciences, Department of Mechanical, Materials, and Aerospace Engineering, Program in Mechanical Engineering, Orlando, FL 32816

AWARDS MSME, PhD, Certificate.

Faculty: 19 full-time (1 woman), 5 part-time/adjunct (0 women).
Students: 35 full-time (3 women), 40 part-time (8 women); includes 19 minority (12 Asian Americans or Pacific Islanders, 7 Hispanic Americans), 33 international. Average age 29. 119 applicants, 60% accepted, 26 enrolled. In 2001, 10 master's, 7 doctorates awarded.
Degree requirements: For master's, thesis or alternative; for doctorate, thesis/dissertation, candidacy exam, departmental qualifying exam.
Application deadline: For fall admission, 7/15 (priority date); for spring admission, 12/1 (priority date). *Application fee:* $20. Electronic applications accepted.
Expenses: Tuition, state resident: part-time $162 per hour. Tuition, nonresident: part-time $569 per hour.
Financial support: In 2001–02, 23 fellowships (averaging $6,766 per year), 79 research assistantships (averaging $3,023 per year), 30 teaching assistantships (averaging $4,390 per year) were awarded. Career-related internships or fieldwork, institutionally sponsored loans, scholarships/grants, tuition waivers (partial), and unspecified assistantships also available.
Application contact: Dr. A. J. Kassab, Coordinator, 407-823-2416, *Fax:* 407-823-0208, *E-mail:* kassab@mail.ucf.edu.

Find an in-depth description at www.petersons.com/gradchannel.

■ UNIVERSITY OF CINCINNATI

Division of Research and Advanced Studies, College of Engineering, Department of Mechanical, Industrial and Nuclear Engineering, Program in Mechanical Engineering, Cincinnati, OH 45221

AWARDS MS, PhD. Evening/weekend programs available. Terminal master's awarded for partial completion of doctoral program.

Degree requirements: For master's, oral exam or thesis defense; for doctorate, variable foreign language requirement, thesis/dissertation.

Entrance requirements: For master's and doctorate, GRE General Test, TOEFL, TSE. *Application deadline:* For fall admission, 2/1 (priority date). *Application fee:* $40. Electronic applications accepted.
Expenses: Tuition, state resident: part-time $2,698 per quarter. Tuition, nonresident: part-time $4,977 per quarter.
Financial support: Fellowships, career-related internships or fieldwork, tuition waivers (partial), and unspecified assistantships available. Financial award application deadline: 2/1.
Faculty research: Signature analysis, structural analysis, energy, design, robotics.
Application contact: Dr. David Thompson, Graduate Program Director, 513-556-3693, *Fax:* 513-556-3390, *E-mail:* david.thompson@uc.edu. *Web site:* http://www.min.uc.edu/

■ UNIVERSITY OF COLORADO AT BOULDER

Graduate School, College of Engineering and Applied Science, Department of Mechanical Engineering, Boulder, CO 80309

AWARDS ME, MS, PhD. Part-time programs available.

Faculty: 15 full-time (2 women).
Students: 57 full-time (7 women), 8 part-time; includes 4 minority (2 Asian Americans or Pacific Islanders, 1 Hispanic American, 1 Native American), 30 international. Average age 28. 106 applicants, 48% accepted. In 2001, 16 master's, 11 doctorates awarded. Terminal master's awarded for partial completion of doctoral program.
Degree requirements: For master's, thesis optional; for doctorate, thesis/dissertation, final, and preliminary exams, comprehensive exam.
Entrance requirements: For master's and doctorate, TOEFL, minimum undergraduate GPA of 3.0. *Application deadline:* For fall admission, 1/15 (priority date); for spring admission, 9/1. Applications are processed on a rolling basis. *Application fee:* $50 ($60 for international students).
Expenses: Tuition, state resident: full-time $3,474. Tuition, nonresident: full-time $16,624.
Financial support: In 2001–02, 37 students received support, including 1 fellowship with full tuition reimbursement available (averaging $3,061 per year), 16 research assistantships with full tuition reimbursements available (averaging $20,278 per year), 5 teaching assistantships with full tuition reimbursements available (averaging $16,321 per year); career-related internships or fieldwork also available. Financial award application deadline: 2/15.
Faculty research: Thermal science, fluid mechanics, solid mechanics, materials science, interactive design and manufacturing. *Total annual research expenditures:* $2.8 million.

Subhendu K. Datta, Chair, 303-492-0287, *Fax:* 303-492-3498, *E-mail:* subhendu.datta@colorado.edu.
Application contact: Rachel Knapp, Graduate Program Assistant, 303-492-7444, *Fax:* 303-492-3498, *E-mail:* rachel.knapp@colorado.edu. *Web site:* http://me-www.colorado.edu/

■ UNIVERSITY OF COLORADO AT COLORADO SPRINGS

Graduate School, College of Engineering and Applied Science, Department of Mechanical and Aerospace Engineering, Colorado Springs, CO 80933-7150

AWARDS Engineering management (ME); information operations (ME); manufacturing (ME); mechanical engineering (MS). Software engineering (ME). Space operations (ME). Part-time and evening/weekend programs available.

Faculty: 7 full-time (0 women), 5 part-time/adjunct (3 women).
Students: 16 full-time (3 women), 14 part-time (1 woman); includes 1 minority (Asian American or Pacific Islander), 1 international. Average age 35. In 2001, 26 degrees awarded.
Degree requirements: For master's, thesis optional.
Entrance requirements: For master's, GRE General Test, TOEFL, bachelor's degree in engineering or related degree, minimum GPA of 3.0. *Application deadline:* For fall admission, 7/15; for spring admission, 12/10. Applications are processed on a rolling basis. *Application fee:* $60 ($75 for international students).
Expenses: Tuition, state resident: full-time $2,900; part-time $174 per credit. Tuition, nonresident: full-time $9,961; part-time $591 per credit. Required fees: $14 per credit. $141 per semester. Tuition and fees vary according to course load, program and student level.
Faculty research: Neural networks, artificial intelligence, robust control, space operations, space propulsion.
Dr. Peter Gorder, Chair, 719-262-3168, *Fax:* 719-262-3589, *E-mail:* pgorder@eas.uccs.edu.
Application contact: Siew Nylund, Academic Adviser, 719-262-3243, *Fax:* 719-262-3042, *E-mail:* snylund@uccs.edu. *Web site:* http://mepo-b.uccs.edu/newsletter.html

■ UNIVERSITY OF COLORADO AT DENVER

Graduate School, College of Engineering and Applied Science, Department of Mechanical Engineering, Denver, CO 80217-3364

AWARDS MS. Part-time and evening/weekend programs available.

Faculty: 9 full-time (0 women).

Students: 3 full-time (0 women), 25 part-time (6 women); includes 8 minority (1 African American, 3 Asian Americans or Pacific Islanders, 2 Hispanic Americans, 2 Native Americans), 4 international. Average age 30. 17 applicants, 53% accepted, 3 enrolled. In 2001, 8 degrees awarded.
Degree requirements: For master's, thesis optional.
Entrance requirements: For master's, GRE. *Application deadline:* For fall admission, 5/1; for spring admission, 11/1. Applications are processed on a rolling basis. *Application fee:* $50 ($60 for international students). Electronic applications accepted.
Expenses: Tuition, state resident: full-time $3,284; part-time $198 per credit hour. Tuition, nonresident: full-time $13,380; part-time $802 per credit hour. Required fees: $444; $222 per semester.
Financial support: Research assistantships, teaching assistantships, career-related internships or fieldwork and Federal Work-Study available. Financial award application deadline: 3/1; financial award applicants required to submit FAFSA. *Total annual research expenditures:* $238,554. James Gerdeen, Chair, 303-556-2781, *Fax:* 303-556-6371, *E-mail:* jgerdeen@castle.cudenver.edu.
Application contact: Loretta Duran, Program Assistant, 303-556-8516, *Fax:* 303-556-6371, *E-mail:* lduran@carbon.cudenver.edu. *Web site:* http://carbon.cudenver.edu/public/engineer/medept.html

■ UNIVERSITY OF CONNECTICUT

Graduate School, School of Engineering, Department of Mechanical Engineering, Field of Mechanical Engineering, Storrs, CT 06269

AWARDS MS, PhD.

■ UNIVERSITY OF DAYTON

Graduate School, School of Engineering, Department of Mechanical and Aerospace Engineering, Dayton, OH 45469-1300

AWARDS Aerospace engineering (MSAE, DE, PhD); mechanical engineering (MSME, DE, PhD). Part-time programs available.

Faculty: 14 full-time (0 women), 10 part-time/adjunct (1 woman).
Students: 38 full-time (4 women), 18 part-time (4 women); includes 9 minority (2 African Americans, 1 Asian American or Pacific Islander, 6 Hispanic Americans), 16 international. Average age 26. In 2001, 10 master's, 5 doctorates awarded.
Degree requirements: For doctorate, variable foreign language requirement, thesis/dissertation, departmental qualifying exam.
Entrance requirements: For master's, TOEFL. *Application deadline:* For fall

admission, 8/1 (priority date). Applications are processed on a rolling basis. *Application fee:* $30.
Expenses: Tuition: Full-time $5,436; part-time $453 per credit hour. Required fees: $50; $25 per term.
Financial support: In 2001–02, 1 fellowship with full tuition reimbursement (averaging $18,000 per year), 20 research assistantships with full tuition reimbursements (averaging $13,500 per year), 1 teaching assistantship with full tuition reimbursement (averaging $9,000 per year) were awarded. Institutionally sponsored loans and tuition waivers (full and partial) also available.
Faculty research: Turbine blade convection, jet engine combustion, energy storage, heat pipes surface transfer, surface coating friction and wear. *Total annual research expenditures:* $400,000.
Dr. Kevin Hallinan, Chairperson, 937-229-2835, *Fax:* 937-229-2756, *E-mail:* khallinan@engr.udayton.edu.
Application contact: Dr. Donald L. Moon, Associate Dean, 937-229-2241, *Fax:* 937-229-2471, *E-mail:* dmoon@notes.udayton.edu.

■ UNIVERSITY OF DELAWARE

College of Engineering, Department of Mechanical Engineering, Newark, DE 19716

AWARDS MEM, MSME, PhD. Part-time programs available.

Faculty: 20 full-time (1 woman).
Students: 58 full-time (8 women), 4 part-time, 47 international. Average age 28. 237 applicants, 21% accepted, 25 enrolled. In 2001, 9 master's, 4 doctorates awarded. Terminal master's awarded for partial completion of doctoral program.
Degree requirements: For master's, thesis (for some programs); for doctorate, thesis/dissertation.
Entrance requirements: For master's and doctorate, GRE General Test, TOEFL. *Application deadline:* For fall admission, 7/1 (priority date); for spring admission, 1/16. Applications are processed on a rolling basis. *Application fee:* $50. Electronic applications accepted.
Expenses: Tuition, state resident: full-time $4,770; part-time $265 per credit. Tuition, nonresident: full-time $13,860; part-time $770 per credit. Required fees: $414.
Financial support: In 2001–02, 46 students received support, including 4 fellowships with full tuition reimbursements available (averaging $16,980 per year), 34 research assistantships with full tuition reimbursements available (averaging $16,980 per year), 13 teaching assistantships with full tuition reimbursements available (averaging $16,980 per year) Financial award application deadline: 3/1.
Faculty research: Biomechanics, composites, design and manufacturing processing, environmental and nonlinear

dynamics, chaos. *Total annual research expenditures:* $2.1 million.
Dr. Tsu Wei Chou, Chair, 302-831-2423, *Fax:* 302-831-3619, *E-mail:* chou@me.udel.edu.
Application contact: Hai Wang, Graduate Coordinator, 302-831-2423, *Fax:* 302-831-3619, *E-mail:* hwang@me.udel.edu. *Web site:* http://me.udel.edu

Find an in-depth description at www.petersons.com/gradchannel.

■ UNIVERSITY OF DENVER

Graduate Studies, Faculty of Natural Sciences, Mathematics and Engineering, Department of Engineering, Denver, CO 80208

AWARDS Computer science and engineering (MS); electrical engineering (MS); management and general engineering (MSMGEN); materials science (PhD); mechanical engineering (MS). Part-time and evening/weekend programs available.

Faculty: 13 full-time (2 women), 3 part-time/adjunct (0 women).
Students: 17 (6 women) 11 international. 50 applicants, 62% accepted. In 2001, 11 degrees awarded. Terminal master's awarded for partial completion of doctoral program.
Degree requirements: For master's, thesis (for some programs); for doctorate, thesis/dissertation.
Entrance requirements: For master's and doctorate, GRE General Test, TOEFL, TSE. *Application deadline:* Applications are processed on a rolling basis. *Application fee:* $45.
Expenses: Tuition: Full-time $21,456.
Financial support: In 2001–02, 11 students received support, including 6 research assistantships with full and partial tuition reimbursements available (averaging $9,999 per year), 7 teaching assistantships with full and partial tuition reimbursements available (averaging $10,782 per year); fellowships with full and partial tuition reimbursements available, career-related internships or fieldwork, Federal Work-Study, institutionally sponsored loans, and scholarships/grants also available. Financial award application deadline: 3/1; financial award applicants required to submit FAFSA.
Faculty research: Microelectrics, digital signal processing, robotics, speech recognition, microwaves, aerosols, x-ray analysis, acoustic emissions. *Total annual research expenditures:* $1 million.
Dr. James C. Wilson, Chair, 303-871-2102.
Application contact: Susie Montoya, Assistant to Chair, 303-871-2102. *Web site:* http://littlebird.engr.du.edu/

■ UNIVERSITY OF DETROIT MERCY

College of Engineering and Science, Department of Mechanical Engineering, Detroit, MI 48219-0900

AWARDS Automotive engineering (DE); manufacturing engineering (DE); mechanical engineering (ME, DE). Evening/weekend programs available.

Faculty: 8 full-time (1 woman).
Students: 5 full-time (0 women), 28 part-time (3 women); includes 1 minority (Asian American or Pacific Islander), 23 international. Average age 31. In 2001, 12 degrees awarded.
Degree requirements: For doctorate, thesis/dissertation.
Application deadline: For fall admission, 8/1 (priority date). Applications are processed on a rolling basis. *Application fee:* $30 ($50 for international students).
Expenses: Tuition: Full-time $10,620; part-time $590 per credit hour. Required fees: $400. Tuition and fees vary according to program.
Faculty research: CAD/CAM.
Mark Schumak, Chairman, 313-993-3370, *Fax:* 313-993-1187, *E-mail:* schumamr@ udmercy.edu.

■ UNIVERSITY OF FLORIDA

Graduate School, College of Engineering, Department of Mechanical Engineering, Gainesville, FL 32611

AWARDS ME, MS, PhD, Certificate, Engr. Part-time programs available.

Degree requirements: For master's, thesis (for some programs); for doctorate and other advanced degree, thesis/dissertation.
Entrance requirements: For master's and doctorate, GRE General Test, TOEFL, minimum GPA of 3.0; for other advanced degree, GRE General Test, TOEFL.
Expenses: Tuition, state resident: part-time $164 per hour. Tuition, nonresident: part-time $571 per hour. Tuition and fees vary according to course level and program.
Faculty research: Thermal sciences, design, controls and robotics, manufacturing, energy transport and utilization. *Web site:* http://www.me.ufl.edu/

Find an in-depth description at www.petersons.com/gradchannel.

■ UNIVERSITY OF HAWAII AT MANOA

Graduate Division, College of Engineering, Department of Mechanical Engineering, Honolulu, HI 96822

AWARDS MS, PhD.

Faculty: 16 full-time (1 woman), 5 part-time/adjunct (0 women).

Students: 11 full-time (4 women), 3 part-time; includes 3 Asian Americans or Pacific Islanders. Average age 30. 28 applicants, 75% accepted, 3 enrolled. In 2001, 5 master's awarded.
Degree requirements: For master's, thesis; for doctorate, thesis/dissertation, exams. *Median time to degree:* Master's–3 years full-time; doctorate–5 years full-time. *Application deadline:* For fall admission, 1/15; for spring admission, 9/1. Applications are processed on a rolling basis. *Application fee:* $25 ($50 for international students).
Expenses: Tuition, state resident: full-time $2,160; part-time $1,980 per year. Tuition, nonresident: full-time $5,190; part-time $4,829 per year.
Financial support: In 2001–02, 6 research assistantships (averaging $15,482 per year), 5 teaching assistantships (averaging $13,097 per year) were awarded. Tuition waivers (full) also available. Financial award application deadline: 8/31; financial award applicants required to submit FAFSA.
Faculty research: Materials and manufacturing; mechanics, systems and control; thermal and fluid sciences. *Total annual research expenditures:* $2 million.
Dr. Hi Chang Chai, Chairperson, 808-956-7167, *Fax:* 808-956-2373.
Application contact: Ronald Knapp, Graduate Chairperson, 808-956-6592, *Fax:* 808-956-2373, *E-mail:* knapp@ eng.hawaii.edu. *Web site:* http://www.eng.hawaii.edu/MEI

■ UNIVERSITY OF HOUSTON

Cullen College of Engineering, Department of Mechanical Engineering, Houston, TX 77204

AWARDS Aerospace engineering (MS, PhD); biomedical engineering (MS); computer and systems engineering (MS, PhD); environmental engineering (MS, PhD); materials engineering (MS, PhD); mechanical engineering (MME, MSME); petroleum engineering (MS). Part-time and evening/weekend programs available.

Faculty: 16 full-time (0 women), 1 part-time/adjunct (0 women).
Students: 34 full-time (4 women), 26 part-time (2 women); includes 7 minority (3 Asian Americans or Pacific Islanders, 4 Hispanic Americans), 32 international. Average age 28. 114 applicants, 64% accepted. In 2001, 20 master's, 3 doctorates awarded. Terminal master's awarded for partial completion of doctoral program.
Degree requirements: For master's, thesis (for some programs); for doctorate, thesis/dissertation, departmental qualifying exam.
Entrance requirements: For master's and doctorate, GRE General Test, TOEFL. *Application deadline:* For fall admission, 7/3 (priority date); for spring admission, 12/4. Applications are processed on a rolling

basis. *Application fee:* $25 ($75 for international students).
Expenses: Tuition, state resident: full-time $1,512. Tuition, nonresident: full-time $5,310. Required fees: $1,308. Tuition and fees vary according to program.
Financial support: In 2001–02, 20 research assistantships (averaging $14,400 per year), 13 teaching assistantships (averaging $14,400 per year) were awarded. Fellowships, career-related internships or fieldwork and Federal Work-Study also available. Financial award application deadline: 2/15.
Faculty research: Experimental and computational turbulence, composites, rheology, phase change/heat transfer, characterization of superconducting materials. *Total annual research expenditures:* $396,172.
Dr. Lewis T. Wheeler, Interim Chair, 713-743-4500, *Fax:* 713-743-4503.
Application contact: Susan Sanderson-Clobe, Graduate Admissions Analyst, 713-743-4505, *Fax:* 713-743-4503, *E-mail:* megrad@uh.edu. *Web site:* http://www.mc.uh.edu

Find an in-depth description at www.petersons.com/gradchannel.

■ UNIVERSITY OF IDAHO

College of Graduate Studies, College of Engineering, Department of Mechanical Engineering, Program in Mechanical Engineering, Moscow, ID 83844-2282

AWARDS M Engr, MS, PhD.

Students: 25 full-time (3 women), 46 part-time (2 women); includes 4 minority (1 Asian American or Pacific Islander, 2 Hispanic Americans, 1 Native American), 6 international. In 2001, 14 master's, 1 doctorate awarded.
Degree requirements: For master's, thesis or alternative; for doctorate, thesis/dissertation.
Entrance requirements: For master's, TOEFL, minimum GPA of 2.8; for doctorate, TOEFL, minimum undergraduate GPA of 2.8, graduate GPA of 3.0. *Application deadline:* For fall admission, 8/1; for spring admission, 12/15. *Application fee:* $35 ($45 for international students).
Expenses: Tuition, state resident: full-time $1,613. Tuition, nonresident: full-time $3,000.
Financial support: Application deadline: 2/15.
Dr. Ralph S. Budwig, Chair, Department of Mechanical Engineering, 208-885-7454.

Find an in-depth description at www.petersons.com/gradchannel.

■ UNIVERSITY OF ILLINOIS AT CHICAGO

Graduate College, College of Engineering, Department of Mechanical Engineering, Chicago, IL 60607-7128

AWARDS Industrial engineering (MS), including industrial engineering; industrial engineering and operations research (PhD); mechanical engineering (MS, PhD), including fluids engineering, mechanical analysis and design, thermomechanical and power engineering.

Faculty: 24 full-time (0 women).
Students: 80 full-time (7 women), 52 part-time (12 women); includes 18 minority (5 African Americans, 8 Asian Americans or Pacific Islanders, 5 Hispanic Americans), 84 international. Average age 29. 276 applicants, 32% accepted, 40 enrolled. In 2001, 24 master's, 5 doctorates awarded.
Degree requirements: For doctorate, thesis/dissertation.
Entrance requirements: For master's and doctorate, GRE General Test, TOEFL, minimum GPA of 3.75 on a 5.0 scale. *Application deadline:* For fall admission, 6/1; for spring admission, 11/1. Applications are processed on a rolling basis. *Application fee:* $40 ($50 for international students). Electronic applications accepted.
Expenses: Tuition, state resident: full-time $3,060. Tuition, nonresident: full-time $6,688.
Financial support: In 2001–02, 70 students received support; fellowships with full tuition reimbursements available, research assistantships with full tuition reimbursements available, teaching assistantships with full tuition reimbursements available, Federal Work-Study and tuition waivers (full) available. Financial award application deadline: 3/1; financial award applicants required to submit FAFSA.
Thomas Royston, Head, 312-996-7951, *E-mail:* troyston@uic.edu.
Application contact: Mun Young Choi, Director of Graduate Studies.
Find an in-depth description at www.petersons.com/gradchannel.

■ UNIVERSITY OF ILLINOIS AT URBANA–CHAMPAIGN

Graduate College, College of Engineering, Department of Mechanical and Industrial Engineering, Champaign, IL 61820

AWARDS Industrial engineering (MS, PhD); mechanical engineering (MS, PhD).

Faculty: 43 full-time.
Students: 240 full-time (20 women); includes 22 minority (4 African Americans, 14 Asian Americans or Pacific Islanders, 4 Hispanic Americans), 135 international. 778 applicants, 12% accepted. In 2001, 70 master's, 29 doctorates awarded. Terminal master's awarded for partial completion of doctoral program.
Degree requirements: For master's, thesis, non-thesis available by petition; for doctorate, thesis/dissertation.
Entrance requirements: For master's, GRE General Test, TOEFL, minimum GPA of 3.25; for doctorate, GRE General Test, TOEFL. *Application deadline:* For fall admission, 2/15; for spring admission, 10/1. Applications are processed on a rolling basis. *Application fee:* $40 ($50 for international students).
Expenses: Tuition, state resident: part-time $3,227 per degree program. Tuition, nonresident: part-time $7,169 per degree program. Tuition and fees vary according to program.
Financial support: In 2001–02, 9 fellowships, 168 research assistantships, 37 teaching assistantships were awarded. Federal Work-Study, institutionally sponsored loans, and tuition waivers (full and partial) also available. Financial award application deadline: 3/1.
Faculty research: Combustion and propulsion, design methodology, dynamic systems and controls, energy transfer, materials behavior and processing, manufacturing systems operations, management. *Total annual research expenditures:* $8 million.
Dr. Richard O. Buckius, Head, 217-333-1079, *Fax:* 217-244-6534, *E-mail:* buckius@uiuc.edu.
Application contact: Karen Bryan, Administrative Secretary, 217-244-4539, *Fax:* 217-244-6534, *E-mail:* k-bryan@uiuc.edu. *Web site:* http://www.mie.uiuc.edu/academic-programs/
Find an in-depth description at www.petersons.com/gradchannel.

■ THE UNIVERSITY OF IOWA

Graduate College, College of Engineering, Department of Mechanical Engineering, Iowa City, IA 52242-1316

AWARDS MS, PhD.

Faculty: 16 full-time, 3 part-time/adjunct.
Students: 68 full-time (9 women); includes 2 minority (1 Asian American or Pacific Islander, 1 Hispanic American), 54 international. Average age 28. 193 applicants, 17% accepted, 12 enrolled. In 2001, 11 master's, 8 doctorates awarded.
Degree requirements: For master's, exam, oral if no thesis, thesis optional; for doctorate, thesis/dissertation, comprehensive exam. *Median time to degree:* Master's–2 years full-time; doctorate–4 years full-time.
Entrance requirements: For master's and doctorate, GRE, TOEFL. *Application deadline:* For fall admission, 1/15 (priority date); for spring admission, 7/15 (priority date). *Application fee:* $30 ($50 for international students). Electronic applications accepted.
Expenses: Tuition, state resident: full-time $3,702; part-time $206 per semester hour. Tuition, nonresident: full-time $11,924; part-time $206 per semester hour. Required fees: $101 per semester. Tuition and fees vary according to course load and program.
Financial support: In 2001–02, 2 fellowships (averaging $14,718 per year), 47 research assistantships (averaging $14,718 per year), 19 teaching assistantships (averaging $14,718 per year) were awarded. Traineeships and unspecified assistantships also available. Financial award applicants required to submit FAFSA.
Faculty research: Computational mechanics, fluid mechanics, heat transfer, materials processing. *Total annual research expenditures:* $4.6 million.
Dr. Jeffrey S. Marshall, Departmental Executive Officer, 319-335-5817, *Fax:* 319-335-5669, *E-mail:* jeffrey-marshall@uiowa.edu.
Application contact: Phyllis Huston, Secretary, 319-335-5668, *Fax:* 319-335-5669, *E-mail:* mech_eng@engineering.uiowa.edu. *Web site:* http://www.mie.engineering.uiowa.edu

■ UNIVERSITY OF KANSAS

Graduate School, School of Engineering, Department of Mechanical Engineering, Lawrence, KS 66045

AWARDS MS, DE, PhD.

Faculty: 13.
Students: 25 full-time (4 women), 12 part-time (2 women), 26 international. Average age 26. 145 applicants, 46% accepted, 13 enrolled. In 2001, 4 master's, 5 doctorates awarded.
Degree requirements: For master's, thesis or alternative, exam; for doctorate, thesis/dissertation, comprehensive exam.
Entrance requirements: For master's, Michigan English Language Assessment Battery, TOEFL, minimum GPA of 3.0; for doctorate, Michigan English Language Assessment Battery, TOEFL, minimum GPA of 3.5. *Application deadline:* Applications are processed on a rolling basis. *Application fee:* $40.
Expenses: Tuition, state resident: full-time $2,722; part-time $113 per credit. Tuition, nonresident: full-time $8,586; part-time $358 per credit. Required fees: $551; $46 per credit. Tuition and fees vary according to campus/location, program and reciprocity agreements.
Financial support: In 2001–02, 10 research assistantships with partial tuition reimbursements (averaging $7,264 per year), 4 teaching assistantships with full and partial tuition reimbursements (averaging $6,300 per year) were awarded. Fellowships, career-related internships or fieldwork also available.

University of Kansas (continued)
Faculty research: Heat transfer, energy analysis, computer-aided design, biomedical engineering.
Ronald Dougherty, Chair, 785-864-2981.

■ UNIVERSITY OF KENTUCKY

Graduate School, Graduate School Programs from the College of Engineering, Department of Mechanical Engineering, Lexington, KY 40506-0032

AWARDS MSME, PhD.

Faculty: 47 full-time (2 women).
Students: 94 full-time (10 women), 23 part-time (3 women); includes 1 minority (Asian American or Pacific Islander), 72 international. 175 applicants, 73% accepted. In 2001, 11 master's, 1 doctorate awarded.
Degree requirements: For master's, thesis optional; for doctorate, thesis/dissertation, comprehensive exam.
Entrance requirements: For master's, GRE General Test, minimum undergraduate GPA of 2.8; for doctorate, GRE General Test, minimum graduate GPA of 3.0. *Application deadline:* For fall admission, 7/19. Applications are processed on a rolling basis. *Application fee:* $30 ($35 for international students).
Expenses: Tuition, state resident: full-time $4,075; part-time $213 per credit hour. Tuition, nonresident: full-time $11,295; part-time $614 per credit hour.
Financial support: In 2001–02, 2 fellowships, 59 research assistantships, 13 teaching assistantships were awarded. Federal Work-Study and institutionally sponsored loans also available. Support available to part-time students.
Faculty research: Combustion, computational fluid dynamics, design and systems, manufacturing, thermal and fluid sciences.
Dr. George Huang, Director of Graduate Studies, 859-257-9313, *Fax:* 859-257-3304, *E-mail:* ghuang@pop.uky.edu.
Application contact: Dr. Jeannine Blackwell, Associate Dean, 859-257-4905, *Fax:* 859-323-1928.

■ UNIVERSITY OF LOUISIANA AT LAFAYETTE

Graduate School, College of Engineering, Department of Mechanical Engineering, Lafayette, LA 70504

AWARDS MSE. Evening/weekend programs available.

Faculty: 6 full-time (0 women).
Students: 19 full-time (1 woman), 3 part-time, 18 international. Average age 25. 101 applicants, 53% accepted, 10 enrolled. In 2001, 6 degrees awarded.
Degree requirements: For master's, thesis or alternative, comprehensive exam.

Entrance requirements: For master's, GRE General Test, BS in mechanical engineering, minimum GPA of 2.85. *Application deadline:* For fall admission, 5/15. *Application fee:* $20 ($30 for international students).
Expenses: Tuition, state resident: full-time $2,317; part-time $79 per credit. Tuition, nonresident: full-time $8,882; part-time $369 per credit. International tuition: $9,018 full-time.
Financial support: In 2001–02, 4 research assistantships with full tuition reimbursements (averaging $5,500 per year) were awarded; Federal Work-Study and tuition waivers (full and partial) also available. Financial award application deadline: 5/1.
Faculty research: CAD/CAM, machine design and vibration, thermal science.
Dr. William Simon, Head, 337-482-6517.
Application contact: Dr. M. A. Elsayed, Graduate Coordinator, 337-482-5363.

■ UNIVERSITY OF LOUISVILLE

Graduate School, Speed Scientific School, Department of Mechanical Engineering, Louisville, KY 40292-0001

AWARDS M Eng, MS.

Students: 34 full-time (7 women), 49 part-time (5 women); includes 8 minority (2 African Americans, 5 Asian Americans or Pacific Islanders, 1 Hispanic American), 15 international. Average age 28. In 2001, 14 degrees awarded.
Degree requirements: For master's, thesis.
Entrance requirements: For master's, GRE General Test. *Application deadline:* Applications are processed on a rolling basis. *Application fee:* $25.
Expenses: Tuition, state resident: full-time $4,134. Tuition, nonresident: full-time $11,486.
Financial support: In 2001–02, 4 fellowships with full tuition reimbursements (averaging $18,000 per year), 13 research assistantships with full tuition reimbursements (averaging $15,720 per year), 5 teaching assistantships with full tuition reimbursements (averaging $16,800 per year) were awarded.
Dr. Glen Prater, Chair, 502-852-6331, *Fax:* 502-852-6053, *E-mail:* gprater@louisville.edu.

■ UNIVERSITY OF MAINE

Graduate School, College of Engineering, Department of Mechanical Engineering, Orono, ME 04469

AWARDS MS, PhD.

Faculty: 9 full-time.
Students: 11 full-time (3 women), 1 part-time, 4 international. 7 applicants, 71% accepted, 2 enrolled. In 2001, 3 degrees awarded.
Degree requirements: For master's, thesis (for some programs).

Entrance requirements: For master's and doctorate, GRE General Test, TOEFL. *Application deadline:* For fall admission, 2/1 (priority date). Applications are processed on a rolling basis. *Application fee:* $50. Electronic applications accepted.
Expenses: Tuition, state resident: full-time $3,780; part-time $210 per credit hour. Tuition, nonresident: full-time $10,782; part-time $599 per credit hour. Required fees: $9.5 per credit hour. $32 per semester. Tuition and fees vary according to reciprocity agreements.
Financial support: In 2001–02, 8 research assistantships with tuition reimbursements (averaging $15,000 per year), 4 teaching assistantships with tuition reimbursements (averaging $9,540 per year) were awarded. Federal Work-Study and tuition waivers (full and partial) also available. Financial award application deadline: 3/1.
Faculty research: Higher order beam and plate theories, dynamic response of structural systems, heat transfer in window systems, forced convection heat transfer in gas turbine passages, effect of parallel space heating systems on utility load management.
Dr. Donald Grant, Chair, 207-581-2120, *Fax:* 207-581-2379.
Application contact: Scott G. Delcourt, Director of the Graduate School, 207-581-3218, *Fax:* 207-581-3232, *E-mail:* graduate@maine.edu. *Web site:* http://www.umaine.edu/graduate/

■ UNIVERSITY OF MARYLAND, BALTIMORE COUNTY

Graduate School, College of Engineering, Department of Mechanical Engineering, Baltimore, MD 21250-5398

AWARDS MS, PhD. Part-time and evening/weekend programs available.

Degree requirements: For doctorate, thesis/dissertation.
Entrance requirements: For master's, GRE General Test, TOEFL, minimum GPA of 3.0; for doctorate, GRE General Test, TOEFL, minimum GPA of 3.25.
Faculty research: Theoretical and applied mechanics, mechatronics (controls, sensors and actuators), dynamic plasticity, fluid mechanics, biomechanics.

■ UNIVERSITY OF MARYLAND, COLLEGE PARK

Graduate Studies and Research, A. James Clark School of Engineering, Department of Mechanical Engineering, College Park, MD 20742

AWARDS Electronic packaging and reliability (MS, PhD); manufacturing and design (MS, PhD); mechanics and materials (MS, PhD); thermal and fluid sciences (MS, PhD). Part-time and evening/weekend programs available. Postbaccalaureate distance learning degree programs offered.

Faculty: 69 full-time (6 women), 15 part-time/adjunct (2 women).
Students: 142 full-time (18 women), 67 part-time (5 women); includes 13 minority (5 African Americans, 6 Asian Americans or Pacific Islanders, 2 Hispanic Americans), 134 international. 519 applicants, 14% accepted, 40 enrolled. In 2001, 49 master's, 21 doctorates awarded.
Degree requirements: For master's, thesis optional; for doctorate, thesis/dissertation, qualifying exam.
Entrance requirements: For master's and doctorate, GRE General Test, minimum GPA of 3.0. *Application deadline:* For fall admission, 8/1; for spring admission, 12/1. Applications are processed on a rolling basis. *Application fee:* $50 ($70 for international students). Electronic applications accepted.
Expenses: Tuition, state resident: part-time $289 per credit hour. Tuition, nonresident: part-time $448 per credit hour. One-time fee: $436 part-time. Full-time tuition and fees vary according to course load, campus/location and program.
Financial support: In 2001–02, 5 fellowships with full tuition reimbursements (averaging $4,406 per year), 123 research assistantships with tuition reimbursements (averaging $14,539 per year), 36 teaching assistantships with tuition reimbursements (averaging $11,663 per year) were awarded. Federal Work-Study and scholarships/grants also available. Support available to part-time students. Financial award applicants required to submit FAFSA.
Faculty research: Decomposition-based design, powder metallurgy, injection molding, kinematic synthesis, electronic packaging, dynamic deformation and fracture, turbulent flow.
Dr. Avi Bar-Cohen, Chairman, 301-405-5294, *Fax:* 301-314-9477.
Application contact: Dr. James M. Wallace, Graduate Director, 301-405-4216.

■ **UNIVERSITY OF MARYLAND, COLLEGE PARK**

Graduate Studies and Research, A. James Clark School of Engineering, Professional Program in Engineering, College Park, MD 20742

AWARDS Aerospace engineering (M Eng); chemical engineering (M Eng); civil engineering (M Eng); electrical engineering (M Eng); fire protection engineering (M Eng); materials science and engineering (M Eng); mechanical engineering (M Eng); reliability engineering (M Eng). Systems engineering (M Eng). Part-time and evening/weekend programs available. Postbaccalaureate distance learning degree programs offered.

Faculty: 11 part-time/adjunct (0 women).
Students: 19 full-time (4 women), 144 part-time (31 women); includes 41 minority (17 African Americans, 18 Asian

Americans or Pacific Islanders, 6 Hispanic Americans), 27 international. 71 applicants, 80% accepted, 50 enrolled. In 2001, 64 degrees awarded.
Application deadline: For fall admission, 8/15; for spring admission, 1/10. Applications are processed on a rolling basis.
Application fee: $50 ($70 for international students). Electronic applications accepted.
Expenses: Tuition, state resident: part-time $289 per credit hour. Tuition, nonresident: part-time $448 per credit hour. One-time fee: $436 part-time. Full-time tuition and fees vary according to course load, campus/location and program.
Financial support: In 2001–02, 1 research assistantship with full tuition reimbursement (averaging $20,655 per year), 5 teaching assistantships with tuition reimbursements (averaging $11,114 per year) were awarded. Fellowships, Federal Work-Study and scholarships/grants also available. Support available to part-time students. Financial award applicants required to submit FAFSA.
Dr. George Syrmos, Acting Director, 301-405-5256, *Fax:* 301-314-9477.
Application contact: Trudy Lindsey, Director, Graduate Admissions and Records, 301-405-6991, *Fax:* 301-314-9305, *E-mail:* grschool@deans.umd.edu.

■ **UNIVERSITY OF MASSACHUSETTS AMHERST**

Graduate School, College of Engineering, Department of Mechanical and Industrial Engineering, Program in Mechanical Engineering, Amherst, MA 01003

AWARDS MS, PhD.

Students: 35 full-time (6 women), 27 part-time (2 women); includes 2 minority (1 Asian American or Pacific Islander, 1 Hispanic American), 44 international. Average age 27. 335 applicants, 34% accepted. In 2001, 16 master's, 4 doctorates awarded.
Degree requirements: For master's, thesis, project; for doctorate, thesis/dissertation.
Entrance requirements: For master's and doctorate, GRE General Test. *Application deadline:* For fall admission, 2/1 (priority date); for spring admission, 10/1. Applications are processed on a rolling basis. *Application fee:* $40 ($50 for international students).
Expenses: Tuition, state resident: full-time $1,980; part-time $110 per credit. Tuition, nonresident: full-time $7,456; part-time $414 per credit. Required fees: $4,112. One-time fee: $115 full-time.
Financial support: Fellowships with full tuition reimbursements, research assistantships with full tuition reimbursements, teaching assistantships with full tuition reimbursements, career-related internships or fieldwork, Federal Work-Study, scholarships/grants, traineeships, and

unspecified assistantships available. Support available to part-time students. Financial award application deadline: 2/1.
Dr. Ian Grosse, Director, 413-545-2505, *Fax:* 413-545-1027. *Web site:* http://www.ecs.umass.edu/MIE/

■ **UNIVERSITY OF MASSACHUSETTS DARTMOUTH**

Graduate School, College of Engineering, Program in Mechanical Engineering, North Dartmouth, MA 02747-2300

AWARDS MS. Part-time programs available.

Faculty: 12 full-time (1 woman), 1 (woman) part-time/adjunct.
Students: 10 full-time (0 women), 4 part-time; includes 1 minority (African American), 8 international. Average age 28. 38 applicants, 68% accepted, 4 enrolled. In 2001, 2 degrees awarded.
Degree requirements: For master's, thesis or alternative.
Entrance requirements: For master's, GRE General Test, TOEFL, minimum undergraduate GPA of 3.0. *Application deadline:* For fall admission, 4/20 (priority date); for spring admission, 11/15 (priority date). Applications are processed on a rolling basis. *Application fee:* $25 ($45 for international students).
Expenses: Tuition, state resident: full-time $2,071; part-time $86 per credit. Tuition, nonresident: full-time $8,099; part-time $337 per credit. Part-time tuition and fees vary according to course load and reciprocity agreements.
Financial support: In 2001–02, 9 research assistantships with full tuition reimbursements (averaging $10,056 per year), 2 teaching assistantships with full tuition reimbursements (averaging $7,500 per year) were awarded. Federal Work-Study and unspecified assistantships also available. Support available to part-time students. Financial award application deadline: 3/1.
Faculty research: Ground source heat pump laboratory, optimal control of recirculating fish tanks, bio-active fabrics, production line redesign. *Total annual research expenditures:* $256,000.
Dr. Alex Fowler, Director, 508-999-8542, *E-mail:* afowler@umassd.edu.
Application contact: Maria E. Lomba, Graduate Admissions Officer, 508-999-8604, *Fax:* 508-999-8183, *E-mail:* graduate@umassd.edu.

■ **UNIVERSITY OF MASSACHUSETTS LOWELL**

Graduate School, James B. Francis College of Engineering, Department of Mechanical Engineering, Lowell, MA 01854-2881

AWARDS MS Eng, D Eng. Part-time programs available. Terminal master's awarded for partial completion of doctoral program.

University of Massachusetts Lowell (continued)

Degree requirements: For master's, thesis or alternative; for doctorate, 2 foreign languages, thesis/dissertation. **Entrance requirements:** For master's and doctorate, GRE General Test.

■ THE UNIVERSITY OF MEMPHIS

Graduate School, Herff College of Engineering, Department of Mechanical Engineering, Memphis, TN 38152

AWARDS Design and mechanical engineering (MS); energy systems (MS); mechanical engineering (PhD); mechanical systems (MS); power systems (MS). Part-time programs available. Terminal master's awarded for partial completion of doctoral program.

Degree requirements: For master's and doctorate, thesis/dissertation, comprehensive exam. **Entrance requirements:** For master's, GRE General Test, BS in mechanical engineering, minimum undergraduate GPA of 3.0. **Expenses:** Tuition, state resident: full-time $2,026. Tuition, nonresident: full-time $4,528. **Faculty research:** Computational fluid dynamics, fracture mechanics, computational mechanics, composites, phase change. *Web site:* http://www.memphis.edu/

■ UNIVERSITY OF MIAMI

Graduate School, College of Engineering, Department of Mechanical Engineering, Coral Gables, FL 33124

AWARDS MS, MSME, DA, PhD. Part-time programs available.

Faculty: 9 full-time (0 women). **Students:** 19 full-time (3 women), 2 part-time (1 woman); includes 1 minority (Hispanic American), 14 international. In 2001, 4 master's, 4 doctorates awarded. **Degree requirements:** For master's, thesis (for some programs), registration; for doctorate, thesis/dissertation, registration. *Median time to degree:* Master's–2 years full-time, 4 years part-time; doctorate–3.5 years full-time. **Entrance requirements:** For master's and doctorate, GRE General Test, TOEFL. *Application deadline:* Applications are processed on a rolling basis. *Application fee:* $50. Electronic applications accepted. **Expenses:** Tuition: Part-time $960 per credit hour. Required fees: $85 per semester. Tuition and fees vary according to program. **Financial support:** In 2001–02, 15 students received support, including 1 fellowship with tuition reimbursement available (averaging $17,000 per year), 7 research assistantships with tuition reimbursements available (averaging

$12,000 per year), 7 teaching assistantships with tuition reimbursements available (averaging $9,000 per year); career-related internships or fieldwork, Federal Work-Study, tuition waivers (partial), and unspecified assistantships also available. Financial award application deadline: 2/1. **Faculty research:** Internal combustion engines, heat transfer, hydrogen energy, controls, mechanics.
Dr. Singiresu S. Rao, Chairman, 305-284-2571, *Fax:* 305-284-2580, *E-mail:* srao@miami.edu. *Web site:* http://www.eng.miami.edu/

■ UNIVERSITY OF MICHIGAN

Horace H. Rackham School of Graduate Studies, Department of Mechanical Engineering, Program in Mechanical Engineering, Ann Arbor, MI 48109

AWARDS MSE, PhD. Part-time programs available.

Faculty: 54 full-time (7 women), 5 part-time/adjunct (0 women). **Students:** 345 full-time (55 women), 48 part-time (7 women); includes 132 minority (14 African Americans, 117 Asian Americans or Pacific Islanders, 1 Hispanic American), 114 international. Average age 26. 860 applicants, 45% accepted, 149 enrolled. In 2001, 94 master's, 45 doctorates awarded. Terminal master's awarded for partial completion of doctoral program. **Degree requirements:** For master's, thesis optional; for doctorate, oral defense of dissertation, preliminary and qualifying exams. **Entrance requirements:** For master's, GRE General Test, undergraduate degree in same or relevant field; for doctorate, GRE General Test. *Application deadline:* For fall admission, 1/15 (priority date); for winter admission, 10/15 (priority date). Applications are processed on a rolling basis. *Application fee:* $55. Electronic applications accepted. **Financial support:** In 2001–02, 35 fellowships with full tuition reimbursements (averaging $20,000 per year), 179 research assistantships with full tuition reimbursements (averaging $21,000 per year), 24 teaching assistantships with full tuition reimbursements (averaging $20,000 per year) were awarded. Institutionally sponsored loans and tuition waivers (full) also available. Financial award application deadline: 1/15. **Faculty research:** Design and manufacturing; kynaomies, systems and controls; materials, and solid mechanics; thermal and fluid sciences. *Total annual research expenditures:* $24.5 million. **Application contact:** Cynthia T. Quann-White, Academic Services Office, Student Services Associate, 734-763-9223, *Fax:* 734-647-7303, *E-mail:* cynthiag@umich.edu. *Web site:* http://www.engin.umich.edu/dept/meam/

■ UNIVERSITY OF MICHIGAN– DEARBORN

College of Engineering and Computer Science, Department of Mechanical Engineering, Dearborn, MI 48128-1491

AWARDS MSE. Part-time programs available.

Faculty: 15 full-time (1 woman), 6 part-time/adjunct (0 women). **Students:** 2 full-time (1 woman), 164 part-time (29 women); includes 23 minority (5 African Americans, 11 Asian Americans or Pacific Islanders, 7 Hispanic Americans). Average age 30. 41 applicants, 98% accepted. In 2001, 45 degrees awarded. **Degree requirements:** For master's, thesis optional. **Entrance requirements:** For master's, bachelor's degree in applied mathematics, computer science, engineering, or physical science; minimum GPA of 3.0. *Application deadline:* For fall admission, 8/1; for winter admission, 12/1 (priority date); for spring admission, 4/1 (priority date). Applications are processed on a rolling basis. *Application fee:* $55. Electronic applications accepted. **Expenses:** Tuition, state resident: part-time $300 per credit hour. Tuition, nonresident: part-time $756 per credit hour. Required fees: $90 per semester. Tuition and fees vary according to course level, course load and program. **Financial support:** In 2001–02, 4 research assistantships (averaging $12,800 per year), 2 teaching assistantships were awarded. Fellowships, Federal Work-Study also available. Financial award application deadline: 4/1; financial award applicants required to submit FAFSA. **Faculty research:** Combustion, fatigue, fracture/damage mechanics, noise and vibration, vehicle climate control.
Dr. C. L. Chow, Chair, 313-593-5241, *Fax:* 313-593-3851, *E-mail:* clchow@umich.edu. **Application contact:** Ramona Borne, Graduate Secretary, 313-593-5241, *Fax:* 313-593-3851, *E-mail:* rlborne@umd.umich.edu. *Web site:* http://www.engin.umd.umich.edu/

■ UNIVERSITY OF MINNESOTA, TWIN CITIES CAMPUS

Graduate School, Institute of Technology, Department of Mechanical Engineering, Minneapolis, MN 55455-0213

AWARDS Industrial engineering (MSIE, PhD); mechanical engineering (MSME, PhD). Part-time programs available.

Degree requirements: For doctorate, thesis/dissertation. **Entrance requirements:** For master's, GRE General Test, minimum GPA of 3.0; for doctorate, GRE General Test. **Expenses:** Tuition, state resident: full-time $2,932; part-time $489 per credit. Tuition, nonresident: full-time $5,758; part-time $960 per credit. Part-time tuition and fees vary according to course load, program and reciprocity agreements. *Web site:* http://www.me.umn.edu/

Find an in-depth description at www.petersons.com/gradchannel.

■ UNIVERSITY OF MISSOURI–COLUMBIA

Graduate School, College of Engineering, Department of Mechanical and Aerospace Engineering, Columbia, MO 65211

AWARDS MS, PhD.

Faculty: 18 full-time (1 woman).
Students: 44 full-time (3 women), 12 part-time (1 woman); includes 4 minority (2 African Americans, 2 Hispanic Americans), 36 international. 23 applicants, 52% accepted. In 2001, 18 master's, 3 doctorates awarded.
Degree requirements: For master's, thesis; for doctorate, one foreign language, thesis/dissertation.
Entrance requirements: For master's and doctorate, GRE General Test, TOEFL, minimum GPA of 3.0. *Application deadline:* Applications are processed on a rolling basis. *Application fee:* $25 ($50 for international students).
Expenses: Tuition, state resident: part-time $179 per credit hour. Tuition, nonresident: part-time $539 per credit hour. Required fees: $122 per semester. Tuition and fees vary according to program.
Financial support: Research assistantships, teaching assistantships, institutionally sponsored loans available.
Dr. Uee Wan Cho, Director of Graduate Studies, 573-882-3778, *E-mail:* chou@ missouri.edu. *Web site:* http:// www.engineering.missouri.edu/ mechanical.htm

■ UNIVERSITY OF MISSOURI–ROLLA

Graduate School, School of Engineering, Department of Mechanical and Aerospace Engineering and Engineering Mechanics, Program in Mechanical Engineering, Rolla, MO 65409-0910

AWARDS MS, DE, PhD. Part-time programs available.

Degree requirements: For master's, thesis (for some programs); for doctorate, thesis/dissertation.
Entrance requirements: For master's, GRE General Test, TOEFL, minimum GPA of 3.0; for doctorate, GRE General Test, TOEFL, minimum GPA of 3.5. Electronic applications accepted.
Faculty research: Fluid mechanics, thermal science, CAD/CAM and CAE, dynamics and vibrations, HVAC. *Web site:* http://www.maem.umr.edu/~grad/

■ UNIVERSITY OF NEBRASKA–LINCOLN

Graduate College, College of Engineering and Technology, Department of Mechanical Engineering, Lincoln, NE 68588

AWARDS Engineering (PhD); mechanical engineering (MS), including materials science engineering.

Faculty: 21.
Students: 35 (2 women); includes 1 minority (Hispanic American) 22 international. Average age 28. 205 applicants, 30% accepted, 14 enrolled. In 2001, 7 degrees awarded.
Degree requirements: For master's, thesis optional; for doctorate, thesis/ dissertation, comprehensive exam.
Entrance requirements: For master's and doctorate, GRE General Test, TOEFL. *Application deadline:* For fall admission, 3/1 (priority date). Applications are processed on a rolling basis. *Application fee:* $35. Electronic applications accepted.
Expenses: Tuition, state resident: full-time $2,412; part-time $134 per credit. Tuition, nonresident: full-time $6,223; part-time $346 per credit. Tuition and fees vary according to course load.
Financial support: In 2001–02, 15 research assistantships, 4 teaching assistantships were awarded. Fellowships, Federal Work-Study, health care benefits, and unspecified assistantships also available. Support available to part-time students. Financial award application deadline: 2/15.
Faculty research: Robotics for planetary exploration, vehicle crashworthiness, transient heat conduction, laser beam/ particle interactions.
Dr. David Lou, Chair, 402-472-2375. *Web site:* http://www.engr.unl.edu/me/ index.html/

Find an in-depth description at www.petersons.com/gradchannel.

■ UNIVERSITY OF NEVADA, LAS VEGAS

Graduate College, Howard R. Hughes College of Engineering, Department of Mechanical Engineering, Las Vegas, NV 89154-9900

AWARDS MSE, PhD. Part-time programs available.

Faculty: 20 full-time (0 women).
Students: 22 full-time (7 women), 20 part-time (2 women); includes 4 minority (1 African American, 3 Asian Americans or Pacific Islanders), 18 international. 30 applicants, 60% accepted, 13 enrolled. In 2001, 7 master's, 1 doctorate awarded.
Degree requirements: For master's, thesis (for some programs), project, comprehensive exam; for doctorate, thesis/ dissertation, comprehensive exam. *Median time to degree:* Doctorate–5 years full-time.

Entrance requirements: For master's, minimum GPA of 3.0; for doctorate, GRE General Test, minimum GPA of 3.2. *Application deadline:* For fall admission, 6/15; for spring admission, 11/15. *Application fee:* $40 ($55 for international students).
Expenses: Tuition, state resident: full-time $1,926; part-time $107 per credit. Tuition, nonresident: full-time $9,376; part-time $220 per credit. Tuition and fees vary according to course load.
Financial support: In 2001–02, 24 research assistantships with full and partial tuition reimbursements (averaging $10,687 per year), 10 teaching assistantships with partial tuition reimbursements (averaging $11,000 per year) were awarded. Financial award application deadline: 3/1.
Dr. Mohamed Trabia, Chair, 702-895-1331.
Application contact: Graduate College Admissions Evaluator, 702-895-3320, *Fax:* 702-895-4180, *E-mail:* gradcollege@ ccmail.nevada.edu. *Web site:* http:// www.me.unlv.edu/

■ UNIVERSITY OF NEVADA, RENO

Graduate School, College of Engineering, Department of Mechanical Engineering, Reno, NV 89557

AWARDS MS, PhD.

Faculty: 13.
Students: 25 full-time (4 women), 5 part-time (1 woman), 20 international. Average age 27. In 2001, 5 master's, 2 doctorates awarded. Terminal master's awarded for partial completion of doctoral program.
Degree requirements: For master's, thesis optional; for doctorate, thesis/ dissertation.
Entrance requirements: For master's, GRE General Test, TOEFL, minimum GPA of 2.75; for doctorate, GRE General Test, TOEFL, minimum GPA of 3.0. *Application deadline:* For fall admission, 3/1 (priority date); for spring admission, 11/1. Applications are processed on a rolling basis. *Application fee:* $40.
Expenses: Tuition, state resident: full-time $2,067; part-time $108 per credit. Tuition, nonresident: full-time $9,282; part-time $109 per credit. Required fees: $57 per semester. Tuition and fees vary according to course load.
Financial support: In 2001–02, 12 research assistantships, 5 teaching assistantships were awarded. Federal Work-Study and institutionally sponsored loans also available. Financial award application deadline: 3/1.
Faculty research: Composite, solid, fluid, thermal, and smart materials.
Dr. Yanyoa Jiang, Graduate Program Director, 775-784-4510.

■ UNIVERSITY OF NEW HAMPSHIRE

Graduate School, College of Engineering and Physical Sciences, Department of Mechanical Engineering, Durham, NH 03824

AWARDS Mechanical engineering (MS, PhD). Systems design (PhD). Part-time programs available.

Faculty: 10 full-time.
Students: 11 full-time (2 women), 15 part-time (2 women), 12 international. Average age 27. 25 applicants, 88% accepted, 6 enrolled. In 2001, 5 master's, 5 doctorates awarded.
Degree requirements: For master's, thesis or alternative; for doctorate, thesis/dissertation.
Entrance requirements: For master's and doctorate, GRE. *Application deadline:* For fall admission, 4/1 (priority date); for winter admission, 12/1 (priority date). Applications are processed on a rolling basis. *Application fee:* $50. Electronic applications accepted.
Expenses: Tuition, state resident: full-time $6,300; part-time $350 per credit. Tuition, nonresident: full-time $15,720; part-time $643 per credit. Required fees: $560; $280 per term. One-time fee: $15 part-time. Tuition and fees vary according to course load.
Financial support: In 2001–02, 1 fellowship, 7 research assistantships, 6 teaching assistantships were awarded. Federal Work-Study, scholarships/grants, and tuition waivers (full and partial) also available. Support available to part-time students. Financial award application deadline: 2/15.
Faculty research: Solid mechanics, dynamics, materials science, dynamic systems, automatic control.
Dr. Barbaros Celikkol, Chairperson, 603-862-1940, *E-mail:* celikkol@cisanix.edu.
Application contact: Dr. James Krzanowski, Graduate Coordinator, 603-862-2315, *E-mail:* jamesk@cisunix.unh.edu.
Web site: http://www.unh.edu/mechanical-engineering/

■ UNIVERSITY OF NEW HAVEN

Graduate School, School of Engineering and Applied Science, Program in Mechanical Engineering, West Haven, CT 06516-1916

AWARDS MSME.

Students: In 2001, 1 degree awarded.
Degree requirements: For master's, thesis or alternative.
Application deadline: Applications are processed on a rolling basis. *Application fee:* $50.
Expenses: Tuition: Full-time $12,015; part-time $445 per credit hour. Required fees: $30. One-time fee: $100 full-time.
Financial support: Federal Work-Study available. Support available to part-time

students. Financial award application deadline: 5/1; financial award applicants required to submit FAFSA.
Dr. Konstantine Lambrakis, Coordinator, 203-932-7408.

■ UNIVERSITY OF NEW MEXICO

Graduate School, School of Engineering, Department of Mechanical Engineering, Albuquerque, NM 87131-2039

AWARDS Engineering (PhD); mechanical engineering (MS). MEME offered through the Manufacturing Engineering Program. Part-time programs available.

Faculty: 18 full-time (2 women), 3 part-time/adjunct (0 women).
Students: 60 full-time (7 women), 29 part-time (4 women); includes 23 minority (3 African Americans, 2 Asian Americans or Pacific Islanders, 16 Hispanic Americans, 2 Native Americans), 29 international. Average age 31. In 2001, 14 master's, 2 doctorates awarded.
Degree requirements: For master's, thesis (for some programs); for doctorate, thesis/dissertation, comprehensive exam.
Entrance requirements: For master's, GRE General Test, minimum GPA of 3.0 in last 2 years of BS program; for doctorate, GRE General Test, minimum GPA of 3.0. *Application deadline:* For fall admission, 7/30; for spring admission, 11/30. *Application fee:* $40.
Expenses: Tuition, state resident: full-time $2,771; part-time $115 per credit hour. Tuition, nonresident: full-time $11,207; part-time $467 per credit hour. Required fees: $570; $24 per credit hour. Part-time tuition and fees vary according to course load and program.
Financial support: In 2001–02, 32 students received support, including 12 fellowships (averaging $2,900 per year), 30 research assistantships with full and partial tuition reimbursements available (averaging $16,117 per year), 14 teaching assistantships with full and partial tuition reimbursements available (averaging $12,964 per year); career-related internships or fieldwork, scholarships/grants, health care benefits, tuition waivers (full), and unspecified assistantships also available. Financial award application deadline: 3/1; financial award applicants required to submit FAFSA.
Faculty research: Multiscale fluid mechanics, advanced mechanics of materials, robotics/mechatronics, modeling and simulation. *Total annual research expenditures:* $697,595.
Dr. Marc S. Ingber, Chair, 505-277-2761, *Fax:* 505-277-1571, *E-mail:* ingber@me.unm.edu.
Application contact: Brent Lambert, Graduate Coordinator, 505-277-2761, *Fax:* 505-277-1571, *E-mail:* brent@unm.edu.
Web site: http://www.me.unm.edu/

Find an in-depth description at www.petersons.com/gradchannel.

■ UNIVERSITY OF NEW ORLEANS

Graduate School, College of Engineering, Concentration in Mechanical Engineering, New Orleans, LA 70148

AWARDS MS.

Faculty: 7 full-time (1 woman).
Students: 34 full-time (6 women), 8 part-time (1 woman); includes 1 minority (African American), 34 international. Average age 24. 165 applicants, 45% accepted, 14 enrolled. In 2001, 9 degrees awarded.
Degree requirements: For master's, thesis optional.
Entrance requirements: For master's, GRE General Test, minimum GPA of 3.0. *Application deadline:* For fall admission, 7/1 (priority date); for spring admission, 11/15 (priority date). Applications are processed on a rolling basis. *Application fee:* $20. Electronic applications accepted.
Expenses: Tuition, state resident: full-time $2,748; part-time $435 per credit. Tuition, nonresident: full-time $9,792; part-time $1,773 per credit.
Financial support: Research assistantships, teaching assistantships available. Financial award applicants required to submit FAFSA.
Faculty research: Two-phase flow instabilities, thermal-hydrodynamic modeling, solar energy, heat transfer from sprays, boundary integral techniques in mechanics.
Dr. Edwin Russo, Chairman, 504-280-6652, *Fax:* 504-280-5539, *E-mail:* erusso@uno.edu.
Application contact: Dr. Kazim Akyuzlu, Graduate Coordinator, 504-280-6186, *Fax:* 504-280-7413, *E-mail:* kakyuzlu@uno.edu.

■ THE UNIVERSITY OF NORTH CAROLINA AT CHARLOTTE

Graduate School, The William States Lee College of Engineering, Department of Mechanical Engineering and Engineering Science, Charlotte, NC 28223-0001

AWARDS MS, MSME, PhD. Evening/weekend programs available.

Faculty: 19 full-time (1 woman), 3 part-time/adjunct (0 women).
Students: 35 full-time (6 women), 41 part-time (1 woman); includes 7 minority (2 African Americans, 5 Asian Americans or Pacific Islanders), 37 international. Average age 27. 99 applicants, 89% accepted, 23 enrolled. In 2001, 11 master's, 6 doctorates awarded.
Degree requirements: For master's, thesis.
Entrance requirements: For master's, GRE General Test, minimum GPA of 3.0 in undergraduate major, 2.75 overall. *Application deadline:* For fall admission,

7/15; for spring admission, 11/15. Applications are processed on a rolling basis. *Application fee:* $35. Electronic applications accepted.

Expenses: Tuition, state resident: full-time $1,483; part-time $371 per year. Tuition, nonresident: full-time $9,850; part-time $2,463 per year. Required fees: $1,043; $277 per year. Tuition and fees vary according to course load.

Financial support: In 2001–02, 1 fellowship (averaging $4,000 per year), 26 research assistantships, 13 teaching assistantships were awarded. Career-related internships or fieldwork, Federal Work-Study, institutionally sponsored loans, scholarships/grants, and unspecified assistantships also available. Support available to part-time students. Financial award application deadline: 4/1; financial award applicants required to submit FAFSA.

Faculty research: Precision metrology, high speed machining, bioengineering, computational modeling, motorsports engineering.

Dr. Jayaraman Raja, Chair, 704-687-2301, *Fax:* 704-687-2352, *E-mail:* jraga@email.uncc.edu.

Application contact: Kathy Barringer, Director of Graduate Admissions, 704-687-3366, *Fax:* 704-687-3279, *E-mail:* gradadm@email.uncc.edu. *Web site:* http://www.uncc.edu/gradmiss/

■ UNIVERSITY OF NORTH DAKOTA

Graduate School, School of Engineering and Mines, Department of Mechanical Engineering, Grand Forks, ND 58202

AWARDS M Engr, MS. Part-time programs available.

Faculty: 6 full-time (0 women).
Students: 7 full-time (0 women), 3 part-time. 13 applicants, 100% accepted, 4 enrolled.
Degree requirements: For master's, thesis or alternative, final comprehensive exam.
Entrance requirements: For master's, GRE General Test, GRE Subject Test, TOEFL, minimum GPA of 3.0 (MS), 2.5 (M Engr). *Application deadline:* For fall admission, 3/1 (priority date); for spring admission, 10/15 (priority date). Applications are processed on a rolling basis. *Application fee:* $30.
Expenses: Tuition, state resident: full-time $3,298. Tuition, nonresident: full-time $7,998.
Financial support: In 2001–02, 3 students received support, including 3 teaching assistantships with full tuition reimbursements available (averaging $9,500 per year); fellowships, research assistantships, career-related internships or fieldwork, Federal Work-Study, institutionally sponsored loans, scholarships/grants, and tuition waivers (full and partial) also available. Support available to part-time

students. Financial award application deadline: 3/15; financial award applicants required to submit FAFSA.

Faculty research: Energy conversion, dynamics, control, manufacturing processes with special emphasis on machining, stress vibration analysis.

Dr. Donald A. Moen, Chairperson, 701-777-2571, *Fax:* 701-777-4838, *E-mail:* donald_moen@mail.und.nodak.edu. *Web site:* http://www.und.edu/dept/sem/html/mechanical_engineering.html

■ UNIVERSITY OF NOTRE DAME

Graduate School, College of Engineering, Department of Aerospace and Mechanical Engineering, Notre Dame, IN 46556

AWARDS Aerospace and mechanical engineering (PhD); aerospace engineering (MS); mechanical engineering (MEME, MS). Part-time programs available.

Faculty: 27 full-time (0 women).
Students: 75 full-time (10 women), 4 part-time (1 woman); includes 2 minority (both Asian Americans or Pacific Islanders), 54 international. 147 applicants, 50% accepted, 24 enrolled. In 2001, 26 master's, 5 doctorates awarded. Terminal master's awarded for partial completion of doctoral program.
Degree requirements: For master's, thesis or alternative, comprehensive exam; for doctorate, thesis/dissertation. *Median time to degree:* Doctorate–6.2 years full-time.
Entrance requirements: For master's and doctorate, GRE General Test, TOEFL. *Application deadline:* For fall admission, 2/1 (priority date); for spring admission, 10/15. Applications are processed on a rolling basis. *Application fee:* $50. Electronic applications accepted.
Expenses: Tuition: Full-time $24,220; part-time $1,346 per credit hour. Required fees: $155.
Financial support: In 2001–02, 73 students received support, including 8 fellowships with full tuition reimbursements available (averaging $18,000 per year), 32 research assistantships with full tuition reimbursements available (averaging $13,100 per year), 22 teaching assistantships with full tuition reimbursements available (averaging $13,100 per year); tuition waivers (full) and unspecified assistantships also available. Financial award application deadline: 2/1.
Faculty research: Aerodynamics/fluid dynamics, design and manufacturing, controls/robotics, solid mechanics/biomechanics. *Total annual research expenditures:* $3.4 million.
Dr. Robert C. Nelson, Chair, 574-631-5430, *Fax:* 574-631-8341, *E-mail:* amedept.1@nd.edu.
Application contact: Dr. Terrence J. Akai, Director of Graduate Admissions, 574-631-7706, *Fax:* 574-631-4183, *E-mail:*

gradad@nd.edu. *Web site:* http://www.nd.edu/~ame/

Find an in-depth description at www.petersons.com/gradchannel.

■ UNIVERSITY OF OKLAHOMA

Graduate College, College of Engineering, School of Aerospace and Mechanical Engineering, Program in Mechanical Engineering, Norman, OK 73019-0390

AWARDS MS, PhD. Part-time programs available.

Students: 47 full-time (7 women), 18 part-time (3 women); includes 4 minority (2 African Americans, 1 Asian American or Pacific Islander, 1 Native American), 42 international. 65 applicants, 78% accepted, 13 enrolled. In 2001, 17 master's, 5 doctorates awarded. Terminal master's awarded for partial completion of doctoral program.
Degree requirements: For master's, thesis or alternative, comprehensive exam; for doctorate, departmental qualifying exam, thesis/dissertation optional.
Entrance requirements: For master's, GRE General Test, TOEFL, BS in engineering or physical sciences; for doctorate, GRE General Test, TOEFL, MS in mechanical engineering or equivalent. *Application deadline:* For fall admission, 6/1 (priority date). Applications are processed on a rolling basis. *Application fee:* $25.
Expenses: Tuition, state resident: full-time $2,208; part-time $92 per credit hour. Tuition, nonresident: part-time $297 per credit hour. Tuition and fees vary according to course level, course load and program.
Financial support: In 2001–02, 10 students received support; research assistantships with partial tuition reimbursements available, teaching assistantships with partial tuition reimbursements available, career-related internships or fieldwork, Federal Work-Study, scholarships/grants, and tuition waivers available. Financial award application deadline: 3/1; financial award applicants required to submit FAFSA.
Application contact: Dr. Ronald Kline, Graduate Coordinator, 405-325-5011.

Find an in-depth description at www.petersons.com/gradchannel.

■ UNIVERSITY OF PENNSYLVANIA

School of Engineering and Applied Science, Department of Mechanical Engineering and Applied Mechanics, Philadelphia, PA 19104

AWARDS Applied mechanics (MSE, PhD); mechanical engineering (MSE, PhD). Part-time programs available.

University of Pennsylvania (continued)

Degree requirements: For master's, thesis optional; for doctorate, thesis/dissertation.

Entrance requirements: For master's and doctorate, TOEFL. Electronic applications accepted.

Faculty research: Heat transfer, fluid mechanics, energy conversion, solid mechanics, dynamics of mechanisms and robots. *Web site:* http://www.seas.upenn.edu/meam/

■ UNIVERSITY OF PITTSBURGH

School of Engineering, Department of Mechanical Engineering, Pittsburgh, PA 15260

AWARDS MSME, PhD. Part-time and evening/weekend programs available.

Faculty: 17 full-time (2 women), 4 part-time/adjunct (0 women).
Students: 38 full-time (4 women), 27 part-time (2 women); includes 5 minority (2 African Americans, 3 Asian Americans or Pacific Islanders), 27 international. 229 applicants, 29% accepted, 15 enrolled. In 2001, 10 master's, 5 doctorates awarded. Terminal master's awarded for partial completion of doctoral program.
Degree requirements: For master's, thesis optional; for doctorate, thesis/dissertation, final oral exams, comprehensive exam.
Entrance requirements: For master's and doctorate, TOEFL, minimum QPA of 3.0. *Application deadline:* For fall admission, 8/1 (priority date); for spring admission, 12/1 (priority date). Applications are processed on a rolling basis. *Application fee:* $40.
Financial support: In 2001–02, 32 students received support, including 1 fellowship with full tuition reimbursement available (averaging $23,196 per year), 17 research assistantships with full tuition reimbursements available (averaging $18,216 per year), 14 teaching assistantships with full tuition reimbursements available (averaging $18,228 per year). Scholarships/grants and tuition waivers (full and partial) also available. Financial award application deadline: 2/15.
Faculty research: Smart materials and structure solid mechanics, computational fluid dynamics, multiphase bio-fluid dynamics, mechanical vibration analysis. *Total annual research expenditures:* $1.1 million.
Dr. Fred S. Pettit, Interim Chairman, 412-624-9784, *Fax:* 412-624-4846, *E-mail:* pittitfs@pitt.edu.
Application contact: Dr. Patrick Smelinski, Graduate Coordinator, 412-624-9788, *Fax:* 412-624-4846, *E-mail:* pat.smel@pitt.edu. *Web site:* http://www.engrng.pitt.edu/~mewww/

■ UNIVERSITY OF PUERTO RICO, MAYAGÜEZ CAMPUS

Graduate Studies, College of Engineering, Department of Mechanical Engineering, Mayagüez, PR 00681-9000

AWARDS MME, MS. Part-time programs available.

Degree requirements: For master's, thesis, comprehensive exam.
Entrance requirements: For master's, minimum GPA of 2.5, proficiency in English and Spanish.
Faculty research: Metallurgy, hybrid vehicles, manufacturing, thermal and fluid sciences, HVAC.

■ UNIVERSITY OF RHODE ISLAND

Graduate School, College of Engineering, Department of Mechanical Engineering and Applied Mechanics, Kingston, RI 02881

AWARDS Design/systems (MS, PhD); fluid mechanics (MS, PhD). Solid mechanics (MS, PhD); thermal sciences (MS, PhD).

Students: In 2001, 5 master's, 3 doctorates awarded.
Entrance requirements: For master's and doctorate, GRE General Test (international applicants). *Application fee:* $25.
Expenses: Tuition, state resident: full-time $3,756; part-time $209 per credit. Tuition, nonresident: full-time $10,774; part-time $599 per credit. Required fees: $1,586; $76 per credit. $76 per credit. One-time fee: $60 full-time.

■ UNIVERSITY OF ROCHESTER

The College, School of Engineering and Applied Sciences, Department of Mechanical Engineering, Rochester, NY 14627-0250

AWARDS MS, PhD. Part-time programs available.

Faculty: 14.
Students: 21 full-time (2 women), 7 part-time (1 woman), 12 international. 110 applicants, 26% accepted, 5 enrolled. In 2001, 11 master's, 3 doctorates awarded. Terminal master's awarded for partial completion of doctoral program.
Degree requirements: For master's, thesis optional; for doctorate, thesis/dissertation, preliminary and qualifying exams.
Entrance requirements: For master's and doctorate, GRE, TOEFL. *Application deadline:* For fall admission, 2/1. *Application fee:* $25.
Expenses: Tuition: Part-time $755 per credit hour.
Financial support: Fellowships, research assistantships, teaching assistantships,

tuition waivers (full and partial) available. Financial award application deadline: 2/1. Stephen Burns, Chair, 585-275-4071.
Application contact: Donna Derks, Graduate Program Secretary, 585-275-2849.

■ UNIVERSITY OF SOUTH ALABAMA

Graduate School, College of Engineering, Department of Mechanical Engineering, Mobile, AL 36688-0002

AWARDS MSME.

Faculty: 8 full-time (0 women).
Students: 28 full-time (2 women), 7 part-time (1 woman). 75 applicants, 63% accepted. In 2001, 2 degrees awarded.
Degree requirements: For master's, project or thesis.
Entrance requirements: For master's, GRE General Test, BS in engineering, minimum GPA of 3.0. *Application deadline:* For fall admission, 9/1 (priority date). Applications are processed on a rolling basis. *Application fee:* $25.
Expenses: Tuition, state resident: full-time $3,048. Tuition, nonresident: full-time $6,096. Required fees: $320.
Financial support: In 2001–02, 2 research assistantships were awarded; career-related internships or fieldwork and institutionally sponsored loans also available. Support available to part-time students. Financial award application deadline: 4/1.
Dr. Ali Engin, Chair, 334-460-6168.
Application contact: Dr. Russell M. Hayes, Director of Graduate Studies, 334-460-6117.

■ UNIVERSITY OF SOUTH CAROLINA

The Graduate School, College of Engineering and Information Technology, Department of Mechanical Engineering, Columbia, SC 29208

AWARDS ME, MS, PhD. Part-time and evening/weekend programs available. Postbaccalaureate distance learning degree programs offered.

Faculty: 18 full-time (1 woman), 2 part-time/adjunct (0 women).
Students: 33 full-time (5 women), 41 part-time (4 women); includes 36 minority (2 African Americans, 31 Asian Americans or Pacific Islanders, 3 Hispanic Americans). Average age 32. 69 applicants, 48% accepted. In 2001, 12 master's, 4 doctorates awarded.
Degree requirements: For master's, thesis (for some programs); for doctorate, thesis/dissertation.
Entrance requirements: For master's and doctorate, GRE General Test, TOEFL. *Application deadline:* For fall admission, 3/1 (priority date); for spring admission, 11/1.

Applications are processed on a rolling basis. *Application fee:* $40. Electronic applications accepted.
Expenses: Tuition, state resident: full-time $4,434. Tuition, nonresident: full-time $9,854. Tuition and fees vary according to program.
Financial support: In 2001–02, 30 research assistantships with partial tuition reimbursements (averaging $12,500 per year), 12 teaching assistantships with partial tuition reimbursements (averaging $12,500 per year) were awarded. Fellowships with partial tuition reimbursements, career-related internships or fieldwork also available.
Faculty research: Heat exchangers, computer vision measurements in solid mechanics and biomechanics, robot dynamics and control. *Total annual research expenditures:* $2.2 million.
Dr. Abdel Moez Bayoumi, Chair, 803-777-4185, *Fax:* 803-777-0106, *E-mail:* ambayoum@engr.sc.edu.
Application contact: R. Renee Jenkins, Administrative Assistant, 803-777-4185, *Fax:* 803-777-0106. *Web site:* http://www.me.sc.edu/

Find an in-depth description at www.petersons.com/gradchannel.

■ UNIVERSITY OF SOUTHERN CALIFORNIA

Graduate School, School of Engineering, Department of Aerospace and Mechanical Engineering, Los Angeles, CA 90089

AWARDS MS, PhD, Engr. Part-time and evening/weekend programs available. Postbaccalaureate distance learning degree programs offered. Terminal master's awarded for partial completion of doctoral program.

Degree requirements: For master's, thesis optional; for doctorate, thesis/dissertation.
Entrance requirements: For master's, doctorate, and Engr, GRE General Test, GRE Subject Test.
Expenses: Tuition: Full-time $25,060; part-time $844 per unit. Required fees: $473.
Faculty research: Aerodynamics of air/ground vehicles, gas dynamics; astronautics and space science; geophysical and microgravity flows, planetary physics; power MEMs and MEMS.

Find an in-depth description at www.petersons.com/gradchannel.

■ UNIVERSITY OF SOUTH FLORIDA

College of Graduate Studies, College of Engineering, Department of Mechanical Engineering, Tampa, FL 33620-9951

AWARDS ME, MME, MSME, PhD. Part-time programs available.

Faculty: 10 full-time (0 women).
Students: 24 full-time (4 women), 25 part-time (1 woman); includes 6 minority (1 African American, 1 Asian American or Pacific Islander, 3 Hispanic Americans, 1 Native American), 25 international. Average age 27. 131 applicants, 53% accepted, 22 enrolled. In 2001, 3 degrees awarded. Terminal master's awarded for partial completion of doctoral program.
Degree requirements: For master's, thesis or alternative; for doctorate, thesis/dissertation, 2 tools of research as specified by dissertation committee.
Entrance requirements: For master's, GRE General Test, minimum GPA of 3.0 during previous 2 years; for doctorate, GRE General Test. *Application deadline:* For fall admission, 6/1; for spring admission, 10/15. *Application fee:* $20. Electronic applications accepted.
Expenses: Tuition, state resident: part-time $166 per credit hour. Tuition, nonresident: part-time $573 per credit hour. Required fees: $17 per term.
Financial support: Fellowships with full tuition reimbursements, research assistantships with full tuition reimbursements, teaching assistantships with full tuition reimbursements, career-related internships or fieldwork, Federal Work-Study, institutionally sponsored loans, and tuition waivers (partial) available. Financial award applicants required to submit FAFSA.
Faculty research: Aerodynamics, heat transfer, energy systems for space applications, building energy systems, robot sensors. *Total annual research expenditures:* $605,002.
Dr. Rajiv Dubey, Chairperson, 813-974-2280, *Fax:* 813-974-3539, *E-mail:* dubey@eng.usf.edu.
Application contact: Dr. Jose L. F. Porteiro, Information Contact, 813-974-5644, *Fax:* 813-974-3539, *E-mail:* megrad@eng.usf.edu. *Web site:* http://www.eng.usf.edu/ME/mechanical.html

■ THE UNIVERSITY OF TENNESSEE

Graduate School, College of Engineering, Department of Mechanical and Aerospace Engineering and Engineering Science, Program in Mechanical Engineering, Knoxville, TN 37996

AWARDS MS, PhD, MS/MBA. Part-time programs available.

Students: 33 full-time (5 women), 33 part-time (1 woman); includes 5 minority (2 African Americans, 2 Asian Americans or Pacific Islanders, 1 Hispanic American), 17 international. 107 applicants, 55% accepted. In 2001, 15 master's, 9 doctorates awarded.
Degree requirements: For master's, thesis or alternative; for doctorate, thesis/dissertation.
Entrance requirements: For master's and doctorate, TOEFL, minimum GPA of 2.7.

Application deadline: For fall admission, 2/1 (priority date). Applications are processed on a rolling basis. *Application fee:* $35. Electronic applications accepted.
Expenses: Tuition, state resident: full-time $4,280; part-time $233 per hour. Tuition, nonresident: full-time $12,066; part-time $666 per hour. Tuition and fees vary according to program.
Financial support: Application deadline: 2/1.
Application contact: Dr. Majid Keyhani, Graduate Representative, 865-974-4795, *E-mail:* keyhani@utk.edu.

■ THE UNIVERSITY OF TENNESSEE SPACE INSTITUTE

Graduate Programs, Program in Mechanical Engineering, Tullahoma, TN 37388-9700

AWARDS MS, PhD. Part-time programs available.

Faculty: 3 full-time (0 women), 1 part-time/adjunct (0 women).
Students: 6 full-time (1 woman), 15 part-time (1 woman); includes 2 minority (1 Asian American or Pacific Islander, 1 Hispanic American), 3 international. 16 applicants, 44% accepted, 1 enrolled. In 2001, 3 master's, 1 doctorate awarded. Terminal master's awarded for partial completion of doctoral program.
Degree requirements: For master's, thesis (for some programs); for doctorate, one foreign language, thesis/dissertation.
Entrance requirements: For master's and doctorate, GRE General Test. *Application deadline:* Applications are processed on a rolling basis. *Application fee:* $35.
Expenses: Tuition, state resident: full-time $4,730; part-time $208 per semester hour. Tuition, nonresident: full-time $15,028; part-time $627 per semester hour. Required fees: $10 per semester hour. One-time fee: $35.
Financial support: Fellowships with full and partial tuition reimbursements, research assistantships with full tuition reimbursements, career-related internships or fieldwork and Federal Work-Study available. Financial award applicants required to submit FAFSA.
Dr. Roy Schulz, Degree Program Chairman, 931-393-7425, *Fax:* 931-393-7530, *E-mail:* rschuhlz@utsi.edu.
Application contact: Dr. Alfonso Pujol, Assistant Vice President and Dean for Student Affairs, 931-393-7432, *Fax:* 931-393-7346, *E-mail:* apujol@utsi.edu.

■ THE UNIVERSITY OF TEXAS AT ARLINGTON

Graduate School, College of Engineering, Department of Mechanical and Aerospace Engineering, Program in Mechanical Engineering, Arlington, TX 76019

AWARDS M Engr, MS, PhD. Part-time and evening/weekend programs available. Postbaccalaureate distance learning degree programs offered (no on-campus study).

Students: 64 full-time (5 women), 46 part-time (2 women); includes 14 minority (3 African Americans, 6 Asian Americans or Pacific Islanders, 5 Hispanic Americans), 66 international. 179 applicants, 96% accepted, 43 enrolled. In 2001, 16 master's, 2 doctorates awarded. Terminal master's awarded for partial completion of doctoral program.
Degree requirements: For master's, thesis optional; for doctorate, thesis/dissertation, comprehensive exam.
Entrance requirements: For master's, GRE General Test, TOEFL, minimum GPA of 3.0; for doctorate, GRE General Test, TOEFL, minimum GPA of 3.5. *Application deadline:* For fall admission, 6/16. Applications are processed on a rolling basis. *Application fee:* $25 ($50 for international students).
Expenses: Tuition, area resident: Full-time $2,268. Tuition, nonresident: full-time $6,264. Required fees: $839. Tuition and fees vary according to course load.
Financial support: In 2001–02, 10 fellowships (averaging $1,000 per year), 2 research assistantships (averaging $12,000 per year), 18 teaching assistantships (averaging $14,000 per year) were awarded. Financial award application deadline: 6/1; financial award applicants required to submit FAFSA.
Application contact: Dr. Bo P. Wang, Graduate Adviser, 817-272-3426, *Fax:* 817-272-5010, *E-mail:* wang@mae.uta.edu.
Find an in-depth description at www.petersons.com/gradchannel.

■ THE UNIVERSITY OF TEXAS AT AUSTIN

Graduate School, College of Engineering, Department of Mechanical Engineering, Austin, TX 78712-1111

AWARDS Manufacturing systems engineering (MSE); mechanical engineering (MSE, PhD); operations research and industrial engineering (MSE, PhD).

Students: 162 full-time (14 women), 45 part-time (7 women); includes 11 minority (4 African Americans, 7 Hispanic Americans), 109 international. 501 applicants, 43% accepted. In 2001, 35 master's, 16 doctorates awarded.

Entrance requirements: For master's, GRE General Test, TOEFL; for doctorate, GRE General Test. *Application fee:* $50 ($75 for international students).
Expenses: Tuition, state resident: full-time $3,159. Tuition, nonresident: full-time $6,957. Tuition and fees vary according to program.
Financial support: Fellowships, research assistantships, teaching assistantships available. Financial award application deadline: 2/1.
Dr. Joseph J. Beaman, Chairman, 512-471-3058, *Fax:* 512-471-8727.
Application contact: Dr. David G. Bogard, Graduate Advisor, 512-471-3128, *Fax:* 512-471-8727.

■ THE UNIVERSITY OF TEXAS AT EL PASO

Graduate School, College of Engineering, Department of Mechanical and Industrial Engineering, Program in Mechanical Engineering, El Paso, TX 79968-0001

AWARDS MS. Part-time and evening/weekend programs available.

Students: 46 (6 women); includes 17 minority (all Hispanic Americans) 22 international. Average age 34. In 2001, 10 degrees awarded.
Degree requirements: For master's, thesis optional.
Entrance requirements: For master's, GRE General Test, TOEFL, minimum GPA of 3.0 in major. *Application deadline:* For fall admission, 7/1 (priority date); for spring admission, 11/1 (priority date). Applications are processed on a rolling basis. *Application fee:* $15 ($65 for international students). Electronic applications accepted.
Expenses: Tuition, state resident: full-time $2,450. Tuition, nonresident: full-time $6,000.
Financial support: In 2001–02, research assistantships with partial tuition reimbursements (averaging $21,125 per year), teaching assistantships with partial tuition reimbursements (averaging $16,900 per year) were awarded. Fellowships with partial tuition reimbursements, Federal Work-Study, institutionally sponsored loans, scholarships/grants, and tuition waivers (partial) also available. Financial award application deadline: 3/15; financial award applicants required to submit FAFSA.
Faculty research: Solar/wind energy, environment machine design.
Dr. Michael Huerta, Graduate Adviser, 915-747-5450, *Fax:* 915-747-5019, *E-mail:* mhuerta@utep.edu.
Application contact: Dr. Charles H. Ambler, Dean of the Graduate School, 915-747-5491 Ext. 7886, *Fax:* 915-747-5788, *E-mail:* cambler@miners.utep.edu.

■ THE UNIVERSITY OF TEXAS AT SAN ANTONIO

College of Engineering, Department of Mechanical Engineering and Biomechanics, San Antonio, TX 78249-0617

AWARDS Mechanical engineering (MSME). Part-time and evening/weekend programs available.

Faculty: 7 full-time (0 women), 2 part-time/adjunct (0 women).
Students: 9 full-time (1 woman), 13 part-time (3 women); includes 5 minority (1 African American, 1 Asian American or Pacific Islander, 3 Hispanic Americans), 8 international. 22 applicants, 86% accepted, 11 enrolled. In 2001, 3 degrees awarded.
Degree requirements: For master's, thesis optional.
Entrance requirements: For master's, GRE General Test, minimum GPA of 3.0 in last 60 hours of undergraduate degree. *Application deadline:* For fall admission, 7/1; for spring admission, 12/1.
Expenses: Tuition, state resident: full-time $2,268; part-time $126 per credit hour. Tuition, nonresident: full-time $6,066; part-time $337 per credit hour. Required fees: $781. Tuition and fees vary according to course load.
Financial support: Research assistantships, teaching assistantships, career-related internships or fieldwork and institutionally sponsored loans available. Support available to part-time students. Financial award application deadline: 3/31. *Total annual research expenditures:* $196,726.
Dr. Amir Karimi, Chair, 210-458-5514.

■ UNIVERSITY OF TOLEDO

Graduate School, College of Engineering, Department of Mechanical, Industrial, and Manufacturing Engineering, Toledo, OH 43606-3398

AWARDS Engineering sciences (PhD); industrial engineering (MS); mechanical engineering (MS). Part-time programs available. Postbaccalaureate distance learning degree programs offered (minimal on-campus study).

Faculty: 23 full-time (1 woman).
Students: 121 full-time (26 women), 76 part-time (6 women); includes 2 minority (both African Americans), 158 international. Average age 27. 673 applicants, 25% accepted. In 2001, 67 master's, 2 doctorates awarded.
Degree requirements: For master's, thesis optional; for doctorate, thesis/dissertation.
Entrance requirements: For master's, GRE General Test, TOEFL, minimum GPA of 2.7; for doctorate, GRE General Test, TOEFL, minimum GPA of 3.3. *Application deadline:* For fall admission, 5/31 (priority date). Applications are

processed on a rolling basis. *Application fee:* $30. Electronic applications accepted.

Expenses: Tuition, state resident: full-time $7,278; part-time $303 per hour. Tuition, nonresident: full-time $15,731; part-time $699 per hour. Required fees: $43 per hour.

Financial support: In 2001–02, 188 students received support, including 1 fellowship with full tuition reimbursement available, 61 research assistantships with full tuition reimbursements available, 43 teaching assistantships with full tuition reimbursements available; Federal Work-Study, scholarships/grants, tuition waivers (full), and unspecified assistantships also available. Financial award application deadline: 4/1.

Faculty research: Computational and experimental thermal sciences, manufacturing process and systems, mechanics, materials, design, quality and management engineering systems. *Total annual research expenditures:* $2.7 million.

Dr. Abdollah A. Afjeh, Interim Chairman, 419-530-8210, *Fax:* 419-539-8214, *E-mail:* aafjeh@eng.utoledo.edu.

Application contact: Dr. M. Samir Hefzy, Director of Graduate Program, 419-530-8234, *Fax:* 419-530-8206, *E-mail:* mhefzy@eng.utoledo.edu. *Web site:* http://www-mime.eng.utoledo.edu/

Find an in-depth description at www.petersons.com/gradchannel.

■ **UNIVERSITY OF TULSA**

Graduate School, College of Business Administration and College of Engineering and Natural Sciences, Department of Engineering and Technology Management, Tulsa, OK 74104-3189

AWARDS Chemical engineering (METM); computer science (METM); electrical engineering (METM); geological science (METM); mathematics (METM); mechanical engineering (METM); petroleum engineering (METM). Part-time and evening/weekend programs available.

Students: 2 full-time (1 woman), 1 part-time, 2 international. Average age 26. 3 applicants, 100% accepted, 1 enrolled. In 2001, 2 degrees awarded.

Entrance requirements: For master's, GRE General Test, TOEFL. *Application deadline:* Applications are processed on a rolling basis. *Application fee:* $30. Electronic applications accepted.

Expenses: Tuition: Full-time $9,540; part-time $530 per credit hour. Required fees: $80. One-time fee: $230 full-time.

Financial support: Fellowships, research assistantships, teaching assistantships, Federal Work-Study, scholarships/grants, tuition waivers (partial), and unspecified assistantships available. Support available to part-time students. Financial award application deadline: 2/1; financial award applicants required to submit FAFSA.

Application contact: Information Contact, *E-mail:* graduate-business@utulsa.edu. *Web site:* http://www.cba.utulsa.edu/academic.asp#graduate_studies/

■ **UNIVERSITY OF TULSA**

Graduate School, College of Engineering and Natural Sciences, Department of Mechanical Engineering, Tulsa, OK 74104-3189

AWARDS ME, MSE, PhD. Part-time programs available.

Faculty: 7 full-time (0 women), 1 part-time/adjunct (0 women).

Students: 22 full-time (3 women), 12 part-time; includes 2 minority (both Asian Americans or Pacific Islanders), 23 international. Average age 28. 55 applicants, 58% accepted, 9 enrolled. In 2001, 3 master's, 2 doctorates awarded.

Degree requirements: For master's, thesis (MSE), thesis optional; for doctorate, thesis/dissertation.

Entrance requirements: For master's and doctorate, GRE General Test, TOEFL. *Application deadline:* Applications are processed on a rolling basis. *Application fee:* $30. Electronic applications accepted.

Expenses: Tuition: Full-time $9,540; part-time $530 per credit hour. Required fees: $80. One-time fee: $230 full-time.

Financial support: In 2001–02, 1 fellowship with full and partial tuition reimbursement (averaging $6,000 per year), 11 research assistantships with full and partial tuition reimbursements (averaging $9,800 per year), 7 teaching assistantships with full and partial tuition reimbursements (averaging $8,500 per year) were awarded. Career-related internships or fieldwork, Federal Work-Study, scholarships/grants, tuition waivers (partial), and unspecified assistantships also available. Support available to part-time students. Financial award application deadline: 2/1; financial award applicants required to submit FAFSA.

Faculty research: Erosion and corrosion, solid mechanics, composite material, fatigue analysis, CAD/CAM, manufacturing. *Total annual research expenditures:* $1.3 million.

Dr. Edmund F. Rybicki, Chairperson, 918-631-2996, *Fax:* 918-631-2397, *E-mail:* ed-rybicki@utulsa.edu.

Application contact: Dr. Siamack A. Shirazi, Adviser, 918-631-3001, *Fax:* 918-631-2397, *E-mail:* grad@utulsa.edu. *Web site:* http://www.me.utulsa.edu/

■ **UNIVERSITY OF UTAH**

Graduate School, College of Engineering, Department of Mechanical Engineering, Salt Lake City, UT 84112-1107

AWARDS Environmental engineering (ME, MS, PhD); mechanical engineering (ME, MS, PhD). Part-time programs available.

Faculty: 16 full-time (1 woman).

Students: 64 full-time (6 women), 51 part-time (4 women); includes 34 minority (3 African Americans, 26 Asian Americans or Pacific Islanders, 4 Hispanic Americans, 1 Native American), 19 international. Average age 29. 169 applicants, 55% accepted. In 2001, 22 master's, 9 doctorates awarded. Terminal master's awarded for partial completion of doctoral program.

Degree requirements: For doctorate, thesis/dissertation, comprehensive exam.

Entrance requirements: For master's, GRE General Test, TOEFL, minimum GPA of 3.0; for doctorate, GRE, TOEFL, minimum GPA of 3.0. *Application deadline:* For fall admission, 7/1. *Application fee:* $40 ($60 for international students).

Expenses: Tuition, state resident: part-time $320 per semester hour. Tuition, nonresident: part-time $1,135 per semester hour. Required fees: $143 per semester hour. Tuition and fees vary according to course load, degree level and program.

Financial support: Fellowships, research assistantships, teaching assistantships, institutionally sponsored loans available. Financial award applicants required to submit FAFSA.

Faculty research: Thermal science, heat transfer, design fatigue, automated manufacturing, robotics.

Dr. Robert B. Roemer, Chair, 801-581-6441, *Fax:* 801-585-9826, *E-mail:* roemer@me.mech.utah.edu.

Application contact: Dr. Joseph C. Klewicki, Director of Graduate Studies, 801-581-7934, *Fax:* 801-585-9826, *E-mail:* klewicki@me.mech.utah.edu. *Web site:* http://www.coe.utah.edu/

■ **UNIVERSITY OF VERMONT**

Graduate College, College of Engineering and Mathematics, Department of Mechanical Engineering, Burlington, VT 05405

AWARDS MS, PhD.

Degree requirements: For master's and doctorate, thesis/dissertation.

Entrance requirements: For master's and doctorate, TOEFL.

Expenses: Tuition, state resident: part-time $335 per credit. Tuition, nonresident: part-time $838 per credit.

Find an in-depth description at www.petersons.com/gradchannel.

■ **UNIVERSITY OF VIRGINIA**

School of Engineering and Applied Science, Department of Mechanical and Aerospace Engineering, Charlottesville, VA 22903

AWARDS ME, MS, PhD.

Faculty: 30 full-time (1 woman).

Students: 51 full-time (6 women), 3 part-time (1 woman), 24 international. Average age 26. 160 applicants, 14% accepted, 11

University of Virginia (continued)
enrolled. In 2001, 19 master's, 4 doctorates awarded.

Degree requirements: For master's, thesis (MS); for doctorate, thesis/dissertation, comprehensive exam.

Entrance requirements: For master's, GRE General Test; for doctorate, GRE General Test, TOEFL. *Application deadline:* For fall admission, 8/1 (priority date); for spring admission, 12/1. Applications are processed on a rolling basis. *Application fee:* $40. Electronic applications accepted.

Expenses: Tuition, state resident: full-time $3,988. Tuition, nonresident: full-time $17,078. Required fees: $1,190.

Financial support: Fellowships, research assistantships, teaching assistantships available. Financial award application deadline: 2/1; financial award applicants required to submit FAFSA.

Joseph A.C. Humprey, Chair, 434-924-7422, *Fax:* 434-982-2037, *E-mail:* mae-adm@virginia.edu.

Application contact: Kathryn Thornton, Assistant Dean, 434-924-3897, *Fax:* 434-982-2214, *E-mail:* inquiry@cs.virginia.edu. *Web site:* http://www.mae.virginia.edu/

Find an in-depth description at www.petersons.com/gradchannel.

■ UNIVERSITY OF WASHINGTON

Graduate School, College of Engineering, Department of Mechanical Engineering, Seattle, WA 98195

AWARDS MSE, MSME, PhD. Part-time programs available. Postbaccalaureate distance learning degree programs offered (minimal on-campus study).

Degree requirements: For master's, thesis (for some programs); for doctorate, one foreign language, thesis/dissertation.

Entrance requirements: For master's, GRE General Test, TOEFL, minimum GPA of 3.2 in last 2 years; for doctorate, GRE General Test, TOEFL, minimum GPA of 3.5. Electronic applications accepted.

Expenses: Tuition, state resident: full-time $5,539. Tuition, nonresident: full-time $14,376. Required fees: $390. Tuition and fees vary according to course load and program.

Faculty research: Manufacturing, automation, and controls; fluid and solid mechanics; heat transfer and combustion; fracture mechanics and composites.

■ UNIVERSITY OF WISCONSIN–MADISON

Graduate School, College of Engineering, Department of Mechanical Engineering, Madison, WI 53706-1380

AWARDS Mechanical engineering (MS, PhD); polymers (ME). Part-time programs available.

Postbaccalaureate distance learning degree programs offered (no on-campus study).

Faculty: 33 full-time (3 women).
Students: 142 full-time (8 women), 21 part-time. Average age 23. 335 applicants, 22% accepted, 31 enrolled. In 2001, 35 master's, 22 doctorates awarded. Terminal master's awarded for partial completion of doctoral program.

Degree requirements: For master's, thesis optional; for doctorate, thesis/dissertation, qualifying exam, preliminary exam.

Entrance requirements: For master's, GRE, TOEFL, BS in mechanical engineering or related field, minimum GPA of 3.0 in last 60 hours; for doctorate, GRE, TOEFL, BS in mechanical engineering or related field, minimum undergraduate GPA of 3.0 in last 60 hours. *Application deadline:* Applications are processed on a rolling basis. *Application fee:* $45. Electronic applications accepted.

Expenses: Tuition, state resident: full-time $7,361; part-time $399 per credit. Tuition, nonresident: full-time $20,499; part-time $1,282 per credit. Required fees: $34 per credit. Full-time tuition and fees vary according to course load, program, reciprocity agreements and student level.

Financial support: In 2001–02, 5 fellowships with tuition reimbursements (averaging $17,940 per year), 94 research assistantships with tuition reimbursements (averaging $16,350 per year), 20 teaching assistantships with tuition reimbursements (averaging $6,593 per year) were awarded. Institutionally sponsored loans and scholarships/grants also available.

Faculty research: Dynamics, vibrations and acoustics, mechatronics, robotics and automation, design and manufacturing, materials processing, solar energy, combustion, fluids. *Total annual research expenditures:* $10.3 million.

Neil A. Duffie, Chair, 608-262-9457, *Fax:* 608-265-2316, *E-mail:* duffie@engr.wisc.edu.

Application contact: Linda S. Aaberg, Student Status Examiner, 608-262-0666, *Fax:* 608-265-2316, *E-mail:* aaberg@engr.wisc.edu. *Web site:* http://www.engr.wisc.edu/me/

Find an in-depth description at www.petersons.com/gradchannel.

■ UNIVERSITY OF WYOMING

Graduate School, College of Engineering, Department of Mechanical Engineering, Laramie, WY 82071

AWARDS MS, PhD.

Faculty: 13 full-time (0 women), 1 (woman) part-time/adjunct.
Students: 14 full-time (1 woman), 7 part-time (1 woman); includes 1 minority (Hispanic American), 6 international. 22 applicants, 50% accepted. In 2001, 7

degrees awarded. Terminal master's awarded for partial completion of doctoral program.

Degree requirements: For master's and doctorate, thesis/dissertation.

Entrance requirements: For master's and doctorate, GRE General Test, minimum GPA of 3.0. *Application deadline:* For fall admission, 3/1. Applications are processed on a rolling basis. *Application fee:* $40. Electronic applications accepted.

Expenses: Tuition, state resident: full-time $2,895; part-time $161 per credit hour. Tuition, nonresident: full-time $8,367; part-time $465 per credit hour. Required fees: $491; $10 per credit hour. $2 per credit hour. Tuition and fees vary according to course load and program.

Financial support: In 2001–02, 8 research assistantships with full tuition reimbursements (averaging $12,000 per year), 9 teaching assistantships with full tuition reimbursements (averaging $12,000 per year) were awarded. Financial award application deadline: 3/1.

Faculty research: Composite materials, thermal and fluid sciences, continuum mechanics, material science. *Total annual research expenditures:* $591,957.

Dr. Demitris A. Kouris, Head, 307-766-2122, *Fax:* 307-766-2695, *E-mail:* kouris@uwyo.edu.

Application contact: Louise Abe, Assistant Coordinator, 307-766-2122, *Fax:* 307-766-2695, *E-mail:* louise@uwyo.edu.

■ UTAH STATE UNIVERSITY

School of Graduate Studies, College of Engineering, Department of Mechanical and Aerospace Engineering, Logan, UT 84322

AWARDS Aerospace engineering (MS, PhD); mechanical engineering (ME, MS, PhD).

Faculty: 14 full-time (0 women), 3 part-time/adjunct (1 woman).
Students: 31 full-time (4 women), 18 part-time (5 women), 27 international. Average age 25. 186 applicants, 24% accepted. In 2001, 11 degrees awarded. Terminal master's awarded for partial completion of doctoral program.

Degree requirements: For master's, thesis (for some programs); for doctorate, thesis/dissertation.

Entrance requirements: For master's, GRE General Test, TOEFL, minimum GPA of 3.0; for doctorate, GRE General Test, GRE Subject Test, TOEFL, minimum GPA of 3.0. *Application deadline:* For fall admission, 3/15 (priority date); for spring admission, 10/15. Applications are processed on a rolling basis. *Application fee:* $40.

Expenses: Tuition, state resident: full-time $1,693. Tuition, nonresident: full-time $4,233. Required fees: $501. Tuition and fees vary according to program.

Financial support: In 2001–02, 25 students received support, including 1 fellowship with partial tuition reimbursement

available (averaging $12,000 per year), 20 research assistantships with partial tuition reimbursements available (averaging $12,000 per year), 5 teaching assistantships with partial tuition reimbursements available (averaging $10,000 per year); Federal Work-Study and institutionally sponsored loans also available. Financial award application deadline: 3/15.
Faculty research: In-space instruments, cryogenic cooling, thermal science, space structures, composite materials.
Dr. J. Clair Batty, Head, 435-797-2868, *Fax:* 435-797-2417.
Application contact: Joan P. Smith, Graduate Student Adviser, 435-797-0330, *Fax:* 435-797-2417, *E-mail:* jpsmith@ mae.usu.edu. *Web site:* http:// www.mae.usu.edu/

■ VANDERBILT UNIVERSITY

School of Engineering, Department of Mechanical Engineering, Nashville, TN 37240-1001

AWARDS M Eng, MS, PhD. MS and PhD offered through the Graduate School. Part-time programs available.

Faculty: 16 full-time (1 woman), 3 part-time/adjunct (0 women).
Students: 43 full-time (4 women), 3 part-time (1 woman); includes 3 minority (2 African Americans, 1 Asian American or Pacific Islander), 26 international. Average age 24. 95 applicants, 43% accepted, 11 enrolled. In 2001, 8 master's, 5 doctorates awarded. Terminal master's awarded for partial completion of doctoral program.
Degree requirements: For master's and doctorate, thesis/dissertation, comprehensive exam, registration.
Entrance requirements: For master's and doctorate, GRE General Test. *Application deadline:* For fall admission, 1/15; for spring admission, 11/1. Applications are processed on a rolling basis. *Application fee:* $40. Electronic applications accepted.
Expenses: Tuition: Full-time $28,350.
Financial support: In 2001–02, 39 students received support, including 5 fellowships with full tuition reimbursements available (averaging $16,500 per year), 15 research assistantships with full tuition reimbursements available (averaging $17,300 per year), 19 teaching assistantships with full tuition reimbursements available (averaging $15,600 per year); institutionally sponsored loans and tuition waivers (full) also available. Support available to part-time students. Financial award application deadline: 1/15.
Faculty research: Active noise and vibration control, robotics, microscale heat transfer, laser diagnostics, combustion. *Total annual research expenditures:* $2.7 million.
Dr. Robert W. Pitz, Chair, 615-322-2413, *Fax:* 615-343-6687, *E-mail:* robert.w.pitz@ vanderbilt.edu.

Application contact: Dr. Arthur M. Mellor, Director of Graduate Studies, 615-343-6214, *Fax:* 615-343-8730, *E-mail:* puccini@vuse.vanderbilt.edu. *Web site:* http://www.vuse.vanderbilt.edu/meinfo/ me.htm

■ VILLANOVA UNIVERSITY

College of Engineering, Department of Mechanical Engineering, Villanova, PA 19085-1699

AWARDS Composite engineering (Certificate); machinery dynamics (Certificate); manufacturing (Certificate); mechanical engineering (MME); thermofluid systems (Certificate). Part-time and evening/weekend programs available. Postbaccalaureate distance learning degree programs offered (no on-campus study).

Faculty: 11 full-time (1 woman), 1 part-time/adjunct (0 women).
Students: 15 full-time (2 women), 27 part-time (1 woman); includes 8 minority (1 African American, 7 Asian Americans or Pacific Islanders). Average age 27. 16 applicants, 81% accepted, 6 enrolled. In 2001, 9 degrees awarded.
Degree requirements: For master's, thesis (for some programs).
Entrance requirements: For master's, GRE General Test (applicants with degrees from foreign universities), TOEFL, BME, minimum GPA of 3.0. *Application deadline:* For fall admission, 7/1 (priority date); for spring admission, 11/1. Applications are processed on a rolling basis. *Application fee:* $40. Electronic applications accepted.
Expenses: Tuition: Part-time $340 per credit. One-time fee: $115 full-time. Tuition and fees vary according to program.
Financial support: In 2001–02, 5 research assistantships with full tuition reimbursements (averaging $10,400 per year), 6 teaching assistantships with full tuition reimbursements (averaging $10,265 per year) were awarded. Federal Work-Study and tuition waivers (full) also available. Financial award application deadline: 3/15.
Faculty research: Composite materials, power plant systems, fluid mechanics, automated manufacturing, dynamic analysis.
Dr. Gerard F. Jones, Chairperson, 610-519-4980, *Fax:* 610-519-7312, *E-mail:* gerard.jones@villanova.edu.
Application contact: 800-338-7927, *Fax:* 610-519-6450. *Web site:* http:// www.engineering.villanova.edu/me/ index.html

Find an in-depth description at www.petersons.com/gradchannel.

■ VIRGINIA POLYTECHNIC INSTITUTE AND STATE UNIVERSITY

Graduate School, College of Engineering, Department of Mechanical Engineering, Blacksburg, VA 24061

AWARDS M Eng, MS, PhD. Part-time programs available. Postbaccalaureate distance learning degree programs offered (minimal on-campus study).

Faculty: 38 full-time (3 women).
Students: 145 full-time (11 women), 24 part-time (1 woman); includes 7 minority (3 African Americans, 2 Asian Americans or Pacific Islanders, 2 Hispanic Americans), 57 international. Average age 24. 400 applicants, 35% accepted. In 2001, 40 master's, 10 doctorates awarded. Terminal master's awarded for partial completion of doctoral program.
Degree requirements: For master's, thesis (MS); for doctorate, thesis/ dissertation.
Entrance requirements: For master's and doctorate, GRE General Test, TOEFL. *Application deadline:* For fall admission, 12/1 (priority date); for spring admission, 8/1 (priority date). Applications are processed on a rolling basis. *Application fee:* $45. Electronic applications accepted.
Expenses: Tuition, state resident: part-time $241 per hour. Tuition, nonresident: part-time $406 per hour. Tuition and fees vary according to program.
Financial support: In 2001–02, 25 fellowships with full and partial tuition reimbursements (averaging $4,000 per year), 91 research assistantships with full and partial tuition reimbursements (averaging $17,400 per year), 28 teaching assistantships with full and partial tuition reimbursements (averaging $17,400 per year) were awarded. Career-related internships or fieldwork, scholarships/grants, traineeships, and unspecified assistantships also available. Financial award application deadline: 4/1.
Faculty research: Turbomachinery, CAD/ CAM, thermofluid sciences, controls, mechanical system dynamics. *Total annual research expenditures:* $5.3 million.
Dr. Walter O'Brien, Head, 540-231-6661, *Fax:* 540-231-9100, *E-mail:* walto@vt.edu.
Application contact: Enrollment Services Coordinator, *E-mail:* megrad@vt.edu. *Web site:* http://www.me.vt.edu/

■ WASHINGTON STATE UNIVERSITY

Graduate School, College of Engineering and Architecture, School of Mechanical and Materials Engineering, Program in Mechanical Engineering, Pullman, WA 99164

AWARDS MS, PhD.
Faculty: 24 full-time (2 women).

Washington State University (continued)

Students: 30 full-time (3 women), 5 part-time; includes 1 minority (Asian American or Pacific Islander), 21 international. Average age 25. 353 applicants, 57% accepted. In 2001, 5 master's, 8 doctorates awarded.
Degree requirements: For master's, oral exam, thesis optional; for doctorate, thesis/dissertation, oral exam, qualifying exam, prelim.
Entrance requirements: For master's, minimum GPA of 3.0; for doctorate, minimum GPA of 3.4. *Application deadline:* For fall admission, 3/1 (priority date); for spring admission, 9/1 (priority date). Applications are processed on a rolling basis. *Application fee:* $35. Electronic applications accepted.
Expenses: Tuition, state resident: full-time $6,088; part-time $304 per semester. Tuition, nonresident: full-time $14,918; part-time $746 per semester. Tuition and fees vary according to program.
Financial support: In 2001–02, 1 fellowship (averaging $3,000 per year), 18 research assistantships with full and partial tuition reimbursements (averaging $10,688 per year), 17 teaching assistantships with full and partial tuition reimbursements (averaging $10,707 per year) were awarded. Career-related internships or fieldwork, Federal Work-Study, institutionally sponsored loans, and teaching associateships also available. Financial award application deadline: 4/1; financial award applicants required to submit FAFSA.
Faculty research: Thermal fluids and heat transfer, combustion, solid mechanics virtual reality as applied to advanced manufacturing, advanced manufacturing and rapid prototyping. *Total annual research expenditures:* $1.3 million.
Application contact: Mary Simonsen, Program Coordinator, 509-335-4546, *Fax:* 509-335-4662, *E-mail:* gradapp@mme.wsu.edu. *Web site:* http://www.mme.wsu.edu/

■ WASHINGTON UNIVERSITY IN ST. LOUIS

Henry Edwin Sever Graduate School of Engineering and Applied Science, Department of Mechanical Engineering, St. Louis, MO 63130-4899

AWARDS MS, D Sc. Part-time programs available.

Faculty: 15 full-time (1 woman), 14 part-time/adjunct (0 women).
Students: 27 full-time (3 women), 17 part-time (3 women); includes 2 minority (both Hispanic Americans), 16 international. 102 applicants, 24% accepted, 17 enrolled. In 2001, 20 master's, 5 doctorates awarded. Terminal master's awarded for partial completion of doctoral program.
Degree requirements: For master's and doctorate, thesis optional.
Entrance requirements: For doctorate, departmental qualifying exam. *Application*

deadline: Applications are processed on a rolling basis. *Application fee:* $20.
Expenses: Tuition: Full-time $26,900.
Financial support: In 2001–02, 16 research assistantships with full tuition reimbursements, 10 teaching assistantships with full tuition reimbursements were awarded. Tuition waivers (full) also available.
Faculty research: Materials, combustion, flow control, biomechanics, nonlinear dynamics, aerosols. *Total annual research expenditures:* $1.8 million.
Dr. David A. Peters, Chairman, 314-935-4337, *Fax:* 314-935-4014, *E-mail:* dap@me.wustl.edu.
Application contact: Mary C. Molloy, Graduate Admissions Secretary, 314-835-7096, *Fax:* 314-935-4014, *E-mail:* mcm@me.wustl.edu. *Web site:* http://www.me.wustl.edu/

Find an in-depth description at www.petersons.com/gradchannel.

■ WAYNE STATE UNIVERSITY

Graduate School, College of Engineering, Department of Mechanical Engineering, Detroit, MI 48202

AWARDS MS, PhD.

Faculty: 18 full-time.
Students: 421. 769 applicants, 59% accepted, 144 enrolled. In 2001, 157 master's, 8 doctorates awarded.
Degree requirements: For master's, thesis optional; for doctorate, thesis/dissertation.
Entrance requirements: For master's, minimum undergraduate GPA of 3.0; for doctorate, minimum graduate GPA of 3.5. *Application deadline:* For fall admission, 7/1 (priority date); for spring admission, 3/15. Applications are processed on a rolling basis. *Application fee:* $20 ($30 for international students). Electronic applications accepted.
Expenses: Tuition, state resident: full-time $3,764. Tuition and fees vary according to degree level and program.
Financial support: In 2001–02, 1 fellowship, 19 research assistantships, 10 teaching assistantships were awarded. Career-related internships or fieldwork, Federal Work-Study, and tuition waivers (full and partial) also available. Financial award application deadline: 2/28.
Faculty research: Acoustic vibrations and noise control, trauma biomechanics, combustion, computational fluid mechanics, behavior of composite materials.
Dr. Kenneth Kline, Chairperson, 313-577-3843, *Fax:* 313-577-8789, *E-mail:* kline@eng.wayne.edu.
Application contact: Victor Berdichevsky, Graduate Director, 313-577-3905, *E-mail:* vberd@eng.wayne.edu.

■ WESTERN MICHIGAN UNIVERSITY

Graduate College, College of Engineering and Applied Sciences, Department of Mechanical and Aeronautical Engineering, Kalamazoo, MI 49008-5202

AWARDS Mechanical engineering (MSE, PhD). Part-time programs available.

Faculty: 17 full-time (0 women).
Students: 47 full-time (4 women), 22 part-time (1 woman); includes 4 minority (all Asian Americans or Pacific Islanders), 39 international. 213 applicants, 59% accepted, 31 enrolled. In 2001, 13 master's, 2 doctorates awarded.
Degree requirements: For master's, thesis optional; for doctorate, thesis/dissertation, oral exam.
Entrance requirements: For master's, minimum GPA of 3.0; for doctorate, GRE General Test, minimum GPA of 3.0. *Application deadline:* For fall admission, 2/15 (priority date). Applications are processed on a rolling basis. *Application fee:* $25.
Expenses: Tuition, state resident: part-time $186 per credit hour. Tuition, nonresident: part-time $442 per credit hour. Required fees: $602. One-time fee: $132 part-time. Tuition and fees vary according to course load.
Financial support: Fellowships, research assistantships, teaching assistantships, career-related internships or fieldwork and Federal Work-Study available. Financial award application deadline: 2/15; financial award applicants required to submit FAFSA.
Faculty research: Computational fluid dynamics, manufacturing process designs, composite materials, thermal fluid flow, experimental stress analysis.
Dr. Parviz Merati, Chair, 616-387-3366.
Application contact: Admissions and Orientation, 616-387-2000, *Fax:* 616-387-2355.

■ WESTERN NEW ENGLAND COLLEGE

School of Engineering, Department of Mechanical Engineering, Springfield, MA 01119-2654

AWARDS MSME. Part-time and evening/weekend programs available.

Faculty: 6 full-time (0 women).
Students: Average age 29. 3 applicants, 33% accepted. In 2001, 2 degrees awarded.
Degree requirements: For master's, thesis optional.
Entrance requirements: For master's, GRE, bachelor's degree in engineering or related field. *Application deadline:* Applications are processed on a rolling basis. *Application fee:* $30.
Expenses: Tuition: Part-time $429 per credit. Required fees: $9 per credit. $20 per semester.

Financial support: Teaching assistantships available. Support available to part-time students. Financial award application deadline: 4/1; financial award applicants required to submit FAFSA.
Faculty research: Low-loss fluid mixing, flow separation delay and alleviation, high-lift airfoils, ejector research, compact heat exchangers.
Dr. Said Dini, Chair, 413-782-1498, *E-mail:* sdini@wnec.edu.
Application contact: Dr. Janet Castleman, Director of Continuing Education, 413-782-1750, *Fax:* 413-782-1779, *E-mail:* jcastlem@wnec.edu.

■ WEST VIRGINIA UNIVERSITY

College of Engineering and Mineral Resources, Department of Mechanical and Aerospace Engineering, Program in Mechanical Engineering, Morgantown, WV 26506

AWARDS Engineering (MSE); mechanical engineering (MSME, PhD). Part-time programs available.

Students: 69 full-time (6 women), 6 part-time; includes 1 minority (Asian American or Pacific Islander), 48 international. Average age 24. 166 applicants, 57% accepted. In 2001, 18 master's, 6 doctorates awarded. Terminal master's awarded for partial completion of doctoral program.
Degree requirements: For master's, thesis/dissertation; for doctorate, thesis/dissertation, comprehensive exam.
Entrance requirements: For master's and doctorate, GRE Subject Test, TOEFL, minimum GPA of 3.0. *Application deadline:* For fall admission, 4/1 (priority date); for spring admission, 10/1. Applications are processed on a rolling basis. *Application fee:* $45.
Expenses: Tuition, state resident: full-time $2,791. Tuition, nonresident: full-time $8,659. Required fees: $1,002. Tuition and fees vary according to program.
Financial support: In 2001–02, 43 research assistantships, 4 teaching assistantships were awarded. Fellowships, Federal Work-Study, institutionally sponsored loans, and tuition waivers (partial) also available. Financial award application deadline: 2/1; financial award applicants required to submit FAFSA.
Faculty research: Fluid mechanics, combustion, multiphase flow, solid mechanics, structures, engines, alternate fuels.
Application contact: Dr. Gary J. Morris, Graduate Director and Interim Chair, 304-293-4111 Ext. 2342, *Fax:* 304-293-8823, *E-mail:* gary.morris@mail.wvu.edu. *Web site:* http://www.cemr.wvu.edu/

■ WICHITA STATE UNIVERSITY

Graduate School, College of Engineering, Department of Mechanical Engineering, Wichita, KS 67260

AWARDS MS, PhD. Part-time programs available.

Faculty: 9 full-time (1 woman).
Students: 75 full-time (2 women), 65 part-time (5 women); includes 23 minority (1 African American, 21 Asian Americans or Pacific Islanders, 1 Native American), 92 international. Average age 27. 222 applicants, 74% accepted, 48 enrolled. In 2001, 23 master's, 4 doctorates awarded.
Degree requirements: For master's, thesis or alternative, oral exam; for doctorate, one foreign language, thesis/dissertation, comprehensive, departmental qualifying, and oral exams, comprehensive exam.
Entrance requirements: For master's and doctorate, GRE, TOEFL, minimum GPA of 3.0 in last 2 years. *Application deadline:* For fall admission, 7/1 (priority date); for spring admission, 1/1. Applications are processed on a rolling basis. *Application fee:* $25 ($40 for international students). Electronic applications accepted.
Expenses: Tuition, state resident: full-time $1,888; part-time $105 per credit. Tuition, nonresident: full-time $6,129; part-time $341 per credit. Required fees: $345; $19 per credit. $17 per semester. Tuition and fees vary according to course load and program.
Financial support: In 2001–02, 24 research assistantships (averaging $3,660 per year), 13 teaching assistantships with full tuition reimbursements (averaging $4,111 per year) were awarded. Fellowships, Federal Work-Study, institutionally sponsored loans, and unspecified assistantships also available. Financial award application deadline: 4/1; financial award applicants required to submit FAFSA.
Faculty research: Materials science, fluid mechanics, manufacturing systems, thermal science, combustion.
Dr. Jharna Chaudhuri, Chairperson, 316-978-6368, *Fax:* 316-978-3236, *E-mail:* chaudhur@me.twsu.edu. *Web site:* http://www.wichita.edu/

■ WIDENER UNIVERSITY

School of Engineering, Program in Mechanical Engineering, Chester, PA 19013-5792

AWARDS ME, ME/MBA.

Degree requirements: For master's, thesis optional.
Entrance requirements: For master's, GMAT (ME/MBA).
Expenses: Tuition: Part-time $500 per credit. Required fees: $25 per semester.
Faculty research: Computational fluid mechanics, thermal and solar engineering, energy conversion, composite materials, solid mechanics.

■ WOODS HOLE OCEANOGRAPHIC INSTITUTE

Joint Program with Massachusetts Institute of Technology in Oceanography/Applied Ocean Science and Engineering, Woods Hole, MA 02543

AWARDS Applied ocean sciences (PhD); biological oceanography (PhD, Sc D); chemical oceanography (PhD, Sc D); civil and environmental and oceanographic engineering (PhD); electrical and oceanographic engineering (PhD); geochemistry (PhD); geophysics (PhD); marine biology (PhD); marine geochemistry (PhD, Sc D); marine geology (PhD, Sc D); marine geophysics (PhD); mechanical and oceanographic engineering (PhD); ocean engineering (PhD); oceanographic engineering (M Eng, MS, PhD, Sc D, Eng); paleoceanography (PhD); physical oceanography (PhD, Sc D). MS, PhD, and Sc D offered jointly with Woods Hole Oceanographic Institution.

Faculty: 185 full-time (60 women).
Students: 119 full-time (59 women); includes 4 minority (2 African Americans, 2 Asian Americans or Pacific Islanders), 27 international. Average age 27. 125 applicants, 30% accepted, 24 enrolled. In 2001, 10 master's, 11 doctorates awarded. Terminal master's awarded for partial completion of doctoral program.
Degree requirements: For master's and Eng, thesis (for some programs); for doctorate, thesis/dissertation. *Median time to degree:* Master's–2.9 years full-time; doctorate–5.8 years full-time.
Entrance requirements: For master's, GRE General Test; for doctorate, GRE General Test, GRE Subject Test. *Application deadline:* For fall admission, 1/15 (priority date). *Application fee:* $60. Electronic applications accepted.
Expenses: Tuition: Full-time $26,960. Full-time tuition and fees vary according to program.
Financial support: In 2001–02, 13 fellowships (averaging $35,948 per year), 69 research assistantships (averaging $35,948 per year) were awarded. Teaching assistantships, institutionally sponsored loans, health care benefits, and unspecified assistantships also available. Financial award application deadline: 1/15.
Prof. Paola Rizzoli, Director, 617-253-2451, *E-mail:* rizzoli@mit.edu.
Application contact: Ronni Schwartz, Administrator, 617-253-7544, *Fax:* 617-253-9784, *E-mail:* mspiggy@mit.edu. *Web site:* http://www.whoi.edu/education/graduate/jp.html

Find an in-depth description at www.petersons.com/gradchannel.

■ WORCESTER POLYTECHNIC INSTITUTE

Graduate Studies, Department of Mechanical Engineering, Worcester, MA 01609-2280

AWARDS M Eng, MS, PhD, Advanced Certificate. Part-time and evening/weekend programs available.

Faculty: 29 full-time (1 woman), 2 part-time/adjunct (0 women).
Students: 46 full-time (8 women), 17 part-time (1 woman); includes 1 minority (Asian American or Pacific Islander), 24 international. Average age 25. 191 applicants, 51% accepted, 26 enrolled. In 2001, 20 master's, 2 doctorates awarded.
Degree requirements: For master's, thesis optional; for doctorate, thesis/dissertation.
Entrance requirements: For master's and doctorate, TOEFL. *Application deadline:* For fall admission, 2/1 (priority date); for spring admission, 10/15 (priority date). Applications are processed on a rolling basis. *Application fee:* $60. Electronic applications accepted.
Expenses: Tuition: Part-time $796 per credit. Required fees: $20; $752 per credit. One-time fee: $30 full-time.
Financial support: In 2001–02, 44 students received support, including 4 fellowships with full tuition reimbursements available (averaging $10,950 per year), 18 research assistantships with full tuition reimbursements available (averaging $17,250 per year), 16 teaching assistantships with full tuition reimbursements available (averaging $12,942 per year); career-related internships or fieldwork, institutionally sponsored loans, and scholarships/grants also available. Financial award application deadline: 2/15; financial award applicants required to submit FAFSA.
Faculty research: Thermal fluid engineering, aerospace and biomechanical engineering, heat transfer/laser holography/reliability and controls, dynamics and vibrations, computational and probabilistic methods. *Total annual research expenditures:* $4.1 million.
Dr. Gretar Tryggvasor, Head, 508-831-5759, *Fax:* 508-831-5680, *E-mail:* gretar@wpi.edu.
Application contact: Dr. Mark Richman, Graduate Coordinator, 508-831-5556, *Fax:* 508-831-5680, *E-mail:* mrichman@wpi.edu. *Web site:* http://www.wpi.edu/Academics/Depts/ME/

Find an in-depth description at www.petersons.com/gradchannel.

■ WRIGHT STATE UNIVERSITY

School of Graduate Studies, College of Engineering and Computer Science, Programs in Engineering, Program in Mechanical and Materials Engineering, Dayton, OH 45435

AWARDS Materials science and engineering (MSE); mechanical engineering (MSE).
Students: 32 full-time (1 woman), 21 part-time (3 women); includes 3 minority (1 African American, 1 Asian American or Pacific Islander, 1 Hispanic American), 22 international. Average age 29. 176 applicants, 56% accepted. In 2001, 10 degrees awarded.
Degree requirements: For master's, thesis or course option alternative.
Entrance requirements: For master's, TOEFL. *Application fee:* $25.
Expenses: Tuition, state resident: full-time $7,161; part-time $225 per quarter hour. Tuition, nonresident: full-time $12,324; part-time $385 per quarter hour. Tuition and fees vary according to course load, degree level and program.
Financial support: Fellowships, research assistantships, teaching assistantships, unspecified assistantships available. Support available to part-time students. Financial award application deadline: 3/15; financial award applicants required to submit FAFSA.
Dr. Richard J. Bethke, Chair, 937-775-5040, *Fax:* 937-775-5009, *E-mail:* richard.bethke@wright.edu.

■ YALE UNIVERSITY

Graduate School of Arts and Sciences, Programs in Engineering and Applied Science, Department of Mechanical Engineering, New Haven, CT 06520

AWARDS Applied mechanics and mechanical engineering (M Phil, MS, PhD). Terminal master's awarded for partial completion of doctoral program.
Degree requirements: For doctorate, thesis/dissertation, exam.
Entrance requirements: For master's and doctorate, GRE General Test, TOEFL.

■ YOUNGSTOWN STATE UNIVERSITY

Graduate School, William Rayen College of Engineering, Department of Mechanical and Industrial Engineering, Youngstown, OH 44555-0001

AWARDS MSE. Part-time and evening/weekend programs available.
Degree requirements: For master's, thesis optional.
Entrance requirements: For master's, TOEFL, minimum GPA of 2.75 in field.
Faculty research: Kinematics and dynamics of machines, computational and

experimental heat transfer, machine controls and mechanical design.

MECHANICS ....

■ BROWN UNIVERSITY

Graduate School, Division of Engineering, Program in Mechanics of Solids and Structures, Providence, RI 02912

AWARDS Sc M, PhD.
Degree requirements: For doctorate, thesis/dissertation, preliminary exam.

■ CALIFORNIA INSTITUTE OF TECHNOLOGY

Division of Engineering and Applied Science, Option in Applied Mechanics, Pasadena, CA 91125-0001

AWARDS MS, PhD.
Faculty: 2 full-time (0 women).
Students: 14 full-time (2 women); includes 1 minority (Hispanic American), 10 international. 24 applicants, 25% accepted, 4 enrolled. In 2001, 1 master's, 1 doctorate awarded.
Degree requirements: For doctorate, thesis/dissertation.
Application deadline: For fall admission, 1/15. *Application fee:* $0.
Financial support: In 2001–02, 2 fellowships, 3 research assistantships, 5 teaching assistantships were awarded.
Faculty research: Elasticity, mechanics of quasi-static and dynamic fracture, dynamics and mechanical vibrations, stability and control.
Dr. John Hall, Executive Officer, 626-395-4160.

■ CALIFORNIA STATE UNIVERSITY, FULLERTON

Graduate Studies, College of Engineering and Computer Science, Department of Civil Engineering and Engineering Mechanics, Fullerton, CA 92834-9480

AWARDS MS.
Faculty: 7 full-time (0 women), 8 part-time/adjunct.
Students: 10 full-time (2 women), 19 part-time (5 women); includes 15 minority (2 African Americans, 11 Asian Americans or Pacific Islanders, 2 Hispanic Americans), 5 international. Average age 32. 27 applicants, 48% accepted, 6 enrolled. In 2001, 7 degrees awarded.
Degree requirements: For master's, project or thesis.
Entrance requirements: For master's, minimum undergraduate GPA of 2.5. *Application fee:* $55.
Expenses: Tuition, nonresident: part-time $246 per unit. Required fees: $964.

Financial support: Career-related internships or fieldwork, Federal Work-Study, institutionally sponsored loans, and scholarships/grants available. Support available to part-time students. Financial award application deadline: 3/1.
Faculty research: Soil-structure interaction, finite-element analysis, computer-aided analysis and design.
Dr. Chandra Putcha, Head, 714-278-3012.

■ CALIFORNIA STATE UNIVERSITY, NORTHRIDGE

Graduate Studies, College of Engineering and Computer Science, Department of Civil and Manufacturing Engineering, Northridge, CA 91330

AWARDS Applied mechanics (MSE); civil engineering (MS); engineering and computer science (MS); engineering management (MS); industrial engineering (MS); materials engineering (MS); mechanical engineering (MS), including aerospace engineering, applied engineering, machine design, mechanical engineering, structural engineering, thermofluids; mechanics (MS). Part-time and evening/weekend programs available.

Faculty: 14 full-time, 2 part-time/adjunct.
Students: 25 full-time (4 women), 72 part-time (9 women). Average age 31. 64 applicants, 77% accepted, 22 enrolled. In 2001, 34 degrees awarded.
Degree requirements: For master's, thesis.
Entrance requirements: For master's, GRE General Test, TOEFL, minimum GPA of 2.5. *Application deadline:* For fall admission, 11/30. *Application fee:* $55.
Expenses: Tuition, nonresident: part-time $631 per semester. Required fees: $246 per unit.
Financial support: Teaching assistantships available. Financial award application deadline: 3/1.
Faculty research: Composite study.
Dr. Stephen Gadomski, Chair, 818-677-2166.
Application contact: Dr. Ileana Costa, Graduate Coordinator, 818-677-3299.

■ CASE WESTERN RESERVE UNIVERSITY

School of Graduate Studies, The Case School of Engineering, Department of Civil Engineering, Cleveland, OH 44106

AWARDS Civil engineering (MS, PhD); engineering mechanics (MS). Part-time programs available. Postbaccalaureate distance learning degree programs offered (minimal on-campus study).

Faculty: 10 full-time (1 woman), 6 part-time/adjunct (2 women).
Students: 13 full-time (3 women), 7 part-time (3 women), 14 international. Average

age 24. 149 applicants, 52% accepted, 4 enrolled. In 2001, 6 master's, 2 doctorates awarded.
Degree requirements: For master's, thesis (for some programs); for doctorate, thesis/dissertation, qualifying exam, teaching experience.
Entrance requirements: For master's, TOEFL; for doctorate, GRE, TOEFL. *Application deadline:* For fall admission, 8/1 (priority date); for spring admission, 1/1. *Application fee:* $25.
Financial support: In 2001–02, 8 fellowships with full and partial tuition reimbursements (averaging $16,200 per year), 6 research assistantships with full and partial tuition reimbursements (averaging $16,200 per year) were awarded. Institutionally sponsored loans also available. Financial award application deadline: 8/1; financial award applicants required to submit FAFSA.
Faculty research: Environmental engineering. Structural engineering; geotechnical engineering; engineering mechanics. *Total annual research expenditures:* $684,122.
Dr. Robert L. Mullen, Chairman, 216-368-2427, *Fax:* 216-368-5229, *E-mail:* rlm@po.cwru.edu.
Application contact: Kathleen Ballou, Secretary, 216-368-2950, *Fax:* 216-368-5229, *E-mail:* kad4@po.cwru.edu. *Web site:* http://ecivwww.cwru.edu/civil/

■ THE CATHOLIC UNIVERSITY OF AMERICA

School of Engineering, Department of Mechanical Engineering, Washington, DC 20064

AWARDS Design (D Engr, PhD); design and robotics (MME, D Engr, PhD); fluid mechanics and thermal science (MME, D Engr, PhD); mechanical design (MME); ocean and structural acoustics (MME, MS Engr, PhD). Part-time and evening/weekend programs available.

Faculty: 6 full-time (1 woman).
Students: 7 full-time (0 women), 16 part-time (3 women); includes 4 minority (2 African Americans, 2 Asian Americans or Pacific Islanders), 8 international. Average age 34. 14 applicants, 36% accepted, 2 enrolled. In 2001, 3 master's, 3 doctorates awarded.
Degree requirements: For master's, thesis optional; for doctorate, thesis/dissertation, oral exams, comprehensive exam.
Entrance requirements: For master's, minimum GPA of 3.0; for doctorate, minimum GPA of 3.5. *Application deadline:* For fall admission, 8/1 (priority date); for spring admission, 12/1. Applications are processed on a rolling basis. *Application fee:* $55. Electronic applications accepted.
Expenses: Tuition: Full-time $20,050; part-time $770 per credit. Required fees: $430 per term. Tuition and fees vary according to program.

Financial support: Research assistantships, teaching assistantships, career-related internships or fieldwork, Federal Work-Study, institutionally sponsored loans, and tuition waivers (full and partial) available. Support available to part-time students. Financial award application deadline: 2/1.
Faculty research: Automated engineering.
Dr. Ji Steven Brown, Chair, 202-319-5170.

■ COLORADO STATE UNIVERSITY

Graduate School, College of Engineering, Department of Mechanical Engineering, Fort Collins, CO 80523-0015

AWARDS Bioengineering (MS, PhD); energy and environmental engineering (MS, PhD); energy conversion (MS, PhD); engineering management (MS); heat and mass transfer (MS, PhD); industrial and manufacturing systems engineering (MS, PhD); mechanical engineering (MS, PhD); mechanics and materials (MS, PhD). Part-time programs available.

Faculty: 17 full-time (2 women).
Students: 36 full-time (6 women), 63 part-time (11 women); includes 5 minority (2 Asian Americans or Pacific Islanders, 2 Hispanic Americans, 1 Native American), 22 international. Average age 32. 234 applicants, 83% accepted, 32 enrolled. In 2001, 10 master's, 3 doctorates awarded. Terminal master's awarded for partial completion of doctoral program.
Degree requirements: For doctorate, thesis/dissertation.
Entrance requirements: For master's and doctorate, GRE General Test, TOEFL, minimum GPA of 3.0. *Application deadline:* For fall admission, 2/1 (priority date). Applications are processed on a rolling basis. *Application fee:* $30. Electronic applications accepted.
Expenses: Tuition, state resident: full-time $2,880; part-time $160 per credit. Tuition, nonresident: full-time $11,412; part-time $634 per credit. Required fees: $750; $34 per credit.
Financial support: In 2001–02, 2 fellowships, 15 research assistantships (averaging $15,792 per year), 14 teaching assistantships (averaging $11,844 per year) were awarded. Traineeships also available.
Faculty research: Space propulsion, controls and systems, engineering and materials. *Total annual research expenditures:* $2.1 million.
Dr. Allan T. Kirkpatrick, Head, 970-491-6559, *Fax:* 970-491-3827, *E-mail:* allan@engr.colostate.edu. *Web site:* http://www.engr.colostate.edu/depts/me/index.html

■ COLUMBIA UNIVERSITY

Fu Foundation School of Engineering and Applied Science, Department of Civil Engineering and Engineering Mechanics, New York, NY 10027

AWARDS Civil engineering (MS, Eng Sc D, PhD, Engr); mechanics (MS, Eng Sc D, PhD, Engr). Part-time programs available.

Faculty: 11 full-time (0 women), 8 part-time/adjunct (0 women).
Students: 25 full-time (2 women), 23 part-time (3 women); includes 18 minority (15 Asian Americans or Pacific Islanders, 3 Hispanic Americans), 18 international. Average age 27. 168 applicants, 23% accepted, 16 enrolled. In 2001, 3 master's, 13 doctorates awarded. Terminal master's awarded for partial completion of doctoral program.
Degree requirements: For doctorate, thesis/dissertation, qualifying exam. *Median time to degree:* Master's–1 year full-time; doctorate–2.5 years full-time.
Entrance requirements: For master's, doctorate, and Engr, GRE General Test, TOEFL. *Application deadline:* For fall admission, 1/5; for spring admission, 10/1. *Application fee:* $55. Electronic applications accepted.
Expenses: Tuition: Full-time $27,528. Required fees: $1,638.
Financial support: In 2001–02, 16 students received support, including 3 fellowships with full tuition reimbursements available (averaging $23,000 per year), 6 research assistantships with full tuition reimbursements available (averaging $22,000 per year), 7 teaching assistantships with full tuition reimbursements available (averaging $22,000 per year); Federal Work-Study, scholarships/grants, and health care benefits also available. Financial award application deadline: 1/5; financial award applicants required to submit FAFSA.
Faculty research: Structural deterioration and control, structural materials, multihazard and risk assessment, geoenvironmental engineering, construction engineering. *Total annual research expenditures:* $720,000.
Rimas Vaicaitis, Chairman, 212-854-2396, *Fax:* 212-854-6267, *E-mail:* rimas@civil.columbia.edu.
Application contact: Carolyn Waldo, Administrative Assistant, 212-854-3143, *Fax:* 212-854-6267, *E-mail:* clw1@columbia.edu. *Web site:* http://www.civil.columbia.edu/

■ CORNELL UNIVERSITY

Graduate School, Graduate Fields of Engineering, Field of Theoretical and Applied Mechanics, Ithaca, NY 14853-0001

AWARDS Advanced composites and structures (M Eng); dynamics and space mechanics (MS, PhD); fluid mechanics (MS,

PhD); mechanics of materials (MS, PhD). Solid mechanics (MS, PhD).

Faculty: 22 full-time.
Students: 28 full-time (1 woman); includes 1 minority (Hispanic American), 19 international. 66 applicants, 30% accepted. In 2001, 6 master's, 7 doctorates awarded.
Degree requirements: For master's, thesis (MS); for doctorate, one foreign language, thesis/dissertation, teaching experience.
Entrance requirements: For master's, GRE General Test), TOEFL, 3 letters of recommendation; for doctorate, GRE General Test, TOEFL, pre-application in not enrolled at a US or Canadian university, 3 letters of recommendation. *Application deadline:* For fall admission, 1/15. *Application fee:* $65. Electronic applications accepted.
Expenses: Tuition: Full-time $25,970. Required fees: $50.
Financial support: In 2001–02, 8 fellowships with full tuition reimbursements, 8 research assistantships with full tuition reimbursements, 13 teaching assistantships with full tuition reimbursements were awarded. Institutionally sponsored loans, scholarships/grants, and unspecified assistantships also available.
Faculty research: Nonlinear dynamics, experimental mechanics, biomathematics, bio-fluids, animal locomotion, probabilistic, non-linear and solid mechanics; nano- and micro-mechanics and systems.
Application contact: Graduate Field Assistant, *Fax:* 607-255-2011, *E-mail:* tam_grad@cornell.edu. *Web site:* http://www.gradschool.cornell.edu/grad/fields_1/tam.html

■ DREXEL UNIVERSITY

Graduate School, College of Engineering, Mechanical Engineering and Mechanics Department, Philadelphia, PA 19104-2875

AWARDS Manufacturing engineering (MS, PhD); mechanical engineering and mechanics (MS, PhD). Part-time and evening/weekend programs available.

Faculty: 22 full-time (0 women), 1 part-time/adjunct (0 women).
Students: 19 full-time (2 women), 69 part-time (7 women); includes 15 minority (4 African Americans, 8 Asian Americans or Pacific Islanders, 2 Hispanic Americans, 1 Native American), 32 international. Average age 30. 124 applicants, 88% accepted, 14 enrolled. In 2001, 20 master's, 2 doctorates awarded. Terminal master's awarded for partial completion of doctoral program.
Degree requirements: For master's, thesis optional; for doctorate, thesis/dissertation.
Entrance requirements: For master's, TOEFL, minimum GPA of 3.0, BS in engineering or science; for doctorate, TOEFL, minimum GPA of 3.5, MS in

engineering or science. *Application deadline:* For fall admission, 8/21. Applications are processed on a rolling basis. *Application fee:* $50. Electronic applications accepted.
Expenses: Tuition: Full-time $20,088; part-time $558 per credit. Required fees: $78 per term. One-time fee: $200. Tuition and fees vary according to course load, degree level and program.
Financial support: Research assistantships, teaching assistantships, unspecified assistantships available. Financial award application deadline: 2/1.
Faculty research: Composites, dynamic systems and control, combustion and fuels, biomechanics, mechanics and thermal fluid sciences.
Dr. Mun Young Choi, Acting Head, 215-895-2284, *Fax:* 215-895-1478, *E-mail:* mem@drexel.edu.
Application contact: Director of Graduate Admissions, 215-895-6700, *Fax:* 215-895-5939, *E-mail:* enroll@drexel.edu.

Find an in-depth description at www.petersons.com/gradchannel.

■ GEORGIA INSTITUTE OF TECHNOLOGY

Graduate Studies and Research, College of Engineering, School of Civil and Environmental Engineering, Program in Engineering Science and Mechanics, Atlanta, GA 30332-0001

AWARDS MS, MSESM, PhD. Part-time programs available. Terminal master's awarded for partial completion of doctoral program.

Degree requirements: For doctorate, thesis/dissertation.
Entrance requirements: For master's, GRE, TOEFL; for doctorate, GRE, TOEFL, minimum GPA of 3.2.
Faculty research: Bioengineering, structural mechanics, solid mechanics, dynamics.

■ IDAHO STATE UNIVERSITY

Office of Graduate Studies, College of Engineering, Pocatello, ID 83209

AWARDS Engineering and applied science (PhD); engineering structures and mechanics (MS); environmental engineering (MS); measurement and control engineering (MS); nuclear science and engineering (MS); waste management and environmental science (MS). Part-time programs available.

Faculty: 13 full-time (0 women), 1 part-time/adjunct (0 women).
Students: 34 full-time (8 women), 18 part-time (1 woman); includes 7 minority (1 African American, 5 Asian Americans or Pacific Islanders, 1 Hispanic American), 15 international. Average age 34. In 2001, 12 master's, 1 doctorate awarded.
Degree requirements: For master's and doctorate, thesis/dissertation.
Entrance requirements: For master's and doctorate, GRE General Test, TOEFL.

Application deadline: For fall admission, 7/1 (priority date); for spring admission, 12/1. Applications are processed on a rolling basis. *Application fee:* $35.
Expenses: Tuition, area resident: Full-time $3,432. Tuition, state resident: part-time $172 per credit. Tuition, nonresident: full-time $10,196; part-time $262 per credit. International tuition: $9,672 full-time. Part-time tuition and fees vary according to course load, program and reciprocity agreements.
Financial support: In 2001–02, 7 research assistantships with full and partial tuition reimbursements (averaging $10,740 per year), 16 teaching assistantships with full and partial tuition reimbursements (averaging $6,775 per year) were awarded. Federal Work-Study and institutionally sponsored loans also available. Support available to part-time students. Financial award application deadline: 2/15.
Faculty research: Isotope separation, control technology, two-phase flow, photosonolysis, criticality calculations. *Total annual research expenditures:* $293,915.
Dr. Jay Kunze, Dean, 208-282-2902, *Fax:* 208-282-4538. *Web site:* http://www.coe.isu.edu/engrg/

■ IOWA STATE UNIVERSITY OF SCIENCE AND TECHNOLOGY

Graduate College, College of Engineering, Department of Aerospace Engineering and Engineering Mechanics, Ames, IA 50011

AWARDS Aerospace engineering (M Eng, MS, PhD); engineering mechanics (M Eng, MS, PhD).

Faculty: 34 full-time.
Students: 47 full-time (11 women), 7 part-time; includes 3 minority (2 African Americans, 1 Asian American or Pacific Islander), 40 international. 83 applicants, 34% accepted, 17 enrolled. In 2001, 7 master's, 2 doctorates awarded.
Degree requirements: For master's, thesis (for some programs); for doctorate, thesis/dissertation. *Median time to degree:* Master's–2.2 years full-time; doctorate–4.2 years full-time.
Entrance requirements: For master's and doctorate, GRE General Test, TOEFL, or IELTS. *Application deadline:* For fall admission, 3/1 (priority date); for spring admission, 10/1 (priority date). *Application fee:* $20 ($50 for international students). Electronic applications accepted.
Expenses: Tuition, state resident: full-time $1,851. Tuition, nonresident: full-time $5,449. Tuition and fees vary according to program.
Financial support: In 2001–02, 18 research assistantships with partial tuition reimbursements (averaging $11,139 per year), 28 teaching assistantships with partial tuition reimbursements (averaging

$11,144 per year) were awarded. Fellowships, scholarships/grants, health care benefits, and unspecified assistantships also available.
Dr. Thomas J. Rudolphi, Chair, 515-294-5666, *E-mail:* aeem_info@iastate.edu.
Application contact: Dr. Ambar Mitra, Director of Graduate Education, 515-294-2694, *E-mail:* aeem_info@iastate.edu. *Web site:* http://www1.eng.iastate.edu/coe/grad.asp

■ JOHNS HOPKINS UNIVERSITY

G. W. C. Whiting School of Engineering, Department of Mechanical Engineering, Baltimore, MD 21218-2699

AWARDS Mechanical engineering (MS, MSE, PhD), including mechanical engineering (MS), mechanics (MSE, PhD). Part-time programs available.

Faculty: 14 full-time (2 women), 6 part-time/adjunct (0 women).
Students: 49 full-time (10 women); includes 2 minority (1 African American, 1 Asian American or Pacific Islander), 36 international. Average age 28. 279 applicants, 10% accepted, 9 enrolled. In 2001, 9 master's, 5 doctorates awarded. Terminal master's awarded for partial completion of doctoral program.
Degree requirements: For master's, thesis (for some programs); for doctorate, thesis/dissertation, oral exam.
Entrance requirements: For master's and doctorate, GRE General Test, TOEFL. *Application deadline:* 1/15 (priority date). *Application fee:* $0. Electronic applications accepted.
Expenses: Tuition: Full-time $27,390.
Financial support: In 2001–02, 49 students received support, including 3 fellowships with full tuition reimbursements available (averaging $18,996 per year), 39 research assistantships with full tuition reimbursements available (averaging $18,996 per year); teaching assistantships, Federal Work-Study, institutionally sponsored loans, scholarships/grants, tuition waivers (full), and unspecified assistantships also available. Support available to part-time students. Financial award application deadline: 1/15.
Faculty research: Mechanical behavior of materials, robotics, heat and mass transfer, fluid mechanics, biomechanics. *Total annual research expenditures:* $4 million.
Dr. K. T. Ramesh, Chair, 410-516-7735, *Fax:* 410-516-7254, *E-mail:* ramesh@jhu.edu.
Application contact: Dr. Shiyi Chen, Chair, Graduate Admissions Committee, 410-516-7154, *Fax:* 410-516-7254, *E-mail:* megrad@titan.me.jhu.edu. *Web site:* http://www.me.jhu.edu/

Find an in-depth description at www.petersons.com/gradchannel.

■ LEHIGH UNIVERSITY

P.C. Rossin College of Engineering and Applied Science, Department of Mechanical Engineering and Mechanics, Bethlehem, PA 18015-3094

AWARDS Applied mathematics (MS, PhD); mechanical engineering (M Eng, MS, PhD); mechanics (M Eng, MS, PhD). Part-time programs available.

Faculty: 28 full-time (0 women).
Students: 64 full-time (7 women), 7 part-time; includes 2 minority (1 African American, 1 Hispanic American), 39 international. 577 applicants, 31% accepted, 12 enrolled. In 2001, 14 master's, 5 doctorates awarded. Terminal master's awarded for partial completion of doctoral program.
Degree requirements: For master's and doctorate, thesis/dissertation.
Entrance requirements: For master's and doctorate, TOEFL. *Application deadline:* For fall admission, 7/15; for spring admission, 12/1. Applications are processed on a rolling basis. *Application fee:* $50.
Expenses: Tuition: Part-time $468 per credit hour. Required fees: $200; $100 per semester. Tuition and fees vary according to program.
Financial support: In 2001–02, 5 fellowships with full and partial tuition reimbursements (averaging $10,380 per year), 27 research assistantships with full and partial tuition reimbursements (averaging $14,475 per year), 8 teaching assistantships with full and partial tuition reimbursements (averaging $12,330 per year) were awarded. Financial award application deadline: 1/15.
Faculty research: Thermofluids, dynamic systems, CAD/CAM. *Total annual research expenditures:* $2.5 million.
Dr. Charles R. Smith, Chairman, 610-758-4102, *Fax:* 610-758-6224, *E-mail:* crs1@lehigh.edu.
Application contact: Donna Reiss, Graduate Coordinator, 610-758-4139, *Fax:* 610-758-6224, *E-mail:* dmr1@lehigh.edu. *Web site:* http://www.lehigh.edu/~inmem/

Find an in-depth description at www.petersons.com/gradchannel.

■ LOUISIANA STATE UNIVERSITY AND AGRICULTURAL AND MECHANICAL COLLEGE

Graduate School, College of Engineering, Department of Civil and Environmental Engineering, Baton Rouge, LA 70803

AWARDS Environmental engineering (MSCE, PhD); geotechnical engineering (MSCE, PhD). Structural engineering and mechanics (MSCE, PhD); transportation engineering (MSCE, PhD); water resources (MSCE, PhD). Part-time programs available.

Faculty: 30 full-time (1 woman).

Louisiana State University and Agricultural and Mechanical College (continued)

Students: 78 full-time (19 women), 26 part-time (11 women); includes 4 minority (2 African Americans, 1 Hispanic American, 1 Native American), 67 international. Average age 29. 133 applicants, 41% accepted, 22 enrolled. In 2001, 15 master's, 7 doctorates awarded.
Degree requirements: For master's, thesis optional; for doctorate, one foreign language, thesis/dissertation.
Entrance requirements: For master's and doctorate, GRE General Test, TOEFL, minimum GPA of 3.0. *Application deadline:* For fall admission, 1/25 (priority date). Applications are processed on a rolling basis. *Application fee:* $25.
Expenses: Tuition, state resident: full-time $2,551. Tuition, nonresident: full-time $5,551. Required fees: $854. Part-time tuition and fees vary according to course load.
Financial support: In 2001–02, 5 fellowships (averaging $15,800 per year), 51 research assistantships with partial tuition reimbursements (averaging $12,089 per year), 2 teaching assistantships with partial tuition reimbursements (averaging $12,500 per year) were awarded. Career-related internships or fieldwork, institutionally sponsored loans, and scholarships/grants also available. Financial award application deadline: 3/1; financial award applicants required to submit FAFSA.
Faculty research: Solid waste management, electrokinetics, composite structures, transportation planning, river mechanics. *Total annual research expenditures:* $1.7 million.
Dr. George Z. Voyiadjis, Interim Chair/ Boyd Professor, 225-578-8668, *Fax:* 225-578-8652, *E-mail:* cegzv@lsu.edu. *Web site:* http://www.ce.lsu.edu/

■ MICHIGAN STATE UNIVERSITY

Graduate School, College of Engineering, Department of Chemical Engineering and Materials Science, East Lansing, MI 48824

AWARDS Chemical engineering (MS, PhD), including environmental toxicology (PhD); engineering mechanics (MS, PhD); materials science and engineering (MS, PhD); mechanics (PhD); metallurgy (MS, PhD). Part-time programs available.

Faculty: 22.
Students: 41 full-time (10 women), 5 part-time (1 woman); includes 9 minority (2 African Americans, 4 Asian Americans or Pacific Islanders, 3 Hispanic Americans), 21 international. Average age 26. 99 applicants, 14% accepted. In 2001, 8 master's, 6 doctorates awarded. Terminal master's awarded for partial completion of doctoral program.
Degree requirements: For doctorate, thesis/dissertation.

Entrance requirements: For master's, GRE, TOEFL, minimum GPA of 3.0; for doctorate, GRE, TOEFL. *Application deadline:* For fall admission, 1/15 (priority date); for spring admission, 11/1. Applications are processed on a rolling basis. *Application fee:* $30 ($40 for international students). Electronic applications accepted.
Expenses: Tuition, state resident: part-time $244 per credit hour. Tuition, nonresident: part-time $494 per credit hour. Required fees: $268 per semester. Tuition and fees vary according to course load, degree level and program.
Financial support: In 2001–02, 26 fellowships with tuition reimbursements (averaging $3,950 per year), 49 research assistantships with tuition reimbursements (averaging $14,052 per year), 19 teaching assistantships with tuition reimbursements (averaging $12,741 per year) were awarded. Financial award applicants required to submit FAFSA.
Faculty research: Agricultural bioprocessing, impact resistance of thermoplastic composite materials, durability of polymer composites. *Total annual research expenditures:* $989,316.
Dr. Martin Hawley, Interim Chair, 517-355-5135, *Fax:* 517-353-9842.
Application contact: Information Contact, 517-355-5135, *Fax:* 517-432-1105, *E-mail:* chems@egr.msu.edu. *Web site:* http://www.chems.msu.edu/

■ MICHIGAN TECHNOLOGICAL UNIVERSITY

Graduate School, College of Engineering, Department of Mechanical Engineering-Engineering Mechanics, Program in Engineering Mechanics, Houghton, MI 49931-1295

AWARDS MS. Part-time programs available.

Degree requirements: For master's, thesis.
Entrance requirements: For master's, GRE General Test, TOEFL. Electronic applications accepted. *Web site:* http://www.me.mtu.edu/

Find an in-depth description at www.petersons.com/gradchannel.

■ MISSISSIPPI STATE UNIVERSITY

College of Engineering, Department of Aerospace Engineering, Mississippi State, MS 39762

AWARDS Aerospace engineering (MS); engineering mechanics (MS). Part-time programs available.

Faculty: 15 full-time (0 women).
Students: 12 full-time (3 women), 5 part-time (1 woman), 5 international. Average age 26. 31 applicants, 94% accepted, 4 enrolled. In 2001, 1 degree awarded.
Degree requirements: For master's, thesis optional.

Entrance requirements: For master's, GRE General Test, TOEFL, minimum GPA of 2.75. *Application deadline:* For fall admission, 7/1; for spring admission, 11/1. Applications are processed on a rolling basis. *Application fee:* $25 for international students. Electronic applications accepted.
Expenses: Tuition, state resident: full-time $3,586; part-time $150 per credit hour. Tuition, nonresident: full-time $8,128; part-time $339 per credit hour. Tuition and fees vary according to course load and campus/location.
Financial support: In 2001–02, 11 research assistantships with partial tuition reimbursements (averaging $12,000 per year), 1 teaching assistantship with partial tuition reimbursement (averaging $12,000 per year) were awarded. Federal Work-Study, institutionally sponsored loans, and unspecified assistantships also available. Financial award applicants required to submit FAFSA.
Faculty research: Computational fluid dynamics, flight mechanics, aerodynamics, composite structures, prototype development. *Total annual research expenditures:* $5.1 million.
Dr. John C. McWhorter, Head, 662-325-3623, *Fax:* 662-325-7730, *E-mail:* mcwho@ae.msstate.edu.
Application contact: Jerry B. Inmon, Director of Admissions, 662-325-2224, *Fax:* 662-325-7360, *E-mail:* admit@admissions.msstate.edu. *Web site:* http://www.ae.msstate.edu/

■ NEW MEXICO INSTITUTE OF MINING AND TECHNOLOGY

Graduate Studies, Program in Engineering Science in Mechanics, Socorro, NM 87801

AWARDS MS.

Faculty: 5 full-time (0 women).
Students: 9 full-time (1 woman), 20 part-time; includes 2 minority (both Hispanic Americans), 3 international. Average age 25. 44 applicants, 73% accepted, 25 enrolled.
Degree requirements: For master's, thesis.
Entrance requirements: For master's, GRE General Test, TOEFL. *Application deadline:* For fall admission, 3/1 (priority date); for spring admission, 6/1. Applications are processed on a rolling basis. *Application fee:* $16 ($30 for international students).
Expenses: Tuition, state resident: part-time $1,084 per semester. Tuition, nonresident: part-time $4,367 per semester. Required fees: $429 per semester.
Financial support: In 2001–02, 2 research assistantships (averaging $13,505 per year), 4 teaching assistantships with full and partial tuition reimbursements (averaging $12,714 per year) were awarded. Fellowships, Federal Work-Study and institutionally sponsored loans also available.

Financial award application deadline: 3/1; financial award applicants required to submit CSS PROFILE or FAFSA.
Faculty research: Vibrations, fluid-structure interactions.
Dr. Harold C. Walling, Chairman, 505-835-5636, *E-mail:* hcwalli@nmt.edu.
Application contact: Dr. David B. Johnson, Dean of Graduate Studies, 505-835-5513, *Fax:* 505-835-5476, *E-mail:* graduate@nmt.edu. *Web site:* http://www.nmt.edu/~genengr

■ NORTH DAKOTA STATE UNIVERSITY

The Graduate School, College of Engineering and Architecture, Department of Mechanical Engineering and Applied Mechanics, Fargo, ND 58105

AWARDS MS. Part-time and evening/weekend programs available.

Faculty: 13 full-time (0 women).
Students: 10 full-time (0 women), 7 part-time, 6 international. Average age 25. 9 applicants, 100% accepted, 6 enrolled. In 2001, 3 degrees awarded.
Degree requirements: For master's, thesis.
Entrance requirements: For master's, TOEFL, minimum GPA of 3.0. *Application deadline:* For fall admission, 7/1 (priority date); for spring admission, 12/1 (priority date). Applications are processed on a rolling basis. *Application fee:* $35.
Expenses: Tuition, state resident: part-time $124 per credit. Tuition, nonresident: part-time $325 per credit. Required fees: $22 per credit. Tuition and fees vary according to reciprocity agreements.
Financial support: In 2001–02, 9 students received support, including research assistantships with full tuition reimbursements available (averaging $9,000 per year), teaching assistantships with full tuition reimbursements available (averaging $9,000 per year); career-related internships or fieldwork, Federal Work-Study, and institutionally sponsored loans also available. Financial award application deadline: 2/15.
Faculty research: Thermodynamics, finite element analysis, automotive systems, robotics.
Dr. Robert V. Pieri, Chair, 701-231-8671, *Fax:* 701-231-8913, *E-mail:* robert.pieri@ndsu.nodak.edu.

■ NORTHWESTERN UNIVERSITY

McCormick School of Engineering and Applied Science, Department of Civil and Environmental Engineering, Evanston, IL 60208

AWARDS Environmental engineering and science (MS, PhD); geotechnical engineering (MS, PhD); mechanics of materials and solids (MS, PhD); project management (MPM). Structural engineering and materials (MS,

PhD); theoretical and applied mechanics (MS, PhD); transportation systems analysis and planning (MS, PhD). MS and PhD admissions and degrees offered through The Graduate School. Part-time programs available.

Faculty: 26 full-time (3 women), 9 part-time/adjunct (2 women).
Students: 80 full-time (32 women), 1 part-time; includes 2 Asian Americans or Pacific Islanders, 1 Hispanic American, 38 international. 282 applicants, 7% accepted. In 2001, 20 master's, 14 doctorates awarded. Terminal master's awarded for partial completion of doctoral program.
Degree requirements: For master's, thesis (for some programs); for doctorate, thesis/dissertation.
Application deadline: For fall admission, 8/1.
Application fee: $50 ($55 for international students). Electronic applications accepted.
Expenses: Tuition: Full-time $26,526.
Financial support: In 2001–02, 10 fellowships with full tuition reimbursements (averaging $13,338 per year), 66 research assistantships with partial tuition reimbursements (averaging $18,000 per year), 7 teaching assistantships with full tuition reimbursements (averaging $13,329 per year) were awarded. Career-related internships or fieldwork, institutionally sponsored loans, and scholarships/grants also available. Financial award application deadline: 1/15; financial award applicants required to submit FAFSA.
Faculty research: Environmental engineering and science, geotechnics, mechanics of materials and solids, structural engineering and materials, transportation systems analysis and planning. *Total annual research expenditures:* $8.4 million.
Joseph L. Schofer, Chair, 847-491-3257, *Fax:* 847-491-4011, *E-mail:* j-schofer@northwestern.edu.
Application contact: Janet Soule, Academic Coordinator, 847-491-3176, *Fax:* 847-491-4011, *E-mail:* civil-info@northwestern.edu. *Web site:* http://www.civil.northwestern.edu/

Find an in-depth description at www.petersons.com/gradchannel.

■ NORTHWESTERN UNIVERSITY

McCormick School of Engineering and Applied Science, Program in Theoretical and Applied Mechanics, Evanston, IL 60208

AWARDS Fluid mechanics (MS, PhD). Solid mechanics (MS, PhD). Admissions and degrees offered through The Graduate School.

Faculty: 11 full-time (2 women).
Students: 8 full-time (2 women). Average age 27. 26 applicants, 23% accepted. In 2001, 5 doctorates awarded.
Degree requirements: For doctorate, thesis/dissertation.
Application deadline: For fall admission, 8/1.
Application fee: $50 ($55 for international students).

Expenses: Tuition: Full-time $26,526.
Financial support: In 2001–02, 1 fellowship with full tuition reimbursement (averaging $13,338 per year), 9 research assistantships with partial tuition reimbursements (averaging $16,285 per year), 1 teaching assistantship with full tuition reimbursement (averaging $12,843 per year) were awarded. Federal Work-Study and institutionally sponsored loans also available. Financial award application deadline: 1/15; financial award applicants required to submit FAFSA.
Faculty research: Composite materials, computational mechanics, fracture and damage mechanics, geophysics, nondestructive evaluation. *Total annual research expenditures:* $4 million.
Issac Daniel, Director, 847-491-5649, *Fax:* 847-491-5227, *E-mail:* imdaniel@northwestern.edu.
Application contact: Secretary, 847-491-3176, *Fax:* 847-491-4011, *E-mail:* k-kerwell@northwestern.edu. *Web site:* http://www.tam.northwestern.edu/

■ THE OHIO STATE UNIVERSITY

Graduate School, College of Engineering, Department of Mechanical Engineering, Program in Engineering Mechanics, Columbus, OH 43210

AWARDS MS, PhD.

Degree requirements: For master's, thesis optional; for doctorate, thesis/dissertation.
Entrance requirements: For master's and doctorate, GRE General Test (international applicants).

■ OLD DOMINION UNIVERSITY

College of Engineering and Technology, Program in Aerospace Engineering, Norfolk, VA 23529

AWARDS Aerospace engineering (ME, MS, PhD); aerospace engineering mechanics (ME, MS, PhD), including experimental methods (ME). Part-time and evening/weekend programs available. Postbaccalaureate distance learning degree programs offered (no on-campus study).

Faculty: 10 full-time (0 women).
Students: 42 full-time (3 women), 12 part-time (1 woman); includes 3 minority (1 African American, 2 Asian Americans or Pacific Islanders), 38 international. Average age 29. 55 applicants, 80% accepted. In 2001, 8 master's, 6 doctorates awarded.
Degree requirements: For master's, thesis, comprehensive exam; for doctorate, thesis/dissertation, candidacy exam.
Entrance requirements: For master's, minimum GPA of 3.0; for doctorate, minimum GPA of 3.25. *Application deadline:* For fall admission, 7/1; for spring admission, 10/1. Applications are processed on a rolling basis. *Application fee:* $30. Electronic applications accepted.

Old Dominion University (continued)

Expenses: Tuition, state resident: part-time $202 per credit. Tuition, nonresident: part-time $534 per credit. Required fees: $76 per semester.

Financial support: In 2001–02, 2 fellowships with tuition reimbursements (averaging $16,000 per year), 31 research assistantships with tuition reimbursements (averaging $15,000 per year) were awarded. Teaching assistantships, career-related internships or fieldwork, scholarships/grants, and tuition waivers (partial) also available. Support available to part-time students. Financial award application deadline: 2/15; financial award applicants required to submit FAFSA.

Faculty research: Computational fluid dynamics, experimental fluid dynamics, structural mechanics, dynamics and control, multidisciplinary problems. *Total annual research expenditures:* $1 million.
Dr. Brett Newman, Graduate Program Director, 757-683-5860, *Fax:* 757-683-3200, *E-mail:* aeroinfo@aero.odu.edu. *Web site:* http://www.odu.edu/aero/

■ OLD DOMINION UNIVERSITY

College of Engineering and Technology, Program in Mechanical Engineering, Norfolk, VA 23529

AWARDS Design manufacturing (ME); engineering mechanics (ME, MS, PhD); mechanical engineering (ME, MS, PhD). Part-time and evening/weekend programs available. Postbaccalaureate distance learning degree programs offered (no on-campus study).

Faculty: 13 full-time (0 women).
Students: 46 full-time (4 women), 58 part-time (4 women). Average age 28. 154 applicants, 90% accepted. In 2001, 32 master's, 2 doctorates awarded.
Degree requirements: For master's, thesis optional; for doctorate, thesis/dissertation, candidacy exam.
Entrance requirements: For master's, GRE, TOEFL, minimum GPA of 3.0; for doctorate, GRE, TOEFL. *Application deadline:* For fall admission, 7/1; for spring admission, 10/1. Applications are processed on a rolling basis. *Application fee:* $30. Electronic applications accepted.
Expenses: Tuition, state resident: part-time $202 per credit. Tuition, nonresident: part-time $534 per credit. Required fees: $76 per semester.
Financial support: In 2001–02, 61 students received support, including 2 fellowships (averaging $10,000 per year), 40 research assistantships with tuition reimbursements available (averaging $8,433 per year); teaching assistantships, career-related internships or fieldwork, institutionally sponsored loans, scholarships/grants, and tuition waivers (partial) also available. Support available to part-time students. Financial award application deadline: 2/15; financial award applicants required to submit FAFSA.

Faculty research: Computational applied mechanics, manufacturing, experimental stress analysis, systems dynamics and control, mechanical design, computational fluid dynamics, optimization. *Total annual research expenditures:* $1.5 million.
Dr. Jen-Kuang Huang, Graduate Program Director, 757-683-6363, *Fax:* 757-683-5344, *E-mail:* megpd@odu.edu. *Web site:* http://www.mem.odu.edu/

■ THE PENNSYLVANIA STATE UNIVERSITY UNIVERSITY PARK CAMPUS

Graduate School, College of Engineering, Department of Engineering Science and Mechanics, Program in Engineering Mechanics, State College, University Park, PA 16802-1503

AWARDS M Eng, MS.

Students: 20 full-time (3 women), 2 part-time. In 2001, 10 degrees awarded.
Entrance requirements: For master's, GRE General Test. *Application fee:* $45.
Expenses: Tuition, state resident: full-time $7,882; part-time $333 per credit. Tuition, nonresident: full-time $16,142; part-time $673 per credit. Required fees: $124 per semester.
Dr. Salik I Hayek, Chair, 814-865-4523.

■ THE PENNSYLVANIA STATE UNIVERSITY UNIVERSITY PARK CAMPUS

Graduate School, College of Engineering, Department of Engineering Science and Mechanics, Program in Engineering Science and Mechanics, State College, University Park, PA 16802-1503

AWARDS PhD.

Students: 56 full-time (11 women), 8 part-time (2 women).
Degree requirements: For doctorate, one foreign language, thesis/dissertation.
Entrance requirements: For doctorate, GRE General Test. *Application fee:* $45.
Expenses: Tuition, state resident: full-time $7,882; part-time $333 per credit. Tuition, nonresident: full-time $16,142; part-time $673 per credit. Required fees: $124 per semester.
Dr. Salik I Hayek, Chair, 814-865-4523.

■ RENSSELAER POLYTECHNIC INSTITUTE

Graduate School, School of Engineering, Department of Mechanical, Aerospace, and Nuclear Engineering, Program in Mechanics, Troy, NY 12180-3590

AWARDS M Eng, MS, PhD. Part-time and evening/weekend programs available.

Faculty: 29 full-time (2 women), 2 part-time/adjunct (0 women).
Students: 2 full-time (0 women), 1 part-time; includes 1 minority (Hispanic American), 1 international. 10 applicants, 10% accepted. In 2001, 1 master's, 1 doctorate awarded.
Degree requirements: For doctorate, thesis/dissertation.
Entrance requirements: For master's and doctorate, GRE, TOEFL. *Application deadline:* For fall admission, 1/15 (priority date). Applications are processed on a rolling basis. *Application fee:* $45. Electronic applications accepted.
Expenses: Tuition: Full-time $26,400; part-time $1,320 per credit hour. Required fees: $1,437.
Financial support: Fellowships, research assistantships, teaching assistantships, career-related internships or fieldwork, institutionally sponsored loans, and tuition waivers (partial) available. Financial award application deadline: 2/1.
Faculty research: Biomechanics, applied and theoretical mechanics, mechanics of materials, fluid mechanics. *Total annual research expenditures:* $2.5 million.
Application contact: Dr. Kevin C. Craig, Director, 518-276-6620, *Fax:* 518-276-4860, *E-mail:* craigk@rpi.edu. *Web site:* http://www.rpi.edu/dept/meaem/
Find an in-depth description at www.petersons.com/gradchannel.

■ RUTGERS, THE STATE UNIVERSITY OF NEW JERSEY, NEW BRUNSWICK

Graduate School, Program in Mechanics, New Brunswick, NJ 08901-1281

AWARDS MS, PhD. Part-time programs available. Terminal master's awarded for partial completion of doctoral program.

Degree requirements: For master's, qualifying exam, thesis optional; for doctorate, thesis/dissertation, qualifying exam.
Entrance requirements: For master's and doctorate, GRE General Test, GRE Subject Test (recommended), TOEFL.
Faculty research: Continuum mechanics, constitutive theory, thermodynamics, visolasticity, liquid crystal theory.

■ SAN DIEGO STATE UNIVERSITY

Graduate and Research Affairs, College of Engineering, Department of Aerospace Engineering and Engineering Mechanics, San Diego, CA 92182

AWARDS Aerospace engineering (MS); engineering mechanics (MS); engineering sciences and applied mechanics (PhD); flight dynamics (MS); fluid dynamics (MS).

Terminal master's awarded for partial completion of doctoral program.

Degree requirements: For doctorate, thesis/dissertation.

Entrance requirements: For master's, GRE General Test, TOEFL.

Faculty research: Organized structures in post-stall flow over wings/three dimensional separated flow, airfoil growth effect, probabilities, structural mechanics.

■ SOUTHERN ILLINOIS UNIVERSITY CARBONDALE

Graduate School, College of Engineering, Department of Civil Engineering and Mechanics, Carbondale, IL 62901-6806

AWARDS MS.

Faculty: 10 full-time (1 woman).
Students: 13 full-time (2 women), 19 part-time (3 women); includes 2 minority (1 African American, 1 Asian American or Pacific Islander), 7 international. Average age 26. 11 applicants, 55% accepted. In 2001, 17 degrees awarded.
Degree requirements: For master's, thesis, comprehensive exam.
Entrance requirements: For master's, TOEFL, minimum GPA of 2.7. *Application deadline:* Applications are processed on a rolling basis. *Application fee:* $20.
Expenses: Tuition, state resident: full-time $3,794; part-time $154 per hour. Tuition, nonresident: full-time $6,566; part-time $308 per hour. Required fees: $277 per hour.
Financial support: In 2001–02, 21 students received support, including 5 research assistantships with full tuition reimbursements available, 9 teaching assistantships with full tuition reimbursements available; fellowships with full tuition reimbursements available, Federal Work-Study, institutionally sponsored loans, and tuition waivers (full) also available. Support available to part-time students. Financial award application deadline: 7/1.
Faculty research: Composite materials, wastewater treatment, solid waste disposal, slurry transport, geotechnical engineering. *Total annual research expenditures:* $230,856. Dr. Bruce DeVantier, Interim Chair, 618-453-7819.

Find an in-depth description at www.petersons.com/gradchannel.

■ SOUTHERN ILLINOIS UNIVERSITY CARBONDALE

Graduate School, College of Engineering, Program in Engineering Sciences, Carbondale, IL 62901-6806

AWARDS Electrical systems (PhD); fossil energy (PhD); mechanics (PhD).

Faculty: 55 full-time (3 women), 3 part-time/adjunct (0 women).

Students: 22 full-time (3 women), 18 part-time (4 women); includes 2 minority (1 African American, 1 Asian American or Pacific Islander), 30 international. 31 applicants, 19% accepted. In 2001, 3 degrees awarded.
Degree requirements: For doctorate, thesis/dissertation.
Entrance requirements: For doctorate, GRE General Test, TOEFL, minimum GPA of 3.5. *Application fee:* $20.
Expenses: Tuition, state resident: full-time $3,794; part-time $154 per hour. Tuition, nonresident: full-time $6,566; part-time $308 per hour. Required fees: $277 per hour.
Financial support: In 2001–02, 13 students received support; fellowships with full tuition reimbursements available, research assistantships with full tuition reimbursements available, teaching assistantships with full tuition reimbursements available, Federal Work-Study, institutionally sponsored loans, and tuition waivers (full) available. Support available to part-time students.
Dr. Hasan Sevim, Interim Chairperson, 618-536-6637, *Fax:* 618-453-4235.

■ THE UNIVERSITY OF ALABAMA

Graduate School, College of Engineering, Department of Aerospace Engineering and Mechanics, Tuscaloosa, AL 35487

AWARDS MSAE, MSESM, PhD. Part-time programs available. Postbaccalaureate distance learning degree programs offered (no on-campus study).

Faculty: 12 full-time (1 woman).
Students: 21 full-time (2 women), 18 part-time (2 women); includes 3 minority (1 African American, 2 Asian Americans or Pacific Islanders), 22 international. Average age 28. 46 applicants, 46% accepted, 13 enrolled. In 2001, 13 master's, 3 doctorates awarded. Terminal master's awarded for partial completion of doctoral program.
Degree requirements: For master's, thesis or alternative; for doctorate, thesis/dissertation.
Entrance requirements: For master's and doctorate, GRE General Test. *Application deadline:* For fall admission, 7/6 (priority date). Applications are processed on a rolling basis. *Application fee:* $25.
Expenses: Tuition, state resident: full-time $3,292; part-time $183 per credit hour. Tuition, nonresident: full-time $8,912; part-time $495 per credit hour. Tuition and fees vary according to course load, campus/location and program.
Financial support: In 2001–02, 25 students received support, including 5 fellowships with full tuition reimbursements available, 12 research assistantships with full tuition reimbursements available, 8 teaching assistantships with full tuition reimbursements available; Federal Work-Study and institutionally sponsored loans

also available. Financial award application deadline: 7/6.
Faculty research: Flight simulation, advanced mechanical behavior in materials, fluid and solid computational mechanics, hypersonic aerodynamics, intelligent systems. *Total annual research expenditures:* $3.8 million.
Dr. Charles L. Karr, Associate Professor, Interim Head, 205-348-0066, *Fax:* 205-348-7240, *E-mail:* ckarr@coe.eng.ua.edu.
Application contact: Dr. Amnon Katz, Information Contact, 205-348-7300, *Fax:* 205-348-7240.

■ THE UNIVERSITY OF ARIZONA

Graduate College, College of Engineering and Mines, Department of Civil Engineering and Engineering Mechanics, Program in Engineering Mechanics, Tucson, AZ 85721

AWARDS MS, PhD. Part-time programs available.

Faculty: 3 full-time (0 women).
Students: 8 full-time (0 women), 3 part-time; includes 2 minority (both Asian Americans or Pacific Islanders), 5 international. Average age 34. 4 applicants, 75% accepted, 1 enrolled. In 2001, 1 master's, 3 doctorates awarded.
Degree requirements: For master's, thesis; for doctorate, thesis/dissertation, departmental qualifying exam.
Entrance requirements: For master's, TOEFL, minimum GPA of 3.0; for doctorate, TOEFL, minimum GPA of 3.5. *Application deadline:* For fall admission, 8/1. Applications are processed on a rolling basis. *Application fee:* $45.
Expenses: Tuition, state resident: full-time $2,490; part-time $436 per unit. Tuition, nonresident: full-time $10,300; part-time $436 per unit. Full-time tuition and fees vary according to degree level and program.
Financial support: Research assistantships, teaching assistantships available. Financial award application deadline: 3/1.
Faculty research: Constitutive modeling of solids and discontinuities, computational mechanics, fracture and composites stability, laboratory testing.
Dr. Juan B. Valdes, Department Head, 520-621-2266, *E-mail:* jvaldes@u.arizona.edu.
Application contact: Olivia Hanson, Graduate Coordinator, 520-621-2266, *Fax:* 520-621-2550, *E-mail:* ceem@engr.arizona.edu. *Web site:* http://w3.arizona.edu/~civil/

■ UNIVERSITY OF CALIFORNIA, BERKELEY

Graduate Division, College of Engineering, Department of Civil and Environmental Engineering, Berkeley, CA 94720-1500

AWARDS Construction engineering and management (M Eng, MS, D Eng, PhD);

University of California, Berkeley (continued)

environmental quality and environmental water resources engineering (M Eng, MS, D Eng, PhD); geotechnical engineering (M Eng, MS, D Eng, PhD). Structural engineering, mechanics and materials (M Eng, MS, D Eng, PhD); transportation engineering (M Eng, MS, D Eng, PhD).

Degree requirements: For master's, comprehensive exam or thesis (MS); for doctorate, thesis/dissertation, qualifying exam.
Entrance requirements: For master's, GRE General Test, minimum GPA of 3.0; for doctorate, GRE General Test, minimum GPA of 3.5.
Expenses: Tuition, nonresident: full-time $10,704. Required fees: $4,349.

Find an in-depth description at www.petersons.com/gradchannel.

■ UNIVERSITY OF CALIFORNIA, SAN DIEGO

Graduate Studies and Research, Department of Mechanical and Aerospace Engineering, Program in Applied Mechanics, La Jolla, CA 92093
AWARDS MS, PhD. Part-time programs available.

Degree requirements: For master's, comprehensive exam or thesis; for doctorate, thesis/dissertation, qualifying exam.
Entrance requirements: For master's and doctorate, GRE General Test, TOEFL, minimum GPA of 3.0.
Expenses: Tuition, nonresident: full-time $10,434. Required fees: $4,883.
Faculty research: Combustion engineering, environmental mechanics, magnetic recording, materials processing, computational fluid dynamics. *Web site:* http://www-ames.ucsd.edu/

Find an in-depth description at www.petersons.com/gradchannel.

■ UNIVERSITY OF CONNECTICUT

Graduate School, School of Engineering, Field of Applied Mechanics, Storrs, CT 06269
AWARDS PhD.

Degree requirements: For doctorate, thesis/dissertation.
Entrance requirements: For doctorate, GRE General Test.

■ UNIVERSITY OF CONNECTICUT

Graduate School, School of Engineering, Field of Fluid Dynamics, Storrs, CT 06269
AWARDS PhD.

Degree requirements: For doctorate, thesis/dissertation.
Entrance requirements: For doctorate, GRE General Test.

■ UNIVERSITY OF DAYTON

Graduate School, School of Engineering, Department of Civil Engineering, Program in Engineering Mechanics, Dayton, OH 45469-1300
AWARDS MSEM.

Students: In 2001, 1 degree awarded.
Degree requirements: For master's, thesis or alternative.
Entrance requirements: For master's, TOEFL. *Application deadline:* For fall admission, 8/1. Applications are processed on a rolling basis. *Application fee:* $30.
Expenses: Tuition: Full-time $5,436; part-time $453 per credit hour. Required fees: $50; $25 per term.
Dr. Joseph E. Saliba, Chairperson, 937-229-3847, *E-mail:* jsaliba@engr.udayton.edu.
Application contact: Dr. Donald L. Moon, Associate Dean, 937-229-2241, *Fax:* 937-229-2471, *E-mail:* dmoon@notes.udayton.edu.

■ UNIVERSITY OF FLORIDA

Graduate School, College of Engineering, Department of Aerospace Engineering, Mechanics, and Engineering Science, Program in Engineering Science and Engineering Mechanics, Gainesville, FL 32611
AWARDS ME, MS, PhD, Engr.

Degree requirements: For master's and Engr, thesis optional; for doctorate, thesis/dissertation.
Entrance requirements: For master's and doctorate, GRE General Test, TOEFL, minimum GPA of 3.0; for Engr, GRE General Test. Electronic applications accepted.
Expenses: Tuition, state resident: part-time $164 per hour. Tuition, nonresident: part-time $571 per hour. Tuition and fees vary according to course level and program.

■ UNIVERSITY OF FLORIDA

Graduate School, Graduate Engineering and Research Center (GERC), Gainesville, FL 32611
AWARDS Aerospace engineering (ME, MS, PhD, Engr); electrical and computer engineering (ME, MS, PhD, Engr); engineering mechanics (ME, MS, PhD, Engr); industrial and systems engineering (ME, MS, PhD, Engr). Part-time programs available. Postbaccalaureate distance learning degree programs offered. Terminal master's awarded for partial completion of doctoral program.

Degree requirements: For master's, thesis optional; for doctorate and Engr, thesis/dissertation.
Entrance requirements: For master's, GRE General Test, TOEFL, minimum GPA of 3.0; for doctorate, GRE General Test, written and oral qualifying exams, TOEFL, minimum GPA of 3.0, master's

degree in engineering; for Engr, GRE General Test, TOEFL, minimum GPA of 3.0, master's degree in engineering. Electronic applications accepted.
Expenses: Contact institution.
Faculty research: Aerodynamics, terradynamics, and propulsion; composite materials and stress analysis; optical processing of microwave signals and photonics; holography, radar, and communications. System and signal theory; digital signal processing. *Web site:* http://www.gerc.eng.ufl.edu/

■ UNIVERSITY OF ILLINOIS AT URBANA–CHAMPAIGN

Graduate College, College of Engineering, Department of Theoretical and Applied Mechanics, Champaign, IL 61820
AWARDS MS, PhD.

Faculty: 18 full-time.
Students: 50 full-time (4 women); includes 2 minority (1 Asian American or Pacific Islander, 1 Hispanic American), 36 international. 50 applicants, 20% accepted. In 2001, 4 master's, 11 doctorates awarded.
Degree requirements: For master's, thesis or alternative; for doctorate, thesis/dissertation.
Entrance requirements: For master's and doctorate, GRE General Test, TOEFL, minimum GPA of 3.0. *Application deadline:* For fall admission, 1/15. Applications are processed on a rolling basis. *Application fee:* $40 ($50 for international students). Electronic applications accepted.
Expenses: Tuition, state resident: part-time $3,227 per degree program. Tuition, nonresident: part-time $7,169 per degree program. Tuition and fees vary according to program.
Financial support: In 2001–02, 1 fellowship, 37 research assistantships, 9 teaching assistantships were awarded. Financial award application deadline: 2/15.
Faculty research: Solid mechanics and materials, acoustics, computational mechanics. *Total annual research expenditures:* $1.8 million.
Hassan Aref, Head, 217-333-2329, *Fax:* 217-244-5707.
Application contact: Barbara Kirts, Administrative Secretary, 217-333-0087, *Fax:* 217-244-5707, *E-mail:* b-kirts@uiuc.edu. *Web site:* http://www.tam.uiuc.edu/

Find an in-depth description at www.petersons.com/gradchannel.

UNIVERSITY OF MARYLAND, COLLEGE PARK

Graduate Studies and Research, A. James Clark School of Engineering, Department of Mechanical Engineering, College Park, MD 20742

AWARDS Electronic packaging and reliability (MS, PhD); manufacturing and design (MS, PhD); mechanics and materials (MS, PhD); thermal and fluid sciences (MS, PhD). Part-time and evening/weekend programs available. Postbaccalaureate distance learning degree programs offered.

Faculty: 69 full-time (6 women), 15 part-time/adjunct (2 women).
Students: 142 full-time (18 women), 67 part-time (5 women); includes 13 minority (5 African Americans, 6 Asian Americans or Pacific Islanders, 2 Hispanic Americans), 134 international. 519 applicants, 14% accepted, 40 enrolled. In 2001, 49 master's, 21 doctorates awarded.
Degree requirements: For master's, thesis optional; for doctorate, thesis/dissertation, qualifying exam.
Entrance requirements: For master's and doctorate, GRE General Test, minimum GPA of 3.0. *Application deadline:* For fall admission, 8/1; for spring admission, 12/1. Applications are processed on a rolling basis. *Application fee:* $50 ($70 for international students). Electronic applications accepted.
Expenses: Tuition, state resident: part-time $289 per credit hour. Tuition, nonresident: part-time $448 per credit hour. One-time fee: $436 part-time. Full-time tuition and fees vary according to course load, campus/location and program.
Financial support: In 2001–02, 5 fellowships with full tuition reimbursements (averaging $4,406 per year), 123 research assistantships with tuition reimbursements (averaging $14,539 per year), 36 teaching assistantships with tuition reimbursements (averaging $11,663 per year) were awarded. Federal Work-Study and scholarships/grants also available. Support available to part-time students. Financial award applicants required to submit FAFSA.
Faculty research: Decomposition-based design, powder metallurgy, injection molding, kinematic synthesis, electronic packaging, dynamic deformation and fracture, turbulent flow.
Dr. Avi Bar-Cohen, Chairman, 301-405-5294, *Fax:* 301-314-9477.
Application contact: Dr. James M. Wallace, Graduate Director, 301-405-4216.

UNIVERSITY OF MASSACHUSETTS LOWELL

Graduate School, College of Arts and Sciences, Department of Physics and Applied Physics, Program in Applied Physics, Lowell, MA 01854-2881

AWARDS Applied mechanics (PhD); applied physics (MS, PhD), including optical sciences (MS). Terminal master's awarded for partial completion of doctoral program.

Degree requirements: For master's, thesis; for doctorate, 2 foreign languages, thesis/dissertation.
Entrance requirements: For master's and doctorate, GRE General Test.
Find an in-depth description at www.petersons.com/gradchannel.

UNIVERSITY OF MINNESOTA, TWIN CITIES CAMPUS

Graduate School, Institute of Technology, Department of Aerospace Engineering and Mechanics, Minneapolis, MN 55455-0213

AWARDS Aerospace engineering (M Aero E, MS, PhD); mechanics (MS, PhD). Part-time programs available.

Faculty: 17 full-time (2 women).
Students: 65 full-time (12 women), 1 part-time, 44 international. Average age 24. 141 applicants, 57% accepted, 23 enrolled. In 2001, 7 master's, 2 doctorates awarded.
Degree requirements: For doctorate, thesis/dissertation. *Median time to degree:* Master's–2 years full-time; doctorate–5 years full-time.
Application deadline: For fall admission, 6/15; for spring admission, 10/15. Applications are processed on a rolling basis. *Application fee:* $50 ($55 for international students). Electronic applications accepted.
Expenses: Tuition, state resident: full-time $2,932; part-time $489 per credit. Tuition, nonresident: full-time $5,758; part-time $960 per credit. Part-time tuition and fees vary according to course load, program and reciprocity agreements.
Financial support: In 2001–02, 1 fellowship with full tuition reimbursement (averaging $13,500 per year), 43 research assistantships with full and partial tuition reimbursements (averaging $13,500 per year), 13 teaching assistantships with full and partial tuition reimbursements (averaging $13,500 per year) were awarded. Partial departmental scholarships also available. Financial award application deadline: 1/31.
Faculty research: Fluid mechanics, solid and continuum mechanics, computational mechanics, dynamical systems and controls. *Total annual research expenditures:* $4.5 million.
William L. Garrard, Head, 612-625-8000, *Fax:* 612-626-1558, *E-mail:* dept@aem.umn.edu.

Application contact: Ruth A. Robinson, Graduate Program Coordinator, 612-625-5000, *Fax:* 612-626-1558, *E-mail:* dept@aem.umn.edu. *Web site:* http://www.aem.umn.edu/
Find an in-depth description at www.petersons.com/gradchannel.

UNIVERSITY OF MISSOURI–ROLLA

Graduate School, School of Engineering, Department of Civil Engineering, Program in Fluid Mechanics, Rolla, MO 65409-0910

AWARDS MS, DE, PhD.

Degree requirements: For master's, thesis or alternative; for doctorate, thesis/dissertation.
Entrance requirements: For master's and doctorate, GRE General Test, TOEFL, minimum GPA of 3.0.

UNIVERSITY OF MISSOURI–ROLLA

Graduate School, School of Engineering, Department of Mechanical and Aerospace Engineering and Engineering Mechanics, Program in Engineering Mechanics, Rolla, MO 65409-0910

AWARDS MS, PhD. Part-time and evening/weekend programs available. Terminal master's awarded for partial completion of doctoral program.

Degree requirements: For master's, thesis (for some programs); for doctorate, thesis/dissertation.
Entrance requirements: For master's, GRE General Test, TOEFL, minimum GPA of 3.0; for doctorate, GRE General Test, TOEFL, minimum GPA of 3.5. Electronic applications accepted.
Faculty research: Composite materials, finite element analysis, smart structures, solid mechanics. *Web site:* http://www.maem.umr.edu/~grad/

UNIVERSITY OF NEBRASKA–LINCOLN

Graduate College, College of Engineering and Technology, Department of Engineering Mechanics, Lincoln, NE 68588

AWARDS Engineering (PhD); engineering mechanics (MS).

Faculty: 17.
Students: 8 (2 women) 6 international. Average age 31. 8 applicants, 25% accepted, 2 enrolled. In 2001, 4 degrees awarded.
Degree requirements: For master's, thesis optional; for doctorate, thesis/dissertation, comprehensive exam.
Entrance requirements: For master's and doctorate, GRE General Test, TOEFL.

University of Nebraska–Lincoln (continued)

Application deadline: For fall admission, 3/1 (priority date). Applications are processed on a rolling basis. *Application fee:* $35. Electronic applications accepted.

Expenses: Tuition, state resident: full-time $2,412; part-time $134 per credit. Tuition, nonresident: full-time $6,223; part-time $346 per credit. Tuition and fees vary according to course load.

Financial support: In 2001–02, 6 research assistantships, 1 teaching assistantship were awarded. Fellowships, Federal Work-Study, health care benefits, and unspecified assistantships also available. Support available to part-time students. Financial award application deadline: 2/15.

Faculty research: Polymer mechanics, piezoelectric materials, meshless methods, smart materials, fracture mechanics.
Dr. Lorraine Olson, Interim Chair, 402-472-2377, *Fax:* 402-472-8292. *Web site:* http://www.unl.edu/emhome/dept.html/

Find an in-depth description at www.petersons.com/gradchannel.

■ UNIVERSITY OF PENNSYLVANIA

School of Engineering and Applied Science, Department of Mechanical Engineering and Applied Mechanics, Philadelphia, PA 19104

AWARDS Applied mechanics (MSE, PhD); mechanical engineering (MSE, PhD). Part-time programs available.

Degree requirements: For master's, thesis optional; for doctorate, thesis/dissertation.

Entrance requirements: For master's and doctorate, TOEFL. Electronic applications accepted.

Faculty research: Heat transfer, fluid mechanics, energy conversion, solid mechanics, dynamics of mechanisms and robots. *Web site:* http://www.seas.upenn.edu/meam/

■ UNIVERSITY OF RHODE ISLAND

Graduate School, College of Engineering, Department of Mechanical Engineering and Applied Mechanics, Kingston, RI 02881

AWARDS Design/systems (MS, PhD); fluid mechanics (MS, PhD). Solid mechanics (MS, PhD); thermal sciences (MS, PhD).

Students: In 2001, 5 master's, 3 doctorates awarded.

Entrance requirements: For master's and doctorate, GRE General Test (international applicants). *Application fee:* $25.

Expenses: Tuition, state resident: full-time $3,756; part-time $209 per credit. Tuition, nonresident: full-time $10,774; part-time $599 per credit. Required fees: $1,586; $76

per credit. $76 per credit. One-time fee: $60 full-time.

■ UNIVERSITY OF SOUTHERN CALIFORNIA

Graduate School, School of Engineering, Program in Applied Mechanics, Los Angeles, CA 90089

AWARDS MS.

Degree requirements: For master's, thesis optional.

Entrance requirements: For master's, GRE General Test.

Expenses: Tuition: Full-time $25,060; part-time $844 per unit. Required fees: $473.

Find an in-depth description at www.petersons.com/gradchannel.

■ THE UNIVERSITY OF TENNESSEE

Graduate School, College of Engineering, Department of Mechanical and Aerospace Engineering and Engineering Science, Program in Engineering Science, Knoxville, TN 37996

AWARDS Applied artificial intelligence (MS); biomedical engineering (MS, PhD); composite materials (MS, PhD); computational mechanics (MS, PhD); engineering science (MS, PhD); fluid mechanics (MS, PhD); industrial engineering (PhD); optical engineering (MS, PhD); product development and manufacturing (MS). Solid mechanics (MS, PhD). Part-time programs available.

Students: 25 full-time (5 women), 16 part-time (2 women); includes 6 minority (2 African Americans, 2 Asian Americans or Pacific Islanders, 1 Hispanic American, 1 Native American), 9 international. 20 applicants, 70% accepted. In 2001, 6 master's, 6 doctorates awarded.

Degree requirements: For master's, thesis or alternative; for doctorate, thesis/dissertation.

Entrance requirements: For master's and doctorate, TOEFL, minimum GPA of 2.7. *Application deadline:* For fall admission, 2/1 (priority date). Applications are processed on a rolling basis. *Application fee:* $35. Electronic applications accepted.

Expenses: Tuition, state resident: full-time $4,280; part-time $233 per hour. Tuition, nonresident: full-time $12,066; part-time $666 per hour. Tuition and fees vary according to program.

Financial support: Career-related internships or fieldwork, Federal Work-Study, and institutionally sponsored loans available. Financial award application deadline: 2/1; financial award applicants required to submit FAFSA.

Application contact: Dr. Majid Keyhani, Graduate Representative, 865-974-4795, *E-mail:* keyhani@utk.edu.

■ THE UNIVERSITY OF TENNESSEE SPACE INSTITUTE

Graduate Programs, Program in Engineering Sciences and Mechanics, Tullahoma, TN 37388-9700

AWARDS Engineering sciences (MS, PhD); mechanics (MS, PhD).

Faculty: 8 full-time (1 woman), 2 part-time/adjunct (0 women).

Students: 7 full-time (0 women), 4 part-time (1 woman), 3 international. In 2001, 2 degrees awarded.

Degree requirements: For master's, thesis (for some programs); for doctorate, one foreign language, thesis/dissertation. *Application deadline:* Applications are processed on a rolling basis. *Application fee:* $35.

Expenses: Tuition, state resident: full-time $4,730; part-time $208 per semester hour. Tuition, nonresident: full-time $15,028; part-time $627 per semester hour. Required fees: $10 per semester hour. One-time fee: $35.

Financial support: Research assistantships, career-related internships or fieldwork, Federal Work-Study, and tuition waivers (full and partial) available. Financial award applicants required to submit FAFSA.
Dr. Roy Schulz, Degree Program Chairman, 931-393-7425, *Fax:* 931-393-7530, *E-mail:* rschuhlz@utsi.edu.

Application contact: Dr. Alfonso Pujol, Assistant Vice President and Dean for Student Affairs, 931-393-7432, *Fax:* 931-393-7346, *E-mail:* apujol@utsi.edu.

■ THE UNIVERSITY OF TEXAS AT AUSTIN

Graduate School, College of Engineering, Department of Aerospace Engineering and Engineering Mechanics, Program in Engineering Mechanics, Austin, TX 78712-1111

AWARDS MSE, PhD.

Students: 28 full-time (4 women), 2 part-time (1 woman), 27 international. 44 applicants, 36% accepted, 6 enrolled. In 2001, 2 master's, 2 doctorates awarded.

Degree requirements: For doctorate, one foreign language, thesis/dissertation, qualifying exam.

Entrance requirements: For master's and doctorate, GRE General Test. *Application deadline:* For fall admission, 1/15 (priority date); for spring admission, 10/1 (priority date). Applications are processed on a rolling basis. *Application fee:* $50 ($75 for international students).

Expenses: Tuition, state resident: full-time $3,159. Tuition, nonresident: full-time $6,957. Tuition and fees vary according to program.

Financial support: In 2001–02, 23 students received support, including 18 research assistantships with tuition reimbursements available, 13 teaching assistantships with tuition reimbursements

available; fellowships Financial award application deadline: 2/1.
Prof. Stelios Kyriakides, Graduate Advisor, 512-471-4167, *E-mail:* skk@ mail.utexas.edu.
Application contact: Nita Pollard, Graduate Coordinator, 512-471-7595, *Fax:* 512-471-3788, *E-mail:* ase.grad@ mail.ae.utexas.edu. *Web site:* http:// www.ae.utexas.edu/

Find an in-depth description at www.petersons.com/gradchannel.

■ UNIVERSITY OF VIRGINIA

School of Engineering and Applied Science, Department of Civil Engineering, Program in Applied Mechanics, Charlottesville, VA 22903

AWARDS MAM, MS. Part-time programs available.

Faculty: 5 full-time (0 women).
Students: 4 full-time (2 women). Average age 25. 15 applicants, 47% accepted, 3 enrolled. In 2001, 2 degrees awarded.
Degree requirements: For master's, thesis (for some programs).
Entrance requirements: For master's, GRE General Test. *Application deadline:* For fall admission, 2/1 (priority date); for spring admission, 8/1 (priority date). Applications are processed on a rolling basis. *Application fee:* $40. Electronic applications accepted.
Expenses: Tuition, state resident: full-time $3,988. Tuition, nonresident: full-time $17,078. Required fees: $1,190.
Financial support: In 2001–02, 4 fellowships with full tuition reimbursements (averaging $17,000 per year), 4 research assistantships with full tuition reimbursements (averaging $17,000 per year), 4 teaching assistantships with full tuition reimbursements (averaging $17,000 per year) were awarded. Financial award application deadline: 2/1.
Faculty research: Fluid mechanics, mechanics of composites, damage mechanics, finite element analysis, shell theory. *Total annual research expenditures:* $150,000.
Dr. Thomas T. Baber, Associate Professor, 434-924-7464, *Fax:* 434-982-2951, *E-mail:* ttb@virginia.edu.

■ UNIVERSITY OF WISCONSIN–MADISON

Graduate School, College of Engineering, Department of Engineering Physics, Madison, WI 53706-1380

AWARDS Engineering mechanics (MS, PhD); nuclear engineering and engineering physics (MS, PhD). Part-time programs available. Postbaccalaureate distance learning degree programs offered (minimal on-campus study).

Faculty: 24 full-time (2 women), 4 part-time/adjunct (0 women).
Students: 62 full-time (8 women), 2 part-time. Average age 25. 125 applicants, 20% accepted. In 2001, 12 master's, 9 doctorates awarded. Terminal master's awarded for partial completion of doctoral program.
Degree requirements: For master's, thesis optional; for doctorate, thesis/ dissertation.
Entrance requirements: For master's and doctorate, GRE General Test, minimum GPA of 3.0 in last 60 hours, appropriate bachelor's degree. *Application deadline:* For fall admission, 1/15 (priority date). Applications are processed on a rolling basis. *Application fee:* $45. Electronic applications accepted.
Expenses: Tuition, state resident: full-time $7,361; part-time $399 per credit. Tuition, nonresident: full-time $20,499; part-time $1,282 per credit. Required fees: $34 per credit. Full-time tuition and fees vary according to course load, program, reciprocity agreements and student level.
Financial support: In 2001–02, 47 students received support, including 4 fellowships with full tuition reimbursements available (averaging $17,400 per year), 34 research assistantships with full tuition reimbursements available (averaging $15,792 per year), 9 teaching assistantships with full tuition reimbursements available (averaging $15,800 per year); career-related internships or fieldwork, Federal Work-Study, and institutionally sponsored loans also available. Support available to part-time students. Financial award application deadline: 1/15.
Faculty research: Fission reactor engineering and safety, plasma physics and fusion technology, plasma processing and ion implantation, applied superconductivity and cryogenics, engineering mechanics and astronautics. *Total annual research expenditures:* $6.5 million.
Dr. Michael L. Corradini, Chair, 608-263-1646, *Fax:* 608-263-7451, *E-mail:* corradini@engr.wisc.edu. *Web site:* http:// www.engr.wisc.edu/ep/

Find an in-depth description at www.petersons.com/gradchannel.

■ VIRGINIA POLYTECHNIC INSTITUTE AND STATE UNIVERSITY

Graduate School, College of Engineering, Department of Engineering Science and Mechanics, Blacksburg, VA 24061

AWARDS Engineering mechanics (M Eng, MS, PhD). Postbaccalaureate distance learning degree programs offered (minimal on-campus study).

Faculty: 30 full-time (0 women), 12 part-time/adjunct (1 woman).

Students: 75 full-time (9 women), 13 part-time (3 women); includes 5 minority (1 African American, 2 Asian Americans or Pacific Islanders, 2 Hispanic Americans), 42 international. Average age 26. 65 applicants, 83% accepted, 24 enrolled. In 2001, 16 master's, 13 doctorates awarded. Terminal master's awarded for partial completion of doctoral program.
Degree requirements: For master's, thesis optional; for doctorate, thesis/ dissertation.
Entrance requirements: For master's and doctorate, GRE General Test, TOEFL. *Application deadline:* For fall admission, 12/1 (priority date). Applications are processed on a rolling basis. *Application fee:* $45. Electronic applications accepted.
Expenses: Tuition, state resident: part-time $241 per hour. Tuition, nonresident: part-time $406 per hour. Tuition and fees vary according to program.
Financial support: In 2001–02, 19 fellowships, 50 research assistantships with full tuition reimbursements (averaging $13,000 per year), 25 teaching assistantships with full tuition reimbursements (averaging $13,000 per year) were awarded. Career-related internships or fieldwork, Federal Work-Study, institutionally sponsored loans, tuition waivers (full and partial), and unspecified assistantships also available. Support available to part-time students. Financial award application deadline: 4/1.
Faculty research: Solid mechanics and materials, fluid mechanics, dynamics and vibrations, composite materials, computational mechanics and finite element methods. *Total annual research expenditures:* $6.5 million.
Dr. Edmund G. Henneke, Head, 540-231-6651, *Fax:* 540-231-4574, *E-mail:* henneke@vt.edu.
Application contact: Loretta M. Tickle, Graduate Records Administrator, 540-231-6743, *Fax:* 540-231-4574, *E-mail:* ltickle@ vt.edu. *Web site:* http://www.esm.vt.edu/ esm.html

Find an in-depth description at www.petersons.com/gradchannel.

■ YALE UNIVERSITY

Graduate School of Arts and Sciences, Programs in Engineering and Applied Science, Department of Mechanical Engineering, New Haven, CT 06520

AWARDS Applied mechanics and mechanical engineering (M Phil, MS, PhD). Terminal master's awarded for partial completion of doctoral program.

Degree requirements: For doctorate, thesis/dissertation, exam.
Entrance requirements: For master's and doctorate, GRE General Test, TOEFL.

Ocean Engineering

OCEAN ENGINEERING

■ FLORIDA ATLANTIC UNIVERSITY

College of Engineering, Department of Ocean Engineering, Program in Ocean Engineering, Boca Raton, FL 33431-0991

AWARDS MS, PhD. Part-time and evening/weekend programs available.

Faculty: 14 full-time (0 women), 3 part-time/adjunct (0 women).
Students: 40 full-time (10 women), 7 part-time; includes 4 minority (2 African Americans, 2 Hispanic Americans), 29 international. Average age 27. 55 applicants, 82% accepted, 25 enrolled. In 2001, 27 degrees awarded. Terminal master's awarded for partial completion of doctoral program.
Degree requirements: For master's, thesis (for some programs); for doctorate, thesis/dissertation, qualifying exam.
Entrance requirements: For master's and doctorate, GRE General Test, TOEFL, minimum GPA of 3.0. *Application deadline:* For fall admission, 3/1 (priority date); for spring admission, 7/1. Applications are processed on a rolling basis. *Application fee:* $20.
Expenses: Tuition, state resident: full-time $3,098; part-time $172 per credit. Tuition, nonresident: full-time $10,427; part-time $579 per credit.
Financial support: In 2001–02, 44 research assistantships were awarded; career-related internships or fieldwork, Federal Work-Study, and unspecified assistantships also available. Financial award applicants required to submit FAFSA.
Faculty research: Marine materials and corrosion, marine vehicles, autonomous underwater vehicles, acoustics and vibrations, hydrodynamics.
Application contact: Patricia Capozziello, Graduate Admissions Coordinator, 561-297-2694, *Fax:* 561-297-2659, *E-mail:* capozzie@fau.edu. *Web site:* http://www.oe.fau.edu/

■ FLORIDA ATLANTIC UNIVERSITY, FT. LAUDERDALE CAMPUS

College of Engineering, Programs in Ocean Engineering, Ft. Lauderdale, FL 33301

AWARDS MS, PhD.

■ FLORIDA INSTITUTE OF TECHNOLOGY

Graduate Programs, College of Engineering, Department of Marine and Environmental Systems, Program in Ocean Engineering, Melbourne, FL 32901-6975

AWARDS MS, PhD. Part-time programs available.

Students: Average age 29.
Degree requirements: For master's, thesis optional; for doctorate, thesis/dissertation, departmental qualifying exams, comprehensive exam.
Entrance requirements: For master's, minimum GPA of 3.0; for doctorate, minimum GPA of 3.3, resumé. *Application deadline:* Applications are processed on a rolling basis. Electronic applications accepted.
Expenses: Tuition: Part-time $650 per credit.
Financial support: Research assistantships with full and partial tuition reimbursements, teaching assistantships with full and partial tuition reimbursements, career-related internships or fieldwork and tuition remissions available. Financial award application deadline: 3/1; financial award applicants required to submit FAFSA.
Faculty research: Underwater technology, materials and structures, coastal processes and engineering, marine vehicles and ocean systems, naval architecture. *Total annual research expenditures:* $645,441.
Dr. Andrew Zborowski, Chair, 321-674-7304, *Fax:* 321-674-7212, *E-mail:* zborowsk@fit.edu.
Application contact: Carolyn P. Farrior, Director of Graduate Admissions, 321-674-7118, *Fax:* 321-723-9468, *E-mail:* cfarrior@fit.edu. *Web site:* http://www.fit.edu/

Find an in-depth description at www.petersons.com/gradchannel.

■ MASSACHUSETTS INSTITUTE OF TECHNOLOGY

School of Engineering, Department of Ocean Engineering, Cambridge, MA 02139-4307

AWARDS Naval architecture and marine engineering (SM); naval engineering (Naval E); ocean engineering (M Eng, SM, PhD, Sc D, Ocean E); ocean systems management (SM).

Faculty: 14 full-time (0 women).
Students: 102 full-time (13 women); includes 2 minority (1 Asian American or Pacific Islander, 1 Hispanic American), 48 international. Average age 28. 92 applicants, 52% accepted, 35 enrolled. In 2001, 32 master's, 14 doctorates awarded. Terminal master's awarded for partial completion of doctoral program.
Degree requirements: For master's, thesis/dissertation; for doctorate, thesis/dissertation, comprehensive exam.
Entrance requirements: For master's and doctorate, GRE General Test, TOEFL. *Application deadline:* For fall admission, 1/15 (priority date); for spring admission, 11/1. *Application fee:* $60. Electronic applications accepted.
Expenses: Tuition: Full-time $26,960. Full-time tuition and fees vary according to program.
Financial support: In 2001–02, 77 students received support, including 18 fellowships, 34 research assistantships, 7 teaching assistantships; career-related internships or fieldwork, Federal Work-Study, institutionally sponsored loans, scholarships/grants, health care benefits, and unspecified assistantships also available. Financial award application deadline: 1/15; financial award applicants required to submit FAFSA.
Faculty research: Computer-aided engineering, marine hydrodynamics, marine resource and environmental management, ocean instrumentation and measurement for environmental monitoring, ocean-related acoustics. *Total annual research expenditures:* $6.1 million.
Dr. C. Chryssostomidis, Head, 617-253-4330, *Fax:* 617-258-5730, *E-mail:* chrys@deslab.mit.edu.
Application contact: Tammy Lynch, Admissions Coordinator, 617-258-6157. *Web site:* http://oe.mit.edu/

Find an in-depth description at www.petersons.com/gradchannel.

■ OREGON STATE UNIVERSITY

Graduate School, College of Engineering, Department of Civil, Construction, and Environmental Engineering, Program in Ocean Engineering, Corvallis, OR 97331

AWARDS M Oc E. Part-time programs available.

Degree requirements: For master's, thesis or alternative.
Entrance requirements: For master's, GRE General Test, TOEFL, minimum GPA of 3.0 in last 90 hours. *Application deadline:* For fall admission, 3/1 (priority date). *Application fee:* $50.
Expenses: Tuition, area resident: Full-time $15,933. Tuition, state resident: full-time $28,937.
Financial support: Fellowships, research assistantships, teaching assistantships, career-related internships or fieldwork and institutionally sponsored loans available.

Support available to part-time students. Financial award application deadline: 2/1. **Faculty research:** Beach erosion and coastal protection, loads on sea-based structures, ocean wave mechanics, wave forces on structures, breakwater behavior. Robert T. Hudspeth, Director, 541-737-6883, *Fax:* 541-737-0485, *E-mail:* robert.hudspeth@orst.edu.

■ STEVENS INSTITUTE OF TECHNOLOGY

Graduate School, Charles V. Schaefer Jr. School of Engineering, Department of Civil, Environmental, and Ocean Engineering, Program in Maritime Systems, Hoboken, NJ 07030

AWARDS M Eng.

■ STEVENS INSTITUTE OF TECHNOLOGY

Graduate School, Charles V. Schaefer Jr. School of Engineering, Department of Civil, Environmental, and Ocean Engineering, Program in Ocean Engineering, Hoboken, NJ 07030

AWARDS M Eng, PhD.

Degree requirements: For master's, thesis optional; for doctorate, variable foreign language requirement, thesis/dissertation.
Entrance requirements: For master's, TOEFL; for doctorate, GRE, TOEFL. Electronic applications accepted.
Expenses: Tuition: Full-time $13,950; part-time $775 per credit. Required fees: $180. One-time fee: $180 part-time. Full-time tuition and fees vary according to degree level and program.
Faculty research: Estuarine oceanography, hydrodynamic and environmental processes, wave/ship interaction.

■ TEXAS A&M UNIVERSITY

College of Engineering, Department of Civil Engineering, Program in Ocean Engineering, College Station, TX 77843

AWARDS M Eng, MS, D Eng, PhD. D Eng offered through the College of Engineering.

Students: 40, 20 international. Average age 29. 49 applicants, 57% accepted. In 2001, 6 master's, 4 doctorates awarded.
Degree requirements: For master's, thesis (MS); for doctorate, dissertation (PhD), internship (D Eng).
Entrance requirements: For master's and doctorate, GRE General Test, TOEFL. *Application fee:* $50 ($75 for international students).
Expenses: Tuition, state resident: full-time $11,872. Tuition, nonresident: full-time $17,892.
Financial support: Fellowships, research assistantships, teaching assistantships available. Financial award application deadline:

4/15; financial award applicants required to submit FAFSA.
Faculty research: Wave-structure interaction, marine mining and dredging, offshore pipelines.
Dr. Billy L. Edge, Head, 979-845-4515, *Fax:* 979-862-2800, *E-mail:* ce-grad@ tamu.edu.
Application contact: Dr. Hamm-Ching Chen, Information Contact, 979-845-2498, *Fax:* 979-862-2800, *E-mail:* ce-grad@ tamu.edu. *Web site:* http:// www.civil.tamu.edu/

■ UNIVERSITY OF CALIFORNIA, BERKELEY

Graduate Division, Group in Ocean Engineering, Berkeley, CA 94720-1500

AWARDS M Eng, MS, D Eng, PhD.

Degree requirements: For doctorate, thesis/dissertation.
Entrance requirements: For master's and doctorate, GRE General Test, minimum GPA of 3.0.
Expenses: Tuition, nonresident: full-time $10,704. Required fees: $4,349. *Web site:* http://www.oe.berkeley.edu/

Find an in-depth description at www.petersons.com/gradchannel.

■ UNIVERSITY OF CALIFORNIA, SAN DIEGO

Graduate Studies and Research, Department of Electrical and Computer Engineering, La Jolla, CA 92093

AWARDS Applied ocean science (MS, PhD); applied physics (MS, PhD); communication theory and systems (MS, PhD); computer engineering (MS, PhD); electrical engineering (M Eng); electronic circuits and systems (MS, PhD); intelligent systems, robotics and control (MS, PhD); photonics (MS, PhD). Signal and image processing (MS, PhD).

Faculty: 35.
Students: 334 (44 women). 1,149 applicants, 20% accepted, 114 enrolled. In 2001, 51 master's, 12 doctorates awarded.
Entrance requirements: For master's and doctorate, GRE General Test. *Application deadline:* For fall admission, 1/12. *Application fee:* $40. Electronic applications accepted.
Expenses: Tuition, nonresident: full-time $10,434. Required fees: $4,883.
Charles Tu, Chair.
Application contact: Graduate Coordinator, 858-534-6606.

■ UNIVERSITY OF CALIFORNIA, SAN DIEGO

Graduate Studies and Research, Department of Mechanical and Aerospace Engineering, Program in Applied Ocean Science, La Jolla, CA 92093

AWARDS MS, PhD. Part-time programs available.

Degree requirements: For master's, comprehensive exam or thesis; for doctorate, thesis/dissertation, qualifying exam.
Entrance requirements: For master's and doctorate, GRE General Test, TOEFL, minimum GPA of 3.0.
Expenses: Tuition, nonresident: full-time $10,434. Required fees: $4,883. *Web site:* http://www-ames.ucsd.edu/

Find an in-depth description at www.petersons.com/gradchannel.

■ UNIVERSITY OF CONNECTICUT

Graduate School, School of Engineering, Department of Mechanical Engineering, Field of Ocean Engineering, Storrs, CT 06269

AWARDS MS, PhD. Terminal master's awarded for partial completion of doctoral program.

Degree requirements: For master's, thesis or alternative.
Entrance requirements: For master's, GRE General Test, GRE Subject Test, TOEFL.

■ UNIVERSITY OF DELAWARE

College of Engineering, Department of Civil and Environmental Engineering, Program in Ocean Engineering, Newark, DE 19716

AWARDS MAS, MCE, PhD. Terminal master's awarded for partial completion of doctoral program.

Degree requirements: For master's and doctorate, thesis/dissertation.
Entrance requirements: For master's and doctorate, GRE General Test, TOEFL.
Expenses: Tuition, state resident: full-time $4,770; part-time $265 per credit. Tuition, nonresident: full-time $13,860; part-time $770 per credit. Required fees: $414.
Faculty research: Shoreline erosion, pollution of estuaries, offshore and near-shore wave motions, water and wave water mechanics, theoretical and experimental analysis.

Find an in-depth description at www.petersons.com/gradchannel.

■ UNIVERSITY OF FLORIDA

Graduate School, College of Engineering, Department of Civil and Coastal Engineering, Program in Coastal and Oceanographic Engineering, Gainesville, FL 32611

AWARDS ME, MS, PhD, Engr.

Degree requirements: For master's and Engr, thesis optional; for doctorate, thesis/dissertation.
Entrance requirements: For master's and doctorate, GRE General Test, TOEFL, minimum GPA of 3.0; for Engr, GRE General Test. Electronic applications accepted.
Expenses: Tuition, state resident: part-time $164 per hour. Tuition, nonresident: part-time $571 per hour. Tuition and fees vary according to course level and program.
Faculty research: Coastal processes, ocean process, coastal structures, ocean structure, wave forces. *Web site:* http://www.coastal.ufl.edu/

■ UNIVERSITY OF HAWAII AT MANOA

Graduate Division, School of Ocean and Earth Science and Technology, Department of Ocean and Resources Engineering, Honolulu, HI 96822

AWARDS MS, PhD.

Faculty: 16 full-time (2 women), 4 part-time/adjunct (0 women).
Students: 17 full-time (4 women), 5 part-time (1 woman); includes 3 Asian Americans or Pacific Islanders, 1 Native American. Average age 33. 102 applicants, 25% accepted, 12 enrolled. In 2001, 3 degrees awarded.
Degree requirements: For master's and doctorate, thesis/dissertation, exams. *Median time to degree:* Doctorate–4 years full-time.
Entrance requirements: For master's and doctorate, GRE General Test, TOEFL. *Application deadline:* For fall admission, 3/1; for spring admission, 9/1. *Application fee:* $25 ($50 for international students).
Expenses: Tuition, state resident: full-time $2,160; part-time $1,980 per year. Tuition, nonresident: full-time $5,190; part-time $4,829 per year.
Financial support: In 2001–02, 12 students received support, including 12 research assistantships (averaging $16,607 per year), 2 teaching assistantships (averaging $15,003 per year); institutionally sponsored loans and tuition waivers (full) also available. Financial award application deadline: 3/1.
Faculty research: Coastal and harbor engineering, near shore environmental ocean engineering, marine structures/naval architecture. *Total annual research expenditures:* $436,100.

Alexander Malahoff, Chairperson, 808-956-8765, *Fax:* 808-956-3498, *E-mail:* ralph@soest.hawaii.edu.
Application contact: Kwok Fal Cheung, Graduate Chairperson, 808-956-3485, *Fax:* 808-956-3498, *E-mail:* cheung@hawaii.edu. *Web site:* http://www.oceaneng.eng.hawaii.edu/

■ UNIVERSITY OF MIAMI

Graduate School, Rosenstiel School of Marine and Atmospheric Science, Division of Applied Marine Physics, Coral Gables, FL 33124

AWARDS Applied marine physics (MS, PhD), including coastal ocean circulation dynamics, ocean acoustics and geoacoustics (PhD), small-scale ocean surface dynamics and air-sea interaction physics (PhD); ocean engineering (MS). Part-time programs available.

Faculty: 11 full-time (0 women), 14 part-time/adjunct (3 women).
Students: 11 full-time (3 women), 6 international. Average age 30. 15 applicants, 47% accepted, 4 enrolled. Terminal master's awarded for partial completion of doctoral program.
Degree requirements: For master's and doctorate, thesis/dissertation, comprehensive exam, registration.
Entrance requirements: For master's and doctorate, GRE General Test, TOEFL. *Application deadline:* For fall admission, 1/1 (priority date). Applications are processed on a rolling basis. *Application fee:* $50. Electronic applications accepted.
Expenses: Tuition: Part-time $960 per credit hour. Required fees: $85 per semester. Tuition and fees vary according to program.
Financial support: In 2001–02, 8 students received support, including 1 fellowship with tuition reimbursement available (averaging $18,000 per year), 5 research assistantships with tuition reimbursements available (averaging $18,000 per year), 2 teaching assistantships with tuition reimbursements available (averaging $18,000 per year); institutionally sponsored loans also available. Financial award application deadline: 3/1; financial award applicants required to submit FAFSA. *Total annual research expenditures:* $2.5 million.
Dr. Michael G. Brown, Chair, 305-361-4640, *E-mail:* mbrown@rsmas.miami.edu.
Application contact: Dr. Frank Millero, Associate Dean, 305-361-4155, *Fax:* 305-361-4771, *E-mail:* gso@rsmas.miami.edu. *Web site:* http://www.rsmas.miami.edu/

■ UNIVERSITY OF MICHIGAN

Horace H. Rackham School of Graduate Studies, College of Engineering, Department of Naval Architecture and Marine Engineering, Ann Arbor, MI 48109

AWARDS Concurrent marine design (M Eng); naval architecture and marine engineering

(MS, MSE, PhD, Mar Eng, Nav Arch). Part-time programs available.

Faculty: 12 full-time (2 women), 9 part-time/adjunct (0 women).
Students: 51 full-time (5 women), 4 part-time; includes 3 minority (2 Asian Americans or Pacific Islanders, 1 Hispanic American), 35 international. Average age 28. 75 applicants, 80% accepted, 50 enrolled. In 2001, 21 master's, 6 doctorates awarded. Terminal master's awarded for partial completion of doctoral program.
Degree requirements: For master's, thesis (for some programs); for doctorate, thesis/dissertation, oral defense of dissertation, preliminary exams (written and oral); for other advanced degree, thesis, oral defense of thesis, comprehensive exam.
Entrance requirements: For master's, GRE General Test (financial award applicants only); TOEFL or Michigan English Language Assessment Battery; for doctorate, GRE General Test, master's degree; for other advanced degree, GRE General Test. *Application deadline:* For fall admission, 2/1. Applications are processed on a rolling basis. *Application fee:* $55. Electronic applications accepted.
Financial support: In 2001–02, 17 students received support, including 3 fellowships with full tuition reimbursements available (averaging $12,832 per year), 15 research assistantships with full tuition reimbursements available (averaging $10,972 per year), 2 teaching assistantships with full tuition reimbursements available (averaging $10,972 per year); career-related internships or fieldwork, Federal Work-Study, institutionally sponsored loans, scholarships/grants, and unspecified assistantships also available. Financial award application deadline: 2/1.
Faculty research: Marine mechanics including hydrodynamics, structures, marine environmental engineering, marine design analysis, concurrent marine design. *Total annual research expenditures:* $5.3 million.
Dr. Michael M. Bernitsas, Chair, 734-936-7636, *Fax:* 734-936-8820, *E-mail:* kdrake@engin.umich.edu.
Application contact: Sandra Schippers Miller, Graduate Program Coordinator, 734-936-0566, *Fax:* 734-936-8820, *E-mail:* sschippe@engin.umich.edu. *Web site:* http://www.engin.umich.edu/dept/name

■ UNIVERSITY OF NEW HAMPSHIRE

Graduate School, College of Engineering and Physical Sciences, Department of Ocean Engineering, Durham, NH 03824

AWARDS Ocean engineering (MS, PhD); ocean mapping (MS).

Faculty: 13 full-time.
Students: Average age 32. 6 applicants, 100% accepted, 2 enrolled. In 2001, 4 master's, 1 doctorate awarded.

Degree requirements: For master's, thesis.
Application deadline: For fall admission, 4/1 (priority date); for winter admission, 12/1. Applications are processed on a rolling basis. *Application fee:* $50. Electronic applications accepted.
Expenses: Tuition, state resident: full-time $6,300; part-time $350 per credit. Tuition, nonresident: full-time $15,720; part-time $643 per credit. Required fees: $560; $280 per term. One-time fee: $15 part-time. Tuition and fees vary according to course load.
Financial support: In 2001–02, 2 research assistantships were awarded; teaching assistantships, Federal Work-Study, scholarships/grants, and tuition waivers (full and partial) also available. Support available to part-time students. Financial award application deadline: 2/15.
Dr. Kenneth Baldwin, Chairperson, 603-862-1898, *E-mail:* kcb@christa.unh.edu.

■ UNIVERSITY OF RHODE ISLAND

Graduate School, College of Engineering, Department of Ocean Engineering, Kingston, RI 02881

AWARDS MS, PhD.

Students: In 2001, 5 master's, 1 doctorate awarded.
Application deadline: For fall admission, 4/15 (priority date). Applications are processed on a rolling basis. *Application fee:* $35.
Expenses: Tuition, state resident: full-time $3,756; part-time $209 per credit. Tuition, nonresident: full-time $10,774; part-time $599 per credit. Required fees: $1,586; $76 per credit. $76 per credit. One-time fee: $60 full-time.
Dr. Malcolm Spaulding, Chairman.

■ UNIVERSITY OF SOUTHERN CALIFORNIA

Graduate School, School of Engineering, Department of Civil Engineering, Program in Ocean Engineering, Los Angeles, CA 90089

AWARDS MS.

Degree requirements: For master's, thesis optional.
Entrance requirements: For master's, GRE General Test.

Expenses: Tuition: Full-time $25,060; part-time $844 per unit. Required fees: $473.

■ VIRGINIA POLYTECHNIC INSTITUTE AND STATE UNIVERSITY

Graduate School, College of Engineering, Department of Aerospace and Ocean Engineering, Department of Ocean Engineering, Blacksburg, VA 24061

AWARDS MS. Part-time programs available. Postbaccalaureate distance learning degree programs offered.

Faculty: 4 full-time (0 women), 1 part-time/adjunct (0 women).
Students: 5 full-time (1 woman), 7 part-time, 2 international. 3 applicants, 67% accepted. In 2001, 3 degrees awarded.
Degree requirements: For master's, thesis.
Entrance requirements: For master's, GRE, TOEFL. *Application deadline:* For fall admission, 12/1 (priority date). Applications are processed on a rolling basis. *Application fee:* $45. Electronic applications accepted.
Expenses: Tuition, state resident: part-time $241 per hour. Tuition, nonresident: part-time $406 per hour. Tuition and fees vary according to program.
Financial support: In 2001–02, 3 research assistantships with full tuition reimbursements (averaging $1,450 per year) were awarded; institutionally sponsored loans and unspecified assistantships also available. Financial award application deadline: 4/1.
Faculty research: Ship structures, collision analysis.
Application contact: Dr. Frederick H. Lutze, Chairman, Graduate Committee, 540-231-6409, *Fax:* 540-231-9632, *E-mail:* lutze@aoe.vt.edu.

■ WOODS HOLE OCEANOGRAPHIC INSTITUTE

Joint Program with Massachusetts Institute of Technology in Oceanography/Applied Ocean Science and Engineering, Woods Hole, MA 02543

AWARDS Applied ocean sciences (PhD); biological oceanography (PhD, Sc D); chemical oceanography (PhD, Sc D); civil and environmental and oceanographic engineering (PhD); electrical and oceanographic engineering (PhD); geochemistry (PhD); geophysics (PhD); marine biology (PhD); marine geochemistry (PhD, Sc D); marine geology (PhD, Sc D); marine geophysics (PhD); mechanical and oceanographic engineering (PhD); ocean engineering (PhD); oceanographic engineering (M Eng, MS, PhD, Sc D, Eng); paleoceanography (PhD); physical oceanography (PhD, Sc D). MS, PhD, and Sc D offered jointly with Woods Hole Oceanographic Institution.

Faculty: 185 full-time (60 women).
Students: 119 full-time (59 women); includes 4 minority (2 African Americans, 2 Asian Americans or Pacific Islanders), 27 international. Average age 27. 125 applicants, 30% accepted, 24 enrolled. In 2001, 10 master's, 11 doctorates awarded. Terminal master's awarded for partial completion of doctoral program.
Degree requirements: For master's and Eng, thesis (for some programs); for doctorate, thesis/dissertation. *Median time to degree:* Master's–2.9 years full-time; doctorate–5.8 years full-time.
Entrance requirements: For master's, GRE General Test; for doctorate, GRE General Test, GRE Subject Test. *Application deadline:* For fall admission, 1/15 (priority date). *Application fee:* $60. Electronic applications accepted.
Expenses: Tuition: Full-time $26,960. Full-time tuition and fees vary according to program.
Financial support: In 2001–02, 13 fellowships (averaging $35,948 per year), 69 research assistantships (averaging $35,948 per year) were awarded. Teaching assistantships, institutionally sponsored loans, health care benefits, and unspecified assistantships also available. Financial award application deadline: 1/15.
Prof. Paola Rizzoli, Director, 617-253-2451, *E-mail:* rizzoli@mit.edu.
Application contact: Ronni Schwartz, Administrator, 617-253-7544, *Fax:* 617-253-9784, *E-mail:* mspiggy@mit.edu. *Web site:* http://www.whoi.edu/education/graduate/jp.html

Find an in-depth description at www.petersons.com/gradchannel.

Paper and Textile Engineering

PAPER AND PULP ENGINEERING

■ GEORGIA INSTITUTE OF TECHNOLOGY

Graduate Studies and Research, College of Engineering, School of Chemical Engineering, Pulp and Paper Engineering Program, Atlanta, GA 30332-0001

AWARDS Certificate.

Faculty research: Black liquor, oxygen delignification, high-yield pulping, synthetic fiber application, colloid-polymer flocculation.

■ INSTITUTE OF PAPER SCIENCE AND TECHNOLOGY

Graduate Programs, Atlanta, GA 30318-5794

AWARDS MS, PhD. Part-time programs available. Terminal master's awarded for partial completion of doctoral program.

Degree requirements: For master's, industrial experience, research project; for doctorate, thesis/dissertation.
Entrance requirements: For master's and doctorate, GRE, minimum GPA of 3.0. Electronic applications accepted.
Faculty research: Bleaching; chemical pulping, impulse drying, biotechnology, physics of fluid flow; environmental improvement, recycling, closed mill technology; black liquor recovery. *Web site:* http://www.ipst.edu/

■ MIAMI UNIVERSITY

Graduate School, School of Engineering and Applied Science, Department of Paper Science and Engineering, Oxford, OH 45056

AWARDS MS.

Faculty: 5 full-time (0 women), 1 part-time/adjunct (0 women).
Students: 5 full-time (0 women), 4 international. 17 applicants, 71% accepted, 3 enrolled. In 2001, 4 degrees awarded.
Degree requirements: For master's, thesis, final exams, comprehensive exam.
Entrance requirements: For master's, GRE General Test, MAT, minimum undergraduate GPA of 3.0 during previous 2 years or 2.75 overall. *Application deadline:* For fall admission, 3/1 (priority date); for spring admission, 12/1. Applications are processed on a rolling basis. *Application fee:* $35.
Expenses: Tuition, state resident: full-time $7,155; part-time $295 per semester hour.

Tuition, nonresident: full-time $14,829; part-time $615 per semester hour. Tuition and fees vary according to degree level and campus/location.
Financial support: In 2001–02, 7 fellowships (averaging $11,176 per year) were awarded; research assistantships, teaching assistantships, Federal Work-Study and tuition waivers (full) also available. Financial award application deadline: 3/1.
Faculty research: Papermaking and pulping, wet end chemistry, environmental control in the pulp and paper industry. Dr. Martin Sikora, Director of Graduate Studies, 513-529-2200, *Fax:* 513-529-2201, *E-mail:* paper@muohio.edu.
Application contact: Dr. Allan Springer, Director of Graduate Studies, 513-529-2200, *Fax:* 513-529-2201, *E-mail:* paper@muohio.edu. *Web site:* http://www.sas.muohio.edu/pps/

Find an in-depth description at www.petersons.com/gradchannel.

■ NORTH CAROLINA STATE UNIVERSITY

Graduate School, College of Natural Resources, Department of Wood and Paper Science, Raleigh, NC 27695

AWARDS MS, MWPS, PhD.

Faculty: 21 full-time (2 women), 12 part-time/adjunct (0 women).
Students: 14 full-time (2 women), 13 part-time (3 women); includes 3 minority (2 African Americans, 1 Asian American or Pacific Islander), 13 international. Average age 31. 27 applicants, 52% accepted. In 2001, 2 master's, 3 doctorates awarded.
Degree requirements: For master's and doctorate, thesis/dissertation.
Entrance requirements: For master's and doctorate, GRE General Test, TOEFL. *Application deadline:* For fall admission, 6/25; for spring admission, 11/25. Applications are processed on a rolling basis. *Application fee:* $45.
Expenses: Tuition, state resident: full-time $1,748. Tuition, nonresident: full-time $6,904.
Financial support: In 2001–02, fellowships (averaging $7,175 per year), 12 research assistantships (averaging $5,796 per year) were awarded. Financial award application deadline: 2/15.
Faculty research: Pulping, bleaching, recycling, papermaking, drying of wood. *Total annual research expenditures:* $1.2 million.
Dr. Michael J. Kocurek, Head, 919-515-5807, *Fax:* 919-515-6302, *E-mail:* mike_kocurek@ncsu.edu.
Application contact: Dr. Richard D. Gilbert, Director of Graduate Programs, 919-515-7711, *Fax:* 919-515-6302, *E-mail:*

richard_gilbert@ncsu.edu. *Web site:* http://www.cfr.ncsu.edu/wps/

■ OREGON STATE UNIVERSITY

Graduate School, College of Forestry, Department of Forest Products, Corvallis, OR 97331

AWARDS Forest products (MAIS, MF, MS, PhD); wood science and technology (MF, MS, PhD). Part-time programs available.

Faculty: 15 full-time (1 woman), 1 part-time/adjunct (0 women).
Students: 24 full-time (5 women); includes 3 minority (all Asian Americans or Pacific Islanders), 10 international. Average age 30. In 2001, 3 master's, 1 doctorate awarded.
Degree requirements: For master's, thesis (for some programs); for doctorate, thesis/dissertation.
Entrance requirements: For master's and doctorate, GRE General Test, TOEFL, minimum GPA of 3.0 in last 90 hours. *Application deadline:* For fall admission, 3/1 (priority date). Applications are processed on a rolling basis. *Application fee:* $50.
Expenses: Tuition, area resident: Full-time $15,933. Tuition, state resident: full-time $28,937.
Financial support: Fellowships, research assistantships, career-related internships or fieldwork, Federal Work-Study, and institutionally sponsored loans available. Support available to part-time students. Financial award application deadline: 2/1.
Faculty research: Biodeterioration and preservation, timber engineering, process engineering and control, composite materials science, anatomy, chemistry and physical properties.
Dr. Thomas E. McLain, Head, 541-737-4224, *Fax:* 541-737-3385, *E-mail:* thomas.mclain@orst.edu.
Application contact: George Swanson, Program Support Coordinator, 541-737-4206, *Fax:* 541-737-3385, *E-mail:* george.swanson@orst.edu. *Web site:* http://www.cof.orst.edu/cof/fp/

■ STATE UNIVERSITY OF NEW YORK COLLEGE OF ENVIRONMENTAL SCIENCE AND FORESTRY

Faculty of Paper Science and Engineering, Syracuse, NY 13210-2779

AWARDS Environmental and resources engineering (MS); evironmental and resources engineering (PhD).

Faculty: 7 full-time (0 women).
Students: 7 full-time (3 women), 7 part-time (3 women), 11 international. 10

applicants, 80% accepted, 2 enrolled. In 2001, 2 degrees awarded.

Degree requirements: For master's, thesis/dissertation, registration; for doctorate, thesis/dissertation, comprehensive exam, registration.

Entrance requirements: For master's and doctorate, GRE General Test, minimum GPA of 3.0. *Application deadline:* For fall admission, 2/1 (priority date); for spring admission, 11/1 (priority date). Applications are processed on a rolling basis. *Application fee:* $50.

Expenses: Tuition, area resident: Part-time $213 per credit hour. Tuition, state resident: full-time $5,100. Tuition, nonresident: full-time $8,416; part-time $351 per credit hour. Required fees: $250. One-time fee: $43 full-time.

Financial support: In 2001–02, 12 students received support, including 2 fellowships with full tuition reimbursements available (averaging $8,817 per year), 8 research assistantships with full tuition reimbursements available (averaging $10,000 per year), 2 teaching assistantships with full tuition reimbursements available (averaging $8,817 per year); career-related internships or fieldwork, Federal Work-Study, institutionally sponsored loans, scholarships/grants, health care benefits, and unspecified assistantships also available. Support available to part-time students. Financial award applicants required to submit FAFSA. *Total annual research expenditures:* $885,627.

Dr. Thomas E. Amidon, Chair, 315-470-6524, *Fax:* 315-470-6945, *E-mail:* teamidon@syr.edu.

Application contact: Dr. Robert H. Frey, Dean, Instruction and Graduate Studies, 315-470-6599, *Fax:* 315-470-6978, *E-mail:* esfgrad@esf.edu. *Web site:* http://www.esf.edu/pse/

■ UNIVERSITY OF WASHINGTON

Graduate School, College of Forest Resources, Seattle, WA 98195

AWARDS Forest economics (MS, PhD); forest ecosystem analysis (MS, PhD); forest engineering/forest hydrology (MS, PhD); forest products marketing (MS, PhD); forest soils (MS, PhD); paper science and engineering (MS, PhD); quantitative resource management (MS, PhD). Silviculture (MFR). Silviculture and forest protection (MS, PhD). Social sciences (MS, PhD); urban horticulture (MFR, MS, PhD); wildlife science (MS, PhD).

Faculty: 57 full-time (12 women), 16 part-time/adjunct (2 women).

Students: 160 full-time (77 women), 186 part-time (158 women); includes 16 minority (1 African American, 10 Asian Americans or Pacific Islanders, 4 Hispanic Americans, 1 Native American). Average age 31. 172 applicants, 52% accepted, 47 enrolled. In 2001, 38 master's, 12 doctorates awarded.

Degree requirements: For master's, thesis (for some programs), registration;

for doctorate, thesis/dissertation, comprehensive exam (for some programs), registration.

Entrance requirements: For master's and doctorate, GRE, TOEFL, minimum GPA of 3.0. *Application deadline:* For fall admission, 1/15 (priority date); for winter admission, 9/1; for spring admission, 11/1. Applications are processed on a rolling basis. *Application fee:* $50. Electronic applications accepted.

Expenses: Tuition, state resident: full-time $5,539. Tuition, nonresident: full-time $14,376. Required fees: $390. Tuition and fees vary according to course load and program.

Financial support: In 2001–02, 140 students received support, including 15 fellowships with full tuition reimbursements available (averaging $14,000 per year), 98 research assistantships with full tuition reimbursements available (averaging $14,000 per year), 27 teaching assistantships with full tuition reimbursements available (averaging $14,000 per year); career-related internships or fieldwork, Federal Work-Study, institutionally sponsored loans, scholarships/grants, traineeships, health care benefits, tuition waivers (full), and unspecified assistantships also available. Financial award application deadline: 1/15.

Faculty research: Ecosystem analysis, silviculture and forest protection, paper science and engineering, environmental horticulture and urban forestry, natural resource policy and economics. *Total annual research expenditures:* $7 million.

Dr. B. Bruce Bare, Dean, 206-685-0952, *Fax:* 206-685-0790, *E-mail:* bare@u.washington.edu.

Application contact: Michelle Trudeau, Student Services Manager, 206-616-1533, *Fax:* 206-685-0790, *E-mail:* michtru@u.washington.edu. *Web site:* http://www.cfr.washington.edu/

Find an in-depth description at www.petersons.com/gradchannel.

■ WESTERN MICHIGAN UNIVERSITY

Graduate College, College of Engineering and Applied Sciences, Department of Paper and Printing Science and Engineering, Kalamazoo, MI 49008-5202

AWARDS MS, PhD.

Faculty: 11 full-time (2 women).

Students: 22 full-time (3 women), 5 part-time (4 women); includes 1 minority (Asian American or Pacific Islander), 22 international. 34 applicants, 59% accepted, 12 enrolled. In 2001, 7 degrees awarded.

Degree requirements: For master's, thesis optional; for doctorate, one foreign language, thesis/dissertation, comprehensive exam.

Entrance requirements: For master's, minimum GPA of 3.0. *Application deadline:*

For fall admission, 2/15 (priority date). Applications are processed on a rolling basis. *Application fee:* $25.

Expenses: Tuition, state resident: part-time $186 per credit hour. Tuition, nonresident: part-time $442 per credit hour. Required fees: $602. One-time fee: $132 part-time. Tuition and fees vary according to course load.

Financial support: Fellowships, research assistantships, teaching assistantships, Federal Work-Study available. Financial award application deadline: 2/15; financial award applicants required to submit FAFSA.

Faculty research: Fiber recycling, paper machine wet end operations, paper coating.

Dr. Said AbuBakr, Chairperson, 616-387-2775.

Application contact: Admissions and Orientation, 616-387-2000, *Fax:* 616-387-2355.

TEXTILE SCIENCES AND ENGINEERING

■ AUBURN UNIVERSITY

Graduate School, Interdepartmental Programs, Interdepartmental Program in Integrated Textile and Apparel Sciences, Auburn University, AL 36849

AWARDS MS, PhD.

Students: 26 full-time (13 women), 11 part-time (5 women); includes 1 minority (African American), 29 international. 69 applicants, 46% accepted. In 2001, 3 degrees awarded.

Entrance requirements: For master's, GRE General Test. *Application deadline:* For fall admission, 7/7; for spring admission, 11/24. Applications are processed on a rolling basis. *Application fee:* $25 ($50 for international students).

Financial support: Research assistantships, Federal Work-Study available. Support available to part-time students. Financial award application deadline: 3/15.

Faculty research: Design and utilization of textile products, engineering and technology of textile production, textile material science, textile chemistry, use of resources.

Dr. Royall M. Broughton, Graduate Program Officer, 334-844-4123, *E-mail:* royalb@eng.auburn.edu.

Application contact: Dr. John F. Pritchett, Dean of the Graduate School, 334-844-4700, *E-mail:* hatchlb@mail.auburn.edu. *Web site:* http://www.eng.auburn.edu/department/te/grad.programs/ms.html

■ CLEMSON UNIVERSITY

Graduate School, College of Engineering and Science, Department of Textiles, Fiber and Polymer Science, Clemson, SC 29634

AWARDS MS, PhD. Part-time programs available.

Students: 30 full-time (11 women), 2 part-time, 27 international. 72 applicants, 49% accepted, 8 enrolled. In 2001, 5 master's, 1 doctorate awarded.
Degree requirements: For doctorate, thesis/dissertation.
Entrance requirements: For master's and doctorate, GRE General Test, TOEFL. *Application fee:* $40.
Expenses: Tuition, state resident: full-time $5,310. Tuition, nonresident: full-time $11,284.
Financial support: Fellowships, research assistantships, teaching assistantships, career-related internships or fieldwork, institutionally sponsored loans, and unspecified assistantships available. Financial award applicants required to submit FAFSA.
Dr. D. V. Rippy, Director, 864-656-3176, *Fax:* 864-656-5973, *E-mail:* rippyd@clemson.edu. *Web site:* http://www.eng.clemson.edu/textiles/Textiles.html

■ CORNELL UNIVERSITY

Graduate School, Graduate Fields of Human Ecology, Field of Textiles, Ithaca, NY 14853-0001

AWARDS Apparel design (MA, MPS); fiber science (MS, PhD); polymer science (MS, PhD); textile science (MS, PhD).

Faculty: 12 full-time.
Students: 13 full-time (7 women), 12 international. 29 applicants, 34% accepted. In 2001, 4 degrees awarded.
Degree requirements: For master's, thesis (MA, MS), project paper (MPS); for doctorate, thesis/dissertation.
Entrance requirements: For master's, GRE General Test, TOEFL, 2 letters of recommendation, portfolio (functional apparel design); for doctorate, GRE General Test, TOEFL, 2 letters of recommendation. *Application deadline:* For fall admission, 3/1. *Application fee:* $65. Electronic applications accepted.
Expenses: Tuition: Full-time $25,970. Required fees: $50.
Financial support: In 2001–02, 12 students received support, including 2 fellowships with full tuition reimbursements available, 2 research assistantships with full tuition reimbursements available, 8 teaching assistantships with full tuition reimbursements available; institutionally sponsored loans, scholarships/grants, tuition waivers (full and partial), and unspecified assistantships also available. Financial award applicants required to submit FAFSA.
Faculty research: High performance fibers and composites. Surface chemistry of fibers; geosynthetics; mechanics of fibrous assemblies/ biopolymers; biological tissue engineering, detergency, protective clothing.
Application contact: Graduate Field Assistant, 607-255-8065, *E-mail:* textiles_grad@cornell.edu. *Web site:* http://www.gradschool.cornell.edu/grad/fields_1/textiles.html

■ GEORGIA INSTITUTE OF TECHNOLOGY

Graduate Studies and Research, College of Engineering, School of Textile and Fiber Engineering, Atlanta, GA 30332-0001

AWARDS Biomedical engineering (MS Bio E); polymers (MS Poly); textile chemistry (MS, MST Ch); textile engineering (MS, MSTE, PhD); textiles (MS, MS Text).

Degree requirements: For master's, thesis (for some programs); for doctorate, thesis/dissertation.
Entrance requirements: For master's and doctorate, TOEFL, minimum GPA of 2.7.
Faculty research: Energy conservation, environmental control, engineered fibrous structures, polymer synthesis and degradation, high performance organic-carbon-ceramic fibers.

■ INSTITUTE OF TEXTILE TECHNOLOGY

Program in Textile Technology, Charlottesville, VA 22903-4614

AWARDS MS.

Faculty: 17 full-time (2 women), 5 part-time/adjunct (2 women).
Students: 16 full-time (6 women); includes 2 minority (1 African American, 1 Hispanic American). Average age 25. 35 applicants, 31% accepted. In 2001, 12 degrees awarded.
Degree requirements: For master's, thesis, comprehensive exam.
Application deadline: For fall admission, 3/15. Applications are processed on a rolling basis. *Application fee:* $0. Electronic applications accepted.
Expenses: All students automatically receive a full fellowship which covers tuition and fees.
Financial support: In 2001–02, 16 fellowships with full tuition reimbursements (averaging $20,000 per year) were awarded; career-related internships or fieldwork and tuition waivers (full) also available. Financial award application deadline: 2/15; financial award applicants required to submit FAFSA.
Faculty research: Computer-aided manufacturing, raw materials, manufacturing process innovation.
Dan J. McCreight, Executive Vice President and Dean of Academic Affairs, 434-296-5511 Ext. 266, *Fax:* 434-297-3873, *E-mail:* danm@itt.edu.

Application contact: Peggy S. Ehrenberg, Administrative Assistant to Academic Affairs, 434-296-5511 Ext. 275, *Fax:* 434-296-2957, *E-mail:* peggye@itt.edu. *Web site:* http://www.itt.edu/

■ NORTH CAROLINA STATE UNIVERSITY

Graduate School, College of Textiles, Program in Fiber and Polymer Sciences, Raleigh, NC 27695

AWARDS PhD.

Faculty: 37 full-time (3 women), 22 part-time/adjunct (0 women).
Students: 30 full-time (9 women), 6 part-time (4 women); includes 1 minority (African American), 25 international. Average age 32. 19 applicants, 37% accepted. In 2001, 6 degrees awarded.
Degree requirements: For doctorate, one foreign language, thesis/dissertation, cumulative exams.
Entrance requirements: For doctorate, GRE. *Application fee:* $45.
Expenses: Tuition, state resident: full-time $1,748. Tuition, nonresident: full-time $6,904.
Financial support: In 2001–02, fellowships (averaging $7,175 per year), 24 research assistantships (averaging $5,892 per year) were awarded.
Faculty research: Polymer chemistry, fiber mechanics, process automation, globalization, systems.
Dr. William Oxenham, Associate Dean, 919-515-6573, *Fax:* 919-515-3733, *E-mail:* william_oxenham@ncsu.edu. *Web site:* http://www.tx.nscu.edu/academic/graduate/programs.html

■ NORTH CAROLINA STATE UNIVERSITY

Graduate School, College of Textiles, Program in Textile Chemistry, Raleigh, NC 27695

AWARDS MS, MT.

Faculty: 25 full-time (1 woman), 27 part-time/adjunct (2 women).
Students: 6 full-time (3 women), 3 international. Average age 26. 4 applicants, 75% accepted. In 2001, 5 degrees awarded.
Degree requirements: For master's, thesis.
Entrance requirements: For master's, GRE. *Application fee:* $45.
Expenses: Tuition, state resident: full-time $1,748. Tuition, nonresident: full-time $6,904.
Financial support: In 2001–02, 4 research assistantships (averaging $5,227 per year) were awarded.
Faculty research: Textile machine/process design, textile production design, polymer/fiber engineering, chemistry of dyes and finishes.
Dr. Harold S. Freeman, Director of Graduate Programs, 919-515-6532. *Web site:* http://www.tx.ncsu.edu/tecs/

■ NORTH CAROLINA STATE UNIVERSITY

Graduate School, College of Textiles, Program in Textile Engineering, Raleigh, NC 27695

AWARDS MS.

Faculty: 25 full-time (1 woman), 27 part-time/adjunct (2 women).
Students: 9 full-time (1 woman), 5 part-time (1 woman), 7 international. Average age 26. 20 applicants, 15% accepted. In 2001, 6 degrees awarded.
Degree requirements: For master's, thesis.
Entrance requirements: For master's, GRE. *Application fee:* $45.
Expenses: Tuition, state resident: full-time $1,748. Tuition, nonresident: full-time $6,904.
Financial support: In 2001–02, fellowships (averaging $6,428 per year), 8 research assistantships (averaging $4,414 per year) were awarded.
Dr. Harold S. Freeman, Director of Graduate Programs, 919-515-6532. *Web site:* http://www.tx.ncsu.edu/academic/graduate/programs.html

■ NORTH CAROLINA STATE UNIVERSITY

Graduate School, College of Textiles, Program in Textile Management and Technology, Raleigh, NC 27695

AWARDS MS, MT.

Faculty: 15 full-time (2 women), 15 part-time/adjunct (3 women).
Students: 28 full-time (16 women), 9 part-time (4 women); includes 4 minority (1 African American, 3 Asian Americans or Pacific Islanders), 17 international. 17 applicants, 76% accepted. In 2001, 19 degrees awarded.
Degree requirements: For master's, thesis.
Entrance requirements: For master's, GRE. *Application fee:* $45.
Expenses: Tuition, state resident: full-time $1,748. Tuition, nonresident: full-time $6,904.
Dr. William Oxenham, Associate Dean, 919-515-6573, *Fax:* 919-515-3733, *E-mail:* william_oxenham@ncsu.edu. *Web site:* http://www.tx.ncsu.edu/academic/graduate/programs.html

■ NORTH CAROLINA STATE UNIVERSITY

Graduate School, College of Textiles, Program in Textile Materials Science, Raleigh, NC 27695

AWARDS MS, MT.

Faculty: 25 full-time (1 woman), 27 part-time/adjunct (2 women).
Students: 2 full-time (0 women), 1 international. Average age 26. 1 applicant, 0% accepted.
Degree requirements: For master's, thesis.
Entrance requirements: For master's, GRE. *Application fee:* $45.
Expenses: Tuition, state resident: full-time $1,748. Tuition, nonresident: full-time $6,904.
Financial support: In 2001–02, 1 research assistantship (averaging $3,025 per year) was awarded
Dr. Harold S. Freeman, Director of Graduate Programs, 919-515-6532. *Web site:* http://www.tx.ncsu.edu/academic/graduate/programs.html

■ PHILADELPHIA UNIVERSITY

School of Textiles and Materials Science, Program in Textile Engineering, Philadelphia, PA 19144-5497

AWARDS MS. Part-time programs available.

Faculty: 9 full-time (3 women), 5 part-time/adjunct (2 women).
Students: 12 full-time (4 women), 3 part-time (all women), 12 international. 44 applicants, 75% accepted, 8 enrolled. In 2001, 2 degrees awarded.
Entrance requirements: For master's, GRE, minimum GPA of 2.80. *Application deadline:* Applications are processed on a rolling basis. *Application fee:* $35. Electronic applications accepted.
Expenses: Tuition: Part-time $517 per credit.
Financial support: Research assistantships, career-related internships or fieldwork, Federal Work-Study, and unspecified assistantships available. Support available to part-time students. Financial award applicants required to submit FAFSA.
Dr. Muthu Govindaraj, Director, 215-951-2684, *Fax:* 215-951-2651, *E-mail:* govindarajm@philau.edu.
Application contact: William H. Firman, Director of Graduate Admissions, 215-951-2943, *Fax:* 215-951-2907, *E-mail:* gradadm@philau.edu. *Web site:* http://www.philau.edu/

■ UNIVERSITY OF MASSACHUSETTS DARTMOUTH

Graduate School, College of Engineering, Department of Textile Sciences, North Dartmouth, MA 02747-2300

AWARDS Textile chemistry (MS); textile technology (MS). Part-time programs available.

Faculty: 6 full-time (0 women), 1 part-time/adjunct (0 women).
Students: 15 full-time (3 women), (all international). Average age 24. 38 applicants, 71% accepted, 9 enrolled. In 2001, 2 degrees awarded.
Degree requirements: For master's, thesis.
Entrance requirements: For master's, GRE General Test, TOEFL. *Application deadline:* For fall admission, 4/20 (priority date); for spring admission, 11/15 (priority date). Applications are processed on a rolling basis. *Application fee:* $25 ($45 for international students).
Expenses: Tuition, state resident: full-time $2,071; part-time $86 per credit. Tuition, nonresident: full-time $8,099; part-time $337 per credit. Part-time tuition and fees vary according to course load and reciprocity agreements.
Financial support: In 2001–02, 12 research assistantships with full tuition reimbursements (averaging $9,403 per year), 3 teaching assistantships with full tuition reimbursements (averaging $7,667 per year) were awarded. Federal Work-Study and unspecified assistantships also available. Support available to part-time students. Financial award application deadline: 3/1; financial award applicants required to submit FAFSA.
Faculty research: Ultrathick cross-section, electrostatic spinning, nano composite fibers, brain induced morphology fibers architecture affluents, substrate-coating interaction in coated fabrics. *Total annual research expenditures:* $659,000.
Dr. Yong Ku Kim, Director, 508-999-8452, *Fax:* 508-999-9139, *E-mail:* ykim@umassd.edu.
Application contact: Maria E. Lomba, Graduate Admissions Officer, 508-999-8604, *Fax:* 508-999-8183, *E-mail:* graduate@umassd.edu.

Telecommunications

TELECOMMUNICATIONS

■ AZUSA PACIFIC UNIVERSITY

College of Liberal Arts and Sciences, Department of Computer Science, Azusa, CA 91702-7000

AWARDS Applied computer science and technology (MS), including client/server technology, computer information systems, end-user support, inter-emphasis, technical programming, telecommunications; client/server technology (Certificate); computer information systems (Certificate); computer science (Certificate); end-user training and support (Certificate). Software engineering (MSE); technical programming (Certificate); telecommunications (Certificate). Part-time and evening/weekend programs available.

Students: 34 full-time (8 women), 98 part-time (30 women); includes 44 minority (6 African Americans, 28 Asian Americans or Pacific Islanders, 10 Hispanic Americans), 57 international. 126 applicants, 94% accepted. In 2001, 51 degrees awarded. **Degree requirements:** For master's, thesis or alternative, project. **Entrance requirements:** For master's, minimum GPA of 3.0; proficiency in 1 programming language, college-level algebra, and applied calculus. *Application deadline:* For fall admission, 9/1 (priority date). Applications are processed on a rolling basis. *Application fee:* $45 ($65 for international students). **Expenses:** Contact institution. **Financial support:** Teaching assistantships, career-related internships or fieldwork available. Support available to part-time students. **Faculty research:** Applied artificial intelligence, programming languages, engineering, database systems. Dr. Samuel Sambasivam, Acting Chairman, 626-815-5310, *Fax:* 626-815-5323, *E-mail:* ssambasivam@apu.edu. *Web site:* http://www.apu.edu/~cs/

Find an in-depth description at www.petersons.com/gradchannel.

■ BOSTON UNIVERSITY

Metropolitan College, Program in Computer Science, Boston, MA 02215

AWARDS Computer information systems (MS); computer science (MS); telecommunications (MS). Part-time and evening/weekend programs available.

Faculty: 8 full-time (1 woman). **Students:** 34 full-time (12 women), 341 part-time (87 women); includes 73 minority (5 African Americans, 65 Asian Americans or Pacific Islanders, 3 Hispanic Americans), 50 international. Average age 34. 113 applicants, 99% accepted, 112 enrolled. In 2001, 64 degrees awarded. *Application deadline:* For fall admission, 6/1 (priority date); for winter admission, 10/1 (priority date); for spring admission, 3/1 (priority date). Applications are processed on a rolling basis. *Application fee:* $60. **Expenses:** Tuition: Full-time $25,872; part-time $340 per credit. Required fees: $40 per semester. Part-time tuition and fees vary according to class time, course level and program. **Financial support:** In 2001–02, 21 students received support, including 21 research assistantships with partial tuition reimbursements available; career-related internships or fieldwork, Federal Work-Study, and tuition waivers (full and partial) also available. Support available to part-time students. **Faculty research:** Software engineering, information systems architecture, process control, operating systems, parallel processing. Dr. Tanya Zlateva, Chairman, 617-353-2566, *Fax:* 617-353-2367, *E-mail:* csinfo@bu.edu. **Application contact:** Sarah-Grace H. Thomas, Administrative Secretary, 617-353-2566, *Fax:* 617-353-2367, *E-mail:* csinfo@bu.edu. *Web site:* http://bumetb.bu.edu/compsci.html

■ COLUMBIA UNIVERSITY

Fu Foundation School of Engineering and Applied Science, Department of Electrical Engineering, New York, NY 10027

AWARDS Electrical engineering (MS, Eng Sc D, PhD, EE). Solid state science and engineering (MS, Eng Sc D, PhD); telecommunications (MS). PhD offered through the Graduate School of Arts and Sciences. Part-time programs available. Postbaccalaureate distance learning degree programs offered (no on-campus study).

Faculty: 20 full-time (0 women), 13 part-time/adjunct (1 woman). **Students:** 136 full-time (20 women), 87 part-time (11 women); includes 30 minority (2 African Americans, 28 Asian Americans or Pacific Islanders), 136 international. Average age 23. 882 applicants, 27% accepted, 53 enrolled. In 2001, 59 master's, 8 doctorates awarded. Terminal master's awarded for partial completion of doctoral program. **Degree requirements:** For doctorate, thesis/dissertation, qualifying exam. **Entrance requirements:** For master's and doctorate, GRE General Test, TOEFL. *Application deadline:* For fall admission, 1/5; for spring admission, 10/1. *Application fee:* $55. Electronic applications accepted. **Expenses:** Tuition: Full-time $27,528. Required fees: $1,638. **Financial support:** In 2001–02, 2 fellowships (averaging $19,800 per year), 49 research assistantships with full tuition reimbursements (averaging $20,550 per year), 17 teaching assistantships with full tuition reimbursements (averaging $20,550 per year) were awarded. Federal Work-Study and readerships, preceptorships also available. Financial award application deadline: 1/5; financial award applicants required to submit FAFSA. **Faculty research:** Communications/networking, signal/image processing, microelectronic circuits/VLSI design, microelectronic devices/optoelectronics/electromagnetics/plasma physics. *Total annual research expenditures:* $6.5 million. Prof. Charles Zukowski, Chairman, 212-854-5019, *Fax:* 212-932-9421, *E-mail:* caz@ee.columbia.edu. **Application contact:** Marlene Mansfield, Student Coordinator, 212-854-3104, *Fax:* 212-932-9421, *E-mail:* mansfield@ee.columbia.edu. *Web site:* http://www.ee.columbia.edu/

Find an in-depth description at www.petersons.com/gradchannel.

■ DEPAUL UNIVERSITY

School of Computer Science, Telecommunications, and Information Systems, Program in Telecommunications Systems, Chicago, IL 60604-2287

AWARDS MS. Part-time and evening/weekend programs available. Postbaccalaureate distance learning degree programs offered.

Faculty: 9 full-time (0 women), 18 part-time/adjunct (2 women). **Students:** 132 full-time (35 women), 154 part-time (35 women); includes 118 minority (39 African Americans, 59 Asian Americans or Pacific Islanders, 20 Hispanic Americans), 65 international. Average age 32. 344 applicants, 64% accepted, 114 enrolled. In 2001, 76 degrees awarded. **Degree requirements:** For master's, comprehensive exam. *Application deadline:* For fall admission, 8/1 (priority date); for winter admission, 11/15 (priority date); for spring admission, 3/1 (priority date). Applications are processed on a rolling basis. *Application fee:* $25. Electronic applications accepted. **Expenses:** Tuition: Part-time $362 per credit hour. Tuition and fees vary according to program. **Financial support:** Fellowships, research assistantships, teaching assistantships,

Federal Work-Study, tuition waivers (full and partial), and unspecified assistantships available. Support available to part-time students. Financial award application deadline: 4/1; financial award applicants required to submit FAFSA.

Faculty research: Data communications, performance analysis.

Dr. Greg Brewster, Director, 312-362-6587, *Fax:* 312-362-6116, *E-mail:* gbrewster@cs.depaul.edu.

Application contact: Genaro Balcazar, Director of Admissions, 312-362-8714, *Fax:* 312-362-6116, *E-mail:* ctiadmissions@cs.depaul.edu. *Web site:* http://www.cs.depaul.edu/

■ DREXEL UNIVERSITY

Graduate School, College of Engineering, Department of Electrical and Computer Engineering, Program in Telecommunications Engineering, Philadelphia, PA 19104-2875

AWARDS MSEE.

Faculty: 32 full-time (4 women), 3 part-time/adjunct (0 women).

Students: 7 full-time (1 woman), 13 part-time (1 woman); includes 2 minority (1 African American, 1 Asian American or Pacific Islander), 4 international. Average age 33. 81 applicants, 49% accepted, 6 enrolled. In 2001, 7 degrees awarded.

Entrance requirements: For master's, TOEFL, BS in electrical engineering or physics, minimum GPA of 3.0. *Application deadline:* For fall admission, 8/21. Applications are processed on a rolling basis. *Application fee:* $50. Electronic applications accepted.

Expenses: Tuition: Full-time $20,088; part-time $558 per credit. Required fees: $78 per term. One-time fee: $200. Tuition and fees vary according to course load, degree level and program.

Financial support: Research assistantships, teaching assistantships, unspecified assistantships available. Financial award application deadline: 2/1.

Application contact: Director of Graduate Admissions, 215-895-6700, *Fax:* 215-895-5939, *E-mail:* enroll@drexel.edu.

Find an in-depth description at www.petersons.com/gradchannel.

■ GEORGE MASON UNIVERSITY

College of Arts and Sciences, Program in Telecommunications, Fairfax, VA 22030-4444

AWARDS MA. Part-time and evening/weekend programs available.

Faculty: 2 full-time (0 women).

Students: 10 full-time (6 women), 42 part-time (17 women); includes 15 minority (9 African Americans, 4 Asian Americans or Pacific Islanders, 2 Hispanic Americans), 5 international. Average age 34. 37 applicants, 62% accepted, 17 enrolled. In 2001, 30 degrees awarded.

Degree requirements: For master's, thesis optional.

Entrance requirements: For master's, minimum GPA of 3.0 in last 60 hours. *Application deadline:* For fall admission, 5/1; for spring admission, 11/1. *Application fee:* $30. Electronic applications accepted.

Expenses: Tuition, state resident: full-time $3,168; part-time $132 per credit hour. Tuition, nonresident: full-time $11,280; part-time $470 per credit hour. Required fees: $1,416; $59 per credit hour.

Financial support: Career-related internships or fieldwork available. Financial award application deadline: 3/1; financial award applicants required to submit FAFSA.

Dr. Michael R. Kelley, Chairman, 703-993-1314, *Fax:* 703-993-1096, *E-mail:* telecom@gmu.edu.

■ THE GEORGE WASHINGTON UNIVERSITY

Columbian College of Arts and Sciences, Program in Telecommunication Studies, Washington, DC 20052

AWARDS MA.

Faculty: 2 full-time (0 women), 2 part-time/adjunct (0 women).

Students: 9 full-time (2 women), 21 part-time (7 women); includes 4 minority (2 African Americans, 2 Asian Americans or Pacific Islanders), 6 international. Average age 35. 15 applicants, 80% accepted. In 2001, 17 degrees awarded.

Degree requirements: For master's, thesis or alternative, comprehensive exam.

Entrance requirements: For master's, GRE General Test, minimum GPA of 3.0. *Application deadline:* For fall admission, 5/1. *Application fee:* $55.

Expenses: Tuition: Part-time $810 per credit. Required fees: $1 per credit.

Financial support: Federal Work-Study and institutionally sponsored loans available. Financial award application deadline: 2/1.

Dr. Chris Sterling, Director, 202-994-5100. *Web site:* http://www.gwu.edu/~gradinfo/

■ ILLINOIS INSTITUTE OF TECHNOLOGY

Graduate College, Armour College of Engineering and Sciences, Department of Computer Science, Chicago, IL 60616-3793

AWARDS Computer science (MS, PhD); teaching (MST); telecommunications and software engineering (MTSE). Part-time and evening/weekend programs available. Postbaccalaureate distance learning degree programs offered (no on-campus study).

Faculty: 18 full-time (3 women), 14 part-time/adjunct (1 woman).

Students: 378 full-time (78 women), 425 part-time (105 women); includes 86 minority (9 African Americans, 67 Asian Americans or Pacific Islanders, 9 Hispanic Americans, 1 Native American), 595 international. Average age 28. 1,741 applicants, 57% accepted. In 2001, 249 master's, 9 doctorates awarded. Terminal master's awarded for partial completion of doctoral program.

Degree requirements: For master's, thesis (for some programs), comprehensive exam; for doctorate, thesis/dissertation, comprehensive exam.

Entrance requirements: For master's and doctorate, GRE General Test, TOEFL, minimum undergraduate GPA of 3.0. *Application deadline:* For fall admission, 7/1; for spring admission, 11/1. Applications are processed on a rolling basis. *Application fee:* $30. Electronic applications accepted.

Expenses: Tuition: Part-time $590 per credit hour.

Financial support: In 2001–02, 1 fellowship, 9 research assistantships, 46 teaching assistantships were awarded. Federal Work-Study, institutionally sponsored loans, scholarships/grants, and unspecified assistantships also available. Support available to part-time students. Financial award application deadline: 3/1; financial award applicants required to submit FAFSA.

Faculty research: Artificial intelligence, computer architecture, medical imaging, concurrent programming, distributed systems. *Total annual research expenditures:* $214,441.

Dr. Edward Reingold, Chairman, 312-567-3309, *Fax:* 312-567-5067, *E-mail:* reingold@iit.edu.

Application contact: Dr. Ali Cinar, Dean of Graduate College, 312-567-3637, *Fax:* 312-567-7517, *E-mail:* gradstu@iit.edu. *Web site:* http://www.csam.iit.edu/

■ IONA COLLEGE

School of Arts and Science, Program in Telecommunications, New Rochelle, NY 10801-1890

AWARDS MS, Certificate. Part-time and evening/weekend programs available.

Faculty: 5 full-time (0 women), 1 part-time/adjunct (0 women).

Students: 1 (woman) full-time, 19 part-time (9 women); includes 5 minority (2 African Americans, 2 Asian Americans or Pacific Islanders, 1 Hispanic American). Average age 32. In 2001, 6 master's, 2 other advanced degrees awarded.

Degree requirements: For master's, thesis.

Entrance requirements: For master's, minimum GPA of 3.0. *Application deadline:* Applications are processed on a rolling basis. *Application fee:* $25.

Expenses: Contact institution.

Financial support: Unspecified assistantships available.

Dr. Robert Schiaffino, Chair, 914-633-2338, *E-mail:* rschiaffino@iona.edu.

Iona College (continued)

Application contact: Alyce Ware, Associate Director of Graduate Recruitment, 914-633-2420, *Fax:* 914-633-2023, *E-mail:* aware@iona.edu. *Web site:* http://www.iona.edu/

■ MICHIGAN STATE UNIVERSITY

Graduate School, College of Communication Arts and Sciences, Department of Telecommunication, East Lansing, MI 48824

AWARDS Digital media arts and technology (MA); information and telecommunication management (MA); information policy and society (MA); mass media (PhD); telecommunication (MA).

Faculty: 14 full-time (3 women).
Students: 21 full-time (11 women), 61 part-time (24 women); includes 8 minority (4 African Americans, 3 Asian Americans or Pacific Islanders, 1 Hispanic American), 49 international. Average age 28. 98 applicants, 49% accepted. In 2001, 38 degrees awarded.
Degree requirements: For master's, thesis (for some programs); for doctorate, thesis/dissertation.
Entrance requirements: For master's, GRE General Test, TOEFL, minimum GPA of 3.25. *Application deadline:* Applications are processed on a rolling basis. *Application fee:* $30 ($40 for international students).
Expenses: Tuition, state resident: part-time $244 per credit hour. Tuition, nonresident: part-time $494 per credit hour. Required fees: $268 per semester. Tuition and fees vary according to course load, degree level and program.
Financial support: In 2001–02, 7 fellowships (averaging $2,971 per year), 12 research assistantships with tuition reimbursements (averaging $11,283 per year), 12 teaching assistantships with tuition reimbursements (averaging $10,436 per year) were awarded. Career-related internships or fieldwork and institutionally sponsored loans also available. Support available to part-time students. Financial award applicants required to submit FAFSA.
Faculty research: New telecommunication technologies, cable, international communication, children and television, minority ownerships and programs, mass media. *Total annual research expenditures:* $452,985.
Dr. Mark Levy, Chair, 517-355-8372, *Fax:* 517-355-1292.
Application contact: Director of Graduate Studies, 517-355-8372, *Fax:* 517-355-1292. *Web site:* http://tc.msu.edu/

■ NEW JERSEY INSTITUTE OF TECHNOLOGY

Office of Graduate Studies, College of Computing Science, Newark, NJ 07102

AWARDS Computer science (MS, PhD); information systems (MS, PhD); telecommunication (MS). Part-time and evening/weekend programs available.

Faculty: 62 full-time (10 women).
Students: 466 full-time (166 women), 529 part-time (132 women); includes 238 minority (25 African Americans, 186 Asian Americans or Pacific Islanders, 26 Hispanic Americans, 1 Native American), 513 international. Average age 29. 1,942 applicants, 40% accepted, 278 enrolled. In 2001, 392 master's, 5 doctorates awarded. Terminal master's awarded for partial completion of doctoral program.
Degree requirements: For master's and doctorate, thesis/dissertation.
Entrance requirements: For master's, GRE General Test; for doctorate, GRE General Test, minimum graduate GPA of 3.5. *Application deadline:* For fall admission, 6/5 (priority date); for spring admission, 10/15. Applications are processed on a rolling basis. *Application fee:* $50. Electronic applications accepted.
Expenses: Tuition, state resident: full-time $7,812; part-time $434 per credit. Tuition, nonresident: full-time $10,746; part-time $597 per credit. Required fees: $47 per credit. $76 per semester.
Financial support: Fellowships with full and partial tuition reimbursements, research assistantships with full and partial tuition reimbursements, teaching assistantships with full and partial tuition reimbursements, career-related internships or fieldwork, Federal Work-Study, institutionally sponsored loans, and unspecified assistantships available. Financial award application deadline: 3/15.
Faculty research: Computer systems, communications and networking, artificial intelligence, database engineering, systems analysis. *Total annual research expenditures:* $2 million.
Dr. Stephen B. Seidman, Dean, 973-596-5488, *E-mail:* stephen.siedman@njit.edu.
Application contact: Kathryn Kelly, Director of Admissions, 973-596-3300, *Fax:* 973-596-3461, *E-mail:* admissions@njit.edu. *Web site:* http://www.njit.edu/

■ NORTH CAROLINA STATE UNIVERSITY

Graduate School, College of Management, Program in Management, Raleigh, NC 27695

AWARDS Biotechnology (MS); computer science (MS); engineering (MS); forest resources management (MS); general business (MS); management information systems (MS); operations research (MS). Statistics (MS); telecommunications systems engineering (MS); textile management (MS); total

quality management (MS). Part-time programs available.

Faculty: 14 full-time (6 women), 3 part-time/adjunct (0 women).
Students: 60 full-time (18 women), 138 part-time (47 women); includes 27 minority (12 African Americans, 13 Asian Americans or Pacific Islanders, 2 Hispanic Americans), 17 international. Average age 32. 225 applicants, 44% accepted. In 2001, 67 degrees awarded.
Entrance requirements: For master's, GMAT or GRE, TOEFL, minimum undergraduate GPA of 3.0. *Application deadline:* For fall admission, 6/25; for spring admission, 11/25. Applications are processed on a rolling basis. *Application fee:* $45.
Expenses: Tuition, state resident: full-time $1,748. Tuition, nonresident: full-time $6,904.
Financial support: In 2001–02, fellowships (averaging $3,551 per year), 32 teaching assistantships (averaging $3,027 per year) were awarded. Research assistantships Financial award application deadline: 3/1.
Faculty research: Manufacturing strategy, information systems, technology commercialization, managing research and development, historical stock returns. *Total annual research expenditures:* $69,089.
Dr. Stephen G. Allen, Head, 919-515-5584, *Fax:* 919-515-5073, *E-mail:* steve_allen@ncsu.edu. *Web site:* http://www.mgt.ncsu.edu/facdep/bizmgmt/bizman.html

■ NORTHWESTERN UNIVERSITY

The Graduate School, Program in Telecommunications Science, Management, and Policy, Evanston, IL 60208

AWARDS Certificate.

Expenses: Tuition: Full-time $26,526.
Rick Morris, Director, 847-467-1168, *Fax:* 847-467-1171.

■ PACE UNIVERSITY

School of Computer Science and Information Systems, New York, NY 10038

AWARDS Computer communications and networks (Certificate); computer science (MS); computing studies (DPS); information systems (MS); object-oriented programming (Certificate); telecommunications (MS, Certificate). Part-time and evening/weekend programs available.

Faculty: 23 full-time, 9 part-time/adjunct.
Students: 210 full-time (70 women), 446 part-time (165 women); includes 129 minority (49 African Americans, 61 Asian Americans or Pacific Islanders, 19 Hispanic Americans), 197 international. Average age 28. 474 applicants, 72% accepted. In 2001, 112 master's, 6 other advanced degrees awarded.

Entrance requirements: For master's, GRE General Test. *Application deadline:* For fall admission, 7/31 (priority date); for spring admission, 11/30. Applications are processed on a rolling basis. *Application fee:* $65. Electronic applications accepted.
Expenses: Contact institution.
Financial support: Research assistantships, career-related internships or fieldwork available. Support available to part-time students. Financial award applicants required to submit FAFSA.
Dr. Susan Merritt, Dean, 914-422-4375.
Application contact: Joanna Broda, Director of Admissions, 212-346-1652, *Fax:* 212-346-1585, *E-mail:* gradnyc@ pace.edu. *Web site:* http://www.pace.edu/
Find an in-depth description at www.petersons.com/gradchannel.

■ PACE UNIVERSITY, WHITE PLAINS CAMPUS

School of Computer Science and Information Systems, White Plains, NY 10603

AWARDS Computer communications and networks (Certificate); computer science (MS); computing studies (DPS); information systems (MS); object-oriented programming (Certificate); telecommunications (MS, Certificate). Part-time and evening/weekend programs available.

Faculty: 14 full-time, 6 part-time/adjunct.
Students: 73 full-time (30 women), 307 part-time (117 women); includes 122 minority (37 African Americans, 60 Asian Americans or Pacific Islanders, 25 Hispanic Americans), 50 international. Average age 31. 262 applicants, 65% accepted, 117 enrolled. In 2001, 65 master's, 9 other advanced degrees awarded.
Entrance requirements: For master's, GRE General Test. *Application deadline:* For fall admission, 8/1 (priority date); for spring admission, 12/1 (priority date). Applications are processed on a rolling basis. *Application fee:* $65. Electronic applications accepted.
Expenses: Contact institution.
Financial support: Research assistantships, career-related internships or fieldwork available. Support available to part-time students. Financial award applicants required to submit FAFSA.
Dr. Susan Merritt, Dean, 914-422-4375.
Application contact: Joanna Broda, Director of Admissions, 914-422-4283, *Fax:* 914-422-4287, *E-mail:* gradwp@ pace.edu. *Web site:* http://www.pace.edu/

■ THE PENNSYLVANIA STATE UNIVERSITY UNIVERSITY PARK CAMPUS

Graduate School, College of Communications, Department of Telecommunications Studies, State College, University Park, PA 16802-1503

AWARDS MA.

Students: 4 full-time (1 woman), 1 part-time.
Entrance requirements: For master's, GRE General Test. *Application deadline:* For fall admission, 3/30. *Application fee:* $45.
Expenses: Tuition, state resident: full-time $7,882; part-time $333 per credit. Tuition, nonresident: full-time $16,142; part-time $673 per credit. Required fees: $124 per semester.
Dr. Richard Barton, Associate Dean, 814-865-3070.

■ POLYTECHNIC UNIVERSITY, BROOKLYN CAMPUS

Department of Electrical Engineering, Major in Telecommunication Networks, Brooklyn, NY 11201-2990

AWARDS MS. Part-time and evening/weekend programs available.

Degree requirements: For master's, thesis optional.
Entrance requirements: For master's, BS in electrical engineering. Electronic applications accepted.
Find an in-depth description at www.petersons.com/gradchannel.

■ POLYTECHNIC UNIVERSITY, LONG ISLAND GRADUATE CENTER

Graduate Programs, Department of Electrical Engineering, Major in Telecommunication Networks, Melville, NY 11747

AWARDS MS.

Degree requirements: For master's, thesis (for some programs).
Electronic applications accepted.

■ POLYTECHNIC UNIVERSITY, WESTCHESTER GRADUATE CENTER

Graduate Programs, Department of Electrical Engineering, Major in Telecommunication Networks, Hawthorne, NY 10532-1507

AWARDS MS.

Degree requirements: For master's, thesis (for some programs).

■ REGIS UNIVERSITY

School for Professional Studies, Program in Computer Information Technology, Denver, CO 80221-1099

AWARDS Database technologies (MSCIT, Certificate), including database administrator (Certificate), Oracle application development (Certificate), Oracle e-commerce enterprise and Web/Internet Protocol programming (Certificate); e-commerce engineering (MSCIT, Certificate), including advanced e-commerce (Certificate), management of technology (Certificate), Oracle e-commerce enterprise and Web/Internet Protocol programming (Certificate), portal management (Certificate); management of technology (MSCIT); networking technologies (MSCIT); networking technology (Certificate), including e-commerce, network engineering, telecommunications; object-oriented technologies (MSCIT); object-oriented technology (Certificate), including C++ programming, Java programming, Visual Basic programming. Offered at Boulder Campus, Northwest Denver Campus, Southeast Denver Campus, Fort Collins Campus, Colorado Springs Campus, and Broomfield Campus. Part-time and evening/weekend programs available. Postbaccalaureate distance learning degree programs offered (no on-campus study).

Students: 343. Average age 36. In 2001, 40 degrees awarded.
Degree requirements: For master's and Certificate, final research project.
Entrance requirements: For master's and Certificate, GMAT, TOEFL, or university-based test (international applicants), 2 years of related experience, résumé. *Application deadline:* Applications are processed on a rolling basis. *Application fee:* $75.
Expenses: Contact institution.
Financial support: Federal Work-Study available. Support available to part-time students. Financial award applicants required to submit FAFSA.
Don Archer, Chair, 303-458-4302, *Fax:* 303-964-5538.
Application contact: 800-677-9270 Ext. 4080, *Fax:* 303-964-5538, *E-mail:* masters@regis.edu. *Web site:* http:// www.regis.edu/spsgraduate/

■ ROOSEVELT UNIVERSITY

Graduate Division, College of Arts and Sciences, School of Computer Science and Telecommunications, Program in Telecommunications, Chicago, IL 60605-1394

AWARDS MST. Part-time and evening/weekend programs available.

Entrance requirements: For master's, GRE. *Application deadline:* For fall admission, 6/1 (priority date). Applications are processed on a rolling basis. *Application fee:* $25 ($35 for international students).

Roosevelt University (continued)

Expenses: Tuition: Full-time $9,090; part-time $505 per credit hour. Required fees: $100 per term.

Financial support: Application deadline: 2/15.

Faculty research: Coding theory, mathematical models, network design, simulation models. *Total annual research expenditures:* $40,000.

Application contact: Joanne Canyon-Heller, Coordinator of Graduate Admissions, 312-281-3250, *Fax:* 312-341-3523, *E-mail:* applyru@roosevelt.edu. *Web site:* http://www.roosevelt.edu/academics/scst/

■ SAINT MARY'S UNIVERSITY OF MINNESOTA

Graduate School, Program in Telecommunications, Winona, MN 55987-1399

AWARDS MS, MS/MA. Part-time and evening/weekend programs available.

Degree requirements: For master's, thesis, colloquium.

Entrance requirements: For master's, interview, minimum GPA of 2.75.

■ SOUTHERN METHODIST UNIVERSITY

School of Engineering, Department of Electrical Engineering, Dallas, TX 75275

AWARDS Electrical engineering (MSEE, PhD); telecommunications (MS). Part-time and evening/weekend programs available. Postbaccalaureate distance learning degree programs offered (no on-campus study).

Faculty: 18 full-time (1 woman).

Students: 98 full-time (21 women), 272 part-time (49 women); includes 114 minority (20 African Americans, 76 Asian Americans or Pacific Islanders, 18 Hispanic Americans), 91 international. Average age 33. 370 applicants, 49% accepted. In 2001, 96 master's, 6 doctorates awarded. Terminal master's awarded for partial completion of doctoral program.

Degree requirements: For master's, thesis optional; for doctorate, thesis/dissertation, oral and written qualifying exams, oral final exam.

Entrance requirements: For master's, GRE General Test, TOEFL, minimum GPA of 3.0 in last 2 years; bachelor's degree in engineering, mathematics, or sciences; for doctorate, preliminary counseling exam, minimum GPA of 3.0, bachelor's degree in related field. *Application deadline:* For fall admission, 7/1 (priority date); for spring admission, 11/15. Applications are processed on a rolling basis. *Application fee:* $50.

Expenses: Tuition: Part-time $285 per credit hour.

Financial support: In 2001–02, 19 research assistantships (averaging $15,000 per year), 3 teaching assistantships (averaging $9,000 per year) were awarded. Institutionally sponsored loans and tuition waivers (full) also available. Financial award applicants required to submit FAFSA.

Faculty research: Mobile communications, optical and millimeter wave communications, solid state devices and materials, digital signal processing. Mandyam Srinath, Head, 214-768-3114, *Fax:* 214-768-3573.

Application contact: Jim Dees, Director, Student Administration, 214-768-1456, *Fax:* 214-768-3845, *E-mail:* jdees@engr.smu.edu. *Web site:* http://www.seas.smu.edu/ee/

Find an in-depth description at www.petersons.com/gradchannel.

■ STATE UNIVERSITY OF NEW YORK INSTITUTE OF TECHNOLOGY AT UTICA/ROME

School of Information Systems and Engineering Technology, Program in Telecommunications, Utica, NY 13504-3050

AWARDS MS. Part-time and evening/weekend programs available.

Faculty: 3 full-time (0 women), 2 part-time/adjunct (0 women).

Students: 21 full-time (8 women), 20 part-time (6 women); includes 3 minority (2 African Americans, 1 Asian American or Pacific Islander), 19 international. Average age 31. 45 applicants, 84% accepted. In 2001, 4 degrees awarded.

Degree requirements: For master's, thesis, project or capstone.

Entrance requirements: For master's, GRE General Test, TOEFL, minimum GPA of 3.0, letters of recommendation (3). *Application deadline:* For fall admission, 6/15 (priority date). Applications are processed on a rolling basis. *Application fee:* $50.

Expenses: Tuition, state resident: full-time $5,100; part-time $213 per credit hour. Tuition, nonresident: full-time $8,416; part-time $351 per credit hour. Required fees: $525; $21 per credit hour. Tuition and fees vary according to course load.

Financial support: In 2001–02, 24 students received support. Federal Work-Study, scholarships/grants, and unspecified assistantships available. Financial award applicants required to submit FAFSA.

Faculty research: Network design/simulation/management, wireless telecommunication systems, international telecommunications policy and management, information assurance, disaster recovery. Dr. Eugene Newman, Coordinator, 315-792-7230, *Fax:* 315-792-7800, *E-mail:* fejn@sunyit.edu.

Application contact: Marybeth Lyons, Director of Admissions, 315-792-7500, *Fax:* 315-792-7837, *E-mail:* smbl@sunyit.edu.

Find an in-depth description at www.petersons.com/gradchannel.

■ SYRACUSE UNIVERSITY

Graduate School, School of Information Studies, Program in Telecommunications and Network Management, Syracuse, NY 13244-0003

AWARDS MS. Part-time and evening/weekend programs available. Postbaccalaureate distance learning degree programs offered (minimal on-campus study).

Faculty: 33 full-time (12 women), 42 part-time/adjunct (12 women).

Students: 20 full-time (1 woman), 62 part-time (12 women); includes 3 minority (2 African Americans, 1 Hispanic American), 44 international. Average age 31. In 2001, 59 degrees awarded.

Degree requirements: For master's, internship or research project.

Entrance requirements: For master's, GRE General Test. *Application deadline:* For fall admission, 2/15 (priority date); for spring admission, 11/1 (priority date). *Application fee:* $50. Electronic applications accepted.

Expenses: Tuition: Full-time $15,528; part-time $647 per credit. Required fees: $420; $38 per term. Tuition and fees vary according to program.

Financial support: Fellowships, research assistantships, teaching assistantships, career-related internships or fieldwork, Federal Work-Study, and tuition waivers (partial) available.

Faculty research: Multimedia, information resources management.

Find an in-depth description at www.petersons.com/gradchannel.

■ TEXAS TECH UNIVERSITY

Graduate School, Jerry S. Rawls College of Business Administration, Area of Information Systems and Quantitative Sciences, Lubbock, TX 79409

AWARDS Business statistics (MSBA, PhD); management information systems (MSBA, PhD); production and operations management (MSBA, PhD); telecommunications (MSBA). Part-time programs available.

Faculty: 16 full-time (1 woman).

Students: 64 full-time (15 women), 16 part-time (5 women); includes 1 minority (Hispanic American), 64 international. Average age 29. 71 applicants, 49% accepted, 18 enrolled. In 2001, 32 degrees awarded.

Degree requirements: For master's, comprehensive exam or capstone course; for doctorate, thesis/dissertation, qualifying exams.

Entrance requirements: For master's and doctorate, GMAT, holistic profile of academic credentials. *Application deadline:* For fall admission, 3/1 (priority date); for spring admission, 9/1 (priority date). Applications are processed on a rolling basis. *Application fee:* $25 ($50 for international students). Electronic applications accepted.
Expenses: Tuition, state resident: full-time $1,926; part-time $107 per credit hour. Tuition, nonresident: full-time $5,724; part-time $318 per credit hour. Required fees: $779; $737 per year. Tuition and fees vary according to course level, course load and program.
Financial support: In 2001–02, 18 research assistantships (averaging $5,500 per year), 4 teaching assistantships (averaging $14,816 per year) were awarded. Federal Work-Study also available.
Faculty research: Database management systems, systems management and engineering, expert systems and adaptive knowledge-based sciences, statistical analysis and design.
Dr. Surya B. Yadav, Coordinator, 806-742-3192, *Fax:* 806-742-3193, *E-mail:* odsby@ba.ttu.edu.
Application contact: Janet L. Hubbert, Director, Graduate Services Center, 806-742-3184, *Fax:* 806-742-3958, *E-mail:* bagrad@ba.ttu.edu. *Web site:* http://is.ba.ttu.edu

■ TEXAS TECH UNIVERSITY

Graduate School, Jerry S. Rawls College of Business Administration, Programs in Business Administration, Lubbock, TX 79409

AWARDS Agricultural business (MBA); e-business (MBA); entrepreneurial family studies (MBA); entrepreneurial skills (MBA); finance (MBA); general business (MBA); global entrepreneurship (MBA); high performance management (MBA); international business (MBA); management information systems (MBA), including systems, technology, telecom and network management; marketing (MBA). Part-time and evening/weekend programs available.
Students: 138 full-time (38 women), 25 part-time (10 women); includes 14 minority (3 African Americans, 2 Asian Americans or Pacific Islanders, 8 Hispanic Americans, 1 Native American), 23 international. Average age 25. 201 applicants, 49% accepted, 55 enrolled. In 2001, 82 degrees awarded.
Degree requirements: For master's, capstone course.
Entrance requirements: For master's, GMAT, holistic review of academic credentials. *Application deadline:* For fall admission, 3/1 (priority date); for spring admission, 9/1 (priority date). Applications are processed on a rolling basis. *Application fee:* $25 ($50 for international students). Electronic applications accepted.

Expenses: Tuition, state resident: full-time $1,926; part-time $107 per credit hour. Tuition, nonresident: full-time $5,724; part-time $318 per credit hour. Required fees: $779; $737 per year. Tuition and fees vary according to course level, course load and program.
Financial support: In 2001–02, 10 research assistantships (averaging $5,500 per year) were awarded; teaching assistantships, career-related internships or fieldwork, Federal Work-Study, scholarships/grants, health care benefits, and unspecified assistantships also available. Support available to part-time students. Financial award applicants required to submit FAFSA.
Dr. W. Jay Conover, Director, 806-742-1546, *Fax:* 806-742-3958, *E-mail:* conover@ba.ttu.edu.
Application contact: Janet L. Hubbert, Director, Graduate Services Center, 806-742-3184, *Fax:* 806-742-3958, *E-mail:* bagrad@ba.ttu.edu. *Web site:* http://grad.ba.ttu.edu/

■ UNIVERSITY OF ARKANSAS

Graduate School, College of Engineering, Department of Electrical Engineering, Program in Telecommunications Engineering, Fayetteville, AR 72701-1201

AWARDS MS Tc E.
Students: 1 full-time (0 women), 1 international. 3 applicants, 100% accepted. *Application fee:* $40 ($50 for international students).
Expenses: Tuition, state resident: full-time $3,553; part-time $197 per credit. Tuition, nonresident: full-time $8,411; part-time $467 per credit. Required fees: $42 per credit. Tuition and fees vary according to course load and program.
Financial support: Application deadline: 4/1.
Dr. J. S. Charlton, Head, 479-575-6048.

■ UNIVERSITY OF CALIFORNIA, SAN DIEGO

Graduate Studies and Research, Department of Electrical and Computer Engineering, La Jolla, CA 92093

AWARDS Applied ocean science (MS, PhD); applied physics (MS, PhD); communication theory and systems (MS, PhD); computer engineering (MS, PhD); electrical engineering (M Eng); electronic circuits and systems (MS, PhD); intelligent systems, robotics and control (MS, PhD); photonics (MS, PhD). Signal and image processing (MS, PhD).
Faculty: 35.
Students: 334 (44 women). 1,149 applicants, 20% accepted, 114 enrolled. In 2001, 51 master's, 12 doctorates awarded.
Entrance requirements: For master's and doctorate, GRE General Test. *Application*

deadline: For fall admission, 1/12. *Application fee:* $40. Electronic applications accepted.
Expenses: Tuition, nonresident: full-time $10,434. Required fees: $4,883.
Charles Tu, Chair.
Application contact: Graduate Coordinator, 858-534-6606.

■ UNIVERSITY OF COLORADO AT BOULDER

Graduate School, College of Engineering and Applied Science, Interdisciplinary Telecommunications Program, Boulder, CO 80309

AWARDS ME, MS, MBA/MS. Part-time programs available. Postbaccalaureate distance learning degree programs offered.
Faculty: 5 full-time (0 women).
Students: 120 full-time (36 women), 38 part-time (11 women); includes 26 minority (6 African Americans, 17 Asian Americans or Pacific Islanders, 3 Hispanic Americans), 64 international. Average age 30. 113 applicants, 73% accepted. In 2001, 137 degrees awarded.
Degree requirements: For master's, thesis or alternative, comprehensive exam.
Entrance requirements: For master's, minimum undergraduate GPA of 3.0. *Application deadline:* For fall admission, 3/1 (priority date). Applications are processed on a rolling basis. *Application fee:* $50 ($60 for international students).
Expenses: Tuition, state resident: full-time $3,474. Tuition, nonresident: full-time $16,624.
Financial support: In 2001–02, 15 fellowships (averaging $4,487 per year), 10 teaching assistantships with full tuition reimbursements (averaging $18,789 per year) were awarded. Career-related internships or fieldwork also available. Financial award application deadline: 1/1.
Faculty research: Optical and wireless telecommunication. *Total annual research expenditures:* $376,245.
Dr. Dale Hatfield, Director, 303-492-8916, *Fax:* 303-492-1112.
Application contact: Eydie Mitchel, Graduate Secretary, 303-492-8475, *Fax:* 303-492-1112, *E-mail:* mitchee@spot.colorado.edu. *Web site:* http://morse.colorado.edu/

Find an in-depth description at www.petersons.com/gradchannel.

■ UNIVERSITY OF DENVER

University College, Denver, CO 80208

AWARDS Applied communication (MSS); computer information systems (MCIS); environmental policy and management (MEPM); healthcare systems (MHS); liberal studies (MLS); library and information services (MLIS); public health (MPH); technology management (MoTM); telecommunications (MTEL). Part-time and evening/weekend programs available.

University of Denver (continued)
Postbaccalaureate distance learning degree programs offered (no on-campus study).

Faculty: 167 part-time/adjunct (52 women).
Students: 1,244 (618 women); includes 177 minority (65 African Americans, 53 Asian Americans or Pacific Islanders, 54 Hispanic Americans, 5 Native Americans) 76 international. 54 applicants, 85% accepted. In 2001, 274 degrees awarded.
Entrance requirements: For master's, minimum undergraduate GPA of 3.0. *Application deadline:* For fall admission, 7/15 (priority date); for winter admission, 10/14 (priority date); for spring admission, 2/10 (priority date). Applications are processed on a rolling basis. *Application fee:* $25.
Expenses: Contact institution.
Financial support: In 2001–02, 174 students received support. *Total annual research expenditures:* $59,206.
Mike Bloom, Dean, 303-871-3141.
Application contact: Cindy Kraft, Admission Coordinator, 303-871-3969, *Fax:* 303-871-3303. *Web site:* http://www.du.edu/ucol/

■ UNIVERSITY OF LOUISIANA AT LAFAYETTE

Graduate School, College of Engineering, Department of Electrical and Computer Engineering, Program in Telecommunications, Lafayette, LA 70504

AWARDS MSTC.

Faculty: 5 full-time (1 woman).
Students: 25 full-time (8 women), 16 part-time (3 women); includes 3 minority (all African Americans), 25 international. 88 applicants, 56% accepted, 12 enrolled. In 2001, 22 degrees awarded.
Degree requirements: For master's, thesis or alternative.
Entrance requirements: For master's, GRE General Test, minimum GPA of 2.75. *Application deadline:* For fall admission, 5/15. *Application fee:* $20 ($30 for international students).
Expenses: Tuition, state resident: full-time $2,317; part-time $79 per credit. Tuition, nonresident: full-time $8,882; part-time $369 per credit. International tuition: $9,018 full-time.
Financial support: In 2001–02, 3 research assistantships with full tuition reimbursements (averaging $5,500 per year) were awarded; fellowships Financial award application deadline: 5/1.
Dr. Robert Henry, Head, 337-482-6568.
Application contact: Dr. George Thomas, Graduate Coordinator, 337-482-5365.

■ UNIVERSITY OF MARYLAND, COLLEGE PARK

Graduate Studies and Research, A. James Clark School of Engineering, Department of Electrical and Computer Engineering, Program in Telecommunications, College Park, MD 20742

AWARDS MS. Part-time and evening/weekend programs available.

Students: 53 full-time (8 women), 28 part-time (7 women); includes 15 minority (9 African Americans, 5 Asian Americans or Pacific Islanders, 1 Hispanic American), 54 international. 152 applicants, 38% accepted, 32 enrolled. In 2001, 21 degrees awarded.
Degree requirements: For master's, thesis or alternative.
Entrance requirements: For master's, GRE General Test, minimum GPA of 3.0, professional experience. *Application deadline:* For fall admission, 8/1; for spring admission, 12/1. Applications are processed on a rolling basis. *Application fee:* $50 ($70 for international students). Electronic applications accepted.
Expenses: Tuition, state resident: part-time $289 per credit hour. Tuition, nonresident: part-time $448 per credit hour. One-time fee: $436 part-time. Full-time tuition and fees vary according to course load, campus/location and program.
Financial support: Fellowships, research assistantships, teaching assistantships available. Financial award applicants required to submit FAFSA.
Asante Shakour, Associate Director, 301-405-3683, *Fax:* 301-314-9281.
Application contact: Trudy Lindsey, Director, Graduate Admissions and Records, 301-405-6991, *Fax:* 301-314-9305, *E-mail:* grschool@deans.umd.edu.
Find an in-depth description at www.petersons.com/gradchannel.

■ UNIVERSITY OF MISSOURI–KANSAS CITY

School of Interdisciplinary Computing and Engineering, Kansas City, MO 64110-2499

AWARDS Computer networking (MS, PhD). Software engineering (MS); telecommunications networking (MS, PhD). PhD offered through the School of Graduate Studies. Part-time programs available.

Faculty: 26 full-time (3 women), 18 part-time/adjunct (1 woman).
Students: 105 full-time (37 women), 103 part-time (27 women); includes 12 minority (3 African Americans, 8 Asian Americans or Pacific Islanders, 1 Hispanic American), 171 international. Average age 29. In 2001, 37 degrees awarded.
Degree requirements: For doctorate, thesis/dissertation.

Entrance requirements: For master's, GRE General Test, minimum GPA of 3.0; for doctorate, GRE General Test, minimum GPA of 3.5. *Application deadline:* For fall admission, 3/1 (priority date); for spring admission, 10/1. Applications are processed on a rolling basis. *Application fee:* $25.
Expenses: Tuition, state resident: part-time $233 per credit hour. Tuition, nonresident: part-time $623 per credit hour. Tuition and fees vary according to course load.
Financial support: In 2001–02, 15 research assistantships, 15 teaching assistantships were awarded. Career-related internships or fieldwork, Federal Work-Study, institutionally sponsored loans, and tuition waivers (partial) also available. Support available to part-time students. Financial award application deadline: 3/1.
Faculty research: Multimedia networking, distributed systems/databases, data/network security.
Dr. William Osbourne, Dean, 816-235-1193, *Fax:* 816-235-5159. *Web site:* http://www.cstp.umkc.edu/
Find an in-depth description at www.petersons.com/gradchannel.

■ UNIVERSITY OF PENNSYLVANIA

School of Engineering and Applied Science, Telecommunications and Networking Program, Philadelphia, PA 19104

AWARDS MSE. Part-time programs available.
Electronic applications accepted. *Web site:* http://www.seas.upenn.edu/PROFPROG/tcom/
Find an in-depth description at www.petersons.com/gradchannel.

■ UNIVERSITY OF PITTSBURGH

School of Information Sciences, Department of Information Science and Telecommunications, Program in Telecommunications, Pittsburgh, PA 15260

AWARDS MST, Certificate. Part-time and evening/weekend programs available.

Faculty: 5 full-time (0 women), 4 part-time/adjunct (1 woman).
Students: 59 full-time (14 women), 28 part-time (4 women); includes 5 minority (3 African Americans, 2 Asian Americans or Pacific Islanders), 51 international. 115 applicants, 80% accepted, 20 enrolled. In 2001, 39 degrees awarded.
Degree requirements: For master's, thesis optional. *Median time to degree:* Master's–1.3 years full-time, 2.5 years part-time.
Entrance requirements: For master's, GRE General Test, previous course work in computer programming calculus, and probability. *Application deadline:* For fall

admission, 6/1; for winter admission, 10/1; for spring admission, 2/1. Applications are processed on a rolling basis. *Application fee:* $40.

Expenses: Tuition, state resident: full-time $9,410; part-time $385 per credit. Tuition, nonresident: full-time $19,376; part-time $797 per credit. Required fees: $480; $90 per term. Tuition and fees vary according to program.

Financial support: In 2001–02, 45 students received support, including 4 fellowships with full and partial tuition reimbursements available, 16 research assistantships with full and partial tuition reimbursements available (averaging $16,500 per year), 29 teaching assistantships with full and partial tuition reimbursements available (averaging $14,670 per year); career-related internships or fieldwork, scholarships/grants, and tuition waivers (full and partial) also available. Financial award application deadline: 1/15.

Faculty research: Telephony, photonic switching, telecommunications policy, network management, wireless information systems. *Total annual research expenditures:* $447,542.

Dr. Richard A. Thompson, Director, 412-624-9423, *Fax:* 412-624-2788, *E-mail:* rat@tele.pitt.edu.

Application contact: Ninette Kay, Admissions Coordinator, 412-624-5146, *Fax:* 412-624-5231, *E-mail:* nkay@mail.sis.pitt.edu. *Web site:* http://www.tele.pitt.edu/

■ THE UNIVERSITY OF TEXAS AT DALLAS

Erik Jonsson School of Engineering and Computer Science, Programs in Electrical Engineering, Richardson, TX 75083-0688

AWARDS Electrical engineering (MSEE, PhD); microelectronics (MSEE); telecommunications (MSEE, MSTE). Part-time and evening/weekend programs available.

Faculty: 26 full-time (1 woman), 5 part-time/adjunct (1 woman).

Students: 195 full-time (38 women), 126 part-time (18 women); includes 52 minority (6 African Americans, 38 Asian Americans or Pacific Islanders, 8 Hispanic Americans), 212 international. Average age 28. 950 applicants, 29% accepted. In 2001, 68 master's, 7 doctorates awarded.

Degree requirements: For master's, thesis or major design project; for doctorate, thesis/dissertation.

Entrance requirements: For master's, GRE General Test, TOEFL, minimum GPA of 3.0 in related bachelor's degree; for doctorate, GRE General Test, TOEFL, minimum GPA of 3.5. *Application deadline:* For fall admission, 7/15; for spring admission, 11/15. Applications are processed on a rolling basis. *Application fee:* $25 ($75 for international students). Electronic applications accepted.

Expenses: Tuition, state resident: full-time $1,440; part-time $84 per credit. Tuition, nonresident: full-time $5,310; part-time $295 per credit. Required fees: $1,835; $87 per credit. $138 per term.

Financial support: In 2001–02, 4 fellowships (averaging $3,000 per year), 40 research assistantships with full tuition reimbursements (averaging $5,288 per year), 35 teaching assistantships with full tuition reimbursements (averaging $5,256 per year) were awarded. Federal Work-Study, institutionally sponsored loans, and scholarships/grants also available. Support available to part-time students. Financial award application deadline: 4/30; financial award applicants required to submit FAFSA.

Faculty research: Communications and signal processing, solid-state devices and circuits, digital systems, optical devices, materials and systems, lasers and photonics.

Dr. Gerry Burnham, Head, 972-883-6755, *Fax:* 972-883-2710, *E-mail:* burnham@utdallas.edu.

Application contact: Kathy Gribble, Secretary, 972-883-2649, *Fax:* 972-883-2710, *E-mail:* ee-grad-info@utdallas.edu. *Web site:* http://www.utdallas.edu/dept/ee/

■ WESTERN ILLINOIS UNIVERSITY

School of Graduate Studies, College of Education and Human Services, Department of Instructional Technology and Telecommunications, Macomb, IL 61455-1390

AWARDS Distance learning (Certificate); graphics application (Certificate); instructional technology and telecommunications (MS); multimedia (Certificate); technology integration in education (Certificate); training development (Certificate). Postbaccalaureate distance learning degree programs offered (no on-campus study).

Faculty: 6 full-time (2 women).

Students: 17 full-time (11 women), 82 part-time (46 women); includes 6 minority (3 African Americans, 3 Hispanic Americans), 5 international. Average age 37. 26 applicants, 73% accepted. In 2001, 33 master's, 5 other advanced degrees awarded.

Degree requirements: For master's, thesis or alternative.

Application deadline: Applications are processed on a rolling basis. *Application fee:* $0 ($25 for international students). Electronic applications accepted.

Expenses: Tuition, state resident: part-time $108 per credit hour. Tuition, nonresident: part-time $216 per credit hour. Required fees: $33 per credit hour.

Financial support: In 2001–02, 5 students received support, including 5 research assistantships with full tuition reimbursements available (averaging $5,720 per year)

Financial award applicants required to submit FAFSA.

Faculty research: Distance learning, educational technology.

John Jamison, Interim Chairperson, 300-298-1952.

Application contact: Dr. Barbara Baily, Director of Graduate Studies, 309-298-1806, *Fax:* 309-298-2345, *E-mail:* grad-office@wiu.edu.

■ WIDENER UNIVERSITY

School of Engineering, Program in Electrical/Telecommunication Engineering, Chester, PA 19013-5792

AWARDS ME, ME/MBA. Part-time and evening/weekend programs available.

Degree requirements: For master's, thesis optional.

Entrance requirements: For master's, GMAT (ME/MBA).

Expenses: Tuition: Part-time $500 per credit. Required fees: $25 per semester.

Faculty research: Signal and image processing, electromagnetics, telecommunications and computer network.

TELECOMMUNICATIONS MANAGEMENT

■ ALASKA PACIFIC UNIVERSITY

Graduate Programs, Business Administration Department, Program in Telecommunication Management, Anchorage, AK 99508-4672

AWARDS MBATM. Part-time and evening/weekend programs available.

Faculty: 1 full-time (0 women), 2 part-time/adjunct (0 women).

Students: 4 full-time (1 woman), 21 part-time (5 women); includes 7 minority (2 African Americans, 1 Asian American or Pacific Islander, 1 Hispanic American, 3 Native Americans). Average age 37. In 2001, 13 degrees awarded.

Degree requirements: For master's, thesis (for some programs), comprehensive exam (for some programs).

Entrance requirements: For master's, GMAT or GRE, minimum GPA of 3.0. *Application deadline:* For fall admission, 4/1 (priority date); for spring admission, 12/15. Applications are processed on a rolling basis. *Application fee:* $25.

Expenses: Tuition: Full-time $9,600; part-time $400 per semester hour. Required fees: $80; $40 per semester. Tuition and fees vary according to program.

Financial support: In 2001–02, 4 research assistantships were awarded; career-related internships or fieldwork, Federal Work-Study, and scholarships/grants also available. Support available to part-time students. Financial award application deadline: 3/15; financial award applicants required to submit FAFSA.

Alaska Pacific University (continued)
Dr. Dale Lehman, Director, 907-564-8271, *Fax:* 907-562-4276, *E-mail:* dlehman@ alaskapacific.edu.
Application contact: Ernie Norton, Director of Admissions, 907-564-8248, *Fax:* 907-564-8317, *E-mail:* ernien@ alaskapacific.edu. *Web site:* http:// www.alaskapacific.edu/

■ CANISIUS COLLEGE

Graduate Division, Richard J. Wehle School of Business, Program in Telecommunications Management, Buffalo, NY 14208-1098

AWARDS MTM.

Faculty: 7 full-time (1 woman), 4 part-time/adjunct (1 woman).
Students: 1 (woman) full-time, 21 part-time (5 women); includes 1 minority (Asian American or Pacific Islander). Average age 29. 10 applicants, 80% accepted, 7 enrolled. In 2001, 8 degrees awarded. *Median time to degree:* Master's–2 years full-time, 3 years part-time.
Entrance requirements: For master's, GRE. *Application deadline:* For fall admission, 7/1 (priority date); for spring admission, 11/1 (priority date). Applications are processed on a rolling basis. *Application fee:* $25. Electronic applications accepted.
Expenses: Tuition: Full-time $11,640; part-time $485 per credit hour. Required fees: $234. Tuition and fees vary according to program.
Financial support: Research assistantships, career-related internships or fieldwork, scholarships/grants, and unspecified assistantships available. Support available to part-time students. Financial award application deadline: 6/15; financial award applicants required to submit FAFSA.
Dr. Linda Volonino, Head, 716-888-2219, *E-mail:* volonino@canisius.edu.
Application contact: Laura McEwen, Director, 716-888-2140, *Fax:* 716-888-3211, *E-mail:* gradubus@canisius.edu. *Web site:* http://www.canisius.edu/

■ CAPITOL COLLEGE

Graduate Programs, Laurel, MD 20708-9759

AWARDS Computer science (MS); electrical engineering (MS); electronic commerce management (MS); information and telecommunications systems management (MS); information architecture (MS); network security (MS). Part-time and evening/weekend programs available. Postbaccalaureate distance learning degree programs offered (no on-campus study).

Faculty: 3 full-time (0 women), 34 part-time/adjunct (4 women).
Students: 6 full-time (3 women), 625 part-time (175 women). Average age 35. 400 applicants, 75% accepted, 275 enrolled. In 2001, 52 degrees awarded. *Median time to degree:* Master's–2 years part-time.

Entrance requirements: For master's, GRE General Test and TOEFL (for international students), minimum GPA of 2.5. *Application deadline:* For fall admission, 7/1 (priority date); for winter admission, 12/1 (priority date); for spring admission, 3/1 (priority date). Applications are processed on a rolling basis. *Application fee:* $100 for international students. Electronic applications accepted.
Expenses: Tuition: Part-time $354 per credit.
Financial support: In 2001–02, 2 students received support. Available to part-time students. Applicants required to submit FAFSA.
Pat Smit, Dean of Academics, 301-369-2800 Ext. 3044, *Fax:* 301-953-3876, *E-mail:* gradschool@capitol-college.edu.
Application contact: Ken Crockett, Director of Graduate Admissions, 301-369-2800 Ext. 3026, *Fax:* 301-953-3876, *E-mail:* gradschool@capitol-college.edu. *Web site:* http://www.capitol-college.edu/

■ DEVRY UNIVERSITY-KELLER GRADUATE SCHOOL OF MANAGEMENT

Graduate Program, Oakbrook Terrace, IL 60181

AWARDS Accounting and financial management (MAFM); business administration (MBA); human resources management (MHRM); information systems management (MISM); project management (MPM); telecommunications management (MTM). Part-time and evening/weekend programs available. Postbaccalaureate distance learning degree programs offered (no on-campus study).

Faculty: 33 full-time, 719 part-time/adjunct.
Students: 1,773 full-time (942 women), 5,169 part-time (2,691 women); includes 2,621 minority (1,818 African Americans, 483 Asian Americans or Pacific Islanders, 320 Hispanic Americans). In 2001, 1373 degrees awarded.
Degree requirements: For master's, business plan (MBA), capstone project (MHRM, MPM, MTM, MAFM).
Entrance requirements: For master's, GMAT, GRE General Test, or institutional assessment, interview. *Application deadline:* Applications are processed on a rolling basis. *Application fee:* $0.
Expenses: Tuition: Full-time $11,850; part-time $297 per quarter hour. Tuition and fees vary according to campus/location.
Dr. Sherril Hoel, Academic Dean of Administration and Accreditation, 630-574-1894.
Application contact: Peggy Simpson, Director, Central Services, 630-706-3243, *E-mail:* psimpson@keller.edu. *Web site:* http://www.keller.edu/

■ GOLDEN GATE UNIVERSITY

School of Business, San Francisco, CA 94105-2968

AWARDS Accounting (M Ac, MBA); business administration (EMBA, DBA); economics (MS); finance (MBA, MS); financial planning (Certificate); human resource management (MS); human resources management (Certificate); information systems (MBA); international business (MBA); management (MBA); marketing (MBA, MS); operations management (MBA); public relations (MS, Certificate); telecommunications (MBA). Part-time and evening/weekend programs available.

Degree requirements: For doctorate, thesis/dissertation.
Entrance requirements: For master's, GMAT (MBA), TOEFL, minimum GPA of 2.5 (MS). *Web site:* http://www.ggu.edu/schools/business/home.html

■ GOLDEN GATE UNIVERSITY

School of Technology and Industry, San Francisco, CA 94105-2968

AWARDS Hospitality administration and tourism (MS); information systems (MS, Certificate); telecommunications management (MS, Certificate). Part-time and evening/weekend programs available.

Entrance requirements: For master's, GMAT (MBA), TOEFL, minimum GPA of 2.5.

■ HOFSTRA UNIVERSITY

College of Liberal Arts and Sciences, Division of Humanities, Department of Speech Language-Hearing Sciences, Hempstead, NY 11549

AWARDS Audiology (MA); audiology and speech-language pathology (MA); biological extension of speech-language pathology (MA). Speech-language pathology (MA); teachers of speech and hearing handicapped (MA). Part-time programs available.

Faculty: 6 full-time (4 women), 5 part-time/adjunct (3 women).
Students: 23 full-time (21 women), 62 part-time (61 women). Average age 27. In 2001, 32 degrees awarded.
Degree requirements: For master's, 3 off-campus externships.
Entrance requirements: For master's, GRE General Test, minimum GPA of 3.0, academic letters of recommendation (3). *Application deadline:* For fall admission, 2/1 (priority date). Applications are processed on a rolling basis. *Application fee:* $40 ($75 for international students).
Expenses: Tuition: Full-time $12,408. Tuition and fees vary according to course load and program.
Financial support: In 2001–02, 12 fellowships were awarded; research assistantships, career-related internships or fieldwork, Federal Work-Study, and scholarships/grants also available. Support available to

part-time students. Financial award application deadline: 3/1.
Faculty research: Acoustic aspects of speech production, emotional and pragmatic aspects of aphasia, learning disorders and literacy, second language acquisition, hearing aids. *Total annual research expenditures:* $2,700.
Dr. Ronald L. Bloom, Chairperson, 516-463-5308, *Fax:* 516-463-5260, *E-mail:* sphrlb@hofstra.edu.
Application contact: Mary Beth Carey, Vice President of Enrollment Services, *Fax:* 516-560-7660, *E-mail:* hofstra@ hofstra.edu.

■ ILLINOIS INSTITUTE OF TECHNOLOGY

Stuart Graduate School of Business, Program in Business Administration, Chicago, IL 60616-3793

AWARDS Finance (MBA); information management (MBA); international business (MBA); management science (MBA); marketing (MBA); operations management (MBA); organization and management (MBA). Strategic management (MBA); telecommunications management (MBA). Part-time and evening/weekend programs available.

Students: 97 full-time (31 women), 181 part-time (45 women); includes 44 minority (11 African Americans, 30 Asian Americans or Pacific Islanders, 3 Hispanic Americans), 121 international. Average age 31. 274 applicants, 65% accepted. In 2001, 84 degrees awarded.
Entrance requirements: For master's, GMAT or GRE, TOEFL. *Application deadline:* For fall admission, 8/1; for spring admission, 4/15. Applications are processed on a rolling basis. *Application fee:* $50. Electronic applications accepted.
Expenses: Tuition: Part-time $590 per credit hour.
Financial support: Institutionally sponsored loans, scholarships/grants, and unspecified assistantships available. Support available to part-time students. Financial award applicants required to submit FAFSA.
Application contact: Lynn Miller, Director, Admission, 312-906-6544, *Fax:* 312-906-6549, *E-mail:* degrees@stuart.iit.edu. *Web site:* http://www.stuart.iit.edu/mba/ index.html
Find an in-depth description at www.petersons.com/gradchannel.

■ MICHIGAN STATE UNIVERSITY

Graduate School, College of Communication Arts and Sciences, Department of Telecommunication, East Lansing, MI 48824

AWARDS Digital media arts and technology (MA); information and telecommunication management (MA); information policy and society (MA); mass media (PhD); telecommunication (MA).

Faculty: 14 full-time (3 women).
Students: 21 full-time (11 women), 61 part-time (24 women); includes 8 minority (4 African Americans, 3 Asian Americans or Pacific Islanders, 1 Hispanic American), 49 international. Average age 28. 98 applicants, 49% accepted. In 2001, 38 degrees awarded.
Degree requirements: For master's, thesis (for some programs); for doctorate, thesis/dissertation.
Entrance requirements: For master's, GRE General Test, TOEFL, minimum GPA of 3.25. *Application deadline:* Applications are processed on a rolling basis. *Application fee:* $30 ($40 for international students).
Expenses: Tuition, state resident: part-time $244 per credit hour. Tuition, nonresident: part-time $494 per credit hour. Required fees: $268 per semester. Tuition and fees vary according to course load, degree level and program.
Financial support: In 2001–02, 7 fellowships (averaging $2,971 per year), 12 research assistantships with tuition reimbursements (averaging $11,283 per year), 12 teaching assistantships with tuition reimbursements (averaging $10,436 per year) were awarded. Career-related internships or fieldwork and institutionally sponsored loans also available. Support available to part-time students. Financial award applicants required to submit FAFSA.
Faculty research: New telecommunication technologies, cable, international communication, children and television, minority ownerships and programs, mass media. *Total annual research expenditures:* $452,985.
Dr. Mark Levy, Chair, 517-355-8372, *Fax:* 517-355-1292.
Application contact: Director of Graduate Studies, 517-355-8372, *Fax:* 517-355-1292. *Web site:* http://tc.msu.edu/

■ MORGAN STATE UNIVERSITY

School of Graduate Studies, College of Liberal Arts, Department of Telecommunications Management, Baltimore, MD 21251

AWARDS MS.

Degree requirements: For master's, comprehensive exam.
Entrance requirements: For master's, GRE, TOEFL. *Application deadline:* For fall admission, 2/1; for spring admission, 10/1. Applications are processed on a rolling basis. *Application fee:* $0.
Expenses: Tuition, state resident: part-time $193 per credit. Tuition, nonresident: part-time $364 per credit. Required fees: $40 per credit.
Financial support: Application deadline: 4/1.
Dr. Allan J. Kennedy, Graduate Coordinator, 443-885-3502.

Application contact: Dr. James E. Waller, Admissions and Programs Officer, 443-885-3185, *Fax:* 443-319-3837, *E-mail:* jwaller@moac.morgan.edu.

■ MURRAY STATE UNIVERSITY

College of Business and Public Affairs, Program in Telecommunications Systems Management, Murray, KY 42071-0009

AWARDS MS.

Students: 47 full-time (12 women), 16 part-time (6 women); includes 2 minority (both Asian Americans or Pacific Islanders), 37 international. 17 applicants, 94% accepted.
Application deadline: Applications are processed on a rolling basis. *Application fee:* $25.
Expenses: Tuition, state resident: full-time $1,440; part-time $169 per hour. Tuition, nonresident: full-time $4,004; part-time $450 per hour.
Financial support: Application deadline: 4/1.
Dr. Gerry Muuka, Coordinator, 270-762-4190, *Fax:* 270-762-3482, *E-mail:* gerry.muuka@murraystate.edu.

■ NATIONAL UNIVERSITY

Academic Affairs, School of Business and Technology, Department of Technology, La Jolla, CA 92037-1011

AWARDS Biotechnology (MBA); electronic commerce (MBA, MS); environmental management (MBA). Software engineering (MS). Space commerce (MBA); technology management (MBA, MS); telecommunications systems management (MS). Part-time and evening/weekend programs available. Postbaccalaureate distance learning degree programs offered (minimal on-campus study).

Faculty: 9 full-time (0 women), 148 part-time/adjunct (20 women).
Students: 349 full-time (108 women), 130 part-time (44 women); includes 145 minority (45 African Americans, 76 Asian Americans or Pacific Islanders, 21 Hispanic Americans, 3 Native Americans), 138 international. 82 applicants, 100% accepted. In 2001, 250 degrees awarded.
Entrance requirements: For master's, interview, minimum GPA of 2.5. *Application deadline:* Applications are processed on a rolling basis. *Application fee:* $60 ($100 for international students).
Expenses: Tuition: Part-time $221 per quarter hour.
Financial support: Institutionally sponsored loans, scholarships/grants, and tuition waivers (full and partial) available. Support available to part-time students. Financial award application deadline: 5/1; financial award applicants required to submit FAFSA.
Dr. Leonid Preiser, Chair, 858-642-8425, *Fax:* 858-642-8716, *E-mail:* lpreiser@ nu.edu.

National University (continued)

Application contact: Nancy Rohland, Director of Enrollment Management, 858-642-8180, *Fax:* 858-642-8710, *E-mail:* advisor@nu.edu. *Web site:* http://www.nu.edu/

■ NORTHWESTERN UNIVERSITY

The Graduate School, Program in Telecommunications Science, Management, and Policy, Evanston, IL 60208

AWARDS Certificate.

Expenses: Tuition: Full-time $26,526. Rick Morris, Director, 847-467-1168, *Fax:* 847-467-1171.

■ OKLAHOMA STATE UNIVERSITY

Graduate College, College of Business Administration, Program in Telecommunications Management, Stillwater, OK 74078

AWARDS MS.

Students: 56 full-time (20 women), 119 part-time (36 women); includes 15 minority (3 African Americans, 8 Asian Americans or Pacific Islanders, 1 Hispanic American, 3 Native Americans), 57 international. Average age 31. 120 applicants, 68% accepted. In 2001, 93 degrees awarded.
Entrance requirements: For master's, GMAT or GRE, TOEFL. *Application fee:* $25.
Expenses: Tuition, state resident: part-time $92 per credit hour. Tuition, nonresident: part-time $297 per credit hour. Required fees: $21 per credit hour. $14 per semester. One-time fee: $20. Tuition and fees vary according to course load.
Financial support: In 2001–02, 25 research assistantships (averaging $6,236 per year), 3 teaching assistantships (averaging $764 per year) were awarded.
Dr. Mark Weiser, Director, 405-744-9000.

■ POLYTECHNIC UNIVERSITY, BROOKLYN CAMPUS

Department of Management, Major in Telecommunications and Information Management, Brooklyn, NY 11201-2990

AWARDS MS.

Degree requirements: For master's, thesis or alternative.
Entrance requirements: For master's, GMAT, minimum B average in undergraduate course work. Electronic applications accepted.

■ REGIS UNIVERSITY

School for Professional Studies, Program in Computer Information Technology, Denver, CO 80221-1099

AWARDS Database technologies (MSCIT, Certificate), including database administrator (Certificate), Oracle application development (Certificate), Oracle e-commerce enterprise and Web/Internet Protocol programming (Certificate); e-commerce engineering (MSCIT, Certificate), including advanced e-commerce (Certificate), management of technology (Certificate), Oracle e-commerce enterprise and Web/Internet Protocol programming (Certificate), portal management (Certificate); management of technology (MSCIT); networking technologies (MSCIT); networking technology (Certificate), including e-commerce, network engineering, telecommunications; object-oriented technologies (MSCIT); object-oriented technology (Certificate), including C++ programming, Java programming, Visual Basic programming. Offered at Boulder Campus, Northwest Denver Campus, Southeast Denver Campus, Fort Collins Campus, Colorado Springs Campus, and Broomfield Campus. Part-time and evening/weekend programs available. Postbaccalaureate distance learning degree programs offered (no on-campus study).
Students: 343. Average age 36. In 2001, 40 degrees awarded.
Degree requirements: For master's and Certificate, final research project.
Entrance requirements: For master's and Certificate, GMAT, TOEFL, or university-based test (international applicants), 2 years of related experience, resumé. *Application deadline:* Applications are processed on a rolling basis. *Application fee:* $75.
Expenses: Contact institution.
Financial support: Federal Work-Study available. Support available to part-time students. Financial award applicants required to submit FAFSA.
Don Archer, Chair, 303-458-4302, *Fax:* 303-964-5538.
Application contact: 800-677-9270 Ext. 4080, *Fax:* 303-964-5538, *E-mail:* masters@regis.edu. *Web site:* http://www.regis.edu/spsgraduate/

■ SAN DIEGO STATE UNIVERSITY

Graduate and Research Affairs, College of Professional Studies and Fine Arts, School of Communication, Programs in Communication, San Diego, CA 92182

AWARDS Advertising and public relations (MA); critical-cultural studies (MA); interaction studies (MA); intercultural and international studies (MA); new media studies (MA); news and information studies (MA); telecommunications and media management (MA).

Entrance requirements: For master's, GRE General Test, TOEFL.

■ SOUTHERN NEW HAMPSHIRE UNIVERSITY

School of Business, Graduate Programs, Program in Business Administration, Manchester, NH 03106-1045

AWARDS Accounting (Certificate); artificial intelligence (Certificate); business administration (MBA); computer informations systems (Certificate); database management (Certificate); finance (Certificate); health administration (Certificate); human resource management (Certificate); international business (Certificate); marketing (Certificate); operations management (Certificate). School business administration (Certificate); taxation (Certificate); telecommunications and networking (Certificate); training and development (Certificate). Part-time and evening/weekend programs available.

Faculty: 29 full-time (3 women), 104 part-time/adjunct (28 women).
Students: 122 full-time (45 women), 1,003 part-time (438 women), 95 international. Average age 32. In 2001, 411 degrees awarded.
Degree requirements: For master's, thesis or alternative.
Entrance requirements: For master's, minimum GPA of 2.7 during previous 2 years, 2.5 overall. *Application deadline:* Applications are processed on a rolling basis. *Application fee:* $0.
Expenses: Tuition: Full-time $11,340; part-time $1,260 per course. One-time fee: $540 full-time. Full-time tuition and fees vary according to course load, degree level and program.
Financial support: In 2001–02, 4 research assistantships were awarded; career-related internships or fieldwork, Federal Work-Study, and institutionally sponsored loans also available. Support available to part-time students.
Application contact: Patricia Gerard, Assistant Dean, Academic Services, School of Business, 603-644-3102, *Fax:* 603-644-3144, *E-mail:* p.gerard@snhu.edu.
Find an in-depth description at www.petersons.com/gradchannel.

■ STEVENS INSTITUTE OF TECHNOLOGY

Graduate School, Wesley J. Howe School of Technology Management, Program in Information Systems, Telecommunications Management Track, Hoboken, NJ 07030

AWARDS MS.

Expenses: Tuition: Full-time $13,950; part-time $775 per credit. Required fees: $180. One-time fee: $180 part-time. Full-time tuition and fees vary according to degree level and program.

■ STEVENS INSTITUTE OF TECHNOLOGY

Graduate School, Wesley J. Howe School of Technology Management, Program in Telecommunications Management, Hoboken, NJ 07030

AWARDS Information management (MS, PhD); network planning and evaluation (MS, PhD); project management (MS, PhD); technology management marketing (MS, PhD); telecommunications management (Certificate). Offered in cooperation with the Program in Electrical Engineering.

Degree requirements: For master's, thesis optional; for doctorate, thesis/dissertation.
Entrance requirements: For master's and doctorate, GMAT, GRE, TOEFL. Electronic applications accepted.
Expenses: Tuition: Full-time $13,950; part-time $775 per credit. Required fees: $180. One-time fee: $180 part-time. Full-time tuition and fees vary according to degree level and program. *Web site:* http://www.stevens-tech.edu/

■ SYRACUSE UNIVERSITY

Graduate School, School of Information Studies, Program in Telecommunications and Network Management, Syracuse, NY 13244-0003

AWARDS MS. Part-time and evening/weekend programs available. Postbaccalaureate distance learning degree programs offered (minimal on-campus study).

Faculty: 33 full-time (12 women), 42 part-time/adjunct (12 women).
Students: 20 full-time (1 woman), 62 part-time (12 women); includes 3 minority (2 African Americans, 1 Hispanic American), 44 international. Average age 31. In 2001, 59 degrees awarded.
Degree requirements: For master's, internship or research project.
Entrance requirements: For master's, GRE General Test. *Application deadline:* For fall admission, 2/15 (priority date); for spring admission, 11/1 (priority date). *Application fee:* $50. Electronic applications accepted.
Expenses: Tuition: Full-time $15,528; part-time $647 per credit. Required fees: $420; $38 per term. Tuition and fees vary according to program.
Financial support: Fellowships, research assistantships, teaching assistantships, career-related internships or fieldwork, Federal Work-Study, and tuition waivers (partial) available.
Faculty research: Multimedia, information resources management.

Find an in-depth description at www.petersons.com/gradchannel.

■ UNIVERSITY OF COLORADO AT BOULDER

Graduate School, College of Engineering and Applied Science, Interdisciplinary Telecommunications Program, Boulder, CO 80309

AWARDS ME, MS, MBA/MS. Part-time programs available. Postbaccalaureate distance learning degree programs offered.

Faculty: 5 full-time (0 women).
Students: 120 full-time (36 women), 38 part-time (11 women); includes 26 minority (6 African Americans, 17 Asian Americans or Pacific Islanders, 3 Hispanic Americans), 64 international. Average age 30. 113 applicants, 73% accepted. In 2001, 137 degrees awarded.
Degree requirements: For master's, thesis or alternative, comprehensive exam.
Entrance requirements: For master's, minimum undergraduate GPA of 3.0. *Application deadline:* For fall admission, 3/1 (priority date). Applications are processed on a rolling basis. *Application fee:* $50 ($60 for international students).
Expenses: Tuition, state resident: full-time $3,474. Tuition, nonresident: full-time $16,624.
Financial support: In 2001–02, 15 fellowships (averaging $4,487 per year), 10 teaching assistantships with full tuition reimbursements (averaging $18,789 per year) were awarded. Career-related internships or fieldwork also available. Financial award application deadline: 1/1.
Faculty research: Optical and wireless telecommunication. *Total annual research expenditures:* $376,245.
Dr. Dale Hatfield, Director, 303-492-8916, *Fax:* 303-492-1112.
Application contact: Eydie Mitchel, Graduate Secretary, 303-492-8475, *Fax:* 303-492-1112, *E-mail:* mitchee@spot.colorado.edu. *Web site:* http://morse.colorado.edu/

Find an in-depth description at www.petersons.com/gradchannel.

■ UNIVERSITY OF DENVER

Daniels College of Business, General Business Administration Program, Denver, CO 80208

AWARDS Business administration (MBA); education management (MSM); health care management (MSM); management and communications (MSMC); management and general engineering (MSMGEN); management and telecommunications (MSMC); public health management (MSM). Sports management (MSM). Part-time and evening/weekend programs available.

Faculty: 76.
Students: 363 (128 women); includes 24 minority (3 African Americans, 7 Asian Americans or Pacific Islanders, 12 Hispanic Americans, 2 Native Americans) 48 international. Average age 28. 386

applicants, 77% accepted. In 2001, 247 degrees awarded.
Entrance requirements: For master's, GMAT, LSAT (JD/MBA). *Application deadline:* For fall admission, 5/1 (priority date); for spring admission, 1/1. Applications are processed on a rolling basis. *Application fee:* $50.
Expenses: Tuition: Full-time $21,456.
Financial support: In 2001–02, 91 students received support, including 8 teaching assistantships with full and partial tuition reimbursements available (averaging $6,273 per year); research assistantships with full and partial tuition reimbursements available, career-related internships or fieldwork, Federal Work-Study, institutionally sponsored loans, and scholarships/grants also available. Support available to part-time students. Financial award application deadline: 2/15; financial award applicants required to submit FAFSA.
Faculty research: International business, privatization, alternative energy models, balancing economic growth in emerging economies.
Dr. Tom Howard, Director, 303-871-4402.
Application contact: Becca Cannon, Executive Director, Student Services, 303-871-3421, *Fax:* 303-871-4466, *E-mail:* dcb@du.edu.

■ UNIVERSITY OF MARYLAND UNIVERSITY COLLEGE

Graduate School of Management and Technology, Program in Telecommunications Management, Adelphi, MD 20783

AWARDS Exec MS, MS. Offered evenings and weekends only. Part-time and evening/weekend programs available. Postbaccalaureate distance learning degree programs offered (no on-campus study).

Students: 11 full-time (3 women), 265 part-time (72 women); includes 125 minority (87 African Americans, 25 Asian Americans or Pacific Islanders, 11 Hispanic Americans, 2 Native Americans), 19 international. 74 applicants, 99% accepted. In 2001, 61 degrees awarded.
Degree requirements: For master's, thesis or alternative.
Entrance requirements: For master's, previous course work in calculus and statistics. *Application deadline:* Applications are processed on a rolling basis. *Application fee:* $50. Electronic applications accepted.
Expenses: Tuition, state resident: full-time $5,418; part-time $301 per credit hour. Tuition, nonresident: full-time $8,892; part-time $494 per credit hour.
Financial support: Federal Work-Study and scholarships/grants available. Support available to part-time students. Financial award application deadline: 6/1; financial award applicants required to submit FAFSA.

University of Maryland University College (continued)
Dr. Donald Goff, Chair, 301-985-7200, *Fax:* 301-985-4611, *E-mail:* dgoff@umuc.edu.
Application contact: Coordinator, Graduate Admissions, 301-985-7155, *Fax:* 301-985-7175, *E-mail:* gradinfo@nova.umuc.edu. *Web site:* http://www.umuc.edu/prog/gsmt/tlmn.html

■ UNIVERSITY OF MIAMI

Graduate School, School of Business Administration, Department of Computer Information Systems/Telecommunications, Coral Gables, FL 33124

AWARDS Computer information systems (MS); telecommunications management (Certificate). Certificate offered jointly with MBA or MS program, or as a 15 credit hour program for applicants with an undergraduate or master's degree. Part-time and evening/weekend programs available.

Faculty: 8 full-time (1 woman), 5 part-time/adjunct (2 women).
Students: 32 full-time (15 women), 78 part-time (33 women). In 2001, 28 master's, 10 other advanced degrees awarded.
Entrance requirements: For master's, GMAT or GRE, TOEFL; for Certificate, TOEFL. *Application deadline:* For fall admission, 6/30 (priority date); for spring admission, 10/31. Applications are processed on a rolling basis. *Application fee:* $40. Electronic applications accepted.
Expenses: Tuition: Part-time $960 per credit hour. Required fees: $85 per semester. Tuition and fees vary according to program.
Financial support: In 2001–02, 5 research assistantships with partial tuition reimbursements were awarded; career-related internships or fieldwork, Federal Work-Study, institutionally sponsored loans, and scholarships/grants also available. Financial award application deadline: 3/1.
Faculty research: Database management, expert systems, systems analysis and design, information systems and strategic management, e-commerce.
Dr. Joel Stutz, Chairman, 305-284-6294, *Fax:* 305-284-5161, *E-mail:* jstutz@miami.edu.
Application contact: Ania Nozewnik-Green, Director, Graduate Business Recruiting and Admissions, 305-284-4607, *Fax:* 305-284-1878, *E-mail:* mba@miami.edu. *Web site:* http://www.bus.miami.edu/cis/

■ UNIVERSITY OF MISSOURI–ST. LOUIS

Graduate School, College of Arts and Sciences, Department of Mathematical Sciences, St. Louis, MO 63121-4499

AWARDS Applied mathematics (MA, PhD); computer science (MS); telecommunications science (Certificate). Part-time and evening/weekend programs available.

Faculty: 18.
Students: 36 full-time (22 women), 59 part-time (17 women); includes 10 minority (all Asian Americans or Pacific Islanders), 46 international. In 2001, 4 degrees awarded.
Degree requirements: For master's, thesis optional; for doctorate, thesis/dissertation.
Entrance requirements: For master's, GRE if no BS in computer science; for doctorate, GRE General Test. *Application deadline:* For fall admission, 5/1 (priority date); for spring admission, 12/1. Applications are processed on a rolling basis. *Application fee:* $25 ($40 for international students). Electronic applications accepted.
Expenses: Tuition, state resident: part-time $231 per credit hour. Tuition, nonresident: part-time $621 per credit hour.
Financial support: In 2001–02, 1 fellowship with full tuition reimbursement (averaging $12,000 per year), 2 research assistantships with full tuition reimbursements (averaging $12,884 per year), 13 teaching assistantships with full and partial tuition reimbursements (averaging $11,787 per year) were awarded.
Faculty research: Applied mathematics, statistics, algebra, analysis, computer science. *Total annual research expenditures:* $402,989.
Dr. Haiyun Cai, Director of Graduate Studies, 314-516-5741, *Fax:* 314-516-5400, *E-mail:* caih@msx.umsl.edu.
Application contact: Graduate Admissions, 314-516-5458, *Fax:* 314-516-5310, *E-mail:* gradadm@umsl.edu.

■ UNIVERSITY OF MISSOURI–ST. LOUIS

Graduate School, College of Business Administration, Program in Management Information Systems, St. Louis, MO 63121-4499

AWARDS Electronic commerce (Certificate); information resources management (Certificate); management information systems (PhD, Certificate); telecommunications management (Certificate). Part-time and evening/weekend programs available.

Faculty: 13.
Students: 41 full-time (15 women), 64 part-time (22 women); includes 3 minority (1 African American, 2 Asian Americans or Pacific Islanders), 39 international. In 2001, 33 degrees awarded.

Entrance requirements: For master's, GMAT. *Application deadline:* For fall admission, 7/1; for spring admission, 11/1. Applications are processed on a rolling basis. *Application fee:* $25 ($40 for international students). Electronic applications accepted.
Expenses: Tuition, state resident: part-time $231 per credit hour. Tuition, nonresident: part-time $621 per credit hour.
Financial support: Career-related internships or fieldwork, Federal Work-Study, and institutionally sponsored loans available. Support available to part-time students. Financial award application deadline: 4/1; financial award applicants required to submit FAFSA.
Faculty research: International information systems, telecommunications, electronic commerce, systems development, information systems sourcing.
Karl Kottemann, Assistant Director, 314-516-5885, *Fax:* 314-516-6420, *E-mail:* mba@umsl.edu.
Application contact: Jeff Headtke, Graduate Admissions, 314-516-6928, *Fax:* 314-516-5310, *E-mail:* gradadm@umsl.edu. *Web site:* http://www.umsl.edu/business/busgrad/sobagrad.htm

■ UNIVERSITY OF PENNSYLVANIA

School of Engineering and Applied Science, Telecommunications and Networking Program, Philadelphia, PA 19104

AWARDS MSE. Part-time programs available.
Electronic applications accepted. *Web site:* http://www.seas.upenn.edu/PROFPROG/tcom/

Find an in-depth description at www.petersons.com/gradchannel.

■ UNIVERSITY OF SAN FRANCISCO

Graduate School of Management, Program in Business Administration, San Francisco, CA 94117-1080

AWARDS Finance and banking (MBA); international business (MBA); management (MBA); marketing (MBA); telecommunications management and policy (MBA).

Faculty: 35 full-time (4 women), 33 part-time/adjunct (7 women).
Students: 273 full-time (120 women), 172 part-time (70 women); includes 92 minority (9 African Americans, 65 Asian Americans or Pacific Islanders, 15 Hispanic Americans, 3 Native Americans), 184 international. Average age 28. 488 applicants, 93% accepted, 155 enrolled. In 2001, 197 degrees awarded.
Entrance requirements: For master's, GMAT, TOEFL, minimum undergraduate GPA of 3.2. *Application deadline:* For fall admission, 7/1 (priority date); for spring

admission, 11/30. Applications are processed on a rolling basis. *Application fee:* $55 ($65 for international students).
Expenses: Tuition: Full-time $14,400; part-time $800 per unit. Tuition and fees vary according to degree level, campus/location and program.
Financial support: In 2001–02, 135 students received support; fellowships available. Financial award application deadline: 3/2; financial award applicants required to submit FAFSA.
Faculty research: International financial markets, technology transfer licensing, international marketing, strategic planning. *Total annual research expenditures:* $50,000.
Cathy Fusco, Director, 415-422-6314, *Fax:* 415-422-2502, *E-mail:* mbausf@usfca.edu.

■ WEBSTER UNIVERSITY

School of Business and Technology, Department of Business, St. Louis, MO 63119-3194

AWARDS Business (MA, MBA); computer resources and information management (MA, MBA); computer science/distributed systems (MS); environmental management (MS); finance (MA, MBA); health care management (MA); health services management (MA, MBA); human resources development (MA, MBA); human resources management (MA); international business (MA, MBA); management (MA, MBA); marketing (MA, MBA); procurement and acquisitions management (MA, MBA); public administration (MA); real estate management (MA, MBA). Security management (MA, MBA). Space systems management (MA, MBA, MS); telecommunications management (MA, MBA).
Students: 1,415 full-time (661 women), 3,483 part-time (1,566 women); includes 1,604 minority (1,183 African Americans, 166 Asian Americans or Pacific Islanders, 220 Hispanic Americans, 35 Native Americans), 606 international. Average age 33. In 2001, 1439 degrees awarded. *Application deadline:* Applications are processed on a rolling basis. *Application fee:* $25 ($50 for international students).
Expenses: Tuition: Full-time $7,164; part-time $398 per credit hour.
Financial support: Federal Work-Study available. Support available to part-time students. Financial award application deadline: 4/1; financial award applicants required to submit FAFSA.
Steve Hinson, Chair, 314-968-7017, *Fax:* 314-968-7077.
Application contact: Denise Harrell, Associate Director of Graduate and Evening Student Admissions, 314-968-6983, *Fax:* 314-968-7116, *E-mail:* gadmit@webster.edu.

School Index

School Index

Index of
Directories in This Book

Your everything education destination... the *all-new* Petersons.com

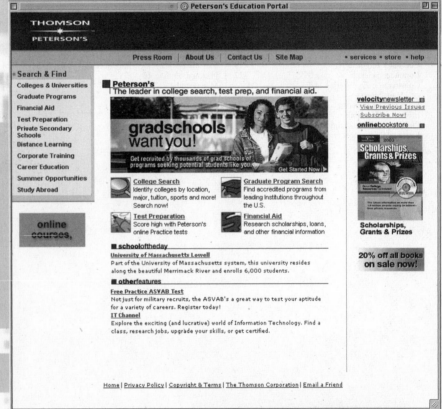